In memory of
Eli M. Savanick

by

Lynda
&
the family

THE
Mennonite Encyclopedia

A Comprehensive Reference Work
on the
Anabaptist-Mennonite Movement

VOLUME V
A-Z

HERALD PRESS
Scottdale, Pennsylvania
Waterloo, Ontario

Library of Congress Cataloging-in-Publication Data
(Revised for vol. 5)

The Mennonite encyclopedia.

Vol. 5 edited by Cornelius J. Dyck and Dennis D. Martin.
1. Mennonites—Encyclopedias.   I. Dyck, Cornelius J.   II. Martin, Dennis D., 1952-
BX8106.M37   289.7′03   55-4563
ISBN 0-8361-3105-3 (V. 5)

THE MENNONITE ENCYCLOPEDIA, VOLUME V
Copyright © 1990 by Herald Press, Scottdale, Pa. 15683
    Published simultaneously in Canada by Herald Press,
    Waterloo, Ont. N2L 6H7. All rights reserved.
Library of Congress Catalog Number: 55-4563
International Standard Book Number: 0-8361-3105-3
Printed in the United States of America

2 3 4 5 6 7 8 9 10 96 95 94 93 92 91

THE EDITORS

Cornelius J. Dyck studied history at Wichita State University (MA, 1955) and historical theology at the University of Chicago (BD, 1959; PhD, 1962). He was director of the Institute of Mennonite Studies, Elkhart, Indiana, from 1958-1979 and also taught at the Associated Mennonite Biblical Seminaries. From 1980-1989 he served at AMBS as Professor of Anabaptist and Sixteenth Century Studies.

Dennis D. Martin studied Reformation history at the University of Waterloo (PhD, 1982). He is a scholar of the history of monastic life, theological education, pastoral leadership, and Mennonite and Anabaptist spirituality.

CONTENTS

PREFACE

One philosopher in the twentieth century has said that *farce* is the mode of consciousness in which a people take leave of their history. False consciousness, in other words, is being cut off from one's past, both corporate and individual. It is the failure to recognize what has gone before or, perhaps as problematic, to distort the realities of the past—both good and bad.

The past, of course, is not a static reality. Because time presses on, there is ever more to remember and to reflect upon. The adding of epoch to epoch assures that the work of the historian is never done. However, there is another reason why history is never finished. New and creative work is demanded of the discipline of history because of an ongoing dialectical tension between past and present. History as a discipline is not a "progressive science," one which moves towards ever higher levels of perfection. Rather, it is an interpretative science (or art?)—it is a way of understanding the past in order to deal with the present and to gain some direction for the future. As the nineteenth-century historian-philosopher Wilhelm Dilthey put it, every new present has in it the possibility of a new past. Our current situation presents both an obligation and an opportunity—it forces us to look anew at our history and provides us a new angle of vision from which to view it.

It is for these reasons that a new volume must be added to the monumental *Mennonite Encyclopedia* published in the 1950s. A whole generation of Mennonites and others interested in Mennonite and Anabaptist history and life—scholars, students, and lay people alike—are indebted to the original work edited by H. S. Bender, Cornelius Krahn, Melvin Gingerich, and, in the planning stages, C. Henry Smith. The first four volumes of the *Mennonite Encyclopedia* cannot yet be superseded. But they must be supplemented. This volume stands as that supplement. Its purpose is to fill in the intervening years since the appearance of the first four volumes, to deal with some themes which were not dealt with in that earlier era, and to provide coverage beyond what was done in the first four volumes, especially of *global* Mennonitism.

Many people, agencies, and Mennonite groups deserve credit for helping to make this volume possible. Cornelius J. Dyck gives more complete acknowledgements in his introduction to this volume. Nevertheless, it is in order for me here to give a word of appreciation to the editors of this volume. Without the vision and editorial oversight of Cornelius J. Dyck and the capable assistance of his associate, Dennis Martin, this work would never have been possible. "Midnight oil" became more than a proverbial description of the lengthy hours which they put into this project. It was rather the lubricant which kept the editorial wheels spinning in order for the project to see the light of day. This they did while carrying out teaching and other duties. Credit should also be given to Willard M. Swartley, who as director of the Institute of Mennonite Studies from 1979-88, gave supervision and support to the work of editors Dyck and Martin.

The Institute of Mennonite Studies sponsored this supplementary volume with the sincere desire that it will contribute toward greater awareness, appreciation, and appropriation of the Mennonite past. Obviously, from a Christian perspective, neither things Mennonite nor events past should be an "end" in themselves. Hence, it is our prayer and hope that in some small measure this volume will help the church live more faithfully towards that vision of God's end and purpose (*telos*) for history—a world of shalom (peace, justice, and well-being) for all God's creation.

Richard A. Kauffman, Interim Director, 1988-89
Institute of Mennonite Studies
Associated Mennonite Biblical Seminaries

INTRODUCTION

Background

The four-volume *Mennonite Encyclopedia* (*ME*) has established itself as an almost indispensable reference tool for research and general use by a wide variety of people. Initial steps toward its production were undertaken soon after Harold S. Bender established contact with European Mennonites in 1945. They had begun their own *Mennonitisches Lexikon* in 1913 (completed in four volumes in 1967).

The basic organization for the *Mennonite Encyclopedia* (*ME*) was set up in 1946. The first volume appeared in 1955, the second in 1956, the third in 1957, and the fourth in 1959. A revision, without changing the number of lines in the columns, was undertaken later with Cornelius Krahn as editor, Melvin Gingerich as managing editor, and Orlando Harms as associate editor. The first revised volume appeared in 1969, the second in 1972, and the third and fourth volumes in 1973.

Despite all the strengths of this original set, the need for additional resources of this kind became increasingly apparent. The tempo of Anabaptist and Mennonite studies had increased considerably since the 1950s. Topics not included in *ME* needed encyclopedic treatment. This need was reported in a preliminary way to the executive council of the Institute of Mennonite Studies (IMS) and IMS associates by the IMS director (Cornelius J. Dyck) in 1976. It was then agreed that IMS would be a logical agency to pursue this issue further and to consider the possibility of adding a fifth volume to the set.

This conclusion was confirmed by a meeting of historians present at the Mennonite World Conference sessions in Wichita, Kansas, in 1978. In 1980, after further study, the Administrative Committee of the Associated Mennonite Biblical Seminaries (AMBS) at Elkhart, Indiana, invited the IMS director to assume editorial responsibility for the production of a fifth volume. He agreed to this and began conversation with the publisher of the earlier set as well as with potential financial supporters for the project.

In September, 1983 arrangements were also made with Dennis Martin, who was nearing completion of his assignment as assistant editor of the *Brethren Encyclopedia* (Philadelphia and Oak Brook, Ill.: Brethren Encyclopedia, 1983), to join the *ME* project in the same capacity. Carol A. N. Martin was invited to join as editorial assistant and copy editor.

The IMS executive council appointed an editorial council consisting of the following members: Wilma Bailey, Nashville, Tenn.; Lois Barrett, Wichita, Ks.; John Friesen, Winnipeg, Man.; Daniel Schipani, Elkhart, Ind.; Beulah Hostetler, Willow Grove, Pa.; Harry Loewen, Winnipeg; Howard Loewen, Fresno, Cal.; John S. Oyer, Goshen, Ind.; and Rodney Sawatsky, Waterloo, Ont. Willard M. Swartley, the new IMS director, was appointed exofficio member.

Selection of Topics

Compilation of a possible topic list began with the initial study of the original set by the editors, in which omissions and the need for updating were identified. For example, an analysis of 441 pages in *ME* (comprising about 12 percent of the total) showed that 29 percent of the biographical material deals with people who were neither Anabaptist nor Mennonite (but believed to be contextually necessary). It further shows that these biographies are often longer than the Anabaptist or Mennonite entries.

Five hundred biographies are in *ME I-IV*, comprising 24 percent of total lines. Of these, 93.5 percent of the space was given to men and only 6.6 percent to women, most of whom where martyrs. (At least one-third of sixteenth-century Anabaptist martyrs were women). Slightly over 11 percent of the space was given to cities, towns and villages, 7.4 percent to congregations, 5.4 percent to Anabaptist cultural and social activities, etc. Only about 2 percent of total lines were given to specifically theological issues.

A second step in preparing the topic list was the mailing of a request for help to some 100 select individuals, asking them to list items which, in their judgment, needed treatment. A third major step was to work through many key Mennonite and Brethren in Christ publications since the 1950s, including books, periodicals, yearbooks, directories, conference reports, catalogs, and other literature, noting whatever items or issues seemed to be important to that group or individual.

At the same time, Reynold Sawatzky, a trained historian and researcher, carried out a similar search in the holdings of the Mennonite Historical Library (MHL) and the Archives of the Mennonite Church at Goshen. He gave particular attention to women and the organizations pertaining to the smaller Mennonite bodies. He was involved in this during most of 1985 and the first six months of 1986.

As these lists developed, they were measured against the parameters and guidelines established. It was agreed, for example, to use collective (umbrella) articles and charts to update institutions and agencies. District and provincial conferences seemed important, as did the need for an article on each country with Mennonite involvement (a goal not fully met). A central axiom was that no article should be included unless it had a direct linkage to some aspect of present or past Mennonite or Anabaptist life and thought.

Biographies chosen were to be of persons who, according to the records available, had made a significant contribution to the life and work of the church. In view of the very large number of persons who fit these criteria, we were forced to include only the deceased and those 80 years of age or older. This age criteria was applied only to North America. The list of martyrs was not updated because it seemed impossible to do justice to it, given the limitations of time and resources, particularly as we thought of martyrs since the sixteenth-century to the present. This subject is one among many which would benefit from depth treatment and analysis.

The guidelines cannot all be listed. It was agreed not to include congregations since most of them are listed with statistics in annual denominational yearbooks. Some maps and charts have been provided to facilitate orientation. More maps had been projected but were dropped for financial reasons. Richard H. Beyler, presently a doctoral student at Harvard University, did excellent work in researching and compiling the necessary information for artist Harriet Miller of Goshen to draw the maps. We are indebted to both of them, and also to John S. Oyer, the MHL staff, and Goshen College for helping to expedite their preparation. The initial plan to use pictures extensively had to be dropped for lack of space.

In working with worldwide, non-North American topics, it was our policy to prepare initial lists and to submit them to the respective country or regional representative(s) for analysis in consultation with others. We urged them to add or subtract topics as seemed best to them, and to assign them to writers of their choice. This worked well for the most part.

Another related problem, however, should be identified here. While the editors and editorial council are fully aware that the primary use of this volume will be in North America and Western Europe, it has been their aim to achieve maximum global coverage. However, many writers were dismayed at their own inability to secure significant amounts of global information on a given topic. They had to be encouraged by the editors to do their best under the circumstances. This explanation is given on behalf of the many writers who felt their information base was more national and local than they desired. It was in this connection also that writers were reminded of the strong emphasis the editors placed on the importance of bibliographies, particularly because space limits led to shorter articles in *ME V* than in *ME I-IV*.

Acknowledgements

Finances

Initial financial support was committed by the Mennonite Church, the General Conference Mennonite Church, the Mennonite Brethren Church of North America, and the Mennonite Publishing House. They pledged annual amounts of $10,000, $8,000, $6,000, and $7,000 respectively for three years. The Associated Mennonite Biblical Seminaries provided a subsidy of $20,000, a necessary line of credit, accounting services, and continuing strong moral support to the project and editors. All of this provided the necessary financial base and a vote of confidence in IMS and the project.

In the following years, grants were also received from Mennonite Central Committee, Mennonite Mutual Aid (Fraternal Funds), the Schowalter Foundation, Mennonite Indemnity, Inc., the Illinois Mennonite Conference, the Eastern Mennonite Associated Libraries and Archives (Maryland), and the Mennonite Historical Society (Goshen), plus a significant number of contributions from interested individuals. This support is gratefully acknowledged.

People Involved

It may be appropriate to begin by thanking the writers of the articles for their work, done carefully, probably under the pressure of time, and often involving extensive research and correspondence. Except for a few freelance writers who earn their living by writing and received a very modest honorarium, all writers wrote without payment. We are most grateful for the fact that a considerable number of writers welcomed the opportunity to do certain articles as the beginning of further work in the field of their article. *ME V* seems to have started a fresh wave of research interest which will, we hope, bear fruit in eventual journal articles and books.

At the risk of making omissions, appreciation is also expressed to the following: retired missionaries John A. Friesen of Goshen, Ind.; Harold and Ruth Ratzlaff of Newton, Ks.; James and Jenny Bertsche of Elkhart, Ind.; and Mahlon Hess of Lititz, Pa., who collected materials on India and on Zaire, Tanzania, Kenya, and other areas in Africa. As Mennonite groups in some of these areas enter their second, third, and fourth generations, the process of recording their history is beginning. Writing articles for *ME V* has helped stimulate this work and encouraged the collecting and preserving of material that might otherwise have been lost. The personal memories, files, and contacts of these retired missionaries became indispensable, as their articles indicate.

We are also particularly grateful to the following: Lawrence M. Yoder of Harrisonburg, Va., who wrote many articles on Indonesia; Peter Hamm of Winnipeg, Man., and Wilbert R. Shenk of Elkhart, Ind., for their counsel on two-thirds world issues; Walter Sawatsky of Winnipeg, for help on issues relating to the Soviet Union; Gundolf Niebuhr of Filadelfia, Paraguay, for counsel on Latin America; Amzie Yoder of Guatemala City and Goshen, Ind., for articles on Central America; Dorothy Yoder Nyce of Goshen, Ind., for her counsel and articles; John Friesen of Winnipeg, who served as primary advisor for Canada, and Adolf Ens, also of Winnipeg, for his counsel, charts, and articles.

Sjouke Voolstra of Amsterdam, Dieter Goetz Lichdi of Heilbronn (West Germany), Isaac Zuercher of Bern (Switzerland), Fritz Sprunger of Tokyo, Peter Wiens of Filadelfia (Paraguay), Martin W. Friesen of Loma Plata (Paraguay), and Enrique Ens of Witmarsum (Brazil) coordinated the writing of articles in their areas and wrote many articles themselves. E. Morris Sider and Martin H. Schrag of Grantham, Pa., helped greatly by assuming responsibility for Brethren in Christ articles and giving other helpful counsel.

Reference has already been made to the help of the staff members of MHL and the Mennonite Church archives at Goshen College and to Richard H. Beyler and Harriet Miller. Particular appreciation is here expressed also to John S. Oyer and to Robert S. Kreider for their ready counsel and encouragement from the very beginning. Kreider capped his own contributions by spending a week with the editors as the countdown began, writing articles, adding bibliographical references, and editing. Similar appreciation is also expressed to Paul M. Schrock and Loren Johns for support in items relating to publication. (At an April 1979 meeting of Mennonite and Brethren in Christ publishers in Chicago it was agreed that Herald Press alone would be the publisher of any further *ME* volumes.)

Deep appreciation is hereby also expressed to IMS director Willard M. Swartley for help and encouragement, but also for taking primary responsibility for things financial after the initial financial arrangements had been made. Richard A. Kauffman, interim IMS director for 1988-90, ably continued this service. So also the support and understanding of the IMS executive council are gratefully acknowledged, and with this the chairpersons of those sessions, Marlin E. Miller and Henry Poettcker, presidents of Goshen Biblical Seminary and Mennonite Biblical Seminary, respectively.

The efficient help of the editor C. J. Dyck's "scribe," Sue DeLeon, a skilled word processor operator, is gratefully acknowledged. The help of Rosemary Wyse and Margaret Schipani in translating Spanish-language manuscripts made an important contribution. All other translations were done by the editor. Reynold Sawatzky has already been referred to above for 1985-86. From July 15, 1986, he skillfully managed the *ME* computer, entering each article, sorting files, entering most editorial corrections, providing information as needed, preparing mailings, working *gratis* during 1985 and through July 15, 1986, after which he would accept only minimal remuneration.

Last, but certainly not least, Dennis and Carol Martin brought not only important skills from their earlier assignment, but also considerable research and historical skills, as well as linguistic and organizational abilities, to their tasks. Together they set up editorial and recordkeeping procedures, with Carol carrying the main responsibility for all aspects of computerization until she terminated her work in July 1986 to pursue doctoral studies. As assistant editor, Dennis functioned as managing editor for a wide range of planning and production. He and the editor shared responsibility for editing the articles for content. Dennis later assumed the duties of copy editing and supervising computer operations.

Cornelius J. Dyck
The Institute of Mennonite Studies
Elkhart, Indiana

A READER'S GUIDE TO MENNONITE ENCYCLOPEDIA, VOLUME 5

Principles of Topic Selection and Organization. In many instances *ME V* entries deal with subjects for which relatively little research has been carried out. Ideally, encyclopedia entries are summaries of an extensive body of detailed research. Anabaptist and Mennonite studies have mined some areas thoroughly and virtually ignored other areas. Rather than leave these areas completely untouched, the editorial council asked scholars to contribute articles summarizing the limited research already done and outlining avenues for future research. In a few instances authors were unable to provide even this minimal entry. In these cases cross references to related articles and suggestions for further reading have been added by the editors in lieu of a full entry.

A basic principle for inclusion was that no biographical entries about people still living should be included. Exceptions were made to this principle for North American and European Mennonite leaders over the age of 80 as of 1984. Younger Mennonite leaders from non-Western countries were included because many Mennonite churches outside Europe and North America are themselves of recent origin and their leadership would not be represented at all if leaders younger than 80 years of age were excluded. For North America and Europe this policy means that prominent leaders of the generation from 1960-1990 do not receive biographies. The *ME V* biographies give the story of Mennonite life between 1920 and 1960. Most of these people were still active when *ME I-IV* was published and were not included in its biographies. In terms of biographies, the encyclopedia thus lags twenty to thirty years behind. However, references to active leaders from the period 1960-1990 are found in articles on the various topics and types of institutions in *ME V*. The reader will look to *ME I-IV* for birth and death dates of many Anabaptist and Mennonite personages mentioned in *ME V*.

Human interest features provide valuable insight and information about Mennonite life around the world. They do not correspond to the typical encyclopedia entry and have not been placed where they might be expected to fit alphabetically. Rather, they have been placed near related standard entries in the hope that readers will find the juxtaposition stimulating and attractive. A list of these feature articles is found below.

Names, Numbers, and Terms. Because the comma following the initial name in a biographical entry indicates that the normal Western order of the name has been inverted (i.e., the "last" name or surname is given first), this comma has been omitted for individuals from cultures in which it is normal to give the "surname," or family name, first. At the suggestion of Japanese contributors, the order of Japanese names has frequently been westernized. Readers should keep in mind that the name given last in *ME V* is customarily given first in Japan. For the sake of clarity, the "surname," or "family name," has been italicized in most instances.

The word-by-word alphabetization pattern used in *ME V* ignores umlauts and diacritical marks, e.g., Münster is treated as if it were spelled Munster and thus follows Mumaw, rather than being treated as if it were spelled Muenster and thus coming between Mudenda and Muganda. Word-by-word alphabetization compares the letters of a word up to the first space or mark of punctuation. Hyphenated compounds are treated as if they were single words. Acronyms are alphabetized as if they were words.

Amish-Mennonite is used occasionally to refer to groups that are neither Old Order Amish nor Mennonite nor Beachy Amish Mennonite. The latter three specific groups are always identified as such with "Amish-Mennonite" reserved for instances that do not fit any of the specific groups. *Amish Mennonite* was used in *ME I-IV* in part to refer to what *ME V* calls the Conservative Mennonite Conference; it was also used in *ME I-IV* to refer to the nineteenth-century Amish. Some descendants of the nineteenth-century Amish-Mennonites are now Old Order Amish; other descendants have now been absorbed by the Mennonite Church (MC), Beachy Amish Mennonites, and Conservative Mennonite Conference. The term *Old Order Amish* is used in *ME V* only in the titles of articles. Elsewhere, in keeping with general popular usage in recent years, the word *Amish* is used to refer to Old Order Amish. Population figures in entries on major Amish settlements refer to total Christian community and are not limited to baptized (adult) members.

Because the *Mennonite Encyclopedia* includes information about a wide variety of groups, *Mennonite* is used on occasion to refer collectively to Mennonites, Brethren in Christ, Hutterites, and Amish. Where it refers only to groups with "Mennonite" in their name, the context will usually make this clear. The term *Anabaptist* has been reserved for sixteenth- and early seventeenth-century groups. *Anabaptist and Mennonite,* (or occasionally, *Anabaptist-Mennonite*) has been used to refer to the entire 450-year history of the Mennonite, Amish, Hutterite, and Brethren in Christ family. Related "historic peace church" groups (Church of the Brethren and Friends) are not included under the labels *Mennonite* and *Anabaptist*. They are included, along with Baptists and others, in the collective term *Believers Church*.

In most instances, names of the various Mennonite groups are given in the language of the country or culture in which they are located. English translations of these names are usually given in parentheses. Names normally written with non-Roman alphabets (such as Japanese and Cyrillic) have been transliterated. In a few exceptional cases only English equivalents have been used.

North American readers accustomed to °evangelicalism as a particular type of Protestant Christianity should note that names of Mennonite groups incorporating the words *evangélica* (Spanish, Portuguese), *evangélique* (French), and *evangelisch* (German) and their derivatives, usually simply mean "Protestant," even though, in *ME V*, they have often been translated "evangelical."

Readers accustomed to British English should note that *corn* as used in *ME V* refers to maize, not to grain in general. Readers accustomed to Canadian usage should note that, solely for the sake of editorial consistency, American (i.e., United States) spellings are used, except in references to proper names of Canadian or British institutions (e.g., "Centre for Mennonite Brethren Studies" in Winnipeg; "Center for Mennonite Brethren Studies" in Fresno; but "community center" elsewhere in *ME V*, where a proper name is not used.)

Most references to Mennonite-related places in Russia and the Union of Soviet Socialist Republics are given in the form used in *ME I-IV*. Those that are given in a different form are included in a concordance to Russian orthography that appears below.

Cross References. *ME V* uses asterisks to indicate to the reader that a related article appears elsewhere in *ME V*. A double asterisk points to a related article in the main body of *ME I-IV*. References to the supplementary alphabetical sequence in *ME IV* are given by means of *ME IV* page numbers. Readers should keep in mind that single-asterisk cross-references to an *ME V* article frequently point farther afield to the earlier article under the same heading in *ME I-IV*. This is indicated by a reference to *ME I-IV* in parenthesis immediately following the *ME V* entry title. Occasionally the *ME I-IV* article is more relevant to the discussion at hand, and the reader is directed via a double asterisk to the earlier article, not to the *ME V* article of the same name.

Specific countries mentioned within *ME V* articles have no asterisks. With a few exceptions, *ME V* contains entries on each country, state, or province in which Mennonites have been active and on each conference or group in the Mennonite Central

Committee and Mennonite World Conference families. Readers should not forget to turn to these articles for further information. In a few instances articles planned on countries, states, provinces, or denominations failed to materialize. In other instances an entry on a Mennonite conference doubles as an entry on the country in which it is located or vice versa. In the case of France, editors were unable to secure articles on either the country or on Mennonite conferences or institutions within France. Mennonite Central Committee is referred to in countless articles but is not preceded by an asterisk. Mennonite World Conference, likewise, is normally not preceded by an asterisk.

No asterisked cross-references are given to articles that appear directly above or below the one being read, i.e., in the article on Humanitarianism, there will be no cross reference to Humanism, since this will appear directly above Humanitarianism, and the reader can be expected to notice the related article. This also applies to spouses whose entries often appear next to each other. Asterisks have been placed in front of names that vary slightly from the grammatical form actually used for the *ME V* entry. Readers are expected to realize that the actual entry *Legalism* is what was intended by °legalists, that °migrated refers to the actual entry *Migrations,* and that °°Denck refers to Hans *Denck,* since nothing appears under *Migrated, Legalists,* or *Denck.*

Bibliographies. At the end of articles bibliographies are often arranged alphabetically. Those that are not arranged alphabetically are ranked in order of decreasing importance (importance meaning breadth of coverage or quality of information). Frequently used bibliographical citations have been abbreviated. A "Key to Bibliographical Abbreviations" appears below. Not all periodical titles are abbreviated. Some periodicals that are cited in full may nonetheless not be familiar to readers outside the group publishing the periodical. Readers should consult *Mennonite Bibliography* (Menn. Bib. in the key below) for information about when and by whom these are or were published. Nonabbreviated book citations are intended to give enough information to permit readers to locate them easily—thus cryptic citations of books should cause the reader to consult the key to bibliographical abbreviations for additional information needed to locate the book or article in question.

In the bibliographies appended to articles on states and provinces in United States and Canada, references are given for the *MC Yearbook* (see the key below) only. Additional information on Mennonites in a given state or province is found in the directories and yearbooks of other Mennonite groups (GCM, MB, BIC, EMCh), but space and editorial time did not permit all these to be listed. A listing of such directories and yearbooks is found in the article °"Yearbooks and Directories." The *MC Yearbook* was cited because it is the single most inclusive listing.

Unless specified, "Scottdale" as a place of publication refers to Herald Press as publisher. Many Herald Press publications also carry Kitchener, Ontario, as place of publication. This was omitted to save space. Where a Scottdale publication was by Mennonite Publishing House rather than Herald Press, Scottdale is always followed by "MPH." Likewise, "Newton" as a place of publication always refers to Faith and Life Press. Where the publisher was one of the General Conference Mennonite Church agencies in Newton, that will be specified. Mennonite Press in North Newton is indicated by "North Newton: MP." Likewise, "Nappanee" always refers to Evangel Press or its predecessors (e.g., Evangelical Visitor Publishing House). Multiple locations are not given for major publishers, e.g., only New York or Oxford is given as the city of publication for Oxford University Press titles, instead of the large number of cities in which this press (and similar major publishers) maintain offices and publish books.

HUMAN INTEREST FEATURES IN ME V

CHARTS

MAPS

KEY TO SYMBOLS AND ABBREVIATIONS

General Abbreviations

A.D. = Anno Domini (in the year of the Lord)
b. = born
BA = Bachelor of Arts degree
B.C. = Before Christ
BSL = Bachelor of Sacred Literature degree
ca. = circa, approximately, thereabouts
cf. = compare, consult
Co. = County or Company
Cos. = Counties
d. = died
desiatin (dessiatine) = 2.67 acres (=1.09 hectares)
e.g. = *exempli gratia*, for example
esp. = especially
fl. = floruit or flourished
ft. = foot
Jr. = junior
KJV = King James or Authorized Version of the Bible (1611)
km. = kilometers (=.62 miles)
m. = married
MA = Master of Arts degree
MCC = Mennonite Central Committee

mi. = miles
ne. = northeast, northeastern
NIV = New International Version of the Bible (Zondervan, 1978)
nw. = northwest, northwestern
PhD = Doctor of Philosophy degree
RN = Registered Nurse
RSV = Revised Standard Version of the Bible
se. = southeast, southeastern
sect. = section
sp. = special
sw. = southwest, southwestern
Twp. = Township
U. = University
U.S. = United States
vs. = versus
WMSC = Women's Missionary and Service Committee (MC), formerly MWMS (1922-33); GSCC (1933-47), WMSCO (1947-55), WMSA (1955-61). See *ME IV*: 974 for details
YMCA = Young Men's Christian Association
YWCA = Young Women's Christian Association

Provinces and States

Alta. = Alberta
B.C. = British Columbia (also used for Before Christ)
Man. = Manitoba
Ont. = Ontario
N.B. = New Brunswick
Nfld. = Newfoundland
N.S. = Nova Scotia
P.E.I. = Prince Edward Island
P.Q. = Province Quebec
Sask. = Saskatchewan

Ala. = Alabama
Alaska = Alaska
Ariz. = Arizona
Ark. = Arkansas
Cal. = California
Col. = Colorado
Conn. = Connecticut
Del. = Delaware
D.C. = District of Columbia
Fla. = Florida

Ga. = Georgia
Hi. = Hawaii
Idaho = Idaho
Ill. = Illinois
Ind. = Indiana
Iowa = Iowa
Ks. = Kansas
Ky. = Kentucky
La. = Louisiana
Maine = Maine
Md. = Maryland
Mass. = Massachusetts
Mich. = Michigan
Minn. = Minnesota
Miss. = Mississippi
Mo. = Missouri
Mont. = Montana
Nebr. = Nebraska
Nev. = Nevada
N.H. = New Hampshire
N.J. = New Jersey
N.M. = New Mexico

N.Y. = New York
N.C. = North Carolina
N.D. = North Dakota
Ohio = Ohio
Okla. = Oklahoma
Ore. = Oregon
Pa. = Pennsylvania
P.R. = Puerto Rico
R.I. = Rhode Island
S.C. = South Carolina
S.D. = South Dakota
Tenn. = Tennessee
Tex. = Texas
Utah = Utah
Vt. = Vermont
Va. = Virginia
Wash. = Washington
W.Va. = West Virginia
Wis. = Wisconsin
Wyo. = Wyoming

Concordance to Russian Terms

ME V	ME I-IV
desiatin (both sing. and pl.)	dessiatine
Kitchkass (Orenburg)	Kitchkas
Pleshanov	Pleshanovo
Taurida	Taurida, Taurien
Tschongraw	Tchongrav
Tsar	Czar

Denominational Abbreviations

AM = Amish Mennonite (as merged into Mennonite Church [MC])

BAM = Beachy Amish Mennonite

BIC = Brethren in Christ

CBreth = Church of the Brethren

CGC = Church of God in Christ, Mennonite (Holdeman)

CM = Conservative (Amish) Mennonite

EMB = Evangelical Mennonite Brethren Conference (since 1987: Fellowship of Evangelical Bible Churches)

EMCh = Evangelical Mennonite Church (United States)

EMCon = Evangelical Mennonite Conference (Canada, formerly Kleine Gemeinde)

EMMC = Evangelical Mennonite Mission Conference (Canada)

EP = Eastern Pennsylvania Mennonite Church

GCM = General Conference Mennonite Church

MB = Mennonite Brethren

MC = (Old) Mennonite Church

Miss = Missionary Church (includes Mennonite Brethren in Christ; United Missionary Church)

OOA = Old Order Amish

OOM = Old Order Mennonite

Bibliographical Abbreviations

AMBS = refers to library holdings at Associated Mennonite Biblical Seminaries, Elkhart, Ind.

Amer. = American (in journal titles)

Annual Report. See *Minutes (EMCh)*; *Minutes (EMB)*

ARG = *Archiv für Reformationsgeschichte*

Lois Barrett, *Vision* (1983) = Lois Barrett, *The Vision and the Reality: The Story of Home Missions in the General Conference Mennonite Church* (Newton: Faith and Life, 1983)

Bender, "Vision" = Harold S. Bender, "The Anabaptist Vision," *Church History*, 13 (March 1944), 3-24, reprinted with slight changes in *MQR*, 18 (1944), 67-88; and reprinted in *The Recovery of the Anabaptist Vision*, ed. Guy F. Hershberger (Scottdale, 1957), 29-54

Bibl. on War and Peace (1987) = *An Annotated Bibliography of Mennonite Writings on War and Peace, 1930-1980*, ed. Willard Swartley and Cornelius J. Dyck (Scottdale: Herald Press, 1987)

BIC Hist. Life = *Brethren in Christ History and Life* (1978-)

Brethren Encyclopedia (1983) = *The Brethren Encyclopedia*, 3 vols. (Philadelphia and Oak Brook, Ill.: Brethren Encyclopedia, Inc., 1983)

BRN 2 = *Bibliotheca Reformatoria Neerlandica*, vol. 2 (The Hague, 1904)

BRN 5 = *Bibliotheca Reformatoria Neerlandica*, vol. 5 (The Hague, 1909)

BRN 10 = *Bibliotheca Reformatoria Neerlandica*, vol. 10 (The Hague, 1914)

Builder = *Builder*, published monthly as teacher's guide for Sunday Schools in General Conference and Mennonite Church congregations (Scottdale and Newton, 1960-)

CGR = *Conrad Grebel Review* (Waterloo, Ontario, 1983-)

Chr. Evangel = *Christian Evangel* (Central Conference Mennonite Church, Chicago and elsewhere, 1910-)

Chr. Leader = *Christian Leader* (MB; Hillsboro, 1937-)

Chr. Living = *Christian Living* (MC; Scottdale, 1954-)

Chr. Monitor = *Christian Monitor* (MC; Scottdale, 1909-53)

CMBC = Canadian Mennonite Bible College (as publisher of books)

Concern Pamphlets = independently published series of pamphlets, 1954-1971 (nos. 1-18)

Courier = *Courier* (Mennonite World Conference, 1986-)

CRR 1 = John H. Yoder, ed. and trans., *The Legacy of Michael Sattler*, Classics of the Radical Reformation, vol. 1 (Scottdale, 1973)

CRR 2 = William Klassen and Walter Klaassen, eds. and trans., *The Writings of Pilgram Marpeck*, Classics of the Radical Reformation, vol. 2 (Scottdale, 1978)

CRR 3 = Walter Klaassen, ed., *Anabaptism in Outline: Selected Primary Sources*, Classics of the Radical Reformation, vol. 3 (Scottdale, 1981); Spanish translation by C. Arnold Snyder, *Selecciones Teológicas Anabautistas* (Scottdale, 1985); all citations in *ME V* are to the English edition

CRR 4 = Leland Harder, ed., *The Sources of Swiss Anabaptism: The Grebel Letters and Related Documents*, Classics of the Radical Reformation, vol. 4 (Scottdale, 1985)

Denck, *Schriften II* = W. Fellmann, ed., *Hans Denck Schriften*, vol. 2: *Religiöse Schriften* (= Quellen zur Geschichte der Täufer, vol. 6, pt. 2), Quellen und Forschungen zur Reformationsgeschichte, 24 (Gütersloh, 1956)

Directory of the Fellowship Churches = *Directory of the Fellowship Churches* (Farmington, N.M.: Lamp and Light Publishers)

Dirk, *Enchiridion*, trans. Kolb (1910) = Dirk Philipszoon, *Enchiridion*, trans. A. B. Kolb (1910, frequent reprintings, e.g., Aylmer, Ontario: Pathway Publishers, 1978)

diss. = dissertation

Doops. Bijdr. = *Doopsgezinde Bijdragen*, n.r. (1975-)

Doops. Jaar. = *Doopsgezind Jaarboekje*, yearbook and directory of the Algemene Doopsgezinde Sociëteit

D. F. Durnbaugh, *Believers' Church* (1968) = Donald F. Durnbaugh, *The Believers' Church: The History and Character of Radical Protestantism* (New York: Macmillan, 1968; reprinted Scottdale, 1985)

C. J. Dyck, *Twelve Becoming* (1973) = Cornelius J. Dyck, *Twelve Becoming: Biographies of Mennonite Disciples from the Sixteenth to the Twentieth Century* (Newton, 1973)

C. J. Dyck, ed., *Intro. Menn. Hist.* (1967, 1981) = Cornelius J. Dyck, ed., *Introduction to Mennonite History* (Scottdale, 1967, 1981)

ed. = edited, edition

EMBMC = Eastern Mennonite Board of Missions and Charities, Salunga, Pa. (as publisher)

EMC = Eastern Mennonite College (as publisher)

Encyclopedia Britannica = *Encyclopedia Britannica*, 11th ed. (1910-11), 14th ed. (1929-73), 15th ed. (1974) (Chicago)

Engl. trans. = English translation

F. H. Epp, *Mennonites in Canada I* = Frank H. Epp, *Mennonites in Canada, 1786-1920: The History of a Separate People* (Toronto: Macmillan, 1974)

F. H. Epp, *Mennonites in Canada II* = Frank H. Epp, *Mennonites in Canada, 1920-1940: A People's Struggle for Survival* (Toronto: Macmillan, 1982)

Essays on Biblical Interpretation (1984) = Willard M. Swartley, ed., *Essays on Biblical Interpretation: Anabaptist-Mennonite Perspectives*, Text-Reader Series, 1 (Elkhart, Ind.: IMS, 1984)

et al. = et alia (and others)

et passim = here and there, throughout

EV = *Evangelical Visitor* (BIC; Nappanee, Ind., 1887-)

Fam. Life = *Family Life* (Aylmer, Ont.: Pathway Publishers)

ff. = and following

FQ = *Festival Quarterly* (Intercourse, Pa., 1974-)

P. M. Friesen, *Brotherhood* (1911, 1980) = Peter M. Friesen, *The Mennonite Brotherhood in Russia (1789-1910)*, trans. J. B. Toews and others (Fresno, Cal.: Board of Christian Literature [M.B.], 1978, rev. ed. 1980)

P. M. Friesen, *Brüderschaft* (1911) = Peter M. Friesen, *Alt-Evangelische Mennonitsche Brüderschaft in Rußlland (1789-1910)* (Halbstadt: Raduga Verlag, 1911), normally the English translation is cited in *ME V*

GCMC = General Conference Mennonite Church (as publisher)

GCM Handbook (year) = *Handbook of Information, General Conference Mennonite Church* (Newton, Ks.)

Gemeinde Unterwegs = former periodical of Verband deutscher Mennonitengemeinden, merged with *Brücke* in 1986

GH = *Gospel Herald* (MC; Scottdale; 1908-)

Esther Rose Graber, comp., "MBM Missionary Directory" (1983, 1984) = Esther Rose Graber, compiler, "Mennonite Board of Missions Missionary Directory" (unpublished, MBM offices, Elkhart, 1983, 1984)

John A. Hostetler, *Amish Society* (1980) = John A. Hostetler, *Amish Society*, 3rd ed. (Baltimore: Johns Hopkins U. Press, 1980)

John A. Hostetler, *Hutterite Society* (1974) = John A. Hostetler, *Hutterite Society* (Baltimore: Johns Hopkins U. Press, 1974)

Hubmaier, *Schriften* = G. Westin, Torsten Bergsten, eds., *Balthasar Hubmaier Schriften* (Gütersloh: Gerd Mohn, 1962); translation in CRR series, *Balthasar Hubmaier: Theologian of Anabaptism* (Scottdale, 1989)

ibid. = in the same place (i.e., in book or periodical)

idem = the same person

i.e. = id est, that is

IMS = Institute of Mennonite Studies, Elkhart, Ind. (as publisher)

India Calling. See *ME III*

J. = Journal (for periodical titles)

Jb. = Jahrbuch (in periodical titles)

Jg. = Jahrgang (an annual volume of a serial publication)

JMS = *Journal of Mennonite Studies* (Winnipeg, 1983-)

Juhnke, *Mission* (1979) = James C. Juhnke, *A People of Mission: A History of General Conference Mennonite Overseas Missions* (Newton: Faith and Life, 1979)

Kauffman, ed., *Bible Doctrines* (1914) = Daniel Kauffman, ed., *Bible Doctrines* (Scottdale: MPH, 1914)

Kauffman, ed., *Doctrines of the Bible* (1929) = Daniel Kauffman, ed., *Doctrines of the Bible: A Brief Discussion of the Teachings of God's Word* (Scottdale: MPH, 1929), revised edition of *Bible Doctrines* (1914); reprinted 1949

Kauffman/Harder, *Anabaptists Four C. Later* (1975) = J. Howard Kauffman and Leland Harder, eds., *Anabaptists Four Centuries Later: A Profile of Five Mennonite and Brethren in Christ Denominations* (Scottdale, 1975)

KG = Kirchengeschichte (in journal titles)

Kingdom, Cross, Community (1976) = N.N., "N.N." in *Kingdom, Cross, and Community: Essays in Honor of Guy F. Hershberger*, ed. J. R. Burkholder and Calvin Redekop (Scottdale, 1976)

John A. Lapp, *India* (1972) = John Allen Lapp, *The Mennonite Church in India, 1897-1962*, Studies in Anabaptist and Mennonite History, vol. 14 (Scottdale, 1972)

Loewen, *Confessions* = Howard John Loewen, ed., *One Lord, One Church, One Hope, One God: Mennonite Confessions of Faith*, Text-Reader Series, 2 (Elkhart: Institute of Mennonite Studies, 1985) (note that this was reprinted in 1985 to correct flaws in the first edition; because of the resulting differences in pagination, *ME V* citations will on occasion carry dual pagination, where the first set of page numbers refers to the reprinting and the second set of numbers refers to the original printing)

Luthy, *Amish* (1986) = David Luthy, *The Amish in America: Settlements that Failed, 1840-1960* (Aylmer, Ont.: Pathway Publishers, 1986)

Luthy, *Amish Settlements* (1985) = David Luthy, *Amish Settlements Across America* (Aylmer, Ont.: Pathway, 1985)

P. J. Malagar *MC India* (1981) = Pyarelal Joel Malagar, *The Mennonite Church in India* (Nagpur: National Council of Churches in India, 1981; Hindi version published at Dhamtari: Mennonite Coordinating Committee, 1986)

Marketplace = *Marketplace* (published by Mennonite Economic Development Associates, 1971-)

Marpeck, *Verantwortung* in *Marbeck-Schwenckfeld,* ed. Loserth (1929) = Pilgram Marpeck, *Verantwortung* in *Pilgram Marbecks Antwort auf Kaspar Schwenckfelds Beurteilung der Bundesbezeugung von 1542*, ed. J. Loserth (Vienna: Carl Fromme, 1929)

Marpeck, *Vermanung* in *Gedenkschrift,* ed. C. F. Neff (1925) = Pilgram Marpeck, *Vermanung,* ed. Christian Hege in *Gedenkschrift zum 400-jährigen Jubiläum der Mennoniten oder Tauf-*

gesinnten, ed. C. F. Neff (Ludwigshafen: Konferenz der Süddeutschen Mennoniten, 1925), 185-282

Martyrs Mirror = usually cited by page numbers according to English translation (Elkhart, 1886, reprinted frequently at Scottdale, e.g., 1951, 1964, 1968, 1972, 1975, 1977 with improved illustrations), see *ME III*: 527 for listing of various editions in various languages

MBBS = Mennonite Brethren Biblical Seminary, Fresno, Cal. (as publisher)

MB Herald = *Mennonite Brethren Herald* (1962-)

MBM = Mennonite Board of Missions, Elkhart, Ind. (as publisher)

MB Profile, 1972-1982 in *Direction*, 14, no. 2 (1985), sp. issue = John E. Toews, Abram B. Konrad, Alvin Dueck, *Mennonite Brethren Membership Profile, 1972-1982* in *Direction* (Fresno, MBBS), 14, no. 2 (Fall 1985), special issue

MB Yearbook = Mennonite Brethren General Conference Yearbook (includes General Conference minutes), published triennially, same as *Minutes (MB)*

MC Archives (Goshen) = Archives of the Mennonite Church (MC) (Goshen, Ind.)

MC Census. See Yoder, *MC Census* below.

MC Yearbook (date) = *Mennonite Yearbook and Directory*, ed. James E. Horsch (Scottdale: MPH, published annually until 1986; after that in alternate years; vol. 77 = 1986-87)

MCC = Mennonite Central Committee (as publisher)

MCC Story = Cornelius J. Dyck, ed., with Robert Kreider, John A. Lapp, and others, *The Mennonite Central Committee Story*, 5 vols. (Scottdale, 1980-87)

MCC Story, 1 = *The Mennonite Central Committee Story*, vol. 1: *From the Files of MCC* (Scottdale, 1980)

MCC Story, 2 = *The Mennonite Central Committee Story*, vol. 2: *Responding to Worldwide Need* (Scottdale, 1980)

MCC Story, 3 = *The Mennonite Central Committee Story*, vol. 3: *Witness and Service in North America* (Scottdale, 1980)

MCC Story, 4 = *The Mennonite Central Committee Story*, vol. 4: *Biographies: Something Meaningful for God* (Scottdale, 1981)

MCC Story, 5 = *The Mennonite Central Committee Story*, vol. 5: *Hungry, Thirsty, a Stranger* (Scottdale, 1988)

MCCC = Mennonite Central Committee, Canada (Winnipeg) (as publisher)

MEA 1 = Richard K. MacMaster, *Land, Piety, Peoplehood: The Establishment of Mennonite Communities in America, 1683-1790*, The Mennonite Experience in America, vol. 1 (Scottdale, 1985)

MEA 2 = Theron Schlabach, *Peace, Faith, Nation: Mennonites and Amish in Nineteenth-Century America*, The Mennonite Experience in America, vol. 2 (Scottdale, 1988)

MEA 3 = James C. Juhnke, *Vision, Doctrine, War: Mennonite Identity and Organization in America, 1890-1930* The Mennonite Experience in America, vol. 3 (Scottdale, 1989)

Menn. Bib. = Nelson Springer and A. J. Klassen,

compilers, *Mennonite Bibliography, 1631-1961*, 2 vols. (Scottdale, 1977)

Menn. Geschbl. = *Mennonitische Geschichtsblätter* (1936-), n.F. 1 (1949) = Jahrgang 6

Menn. Historian (Winnipeg) = *Mennonite Historian* (Winnipeg: Mennonite Heritage Center and Centre for Mennonite Brethren Studies)

Menn. Jahrbuch = *Mennonitisches Jahrbuch*

Menn. Life = *Mennonite Life* (North Newton: Bethel College, 1946-)

Menn. Rep = *Mennonite Reporter* (Waterloo, 1971-; continuation of *The Canadian Mennonite* [Altona, Man., 1953-])

Menn. Rund. = *Mennonitische Rundschau* (1880-)

Menno, Writings = *The Complete Writings of Menno Simons, c. 1496-1561*, trans. Leonard Verduin, ed. J. C. Wenger (Scottdale, 1956)

Menno, Writings (1870) = Menno, *Complete Writings*, Engl. trans. (Elkhart: John Funk, 1870)

Mennonite = *The Mennonite* (GCM; Newton and Winnipeg, 1885-)

MHB = *Mennonite Historical Bulletin* (Goshen, Ind.: Historical Committee [MC], (MC Archives)

MHL (Goshen) = Mennonite Historical Library (Goshen, Ind.)

Minutes (BIC) (1871-1904) = *Minutes of General Conferences of Brethren in Christ (River Brethren) from 1871-1904 in Condensed Form*, comp. H. K. Kreider, Eli M. Engle, S. R. Smith (Harrisburg, Pa., 1904)

Minutes (BIC) (1986) = *Minutes of the 109th [Seventh Biennial] General Conference, Brethren in Christ Church, July 5 - July 10, 1986* (Nappanee, Evangel Press), with minutes of earlier General Conference cited with corresponding changes in dates

Minutes (MB) = *Yearbook* of the Mennonite Brethren General Conference (same as *MB Yearbook*)

Minutes (EMB) = Annual Report of the Evangelical Mennonite Brethren Conference, later renamed Fellowship of Evangelical Bible Churches

Minutes (EMCh) = Annual Report and Directory of the Evangelical Mennonite Church (Fort Wayne, Ind.: Evangelical Mennonite Church)

Minutes (GCM) = Minutes of the general conferences of the General Conference Mennonite Church

Miss. Focus = *Mission Focus* (Elkhart, Ind.: MBM, 1972-)

Miss. Mess. (EMBMC) = *Missionary Messenger* (EMBMC, 1924-)

Miss. News and Notes = publication of women's missionary auxiliary (GCM)

ML = *Mennonitisches Lexikon*, vol. 1 to vol. 3, fasc. 6, ed. Christian Hege and Christian Neff (Frankfurt a. M. and Weierhof, 1913-42); vol. 3, fasc. 7-12, ed. Ernst Crous and Harold S. Bender (1958); vol. 4, ed. Ernst Crous and Gerhard Hein (Karlsruhe: Heinrich Schneider, 1967)

MLA (North Newton) = Mennonite Library and Archives, Bethel College (North Newton, Ks.)

MM = *Mennonite Mirror* (Winnipeg; Oct. 1971-)

MP = Mennonite Press, North Newton, Ks.

MPH = Mennonite Publishing House, Scottdale, Pa.

MPO = Mennonite Publications Office, Newton, Ks.

MQR = *Mennonite Quarterly Review* (Goshen; 1927-)

MRJ = *Mennonite Research Journal* (1960-)

MS = manuscript (plural: MSS)

MWH (1978) = *Mennonite World Handbook*, ed. Paul N. Kraybill (Lombard, Ill.: Mennonite World Conference, 1978)

MWH (1984) = supplement to the *Mennonite World Handbook* (Strassbourg, France, and Lombard, Ill.: Mennonite World Conference, 1984)

MWR = *Mennonite Weekly Review* (Newton, 1923-)

NCE = *The New Catholic Encyclopedia* (New York: McGraw-Hill, 1967)

n.d. = no date of publication indicated

n.F. = neue Folge (new series—German)

n.p. = no place of publication indicated; no publisher indicated

n.r. = nieuwe reeks (new series—Dutch)

n.s. = new series (periodicals)

S. F. Pannabecker, *Open Doors* (1975) = Samuel Floyd Pannabecker, *Open Doors: History of the General Conference Mennonite Church* (Newton, 1975)

Plough = *The Plough* (Rifton, N.Y.: Plough Publishing, 1983-); also appeared earlier in England

PMH = *Pennsylvania Mennonite Heritage* (Lancaster Mennonite Historical Society, 1978-)

Recovery = Guy F. Hershberger, ed., *The Recovery of the Anabaptist Vision* (Scottdale, 1959)

Reimer, *Quilt* (1983) = Margaret Loewen Reimer, ed., *One Quilt, Many Pieces* (Waterloo, Ont.: Mennonite Publishing Service, 1983)

repr. = reprinted or reprint edition

Rich, *Mennonite Women* (1983) = Elaine Sommers Rich, *Mennonite Women: A Story of God's Faithfulness, 1683-1983* (Scottdale, 1983)

SAW = George H. Williams and Angel M. Mergal, eds., *Spiritual and Anabaptist Writers: Documents Illustrative of the Radical Reformation*, Library of Christian Classics (Philadelphia: Westminster Press, 1957)

J. W. Shank, *Southern Cross* (1943) = Josephus Ward Shank, *The Gospel Under the Southern Cross: A History of the Argentine Mennonite Mission of South America Celebrating Its 25th Anniversary, 1917-1942* (Scottdale: MPH, 1943)

J. M. Stayer, *Sword* (1972, 1976) = James M. Stayer, *Anabaptists and the Sword* (Lawrence, Ks.: Coronado Press, 1972; revised ed. 1976)

TA Baden/Pfalz = M. Krebs, ed., *Quellen zur Geschichte der Täufer*, vol. 4: *Baden und Pfalz*, Quellen und Forschungen zur Reformationsgeschichte, 22 (Gütersloh, 1951)

TA Bayern, I: *Brandenberg* = K. Schornbaum, ed., *Quellen zur Geschichte der Täufer*, vol. 2: *Markgraftum Brandenburg (Bayern I)*, Quellen und Forschungen zur Reformationsgeschichte, 16 (Leipzig, 1934)

TA Bayern, II = K. Schornbaum, ed., *Quellen zur Geschichte der Täufer*, vol. 5: *Bayern II*, Quellen und Forschungen zur Reformationsgeschichte, 23 (Gütersloh, 1951)

TA Elsaß I = M. Krebs and H. G. Rott, eds., *Quellen zur Geschichte der Täufer*, vol. 7: *Elsaß*, vol. 1: *Stadt Straßburg, 1522-32*, Quellen und Forschungen zur Reformationsgeschichte, 26 (Gütersloh, 1959)

TA Elsaß II = M. Krebs and H. G. Rott, eds., *Quellen zur Geschichte der Täufer*, vol. 8: *Elsaß*, vol. 2: *Stadt Straßburg, 1533-35*, Quellen und Forschungen zur Reformationsgeschichte, 27 (Gütersloh, 1960)

TA Elsaß III - Marc Lienhard, Stephen F. Nelson, and Hans Georg Rott, *Elsaß III. Teil: Stadt Straßburg, 1536-1542* (Gütersloh: G. Mohn, 1986)

TA Hessen = G. Franz, ed., *Urkundliche Quellen zur hessischen Reformationsgeschichte*, 4. Band: *Wiedertäuferakten 1527-1626* (Marburg, 1951)

TA Oberdtsch. I = Lydia Müller, ed., *Quellen zur Geschichte der Täufer*, vol. 3: *Glaubenszeugnisse oberdeutscher Taufgesinnter*, vol. 1, Quellen und Forschungen zur Reformationsgeschichte, 20 (Leipzig, 1938)

TA Oberdtsch. II = Robert Friedmann, ed., *Quellen zur Geschichte der Täufer*, vol. 12: *Glaubenszeugnisse oberdeutscher Taufgesinnter*, vol. 2, Quellen und Forschungen zur Reformationsgeschichte, 34 (Gütersloh, 1967)

TA Österreich I = Grete Mecenseffy, ed., *Quellen zur Geschichte der Täufer*, vol. 11: *Österreich*, vol. 1, Quellen und Forschungen zur Reformationsgeschichte, 31 (Gütersloh, 1964)

TA Österreich II = Grete Mecenseffy, ed., *Quellen zur Geschichte der Täufer*, vol. 13: *Österreich*, vol. 2 (1973)

TA Österreich III = Grete Mecenseffy, ed., *Quellen zur Geschichte der Täufer*, vol. 14: *Österreich*, vol. 3 (1983)

TA Schweiz I: (Zürich) = L. von Muralt, W. Schmidt, eds., *Quellen zur Geschichte der Täufer in der Schweiz*, vol. 1 (Zürich: S. Hirzel, 1952)

TA Schweiz II (Ostschweiz) = Heinold Fast, ed., *Quellen zur Geschichte der Täufer in der Schweiz*, vol. 2: *Ostschweiz* (1974)

TA Schweiz III (Bern, Aargau) = Martin Haas, ed., *Quellen zur Geschichte der Täufer in der Schweiz*, vol. 3: *Bern, Aargau* (1974)

TA Württemberg = G. Bossert, Sr., and G. Bossert, Jr., eds., *Quellen zur Geschichte der Täufer*, vol. 1: *Herzogtum Württemberg*, Quellen und Forschungen zur Reformationsgeschichte, 13 (Leipzig, 1930)

John A. Toews, *History MB* (1975) = John A. Toews, *History of the Mennonite Brethren Church*, ed. A. J. Klassen (Fresno, Cal.: Mennonite Brethren Board of Literature and Education, 1975)

trans. = translated, translator, translation

Umstrittenes Täufertum (1975) = Hans-Jürgen Goertz, ed., *Umstrittenes Täufertum, 1525-1975* (Göttingen: Vandenhoeck und Ruprecht, 1975; 2nd ed., 1977)

Ruth Unrau, *Encircled* (1986) = Ruth Unrau, *Encircled: Stories of Mennonite Women* (Newton, 1986)

Who's Who Mennonites (1943) = A. Warkentin and Melvin Gingerich, compilers, *Who's Who Among the Mennonites* (North Newton: Bethel College, 1943)

K. F. Wiebe, ed., *Women Among the Brethren* (1979) = Katie Funk Wiebe, ed., *Women Among the Brethren* (Hillsboro, Ks.: General Conference of MB Churches, 1979)

With = *With* (Scottdale, 1968-)

Wittlinger, *Piety and Obedience* (1978) = Carlton O. Wittlinger, *Quest for Piety and Obedience: The Story of the Brethren in Christ* (Nappanee: Evangel Press, 1978)

WMSC Voice = *Women's Missionary and Service Commission Voice* (formerly *Missionary Sewing Circle Letter*, 1930-)

YCC = *Youth's Christian Companion* (MC; Scottdale, 1920-1956)

Yoder, *MC Census* (1985) = Michael L. Yoder, "Findings from the 1982 Mennonite Census," *MQR*, 59 (1985), 307-49

Z. = Zeitschrift (in journal titles)

WRITERS' INITIALS

AB Atlee Beechy, Goshen, Indiana
ABH Amos B. Hoover, Denver, Pennsylvania
ABos Abram Boschmann, Filadelfia, Paraguay
ACS† Arnold C. Schultz, Tucson, Arizona
AD Anna Dyck, Sadowara Cho, Miyazaki Ken, Japan
ADue Alvin Dueck, Fresno, California
AE Adolf Ens, Winnipeg, Manitoba
AEM Anna Eby Millar, Kitchener, Ontario
AES Alta E. Schrock, Grantsville, Maryland
AF Abram Funk, Volendam Colony, Paraguay
AGK Abram G. Konrad, Edmonton, Alberta
AGW A. Grace Wenger, Lititz, Pennsylvania
AH Abner Hershberger, Goshen, Indiana
AHcht Alfred Hecht, Waterloo, Ontario
AHE Albert H. Epp, Henderson, Nebraska
AJD Abe J. Dueck, Winnipeg, Manitoba
AJM A. J. Metzler, Goshen, Indiana
AJR A. James Reimer, Waterloo, Ontario
AK Alan Kreider, London, England
AKH Anne K. Hershberger, Goshen, Indiana
AM Albert Märki, Zürich, Switzerland
AMC Arthur M. Climenhaga, Mechanicsburg, Pennsylvania
AN Asao *Nishimura*, Nagato Shi, Yamaguchi Ken, Japan
ANK Albert N. Keim, Harrisonburg, Virginia
AP Arnold Prieb, Fresno, California
AR Al Reimer, Winnipeg, Manitoba
ARR Alice Ruth Ramseyer, Hiroshima Shi, Japan
ASchn Adolf Schnebele, Karlsruhe, West Germany
AW Anneke Welcker, Amsterdam, The Netherlands
AWB Ann Weber Becker, Kitchener, Ontario
AWL Alice Lapp, Akron, Pennsylvania
AY Amzie Yoder, Goshen, Indiana
BCS Barbara Claassen Smucker, Waterloo, Ontario
BF Bert Friesen, Winnipeg, Manitoba
BFH Bertha Fast Harder, N. Newton, Kansas
BHH Beatrice Hershey Hallman, Goshen, Indiana
BKR Barbara K. Reber, Goshen, Indiana
BN Benjamin Noll, Spring Grove, Pennsylvania
BO Bernhard Ott, Bienenberg/Liestal, Switzerland
BR Barbara Risser, Greencastle, Pennsylvania
BS Brenda Stauffer, Akron, Pennsylvania
BSH Beulah Stauffer Hostetler, Elizabethtown, Pennsylvania
BW Bernie Wiebe, Winnipeg, Manitoba
CA Clayton Auernheimer, Reedley, California
CAP Calvin A. Pater, Toronto, Ontario
CAS C. Arnold Snyder, Waterloo, Ontario
CBL Clair B. Lehman, Chambersburg, Pennsylvania
CCB Carl C. Beck, Tokyo, Japan
CCW Carolyn C. Wenger, Lancaster, Pennsylvania
CDH C. Douglas Hostetter, Nyack, New York

CFB C. F. Brüsewitz, Bunnik, The Netherlands
CGB Conrad G. Brunk, Waterloo, Ontario
CH Clarence Hiebert, Hillsboro, Kansas
CJD Cornelius J. Dyck, Elkhart, Indiana
CJM Cornelius J. Martens, Kleefeld, Manitoba
CLD C. Lorne Dick, Medicine Hat, Alberta
CNH C. Nelson Hostetter, Akron, Pennsylvania
CRW Christine R. Wiebe, Chicago, Illinois
CRY Carl R. Yusavitz, Nairobi, Kenya
CTK Catherine Thiessen Klassen, Winnipeg, Manitoba
CWR Calvin W. Redekop, Waterloo, Ontario
DAH David A. Haury, N. Newton, Kansas
DAP-B Dean A. Preheim-Bartel, Elkhart, Indiana
DB Donald Brenneman, Greensboro, North Carolina
DBK Donald B. Kraybill, Elizabethtown, Pennsylvania
DBru Dave Brubaker, Akron, Pennsylvania
DByl Dan Byler, West Liberty, Ohio
DCB Doyle C. Book, Kitakyushu Shi, Fukuoka Ken, Japan
DD David Diller, San Jose, Costa Rica
DDK Donald D. Kaufman, N. Newton, Kansas
DDM Dennis D. Martin, Elkhart, Indiana
DE David Ewert, Winnipeg, Manitoba
DEK Daniel E. Kauffman, Goshen, Indiana
DES Donovan E. Smucker, Waterloo, Ontario
DF Delton Franz, Washington, D.C.
DFD D. F. Durnbaugh, Huntington, Pennsylvania
DFDueck D. F. Dueck, Spanish Lookout Colony, Belize
DFH Doreen F. Harms, Akron, Pennsylvania
DFl David Fluery, Waterloo, Ontario
DGL Diether Götz Lichdi, Heilbronn, West Germany
DGr Delbert Gratz, Bluffton, Ohio
DH Daniel Hertzler, Scottdale, Pennsylvania
DHa David L. Habegger, Urbana, Illinois
DHS Dale H. Schumm, Elkhart, Indiana
DHSh Douglas H. Shantz, Langley, British Columbia
DJ David Janzen, Niagara on the Lake, Ontario
DJRS David J. Rempel Smucker, Lancaster, Pennsylvania
DK Dan Kauffman, Hutchinson, Kansas
DKF David K. Friesen, Orange Walk Town, Belize
DKla Dietrich Klassen, Neuland Colony, Chaco, Paraguay
DL Daniel Liechty, Philadelphia, Pennsylvania
DLR Dennis L. Rempel, Upland California
DLW Daniel L. Wenger, Lancaster, Pennsylvania
DM/JM Daniel and Joyce Maxwell, Kampala, Uganda
DMM Dorothy M. Martin, Mechanicsburg, Pennsylvania
DoKla Doreen Klassen, Steinbach, Manitoba
DPH Dennis P. Hollinger, Elkhart, Indiana

DPM David P.McBeth, Grantham, Pennsylvania
DR-H Duane Ruth-Heffelbower, Fresno, California
DRK Dennis R. Kuhns, Gettysburg, Pennsylvania
DRM D. Richard Martin, Hagerstown, Maryland
DRS Dale R. Schrag, N. Newton, Kansas
DRY Delmar R. Yoder, Atlanta, Georgia
DRZ Donald R. Zook, Mt. Joy, Pennsylvania
DS Daniel S. Schipani, Elkhart, Indiana
DSchr Dan Schrock, Hayward, Wisconsin
DSchroed David Schroeder, Winnipeg, Manitoba
DSh David Shelly, Newton, Kansas
DSR David S. Russell, Bristol, England
DWA David W. Augsburger, Goshen, Indiana
DWM David W. Mann, Phoenix, Arizona
DWP David W. Powell, Goshen, Indiana
DWS David W. Shenk, Salunga, Pennsylvania
DYN Dorothy Yoder Nyce, Goshen, Indiana
DZU Diane Zimmerman Umble, Lancaster, Pennsylvania
EAM Elmer A. Martens, Pasadena, California
EB Ervin Beck, Goshen, Indiana
EBM Eve B. MacMaster, Bluffton, Ohio
EBo Ed Boldt, Kitchener, Ontario,
EDZ† Ellrose D. Zook, Goshen, Indiana
EE-T Esther Epp-Tiessen, Kitchener, Ontario
EEA Ethel Ewert Abrahams, Hillsboro, Kansas
EG Ewald Goetz, Filadelfia, Fernheim Colony, Paraguay
EGr Erma Grove, Goshen, Indiana
EH Emery Hochstetler, Oxford, Iowa
EITB E. I. T. Brussee-van der Zee, Voorburg, The Netherlands
EJ Esther Jost, Reedley, California
EKE Eugene K. Engle, Manheim, Pennsylvania
EL Elfriede Lichdi, Heilbronn, West Germany
EM Earl Martin, Akron, Pennsylvania
EME Eva M. Eberly, Harrisonburg, Virginia
EMS E. Morris Sider, Grantham, Pennsylvania
EmSR Emma Sommers Richards, Lombard, Illinois
EN Elmer Neufeld, Bluffton, Ohio
ENe Ernest Neufeld, Fargo, North Dakota
EP Esther Patkau, Saskatoon, Saskatchewan
ERK Edna Ramseyer Kaufman, Hesston, Kansas
ES Edgar Stoesz, Akron, Pennsylvania
ESB E. Stanley Bohn, Newton, Kansas
ESR Elaine Sommers Rich, Raleigh, N.C.
ESto Eldon Stoltzfus, Port-au-Prince, Haiti
EStr Ernest Strubhar, Farmington, New Mexico
ESY Elmer S. Yoder, Hartville, Ohio
EW Erland Waltner, Elkhart, Indiana
EWB Eby W. Burkholder, Ephrata, Pennsylvania
EWN E. Wayne Nafziger, Manhattan, Kansas
FAS† Felonito A. Sacapano, Laguna, Philippines
FASchr Freeman A. Schrock, Goshen, Indiana
FB Foppe Brouwer, New South Wales, Australia
FE Franz Esau, Freiburg, West Germany
FG Francisco Galmes, Santa Rosa, La Pampa, Argentina
FK Frank Kroeker, Manitoba, Canada
FM Frank Martens, Clearbrook, British Columbia
GB George Brenneman, Anchorage, Alaska
GCS Gerald C. Studer, Hatfield, Pennsylvania
GCW Gayle C. Wiebe, Elkhart, Indiana
GD George Dyck, Newton, Kansas
GE Gerhard Ens, Winnipeg, Manitoba
GeoRBrII George R. Brunk II, Harrisonburg, Virginia

GeoRBrIII George R. Brunk III, Harrisonburg, Virginia
GFH† Guy F. Hershberger, Goshen, Indiana
GG Gladys Goering, Moundridge, Kansas
GGK Gayle Gerber Koontz, Elkhart, Indiana
GH Gary Harder, Edmonton, Alberta
GHil Gerhard Hildebrandt, Göttingen, West Germany
GJ Galen Johns, New Paris, Indiana
GKE George K. Epp, Winnipeg, Manitoba
GKla Glen Klassen, Winnipeg, Manitoba
GKW Gary K. Waite, Fredericton, New Brunswick
GM Gerald Mumaw, Elkhart, Indiana
GN Gloria Nussbaum, Akron, Pennsylvania
GNie Gundolf Niebuhr, Filadelfia, Paraguay
GR Gerhard Ratzlaff, Filadelfia, Paraguay
GRB Gerald R. Brunk, Harrisonburg, Virginia
GS Griselda Shelly, Newton, Kansas
GT Grace Tiessen, Kalona, Iowa
GW George Wiebe, Winnipeg, Manitoba
GWö Gerhard Wölk, Frankenthal, West Germany
HA Helen Alderfer, Goshen, Indiana
HaFr Harry Friesen, Okeda Shi, Osaka, Japan
HaL Harry Loewen, Winnipeg, Manitoba
HAP Harold A. Penner, Akron, Pennsylvania
HB Hubert Brown, Inglewood, California
HBon Herman Bontrager, Akron, Pennsylvania
HBr Heinz Braun, Neuland Colony, Paraguay
HDueck Henry Dueck, Winnipeg, Manitoba
HE Harold Ens, Hillsboro, Kansas
HEB Harold E. Bauman, Goshen, Indiana
HeFu Helmut Funck, Eichstöck-Vierkirchen, West Germany
HEid Helen Eidse, Steinbach, Manitoba
HenEns Henrique Ens, Curitiba, Paraná State, Brazil
HEns Helen Ens, Cuauhtemoc, Chihuahua, Mexico
HES Herbert E. Schultz, Cambridge, Ontario
HFa Henry Fast, Steinbach, Manitoba
HFas Heinold Fast, Emden, West Germany
HFr Herb Friesen, Peshawar, Pakistan
HFT Hildi Froese Tiessen, Waterloo, Ontario
HG Horst Gerlach, Weierhof, Post Bolanden, West Germany
HGK Horst Gunther Kliewer, Witmarsum Colony, Brazil
HGra Harold Graber, Buhler, Kansas
HGVV Héctor G. Valencia V., Bogota, Colombia
HH Henry Hostetler, Red Lake, Ontario
HHa Helmut Harder, Winnipeg, Manitoba
HHau Helmut Haury, Weierhof, West Germany
HHue Harry Huebner, Winnipeg, Manitoba
HI Hiroshi *Isobe*, Miyakonojo Shi, Miyazaki Ken, Japan
HJ Harold Jantz, Winnipeg, Manitoba
HJB Herbert J. Brandt, Kelowna, British Columbia
HJeck Hanspeter Jecker, Liestal, Switzerland
HJG Henry J. Gerbrandt, Winnipeg, Manitoba
HJL Howard John Loewen, Fresno, California
HJS Harold J. Schmidt, Baden, Ontario
HJW Hans Joachim Wienss, Enkenbach-Alsenborn, West Germany
HK Hans Kasdorf, Fresno, California
HKaw Hiroshi *Kawakatsu*, Kobe Shi, Hyogo Ken, Japan
HKL Hope Kauffman Lind, Eugene, Oregon
HKla Henry Klassen, Steinbach, Manitoba
HKor Helen Kornelsen, Watrous, Saskatchewan

HlnaEns Helena Ens, Curitiba, Paraná State, Brazil
HLS H. Leonard Sawatzky, Winnipeg, Manitoba
HM Harold Miller, Irwin, Ohio
HMa Helen Martens, Waterloo, Ontario
HMei Hans Meier, Hutterian Society of Brothers, Norfolk, Connecticut
HMF Herta Marie Funk, Suzhou, Jiangsu Province, People's Republic of China
HMo Hiroshi *Mori,* Asahigawa Shi, Hokkaido, Japan
HN Horst Neufeld, Espelkamp, West Germany
HP Henry Poettcker, Elkhart, Indiana
HPaet Henry Paetkau, St. Catharines, Ontario
HPF Heinrich P. Friesen, San Ignacio, Belize
HR Harold Ratzlaff, Newton, Kansas
HRC† H. Raymond Charles, Lancaster, Pennsylvania
HRe Henry Rempel, Winnipeg, Manitoba
HRP Hubert R. Pellman, Harrisonburg, Virginia
HRS Harvey R. Sider, Fort Erie, Ontario
HRT Helen R. Tieszen, Seoul, Republic of Korea
HT Hiroshi *Takahashi,* Sapporo Shi, Hokkaido, Japan
HU Harlan Unrau, Lakewood, Colorado
HvN Hans von Niessen, Neuwied, West Germany
HW Hans Wiens, Asunción, Paraguay
HWH Harry W. Hertzler, Salisbury, Maryland
HWö Heinrich Wölk, Frankenthal, West Germany
HY Hiroshi *Yanada,* Miyazaki Shi, Miyazaki Ken, Japan
HZ Hugo Zorrilla, Madrid Spain
IDV Irvin D. Voth, Newton, Kansas
IET Ivan E. Troyer, Beemer, Nebraska
IHie Isbrand Hiebert, Steinbach, Manitoba
IJM Ivan J. Miller, Grantsville, Maryland
ILF Irvin L. Friesen, Reedley, California
IRH Isaac R. Horst, Mt. Forest, Ontario
IZ-G Isaac Zürcher-Geiser, Bern, Switzerland
J-RT Jean-Raymond Théorèt, Ville St. Lalurent, Quebec
JAE John A. Esau, Newton, Kansas
JAF John A. Friesen, Goshen, Indiana
JAL John A. Lapp, Akron, Pennsylvania
JAP-V James Adrián Prieto-Valladares, Hamburg, West Germany
JAS James A. Steiner, Orrville, Ohio
JB Joseph Bontrager, Musoma, Tanzania
JBau Jacques Baumann, Liestal, Switzerland
JBe Johannes Bergmann, Montivideo, Uruguay
JBL John B. Loewen, Belize City, Belize
JCJ James C. Juhnke, N. Newton, Kansas
JCL James C. Liu, Hengyang, Hunan Province, People's Republic of China
JCM Joyce Clemmer Munro, Harleysville, Pennsylvania
JCW John C. Wenger, Goshen, Indiana
JD John Dyck, Winnipeg, Manitoba
JDH J. Daniel Hess, Goshen, Indiana
JDR John D. Rempel, Waterloo, Ontario
JDRi John D. Risser, Dayton, Virginia
JDW J. Denny Weaver, Bluffton, Ohio
JEB James E. Bertsche, Elkhart, Indiana
JeB Jewell Brenneman, Anchorage, Alaska
JEH James E. Horsch, Scottdale, Pennsylvania
JEM James E. Metzler, Goshen, Indiana
JF John Friesen, Winnipeg, Manitoba
JFF Justine F. Foxall, Akron, Pennsylvnia
JG José Gallardo, Quintanadueñas (Burgos), Spain
JGH Justus G. Holsinger, Hesston, Kansas

JGies Jacob Giesbrecht, Loma Plata, Paraguay
JGing James Gingerich, Moundridge, Kansas
JGray John Graybill, Nagoya Shi, Aichi Ken, Japan
JH Jack Heppner, Steinbach, Manitoba
JHF J. Herbert Fretz, Goshen, Indiana
JHK J. Howard Kauffman, Goshen, Indiana
JHo John Hofer, James Valley Colony, Elie, Manitoba
JHR John H. Redekop, Waterloo, Ontario
JHU Jenifer Hiett Umble, Parkesburg, Pennsylvania
JHW James H. Waltner, Goshen, Indiana
JHY John Howard Yoder, Elkhart, Indiana
JIS John I. Smucker, Flushing, New York
JJB John J. Bergen, Edmonton, Alberta
JJE Jacob J. Enz, Elkhart, Indiana
JK Jess Kauffman, Brooksville, Florida
JKH John K. Hershberger, Goshen, Indiana
JKS John K. Stoner, Akron, Pennsylvania
JL Julia Leatherman, Goshen, Indiana
JLB J. Lawrence Burkholder, Goshen, Indiana
JLo Joy Lovett, Villa Park, Illinois
JLP J. Lorne Peachey, Scottdale, Pennsylvania
JMB John M. Bender, Elkhart, Indiana
JMBren Janet M. Breneman, Lancaster, Pennsylvania
JMD John M. Drescher, Harrisonburg, Virginia
JMH Joseph M. Haines, Pillipsburg, New Jersey
JMJ John M. Janzen, N. Newton, Kansas
JMK John M. Klassen, Langley, British Columbia
JMO José M. Ortiz, Goshen, Indiana
JMS James M. Stayer, Kingston, Ontario
JMW J. M. Welcker, Amsterdam, The Netherlands
JN Jesse Neuenschwander, Lititz, Pennsylvania
JNK John N. Klassen, Bielefeld, West Germany
JNKr J. Nelson Kraybill, Richmond, Virginia
JOLe James O. Lehman, Harrisonburg, Virginia
JoTh John Thiessen, Altona, Manitoba
JP Jake Peters, Winnipeg, Manitoba
JPl Johann Plett, Bechterdissen, West Germany
JPM J. Paul Martin, Annville, Pennsylvania
JR Johannes Reimer, Bielefeld, West Germany
JRB John R. Burkholder, Goshen, Indiana
JRC James R. Coggins, Winnipeg, Manitoba
JRK James R. Krabill, Birmingham, England
JRKla James R. Klassen, Broken Arrow, Oklahoma
JRS John R. Schmidt, Goessel, Kansas
JRW James R. Wenger, Fresno, California
JS James Sauder, Santo Domingo, Dominican Republic
JShow Jewel Showalter, Irwin, Ohio
JSN J. Samuel Nisley, Belize City, Belize
JSO John S. Oyer, Goshen, Indiana
JT Jacob Tilitzky, Abbotsford, British Columbia
JTh Jack Thiessen, Winnipeg, Manitoba
JU James Urry, Wellington, New Zealand
JVH John V. Hinde, Pleasant View Bruderhof, Ulster Park, New York
JWF J. Winfield Fretz, N. Newton, Kansas
JWH J. Wilmer Heisey, Akron, Pennsylvania
JWS James W. Shenk, Akron, Pennsylvania
JY Janet Yoder, Goshen, Indiana
JZH Judy Zimmerman Herr, Gaborone, Botswana
K-DW Klaus-Dieter Wahl, Kaiserslautern, West Germany
KB Kornelius Boschmann, Asunción, Paraguay
KE-R Kevin Enns-Rempel, Fresno, California
KFW Katie Funk Wiebe, Hillsboro, Kansas
KK Kazuko *Kanaya,* Sapporo Shi, Hokkaido

KKB Kenton K. Brubaker, Harrisonburg, Virginia
KKlaa Kurt Klaassen, Espelkamp, West Germany
KLJ† Kathryn L. Jantzen, Alhambra, California
KLS Keith L. Sprunger, North Newton, Kansas
KMN Kenneth M. Nissley, Mt. Joy, Pa.
KR Ken Reddig, Winnipeg, Manitoba
KT Kazunari *Tamura*, Sapporo Shi, Hokkaido, Japan
LB Lois Barrett, Wichita, Kansas
LBe Lorna L. Bergey, New Hamburg, Ontario
LBo Lloyd Bowman, Grantham, Pennsylvania
LD Leonard Doell, Warman, Saskatchewan
LDe Lois Deckert, N. Newton, Kansas
LDet Lowell Detweiler, Akron, Pennsylvania
LDH Leland D. Harder, N. Newton, Kansas
LDr Leo Driedger, Winnipeg, Manitoba
LDS Leroy D. Saner, Freeman, South Dakota
LDW Lawrence D. Warkentin, Traunstein, West Germany
LF Lauren Friesen, Goshen, Indiana
LG Leonard Gross, Goshen, Indiana
LHab Loris Habegger, N. Newton, Kansas
LHG Lawrence H. Greaser, Goshen, Indiana
LK Lawrence Klippenstein, Winnipeg, Manitoba
LKei Levi Keidel, Clearbrook, British Columbia
LLau Leo Laurense, Zutphen, The Netherlands
LLK Luke L. Keefer, Jr., Ashland, Ohio
LM Levi Miller, Scottdale, Pennsylvania
LMW Linden M. Wenger, Harrisonburg, Virginia
LMY Lawrence M. Yoder, Harrisonburg, Virginia
LN Lloyd Nightingale, Plains, Kansas
LO Lewis Overholt, Berlin, West Germany
LP Laban Peachey, Goshen, Indiana
LS Laura Schumm, Elkhart, Indiana
LSM Luke S. Martin, Allentown, Pennsylvania
MAS M. A. Solomon, Mahbubnagar, Andhra Pradesh, India
MB Myrna Burkholder, Goshen, Indiana
MD Martin Durksen, Winnipeg, Manitoba
MDS Myron D. Schrag, Minneapolis, Minnesota
MDyck Margaret Dyck, Winkler, Manitoba
ME Menno Ediger, Santa Cruz, Bolivia
MEB Mary E. Bauman, Berne, Indiana
MEM Marlin E. Miller, Elkhart, Indiana
MG Millard Garrett, Salunga, Pennsylvania
MGa Mike Garde, Dublin, Republic of Ireland
MGP Marilyn G. Peters, Fresno, California
MGS Marcus G. Smucker, Elkhart, Indiana
MH Marian Hostetler, Mogadishu, Somalia
MHei Menno Heinrichs, East Syracuse, New York
MHein Marvin Hein, Fresno, California
MHS Martin H. Schrag, Grantham, Pennsylvania
MHSh Michael H. Shank, Madison, Wisconsin
MJ Marlin Jeschke, Goshen, Indiana
MJH Mary Jane Hoober, Elkhart, Indiana
MJLH Mary Jane Lederach Hershey, Harleysville, Pennsylvania
MJo Martin Johnson, Woodcrest Bruderhof, Rifton, New York
MK Melva Kauffman, Hesston, Kansas
MKM Marilyn Kauffman Miller, Boulder, Colorado
MKP Marion Keeney Preheim, Newton, Kansas
MKr Marlene Kropf, Elkhart, Indiana
ML Millard Lind, Goshen, Indiana
MLY Michael L. Yoder, Orange City, Iowa
MMH Mahlon M. Hess, Lititz, Pennsylvania
MMMat M. M. Mattijssen-Berkman, Doorwert, The

Netherlands
MO Michio *Ohno*, Toke Shi, Chiba Ken, Japan
MOk Masaharu *Okano*, Hagi Shi, Yamaguchi Ken, Japan
MR Milka Rindzinski, Montevideo, Uruguay
MS Mikio *Shimizu*, Tokyo, Japan
MSA Myron S. Augsburger, Washington, D.C.
MSe Manuel Sepulveda, Santo Domingo, Dominican Republic
MSh Maynard Shelly, Newton, Kansas
MTS Muriel T. Stackley, Newton, Kansas
MW Menno Wiebe, Winnipeg, Manitoba
MWe Malcolm Wenger, Newton, Kansas
MWei Mark Weidner, Bluffton, Ohio
MWF Martin W. Friesen, Menno Colony, Paraguay
MWL Martin W. Lehman, Sarasota, Florida
MWS Maynard W. Shetler, Scottdale, Pennsylvania
NEL Naomi E. Lehman, Berne, Indiana
NG Noah Good, Lancaster, Pennsylvania
NGS N. Gerald Shenk, Zagreb, Yugoslavia
NH Nathan Hege, Salunga, Pennsylvania
NJK Nancy J. Kreider, Grantham, Pennsylvania
NJW Norma Jean Weldy, Goshen, Indiana
NLP Nancy-Lou Patterson, Waterloo, Ontario
NNK Nancy N. Kreider, Mechanicsburg, Pennsylvania
NPS Nelson P. Springer, Goshen, Indiana
NRH Nancy R. Heisey, Akron, Pennsylvania
OD Otto Driedger, Regina, Saskatchewan
OEH Otis E. Hochstetler, Palmeira, Paraná State, Brazil
OG Orland Gingerich, Kitchener, Ontario
OHA Owen H. Alderfer, W. Milton, Ohio
OHG Oswald H. Goering, N. Newton, Kansas
OJG Orlando J. Goering, Vermillion, South Dakota
OJW O. J. Wall, Frazer, Montana
OS Orlando Schmidt, Elkhart, Indiana
OW Oskar Wedel, Hannover/Nenndorf, West Germany
OY Orville Yoder, Goshen, Indiana
PCE Peter C. Erb, Waterloo, Ontario
PDW Paul D. Wiebe, St. Paul, Minnesota
PDZ Peter D. Zacharias, Gretna, Manitoba
PFK Peter F. Kornelsen, Orange Walk, Belize
PGH Paul G. Hiebert, Pasadena, California
PHM Pat Hostetter Martin, Akron, Pennsylvania
PJD Peter J. Dyck, Akron, Pennsylvania
PJFo Peter J. Foth, Hamburg, West Germany
PJK Peter J. Klassen, Fresno, California
PJM Pyarelal J. Malagar, Dhamtari, Madhya Pradesh, India
PK Peter Kehler, Sumas, Virginia
PLG Paul L. Goering, Goshen, Indiana
PLK Paul L. Kratz, Harrisonburg, Virginia
PM Paul Myers, Akron, Pennsylvania
PMH Peter M. Hamm, Winnipeg, Manitoba
PML Paul M. Lederach, Franconia, Pennsylvania
PMM Paul M. Miller, Lititz, Pennsylvania
PMS Paul M. Schrock, Scottdale, Pennsylvania
PMZ Paul M. Zehr, Lancaster, Pennsylvania
PNK Paul N. Kraybill, Carol Stream, Illinois
PP,Jr. Peter Pauls, Jr., Palmeira, Witmarsum Colony, Brazil
PPe Peter Penner, Sackville, New Brunswick
PPea Paul Peachey, Harpers Ferry, W. Virginia
PPen Peter Penner, Winnipeg, Manitoba
PPK Peter P. Klassen, Filadelfia, Chaco, Paraguay

PS-F Peter Sprunger-Froese, Colorado Springs, Colorado
PS-K Priscilla Stuckey-Kauffman, Oakland, California
PSD Premnath S. Dick, Millersville, Pennsylania
PT Paul Toews, Fresno, California
PV Paul Voegtlin, Edson, Alberta
PVis Piet Visser, Amsterdam, The Netherlands
PW Peter Wiens, Fernheim Colony, Paraguay
PY Perry Yoder, Elkhart, Indiana
RAK Richard A. Kauffman, Goshen, Indiana
RAL Russel A. Liechty, Goshen, Indiana
RAS Rachel A. Shenk, Goshen, Indiana
RB Robert J. Baker, Elkhart, Indiana
RC Robert Charles, Somerville, Massachusetts
RDS Ronald D. Sawatzky, Elkhart, Indiana
RDSh R. Donald Shafer, Upland, California
RE Robert Enns, Fresno, California
REP Ralph E. Palmer, Ashland, Ohio
RFal Rafael Falcón, Goshen, Indiana
RFK Richard F. Keeler, Harrisonburg, Virginia
RFl Ron Flickinger, Indianapolis, Ind.
RH Rebecca Haarer, Shipshewana, Indiana
RHof R. Hofman, Bilthoven, The Netherlands
RHul Robert Hull, Newton, Kansas
RJ Rufus Jutzi, Cambridge, Ontario
RJH Ronald J. Hunsicker, Putnam Valley, New York
RJP Ronald J. Penner, Madrid, Spain
RJS Rodney J. Sawatsky, Waterloo, Ontario
RK Robert S. Kreider, N. Newton, Kansas
RKH Richard K. Herr, Gettysburg, Pennsylvania
RL Ralph A. Lebold, Waterloo, Ontario
RLG Rebecca L. Gates, Fort Wayne, Indiana
RLR Robert L. Ramseyer, Hiroshima Shi, Japan
RM Ruth Mellinger, Orange Walk Town, Belize
RM-K Robert Martin-Koop, Montreal, Quebec
RMG Roy M. Geigley, Phoenix, Arizona
ROG Raul O. García, Buenos Aires, Argentina
ROZ Robert O. Zehr, Des Allemands, Lousiana
RR Ruth Ratzlaff, Newton, Kansas
RRe Ron Rempel, Waterloo, Ontario
RRK Russell R. Krabill, Elkhart, Indiana
RRo Ron Ropp, Bloomington, Illinois
RS Rueben Short, Fort Wayne, Indiana
RSA Aseervadam Rampogu, Malakpet, Hyderabad, India
RSa Reynold Sawatzky, Goshen, Indiana
RSK Roelf S. Kuitse, Eklhart, Indiana
RSL Rampogu Sampson Lemuel, Jadcherla, Andhra Pradesh, India
RSl Rebecca Slough, El Cerrito, California
RT Raul Tadeo, Ahome Sinaloa, Mexico
RTB Ross T. Bender, Elkhart, Indiana
RU Ruth Unrau, N. Newton, Kansas
RW Ruth Wiens, Minoo Shi, Osaka, Japan
RWB Rainer W. Burkart, Ludwigshafen, West Germany
RWG Rachel Waltner Goossen, Goessel, Kansas
SAK Stanley A. Kaufman, Berlin, Ohio
SBB Stephen B. Boyd, Winston Salem, North Carolina
SBJZ S. B. J. Zilverberg, Amstelveen, The Netherlands
SC Sandra Cronk, Princeton, New Jersey
SCS Stanley C. Shenk, Goshen, Indiana
SES Stephen E. Scott, Columbia, Pennsylvania
SG Sue Goerzen, Windsor, Ontario
SGer Samuel Gerber, Nuglar, Switzerland
SGG Simon G. Gingerich, Elkhart, Indiana
SGS† Sanford G. Shetler, Hollsopple, Pennsylvania
SKS Steven K. Smith, Monterey, Massachusetts
SL Sinecio Lezcano, Asunción, Paraguay
SLH Samuel L. Horst, Harrisonburg, Virginia
SLK Sharon L. Klingelsmith, Philadelphia, Pennsylvania
SLY Samuel L. Yoder, Goshen, Indiana
SM Sam Myovich, Bloomington, Indiana
SN Stan Nussbaum, Birmingham, England
SNS S. N. Solomon, Dhamtari, Madhya Pradesh, India
SPM S. Paul Miller, Goshen, Indiana
SR Sara Regier, N. Newton, Kansas
SRE Steven R. Estes, Hopedale, Illinois
SS Shozo *Sato*, Miyazaki Shi, Miyazaki Ken, Japan
SSchär Sieghard Schärtner, Filadelfia, Paraguay
SSI Sally Schroeder Isaak, Clearbrook, British Columbia
SSt Sam Steiner, Waterloo, Ontario
SV Sjouke Voolstra, Landsmeer, The Netherlands
SVS Sheldon V. Sawatzky, Taichung, Taiwan
SWS Stuart W. Showalter, Goshen, Indiana
SZ S. Zijlstra, Groningen, The Netherlands
TB Terry Burkhalter, Brooksville, Florida
TBurk Timothy Burkholder, Edmonton, Alberta
TDR Ted D. Regehr, Saskatoon, Saskatchewan
TFS Theron F. Schlabach, Goshen, Indiana
TGlü Theo Glück, Karlsruhe-Bad Herrenalb, West Germany
ThSchm Theo Schmidt, Munich, West Germany
TJK Theodore J. Koontz, Elkhart, Indiana
TJM Thomas J. Meyers, Goshen, Indiana
TMG Thelma Miller Groff, Goshen, Indiana
TN Takeji *Nomura*, Kobe Shi, Hyogo Ken, Japan
TNF Thomas N. Finger, Bronx, New York
TR Thomas Rutschman, Jokkmokk, Sweden
TRS Tilman R. Smith, Goshen, Indiana
TSJ Timothy Stoltzfus Jost, Columbus, Ohio
TTan Takio *Tanase*, Tokyo, Japan
TTo Takanobu *Tojo*, Shimonoseki Shi, Yamaguchi Ken, Japan
TY Takashi *Yamada*, Kobayashi Shi, Miyazaki Ken, Japan
UP Urbane Peachey, Ephrata, Pennsylvania
VAM Vesta A. Miller, Goshen, Indiana
VC Virgil Claassen, Elkhart, Indiana
VGD Victor G. Doerksen, Winnipeg, Manitoba
VH Volker Horsch, Neuwied, West Germany
VMG Virgil M. Gerig, Goshen, Indiana
VMi Vern Miller, Cleveland, Ohio
VP Vern Preheim, Newton, Kansas
VR Vernon Ratzlaff, Winnipeg, Manitoba
VU Verney Unruh, Newton, Kansas
VV Virgil Vogt, Evanston, Illinois
WB Wesley Berg, Edmonton, Alberta
WDH William D. Hooley, New Paris, Indiana
WER Willard E. Roth, Elkhart, Indiana
WH Wilbur Hostetler, Goshen, Indiana
WHD Walter H. Dyck, Normal, Illinois
WHS Willard H. Smith, Goshen, Indiana
WIM Wilma I. Musser, Mechanicsburg, Pennsylvania
WIN William I. Neufeld, Winnipeg, Manitoba
WJ Wallace Jantz, Monument, Colorado
WK William Keeney, Kent, Ohio
WKla William Klassen, Waterloo, Ontario
WKlaa Walter Klaassen, Vernon, British Columbia

WKr Wally Kroeker, Winnipeg, Manitoba
WMS Willard M. Swartley, Elkhart, Indiana
WN Wayne North, Harrisonburg, Virginia
WNo Wayne Northey, Port Moody, British Columbia
Woodcrest Bruderhof members of Woodcrest Bruderhof archives staff, Douglas A. Moody and others, Rifton, New York
WOP Werner O. Packull, Waterloo, Ontario
WP Wesley Prieb, Hillsboro, Kansas
WRE, Jr. William R. Estep, Jr., Fort Worth, Texas
WRS Wilbert R. Shenk, Elkhart, Indiana
WS Wilford Stutzman, Keota, Iowa
WSK Willard S. Krabill, Goshen, Indiana

WU Walter Unger, Clearbrook, British Columbia
WUnr Willard Unruh, N. Newton, Kansas
WWG Weyburn W. Groff, Goshen, Indiana
WWS Walter W. Sawatsky, Winnipeg, Manitoba
YI Yoshihira *Inamine*, Urawa Shi, Saitama Ken, Japan
YS Yosuke *Sonoyama*, Osaka, Japan
YT Yoshiaki *Tamura*, Furano Shi, Hokkaido, Japan
YY Yorifumi *Yaguchi*, Sapporo Shi, Hokkaido, Japan

† = deceased; Shi = city; Ken = prefecture

Frederick H. Liechty, Berne, Indiana, wrote "A Letter from a Small-Town Banker."

THE
MENNONITE ENCYCLOPEDIA

A

Abortion is for some a means of °birth control, for some a way to manage a dilemma, for others never an option because it ends life. Abortion is not new, nor is the debate about it likely to end.

While a relatively small sample of French Mennonites reflect divergence of opinion (fewer are in favor of abortion), the reason is likely personal. Women, more directly involved, prove less rigid. Japanese culture is less driven to reproduction, so abortion can be more routine. Opposing all birth control, Russian Mennonites are also sparse with sex education. Old Colony and or Kleine Gemeinde members in Belize long to have children and see birthing as a woman's prime reason for being. For her to be pregnant every year is common and God-willed. Having a child out of wedlock is not unusual in Zaire; having a child there is what makes a woman a woman. Abortion would be strongly opposed among Mennonites in both Switzerland and India.

The 1973 United States Supreme Court decision that no state may interfere with a woman's right to obtain an abortion during the first 12 weeks of pregnancy highlighted the topic for Mennonites in the United States. A decision by Canada's Supreme Court in 1988 heightened the debate for Canadian Mennonites. As with other °sexual matters, men have given primary input and shaped statements. That in itself is an ethical problem never owned up to. Nor have men, for example, via Mennonite Medical Association, duly noted male involvement with conception that leads to abortion trauma.

Instead, focus and debate have been on when life begins, ideal church care, biblical principles, and moral factors of ending life. Mennonites tend to compare war and abortion, ignoring points of difference. Critique of "abortion on demand" is seldom connected to socialized "sex on demand." Responsible sexual activity, beginning with due credit of woman's worth and mutual esteem, has yet to become primary. Economic justice for people worldwide needs to follow that.

Responses to a questionnaire indicate that, while the majority of North American Mennonites favor abortion when a mother's health is a risk, one-half approve legalizing abortion if rape was involved or if the baby would likely be defective. Believing that human life is a divine gift created in God's image, that each is responsible to care for the sacred in those who are defenseless, and that what is required of believers is not expected of society in general, early Anabaptists and Mennonites today realize that abortion is not an ideal solution to problem pregnancy. Churches need to establish more genuine community with those confronting abortion.   DYN

Kauffman/Harder, *Anabaptists Four C. Later* (1975), 180-82;

George Brenneman, "Abortion: Review of Mennonite Literature, 1970-1977," *MQR,* 53 (1979), 160-72; Edwin and Helen Alderfer, eds., *Life and Values* (Scottdale: MPH, 1974); General Conference Mennonite Church Family Life Committee, *Abortion Packet* (Newton, 1979); Duane K. Friesen, *Moral Issues in the Control of Birth,* and Muriel T. Stackley, *A Leader's Guide for Moral Issues in the Control of Birth* (Newton, 1974); papers from a conference on life and human values (with particular reference to abortion), sponsored by Mennonite Medical Association, Chicago, Oct. 5-6, 1973); Brenda D. Hofman, "Political Theology: The Role of Organized Religion in the Anti-Abortion movement," *J. of Church and State,* 28, no. 2 (Spring 1986), 225-4; *Minutes (EMCh* (1984), 34-35. Conference statements on abortion are available from the Evangelical Mennonite Conference; General Conference Mennonite Church; MCC Committee on Women's Concerns; Executive Committee and Peace and Social Concerns Committee of MCC Canada; Mennonite Brethren; and Mennonite Church (MC)7.

See also Bioethics; Children.

Aburatani Seiichiro, a resident of Hagi, Yamaguchi Prefecture, Japan, Seiichiro Aburatani appeared at the door of missionaries Peter and Mary Willms soon after they began the Brethren in Christ work in that city. He came in response to an advertisement for an interpreter, and he became a loyal supporter of the mission and one of the first lay leaders of the Hagi Church. When illness forced him to quit his job, he started a private English school in his home. He was helped in this venture by volunteer English teacher, Doyle Book. Aburatani was baptized in the second baptismal service of the new church in September 1955. He was appointed a member of the original board of the church incorporation in 1959. A detailed recordkeeper, from 1962 to 1970 he tabulated responses to the radio broadcast sponsored by the mission. He assisted in the leadership of the Hagi Church meetings and led a home meeting in his mother's house in Agawa. With his wife, he retired to a small house in Shimonoseki in 1982.   DCB

Doyle C. Book, *The Threshold Is High: The Brethren in Christ in Japan* (Nappanee, 1986), index.

Acculturation. The explication of acculturation among Mennonites and related groups is a conceptual part of the "Christ and Culture" problem as analyzed in the book with that title by H. Richard °Niebuhr. Mennonites, according to Niebuhr, represent a radical "Christ *against* culture" solution, in distinction to four other types of solution: the Christ *of* culture, Christ *above* culture, Christ *in paradox with* culture, and Christ *the transformer of* culture. Although the fourth and sixth °Schleitheim articles of faith (1527) and numerous articles by H. S. °Bender in the *Mennonite Encyclopedia* (°°nonconformity, °°worldliness, °°language problem) would seem to verify Niebuhr's characterization, all five types of solution have been espoused within Mennonitism in its pluralism. In the limited space for this article, the main focus will be the sociology of Mennonite acculturation, followed by a few concluding theological reflections in view of Niebuhr's typology.

From a purely °sociological perspective, the terms "culture" and "acculturation" do not carry the negative connotations they often have in sectarian theological discourse. *Culture* refers to the total way of life of a human group or society, including its material products (tools, dwellings, clothing, etc.) and its nonmaterial products (language, ceremonies, beliefs, etc.). Every group, including the original group of Christ's disciples, has a culture, or subculture, e.g., the way the disciple group rooted its kingdom lifestyle in its Jewish heritage.

The most basic element and spearhead of human culture is learned speech and the group's vehicle of language. Culture is shared by its members because it is useful. It is transmitted to its younger members as they mature (the process called "socialization") and to members of other groups who can use it (the process called "acculturation"). Acculturation is simply the acceptance of culture traits by one group from another. Acculturation should be distinguished from *assimilation*, which refers to the fusion of two or more cultures, usually a one-sided process by which the members of a minority group are integrated into the host society with some permanent loss to the group accepting the majority culture. Acculturation should also be distinguished from *secularization*, which refers to the church's assimilation of the "world," defined theologically as a fallen profane social and structural way of life (Gal 1:4, Jas 1:27, 1 Jn 5:19, etc.). The acculturation of Mennonites leads to assimilation and secularization only if the ways and values adopted require a fundamental compromise with the world and result in detrimental changes in Mennonite ethics and lifestyle.

Certain studies of Mennonite culture-borrowing have concluded that acculturation in some aspects of its adaptation to a host society does not lead to assimilation and secularization, while in other aspects it does. Calvin Redekop refers to adoption of farm machinery by Mennonites as an instance of acculturation that need not lead to assimilation, while attendance at °public schools will more likely lead to assimilation as alien ideas and values are accepted. Whether or not these types of acculturation lead to secularization depends on whether the techniques or values adopted are compatible with historic Mennonite norms. For instance, the adoption of a concept of an organized °voluntary service program may well require some degree of assimilation because it involves identification and a sense of interdependence with persons and groups served; but, inasmuch as this program has led to a revitalization of the normative Anabaptist vision by providing a valid expression of it, members who have served in Mennonite voluntary service may have found new ways to resist conformity to the world.

In his study of the Mennonites of Manitoba, E. K. Francis observed many indications of acculturation which had not had detrimental effects, and he explains this by reference to "a core of religious principles and practices which differentiates all branches of the Mennonite church from non-Mennonite religious bodies and thus necessarily draws them together, once the chips are down."

These finer concepts can be further illustrated from Mennonite history by reference to two indices of Mennonite social change. The first has to do with changes in the languages used. It was the prevalent view of the newly arrived immigrants that their language of origin was a necessity for the perpetuation of their socioreligious way of life insofar as it reinforced their sense of separation from the pervading culture and strengthened their nonconformity to the pagan world. Learning and using the language of the host society opened countless channels for assimilation and secularization, but to the extent that the Mennonite norms of an aggressive missionary witness and prophetic ministry require communication with those outside of the ethnic community, opposition to a language change on the basis of value preservation is undermined. For a group like the Mennonites, who define themselves as a church of voluntarily committed believers, there must come a point in their acculturation when they can be said to have acquired enough proficiency in the language of their adopted society to be able to bear effective witness to their faith, not only to outgroup persons, but also to their own acculturated children.

In the 450 years of their history, the Anabaptists and Mennonites have faced the language-change problem with almost every new °migration: (1) Dutch to German for the emigrants from The Netherlands who resettled in nw. Germany and Prussia (1535 ff.); (2) German to French for the Swiss-Mennonite settlers in the Jura mountains and valleys and in Alsace-Lorraine (1700 ff.); (3) German to Russian for the emigrants from Prussia to Russia (1788 ff.); (4) Dutch or German to English for the immigrants to America (1690 ff.); (5) German to Spanish or Portuguese for the Russian Mennonite immigrants to Paraguay, Bolivia, and Brazil, (1926 ff. and 1930 ff.); and other lesser-scale resettlements.

Cases 1 and 3, above, represent contrasting characteristics and consequences of acculturation. In northern Germany and Prussia, the use of the Dutch language persisted longest in the conservative Flemish congregations of Emden and Danzig, but everywhere else the language shift was fairly rapid, accompanied by a rather thoroughgoing adaptation to the dominant intellectual, political, and socioreligious norms of the surrounding rural-urban, nationalistic culture. The acculturation process was not entirely one-sided insofar as the Mennonites contributed flood control and °water drainage methods in the marshlands, a new water and sewage system in the city of Danzig, and many other skills and resources; but in order to resolve the conflicts caused by their alleged heretical faith and ethics, the Prussian Mennonites largely rescinded their historic principle of nonresistance by the middle of the 19th c.

In case 3, on the other hand, the Russification of the Mennonite immigrants was resisted much longer because of their explicit entrance °privileges; and here the result was their separation into isolated colonies with a marked degree of religious and cultural impoverishment *from within*, i.e., the near loss of their missionary motive. Thus, in the sequence of resettlement, Mennonites have faced the choice of adjusting their language and socioreligious norms to the dominant secularized culture or living in semi-isolation from that culture. Case 1 illustrates the first horn of the dilemma, i.e., adaptation at the risk of secularization; and case 3 illustrates the other, i.e., the risk of an unconcerned, aloof irrelevance.

The other index of change that illustrates both of these risks is the degree of Mennonite adherence to their historic °peace ethic. The classic illustration of acculturation in sociology textbooks is the adoption of firearms by the American Indians; and in the Mennonite sociology classroom we could refer to the acceptance of the duties of °military service in Prussia or the adoption of firearms by certain Russian Mennonites (the °*Selbstschutz* or self-defence units) when their communities were being ravaged by marauding revolutionists following the °Russian Revolution. As was often true in Mennonite history, the greatest interaction with the Russian people occurred in wartime when the Mennonites contributed to the war effort in ways both consistent (hospital and medical corps) and inconsistent (implements actually used for warfare) with their traditional pacifist norms.

North American Mennonites have had a severe sequence of tests in this regard: the American Revolution, the °American Civil War, °World War I, °World War II, and the period after World War II with the first "peacetime" °conscription in United States history. While their formal position during all of these periods was that of nonparticipation in military service, it is a known fact that in the 20th c., for all the Mennonite groups, more than half of the younger members who were conscripted were willing to serve in combatant or noncombatant roles within the military system.

Following World War II, however, there was a vigorous group introspection concerning this discrepancy between principle and practice. The self-study had two facets. The first concerned the conscription data that was collected. Howard Charles observed a curvilinear correlation between strict adherence to the norm of nonresistance and the amount of education of the draftee, i.e., the proportion of drafted men willing to enter military service increased with the amount of education through grade 12 in school; but with additional education beyond high school, the proportion steadily decreased. In his interpretation, Charles wrote: "We may safely say that the majority of draftees having only a grade school education are of rural extraction, and consequently have been sheltered somewhat from the secularizing influence which would predispose them to military service. Furthermore, the grade school psychologically and sociologically plays a less dominant role in the forging of a favorable attitude toward military service than does the high school. The high percentage of college men in CPS [°°Civilian Public Service] may be due partially to the influence of our church colleges." Charles concluded that "social influence is the most important single factor which was responsible for men going into military service. . . a sobering comment on the influence of environment on Christian ideals and conduct."

As convincing as the acculturation explanation appears, one still needs to account for the fact that societal pressures failed to conscript nearly 5,000 men from all Mennonite bodies for military service during World War II. While a person's behavior is influenced by the total cultural environment in which one lives, it is also influenced by one's primary group and its subculture. Reflecting on such intervening influences, Robert Kreider wrote: "Implied in our faith is the belief that man is [indeed] molded by his environment. Mennonites of all ages have been deeply concerned about the type of home, community, church, and economy within which the young generation is nurtured." Kreider analyzed the principal forms of "internal" environment which support the adherence to the norm of pacifism. Congregations which are known to have cultivated and cherished the norm of pacifism have a high percentage of °conscientious objectors (COs). Congregations which are known to have become imitative of modern Protestantism in theology and ethics have produced relatively few COs. The presence or absence of a viable discipline in the local congregation is directly related to the presence or absence of overt conscientious objection. Kreider concluded that "the hour of decision for young men of these traditional, disciplinary groups is not the time of the [conscription] questionnaire's arrival, but the day of union with the church."

The other facet of the self-study after World War II concerned the dysfunctions of the °alternative service program, i.e., the legal arrangement with the government at those periodic occasions of national military preparedness when Mennonites seek exemption. Many Civilian Public Service men felt that the government had deliberately isolated them in order to restrict their influence on public opinion, that this was the reason Congress had denied them the right to serve in foreign relief work. They would have preferred to do something that seemed more relevant to the world's crises. The traditional Mennonite strategy of refusing any involvement in the conflict seemed to be too complacent and legalistic, if not irresponsible.

Since the publication of Niebuhr's book in 1951, it is doubtful that Mennonites as a whole still represent the "Christ against culture" position. While continuing to affirm those teachings of Jesus and the apostles that confront societal culture with the hard challenges of an alternative kingdom (Mt 5-7, Rom 12, Gal 1, 1 Pet 2, 1 Jn 5, etc.), they also often recite the prayer of the Johannine Christ that his disciples will be *in* the world, while not *of* the world (Jn 17:11-16). The implication of this prayer is that, while they still maintain a clear distinction between Christ and culture, they believe it is possible, under the lordship of Christ, to hold them together in some type of unity. In Niebuhr's typology, Mennonites would find some truth to all of the options he described. Separation from the world in the geographic sense is no longer possible, and it is now being affirmed that the New Testament call to separation (2 Cor 6:17) is an ethical, rather than a geographical, injunction and that the Christian's place is in the world. Knowing that society and its culture is fallen, Mennonites, nevertheless, should covenant in local congregations to fulfil Christ's commission to evangelize and prophesy, using the cultural resources of the world to that end, insofar as they are compatible with evangelical goals. In this perspective, acculturation is not only inevitable, it is mandated (1 Cor 9:20-24).　　　　　　　　LDH

L. Broom and J. I. Kitsuse, "The Validation of Acculturation: A Condition to Ethnic Assimilation," *American Anthropologist* (Feb. 1955), 44ff.; Howard Charles, "A Presentation and Evaluation of MCC Draft Status Census," *Proceedings of the Fourth Annual Conference on Mennonite Cultural Problems* (Bluffton College, 1945), 83-106; E. K. Francis, *In Search of Utopia* (Glencoe: Free Press, 1955); Leland Harder, "The Quest for Equilibrium in an Established Sect: A Study of Social Change in the GCMC" (PhD diss., Northwestern U., 1962); Peter J. Klassen, "Faith and Culture: Mennonites in the Vistula Delta," *MQR*, 57 (1983), 194-205; Robert Kreider, "Environmental Factors Influencing Decisions of Men of Draft Age," *Proceedings of the First Conference on Mennonite Cultural Problems* (Bethel College, 1942), 75-88; H. Richard Niebuhr, *Christ and Culture* (New York: Harper and Brothers, 1951); Calvin Redekop, "Patterns of Cultural Assimilation among Mennonites," *Proceedings of the Eleventh Conference on Mennonite Educational and Cultural Problems* (Bethel College, 1957), 99-112; John B. Toews, *Czars, Soviets, and Mennonites* (Newton, 1982).

See also Dialect Literature and Speech; Mennonite Studies; Names, Personal; Nonconformity; Philanthropy; Professions; Urbanization.

Johann Funk and John F. Funk: Brothers in the Faith

On April 6, 1835, a certain John Fretz °°Funk was born in Bucks Co., Pa. A little over one year later, on Dec. 26, 1836, a Johann Funk was born in the Mennonite colony of °°Bergthal in South Russia. John F. and Johann were to become influential men and outstanding leaders in the years to come. Their lives, different in so many ways, were to cross paths briefly as they both sought to be faithful disciples and to encourage and challenge the church to be faithful.

John F. began his career as a public school teacher in his home community but after two years entered the lumber business in Chicago. He married Salome Kratz in 1864, and they had two daughters. John F.'s years in Chicago were significant in his development as a Christian, as a pacifist, and as a believer in the importance of Sunday schools and mission work. It was also in Chicago that John F. founded the publication °°*The Herald of Truth*, a religious newspaper that was forthrightly nonresistant in its perspective. (It was later to be merged with *Gospel Witness* to form the °°*Gospel Herald*.)

In April of 1867 John F. moved to Elkhart, Ind., where he continued to publish the *Herald* and develop the printing and publishing business he had begun in Chicago. In 1865 John F. was ordained to the ministry, and in 1892 he was ordained to the office of °bishop. These responsibilities he combined with his publishing business. John F.'s contributions as a publisher include Menno Simons complete works, both in English and German, as well as *Martyrs Mirror*.

Upon his arrival in Elkhart, John F. became actively involved in the °°Yellow Creek congregation

and served as one of its ministers for several years. It was here that John F. found himself in the midst of controversy between those who were more conservative in their understandings of church practices (led by Bishop Jacob °°Wisler) and the more progressive element. John F. was appealed to many times as a person best able to achieve reconciliation between the two factions, but his own progressive tendencies did not allow him to support Bishop Wisler's rejection of evening meetings and °Sunday school. In 1872 John F. declared that Jacob Wisler was no longer a member of the Yellow Creek congregation, and Wisler left to form a more conservative Mennonite group, often called the Wisler Mennonites or the °Old Order Mennonites. At the same time, John F. spoke against those who, led by Daniel °°Brenneman, had progressive, evangelistic leanings and did not agree with many of the practices of church order. In 1874 Brenneman was excommunicated from the Yellow Creek congregation and formed what eventually became the (°°United) Missionary Church.

John F. considered his congregation to be the more neutral group between the two extremes and to a large extent, continued to develop the Mennonite Church's characteristic of working at the middle ground between tradition and progress. Due in large part to John F.'s publishing company, which attracted many progressive thinkers who became influential church leaders, and his own leadership abilities, Elkhart became a center of Mennonite Church (MC) activity. John F. became actively involved in building and leading °°Prairie Street Mennonite Church in Elkhart. It was here that the first young people's meeting and one of the first Sunday schools were established. Much of this growth and change was directed and aided by John F.'s leadership, vision, and his publications. As he had discovered in the Yellow Creek congregation, change was not always easy, and in the later years of his life, he found himself in the midst of congregational conflict once more, this time in the Prairie Street congregation. This conflict resulted in part of the congregation withdrawing, and in 1902 John F. was asked to suspend his activity as a bishop.

Just as congregational controversy seemed a significant aspect of John F.'s church life, so it was a major component of Johann Funk's experience as a church leader. At the age of 38 Johann, along with his family, migrated to Canada and settled in Bergthal on the °°East Reserve in Manitoba. Three years later, in 1877, he was elected and ordained to the ministry. In 1882 he was ordained as *Ältester* (°elder) and in this capacity assumed much of the leadership responsibility for the °Bergthal Mennonite Church.

The history of the Bergthalers is a rather stormy one. At that time in Manitoba, "Bergthaler" was equated with "progressive." While other Mennonite churches emphasized strict discipline and avoidance of worldly ways, the Bergthalers were known to drive buggies and bicycles, take part in civic elections, and allow their children to attend public schools. Many of the immigrants coming to Canada at the time chose to settle on farms rather than stay in the village groups they had come from in Russia.

According to the more °conservative Mennonite leaders, this was against church order and such people were banned. These settlers then went to Johann, who believed this to be insufficient reason for the ban and so accepted them into the Bergthaler church. This resulted in severe discord between the two Mennonite groups.

In addition, Johann supported the home, mission work of the General Conference Mennonites, which sought to meet the needs of immigrant settlements. Many of the Mennonite groups at that time did not support this type of mission work, and so conflict continued. Johann looked to higher education as the means of survival for the Mennonites in Manitoba and by 1888 was advocating the formation of a teacher-training school. Johann was intrumental in the beginning of the Mennonite continuation school, which first opened its doors in 1889 in Gretna, Man. Eventually the school was named Mennonite Educational Institute and, in 1988, is known as Mennonite Collegiate Institute. The school was the object of major opposition from many in the Bergthaler Church, resulting in two-thirds of the group leaving Johann's church to form a new congregation, which eventually came to be known as the °Sommerfelder church. This was not the end of conflict for Funk, however. Controversy continued with the various Mennonite groups in southern Manitoba. Finally in 1910 Johann was asked to submit his resignation as Ältester, which he did.

Did John F. and Johann, who lived in two different countries and led two very different lives, ever discuss their similar struggles? It is clear that they knew of one another. John F. was instrumental in helping Mennonites to settle in Manitoba. When Johann was concerned about church renewal, John F. made many contacts for special speakers to come to the Manitoba churches, as well as making several trips to Manitoba himself. Johann advocated relations with the Mennonites in the United States and used educational and religious materials published by John F. But did John F., the wealthy businessman, and Johann, the Russian Mennonite immigrant, ever find a sympathetic ear in the other? Two great leaders, with such a love for the church, such a vision for its future, and so many struggles along the way, might well have benefited by the knowledge that their struggle was not entirely unique, that it was part of the growth and development of the Mennonite church and that, at a later date, the significance of their contributions would be recognized. GCW

Esther Epp, "Ältester Johann Funk: His Life and Work," in *Ältester Johann Funk: A Family Tree,* ed., Mary Dueck Jeffery (Grafton, N. D.: Associated Printers, 1980), 1-15; F. H. Epp, *Mennonites in Canada II* (1974); Henry J. Gerbrandt, *Adventure in Faith* (Altona, Man.: D. W. Friesen and Sons, 1970); Lawrence Klippenstein, and Julius G. Toews, ed., *Mennonite Memories: Settling in Western Canada* (Winnipeg: Centennial Publications, 1977); Aaron C. Kolb, "John Fretz Funk, 1835-1930: An Appreciation," *MQR,* 6 (1932), 144-55, 250-63; Joseph Liechty and James O. Lehman, "From Yankee to Nonresistant: John F. Funk's Chicago Years, 1857-1865," *MQR,* 59 (1985), 203-47; Kempes Schnell, "John F. Funk, 1835-1930, and the Mennonite Migration of 1873-1875," *MQR,* 24 (1950), 199-229; J. C. Wenger, ed., "Documents on the Daniel Brenneman Division," *MQR,* 34 (1960), 48-56; idem, "Jacob Wisler and the Old Order Mennonite Schism of 1872 in Elkhart County, Ind," *MQR,* 33 (1959), 108-31, 215-40).

ACCULTURATION CHART
MENNONITES IN WESTERN CANADA - THE 1870s IMMIGRANTS

Researched by Adolf Ens

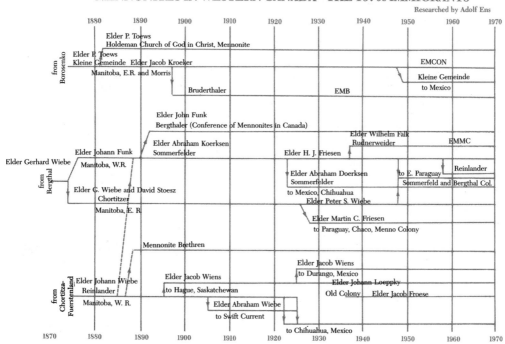

Mennonites in Western Canada: The 1870s Immigrants

The 6,931 Mennonites who emigrated from Russia to Manitoba between 1874 and 1880 came almost entirely from three sources: 83 percent of the entire Bergthal Colony (ca. 3,000 people), the major part of the Kleine Gemeinde from Borosenko Colony (ca. 700 people), and a large group from Chortitza Colony and its relatively new daughter colony, Fürstenland (ca. 3,200 people). In Canada all three groups were divided by migration and church splits, as indicated in the chart above. Separations shown by solid lines indicate movement of a group; broken lines indicate the movement of individuals. The elder (*Ältester*) of a group is named in some cases, serving as one indicator of lines of continuity or discontinuity. The Reinländer Church in Manitoba and Saskatchewan discontinued after the emigration to Mexico and was reorganized after an interval as the Old Colony church in Manitoba.   AE

Adams Co., Ind., Old Order Amish Settlement. See Berne, Ind., Old Order Amish Settlement.

Africa (ME I:21). Though a single continent, Africa in reality combines two very different worlds, i.e., the Arabic Muslim world of the north and the black animistic world of central and southern Africa. While the former has been part of Mediterranean and European history across the centuries, sub-Saharan Africa has been a world apart, which has experienced its own unique history.

With the dramatic exploratory treks of Livingstone and Stanley in the 1860s and 1870s, Africa below the Sahara Desert quickly became the focus of attention for the European powers and the Christian world of that era. As Europeans scurried to establish colonial holdings on that continent, Christians in widely scattered areas of the world also organized themselves to undertake missions of witness and service. Already before 1900, Mennonites and Brethren in Christ missionary pioneers were arriving on the continent.

In 1890 Eusebius Hershey of the °°Mennonite Brethren in Christ Church ([°°United] Missionary Church) went to Liberia on his own to engage in missionary work. He soon sickened and died there, but his example prompted others from his church to volunteer. In 1920 the Mennonite Brethren in Christ organized the United Missionary society and subsequently took charge of the missionary endeavor of its personnel in West Africa, notably in Nigeria.

In 1896 the Defenseless Mennonite Church (later known as the Evangelical Mennonite Church) sent Mathilda °Kohm as its first missionary to the Congo Free State (Zaire) to work with the Christian and Missionary Alliance Mission. A second woman, Alma °Doering, was sent in 1900 to join her, this time to work with the Swedish Baptists.

In 1906 the Defenseless Mennonite Church sent six missionaries to British East Africa (Kenya, Uganda, and Tanzania) to work under the auspices of the Africa Inland Mission. In that same year, the °°Central Conference Mennonite Church sent its first missionary couple, Lawrence and Rose °Haigh, also to work in East Africa with the Africa Inland Mission. By 1910 the missionaries of these two conferences persuaded their sponsoring bodies to dispose of their work in East Africa and engage in pioneering efforts elsewhere. In January 1911 the two conferences created the United Mennonite Board of Missions which envisioned a cooperative effort in Africa. In 1912 this new inter-Mennonite organization commissioned its first missionaries, Lawrence and Rose Haigh and Alma Doering. By mid-year the Haighs were in the Belgian Congo (Zaire), engaged in exploratory travel for their board. In January 1912, the home board changed its name to the Congo Inland Mission (known as Africa Inter-Mennonite Mission since 1971). Across the years the ministry of Africa Inter-Mennonite Mission (AIMM) in Africa has been broadened. After working until 1972 exclusively in Zaire, mission workers were placed in Lesotho in 1973, in Botswana in 1975, in Burkina Faso in 1978, and in the Transkei in 1982. In North America, AIMM's supporting base of conferences, working in partnership, has increased from two to six.

In 1898 the first Brethren in Christ missionaries arrived in Southern Rhodesia (Zimbabwe) followed by other recruits in 1906 in Northern Rhodesia (Zambia). The Brethren in Christ have maintained a continuous witness and ministry in these areas to the present (1988).

In 1934 the Eastern Mennonite [MC] Board of Missions and Charities (EMBMC) sent Elam and Elizabeth °Stauffer, and John and Ruth °Mosemann to Tanganyika (Tanzania), where they opened a work at Shirati in the Musoma district. Stations at Bukiroba, Mugango, Bumani, and Nyabisi were soon added. Later personnel was placed in Ethiopia (1948), Somalia (1953), Kenya (1964), Swaziland (1971), Southern Sudan (1972) and Mozambique (1978-86). Along the way Nairobi has become the administrative center for both EMBMC and Mennonite Central Committee in East Africa.

Already in 1921, Mennonite Brethren missionaries Aaron and Ernestina °Janzen opened an independent work at Kafumba in the Kwilu area of the Belgian Congo (Zaire). After World War II, several smaller independent missions in Kwilu and Kwango disbanded and appealed to other organizations to take over responsibility. The Mennonite Brethren Board of Missions then became heavily involved in this area. They took over Janzen's work at Kafumba and sent personnel to °Kikwit, Lusemvu, Panzi and Kajiji. The Mennonite Brethren also placed people in °Kinshasa early in their mission work and continue to maintain a strong emphasis on church planting and the creation of Christian literature in the major languages of the region.

In the late 1950s the Mennonite [MC] Board of Missions and Charities (MBM) received inquiries from western Africa in response to radio programs which the board sponsored. In 1959 Ed and Irene Weaver went to Nigeria to ascertain whether a ministry among these inquirers was feasible. Thus Mennonites became involved with °African independent churches, a ministry which expanded to Ivory Coast (1978), and Benin (1986). In addition the Menno-

AFRICA

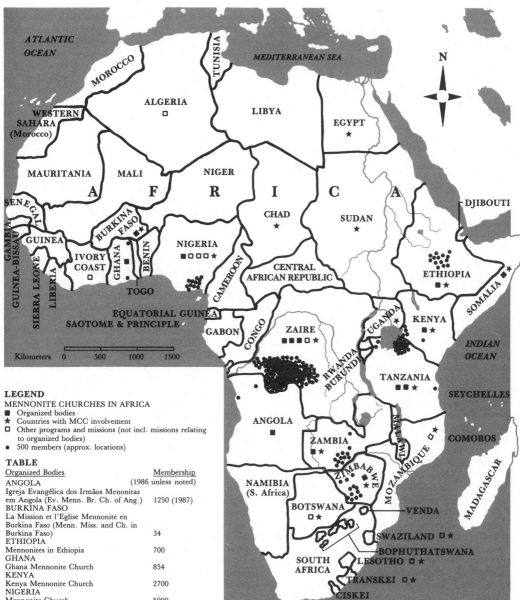

LEGEND

MENNONITE CHURCHES IN AFRICA
- ■ Organized bodies
- ★ Countries with MCC involvement
- ◻ Other programs and missions (not incl. missions relating to organized bodies)
- ● 500 members (approx. locations)

TABLE

Organized Bodies	Membership
	(1986 unless noted)
ANGOLA	
Igreja Evangélica dos Irmãos Menonitas em Angola (Ev. Menn. Br. Ch. of Ang.)	1250 (1987)
BURKINA FASO	
La Mission et l'Eglise Mennonite en Burkina Faso (Menn. Miss. and Ch. in Burkina Faso)	34
ETHIOPIA	
Mennonites in Ethiopia	700
GHANA	
Ghana Mennonite Church	854
KENYA	
Kenya Mennonite Church	2700
NIGERIA	
Mennonite Church	5000
SOMALIA	
Somalia Mennonite Believers Fellowship	ca. 100
TANZANIA	
Kanisa la Mennonite Tanzania (Tanzania Menn. Ch.)—North Mara Diocese	4183
South Mara Diocese	10258
ZAIRE	
Communauté des Eglises de Frères Mennonites au Zaïre (Menn. Br. Community of Zaire)	35000 + (1987)
Communauté Evangélique Mennonite (Menn. Evan. Community)	7583
Communauté Mennonite au Zaïre (Menn. Community of Zaire)	ca. 50000
ZAMBIA	
Mbungano Yabunyina Muli Kristo (Br. in Christ Ch.)	6000
ZIMBABWE	
Ibandla Labazalwane e-Zimbabwe (Br. in Christ Ch. in Zimbabwe)	7718

Other missions and programs (not incl. missions relating to organized bodies):
ALGERIA: MBM
BOTSWANA: AIMM
CHAD: EMEK
IVORY COAST: MBM
LESOTHO: AIMM
MOZAMBIQUE: EMBMC
NIGERIA: Ch. of God in Christ, Menn.; Fell. Churches
ZAIRE: MBM

Notes

No country except S. Africa has recognized the independence of the "homelands" of Bophuthatswana, Ciskei, Transkei, and Venda.

nite Board of Missions has planted Mennonite churches in Ghana and Nigeria.

French and Swiss Mennonites have sponsored missionaries for many years under °Europäisches Mennonitisches Evangelisationskomitee (EMEK) in Chad, where they worked in partnership with the United Evangelical Mission, an umbrella organization for four different mission groups. In 1986 EMEK appointed a missionary couple to work in partnership with AIMM in Burkina Faso.

Africa has, since World War II, been a major area of involvement for the Mennonite Central Committee (MCC). Since the early 1960s, MCC has responded to refugee needs and famine caused by political instability and severe drought in a number of areas. Many volunteers have also served in Africa under MCC's °°Pax Program and its Teachers Abroad Program (TAP), which was launched in Botswana. While working out formal partnership arrangements with the Eastern Mennonite Board of Missions and Charities and with Africa Inter-Mennonite Mission in Botswana, MCC has always sought to maintain a supportive and cooperative role with the Mennonite missions in the areas where MCC personnel are located. In January 1988, MCC had 175 volunteers in 17 different countries in Africa.   JEB

MWH (1978), 35-37, 75-120; *MWH* (1984), 10-24.

Africa Mennonite and Brethren in Christ Fellowship. The first Africa-wide gathering of representatives of Mennonite and Brethren in Christ churches was sponsored by the Mennonite Central Committee in 1962 in Limuru, Kenya. Thanks to this meeting, church leaders from a variety of countries for the first time were able to meet their counterparts and to think together seriously about their common interests, problems, and witness as Anabaptist Christians in Africa. By formal action the Africa Mennonite and Brethren in Christ Fellowship (AMBCF) was organized and officers were elected. Plans were made for the next meeting to be held in 1965 in °Bulawayo, Zimbabwe.

Estimated combined membership of Mennonite and Brethren in Christ conferences in Africa reached 137,000 in 1986, but the churches are widely separated by distance and national boundaries. Travel costs are high and visas sometimes not readily available. While the executive committee has been able to meet with some regularity, the general meetings of AMBCF have been sporadic. Sessions of the Mennonite World Conference (MWC) General Assembly and meetings of the MWC's General Council have served as vehicles for AMBCF meetings outside Africa (Wichita, 1978, and Strasbourg, 1984).

The fellowship has produced a significant peace statement (1979) and has formulated guidelines for the development of study materials with a clear Anabaptist orientation (1985) to be made available to all member churches for leadership training.   JEB

See also Regional Mennonite Conferences.

African Independent Churches. Most Western Christians are accustomed to dividing world Christianity into three branches, Roman Catholic, Orthodox, and Protestant. It would now appear, however, with the recent rise and rapid growth of religious movements in Africa, the Pacific, and the Americas, that identifiable new forms of the Christian tradition are taking shape. A 1984 survey indicates that in Africa alone nearly 7,000 distinct indigenous denominations have come to life in 43 countries. All together they claim 71,000 places of worship and a total membership approaching 28 million, with more than 800,000 new members joining each year.

These movements—in many ways the "stepchildren" of the modern missionary era—are almost entirely local and indigenously African in polity, program, leadership, and finance. There exists among them a wide spectrum of religious understanding, ranging from neotraditional (African traditional) movements to christocentric, biblically-oriented independent churches.

American Mennonites have since 1959 responded to calls from a variety of these churches requesting recognition, fraternal relationships, and opportunities for Bible study and leadership training. The Mennonite Board of Missions (MC), beginning with the pioneer efforts of Edwin and Irene Weaver, has worked primarily in West African settings (Nigeria, Ghana, *Côte d'Ivoire* [Ivory Coast], Liberia, and Benin). Mennonite Central Committee, the Africa Inter-Mennonite Mission, and the Eastern Mennonite Board of Missions and Charities have variously carried on both separate and combined ministries with churches in Central and Southern Africa (Zaire, Botswana, Lesotho, Swaziland, and Transkei).

Equipping leaders through biblical instruction has been the major Mennonite thrust in most of these ministries. Teaching patterns, determined by local needs and context, have varied greatly, ranging from the more formal seminary and training-center approach to itinerant village-based °theological education by extension (TEE). Retreat days, weekend outings, and week-long seminars have been particularly popular in many settings.

Other significant Mennonite ministries have included medical and educational work, agricultural and water development, translation projects, sewing classes, °literacy programs, literature development and distribution, the compilation of liturgical materials (hymnbooks, catechisms, etc.), and the collection of documentation and resources for use by churches being served.

Independent churches in increasing numbers express the desire to be a part of the larger world Christian fellowship. Yet many remain suspicious of outside overtures, fearing loss of identity or even takeover. It has been important in Mennonite initiatives to abandon all empire-building intentions, to respect and serve local structures, and to develop models of ministry based on mutual sharing, where the teacher becomes the learner and the learner becomes the teacher.   JRK

Harold W. Turner, *Bibliography of New Religious Movements in Black Africa* (Boston: G. K. Hall, 1977); idem, *Religious Innovation in Africa* (Boston: G. K. Hall, 1979), collected essays; Gottfried Oosterval, *Modern Messianic Movements* (Elkhart: IMS, 1973); David B. Barrett, *Schism and Renewal in Africa* (Nairobi, Addis Ababa, Lusaka: Oxford Press, 1968); Bengt Sundkler, *Bantu Prophets in South Africa* (London: Lutterworth Press, 1948; David A. Shank, "Mission Relations with the Independent Churches of Africa," *Missiology*, 13 (Jan. 1985), 24-44; idem, "A Survey of American Mennonite Ministries to African Independent Churches," *Mission Focus*, 13 (March 1985), 1-5; David A. Shank, ed., *Ministry of Missions to African Independent Churches* (Elkhart: MBM, 1987); Wilbert R. Shenk, "Mission Agency and African Independent Churches," *International Review of Mission*, 63, no. 251 (Oct. 1974), 475-91; Edwin and Irene Weaver, *The Uyo Story* (Elkhart: MBM, 1970); idem, *From Kuku Hill* (Elkhart: IMS, 1975); Stan W. Nussbaum, "Toward Theological Dialogue with Independent Churches: A Study of Five Congregations in Lesotho" (PhD thesis, U. of South Africa, 1985); unpublished papers presented at the Abidjan (Ivory Coast) Pan-African Interdenominational Conference of Mission Agencies Relating to AICs, July 14-19, 1986 (duplicated by and available from MBM), the first forum of its kind, making it possible to compare over a dozen models from ten different agencies (including Mennonite) at work in ten African nations; field reports and press releases describing various Mennonite ministries to AICs in: *AIMM Messenger*, 48, no. 3 (1981), 4-5; 49, no. 1 (1981), 8-10; 50, no. 3 (1983), 7-9; 50, no. 4 (1983), 6-8; 51, no. 1 (1984), 10-11; and 53, no. 2 (1986), 10-12; *GH* (July 20, 1982), 489-91; (May 21, 1985), 362; *Miss. Mess.* (Dec. 1976), 10, (Jan. 1979), 8, (Aug. 1981), 14-15, (Aug. 1983), 6; *MWR* (Dec. 5, 1985), 6; *Sent* (Feb. 1979), 8-11, (Apr. 1983), 1-3, (Sept. 1986), 1-5.

Afro-American Mennonite Association The Afro-American Mennonite Association (AAMA) is an organization, within the Mennonite church structure, whose membership is comprised of black and integrated congregations (80-100 percent black membership), associate congregations (less than 20 percent black membership), individuals committed to the goals of AAMA, and various groups within congregations, including youth groups and church agencies. Black and integrated congregations of the General Conference Mennonite Church are also members of AAMA. Sixty-seven black, integrated, and associate congregations are listed as members of AAMA. In 1988 there were 72 black, integrated, and associate congregations.

Approximately 4,500 blacks hold membership or regularly worship in a black or integrated congregation. This number does not reflect blacks who are participating in associate congregations. The average growth rate of black and integrated congregations has exceeded five percent per year during the last six years. The rate of growth is well above that of the denominations as a whole. Ninety-five percent of the black and integrated congregations are located in highly urbanized areas. In many locations most members of inner-city churches live in the suburbs.

AAMA was formed as a successor to the Black Caucus of the Mennonite Church (MC) in 1982 by virtue of the vote of delegates to the annual assembly of the Black Caucus. The AAMA provides a base from which scattered black and integrated congregations support and encourage one another. It provides special expertise to the larger church in dealing with the problems and needs of black and integrated congregations and communities, and provides direct services to its members if such services cannot be obtained elsewhere.

The move to an association structure brought about the following changes: (1) voluntary membership in the association, rather than automatic membership (in the Black Caucus) by virtue of a congregation's existence; (2) provision of membership for individuals who are not residing near a Mennonite church; (3) direct responsibility to the membership, rather than operating as a standing committee of the General Board (MC); (4) the virtual elimination of subsidies for the members to attend annual assemblies (formerly such subsidies reached $7,000), thus encouraging constituencies to support their own priorities; (5) change of priorities from contending for a "place" within the denomination and "fair" treatment to enabling congregations to grow, become self-sufficient, and develop new congregations; (6) establishment of formal working relationships with each of the program boards and conferences of the Mennonite Church, as well as involvement in joint goal setting and implementation of efforts, thus creating a cooperative work environment rather than the earlier adversarial relationships; (7) engagement in developing programs to fill gaps in the services provided by the program boards of conferences in order to meet congregational and individual needs, instead of being restricted to "fellowship activities."

The work of the AAMA, as well as the Black Caucus before it, was carried out by the Associate Secretary for Black Concerns of the General Board (MC). However, at the inception of the organization plans were approved by the General Board (MC) and AAMA for providing a separate executive director for AAMA.

At the beginning AAMA assessed needs and developed goals and strategies for accomplishing the goals. In the late 1980s, the association is in the process of implementing the goals based on annual review of the needs and strategy. Current priorities include leadership development, self-sufficiency, church growth, and church planting. A primary concern centers upon becoming acquainted with one another as pastors and congregations, finding ways to support and encourage one another over long distances, as well as working closely together to achieve greater results in shorter periods of time. The AAMA Board of Directors is responsible for the relational goals.

The organization operates with an eight-member board of directors which meets quarterly. The membership of AAMA mets annually to review and approve the work of the board of directors, give direction for the coming year, and provide fellowship and worship. Members of the board of directors may serve up to three three-year terms.

In producing resources to aid the congregations in the achievement of the goals and priorities, the AAMA assembly requested that first priority be given to developing leadership among black men and youth. Examples of resources which have been produced since AAMA's inception include: (1) a job description and qualifications for pastors of black and integrated congregations—an ideal model from which to develop a realistic expectation; (2) a correspondence training course for pastors (for use by the entire denomination, not limited to minorities); (3) a resource manual to aid pastors in evangelizing and nurturing black men; (4) a resource manual to assist volunteer youth directors; (5) aids for organizing and conducting administrative responsibilities within the church; (6) retreats targeting either black women or black men in black and integrated congregations; (7) national conferences addressing the °justice (°peace) concern from the perspective of black Mennonites and targeting black evangelicals in other denominations; (8) demonstration projects in congregational economic development in Philadelphia and in the Bronx, N.Y. (9) *United Action Newsletter,* published quarterly, a communication linkage among the black and integrated congregations, which emphasizes the achievements of congregations and individuals and other positive news.

Black pastoral leadership has steadily increased over the past 10 years until half of the black and integrated congregations are led by black pastors. Less than one-third of the congregations were pastored by blacks before the Black Caucus came into being. In 1986 the Virginia Mennonite Conference commissioned Leslie Francisco III (pastor of Calvary Community Church in Hampton, Va.) to become the second black bishop in the history of the Mennonites in North America. James °Lark, the first black bishop, and his wife were recognized as leaders before their time in developing new congregations and planning for long term developments.

Membership within black and integrated congregations includes a growing number of professionals with leadership abilities and skills brought from "secular" job training. However, this number remains fairly small in comparison to the resources available in the denominational sphere. A pastoral and lay leadership training program on the collegiate level was named after James Lark and is located in Philadelphia and Chicago.

The organization also continues to work for full acceptance of the cultural and religious traditions of its membership. AAMA operates with the belief that the unity Christ desired in his body, the church, incorporates diversity. The beauty within the body comes from the rainbow of colors and customs, which are free to mix and separate at will, while pursuing the same goals of service and evangelism.　　　　　　　　　　　　　　　　　　JLo

Leroy Bechler, *The Black Mennonite Church in North America, 1886-1986* (Scottdale, 1986); *MC Yearbook* (1988-89), 105.

Age, Respect for. See Aged, Care for; Ancestors, Respect for; Genealogy.

Age of Baptism. See Baptism, Age of.

Aged, Care for. Among those with special needs have always been the poor, the sick, the afflicted, and the widowed. Older persons, particularly women, have often fallen into one or more of the above categories. In North America over 60 percent of those above 65 years are female. The population is becoming older and more female. The fastest growing age group is women over 85. More than half of the older women are widows, and there are five times as many widows as widowers in North America.

Christ spoke most frequently about his concerns for the poor, the orphans, the oppressed, the brokenhearted, and the widows. There was good reason. "In every code except Hebrew the widow had rights of inheritance but in Hebrew law she was

completely ignored" (Interpreter's Dictionary of the Bible, vol. 4:842). The widow's plight was often the older person's plight, male or female. Even on the cross Jesus thought about his mother. He told John, "Behold, your mother!" And from that hour the disciple took her into his own home (Jn 19:27). The early church continued a mission and ministry of compassion.

The early Anabaptists were people of deep compassion. °Menno Simons stated, "True evangelical faith cannot lie dormant. . . . It clothes the naked. It feeds the hungry. It comforts the sorrowful. It shelters the destitute. It serves those who harm it. It binds up that which is wounded. It becomes all things to all men." The °°Dordrecht Confession (1632), art. 9, states that deacons are "to look after and care for the poor and honorable aged widows." The ministry of °°deacons and °°deaconesses found expression first among the Dutch Mennonites, and it was continued among the Mennonites in Russia and in America. °Homes for the aged were established in The Netherlands in the 17th and 18th c. These homes provided shelter and care primarily for the poor of the faith community. During the late 16th c. and through the 17th c., prosperous Dutch Mennonites contributed money and provisions to persecuted brethren in Switzerland and Germany, as well as to charitable causes not involving fellow Mennonites (Smith, *Mennonites of America,* 66).

In early North American history, the elderly were highly respected as persons of authority and power. They were few in number—two percent of the population in 1775 compared to 12 percent of the population in the 1980s. Also, the elderly were equal in education, and far ahead in experience, of the younger generations of that time. The population of the 13 colonies in 1775 was 90 percent rural, and the elderly controlled the means of production for more than a century. A certain degree of deference had to be shown the elderly if younger persons were to achieve later independence.

In 1900 and somewhat after, families were large, and typically one parent died before the last child left home. Life expectancy at birth was 47 years. Older parents expected care from the family, particularly in the case of a surviving spouse. Children felt a sense of duty and responsibility toward parents, and the parent or parents remained in the family home, with one or more of the children responsible to extend care generally until death of the parent. Education, broader employment opportunities, smaller families, greater life expectancy, and financial independence of parents (through government social insurance programs and children who had broader job opportunities) changed this. Accordingly, institutions began to develop to meet the needs of the elderly, needs formerly met by the family.

The Mennonite churches in North America were very slow in going beyond the family and the local congregation in caring for the elderly, sick, mentally and physically handicapped, widows, poor, and orphans. Local congregations did have alms funds to which members contributed, particularly at the time of °communion services, but these funds were very limited and very cautiously administered. This was the general pattern until the end of the 19th c.. However, those who can remember the early 20th c. recognize the tremendous discrepancy between, on the one hand, the kind words and thoughts about God and the church taking care of the widows, the poor, and the aged, and, on the other hand, what actually happened, particularly to widows.

The first home for the elderly sponsored by American Mennonites was the Salem Home at Hillsboro, Ks., opened in 1894. This was only 10 years after the Krimmer Mennonite Brethren had come from Russia, where Mennonites for many years had made many significant contributions to aging persons and to health care in general. The second home was the General Conference Mennonite home at Frederick, Pa., established in 1896; the third was the Welsh Mountain Samaritan Home established by the Lancaster Mennonite Conference in 1898, and the fourth was the Bethesda Home (GCM), at Goessel, Ks., in 1899. Only seven homes were added in the next 40 years. These early homes were operated for the care of older persons who were unable to care for themselves, but who did not require hospital attention. The primary purpose was to provide care for older members of the churches in a Christian atmosphere. Generally these homes provided for Mennonite indigents who had no responsible relatives or other persons willing to take care of them. By 1940 there were only 12 homes among all the Mennonites in North America established for older persons.

Since 1940 the development of church-administered facilities for aging persons has increased more than 800 percent. In 1987 there were more than 100 Mennonite-related homes for older persons in the United States and Canada. An aspect more important than taking care of material needs has also emerged. In many places Mennonites are attempting to capitalize on the total resources of older persons and to use these resources to benefit the church and the community.

Mennonites recognize that the needs of all people for food, clothing, and shelter are only a part of wholeness and wellness. This broadened concept has led to the development of a wide range of health ministry services which carries Mennonites far beyond the "Orphan's Homes" and "Old People's Homes" approach. It takes into account that aging is growth toward maturity from conception to physical death. In preparation for wellness in the later years, a healthy life-style must begin early. The congregation, with the larger conference or denomination, must provide a variety of °mutual aid and wellness ministries which will help older people to live independently longer. The broad sweep of services now organized under the Mennonite Health Association (Elkhart, Ind.) offers programs of wholeness and wellness, which should enable each to realize that, regardless of our birth dates we are, at any given time, determining what kinds of older persons we will be. The Mennonite council for Aging Ministries still carries an important role for older persons who need long term care, nursing services, and retirement programs.

However, other ancillary organizations are considered necessary and are in place: Inter-Mennonite Council on Aging, Mennonite Mental Health Services, Mennonite Council for Hospitals, Mennonite Developmental Disability Services, Mennonite Child Care Association, Mennonite Medical Association, Mennonite Nurses Association, Mennonite Chaplains Associates, Mennonite Mutual Aid, Canadian Mennonite Mental Health Assembly.

Mennonite formal institutional programs for older persons will continue to grow because of the sheer potential in numbers. In 1988 there are 32,000,000 persons 65 and above in Canada and the United States. That number is conservatively projected to be 67,000,000 in 2030. Mennonite norms presently follow the national norms quite closely.

It would be injudicious and extremely difficult economically to double the number of Mennonite retirement homes. A better use of ancillary services now in place and a creative approach to techniques not yet known or tried could help Mennonites tap the resources of older persons more intensively and extend their independence more appropriately. TRS

American Association of Retired Persons, "A Profile of Older Americans, 1986"; Edwin F. Rempel, ed., *Congregational Health Ministries Handbook* (Elkhart, Ind.: Mennonite Health Association, 1987); C. Henry Smith, *Mennonites of America* (Goshen, 1909); Yoder, *MC Census* (1985); *Gemeinde Unterwegs* (Nov. 1984), sp. issue.

See also Ancestors, Respect for; Homes, Retirement and Nursing.

Agencies, Church. See Institutions, Church.

Agriculture. See Bankruptcy ("A Letter from a Small-Town Banker" [feature]); Development Work; Geography; Industrialization; Occupations; Rural Life; Sciences, Natural.

Agua Azul Colony, Paraguay, was founded in 1970 by American Mennonites on 1,900 hectares (4,700 acres) located 375 km. (230 mi.) northeast of Asunción, some 80 km. (50 mi.) from the Brazilian border near Saltos de Guairá. They came both to preserve their traditional faith and to do missionary work among the Paraguayan people. The colony's name means "Blue Water."

Paraguayans living in the area have been won to the faith and baptized, upon which they are incorporated into the life of the congregation and the colony. Only members of the congregation may own land in the colony. Worship services and instruction in the school is carried on in both English and Spanish. Instructional materials are obtained from the *Rod and Staff* °publishing house in North America. A loose relationship is maintained to the Eastern Pennsylvania Mennonite Church. The churches in Agua Azul, °Rio Corrientes, and °Luz y Esperanza colonies together constitute the Mennonite Christian Brotherhood. In 1986 the colony comprised 25 families (172 persons). The congregation numbers 65 members, of which 33 were Paraguayans and 32 were Americans or Canadians. In 1980 some people from Agua Azul left to establish La °Montana Colony. GR

MWH (1978), 252; *MWH* (1984), 100.

Agua de Dios. See Iglesia Evangélica Menonita, Colombia.

Aibonito, Puerto Rico (ME IV: 1057), is located on the old military highway which joins San Juan, 80 km. (50 mi.) to the north, and Ponce, 50 km. (30 mi.) to the south. With an altitude of 2,000 feet (615 meters), it is the highest city in Puerto Rico. It is the seat of the municipality of Aibonito and has a population of more than 22,000. The municipality is divided into eight rural *barrios,* one of which is La Plata, where the first Mennonite Central Committee program began in July 1943. The municipality, of Aibonito is noted for its two most important products, poultry and flowers, both introduced to Puerto Rico by the Mennonites.

The central office of the Convención de las Iglesias Evangélicas Menonitas de Puerto Rico, Inc. (Convention of Mennonite Evangelical Churches) is located in Aibonito. The Aibonito Mennonite Church is the largest Mennonite congregation in Puerto Rico, with a membership of 80. Two other congregations in the municipality have 48 members. *Hospital General Menonita,* recognized on the island for its quality medical services, provides the following services for the people of the interior of the island: physical and respiratory therapy, orthopedics, pediatrics, gynecology, and surgery (131 beds). *Academia Betania,* located in Barrio Pulguillas, is an accredited four-year secondary school of 260 students. It is administered by the Puerto Rico Mennonite Convention.   JGH

Alabama (ME I:30). In 1988 there were 13 Mennonite congregations in Alabama, representing five different conferences. The Lancaster Mennonite Conference (MC) had eight congregations with total membership of 242. Two of the congregations were also members of the Afro-American Mennonite Association. In addition this conference had begun planting three more congregations in Birmingham and Montgomery. Gulf States Mennonite Fellowship (MC; 42 members), Brethren in Christ, and Beachy Amish Mennonite Fellowship (39 members) each had one congregation; the Church of God in Christ Mennonite (Holdeman) had two congregations. The Eastern Mennonite Board of Missions (MC) administered voluntary service units in Birmingham and Mobile; the Conservative Mennonite Board of Missions operated one in Boykin. An elementary and high school at Atmore sponsored by the Mennonite Christian Fellowship had 46 students.   RSa

MC Yearbook (1988-89), 18, 58, 66-70, 166-68, 121, 142, 150; Paul Dagen, *Seedtime and Harvest* (Lancaster, Pa.: the author, 1988).

See also Indian Ministries, North America.

Alaska (ME I:31). In 1947, Linford Hackman, pilot and beloved Alberta Mennonite minister, saw mission possibilities in Alaska. Self-supporting church workers Mahlon and Hilda Stoltzfus collaborated with the Covenant Church at the village of Fortuna Ledge (Marshall) (1952-57) and led a °°voluntary service unit at the village of Russian Mission until 1961. In 1978 Hackman encouraged Mennonites in Anchorage to form the Anchorage Mennonite Fellowship (21 members, 1984) which affiliated in 1981 with the Northwest Mennonite Conference (formerly

Alberta-Saskatchewan Conference). In 1986 Ray Horst and Timothy Burkholder assessed potential church planting at Homer, Kenai, and Fairbanks.   GB/JeB

Alberta (ME I:31). In 1988 there were 74 Mennonite congregations in Alberta, representing 10 different conferences as follows (number of congregations followed by membership in parenthesis): Brethren in Christ ([1986 statistics] 2, 26); Church of God in Christ Mennonite (9, 1,007); Conference of Mennonites in Canada ([GCM], 18, 1,933); Evangelical Mennonite Conference of Canada (3 congregations); Fellowship Churches (5, 94); Fellowship of Evangelical Bible Churches (formerly Evangelical Mennonite Brethren, 1 congregation); Midwest Mennonite Fellowship (1, 20); Mennonite Brethren (19, 2,476); Northwest Conference ([MC], 15, 825); Western Conservative Mennonite Fellowship (2 congregations). Two congregations were members of more than one conference. The Mennonite Brethren Church of Alberta and the Conference of Mennonites in Alberta (GCM) each sponsored a camping program. The Northwest Mennonite Conference (MC) had begun planting churches at Edmonton, Medicine Hat, and Sherwood Park. Since 1983 Mennonites in Calgary sponsored Menno Simons Christian school (kindergarten through grade 9) with 90 students and 6 teachers in 1988. There were six Mennonite Central Committee (MCC) Thrift and °SELFHELP Crafts outlets in the province (1988) and MCC also had five voluntary service units. As of 1982, there were 108 Hutterian colonies in the province.

Among several of the Mennonite bodies in the province, there has been a decided shift from rural to urban residence For example, only 14 percent of Alberta Mennonite Brethren lived in urban centers in 1959, compared to 52 percent in 1986. CLD/RSa

MC Yearbook (1988-89), 11-12, 73, 94, 96, 100, 120, 121, 142, 149, 150; *GCM Handbook* (1988), 5, 146; *Minutes (BIC)* (1986), 243.

Alberta Provincial Conference of the Mennonite Brethren Church (ME I:33). The first Mennonite Brethren church in Alberta was established by immigrants from Russia in 1926 in Coaldale, a southern farming community. Three years later several churches united to form a provincial conference to assist local churches in proclaiming the kingdom of God, unifying faith, stimulating vision, and enabling common ministries in areas of education and mission.

To provide young people access to educational opportunities, both local Bible schools and an Alberta Mennonite High School were established. As communities expanded and °urbanization increased, the high school was closed in 1964, and in 1968 the Bible school thrust was merged with that of the Saskatchewan Conference of Mennonite Brethren churches, as both conferences assumed sponsorship of Bethany Bible Institute.

In 1987 the conference consisted of 19 churches with a total membership of more than 2,250 scattered across the province. With more than 50 percent of the members located in urban centers, the churches also minister to the communities in which

ALBERTA

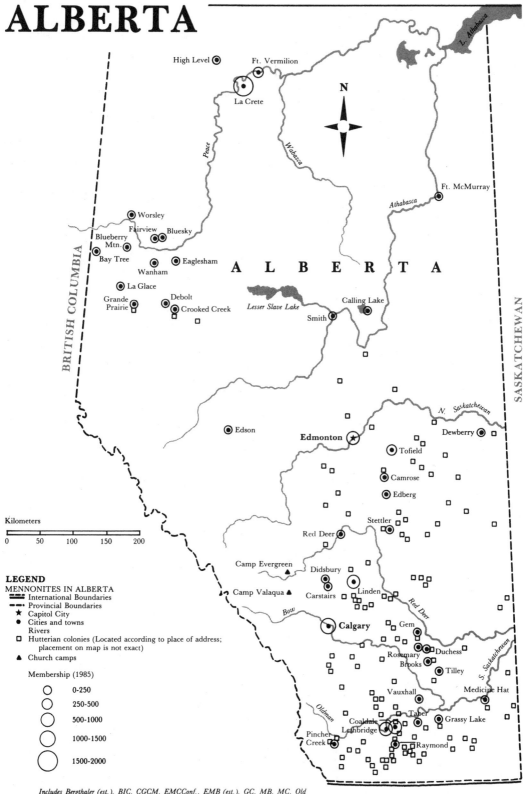

N

High Level
Ft. Vermilion
La Crete

Peace
Wabasca

Ft. McMurray

Athabasca

Worsley
Fairview   Bluesky
Blueberry
Mtn.
Bay Tree
Wanham   Eaglesham

A L B E R T A

La Glace
Grande   Debolt
Prairie   Crooked Creek
Lesser Slave Lake   Calling Lake
Smith

N. Saskatchewan

Edson
Edmonton   Dewberry
Tofield
Camrose
Edberg
Stettler
Red Deer

Kilometers
0   50   100   150   200

Camp Evergreen
Didsbury
Camp Valaqua   Carstairs   Linden
Bow   *Red Deer*

Calgary   Gem
Rosemary   Duchess
Brooks   Tilley
S. Saskatchewan
Vauxhall   Medicine Hat
Oldman   Taber   Grassy Lake
Coaldale
Pincher   Lethbridge
Creek   Raymond

LEGEND

MENNONITES IN ALBERTA
≡≡≡ International Boundaries
–·–· Provincial Boundaries
★   Capitol City
●   Cities and towns
     Rivers
□   Hutterian colonies (Located according to place of address;
     placement on map is not exact)
▲   Church camps

Membership (1985)

○   0-250
○   250-500
○   500-1000
○   1000-1500
○   1500-2000

BRITISH COLUMBIA

SASKATCHEWAN

Includes Bergthaler (est.), BIC, CGCM, EMCConf., EMB (est.), GC, MB, MC, Old Colony (est.), and Sommerfelder (est.) congregations.

they are found through Camp Evergreen and a Mailbox Bible Club. Ministries to native peoples (°Indian ministries) are pursued at Hobbema. In Calgary and Edmonton the churches also minister to East Asian people. Together the churches experience rich blessings in worship and service.   AGK

Alberta-Saskatchewan Mennonite Conference. See Northwest Conference of the Mennonite Church.

Algemene Doopsgezinde Sociëteit (ME I:52). Immediately following World War II, the Algemene Doopsgezinde Sociëteit (ADS) played a central role among the Dutch congregations, a leadership role occasioned by the difficulties of the war years and the German occupation. During the 1960s and later, Dutch Mennonite leaders became aware of a growing desire for change in the function of this central agency. This led to a meeting of the directors of the ADS and congregational representatives at Elspeet in April 1970 to reflect on the functioning of the ADS and on congregational renewal. A list of recommendations was drawn up, beginning with a concern that greater unity and fraternal relationships should transcend local congregational autonomy. Beyond this, it was felt that the several agencies e.g., the mission board, (Doopsgezinde Zendingsraad), youth office (Doopsgezinde Jeugdcentrale), fellowship committee (Gemeenschap voor Doopsgezind °°Broederschapswerk), and the relief and service committee (Stichting voor Bijzondere Noden), should have a place in the administrative structure of the ADS.

These recommendations led to the appointment of a structures review committee following intense review of issues in all congregations across the land. During a period of several years, a new structure for the ADS was recommended; it was adopted on June 3, 1975. In this agreement, the primary purpose of the ADS was stated as being the strengthening of congregational life and faith, with particular concern for the evangelism and proclamation of the word. The ADS was commissioned to increase support of congregational activities, while the congregations committed themselves to increased spiritual and material fellowship and support. The structure for achieving these objectives consists in the brotherhood meeting (conference), in which all congregations are equally represented, and in two agencies to implement decisions: the brotherhood council (Broederschapsraad), organized regionally with local agency participation, and the general board (Dagelijks Bestuur committee).

While the congregations were more actively related to the ADS after 1975, the freedom of the ADS to take new initiatives remained too limited. At the same time, the tendency to return to earlier patterns of congregational autonomy became apparent. Nevertheless, the discussion about renewal continued, particularly as congregations and the ADS became aware of the decline in total membership. This led in 1976 to the establishing of the BOLT (Broederschap op langere termijn) commission, which was to concern itself with the study and analysis of longer range trends within the brotherhood. Based upon a sociological study, this group made a recommendation in 1979 for the strengthening of leadership training and a broadening of the mandate of the seminary. In view of the urgent need for more pastors and leaders, the seminary received the assignment to provide an alternative two-year course in Anabaptist theology and congregational leadership for persons who, for one reason or another, could not pursue the full university-seminary curriculum. Two faculty members were added to the seminary in 1981 to make this program, known as the "Second Way," possible.

In keeping with the earlier study, the ADS mandate was also increased considerably and, since 1986, the ADS is better prepared organizationally to support congregational and other activities. At the same time, the declining membership has led to financial concerns. Fortunately, the merging of the ADS ministers pension fund with the larger national fund in 1986, together with additional federal funds received on the basis of longstanding obligations, resolved the earlier financial concerns.

Ecumenical cooperation with other denominations remains a significant task for the ADS. One visible sign of this cooperation was the publication of a new joint hymnal in 1973. Most Protestant congregations in The Netherlands now use this hymnal.

Chairmen of the ADS have been: H. Craandijk (to 1959), S. M. A. Daalder (1959-63), J. J. J. van Sluijs (1963-70), S. C. Dierdorp (1970-71), C. F. Brüsewitz (1971-79), J. A. van Ingen Schenau-Elsen (the first woman in this office; 1979-83), and S. A. Vis (1983-). R. de Zeeuw was executive secretary until 1979, when he was succeeded by E. van Straten. G. H. Rahusen (to 1971), A. C. Bakker (1971-83), P. Krom (1983-86), and G. Witteveen (1986-) served as treasurer.   CFB

S. A. Vis, "175 jaar ADS," in *Doops. Jaar.* (1986), 24-32; *MWH* (1978), 303-6; *MWH* (1984), 123.

Algeria (ME IV:1058). A group of °°Pax volunteers, under the °°Mennonite Relief and Service Committee, was sent to Algeria in 1955 to assist with reconstruction after an earthquake. In 1957 the Mennonite Board of Missions (MC) founded the Algeria Mennonite Mission and sent its first missionaries. A small group of Mennonite Board of Missions (MBM) missionaries was present in Algeria until 1977, and until her retirement in 1988 in Algeria, the board continued to support a French Mennonite missionary nurse, Annie Haldemann, who has been in Algeria since 1957.

Mennonite Central Committee (MCC) entered Algeria late in 1961. In the summer of 1962, Algeria gained independence after a seven-year war with France, and that fall the number of MCC workers greatly increased. MCC worked through Christian Committee for Service in Algeria (organized by the World Council of Churches) in reconstruction, food and clothing distribution, demonstration farming, medical work, mechanics and agriculture instruction, and teaching. Besides North Americans, Mennonites from Switzerland, Germany, The Netherlands, and France were part of the MCC team. The highest number of workers was 23 adults in 1966. By 1971 MCC work was limited to high school teachers, the last of whom left in 1978.   MH

MCC annual reports, 1960-78; MBM annual reports, 1955-

77; Algeria newsletters from 1963 to 1980, and personal letters of Marian Hostetler, 1961-70 (Hist. MS 1-736, MC Archives, Goshen).

Alianza Evangélica Menonita de la Argentina (Evangelische Mennonitische Alianzgemeinde in Argentinien / Evangelical Mennonite Brethren Church in Argentina). Early in the 1940s, individuals from Paraguayan Mennonite colonies moved to Buenos Aires, looking for work. In 1947 about 150 (out of ca. 2,000) Russian-Mennonite immigrants to Paraguay on the first *Volendam* transport stayed in Buenos Aires, hoping for better living conditions. Hundreds of the others soon returned to Buenos Aires from Paraguay.

Mennonite Central Committee (MCC), by request of various Mennonite mission boards of North America, established a religious and social center in Buenos Aires in 1949 (°ME I:154). After three years of pastoral ministry, a believers' fellowship organized with sanction from the various Paraguayan churches and North American mission boards. From its outset, this fellowship was intended to be an "alliance" between the various Mennonite conferences—thus the name *Alianza Evangélica Menonita de la Argentina.* Members are baptized upon their faith by either immersion or sprinkling.

In 1962, once the congregation was established and had its own building, MCC ended its involvement. This German-speaking congregation then joined the Evangelical Mennonite Brethren (°Fellowship of Evangelical Bible Churches) conference, being cared for primarily by the Paraguayan Evangelische Mennonitische Brüderschaft (°Konferenz der Evangelischen Mennonitischen Brüderschaft von Südamerika). conference. The congregation is continually weakened by emigration to Europe and North America, due to Argentinian political and economical upheavals. The congregation has established a Spanish-speaking congregation at Delviso, near Buenos Aires.   MD

MC Yearbook (1986-87) 164; *Minutes EMB* (1984), 55-56; *MWH* (1978), 247-48, (1984), 97.

Allebach, Ann Jemima (May 8, 1874–Apr. 27, 1918), has the distinction of being the first Mennonite woman on record to be ordained a minister by Mennonites in North America. She was ordained Jan. 15, 1911, at First Mennonite Church, Philadelphia, by minister N. B. Grubb, assisted by her pastor, J. W. Schantz, of Eden Mennonite Church, Schwenksville, Pa.

Ann was born to Jacob R. and Sarah Markley Allebach of Green Lane, Pa. Her parents were successful merchants, and her father, in addition, became the banker and postmaster of the town. She was baptized in the Eden congregation and became active in the Christian Endeavor movement, founding the first group in her area. In 1893 she became principal of the East Orange, N.J., Collegiate School and attended classes at New York U., Columbia U., and Union Theological Seminary in New York City. During these years in New York, she was engaged in the women's suffrage movement and served among the poor, teaching Sunday school in an Episcopal chapel and interviewing job applicants. At one point, at the request of the New York mayor, she arranged conferences on home religion and other social services.

It was during these years that she approached her mentor, N. B. Grubb, pastor of the First Mennonite Church in Philadelphia, and her own pastor, about ordination. It appears that they, more or less on their own, were open to her convictions and proceeded with the service in the company of a large audience of church members, friends, and family. Even though it may have been done at that time with little conference support, there did develop some openness in the conference to have her return as guest preacher from time to time. Her Christian commitment and fervent oratory drew large and curious audiences. One September Sunday in 1912 she preached in the morning on Job 23:8, 9 at her home congregation at Eden; in the afternoon at Zion congregation in Souderton on Jn 14:6; and in the evening at Harleysville Chapel on Acts 1:8, all to overflow audiences. From 1911 to 1918, her name appeared on the annual roster of Eastern District Conference ministers in *Mennonite Yearbook and Almanac.*

In 1916 she accepted a call to ministry at the Sunnyside Reformed Church, Long Island. Here, as elsewhere, people were drawn by her enthusiasm and earnestness, until a sudden heart attack ended her short, but intense life.   JHF

"Biography," *Mennonite Yearbook and Almanac* (1919); "Sketch of Miss Annie J. Allebach," *Mennonite* (Jan. 19, 1911); Mary Lou Cummings, *Full Circle* (Newton, 1978); John L. Ruth, *Maintaining the Right Fellowship* (Scottdale, 1984).

Allebach, Harvey G. (Feb. 18, 1869–Dec. 3, 1921). Harvey Allebach's modest life, interrupted often by ill health, does not do justice to his ministry as gifted student, teacher, preacher, poet, pastor, editor, and naturalist.

Harvey was born to Jacob R. and Elizabeth Gottshall Allebach, in Lower Salford Township, Montgomery Co., Pa. When he was two, his mother died from smallpox, and for several years he lived with his maternal grandparents, Mose and Mary Gottshall. When his father married Sarah Markley in 1873, he went to their new home in Green Lane, Pa., where he and his half-sister, Ann Jemima, grew up. He was educated at Ursinus College and graduated with honors from the U. of Pennsylvania. He was a teacher and principal at several high schools in his native county and taught for one year at the East Orange, N.J., Collegiate Institute for women, a school conducted by his half-sister.

Early in life, he felt called into the ministry and was licensed, and later ordained, by his uncle, William S. Gottshall. He served in his home congregation at Schwenksville and frequently preached at the First Mennonite Church, Philadelphia, where he was active in Christian Endeavor during his university days. He was pastor of Mennonite churches at Eicher and Wayland, Iowa, for several years beginning in 1894; taught at the Araphaho Mission School, Darlington, Oklahoma Territory, for one year; and was pastor of the Pottstown and Boyertown, Pa., Mennonite congregations (GCM). He edited *The Mennonite* at Berne, Ind., 1902-05. From 1914 to 1921, he was pastor of the East and West

Swamp congregation, as well as the Bethany and Flatland congregations in Pennsylvania. After a long struggle with tuberculosis, he succumbed to pneumonia. His body was buried in the Mennonite Cemetery high on Mine Hill at Schwenksville.   JHF

"Biography," *Mennonite Yearbook and Almanac* (1923); H. G. Allebach, *Echoes from Parnassus* (Berne, Ind., 1902); John L. Ruth, *Maintaining the Right Fellowship* (Scottdale, 1984), 411, 412, 423, 424, 439; Freeman H. Swartz, "Contemporaries in 1921," *Messenger, Eastern District Conference [GCM]*, 7, no. 4 (Summer 1954).

Echoes from Parnassus

Harvey Allebach was an enthusiastic botanist, astronomer, and ornithologist, who frequently led parties to the hills and valleys of his home town, where he was aquainted with song birds, rare plants, and the planets and constellations. While editor of *The Mennonite* at Berne, Ind., he published a booklet of poems, titled "Echoes from Parnassus." John L. Ruth calls this volume "impressive evidence of genuine literary powers" and adds "[he] would later be called 'the best preacher in the conference' and a man of rare spirituality. The forced retirement, for reasons of health, of this lanky, intellectual, and devout preacher left his congregation in tears." Lines from his 1897 poem, titled "My Legacy", were indeed prophetic:

". . . he lived the life of every day
Unknown to fame, content to be obscure;
Perfectly happy, feeling all was pure, . . ."   JHF

Allegheny Mennonite Conference (MC) (ME IV:589) has congregations in Delaware, Maryland, Pennsylvania, and West Virginia. Its principal membership concentrations are within a triangle bordered roughly by Lewistown, Pittsburgh, and Cumberland. The 1987 membership was 3,775 in 36 congregations.

A constitution adopted in 1981 provides for five commissions: Leadership; Finance and Stewardship; Nurture and Education; Missions and Service; Faith, Life and Procedures. Related organizations are Women's Missionary and Service Auxiliary, Allegheny Conference Laymen's Fellowship, and Mennonite Disaster Service. The Missions and Service Commission sponsors the development of new congregations. It has also been involved with International Guest House in Washington, D.C.; World's Attic in Somerset, Pa.; and Diakonia at Ocean City, Md.

Between sessions of the conference assembly, the work of the conference is monitored by a coordinating council comprising the chairs of the five commissions plus the moderator and the moderator-elect. The council employs the conference minister. The conference publication is *Allegheny Conference News,* published 10 times a year.   DH

Sanford G. Shetler, *Two Centuries of Struggle and Growth* (Allegheny Mennonite Conference, 1963); *MC Yearbook* (1988-89), 46-47.

Allegiance, Pledge of. See Civil Religion; Flag; Patriotism.

Allen Co., Ind., Old Order Amish Settlement. See

Grabill-New Haven, Ind., Old Order Amish Settlement.

All-India Mennonite Women's Conference was organized by the °Mennonite Christian Service Fellowship of India (MCSFI). P. J. °Malagar organized a committee of women from the MCSFI constituency. The following committee members helped to get the organization started: coordinator, P. J. Malagar (Mennonite Church in India [MCI], Dhamtari); chairperson, Mrs. H. Bhelwa (MCI, Dhamtari); vice-chairperson, Mrs. Kriparam (MB, Andhra Pradesh); secretary, Mrs. K. Martin (MCI, Dhamtari); treasurer, Mrs. E. Kniss, (Bihar Mennonite Mandli, Bihar); other members: Mrs. U. Sona, (GCM, Madhya Pradesh); Miss Leah Sonwani (GCM, Madhya Pradesh); Mrs. Irene Roy (BIC, Bihar); Mrs. Premlata John (MB, Andhra Pradesh); and Mrs. P. Sarkar (United Missionary Church of India, Calcutta).

The first conference was held Nov. 1-6, 1977, at the Sunderganj Mennonite Church, Dhamtari. About 250 women from outside Dhamtari were present. They experienced a wonderful and warm fellowship with Mennonite women from a variety of places in India. They decided to retain most of the original committee to plan for the next meeting. Mrs. U. Sona replaced Mrs. E. Kniss as treasurer. The committee met and decided the conference should support one nurse in training at Dhamtari Christian Hospital.

The second All-India Mennonite Women's Conference was held at Shamshabad, Andhra Pradesh (Oct. 14-18, 1983). This conference, was coordinated by the director of MCSFI, R. S. Lemuel (MB). At this conference 262 women registered. They made decisions which should give stability for continuation of the organization. They accepted the following goals: (1) to bring unity between Mennonite women in India; (2) to understand their common Anabaptist heritage; (3) to make it possible for Mennonite women in India to meet together for fellowship and mutual understanding; (4) to discuss the status of women in the church and community and to seek solutions to common problems.

The second conference formalized the organization with decisions to meet every five years; require each registered member to contribute six rupees per year; require the treasurer's report be sent to each constituency; and circulate a newsletter every six months. Two women were chosen from each constituency to carry on the business of the organization between meetings. The first officers under this permanent plan are: president, Mrs. K. Martin (MCI); vice-president, Mrs. Arnold (MB); secretary, Mrs. S. Paul (MB),treasurer, Mrs. U. Sona (GCM); and news editor, Mrs. N. Das (MCI).   VAM

All-Union Council of Evangelical Christians–Baptists (AUCECB) The AUCECB is the only church body, apart from the Russian Orthodox church, that is recognized as a church existing throughout the Soviet Union, other confessions having only regional or local recognition. At a congress in Moscow in October 1944, under wartime conditions, former representatives of the Evangelical Christian and Baptist Unions, which had collapsed before the war, agreed to unite. In 1945 the state gave several Pentecostal groups the option of joining the AUCECB or ceasing to function. An "August Agreement" spelled out the conditions of union, requiring Pentecostals to forego the practice of glossalalia and other distinctives, except in private. Mennonites were officially invited to join in 1963, and an agreement of union was approved at an All-Union Congress in December 1966.

At that time about 16,000 Mennonites were said to have joined. The number increased to 25,000-30,000 by the mid-1980s. This means that about half of the believing Mennonites in the Soviet Union are part of the AUCECB, where fusion has reached the point that individuals refer to themselves as "Evangelical Christians-Baptists" (ECB). Nevertheless, spokesperson Emil Baumbach strongly affirmed a sense of Anabaptist-Mennonite identity when questioned during a visit to Canada in July 1987.

Ties between Soviet evangelicals and the Mennonites have existed for a long time and involve mutual influence (°°Baptists). The fact that Mennonites officially joined after 1963 probably had much to do with creating an image of unity for the AUCECB at a time when they were losing nearly half their supporters to a separating renewal movement, now known as the °Council of Churches of Evangelical Christians-Baptists (CCECB). At the All-Union Congress in 1963, the first permitted by the state since 1944, four persons of Mennonite origin were present. They were Jacob Fast, Johann Martens, G. K. Alert, and Traugott Kviring. All were preachers in AUCECB churches. Alert, from °Karaganda, where Mennonites were divided on how to relate to Baptists, addressed the congress delegates (this time elected but often with uncertain mandates) as follows: "I fail to see the difference between you and us and request the congress to accept Mennonite congregations into the Union of Evangelical Christians-Baptists." At its July 1964 session, the AUCECB presidium, in part presumably at the instigation of a senior member I. I. Motorin, who was enthusiastic about his encounter with North American Mennonites, took four decisions: (1) to determine the number and location of all Mennonites in the Soviet Union; (2) to accept all immersed Mennonite Brethren unconditionally into ECB congregations; (3) to secure the right for Mennonites joining AUCECB churches to have their own services in German; and (4) to request state registration of Mennonite Brethren groups in those locations where there were no registered ECB congregations.

Several local unofficial consultations of Mennonites took place and, at the 1966 congress, where 74 of the 400 delegates were Mennonite Brethren, these representatives (with the exception of four from Karaganda) presented a signed application for membership. By this time such Mennonite distinctives as pacifism and feetwashing had not been practiced by Mennonites for many decades; now they were no longer part of their confession of faith, either. Nevertheless, Mennonites (and with them German Baptists) received the cultural concession of German-language services. In practice this often also meant a separate organizational structure within a local church, different in style from that of the Russians. Since local Mennonite groups had not met to vote on the proposed union, it now remained for the Mennonite leaders to persuade the members to support the union.

Mennonite representatives were named to the headquarters staff in Moscow (Viktor Kriger, who had been sent by the AUCECB for two years of theological study in Hamburg), and to the major decision-making bodies. In 1966 Jacob Fast of Novosibirsk was elected to the All-Union Council; Kriger was a candidate member. A further increase in Mennonite representation came in 1974, when Kriger, who remained a staff member in Moscow, did not stand for reelection. Traugott Kviring replaced him, with Philip P. Wirtz as candidate member. Another Volhynian German, V. A. Schultz, was elected to the finance, or revision, committee. Jacob Fast was now also elected into the 10-member presidium. Mennonites were also elected as assistant regional superintendents, with Kviring, in 1977, becoming the first German elected as senior presbyter of a large region encompassing three Central Asian republics. In 1979 Fast was also elected as deputy senior presbyter for the vast °Russian Soviet Federated Socialist Republic and given the task of administrative oversight of all Germans in that area.

With each passing congress, it became evident that the Mennonites exerted some influence as a voting bloc, often siding with the Ukrainian contingent in expressing anxiety about the AUCECB's role ecumenically. It also became apparent that the Mennonites, in general, were theologically conservative. The elected representatives usually received near unanimous support during the All-Union elections, which was certainly not the case for many of the other council and presidium members. The Moscow leadership also called regular meetings with a dozen of the leaders to review the relationship every several years.

It was only after 1966 and the consummation of the union with the AUCECB that it became possible for Mennonite Brethren and °"Kirchliche" Mennonites to obtain local autonomous registration as Mennonites, albeit without a nonresistant clause in their constitution. This government-imposed difficulty had prompted Mennonite World Conference President Harold S. °Bender to urge Mennonites whom he met during a visit to the Soviet Union in 1956 to seek protection under the AUCECB umbrella. He, as did most Mennonite representatives from North America who visited subsequently, discussed with the Moscow leadership the possibilities for an amicable relationship. The Moscow AUCECB leaders, especially Alexander Karev, the general secretary, were supportive, even sending out a circular in 1964 urging local congregations to accept Kirchliche Mennonites (who were not immersed) for communion. The second-class role of the Kirchliche Mennonites remained a persistent point of contention. Moscow leaders often suggested that local Mennonite Brethren leadership resisted a compromise solution with Mennonites most strongly.

During the past two decades, relationships with Mennonite World Conference and Mennonite Central Committee have become regularized. A delegation of six from the AUCECB attended the Mennonite World Conference in Wichita (1978), two of whom (Kviring and Fast) were Mennonites. Heinrich Gertsen and Bernhard Sawadsky represented an autonomous Mennonite Brethren church in Karaganda and a Mennonite church in Novosibirsk at the same assembly. In 1984 in Strasbourg, the four-person delegation to the Mennonite World Conference included Fast, plus Daniel Janzen and Diedrich Thiessen of autonomous Mennonite Brethren and Mennonite churches respectively. Mennonite Central Committee had developed a more intimate relationship through its administration of a cooperative project to produce the Barclay commentaries on the New Testament in Russian.

Currently (1987), slightly more than half of all Mennonites are claimed by the AUCECB. There have been significant personnel changes recently. Jacob Fast was removed from all offices after August 1986, at the request of his local church, which was disciplining him, and Traugott Kviring had emigrated to West Germany. They were succeeded by Emil Baumbach of Karaganda, also appointed to the presidium in 1987 and made an assistant senior presbyter. He too was excommunicated in July 1988 for adultery. The current spokespersons are Peter P. Ens of Orenburg, assisted by a half-dozen regional representatives, and Johannes P. Dyck, AUCECB staff specialist for Mennonites, who has become an authority on Anabaptist as well as AUCECB history. During the past decade, there have been many new registrations of churches in the °Orenburg region, most of which maintain a fraternal relationship to the AUCECB (if they are Mennonite Brethren) but have not joined formally. More than 54 local AUCECB congregations are heavily Mennonite/German. Most of these are located in °Kazakhstan and °Kirgizia, but detailed statistics are still only sporadically available as is true for the AUCECB churches in general.   WWS

Walter Sawatsky, *Soviet Evangelicals Since World War II* (Scottdale, 1981); idem, "What Makes Russian Mennonites Mennonite?" *MQR*, 53 (1979), 5-20; "Presidium Report," *Bratskii Vestnik*, no. 4 (1987); *MWH* (1978), 310; *MWH* (1984) 126.

See also Union of Soviet Socialist Republics.

Altar Call. Mennonites, in the main, do not use the altar call, that is, the calling of persons to the front of the church by an invitation to repentance and faith, °conversion, or for special ministering to some need through prayer and counseling. This means that one can go to many Mennonite congregations and never hear such an invitation given. The altar call originated in the "new measures" of Charles Finney (1792-1875) and in frontier and °holiness camp meetings (°ME I:499). Many Mennonites, particularly in the "Old Mennonite" (MC) tradition opposed such °revival techniques, including the "anxious bench" and altar call. Some Mennonites and Brethren in Christ, particularly those open to holiness teaching were more ready to accept them. Some Mennonites largely ignored the issue.

With the coming of an emphasis on spiritual renewal, particularly °evangelistic tent campaigns and congregational revival meetings (late 19th c. and early 20th c.), people were invited to respond to the message by coming to the front of the tent or church, to kneel or stand there in order to be ministered to by a counselor. Sometimes people were invited to move from the front to a prayer room provided for counsel and prayer.

Some Mennonite groups which emphasize more evangelistic and revivalistic preaching use the altar call more consistently. Invitations to public confession of faith or to a fresh step of commitment are not uncommon, particularly in a series of renewal or revival services. There are some congregations which call for response regularly in the service. Many times the invitation is to stand or to raise the hand to make the response known, with the invitation to talk to with the pastor or a special counselor following the service.

One of the influences of the °charismatic movement is that the use of the altar call is prominent in newer congregations, which are more open to change. This call to the altar is many times for persons who desire prayer, a greater fullness of the Spirit, or greater surrender to °service.   JMD

Wittlinger, *Piety and Obedience* (1978), 204-5.

Alternative Service (ME I:604; I:76). It was 1918. Rufus °Jones, chairman of the °°American Friends Service Committee had just returned from yet another fruitless mission to Washington, D.C. "It apparently did not occur to the Washington people that our objection to war was anything more than an objection to the direct killing of people. They do not seem to understand that we are opposed to the military system. . . ." Jones had hoped the War Department would be willing to help design a program of alternative service for World War I °conscientious objectors (COs). The model he had in mind was already functioning as the Friends reconstruction work behind the lines in war-torn France. The problem was that COs were not allowed to enroll for the work.

The unfortunate experiences of °historic peace church (HPC) objectors in °World War I lent special urgency to the development of alternative service plans at the onset of °World War II. The result was the °°Civilian Public Service program (CPS). Both the US military °conscription administrators and the historic peace churches desired an alternative service program.

For military's Selective Service System, COs were a practical nuisance: they obstructed the conscription machinery. So Selective Service System welcomed a relatively simple solution—Civilian Public Service—which solved many of their administrative problems and met the political need of Congress to require a level of sacrifice from the objector sufficient to satisfy the public in time of war.

For most peace church members, CPS was a positive statement of their desire to emphasize Christian service as an alternative to °military service. On the practical level, it represented the most that was politically possible for COs in the context of World War II. Complete deferment was politically impossible. Imprisonment was not an option most peace church COs were prepared to accept.

No one captured the essence of the alternative

service idea better than Guy Hershberger, in a 1935 essay entitled "Is Alternative Service Desirable and Possible?" War is a time of suffering and it behooves Christians to serve those who suffer, he argued. Alternative service offers a Christian witness; a graphic alternative way of behaving in wartime.

When conscription began again in 1948, Congress, in a fit of amnesia, provided for a simple deferment for COs. With the high casualties of the Korean War in 1951, public opinion forced termination of the deferment clause, and a new era of alternative service was ushered in.

The new program, I-W service, which existed with little change from 1951 to 1973, was quite different from CPS. Objectors were employed in government and nonprofit organizations engaged in charitable, health, social welfare, educational, and scientific work. They could volunteer and choose their service job. They could serve abroad. And they were paid wages comparable to those of non-CPS fellow workers. Immediate supervision of the program, was placed with state Selective Service directors. In the 22 years of the program approximately 15,000 Mennonite and Brethren in Christ men participated in the I-W service.

Alternative service is an attractive possibility for many COs, for it meets a minimal obligation of citizenship in a democracy in time of war—public service. While some COs have opted for exile or imprisonment as a Christian and moral protest against war, especially during the °Vietnam War (1965-74), most Mennonites prefer alternative service because it has the potential for a positive witness against war in the form of acts of love and goodwill.

During the 1970s, the idea of a National Service program which would require all young persons to serve the nation for a year or two years, either in a military or a civilian assignment, was proposed in the United States. Despite some perceived advantages, Mennonites have not endorsed the idea for two reasons. One is a growing conviction that conscientious objection to war should more directly challenge the military system. Alternative service, as an aspect of national service, would confront public awareness even less directly than it has in the past. A second reason is suspicion of the government's right to a claim on an individual's life. The national service idea has a proto-fascist connotation which promotes nationalism and becomes another military wedge into civilian life.

Alternative service is an idea which has great appeal to many pacifists. The Federal Republic of Germany (West Germany) has an alternative service plan modeled on the earlier I-W program in the United States, and a recent United Nations draft proposal for universal recognition of conscientious objectors to war has a suggestion for alternative service as one means by which conscientious objectors could meet citizenship obligations.   ANK

Albert Keim and Grant M. Stoltzfus, *The Politics of Conscience* (Scottdale, 1988); Hans Rempel, ed., *Waffen der Wehrlosen. Ersatzdienst der Mennoniten in der USSR* (Winnipeg, CMBC Publications, 1980); Wittlinger, *Piety and Obedience* (1978), 379-81, index; Lawrence Klippenstein, "Mennonite Pacifism and State Service in Russia" (PhD diss., U. of Minnesota, 1984).

See also Associação das Igrejas Menonitas do Brasil;

Forsteidienst; Medical Service; Nazarenes; Privileges.

Ältester. See Elder.

Altkolonier Mennoniten Gemeinden. See Old Colony Mennonites.

American Civil War. The "brothers war" of 1861 to 1865, when 31 million people of the United States turned upon each other in terrible strife, affected Mennonites and Amish in varied and complex ways. Unprepared for intense war hysteria and military °conscription, many found little room remaining for neutrality. No war had arrested their attention for three generations.

Many had become comfortably established in America. Caught up in the spirit of building America or moving west with the frontier, their quiescent piety had little room for Christian education or even church periodicals. Calls for enlistees to "save the Union" found numerous unbaptized young men joining local regiments and marching off to war. Most Mennonites and Amish, however, tried to avoid °military service, as °nonresistance remained the official position of their churches. Large and strong churches and communities sometimes found that easier to maintain than weaker frontier communities.

From their own records, we learn only a little about how Mennonites and Amish were jolted by feverish and rabid patriotism. Local newspapers and government records here and there reveal more. By the 1860s, many Mennonites had become used to the idea of °°voting, serving as school directors, and even holding local offices. Generally, Republican Party candidates got the Amish and Mennonite vote. Two notable exceptions were the Hessian Amish at Danvers, Ill., and the Amish of Holmes Co., Ohio, where German Township had a nearly unanimous Democrat Party voting pattern.

Mennonite and Amish historic teachings on nonresistance, paying of °taxes, and being loyal to government sometimes became verbal flash points in local communities. After a year of war, by the summer and fall of 1862, there was alarm when the first draft threatened. Many Pennsylvania Mennonites scrambled to file °conscientious objector depositions permitted by that state, or they sought physical exemptions. Franconia area ministers went to visit the Pennsylvania governor. In Ohio John M. °°Brenneman drafted a petition to President Lincoln and tried to get a fellow minister to take it to Washington. No evidence has been found that it reached Lincoln. Mennonites favored the Union, abhorred rebellion, and were glad to pay a fine, said Brenneman. In Wayne Co. the Sonnenberg congregation held a special meeting to discuss "the present sad state of the country," then sent resolutions to Ohio's governor, offering money and suggesting a commutation fee in lieu of military service. Within several months, a large majority of family heads had given a total of over $1,500 to the local military committee. Fellow Swiss Mennonites at Bluffton petitioned Ohio's governor to levy a reasonable military tax. The Amish of Holmes Co., as described by several letters, were said to be wholly nonresistant and would not fight, but they would be happy to pay liberally for substitutes.

Pro-union sentiments tend to be obvious. Amish mothers in the Peoria, Ill., area even sang a derisive ditty to their children about Jefferson Davis. Samuel Hage's letter from Washington, Iowa, expressed chagrin at southern sympathizers. Minister Peter Nissley of Marietta in Lancaster Co., Pa., had this same opinion. He heard the cannon and watched the burning of the long and magnificent 40-foot wide Columbia bridge across the Susquehanna—a fire set by "our few men" to stop the "Rebels." Throughout the war, Mennonites in Lancaster Co. were assaulted verbally in the newspapers. Many were successful farmers, and some neighbors failed to understand how Mennonites could vote for Thaddeus Stevens, Republican leader of the House of Representatives—a fire-breathing warmonger—then insist on avoiding military duty by buying substitutes or paying the $300 commutation fee.

John F. °°Funk, a baptized Mennonite and a Chicago businessman, joined the Wide Awakes Republican Club and at one point considered joining the military, if drafted. After a crucial visit to Indiana Mennonites, he turned from political interests to begin the °°Herald of Truth, to write Warfare: Its Evils, Our Duty in 1864, and to publish John M. Brenneman's booklet, Christianity and Warfare. Toward the end of the war a few voices began to question whether nonresistant Mennonites should be buying substitutes and paying money so freely.

Virginia Mennonites have a considerably different story, as outlined in Samuel Horst's Mennonites in the Confederacy (Scottdale, 1967). Most were pro-Union, but under duress of life and limb some voted in favor of Virginia seceding from the Union. A few risked voting against it. Some were forced into the military but then refused to shoot at people. Arrests, prison, high fines, and other pressures finally drove quite a few to take flight to the North. Mennonite farmers saw their horses pressed into service, and raiding soldiers took food and supplies. The final and worst outrage came when General Sheridan's raid through the Shenandoah Valley torched more than 2,000 barns, more than 70 mills, and a few houses and devastated food supplies. Numerous families secured passes and transportation northward.   JOLe

John M. Brenneman, "A Civil War Petition to President Lincoln," MHB, 34 (Oct. 1973), 2-3; Steven R. Estes, A Goodly Heritage: A History of the North Danvers Mennonite Church (Danvers: North Danvers Mennonite Church, 1982), 47-52; idem, Living Stones: A History of the Metamora Mennonite Church (Metamora: Metamora Mennonite Church, 1984), 83-88; Samuel Hage, "A Civil War Letter," MHB, 27 (July 1966), 5; Joseph Liechty and James O. Lehman, "From Yankee to Nonresistant: John F. Funk's Chicago Years, 1857-1865," MQR, 59 (1985), 203-47; James O. Lehman "Conflicting Loyalties of the Christian Citizen: Lancaster Mennonites and the Early Civil War Era," PMH, 7 (Apr. 1984), 2-15; idem, "Duties of the Mennonite Citizen: Controversy in the Lancaster Press Late in the Civil War," PMH, 7 (July 1984), 5-21; idem, "Mennonites in the North Face the Crises of the Civil War," (unpubl. manuscript in possession of the author, 562 pp.); idem, Sonnenberg: A Haven and a Heritage (Kidron: Kidron Community Council, 1969), 88-95; John L. Ruth, Maintaining the Right Fellowship (Scottdale, 1984), 326-27.

American Friends Service Committee (AFSC (ME I:87). In 1947 the American Friends Service Com-

mittee, along with Friends Service Council of London, received the Nobel Peace Prize for their work among °refugees during World War II. Although the AFSC and Mennonite Central Committee (MCC) no longer share the close working relationship of earlier years, when working in areas of international conflict, the organizations still tend to cooperate. During the Nigerian Civil War AFSC and MCC jointly administered a project in Biafra (1969-1971). Field staff of both organizations have assisted each other in logistics and planning in postwar Indochina (°Vietnam, °Kampuchea, and °Laos) and the war-torn Horn of Africa (°Ethiopia, °Somalia) during the 1970s and 1980s.   CDH

Clarence E. Pickett, For More Than Bread (Boston: Little, Brown, 1953); John Forbes, The Quaker Star under Seven Flags, 1917-27 (Philadelphia: U. of Pennsylvania Press, 1962); Marvin R. Weisbord, Some Form of Peace (New York: Viking, 1971); Gerald Jonas, On Doing Good (New York: Scribner's, 1971); C. H. Mike Yarrow, Quaker Experiences in International Conciliation (New Haven: Yale U. Press, 1978).

Amish. (ME IV:43; I:90-97). The Old Order Amish are among the most conservative descendants of the 16th c. Anabaptists. The Old Order are usually distinguished from the Amish Mennonites (now largely absorbed into the Mennonite Church [MC] or various °conservative Mennonite groups), °Beachy Amish and the °New Order Amish by their strict adherence to the use of horses on the farm and as a source of transportation, their refusal to allow electricity or telephones in their homes, and their more traditional standard of °dress, including the use of hooks-and-eyes fasteners on some articles of clothing. For all practical purposes, "Amish" has come to be synonymous with "Old Order Amish" in the eyes of most observers in North America (see ME I: 97).

Old Order settlements exist in twenty states and one province in the United States and Canada. Settlements are defined geographically and culturally; i.e., a settlement consists of all individual church districts (congregations) that are contiguous in a given region. Districts within settlements are usually, but not always, in agreement on basic principles of church life and discipline. In 1984 there were 40 settlements in Pennsylvania, 23 in Ohio, 18 in Michigan, 14 in Wisconsin, and 13 in Indiana. Missouri and New York each had 12 settlements; Kentucky and Ontario had 7 apiece, Iowa and Minnesota had 5 each, Tennessee had 4, Kansas and Texas had 3, Maryland and Oklahoma had 2, and Arkansas, Delaware, Florida, Illinois, and Montana each had 1. As a result of genetic research, which required a complete settlement census in order to trace the history of a disease through family lines, many of these communities are producing directories which include information such as addresses, birth dates, church membership status, and the occupation of the head of the household. More than 70 directories have been published. In some settlements as many as three editions have been produced over a period of 15 years.

The largest settlements in 1984 were in Holmes-Wayne Co., Ohio (111 districts), Lancaster-Chester Co., Pa. (77 districts), Elkhart-Lagrange Co, Ind. (54 districts) and Geauga-Trumbull Co., Ohio (42 districts). In these large settlements there is much of diversity from district to district in °Ordnung (church discipline).

In this century the Old Order Amish population has grown very rapidly. In 1900 there were approximately 3,700 Amish in North America. By 1979 the estimated figure had increased to 85,000 (adult membership ca. 35,000). According to sociologist Julia Erickson and her colleagues, the Amish are among the fastest-growing populations in the world. They prohibit the use of contraception and have low infant mortality rates. The average Amish woman can expect to have at least seven live births.

A rapid increase in the Amish population is one factor that has led to gradual change and innovation in Amish society. Population pressures have increased the price of land and led to shortages of available farmland in some settlements. The Amish respond to this pressure by adopting farm management strategies of the larger society such as reducing the farm size and field crop production, placing more emphasis on the production of milk by increasing the size of a dairy herd, or specializing in the production of hogs for market.

Another response to demographic and economic pressure is to migrate to a new area of the country. In one decade (1974-84) Amish established 71 new settlements. However, not all attempts to establish a new settlement are successful. In the same decade 11 settlements ceased to exist, including 2 experimental settlements in Honduras and Paraguay. (Some members of the °Honduras settlement affiliated with Beachy Amish Mennonites).

An alternative to migration for many young Amish people is to seek employment outside agriculture. In the three largest settlements fewer than half of the heads of households are farmers. Many Amish are working in small businesses which specialize in the construction of horse-drawn farming implements, °buggies, blacksmithing, construction work, cabinetry, etc. Others seek employment in industry. In the large settlements certain industries, particularly recreational vehicle and mobile home industries, have consciously decided to seek Amish employees who are reliable workers and refuse to join °labor unions. While Amish factory workers do not typically live in towns, they do live on smaller plots of land, have more leisure time and more cash available than their agricultural counterparts.

In many states changes in Amish life have occurred as a result of government intervention. When local polities decided to consolidate °public schools, many Amish chose to develop their own °private schools. This development of Amish schools, where young Amish teachers with an eighth-grade education are supervised by a school board composed entirely of Amish men, has met with a great deal of opposition in some communities. In 1972 the United States Supreme Court ruled in *Wisconsin vs. Yoder* that states could not legally insist that Amish children attend public schools. As Amish schools have become more numerous, settlement, state, and regional structures have been established to supervise the operation of Amish schools. These organizations hold annual teachers meetings designed to be informative and to provide training to teachers.

The state has also made inroads into agriculture.

In many states the government has established regulations concerning acceptable substances used to shoe horses, or has ruled that all slow-moving vehicles used on public highways must have prescribed symbols attached to them. Other state governments have insisted that grade-A milk which is used for direct human consumption may not be cooled using the traditional method of immersing milk cans in very cold water. Reactions to these intrusions in Amish life have not been uniform, but in many instances the Amish have used "the ways of the world to withdraw from the world" (Huntington). In several states, rather than introducing mechanically powered bulk milk tanks, the traditional cooling method is used to produce milk for indirect human consumption in the form of cheese. In some settlements Amish-run cheesemaking operations have made it possible for Amish farmers to continue to make a living in the preferred manner.

There have been situations in which solutions to governmental intervention have required nationwide discussions. When such issues as °conscription or the payment of social security taxes needed to be addressed, a Steering Committee composed of representatives from settlements across the country was convened. The leader of the committee has, on occasion, negotiated directly with government officials on behalf of his constituency. There are also steering committees at the state level. At annual committee meetings, important issues that the Amish are confronting are discussed.

Some external intervention into Amish life cannot be dealt with directly and must be simply tolerated. °Tourism, for example, has become a burden for Amish in many settlements. While tourists purchase products produced by the Amish (e.g., baked goods or quilts), they also congest country roads, interrupt schools and small businesses and, perhaps most obtrusively, take photographs. Many tourists are simply unaware of the Amish prohibition against being photographed. The Amish response to these intruders is to accept them as unavoidable. Furthermore, tourism has, at least indirectly, created additional nonagricultural employment for Amish.

An important voice of the Amish are publications. A non-Amish publisher in Sugarcreek, Ohio, has published *The Budget*, a weekly newspaper, since 1890. Amish scribes from nearly every settlement report about important events in their locality to the nationwide Amish readership of this paper. Amish-produced publications with a large readership are *Die Botshaft* and *The Diary* published in Lancaster County, Pa., and three monthly periodicals (*Family Life*, *Young Companion*, and *Blackboard Bulletin*) published in Aylmer, Ont., by °Pathway Publishers. Recently settlements have begun to establish their own periodicals with information such as where church services are to be held, funeral and wedding notices, and reports of accidents. These include *Die Blatt*, established in Lagrange Co., Ind., in 1977; *Die Gemeinde Register*, established in Holmes Co., Ohio, in 1979; *Echos*, established in Arthur, Ill., in 1981; and the *Gemeinde Brief*, established in Geauga Co., Ohio, in 1985.

One extension of the work of Pathway Publishers has been to establish a °historical library (1972).

The stated goal of the library is to collect all materials written by, for, and about the Amish.

Finally, in many communities the Amish have acculturated into the dominant culture to some extent. They have borrowed technology as well as ideas from their non-Amish neighbors. Examples of the former include the increase in the use of diesel or gasoline engines to provide power for machinery. Indoor plumbing, gas stoves, and refrigerators are found in more and more Amish homes. In some Amish homes secular as well as non-Amish religious print materials are found. Ideas which are not part of their culture are making their way into the Amish community. These include ideas such as fear of °communism or a need for assurance of salvation.

While °acculturation is occurring, there is no evidence that Amish culture is on the verge of disappearing. Amish people clearly understand the boundary between their culture and the non-Amish world. While change may be necessary and, in some instances unavoidable, it is made cautiously and with a great deal of discussion.   TJM

John A. Hostetler, *Amish Society* (1980); David Luthy, *Amish Settlements Across America* (Alymer, Ont.: Pathway Publishers, 1985); idem,, *The Amish in America: Settlements that Failed, 1840-1960* (Aylmer,Ont.: Pathway Publishers, 1986); John A. Hostetler and Gertrude Huntington, *Children in Amish Society: Socialization and Community Education* (New York: Holt, Rinehart and Winston, 1971); Thomas J. Meyers, "Stress and the Amish Community in Transition," (PhD diss., Boston University, 1983); Eugene P. Erickson, Julia A. Erickson, John A. Hostetler, "The Cultivation of the Soil as a Moral Directive: Population Growth, Family Ties, and the Maintenance of Community Among the Old Order Amish," *Rural Sociology,* 45 (1980), 49-68; Julia A. Erickson, Eugene P. Erickson, John A. Hostetler and Gertrude E. Huntington, "Fertility Patterns and Trends Among the Old Order Amish," *Population Studies,* 3 (1979), 255-76; Henry Troyer and Lee Willoughby, "Changing Occupational Patterns in the Holmes County Ohio Amish Community," in *Aspects of Amish Mennonite History: Religious, Social, Linguistic and Symbolic Dimensions,* ed. Werner Enninger (Essen, West Germany: Essen University Press, 1984) 52-77; Victor Stoltzfus, "Reward and Sanction: The Adaptive Continuity of Amish Life," *Rural Sociology,* 38 (1976), 196-205; Roy C. Buck, "Boundary Maintenance Revisited: Tourist Experience in an Old Order Amish Community," *Rural Sociology,* 43 (1978) 221-34; William Crowley, "Old Order Amish Settlement Diffusion and Growth," *Annals of the Association of American Geographers,* 68 (1978) 249-64; Albert Keim, *Compulsory Education and the Amish* (Boston: Beacon Press, 1975); Joseph F. Beiler, *Old Order Shop and Service Directory of the Old Order Society in United States and Canada* (Gordonville, Pa.: Pequea Publishers, 1977); Reimer, *Quilt* (1983), 9; *MWH,* (1978), 363-65; *MWH,* (1984), 143.

See also Brauche; Conservative Mennonites; Ohio; Old Colony Mennonites; Arthur, Ill.; Ashland, Ohio; Belleville, Pa.; Berne, Ind.; Bowling Green, Mo.; Cashton, Wis.; Centreville, Mich.; Clark, Mo.; Conewango Valley, N.Y.; Dover, Del.; Ethridge, Tenn.; Geauga-Trumbull Cos., Ohio; Grabill-New Haven, Ind.; Hazleton, Iowa; Holmes-Wayne-Tuscarawas Cos., Ohio; Jamesport, Mo.; Kalona, Iowa; Lagrange-Elkhart, Ind.; Lancaster-Chester Cos., Pa.; Medford, Wis.; Meyersdale-Springs, Pa.; Milverton, Ont.; Montgomery, Ind.; Nappanee, Ind.; New Wilmington, Pa.; Smicksburg, Pa.; Spartansburg, Pa.; Tradition.

Ammann, Jakob (ME I:90, 98), early leader of the Amish. Biographical information on Ammann continues to be incomplete and speculative. It is doubtful he was the son of Michael and Anna Rupp Ammann (this person was born Feb. 12, 1644), as this contradicts Hans °°Reist's description of him as a "young fellow" at the time of the Amish division in 1693. An alternate theory suggests he was born Feb. 19, 1656 to Jacob and Katharina Leuenberger Ammann in the Madiswil area of the canton of Bern, Switzerland. This Jakob Ammann, baptized as an infant, was known to be religiously zealous in school and to be a diligent student. He disappeared from the community after his schooling and was said to have moved to the Alsace. John A. Hostetler suggests this indicates Ammann may have been a convert from the Reformed Church to Anabaptism. As a new convert Ammann might have become more committed to traditional forms. His authoritarian approach to church polity and °discipline could also reflect a Reformed background. While this thesis better fits the known facts than earlier theories, the search for confirmed historical linkages continues.   SSt

John A. Hostetler, *Amish* (1980), 41-47.

Amor Viviente (Living Love) Movement, Honduras, is an organized church which resulted from a °charismatic youth ministry in Tegucigalpa, Honduras, from 1973 to 1983. Eastern Mennonite Board of Missions and Charities (MC) missionaries, Ed and Gloria King, had a burden and vision for reaching youth caught up in drugs, alcohol, and prostitution, and youth abandoned by parents. The established churches did not seem to be reaching these socially rejected youth. An informal, friendly coffee shop setting was appealing to the youth. Among the first few attending, several testified of being healed, liberated, and having relationships restored. Word spread rapidly among other youth, and the Kings were soon overwhelmed with requests for prayer and personal counseling. Many of the youth had high school and university training. They learned rapidly from the Kings' personal leadership, and soon became involved in ministry to others. Weekend rallies were held in local school facilities and parks. Contemporary music kept attracting new followers. Parents who were impressed by the changes in their own daughters and sons soon joined. A Christian bookstore was established in Tegucigalpa, and the campus of the Eastern Board's former missionary children's school outside the capital city became an alcoholic rehabilitation center staffed partially by Amor Viviente personnel.

Some of these redeemed youth and couples were commissioned to begin work in other Honduran cities and towns. Amor Viviente groups were established in Puerto Cortez in 1977, Danli and Choluteca in 1978, San Pedro Sula in 1980, El Paraiso in 1981, and La Ceiba and Progreso in 1984. The first group in a rural community was at Moroceli in 1986. In 1981 the Child Feeding Center, "Ebenezer," was set up in an impoverished area of Tegucigalpa. In August 1985, in coordination with the Eastern Mennonite Mission Board, Amor Viviente commissioned a pastoral couple to go as missionaries to New Orleans to work with Ed and Gloria King in reaching out to the 40,000 Hondurans there. Amor Viviente held large public meetings in public school facilities and used rented office facilities until 1985. With the help of a loan from the Eastern Board, they built an attractive building that includes an auditorium that seats 1,200 people, and space for a video-audio recording studio, a print shop, and administrative and counseling offices.

Amor Viviente continues to have a strong centralized leadership structure. Since 1983 when the Kings left Honduras, Rene Peñalva is both pastor of the Tegucigalpa congregation and national director of this movement of about 2,500 members in 15 congregations. Each congregation follows the pattern of having a limited number of large meetings and many small growth and discipleship groups. The movement is associated with Mennonite World Conference but continues to have very limited contact and interaction with all other church groups in Honduras.   AY

MWH (1978), 221-24; *MWH* (1984), 80.

Amusements and Entertainment (ME I:112). In the first half of the 20th c., many Mennonites condemned various types of worldly amusements—card playing; °dancing; °television; attendance at fairs, farm shows, political rallies, theaters, circuses, °motion pictures, carnivals, public sporting events; participation in bowling, rollerskating, and gambling; and swimming at public beaches. Restrictions on these activities provided an effective means of limiting social interaction with the larger society, thus preserving a rural and separatist religious subculture (°nonconformity). The word *amusement* had a pejorative ring in the ears of conservative ʼMennonites, for it contradicted the strong Mennonite °work ethic, and implied pleasure-seeking, idleness, vanity, waste, and worldliness. Many of the activities listed above continue to be forbidden by Old Order Mennonite and Amish groups in the 1980s. Amusements permitted by these more conservative groups are typically informal, noncommercial, familial, and local in orientation, e.g., baseball and volleyball played in a pasture, skating and sledding on the family farm, as well as barn dances, singings, and table games. Members of Old Order groups may occasionally go on a deep-sea fishing trip, visit a public zoo, or go camping, but the bulk of their entertainment revolves around home, church, and neighborhood.

The encounter with °modernity transformed the entertainment patterns of the major Mennonite denominations in the last half of the 20th c. As they exchanged their plows for °professions and careers in public life, Mennonites began to enjoy the forms of amusement and entertainment typical of modern culture. In fact, the term *amusement* has largely slipped from the vocabulary of mainstream Mennonite groups. A national survey of five Mennonite denominations in 1972, conducted by Kauffman and Harder, revealed the percent of respondents who considered the following activities "always wrong": drinking °alcoholic beverages (50 percent), smoking tobacco (64 percent), using hard °drugs (97 percent), attending movies rated for adults and children (18 percent), attending movies rated for adults only (48 percent), gambling (75 percent), and social dancing (43 percent). The type of entertainment embraced by Mennonites varies according to the region of the country and the religious tradition of

their particular group. The following forms of entertainment are widely accepted by many Mennonites today: television, motion pictures, theater (°dramatic arts), fairs, symphony concerts, art shows, farm shows, bowling, pool (billiards), public °sporting events, golfing, international travel, tours, cruises, camping, hunting, fishing, surfing, tennis, and hockey, to name just a few. Family vacations have become an annual ritual in most Mennonite families, including those that are still farming. Eating in public restaurants, some of which are Mennonite-owned, became a fashionable pastime in the 1970s. Table games, family reunions, and television viewing are important forms of family-based entertainment. Local congregations often sponsor sports teams, camping trips, and other forms of leisure activities for their members.

For the most part, Mennonite patterns of entertainment differ little from the surrounding culture. Alcohol and drug use, gambling, and participation in lotteries are strongly discouraged. Mennonite °wedding receptions, for example, typically do not include dancing and alcohol, although folk dancing does occasionally occur. Mennonite high schools generally do not have football teams nor do they sponsor dances. Two colleges owned by the Mennonite Church (MC), Goshen College and Eastern Mennonite College, permitted dancing for the first time in the 1980s. Although few restrictions remain in the main Mennonite groups, the cost of certain activities, as well as the content of television programs, movies, and other forms of entertainment touted by popular culture, are ethical concerns in many congregations.   DBK

Kauffman/Harder, *Anabaptists Four C. Later* (1975), 122-129; C. F. Derstine, "Popular Amusements: Their Danger," *Christian Monitor* (July 1918), 581-82; Pauline Cline, "Why Worldly Amusements Do Not Amuse the Christian," *GH* (Oct. 15, 1942), 618; James O. Lehman, *Sonnenberg: A Haven and a Heritage* (Kidron, Ohio: Kidron Community Council, 1969), 288-89; Ella May Miller, "Sick Movies and Dancing," *GH* (May 21, 1968), 454-55; Melvin Gingerich, *The Mennonites in Iowa* (Iowa City: State Historical Society, 1939), 170-71, 234-35, 240-45, 316-17; Henry H. Ness, "Questionable Amusements," *Youth's Christian Companion* (Feb. 11, 1951), 471-72; "Bowling: Right or Wrong," (Salunga Pa.: Bishop Board of Lancaster Mennonite Conference, 1962), pamphlet; Joanne Hess Siegrist, "Friendship Gatherings of Lancaster Mennonite Women, 1890-1950," *PMH*, 11 (Apr. 1988), 2-15.

See also Eastern Pennsylvania Mennonite Church; Folklore; Nonconformity; Radio; Recreation; Sports.

Anabaptism. The article in ME I:113ff. is a summary of the perception of what Anabaptism was after the revision carried out by Harold S. °Bender and others. It ends with Robert °Friedmann's assertion that Anabaptists were "nearer to the spirit of Christ's exemplary life and teaching . . ." than were Protestants, °°*Schwärmer*, ("enthusiasts") and millennialists, and that Bender's °"Anabaptist vision" might supply "delineation of the idea of evangelical Anabaptism." This had, in fact, already happened by the time Friedmann wrote. "Evangelical Anabaptism" was identified by insistence on °discipleship as the essence of Christianity, on the church as a brotherhood, and on an ethic of °love and °nonresistance. This became the normative description of Anabaptism. In this view, evangelical Anabaptism arose with the Swiss Brethren, and by transmission became part of Netherlands Anabaptism and of the Hutterites. Thus was Anabaptism given unity and clearly distinguished from Catholics, Protestants, and other 16th-c. dissenters.

A revision of this portrayal began about 1960. Heinold Fast warned in a 1967 article that the Mennonite revision of four centuries of negative historiography was too tidy, too ideal, and that reaction would come. Indeed, reaction was already under way as part of a major shift in Reformation studies from systematic theology to history of ideas and from confessional history to social history. This shift strongly modified the traditional confessional (Lutheran, Reformed, Catholic, Mennonite, etc.) orientation and opened the door to consideration of the dialectic between social and political developments, on the one hand, and the development of theological positions in the various reinterpretations of Christian faith, on the other. For Anabaptist studies it meant the entry into the field of a number of non-Mennonite historians who studied Anabaptism not as the ancestral movement of the 20th-c. church communion, but as part of the general history of western Europe in the 16th c. It produced a new picture of Anabaptism not only socially but also in theology.

Definition of Anabaptism. The word Anabaptism is normally used today to denote the mosaic of groupings of dissenters without at the same time making claims to uniformity. In his 1972 work *Anabaptists and the Sword,* James M. Stayer used the term with great care in order to avoid giving the impression that he was writing about a single unified movement across Europe. He wrote about Anabaptists and defined them as those who rebaptized persons already baptized in infancy. Walter Klaassen had already used this definition in his Oxford dissertation in 1960. Calvin Pater (1984) broadened the definition by including those who, before 1525, rejected the baptism of infants, but this is perhaps too broad to be useful. These definitions were meant to avoid such confessional definitions as "evangelical Anabaptism." Thus, all those rebaptizers who have in the past been classified as *Schwärmer* (Melchior °Hoffmen), spiritualists (Hans °°Denck), and revolutionaries (the °Münsterites) are now considered to be genuine Anabaptists.

Despite the variety of viewpoints among 16th-c. Anabaptists, despite important differences of nuance even where Anabaptists appear to be similar, one may hazard to identify some themes held in common following the crystalization of the movement between 1527 and 1540. (1) All shared a basically synergistic view of °salvation (human and divine "cooperation"). °Justification was seen as progression in °holiness; the ethic of the °Sermon on the Mount was the guide to it. (2) Baptism was considered to be the sign of lay emancipation from clerical control and the spiritual enfranchisement of lay people (°priesthood of all believers). (3) Anabaptists developed a *Gemeindechristentum* centered on the congregation, in contrast to the clericalized territorial churches, both Catholic and Protestant.

Anabaptism and Anabaptists. However, the open definition of *Anabaptist* now in use emphatically does not imply uniformity. Anabaptism was pluralistic. Claus-Peter Clasen identified six major groupings often hostile to each other, and then cited contemporary literature to show that there were actually many more (1972). The 1975 article "From Monogenesis to Polygenesis," by James M. Stayer, Werner O. Packull, and Klaus Deppermann, has become the accepted statement on Anabaptist plurality. The essay disputed the older view that Anabaptism had its origins solely in Zürich, and that Swiss Brethren Anabaptism was transmitted to South Germany and Austria (°°Blaurock, °Hubmaier) and to The Netherlands-North Germany (Hoffman), where it developed into the °Hutterian and Mennonite branches respectively. The authors showed that each of the three in fact had a distinctive character and therefore a distinct source. For South German-Austrian Anabaptism it was a diluted form of Rhineland mysticism (Packull, 1977). Social unrest and the °apocalyptic visions of Melchior Hoffman put their stamp on Netherlands Anabaptism (Deppermann, 1979; 1987). Swiss Anabaptism arose out of Reformed congregationalism (Stayer, 1975).

Numerous individual studies demonstrating links and relationships between Anabaptists have gradually led to the abandonment of the °Schleitheim Confession as a norm for all "true" Anabaptists. As long ago as 1956 Frank J. Wray showed that Pilgram °Marpeck had borrowed the bulk of his *Vermanung* (1542) from the despised Münster theologian Bernhard °Rothmann's *Bekenntnisse* of 1533. Quite as surprising was the demonstration that Melchior Hoffman's commentary on the Apocalypse (1530) was used by the Hutterites soon after Hoffman wrote it, but with no acknowledgement of authorship (Packull, 1982).

°David Joris had for long been a pariah, especially for North American Mennonite historians, and was condemned by relative inattention. Two major dissertations have shown Joris to have been the most important Anabaptist leader in The Netherlands before 1540, even more so than °Menno Simons (Zijlstra, 1983; Waite, 1986). He was an influential figure in Anabaptism's consolidation period following the fall of Münster.

Most significant is the integrative rewriting of the history of Anabaptism in The Netherlands. Melchior Hoffman is acknowledged as the progenitor, as the person who gave the movement its basic apocalyptic stamp. The differences that appear along the "peaceful" to "revolutionary" spectrum can be accounted for by differing nuances in the era's widespread apocalyptic expectation (Klaassen, 1986). A clear line stretches from Hoffman to Rothmann, Menno Simons, and David Joris on apocalyptic anticipation. Very similar formulations of apocalyptic views on secular government and on the °°incarnation are found in Hoffman, Rothmann, and Menno Simons (Voolstra, 1982; Stayer, 1972, 1978, 1986). The work of these scholars has therefore shown that in some important respects there was a single movement from Hoffman to Menno.

Anabaptism and Radical Dissent. George H. Williams' massive volume, *The Radical Reformation* (1962), presented for the first time a comprehensive portrayal of radical dissent in the 16th c. Moving across his stage are the whole cast of characters, from Andreas Karlstadt (°°Carlstadt) and the Zwickau Prophets through Conrad °Grebel and the St. Gall fanatics, Hans °Hut and Jacob °°Hutter, Menno Simons and the °°Batenburgers, to Michael °°Servetus and Faustus °°Socinus, with all the intricate linkages between them.

Clear links between Thomas °Müntzer and Hans Hut had been established by Grete Mecenseffy (1956) and Walter Klaassen (1960, 1962), but the most important study on this relationship was done by Gottfried Seebaß (1972). His work and the work of Werner Packull (1977) established beyond question the formative influence of Thomas Müntzer on South German Anabaptism, both in its °mysticism and its apocalyptic cast. By means of the thesis that mystical theology was a theology of dissent in the 16th c., Steven Ozment linked the Anabaptists Hans Denck and Hans Hut with Müntzer, Sebastian °°Franck, and others. The central thrust of this mysticism was that ultimately God could communicate his will to men and women directly in disregard of ecclesiastical channels, a kind of democratization of revelation. Later Calvin Pater (1984) convincingly showed that Andreas Karlstadt significantly influenced Swiss Anabaptism. Versions of Karlstadt's view and use of Scripture, his doctrine of the church, and his views on baptism, all found their way into Anabaptism.

Building on earlier work, Hans-Jürgen Goertz (1980) offered the first extended discussion of the thesis that anticlericalism was a prime motive for dissent, and that this factor provided close links between Anabaptism and other movements of the "common man," such as the peasant uprisings of 1524-26, also extensively motivated by anticlericalism. Among Anabaptists this expressed itself in contrasts between the Good Shepherd and the self-indulgent clergy, the simple reading of Scripture and its use as a means of oppression, and the improvement of life and the fruitless life of the new Protestant teachers of justification by faith alone. Other expressions of anticlericalism were the involvement of the Zürich radicals in opposition to °tithes and the demand for congregational autonomy. Both central issues for °peasants have been clearly documented by Haas (1975) and Stayer 1975A). Werner Packull (1985) and Arnold Snyder (1984, 1985) have provided further evidence for these links.

Finally, the relationship of Anabaptists to Caspar °Schwenckfeld has also been extensively studied in recent years. Neal Blough's work on Pilgram Marpeck (1984) demonstrates dependence of Marpeck on Schwenckfeld especially relating to their understanding of the Incarnation. A complex set of relationships of Schwenckfeld with Melchior Hoffman and Pilgram Marpeck was described by R. Emmet McLaughlin (1985). The lure of Schwenckfeld's spiritualism for South German Anabaptists was clearly shown by George H. Williams in his *Radical Reformation*. Anabaptists and Schwenckfeld agreed on many important issues (Klaassen, 1986).

Anabaptists must now therefore be seen as an integral part of the larger phenomenon of religious and social dissent in 16th-c. Europe from the °°Zwickau Prophets to Sebastian °°Castellio.

Anabaptism and the Reformation. Anabaptism arose out of the religious and social ferment of the °Reformation period. That Anabaptists everywhere should have been influenced in numerous ways by the Reformers, is established. That they were the most consistent Protestants carrying the reforms of Luther and Zwingli to their logical conclusion as earlier Mennonite interpreters such as Cornelius H. °°Wedel and John °°Horsch held, is a view that can no longer be sustained. For Anabaptists differed with the major Reformers both on the principles of *sola scriptura* (by Scripture alone), and even more radically on *sola fidei* (by faith alone). Because of their profound concern for ethics, they adopted variants of a synergistic soteriology which bore resemblance to some late medieval views. But there was also ambivalence among Anabaptists as to whether they were reformist or °restitutionist (Wray, 1954; Meihuizen, 1970). As Hans J. Hillerbrand (1971) pointed out, restitutionists have great difficulty dealing with past history. This point has also been made by Dennis Martin (1987), who argued that restitutionists, in contrast to reformers, can really build no lasting traditions since their revolt against a corrupt immediate past makes them suspicious even of any new institutions or traditions they may establish.

Finally, the question as to whether Anabaptism was medieval or modern has been vigorously debated. The link of Anabaptism to mysticism, its synergistic soteriology, and its version of *imitatio Christi*, all point to pre-Reformation forms of piety (Ozment, 1972; Davis, 1-974; Packull, 1977). Alternatively, it has been argued that Anabaptism was the true harbinger of °modernity in its emphasis on voluntarism, toleration, and pluralism in religion (Bender, 1955, Zeman, 1976). The early Swiss Brethren, claimed Fritz Blanke, were a vanguard striving toward a new dawn (Blanke, 1961). A carefully nuanced statement on this subject describes social tendencies in Anabaptism that moved in the direction of modernity (Goertz, 1985).   WKlaa

Harold S. Bender, "The Anabaptists and Religious Liberty in the 16th Century," *MQR*, 29 (1955), 83-100; Fritz Blanke, *Brothers in Christ* (Scottdale, 1961); Neal Blough, *Christologie Anabaptiste: Pilgram Marpeck et l'humanité du Christ* (Genève: Éditions Labor et Fides, 1984); cf. *MWR* 61 (1987) 203-13; Claus-Peter Clasen, *Anabaptism: A Social History 1525-1618* (Ithaca: Cornell U. Press, 1972); Kenneth R. Davis, *Anabaptism and Asceticism* (Scottdale, 1974); Klaus Deppermann, *Melchior Hoffman: Soziale Unruhen und apokalyptische Visionen im Zeitalter der Reformation* (Göttingen: Vandenhoeck und Ruprecht, 1979; English translation, Edinburgh: T. and T. Clark, 1987); Heinold Fast, "Europäische Forschungen auf dem Gebiet der Täufer-und Mennonitengeschichte (1962-1967)," *Menn. Geschbl.*, 24 (1967), 19-30; Hans-Jürgen Goertz, *Die Täufer: Geschichte und Deutung* (Munich: C. H. Beck, 1980), 41-76; idem, "Das Täufertum—ein Weg in die Moderne?" in *Zwingli und Europa*, ed. Peter Blickle et al. (Zürich: Vandenhoeck und Ruprecht, 1985), 165-81; J. F. Gerhard Goeters, "Die Vorgeschichte des Täufertums in Zürich," *Studien zur Geschichte und Theologie der Reformation: Festschrift für Ernst Bizer*, ed. Louise Abramowski und J. F. Gerhard Goeters (Neukirchen/Vluyn: Neukirchener Verlag, 1969), 239-81; Martin Haas, "Der Weg der Täufer in die Absonderung: Zur Interdependenz von Theologie und sozialem Verhalten," in *Umstrittenes Täufertum* (1975), 50-78; Hans J. Hillerbrand, "Anabaptism and History," *MQR*, 45 (1971), 107-22; Walter Klaassen, "Word, Spirit, and Scripture in Early Anabaptist Thought" (PhD diss., U. of Oxford, 1960); idem, "Hans Hut and Thomas Müntzer," *The Baptist Quarterly*, 19 (1962), 209-27; idem, "Eschatological Themes in Early Dutch Anabaptism," in *The Dutch Dissenters*, ed. Irvin B. Horst (Leiden: Brill, 1986), 15-31; idem, "Schwenckfeld and the Anabaptists," in *Schwenckfeld and Early Schwenkfeldianism*, ed. Peter C. Erb (Pennsburg: Schwenkfelder Library, 1986), 389-400; Dennis D. Martin, "Nothing New under the Sun: Mennonites and History," *CGR*, 5 (1987), 1-27; R. Emmet McLaughlin, "Schwenckfeld and the Strasbourg Radicals," *MQR*, 59 (1985), 268-78; Grete Mecenseffy, "Die Herkunft des oberösterreichischen Täufertums," *ARG*, 47 (1956), 252-59; Hendrik W. Meihuizen, "The Concept of Restitution in the Anabaptism of Northwestern Europe," *MQR*, 44 (1970), 141-58; Steven E. Ozment, *Mysticism and Dissent: Religious Ideology and Social Protest in the Sixteenth Century* (New Haven: Yale U. Press, 1972); Werner O. Packull, *Mysticism and the Early South German-Austrian Anabaptist Movement 1525-1531* (Scottdale, 1977); idem, "The Origins of Swiss Anabaptism in the Context of the Reformation of the Common Man," *JMS*, 3 (1985), 36-59; idem, "A Hutterite Book of Medieval Origin' Revisited," *MQR*, 56 (1982), 147-168); Calvin A. Pater, *Karlstadt as the Father of the Baptist Movements: The Emergence of Lay Protestantism* (Toronto: U. of Toronto Press, 1984); Gottfried Seebaß, "Müntzers Erbe: Werk, Leben und Theologie des Hans Hut" (unpub. Habilitationsschrift, Erlangen, 1972); C. Arnold Snyder, *The Life and Thought of Michael Sattler* (Scottdale, 1984); idem, "The Schleitheim Articles in the Light of the Revolution of the Common Man," *Sixteenth Century J.*, 16 (1985), 419-430; James M. Stayer, "The Anabaptists," in *Reformation Europe: A Guide to Research*, ed. Steven Ozment (St. Louis: Center for Reformation Research, 1982), 135-59; James M. Stayer, Werner Packull, and Klaus Deppermann, "From Monogenesis to Polygenesis: The Historical Discussion of Anabaptist Origins," *MQR*, 49 (1975), 83-121; James M. Stayer, "Die Anfänge des schweizerischen Täufertums im reformierten Kongregationalismus," in *Umstrittenes Täufertum* (1975), 19-49; idem, "Menno and Oldeklooster," *Sixteenth Century J.* 9 (1978), 51-67; idem, "Was Dr. Kühler's Conception of Early Dutch Anabaptism Historically Sound? The Historical Discussion of Münster 450 Years Later," *MQR*, 60 (1986), 261-88; Sjouke Voolstra, *Het Woord is Vlees Geworden: De Melchioritisch-Menniste Incarnatieleer* (Kamkpen: Kok, 1982); Gary K. Waite, "Spiritualizing the Crusade: David Joris in the Context of the Early Reform and Anabaptist Movements in the Netherlands 1524-1543," (PhD diss. U., of Waterloo, 1986); Frank J. Wray, "The Anabaptist Doctrine of the Restitution of the Church," *MQR*, 28 (1954), 186-96; Jarold K. Zeman, "Anabaptism: A Replay of Medieval Themes or a Prelude to the Modern Age," *MQR*, 50 (1976), 259-71; Samme Zijlstra, *Nicolaas Meyndertsz. van Blesdijk: Een Bijdrage tot de Geschiedenis van het Davidjorisme* (Assen: Van Gorcum, 1983).

See also Christology; Historiography; Mennonites.

Anabaptist Vision, The, was the title of Harold S. °Bender's presidential address to the American Society of Church History in 1942. Bender posited °discipleship, i.e., following Jesus in life and under the cross, as the essence of Anabaptism, especially by comparison with Protestantism. He contrasted discipleship to faith (°°Luther), the first leading to patterns of Christian life, the second to °theology. Second, the "Anabaptist Vision" meant a new church, with voluntary membership, separation from the world, °persecution, and the exercise of brotherhood and sisterhood in economic affairs (°mutual aid). Third, °love and °nonresistance applied to all human relationships.

Historians of Bender's time emphasized synthesis and especially the search for essence, e.g., trying to define the essence of the Renaissance. Secular scholars, as well as Christians, especially Mennonites, warmly accepted his formulation of Anabaptist essence. It fitted the historiographical mood, and its evidence made it credible. European scholars saw Anabaptist discipleship in the prior work of Johannes °°Kühn. And many Christians were reading the writings of Dietrich °Bonhoeffer.

In the 1960s and 1970s the "Anabaptist Vision" has come under attack, usually indirectly, on grounds of over-idealization. Did Bender denigrate too many bona fide Anabaptists as marginal because they did not fit his discipleship definition? The "Anabaptist Vision" continues to inspire many Mennonites.   JSO

Harold S. Bender, "The Anabaptist Vision," *Church History*, 13 (1944), 3-24; and *MQR*, 18 (1944), 67-88, many reprints in several languages; Guy F. Hershberger, ed., *The Recovery of the Anabaptist Vision* (Scottdale, 1957), including Franklin H. Littell's answer to Bender on discipleship vs. the church as essence of Anabaptism; Kauffman/Harder, *Anabaptists Four C. Later* (1975), 114ff; Werner O. Packull, "Some Reflections on the State of Anabaptist History: The Demise of a Normative Vision," *Studies in Religion*, 8 (1979), 313-23; J. Denny Weaver, "The Work of Christ," *MQR*, 59 (1985), 107-29; Leonard Gross, "Recasting the Anabaptist Vision," *MQR*, 60 (1986), 352-63; Johannes Kühn, *Toleranz und Offenbarung* (Leipzig: Meiner, 1923).

See also Historiography.

Anarchists. See Sociopolitical Activism ("Anarchy and Activism: The Isaak Story" [feature]).

Ancestors, Respect for. Attitudes toward elderly and deceased members of the family, church, and community are reflected in a variety of articles in this encyclopedia, including °burial customs, care for the °aged, °°cemeteries, °death and dying, °eternity, °funerals, °genealogy, and martyrs. The °family, with the assistance of the church, has provided the context for many of these practices through most of the history of the Mennonite communities. Along with most other branches of Protestantism, Mennonites have rejected sacramental rites performed on behalf of the dead, as well as veneration of the deceased as special mediators of God's grace. The dead have been memorialized, rather, as personal and collective expressions of gratitude and affection. Memories of the deceased (the martyrs in particular) have also been preserved to serve as examples to be emulated by posterity.

In many Asian and some African societies, ancestor veneration plays a crucial role in consolidating family and community relationships. Ritual care for the ancestors is, in these societies, both a social obligation and a religious practice. The commemoration of death is intimately related to the entire structure of one's larger family, which includes a strong sense of continuity between the dead, the living, and the not-yet-born.

In China, Korea, and Japan, remembering people after death is an important factor in enhancing a sense of communal solidarity. It is in this sense of community, rather than in individuality, that people find meaning in life. The community provides a framework which, on the one hand, provides protection and security and on the other hand, demands allegiance and loyalty. This reciprocal relationship balances the "bestowal of favor" with obligations to "return a favor." Although petitioning the dead for favors and for protection from misfortunes cannot be ignored as factors in the preservation of ancestor veneration, memory is at the heart of the rites. Memorial rituals are performed in order to maintain a sense of continuity in relationships between the dead and the living.

In many Asian societies, commemoration of the dead is not limited to burial rites. Funerals are followed by a series of memorial services and rites, usually conducted in homes and at gravesites. These rites may include gatherings of relatives and friends and offerings of food, water, incense, and flowers. In this way, the ancestors and their descendants remain linked together in a circle of obligation, reciprocity, and loyalty.

In Japan, ancestor rites are closely associated with °Buddhism. Though they have also been influenced by Confucianism, mystical elements of °Shinto, and folk religions, Japanese generally view ancestor veneration as standing outside of any particular religious tradition. Many Japanese do not view ancestral rites as "religious" at all since respect for the dead transcends and encompasses all religious traditions.

The ancestral system has been susceptible to manipulation by political leaders for nationalistic and militaristic ends. In Japan, the Tokugawa government (1603-1868) made ancestral veneration compulsory, as a means to expose the "hidden Christians" who refused to "worship" in accordance with the rites as prescribed by the government. Their willingness to accept martyrdom, rather than engage in ancestor "worship," indicates that many Christians in Japan have equated ancestor veneration with idolatry.

However, ancestor veneration may also be viewed as an appropriate human symbol of honor, respect, and gratitude towards one's parents. The specific forms may vary with the culture, but the respect paid to ancestors in West and East may not be fundamentally different. Rites of commemoration and respect for the dead need not mean that the deceased are regarded as "gods" or are the object of "worship." If God is truly known and worshiped as God, lessor priorities will be relegated to subordinate positions. This is the interpretation which has generally been adopted by the Roman Catholic church in Japan during the modern period, as well as by many of the groups within the ecumenical United Church of Christ in Japan.

A 1986 church member profile of Mennonites and Brethren in Christ in Japan shows that a majority of the members reject "worship" (*matsuru*) at a household ancestral altar (*butsudan*) or shrine (*kamidana*) and disapprove of sponsorship of the traditional Buddhistic memorial services (*hoji*). Regarding the appropriateness of attendance and participation in Buddhist funerals, memorial rites, and activities associated with the *Bon* festival for the dead, a majority are uncertain or say it depends upon specific circumstances. Only a few members categorically disapprove of attendance or participation in any Buddhist funerals or memorial rites. On the other hand, a few members also indicate that they see no problems in attending and participating in these rituals. Many respondents view at least some of these activities as "cultural" rather than "religious" (*shukyo*).

Comparable data for other Protestant groups in Japan are not available, but earlier studies support the observation made by Mennonite pastor Hiroshi °Yanada: "We are not so different from other conservative groups concerning this issue."

There is no single, universal Christian answer to the question of the right way to express honor to and gratitude for deceased members of the family, church, and community. Christians in each cultural situation must deal with this question responsibly, constructively, and with personal, political, and religious sensitivity. TN/RE

Kiyomi Morioka, *Ie No Henbo To Senzo No Matsuri* (Transformation of the Household and the Celebration of Ancestors in Japan), (Tokyo: The Board of Publications, UCC in Japan, 1984); Robert J. Smith, *Ancestor Worship in Contemporary Japan* (Stanford: Stanford U., Press, 1974); various articles in *Japanese Religions* (1983-84) and in *The Japan Missionary Bulletin*, 39 (1985); Juhnke, *Mission* (1979), 54-55; Bong Rin Ro, ed., *Christian Alternatives to Ancestor Practices*, Asian Evangelical Theological Library, 1 (Taichung, Taiwan: Asia Theological Association, 1985).

Andersson, Oscar (1886-1979) was born in Ubby, Sweden, and became a member of the Swedish Baptist Church. Alma °Doering visited his community and recruited him for work with the °°Congo Inland Mission (Africa Inter-Mennonite Mission). He joined a pioneering team at Djoko Punda on the Kasai River in 1914.

In his diary Andersson wrote about loneliness while supervising firing of kilns of raw clay bricks; of encounters with African people, language, and culture; and thoughts of how they might best be reached with the Gospel. He also mentioned disagreements among the multinational team over questions of missiology, and personality clashes. He married one of the team members, Sarah Kroeker, a trained nurse and midwife from the Evangelical Mennonite Brethren Church (°Fellowship of Evangelical Bible Churches) at Henderson, Nebr. They buried a stillborn son in Africa.

Differing opinions within the missionary team eventually induced the Anderssons to transfer in 1916 to a mission of Oscar's home church in Kwilu Province west of Djoko. They continued in their service until 1948 when they returned to Sweden. JEB

An English translation of Oscar Andersson's diary is found in the AIMM archives at the Mennonite Historical Library, Bluffton College.

Andhra Pradesh, India, is the fifth largest state in India, both in area and population (275,068 sq. km. [106,200 sq. mi.]; 53,549,673 people). Hyderabad is the capital; languages spoken are Telugu and Urdu. Christians make up 5.25 percent of the population. Andhra Pradesh forms the major link between northern and southern parts of India. The climate is generally hot and humid. The Krishna and the Godavari are the major river systems in the state. Andhra Pradesh has 23 districts and three distinct regions (coastal, called Andhra; interior called Rayalaseema; and Telengana consisting of the city of Hyderabad)

About 42 million people live in rural settings, and 70 percent of them are engaged directly in agriculture. Andhra Pradesh is the historic land of temples and mosques, which combines age-old traditions of Hindu and Muslim culture.

Mennonite Brethren congregations (40,000 members) are located in five districts of the Rayalaseema and Telengana regions with headquarters in Mahabubnager District. Mennonite Brethren influence is felt throughout the entire state through

°Mennonite Christian Service Fellowship of India, Mennonite Central Committee, Mennonite Brethren Medical Centre, and Mennonite Brethren Bible Institute. Recently, Mennonite Brethren churches were established at Gangavathy in Karnataka State and at Bombay.   RSL

Rampogu S. Asservadam, "The Mennonite Brethren in Andhra Pradesh: A Historical Treatise" (PhD thesis, Hyderabad Osmania U., 1980); Rampogu S. Lemuel, "The Mennonite Brethren Medical Centre, Jadcherla, Provides Avenues for Evangelism to Mennonite Brethren Churches of India" (MA research project, Mennonite Brethren Biblical Seminary, Fresno, 1977); Paul D. Wiebe, *Christians in Andhra Pradesh: The Mennonites of Mahbubnagar* (Bangalore: Christian Institute for the Study of Religion and Society, 1987).

Angola. See Igreja Evangélica dos Irmãos Menonitas em Angola (IEIMA).

Animism. The word *animism* was used for the first time by E. B. Tylor (1832-1917) in his theory, about the origin of religion. According to this theory religion finds its origin in the application of the idea of the soul (Latin: *anima*) to all the phenomena that appear in human existence. Everything is seen as caused by personal, supranatural powers. Tylor's theory has met much opposition from cultural anthropologists and historians of religion. The word *animism*, however, continues to be used to point to those religions that do not belong to the large group of "world religions"—°Hinduism, °Buddhism, °Judaism, Christianity and °Islam. Animistic religions are also referred to as tribal, or primal, religions.

These "animist" religions neither have holy Scriptures nor do they trace their existence to a historical founder or prophet. In general, they are tied to a certain social group in a specific region, and there are no attempts to spread the religion to people of other groups or regions. Reality is seen and experienced as permeated by superhuman powers, which can manifest themselves in different ways in things, in natural phenomena, and in special persons. The deceased °ancestors are believed to have special power. Above the spirits and deities, there is believed to be the High God, the distant God, who does not play an important role in daily human existence. Central in religious life is the ritual (purification, sacrifice, and so on), performed in order to remain in contact with the supranatural powers, to intensify life and to ward off evil powers, especially during the transition from one stage of life to another. A substratum of animistic ideas can still be found among many adherents of world religions.

Christian missions have gained most of their converts among "animists." That is also true in regard to Mennonite mission work. The largest Mennonite churches outside of Europe and North America are located in regions of primal religions (Zaire and rural India). The primal religions have not been able to resist the destructive influence of the modern, secularizing western civilization. The encounter between Christianity and primal religion has contributed also to the birth of the new religious movements, such as the °African independent churches.   RSK

E. B. Tylor, *Primitive Culture*, 2 vols. (New York: G. P. Putnam's Sons, 1920); J. V. Taylor, *The Primal Vision* (London: S.C.M Press, 1963); J. S. Mbiti, *African Religions and Philosophy* (New York: Anchor Books, 1970).

Anthropology aims to describe in the broadest sense what it means to be human. It is the study of human nature, human society, and human history, trying to integrate all that is known about human beings and their activities at the highest and most inclusive levels. Anthropologists study and compare human societies across space and time, in order to formulate generalizations about what it means to be human.

Although the concerns of anthropology are as old as human history, anthropology as an academic discipline dates only from the late 19th c. Anthropology is divided into the following four subdisciplines: physical anthropology, cultural anthropology, anthropological linguistics, and archaeology. Cultural anthropology is also called social anthropology and ethnology.

Mennonite interest in anthropology has come largely through experiences in cross-cultural ministries of the church, in °mission and °service activities. Anthropology has been introduced into the curricula of Mennonite schools as part of training for such service. Since the 1950s, Mennonites have pursued graduate studies in cultural anthropology and anthropological linguistics as preparation for mission service, for Bible translation, for training others for such ministries, and for academic careers in university departments of anthropology. Mennonites have also published definitive and respected works on a wide variety of anthropological topics.   RLR

See also Contextualization; Geography; Sociological Studies.

Anti-Anabaptist Polemics. See Polemics, Anti-Anabaptist.

Anticatholicism. See Roman Catholic Church.

Anticlericalism. See Anabaptism; Menno Simons; Müntzer, Thomas.

Anticommunism. See Communism.

Antisemitism. See Judaism and Jews.

Apocalypticism (ME I:557) is a stream of thought and a symbolic language, developed in Christianity from Jewish models, concerned to interpret the course of human history and to uncover (*apokaluptein*) the secrets of the end of history. From the beginning, Christians expected the early return of Christ in glory to judge the world. Christian apocalyptic literature, especially the book of Revelation, ensured the continuation of endtime expectation and unremitting attempts by virtually every generation to identify events of its time as those of the end. A central element in these speculations was the figure of the antichrist who was sometimes identified as a specific historical figure, sometimes serving as a corporate figure symbolizing all opposition to Christ. During the great struggle between pope and emperor beginning in the 11th c., both emperor and pope were identified as the antichrist, as also were the Saracens (Arabs) and the Turks. Since the 14th c., it became common in some circles to refer to the papacy as the antichrist.

Hence Martin °°Luther's use of the image was a standard component in an ongoing polemic against the corruptions of the papacy. Apocalyptic speculation and imagery in Reformation times was a continuation of earlier traditions. Thomas °Müntzer, more than any other person, served as a transmitter of apocalyptic expectation and imagery to the Anabaptists. From him also come some of the more sensational elements, such as a sense of being an identifiable actor in the endtime scenario.

It was therefore to be expected that Anabaptists too would use this powerful medium to express their convictions about the tumultuous events of their time. Earlier Mennonite historians denied that apocalyptic expectations were an important part of Anabaptist life and thought. They played down its influences in the case of Hans °Hut, and simply rejected it as non-Anabaptist in the case of °Münster. Extensive study of endtime expectation in Reformation Europe yields a different picture, namely, that apocalyptic thought was a standard feature of the 16th c. theological furniture. Of the major Protestant leaders, only Huldrych °°Zwingli and Andreas Karlstadt (°°Carlstadt) did not use it.

It has often been observed that apocalyptic thought forms make their appearance in times of crisis, when they provide language and images commensurate with the magnitude of the emergency. For the first six decades of its life, Anabaptism was threatened with extinction. Fierce persecution was, according to Jesus' words, a sign of the nearness of the end. The renewal which had begun with Martin Luther was understood to be the preaching of the gospel of the kingdom which was to come just before the end. These were the times of restitution of all that God had promised by his prophets. These sentiments were not incidental to the Anabaptist vision of discipleship. They were fundamental to their self-perception and to their readiness for martyrdom.

All Anabaptists were united in their conviction that the return of Christ was near, and that their overriding concern was to remain faithful to the end and thus survive the judgment. In that judgment justice would be irreversibly rendered. All the powerful, persecuting enemies of God would stand to the left, and all the faithful martyrs on the right. (Mt 25:31ff.) The judgment would confirm that God had always been on the side of the little, despised, persecuted, faithful flock. The anticipation of that grand reversal steeled the resolve and fueled the ecstasy of many a martyr in those years.

Certain themes characterized apocalyptic expectation among Anabaptists. The first of these was the conviction of living in the "times of restitution" which were especially associated with a renewed outpouring of the Holy Spirit and with it of the restoration of the purity of the gospel. In the early days of the movement there was therefore frequent appeal to the direct guidance of the Holy Spirit. Thomas Müntzer, Hans Hut, and Melchior °Hoffman all proclaimed that in this last age an ordinary un-

educated believer to whom God had given the Spirit was a more reliable guide to truth than the educated clergy and sacramentally ordained priests. As in the early chapters of Acts of the Apostles, so now, the outpouring of the Spirit led to aggressive missionary work. Both Hut and Hoffman believed themselves to be actors in the endtime events and took their baptizing to be the sealing of the 144,000, the faithful, pure church of the last times. As could be expected, these two men also produced timetables for the succession of the final events of history. The age of the Spirit was also conceived of as a time when many of the older practices and conventions of the church were suspended. People who believed themselves guided by the Spirit (but virtually always constrained by the biblical text) found it easy to break with the venerable sacramental teachings of the church, especially since they were sure that there was little time left.

A second theme was that, while they lived in the age of the Spirit, they were also at the same time living in the age of the antichrist. At no time in Christian history had the work of the antichrist been so clearly in evidence. While Martin Luther saw in the papal antichrist primarily the perverter of pure doctrine, Anabaptists saw his work primarily in the destruction of the two sacraments instituted by Christ. By destroying the true baptism of confessing believers, the antichrist had subjected everyone to the tyranny of the priests, who told Christians what to believe and do, and who would allow no infringement of their absolute °authority. The restoration of baptism meant the liberation from clerical tutelage. The destruction of the true Lord's Supper consisted of the Catholic claim that the bread itself was the Lord. The doctrine of the real presence was the erecting of the "abomination of desolation" in the holy place. The adoration of the eucharistic bread was therefore idolatry.

Christ and antichrist were locked in the final struggle, the truth was struggling against the lie, but the outcome was never in doubt. antichrist might kill the faithful witnesses of Christ, but, provided they remained pure and faithful, they would eventually reign with Christ after the antichrist had been finally destroyed.

Generally the antichrist was regarded as the total of everything that opposed Christ. Occasionally, as the great cosmic struggle became personal, the persecutors themselves were called antichrist. Apart from a few instances in which the antichrist was identified with the Turks, the antichrist was not directly identified with an individual human actor.

The third theme was the call to perfection, or the striving to present the church as a bride without spot or wrinkle to the returning bridegroom Christ. It intersected with the strongly ethically oriented °discipleship motif which characterized all segments of Anabaptism and which was rooted in the New Testament writings. But this linkage between eschatology and ethics is characteristic of the biblical materials also; hence it was not accidental in Anabaptism. The call to holiness in personal life and in the life of the church, and the emphasis on church discipline to retain that purity in view of the approaching end is clearly visible in the °Schleitheim

Articles, and in Anabaptist writings everywhere in the first generation. It was especially strong in the writings of Melchior °Hoffman, and of his immediate progeny, the Münsterites and the Mennonites. It has often been pointed out that the docetic °Christology of Hoffman and °Menno Simons, with its insistence that Christ had no blemish of terrestrial materiality, meshed flawlessly with the doctrine of the °church as the bride without spot or wrinkle.

The recognition of the vital part endtime expectation played in Anabaptism has in the past been obscured by the Mennonite abhorrence of the "excesses" of apocalyptic expectation. These manifestations are found in all segments of Anabaptism and cannot be seen as an aberration but as indicators of the intensity of the longing for vindication of the faithful witnesses and of retribution upon the godless. Followers of Hut and Hoffman believed themselves to be the executors of God's vengeance as described in Ps 149. When the end did not come as expected and the fury of the persecution continued, Anabaptists adopted a stance of separation from all defilement, waiting quietly for the salvation of the Lord.

There were to be periodic revivals of the certainty of the nearness of the end with the accompanying concern for the purity of the church. The 19th c. in particular provides both specific cases of apocalyptic belief and action as well as an upsurge of apocalyptic consciousness in general. The French Revolution and its aftermath (1789-1815) were interpreted by German °Pietists as the beginning of the rule of the antichrist. This interpretation profoundly influenced Mennonites in Russia through the preaching of Eduard °Wüst and contributed to the emergence of the Mennonite Brethren. A few decades later, under the influence of the writings of °°Jung-Stilling and S. G. C. Clöter, a group of Mennonites from the Trakt (Am Trakt) and Molotschna settlements left under the leadership of Claas °°Epp for Central Asia (°°Asiatic Russia), there to await the second coming of Christ. Radical separation from the world and the determination to keep God's little flock pure were fundamental features of these events. Similar influences prompted some Mennonites to join the °Templar movement which was related to the place of the Jews and their homeland in the endtime events.

North American Mennonites too were caught up in the excitement of apocalyptic expectation which, primarily in the form of premillennialism (°dispensationalism), was part of the °Fundamentalist reaction to the optimistic °liberalism of the turn of the 20th c. Mennonite support for popular radio and television preachers beginning in the 1950s produced a Mennonite literary response setting forth a restrained and sober form of endtime expectation. It is possible that the deliberate revival and enforcement of plain °dress and the °prayer veil in the Mennonite Church (MC) in the early 1900s were evidence that the original Anabaptist tradition of the call to perfection to be ready for the returning Bridegroom was alive and well.

Wherever apocalyptic expectations were articulated within Anabaptist and Mennonite history, the book of Revelation played a major part. Preoccupation with it is found in all of the three major Anabaptist groupings but with both literal and symbolic interpretations. In the 19th and 20th c. more literalistic interpretations were prominent, reflecting the prevailing Pietist and Fundamentalist uses of the book. Beginning with the 1960s, a strong swing to a position resembling earlier postmillennialism became noticeable among Mennonites as they were drawn into civil rights, antiwar, and social justice causes.　　　　　　　　　　　　　　　WKlaa

"Apokalyptik," in *Die Religion in Geschichte und Gegenwart*, 3rd ed. (Tübingen: Mohr, 1957) 1: 463-72; Franz Bartsch, *Unser Auszug nach Mittelasien* (North Kildonan, Man.: Echo Verlag, 1948; Fred R. Belk, *The Great Trakt of the Russian Mennonites to Central Asia 1880-1884* (Scottdale, 1976); idem, "The Emergence of Millennialism Among the Russian Mennonites," *MQR*, 49 (1975), 217-25; Klaus Deppermann, *Melchior Hoffman: Soziale Unruhen und apokalyptische Visionen im Zeitalter der Reformation* (Göttingen: Vandenhoeck und Ruprecht, 1979; English trans. Edinburgh: T. and T. Clark, 1987); idem, "Pennsylvanien als Asyl des frühen deutschen Pietismus," *Pietismus und Neuzeit*, 10 (1984), 190-212; Victor G. Doerksen, "Mennonite Templars in Russia," *JMS*, 3 (1985), 128-137; A. J. Dueck, "Claas Epp and the Great Trakt Reconsidered," *JMS*, 3 (1985), 139-47; Paul Erb, *The Alpha and the Omega* (Scottdale, 1955); idem, *Bible Prophecy: Questions and Answers* (Scottdale, 1978); David Ewert, *And Then Comes the End* (Scottdale, 1980); Melvin Gingerich, "Change and Uniformity in Mennonite Attire," *MQR*, 40 (1966), 243-59; Waldemar Janzen, "The Great Trakt: Episode or Paradigm," *MQR*, 51 (1977), 127-39; Martin Klaassen, *Geschichte der Wehrlosen Taufgesinnten Gemeinden* (Danzig: Edwin Groening, 1873); Walter Klaassen, "Eschatological Themes in Early Dutch Anabaptism," in *The Dutch Dissenters*, ed. Irvin B. Horst (Leiden: Brill, 1986), 15-31; idem, "Visions of the End in Reformation Europe," in *Visions and Realities*, ed. Harry Loewen and Al Reimer (Winnipeg: Hyperion Press, 1985), 11-57; idem, "A Belated Review: Martin Klaassen's 'Geschichte der Wehrlosen Taufgesinnten Gemeinden' Published in 1873" *MQR*, 49 (1975), 43-52; idem, "The Abomination of Desolation: Schwenckfeld's Christological Apocalyptic," in *Schwenckfeld and Early Schwenkfeldianism*, ed. Peter C. Erb (Pennsburg: Schwenkfelder Library, 1986), 27-46; idem, "'The Schleitheim Articles' and 'The New Transformation of Christian Living': Two Responses to the Reformation," *Historical Reflections*, 14 (1987), 95-111; Ira Landis, *The Faith of Our Fathers on Eschatology* (Lititz, Pa.: the author, 1946); Werner O. Packull, *Mysticism and the Early South German-Austrian Anabaptist Movement 1525-1531* (Scottdale, 1977), chapters 3, 4, 5; idem, "'A Hutterite Book of Medieval Origin' Revisited: An Examination of the Hutterite Commentaries on the Book of Revelation and Their Anabaptist Origin," *MQR*, 56 (1982), 147-68; idem, "Anna Jans of Rotterdam: A Historical Investigation of an Early Anabaptist Heroine," *ARG*, 78 (1987), 147-73; idem, "The Schwenkfeldian Commentary on the Apocalypse," *Schwenckfeld and Early Schwenkfeldianism*, ed. Peter C. Erb, (Pennsburg: Schwenkfelder Library, 1986), 47-86; Gottfried Seebaß, "Apokalyptik: Reformation und Neuzeit," *Theologische Realenzyklopädie*, ed. Gerhard Krause und Gerhard Müller (Berlin: De Gruyter, 1978), vol. 3, pp. 280-89; John H. Yoder, *Peace Without Eschatology?* Concern Reprint, (Scottdale: MPH, 1959).

See also Biblical Interpretation; Ordinances; Prophecy.

Apologetics. The Anabaptists did not see themselves as theologians, certainly not as formal theological apologists. They looked with great suspicion on learned theologians who could give erudite arguments on doctrine, but whose lives were not in harmony with the spirit of Christ. They did, however, engage in polemics and in apologetic discourse for several significant reasons. (1) They were forced to do so by their opponents who brought charges of heresy against them. (2) They were enjoined by Scriptures (1 Pet 3:15) to give an answer for their faith to anyone who asked. (3) They made universal claims for the gospel they preached. They engaged freely in normative discourse and sought to confront all people with the claims of the gospel. (4) They felt a sense of mission to all who named the name of Jesus and were free to engage any and all Christians in mutual discussion, study, exhortation, warning, and action on the basis of the Word of God. (5) Such exhortation, discussion and mutual exhortation was seen as necessary in arriving at an understanding of God's will. (6) They tried, often in vain, to answer gross misunderstandings and misrepresentations about themselves, and (7) they sought to answer such false charges so that they could convince people of their biblical orthodoxy and thus avoid being executed for sound biblical faith and life.

The Anabaptists did not try to explicate a rationally coherent body of propositional truths. They sought rather to understand and proclaim God's work in the world; to proclaim the way of salvation as they understood it and to live as disciples of Jesus Christ. They tried in all simplicity to give a reason for their faith (1 Pet 3:15).

From the beginning and throughout the 16th c., the Anabaptists had to defend themselves against °polemical attacks from four different directions—Roman Catholics, Lutherans, Reformed, and from within. Though the Catholics saw them as one with all Protestants, adult baptism was the central issue in the Roman Catholic debate with the Anabaptists. Johannes °°Faber challenged Balthasar °Hubmaier who yielded to Faber on many of the issues raised, but not on °baptism and °communion. Other exchanges were between Martinus °°Duncanus and the Anabaptists; Christoph °°Erhard against the Hutterites, to which Klaus °°Braidl replied; Franciscus Casterns against Jacob P. van der °°Meulen, who also replied. The Hutterites were particularly hard pressed by the Catholics because of the strength of the Counter Reformation in Moravia during the 1600s. Leonhard °°Dax, a Hutterite, wrote *Noble Lessons and Instructions* in the 1560s in answer to Catholic charges. °Menno Simons devoted a section to the refutation of Roman Catholic doctrine in his *Foundations of Christian Doctrine* (1539, *Writings*, 142-90).

A second line of defense was against Lutheran attacks. Though Martin °°Luther himself had little to do with the Anabaptists, and was not at all well informed about them, he nevertheless advised two pastors on how to answer the Anabaptists' teaching on baptism (1528). Philip °°Melanchthon also wrote against the Anabaptists in 1528 and 1535 on topics of baptism, the Lord's Supper and °°community of goods. In 1557 the Lutherans and Catholics consulted together at Worms on how to answer the Anabaptist threat. Their findings were given in a document signed by Melanchthon, Johannes °°Brenz, Jacob °°Andreae, and others. Anabaptists responded to it through Leonhard Dax's *Refutations*, a 107-page booklet that systematically refuted each of the charges.

The main line of defense of the Anabaptists was against the Reformed, since they were the dominant group in Switzerland and The Netherlands. Two of Calvin's books were directed against the Anabaptists: *Psychopannychia* (1542), in which Calvin wrote against the doctrine of soul °°sleep, widely held among the French Anabaptists; and *Brieve Instruction....* (1544), which sought to refute the seven articles of the °Schleitheim Confession, soul sleep, and the Anabaptists' view of the °°incarnation. The Anabaptists, on their part, spoke against °°infant baptism, oaths, bearing of arms, service in government office, and in favor of °°avoidance, or the ban. Taking part on the Reformed side were Ulrich °°Zwingli, especially on baptism; Heinrich °°Bullinger; Gellius °°Faber; John à °°Lasco; and Martinus °°Micronius. Anabaptists who answered were Menno Simons, Balthasar Hubmaier, Pilgram °Marpeck and Leonhard Dax.

A further line of defense was directed against error from within their own ranks and from other "sectarian" groups. Pilgram Marpeck wrote *Verantwortung* as a reply to Caspar von °Schwenckfeld, a spiritualist, emphasizing the humanity of Christ which Schwenckfeld neglected; Balthasar Hubmaier wrote *On the Sword* to differentiate his views from the °°Stäbler groups in °°Nikolsburg; Menno Simon's *Confessions of the Triune God* (1550, *Writings*, 489-98) was directed against Adam °°Pastor's views of Christ, and Menno's *Reply to Sylis and Lemke* (1560, *Writings*, 1001-15) was directed against those south German Mennonites who disagreed with Menno on the ban, and especially on marital avoidance.

Beyond this, the Anabaptists had to defend themselves against other common accusations and misrepresentations: that they were revolutionaries, like the °Münster Anabaptists; that they practiced polygamy, held things in common, were too severe in church °discipline; that they were schismatic; and that they were °legalists. These and other accusations were dealt with in Menno Simons' *Reply to False Accusations* (1552, *Writings*, 541-78).

During the 17th c. the main apologetic activity was centered in The Netherlands, where Anabaptists still needed to defend themselves against Calvinism. Calvinist books against Anabaptists were published from 1565 to 1671 and as late as 1757. Anabaptism was defended by Claes Claesz, Anthoni °°Jacobsz Roscius, E. A. van °°Dooresgeest, and °°Galenus Abrahamsz (*ME* I:498). Hans de °°Ries wrote his *Apologia* in 1626 and earlier published 40 articles of faith together with Lubbert °°Gerritsz (1618). He had already helped to draw up articles of faith (38 articles), which were published in 1561 (*ME* I:681). The period from 1615 to 1665 was immensely productive of °confessions of faith by the Dutch Mennonites. They were attempts to heal °schisms among them and to unite the fellowship. At the same time, they were meant to differentiate the Mennonite understanding of faith from the predominant Calvinist view. Of special note is T. T. von °°Sittert's apology for the Anabaptist-Mennonite tradition in 1664. He made a strong defense for adult baptism, °nonresistance, the refusal to swear oaths, subjection to the state, and a plea for tolerance (trans. and ed. by Wenger in *MQR*, 49 [1975], 5-21).

In the 18th and 19th c., there is very little that could be called apologetic writing or discussion by Mennonites. With increasing toleration and the shifting of concern for the faith to questions of the Enlightenment, the parties that earlier debated against each other, now had to defend themselves against a totally new front, and were, in a sense, allies rather than opponents.

So also The *Martyrs Mirror* of 1660 was designed to inspire the Mennonite Christians to consider their own faith, probably because that faith was no longer sustained by overt °persecution. Theological disputations were no longer held, Calvinist books against Anabaptists were few, and complaints to the government decreased. The most frequent charge against Mennonites was that they were °°Socinians. The Mennonites in the 18th-19th c. did not concern themselves with the challenges to orthodoxy coming from the universities of that time: historical-critical interpretation, the relation of science and Scripture, and other issues arising out of the Enlightenment.

At the turn of the 19th-20th c., during the Modernist-°Fundamentalist controversy, Mennonite scholars were forced to differentiate themselves both from °Liberal theology and from Fundamentalist °dispensationalist theology, both of which had made some inroads into Mennonite thought and practice. John °°Horst wrote *The Failure of Modernism*, and Daniel °Kauffman wrote *Doctrines of the Bible* to affirm an evangelical faith and yet state clearly Mennonite teachings on adult baptism, nonresistance, the non-swearing of oaths, and other doctrines not emphasized by the Fundamentalists.

In the 20th c. the main polemical and apologetic writings have come from J. H. Yoder. He offered a strong emphasis on °peace and nonresistance as the heart and center of a true understanding of the saving work of Christ. His apologetics for a new understanding of the faith, in harmony with the Anabaptist and Mennonite tradition, addressed the entire spectrum of theological positions in North America and abroad.

The disputes or apologies were inevitable. Disputants came with their own presuppositions, biblical principles, and approach to the Scriptures. The Anabaptists began with a set of presuppositions not shared by the Protesetant Reformers or the Catholic theologians. Basic to their apologetics were the following: (1) Jesus Christ is the full and final revelation of God. Jesus is Lord and is to be followed in life. (2) An important distinction is to be made between the Old Testament and the New Testament. They relate as promise and fulfillment, shadow and reality, preparation and actualization. (3) The church is the body of Christ; i.e., the visible embodiment of Christ in the world. Thus Christians must live a Christ-like life, and follow the Lord in his obedience, suffering and, if necessary, death. (4) The church is the community in which the will of God is discerned—a hermeneutic community. The word of God is not established by papal decree, or by theologians, but by the corporate community directed by the °Holy Spirit of God. (5) The Scriptures best interpret the sense of Scripture and no extra-biblical appeals to nature, philosophy, or the state can be made. (6) The end of the age is at hand, when the works of all humans will be rewarded according to their faith and works.

The Anabaptists insisted on certain prerequisites in understanding the Bible and the will of God. (1) Apart from regeneration by the Holy Spirit, the new birth, no one can rightly understand and interpret the Scriptures. This new birth was seen as a commitment to Christ made by adults, on the basis of repentance and faith, and, therefore, could not be made by an infant. (2) People have to come to the Scriptures in a proper spirit in order to understand its messsge and call. Only those who truly wish to know the will of God, and open themselves to the leading of the Spirit will hear the word of God. (3) Only those who are obedient to Christ and follow him in newness of life will be led by the Spirit into all truth. (4) The church must be willing to preach the word of God and to exhort on the basis of that word if the Spirit is to work in the fellowship. Only as the church is willing to actually loose and bind (discipline) its members, can it fully know the truth of God.

Specific principles of interpretation also set the Anabaptists apart from their contemporaries. (1) Christocentrism in interpretation was not new, but it was applied differently by the Anabaptists. They did not ask "What promotes Christ" (*was Christum treibet*) so as to make judgments about which Scriptures promoted Christ, but rather evaluated all of Scripture through the revelation received in Christ. The controlling principle of °biblical interpretation was the proper understanding of the life and ministry of Jesus. (2) A clear distinction had to be made between the Old and the New Testaments. The Old Testament history and revelation was preparatory and culminated in Jesus, who was the fulfillment of the Old Testament prophecies and of God's actions in Israel's history. A new reality came into being through Christ. The Anabaptists acknowledged that there was a progressive understanding of the work of God culminating in God's revelation in Jesus Christ. (3) The word of God was not restricted to or confined to the Bible. The Bible was God's chief way of sharing the word of God with humankind, but the Spirit could speak directly to people, and the word of God could be proclaimed by others in preaching and admonition. Nevertheless, all such revelations remained subject to and had to be judged by the revelation of Christ as given in Scripture. (4) This necessitated making a distinction between the "inner" and "outer" word; to distinguish letter and spirit. The Anabaptists were accused of being literalists (for they insisted that the simplicity and clarity of the text did not require professional interpreters) and of relying too much on the Spirit (because of the insistence that all interpretation must be guided by the Holy Spirit). The interpretation of Scripture without the personal appropriation of its message and truth, would result in a dead letter. There had to be an inner response to the message. (5) The Anabaptists insisted on corporate discerning of the will of God. Each person had to be encouraged and supported to follow Christ in life. Each person's spirit, insight, and life had to be tested to see if it conformed to the Spirit of Christ. The details of what it meant to follow Christ were discerned in the fellowship of believers. The loosing (freeing from bondage) and binding (binding to the will of God) function of the church was seen as part of being the church of Christ.   DSchroed

John Calvin: Treaties against the Anabaptists and against Libertines, trans. B. W. Farley (Grand Rapids: Baker, 1982); Willem Balke, *Calvin and the Anabaptist Radicals* (Grand Rapids: Eerdmans, 1981); Walter Klaassen, ed., *Sixteenth Century Anabaptism: Defences, Confessions, Refutations*, trans. Frank Friesen (Waterloo, Ont.: Conrad Grebel College, 1982); CRR 1; CRR 2; *TA Elsaß I, II* ; *TA Baden/Pfalz*; J. Loserth, *Quellen und Forschungen zur Geschichte der oberdeutchen Taufgesinnten im 16. Jahrhundert* (Leipzig, 1929); Dirk (Dietrich) Philips, *Regeneration and the New Creature, Spiritual Restitution and the Church of God* (Berne: Light and Hope, 1958); Peter Riedemann, *Account of Our Religion, Doctrine and Faith*, trans. Kathleen E. Hasenberg (London: Hodder and Stoughton, and Plough Publishing House, 1938, 1950, 1970); Robert Stupperich, ed., *Die Schriften Bernhard Rothmanns* (Münster in W.: Aschendorff, 1970); Menno, *Writings*; Hubmaier, *Schriften*; John H. Yoder, *The Priestly Kingdom* (U. of Notre Dame Press, 1984); idem, *The Christian Witness to the State* (Newton, 1964); idem, *The Politics of Jesus* (Grand Rapids: Eerdmans, 1972), cf. Gayle Gerber Koontz, "Confessional Theology in a Pluralistic Age: A Study of the Theological Ethics of H. Richard Niebuhr and John Howard Yoder" (PhD diss., Boston U. 1985); H. S. Bender, "The Discipline Adopted by the Strasburg Conference of 1568," *MQR*, 1 (1927), 61-90; Wilhelm Ewert, "A Defense of the Ancient Mennonite Principle of Non-resistance by a Leading Russian Mennonite Elder in 1873," *MQR*, 11 (1937), 284-90; Jan P. Matthijssen, "The Bern Disputation of 1538," *MQR*, 22 (1948), 19-33; "Pilgram Marpeck's Confession of Faith, 1531," *MQR*, 12 (1938), 167-202, cf. CRR 2: 107-57; Paul Peachy, ed., "Answer of Some Who Are Called (Ana) Baptists; Why They Do Not Attend the Churches; A Swiss Brethren Tract," *MQR*, 45 (1971), 5-32; John C. Wenger, trans. and ed., "T. T. Van Sittert's Apology for the Anabaptist-Mennonite Tradition, 1664," *MQR*, 49 (1975), 5-21; idem, "The Schleitheim Confession of Faith," *MQR*, 19 (1945), 243-53, cf. CRR 1:28-54; idem, "Martin Weninger's Vindication of Anabaptism, 1535," *MQR*, 22 (1948), 180-87; J. R. Burkholder and Calvin Redekop, eds., *Kingdom, Cross and Community* (Scottdale, 1976); Leonard Gross, *The Golden Years of the Hutterites* (Scottdale, 1980), cf. *MQR*, 49 (1975), 284-334; *Recovery*; John Horsch, *The Failure of Modernism. A Reply to Harry Emerson Fosdick* (Chicago, 1925); Walter Klaassen, *Anabaptism: Neither Catholic nor Portestant* (Waterloo: Conrad Grebel Press, 1973); William Klaassen, "The Hermeneutics of Pilgram Marpeck" (diss., Princeton Theological Seminary, 1960), cf. idem, *Covenant and Community: The Life, Writings, and Hermeneutics of Pilgram Marpeck* (Grand Rapids: Eerdmans, 1968), cf. *MQR*, 40 (1966), 97-115; Cornelius Krahn, *Dutch Anabaptism* (Scottdale, 1981); Franklin Hamlin Littell, *The Anabaptist View of the Church* (American Society of Church History, 1952); John S. Oyer, *Lutheran Reformers Against Anabaptists* (The Hague: Martinus Nijhoff, 1964), cf. *MQR*, 26 (1952), 259-79, and 27 (1953), 100-110; Henry Poettcker, "The Hermeneutics of Menno Simons" (ThD diss., Princeton Theological Seminary, 1961), cf. *MQR*, 40 (1966), 112-26; Willard Swartley, ed., *Essays on Biblical Interpretation* (Elkhart, Ind.: IMS, 1984); C. J. Dyck, "The Suffering Church in Anabaptism," *MQR*, 59 (1985), 5-23; Hans Georg Fischer, "Lutheranism and the Vindication of the Anabaptist Way," *MQR*, 28 (1954), 27-38; Robert Friedmann, "Claus Felbinger's Confession of 1560," *MQR*, 29 (1955), 141-61; Hans J. Hildebrand, "Thomas Müntzer's Last Tract Against Martin Luther," *MQR*, 38 (1964), 20-36; Walter Klaassen, "Speaking in Simplicity: Balthasar Hubmaier," *MQR*, 40 (1966), 139-47; idem, "The Berne Debate of 1538: Christ the Center of Scripture," *MQR*, 40 (1966), 148-56; William Klaassen, "The Limits of Political Authority as Seen by Pilgram Marpeck," *MQR*, 56 (1982), 342-64; Cornelius Krahn, "The Emden Disputations," *MQR*, 30 (1956), 256-58; Wilhelm Wiswedel, "The Anabaptists Answer Melanchthon," *MQR*, 29 (1955), 212-23; Jessie Yoder, "The Frankenthal Debate with the Anabaptists in 1571: Purpose, Procedure, Participants," *MQR*, 36 (1962), 14-35, 116-46; N. van der Zijpp, "The Confessions of Faith of the Dutch Mennonites," *MQR*, 29 (1955), 171-87; *ME* I:532-35, 598, 679-86, II:247-48, 286, III:70-74, 527-31.

See also Pfeddersheim Disputation; Polemics, Anti-Anabaptist; Recantation; Sectarianism.

Appropriate Technology is a term most often used in reference to the introduction of °technology from developed nations to less developed ones. Technology that is appropriate produces a new machine or process for use in the local community, requires skills known or easily taught, and is made of materials readily available, with little or no importing of material, tools, or capital from the outside. In practice, some items usually need to be imported: hardware, sheet metal, plastic sheet or pipe, simple bearings (e.g., from bicycles), etc. Since the technology is produced locally, it can be maintained rather than discarded when it breaks down. Examples of appropriate technology designed by Mennonite Central Committee workers include a human-powered irrigation pump (Bangladesh) and an earthen stove with improved fuel economy (Mexico and Central America). Appropriate technology carries with it the ideas of self-sufficiency and self-improvement. Skills are upgraded, and arduous tasks are eased. The quality of life improves, and resources kept in the community raise the standard of living.   WUnr

See also Development Work.

Arapaho People. See Indians, North America.

Arbeitsgemeinschaft der Mennonitengemeinden zur geistlichen Betreuung der Umsiedler (Mennonite Churches Task Force for the Pastoral Care of Resettlers). See *Umsiedler*.

Arbeitsgemeinschaft deutscher Mennonitengemeinden (AdM) (Task Force of the German Mennonite Churches). The *Arbeitsgemeinschaft deutscher Mennonitengemeinden* (AdM), is an organization seeking ways to increase cooperation among German Mennonites, specifically the °Verband deutscher Mennonitengemeinden and the °Vereinigung der deutschen Mennonitengemeinden. Already in 1934, representatives of the Mennonite youth had declared "We, the young Mennonites, are at a loss to understand how our responsible brethren have been unable to come to a mutual understanding. We pray to the Lord for clarity, courage, and obedience in the decisions that lie ahead." In the *Mennonitisches Jahrbuch 1976*, Hans-Adolf Hertzler wrote: "There should be possibilities to meet each other, favorable moments for talking and thinking together." These ideas did not remain unnoticed. In 1980, Paul Schwan, from Stuttgart, suggested that an institution responsible for the interests of all Mennonites be established. The first contacts between representatives of the *"Verband"* and *"Vereinigung"* took place May 27, 1981; at a second meeting in °Neuwied a year later (June 4-6, 1982), Bernd Dyck submitted new ideas for a renewed approach. The most important part of his remarks was the assertion that "the witness of brotherly love that is lived out counts more than the best confession of faith. Without active brotherly love we are liars and hypocrites."

Two inter-Mennonite meetings of German Mennonites are evidence of successful attempts for further approach. One took place in 1983 at Espelkamp under the theme, "There is Only One Lord, but We are Sisters and Brothers." At the other one, in 1985 at Neuwied, the topic was "Live Differently." The merger of two periodicals, *Gemeinde Unterwegs* (Verband), and the *Mennonitische Blätter* (Vereinigung) followed: *Brücke - Mennonitisches Gemeindeblatt* (*Bridge*) has been published since January 1985.

Regular meetings between seven representatives each of the *Verband* and the *Vereinigung* have been held since 1982. The AdM was incorporated in June 1986. It serves not only the purpose of cooperation between the *Verband* and the *Vereinigung*, but also among other Mennonite groups of the Federal Republic of Germany and West Berlin, aiming toward the establishment of a comprehensive conference of German Mennonite churches.

The *Arbeitsgemeinschaft zur geistlichen Unterstützung in Mennonitengemeinden*, a task force for the spiritual support in resettler (°*Umsiedler*) churches, has withdrawn from the AdM. This is one of the reasons for the resignation of Gerhard Hildebrand one of the AdM's two chairpersons, in April 1980. Adolf Schnebele, president of the *Verband*, and Heinold Fast, president of the *Vereinigung*, are presently chairpersons of the AdM.   OW
Menn. Jahrbuch (1984-86).

See also Konferenz Süddeutscher Mennonitengemeinden.

Arbeitsgemeinschaft Mennonitischer Brüdergemeinden in Deutschland. See Bund Europäischer Mennonitischer Brüdergemeinden.

Arbeitsgemeinschaft Mennonitischer Brüdergemeinden in Österreich und Bayern (Task Force of the Mennonite Brethren Churches in Austria and Bavaria). See Bund Europäischer Mennonitischer Brüdergemeinden.

Arbeitsgemeinschaft südwestdeutscher Mennonitengemeinden (Task Force of Southwest German Mennonite Churches). In existence since 1974, this task force is the successor to the Konferenz pfälzisch-hessischer Mennonitengemeinden (ME I:677) and the Mennonitische Hilfskasse. The task force is made up of the Altleiningen, Enkenbach, Eppstein, Friedelsheim, Ibersheim, Kohlhof, Kühbörnscheshof, Ludwigshafen, Monsheim, Neudorferhof, Obersülzen, Sembach, Weierhof, and Zweibrücken congregations (2,305 members). Its purpose is to work together in the encouragement and support of Christian and Mennonite faith in mission and social projects. A general business meeting is held once a year. The task force offers regular courses for volunteers, a yearly fellowship meeting, and a mission day. The preachers' conference takes place six times a year and is attended not only by full-time church workers, but also by members of the board. Theological and administrative questions are discussed during these meetings. The organization owns the Mennonitenhaus in Kaiserslautern, which was built by the Mennonite Central Committee in 1956 and is used as retreat and conference center. In 1982, the task force began missionary work in cooperation with the °Deutsches Mennonitisches Missionskomitee in Kaiserslautern.   K-DW

Menn. Jahrbuch (1951-); published congregational histories from Enkenbach, Ibersheim, Ludwigshafen, and Weierhof.

Architecture (ME I:146). In the decades following World War II, North American Mennonites experienced an outburst of church building and institutional construction (colleges, °hospitals, retirement and nursing °homes, °camps, etc.) unprecedented in their history. Construction of church buildings had been postponed by the Great Depression of the 1930s and the war years of the 1940s. After the war, Mennonites found themselves with increased financial resources and ideas for expanded °institutional programs. This was accompanied by much residential construction and movement into more urban areas.

With radical changes in agriculture, the appearance of Mennonite farmsteads changed. Many special-purpose small farm buildings were torn down as agricultural enterprises became less diversified. With less need for the storage of large quantities of hay, many Mennonite-owned barns fell into disuse and were razed.

In the 1950s and 1960s many small churches or meetinghouses of simple design were replaced by more spacious and complex church structures. Many of these were built at comparatively low cost with much contributed labor under the direction of local contractors and without benefit of architectural services. Educational wings were often added to existing older church buildings to accommodate expanded church programs.

This period brought to an end the simple "meetinghouse" era. Mennonites were now inclined to borrow architectural ideas from their Protestant neighbors. Often church design reflected the pragmatic decisions of those experienced in building for farm and business purposes. Churches often reflected the "L-shaped" ranch-style residential or pole-shed industrial patterns of the era.

As new church buildings were constructed, a wide range of questions evoked congregational discussion and even conflict. Many of the questions were laden with concerns related to Mennonite traditions and values, i.e., questions of simplicity, °wealth, replication of conventionaal non-Mennonite architecture, expanding church programs, °technology, and °acculturation. A list of some of these questions follows: How shall the building be identified so that it is recognized as a church? Should it have a steeple, cross, a name on the building, or a free-standing sign? Should it have a central pulpit or a divided chancel? In other words, should the church building be pulpit-centered or chancel-oriented or congregation-oriented? Should the building have plain windows, stained glass windows, a public address system, provision for showing °motion pictures, a piano or organ (and where should these °musical instruments be located)? Should a loft for a choir be included? Questions about the use of works of art in the church building; choice of furniture, chairs, pews (with or without padded seats), carpeting; and provision for a fellowship hall, a kitchen, even a gymnasium, were raised. Additional issues involved the arrangment of classrooms (for different age groups), the size of the foyer (i.e., provision for visiting before and after services), space for a library, access for those with °disabilities, retention or razing of °buggy sheds, and landscaping and parking lots (paved or unpaved). Some congregations debated whether to design buildings for multiple use—as day-care centers and for after-school youth activities, etc. Even the decision on location of a new building—whether to move into town or not, a move that might mean leaving behind the historic congregational cemetery—could be controversial.

Significant and varied examples of architect-designed church buildings, which involved substantial dialogue between the architect and the congregation, have appeared. These discussions have focused on some of the above questions, but more importantly, on questions of congregational °identity and self-image, heritage motifs, sense of congregational vocation, etc. Several notable examples of such collaboration between architects and congregations are (architect's name in parenthesis) Zion Mennonite Church, Souderton, Pa. (Edward Sovik); Normal Mennonite Church, Normal, Ill. (LeRoy Troyer); Bahia Vista Mennonite Church, Sarasota, Fla. (Orus Eash); and Prince of Peace Chapel, Aspen, Col. (Ron Birkey).

College and seminary campuses have reflected new architectural patterns and trends. Recent construction of note on Mennonite campuses includes the following: College Church at Goshen College, Ind. (Orus Eash); Mennonite Heritage Centre at Canadian Mennonite Bible College, Winnipeg (Sig Toews); Chapel of the Sermon on the Mount at the Associated Mennonite Biblical Seminaries, Elkhart, Ind. (Charles Stade); Marbeck Center at Bluffton College, Ohio (Jack Hodell); John S. Umble Center, Goshen College (Weldon Pries); Administration Building, Eastern Mennonite College, Harrisonburg, Va. (LeRoy Troyer).

A growing number of Mennonites have been entering the professions of architecture and landscape architecture. More Mennonite congregations are making use of the services of professional architects. This promises to change the face of North American Mennonite church buildings in the years to come. RK

Wittlinger, *Piety and Obedience* (1979), 492-95.

See also Worship.

Archives (ME I:151). During the 30 years ca. 1955-87, Mennonite archives have developed, broadly speaking, in two major dimensions. One is the stabilization and internal refinement of four older archival institutions which led the way among Mennonites of the western world. The other has to do with the emergence of several dozen new centers, both large and small, that did not exist, for the most part, in the early 1960s.

To begin with, there were the document centers developed at Goshen, Ind., and North Newton, Ks., in the United States, at the Weierhof in West Germany, and in Amsterdam, The Netherlands. The Dutch Mennonite materials have become accessible to other communities through a massive microfilming project which was completed in the 1950s and 1960s. A comprehensive catalog, produced in 1983-84 is still a significant general finding aid to this collection.

In Goshen the Mennonite Church (MC) archives had been relocated to the former seminary building on the Goshen College campus even before pioneer archivist and historian Harold S. °Bender died in 1962. Since then this center has become the official depository for the records of the Mennonite Church, Mennonite World Conference, Mennonite Central Committee, and the Council of International Ministries, among others. The wide-ranging personal collections of a number of leading persons (e.g., H. S. Bender, Melvin °Gingerich, Paul °Erb, Robert °Friedmann, J. C. Wenger, S. C. °Yoder, and Guy F. °Hershberger have added much to the manuscript holdings here. The total number of personal collections is 1,800, with the number of documents estimated to be ten million or more.

Similar developments have taken place at Mennonite Library and Archives in Kansas. With the retirement of historian Cornelius °Krahn and archivist John Schmidt, the archives at Bethel College shifted from an emphasis on collection to organization and cataloging, under the guidance of director Robert Kreider and more recently, David Haury. The materials of MLA have very recently gained a more spacious home, with the construction of a new library building on the campus.

The Mennonitische Forschungstelle (Mennonite Research Center) at the Weierhof in West Germany has gained some permanence at this location. Its long-time director, Gary Waltner, has sought to organize the older deposits, and to make the collection more accessible to researchers at home and abroad.

One can summarize some of the more recent major developments in archival work under four regional headings: (a) Mennonite Brethren research centers in North America; (b) emerging archives in the eastern United States; (c) archival work in Canada; (d) new depositories in Latin America and the Far East.

Three Mennonite Brethren archive and research centers came into being in the mid-1970s—at Fresno, Cal. (Mennonite Brethren Biblical Seminary); Hillsboro, Ks. (Tabor College); and Winnipeg, Man. (Mennonite Brethren Bible College). These centers received a strong mandate to gather Mennonite Brethren congregational and conference materials, and to further research on church-related themes.

Other new centers in Ohio, Illinois, Pennsylvania, and Virginia have tended to favor collection in Swiss-Pennsylvania Mennonite communities. Among these are the Illinois Mennonite Historical and Genealogical Society archives at Metamora, the archives at Bluffton College (Ohio), the Lancaster (Pa.) Mennonite Historical Society archives, the Mennonite Historical Library and Archives of Eastern Pennsylvania at Lansdale, and the Menno Simons Historical Library and Archives at Eastern Mennonite College in Harrisonburg, Va. The collection of the Archives of the Brethren in Christ Church (United States and Canada) and Messiah College, located at Messiah College, Grantham, Pa. (1952-), contains denominational, congregational, and personal documents as well as museum artifacts. A number of smaller conference or regional collections are maintained at Mennonite high schools, junior colleges, and Bible institutes in the United States and Canada.

Archival work in Canada has been concentrated mainly in the growing depositories at Conrad Grebel College (emphasis again on Swiss Mennonites in Ontario), the Centre for Mennonite Brethren Studies in Winnipeg, and the Mennonite Heritage Centre, also located in Winnipeg, on the campus of Canadian Mennonite Bible College. Russian Mennonite studies have become a strong secondary emphasis at these three centers. All date the serious beginnings of their general programs to the period 1974-76, when Mennonite centennial celebrations in Canada helped to emphasize the importance of records for history writing and related work. The Evangelical Mennonite Conference began its collection at Steinbach, Man., around 1980, and Columbia Bible College in Clearbrook, B.C., has begun to build up an archives for British Columbia Mennonites as well. Saskatchewan Mennonites made a similar beginning in the late 1970s at Rosthern Junior College. Congregational records are central to the collection policies of all Canadian Mennonite archival centers.

Begun in the late 1970s, the Mennonite archival centers of Brazil (Curitiba) and Paraguay (Fernheim and Loma Plata in the Chaco) collect church data and give much attention to community records generally. The Archives of Chaco Indian Cultures in Filadelfia holds materials on the Chaco Indians. The Gereja Injili di Tanah Jawa (Evangelical Church of Java) has archives at Pati, Indonesia, and there is important material for Japanese Mennonites at the Anabaptist Center Library and Archives in Tokyo. LK

Periodicals published by various Mennonite archives include *The Mennonite Librarian and Archivist Newsletter* (1984); *MHB*; *Menn. Life* (1946-); *Menn. Historian* [1975-]; *Mennonite Brethren Historical Society of Canada Newsletter* (1979-86); *Brethren in Christ History and Life*. Current statistics are found in *MC Yearbook* (biennial); cf. Lawrence Klippenstein, ed., *Directory of Mennonite Archives and Historical Libraries* (Winnipeg: Mennonite Heritage Centre, 1984). See also David A. Haury, "The Mennonite Library and Archives, A Brief History," *Menn. Life*, 42 (Sept., 1987), 26-29; Lawrence Klippenstein, and John Friesen, "The Mennonite Heritage Centre for Research and Study," *Menn. Life*, 33 (Dec., 1978), 19-22; Ken Reddig, "The Mennonite Brethren Archives in Winnipeg," *Menn. Life*, 34 (Dec., 1979), 11-14; Ted Regehr, "Mennonite Archives in Canada," *Archivaria*, no. 5 (Winter, 1977/78), 164-65; Gary Waltner, "Leidvolle Geschichte-dokumentiert in der Mennonitischen Forschungsstelle Weierhof," *Donnersberg Jahrbuch* (1979), 173-78; *Menn. Rep.* (Sept. 14, 1987), 10; Wittlinger, *Piety and Obedience* (1978), 547.

See also Conservative Mennonite Conference; Historical Libraries; Historical Writing; Historical Societies.

Arcola-Arthur, Ill., Old Order Amish Settlement. See Arthur, Ill., Old Order Amish Settlement.

Argentina. See Iglesia Evangélica Menonita, Argentina (Argentine Mennonite Church); Remeco-Guatrache Mennonite Colony.

Martin's Mission to Bartolomé

Martin Esteban stepped out of his small house made of split palm trunks and sticks plastered with mud. Chickens were scratching in the yard, and in the distance a dog barked. But Martin did not hear them. He was thinking about his dream last night. In it, God had told him to leave the small Toba Indian reservation in northern Argentina where he lived and to travel to the village of Bartolomé to take the gospel to the Pilaga Indians who lived there.

Martin was troubled because there was hatred and sometimes violence between the Toba Indians and the Pilaga tribe. Would it be safe for him, a Toba, to go to the Pilaga and tell them about Jesus? But then Martin thought, "My mother was a Pilaga and taught me the Pilaga language. This will help me greatly. And besides, if God has called me, he will protect me."

Martin felt excited to be worthy of the call from God and began to make plans to sell his small farm. He thought about the long trip—it would take four or five days by foot to go the 160 miles to Bartolomé.

When the farm was sold, Martin packed his few belongings in a bag: a blanket, mosquito netting, bow and arrows and knife for hunting, and machete for clearing a path through thick grass or weeds. He also packed a small teakettle, a small bag of *yerba maté* tea leaves, his *bombilla* (a metal straw), and a teacup. With these he could brew and drink his favorite strong tea.

As he went along the hot, dry path, Martin gathered fruit, bean pods from the carob plant, berries, and nuts. He would stop early in the afternoon and hunt some meat for his supper—perhaps a bird or a wild animal. Martin was strong and taller than many men in his village. He was also an expert hunter. He felt content as he realized that as he traveled and hunted, he was living as his family had lived not so many years ago.

The next day he met a man with a wagon and horses, and Martin rode several hours on the wagon. By evening he reached the Bermejo River, and that night his supper was fish caught from the river with his bow and arrows. Martin took his tinderbox, made from the hard tail of an armadillo, and started a fire to roast the fish and prepare his *maté* tea.

The next day he had to wade and swim across the Bermejo River, then go through a swampy area with many insects. After that came the scrub forest with thorn trees, many with thorns five or six inches long. The fourth day Martin joined with some men going ostrich hunting. They were able to get an ostrich by disguising themselves with leafy branches. Then each one had some ostrich meat plus some beautiful plumes, which they could sell at the market.

Martin knew he would reach Bartolomé the next day, and prayed for God's direction and protection. When he finally approached the Pilaga settlement the chief and several men came out to meet him. Speaking in Pilaga, Martin told them who he was and that his mother was Pilaga. He also explained to them why he had come—to tell them about Christ.

The men looked sternly at him. For a few seconds Martin didn't know what would happen. Then the chief's face softened, and he invited Martin to sit down in the shade near his house. As the chief's wife prepared some *maté* tea, the men asked Martin about his long journey. He told them of his travels but also about God and his son, Jesus.

As the days went by, many persons listened to Martin's message. Some of them believed, soon a church was formed in the town. People came to the church to worship, to be healed, and to be together as believers in Christ. They sang songs and praises, accompanied by guitars and tambourines. Some waved pom-poms, and others made a rhythmic noise with *guiros* (notched sticks rubbed with other sticks). Those who didn't have instruments clapped their hands and stamped their feet to the rhythm of the music.

As time went on, the church grew. Martin became restless; he wanted to go on to other Pilaga villages. Two leaders from the new Bartolomé church went with Martin, and they visited 10 other settlements. Many people believed, and several churches were begun before Martin died in 1978.   MH

Adapted from "The Obedient Messenger" in Marian Hostetler and Ruth Liechty, *God's Messengers* (copyright Mennonite Publishing House, Scottdale, Pa., 1985), 42-44. Used by permission.

Arita Masaru (b. Jan. 8, 1930), the first baptized member of the Nihon Menonaito Burezaren Kyodan (Japan Mennonite Brethren Conference), was born in Hyogo Prefecture. After graduating from Osaka Municipal University in 1956, he taught high school English at the Episcopal Momoyama Mission School until 1961. He was baptized in July 1951; entered Osaka Biblical Seminary, which was sponsored by the Mennonite Brethren Mission, in 1961; became pastor of the Ishibashi Church in 1964; and was ordained in Sept. 1971. In 1958 he married Teiko *Wakizaka*. They have three children.

While pastoring the Ishibashi church, he also served as moderator of the Japan Field Council for six years. After the Japan Mennonite Brethren Conference reorganized the seminary training program in 1971, he served as the first principal; later he was dean of education. In 1987 he continues to teach New Testament studies, church history, and other courses.

In the early years of the Japan Mennonite Brethren Conference, he worked diligently to establish an indigenous church with strong national leadership, to formulate a constitution and doctrinal statement for organization, and to produce a handbook for members. These guiding principles are based on evangelical, fundamentalist, and Anabaptist teachings.

In Mennonite Brethren circles, he is widely known and loved as an evangelist, pastor, Bible teacher, and leader.   RW

Arizona (ME I:156). Eleven Amish families from Kansas and Oregon moved to Glendale, Ariz., in 1909, living on small irrigated farms. By 1916, all of these families had left Arizona. Sunnyslope, the first organized Mennonite congregation, began in Phoenix in 1946. Families who moved to Arizona for health reasons found each other and gathered for worship in the home of Harold and Mae Brooks.

As Mennonites continued to move to Arizona for health, climate, and employment, the number and variety of Mennonite churches increased. Of the hundreds of people who came to Arizona since 1950 to serve in Voluntary Service and its Discipleship Program, many decided to stay and become part of the life and witness of the church.

By 1987 there were more than 1,300 members in 18 congregations: 12 in the Phoenix area, 1 each in Tucson and Prescott, 2 on the Navajo reservation and 2 on the Hopi reservation. These represent six Mennonite denominational groups: Mennonite Church (MC); General Conference Mennonite Church; Mennonite Brethren; Conservative Mennonite Conference; Western Conservative Mennonite Fellowship; Church of God in Christ, Mennonite; and several unaffiliated Mennonite congregations.

The Glencroft Retirement Community, sponsored by Mennonites, Apostolic Christian Church, Friends, and the Church of the Brethren, began in 1972. It has 1,000 residents on the Glendale campus and has built a second facility on the northeast side of Phoenix.   DWM

MC Yearbook (1986-87), 20; Henry D. Esch, *Mennonites in Arizona* (Phoenix: the author, 1985); Daniel Hertzler, *From Germantown to Steinbach* (Scottdale, 1981); David Luthy, "Amish in the 48th State," *Fam. Life* (May 1975), 13; Wittlinger, *Piety and Obedience* (1978), 147.

Arkansas (ME I:158). In 1988, there were 16 Mennonite congregations in the state belonging to the following six conferences (number of congregations and membership in parentheses): Beachy Amish Mennonite Fellowship (2, 42); Conservative Mennonite Conference (1, 29); South Central Conference (MC, 3, 44 plus one church planting effort); unaffiliated Mennonite congregations (6, 147); Church of God in Christ Mennonite (1 congregation); Mennonite Brethren (3 congregations). Two congregations belong to more than one conference. There was one Amish settlement (one congregation) in White Co. Mennonites sponsored a 26-bed hospital and outpatient clinic at Calico Rock, one skilled nursing facility (108 beds) at El Dorado, and one nursing home (67 beds) at Harrison.   RSa

MC Yearbook (1988-89), 18-19, 51, 78-79, 98-99, 121, 126, 127, 167-168; Luthy, *Amish Settlements* (1985), 7.

Arnold, Emmy von Hollander (Dec. 25, 1884–Jan. 15, 1980), was born in Riga, Latvia, the daughter of Heinrich von Hollander, a professor of law, and his wife Monika. Soon after, the family emigrated to Germany and eventually settled in Halle a. d. Saale. Emmy grew up there and, in 1909, married Eberhard °°Arnold. In 1920, after many years of active evangelistic work and search for full Christian discipleship, they started to live in community with their children, Emmy's sister Else von Hollander and others. Emmy's other two sisters joined them. Later they adopted the name *Bruderhof* from the °°Hutterian Anabaptists. Eberhard acknowledged his indebtedness to Emmy on this journey of faith. The *Bruderhof* movement recognizes her important contribution to their life and history to this day. Emmy died in the °°Woodcrest Bruderhof, in New York state. She was faithful, courageous, and possessed childlike joy into her 96th year.   MJo

The following items were all published by Plough Publishing, Rifton, N.Y.: Emmy Arnold, *Torches Together* (1971), also published in Germany and Sweden; idem, *Inner Words for Every Day of the Year* (1963); idem, "Eberhard Arnold's Life and Work," in *Eberhard Arnold: A Testimony to Church Community from his Life and Writings* (1973); idem, "Christmas Joy" and "Expectation and Fulfillment," in *When the Time was Fulfilled* (1965); Eberhard and Emmy Arnold, *Seeking for the Kingdom* (1973).

Arnold, Eberhard C. H. ("Hardy") (Aug. 18, 1912-Nov. 2, 1987). Born in Halle a. d. the Saale, Germany, Hardy Arnold was the eldest son of Eberhard °°Arnold and Emmy (von Hollander) °Arnold. He died at the °°New Meadow Run Bruderhof. He was raised in Berlin, Sannerz, and the °°Rhönbruderhof, and studied at universities in Tübingen, Zürich, and Birmingham, England. He lived at Primavera, Paraguay, then immigrated to the United States in 1958. He was married to Edith Boecker; they had four children. After Edith's death he married Martha (Sekunda) Kleiner. He was confirmed in the Service of the Word (°°*Diener am Wort*), by the visiting °°Schmiedeleut Hutterite Servant of the Word, David Hofer of James Valley (Man.) Bruderhof, on Sept. 13, 1937, at the °°Cotswold Bruderhof in England. He was editor at the Plough Publishing House, where his responsibilities included the periodicals *Der Pflug* (1938-39), and *The Plough* (1938-40). He served the eastern Hutterian Brethren (Society of Brothers) as a prolific translator and editor until his death. The most important published works that he edited and translated were: *Rechenschaft unserer Religion, Lehr und Glaubens . . . durch Peter Riedemann* (Ashton Keynes, England, 1938), which he also translated as *Confession of Faith: Account of Our Religion, Doctrine and Faith, Given by Peter Riedemann . . .* (Hodder and Stoughton, Great Britain, 1950); *The Early Christians After the Death of the Apostles* (Rifton, N.Y., 1970), a translation of Eberhard Arnold's *Die ersten Christen nach dem Tode der Apostel* (Sannerz and Berlin, 1926); *Am Anfang war die Liebe: Dokumente, Briefe und Texte der Urchristen* (Wiesbaden, 1986), a new edition of *Die ersten Christen*. He was coeditor of Eberhard and Emmy Arnold, *Seeking for the Kingdom of God: Origins of the Bruderhof Communities* (Rifton, N.Y., 1974); wrote "Eberhard Arnold, 1883-193(5): A Short Biography," *MQR*, 25 (1951), 219-21; edited Eberhard Arnold, "On the History of the Baptizer Movement in Reformation Times," *MQR*, 43 (1969), 213-33; and coauthored *For the Sake of Divine Truth* (Rifton, N.Y., 1974).   Woodcrest Bruderhof

Arnold, Johann Heinrich ("Heini") (Dec. 23, 1913-July 23, 1982). Born in Oberbozen in the Tirol, Heini Arnold was the son of Eberhard °°Arnold and Emmy (von Hollander) °Arnold. He died at the °°Woodcrest Bruderhof, Rifton, N.Y. He was elder (*Vorsteher*) for the eastern Hutterian Brethren (Society of Brothers) from July 13, 1962, until his death. He was raised in Berlin, Sannerz, and the °°Rhönbruderhof in Germany; lived in England and at Primavera, Paraguay; then immigrated to the United States in 1955. He was married to Annemarie Wächter; they had nine children. He was confirmed

as Servant of the Word (°°*Diener am Wort*) on Oct. 23, 1939, at the °°Cotswold Bruderhof. He was devoted to his father's early Christian witness and last request for the "uniting of genuine old Hutterianism with the attitude of faith of the Blumhardts [Johann Christoph Blumhardt, 1805-80; Christoph Blumhardt, 1842-1919] and the life-attitude of the true Youth Movement." The direction taken by members of the Paraguayan Bruderhofs led to a break with the Hutterian Brethren in western North America in 1955. After years of prayer, his humility and self-sacrifice were instrumental for the forgiveness and reuniting that took place in 1974. His love for Christ led the Bruderhof back to unity in living and proclaiming the Word, as recorded in numerous letters and transcripts of meetings. His most important works (all published by Plough Publishing at Rifton, N.Y.) are: *Freedom from Sinful Thoughts: Christ Alone Breaks the Curse* (1973) (= *Freiheit von Gedankensünden: Nur Christus bricht den Fluch*, 1973); editor, with Annemarie Arnold, of Eberhard and Emmy Arnold, *Seeking for the Kingdom of God: Origins of the Bruderhof Communities* (1974); *In the Image of God: Marriage and Chastity in Christian Life* (1977); *Purity of Childhood* (1973); *Man the Image of God and Modern Psychology* (1973); *Living in Community: A Way to True Brotherhood* (1974), with Annemarie Arnold (= *Gemeinsames Leben, ein Weg zu wahrer Brüderlichkeit*, 1977); *Gifts and Saving Grace* (1979).   Woodcrest Bruderhof

Art. See Ceramics; Dramatic Arts; Filmmaking; Folk Arts; Graphic Design; Interpretation and Information Centers; Literature; Mennonite Studies; Museums; Music; Painting and Printmaking; Photography; Sculpture.

Arthur, Ill., Old Order Amish Settlement (ME I: 173) was founded in 1865 by several families from Somerset Co., Pa. Located in Douglas and Moultrie Cos. in east central Illinois, 30 mi. (50 km.) west of Decatur, the Arthur settlement is the only surviving Amish community in the state. Four other settlements established in the middle and late 1800s have long become extinct (Luthy, *Amish* [1986], 74-91). In 1936, a group left the Amish church to establish the Arthur Mennonite Church (MC) and some 10 years later (1945) a smaller group of Amish families formed the Conservative Mennonite Church. Otherwise, the Arthur Amish community has experienced long and steady growth with 18 districts (congregations) serving more than 3,000 people (1986).

The survival and steady growth of the Arthur community can be attributed to excellent farming conditions and to the strong leadership among the bishops and ministers. High land prices and an increased tolerance by the church of nonfarming occupations have resulted in many factory and farm-related jobs for young men in the community. This has affected Amish lifestyle, and challenges some of the traditional cultural patterns of this rural farm community. In 1986 the Arthur-Arcola community was one of the 10 largest Amish settlements in the United States.   SLY

D. Paul Miller, *The Illinois Amish* (Gordonville, Pa.: Pequea

Publishers, 1980); Lois F. Fleming, "The Old Order Amish Community of Arthur, Illinois" (unpubl. MS Ed. paper, Eastern Illinois State U., 1962), copy at AMBS.

Ashland, Ohio, Old Order Amish Settlement is located in north central Ohio, approximately 40 mi. (65 km.) nw. of the Holmes Co. community. The first Amish settlement, made up of Holmes and Wayne Co. families, lived amidst the four Mennonite churches in the same area. Within several decades, Amish farmers moved away or affiliated with the Mennonite Church (MC), and the settlement became extinct. In 1954, a new Amish settlement began. In its 30-year history, the Ashland community has seen steady growth. In 1986 it had five church districts (congregations) with more than 700 people and maintained seven Amish schools. The Ashland Amish pioneered new settlements in Greenwood, Wis. (1975), and Stanwood, Mich. (1982).   SLY

Asia. See Bangladesh; Hong Kong; India; Indonesia; Japan; Kampuchea; Korea; Laos; Nepal; Pakistan; Philippines; Peoples Republic of China; Taiwan; Thailand; Union of Soviet Socialist Republics; Vietnam; Work Camps.

Asna, Mohansingh Rufus (Dec. 3, 1883–Apr. 30, 1960), came to the mission at Janjgir from the German Lutheran Mission in Bihar Province, India. After some years of resisting the claim of Christ on his life, he finally said yes to go to the Mennonite Mission in Madhya Pradesh (Central Province) to become an evangelist.

In July 1903 he and his wife arrived in Janjgir where they were warmly welcomed. Soon he became a dedicated Christian worker. He was ordained as a deacon in the Janjgir congregation in 1914. In 1929 he became the first Indian evangelist to be ordained an elder in the General Conference Mennonite Church.

His first wife died in 1912 and his second wife died of cholera in 1914 after a brief marriage. In 1918 he married again. Through it all he never lost his love for people and he showed many a young person the path of life which leads to faith in and commitment to Christ.   HR

Twenty-five Years With God In India (Berne, Ind.: Mennonite Book Concern, 1929), 48-54; letter from P. Lader (Aug. 7, 1987) trans. by Harold Ratzlaff.

Asociación de Iglesias Hermanos Menonitas, Colombia (Association of Mennonite Brethren Churches). In April 1945 the Mennonite Brethren sent their first missionaries to Colombia, the Daniel Wirsche family. They established a headquarters in the mountain town of La Cumbre, Valle, near Cali. From there missionaries moved out into the steamy rain forests of the Chocó in nw. Colombia, where medical and evangelistic work was begun among both the black and the Indian population. Persecution led to the closing of the Indian work in Noanamá some ten years later. The work begun among blacks in Istmina and among the rural people in La Cumbre also suffered setbacks through persecution in the 1950s, but has continued.

The year 1958 brought political changes to Colombia which resulted in an open door for evangelism and church planting by Mennonite Brethren

missionaries. Two other events that year also proved significant for the future of the Mennonite Brethren in Colombia. The Association of Mennonite Brethren Churches was officially organized, and a decision was made to begin church planting in the city of Cali, which became the headquarters for the national Mennonite Brethren conference.

By 1971 the conference had grown to 24 congregations including those in Cali, rural areas of the Valle, and in the Chocó. New outreach since that time has added one congregation each in the major cities of Medellín and Bogota and several new congregations in Cali.

The Mennonite Brethren in Colombia have been involved with education from the beginning. Schools were part of the early work in the Chocó. A primary and a secondary school were established in La Cumbre. The primary school was eventually turned over to Colombian leadership. It operated until 1969. The high school, Colegio Américas Unidas, was moved to Cali in 1966, and has done well in recent years under a Colombian director. Theological education has also played an important part in the nationalization of the Mennonite Brethren Church in Colombia. The first organized attempt was a small Bible institute in Cali, 1959-68. In 1968 the Mennonite Brethren, together with eight other groups, merged their program into the extension seminary known as the United Biblical Seminary of Colombia. Though considered an innovative approach, it did not meet all the needs of the denomination, and today the Association of Mennonite Brethren churches again operates a residence program in Cali known as the Seminario Bíblico Tecnológico. The school has been directed by Colombians since 1986.

Despite a turbulent beginning, the Mennonite Brethren church in Colombia has grown and matured. With its roots in the jungles and rural areas, its major challenge today seems to be the cities. The three cities of Cali, Bogotá, and Medellín have a combined population of more than 12 million people. In Cali, the newest church, Comunidad Bethel, joined the conference in 1986 with 100 members. The church's goal is to reach 1,000 members by 1990 (conference in 1987 was 820). Though only five missionaries remained in 1986, all in Cali, Mennonite Brethren Board of Missions and Services has agreed to send twelve additional missionaries by 1988. Most of these will go to the cities of Bogotá and Medellín where new church planting thrusts are envisioned. The goal is to have five churches in each of those cities by the time of the 50th anniversary of the Mennonite Brethren church in Colombia in 1995.   HE

Phyllis Martens, *The Mustard Tree* (Fresno: M.B. Board of Christian Education, 1971), 174-88; John A. Toews, *History MB* (1975), 427-29; *Mennonite Brethren in World Mission*, 2, no. 1 (Jan./Feb. 1986), 3; *MWH* (1978), 211-12.

See also Panama.

Asociación de Servicios de Cooperación Indigena-Menonita (Association for Indian and Mennonite Cooperation). See Chaco Mission.

Associação das Igrejas Irmãos Menonitas do Brasil (AIIMB; Conference of the Mennonite

Brethren Churches in Brazil) was founded in 1960 with the union of seven German-speaking Mennonite Brethren congregations in °Curitiba, °Witmarsum, Lapa, São Paulo, and Colônia Nova-Bagé. Through missionary work begun in 1963 among German-speaking Brazilians, an additional 10 congregations have been added to the AIIMB. The purpose of the conference is to promote felowship, unity of doctrine, and Christian service. Conference sessions are held annually. Membership in 1987 was 1,954, with 49 ministers, 49 deacons, 71 youth workers, 154 Sunday school teachers, and 364 choir members. Mission outreach has become the most important branch of conference work.

The official conference organ is the *Informationsblatt,* published monthly in Curitiba since 1967. It offers articles in both German and Portuguese. For a number of years the paper had an insert *Licht auf dem Wege,* which served as a theological help to ministers and church workers. Another paper, *Bausteine,* was published from 1973 to 1983, providing encouragement and useful materials for German-speaking Sunday school teachers, youth workers, and others. AIIMB also supports Bethel, near Curitiba, a center used for retreats, seminars, and summer Bible courses. A theological program of study for the preparation of ministers and other workers is maintained in the Instituto Seminário Bíblico Irmãos Menonitas (Mennonite Brethren Bible Institute and Seminary), likewise located in Curitiba. The Bible institute also coordinates and carries on Bible studies in the congregations. The Colégio Erasto Gärtner in Curitiba is supported jointly with the Associação das Igrejas Menonitas do Brasil (AIMB, Conference of the Mennonite Churches [GCM] in Brazil), as is the retirement center Lar Betesda. Other projects such as historical research, evangelism, and service are coordinated between the two conferences by a joint committee.

Women's church activities in the AIIMB were formally organized in 1971. They have various branches and projects within the congregations. A love treasury gives help in emergency situations.

The AIIMB works closely with the South American Conference of the Mennonite Brethren Church of North America. The AIIMB is not to be confused with the Convenção das Igrejas Irmãos Menonitas do Brasil (CIIMB, Conference of Mennonite Brethren Churches in Brazil) which is the conference of the Portuguese-speaking mission congregations.

PP,Jr./HenEns

MWH (1978), 196-200.

Associação das Igrejas Menonitas do Brasil (AIMB, Association of the Mennonite Churches [GCM] in Brazil). In 1987 the AIMB consists of congregations in Curitiba (Boqueirão and Vila Guaira) and the Free Evangelical Mennonite Church (GCM) of Witmarsum. The conference consists of 800 members, 18 ministers, 11 deacons, 46 Sunday school teachers, and 6 choirs. The conference was founded in 1952 with Curitiba as its administrative center. It is a member of the Conference of Mennonites in South America and of the General Conference Mennonite Church (GCM) in North America. The stated purpose of AIMB is to nurture the faith and facilitate programs in mission, youth work, ministerial exchange, and Sunday school work and to publish *Bibel und Pflug* (1,000 subscriptions). Missionary activity was begun in the 1950s, leading to congregations in the Vila Lindoia and Xaxím suburbs of Curitiba, as well as in the city of Palmeira near Witmarsum. In the 1960s close cooperation began with missionaries of the Mennonite Board of Missions (MC) from North America, which had been working in the states of São Paulo and Goiás since 1954. A united agency, the Associação Evangélica Menonita (AEM, Mennonite Evangelical Association) was created to facilitate this cooperation. In 1987 six AIMB missionaries are serving in AEM. The congregation in Boqueirão includes numerous couples not of ethnic Mennonite background. The congregation in Vila Guaira is likewise actively involved in working with people in the community. An autonomous Portuguese-speaking congregation has arisen in Witmarsum, consisting primarily of employees of the settlement.

Additional work is carried on in prison ministries, marriage enrichment seminars, retreats, and a radio program on station HCJB, Quito, Ecuador. A joint committee with the Associação das Igrejas Irmãos Menonitas do Brasil (AIIMB, Mennonite Brethren) has been established to facilitate cooperation.

The congregations in Vila Guaira and Boqueirão are founders and strong supporters of the Mennonite Colégio Erasto Gärtner school in Curitiba. This school has promoted biblical and Mennonite values in faith and ethics and encouraged an openness to new contemporary issues in society and faith.

Next to the work with AEM the largest undertaking of AIMB is the social welfare work carried on by the Associação Menonita de Assistência Social (AMAS, Mennonite Relief Organization in Brazil). AMAS was founded in 1970 as a nonprofit welfare agency. It works closely such international agencies as Mennonite Central Committee and the °International Mennonite Organization (IMO), and receives funding from the West German government for children's aid. AMAS work is not only supported by the congregations, but also by their auxiliaries, especially the women's organizations and Mennonite business enterprises. Some of its work is also carried on with AEM and the AIIMB (Mennonite Brethren) congregations.

The largest project of AMAS is the day-care center in Palmeira, where more than 200 children under the age of 14 years are cared for, and a vocational training center, which has an enrollment of ca. 200, has been established. Two congregations have arisen as a result of this work. A large, beautiful building has been erected, which is also used for retreats, seminars, and mission conferences.

Since 1978 AMAS has been responsible for the Araguacema mission project in the Amazon region's Goiás State. It includes a school for grades 1-8, with 350 pupils in 1987, a clinic, and a second school "Cidade Leer" (named after support it receives from benefactors in Leer, West Germany), with an enrollment of 150 pupils. Technical and financial help from AMAS and IMO has made the establishing of a °cooperative possible. This in turn has aided agricultural production and income enormously.

AMAS facilitates children's retreat centers, schools, health and development programs, and catastrophe help wherever it may be needed. The agency also coordinated exchange programs for trainees and others from Europe and North America, and is legally responsible for the °development projects in Recife/Pernambuco and Paraíba. AMAS also assumes responsibility for securing visas for voluntary service workers, and was involved in discussions which led to an °alternative service program in lieu of military service (1988). A board of 15 members, chosen from the AIMB congregations, is responsible for the AMAS work.   HenEns

MWH (1978), 201-3; *MWH* (1984), 61.

Associação Evangélica Menonita, Brazil (AEM, Evangelical Mennonite Association) is the Portuguese-speaking conference of Mennonites in Brazil. It began when the Mennonite Board of Missions and Charities (MC) sent Peter and Alice Sawatsky, and J. Richard and Susan Burkholder, to São Paulo state in 1954. They were joined by Glenn and Lois Musselman, and David and Rose Hostetler, in 1956. Church planting ministries were started in three locations in São Paulo state.

About the same time Howard Hammer, Richard Kissell, Mildred Eichelberger, and others went to north Brazil, where they initiated evangelistic work in Araguacema, Goiás state, and also started medical and educational work. This mission was called the Amazon Valley Indian Mission.

In 1957 the Associação Evangélica (AEM) was formed as a legal entity to hold property titles for the churches established in the cities of São Paulo, Valinhos, and Sertaozinho. Contacts were also made with German-speaking Mennonites in the Curitiba area, where the Associação das Igrejas Menonitas do Brazil (AIMB) was also reaching out in evangelism. Over the years AEM and AIMB have cooperated in outreach, and three congregations in 1986 were affiliated with both conferences.

Literature work was begun in 1957 with a bookstore in Campinas, expanding to include bookstores in Brasilia (1962), Taguatinga (1963), and Ribeirao Preto (1964). The stores use the name Livraria Crista Unida (United Christian Bookstore). The stores are unique because they carry a broad selection of materials to serve all denominations. More than 20 titles have been published under Mennonite auspices. In 1973 the bookstores were incorporated as branches of AEM. In 1983 the Literature Commission was formed to administer the literature program. All managers are Brazilian Mennonites.

The work begun in Araguacema came under the administration of AEM in 1960, and it expanded into other towns in the area. In 1976, 1977, and 1982 strategy conferences were held to plan for future expansion and to set priorities for the churches. In 1976 the Commission for Overseas Mission (GCM) began working in cooperation with the Mennonite Board of Missions (MBM) and AEM.

In 1986 AEM had 1,001 members in 25 congregations. These are organized into four geographical regions: region 1 in São Paulo state with nine churches; region 2 in Paraná state with seven churches; region three in the Federal District and adjacent state of Goiás with four churches; and region four in northern Goiás around Araguacema with five churches. Region five in ne. Brazil has fraternal relationships with AEM, but is administered by the Commission on Overseas Missions COM. MBM, COM and AIMB support AEM with funds and personnel. Teodoro Penner is executive secretary in 1987. The conference publishes *Intercambio Menonita* (Mennonite Exchange).

Each year in July, AEM meets for a three-day conference. The assembly meets for a half-day session of formal business. The AEM executive committee is elected biennially. The remainder of the time is given to worship and the Word. It also provides a time for renewing friendship and fellowship for churches which are scattered over long distances. The four regions take turns hosting the conference.

Centro Menonita de Teologia (CEMTE) is the leadership training program of AEM. After an extensive survey in 1982, a program was designed to instruct leaders through an open seminary format. The basic course of °theological education by extension had 173 students in 1987. More advanced courses are being developed. CEMTE is administered from Campinas, São Paulo state.   OEH

MWH (1974), 204-8; *MWH* (1984), 62; *MC Yearbook* (1986-87), 154; *GCM Handbook* (1988), 87, 91.

Associação Menonita de Assistência Social, Brazil (Mennonite Association for Social Assistance). See Associação das Igrejas Menonitas do Brasil; Brazil.

Association Mennonite Luxembourgeoise (Luxembourg Mennonite Association) was organized in 1953. It assumed responsibility for the mission activity of Luxembourg Mennonites in 1964. From 1965 until 1978, the Association operated a Christian bookstore in downtown Luxembourg City. Association workers continued to sell Christian books and literature from a bookmobile at outdoor markets. In 1969, land was purchased, and a chalet was built near Scheidgen for a °camping program. The association took full charge of the mission outreaches in Dudelange and Esch in 1971. A chapel was dedicated in Dudelange in March 1961. The congregation organized a church council in 1971. The members of this congregation come from the vicinities of Esch and Dudelange.

Regular Sunday services continued in Diekirch until the Rosswinkel chapel was dedicated in 1954. The association began work again in Diekirch in 1981, when the Henk de Fijter family, from Belgium, moved into the area to begin home Bible studies.

In 1986 there were 105 members in the Rosswinkel and Dudelange congregations. Children's Sunday school, weekly Sunday worship services and midweek Bible studies are held in each congregation. They fully support Jean Marcus, a Luxembourg Mennonite physician serving in Zaire. The congregations maintain contact with the Association des Églises Evangéliques Mennonites de France (Association of the Evangelical Mennonite Churches of France), but are not members. They also maintain relationships with other °believers churches in Luxembourg.   MG

MWH (1984), 122.

Association of Evangelical Mennonites (AEM) was founded at Wilmot, Ohio, in 1983 by a group of pastors and lay leaders concerned about "the damaging liberal drift in theology and the consequent erosion of faith and of our Anabaptist biblical orthodoxy in the Mennonite Church, Conferences and Institutions." AEM is not a conference, but a tax-exempt religious organization dedicated to promote faithfulness to the "inerrant and divinely inspired Scriptures as originally held by our Anabaptist forefathers."

An eight-point statement of doctrine or polity was adopted which (1) affirms the separation of church and state, and allows qualified civil disobedience; (2) rejects abortion, and affirms the right of the state to exercise capital punishment; (3) affirms the use of grammatically masculine pronouns to refer to God, and the traditional roles of male and female in leadership and the family; (4) affirms the priority of soul and spirit without neglecting the secondary needs of the body; (5) advocates congregational autonomy and (6) the priesthood of believers as a key to witness; (7) affirms the chastity of single men and women and heterosexual marriage; and (8) advocates a witness against apostasy and the misuse of the Scriptures. Headquarters in 1987 were in Sugarcreek, Ohio.   CJD

See also Evangelicalism; Fellowship of Concerned Mennonites; Fundamentalism.

Association of Mennonite Churches of Paraguay. See Vereinigung der Mennonitengemeinden von Paraguay.

Association of the Mennonite Brethren Churches of Brazil. See Associação das Igrejas Irmãos Menonitas do Brasil.

Association of the Mennonite Brethren Churches of Colombia. See Associação de Iglesias Hermanos Menonitas, Colombia.

Association of the Mennonite Churches of Brazil. See Associação das Igrejas Menonitas do Brasil.

Asunción, the capital and largest city of Paraguay, is located roughly 1,500 km. (930 mi.) up the Parana-Paraguay River from Buenos Aires, Argentina. In 1537 Spaniards, eager to find a route to the legendary goldfields in Peru, navigated up the river system and established a small fort, on the site of what later became the city of Asunción. Because of its strategic position, Asunción flourished initially, but later its growth stagnated. A new spurt of growth developed after the Chaco War (1935), and especially in the 1950s. Within the last 30 years the city's appearance has changed considerably. The colonial heritage is still evident, but the invasion of technology is noted in the considerable number of high-rise office buildings in the old center of the city. In the years immediately prior to 1987, many connecting roads to other parts of the country have been paved, making travel easier and predictable. The city houses government offices, the central bank, a number of hotels and theaters, and several universities. Most of the commercial activity in Paraguay is centered in Asunción, a city of 500,000 residents in 1987.

Mennonites have lived in Asunción since the early 1930s. The Mennonite colonies established in the °°Chaco region, sent representatives to the capital. Other Mennonites were attracted to the city by business opportunities or to study Spanish. Economic survival in the early years was easier in Asunción than in the colonies. In the 1940s, the Mennonite Home was established by the Mennonite Central Committee, and soon became the center of activities for Mennonites in the city. It remains a popular center, where visitors from the colonies can lodge. Many foreign tourists also stay there.

The German-speaking Mennonites in the city have established a Mennonite Brethren and a General Conference Mennonite congregation. Both congregations share the same facility. They also operate a private school ("Concordia"), which offers classes from first through twelfth grade.

Since the late 1950s, mission work, mainly by the Mennonite Brethren, has been carried out among Spanish-speaking citizens in the city and its environs. A number of Spanish- and Guarani-speaking congregations have been established. These congregations have organized into two separate conventions and take an active part in Mennonite activities throughout Paraguay. They help sponsor a missionary effort and °voluntary service work. They also participate in the two theological institutions that have been established in the city to serve both Spanish- and German-speaking Mennonite churches throughout the country, in the task of leadership training (Centro Evangélico Menonita de Teología Asunción; Instituto Biblico Asunción).

The headquarters of the Paraguayan Mennonite voluntary service program are also located in Asunción. Most Mennonite congregations in the country now participate in this program, as they try to respond to the growing socio-economic needs of large sectors of the population.   GNie

Athletics. See Sports.

Atlantic Coast Conference of the Mennonite Church (MC) was originally the eastern section of the Ohio and Eastern Conference (MC). The congregations forming the eastern section were part of two mission districts of the Ohio and Eastern Conference known as the Conestoga-Maple Grove and the Atlantic States districts.

On Nov. 4, 1978, members of congregations in the eastern section took action to approve a constitution forming a new sister conference, called the Atlantic Coast Conference of the Mennonite Church. The primary purpose for organizing a new conference was to bring more continuity to mission, leadership, and youth activities. The new conference held its first full session in March 1979. The constitution was adopted on Mar. 28, 1980, and revised on Mar. 22, 1986.

At the time of its formation, the Atlantic Coast Conference was composed of 36 congregations and had a reported membership of 3,887. In 1986 there were 44 congregations and a membership of 4,630. The congregations are divided into eight overseer districts, spanning an area from New York to North Carolina, and from the Atlantic Coast to the Appalachian Mountains. The majority of congregations are concentrated in the mid-Atlantic region, thus the name Atlantic Coast Conference.

The *Atlantic Coast Conference Currents* is the bimonthly organ of the Atlantic Coast Conference. It is published in a newspaper format, carrying conference and churchwide news.   DRK

MC Yearbook (1986-87), 49-51; Glenn Lehman, "Pennsylvania Seeds, Ohio Fruit" *GH* (July 14, 1987), 488-500.

Atlantic Provinces are the four eastern provinces of Canada: New Brunswick, which borders on Maine and Quebec, Nova Scotia, Prince Edward Island, and Newfoundland. The term *Maritime Provinces* does not normally include Newfoundland. New Brunswick and Nova Scotia became part of the Dominion of Canada in the Confederation of 1867. Prince Edward Island joined Canada in 1873, and Newfoundland in 1949. The Atlantic Provinces are noted for their deep-sea fisheries, good farming areas, and exceptional tourist attractions. The combined population in 1951 was 1,215,872. In 1985, it was 2,908,425, an average annual increase of about 40,000.

Mennonites first came to the Atlantic Provinces in 1954, when Harvey Taves brought Mennonite Central Committee (MCC) Voluntary Service workers to Newfoundland as teachers and nurses. In the same year Siegfried and Margaret Janzen brought their family to Nova Scotia. In 1988 there were four Mennonite churches. Three were related to the Mennonite Brethren (Dartmouth, N.S., and Moncton and Campbellton, N.B.), and one, at Petitcodiac, N.B., was related to the Western Ontario Mennonite Conference (MC). In 1988 it became part of the Mennonite Conference of Eastern Canada.

In the 1980s two colonies of conservative Mennonites planted themselves in Nova Scotia. More then 30 families of the °°Kleine Gemeinde from Belize settled at Northfield (25 mi./42 km. from Truro). Several families of the Church of God in Christ, Mennonite, bought farms near Tatamagouche.

Other Mennonite institutions are in place also. MCC (Canada) has supported MCC services in the Maritimes since 1982, under Brian Elliot as director. At the same time MCC renewed an earlier mandate to serve needy areas in Newfoundland and Labrador.

MAP (Mennonites in the Atlantic Provinces) was launched by the writer in 1975 in order to provide an informal association for an annual retreat designed for fellowship and inspiration around a common Anabaptist and Mennonite heritage. It has met for one weekend every year since then.   PPe

Menn. Rep. (July 8, July 22, Aug.5, 1974), (Mar. 3, 1975).

Atonement, Anabaptist Theology of. Literally, this word means *at-one-ment*. It can refer to all the ways in which God and humans have been reconciled through Jesus Christ. Often, however, discussions of atonement focus on the meaning of Jesus' death. Historically, three theories of atonement have been especially influential. Each has some biblical basis and can be found among the writing of the early church fathers.

Anselm of Canterbury (1033-1109) first gave the substitutionary theory a systematic formulation. This view was emphasized by the Protestant Reformers, and more so by post-Reformation Protestant orthodoxy and °Fundamentalism. According to this theory, the main evil from which Christ saves us is the penalty of sin: eternal death. Humans were created to merit eternal life through perfect °°obedience to God. But since everyone has disobeyed, no one has attained this reward. Moreover, since sin violates God's law, it carries the penalty of eternal death. Jesus' saving work, then, consisted in a life of perfect obedience, which merited eternal life for us; and in bearing God's judgment on the cross, which paid the penalty of eternal death in our place. According to the substitutionary theory, the high point of Jesus' atoning work is his death.

Peter Abelard (1079-1142) first gave detailed expression to the moral influence theory. It has been emphasized by Protestant °liberalism. According to this theory, the main evil from which we need °salvation is the power of sin in our lives. Jesus' life, therefore, was primarily devoted to showing us how to live. Jesus' death reveals a God who is loving. Through the moral influence of Jesus' life and death, we are inwardly transformed and thereby brought into fellowship with God. According to this theory, the high point of Jesus' atoning work is his earthly teaching and example.

The *Christus Victor* motif was especially popular among the early church fathers. It has been prominent in Eastern Orthodox Christianity, but has had comparatively little influence in the West. According to this theory, the main evil from which we need salvation is bondage to hostile forces. These include spiritual powers such as the devil, sin, and death. In the pre-Constantinian era (before A.D. 300), pagan religions and governments were often thought to be their agents. Jesus' obedient life was, on one hand, a struggle against these powers; on the other, it established communion between God and humans in his person. Jesus' death was the powers' apparent victory over him. Jesus' resurrection, however, forms the high point of his atoning work: it is the triumph of the divine life over the powers, in which all who are united with him can participate.

Because the Anabaptists emphasized Jesus' teachings and example, some feel that they understood atonement along the lines of the moral influence theory. Unlike most other Protestant reformers, Anabaptists insisted that following in Jesus' earthly footsteps is essential to salvation. Accordingly, the life through which he provided this pattern was not secondary, but central to, his atoning work. Moreover, many Anabaptists stressed that Jesus' entire life, culminating in his death, was an outpouring and demonstration of love.

However, numerous themes expressed in the substitutionary and *Christus Victor* theories also appear in Anabaptist writers. Anabaptists often emphasized Jesus' example and its continuing significance not along moral influence lines, but in ways which supplement or give concrete focus to these other themes.

Substitutionary language occurs particularly among Dutch Anabaptists. They rejected the idea that Jesus' flesh could have come from Mary, and therefore ultimately from Adam, insisting that if it had, this corrupt flesh could not have "paid" the price for sin. When Anabaptists maintained that Christ's atoning work is imputed to infants, to the previous sins of believers, or to the continuing sinfulness of their flesh, substitutionary notions of payment and acquittal were at least implicitly present.

Nevertheless, Anabaptists did not regard Christ's merits and sufferings as entirely past accomplishments. They denied that atonement would be obtained merely by believing in Christ's previous work, without transformation of life. They insisted that Jesus' active righteousness, and especially his sufferings, also continue in his members, sanctifying them and delivering them from present sin as they walk in the way which he walked.

Through their sharp sense of conflict with the world, the flesh, the devil, and with the religious and political powers through which these assailed them, many Anabaptists remind one of the *Christus Victor* motif. Melchior °Hoffman and Bernhard °Rothmann regarded humanity as the devil's property, and Christ's atonement as bringing liberation from this bondage. Peter °°Riedemann spoke of sins as chains by which the devil binds people, and of governments as executors of the curse under which sin places people.

Moreover, most Anabaptists emphasized another central *Christus Victor* theme: that Christ brought humanity into communion with the divine life. Salvation involved "divinization": transformation through participation in the divine nature. Nonetheless, this did not raise one above earthly reality. Instead, as Menno Simons wrote, we participate in the divine life when we "understand, grasp and follow and emulate [Christ], not according to his divine nature . . . but according to his life and conversation here on earth, shown forth among men in his words and deeds as an example set before us to follow. . . ." (*Writings*, 55)

In conclusion, Jesus' teaching and example and our present participation in his earthly task of obedience and °suffering play a greater role in Anabaptist understandings of atonement than in most others. Yet, while some of these emphases parallel the moral influence theory, others are more compatible with substitutionary or *Christus Victor* perspectives. In the final analysis, Anabaptist understandings overflow any and all of the three traditional theories, and suggest a variety of angles from which to consider atonement.

For Mennonite theologies of atonement, particularly in the 19th c. and 20th c., see J. Denny Weaver, "The Quickening of Soteriology: Atonement from Christian Burkholder to Daniel Kauffman," *MQR*, 61 (1987), 5-45.   TNF

John Driver, *Understanding the Atonement for the Mission of the Church* (Scottdale, 1986); Thomas Finger, *Christian Theology: an Eschatological Approach*, vol. I (Nashville: Nelson, 1985), 303-67; Gustav Aulen, *Christus Victor* (New York: MacMillan, 1960); Anselm, *Why God Became Man and the Virgin Conception and Original Sin*, trans. J. M. Colleran (Albany, 1969); Horace Bushnell, *The Vicarious Sacrifice*, vol. I (New York: Scribner's 1903); William Keeney, "The Incarnation" in *A Legacy of Faith*, ed. C. J. Dyck (Newton, 1962), 55-68; CRR 3:23-100; Menno Simons, "The Incarnation of our Lord," in Menno, *Writings*, 785-834; idem, "Brief and Clear Confession," ibid., esp. 422-40; idem, "The Cross of the Saints" ibid., esp. 614-22; idem, "The Spiritual Resurrection" *ibid.*, 53-62; Pilgram Marpeck, "Concerning

the Lowliness of Christ" in CRR 2:428-63, idem, "Judgment and Decision," in CRR 2, esp. 314-23; Peter Riedemann, *Account of Our Religion, Doctrine, and Faith*, trans. Kathleen E. Hasenberg (London: Hodder and Stoughton, 1938; Rifton, N.Y.: Plough Publishing House, 1970), esp. 28-68, 102-11, 205-23; Michael Sattler, "On the Satisfaction of Christ," in CRR 1:108-120; John H. Yoder, *Preface to Theology* (Elkhart: Goshen Biblical Seminary, n.d., ca. 1982), 206-43.

Attendance. See Church Attendance.

Australian Conference of Evangelical Mennonites. Foppe Brouwer, a Dutch Mennonite, moved to New South Wales, Australia, in 1952. He and his wife Aaltje (Hazenberg) were ordained in their home church of Hollum op Ameland, The Netherlands, in 1978 and sent by the Europäisches Mennonitisches Evangelisations-Komitee (European Mennonite Evangelism Committee), to plant a Mennonite church and outreach in Australia.

Initially the Brouwers developed a newsletter (*De Mennist*) and sent it to Mennonite Dutch immigrants living in Australia. Their aim was to locate and bring together the Mennonites of that continent. At the same time, an outreach was begun at Fennell Bay, a small village on the shores of Lake Mcquarie, on the East Coast of New South Wales. They opened a "Care and Share" fruit and vegetable shop, in which fruit and vegetables purchased every Thursday from the wholesale market, were sold locally at budget prices. The friendships developed in this shop resulted in the beginning of a Sunday school (attendance 40-50 in 1987). Eventually, a church fellowship, the Mennonite Church of Hope, developed from this outreach. By 1987, 25 adult members had been baptized (average attendance 15 to 35 adults). This church was officially recognized by the federal and state governments in Jan. 1980. In addition to the local outreach, the Mennonite Church of Hope has been working in the city of Newcastle since 1985. Two of its members, Derek and July Bernardson, have opened a Mennonite Information center in the city of Melbourne. In Perth in western Australia, the Eastern Mennonite Board of Missions and Charities (MC) has begun planting a church under the leadership of Ian and Anne Duckham. FB

MC Yearbook (1986-87), 153; *MWH* (1978), 43-44; *MWH* (1984), 43.

Austria (ME I:193). After World War II the Mennonite Central Committee's response to the need for relief paved the way for Mennonite Brethren mission work in Austria. In 1953 J. W. and Martha Vogt and the John Goosen family began a ministry in the refugee camps where they found a positive response to the gospel. Linz, the capital of Upper Austria, became the first church center. Abe and Irene Neufeld continued evangelizing and church planting. A church building was erected in 1958. Expansion led to new church centers, and additional workers were sent through Mennonite Brethren Board of Missions and Services. Gerhard and Anna Jantz led the congregations in Linz, and Lawrence and Selma Warkentin gave leadership in Wels. The Vienna and Steyr congregations were led by Helmut Funck and Wolfgang Rüschhoff. These congregations formed the Austrian Conference as part of the Bund Europäischer Mennoniten Brüdergemeinden. Joint projects were the radio ministry over Radio Luxembourg; the conference paper, *Quelle des Lebens*; and participation in the °International Mennonite Organization, the Europäische Mennonitische Bibelschule at Bienenberg in Switzerland, and Mennonite Brethren mission work in Spain.

Expansion through the Austrian churches continued in the late 1960s when the Lawrence Warkentin family established new congregations in Salzburg and in Traunreut, Bavaria. A Mennonite Brethren witness had thus been established in five strategic Austrian cities: Vienna, Linz, Wels, Steyr, and Salzburg. They experienced a slow growth, but expanded their ministry to Amstetten, Liezen, Braunau, and Gmunden, where new churches developed.

In 1972 a new group of churches, closely connected to the Austrian conference, developed in Vienna under the ministry of Abe and Irene Neufeld. This work is best known as "Tulpengasse," the location of the first church. The church in Cottagegasse dissolved, and the building was later used by the Tulpengasse congregation.

A Christian book store, Christliche Bücher-Zentrale, was started in Wels in 1966. It started as a ministry of the Wels church, but subsequently became a private business of Georg Emrich, who is a member of the church. It has become one of the most prominent Christian bookstores in Austria. Tent ministries proved effective in evangelism, so the Austrian churches bought a tent with a seating capacity of 150. It was used from 1966 to 1974 and then sold to another mission.

The need for biblical training led to the development of a Bible School in Linz, 1975-80. In 1983 a joint Bible school of the evangelical churches in Austria was established in Ampfelwang, with Mennonite Brethren Board of Missions and Services supplying teachers. In this way the Austrian churches trained workers to serve the Austrian churches, and to reach out into other cities in Austria. Total membership in 1988 in Austria was 197.　　LDW

John A. Toews, *History MB* (1975), 434-36; *MWH* (1978), 282-84; Margaret Epp, *Eight Tulpengasse: A Church Blossoms in Vienna* (Scottdale, 1978).

Authority. Challenging, and even negating, particular authorities and even authority in general, in the name of individual freedom and personal autonomy, has been the Western liberal project at least from the time of the Protestant Reformation, through the 17th-c. and 18th-c. Enlightenment, the national revolutions, and 20th-c. liberation movements. Authority became, in this process, a negative category to the degree that in the late 20th c. it is for many a pejorative term equated with authoritarianism. The tyrannies of totalitarian dictatorships in this century have particularly added credence to this perspective.

The consequent juxtaposition of freedom and authority is, however, problematical. While the pursuit of freedom is a Christian goal, and much of the liberal project has contributed immensely to the emancipation of individuals and groups of people from dehumanizing forces, it is wrong to assume that either individuals or communities can exist without some defining authority. Freedom requires authority.

Authority is that which grounds our being, beliefs, and actions, and that which legitimates who we are, what we believe, and how we live. This is true for individuals and groups alike. Such authority can be chosen freely, or imposed by overt or covert means. Some students of the subject argue that an authority is truly authoritative only when freely chosen. While this may generally be true, the question remains: what do we really choose freely? But even those authorities chosen relatively freely can lead to either bondage or freedom. From a Christian perspective, true freedom results only when chaos, fear, and self-centeredness are replaced by purpose, love, and service; all else is bondage. The merits of any authority, to whatever degree chosen or coerced, are judged by this standard: does it produce freedom or bondage?

God is the ultimate authority, and all that is truly authoritative is derivative from God. This Christian affirmation implies not least that authority is good, even as God is good, but in order to be good it must be in keeping with the nature of God as revealed most perfectly in Jesus Christ. Those authorities which do not contribute to understanding humanity, or ordering the world as intended by the Creator and incarnated by the Re-creator are merely temporal or temporary. From an Anabaptist and Mennonite perspective, all authorities must be relativized by this standard. Mennonite history accordingly is replete with examples of saying "no!" to authority. How consistent and persistent Mennonites are on this issue is another matter.

How is God known authoritatively? God the Father is known in Jesus the Son through the work of the Holy Spirit. Wherever this Spirit rules, God's authority is present. This same Spirit authorized and authorizes the °°Bible, the most authoritative witness to God's being and activity.

The Anabaptists and their Mennonite heirs share in the Protestant principle: *sola scriptura* ("by Scripture alone." As such their primary authoritative referent is the Bible, rather than Scripture plus tradition as understood by Roman Catholicism and Eastern Orthodoxy. In turn, Mennonites also share in the Protestant problem: whose reading of Scripture is authoritative? The absence of an authoritative adjudicator to rule on contesting claims, is a major reason both for the divisions within Protestantism as well as the numerous subdivisions within the Mennonite family. Additionally, the Mennonite quest for a pure church made the Protestant problem greater, since authoritative definitions of purity in each unique cultural context were lacking.

Authority accordingly is a problem for Mennonites, not only on the larger theoretical level, but also on the operational level. Operationally, among Mennonites, authority is sometimes identified but more frequently is not identified; it is sometimes formulated, but typically only implied. A discussion of Mennonite understandings of authority, such as this, is largely a matter of identifying the implied.

Scripture. While all Anabaptists in the 16th c. and Mennonites since then have agreed that the Bible is uniquely authoritative, a series of issues remain. Firstly, is authority vested in the words of Scripture or in the spirit of the Word? The °°Swiss Brethren and °Menno Simons tended to the former or biblicist stance (words of Scripture) when they maintained, for example, that what the Scriptures do not positively teach and command is forbidden. Hans °°Denck represented the latter approach. For him the Bible was not identical to the Word of God— even as the material world is secondary to the spiritual world, so the outer word (Bible) serves the inner word (spirit). Pilgram °Marpeck and Hans de °°Ries sought a balance to avoid either extreme. This balance continues to be a challenge as the options are redefined, for example, by the more °fundamentalist and more °liberal currents within modern Protestantism.

A second issue is the relationship between the Old and New Testaments. Pilgram Marpeck again provided a model here that has gained considerable currency among contemporary Mennonites. To oversimplify, the New Testament fulfills what the Old Testament promises. In turn, Jesus Christ in his life and teaching, death and resurrection, is the interpretive (hermeneutical) key to all Scriptures both Old and New. Biblical authority, then, is nuanced to recognize that the Incarnate Word revealed in biblical words and by the Spirit is the judge of the relative authority of those words. Yet, to continue the circle, the biblical words establish the norms for our understanding of both the Incarnate Word and the Holy Spirit. Biblical authority is dynamic, not static; it is a living force, not a dead letter.

Leaders. While the Scriptures are authoritative, leaders called to interpret the Scriptures have been granted a derivative authority throughout Mennonite history. The nature and degree of that authority, especially in relation to the church community, remains controversial.

Anabaptist and Mennonite leaders gained authority at various times and places either by their charismatic urgency, by their faithfulness to a tradition, or by successfully fulfilling a functionally defined role (to use Max Weber's categories). Most early Anabaptist leaders were protestors against the status quo and frequently did not gain formal legitimation from a church community. More recently some evangelists and other leaders who have urgent messages, powerful personalities, and are skilled communicators have similarly gained authority more charismatically than through formal authorizing means.

By contrast, at least from the time of °Menno Simons, a more traditional °leadership pattern emerged. °Bishops or °elders, preachers or shepherds, and °°deacons were authorized through °ordination. Called by the community and confirmed by the Spirit, frequently through the vehicle of the °°lot, the leader's authority rested more in the position than the person. Today this type of authority is fully operative primarily in the traditionalist (°conservative) Mennonite communities, such as the Old Order Mennonites, Old Colony Mennonites, and Amish, where the office of bishop remains both the authoritative and organizational center of the community.

With the adoption of denominational structures beginning in the mid-19th c., the more "progressive" Mennonite groups gradually shifted from the authority of bishops to that of °democratic and bureaucratic structures, from the authority of tradition to that of °education, and from the authority of office to that of function. Individuals now volunteered for leadership roles, typically by pursuing theological education, or gained leadership through employment in one of the many agencies and °institutions of the church. Congregations increasingly called leaders from this pool of volunteers. The selection, ordination, and evaluation of these candidates, in turn, were premised on functional criteria rather than on the authority of office. Ministry was thus professionalized. The old threefold ministry structure largely disappeared, to be replaced by professional pastors.

Pastors, in this most recent model, are hired to serve as the leaders of those who have hired them. Their authority is at best ambiguous! The 1960s credo "Question authority!" challenged the church and its ministers. Correlatively, a new emphasis on the °priesthood of all believers suggested not only that all Christians are called to minister according to their gifts, but also, by extension, that those called to lead can claim no unique authority. Hence, pastors have the responsibility but not the authority to lead. Authority theoretically resides with the congregation, but functionally frequently devolves to particular boards or committees whose expertise is not necessarily in ecclesiological matters. The issue of the relationship of leadership and authority accordingly remains ambiguous in this most recent leadership model.

Congregation. In important ways both the Bible and leaders are secondary authorities to the church, even though the Bible is normative for both the church and its leaders. Devoted students of Yahweh and followers of Christ wrote and edited the various books of the two testaments, and the church adopted the Jewish canon and established the canon of the New Testament writings. The Bible is thus product of the people of God—the church. Leaders, too, are chosen by the church from within the church; they are nurtured by the church and subject to the church.

Church authority for Mennonites is ultimately congregational authority. The local congregation, rather than supracongregational structures or leaders, is the final arbiter on all matters, be they internal or external to the congregation. This localized authority is premised on the responsible actions of each Christian. Even as each Christian comes to faith individually and voluntarily joins a congregation through adult baptism, it is assumed that each Christian hears the word of God and is responsible to act upon that hearing in and through a congregation. The Bible is thus read and understood within the context of the congregaiton. This is the "hermeneutical community." In more recent Mennonite history, ministers and scholars might be seen as specialized authorities on °biblical interpretation, yet the Anabaptists were distrustful of the learned, who allegedly distorted the "plain and simple word." A populist distrust of the educated remains to this day among Mennonites. Even biblical scholars must remain subservient to the discerning and admonishing authority of the church. Each member is thus subservient to the authority of the congregation and subject to its °discipline.

Beliefs, Experience, Practice. Despite their congregational polity, most Mennonite congregations belong to larger intercongregational bodies, which define their commonality in various authoritative ways. Here only the common definitions of orthodoxy, orthopraxis and orthoexperience can be noted.

The Mennonite tradition is strongly confessional even if not creedal. Creedalism is frequently seen by Menonites to emphasize correct doctrinal formulation at the expense of personal transformation. Mennonite °confessions, such as the °°Dordrecht Confession of 1632, by contrast, function as the authoritative indicators of the community's common mind on numerous doctrinal and ethical issues. Although not liturgically recited, they serve as the basis for inclusion (defining necessary beliefs for baptismal candidates), and for exclusion (by their implicit definition of heterodoxy).

At certain times and places confessional orthodoxy was augmented and possibly even superseded by orthoexperience. Certain normative religious experiences surrounding °conversion, or at least a normative expression of those experiences, became authoritative. Especially under the influence of various °revivalistic and °charismatic currents, authority for some is located experientially.

Orthopraxis has served as a primary authority throughout Mennonite history. Correct action defined either negatively (what ought not to be done), or positively (what ought to be done), are constants in defining normative Mennonitism. Such formulations of orthopraxis, in turn, can be powerfully authoritative.

Tradition. History, or better said, tradition, has further served as an authoritative referent for Mennonites. Mennonites have defined themselves consistently by recounting their particular history. Beliefs, action, and change are tested against tradition to determine legitimacy. In this century, appeal has particularly been made to 16th-c. Anabaptism as the historical norm to judge the Mennonitism that followed.

Interestingly, despite their theoretical stance of *sola scriptura*, Mennonites have in fact retained tradition as authoritative. The Christian community over time read the Bible, interpreted and applied it, and accordingly created a normative tradition of interpretation. This tradition is not closed; rather it is open to renewal and new readings, but the tradition using code concepts such as "is it Anabaptist?" still determines authoritatively if new perspectives are legitimate. Tradition thus joins Scripture as authoritative.

Do Scripture and tradition, community and leaders, orthodoxy, orthoexperience and orthopraxis as understood and implemented by Mennonites, free or bind according to the norm of freedom provided by the incarnation? This is the test of legitimate authority for Mennonites.   RJS

William Klassen, *Covenant and Community: The Life, Writings and Hermeneutics of Pilgram Marpeck* (Grand Rapids: Eerdmans, 1968); Cornelius J. Dyck, "Early Ideas of Authority" in *Studies in Church Discipline* (Newton: MPO, 1958), 35-56; Rodney J. Sawatsky, "Defining Mennonite Diversity and Unity," *MQR*, 57 (1983), 282-92; idem, *Authority and Identity: The Dynamics of the General Conference Mennonite Church* (North Newton, Ks: Bethel College, 1987); Paul H. Harrison, *Authority and Power in the Free Church Tradition: A Social Case Study of the American Baptist Convention* (Carbondale, Ill.: Southern Illinois U. Press, 1959); John R. Burkholder and Calvin Redekop, eds., *Kingdom, Cross and Community* (Scottdale, 1976).

See also Christology; Church-State Relations; Law, Attitudes toward Civil and Criminal; Institutions; Law, Theology of; *Ordnung*; Polity; Revolution; Theology.

Automobile. A commission appointed by the president of the United States concluded in 1933 that no other invention was diffused so rapidly in American life with such profound and far-reaching consequences as the car. With its speed and automatic mobility, the automobile became the symbol par excellence of modern life. The Mennonite and Amish reception of this modern contraption is a fascinating and diverse story. Reactions were mixed and heated in the first two decades of the 20th c. The more progressive and °acculturated Mennonites welcomed the car with delight—some were even the first in their communities to own one. The Amish and Old Order Mennonites rejected the "devil's machine" outright as a symbol of worldliness and pride. In most Mennonite groups, members gradually purchased automobiles while more conservative members resisted the new contraption for several years. By 1915 even bishops in the conservative Lancaster Conference of the Mennonite Church (MC) were buying cars, and by the early 1920s it was widely accepted in the majority of Mennonite conferences.

In the third decade of the 20th c., the automobile became a divisive wedge in a number of °schisms in Old Order Mennonite groups in the United States and Canada. The Old Order division between the Weaverland Conference and the Groffdale Conference in the Lancaster area in 1927 hinged largely on the car. In the 1980s, some Old Order Mennonite groups accept the car, others permit it if the bumpers are painted black to guard against pride, and still other Old Order groups cling to horsedrawn transportation. The Old Order Amish continue to prohibit car and truck ownership; however, expanding settlements and economic pressures have produced a compromise in which the hiring of cars and trucks is permitted for business and travel between settlements. Some "new order" Amish groups allow their members to purchase cars.

The debate over car ownership in Mennonite circles in the first two decades of the century was not an idle one. The car symbolized individualism, independence, *auto*matic *mobili*ty (automobile), freedom, speed, accelerated lifestyles, leisure, social status, and prestige. Such values were a threat to a sectarian subculture that heralded °humility, submission, caution, simplicity, modesty, and separation from the world (°nonconformity). The car, the child, and charm of modernity, menaced groups that hoped to preserve a pure, undefiled, and separated religious subculture. Hence, the acceptance and rejection of the automobile became a key indicator of modernization among Amish and Mennonite groups. Over the years, the car symbolized a firm boundary line between the groups that preferred the slow pace of °tradition sharply separated from the world, and those willing to negotiate with the relentless forces of modernization. Members of Old Order groups, dissatisfied with the slow pace of change, would often join a more progressive Mennonite group in order to have a car. In the words of one Amishman, "The first thing people do when they leave our church is go out and buy a car."

The car transformed congregational life in profound ways for those groups that accepted it. The older pattern of congregational life that was geographically anchored in a local neighborhood was eroded by automobile transportation. With their new automatic mobility, members could drive to the church of their choice, regardless of distance. Informal social control diminished as members drove out of their immediate community to worship. Moreover, such mobility divorced public worship from the routines of daily life and the watchful eye of local church elders. The automobile enabled congregations to increase both the number of their members and the size of the meetinghouse since members could drive from a distance. In some cases small congregations closed and their members joined larger congregations outside their local community. In other cases, the ease of transportation permitted services to be held every Sunday instead of the older pattern of every other Sunday. The car transformed congregational life by diversifying its membership, eroding social control, increasing the size of membership and buildings, and by detaching it from a local geographical base. The car also enhanced opportunities for interaction with the larger culture in social, business, and leisure activities, shattering once and for all, rural isolation. Rejection of car ownership by the Amish has been a key factor in their ability to maintain small, locally based congregations that are essential for preserving their culture and deterring modernization.

The car increased interconference communications and enabled the development of strong conference structures among the Mennonites in the 20th c., structures that had begun to develop in the late 19th c. with the aid of reliable and relatively affordable railroad transportation. Auto transportation facilitated home mission activity in the United States and Canada as well as overseas. While the car shrank geographical distance in many missionary efforts, it sometimes increased the social distance between missionaries and native populations who were still walking and using ox carts.   DBK

Francis R. Allen, "The Automobile," in *Technology and Social Change,* ed. Allen and others (N.Y.: Appleton, Century, Crofts, Inc., 1957), 107-32; James J. Flink, *The Car Culture* (Cambridge, Mass.: MIT Press, 1975); David Wagler, *Are All Things Lawful?* (Aylmer, Ont.: Pathway Publishers, n.d.); James E. Landing, "The Amish, The Automobile and Social Interaction," *J. of Geography,* 71 (Jan. 1972), 52-57; John A. Hostetler, *Amish Society* (1980), 85, 340, 357-60; Donald B. Kraybill, *The Riddle of Amish Culture* (Baltimore: Johns Hopkins U. Press, 1989); Stephen Scott, *Plain Buggies* (Intercourse, Pa.: Good Books, 1981), 6-9; James O. Lehman, *Sonnenberg: A Haven and A Heritage* (Kidron, Ohio: Kidron Community Council Inc., 1969), 196-203, 218-19, 288-89; J. Allan Ruth, "The Effect of the Automobile on the Franconia Mennonite Conference," unpublished paper (1968), copy at Lancaster Mennonite Historical Society; F. H. Epp, *Mennonites in Canada II:* 79, 249, 380, 430-33; Elmer S. Yoder, *The Beachy Amish Mennonite Fellowship Churches* (Hartville, Ohio: Diakonia Ministries, 1987), 126-29, 354; H. C. Early, "A New Source of Expense," *GH* (Apr. 7, 1927), 20-21; H. K. Martin, "Automobile Insurance," *GH* (June 29, 1933), 261-62; Menno D. Sell, "Automobile Insurance," *GH* (Oct. 5, 1933), 570-71; Moses Slabaugh, "The Christian Driver," *GH* (Aug. 19, 1958), 778; John L. Ruth, *Maintaining the Right Fellowship* (Scottdale, 1984), 422, 433, 461-62, 514; John A. Lapp, *India* (1972), 75; Wittlinger, *Piety and Obedience* (1978), 343-44; Melvin Gingerich, *The Mennonites in Iowa* (Iowa City: State Historial Society, 1939), 173, 258-59; Arlene Yousey, *Strangers and Pilgrims: History of Lewis County Mennonites* (Croghan, N.Y.: the author, 1987), 174-75.

See also Buggies; Technology.

B

Baden-Württemberg Federal State, Germany (ME I:205; IV:991). The state of Baden-Württemberg was formed from areas of the French and American occupation zones after World War II. After a short period of recovery from the war's devastation, the state has become, with its modern industry, one of Germany's most prosperous states. The 12 Mennonite congregations of Baden-Württemberg belong to the Verband deutscher Mennonitengemeinden. They are the following: Backnang, Freiburg (until 1965 Schopfheim), Hasselbach, Heidelberg, Heilbronn (the Nesselbach congregation joined Heilbronn in 1975), Karlsruhe-Thomashof (formerly Durlach), Möckmühl (Adelsheim joined Möckmühl in 1980), Reutlingen, Sinsheim, Stuttgart, Überlingen and Wössingen-Bretten. Baptized membership in Baden-Württemberg congregations was 1,012 in 1986. This constitutes two-thirds of the entire membership of the Verband.

Preaching is done by 28 lay preachers and 2 salaried preachers. In the past 30 years, congregational life has become more active, and activities have become more varied. Numerous meetings in groups and circles are held. Women's involvement is increasing. Young people determine for themselves when they are baptized. The small congregation of Hasselbach, together with the Evangelische Landeskirche (Protestant State Church), annually organizes a children's camp, which is well attended. The old congregational meetingplace of Hasselbach has been expanded. The neighborhood center, presented to the Heilbronn congregation by American Mennonites in 1948, has been replaced by a newly constructed building in Kochendorf. The church in Möckmühl intends to build its own meetingplace.

Although there is a tendency to give up farming due to changes in economic conditions, in 1986 there were still 42 Mennonite farms in Baden-Württemberg.   EL

Menn. Jahrbuch (1965-).

Baker, Charles (1844-1929), a Brethren in Christ minister and bishop, was born near Magdeburg, Germany. In 1855 he migrated with his family to Canada and settled near Collingwood, Ont. Baker, a Lutheran, became a member of the local Brethren in Christ congregation, and, in 1890, was elected to the ministry. Six years later, he was chosen bishop of his district (2 congregations). He also served for many years as the non-resident bishop of the Waterloo district. From 1899 to 1911, he was a member of the Examining Board of the denomination.

Progressive in much of his thinking, Baker was influential in introducing Sunday schools and revival meetings into the denomination. He also played a significant role in the founding of the church's first

school, which eventually became Messiah College. He was opposed, however, to the doctrine of °sanctification as a second work of grace that, by the turn of the century, was being received with increasing favor among the Brethren in Christ. Baker argued the historic position of the church that sanctification was a progressive action. Despite his strong leadership against it, the doctrine of the second work of grace was formally accepted by General Conference in 1910.   EMS

E. Morris Sider, *Nine Portraits* (Nappanee, Ind., 1978), 85-119; Wittlinger, *Piety and Obedience* (1978), e.g., 215-16, 246-48; *EV* (June 10, 1929), 4.

Bakker, Adolfina Henrietta Annette (July 27, 1907–Oct. 8, 1983). Following the writing of her New Testament dissertation ("The Study of Codex Evang. Bobbiënsis (K)") in 1933, Bakker lectured at the National University in Utrecht until 1940. In October of that year she became pastor of the Mennonite congregations in Middleburg and Goes. She served until her retirement in August 1972, meanwhile also having added the congregation at Vlissingen in 1968.

Bakker continued her academic work by collaborating with D. Plooij and C. A. Phillips on an edition of the *Liège Diatessaron*, a medieval Scripture manuscript. From 1960 to 1968 she was a member of the executive committee of the Algemene Doopsgezinde Sociëteit (ADS), and from 1969 to 1981 was chairperson of the educational center "Van Eeghenhuis." She also served as editor of the newsletter of the Union of Mennonite Retreat Centers, 1936-1942, and of the Doopsgezinde Vredesgroep's (Dutch Mennonite Peace Group) newsletter, 1947-48.

Bakker was also active outside of the Mennonite fellowship. From 1949 to 1978 she served on the executive committee of the foundation responsible for the care of rest homes in Zeeland, serving as chairperson for 20 years.   RHof

Doops. Jaar. (1984), 13-16.

Bakker, Pieter Huisinga (Mar. 24, 1713–Oct. 22, 1801), married Elisabeth Wagenaar in 1749. He was the son of a Mennonite family and a Collegiant. An exporter by trade, he was also a poet, writing his *Poëzy* in three parts (Amsterdam 1773, 1782, 1790). He also translated the writings of John Milton (1608-74). In 1768 he was named a member of the Dutch Literary Society, founded in Leiden in 1766, in whose *Werken* (works) he published a remarkable study of Dutch poetry titled *Beschouwing van den ouden gebrekkelyken en sedert verbeterden trant onzer Nederduitsche versen* (vol. 5 [1781], pp. 83-130). The biography, *Het leven van Jan Wagenaar, beneevens eenige brieven van en aan denzelven* (Amsterdam, 1776), of his brother-in-law and well-known °°Collegiant, remains of enduring significance.   SBJZ

Steven Blaupot ten Cate, *Geschiedenis der Doopsgezinden in Holland*, vol. 2 (Amsterdam, 1847), 162; J. te Winkel, *De Ontwikkelingsgang der Nederlandsche Letterkunde*, vol. 5, 2nd ed. (Haarlem, 1924), 463; F. K. H. Kossmann, *Opkomst en voortgang van de Maatschappij der Nederlandse Letterkunde te Leiden* (Leiden, 1966), 87-92 passim; P. C. Molhuysen, and others, eds., *Nieuw Nederlandsch Biografisch Woordenboek* (Leiden, 1911-37), vol. 1, p. 67 (inaccurate); *ME* II:837.

Baksh, Isa (ca. 1890-1970), was the first ordained national minister in the Mennonite Church (MC) in India. He came from a humble Hindu family and was admitted to the boys orphanage of the American Mennonite Mission (MC) in °Dhamtari, Madhya Pradesh, during the famine days of 1899 and 1900. Here he received his education through high school, and here he also embraced the Christian faith. In the early 1920s he worked as a Bible teacher in the mission middle school in Dhamtari and was warden of the boy's orphanage there.

In 1927 he was ordained to the Christian ministry and became pastor of the Sunderganj Mennonite congregation, continuing there until 1914, when the conference transferred him to Sankra. His ministry at Sankra ended in 1943, when the conference revoked his ordination and ministry. He left the church in bitterness and humiliation, deserting his family. He lived in near obscurity in Jagdalpur until his death from tuberculosis. Before his death at the Dhamtari Christian Hospital, he once again affirmed faith in Christ and was reconciled to his family. JAF

Annual reports of American Mennonite Mission (MC), 1922, 1928, 1935, 1942.

Ballads. In light of the great interest that folklorists have shown in ballads, it is interesting that 21 martyr ballads from early Anabaptism were included in the 1583 °°*Ausbund* (hymnbook). All depict the martyrdom of a particular person.

Hymns 9 and 29, by Hans Buchel, are romantic stories of a young maiden and knight, respectively, who die in distant places, the maiden also in the far distant past. The remaining hymns (10 through 28) depict actual 16th-c. Anabaptist martyrs from commonplace backgrounds. The typical plot follows a sequence of arrest, trial, and execution. The trial scenes usually include much dialogue, sometimes on such Anabaptist issues as baptism, rejection of the sacraments (eucharist and confession), the oath, the papacy, the church, and the ban. The narration is simple and understated; the concluding martyrdom stresses the grace of God that enables the believer to be strong to the end.

Victor G. Doerksen, who has made the closest study of the formal qualities of these songs, emphasizes their differences from the ballads admired by poets of the Romantic Era. However, he says little about their relationship to other Protestant martyr ballads of their day and does not speculate on whether or not the Anabaptist ballads circulated orally before they were written down (and, are therefore, truly "folk") or, instead, were written for publication (and are therefore "literary"). Available evidence supports the latter case.   EB

Victor G. Doerksen, "The Anabaptist Martyr Ballad," *MQR*, 51 (Jan. 1977), 5-21; William I. Schreiber, "The Hymns of the Amish *Ausbund* in Philological and Literary perspective," *MQR*, 36 (Jan. 1962), 36-60.

Baltic Soviet Socialist Republics of Latvia, Estonia, and Lithuania, which were independent states from 1918 to 1940, were incorporated into the Soviet Union in 1940. A German invasion in 1941 was repulsed four years later, and all three areas have been part of the Soviet Union since then.

Both Lutheran and Catholic churches hold significant membership in the population of these republics. The Mennonite presence in these republics has been brief and hardly exists at all in the late 1980s. Large numbers originally moved to Estonia and Latvia in the period from 1965 to 1975, looking generally for better living conditions and a more congenial cultural climate. In particular, many who moved hoped that here they might have better opportunities to emigrate than they had in Central Asia and other regions. Their discovery rather early that repressive measures seemed to be lighter in the Baltic RSRs also attracted settlers.

The first families to come were often scattered, and there were too few in any particular locality to form their own congregations. Some families, for example, moved to Kokhta Jarve in Latvia, and joined a registered Baptist congregation. For a while they were able to hold their own German services, but state influence caused the local Baptists to restrict their activities, so all the Germans and a number of Russians moved away.

In 1972, this group was able to secure its own church building, and register as a Methodist affiliate. This mixed Mennonite group became a Methodist congregation this way. Eventually, however, all the Germans in this group emigrated to West Germany.

In Valga, too, the congregation met in a Latvian Baptist church building, holding separate German services on Sundays, and Bible study meetings during the week. A group at Priekul had 130 members, while the one at Valga had 150. Congregations were usually mixed in membership. One collective farm had eight German families belonging to Mennonite, Mennonite Brethren, and Pentecostal denominations.

For a time these groups were able to send Bibles to their relatives in Central Asia. Where they fellowshipped with local Estonian or Latvian groups, the Mennonite dynamism would become contagious.

When the Soviet government began to hinder movement to the Baltic States by refusing to provide residence permits, many turned to °Moldavia, where they hoped for advantages similar to those found in the Baltics. At present (1987) virtually all Germans have left the Baltic republics. The advantages for emigration have disappeared, and there are few signs that the earlier movement to this area will be resumed.   LK

Ressi Kaera, *Estland* (Moscow: APN Verlag, 1987); Walter Sawatsky, "Mennonite Congregations in the Soviet Union Today," *Menn. Life*, 33 (March, 1978), 12-26.

Balzer, Peter V., (May 22, 1891–July 6, 1985). Born at Inman, Ks., Peter Balzer was the son of Henry Balzer. Peter was a Mennonite Brethren missionary in India for 38 years. A graduate of Tabor College (BA) and Central Baptist Seminary (ThB), he later completed an MA degree at Phillips University, Enid, Okla. Following several years of evangelistic ministry, he married Elizabeth Kornelsen on Jan. 1, 1922, and was ordained in 1923 before leaving for India. His ministry at Devarakonda, Wanaparty, Narayanpet, and Shamshabad consisted of village evangelism and Bible training, the latter in Devarakonda and Shamshabad. After his formal retirement in 1961, Elizabeth Balzer's death, and his marriage to Margaret Willems (1967), former missionary to India, he returned with her to India to develop a new work among the caste converts at Kavitam in the coastal part of °Andhra Pradesh State. PMH

Christian Leader (July 23, 1985) 11.

Bangladesh. °°Pax workers served in East Pakistan in the 1960s with the East Pakistan Council of Churches. In 1970 Mennonite Central Committee (MCC) provided emergency material aid following the tidal bore which killed more than 300,000 people in Noakhali district. Immediately following the bloody emergence of the new nation, Bangladesh, late in 1971, MCC workers returned to Noakhali district to provide emergency assistance there and to assist many other institutions and Bihari communities throughout the country.

In 1973 and 1974, after the emergency phase, MCC began a major food production effort under the leadership of Arthur DeFehr, using the theme "nutritional self-sufficiency." This resulted in MCC receiving, in 1975, one of the first three gold "Bangabandhu" medals awarded by the country. Family planning, maternal child health care, and job creation programs soon became important foci. In 1987 there were 35 MCC volunteers plus approximately 175 Bangladeshi staff members, making it one of MCC's largest programs in any country. Mennonite Brethren Board of Missions and Services personnel worked with the MCC program for a number of years. PM

MC Yearbook (1986-87), 153; *MB Yearbook* (1981), 104.

Bankruptcy is variously defined and understood, but for purposes of this article it is "the status of a debtor who has been declared by judicial process to be unable to pay his debts" (*Encyclopedia Britannica*, 120). It is different from insolvency, which refers to the person who is unable to meet her °debts as they mature, but does not undergo legal procedures of dissolving the business.

Although evidence is almost nonexistent, it is fair to say that bankruptcy was exceedingly rare among Anabaptists and Mennonites until recent times. For early Anabaptists, property was closely related to °mutual aid; hence if there was insolvency, the Mennonite community stepped in to assist (Klassen, 42ff.). Mennonite doctrines and confessions of faith make no direct statements about on economic issues, including bankruptcy, because of the strong church and world dualism (separation from or °nonconformity to political and economic activity). The spiritual leaders of Anabaptism, such as °Menno Simons and Peter °°Riedemann, stress honesty, frugality, simplicity, mutuality, and sharing of profits,

but do not refer to specific economic activity.

Hence an encounter with bankruptcy is a direct function of Mennonite entrance into the °capitalist economic and political system, and is becoming an increasingly relevant concept with the passing of time (Kreider, 1980). The most extensive treatment has recently appeared in the periodical *Marketplace*, sponsored by °Mennonite Economic Development Associates (MEDA), especially after 1980. Church periodicals are also dealing increasingly with the issue.

Although the evidence is weak, it is apparent that the rate of bankruptcy among Mennonite and Brethren in Christ members is alarmingly high, and includes agriculture as well as other types of businesses. This has been accelerated by the economic stresses of the 1980s, especially the high cost of borrowing money (interest payment).

Mennonites have traditionally been very stringently opposed to declaring insolvency or bankruptcy. Sources of this are the tradition of nonswearing of oaths, interpreted to mean that a person's word is his bond, and that debts are always paid; the Mennonite disinclination toward becoming involved in economic activities of usury, merchandising for profit, risk taking, and competition; and the Mennonite "communalistic brotherhoods ethic," (Nelson, 133). Although pioneer sociologist Max Weber (1864-1920) assumed Mennonites were part of the capitalistic ethic, Troeltsch, Nelson, Tolles, Klassen, Vogt, and others emphasize more the mutual aid and brotherhood economics, which downplayed the risks of bankruptcy. Insolvency and bankruptcy would, in this context, have been interpreted as the results of a deviant economic practice, which on some occasions would result in church °discipline or °°excommunication. Hence innumerable warnings have emanated from Mennonite spiritual leaders about the temptations of seeking wealth and the threat to spirituality and nonconformity (cf. Hershberger, 290).

In this view, insolvency and bankruptcy would result from attitudes and practices that are at odds with the traditional Mennonite understanding of the two kingdoms—the kingdom of God and the secular, selfish kingdom of the world. This understanding may be less characteristic of those members who are on the fringes of the community, and who are entering nontraditional economic activities where the temptations or needs of acquisition, risk taking, entrepreneurship are encouraged (Kreider). In this way the Anabaptist and Mennonite tradition, including related groups such as the Church of the Brethren and Friends, is different from the rest of the sectarian, Free Church, Puritan, and evangelical wing of Protestantism, which is more directly the result of the Lutheran or Reformed tradition and which stress individual effort and the idea of working in this world as part of God's calling.

Each bankruptcy is unique, and no general formula can be given; clearly, bankruptcy is the result of risk taking which is at the heart of the capitalistic entrepreneurial spirit. Not being able to predict future economic conditions is another major factor. Unusually difficult times for certain sectors of the economy also play a role. For Mennonites, another very significant factor is their recent entry into the business world, and the loss of community guidance and assistance which was available to the traditional family provider in the rural and village Mennonite society and economy.   CWR

Guy F. Hershberger, *The Way of the Cross in Human Relations* (Scottdale, 1958); Peter J. Klassen, *The Economics of Anabaptism* (The Hague: Mouton and Co., 1964); Carl Kreider, *The Christian Entrepreneur* (Scottdale, 1980); Loewen, *Confessions*; Benjamin Nelson, *The Idea of Usury from Tribal Brotherhood to Universal Brotherhood* (U. of Chicago Press, 1969); Ernst Troeltsch, *The Social Teachings of the Christian Churches* (German ed., 1911; English trans., 1931); Roy Vogt, "Economic Questions and the Mennonite Conscience," in *Call to Faithfulness*, ed., Henry Poettcker and Rudy A. Regehr (Winnipeg: CMBC, 1972); "Bankruptcy," *Encyclopedia Britannica*, 14th ed. vol. 3 (Chicago 1966); *Marketplace*, (Winnipeg: Mennonite Economic Development Associates, published quarterly, 1971-).

A Letter from a Small-Town Banker

Our bank is called "First Bank of Berne" and is located in a rural community of 3,000 residents. I am the president of the bank; I am also a Mennonite who has been associated with the bank for 37 years. When I came to the bank, about 70 percent of its clientele were farmers. Today only 40 percent of the bank's borrowers are farmers. The bank is a 95-year-old shareholder-owned bank. At its inception there were no investors from outside the community. In 1987, most of the bank shares are still held by local residents or people who have or have had roots in the Berne community. The bank is run by an elected board of seven directors, five of whom are members of the local General Conference Mennonite Church. The president of the bank is the chief executive officer, actively runs the day-by-day operation, and has authority to make all loan operation decisions. He then reports to the board at monthly meetings.

In 1950, the average cost of an acre of land in the Berne area was $300. This escalated in an almost uninterrupted inflationary spiral until it reached a pinnacle of $4,000 per acre in the late 1970s. Equipment costs followed a similar spiral. For example, a combine harvester that sold for about $4,000 in the early 1950s now sells for $80,000 to $100,000. A bushel of soybeans went from $2.00 to a high of $11.00, and corn rose from $1.25 to $7.50 per bushel. Cattle and hog prices followed the same pattern. As a result of this strong progressive inflationary spiral, many farmers mortgaged all the land they owned in order to purchase as much additional ground as they could. In the late 1970s, land, grain, and livestock values decreased drastically. Farmers found their debt load schedule impossible to maintain. As a result, the First Bank of Berne finds itself caught in the web of this farming financial squeeze, with many of its agriculture loans in jeopardy.

The policy of the First Bank of Berne has been to help farmers work their way out of precarious situations, with foreclosure as a last resort. In the 37 years of my banking experience, we have yet to carry out a foreclosure. The First Bank of Berne has generally taken the following position on all delinquent farm and small business loans: First, we call in the borrower to see if there is any possible way of working out the delinquency. This might be accomplished by restructuring the loan or suspending principal payments. In addition, we may lower the interest rate by 2 to 3 percent. If this is unsuccessful, we might suggest a liquidation of some of the assets in order to reduce the loan principal. This could mean selling some of the land or equipment quietly, rather than selling all of it at a forced sale. This usually leads to a higher sale price. Often, by this partial liquidation, it is possible for the borrower to restructure and have a greater chance to work out of the debt load.

Often we find that, if we are willing to forgive or "charge-off," some of the debt load and get it down to a manageable amount, the farmer can continue to meet the scheduled payments. Our hope is that the borrower may sometime in the future be able to pick up the charged-off principal. So far, this policy has been our loss entirely, but as long as we can absorb these losses, we feel comfortable with this procedure to prevent foreclosure. If the borrower still cannot pay interest on the remaining debt, we may encourage enlistment of family members or friends to aid with additional collateral. Occasionally, a parent or grandparent may come to the rescue. As a preface to all of these situations, the First Bank of Berne offers financial counseling in regard to cash flow sheets, balance sheets, and other financial management measures. So far we have threatened foreclosure a few times, but have yet to carry out these threats. It is our hope that we will not have to resort to this, which would be our very last option.

Another area of banking that might create a conflict of conscience for a Mennonite banker is the area of investments. All banks are regulated by state and federal agencies. First Bank of Berne is therefore subject to certain requirements. For instance, the bank must maintain a certain percent of liquidity in order to accommodate a quick or massive drop in deposits, panic deposit "runs," or heavy withdrawals. In order to keep a certain amount of funds liquid for this possibility, we are required to maintain certain types of short-term investments. One of the best sources of this type of investment is United States government bonds. Government bonds are both safe and readily marketable and therefore a good source of liquidity. However, the thought of investing in the United States government, where a high percent will be used for war and military preparation, does present an immense problem for an Mennonite believer. Our solution is to invest a large percentage of our excess funds in municipal and government agency bonds that are used for expenses such as city sewer works, schools, water projects, federal housing projects, interstate highways, and airports. Although not as liquidable as federal government bonds and therefore riskier if an immediate liquidation should be necessary, these kinds of bonds are allowed by the regulators, and we have invested a high percent of our excess funds in them so as not to invest directly in government activities we disapprove of.

Another area that has been satisfying for me as a Mennonite in the banking field is that we have been able to share our profits with our customers. One of the ways we have been able to do this is to lower our interest rates voluntarily, even though our borrowers had previously committed themselves to long-term mortgage loans. During the past five or six years, we have voluntarily lowered rates on existing mortgage loans four different times. So far as we know, we are the only bank in the state of Indiana voluntarily to initiate this plan. As a Mennonite, I feel good about being able to carry out such sharing policies.

There is one final way in which I might respond in regard to the positive opportunities I've found as a Mennonite banker. In a small community such as ours, the bank and bank employees often serve as financial advisors. People come to us for financial counseling in regard to debts and investments. In both areas we often find ourselves in a position to have a positive influence. In addition, I often find that people with multiple financial problems may have a family problem or a spiritual problem. It is very natural to counsel on financial issues and end up talking about spiritual things. I don't want to overplay this aspect of the community bank, but the opportunity is there. Working out financial problems can help resolve marriage or personal spiritual problems.

In summary, I would say that the opportunity for a Mennonite to be in a position to exercise an Anabaptist faith in a small community bank is very real. Perhaps First Bank of Berne is a unique institution in the banking profession, yet as I talk to other small-town bankers, I feel that we are not a totally isolated case. Banking, like many other °businesses, can be ruthless, greedy, and very demanding. On the other hand, it can offer service, opportunities, and encouragement to a community. *Sincerely yours, Frederick H. Liechty, February 16, 1987.*

Banwar, Puran A. (Feb. 2, 1912–May 21, 1971), was employed as a young man as "caretaker" of the Bethesda Leprosy Home, °Champa, Madhya Pradesh, India. He took an active interest in the church and soon became one of the conference leaders. In 1946 he received the distinction of being the first Indian national to come to the United States from the Bharatiya General Conference Mennonite Church in India. In the United States, he visited many churches and earned a BA degree from Bethel College (Ks.) in 1948.

Back in India, he taught in the Union Bible School in Janjgir, was ordained as elder, and quickly established a reputation for being an excellent teacher and preacher. In 1954 Puran was appointed the first resident evangelist-in-charge in the Surguja District. He and his wife endured much opposition and persecution. During their 17-year ministry in Surguja 600 people were baptized, and the Calvary Mennonite Church was planted and became a member church in the Bharatiya General Conference Mennonite Church conference. The number of evangelists increased from 2 to 13; three church buildings were erected; a hostel for students and one primary school were opened.

Puran was married to Lily King on June 13, 1936. They had three children, Pramod, Nawal, and Purnima. HR

Baptism, Age at. There are two dimensions to the subject of the age of baptism: the question of a minimum age at which reception into church membership is viable; and the question of the attenuation and loss of persons when baptism is unduly postponed.

The Minimum Age of Baptism. For Protestant denominations opposed to baptizing infants, the tendency for the age of baptism to become lower over time presents a concern for the renewal of the normative vision for a °believers church of truly committed adults. The estimated average age of baptism for 10 representative Anabaptist men and women, 1525-1536, was 36.4, with none under the age of 20, two between the ages of 20 and 29, four between 30 and 39, and four between 40 and 49. In 1973 the median age of baptism for four Mennonite denominations (MC, GCM, MB, EMCh) plus the Brethren in Christ (BIC) was 14.9. By its very nature, the voluntaristic character of a believers church is valid only for one generation and must be repeatedly renewed as the faith is transmitted to the next generation. The problem is that the fervency and diligence of the first generation is seldom equaled by the succeeding generations. In order to bring the children of the voluntary members of any given generation into conformity with the normative vision, they are usually programmed by an educational process to make their own commitments preparatory to baptism. Communal and peer-group pressures to conform set in, and the corresponding parental or congregational obligations to guide them through the "rite of passage" seem to be most applicable at the lowest possible age of discretion.

The Kauffman-Harder study of five Mennonite-related denominations (1973) documented the downward trend in the age of baptism. For the oldest generation of members (over 50), it was 16.3; for the middle generation (30-49), it was 14.9; and for the youngest generation (under 30), it was 14.0. The median age for women (14.7) was significantly lower than for men (15.2), reflecting the fact that women reach puberty and, presumably, the age of maturity (i.e., discretion) at an earlier age than men. The spread ranged from age 8 or less at baptism (109 cases) to 40 plus years at baptism (49 cases). Thirteen percent of all members had been baptized before the age of 12. Moreover, the 1973 data revealed significant differences between the five denominations. The median age of baptism was lowest in the Mennonite Church (MC, 14.0) and highest among General Conference Mennonites and Mennonite Brethren (16.4), with the Evangelical Mennonite Church and Brethren in Christ (14.1 and 14.5) more like the Mennonite Church (MC) practice.

Mennonite Brethren work at this issue by stressing their historic qualification of the °conversion experience, with baptism following the candidate's conversion testimony before the congregation, on the basis of which the person is certified as ready for membership. The concept of the conversion experience is not totally absent in the other groups but is not as explicitly emphasized. Among General Conference Mennonites, only 65 percent of the members can identify a personal experience of conversion (compared to 93 percent for the Mennonite

Brethren). The higher age of baptism among General Conference Mennonites is the consequence of a tradition in the Canadian churches (comprising 42 percent of the GCM) of postponing baptism to an age several years beyond adolescence.

It is not surprising that the greatest concern for the lowering age of baptism has been expressed in the Mennonite Church (MC). In 1963 Melvin Gingerich reported his findings from the second Mennonite Family Census. He found the median age of baptism to be 14.6. He also found that of 3,150 young people living in the Mennonite Church homes studied, 399 (12.6 percent) had been baptized before the age of 10. "What does this mean," he asked, "in the context of the responsible decision demanded of those who accept the Christian life?" (Gingerich, *Family Census*, 4). He referred his readers to Gideon Yoder's book, *The Nurture and Evangelism of Children* (Scottdale, 1959), which argued that parents and congregations in the Anabaptist tradition should seek to guide their children in their faith at their own maturational levels of understanding until they arrive at the age of accountability. Then they are mature enough to make their own decisions and understand their own need for God's salvation and what it means to be truly converted and committed to Christ. A position statement adopted by the Mennonite Church's general conference in 1959 carried the same title as Yoder's book and identified the criteria for determining the age of accountability, but it was a regression in one respect: it legitimized early adolescence as the age when children normally reach the age of accountability. Critics of the practice of such an early baptism argued that many MC young people who are baptized have not been converted. They assented to their parents' beliefs with their minds, but were not deeply convinced in their hearts. One woman, who was baptized at the age of 12, admitted that she joined the church because all of her girl friends were doing it. At the age of 20 she really became converted and expressed the wish that she had waited for baptism until it really meant something to her. A minister related that his parents pushed him into baptism at an early age, before he understood what it was all about, and asserted that this was little better than infant baptism (Martha Wagner in *GH* [Sept. 8, 1964], 788).

Similar concerns have been expressed in the other denominations. Norman Bert wrote that in the Brethren in Christ tradition, "'maturity' meant twenty to twenty-five years old. In some conservative parts of the [BIC] church, young people were not expected to 'make a start' until they were married. The Brethren held to this late age for conversion [not] in order to give their young people a chance to sow their wild oats before joining the church. They expected conversion to happen at a mature age because it demanded a serious, responsible decision." (Bert, *Adventure*, 37-38). In the General Conference Mennonite study conference on the believers church in 1955, delegates meeting in small groups expressed concerns like the following: "The Anabaptists took a stand for adult baptism, while we are in danger of swinging back toward infant baptism, especially if we baptize seven-year-olds. How can such a child become a part of the church fellowship and would he be eligible for the office of deacon? Not only do we have the problem of knowing when children are old enough to join the church, but there is also the problem of allowing age alone to become the only criterion. Upon reaching this age they more or less automatically join the church. Some churches start too young and find that when the person grows older he has another and more meaningful experience." (Regier, *Proceedings*, 229-30). The statement of findings adopted by the conference delegates reiterated these concerns and encouraged "a careful study of the Scriptures in the light of the requirements of church membership suggested in this [believers' church] statement." (Regier, *Proceedings*, 10).

A recent, reasoned study of this issue in the light of biblical and historical theology is found in the book by Marlin Jeschke, *Believers' Baptism for Children of the Church* (Scottdale, 1983). The author's thesis is that the New Testament pattern for the baptism of adult converts entering the messianic community from a fallen world cannot be applied in the same way to the children of the church, who should be expected to grow up under the nurture and influence of the Christian community and should not be expected to have the radical conversion of their first-generation ancestors. Their experience will rather be one of appropriation and ownership of the faith in which they have been raised. Jeschke argues for a new perspective on this issue: "to move children from [their childhood] innocence to the Christian way in adolescence" and to baptize them at this point in their lives " as a sign of their crossing-over from innocence into an owned faith" (p. 146).

The Loss of Unbaptized Persons. Although the second dimension to the age of baptism issue has received much less attention, there is much reason to be concerned about the attenuation and loss of persons when baptism is postponed or rejected. This is the problem of seepage from our churches as a result of the ineffective nurture and evangelism of children and the inept transmission of a meaningful self-identity.

The decennial census of members, children, and ex-members (GCM) reveals some startling statistics in this regard. From 1960 to 1970, a total of 17,530 people were received into membership in 222 reporting churches, 51 percent by baptism (mostly teenagers), 43 percent by transfer from another church, and 5 percent by reaffirmation of faith. During the same decade 15,956 memberships were terminated by death, transfer, or deletion from membership roles. Thus, the ratio of receptions to losses was a bare 1.1. Only 45 percent of the children between the ages of 15 and 19 had been baptized; and about one-fifth of the children over 20 years of age had still not been baptized and received as members. It is especially in the Canadian churches, where the median age of baptism is the highest of any area conference, that a significantly lower percentage of teen-age children are ever baptized and received into membership. In the Conference of Mennonites in British Columbia, only 28 percent of the children aged 15-19 had been baptized, compared to 93 percent for the Western District Conference. Moreover, there was a much greater seepage of men than of women. In the British Columbia provincial conference, only 36 percent of the male children (aged 20-24) of members had ever been baptized, compared to 69 percent of the women. Among General Conference Mennonites as a whole, it appears that about 15 percent of the offspring of members are never baptized and are thus lost to the General Conference Mennonite Church, if not to the wider Christian church.

This discussion of the age of baptism question leads to the conclusion that the problem is not primarily one of some ideal modal age of baptism, but rather a question of effective evangelism and teaching in the process of leading people to wholehearted Christian discipleship. This requires a theory of °Christian education that takes seriously the developmental sequence in the maturational process and its correlation with authentic Christian response.   LDH

Norman A. Bert, *Adventure in Discipleship* (Nappanee, 1968); Melvin Gingerich, *The Mennonite Family Census* (Goshen, Ind.: Mennonite Research Foundation, 1963); CRR 4: 527-75; Kauffman/Harder, *Anabaptists Four C. Later* (1975), 70-73; Maurice Martin, *Identity and Faith* (Scottdale, 1981); Mennonite Church (MC) Position Statement on the "Nurture and Evangelism of Children," adopted by general conference (MC) on Aug. 27, 1959, and published in Ernest D. Martin, *The Story and Witness of the Christian Way* (Scottdale: MPH, 1971), 81-83; P. K. Regier, ed., *Proceedings of the Study Conference on the Believers' Church* (Newton: GCMC, 1955), 10, 25, 93, 113, 118ff., 228-30.

See also Church Membership; Dedication of Infants; Revivalism.

Baptismal Instruction, North America (ME I:527, 529). The Kauffman and Harder study, *Anabaptists Four C. Later* (1975) reported that the median age of baptism was 14.0 in the Mennonite Church (MC) and 16.4 in the General Conference Mennonite Church. A survey in the Mennonite Conference of Ontario and Quebec (MC) in 1979 indicated a median age of 17.5.

Accompanying a trend toward °baptism at a later age, many congregations have moved from baptismal instruction during the Sunday school hour to a period of instruction at a separate time for those who are ready to step forward in the public act of confession of faith in Christ and identity with the church. Baptism continues to be understood as a entry ritual into the faith community.

A greater understanding of faith development and covenant-making in the midst of the congregation underlies *The Foundation Series* °Sunday School curriculum produced by the General Conference Mennonite Church, the Mennonite Church (MC), and the Brethren in Christ. Greater attention is being given baptism as a conscious decision of "crossing over" to saving faith for those who have been nurtured by the congregation.

Baptismal instruction classes vary in length from four or five sessions to 13 weeks or a year. Bible study, other reading materials, group discussion, and personal visits are used, with attention given to the relational aspects of °church membership. Often a mentor or partner-in-faith from the congregation, as well as the pastor, is involved. The content of in-

struction includes key themes in biblical theology, basic understandings of Christian faith, unique perspectives of the Anabaptist movement, historic confessions, and contemporary statements of faith.

The article on °°catechism traces the influence of the Elbing catechism on baptismal instructional material for the Amish in America, the Mennonites (MC), the General Confernce Mennonites, the Fellowship of Evangelical Bible Churches (formerly Evangelical Mennonite Brethren), and the Evangelical Mennonites.

Widely used baptismal instruction materials include: Russell Krabill *Beginning the Christian Life* (Scottdale, 1958), a 12-lesson book for upper elementary grades; James H. Waltner, *This We Believe* (Newton, 1968), a reading book for high school age youth on the basic doctrines of the Christian faith; Paul Erb, *We Believe* (Scottdale, 1969), a commentary on the 20 articles of the Mennonite Church (MC) Confession of Faith; *Preparing for Church Membership* (Scottdale, 1971), materials including a devotional guide (*Off to a Good Start*), a historical and doctrinal resource book (*Experiencing Christ in the Church*), and a study of the Sermon on the Mount (*The Christian Way*); *Focus on Faith* (Newton, 1978), a loose-leaf manual of materials from catechism classes of 12 General Conference Mennonite Church pastors; Helmut Harder, *Guide to Faith* (Newton, 1979), a reading book on concepts of the Christian faith written for grades 11 and 12; Frank Keller, *Preparation for Covenant Life* (Newton, 1979), a study book on the Bible as the salvation story of God's people, for the young adult level; Paul Lederach, *A Third Way* (Scottdale, 1980), a reading book on Mennonite understandings of Christian faith; Bruce Yoder, *Choose Life* (Scottdale, 1984), a study book for youth on basic faith and discipleship issues; and Kenneth G. Bauman, *Invitation to Life* (Newton, 1986), a leader's guide with student worksheets.   JHW

Maurice Martin, *Identity and Faith* (Scottdale, 1981), 77-97; Maurice Martin with Helen Reusser, *In the Midst of the Congregation* (Scottdale, 1983), 12-19, 70-81; Marlin Jeschke, *Believers Baptism for Children of the Church* (Scottdale, 1983); James H. Waltner, *Baptism and Church Membership* (Newton, 1979), 23-26; Merle D. Strege, ed., *Baptism and Church* (Grand Rapids: Sagamore Books, 1986); Gideon G. Yoder, *The Nurture and Evangelism of Children* (Scottdale, 1959); Henry Poettcker, *A Study on Baptism* (Newton, 1963).

See also Christian Education.

Baptismal Theology (ME I:224). Believers baptism is without question one of the most central articles of faith of the Anabaptist and Mennonite heritage. One portion of the Anabaptist movement began in Zürich in 1525 with a historic act of believers baptism, and the tenet on believers baptism leads the list of seven °Schleitheim articles of 1527.

In 1966 there appeared the first book-length study on Anabaptist baptism (Armour), which examines the baptismal theology of Balthasar °Hubmaier, Thomas °Müntzer, Hans °°Denck, Hans °Hut, Melchior °Hoffman, and Pilgram °Marpeck. These Anabaptists "differed somewhat in their view of the time and manner of inner transformation," but "they were at one in saying that the only legitimate basis for receiving baptism and entering the baptismal covenant was the experience of regeneration within, a regeneration which gave the believer power to make a valid confession of faith. . . ."

Recent confessions of faith continue to reaffirm the principle of believers baptism. The 1963 Mennonite Church (MC) Confession of Faith says, "In order to qualify for baptism one must repent, turn to Christ in sincere faith, and accept Him as Lord." Similarly, the 1975 Mennonite Brethren Confession of Faith says, "To qualify for baptism, one must repent of sin and trust Jesus Christ as personal Savior and Lord."

A study of five Mennonite groups in 1972 (Kauffman/Harder, *Anabaptists Four C. Later*, 1975) found 82 percent of the respondents agreeing that "baptism is neither necessary nor proper for infants and small children." Seventeen percent of the respondents were uncertain or disagreed. The Kauffman/Harder study found the median age of baptism in the Mennonite Church (MC) to be 14 years, in the General Conference Mennonite Church 16.5, in the Mennonite Brethren Church 16.3, and overall 14.9.

In the last several decades Mennonite baptismal theology has moved from a restatement of objections to infant baptism to the question of the appropriate age of baptism of °children and youth reared within the sphere of the church. It has also addressed the related question of the appropriate kind of religious experience to be expected of those coming to baptism who have been reared within the church.

In his 1956 Conrad Grebel Lectures, Gideon Yoder anticipated the later interest in "faith development" by speaking of a "religion of childhood"—that is, of a preadult understanding of faith. Yoder invited respect for such a "religion of childhood" and sought to resist tendencies to impose upon innocent children in the church the radical kind of conversion more usually characteristic of adult sinners. Similarly, J. C. Wenger in *Introduction to Theology* (1954) wrote, "It is cruel and unchristian to attempt to precipitate a conversion experience on those who are not sufficiently mature to experience conversion. Furthermore it is actually impossible to bring an individual to Christ when the Holy Spirit is not working in his heart."

James H. Waltner claims "it is . . . important to distinguish between the religion of childhood . . . and a Christian experience which is based on faith and repentance. . . . If we understand salvation as acceptance also of the lordship of Christ to lead us into a life of discipleship, then a child may not be ready for the commitment implied in baptism. . . . We should be cautious about using baptism as a device to hold the children while they are young so that they don't get away unbaptized when they are older. That kind of baptism has little meaning and may innoculate them against a more meaningful experience later."

In *Believers Baptism for Children of the Church* (1983), Marlin Jeschke calls for careful notice of the special situation of children of the church. An unreflective and singleminded fixation upon believers baptism, reinforced by an idealization of the sensational conversions of modern evangelism and missions, is in danger of blinding people to the quite different circumstances of those born and reared within the community of faith. Because children of believers are instructed in Christian homes and within the Christian congregation, their responsibility when they reach the age of discretion is to appropriate and make their own the faith in which they were reared. They should not be expected, as pagan adults would be, to leave a sinful world in which they were reared in order to cross over into the Christian church.

Someone privileged to have been reared in a Christian community will not likely have as dramatic a conversion as a notorious sinner. But the experience of one brought up "in the discipline and instruction of the Lord" (Eph 6:4) such as a Timothy, who from his childhood knew the holy Scriptures, is not to be considered inferior. Indeed, it is "the more excellent way" of coming to faith, the way intended in God's institution of the Christian home and church. Two recent books by Maurice Martin offer helpful counsel to a congregation on how to minister to its children in their faith development.

A subject that Mennonite baptismal theology has not sufficiently addressed, likely because of Mennonite suspicion of sacramentalism, is that of the timing of baptism—connecting the sign with the reality signified. In marriage the timing of a wedding is usually deemed important, because a wedding is not just a *sign* of marriage but also the rite that *effects* the marriage. As a sign of faith, is baptism chiefly a report of a past decision of faith or, as in the New Testament, the effectual sign by which someone coming to faith is actually incorporated into the body of Christ? Mennonite baptismal practice has always employed the authoritative classic formula, "I baptize you in the name of the Father and of the Son and of the Holy Spirit," which many take to imply that the act of baptism effects what it signifies (°ordinances).

The mode of baptism (affusion or °immersion) has become a less controversial issue in recent years. Affusionist congregations occasionally grant immersion baptism to those desiring it. Some immersionists, the Mennonite Brethren at least, are accepting by transfer of membership those believers earlier baptized by affusion. A number of Mennonite Church (MC) and General Conference Mennonite Church congregations are also beginning to accept by transfer of membership believers who were baptized as infants without requiring them to be rebaptized.   MJ

Rollin Armour, *Anabaptist Baptism* (Scottdale, 1966); Marlin Jeschke, *Believers Baptism for Children of the Church* (Scottdale, 1983); Maurice Martin, *In the Midst of the Congregation* (Scottdale, 1983); Marlin E. Miller, "The Mennonites," in *Baptism and Church*, ed. Merle D. Strege (Grand Rapids: Sagamore Books, 1986); Henry Poettcker, *Baptism in the New Testament* (Newton, 1963); James H. Waltner, *Baptism and Church Membership* (Newton and Scottdale, 1979); Gideon Yoder, *The Nurture and Evangelism of Children* (Scottdale, 1959); *Menn. Bib. II*, p. 536.

See also Church Membership; Discipline; Dedication of Infants; Exorcism.

Baptists (ME I:228). It is generally agreed that the Baptist tradition began about 1609 in the John °Smyth congregation of English Separatists (a radical group that broke away from the Puritans). While in exile in Amsterdam, this congregation was influenced to some extent by Dutch Mennonites. There are similarities of position between Baptists and Anabaptists which cannot all be attributed to Mennonite influence: an emphasis on the °believers church, believers baptism and biblicism, and opposition to hierarchy and state interference in religious matters. However, when the majority of Smyth's congregation decided to unite with the Mennonites and a minority returned to England, the two traditions diverged. In *An Advertisement or admonition unto the Congregations, which men call the New Fryelers* (1611), Thomas °°Helwys, leader of the Baptist minority, outlined four reasons for the division: unorthodox Mennonite views of the °°Incarnation; Mennonite laxity on Sabbath (Sunday) observance; Mennonite insistence on "succession" in the church; and Mennonite damning of the magistracy (°church-state relations), including the refusal to bear arms or otherwise participate in °government. The Incarnation issue disappeared when Mennonites quietly dropped their unique interpretation in the 18th c. The Sabbath issue has also ceased to be prominent, but questions related to "succession" and church-state relations continue to separate Anabpatists and Baptists. Helwys insisted that each congregation has the right to initiate baptism and ordain pastors and accused Smyth and the Mennonites of accepting the successionist error of Catholics and magisterial Reformers. Smyth replied that °baptism and °ordination should be passed on in succession *where possible*. The issue was one of degree, and the differences have remained. While Baptists and Mennonites have a similar church °polity, Baptists, particularly in North America, have tended to place more stress on congregational autonomy, while Mennonites have usually been more conscious of the larger brotherhood.

The big difference between Mennonites and Baptists remains the attitude toward the state and society. Baptists in the United States have often been ardent nationalists and promoters of the military, while Mennonites have frequently been pacifists and at odds with the state. Baptists have tended to separate church and state while participating fully in both spheres, in Helwys' words, serving God with their souls and the state with their bodies. Mennonites have taken a more wholistic view of persons, separating the church, body and soul, from society. The same tendencies are evident in the Soviet Union, despite state pressure for both groups to amalgamate in the °All-Union Council of Evangelical Christians-Baptists (AUCECB). Mennonite Brethren, whose position has been revised by Baptist, °evangelical, and °pietist influence, have tended to join the AUCECB, while other Mennonites have preferred to remain independent. Among Mennonites absorbed by the AUCECB, there has been a disproportionate number of former Mennonites among the breakaway Reformed Baptists, who refuse all involvement with the state.

On the other hand, external influences have revised Baptist positions on other issues since 1609. A second branch of English Baptists, the Particular Baptists (independent origins, 1633), introduced a Calvinist strain into the Baptist tradition. The Baptists were also forerunners and beneficiaries of the evangelical and Pietist movements of the 18th and 19th c. This has increased Baptist stress on individual °conversion, in contrast to the Mennonite stress on °discipleship and lifelong commitment. The differences between Baptists and Mennonites are thus part of the larger distinction between the evangelical and Anabaptist traditions. Nevertheless, the close ties and similarities between the two groups have generated a long debate among Baptists, particularly in the United States, over whether Baptists are Anabaptists or Protestants. JRC

B. R. White, *The English Baptists of the Seventeenth Century* (London: The Baptist Historical Society, 1983); two more volumes are projected by the same publisher; Raymond Brown, *The English Baptists of the Eighteenth Century* and J. H. Y. Briggs, *The English Baptists of the Nineteenth Century*; B. R. White, *The English Separatist Tradition* (Oxford University Press, 1971); Walter Sawatsky, *Soviet Evangelicals Since World War II* (Scottdale, 1981); James R. Coggins, "John Smyth's Congregation: English Separatism, Dutch Mennonites and the Elect Nation" (PhD diss., U. of Waterloo, 1986); Lonnie D. Kliever, "General Baptist Origins: The Question of Anabaptist Influence," *MQR*, 36 (1962), 291-321; Goki Saito, "An Investigation into the Relationship between the Early English General Baptists and The Dutch Anabaptists" (PhD diss., Southern Baptist Theological Seminary, 1974); Keith L. Sprunger, *Dutch Puritanism* (Leiden: E. J. Brill, 1982), 76-90; William R. Estep Jr., "Thomas Helwys: Bold Architect of Baptist Policy on Church-State Relations," *Baptist History and Heritage* 20 (July 1985), 24-34; Timothy George, "Between Pacifism and Coercion: The English Baptist Doctrine of Religious Toleration," *MQR*, 58 (1984), 30-49; James E. Tull, *Shapers of Baptist Thought* (Valley Forge, Pa.: Judson Press, 1972). A series of articles in *The Chronicle* 14 (1951), 16 (1953), 20 (1957) debated whether Baptists were Anabaptists or Protestants; Joseph D. Ban took up the question in *In the Great Tradition* (Valley Forge, Pa.: Judson Press, 1982), 91-106. See also D. F. Durnbaugh, *Believers' Church* (1963); Calvin Augustine Pater, *Karlstadt as the Father of the Baptist Movements* (U. of Toronto Press, 1984), 253-78; Benjamin Evans, *The Early English Baptists* (London, 1862); William L. Lumpkin, *Baptist Confessions of Faith* (Valley Forge, Pa.: Judson Press, 1969. The writings of Will D. Campbell, particularly *Cecelia's Sin* (Macon, Ga.: Mercer U. Press, 1986), and *Brother to a Dragonfly* (New York: Seabury, 1972), represent a direct appropriation by a 20th c. Southern Baptist of the 16th c. Anabaptist heritage without addressing the issue of historical continuity. Dissertations on Anabaptist and Hutterite themes have been written at leading Baptist seminaries (see *MQR*, 54 (1980), 64-65, 60 (1986), 200-201). See also James R. Hertzler, "English Baptists Interpret Continental Mennonites in the Early 19th Century," *MQR*, 54 (1980), 42-52; William R. Estep, Jr., *The Anabaptist Story* (Nashville: Broadman, 1963; reprinted, Grand Rapids, 1975), and John A. Moore, *Anabaptist Portraits* (Scottdale, 1984).

See also Hubmaier, Balthasar; Oncken, Johann Gerhard; *Umsiedler.*

Barents, Christiana Michiel (ME I:584). Born ca. 1489, Christiana Barentsdochter married the medical doctor Mathijs' van der Donck. She was baptized in 1534 by °°Jan Smeetgen (Smeitgen) of Maastricht. A zealous disciple of °David Joris, she fled to England with °°Anneken Jans. In November 1538 both returned to visit David Joris. During their wagon journey from Ijsselmonde to Rotterdam, they sang a spiritual song which became their undoing. When they later waited for a connection to Delft, they were both arrested. They were interrogated on December 24, following which their confession led to the arrest of numerous followers of David Joris in

Delft. On Jan. 24, 1539, both women were executed by drowning. Christina's daughter °°Anna Mathijs van der Donck experienced the same fate on June 11, 1539, at Utrecht.   SBJZ

W. J. Kühler, *Geschiedenis der Nederlandsche Doopsgezinden in de Zestiende Eeuw* (Haarlem, 1932), 227; A. F. Mellink, *De Wederdopers in de Noordelijke Nederlanden* (Groningen, 1953), 225, 399, 401; Irvin B. Horst, *Anabaptism and the English Reformation to 1558* (Nieuwkoop, 1966), 36.

Bargen, Bernhard ("Benny") (Dec. 10, 1901–Nov. 14, 1972), was the son of German Mennonite parents who immigrated to the United States from the Russian Ukraine. A polio attack at age one left him handicapped for life. Crutches were no hindrance to him. His handicap fueled a brilliant and innovative mind, and a lifelong love for education was the result. He studied at Bethel College, Friends University (BA) and the University of Kansas (MA). Bargen married Esther Kliewer on June 12, 1924; their three children are Ralph, Eldon, and Joyce.

He was a teacher throughout his life, beginning as a high school instructor in the Kansas towns of Oxford and Buhler. He came to Bethel College as an instructor in business courses in 1935. He remained there as a professor until 1965, except for three years which he spent as a visitor and member of the °°Woodcrest Bruderhof (°Hutterian Brethren) community at Rifton, N.Y. (1955-57). He was alumni secretary at Bethel College from 1965 to 1970 when he retired. A return to the Hutterian Society of Brothers at New Meadow Run Bruderhof, Farmington, Pa., in 1972 closed out the last four months of his life.   LHab

Barnaul, USSR. See Russian Soviet Federated Socialist Republic.

Barrefelt, H. Jansen van (ca. 1520–ca. 1594). See Family of Love.

Bartel, Henry Cornelius, and Bartel, Nellie Schmidt, were founders of two Mennonite missions in China. Henry Bartel (1873-1965) was born in Gombin, Poland (under Russian rule), and immigrated with his parents to Hillsboro, Ks., at age three. He was converted at eighteen and joined the Gnadenau Krimmer Mennonite Brethren Church. In 1899 he answered the call to serve Christ by going to work at the Light and Hope Society orphanage, Berne, Ind. (ME IV:1102). Nellie Schmidt (1876-1946) was born in Avon, S.D., shortly after her parents arrived from Russia, the third of fifteen children. She was converted and baptized in the Evangelical Mennonite Brethren Church at the age of 16. In 1898 she went to serve at the Light and Hope orphanage. The Bartels were married Nov. 4, 1900.

In 1901 Henry and Nellie Bartel went to China as missionaries with Horace Houlding of the South Chihli Mission. In 1905 they founded the first Mennonite mission in China, later known as the °°China Mennonite Mission Society. This was an independent faith mission organization with a board made up of a few friends and supporters. It drew both its missionaries and its support from members of the Krimmer Mennonite Brethren, Mennonite Brethren, Evangelical Mennonite Brethren, and °°Missionary Church Association. The mission was located in Shandong (Shantung) and Henan (Honan) provinces with its center in Caoxian, Shandong (ME I:560).

In 1941 the Bartels began work in West China along the Sichuan-Gansu-Shaanxi border; this became the West China field of the Mennonite Brethren Church in 1945. Nellie Bartel died in Shaanxi Province in 1946; Henry Bartel continued to work in China until 1952. He died in Hillsboro, Ks. The Bartels also assisted Henry and Maria Miller °Brown in the beginnings of the General Conference Mennonite Mission in an area adjacent to that of the China Mennonite Mission Society. They also assisted Frank V. and Agnes Ebel Wiebe in founding the Krimmer Mennonite Brethren mission in Inner °°Mongolia (1923; ME I:562).

The Bartels were parents of Loyal, Paul, Agnes (Wieneke), Elsie (Eisenbraun) and Jonathan; all but Jonathan served as missionaries in China. Paul was a long term missionary in Hong Kong and Jonathan in Japan. Loyal remained in China until his death in 1971.   ARR

H. C. Bartel, *A Short Review of the First Mennonite Mission in China* (Tsao Hsien, Shantung Province, China, 1913); idem, *China Mennonite Mission Society* (Tsao Hsien, 1927); Jonathan Bartel, "The China Mennonite Mission Society" (unpublished term paper, Tabor College, Hillsboro, Ks, 1949); Margaret Epp, *This Mountain Is Mine* (Chicago: Moody Press, 1969); Robert and Alice Ramseyer, *Mennonites in China* (Winnipeg: China Educational Exchange, 1988); for additional writings by the Bartels see *Menn. Bib.*, 14890-91, 14921-22, 14927, 14967.

See also People's Republic of China ("Committed to China" [feature]).

Bartsch, Henry G. and Bartsch, Anna Funk, were missionaries in Africa and Mennonite Brethren church workers in Canada. Henry Bartsch (1896-1966) was born in Sparrau, and Anna Funk (b. 1897) in Katerinovka, both Mennonite villages in the Ukraine. They grew up in devout Christian homes; he had 6, she 17 brothers and sisters. Both attended village schools. Anna continued her education, became a private teacher, and later attended Bible school in the Crimea. Henry was drafted in 1915 and served as a noncombatant in the Red Cross medical corps in World War I. Both experienced much violence and saw entire villages destroyed during the °Russian Revolution and Civil War (1917-20) and the subsequent epidemic and famine (1920-22). They personalized their faith in Christ, were baptized, and joined the Mennonite Brethren Church.

Henry immigrated to Canada in 1923, and Anna arrived in 1927, settling near Dalmeny, Sask. They were married in 1928 and went to Winkler Bible School, pursuing one goal: mission in Africa. The call had come through reports given by missionaries Aaron and Ernestine °Janzen. Upon ordination in 1931, the Bartsches left "by faith" for the Belgian Congo (Zaire) to join the Janzens at Kafumba 1932. Urged by a call to pioneer evangelism and accompanied by four missionaries, they set foot with their children on an untrodden path to an unknown land of the Dekese people in Bololo, 750 km. (450 mi.) ne. of Kafumba. More missionaries joined them later.

"We did not know where we were going, but knew that God was leading," wrote Anna. As they began their evangelism work, they felt they "were talking to the trees in the wood." Having neither church nor conference behind them, their support came from the small Africa Mission Society founded by friends in Winkler Bible School. The *Kleine Afrika-Bote* (1935-43) was their official organ. Although their courage was as undaunted as their hardships were severe, they found it necessary to return to Canada in 1938. Henry went back to Bololo the following year, staying alone until the field had to be vacated in 1942. Most missionaries left earlier. Remnants of the work came under Mennonite Brethren mission auspices in 1943. Henry and Anna Bartsch and their four children made their home on a small farm in Yarrow, B.C., until 1966. Anna Bartsch lives in Clearbrook, B.C., in 1988. She published their story, *Die verborgene Hand*, in 1982.   HK

J. B. Toews, *Mennonite Brethren Church in Zaire* (Fresno: MB Board of Christian Literature, 1978), 57-70, 229, index; *Menn. Bib.*, nos. 15477, 15482-83.

Basel, Switzerland (ME I:241). The results of recent research on 16th-c. Anabaptism in the Basel area might be summarized as follows: (1) While Zürich clearly remains the primary center of Swiss Brethren origin, we can no longer speak of the Basel area as marginal to the early movement. During the period of the °Schleitheim Confession, ca. 1526-1529, Basel was certainly a center, if not *the* center, of the new Swiss Brethren movement. (2) The continuity between late medieval and Reformation movements, as well as between pre-Reformation folk piety and Anabaptism is greater than has generally been assumed. (3) In the same way there is a close relationship between incipient Anabaptism and radi-cal Reformation social unrest in the rural hinterlands, particularly in relation to latant anticlericalism, iconoclasm, and the common people's resistance to paying the °tithe. (4) Anabaptist separatism was not due only to external pressures, but also to a mixture of other motives—the survival impulse, the result of °Bible study, and the Anabaptists' concern for °discipleship as evidence of faith. Thus Anabaptist separatism was ultimately the consequence of an understanding of the church as a body of faithful followers of Jesus.   HJeck

Hanspeter Jecker, *Die Basler Täufer: Studien zur Vor- und Frühgeschichte*, special printing from *Basler Zeitschrift für Geschichte und Altertumskunde*, 80 (Basel, 1980); Markus Mattmueller, "Die Basler Täufer. Überblick über den Stand der Forschung," *Zwingliana*, 12, no. 7 (Zürich, 1967), 510-21.

Batea Colony, La. See Zacatecas Colonies.

Bauman, Ella Garber (b. May 31, 1895), was born in Versailles, Mo., to Daniel A. and Anna D. Loganbill Garber, a Mennonite farming family. Ella graduated from Bluffton College in 1919. She attended the U. of Missouri Medical School and received her degree from Women's Medical College in Pennsylvania in 1924. She married Harvey R. Bauman in 1924. In 1925 they sailed to India and together established the first General Conference Mennonite hospital in °Champa, Madhya Pradesh. The Baumans had five children: Kenneth, Clara Ann Stauffer, Albert, Har-

vella Stutzman, and Elizabeth Shelly. Ella served as Woodstock School doctor for an interim. During the 1947 uprising in India, Ella was called to work at a refugee camp near New Delhi. After retirement she and her husband were physicians at camp Men-O-Lan in Pennsylvania (1963-76). They also worked in a cancer clinic in Allentown, Pa., and later served as interim chaplains at Mennonite Hospital, Bloomington, Ill.   MEB

Juhnke, *Mission* (1979), 33, 252, 223.

Bauman, Harvey Rosenberger (Feb. 26, 1897–Oct. 4, 1970), was born to farming parents, Samuel W. and Clara Rosenberger Bauman in Congo, Pa. He graduated from Bluffton College, (1919) and from Jefferson Medical School, Philadelphia (1923). On June 11, 1924, he married Ella Garber, also a physician. They served as medical missionaries in India for 35 years (1925-1961). Harvey and Ella founded the Christian Hospital in °Champa, Madhya Pradesh, India; he was its medical superintendent. He was medical superintendent of the Bethesda Leprosy Hospital, Champa, India, from 1947-53. Harvey was secretary and treasurer of the General Conference Mennonite Mission in India for the 35 years he worked there. He also served as pastor, deacon, and Sunday School teacher, and supervised building and maintenance. In his medical work he trained compounders, nurses, and paramedics. Harvey served on the board of Woodstock School, Mussoorie, Utter Pradesh, where his five children attended boarding school.   MEB

Juhnke, *Mission* (1979), 33, 252, 223.

Bauman, Kenneth Garber (Apr. 6, 1926–Dec. 21, 1986), was born in Champa, Madhya Pradesh, India, to Harvey R. and Ella (Garber) Bauman. He was a graduate of Bluffton College and Mennonite Biblical Seminary (1953), having also studied at °New York Biblical (Theological) Seminary. He graduated with the MTh degree from Princeton Theological Seminary in 1962. He and Mary Gallagher were married in 1950. He was the father of five children.

In 1954 the Baumans went to India, where they served for 18 years under the Commission on Overseas Mission (GCM), first at Korba, where he worked as Bible teacher and church planter (1954-61), then at Union Biblical Seminary, Yavatmal, teaching primarily in homiletics and pastoral care. From 1968 to 1972 he also served as president of the seminary.

During their 1972 leave in North America, Bauman was invited to serve as senior pastor of the First Mennonite Church, Berne, Ind., and accepted the call, serving from 1973 until his death. He was widely known for his dynamic, Bible-centered preaching and his concern for evangelism. In July 1986 he was elected president of the General Conference Mennonite Church. He had served 12 years on the General Board of the conference and on the board of trustees of Bluffton College (1974-83). His catechism *Invitation to Life* (1982) has found wide use in many congregations. His hobbies were playing violin, classical music, collecting stamps, and bird watching.   CJD

MWR (Dec. 25, 1986), 1; *Mennonite* (Jan. 27, 1987), 44-45.

Bayanganga Samuele was born in the early 1920s in Banga Ibundula among the Bashilele people in western Kasai Province of what later became Zaire. His people were headhunters, primitive, fearless, and hostile to outsiders. Samuele was an early convert to Christianity from missionary work of the °°Congo Inland Mission. He was permanently disowned by his people after he renounced many of his traditional customs which were incompatible with Christianity. He married and reared his family in Muanza Mukala, the village of a neighboring tribe.

Bayanganga was the first Mennonite church leader to emerge from the Bashilele people. With a minimum of formal Bible education, he served first as as resident village evangelist and then as an overseer of a cluster of village churches. He remained faithful in his ministry until his death in the early 1970s.   LKei

Bayern (Bavaria) Federal State, Germany (ME I:251). In 1987 Bavarian Mennonites were represented in eight congregations whose numbers range from 28 to 137; total membership was 521.

Members are scattered widely. Some, who live too far away to attend Mennonite worship regularly, worship with other denominations. A number of people take part in the life of a Mennonite congregation while retaining membership in other churches. Five congregations rent facilities in which to worship. One group, which has owned a meeting-house since 1841, built a youth retreat center nearby in 1967. Two congregations built their own facilities in 1965 and 1982 respectively. Members also gather in homes for small-group meetings.

There is a clear tendency toward team ministry; 20 lay ministers serve in the congregations, four churches have salaried part-time pastors also. The traditional mode of baptism is by pouring, although some congregations are willing to perform °immersion upon request. Once a year the Bavarian Mennonites gather for a one-day conference.   RWB

See also Vereinigung bayerischen Mennonitengemeinden.

Beachy Amish Mennonite Fellowship (ME I: 254) is composed of about 100 congregations located in 23 states and six countries in the Americas. Its name is taken from that of Bishop Moses M. °Beachy (1874-1946) of Salisbury, Pa. (Somerset Co.). Beachy served as the Old Order Amish bishop from 1916 until 1927, and maintained a moderate position on the application of the *Meidung* (°°avoidance), especially in regard to those transferring to the neighboring °Conservative (Amish) Mennonite congregation, which had been Old Order Amish until 1895. About one-half of the congregation, which favored application of the *Streng-Meidung* (strict banning), withdrew from Beachy's bishop district in June 1927. Also in the mid-1920s, Bishop John A. °Stoltzfus of Lancaster Co., Pa., was leading what came to be known as the Weavertown Amish Mennonite Church. The roots of this congregation grew out of disagreements over the use of the *Streng-Meidung* as applied to Moses Hartz, Sr., in the 1890s. These two congregations were the leaders of the emerging

Beachy Amish Fellowship for nearly three decades.

Growth prior to 1947 was slow, but the tempo increased during the 1950s. By 1959 the three-decade period of consolidation was completed with the inclusion of several key congregations, including Oak Grove of Virginia, Woodlawn of Indiana, Center in Kansas, and Bethel in Ohio. These were pivotal and influential congregations within the fellowship in regard to missions, language, and spiritual vitality and expression. By 1959 the 27 congregations were located in 11 states and Ontario and included a membership of 2,446. Growth of these churches during the second 30-year period has been far greater than the first 20 years. Membership in 1987 stands at 6,530.

The Beachy Amish were influenced by the spiritual awakening in the larger Mennonite Church that followed World War II as it filtered into Beachy and Old Order Amish circles. Out of this awakening developed the Amish Mission Interests Committee (MIC). Russell Maniaci, a former Roman Catholic of Detroit, had initiated several national meetings of Amish in the interest of missions. The emerging Mission Interests Committee came under the control of the Beachy Amish by 1959. The committee has concentrated on projects within the United States and Ontario. These included °Indian schools and missions in Ontario, and supervision of Hillcrest Home in Arkansas, Faith Mission Home in Virginia, and Fellowship Haven in Washington, D.C. The latter two are joint projects with Amish Mennonite Aid.

Amish Mennonite Aid (AMA) resulted from interest in °relief work, especially to °refugees in West Berlin. Minister Joseph Roth had served in Europe under Mennonite Central Committee and the Conservative Mennonite Board of Missions. Roth urged the formation of an organization by which Beachy Amish young people could serve under Beachy Amish supervision. Bishops John A. Stoltzfus and Eli D. Tice were instrumental in calling the historic meeting in 1955 at the Weavertown Amish Mennonite church, during which AMA was organized. Jacob J. Hershberger was the first secretary-treasurer, Norman Beachy was chairman, and Elam Kauffman was the board's third member.

Simon Schrock, who succeeded Roth, led in the dedication of Friedensheim, a refugee center in Berlin. Lewis Overholt was the first minister ordained (1963) by the Amish for work on a foreign field, which was Friedensheim. The Berlin Wall (1961) sealed off the flight of refugees and changed the emphasis from relief to church planting. The Fellowship at Friedensheim became autonomous in 1977, thus closing AMA work in Berlin.

Hurricane Hattie devastated the coastal region of Belize in 1961. The initial Beachy Amish response to the cleanup and assistance of the homeless led to continued involvement in rebuilding. In addition, it led to a gradual shift from relief work to mission work. Six Beachy Amish congregations now dot the countryside of Belize.

The Beachy Amish were also interested in putting to use the agricultural skills of their young people. This led to involvement in El Salvador in 1962. The agricultural projects gave way to more direct mission and community work. The three congregations and the out-stations have suffered during the internal strife in the country, but there have been Beachy workers in the country during the troubled years, notably the Eli Glick family. An Old Order Amish colony in Honduras, located in Guaimaca, has been affiliated with Beachy Amish and Fellowship Churches since the late 1970s (°Honduras).

The Paul Eichorn family pioneered the °Luz y Esperanza Colony (Light and Hope) in Paraguay in 1967. The location was a tract of land of 5,300 acres (2,147 hectares), which they hoped could be divided among 25 familes. Plans were for the church and colony to be one. Two congregations have resulted—Light and Hope and Florida. In 1970 the Light and Hope Clinic was constructed and is operated by AMA. Land transfer in the colony has proven a problem, since if not handled properly, it might lead to the loss of military exemption for the Beachy Amish who came to Paraguay from the United States. Christians born in Paraguay who join the Beachy Church are not granted such privileges. Another effort at evangelization by colonization was led by minister Sanford Yoder and several families who pioneered the settlement in Costa Rica in 1968. There were six Beachy Amish congregations in Costa Rica by 1987.

Motorized vehicles, electricity, telephones, and use of meetinghouses have characterized Beachy Amish Mennonite churches since 1930. The names *Amish* and *Mennonite* deserve to be part of the full name, since both influences are visible. Amish influence is reflected in organizational structure, the strong congregationalism, the small size of the congregations, the °*Ordnung* (discipline), and the sharing of ministry leadership by several men (plural ministry). Mennonite influence is evident in °°Sunday schools, preaching in each Sunday morning service, midweek Bible studies, °summer Bible schools, °°revival meetings, and winter Bible schools (°Bible conferences). All except about six of the congregations have made the transition from German to English as the language used during public worship services.

The Beachy Amish subscribe to and use the °°Dordrecht Confession. Except in rare cases, ministers are selected by use of the °°lot. The ideal "bench" (ministerial team) is composed of a bishop, one or two ministers, and a deacon in each congregation. The educational level of ministers is the same as that of the congregations they lead, with very few ministers pursuing higher education.

Beachy Amish publishing falls into two periods. The first, from 1955-69, involved the °°*Herold der Wahrheit*, an independent Amish publication. Ervin N. Hershberger, Beachy Amish, served as editor of the English part which was devoted to Beachy Amish interests. In 1970 *Calvary Messenger* appeared, designed to meet more adequately the needs of the Beachy constituency, including youth and children. Ervin N. Hershberger has served as editor since 1970. It is a monthly publication of about 25 pages and is under the supervision of Calvary Publications, Inc., incorporated in the state of Ohio.

Calvary Bible School at Calico Rock, Ark., opened for the first term in 1970 with two three-week terms. By 1975 a pattern of four three-week terms

was introduced and has been continued. The Bethel Springs property was purchased in 1973 and considerable new construction and renovation has taken place. Hundreds of students each year drive thousands of miles to study under a wide range of Beachy Amish ministers who serve as faculty members. Principals have been Lester Hershberger (1970), William Wagler (1971-80), and Ervin N. Hershberger (1981-). The school was an attempt by Beachy leaders to provide Bible school training for their own young people, rather than have them attend other schools.

Ministers' meetings have been held annually since 1964. The annual youth meetings have continued since 1953. In 1962 the youth meetings were divided into an eastern and a western section because of the large numbers of young people attending. Among the groups on the Amish-Mennonite spectrum, the Beachy Amish rank among the strongest supporters of Christian elementary schools, with a 90 percent participation. They have been discouraging higher education.

Amish Mennonite Aid and Mission Interests Committee are the official Beachy mission and service organizations. In the late 1970s and early 1980s a growing number of parachurch organizations drew off increasing amounts of funds and personnel from the Beachy churches. A number of these organizations are operated or headed by Beachy Amish persons.

The Beachy Amish churches are appropriately called a fellowship. They have deliberately avoided the degree of centralization that they associate with a conference. They are organized well enough to function, and yet at the same time, preserve the congregationalism they value so highly.   ESY

Elmer S. Yoder, *The Beachy Amish Mennonite Fellowship Churches* (Hartville, Ohio: Diakonia Ministries, 1987); Alvin J. Beachy, "The Rise and Development of the Beachy Amish" *MQR*, 29 (1955), 118-40; *MWH* (1978), 366-69; *MWH* (1984), 100, 136; *MC Yearbook* (1986-87), 168-74.

Beachy, Moses M. (Dec. 3, 1874–July 7, 1946), was born near Salisbury, Pa., and was a lifelong resident of that community. His father, two brothers, and two sons were Amish ministers. Moses was ordained minister (May 19, 1912) and bishop (Oct. 1, 1916) in the Old Order Amish church. He and Lucy S. Miller were married Feb. 17, 1895, and became the parents of 14 children. Lucy died Nov. 25, 1927. Moses married Mary E. Hershberger on Nov. 12, 1928.

Meidung (°°avoidance of members under °discipline) was an issue in Beachy's congregation, and Moses held a moderate position. After a decade of tension, about one-half of his congregation, calling for stricter application of the *Meidung*, withdrew in June 1927. Within two years Beachy's congregation approved the use of °automobiles, electricity, and telephones. Moses Beachy and Bishop John A. °Stoltzfus of Lancaster, Co., Pa., began fraternal visits in 1929, and their two congregations became the leaders of the emerging °Beachy Amish Mennonite Fellowship.

Moses was compassionate and ready to respond to requests for assistance from scattered congregations. He helped organize numerous "Beachy" congregations within a radius of 500 miles of his home. His influence and travels gave impetus to the use of the name "Beachy Church."

At the time of his death at age 71, Moses had served the Beachy Amish Mennonites 19 years. One indication of his stature among ministers was the presence of 23 Beachy ministers at his funeral.   ESY

Elmer S. Yoder, *The Beachy Amish Mennonite Fellowship Churches* (Hartville, Ohio: Diakonia Ministries, 1987), 253-54, 311-12, 360-67.

Beare, George Henry, and Swartzendruber, Ida May. George H. Beare, minister, and missionary to India under the Mennonite Board of Missions (MC), was born Nov. 25, 1898, in North Platte, Nebr., the youngest of four sons born to Robert and Ellen (Jay) Beare.

While still very young, George moved with his parents to Modesto, Cal., where the family related to the Free Methodist Church. George did not complete high school, but was an avid reader and Bible student. In 1933 he studied as a Bible student at Hesston College. In 1920 he was baptized and became a member of the Los Angeles Mennonite Church. On July 20, 1920, he married Ida May Swartzendruber, daughter of Benjamin P. and Mary (Zimmerman) Swartzendruber of Upland, Cal., who operated a citrus farm. George and Ida had two daughters: Allene (b. 1921) and Evelyn (b. 1924).

The Beares served as missionaries in India from 1926 to 1951. At Balodgahan George served as *malguzzar* (administrator of the mission-owned village). Ida was in charge of the widows' home and babyfold. George also served as field secretary of the American Mennonite Mission for several terms, was a regular member of the mission's Managing Committee, and directed the evangelistic work of Balodgahan station. In 1932 he served as pastor of the Bethel Mennonite congregation at Balodgahan. In 1944 he was sent by the mission board to assist Mennonite Central Committee on a special four-month relief assignment in Calcutta.

From 1955 to 1956 George served as field representative for Hesston College. He was then pastor of Seventh Street Mennonite Church, Upland, Cal. (1956-64). He was also interim pastor at Faith Mennonite Church, Downey, Cal., and Plainview Mennonite Church, Shedd, Ore. In 1973 the Beares moved to Albany Retirement Village, Albany, Ore. where they remained until death.

As an administrator George was forthright and utterly frank, and at times was misunderstood, especially by the Asian mind. As a minister of the good news he believed with intensity in the transforming power of the gospel of Christ for all people and sought to see the simplest person become a responsible creature in Jesus Christ.   JAF

Magdalene Swartzendruber and Keith and Mary Brenneman, *Family Record of Peter Swartzendruber and Barbara Hochstetler and their Descendants* (Wellman, Iowa, 1977); obituary of Ida Beare in the *Albany* [Ore.] *Democratic Herald* (Jan. 28, 1988); Esther Rose Graber, "MBM Missionary Directory" (1984); Annual AMM Misson Report, 1932, p. 139.

Becker, Abraham J. (Feb. 25, 1872–Jan. 15, 1953), a Mennonite Brethren missionary to the Commanche people, was born in Russia to Jacob P. and Margaretha Wiens Becker. His public school education was in Hillsboro, Ks. He attended the *Vereins Schule* in Buhler, Ks.; McPherson College, Ks.; and Moody Bible Institute. He married Magdalena Hergert in Fairview, Okla., in 1897. They had six children. Magdalena died in 1938. He married Katharina Poetker in 1941. In 1901 Abraham and Magdalena went to work at the Post Oak mission in Indiahoma, Okla. This was the first Mennonite Brethren Indian mission. Abraham also began evangelistic work with Hispanic people in Commanche Co., Okla. During his 50 years with the mission he interceded with government agencies, always trying to safeguard Indian interests and improve living conditions for the Indians.   LDe

Who's Who Mennonites (1943), 20; A. E. Janzen, "Tribute to Missionary Abraham J. Becker," *Chr. Leader*, 17 (Feb. 1, 1953), 1, 5, 6; A. J. Becker, "Post Oak Mission," MLA (North Newton); *Menn. Bib. II*, p. 419.

Becker, Magdalena Hergert (1878-1938), a pioneer missionary, with her husband, Abraham, spent 37 years working for the Mennonite Brethren Mission board at the Post Oak Mission near Indiahoma, Okla. (1901-38). For 28 years she served half-time as a United States Government field matron to the people. The job of field matron involved record-keeping of land ownership, rent contracts with white farmers, government allotments, and all Department of Interior transactions with Indians. Magdalena was known to the Comanche as the "kind white mother." She became a skilled mediator in family disputes among the Comanches. She taught first aid and hygiene, nursed the sick, and organized sewing, cooking, and flower clubs among the women. The concern she and her husband showed for people extended to the Hispanic community in Lawton, Okla., resulting in the establishment of a church. The Beckers had six children.   LDe

K. F. Wiebe, ed., *Women Among the Brethren*, (1979), 95-104; *Menn. Bib. II*, p. 419.

Behrends, Ernst (May 19, 1891–1982), was a North German writer whose major work, a series of six historical novels titled collectively *Das Volk der Wanderschaft*, deals with the history of the "peaceful" Anabaptists. Earlier literary treatments and literary research on Anabaptists had dealt almost exclusively with the more violent Anabaptists at Münster.

Behrends was a high school teacher in Mölln from 1911 to 1939, with the exception of his brief military service, cut short by a serious head wound. Even though he lived in North Germany close to the "Menno-Kate" (Menno Simons cottage) near Oldesloe, he did not know about the "peaceful" Mennonites until 1929, when 6,000 Russo-Germans (including 4,000 Menonites) were housed in a refugee camp in Mölln. His contact with a type of Christianity which rejected force and revenge (*Gewalt und Rache*) impressed him to such an extent that he spent 1950 to 1966 studying and giving literary shape to Mennonite history, tracing the movement of Mennonites from Holland to North Germany, then to Prussia, later to Russia, then to Germany (Mölln in particular), and from there to North and South America.

The resulting sequence of six novels deals with

the following periods of history: *Der Ketzerbischof* (The Heretic Bishop, 1525-1561); *Die Rose von Wüstenfelde* (The Rose of Wüstenfelde, 1618-1648); *Der rote Tulipan* (The Red Tulip, 1710-1713); *Stromaufwärts* (Upstream, 1786-1806); *Der Steppenhengst* (The Prairie Stallion, 1848-1906); and *Wir trotzen dem Irrlicht* (We Spite the False Light, 1929-1935, 1948-1961). The six novels were published between 1966 and 1977 (details under °literature, Mennonites in).

Behrends published at least five additional novels, four short stories, nine books of poetry, and many articles (including several about Mennonites). The Mennonite Library and Archives in North Newton, Ks., has the most complete collection of his works, including typed manuscripts of several of his novels.　　　　　　　　　　　　　　HMF

Obituary in *Menn. Geschbl.*, 39, n.F. 34 (1982), 96-105. For a list of Behrends' writings, manuscripts, and reviews of his works see Herta Marie Funk, "Die religiöse Weltanschauung in Ernst Behrends Romanreihe, *Das Volk der Wanderschaft*," (PhD diss., University of Kansas, 1982). In addition see Harry Loewen, "Themes and Symbols in the 'Mennonite' Novels of Ernst Behrends," *Menn. Life*, 37, no. 1 (1982), 14-18.

Belgium (ME I:270). In Oct. 1950, five years of Mennonite Relief Committee efforts ended and mission work was begun by David and Wilma Shank under the Belgium Mennonite Mission of Mennonite Board of Missions (MC).

The first Mennonite congregation was organized in Brussels in 1953 under the leadership of Belgian evangelist Jules Lambotte, Jr. A second congregation emerged in 1955 in Rixensart. In 1957, Mauro Sbolgi began a ministry among Italian and Spanish miners near Charleroi that led to the creation of the Brussels Spanish-speaking congregation in the early 1960s. In 1960, Jules Lambotte founded Lighthouse Publications, located in Flavion since 1965.

In addition to personnel and financial involvement in these efforts, Mennonites administered the Home of Hope orphanage in Ohain during the 1950s and helped establish the Protestant Social Center in Brussels in the early 1960s. Vasil Magal of La Louvière has produced radio programs for broadcast to Russia through Mennonite Board of Missions Media Ministries since 1958.

Mennonite Central Committee volunteers served in Brussels from 1969 to 1983 in the Foyer International David Livingstone, directed from 1973 to 1979 by Robert and Wilda Otto. Other Mennonite Board of Missions workers in 1987 were Stephen and Jean Gerber Shank, and Robert and Sylvia Shirk Charles. The Missions Interests Committee of the Beachy Amish Mennonite Fellowship began work in Poperinge late in 1986.　　　　　　　　　　　RC

David A. Shank, "Discovering the Strategy of the Spirit," in *Being God's Missionary Community* (Elkhart, Ind.: MBM, 1975), 23-30; Wilma Shank, "A Voice for the Voiceless," *Miss. Focus*, 8, no. 1 (March 1980), 9-10; *Annual Reports of Mennonite Board of Missions* (1951ff.); *MWH* (1978), 288-89; *MWH* (1984), 113; Jean Séguy, *Les Assemblées Anabaptistes-Mennonites de France* (Paris: Mouton, 1977), 661-63.

See also Conseil Mennonite Belge.

Believers Church is a term that emerged after 1955 to define those religious groups with direct or indirect foundation in the Radical Reformation (ME IV:242). The term was evidently coined by the German sociologist of religion Max Weber (1864-1920) to describe radical Protestants who distanced themselves from the state-sponsored church establishments or other socially dominant ecclesial bodies. Some writers have used the phrases "Free Churches," "Nonconformists," or "Dissenters" to characterize radical Protestantism, thus emphasizing the determination of its adherents to maintain their religious beliefs independent from government control. Increasingly, however, others are preferring *believers church* as a more precise designation, pointing out that in the United States and some other nations, all religious bodies are technically free churches, because of the practice of separation of church and state.

Characteristics of believers churches are held to include: scriptural (especially New Testament) °authority; °discipleship to Christ as Lord; regenerate °church membership; covenant of voluntarily-gathered believers; adult °baptism (often by immersion); separation from the world (°nonconformity); °mutual aid and Christian °service; a nonorganizational view of church unity. Among the denominational families considering themselves largely within this tradition are: Baptists, Brethren, Christian Church (Disciples of Christ), Churches of Christ, Churches of God, Friends, Mennonites, Pentecostals, and others.

An early study conference on the concept was sponsored by the General Conference Mennonite Church in August 1955 in Chicago, Ill. A large and carefully planned conference at the Southern Baptist Theological Seminary, Louisville, Ky., in June 1967, was influential in making the term known in churchly and academic circles. Leading scholars, church executives, and pastors attended the conference, the theme of which was "The Concept of the Believers Church"; it was extensively reported in the church press. The conference proceedings were published in a widely used volume edited by the conference organizer, James Leo Garrett, Jr.

The momentum created by the Louisville conference led to a series of further meetings, called at the initiatives of denominations and institutions. A loosely organized Committee of Continuing Conversations, coordinated by John Howard Yoder and D. F. Durnbaugh, offered guidance to these successive independent initiatives during the planning processes. The next conference was held in Chicago in June and July 1970, sponsored by Chicago Theological Seminary (United Church of Christ); its themes were Christian witness and lifestyles. In May 1972 the Laurelville Mennonite Church Center, Mount Pleasant, Pa., convened a conference for lay members to familiarize them with the concept of the believers church. Pepperdine College (Churches of Christ) in Malibu, Cal., held the next in the informal series in June 1975, with the focus on °restitution of apostolic Christianity.

Canadian Baptists and Mennonites sponsored an elaborately planned and well attended conference in Winnipeg in May 1978. Its proceedings were published in 1979, accompanied by a study guide. The focus of the Canadian meeting was the relevance of the believers church concept to the religious situation in Canada. Bluffton College (General Conference Mennonite) organized the next meeting in October 1980, to investigate the Christology of the believers churches. This was followed by a conference at Anderson, Ind. (Church of God), in June 1984, at which participants reacted to the ecumenical document on "Baptism, Eucharist, and Ministry (Faith and Order Commission of the World Council of Churches, 1982), with particular attention to the issue of baptism. These proceedings were also published. An eighth conference, on ministry in believers church perspective, was held in September 1987 at Bethany Theological Seminary, Oak Brook, Ill. (Church of the Brethren).

Mennonites have been at the center of this series of meetings. One of the initiators of the series was Johannes A. Oosterbaan, professor of the Amsterdam Mennonite Theological Seminary. As a result of his ecumenical involvements with the World Council of Churches, Oosterbaan was convinced that descendants of the Radical Reformation needed to be aware of their common heritage in order to enter the ecumenical dialogue. Following the 1963 meeting of the Faith and Order Commission in Montreal, he gathered support for his vision in conversations with colleagues in Canada and the United States. This was an immediate catalyst for the landmark Louisville conference in 1967. Another precipitant was a meeting of representatives of Mennonites, Friends, and Brethren (°historic peace churches) held at Richmond, Ind., in June 1964, the immediate forerunner of the Louisville meeting of 1967. Franklin H. Littell, the Methodist author of *The Anabaptist View of the Church* (1952, 1958, 1964) and *The Free Church* (1957), was a leading participant in both the Richmond and Louisville gatherings; in many speeches and articles he had delineated the significance of the "Left Wing" of the Reformation for modern church life. John Howard Yoder has provided incisive theological leadership in shaping the conferences and in delivering major papers at them.

Mennonites from several branches have found the concept of the believers churches helpful in providing self-understanding. They have used it as an organizing principle for curricula or courses in several academic institutions (Associated Mennonite Biblical Seminaries, Goshen College, Eastern Mennonite College, Bluffton College), and have used the term as a theological basis for °Christian education materials (Foundation Series) and a series of Bible commentaries. Other educational institutions have also found the concept useful as a theme for course offerings.

Some Mennonite writers have pointed out that although the defining characteristics of the believers church correspond with Mennonite self-understandings and actual practice in many cases, there are aspects of Mennonite history which do not fit well at all. Notable here are the experiences of Mennonite colonies in the Ukraine and in Latin America. Also, those Mennonites in northern Germany and The Netherlands who became increasingly urbanized and acculturated in the 19th and 20th c. fail to see their churches best interpreted by this phrase.

Related to the constituency of the believers churches is the work of the North American Committee for the Documentation of Free Church Origins (NACDFCO). It was initiated in 1963 (constituted in 1966 with bylaws) at the suggestion of the Täuferakten-Kommission of Germany to further that body's work of publishing sources of Anabaptism. Leading figures in the work of the NACDFCO were George H. Williams and Franklin H. Littell; Cornelius Krahn was the first executive secretary, succeeded in 1971 by Walter Klaassen. The ambitious plans of the original committee were never realized, although its work did result in several publications. The never-completed series of sources in translation, Documents in Free Church History Series, edited by Williams and Littell, resulted in two volumes: D. F. Durnbaugh, ed., *Every Need Supplied* (1974), on mutual aid and Christian community; and Lowell H. Zuck, ed., *Christianity and Revolution* (1975). A volume compiled by Clyde L. Manschreck on religious liberty was never published and a fourth in the series, titled *Womanhood in Radical Protestantism*, ed. Joyce L. Irwin, was published independently in 1979. The series Classics of the Radical Reformation (Institute of Mennonite Studies and Herald Press, 1973ff.) was inspired in part by the committee. In 1973 NACDFCO participants agreed to meet more informally as a fellowship of historians.   DFD

Donald F. Durnbaugh, *The Believers' Church: The History and Character of Radical Protestantism* (New York: Macmillan Co., 1968, 1970, reprinted Scottdale, 1985); Franklin H. Littell, *The Free Church: The Significance of the Left Wing of the Reformation for Modern American Protestantism* (Boston: Starr King Press, 1957); idem, "The Historic Free Church Defined," *Brethren Life and Thought*, 9 (Autumn 1964), 78-90; Gunnar Westin, *The Free Church Through the Ages* (Nashville: Broadman Press, 1958); J. Gordon Melton, *Encyclopedia of American Religions*, 2nd ed. (Detroit: Gale Research Co. 1987), 47-67; James Leo Garrett, Jr., *The Concept of the Believers' Church* (Scottdale, 1969); *Chicago Theological Register*, 60 (Sept. 1970), 1-59; *GH* (June 20, 1972), 535-36; *J. of the American Academy of Religion*, 44 (Mar. 1976), 7-113; Jarold K. Zeman and Walter Klaassen, eds., *The Believers' Church in Canada* (Waterloo, Ontario: Baptist Federation of Canada and Mennonite Central Committee Canada, 1979); J. Denny Weaver, "A Believers' Church Christology," *MQR*, 77 (1983), 112-31 [with footnote references to places of publication of conference papers]; Merle D. Strege, ed., *Baptism and Church: A Believers' Church Vision* (Grand Rapids: Sagamore Books, 1986); *Menn. Bib. II*, p. 537.

Belize (ME IV:1094). In this relatively small country with its wide range of Latin-American, African, European, and Asian cultures, it is fitting that the Mennonites appear on the scene in many phases as they make up four percent of the total population, the highest percentage of any country in which Mennonites live. Total Mennonite membership in Belize in 1987 was 2,236 in 37 congregations.

The general public considers the conservative attitude of the Mennonites unnecessarily backward because they shun so many conveniences in life. On the other hand the non-Mennonite people envy the Mennonites, noticing how they receive preference among the elite and from financial institutions. The government's agricultural ministry turns to the Mennonites for advice on such subjects as issuing importation licenses for agricultural products. This is logical because there are no other statistics as dependable as those of the Mennonites on food production. The government's dependence on Mennonite data does not always meet with the approval of the local merchants.

Mennonites are well recognized for their skill in carpentry and mechanics and for their prompt and dependable service in these areas. Mennonites have also developed service projects for needy people in the larger community. This work includes preparation of land for planting and, sometimes, machine harvesting. At other places, small, simple structures have been erected as modest living quarters for workers at these projects. Corn and beans have been supplied to distribution centers to help the most needy. Eggs have been supplied free for years to the government hospital in Belize City and some to the Cayo Hospital. In some instances money was loaned toward a common cause so that a tractor or other implement could be supplied to a group of native Belizian farmers. These farmers are expected to pay for the machines on easy terms.

Recently a government official asked one of the more responsible brothers for the secret of our success in agriculture. "I don't know of any special secret," answered the brother, "but it might be striving to live according to scriptural standards, and 'Zusammenarbeit' (working together)."

Whenever Mennonites have to deal with the bureaucracy, e.g., when a Mennonite family wants to emigrate, they have to worry about corruption and thievery, although governmental security forces offer some protection. Most of the Mennonites, however, are making permanent commitments to life in Belize and are generally tolerant of conditions. Non-Mennonite laborers adjust easily to their Mennonite employers, and Mennonite businessmen adjust to the legal requirements for importing and exporting merchandise. Some Mennonites are considering joining national agricultural associations. Non-Mennonite missionaries from North America look to the Mennonites for financial support and are not disappointed.

Young Mennonite women tend to be more controlled and loyal to the Mennonite traditions. More young men than women marry outside the Mennonite community. Belizian parents seem to encourage their daughters to marry Mennonite men because of the economic and domestic stability evident in the Mennonite community. Most of the couples in the mixed marriages, however, do not join the Mennonite church.

Government officials are generally tolerant in their attitudes toward the Mennonites, even though the officials know that the Mennonites do not involve themselves in politics and are, therefore, neither threat nor asset to the officials' tenure. In general, the Mennonites have not adopted local culture, and some of the smaller, more conservative groups are quite isolated from the general population.   JBL

MWH (1978), 192-95; *MWH* (1984), 49-53; Hannah B. Lapp, *To Belize with Love* (Lawrenceville, Va.: Brunswick Pub. Co., 1986).

See also Belize Evangelical Mennonite Church; Blue Creek Colony; Caribbean Light and Truth; Central America; Evangelical Mennonite Mission Conference; Old Colony Mennonites; Pilgrim Fellowship Missions; Richmond Hill Colony; Shipyard Colony; Spanish Lookout Colony.

Belize Evangelical Mennonite Church. Belize is a small Central American country of approximately 150,000 people. Old Colony Mennonites first arrived in Belize in 1958. In 1988 they continue to live in colonies.

Outreach to the Old Colony Mennonites was begun in 1960 by Mennonite Central Committee. In 1963 this was transferred to Eastern Mennonite Board of Missions and Charities (MC). During this time and up to the mid-1970s, medical and agricultural work was carried out by missionaries in the Orange Walk District. As a result, outreach to the local Belizians began in place of continuing to help the colonies, which were now self-sufficient. Emphasis was placed on evangelism and church growth.

By 1973 the Belize Evangelical Mennonite Church General Church Council was established, consisting of pastors and deacons from each congregation. The church was incorporated in 1981. In 1987 the Belize Evangelical Mennonite Church had 14 congregations and approximately 400 members, worshiping in English, Spanish, and Garifuna (the language of an ethnic group descended from African slaves who intermarried with indigenous peoples), or often in a combination of two of these languages. All of these churches have Belizian pastors. A yearly countrywide conference helps to unify the congregations. Pastors also unite for leadership training.

Three missionary families working under the Eastern Board are serving the churches in leadership training in the districts of Orange Walk, Belize and Cayo, and Stann Creek. Approximately 40 pastors or potential leaders are involved in weekly Bible studies and leadership training courses as well as three or four regional seminars per year. In 1987 three of these leaders are also enrolled in SEMILLA, the Mennonite extension seminary for Central America (°Consulta Anabautista Menonita de Centroamericana).   RM

MWH (1978), 192-93; *MWH* (1984), 49; *MC Yearbook* (1988-89), 153.

Belleville, Pa., Old Order Amish Settlement (ME III:683) is located in Mifflin Co., in the picturesque Kishacoquillas Valley between the Jacks and Stone Mountain ranges of central Pennsylvania. Belleville lies in the central portion of the Big Valley and serves as one of the main shopping towns for the Amish community. Amish settlers moved into this area in the early 1790s from °Lancaster Co., Pa. The Mifflin Co. settlement figured largely in the western movement of the Amish. Mifflin, along with Somerset Co. (°Meyersdale), provided many settlers in the new communities in Ohio, Indiana, and Iowa.

The mobility of Mifflin Co. Amish can be attributed in part to strong personalities with settled convictions among its bishops and ministers. In 1986 there were at least 12 Amish-related groups springing from tensions and differences on such matters as the use of meetinghouses, mode of baptism, dress codes, °buggy tops, and *Meidung* (shunning, °°avoidance). Many older Amish communities have become extinct by moving on to Amish-Mennonite affiliations (°conservative Mennonites) or moving to another one of Pennsylvania's 40 Amish settlements. In 1986 the Belleville settlement had 12 church districts (congregations) with a total Amish population of about 2,000. Sociologists identify the Belleville community, with its many different Amish and Mennonite groups, as the largest single community of diverse expressions of Anabaptist culture found anywhere in North America.   SLY

Bender, Elizabeth Horsch (Feb. 7, 1895–Mar. 24, 1988), is best known to the world of scholarship for her editing and translating skills and for her studies of the Mennonites as found in German and American literature. She was born to John and Christine (Funck) Horsch, in Elkhart, Ind. She graduated from the Scottdale, Pa., high school in 1913. She attended Hesston College (Ks.) and Goshen College (1915-18, BA).

Elizabeth Horsch taught two years, 1918-20, at Eastern Mennonite School, Harrisonburg, Va., teaching Latin, Greek, Spanish, geometry, psychology, and physical education. During the year 1920-21 she taught at Hesston College. She set linotype for a year in Pittsburgh, after which she taught a year at the public high school in Johnstown, Pa. (1922-23). She married Harold S. Bender in 1923 (children: Mary Eleanor and Nancy Elizabeth). Bender taught at Goshen College most of the years from 1924 until her retirement in 1963. She taught German, but also Latin, English, and math (including analytic geometry and calculus). In 1943 she earned an MA in German literature at the U. of Minnesota. Her thesis was a study of "The Mennonites in German Literature."

Elizabeth Bender edited almost all of Harold S. Bender's published books and articles, from the 1920s to 1962. She was a master translator, able to translate from Dutch, French, Spanish, Latin, and German into English, and into German. In the 1950s she translated into English the whole of the then-published volumes of the *Mennonitishes Lexikon*. These 1,700 pages emerged as the core of the °*Mennonite Encyclopedia* (4 vols., 1955-59). As assistant editor, she also edited every *ME* article at every stage of the project. Bender was also a major office editor for the *Mennonite Quarterly Review*, 1927-85. From 1970 to 1985 she worked half-time for the Historical Committee of the Mennonite Church (MC), transcribing and translating German-language materials and editing manuscripts.   LG

Elizabeth Horsch, "The Quest of an Ideal," valedictory address, 1913, published in *Christian Monitor* (Sept. 1913); reprinted in *MHB*, (Jan. 1986); Rich, *Mennonite Women* (1983), 50-54; *MHB* (Jan. 1985), sp. issue for 90th birthday; see also the series of "Conversations with Elizabeth Bender" in *MHB* (Jan. and July 1985, Apr. and July 1986, Jan. 1987); *MQR*, 60 (July 1986), sp. issue; *Menn. Bib.* II: 420; Elizabeth Horsch Bender collection, MC Archives (Goshen).

Bender, Harold Stauffer (July 19, 1897–Sept. 21, 1962), was the leading worldwide Mennonite spirit in his time, ca. 1930-62. He remains best known for his essay, the "Anabaptist Vision" (1944)—a vision of faithful disciples, gathered in the name and spirit of the Christ of peace. This vision permeated Bender's life and thought throughout his lifetime (see G. F. Hershberger, ed., *The Recovery of the Anabaptist Vision*, Scottdale, 1957).

Bender was born in Elkhart, Ind., to George Lewis and Elsie (Kolb) Bender. At the time, Elkhart was at the hub of the Mennonite Church (MC), thanks to John F. °°Funk's *Herald of Truth* and the other programs in °publishing, °relief work, °mission work, °mutual aid, and °education that developed there in the 1880s and 1890s.

Bender graduated from Elkhart High School (1914), Goshen College (BA, 1918), Garrett Biblical Institute (BD, 1922), Princeton Theological Seminary (ThM, 1923), Princeton U. (MA, 1923), and the U. of Heidelberg (ThD, 1935). He attended the U. of Tübingen, 1923-24. In 1923 he married Elizabeth Barbara Horsch; their children were Mary Eleanor (1927) and Nancy Elizabeth (1933).

Bender taught one year at the Thorntown, Ind., high school (1916-17) and two years at Hesston College (1918-20). From 1924 to 1962 he was professor at Goshen College in church history, Bible, and sociology. He was dean of Goshen College, 1931-44, and dean of Goshen College Biblical Seminary, 1944-62.

Bender's birth coincided with the Mennonite °renaissance or awakening of the 1880s and 1890s, which was, in part, the result of a shift in language from German to English. Mennonites during this era began accepting much within their new English-speaking, North American culture, including higher education and a renewed interest in missions, at home and abroad. Bender's own interest in education should be understood in this light.

Bender's formative years, on the other hand, came during the time of a new era of Mennonite Church (MC) leaders who attempted to establish a new Mennonite orthodoxy, in doctrine and °dress, with a certain codification of both, and imbued to some degree by °Fundamentalism. Daniel °Kauffman was the major leader at the time (ca. 1898-1930). His *Manual of Bible Doctrines* (1898, 1914, 1929) became the definitive word for many within the church at that time.

The significance of Bender may be seen in part in terms of how he dealt with these new trends, both Fundamentalist and °Liberal, within the church. Bender chose a route and approach to vision that differed from both. It stood in contrast to the Kauffman view of doctrine and dress, not so much in criticizing it directly, but rather by circumventing it. Bender chose to express the Christian faith through the historical process and attempted to rediscover the Anabaptist vision of biblical faith and life. Bender believed he was not creating a new theology but was returning to and recovering an old faith: that of his own forebears. In 1927 he created a journal, the *Mennonite Quarterly Review* (*MQR*), and in 1929 he founded a scholarly series, Studies in Anabaptist and Mennonite History, writing the first volume himself (*Two Centuries of American Mennonite Literature*). A dissertation on Conrad Grebel, one of the founders of Anabaptism (1935, published 1950); a biography of Menno Simons (1936); *Menno Origins in Europe* (1942); "The Anabaptist Vision" (1944); the *Mennonite Encyclopedia* (4 vols., 1955-59); *Biblical Revelation and Inspiration* (1959); and *These Are My People* (1962), indicate the scope of his efforts to bring about a return to the Anabaptist faith as he understood it. Throughout all these decades he edited the *MQR* and published many shorter essays therein, in other scholarly journals, and in church papers.

Bender's leadership in the life of the Mennonite Church (MC), worldwide Mennonitism, and in ecumenical contacts was evident, in part, through the long list of committees and organizations in which he was active (see bibliographical references for details). Central in Bender's vision, on all levels of interaction, was his concern for the way of °peace and °love as being integral to the path Christians should take.   LG

MQR, 38 (Apr. 1964), sp. memorial issue; G. F. Hershberger, "Harold S. Bender," in *A Cloud of Witnesses*, ed., J. C. Wenger (Harrisonburg, Va: EMC, 1981); *GH* (Sept. 15, 1987), 649-54; H. S. Bender, "The Anabaptist Vision," *Church History*, 13 (Mar. 1944), 3-24, reprinted in *MQR*, 18 (Apr. 1944), 67-88, and in Hershberger, *Recovery*, 29-54; *ME* IV: 1149; *Who's Who Mennonites* (1943), 21-22; Ernst Crous, "Harold S. Bender," *Menn. Geschbl.*, 20, n.F. 15 (1963), 2-8; MennBib II:420 and entry no. 227; Harold S. Bender collection, MC Archives (Goshen).

See also Anabaptist Vision; Historiography.

Bergthal Colony, Bolivia, is located about 30 km. (19 mi.) ne. of Santa Cruz or about 8 km. east of the Canadiense colony. It was founded in 1963 by about 25 families from the Menno colony in Paraguay, who were joined by some 20 families from Canada. The group belongs to the Saskatchewan Bergthal Mennonites (closely related to °Sommerfeld Mennonites). In 1986 there were 127 members belonging to the church with a total population of 306 inhabitants. Both groups, the one from Paraguay as well as those from Canada, left their home countries because of modern religious and educational trends in their home communities. People in this small farming community are generally quite poor.   IHie

See also Bergthal Mennonites.

Bergthal Colony, Paraguay (ME I:282). See °Sommerfeld Colony, Paraguay for origins of this settlement in 1948. The colony's lands consist of 10,297 hectares (25,433 acres) populated by 1,478 settlers, of whom 495 were church members in 1986. A shortage of land has led many from this settlement to return to Canada in recent years.   GR

MWH (1978), 252.

See also Bergthal Mennonites; Sommerfeld Mennonites.

Bergthal Mennonites (ME I:282) comprise the following three groups in Canada: (A) the congregations which belonged to the Bergthal Church (congregation) of Manitoba until it was dissolved in 1972 and which have since functioned autonomously (in part also in affiliation with General Conference Mennonites); (B) the °Chortitzer Mennonite Conference, based in the former °°East Reserve; and (C) the °Sommerfeld Mennonites, based in the °°West Reserve. The Sommerfeld Mennonites also have settlements in Saskatchewan (Herbert and Hague areas), where they are known as Bergthaler Mennonites of Saskatchewan—these will be designated

here as Saskatchewan Berthaler (Sommerfelder) for clarity. Sommerfeld Mennonites and Chortitzer Conference Mennonites are also found in Paraguay, Mexico, and Bolivia. Largely of Bergthal background is the °Evangelical Mennonite Mission Conference, formerly known as the °°Rudnerweide Mennonites, which grew out of a renewal movement among the Sommerfeld Mennonites in 1936, and the °Reinländer Mennoniten Gemeinden (Reinland Mennonite Church), which also grew out of the Sommerfeld Mennonites in 1958.

In 1922 a small group of Sommerfeld Mennonites settled in the Santa Clara region of Mexico. A further movement (comprising almost half of the Chortitz group) immigrated to the Chaco area of western Paraguay in 1926. They were joined by a small number of Manitoba Sommerfelder and most of the small Saskatchewan Bergthaler (Sommerfelder). In 1948 a Sommerfeld group emigrated from Canada to East Paraguay where they founded the °Sommerfeld Colony. In that same year a group of Chortitzer Conference Mennonites left for East Paraguay, founding the Bergthal Colony and church. In 1963 a group of Saskatchewan Bergthaler (Sommerfelder) immigrated to Bolivia and founded the °Bergthal Colony. They were soon joined by settlers from the Menno Colony of Paraguayan Chaco. A group of Sommerfeld Mennonites from Mexico founded the °Sommerfeld Colony in Bolivia in 1968, and another group left Mexico for East Paraguay in 1972, founding the Santa Clara settlement. Reinländer Mennonites also participated in the 1963 movement to Bolivia. In 1983 members of the Sommerfeld churches in Manitoba founded Nueva Holanda Colony in Bolivia together with settlers from Menno Colony in the Chaco.

During the 1960s many Mennonites left Menno Colony in the Chaco for Bolivia because church and school activities seemed too progressive, and because of objections to the cooperative economic practices in the colony. A large group founded °Canadiense Colony there.   MWF/CJD

Manitoba (ME I:280). In 1837 the Chortitza colony in Russia established its first daughter colony, Bergthal, consisting of five villages, Schoenthal, Schoenfeld, Heuboden, Friedensthal, and Bergthal, with Bergthal as worship center. The widespread religious, educational, and agrarian renewal movements of the nineteenth century left Bergthal largely untouched. When new pressures from the Russian government threatened through proposed educational and noncombatant-service legislation, the majority of the Bergthal colony migrated to the Canadian prairies (1874-76), settling east of the Red River in Manitoba, on land known as the East Reserve. After 1880 many homesteaders from the East Reserve relocated to the West Reserve because of better soil conditions.

The first West Reserve elder, Johann Funk (ordained 1882 by East Reserve Elder David Stoesz), lived in the village of Alt-Bergthal. In 1885 Funk and other leaders began to lay the groundwork for the establishing of the first western Canadian Mennonite secondary school, Mennonite Educational Institute, built in Gretna in 1889. In 1891 H. H. Ewert, a highly motivated Prussian Mennonite from

BERGTHAL COLONY AND ITS DESCENDANTS

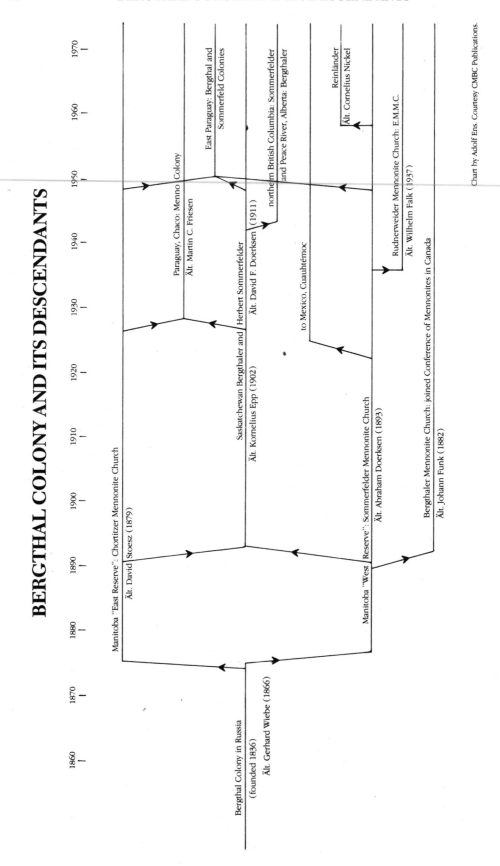

Chart by Adolf Ens. Courtesy CMBC Publications.

Kansas, was called to give new life to the faltering school concept. Ewert, a charismatic leader, made far-reaching contributions to the educational, cultural, and spiritual renewal of the West Reserve Mennonites. Funk worked closely with Ewert for a parallel renewal in the church.

In 1892 Funk proposed a new direction in church activity. His proposal included an affirmation of the "old and tried foundation which is Jesus Christ," obedient discipleship, spiritual renewal, training of teachers, progressive schools, fellowship with other believers, the opening of the pulpits to ministers of other churches, and the preaching of the Gospel to the "heathen." Reaction against Funk and his co-workers was resolute. Already in the spring of 1892 an elder from the East Reserve was invited to baptize in the West Reserve churches, and by the spring of 1893 Abraham Doerksen was ordained in the village of Sommerfeld to give leadership to the conservative majority of West Reserve families, who came to be called the °Sommerfeld Mennonite Church (ME IV:576). Funk was left stranded with a few ministers, one church building, and about sixty families, a group that became known as Bergthal Mennonite Church of Manitoba (A).

Under Funk's leadership the Manitoba Bergthal Mennonites moved forward slowly. Progress during the first quarter century was hampered by various tensions: Mennonite Educational Institute location and direction, relationship to the General Conference Mennonite Church (GCM) Home Mission Board, and leadership difficulties. After 1926, with the leadership of Elder David Schulz, the church grew rapidly, reaching its peak of 3,500 members in 20 worship centers in 1972. Technically it was still a single congregation, according to the pattern that characterized Mennonite colonies in Russia and Latin America; functionally it had become in many ways a multi-congregation conference. At its peak the church had 44 ministers and 35 deacons. All but the leading elders were elected locally.

The leading elders were Johann Funk, 1892-1917; Jacob Hoeppner, 1910-1936; David Schulz, 1927-1972; Jacob F. Pauls, 1964-1967; and Ernest Wiebe, 1967-1972. The overlapping years indicate that younger men were called before the officiating elder passed away or retired. In 1950 J. M. Pauls was called as assisting elder, and in 1961 D. D. Klassen, J. F. Pauls, and Ernest Wiebe were called as assistants. By 1968 all leading minsters were ordained as elders.

The 20 "congregations" developed as follows (the earlier date suggests when work began and the later date when the congregation was fully developed with a church building): Altona, 1892, 1912; Gretna, 1892, 1958; Winkler, 1892, 1895; Lowe Farm, 1898, 1928; Halbstadt, 1892, 1955; Plum Coulee, 1900, 1926; Rosenfeld, 1902, 1942; Carman, 1937, 1954; Grunthal, 1936; Steinbach, 1948, 1950; Winnipeg, 1921, 1958; MacGregor, 1950; Gladstone, 1946, 1953; Arden, 1951; Kane, 1937, 1948; Bethel Bergthaler, 1966.

The founding of the Mennonite Educational Institute, the calling of H. H. Ewert, and the emphasis on public schools created the environment in which the Bergthaler Mennonite Church had its beginning. The church continued to support education in a Christian context. Schisms in the church brought forth two schools in 1908: the Mennonite Educational Institute (rebuilt in Altona), and a new school, the Mennonite Collegiate Institute, in Gretna. The church was largely responsible for the founding of Elim Bible School and was involved with the development of Canadian Mennonite Bible College, though with less enthusiasm.

The church supported mission work from its beginning, and during the 1940s established Mennonite Pioneer Mission for work in Mexico and later with native people in Canada. The latter work was transferred to the Conference of Mennonites in Canada in 1957.

The ordaining of elders for the local congregations; the localization of finances; the younger church workers serving in the enlarging context of the provincial, Canadian, and international conferences and service agencies; and the developing competitiveness with its sister conferences accelerated the dissolution of the central church structure.

In the process of dissolution, Bergthal Mennonite radio work and scholarship funds were transferred to the Conference of Mennonites in Manitoba. The dissolution became final in 1972, although legal matters, including transfer of property titles, kept the official corporation alive until 1983.

Two congregations have closed doors: Kane, which amalgamated with Lowe Farm, and Arden, which dissolved. The Morris congregation joined the Evangelical Mennonite Brethren Conference (°Fellowship of Evangelical Bible Churches), and the Steinbach congregation severed relations with the various conferences. The remaining congregations continue with relationships to the General Conference Mennonites on the provincial and Canadian or General Conference (or both) levels. Some have dropped, and some are in the process of dropping, the "Bergthaler" prefix.   HJG

Saskatchewan Bergthaler (ME I:281). Many of the Mennonites who settled near Rosthern, Sask., in 1891 and 1892 later became part of the Saskatchewan Bergthal Mennonite Church (C). Some of these settlers came directly from Russia, others came from Manitoba, and one group came from Manitoba via Gleichen, Alta., in 1891. Among these settlers was a nucleus that had come from the Bergthal Colony in Russia and had left the overcrowded West Reserve for land in Saskatchewan. This latter group left the mother Bergthal church in Manitoba before the division that created the Sommerfeld Mennonites in 1894 (ME IV:576). Therefore, the Saskatchewan group retained the name *Bergthal* yet bore closer ties to the Sommerfeld group in Manitoba than to the Manitoba Bergthal Mennonites.

Elder David Stoesz of the Manitoba Chortitzer Mennonite (B) church of the East Reserve came to Saskatchewan in 1893 to organize the Bergthal Church. The Manitoba Chortitzer church was closely tied with the Sommerfeld Mennonites of the West Reserve until about 1958. Elder Stoesz ordained Kornelius Epp (1861-1936) as the first Saskatchewan Bergthal minister in 1893 at Rosthern. The church dissolved in 1896 when the group at Rosthern could not agree about who should serve them as elder. Some preferred the local elder Peter Regier of the Rosenort (GCM) Church. Kornelius

Epp was ordained as elder in 1902 and served the group until 1908, when the church split because of differences over wedding ritual. Epp formed his own church, first at Lost River and later at Hague, Sask. He eventually moved to Mexico in the 1920s with a Sommerfeld group from Herbert. The remaining group was then led by Elder Aaron Zacharias who served the church until 1926. He died in Paraguay where he led a number of his followers in 1926. They, like Elder Epp, left Canada because the Canadian government refused to allow them to operate their own private schools as it had promised these Mennonites in 1873.

The members that remained in Canada were reunited under Elder Cornelius Hamm (1878-1947). This era brought many changes. The °°*Waisenamt* (widows' and orphans' fund) fell apart in the 1930s, largely as a result of the economic Depression. To help relieve the effects of poverty many Saskatchewan Bergthaler were resettled to northern Saskatchewan. A Sunday school program began in the 1940s as well as a change from High German to Low German in the worship services.

There have been three major migrations of Saskatchewan Bergthaler since the 1940s: one to Paraguay in 1948; another to Honduras under minister Jacob B. Guenter in 1951 (this group was refused entry and forced to return home); and a third in 1962, when a small group moved to Bolivia. The concern in each has been the desire to resist accommodation to the world (°nonconformity).

The Saskatchewan Bergthaler participated in three church conferences held with Manitoba Sommerfeld and Chortitzer Mennonites and related groups from Swift Current, Sask.; LaCrete, Alta.; and Vanderhoof, B.C. These took place in 1952, 1955, and 1957. In 1958, two church schisms ended this unity, namely the Reinländer group leaving the Manitoba Sommerfeld Mennonites and the Evangelical Mennonite Missions Conference (Rudnerweider) church forming from the Swift Current Sommerfeld group.

The Bergthal Mennonites have recalled their historic peace position at least three times—in World War I, in World War II, and again in 1980, when a uranium refinery was proposed for the Warman, Sask., area. The latter was opposed because of a relation between uranium and nuclear arms.

There have been two further divisions: one in 1979 when minister Jacob D. Peters formed a Sommerfeld church at Hague because of concern about too much English in church services; another in 1983, when the leadership of the church was divided over the amount of accommodation to the world. A group of four ministers and one deacon left to form a church at Reinland.

Education has been a key factor in the migrations to Paraguay in 1926 and 1948 and later to Honduras and Bolivia. Two °private schools have also been set up locally in Saskatchewan in opposition to the °public school system. A two-room private school started in 1979 by 14 Saskatchewan Bergthal and °Old Colony families is located at Reinland, Sask. Another opened in the fall of 1986 near Osler, Sask., led by Elder John D. Redekopp. It pulled 200 students out of the public school system to form a church school. Each school has a different approach and emphasis, and yet both share similar frustration with the public school system.

The Saskatchewan Bergthal Mennonites became a member of Mennonite Central Committee (Canada) in 1984. The group had a membership of approximately 1,000 persons in 1986.   LD

Henry J. Gerbrandt, *Adventure in Faith: The Background in Europe and the Development in Canada of the Bergthaler Mennonite Church of Manitoba* (Altona: D. W. Friesen for Bergthaler Mennonite Church of Manitoba, 1970); idem, *Postscript to Adventure in Faith* (Winnipeg: CMBC, 1986); Leonard Doell, *The Bergthaler Mennonite Church of Saskatchewan* (Winnipeg: CMBC, 1987); Klaas Peters, *The Bergthaler Mennonites* (Winnipeg: CMBC, 1988), trans. by Margaret Loewen Reimer from a series of articles in *Der Bote*, 1890, reprinted in German as a book in 1925, 1983; Martin W. Friesen, *Neue Heimat in der Chacowildnis* (Altona: D. W. Friesen, 1986); William Schroeder, *The Bergthal Colony* (1974; rev. ed. Winnipeg: CMBC, 1986); *MWH* (1978), 313-14.

See also Acculturation ("Funk and Funk" feature); Conservative Mennonites (Dutch-Prussian-Russian); Riva Palacio Colony; Swift Colony; Paurito Colony; Las Piedras Colony; San Jose de Pequina Colony; Bergthal Colony; Canadiense Colony; del Norte Colony; Nueva Colony; Reinland Colony; Santa Rita Colony; Schisms; Sommerfeld Colony; Tres Cruces Colony; Valle Esperanza Colony.

Bergthold, Anna G. Suderman (1875-1957) was the first American Mennonite Brethren missionary to go to India (1898), working first under the auspices of the Christian and Missionary Alliance Church in North India. She had received her Bible training at Moody Bible Institute and Berne, Ind., and was trained as a nurse at Cook County Hospital, Chicago. She had also served in a mission to °Indians in Oklahoma and at the Light and Hope Mission in Chicago. In 1896 she was ordained as a deaconess.

In 1899 she joined the N. N. Hiebert family and Elizabeth Neufeld, who had recently come from America to establish the first Mennonite Brethren mission in India at Mulkapet. She worked among women and in medical work, becoming the first Mennonite Brethren medical missionary. Later she worked in the first Mennonite Brethren hospital, established in Nagarkurnool in 1912. In 1911, when the plague killed many in Hyderabad City and surrounding villages, she worked daily with the sick. In 1916 in India, she married D. F. °°Bergthold, a widower with five children. One son was born to them. Together they continued in evangelism, church building, and Bible instruction, once being pelted with stones and barely escaping with their lives. They retired to the United States in 1946. KFW

Obituary in *Zionsbote* (June 12, 1957), 5; Mrs. H. T. Esau, *First Sixty Years of MB Missions* (Hillsboro, Ks.: Mennonite Brethren Publishing House, 1954); *Missionary Album 1889-1963 Mennonite Brethren and Krimmer Mennonite Brethren Conferences* (Hillsboro, Ks.: Board of Missions of MB Church, 1963).

Bern, Switzerland (ME I:287) is the capital of the canton of Bern and, since 1848, also of Switzerland. It was founded in 1191 on the site of earlier Frankish (Merovingian) settlements.

The Reformation came later in Bern than in °°Zürich. Images and the mass were abolished only in 1528. Monasteries and other ecclesiastical establishments, of which there were 12 in the city, were secularized and became the property of the town government. Endowment and other property gifts were not returned to the original donors, which led to considerable resistance to the new faith and, possibly, to greater receptivity to Anabaptism. Troubling memories are associated with the old city: Jews were persecuted here long after they had received toleration in other areas; here also the Anabaptists suffered imprisonment and persecution.

Documents in the Bernese state archive bear witness to the depth of Bern involvement with Swiss Anabaptism. Several places where Anabaptists of the 16th century gathered are located near the city. Bernese nobles can also be found among the Anabaptists. Prominent 17th-c. leaders in the °Ammann-Reist schism lived in the area; for example, Niclaus Balzli, Durs Rohrer, and Ulrich Balzli of Bolligen and Habstetten near Bern.

According to the documents, the following are some of the detention centers, dungeons, and prisons in which Anabaptists were incarcerated: the *Chorhaus* near the cathedral; the *Frauengefängnis* or *Wyberchefi* (women's prison) in the tower of the West Gate to the city (a Mennonite congregation was founded nearby in 1959); a house called *Hohliebe*, used particularly for the imprisonment of Anabaptist women, located near the present university buildings; the *Inselspital*, and the *Täuferhaus* (the fact that it was actually called an "Anabaptist House" indicates its use); the *Obere Spital*, located near the present *Heiliggeistkirche*; the *Kreuzgasse*, a cross street to the main city thoroughfare, located below the cathedral, mentioned numerous times in connection with judgment of Anabaptists; the *Predigerkloster* (Dominican monastery), used not only to incarcerate Anabaptists, but also to lodge those who came for the disputation of 1528; the *Ratshaus* (city council chambers), which presumably also included the *Täuferkammer* (Anabaptist room); the *Schallenhaus*, or *Schallenwerk*, a disciplinary institution for dangerous criminals mentioned several times in connection with Anabaptist men and women. The *Schiffländte*, or *Schifflaube* was the harbor from which the Anabaptists were deported. The Waisenhaus was used as a kind of penitentiary in 16th-17th century. Numerous Anabaptists are mentioned in connection with this location. There were 20 towers in the city of Bern in the 16th century, many of which were used to interrogate Anabaptists. These interrogations usually involved torture. The *Kafigturm* (cage tower) is the only one still standing in the 1980s.

The Bern congregation, mentioned earlier, consists of ca. 150 members, most of whom have moved to the city from the °Emmental and the Jura areas. The congregation has a full-time pastor, an elder who preaches once monthly, and a team of deacons, including three women.   IZG

Historisch-Biographisches Lexikon der Schweiz, vol. 2 (Neuchatel, 1924); *Historisch-Topographisches Lexikon der Stadt Bern* (Bern 1976); Isaac Zürcher, "Die Täufer um Bern," *Informationsblatter: Organ des Schweizerischen Vereins für Täufergeschichte*, no. 9 (Bern 1986); Walter Laedrach, *Bern die Bundesstadt*, Berner Heimatbucher, no. 33 (Bern 1963); Peter Sommer, *Scharfrichter von Bern* (Bern 1969); J. B. Mast, ed., *The Letters of the Amish Division, 1693-1711* (Oregon City, Ore.: C. J. Schlabach, 1950); various documents and materials from the Staatsarchiv Bern.

Berne, Ind., Old Order Amish Settlement (ME I: 11) is located in Adams County in east central Indiana, 30 mi. (50 km.) south of Ft. Wayne. Henry Egli and family moved into this area from Ohio in 1850. Egli later left the group to establish other Amish-Mennonite communities in Illinois and Indiana. The Berne Amish community is made up primarily of descendants of settlers who came to Indiana directly from Switzerland and Alsace in the 19th c. Amish and Mennonite (Swiss Brethren) immigration wave. The Swiss-German language, which provides a degree of separation from other Amish settlements in northern Indiana, is maintained. The 16 congregations, with more than 2,000 people, constitute a tightly knit community, with strict church °discipline in °dress and transportation. Uniquely, Berne Amish are allowed only open buggies with backless seats. The community, more than most other Amish communities, has experienced open conflicts with the outside world on such issues as medical care, schools, and building regulations. The Adams Co. Amish thrive in the shadows of the much larger Mennonite Church (GCM) in Berne, generally listed as the largest Mennonite congregation in the United States. While family names and ethnic backgrounds are similar, there is only minimal interaction between the two groups. Amishville, a °tourist attraction, owned and operated by "outsiders" and located five miles se. of Berne, has been an annoyance to many Amish families by its invasion of an otherwise peaceful, rural community.   SLY

Bert, Sarah Hoover (1860-1948) was the daughter of Peter Bert, an early 19th-c. German immigrant of Waldensian descent, who was part of the group of Brethren in Christ who settled near Abilene, Ks., in 1879. In 1894 Sarah Bert visited relatives in Chicago and remained to help found the first °urban mission of the Brethren in Christ Church. In 1905 she became superintendent of the mission, a position that she relinquished in 1941 at the age of 81. She conducted programs to assist the needy of the area. These included sewing classes to teach young women a trade and to provide them with pocket money; instruction in housekeeping to enable girls to obtain positions as maids and take better care of their own houses; and distribution of food and clothing. These were the first activities of this kind in the denomination. The first organ and choir in the Brethren in Christ Church were also introduced by Sarah Bert, in an effort to attract young people to the mission services.   EMS

E. Morris Sider, *Nine Portraits* (Nappanee, 1978), 15-45; Wittlinger, *Piety and Obedience* (1978), 174-76; *History and Genealogy of Peter Bert* (Nappanee, Ind., n.d.); *EV* (Feb. 23, 1948), 69.

Bertsche, Harry (1897-1971) was born near Flanagan, Ill., but spent his childhood on a farm near Centralia, Mo., where his parents had joined other Mennonite families from Illinois. He was a good student, but was not allowed to attend high school because this entailed boarding away from home. A sympathetic elementary teacher gave him an extra year of instruction at his country school. Crop failures in Missouri prompted a move by the family to a farm one mile east of Bluffton, Ohio, where they joined the local Evangelical Mennonite Church. Here Harry met Emma Steiner (1897-1980), to whom he was married in June 1920. Harry pursued further formal education at Marion Academy and

College, Marion, Ind., but had to return to the family farm after two years because of the death of his father.

After renting out the farm, Harry began serving in 1933 as pastor at Salem Evangelical Mennonite Church near Gridley, Ill. He continued in pastoral work in the Evangelical Mennonite Conference into the mid-1970s. He served at various times as conference president, editor of the conference periodical, and as a member of a variety of conference boards. In 1928 he was named a representative of the Evangelical Mennonite Church to the board of the °°Congo Inland Mission (Africa Inter-Mennonite Mission), a position he held without interruption until his death. The Africa Inter-Mennonite Mission is greatly indebted to the service of time, resources, and prayers of Harry Bertsche.   JEB

Bestvater, William J. (July 26, 1879–1969) was well-known pastor, teacher, and itinerant Mennonite Brethren minister. He was born in Alexanderthal in Russia to Jacob and Katherina (Penner) Bestvater. He migrated to Mountain Lake, Minn., in 1894. After his conversion he was baptized and became a member of the Bethel Mennonite Church. He married Helena Janzen in 1900; together they attended Light and Hope Bible Institute in Cleveland. They were rebaptized by immersion in Lake Erie and joined the Mennonite Brethren Church on their return to Mountain Lake. Subsequent years were spent in a variety of pastoral, itinerant Bible teaching, and school teaching assignments. These included approximately eight years in the Winnipeg Mennonite Brethren city mission and nine years as instructor at the Herbert Bible School. He wrote several textbooks for °Bible schools, an exposition of the book of Revelation, numerous articles in the *Zionsbote*, and a pamphlet called *Zeugnis der Schrift*. Bestvater was probably best known for his strong °dispensational eschatology, and his influence on North American Mennonite Brethren in this regard was considerable.   AJD

William J. Bestvater, *Textbüchlein in Bible-kunde für Deutsche Bibelschulen* (Regina, Sask.: Courier Press, n.d.); idem, *Textbüchlein für Glaubenslehre für die Herbert Bibelschule* (Regina, Sask.: Courier Press, n.d.); idem, *Betrachtungen über das letzte Buch der Bibel* (Hillsboro, Ks.: Mennonite Brethren Publishing House, 1919); Anna Rose Redekop, "Amazing Grace: Biography of William J. Bestvater" (unpubl. MS, n.d.); F. H. Epp, *Mennonites in Canada II*, pp. 55, 84-85; *Menn. Bib. II,*, p. 421 and entry no. 309.

Bharatiya General Conference Mennonite Kalisiya (India General Conference Mennonite Church) came to birth in July 1904 with the baptism of P. A. °°Penner's first convert, Sirkanti Bai, a patient suffering from Hansen's disease (leprosy). She died soon after. Less than six months later, four orphan girls and eight boys were baptized. The nucleus for Bethesda (Leprosy) Church was formed in February 1905, when eight lepers accepted baptism.

By 1916, the small mission congregations of °Champa, Janjgir, Korba, and Mauhadih, together with Bethesda, met annually for fellowship, Bible study, and sharing. These congregations were shepherded by missionaries, assisted by national workers imported from other missions. One of these, M. R. °Asna, was later to become the first ordained elder in the "Hindustani Conference," which was organized formally in 1922 by these five churches. It became the forerunner of the Bharatiya General Conference Mennonite Kalisiya. C. H. °Suckau, its first chairman, served two terms; after that Indian leadership took over.

One of the congress's early objectives was evangelism. The choice of a home mission station fell on Kendai, in the state of Surguja, 40 mi. (65 km.) north of Korba. Not much could be accomplished until Surguja state became open to Christian witness after India's independence in 1947. Puran and Lily °Banwar were commissioned as the conference's first missionaries to Surguja in 1959. Calvary Church came into being two years later.

Exciting things were happening in the southern end of the General Conference Mennonite Mission area. As early as 1918, evangelistic work gained momentum in Sukhri, where Isa °Das and Mathuria Bai were stationed as evangelistic workers. In Basna, S. T. and Metta °Moyer opened the Jagdeeshpur station in 1921. When, in 1938, the English Baptist Mission ceded the Basna-Saraipali area of its opertion to the General Conference Mennonite Mission, a large number of Christians were added to an already rapidly growing group of new Christians. This required a reorganization of 17 evangelistic outposts in an area of 700 sq. mi. so as to better nurture the new converts and bring together scattered Christian communities. This reorganization found concrete form in the *Phuljhar-Deori Sammelan* (Assembly), thanks to the vision and genius of W. F. Unruh, followed by J. R. Duerksen.

The Sammelan was organized in Sirko, on July 20, 1938, with 40 delegates present from the 17 village "churches." It was named the "Sammelan of the Phuljhar-Deori Mennonite Churches." A simple constitution, revised several times during its brief but significant history, stated its objectives as providing a channel for teaching God's Word, and for exercising necessary discipline. These 17 church groups became six large district churches, some containing as many as 37 villages. They adopted the names of Bethel, Bethany, Antioch, Salem, Emmanuel, and Eden. In a later reorganization, Philippi was formed out of parts of Antioch and Salem, and Ephesus from parts of Emmanuel and Eden. Each church was so set up as to later fit into the Hindustani Conference as recognized member churches.

Representatives, called "members," from the various churches, gathered monthly for spiritual refreshing, consultation, and planning. Sermons were outlined and prepared. Bible stories were studied and prepared for use in evening village worship. Eventually these monthly meetings became semiannual events with the Palak Sabha (Council of Shepherds) assuming responsibility between sessions. The Palak Sabha became the administrative body and was composed of all ordained elders, deacons, and one missionary.

The need for the Sammelan ended when the Hindustani Conference in 1951 assumed the full national support of all ordained pastors of the eleven member churches. This was a significant step towards becoming indigenous. The Hindustani Congress had become the "Hindustani Conference of the General Conference Mennonite Congregations in India" with the adoption of a revised constitution in 1943. This constitution included a provision for a governing body which acted both as an executive committee and as the final authority on conference matters. It consisted of 10 Indian and 7 missionary members.

Foreign support of evangelists ceased in 1959. With it came a drastic reduction of °lay evangelists and Bible women. Indigenization, understood to mean the achievement of a self-supporting, self-governing, and self-propagating church, a goal that had existed from the beginning, was accepted as a challenge by the Hindustani Conference. Beginning with 1960, the conference began to carry the full support of its own appointed evangelists. With the 1960 revision of the constitution, the term *missionary* no longer appeared. Missionaries became members of committees and the conference governing body by election. Within seven years provision was made for a central treasury. The conference also undertook partial support of its students in seminary training. The Hindustani Conference thus became the Bharatiya General Conference Mennonite Kalisiya, indigenous in its existence and functions.   HKor

MWH (1978), 125-29; *MWH* (1984), 27; Mrs. Harold [Ruth R.] Ratzlaff, *Fellowship in the Gospel* (Newton: MPO, 1950); Harold Ratzlaff, "Planting a Church in India" (MTh thesis, Bethany Biblical Seminary and Mennonite Biblical Seminary, 1950).

Bharatiya Jukta Christa Prachar Mandali (India United Missionary Church). See Calcutta; India.

Bhelwa, Mukut and Sonya Bai. Mukut Bhelwa, an ordained minister of the Mennonite Church in India (MC), was born Apr. 4, 1884, in Khairagarh village, Madhya Pradesh. His father, Atma Ram Bhelwas, was a Hindu and a farmer. During the famine of 1900 Mukut was admitted to the boys' orphanage of the American Mennonite Mission in °Dhamtari. Here Mukut was led to Christ, being deeply influenced by the prayer life of Jacob Burkhard.

He was educated through middle school at the mission and also studied in Bible school. His interest in evangelism and village preaching led to Mukut's full-time appointment as an evangelist with the American Mennonite Mission in 1906. In 1915 he began serving at the evangelistic station at Ghatula where he helped George and Esther Lapp pioneer in village evangelism. In 1916 he was ordained deacon for the Ghatula congregation. He was married twice; his first wife died ca. 1918. In 1920 he married Sonia Bai, a trained nurse. From 1933 to 1936 he served as manager of the evangelistic outstation at Likhma, 18 mi. (30 km.) from Ghatula. In 1936 he was ordained by the Mennonite Church in India to the Christian ministry and served in pastorates at Balodgahan and Ghatula.

Sonai was born Feb. 12, 1894, to Hindu parents, Dasrath Ram Sahu and Budhiyarin Bai, farmers in Balod Tahsil of Durg District, Madhya Pradesh. Sonai was admitted to the girls' orphanage of the American Mennonite Mission in Dhamtari during the famine of 1900. She was educated through middle school in the mission schools in Dhamtari and Balodgahan, came to faith in Christ, and became a member of the Mennonite Church in India. She was sponsored by the mission for nurses training at the Christian Hospital in Ludhiana, Punjab. In 1916, she

along with a second student, Asra Bai, became the first trained nurses in the Mennonite Church in India.

After their marriage Mukut and Sonai continued in their individual service until 1932, when Sonai gave up full-time mission employment to help Mukut in his work at Ghatula. Here she continued to serve the people with her gifts in healing. The Bhelwas retired in Ghatula on their farm in 1948, continuing their interest and support of the local congregations until their deaths. Mukut died on Aug. 4, 1959; Sonai died on Jan. 12, 1962. They had six sons and three daughters.   JAF

J. M. Bhelwa, Dhamtari, M.P., India furnished biographical information on the Bhelwas; annual report of American Mennonite Mission (1916-17), 35 (1933), 78 (1936), 116, 121; American Mennonite Mission, *Building on the Rock* (Scottdale: 1926), 190.

Bible Colleges and Institutes (ME I:330, 332) are training schools for Christian workers. Bible institutes usually operate on a lower academic level than do Bible colleges, have programs of shorter duration, and usually do not offer degrees nor have professional accreditation.

North America. The American Association of Bible Colleges, founded in 1947, defines Bible college training as education at the college level whose distinctive function is to prepare students for Christian ministries or church vocations through a program of biblical, general, and professional studies. Bible colleges also provide training for lay or avocational ministries and prepare students for more advanced studies at °seminary.

The oldest Bible institute in Europe is St. Chrischona, near Basel, Switzerland, founded in 1840 by C. F. Spitteler. Bible institutes and colleges did not develop in Europe with the same rapidity nor did they have as great an impact as they did in North America.

The English antecedent to the first American Bible training school was the East London Institute for Home and Foreign Missions founded in 1872 by Grattan Guiness. The purpose of the institute was to prepare missionaries, and, in its first 16 years, 500 young men completed their training to become workers at home and abroad. Guiness' school became a model for A. B. Simpson in establishing what became Nyack Missionary College, the first Bible college in North America (1882). From the first North American school with score of students, the movement has grown to over 500 institutes and colleges in the United States and Canada.

Moody Bible Institute, which was to become the leading school in the Bible institute and Bible college movement, was founded in Chicago in 1886 by evangelist Dwight L. Moody, to prepare "gap-men— men to stand between the laity and the ministers; men who are trained to do city mission work." In 1889 Baptist pastor and missionary statesman A. J. Gordon established the Boston Missionary Training School, whose aim was not only to furnish men and women with a thoroughly biblical training, but also to engage them in practical religious work in the neglected parts of the city. Toronto Bible College (later Ontario Bible College and Theological Seminary) was the first Bible college in Canada (1894).

The aim of the school was to train men and women for Christian ministries at home and abroad.

The North American Bible institute and Bible college movement grew rapidly in the 20th c., and the schools became powerful expressions of the conservative Protestant movement commonly known as *Fundamentalism. By 1930 the Fundamentalist weekly *Sunday School Times* endorsed more than 50 Bible schools, most of which were in major cities. In addition to Moody Bible Institute, Northwestern Bible and Missionary Training School (founded by William B. Riley) and the Bible Institute of Los Angeles (founded by R. A. Torrey) were very influential. In Canada, Prairie Bible Institute, Three Hills, Alta.; Briercrest Bible Institute, Caronport, Sask.; and Prophetic Bible Institute, Calgary, Alta.,

BIBLE COLLEGES AND INSTITUTES
Compiler: Walter Unger (author of article)

Table1. Canadian Bible Schools and Institutes 1900 - 1940

Date	Place	Name	Affiliation
1907	Kitchener, Ont.	Ontario Mennonite School	MC
1913	Herbert, Sask.	Herbert Bible School	MB
1913	Markham, Ont.	Winter Bible School	MC
1921	Didsbury, Alta.	Mountain View Bible School	Miss.
1925	Winkler, Man.	Peniel Bible School	MB
1927	Hepburn, Sask.	Bethany Bible School	MB
1928	Dalmeny, Sask.	Tabor Bible School	MB
1929	Gretna, Man.	Elim Bible School	GCM
1929	Coaldale, Alta.	Coaldale Bible School	MB
1930	Winnipeg, Man.	Winnipeg Bible School	MB
1930	Yarrow, BC	Elim Bible School	MB
1932	Glenbush, Sask.	Glenbush Bible School	MB
1932	Rosthern, Sask.	Rosthern Bible School	GCM
1932	Rosemary, Alta.	Rosemary Bible School	GCM
1932	Tavistock, Ont.	Winter Bible School	AM
1933	Steinbach, Man.	Steinbach Bible School	MB
1933	LaGlace, Alta.	La Glace Bible School	MB
1933	Gem, Alta.	Bethesda Bible School	MB
1933	New Hamburg, Ont.	Winter Bible School	AM
1934	Aberdeen, Sask.	Aberdeen Bible School	MB
1934	Winnipeg, Man.	Mennonite Bible School	GCM
1934	Wembley, Alta.	Wembley Bible School	GCM
1935	Springridge, Alta.	Springridge Bible School	GCM
1935	Coaldale, Alta.	Mennonite Bible School	GCM
1936	Abbotsford, B.C.	South Abbotsford Bible School	MB
1936	Crowfoot, Alta.	Crowfoot Bible School	MB
1936	Leamington, Ont.	Leamington Bible School	GCM
1936	Vineland, Ont.	Vineland Bible School	GCM
1936	Swift Current, Sask.	Swift Current Bible School	GCM
1936	Didsbury, Alta.	Menno Bible Institute	GCM
1937	Vauxhall, Alta.	Vauxhall Bible School	MB
1937	St. Elizabeth, Man.	St. Elizabeth Bible School	GC
1938	Virgil, Ont.	MB Bible Institute	MB
1938	Sardis, B.C.	Greendale Bible Institute	MB
1939	Vineland, Ont.	Vineland Bible School	MB
1939	Coughlan, B.C.	Bethel Bible Institute	GCM
1939	Countess, Alta.	Countess Bible School	GCM
1939	Drake, Sask.	Drake Bible School	GCM
1939	Sardis, B.C.	Mennonite Bible School	GCM
1939	Yarrow, B.C.	Mennonite Bible School	GCM
1940	Kitchener, Ont.	Emmanuel Bible College	Miss.

emerged in the 1920s and 1930s as leading schools. Large numbers of Mennonite and Brethren in Christ students attended and continue to attend these schools.

Among Mennonites in North America, the Mennonite Brethren in Christ (later Missionary Church) attempted to establish a Bible institute at Elkhart, Ind., in 1903, but this effort failed after a short time. In 1905, the °°Missionary Church Association established Fort Wayne Bible Institute (later Fort Wayne Bible College).

Grace College of the Bible was established in 1943 with six Mennonite conferences represented on the first board of directors. Located in Omaha, Nebr., the school became an independent Bible college with board members representing several denominations.

Pacific Bible Institute was established by Mennonite Brethren at Fresno, Cal., in 1944 to prepare students for Christian service at home and abroad. In the early 1960s the institute became a junior college and, by 1965, a fully accredited four-year liberal arts college (Fresno Pacific College), rather than a Bible college.

Conservative Mennonite Bible School began in 1952 near Berlin, Ohio. It was relocated in Irwin, Ohio, in 1964 and renamed Rosedale Bible Institute. It is owned and operated by the Conservative Mennonite Conference.

Brethren in Christ Bible schools and colleges in the United States (Upland College, Jabbok Bible School, Beulah College and Bible Training School, Messiah Bible School and Missionary Training Home, Ontario Bible School [Niagara Christian College], were not included in ME I-IV. Those in the United States have all been consolidated into Messiah College, a four-year liberal arts college at Grantham, Pa. Niagara Christian College has become a secondary school, with public funding as permitted by Ontario law relating to parochial schools. (Details are found in Wittlinger, *Piety and Obedience*, 284-317.)

The Bible institute movement among Mennonites in Canada saw a proliferation of schools in its early history. In the first four decades of the 20th c. more than 40 Bible institutes were established (Table 1). Many were local Bible schools started by individual congregations. These schools were then merged into larger institutes. In 1987 there were 10 Mennonite Bible institutes or colleges in Canada and one in the United States.

The first Mennonite-related Canadian institution established as a Bible college, rather than Bible institute, was Emmanuel Bible College in Kitchener, Ont. The school was operated by the Ontario Conference of the Mennonite Brethren in Christ (Missionary Church) and was founded in 1940. Emmanuel is accredited with the American Association of Bible Colleges.

The next two Mennonite Bible colleges in Canada were both begun in Winnipeg. The Canadian Mennonite Brethren Conference established Mennonite Brethren Bible College (MBBC) in 1944, and the Conference of Mennonites in Canada established Canadian Mennonite Bible College (CMBC) in 1947. They are affililated with the University of Winnipeg (MBBC) and the University of Manitoba (CMBC).

More recently, two Mennonite institutions which achieved Bible college status are Steinbach Bible College, Steinbach, Man. (Steinbach Bible Institute until 1979), and Columbia Bible College, Clearbrook, B.C. (Columbia Bible Institute until 1985). Both schools are inter-Mennonite and are affiliated with the American Association of Bible Colleges for purposes of accreditation.

Steinbach Bible College is operated by five Mennonite groups—The Evangelical Mennonite Conference of Canada, the Chortitzer Mennonite Conference of Canada, the Evangelical Mennonite Mission Conference of Manitoba, the Christian Fellowship Church of Steinbach (formerly Bergthal Church), and the Steinbach Evangelical Mennonite Brethren Church (°Fellowship of Evangelical Bible Churches).

Columbia Bible College is owned and operated by the British Columbia Mennonite Brethren Conference and by the Conference of Mennonites in British Columbia (GCM). Columbia is a 1970 merger of the Bethel Bible Institute of Abbotsford (GCM) and the Mennonite Brethren Bible Institute of Clearbrook.

As noted earlier, most North American Bible colleges and institutes have, to varying degrees, been expressions of Fundamentalism. Down through the years many Mennonite and Brethren in Christ students have attended schools such as Moody Bible Institute, the Bible Institute of Los Angeles, Prairie Bible Institute, and Briercrest Bible Institute (College). This has left a marked influence in Mennonite and Brethren in Christ circles. While furthering Bible knowledge and instilling a vision for missions and evangelism, Fundamentalist and Fundamentalist-oriented schools have also developed a defensive mentality in students.

Non-Mennonite Bible colleges and institutes have a tendency to build theology on narrow premises (i.e., a list of creedal statements or "points" to be defended). They generally do not adhere to the Anabaptist emphasis on biblical as opposed to systematic °theology. Other Anabaptist distinctives regarding °discipleship, the church, and the ethic of love and °nonresistance generally fare badly in these schools.

Mennonites and Brethren in Christ students coming through such institutions of learning often suffer a loss of denominational loyalty, and many serve in a variety of non-Mennonite denominations and parachurch organizations. Some congregations and even whole branches of Mennonite and Brethren in Christ conferences have been brought into the orbit of Fundamentalism as as result of the impact of non-Mennonite Bible colleges and institutes.

The increasing drift of Mennonite and Brethren in Christ students to a wide variety of Fundamentalist and Fundamentalist-oriented Bible colleges and institutes stimulated Mennonites to develop comparable schools which would uphold an Anabaptist understanding of the Scriptures, Christian discipleship, and the church. The record of Mennonite Bible colleges and institutes is excellent. These schools have trained thousands of workers for leadership roles in word and deed ministries of the Gospel around the world.

BIBLE COLLEGES AND INSTITUTES
Compiler: Walter Unger (Author)

Table 2. Mennonite Bible Colleges and Bible Institutes in North America (1987)

School	Place	Affiliation	1987-88 Enrollment
Aylmer Bible School	Aylmer, Ont.	EMMC	14 FT
			30 PT
Bethany Bible Institute	Hepburn, Sask.	MB	104 FT
			1 PT
Canadian Mennonite Bible College	Winnipeg, Man.	GCM	176 FT
			49 PT
Columbia Bible College	Clearbrook, B.C.	MB/GC	161 FT
			129 PT
Elim Bible Institute	Altona, Man.	GCM	15 FT (85-86)°
Institut Biblique Laval	St. Laurent, Que.	MB	6 FT
			55 PT
Mennonite Brethren Bible College	Winnipeg, Man.	MB	96 FT
			117 PT
Rosedale Bible College	Irwin, Ohio	CM	208 FT
			8 PT
Steinbach Bible College	Steinbach, Man.	Inter-Mennonite°°	67 FT
			6 PT
Swift Current Bible Institute	Swift Current, Sask.	GCM	28 FT
Winkler Bible Institute	Winkler, Man.	MB	96 FT
			3 PT

FT - Full-time students

PT - Part-time students

° No full-time on campus students after 1985-86; extension courses offered.

°°Operated by Evangelical Mennonite Conference of Canada, Chortitzer Mennonite Conference of Canada, Evangelical Mennonite Mission Conference of Manitoba, Christian Fellowship Church of Steinbach (formerly Bergthal) and Steinbach Evangelical Mennonite Brethren Church (now member of Fellowship of Evangelical Bible Churches).

Asia and Africa. Mennonite and Brethren in Christ Bible training programs outside of Europe and North America are difficult to categorize as being either Bible institutes, Bible colleges, or Bible schools. Methodology in training leaders in these countries is fluid and experimental. There is a marked trend away from residential institutions to training while in service (°theological education by extension [TEE]). Mennonites, Mennonite Brethren, and Brethren in Christ in Japan have participated in a variety of Bible institutes, including the extension courses of the Eastern Hokkaido Bible School (Nihon Menonaito Kirisuto Kyokai Kyogikai [Hokkaido]), founded in 1965, and the Evangelical Biblical Seminary in Osaka (Nihon Menonaito Burezaren Kyodan), founded in 1957. Mennonites in Indonesia participate in several schools and °seminaries, some of which are related to Christian universities. Mennonite Brethren in India have had a Bible institute at Shamshabad; Bihar Mennonite Mandli operated a Bible school at Chandwa for a time. In Africa programs range from theological education by extension to seminaries. Mennonite- and Brethren in Christ-related residential Bible schools have existed in Ethiopia (Dresser Bible School), Zaire, Tanzania, Zambia (Choma Bible Institute, BIC), and Zimbabwe (Ekuphileni Bible Institute [formerly Wanezi Bible School] at Mtshabezi, BIC). See articles on these countries for additional information.   WU

Latin America. Mennonites migrating to Brazil, Paraguay, Argentina, and Uruguay in the first half of the 20th c. brought with them a concern for proper training of preachers, missionaries, and other church workers. During the first decades of settlement, the struggle for survival did not allow for the establishment of full-fledged Bible institutes, but evening, weekend, or even week-long Bible courses were conducted throughout the churches.

The Mennonite Board of Missions and Charities (MC), working in Argentina, took the initiative in 1926 by establishing the Bragado Bible Institute. In 1955 it was transferred to Montevideo, Uruguay, and renamed Mennonite Biblical Seminary of Montevideo. A considerable number of students from the German- and Spanish-speaking churches of the above-mentioned countries attended this school until its closing in 1975. In 1987 a Centro de Estudios y Retiros (Study and Retreat Center), located in the building used by the la Floresta congregation, was inaugurated. It offers a three-year certificate program through a series of evening classes.

The Konferenz der Mennoniten Brüdergemeinden (Mennonite Brethren Conference) in Paraguay started the Institito Biblico Asunción (Asunción Bible Institute) in 1964-65, with the aim of training workers for church and mission. Its emphasis and impact on mission work in Paraguay has been marked. Its enrollment in 1987 averages about 45-50 students, and it offers several programs of study.

In Brazil, the German- and Portugese-speaking Mennonite Brethren conferences together have operated the Instituto e Seminário Bíblico dos Irmçãos Menonitas (Mennonite Brethren Bible Institute and Seminary) since 1972, with an enrollment of about 100 students (1986). Regular extension courses in the local churches are also coordinated by this school, located at Curitiba.

In 1977 the library resources of the former Mennonite Biblical Seminary of Montevideo were transferred to Asunción, Paraguay. Under the auspices of the Conference of Mennonites in South America, a school by the name of Centro Evangélico Menonita de Teología, Asunción (CEMTA; Evangelical Mennonite Theological Center) was established. Initially it offered a three-year program in both theology and church music. Both programs of study were lengthened to four years in 1980. With an enrollment of ca. 65 students in 1987, CEMTA serves German- and Spanish-speaking Mennonite churches of Uruguay, Brazil, and Paraguay. See also Asociación de Iglesias Hermanos Menonitas, Colombia; Concilio de las Iglesias Evangélicas Menonitas, Venezuela; Iglesia Evangélica Menonita, Honduras; Convención Evangélica Menonita de Costa Rica; and Central America (Seminario Ministerial de Liderazgo Anabautista [SEMILLA], a TEE program. GNie

Europe. The conviction that it is important to uphold an Anabaptist understanding of the Scriptures, Christian discipleship, and the church led European Mennonites in 1950 to found the European Mennonite Bible School. Due to significant participation of North American Mennonites, the first courses took place in Basel until 1957 and after that at Bienenberg near Liestal, Switzerland. The bilingual school (German and French) is supported by the Mennonite conferences of Germany, France, and Switzerland; the Mennonite Brethren church in Europe (°Bund Europäishen Mennonitischen Brüdergemeinden); Mennonite Central Committee; the Mennonite Board of Missions (MC); and Eastern Mennonite Board of Missions and Charities (MC). The course offerings include a two-year general course and various shorter courses on diverse subjects. The annual enrollment for the general course is approximately 70 students, coming from Europe and overseas. Half of them are from Mennonite background. Their average age is 25 and they are presently (1988) taught by four full-time and several part-time instructors.

European Mennonite Brethren cosponsor a nondenominational Bible school at Ampflwang in Austria (1984). In addition, the Haarlem Mennonite Church in The Netherlands has initiated a Bible school in 1988 in their own city. Finally, it should be mentioned that due to geographical, professional, and theological considerations, a number of European and South American Mennonites relate to non-Mennonite schools and seminaries as well, e.g.,

Bibelschule Brake and Bibelschule Bergstraße in West Germany; the Freie Evangelische Theologische Akademie (Basel) and Bibelschule Sankt Chrischona in Switzerland; the Institute Biblique at Nogent-sur-Marne in France; and the school at Heverlee in Belgium. HJeck

S. A. Witmar, *The Bible College Story* (Manhasset, N.Y.: Channel Press, 1962); F. H. Epp, *Mennonites in Canada II,* ch. 10; John A. Toews, *History MB* (Fresno, Ca.: Board of Christian Literature, 1975), ch. 16; J. C. Wenger, *The Mennonite Church in America* (Scottdale, 1966), 210-12; Phil Bender, "What's Unique About the Mennonite Bible Institute?" *Menn. Rep.* (Oct. 18, 1982), 15; idem, in *MM* (Apr. 1988), 9-10 on the distinction between Bible colleges and Bible schools; *Mennonite* (Aug. 13, 1985), 381-83; J. B. Toews, "The Influence of Fundamentalism on Mennonite Brethren Theology," *Direction,* 10, no. 3 (July 1981), 20-29; Wittlinger, *Piety and Obedience* (1978), 284-317, 459-60.

See also Bible Conferences; Kroeker, Susanna Schowalter; Ohio.

Bible Conferences, North America (ME I:328).
   United States. While Bible conferences of the format discribed in ME I were no longer a major part of Mennonite life in the United States by the 1950s, this does not suggest that they had become extinct or that there are no similar activities in the 1980s. While there are other types of Bible instruction in various settings (e.g., winter and summer Bible schools for adults and children and Bible instruction in the many church-controlled elementary and °secondary schools and colleges), there is still much to be said for the original Bible conference pattern, where large segments of the church population, at all age levels, gathered for a week or more in two or three daily sessions to hear the Bible expounded and current issues discussed by a team of well-known ministers. At the peak of the Bible conference movement, there were conferences in 24 areas of the Mennonite Church (MC).

There are several areas where the original pattern has changed little, except in length. These include an area in northern Indiana surrounding the Shore Mennonite Church where seven congregations participate annually in a series of four sessions, and the Johnstown, Pa., area where eight congregations participate in a series of five sessions. The 91st conference in the Johnstown area, in 1987, followed the original pattern except in length and drew a sizable attendance.

Among the various types of Bible study which have become a part of congregational life, in addition to that of the schools and colleges, are weekend Bible and spiritual life conferences, institutes, and retreats at church °camps for the different age groups. Church camps also hold numerous seminars dealing with church and family life.

Two outstanding institutes include a series held at Rosedale Bible Institute in Ohio (a series of five six-week sessions); the Keystone Bible Institute of the Lancaster Mennonite Conference (MC), held at various locations during the winter months; and a similar institute held at Sarasota, Fla., during January and February, involving a number of churches. Winter Bible schools were also held in various areas of the church. The one at Johnstown, begun in 1922 and operating for years as a six-week day school, now functions as a night school two nights a week for a month.

Most of the °conservative Mennonite conferences and fellowships have regular or occasional Bible conferences, or winter or summer Bible institutes.   SGS

Canada. In 1899 the Canada Conference (the forerunner to the Mennonite Conference of Ontario [and Quebec]) decided to hold an annual Bible conference. That same year, a three-day Bible conference was held after Christmas in the Weber's Church at Strasburg, Ont. Speakers at these conferences were such persons as L. J. °°Burkholder, Jonas Snider, Jacob Woolner, Samuel R. Hoover, Solomon Gehman, Noah °°Stauffer, Abraham Gingrich, Eli S. °°Hallman, Enoch S. Bauman, and Samuel F. °°Coffman.

In 1906 the Canada Conference (at the Moyer Church, Vineland) decided to augment the Bible conference by adding a two-week period of Bible study at the end of the Bible conference. Classes were held Jan. 7-11, 1907, with J. Buckwalter from Ohio as the main speaker. In 1909 a Bible Conference and Bible Study Board was appointed (Isaiah Wismer, 1909-1916; Urias K. Weber, 1909-1917; Absalom B. Snyder, 1909-1918). The school term by 1909 was a four-week course and well on the way to becoming the °°Ontario Mennonite Bible School. Bible conferences, however, continued at many places even after the organization of the Ontario Mennonite Bible School. S. F. Coffman was one of the favorite speakers.

In the West, the early Bible conferences were held at Eigenheim, Sask., usually during the first week in March. People from as far as Drake, Sask., came to the meetings. Horses were sheltered on the farms near the church. The meetings lasted all week. The speakers at the 1919 conference (Mar. 10-14) were H. Neufeld from Herbert, Sask.; and David °°Toews, from Rosthern. Other leaders were Gerhard Buhler, J. Buller, Johann J. °Klassen, Johann Peter Klassen, Jacob H. °°Janzen, J. J. Nickel, and Jacob Wilhelm °°Reimer. Later these were held at other places in Saskatchewan (e.g., Herbert, Mar. 21-25, 1926) and in other provinces. Speakers from the Mennonite Brethren churches were often invited to participate in these conferences.

One of the well-known Bible conferences was started at the North-End Mennonite Brethren Church in Winnipeg in 1926. It was held for three days between Christmas and New Year's Day and was attended by ministers and deacons from the various Mennonite conferences. A. H. °Unruh, H. H. °Janzen, J. W. Reimer, and teachers at Mennonite Brethren Bible College were frequent speakers at the conference. A similar conference was established in the late 1940s in Virgil, Ont., and met during the Easter week.

The legacy of these Bible conferences is still evident in the special lecture series in Bible schools and colleges, and in the Deeper Life Meetings held in various churches. They became popular also in the Evangelical Mennonite Missions Conference and Evangelical Mennonite Conference congregations in western Canada. Similar Bible conferences are common in Mennonite colonies in Latin America.   DSchroed

Sanford G. Shetler, *Preacher of the People* (Scottdale, 1982), 102-10; Clarence Fretz, "A History of Winter Bible Schools

in the Mennonite Church," *MQR*, 16 (1942), 51-81, 178-95; *Mission Completed: History of the Ontario Mennonite Bible School and Ontario Mennonite Bible Institute* (n.d.); H. T. Klaassen, *Birth and Growth of Eigenheim Mennonite Church, 1992-1874* (Rosthern, Sask.: Valley Printers, 1974); H. P. Toews, *A. H. Unruh's Lebensgeschichte* (Winnipeg, 1961); David Ewert, *Stalwart for the Truth: The Life and Legacy of A. H. Unruh* (Hillsboro and Winnipeg, 1975); indexes to *Der Bote* and *Canadian Mennonite*.

See also Beachy Amish Mennonite Fellowship; British Columbia Provincial Conference of Mennonite Brethren Churches; Eastern Pennsylvania Mennonite Church; Fellowship of Concerned Mennonites; Ohio.

Bible Institutes. See Bible Colleges and Institutes.

Bible Mennonite Fellowship is a loose confederation of two congregations, one in Brownsville, Ore. (organized 1958), the other in Corvallis, Mont. (organized 1966). The fellowship has a common statement of faith, discipline, and constitution, and sponsors mission work in northwestern Mexico. Total membership of the fellowship in 1988 was 79.   RSa

MC Yearbook (1988-89), 92.

Bible Quizzing in North America began at a Kansas City chapter of Youth for Christ (YFC) in the late 1940s. Designed to involve young people in Bible study, YFC quizzing featured a 20-question quiz with five quizzers on each team. As of 1987, Mennonite and Brethren in Christ Bible quiz programs permitted four quizzers on each team (plus substitutes) and used the New International Version for study and question-writing.

Conferencewide Bible quiz programs were established in the Brethren in Christ (BIC) Church in 1957, the Evangelical Mennonite Church (EMCh) in 1961, and several conferences of the Mennonite Church (MC) in 1970. Mennonite Church conferences with quizzing programs in 1987 included the Atlantic Coast Conference, Iowa-Nebraska Conference, Lancaster Conference, Ohio Conference, and the Ontario and Quebec Conference. Quiz teams from local congregations are generally organized by region or by conference, reflecting the denominational structure. In the EMCh and BIC programs, the teams from each region or conference meet at the denominational playoffs, which are often scheduled for an annual conference or youth convention.

The General Conference Mennonite Church, Mennonite Brethren, and Evangelical Mennonite Brethren churches do not sponsor quizzing programs. However, a few individual congregations do have quiz teams which compete interdenominationally. The World Bible Quiz Association, with headquarters in Washington, Pa., was established in 1974 for the purpose of bringing together the various denominations and organizations involved in quizzing.   DBru

Numerous articles in *EV*, e.g., Ernest L. Boyer, "The Quiz in Prospect," *EV*, (Oct. 22, 1959); A. C. Burkholder, "The Bible Quiz Program," *EV*, (Oct. 22, 1959), cf. (Feb. 10, 1976), 31; Wittlinger, *Piety and Obedience* (1978), 426; *Menn. Rep.*, e.g., Feb. 3, 1986, p. 20; Jan. 19, 1987, p. 16; *Minutes (BIC)* (1986), 21.

Bible Schools. See Bible Colleges and Institutes.

Bible Study. The study of the Bible was a focal activity of early Anabaptist gatherings. This focus was due to several interlocking aspects of their beliefs. First was their contention that the Bible, not the central institutions of state and established church, was the ultimate authority for Christian people. They counterbalanced the demands of these institutions with those of the Bible. In this strategy the early Anabaptists were themselves in continuation with other reformers. "We do not admit that we have acted counter to the imperial mandates; for it says that one should not adhere to the Lutheran doctrine and sedition, but only to the gospel and the Word of God; this we have held to. Counter to the gospel and the Word of God I do not know that I have done anything; in witness thereto I appeal to the words of Christ" (Michael Sattler, CRR 1:93).

Second, the Bible must be taught and studied in the church so that its members can know true faith and experience God: "Since all people by nature do not understand the things of God they are taught the true faith and knowledge of God through the Word. Moreover the Scriptures offer us no other way. Therefore the first thing which all people, and each one in particular, who are to be brought into the knowledge of God and the holy church of God (so far as it is proper for us to judge this) must encounter is the preaching and hearing of the divine word" (Bernhard Rothmann, CRR 3:105).

Third, the true church is the church which knows the Bible and follows it as a guide in faith and life. Especially this last aspect was stressed as the true mark of the church; the true church is the church which ". . . holds only to [God's] words and seeks to fulfill his whole will and his commandments. A gathering thus constituted is truly a congregation of Christ" (CRR 3:106). This was not a form of works righteousness, as if reading and knowing the Bible alone were sufficient. Rather, Bible study was to lead to a transformation of the person through meeting God, who stood behind the Scriptures. As Ulrich Stadler writes, "I value the Holy Scriptures above all human treasures but not as high as the Word of God, which is living, powerful and ,eternal, and which is free and unencumbered by all the elements of this world. For insofar as it is God Himself it is spirit and no letter, written without pen and paper that it may never be expunged. Therefore also salvation cannot be tied to the Scriptures, however important and good they may be with respect to it. The cause is that it is not possible for the Scriptures to improve an evil heart even if it is highly learned. A pious heart, however, that is a heart in which there is a true spark of godly zeal, will be improved through all things" (CRR 3:142).

In Anabaptist meetings, much time was given over to Bible study and exposition. It was said of their meetings that, "They have not special gathering places. When there is peace and unity and when none of those who have been baptized are scattered they come together wherever the people are. They send messages to each other by a boy or girl. When they have come together they teach one another the divine Word" (CRR 3:124). The process of study is described by Michael Sattler, "When brothers and sisters are together, they shall take up something to read together. The one to whom God has given the best understanding shall explain it, the others should be still and listen, so that there are not two or three carrying on a private conversation, bothering the others. The Psalter shall be read daily at home" (CRR 1:44). These meetings might go on for some time. In a description of a night meeting it is reported that five leaders took their place in the center of the group. "Each one in turn read a passage from the New Testament and then preached for about 15 minutes. Prayer then followed these five sermons, lasting for about 30 minutes. Then there was a call for those who did not understand to come and be instructed by the elders. Or if God's Spirit led, one could address the whole group" (Schad, "True Account" 292-95).

In the first generation of Anabaptists, the leaders who were educated could lead Bible studies from the biblical text itself, rather than from a translation; e.g., Felix °Mantz taught from the Hebrew text and Conrad °Grebel from the Greek. Other Anabaptists emphasized lay Bible study and preaching under the anointing of the Holy Spirit, which drew a vehement response from Ulrich °°Zwingli (CRR 4:385-409). With persecution, leaders conversant with Greek and Hebrew passed from the scene, and the movement became more rural and underground. In this circumstance, since their opponents also affirmed the Scriptures as the sole authority (*sola scriptura*), the early Anabaptists developed a suspicion of scholars learned in Scripture. These scholars seemed to twist things to suit their needs and thereby take the "sting" out of it. Thus Mennonite Bible study became characterized by a literalistic reading and understanding of the text. In this situation a great gap developed between study in the church and the study of the Bible in the academic community.

Because of this emphasis on Bible study, the early Mennonites, although often not as educated as their opponents, showed an astonishing grasp of the contents of Scripture. This tradition of Bible study in the congregation continued in the 17th and 18th c., at least among the Dutch, who had regular Bible study hours in the congregation.

In Russia, the Bible study movement, fostered by °Pietism, found its way into Mennonite life by 1815. Through this development Pietist writings became widely known among Mennonite writers, and there was a reawakening of Bible study. °Bible conferences also came to be held in local churches, but usually Bible studies were conducted in homes by the pastor of the congregation.

In North America, when a renewed interest in Bible study appeared, it took the form of Winter Bible Schools, Young People's Bible Meeting, °Bible conferences, and Bible institutes. Winter Bible Schools began in North America at the turn of the century, the first being held at Elkhart Institute (later to become Goshen College) beginning Jan. 24, 1900. These Bible schools were held for a term of 2 to 12 weeks, with 4 and 6 week terms being the most popular. At one time or another these Bible schools were held in all sections of the Mennonite Church (MC). The earliest ones were sponsored by conferences or districts, but later individual congregations held their own schools, usually for a two-week period when a visiting teacher would come and give classes. These were especially promoted by

Sanford Shetler in the 1930s, when about a dozen such congregational programs were begun.

The Young People's Bible Meeting along with Youth Endeavor sprang up in various places, beginning in the 1870s. These meetings were a regular part of the congregations's Sunday program and provided an opportunity for study, reflection, and articulation of beliefs by lay people. The "young" in the name of these groups is misleading because members of all ages participated in these sessions. This program played an important role in the ongoing Bible study taking place within Mennonite congregations.

Church colleges were also founded at this time, Bethel College in Kansas being the earliest (1887). Bible courses were an integral part of the curriculum of these schools. Here Bible teachers, who had pursued academic study of the Bible, began teaching some of the findings of biblical scholarship in their courses. With the rise of Mennonite °seminaries (1930s), this development increased in strength.

This development brought tensions between the churches and the colleges, with faculty members becoming casualties; some were dismissed or left because of pressures brought to bear on the schools. By the 1970s, however, the academic study of the Bible was widely accepted in most Mennonite schools of higher education and with it the use of historical-linguistic tools of study, commonly called "higher criticism." However, the study of the Bible in the congregations largely proceeds along traditional lines.

As a result of the rise of colleges and seminaries, Mennonite Bible scholars in North America are beginning to contribute to the broader, ecumenical world of biblical studies. This has been true in the area of °biblical theology, e.g., Elmer Martens and Ben Ollenburger, to name two scholars. In the area of exegetical and general studies one might name others, including Clarence Bauman, John W. Miller, Waldemar Janzen, David Schroeder, William Klassen, Devon Wiens, and Willard Swartley.

In addition, the Institute of Mennonite Studies at the Associated Mennonite Biblical Seminaries (Elkhart, Ind.) has supported biblical studies. The institute has begun a Shalom Biblical Theology and Ethics research seminar in which several biblical scholars gather for the month of June to work on research related to this theme. Further, an editorial council has been appointed to oversee the publication of monographs on biblical topics which can contribute to the wider scholarly community.

In conjunction with this project, the Institute of Mennonite Studies has sponsored a meeting of Mennonite biblical scholars in conjunction with annual professional meetings (Society of Biblical Literature). These sessions have attracted 25-40 people yearly since they began in 1983. This is in contrast to the small number of Mennonite scholars who attended the annual meetings until the mid-1970s.

While in North America scholarly work in biblical studies is fairly recent, in The Netherlands, Mennonite scholars have been making a contribution for much of the church's history, and the church has been in touch with contemporary study of the Bible. Pieter Jansz °°Twisck published a concordance of the Bible in 1648. In the 19th c. °°Harting and

Hertog, among others, were active. From the 20th c. one can name F. van der Wissel, A. J. Elhorst, and F. Dijkema.

In addition to scholarly activities Mennonites have also been active in translation projects. To mention only a few, Rudolphe °°Petter was a pioneer in the analysis of the Cheyenne language and translation of parts of the Bible into Cheyenne. In Africa the tireless efforts of Agnes Sprunger resulted in the translation of the Bible into Gipende (Kipende). Jacob Loewen has worked extensively as an anthropology and linguistic consultant for Bible translation projects in many countries.   PY

"AIMM Notes 50th Anniversary of Gipende New Testament in Zaire," *MWR,* (Sept. 12, 1985), 7; Kenneth H. Berg, "Case Studies in Hermeneutics," *Direction,* 6 (1977), 32-35; Clarence Fretz, "A History of Winter Bible Schools in the Mennonite Church," *MQR,* 16 (1942), 51-81, 178-95; Silas Hertzler, "Early Mennonite Sunday Schools," *MQR,* 2 (1928), 123-24, 205; A. J. Klassen, "The Bible in the Mennonite Brethren Church," *Direction,* 2 (1973), 34-57; Paul M. Lederach, "The History of the Young People's Bible Meeting in the Mennonite Church," *MQR,* 26 (1952), 216-31; Ben Ollenburger, "The Hermeneutics of Obedience: A Study of Anabaptist Hermeneutics," *Direction,* 6 (1977), 19-31; Elias M[aster] Schad, "True Account of an Anabaptist Meeting at Night in a Forest and a Debate Held There with Them," trans. Elizabeth Bender, *MQR,* 58 (1984), 292-95; Devon Wiens, "Biblical Criticism: Historical and Personal Reflections," *Direction,* 1 (1972), 107-11; Willard M. Swartley, *Slavery, Sabbath, War and Women: Case Issues in Biblical Interpretation* (Scottdale, 1983), proposes guidelines for personal and scholarly Bible study; Perry Yoder, *From Word to Life: A Guide to the Art of Bible Study* (Scottdale, 1982); *GH* (Jan. 26, 1988), 52-58, regarding a lay-oriented approach to the use of Greek in Bible study; for numerous other articles, see *Menn Bib.* II:538-40.

See also Scholarship.

Bible Translations. See Bible Study.

Bible Women. See Lay Evangelists.

Biblical Interpretation (hermeneutics) is the task and process whereby Christians come to understand the Bible, accept its claims, and live according to its teachings. As stated in *Biblical Interpretation in the Life of the Church,* (approved by the Mennonite Church [MC], 1977) "The *ultimate goal* in interpretation is to allow the Bible to speak its own message with a view to worship and obedience." The same statement emphasizes that the "Bible is the Book *of the people of God,"* i.e., the understanding and credibility of its message are to be found in the community of faith. The statement also outlines in nine steps a method for interpretation and identifies four theological convictions which should guide Mennonite study of the Bible. An expanded set of theological assumptions and a method of study are described in Swartley, *Slavery* (1982), 215-228.

Interpretation of biblical tradition takes place already within the Bible itself, on a variety of levels: Isaiah's understanding and use of the exodus to describe God's new actions in history (43:15-21); Ezra's paraphrasing, presumably in Aramaic, of the Hebrew reading of the law so the people could understand (Neh 8:8); four Gospel interpretations of the life and mission of Jesus; and 2 Peter's comment that some of Paul's writings are hard to understand (3:16).

Biblical interpretation becomes important, especially in situations of religious pluralism when people become aware of differing and competing understandings of Scripture, both in belief and practice. While differences in interpretation were present in the 3rd- and 4th-c. church, e.g., the Alexandrian allegorical method versus the Antiochian historical method, differences in interpretation during the Protestant Reformation produced more serious results since confessional identities were formed and defended by these differences.

The Reformation Era. Scripture interpretation among the Anabaptists resembled that of the other Protestant reformers in many ways, but also showed distinctive elements. All Protestant and Anabaptist leaders agreed that the Bible was the final °authority; all emphasized the literal-historical method of interpretation—in contrast to the allegorical method in use since the 2nd c. A.D.; all followed the Christ-principle and used Scripture to interpret Scripture. Significant areas of disagreement were in the understandings of the relation between the testaments, which were correlated with the Christ-principle; in the relation of the letter and Spirit, and inner and outer word; in the role of all believers in interpretation and testing of interpretation (°priesthood of all believers); and, perhaps most important of all, in the relation of °discipleship and obedience to insight and knowledge.

While all the Protestant Reformation groups stressed christocentric interpretation, the outcome of this emphasis differed because of the way it was correlated with a particular doctrinal or ethical perception. Martin °°Luther's doctrinal priority of salvation by faith alone resulted in a comparative evaluation of biblical literature, ranking most highly those books which emphasize salvation by faith; thus Genesis, Psalms, Galatians, and Romans ranked more highly than Leviticus, Ezra-Nehemiah, and James. John °°Calvin's doctrinal priority of God's sovereignty and elective purpose together with Calvin's view that authority resides objectively in the text itself led to the emphasis that all Scripture bears witness to the elective and salvific purpose of God. The Anabaptists stressed following the way of Jesus; they believed that all Scripture culminates in the gospel story, thus witnessing to Jesus' life, death, and resurrection power.

Seen within these theological distinctives, other differences in Scripture interpretation are readily understood. Accenting personal commitment to follow Jesus, Anabaptists held to believers °°baptism, refused participation in war on the basis of Jesus' teaching of °nonresistance and "love of enemy," and practiced rigorous church °discipline following Jesus' instructions on "binding and loosing" (Mt 18:15-18). Because of differences between the testaments, especially in the divine sanctioning of believers' participation in war, the Anabaptists regarded the Old Testament as preparatory to the New Testament and characterized by pre-Christian practices. The fullness and completeness of revelation in and through Jesus Christ means, a new time, a new reality, and a new possibility for living according to God's way. To describe the *real* differences in time and revelation, Pilgram °Marpeck used the images of "summer and winter," "figure

and essence." The extent of divine knowledge and saving faith in one time cannot be confused with that of another time. In the Old Testament Christ had not yet come, had not yet died for human sin, and had not yet brought the reality of the °kingdom of God. In an 800-page treatise, *Testamentserleutterung* (Explanation of the Testaments, ca. 1544-50), Marpeck and his colleagues illustrated how the two testaments are to be understood in relation to each other.

Eight articles on Anabaptist hermeneutics, republished in *Essays on Biblical Interpretation* (1984), highlight several other distinctive emphases. Committed to the Rule of Paul (1 Cor 14:29), Anabaptist leaders held that Scripture was plain and that the gathered believers could understand the Scriptures. In debate against John °°Eck, Balthasar °Hubmaier called for the gathered believers to decide who speaks more clearly the truth of the Scripture. John H. Yoder thus claims, "It is a basic novelty in the discussion of hermeneutics to say that a text is best understood in a congregation" (*Essays*, 20-21). Accordingly, Anabaptist leaders generally criticized the "schoolmen" (although some of the Anabaptist leaders were themselves well educated as humanists, only Hubmaier had a scholastic theological education) for perverse interpretation, since with clever arguments they obscured and evaded the clear teaching of the word of God (Klaassen, *Anabaptism: Neither Catholic Nor Protestant*, 37-48).

Anabaptists would often appeal to the Holy Spirit as the source of insight and illumination in understanding Scripture (Dyck in *Essays*, 35-38). Hans °°Denck, more than other writers, stressed the primacy of "the inner word," referring to the testimony of the Spirit in illuminating the text and revealing the truth. In argument against °°Spiritualists, however, Marpeck upheld the primacy of Word over Spirit, the outer word over the inner (ME I:324-28); but in argument against legalists the same writers, e.g., Marpeck, would appeal to the Spirit over the letter (Klaassen in *Essays*, 81-87). On this particular point it is important to recognize significant diversity among the Anabaptist leaders and writers, occasioned often by the context of argument and issues put forth by their opponents.

Most distinctive was the strong position of Anabaptism on the connection between obedience and knowledge. As Denck put it, "No one can know Christ except by following him in life, and no one can follow him except by knowing him." Hence, only the person "who is committed to the direction of obedience can read the truth so as to interpret it in line with the direction of God's purposes" (Yoder in *Essays*, 27). This emphasis on obedience and discipleship, as necessary to understand the Word, has been described as an epistemological principle, a distinctive emphasis within the 16th c. on the nature and method of knowing (I. B. Horst, Proposition V of the theses appended to his doctoral dissertation for its defence, later published, minus the theses, as *The Radical Brethren: Anabaptism and the English Reformation to 1558* [Nieuwkoop: B. de Graaf, 1972]). This insight has much in common with current hermeneutical developments in °liberation theology and more broadly in interpretation theory (Harder, "Hermeneutic Community"). A significant dimension of this hermeneutical insight was the conviction that biblical truth and believers' obedience to it must be applied to all dimensions of life (Ollenburger in *Essays*, 48). In contrast to positions taken by other Protestant reformers, the Anabaptists would not allow the civil magistrates to preempt the authority of the Word over their lives. Their understanding of Scripture required obedience in all spheres of their lives, even to the point of forbidding vocations which jeopardized obedient discipleship.

Aberrations within Anabaptism from the above hermeneutical characteristics must also be recognized. The shift from a nonresistant, peacemaking stance to a dominating, violent position in the city of °Münster (1531-35) represents a deviant hermeneutical strand. Not unlike Marpeck's view that the conduct of God's people must accord with the distinctive time and content of divine revelation, the theological and political perception of the leaders at Münster (Melchior °Hoffman's eschatology and °Jan van Leyden's political ideology) shifted from nonresistance to violence because they regarded their time as the endtime, the time of God's wrath to be meted out upon the wicked—and through them as God's agents. Hence this eschatological perception introduced a new hermeneutic, calling for Davidic-type kingship, rule by twelve elders, holy war, the death penalty, and polygamy.

Mennonite Biblical Interpretation. The chief influences upon later European and North American Mennonite interpretation of the Bible have been °Pietism; European Protestant orthodoxy or scholasticism, which developed, in part, into later American °Fundamentalism; and historical-critical methods of Bible interpretation, arising for the most part from universities where faith is not determinative for interpretation.

Pietism in its many expressions over the last four centuries influenced Mennonite faith in Europe, Russia, and North America through °revivalism, emphasis on the devotional life, and in the tendency to give inner spirituality priority over ethical obedience in the public sphere. During the 18th and 19th c., conflict between the relative authority of °tradition and Scripture influenced Mennonite thought, playing a role in the °Oberholtzer schism of 1847 and in other °schisms as well. The influence of Protestant orthodoxy and Fundamentalism, partly in reaction to °liberal influences, introduced specific language about the authority of the Bible, such as "inerrant, infallible, plenary inspiration" (Kraus in *Essays*, 131-50). Through study at institutions of higher learning, both European and, then later, North American Mennonite leaders absorbed historical-critical views and approaches to the Bible. This diversity of influence has led to a common recognition that biblical interpretation has been the crux of many Mennonite church disputes in the 20th c. The inductive method of Bible study, which put more emphasis on direct study of the text than on the historical and cultural backgrounds, has been a mediating influence and has been employed widely in classroom instruction in Mennonite schools. From 1960 onward the number of North American Mennonites in doctoral-level biblical studies vastly increased (to more than 75 by 1986), so that a variety of methods (historical-critical, sociological, literary compositional, etc.) influenced Mennonite scholars as they became immersed in advanced biblical studies.

Mennonites beyond this Western circle of influence have reflected these trends in varying degrees through missionary teaching. African Mennonite use of the Bible shares in its African contextual reality, using allegorical interpretation in preaching and often spiritualizing Old Testament narratives in instruction. Mennonites in Latin America and other countries of the "two-thirds world" have been influenced by emphases from liberation hopes and theologies.

Recognizing the tensions produced by the liberal and Fundamentalist influences upon Mennonite teaching, especially at the seminary level, H. S. °Bender wrote the booklet, *Biblical Revelation and Inspiration* (1958), to set a direction that affirms biblical authority and discriminatingly allows for some of the approaches of higher criticism. Similarly, in 1962 the General Conference Mennonite Church produced a statement, *The Authority of the Bible*. In 1966 the Mennonite Church and General Conference Mennonite churches produced a primer in Bible study for use in the congregations, *Learning to Know the Bible*, by David Schroeder. In the early 1960s the Conrad Grebel Lectureship Committee commissioned a series of lectures by J. C. Wenger (*God's Word Written*), and in the mid-1970s commissioned another series, utilizing a case-issue approach (Swartley, *Slavery, Sabbath, War and Women*). A year later the committee commissioned a companion series on Bible study method (Perry Yoder, *From Word to Life*). In 1973 the Mennonite Church (MC) General Assembly commissioned and later adopted the statement, *Biblical Interpretation in the Life of the Church* (1977). In 1977 the Council of Mennonite Seminaries sponsored a consultation on biblical hermeneutics (most of the papers appear in *Essays*, in which the use of the historical-critical method was extensively examined. Numerous publications appeared on biblical interpretation in the 1980s, and churchwide consultations on biblical interpretation were held by the major bodies of North American Mennonites.

Throughout this period significant commentary work on the Bible appeared: two studies of the °Sermon on the Mount: John W. Miller, *The Christian Way* (Scottdale, 1969) and John Driver, *Kingdom Citizens* (Scottdale, 1980); Willard M. Swartley, *Mark: The Way for All Nations* (Scottdale, 1979); John W. Miller, *Step by Step Through the Parables* (New York: Paulist, 1981); Myron Augsburger, *Commentary on Matthew*, Communicator's Commentary Series (Word: Waco, Tex.: 1982) and Elmer Martens, *Jeremiah* (Scottdale, 1986), the first volume in the Believers Church Bible Commentary project, sponsored by five Mennonite and related denominations. Under the auspices of the Institute of Mennonite Studies (Elkhart), both a biblical monograph and essay series was begun in the late 1980s. Of note also are Elmer Martens, *God's Design: A Focus on Old Testament Theology* (Grand Rapids: Baker, 1981); Waldemar Janzen, *Still in the Image: Essays on Biblical Theology and Anthropology* (Faith and Life, 1982), and David Ewert, *From Ancient Tablets to Modern Translations: A General Introduction to the Bible* (Grand Rapids: Zondervan, 1983). Specialized interpretive studies of selected parts of Scripture are Millard Lind's *Yahweh Is A Warrior* (Scottdale, 1980) and John Howard Yoder's, *The Politics of Jesus* (Grand Rapids: Eerdmans, 1972). WMS

Biblical Interpretation in the Life of the Church: A Summary Statement (Scottdale, 1977); *A Christian Declaration on the Authority of Scripture* (Newton: GCMC, 1962); Willard M. Swartley, ed., *Essays on Biblical Interpretation: Anabaptist-Mennonite Perspectives* (Elkhart: IMS, 1984): eight essays on 16th-c. Anabaptist hermeneutics, two on developments in Mennonite history, seven on Mennonite scholarly response to contemporary hermeneutical methods and trends, and three on the Bible's use in the congregation, plus a bibliography; Perry Yoder, *From Word to Life: A Guide to the Art of Bible Study* (Scottdale, 1982): selects four biblical texts and shows how the main steps in the historical-critical method illumine these texts; David Schroeder, *Learning to Know the Bible* (Newton, and Scottdale, 1966): well-suited for congregational use; Willard M. Swartley, *Slavery, Sabbath, War and Women: Case Issues in Biblical Interpretation* (Scottdale, 1982); Lydia Harder, "Hermeneutic Community: A Study of the Contemporary Relevance of an Anabaptist-Mennonite Approach to Biblical Interpretation" (ThM thesis, Newman Theological College, Edmonton, Alta., 1984); Myron S. Augsburger, *Principles of Biblical Interpretation in Mennonite Theology* (Scottdale, 1967); William Klassen, *Covenant and Community: The Life, Writings and Hermeneutics of Pilgram Marpeck* (Grand Rapids: Eerdmans, 1968); Henry Poettcker, "The Hermeneutics of Menno Simons: An Investigation of the Principles of Interpretation which Menno Brought to his Study of Scripture" (ThD diss., Princeton Theological Seminary, 1961); J. C. Wenger, *God's Word Written: Essays on the Nature of Biblical Revelation, Inspiration and Authority* (Scottdale, 1966); Harold S. Bender, *Biblical Revelation and Inspiration* (Scottdale, 1959, repr. 1986); Paul M. Zehr, *Biblical Criticism in the Life of the Church* (Scottdale, 1986); John R. Martin, *Keys to Successful Bible Study* (Scottdale, 1981); Robert Charles Holland, *The Hermeneutics of Peter Riedemann* (Basel: Friedrich Reinhardt Kommission, 1970); Walter Klassen, *Anabaptism: Neither Catholic Nor Protestant* (Waterloo, Ont.: Conrad Grebel Press, 1973), 37-47. On Alexandrian and Antiochene exegesis see James L. Kugel and Rowan A. Greer, *Early Biblical Interpretation* (Philadelphia: Westminster, 1986), 177-99.

See also Biblical Theology; Inerrancy; Scholarship.

Biblical Seminary in New York. See New York Theological Seminary.

Biblical Theology sometimes means a theology that accords with the Bible, but usually refers to the theology that lies within the Bible. Since 1787 biblical theology has been regarded as a specific academic (scientific) discipline of describing and laying bare the theology of the Old and New Testament and the relationship between the two. While building on exegesis, biblical theologians work wholistically with the text blocks, trying to get to the essence or heart of the Bible theologically.

The closely related term, "Biblical Theology Movement," (1940s and onward) applies to a mood or school of thought which was marked by a "fresh" sense of the Bible's unity, an emphasis on revelation in history, and focus on the Bible's immediate relevance for modern life. Impetus for such belief came in part from Europe where, in protest against the "liberal" study of the Scripture, often characterized as arid, the Bible was viewed as God's direct address to human beings (e.g., Karl Barth).

The Biblical Theology Movement, which promised renewal and healing of divisions in the church, contributed on the academic level to several attempts to write a synthesis of the Bible's message. On the popular level, a mood was set for greater personal and group °Bible study. In the younger churches outside Europe and North America this approach, more than western systematic theology, seemed fruitful for theologizing contextually. The Biblical Theology Movement began to wane in the late 1950s because of problems surrounding the notion of God's revelation in history (ancient peoples made similar claims; how was history a medium of revelation?) and because of the emergence of vigorous systematic theologies (e.g., process theology).

The more specific attempt within biblical studies to get at the Bible's theological heart also sputtered somewhat, partly over such problems as (1) how history and theology were related, (2) by what method a theological summary was to be achieved, (3) whether there was a center around which such a theology should be organized, and (4) how the dynamic within the Bible could be maintained when one systemizes concepts. Despite these problems, in addition to classic syntheses (e.g., Eichrodt, von Rad), other attempts to offer theological summaries of the Bible continued—even with vigor (e.g. Terrien, Hanson, Kümmel, and Morris).

Mennonites felt comfortable with the stress on biblical theology, for as a noncreedal group, they welcomed "theologizing" which used biblical, rather than philosophical categories (cf., Pilgram °Marpeck, 16th c. as described by Klassen, 1968). Specifically, Mennonite °seminaries (deliberately named "biblical" rather than "theological") and religion departments in Mennonite colleges gave pride of place to biblical theology courses over systematic theology courses. °Sunday school curricula (e.g., Foundation series) branched into electives which explored biblical themes (e.g., people of God), and writers were briefed on biblical theology. The Believers Church Bible Commentary series, begun in the mid-1980s deliberately incorporated a more "theological" approach.

Mennonites also contributed to the biblical theology movement. Monographs include studies on such themes as love of enemies (Klassen), atonement (Driver), Holy Spirit (Ewert), war (Lind, Janzen) and shalom (Yoder). Full-blown "biblical theologies" include a two-volume work which embraced both Testaments (Lehman), and a theology of the Old Testament (Martens). Mennonites also joined in writing about the history of biblical theology as a specific discipline (Ollenburger). EAM

Brevard S. Childs, *Biblical Theology in Crisis* (Philadelphia: Westminster, 1970); Krister Stendahl, "Biblical Theology, Contemporary," in *The Interpreter's Dictionary of the Bible*, vol. 1 (Nashville: Abingdon, 1962), 418-32; John H. Hayes and F. Prussner, *Old Testament Theology: Its History and Development* (Atlanta: John Knox Press, 1985), 209-18; Gerhard F. Hasel, *New Testament Theology: Basic Issues in the Current Debate* (Grand Rapids: Eerdmans, 1978); Henning Graf Reventlow, *Problems of Old Testament Theology in the Twentieth Century* (Philadelphia: Fortress, 1985); William Klassen, *Covenant and Community: The Life, Writings and Hermeneutics of Pilgram Marpeck* (Grand Rapids: Eerdmans, 1968), 50-53; Ben C. Ollenburger, "Biblical Theology: Situating the Discipline," in *Understanding the Word: Essays in Honour of Bernhard W. Anderson*, ed. J. T. Butler, E. W. Conrad, and B. C. Ollenburger, *J. for the Study of the Old Testament*, Supplement series, 37 (Sheffield: JSOT Press, 1985), 37-62; Ben C. Ollenburger, "Old Testament Theology (since 1800)," *Dictionary of Biblical Interpretation* (forthcoming); Walther Eichrodt, *Theology of the Old Testa-*

ment, 2 vols (Philadelphia: Westminister, 1961, 1967); Gerhard von Rad, *Old Testament Theology,* 2 vols. (New York: Harper and Row, 1962, 1965); John Bright, *The Kingdom of God* (Nashville: Abingdon-Cokesbury, 1953); George E. Wright, *God Who Acts: Biblical Theology as Recital* (Chicago: Regnery, 1952); Walther Zimmerli, *Old Testament Theology in Outline* (Atlanta: John Knox, 1978); Walter Kaiser, *Toward an Old Testament Theology* (Grand Rapids: Zondervan, 1978); Brevard Childs, *Old Testament Theology in a Canonical Context* (Philadelphia: Fortress, 1986); Paul Hanson, *The People Called: The Growth of Community in the Bible* (San Francisco: Harper and Row, 1986); Rudolph Bultmann, *Theology of the New Testament,* 2 vols. (New York: Scribner, 1951, 1955); Leonhard Goppelt, *Jesus, Paul and Judaism: An Introduction to New Testament Theology* (New York: Thomas Nelson, 1964); Werner G. Kümmel, *The Theology of the New Testament* (Nashville: Abingdon, 1973); George Ladd, *A Theology of the New Testament* (Grand Rapids: Eerdmanns, 1974); Leon Morris, *New Testament Theology* (Grand Rapids: Zondervan, 1985); Samuel Terrien, *The Elusive Presence: Toward a New Biblical Theology* (San Francisco: Harper and Row, 1978); Edmund Jacob, *Theology of the Old Testament* (New York: Harper & Row, 1958, rev. ed., 1968); Harold S. Bender, *These Are My People: The Nature of the Church and its Discipleship according to the New Testament* (Scottdale, 1962); John Driver, *Becoming God's Community* (Elgin, Ill.: Brethren Press, 1981); idem, *Understanding the Atonement for the Mission of the Church* (Scottdale, 1986); Jacob J. Enz, *The Christian and Warfare: The Roots of Pacifism in the Old Testament* (Scottdale, 1972); David Ewert, *The Holy Spirit in the New Testament* (Scottdale, 1982); idem, *And Then Comes the End* (Scottdale, 1980); Waldemar Janzen, *Still in the Image: Essays in Biblical Theology and Anthropology* (Newton, 1982); William Klassen, *Love of Enemies: the Way to Peace,* Overtures to Biblical Theology, 15 (Philadelphia: Fortress, 1984); idem, *The Forgiving Community* (Philadelphia: Westminster, 1966); Chester Lehman, *Biblical Theology,* 2 vols. (Scottdale, 1971, 1974); Millard Lind, *Yahweh Is a Warrior: The Theology of Warfare in Ancient Israel* (Scottdale, 1980); Elmer A. Martens, *God's Design: A Focus on Old Testament Theology* (Grand Rapids: Baker, 1981; published in England as *Plot and Purpose in the Old Testament,* Leicester: University Press, 1981); Ben Ollenburger, *Zion: The City of the Great King, J. for the Study of the Old Testament,* Supplement series, vol. 41 (Sheffield: JSOT Press, 1987); David Schroeder, *Invited to Faith,* Foundation Series (Elgin, Ill,: Brethren Press, 1981); Perry Yoder, *Shalom: the Bible's Word for Salvation, Justice, and Peace* (Newton, 1987).

See also Biblical Interpretation.

Bielefeld, in the ne. part of the Bundesrepublik Deutschland (Federal Republic of Germany), first became a home to Mennonites after World War II. Many families from °West Prussia and other East European areas had fled westward ahead of the advancing Soviet army. The first permanent Mennonite settlement in the area formed in 1956 near the old village of Bechterdissen, not many miles from the city. By 1960 this group was worshiping in its own church building. Families returning from Paraguay, and others beginning to emigrate from the Soviet Union later in the decade (°*Umsiedler*) had begun to increase the membership significantly. By 1980 this °"Kirchliche" body numbered more than 1,000 members. A part of the group had begun to meet independently in the city six years earlier.

Mennonite Brethren congregations began to form around 1977. In 1987 there were three in all. With the Bechterdissen-Bielefeld "Kirchliche" group subdividing twice, the city and environs had seven Mennonite and Mennonite Brethren congregations, including Lage, Brockwede, Stieghorst, Oldentrup, with a total membership of about 2,000. Many more families continue to come here as the emigration from the Soviet Union again gained momentum in the late 1980s.   LK/JPl

Bechterdissen congregation, *25 Jahre Mennonitengemeinde Bechterdissen* (Bielefeld/Bechterdissen, 1981); *Menn. Jahrbuch* (1988).

Bihar Mennonite Mandli (Bihar Mennonite Church). The Mennonite Church in Bihar has 621 members in 19 congregations, led by 15 pastors (1985). The congregations are located in Palamau and Ranchi districts. The conference headquarters is in Chandwa, Palamau District.

The conference operates student hostels in Latehar, Palamau District, and in Ranchi for rural young people attending secondary schools. Nav Jivan (New Life) Hospital was established in 1961 near Satbarwa, Palamau District. This location was chosen for its lack of medical services. Nav Jivan has 166 beds and is staffed by four doctors (1986).

°Mennonite Service Agency, with headquarters in Chandwa, is a development program which grew out of famine needs in 1960. Funded by Mennonite Central Committee, needy persons are employed in water resource projects, e.g., well digging and dam construction. The agency promotes agricultural improvement by introducing new seeds, fertilizers, and pesticides.

Good Books is a chain of bookstores with headquarters in Ranchi. Religious literature and school books are made available to the public. Paul and Esther Kniss, North American missionaries since 1950, founded and manage Good Books. They also publish *Masihi Awaz* (Christian Voice), a monthly magazine for Christian families. They have begun recording the Scriptures in Hindi for radio broadcast in Sri Lanka. The broadcast area includes all of Hindi-speaking India.

Chandwa Bible School was designed to develop leaders among the new Christians. Because of dwindling attendance the school was discontinued. However, most pastors in the Bihar Mennonite Mandli as of 1986 studied at the school, and one of them, George Khakha, became the conference youth minister.

The Bihar Mennonite Mandli grew out of work begun in 1940 by the Mennonite Board of Missions and Charities (MC), through the American Mennonite Mission (later Mennonite Church in India), °Dhamtari, Madhya Pradesh. The first witness was made in Hazaribagh District, where several Christians lived, the products of previous work by another mission. When the number of Christians increased, severe persecution scattered the old and the new Christians, and the church has lost contact with them. In 1947 a mission in Palamau District which was understaffed, invited the Mennonite missionaries to occupy its area. Most of the Mennonites are now located in Palamau Dstr.

The churches formed a conference in 1947. Bihar Mennonite Mandli is independent of, but has fraternal relationship with the Mennonite Board of Missions.   WH

MWH (1978) 122-24; (1984) 29; John A. Lapp, *India* (1972), ch. 22.

Bihar State, India. Bihar, 100 miles northwest of Calcutta, is one of the 22 states of India. The capital is Patna. The land area is 67,164 sq. mi. (174,626 sq. km.), slightly more than half the size of Italy. The population was 61.9 million in 1976, about the same as that of Italy and one-fourth of the entire population of the United States.

Bihar is rich in minerals. More than half of the world's supply of mica comes from Hazaribagh District, which includes Kodarma, site of the first Mennonite witness in Bihar. The abundance of coal and iron contributes to Bihar's considerable manufacturing. Chakradharpur (City of Wheel Mounting), on the Bengal and Nagpur Railroad, derives its name from its locomotive works.   WH

Bioethics and Medical Ethics, which emerged in the 1970s as a subject of broad societal study and concern, increasingly command the attention of North American Mennonites. In 1985 °Mennonite Mutual Aid called together a Heath Ethics Review Committee which resulted in the publication of *Medical Ethics, Human Choices,* edited by John Rogers (Scottdale, 1988).

Issues of bioethics have ceased to be of concern primarily to medical professionals, and responding to them is no longer the prerogative of medical professionals. These issues have drawn the interest and intervention of government, a wide range of professions, interest groups, the mass media, and the general public. Reasons for the upsurge of interest are many. First, many new medical technologies have been introduced; respirators, kidney dialysis, sperm banks and artificial insemination, genetic engineering, computerized data processing, complex life support systems, heart and organ trnsplantation, new and expensive wonder drugs, and much more.

Second, medical services have become more sophisticated and concentrated in clinics and large medical institutions with accompanying increases in costs. Third, standards of medical and nursing care have risen and are more carefully monitored by public agencies. Fourth, new lay movements have arisen, beginning in the 1960s—civil rights, feminism, environmental action, advocacy groups for the elderly, etc.—all of which have empowered groups heretofore relatively silent on concerns of cost, equity, quality, and public policies relating to medical care.

Bioethical issues can be divided into micro and macro issues. Micro or personal and familial issues include the following: °abortion, °birth control, organ transplants, prolongation of life, heroic measures for severely impaired infants, AIDS (acquired immune deficiency syndrome), homosexuality, sperm banks, surrogate motherhood, alcoholism, and °drug abuse.

Macro issues are broader in scope and invite public policy decisions and action. Some of these issues are both macro and micro in scale: abortion, birth control, alcoholism, etc. Larger bioethical issues, which increasingly have claimed the attention of Mennonites, are the following: world hunger, environmental pollution (acid rain, nuclear radiation, etc.), population controls, genetic engineering, sex education, equity in the availability of medical services, allocation of limited medical resources (e.g., organs, expensive medicines, scarce equipment, limited hospital space), governmental health care coverage, public campaigns against drug sales and use, etc.

Increasingly it is being recognized that the many vexing issues of bioethics are not resolved by simple technical professional answers. They are invariably complex human problems which require the wisdom and insights of medical professionals and laity, and the discernment of congregations and public agencies. These issues are now on the agendas of Mennonite congregations and conferences.   RK

In addition to the book mentioned above, see Graydon F. Snyder, *Tough Choices* (Elgin, Ill.: Brethren Press, 1988).

See also Ethics; Health Services; Hospitals, Clinics, and Dispensaries; Medicine.

Birth Control. Mennonites regard °children as gifts from God, a heritage of the Lord; and to bear and rear children is an expected reality of °marriage. However, in the late 20th c. many believe responsible Christian behavior includes using birth control to space children, to prevent unwanted pregnancies, or both.

A study published in 1975 asked about the use of birth control devices or pills by married spouses in Mennonite and Brethren in Christ congregations. Of the respondents, 11 percent thought the use of birth control was always wrong, 25 percent thought it was sometimes wrong, 47 percent considered it never wrong and 17 percent were uncertain (Kauffman/Harder, *Anabaptists Four C. Later,* 180). Apparently about half of these people were unwilling to give blanket approval to the practice of contraception despite the fact that the Mennonite Church (MC) and the General Conference Mennonite Church (GCM) had adopted statements indicating approval of contraception by methods approved by the medical profession.

These percentages reflect a more accepting attitude regarding the use of birth control than that found in a resolution adopted by a district of the Virginia Conference (MC) in 1940, an official statement of belief about marriage and marital relations. This resolution reflects the belief that artificial devices and the general practice of birth control are injurious to the moral and spiritual welfare of the home, and they may lead to harmful physical results. A later, even stronger, statement in the same document calls attempts to avoid parenthood by use of artificial devices sinful and contrary to the will of God.

Greater °acculturation of Mennonites with the broader society may be promoting more liberal attitudes toward birth control. Research among the general population has shown that the higher the level of education of the wife or husband, the more likely is the use of contraception. Farm workers consistently have a lower proportion of birth control users than the general population and wives working outside the home are much more likely to have completely planned fertility. As greater numbers of Mennonites increase their level of education, leave the farm, and have families in which the wife works outside the home, it is likely that greater numbers are using birth control methods.

The Old Order °Amish, who still reject higher education, remain primarily an agricultural society in which women do not work outside the home and show no indication of reducing their growth rate by birth control. In 1981, the mean complete Amish family size was 6.8 children, more than twice the mean for the American family. Abstaining from sexual intercourse is their only accepted form of birth control, but some Amish families concede to using the rhythm method. Some reluctantly use other methods upon medical advice. In Amish circles birth control is not commonly discussed, even among Amish women. °Old Colony Mennonites also do not practice birth control.   AKH

John R. Mumaw, *Marriage, Marital Relations and the Home* (Scottdale, 1940), 19; Duane K. Friesen, *Moral Issues In the Control of Birth* (Newton, 1974), 67; Mennonite Church (MC) General Conference statement, *The Christian View of Marriage and Christian Parenthood* (Scottdale, 1959), 7; John A. Hostetler, *Amish Society* (1980), 104; Julia Ericksen, Eugene Ericksen, John A. Hostetler, and Gertrude Huntington, "Fertility Patterns and Trends Among the Old Order Amish," *Population Studies,* 33, no. 2, p. 275; A. Frances Wenger, "Acceptability of Perinatal Services Among the Amish," presented at Nurses' Symposium on Future Direction in Perinatal Care, (Baltimore, Md., Oct. 1, 1980).

See also Abortion; Bioethics; Demography; Development Work.

Birth Rate. See Demography.

Bishop (Swiss-Pennsylvania) (ME I:347-49). The term *bishop* was not common among the Swiss-South German Anabaptists, who developed a congregational °polity, modified by a synodal element that helped bring unity to the larger group—the first major synod being the Schleitheim Conference of 1527. The Hutterites had a *Vorsteher,* or head elder, from the time of Jakob Hutter (1530s) to 1687; this leader helped coordinate all aspects of faith and life among all the various Hutterian communities in Moravia and Slovakia.

From 1530 onward Anabaptism in the Low Countries, as a free church movement, took on a congregational polity. During the time of Menno Simons, however, four leaders—°°Dirk Philips, °Menno Simons, °°Gillis van Aken, and °°Leenaert Bouwens—each apparently agreed to oversee a definite territory. Each geographic district contained a number of congregations, and one of the four individuals carried ongoing responsibility for that area in pastoral care and oversight, exercising °discipline, baptizing, etc. Although °*elder* was the usual term used, the term *bishop* also came to be used, as can be seen in the Dordrecht Confession of Faith of 1632. The Dutch Mennonites, in later generations, adopted a congregational polity, and the idea of bishop has long since disappeared from the Dutch Mennonite scene.

In North America, the usual German term in use for the senior minister was "*voller (volliger) Diene(r)*"; such a "full servant (of the Word)" was empowered by the congregation to baptize, to preside at the congregation's °communion services, and to handle matters of discipline, etc., in consultation with the congregation.

The full servant, however, was often simply the congregation's leader, and not a "bishop," in the sense of having oversight over a district of congregations. In some area conferences, e.g., Franconia Conference, one "full servant" could, and often did,

have oversight over several congregations that had developed out of the various meetingplaces of what earlier had been a single congregation.

In other area conferences, e.g., Franklin, Lancaster, and Virginia, the idea of bishop as having official oversight over a definite district has a more formal and long-standing tradition that probably shows a more direct influence of the Low-Country Mennonite pattern as established in the time of Menno Simons. These same conferences—Franklin, Lancaster, and Virginia—still (1988) maintain a formal bishop's office, including bishop districts. A few other independent conferences also fit in here, such as the Cumberland Valley Mennonite Church, the Eastern Pennsylvania Mennonite Church, the Mid-Atlantic Mennonite Fellowship, and the Southeastern Mennonite Conference. Most Old Order Mennonite groups in Pennsylvania, Virginia, Ontario, Ohio, Indiana, and Missouri also fit this scheme, again probably due to the Low-Country Mennonite influence. This came, most likely, through Jakob °°Ammann's overt interest in Menno Simons and Dirk Philips and their approach to church government. Later, the Old Order Amish generally rejected the bishop district idea, having instead only a *volliger Diene(r)* (full servant) with authority to serve the interests of one congregation only.

Since the 1960s, almost all other area conferences of the larger Mennonite groups have moved away from the idea of bishop; in the 1980s the term *overseer* is becoming the term used for the area-conference coordinator for most such conferences—a term more in line with the traditional (modified) congregationalism of most Anabaptist and Mennonite groups over the centuries.

This represents a return to a traditional Swiss-South German and Dutch (before and after the Menno Simons and Dordrecht Confession era) denominational structure for most Mennonite congregations and areas: a congregational pattern, modified by a synodal element (triennial general conferences [GCM] and biennial general assemblies [MC]). For the Mennonite Church (MC), an important shift away from the bishop idea came at the time of a major denominational restructuring in 1971. The several regional conferences that still hold on to the bishop district, as noted above, in effect continue to maintain the church government of the Dutch Mennonites as established during Menno Simons' time.   LG

See also Conservative Mennonites; Mid-Atlantic Mennonite Fellowship; Northwest Conference of the Mennonite Church; Old Order River Brethren; South Central Mennonite Conference (ME IV:584); Western Ontario Mennonite Conference.

My Good Bishop

I was contently, perhaps lackadaisically, reading in the New International Version of the Bible, when I bumped into Ps 78:72. It was like hitting a specially prepared section on the toll road, where the pavement has been surfaced so your tires rumble, warning of the approaching collection booths. Immediately I went on a red alert, knew there was something special in that phrase, "And David shepherded them with integrity of heart." I said to myself, "Yes, he was like that. His name was David, and he tended us in the church with honesty, loving us from the heart—a true shepherd."

I was not thinking of David, son of Jesse. I was thinking of David, son of Peter, a longtime bishop in Elkhart County, Indiana—D. A. Yoder.

I know the word "bishop" raises the hackles of some, but not mine. Perhaps it was because David A. Yoder was one of the few bishops I knew intimately, and I must say that my relationship to him was always one in which he treated me with tenderness, with love, never harshly.

For me, this bishop was a beautiful person. He saw me at my best, he saw me at my worst. He baptized me as a lad of 12, he helped me back into full fellowship with the Mennonite Church [MC] in 1947. That was after four years of participation in the military during World War II. He ministered to me in 1950 and in 1951, when I was seeking release from the United States Naval Inactive Reserve during the Korean War. Twice he helped me walk to the front of Belmont Mennonite Church and seek forgiveness from the brotherhood, both difficult experiences.

I have vivid memories of this brother, this leader—some humorous, some very serious. I remember looking at his patched rubber boots as I knelt in the Elkhart River at Studebaker Park the Sunday morning he baptized me. The day was sunny, but the water was cold, and I envied his dry feet as I knelt in that early spring water, wet nearly to my waist. At that time I was 12, he was just next to 50. As I look back from 66, I think he deserved to keep his feet dry.

I recall his congregational prayers—always long, substantial, effective, his wide open eyes sweeping over the benches as he took his flock to God. D. A. Yoder always prayed with eyes open, beholding the object of his prayers. The fact that I know tells you that I peeked, but never for long. I never wanted our eyes to meet as they swept down each row, touching each person. It was as if he was introducing his flock to God, bringing each of us to the throne for healing. I stood in awe of the man as he graced the pulpit, yet always sensed his common, "we are brothers" spirit, when dealing with him on a one-to-one basis. For me, he was God's man in contact with the heavenly Boss. We had special connections.

I remember him at communion time in those bishop days. There was no communion unless he could be there, massive brother, powerful leader, but to me, at that time and always, a saint. Our minister at Belmont carried the plate of pure white bread, cut into those neat, squared-off loglike planks, trailing Bishop D. A. Yoder down the church aisles where he pinched off a tiny piece for each of us, placing it directly in our hand.

And always those eyes, those large eyes that looked deep into your soul, made you shiver with a delicious mixture of fear and happiness. You knew better than to take communion unworthily. It seemed to me as a boy that the bread came from God himself, and I say it with deep respect for this brother. I can still hear him say those soft-spoken words, "Take, eat, this is my body which is broken for you." Then came the common cup, this time passed down the rows with accompanying words that reminded you of the shed blood of Christ. Spring and fall communion became real, special—the bishop was there.

D. A. was not without humor. At times as president of the Mennonite Board of Education [MC], he would stop at Goshen College and enjoy a meal with the students as they ate in the basement of Kulp Hall. At that time they ate family-style, six or so at a table. Once, as he sat there enjoying a meal that featured beans, an interesting comment was made by the student serving as hostess. Evidently beans were not her favorite choice of food, and she so expressed herself. Then she added, "I understand that some benefactor of the college gives 100 pounds of these beans to the school each year." With the inference that she would really like to tell the giver off, she commented with some vehemence, "I would certainly like to know who it is!"

Bishop Yoder, at the other end of the table, and the donor of 100 pounds of beans to the college annually, looked up, smiled, and said, "Well, there is no better time than now, for it is me." It is my understanding that a hole opened in the cement floor beneath the bean-complaining student and she dropped into a subbasement.

Mary Mishler met D. A. once at Elkhart General Hospital. She wondered whom he was visiting. He said, "Well, it depends. I come here, check with those in charge as to persons who never receive visitors, then I visit them." That was D. A. Yoder.

Later, as the bishop's health faded, I would visit him at various nursing homes. At Greencroft in Goshen, I especially remember some of those visits, our sharing of the past, the present, the future. He knew where he was going. I recall holding his hand and leaning over the bed to unashamedly embrace the man, to give him back the kiss of love he gave so often to me as a young, learning, struggling Christian.

My last visit to him was at the funeral home, paying my last respects to my beloved, plain-coated bishop. Well, that was not quite the last visit.

Today, January 3, 1987, I visited the Olive Mennonite Church cemetery. I found the gray granite stone marking his grave and ran my fingers over the deeply etched initials and name, over the dates 1883-1980. A milkweed plant had sprouted from a small evergreen shrub next to the stone, the stem arching over the stone, only empty husks upon it, the seed scattered. It was symbolic. What was under that stone—wife Frances and D. A. Yoder—was not what mattered. They had scattered the good seed. It would grow again.

Today was a gray day, the sun shining only this morning, not while I was at the grave. It was near freezing. I wanted to do something in that empty cemetery. Nor did I care if those in passing cars saw me. I knelt, took off my hat as I always do when I pray. I sensed God close, and with eyes wide open, thanked him for the man who was once in the body that lay beneath me. D. A. Yoder was one of several men who profoundly influenced my life.

Only then could I come home, finish this article, and write the concluding sentence. I think it's time that someone says something good about the time when bishops roamed, shepherding their sheep with hearts of integrity.   RB

Adapted from *GH* (Feb. 24, 1987), 126-27. Used by permission.

Biswas, Fredrick Amarendra Kumar (Freddie) (Jan. 3, 1909–Jan. 6, 1972), Mennonite educator, and lay church leader in the Mennonite Church in India (MC), was born in Itarsi, Madhya Pradesh. He was the youngest of three sons born to Chunilal and Kamolini (Ganguli) Biswas, a Bengali Christian family serving with the British Friends Mission in Itarsi. In 1919 he came to °Dhamtari to live with his older brother R. N. K. Biswas, who had received a position as headmaster of the American Mennonite Mission English school. Here A. K. also joined the Mennonite Church in India and received his education in the mission schools. After completing high school he earned a BA degree from Allahabad U., and a BT degree from Spence Training College in Jabalpur, Madhya Pradesh. In 1932 he joined the staff of the Dhamtari Christian Academy (later named Mennonite Higher Secondary School) in Dhamtari, where he taught, served as warden of the boys' hostel, and later as assistant headmaster, until he succeeded J. W. °Samida as principal in 1962. He retired from the school in 1963. In 1934 A. K. Biswas married Rachel Haidar. They had five children, of whom one died in infancy.

A. K. was dynamic, a natural leader, and an aggressive and courgeous voice in the Mennonite Church in India. He championed the cause of the poor and challenged missionary paternalism, working to lift the church out of its "orphan" legacy to active maturity. He was treasurer of the conference, a regular member of its executive committee, and a member of the Mennonite Educational Board and the Mennonite Medical Board.   JAF

John A. Lapp, *India* (1972), ch. 17, 19; AMM Annual Reports (1945, 1962); biographical information supplied by Mrs. Kamolini (Biswas) Martin; interview with Minnie Graber, Irene Weaver, and S. Paul Miller.

Biswas, Reginald Nolendra Kumar (Aug. 24, 1895–Dec. 4, 1975) was born at Gorakhpur, Uttar Pradesh, India, the second of four sons born to Chunilal and Kamolini (Ganguli) Biswas. After his family moved to Itarsi, Madhya Pradesh, R. N. K. Biswas was able to complete his education through college there (BA and BT degrees). He joined the British Quakers and was sponsored to study in England for a year. He returned in 1919 to work for the American Mennonite Mission in °Dhamtari, Madhya Pradesh, as headmaster of the mission's English school.

R. N. K. was a daring visionary. He purchased the village of Maradev to become the first Mennonite landlord. In 1929 he retired from his headmaster position to devote himself entirely to his farm. In 1938 he had a life-transforming experience through the preaching of Sadhu Bhakt Singh, a converted Sikh. Biswas now was committed to tithing, to a deep devotional life, to renewal among other Indian Christians, and to lifting living standards among his neighbors. Through his efforts, the Economic Ser-

vice Council was formed in 1952. He challenged Indian Christians to maturity and made missionaries aware of the perils of paternalism. He died at Dhamtari.   JAF

Biographical data supplied by Kamolini (Biswas) Martin; AMM Annual Report (1919); John A. Lapp, *India* (1972), ch. 18.

Blackfeet People. See Indians, North American.

Blanke, Fritz (1900-1967), church historian, first at Königsberg (1926-29), then Zürich (1929-67), is best known among students of Anabaptism for his pioneering studies of Zürich Anabaptism, as published in *Brothers in Christ* (1955, German; 1961 English). He wrote some 27 articles, reviews, and books on the theme of Anabaptism and Mennonitism, attempting to understand the movement within the broader European religious context. As a true friend and sympathetic interpreter of many religious groups, he always attempted to allow the true Anabaptist genius to show through. Blanke also pioneered in the redefining of the word *sect*: he listed the Anabaptists under the category of "free churches," and not under "sects" (see his *Kirchen und Sekten*, 4th ed., 1963). In a very real sense, Blanke continued within his generation what two other Swiss historians, Emil °°Egli and Walther °°Köhler, had done for their generations (Zürich professors in church history from 1893 to 1908, and 1909 to 1929 respectively), in taking seriously the variegated Anabaptist movement.

Blanke's major attempt to interpret Anabaptism within the broader Reformation context is his article, "Anabaptism and the Reformation," in *The Recovery of the Anabaptist Vision*, ed. by Guy F. Hershberger (Scottdale, 1957), 57-68. Blanke found within early Zürich Anabaptism a close connection to Zwingli, especially in the group's desire to be faithful to the Scriptures—so central to Zwingli's thought. Late in his life, apparently through Harold S. Bender's influence, Blanke gave increasing room to a shift in Zwingli's view of the church, so that in effect, the Zürich Anabaptist circle simply continued to hold to Zwingli's earlier ecclesiastical position, including that of nonviolence (see Heinold Fast, "Fritz Blanke's Contribution to the Interpretation of Anabaptism," *MQR*, 43 [1969], 64-65).   LG

For a general biography on Blanke, see the "Fritz Blanke Memorial Issue," *MQR*, 43 (January 1969); *Aus der Welt der Reformation* (five essays by Fritz Blanke, with a list of the author's publications, 1960); Ulrich Gäbler, "Verzeichnis der Veröffentlichungen von Fritz Blanke, 1960-67," *Zwingliana*, 12, no. 1 (1968), 677-82.

Block Settlement. The experience of living in geographically separate colonies in Russia and the group nature of the emigration from Russia to North America in the 1870s led Mennonites to look for large tracts of unoccupied °land suitable for block settlement in the United States and Canada. The central plains offered the best opportunities for this.

The Canadian government, having just created the new province of Manitoba on land obtained from the aboriginal Indian nations, sought to attract European settlers by offering to reserve contiguous blocks of land and hold them for a period of time for homesteading exclusively by members of the group apply-ing for such a reserve. In the United States the °rail-road companies owned sufficient lands to make pos-sible concentrated Mennonite settlments in Kansas, Minnesota, and South Dakota.

In this way Mennonites from Russia obtained the East and West Reserves in Manitoba (1873-75) and the Hague and Swift Current Reserves in Saskatch-ewan (1894 and 1905). This allowed them in the next 50 years to maintain almost unchanged the or-ganizational patterns of church, school, local govern-ment, fire insurance, inheritance regulations, etc., that they had developed in Russia.   AE

C. A. Dawson, *Group Settlement: Ethnic Communities in Western Canada* (Toronto: Macmillan, 1936), 95-117; C. Henry Smith, *The Coming of the Russian Mennonites* (Berne: Mennonite Book Concerns, 1927), ch. 7-12.

Blood People. See Indians, North American.

Blue Creek Colony, Belize. Located in northern Belize, this colony was founded in 1958 by 80 Old Colony Mennonite families from Mexico. Though there was much illness and infant mortality, the population rapidly increased to 200 families. Dis-unity, however, soon led to the founding of an Evan-gelical Mennonite Mission Conference congregation as well as to the departure of an increasing number of families to Bolivia, Mexico, and Canada during the 1960s. Eventually the leaders of the Old Colony church also left, forcing members to decide whether they would leave with them or join other groups. In 1978 several families of the Kleine Gemeinde con-gregation in the Spanish Lookout Colony moved to Blue Creek, especially to be of help in the school and congregation. At that time 120 families were still living there; in 1987 only 80 families remained.

Economic circumstances remain difficult. Initially, the sale of lumber was the primary source of in-come, but corn, beans, peanuts, and vegetables soon helped the economy. Finding markets remains dif-ficult. Some have turned to cattle-raising, others to raising broiler hens or doing custom work in clear-ing land and building roads. The Blue Creek credit union has been of considerable help in these economic ventures.   PFK

Boehr, Frieda Nettie Sprunger (Feb. 13, 1890–Jan. 15, 1982), missionary to China, was born in Berne, Ind. Her parents were David C. Sprunger and Verena Sprunger Sprunger. She chose nursing as her career, and in 1914-15 she joined the °°deaconess movement. She went to China in 1921 to assist in the medical work of the General Conference Men-nonite mission. Seeing the need for outpatient clinics, the mission released her from full-time hospital duties. She managed country clinics with the help of two Chinese workers and a Chinese °lay evangelist. She married Peter J. Boehr, also a mis-sionary in China, on Jan. 30, 1937. Together they worked in medicine and evangelism. After World War II Peter and Frieda were the first General Con-ference Mennonite missionaries to return to China. They began a new work in western China, where their last years were productive ones. They lived through the hardships of a country in revolution, being the last General Conference Mennonite mis-

sionaries to leave China (1951). Following service in various locations in the United States, Frieda and Peter retired in Berne, Ind.   LDe

Naomi Lehman, *Pilgrimage of a Congregation* (Berne, Ind. First Mennonite Church, 1982); H. C. Brown, *The General Conference China Mennonite Mission* (Taming-fu, China: the author, 1940), 84, 91, 93, 126.

Boehr, Peter J. (Apr. 2, 1886–Dec. 22, 1973), was born to John and Anna Regier Boehr in Henderson, Nebr. He attended public school in Henderson, received his state teacher's certificate from York College in 1908, and attended a Bible training school in Fort Wayne, Ind. He graduated from Bethel Academy (1910) and Bethel College (AB, 1913), Ks. He obtained a graduate certificate from McCormick Theological Seminary in 1925. He mar-ried Jennie Gottshall, from Bluffton, Ohio, in 1915. Peter and Jennie went to China as missionaries in 1915. They had six children. Jennie died in 1936. Peter married Frieda Sprunger from Berne, Ind., in 1937. Peter's mission work included educational and evangelistic endeavors.   LDe

Who's Who Mennonites (1943), 26; GCM Handbook (1952-1962); H. C. Brown, *The General Conference China Menno-nite Mission* (Taming-fu, China: the author, 1940), 65, 86, 104, 126.

Bogotá, Colombia, the capital of the Republic of Colombia, is located on an extensive plateau on the eastern range of the Colombian Andes at an altitude of nearly 9,000 feet (2,700 meters). At the time of the conquest by the Spaniards in the 16th c., Bacatá (Bogotá), was one of the main seats of worship and government of the Chibcha Indian civilization. In the 1980s, with a population of more than 5 million, Bogotá is the cultural, economic, and political center of the country. Like most Latin American cities, Bo-gotá is growing at a fast rate. Such population growth causes hardships for the already over-burdened system of public services and housing.

The Iglesia Evangélica Menonita (General Confer-ence Mennonite Church) of Colombia began work in the city in Jan. 1964. Since then three active Men-nonite churches have emerged with a total member-ship of 417. The Centro Cristiano Menonita (Menno-nite Christian Center), established in 1982, is an at-tractive three-story building located downtown, which houses the Teusaquillo Mennonite Church, a Mennonite bookstore, the Mennonite Development Foundation (MENCOLDES), an audio-visual office, a Christian family agency, and the office of the church's executive secretary. Other Mennonite and Christian agencies use the Mennonite Christian Center for seminars, lectures, and other programs.

More recently three other Anabaptist-related groups have come to work in the city: the Asocia-ción de Iglesias Hermanos Menonitas (Mennonite Brethren), the Comunidad Cristiana Hermandad de Cristo (Brethren in Christ), and the Iglesia Colombi-ana de los Hermanos (related to the Brethren Church, Ashland, Ohio). There is a National Anabap-tist Committee which cooperates on specific issues, e.g., voluntary service programs, °conscientious ob-jection, and Anabaptist identity.   HGVV

Bolivia (ME IV:1067). This republic, located in central South America, is one of the least industrialized and least developed countries of the continent. Mennonite settlement in Bolivia began in 1954 when 11 families from the Fernheim Colony and one family from Menno Colony, both in Paraguay, located near Santa Cruz. Mennonite settlements in Bolivia are all located in the Santa Cruz region of the Bolivian lowlands and comprise the following: (1) Descendants of the immigrants to Manitoba from the Bergthal Colony in Russia (°Sommerfeld Mennonites, the °Chortitzer Mennonite Conference-related Grünthal Mennonites—see °Reinländer Mennoniten Gemeinden, and Saskatchewan °Bergthal Mennonites) have migrated to Bolivia and form seven colonies (all statistics as of 1986): Canadiense (founded 1956, from Paraguay, 807 inhabitants and 329 church members belonging to the Grüntal Mennonites) and its branch colony Morgenland (founded 1975, 280 inhabitants and 104 members, Grünthal Mennonites); Bergthal (founded 1963, from Paraguay and Canada, 306 inhabitants and 127 members); Reinland (also called Las Pavas, founded 1963, from Paraguay and Canada, disbanded 1987) and its branch colony Rosenort (founded 1975, ca. 350 inhabitants and 140 members, including some recently arrived from Reinland); Sommerfeld (founded 1968, from Mexico, 419 inhabitants and 132 members); Neuva Holanda (founded 1983, from Reinland colony, 394 inhabitants and 157 members). In 1986 there were thus ca. 2,500 Mennonites from the Bergthaler-Sommerfelder Mennonite family in Bolivia (989 church members).

(2) Old Colony Mennonites are located in 9 colonies: Swift Current (founded 1967, from Mexico, 2,510 inhabitants with 840 church members in 1986); Rivas Palacios (founded 1967 from Mexico, 5,686 inhabitants and 1,900 members) and its branch colony, Tres Cruces (founded 1982, 785 inhabitants and 285 members); Santa Rita (also called Paurito, founded 1967, from Mexico and Belize, 1,505 inhabitants and 482 members); Las Piedras (founded 1968, from Canada, 594 inhabitants and 218 members) and its branch colony Las Piedras II (founded 1984, 382 inhabitants and 115 members); Valle Esperanza, or Hoffnungstal (founded 1975, from Mexico, 1,400 inhabitants and 607 members); Colonia del Norte (founded 1980, from Mexico, 400 inhabitants and 143 members); San José de Chiquitos (founded 1974, from Mexico and Belize, 1,668 inhabitants and 543 members). Old Colony Mennonites in Bolivia thus numbered nearly 15,000 in 1986 (ca. 5,000 church members). MWF/ME/IHie

Most Mennonites came to Bolivia with more experience in colonizing than in similar ventures elsewhere. Some had sufficient money to purchase machinery helpful in carving a settlement out of the forest. Rainfall and temperature are especially favorable for soya beans, corn, and wheat, with Mennonites growing some 75 percent of Bolivia's soya crop in the Santa Cruz region, as well as producing a large percentage of Bolivia's cheese. Economic conditions worsened markedly in the mid-1980s. With the exception of a few small cheese °cooperatives, Mennonites in Bolivia have not organized °credit unions or colonywide economic cooperatives, as is customary in many Latin American Mennonite colonies. Each group has, however, established a °°Waisenamt (orphan's agency) to take care of

widows and orphans. In some colonies organized °mutual aid provides a type of storm and fire °insurance.

Colony Mennonites in Bolivia have largely maintained an attitude of social distance from non-Mennonite Bolivians. One index of °acculturation is the growing use of the host country's language, Spanish, especially to negotiate business. (Old Colony schools do not teach Spanish.). Children attend school about six months each year to the age of 12 (girls) or 14 (boys). Instruction is in high German, which is not used outside of church and school. There are no Bible schools. Church and colony leadership plan no specific youth activities and no °sports are allowed. Church life remains a predictable, traditional source of deep strength and character for many. Social problems such as alcohol and drug abuse are not unknown. Church °discipline is administered through the °°ban and excommunication, as well as corporal punishment in some instances. Health-care expense is an increasing concern for colony Mennonites. Both well-trained physicians and more informally trained practitioners of °folk medicine are consulted. Marriages occur within the colonies; the consequences of genetic inbreeding have not yet been studied.

Bergthal (Sommerfeld) and Old Colony Mennonites have lived in Bolivia for 30 years. Some signs of an exodus from Bolivia are apparent. The original colony, Tres Palmas, disbanded in 1985; Reinland colony is in decline. Some Old Colony Mennonites moved to Argentina and began the Remeco-Guatrache Colony there. Colony Mennonites have been challenged by difficult conditions to respond nonresistantly to violence and attacks on property. In spite of problems and an uncertain future, most Mennonites are content to live in Bolivia. The country has been good to them; they have been good for Bolivia. Bolivia has its own unique history— how the colonists will fare in that continuing history depends on their willingness and ability to relate to the larger Bolivian society. ME/IHie

Information about the Spanish-speaking Mennonite congregations in Bolivia is found in two related articles. The °Iglesia Menonita de Bolivia (Mennonite Church in Bolivia) resulted from mission work begun in 1971. It was officially organized in 1983 and had four congregations in 1986. In 1988 it is known as Iglesia Evangélica Menonita Boliviana (Bolivian Evangelical Mennonite Church). It is related to both General Conference Mennonite Church and Mennonite Church (MC) mission agencies. The °Misión Evangélica Menonita (Evangelical Mennonite Mission Conference) grew out of mission work begun by Evangelical Mennonite Mission Conference radio broadcasts, 1965-68. It had ca. 125 members in two congregations in 1986.

Mennonite Central Committee (MCC) began work in Bolivia in 1960 in response to a request from the Mennonite colonies to assist in agriculture and health. A clinic constructed in the Tres Palmas colony operated until 1970. During the 1960s the program grew by loaning volunteers to other church agencies.

In 1968-70, a rural-based, integrated development program involving village public health care, education, and agriculture development began in the

BOLIVIA

LEGEND

MENNONITE CHURCHES IN BOLIVIA
≡ National boundary
★ Capitol city
○ Towns and villages with Iglesia Menonita
   de Bolivia (IM) and Mision Evangélica
   Menonita (MEM) congregations
● Other towns and cities
◆ Mennonite colonies: Old Colony (OC),
   Bergthaler (Berg), Reinlaender (Rein),
   Sommerfelder (Somm)
— Selected roads
〜 Rivers

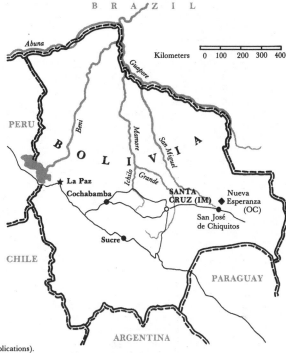

Based in part on map by Bill Schroeder & Bruce Wiebe (CMBC Publications).

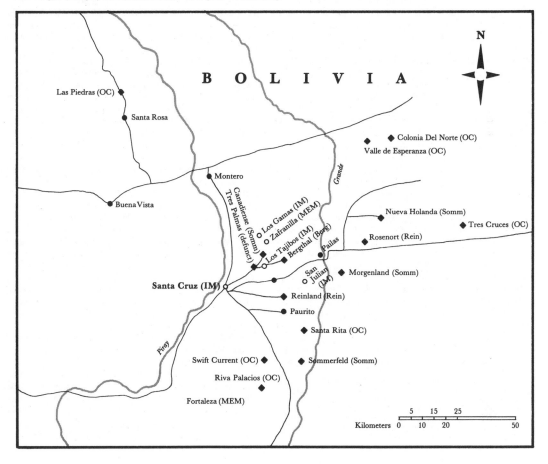

Santa Cruz region and in the San Julian region (the latter in cooperation with the Methodists, Maryknoll missioners, and the Bolivian government). A farm located on the southwest outskirts of Santa Cruz has served since 1972 as a base for crop experimentation, °appropriate technology shop, animal traction experimentation, and Heifer Project International (HPI) animal holding grounds. The farm also has facilities for week-long workshops, seminars, and retreats for a variety of organizations, including the two organized Spanish-speaking Mennonite groups.

In 1976 a conscientious effort to build relationships with the Mennonite colonies was augmented with the appointment of workers specifically for this task. MCC workers have also carried out a tuberculosis program (1975-80); promoted well drilling with hand equipment and placement of HPI animals; conducted nonformal education and a village teachers training program; distributed material aid; and organized disaster relief efforts.

Training materials developed by MCC for preventive health care workers and an orientation program for village colonists coming to the tropics from various parts of Bolivia were adopted by the Bolivian government in 1977 and 1976, respectively.

MCC volunteers have been instrumental in the formation of the Iglesia Menonita de Bolivia since its beginning. In many other communities MCC workers have strengthened struggling Baptist, Assemblies of God, Plymouth Brethren, and other congregations instead of attempting to start competing Mennonite congregations. In some settings dynamic Roman Catholic Bible study groups have also been supported. More than 300 North American and South American volunteers have served in more than 100 Bolivian communities, 1960-85, making it the largest MCC program in any country over that period—in terms of total volunteers.

°Mennonite Economic Development Associates (MEDA) first became active in Bolivia in the early 1970s through MCC. After several smaller loans, including several to Mennonite colonists, in 1974 MEDA loaned $25,000 to La Merced Cooperative, the largest savings and loan cooperative in Santa Cruz. These funds were for small farmers from MCC-related villages who previously had been unable to obtain credit. The first MEDA overseas country director in any country was placed in Bolivia in 1976. MEDA seeks out funding for suitable projects; teaches economic, bookkeeping, and accounting principles on an individual and short course basis; promotes production-oriented cooperatives; gives economic counsel and supervision; and provides funds for small loans. MEDA works closely, although not exclusively, with MCC and has seen itself as the "economic °development arm of MCC in Bolivia."   GM

J. W. Fretz, "A Visit to the Mennonites in Bolivia," *Menn. Life*, 15 (Jan. 1960), 13-17; James Walter Lanning, "The Old Colony Mennonites of Bolivia: A Case Study" (MSc thesis, Texas A and M University, 1971); Richard Plett, *The Colony Mennonites in Bolivia* (Winnipeg: MCC Canada and Die Mennonitische Post, 1980); George Reimer, *A Survey of Mennonites in Mexico, Belize, Bolivia, and Paraguay* (Winnipeg: MCC Canada, 1980ff); letters in *Die Mennonitische Post*, 1977-87; Helen Liechty Glick, *Spiritsong: Mennonite Central Committee's Twenty-five Years in Bolivia* (Akron, Pa.: MCC, 1985); *MWR* (Aug. 8, 1985), 12; (Feb. 19, 1987), 7.

See also articles on specific colonies mentioned above; Old Colony Mennonites.

Bolivian Mennonite Church. See Iglesia Menonita de Bolivia.

Bonhoeffer, Dietrich (Feb. 4, 1906–Apr. 9, 1945), made a profound impact upon Mennonite life and thought. Although in later life he participated in violent resistance against Hitler, the English translation of his book, *Nachfolge* (first published in German in 1937; translated as *The Cost of Discipleship*, 1949), was used as a text in H. S. °Bender's class on °discipleship at Goshen College and Goshen College Biblical Seminary for many years. It helped to make *discipleship* the key term used to describe Anabaptist piety. Together with Johannes °Kühn, he gave the impetus, more than any Anabaptist sources, to Bender's formulation of the °Anabaptist Vision. (Yet Kühn, not Bonhoeffer, was included in ME I-IV). No doubt others, e.g., Robert °Friedmann, whose interest in Kühn was strong, also had an impact on the formulation of the Anabaptist Vision (Gross, "Recasting," 358-59). Allusions and quotes from the Bonhoeffer book appear in Harold Bender's sermons and speeches, and, through Bender's gifted teaching, the life and words of Bonhoeffer inspired several generations of students.

In recent years courses on discipleship and on Bonhoeffer himself have been offered at the Mennonite seminaries in Elkhart and Fresno. As the facts of Bonhoeffer's life became better known, a critical engagement with Bonhoeffer has taken place, with at least two Mennonites writing doctoral dissertations on him (A. J. Klassen, Leroy Friesen). Extensive attention is given to his interpretation of the °Sermon on the Mount, e.g., by Clarence Bauman, who devotes more space to Bonhoeffer than to any other single individual. Factors that have made Bonhoeffer attractive to Mennonites are his concern with the church, the way in which he sought to apply the costly aspects of the gospel in a time of "cheap grace," and, perhaps above all, the concern that he had with making the words of Jesus apply to life here and now. Once the "whole" Bonhoeffer emerged, it was not possible to appropriate his ethical complexity, but there is no doubt that the direct simplicity of *The Cost of Discipleship* and, above all, the profundity of *Life Together* have made a deep and wholesome contribution to Mennonite church life. The most difficult aspect of his position is the devotion he showed to the *Volk* concept (Bauman, 265-66). It seemed as if his devotion to his *Volk* led to an attenuation of his allegiance to Christ as Lord, when he plotted the death of Hitler. Such an act is clearly always in fundamental conflict with Mennonite faith in the lordship of Christ, who calls to a life of love and self-sacrifice. As Bonhoeffer himself said: "When Jesus bids a man come and follow him he bids him come and die" (not kill). Mennonites have had their temptations in this regard, and Bonhoeffer has helped Mennonites to recover the ideal that following Christ means saying farewell to other attachments.   WKla

Eberhard Bethge, *Dietrich Bonhoeffer*, trans. E. Robertson and others (Evanston: Harper and Row, 1970); Clarence

Bauman, *The Sermon on the Mount: The Modern Quest for its Meaning* (Macon, Ga.: Mercer U. Press, 1985), 249-74; Leonard Gross, "Recasting the Anabaptist Vision: The Longer View," *MQR,* 60 (1986), 352-63; Johannes Kühn, *Toleranz und Offenbarung* (Leipzig, 1923).

See also Ethics; National Socialism.

Bookstores, Mennonite. See Associação Evangélica Menonita, Brazil; Austria; Bihar Mennonite Mandli; Bogotá, Colombia; Conferencia de las Iglesias Evangélicas Menonitas, Dominican Republic; Iglesia Evangélica Menonita, Colombia; Konferenz der Mennonitengemeinden in Uruguay; Publishing; Tanzania; Tshikapa, Zaire.

Bote, Der. **See General Conference Mennonite Church; Conference of Mennonites in Canada.**

Botschaft, Die. **See Amish.**

Botswana. Botswana gained independence in 1966; Mennonite presence began soon after, with the arrival of Mennonite Central Committee (MCC) workers in 1968. Initially emphasis was placed on secondary education and teacher training. The MCC program expanded into agriculture and the training of skilled laborers, e.g., mechanics and bricklayers. Later it moved into the area of community development. As MCC workers became more involved in the community they became increasingly aware of °African Independent Churches. Africa Inter-Mennonite Mission (AIMM) began work with these churches in 1975. In 1981 the administration of MCC and AIMM programs was united under Mennonite Ministries in Botswana. In 1986 Mennonite Ministries had personnel working in the areas of community development, education, Bible teaching, and health. A total of 27 workers was anticipated for 1987.   RDS

Bowling Green, Mo., Old Order Amish Settlement (ME IV:180), is located in Pike Co., 50 mi. (80 km.) nw. of St. Louis. It was founded in 1947 by Amish families from °°Jay Co., Ind. The Pike Co. settlement is the oldest and third largest Amish community in the state. Its growth has been slow in its 40-year history. Several newer locations in the state have attracted more Amish families because of better farmland in more ideal locations. All of Missouri's 12 settlements were established after World War II as young families sought cheaper land in the postwar industrial expansion. With less stringent state regulations on the schooling of their children, Amish found the state of Missouri to be ideal for new settlements.   SLY

Branham, John C. (Feb. 12, 1925–Aug. 20, 1984), was born to John Earl and Pearl Branham at Cleveland, Ohio. He was educated in the Cleveland public schools and served in the Navy during World War II, returning to Cleveland after the war. On Nov. 4, 1950, he married Margaret Underwood of Marion, Ala. They had one daughter, Deanna. John worked for Warner and Swasey Co. for 20 years and was member of the Elim Gospel Chapel until 1960 when he joined the Lee Heights Community Church (MC). He was senior presiding elder of this congregation (1962-65) and a member of its board of

directors (1962-84). He helped form the Inter-Church Youth Fellowship of Greater Cleveland in the 1950s and was active on its board. He began chaplaincy work at the House of Correction and at the county jail in 1969; he was ordained a chaplain by Ohio Mennonite Conference in 1971. He opened a halfway house with help of the Ohio Mennonite Evangelism Commission (1973) and continued to lead group sessions for prisoners and ex-offenders weekly. He disappeared on Aug. 20, 1984, after a counseling session. Five days later his body, with a single gunshot wound, was found along Interstate 71 in Medina Co., Ohio. The murder remains unsolved.   VMi/RSa

Obituary from funeral program, Lee Heights Community Church, Cleveland, Ohio, Aug. 30, 1984; James Neff, "The Samaritan," *Cleveland Plain Dealer* (Sept. 12, 1984), 19-A; Katherine L. Siemon, *Plain Dealer* (Aug. 29, 1984).

Brauche, also called *powwowing,* is the practice of customary healing (from *Bräuche,* i.e., "customs") transplanted to America by emigrants from South Germany, Alsace, and Switzerland, and practiced by many settlers in Pennsylvania Dutch country. Powwowing comes in various forms, depending on the geographical location and cultural traditions of the community. Some *Brauchers* use magical words and charms as they apply their art at the bedside of the ill. Other practitioners rely exclusively on the gift of "electric" in the hand. By rubbing and massaging and even following nerve routes through the body, pain can be located and treated. Some *Brauchers* learn their skills from local chiropractors and manipulate the body to relieve pain and pressure. All authentic Amish powwowers agree that the art of *Brauche* is a gift of God and not self-induced. The practice is usually carried out in the home. Treatments are free, but a modest contribution is accepted. *Brauche* has been the subject of debate for centuries. It has nearly vanished in some Amish communities. Many young people know little about this healing art, except for the glowing stories handed down by their elders.   SLY

See also Folk Medicine.

Braun, Bernhard J., and Braun, Linda Marie Ewert, were active in pastoral, educational, and missionary ministries of the Mennonite Brethren in North America and Europe for nearly 50 years. Bernhard Braun (1907–July 9, 1985) grew up in the Orenburg Mennonite settlement near the Ural foothills of central Russia, where Mennonites had pioneered since 1898. The youngest of 14 children, he saw and felt family struggles for existence, uncertainties during World War I, and the terrors of the °Russian Revolution and ensuing unrest in the land. These experiences contributed to his knowledge of God's sovereign love and grace and helped shape his cultural, moral, and spiritual values as a discipline of life. At age 19, he immigrated to Canada. He worked as a farm laborer to pay the debt incurred through that move.

Sensing the call to Christian service, Braun trusted God for resources to acquire needed education. He went to Tabor Academy and then studied at Tabor College. In 1934 he married Linda Marie

Ewert (1908-83) of Mountain Lake, Minn. They became parents of five children. Braun entered social work and business ventures. Things went well and "the treasures of Egypt" (Heb 11:26) were attractive. But the call of the Lord was heavy upon the young couple. After one year of studies at the Baptist Theological Seminary in Fort Worth, Tex., the Brauns accepted the pastorate of the Carson Mennonite Brethren Church, Delft, Minn., in 1939. They were both gifted servants, complementing each other. While Linda used her gifts of caregiving in quiet, tender ways, Bernhard's ministry was more public in nature. With short intervals of graduate studies, he served on all levels of denominational leadership, including 27 years as pastor in Minnesota and California, 10 years as president of Pacific Bible Institute (1947-50) and the Mennonite Brethren Biblical Seminary (1955-62), and concurrently 14 years on the Board of Reference and Counsel. The Brauns also worked together as missionaries in Europe under Mennonite Brethren Missions and Services for 13 years (1964-77), evangelizing, preaching, and teaching. Students there speak with fondness of "Mama Braun" and "Papa Braun." After Linda Ewert Braun's death in 1983, Bernhard Braun married Mary Brandt a year later, one year before his sudden death in 1985.   HK

Chr. Leader (July 23, 1985) 22; *MBHerald* (Sept. 20, 1985) 21.

Brazil (ME 1:408-10). Two hundred Mennonite families found a new home in Brazil in 1930. Until 1960 these settlers were concentrated in the areas of Curitiba, Paraná State; Colônia Nova (Bagé), Rio Grande do Sul State; São Paulo, São Paulo State; °Witmarsum, Paraná State; and the Krauel Valley, Santa Catarina State. The last named settlement dissolved in the 1950s, with settlers going to Colônia Nova near Bagé and Witmarsum in Paraná State.

During the two decades from the 1960s to the 1980s, Mennonites have scattered across Brazil establishing new settlements, business ventures, missionary centers, and other activities. Large plywood factories were established in Manaus and Pará states as subsidiaries to the factories in Curitiba. Other Mennonites moved to Mato Grosso State. Mission congregations arose in Goiás, São Paulo, and other states. In 1987 a new settlement was begun in the state of Bahia in ne. Brazil, some 2,500 km. (1,500 mi.) from Curitiba.

The largest concentration of Mennonites is in three suburbs of Curitiba: Boqueirão, founded in 1935; Vila Guaíra/Agua Verde, founded 1934; and Xaxím, founded in 1936. The Witmarsum (Paraná) and Colônia Nova (Bagé) are flourishing diversified agricultural colonies, with dairy production taking a central place in 1987. The Auhagen-Stolzplateau settlement (in Santa Catarina State), begun in 1930, had dissolved by 1935, with most settlers moving to the Curitiba area. The Guarituba (Paraná) settlement has also been largely terminated (°Witmarsum). The Clevelândia (Paraná) settlement existed, 1953-60 (°Witmarsum). A mission congregation remains active there. Colônia Médici is a daughter colony of Colônia Nova (Bagé). The most recent settlement is Concórdia, comprising an area of nearly 50,000 acres (20,000 hectares), located in the northern state of Bahia (°Witmarsum). It was begun in 1986. Sinop in Mato Grosso state and Rio Verde (Church of God in Christ, Mennonite) in Goias State are small agricultural developments.

Belém, Manaus, and Xinguara in the Amazon region of northern Brazil are regional branches of the plywood factories of Curitiba. Recife (Pernambuco State), located in ne. Brazil, is a development project center begun by Mennonite Central Committee and Brazilian Mennonites in 1968. The Mennonite Church (MC) began work in Brazil in 1954. The Associação das Igrejas Menonitas do Brasil (AIMB, Mennonite Church [GCM] of Brazil) has undertaken missionary activity since 1966 through the Associação Evangélica Menonita (AEM, Mennonite Evangelical Association). In 1975 the Mennonite Board of Missions (MC), the Commission on Overseas Mission (GCM), and the AEM began cooperative work. This included evangelism among existing congregations, founding new congregations in Portuguese-speaking areas, developing leadership and Christian literature, and, especially, work with young people. In 1987, 25 congregations, with a membership of 1,001, were related to AEM, particularly in the state of São Paulo and the Amazon region. Related to the Associação das Igrejas Irmãos Menonitas do Brasil (AIIMB, Conference of Mennonite Brethren Churches in Brazil, German-speaking, 13 congregations, 1,879 members) are 27 Portuguese-speaking congregations of the Convenção das Igrejas Irmãos Menonitas do Brasil (CIIMB, Convention of Mennonite Brethren Churches of Brazil). Total membership in the CIIMB was 1,954. This work is concentrated in southern Brazil, but also takes place in Mato Grosso State, and is done in cooperation with the Mennonite Brethren Board of Missions and Services.

The descendants of Mennonite immigrants from Europe have largely retained their social and community structures. They have relative autonomy in the administration of their economic and other institutions. Great emphasis is placed upon elementary and secondary schools, which are conducted in Portuguese with German as the first foreign language. Colégio Erasto Gaertner in Curitiba has an enrollment of 1,200 students in levels kindergarten–grade 11. Forty percent of the pupils are Mennonite. Colégio Fritz Kliewer in Witmarsum has 350 students enrolled at the same levels. Colégio Erasmo Braga operated in Curitiba from 1956-80, and since then is the location of Instituto e Seminário Bíblico Irmãos Menonitas (Mennonite Brethren Bible Institute and Seminary). The Centro Evangélico Menonita de Teologia por Extensão (Evangelical Mennonite Center of Theology by Extension, CEMTE) is the school of the AEM, which also cooperates with the Centro Evangélico Menonita de Teología Asunción (CEMTA, Evangelical Mennonite Theological Center in Asunción) in Paraguay. Elementary and secondary schools are also maintained by Mennonites in a number of the other settlements in Brazil. As a result of this strong interest in education, Mennonites are active in many vocations throughout the land, as teachers, doctors, lawyers, technicians, business owners, industrialists, etc. In 1986 the total number

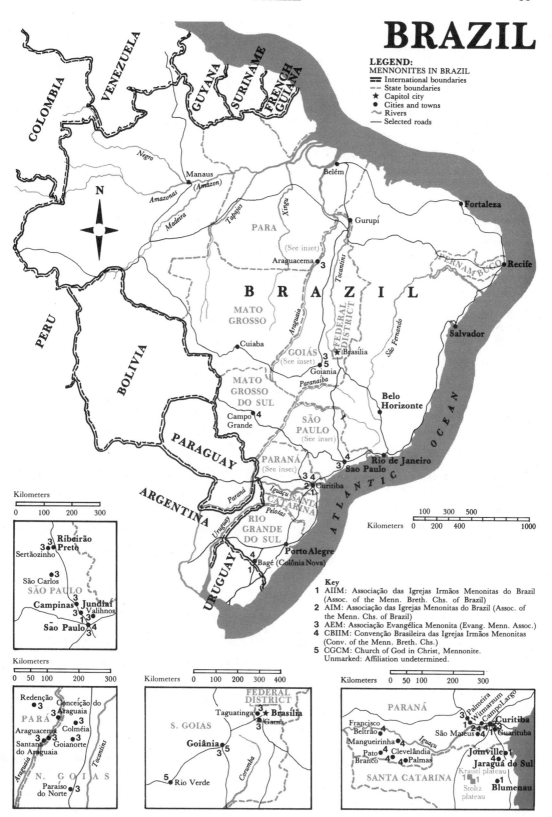

BRAZIL

LEGEND:
MENNONITES IN BRAZIL
- International boundaries
- State boundaries
- ★ Capitol city
- ● Cities and towns
- ~ Rivers
- Selected roads

Key
1 **AIIM:** Associação das Igrejas Irmãos Menonitas do Brazil (Assoc. of the Menn. Breth. Chs. of Brazil)
2 **AIM:** Associação das Igrejas Menonitas do Brazil (Assoc. of the Menn. Chs. of Brazil)
3 **AEM:** Associação Evangélica Menonita (Evang. Menn. Assoc.)
4 **CBIIM:** Convenção Brasileira das Igrejas Irmãos Menonitas (Conv. of the Menn. Breth. Chs.)
5 **CGCM:** Church of God in Christ, Mennonite.
Unmarked: Affiliation undetermined.

of baptized Mennonites in Brazil, including those in mission congregations, was 6,000.

Mennonites have become well established economically in Brazil. All agricultural enterprises are fully mechanized. Various business and industrial enterprises are located in Curitiba and São Paulo, including three travel agencies. Mennonites have also founded the Associação Menonita de Assistência Social (Mennonite Association for Social Welfare), which carries on numerous projects, some also in cooperation with MCC, the °International Mennonite Organization, and the °Europäisches Mennonitisches Evangelisations-Komitee. Lar Betesda, a Mennonite retirement center, is maintained in Curitiba. The Bethel Bible Center at Araucária, near Curitiba, serves as a retreat, conference, and vacation center. °Cooperatives have been operating successfully in Curitiba, Witmarsum, and Bagé, being responsible for all business activities of these settlements.

Mennonites feel themselves fully integrated into Brazilian society and are aware of their responsibilities as citizens for the development of the country. Much is being done in economics, socially, and culturally. The Anabaptist witness is present in 10 states of the nation.

Publications include *Bibel und Pflug* (AIMB), *Informationsblatt* (AIIMB), and *Intercâmbio Menonita*, a publication of AEM. *Bausteine* was published 1973-83 by the German-speaking Mennonite Brethren conference.   HenEns/PP,Jr.

MWH (1978), 196-210; *MWH* (1984), 60-63; Peter Pauls, Jr., ed. *Mennoniten in Brasilien: Gedenkschrift zum 50 Jahr-Jubiläum ihrer Einwanderung, 1930-1980* (Witmarsum: n.p., 1980).

See also articles on the conferences named above.

Brazilian Conference of the Mennonite Brethren Churches. See Convenção Brasileira das Igrejas Irmãos Menonitas.

Brethren in Christ Church, Cuba. See Iglesia de los Hermanos en Cristo, Cuba.

Brethren in Christ Church, Nicaragua. See Iglesia Hermanos en Cristo, Nicaragua.

Brethren in Christ Church in Zambia. See Mbungano Yabunyina Muli Kristo.

Brethren in Christ Church in Zimbabwe (Southern Rhodesia). See Ibandla Labazalwane Kukristu e-Zimbabwe.

Brethren in Christ Church Society, India. The Brethren in Christ Church established its first mission station in India near the site of the later Madhipura Christian Hospital in Saharsa District, Bihar State, in 1914. This area of India, lacking a Protestant witness, was designated for the denomination by the Comity Committee (a cross-section of churches and missions already established in India, °comity).

Over the next 35 years, a number of mission stations developed, including Madhipura, Supaul, Bajora, Monghyr, and Saharsa. Saharsa served as the

headquarters for more than 50 years. The erratic Kosi (Koshi) River destroyed Supaul, which was then replaced by Barjora. A ministry was conducted in Monghyr, a former Baptist mission center, for less than a decade.

Orphanages and schools were established at Saharsa and Barjora. After 1950 no new orphans were accepted and, by attrition, this ministry was eliminated by 1965. Dispensaries and a widows' home served needs during the early days of mission activity. The farm at Barjora began as a labor relief project during the local famine of 1957. It soon became a bridge that built excellent rapport with both government officials and the local people. Madhipura Christian hospital had its origin in the mid-1950s, experienced expansion in the 1960s and 1970s, and continues to provide excellent services under the auspices of the Emmanuel Hospital Association (see below).

In the late 1940s a new work was begun among tribal peoples in neighbouring Purnea District to the east. Two stations were established, one in Banmankhi and one in Purnea. For the first time, Christians remained in their own villages. Three groups were reached by the gospel: the Santal, Uraon, and Munda people. The larger Santal and Uraon groups now have their own regional conferences. The Munda people who live in Purnea work with the Uraon conference.

The upheaval during and after World War II emphasized the need for the church to become indigenous. Along with this was the growing awareness that the purpose of mission was to produce a truly national church. It was not until 1967, however, that a constitution was implemented and the first Indian national became chairman of the church. In 1973 the church became a registered charity, and in 1974 property held by the mission was deeded to the church.

Since 1970 the church among the tribal peoples continued to experience growth in Purnea District and beyond. New villages were constantly being contacted and new churches established. Some of the migrant Santal people found affordable land in nearby Nepal and began to establish new churches. Lay pastors have provided much of the leadership for the churches in both Purnea and Nepal. In 1982 a new ministry was initiated in Orissa. In the late 1980s, steps were taken to capitalize on church planting opportunities in West Bengal and Assam.

In 1987 there were 1,944 communicant members recorded with more than 3,000 people in the Christian community. These were scattered throughout 90 villages over approximately 4,000 square miles (10,000 sq. km.). There were 48 places of worship, fewer than half of which had church buildings. Church planting is a definite, direct thrust reaching new villages, both in the area of the established churches and beyond.

Institutions continue to be the primary ministry among the Bihari people of Saharsa District. The church operates two elementary schools, at Barjora and Saharsa, both of high caliber. There are three hostels, one at Barjora and two at Purnea. The children at the latter attend nearby government schools. Madhipura Christian Hospital has developed into a significant institution. In addition to serving up to 40,000 patients a year, it has initiated a rural °health program in an attempt to heighten preventive medical care in the community and beyond. In cooperation with Mennonite Central Committee, the church initiated a rural °development program. The Brethren in Christ Church has been involved with °Mennonite Christian Service Fellowship of India since its inception in the 1960s.

Leadership training is a significant facet of church life. This occurs at various levels, including seminary and Bible college opportunities. Recently, church growth training is being provided to some leaders through the Haggai Institute in Singapore. Because many of the new tribal Christians are semiliterate, significant lay leadership and °literacy training occurs at the Banmankhi Centre. The village lay leaders who provide spiritual oversight in their local villages come together periodically for training by the more adequately trained pastoral leadership. Former missionaries return to share in leadership training seminars during short visits to India.   HRS

A. Engle, J. Climenhaga, L. Buckwalter, *There is No Difference* (Nappanee, 1950); William Hoke, *Each One Win One* (Delhi: Pioneer Fine Arts Press, n.d., ca. 1971); Harvey Sider, *The Church in Mission* (Nappanee, 1975); Wittlinger, *Piety and Obedience* (1978).

Brethren in Christ Churches, General Conference of (ME I:424), a movement which began around 1780 in Lancaster County, Pa. The founders, largely of Anabaptist background (probably mainly Mennonite), were deeply influenced by the °pietistic revival movements of the period which emphasized a crisis °conversion experience, with an attendant belief in a personal, "heartfelt" relationship to God. Some of the founders received a conversion experience in the revivals, while others came to believe in what the revivals emphasized. They began to meet in their homes to discuss their experiences and to study the Bible for new insights it might give them.

Their discussion led eventually to their formal organization as a separate group. As Anabaptists they were firm in their views of °discipleship and of the church as the visible, called-out body of believers. But they were also convinced of the need for the crisis conversion experience. Thus they did not feel comfortable with the Anabaptist groups from which they came or with various other pietistic groups in the area. As a result, they organized themselves into a new group where the principles of baptism and pietism were combined.

The catalyst for their decision to organize appears to have been the issue of the correct mode of baptism. The founders became convinced from their reading of the Bible that baptism should be by trine °immersion. Their Mennonite ministers, however, would not baptize in this mode. The German Baptists Brethren (later known as Church of the °°Brethren), from whom some of the founders probably came, did practice trine immersion, but would baptize the group in the manner requested only if they became German Baptists Brethren. In their impasse, the group, led by Jacob Engel, decided to baptize each other. The site of their baptism was near Marietta in the Convoy Creek that ran past the Engel farm, located near the Susquehanna River. This action served to reinforce the stance of the founders as a separate group.

The new body called itself the Brethren. They soon became known, however, as River Brethren. Probably the name was given to them by others to distinguish them from other Brethren groups in the area. At the time of the Civil War, when it became necessary to register with the federal government as a nonresistant group, they named themselves Brethren in Christ. In Canada, members were first called Tunkers (from the German verb *tunken*, meaning to dip); according to tradition it was a name given to them by their neighbors who observed them immersing converts in baptism. This name was officially retained until 1933, although the term Brethren in Christ had already been used for some years in conjunction with Tunker.

Shortly after their organization, members began to spread out from their base in Lancaster County. A few went to Canada (primarily Ontario) as early as 1788, and during the course of the 19th c. they also settled in Ohio, Indiana, Illinois, Michigan, Iowa, Kansas, Oklahoma, and California. For the most part, these areas remain the main centers of the Brethren in Christ Church in North America in the 1980s.

Two schisms occurred in the mid-19th c. A small progressive group in Pennsylvania was expelled for constructing a church building rather than continuing to worship in homes and barns. The new group became known as the United Zion's Children (later °United Zion Church). At about the same time, a more conservative group broke from the main body, in part because the latter did not appear aggressive enough in °disciplining those who had built a meetinghouse. This more conservative group called themselves the °Old Order River Brethren (sometimes referred to as Yorkers, but now preferably Old Order Brethren).

During their first century the Brethren in Christ worked out a synthesis of their Anabaptist-pietistic beliefs. Their emphasis on a two-kingdom theology (°nonconformity) made them one with other Anabaptist groups in such matters as °nonresistance and nonparticipation in politics. They wore simple, or plain, clothing, and they practiced brotherhood, including in such matters as church discipline and caring for one another. Their love feasts, adopted from the Church of the Brethren, were an expression of their brotherhood concerns. Their pietism was expressed, among other ways, in testimony meetings (or experience meetings), and in the continued insistence on the crisis conversion experience.

Beginning in the later part of the 19th c., the Brethren in Christ came into contact with new movements and ideas, and during a 30-year period grafted them onto their traditional life and thought. This period may be seen as the first transitional period. It was similar in some ways to the awakening or °renaissance occurring among Mennonites at the same time.

During this transitional period the Brethren in Christ adopted a more aggressive approach to °evangelism. They established missions in Canada, the United States, and in Africa, in what eventually became Zimbabwe and Zambia. They also adopted some of the °revivalist methods then current. Revival meetings at least once a year became an important part of each congregation's yearly activities. °Sunday schools, with their emphasis on the salvation and instruction of youth and °children, also became an aggressive means of evangelism.

In the same period, the Brethren in Christ established a number of institutions. In 1887 they began a church paper, the *Evangelical Visitor*, which became a useful medium for evangelism and the spread of new ideas. They began °°orphanages in Oklahoma, Illinois, and Pennsylvania, and, also in Pennsylvania, a home for the elderly. Messiah Bible School and Missionary Training Home (later Messiah College) was chartered in Pennsylvania in 1909; Beulah (later Upland) College in California in 1920; and Ontario Bible School (later Niagara Christian College) in 1931.

A formal merger of the church in Canada with the church in the United States occurred in 1879. The governing body (General Conference) created by this merger, met annually until 1972, when it began to meet biennially. These institutions, together with the structures needed to conduct missions, gave the Brethren in Christ a more organized structure, in contrast to an earlier informal approach to church life.

At the same time, Wesleyan °holiness theology, with its emphasis on the sanctified life, gradually worked its way into the church to become an official doctrine in 1910. Although in some ways pietistic in nature, the doctrine was essentially a new teaching. The emphasis was now less on the work of the Holy Spirit leading the Christian to a more perfect spiritual state and more on a second work of grace in which the Holy Spirit filled the heart, cleansed it from its carnal nature, and enabled the Christian to live the life of obedience more successfully. By the 1930s holiness camps began to appear—at Roxbury, Pa., in 1936, followed by others in Ohio, Ontario, Kansas, California, and Florida.

Beginning in the early 1950s, a second period of transition brought more significant changes to the Brethren in Christ. In part, this was owing to the increasing °urbanization and °professionalism of members of the church, which brought them into contact with new people and ideas; in part, it grew out of a growing concern to be more effective in changing conditions in which the church was finding itself. Standards for plain dress were relaxed and eventually disappeared, although an emphasis on modesty remained. °Musical instruments, once forbidden in both homes and churches, became widely used, even for worship services. A strong youth program was developed which included youth °camps, °Bible quizzing competitions, and athletic events. Absolute restrictions against membership for °divorced and remarried people were officially relaxed by General Conference and in a growing number of congregations.

At the same time, the Brethren in Christ became more ecumenical. In 1949 they became official members of the National Association of Evangelicals, and in 1950 joined the National Holiness Association (later Christian Holiness Association). Brethren in Christ have held leadership positions in both organizations. Beginning in World War II, the Brethren in Christ Church has been a member of Mennonite Central Committee, and have cooperated closely with Mennonites in peace witness and relief service.

A structural reorganization accompanied this second transitional period. Many small districts (some with only one congregation), each with its own °bishop, were replaced with six regional conferences with a bishop for each conference. Greater freedom was given to local congregations to interpret the decisions of General Conference and its doctrinal statements. A further structural reorganization in the early 1980s (known as Renewal 2000) consolidated many boards, committees, and commissions into several boards. It also instituted Cooperative Ministries, a brotherhood concept of financing the sevices of the church in which money given in congregational offerings goes in proportional amounts to congregational, regional, and General Conference ministries.

The continuing strong missions orientation of the Brethren in Christ Church is illustrated in the Board for World Missions receiving (in 1986) nearly 50 percent of the Cooperative Ministries budget. Since 1945 the mission areas of the church have been expanded beyond Africa and India to include Japan, Cuba, Nicaragua, Venezuela, Colombia, England, and Malawi. In recent years. representatives from each area have come together periodically for a conference, as in 1984 in Hagenau, France. In its mission program, the church has endeavored to provide wholistic ministry. Along with preaching and building churches, it has established orphanages and homes for children, medical clinics, and hospitals.

Other ministries of the Brethren in Christ Church in North America speak to similar concerns. Messiah Village in Pennsylvania and Upland Manor in California are retirement °homes. Timber Bay Children's Home in Saskatchewan, Canada, cares for North American Indian children during the school year. Paxton Street Home in Harrisburg, Pa., provides food and housing for disadvantaged people. Camping programs at Kenbrook and the Christian Retreat Center (both in Pennsylvania), Camp Kahquah in Ontario, Camp Lakeview in Michigan, and Mile High Pines in California focus on children, youth, and families.

The membership of the Brethren in Christ Church in North America in 1986 was approximately 18,000. Total membership in Brethren-in-Christ-related churches outside North America was approximately 16,000.   EMS

Wittlinger, *Piety and Obedience* (1978); Asa W.Climenhaga, *History of the Brethren in Christ Church* (Nappanee, 1942); Norman A. Bert, *Adventure in Discipleship* (Nappanee, 1968); E. Morris Sider, *Nine Portraits* (Nappanee, 1978); idem, *The Brethren in Christ in Canada: Two Hundred Years of Tradition and Change* (Nappanee, 1988); Owen H. Alderfer, *Called to Obedience* (Nappanee, 1975).

"Brinser Brethren." See United Zion Church.

British Columbia. By 1911 a Mennonite settlement had taken root at Renata along the Arrow lakes in se. British Columbia. The settlers' source of livelihood was fruit growing and timber processing. They built a school and organized Sunday school classes and church services in which lay and visiting ministers played a leading role. In the mid-1960s the community was relocated when a nearby hydroelectric dam flooded the valley.

Today Mennonites in British Columbia worship in about 90 congregations from the ne. Peace River valley to Vancouver Island. Most reside in the Fraser Valley and the city of Vancouver. Fifty-eight congregations are affiliated with the °British Columbia Provincial Conference of Mennonite Brethren Churches and 26 with the Conference of Mennonites in British Columbia (GCM). There is a Church of God in Christ, Mennonite (Holdeman), congregation, an Evangelical Mennonite Brethren (°Fellowship of Evangelical Bible Churches), and several Evangelical Mennonite Conference (EMCon) congregations. Mennonites worship in a variety of languages, including German, English, Mandarin, Cantonese, Vietnamese, and Punjabi. The conferences see church planting as a high priority.

Since the 1950s Mennonites have become more urbanized as the Fraser valley as far as Abbotsford has acquired suburban characteristics. Dairy farming, fruit growing, and poultry raising are still important ways of making a living, but British Columbia Mennonites are increasingly entering the commercial and professional fields. Growing material success seems to be muting the traditional Anabaptist renunciation of secular society (°nonconformity).

Mennonites are relating more to °evangelical Christian groups. They share with them an emphasis on regeneration, evangelism, and personal piety, characteristics also of the 16th-c. Anabaptists. At the same time some evangelicals are recognizing that the gospel confronts social and economic injustice and militarism. Interaction between Mennonites and the broader evangelical movement may therefore help both to speak directly to °peace and °justice issues.

British Columbia Mennonites serve society jointly and as congregations. Since the 1950s, the Mennonite Brethren and the Conference of Mennonites have cooperated through Mennonite Central Committee (MCC B.C.) and through educational ventures.

MCC B.C. was established in the 1940s. Siegfried Bartel has served as chair for the last 15 years, and before him George Thielmann served for 17 years. In addition to MCC's global and national program it is involved in supportive care services for the developmentally °disabled. MCC B.C. has established three group homes as well as a Community Living Program in which MCC staff provide assistance to mentally handicapped people living in their own homes. It also provides a day school and a self-help craft program for the handicapped. Through its Peace and Service Committee, MCC B.C. has organized annual children's festivals to introduce children, within the context of their family, to their Mennonite heritage and to the MCC program. In 1986 MCC B.C.'s Social Housing Society opened the doors of an apartment building in Vancouver with the goal of providing affordable housing for the poor. MCC B.C. sponsors a number of °voluntary service units and a growing number of annual °relief sales.

Initiatives also come from individual congregations. Langley Mennonite Fellowship in 1982 launched its Victim Offender Reconciliation Program. It seeks to reconcile the victim of a crime with the offender in such a way that offenders recognize the effects of their actions on victims, and in some way make restitution.

Mennonite women are active in British Columbia. They meet monthly in individual congregations for fellowship, meditation, sewing, knitting, and quilting. The sale of their products provides MCC B.C. with a substantial part of its annual budget. After World War II, General Conference Mennonite women operated the Mary-Martha Home for young women in Vancouver, which took in those recently arrived in the city and put them in touch with employers. In 1985 the Open Door in Aldergrove was established by women to serve economically deprived single mothers.

In 1970-71 the two major conferences agreed to operate one Bible school. Because attendance at Bethel Bible Institute in Abbotsford diminished in the 1960s, the Conference of Mennonites (GCM) held a special study conference in 1967 on the future of their school. As a result of discussions with the Mennonite Brethren, whose Mennonite Brethren Bible Institute (MBBI) had been growing during the 1960s, it was decided to close Bethel and join forces with MBBI in nearby Clearbrook. The result was Columbia Bible Institute (CBI), with students and faculty from both conferences. In 1982 the Conference of Mennonites in British Columbia joined the Mennonite Brethren provincial conference as owners and governors of CBI. It is the first inter-Mennonite Bible institute in North America and has as its goal "to actively promote and teach a strong evangelical, Anabaptist (Mennonite) theology. . . ." In 1985 the school was renamed Columbia Bible College. It is accredited by the American Association of Bible Colleges and has applied to the province for the right to grant degrees.

Mennonites in British Columbia also cooperate in ministering to university students. In 1986 the Menno Simons Centre was established near the campus of the U. of British Columbia. The center consists of a residence for some 20 students with a small chapel. It also serves as headquarters for student ministry for other students enrolled in the province's institutes of higher learning and as a retreat center.

Mennonite Educational Institute in Clearbrook is also a cooperative venture, run by a society of six Mennonite Brethren and four General Conference Mennonite congregations. It provides education for students from grades eight to twelve. It was founded in 1944 and in 1987 is filled to capacity with 640 students.   JMK

George G. Baerg, *A Brief History of Mennonites in British Columbia* (Yarrow: Columbia Press, 1967); idem, "The Mennonites" in *Strangers Entertained: A History of Ethnic Groups in British Columbia*, ed., John Norris (Vancouver: B.C. Centennial Committee, 1971), 185-90; *Die Vereinigten Mennonitischen Gemeinden in British Columbia* (Yarrow: Columbia Press, 1959); John J. Krahn, "A Social History of Mennonites in British Columbia" (MD thesis, School of Medicine, U. of British Columbia, 1955); Adina Janzen and Winnie Dueck, eds., *History of B.C. Mennonite Women in Mission 1939-1976* (Chilliwack, n.d.); Abram J. Klassen, ed., *The Bible School Story (1913-1963)*, (Clearbrook: General Board of Education, MB Conference, 1963); Agatha Klassen, ed., *Yarrow: Portrait in Mosaic* (Yarrow: A. E. Klassen, 1976); Lawrence Klippenstein, "Early Mennonites in B.C.: Renata, 1907-1965," in *Menn. Historian* (Winnipeg), 7, no. 3, pp. 1-2, and no. 4, p. 2; Gerhard Lohrenz, *The Mennonites in Western Canada* (Steinbach: Duerksen Printers, 1974); Mary Warkentine and Rose Ann Rahn, eds., *The Story of*

BRITISH COLUMBIA

MENNONITES IN BRITISH COLUMBIA

LEGEND

- ● Cities and towns
- ★ Capitol city
- ▲ Church camps
- ~ Rivers
- ═ National boundary
- -- Provincial boundary

Church Membership

- ○ 0-250
- ○ 250-500
- ○ 500-1000
- ○ 1000-1500
- ○ 1500-2000
- ○ 2000-2500
- ○ 2500-5000

Membership figures include Chortitzer (est.), CGCM, E. Pennsylvania, EMB (est.), EMC (Canada), EMMC (est.), GC, MB, MC, Old Colony (est.), and Sommerfelder (est.) congregations.

Totals based on the congregations' addresses.

Kilometers 0   45   90

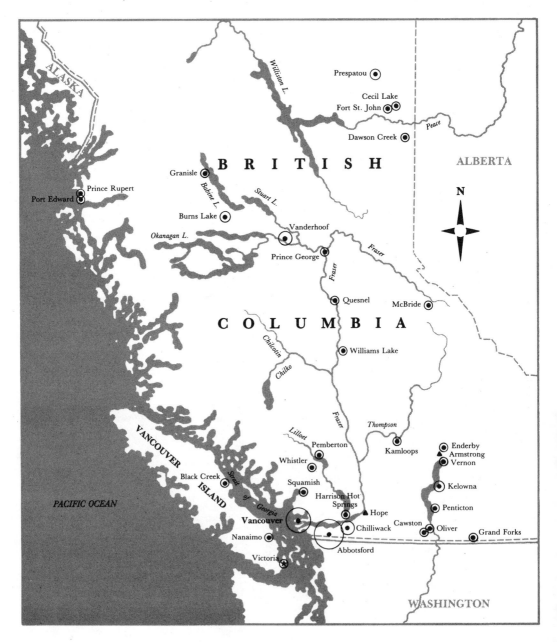

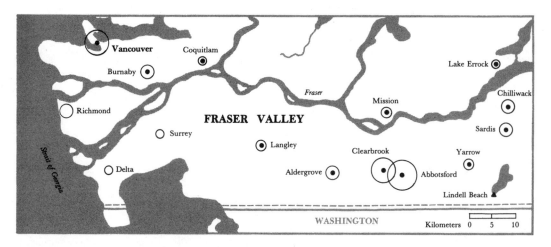

Renata (Renata, B.C. 1965); *MC Yearbook* (1988-89), 12-13; Daniel Hertzler, *From Germantown to Steinbach* (Scottdale, 1981), 186-97.

British Columbia Provincial Conference of Mennonite Brethren Churches (ME I:431) was organized in 1931. John Harder, Peter D. Loewen and C. C. Peters significantly shaped the Conference in its formative years. By 1986 the Mennonite Brethren conference had become one of the largest evangelical denominations in British Columbia, with 56 congregations and a membership of 9,787.

From its inception, the conference emphasized °evangelism and °Christian education. The earliest outreach activities included establishing a city mission in Vancouver, and by 1945, support of the West Coast Children's Mission. Simultaneously, much emphasis was placed on °Bible conferences, Sunday School conventions, and music festivals.

During the 1970s and 1980s, priority has been given to church planting, including congregations among six non-English ethnic groups. The conference also supports Columbia Bible Camp, and together with the Conference of Mennonites in British Columbia (GCM), cosponsors Columbia Bible College in Clearbrook.   HJB

Minutes of the Annual Meetings (1931-1986) (Clearbrook: B.C. Conference of Mennonite Brethren Churches, published annually); Agatha E. Klassen, *Yarrow A Portrait in Mosaic* (Yarrow: A. E. Klassen, 1976); Peter Penner, *Reaching the Otherwise Unreached* (Clearbrook: West Coast Children's Mission, 1959); John A. Toews, *History MB* (1975), index, esp. 167-71.

British Honduras. See Belize.

Broadcasting, Radio and Television (ME IV:244). Religious programs have been a part of the broadcasting environment since the early 1920s. Mennonites have offered both condemnation and praise of broadcasting. On one hand, °radio and °television programs were condemned as dangerous to spiritual life and as promoting materialism, immorality, and questionable theology. On the other hand, Mennonites recognized the potential for evangelism, inspiration, and nurture through broadcasting. The earliest radio programs produced by Mennonites in North America featured sermons and singing. Some were broadcasts of church services. Two of the earliest programs continue in the 1980s. In 1936 pioneer broadcaster, pastor William Detweiler, began "The Calvary Hour." The program, carried on by his sons, can be heard on over 30 stations in North and South America in 1988. In 1939 Theodore °Epp, a former General Conference Mennonite minister, founded Back to the Bible, Inc., an independent, nondenominational broadcast ministry based in Nebraska. The program, "Back to the Bible," is heard on nearly 600 stations around the world in 1988.

During the 1950s, Mennonite broadcast activity expanded. Mennonites in Manitoba established a Mennonite-owned and operated radio station, CFAM. Three Mennonite colleges operated FM radio stations during the 1950s: Bethel College, Goshen College, and Eastern Mennonite College. Numerous local broadcasts were produced by General Conference Mennonite Church, Mennonite Brethren, and Mennonite Church (MC) congregations and colleges in the United States and Canada (Shelly, 1952; Rempel, 1952).

During the decade, various Mennonite conferences and mission boards became active in broadcasting. In 1951 the Mennonite Church (MC) authorized the Mennonite Board of Missions and Charities to establish a national Mennonite broadcast. In association with Mennonite Crusader, Inc., a Harrisonburg, Va., group, Mennonite Broadcasts, Inc. (MBI) was founded to continue the operation of the "Mennonite Hour," with B. Charles Hostetter as speaker. (By 1988 Mennonite Broadcasts, Inc., had become Mennonite Board of Missions Media Ministries.) By the end of the decade of the 1950s, MBI was producing programs in English, Spanish, Japanese, Italian, Navajo, German, French, and Russian. They also sponsored a weekly women's program, "Heart to Heart," established by Ruth Brunk Stoltzfus in 1950 and carried on by Ella May Miller from 1958 to 1977.

The Canadian Mennonite Brethren also embraced a broadcast. In 1954 they officially sanctioned the "Gospel Light Hour," a broadcast begun at Mennonite Brethren Bible College in the late 1940s. Gospel Light (later known as Mennonite Brethren Communications) developed programs in English, German, Low German, and Russian for adults and children.

The General Conference Mennonite Church expanded a local devotional broadcast in Newton, Ks., called "Faith and Life," to a conferencewide project in 1953. The General Conference Mennonite Church effort was ultimately lodged with the Commission on Home Ministries. It became known as Faith and Life Radio and Television in the late 1960s, and as the Media Division in the 1980s.

During the 1960s Mennonite organizations and independent producers concentrated on refining production techniques and expanding distribution of the programs. Many of the ongoing programs featured choirs or quartets in addition to speakers. Music and speaking tours in the churches were common, along with the distribution of printed messages and other literature to listeners through the mail. Staff sometimes purchased air time, often sought free time, or found local congregational or business sponsorship.

By the mid-1970s, the North American broadcast industry presented religious broadcasters with several challenges: free or sustaining time was hard to find or available only for undesirable hours; the cost of air time was increasing; broadcasters were interested in shorter programs; television presented a challenge that could no longer be ignored.

MBI began experimenting with seasonal specials and radio spots in 1964. The first series of 30 to 60-second spots were designed to speak to the pressures and problems facing men. "Minutes for Women" spots, released in 1966, spoke to the needs of women and families. The "Choice" spots, developed by David Augsburger, grew out of this initial experimentation. "Choice" was designed to fit a 13-week block of station programming with daily spots, five days a week. These spots were well received because they were issue-oriented and fit the flow of commercial radio formats. In the 1970s "Choice" was used on 300-500 stations. In the late 1980s, up to 1,000 stations were using the program. The 11th edition of "Choice" was produced in 1988. Most "Choice" series were interdenominational productions with participation from the General Conference Mennonite Church, Mennonite Brethren, and Church of the Brethren.

Mennonites also experimented with television spots for the first time in the late 1960s. The Mennonite Church and the General Conference Mennonite Church together produced four 60-second spots on family life in 1969. By 1970 the Mennonite Brethren joined them to produce a second series of "Family Life" spots. In 1975 the Inter-Mennonite Media Group (IMMG) was formed to carry out inter-Mennonite broadcast activities. IMMG spearheaded the joint production of such multimedia campaigns as "Invitation to Live" (1976-77). In addition to radio and television spots, "Invitation to Live" messages were carried through posters, paperback books, newspaper advertisements, calendars, post cards, T-shirt transfers, pens, and stickers. A *Media Handbook* for congregations accompanied the media materials, offering ideas and suggestions for how congregations might use the materials in their local communities.

The 1970s were thus characterized by inter-Mennonite cooperation and a growing emphasis on spot production, along with the production of ongoing radio programs. The only ongoing television program from this era appears to be the children's program, "Third Story," produced by Mennonite Brethren Communications for release on Canadian television. With the exception of television spots, Mennonites have generally been unable to afford to do full-length television program production for commercial markets.

The 1970s were also characterized by growing concerns about the impact of television programs on traditional Mennonite values (see °mass media; television). These concerns were renewed in the 1980s with the penetration of video cassette recorders into Mennonite homes.

During the 1970s, philosophies of mission underwent a metamorphosis that had direct impact on broadcast activities by Mennonite mission boards in North America and beyond for the next decade. Concerns about cultural imperialism and indigenous leadership development led to increased sensitivity about exporting North American programs overseas and to production partnerships with local churches and conferences around the world. In 1977, for example, Europäische Mennonitische Radiomission was formed to carry responsibility for the German broadcasts conducted by the Mennonite Board of Missions ("Worte des Lebens" [Words of Life] founded in 1959; "Quelle des Lebens" [Fountain of Life] founded in 1976). The committee was formed with representation from the Swiss, German, and French (Alsace) conferences and the European Mennonite Bible School (Bienenberg) board. In 1988 it includes members from Mennonite and Mennonite Brethren churches in West Germany, Switzerland, Austria, and France.

Mennonite Board of Missions Spanish broadcast ministries were initiated through missionary efforts in Puerto Rico in 1947 ("Luz y Verdad" [Light and Truth] founded in 1947; "Corazon a Corazon" [Heart to Heart] founded in 1964). In 1972 the 10 Latin American conferences took responsibility for the expanded broadcast and literature ministries with the organizing of Junta Ejecutiva Latinoamericana de Audiciones Menonitas (JELAM; Latin American Executive Council for Mennonite Broadcasts). JELAM produced and distributed internationally radio, television, and print materials until 1984. With a shift in conference activities, Agrupacion Menonita Lationamerica de Comunicaciones (AMLAC; Latin American Mennonite Consortium for Communications) replaced JELAM in 1983 to provide resources and consultation for conferences and congregations who were involved in program production in their local communities. Programs were local and national instead of international. AMLAC holds regular conferences for Latin American communicators and publishes a newsletter, *Informa,* to offer resources and to promote the use of media among Latin American churches.

With the 1980s came sweeping changes in the configuration of the communications scene. The diffusion of cable television offerings and the addition of home video recorders gave North American consumers more choices and more control over what they could watch. In the United States, radio and television were deregulated and broadcasters were no longer obligated to offer free time for public service programs and spots. Sponsored broadcast time became increasingly expensive. Instead of mass audiences, programs were targeted to specific audiences for specific purposes. The "electronic church" was rocked by a series of scandals, precipitating a decline in both viewers and in support, as well as a decline of the public image of religious broadcasting in general.

On the Mennonite front, both the General Conference Mennonite Church and Mennonite Brethren in the United States closed their media divisions because of budget squeezes and shifting institutional priorities. As a result, inter-Mennonite production activities declined, and IMMG was replaced with the Council on Church and Media (CCM) in 1985. CCM holds an annual conference; serves as a media think-tank and clearing house for ideas and plans; and brings together both audiovisual and print communicators from church agencies, schools, and publications. Increasingly sophisticated marketing techniques have also influenced program planning and philosophy. Broadcast productions are now considered part of an overall communications strategy, often combining print and other communications media to accomplish specific tasks, including evangelism, training, nurture, inspiration, interpretation, promotion, and fundraising.

Internationally, MBM in 1988 produces just two international broadcasts. Both are Russian-language programs. All other Mennonite programs outside North America are produced by national church organizations in various regions of the world. MBM's focus is now on training, consultation, and financing in partnership with local groups. For example, Indonesian Mennonites own and operate a radio station that serves their region of the world. Japanese Mennonites are involved with two ecumenical broadcast operations and have placed their first missionary in the Japanese department of the international station, HCJB, in Quito, Ecuador. Many national church media projects are inter-Mennonite in sponsorship. (Descriptions of current activity are found in the annual reports of the °mission boards.) Domestically, MBM's focus has shifted from doing radio evangelism for the denomination to helping congregations use the media to enhance their local evangelism activities. Ongoing broadcasts have given way to the production of special packages that are designed to help congregations with local outreach. "Art McPhee in Touch," the program that succeeded the "Mennonite Hour," ceased production in 1984. "Your Time," the program that succeeded "Heart to Heart," ended production in 1987. Media staff in 1988 are devoting energies to training local congregations to use local media, to creating packages of spots and other resources for congregations to use in their local communications efforts, and to producing video resources for the church. Video recordings are perceived to be the medium of the future. Neverthe-

less, programs that identify who Mennonites are and what they believe (see °mass media) continue to be produced for the public media.

The number of evangelistic radio programs produced by Mennonite mission agencies and Mennonite-affiliated parachurch organizations has declined since flourishing in the 1950s. While a number remain in 1988, listed in *MC Yearbook* (1988-89), mission agencies have expanded their media activities beyond broadcasting, sometimes using radio for news and information, and sometimes combining broadcast activities with other media efforts in a multimedia approach. Denominational resources in the late 1970s and 1980s have emphasized church planting and church growth. Rather then producing programming in the name of the denomination, media agencies have reflected denominational priorities, increasingly becoming consultants and producers for local congregations. They attempt to match what is produced with the needs and priorities of the local congregational activities, both in North America and around the world. While radio production continues, denominational resources have shifted toward multimedia approaches with an increasing emphasis on the production of video resources. Ongoing broadcasts with an evangelistic emphasis are produced mainly by parachurch organizations with both formal and informal relationships to denominational agencies. The productions of Mennonite agencies have diversified in purpose, in audience, in language, and in form in the 1980s. DZU

Mennonite (Mar. 26, 1985), 130-31; *GH* (June 25, 1985), 448; Frank H. Epp, "Radio as It Should Be," *Menn. Life*, 14 (January 1959), 39-40; *GH* (Mar. 11, 1985), 202; *GH* (Oct. 28, 1986), 736-38; *Mennonite Board of Missions Annual Report* (Elkhart, Ind.: MBM, annually); *MC Yearbook* (Scottdale, MPH, biennially); Hubert R. Pellman, *Mennonite Broadcasts: The First 25 Years* (Harrisonburg, Va.: Mennonite Broadcasts, 1979); J. G. Rempel, "Mennonites on the Air in Western Canada," *Menn. Life*, 7 (1952), 125-27; Andrew R. Shelly, "Mennonites on the Air," *Menn. Life*, 7 (April 1952), 65-70; Eugene K. Souder, "Ventures in Radio Broadcasting," *Menn. Life*, 18 (January 1963), 35-38; Wittlinger, *Piety and Obedience* (1978), 509-12; James Metzler, *Saigon to Shalom* (1985); Justus G. Holsinger, *La Obra Menonita en Puerto Rico/Mennonite Work in Puerto Rico, 1943-1981*, passim; John A. Toews, *History MB* (1975), index; David Nightingale, "Radio and Literature in World Missions," in *The Church in Mission*, ed. A. J. Klassen (Fresno: MB Board of Christian Literature, 1967), 329-44.

See also Bihar Mennonite Mandli; Canadian Conference of Mennonite Brethren Churches; Chiesa Evangelica Mennonita Italiana; Mennonite Church of Trinidad and Tobago.

Broederschapshuizen (Brotherhood Houses). See Camps and Retreat Centers.

Brotherhood Auto Aid. See Insurance; Mutual Aid; Church of God in Christ.

Brown, Henry Jacob (Dec. 9, 1879–Sept. 18, 1959), went to China in 1909 with his wife, Maria Miller Brown, to begin mission work in the city of Kai Chow (later known as Puyang), Hopei Province. An early ministry for them was a medical dispensary in which Brown, with limited training, performed minor surgeries because of the dire needs of the people. In 1914 their initiative was approved as a mission field for the General Conference Mennonite Church. The son of Jakob and Elizabeth Penner Braun of Mountain Lake, Minn., Henry was a traveling evangelist in the United States and Canada for two years before leaving for China. In 1922 he proposed a plan to share leadership of the church and mission with the Chinese Christians. In 1941 the Browns were interned near Beijing by the Japanese in their invasion of China. They were released in 1943 and returned home. After World War II, they served in Kaifeng and Shanghai. They retired in 1949.   MSh

Juhnke, *Mission* (1979), 45-64; Edmund G. Kaufman, *The Development of the Missionary and Philanthropic Interest Among the Mennonites* (Berne, Ind.: Mennonite Book Concern, 1931), 160, 323-326; idem, "Henry J. Brown, 1879-1959," in *General Conference Mennonite Pioneers* (North Newton, Ks.: Bethel College, 1973), 347-353. Books by H. J. Brown include: *Chips of Experience* (n.p., n.d.); *The General Conference China Mennonite Mission* (Taming-fu: author, 1940); *In Japanese Hands* (North Newton, Ks.: author, 1943).

Brown, Maria Miller (Oct. 16, 1883–Dec. 10, 1975). With her husband, Henry Jacob Brown, Maria Miller Brown founded a mission program in Hopei Province, China, in 1909, with the support of their families and a number of Mennonite congregations in North America. Her husband had wanted to take up work in Africa, but she suggested China because her family had ties with people doing mission work in China. Their first point of contact in China was with her cousin, Jonathan J. Schrag, Freeman, S.D., who was part of a mission society founded earlier by Henry C. and Nellie Schmidt °Bartel. Born in Marion, S.D., she helped to develop the first mission station at Kai Chow (later known as Puyang). In the early years, before the General Conference mission board took on the support of their program, she assisted her husband in operating a medical dispensary. She led in women's work and engaged in village evangelism and church visitation. A son, Roland, entered mission work in Taiwan in 1956.   MSh

Jesse Brown Gaeddert, "At Home in Two Worlds: Maria Miller Brown, 1883-1975," in *Full Circle*, ed. Mary Lou Cummings (Newton, 1978), 48-58; Maria Miller Brown, *Praise the Lord* (Freeman, S.D.: Pine Hill Printery, 1963).

Brubaker, Henry Heisey (July 21, 1900–Aug. 20, 1972), a distinguished Brethren in Christ Church leader and missionary statesman, was born near Mechanicsburg, Pa., the son of Henry B. and Annie Heisey Brubaker. He attended Messiah Bible School (later Messiah College) and went to Africa in August 1922. In 1926 he married Grace Book, and they had two children: Ronald and Edna, wife of Lee Schroeder.

Brubaker served 29 years in Africa and was General Superintendent and Bishop of the Northern and Southern Rhodesia mission fields (Zambia and Zimbabwe respectively). During that time he was also president of the Southern Rhodesia Missionary Conference and the church's representative on the government Advisory Board for African Education.

When he retired from the mission field, he served his church as president of Niagara Christian College in Ontario and as superintendent of the Messiah Home, Harrisburg, Pa. For 10 years he was secretary

for the General Conference (BIC) and made a vital contribution to the development of its structure. He died in Upland, Cal.   NJK

Anna R. Engle, and others, *There Is No Difference* (Nappanee, 1950), 76-109, 371-72; *EV*, (Sept. 25, 1972), 2, 15; Wittlinger, *Piety and Obedience* (1978), index.

Bruderhof. See Hutterian Brethren.

Brüderliche Vereinigung. See Schleitheim Confession.

Brunk, Aldine Carpenter (Oct. 25, 1886–Dec. 23, 1969), was one of five children born to John and Lilly Carpenter Brunk in Broadway, Va. He received his formal education from Goshen College, where he graduated from the academy in 1908 and received a BA degree in 1912.

During his years at Goshen College he was challenged to offer himself for foreign missions and was appointed by the Mennonite Board of Missions and Charities (MC) in 1912 to serve in India. In 1913 he married Eva Harder, who was also serving in the mission. In 1921 he earned an MA degree from the College of Missions, Indianapolis, Ind.

Though not an eloquent speaker, A. C. Brunk was an effective evangelist and able administrator. In India he served in many leadership roles. He was manager of the Balodgahan village, opened the Dondi station, engaged in extensive village evangelism, and served as field secretary, pastor, and superintendent of Shantipur Leprosy Home and Hospital.

Aldine and Eva retired from mission service in 1947 and lived in Elkhart, Ind., until Eva's death in 1949. Then Aldine moved to Colorado Springs, Col., where he helped organize the Beth-el Mennonite congregation. In Colorado he married Eva's sister Melva Harder, and they moved to Hesston, Ks. for their final retirement years.   JAF

John A. Lapp,*India* (1972), index; *Building on the Rock* (Scottdale, 1926), 183; Esther Rose Graber, comp., "MBM Missionary Directory" (1984); *GH* (Feb. 30, 1970), 111; (Oct. 23, 1951), 1017-18.

Brunk, Eva Harder (July 22, 1883–Apr. 15, 1949), was born in Latham, Mo., the third of eleven children born to Charles and Helena Harder. With the death of her mother when she was 20 years old, Eva assumed the responsibilities of running the home.

Eva taught public school for a number of years before enrolling in Goshen College, where she graduated in 1908. That same year she was appointed by the Mennonite Board of Missions and Charities (MC) to serve in India. In 1913 she and A. C. Brunk, a fellow missionary, were married.

In India, Eva served as a practical nurse. She was a creative worker, teaching self-help skills to the widows and ministering to orphaned and neglected children. During her last seven years of service she directed the medical program at the Shantipur Leprosy Home and Hospital.

Eva retired with her husband to Elkhart, Ind., in 1947 where she lived until her death.   JAF

GH (May 31, 1949), 534; Esther Rose Graber, comp. "MBM Missionary Directory" (1984); interviews with Minnie Graber, Elizabeth Kniss, and Ida Beare.

Buckwalter, Ralph Earl (Aug. 20, 1923–Jan. 10, 1980), a pioneer missionary to Japan under the Mennonite Board of Missions (MC), was born at Hesston, Ks. During World War II, as a conscientious objector, he spent three years in °°Civilian Public Service. He married Genevieve Lehman in 1947. They had four children. After graduating from Goshen College in 1949, Ralph and Genevieve studied Japanese in Tokyo, then moved to Hokkaido in 1951.

He founded the Tsurugadai Church in Kushiro, and later served in Hombetsu, Obihiro, Asahikawa, and Furano until 1979. He helped organize the Nihon Menonaito Kirisuto Kyokai Kyogikai (Hokkaido) (Japan Mennonite Christian Church Conference). He received a MDiv degree from Associated Mennonite Biblical Seminaries in 1972. Much loved and respected, he died at Upland, Cal., after a long battle with cancer. A collection of his poetry was translated and published in Japanese in 1986 under the title *Bye, Bye, Ojichan* (Uncle). Another collection of poems, titled *I Saw Jesus Today* was privately published in the United States in 1987.   YT

Buddhism, one of Asia's major religions, came to Japan from Korea in A.D. 552. Most Japanese are nominally Buddhists. They observe such Buddhist customs as visiting cemeteries to communicate with and pray for their °ancestors, especially during the summer *Obon* (Festival of Souls). They install mortuary tablets in the family altars at their homes. On the whole, however, they are not well-instructed about their own beliefs, and many of them are °Shintoists as well. Many different kinds of Buddhism exist.

When Christians have contact with Buddhists, they do not discuss differences of belief. They simply try to share the gospel, which might seem to be conveyed in Western garb. Nominal Buddhists may come to church or home meetings if they are interested in Christianity.

Buddhism teaches its adherents to be in harmony with society. Problems often occur at baptism, or when new converts realize that Jesus Christ is not only a soul savior but also their Lord, to be obeyed in daily life. When they try to follow Christ and to witness about peace and justice, this naturally results in conflict and a break in harmony. Buddhism is basically a "funeral religion," having little relation to everyday life.

There are occasions when Japanese Christians are put to the test in connection with Buddhist customs. For example, sometimes Christians must attend Buddhist funeral services, where they are expected to burn incense for and do obeisance to the dead. To refrain (from this near worship of the deceased) would be to show great disrespect to the family and may cause alienation.

For some Christians, the mortuary tablet is still so important that they leave the church when told to throw it away. One of the criticisms that Buddhists have against Christianity is that Christians do not care for and revere their deceased ancestors.

There have been few contacts between Mennonite leaders and Buddhist monks—they each go their own way. *Soka Gakkai,* a militantly evangelistic sect of Nichiren Buddhism, which tries aggressively to win even Christians, is an exception. *Soka Gakkai* members seek to engage others in argument, defending their positions.

Many Christian groups in recent years have been protesting efforts by the Japanese government to reinstate the Yasukuni Shrine, a Shinto shrine dedicated to the war dead, to a position of national and religious prominence. Peace-loving Buddhist monks, from the Pure Land sect in particular, also support this opposition. The national shrine issue is an opportunity for Mennonites to express their Anabaptist views of peace. It may provide a point from which dialogue with other groups can begin.   YY

Budget, The. See Amish.

Buena Vista Colony, Mexico. See Casas Grandes Colonies, Mexico.

Buenos Aires, Argentina, is the capital city of the Argentine Republic. Its population is about 10,000,000, including greater Buenos Aires.

The policy of the Mennonite Board of Missions and Charities (MC) as it began witness in Argentina was to work mainly in the rural areas. Due to the critical economic situation of the 1930s, many church members began to move to the Buenos Aires area, and it was evident that something had to be done to care for the church members moving to the city. For that reason, the missionary council decided to recommend periodic visits to the church members scattered all over the city. The first Mennonite congregation was established ca. 1940 in the Parque Chacabuco neighborhood. Later that property was sold, and land in Mercedes 149 (Floresta) was purchased. This became the permanent location of the first Mennonite congregation established in Buenos Aires.

A few years later, Albano Luayza, the first national worker, moved to Ramos Mejía and established the second Mennonite congregation. Pastor Luayza visited Morón regularly since 1954, and in 1967 a new chapel was dedicated. This same pattern followed in Ituzaingó, where, in 1988, the congregation is pastored by Rubén Darino and owns its meetingplace. Mennonite witness was begun in Villa Adelina in 1961 by Mario and Barbara Snyder. This congregation has had its own chapel since 1968 and has been pastored by Néstor Comas since 1964. Haedo was started as an branch of the Ramos Mejía church in 1961; in 1988 this congregation has completed the building of a new chapel as a meetingplace. Kilómetro 30 (later Adolfo Sourdeaux) began in 1964 in the home of Boris Janzen, led by Mario Snyder and the members of the Villa Adelina church. Alicia Neufeld was a faithful worker until her death in 1967. It has become the largest congregation in Buenos Aires (200 members). Its pastor is the well-known evangelist Delfin Soto. San Pablo is a church planting effort of the Adolfo Sourdeaux congregation that has become a a growing and established congregation. The administrative center for the °Iglesia Evangélica Menonita Argentina (Argentine Evangelical Mennonite Church) is at the Floresta church. It contains the files for the Argentine church and the Centro Evangélica Menonita de Estudios Bíblicos (Mennonite Center for Bible Studies). Juan A. Gutiérrez is the pastor (1988).

Several theological educational institutes are located in Buenos Aires, representing diverse denominations. Some of them serve partially in the leadership training of Mennonites, and they also welcome and sometimes hire Mennonite teachers and lecturers.   ROG

Buenos Aires Colony, Mexico. See Casas Grandes Colonies, Mexico.

Buggies (ME I:464). Horse-drawn transportation has been maintained as a matter of Christian °discipleship by the most conservative elements in the Anabaptist family. The Old Order Amish, and over half of those identified as Old Order Mennonites and Old Colony Mennonites, forbid ownership and driving of automobiles. Small groups of Old Order River Brethren and Old Order German Baptists have the same rule. In the 1980s the membership of these groups totaled about 80,000, with a total population of about twice that number.

The Old Order people see the °automobile as a disintegrating force affecting the family, church, and community. They feel that cars are an object of pride, not conducive to self-denial. The Old Orders also avoid involvement with the evil of °insurance by using buggies rather than cars. The Old Orders do not feel the car is evil in itself. By forbidding ownership of cars, it is felt mobility is limited and thus many temptations are avoided. Old Orders will make use of public transportation (as they did in the preautomobile age) and permit hiring cars and vans for special needs. In many communities, mobility is also limited by insisting on steel wheels on tractors (so they cannot be used for transportation on the road) and by forbidding bicycles.

Since the demise of the buggy in the larger society, the manufacture of horse-drawn vehicles, as well as the related harness and farrier trades, have largely fallen into the hands of the Old Orders. Many shops specialize in certain aspects of buggy-making: wheels, axles, shafts, tops, hardware, etc. Amish and Mennonite craftsmen have introduced a number of improvements in buggy construction, including the use of fiberglass, roller-bearing axles, and hydraulic brakes. Old Colony Mennonites make extensive use of pneumatic tires. Other innovations which individual groups may accept or reject are sliding doors, hard rubber tires, and battery-operated lights. Buggy drivers have been persuaded by state governments to adopt various kinds of safety devices to increase the visibility of their vehicles on the roads. These include large, orange "slow-moving-vehicle" triangles, flashing red lights, and luminous tape.

There are a great many regional and group vehicle styles among the various Old Order communities. Most Amish vehicles have black tops; however, in Pennsylvania gray tops are most common, and a minority use white and yellow tops. Amish communities in Adams and Montgomery Co., Ind., permit only open buggies. Old Order Mennonite youth in Pennsylvania and Indiana and adults in Virginia have traditionally used buggies with fold-down tops. This style is being replaced by vehicles with stationary tops. Old Colony Mennonites in Mexico and other Latin American countries have constructed trailer-like vehicles on auto chassis.   SES

Stephen E. Scott, *Plain Buggies, Amish, Mennonite, and Brethren Horse-drawn Transportation* (Lancaster, Pa.: Good Books, 1981); David Wagler, *Are All Things Lawful* (Aylmer, Ontario: Pathway Publishers, n.d.); Werner Enninger and Stephen Scott, "Kutschen als Dinge und Zeichen. Zur Semiotik des Fahrzeug-Designs," *Zeitschrift fur Semiotik*, 7. Heft 4 (1985), 367-382, a study of symbolism in buggy designs.

Bukungu Mishumbi was born at Banga Makonda of the Bashilele tribe in western Kasai Province (Zaire). The Bashilele, former headhunters, were fiercely independent and submitted to Belgian administration only in the late 1940s. In 1950 Russell and Helen Schnell of the Congo Inland Mission began work among the Bashilele at Banga. Bukungu attended primary school there and was converted and baptized. Graduating with high marks, he went to Nyanga Station where he was the first Mennonite believer of his tribe to complete a three-year teachers' training course. Back at Banga he took a leadership role in the eduational system and held that position until political independence of Zaire in 1960.

During the transfer of responsibilities to national leaders after independence, Bukungu learned accounting from missionary Art Janz and was elected the General Treasurer of the Église du Christ au Zaire, Communauté Mennonite au Zaire (CMZA; Zaire Mennonite Church) in 1966. He served in this capacity with total honesty for 15 years. After 1980 he moved to the port city Ilebo and developed a successful business there while making a strong contribution to the local Mennonite congregation as a layman. He later was chosen to be a deacon, then was ordained as a pastor.   LKei

Bulawayo, Zimbabwe, a transportation and commercial center with a population of 550,000, is located in Matabeleland, South Province, in sw. Zimbabwe. It is the second largest city in that country. It was an important source of supplies and transportation for the early mission work of the Brethren in Christ (in 1898 in the Matopo Hills se. of the city), but no mission work was started in Bulawayo before 1956. In 1987 there were nine congregations of the Ibandla Labazalwane Kukristu e-Zimbabwe (Brethren in Christ Church in Zimbabwe) in the city: Bulawayo Central, Entumbane, Hillside, Lobengula, Mpopoma, Nkulumane, Pumula, Ngubuyenja, and Rangemore. In addition, there were some small group meetings that might become congregations. Lobengula was the largest congregation with some 1,500 people attending Sunday morning services. Bulawayo, with more than 2,200 Brethren in Christ members, had the largest concentration of this denomination of any city in the world.

Church planting in Bulawayo began in 1955 with visitation of former Brethren in Christ students employed in the city. Don Zook and Sandi Vundla began making weekend trips to Bulawayo and organized Sunday schools and worship services in two different townships. The first church was dedicated in 1957 at Mpopoma with Sandi Vundla as resident pastor. He also gave leadership in weekly released-time Bible classes in public schools, Bible study sessions for adults, and a growing hospital visitation program.

The headquarters for the Ibandla Labazalwane Kukristu e-Zimbabwe are located in Bulawayo as well as the office of the church's bishop. Related to that office is Acagugu Evangeli, the Ndebele radio station, and the publication of *Amazwi Amahle*, the church paper. The Matopo Book Center is also located in Bulawayo. DMM

Velma R. Brillinger, "Development of Brethren in Christ Church Work in Bulawayo," *Look on the Fields* published with the *Evangelical Visitor*, 70 (June 17, 1957), 2; *Brethren in Christ Handbook of Missions* (1956, 1957, 1958); Dorothy M. Martin, *Memoirs* at BIC Archives (Grantham, Pa.).

Bund Europäischer Mennonitischer Brüdergemeinden (Federation of European Mennonite Brethren Churches) is an association of 13 autonomous congregations in Austria (4) and West Germany (9). Most of the purposes and tasks of these churches are carried out on the local and national level. Six of the German Mennonite Brethren (MB) churches are united as a "working association" called Arbeitsgemeinschaft der Mennonitischen Brüdergemeinden in Deutschland (AMBD). The three MB churches in Bavaria (south Germany) are working together with the churches in Austria (Arbeitsgemeinschaft der Mennonitischen Brüdergemeinden in Österreich und Bayern, AMBÖB).

The first Mennonite Brethren congregation in western Europe was organized in 1950. About 30 Mennonite Brethren refugees from Russia and Poland—who could not or who did not want to migrate to South America or Canada—united as a congregation in °Neuwied. Ten years later a second Mennonite Brethren congregation was formed in Neustadt a. d. Weinstrasse with native believers. In 1966 some 30 Mennonite Brethren returning from South America organized themselves as an autonomous church in Lage (Müssen). Through evangelistic efforts of the Lage congregation, and through division of the membership, three more congregations had been formed in °Bielefeld by 1985. In Austria all congregations originated through longterm efforts of evangelism and by baptism upon confession of faith in Christ Jesus—beginning in Linz in 1951, followed by Steyr in 1959, Wels in 1960, and Salzburg in 1969. Finally, Mennonite Brethren missionary extension reached Bavaria. Work began in Traunreut, 1969; in Traunstein, 1982; and in Burghausen, 1983.

In addition, in Germany are five °*Umsiedler* Mennoniten Brüdergemeinden. These congregations were formed by "resettlers" coming from the Soviet Union, 1972-79. For various reasons these Mennonite Brethren believers chose not to become part of the existing Mennonite Brethren churches. In Vienna, a growing Evangelical Free Church came into being by the grace of God and the testimony of Abe and Irene Neufeld during the 1970s. This "TUGA" (Tulpengasse) church has divided and developed into four indigenous congregations. They all have a good relationship to the Austrian MB churches, but are not part of the AMBÖB.

Since Mennonite Brethren missionary endeavors and church work were initiated and supported by North American personnel and, to some extent, financed by the Mennonite Brethren Board of Missions and Services, there was from the beginning a feeling of belonging together among workers and congregations. However, there was and is no organizational structure that ties the European churches to the larger North American or any other conference of Mennonite Brethren churches. Some of the pioneer missionaries and church planters were H. H. °Janzen, J. N. C. °Hiebert, C. C. °Wall, J. W. Vogt, G. H. Jantzen, and B. J. °Braun. In 1987 there was one couple from Canada working with the German Mennonite Brethren churches and there were seven couples in Bavaria and Austria.

Beginning in 1960 and continuing for 20 years, members and delegates of all congregations from Austria and Germany met annually (except 1974) for a faith conference, with a minimum of business on the agenda, alternating between German and Austrian churches as a place of meeting. Since 1982 this Pentecost-Faith-Conference convenes every second year.

In Germany other Mennonite church bodies outnumber the Mennonite Brethren membership by about ten to one. In several communities they work and worship side-by-side. In Austria there are no other Anabaptist-Mennonite churches represented. The °International Mennonite Organization, a counterpart to the North American MCC for social and relief work, is a forum where all Mennonite groups in Western Europe are working together. By and large, Mennonite Brethren have a good relationship with other evangelical churches. On the local level, they work with the Evangelische Allianz in united prayer meetings, Bible studies and evangelistic outreach. In several places, Mennonite Brethren have given leadership to such united Christian ministries.

Mennonite Brethren young people and leaders have had their training in various °Bible schools and °seminaries, e.g. in Basel, Bienenberg, Brake, Giessen, Seeheim, Walzenhausen, and lately in Ampfelwang. So far the churches have not identified with only one of these learning institutions nor have they found it necessary to create their own training center.

A weekly radio program *Quelle des Lebens* was first broadcast by H. H. Janzen in 1957. A follow-up letter by the same title was sent to those listeners who asked for help. *Quelle des Lebens* can still be heard from Luxembourg and Quito, produced by the European all-Mennonite Radiomission at the European Mennonite Bible School at Bienenberg in Switzerland. The *Quelle des Lebens* newsletter has become the bimonthly publication of the European Mennonite Brethren Churches. The AMBD has translated and published the confession of faith of the North American Mennonite Brethren Churches and the brochure "The Ministry of Reconciliation in a Broken World" by J. A. Toews. *Die Mennonitische Brüdergemeinde - eine kurze Selbstdarstellung*, originally written by H. H. Janzen, was being revised and enlarged in 1987.

Even though the European Mennonite Brethren are not known for being outstanding in bringing the gospel of Jesus Christ to unreached people, they always have professed to be a missionary-minded church. Dorli Schnitzler, a graduate of the Brake Bible School, was commissioned to work among the Tambira Indians in Brazil in 1968. Church growth by evangelism was slow during the first decades. In Germany the congregations in Lage and Neuwied grew primarily through returnees from South America and by the arrival of the *Umsiedler* from the

Soviet Union. However, during the 1980s new members have increasingly come from the unreached German population. At the end of 1986, church planting in areas with no evangelical free church seems to have become part of the vision of many Mennonite Brethren in Austria and Germany. At the end of 1986, the Federation of European Mennonite Brethren churches counted 1,200 members, with 22 full-time and 4 part-time ministers, missionaries, and teachers, 8 of whom are financially supported by the North American Mennonite Brethren Board of Missions and Services.   JNK

J. A. Toews, *History MB* (1975), 433-36; *Quelle des Lebens,* 1966 (no. 1), 1974 (no. 6), 1976 (no. 6), 1977 (no. 3), 1978 (no. 3); *MWH* (1978), 282-84; *MWH* (1984), 112.

Bundesrepublik Deutschland (BRD; Federal Republic of Germany). Mennonites in the Federal Republic of Germany (West Germany) can be divided into six groups: (1) "urban Mennonites" of the north and west; (2) descendants of Swiss immigrants in the south; (3) West Prussian refugees, who for the most part are living in northern Germany in their second generation; (4) approximately 700 return emigrants, who came from Paraguay and Uruguay since the 1960s; (5) more than 3,000 °*Umsiedler* (resettlers), who arrived from the Soviet Union in the 1970s; (6) ca. 800 Mennonites in congregations resulting from Mennonite Brethren and °Mennonitische Heimatsmission (MHM) mission work. The differing backgrounds of these groups has made "coming together" difficult.

The four German Mennonite conferences vary in the roles they fill. In general, their functions include: publication of periodicals; continuing education for church workers; organization of conferences; support and encouragement of congregations, missions, and social projects; the peace witness; and representation before state, society, and other denominations.

The Vereinigung Deutscher Mennonitengemeinden (VdM; Union of German Mennonite Congregations) includes 34 congregations, with 7,248 members in the north and west as well as in the °°Palatinate. The Verband deutscher Mennonitengemeinden (VdM; Federation of German Mennonite Congregations) has 22 congregations and 1,617 members in °Baden-Württemberg, °Bayern (Bavaria), and the Palatinate. The two Mennonite Brethren conferences (Arbeitsgemeinschaft Mennonitischer Brüdergemeinden in Deutschland and Arbeitsgemeinschaft Mennonitischer Brüdergemeinden in Österreich and Bayern) include 938 members in eight congregations within the Federal Republic. Ten *Umsiedler* congregations, with 2,183 members, have neither joined an existing conference nor organized their own; they are connected among themselves and with other congregations through the Arbeitsgemeinschaft zur geistlichen Unterstützung in Mennonitengemeinden (Task Force for Spiritual Aid in Mennonite Congregations).

For 1987, the *Mennonitisches Jahrbuch* lists 81 Mennonite congregations and three mission projects by MHM, two by °Deutsches Mennonitisches Missionskomitee (DMMK), and one by Rosedale Mennonite Mission (°Conservative Mennonite Conference). Altogether, these add up to 11,335 members, not including children or guests. Congregational size varies from 15 to 1,170 members. Geographical concentrations exist in the Palatinate (18 congregations, 2,600 members), the °Bielefeld area (5 congregations, 1,858 members), °Espelkamp (3 congregations, 1,555 members), and °Neuwied (4 congregations, 1,078 members). Roughly calculated, Mennonites in the Bundesrepublik can be categorized as one-fourth "West Prussian," one-fourth "Swiss," one-third "Russian," one-twelfth urban, and one-twelfth not of Mennonite background. If the total figure is compared with that of 1933, a one-third decline is revealed; however, if those of Russian Mennonite heritage are not figured in, it becomes evident that Mennonites in Germany declined by more than one-half during that period. Every sector of German Mennonites is faced with this.

Along with this dramatic decline, structural changes have taken place since World War II. After the flight and expulsion of West Prussians and during the beginnings of return emigration from South America and resettlement from the Soviet Union, more and more rural Mennonites in the southern Bundesrepublik left their villages and farms for the cities. Opportunities for young people in agriculture diminished due to structural shifts in that field; at the same time, the educational system improved, broadening the spectrum of professional opportunities. The demands of professional mobility brought many young Mennonites to cities without Mennonite congregations. The customary relationship of profession and congregation was lost; a steady shrinking of congregations resulted. In addition, the number of marriages in which one partner either was a stranger to the Mennonite world or had other confessional ties increased. As patriarchal structures weakened, the extended family lost its hold. The Mennonite "family church" was no longer the natural home, no longer provided the sought-after shelter and protection. Most young Mennonites were finding themselves on their own in a strange environment.

Due to these shifts, numerous congregations have been founded in small and middle-sized cities since 1945. In the late 1980s, there were as many "new" congregations (40 with 5,468 members) as "old" ones (41 with 5,867 members). In recent years, many congregations have been able to buy or build meetingplaces; in 1986 more than half of the congregations owned the building in which they met. Based on the frequency of congregational events, on involvement reaching outside the congregation, and on the findings of church workers, congregations with their own buildings are especially active.

More than 100 lay preachers (119, not including MHM) and 23 salaried ministers serve Mennonite congregations; eight church workers are also employed in various projects (not including the staff of the four homes for the elderly in Thomashof, Burgweinting, Enkenbach, and Bad Oldesloe). The training of the salaried pastors varies considerably: some have attended a Bible school, others have studied at independent theological academies, and eight have university degrees in theology. Seven also supplemented their ministerial training through courses at Mennonite °seminaries or colleges in North America. Forty-seven of the lay ministers are with VdM, and

GERMANY

Kilometers 0 50 100 200

LEGEND

MENNONITE CHURCHES IN GERMANY
- ═══ International boundary
- --- State boundary
- ● Cities with Mennonite congregations
- ● Mennonite missions
- ∿ Rivers

KEY

IN WEST GERMANY
1. VDM   Vereinigung der Deutschen Mennoniten-Gemeinden (United German. Menn. Congs.)
2. VdM   Verband deutscher Mennoniten-Gemeinden (Union of Menn. Churches in Germany)
3. BEMB Bund Europaischer Mennonitischen Brüdergemeinden (European M. B. Ch.)
4. MBI   Mennoniten Brüdergemeinden (Independent Umsiedler)
5. EMBI Evangelische Mennoniten-Brüdergemeinden (Ind. Umsiedler)
6. MGI   Mennonitengemeinden (Ind. Umsiedler)
7. MKI   Mennoniten-Kirchengemeinden (Ind. Umsiedler)
8. EF   Evangeliche Freikirche (Independent)
9. CM   Conservative Menn. Board of Missions and Charities
10. EMC Evangelical Menn. Conf. Board of Misions

IN EAST GERMANY
11. MDDR Mennonitengemeinden in der Deutschen Demokratischen Republik (Mennonites in the Germ. Dem. Rep.)

28 are with the *Umsiedler* congregations. In recent
years, the readiness of laity to deliver sermons has
also been increasing in many predominantly West
Prussian congregations. An important task in coming
years will be further training of lay ministers.
However, many congregations still have difficulty
finding lay persons who will preach. Some smaller
congregations no longer have a minister, and others
have no replacement leadership under training. A
number of congregations meet for worship only
every two to four weeks. Nine of the salaried ministers serve two or more congregations. There are
many other congregations in which the number of
weekly events has increased, and in which consistent work with congregational subgroups (the
elderly, youth, young adults, etc.) has been growing.
Such a variety of offerings in a congregation is not
possible without strong lay involvement.

Because of their diverse backgrounds and situations, Mennonites in the Bundesrepublik present a
picture rich in variety. There are "conservative"
Mennonites as well as those looking for new forms
and directions; here a congregation influenced by
evangelistic renewal, and there one more interested
in the °peace witness. The social spectrum has
changed; the number of farmers has gone down and
social and service professions have become more
popular, while the *Umsiedler*—due to their background—frequently find employment as industrial
workers.

Nonetheless, such insecurity about the position of
Mennonites in the modern world or about the
relationship of congregation to believers as may
exist, has not led to resignation or indifference. Instead, we find a reflective "backwards look" toward
the Anabaptist heritage, and a deepening consideration of the task of Mennonites in the Bundesrepublik of today. German Mennonites—in all their
variety—are pursuing a new identity. This can be
seen in Mennonite publications, discussions at the
conference level, and the offerings of church workshops and conferences. In the following ways the
German Mennonite identity has been strengthened
since 1945: (1) With three exceptions, salaried ministers come from Mennonite ranks, and there are
currently a number of Mennonite theology students
who can provide for future needs. (2) Youth work,
in the north as well as south, is being intensified
through full-time staff; non-Mennonites are also attending youth conferences and retreats. (3) The
peace witness, and its implications, has become a
determining factor for many Mennonites, and is
beginning to mold their thinking and the manner in
which they lead their lives. (4) There is a
heightened interest in °missions (including home
missions) and social responsibility, expressed
through contributions and personal involvement. (5)
The tendency toward °inter-Mennonite cooperation
at many levels, and the desire to stay together and
come closer to each other, are both increasing. (6)
In evidence is an increasing commitment of sisters
and brothers who expect more than Sunday worship,
and who are ready to be involved in congregational
activities.   DGL

Horst Penner/Horst Quiring/Horst Gerlach, *Weltweite
Bruderschaft*, 2nd ed. (Weierhof, 1985); D. G. Lichdi, *Über

*Zürich und Witmarsum nach Addis Abeba: Die Mennoniten
in Geschichte und Gegenwart* (Maxdorf, 1983); Peter J. Foth,
"Mit hundert Jahren noch ein Kind—Wege und Umwege zur
mennonitischen Einheit," *Brücke*, 4 (1986); "Konferenzen
Woher? Wohin?" in *Menn. Jahrbuch* (1986); *MWH* (1978),
293-99; *MWH* (1984) 115-17.

Burial Customs (ME I:473). There does not appear
to be an Anabaptist and Mennonite standard for
burial. As with some other areas of life, Mennonite
patterns for the handling of the physical remains of
the deceased reflect wider cultural practices and responses to laws or historic settings. The most common Mennonite burial forms, worldwide, articulate
the kin group or family, town or community of
residence, and congregational affiliation.

In Europe during 16th c., Anabaptists buried their
dead in public or church cemeteries. Where possible, this continued. The break with the state
church and banning of Anabaptists from public roles,
meant that they were sometimes refused burial in
public cemeteries. In Switzerland some Anabaptists
are reported to have been buried in places reserved
for criminals and non-Christians. The unbaptized
deceased children of Mennonites were sometimes
buried separately, or in special sections of common
cemeteries. Where Mennonites developed their own
settlements and congregations in the mountains of
Switzerland, the Palatinate, and the Vistula Delta
(°°West Prussia), they had their own cemeteries and
burial practices.

As distinctive traditions emerged among those
Mennonites who had emigrated from their original
16th-c. homes and cities, family, village, and congregational burial arrangements became the most
common.

A study in central Kansas (Janzen) identified the
burial patterns of linked Old and New World Mennonite traditions: the Amish of Eastern United States
and Swiss-Alsatian-Palatinate origin; the Swiss-
°°Volhynian, i.e., "Old World" Amish, who emigrated
to Kansas in 1874 via Poland; Dutch-Prussian-
German immigrants with ancestry in the Vistula
Delta "Old Flemish" congregation of Prezchowka
(later, in Molotschna, Alexanderwohl).

The Amish practice congregational and community
burial with patrilineal family rows, based on order of
death of family members. Some conjugal pairs are
recognized in that a place is reserved for the spouse
beside the deceased, usually within the man's family
row. An emphasis on Amish "plainness" is clearly
evident in burial, with the use of wooden coffins,
the absence of embalming, and uniform, simple,
hand-cut limestone or concrete markers with name
and birth/death dates.

In the Swiss-Volhynian congregations of Hopefield
and Eden, burial reflects age-grading within the
congregation. Adults and children are buried in adjacent rows, in order of death within the congregation, regardless of family membership. Conjugal
pairs are recognized by reserving a burial place beside the first-deceased spouse. A variety of commercial tomb markers are used, with the largest identifying community leaders.

Low-German-speaking immigrants from the Molotschna colony brought their village settlement system to the North American plains. At first, as in the
Ukraine, each village had its own cemetery, although

some families buried in family plots. The village cemeteries of Alexanderwohl tended to practice age-segregated burial, as the Swiss Volhynian above, with children's rows and adult rows, within patrilineal family plots. Later, when the villages were dissolved, and the people began to bury in congregational cemeteries, they practiced an egalitarian pattern of burial, filling row after row without distinction for age or family. Only the conjugal unit was recognized, by leaving room for the spouse beside the deceased.

In the Prussian-German tradition, both congregational and patrilineal family lines were articulated in burial, as had been the case in Heubuden's cemetery in the Vistula Delta. The burial practices of Emmaus and Zion congregations were based on family plots demarcated within the cemetery. The historic practice of cousin marriage between landed families in this tradition—in the face of restrictive land-owning conditions imposed by the Prussian military state—carried over in a few cases into the New World, and was reflected in partner-family sections in congregational cemeteries, or in private family cemeteries such as the Bergman-Harder cemetery of rural Whitewater. Here a variety of commercial tombstones was used, with some reflecting the *Grabschrift* song and verse tradition of Europe (°funerals). An urban congregation in this tradition utilized a city public cemetery.

Non-Western Mennonites have utilized a combination of wider cultural practices and more self-consciously "Christian" burial forms. In India, Christians, as well as Muslims, practice burial, in contrast to the Hindu practice of cremation. Indian Mennonites of °Madhya Pradesh utilize a congregational cemetery; the separate identity of the family is minimal. In the Zaire Mennonite Church, located mainly in Kasai and Bandundu provinces, burial is either in the village, lineage, or family plot, or in the church cemeteries found on some of the mission stations.

Indonesian Mennonites, whose origins go back to Dutch Mennonite missions of 1850, are drawn from both Chinese and Javanese ethnic groups. Both practice burial in public Christian cemeteries following services in the home with family and friends. The conjugal unit is acknowledged by reserving a place for the spouse beside the first-deceased. The tomb is marked with a simple marble tablet. Because of limited space for cemeteries, and cost of burial, °cremation has been approved by the °Persatuan Gereja-Gereja Kristen Muria (United Muria Indonesia Christian Church, largely drawn from ethnic Chinese).   JMJ

John M. Janzen, "The Early Midwestern [US] Mennonite Cemetery as a Social Document," *Yearbook of the American Philosophical Society* (Philadelphia: American Philosophical Society, 1968), 605-7; information on Indian, Zairian, and Indonesian Mennonites supplied by Lubin Janzen, Fremont Regier, and Mesach Krisetiya.

See also Death and Dying; Folk Art (including bibliography).

Burkhalter, Martha Rose (Oct. 12, 1889–Oct. 4, 1965), was born on a farm near Berne, Ind., and received a BA degree from Bluffton College (Ohio). She was sent by the General Conference Mission Board to India, arriving there in December 1917.

After language study she served as principal of the Annie Funk Memorial Girls' School for 10 years. The enrollment grew from 22 to 100 during Martha's tenure while she upgraded staff and buildings. The school received official government recognition during this time.

Martha attended the Biblical Seminary in °New York for two years during a three-year furlough (1932-35). She was a popular mission speaker who excelled in storytelling and fundraising.

In 1936 Martha became principal of the Bible school in Janjgir, which trained rural Christian leaders. Two months of the school year were spent in intensive evangelistic campaigns for practical training. Here Martha also initiated improvement of plant and facilities. When the interdenominational theological seminary was founded at Yavatmal, Maharashtra State, in 1951, Martha was the first General Conference Mennonite Mission representative on the staff. She continued to excel in Bible teaching.

After 30 years in India, Martha adopted an Indian child (Dilasie) and raised her to adulthood. When Martha retired in 1950, Dilasie remained in Yavatmal with friends. Martha returned to India later for Dilasie's wedding, where she (Martha) contracted amoebic dysentery which eventually caused her death in Fort Wayne, Ind.   HR/RR

Mary Lou Cummings, ed., *Full Circle* (Newton, 1978), 60-68; Samuel T. Moyer, *They Heard the Call* (Newton, 1970), 94-105; *Twenty-Five Years With God in India* (Berne, Ind.: Mennonite Book Concern, 1929), 232-35; Mrs. Harold [Ruth R.] Ratzlaff, ed. and compiler, *Fellowship in the Gospel India: 1900-1950* (Newton, Ks.: MPO, 1950), 25-35, 128.

Burkhard, Mary Yoder (Feb. 2, 1880–Sept. 7, 1957) was missionary in India, author and Women's Missionary Society (MC) leader. Born near West Liberty, Ohio, she studied at Elkhart Institute, then married Jacob Burkhard of Roseland, Nebr. They had three children, all born in India. Burkhard and her husband served in the Central Provinces (later °Madhya Pradesh), under appointment of what later became Mennonite Board of Missions and Charities (MC), beginning in 1900. After Jacob's death in 1906 and a furlough, Mary continued directing a program of Bible women (°lay evangelists) at °Dhamtari until 1915. She returned to India in 1924-31 under the General Conference Mennonite Board of Missions, working in the °Champa region 100 miles north of Dhamtari.

She was an articulate advocate for the cause of °missions. In India she served on the mission executive committee and, when on furlough, she was a widely used speaker. From 1916 to 1923 she served as president of the Women's Missionary Society. In 1936 she published *The Life and Letters of Jacob Burkhard*.   JAL

Rich, *Mennonite Women* (1983), 5; Sharon Klingelsmith, "Women in the Mennonite Church, 1900-1930," *MQR*, 54 (1980), 163-207.

Burkholder, Christian Charles (1865-1931) was born of Mennonite parents in New Danville, Pa. In 1885 he moved to Kansas, where he married Fannie Zook, a daughter of Brethren in Christ bishop Samuel °Zook. He was elected a deacon of the local

Brethren in Christ Church in 1891, and became a minister four years later.

In 1896 the couple moved near Glendale, Ariz., to pastor a small group of Brethren in Christ who had settled there a few years earlier. Five years later they moved to Upland, Cal., where he became a building contractor, organized a Brethren in Christ congregation, and became its bishop in 1904. Under his leadership, several other congregations were established in the state, and a mission was begun in San Francisco (1910). He helped to found a church school, Beulah College (later Upland College) in 1920 and served as its first president until his death.

Burkholder was an active churchman, a much requested evangelist, a member of the Home Mission Board and the Examining Board, and moderator of General Conference nine times. He was one of the leading exponents of the doctrine of °sanctifcation as a second work of grace that came into his denomination in the early years of his ministry.   EMS

E. Morris Sider, *Nine Portraits* (Nappanee, 1978), 278-307; Wittlinger, *Piety and Obedience* (1978), 303-4; *EV* (Oct. 26, 1931), 344.

See also Holiness Movement.

Burkina Faso (formerly Upper Volta). Mennonite Central Committee (MCC) began work in Burkina Faso in the early 1970s. The main relief efforts and water projects were located near Djibasso and Tougan in the nw. part of the country. Through MCC contacts with Christian and Missionary Alliance congregations and missionaries, Mennonite missionaries were invited to plant churches in the sw. part of the country. Two couples were sent there by Africa Inter-Mennonite Mission (AIMM) in 1978. They settled in the town of Orodara in the province of Kenedougou. Because of the diversity of language groups in that area, linguists were needed, and the first such team arrived in 1982 and settled in Kotoura, ca. 50 km. (30 mi.) west and south of Orodara. Since 1982 three more couples joined the first linguistic team. Each has entered a new language group.

The AIMM mission has expanded to six villages, of which four have church groups meeting regularly with a total of more than 40 members. Several national members give leadership to their respective congregations.

Volunteers for MCC and AIMM workers have strong fraternal ties. MCC has expanded its program into the southern and eastern regions of the country and in 1987 had 20 workers.   DLR

Menn. Rep. (Oct. 1, 1984); *MWH* (1984), 18.

See also Mission et l'Église Mennonite en Burkina Faso.

Chaybah Speaks

(Chaybah, the first person to become a Christian in the Senoufo village of Kotoura, Burkina Faso, tells of some of his experiences.)

Before I was a Christian, Karidja, my second wife, had had a very difficult pregnancy with four days of labor. When she became pregnant again (after I was a Christian), she wanted me to sacrifice so that she wouldn't have such a difficult time. While I was wondering what to do, I saw a cock crow at the door of her hut. To us Senoufo people, this is a sign of death. I went to tell Gail (the Africa Inter-Mennonite Mission missionary living in the village), and she prayed with me. But a second time a cock came and crowed at Karidja's door. I prayed again. I felt some reassurance, and yet I wondered. Then Karidja's time came and she went to the clinic, and Gail and I prayed. Everything went well! I could see now how God was helping me and my wives. Because of the changes that Mariam and Karidja saw in my life and because both gave birth safely without my having offered sacrifices, they became Christians too.

However, their families are unhappy that they are Christians. Both Mariam and Karidja's fathers have told them, "Either you must leave this Christian way or you must leave Chaybah and return home." I do not know what will happen. If their fathers command them to return home and they refuse, they will be cut off from their families.

The next planting time after I was a Christian, I went to our fields to cut down some trees. I didn't know the belief that if the branches of this certain tree are put on the ground, the rains will not come. When my older brother saw that I had put the branches on the ground, he went and told my father. My father said, "You must go early tomorrow morning and gather up those branches. If it still doesn't rain, you will have to sacrifice a goat." I went and gathered up the branches, but it didn't rain. So one morning I got up very early and prayed until 8:00 for rain. By 10:00 the sky had become dark and the rain began and continued for several days. I knew that God had helped me and kept me, because if it hadn't rained, my life could have been in danger from the other villagers.

In our tribe we do not have a day of rest, but I wanted to have Sunday for worship and for rest for me and my wives. My older brother was unhappy about this, because everyone in the family helps in everyone else's fields. Finally, he agreed that we would not have to work on Sunday. In our family everything was harvested without problems, even though my immediate family didn't work on Sundays. Karidja is pregnant now, and after she was baptized last Sunday, my older brother said to her, "When are you going to have your baby? What will you do if it comes on Sunday, on your day of rest?"

Once we realized that someone had been stealing from us. Then the women told me that they had seen who it was—they had seen our neighbor take some sorghum from our granary. I was so angry that I couldn't sleep that night. Then the Bible made me think that I should do something *for* him rather than something against him. So the next day I went to his house with some sorghum and said, "This is a present for you—take it." He took it, but was so ashamed that he wouldn't talk to me. My mother was unhappy with what I'd done. She said, "Why didn't you come and give the grain to me if you've got extra?" But since then, my neighbor has never stolen from me. Sometimes he even comes to buy grain from me!

In my two and a half years as a Christian, I have changed. I regard my wives differently. I am not mean to my children. In the fields, if there are disagreements, I don't quarrel and fight. It's God who changes these things. If you want to do it yourself, it won't work.   MH

Based on an unpublished article, used by permission of Africa Inter-Mennonite Mission.

Business (ME I:480) has been one of the most underrated, ignored, and misunderstood topics in Mennonite life. Although Mennonites have always been deeply involved in business, there is little explicit discussion of business in writings by or about Mennonites. In fact, Mennonites have been described as antipathetic toward business (ME I:481). Business is an aspect of °economics which has been defined as the procedures by which "Men and society choose, with or without the use of money, to employ scarce productive resources to produce various commodities over time and distribute them for consumption, now and in the future, among various people and groups in society" (Samuelson, p. 6). Business is not easily defined; it usually includes activity for profit which is dependent on production of goods and services but may consist solely of transactions. Business usually involves dealing with people to achieve goals and is circumscribed by its own language and normative system of duties and obligations (Solomon and Hanson). Business also normally assumes an entrepreneurial dimension, i. e., someone must initiate or manage the business, and this is distinguished from employment, vocation, °profession, °occupation, and job. It is thus apparent that Mennonites, from earliest times to the present, have been involved in °economic activity, and many of them, in business activities as well.

Business activity on the part of Christians has created some of the greatest concern for the church. Early Christian leaders such as Augustine (354-430) and Tertullian (ca. 160-220), were quite restrictive; later theologians such as Thomas Aquinas (1225-74), approved of business, but insisted on a just price, just profit, and generous charity to the poor. Protestant leaders such as Martin Luther (1483-1546) and John Calvin (1509-64), "sanctified" business activities and suggested that they could be a calling by which God's kingdom might be enhanced. There is clearly discernable an emphasis on poverty and the responsible use of °wealth in the Catholic tradition, and an emphasis on Christian stewardship to exercise the God-given talents to acquire wealth in Protestantism (Mullin, 1984). The Anabaptist tradition has espoused yet another approach (the communal ethic).

Social theorists have proposed that Catholicism has promoted a "traditional" economic and business ethic, where individual gain was regulated by the church; Protestantism, being more concerned about individual salvation, has tended to encourage individual effort and has been more amenable to °capitalism, as propounded in a well-known book, *The Protestant Ethic and the Spirit of Capitalism* (1904-5) by Max Weber (1864-1920). Much literature is now appearing from both Catholic and Protestant circles, promoting Christian faithfulness in the world of economics, especially business.

Mennonite Experience in Business. The early Anabaptists in Switzerland, North Holland, and Germany came from various occupations, professions, and social classes (Clasen, Peachey, Klassen, Stayer, Goertz, and others) but they were not wealthy land owners or business owners. They were part of the revolution of the "common man" (Packull, Goertz) and were concerned about social, religious, and economic oppression. This does not mean that they were uninvolved in business, for many were, as can be inferred from their professional and occupational titles. The early period is difficult to describe further because of the massive dislocation, disruptions, and oppression which Mennonites faced from the church and the municipal and territorial rulers. It is probably safe to say that some Anabaptists were active in business in this early period but that their activities were frequently disrupted.

Since Mennonite activity on farms (most of them rented) in the Swiss and Alsatian Jura Mountains, as well as Germany, Austria, and elsewhere, can be defined as business, then Mennonites were clearly active in business by 1550. Their survival as a religious group depended upon shrewd and competent management of farming and related activities. These skills they developed remarkably well. Examples are shown in Jean Séguy's account of the French Mennonites; and in the Hutterite management of noble lands, including clockmaking and pottery (Hostetler).

The Dutch Mennonites are the best example of business involvement after 1588. This ran the gamut from lumber trading, fishing and whaling, shipping, and shipbuilding to banking and distilleries (ME I:483; see especially Groenveld and others). No business activity was foreign to the Dutch Mennonites. They numbered among their membership some of the foremost business people in Holland, one of Europe's leading commercial centers during the 17th c. In Germany, Alsace, Austria, Switzerland, and subsequently in Prussia, the more limited business involvements of Mennonites were a function of their lack of freedom to establish themselves in business and their relative lack of opportunity to work the land. Later, especially in Prussia and Russia, the manufacturing and industrial growth of Mennonite business was a consequence of the increasing paucity of land for farming, which had become a major form of economic activity among Mennonites (ME I:484).

By 1850, however, Mennonites were engaged in business to a degree verging on industrialism. In Russia, the development of the Agricultural Association in 1831 initiated a modernizing of agriculture and related activities which finally resulted in several "commerce schools" (*Kommerzschule*). In North America, the predominant economic activity was farming, which represented both a way of life and making a living. No statistics are available before the turn of the present century regarding the proportion of Mennonites involved in business and professional activities in Europe, Russia, or North America (Smucker).

The year 1850, although arbitrary, can be taken as the beginning of a shift in Mennonite involvement in business. Unoccupied lands became much scarcer, and °urbanization was accelerating. The Industrial Revolution, beginning in England in the 18th c., spread to western Europe and North America between 1800 and 1850. The Dutch Mennonites were already well advanced in both urbanization and °industrialization by 1850. Although the German Mennonites and Swiss remained largely rural and agricultural, the Russian Mennonites made great strides, including the development of flour milling, foundries, implement manufacturing and a host of commercial and merchant activities, all well developed by the end of the 19th c. (D. G. Rempel, David H. Epp).

By 1940, a half-century after the American frontier was "closed," the "agricultural phase" of Mennonites in North America had begun its decline. The Russian Mennonites have been forcibly dispersed, so it is no longer possible to include them in the general characterization. Of course the more conservative or "communal" groups of Mennonites have retained their rural and agricultural patterns. This category includes a signifcant percentage of Mennonites in the 1980s (Hutterites, Amish of all branches, Old Order Mennonites and related smaller groups, Old Colony, Sommerfelder and related groups), but they are fighting an increasingly difficult battle.

Mennonites, including now the recent non-Germanic additions through missionary activity, can be defined as being basically urban, well-educated, and tending toward middle class status. Many are conducting their own businesses, including barbershops; saw-sharpening shops; implement sales and services; woodworking shops; and factories; massive °furniture manufacturing; wood processing (North and South America, especially Brazil); machinery, food, and housing production; and the building of railroads in Canada. The description of Mennonite businesses in *Mennonite Encyclopedia*, vol. 1 is fairly adequate until the 1950s, but, if anything, it understates the case. Certainly since 1950, Mennonite business activity has grown explosively in all parts of the world. In fact, according to the Kauffman and Harder profile published in 1975 (the only adequate source so far), Mennonites are above the United States average by 29 percent in three areas: professional and technical, business owners and managers, and farm owners and managers (Smucker; Nafziger).

Although adequate specific and concrete data and information is not available, the general evidence is overwhelming that the Mennonites never eschewed business; in fact, they seemed to have gone into it with zest (Epp-Tiessen). Mennonites have entered all manner of economic activity and have been generally known as very good farmers. They have, in fact, succeeded better than many artisans and shrewd and aggressive business people, according to Kauffman and Harder income statistics. Whether this factor has been consistent with Mennonite theology and practice, and whether Mennonite activity in business has affected their theology and practice in return, is another matter, to which we now turn.

The Mennonite People in Business. *Theology.* Mennonite thinking about the role of the Christian in business is weak. One looks in vain for any reference to business, commerce, trade, or economic activity in the writings of the early Anabaptist leaders. Similarly, Mennonite confessions from the Schleitheim Confession (1527) statements to the most re-

cent have no reference to economic behavior and its role in the Christian life. Discussions of °stewardship come the closest by referring to resources and wealth. Judging from Anabaptist writings, Anabaptist theology seemed limited to concern about the status of property in the community, and about its use in the community and outside. A Christian stewardship of °creation and material goods implied a mutual sharing and caring (Klassen, Hershberger, Smucker). Peter Klassen describes the Anabaptist understanding of economics as "The Economics of Mutual Aid" (p. 28ff.). Anabaptists never developed any coherent discussion or theology of economic behavior; hence, business has never figured in Anabaptist-Mennonite churchly discourse.

There has been some discussion and writing recently on the issue of economics and business. One of the first concerted efforts in North America was the °°Committee on Economic and Social Relations, which was formed in 1939, spearheaded by Guy F. °Hershberger, who was a pioneer in the field. This committee sponsored conferences and published position papers on labor-mangagment relations, race relations, etc. The °°Conference on Mennonite Cultural Problems, formed in December 1941, also included economic subjects in its program, although in a more descriptive than normative manner. The most concerted writings on economics (and business indirectly) have come from Guy F. Hershberger and are summarized best in his book *The Way of the Cross in Human Relations* (1958). *The Mennonite Community* magazine (ME III:619) included some allusions to normative economic and business relationships. *The Marketplace*, published by °Mennonite Economic Development Associates since 1971, is the most conscious attempt to relate Mennonite theology, economics, and business. That the leadership in Mennonite pulpits has not stressed economic behavior is surprising. Until the advent of the professional ministry, the lay ministers were almost always engaged in business or farming (or both) and would have had reasons to concern themselves with the subject. In summary, it must be said that Mennonites had an implicit theology of economics and business, expressed in their °discipleship and °nonconformity emphases.

The Congregation and Business Activities. Lacking an explicit theology of economics and business, Mennonites have controlled it by emphasizing a way of life which tended to promote agriculture and related activities as most consistent with nonconformity to the world. Thus, valuing °land and its use has become an identifiable characteristic of Mennonites (Séguy, Redekop, 1985, Nafziger). In this way economic activity, especially business, was monitored and sanctioned by the congregational emphasis on nonconformity, °nonresistance, honesty, fairness, etc. Menno Simons castigated the avarice and dishonesty of merchants and others, but has nothing further to say about how business relates to the church (*Writings*, 368ff.).

There is limited evidence that congregations, including those in The Netherlands, specifically admonished or disciplined members for immoral business practices. Often, especially among the Hutterites, Amish, and Old Colony Mennonites, individuals who deviated from the congregation's principles voluntarily left the church (Hostetler, Redekop, 1969).

Unfortunately, the business owners in the typical Mennonite congregation often felt alienated from other members, and their success was often resented. Some complained that "the church only appreciates the business community when it needs money." This ambiguity has been further exacerbated by the fact that the Mennonite church has become deeply involved in the establishment of myriad fraternal organizations, agencies, and °institutions that make use of business practices or, in fact, have become businesses. Thus, the °educational enterprise (including grade schools, high schools, and colleges), °publishing houses, °mutual aid organizations, and °health care systems, to name a few, have become deeply enmeshed in business activities, including making of profits. But Mennonites have not openly evaluated these institutions as part of the economic stream. The promotion of economic and business activity has emerged almost by default. Most pertinent and ironic are probably the college economics and business departments, which prepare young people for careers in economics and business. This is done without a clear framework, since Mennonites have only an implicit religious belief system in the area of economics and business. Mennonite colleges were basically initiated for the propagation of the faith of their forebears, best expressed for a time in preparing for the "service professions," which seemed consistent with Mennonite beliefs. Business and economics departments, now among the most popular in North America, are more difficult to harmonize with this Mennonite ethos.

Church Agencies in Economics. Because economic activity, especially business, has not been self-consciously promoted and evaluated, it is the "parachurch" structures that have attempted to come to grips with the problem. Beginning with the mutual aid work of the °°*Waisenamt*, although there may have been other less formal earlier activities, Mennonites have begun to attempt to put in practice their religious faith in the economic sphere in specific organizations such as the °cooperatives (especially in South America, Canada, and parts of the United States). The °credit union movement, now one of the fastest growing parachurch movements; the °Mennonite Foundation; the numerous Mennonite mutual aid organizations, (some of which actually are °insurance companies); professional organizations, such as the Mennonite Medical Association, and Mennonite Economic Development Associates, are examples of Mennonites committed to applying the Christian gospel in economics and business. Almost all of these have emerged without official congregational or conference support or initiative, often facing opposition.

But the inference is clear: Mennonites in economic activity, especially business, need help in charting a course in dangerous waters. The temptations, dangers, costs, and demands of the economic arena are heavy. And there are many casualties—many business and professional people live at the margins of congregational life and feel alienated from the congregation. This is not to say the fault lies solely with those not involved in business. Both sides in the alienation carry responsibility to attempt to hold the poles together.

The issues of profits, accumulation of wealth (actually power), private property, charging interest, speculation and wheeling and dealing, debt versus equity financing in business, doing business with, or joining with, nonbelievers (the traditional Mennonite nonconformity theology that rejected being "yoked with unbelievers" [2 Cor 6:14-15]), and many more similar issues are confronting Mennonites around the globe with serious implications. The reason why this entire issue is relatively neglected may well be because the membership in the pews has accepted rather fully the western "capitalistic ethic" as Hershberger so eloquently states in *The Way of the Cross* (esp. pp. 285ff).

Recent scholarship is redefining much of the Anabaptist-Mennonite movement as a utopian revolt (Goertz) that was concerned about reestablishing the communal life of the early church, and hence strongly eschewed private property and personal acquisition. As a general movement, Anabaptism was concerned about utilizing natural resources for the good of all. In some wings of Anabaptism, property was to be held in common, while in others private property was permissible, but it was to be at the disposal of others and for the common good. Hence, the world of economics and business challenges the Anabaptist comunal ethic directly, and the record of Mennonite response so far is uneven and at times tragic. This is one of the most critical issues facing the world fellowship of Christian faith as well as Mennonites in the late 20th c.   CWR

"The Christian in Business," a report of the General Conference Study Conference, Hillsboro, Ks., April 15-16, 1955 (mimeographed, 1955); Claus-Peter Clasen, *Anabaptism: A Social History* (Ithaca: Cornell University Press, 1972); Robert G. Clouse, ed., *Wealth and Poverty: Four Christian Views* (Downers Grove, Ill.: Inter Varsity, 1984); David H. Epp, "The Emergence of German Industry in the South Russian Colonies," *MQR,* 55 (1981), 289-371; Esther Epp-Tiessen, *Altona: The Story of a Prairie Town* (Altona: D. W. Friesen and Sons, 1982); Hans-Jürgen Goertz, *Alles gehört Allen* (Munchen: C. H. Beck, 1984); S. Groenveld, J. P. Jacobszoon, S. L. Verheus, *Wederdopers Menisten, Doopsgezinden in Nederland, 1530-1980* (De Walburg Pers, 1980), esp. ch. 11; Guy F. Hershberger, *The Way of the Cross in Human Relations* (Scottdale, 1958); John A. Hostetler, *Hutterite Society* (1974); Kauffman/Harder, *Anabaptists Four C. Later* (Scottdale, 1975); Karl Kreider, *The Christian Entrepreneur* (Scottdale, 1980); Redmond Müllin, *The Wealth of Christians* (Maryknoll: Orbis, 1984); E. Wayne Nafziger, "The Mennonite Ethic and Weber's Thesis," in Nafziger, *Entrepreneurship, Equity, and Economic Development* (Greenwich: JAI Press, 1986); Werner Packull, "The Image of the 'Common Man' in the Early Pamphlets of the Reformation (1520-1525)," *Historical Reflections,* 12 (1985), 253-78; Paul Peachey, "Social Background and Social Philosophy of the Swiss Anabaptists," 1525-1540, *MQR,* 28 (1954), 102-27; Calvin Redekop, *The Old Colony Mennonites* (Baltimore: Johns Hopkins, 1969); idem, "The Mennonite Romance with the Land," in *Visions and Realities,* ed. Harry Loewen (Winnipeg: Hyperion Press, 1985); David G. Rempel, "The Mennonite Colonies in New Russia: A Study of their Settlement and Economic Development, from 1789 to 1914" (PhD diss., Stanford U., 1933), cf. *MQR,* 47 (1973), 259-308; 48 (1974), 5-54; Paul A. Samuelson, *Economics* (New York: McGraw-Hill, 1961); Donovan Smucker, "*Gelassenheit,* Entrepreneurs, and Remnants: Socio-economic Models among the Mennonites," in *Kingdom, Cross and Community,* ed. J. R. Burkholder and Calvin Redekop (Scottdale, 1976); Jean Séguy, *Les Assemblées Anabaptistes-Mennonites de France* (The Hague: Mouton and Co., 1977); Robert C. Solomon and Kristine R. Hanson, *Above the Bottom Line: An Introduction to Business Ethics* (New York: Harcourt, Brace Jovanovich, Inc. 1983); *Who's Who Mennonites* (1943), 300-314.

See also Bankruptcy; DeFehr, Cornelius A.; Historiography; Idleness; Investments; Lawsuits; Loevenich, Sybille (von der Leyen) von; Shantz, Jacob Yost; Smith, Samuel Roger; Work Ethic.

Byers, Noah E. (July 26, 1873–June 15, 1962), was born at Sterling, Ill., to John J. and Esther Ebersole Byers. In 1898 he married Emma Lefevre of Sterling. Two sons, C. Floyd and Robert, were born to this union. As a pioneer in Mennonite higher °education, Byers spent his active life as a teacher and administrator. One of the first members of the Mennonite Church (MC) to attend high school and college, he received a BS degree from Northwestern U. (1898), an MA degree from Harvard (1903), and took additional graduate work at other universities. He served as principal of Elkhart Institute, Elkhart, Ind., (1898-1903), president of Goshen College (1903-13), and dean and professor at Bluffton College (1913-38).

Emma Lefevre Byers died in 1946. Later Noah married Edna Hanley of Decatur, Ga., where he lived until his death. In addition to pioneering work in Mennonite higher education, he gave leadership to the movement for °inter-Mennonite cooperation and unity. **WHS**

John S. Umble, *Goshen College 1894-1954* (Goshen College, 1955); C. Henry Smith and E. J. Hirschler, eds., *The Story of Bluffton College* (Bluffton College, 1925); C. Henry Smith, "A Pioneer Educator, N. E. Byers," *Menn. Life*, 3 (Jan. 1948), 44-46; N. E. Byers, "The Times in Which I Lived," *Menn. Life*, 7 (Jan. 1952), 44-47; (Apr. 1952), 77-81; (July 1952), 138-41; idem, "Reminiscences," address given at 50th anniversary of Goshen College, Jan. 1954, copy in MC Archives (Goshen); *Who's Who Mennonites* (1943), 37; obituaries in *Bluffton College Bulletin* (July 1962) and *MWR* (June 21, 1962), 12.

Byler, Edna Ruth (May 22, 1904–July 6, 1976), daughter of Benjamin Miller and Anna May Weaver, grew up near Hesston, Ks. She attended a one-room school, and a Mennonite church made up mostly of Pennsylvania Dutch people. She graduated from Hesston College in 1923. While at the college, Professor J. N. Byler (d. Feb. 14, 1962) noticed her, and they were married in 1925. He was 30, she was 21. By 1928 they had their first child, Donna Lou. Delmar was born in 1930.

In 1939 they moved to Boulder, Col., where J. N. Byler pursued a PhD degree. They returned to Hesston in 1941, then traveled to the East, where Mennonite Central Committee (MCC) administrators asked J. N. Byler to oversee what eventually became °relief work in unoccupied France. Edna stayed behind with the two children and became housemother for the unit workers at MCC headquarters in Akron, Pa. When her husband returned in 1942, the workers were calling her "Mrs. B."

On a trip to Puerto Rico with her husband, Edna saw the needlework of poor women and agreed to market it. With crafts added later, this became the MCC °SELFHELP Crafts program. She also operated a gift shop until her death. **MKP**

C

Calcutta, India, is the nerve center of eastern India. In 1650 Job Charnock, as agent of the East India Company, chose this site for a British trade settlement. The three villages of Sutanuti, Govindapur, and Kalikutta on the east bank of the Ganges (Hooghley) River formed the nucleus of the present city. It is the center of business and industry, art and culture, and is the largest city in India and second only to London in the Commonwealth. It handles almost half of the sea-borne trade of India. Calcutta has a population of 10 million spread over an area of 104 sq. km. (40 sq. mi.). It is the center for manufacturing textiles, leather goods, plastics, and iron and steel products and is the commercial center for East India.

Offices of Mennonite Central Committee and Bharatiya Jukta Christa Prachar Mandali (India United Missionary Church), are located in Calcutta. The latter is a member of Mennonite World Conference. (The Missionary Church in North America [ME III:603; IV:774] is not.) The India United Missionary Church had 2,500 members in 28 congregations in 1988. PJM

MWH (1984), 28.

California (ME I:491) has seen substantial growth in the various Mennonite groups since the early 1950s. The following Mennonite Brethren congregations have emerged since 1952: South Shafter (1955), Arleta (1957), Butler (1957), El Camino (1958), Wasco (1958), Neighborhood (1960), Kingsburg (1962), College Community (1963), Temple LePaz (1963), El Faro (1963), Parlier (1963), Temple De Calvario (1964), Green Haven (1964), Faith (1965), Orange Cove (1965), Cliffwood (1965), Blossom Valley (1968), North Fresno (1969), Raisin City (1971), Fremont (1977), Laurelglen Bible (1978), Fig Garden (1981), and Church of Acts (1984). The General Conference Mennonite Church (GCM) established six new congregations: Atwater (1964), Santa Fe Springs (1965), San Francisco Chinese (1980), Santa Clara Ethnic Chinese (1981), Santa Clara Mennonite (1982), and Trinity (1985). Eight new Mennonite Church (MC) congregations are Los Angeles Mennonite Fellowship (1958), Faith (1961), Monte Sinai (1979), Family (1980), House of the Lord Fellowship (1980), New Jerusalem (1982), Indonesian Christian Fellowship (1983). Two new congregations, First Mennonite in San Francisco (1976) and Mennonite Community of Fresno (1954), are members of both GCM and MC conferences. The Atwater Mennonite Church (GCM) is made up of former General Conference, Mennonite Church (MC), and Mennonite Brethren (MB) members. The Church of God in Christ Mennonite started one new congrega-

tion, Glenn (1953). Brethren in Christ (BIC) remain very active in California, primarily in the Greater Los Angeles area.

The following congregations are no longer active: Escondido (MB); Victor Chapel, Fresno (MB); Sunset Gardens, Fresno (MB); Natomas, Sacramento (MB); Community Chapel, London (MB); Clayton Park, Concord (MB); Bethania, Escondido (MB); Woodlake (GCM); First Mennonite, Shafter (GCM); San Marcos, Paso Robles (GCM); Willow Creek, Paso Robles (GCM); Winton Mennonite (MC); Bethel, Westminister (GMC).

Total membership and number of congregations in the various groups in 1986-87 was: Mennonite Brethren (6603; 27); General Conference Mennonite Church (1167; 11); Mennonite Church (625; 11); Church of God in Christ, Mennonite (742; 3); Brethren in Christ (1,506; 17). The Evangelical Mennonite Brethren (°Fellowship of Evangelical Bible Churches) had three churches in California— Sun Valley (1942-68), Grace at Reedley (1952-83), and Orange Co. (1945-64). The Krimmer Mennonite Brethren Church of Dinuba is now part of the Mennonite Brethren Conference

California Mennonites were farmers and many still are closely linked with the soil. More than one-half of all California Mennonites live in the Reedley-Dinuba-Fresno area, the center of the world's largest fruit-growing district. There is, however, a movement from farm to city as the result of young people seeking employment and °business opportunities and older people retiring from farm life. Most new congregations since 1940 have been located in °urban areas. Along with this movement there is a corresponding tendency to adopt urban ways of life. In some areas the distinctive Mennonite way of life has all but disappeared. Many of the Mennonite Brethren churches no longer have "Mennonite" in their names.

Many of the new churches of all conferences are non-English speaking. There are 10 Spanish-speaking congregations (7 MB, 1 GCM, and 2 MC). Four General Conference congregations are Chinese-speaking, and one Mennonite Church congregation is made up of people from Indonesia.

Among Mennonite Brethren institutions in California, Immanuel High School (1912) continues in operation. Pacific Bible Institute of Fresno (MB, 1944) is called Fresno Pacific College in 1987 and offers baccalaureate and masters' degrees. Mennonite Brethren Biblical Seminary and the Mennonite Brethren conference offices are located adjacent to the college. Upland College (BIC) achieved regional accreditation in 1959; it ceased to exist when it merged with Messiah College, Grantham, Pa., in 1965.

The Mennonite Aid Plan (1922) and Mennonite Aid Society (1941) in Reedley enjoy wide support from various Mennonite groups. Kings View Hospital is also continuing its °mental health services in 1987. Mennonite Brethren Homes (1942) is a multilevel institution in 1987. It has 99 skilled nursing beds, 100 board and care beds, and 43 independent living apartments. Other Mennonite health and retirement institutions in the state: Kern Crest Manor retirement home (MB, 1960) in Shafter has expanded from the original 15 housing units; Grace Nursing Homes (GCM, 1958) in Livingston is a 33-bed skilled nursing facility; Lincoln Glen Manor (MB, 1965) in San Jose has 59 intermediate-care beds and 80 housing units; Sierra View Homes (GCM, 1968) in Reedley is a 59-bed skilled nursing facility with 27 independent living apartments.

Many of the churches sponsor and operate daycare and preschool services for community children. The General Conference Mennonite Church began a camping program in 1927 using YMCA facilities. In 1967 they acquired Camp Keola at Huntington Lake in the High Sierras. The Mennonite Brethren camping program has been carried on at Hartland Camp, Badger, Cal., since 1948.

The First Mennonite Church in Reedley, has an active °voluntary service unit serving the elderly since 1983. Various other voluntary service activities have taken place over the years, including units at Kings View Homes, the Hoopa Indian Reservation, and migrant labor camps. Brethren in Christ °rescue mission work in San Francisco and Riverside has developed into more general family services programs.

Two Mennonite Disaster Service units, one in the north and the other in the south, function in California. The clothing and relief center and administrative offices of the West Coast Mennonite Central Commmittee (MCC) are located in Reedley. There are Nearly New shops and SELFHELP Crafts stores, under the auspices of local congregations and MCC throughout the state. CA

MC Yearbook (1986-87), 21; Stephen Intagliata, "An Accurate Picture of the Pacific District Conference of the General Conference Mennonite Church, 1975-1985" (Fuller Theological Seminary, 1986); Wittlinger, *Piety and Obedience* (1978), 147, 149, 306; Daniel Hertzler, *From Germantown to Steinbach* (Scottdale, 1981), 118-60.

Cambodia. See Kampuchea.

Campeche Colonies, Mexico. Land shortage led the Old Colony Mennonites of the Durango Colony at Nuevo Ideál, Durango State, to look for new tracts of land in the early 1980s. A number of states made offers, but always problems with "ejido" lands (communal land destined to be cultivated by landless Mexicans) loomed on the horizon. When in 1983 the State of Campeche offered several thousand hectares and conditions seemed favorable, the mother colony in Durango decided to buy the land. Immediately settlement began with 88 familes near the town of Hopelchen. By 1987 the new colony had 737 inhabitants, of which 211 were church members. Six schools, with as many teachers, are in operation. Two of them also serve as meetinghouses for Sunday morning worship services.

The two colonies in Zacatecas State, La Batea and La Honda, also have daughter colonies in Campeche, the former consisting of about 30 families, adjacent to the "Durango" colony; the latter, consisting of ca. 40 families and located 50 km. (30 mi.) to the southeast. The La Honda colony, begun in 1987, is optimistic about the choice of terrain and more families are expected to follow.

In all colonies High and Low German only are used in church and school. Agriculture, with accommodations to the regional climatic and soil conditions, is the main occupation. HEns

Camps and Retreat Centers (ME IV:1070). The first references to camping and retreats among Mennonites were in connection with the General Conference Mennonite mission to the Hopi Indians as early as 1903. Mennonites and Brethren in Christ recognized the impact that retreats and camps were making on youth and children. The early programs emphasized evangelism and spiritual growth in the Christian faith. The first Mennonite camps and retreats in North Amnerica were closely related to and influenced by the events and movements both within the church and in society at large.

During the period prior to World War I, Mennonites and Brethren in Christ were still a basically rural people. As such their needs were not the same as those of their urban neighbors. An outdoor ministry such as Christian camping was not part of their thinking because it did not seem needed.

The movement did not start at one place or with one group of persons. Each beginning had its own reasons and objectives. These facilities and programs were equally distributed across the map where there were Mennonite fellowships. By 1960 there was no area with a concentration of Mennonites that did not have access to a camping or retreat program and the development of permanent sites was on the increase.

If a specific decade were to be chosen as the beginning of the outdoor ministry of Christian camping and retreats in the Mennonite conferences, it would be the 1920s. An important phase of the youth movement during this period was the introduction of retreats for youth of high school and college age. The need for something to challenge this age group was felt throughout the churches.

The beginning of the retreat movement in the Mennonite Church came through the Young People's Problems Committee (1921ff.). Intended as a study committee to determine what activities there were in the church for youth, and to isolate problems that might be resulting from them, it acquired the status of a standing committee in 1927.

In 1928 a churchman wrote to Orie °Miller and O. N. °Johns, members of the Problems Committee, as follows: "I have also noted a strong emphasis given by the brethren on nature studies. I cannot see how such a program will fit into our rural congregations. This sectional conference idea may appeal to some of our young people, and it may be possible to conduct such conferences on a religious basis. . . . By the time this is done there will be other influences at work that must be counteracted. . . . There is danger in having something separate for a small group of believers within the church. This is a departure from the common practice in all our church activities." He remarked that the Sunday school and the Young People's Bible meetings had always been shared by the entire church and all ages.

The youth movement among the Mennonite Brethren during this time was also undergoing the changes characteristic of the time. J. A. °Toews, noted, "In the first two decades of the 20th c., youth fellowship groups became generally accepted in the Mennonite Brethren churches of Russia. It should be noted, however, that there was a separate organization for the young men and the young women. These fellowship meetings were not only attended by members of the church, but also by the unsaved relatives, friends, and members. The purpose of these meetings was to promote spiritual growth of believers and to influence the unsaved to made a personal commitment to Christ."

The retreats of the General Conference Mennonites; the Young People's Institutes of the Mennonite Church (MC); and the *Jugendvereine* (youth fellowships) for the Mennonite Brethren had much in common, and all were in the interests of the youth. They provided an opportunity for young people to become a part of the church and to interact with church leaders.

A letter from one of the youth leaders, Orie Miller, to Paul Mininger in 1934 states his concern, "Our young people are in need of help; and in most communities are not getting it. They need help in meeting perplexing problems and temptations of the modern world."

Coming to the 1930s, it is easy to detect a growing interest and participation on the part of the young people in church activities. As the curtain dropped on the 1930s, camping for boys and girls and retreats and institutions for young people had found their way into eight states in the United States and three provinces of Canada.

The expansion of this outdoor ministry in the 1940s was phenomenal as compared to previous decades. Nineteen additional camps and retreat centers had been established by the end of the decade. There was little or no sharing between the leaders of these scattered programs. Each group was left to its own ingenuity and resourcefulness. Those whose background was retreats and institutes were programming primarily for the youth within the churches, and with few exceptions were not thinking in terms of outreach. There were others who were concerned with the plight of inner-city children, or children with physical and emotional handicaps. Vacationing and °recreational trends in a changing society were the concern of another group, which saw the development of campsites as a solution for Christians' vacations. In spite of this wide scope of rationale behind the movement, there were many common features. It was also a new era for youth within the Mennonite conferences. Positive trends were established that have continued. Youth were included in the mainstream of the church. Organized youth teams traveled from community to community to organize and encourge local youth groups. Christian camping was experiencing rapid growth, and was becoming a significant part of the total camping movement in America.

During the 1950s Mennonite camps and retreats experienced a record growth as widespread interest was developing in welfare camping and specialized programming for underprivileged children or those with emotional or physical handicaps. Other groups were involved in °missions and church planting and saw camping as a tool for outreach and evangelism. Minority and ethnic groups were included.

Building facilities, developing programs, and philosophy were producing some unforseen blessings. It was now possible to include groups and interests that were not included in the original plans, e.g., family camps and camps for other special interest groups. Conferences, local congregations, and other organizations began to use the facilities to augment their programs of nurture (°Christian education) and evangelism. Camps and retreats were an established tradition in all of the Mennonite conferences.

Camping in the Mennonite and Brethren in Christ conferences experienced a steady growth of new facilities and programs. In the camping community much of the emphasis in the 1960s was on mission outreach, both to children of the community and to children from local congregations and missions. During the decade two programs were established on a year-round basis for the rehabilitation of delinquent youth: Frontier Forest Camp in Ontario and Frontier Boys Camp in Colorado. Both programs were successful. The Mennonite Board of Missions sponsored the cycling program known as OutSpokin', founded by Terry Burkhalter, which sponsored and organized bicycle trips throughout the United States, Canada, and overseas.

The outdoor ministry of the church was especially valuable in these times. Many camps that had been developed previously were expanding. In the earlier development it was usually anticipated that the camps would be used only during the summer months. As winter programming became popular, especially where snowfall permitted winter sports, camp facilities were modified to permit year-round occupancy.

The 1970s saw the camps enlarging, winterizing, and expanding programs to include more groups, programs for the handicapped, ethnic and minority groups. Camping had found its way into the mainstream of church life and Christian education.

Several decades ago the camping movement was compared to a grain of mustard seed. The beginnings were small, but over the years the camping movement in the Mennonite and Brethren in Christ community of camps and retreats has grown steadily. The program had proven its worth and was making its contribution in Christian education and evangelism.

Camping programs that included both girls and boys, men and women, had become the accepted practice. Programs that were originally tailored for the children and youth of the church were finding themselves including many children from the general communities in which they were located. Many camps were reporting a ratio of Mennonite to non-Mennonite or unchurched campers as much as fifty-fifty. Friendship evangelism was apparent as campers brought friends with them, often these who would later attend the functions of the traditional church.

The visionary founders of the camping movement in the Mennonite conferences were not aware of the impact the program would have, or of the unexpected happenings that would result from the simple beginnings. They did not dream of establishing a chain of camps across the churches.

It soon became apparent that the facilities developed for camping were a gift to the church for the purpose of °retreats. Congregations and conferences became aware of the advantages of sponsoring activities in the atmosphere of the outdoors and natural surroundings, away from the everyday world. Retreating had become a necessary function in the lives of many individuals and of the church. Thus many camps developed a two-pronged ministry. They provided facilities and program both for youth camps and for retreats where youth and adults with specialized interests could come for study and fellowship.

The movement's contribution to evangelism and outreach far exceeded the expectations of its founders. Some camps were founded with this as an objective, but for the most part they were denominationally oriented, and programs were tailored for the youth already within the church. Evangelism was natural in the outdoor setting where living was relaxed and where one was removed from the everyday schedule. Through the years literally thousands of youth have experienced their first opportunities at Christian service at the church camp (°work camps).

Interracial and intercultural camps became common early in the program. Persons with physical and emotional handicaps were included. This provided the church an opportunity to extend its witness beyond what was possible prior to the outdoor ministry of Christian camping. The genius of camping was that its informal setting away from the camper's live-a-day-world contributed to understanding and acceptance of people who were different.

In 1977 Virgil Brenneman, then executive secretary for the Mennonite Camping Association, noted that the camping ministries represent a sizeable investment of the funds and personnel resources of the church. He summarized their value as follows: (1) Church camping is education. It is a setting for Christian nurture and evangelism in providing living situations. (2) The church camp is an extraordinary leadership training resource for the church. Youth receive training and experience in counseling, teaching, experiential education, as well as other skills which can be used in other nurture and evangelism settings. (3) The Christian camp is a resource to help the church to meet the opportunities and challenges of the "new leisure." (4) The camping program is uniquely suited to model the church's goals with regard to the simple life-style, conflict resolution, the building of the community, the teaching of the stewardship of creation, and an awareness of a responsibility regarding natural resources.

The pioneers of Mennonite camping were men and women of quality and perseverance. They had a sense of direction and a call from God.

The freedom of the camping movement to experiment with new ideas in program has been one of the factors in its success and growth. It has used this freedom in a responsible way. It has had the opportunity to reach out and test methods of Christian service and witness.

The Mennonite Camping Association was born out of a need that was felt among camping people early in the movement. As each group of Mennonites wrestled with the problem of leadership training and the sharing of techniques, a beautiful thing was happening that was not visible at the time. There were a few who had the vision of an inter-Mennonite fellowship of camps and camping people. They had so much in common. Why not get together to share and affirm each other? The inter-Mennonite fellowship known as the Mennonite Camping Association took shape over a period of several years. It is primarily supported by the Mennonite Brethren, Mennonite Church, and the General Conference Mennonite Church. It is dependent entirely on contributions of volunteer staff and officers.   JK/TB

Since 1960, Dutch Mennonites have expanded facilities, notably with the addition of new retreat houses in Giethoorn (1964, 1983) and a new retreat center (*Broederschapshuis*), and education center at Aardenburg (1965). Most of the other Dutch Mennonite retreat centers have undergone remodeling to make winter occupancy possible. Campsites for individual recreation have been provided at Aardenburg and Elspeet. Between 1959 and 1963 the camping center "Valkeveen" operated near Naarden. The retreat house at Bilthoven closed in 1971. In 1961 an effort was made to found a center in Noordwijk near Groningen. After several years it was turned into a hotel, but was forced to close in 1968. The Mennonite Central Committee founded an international retreat center at Heerewegen near Zeist. Dutch Mennonites assumed responsibility for it in 1957, but it was forced to close in 1963. Most of the retreat centers in The Netherlands serve as places for vacationing Mennonites, although the individual centers also host conferences and develop some organized programs.   LLau

Retreats (*Freizeiten*) are common among German Mennonite congregations, youth groups, and other interest groups. Church-owned facilities are found at the °Weierhof and at the Thomashof near °Karlsruhe; some congregations also own retreat centers. The Association Mennonite Luxembourgeoise uses a retreat center at Scheidgen. Mennonites in Brazil established a retreat center "Bethel" near Araucária (Curitiba) in the early 1970s under the direction of the Sociedade Educativa Cristã Irmãos Menonitas (Mennonite Brethren Christian Education Society). The Centro de Estudios y Retiros and Camp Maranatha serve Mennonites in Uruguay. Japanese Mennonite Brethren (°Nihon Menonaito Burezaren Kydoan) also have a camping program. Camps and retreat programs figure minimally in other Mennonite groups around the world, for the most part, however, without the purchase and development of permanent, Mennonite-owned facilities.   Staff

The best collection of documents and information about the history of the Mennonite camping movement and about individual camps is found at the MC Archives (Goshen). See also Jess Kauffman, *A Vision And A Legacy* (Newton, 1984).

Current listings for North America are found in *MC Yearbook*, issued biennially since 1986, and other °yearbooks and directories. For Dutch Mennonite camps see *Doops. Jaar.*.

See also Conferencia de las Iglesias Evangélicas Menonitas, Dominican Republic; Iglesia Evangélica Menonita, Colombia; Fraternidad de Iglesias Evangélicas Menonitas de Nicaragua; Iglesia Evangélica Menonita, Colombia; Holiness Camps; Leendertz, Johannes Matthias; Recreation; West Virginia; Work Camps. Articles on various states and regional conferences in ME V contain additional information about church-owned camps and retreat centers.

Canada (ME I:501), once known as British North America, has been home to Mennonites since 1786. The first Canadian Mennonites came from Pennsylvania and were followed by an intermittent stream of immigrants which swelled on at least three other occasions into major movements of Mennonites to Canada.

The first group of Mennonites that came to Canada were pushed in part by hostility at home arising from their pacifism during the American Revolution. But they were also pulled by the promises and opportunities of a new western agricultural frontier where minority rights seemed better protected than in revolutionary America.

It is estimated that approximately 2,000 Mennonites came from Pennsylvania to Ontario between 1786 and 1825. A detailed Canadian census in 1841 enumerated 5,379 Mennonites, of whom 3,022 lived in the Niagara District, 933 in the Wellington (Waterloo) district, and 859 in the Home (Markham) district.

A second major migration of Mennonites to Canada occured in the 1870s, when thousands of Mennonites living in Russia sought new homes on North American prairie frontiers. Both American and Canadian authorities were eager to recruit successful settlers and offered major religious, military, and educational concessions (°privileges). Canada promised more concessions, but economic prospects seemed better on the American frontier. As a result, approximately 7,000 Russian Mennonites migrated to Manitoba in the 1870s, while about 10,000 went to Kansas and Nebraska.

In Manitoba two large land reserves were set aside for the Mennonites in the 1870s, and two more in Saskatchewan in the 1890s (°block settlement). None of these reserves were ever completely filled by Mennonite settlers, and all were eventually thrown open to non-Mennonites. Many other Mennonites moving west from Manitoba, Ontario, the United States, Germany, and Russia chose to take up individual homesteads rather than to occupy land or establish traditional Mennonite villages in the reserved tracts. Mennonite land ownership in Canada therefore developed a rather diverse character.

The third major influx of Mennonites into Canada came as a direct result of the °Russian Revolution and Civil War. Approximately 22,000 Russian Mennonites were able to emigrate to Canada between 1923 and 1929, thanks largely to the active support and assistance of Canadian Mennonites, who worked closely with the Canadian Pacific Railway, and with Prime Minister William Lyon Mackenzie King, who had learned to know the Mennonites while growing up in Waterloo, Ontario. The immigrants of the 1920s made no attempt to achieve a geographical separation from the rest of Canadian society and sought no exclusive land grants or reserves.

CANADA

Compiler: T. D. Regehr (author of Canada article)

Table 1. Mennonites in Canada Census Figures

Prov.	1901	1911	1921	1931	1941	1951	1961	1971	1981
Nfld.	-	-	-	-	-	3	39	45	90
P.E.I.	-	-	3	2	-	6	1	15	5
N.S.	9	18	2	1	23	23	31	90	220
N.B.	-	1	4	-	5	30	5	90	180
P.Q.	50	51	6	8	80	220	197	655	1,075
Ont.	12,257	12,861	13,665	17,683	22,256	25,796	30,948	40,115	46,485
Man.	15,289	15,709	21,321	30,375	39,395	44,667	56,823	59,555	63,490
Sask.	3,787	14,586	20,568	31,372	32,553	26,270	28,174	26,315	26,265
Alta.	546	1,555	3,131	8,301	12,119	13,528	16,269	14,645	20,540
B.C.	11	191	173	1,095	5,119	15,387	19,932	26,520	30,895
Y. & N.W.T.	-	-	1	-	4	8	33	100	125
Totals	31,949	44,972	58,874	88,837	111,554	125,938	152,452	168,150	189,370

Source: Census of Canada for each of the above years. In 1871, 1881, and 1891, no separate figures were given for Mennonites. In 1871 and 1881 they were included with Baptists, and in 1891 they were included with other denominations. These figures include Amish, Hutterites, and Brethren in Christ, to the degree that they identified themselves as Mennonite to census workers. Figuresinclude children, i.e., are not limited to baptized church members.

World War II set in motion the last major wave of Mennonite immigrants to Canada. These were Mennonite war refugees and displaced persons from eastern Europe, of whom about 7,000 came to Canada in the late 1940s. Few of these displaced persons took up farming in Canada on a permanent basis. Instead, they pursued new economic opportunities, usually in the cities, and played a key role in the °urbanization and integration of Canadian Mennonites into Canadian economic, social, cultural, and educational life.

Canadian Mennonites are a rather divided and fragmented denomination. Major historical distinctions can be made between those who came from Swiss and South German Anabaptist stock, and those from Dutch and North German backgrounds. Most of the former came to Canada from Pennsylvania in the late 18th and early 19th c., while most of the latter came from Russia and eastern Europe after 1870. Theologically, these two main streams of Mennonitism have remained close, and after World War II historical and cultural differences have decreased.

Mennonites initially organized themselves into small, local, and relatively autonomous communities and congregations, but in 1825 the first Ontario Mennonite Conference was established. In western Canada some of the Mennonites who had come to western Canada from Russia and northern Germany after 1870 organized their own conference, the Conference of Mennonites in Central Canada, in 1903. The Mennonite Brethren, a group that had already organized separately in Russia in 1860, organized their own conference in the United States in 1879, with Canadian congregations included in a "Northern District" of the conference. The Mennonite Church (MC, sometimes also known as the "Old Mennonites"), the Conference of Mennonites in Canada (often referred to as "General Conference Mennonites") and the Mennonite Brethren are the three largest Canadian Mennonite groups. The other, smaller conferences and groups manifest much diversity.

Despite the °schisms and differences among various Canadian Mennonite groups, they have all joined together to undertake joint °relief, immigration, and economic assistance programs. They do so through the Mennonite Central Committee, which was first organized in North America in 1920 to extend economic assistance to Russian Mennonites then hard pressed by war, revolution and civil disorder. °Mennonite Central Comittee Canada was organized in 1963. Other joint ventures, such as the Conference of °Historic Peace Churches, the Non-Resistant Relief Organization, and the Canadian Mennonite Board of Colonization were organized for specific purposes and then disbanded.

While relief and economic assistance to those in need could be undertaken jointly, Canadian Mennonites have not been able to achieve a similar unity in their various foreign and home mission ventures. All the major and many of the smaller Mennonite groups have committed considerable effort and resources to missionary activities, which have added many new members. Canadian Mennonites have, however, also suffered high attrition rates as various missionary and revival movements have drawn many persons of Mennonite background into other denominations.

Two unique circumstances have greatly influenced the Canadian Mennonite experience. Canada was and remained British, placing high value on loyalty, conservatism, respect for parliamentary institutions, and tolerance of minorities. These were values that Mennonites shared, and many of the confrontations with civil authorities that mark the histories of Mennonites in other countries were muted or did not happen at all in Canada. If the Mennonites sought separation, the authorities, with only sporadic exceptions, did little to coerce them into the mainstream of Canadian life. However, when the Mennonites were ready to take a more active role, there were few major barriers or obstacles.

Canada was also the home of a substantial and politically powerful French Canadian minority. Mennonites and French Canadians rarely agreed on major policy issues, but they did reinforce one another, often inadvertently, on the two important issues of military °conscription and °public school policies.

The French Canadians were a conquered people, cut off militarily from their former homeland in 1759, and also philosophically and spiritually after the French Revolution (1789). They had little interest in remote imperialist conflicts, and strongly opposed any compulsory military service except that required to defend their own homes. Conscription for military service overseas was therefore a hot political issue in Canada. British parliamentary concerns about minority rights led to a search for acceptable alternatives. French Canadians were willing to serve in home defence units, Mennonites in a variety of restricted and °alternative services.

Mennonites and French Canadians also shared a strong commitment to separate or °private schools. Both had strong legal claims to such schools, the French Canadians and Ontario Mennonites on the basis of terms included in the British North America Act, and the Mennonites in western Canada on the basis of a federal Order in Council passed in 1873.

After 1890, and particularly during and immediately after World War I, some Canadian reformers hoped to eliminate all separate schools and to make the public schools major instruments of assimilation and Anglo-conformity. Educational legislation governing school curricula, patriotic exercises, teacher qualifications, and compulsory school attendance were passed in most Canadian provinces. This offended both Mennonites and French Canadians. The latter resorted to political measures, but at least 7,000 Saskatchewan and Manitoba Mennonites sold their farms and emigrated to Mexico and Paraguay (°Old Colony Mennonites). In this dispute the Mennonites found that the °privileges and concessions they had obtained from the federal government in 1873 were of little value, since education in Canada is under provincial jurisdiction.

Canadian school legislation between 1890 and 1920 severely restricted what could be done in private or separate schools, but it did not abolish them entirely. The Canadian Mennonites who stayed accommodated themselves as best they could to the new state of affairs, accepting what could not be avoided while retaining and strengthening their own educational institutions within the changed Canadian context. In the years since the World War I hysteria, and particularly since World War II, Canadian

CANADA

Table 2. Mennonite Groups In Canada (1981-82)

Name of Group	Members	Congregations
Old Order Amish	725	14
Old Orer Mennonites	1,387	10
Waterloo-Markham Conference	935	7
Beachy Amish Church	314	5
Conservative Mennonite Fellowship	95	2
Conservative Mennonite Church of Ontario (CMCO)	325	8
Fellowship Churches	520 (325°)	14 (8°)
Midwest Fellowship	263	4
Other Conservative Groups	376	10
Northern Light Gospel Missions	287	21
Reformed Mennonites	162	2
Mennonite Conference of Ontario and Quebec	5,292 (543°)	42 (4°°)
Western Ontario Mennonite Conference	3,111	16
Northwest Mennonite Conference	1,000 (48°°)	17 (1°°)
Chortitzer Mennonite Conference	2,300	11
Sommerfelder Church of Manitoba	4,000	14
Other Sommerfelder Groups	1,675	5
Bergthaler Churches in Saskatchewan	1,002	6 (1°°°)
Reinlaender Mennonite Church	800	6
Old Colony Mennonite Church	4,500	18
Evangelical Mennonite Mission Conference	2,658	23
Evangelical Mennonite Conference	5,000	45
Evangelical Mennonite Brethren Conference	1,935	17
Church of God in Christ, Mennonite	2,500	30
Conference of Mennonite in Canada	28,152 (591°°)	147 (5°°)
Canadian Conference of Mennonite Brethren Churches	23,248	157
Totals	**91,646**	**638**

°Conservative Mennonite Church of Ontario
°°Dual Conference
°°°Independent

Source: Margaret Loewen Reimer, *One Quilt Many Pieces* (Waterloo: Mennonite Publishing Service, 1983), 56.

Mennonites have built their own high schools and several colleges, which have achieved high academic standards that are widely recogized by secular colleges and universities.

Early Canadian Mennonite immigrants sought isolation, religious freedom, and economic security. In the early years almost all Canadian Mennonites were rural farmers. They have not, however, escaped the influences and events which have shaped Canadian society. Gradually, but at a rapidly accelerating rate after World War II, they have moved into the cities, where most have adopted a social, economic, and cultural lifestyle that is neither separatist nor distinctive. They have sought to redefine and refocus their distinctive beliefs in a manner which permits much greater accommodation but not complete as-similation into Canadian society. Some distinctive and colorful rural remnants remain, particularly in Ontario, but the Canadian census of 1981 showed that only 23 percent of Canadian Mennonites still lived on farms. Fifty-two percent were listed as living in urban centers with the remaining 25 percent being rural nonfarm people. For most Canadian Mennonites traditional separation, with its special life-encompassing value system, has given way to a more accommodative and integrated role in Canadian society.   TDR

Frank H. Epp, *Mennonites in Canada* vol I: *1786-1920: The History of a Separate People* (Toronto: Macmillan, 1974), vol. II: *1920-1940: A People's Struggle for Survival* (Toronto: Macmillan, 1982); Reimer, *Quilt* (1983); *MWH* (1978), 312-81; Peter Penner, *No Longer at Arm's Length: A History of Mennonite Brethren Home Missions in Canada* (Winnipeg:

Kindred, 1986); E. Morris Sider, *The Brethren in Christ in Canada: Two Hundred Years of Tradition and Change* (Nappanee, 1988). Current statistics for many groups are found in the biennial *MC Yearbook*.

See also Amish; Beachy Amish; Bergthal Mennonites; Brethren in Christ; Chortitzer Mennonite Conference; Church of God in Christ, Mennonite (Holdeman); Conservative Mennonite Church of Ontario; Conservative Mennonite Fellowship; Evangelical Mennonite Conference; Evangelical Mennonite Mission Conference; Fellowship Churches; Fellowship of Evangelical Bible Churches; Hutterian Brethren; Mid-West Mennonite Fellowship; New Reinland Mennonite Church of Ontario; Northern Light Gospel Mission Conference; Old Colony Mennonites; Reformed Mennonites; Reinländer Mennoniten Gemeinden; Sommerfeld Mennonites; Zion Mennonite Church; Alberta Provincial Conference of Mennonite Brethren Churches; British Columbia Provincial Conference of Mennonite Brethren Churches; Canadian Conference of Mennonite Brethren Churches; Conference of Mennonites in Alberta; Conference of Mennonites in British Columbia; Conference of Mennonites in Canada; Conference of Mennonites in Manitoba; Conference of Mennonites in Saskatchewan; Conference of United Mennonite Churches of Ontario; Manitoba Conference of Mennonite Brethren Churches; Mennonite Conference of Eastern Canada; Mennonite Conference of Ontario and Quebec; Western Ontario Mennonite Conference; Northwest Conference of the Mennonite Church; Ontario Conference of Mennonite Brethren Churches; Quebec Conference of Mennonite Brethren Churches; Alberta; Atlantic Provinces; British Columbia; Manitoba; Ontario; Quebec; Saskatchewan.

Canadian Conference of Mennonite Brethren Churches (ME I:505). Sometime in late 1947 or early 1948, Mennonite Brethren in Canada began to outnumber their United States parent church. That shift signaled important changes within Canadian Mennonite Brethren (MB) churches between 1955 and 1985. Migrations of displaced Mennonite refugees from Europe after World War II and of other Mennonites from South America aided the growth of the church. Beginning in the early 1950s a movement from the farm to the city began. In 1950 the three largest congregations in the conference were all rural. By 1986, in every province except Alberta the biggest congregations were in °urban settings, and in several places Mennonite Brethren could claim to be one of the major evangelical church communities (Abbotsford, Vancouver, Winnipeg, St. Catharines, and Saskatoon). In 1986, there were 16 congregations in Winnipeg alone. Between 1955 and the end of 1985 Canadian membership nearly doubled (12,884 to 25,152).

As the Canadian church (MB) grew, a number of changes followed. The head office of Missions and Services (MB) was moved from Hillsboro, Ks., to Winnipeg. A decision to support one seminary (in Fresno, Cal.) for both the United States and Canada was finalized in 1975. Most of the teachers at the seminary in 1986 were former Canadians.

Canadian Mennonite Brethren have been characterized by a strong sense of their identity, aided by annual national conventions. Nationally, they have

supported the Mennonite Brethren Bible College in Winnipeg, publications (*Mennonite Brethren Herald*, *Mennonitische Rundschau*, and *Le Lien*), and the Board of Evangelism church planting work in Quebec. The latter began in 1961 and became a provincial conference in 1984. Christian education programs and the Board of Spiritual and Social Concerns' leadership in doctrinal and ethical issues have also been supported. Total giving for 1985 totaled $24.5 million, and per member giving was $976. Among evangelicals in Canada, Mennonite Brethren were well known, providing leadership and funds to many causes. Frank C. Peters, Victor Adrian, and John H. Redekop, along with David E. Redekop and Jacob M. Klassen, have given national leadership far beyond the Mennonite Brethren Church.

Between 1955 and 1985 Mennonite Brethren became culturally a Canadian church. In 1986, 24 of the 180 congregations still used some German, a third of these for services and the rest for Sunday school classes. (In 1940 all Canadian MB congregations used German for worship.) Mennonite Brethren congregations were worshiping in at least nine languages, including French, German, and Hindi. Understanding for church growth gradually changed, from outreach through vacation Bible schools and mission Sunday schools to church planting and church extension in the early 1980s. Growth has come increasingly through local church outreach.

In 1986, each of the provinces from Quebec westward had strong provincial conferences. Three high schools were supported by conferences in Ontario, Manitoba, and British Columbia, and three Bible institutes in Quebec, Manitoba, and Saskatchewan-Alberta. The British Columbia conference supported a Bible college, and the Mennonite Brethren Bible College in Winnipeg was supported by the entire Canadian Conference. All provincial conferences had mission programs, with especially strong efforts in British Columbia and Manitoba. The Manitoba conference carried on a strong radio and television ministry, one of the largest denominationally supported °broadcasting programs in Canada. By 1986, 40 percent of all Canadian Mennonite Brethren as well as the two largest churches, Willingdon in Burnaby and Central Heights in Abbotsford, were located in British Columbia.

Canadian Mennonite Brethren in the mid-1980s were increasingly viewing themselves as evangelical rather than Mennonite, and indicating it by using such names as "community church" or simply dropping the "Mennonite Brethren" name. Church °polity was becoming more presbyterial. Support for Mennonite Central Committee (MCC) and other inter-Mennonite causes continued to come from a large part of the Canadian Mennonite Brethren community. Of 486 workers serving in various ministries in 1984, 112 were with Mennonite Brethren Board of Missions and Services, 71 were with MCC, and 303 were with non-Mennonite Brethren mission boards.

Yet a strong common vision bound most of the churches together. Life as a fellowship of churches continued to be important. Holding common positions on social and ethical issues was considered important. Leadership had the respect of the churches. A strong sense of mission was evident. Cooperation was cultivated both with the wider Mennonite fellowship as well as with the evangelical fellowship. HJ

The *Canadian Conference of MB Churches Yearbook*, published annually, contains minutes and statistics; John A. Toews, *History MB* (1975), index.

See also Mennonite Brethren Church of North America.

Canadian Foodgrains Bank. See Development Work; Dyck, John R.; Mennonite Central Committee, Canada.

Canadiense Colony, Bolivia, founded in 1956 by a group of 48 families from the Menno Colony in Paraguay, is located about 20 km. (12 mi.) ne. of Santa Cruz. The original settlers were joined by another 15-20 families from Paraguay in 1963-64. Many of these families left Paraguay due to the establishment of a producer-consumer °cooperative in the Menno colony, the modernization trends of the schools, the founding of a high school, and changes in the church. The church in the Canadiense colony is called Grünthaler and resembles the °Sommerfelder church.

A daughter colony, Morgenland, was founded in 1975 about 80 km. (50 mi.) se. of the town of Santa Cruz, 30 km. (18 mi.) south of Pailón. In 1986 Canadiense had a population of 807 inhabitants, of which 329 were baptized church members; Morgenland had 280 inhabitants with 104 members.

Although it became the oldest Mennonite colony in Bolivia after Tres Palmas was disbanded in 1986, Canadiense is still one of the poorer ones. Farms are generally mechanized, and some farmers own light trucks, jeeps, or other small trucks. Radios and tape recorders are not prohibited in Canadiense.

Several individual men and families have been involved in making harnesses for Mennonite Central Committee (MCC), which MCC workers pass on to poor Bolivian farmers. Several women from the colony have been working at the adjacent Chorovi clinic, operated by the Evangelical Mennonite Mission Conference of Canada (Misión Evangélica Menonita, Bolivia).   IHie

See also Bergthal Mennonites.

Capital Punishment. The conviction that human life is sacred has generally but not uniformly meant that Mennonites sanctioned neither war nor capital punishment. Opposition to capital punishment is based on biblically oriented arguments. The stipulation of "life for life," was not enforced with Cain, the first murderer (Gn 4:8-15), nor with David (2 Sm 11:1-12:23). Jesus refused to advocate stoning for the woman caught in adultery (Jn 8:12-11), though biblical law so prescribed. The direction in the Bible, it is claimed, is from an older severity to a stance of grace, from retribution to rehabilitation. Genesis 9:6, which on the face of it calls for the death penalty for murderers, is explained as being in the nature of an atonement. With Christ's satisfactory atonement, such demands fall away.

Other arguments against capital punishment draw on judicial, sociological, and psychological considerations. The legal system is not foolproof, and innocent persons have been convicted and executed.

Frequently, members of minority groups suffer the ultimate penalty, while wealthy or influential people do not. According to some sociological studies, the enforcement of capital punishment has not been a deterrent to crime. Life imprisonment, rather than the death penalty, is a more humane form of punishment. To cut short a criminal's life is to cut short the opportunity to repent. Psychologically, capital punishment is evil because it feeds the desire for revenge. The death penalty is a form of retaliation. Moreover, by putting the criminal to death, society commits the very evil it protests.

Mennonites who favor retaining capital punishment have argued that sociological surveys are flawed. The Bible substantiates that the death penalty is a deterrent (Dt 13:10-11). Capital punishment is not venting one's vengeance; there is a large difference between proper judicial process and revenge. As for cutting short the criminal's opportunity for repentance, the criminal, since he knows the time of his end, has greater reason for immediate repentance. If the legal system is faulty and innocent people are consigned to execution, then the solution is not the abolition of the death penalty but the reform of the legal system.

The interpretation of Scripture has for Mennonites been the center of the debate. Those who support capital punishment also stress the sacredness of life. It is precisely because men and women are made in God's image—a permanent factor in the creation order—that anyone taking human life forfeits his own right to life (Gn 9:6). The directive in Gn 9:6 has *not* an atonement context, but is intended to restrain disorder in society. Nor has this command been rescinded or revoked. Those who do wrong have reason to fear, for the governmental authority "does not bear the sword for nothing" (Rom 13:4). Nor did Jesus' statement to the woman caught in adultery (Jn 8:1-11) set aside the death penalty. Had they indeed observed protocol, the accusers would have brought the male offender also, as the law stipulated (Lev 20:10). The reason Cain and David were not summarily dealt with shows that these laws are not to be mechanically or routinely enforced. There is a place for leniency, grace, even forgiveness. The death penalty could be incurred for 18 different offenses, yet the law was tempered by its provision of cities of refuge. For all offenses except murder (Num 35:31), a redemptive alternate was in place. Since the laws calling for capital punishment were tempered in this way, some Mennonites have argued that the death penalty is required and right.   EAM

Larry Kehler, and others, *Capital Punishment Study Guide* (Winnipeg: MCC, 1985); John H. Redekop and Elmer Martens, *On Capital Punishment* (Winnipeg: Kindred Press, 1987), 31 pp.; *MQR* 48 (1974), 104-5; *The Church, the State, and the Offender* (Newton); John H. Yoder, *The Christian and Capital Punishment* (Newton, 1961), 24 pp.; Howard Zehr, *Death as a Penalty* (Elkhart, Ind.: MCC U.S. Office of Criminal Justice).

See also Peace; Politics; Reconciliation.

Capitalism, along with °*communism*, is a familiar word in much of the modern world; the ideologies these two words imply have contributed to some of the greatest crises in history. *Capitalism* has no precise meaning, but it can be assumed to depend upon, or be constituted by "self interest as ultimately the servant of society, the minimization of the role of the state, and the institution of private property . . ." (Hoover, 294-5). Adam Smith (1723-90) proposed that the seeds of capitalism derive from the tendency of human nature to "truck, barter, and exchange one thing for another" (Smith [1776] 1952, p. 6).

While the above characteristics have existed in most human societies, the entrepreneur has focused and energized the "capitalistic" emphasis in western Europe and North America during the last two centuries. The entrepreneur's own energy and °wealth, and that of others, has sparked the growth of capitalism. Capitalism has undergone a great transformation from the time of Adam Smith. Capitalism emerged gradually, and did not necessarily follow upon feudalism nor need much technology, but it needed a free market (Polanyi) and stable governmental support. Max Weber (1864-1920) maintained that capitalism required entrepreneurial organization of capital, rationalized technology, free labor, and unrestricted markets. Modified capitalism is said to have developed from the internal contradictions between private property and self-interest as being best for society and reality. Restraints against the uninhibited promotion of self-interest were the natural result.

Contrary to Marxist theory, modern pluralistic modified capitalism (i.e., modified to suit the various national and historic conditions) is not doomed to self-destruction, unless it will be overthrown with violence. The real possibility for this hinges on the nuclear weapons confrontation between the two great proponents of each ideology, the Soviet Union and the United States.

Anabaptists, Mennonites, and Capitalism in Theory. Anabaptist-Mennonite beliefs have promoted respect for °government, peace, and integrity in social and human relations, but have been diametrically opposed to two basic tenets of capitalism, namely, the centrality of self-interest in human action and the respect for the sanctity of private property. Anabaptists and Mennonites have had a belief system or °theology that stressed regeneration of the individual and made self-interest and self-will submissive to God's will and the welfare of the neighbor. This belief system has been termed *"Gelassenheit"* (Cronk). In this view human energies should be directed to helping the neighbor and sharing natural resources with them. The "Sermon on the Mount," "following Jesus," the "way of the cross" and other phrases refer to the *"Gelassenheit"* or communal ethic, which best typifies the attitude of Mennonites regarding the two cardinal ideas of capitalism, namely, self-interest and private property.

That Anabaptists and Mennonites must be seen historically as a part of a general confrontation and rejection of the emerging capitalist orientation is indicated by the many antagonists and theoreticians who defined Mennonites as "communistic" (Kautzky, Zschäbitz) or °socialistic, both in the 16th c. and in later eras. The actual communistic organization in economic life for example, among the °Münster Anabaptists or the °Hutterian Brethren and the many anti-self-interest and anti-private property activities which have defined Mennonites, as discussed briefly below, indicate the direction of Mennonite and Anabaptist theology.

Anabaptism-Mennonitism and Capitalism in Practice. Mennonites, with the exception of those in the Soviet Union after 1917, in China during the Maoist revolution, and in eastern European countries since World War II, have operated almost exclusively in a capitalistic environment. Hence they have adapted and adjusted to the capitalistic economic institutions in which they operated. But this does not automatically make them capitalistic in orientation or commitment.

It must be admitted, however, that a substantial and increasing percentage of European and North American Mennonites, including pockets of Mennonites in Brazil and Paraguay, have become rather completely involved in the capitalistic free enterprise system. °Businesses of great size developed early in The Netherlands, Germany, Russia before the Revolution, Canada, the United States, Brazil, and Paraguay. Statistical information is not readily available on the incomes and the wealth held by Mennonites, but most concentrations of Mennonite congregations contain a substantial number of millionaires, owners of various business, investors, and participants in industrial and commercial establishments. One writer estimates that there were nearly 1,000 Mennonite millionaires in Canada and the United States in 1979 (*Marketplace*, 1979). It can be assumed that the Mennonites who have entered the entrepreneurial arena often become politically and religiously conservative. Kauffman and Harder's study indicates that 74 percent of United States Mennonites chose the Republican Party in 1972, but we have no breakdown by °occupation or wealth. On the basis of interviewing conducted by the present writer, it is clear that the more successful financially, the more conservative politically the Mennonite entrepreneur generally is.

There are, however, sectors of Mennonites who have resisted becoming ideologically captivated by capitalism. The best example is the Hutterite sector. Although it could be demonstrated that they are a type of "church capitalism," the Hutterites believe that "community of goods (*Gütergemeinschaft*) is the will of God, who from the beginning created all things common for common use" (Hostetler, 146). The "semicommunal" sector of Mennonitism, including the Old Colony Mennonites, the Sommerfelder Mennonites, the Old Order Mennonites, the Amish, and related smaller groups do not generally promote a capitalistic ideology which stresses self-interest and the sanctity of private property. Their practice of °mutual aid and communal ownership of the land (the latter among the Sommerfelder and Old Colony Mennonites) and their stress on simple living, which downgrades self-enhancement and the accumulation of private property, strongly indicate the rejection of the classic capitalistic ethos. Further and intriguing proof of the underlying "communal" ethos in the mainstream Mennonite tradition is the emergence of the modern intentional communities. More than 30 such communities (Fretz 1979, p. 116) provide evidence for this strand of residual communalism in Mennonitism.

Furthermore, almost everywhere in Mennonite congregations are found individual families, couples, and persons, who in various forms reject classical capitalist activity. Some have joined intentional communities, while others have given substantial amounts of time in °voluntary service to various church and secular organizations, especially Mennonite Central Committee. Some comparative data suggest that Mennonites spend a much higher amount of time in voluntary service to other people than do most of their neighbors. This does not prove an anticapitalistic bias, but it shows that their "self-interest" is not actively directed toward amassing private property, the heart of the capitalistic effort.

As indicated in the article on °business, one, if not *the* greatest, battleground for the survival of the Anabaptist faith is the role of °economics in religious life. The values of classical capitalism collide head-on with Anabaptist values. The question before Mennonites is: how can Christians participate in the necessary economic life without being seduced and captured by the lures of self-interest and the sanctity of private ownership of property?   CWR

Randall Collins, "Weber's Last Theory of Capitalism: A Systematization," *American Sociological Review*, 45, no. 6 (Dec. 1980), 925-942; Sandra Cronk, "Gelassenheit: The Rites of the Redemptive Process in the Old Order Amish and Old Order Mennonite Communities:" (PhD diss., U. of Chicago, 1977), cf. *MQR*, 55 (1981), 5-44; J. Winfield Fretz, "Newly Emerging Communes in Mennonite Communities," in *Communes: Historical and Contemporary*, ed. Ruch Shonle Cavan (New Delhi: Vikas Publishing House, 1979); John A. Hostetler, *Hutterite Society* (1974); Calvin Hoover, "Capitalism," *International Encyclopedia of the Social Sciences* (New York: Macmillan, 1968); Kauffman/Harder, *Anabaptists Four C. Later* (1975); Karl Kautsky, *Communism in Central Europe in the Time of the Reformation* (London: T. Fisher Unwin, 1897); Peter J. Klassen, *The Economics of Anabaptism, 1525-1560* (London: Mouton, 1964); Karl Polanyi, *The Great Transformation* (Boston: Beacon Press, 1944); Adam Smith, *The Wealth of the Nations* (London, 1952; originally published 1776); Gerhard Zschäbitz, *Zur mitteldeutschen Wiedertäuferbewegung nach dem großen Bauernkreig* (Berlin, 1958).

See also Economics; Marxism; Political Attitudes; Socialism.

Caribbean Light and Truth had its beginning in 1974 as a missionary endeavor of Salem Mennonite Church of Keota, Iowa. The purpose of the organization is to bring the gospel message to the people of the Caribbean Basin. The name is derived from Ps 43:3: "O send out thy light and thy truth: let them lead me." The first workers, sent by the church in July 1974, were David and Nancy Stutzman and Daniel Stutzmen, members of the Keota congregation. Daniel later married Judy Miller. Chosen by the church in Belize, Daniel was ordained to the ministry in 1976. As the number of believers increased, there was need for more ordained leaders, so in 1980 three native Belizean ministers were ordained. One more was ordained in 1987 and two in 1988. There were 14 ordained and lay leaders in 1987, with a total membership of 151. Services are held on a regular basis in 14 different areas. There are three schools organized and supported by Caribbean Light and Truth. To meet some legal requirements the organization has become incorporated in the state of Iowa as a nonprofit corporation, with the board of directors from the local congregation.   WS

MWH (1984), 51.

Casas Grandes Colonies, Mexico. Buenos Aires Colony, the first of several Casas Grandes colonies, was founded in 1960 in the municipality of Janos in nw. Chihuahua State. It is a daughter colony of the Manitoba Colony near Cuauhtémoc and was founded not only because of land shortage but also because there was a fear that the Manitoba Colony would lose its isolation as a result of the paved road passing through the colony. About 50 families formed the first settlement at Janos. In 1962 another tract of land 50 km. (30 mi.) to the east was purchased; this became the El Capulin colony. Both colonies were served by the same bishop until 1981. The Buenos Aires, colony bought another tract of land 125 km. (15 mi.) se. of Buenos Aires where the El Cuervo colony was founded in 1979. The El Cuervo and Buenos Aires colonies form one church body, having the same bishop. There is one meetinghouse in each colony. In 1987 the Buenos Aires colony had 330 baptized members and 945 inhabitants. El Cuervo had 160 members and 560 inhabitants.

Congregations meet Sunday mornings and on church holidays. The High German language predominates in their services, but some Low German is used. Average Sunday morning attendance in Buenos Aires and El Cuervo is 175 and 125 respectively. There are six schools in the Buenos Aires Colony and four at El Cuervo, with one teacher for each school. These colonies still do not have any °television, °radio, or telephone, and transportation within the colony is still by means of horsepower. Agriculture is the main occupation. Cotton, sorghum, and some wheat and oats are raised, all under irrigation.

In 1981 the Manitoba Colony bought more land 30 km. (18 mi.) nw. of Buenos Aires where the Las Virginias colony was established. In 1987 it had 418 church members and 1,279 inhabitants. The latest colony is Buena Vista, located 60 km. (36 mi.) ne. of Buenos Aires. Climate and vegetation correspond to semiarid conditions. All farmland is irrigated by water pumped from wells. Despite their efforts to isolate themselves, these colonies have adapted to climatic and agricultural conditions rapidly. Each colony is relatively small and must have continued contact with the non-Old Colony world.

In 1986 the Casas Grandes colonies began efforts to find land in Argentina, and in 1987 a settlement was begun at °Remecó, in La Pampa State.   HEns

Cashton, Wis., Old Order Amish Settlement is located in the sw. part of the state. Wisconsin has been an attraction to the Amish because of its rural character and reputation as the "Dairy State." The Supreme Court ruling in Wisconsin v. Yoder (1972), deciding that no state could require Amish children to attend high school, drew attention to this part of the country and triggered small migrations from Ohio and Indiana. In 1986 there were 14 Amish settlements in Wisconsin. Most of these are one-congregation communities and need more time to test their survival. The Cashton settlement was founded in 1966. It had four congregations in 1984 and is still growing by virtue of families moving in from smaller settlements. The Amish community at Cashton had fewer than 800 persons after 20 years, but seemed to have the foundations to become a permanent settlement.   SLY

Caste systems assign individuals permanently to social positions purely on the basis of race, religion, or some other ascribed characteristic. South Africa's *apartheid* is a caste system based on racial segregation. So are the systems of slavery and Jim Crow segregation in the history of the United States.

Caste in India may be described in reference to *varnas* and *jatis. Varnas* are the broad, classificatory levels of Indian civilization and typically include *Brahmins* (priests and teachers) at the top, *Kshatriyas* (warriors) at the second level, *Vaisyas* (merchants) next, followed by *Sudras* (laborers). Below are the Untouchables or, as Gandhi referred to them, the *Harijans* (children of God).

Jatis are endogamous groupings, i.e., members are expected to marry within the group. Historically they have also defined the occupations and lifestyles of their members. *Jati* prescriptions and proscriptions are religiously reinforced, meaning that, within the Hindu system of interpretation, it makes a difference for this and all future lives whether or not a person lives up to the definitions of his or her *jati* position. From 15 to 20 *jatis* can be found in most larger Indian villages; from 200 to 300 can be associated with each of the general language regions of India.

Indian churches today, particularly in the cities, include members from many different backgrounds. Yet the strengths, outlines, problems, and prospects of the church in India, in general, can only be well understood if caste considerations are taken into account. Recruitment of new Christians over the years has followed *jati* lines rather closely, or has occurred primarily at the "edges" of Indian civilization, where *jati* lines are not as clearly drawn as they are closer in. Another important source of Christian converts has been the *Harijans,* the level of Indian society at which converts have had the least to lose socially in leaving the Hindu system. Church rivalries frequently follow *jati* lines.   PDW

Stephen Neill, *The Story of the Christian Church in India and Pakistan* (Grand Rapids: Eerdmans, 1970); Louis Dumont, *Homo Hierarchicus: The Caste System and Its Implications* (Chicago: U. of Chicago Press, 1970); Donald A. McGavran, *Ethnic Realities and the Church: Lessons from India* (Pasadena: William Carey, 1979); Paul D. Wiebe, *Christians in Andhra Pradesh: The Mennonites of Mahbubnagar* (Bangalore: Christian Institute for the Study of Religion and Society, 1987); William and Charlotte Wiser, *Behind Mud Walls, 1930-1960* (Berkeley: U. of California Press, 1963); Paul G. Hiebert, *Konduru: Structure and Integration in a South Indian Village* (Minneapolis: U. of Minnesota Press, 1971).

See also Social Class.

Castelberger, Andreas (ME I:523). Resident in Zürich since late 1521 or early 1522, Castelberger plied the trade of bookseller between Glarus, Basel, and Einsiedeln. As supplier of radical Reformation °pamphlets in and around Zürich, he became the liaison between the rural and urban radicals, made contact with Andreas Karlstadt (°°Carlstadt), and was one of the signatories of Conrad Grebel's letter to Thomas °Müntzer. J. F. G. Goeters considered Castelberger's study meetings for lay people to have been the cradle of Zürich Anabaptism. Here biblical opinions were sought on such topics as church benefices, usury, payment of the tithe, war, images, and infant baptism. On Jan. 21, 1525, the day of the first Zürich Anabaptist baptisms, the city council ordered him to cease all private meetings and to leave within eight days. Petitions pleading ill health secured temporary extensions. On June 12, 1525, the council learned that Castelberger was reading Zwingli's *Taufbüchlin* (published May 27, 1525) to peasant visitors, explaining "that Zwingli had written falsely . . . strengthening them in Anabaptism, holding the opinion that one should have no authority and need not pay the tithe." Without further delay, Castelberger, his wife, children, books and belongings were loaded on a boat and deported. Among the books were presumably holdings from Grebel's library. Only a few weeks earlier Grebel, seeking to cover his debts, had consigned his library to Castelberger.

From Zürich, Castelberger returned to his home area of Graubünden (Grisons). On March 17, 1528, the reformer of Chur, Johannes Comander, complained that "limping Andreas" was sowing dissent among his parishoners. A Castelberger, presumably our Andreas, obtained citizenship at Chur in 1531. Thereafter our sources fall silent.   WOP

TA Schweiz I (Zürich), 37, 55-56, 386-88; Emil Egli, ed., *Aktensammlung zur Geschichte der Züricher Reformation in den Jahren 1519-1533* (reprint Nieuwkoop, 1973), 66-67, 72-73, 83, 85-86; *TA Schweiz II (Ostschweiz),* 502, 504,, 509, no. 7; J. F. G. Goeters, "Die Vorgeschichte des Taüfertums in Zürich," in *Studien zur Geschichte und Theologie der Reformation,* ed. by Louise Abramowski and J. F. G. Goeters (Neukirchen-Vlyn: Neukirchner Verlag, 1969), 255; Werner O. Packull, "The Origins of Swiss Anabaptism in the Context of the Reformation of the Common Man," *JMS,* 3 (1985), 38-43, 47; CRR 4: 357-58, 203-204, 533-34, 715-18.

Casting Out Demons. See Exorcism.

Catechism. See Baptismal Instruction; Christian Education.

Central America is the relatively narrow isthmus of land that extends over slightly more than 2,000 kilometers from the se. border of Mexico to Colombia on the north coast of South America. Historically, Central America consisted of the five countries Guatemala, El Salvador, Honduras, Nicaragua, and Costa Rica, but now Belize on the northeast and Panama on the south are also seen as part of Central America. In the 1980s this whole area with the inclusion of Mexico is referred to as Mesoamerica.

The first Mennonites to live in Mesoamerica were the Old Colony Mennonites who migrated to Mexico from Canada in the early 1920s. Less than 40 years later about 4,000 of these Mennonites moved from Mexico to Belize, again in search of guaranteed freedoms for their agriculture-based, isolated religious communities.

Mennonite mission activities in the Mesoamerican region began in 1950, when the Eastern Mennonite Board of Missions and Charities of Lancaster Mennonite Conference (MC) began a mission in Trujillo, Honduras. Beginning the following year the board also sent nurses to operate medical clinics and North American youths for °development work. These became known as Overseas Voluntary Service Units that continued for more than a decade. A similar strategy was followed when other Mennonite

CENTRAL AMERICA

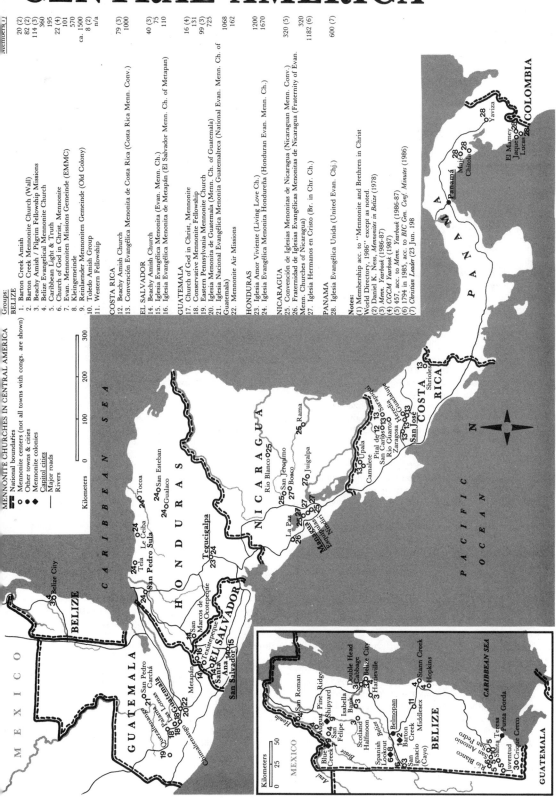

mission boards opened work in neighboring countries. In the late 1950s the Franconia Mennonite Conference (MC) sent missionaries to Mexico City and the Pacific Coast Mennonite Conference (MC) mission board opened work in Sinaloa in ne. Mexico.

In the decade of the 1960s and the early 1970s there was a flurry of Mennonite mission activity in Central America. Many Mennonite mission efforts included personnel to minister to both spiritual and social needs. Rosedale Mennonite Missions of the Conservative Mennonite Conference (MC) began in Costa Rica with both missionaries and °voluntary service units. In Nicaragua nurses and volunteer workers preceded missionaries, who then worked with the new groups of believers already begun. The Conservative Mennonite Fellowship assigned missionaries to work among Cachiquel Indians in western Guatemala. A few years later some of these workers organized a separate program under the name Mennonite Air Missions. A similar group, Caribbean Light and Truth, began in southern Belize. Eastern Mennonite Board of Missions and Charities sent personnel to Belize to work with the Old Colony Mennonites and to start new Mennonite churches. They also assigned workers to establish Spanish churches in Guatemala City and among the K'ekchi Indians in northern Guatemala. The Brethren in Christ transferred their first missionaries from Cuba to Nicaragua. The Evangelical Mennonite Conference of Manitoba, Canada, sent both missionaries and voluntary service workers to Nicaragua. The Mennonite Brethren sent missionaries to work in Panama as an outgrowth of their program in Colombia. The Beachy Amish Mennonite mission and development board, Amish Mennonite Aid, sent volunteer workers to El Salvador and later sent their first missionaries to El Salvador and Belize to establish an orphanage and churches. Single short-term volunteers generally worked in supportive roles with their missionaries. Beachy Amish groups also established small self-supporting communities in El Salvador, Belize, Honduras, and Costa Rica.

In the early 1970s Eastern Board missionaries, Ed and Gloria King, began a youth ministry, Amor Viviente, in the capital of Honduras. Following relief work after the 1976 Guatemala earthquake, the Church of God in Christ Mennonite (Holdeman) mission board sent missionaries to establish churches north and east of Guatemala City. The Iglesia Evangélica Menonita del El Salvador [Metapán] (Evangelical Mennonite Church) in northern El Salvador was started in the early 1980s by former members of the Iglesia Evangélica Menonita Hondurena (Honduran Mennonite Church) who migrated to El Salvador and by Honduran Eastern board missionaries and pastors.

Most of these missionary efforts included efforts to train national church leaders as they participated in the different aspects of ministry. After the three consecutive natural disasters in the 1970s (an earthquake in Nicaragua, hurricane Fifi in Honduras, and another earthquake in Guatemala), Central American Mennonites, including Old Colony Mennonites from Belize, worked alongside their North American sisters and brothers in °relief efforts. This relief work, the earlier service projects and teaching, and continuing Mennonite Central Committee (MCC) involvement in development work in the region have encouraged the conferences to develop a wholistic concept of the gospel. Several of the conferences now have their own social service committees and are coordinating their involvement with various international organizations in working in service projects and with refugees.

Since 1973 an annual °Consulta Anabautista Menonita Centroamericana (CAMCA; Central American Anabaptist Mennonite Consultation) has been held by national and missionary church leaders. This regular interchange in alternating countries of the region has provided a significant opportunity for the development of an area ministers' manual, Bible lessons for new believers, and a hymnbook. CAMCA also served as a forum for the development of a regional leadership training program beyond the level of Bible institute studies. It is known as the Seminario Ministerial de Liderazgo Anabautista (Anabaptist Ministerial Leaders Seminary), SEMILLA. This extension Bible training program begun in 1983 has a regional board of directors made up of national, rather than expatriate, members and is helping the different groups of Anabaptist origin to develop a common vision and identity.

As a result of these missionary and church activities, in 1988 there are a dozen organized national church conferences and several more recognized mission groups. The total of all these, not including the colony Mennonites, exceeds 13,000 baptized members. These are in approximately 335 congregations which are, with a few exceptions, led by national pastors who have only occasional contact with foreign missionary personnel.   AY

MWH (1978), (1984).

See also El Salvador; Guatemala; Panama; Nicaragua; Honduras; Dominican Republic; Haiti; Jamaica; Trinidad and Tobago; Cuba; Puerto Rico.

Central American Anabaptist-Mennonite Conference. See Consulta Anabautista Menonita Centroamericana (CAMCA).

Central District Conference (GCM). The second largest district of the General Conference Mennonite Church in the United States was created by a merger of the °°Central Conference Mennonite Church and the Middle District (GCM) at a joint session in Normal, Ill., April 27, 1957. It had 41 congregations from Ohio, Michigan, Indiana, Illinois, Iowa, and Missouri, and a membership of 8,361. Its original purpose, to promote unity, offer guidance, and provide a channel for the united mission efforts among its constituent churches, continues to be a focus of the conference in the late 1980s.

Each member congregation has one delegate vote for every 30 members. Delegates meet yearly for a three-day session of business, worship, seminars, and fellowship at various locations around the district. An elected president, president-elect, treasurer, secretary, and two members-at-large make up the board of directors. Forty other elected people make up the standing committees: Ministerial; Program; Historical; Missions; Education and Publication;

Camp Friedenswald; and Peace, Service, and Justice. A nominating committee is appointed. The district also elects six Bluffton College board members, three General Conference commission members, and five board members of the Chicago Mennonite Learning Center. The district board and committees guide ministries in church planting and evangelism, prison and law offenders, youth, Christian camping, teacher training, marriage and family, leadership development, worship and music, and peace education. The budget for 1987 was $242,000. *The Reporter*, the monthly conference paper, is published 11 times each year.

The following have served as conference ministers: Raymond L. °Hartzler, 1957-64; Gordon Dyck, 1964-69; Jacob T. Friesen, 1970-75; Stanley Bohn, 1975-79; and Mark Weidner, 1980-. Membership in 1987 was 62 congregations with 8,247 members. Twenty-six of the congregations were also affiliated with other conferences, primarily those of the Mennonite Church (MC). MWei

Central District Yearbook, annual reports, conference minutes, directory, and statistics; Samuel F. Pannabecker, *Faith and Ferment: The History of the Central District Conference* (Newton, 1968); minutes, correspondence, records, etc., are retained in the Bluffton College Archives, Bluffton, Ohio; *GCM Handbook* (1988), 111-12, 139-40.

Central District Conference (MB) (ME I:541) consists of 28 churches in the states of Nebraska, South Dakota, North Dakota, Montana, Minnesota, and Illinois. In 1960, when the °°Krimmer Mennonite Brethren and Mennonite Brethren churches merged, the Central District received 800 new members in South Dakota and from missions in Chicago and Omaha; the merger thus affected the Central District more than any other Mennonite Brethren conference. In 1987 the total membership was 2,350.

The conference is organized into six committees coordinated through an executive committee and a district minister. The first district minister was Waldo Wiebe (1978-86). He was succeeded by J. J. Toews. The other committees are: Reference and Counsel, Pulpit, Home Missions Board, Youth, Board of Trustees, and Women's Missionary Service. The Central District, together with the Southern, Latin American, and North Carolina districts, operates Tabor College through the Tabor College Senate. The college makes annual reports to the Central District.

The Central District is known for its deep commitment to foreign missions, home missions, and youth work. Work with Native American peoples (°Indian ministries) began in 1948 at the Pineridge Indian Reservation of South Dakota. In 1987 home mission churches were located in Sioux Falls and Rapid City, S.D.; Bismark, N.D.; and Millard, Nebr. WP

MB Yearbook (1981), 172, 187-89.

Centreville, Mich., Old Order Amish Settlement, in St. Joseph Co., Mich., was founded in 1910 by families from Allen and Adams Cos. (°Grabill, °Berne) near Ft. Wayne, Ind. Later, Amish from °Lagrange Co., Ind., joined these early settlers, making this the largest and oldest of the 18 Amish settlements in Michigan. This community is unique in that the five congregations of approximately 800

people are a mixture of descendants of 18th-and 19th-c. immigrants from °°Alsace and Switzerland. Although founded by the Swiss Amish, the community fellowships closely with the large Elkhart-Lagrange, Ind., community, less than 20 mi. (30 km.) away, with frequent exchange of ministers and sometimes sharing the same bishop oversight. For 46 years, the Centreville settlement was the only Amish community in Michigan. Since the mid-1950s, 17 new settlements have developed in the state. Fourteen of these are single-congregation communities, and only time will tell whether or not these will survive. SLY

Ceramics (ME I:543). European Mennonite and Hutterite ceramics are discussed in the ME I-IV, including Habaner pottery and the tile produced by the °°Tichelaar family in °°Makkum, Friesland.

Research on 19th-c. North American Mennonite potters began in the 1970s. Four potters in Canada and two in the United States have been documented.

The earliest of these potters was Jacob Bock (1789-1867), who was born in Lancaster Co., Pa., and came to Waterloo Co., Ont., as a young boy. In 1832 he was elected township clerk, and in 1850 he helped found the Blenheim Mennonite Church, where he served as deacon from 1841 until his death. His 1865 will has been found, and his pottery shop is known to have been located in Waterloo. The three known pieces of his work, each dated 1825, are the earliest dated pieces of Ontario pottery known. They are covered earthenware tobacco jars, each decorated with four relief plaques of St. Ambrose (ca. 240-397).

Cyrus Eby (1844-1906) was a potter in Markham Twp., York Co., Ont. He was producing ware in 1862. His grandfather was a Mennonite pioneer from Pennsylvania. His father was known as "Potter Sam," and it was from him that he and his brother likely learned the trade. Cyrus's older brother, William K. Eby (1831-1905), was a potter in Conestogo, Waterloo Co., Ont. The pottery was located just south of Conestogo and east of St. Jacobs. Earlier, in 1855, he had operated a pottery in Markham for two years. He then bought an existing pottery from potter Burton Curtis. Eby was a part-time potter, also supporting himself with farming. An 1890s price list indicates that he produced crocks, pans, jugs, pitchers, flower pots, chamber pots, spittoons, stove tubes, and pie plates "of common earthenware." After 1900, he was assisted by his son, William, Jr. Twin-stemmed cherries are a distinguishing decoration on Eby's pie plates and tableware. His was the last Pennsylvania German pottery in Ontario.

Two potters operating in the United States at about the same time as the Ebys in Canada, were John D. Heatwole (1826-1907) and his cousin, Emanuel Suter (1833-1902). According to family tradition, Suter became an apprentice to Heatwole in 1851. Several pieces survive by each man, dated 1851. Both potteries were located in Rockingham County's Central District, near Harrisonburg, Va. In 1848, Heatwole was married to Elizabeth Coffman. In 1852, they became members of the Bank Mennonite Church, one mile from his pottery.

According to tradition, Heatwole learned the trade from his wife's brother-in-law, Lindsay Morris. Their common father-in-law was Andrew Coffman, another potter of Mennonite ancestry, who was not a member of the church himself. His son and grandson served together in the same regiment in the Civil War. Two signed pieces of Coffman's blue decorated stoneware have survived. His 1853 stoneware tombstone, apparently made by his son, John Coffman, is one of only two examples known. John Heatwole produced the other one.

Heatwole was already listed as a potter in the 1850 census. His pottery was a one-man operation, except for a brief partnership with Joseph Silber in 1866. Silber (d. 1890), a recent immigrant from Baden, Germany, also collaborated with Suter in the same year.

Heatwole's shop was a small frame building resting on four cornerstones with a dirt floor, near a small two-story log house of four rooms and a mule stable. He produced both lead-glazed earthenware and stoneware. Many of his crocks are highly decorated individual creations; his operation never reached the large commercial proportions of Suter's.

Heatwole's avoidance of military service is legendary. After initially joining the militia in June 1861, he went into hiding after being allowed to return home for fall planting. While in what is now West Virginia, he sowed the seeds of the Mennonite faith there. He was finally able to return to his family in 1865. In the 1880 census he was still listed as a potter.

Emanuel Suter (1833-1902) married Elizabeth Swope in 1855, and they settled on the Swope family farm three miles west of Harrisonburg. There he built a small kiln, which he apparently operated until 1866. In 1864, he fled northward, a refugee with his family from the Civil War. This brought to a close the early period of his pottery-making, during which he made both earthenware and stoneware. His few known pieces from this period are most highly decorated. Suter was exempt from military service because his potter skills were needed to make tableware. Heatwole had not applied for the exemption. As he fled northward, Suter began a daily account of his experiences. This ongoing practice resulted in a set of diaries reaching to 1902, constituting a unique record of the life of an American potter.

While in Pennsylvania, Suter worked for a few months for the large Cowden and Wilcox Pottery Company in Harrisburg. In 1866, back in Virginia, he began building a much larger kiln and pottery shop for his New Erection Pottery. The new shop was two stories high. This new operation was very successful for 25 years. It produced large quantities of utilitarian stoneware and earthenware, generally undecorated. More than 75 different kinds of ware are listed in his account books. The most common were crocks, flower pots and saucers, preserve jars, butter churns, milk pans, and spittoons. In 1890 Suter moved his operation to town near the railroad, where it was known as the Harrisonburg Steam Pottery Company. In preparation for building the new pottery, Suter had spent the summer of 1890 visiting potteries in Pennsylvania and Ohio to learn the latest methods. The undecorated stoneware produced here was covered with gray or tan slip outside and Albany slip inside. By 1897, internal administrative problems prompted Suter to sell out. The operation failed soon after that.

Active in the church, Suter was secretary of the Virginia Mennonite Conference (MC) for many years and was influential in promoting Sunday schools. Suter's 1902 obituary did not mention that he had been a potter.

Two potters who came to the craft late in life are to be noted. Born in 1892 in Old Oraibi Hopi village on Third Mesa in Arizona, Polingaysi Qoyawayama, also known as Elizabeth Q. White, completed a distinguished career as a teacher before she retired in 1954 and became a potter. After taking course work at Northern Arizona U., she was known for developing new techniques and working with unusual clays. She produced corn maiden wind bells and decorated pots with raised ears of corn. Her work was highly prized; even broken pieces were saved.

John P. Klassen, a Russian Mennonite, was instrumental in leading a group of Mennonite immigrants to Canada in 1923. He had had art training in Munich and Berlin. In 1924, he joined the Bluffton College faculty as a sculptor and painter. In the 1930s and 1940s, he introduced ceramic casting and thrown pottery to the curriculum. Klassen influenced many people to become potters, including American potters Darvin Luginbuhl, Jack Earl, and Paul Soldner. Soldner, of international reputation, is the son of Mennonite pastor G. T. Soldner of Bluffton.

Pottery seems to have special appeal for Mennonites in the 20th c. Ceramic work usually outsells the purely aesthetic media with Mennonite purchasers (°painting and printmaking; °sculpture); perhaps the functional aspect gives it an edge. But like many Mennonite artists of the past, those of today still have to look beyond the church for most of their support. Ceramics classes at Mennonite colleges are popular, and at least 30 Mennonite potters are currently producing work in the United States alone. These express in their work diverse influences ranging from abstract expressionism to traditional °folk art and from one-of-a-kind abstract sculptural forms to functional production ware. SAK

David L. Newlands, *Early Ontario Potters: Their Craft and Trade* (Toronto: McGraw-Hill Ryerson Ltd., 1979), 106-8; Michael Bird and Terry Kobayashi, *A Splendid Harvest; Germanic Folk and Decorative Arts in Canada* (Toronto: Van Nostrand Reinhold Ltd., 1981), 76-79, 157-59, 161; Stanley A. Kaufman, *Heatwole and Suter Pottery* (Harrisonburg, Va.: Eastern Mennonite College, 1978); Reginald Good, "I. Jacob Bock and his Folk Art," *Menn. Life*, 35 (Dec. 1980), 20-23; Ruth Unrau, ed., *Encircled* (1986), 163-75.

Chaco Mission. The Spanish conquest of lower and western South America in the 16th and 17th centuries included east Paraguay, but not the °°Chaco region (west Paraguay). A 17th-c. Jesuit attempt to establish mission stations in the Chaco failed. The first continuing missionary presence in the Chaco began ca. 1890 with the work of the South American Missionary Society of the Anglican Church. The first missionary, Barbrooke Grubb, who entered the Chaco opposite the town of Concepcion, was eventually successful among the South Lengua people, though he endured many hardships, including an attempt on his life. During the 1920s the Roman Catholic church also established mission stations in various parts of the Chaco.

In 1927 the first Mennonite settlers from Canada entered the Chaco in the region of the North Lengua people. Fred Engen, an American pacifist, had earlier established himself in that region and cultivated friendly relationships with the Lengua. In introducing the Mennonites to the Lengua tribes, he identified them as people who, like himself, would not kill other people. This was soon understood and appreciated by the Indians, whose contacts with other white people had not been positive. The Mennonite settlers initially had no intention of carrying on missionary activity. They assumed that the government would place the Indians into reservations, as had been the pattern in Canada. This did not take place, however, and Mennonites and Indians continued to live side by side.

As contacts with the °°Lengua people continued, some Mennonite young people learned to speak the Lengua language, which had not yet been reduced to writing, and a low-key witness did take place. Planned missionary activity, initiated by Menno Colony people and supported by the General Conference Mennonite church of North America, began only in the 1950s. Early in the 1960s the various Mennonite groups in the Chaco united to form the °Mennonitisches Missions-Komitee für Paraguay (Mennonite Missions Committee for Paraguay), acknowledging John M. Funk, who had already begun his work in 1952, as missionary. He was soon joined by Bernhard W. Toews. By 1986 this work also included the Toba tribe, which, together with the Lenguas, comprised ca. 1,500 baptized members in six congregations (°Convención . . . Lengua). The congregations are autonomous and select their own leaders. Small mission congregations have also arisen among the native Paraguayan people at various places.

Meanwhile the Mennonite immigrants from Europe attempted to begin missionary work soon after their arrival in 1932, but were prevented by the Chaco War. By 1936, however, they were able to proceed and had organized the mission agency °Licht den Indianern, initially supported primarily by Mennonite Brethren, but eventually including other Chaco Mennonite groups also. In addition to the Lengua people the Chulupí people were also included. By 1986 they had ca. 1,500 baptized members, organized into independent, autonomous congregations (°Convención . . . Chulupí).

In 1951 the New Tribes Missions also began work in the Chaco, particularly with the Ayoreo (Moro) people located north of the Mennonite settlements. New Tribes Mission personnel worked closely with the Mennonites, including Kornelius °Isaak of Filadelfia, who was killed in his attempt to establish contact with the the Ayoreo people. Both the New Tribes Mission and the Mennonites are continuing their work with the Ayoreo people in 1986, accompanied by considerable success. (For Mennonite Church [MC] work in the Argentine Chaco, see ME I:545.) MWF

W. Barbrooke Grubb, *An Unknown People in an Unknown*

Land (London: Seeley Service and Co., 1913, 1932); R.J. Hunt, *The Livingstone of South America* [B. Grubb] (London: Seeley Service and Co., 1932); C. L. Graber, *The Coming of the Moros* (Scottdale, 1964); *Wer ist mein Nächster? Indianermission im zentralen Chaco von Paraguay, 1936-1986* (Fernheim: Licht den Indianern, 1986); Martin W. Friesen, *Neue Heimat in der Chacowildnis* (Altona, Man.: D. W. Friesen, and Menno Colony: Chortitzer-Komitee, 1987); *Kanadische Mennoniten bezwingen eine Wildnis: 50 Jahre Kolonie Menno* (Menno Colony, 1977); *50 Jahre Kolonie Fernheim* (Fernheim Colony, 1980).

See also Giesbrecht, Gerhard Benjamin.

Chaco War (1932-35), between Paraguay and Bolivia, was the outgrowth of a boundary dispute in the northern part of the Gran °°Chaco. From 1870 both countries claimed the same territory, Paraguay to the Parapiti River and Bolivia to the Paraguay River. Repeated boundary treaties did not provide a permanent solution. Increasing skirmishes along the border finally led to the three-year war and to the eventual victory of the Paraguayan army. In the Peace of Buenos Aires (1938), Paraguay received by far the largest portion of the Chaco.

The immigration of the Mennonites to this area played a considerable role in the conflict. The establishing of °Menno Colony (1927) and °Fernheim Colony (1930) strengthened the Paraguayan claim to this territory and added considerably to its potential value. The Mennonite immigration was protested by Bolivia at the League of Nations. Initially the Mennonite colonies were in a no-man's-land between the opposing armies, but the battles soon came much nearer. The colonies played a considerable role as supply centers for the Paraguayan army. PPK

David Zook, "The Conduct of the Chaco War" (1962); Peter P. Klassen, *Kaputi Mennonita* (Asunción, 1976); José Félix Estigarribia, *The Epic of the Chaco: Marshal Estigarribia's Memoirs of the Chaco War, 1932-1935* (Austin: U. of Texas Press, 1950; originally published in 3 volumes in Spanish).

Chad. French and Swiss Mennonite missionaries began work in Chad in the early 1950s under the °Europäisches Mennonitisches Evangelisationskomitee (EMEK; European Mennonite Evangelization Committee) and Sudan United Mission (SUM). They work with the Église Evangélique au Tchad (Evangelical Church of Chad) in cooperation with three other, non-Mennonite, mission boards. Mennonite missionaries have taught Bible and theology; taught high school courses; and have worked as medical personnel, Bible translators, evangelists, and maintenance personnel. In 1986 EMEK and SUM were sponsoring a Bible and theology teacher, a rural development worker, an evangelist, and two nurses in Chad. Mennonite missionaries have not established a Mennonite church nor emphasized Anabaptist theology in particular.

Mennonite Central Committee (MCC) became involved in 1973, but stopped working temporarily from March 1980 to August 1982 during the worst of the civil war. In 1986 nine MCC workers in Chad were engaged in rural communities through agriculture, health classes, and water resources activities. JFF

Reports in *Christ Seul; Gemeinde Unterwegs; Brücke; Mennonitische Blätter; Zionspilger.*

Champa, India (ME I:547). In ME I Harvey R. °Bauman described the Champa Mission Station in three parts: the mission compound, the leprosy home and hospital, and the medical station. In 1987 the original bungalows, constructed by P. A. °°Penner, have been sold. The first church building is a part of the school complex. The primary school has been upgraded to a middle school and is housed in a new building since 1982. The Menno Christian Education Society, organized in 1987, has replaced the General Conference Mennonite Mission as sponsor. The medical station—hospital, bungalow, and property—was turned over to a recognized non-denominational Christian organization (Emmanuel Hospital Association) in 1975. Under this association the hospital continues to uphold Christian principles upon which it was founded. The Leprosy Mission, based in London, England, administers the Bethesda Leprosy Home and Hospital.

Many employees of these institutions are Mennonites, and a large Mennonite community continues to reside in the Champa area. Two congregations, the Bethesda church (200 members) and the Champa church (350 members), are affiliated with the Bharatiya General Conference Mennonite Conference and continue to provide a church home for these Christians.   HR/RR

Chaplaincy. The 16th c. was a volatile age which produced changes of the largest magnitude. It was a time of change in the social, political, economic, and religious arenas of life. Arising out of this dynamic crucible was a religious sect which came to bear the title "Anabaptist." The Anabaptists attempted to recover the essential principles of the primitive church and of the literal teachings of Jesus. Two distinctive marks of the early Anabaptists surfaced. The first emphasized the basic nature of Christianity as °discipleship; the second focus saw the church as a voluntary brotherhood of °love and °nonresistance, with °nonconformity and °suffering as corollary concepts. Discipleship, for the radical Anabaptist, implied the life and teaching of Jesus Christ as the basis for action. The disciple is one who follows Christ—*Nachfolge Christi*.

This concept of discipleship, along with the radical commitment to taking seriously the teachings found within the New Testament, inevitably led the Anabaptists to a position where they demonstrated compassion toward those who were often rejected by others. This allowed the Anabaptists, in an experiential way, to identify with those persons who were abused, mistreated, and isolated. The Anabaptists became attracted to those who today are institutionalized.

Anabaptist and Mennonite involvement in institutional settings was not, however, developed by "the pastor," but rather grew out of a commitment to compassion and to the healing of those persons who were in need. Therefore, the church viewed its involvement in institutions as a logical extension of itself in the area of helping, compassion, and responding. Involvements in the 1940s and 1950s by Mennonites in °hospitals and °mental health centers were both an expression of compassion and an extension of the church's earlier institutional involvement, particularly its Russian experience.

The emergent "chaplains" and the "chaplaincy" occurred much later than the actual development of hospitals and centers themselves. When the Mennonites became involved in these institutions, they found it difficult to visualize a pastor operating in any situation other than a local congregation. The only possible exception to the local congregation was the mission field. Consequently, some of the early chaplains within Mennonite hospitals and mental health centers were, in fact, appointed by and responsible to the mission board. Rather than create chaplaincy departments, Mennonites have historically wanted to see the hospital or the center as the ministry. Oftentimes administrators of such institutions were also ordained ministers.

The 1980s have brought with them significant shifts. More and more Mennonite ministers are being trained for and employed as chaplains in hospitals, retirement centers, prisons, factories, and mental health facilities. Ordained Mennonite women clergy have more readily found positions as chaplains than as pastors of congregations. Several Mennonites have become certified supervisors of °clinical pastoral education, which has opened up new employment opportunities.

In hospitals, correctional institutions, mental health centers, state mental hospitals, and factories, Mennonite chaplains are, on a day-to-day basis, living out the ministry of compassion. In so doing, however, many Mennonite chaplains find themselves employed in locations where no Mennonite congregations exist and their worshiping community is therefore often "non-Mennonite." Likewise, Mennonite chaplains have struggled to determine if they are real Mennonite pastors. To whom are they accountable? What standards should guide their practice? The Mennonite Chaplains Association has been organized as an annual gathering of individuals involved in institutional ministry. This support group remains the only official umbrella organization which provides Mennonites an opportunity for such dialogue.

Chaplaincy remains one of the church's expressions of compassion. Chaplains often find their loyalties divided between the church and the institution. There is a need for Mennonites to embrace chaplaincy and see their ministry as an extension of the church's life, not just an extension of the pastor's training.   RJH

Lawrence E. Holst, ed., *Hospital Ministry: The Role of The Chaplain Today* (New York, 1985); *idem*, ed., *Toward a Creative Chaplaincy* (Springfield, Ill., 1973); William B. Oglesby, Jr., *Biblical Themes for Pastoral Care* (Nashville, Tenn., 1980); Heije Faber, *Pastoral Care in the Modern Hospital* (Philadelphia, 1971); Erland Waltner, "Toward an Anabaptist Theology of Chaplaincy in Health Care Institutions" (unpub. paper presented at Mennonite Health Assembly, St. Louis, March 1980).

Charismatic Movement. The term *charismatic* comes from the Greek word *charismata*, which means spiritual gifts. It is the informal name given to the movement which is calling the Christian church back to a fuller recognition of the Holy Spirit in Christian experience and in the life and mission of the church, including the exercise of all the spiritual gifts described in the New Testament.

The modern Pentecostal movement which began

in 1906 did not make much of an impact on the mainline denominations, affecting mainly the lower classes of society. What is called the charismatic movement emerged in the early 1960s in the mainline denominations and has had an impact on most denominations. It holds that being a Christian includes having a definite experience with the Spirit and the exercise of spiritual gifts, often speaking in tongues.

In the Mennonite Church (MC), in 1906 the Pacific Coast Conference resolved that all ministers, evangelists, and all members having the baptism of the Holy Ghost encourage everywhere that believers seek a definite experience of the baptism of the Holy Ghost.

In 1954 and 1955 Gerald Derstine, pastor, and a number of young people of the Strawberry Lake Mennonite Church (MC), Ogema, Minn., experienced unusual signs of the Spirit, such as speaking in tongues and being slain in the Spirit. Conference officials asked Derstine to say that at least some of the activities were of the devil, but he refused. In 1956 the conference withdrew his ministerial credentials and he left. In 1977 the officials apologized for what they had done to Gerald and welcomed him back into the Mennonite Church. He has continued his independent ministries from Christian Retreat Center, Bradenton, Fla. Other pastors and members had the "baptism with the Spirit" during the 1950s and 1960s, often without revealing it publicly. In 1970 retired missionary Nelson °Litwiller experienced the baptism with the Spirit in a Catholic charismatic prayer meeting in South Bend, Ind. He exercised significant leadership in the charismatic movement in the Mennonite Church until his death in 1987.

The official response of the church came in several ways. In 1972 a consultation was held on the person and work of the Spirit at Eastern Mennonite Seminary, Harrisonburg, Va. Festivals of the Spirit were held at Goshen College in 1972 and 1973 with an attendance of several thousand persons. In 1974 the General Board (MC) appointed a task force to develop a statement on "The Holy Spirit in the Life of the Church" to be brought to Mennonite Church (MC) General Assembly in 1975. The assembly commended the statement to congregations for study and to return counsel to improve the statement. With some changes it was adopted in 1977 as a resource for teaching throughout the church, giving a favorable response to the charismatic movement.

Some lay leaders and ministers planned a churchwide charismatic conference in 1974, held at the Landisville (Pa.) campgrounds and a second one at the Missionary Church campgrounds (Goshen) in 1975. Kevin Ranaghan, executive director of the Conference on Christian Renewal among the churches, wrote Nelson Litwiller and Harold Bauman, asking whether the Mennonite Church would help in planning the event.

A group of 32 people met in Youngstown, Ohio, in October 1975 and formed Mennonite Renewal Services (MRS). The purposes were to provide consultative and liaison services to individuals and conferences, to represent charismatic Mennonites to groups within and beyond the denomination, to converse with leaders of the Mennonite Church, to provide information and referral services, and to sponsor teaching ministries and conferences. Nelson Litwiller represented MRS on the planning for the Conference on Christian Renewal (interdenominational charismatic conference) at Kansas City in 1977 and for the North American Congress on the Spirit and World Evangelization, held in New Orleans in 1987. Mennonite Renewal Services has reported to each Mennonite Church (MC) General Assembly and has been affirmed in its work by Mennonite Church General Board. The leaders of MRS seek to renew the church and to encourage renewed members to stay with the church and not to leave it. A significant factor in the renewal in the Mennonite Church (MC) has been renewal conferences. Mennonite Renewal Services continued holding churchwide conferences until 1978. Annual regional conferences emerged in 10 to 12 areas across North America. The MRS organization has also held annual consultations involving persons active in renewal ministries throughout the church. People from other Anabaptist and Mennonite groups were invited to participate in the early stages of this development. While some members of other groups joined MRS, no official delegates were sent more than a few times.

In Apil 1987 MRS decided to change its name to Believers Church Renewal Ministries and incorporate people from the Church of the Brethren renewal ministries. This was the result of working with these leaders for several years. In the same month an Apostolic and Prophetic Council was established as an aid to charismatic congregations which needed a different kind of ministry than what their conference leaders were able to provide. In November 1987 a consultation brought together leaders of charismatic congregations and conference leaders to work at strengthening relationships. Sponsored by the Mennonite Board of Congregational Ministries, the consultation developed practical steps to strengthen relationships.

In a survey of one of every three Mennonite Church (MC) congregations in 1986, pastors reported 10 to 15 percent of the members called themselves charismatic. Between 25 to 30 percent of the pastors identified themselves as charismatic.

The General Conference Mennonite Church has been affected less by the charismatic movement in the United States than in Canada. A number of Canadian Mennonite congregations in the western provinces have a significant number of people with the charismatic experience. Some congregations have been able to minister to these persons while in others there have been tensions. Some members have left to join Pentecostal groups.

Some of the issues the charismatic movement has brought to congregations include whether the baptism with the Spirit is another name for the new birth, or is a definite experience with the Spirit as a part of °conversion, or is an experience subsequent to conversion. Other issues involve °worship: the raising of hands, speaking in tongues, prophecy, and the use of Scripture songs. Some charismatics have borrowed views of central leadership authority from other charismatic groups. Some of the contributions of the charismatic movement have been renewed vigor in worship, renewed interest in releasing spiritual gifts in congregational life, and new motivation for °evangelism and °missions.   HEB

Wittlinger, *Piety and Obedience* (1978), 527ff.; Harold E. Bauman and Ernest Hershberger in *GH* (Jan. 27, 1987), 52-55.

See also Amor Viviente, Honduras; Holy Spirit; Sanctification.

Cheliabinsk. See Russian Soviet Federated Socialist Republic (RSFSR).

Chester Co., Pa, Old Order Amish Settlement. See Lancaster-Chester Counties, Pa., Old Order Amish Settlement.

Cheyenne People. See Indians, North America.

Julia Yellow Horse Shoulderblade: Cheyenne Minister

The ministry of Julia Shoulderblade, born May 1, 1913, bridged two cultures, Native American and white. Her mother, Rose Coal Bear from Lame Deer, Montana, came from a family with some prestige, as they were Keepers of the Sacred Hat, a bundle of sacred objects that had meaning in religious ceremonies of the Northern Cheyenne. Julia's father, John Yellow Horse, came from Birney, Montana.

Julia's father died when she was three. Her mother married Milton Whiteman, who became one of the two ministers that missionary Rodolphe Petter ordained among the Northern Cheyenne. Rose and Milton were strong spiritual leaders in the church, and Julia was always a part of the Christian community. In spite of objections from the church community, she married James Shoulderblade on March 19, 1946. After two years, James was converted and later called to the ministry by the church at Birney. Their children were Timothy, Wendaline Valdo, Mary Magdaline, and Titus.

Julia and James were among the first in Montana to sing openly the indigenous Cheyenne spiritual songs along with hymns taught by the missionaries. The use of these songs had been forbidden by the missionaries because they used Cheyenne tunes with words composed by the Cheyenne Christians. But the Shoulderblades introduced the songs as their way of saying what God meant to them. Recordings were made, and eventually the songs were included in a hymnbook *Tsese-Ma'heone'Nemeototse*, which was published in 1982.

Julia's gifts lay in her formal and informal participation in the work of the church. Especially appreciated was her ability to read Scripture in Cheyenne. She was one of the few Cheyenne Christians who could read fluently Rodolphe Petter's translations. Julia taught Sunday school to the older Cheyenne in their language and was active in home Bible study groups. She also visited in the homes of those who never attended church. Julia brought to the church the idea of caring for God's family with the old Cheyenne way of gift giving. She and the church women arranged showers for young mothers

and brides, drawing into the circle those on the edge of the church community. They made comforters for themselves and for those who were sick or cold.

Ill health plagued Julia for much of her life. Diabetes, cancer, and arthritis sapped her energy. But even during the times she was bedridden, she was active in intercessory prayer. She died on May 16, 1973. At her memorial service in the Birney church, a group from Petter Memorial Church at Lame Deer sang hymns in Cheyenne, and a quartet of Cheyenne women from Birney Mennonite Church sang hymns in English. She had asked that the Cheyenne custom of burying the deceased's belongings with the body not be observed, as she would not need them in her next life. Julia bridged the two cultures, her Cheyenne past with its tradition of the spirit of the Sacred Hat and the Christian present with its faith in God.   RU

Based on the story in Ruth Unrau, ed., *Encircled* (Newton, 1986), pp. 317-23. Used by permission.

Chiesa Evangelica Mennonita Italiana (Italian Mennonite Church) (ME III:55). Faith was born in Franca Ceraulo through reading a New Testament sent in a relief package to Palermo, (Sicily) Italy, by American friends. In 1949, Lewis Martin and Jason Weaver traveled to Europe in the interest of relief efforts by the Mennonite Church (MC). Franca's friends suggested they stop to visit her. On that occasion she requested baptism. Through Franca's dynamic testimony and leadership in the following years, a congregation began to emerge.

George R. Brunk III and his wife Erma were sent to Palermo in 1964 by the Virginia Mennonite Board of Missions (MC) as the first resident missionaries. Other missionaries to Italy in the 1960s were Paul and Naomi Lehman. They were primarily involved in a music ministry, producing music for an Italian radio broadcast, *Parola di Vita* (Word of Life). Elio Milazzo, an Italian pastor, was director and speaker on this broadcast from 1960 until 1980, when it was discontinued.

The period following 1970 marked the beginning of slow but steady expansion of the Mennonite witness with gradual buildup of missionary presence to four families. In 1987 there were five fellowship groups in the highly populated province of Palermo, three of which were led by Italian pastors—Francesco and Martha Picone, Francesco and Helen Sapienza. Several Italian lay assistants were preparing for ordination.

Since 1981 the Virginia Mennonite Board of Missions (VMBM) has related officially to the Italian Church through the ministerial council of Chiesa Evangelica Mennonita Italiana (CEMI). This council functions autonomously as the governing body of the Italian church, acting as a fraternal partner with Virginia Mennonite Board of Missions in evangelism, church planting, and leadership training. In 1987 the Mennonite Church was recognized only locally as a nonprofit religious association; however, application was being made for recognition at the national level.

In the earthquakes of 1976 (Friuli) and 1980 (Naples), Mennonite Central Committee participated with other European evangelical groups in emergency aid and rebuilding projects. EME

MWH (1978), 300-302; *MWH* (1984), 121; Virginia Mennonite Board of Missions, *Missionary Light* (1967-87); E. Richard Good, *Enlarging the Borders* (Virginia Mennonite Conference, 1985), 38-39; *Holding Forth the Word of Life* (VMBM, 1969), 31-36; *Go Ye . . .* (presentation of VMBM), 8-9.

Child Dedication. See Dedication of Infants.

Childrearing.

The process by which the child gains the knowledge and skills needed to function successfully in adult society is called socialization. The chief agency of socialization in modern western societies is the °family, since it has full and nearly exclusive access to the child duing the early, most formative years. Other agencies, particularly the school and the church, supplement the family's socialization role.

Childrearing is therefore a function of all those agencies and °institutions that affect a child's learning process: school, church, peer groups, family, °television, °motion pictures, and all other settings that provide educational experiences. Nevertheless, the most basic learnings—language, personal habits, °work skills, values, etc.—are gained in the family context before other agencies have much access to the child. Although it is generally agreed that the family is still the primary socializing agency, social scientists have noted that many family functions are being transferred to other agencies, in part at least. Nurseries and child-care centers are only the most recent of 20th-c. agencies to take over aspects of child training. A major issue is whether the shift of childrearing functions away from the family enhances or impedes the process of preparing children for adult life (Bender, 90).

At the heart of the socialization process is the inculcation of the basic beliefs, values, attitudes, and social mores that will guide the individual into socially accepted and responsible adult roles. That is, a well-socialized individual will accept, rather than reject, the values of society, and not become a social deviant.

Within a religious context, the highest values are those centered in doctrinal beliefs and in the ethical and moral standards advanced by the churches. Therefore, the goal of childrearing within religious groups, Mennonites as well as others, is to help each generation of children and young people to reach a level of spiritual maturity that will cause them to accept and remain within the framework of their religious heritage. It appears that parents in all societies hope their children will adopt and support the faith of their fathers and mothers in general, if not in all particulars. If the children reject the faith, it is somehow a reflection upon the process of parenting.

Since within the Mennonite context individuals are not incorporated into the body of the church through °°infant baptism, it becomes doubly important that the religious socialization process be successful. Otherwise the developing youth will not accept through individual choice membership in their parents' °church. Mennonites have thus supported a strong teaching program, both within the home and the church, that emphasizes the spiritual values to be inculcated.

To understand the Mennonite context, it may be helpful to posit two contrasting approaches to childrearing: a conservative view and a liberal view. The conservative view holds that the body of religious knowledge has already been given and it is the task of each generation of parents to "train up children in the way they should go," so that when the children are older (i.e., adults) they will "not depart from it" (Prv 22:6). It is assumed that the desired results will be achieved through a strong indoctrination program. This is a somewhat pessimistic view which holds that, left their own devices, i.e., to the freedom of self-determination, children will go wrong. The time-tested standards of right and wrong have been determined by religious authority of the Bible and the church leadership, and are not to be questioned or altered. The child will become a responsible adult only if properly trained and, if necessary, disciplined. Certain social boundaries are imposed so that the child will not be faced by "the temptations of the world." In its more extreme manifestations, child training and discipline is embedded in a doctrine of "spare the rod and spoil the child." If the child shows tendencies to rebelliousness, his "will must be broken." The authority of parent over child is buttressed by a larger system of authority figures, normally male, who administer the "rules and discipline" and order the social structures of church and community beyond the family.

The liberal approach posits a more optimistic view of the individual, rooted in the findings of mid-20th-c. social psychology and psychiatry. This argues that, given an emotional climate of love, trust, and acceptance in the home, the developing individual will come to accept the values of the social system, not because he is *required* to do so under pain of punishment if he does not, but because he has warm and kindly feelings toward those people (parents, teachers, etc.) who model and teach the system's prevailing values. There is an emphasis on the need for the individual to accept these values on the basis of mature personal choice rather than imposition by authorities. Imposition by authorities, in this view, is thought more likely to lead to a child's perceived lack of freedom and consequent rebelliousness.

Hutterite, Amish, and Mennonite families are ranged along a continuum between these contrasting philosophies of childrearing. The Hutterite, Old Order Amish, Old Order Mennonite, and Old Colony Mennonite family systems reflect the conservative view. Various social and cultural boundaries (language, church-operated schools, denial of radio, television, etc.) are maintained in order to limit the child's contact with the outside world. Few occupational choices beyond farming or closely related trades are available. Travel is limited. The whole socialization process is based on the assumption that the outside world is evil, and children can be safely reared only within the limits of the isolated colony or religious community in which the children receive clearly defined and unmixed messages as to what is right and what is wrong with respect to how life is to be lived and how one should think and believe.

The more °modernized Mennonite groups reflect the liberal view of child development, being influenced by the social sciences (psychology, professional education, family sociology) and the philosophies of individualism and personal freedom. Mennonite educators stress the importance of positive reinforcement rather than negative sanctions; parental guidance by word and example, rather than corporal punishment; and the child's assumption of responsibility for her own choices and decisions as early as her age and maturity will permit. The qualities of love, acceptance, security, and a sense of belongingness are emphasized ("Christian Family Relationships," 1959). A Mennonite psychiatrist found that rigidities and strict discipline of children in some families yields parent-child conflicts that result in alienation, depression, and other child personality disorders (Loux, 1961).

In support of these views, Kauffman's survey of Midwest Mennonite families indicated that teenagers were more likely to accept Mennonite values when the parents themselves had a high acceptance of those values and when the quality of emotional relationships between child and the parents was higher (Kauffman, 1960). The same study revealed that the quality of interpersonal relationships (child-parent, husband-wife) was somewhat greater when authority was shared more equally between father and mother than when one parent dominated the other. Thus childrearing outcomes appear to be improved when traditional patriarchal models of family organization and discipline are replaced with more democratic, authority-sharing patterns. Subsequent research indicated that the quality of child-parent relationships is best when the child perceives a high level of affection from parents, combined with a perceived low level of disciplinary control. Child rebelliousness is more likely to result when the child experiences a high level of parental control and a low level of parental affection.

Mennonite doctrine holds that the infant or small child is not sinful by nature, but that at "the age of accountability" the child should acknowledge his sin, accept the sacrificial atonement of Christ for his sin through confession and forgiveness, and be baptized into the fellowship of the church (Mennonite Confession of Faith, 1963). In the absence of infant baptism, in some congregations it is customary for parents to present themselves and their infant in a service of °dedication in which they pledge themselves to rear the child in the Christian faith. The appropriateness of this ceremony is stated in the 1963 Mennonite (MC) Confession of Faith.

Baptism is one evidence of parental success in childrearing, since the major goal of bringing the child to acceptance of the parents' faith is thereby signified. Among the more conservative groups, baptism occurs just prior to °marriage, signifying the individual's readiness to come under the rules and discipline of the church. Among the more °acculturated Mennonite groups, baptism usually occurs in the teen years. The 1972 church member survey indicated that the age of °baptism is as early as nine or ten years in a few cases, but with median ages as follows: Mennonite Church (MC), 14.0 years; General Conference Mennonite Church, 16.4; Mennonite

Brethren, 16.4; Brethren in Christ, 14.1; Evangelical Mennonite Church, 14.9 (Kauffman and Harder, 70). The higher age at baptism of the Mennonite Brethren and General Conference Mennonites appears to reflect the older age at baptism typical of more recent immigrants from Europe.

During the era of revival meetings in the United States and Canada (ca. 1920 to 1960), greater emotional pressures were put upon children and teenagers to make "commitments to Christ," and this resulted in a gradual lowering of the age at baptism, so much so that by the 1960s there was concern among these groups that children were joining the church before they were mature enough to understand the seriousness and significance of the act. Subsequently there has been a gradual increase in the age at baptism (Harder, 1971, p. 37).

Among Mennonite and related groups, it appears that the Hutterites have the lowest rate of defection of youth from their religious heritage. Hostetler reports that less than two percent of the total population, but about seven percent of males over 15 years of age, defected between 1918 and 1950. Thus the socialization of Hutterite children and youth appears to be very effective. Also the rate of mental disorders is reported to be unusually low among Hutterites (Eaton and Weil, 1955).

Among the Old Order Amish of Lancaster Co., the loss rate for persons born prior to 1940 was 22 percent (Hostetler, 1980, p. 106). Data on 554 children born to Mennonite (MC) parents between 1938 and 1964, indicated that in 1979, 30 percent were not members of Mennonite churches. Twenty-four percent were members of other Christian denominations, while six percent were not members of any church, three percent having never been baptized. Other studies of membership losses, and reasons therefore, were made by Hostetler (1954) and Harder (1971, 1982), but comparable loss rates by birth cohorts were not obtained.

If success in childrearing is measured by success in the retention of offspring within the religious body, it appears that the more conservative groups have the most success. Quite different conclusions might be reached if other criteria of successful childrearing are used; for example, the proportion of youth who enter missionary, evangelistic, or service programs. Further studies need to be made before more general conclusions can be reached as to what patterns of childrearing yield the most desired results.   JHK

Ross T. Bender, *Christians in Families* (Scottdale, 1982), 78-105; H. Clair Amstutz, *Becoming Parents* (Scottdale, 1952); "Christian Family Relationships," Proceedings of the Study Conference on Home Interests Sponsored by the Mennonite Commission for Christian Education, held at Goshen College, Aug. 28-31, 1959, unpublished, copy at MHL (Goshen); J. Howard Kauffman, "A Comparative Study of Traditional and Emergent Family Types Among Midwest Mennonites" (PhD diss., U. of Chicago, 1960), 126-34; John A. Hostetler, *Hutterite Society* (1974), 201-20, 273; Hutterian Brethren, ed., *Children in Community* (Rifton, N.Y.: Plough, 1963); John A. Hostetler, *Amish Society* (1980), 172-77, 106; Kauffman/Harder, *Anabaptists Four C. Later* (1975), 71; John A. Hostetler, *The Sociology of Mennonite Evangelism* (Scottdale, 1954), 175-83, 220-46; Norman Loux, "The Home and Personality," *Chr. Living* (Mar. 1961), 28-30; Leland Harder, *Fact Book of Congregational Membership* (GCM) (the author, 1971), 20-29; idem, *Fact Book of Congregational Membership, 1980-81* (GCM) (the author, 1982);

Joseph W. Eaton and Robert J. Weil, *Culture and Mental Disorders* (Glencoe, Ill.: The Free Press, 1955), 46-54; *The Sword and Trumpet*, e.g., "The Responsibility of Training Children," in vol. 55, no. 3 (Harrisonburg, Va., March 1988); *Glimpses of Amish-Mennonite Homes* (ca. 1906).

See also Children; Christian Education.

Children. For the purposes of this article, the noun will be used to refer to the years of a person's life from birth to the so-called age of accountability or responsibility or discretion. This is a theological definition to be tested by biblical, psychological, and sociological data. It was a conception especially proposed by the 16th-c. Anabaptist dissenters, who, on this issue, were reacting to the Augustinian view of °°original °sin. The Augustinian view was that the sin of Adam and Eve was transmitted from one generation to another and that children without the regenerational efficacy of the baptismal sacrament are lost. Although the Zürich Reformer Ulrich °°Zwingli first denied the necessity of baptism for salvation, he vehemently opposed the Anabaptist rejection of °°infant baptism, fearing that these radicals would abandon the proper °Christian education of their children and regard their children as infidels prior to the alleged age of accountability. In response to the latter charge, Conrad °Grebel wrote that "all children who have not attained the knowledge to discern between good and evil and have not eaten of the tree of knowledge are surely saved through the suffering of Christ, the new Adam," a view further explicated by Balthasar °Hubmaier, Sebastian °°Franck, °°Dirk Philips, °Menno Simons, Pilgram °Marpeck, Ulrich °°Stadler, Peter °°Riedemann, Peter °°Walpot, Klaus °°Felbinger, and other Anabaptists.

Zwingli and the Anabaptists substantially agreed that children in biblical perspective were surely included in the covenant people of God (Gen 12:1-4; 17:9-27; Ex 24:7; Dt 1:34-39; 6:5-8; 20-25; 31:12; Mt 14:21; Mk 10:13-16; Acts 16:30-33; 2 Tim 1:5; etc.). Some of the same texts from the two Testaments cited by Zwingli to prove that infant baptism superseded circumcision were used by the Anabaptists to prove that children were covered by Christ's universal atonement whether baptized or not. The latter celebrated this affirmation in a rite of child °dedication, for which Marpeck included some suggestions in his confession of 1531 (CRR 2: 147).

For Marpeck, however, this was not a naive insistence on the moral impotence of children, who are nevertheless affected by the consequences of the fall of Adam and Eve and can express harmful self-will from an early age. Yet, until they are fully responsible for their behavior, original sin is not imputed unto them damnation. Thus, before the use of their reason children have no sin but only the proclivity to sin.

Support for this view can be found in modern theories of child development (e.g., Jean Piaget, Lawrence Kohlberg, Eric Erikson, etc.). Some of their implications are the following: Children cannot be expected to behave or think at a level beyond their stage of development. Children perceive God first by experiencing a parent-figure and particularly by observing how adult mentors relate to God affective-ly. Children think concretely in relation to the immediate experience, and only at a later stage of development can they generalize from the immediate experience to the human predicament. Moral reasoning also develops by stages from what Kohlberg called the premoral to the principled levels, with the implication that free voluntary obedience to the laws of God motivated by a love from within is a more mature response than an externally motivated obedience based on the fear of God and divine punishment.

Among the various surviving Anabaptist groups, the Hutterian Brethren, with their communal type of living, have seemed to understand best the nature of child development. Peter Riedemann's *Rechenschaft* (1545) and Peter Walpot's *Schulordnung* (1578) reveal a deep sense of responsibility for child nurture and outline relatively advanced methods whereby children were to be trained with kindness and firmness according to their respective abilities. For instance, the teachers were supposed to teach the art of prayer to boys and girls in their teens and "not to occupy the time of the children with long preaching since much reading and many quotations cannot be understood and grasped by them" (*Schulordnung*). Again, the teachers were admonished not to be harsh with little children "but rather to be sympathetic and longsuffering with them on account of their innocence and lack of understanding."

Following the harsher realism of Menno and Marpeck, the less-communal-type Anabaptist and Mennonite groups expressed more concern for programming a °conversion experience marking the age of accountability in a child's maturation. In the 1980s, in Mennonite and Brethren in Christ circles, about 80 percent of the members have experienced an identifiable occasion or period in life when Christ was accepted as Savior and a personal commitment to following him as Lord was made. The median age at which this commitment is made is 13.8 years for five contemporary groups, all of which have published statements on the conversion phenomenon in question. For instance, the statement on "The Nurture and Evangelism of Children" adopted by the Mennonite General Assembly (MC) in 1959 states: "When the age of accountability arrives, a totally new spiritual situation arises. The individual now has a new sense of restlessness and guilt. He recognizes himself as a sinner. He stands in need of repentance, faith, and the new birth. As the Holy Spirit convicts, he may either yield to Christ or reject Him. Those receiving Christ are born again. Those rejecting Him lose their former saved status and are lost persons spiritually."

In sociological perspective, children tend to have the type of "conversion experience" for which they have been prepared and conditioned, and they tend to have this experience at the time this "rite of passage" is conventionally expected. With considerably more sensitivity to individual differences than the sociological perspective implies, the Anabaptist-oriented "Foundation Series" °Sunday school curriculum (1977) emphasizes the nurture and instruction of children from preschool to adulthood in the constant and continuing context of the ongoing life of the congregation, to the end that "the children individually and corporately will freely respond to Jesus Christ in love, in faith, and in obedience, to the full extent of their ability."   BFH/LDH

William Klassen, "The Role of the Child in Anabaptism," in *Mennonite Images*, ed. Harry Loewen (Winnipeg: Hyperion, 1980), 17-32; Marlene Kropf, Bertha Harder, and Linea Geiser, *Upon These Doorposts: How Children Grow in Faith* (Newton, 1980); Cornelia Lehn, "The Education and Conversion of Children," [pamphlet] (Newton, n.d.); Gideon G. Yoder, *The Nurture and Evangelism of Children* (Scottdale, 1959); Marlin Jeschke, *Believers Baptism for Children of the Church* (Scottdale, 1983); Maurice Martin, *Identity and Faith: Youth in a Believers' Church* (Scottdale, 1981); Marvin K. Yoder, *What We Believe About Children* (Scottdale, 1984).

See also Abortion; Birth Control; Christian Education; Family; Marriage; Rhymes.

Children's Work. Within the Anabaptist and Mennonite tradition church membership has been theologically limited to adults (mature believers), but from the beginning children have played a special role in the community of faith.

On the basis of the following Scriptures: Mennonites hold that all children who have not attained the knowledge to discern between good and evil and have not eaten of the tree of knowledge are surely saved through the suffering of Christ: Gn 8; Dt 1:30-31; 1 Cor 14; Wis 12; 1 Pet 2; Rom 1,2,7,10; Mt 18-19; Mk 9-10; Lk 18.

Pilgram Marpeck was one of the first Anabaptists to develop this theme, basing his discussion on the principle that "where man has no knowledge (of good and evil) there is no sin." Marpeck argued that infants are without guilt, for they lack the knowledge of good and evil requisite for the reckoning of guilt. When the children come of age, that knowledge comes to life in them, knowledge inherited from Adam and Eve; but until then they remain in "creaturely innocence." To this day Mennonites consider children to be pure and innocent.

Up to the turn of the 20th c. the °°catechism was a traditional way of passing on the biblical and Anabaptist faith. Balthasar °Hubmaier's may be the oldest published Anabaptist catechism (1526). The Dutch Mennonites, the first Mennonites known to use a catechism, produced extensive catechetical literature. In America the Elbing catechism was first printed in Ephrata, Pa., in 1824.

Traditional European and North American patterns of baptism at the age of accountability continue to the present time, although in Europe there was a shift in this pattern because of the outside influences of °Pietism and the °Sunday school movement. Some areas of North American churches were drawn into child evangelism, baptizing children as young as six years of age. Gideon Yoder, author of *The Nurture and Evangelism of Children* (Scottdale, 1959) raised serious questions about such practices and was influential in a return to a more mature age for °baptism.

The Mennonite churches continue to teach discipleship based on freedom of the will and the belief that each person is accountable before God for his or her own decisions. Mennonites teach mutual responsibility, the ethics of love and °peace, and response to Christ's life and teaching as identifying features of faithfulness.

Education for children has been a high priority for Anabaptists, beginning with special schools for Mennonite children in Switzerland as early as 1840. In North America, in 1718, the school teacher Christopher °°Dock was teaching a subscription elementary school among the largely Mennonite population of the Skippack settlment north of Germantown, Pa. His essay, *School Management* (1750) was influential with teachers of that time. In 1986 there were 95 elementary Christian schools listed in the *MC Yearbook*. The General Conference Mennonite Church and the Mennonite Brethren have been less inclined to build their own elementary schools, although soon after the Mennonites immigrated to Canada from Russia they organized Saturday schools to teach the children the German language. This was important to the congregations at that time because German was used in all services and in the Sunday school. These schools included religious instruction as well. The Hutterites have expended great effort for schools for children as well as in writing material for them.

Mission work of the Mennonite Church often included schools. In India, after °°orphanages were established, °mission schools followed, then industrial and vocational schools. In family-oriented Japan, church planting called for an outreach that would include family units, so childrens' classes, youth work, and women's gatherings were included. In Indonesia, European missionaries founded schools early on. Schools were included in work in Puerto Rico, South America, Africa, and almost every place mission work has been done. The General Conference Mennonite Church includes in its mission to children in foreign countries, activities such as: Sunday school in each of the Asian countries, a center for developmentally disabled children in Taiwan, preschool and kindergartens in Japan and Taiwan, elementary and °secondary schools in India, a youth study and tutoring center in Hong Kong. They also have schools in Colombia, Paraguay, and Zaire. There are Bible and music classes, craft activities, children's camping, and retreat programs in Bolivia, Brazil, and Costa Rica. Early mission work in such cities as Chicago, Kansas City, and Detroit always included children in after-school club activities and Bible classes.

Sunday schools were started reluctantly, sometimes so that Mennonite young people would not attend the Sunday schools of other denominations. The first permanent Sunday school in the Amish-Mennonite Church was started June 7, 1863, at the South Union Church in Logan Co., Ohio. The first Sunday school classes for children were largely devoted to memory exercises. Teaching used the question-and-answer method. Between 1874 and 1888 the Sunday school became a regular institution in all Mennonite Brethren congregations. The Amish church has never included Sunday school for children, believing that children learn by the modeling of adults in worship.

More recently Mennonite worship services have included narrative in the form of a story for children; sometimes the focus for children was an object lesson. Children also participate in reading Scripture and in special singing goups. In 1982 *In-*

volving Children and Youth in Congregational Worship, the eleventh in a series of booklets on worship and the arts, was written by Cornelia Lehn and published jointly by Faith and Life Press, and the Mennonite Publishing House (MC; Scottdale).

In some parts of the church there was reluctance to accept the use of °television. In 1954 the Commission of Reference and Council of the Mennonite Brethren Church warned the brotherhood against this new threat to the faith and morals of the church by issuing a lengthy declaration. Included in it was item 6: "Children will early be poisoned (in their minds) and will not have any time for school assignments."

°Summer Bible schools were started in Mennonite churches in the United States in 1923. The General Conference Mennonite Church organized summer Bible schools in Canada in the 1940s with youth teaching in the far outlying northern areas of Saskatchewan. In the 1980s most congregations in Canada and the United States conduct Bible schools in their own communities.

Boys' and girls' clubs were started in the 1950s. Both the General Conference Mennonite Church and the Mennonite Church had such clubs. Some material was printed for their use, including a *Program Guide for Girls* (1957-64) accompanied by a manual for junior leaders. A *Wayfarer's Guide* was begun in 1957 for use in girls' clubs; *Torchbearers* was published for boys' clubs beginning in 1958. The Mennonite Church began °camping and retreat programs in the 1920s with additions each year until there were almost 150 by 1987. The General Conference Mennonite Church first held children's camps at the Youth Farm in Rosthern, Sask. Later all provincial Mennonite conferences acquired retreat grounds and had children's programs every summer. In the United States camps for children were held at the camp or retreat grounds in the various districts. The Mennonite Brethren Church also started a camp program in the early 1940s.

Periodic publications for children began as early as 1876 with *Words of Cheer* for juniors (called *On the Line* since its merger with *Junior Messenger* [GCM] in 1970). *Junior Messenger* was published by the General Conference Mennonite Church beginning in 1939. Beginning in 1886 they also published *Der Kinderbote,* which was later transferred to Brazil (1967), where it was published until it was discontinued in 1981. *Beams of Light* (later *Story Friends*) for younger children was begun in 1905 and published by the Mennonite Church. A few books for children, such as *Bible Stories of Little Children* by Clara Eby °Steiner (Scottdale, 1908) were published early in this century. Since World War II Herald Press (MC; Scottdale) has developed a large list of children's literature and has frequently won awards in this field.

Singing has been important throughout Anabaptist and Mennonite history. As early as 1878 *South Russian Songs for Children* was published. In 1924 the Mennonite Publishing House (MC) printed *Children's Hymns and Songs.*

In 1972 a Missions Committee made up of members from the Mennonite Church, General Conference Mennonite Church, and the Brethren in Christ Church planned mission material for children which was published and used in many churches. More recently the Commission on Education (GCM) has published materials called *Neighbors Near and Far* on Asians in Asia and North America, and similar materials on Hispanics. In 1979 the Peace and Social Concerns offices of the General Conference Mennonite Church and the Mennonite Church commissioned Cornelia Lehn to write peace stories for children. *Peace Be With You* was published in 1980 and *The Sun and the Wind* in 1983. In 1983 a book of mission stories was published: *I Heard Good News,* written by Cornelia Lehn.

The Amish and Old Order Mennonite groups are served by Pathway Publishers, a source for school books, periodicals, and a children's and youth paper, *Young People's Companion.* They also reprint and sell novels and storybooks not written by Amish or Old Order Mennonites, but acceptable to them. Rod and Staff Publishers provides similar literature for a variety of conservative Mennonite groups.   HA

For current listings of Mennonite-related children's homes, homes for developmentally disabled children, and ministries with delinquent children, see *MC Yearbook.*

See also British Columbia Provincial Conference of Mennonite Brethren Churches (West Coast Children's Mission).

Chile. Mennonite work in Chile had its beginning among a group of Chilean refugees in Alberta, Canada. The refugee group had formed a Spanish-speaking Evangelical Church in Edmonton under the leadership of Jorge Vallejos. Vallejos had been the leader of a group in Chile known as Iglesia Evangélica Misionera. As a result of contacts and relationships with Mennonites of the Northwest Mennonite Conference (MC) and specifically with Nancy Hostetler and the Holyrood congregation, the group requested and were accepted as members in the Northwest Mennonite Conference in 1980. In 1981 the °Iglesia Evangélica Misionera of Chile requested relationships and official recognition as Mennonites. They also requested that Mennonite Board of Missions (MC; MBM) appoint Keith and Nancy Hostetler as Bible teachers and leadership trainers.

After extensive investigation and dialogue the group in Chile was officially recognized as a part of the Mennonite Church by action of the General Board of the Mennonite Church. The Hostetlers were appointed by MBM and arrived in Santiago, Chile, in 1983. In 1984 Donald and Marilyn Brenneman were appointed by the mission board to work in Chile.

In 1984 new leadership came into place. The original requests for assistance were altered. It became obvious that theological perspectives and practices and the vision of the leaders of the group were incompatible with the Mennonite Church and MBM. In 1985, following extended deliberation with the group, official relationships were terminated. Mennonite Board of Missions continued to send missionaries to Chile for church planting and related ministries. Following the 1985 earthquake, MBM and Mennonite Central Committee worked cooperatively in relief and reconstruction ministries.   LHG

Rafael Falcón, *Hispanic Mennonite Church in North America* (Scottdale, 1986), 137-38; *GH* (Oct. 22, 1985), 737; *MWR* (Aug. 15, 1985), 2.

See also Iglesia Evangélica Menonita, Chile.

China. See People's Republic of China; Taiwan.

China Educational Exchange. See International Exchanges.

Choco People. See Iglesia Evangélica Unida, Panama.

Choctaw People. See Indians, North America.

Choirs, Canada (ME I:563). Choral singing among Russian Mennonites developed after the Mennonite Brethren church was established in 1860, spreading to most Mennonite colonies by the early 20th c. The Mennonites who emigrated to Canada in 1874 did not encourage choral singing, with the exception of the Bergthal Mennonites, who organized some choirs as early as 1890. The Mennonites who moved to the United States adopted choral singing more quickly. Choral festivals as part of Sunday school conventions began in 1889 in Kansas and Oklahoma, and were held independently by 1902. Among the Mennonites of Swiss ancestry, choral singing was practiced in the singing schools, but was not an essential part of the worship service as it was in Russian Mennonite churches.

Mennonite Brethren who moved to Saskatchewan after 1902 formed a choral society (1906-1923) with members in Saskatchewan, Manitoba, Minnesota, North Dakota, Kansas, Oklahoma, Oregon, and California. The society published a periodical and a collection of hymns, many by its most important leader, Aron G. Sawatzky (1871-1935).

Choral singing in Canadian Mennonite congregations was stimulated by Russian Mennonite immigrants of the 1920s—K. H. °Neufeld, John Konrad, Franz °Thiessen, David Paetkau, Nikolai Fehderau—who brought the Russian tradition to North America. Especially noteworthy are the provincial choir festivals and conductor's workshops organized by the Conference of Mennonite Brethren in Canada and the provincial General Conference Mennonite conferences in Ontario and the western provinces.

The most important developments since 1950 have been the result of °urbanization and education. The choirs of Bethel College under William Hohman, Tabor College under Herbert Richert, Rosthern Junior College under David Paetkau, and the Bible college choirs in Winnipeg under John Konrad, Ben °Horch, George Wiebe, and William Baerg have provided examples of choral excellence and a training ground for many conductors and singers. The combined oratorio choirs of Canadian Mennonite Bible College and Mennonite Brethren Bible College, both in Winnipeg, sing regularly on national radio broadcasts. Mennonite oratorio choirs have been established in Winnipeg, southern Manitoba, Saskatchewan, the Fraser Valley (B.C.), and the Kitchener-Waterloo (Ont.) area. Well-known mass male choirs are found in Kansas, the Pacific region of the United States, and Winnipeg.

Alongside the growth of professionalism and high standards of performance and repertoire in the 1970s and 1980s, choirs in many North American Mennonite churches have dwindled as families grow smaller and young people no longer automatically sing in the choir. On the other hand, visitors to the Soviet Union have reported that vigorous choral singing by young people can once more be heard in Mennonite Churches.   WB

Wesley Berg, *From Russia With Music: A Study of the Mennonite Choral Singing Tradition in Canada* (Winnipeg: Hyperion Press, 1985); Calvin Buller, "Brotherly Love," *The Choral Journal*, 18 (Dec. 1977), 30-31; Paul W. Wohlgemuth, "Singing the New Song," in J. A. Toews, *History MB* (1975); Paul Marvin Yoder, "Nineteenth Century Sacred Music of the Mennonite Church in the United States" (PhD diss., Florida State U., 1961); *PMH*, 8 (Apr. 1987), 6-17.

See also Menno Colony; Music (choirs in the United States).

Chortitzer Mennonite Conference (ME I:566), officially known as "Die Mennonitische Gemeinde zu Chortitz," is a conference of nine congregations in se. Manitoba, one in Osler, Sask., and one in Prespatou, B.C.).

This group came from Russia to Manitoba in 1874 and settled in the °°East Reserve. At that time they were known as "Bergthalers." The bishop, Gerhard °°Wiebe (1827-1900), lived near the small village of Chortitz and therefore his church came to be known as "the Chortitzer Church."

At the time of settlement in Manitoba this Mennonite group was very conservative, with strict rules forbidding harmony singing, evening services, Sunday schools, and other functions of similar nature. The German language was used in all church services. The administrative structure vested most of the control in the bishop (°elder). The collective body of ministers kept strict control of the affairs of the conference.

In 1948 a large number of families, some 1,700 persons in all, emigrated to Paraguay. This opened the doors for changes in the conference as the more conservative element had left, with the more progressive families remaining.

Since that time the Chortitzer conference has undergone many changes. Under the tactful leadership of Bishop H. K. Schellenberg (b. 1914), who held this office from 1962 to 1983, English was adopted, first in the Sunday School, and then in the morning services. In 1987, all but one of the congregations had both an English and a Low German service.

°Christian education has become an important emphasis in each of the congregations. This education manifests itself in young people's programs, Sunday school, evening services, and Bible studies.

Missions has become an important thrust of this conference. In the late 1950s interest in missions began as John Funk, missionary to Indian peoples in Paraguay, conducted meetings in the Grunthal area. Since then a board of missions has been set up with a hired executive secretary to conduct the mission outreach of the conference. Numerous members of the conference are found in different parts of the world, serving either directly under the Chortitzer conference missions, with other church conferences, or with faith missions.

In 1987 the Chortitzer Mennonite Conference consisted of some 2,000 baptized members attending services in 11 different congregations. These congregations are served by 16 preachers, some of them graduates of Bible schools. There is one bishop (Bill Hildebrand, b. 1936). The individual congregations have gained considerable local autonomy and show distinct characteristics in their worship services. The bishop presides over the ministerial meetings and continues to function as the spiritual leader of the whole conference. He, or his assistant, does all the baptizing within the conference. The bishop also is responsible for communion in all of the congregations. Elections and ordinations (for life) of ministers and deacons are his responsibility. The ministers continue to itinerate in the Manitoba congregations, but on a limited basis only. The pastors are unpaid and therefore must have a job or farm to provide their daily necessities. Only the congregation in Prespatou, B.C., operates with a full-time, fully paid pastor. The conference's official publication is the *CMC Chronicle*. CJM

MWH (1978), 313-14; *MWH* (1984), 130; Reimer, *Quilt* (1983), 35.

Choruses. See Choirs.

Christ Foundation Church. See Ethiopia.

Christian Calendar (ME II:789). The Christian calendar developed in the church of the 2nd-4th c. as (1) an elaboration of the Jewish religious holidays and (2) a deliberate effort to offer an alternative to pagan festivities. The Christian calendar was the universal calendar used for dating documents and setting work and school schedules in Europe until the modern era. It was attacked by radical Protestant groups, e.g., the °Puritans in England, whose refusal even to celebrate Christmas left its mark. This is particularly evident in the United States, where the Puritan antipathy to religious holidays combined with the doctrine of separation of church and state and religious pluralism to produce a secular, nationalistic calendar. In Europe, the general secularization that followed upon the French Revolution (1789) never completely eliminated traditional religious holidays, although they were emptied of most religious meaning.

Although Anabaptists opposed special commemorations of saints, they used the calendar of Christian feasts and saints' days, as did all of society in the 16th c., as a way of marking time. (See, e.g., *Martyrs Mirror*, 448-49, 651, 963-65.)

As outlined in ME II, the traditionalist Mennonite groups (Amish, Old Colony Mennonites, Sommerfeld Mennonites, Hutterites) continued to celebrate the main festivals of the Christian year with special worship services, fasting, and other practices at the same time that the more °acculturated groups abandoned them. The Amish "Alt-Christtag" on January 6, mentioned in ME II, corresponds to the feast of Epiphany, the oldest form of celebrating Christ's birth and one of the four main festivals of the traditional church year (Easter, Pentecost, Christmas, Epiphany). The most extensive cycle of holidays is

maintained by the Hutterian Brethren, who, in addition to the above, also observe January 1 as the day of Christ's circumcision; March 25, or the nearest Sunday, as Annunciation Day (Schmiedeleut); Ascension Day; and Palm Sunday as a baptismal day (Hostetler, [1974], 347-48).

The continued celebration of Pentecost, Ascension Day, Easter Monday (and Tuesday by Hutterites), and Pentecost Monday by traditionalist Mennonite groups may be related to the retention of the German language and the traditional culture that went with it (Toews, 85-104). In 1987 Old Order Mennonites in the Mt. Forest, Ont., area, finding themselves to be the only church still holding Ascension Day services, invited their non-Mennonite neighbors to join them. Christmas and Easter were never lost by any of the Mennonite groups, although special services on Christmas Day or Christmas Eve (which usually do not fall on a Sunday) were largely dropped by the more acculturated groups.

In the 1980s special services on festival weekdays at Christmas and Easter (Christmas Eve, Christmas Day, Maundy Thursday, Good Friday) have begun to return in a few congregations. For many Mennonite groups a °communion service before Easter remained traditional, keeping the Maundy Thursday or Good Friday commemoration visible. Some congregations participate in community-wide, interdenominational Good Friday services. Mennonite periodicals take some account of the themes of the church year but do so intermittently.

Some traditional elements of the Christian calendar were modified even as they were retained. Russian Mennonites continued to observe Epiphany and baptized new members at Pentecost (*MQR*, 58 [1984], 101, 116). The traditional practice of the early church was to baptize primarily at Easter, with Pentecost and Epiphany as secondary times of baptism. Hutterites also gave great prominence to Pentecost and Ascension Day. Sommerfeld Mennonites in Paraguay continue this practice, holding °baptismal instruction classes from Easter to Pentecost, a modification of the early church practice, in which Lent was the period of baptismal instruction leading to baptisms during the Easter Vigil service at midnight on Holy Saturday-Easter Sunday.

The more acculturated Mennonite groups in North America print church calendars in the front of their yearbooks and directories. The main Christian holidays are listed but they are outnumbered by a great variety of days of special emphasis for church boards and °institutions. Renewed interest in public °worship has led to a variety of efforts to restore observance of the church year in Mennonite congregations. Ironically, of the four main seasons of the Christian year, the preparation seasons of Lent and Advent have been the most popular, with much less attention given to restoration of the celebrative Christmas (December 25-January 6) and Easter (seven weeks from Easter to Pentecost) seasons. Some congregations, often those in urban settings or in Mennonite college towns, have begun to follow the three-year lectionary cycle of Scripture readings adopted by the main Protestant and Catholic denominations in the 1970s. Hutterites and Amish traditionally follow their own lectionary cycles (Hostetler, [1974], 349-51; Fretz). The series of pamphlets on worship resources published by North American Mennonites in the late 1970s and 1980s had, as of 1988, devoted no specific pamphlet to explaining and implementing the church calendar, although a portion of one pamphlet offered special prayers and litanies for parts of the church year (Mark, 19-22, 46-59).

Mennonite emphasis on biblical authority at the expense of °tradition, or, in some cases, an extreme form of °restitutionism that rejects the development of the Christian calendar as a corruption of apostolic teaching, has led some to advocate following the Jewish cycle of festivals (Passover, Pentecost [Feast of Weeks], Feast of Tabernacles or Succoth). Mennonite missionaries on occasions sought to establish Christian festivals to replace the Hindu, Muslim, or Buddhist festivals they encountered (Juhnke); more often their own ambivalence toward the legitimacy of a cycle of religious holidays inclined them to denounce non-Christian festivals as pagan, superstitious, and immoral without offering Christian alternatives.   DDM

Abraham P. Toews, *American Mennonite Worship: Its Roots, Development and Application* (New York: Exposition Press, 1960; originally an MST thesis, Concordia Seminary, St. Louis, 1958); F. H. Epp, *Mennonites in Canada II*, 285; *Glimpses of Amish-Mennonite Homes* (ca. 1906), 73-80; John A. Hostetler, *Amish Society* (1980), 220-22; idem, *Hutterite Society* (1974), 148, 159-61, 347-51; James Russell Anderson, "Pentecost Preaching of Acts 2: An Aspect of Hutterite Theology" (PhD thesis, U. of Iowa School of Religion, 1972); Clarence Y. Fretz, "The Church Year?" *GH* (Dec. 29, 1981), 960-62; Arlene Mark, *Worship Resources*, Worship Series, 12 (Scottdale and Newton, 1982); Dennis D. Martin, in *GH* (Feb. 11, 1986), 89-91; Cornelia Lehn, *Involving Children and Youth in Congregational Worship* (Newton and Scottdale, 1982), 40-41, on Pentecost observance in Western Canada; Gerald Peters, trans. and ed., *Diary of Anna Baerg, 1916-1924* (Winnipeg: CMBC Publications, 1985), 20, 24, 40, 61, 62, 72, 100, 124 on Advent, Pentecost, Easter Octave, and Ascension Day among Mennonites in Russia; *GCM Handbook*; *MC Yearbook*; *MQR*, 48 (1974), 83, 99; *MWR* (Jan. 14, 1988), 6; Juhnke, *Mission* (1979), 34; *Menn. Bib.*, 4612, 15239, 21102, 25443, 27664; Stephen Scott, *The Amish Wedding and Other Special Occasions of the Old Order Communities* (Good Books, 1988).

See also Denner, Jacob (ME II:36-37).

Christian Community, Spain. See Comunidad Cristiana.

Christian Disaster Relief. See Church of God in Christ Mennonite; Disaster Services.

Christian Day Schools. See Private Christian Schools.

Christian Education (ME I:378). As a ministry mandated by Jesus, Christian education is essentially (but not exclusively) the ongoing unfolding of his gospel to believers and their children, "teaching them to observe all that I have commanded you" (Mt 28:20). As used in this article it refers to all the provisions made by Mennonite Christians through church and home for persons of all ages to grow into the Christian life and to mature in commitment to Christ and his kingdom. The educational methods have included °family nurture, formal instruction, prebaptismal experience, and postbaptismal discipling.

Developments in the general field of Christian education in the 20th c. have given Mennonite educators new resources by which to review the validity and improve the effectiveness of their teaching methods. First, there have been new designs for the teaching curriculum, e.g., the Cooperative Curriculum Project, begun in 1960 (°Sunday School literature). These designs generated the standard curricular principles of comprehensiveness, balance, and sequence that guided the production of many denominational curriculum projects, including for Mennonites the Living Faith Guided Sunday School Series (1960-72) and its successor, The Foundation Series (1972-).

Second, behind the new designs was a more integrative body of theory of how learning which may be called Christian is guided. For Mennonites as well as for other groups, Christian education has become a self-conscious academic discipline, especially in theological schools and denominational commissions. This is largely the fruit of the recovery of Biblical and historical theology since 1941 when H. Shelton Smith published his work on *Faith and Nurture*.

For Mennonite educators the integrative principle of Christian education is a doctrine of °discipleship that incorporates those processes that are valid in family nurture, formal schooling, and the supervised experience of the learner. Nurture, instruction, and experience do not always imply discipleship, but discipleship always incorporates these other educational processes into a more integrative whole.

Family Nurture. Like the ancient Hebrew people after their exodus from Egypt, the Mennonites emerging from the Anabaptist wing of the Reformation carried on an informal religious nurture that transmitted the faith to each succeeding generation of members. The context of Christian nurture for adults as well as children may be the church or °community in which religion is intertwined with all the other affairs of communal life; but predominantly it is the smaller, more intimate, circle of the Christian family. During its long formative period under persecution, Anabaptists developed a "family school" type of education that was unique in two ways.

First, it developed a view of °children that was new in Reformation history. In refutation of the Reformers' charge that their rejection of infant °baptism would cause them to abandon child training and treat their unbaptized children as unbelievers, the Anabaptist developed and explicated the belief that prior to the age of accountability, children are covered by the atonement of Christ and are thus saved in the life to come, whether baptized or not.

Second, it emphasized the parental-communal responsbility for bringing up children so that they would voluntarily choose the way of faith and discipleship. Writing to underground churches in a tract entitled, "The Nurture of Children" (ca. 1557), °Menno charged the elders of the Dutch and North German Anabaptist congregations as well as the parents to teach their children as the ancient Hebrews had taught theirs, by binding the words of the Lord as frontlets between their eyes and as inscriptions on the doorposts of their houses, talking about them when they sit in their houses and when they walk by the way (Dt 6:7-9). They were first to show themselves as "patterns and examples," but Menno also stressed the need for moral formation in the home so that children both fear and love the Lord and behave according to the purest moral values of the community. This early Anabaptist concept of nurture was developed further by Pilgram °Marpeck for the South German Anabaptists and by Peter °°Riedemann and Peter °°Walpot for the Hutterian communities in Moravia (ME II:149).

In certain respects the early Anabaptist nurture system anticipated the 19th-c. work on *Christian Nurture* by Horace Bushnell, except that in their isolated circumstances the Mennonites and Hutterites were unable to be as perceptive and self-critical as Bushnell was in seeking to evaluate and improve the Christian family nurture of his time. For Bushnell, Christian nurture is essentially a fostering relationship in which the highest values and best way of life of the fostering group are propagated in their children as naturally and by a law as truly organic as when the sap of the trunk flows into a limb. From a 20th c. perspective the early nurture concepts of Menno and his Anabaptist contemporaries suffered from too much moralism and excessively harsh discipline. Both of these weaknesses stemmed from the assumption that the conduct of children was the highest end of nurture rather than the attitudes of faith, hope, and love. For Menno "an unrestrained child becomes as headstrong as an untamed horse. Give him no liberty in his youth and wink not at his follies. Bow down the neck while he is young, lest he wax stubborn and be disobedient." The main objectives in early Mennonite and Hutterite °childrearing were submission and obedience to elders, with the rooting out of self-will. Disobedience required punishment, often with the rod and often with the intention of "breaking the will." In spite of these faults, Mennonites continue to emphasize family nurture, more recently through conference-wide commissions on family life education.

Formal Instruction. From the beginning of the movement, no doubt in part because of the inherent limitations of family nurture, there was a tendency to supplement the latter with more formal instruction in schools sponsored by the churches. This shift was already at work in the Hutterian communities in which most of the functions of nurturing the children were transferred from the parents to selected female teachers for ages 2-5 (the so-called "Little School") and male teachers for ages 6-12 (the "Big School"). In their separatist school system, emigrant Mennonite groups in Prussia and Russia were also compelled to provide for the total °education of their children, which over time meant the development of a more elaborate school system on the elementary, °secondary, and higher levels of education.

In North America, with its separation of church and state and its free °public schools, the Mennonites could concentrate more on specifically religious education with particular reference to a more systematic teaching of the Bible, which had always been accepted as the divinely inspired, authoritative, trustworthy guide to faith and discipleship. This took the form of church-sponsored °Bible schools of various types, but in time chiefly of the congregational °Sunday school, an agency borrowed from the broader Protestant Sunday school movement. The adoption of this method was not without internal opposition, but in-group leaders prevailed by working constantly to give it a content and form congenial to Anabaptist-Mennonite theology and practice.

This was especially the character of the closely graded cooperative Anabaptist Sunday school curriculum called The Foundation Series, jointly published in the 1970s and 1980s by the Mennonite Church, General Conference Mennonite Church, and Brethren in Christ, with the Church of the Brethren joining as a "cooperative user." The initial series was designed for children through grade 8, including preschool and kindergarten. It was then enlarged to include youth, grades 9-12, and adults (see below). The Church of the Brethren became a "publishing partner" in these additional series with the Mennonite Brethren Church participating as a "cooperative user."

The Foundation Series, designed to emphasize the distinctive qualities of an Anabaptist (°believers church) heritage from a biblical perspective, was thoroughly revised in 1985-86. Regional and congregational teacher-training workshops were planned and administered by the respective participant denominational Christian education commissions.

Partly because the new series placed high demands on teacher preparation, some churches within these groups and most other Mennonite groups prefer to use other Sunday school materials. For groups not using The Foundation Series, the next most frequently used curriculum for adults is the older International Uniform Series, adapted by many denominational and nondenominational publishers. For children a variety of nondenominational lessons have been used.

The Mennonite Church and General Conference Mennonite Church together publish *Builder: An Educational Magazine for Congregational Leaders* in two editions: a Uniform Series edition with Sunday-to-Sunday teaching aids and a general edition for Foundation Series teachers and congregational leaders. The latter edition is made available through each of the participant denominations in the series.

The weakness of formal instruction, like that of family nurture, comes at the point where it is supposed to carry the total function of Christian education in the congregation. Then it tends to degenerate into transmitting precertified content without necessarily contributing to the larger purpose of the person's continuing relationship to Christ as Lord. Some teachers complain that The Foundation Series is difficult to teach and demands too much of lay teachers; and they are tempted to take shortcuts or revert to the easier-to-teach Uniform Series, with the constant temptation to moralize every lesson. The superficiality of many Sunday school classes is offset in part by an improved °Summer (Vacation) Bible School program of one- or two-week duration. It is a popular time of focused study and creative expression for children of all ages, sometimes sponsored by a group of cooperating churches with their best lay leadership.

The perils of formalized instruction require a third motif in Christian education, which leaders with Anabaptist (believers church) perspective usually conceptualize as "discipleship"—a personal relationship with Jesus Christ as Lord in the fellowship of the church through which one learns not only by informal nurture and formal instruction but also by firsthand experience of living in God's kingdom with mature mentoring in the Christian fellowship. As Jesus taught, "Take my yoke upon you, and learn from me" (Mt 11:29).

Prebaptismal Experience. Given the inherent difficulties of family nurture and school instruction, 20th-c. Mennonite educators have recast °baptismal instruction into a mold more flexible and discipleship-oriented than the older rote forms of catechism (ME I:527). Newer manuals have been published, for example, *Experiencing Christ in the Church: A Resource Book for Youth and Adults Preparing for Church Membership* by Ernest Martin (MC) and *Preparation for Covenant Life* by Frank Keller (GCM). Moreover, The Foundation Series for youth, with its educational materials on basic Christian beliefs and the enduring emphases of the Anabaptist vision, has been largely oriented toward the imminent commitment of youth to Christ as Savior and Lord in the context of the church as people of God.

Preparation for baptism is further augmented by youth-group work and the church °camping program. Work with youth groups has shifted from an auxiliary program with the traditional three-phase approach of °worship, °service, and fellowship, to a type of apprenticeship. In this approach mentors guide teenagers in a kind of parachurch experience in which issues are discerned and tentative commitments are made. Members of local youth groups then gather at all-church youth conferences connected with the North American denominational assemblies.

Moreover, district and provincially owned church camps have come to be significant centers for the more informal study of the Bible and the deeper meaning of the Christian faith. The experience of "coming apart" into a nature setting for a continuous period of time is especially effective during campfire services of decision and commitment.

Postbaptismal Discipling. For adults The Foundation Series provides a continuing succession of study books designed as aids to a more wholistic discipling process. They reflect the distinctive aspects of the Anabaptist vision of the Christian faith, e.g., "the agenda of the people of God," "faith pilgrimage through life's stages," and "living in the Spirit." The trend in adult education in Mennonite congregations is to move from knowledge and information *about* the Word of God to application in the human life situations of believers in congregation and community beyond the bounds of the Sunday school classroom. To accomplish the larger goal, church members are being pushed to a more transformational personal and corporate discernment of what the Lord expects of followers in all facets of daily life. One key to this discipling process is accountability, another theme being incorporated into study guides

for adults.

Implicit in the foregoing paragraphs are numerous problems for the modern theology of Christian education, the discussion of which are beyond the scope of the present article, e.g., the doctrine of the church as the structured context in which learning from Jesus takes place. Although the nature of authentic Christian descipleship is subject to considerable mystery and ambiguity in the church today, any curriculum for an education that is truly Christian must incorporate this dimension in ongoing and transformational ways. This is the most formidable task confronting Mennonite educators as they work in the last quarter of the 20th c. and beyond.　　　　　　　　　　　　　　　BFH/LDH

Kauffman/Harder, *Anabaptists Four C. Later* (1975), 199-218; Marlene Kropf, Bertha Harder, and Linea Geiser, *Upon These Doorposts: How Children Grow in Faith* (Newton, 1980); Virginia Hostetler and Laurence Martin, eds., *The Foundation Series Handbook* (Scottdale: MPH, 1986); Ernest Martin, ed., *Experiencing Christ in the Church: A Resource Book for Youth and Adults Preparing for Church Membership* (Scottdale: MPH, 1971); Frank R. Keller, *Preparation for Covenant Life* (Newton, 1979); Leland Harder, "The Concept of Discipleship in Christian Education," *Religious Education*, 58 (1963), 347-358; Jess Kauffman, *A Vision and a Legacy: The Story of Mennonite Camping* (Newton, 1984); John H. Westerhoff III, *Will Our Children Have Faith?* (New York: Seabury, 1976).

See also Baptismal Instruction; Camps and Retreat Centers; Dedication of Infants; Erb, Alta Mae Eby; Private Christian Schools; Spiritual Formation; Sunday School; Sunday School Curriculum; Yake, Clayton F.

Christian Peace Conference. Since the early 1960s, the Christian Peace Conference (CPC), headquartered in Prague, Czechoslovakia, has been an actor in the global °ecumenical arena. Concerned initially with the quest for peace in Europe, the CPC quickly turned also to the problems of imperialism, liberation, and development in countries of Africa, Asia, and Latin America, addressing also North America.

The conference expressed the deep yearning for peace engendered by the enormous suffering inflicted by World War II in eastern and central Europe. It served the churches of eastern Europe as a channel for expression and fellowship during the early years of the ecumenical movement (World Council of Churches, 1948), when their membership in the council had not yet been realized. It provides an opportunity for churches in eastern Europe to bargain for more breathing space with their governments. On the other hand, the CPC is beholden enough to government control that its roots in some of those churches, particularly among the laity, are relatively shallow.

Activity and organization have expanded continuously since the beginning. Local chapters ("regional committees") have been formed in many lands. In recent years these have been drawn together into continental conferences. A "North American Christian Peace Conference" was formed in Oct. 1987. Until then, °Christians Associated for Relationships with Eastern Europe had channeled the communications between the churches in the United States and the CPC, serving in lieu of a regional group.

The CPC is both a delegate and a membership organization. In eastern Europe, most, though not all, non-Roman Catholic church bodies belong; in other parts of the world, membership is by individuals, mediated by regional groups. An All-Christian Assembly, meeting at five-year intervals, is the governing body. A smaller group of 100 or more persons, known as the Committee for the Continuation of the Work, meets twice during the interim. A still smaller Working Committee is the executive body.

Numerous standing and special committees and commissions deal with specific problem areas. Representatives are sent to a variety of international conferences around the world. The CPC maintains a standing representative at the United Nations in New York (non-Governmental Organizations). Churches in central Europe and eastern Europe, especially the Soviet Union, carry most of the financial burden.

Mennonites from Europe and North America have attended many CPC events, chiefly as observers. The political ambiguities surrounding the CPC have inhibited greater Mennonite participation, as has the conference's disinterest (somewhat softened in recent years) in Christian pacifism.

The Christian Peace Conference is theologically serious. In application, given the political context, it publicly endorses Soviet foreign policy, socialism as an economic system, and the renunciation of colonialism and imperialism in the Third World. Given the weight of Western global influence, these may be needed correctives, but may also accentuate the brokenness of the church ecumenical. PPea

Christian Peacemaker Teams (CPT). See Peace.

Christians Associated for Relations with Eastern Europe (CAREE) is an independent membership organization affiliated with the National Council of Churches (NCC) in New York, where its secretariat is maintained. As an independent volunteer agency, CAREE facilitates communications between the °Christian Peace Conference (CPC) and the churches in the United States, as well as other ecumenical endeavors. Initially formed as the United States Committee for the Christian Peace Conference in 1965, CAREE was constituted in 1972, and incorporated in New York State. In 1980 CAREE established the Institute for Peace and Understanding, an independent agency incorporated in the Commonwealth of Pennsylvania, to facilitate the participation of the CAREE constituency in Christian-Marxist dialogue events, and other academic exchanges. CAREE operates with a modest budget, raised by contributions from denominations in the NCC. The Mennonite Central Committee has actively supported the effort from the outset. PPea

Christina Michiel Barents. See Barents, Christina Michiel.

Christology (ME III:18). The responses to Jesus' question "Who do you say that I am" have been decisive for Christian faith and witness ever since Peter's first answer that Jesus is the Messiah (Mt 16:16 and parallels). In many additional ways and with a rich variety of images and concepts, the New Testament recounts, testifies, describes, and teaches who Jesus is, what he has done, and what he shall yet do.

Since New Testament times, Christian churches have usually summarized this variety by speaking about both the divinity and the humanity of Jesus Christ (his person) and about what he has already done and will yet do for the °salvation of human beings and the renewal of °creation (his work). Christology addresses both major concerns. It thus seeks to articulate, in a disciplined way, a coherent and comprehensive account of the person and work of Jesus Christ for the church's life and witness, an account which is based on the Scriptures, learns from the church's teachings through the centuries, and meets the contemporary challenges to confessing him as Savior and Lord.

Because of its fundamental importance, Christology has been a focus of intense concern as well as controversy in church history. Especially from the 2nd through the 7th c., the churches hammered out basic formulations (dogmas) meant to establish guidelines for orthodox teaching and guard against heretical doctrines about the person of Jesus Christ. They sought to correct views which overemphasized his divinity at the expense of his humanity (sometimes called Docetism) or his humanity at the expense of his divinity (sometimes called adoptionism). Particularly the creeds of Nicaea (325) and Chalcedon (451) have been seen as foundational references for orthodox doctrine.

Throughout the centuries there has been less dogmatic unanimity about the work of Christ. Mainstream Western orthodox theology has generally adopted some form of the "satisfaction" view originally associated with Anselm of Canterbury (11th c.). Other major views of the °atonement have included the "moral influence" theory, originally elaborated by Peter Abelard (12th c.), and the classical or "victory over the powers" motif, most popular in western Christianity from the 2nd through the 7th c., and revived more recently in revised forms.

Prior to the 19th c., Protestant theology generally adopted traditional Western Christian christological views. In addition, it placed great emphasis upon the Christian's appropriation of Christ's benefits through faith, rather than through a sacramental system (°ordinances). And particularly in the Calvinist tradition, Protestant orthodoxy elaborated an understanding of Christ's work according to his threefold prophetic, priestly, and kingly "office."

Sixteenth-century Anabaptist and Mennonite Christologies were generally compatible with orthodox understandings in the sense that they affirmed both the divinity and humanity of Jesus Christ and salvation through his atoning death on the cross. However, they usually couched these affirmations in selected biblical categories and made little constructive use of the traditional dogmatic vocabulary. This preference for biblical terms has had both positive and problematic consequences for Mennonite °theology and ethics since the 16th c.

On the positive side, this preference contributed to the Anabaptist and Mennonite teaching about Jesus as the model and example for believers. While affirming his divinity they also emphasized Jesus' humanity, teaching, and actions. While teaching his atoning work on the cross, they also emphasized Jesus' way of the cross as the model for Christian °discipleship. These emphases had tended to recede into the shadows of orthodox Christology since the controversies of earlier centuries. To be sure, Protestants and Roman Catholics also found ways of considering Jesus Christ normative for Christian life. But these ways fit predominantly within the patterns of Constantinian Christendom. For the Anabaptists and Mennonites, following Jesus Christ and his teaching in life resulted in an alternative pattern of Christian and church life.

On the problematic side, this preference contributed to some deviations from traditional orthodoxy as well as from scriptural balance and most likely contradicted either one or both. These included the "heavenly flesh" teaching, adopted by °Menno Simons and °°Dirk Philips largely from Melchior °Hoffman's °apocalypticism, and the Logos Christology represented especially by Hans °°Denck.

Menno and Dirk asserted that Jesus' humanity (flesh) was nourished in Mary, but that it originated in heaven and did not receive its substance from Mary. They based this position partly on Jn 6 and 1 Cor 15, and partly on the Aristotelian view that the mother's seed is entirely passive. By emphasizing that Jesus' humanity came down from heaven in the Incarnation as an entirely new creation, they intended to support their distinctive views on salvation and the church. Through faith in the new Adam descended from heaven, human beings can be born anew and recreated to a new state of obedience. And this new creation manifests itself in the church without spot and wrinkle, the new community of those who are reborn and separated from the sinful world, having cast aside the weapons of violence and war.

The heavenly flesh doctrine became a major point of controversy between Mennonites and Protestants as well as between several Mennonite and Anabaptist groups in the 16th and into the early 17th c. Some maintained it until the middle of the 18th c. But it may have influenced some Mennonite concepts of church, salvation, and Christian ethics considerably longer, perhaps even until the present. The concept of the pure church, linked originally with the heavenly flesh Christology, has most likely contributed to both perfectionism and divisions among Anabaptists and Mennonites throughout their history.

In terms of traditional dogma, the celestial-flesh Christology emphasizes the divinity of Jesus Christ at the expense of his humanity. It has therefore been accused of being gnostic in the sense of assuming that matter and spirit are irreconcilable. It has also been considered docetic. Contemporary scholars differ in their assessments: the Melchiorite-Mennonite teaching is docetic (Klaassen in CRR 3), has docetic tendencies (Beachy), cannot be adequately described as docetic (Voolstra), or is not docetic (Keeney). Judgments differ along a similar scale on whether it is basically gnostic, has gnostic tendencies, or does not fall into gnosticism.

Denck's Christology has been markedly less influential. As are other areas of his thought, Denck's Christology is complex and difficult to categorize. Nonetheless, it had a mystical and universalizing tendency. It focused on the incarnate Word more than on the incarnate Christ. The eternal or inner Word suffered not only in the incarnate Lamb Jesus Christ, but had also suffered before and suffers since in the elect. Similarly, the eternal Logos which was victorious in Jesus Christ, has been victorious in the elect from the beginning and shall be so until the end.

This Logos Christology provides the basis for the theology of the divine in every human. Although the humanity as well as the divinity of Jesus is important for Denck, the two natures seem to remain somewhat separated from each other. The historical Jesus or the outer Word is important primarily as the teacher and example, namely, as the witness to the inner Word, which provides the means of deification for the disciple. Denck emphasized the unity of Christ's will with God's will, and the freedom of the will to be one with God. Some of his followers found his synthesis difficult to maintain and seriously questioned orthodox Christological and trinitarian doctrines.

Another Anabaptist theologian and church leader during the 16th c. was Pilgram °Marpeck. His influence at the time may have almost equaled that of Menno Simons. Although he shared an interest in relating Christology to the concepts of salvation and the church, he rejected the heavenly flesh Christology and articulated a distinctive view of Christ's humanity and its relation to his divinity.

Marpeck developed his views on the humanity of Christ partly as correctives to Lutheran and spiritualist (°Schwenckfeld) Christologies. At the heart of Marpeck's thought is his view of the unity between the divine and the human natures in Jesus Christ. The essence (*wesen*) of reality is the unity between its inner and the outer dimensions. In Jesus Christ, the human (outer) serves the divine (inner). Simultaneously, the human (outer) also makes the divine (inner) visible and corresponds to it. In parallel fashion, the church as the visible and nonglorified body of Christ is enabled and called to correspond to the glorified and reigning Christ, who is the head of the body. Marpeck also extended this structure of thought to Christian discipleship, the sacraments, Christian liberty, and anthropology.

Contemporary scholars have devoted little attention to christological developments among Mennonites from the 17th through the 19th c. During that time, Mennonite °confessions of faith generally perpetuated nondogmatic views of Christ's person and work, which they nevertheless gradually adapted to traditional orthodox and Protestant concepts. This tendency is most pronounced in the major 20th-c. North American Mennonite confessions from the early 1920s through the mid-1970s. These confessions have also been influenced by °Fundamentalist and conservative reactions to modernism, reactions that emphasized Christ's divinity and sacrificial atonement and tended toward doceticism. Simultaneously, Mennonites have continued to preach and teach that Jesus Christ exemplifies how Christians are called to live. This has both tempered the Fundamentalist and traditional orthodox influences and opened Mennonites to modern christological views which begin with the historical Jesus, emphasize his humanity and ethical significance, and frequently have adoptionist tendencies.

A representative voice for the conservative view tempered with a nondogmatic biblicism and Jesus as the example for Christian discipleship is J. C. Wenger. He generally adopts traditional orthodox and Protestant views on Jesus Christ's humanity and divinity and his three-fold office as the framework for interpreting New Testament Christology. Wenger summarizes several biblical concepts for the atonement rather than attempting to develop a comprehensive synthesis. He also accepts several affirmations of conservative Christologies, including the preexistence, the virgin birth, the sacrifical death, and the bodily return of Jesus Christ. Wenger assumes the bodily resurrection without mentioning it in his account of Christology. His concept of discipleship appears not to imply any basic modifications of traditional christological assumptions, but belongs to an understanding of Christian life and holy living. This includes an emphasis on °nonresistance and °nonconformity.

The most influential book related to Christology by a 20th-c. Mennonite theologian to date is likely John Howard Yoder's *The Politics of Jesus,* which has been translated into several languages since the mid-1970s. In contrast to Wenger, it adopts current emphases on Jesus' humanity and his ethical significance. Yoder first put forth its major thesis in the context of conversations between the °historic peace churches and mainstream Protestants in the late 1950s (°Puidoux Conferences). It seeks to correct traditional theological ways of avoiding the pacifist content of Scriptures and rejects modern systematic divisions between the Jesus of faith and the real Jesus.

For Yoder, Jesus' life, his calling of an alternative community, teaching, and crucifixion reveal and incarnate a qualitatively new possiblity of human, social, and political relations. Jesus' life, calling of alternative community, teaching, and crucifixion therefore remain normative for Christian social ethics. Although Yoder does not attempt to construct a comprehensive Christology, he claims to take Chalcedon's affirmation of Jesus' humanity more seriously than mainstream theologies which circumvent biblical pacifism and the way of the cross. In other writings, Yoder emphasizes Jesus' lordship and affirms that the ordinariness of Jesus' humanness and crucifixion, as well as his resurrection, demonstrates the general application of Jesus' work of reconciliation. Simultaneously, he criticizes theological and ethical approaches which limit the distinctiveness of Jesus, discipleship, and the church entirely to modern historicist and moral categories.

More than any other Mennonite author, Gordon Kaufman has attempted to reformulate theology from an historicist perspective. Rather than beginning with a conservative framework for Mennonite concerns like Wenger or with the christological foundations for Christian pacifism in a biblical realist and Barthian vein like Yoder, Kaufman comes to Christology from modernist systematic and epistemological considerations and grounds Christology in an understanding of the humanness of Jesus compatible with critical New Testament scholarship and contemporary historicism (the view that all of reality is essentially historical rather than based on supernatural, transcendent reality).

Kaufman therefore fundamentally reformulates most christological concepts. Instead of focusing upon the person of Christ as the unity of divine and human natures, he speaks about Jesus as the Servant, the Word, and the Son understood in historical-personal terms. Instead of adopting any traditional view of the atonement, he interprets the Christ-event as having established a community of authentic love and thus inaugurating a historical process which is transforming human existence into God's °kingdom. Instead of the resurrection referring to an experienced event, it is a theological interpretation of Christ's appearances and means that God is Lord of history regardless of what human beings may do. Instead of the virgin birth being a touchstone for the doctrine of the incarnation, it represents a crude attempt to express the belief that Jesus is God's Son.

The most recent christological proposals from Mennonite theologians are being made by John Driver, Thomas Finger, and C. Norman Kraus. Finger reconstructs theology by adopting an eschatological orientation for the entire range of doctrine. Within this perspective, he understands Christ as the fulfillment of the promise of God's righteousness. He then develops a Christology around the life, death, and resurrection of Jesus Christ, rather than with traditional dogmatic categories.

Driver has focused on the work of Christ. His radical evangelical approach to the doctrine of atonement has arisen in the context of cross-cultural mission (in Spain and Latin America) seeking to disengage itself from the Constantinian assumptions of traditional theories and to do justice to the multiple biblical images of the atonement. Driver discovers even more biblical concepts for the atonement than Wenger and suggests that they reflect the contexts in which the early church carried out the missionary mandate of its Lord. Rather than reducing the multiple biblical images to one system, Driver recommends using them to enrich the understanding of the entire work of Christ. This pluralism of motifs also means that the saving work of Christ includes his ministry, his resurrection, and the actualizing power of the Spirit, as well as his death.

Kraus may be the first North American Mennonite theologian who attempts to construct, as an alternative to conservative as well as liberal Protestant approaches, a comprehensive Christology from a modern reinterpretation of Anabaptism. Like Driver, Kraus' approach has also been influenced by cross-cultural mission (in Japan). He contends that Christology in a historical and social-psychological mode best reflects the biblical and Anabaptist understandings of Jesus Christ and fits a missionary theology.

Kraus replaces the traditional metaphysical concepts of person and work of Jesus Christ with the identity and mission of Jesus, the Messiah. The identity of Jesus is described in terms of the man Jesus, the Son of the Father and the Self-Disclosure of God. Kraus's account of Jesus' mission focuses on how Jesus as Lord overcomes sin with love by having taken the way of the cross, on salvation as the renewal of the image of God, and on the appropriation of salvation through Jesus' identification with us and our solidarity with him. In contrast to Western theological emphases on salvation from guilt, Kraus argues that reconciliation to God through the cross of Christ deals with shame as well as with guilt.

Driver and Kraus thus contribute crosscultural mission concerns to current christological discussions. In addition to such attempts to address Christology from a missionary stance, contemporary Mennonite teaching, preaching, and piety reflect both diverse motifs and some common interests. The diversity ranges from classical orthodox views filtered through °pietist and °evangelical lenses to modern images seen in historical and social perspectives. The common interests focus on discipleship and the community which confesses Jesus as the Christ. Some 16th-c. Anabaptists couched these common interests in terms vulnerable to Docetism. Some contemporary Mennonites express them in categories vulnerable to adoptionism. Christology therefore remains at the center of both doctrinal and ethical, as well as soteriological and ecclesiological discussion and debate, both among Mennonites and between Mennonite and other Christians.   MEM

Alvin J. Beachy, *The Concept of Grace in the Radical Reformation* (Nieuwkoop: B. de Graaf, 1977), 79-86, 178; Neal Blough, *Christologie Anabaptiste: Pilgram Marpeck et l'humanité du Christ* (Genève: Labor et Fides, 1984); cf. *MQR*, 61 (1987), 203-12; Mitchell Brown, "Jesus: Messiah, Not God," *CGR*, 5 (1987), 233-52, with responses *CGR*, 6 (1988), 65-71; John Driver, *Understanding the Atonement for the Mission of the Church* (Scottdale, 1986); Thomas N. Finger, *Christian Theology: An Eschatological Approach* (Nashville: Thomas Nelson Sons, 1985; Scottdale, 1985 idem, "The Way to Nicea: Some Reflections from a Mennonite Perspective," *J. of Ecumenical Studies*, 24 (1987), 212-31; cf. *CGR*, 3 (1985), 231-49; Edmund G. Kaufman, *Basic Christian Convictions* (North Newton: Bethel College, 1972) 125-63; Gordon D. Kaufman, *Systematic Theology: A Historicist Perspective* (New York: Scribner's, 1978); William E. Keeney, *The Development of Dutch Anabaptist Thought and Practice from 1539-1564* (Nieuwkoop: B. de Graaf, 1968), 89-113, 191-221; idem, "The Incarnation: A Central Theological Concept," in *A Legacy of Faith*, ed. C. J. Dyck (Newton, 1962), 55-68; *CRR* 3:23-40; C. Norman Kraus, *Jesus Christ Our Lord: Christology from a Disciple's Perspective* (Scottdale, 1987); John H. Leith, editor, *Creeds of the Churches: A Reader in Christian Doctrine from the Bible to the Present* (Atlanta: John Knox Press, 1977), with confessional and creedal statements, including New Testament, Protestant and Roman Catholic, Anabaptist and Mennonite; cf. Loewen, *Confessions*; J. S. Oosterbaan, "Een doperse christologie," *Nederlands theologisch Tijdschrift*, 35 (1981), 32-47; Sjouke Voolstra, *Het Woord Is Vlees Geworden: De Mechioritisch-Menninste Incarnatieleer* (Kampen: Uitgeversmaatschappij J. H. Kok, 1982); cf. idem, "The Word has Become Flesh, the Melchiorite-Mennonite Teaching on the Incarnation," *MQR*, 57 (1983), 155-60; J. Denny Weaver, "A Believers' Church Christology," *MQR*, 57 (April 1983), 112-31; idem, "The Work of Christ: On the Difficulty of Identifying an Anabaptist Perspective," *MQR*, 59 (1985), 107-29; John C. Wenger, *Introduction to Theology* (Scottdale, 1954), 62-70, 193-211, 334-59; John Howard Yoder, *The Politics of Jesus* (Grand Rapids: Eerdmans, 1972); idem, "But We Do See Jesus: The Particularity of Incarnation and the Universality of Truth," in *The Priestly Kingdom* (Notre Dame: U. of Notre Dame Press, 1984) 46-62.

See also Judaism and Jews; Science, Natural.

Chulupí Evangelical Conference. See Convención de las Iglesias Evangélicas Chulupí.

Church, Doctrine of (ME I:594). Scripture describes the church as the community of the people of God through whom God acts and is glorified (1 Pet 2:9-10), as the body of Christ (Eph. 4:15-16); Rom 12:5), the community of the Holy Spirit (1 Cor 12), as both locally and universally complete (Acts 15; Jn 17:21); and with love as its primary mark (1 Cor 13; Phil 2; Gal 5:22). The church is also a sociological reality, both human and divine.

The ME I article is a powerful and comprehensive statement which need not be repeated here. The following paragraphs will identify new developments which have occurred in understanding the nature of the church in 16th c. Anabaptism and in Mennonitism since the 1950s in theory and, to some extent, in practice.

A variety of new, in part revisionist, interpretations of the origins of Anabaptism have been proposed since the 1950s (°historiography). The earlier account of Zürich as the only place of origin has been superseded by studies showing the multiple roots of Anabaptism in °mysticism (Packull), asceticism (Davis), °monasticism (Snyder), and peasant unrest even in Switzerland (Stayer). While the Anabaptists were not the outgrowth of the Peasants' War of 1525, as many historians have thought for centuries, they were influenced by its primary ideological leader, Thomas Müntzer. They also owed a great deal to Martin Luther, in part through his former colleague Andreas Karlstadt (°°Carlstadt), who has been called ". . . the Father of the [Ana]Baptist Movements" (Pater).

All of these influences helped to shape the early Anabaptist understandings of the nature of the church. These Anabaptist self-understandings are now seen in the broad social context in which they lived. The movement was quite diverse, but there was also a common core. Without intending in any way to restore the prerevisionist image of a purely peaceful movement trying to "complete the Reformation," one may note that the overwhelming evidence still is that most Anabaptists, in most places, most of the time were, in fact, peaceful, missionary, and willing to suffer, seeking to shape their life together after the New Testament church.

According to studies since the 1950s this church did not intend to separate itself from society (Klaassen, Haas, Stayer). It was expelled from church and society because of its call for a church of believers only, separate from state authority, a people who had experienced conversion to Christ and committed themselves to obedience, which came to be called °discipleship.

Separation and persecution heightened discipline to achieve the pure body of Christ "without spot or wrinkle" (Menno; cf. Eph 5:27). Discipline, in turn, tended to look for perfection in the disciple rather than in Christ, leading to many schisms. Political, economic, social and, eventually, religious tolerance came first in the Lowlands in late 16th c. but not until the 19th c. in Switzerland. Consequently, °migrations to escape persecution occurred in all directions (frontier). In new locations and cultures reliance on traditional ways of doing things and of believing often led to sterile spirituality and worship. Old forms provided needed security and protection against the new.

The proliferation of groups originally caused by historical, geographical, and theological factors in the 16th c. was fostered further through migrations. The Amish schism of 1693-97 added a new separate group. Numerous °confessions were written later by the 16th-c. Dutch groups to promote unity, and they were helpful to that end, but they thereby also alienated others. The first major union of all national Mennonite (Doopsgezinde) bodies occurred in The Netherlands in 1811 (°°Algemene Doopsgezinde Sociëteit). In the 19th c. renewal movements in Russia led to further divisions.

Proliferation of Mennonite groups continued in the North American environment into late 20th c., because of historical, cultural, geographic, doctrinal, and polity factors, though there were modest unitive signs in the late 1980s. Most of these divisions were also transplanted onto mission fields globally. Considerable erosion of 16th-c. Anabaptist values did occur hrough °acculturation. The °charismatic movement provided freedom to form new fellowships without serious disunity. Mennonites found it easier to work together in °Mennonite Central Committee than to worship together. °Mennonite World Conference illustrated clearly the preference for spiritual unity over organizational unity.

While some Mennonite groups had joined the National Association of Evangelicals in North America and two European groups had joined the World Council of Churches, most Mennonite groups joined neither of these, nor the National Council of Churches, though in 1988 the Conference of Mennonites in Canada was seriously considering joining both the Canadian Council of Churches and the Evangelical Federation of Canada (see °ecumenism).

Mennonites played an active part in facilitating a series of meetings known as the believers church conferences, of which the first was held in Louisville in 1967 and the most recent (eighth) in Oak Brook, Ill., in 1988. The fifth of these conferences was held at Canadian Mennonite Bible College in Winnipeg in 1978, sponsored jointly by Baptists and Mennonites. The report of the findings committee for the 1967 conference lists numerous characteristics and problems, of °believers church congregations in some detail under four general headings: (1) ". . . the most visible manifestation of the Grace of God is His calling together a believing people," (2) ". . . the particular local togetherness of the congregation is the primordial form of the church," (3) ". . . the Word of God creates, judges, and restores the church," and (4) ". . . the mission of the church in the world is to work out her being as a covenant community in the midst of the world."

This report is followed by a "Summary of Believers' Church Affirmations," under eight categories, prepared by Donald F. Durnbaugh, secretary of the conference: (1) lordship of Christ, (2) authority of the Word, (3) °restitution (restoration) of the church, (4) separation from the world (°nonconformity), (5) living for the world (°service), (6) covenant of believers (°church membership, °discipline), (7) fellowship of saints, and (8) relation to other Christians (Garrett, 322-23). Other volumes in the Believers Church Conference series, listed in the bibliography (Strege; Zeman/Klassen), provide further materials on the themes considered.

Questions about governance (°polity) continued to be central agenda for Mennonites. The more hierarchical pattern of the Mennonite Church, and the congregational pattern of the General Conference Mennonite Church, both seemed to move to more common ground. The authority of bishops and regional conferences was being replaced by overseers and a General Assembly in the Mennonite Church, while General Conference Mennonites were ready for more conference authority and direction, particularly in Canada. The question of leadership and °authority, including the role of °women (feminism), continued to engage most congregations and conferences. For some reason the nature of °worship seemed to be less of an issue. A new hymnal, to be released in 1992, was being prepared jointly by several conferences. The Amish, Old Order Mennonite, and Old Colony groups continued with strong centralized leadership as before.

Dialogue about the nature of the church was also stimulated by John H. Redekop's book *A People Apart: Ethnicity and the Mennonite Brethren* (1987), which described °ethnicity as a barrier to witness and proposed that the Conference of Mennonite Brethren Churches in Canada call itself the "Canadian Conference of Evangelical Anabaptist Churches." It triggered discussion far beyond his own conference.   CJD

Harold S. Bender, *These Are My People* (Scottdale, 1962); Claus-Peter Clasen, *Anabaptism: A Social History, 1525-1618* (Ithaca: Cornell, 1972); Kenneth R. Davis, *Anabaptism and Asceticism* (Scottdale, 1974); Leo Driedger, *Mennonite Identity in Conflict* (Queenston, 1988); Donald F. Durnbaugh, *The Believers' Church* (New York; Macmillan, 1968; Scottdale, 1985); idem, ed., *Every Need Supplied: Mutual Aid and Christian Community in the Free Churches, 1525-1675* (Philadelphia: Temple U. Press, 1974); Cornelius J. Dyck, ed., *The Lordship of Christ: Proceedings of the Seventh Mennonite World Conference* (Elkhart: MWC, 1962); James L. Garrett, ed., *The Concept of the Believers' Church* (Scottdale, 1969); Martin Haas, "Der Weg der Täufer in die Absonderung," in *Umstrittenes Täufertum* (1975), 50-78; Hans Hillerbrand, "Andreas Bodenstein of Carlstadt, Prodigal Reformer," *Church History*, 35 (1966), 379-98; Marlin Jeschke, *Believers Baptism for Children of the Church* (Scottdale, 1983), James C. Juhnke, *Dialogue with a Heritage: Cornelius H. Wedel and the Beginnings of Bethel College* (North Newton: Bethel College, 1987); Kauffman/Harder, *Anabaptists Four C. Later* (1975); Walter Klaassen, "The Nature of the Anabaptist Protest," *MQR*, 55 (1971), 291-311; idem, "The Anabaptist Understanding of the Separation of the Church," *Church History*, 47 (1977), 421-36; idem, *Anabaptism: Neither Catholic Nor Protestant* (Waterloo: Conrad Press, 1973); CRR 3; C. Norman Kraus, *The Authentic Witness* (Grand Rapids: Eerdmans, 1979); Loewen, *Confessions* (1985); Paul Minear, *Images of the Church in the New Testament* (Philadelphia: Westminster, 1960); Werner O. Packull, *Mysticism and the Early South German-Austrian Anabaptist Movement 1525-1531* (Scottdale, 1977); Calvin A. Pater, *Karlstadt as the Father of the Baptist Movements: The Emergence of Lay Protestantism* (Toronto: U. of Toronto Press, 1984); Dirk Philips, "Van de Gemeynte Godts. . . ," *BRN*, 10: 377-414; John H. Redekop, *A People Apart* (Winnipeg, 1987); James M. Stayer, Werner O. Packull, Klaus Deppermann, "From Monogenesis to Polygenesis: The Historical Discussion of Anabaptist Origins," *MQR*, 49 (1975), 83-121; Rodney J. Sawatzky, *Authority and Identity: The Dynamics of the General Conference Mennonite Church* (North Newton: Bethel College, 1987); Menno, *Writings*, 87-102, 734-44; James M. Stayer, "Die Anfänge des schweizerischen Täufertums im reformierten Kongregationalismus," in *Umstrittenes Täufertum* (1975), 19-49; idem, "The Anabaptists," in *Reformation Europe: A Guide To Research*, ed. Steven E. Ozment (St. Louis: Center for Reformation Studies, 1982), 135-59; James M. Stayer and Werner O. Packull, eds., *The Anabaptists and Thomas Müntzer* (Dubuque: Kendall/Hunt, 1980); Merle D. Strege, ed., *Baptism and Church: A Believers'*

Church Vision (Grand Rapids: Sagamore, 1986); Leonard Verduin, *The Reformers and Their Stepchildren* (Grand Rapids, 1964); Jarold K. Zeman and Walter Klaassen, eds., *The Believers' Church in Canada* (Brantford and Winnipeg, 1979); N. Van Der Zijpp, "The Conception of Our Fathers Regarding the Church," *MQR*, 27 (1953), 91-99.

Church Attendance. In the early decades of Anabaptist history, baptism and active participation in the °worship and mission of the church rather than formal technical reception into a °church membership were the marks of adherence. As early as 1526, a document on congregational order that apparently circulated with the °Schleitheim articles of faith specified that "the brothers and sisters should meet at least three or four times a week to exercise themselves in the teaching of Christ and his apostles and heartily to exhort one another to remain faithful to the Lord as they have pledged" (CRR 1: 44). As time passed this early emphasis upon the frequency of the congregational meeting was preserved, although like the meaning of membership, the meetings for worship became more formalized. Still, the edifices were simply called °°meetinghouses, with men sitting on one side of a central aisle and women on the other, a pattern practiced in most of the Mennonite and Brethren in Christ groups well into the 20th c. (It was also common in most churches in traditional, premodern Europe and North America.)

The question, "How often have you attended church worship services (on Sunday morning, evening, and/or other days) during the past two years?" is still a pertinent gauge of Mennonite religious commitment. Seventy percent of all respondents in a study of five Mennonite and Brethern in Christ groups (1973) replied "once a week or more" and an additional 23 percent replied "almost every week." The combined response was highest for the Mennonite Brethren (MB) and lowest for the General Conference Mennonite Church (GCM; 86 percent), but all five groups were significantly higher than for most Protestant denominations and certainly higher than for the United States as a whole. According to an annual Gallup poll, weekly church attendance in America began a slow decline from 47 percent in 1957 to 40 percent in 1980, followed by a slight increase to 42 percent in 1985.

In the same study there was no significant difference between men and women in their regularity of church attendance; and the only difference on the age factor was the decline of attendance from 95 percent "almost weekly" or more for teenagers to 80 percent for the 20-29 age group.

Sunday school attendance of baptized members of the five groups (69 percent "every Sunday possible" plus 11 percent "most Sundays"), while not quite as high as attendance at worship, was also significantly higher than for other Protestant groups, e.g., the American Baptist Convention, which showed a low 28 percent regular attendance.

When these measures of attendance were combined with several related indexes into an associational scale, it was found that this scale ranked 5th out of 15 predictors of the religious commitment of members as measured by 19 moral-ethical and work-of-the-church indexes. Associationalism, moreover, had a "positive" effect on 12 out of the 19 °disciple-ship variables with respect to direction of influence, although the direction of influence was negative on such indexes as anti-Catholicism, anti-Semitism, °ecumenism, shared ministry, role of °women, social concerns, and welfare attitudes (Kauffman/Harder, *Anabaptists Four C. Later* [1975], 324). Evidently church attendance tends to reinforce certain ethnocentric characteristics, while it promotes other more positive commitments.

Although formal reception into church membership continues to be the primary criterion of belonging to a congregation, there are some tendencies toward a de-emphasis on membership among Mennonites. Members who attend worship irregularly or seldom number from 3 percent (MB) to 14 percent (GCM). Membership therefore is not always thought to be the more reliable index of Christian commitment, especially when there are active participants who are not members for whatever reason. In some congregations, leadership roles are no longer restricted to members so long as the candidates are otherwise active participants. Although Mennonite groups are not likely to adopt the practice of the Church of God and Plymouth Brethren, for whom attendance rather than membership is the prior criterion of belonging, they constantly seek to renew the Anabaptist admonition to meet regularly "to exhort one another to remain faithful to the Lord as they have pledged." LDH

Gallup Opinion Poll, Princeton, N.J., "Religion in America" in *The Gallup Report* (periodic); Kauffman/Harder, *Anabaptists Four C. Later* (1975) ch. 4, 20; *MC Yearbook* (1986-87), 180-88.

Church Extension. See Church Planting; Evangelism.

Church Growth Movement. Longstanding interest in °missions and °evangelism have served to open the Mennonite church in North America to the modern church growth movement, which teaches that church growth can be planned through °sociological principles. It began in 1955 when India missionary Donald McGavran published *The Bridges of God*. Later, McGavran established the chair of church growth at the School of World Missions at Fuller Theological Seminary in Pasadena, Cal. In 1981, Peter Wagner replaced McGavran at Fuller Seminary.

McGavran, Wagner, and their colleagues in this field have brought ferment into thinking about church growth worldwide. Some issues Mennonites ponder include: Might rapid growth erode Mennonite °peace and °discipleship commitments? Might a reliance on sociological principles distort the sovereignty of the Holy Spirit? Might an emphasis on receptive people sabotage faithful witness among those who are nonreceptive?

The homogenous principle of church growth suggests that churches grow most rapidly among a similar kind of people. Here the movement has encountered a theological thunderbolt, for some fear this is a sellout to racism. In the late 1980s the movement has shifted to emphasize the need for a congregation to include all the people living within its community. During the 1980s, the movement has included an appreciation for signs and wonders as an encouragement to church growth. Attention to these have been commonplace in some Mennonite communities, e.g., Indonesia, but they are new for most North American Mennonites.

Most of the larger Mennonite denominations in North America have been influenced by the church growth movement. For example, in 1985 the Mennonite Church (MC) adopted ten-year goals which included a commitment to doubling the size of the denomination. Eastern Mennonite Seminary in Harrisonburg, Va., established its Center for Evangelism and Church Planting in 1983. One year later, the Mennonite Brethren Biblical Seminary in Fresno, Cal., established its Center for Training in Missions/Evangelism. Associated Mennonite Biblical Seminaries in Elkhart, Ind., also offers courses on church growth in the context of its Mission Training Center. DWS

MB Herald (Oct. 18, 1985), sp., issue; Wilbert R. Shenk, ed., *Exploring Church Growth* (Eerdmans, 1983); idem, ed., *The Challenge of Church Growth* (Elkhart: IMS, 1973); Floyd G. Bartel, *A New Look At Church Growth* (Newton, 1979), intended for Mennonite congregations; John I. Smucker, "Church Discipline and Church Growth" (DMin thesis, New York Theological Seminary, 1976), a study of the creative tension between Anabaptist commitments to Biblical discipleship and commitment to evangelism and church growth; Henry J. Schmidt, *Witness of a Third Way* (Elgin, Ill.: Brethren Press, 1986); C. Norman Kraus, *Missions, Evangelism, and Church Growth* (Scottdale, 1980); C. Peter Wagner, *Our Kind of People: The Ethical Dimensions of Church Growth in America* (Atlanta: John Knox, 1979), a response to the criticisms about racism and ethnic divisions; Edwin G. Bontrager and Nathan Showalter, *It Can Happen Today: Principles of Church Growth From the Book of Acts* (Scottdale, 1986), helpful for congregations or groups considering evangelistic outreach; Dale Stoll, *Church Planting, From Seed Time to Harvest* (Elkhart, Ind.: MBM; Newton: GCMC, 1986), a handbook for church planters; *Miss. Focus*, 4 (1976), 1-8; vol. 5 (1977), 9-10; vol. 7 (1979), 21-26; and the bibliography in vol. 12 (1984), 70; Juhnke, *Mission*, (1979), 40, 120, 252; Elmo H. Warkentin, "Planning for Church Growth," in *The Church in Mission*, ed. A. J. Klassen (Fresno: MB Board of Christian Literature, 1967), 361-80.

See also Ethnicity.

Church Membership (ME I:13). As Harold Bender's article on °°admission into the church indicated, the concept of church membership among Mennonite-related groups implies a formal, technical act of reception which assumes the more informal, interpersonal engagements related to the candidate's participation in the activities of the congregation. The traditional signs of church membership are the offering of the hand of Christian fellowship (sometimes accompanied by the "holy °°kiss") and the listing of the new name on the roster as maintained in an official handwritten membership book or the printed congregational yearbook, or both. Congregations are requested to make annual statistical reports of membership changes to officials of regional and general conference bodies. These °statistics are then tabulated in conference °yearbooks and used for such purposes as gauging °church growth and decline and specifying denominational per-member fund raising apportionments. The most comprehensive annual all-Mennonite membership statistical reports are published in the *Mennonite Yearbook and Directory* (annually to 1986; biennially since 1986).

There are normally three ways by which persons are admitted to membership: by °baptism on the basis of affirmation of faith; transfer by letter of recommendation from another congregation; and by reaffirmation of faith without rebaptism or letter of transfer, or both. For instance, in the General Conference Mennonite Church (GCM) from 1985 to 1986, a total of 2,164 persons were received as members, 974 (45 percent) by baptism, 1,078 (50 percent) by transfer, and 112 (5 percent) by reaffirmation. Of those baptized, 73 percent were youth from member families and 27 percent were persons from other backgrounds. Of those received by letter, 48 percent were recycled from other GCM congregations, 24 percent transferred from other non-GCM Mennonite churches, and 29 percent transferred from non-Mennonite denominations. The gross gain of 2,164 was offset by a loss through death, transfer, and deletion of 2,502 for a net loss of 338 members (ca. 1 percent of the total membership). This more-or-less static profile has been the gain/loss situation among most Mennonite groups for the past number of decades. In the Mennonite Church (MC) for the same year, 2,428 (42 percent of all received) were received by baptism (70 percent from MC households), 2,076 (36 percent) were received by letter of transfer (59 percent) from other MC congregations), and 1,223 (21 percent) were received by confession or reaffirmation of faith. In the same year this gain of 5,727 new members was offset by a loss of 4,835, which yelded a 1 percent net gain in total membership.

Because of a growing proportion of members who are nonresident or otherwise inactive (from 16 percent in 1970 to 22 percent in 1980, GCM) and of nonmembers who are active participants, some congregations have attempted to redefine and reclassify their memberships. It is a sensitive issue when the category of "inactive member" is added; and churches have sought redemptive ways to reactivate resident members who have quit coming to worship services for various reasons or to drop their names by revision of the roll. Moreover, with an interest in °church planting and °ecumenicity, the nonresident inactive members have been encouraged by some "home congregations" to transfer to a church of their choice where they can be active or to help form a new congregation.

Another new category is that of the associate member, which has both inclusive and exclusive implications in certain congregations. People who have moved to cities where new Mennonite fellowships are emerging and who may not be ready to sever their memberships in their "home church" may be invited to join the new fellowship as associate members with the same rights and privileges as regular members. But in some groups, e.g., certain Brethren in Christ congregations (Wittlinger, *Piety and Obedience* [1978], 487), the associate member category was created for people who could not meet full membership requirements, such as candidates who are °divorced and remarried.

Some emerging urban Mennonite fellowships with a "covenant basis" for membership are practicing an annual covenant renewal service in which everyone's membership is voluntarily either renewed or terminated, hopefully without the negative connotations of arbitrary roll revision and member deletions. Membership defined as a commitment for a specific term subject to annual renewal is thus one method of keeping the roster viable and up-to-date.

As functional as the technical definition of church membership is for record keeping and statistical analysis, it is not the best indication either of a person's faithfulness or involvement in the ongoing Christian mission. For that reason groups like the Church of God and the Plymouth Brethren have tried to de-emphasize official membership and place the emphasis on active participation as the key mark of belonging to a congregation. However, among Mennonites the need to specify more objectively who belongs and who does not will likely keep the more formal procedures for membership accounting intact for the foreseeable future.

The latest demographic descriptions of the total memberships of two Mennonite groups are found in Michael Yoder's report of the 1982 Mennonite Census (MC) and in Leland Harder's *1980-81 Fact Book of Congregational Membership* (GCM). Yoder's summary included the comment that "the general picture revealed . . . is of a church family which is becoming increasingly diverse in many ways—race, church background, education, occupation, residence, and marital status. . . . It is likely that this increasing diversity is related to differences of opinion that sometimes arise in the church over matters of faith and related social issues."

The most comprehensive attitudinal study of the church members of four Mennonite denominations plus the Brethren in Christ Church was published in 1975 (Kauffman/Harder, *Anabaptists Four C. Later*). On seven indexes of religious commitment (Anabaptism, communalism, °conversion, °sanctification, devotionalism, orthodoxy, and °Fundamentalism), the five groups scored very high when compared to other Protestant denominations for whom comparable data was available (Kauffman/Harder, p. 308). Moreover, the commitment to Anabaptism was the second best overall predictor of some 19 moral-ethical and discipleship indexes, second only to Fundamentalism, and Anabaptism was "positive" in its direction of influence on 14 of the later indexes, while Fundamentalism was "negative" in its direction of influence on 12 of the discipleship indexes (Kauffman/ Harder, 324). While Fundamentalism has left the churches with many detrimental effects, commitment to the Anabaptist vision by church members as a whole appears to be significant and wholesome.

Moreover, on a probe of intensity of feeling about their membership in the denomination, only 3 percent of 3,538 respondents replied that they had definite thoughts of joining another denomination or discontinuing membership in any. On the other end of the scale, 75 percent replied either that "I will certainly always want to remain a member of my denomination and I could never feel right being a member af another denomination" (25 percent) or that "Although I prefer my own denomination, there are some other denominations that I would not hesitate to join if occasion arose" (50 percent). Overall, one-fourth of the members of these five groups have a rather weak denominational self-identity, but that denominational self-identity is certainly strong and positive, if not exclusively so, for the other three-fourths of the members.   LDH

Anthony Campolo, *A Denomination [American Baptist Convention] Looks at Itself* (Valley Forge: Judson Press, 1971); Leland Harder, *Fact Book of Congregational Membership, 1980-81* (Newton: GCMC, 1981); Kauffman/Harder, *Anabaptists Four C. Later* (1975); *MC Yearbook* (1986-87), 179-88; Merton P. Strommen, and others, *A Study of Generations: Report of a Study of 5,000 Lutherans* (Minneapolis: Augsburg Publishing House, 1972); Wittlinger, *Piety and Obedience* (1978); Michael Yoder, "Findings from the 1982 Mennonite [MC] Census," *MQR*, 59 (1985), 307-49.

See also Baptism; Discipline, Church; Church Attendance; Sociological Studies.

Church of God in Christ Mennonite (CGC) (ME I: 598), often referred to as the "Holdeman Mennonites," was one of several 19th-c. offshoot movements from (Old) Mennonite (MC) and Amish churches. At that time, Americanizing influences (°acculturation) and internal adjustments and shifts overwhelmed a number of traditionalist, isolation-prone Mennonites, resulting in many frustrated members (see John F. Funk, *The Mennonite Church and Her Accusers,* 1878). True to their Anabaptist moorings, they sought to be °restitutionist (restorationist) and were therefore inclined toward secession.

John °Holdeman, the energetic "prophet-founder" of this group, was born on the newly settled frontier of Wayne Co., Ohio, to (Old) Mennonite parents. His father was interested in "true lineage" aspects of church history and the revival movements of his day—particularly the Methodist-influenced Church of God (Winebrennarians). At midcentury Winebrennarians were strong in some areas where Mennonites resided, but the revivalism associated with the Winebrennerians was largely rejected by North American Mennonites until the turn of the century. Amos Holdeman's interest in this probably stimulated the interest of his son John, who reported having a definite religious experience of new birth and forgiveness of sins at age 12. It is believed that this happened under the revivalistic preaching of Jacob Keller and Thomas Hickernell at a nearby Church of God. By the time he was 20, however, he reported that he had become "a wicked sinner." Following his marriage to Elisabeth Ritter on Nov. 18, 1853, he went through "dark experiences" until 1854, when he finally experienced "release and received joyful light and quiet conscience" and was baptized (October). He reported having visions and dreams, a call to ministry, and "special power and love as never before." This moved him to study the Bible, writings of °Menno and °°Dirk Philips, and *Martyrs Mirror*.

In the decade that followed, he was disturbed by the "decay" he observed in Mennonite churches and conferences that he visited or read about. His exhortations to other Mennonites went unheeded. He was not invited to speak or ever nominated for "the lot" as a candidate for the ministry. Meanwhile, he continued to experience visions and dreams about the nature of the "true church." Discouraged by the lack of response to suggested reforms, he finally called his own meeting in April 1859. This became the beginning of the Church of God in Christ Mennonite—for him a continuation of the "true lineage church" which he now considered the carrier of the "candle-stick."

He stressed the necessity of experiencing genuine rebirth before being baptized (by pouring). Many of his emphases were based on traditional Mennonite teachings—more faithful and consistent church °discipline and °avoiding the excommunicated, the practice of °nonresistance, etc. The twelve books and booklets he authored between 1862 and 1889 (eight in German, four in English) reflect this, as do many exhortations in periodical articles and private letters pertaining to lax practices and the "heresies" of his time. His major work, *Spiegel der Wahrheit* (612 pages), has been available and broadly used by his adherents in an English translation (*Mirror of Truth*) since 1956.

His hoped-for following among Mennonites and Amish was minimal. Only 150 joined in two decades (1860-1880). Some estimated that his movement, like most of the other 19th-c. Mennonite spin-off groups, would soon have ceased to exist, had it not been for a major growth spurt after 1878, when some immigrant Mennonites from Prussia, coming from an ethnically different background, were attracted to him. These came largely from frustrated, landless "Polish Russians" from the Ostrog area, and from some spiritually troubled °°Kleine Gemeinde Mennonites, from South Russia's Molotschna area, who had experienced traumatic, internal divisions.

The Ostrogers were the progeny of the conservative Groningen Old Flemish from Holland. They were semiliterate, financially impoverished, and perceived by others as being "spiritually needy." At the time of their settlement in McPherson Co., Ks., in 1875 they were referred to as the "Destitute Poles." These 500 immigrants found it impossible to assimilate with the existing American General Conference Mennonite Churches in Kansas which most other °"Kirchliche" Mennonite immigrants joined. Differences in culture and lifestyle were too great. John Holdeman was attracted to these Ostrogers. And they seemed to be ripe both for what he had to say and the way he related to them, even though, by this time, most American Mennonites had rejected him. In 1878 he baptized 78 of them.

Three years later he baptized another 118 in Manitoba. These were Kleine Gemeinde Mennonites who had migrated to North America. About two-thirds of these had settled in Manitoba and the other one-third near Janzen, Nebr. (one-third). Disagreements about leadership among themselves had developed in Russia, resulting in this decision to locate at a distance from each other. Those who came to Manitoba with their leading elder, Peter Toews, represented the more progressive of the Manitoba group. This was the portion that joined Holdeman's movement.

This 1878-1881 growth spurt more than tripled the number of Holdeman's followers by 1882. Membership in the CGC in the 1980s still reflects their progeny. About 45-50 percent come from the McPherson Co. group with names like Koehn, Schmidt, Unruh, Jantz, Becker, Nightengale, Wedel, Ratzlaff, Jantzen/Johnson. About 25-30 percent have a Manitoba background with names like Toews, Penner, Friesen, Giesbrecht, Loewen, Isaac, Wiebe, Reimer. About 10-15 percent are from Holdeman's own Swiss-South German background with names like

Holdeman, Leatherman, Litwiller, Yost. Among the remaining 10-15 percent a few names like Fricke and Mastre stand out.

During his lifetime, Holdeman moderated the first seven conferences held by the group. These dealt largely with the shaping of doctrinal emphases and resolving some ongong internal tensions, as well as conflicts with some people outside the CGC. The minutes of the seventh conference (1896) together with minutes from 20 subsequent conferences, continue to be used as the binding directives that guide CGC members.

In the last two decades of his life, Holdeman was plagued by increasing financial indebtedness incurred from his poor farm management and overinvestment in publishing his own writings; a rejection of his movement by his own mother and two of his three living children; and his father's ill health and addiction to tobacco. Leaders who left the group openly contested the validity of Holdeman's ordination, which he claimed needed no human "laying on of hands" since he had already been "ordained by God," A successful lawsuit of $2,000 was won against him and three of his colleagues for their role in encouraging a CGC member in practicing marital avoidance of her excommunicated CGC husband.

A little over two years before his death he began to edit and publish the first conference periodical, *Botschafter der Wahrheit*. Holdeman resided in Wayne Co., Ohio, from 1832 to 1883; Jasper Co., Mo. (1883-97); and McPherson Co., Ks. (1897-1900). It is estimated that he spent the equivalent of 13 years traveling and preaching in 17 states of the United States and two provinces of Canada, visiting at least 112 locations. When he died in 1900 the CGC membership numbered approximately 750.

The decade after Holdeman's death was difficult for the group. No strong leadership emerged until an earlier convert to the CGC, from Lutheran parentage, Fredrick C. Fricke (1867-1947), took leadership in 1909.

During the first half of the 20th c. the CGC faced a number of demanding changes: going through the transition from German to English; facing the compulsory draft and maintaining a strict °conscientious objector stance through the two World Wars; adapting to some Americanization; finding new ways to deal with the emergence of °technology (farm machinery, radios, television, etc.); routinizing the yearly °revival meeting method as the major church disciplining process; establishing conference channels for emerging mission and evangelistic thrusts and publications; and moving away from leadership by °elders.

The Church of God in Christ Mennonite grew from 5,000 to 8,500 members between 1950 and 1970. During these two decades missionary efforts intensified domestically and abroad (Mexico, Nigeria, Haiti, India, Brazil). Service and ministry involvments also developed, including extensive tract dissemination, °relief efforts, and °disaster assistance, leading to the development of the Christian Disaster Relief Board. They developed health care institutions (Grace Nursing Home, Livingston, Cal.; Bethel Home, Montezuma, Ks.; Greenland

Home, Sainte Anne, Man.; Linden Nursing Home, Linden, Alta.; Valhaven Home, Mt. Lehman, B.C.) and moved toward more centralization by erecting a building for conference functions at Moundridge, Ks. Gospel Publishers has offices in Moundridge, Ks., and Sainte Anne, Man. Two °mutual aid organizations, Mennonite Union Aid and Brotherhood Auto Aid, serve the church. Some felt there was serious spiritual "decay." A few groups defected from the CGC, seeking a restitution of John Holdeman's emphases. None of these were large movements, nor did lasting offshoots materialize.

Since 1970 other issues have surfaced. One of the most frequently addressed and demanding was the growing affluence within the membership (a few members had become millionaires). Because of higher land costs and a growing membership more were forced to find °occupations outside agriculture, which increased relationships with people outside the CGC. Many traveled widely and experienced a broadened understanding of the world. The defection level increased with more members and more questioning the central doctrinal emphasis of being "the true church."

By the mid-1970s, frustration about the routinized church disciplining process of yearly revival meetings triggered a "new way" of dealing with deviants. An intensive, highly personal, probing method usually referred to as "paneling" was introduced. Those who observed the often traumatic effects of life-probing thoughts and the sought-after behavior correctives referred to the method as "purging" or even "witch-hunting." An exceptionally large number were "disciplined" and many were excommunicated. The level of bitterness felt by those who had been disciplined, as well as a general emotional depression, was noted by those who lived close to CGC congregations. The steady growth in membership of the CGC declined between 1976 and 1979. The largest drop was experienced in Manitoba, where the "paneling" was most severe. Since then the yearly revival meeting pattern of church discipline has returned.

Another threat felt for many years resulted in the establishment of 87 °private elementary schools by 1987 in response to a formal decision reached at the 1974 conference. The encroaching worldliness of the peer pressures in the °public schools, along with curriculum developments, use of television, and the physical education requirements, triggered this. Virtually the entire North American membership of nearly 12,000 in 98 congregations in 1987 had access to private schooling taught largely by those who had themselves completed the eighth grade.

Church of God in Christ involvement in missionary endeavors by 1987 was evidenced by the fact that more than 150 members were involved in overseas assignments. These assignments took place in the following countries (membership in parenthesis): Belize (24), Brazil (208), Dominican Republic (20); Guatemala (21), Haiti (318), India (27), Mexico (375), Nigeria (203), and the Philippines (183). Additional relief work, tract distribution, and evangelism has taken place in several other countries. Overseas membership of 1,379 in 1988 was about 10 percent of the total worldwide membership of

13,732. Of the 12,353 members in North America, 3,120 were found in Canada (six provinces) and 9,233 in the the United States (23 states). Approximately one-third of the United States membership resided in Kansas; approximately half of the Canadian membership lived in Manitoba. The church's periodical is *Messenger of Truth*.

Church of God in Christ beliefs continue to reflect conservative strains of the Anabaptist and Mennonite traditions. They regard six °confessions of faith important, beginning with the "33 articles" found in *Martyrs Mirror*. The most recent confession was accepted in 1959. Holdeman beliefs pertaining to the supernatural, the °°Bible, °salvation, and eternal destiny are similar to those of evangelical Protestants. Their distinctives are largely those seen among conservative Mennonites of the past four centuries. Beliefs unique to them are the authority they have tended to give to dreams, visions, and revelations and their adherence to the docetic "celestial flesh" °Christology of Menno (and Melchior °Hoffman). Their most often noted doctrinal emphasis is their "true church" doctrine coupled with a carefully defined and monitored lifestyle faithful to their worldview.

Beliefs and accepted practices are carefully defined with little room left for doubt as to what is "right" or "wrong." These begin with an emphasis on being redeemed from sinfulness, which results in an emulation of Christlikeness, focused both on attitudes and outward expressions in appearance, family and community relationships, vocation, and possessions. The decisions reached on these matters at conferences are binding. Unheeded infractions usually result in discipline, particularly during the yearly revival meetings. This has forced a fairly standard outward conformity: men wear relatively plain °dress and beards; they avoid wearing ties. Women also dress simply and wear black headcoverings (either a small cap or a kerchief tied under the chin. These °symbols serve as powerful reminders of religious obligations of being a faithful Holdeman Mennonite. Deviations in appearance signal tendencies toward defection and are dealt with by peer pressures of fellow church members, family, ministers, deacons, and the visiting ministers during their revival meetings. Observers have noted that they have managed to retain one of the most carefully disciplined groups in this respect in North America.

Typical of many evangelical and/or conservative Christians, CGC members normally gather Sunday mornings for Sunday school and worship and Sunday and Wednesday evenings for teaching, fellowship, and music-making. Ministers are chosen from their own ranks without formal training for pastoral ministry. Usually there are several in one congregation. They, together with ordained deacons, comprise the church staff, which takes major responsibility for local church matters. There is no regularly salaried minister. Most members and ministers have traditionally been farmers.

They worship in comfortable, but relatively plain, buildings which may include loudspeaker systems, air-conditioning, padded pews, and carpeted floors, but no °musical instruments. They have no regular °choirs but °sing in four-part harmony, drawing on hymnody that makes heavy use of gospel songs. Ministers tend to preach topically rather than exegetically and seldom use prepared notes.

Erring members are warned. If this goes unheeded they are ultimately excommunicated and avoided (shunned) by fellow members. It is estimated that about 10-25 percent experience excommunication. The fact that about 75-80 percent "repent" and return and are reaccepted attests to the success of their socialization and the feared experience of avoidance. Most important decisions are made at the conclusion of yearly revival meetings after they have observed °feetwashing (symbolizing their revival meeting "cleansing"), °communion, °baptisms, reacceptance of repentant excommunicants, and the calling and ordination of ministers and deacons as needed.

They have a tightly knit, closed system of church member control centered in their "true church" concept; an insistence on unity in doctrine and practice; unquestioned following of their ordained leaders; °decision making relegated basically to the ordained men; and a rigid doctrine and practice of church discipline which is coupled with the threat of eternal penalty. Attendance at other churches and participation in intimate spiritual relationships with nonmembers are regarded as bordering on "spiritual adultery" or listening to "false prophets."

In communities where they reside they are generally respected, particularly for their care and concern, willingness to help, reliability in work, and ethical ways. They are regarded as a people who continue to take their Christian doctrines and responsibilities very seriously, seeking to deal with seductive, world-conforming agendas in every way. CH

Brazil. Expansion of the CGC into Brazil has followed a pattern similar to that in Mexico, beginning as a colonization venture and developing into a mission program. In November 1968, a group of three families of the Church of God in Christ Mennonite moved from the United States to Brazil. They wanted to locate in a rural area where they could raise their families according to biblical principles. A farm near Rio Verde, Goiás State (460 km./285 mi. from Brasilia), was purchased and divided among eight families. More families arrived and bought neighboring farms. They are engaged mainly in farming, raising primarily cattle, corn, and soybeans. In the beginning, services were held in English with Portuguese translation. They have been interested in missions and known for their tract ministry, conscientious objection to military service, and °nonconformity to the world in dress and lifestyle.

In 1988 there were two churches in the rural area, one in the city of Rio Verde, and a new outreach in Goiania, the capital of the State of Goiás. Combined membership is around 220. Ordained ministers are: Reno Hibner, Richard Mininger, John Penner, Mark Loewen, Elias Stoltzfus, and Claudio Silva.   OEH

Clarence Hiebert, *The Holdeman People: The Church of God in Christ, Mennonite, 1859-1969* (South Pasadena, Cal.: William Carey Library, 1973); *Histories of the Congregations of the Church of God in Christ, Mennonite* (Moundridge, Ks.: Gospel Publishers, 1975); Linda Louise Boynton, *The Plain People: An Ethnography of the Holdeman Mennonites* (Salem, Wis.: Sheffield Publishing Company, 1986); *MWH* (1978), 324-27; *MWH* (1984), 136.

See also Église de Dieu en Christ, Mennonite, Haiti; Guatemala; Mexico.

Church of God in Christ Mennonite, Haiti. See L'Église de Dieu en Christ Mennonite, Haiti.

Church Planting brings into clear focus a task that lies at the very core of Christian °mission, the formation of new churches. While the term does not square with some New Testament metaphors for the church—body of Christ, a building—it corresponds well with common New Testament imagery for evangelization: planting, watering, and God making the plant grow. It contributes to the biblical understanding that the church is a living organism. It also serves well to express the process of introducing the gospel into a new community of people, resulting in a new congregation of believers springing forth among them.

The use of this term to give focus to the special task of new church formation is represented in old titles like that of John Nevius' landmark book, *The Planting and Development of Missionary Churches* (1886) and Peill and Rowland's World Dominion Press book, *Church Planting* (n.d.). The term has in recent decades come back into common usage under the influence of the °Church Growth movement. Two important principles of church growth are brought into focus in the use of "church planting." First, there are in the world thousands of unreached peoples, clearly definable communities of people among whom there exists no church and no faithful, culturally relevant expression of the gospel.

Secondly, °evangelism is not evangelism in the biblical sense unless it results in the incorporation of new believers into the church. The obvious implication of these two principles is that many new churches will need to be formed if the gospel is to be proclaimed to every people.

Certain elements inherent within these church growth principles correspond with Anabaptist concerns. First, the gospel is not fully represented simply through verbal communication. It needs to be expressed in a life of obedience together. Secondly, believers are members of a body, not individuals standing alone in their faith. (On the other hand, Church Growth theory does not adequately recognize that the church is a community of reconciliation in and through which is broken down the wall of enmity that separates individual people and groups of people from each other.)

Anabaptist Vision and Church Planting. In their letter to Thomas °Müntzer in September 1524, Conrad °Grebel and his friends reveal that their ideas about the church were changing. They had been faithful colleagues of °°Zwingli, but over the issue of the authority of the government to determine when and how the church was to be reformed, these men had become increasingly doubtful about the authenticity of a church whose very existence was dependent on the decision of the civil government.

After critiquing Müntzer at several points, explaining at the same time their own views, Grebel challenged Müntzer to "go forth with the Word and establish a Christian church," congregations of believers committed together to Christ and his rule. In just a few short months, under threat of imprisonment or banishment from Zürich, they themselves would act on this challenge, caught up in a powerful impulse to go from town to town, from canton to canton, from principality to principality, declaring and sharing their new vision of the kingdom of God and his church.

This impulse comes close to the core of the vision that most Anabaptists were caught up with. The premier task was to "go forth . . . and establish a Christian church," to set out with the intention of forming new cells of people of God, new expressions of the body of Christ—in cities, towns and villages, among groups of people where an authentic church had not yet been planted.

It was a vision and an impulse similar to the one that had captured the imagination of the people from Cyprus and Cyrene who had been to Jerusalem on Pentecost and later went to Antioch to form a fellowship of followers of Jesus the Messiah there. That vision captured the imagination of Paul, who seems to the modern Christian observer almost irresponsible in his urge to press on to yet another town to form a cell of believers in Jesus there.

It might well be said that some elements of this urge to form new fellowships of believers wherever possible were carried over from the clear impulse in Hellenistic Judaism to form new synagogue fellowships wherever they could, having clear criteria in mind as to how that was to be accomplished. But in sharp contrast to synagogue fellowships, these cells of believers in Jesus were to be profoundly assimilative. This impulse, imparted by Jesus to his disciples in both word and action, was to gather peripheral people—the disinherited, the despised, the disregarded, and the disenfranchised of the larger community—making them members of the body of the new community. This impulse springs to life in the work of Paul, a Pharisee of the Pharisees, who takes into his circle people who in Jewish practice had no hope of ever partaking of the feast of the kingdom.

Mennonites and Church Planting. Within the Anabaptist movement the impulse to go forth and establish the church was subverted within a generation or two. On the one hand, there quickly developed an alternative impulse—to gather people out of the threatening, evil world, take them to the safe pastures of Moravia, and form colonies of heaven there. The clear implication of this Hutterian strategy of mission was that the world was not redeemable; one needed to be saved out of the world into a pure, safe, colony of heaven.

On the other hand, within the mainstream of Swiss, German, and Dutch Anabaptism, the impulse to "go forth . . . and establish a church" by forming new congregations in every village and town was subverted when intense persecution and other factors transformed large segments of the Anabaptist community into "the quiet in the land." It was in the lengthening experience as relatively isolated quiet people in the country that a distinct ethnic, subcultural identity became an increasingly pervasive element in their self-consciousness as church.

The mindset of such a Christian subculture becomes in certain respects like the mindset of the Christendom from which the Anabaptist, had separated: The church has already been established. Everyone that counts is already a Christian. This thought certainly applies within the community, but it also easily comes to apply beyond the community. For Luther, sending someone into another principality to proclaim the gospel and form a new church was tantamount to political subversion. In a corresponding way, to many Christian communities with a strong ethnic identity, going to another community to start a new church appears at least presumptuous. To people of such a mindset, the impulse to form a new congregation is reduced to a function of the migration of a significant segment of the community to a new location. So it is that in the Mennonite experience, migration has been the primary model for the formation of new congregations.

Even entering the 20th c., when Mennonites were stirred to launch new efforts to evangelize and plant new churches in North America and overseas, a strong element of the strategy has been to depend on a number of people migrating or commuting to the new area to form the core of the new congregation. In the case of mission in non-Western societies, the method of the mission compound coupled with the mission boarding school was the core of the strategy to mold or enculturate a community of converts into the image of the sending church in a pattern corresponding substantially to the civilizing vision of much of the establishment-oriented Protestant mission movement.

Models for Church Planting. Transplanting—taking a whole plant or a branch and planting it in a new place—is a metaphor that can be helpfully used to describe the process of church formation by migration. It illustrates taking a body of people from one or more existing congregations and gathering them in a new setting to from the core, or even the bulk, of a new congregation. A new congregation formed in this way will have characteristics similar to the congregation(s) of origin. Its capacity for incorporating new people of diverse backgrounds into itself, will not be substantially different from that of the congregation of origin. It is not a foregone conclusion that churches formed in this way will be effectively involved in mission in their surrounding community; the migrating group itself already constitutes a church. If the community into which this group migrates is distinctly different culturally from the migrating group, the possibilities for the new church to become indigenous to the new community are clearly limited.

Hundreds of new Mennonite congregations in cities and rural areas of North America have been started in this way. Many of them have existed for decades, but there is still a clear consciousness of who are the "Mennonites" (that is the immigrants or commuters of Mennonite family background) and who are the "community people" (the members of non-Mennonite background).

Seed-planting—taking a seed of a plant and planting it in a new place to become a new plant—is a metaphor that can helpfully be used to describe the sending of representative missionaries or church planters from existing congregations to a different community or society to work towards the formation of a new church made up of people of that community or society. By sending only a few representatives into the new context, the formation of a new church will be dependent on success in calling people of that community to faith and forming them into a body of believers. Since the number of representatives is so small, leaders for the new congregation will have to be recruited from among the people gathered from the community. The cultural patterns of the communtiy will have a formative effect on the new congregation, thus assuring that it will be more indigenous (°contextualization).

Church Planting Strategy. In the 1980s a number of Mennonite conferences in North America have recognized their need to sharpen their commitment to the mission God has given the church. One form of response has been to set goals for stewardship and mission. Taken together, these conferences have goals to plant well over 1,000 new congregations in a decade. While there is much difference of opinion over the validity of setting goals in Christian ministry, these goals have stimulated the churches to reflection and new activity in mission.

Mennonite churches in other countries may not be setting goals like the North Americans, but in some places there is evident a similar kind of intentionality about church planting. In the mid-1960s a remarkable number of people were coming to faith in Java. Beginning in about 1970 the leaders of the Evangelical Church of Java took deliberate steps to foster the formation of new congregations. They reflected carefully on the stages and criteria for church formation. The number of "mature" congregations in that conference increased from 18 in 1970 to 60 in 1988, with 105 branch congregations still in earlier stages of development.

One of the major challenges of church planting is the selection and training of people to lead. Church planting requires certain abilities not essential for leadership in established congregations. It requires an ability to envision something that does not yet exist and then bring it into being. It requires the ability to adapt quickly and to tolerate sudden change. It requires the ability to enter and thrive in unfamiliar communities. The challenge is to identify and learn how to develop these characteristics in leaders.   LMY

John L. Nevius, *Planting and Development of Missionary Churches* (n.p.: Presbyterian and Reformed Publishing House, 1886); David W. Shenk and Ervin R. Stutzman, *Creating Communities of the Kingdom: New Testament Models of Church Planting* (Scottdale, 1988); Wilbert R. Shenk, ed., *Anabaptism and Mission* (Scottdale, 1984); Dale L. Stoll, *Church Planting from Seed Time to Harvest* (Elkhart, Ind.: MBM, 1986); *SAW*; Wittlinger, *Piety and Obedience* (1978), 505-9.

Church Year. See Christian Calendar.

Church-State Relations (ME IV:611). Although the description of the majority position of Anabaptists toward the state in the ME IV article is basically accurate in the view of most recent interpreters, more would be made of the diversity among early Anabaptists concerning the state. The major work on the subject (Stayer) argues that Anabaptist views on the sword ranged from "crusading" (°Münster), to "Realpolitik" (°Hubmaier, cf. °°Zwingli and °°Cal-

vin) to "Separatist Nonresistance" (the Swiss Brethren, the view which the ME IV article identified as the normative Anabaptist-Mennonite view). The °apocalypticism of Hans °Hut and of Melchior °Hoffman is stressed by Stayer and other recent interpreters. In this view, Anabaptist apocalyptic expectations relativized their nonresistance and made possible a transition from peaceable Anabaptism to the effort to usher in the °kingdom of God with violence (Münster). In Stayer's view, the "separatist °nonresistance" position did not become the norm until around 1560—though it is the position which survived and became dominant. In addition, it seems that a number of Anabaptists, including Pilgram °Marpeck and °Menno Simons, believed firmly that Christians may not kill but—unlike the Swiss Brethren—were not necessarily convinced that this required a full separation from all involvement with °government. If this is true, the difference between "Mennonite" and "Quaker" attitudes toward the state are less systematic and theological, and more situational, shaped by their concrete experiences of the state (Yoder). Stayer sometimes suggests that the "separatist nonresistants" saw the state as being of the devil. On this point the ME IV article is more accurate: "The necessity for the state is human sin, but the ordination of the state expresses both God's wrath against sin and His gracious love" (p. 612).

A related point of updating concerns Mennonites in colonial and revolutionary Pennsylvania (1700s). Mennonites were quite active politically, certainly including voting, generally supporting the Quaker party during the colonial period. Though they did not hold high offices, Mennonite concern in this period had not so much to do with avoiding all government as it did with avoiding direct participation in violence. Only when, especially during the Revolution, they had to choose between political participation and nonviolence, did they chose to forfeit their political rights. They did not see political participation as un-Christian so long as it did not require participation in war.

Church-State Relations in Europe and North America. (a) *Western Europe.* In general terms, the period since World War II has seen some revival of °peace concern among European Mennonites, partly as a result of increased contact with Mennonites from North America, but also because of involvement, particularly among some Dutch and German Mennonites, with the broader religious and secular peace movement. In Germany a gradually increasing number of Mennonites have been °conscientious objectors (COs) since °conscription was reintroduced in 1957. In 1985 the North German Vereinigung der deutschen Mennonitengemeinden (Association of German Mennonite Congregations) approved a new peace concerns statement (the first since 1934) that affirmed COs. In Switzerland since the early 1970s a small minority of Mennonites (about 20) have refused military service, even though there was no legal provision for conscientious objection until 1988.

There has also been interest in witness to government and in a broad program of °peace education. The Dutch, Swiss, and German Mennonite peace committees and the European Mennonite Peace Committee (°Europäisches Mennonitisches Friedenskomitee), have been organizational centers of these efforts. One recent and visible attempt to deal with some of these concerns has been the establishment of Agape Verlag in Germany. Another is a series of discussions with representatives of the North Atlantic Treaty Organization (NATO) on defense policy, together with the establishment of the newsletter *NATO Watch*. Mennonites from the Netherlands, Germany, and Switzerland have also been active in °Church and Peace, an ecumenical European peace organization. The general posture of European Mennonite peace groups toward the state as been one of *witness*, supporting less militaristic policies and greater recognition of conscientious objection (the latter particularly in France and Switzerland). Except for the Netherlands where the °Doopsgezinde Vredesgroep (Mennonite Peace Group) has been comparatively strong, the number of Mennonites actively supporting peace groups is relatively low. Small Mennonite churches, focused centrally around peace witness, have been started in England, Ireland, and Spain.

(b) *Soviet Union.* In the years immediately after the °Russian Revolution (ca. 1918-21) Mennonite life in the Soviet Union was almost totally disrupted due to famine, civil war, and general lawlessness and disorder in the areas of the major Mennonite colonies. A minority of young Mennonite men took up arms to defend the colonies against roving bands of marauders (the °*Selbstschutz*). This experience of anarchy and subsequent experiences with the Soviet government gave many Mennonites who left the Soviet Union a deep appreciation of stable government and a great aversion to °revolution and to °communism.

Since the revolution Mennonites as Christian believers have stood in a basically conflictual relationship with the officially atheistic government, suffering various kinds of °persecution or limitation of freedom. The status of some of them, wealthy farmers or businessmen, also put them in conflict with the new government. During the 1920s more than 20,000 emigrated. During the 1930s and 1940s virtually all Mennonites were sent to labor camps and mines or were otherwise relocated, a process through which many died. Another large emigration, about 12,000, followed World War II. Nevertheless, many others remained. For those who stayed, relations with other German-speaking Christians became increasingly important after World War II. In the decades following the revolution, specifically Mennonite identity waned as the religious institutions which had supported church life were disrupted. Since the mid-1960s most Mennonites have joined the officially recognized °All-Union Council of Evangelical Christians-Baptists while others have rejected it as too compromised. In both cases, a specifically "Mennonite" identity is fading as they find fellowship and identify with other Christians—now often leaving behind the German language also. Since the mid-1970s restrictions on church life have generally been less severe than in earlier decades. Nevertheless, more than 13,000 persons of Mennonite origin emigrated from the Union of Soviet Socialist Republics, primarily to West Germany, since 1970 (°*Umsiedler*).

(c) *North America.* Developments on church-state issues in Canada and the United States since World War II have had important elements of commonality, but with some significant differences as well. In both countries World War II reinforced theologically a sharp church/world dualism and a pessimism about the possibility of the world adopting the way of peace (see the debate about °°"nonresistance" versus °°"pacifism" in the writings of Hershberger and others)—thus strengthening a tendency toward "separation." At the same time, the war helped set in motion changes in °education, °occupations, and geographic patterns (°urbanization) which brought many Mennonites into the mainstream of their societies in important respects. This, together with the development of a positive theology of mission and service (Hershberger), and a corresponding widespread involvement in mission agencies and Mennonite Central Committee, caused Mennonites to become engaged with the world in a new way. This shift lies in the background of a growing acceptance of the state as a proper arena for Christian witness in both countries among most, though not all, Mennonites.

Especially in the United States, the experiences of the civil rights movement and the war in °Vietnam helped overcome the view that Christians should have nothing to do with government. In the civil rights movement, Martin Luther King, Jr., demonstrated that *nonviolent* action could bring significant political change. In addition, the political structures proved to be open to some positive change. In the case of Vietnam, the war was ended partly because of widespread public discontent. In both cases Mennonite peace concerns, theologically grounded, and secular wisdom often coincided and Mennonites had many allies in the broader society, unlike their experience during the 1940s. These experiences suggested that Mennonite concerns were not entirely inapplicable to °politics and that perhaps one did not need to compromise one's convictions to have a political role. Nevertheless, these experiences left a sense of "over againstness" among U.S. Mennonites in their relationship to government. While the government might be brought to change, it was often a major perpetrator of problems. This was somewhat different on the Canadian scene, where Mennonites experienced a government which was more benign (often even positive), especially in terms of world peace.

Also growing out of these experiences and the experiences of Mennonite Central Committee (MCC) and mission workers was a concern for °justice. This was felt on both sides of the border. To avoid war and other sins—or to give "a cup of cold water"—was no longer a sufficient expression of discipleship. Attention began to focus on seeking justice, especially for those who were victims of systemic forces beyond their control, often forces based in the United States (victims such as blacks in America, Vietnamese civilians, Nicaraguan peasants, etc.). Attention began to focus more on the political and economic *causes* of poverty and war. With that came, naturally enough, a stronger need to address those in power.

An additional change was a theological shift

which, in a different way, called into question traditional understandings of the church/world dualism. Beginning in the early 1960s, the idea of "the lordship of Christ" began to be used in Mennonite circles to mean that Christ is objectively Lord of all. He is not only Lord of the church (where his lordship is recognized) but also of the world (though his lordship is not recognized). From this theological perspective "a Christian witness to the state" was a sensible, even mandatory, undertaking—in a way that it was not if the state was conceived of mainly or solely as a mechanism through which God held back the forces of sin and chaos. One should be a "witness" to Christ's lordship over the state by calling the state to approximate more fully the norms which Christ revealed as right for all humankind. John H. Yoder was the most important figure in this development.

On the basis of these experiences and this theology, offices were opened by MCC in Washington (late 1960s) and Ottawa (mid-1970s). They were designed to facilitate a witness to government both by providing to churches information on issues facing governments and by arranging for Mennonites to share their concerns and knowledge with officials (°lobbying). The second function often involves scheduling appointments for returned mission and service workers with appropriate government officials in order to present officials with alternative perspectives on situations about which they must make policy decisions. This kind of witness is seen as being dependent upon substantial direct involvement in situations of conflict and need around the world through mission and service programs. Such involvement provides both the knowledge to make the witness and the integrity which makes it authentic.

This "semiofficial" posture of "witness" to government still assumes that Christians (at least Mennonite Christians) are not themselves "the government." Nevertheless, the sense that government centers are important places if one is interested in pursuing questions of peace and justice has caused an influx of Mennonites into Washington and Ottawa (symbolically and actually). Some work in various lobbies, but many work within government. In Canada there are more Mennonites in high positions (including Parliament) than in the United States, and working within government is more common for Mennonites there, but Mennonite involvement in various government capacities is increasing rapidly in both countries. In addition, MCC Canada has received sizable amounts of government funding since about the mid-1970s.

If those who move from "witness" to "involvement" in government may, at least in some cases, step outside the mainstream of Mennonite thought on church-state relations, there are others who do so by stepping out in different directions. Some, particularly in the United States, take part in more dramatic and controversial kinds of witness to government, such as war °tax resistance, and military draft and draft registration resistance (the General Conference Mennonite Church and the Mennonite Church [MC] have pledged support of draft resisters, but have not called on all members to act like-

wise). Some have also engaged in protests and °civil disobedience opposing the arms race. On the other side are those who reject the idea that the church should witness to government at all, who claim Christians have no business telling governments how to govern, and who see themselves as the true inheritors of the Mennonite heritage.

The dual emphases on the value of justice and the systemic analysis of the causes of injustice, as noted above, have also led some to question the rejection of revolution which has been a part of Mennonite thought. This kind of questioning has grown out of experiences of workers in places like Vietnam, Central America, the Philippines, and South Africa, where meaningful changes seem to be blocked by ruling elites. Along with this has come a certain questioning of pacifism. What *if* justice is apparently best served by violent revolution? While this question is not fully resolved in Mennonite thought, the direction being explored most seriously now is that of nonviolent direct action (witness the interest in the "Christian Peacemaker Teams" idea suggested at the 1984 Mennonite World Conference). Along with a more activist understanding of peacemaking (°sociopolitical activism) has come a widespread rejection of "nonresistance" as an adequate understanding of the positive *peacemaking* task. This interest in a more activist posture, and in social change in the direction of justice, has contributed to a new understanding of the ethic of Jesus. The emerging view rejects "nonresistance" in favor of the use of active (perhaps even "coercive") nonviolent action in pursuit of justice (Duane Friesen).

But all of these approaches are not necessarily widely representative of Mennonites as a whole. It is true that political participation, at least as measured by voting, is increasing at the "grassroots" level. But despite the focus of "official" Mennonite structures dealing with policy questions centered on peace and justice issues, the evidence suggests that Mennonite voting patterns are heavily dependent on the social, economic, and political ethos of their communities. Thus in the United States rural Mennonites, who are more accessible to analysis than urban Mennonites, tend to vote heavily for conservative Republican candidates. Some of this may be explained by the influence of conservative radio and television preachers in parts of the Mennonite world.

It is not clear what the implications of these shifts might be. Evidence does not indicate that greater acceptance of political participation has led, for example, to a decline in pacifist commitment. Nevertheless, in the long term, shifts on that level may also occur, particularly unless some sense of church and world separation is maintained.

Mennonite Churches Outside North America and Europe. The views of the missionary founders of newer Mennonite churches around the world are a crucial factor shaping the churches' attitudes. Generally, Mennonite missionaries carried with them personal convictions affirming nonresistance, separation of church and state, and other distinctively Mennonite views. Sometimes these elements have been consciously included as central to the gospel. Especially in recent years, efforts have been made to articulate and embody an integrated "gospel of peace" (Ramseyer). Nevertheless, such "distinctives" apparently were often seen as secondary and not essential to the gospel message itself. This was especially true among missionaries strongly influenced by °Fundamentalism. Thus these components of the gospel frequently were not stressed or taught systematically. In addition, at least in some areas (e.g., India), missionaries usually cooperated closely with, and identified with, colonial government officials (°colonialism).

Little has been written about the relations of indigenous Mennonites to the state in areas where the church was planted as a result of mission efforts, usually within the last 100 years. It is clear that relations have varied greatly, depending upon the concerns of the missionaries, the culture and history of the country involved, and the attitude of the government toward the churches. Both lack of information and variety make any generalizations hazardous. In most places, it appears that working out a relationship with the state self-consciously within the Anabaptist-Mennonite tradition has not been a high priority, though this appearance may reflect as much the lack of information available in the West as a lack of concern. It seems that often the gospel has been understood largely as dealing with personal piety, ethics, and one's individual relationship to God, without much thought given to its social and political implications. To what extent this indicates a rejection of important strands of historic Mennonite perspectives on the state is not clear. In many places the explanation may be that major problems in this area simply have not yet demanded the attention of the church.

There are some important exceptions to this general picture. The small Mennonite churches in Japan have been deeply concerned with peace questions, have wrestled with relations toward and witness to government, including the "war tax" question, and have sought self-consciously to be Anabaptist. Taiwanese Mennonites have wrestled with the problem of compulsory military service, sometimes serving only with great reluctance. In Ethiopia, since the early 1980s a severe conflict between the Marxist government and the Mennonite church has caused much soul searching. In Argentina and some other parts of Latin America, increased priority is being given to peace education, including perspectives on church-state relations. In some Latin American countries, efforts are being made to secure the right of conscientious objection to military service. In Honduras, Mennonites are responding to refugees from the war in Nicaragua and El Salvador—and coming into conflict with government over the "political" implications of their humanitarian aid. In Nicaragua, Mennonites are struggling with conscription and conscientious objection in a war situation. Other examples could be given, but the story of Mennonite church-state relations among the newer churches is yet to be written.   TJK

Bibl. on War and Peace (1987), esp. 128-77; Peter Brock, *Pacifism in Europe to 1914* (Princeton U. Press, 1972), 59-113, 162-254, 407-441; CRR 3, esp. 244-301; James M. Stayer, *Anabaptists and the Sword*, 2nd ed. (Lawrence, Kansas: Coronado Press, 1976); cf. John H. Yoder, "Anabaptists and the Sword Revisited," *Z. für KG*, 85 (1974), 270-83; Richard K. MacMaster, *Land, Piety, Peoplehood: The Establishment of Mennonite Communities in America, 1683-1790* (Scottdale,

1985); Richard K. MacMaster with Samuel L. Horst and Robert F. Ulle, *Conscience in Crisis: Mennonites and Other Peace Churches in America, 1739-1789* (Scottdale, 1979); John B. Toews, *Czars, Soviets and Mennonites* (Newton, 1982); Walter Sawatsky, "From Russian to Soviet Mennonites, 1941-1985," forthcoming in *Russian Mennonite History: Essays in Memory of Gerhard Lohrenz*, ed. John Friesen; Al Reimer, *My Harp Is Turned to Mourning* (Winnipeg: Hyperion Press, 1985); Walter Sawatsky, *Soviet Evangelicals Since World War II* (Scottdale, 1981); John B. Toews, "The Origins and Activities of the Mennonite Selbstschutz in the Ukraine (1918-1919)," *MQR*, (1972), 5-40; John H. Redekop, "Mennonites and Politics in Canada and the United States," *JMS*, 1 (1983), 79-105; John H. Yoder, *The Christian Witness to the State* (Newton, 1964), the most important book justifying a posture of "witness" to the state, which has become the dominant stance among North American Mennonites; idem, The Politics of Jesus (Grand Rapids: Eerdmans, 1972), the most important modern Mennonite interpretation of the political orientation of Jesus and the early church; Guy F. Hershberger, *War, Peace, and Nonresistance* (Scottdale, 1944); idem, *The Way of the Cross in Human Relations* (Scottdale, 1958), the most important works on these issues from the 1940s and 1950s; Duane K. Friesen, *Christian Peacemaking and International Conflict* (Scottdale, 1986), represents a newer activist "peacemaking" approach which focuses primarily on action in the world, not on ethics for the Christian community itself; *Justice and the Christian Witness* (Joint Statement of the Mennonite Church [MC] and the General Conference Mennonite Church, 1983); *The Christian Witness to the State* (Statement of the Mennonite Church [MC] 1961); Frank H. Epp, *Mennonites in Canada I* and *II*; *Where We Stand: An Index of Peace and Social Concerns Statements by Mennonites and Brethren in Christ in Canada, 1787-1982*, compiled by Bert Friesen (Winnipeg: MCC Canada, 1986); Urbane Peachey, ed., *Mennonite Statements on Peace and Social Concerns, 1900-1978* (Akron: MCC, 1980); *Christian Peacemaker Teams: A Study Document* (Akron: MCC, 1986), reflects the growing interest in activist peacemaking and nonviolent direct action; *Washington Memo*, a bimonthly publication of the MCC Washington office, the best source on current U.S. Mennonite dealings with national policy questions; *Menn. Rep.*, the best source of current reporting on Canadian Mennonites and political issues; William Janzen, "Militarism and the Response of Canadian Mennonites from the 1940s to the 1980s," unpublished MCC Canada discussion paper, Sept. 12, 1986; Kauffman/Harder, *Anabaptists Four C. Later* (1975), 150-169, statistical information on attitudes and actions from a 1972 survey; *God and Caesar*, a newsletter promoting war tax resistance published by the General Conference Mennonite Peace Secretary, Newton, Ks.; *Guidelines for Today* and *The Sword and Trumpet*, major expressions of conservative criticism of the kind of Mennonite political witness which has become prevalent; Theron F. Schlabach, *Gospel Versus Gospel: Mission and the Mennonite Church, 1863-1944* (Scottdale, 1980), focuses on the nature of the gospel taken by North American Mennonite (MC) missionaries as they started new churches; Juhnke, *Mission* (1979); John A. Lapp, *India* (1972); Robert L. Ramseyer, ed., *Mission and the Peace Witness* (Scottdale, 1979); *Miss. Focus*, a quarterly journal; Alle Hoekema, "Pieter Jansz (1820-1904), First Mennonite Missionary to Java," *MQR*, 52 (1978) 58-76; Levi Keidel, *Caught in the Crossfire* (Scottdale, 1979); Lawrence Yoder, "The Church of the Muria: A History of the Muria Christian Church of Indonesia" (PhD Thesis, Fuller Theological Seminary, 1981); Gerald W. Schlabach, "Military Service, Conscientious Objection and Nation-Building: The Case of Revolutionary Nicaragua," unpublished paper available from Mennonite Central Committee.

See also Business; Amish; Development Work; Education; Deutsches Mennonitisches Friedenskomitee; Schweizerisches Mennonitisches Friedens-Komitee/Comité mennonite suisse pour la paix.

Citizenship. See Church-State Relations.

Civil Disobedience (CD) is a dramatic, intentional, and nonviolent confrontation of legally sanctioned violence and injustice. Although CD invests little energy in party politics, the ramifications of its actions are acutely political. It is never an end in itself, seeking always to improve government policy and promote moral and social change. Civil disobedience grows out of cultural resistance—the attempt to serve the poor and to model a counterculture based on peace and justice rather thn militarism and greed.

Civil disobedience honors the variegated legal styles of peacemaking, but challenges prevailing overconfidence in participatory government (voting, °lobbying, advocacy) in which °democratic and other governments claim to be serving their subjects and to be governed by them. Heightened awareness of poverty, political repression, racism, and global over-kill perfidy convinces both secular and religious proponents of CD, especially in the United States, that legal channels of social change have become illusory. The US National Security Council since World War II has become a "second government"—a bureaucratic apparatus which makes legally protected, secret, far-reaching decisions about war, international policy, and the economy (the latter through collusion with the military-industrial complex). Court decisions on behalf of this huge complex repeatedly defy constitutional and international law, as well as the higher moral sense of the citizenry. The legal system protects the arms race and in effect perpetuates the underlying nationalistic worship of military might. To confront these immoral laws is therefore also to confront public propriety and irresponsibility —the same philosophy that ratified the judicious verdict to crucify Jesus.

The term *civil disobedience* is not biblical, but its concept clearly is. For brevity's sake we omit a textual survey to support this claim, and note simply that resistance to a ruler's temptation to be God begins in the Exodus, then continues impellingly throughout the subsequent biblical narrative. Jesus deliberately confronted virtually every level of law and custom of the socio-religious-political power structure of his day—to underscore the absolute authority of the incipient reign of God. His entire servanthood-leadership life embodied a "nonviolent campaign" in collision with prevailing systems: colonial, national, and religious. The cross, a Roman punishment reserved for political dissidents, was the inevitable outcome of his life. Similarly, the apostles are frequently arrested for preaching another authority. Several New Testament letters are written either from prison or political exile, and in some instances (e.g., Rom 13:1-7; 1 Pet 2:11-17; 1 Tim 6:11-16) there is instruction against "antinomian" and gratuitous excesses of a faith discordant with the state. Paul's call to declare God's wisdom to the powers (Eph 3:10) is a seminal admonition, much like 20th-c. acts of civil disobedience, in response to the state's disobedience to God's sovereignty.

Mennonite conversation with contemporary faith-based CD denotes significant theological overlap—particularly in their shared disavowal of the state's ultimate authority. Historically, Mennonites have shown this disavowal in typically *defensive* CD, as in reactive noncompliance with war °tax and °military participation—and indirectly—in their refusal to purchase war bonds and work in war industries. Contemporary CD makes use of all these measures, and adds the *offensive*, more aggressive CD style—trespass, sit-ins, blockades, ploughshare (attacks on weapons manufacturing plants), and even sanctuary actions (illegal protection of political refugees)—to express the same basic disavowal.

This initiatory lack in traditional Mennonite CD rests on a formerly static ethical dualism in which Christian values are viewed as being in stark contrast to those of the world. While it denies any division between the sacred and secular, this Mennonite church/world dichotomy nevertheless tends toward a fairly pessimistic expectation of the state's moral performance. Contemporary CD thought approximates this dichotomy also, but does not share as distinct an ethical dualism. A universal ethic of °love is regarded as a potential here and now and applicable even to statecraft. Romans 13, for instance, is viewed as an instruction in political moral discrimination, but not as an ontological sanction for the existence of government as such. The fact of frequently barbaric human regimes is no reason not to push fully in love's direction.

The moral urgency surrounding today's war-torn and nuclear-hair-trigger world has exhumed a strident this-worldly eschatology in contemporary CD. The danger of existential impatience is therefore constant, and here is where Mennonite thought can deepen the CD movement. Yet here is also where this movement makes a distinct contribution to Mennonites. It assumes the potential to prevent global catastrophe is in God-inspired, human hands—not in reformism and compromise, nor in the futuristic and supraearthly bent that easily tempts Mennonite eschatology in times of crisis. The theology of CD claims that God must not be "counted on," separate from human nonviolent struggle, to save the earth. Jesus has entrusted to us the fate of the new order he lived and died for.   PS-F

Bibl. on War and Peace (1987), 178-200; Daniel Berrigan, *No Bars To Manhood* (New York: Doubleday Press, 1970), 33-123; Martin L. King Jr., *Why We Can't Wait* (New York: Signet Books Press, 1963), 76-109; Bob Campagna, Deb Wiley, Tom Cordaro, *Faith and Resistance* (Mount Vernon: Abbe Creek Press, 1985), 8-66; Ched Myers, "By What Authority? The Bible and Civil Disobedience," *Sojourners,* 12 (May 1983), 11-14; idem, "Jesus and the Practice of Civil Disobedience," *Year One,* 12 (Oct. 1986), 2-4; Geoffrey Gneuhs, "Anarchism and the Church: Are They Compatible?" *Catholic Worker,* 50 (Mar.-Apr. 1980), 3; William Durland, *The Illegality of War* (Colorado Springs: CLP Press, 1983), 1-55; J. Lawrence Burkholder, "Nonresistance, Nonviolent Resistance, and Power," in *Kingdom, Cross, and Community* (1976), 131-37; Walter Wink, "We have met the Enemy," *Sojourners,* 15 (Nov. 1986), 15-18; Thomas G. Sanders, *Protestant Concepts of Church and State* (Garden City: Doubleday Anchor Books, 1964), 25-178; John H. Yoder, *The Priestly Kingdom* (Notre Dame: U. of Notre Dame Press, 1984), 80-195; Joan V. Bondurant, *Conquest of Violence: The Gandhian Philosophy of Conflict* (Berkeley: U. of California Press, 1969), 15-188; Tom Hanks, "Oppressors on the Run," *The Other Side,* 17 (Feb. 1981), 23-35.

See also Church-State Relations; Juridical Procedures (ME III); Law; Persecution.

Civil Religion, United States. The phrase "civil religion," first coined by the 18th-c. French philosopher Jean-Jacques Rousseau (1712-78), was popularized by the American sociologist Robert N. Bellah in 1967. Using President John Kennedy's inaugural address as an example, Bellah described the pervasive presence of civil religion in the United States and argued that it existed as a religion in its own right alongside denominational religions. Although civil religions emerge in other national settings, this article focuses on the American situation.

The symbolic content of American civil religion in the United States is heavily influenced by the Judeo-Christian tradition. The sacred myths, rituals, and symbols that constitute this generic American faith unite a diverse population in a common religious experience. As a "folk" or "generalized" religion, it transcends divisive denominational, racial, economic, political, and ethnic loyalties that fragment the nation, and it enables Protestant and Catholic, Hispanic and Italian, as well as Republican and Democrat, to rise above their differences and join together in singing "God Bless America." A civil religion performs valuable integrative functions for a nation and in rare instances, such as in Martin Luther King's "I Have a Dream" speech, prophetic civil religion can mobilize citizens for social justice.

Although the United States constitution calls for a legal separation of church and state, the two realms blend together informally in the rituals of civil religion—national holidays, Memorial Day parades, patriotic songs, and presidential inaugurations. The symbolic marriage of sacred and political orders is consummated when Bible and flag blend together in the same photograph, when religious pamphlets are printed in red, white, and blue, and when presidents issue Thanksgiving Day proclamations and invoke the name of God in their speeches. Religious leaders of national prominence encourage the church-state romance when they publicly support the political order by attending ceremonial occasions such as "White House Prayer Breakfasts."

The civil religion of a nation provides a sacred canopy that enshrouds the origins and destiny of the state in sacred mysteries. Although American civil religion is imbued with Judeo-Christian language and symbolism, its doctrinal content is diluted with the most vague references to God, e.g., Almighty Power and Divine Providence. References to Christ, sin, and the cross are conspicuously and necesssrily missing, to prevent offense in a pluralistic religious setting. The doctrinal creed of civil religion is inoffensive, polite, and courteous, for it must confer a divine blessing that legitimates national policies and encompasses the entire body politic in bland but common mysteries.

The sometimes subtle and other times explicit fusion of church and state in civil religion has troubled Mennonites for several reasons. From the outset of the Anabaptist movement in the 16th c., Mennonites have insisted that the church is autonomous from the political order. The two-kingdom theology in the early Anabaptist confessions of faith assumed that the church would often be at odds with civil government as well as the dominant culture. The Mennonite conception of the state was somewhat ambiguous, since the civil government was also understood to be ordained of God. The Anabaptists contended however, that the holy Scriptures and the lordship of Christ, not the civil authorities, were the normative standard for the faith and practice of the church. Indeed the church, in the Anabaptist view, was a counterculture, an alternate social order that often found itself in conflict with the state.

Civil religion, in Mennonite eyes, blurs the historical distinction between the political and sacred orders, confers a divine legitimacy on the state, and lures the faithful into a patriotic embrace of °nationalism. Indeed, many Mennonite authors have argued that civil religion fosters national idolatry, a worship of the nation-state and its powerful interests in ways that divert the faithful from the radical demands of the God of the New Testament. Mennonites have argued that the God of American civil religion is a provincial deity, a tribal God who typically blesses the political status quo and frowns sternly on other forms of governments, especially nondemocratic ones. Mennonite authors have contended that the star-spangled God of American tribal religion threatens to usurp the biblical notion of a God who sends rain on the unjust as well as the just and welcomes followers from every tribe, nation, and ethnic enclave. A civil religion that wraps the destiny of a particular nation up with the promises of a tribal God is an affront to the universal character of the God of holy Scripture whose purposes transcend the destiny of particular nations. While this critical view of civil religion prevailed among academicians, many Mennonites were comfortable with the religious flavor of the God-and-country °patriotism.

Mennonite concern with civil religion peaked with the patriotic celebrations surrounding the American bicentennial in July 1976. In the 12 months preceding the bicentennial celebration, the *Gospel Herald*, weekly publication of the Mennonite Church (MC), printed 23 articles, including three editorials, which dealt with civil religion. A variety of authors pointed out the dangers of uncritical national worship and called the readers to repentance and obedience to the God who loves all nations and all cultures. Other Mennonite papers carried articles with similar concerns during this time. The Mennonite Central Committee distributed a "Civil Religion" packet containing 11 articles describing and critiquing civil religion and 9 other articles which discussed appropriate ways to celebrate the bicentennial. A summary pamphlet in the MCC packet warned that the danger of civil religion "lies in being seduced into uncritical celebration of the nation state, forgetting our higher loyalty to God." Several Mennonite regional conferences issued statements criticizing the "strong spirit of nationalism" and calling their members to "reaffirm their allegiance to the Lordship of Christ and his supranational kingdom."

The Herald Press publication of *Our Star-Spangled Faith* provided a Mennonite critique of civil religion that circulated beyond Mennonite circles. In the same manner, the publication of *A Dream for America* offered proposals by a Mennonite scholar for celebrating the national dream without the entrapment of idolatrous nationalism. The common theme in all of these Mennonite publications warned that an untamed civil religion would degenerate into a national idolatry that would not only supplant the prophetic teaching of the New Testament, but would also confer a divine blessing on the state, thereby legitimating militarism and oppression in the name of God.

                                                                    DBK

Donald B. Kraybill, *Our Star-Spangled Faith* (Scottdale, 1976); idem, "Civil Religion vs. New Testament Christianity," *GH* (May 11, 1976), 402-03; John A. Lapp, *A Dream for America* (Scottdale, 1976); idem, "Civil Religion Is But Old Establishment Writ Large," in *Kingdom, Cross and Community*, ed. J. R. Burkholder and Calvin Redekop (Scottdale, 1976), 196-207; idem, "Understanding Civil Religion," *Chr. Living* (Oct. 1973), 15, 24; "Civil Religion and Bicentennial," a resource packet of 20 items (Akron, Pa.: MCC, 1976); Robert Bellah, *The Broken Covenant: American Civil Religion in Time of Trial* (New York: Seabury Press, 1975); Russell E. Richey and Donald G. Jones, eds., *American Civil Religion* (New York: Harper and Row, 1974).

See also Church-State Relations; Shinto.

Civil War (United States). See American Civil War.

Clark, Mo., Old Order Amish Settlement is located in north central Missouri (Randolph Co.). The first Amish families moved into this area in 1953, although church services did not begin until a year later. Settlers were mainly from Iowa who were seeking greater freedom in the education of their children. In 1986 there were six church districts (congregations) serving a population of more than 1,000. The settlement maintains nine Amish schools with nearly all of its school-age children attending these rather than °public schools. The Clark community is unique in that its 124 families live in a tightly knit area with Amish farms adjacent to each other for miles along its country roads. An earlier settlement, also from Iowa, but located 10 mi./16 km. farther east, disbanded in 1918. The Clark community is one of the largest of 12 Amish settlements in Missouri (°Jamesport). SLY

Claszen, Johann Peter (Aug. 4, 1891 - June 1974), noted Canadian hymnologist, was born in South Russia. In 1923, upon completion of his teacher's training, Claszen migrated to Canada. He lived in Winnipeg, earning his livelihood as a carpenter.

Claszen's passion for °hymnology surfaced in the early 1930s. He wrote numerous, frequently controversial, articles for Mennonite publications. Two of Claszen's publications, the *Liederborn* (1932) and the *Choralbuch in Ziffern* (1935) were very useful to the immigrant °choirs and congregations who still used *Ziffern* (numbers) instead of notes (ME IV: 1027).

From 1935 to 1938 Claszen served on the hymnal committee of the Conference of Mennonites in Canada. During the 1950s, he was frequently consulted by scholars, musicians, and historians. From 1960 to 1965 he served as consultant for the new *Gesangbuch der Mennoniten* (1965). His significant influence on this hymnal resulted in further contribution of his hymnological expertise to the *Mennonite Hymnal* (1969). Claszen also conducted significant research into Anabaptist hymnology. His papers and manuscripts are housed in the Mennonite Heritage Centre, Winnipeg, Man. His large library of books on hymnology is part of the library of Canadian Mennonite Bible College and the rare book collection of the Heritage Centre. GW

Wesley Berg, "Gesangbuch, Ziffern und Deutschtum: A Study of the Life and Work of J. P. Claszen, Mennonite Hymnologist," *JMS*, 4 (1986), 8-30; idem, in *MM*, 15 (Sept. 1985), 9-11.

Clevelândia Colony, Brazil. See Brazil.

Clinical Pastoral Education. The idea of learning pastoral ministry by serving the sick in a hospital—which is the central thrust of clinical pastoral education—has been an attractive idea for many Mennonites. It may be that, with their strong emphasis upon °discipleship, they have felt that this is nearest to the way Jesus trained the twelve. He trained them "to do by doing." First, he modeled for them, then sent them to serve and to report back to him. He gave his "lectures" between his ministries to the sick, and discussed faith issues in this milieu of serving the sick.

Although individual Mennonites began to show their interest in CPE alrady in its formative years, they were not among the founders of the movement. In 1925 a medical doctor named Richard Cabot set out to train ministers by supervised practice, somewhat as a medical doctor is trained. In 1930, Anton Boisen, a sociologist of religion who had experienced mental illness himself, pioneered in arranging for pastoral interns to serve the mentally ill and to receive peer and professional supervision. He called it "learning pastoral theology by reading the living human document." Two major denominations, the Lutheran and the Southern Baptist, developed their own clinical education programs for their pastors, and many hospitals developed programs. In 1944, the first National Conference on Clinical Training was held. By 1950, a Council for Clinical Training had developed professional standards.

All of the score or more of clinical pastoral education programs relied upon the action-reflection method. An ecumenical group of six "chaplain interns" were assigned to give pastoral care to sufferers in crises, asked to report back to peers and a professional supervisor, and to discuss the "teaching input sessions" together. Each student used an individualized "contract for learning," to focus the resulting insights toward developing a unique style of ministry in line with his or her gifts.

In 1967, in an amazing ecumenical achievement, a score of separate programs of clinical training for pastoral ministries merged and formed The Association for Clinical Pastoral Education (ACPE). Soon leading hospitals and chaplain associations gave it their endorsement and theological seminaries gave its programs recognition by awarding transcript credit toward their pastoral degree. The movement grew steadily, and the standards have remained constant over the years. The Dec. 1987 ACPE News reported that in the United States alone there were 750 active supervisors, serving in 382 centers (hospitals, etc.) relating to 110 seminaries, representing 20 denominations. ACPE had 1,366 "clinical members."

No records known to this writer have preserved the names of all the Mennonites who have profited from CPE and who have made unique contributions to it. At least 20 Mennonites have served as supervisors. The 1987 directory of ACPE supervisors listed seven who were Mennonite.

Ralph Lebold, in addition to supervising in the London [Ont.] Psychiatric Center, also developed an accredited CPE program in the Valley View Mennonite Church of London, of which he was pastor. This was one of only two congregations in North America to be so accredited.

Bob Carlson, Mennonite CPE supervisor in the Prairie View Psychiatric Center of Newton, Kansas, offered CPE to area pastors as part of a large community education program. In the year 1980 alone, Prairie View offered education and consultation to 80 hospitals, universities, colleges, and church organizations of the area. Elmer Ediger commented, "The CPE program has been the most substantial training contribution of Prairie View" (*If We Can Love,* 141).

At Philhaven Hospital, Mt. Gretna, Pa., John Lederach and Paul Miller developed a program in 1985 to serve pastors of their catchment area. Missionaries returning from years of service overseas, leaders in a mid-life change of career, nurses shifting to °chaplaincy, etc., came for training. The average age of the first 28 pastors and leaders (of whom 14 were women) was 48 years of age.

Chester Raber and Ronald Hunsicker, Mennonite CPE supervisors at Oaklawn Center, Elkhart, Ind., developed a remarkable program of satellite centers. Between 1973 and 1981 they offered CPE in as many as 10 other hospitals, prisons, homes for boys, and geriatric centers of the area. They had 17 students, representing 6 denominations, in CPE at one time.

Myron Ebersole developed the CPE programs at Lancaster General Hospital and the Hershey Medical Center in Pennsylvania. Of the 369 students in programs he has directed and supervised, 26 have been Mennonites or Brethren in Christ. He has been involved at regional and national levels of the ACPE, and he led in the development of a Standing Commitee on Public Issues, with the intention of integrating concerns for peace, social justice, and ethical issues as a aspect of education for pastoral care.　　　　　　　　　　　　　　　　　PMM

See also Mental Health Facilities and Services.

Clocks (ME I:629). The most distinctive tradition in Mennonite clocks is found in the Kroeger wall clocks treasured by the Russian Mennonites in Europe and the Americas. The names of more clockmakers can be added to the information found in ME I.

Kroeger clocks were first made in Rosental near Chortitza by Johann Kroeger (1754-1823), who arrived there from West Prussia in 1804. Kroeger's clockmaking descendants included Abraham (1791-1872); David (1929-1909); Peter (1832-1908); David D. (1860-1920), under whom production reached its peak; and Johann D. (1863-?), the last clockmaker, who moved the business to Dnjeprstrasse. The making of Kroeger clocks has been continued in the Americas by, among others, Cornelius Ens (1884-1960) of Edenburg, Sask., and John W. Peters (active 1980) in Mexico.

Swiss-German Mennonites brought their renowned clockmaking skills (see ME I) to colonial Pennsylvania, where they made works for tall case clocks in the English style. Ira Landis and Stacy B. C. Wood have tentatively identified many Mennonite (but no Amish) clockmakers.

Among those working in eastern Pennsylvania, the most important are Jacob Godschalk (ca. 1735-81) and brothers Benjamin (1740-?) and David (1732-96) Rittenhouse. Apparently the Rittenhouse brothers, from Philadelphia, were not Mennonites themselves, but were the great-grandsons of William Rittenhouse, the first Mennonite preacher in Pennsylvania. From ca. 1755-65 Godschalk made clocks in Towamencin Twp., Montgomery Co., after which he moved his shop to Philadelphia, where he, along with David Rittenhouse and others, was given responsibility for taking care of the clock in the Pennsylvania statehouse (Independence Hall). Godschalk apparently left the Mennonite church, becoming a lieutenant in the Revolutionary War. His stepson Griffith Owen (1773-1780) learned clock-making from Godschalk and became an important clockmaker in his own right. Three generations of Hege clockmakers also worked in eastern Pennsylvania, including Jacob Hege (active 1790-1820), who made over 100 clocks in Lower Salford Twp., Montgomery Co., and Samuel Hege (active 1820s to 1840s), who worked in Franconia and Germantown. Hendrich Heilig (?-1775) emigrated in 1720 from Hannover, Germany to Hanover Twp., Montgomery Co. He was an uncle by marriage to David and Benjamin Rittenhouse.

Even more Mennonite clockmakers worked in Lancaster Co. Anthony W. Baldwin (1783-1867) of Lampeter learned clockmaking from his father-in-law Joseph Bowman, Sr. (?-1811), of New Holland and, in turn, taught clockmaking to John's son Joseph Bowman, Jr. (1799-1892), who was active in Strasburg until ca. 1850. John Erb (1814-ca. 1860) was an apprentice of Joseph Bowman, Jr., and worked in Conestoga Center. Christian Forrer (ca. 1737-1783) and Daniel Forrer (?-1780) were born in Switzerland and settled in Lampeter, where they made clocks for about 20 years, after which Christian moved to York Co. and Daniel (perhaps) to Virginia. Christian Huber (?-1789) worked in Reamstown; Isaac Hunchberger (1804-?) in West Earl; Jacob Hunsecker (1809-?) in East Donegal Twp.; Elias Leinbach (active 1801-16) in Bowmansville; and John Leinbach (active 1792-1798) in Reamstown. Samuel C. Stauffer (1757-1825) of Manheim is known for clocks that strike on the quarter-hour. Isaac Witwer worked in New Holland, ca. 1850-55.

The cabinetmakers who made the cases for these clocks are generally unknown, although apparently a Jacob Bachman (°furniture) occasionally made cases for A. W. Baldwin.　　　　　　　　　　　　　EB

James W. Gibbs, "Religious Sect Clockmakers, Part 1," *National Association of Watch and Clock Collectors Bulletin,* 167 (Dec. 1973), 44-47, and "Part 2" in vol. 168 (Feb. 1974), 168-74; Arthur Kroeger, "Kroeger Clocks," (n.d., n.p., mimeographed); Stacy B. C. Wood and Stephen E. Kramer, *Clockmakers of Lancaster County and their Clocks 1750-1850* (New York: Van Nostrand Reinhold, 1977).

Clothing. See Dress.

Colombia, Republic of (ME I:643), located on the nw. part of South America, was named after Christopher Columbus. The Spaniards discovered and settled it during the first 50 years of the 16th c. The

COLOMBIA

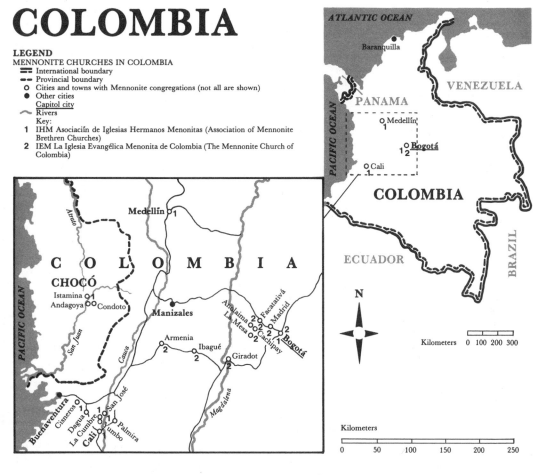

LEGEND

MENNONITE CHURCHES IN COLOMBIA
- ▬▬ International boundary
- ▬▬ Provincial boundary
- ○ Cities and towns with Mennonite congregations (not all are shown)
- ● Other cities
- <u>Capitol city</u>
- ﹏ Rivers

Key:
1 IHM Asociaciín de Iglesias Hermanos Menonitas (Association of Mennonite Brethren Churches)
2 IEM La Iglesia Evangélica Menonita de Colombia (The Mennonite Church of Colombia)

settlers implanted the Spanish language and the Roman Catholic religion, thus establishing cultural patterns and some of the country's ethnic characteristics.

Colombia has an estimated population of 32 million (1986). Its inhabitants are the descendants of white Europeans, black Africans, and native Indians. There is a common language, Spanish, spoken in all of the territory. In the small islands of San Andrés and Providencia in the Caribbean, English is also spoken. The relatively few Indian tribes speak their own dialects. Most of the population lives in urban centers, such as °Bogotá, Medellín, Cali, and Barranquilla. Colombians are by nature open, friendly, religious, and resourceful.

Colombia takes pride in cultivating the use of good Spanish. Many poets, essayists, and novelists have made outstanding contributions to literature. Gabriel García Márquez, a novelist, received the Nobel Prize in literature in 1982. The work of contemporary painters, such as Fernando Botero, Alejandro Obregón, Enrique Grau, and others, are universally recognized. Cartagena, the historic city founded in 1535 on the Atlantic coast, has been declared part of the cultural patrimony of the world by the United Nations. Bogotá, the capital (5 million inhabitants), is the cultural center of Colombia. It has two professional orchestras, several theater groups,

and several colleges and universities. There are several large daily papers (most cities have local papers), broadcasting stations, and three television channels. The rate of literacy in the country is 81 percent.

Colombia is rich in gold, platinum, copper, emeralds (most emeralds on the world market come from this nation), coal, and oil. The main agricultural products are coffee, bananas, and other fruits, flowers, and vegetables. The average yearly income was $1,430 (U.S.) in 1983.

Colombia is a representative democracy. The president is elected by popular vote every four years. He appoints the members of the cabinet, the governors of the different states and territories, and other important functionaries. Members of the two houses of Congress are freely elected by popular vote. A law approved in 1986 authorized the election of municipal mayors by popular vote.

The majority of Colombians have been baptized in the Roman Catholic church at an early age. Marriages and burials are usually performed by this church. However, there is complete freedom to practice any religion that does not endanger Christian morality.

There are no official statistics regarding the Protestant community. The estimates go from 2,500,000 to as few as 250,000. A recent survey conducted by one of the Protestant groups gives 350,000 as a more realistic calculation. This equals 1.16 percent of the total population.

There are four Anabaptist groups working in the country: Iglesia Evangélica Menonita de Colombia (an outgrowth of General Conference Mennonite mission work, begun 1945); Asociación de Iglesias de los Hermanos Menonitas (Mennonite Brethren, 1945); Iglesia Colombiana de los Hermanos (an outgrowth of mission work by the Brethren Church, Ashland, Ohio, 1973); and Comunidad Cristiana Hermandad de Cristo (Brethren in Christ, 1982). Together these groups have an approximate membership of 2,300 in 40 congregations served by 31 pastors. These churches devote themselves to evangelism, education, health, and social services. The Iglesia Evangélica Menonita de Colombia, and Asociación de Iglesias de los Hermanos, work together in the social service agency MENCOLDES (Fundación Menonita Colombiana para el Desarrollo, 1977) in cooperation with Mennonite Central Committee and the °Mennonite Economic Development Associates (MEDA).   HGVV

MWH (1978), 211-15; *GCM Handbook* (1988), 88, 91; *MB Yearbook* (1981), 113-14; Juhnke, *Mission* (1979), 147-61; *Brethren Encyclopedia* (1983), 324.

Colonialism and Foreign Missions. That foreign °missions have been influenced by colonialism is a well-established fact. This was especially true in the late 19th and early 20th c. when colonialism was at its peak and Mennonite foreign mission efforts were being established. Though this association came to have some negative consequences later, it also had some practical advantages. Missionary visas to the host countries were usually easy to obtain since political ties already existed between them and the sending colonial countries. Transportation was readily available, with missionaries sometimes riding on ships which facilitated trade between the two countries. Within the host country itself, compatriots (colonial administrators and missionaries) supported and assisted each other, though their foreign service was prompted by different motives.

In many instances foreign missions were established in African, Latin American, and Asian colonies when they still had a limited infrastructure. Missionaries played a substantial role in opening up the frontier. David Livingstone (1813-73), for example, spent so much time surveying southern and central Africa that his fellow missionaries were not sure if he was one of them or if he was a government surveyor.

To sustain themselves in these remote locations, especially in the early years, missionaries had to construct their own buildings. Labor and materials were relatively cheap, resulting in the construction of some large, even palatial, buildings. These buildings, for a combination of practical reasons, were grouped into what came to be known as compounds, which were not unlike the headquarters used by colonial administrators. Even the style of administration used by some missions was borrowed from colonial models.

The association between early missions and colonial governments also carried over into the area of °church-state relationships. The church was expect-

ed to sanction the acts of the state. In return the state did some favors for the church. Missionaries worked closely with many governments in the establishment of schools (°mission schools) and hospitals. Many officials in postcolonial governments of the late 20th c. were educated in missionary schools. This has had both positive and negative consequences.

Occasionally, missionaries became economic opportunists. This led to coining of the phrase, "They (missionaries) came to do good and ended up doing well."

In 1852, the first foreign Mennonite missionary work was carried out in Indonesia, a Dutch colony, by churches in the Netherlands. Missions which emanated from the Mennonite churches in the United States and Canada were less affected by the colonial association, because they had a tradition of separatist nonresistance, their governments were less involved in the overt colonialism of European countries, and because they did not become active in foreign mission until the early 20th c., when the colonial influence was subsiding. It is nevertheless apparent that North American Mennonite missions borrowed heavily from the models of earlier missionary work.

When colonialism came under severe criticism, particularly following World War II, missions were unavoidably implicated. The transition from colonial to home rule was difficult for missions, missionaries, and national churches. How were the leaders of these relatively young churches to take charge of a process which had been so heavily predicated on outside funding and leadership? At one stage some African churches called for a complete °moratorium on outside funding and staffing. Eventually better understandings were arrived at. In the end it can be said that termination of the colonial era has furthered the estblishment of indigenous churches. These churches are maturing and the former sending churches are increasingly working in a partnership relationship with them.   ES

Juhnke, *Mission* (1979) 26-27, 32-37, 53-54 (on mission compounds).

See also Liberation Theologies; Theologies from Impoverished Peoples.

Colorado (ME I:646). Clear evidence of Mennonite settlement in Colorado dates from ca. 1900. However, since Dunkers (Church of the °°Brethren) were there by the early 1870s, it is likely that small groups of Mennonites had entered the state by the 1880s.

Mennonite migration to Colorado continued to increase after World War II, with the largest concentrations arriving in the early 1950s and the late 1960s when hundreds of conscientious objectors were assigned to hospital work during the Korean conflict and the Vietnam War. By the late 1950s the General Conference Mennonite Church (GCM) and the Mennonite Brethren (MB) had established congregations in the Denver metropolitan area.

In 1987 there were nearly 1,800 baptized members of Mennonite congregations in the state. There were 17 Mennonite Church (MC) congregations with more than 1,100 members, 2 of which were dually affiliated with the General Conference Mennonite Church; 6 General Conference congregations with 300 members; and 4 Mennonite Brethren congregations with 370 members.

Mennonites are active in a variety of outreach ministries in Colorado. In 1987 Mennonite Board of Missions (MC) and Mennonite Health Resources administered or sponsored hospitals, medical centers, and nursing homes in La Junta, La Jara, Walsenburg, and Rocky Ford. A Voluntary Service (VS) unit was located at La Jara. Rocky Mountain Mennonite Camp (established in 1951) is located near Divide, Col. The General Conference Mennonite Church operates three VS units in the Denver area. Mennonite (MC, GCM, MB) congregations in Denver cooperate in sponsoring Mennonite Urban Ministries and an Mennonite Central Committee Thrift Shop and °SELFHELP Crafts store in Lakewood.   HU

MC Yearbook (1988-89), 19; Wittlinger, *Piety and Obedience* (1978), 147-48; *Brethren Encyclopedia* (1983), 324.

Comité Menonita de Acción Evangélica y Social en el Paraguay (Mennonite Committee for Evangelical and Social Action in Paraguay). See Mennonitisches Missions-Komitee für Paraguay.

Comity. Within the context of overseas mission, the term *comity* refers to arrangements mutually agreed upon by the mission organizations working within a given area or country. These agreements specify where each group is to carry out its ministries of witness and service.

Some advantages in such agreements are immediately evident, e.g., the dialogue and mutual respect inherent in the process of establishing comity arrangements; the distribution of missionary personnel and witness over as wide an area as possible; and the avoidance of overlapping and competition between several missions in a given area.

Comity arrangements, however, have also on occasion had some negative dimensions. They may foster an "empire mentality" with regard to a specific area and ethnic population which have become the exclusive domain of ministry for one particular mission. Comity arrangements may also facilitate the uncritical reproduction of a Western form of Christianity which, in a context of isolation, makes comparison and challenge difficult. They may leave people in the area little choice as to the Christian tradition they wish to adopt or follow.

Large scale inter-mission comity arrangements were largely characteristic of the era before World War II. Typical examples were China, India, and a variety of countries in Africa. By 1960, in Zaire (Belgian Congo), for example, there were more than 50 different Protestant missions at work, each with a separate and agreed-upon area of ministry within the country.

With the transition of leadership from missionary personnel to national pastors, however, comity arrangements have been by and large considered as a feature of the missionary era and no longer relevant or helpful for the church in its work. It is particularly in the rapidly growing overseas urban centers that denominations have quickly multiplied as church leaders have sought out fellow believers in the cities and encouraged them to meet and organize into congregations. A variety of Protestant denominations, which in large part reflect the different missions which have been at work in the country, are now usually found in the cities. It is in the rural areas where the impact of comity patterns are still often found. This is not due to commitment on the part of national church leaders to respect them but is simply the legacy left by missions which evangelized significant blocks of rural populations and planted churches of their denomination or tradition in the absence of any other denomination or confession.

There seems to have been a correlation between the presence of active interconfessional Christian councils and fairly detailed comity arrangements. The lack of such arrangements also seems to correlate with the absence of strong councils. It seems clear that comity arrangements have been born of active interdenominational cooperation and not vice versa.

Mennonite mission boards which have fielded personnel in areas where there were active Christian councils with comity agreements in place have generally respected them and have consulted with mission and church groups on the scene regarding their new areas of work. Roman Catholics have typically ignored Protestant comity arrangments they have found around the world. Protestants have usually returned the favor. This course of action has often lent itself in the past to competition and heated confrontation. With the transition from expatriate to national church leadership in more recent years, the interconfessional relations have tended to be less volatile in a number of areas of the world.   JEB

P. J. Malagar, *MC India* (1981), 36, 39.

See also Ecumenism; Inter-Mennonite Cooperation.

Comanche People. See Indians, North America.

Communauté des Frères Mennonites au Zaïre (Mennonite Brethren Church of Zaïre). See Église du Christ au Zaïre, Communauté des Églises de Frères Mennonites au Zaïre (CFMZA).

Communauté Evangélique Mennonite au Zaïre (Evangelical Mennonite Church of Zaïre). See Église du Christ au Zaïre, Communauté Evangélique Mennonite (CEM).

Communauté Mennonite au Zaïre (Mennonite Church of Zaïre). See Église du Christ au Zaïre, Communauté Mennonite au Zaïre (CMZA).

Communidad Cristiana (Christian Community), Spain. The Christian Communities of Burgos started in 1974 as an evangelistic movement among young people, under the leadership of Luis Alfredo Díaz, a Christian artist from Uruguay.

In 1978 José Gallardo came from Belgium, where he was pastor of the Spanish Mennonite Church. With other Christians from Burgos he founded the Communidad Cristiana of Quintanadueñas, a village 16 km. (10 mi.) north of Burgos. Since then it has been a center for the rehabilitation of drug addicts and delinquents. A wooden toy manufacturing enterprise was also started (later incorporated under the name Association of Christian Communities for the Rehabilitation of Marginal People, ACCOREMA) as well as a prison ministry. This Christian community is also part of the communities of Burgos, where Dennis Byler was one of the pastors in 1987. Dennis, with his wife Connie and three children, were sponsored by the Mennonite Board of Missions (MC) and the Shalom Covenant Communities. In 1987 the Christian Communities of Burgos consist of three congregations with a total of 200 baptized members with strong ties to the Mennonite church.   JG

MWH (1984), 124.

Comunidad Cristiana de los Hermanos Menonitas de España (**Mennonite Brethren Christian Community of Spain**) was officially organized in April 1982, with six members. The initial thrust began when Ernie and Elsie Friesen together with their son and his wife, Jim and Patty Friesen, arrived in Madrid in October, 1976. Albert and Margarit Schaberl from Austria joined them. A storefront meetingplace in the city district of Saconia was rented in March, 1977; a second church-planting effort began with the purchase of a storefront in the city district of Bellas Vistas in November 1980; a third church-planting effort began in Tres Cantos, fifteen kilometers to the north of Madrid, in June 1984.

In 1986 there were 12 members and nine missionaries in one congregation in Bellas Vistas, and the two mission points (in Saconia and Tres Cantos). RJP
MWH (1984), 124.

Communion (ME I:651; ME III:394). The primal act of the Christian church is its gathering to eat bread and drink wine in memory of Jesus. This ritual meal originated among the Jewish people as a reenactment of their exodus from Egyptian bondage. The Christian breaking of bread recalls Jesus' meals with seekers and friends before and after his resurrection (Mk 2:18-22; Mk 6:30-44; Lk 24:13-35; Jn 21:9-14) and, supremely, that Passover supper at which the Messiah announced a new covenant to be inaugurated by his death (Mk 14:12-25). The early Christians believed that even after his ascension the repeating of the meal Jesus had instituted at his death was a "communion of the body and blood of Christ" (1 Cor 10:16), i.e., a participation in his person and life.

It was not long before attempts were made to explain this mystery. Some (Irenaeus, fl. ca. 180-200; Cyril of Jerusalem, 315-86) emphasized the physical changing or conversion of the bread and wine as the means by which Christ is present; others (Clement of Alexandria, fl. ca. 200-215; Origen, ca. 185-254) concerned themselves more with the spiritual reality of this communion. At the time of the Protestant °Reformation the former interpretation dominated in the western church. It was one of the central concerns of the Reformation to restore eucharistic practice and belief to their primitive simplicity. This involved a denial that priest and sacrament cause Christ to be present by the performance of the ritual whether or not there was a response of personal faith. All the reformers taught that nothing could or needed to be added sacramentally to Christ's sacrifice on the cross. Many non-Lutheran reformers (Anabaptist, Reformed, Anglican) put forth the claim

that Christ could not be offered again because physically he was in heaven. Since the Lord's Supper was not a sacrifice, it was not to be celebrated at an altar but around a table.

Anabaptism as a separate church community came into existence in a celebration of the Lord's Supper in Zürich in 1525. Its leaders emphasized those medieval and Reformation beliefs concerning communion which they believed to have a basis in Scripture. There were three characteristics and three tendencies which appeared in varying degrees in most Anabaptist understandings of the Lord's Supper. The three characteristics were: (a) "Body of Christ" signifies not only the historical person of Jesus and not only the bread and wine, but also the °church. The church is the body of Christ because it is made up only of those who have personally covenanted with Christ and fellow believers in °baptism. In the breaking of bread this reality is recreated; in it Jesus' incarnation is prolonged through time. (b) The Lord's Supper is, inseparably, an act of remembrance of and thanksgiving for Jesus' suffering sacrifice for the world. It is a visible word by which the church "proclaims the Lord's death until he comes" (1 Cor 11:26). (c) It is a communion of the body and blood of Christ. The elements do not change, but in a gathering of believers who break bread in faith and love, there is an assured participation in Christ's saving presence.

The three tendencies of Anabaptist belief about communion are the following: (a) The relationship between God and humanity is unmediated; °grace cannot be caused by material means. It is the immediate work of the Spirit through the response of faith which unites us to Christ. Bread and wine remain outward signs of an inward relationship. (b) The person of Christ, more than the words of institution, is the source for understanding what happens in communion. The church is the extension of his incarnate life. This presence is renewed in the Lord's Supper. Since his ascension, the Lord's physical body is in heaven. Because he is fully human and fully divine, Christ can be present only in one place at a time in his humanity, but he is present everywhere in his divinity. (c) The Gospel of John is the preeminent source for Anabaptist eucharistic thought. From it comes the emphasis on Christ's ascension, the description of the Lord's Supper as a meal of love, and the inclusion of °feetwashing as the enactment of that love.

Certain of these characteristics and tendencies dominated each of the three regions in which Anabaptism originated. The most far-reaching reformation of the Lord's Supper took place among the °°Swiss Brethren. They placed their emphasis on the body of Christ as the church and on the memorial/thanksgiving character of communion (°Schleitheim Confession, articles 2, 3). Peter °°Walpot turned to rational arguments to prove the impossibility of the Catholic position and removed all mystery from communion (*TA Oberdtsch. II*, "Vom Abentmahl, 126-34, 154ff.). Balthasar °Hubmaier, the most original and sophisticated representative of the Swiss Anabaptist view of communion, argued that the most profound sign function of the Lord's Supper was that it represented the church's pledge to give up its life just as Christ had done (Hubmaier, *Schriften,*

104, 317-18). Thus communion became primarily an ethical event; not so much a means of grace as a response to grace.

Among South German Anabaptists, Hans °°Denck taught a mystical union with Christ which was symbolized by bread and wine but came about in the individual's willingness to suffer with Christ. Pilgram °Marpeck reacted against the emphasis on the exclusively human and inward reality of communion, insisted on divine initiative in the celebration, and emphasized the outward form of the celebration. For him, the Lord's Supper was not a static object but a dynamic event. In it the Holy Spirit takes the gathering of those who come in faith and love to break bread and unites it with Christ. Christ's incarnation is the model of how God reveals himself: he comes to us in outward realities to lead us to inward ones (CRR 2:76, 85, 99). Thus, our faith and the bread we share are made by the Spirit into a participation in Christ (CRR 2:194ff.; Marpeck, *Verantwortung,* in *Marbeck-Schwenckfeld,* ed. Loserth [1929], 501-515).

In Dutch and North German Anbaptism, °Menno Simons taught that it is by faith in the working of the Spirit rather than in the working of the sacrament that one receives Christ. The Supper is a memorial of Jesus' suffering and the renewal of the covenant made in baptism (Menno, *Writings,* 1870, bk. 1, 40-52). Dirk Philipszoon carried forward and expanded these beliefs in a systematic way (*Enchridion,* trans. Kolb, 69-96; *On the Incarnation,* BRN 10, 10-140). He emphasized that the communion we have with Christ is given to us when we are born again. The Lord's Supper is a moment within time and space when visible evidence is given of this communion. Through it the believer is assured of the grace of God. On the basis of Jn 6, Dirk claims that this communion is a spiritual eating and drinking of Christ's body and blood (*Enchiridion,* 57, 141). Though the church must come to the Lord's table forgiven of God and at peace with its own members, its communion is predominantly that of individuals with Christ rather than with each other.

Only fragmentary data exist to describe how these communities observed communion. The one complete order of service from the first generation of Anabaptists was composed by Hubmaier (*Schriften,* 355-64). The first extant minister's manuals with orders of service for communion date from the 19th century (Dahlem, 1807; Eby, 1841).

The second stage in Mennonite eucharistic thought and practice begins with the transition to an established movement. The two most influential °confessions of faith (Dordrecht in 1632 and the West Prussian [Flemish-Frisian-High German, later GCM] in 1660) perpetuate the plurality of Anabaptist eucharistic doctrines. The former articulates the memorial and covenant aspects (Loewen, *Confessions,* 67). The latter includes these but also teaches that Christ, "in his heavenly estate is the life-giving bread, food, and drink of our souls. In the keeping of this spiritual supper, Christ unites himself with all who truly believe" (Loewen, *Confessions,* 121/119). The Dordrecht Confession articulated beliefs which were to be carried to the new world by Swiss Mennonites; the West Prussian confession articulated those which were carried by North German Menno-

nites to Russia and to North America. Both confessions included the °ordinance of feetwashing.

This second period of Mennonite history led to the codifying of practices concerning communion. Hans de °°Ries and J. °°Gerrits van Emden wrote meditations on and instructions for the observance of the Lord's Supper (*Vijf Stichtelijcke Predicatien,* 1650, 37ff.). Leenaerdt °°Clock composed a prayer formulary in 1625 (*Formulier,* 60ff.). Its three communion prayers were used by Mennonites throughout Europe and are still used by the Amish in the late 20th century.

By the 17th c. it had become usual for Mennonites in northern Europe to celebrate communion twice a year while Mennonites in south Germany and Switzerland celebrated it once a year (Mast, *Letters,* 69). There is no extant rationale for the establishment of this practice. The following is an interpretive hypothesis: added to the undercurrent of fear of unworthy communion and obligatory confession beforehand, common through much of Christian history, was the Mennonite stipulation that believers had to be reconciled not only to God but to fellow Christians before they could commune. As communion for Anabaptists was a celebration of the church as the body of Christ, it could be observed only when the whole community was together and of one mind. As persecuted believers went into hiding and differing factions solidified, there could hardly be communion.

The first permanently institutionalized challenge to this practice and to the piety which underlay it came with the formation of the Mennonite Brethren Church (1859-60). Its emphasis on grace and the assurance of salvation as well as its adoption of the Baptist practice of monthly communion counteracted the dread and awe associated with the Lord's table. This spirit and practice have become evident in other Mennonite communities in the mid-20th century.

A description of communion practice and understandings among Mennonites in North America in the late 20th century includes the following: The traditionally °conservative (as opposed to revivalist) groups outside the large conferences have retained conventional forms and piety, often in a stern fashion. In the large conferences there has been a reductionism at work concerning the breaking of bread. The emphasis on mystical union with Christ among Russian Mennonites (Loewen, *Confessions,* MB 1903, 169-170; GCM 1881, 186; GCM 1930, draft 146, final text 306) has receded in both worship and theology (e.g., Loewen, *Confessions,* MB 1975, 177). In these groups, as well as in the Mennonite Church (MC), the teaching of the church as the body of Christ (implying renewal of covenant and church °discipline) has also receded, leaving only the memorial/thanksgiving aspect of the original threefold belief about the Lord's Supper.

This diminution of belief has come about in part due to the rationalism and individualism of both °Fundamentalist and °liberal Protestant influences on Mennonites. It has also come about through protest by church members against the inflexible ritual, legalistic spirit, and morbid tone of many communion services. In the past, ethical conformity in matters of detail was often the precondition of admission to the Lord's table. Intense reflection on Jesus' suffering was practiced by communicants in the hope of thereby becoming worthy of communion. In reaction, considerable change and experimentation have taken place in the mid-20th century. Close communion (limited to members of one's congregation or specific faith community) has all but disappeared, its departure hastened not only by opposition to earlier ethical stringency but also by the ecumenical spirit of the times. Innovative orders of service, characterized by a spirit of freedom and grace, have become common. The contraction of the Lord's Supper from an event unto itself (with a preparatory service) into a brief appendix to a regular Sunday worship service is now commonplace. The demand to admit to communion unbaptized children who are growing up in the care of the church is heard more loudly. Little theological or devotional reflection on a popular or academic level has guided this changing understanding of communion. The teaching of Anabaptist and early Mennonite theologians on the subject has almost been lost to memory. This loss is reflected in all of the theological summaries of the Lord's Supper written by Mennonites in recent years (Wenger, Friedmann, Kaufman, Finger). In the conservative districts of the Mennonite Church (MC) in the United States and in traditionalist General Conference (GCM) and Mennonite Brethren congregations in Canada, longstanding communion rituals have been retained, though often without attention to their shortcomings.

The spiritual and theological work of the °ecumenical movement has transcended 16th-c. formulations as the unassailable norm for how both Protestants and Catholics understood the Bible. Mennonite, like other Protestant, understandings of the Lord's Supper came into being in the controversies of the Reformation. In the late 20th century, Mennonites stand on the threshold of a revolution sure to be as significant for how the church breaks bread as was that of the 16th century.

In summary, the Mennonite interpretation of Christian belief concerning the Lord's Supper has the following traits: It is opposed to speculation about metaphysical changes in the elements, yet often rationalistic in its arguments against such speculations. It has a spiritualistic tendency which is manifest in its inability to make positive claims for the relationship in communion between bread and the presence of Christ. At the same time the traditional piety of participants in communion indicates belief in a mysterious reality beyond what Mennonite teaching can explain. The Mennonite interpretation of communion has emphasized the human more than the divine action of grace. This has sometimes been a way of countering claims for divine action which Mennonites deem to be unbiblical. More often it has issued from the conviction that ethical response is the most profound act of gratitude for grace.   JDR

Primary Sources: V. Dahlem, *Allgemeines und Vollständiger Formularbuch* (Neuwied: J. T. Haupt, 1807); Hans Denck, *Schriften*, 2 vols., ed. Georg Baring and Walter Fellmann (Gütersloh: C. Bertelsmann, 1959-60); Benjamin Eby, *Kurzgefaßte Kirchengeschichte und Glaubenslehre* (Scottdale: Mennonitische Verlagshandlung, n.d.); Peter Walpot, *Vom Abendmahl* in *TA Oberdtsch II*); J. Gerrits, *Vijf Stichtelijcke Predicatien*, 2nd ed. (Amsterdam: Gerrit van Goedesbergh, 1650); L. Clock, "Formulier Ethlicken Christlichen Gebaethe" in *Christliche Glaubens-Bekentnus*, ed. Tieleman Sittert (Amsterdam: Johan Paskovium, 1664); H. Rol, "Die Slotel van dat Secreet des Nachtmalls" in BRN 5; J. B. Mast, ed., *Letters of the Amish Division* (Oregon City, Ore.: C. J. Schlabach, 1950).

Secondary Sources: Torsten Bergsten, "Pilgram Marpeck und seine Auseinandersetzung mit Caspar Schwenckfeld," *Kyrkohistorisk 38 Aaarschrift*, 1957-58; Alvin J. Beachy, *The Concept of Grace in the Radical Reformation* (Nieuwkoop: B. de Graaf, 1977); Thomas N. Finger, *Christian Theology: An Eschatological Approach*, II (Scottdale, 1989); Hans-Jürgen Goertz, *Die Täufer* (Munich: C. H. Beck, 1980); Gordon F. Kaufman, *Systematic Theology: A Historicist Perspective* (New York: Charles Scribner's Sons, 1968); John D. Rempel, "Christology and the Lord's Supper in Anabaptism" (ThD diss., St. Michael's College, Toronto School of Theology, U. of Toronto, 1986); George H. Williams, *The Radical Reformation* (Philadelphia: Westminster, 1962); Christof Windhorst, "Das Gedächtnis des Leidens und Pflichtzeichen brüderlichen Liebe" in *Umstrittenes Täufertum, 1525-1975*, ed. Hans-Jürgen Goertz (Göttingen: Vandenhoeck und Ruprecht, 1975).

See also Bishop ("My Good Bishop" feature); Christology; Evangelical Mennonite Conference; Mennonite Church (MC); Old Order River Brethren; Worship, Public.

Communion Mennonite d'Haiti (Mennonite Communion of Haiti) was organized in 1976. Rodrigue Debrosse is the founder and superintending pastor of the six congregations, which are located in southern Haiti in the rural communities of Mussotte, Masson, Belle Rivière, Bédouze, Chaulette, and Javel. In 1987 these six congregations had a total of 500 baptized members. Two primary schools, in the Mussotte and Masson communities, are a ministry of the Mennonite churches in those communities. The total enrollment has varied between 500 and 700 students since 1985. The Mennonite Communion of Haiti has received some assistance over the years from Mennonite churches and individuals in the United States, including Sonlight Mission, an independently constituted group of Mennonites, largely from Pennsylvania and Ohio, and Mennonite Central Committee.

The Mennonite Communion of Haiti recognizes, in addition to the superintending pastor, seven other pastors as church leaders. Two of these church leaders are also involved as school teachers. The Mennonite Communion of Haiti is a member of the Concile des Églises Evangéliques d'Haiti (Council of Evangelical Churches of Haiti).   ESto

MWH (1984), 78.

See also Église Mennonite Sonlight Mission.

Communism (ME I:655). Writing in the 1950s, when communism was seen in monolithic terms, Cornelius Krahn pointed out that one-third of all Mennonites had been directly affected by communism through the loss of homes, life, and property, and many others were affected indirectly. Further, the communist success in China had meant the end of Mennonite missions there. It is a fair generalization to say that for a major part of the Mennonites of Russian and Prussian background in North America, communism still tends to be equated with anarchy, with Stalinism, with war and suffering.

This perception has remained, due to the continued persecution of "our own people" (relatives and Mennonites in the Soviet Union), due to the information about the Khrushchev campaign to eliminate religion, and the ongoing information about prisoners of conscience and less extreme forms of discrimination. Mennonite perceptions were influenced by the anticommunist movements in North America and popular fears of communist expansion that fed the Cold War.

Initial interpreters of the Soviet communist impact, e.g., B. H. °°Unruh, writing in the 1930s, tended to see in Nazism (°National Socialism) a bulwark against communism, which led him to reformulations of Mennonite distinctives that allowed military participation against this evil. In the 1950s such scholars as J. Lawrence Burkholder, Donovan Smucker, and Melvin Gingerich analyzed communist philosophies in the context of Mennonite efforts to articulate a peace position in the midst of the Cold War. The general Mennonite attitude to communism remains a major obstacle to developing a peace practice with integrity, since the fears engendered by personal and group trauma, plus the propaganda impact of western Sovietology which remains heavily partisan, has caused many Mennonites to vote for politicians of the peace-through-military-and-nuclear-strength school, while seeking personal exemption from military service or supporting peace efforts in Asian, African, and Latin American settings.

Nevertheless, both the communist practice and Mennonite perceptions of it have changed to some extent. Mennonite workers encountered communist societies firsthand through relief and development work, and thus were forced to compare differences between the Soviet Union, East European countries, and Central America. The usual approach was to maintain a political neutrality, for example, to witness to peace in Vietnam by giving aid and being present with personnel before and after the change of government in 1975.

Thus far, Mennonite reflections on communist diversity, or efforts to understand communism's persistent appeal to underprivileged peoples, have resulted in an emphasis on the possibility of Christian witness in word and deed in communist societies, but communist or even other socialist theories of development (an essential part of communist self-understanding) have not been taken seriously by Mennonites working in °development efforts outside Europe and North America. Growing experience in Eastern Europe and China through exchange programs has led to some ecumenical dialogue with churches now forced to be voluntaristic churches in an aggressively secular society. Mennonite congregations are present in the following communist countries in 1988: Soviet Union, German Democratic Republic, Hungary, Ethiopia, Angola, Nicaragua, Cuba, and, as part of the Three Self movement, China.

WWS

Kauffman/Harder, *Anabaptists Four C. Later* (1975), 143-44.

See also Koejemans, Anthoon Johan; Marxism; Political Attitudes; Socialism; Union of Soviet Socialist Republics.

Communities. See Hutterian Brethren; Shalom Covenant Communities.

Community (ME I:656). The phrase, "the Mennonite community," is probably second only to "the Mennonite church" as the most prevalent term used by Mennonites and others to refer to the Mennonite phenomenon. This suggests that the term *community*, however it is defined, has central significance for the Mennonites. A brief review of the term and related concepts, however, is necessary before the subject of "Mennonites and community" is discussed.

Social Science Definition of Community. Even though it has a long and distinguished career in social science, the term *community* has acquired no unified definition (Reiss, Warren, Kasarda, and Janowitz). There is also little agreement on how to conceptualize community (Polsby). One helpful approach is to distinguish between normative and descriptive community types. The normative perspective defines community as a social system characterized by certain types of goals, relationships, and processes ranging from the utopian to the actual. Clearly the criteria for defining and studying community derive from a value system, or a paradigm based on personal preference or value commitment.

The descriptive approach attempts to utilize objective and scientific assumptions and criteria to define, as well as to analyze, the nature and function of community. An exasperating circular dilemma has resulted from this approach, because community has to be defined by the scientist before it can be studied or observed, and as yet, no single theory has succeeded in becoming accepted as the dominant one. Even the attempts to define the various descriptive approaches are in no danger of convergence. The most general descriptive approach assumes that community has: (1) some type of delineation in space and time; (2) a semblance of being a social system, if in miniature; (3) some unified objective, system of objectives, or goals toward which the members of the collectivity strive. The most generally used definitions under this second rubric include: (1) the ecological approach, in which "all individuals, their interrelationships and institutions, and their social systems can be allocated to territorial space" (Reiss, 122), and (2) the social systems approach, defined as "the smallest territorial system which encompasses the major features of society, that is, a society in miniature" (Reiss, 125).

Although a mass of important information and insights have been produced by the descriptive approach, especially by community studies such as *Middletown, USA, Yankee City,* few substantive theories about community have emerged which could be scientifically tested. The only exception to the preceding statement concerns studies of community change, as, for example, Albert Hunter's description of an urban area which had been studied twenty-five years earlier (Hunter, 1975). This latter approach provides a basis for evaluating societal change in general.

Different has been the writing on normative approaches to community, which, though less amenable to scientific testing, has become the dominant sociological literature on community. Here can be listed most of the masters of community theory, including Ferdinand Tönnies, Emile Durkheim, Charles Horton Cooley, Robert Redfield, Charles P. Loomis, and others.

These scholars and many others have subscribed

to a qualitative approach to community, focusing on the quality of human relationships (e.g., personal and intimate), the meaning of the individual in relationship to the group, the way the individual and group influence and create each other, and the way values and traditions function in groups. The normative approach to community is really an attempt to understand more fully the nature of human society, and it uses the concept of community as a metaphorical tool to manage and focus the data. The major conclusion derived from the normative community literature is that community is lost or in danger of being lost. Recent scholars, such as Hunter, retort that neighboring and similar elements of community are not necessarily decreasing in the city.

The Mennonite society has been interpreted by social scientists as a prototype of community usually from the normative point of view. Hence Loomis and Beegle, John C. Bennett, E. K. Francis, and John A. Hostetler, to name a few recent scientists, have studied the Mennonites and described them as retaining the traits of an authentic community, meaning thereby some type of achievement of "primary" type relationships, with mutual support and having a common bond, goals, and history. Driedger and Redekop describe the "Community Study Approach" as one of the major ways that has been used in studying Mennonites in recent years (1983). We turn now to analysis of how Mennonites have related to the concept of community.

Mennonites and Community. *Historically.* Soon after their emergence as a utopian movement, Mennonites began to build enclaves of like-minded persons committed to the same beliefs, ideologies, and goals. Hence the Mennonites in Switzerland, France, Germany, Austria, Holland, Prussia, and Russia proceeded to live in geographically isolated regions. Some of these emerged into full-fledged "commonwealths" in the Mennonite colonies in Russia, Canada, Mexico, and Latin America (Rempel, Kreider, Redekop). The settlements in Pennsylvania, Ohio, and elsewhere have more often been defined as Mennonite communities (Hostetler, Fretz). Recent °sociological studies of Mennonites include Jean Séguy's *Les Assemblées Anabaptistes-Mennonites de France* (1977) and Esther Epp-Tiessen's *Altona* (1982).

A serious conceptual problem emerges, however. Unless one takes a normative approach, it is almost impossible to discuss the Mennonites historically as communities, because of unclarity as to what definition of community one uses. Further, the Mennonites will hardly conform to any scientific definition of community, for they are simultaneously more and less than any sociological definition of community. Mennonites have never been defined by delimited geographical boundaries, nor seen as a microsocial system by scientists or Mennonites.

Mennonites have cohered around an ideological basis (religious system of theology and practice), which provided the dynamic for developing a historical consciousness has been characterized as an ethnic group consciousness, although that term also has its limitations, as will be defined below (Peachey; Redekop, 1984). Hence community can only be utilized, whether by members or outside students, as a metaphor or label when talking about Mennonites.

Ideologically, Mennonites have been concerned about building community, if it is normatively defined. Such concepts as church, congregation, fellowship, *Gemeinde, Gemeinschaft,* colony of heaven, all allude to dimensions of the ideological community which Mennonites have espoused. Menno himself said, "What is the church of Christ?—A community of saints" (Menno, *Writings,* 742). The church, defined as that group of persons which has committed itself by repentance and confession of faith to each other, is thus the "Mennonite community."

Equating the visible, sociological, and especially the rural aspects of Mennonite experience with the church of Christ and the community of saints, however, has been the great temptation in the life of Mennonite peoples, and, we might add, indicates a capitulation to sociological community. Thus the "rural bias" of Mennonite life and faith, as it has expressed itself in the Germanic Mennonite tradition, especially in Europe, Russia, North America, and Latin America; and the assumptions that Mennonite faith could survive best in the rural arena, are illustrative (ME III:619 on "Mennonite Community" and "Mennonite Community Association"; cf. Redekop, 1985).

The bulk of American as well as European Mennonites have lived in rural and village situations, and have formed enclaves of spatially proximate families and congregations. Especially the °conservative Mennonites, such as the Old Order Mennonites or Hutterites in North America, Russian Mennonites living in "commonwealths" in Russia, Paraguay, Canada, Brazil, Mexico, and Bolivia, to name a few, have expressed aspects of the community, but as indicated above, have not done so in a full sense because the ethnic dimension needs to intersect the analysis. The Mennonite movement, from its inception, has been derived from a common religious faith, as transmitted through time by the story of °persecution, °martyrdom, rejection, peculiarity, and concept of biblical °discipleship.

Thus an ethnic dimension has emerged, which possibly describes the Mennonites better than community, if by ethnicity is meant the development of a consciousness of belonging based on an ideological commitment. This consciousness has contributed to the cohesion resulting in such common subcultural aspects as °dress, °architecture, speech (°dialect literature; °German language) and endogamous °marriage patterns, to list only a few (Francis; Redekop, 1984). But this ethnic dimension has always transcended spatial, i.e., local, community boundaries and can be characterized better as a people which knows no boundaries or nationality. Seeking lodging among Mennonites while traveling ("Mennoniting your way") across continents is a contemporary expression of this awareness.

A helpful approach is to observe how community has been used as a modifier of Mennonitism itself. One such is the term "community of discernment" which refers to the fellowship of believers as the source of °biblical interpretation (Burkholder, Lind). Another is "disciple community" or "covenant community," which emphasizes the way the collective group of believers exercises admonition and °discipline upon its members, who "have voluntarily entered into the communion of Christ Jesus" (Menno, *Writings*, 415) (Bauman). The "serving community" has been used to emphasize the °mutual aid, °service, and caring aspect of Mennonite faith. Other terms include the "holy community" (Bender), the "colony of heaven" (Hershberger), or the "gathered community" (Gross, 61).

Although this does not exhaust the list, it illustrates the range of perspectives from which community is defined, and also the metaphorical content. There is no unitary way in which community can be used to describe Mennonites and it is probably precisely because of its wholistic and metaphorical nature that the word *community* continues to be relevant and useful in addressing Mennonite issues. An analytical look at the referents of "community" would be a possible focus for future research.

Community as Metaphor for Anabaptism-Mennonitism. Mennonites have been defined (even accused) as having been communistic, socialistic, communitarian, and utopian (Klassen, Clasen, Goertz). Consequently, the Münsterites are now considered a part of the Anabaptist movement, along with other revolutionary groups (°historiography). These terms, and others described above, all attempt to point to, and explicate, the essential nature of the Anabaptist-Mennonite phenomenon. How is community helpful as a term to help define it? As indicated above, the scientific definition of community has been a cripple from birth. Thus community must be seen more as a metaphor than an exact description. What is the reality it points to?

(1) The church of Christ, as it is expressed in the unique theology and faith of the Anabaptist-Mennonite protest. Here the Mennonite "community of faith" is central, and this orientation is increasingly relevant as new "converts" or members are being brought into the body from various subcultural and nationality groups.

(2) The Mennonite congregation as community. Anabaptism-Mennonitism has been identified as congregational, as insisting that the reality of the Christian faith is structured and expressed in the local congregation. Here the emphasis is on °polity, or how faith is ordered. The local body of believers as the gathered community defines how the term community is used. This dimension comes close to the sociological definition of community, because of its identifiable and spatial references, but it goes beyond either the ecological or social-system definition of community. But it is possible to talk about the Mennonite community when the reference is the congregation in its observable social and religious aspects.

(3) The community of a religious people. The narrow road that Anabaptism has preached has meant that the movement did not spread to all of society as had originally been assumed. Hence a minority structure emerged, which has produced a self-conscious people, determined to live faithfully according to their confession and commitments. As indicated above, this has produced a people conscious of their past, present, and future (Gordon), and thus it is possible to refer to this religious ethnicity as the Mennonite community. But it does not imply that the Mennonites were only an ethnic group; religious

faith has been the hinge of their existence (Redekop, 1984).

(4) Mennonites as a communal people. Anabaptists and Mennonites from the beginning were reported to have resisted being defined as communists. This, however, bears further analysis, since newer research indicated Anabaptism has been motivated by communistic factors, as witness the Hutterites, Münsterites, and the increasing intentional community movement in contemporary North American, European, and Latin American contexts. The evidence is mounting rapidly, that if the Anabaptists were not indeed communistic by definition, they have adhered to a communal ethic from the beginning, with communitarian expressions. This communal ethic informed their personal, social, and religious existence, in which the motivation of the individual was subordinated to the collective, not only in material, but in other areas as well. The central idea seems to have been °°*Gelassenheit* or yieldedness to the will of Christ to love and serve the neighbor, whether a fellow believer or a nonbeliever (Cronk, Smucker). This concept influenced Anabaptist-Mennonites as they adjusted to the major social, political, economic, and educational institutions. Mennonites are consequently, according to this approach, better defined as a religious communal society than as a community.   CWR

Articles by Harold Bauman, Leonard Gross, Millard Lind, and Donovan Smucker in *Kingdom, Cross and Community*, ed. J. R. Burkholder and Calvin Redekop (Scottdale, 1976); Harold S. Bender, *These are My People* (Scottdale, 1962); John W. Bennett, *Hutterian Brethren: The Agricultural Economy and Social Organization of a Communal People* (Stanford U. Press, 1967); J. Lawrence Burkholder, "The Peace Churches as Communities of Discernment," *Christian Century*, 80 (Sept. 4, 1963), 1072-75; Claus-Peter Clasen, *Anabaptism: A Social History* (Ithaca: Cornell U. Press, 1972); Charles Horton Cooley, *Human Nature and the Social Order* (Glencoe: The Free Press, 1922); Sandra Cronk, "*Gelassenheit*: The Rites of the Redemptive Process in the Old Order Amish and Old Order Mennonite Communities:" (PhD diss., U. of Chicago, 1977); cf. *MQR*, 65 (1981), 5-44; Leo Driedger and Calvin Redekop, "Sociology of Mennonites," *JMS*, 1 (1983), 33-63; Emile Durkheim, *The Division of Labor in Society* (Glencoe: The Free Press, 1947); Esther Epp-Tiessen, *Altona: The Story of a Prairie Town* (Altona: D. W. Friesen and Sons, 1982); E. K. Francis, *In Search of Utopia* (Altona: D. W. Friesen and Sons, 1955); Hans-Jürgen Goertz, *Alles gehört Allen* (Munich: C. H. Beck, 1984); John A. Hostetler, *Amish Society* (1980); Guy F. Hershberger, *The Way of the Cross in Human Relations* (Scottdale, 1958); Albert Hunter, "The Loss of Community: An Empirical Test through Replication," *American Sociological Review*, 40, no. 5 (Oct. 1975); John S. Kasarda and Morris Janowitz, "Community Attachments in Mass Society," *American Sociological Review*, 39, no. 3 (June, 1974); James Peter Klassen, *The Economics of Anabaptism* (London and The Hague: Mouton and Co., 1964); Robert Kreider, "Anabaptist Conception of the Church in the Russian Mennonite Environment," *MQR*, 25 (1951), 17-34; Charles P. Loomis and J. Allan Beegle, *Rural Social Systems* (Englewood Cliffs: N. J.: Prentice Hall, 1951); Paul Peachey, "Identity Crisis Among American Mennonites," *MQR*, 42 (1968), 243-59; Nelson W. Polsby, "Community," *International Encyclopedia of the Social Sciences* (New York: Macmillan, 1968); Calvin Redekop, "Anabaptism and the Ethnic Ghost," *MQR*, 58 (1984), 133-46; Calvin Redekop, "The Mennonite Romance with the Land," in *Visions and Realities*, ed. Harry Loewen (Winnipeg: Hyperion Press, 1985); Robert Redfield, *The Little Community* (Chicago: U. of Chicago Press, 1955); Albert J. Reiss, Jr., "The Sociological Study of Communities," *Rural Sociology*, 24 (June 1959); David G. Rempel, "The Mennonite Colonies in New Russia: A Study of their Settlement and Economic Development, from 1789 to 1914," (PhD diss., Stanford University, 1933); Jean Séguy, *Les Assemblées Anabaptistes-Mennonites de France* (The Hague: Mouton and Co. 1977); Ferdinand Tönnies, *Community and Society* (East Lansing: Michigan State University Press, 1957); Roland L. Warren, "Toward a Non-Utopian Normative Model of the Community," *American Sociological Review*, 35, no. 2 (April 1970).

Community Health Work involves much interdisciplinary collaboration. Florence Nightingale (1820-1910), often thought of as the mother of modern nursing, was a true community health worker. She received her training from Theodor Fliedner at Kaiserwerth in Germany and he received his nursing ideas from early Mennonite °°deaconesses of Holland as well as from the work of Elizabeth Fry, a Quaker social worker. Florence Nightingale was not a nurse who just cared for the ill or carried out treatments to cure. She did the interdisciplinary work of community health, both in the hospital and community setting. She was a social worker, caring for patients, spouses, and families; an environmentalist, with her fresh-air policies; a nutritionist, developing central kitchens in hospitals; a statistician, with her data analysis; and a nurse and teacher. These and more are the components of community health work.

Community health work is more than just providing health care in the community setting. Community health work is to improve the health of all in the community through prevention of illness and health promotion, with a focus on the physical, biological, social, psychological, and environmental health of a population group. Primary health care, or essential health care, made universally accessible to individuals and families by acceptable means, with their full participation, and at a cost that the community and country can afford, is the nucleus for the overall social and economic development of the community.

Patterns of community health work should include a minimum of education concerning prevailing health problems and the methods of identifying, preventing, and controlling them; promotion of an adequate food supply and proper nutrition; basic sanitation; promotion of an adequate supply of safe drinking water; basic maternal and child health care, including family planning; prevention and control of locally endemic diseases; immunization against the major infectious diseases; appropriate treatment of common diseases and injuries; and the provision of essential drugs.

Community health workers must in everything they do keep in mind the culture they are serving. This calls for adaptable people, even in North America, where one can serve many different cultures in the same community. Community health workers in all situations must do two things: (1) Take careful account of the current practices and resources of the people, being careful to value and keep all that is good and constructive. (2) As much as possible, work with the people in making necessary changes to help them maintain control of the power for the changes they want. Things that make persons dependent on outside resources instead of making them involved in the process of improving their own health are short-sighted.

Community health workers encounter many situations where °human rights and freedoms are in jeopardy. Assuming health-care is a right, community health workers have the responsibility to be advocates for individuals, families, and groups; to identify and rectify gaps in health-care services; and to influence health and social policies that are inconsistant with this basic right. Communities also have the right and the responsibility to identify their own health needs and to negotiate regarding priorities for intervention and program development.

It is impossible here to describe all the community health work being done today by the many branches of Mennonites. Mennonite four-year colleges that give a BS degree do include community health work as part of nursing, social work, nutrition, and community development curricula.

The Eastern Mennonite Board of Missions first sent missionaries to East Africa in 1934. One of these missionary couples was sent, prior to going to the mission field, to the National Bible Institute for Missions in New York City for one semester to learn first aid, to study anatomy, to learn about health in other countries, and to learn how to meet the simple health-care needs of the missionary families and African people. One year later a physician was sent to open the first medical program. The emphasis, as in the United States, was on curative rather than preventive medicine. This emphasis continued until the 1970s.

The first community health work of the Mennonite Church (MC) took place at the tuberculosis sanitarium in °°La Junta, Col. The first planning for this work is recorded in 1903 in the °°*Herald of Truth*. The Mennonite Church also sent missionaries to India in the late 1800s. Although community health work was not being called by that name then, the events recorded in mission history include harnessing the Mahanadi River for irrigation purposes, constructing a dam, and digging a canal. These activities today would be called community health work.

Mennonite Central Committee and other branches of Mennonites are active in community health and °development work. Over the years many Mennonites trained as physicians, social workers, environmentalists, nurses, agriculturalists, nutritionists, and support personnel have worked in emergency °relief, °disaster aid, medical care, nutrition, °mental health care, °refugee resettlement, community development, and teaching of primary health care in community settings around the world.

Community health activities change according to different situations, changing technology, and changing social values. The goals, however, remain the same throughout the world: to reduce the amount of disease, premature death, discomfort, and disability.   JL

American Nurses Association, *Standards of Community Health Nursing Practice* (Kansas City: American Nurses Association, 1986); Christian Health Declaration, in *Journal of Christian Medical Society* (Brunswick, Ga.: Medical Assistance Program, 1981); Lena Dietz and Arvelia Lehozky, *History and Modern Nursing* (Philadelphia: F. A. Davis Co., 1967); John A. Lapp, *India* (1972); M. Stanhope and J. Lancaster, *Community Health Nursing* (St. Louis, Toronto, Princeton: C. V. Mosby Co., 1984); Maude Swartzendruber, *The Lamp in the West* (Newton: United Printing, 1975); World Health Organization *A Guide to Curriculum Review for Basic Nursing Education, Orientation to Primary Health Care and Community Health* (Geneva: WHO, 1985); World Health Organization, *Primary Health Care: Report of the International Conference on Primary Health Care, Alma-Ata, USSR* (Geneva, Switzerland, 1978).

See also Health Services; Missions.

Concentration Camps (ME I:662). Governments have at all times attempted to suppress and eliminate unpopular persons (through imprisonment, ghetto, exile). At the turn of the 19th to the 20th c., the practice of combining larger groups of people into "concentration camps" for the purpose of dominating them or for misusing them as hostages began (Spain in Cuba, 1895; United States in Mindanao [Philippines], 1900; England in the Boer War, 1901). Whereas concentration camps in countries with a democratic, rule-of-law constitution can be maintained only temporarily, due to the protests of the population, totalitarian states (Soviet Union, Germany from 1933 to 1945, military dictatorships or "one-party-states") grasp at this method permanently in order to isolate or to terrorize (supposed) opponents on racist, idealistic, or political grounds; to exploit labor forces; and, in the worst case, to annihilate entire groups of people (genocide). Concentration camps are just such an instrument of power for depriving the rights of and exterminating opponents and for the intimidation of the people.

In only one case did Mennonites in Germany under °National Socialism come into some contact with a concentration camp. In Stutthof, located approximately 30 km. (20 mi.) east of Danzig (Gdansk), near a main Mennonite settlement area, a concentration camp was set up in 1939. From here, in the later war years, prisoners were sent as laborers to surrounding farms, among them Mennonite farms. According to oral reports, these laborers were as a rule treated fairly by Mennonite employers; on the other hand, Mennonites expressed no concern about the concentration camps, nor did they render resistance of any kind. In the years 1973 and 1980 German Mennonite youth organized work camps on the terrain of this former Stutthof, within the framework of Aktion Sühnezeichen, a German Protestant peace service organization.

Together with millions of other people Mennonites suffered in the concentration camps of the Soviet Union. In the 1920s and 1930s, chiefly men (the more prosperous farmers, preachers, teachers) were arrested; as a rule they never returned. In the World War II and following, Mennonites were exiled into central Asia as members of the German minority; many of them were put into camps. Recently, leading members of Christian church bodies judged to be illegal were sentenced to long and often multiple terms in concentration camps.

Today there are, in many countries of Africa, Asia, and South America, arrangements comparable to concentration camps for the liquidation of alleged political opponents. It is not known whether Mennonites have to suffer in these camps; certainly in some countries Mennonites, as members of an ethnic or tribal minority (Chinese Mennonites in Indonesia, Brethren in Christ in Zimbabwe), are victims of measures of suppression. The internment of people of Japanese ancestry in the United States during World War II, to whom Mennonites, among others, ministered; or the frequently wretched or brutal treatment of prisoners-of-war in World War II by Germans, Japanese, and Allies (in Germany in the summer of 1945); cannot, strictly speaking, be compared to actual concentration camps.   PJFo

Andrzej J. Kamiński, *Konzentrationslager 1896 bis heute* (Stuttgart: W. Kohlhammer, 1982); Eugen Kogon, *Der SS-Staat* (Frankfurt a. Main: Europäische Verlagsanstalt, 1846); Horst Gerlach, "Stutthof und die Mennoniten" in *Mennoniten im Dritten Reich,* ed. D. G. Lichdi (Weierhof, 1977), 237-48; Herta Neufeld, *Im Paradies der Arbeiter und Bauern* (Hannover: Karl-F. Bangemann Verlag, 1986); G. Fast, *Im Schatten des Todes* (Winnipeg: Regehr's Printing, 1956); Hans Rempel, *Waffen der Wehrlosen* (Winnipeg: CMBC, 1976); Gerhard Hamm, *Du hast uns nie verlassen* (Wuppertal: Brockhaus-Verlag, 1978); Anita Priess, *Verbannung nach Sibirien* (Steinbach, Man.: Derksen Printers, 1979); Olga Rempel, *Einer von vielen* (Winnipeg: CMBC, 1979); Gerhard Lohrenz, *Lose Blätter* (Winnipeg: Christian Press, 1974); annual reports and country reports by Amnesty International.

See also Persecution; Spetskomandantura.

Concern Pamphlets Movement. *Concern* is the name given to a series of pamphlets initiated by a group of young American Mennonite graduate students, relief workers, and missionaries who met in Amsterdam in 1952 to address issues confronting the Mennonite church in Europe. Although the "Concern Group" preferred not to be known as an organization or even as a fellowship with defined membership, the initiating participants consisted of Irvin Horst, David Shank, Orley Swartzendruber, John W. Miller, Paul Peachey, Calvin Redekop, and John Howard Yoder. They felt led to further discussions focusing upon the condition of the American Mennonite church in relation to its founding principles as represented by the "Anabaptist Vision."

It is difficult to characterize Concern as a group because of its informal way of working. For a number of years Concern held annual retreats but elected no officers. The Concern pamphlet series appeared without an announced editor, though an editorial secretariat and an editorial council appeared with issue no. 5 in 1958. Concern's reluctance to define itself seems to have been deliberate. It preferred not to add to the organizational structures of the Mennonite church, which were considered excessive. Ambiguity regarding Concern's identity led to recurring internal questions as to what Concern is and gave rise to external fears that it might become an alienating movement or even a dissenting church. Eventually suspicions were allayed somewhat as internal dynamics demonstrated less than unanimity among its participants. As its early supporters scattered and assumed professional duties, and as publication tended to take precedence over fellowship, Concern came to be remembered primarily for its pamphlet series.

In order to understand Concern, we must recall theological developments following World War II. With respect to Mennonite theology, the dominating themes were set by the °"Anabaptist vision" as articulated by the first generation of American Anabaptist-Mennonite scholars, of which Harold S. °Bender may be considered the most influential advocate. Early participants in Concern were young second-generation Mennonite scholars who, having received their undergraduate education at Mennonite institutions, were committed to the extension of theology based upon Anabaptist studies.

Simultaneously, major Protestant denominations in

Europe and America engaged in theological reconstruction with great creativity and intensity. The postwar period produced such famous European theologians as Karl Barth, Emil Brunner, and Rudolf Bultmann, and such outstanding American theologians as Reinhold Niebuhr, H. Richard °Niebuhr, and Paul Tillich. The World Council of Churches as well as major denominations engaged in studies of all aspects of church life from both historical and biblical perspectives. Theological thinking at that time was sweeping and thorough, as the church sought to come to terms with existential philosophies and monumental political developments. It was assumed that Protestant theology only in the grand tradition of theological systems could stand over against such threatening ideologies as fascism, communism, and such cultural tendencies as secularism and empiricism.

The Concern group was affected by theological postwar developments by virtue of the fact that several of its initiating participants studied under Karl Barth, Emil Brunner, and Oscar Cullmann. Others participated in ecumenical discussions about church renewal. Thus within the European theological context, Mennonite students were led to ask fundamental questions about Mennonite theology, questions having to do with the nature of the church, its mission, its polity, and its relation to Christendom and society at large.

An examination of the early issues of the pamphlet series would give some indications of major themes and Concern's point of view. In the first pamphlet (1954), Paul Peachey presented an article titled "Toward an Understanding of the Decline of the West." This article illustrates both the manner and the content of Anabaptist-Mennonite thinking at that time. It was ideological in manner and sectarian in content. It was ideological in the sense that it attempted to bring all relevant considerations together in relatively simple, comprehensible, and uncompromising terms; and it was °sectarian in the sense that it relied upon the methodologies and sharp antitheses of Ernst Troeltsch in *The Social Teachings of the Christian Churches.*

In one grand sweep, Peachey attributed the "Decline of the West," to the "dilution of christianity itself rather than to the secularization of culture in general." Such sectarian interpretation of western history rests upon Troeltsch's typology in which the church-type and the sect-type were thought to represent fundamental and inexorable alternatives facing Christendom. The mission of Concern was to develop a consistent sectarian theology and a practical polity based upon Anabaptist sectarian principles.

In the same pamphlet John Howard Yoder offered a seminal article entitled "The Logic of the Place of the Disciple in Society," in which he set out some of the assumptions of a sectarian ethic, such as the lordship of Christ, °discipleship, and separation from the world. Without apologies and without concessions to those who commonly interpreted withdrawal as personal conviction or "talent," Yoder advocated "social withdrawal" as a consequence of the uncompromising ethic of Christ. "The Anabaptist-Mennonite position of 'dissent' represents an historical incarnation of an entirely different view of the Chris-

tian life, of the work and nature of the church and fundamentally also the meaning of redemption."

Although the development of a consistent Mennonite sectarian theology persisted, a diffusion of interests and points of view characterized later pamphlets. Ideological consistency waned in the 1960s as problems became increasingly practical in nature, and as authors were featured from a rather broad spectrum of Mennonite life. Eventually non-Mennonites found their way into Concern's pages. Reprints from such prominent theologians as Karl Barth, Edmund Perry, and Hans-Rüdi Weber were featured. Even such an occasional problem as "the meaning of Christmas" merited an entire issue (no. 16, 1968). Sometimes articles reflected a tendency toward self-criticism. As reported in pamphlet number 3 (1956), the leaders, having returned from Europe, held a retreat at Camp Luz in Ohio and discussed the meaning of fellowship. Out of this emerged questions as to whether Concern itself should function as a community along New Testament lines.

As a sign of the times, a parallel renewal movement among the Quakers was initiated. It published a quarterly series named *The Call.* This movement sought to encourage the Friends to return more closely to their Christian origins. Concern kept in touch with leaders of *The Call,* since the objectives of both renewal efforts were similar. In fact, Lewis Benson, a Quaker leader of *The Call,* permitted his name to appear on the editorial masthead of Concern. It may be conjectured that the name "Concern" was drawn from traditional Quaker language.

It is impossible to find a rubric by which to epitomize numerous articles that found their way into Concern's 18 issues, the last one appearing in 1971. However, one can delineate two main, interrelated areas. They are (1) the nature and mission of the church, and (2) the relation of the church to society.

With respect to the nature of the church, articles appeared from the outset that expressed disillusionment with the Mennonite church for its alleged conformity to denominational patterns of organization and religious life. Especially offensive was the apparent identification of the church with vertical structures, as represented by conferences, ministerial boards, and °institutions. Also, it was claimed that °ethnicity was frequently confused with spiritual reality. Members of Concern insisted that tendencies, both social and theological, that led historically from New Testament Christianity to the *Corpus Christianum* and from early Anabaptism to Dutch Mennonite formalism, were at work among American Mennonites as well. What emerged was a vision of the church according to which spirit supersedes structure, essence transcends form, and the simple resists the complex. The church is not to be understood as a building or as an institution but as an intimate fellowship of believers within which interaction includes mutual support, Bible study, edification, and discipline. The church is defined as "where two or three are gathered together in the presence of Jesus."

"Intimations of Another Way" is the title that C. Norman Kraus and John W. Miller gave to a seminal article appearing in *Concern* no. 3 (1956), in which the church was defined in singular terms as a fellowship. To "gather" in Jesus' name is to bring together the essentials of what it means to be the church. The church is where Christ is and "not necessarily where the membership rolls are kept, not necessarily where the preacher stands Sunday by Sunday to present his discourse . . . but where Christ is reigning in the midst of His gathered people."

With the church defined as koinonia (community), many questions emerged as to just what the church should do. Subsequent issues filled out the vision of a renewed Mennonite church. Articles supporting small-group dynamics, °Bible study, ethical discernment, °discipline, °mutual aid, caring, vocational counseling, teaching, and preaching appeared. All of these functions were to be located in the local congregation meeting possibly, though not necessarily, in homes (°house churches).

Inevitably, the logic of the mutuality of love led to discussions about "full community," and especially as the leaders of Concern entered into conversations with representatives of the Society of Brothers (°Hutterian Brethren) at Rifton, New York. Given the principles of °nonconformity to world systems, including the capitalistic economic order, and the necessity to break with western individualism, not to speak of the need to "bear one another's burdens," the leaders of Concern wrestled with the Hutterian ideal. Predictably, differences of opinion emerged regarding the structural implications of communal love. Would Concern follow the ideal of community to its logical conclusion? Although, Concern generally stopped short of "full community," one may be justified in making a connection between Concern and the Reba Place fellowship, which was founded in 1957 through the instrumentality of John W. Miller (°Shalom Covenant Communities).

With respect to the second major issue, namely, the relation of the church to society, discussion centered on the concept of "social responsibility." Social responsibility entered ecumenical discussion through the World Council of Churches meeting in Amsterdam in 1948. It served as a comprehensive framework by which to define how the churches should relate to °democratic society.

At the outset leaders of Concern saw "responsibility" as an "unbiblical presupposition" of Christian social ethics because it violated the fundamental division between the "two kingdoms," most clearly delineated by the °Schleitheim Confession. John Howard Yoder in "The Anabaptist Dissent," Concern no. 1 (1954), insisted that the sect is by necessity withdrawn from the world. "The basic 'dissent' of the sect as here spoken of is its refusal to assume responsibility for the moral structure of non-Christian society." He pointed out that "social responsibility" is grounded in the Constantinian Corpus Christianum, within which the church ceases to be an "autonomous moral force." Responsibility is ethically ambiguous since it "says nothing definite about ends and means." To be responsible for society is to compromise especially in the areas of war and the police functions of the state. At that time Yoder seemed to have represented not only the traditional Mennonite position but also the position of most of his contemporaries when he wrote, "Because the work of the church is what gives real meaning to history, we need not be ashamed of our irresponsibility in giving our attention as Christians to the church's peculiar tasks, and thus leaving to the 'good heathen' the functions necessary but nonredemptive, which fail to accord with our particular mission."

This point of view, however, was challenged by Gordon Kaufman in an article entitled 'Non-resistance and Responsibility,' Concern no. 6 (1958). Kaufman upheld responsibility as a "derivative of Christian love." Love drives Christians to the political sphere, since this is where love is most needed. Love means accepting the neighbor where he is "in hope that the neighbor may be transformed and the situation may be redeemed." Willingness to participate in °decisionmaking, even for a military budget, despite one's own personal Christian desires, can be justified as an implication of Christian freedom to love. Kaufman acknowledged the church-world dichotomy in principle, but he refused to define it objectively with discernible boundaries.

Kaufman's article set the agenda for a spirited "Second Look at Responsibility" as Albert Meyer and others responded critically. Their criticism centered upon Kaufman's apparent failure to carry out the implications of the church-world dichotomy. The dichotomy disappears in Kaufman's essay, it was claimed, when the Christian as a moral agent allows his actions to be determined by others. " 'Love' is no longer Christian love when it is supporting every neighbor in terms of his own understanding or misunderstanding," wrote Meyer.

As issue followed issue, leaders throughout the Mennonite Church pondered what to make of Concern. To some it could be interpreted as normal generational conflict, to which the Mennonite church needs to pay attention. Leaders of Concern were young men full of idealism as yet untempered by experiences in life which come to heads of families, business leaders, and professionals, so some declared.

But others saw Concern as unreasonable rebellion against the church and especially against its institutions. Some of the most prominent leaders of the Mennonite Church (MC), including heads of institutions, felt threatened. Suspicions and misunderstandings led to some heated, and in retrospect, tragic correspondence and even broken relationships. The conflict ensued between first- and second-generation advocates of the "Anabaptist vision" over what it means to live as disciples and to bring to order churches in the Anabaptist tradition. In general, the first generation claimed that, despite obvious shortcomings, American Mennonitism maintained continuity with the original vision while Concern saw discontinuity, compromise, social accommodation, materialism, institutional rigidities, apathy, and excessive and manipulative power by a few well-known leaders. The second generation said in effect to the first generation, You led us to the trough (Anabaptist vision), but you won't let us drink.

Problems of misunderstanding were augmented by Concern's uncertainty about its own identity. Was it simply an informal fellowship of concerned Mennonites? Or was it, given its definition of the church as where "two or three are gathered together," an incipient congregation? Was it a reform movement reminiscent of Anabaptism, Methodism, and the Oxford Movement in relation to the religious establishments? Or was it simply a vehicle for publication?

In reality Concern was all of these, yet without the consistency that would grant a clear sense of identity either to its insiders or its observers. Its ambiguity became increasingly evident at Goshen College when some group members dared to conduct communion in the house context without the approval and presence of a minister.

Even in historical perspective it is difficult to measure the impact of Concern upon the Mennonite Church. To be sure, Concern fathered no sectarian children in the pure sense, except possibly Reba Place. But certain Concern ideas found their way into traditional Mennonite congregational life. Some of these would be the transfer of authority from conference leadership to the congregation. In fact, the radical shift toward congregational freedom vis-à-vis conference authority may be attributed in part to Concern's insistence that the congregation is the basic unit of the church of Christ. Also, Concern's emphasis upon primary fellowship found expression, however indirectly, in the development of koinonia groups within existing congregations. And theological education for the pastorate, while proceeding at Mennonite seminaries in the general direction of the professional ministry, included a search for alternative patterns within the tradition of the plural ministry. In summary, it may be said that many of the essential elements of the °"believer's church" concept were set forth initially by Concern.

Furthermore, one of the most significant services of Concern to the Mennonite church was the opportunity it provided for young theologians and potential church leaders to express their thoughts and convictions. Few avenues for expression existed in the 1950s and 1960s except in the field of church history. Although Concern seemed to have lost much of its unity and revolutionary zeal by 1972, as the inner circle branched out into active church work of various kinds, it nevertheless made a mark upon the Mennonite church, along with the inevitable confluence of numerous historical developments.

Concern illustrates the strength and the weakness of ideological thinking. Ideological thinking may be appreciated for its capacity to epitomize essential truths. But it is invariably too simple to communicate the whole truth. The contribution of Concern lies in the fact that it articulated alternative conceptions of the church as represented by sectarian Anabaptism and the *Corpus Christianum* of "placed Christianity." But Concern lacked the imagination and the experience to understand the pathos of its own strengths and weaknesses and the historical logic of the *Corpus Christianum*. Ironically, while some of the most enthusiastic leaders of Concern found their way vocationally into positions of responsibility within the Mennonite church as pastors, teachers, and missionaries, others joined faculties of Catholic and state universities. Still others left the Mennonite church altogether as pastors and missionaries of other denominations, all having matured in the process, including the Mennonite Church (MC) itself.   JLB

Concilio de las Iglesias Evangélicas Menonitas, Venezuela (Council of Mennonite Evangelical Churches of Venezuela), is the name of the conference of churches that developed out of the mission activity of the Eastern Mennonite Board of Missions and Charities (MC). The José Santiago family arrived in Caracas in Nov. 1978 to establish new fellowships of believers. The first congregation was organized in 1979 with 32 believers. The council organized and purchased a building in the San Bernardino district of Caracas that year. That building serves as meetingplace, pastor's residence, council office, and Bible institute classroom. The second congregation was organized in Charallave, an industrial town 70 km. (42 mi.) south of Caracas, in 1982.

The council publishes *El Portavoz Menonita* (The Mennonite Spokesman), a bimonthly church magazine. It operates a nonresident Bible institute and works as a partner with Mennonites from Colombia in annual advanced-level training seminars. The council is a member of the Evangelical Council of Venezuela.

In 1987 two congregations were in formation in addition to the two established congregations. Total membership was 170.   MG

MWH (1984), 107; *MC Yearbook* (1986-87), 162.

Concilio Nacional de Iglesias Menonitas Hispanas (National Council of Hispanic Mennonite Churches. The Concilio Nacional serves the needs of 72 °Hispanic Mennonite congregations with a membership of 2,386 scattered in 17 states of the United States, two Canadian provinces, and three bordering Mexican cities in joint efforts with 14 Mennonite conferences. The seven members of its board represent geographical areas and the youth and women's groups. The board is responsible to help plan, facilitate, and implement the decisions of the biennial convention of the Concilio Nacional; represents Hispanic interests in the program boards of the Mennonite Church (MC); and identifies needs and leaders for the congregations. The board also helps the staff members of the Mennonite Church General Board (MC) represent Hispanic concerns to the program boards and conferences to help the Mennonite Church develop a better understanding of minorities. The Hispanic Mennonites in the General Conference Mennonite Church are invited to the biennial convention and participate as observers in board meetings.

The Concilio Nacional has been instrumental in developing a Hispanic Ministries program at Goshen College (MC); an office to serve migration issues through the Mennonite Central Committee; the production and distribution of Spanish literature through the Mennonite Board of Congregational Ministries (MC), including a periodical, *Ecos Menonitas* (1975-); and media services via the Mennonite Board of Missions (MC). Hispanic Mennonites have experienced rapid numerical growth due to their evangelistic zeal, charismatic pastors, and the responsiveness of Hispanics to the gospel. Peace education, congregationalism, and awareness of Anabaptist themes are the frontiers for the emerging churches. In August 1988 the organization changed its name to Convención de Iglesias Menonitas Hispanas de los Estados Unidos y Canada.   JMO

Rafael A. Falcón, *La Iglesia Menonita Hispana en Norte América, 1932-1982* (Scottdale, 1985); Eng. trans. by Ronald Collins as *The Hispanic Mennonite Church in North America, 1932-1982* (Scottdale, 1986); *MC Yearbook* (1986-87), 109; "General Board Approves New Minority Plan," *GH* (Jan. 1, 1974), 19-20; Mennonite Church General Board Minutes (Sept. 11-12, 1973), 5; José M. Ortiz, "Church Growth Among Spanish-Speaking North American Mennonites." *Miss. Focus,* 5, no. 3 (1977), 2-3.

Concordia Colony, Brazil. See Witmarsum Colony.

Conewango Valley, N.Y., Old Order Amish Settlement in Cattaraugus Co., sometimes called the Oldtown community, 50 mi. (80 km.) south of Buffalo. The Oldtown community is the oldest and largest of the 12 Amish settlements in New York. Founded in 1949 by families from °Holmes Co., Ohio, and the Enon Valley in Pennsylvania who were seeking cheaper farm land and greater freedom to practice certain rules and regulations of the Amish church. There has been slow but steady growth in the Conewango Valley; many families have moved in and out of this settlement. Dairy farming and the building trades are the main occupations. In 1986 there were eight church districts (congregations) with more than 1,000 people. The 11 newest New York settlements were all established after the Supreme Court decision in *Wisconsin Versus Yoder* on school attendance, indicating the migrations to New York may have been the result of liberal state guidelines for the operation of °private church schools.   SLY

Conference. See also Konferenz.

Conférence Mennonite Suisse/Konferenz der Mennoniten in der Schweiz. See Schweizerisches Mennonitisches Evangelisationskomitee; Schweizerisches Mennonitisches Friedenskomitee.

Conference of Mennonite Brethren Churches, Canada. See Canadian Conference of Mennonite Brethren Churches.

Conference of Mennonite Brethren Churches, Paraguay. See Konferenz der Mennonitischen Brüdergemeinden, Paraguay.

Conference of Mennonite Brethren Churches in North America. See Mennonite Brethren Church of North America.

Conference of Mennonites in Alberta. Major changes have taken place in the conference since 1950, when there were seven member congregations, all but one located in the rural areas of the province, and all served by unpaid lay minsters. In 1986 the conference numbered 18 affiliated congregations, with a total membership of 1,913. Each congregation was served by a professionally trained and salaried minister.

The six rural congregations affiliated with the conference in 1950 are, for the most part, little changed in membership and character in 1986. The exception is the Coaldale Mennonite Church, which is so close to a large °urban center that many of its members work in the city. The 11 new congregations are located in urban centers. The lifestyle and form of worship in these congregations differs little from that found in other urban Protestant churches.

°°Menno Bible Institute, formally established in 1935, closed in 1966 for lack of enrollment. It had a profound influence on the conference during its 30-year history. The Alberta Conference then joined the Saskatchewan Conference of Mennonites in support of the Bible School at Swift Current. Interest in camping grew rapidly in the 1950s. In 1958 and 1959, 166 acres (67 hectares) on the Little Red River were purchased to establish a °camp. Camp Valaqua has been developed so that it is suitable for both summer and winter programs. A retirement °home was constructed in Coaldale in 1955 at a cost of $19,500. Most of the work was done by volunteer labor. The facility has been renovated several times since then and houses 14 residents (1987).

The conference shares responsibilities in a number of other projects. Each year it gives financial support to °°Rosthern Junior College and appoints members to its board of directors. It actively participates in Mennonite Central Committee Alberta (MCC) and is directly involved in the Youth Orientation Unity, an MCC project at Warburg, which endeavors to rehabilitate youth offenders placed there by the attorney general's office.   CLD

GCM Handbook (1988), 103-4; Reimer, *Quilt* (1983), 51.

Conference of Mennonites in British Columbia. In November 1936 representatives from five newly formed churches of General Conference Mennonite Church (GCM) background met at Sardis, B.C., to establish the Conference of United Mennonite Churches of British Columbia. From this small body of 5 churches with 266 members, the conference, renamed Conference of Mennonites in British Columbia, has grown to 26 congregations with 4,641 members (1987). The conference's stated threefold purpose was to be a united force in the cause of Christ, to serve as guardian of the faith in the Anabaptist tradition, and to be a beacon to attract and draw together the many lost and straying members of the family of faith.

The following have been or still are major programs and institutions of the conference. A °°girls' home for girls working in the city of Vancouver was established in 1935. A Bible school begun at Aldergrove (1939) later moved to Abbotsford as Bethel Bible Institute, and amalgamated with the Mennonite Brethren Bible Institute to become Columbia Bible Institute (1972) and Columbia Bible College (1985). A Mennonite high school operated at Sardis, 1947-51. Camp Squeah, nestled in the coastal mountains, serves the churches as a year-round retreat center. Sunday school teacher training has found emphasis throughout the years. Mission endeavors include church planting and cross-cultural ministries with Chinese, Laotian, and Indo-Canadian ethnic groups. Peace and justice issues and care for underprivileged has largely been relegated to Mennonite Central Committee (B.C.) of which the conference is an integral part. The youth organization, Women in Mission, and the Ministers and Deacons conference play a vital role in the life of the Conference of Mennonites in British Columbia. In 1976 the conference opened an office in Clearbrook with a full-time conference coordinator, later referred to as the conference minister. The conference continues to maintain close ties with the Conference of Mennonites in Canada and the General Conference Mennonite Church of North America.   JT

Conference of Mennonites in Canada (ME I:671). Since the initial union (1902-03) of congregations from the Rosenorter Mennonites of Saskatchewan and the Bergthaler Mennonites of Manitoba, the Conference of Mennonites in Canada (CMC) has come to include a significant number of new congregations made up of some families who arrived from the United States, along with many more recent immigrants from the Soviet Union. The latter came to Canada first in the 1920s, then in a further wave during the years following World War II, and finally in a smaller group of scattered families who left the Soviet Union in the 1960s and 1970s.

A series of three different name changes led to the present conference name. Known first as "Die Konferenz der Mennoniten im Mittleren Kanada," it became the General Conference of Mennonites in Canada in 1932 (sessions at Laird, Sask.). Restructuring in 1959 brought about some major changes, such as limiting the terms of offices, and giving the organization its present name. At the same time a varying set of committees, which had carried out tasks as they arose, was replaced by five boards: Missions, Education and Publications, Christian Service, Canadian Mennonite Bible College, and Finance. Beginning in the 1950s the first staff members (a part-time treasurer, then a general secretary, and soon also executive secretaries of other boards) took up responsibilities as a central office developed rapidly in the next decade and a half. In the congregations there was a strong move away from leadership by °elders toward the promotion of a professional ministry.

These new directions created a project-oriented agenda. With it came rising budgets and new initiatives of ministry and mission. The Mennonite Pioneer Mission, established and maintained by the °Bergthal Mennonites of Manitoba until 1958, was brought into the conference program. Ultimately it formed the core aspects of Native Ministries as this work is called in 1987 (°Indian ministries). Congregations were given loans to build new church buildings. Canadian Mennonite Bible College (CMBC) expanded its new campus at 600 Shaftesbury Blvd., Winnipeg, where the conference also had its offices. The Board of Education and Publication meanwhile published devotional materials, subsidized conference-related periodicals, and undertook to publish the *Conference Bulletin* and other promotional materials. From time to time certain key theological and other issues rose to the fore. In the beginning years the issues related to problems of assuming public office (°government) and other civic responsibilities. Then the matter of °conversion and the nature of becoming believers caught attention for a time. Eschatology questions had their turn also. In the 1960s there arose the seeming tension between faith and social action, particularly in the years when the

Board of Christian Service drew attention to major social ills erupting in society at the time.

Representation in the delegate sessions and board tended to shift in these years from a predominantly clergy-oriented body to one with a growing lay member involvement—at the first conference session in 1903 there was one lay person present. By 1970 a large number of delegates were lay members, although ministers tended to dominate the executive committee and boards for some time to come. This was no doubt partly because ministers were more readily available, and perhaps better-trained to take up board and other responsibilities. Congregations were more likely to view ministers' attendance at meetings and annual sessions as part of their regular employment than would be true of farmers and the employers of urban workers and professionals.

In 1971 the constitution was revised again. The earlier five boards now became four: General Board, Congregational Resources, Canadian Mennonite Bible College (CMBC), and Mennonite Pioneer Missions (changed to Native Ministries the following year). Another result of the change was a marked reduction of staff, and the general board of the conference assumed responsibility for finances.

The conference celebrated its 75th birthday at the Gretna, Man., sessions in 1978. That year the CMBC board reported a projection of changes and expansion which would allow the college's student body to rise to between 160 and 200. The following decade would see that goal attained as student enrollment stabilized around 180.

Additional issues, such as the place of °women in the church, marital stability (°divorce, °marriage), a conference periodical, a new partnership with a growing number of Chinese and other Asian congregations, several Native churches, relating to the °*Umsiedler* Mennonite churches of the Federal Republic of Germany (emigrants from the Soviet Union), and the development of an °archival center, have come to be important questions for the current (1980s) network of ministries in the conference.

A few new congregations have come into the conference from eastern Canada (Quebec and New Brunswick). Various other, notably urban, congregations have also joined in the last decade. One segment of the conference has accepted a new inter-Mennonite affiliation in Ontario when the Conference of United Mennonite Churches of Ontario became part of Mennonite Conference of Eastern Canada in 1988. Provincial conferences have taken on sizable programs of their own, and reassessments of mutual relationships continue as this occurs. Joint sessions occurred for the first time with the General Conference Mennonite Church (GCM) in 1989.   LK

Bulletin: Conference of Mennonites in Canada, 1965- (Winnipeg, four to six times annually; annually since 1971); *Conference of Mennonites in Canada Yearbook* (Winnipeg, 1928-); Irene Friesen-Petkau, "*Just when we were . . .*," (Winnipeg: History Archives Committee of the Conference of Mennonites In Canada, 1978); Henry J. Gerbrandt, "A History of the Conference of Mennonites in Canada," in *Call to Faithfulness*, ed. Henry Poettcker and Rudy Regehr (Winnipeg: CMBC, 1972), 81-91; Jacob Peters, "Organizational Change Within A Religious Denomination: A Case Study of the Conference of Mennonites in Canada, 1903-1978," (PhD diss., U. of Manitoba, 1987); Rudy A. Regehr and Margaret Franz, ed., *Twenty-Five Years: A Time To Grow* (Winnipeg: CMBC, 1972); J. G. Rempel, *Fuenfzig*

Jahre Konferenz Bestrebungen, 1902-1952: Konferenz der Mennoniten in Canada (Steinbach, 1952); *Totemak* (Winnipeg, Native Ministries program, 1972-79), frequency varies; name changed to *Intotemak* (1980-); Reimer *Quilt* (1983), 49-51; *MWH* (1984), 131; *GCM Handbook* (1988), 100-103.

See also General Conference Mennonite Church; General Conference Mennonite Church (US); Conference of Mennonites in British Columbia; Conference of Mennonites in Alberta; Conference of Mennonites in Saskatchewan; Conference of Mennonites in Manitoba; Conference of United Mennonite Churches of Ontario; Mennonite Conference of Eastern Canada.

Conference of Mennonites in Manitoba. A provincial conference in Canada consisting largely, though not necessarily or entirely, of General Conference Mennonite (GCM) congregations, the Conference of Mennonites in Manitoba had its beginnings in the 1930s as a lay ministers' conference dealing annually with themes and problems common to lay ministers, but without an ongoing program. For a brief period (1936-38) there was also an annual delegates' session, but after 1938 it did not convene again until after World War II.

In 1947 a delegates' session was called which adopted a constitution and began a modest program of home missions. Congregations represented were all Manitoba member congregations of the Conference of Mennonites in Canada. Thirteen congregations were registered as charter members, but these included both the °Bergthal and °°Whitewater multi-congregational organizations, so that the actual number of local congregations was considerably larger.

The home missions program was gradually expanded to include a °camping program (1957) which had been begun by the Manitoba Mennonite Youth Organization, with three Christian campgrounds (Camp Assiniboia [ME IV:1060] at Headingly, Camp Koinonia at Boissevain, and Camp Moose Lake at Sprague, Manitoba); an annual provincial Sunday school convention (1957); and a modest radio program (1956), which was quickly expanded into three weekly half-hour programs on a newly opened local radio station, CFAM, in Altona, a year later.

In 1975 the °°Elim Bible School was made a Manitoba Conference institution. It closed in 1988. While the two private high schools, Westgate Mennonite Collegiate in Winnipeg and Mennonite Collegiate Institute in Gretna, are not conference schools, they move within the orbit of other conference institutions and receive some conference support.

In 1968 the large First Mennonite Church of Winnipeg joined the conference. New congregations formed after the immigration which followed World War II, also joined the conference, making it an organization of 47 congregations and 11 associate congregations, with a total membership of 11,019 in 1987. Its three-pronged program still emphasizes Christian education, home missions, and radio work.   GE

Minutes and Yearbooks of the Conference of Mennonites in Manitoba (1935-1986); *GCM Handbook* (1988) 105-7; Reimer, *Quilt* (1983), 51.

Conference of Mennonites in Saskatchewan. The conference convened Oct. 29, 1959, at Rosthern for its first annual delegate session and applied for incorporation in December 1960. It was preceded by the Ministers and Deacons Conference, which met annually from 1934, and the Saskatchewan Mennonite Youth Organization (SMYO), formed in 1940. The purpose was to link congregations to the Conference of Mennonites in Canada, General Conference Mennonite Church, and Mennonite Central Committee, and to provide a base for a broad spectrum of programs, both existing and new developments. At its sessions reports are heard from the conference pastor; Rosthern and Herbert Nursing Homes; Rosthern Youth Farm; Shekinah, Elim, and Rosthern °camps; Saskatchewan Mennonite Youth Organization; hospital °chaplaincy; corrections chaplaincy; Person-Two-Person (prison ministry); mediation services (offender-victim °reconciliation); Asian Ministries Outreach Services (Chinese, Vietnamese, and Laotion outreach); radio ("Wings of the Evening"); music library; education workships; family ministries; church planting outreach; Rosthern Junior College; and Swift Current Bible Institute.

Since 1959 notable changes have come. The language of worship services has changed from predominantly German to almost exclusively English. Pastoral leadership by men in a nonsalaried, lay ministry of multiple preachers and a single °bishop, or °elder, has been replaced with salaried professional clergy, including women. Some congregations have paid pastoral teams. Highly trained professional lay people contribute significantly in all areas. A strong emphasis on mission and song festivals shifted and waned, but efforts are reviving these areas. An annual °Bible conference has been added. Emphasis has shifted to community involvement and dealing with issues prevalent in society: °family relationships, conflict resolution, °health-care needs of an aging population, and problems of youth.

In 1987 the conference numbered 5,150 members in 45 congregations. One church still has a German worship service, another uses the Chinese language.   EP

Conference of Mennonites of Saskatchewan, Yearbook containing minutes, church directory, conference organization, for the 28th annual session, Feb. 27-28, 1987; Henry Funk, "Reflections," a paper given at the 25th annual session of the Conference of Mennonites of Saskatchewan at Rosthern, Sask., Feb. 24, 1984 (7 pp. typescript); *GCM Handbook* (1988), 109-10; Reimer, *Quilt* (1983), 51.

Conference of Mennonites in Uruguay. See Konferenz der Mennonitengemeinden in Uruguay.

Conference of United Mennonite Churches in Ontario. Several thousand Russian Mennonites immigrated to Ontario after World War I, settling primarily in three areas: Kitchener-Waterloo and vicinity, Essex Co. in the extreme southwest, and the Niagara peninsula. Under the leadership of Bishop Jacob H. Janzen, those of General Conference Mennonite (GCM) affiliation organized themselves as United Mennonite congregations. Developments during World War II underscored the need for a concerted effort in °urban missions and education. Consequently, a provincial conference was organized in 1944. It supported the establishment of a private high school, the United Mennonite Educational Institute (Leamington), and continues to take responsibility for ministry to a growing number of Mennonites in such cities as Toronto, St. Catharines, Hamilton, Ottawa, and Windsor, where new congregations soon emerged. The Hamilton Mennonite Church, in turn, initiated an inner-city ministry, which has since grown into the Welcome Inn Community Centre and Church. More recently, conference mission work has extended to Chinese, Laotian, and Latin American immigrants.

Increasing inter-Mennonite cooperation in education and mission has marked the last 25 years. The conference joined in establishing Conrad Grebel College in 1963 and in forming the Inter-Mennonite Conference of Ontario in 1973. In 1987 the conference agreed to dissolve in favor of the broader Mennonite unity represented by the emerging °Mennonite Conference of Eastern Canada (1988). At the time, the United Mennonite Conference comprised 22 congregations and 5,363 members.   HPaet

Jahrbuch der Vereinigten Mennoniten Gemeinden in Ontario, superseded by *Yearbook of the United Mennonite Churches in Ontario* (1947-); *GCM Handbook* (1988), 108-9; Reimer, *Quilt* (1983), 51.

Conferences on the Concept of the Believers Church. See Believers Church.

Conferencia de las Iglesias Evangélicas Menonitas, Dominican Republic (Evangelical Mennonite Church). The first Mennonite missionary to arrive in the Dominican Repubic was Lucille Rupp in 1945. A year later the Omar Sutton family joined her to begin work in the town of El Cercado, located in the south, near the Dominican-Haitian border.

The first Mennonite church was organized with 13 members in El Cercado in 1948. While the work prospered, there was also opposition, but by 1954 six congregations with a membership of 101 had been organized. Other workers joined the group later, but great emphasis was placed upon the involvement of native Dominicans. By 1959 there were 75 preaching locations. Two bookstores and a school were added to the work. By 1973 membership in all the congregations together had grown to 700.

By 1986 the number of members had increased to 1,070. Many church buildings, a retreat camp, and other institutions had been built. The conference is largely autonomous, but receives some support from North America. Other groups, e.g., the West Indies Mission and the Assemblies of God, have also begun work in the country, as have other Mennonite groups, including the Church of God in Christ, Mennonite.   MSe/JS

MWH (1978), 218; *MWH* (1984), 69.

Confessions, Doctrinal (ME I:679). Confessions have not often been studied by Mennonite scholars, yet the Anabaptists and later the Dutch Mennonites wrote many confessions—more than any of the other Reformation traditions. Confessions were used by individuals, local churches, and church conferences for apologetic purposes, as a major form of witness, and as instruments in the search for unity among the diverse Anabaptist and Mennonite groups.

European and North American Mennonite confessions find their roots in a series of European confessions, including the *Dordrecht Confession* (1632), the *Frisian-Flemish Confessions* (1660), the *Cornelius Ris Confession* (1766), the *Prussian Confession* (1792), the *Prussian Confession* (Elbing edition, 1836), the *Rudnerweide Confession* (1853), and the *Mennonite Brethren Confession* (1902). The complex interrelationship of confessions, and the process of borrowing and building that went on, is well-documented in the article on confessions in ME I.

North American Mennonite confessions derive from these major European Mennonite confessions. They emerge within the main Mennonite groups in North America and also in the smaller, more independent, yet nonetheless related, Mennonite denominations. In many instances these confessions have been adopted by churches begun by Mennonite missionaries in other countries.

The specific occasions and purposes of the confessions are as varied as the times and places in which they emerged. In the Mennonite Church (MC) the *Dordrecht Confession* has functioned more powerfully than any other. In North America it was translated into English in 1725 in order to build unity and clarify the Mennonite theological identity and witness, particularly the Mennonite position on °nonresistance, to the new society. Together with °°catechisms it continued to be used for instruction in °baptism and °church membership. It symbolizes a rich Mennonite theological heritage.

The *Christian Fundamentals* (1921) appeared as a confessional supplement during the period of °Fundamentalist tensions within the Mennonite Church. The *Mennonite Confession* (1963) is a restatement and revision of the Dordrecht confessional tradition in light of issues current at that time. The recovery of the °Anabaptist vision in the 20th c. has refocused attention on the significance of the °*Schleitheim Confession* (1527), the oldest Anabaptist confession. Its articles, originally defining the tenets of the Swiss Brethren, have attained a new confessional status within the Mennonite Church (MC) tradition, and even beyond.

The General Conference Mennonite Church has never formally adopted a confession. The 1896 constitution has a simple paragraph titled, "Our Common Confession," which summarizes the General Conference position. Later revisions of the constitution carry through the same *Common Confession* with little change. Strong recommendations were made in 1905 to accept the *Ris Confession* (1766) as an official confession for the conference. Even though that attempt failed, the *Ris Confession* has been used for instruction within the church and has clarified Mennonite identity to others. In 1933 a revised set of articles was proposed but rejected at the General Conference, although official permission was given for the printing and dissemination of these 1933 *Articles of Faith*. In 1941 a *Statement of Faith* was written in conjunction with the purposes of General Conference Mennonite seminary education. The statement, however, was never officially adopted or widely used.

In contrast to the other Mennonite groups, the General Conference Mennonites gave birth to a series of local church confessions. In 1878 the Turner (Ore.) congregation adopted the *Rudnerweide Con-*

fession (1853). In 1918 the Beatrice (Nebr.) congregations adopted the 1836 *Prussian Confession* (Elbing edition). H. D. °°Penner and P. H. °°Richert merged three European confessions to produce the *Kurzgefasstes Glaubensbekenntnis der N. . . . Mennoniten Gemeinde* (Summary Confession of Faith of the _____ Mennonite Church, n.d.). Intended for use by local congregations, it strongly reflected the content of the *Dordrecht Confession.* P. H °°Unruh authored a shorter confession, *What We Believe* (n.d.), that was printed by resolution of the Alexanderwohl (Ks.) Mennonite Church.

The Mennonite Brethren Church has produced two major confessions. Written originally within the context of southern Russia, the *Mennonite Brethren Confession* of 1902 drew heavily from previous Mennonite confessions. It dealt with differences and agreements with the other Mennonites. The Mennonite Brethren break in 1860 from the Mennonite church (°°Kirchen-Gemeinden) was the occasion for such an emphasis. This note of separation is distinctive among Mennonite confessions. The *Mennonite Brethren Confession* of 1975 was intended to stand in continuity not only with the 1902 Mennonite Brethren confession (which the text clearly reflects), but also with the larger Anabaptist-Mennonite heritage (which is made explicit in the preface and introduction). It therefore reflects a broader identity than the 1902 confession.

A considerable number of confessions have emerged from the smaller Mennonite and Mennonite-related traditions: *The Confession of Faith of the Brethren* (ca. 1780), known also as the *The Eighteenth-Century Confession,* is the earliest confessional statement of the Brethren in Christ, who also published a *Statement of Doctrine* in 1961. The °°Evangelical United Mennonites, precursors of the (°°United) Missionary Church (known as the °°Mennonite Brethren in Christ, 1883-1947), published their *Doctrine of Faith and Church Discipline* in 1967. It was revised in 1951 as *The Doctrines and Discipline of the United Missionary Church.* The Evangelical Mennonite Conference (Kleine Gemeinde) revised their confession in 1954 as the *Historic Articles of Faith of the Evangelical Mennonite Church,* and wrote a brief *Statement of Faith* in 1973. The *Glaubensbekenntnis der Mennoniten in Reinland Manitoba, Nord Amerika* was published in 1881 and reprinted in 1913. This confession contributed significantly to the identity of various Mennonite groups, including the ones associated with the Old Colony Mennonites in Manitoba.

The *Confession of Faith of the Church of God in Christ, Mennonite* was adopted by that group in 1886 and reprinted in 1952. The revised and expanded *Articles of Faith* were adopted in 1961. In 1917 the °Evangelical Mennonite Church (Egly Amish) wrote their *Articles of Faith,* which were reprinted in 1936. They were revised in 1949 and reprinted with minor revisions in 1961 and 1980. In 1923 the Evangelical Mennonite Brethren Conference adopted and printed the *Articles of Faith* which were reprinted in 1950. The °°Krimmer Mennonite Brethren Church adopted and printed their *Articles of Faith* in 1929 and reprinted them in 1940. The Evangelical Mennonite Mission Conference published *A Confession of Faith* in 1973.

Most of the Mennonite confessions reflect a strong sense of continuity with traditional Anabaptist-Mennonite theological convictions. They frequently quote Matthew's gospel and emphasize corporate church life. Mennonite confessions generally reflect the following theological framework: God, Word of God (°biblical interpretation), Jesus Christ (°Christology), °Holy Spirit, human nature, °free will, °conversion, °church and its mission, church offices, baptism, °communion, °feetwashing, °marriage, church °discipline, Christian life and °nonconformity, integrity and oaths, nonresistance and revenge, Christian and the state (°church-state relations), Lord's day and work, last things (eschatology). In addition to their distinctive churchly center, Mennonite confessions consistently revolve around the themes of eschatology, Christology, °theology. In the absence of a systematic theological tradition these confessions have often served an important role in preserving theological unity and identity in the Mennonite communities. They have also been used to reinforce °schisms.   HJL

Loewen, *Confessions* (1987), contains an extensive bibliography.

See also Authority.

Congregationalism (ME I:199). Historically, there have been three major governing patterns in the Christian church: episcopal, presbyterian, and congregational. Each of these can claim some rootage in the New Testament church and each has a tendency to claim that it best represents the original New Testament pattern.

The earliest churches in Jerusalem and environs were governed primarily by the apostles. Several persons emerged as leaders among "the Twelve," notably Peter and John. In due time, James, the brother of the Lord, also became a recognized leader, though he was not one of the Twelve. The episcopal tradition holds that the successors of these original leaders were the bishops (*episkopoi*). This line of development tends to emphasize the offices of the church to which leaders were appointed or elected. The doctrine of °°apostolic succession, so central to the episcopal tradition, refers to an unbroken line of ordination by the bishops who succeeded the bishops (etc.) who succeeded the apostles.

A second line of development emphasizes the gifts of the °Holy Spirit (*charismata*) rather than the offices of the °institutional church. This would be more characteristic of the Gentile churches, largely established by the missionary outreach of Paul. Paul certainly did not depreciate apostleship and appointed offices. Indeed, he went to great pains to establish his own apostolic credentials, and everywhere he went among the emerging churches he appointed elders (Ti 1:5). However, the major emphasis of Paul's teaching about leadership fell on the gifts of the Spirit rather than on fixed offices (Rom 12, 1 Cor 12, Eph 4). Paul recognized the need for order and authority at the same time that he was advocating the exercise of the variety and diversity of the spiritual gifts among all the members.

The fact that Paul uses two different terms in the

first chapter of Titus—elders (*presbyterous*) and bishop (*episkopon*)—creates some confusion. Were these in fact synonyms for the same office, or were they two distinct offices, one plural (elders) and one singular (bishop)? One possibility is that the pattern he was advocating was one in which one of the elders served as the presiding elder, i.e., as the bishop. In any case, there developed in the history of the Christian church two distinct patterns of church polity known as episcopal (governed by the bishop) and presbyterian (governed by a council of elders).

The episcopal pattern as it developed in the Eastern Orthodox and Roman Catholic churches involved a hierarchy of bishops and other clergy who governed the church in a given region. The bishop of Rome claimed apostolic succession to Peter and as such a role of supremacy over the other bishops as first among equals. The Anglican Church has maintained a similar pattern of church governance.

The presbyterian pattern of church government was developed primarily by the Reformed church under the direction of John °°Calvin. A major feature of the presbyterian pattern is the eldership, which consists of ruling elders and teaching elders. The former are lay persons; the latter are the preaching ministers. The ministers are not members of the local congregation but of the presbytery, which is composed of representatives of the local congregations in a given district.

A third pattern of church polity, congregationalism, has its roots in the Reformaton of England. Congregationalism is a type of church government in which each local congregation is self-governing. In its purest form, it insists on the full autonomy of the local congregation in matters of faith and doctrine as well as in all other matters of governance, including the selection of the pastor. It acknowledges no authority outside the local congregation, neither bishop nor presbytery. It is clear that this form of polity emerged in the struggle with the monarchical episcopacy of the Anglican Church but it is rooted as well in the developing democratic idealism of the 17th c. Congregationalists also claim New Testament support for their views on how the church should be governed. They stress the gifts of the Spirit and the °priesthood of all believers.

One of the important issues in the search for the most authentic pattern of church government is whether there is a fixed and normative pattern in the New Testament, or whether the church in every age has the freedom to determine its forms and structures in flexible ways. Congregationalists, while looking to the New Testament as normative, exercise considerable freedom and flexibility in working out the details of the pattern. Since the basic principle of congregationalism is local autonomy, it should not be surprising to discover considerable diversity in the governing patterns of local congregations because there is no central coordinating body to impose a common pattern.

A second issue is the relationship between the ministers and the lay people. It is only in the episcopal tradition that a sacramental distinction is made between the clergy and the laity. It is the clergy who have the primary (in some cases the sole) authority to govern the church. In the presbyterian

and congregational patterns, the laity share governance with the ordained ministers.

These traditions also differ when it comes to the question of the primary unit of the church. In the episcopal tradition it is the diocese, that is, the district or the churches under the jurisdiction of a bishop. It is the presence of the duly ordained and appointed bishop which guarantees the apostolicity of the church. In the presbyterian tradition, the primary unit is the presbytery. The presbytery is composed of ruling and teaching elders, with the ruling elders (lay men and women) constituting a majority. The presbytery has among its functions a judicial one, somewhat akin to that of a lower court. The general assembly as one of its functions convenes as a higher court.

In the congregational tradition, all matters of faith and life, of doctrine and practice, are determined locally, since by definition there is no authority outside the local congregation higher than that of the congregation itself. Nowhere is this more evident than in °worship. Each congregation is free to determine the form and content of its order of worship. There is no fixed liturgy determined by central authorities, such as the bishop or the prayer book. The same is true when it comes to doctrine.

Congregationalists also tend by conviction to insist on separation of church and state. This insistence is inherent in their refusal to accept any outside authority, whether bishop or prince. For Mennonite practices in regard to congregationalism, see °polity and °°autonomy of the congregation.   RTB

Congresos Menonitas Latinoamericanos (Latin American Mennonite Conferences). The first regional conference for Mennonite groups in Latin America was held at Bogotá, Colombia, Feb. 12-18, 1968. It was followed by meetings at Montevideo, Uruguay, July 11-15, 1972; Alajuela, Costa Rica, July 8-12, 1975; San Antonio, Tex., July 1922, 1978; and Bogotá, Colombia, Nov. 5-6, 1982. The theme of the fifth and last conference was "Violence and Peace in Our Midst."

Experience showed that regional conferences for smaller areas of Latin America would prove more beneficial. The first Congreso Menonita Latinoamericano for the Southern Cone (Cono Sur) took place at Bragado, Argentina (Buenos Aires), Dec. 10-13, 1981, under the theme, "The Non-Violent Stance and the Church's Task of Reconciliation." Following conferences were at Palmeira, Paraná, Brazil, Jan. 26-28, 1984 ("How to Live as Mennonite Churches in Today's Latin America"); Baleneario Argentina, Uruguay, Jan. 30-Feb. 2, 1986 ("Principles for the Mission of the Church in Latin America"); and Areguá, Paraguay, July 8-11, 1987 ("The Church as a Visible Sign of the Kingdom").   ROG

See also Regional Mennonite Conferences; Mennonitische Europäische Regional-Konferenz; Africa Mennonite and Brethren in Christ Fellowship.

Connecticut. See New England.

Conscientious Objection. For more than four centuries Mennonites have refused to perform °military service. Their refusal is grounded in a conviction that obedience to Christ means a rejection of violence and willingness to suffer for the cause of truth. The example they cite is Jesus, who chose the cross and °nonresistance as his way in the face of violence. Jesus' command to demonstrate love in all relationships is taken to be normative for all of his followers. The alleviation of human distress and suffering is understood to be the first order of responsibility for the Christian. Not even an overriding "reason of state" can cancel the Christian's commitment to peace and nonviolence. The Mennonite practice on this point has been continued not only over an unprecedented length of time, but at considerable sacrifice. Throughout their history Mennonites have suffered exile, emigration, punishment, and in some cases, death, for their fidelity to °love and nonresistance.

Conscientious objection has been a particularly important issue for Mennonites and their sister °historic peace churches (the °°Society of Friends, Church of the °°Brethren, and °Brethren in Christ) in the context of the totalitarian character of modern warfare. The draconian and democratic character of military °conscription systems demands universal commitment by citizens and rejects individual reservations about war and its purposes. Modern warfare requires not only soldiers, but the mobilization of the entire nation. Thus while the personnel aspects of conscientious objection continue to be at the center of concern, there is growing awareness that conscientious objection must also be seen in relation to °occupations, °taxes, and °investments. As warmaking becomes more technologically sophisticated, the personnel aspect of conscientious objection may diminish, and the financial and societal entanglement of nonresistant Christians in the warfare state will become more urgent and pervasive moral questions.

In the United States the constitutional arrangements regarding arms-bearing has made conscientious objection hostage to political and legislative considerations. In 1789 James Madison submitted an amendment to the Constitution which, if approved, would have protected the rights of those unable to bear arms. It read: "The right of the people to keep and bear arms shall not be infringed. A well armed and well regulated militia being the best security of a free country; but no person religiously scrupulous of bearing arms shall be compelled to render military service in person." Madison intended to protect the conscientious objector (CO) by constitutional right, but a majority of his colleagues in the Congress refused to concede that conscientious objection was a natural right. Rather, as they saw it, Congress has control of the CO as an aspect of its general power over military affairs. The legal status of the CO derives from the will of Congress and is a matter of legislative privilege rather than a constitutional right.

From a military point of view COs are a genuine nuisance. Since the quite disastrous handling of COs by the American War Department in °World War I, American military conscriptors have sought ways to classify efficiently and shunt into a well-defined, publicly acceptable program those who persisted as COs. General Lewis Hershey, long-time Director of Selective Service, in testimony before a congressional committee in 1943, argued that the best solution for COs was to put them in out-of-the-way camps, for, as he put it, "the CO, by my theory, is best handled if no one hears of him."

A recurring problem for Selective Service has been establishing criteria for CO status. The administrator's desire is always for a strict definition lest, in the words of Secretary of War Newton °°Baker (1913-21), too many young men become "conscientious." Hence, religious criteria, augmented by belief in a Supreme Being, and an insistence on membership in a sect officially opposed to military conscription, have usually characterized CO legislation.

Having established criteria for selecting genuine COs, the next problem was to determine what to do with the CO. During the period between World War I and World War II, the historic peace churches came to agreement that some form of °alternative service would be a desirable solution. Service rather than resistance to the draft became the appropriate stance of the historic peace church CO. This was rooted in the belief that the CO as citizen owed the nation and the world some service during wartime as a demonstration of Christian love and alternative form of behavior to war.

The °°Civilian Public Service (CPS) program during World War II was a result of a coincidence of interest between Selective Service and the historic peace churches. Both sought to avoid the debacle of World War I. Selective Service wanted an efficient way to handle the CO problem. The historic peace churches wanted a program to give young COs an opportunity to demonstrate their Christian convictions in action. Both the Selective Service and the historic peace churches needed a program the Congress and the country would tolerate in wartime. Civilian Public Service, with its camps and special social service assignments, met the needs of both parties.

By the end of the war, however, many COs, and especially the American Friends Service Committee, had begun to change their views about CO alternative service. For some, CPS seemed an all-too-easy means to shunt COs into out-of-the-way places, where the ability to witness against war was largely nullified. For most World War II COs, however, CPS was a satisfactory solution to a difficult problem.

In 1948, through an unusual set of circumstances, Congress, in a fit of absentmindedness, offered COs complete exemption from all service in a new draft law passed in response to the anxieties generated by the Cold War. When the Korean War erupted in 1950, public outrage over the CO exemption clause quickly moved Congress to cancel the exemption clause and replace it with a two-year required alternative service for COs.

The I-W program inaugurated in 1951 became a long-term alternative service lasting until conscription ended in 1973 as the conclusion of the Vietnam war drew near. The 1951 regulations built on the experience of the CPS program in World War II. A key change desired by both Selective Service and the historic peace churches was the elimination of the camp program. The churches were also relieved of the administrative (and partial financial) responsibility for drafted COs. Selective Service approved assignments and appointed men to jobs. A wide latitude prevailed in job choices—more than 2,000 agencies were approved for I-W service. Church agencies found the I-W men highly desirable appointees. Thousands of young men filled appointments in °Voluntary Service, °Mennonite Central Committee, °°Pax, and the Teachers Abroad programs.

Assessments of the I-W program have been generally favorable from both the Selective Service and historic peace church perspectives. Selective Service found the program trouble-free to administer. There were few complaints from the public. For the churches, the I-W program enhanced the growth of service tradition among young people, gave young men opportunity to test new careers, planted many new churches, especially in urban areas, often with creative new patterns of congregational organization and worship. The coincidence of the recovery of an Anabaptist theological vision linked with a broad-based service program, resulted in a remarkably generative period in American Mennonite history from 1950 to 1980.

The relative ease with which young men in the historic peace churches could enter I-W alternative service led to lax behavior by some who lacked maturity and deep conscientious convictions regarding war and peace. Some simply melded into the urban landscape after their service and were lost to the church.

The major shortcoming of the I-W program was the continued focus it placed on staying out of military service rather than a more direct confrontation with military conscription. The Vietnam War brought this issue into focus for Mennonites and other religious COs.

The matter came to a crisis for the Mennonite Church (MC) at their general conference at Turner, Ore., in 1969. There the urgent demands of a group of young people requesting a review of Mennonite cooperation with the Selective Service system, placed the issue of how to witness against war squarely at the center of church attention. The response was a movement by the church to acknowledge that refusal of all cooperation with the Selective Service System was legitimate and to offer some church support for such a posture. Widespread endorsement among Mennonites for such a direct challenge by COs to the draft system did not develop.

In 1980 President Carter created mandatory draft registration for all 18-year-old men as a means to send a message to the Soviet Union regarding American commitment to freedom in relation to the Soviet occupation of Afghanistan. The registration law reopened the issue of how COs can best respond to the conscription system. Since there is no actual draft, the matter is focused on whether registration, designed to assert national resolve and military preparedness, is a step appropriate for a CO.

Many Mennonite young men have adopted a stance of nonregistration. In 1982 Mark Schmucker, a 22-year-old from Alliance, Ohio, became the first Mennonite to be tried and found guilty by a jury for violation of the Selective Service Act. He was fined $4,000 and sentenced to serve two years of full-time work at Emmaus House, a facility for retarded adults in Marthasville, Mo.

American Mennonites still overwhelmingly endorse alternative service as the most appropriate form of response to military conscription. A survey made in 1975 showed 71 percent of the Mennonites queried found alternative service their preferred response to military service. Only 3 percent affirmed total refusal of service as an appropriate option (Kauffman/Harder, *Anabaptists Four C. Later*, 133). Greater support for total refusal is evident since renewal of mandatory draft registration. In 1980 an Assembly on The Draft and National Service at Goshen, Ind., sponsored by Mennonite Central Committee Peace Section, summarized what would surely be a contemporary consensus by the church on conscription. It affirmed two options: (1) alternative service, which must be free of all military involvement, and (2) noncooperation (including nonregistration) with any aspect of the conscription system, as a direct challenge to the legitimacy of the military system in all its forms.

In 1982 the General Board of the Mennonite Church wrote a letter to President Reagan on behalf of nonregistrants. Mennonites, by no means in agreement on the matter of nonregistration and draft refusal, nevertheless have moved to a position where the legitimacy of draft refusal is recognized as an appropriate action for draft-age young men.

Since a 1971 Supreme Court decision reversing the Selective Service conviction of boxer Muhammed Ali, three requirements for CO status are in effect: (1) a sincere opposition to war; (2) opposition to war in any form; and (3) CO convictions based on religious training and belief. Sincerity is all-important, but opposition to all wars is also required. Selective objectors are viewed as political rather than religious and are not recognized as legitimate. Since the 1970 Supreme Court case of *Walsh versus United States*, the CO is not required to believe in a deity. A sincere objector may base his claim on moral grounds.

With the end of the draft in 1973, most CO cases have involved military personnel who have developed convictions against military service while serving in the armed forces. In 1981 there were 449 CO claims. Any military person whose conscientious scruples meet the three criteria of the 1971 Supreme Court decision may elect either an I-A-O status (noncombatant), or a I-O classification which carries an automatic honorable discharge.

In the nuclear era with its high-technology volunteer army, new concerns have surfaced regarding conscientious objection in the form of tax resistance. The General Conference Mennonite Church held an unusual session outside the normal triennial pattern to deal with the issue in 1979. Some employees of Mennonite institutions requested their employers to stop withholding tax money from their paychecks, since the employees intend to refuse payment of taxes for war. Because employers are required by law to withhold taxes, such Mennonite institutions find themselves facing contradictory expectations from the government and their Mennonite employees.

Conscientious objection to war has received considerable attention on the international scene during the past decade. In 1978 the United Nations General Assembly passed a resolution recognizing "the right of all persons to refuse service in military and police forces which are used to enforce apartheid," a reference to the plight of COs in South Africa. In 1985 the UN Commission on Human Rights formulated a proposed statement on behalf of COs in connection with the International Youth Year. The proposal is based on article 3 of the Universal Declaration of Human Rights, which guarantees that "Everyone has the right to life," and hence its corollary, the right not to take life. The resolution also invokes the right to freedom of thought, conscience, and religion embodied in article 18 of the Declaration. The proposal enjoins all states to consider legislation which recognizes the right of persons who, for reasons of conscience, cannot perform military service; to release such persons from obligation to perform military service; to develop nonmilitary forms of service; and to refrain from imprisoning COs as punishment for their refusal of military service.

The Federal Republic of Germany had 63,334 applications for CO status in 1983. A new law adopted in February 1983 raised the length of alternative service from 16 to 21 months (the length of military service was 15 months). The new law also replaced test of conscience with proof of sincerity based on acts which validate the CO convictions.

In France a law recognizing COs was passed by the national assembly in 1963. CO status was granted, on the basis of religious and philosophical reasons, to anyone who, in all circumstances, opposed the use of weapons. Alternative civilian service for two years is possible with employment administered through the Ministry of Agriculture. In 1984, 1,866 COs entered alternative service.

Recently Argentina has introduced a bill which offers COs an option to do social and humanitarian work in lieu of military service. A similar provision is in effect in Colombia. Brazil wrote a provision for alternative service for COs into its new constitution, adopted in October 1988.

Most nations in the world do not recognize conscientious objection to military service as a legitimate position. Countries in this category with significant Mennonite populations include the Soviet Union, and, until 1988, Switzerland (see below). In almost no case is total exemption possible. In most cases where the CO position is acknowledged, provisions are also in effect requiring some form of alternative civilian or noncombatant service.

A recent survey of American Mennonites found that only 69 percent would adopt a CO position. That suggests that the issue of conscientious objection to war is not merely a matter between church and world, but an ongoing challenge to the church at the center of its convictional and theological life.

Thus the worldwide Mennonite Church continues to encounter a variety of contexts in which fidelity to conscience and commitment to the way of love and nonresistance continues to be challenged. ANK

Switzerland. Historically all men in the Swiss Confederation were required to do military service. The service program was regionally administered before 1800. While there was no alternative service option, those objecting to military service for reasons of conscience could be freed from it through the payment of a substantial sum of money, or through the securing of an alternate representative. After the political changes in Switzerland ca. 1788, in the wake of the French Revolution, and particularly after the new Swiss constitution was adopted in 1874, these latter options were no longer available.

The present (1987) constitution reads: "Every Swiss male is required to fulfill military service" (article 18); "Freedom of faith and conscience is guaranteed" (article 49, section 1); "Faith convictions do not relieve a person of his responsibilities as a citizen" (article 49).

It is, therefore, the duty of every Swiss man between the ages of 20-50, to render military service. Until 1988, those who refused, served up to three years in prison and were entered in the register of criminals. If the refusal was based on "religious or ethical convictions" and the objector suffers "severe pangs of conscience," he might be required to serve only six months of the prison term. Those who could not serve for health or other reasons were required to pay the full amount for a substitute, including his equipment. Refusal to do this led to imprisonment, listing in the criminal records, and the posting of bond. Military tribunals heard 686 CO cases in 1985. In a modest way consideration was given to COs by the army in assigning them to the medical corps or air defense troops. There was no legal way, however, to avoid military service. Arrangements for alternative service were being introduced for the first time in 1988 (*Brücke* [Mar. 1988], 45).

The Articles of Faith adopted by the Swiss Mennonite Conference in 1983 reaffirmed the historic nonresistant position, stating: "As followers of Jesus we reject the use of force and encourage the witness of peace, beginning in our own personal living." Apparently a considerable majority of Swiss Mennonites wished to be nonresistant, but understandings of what this means differ considerably. As of 1987 it was estimated that one-half of Swiss Mennonite men fulfilled their military obligation, and that the other half did this also within the context of the army, but without weapons. Approximately 24 had refused military service up to 1987.

The numerous different understandings of the meaning of conscientious objection have their roots in theological, sociological, and cultural developments. Originally, many suffered martyrdom because of this conviction. Later, geographical and cultural withdrawal from society gave some respite, but led to theological paralysis. Privileges were purchased at the price of their own identity. Beyond this it may be that those who felt strongest about this issue emigrated to the Palatinate and North America, while those more ready to compromise stayed. Eventually, °pietism and °revivalism entered the congregations and further marginalized the Anabaptist heritage. After centuries of isolation Mennonites increasingly wished to be like others, to be recognized for their hard work, professional achievements, and morality. Thus they were seen as biblical people in the world, but were also increasingly of the world. Remaining convictions about counterculture issues were internalized.

In recent years a new concern for spiritual and social relevance and renewal in keeping with the Anabaptist heritage has emerged. One expression of this is the founding of the commission for military affairs by the Swiss Mennonite Conference in 1970. Since 1982 this has been changed to the °Schweizerisches Mennonitisches Friedenskomitee (SMFK; Swiss Mennonite Peace Committee), which has undertaken further work in this areas.   HJeck

Mark Becker, "Mennonite Resistance to Draft Registration, 1980-1985" (unpublished paper, Bethel College, Ks., (1985); P. Bender, "Kriegsdienstverweigerung aus Gewissensgründen," Menn. Geschbl., Jg. 17, n.F. 12 (1960), 14-28; James Juhnke, A People of Two Kingdoms (Newton, 1972); Al Keim, Conscientious Objection and the Historic Peace Churches (Scottdale, 1987); Melvin Gingerich, Service for Peace (Akron: MCC, 1949); Urbane Peachey and Brenda Hurst, International Provisions for COs (Akron, Pa., MCC Peace Section, 1982); Dirk Eitzen and Timothy Falb, An Overview of the Mennonite I-W Program (Akron, Pa.: MCC Peace Section, 1980); Juhnke, Mission (1979), 120-23 (Japan), 141 (Taiwan); Wittlinger, Piety and Obedience (1978), 366-93; Werner Bauman, Die Entwicklung der Wehrpflicht in der Schweizerischen Eidgenossenschaft, 1803-1874 (Zürich, 1932); Hanspeter Jecker, "Die Militärfrage: Die Haltung der Schweizerischen Täufer zur Entwicklung der Allgemeinen Wehrpflicht" (Basel, 1976; mimeographed, available from Schweizerischer Verein für Täufergeschichte); MWR (Nov. 17, 1988), 1.

See also Nazarenes; Deutsches Mennonitisches Friedenskomitee; Nicaragua; Iglesia Evangélica Menonita, Honduras; Bogotá, Colombia.

Conscription. During the °Vietnam War period, 1960-73, in the United States 171,000 draft-age men were granted the °conscientious objector (CO) classification by the Selective Service System. A larger number, approximately 500,000, had decisions made about the validity of their CO claims. Selective Service officials stated that they do not have a record of how many men filed claims for a CO classification during the Vietnam War period. Including those disqualified for health or other reasons, it is estimated that as many as one million draft-age youth were CO claimants, the largest proportion in any United States war in the 20th c. The total male population of draftable age during the Vietnam War was 27 million.

Selective Service calculations state that 250,000 were nonregistrants during the Vietnam war period. An additional 325,000 draft-law violators existed, but the data is not available to indicate how many of these were COs under the legal definition. The vast majority of Mennonites drafted during the Vietnam War utilized their legal option, alternative civilian service, to avoid military induction. More than 50 draft-age Mennonite men took steps of noncooperation with the Selective Service System for reasons of conscience, some going to Canada, others going to prison for refusing to register with Selective Service.

A statement adopted by the Mennonite Church (MC) in 1969, and a similar statement adopted by the General Conference Mennonite Church in 1971, recognized the validity of noncooooperation as a legitimate witness and pledged to support these young men even in their difficult circumstances.

Amnesty for draft resisters and military resisters was sought by scores of organizations and church bodies following the Vietnam War, as a means of "binding up the wounds" of that divisive war. It was not to be. The legislation introduced to enact a full amnesty proved also to be divisive in the larger American society.

President Gerald Ford introduced in September 1974 a clemency program to restore certain civil rights, with the conditions that participants take an oath of allegiance and perform alternative civilian service as the components of "earned re-entry." The clemency program ended as a failure March 31, 1975, six months after it began. Only 24,847 of the 124,515 eligible applied for the program. Considered punitive, it was rejected by 82 percent of the resisters who had moved to Canada or Europe. An MCC Peace Section statement, "A Christian Declaration on Amnesty" was adopted in January 1973.

The United States Supreme Court decisions of Welsh versus United States (1970) and U.S. versus Seeger (1965) addressed two longstanding issues affecting COs. The Welsh decision broadened the criteria for the CO classification. These criteria had previously insisted on deeply held religious beliefs. The Welsh decision specified "deeply held moral and ethical convictions" as the criteria for conscientious objector status. U.S. versus Sisson (June 29, 1970) held that to qualify as a CO, the registrant must be opposed to participation in all wars, i.e., cannot be a selective objector.   DF

Lawrence Baskir and William A. Strauss, Chance and Circumstance: The Draft, The War and the Vietnam Generation (New York: Knopf, 1978); Melissa Miller and Phil M. Shenk, The Path of Most Resistance (Scottdale, 1982).

See also Beachy Amish Mennonite Fellowship; Church-State Relations; Military Service.

Conseil Mennonite Belge (Belgian Mennonite Council) is a nonlegal, fraternal body responsible for coordinating the Mennonite witness in Belgium emerging from the work of Mennonite Board of Missions (MC), begun in 1950.

The Conseil originated in the late 1960s under the leadership of David A. Shank, followed as president by José Gallardo (1973-77). The president in 1987, Willy Hubinont, has served since 1978, when the Conseil was reorganized through Mennonite Board of Missions (MBM) initiative. Other officers are Jules Lambotte, Jr., vice-president; and Sylvia Shirk Charles, secretary.

The Conseil began as a consultation of workers of different nationalities (United States, Belgian, Italian, Russian, and Spanish) receiving MBM support for evangelistic, social, educational, pastoral, radio, and publishing ministries. While never organized as a Mennonite conference, the council has included persons from five congregations variously related to MBM work: East Brussels, Rixensart, Brussels Spanish, Flavion, and Slavic Evangelical. Total membership in 1984 was 85.

East Brussels, Rixensart, and Flavion belonged to the Groupe des Églises Evangéliques Mennonites de Langue Française (French-Speaking Evangelical Mennonite Conference) until this group's merger in 1979 into the Association des Églises Evangéliques Mennonites de France (Association of Evangelical Mennonite Churches of France, AEEMF). In 1987 Flavion was affiliated with AEEMF. Rixensart joined the United Protestant Church of Belgium in 1983 after an earlier (1972-79) affiliation with the Reformed Church of Belgium. The Brussels Mennonite Center opened in 1982 as a joint Conseil Mennonite Belge and MBM project. RC

David A. Shank, "Discovering the Strategy of the Spirit," in *Being God's Missionary Community* (Elkhart, Ind.: MBM, 1975), 23-30; Annual Reports of MBM, 1951-; *MWH* (1984), 113.

Consejo de las Congregaciónes de los Hermanos Menonitas, Uruguay (Council of Mennonite Brethren Congregations). The Mennonite Brethren church in Uruguay consisted in 1986 of seven established congregations with a combined membership of 180 persons. With the exception of several families, the previously numerous German Mennonite Brethren community had emigrated to Germany and Canada. Mennonite Brethren missionary endeavors among Spanish-speaking Uruguayans began in 1966.

Overall leadership within the conference is provided by an executive council, while each individual church is pastored by a trained couple or committee. A Bible institute was established in 1978. Fifteen students had graduated from the three-year program by 1986.

Periodic rallies bringing the congregations together for celebration and instruction are highlights in the church calendar. A major contribution to the church's life is made by Camp Maranatha, a lovely beach property with room for 60 persons. The facility is also rented to other evangelical groups. The conference's publication is *Faro del Sur* (Southern Beacon).

The Mennonite Brethren Board of Missions and Services works in partnership with the national conference in the areas of evangelism, church planting, and Christian education. In 1986, four missionary couples were serving. New church planting efforts were being made in a suburb of Montevideo and in Paysandu, Uruguay's second largest city.

Church growth has been slow and characterized by reversals. A strong economic and leadership base has been slow in forming and evangelism has often been perceived as the task of the foreign missionary instead of the function and result of a vital church community life. More recently, interest in home Bible study groups and discipleship ministry began to grow, and renewed awareness of the church as the people of God gifted for ministry to one another and to the world, began to revitalize existing congregations. These developments were generating new hope for growth in the future. FM

MWH (1978), 267-69; *MWH* (1984), 105.

Consensus. The consensus pattern of °decisionmaking is reflected in the life of the early church. The consultation procedure followed during the conference at Jerusalem described in Acts 15, included a variety of components: the gathering together of church leaders, identification of the issue, sharing various points of view, an appeal to history and biblical truth, a review of current experiences, summarizing a possible direction based on a new interpretation of Scripture, gaining consensus on key points, and trusted leaders communicating the outcome. This model of decisionmaking appears to have

been followed in the Anabaptist communities according to Peachey, Redekop, and others (see °decisionmaking). The consensus model takes seriously the Anabaptists' understanding of the church as a community in search for truth. It allows for a mutuality in decisionmaking which values the insights and views of the entire body of gathered believers.

In recent decades various interpretations have been given on the meaning of consensus as a form of decisionmaking. Lippitt sees a difference between unanimous decisionmaking and a consensus decision. In the latter case people agree on a course of action, but those who disagree reserve the right to test the intended action which will be evaluated later. This amounts to a provisional decision. This approach is different than compromise, which entails bringing two opposing views together forming a new proposal different from the two original ideas. In consensus, people may not be sure of the right decision but are willing to give the proposal a try.

Others would see consensus more in the direction of an unanimous decision, or coming to a "common mind." The Quaker view is that this is not a "humanistic" process using good group dynamics procedures. It is rather a search for truth to discern "the mind of Christ." Through the use of silence, listening carefully to the insight of community members, the group moves in a direction which reflects the sense of the meeting. The clerk of the meeting possesses the skills to draw together the emerging consensus of the group.

Consensus decisionmaking need not presuppose full unanimity. However, consideration must be given to those people who have not fully made up their mind but are willing to proceed, given a time of testing and evaluation. Futher, there may be those who would choose to go a different direction, but for the sake of the group are prepared to support a decision to move ahead. Various procedures can be used to test whether consensus has been reached, such as a voice or hand vote or outlining the decision and asking whether people disagree.

The consensus approach works well where the group is not too large, is relatively homogenous, has a high level of trust, and is accustomed to interacting with one another. RL

Gordon L. Lippitt, "Improving Decisionmaking With Groups," in *Group Development*, Selected Reading Series One, National Training Laboratories (1961), 90-93; Harold Bauman, *Congregations and Their Servant Leaders* (Scottdale: MPH, 1982), 7-16; Willard Claassen, *Learning to Lead*, Christian Service Training Series (Scottdale and Newton, 1963), 79-90; *Concern Pamphlet*, no. 14 (1967); Howard Brinton, "Reaching Decisions," in *Friends for 300 Years* (New York: Harper, 1952), ch. 6, also published as Pendle Hill Pamphlet, no. 65; Calvin Redekop, *The Free Church and Seductive Culture* (Scottdale, 1970), 70-71.

See also Democracy.

Conservative Mennonite Church of Ontario was established in 1959. Curtis Cressman and Moses Roth, bishops; Moses Baer and Elmer Grove, ministers; Andrew Axt and Clarence Huber, deacons; with their followers, held their first separate church service on Nov. 22, 1959, at the Township Hall, Baden. Services at Baden continued until the New Hamburg Conservative Mennonite church was built in 1960.

The Heidelberg and Fort Stewart congregations were established the same year.

The reason for the group's withdrawal from the Mennonite Conference of Ontario (and Quebec) (MC) was the desire to return to earlier biblical standards of °nonconformity to the unequal yoke in regard to °politics, immodest attire (°dress), women's hair cutting, and wearing of jewelry. They wanted closer adherence and obedience to scriptural church °ordinances. Their appeal to the conference was ineffective, resulting in their withdrawal.

In 1975, issues relating to °radio and °television again surfaced, causing about one-third of the most lenient members to secede and establish the Heidelberg Fellowship Church.

In 1986 there were 11 congregations, with 4 bishops, 17 ministers, and 7 deacons. Membership was 418. Ten schools offer instruction up to grade 10. Under the °Fellowship Churches program, the Conservative Mennonite Church of Ontario supports missions in India, Nigeria, Mexico, Dominican Republic, and the Philippines.   IRH

Mennonite Archives of Ontario, Conrad Grebel College, Waterloo, Ont.; *Constitution and Faith and Practice of the Mennonite Church of Ontario*; *Directory of the Fellowship Churches* (Farmington, N. Mex.: Lamp and Light Publishers, Inc.); Reimer, *Quilt* (1983), 18.

Conservative Mennonite Churches of York and Adams Counties, Pa., consists in 1986 of six congregations: Hanover, Hershey, Kralltown, Mummasburg, North Hartman Street in York, and Winterstown. They were formerly a part of the York-Adams District of the Lancaster Mennonite Conference (MC) and asked to be released in 1975 because of certain trends in the Lancaster Conference. In 1986 Elmer H. Kreider was the bishop. There were nine ministers, seven deacons, and a membership of 221.   BN

MC Yearbook (1988-89), 101.

See also Conservative Mennonites.

Conservative Mennonite Conference (ME I:700), was organized in 1910 as the Conservative Amish Mennonite Conference. The word *Amish* was dropped from the name with the adoption of a revised constitution in 1957. The °°Amish Mennonites were that segment of the °°Swiss Brethren who followed Jakob °Ammann in the Amish division of 1693-97, in part under influence of the strict °discipline of North German and Dutch Mennonites. From their first American settlement in Berks Co., Pa. (1710-20), and strengthened by later immigration, they moved westward with the North American frontier so that by midcentury they were scattered in autonomous congregations from eastern Pennsylvania to Ontario and Iowa. To unify these scattered churches, Amish Mennonite ministers' conferences were held in 1862-78. After 1878 these meetings were discontinued, and three district Amish Mennonite conferences were formed: Eastern A. M., Indiana-Michigan A. M., and Western A. M. Some Amish Mennonite congregations did not join the conference movement, and others withdrew during the ministers' meetings or after their termination. These nonconference churches met for worship in private homes, held to former worship patterns, including the German language, and generally tended to reject

innovations. They came to be known as Old Order Amish, Mennonites and finally as Old Order Amish. The term *Amish* has come to refer nearly exclusively to Old Order Amish as the conference Amish Mennonites merged with Mennonite groups, primarily the Mennonite Church (MC).

Between the Old Order Amish Mennonites and the conference Amish Mennonites were some congregations, interested in missions and social service, publication, use of meetinghouses, Sunday schools, etc., that had not joined the Amish Mennonite conferences. In the early 1900s the *Mennonite Yearbook* (MC) began listing these churches as *Conservative Amish Mennonite*. When these congregations met in their first conference in 1910 they adopted the name as their own.

Since 1950 the Conservative Mennonite Conference has representatives on the major boards of the Mennonite Church (MC) but has declined to be organically affiliated, thus maintaining a rather loose, fraternal relationship with the Mennonite Church (MC) General Assembly (formerly General Conference).

In 1964 the Conservative Mennonite Bible School was moved from the Pleasant View meetinghouse near Berlin, Ohio, to the village of Rosedale on Rosedale-MC Road, Irwin, Ohio. Known as Rosedale, Bible Institute, the school offers courses in Bible, theology, evangelism, teacher training, music, and related subjects on both high school and college levels. Credits are transferable to various colleges and seminaries. The conference missions and service offices, known as Rosedale Mennonite Missions (also known as Conservative Mennonite Board of Missions and Charities), are located on the same campus. So also are the conference °archives.

In 1961 Rosedale Mennonite Mission opened mission work in Costa Rica. By 1974 the Costa Rica Mennonite Conference had been formed, with fraternal ties to the parent conference. The Costa Rica conference in 1986 had 1,053 members in 19 congregations with 20 ordained or licensed ministers. In 1968 mission work was opened in Nicaragua. By 1977 the Nicaragua Mennonite Conference had been formed, with fraternal ties to the parent conference. The Nicaragua conference in 1986 had 723 members in 30 congregations with 21 ordained or licensed ministers. In 1982 mission work was opened in Ecuador. There were 27 members in 1986. The conference launched the *Brotherhood Beacon*, an official monthly periodical in 1971.

The Conservative Mennonite Conference in 1986 had 7,918 members in 99 congregations and mission points, served by 60 bishops, 160 ministers, 11 deacons, and 11 licensed ministers.   IJM

MC Yearbook (1988-89), 49-52; Ivan J. Miller, *History of the Conservative Mennonite Conference* (Grantsville, Md.: the author, 1985); Conservative Mennonite Conference, *Conservative Conference Reports* (Irwin, Ohio, 1910-86).

Conservative Mennonite Fellowship is one of a number of fellowships of conservative-minded independent congregations. It was formed in June 1957 to counteract tendencies toward compromise and apostasy. It operates under a constitution based on the updated Eighteen Articles of Christian Fundamentals (1921; Loewen, *Confessions,* 71) as adopted in 1964 at Hartville, Ohio. The fellowship is strongly °nonresistant and °nonconformed in practice, with uniform plain °dress standards, including uncut, veiled hair for women (prayer veil), and closely cut hair for men. In 1985 it consisted of 5 congregations in Ohio, Ontario, Indiana, and Delaware (174 members).

Itinerant mission activity in Central America, begun in 1961, resulted in the establishment in 1964 of the first Mennonite mission in Guatemala at Chimaltenango. It is operated by a board elected by the fellowship ministers. *The Guatemalan Cry* recounts its first 10 years. A similar board operates an 11-week Bible school (Messiah Bible School) at Carbon Hill, Ohio. A free 12-page monthly, *The Harvest Call,* carries mission, Bible school, and congregational materials.   HWH

Dallas Witmer, *The Guatemalan Cry* (Seymour, Mo.: Edgewood Press, 1974); *The Conservative Mennonite Fellowship, A Brief Account of the First Ten Years* (Hartville, Ohio: The Fellowship Messenger, 1968); *The Harvest Call* (Salisbury, Md.); *MC Yearbook* (1988-89), 92.

See also Ohio.

Conservative Mennonite Fellowship, Guatemala. The Conservative Mennonite Fellowship mission board sent Jacob and Martha Coblentz as their first missionaries to Guatemala in 1964. Chimaltenango, a rural town an hour west of Guatemala City, became the center of operations, and over the next 10 years more than 50 persons coming from North America served in numerous Cachiquel and Quiche Indian villages in the central highlands north and west of Chimaltenango. Various small animal, agriculture, and rural health projects were established. In 1983 missionary John Mast of Michigan was shot to death by unidentified armed men in Palama, where he lived and worked. The first converts were baptized in 1968. By 1987 there were 130 members in three congregations. Small Christian schools are operated for the church families and neighbors. Three ordained ministers and a deacon assist the missionary men in pastoral work. Contacts made in Guatemala related to this mission resulted in work by the Messianic Mission Board (Eastern Pennsylvania Mennonite Church) in the western department of Quetzaltenango.   AY

MWH (1984), 73; *MC Yearbook* (1988-89), 156, 164.

Conservative Mennonites (Dutch-Prussian-Russian). The Anabaptist reform movements of the 16th c. exhibited in the subsequent centuries an amazing capacity to divide and reunite. This article will survey the dividing and the reuniting of one stream of the Mennonite family, namely, the Dutch Mennonites who migrated to Poland (Prussia), Russia, Canada, and Latin America.

The parallel term "Old Orders" is used principally to refer to North American Swiss-Pennsylvania Mennonites and Amish. It refers to the dividing processes among Amish and Mennonites in which some groups separated in order to conserve or maintain the old ways or the old order (Ordnung). Although the term "Old Orders" was not normally used in the stream of Mennonitism being discussed in this article, the process is present. It is this process which will be described here, under the label "conserving" or "conservative Mennonites."

Early Dutch Anabaptists and Mennonites both united and divided. During the time of Menno Simons, the Dutch united into two groups, the Menists or Mennonites, and the °°Waterlanders. The principal issue dividing these two groups was church °discipline. Waterlanders were more lenient and the Menists stricter in exercising church discipline. How church discipline was administered affected their expression of pacifism (°nonresistance), relationships to the surrounding culture, intermarriage with non-Mennonites, lifestyle, etc. In 1567, shortly after these two groups had formed, the Menists divided into the °°Frisian and °°Flemish factions. Again, the main issue was church discipline, with the Frisians more lenient and the Flemish somewhat stricter. Not long after the division, both groups began to divide into factions, again shaped largely by the stance on church discipline. The Old Flemish attempted to retain the stricter views of the past, whereas the "Soft" Flemish moved closer to the less strict Frisians. The Old Frisians, in trying to retain the old ways, moved closer to the Flemish, and the New Frisians moved closer to the more lenient Waterlanders and °°High Germans. The people who were the strictest separated from the Old Flemish and formed the °°Borstentasters, °°Bankroetiers, and °°Jan Lucasvolk factions.

Under the influence of the °°Socinians and the °°Remonstrants, the focus of issues in the Netherlands shifted from church discipline to doctrine. In 1664 practically all the Dutch groups realigned into two groups, one (the °°Zonists) which emphasized the necessity of correct doctrine, and another (the °°Lamists) which emphasized inner personal faith and downplayed the necessity of correct doctrine. These two groupings remained separate until the Napoleonic era, when the central issue shifted to the necessity to educate leaders. Because of serious membership losses by both groups, neither was able to finance the operation of a seminary. Therefore, in 1811 the two groups joined to form the °°Algemeene Doopsgezinde Sociëteit and jointly provided the finances for the °°Amsterdam Mennonite Theological Seminary in Amsterdam. The Dutch church had no subsequent divisions.

The Frisian-Flemish division was imported into Poland by 1569, and this division remained in effect when the churches came under Prussian rule in 1772, and even after the emigration to New Russia in 1788. The same issue, church discipline, was the issue which separated the two. As in the Netherlands, the Frisians were more lenient and the Flemish stricter in the use of church discipline. These two groups remained opposed to each other until after the Napoleonic wars when, due to the influence of Pietism and Prussian nationalism, the antagonism gradually disappeared.

When the Chortitza and Molotschna settlements were established in New Russia, the Frisian and Flemish division was still strong enough to result in the formation of separate churches. However, in both settlements, fraternal relationships developed almost immediately so that this division did not have a major impact upon Mennonite life in Russia.

In New Russia the central issue which caused di-

NETHERLANDS: MENNONITES - DOOPSGEZINDE

Compiled by John Friesen (author of article)

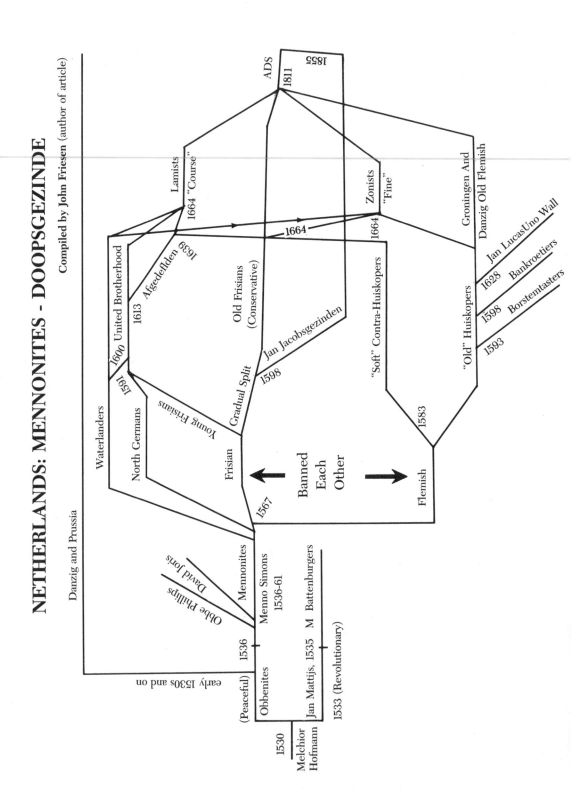

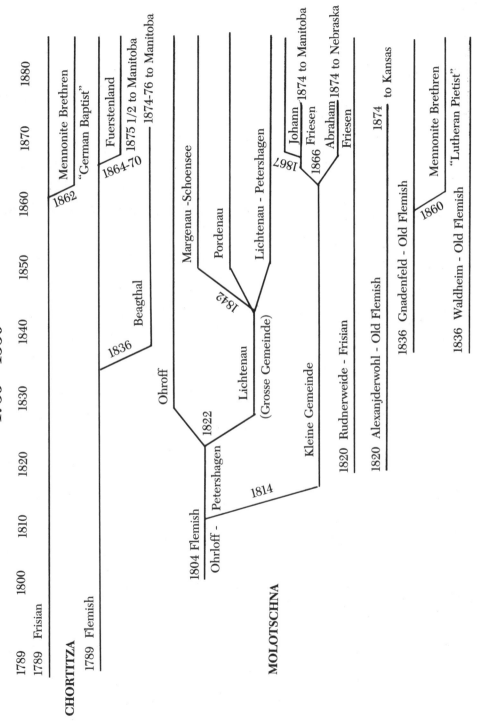

MENNONITES IN RUSSIA
1789 - 1880

visions was the role that civil Mennonite organizations should play within Mennonite communities. This problem arose because the Russian government insisted that Mennonites, like all other foreign colonists, establish local civil organizations which were to be responsible to the Department of the Interior. The local Mennonite civil organizations were responsible for roads, bridges, and other municipal affairs, as well as local administration of justice. During the days of Johann °°Cornies, the civil organizations took control of education from church leaders.

Out of this context, two key issues emerged, namely, who was responsible for administering church discipline, and who controlled °education—the church or civil organizations? The conservers of the "old order" believed that the church should administer church discipline with the traditional patterns of admonition, °°ban, and reacceptance upon confession. They also believed that the church should control the education of children, and that education should prepare them for membership in the church and local village community. The progressives, or innovators, were willing to see the civil administation take over control of the schools, so that in their view the quality of the schools could be upgraded, and the curriculum could be broadened to include studies far beyond what was necessary for life in a Mennonite village and church. In brief, the innovators were willing to allow the civil administrations to play an increasingly important role in shaping the character of Russian Mennonitism.

In the Chortitza settlement many of the conservers were able to separate themselves from the innovators by moving to the new settlements of Bergthal, founded in 1836, and Fürstenland, founded from 1864 to 1870 (°Bergthal Mennonites). In the 1860s the Frisian church in the Chortitza settlement divided, with the formation of a Mennonite Brethren Church under German Baptist influence. The Mennonite Brethren asserted church control over discipline and argued that the old church (°°Kirchen-Gemeinden), from which they were separating, was lax, since, they asserted, everyone was considered a member in good standing, and no test of authentic faith, no discipline was exercised.

The Molotschna settlement suffered more separations than the Chortitza settlement over the issues of how to relate to the civil Mennonite organizations. The first church in the Molotschna colony (founded 1804) was Flemish. Its leaders accommodated to the establishment of civil Mennonite organizations. In 1812 some Mennonites under the leadership of Klaas °Reimer objected to this situation in which the civil authorities were taking over the discipline of Mennonite people through the exercise of civil punishments. They argued that the church should exercise discipline through a process which would lead to forgiveness. When the leaders continued to support the civil organizations, the °°Kleine Gemeinde was formed.

Most members of the Molotschna Flemish Church, even though they did not join the Kleine Gemeinde, nevertheless disagreed with the stance of the leadership, which was accommodating to the civil organizations. Consequently, in 1822 the majority of the Flemish left to form the Lichtenau-Petershagen

church. The smaller group which remained with the accommodating leadership was the Ohrloff Church. This group became the center for most innovations in the Molotschna school settlement. It established the first secondary schools, with their new curriculum, and introduced new farming methods. Through Johann Cornies it attempted to impose its innovations upon the rest of the Russian Mennonites.

The Lichtenau-Petershagen Church, also known as the Grosse (large) church, seriously attempted to retain the old ways of administering discipline through the church. They ran into direct conflict with the Russian government, which supported the civil Mennonite organizations. The result was that in 1842 the Russian government broke up the Lichtenau-Petershagen Church into three smaller factions which could be controlled more easily, and forced the °elder (Ältester) to abdicate his position.

Four additional churches were formed in the Molotschna settlement as a result of immigration from Prussia. One, the Rudnerweider (1820), was Frisian, and the other three were Flemish, namely Alexanderwohl (1820), Gnadenfeld (1836), and Waldheim (1836). These four accommodated themselves to the prevailing pattern in which the civil organizations had control of discipline and education.

The Mennonite Brethren Church originated in 1860 in the Molotschna settlement. The movement began largely in the context of the Gnadenfeld Flemish congregation, a congregation which had immigrated in 1836. The Mennonite Brethren movement soon drew adherents from throughout the Molotschna settlement. The Mennonites who formed the Mennonite Brethren movement especially criticized the Mennonite churches for being unwilling to exercise the necessary discipline. The problems that the Mennonite Brethren pointed out were largely caused by the influence of the civil Mennonite organizations, which had on the one hand caused the church to relax discipline, and on the other had created a civil Mennonite community in which the churches were not free to exclude anyone from the church. The Mennonite Brethren leaders were thus in a sense also conservers, calling the church back to express the discipline of its former days. This critique of the Mennonite churches was, however, not shaped solely by the attempt to restore the old ways. Mennonite Brethren leaders also wanted to implement new ideas learned from Lutheran Pietists or from German Baptists.

Mennonites who migrated to Manitoba, Canada, in the 1870s came primarily from two sources. One group consisted of one-half of the Kleine Gemeinde (the other half of the Kleine Gemeinde settled in Nebraska). The other group consisted of people from the Bergthal and Fürstenland settlements in Russia which, when they were first formed, had drawn conservers from Chortitza. The Bergthal and Fürstenland people were joined in their trek to Manitoba by conservers from their mother colony, Chortitza. They all hoped to establish settlements in Canada in which the church would have control over education and discipline, and in which civil authority would be subordinate to religious authority.

In Canada, however, the situation was quite different from that in Russia. The Mennonite civil organizations, e.g., the village Vorsteher (mayor's office; °°Schulze) and regional *Obervorsteher*, were not supported by the government. These organizations were purely voluntary. Instead of supporting the Mennonite civil organizations, governments proceeded to impose their own civil organizations upon Mennonite settlements. Governments first took over municipal matters and then gradually the education system. Mennonite churches in Manitoba and Saskatchewan found the spheres of community life over which they had authority gradually shrinking. It thus became clear that the policy of the provincial governments was to integrate Mennonites into the Canadian way of life. In Canada °acculturation thus became the issue around which divisions occurred.

Acculturation involved not only questions of authority over schools and community organizations, it involved also faith and beliefs. Those who accommodated usually felt that their earlier theology was inadequate to express their new outlook. In Manitoba two patterns developed for formulating new theologies. Within what became known as the (Manitoba) °Bergthal Mennonites, a new theology was shaped through higher education with the establishment of a secondary school at Gretna in 1889. More than three-quarters of the Bergthal-Fürstenland-Chortitza immigrants rejected this option, chose to retain the old ways, and formed in 1893 what became the °Sommerfeld Mennonites.

The other pattern the acculturating group used was to shape a new theology on the basis of a °revivalist movement. The revivalist movements were rooted in North America and seemed to give better theological expression to a North American way of life. As a result of revivalist influence, half of the Kleine Gemeinde followed its elder into the °Church of God in Christ Mennonite. The other half of the Kleine Gemeinde followed the older ways, eventually becoming the °Evangelical Mennonite Conference. In 1888 a small group of Reinländer Mennonites (Old Colonists) left to form the first Mennonite Brethren Church in Canada. The large Reinländer Church continued to follow the old ways (°Old Colony Mennonites). In 1898 some Kleine Gemeinde members formed the first °°Bruderthaler Mennonite Church in Canada. The Kleine Gemeinde followed the old ways.

The conservers feared that by accommodating to the new ways they would jeopardize their faith in God, which included community and peace witness. By the 1920s many of the conservers felt that they could no longer follow the old ways adequately in Manitoba and Saskatchewan. Many conservers emigrated to Mexico and Paraguay, while other conservers, for various reasons, remained in Canada. By the 1930s the Canadian conserving groups consisted of Chortitzer (Conference), Sommerfelder, Old Colony, and Kleine Gemeinde (°Evangelical Mennonite Conference) in Manitoba; and Sommerfelder, Bergthaler, and Old Colony in Saskatchewan.

The dividing over the issues of acculturation, accommodation, and revivalism continued. In 1936 a group of more accommodating Sommerfelder Mennonites split to form the Rudnerweider Mennonites (later becoming the Evangelical Mennonite Mission Conference). In 1948, because of the new acculturating pressures caused by World War II, a number of groups of conservers moved to Latin America—

some Bergthaler, Sommerfelder, and Chortitzer to Paraguay; some Kleine Gemeinde to Mexico. In the 1960s some conservers emigrated to Bolivia.

In 1959 a group of Sommerfelder Mennonites felt that their church had become too accommodating, and left to form the Reinländer Mennoniten-Gemeinde Church. In 1983 a group of Old Colonists who wanted slightly more accommodation left the Old Colony church in Manitoba to form the Zion Mennonite Church. In 1986 a group of Reinländer felt the church had become too accommodating and left to found a new group, the °Friedensfelder Mennoniten Gemeinde.

The churches which moved to Latin America were not immune to divisions. Not all the people who emigrated were of one mind about how to relate to the surrounding cultures. In Latin America, in contrast to Canada, the churches usually had much stronger control over the affairs of the whole Mennonite community. The greater autonomy of the Mennonite settlements gave the Mennonite churches greater authority over settlement life. For Mennonite churches in Latin America, the role of church leadership became the central issue around which church divisions tended to develop.

The settlements in Paraguay generally were able to evolve leadership patterns which were representative of the wishes of the people. Thus in Paraguay none of the original settlements from Canada experienced divisions.

The situation was quite different in Mexico. In Mexico the leaders in the Mennonite settlements tended to become increasingly authoritarian and were perceived by some to exercise their authority arbitrarily. Thus the divisions frequently represented revolts against the authority of the church leaders. The formation of mission churches, decisions by some of the Old Colonists to join the Kleine Gemeinde, and by others to join the Reinländer, tended to represent a revolt or rejection of the authority of the church leaders. These revolts usually involved not only theological changes, but were accompanied by changed life-style, different clothing styles, changed modes of transportation, and often by the development of better schools. Divisions also happened in the more conserving direction by those who thought that the authority of the church leaders had been eroded too much and that people had gone their own ways too far. These conservers tended to separate by moving to another location to found a new setlement either in Mexico or in some other Latin American country.

Conservers have played an important role in the history of the Mennonite people. They have often intuitively sensed the close interrelationship and interdependence between cultural forms and religious values. They have realized that cultural forms become the carriers and communal symbols for theological values. They have seen that values are not free-floating, but rather are incarnated in cultural forms, and that the values and their cultural incarnations cannot easily be separated without destroying the values themselves.

Conservers have frequently been the pioneers in Mennonite °migrations. They had the vision and the motivation to move because they valued their beliefs highly enough to give up financial security for an

THE DIVISIONS AND DISPERSIONS OF MEXICO MENNONITES

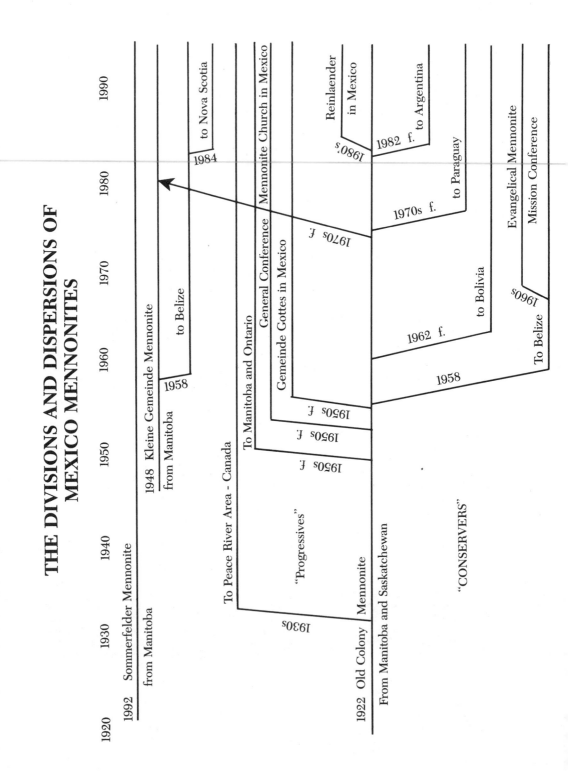

uncertain future. Consequently, they have frequently been the pioneers in new regions in Russia, Canada, and Latin America. Often after they struggled through the pioneer years to build more comfortable settings, the more progressive fellow Mennonites joined them and built on the foundation they had established. Then the progressives frequently, in a mood of ungratefulness, either reviled the conservers for being too conservative, or tried to convert them because they seemed to the progressives to be lacking in spiritual, expressive faith.

From the view of the progressives, the conservers have frequently seemed too strongly inward looking, too closed, and lacking a vision to relate to the larger society. From the conservers' own perspective, they have attempted to emphasize the preeminence of faith for all of life, have tried to maintain the structures of community, have sensed the potentially destructive force of individualism, and have been tenacious in maintaining pacifism. They have played an important role within the larger Mennonite community in continuing to witness to Christian values, beliefs, and practices.   JF

See also Old Colony Mennonites; Hutterian Brethren.

Conservative Mennonites (Swiss-High German, Pennsylvania). The assemblage of congregations and fellowships referred to as "conservative" Mennonites is an elusive group to identify. Some are composed of persons almost exclusively of Amish origin (°Beachy Amish Mennonite Fellowship), while a smaller number are exclusively of Mennonite origin. Still others have a high degree of mixture of Amish and Mennonite elements. The gradual evolution of the names in common usage also contributes to the difficulty. A similar variety of "conserving" or conservative Mennonites in the Dutch and Russian Mennonite tradition clusters around the °Old Colony Mennonites and the branches of the °Bergthal Mennonites, including °Sommerfeld Mennonites and the °Chortitzer Mennonite Conference. The reader should also consult related articles on °Old Colony Mennonites and °Old Order Mennonites (also ME IV:38-48).

Most of the groups using the name *conservative Mennonite* trace their origin to the °Amish rather than to the Mennonites. Those which would best qualify for the conservative *Mennonite* name do not use the term *conservative*; rather, they are usually identified by such names as Old Order Mennonite (Wisler), or by a regional name such as Washington-Franklin or Southeastern Conference. They include the following: °Conservative Mennonite Conference; °Conservative Mennonite Fellowship; °Conservative Mennonite Church of Ontario; °Conservative Mennonite Churches of York and Adams Counties, Pa.; °Cumberland Valley Mennonite Church; °Eastern Pennsylvania Mennonite Church; °Mid-Atlantic Mennonite Fellowship; °Midwest Mennonite Fellowship; °Northern Light Gospel Mission Conference; °Southeastern Mennonite Conference; °Washington-Franklin Mennonite Conference; and °Western Conservative Mennonite Conference. The congregations deriving from Amish roots are much more inclined to use "conservative Mennonite" as part of their name

because it is often Mennonite influence on their programs and methods that accompanied their departure from the Amish. The °Old Order River Brethren are a conservative group that is neither Amish nor Mennonite but rather °Brethren in Christ in origin.

The name *conservative Mennonite* became secure by its usage in the *MC Yearbook* in the early 1900s. It was a name applied to some independent Amish Mennonite churches not ready to affiliate with the three newly organized Amish Mennonite Conferences (1888-1892), which were the °°Ohio and Eastern A.M., the °°Indiana-Michigan A.M., and the °°Western A.M. In 1910-12 the congregations forming a new conference adopted the name used in the *MC Yearbook,* Conservative Amish Mennonite, and added the term "Conference". The name Amish was dropped in 1954 (°Conservative Mennonite Conference).

The pattern established by the Conservative Conference, i.e., using the name *Mennonite* because of program and methods, and eventually dropping the *Amish* name, has been followed by others. For most of those people, using *conservative* Mennonite is more respectable than using the more appropriate term *progressive* Amish. The gradual assimilation into the Mennonite mainstream takes place at greatly differing degrees, as is evident with the Conservative Mennonite Conference.

The difficulty of classifying congregations is evident in the *MC Yearbook*, especially in the two broad groupings listed as "Unaffiliated Mennonite Congregations" and "Fellowship Churches." The first group, covering more than two pages, includes 1 horse-and-buggy Amish congregation, 3 fringe Beachy Amish congregations, and 16 "conservative" Mennonite congregations whose members trace their origin to the Amish and who, for the most part, are one or two generations removed from their Amish connections. At least one of the congregations is an Amish Mennonite group from the Amish schism of the late 1800s. Also included are five Amish Mennonite congregations of the "°°sleeping preacher" tradition. Several of the congregations qualify as truly conservative Mennonite, always having been Mennonite rather than Amish.

The °Fellowship Churches listed in *MC Yearbook* are a combination of conservative Mennonites and progressive Amish. They range from several congregations consisting largely of people from progressive Amish background to those composed of a majority of conservative Mennonites.

The Tennessee Brotherhood Churches are an unusual combination of Old Order Mennonites (Wisler) and people from various Amish groups. These influences show in a highly codified written °discipline which is vigorously applied. There are a total of five congregations in Tennessee and Kentucky, none of which are listed in the *MC Yearbook* (1986-87).

The congregations listed as conservative Mennonite are usually limited in their contacts and fellowship with each other. The working relationships between congregations are not nearly as broad as many people assume. They are not a uniform group any more than are the Amish. There are dozens of fragmentations and subgroups.

The accompanying diagram is an attempt to show

OLD ORDER AMISH MENNONITE SPECTRUM

Two movements: a) To the right - represents forward movement chronologically
b) Downward movement represents "distance" from Old Order Amish

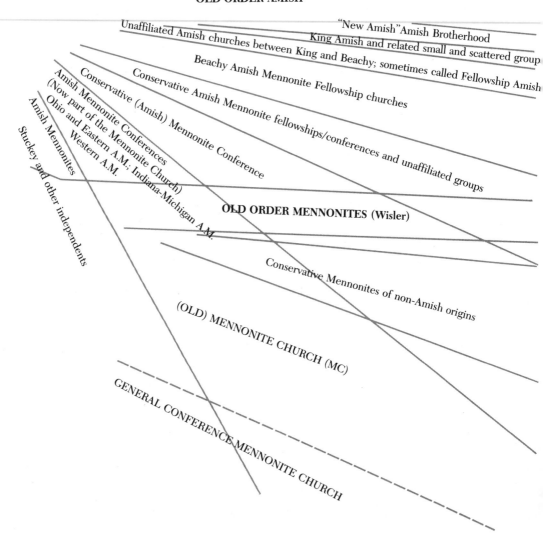

OLD ORDER AMISH

Conservative Mennonites (Swiss-Pennsylvania) chart
Compiled by Elmer S. Yoder 1987 (author of the article)

the general movement and relative location of the groups. It must be remembered that the groups blend into each other and are not as distinctly separated at the margins as the lines might indicate. ESY

MC Yearbook (1986-87), 95-105, 167-78; in addition to histories of the Beachy Amish Mennonites and the Conservative Mennonite Conference cited in articles on those groups, see Isaac R. Horst, *Separate and Peculiar* (Mt. Forest, Ont.: the Author, 1979); Stephen Scott, *The Amish Wedding and Other Special Occasions of the Old Order Communities* (Good Books, 1988).

Consulta Anabautista Menonita de Centroamericana (CAMCA; Central American Mennonite Conference) was born as the result of concerns of various Central American Mennonite leaders who considered it important to share with each other the work of the church, biblical and theological reflection, and pastoral experiences. The first conference took place from July 2-12, 1974, in the Pinares Academy in Tegucigalpa, Honduras. The theme was "The Growth of the Church and the Formation of Leaders." Conferences are held once a year in alternating locations. Participants are official delegates of the Mennonite or Anabaptist churches from Honduras, Costa Rica, Belize, Nicaragua, Guatemala, and lately, Panama.

The organization has been like a seedbed producing a fruitful convergence of Anabaptist reflections and interchange of pastoral experiences. The *Alabanzas de Libertad* (Praises of Liberty) hymnal was produced through CAMCA in 1975 and has contributed to worship renewal not only in the Central American Mennonite Church but also in other evangelical churches in the area. This °regional conference has also provided needed opportunity for dialogue concerning the difficult political, economic, and spiritual situation in which the Central American countries find themselves. The statements formulated in Belize (1978) and Nicaragua (1982) express the Anabaptist witness of concern for the economic, social, and spiritual needs of the Central American peoples, together with a clear peace-oriented position as an alternative to the prevailing violence in the region.

The need for an Anabaptist witness resulted in the creation of the Anabaptist Ministerial Leaders Seminary (SEMILLA) in 1982. Together with CAMCA, SEMILLA constitutes major effort to promote wholistic growth and an Anabaptist identity in Central America.   JAP-V

Programs, proposals, and reports from the churches presented in CAMCA since 1974 are in the collection of the author.

Contextualization is a term introduced around 1972 to supersede the time-honored "indigenous." The phrase "indigenous church" emerged in the 19th c. to describe the goal of °mission. A church was said to be indigenous when it became self-supporting, self-propagating, and self-governing. Increasingly this formulation fell under criticism. First, it assumed that Western forms were normative universally and encouraged attempts to transplant a Western-style church in other cultures. Second, it had no biblical support. Third, it was arbitrary as to what it set up as the standard by which to evaluate the results of missionary work.

Contextualization shifted emphasis to the context or situation in which Christian witness was being given. It called for recognition of the culture, history, and sociopolitical position of the people among whom witness was being made. Theologically, it took the incarnation of Jesus Christ as the foundation for missionary approach and witness.

After vigorous debate during an initial phase, the word *contextualization* and its implications gained wide acceptance among all varieties of Christian traditions. A large body of literature has developed around this theme, and it has become the point of departure for a wide-ranging critique of all missionary work and practice.

Among the advocates of contextualization were prominent non-Western theologians and church leaders. They urged its application to all aspects of church life—structures, worship and ritual, and theology.

Several developments helped prepare the way for the acceptance of contextualization. From the mid-1940s missionary °anthropology came into prominence through the influence of such leaders as Eugene A. Nida and Kenneth L. Pike, both associated with the work of Bible translation. This fostered a more positive evaluation of all cultures, encouraged a deepened understanding of and respect for each culture, acknowledged that no culture is morally superior to another and that each culture falls under judgment of the gospel, asserted that all cultures can be vehicles for receiving the gospel of Jesus Christ, and noted that individuals always express themselves most profoundly in their own—rather than an alien—culture. It is noteworthy that Roman Catholic missionaries first employed vernacular translations of the scriptures and promoted literacy and Bible reading after the Second Vatican Council (1962-65), in part because of the pastoral needs of the newer churches in the non-Western world.

Several Mennonites received advanced training in anthropology and linguistics and have been part of this change in emphasis. Jacob A. Loewen exerted wide influence through his graphic and prolific writings as a missionary anthropologist, especially in the 1960s. Mennonites participated in this conceptual change and have viewed it positively.   WRS

Jacob A. Loewen, *Culture and Human Values: Christian Intervention in Anthropological Perspective* (South Pasadena, Cal.: William Carey Library, 1975), a collection of 29 articles which appeared largely in the 1960s; Albert Widjaja, "Beggarly Theology," *South East Asia Journal of Theology*, 14, no. 2, 39-45; John R. W. Stott and Robert T. Coote, eds., *Down to Earth* (Grand Rapids: William B. Eerdmans, 1980).

Contraception. See Birth Control.

Convenção das Igrejas Irmãos Menonitas do Brasil (CIIMB; Brazilian Conference of the Mennonite Brethren Churches) is the conference of Portuguese-speaking congregations which have arisen through missionary activity of the German-speaking °Associação das Igrejas Irmãos Menonitas do Brasil (Conference of Mennonite Brethren Churches in Brazil, AIIMB). Twenty-seven congregations belonged to the Portuguese-speaking conference in 1986. Administrative offices were located in Curitiba. The goal of CIIMB is to reach a membership of 50,000 by the year 2000. The 1987 membership is 1,954. Thirty-one ministers are active in the conference, as are four missionary couples from North America. Theological training for them is available at the Instituto e Seminário Bíblico Irmãos Menonitas (Mennonite Brethren Biblical Seminary and Institute). Missionary activity is carried on by the CIIMB together with the North American Mennonite Brethren Board of Missions and Service. Congregations are located primarily in the states of Mato Grosso,

Rio Grande do Sul, Paraná, and São Paulo. A spiritual counseling service by telephone was begun in Curitiba in 1985. Thousands of persons have been helped in this way.   PP,Jr./HenEns

MWH (1978), 209-10; cf. J. A. Toews, *History MB* (1975), 418-20; *MWH* (1984), 63.

Convención de Iglesias Menonitas de Costa Rica. See Convención Evangélica Menonita de Costa Rica (Evangelical Mennonite Conference of Costa Rica).

Convención de Iglesias Menonitas Hispanas de los Estados Unidos y Canada. See Concilio Nacional de Iglesias Menonitas Hispanas.

Convención de las Iglesias Evangélicas Chulupí (Chulupí Evangelical Conference), Paraguay (ME I:591). The Chulupí tribe had its original base in the southern °°Chaco region of Paraguay and northern Chaco region of Argentina. Many of them lived along the banks of the Pilcomayo River, the boundary between Paraguay and Argentina. With the coming of the Mennonites to the Chaco, small groups of Chulupí soon found their way to the colonies in search of work and bread. A strong increase in migration to the colony area occurred 1940-47. Mennonites were challenged to begin a new mission work among people whose language and culture was different from the Lengua people with whom they had previously worked (°Convención de las Iglesias Evangélicas de los Hermanos Lenguas). The work with the Chulupí was carried on primarily by Mennonite Brethren.

Intensive teaching and preaching led to the baptism of 21 members in 1958. By 1972 the five Chulupí congregations united to form the Convención de las Iglesias Evangélicas Chulupí. Its membership in 1987 was 1,450 in seven congregations.

Like the Lengua conference, the Chulupí congregations also work autonomously in every respect, including evangelism and courses for the further education of congregational workers. Missionaries collaborate with these leaders and are available for counsel, the securing of materials needed, and other services.   SSchar

MWH (1978), 242-44; *MWH* (1984), 93.

See also Chaco Mission; Licht den Indianern.

Convención de las Iglesias Evangélicas de los Hermanos Lenguas (Conference of the Evangelical Churches of the Lengua Brethren) (ME I:322). Interest in mission work was present among the immigrants to the °°Chaco region in 1930 from the beginning, but delayed by the °Chaco War until 1935. In September of that year a mission organization named °Licht den Indianern (Light to the Indians) was founded. Members of the three conferences represented among the immigrants were free to join this organization, although initially much leadership came from Mennonite Brethren. Missionary activity began immediately on a site selected for that purpose, with primary concentration on food production and language study. For people who were themselves struggling for their very existence and who lacked missionary experience, this was a difficult period.

Nevertheless, the work continued, and in February 1946 the first seven Lengua Christians were baptized. Others soon followed, and a congregation was organized. As missionary work spread to other Indian settlements, new congregations arose there also. Indian agricultural settlements began in 1953. In those locations native leadership took the initiative, with the support of the missionaries. By 1978 these congregations were led to found the Convención, which consisted of 1,400 members in six congregations in 1986. Lengua leaders take full responsibility for their congregational life. The role of the missionary is to counsel in difficult situations, to help with Sunday schools, youth work, women's work, choirs and singing, special courses for congregational workers, etc. All of this is done in closest cooperation with Lengua congregational leadership.   SSchar

MWH (1978), 249-50; *MWH* (1984), 94.

See also Chaco Mission.

Convención de las Iglesias Evangélicas de las Indigenas, Paraguay (United Evangelical Churches). Mennonites from Canada founded Menno Colony in the °°Chaco region of Paraguay in 1927. They were followed in 1930 by Mennonites from Russia, who founded Fernheim Colony. Approximately 600 Lengua Indians lived in the area in which these colonists settled. These were organized into small migratory groups subsisting on hunting and such fruit as the Chaco provided.

In 1953 a member of the Menno Colony began missionary activity among these Lengua Indians on his own initiative. Eventually the Mennonite congregations began to support him. Further developments led to the establishment of a °Mennonitisches Missions-Komitee für Paraguay (MMKFP, Mennonite Missions Committee for Paraguay). This is a united effort of the Mennonite congregations (Vereinigung der Mennonitengemeinden, GCM) and the Evangelische Mennonitische Brüderschaft (EMB-related) of Paraguay. Through this cooperation the Lengua, Toba, and Sanapaná Indians eventually organized their own conference, the Convención de las Iglesias Evangélicas Unidas. In 1987 this conference had a membership of 1,900 in eight congregations.   SSchar

MWH (1984), 96.

See also Chaco Mission; Evangelical Mennonite Conference (Kleine Gemeinde); Licht den Indianern.

Convención de las Iglesias Evangélicas Menonitas de Nicaragua (Nicaragua Mennonite Conference) was founded in 1977 through the mission work of Rosedale Mennonite Missions (Conservative Mennonite Board of Missions and Charities). Their work in Nicaragua began 10 years earlier with a large, rural voluntary service program. The first church planters arrived in 1973, and planted churches in Managua and in rural areas, often related to the voluntary service work.

The (Sandinista) revolution of 1979 brought changes to the structure of the conference. Indigenous leaders took major new responsibilities in the leadership of their own conference, and the churches emerged from the revolution with a new vision for church planting. This, coupled with increased receptivity in the general population, brought a spurt of growth from 1981 to 1983. Foreign missionaries worked in leadership training and gradually phased out their work by 1987. Economic and political difficulties have slowed church growth since then. Several churches were dispersed by armed conflict, and some of the conference leaders left the country. Rampant inflation and scarcity contributed to a loss of vision for starting new churches.

The conference strives to train new leaders to nurture existing congregations and to plant new ones. The key to the future of the conference is in its ability to call and equip new leaders. The revolution has brought many changes in Nicaraguan life, and church leaders are often called upon to make difficult decisions. They must be resourceful in order to carry on the work with limited material resources. A dedicated core of national leaders is working to carry this out.   DByl

MWH (1984), 90; *MC Yearbook* (1986-87), 160.

Convención de las Iglesias Evangélicas Menonitas de Puerto Rico (Puerto Rico Mennonite Conference) (ME IV:231), organized in 1988 as an autonomous Latin American conference, a member of the Mennonite World Conference in the Central and South American region. By 1988 there were 15 congregations affiliated with the conference, with a total membership of about 900, led by 9 ordained ministers and one licensed minister, plus other local leaders.

The conference has become a fully indigenous church with Puerto Rican leadership, pastoral and otherwise. The last missionary couple from the Mennonite Board of Missions (MC) left in 1986, thus ending a period of closer affiliation with that agency. In 1988 the Mennonite Board of Missions contributed financial support designated primarily for leadership training, communications, and specific outreach and mission programs. While maintaining its fraternal relationship with the North American Mennonite church, the Puerto Rican conference has increased its contacts with and participation in regional Latin American events, such as annual conferences and leadership training programs, during the last decades. Further, it has had an active participation in special projects in areas such as communications and curriculum design for Christian education.

Significant changes during the decades of the 1960s, 1970s, and 1980s correlate with the wider sociocultural changes in the island and political and economic developments in the Commonwealth of Puerto Rico (Estado Libre Asociado de Puerto Rico). What was in the beginning a rural Mennonite program in the La Plata valley, expanded through the years into urban communities. What was started as a church-based endeavor to serve largely the lower-income families, focuses in 1988 on serving primarily lower-middle-class and middle-class people. Relatively unstructured service and mission programs operating side-by-side gave way to a more structured and institutionalized program administered under a rather centralized conference. The overall church program operates under the conference with an executive secretary and a conference executive committee. However, each congregation is allowed to develop somewhat autonomously, and no one established model or pattern describes all the congregations.

Institutions and programs in the conference in 1988 included the following: Academa Betania, the conference-sponsored school in Pullguillas (Coamo), with grades kindergarten through senior high school and an enrollment of about 300 students. Another school, Academia Menonita (instruction mainly in English), was started in 1961 and is run by the Summit Hill congregation in the metropolitan area; it had grades prekindergarten through senior high school and about 650 students. A Bible institute offered workshops and courses for congregational leaders and provided assistance for more advanced biblical and theological training in Puerto Rico and elsewhere. The conference also operated a bookstore, an audio-visual center, and a °credit and savings °cooperative. It publishes a monthly bulletin. Further, it appoints three representatives to the community-church board of directors of the Mennonite General Hospital in Aibonito.

Major challenges and goals identified by the conference include the following areas: reassessment of conference structure and organization; pastoral leadership discernment and training; affirmation of an Anabaptist-Mennonite identity and stance in the midst of the Puerto Rican situation; and nurturing and implementing of a wholistic view of mission for the next decades.   DS

Justus G. Holsinger, "Puerto Rico Mennonite Church," *Menn. Life,* 26 (July 1971), 106-13; idem, *La obra menonita en Puerto Rico / Mennonite Work in Puerto Rico, 1943-1981* (PRMC/MBM, 1982); *MWH* (1978), 261-63; *MWH* (1984) 102.

Convención de las Iglesias Evangélicas Unidas, Paraguay (Conference of United Evangelical Churches), is the Paraguayan, Spanish-speaking conference resulting from the work of the °Mennonitisches Mission-Komitee für Paraguay (MMKfP) in Villa Hayes and in East Paraguay. For further information see the article on MMKfP.   Staff

MWH (1984), 96.

Convención de las Iglesias Menonitas en Uruguay (Conference of Mennonite Churches in Uruguay). In 1954, the Mennonite Board of Missions (MC) began a missionary witness in Montevideo. Later the Commission on Overseas Mission (GCM) also cooperated. In 1972 four congregations organized the Convención de las Iglesias Menonitas del Uruguay. In 1986 there were seven Spanish-speaking congregations affiliated in this conference, with a total of 295 active members.

The mission boards continue to contribute to the budget of these churches through the °Evangelization Board of the Mennonite Churches of Uruguay. In the late 1980s the Convención and the Evangelization Board began a process of self-study to determine their respective roles. The congregations were also looking into the future, to discern the kind of churches they were called to be.   MR

MWH (1978), 264-66; *MWH* (1984), 104.

Convención Evangélica de Iglesias Paraguayas Hermanos Menonitas (Evangelical Conference of the Mennonite Brethren of the Paraguayan Churches) is the organization of the Mennonite Brethren churches of Paraguayan culture. It was begun in 1955 through the missionary efforts of the Board of

Missions and Services (BOMAS) of the Mennonite Brethren Church of the United States and Canada. The pioneering missionaries were Albert Enns and Susana Wiens, later Rudolf and Hilda Plett, and Hans Pankratz. At the initiative of the missionaries the conference was organized in 1971 and was made up of four congregations in and around Asunción: Bernardino Caballero, Santa Lucia, Dr. Francia, and San Isidro. The name *Convención Evangélica de Iglesias Paraguayas Hermanos Menonitas* was adopted in May 1986.

The goals of the conference are the formation of Christian missions within and outside the borders of Paraguay, the establishment of charitable and educational institutions, the search for the well-being of the neighbor, and the building of the kingdom of God.

Within the 15 years of the conference's existence, it has grown to 19 congregations. Six are located in Asunción and several in interior cities, along with numerous mission outposts in which the conference continues to work.

The principal authority of the conference is found in the general assembly, made up of representatives from the member churches. The general assembly delegates its authority to an executive committee elected by the assembly. The terms of office are for two years and members may be reelected. The following pastors have been president of the conference: Carlos Chaves (1971-73), Luis Alum (1973-76), Charlos Chaves (1976-78), and Sixto Mencia (1978-80), Juan Silverio Verón (1980-84), Sixto Mencia (1984-86).

The conference maintains fraternal relations with the Konferenz der Mennonitischen Brüdergemeinden (conference of German-speaking Mennonite Brethren). They cooperatively sponsor the Instituto Bíblico Asunción and a studio for preparation of tapes for radio programs.

The conference has the following commissions: Evangelism and Missions Commission with an evangelistic team, Youth Commission, Women's Commission, Publicity Commission, and Christian Education Commission, which also has a teaching team.

The functions of the conference are coordinated through the administrative department, headed by an executive secretary and an office secretary. Headquarters are located at 2150 Juan Díaz de Solís in Asunción.

The conference publishes a monthly bulletin called *La Voz del Rebaño* (The Voice of the Flock). Other publications are the following books: *Documento Commemorative 1983*, *Manual Para la Iglesia Local*, and *Presencia Menonita en el Paraguay* by Rudolf Plett, Asunción (1979). Other media efforts include a daily radio program on a local Asunción station.

The actual administration of the conference programs has been under the leadership and direction of the national church leaders. However, these programs receive a subsidy of almost 90 percent from BOMAS, of the Mennonite Brethren Churches of the United States and Canada. SL

MWH (1978), 255-57; *MWH* (1984), 95.

Convención Evangélica Menonita de Costa Rica (Conference of Evangelical Mennonites of Costa Rica). In August 1961 the Conservative Mennonite Board of Missions and Charities (Rosedale Mennonite Missions) sent two missionary couples, Elmer and Eileen Lehman, and Raymond and Susanna Schlabach, to establish a Mennonite witness in Costa Rica. The Lehman family started a church planting ministry in the city of Heredia, located in the central plateau. The Schlabachs began work translating the Bible into the Bri-Bri Indian language and settled in Talamanca in southern Costa Rica. A voluntary service program in Costa Rica begun by Rosedale Mennonite Missions in 1962 continued until 1983. During the program's existence at least 96 volunteers served two years or more in the country and were involved in community development through agricultural services, °literacy work, and sanitation and health programs. Henry and Esther Helmuth came to Costa Rica as missionaries in 1965 to start a church planting ministry in northern Costa Rica, in the town of Puerto Viejo de Sarapiquí. In 1967 the Helmuths moved to the capital city of San José to plant a congregation in the suburb of Guadalupe. The first decade of church planting ministry in Costa Rica led to a national membership of 87 in three churches, Heredia, Guadalupe, and Talamanca.

On March 30, 1974, six charter member churches with a total membership of 165 united to form the Convención Evangélica Menonita de Costa Rica. Of the seven-member conference executive committee, three were from North America and four were Costa Rican believers. In 1979 a memo of understanding between Rosedale Mennonite Missions and the Costa Rican conference was signed. It recognized the conference as an autonomous body and provided for a gradual year-by-year reduction in the subsidy granted by the mission. By 1980 the executive committee of the Costa Rican conference was composed entirely of national leaders. In 1983 the voluntary service program sponsored by Rosedale Mennonite Missions was terminated and all foreign missionary personnel except for one couple, David and Mayela Diller, left the country.

The Centro para Desarrollo Ministerial (Center for Ministerial Development) was formed in 1979 as a resident Bible institute. In 1982 its program was revised to provide °theological education by extension, with teachers visiting six regional centers around the country to give short seminars to local church leaders. The Costa Rican conference is also affiliated with SEMILLA (Seminario Ministerial de Liderazgo Anabautista [Anabaptist Ministerial Leaders Seminary]), a cooperative effort of the Latin American Mennonite-related churches to train Anabaptist leaders.

The Costa Rican conference is governed by an annual assembly composed of pastors and delegates from each congregation. The executive committee is elected each year during the assembly to carry out the conference program throughout the year. In addition to the executive committee, there are eight auxiliary committees that function in the following areas: Christian education, evangelism, social services, communications, stewardship, youth, music, and investments. As of March 1987 the Costa Rican conference reported 18 churches with 1,212 baptized members, six ordained ministers, one ordained evangelist, nine licensed ministers, and four lay pastors. DD

James A. Prieto-Valladares, "El proyecto Misionero de la Conferencia Menonita Conservadora en Costa Rica, 1960-1985" (Licenciate in Theology thesis, Escuela Ecuménica de Ciencias de la Religion, Facultad de Filosofia Universidad Nacional de Costa Rica, 1985); Ivan J. Miller, *History of the Conservative Mennonite Conference* (Grantsville, Md: Ivan J. and Della Miller, 1985), 205-71; Howard I. Blutstein and others, *Area Handbook for Costa Rica* (Washington, D.C.: The American University, 1970); *MWH* (1978), 216-17; *MWH* (1984), 67.

Convention of Evangelical Indian Churches, Paraguay. See Convención de las Iglesias Evangélica de las Indigenas, Paraguay.

Conversion is a complex term and broad in its usage. It is primarily used in a religious sense, but can be used more widely to describe any profound change of conviction or way of life. In its religious sense, the reference is generally to the initial stage of spiritual experience, as in moving from unbelief to faith in God, or in changing from one religious viewpoint to another. The change involved is perceived to be radical in nature and contains some element of reversal, i.e., a change between opposites. Although sometimes popularly associated with instantaneous change, the experience may take place over a longer period of time and, in any case, is usually preceded by preparatory influences and explorations.

Conversion is not self-defining. Its exact nature and form depend upon the expectations of the belief system to which one is converted and, furthermore, upon the personality characteristics of the convert. Conversion can be described as intellectual, moral, or religious, depending on its focus in the human experience. In Christian conversion all three dimensions come into view, although differing accents appear in the various Christian traditions.

Conversion translates the biblical terms for turn or return. In the Old Testament the concept refers to the return of the people of God after leaving the way of God. The return involves both a spiritual renewal of relationship to God in covenant and a moral change toward upright living. It implies a restored life in community with the people of God. The New Testament takes up this viewpoint while expanding it. Conversion is given a special meaning by its linkage to Jesus' kingdom teaching. All are called to repent, to reorient their outlook in the light of the arriving rule of God in Jesus and his work. Even the pious in Israel must convert to this new reality that Jesus brings. This is the ground for the universal call to conversion that the church directs to people of every religious persuasion. Since the kingdom is identified with the person and work of Jesus the Christ, the call to convert (repent and believe) becomes a call to identify with Jesus Christ and to follow him. Repentance is the principal word in the New Testament to express the human decision to leave the old sinful life and to embrace the way of Jesus. Other concepts such as °regeneration, new birth, new creation, °justification, and °sanctification speak of the divine work to effectuate and empower the new life in the believer. Conversion in the biblical sense is not just an inward, spiritual religious event; it is an event of exodus from an old life in a fallen social order into a new life in a renewed social order, which is the church. The entire person is involved in the change at the intellectual, volitional, affective, and behavioral levels.

The Anabaptists of the 16th c. can well be described as a conversionist movement. They did not assume that people in the Christianized society of Europe were true believers. They directed a strong critique against that society for its moral decay and compromise. Their message was a call to renounce the life of general society and to take up a life of following Christ in the context of a believing community. Each member of the church was expected to exercise personal faith and to manifest the evidence of regeneration by a changed life. The Anabaptists, in contrast to later °Pietism, had little interest in the psychological process and the inner experiences associated with conversion. They focused rather on the changed outlook on self and on the resulting changed behavior. The subjective experience, or the itinerary of the soul, is not explored. This aspect is neither denied nor suppressed; it is simply not seen as determinative. The means of conversion is the active grace of God mediated by the work of the °Holy Spirit in response to faith. They insisted on baptism as a sign that conversion had taken place and rejected the concept of sacraments as the means of grace. The effect of grace was a real change in the self of the believer. Anabaptists were critical of other reformers who spoke of justification by grace as a change of status before God without equal emphasis on a real change in the believer. Neither did they distinguish sharply between justification as the initial experience, and sanctification as the later experience.

Conversion is the indispensable protection of the voluntaristic principle of the believers church. The Anabaptist and Mennonite tradition has not found it easy to preserve the earlier meaning of conversion. For a socially isolated and community oriented people, the depth of personal religious commitment in the new generations can easily be replaced with ethnic identity and cultural forms. Even where religious experience is deeply felt, there is less of a sense of sudden change than of a gradual nurturing of spirituality. The individual is formed by the community to such an extent that a personal spiritual identity can be missing or weak. Thus the meaning of conversion can be modified or lost altogether.

Not surprisingly, therefore, Mennonites have shown considerable openness to renewal influences such as Pietism, the °revival and °holiness movements, and, most recently, the °charismatic movement. All of these movements make a greater distinction than did the Anabaptists between the initial experience (conversion) and later experiences, such as sanctification or baptism with the Spirit. As a result, many Mennonites have been led to a personal encounter of faith that makes conversion a meaningful concept, as in early Anabaptism. However, the close integration of faith and obedience, individual and community, and of new birth and Spirit, characteristic of the early movement, is attenuated or lost because these renewal movements have reflected other theological traditions and claims.

The sociological studies of Kauffman and Harder (1975) document and illustrate the variation of understandings on conversion among the Mennonite subgroups as a reflection of these influences. They also show that all contemporary Mennonite and Brethren in Christ groups continue to emphasize strongly a personal, life-changing faith in their members.   GeoRBrIII

Henry J. Schmidt, ed., *Conversion: Doorway to Discipleship* (Hillsboro, Ks.: Mennonite Brethren Publishing House, 1980); Kauffman/Harder, *Anabaptists Four C. Later* (1975), esp. 84-91; Wittlinger, *Piety and Obedience* (1978); Myron S. Augsburger, "Conversion in Anabaptist Thought," *MQR*, 23 (1962), 243-55; Cornelius J. Dyck, "The Life of the Spirit in Anabaptism," *MQR*, 47 (1972), 309-26; Alvin J. Beachy, *The Concept of Grace in the Radical Reformation* (Nieuwkoop: De Graff, 1977).

See also Baptism, Age at; Salvation.

Cooperatives (ME I:707). The cooperative movement, seen in global perspective, is not languishing; on the contrary, it is one of the fastest growing economic institutions (*Encyclopedia Britannica*). Although still predominantly expressed in the form of consumer cooperatives, producer cooperatives are increasing, and in some countries, combined with consumer cooperatives, are literally remaking communities and regions. Two examples are the Mondragon movement in the Basque region of Spain, and the cooperative movement in Israel, including the kibbutzim. Outside Europe and North America most development initiatives by governmental and nongovernmental organizations operate on the cooperative principle, indicating the power of this form of economic development, which ignores the ideological strictures of °socialism and °capitalism and pragmatically takes advantage of private and collective resources, motivations, and needs, especially those of women (*Development International*, vol. 1; vol. 2, 40ff.). The Mennonite interpretation of and experimentation with cooperatives had been largely described and analyzed by J. Winfield Fretz in ME I. This present article describes developments since the 1950s. (The role of the producer-consumer cooperatives [*Genossenschaften*] in most Mennonite colonies in Paraguay, as described in ME I:708-9, remains central, as indicated in articles on individual colonies elsewhere in ME V.)

Mennonite community participation in agricultural and community cooperatives was seen by Fretz as an expression of the °mutual aid tradition of Mennonites. E. K. Francis, in his monumental study of Manitoba, proposes the opposite—cooperatives expressed the secularization of the sacred Mennonite mutual aid practice (p. 224ff.). He documents further that the cooperative movement itself was in process of losing its influence and power in Manitoba, a fact which has been corroborated in other community studies since that time (Epp-Tiessen, Ens, Redekop). This may well be due to accommodation to the capitalist free-enterprise milieu, as Francis maintains and Fretz suggests.

There are developing, however, several new forms of Mennonite cooperatives, which may be heralding a renewed interest in mutual aid and °economics. One form is found primarily in North America, another in the service and °development work being done in the Two-thirds World.

(1) The emergence of °credit unions in North America. Following the credit union established in Altona in 1939, as part of the larger cooperative movement in Manitoba (J. J. °Siemens), credit unions have slowly begun to be established by and for Mennonites in Canada and the United States, and they promise to be a major area of growth in the near future. Beginning with Crosstown Credit Union in Winnipeg, in 1944, credit unions were organized at the Mennonite Publishing House at Scottdale, Pa. (1955); Hesston, Ks. (1960); Kitchener, Ont. (1964); La Junta, Col. (1965); Harrisonburg, Va. (1964); Kidron, Ohio (1985); and Evanston, Ill. (1988). Canada-United States conferences on Mennonite credit union philosophy, held in 1987 and 1989, assisted in the emergence of a new awareness of Anabaptist-Mennonite theology regarding economic mutual aid and caring.

(2) The support and initiation of cooperatives in underdeveloped countries. The Mennonite Central Committee (MCC) and several Mennonite mission boards have helped establish cooperative ventures in India, East Asia, Africa, and Latin America. The Mencoldes project in Colombia is one such example (Juhnke, 156-58). A new thrust which has enhanced the cooperative movement abroad is the emergence of °Mennonite Economic Development Associates (MEDA), which has promoted economic development including entrepreneurial assistance as well as cooperative organizations where feasible. Thus MEDA has worked alongside MCC, and numerous mission boards, in establishing and expanding cooperative organizations, including credit unions, agricultural, and handicrafts cooperatives, in Haiti, Jamaica, Colombia, Bolivia, Uraguay, Paraguay, India, Zaire, Ethiopia, and Somalia (Fretz, 1947, 1978).

The MEDA program is confronted with the melding of the capitalistic and cooperative dimensions in its foreign program, and its successes and failures show how economics can operate for the benefit of all in the most effective way. What has already been learned is that strict Western capitalistic patterns will not work in most non-North-American settings; this does not even touch the issue of the ethical dimensions of biblical views on economics. The promotion of domestic and international cooperative economic institutions among Mennonites in the future is a part of the larger issue of whether Mennonites are going to retrieve the "communal ethics"; the jury is still out on this critical issue.   CWR

"Cooperatives," *Encyclopedia Britannica*, 14th ed., vol. 6 (Chicago, 1966); "Cooperatives," *International Encyclopedia of the Social Sciences*, vol. 3 (New York, 1968); Esther Epp-Tiessen, *Altona: The Story of a Prairie Town* (Altona, 1982); Gerhard John Ens, *The Rural Municipality of Rhineland* (Altona, 1984); E. K. Francis, *In Search of Utopia* (Glencoe, 1955); J. Winfield Fretz, *The MEDA Experiment* (Waterloo, 1978); idem, *Christian Mutual Aid* (Akron, 1947); Calvin Redekop, "The Cultural Assimilation of the Mennonites of Mountain Lake" (MA thesis, U. of Minnesota, 1954); various accounts by mission and development workers, e.g., *Development International* (Arlington, Va.; Juhnke, *Mission* (1979); S. T. Moyer, *With Christ on the Edge of the Jungle* (Berne: Mennonite Book Concern, 1941), 88-101; *MC Yearbook* (1988-89), 117, 135-136, 149-150.

See also Greece.

Cooprider, Florence. See Friesen, Florence Cooprider.

Coptic Orthodox Churches. See Eastern and Coptic Orthodox Churches.

Correll, Ernst H. (April 5, 1894–June 24, 1982). Born in Heilbronn, Germany, Correll came to newly reopened Goshen College with Harold S. Bender in 1924. Correll taught at American University, Washington, D.C., from 1928 until retirement. Correll and Bender founded the Mennonite Historical Society, the *Mennonite Quarterly Review* (1927-), and Studies in Anabaptist and Mennonite History. Correll contributed scholarly notes for early stages of the Conrad Grebel letters translation project (CRR 4:17-21). An early proponent of socioeconomic interpretation in Anabaptist-Mennonite studies, his dissertation, begun under Max Weber (1864-1920) and directed by Ernst °°Troeltsch, is unsurpassed on 18th c. Mennonite agriculturalists spreading the agricultural revolution, and in defining the legal status of 18th- and 19th-c. Mennonites. He published on sources covering Russian Mennonite immigration into North America, 1874ff., and also on the contributions of family histories (°genealogy) contributions to broader Mennonite history. He died at Salt Lake City. JSO

Ernst H. Correll, *Das schweizerische Täufermennonitentum* (Tübingen: Mohr, 1925); *Goshen College Bulletin*, vols. 19 through 22 (1925-28); a dozen articles by Correll in *MQR* on Russian Mennonite immigration; MC Archives (Goshen), Hist. Mss. 1-28; John S. Oyer in *MQR,* 56 (1982), 400.

Costa Rica. See Convención Evangélica Menonita de Costa Rica.

Costa Rica Mennonite Conference. See Convención Evangélica Menonita de Costa Rica.

Costume. See Dress.

Council of Churches of Evangelical Christians—Baptists (CCECB). Still not legally recognized by the Soviet authorities, this union has gained a reputation for advocating radical separation of church and state, religious liberty, active priesthood of all believers, a thoroughgoing church discipline, and a costly discipleship that includes prison and a few martyrs. Are they the new Anabaptists of the 20th c.? A Soviet sociologist, A. N. Ipatov, warned about the ideological links between Mennonites and these Initsiativniki (an initial designation). Their best known leader, Georgi P. Vins, was of Russian Mennonite lineage, but his grandfather had already cast in his lot with the Baptists. The only other nationally known CCECB leader of Mennonite stock was Kornelius K. Kreker, who led the Siberian branch and served on the national council until the mid-1980s, when differences with the increasingly authoritarian leadership style of the president, Gennadi Kriuchkov, caused him to leave.

Most Mennonite groups in the Soviet Union were just beginning to form as congregations after the upheavals of the 1930s and 1940s, when the major split in Baptist ranks in 1961, precipitated by renewed state pressure, led to the formation of the Initsiativniki movement and its ultimate development into a counter-union to the °All-Union Council of Evangelical Christians-Baptists (AUCECB) in 1965. Hence, Mennonites found themselves choosing between the two unions when seeking broader fellowship and support, including literature. The choice depended on local conditions, since state pressure and the conformity or resistance of local leaders

varied widely. Between 2,500 and 5,000 persons of Mennonite origin chose to support the CCECB morally, even if many remained formally uncommitted, and their congregations remained unregistered in any case. Nor did such supporters of the CCECB develop an explicit sense of being a Mennonite wing of the CCECB, as was true in the AUCECB.

Typical Mennonite names were more frequent than their number warranted in the prisoners' lists that began appearing systematically after 1962, when the Council of Prisoners' Relatives was organized. These were often also the persons active in the secret printing press Khristianin. Since many Mennonite preachers had been in prison, it was emotionally easy for them to identify with Baptists who were ready to be imprisoned for their faith.

After emigration to West Germany through the family reunification program developed (1970s), a disproportionately large contingent of CCECB preachers of Low German stock came to West Germany. There they soon organized more than two dozen large and active congregations and set about establishing the Friedensstimme mission, a name they remembered from turn-of-the-century Mennonite missionary days. This mission, led by persons named Penner, Janzen, Klassen, and Esau, soon became the official representative for the CCECB in Europe, acting as major distributor of the *Samizdat* (underground journals) that the CCECB continued to send with great regularity. Ties to the Mennonites were strained, but family relations to leading Mennonites and a sense of theological affinity invariably prevented a breakdown in relations, even if most Mennonites in the Soviet Union tended to reject their more confrontational style. WWS

Walter Sawatsky, *Soviet Evangelicals Since World War II* (Scottdale, 1981); *25 Jahre auf dem Weg: Kurze Geschichte des Bundes unabhaengiger Evangeliumschristen-Baptisten in der Soujetunion, 1961-1986* (Gummersbach: Missionswerk Friedensstimme, 1987); Albert W. Wardin, Jr., "Jacob J. Wiens: Mission Champion in Freedom and Repression," *Journal of Church and State,* 29 (1986), 495-514; *MWH* (1978), 310; *MWH* (1984), 126.

See also All-Union Council of Evangelical Christians—Baptists; Union of Soviet Socialist Republics.

Council of Mennonite Churches, Venezuela. See Concilio de las Iglesias Evangélicas Menonitas, Venezuela.

Council of Mennonite Seminaries (CMS). See Seminaries.

Council of Mission Board Secretaries (COMBS). See Inter-Mennonite Cooperation.

Council of Moderators and Secretaries (CMS). See Inter-Mennonite Cooperation.

Counseling, Pastoral. See Pastoral Counseling.

Courtship Customs (ME I:318). With the exception of several conservative groups, courtship customs among Mennonites reflect the prevailing customs in the national societies of which they are a part. This appears to be true in Asia, Africa, and Latin America, as well as in Europe and North America. In traditional rural societies in India and Africa, mate selection has been almost totally negotiated and controlled by the parents of the marrying couple, and "courtship" did not really exist. The impact of Christianity has been to shift some of the parental control over mate selection to the church and to the young couple themselves.

Under the aegis of Western missions, Western ideas of mate selection by the marrying individuals, preferably with parental approval and sponsorship, have come to prevail among the more educated members of new churches in India and Africa, among Mennonites as well as others. °Urbanization and education in non-Western countries have precipitated major changes in the mate selection process, since many youth have gone to towns and cities for employment or to study in boarding schools (Kauffman, 1976). These youth, living many miles from their parents in the agricultural villages, meet informally, develop a rudimentary "dating" system, and eventually fall in love and marry, with or without parental consent, and sometimes avoiding the traditional customs of bride price, betrothal rituals, and family-oriented wedding celebrations in the villages. As a result, major tensions and disaffection develop sometimes between traditional parents and their °modernized offspring.

In the European context, Mennonites historically have been accustomed to considerable control by parents over the choice of spouse and °marriage arrangements for a son or daughter (°°betrothal). Recently European youth have more freedom in the choice of a spouse, and customs of dating have developed, although more slowly than in the United States. European youth tend to go out in groups, and pair dating is not likely to begin until the late teens, or until there is serious intent to find a spouse.

The older European customs are reflected still today among the Old Order Amish, Old Order Mennonites, Old Colony Mennonites, Hutterites, and the Church of God in Christ, Mennonite (CGC). Among these groups, dating and boy-girl contacts, prior to engagement, have been restricted, and there is considerable distrust of a young couple out somewhere on a date by themselves. Persons wishing to marry must have the approval of the parents and the church officials.

Traditionally, until recently, among the Old Order Amish "courtship is secretive, and the community at large is not informed of an intended wedding until the couple was 'published' in church, from one to four weeks before the wedding" (Hostetler, 1980, p. 191). Although free to choose whom they wish to marry, Amish youth had to submit to the formality of having a "Schtecklimann" (a go-between, often a deacon) go secretly to the girl's house to obtain her consent and the consent of her parents. While secretly courting, the Amish couple would have opportunities to meet and talk at weddings, funerals, and other gatherings. Although the boy would not take his girl to an evening youth gathering, he could take her home in his buggy afterwards when it was dark. He would also visit her at her home, but only after her parents had gone to bed. In recent decades, however, these traditional strictures have been gradually loosened, and are still found only in the most conservative Amish districts. Elsewhere there is much more openness in dating and courting, and the "Schtecklimann" function is no longer employed. The couple, having decided on marriage, and without any formal engagement, simply go to the minister and ask to initiate the marriage process in the church.

"Hutterite preachers assert that courtship and dating are not allowed on the colony. These terms connote for them romance and carnal pleasure." When boys and girls from one colony visit another, they meet in groups, but a boy can arrange to talk privately with a girl if he wishes and she is willing. Although Hutterite youth "find their marriage partners voluntarily, parents have almost complete veto power over a child's choice." Since spouses usually come from different colonies, their contacts prior to marriage are very infrequent (Hostetler, 1974, p. 223).

Among the "Holdeman" Mennonites (Church of God in Christ, Mennonite), changing courtship customs are evident. Until recent decades, courtship was restricted by limitations on boy-girl contacts and by rigorous parental and church control of choice of spouse. Currently, however, the young people are adopting the courtship and dating patterns of other Mennonites and the general public, but with strong parental and churchly expectations that all behavior be in line with strict moral codes and that the chosen spouse be of the same denomination (Hiebert, 1973, p. 461).

Among the larger and less-conservative Mennonite bodies in North America, the youth tend to follow the prevailing dating and courtship customs of the general society. Dating is a 20th-c. development, particularly enhanced by the emergence of the °automobile and the mushrooming of places to go—restaurants, movies, theatre, school functions, athletic events, concerts, fairs, etc. Dating has been defined as an American invention that emerged after World War I among college students and other young adults (Eshleman, 308). Eshleman describes dating as a form of recreation, a form of socialization, a means of status grading and status achievement, and a form of courtship. The custom of dating has considerably lengthened the courtship period, which may begin as casual dating as early as the age of 14 or 15, and permits "shopping around" until settling on a chosen spouse a number of years later. This modern form of mate selection should result in more compatible marriages, but currently high °divorce rates raise serious question as to whether the romantic idealism and emotionalism associated with the courtship period is an adequate basis for successful mate selection.

In earlier times a date was almost always initiated by the boy, with the girl having the option of accepting or refusing. More recently, with the emphasis on °gender equality, the girl may sometimes take the initiative in asking, although it appears that many are reluctant to do so. In recent decades dating has become more informal, especially on college campuses, and many youth prefer to think of themselves as merely "going out together," without all the formalities of prior arrangements, dress-up, and other niceties associated with dating.

Americans have gone farther than others in promoting individual choice of spouses based on the concepts of romantic love, and parental influence on the choice of spouse has all but disappeared. Thus dating, as a means of compatibility testing, has become all the more important. Whereas in Europe and America pre-20th-c. customs discouraged boy-girl contacts before marriage, and in Latin America chaperonage is still insisted upon, current American and Canadian youth are free to associate unchaperoned over a period of many years before marriage, strongly increasing the possibilities of sexual involvements and premarital pregnancies. Although cultural mores developed to discourage sexual involvements of unchaperoned dating partners, these unfortunately have been breaking down in recent decades. As as result, rates of premarital sexual intercourse and premarital pregnancies have greatly increased, reflecting the "sexual revolution" of the last 30 years. Recent surveys indicate that the proportion of American men and women having intercourse before marriage, some only with their fiancé(e)s, is around 75 percent (Kephart, 288-89). Two studies of Mennonite college students estimate the rates at under 20 percent in the 1960s and under 30 percent in the 1970s, indicating that Mennonite youth tend to follow stricter mores opposing sexual intercourse before marriage. Some youth tend to postpone dating until they are serious about finding a spouse, thus avoiding temptations to physical intimacies as well as the requirements of time and money which dating entails.

Survey data on Mennonite courtship customs is extremely limited. One study of 149 midwest Mennonite (MC) teenagers indicate that dating began, on the average, at age 16 for boys and 15 for girls, about one and one-half years later than indicated by comparable data for American college students at a similar time period. This may simply reflect a greater rurality of Mennonite youth at the time, since dating tended to begin earlier among urban residents. In the same study (Kauffman, 1960), 149 married couples, parents of the above teenagers, indicated that they had been acquainted with each other an average of 4.2 years before marriage, their courtship periods averaged 28 months, and their engagement periods averaged 8 months.

Following general custom, Mennonite couples tend to announce their engagements some months prior to the wedding, often in the local newspaper or occasionally at a party for female friends arranged by the bride-to-be. Typically, the newspaper item specifies that the engagement is announced by the parents of the bride-to-be, although it is often the young couple itself that prepares the notice. Except when required by law in some Canadian provinces, "publishing the banns" in churches (or elsewhere) is not practiced by Mennonites in North America, but it is a regular practice among the Old Order Amish. JHK

J. Ross Eshleman, *The Family: An Introduction*, 3rd ed. (Boston: Allyn and Bacon, Inc., 1981), 308-14; Clarence Hiebert, *The Holdeman People* (South Pasadena, Cal.: The William Carey Library, 1973), 459-61; John A Hostetler, *Amish Society* (1980), 147-52, 191-92; idem, *Hutterite Society* (1974), 223, 237-38; Johann Christoph Arnold and Merrill Mow in *The Plough*, no. 18 (Jan.-Feb. 1988), 12-16; and no. 14 (Feb.-Mar. 1986), 2-4; J. Howard Kauffman, "Sexual Attitudes and Behavior of Mennonite College Youth," unpubl. paper, copy at MHL (Goshen); idem, "A Comparative Study of Traditional and Emergent Family Types Among Midwest Mennonites" (PhD diss., U. of Chicago, 1960); William M. Kephart, *The Family, Society, and the Individual*, 5th ed.

(Boston: Houghton Mifflin Co., 1981), 287-90; J. Howard Kauffman, "An Introduction to African Courtship and Marriage," unpublished paper, 1976, copy at MHL (Goshen); Jean Huntington Phillips Hicks, "Premarital Sexual Intimacy: A Mennonite College Sample" (MS thesis, Purdue U., 1972).

See also Folklore.

Crafts. See Folk Arts.

Crautwald, Valentin (ME I:732), Silesian humanist and admirer of Johannes Reuchlin (1455-1522) and °°Erasmus, colleague of Caspar °Schwenckfeld (described by some scholars as Schwenckfeld's "Melanchthon"), canon and lector in the cathedral seminary in Liegnitz, Silesia, from 1524-37. With Schwenckfeld, Crautwald promoted a unique "spiritualist" ideal of radical religion that minimized the role of external observances. Crautwald's 16th-c. biographer noted that Crautwald "fled as much as possible a famous reputation and the glory of men," preferring the quiet of his study. Not surprisingly, Crautwald's actual significance for Silesian Schwenckfeldianism has only recently been appreciated.

Born of peasant parents in the region of Neisse, Silesia, Crautwald's family derived its name from the region of Krautenwalde in Austria-Silesia. Scholars dispute the exact year of his birth, although Sudermann's suggestion of 1465 seems right (Corpus Schwenckfeldianorum [=CS], vol. 6, 193-94). He joined a host of young Silesians in pursuing studies at the U. of Cracow, encountering °humanist teaching there and becoming a follower of Reuchlin the Hebraist. Crautwald returned to Neisse to teach and soon gained a reputation in Silesia for his gifts in Latin, Greek, and Hebrew. His abilities brought him to the attention of the bishop of Breslau, who appointed him personal secretary and protonotary in 1514.

Under the influence of Erasmus, Karlstadt, and Melanchthon, by 1522 Crautwald was caught up in efforts for church reform. In a dramatic personal gesture, and possibly in imitation of Giovanni Pico della Mirandola (1463-94), Jacques Lefèvre d'Étaples (1455-1536), and Erasmus, he burned all of his previous literary endeavors in philosophy, prose, and poetry, and committed himself to the study and teaching of Scripture. He was given an opportunity to carry out this resolve when in Dec. 1523 Duke Friedrich II of Liegnitz invited him to fill the post of lector in the Cathedral of the Holy Sepulchre in Liegnitz.

For the next 14 years Crautwald fulfilled his duties in Liegnitz as Lector, instructing the public and younger clergy in the Scriptures. He began with the Pauline epistles, teaching them "according to their evangelical meaning."

His association with Schwenckfeld, the influential Silesian nobleman, soon inspired him to write in behalf of a unique program of radical spiritualist religion. Convinced in 1525, by a "revelation" from Christ, that Catholic and Lutheran notions of Christ's real eucharistic presence were in error, Crautwald advocated a temporary suspension of sacramental observances, and diligent catechizing according to the model of Augustine and other early church fathers. Crautwald went on to elaborate distinctively "Schwenckfeldian" doctrines of Christ's noncreaturely origin and deified flesh, of which believers could partake simply by faith. For Crautwald, as with Erasmus, the essence of renewal lay in creation of the "new man" through promoting the true knowledge of Christ. Crautwald sought a *via regia* (royal way) between the Catholic and Lutheran parties of his day, hoping for their eventual reconciliation.

Schwenckfeld's early reliance on Crautwald, and his writings for theological guidance and exegetical help, soon became a pattern that characterized their future reform efforts. The evidence suggests that Crautwald should be recognized as the theological formulator of Silesian spiritualism and Schwenckfeld as essentially the popular proponent of Crautwaldian theology.

In April 1526 Martin Luther addressed a letter to Crautwald, pleading with him to forsake his teaching, or to "leave off calling us brothers." The Strasbourg reformers accused Crautwald of the Eutychian "one-nature" (monophysite) heresy, along with Melchior °Hoffman, whose view of Christ was inspired by Schwenckfeld and Crautwald. However, unlike Hoffman, Crautwald always held to Mary's part in Christ's conception, and recognized in Christ two distinct natures, without confusion or division, consciously following the teaching of the Council of Chalcedon (451), Augustine (354-430), and Cyril of Alexandria (d. 444). Crautwald's view is best understood as an original effort to push the Christology of Chalcedon and Augustine in an Alexandrian direction. He did this to explain how a real partaking of Christ could take place apart from the eucharistic elements.

Crautwald lived out his last years in Liegnitz, devoting himself to study of the scriptures and the church fathers. He never married.   DHSh

Many of Crautwald's works were preserved in manuscript books by the efforts of Adam Reissner (1496-1582) and Daniel Sudermann (1550-1631). These are now housed at Munich in the Bayerische Staatsbibliothek (clm 718) and at Wolfenbüttel in the Herzog August Bibliothek (Cod. Aug. 45.9.2). Crautwald was reluctant to publish, thus only a few of his many works that circulated in manuscript saw publication, and these mainly at the hand of Schwenckfeld. Crautwald works published by Schwenckfeld are contained in early volumes of the *Corpus Schwenckfeldianorum* and listed in CS, vol. 17, 698, 722-23. Crautwald's key works include *De Cognitione Christi* (clm 718, fol. 423-58) and *Novus Homo* (CS, 8:46-72). See also Horst Weigelt, *The Schwenkfelders in Silesia*, trans. Peter C. Erb (Pennsburg, Pa.: Schwenkfelder Library, 1985); idem, "Valentin Krautwald: Der führende Theologe des frühen Schwenckfeldertums," *Bibliotheca Dissidentium, Scripta et Studia, No. 1* (Baden-Baden: Koerner, 1983), 175-90; Peter C. Erb, "Valentin Crautwald," *Bibliotheca Dissidentium*, vol. 6, ed. André Séguenny (Baden-Baden: Koerner, 1985); various articles in *Schwenckfeld and Early Schwenkfeldianism*, ed. Peter C. Erb (Pennsburg, Pa.: Schwenkfelder Library, 1986); Douglas H. Shantz, *Cognitio et Communicatio Christi Interna: The Contribution of Valentine Crautwald to 16th c. Schwenckfeldian Spiritualism*," (PhD thesis, U. of Waterloo, 1986).

Creation, Theology of. A definitive study of Anabaptist and Mennonite theolgies of creation is a much-needed research undertaking. This present article serves merely to comment on several aspects of the topic. Belief in God as Creator was one of the crucial battlegrounds of early church theology. Gnostics had a highly spiritualized view of God; hence they could not conceive of God stooping to create physical matter. Thus they considered the Creator God Yahweh to have been an intermediary divine being. The orthodox Christian defense of God and Christ (the Logos) as Creator—and the Christian identification of this creator God with the Jewish Yahweh and Yahweh's Spirit and Wisdom—was one of the ways the early church retained its Jewish heritage.

The defense of God as creator lies behind the entire sacramental theology of the early and medieval church—the belief that God comes to humans in physical and material life in the incarnate Christ Jesus and thereby redeems all of the created order, led to the belief that created things (bread and wine, water) can serve as vehicles of God's grace. A similar defense of God as Creator lies behind the Augustinian effort to establish a Christian society, since human society and culture also are created, material things that have been corrupted by sin but are redeemed in Christ. The orthodox Christian doctrine that God had created out of nothing, was a way to guard against pantheism: the world was not identical with God. Rather, it had been created by God and now was redeemed in Christ. Creator and creatures were clearly distinct (thereby avoiding pantheism), yet in Christ the Creator had become the Mediator between the fallen creation and God's shalom (meaning the integration, harmony, peace of the original creation and of heaven), was restored, already but not yet.

Anabaptists were suspicious of the sacramental theology of the late medieval church. A thoroughgoing rejection of sacramental mediation is characteristic of all of them, with the exception of Pilgram Marpeck, although even he ultimately abandoned sacramental mediation for a more direct spiritual, °salvation (Rempel, "Christology and Lord's Supper," 182-86). In place of the redemption of the old creation (including human society, the magistracy, warfare), Anabaptists preached the new creation. In Menno's view, people are created after the image of God when they are converted to Christ (Menno, *Writings*, 55-58, 396, 409, 416). Rarely does he refer to the original creation of Adam and Eve after the image of God (*Writings*, 305-6, 503, 804). Traditional Catholic and Eastern Orthodox teaching emphasized the original creation in the image of God and its re-formation as the process of salvation proclaimed by Christ's °incarnation (Ladner). Melchior Hoffman's and Menno's difficulty accepting the full, human enfleshment of Christ and their doctrine of the celestial flesh of Christ, are related to their mistrust of the role of created things in salvation. They preferred to emphasize instead the power of the Holy Spirit to recreate rather than re-form. Menno came close to identifying the original creation with sin itself (Tonkin, 141-42, 164-65; Verduin). Unlike the Augustinian understanding of visible words (God spoke and visible creation existed) underlying sacrament, Menno and most Protestants emphasized the role of the Word (or Word and Spirit) alone. In a broad sense, Protestant and Anabaptist rejection of created things as vehicles of salvation was an overreaction to the idolatrous use of these things. As with Eastern Orthodox icons, classic Christian teaching on the role of created things, in worship and salvation walked a narrow line between idolatrous worship of created things and orthodox use of them because God used them in Christ's incarnation. It was the idolatrous abuse of creation in the church that loomed large on the Anabaptist horizon.

Anabaptists frequently emphasized disjunction between the Old Testament and the New Testament. Faith must be individually and directly appropriated; human society (parents, families, liturgy, schools) cannot mediate faith between generations.

This attitude toward the created order based in theological rejection of a corrupted Christian society, was modified as Mennonites established their own subcultures and their own version of sacramental, cultural faith (Cronk, *"Gelassenheit"*). As farmers, who worked daily with the natural world and its wonders, they intuitively reappropriated a sense of God's working through the created order to bring wholeness, integration, shalom. Mennonites were not ready, for the most part, to articulate a theology of the sacramental nature of created things, whereby the Incarnation serves as the testimony that God is redeeming the sin-corrupted creation, and as testimony that created things, like Christ's physical, human body, serve as vehicles for God's grace. The "Mennonite period" of Anabaptist and Mennonite history, then, was lived in the tension between intuitive reappropriation of created things as means of God's mercy and grace, as signs of God's faithfulness, on the one hand, and suspicion of "merely" cultural faith, or fear of the idolatry that so easily grows out of sacramental religion. Thus renewal among Mennonites has rarely taken the form of sacramental or liturgical or cultural renewal; rather, most renewal movements have emphasized the role of the Holy Spirit or radical, individual, crisis conversion (Brethren in Christ, Mennonite Brethren, °charismatic renewal, °revivalism).

The 20th-c. "recovery of the Anabaptist vision," especially since World War II, likewise has mistrusted enculturated Christianity (Kreider, *Holiness*). It has emphasized the Exodus-prophets trajectory at the expense of the creation-kings trajectory in choosing models for °sociopolitical activism. It has been suspicious of natural theology, which is intimately related to but not identical with a positive theology of creation in classic Christian orthodoxy (John H. Yoder). At the same time, Mennonites have moved into the mainstream cultures, abandoning their subcultures. A variety of forms of enculturated Christianity have been experimented with, but no articulated theology of creation and its re-formation in Christ exists to guide either the older subcultures (nostalgically celebrated, after they disappear) or the new enculturations. The issues are particularly acutely raised in Mennonite °institutions and °businesses. Similar tensions are evident in Mennonite art. Because the modern world, especially the modern, western Protestant world, has shared the Mennonite mistrust of the sacramental use of the created order, the Mennonite venture into the larger culture has rarely brought Mennonites into contact with articulated theologies of creation, culture, and art. Instead, it has contributed to the tension and confusion between intuitive appreciation for God's creation and fear of using it in idolatrous ways. Similarly, the Protestant mistrust of sacral use of created things lies behind the rise of modern technology

and the disastrous modern misuses of the °ecology. Contrary to frequent assertions in the ecology movement, the abusive "domination of nature" is not a necessary outcome of Christian theology. As long as Christian theology was based on sacramental use of creation, limits were placed on the exploitation of the natural world. As nature was reduced to mechanics and desacralized, domination by human machinery triumphed.

Discussions of creation in 20th c. Mennonite °°catechism or doctrinal manuals have often been dominated by an effort to respond to the challenge of °evolution theory (Daniel Kauffman, Wenger, Harder, Waltner).

As Mennonites begin to work with systematic, articulated °theology, the question of creation is being addressed, although there is no consensus on its place in Mennonite life and thought. The reader is referred to the works by Peter C. Erb, Gordon Kaufman, A. James Reimer, and Calvin Redekop in the bibliography below.   DDM

Calvin W. Redekop, "Toward a Mennonite Theology and Ethic of Creation," *MQR,* 60 (1986), 387-403; Peter C. Erb, "Reflections on Mennonite Theology in Canada," *JMS,* 1 (1983), 179-90; A. James Reimer, "The Nature and Possibility of a Mennonite Theology," *CGR,* 1 (1983), 33-55; Gordon Kaufman, *Systematic Theology: A Historicist Perspective* (New York: Scribners, 1968, 1977), ch. 18-23, 31; Daniel Kauffman, ed., *Doctrines of the Bible,* 2nd ed. (Scottdale, 1929, 1949), 35-50, 378-81; J. C. Wenger, *Introduction to Theology* (Scottdale, 1954), esp. 73-85, 107-112, 231-41; James H. Waltner, *This We Believe* (Newton, 1968), 30-44; Helmut Harder, *Guide to Faith* (Newton, 1979), ch. 4; Loewen, *Confessions,* e.g., p. 63 (Dordrecht, art. 1), 80 (Schleitheim, art. 4), 87/85 (GC Ris, 1766/1895, art. 1), 204 (CGC, 1952, art. 1); S. Goudie, ed., *Book of Religious Instruction* (n.p.: S. Goudie for the Executive Committee, Mennonite Brethren in Christ Church, 1930), 23-26; John D. Rempel, "Christology and the Lord's Supper in Anabaptism: A Study in the Theology of Balthasar Hubmaier, Pilgram Marpeck, and Dirk Philips" (ThD diss., St. Michael's College, Toronto School of Theology, University of Toronto, 1986); John Tonkin, *The Church and the Secular Order in Reformation Thought* (New York: Columbia U. Press, 1971); Willis M. Stoesz, "The New Creature: Menno Simons' Understanding of the Christian Faith," *MQR,* 39 (1968), 5-24; Leonard Verduin, "Menno Simons' Theology Reviewed," *MQR,* 24 (1950), 53-64; William E. Keeney, *The Development of Dutch Anabaptist Thought and Practice from 1539-1564* (Nieuwkoop: B. de Graaf, 1968); Sjouke Voolstra, *Het Woord Is Vlees Geworden: De melchioritisch-menniste incarnatieleer* (Kampen: J. H. Kok, 1982); Ben C. Ollenburger, *Zion, the City of the Great King* (Sheffield: JSOT Press, 1987); idem, "Isaiah's Creation Theology," in *Ex Auditu,* 3 (1988), 54-71; Sandra L. Cronk, *"Gelassenheit:* The Rites of Redemptive Process among Old Order Amish and Old Order Mennonite Communities" (PhD diss., U. of Chicago, 1977); Alan F. Kreider, *Journey toward Holiness* (Scottdale, 1987); C. Norman Kraus, "Becoming Who We Are In God (As Christians)," *GH* (Apr. 12, 1988), 249-51; Gerhart B. Ladner, *The Idea of Reform* (Cambridge, Mass.: Harvard U. Press, 1959); Alexander Schmemann, *For the Life of the World: Sacraments and Orthodoxy* (Crestwood, N.Y.: St. Vladimir's Seminary Press, 1963, 1973).

See also Ecology; Ordinances; Philosophy; Salvation; Sciences, Natural.

Credit. See Bankruptcy; Debts.

Credit Unions (ME I:733) can best be described as °cooperatives that offer financial services similar to those found at banks. Credit unions may be small, with services limited to share (savings) accounts and loans. Or they may be large and also offer draft (checking) accounts, certificates of deposit, mortgage loans, credit cards, and facilities for electronic funds transfer.

The credit union idea started in Germany in the mid-19th c. and grew throughout Europe and Asia. It came to North America via Canada and later spread throughout the United States. Credit unions were built around the principles of membership with persons of a common bond having an equal voice regardless of investments, refunds on purchases of goods and services from the cooperative, and the application of surplus income to benefit the organization, not individual directors or stockholders. For the most part directors of credit unions are volunteers.

Many of the basic tenets of the credit union movement are similar to Mennonite values of °mutual aid and sharing. However, credit unions have been slow to catch on among Mennonites, likely because the early credit union movement in North America flourished among °labor unions and military organizations.

Mennonites in Russia became familiar with the credit union idea before World War I, founding mutual credit societies. One of the first Mennonite credit unions in North America, Crosstown Credit Union, was organized in 1944 to serve the Mennonites of Winnipeg, Man. In 1955 the employees of Mennonite Publishing House (MC), Scottdale, Pa., organized a credit union, which changed its charter in 1983 to serve all members and employees of the Mennonite Church who live in the Commonwealth of Pennsylvania. Other Mennonite-related credit unions in North America are located in Hesston, Ks. (Central Kansas Federal Credit Union, 1960); Waterloo, Ont. (Mennonite Credit Union-Ontario, 1964); LaJunta, Col. (Mennonite Federal Credit Union, 1965); Harrisonburg, Va. (Park View Federal Credit Union, 1969); Kidron, Ohio (Ohio Mennonite Federal Credit Union, 1985); and Evanston, Ill. (Illinois Mennonite Federal Credit Union, 1988). Credit unions are also common in Mennonite communities outside North America, including some Latin American colonies. °Mennonite Economic Development Associates, Mennonite Central Committee, and Mennonite Mission and Service agencies have played auxiliary roles in these developments.

Credit unions are one way that Mennonites can put into practice their values of caring, sharing, and bearing each other's burdens. While the movement has been slow to catch on in Mennonite communities, in the middle 1980s there seems to be a new openness to considering credit unions as one way to help each other share wealth and knowledge for the benefit of each other.   JLP

Urie Bender, ed, *Working Together: The Story of Mennonite Credit Union (Ontario), 1964-1984* (1985).

See also Brazil; °°Waisenamt; Witmarsum Colony.

Cree People. See Indians, North America.

Creek People. See Indians, North America.

Cremation, the burning of bodies of the deceased, has been practiced since the dawn of civilization. There is evidence that it was practiced throughout most of Europe by the Neolithic cultures and died out only with the arrival of Christianity in the 5th and 6th c. It was apparently introduced to Asia by the invading Aryans ca. 2000 B.C. The Hindu community continues to perpetuate it as part of sacred Hindu tradition to the present time.

There is no evidence in the Bible to suggest that cremation was practiced by any of the peoples of Bible history. Christian burial customs have grown out of the Jewish background.

Because of the deep religious connotations involved in a Hindu burial ceremony, the Church in India has been reluctant to consider cremation as a burial option for Christians. In China and Japan cremation is not part of the cultural tradition, but due to the need to conserve land, cremation has been secularized and made mandatory for all communities. Thus it is not an issue for Christians.

In the last 50 years attitudes toward cremation have changed in the West, where more and more Christians use it as an acceptable alternative to the high costs of embalming and burial. In a survey taken in 1965, only 9 out of 27 denominations surveyed, prohibited cremation. Mennonites have never taken any official stand for or against cremation, but tend to favor traditional °burial customs.   JAF

Paul Erb, "Funeral Procedures of Religious Groups and Fraternal Organizations—Mennonites," in *Funeral Customs the World Over,,* ed. Haberstein and Lamers, 2nd edition (Milwaukee: Radtke Bros. and Kortsch Co., 1963); Haberstein and Lamers, *The History of Funeral Directing,* esp. ch. 2, rev. ed. (1962); *Encyclopedia Americana,* vol. 18 (1986), 171; A. L. Bosham, "Hinduism," *Concise Encyclopedia of Living Faiths* (Beacon press), 224; Dubois and Beachamp, *Hindu Manners, Customs and Ceremonies,* 3rd ed. (Oxford Press, 1906).

Crete. Mennonite Central Committee (MCC) was first invited to Crete in 1961 by Greek Orthodox Bishop Ireneos to help open a vocational school. MCC sent two volunteers as teachers. Two years later, as enrollment increased, the Greek government supplied and funded the teachers.

In 1965 Bishop Ireneos again invited MCC to Crete to develop an agriculture and demonstration center. MCC workers distributed the offspring of imported improved livestock. They made available improved livestock feed and conducted limited classes in agriculture. Produce from the center was used to provide food for the students, who supported by the bishop, lived in dormitories located in villages with schools. In 1973 the agriculture center was turned over to the bishop. In all of this an attempt was made to build bridges of greater understanding between the Greek Orthodox and the Mennonites.   VC

See also Eastern and Coptic Orthodox Churches; Greece.

Crimean War. The battle zones on the Crimean peninsula were located only about 160 mi. (260 km.) from the mother colonies, Chortitza and Molotschna. All Russians were urged to help in the war effort. Under their colonizing charter of 1800, Mennonites were exempted from active °military duty. Many of them felt, however, that one ought to stand by the tsar somehow. They agreed, therefore, to provide supplies for Russian soldiers marching through the colonies and also for those at the front. In addition, many wounded men were brought back by horse and wagon to be treated in the colony hospitals and homes.

Some felt they had now compromised their °nonresistant beliefs. However, a monument was set up and numerous medals were given to the Mennonites to honor those who had supported the war in these ways.   LK

William Schroeder, *The Bergthal Colony,* 2nd ed. (Winnipeg: CMBC, 1986); James Urry, "The Closed and the Open: Social and Religious Change Amongst the Mennonites in Russia, 1789-1889" (PhD diss., Keble College, Oxford, England, 1978); Lawrence Klippenstein, "Mennonite Pacifism and State Service in Russia: A Case Study in Church-State Relations, 1789-1936" (PhD diss., U. of Minnesota, 1984); John S. Curtiss, *The Russian Army Under Nicholas I (1825-1855)* (Durham, N.C.: Duke U. Press, 1965); *Unterhaltungsblatt für deutsche Ansiedler im Südlichen Russland (1853-1856);* Johann Wall, unpublished diary from Neuendorf, 1825-1866, in the Mennonite Heritage Centre archives (Winnipeg), vol. 1086.

Crossbearing. See Suffering.

Crous, Ernst (Mar. 6, 1882–May 31, 1967). Ernst Crous was a descendent of an old Krefeld Mennonite family. Following his doctoral studies in German history, literature, law, and philosophy, Crous worked in the Prussian state library (Preußische Staatsbibliothek) in Berlin and served as lecturer at the Berlin library school. As head of the *incunabula* section (books printed before 1501) of the library, as well as through his own research, he soon became known internationally as an authority in this field. In 1925 he was elected to the church council of the Berlin Mennonite congregation, and five years later became its chairperson. He was instrumental in gathering the scattered Mennonites of Berlin into a unified congregation. During the era of °National Socialism (Nazism), he and his wife Rose developed a relationship to the Confessing Church. In 1944 the Berlin Library School was transferred to Göttingen, where he also settled.

It was in the Göttingen area that many refugees from West Prussia and Russia found shelter after World War II. Crous played a significant role in providing the refugees in lower Saxony, Westfalia, and North Hesse with spiritual and material help. He became elder of the Mennonite congregation in Göttingen. Soon after World War II he succeeded in convening a conference of Mennonite representatives from Holland, Canada, and North and South Germany in Göttingen to rebuild bridges of understanding which had been destroyed by the war. From 1932 to 1951 Crous served as vice president of the Vereinigung der Deutschen Mennonitengemeinden (Association of [North] German Mennonite Churches), in which capacity he represented German churches in the founding of the World Council of Churches in Amsterdam in 1948. Crous was also instrumental in helping organize in 1947 the Mennonite distribution network for relief assistance coming from North America to the British zone in northern Germany.

He was one of the founders of the Mennonitischer Geschichtsverein (German Mennonite Historical Society) in 1933. From 1947 to 1958 he was editor of the °°*Mennonitisches Lexikon.* He collaborated in the preparation of the four-volume °*Mennonite Encyclo-*

pedia, and the third edition of a standard German theological encyclopedia, *Die Religion in Geschichte und Gegenwart.* He also became chairman of the Täuferaktenkommission (Commission for the Publication of Anabaptist Documents). Research in Anabaptist and Mennonite history remained his preferred academic interest throughout his life. In this connection he wrote more than 380 articles for the *Mennonitisches Lexikon* and the *Mennonite Encyclopedia.* Many articles in a variety of other publications further confirm this interest.   GHil

W. Regehr, "Dr. Ernst Crous zum Gedachtnis," *Mennoblatt,* 16 (1967); J. S. Oyer, "Ernst Crous, 1982-1967," *MQR,* 42 (1968), 301-11; W. Holler, E. Koppen, "Ernst Crous, Historiker der Mennoniten," in *Sie kamen aus Krefeld,* (Krefeld: Joh. van Acken); G. u. J. Hildebrandt, "Ernst Crous (1882-1967) Brückenschlag nach allen Seiten," in *Menn. Jahrbuch* (1987); K. Kauenhowen, "Dr. Ernst Crous zum 70. Geburtstag," *Menn. Geschbl.,* Jg. 10, n.F. 5 (1953) 41-44; G. Hein, "Ernst Crous in memoriam," *Menn. Geschbl.,* Jg. 23, n.F. 18 (1966), 3-14.

Cuauhtémoc, Chihuahua State, (ME I:743), one of the fastest-growing cities in Mexico, has more than 100,000 inhabitants. A four-lane highway, completed in 1986, connects the city with the city of Chihuahua, the state capital. Another highway connects Cuauhtémoc with Col. Anahuac, where a large pulp mill is located. The Gran Visión highway, which is to be continued to the west coast through the Sierra Madre Occidental mountains, joins the city to the western hinterlands, and another highway leaving the city passes through the Mennonite colonies to the north (°Manitoba Colony).

The apple industry, introduced to the area by a former Old Colony Mennonite, Enrique Wiebe, has contributed much to the rapid growth of the city. The influx of American industry in the mid-1980s, is also attracting people from all over the Republic. Doctors, dentists, and lawyers abound. Elementary, secondary, preparatory, and technology schools are numerous. One agricultural school, incorporated with the U. of Chihuahua, is located in Cuauhtémoc, and the one incorporated Mennonite elementary and secondary school, Alvaro Obregon, is located on the outskirts at Quinta Lupita.

Although the city, formerly called San Antonio de los Arenales, only developed after the arrival of the Old Colony Mennonites in 1922, it has practically no Mennonites living in it. However, the streets and the numerous banks teem with them, especially on Monday mornings. Cuauhtémoc is the most important commercial center for Old Colony Mennonites in Chihuahua.

In the early 1930s the recent Mennonite immigrants from the Soviet Union (°Rußländer) formed a Mennonite congregation in the town, but by 1987 it had disintegrated completely. The few Mennonite families and General Conference Mennonite Church and Mennonite Central Committee workers living in the city (5 families and 5 singles) worship mostly at the General Conference congregation at Kilometer 11. Cuauhtémoc was the first city to erect a senior citizens home under public or government jurisdiction. Its first matron was a Mennonite, Maria Giesbrecht, from the Santa Rita Colony (°Nord Colony).   HEns

Cuba (ME IV:1075) is an island in the West Indies.

Many in the population of nearly ten million are nominally Roman Catholic; about two percent are Protestant. Working on the island are two Anabaptist-rooted denominations and the Mennonite Central Committee.

The Brethren in Christ began their work in 1953, establishing a mission program that developed into the °Iglesia de los Hermanos en Cristo. The two congregations formed have weathered difficulties and were active in 1987 as a registered church. The Franconia Mennonite Conference (MC), founded the Cuba Mennonite Mission in 1954. The missionaries worked out of two centers, Rancho Veloz and Sagua la Grande, both located in Santa Clara Province in north central Cuba. Numerous witness points were established. Methods included teaching English, home visitation, home Bible studies, and radio broadcasting. By 1960, six missionaries were on the field. All of them eventually left as a result of the revolution (1959). Because government registration was not obtained, any Mennonite Church gathering became illegal. Therefore, in 1987, Mennonite converts were worshiping with other Protestant groups. After Cuba began to permit some visitation, a few Brethren in Christ and Mennonite leaders visited their respective people.

Since 1981 the Mennonite Central Committee (MCC) has worked through church agencies in Cuba to help Cuban churches carry out their ministries, and to foster understandings between Cubans and North Americans. Examples of MCC work include helping repair a chapel, assisting in refurbishing a Bible study center, and contributing Anabaptist and peace literature to church libraries.   MHS

MWH (1984), 68; Wittlinger, *Piety and Obedience* (1987), 516-18.

Culture. See Acculturation; Creation; Literature; Nonconformity; Niebuhr, Helmut Richard; Mennonite Studies; Sectarianism and Cultural Mandate.

Cumberland Valley Mennonite Church was formed in 1971 by six congregations who ascribe to the °°Dordrecht Confession of Faith (1632). Three congregations are located in Franklin Co., Pa, and three in Washington Co., Md. The three congregations in Pennsylvania are: Rowe, near Shippensburg founded in 1840; Strasburg, near Chambersburg (1812); and Burns Valley near Doylesburg (1953). Burns Valley began as a mission outreach of the Rowe congregation. These congregations were formerly part of the Franklin Mennonite Conference. The three congregations in Maryland are: Mt. Olive near Maugansville (1971); Lanes Run near Clear Spring (1969); and Yarrowsburg near Brownsville (1965). These congregations were made up of former members of the Washington-Franklin Mennonite Conference.   CBL

MC Yearbook (1988-89), 93; Nelson Baer, "A Short History of the Rowe Mennonite Congregation"; Harry Burkholder, "A Brief History of the Strasburg Meeting House"; Amos Strite, "Amos Strite Collection," copies at Mennonite Historical Association of the Cumberland Valley, Maugansville, Md.

Curitiba, Brazil (ME I:747). Founded in 1654 as a goldmining camp, and since 1854 the capital of the State of Paraná in se. Brazil, Curitiba is situated 905 m. (3,000 ft.) above sea level near the Atlantic rim of the Brazilian Highlands and headwaters of the Iguaçu River. Inverted umbrella-like *pinheiros* (pines) and lush *mate* (tea) trees are native to the surrounding subtropical forest and the pride of over one million *curitibanos* (inhabitants of Curitiba).

The population forms a mix of original nationals with Italian, German, and Polish immigrants from the 19th c., and large additions from Syria and Japan in the 20th c.

A modern business center, the city is proud of its uniquely planned and developed industrial district, its many banks, and its more than 14,000 commercial establishments that collectively account for sustained economic growth. Paper, leather goods, furniture, and foods are among the principal manufactured items. All this plus a healthy climate and easy access by road, rail, and air, make Curitiba an attractive place to live.

The first Mennonite family settled there in 1931. Since then until the early 1950s, more than 50 percent of all Brazilian Mennonites moved from the Stolzplateau and Krauel colonies to Curitiba and surrounding areas to enter dairy farming, business ventures, agriculture, or professional careers.   HK

Peter Pauls, Jr., ed. *Mennoniten in Brasilien: Gedenkschrift zum 50 Jahr-Jubiläum ihrer Einwanderung, 1930-1980* (Witmarsum: n.p., 1980).

Currículo Anabautista de Educación Bíblica Congregaciónal, proyecto interamericano e intermenonita (Biblical Anabaptist Curriculum for Congregational Education, Inter-American and Inter-Mennonite Project). See Sunday School Literature.

Customs. See Folklore.

D

Daily Vacation Bible School. See Summer (Vacation) Bible School.

Dance. Dancing continues to be a controversial subject in the Mennonite churches. Social dancing involving the physical contact of men and women is the type of dancing that has caused the most concern. The reasons most frequently cited for this concern include the potential for sexual stimulation, creating an image that weakens the Christian witness, and breaking down the spiritual life of the members of the church.

Theologically, condemnation of the social dance was frequently rooted in the doctrine of °nonconformity. Together with other °amusements, social dancing conformed the Christian to the world instead of the character of Jesus Christ.

Square dancing, though seldom encouraged among Mennonites, has generally been more acceptable. The young people of some Old Order Mennonite and Amish groups have a history of Sunday evening square dancing (Horst, *Heritage*). In 1910 J. E. °Hartzler wrote that, "The square dance, if it were kept square, would not be so bad."

While many Mennonites hold fast to these convictions, many others have recently become more involved in a variety of recreational activities, including social dancing. Youth often participate in high school dances, and a growing number of Mennonite colleges allow social dancing on their campuses.

Numerous leaders who have spoken out against social dancing have also acknowledged that the Bible records positive examples of dance. Frequently cited are the dances of Miriam (Ex 15:20-21) and David (2 Sam 6:14-16), both offered to God in a spirit of thanksgiving and praise.

A growing number of Mennonites are reclaiming sacred dance as an expression of °worship, in the tradition of the Israelites and the early church. In some North American congregations ongoing creative movement or liturgical dance groups offer accompaniment to congregational singing or special music during the Sunday morning service. In some African Mennonite congregations, traditional music and dance have been incorporated into worship. The offering in Zairian Mennonite churches is brought forward in the midst of lively singing, clapping, and dance, all to the glory of God. **AWB**

Carolyn Deitering, *The Liturgy as Dance and the Liturgical Dancer* (New York: Crossroad, 1984); Kauffman/Harder, *Anabaptists Four C. Later* (1975), 122-23, 281, 288, 308; *Menn. Rep.* (Mar. 14, 1988), 8; P. M. Friesen, *Brotherhood* (1911, 1980), index; J. E. Hartzler, *Paths to Perdition* (Scottdale: MPH, 1910), 177-84; Mary Ann Horst, *My Old Order Mennonite Heritage* (Kitchener, Ont, 26-28; Isaac R. Horst, "Should Christians Dance?" (undated pamphlet from MHL, Goshen); Daniel Kauffman, ed., *Bible Doctrine* (Scottdale: MPH, 1914), 514-18; Richard H. Shaner, "The Amish Barn

Dance," *Pennsylvania Folklife*, 13 (Winter 1962-63), 24-26; M. S. Steiner, *Pitfalls and Safeguards* (Elkhart, Ind., 1899), 107-14; J. C. Wenger, *Separated Unto God* (Scottdale: MPH, 1951), 75-87, 113-15, 279-81.

See also Folk Music.

Danzig (Gdansk). See West Prussia.

Das, Isa (1880-1940), the son of a rich Satnami farmer from Kyota Dabri near Mungeli, was an orphan of the 1896-97 famine. He was brought up, educated, and married in the Disciples of Christ mission in Bilaspur. As teacher-preacher, he and his wife, Mathuria, also a famine orphan, served in rural evangelistic work. Because of his great generosity to the poor, Isa could not always account for the mission funds he had spent. These misunderstandings led to his resignation from the Disciples of Christ mission.

At the invitation of P. J. Wiens, Isa and Mathuria joined the General Conference Mennonite Church mission in 1911. They were stationed at Mauhadih first and then moved to the new outstation at Sukhri (1917-23) where Isa ministered in the surrounding villages with great success, baptizing 109 converts in 1919. Isa and Mathuria also worked at Dhabakar and later lived at Basna and Jagdeeshpur.

Characteristic of Isa Das was his close identification with the people. He repudiated the use of a bicycle in favor of walking, talking, and singing his way into the hearts of the people. He chatted freely with farmer, weaver, merchant, or official, and always kept an eye open for children. As with a magnet, he drew them to himself. In the shade of a tree he would sit and sing and tell of Jesus, an effective way of reaching adults as well. His Satnami background, and his wife's Brahmin background, permitted them free access into homes of low and high °caste alike, and enabled them to bring the gospel to those others could not reach. **HKor**

Das, Mathuria (1885-Feb. 2, 1964), the second daughter of orthodox Brahmin parents, Bhagwan Das and Kaushalya Bai, was adopted as an infant by her childless Uncle Maniram and his wife Sumitra. During the famine of 1896 and 1897, Mathuria, her sister Esther, and her brother Dhaniram were taken to the Disciples of Christ mission in Bilaspur.

Mathuria married Isa Das at age 18 and joined him in rural evangelistic work in the Nippania area of Bilaspur. Because of her own Brahmin background, she enjoyed an effective ministry among the women of high caste. After joining the General Conference Mennonite Church mission, Mathuria worked with courage and resourcefulness at Mauhadih, and in the pioneer work at Sukhri she had to cope, often alone, with the strange Oriya speech and customs in crowded living conditions with a growing family. The supreme test came when her youngest child died and her husband was away. Determined to give her child a Christian burial in Mauhadih, many miles away, she made her way, accompanied by Sukhri Christians, through tiger- and snake-infested jungle, in the monsoon downpour, and across the swollen Mahanadi river to Mahadih. ,

After a brief time working in Dhabakar, Isa and Mathuria moved to Basna. Muslim families there invited Mathuria to teach their daughters. Later she was invited to teach the princesses in the Rajkumar palace in Saraipali. The Das family then settled in Jagdeeshpur.

Always hospitable and gracious, Mathuria opened her home to orphans and strangers, sometimes for weeks, sometimes longer, sheltering them, feeding them, sharing whatever she had. She devoted her latter years to teaching and counseling, always present when a crisis of death or tensions in a marriage called for her services. She was honored at the 50th anniversary celebration of Madhkughat Mela.   HKor

David Joris (ME II:17) was by trade a glasspainter whose reform career can be divided into four overlapping phases: Sacramentarian (1524-1530); Melchiorite sympathizer (1531-1534); Anabaptist leader (1534-ca. 1543); and Spiritualist (ca. 1540-1556). As a Melchiorite, Joris was caught up in the °apocalyptic excitement that inspired much of the movement (Melchior °Hoffman), but due to his earlier punishment in 1528 and despite his acceptance into the leadership by °°Obbe Philips and °°Damas von Hoorn at the end of 1534, he remained hesitant to join radical programs. This is borne out by his cautious behavior at the Waterland Conference in the winter of 1534/1535.

After the fall of °Münster, Joris became the most important Anabaptist leader in the Netherlands between 1536 and 1539, concerned primarily with uniting the remnants of Melchiorites and Münsterites by his charisma and a compromise program. As the result of his successful mediation at Bocholt (August 1536) and encouraged by visions experienced in December 1536, Joris came to conceive of himself as the "third David." His consistent advocacy of a peaceful approach may have enhanced his stature in the eyes of those seeking to distance themselves from the Münster fiasco. It also helped some to make a successful transition from revolution to non-violence. Joris' support came largely from Anabaptist artisans who found his option of flight into interior religion ("internal exile") more appropriate for remaining in the urban centers of the Netherlands than the sectarian option of gathered, disciplined congregations presented by °Menno Simons. Joris' leadership campaign led him to conferences in Oldenburg in Westphalia (spring 1538), where he gained briefly the adherence of the remnant Münsterites under the leadership of Heinrich Krechting and in Strasbourg (summer 1538), where his program was rejected by the Strasbourg Melchiorites.

Although retaining contact with many former Mel-chiorites, Joris accelerated his spiritualization of Melchiorite beliefs after he moved to Antwerp in 1539. Moving to Basel in 1544, he found permanent refuge and freedom from the persecution that had hounded him for 15 years—under the name "Jan van Brugge." In Basel his Spiritualism developed fully and his Anabaptist beliefs receded to insignificance.   GKW

A. van der Linde's *David Joris Bibliografie* (Martinus Nijhoff, 1867) is in need of updating. Not only have additional works been discovered by Roland Bainton, *David Joris. Wiedertäufer und Kämpfer für Toleranz* (Leipzig, 1937), 108-9, but there is a large collection of Joris material, called the *Jorislade*, located in the Basel University Archives. One of the 15 volumes, the "Hydeckel" (no. IX), is a manuscript collection of Joris' early letters (1537-1543), including his response to Hans Eysenburg that formerly was thought to have been lost. The record of Joris' debate with the Strasbourg Melchiorites (the "Twistredt") was published in *TA Elsaß III*. Biographical information is found in "David Joris sonderbare Lebens-beschreibung" in Gottfried Arnold, *Unpartheiische Kirchen- und Ketzer Historie*, vol. 2 (Frankfurt, 1729, reprinted Hildesheim: Georg Olms, 1967), 703-37. This anonymous work is so richly detailed and historically accurate that it may have been written by Joris himself. Further information is found in Nicolaas Meyndertsz van Blesdijk, *Historia Vitae, doctrinae ac rerum gestarum Davidis Georgii haeresiarchae* (Deventer, 1642). While the anonymous biography in Arnold's *Ketzer Historie* is slanted in favor of Joris, Blesdijk wrote his account to uncover his father-in-law's heresy. Recent scholarship has gone beyond the preliminary work of Friedrich Nippold, "David Joris van Delft: Sein Leben, seine Lehre und seine Secte," *Z. für historische Theologie* (Gotha, 1863) and Bainton. James M. Stayer has summarized recent literature in "David Joris: A Prolegomenon to Further Research," *MQR*, 59 (1985), 350-66, and detailed the debate between Joris and Menno Simons in "Davidite vs. Mennonite," *MQR*, 58 (1984), 459-76. S. Zijlstra argued that Joris was the most important Anabaptist leader in the Netherlands between 1536 and 1539 in "David Joris en de Doperse Stromingen (1536-1539)," in *Historisch Bewogen*, ed. M. G. Buist and others (Groningen: Wolters-Noordhoff, 1984), 125-38, and in *Nicolaas Meyndertsz van Blesdijk. Een Bijdrage tot de Geschiedenis van het Davidjorisme* (Assen: Van Gorcum, 1983). Zijlstra has also explained the reasons behind Joris' success in winning some followers from Menno in "Menno Simons and David Joris," *MQR*, 62 (1988), 249-56. Gary K. Waite discussed Joris' following, ideology, and contribution in "Spiritualizing the Crusade: David Joris in the Context of the Early Reform and Anabaptist Movements in the Netherlands, 1524-1543" (PhD diss., U. of Waterloo, 1986). See also idem, "Staying Alive: The Methods of Survival as practiced by an Anabaptist Fugitive, David Joris," *MQR*, 61 (1987), 46-57; idem, "David Joris' Thought in the Context of the Early Anabaptist Movement in the Netherlands, 1534-1536," *MQR*, 62 (1988), 296-317. Werner O. Packull, "Anna Jans of Rotterdam, a Sixteenth Century Heroine," *ARG*, 78 (1987), 147-73, is a study of one of Joris' followers. Klaus Deppermann, *Melchior Hoffman* (Göttingen: Vandenhoeck and Ruprecht, 1979), esp. 315-24, analyses Joris' discussions with the Strasbourg Melchiorites, although Deppermann's contention that Joris supported polygamy (317) has been refuted by Zijlstra, "David Joris," p. 134. See also C. W. A. Willemse, "De briefwisseling tussen David Joris en Johannes a Lasco," *Doops. Bijdr.*, n.r. 4 (1979), 9-22.

Davidson, Hannah Frances (1860-1935), was a pioneer Brethren in Christ missionary in Africa. Her father, Henry Davidson, was a minister and the first editor of the denomination's paper, the *Evangelical Visitor*. She attended Ashland College in Ohio and obtained her BA and MA degrees from Kalamazoo College in Michigan, the first member of the Brethren in Christ to earn an academic degree. She taught high school in Michigan and assisted her father in editing the church paper. From 1888 to 1897, except for a year's leave of absence, she was a member of the faculty of McPherson College (CBreth) in Kansas.

While there she responded to a call for missionaries from the mission board of the Brethren in Christ Church. She was among the small group of five missionaries, including Jesse M. °Engle, who sailed for Africa in late 1897 to found Brethren in Christ missions on that continent. She assisted in establishing Matopo Mission in Southern Rhodesia (Zimbabwe), some 30 mi. (50 km.) west of Bulawayo. She organized a school system, surveyed the mission grounds and surrounding land, and served as Bible teacher and preacher (although without ordination).

In 1906 with Adda Taylor and two African young men, Davidson traveled north nearly 500 mi. (800 km.), more than one-third of the way by ox-cart, to found Macha mission in Northern Rhodesia (Zambia). She was superintendent of the mission for most of her remaining years in Africa. Here she again organized a school system which came to include some 30 so-called out-schools. She also managed a large and successful farm which by 1921 had 100 cattle. In addition she assisted Primitive Methodist missionaries in the translation of the Greek New Testament into the local languages which at that time were still unwritten.

On a furlough to the Unites States in 1914, Davidson wrote *South and South Central Africa: A Record of Fifteen Years' Missionary Labors Among Primitive Peoples*. The 481-page book remains the authoritative account of the beginning and first years of Brethren in Christ missions in Africa. From her days at Ashland College she maintained a journal, detailed at times, from which she drew heavily in writing the book. The journal is a valuable source for understanding the difficulties and challenges of missionary work, especially for women.

Davidson left Macha in 1922 and returned to the United States. Following a year of practical nursing in California she joined the faculty of Messiah Bible College (Messiah College) in Grantham, Pa. Here she taught English, Greek, and German, and edited and wrote for the missionary section in the *Evangelical Visitor*. Because of failing health she retired in 1932 at the age of 72 and moved to Abilene, Ks., to live with her sister. She died in December 1935.   EMS

E. Morris Sider, *Nine Portraits* (Nappanee, Ind., 1978), 157-212; Frances Davidson, *South and South Central Africa* (Elgin, Ill.: Brethren Publishing House, 1915), 1-481; Anna R. Engle, John A. Climenhaga, Leoda A. Buckwalter, *There Is No Difference: God Works in Africa and India* (Nappanee, Ind., 1950), 10-129; Carlton O. Wittlinger, *Piety and Obedience* (1978), 182-84; *EV* (December 23, 1935), 8.

See also Mbungano Yabunyina Muli Kristo.

Davidson, Henry (1823-1903), Brethren in Christ °bishop and influential churchman who made major contributions in publication and foreign missions. He was born in Pennsylvania and ordained to the ministry at the age of 23. He moved several times, living in Ohio, Michigan, Kansas, and Pennsylvania, and in each location actively served the church. He was frequently chosen as moderator or assistant moderator of General Conference and served on such important boards as the Publication Board and the Mission Board. He was the chief mover in the Brethren in Christ decision to publish its own paper, the *Evangelical Visitor*, and was the paper's first editor (1887-96). As editor he sought to move the denomination in new ways in keeping with the Brethren heritage. He emphasized °missions, °Sunday schools, and higher °education. He was chairman of the mission board when the decision was made to undertake overseas work. The first person to volunteer was his daughter, H. Frances °Davidson.   MHS

Wittlinger, *Piety and Obedience* (1978), index; *Minutes (BIC) 1871-1904)*, [5-7], 161.

Daviess Co., Ind., Old Order Amish Settlement. See Montgomery, Ind., Old Order Amish Settlement.

Deaf Ministries. See Disabilities.

Death and Dying. The Mennonite understanding of death and dying and attitudes and response to these final life experiences have been influenced by Mennonite faith and the surrounding society.

The Anabaptists were doubtless greatly influenced in this regard by the terrible persecutions and deaths as described by Thieleman von Braght in his *Martyrs Mirror*, published in 1660. Here he tells of the persecution and tragic death of more than 4,000 Christians, beginning with Christ's death. Many of these were during the apostolic period, some in each century until the Reformation period and more in the 16th and 17th c., when there were great slaughters of human life. As the Protestant churches became more accepted by society in Europe and North America, differences in practices related to death diminished in relation to the culture generally. For Christians there was always the emphasis on the resurrection and future life.

Some practices among Mennonites include shrouds, sometimes white; keeping caskets outside church buildings; and conducting a wake. Until the 20th c., families and the church community usually took care of everything associated with death. In the latter part of the 19th c. there was a perfecting of chemicals and techniques which contributed to the more general practice of embalming. This contributed to the beginning of the modern undertaking profession. First these were sidelines to other businesses, such as livery stables, furniture stores, or barbershops. The writer personally remembers at least three furniture store/undertaking establishments and a barbershop/undertaking establishment by Mr. Byers in Woodbury, Pa.

Mennonites seem to be generally unaware of the radical change in their attitude toward death as a result of changing practices. Since the mid-20th c. many deaths occur in hospitals or nursing homes instead of at home in the presence of family; the body is taken to a funeral home by employees, instead of family and friends washing, dressing, and placing it in a homemade coffin; viewing of the body in business establishments has replaced a wake held in the home; the body is conveyed to funeral services and grave site by a luxurious, chauffeured vehicle instead of family-provided vehicle; the grave is opened and closed commercially instead of by friends.

The former practices helped to provide familiarity

with death and had a therapeutic benefit. Now there is a certain fear or revulsion associated with a dead body. Touching or handling it is to be avoided. Death has become a "hush, hush" subject, to be mentioned or talked of only when it has occurred in a family or community.

These attitudes have begun to change during the past two decades. By the 1980s death is spoken of more freely. Literature on the subject is appearing. More families and groups in the Mennonite churches are taking charge of planning their °funerals. Some of them are modest modifications of the conventional patterns and some are more radical. There is a recognition that most of the 20-30 specific services which the modern undertaker is prepared to render could well be the opportunity and responsibility of the Christian family and church.

Churches are beginning to consider this issue. In May 1975 the Mennonite Medical Association sponsored a two-day consultation on "Death and Dying" in Chicago, in which seven papers were presented and discussed. The Virginia Mennonite Conference (MC) under the direction of one of its regular committees and a special committee, had two series of papers prepared.

In 1978, the Mennonite Board of Congregational Ministries (MC) assumed responsibility for giving leadership in the Mennonite Church (MC) to this growing concern. They named a committee which, among other things, planned several consultations, produced two editions (1980 and 1986) of a 160-page study manual, and gave assistance to area workshops, studies, and preparation of articles.

The Christian death has been called the third death/birth experience. The *first* death/birth is when the infant leaves the comfort, security, and provisions of the mother's womb for a new and unknown world. The *second* death/birth is when one leaves (dies to) the known world where the individual has "enjoyed the pleasures of sin" and has been born again into the church, the Body of Christ. Again, one is leaving the known and the comfortable for the unknown. The *third* death/birth means dying to what one has known of one's Christian life on earth and again born into a life which will be far beyond our human comprehension here and now.

For the Christian, death is life's greatest paradox! Christians are told to "rejoice with them that do rejoice and weep with them that weep" (Rom 12:15, KJV). Usually this refers to two totally separate and different occasions; but, in the death of a Christian, these two radically different emotional experiences are at one and the same time, same place, same circumstance, with the same people involved. On the one hand, there is the pain, suffering, and sorrow due to the separation from a loved one. Being of this earth, this is natural. Being a Christian does not change it greatly. On the other hand, death is a time of victory, joy, gladness, and celebration with and for the saint who has gone Home. Since there is joy in heaven over one sinner that repenteth, what a time of celebration there must be when a saint "goes marching in"! The big question is: What is the appropriate Christian attitude toward and response to such an apparently conflicting situation? What a paradox! AJM

Samuel Gerber, *Learing to Die* (Scottdale, 1984) Billy Graham, *Facing Death and the After Life* (Waco Tex.: Word Books, 1987); Janette Klopfenstein, *My Walk with Grief* (Scottdale, 1987); Elizabeth Kübler-Ross, *On Death and Dying* (New York: Macmillan, 1969); Larry Richards and Paul Johnson, *Death and the Caring Community* (Multnomah Press, 1980); Abraham Schmitt, *Dialogue with Death* (Waco: Word Books, 1976); Paul D. Simons, *Birth and Death: Bioethical Decision-Making* (Philadelphia: Westminster Press, 1983); Victor Zora and Rosemary Zora, *A Way to Die* (New York: Alfred A. Knopf, 1980).

See also Hospice Movement; Burial Customs.

The Resurrection According to Matthew

[March 18]. Today, just two weeks before the beginning of Holy Week festivities, death hit the village when our neighbor, Pita, left this world to join the next.

[March 19]. As the tradition of the Dida people of Côte d'Ivoire [Ivory Coast] prescribes, on the night before burial, the body is placed outside on a spacious double bed in the courtyard of the deceased one and the entire community gathers around to pass the night in singing. Mama and Papa [James and Jeanette Neff Krabill] put Matthew and Elisabeth Anne to bed a bit early tonight and left them for several hours in the care of Lassina—a Muslim friend from Mali who sometimes helps with work around the place—in order to attend the "death watch."

[March 20]. This morning was Pita's funeral service and burial and Matthew accompanied his Mama and Papa throughout the entire affair, even walking the long distance in the scorching midday sun to the cemetery and back again. Most folks came dressed in black or dark blue, and before the service assembled quietly around Pita's bed to pay last respects. Pita's sister sat beside her brother on the bed, wiping his brow and chasing away a growing number of flies also drawn to the occasion. "Fight, fight the war for me!" the choir sang in muted voices and without the usual musical instruments. "It is you, my God, who can fight for me!"

When the body had been washed and placed in the casket, the mourners proceeded to the church in two long lines—men on the right, women on the left—on either side of Pita. "Women of Honor," dressed in black uniforms, led the way carrying bouquets of freshly cut flowers to be spread about Pita's grave. We paused for several brief moments at the church to offer final prayers. The middle row of benches had been removed to make way for the casket. Everywhere one looked were signs of sadness. The sanctuary candles remained flameless, the flower pots flowerless, and the floor unswept. Across the altar was draped a large black cloth in place of the usual white one. Preacher Alphonse's comments were short and barely audible; from where he stood, only snatches reached us. Matthew, normally bubbling with questions, was caught up in the solemnity of the occasion. He remained silent and like the rest of us simply moved along with the flow of things until Pita had been lowered into the ground and we had headed for home.

[April 1 — Good Friday]. The practice here on Good Friday is to reenact a funeral—the funeral of

Jesus. And so today we did it all over again. Black dress, muted singing, the symbolic removal of the benches and freshly cut flowers (deposited this time at the foot of the altar). We explained the rerun to Matthew by telling him that Jesus had died and that on this day, all other activity ceased in order to think about His passing. "You mean Jesus is like Pita?" Matthew wanted to know. "He's like Pita lying there on his bed?" "Yes," we said, "Jesus is like Pita lying there on his bed."

[April 3 — Easter Sunday]. Easter morning! We got up and began preparing for church. This day, we knew, would be one of great joy! There would be singing. Dancing. Bright flowers and palm branches decorating the sanctuary. And the musical instruments would be back in full force! We dressed the children in their little white outfits prescribed for today. "Hey, why aren't we wearing dark clothing?" asked Matthew, confused by his revolving wardrobe. "Because Jesus isn't dead any longer," we replied. "He's come back to life!" Matthew stopped, reflected for a moment and then with a burst of inspiration added, "Jesus isn't on the bed anymore!" "No," we said, "Jesus isn't on the bed anymore!" JRK

Adapted from *Festival Quarterly* (Summer 1984), p. 43. Used by permission of *Festival Quarterly*, 3513 Old Philadelphia Pike, Intercourse, PA 17534.

See also African Independent Churches.

Death Penalty. See Capital Punishment.

Debts. Until recently, Mennonites have been highly skeptical about debt and have sought to keep it at arm's length. Ironically, they have become accommodated to it at a time when government indebtedness is at an all-time high, underdeveloped countries are mired in debt, and rampant consumer debt is such that the average North American family is but weeks away from personal bankruptcy.

The early Anabaptists had little to say about debt *per se*, though they avoided charging interest (in accordance with their understanding of Deut 23:19 and Ps 15:5), paid it only reluctantly, and frowned upon any occupation that required charging it. Early writings counseled against being indebted to the world. Debt was dangerous. The word itself had pejorative theological overtones ("Forgive us our *debts*. . .").

Scripture did not prohibit borrowing but seemed to caution against it. There were warnings against pledging surety (Prov 17:18), but lending to someone in need was encouraged (Ps 112:5). More practically, Mennonites saw debt as an enslaving entanglement that could lead to dilemmas such as foreclosure and the use of litigation for collection. It was better to owe no one anything.

One could speculate about psychological dimensions as well. Debt naturally creates guilt for a people who have not always readily accepted gifts, mercy, or grace. When Russian Mennonite immigrants to Canada in the early 20th c. received rail passage on credit from the Canadian Pacific Railway, many were haunted for years by the burden of their *Reiseschuld* (travel debt) until they could finally pay it off. (Some, however, felt little responsibility to repay their travel debt, causing church leaders great concern and embarrassment. This uncharacteristic lapse among the normally meticulous Mennonites was a major economic issue facing Canadian Mennonites of the period.)

Today Mennonites have little if any hesitation about going into debt. They no longer feel as constrained as they once did by the homespun prohibition, "If you can't afford it, don't buy it." A Mennonite without some indebtedness (farm, °business, or student loan, home mortgage, outstanding credit card balance, etc.) is a rarity. Increasing numbers of Mennonites also feel comfortable in the profession of banking.

In some Mennonite circles credit is seen as a potentially useful tool as it was by the 14th-c. English church leaders who established the first °credit unions to provide remedial loans to the poor. In recent years Mennonite and other Christian aid to the poor in underdeveloped countries often has taken the form of credit to peasant farmers or struggling small business people (°development work).

Credit unions have become an accepted fixture of some Mennonite communities (Manitoba and Ontario, for example). By 1987, when the first Mennonite credit union retreat was held, the number of Mennonite credit unions in North America numbered seven, some of which had thousands of members and assets in excess of $50 million. Credit unions see themselves in the context of the economics of caring and °mutual aid, but to many observers and clients they are seen as a more benevolent form of banking, a place to deposit money, carry out financial transactions, and, when necessary or convenient, incur debt.

The prevailing Mennonite sentiment seems to be that debt is an economic reality of contemporary society that can profitably be used by believers if done so carefully. Christians should not be overwhelmed or seduced by it. Being unable to repay obligations still meets with strong disapproval in most Mennonite circles. WKr

J. Winfield Fretz, "Brotherhood and the Economic Ethic of the Anabaptists," *Recovery* (1959), 194-201; Donald F. Durnbaugh, ed., *Every Need Supplied: Mutual Aid and Christian Community in the Free Churches, 1525-1675* (Philadelphia: Temple U. Press, 1974).

See also Bankruptcy.

Decision-making patterns have changed throughout the 400-year history of the Mennonites. Early patterns (Swiss) were generally informal and focused on the *Gemeinde*, the local community of faith (Peachey). Larger gatherings promoted consensus on basic questions of faith and church life through discussion, debate, and eventual agreement (e.g., the °Schleitheim Confession). Dutch and North German Mennonite patterns tended to be more leader-centered, possibly dictated by the need to bring unity to a fragmented people, especially following the °Münster uprising.

Church °polity or patterns of church government and theological orientations influence decision-making procedures. In the first half of the 20th c. decision-making power and °authority was often centralized in strong leaders. In recent decades the

°democratic patterns of government prevalent in society have strongly influenced both expectations and styles found in congregations, district conferences, and denominations.

A renewal group which emerged in the 1950s sought to introduce a community-based consensus form of decision-making particularly among the Mennonite Church (MC) congregations. Drawing on the writings of Lewis Benson, a Quaker writer, they argued for a corporate discernment process which encouraged °consensus rather than voting and engaged the membership of the congregation in a process of discernment. The °"Concern pamphlets" group published a variety of materials encouraging more direct involvement of the laity in decision-making. Calvin Redekop's essay, *The Church Functions With Purpose,* is a good illustration of the focus and tone of the emphasis in that era. In the 1980s writers are also calling for a process of mutual discernment or using New Testament terminology a "binding and loosing model" which takes the community of faith seriously (Retzlaff, Harder, Lederach, Miller, Bauman, Jeschke, etc.).

The Anabaptist and Mennonite concept of the church envisions a community which seeks God's will together. Lederach notes that the New Testament calls Christians "to discern the truth, what is virtuous, what is good and how to behave . . ." (p. 118, NIV). The concept of "binding and loosing" (Mt 18:19-20) is seen not only as a mandate to practice church °discipline but as a decision-making model for the church (Retzlaff, 56). The discernment model will vary depending on the issue under consideration. Identifying church beliefs, choosing leaders, decisions related to organization or program—each will call for variations in procedure.

Two New Testament terms which give substance to the meaning of discernment are *krino* which means to judge, to decide, or to assess, and *dokimazo* which means to be watching or alert. Romans 12:2 encourages a °nonconformed life, the content of which is discovered by a discernment (*dokimazo*) process, "to test and approve what God's will is" (NIV). Rather than going to the law courts Christians should find a solution in the Christian community (*diakimo,* 1 Cor 6:1-8). Paul prays that the Philippian Christians' "love may abound more and more in knowledge and depth of insight, so that you may be able to discern what is best. . ." (Phil 1:9-11). Discernment also happens when the broader church confers together as in Acts 15, permitting a consensus regarding expectations for the Gentile church community to emerge.

The authority for engaging in a process of discernment to discover God's will on various issues of church life is rooted in such passages as Mt 18:18-20 (binding and loosing) and rests in a belief that the gathered community through searching the Scriptures together under the guidance of the Holy Spirit can determine God's leading for a particular time and place (Bauman). An added dimension which gives shape to decisions is the recognition that history and tradition set in the context of current needs and practice are significant factors as well.

Models for decision-making will vary depending on denominational and congregational theology and polity, the nature of the issue to be addressed, the size of the group, previous decision-making experiences and how the decision-making task is perceived. The emphasis may be on the importance of the democratic procedure and the parliamentary process, or on group dynamics, or on community discernment, or on a combination of these foci.

A stress on the importance of the organization and the parliamentary process has its roots in the North American democratic model with its emphasis on the right of each person to participate in running the affairs of the organization. Values are upheld such as the right to vote or to express an opinion, following an orderly procedure (using *Robert's Rules of Order*), the importance of representation in decision-making, having choices in the election of people to offices, in short giving due attention to the parliamentary process including the majority vote. Gaining a majority opinion with majority rule appears to hold more value than achieving a common mind or consensus.

When group dynamics become a central focus in decision-making stress is placed on such issues as the role of the leader, power systems in the group, helping the group to work together, encouraging all people to participate. Consensus rather than voting is employed as a way to arrive at decisions. Group building and group nurture or maintenance are significant values. People often consider the process to be as important as the end result and at times sacrifice substance in favor of attention to process.

The discernment model of decision-making has as a central goal finding God's will for the issue at hand. This model does not ignore good parliamentary procedures, group process, or people, but it emphasizes the importance of finding God's will in relation to the issue in question. The goal of the decision-making process is not to discover the majority opinion but "the mind of Christ." New Testment patterns are cited as illustrations on how decisions can be made and on principles to be used in coming to a decision.

Ideally groups can draw on elements of all three perspectives depending on the issue at hand, on group size, on previous patterns familiar to the group plus other factors. Groups may well develop a range of patterns to serve their varied decision-making needs. Elements in a good decision-making process include the following: (1) a clear statement of the problem or issue which requires action; (2) adequate background information to focus the scope of the decision and to provide a basis upon which to explore alternatives; (3) development of a statement of alternative solutions; (4) an exploration of the various alternatives and their implications; (5) making the decision with a timetable for implementation; (6) depending on the nature of the decision, a review process may be indicated for a later date. Planning a meeting sequence is often helpful as well. The first meeting is a time to define the issue or problem and to give background information. The next meeting is a time to explore options, hear concerns, objections, positive responses, and to prioritize desirable solutions. The final meeting moves to a solution and implementation of the decision. In situations where documents are being written (e.g., position papers) an additional one or two meetings may be needed to review and revise documents. RL

Paul M. Lederach, *A Third Way* (Scottdale, 1980), 114-22; Helmut Harder, *Accountability In the Church: A Study Guide for Congregations* (Winnipeg: Conference of Mennonites in Canada, 1985), esp. Resource Essay II by Peter Retzlaff, "Authority For Binding and Loosing," pp. 54-57; Harold Bauman, *Congregations and Their Servant Leaders* (Scottdale: MPH, 1982), 7-16; Willard Claassen, *Learning To Lead*, Christian Service Training Series (Scottdale, 1963), 79-90; Philip A. Anderson, *Church Meetings That Matter* (Philadelphia and Boston: United Church Press, 1965); Gordon L. Lippitt, "Improving Decision-making With Groups," in *Group Development*, Selected Reading Series One, National Training Laboratories (1961), 90-93; Paul M. Miller, *Leading the Family of God* (Scottdale, 1981), 79-88; Marlin Jeschke, *Discipling the Brother* (Scottdale, 1972), 163-39; *CRR* 3: 118-39; Calvin Redekop, *The Church Functions With Purpose: An Essay on Church Organization*, Focal Pamphlet no. 11 (Scottdale, 1967).

Dedication of Infants

Dedication of Infants (ME I:699). The greatest divine gift that can be bestowed upon men and women is the joy of the kingdom of God. The confession of faith at the beginning of part II of van °°Bracht's *Martyrs Mirror* (English edition, pp. 373ff.) claims that neither faith nor unbelief may be imputed to children. They are well-pleasing to God through his grace alone. Since God nowhere speaks of the regeneration of infants, it is not proper to ascribe this function to °infant baptism or infant dedication. Nor may one hold that infants are regenerated by means of the general redemption of Christ. Since children have never known, served or practiced sin from which they might be converted, they are placed by God in a holy God-pleasing state, through the atonement of Christ.

Pilgram °Marpeck says children are in the kingdom of Christ through promise (CRR 2:112). In dedicating them to God, parents and the church together affirm this belief, and commit themselves to the loving care of bringing up children in the nurture and admonition of the Lord, so that when they reach the age of full accountability, they will through faith in Christ be baptized for the forgiveness and remission of sins. Marpeck says infants shall be named before a congregation and God shall duly be praised for them (CRR 2:147).

Because God did not lay down a command in his Word for parents to dedicate their infants as he did in the case of circumcision in the old covenant, Mennonites have tended to view this ceremony as optional. Conservative Mennonites, e.g., Old Order Mennonites, Sommerfelder, and Old Colony Mennonites, have not practiced it; but former Old Colony Mennonites who have recently joined the Evangelical Mennonite Mission Conference have accepted it. While the practice is still largely regarded as optional, it has become much more common since the 1950s among Brethren in Christ and Mennonite Brethern and within the Mennonite Church (MC) and General Conference Mennonite Church.

There is no uniformity of practice. Some ministers will take the child in their arms, hug it to their heart and cherish it, while blessing it with the laying on of the hand. This would be reminiscent of the gospel record and also of the importance of psychological mothering (Mk 10: 13-16). Others bless the child with the laying on of hands while held by a parent. Still others bless °children and parents with the uplifted hands. Generally children are not blessed individually when they are brought to the church for the first time after birth, but weeks or months later, sometimes in small groups.

While some ministers acknowledge that members who come from a tradition where infant baptism was practiced, will tend to equate infant dedication and infant baptism, they do teach them the Anabaptist view. In general the ministers place greater emphasis on the dedication of parents and the congregation children's Christian upbringing. In view of this commitment many congregations are beginning to devote part of the Sunday morning worship service to the involvement of children.

Recently there is some pressure to allow children to partake of the elements of the Lord's Supper before they are baptized (Lois Thieszen Preheim, *Mennonite*, December 1, 8, 15, 1981). In part this influence comes from those who are not trained in Anabaptist theology. Balthasar °Hubmaier explains that just as faith precedes love, so must water-baptism precede communion (*Schriften*, 364). Similarly the confession in the *Martyrs Mirror* referred to earlier statements of the ordinances of baptism and communion, that no one is commanded to cause them to be administered to another, but each one must desire and receive them on the basis of their own faith (397). In the Anabaptist view children belong to the kingdom of God on the basis of promise and they do not meet the criteria for baptism and communion ceremonies. DJ

Menno, *Writings*, 241, 280-81; Loewen, *Confessions*, 109/107, 146, 169, 177, 218, 238.

See also Baptism, Age of; Baptismal Theology; Baptismal Instruction; Christian Education; Childrearing; Church Membership; Ordinances.

Deelen, Wouter

Deelen, Wouter (Delenus, Gualterus) (ca. 1500-1563), was born in Balen in the province of Antwerp in °°Brabant. He registered at the U. of Leuven (Louvain) on Apr. 4, 1516. He made a trip to Wittenberg in Germany before or during 1522. Following graduation he taught Greek and Hebrew in Haarlem, 1523-27. In July 1533 he was appointed professor in Amsterdam where he taught the biblical languages in the Chambers of Rhetoric on the basis of Old and New Testament exegesis. Through his interpretation of the gospel of John, specifically chapter 6:51b, he was suspected of Lutheran and Anabaptist heresy, and his appointment was terminated on May 1, 1535. It appears that he became involved in the May 10, 1535, uprising in Amsterdam unwittingly through his participation in a secret meeting of significant Anabaptist leaders, including the °Münster Anabaptist leader Jan van Geelen. The purpose of this meeting seems to have been to explore the possibility of finding a peaceful way in which governance of the Anabaptist city of Münster could be transferred to the Habsburg government in Brussels.

He escaped to England via Haarlem, becoming a librarian of sorts to Henry VIII. Various extant theological manuscripts can be traced to his London period. His *Novum Testamentum* appeared in London 1540, being a reworking of Erasmus' Latin translation of the New Testament. In 1550 Edward VI named him, with Martin Micron, deacon of the Dutch refugee congregation in London (Austin Friars). Following the death of Edward VI (1553), Delenus fled England together with other Protestants. He settled in Emden. Here he assisted J. °°Utenhove in the correcting of his translation of the New Testament into Dutch and edited the Dutch translation of Sleidanus' *De statu religionis commentarii.* After Elisabeth I succeeded Mary Tudor in England (1558) Delenus returned to London in 1559 where he died in 1563.   SV

H. F. Wijnman, "Wouter Deelen, de eerste professor in het Hebreeuwsch te Amsterdam," *Jaarboek Amstelodanum,* 22 (1939), 43-65; J. Trapman, "Delenus en de bijbel," *Nederlands Archief voor Kerkgeschiedenis,* 56 (1975), 95-113; H. J. de Jonge, "Caro in spiritum: Delenus en zijn uitleg van Joh. 6:51," in *De Geest in het geding,* Oosterbaan Festschrift, ed. I. B. Horst and others (Alphen aan den Rijn: H. D. Tjeenk Willink, 1978), 145-66.

DeFehr, Cornelius A. (Oct.6, 1881-1979), was a successful Mennonite Brethren businessman in Russia and in Canada who was extensively involved in the affairs of the Mennonite constituency. He was born in Einlage, Chortitza Colony, to Abraham and Helena (Peters) DeFehr. After his conversion through the ministry of Jakob W. Reimer he was baptized and joined the Mennonite Brethren Church in Petrovka. He was married to Elizabeth Dyck in 1903, and six children were born to them, two of whom died in infancy.

DeFehr's first °business venture was a partnership in a manufacturing industry in Millerovo in 1904. This brought prosperity, especially during the years of the Great War (World War I). The °Russian Revolution brought drastic upheaval, however, and eventually the family migrated to Canada. DeFehr soon (1926) established an import business in Winnipeg which became a prosperous family enterprise with branches in Edmonton, Regina, and Saskatoon.

Throughout the years DeFehr was very active in matters pertaining to the Mennonite people. In Russia he was appointed as one of the chief administrators of the massive relief effort during the famine. In Canada he was active in a large number of Mennonite Brethren committees, including the Winnipeg City Mission, the Mary-Martha Girls' Home, Mennonite Brethren Collegiate Institute, Christian Press, and Mennonite Central Committee. He directed the resettlement of Mennonite refugees in Paraguay after World War II. Although DeFehr was perhaps the most successful Mennonite Brethren businessman of his generation, he never lost his capacity to identify with people in many different circumstances. He was a true servant of his people.   AJD

Cornelius A. DeFehr, *Memories of My Life: Recalled for My Family* (Altona, Man: C. A. DeFehr, 1967): articles by Abraham C. DeFehr, Bernhard B. Fast, and John B. Toews in *Mennonite Brethren Historical Society Newsletter,* 5, no. 2 (Dec. 1982), 1-8, and 5, no 3 (April 1983), 1-6.

Del Norte Colony, Bolivia. See Norte Colony, Del.

Delaware (ME II:29). The Conservative Amish Mennonite settlement near Greenwood in Sussex Co. consisted of four congregations with a total member-

ship of 467 in 1986 (Greenwood Laws, Canon Central). The Greenwood congregation established the Greenwood Mennonite School in 1928, when Mennonite students were expelled from the public schools for not saluting the flag. In 1986 this school had 151 students in 12 grades and kindergarten. Central Christian School, founded by the Central congregation in 1975, had grades 1-12 with 69 students. The Country Rest Home, Greenwood, founded in 1954 by Mr. and Mrs. L. L. Swartzentruber is a 32-bed facility for senior citizens owned and operated by Mr. and Mrs. Mark B. Yoder, pastor of the Laws congregation.

In 1987 the Old Order Amish community near Dover had eight church districts serving 261 families with a total population of 1,432. It maintains 11 elementary schools.

Tressler Mennonite Church, Greenwood, organized in 1935, is a member of Allegheny Mennonite Conference. In 1986 it had 113 members. Two congregations affiliated with Eastern Pennsylvania Mennonite Church are Highland, near Bear, in New Castle Co., (26 members) and Kenton, in Kent Co., (41 members). The Kenton Mennonite School had 14 students in 1986.

The Pine Shore Conservative Mennonite Fellowship near Delmar, in southern Sussex Co., withdrew from a congregation just south of the Maryland line and numbers 14 members.

The Wilmington Mission was founded by the Greenwood Conservative Mennonite Church in the 1940s. Later it served Spanish-speaking worshipers, under sponsorship of the Lancaster Mennonite Conference (MC). It was closed and the property sold in 1987.   IJM

MC Yearbook (1988-89), 20.

See also Dover, Del., Old Order Amish Settlement.

Deliverance Ministry. See Exorcism.

Democracy. This term comes from the Greek *demos,* "people," and *kratein,* "to rule." From earliest usage it has been difficult to formulate a general definition. Aristotle, after noting four types of democracy, finally concludes, "It is a democracy whenever the free are sovereign" (*Politics* Bk. 4, ch. 4). Abraham Lincoln's classic words "government of the people, by the people, for the people" highlight the popular character of any government labeled "democratic." Nevertheless the reality is always circumscribed. From Aristotle to Lincoln slaves were not party to democracy. Often there are property and residence qualifications. Only in the past century have women been included in the franchise. Children and the imprisoned rarely participate politically.

Contemporary usage of the term also inhibits clear definitions. Definitions change with evolving political and economic systems. Political scientists point out that the most authoritarian governments still depend on some sort of "consent of the governed" for their power and authority and authoritarian governments frequently call themselves "democratic" or "people's" republics, using democratic strategies such as the nurture of public opinion and holding frequent elections as evidence of their being supported by the people. °Socialist societies emphasize the economic component of democracy or public welfare in comparison to the more narrowly defined process of selecting representation. In other situations, although the formal designation of a government may be as a "monarchy" or "republic," it is also clear that the essential ingredients of "people's rule" are also present: universal suffrage, equality before the law, freedom of speech and discussion, majority rule, representative institutions, civil liberties, protection of minorities, open expression of dissent, skepticism about concentrated authority. Political scientists also counsel caution about exaggerated expectations regarding rule by all the people. There are such phenomena as elites who, with advantages of expertise and status, are able to wield greater influence and hence more power than others. It is difficult to make democratic processes genuinely beneficial to oppressed and marginalized people.

Democracy is a process by which power is derived from the people for directing the institutions of a social order. Such voluntarily delegated authority gives integrity to popular sovereignty but it also requires constant nurture and testing, normally by regular elections or other forms of referendum. The terminology usually relates to the various levels of government but as a process democracy is equally applicable to churches, corporations, educational institutions, and voluntary organizations.

A thriving democracy requires a congenial cultural milieu and sets of convictions which enable the process to have as much integrity as possible. Scholars noting some of the intimate connections between democratic practice and parts of western culture have asked whether there is a special relationship between Christianity and democracy. Such connections cannot be made glibly since democratic governments are a relatively recent historical phenomenon. Furthermore the allied benefits of democratic practice compared to other political traditions require very careful analysis. Freedom has to do with the degree of openness rather than an absolute difference of performance.

Yet noting these qualifications there are ways in which the experience of the Judeo-Christian tradition has contributed to some of the values associated with democracy. The repeated biblical search for a kingdom of righteousness has helped to establish a concern for a peaceful and just social order. The clash of the prophets with ancient Hebrew kings and the subsequent tensions of the Christian era have helped to establish the plural institutional base so essential to an operative democratic society as well as to insure the notion that the presumed sovereignty of rulers is confronted by the sovereignty of God. The conviction that all believers participate in developing the polity of the free churches may, as some scholars suggest, have nurtured the participatory process of governance which was transferred from the congregational meeting to the town meeting. Finally the Christian view of human potential and its limitations, caught in Reinhold Niebuhr's famous epigram "Man's capacity for justice makes democracy possible; but man's inclination to injustice makes democracy necessary," suggests that democratic practice requires a healthy humility about the human condition.

Did the °believers church or free church tradition contribute to the democratic experience? The insistence that the church be made up of individuals who make a personal and voluntary decision undercuts the well entrenched traditional unitary political-religious state. The sheer existence of such a church forces the development of an alternative political theory rooted in the separation of the institutional entities known as church and state. The believers churches' persistent claim to religious freedom, called by William Lee Miller "the first liberty," has helped establish open discussion so essential to democratic process.

These connections notwithstanding, most democratic thought is rooted in the liberal Enlightenment tradition of the 18th- and 19th-c. West which emphasizes natural rights, rational behaviors, optimism about the human situation, and the superiority of modern secularity. John Locke (1632-1704), Jean-Jacques Rousseau (1712-78), and Thomas Jefferson (1743-1826) are more influential in the development of democratic thought than are Augustine (354-430), Martin °°Luther, and John Wesley (1703-91).

Because of °persecution by political structures, the lack of experience in a democratic system and reservations about what priority political activity ought to have for the church, some of the most °sectarian Mennonites and Amish have frowned on any involvement in the democratic process, often admonishing nonparticipation in °°voting and office holding. On the other hand the self-governing structure of Mennonite colonies in Russia and Paraguay included broadly based "male" participation while at the same time holding that constitutional monarchs would more likely grant a *privilegum* (°privileges) to a religious minority.

In recent years there has been a strong argument given that Mennonites should use the democratic system to influence government in positive directions. Mennonites currently hold elective offices in Western Europe and North America and the majority of Mennonites in these regions participate in using the franchise. They also serve in the civil services at many levels. While ambivalence remains about the effectiveness of °political action, there is a considerable consensus that the church must find ways to witness within the political order to the will of God "on earth as it is in heaven."   JAL

Edward McNall Burns, *Ideas in Conflict* (1960); Ralph Buultjens, *The Decline of Democracy* (1978); Harold Lasswell, *Politics: Who Gets What, When, How* (1958).

See also Decision-making; Government; Polity.

Demography. The Anabaptist movement began in 16th-c. Switzerland, Germany, and The Netherlands. However, since then Mennonites have fanned out into 57 countries of the world and are represented on every continent. These world Mennonite population shifts are of great interest to demographers who like to trace population trends, taking into account such changes as births, deaths, and °migration (immigration and emigration). The Mennonite World Conference surveys are not always as complete as one would like, but the 1984 data show interesting demographic patterns.

Mennonite Distribution. Table 1 shows that in 1984 about three-fourths of a million (723,747) Mennonites were located on six continents. Almost half of these were located in North America (46.1 percent), and the other half were located fairly evenly on four continents including Asia (113, 504), Africa (107,221), Europe (92,368) and Latin America (76,936). Only 12 Mennonites were located in Australia. These are adult membership figures; if younger unbaptized offspring were included, these figures would likely double.

DEMOGRAPHY

Compiler: Leo Driedger (author of the article)

Table 1. Distribution of Mennonites
of the World by Continents, 1984

Continents	Countries	Mennonite Membership	% of All Mennonites
North America	2	333,704	46.1
Europe	13	92,368	12.7
Latin America°	23	76,938	10.7
Asia	7	113,504	15.7
Africa	11	107,201	14.8
Australia	1	12	0.0
Totals	**57**	**723,747**	**100.0**

°Includes Caribbean countries
Source: Mennonite World Conference map, 1984

Only about one eighth (92,368; 12.7 percent) of the Mennonites of the world live in Europe, the place of Anabaptist origins. The majority of the European Mennonites are located in the Soviet Union (55,000; 7.6 percent). The 20,000 Mennonites in The Netherlands (2.8 percent) are the second largest group in Europe, one of the two Mennonite groups with continuous links to their 16th-c. origins. Mennonites in West Germany number 11,688 (1.6 percent), and only 2,750 Mennonites remain in Switzerland (.4 percent), the other country with a history of unbroken Anabaptist and Mennonite presence. Many emigrated from the original Anabaptist centers in central Europe which resulted in loss of potential for growth.

Almost half of all Mennonites live in North America (46.1 percent), in United States (232,192) and Canada (101,512). Most of them are descendants of Mennonite immigrants from Europe. The first Mennonites came to America 300 years ago, and to Canada 200 years ago. A large number of Mennonites arrived in both countries in the 1870s, and more immigrants came to Canada in the 1920s and 1950s, mostly from the Soviet Union. In 1984 one-third of all Mennonites live in the United States (32.1 percent), and the second largest number live in Canada (14.0 percent).

The 76,938 Mennonites living in 23 countries of Latin America represent 10.7 percent of all Mennonites. The largest number (31,161 or 4.3 percent) are descendants of those who went to Mexico in the 1920s from Canada; the 13,939 Mennonites living in Paraguay (1.9 percent) are descendants of later immigrants from both Canada and Europe, including the Soviet Union. Mennonites in the other Latin American countries represent small minorities, some who came as immigrants, and others who are converts of mission outreach. Thus, about two-thirds of the Mennonites in Latin America are also descendants of the original European Anabaptists.

The 113,504 Mennonites in seven countries of Asia represent 15.7 percent of all Mennonites. The two oldest and also largest groups of Mennonites reside in Indonesia (62,911 or 8.7 percent) and India (43,998 or 6.1 percent) representing the fourth- and sixth-largest groups in the world respectively. These Mennonites are the outgrowth of late 19th-c and 20th-c. mission outreach, rather than immigration. The same is true of the comparatively small groups of Mennonites in the other five Asian countries.

In Africa, the 66,408 members in Zaire represent about two-thirds of all Mennonites in the 11 countries, and Zaire Mennonites are the third-largest group in the world representing 9.2 percent of all Mennonites. Tanzania, the country with the second-largest Mennonite population in Africa, ranks tenth in the world, but the 13,614 Mennonites there represent only 1.9 percent of all Mennonites. Demographic trends suggest that the growth potential for Mennonites in Africa is great.

Population Growth. What is the potential for the future increase or decrease of the Mennonite population in the various parts of the world? Demographers work with four factors: births and immigration which increase population growth, and deaths and emigration, which decrease the population. Since the Mennonites are an ethno-religious group, two other factors, recruitment and assimilation, enter the equation. Evangelism will add to the numbers, and assimilation will subtract from the population. Data for longer periods of time is not as readily available as might be desired, but some tentative observations and projections can be made.

With respect to births and deaths, industrial countries tend to have low birth and low death rates. This applies to Mennonites in North America and Europe. Small families and better medical care will tend to keep both birth and deaths down, so that population will stabilize. However, in developing countries of Africa and Asia, where birth rates are high, and death rates are beginning to decrease, Mennonite population will likely grow considerably in the future by natural increase. Migration, the other change factor, was important when Mennonites left Europe in large numbers and migrated to North America and South America, decreasing the Mennonite numbers in Europe and adding to growth in the Americas. In the future migrations will most likely not be as important.

Evangelism has greatly increased the Indonesian Mennonite population in recent decades, and Mennonite World Conference projections suggest that it is also an important factor in Africa, especially Zaire, where Mennonite numbers have escalated since 1984. More study is needed to help decide whether the minimal growth in Europe is due to continued out-migration, lack of evangelism, and assimilation, now that birth and death rates are low. The available data suggest that the proportion of world Menno-

DEMOGRAPHY

Table 2. Mennonite Population by Continents and Countries, 1984

Continents	Countries	World Rank	Mennonite Membership	% of All Mennonites
North America	USA	1	232,192	32.1
	Canada	2	101,512	14.0
	2		333,704	46.1
Europe	Russia	5	55,000	7.6
	Netherlands	8	20,200	2.8
	West Germany	11	11,688	1.6
	Switzerland	19	2,750	.4
	France	26	2,000	.3
	East Germany	40	244	12.7
	Austria	41	185	
	Luxembourg	43	105	
	Belgium	47	73	
	Italy	48	66	
	Spain	51	33	
	England	53	15	
	Ireland	56	9	
	13		92,368	
Latin America	Mexico	7	31,161	4.3
	Paraguay	9	13,939	2.0
	Bolivia	13	6,203	.9
	Brazil	17	4,750	.7
	Honduras	18	2,850	.4
	Colombia	22	2,633	.4
	Belize	23	2,591	.4
	Nicaragua	25	2,412	.3
	Dominican Republic	27	1,800	.2
	Guatemala	28	1,789	.2
	Argentina	29	1,576	.2
	Uruguay	31	971	.1
	Puerto Rico	32	909	.1
	Haiti	33	900	.1
	Costa Rica	35	850	.1
	Chile	36	400	.1
	Panama	37	400	.1
	Jamaica	39	385	.1
	Venezuela	45	85	10.7
	El Salvador	46	75	
	Trinidad	49	44	
	Ecuador	52	15	
	Cuba	57	NA	
	23		76,938	
Asia	Indonesia	4	62,911	8.7
	India	6	43,998	6.1
	Japan	20	2,710	.4
	Philippines	24	2,500	.3
	Taiwan	30	1,200	.2
	Vietnam	42	150	15.7
	Hong Kong	50	35	
	7		113,504	
Africa	Zaire	3	66,408	9.2
	Tanzania	10	13,614	1.9
	Ethiopia	12	7,000	1.0
	Zambia	14	6,000	.8
	Zimbabwe	15	5,184	.7
	Nigeria	16	5,000	.7
	Kenya	21	2,653	.4
	Ghana	34	854	.1
	Angola	38	395	14.8
	Somalia	44	100	
	Upper Volta	54	13	
	11		107,221	
Australia	Australia	55	12	
	1		12	0.0
Totals	57		723,474	100%

Source: *MWH* (1984) and Mennonite World Conference map, 1984.

nites will decline in Europe, hold steady in North America, and increase in South America and especially Africa in the next several decades.   LDr

MWH (1978), (1984); David Shelly, "World Membership Now 774,000," *MWR* (Oct. 30, 1986), 1, cf. *Courier*, 1, no. 4 (1986), 9, and MWC directory insert; *Courier*, 2 no. 2 (1987), 9.

See also Sociological Studies; Statistics; Urbanization.

Denlinger, Mary (1867-1958), was a Mennonite Church (MC) missionary in Chicago and Philadelphia for a total of 30 years. She was born to John B. and Elizabeth Shaub Denlinger in Black Horse, Pa., and was converted at Mendon, Mo., under the preaching of John S. °°Coffman. From 1894 to 1899 she was a missionary at the Gospel Mission (MC) in Chicago. There she served with Lina Zook (°Ressler) and Melinda °Ebersole doing visitation, helping with cottage prayer meetings, teaching Sunday school, and working in the medical dispensary. From 1899 to 1924 she served as city missionary for the new Norris Square Mission in Philadelphia.   LB

Ira D. Landis, in *Miss. Mess.* (Apr. 1958), 4; Rich, *Mennonite Women* (1983).

Denominationalism (ME II:37), is the characteristic form of church organization and identity in North America. In contrast to the European pattern of dominant state church and tolerated (or persecuted) sects, American denominationalism accorded legitimate religious status to all kinds of churches. Each church or denomination came to recognize the place of the others in the national religious mosaic. As a religious social system, denominationalism was not the product of an ideology or a plan but rather resulted from the experience of religious pluralism in America. In the 19th c. American denominations fostered identity and gained vitality through voluntary activities for church renewal and world reform—°missions, °Sunday Schools, benevolent institutions, and other activities. The denominations often retained an ethnic quality which helped members sustain distinctive identity in the face of rapid social change.

American denominationalism deeply affected Mennonites who had been °persecuted as °sectarians in a European system which was dominated by established state churches. In times of peace Mennonites in America increased their contacts with non-Mennonite neighbors and sectarian consciousness declined. In times of war and military °conscription, however, Mennonite pacifists refused military participation and lost something of their claim to denominational respectability in the face of a militant °civil religion. The American War for Independence (1775-83) and the American involvement in World War I (1917-18) both had the effect of marginalizing Mennonites after periods of increasing accommodation to American society. In the late 20th c., after the °Vietnam War and the threat of nuclear war, pacifist convictions became more acceptable in America and served as a respected denominational distinctive rather than as a sectarian quirk.

Mennonite historian Paul Toews has suggested

that progressive Mennonite groups (especially the "old" Mennonite Church [MC], the General Conference Mennonite Church, and the Mennonite Brethren) have experienced a denominational revitalization of three successive and overlapping stages in the late 19th c. and the 20th c. The first was a surge of new institutional development before World War I. The new institutions included Sunday schools, °Bible conferences, church periodicals, °mission boards, colleges, and national conference (denominational) organizations. The second stage was a more clearly articulated theology focused on the Anabaptist story. The third stage was an acceleration of inter-Mennonite activity for °relief work, missions, °mutual aid, °historical study, etc. While the progressive groups became denominationalized, the traditionalist or Old Order groups survived and grew by maintaining the boundaries which separated them from the larger society. The Hutterites and Old Order Amish have demonstrated that it is possible to grow and to thrive while resisting pressures of denominationalization (°conservative Mennonites).

There is no commonly accepted theory or definition of denominationalism to determine whether the various Mennonite and Amish groups in North America should be considered one denomination or many, or at what point a sectarian group should be considered a denomination. Nor do the °sociological types of "church" and "sect" adequately describe American Mennonite pluralism. Mennonites of various kinds have sustained a sense of common peoplehood, despite the wide variation of life-style and religious practice from the traditionalist Old Orders to the more °acculturated groups. The fact that nearly all groups cooperate in inter-Mennonite efforts for °peace and °nonresistance, as well as in relief and °development work under Mennonite Central Committee, suggests a shared denominational identity.   JCJ

Winthrop Hudson, "Denominationalism," in *The Encyclopedia of Religion*, vol. 4 (New York: Macmillan, 1987), 292-98; Richard Kyle, *From Sect to Denomination: Church Types and Their Implications for Mennonite Brethren History* (Hillsboro, Ks.: Center for Mennonite Brethren Studies, 1985); *MEA* 1; Russell E. Richey, ed. *Denominationalism* (Nashville: Abingdon, 1977); Paul Toews, "Dissolving the Boundaries and Strengthening the Nuclei," *Chr. Leader* (July 27, 1982), 6-8; James Juhnke, "The Role of Women in the Mennonite Transition from Traditionalism to Denominationalism," *Menn. Life*, 41 (Sept. 1986), 17-20.

Deportation. See Persecution; Russian Soviet Federated Socialist Republic (RSFSR); Spetskomandantura.

Derstine, Clayton Freed (1891-1967), was the son of Mahlon and Mary (Freed) Derstine of Souderton, Pa. Following his conversion in 1911, "C. F." Derstine joined the Souderton Mennonite congregation. His zeal in organizing cottage meetings for Bible study and young peoples' Bible meetings launched him on a lifelong mission of evangelism and teaching throughout the Mennonite Church (MC) and beyond.

Derstine was ordained a minister in 1914. He and his first wife, Gertrude Hangey (m. 1912), served at the Mennonite Mission in Altoona, Pa., 1913-15. Within 13 months of his ordination, C. F. preached

520 sermons, as he accepted invitations from congregations in various states to conduct evangelistic services. He served as pastor of the Roanoke Mennonite Church at Eureka, Ill., 1915-24. He was ordained a bishop in 1921. Derstine moved with his family to Ontario in 1924 in response to a call from First Mennonite Church, Kitchener, where a division had splintered the congregation. During his pastorate (1924-64), membership quadrupled. Derstine continued his evangelistic itineraries throughout Canada and the United States. His pulpit ministry stands as the focal point of his contribution to the church. After the death of his first wife, he married Mary Kolb in 1927.

His assignments in the Mennonite Conference of Ontario (MC) included: conference executive committee, 1925, 1930-33, 1936-39; bishop, Toronto Mission (1938-44), and Central District (1961-66); Mennonite Mutual Benefit Association board (1944-47); Colonization Committee (1953-55); and the Ontario Mennonite Bible School faculty (1929-48). He served the Mennonite Church (MC) general conferences as associate member on the Relief Committee (1944-46) and as editor of the *Youth's Christian Companion* (1927-29; editor of the "World News" section until 1953).

His ministry in the community included founding a °Summer Vacation Bible School for children, the first to be held in any denomination in Canada, and founding of the Kitchener House of Friendship, a ministry for transients, with the support of community churches, and the city of Kitchener.   LBe

Who's Who Mennonites (1943), 43; *Menn. Bib. II,* p. 433; Urie A. Bender, *Four Earthen Vessels* (Kitchener and Scottdale, 1982); minutes of the Mennonite Conference of Ontario and Ontario Mennonite Bible School in Ontario Mennonite Archives, Conrad Grebel College, Waterloo.

Detwiler, George Bechtel (1847-1931), was born near Roseville in Waterloo Co., Ont. A Mennonite, he married Harriet Tyson, a Brethren in Christ from Pennsylvania, in 1870. Four years later he joined her denomination. After teaching school for several years, he moved in 1885 with his family to a farm near Fort Erie, where he became a minister in the Bertie congregation and helped organize the first Sunday school in at least two Ontario Brethren in Christ congregations.

In 1899 the Detwilers moved to Abilene, Ks., where he became first associate editor and a few months later editor of his denomination's paper, the *Evangelical Visitor.* In 1902 the editorial offices and the Detwilers moved to Harrisburg, Pa. Although he did not accept the doctrine of °sanctification that was being increasingly favored in the Brethren in Christ Church, he endeavored in his editing to maintain a balance between opposing positions on the doctrine. This policy, however, led in 1918 to his replacement as editor by Vernon Stump, a strong °holiness advocate. Thereafter under Stump, the *Evangelical Visitor* became a holiness paper.

From 1917 to 1925 he taught Bible at Messiah Bible College (later Messiah College). Throughout his life he was a respected Bible commentator and Bible conference speaker.   EMS

E. Morris Sider, *Nine Portraits* (Nappanee, Ind., 1978), 213-44; Wittlinger, *Piety and Obedience* (1978), 204-5; *EV* (Aug. 17, 1931), 259.

Deutsche Demokratische Republik (DDR; German Democratic Republic [East Germany]. Founded on Oct. 7, 1949, the Deutsche Demokratische Republik comprises the area of the post-World-War-II Soviet zone of occupation. Its social, political, and economic systems were modeled on those of the Soviet Union under Stalin. Since 1949 the Socialist Unity Party (SED), governing according to the principles of democratic centralism, has remained virtually unchallenged in its control. Economically and socially weakened by heavy emigration to West Berlin, the DDR built a wall to seal off West Berlin from the surrounding territory of the DDR (1961). In 1971 the communist party leader, Walter Ulbricht, was replaced by Erich Honecker, who, while strengthening ties to the Soviet Union, was also responsive to the needs of the people. A new treaty with the Bundesrepublik Deutschland (BRD, Federal Republic of Germany [West Germany]), ratified the next year, moved towards normalization of relations and increased contact between the two Germanys at many levels. The economic and social stability of the German Democratic Republic increased significantly during Honecker's time in power. In 1985 the country had a population of 16.7 million.

During the early years of the DDR's existence church-state relations were often confrontational. This situation peaked in 1953 with widespread harassment and some arrests. The state has introduced clubs for children and youth, and also the *Jugendweihe*—a socialist youth initiation at the traditional age of church confirmation. In 1969 the Evangelische Kirche (the main Protestant [Lutheran-Reformed] body) in the DDR separated from the inter-German Protestant union (Evangelische Kirche in Deutschland). The leadership of this church sought to be a "church within socialism," not beside it, and not against it. This stance of critical solidarity was combined with an appeal to the humanistic core of communism.

On Mar. 6, 1978, leaders of the Protestant Church met with Honecker. One result was the expansion of the role of the church in the society. Numerous educational institutions, hospitals, and homes for the elderly and the disabled are supported by the church. The Protestant Church is also known for its active involvement in international ecumenical work.

The cooperation of the church with the state in the celebration of the 500th anniversary of Martin Luther's birth in 1983 was positively evaluated by many. However, the unequal treatment of Christians in the education system, repeatedly addressed at church synods in 1985 and 1986, has not been resolved.

Statistics for 1983 show the Protestant Church with 6,950,000 members, the Roman Catholic Church with 1.2 million, and the free churches and fellowships with 150,000. Membership has declined steadily in the two large churches, and active membership is substantially lower.

Before World War II very few Mennonites resided in what became the DDR. Immediately after the war, many hundreds came from °West Prussia. They scattered widely, and because of their dispersion often associated with the Lutheran-Reformed or Baptist churches in their areas. Beginning in 1961 Walter Jantzen, a businessman in East Berlin, took the initiative to gather and organize the Mennonites in the DDR, and achieved state recognition of the church the following year. Jantzen, ordained in 1965, took much time to visit members and to lead worship services at various meeting places. Since 1980 Knuth Hansen, a Protestant Church pastor, was full-time minister. His main functions were to conduct worship services and to visit the members of the largely elderly congregation. In 1986 the Mennonites met monthly or quarterly in East Berlin, Rostock, Halle, Erfurt, and Freital. Due to death and emigration membership has declined steadily. In 1950 one spoke of 1,100 Mennonites in the DDR. In 1985 the membership stood at 287. Since 1983 the church has sought to strengthen ties to Mennonites in the BRD. In 1984 six delegates attended the Mennonite World Conference, and since then others have attended international Mennonite gatherings. The church is also represented in ecumenical organizations in the DDR. A feeling of togetherness remains even though understanding of the Anabaptist heritage and distinctives is cloudy. The church held its first national congregational meeting in October 1985.   JoTh

Knuth Hansen, "Die Mennoniten-Gemeinde in der DDR" (1986, copy of chapter prepared for future publication in the DDR); idem, "Mennonitengemeinde in der DDR—Bilanz der letzten 5 Jahre," report to the West Berlin Mennonite Church on Feb. 2, 1985; Bill Yoder, "Installation of New Pastor in East Berlin: Time for Reflection on Destiny," *GH* (Oct. 13, 1981); Trevor Beeson, *Discretion and Valour Religious Conditions in Russia and Eastern Europe* (London: Fount Paperbacks, 1982; Philadelphia: Fortress Press, 1982); David Childs, *The GDR: Moscow's German Ally* (London: George Allen and Unwin, 1983); *DDR Handbuch*, 3rd. ed., 2 vols., ed. by Hartmut Zimmermann (Cologne: Verlag Wissenschaft und Politik, 1985); Reinhard Henkys, ed., *Die evangelischen Kirchen in der DDR: Beiträge zu einer Bestandsaufnahme* (Munich: Car. Kaiser Verlag, 1982); idem, *Gottes Volk in Sozialismus: Wie Christen in der DDR leben* (West Berlin: Wichern Verlag, 1983); John Sanford, *The Sword and the Ploughshare: Autonomous Peace Initiatives in East Germany* (London: Merlin Press/European Nuclear Disarmament, 1983); *Travelling Information about the Evangelical Church in the German Democratic Republic* (East Berlin: Press and Information Office of the Federation of Protestant Churches in the GDR, 1981); Hermann Weber, *DDR: Grundriß der Geschichte 1945-1981* (Hannover: Fackelträger, 1982); *MWH* (1978), 290-92; *MWH* (1984), 119.

Deutsches Mennonitisches Friedenskomitee (DMFK; German Mennonite Peace Committee) was established in 1956 as a response to the resumption of °conscription in the wake of the rearmament of the Bundesrepublik Deutschland (Federal Republic of Germany [West Germany]) during the Cold War. The German Mennonite peace witness was stimulated by the German collapse at the end of World War II, the influence of American Mennonites, the recovery of the Anabaptist-Mennonite tradition, and a general change in theological thinking. The DMFK is commissioned by the °Arbeitsgemeinschaft deutscher Mennonitengemeinden to promote the peace witness. Its mission is assisting °conscientious objectors during hearings and in their civilian public service, occasionally publishing pamphlets, and organizing meetings and demonstrations. It employs two staff members. Since 1976 it has become more active because of deepening convictions and growing general awareness of the nuclear arms race. DGL

Dreißig Jahre DMFK, 1956-1986 (Rammental: DMFK, 1986).

See also Peace Education.

Deutsches Mennonitisches Missionskomitee (DMMK; German Mennonite Mission Committee). At a mission conference in The Netherlands, in which the representatives of West Germany, France, Switzerland, and Holland participated, it was agreed that the Mennonites in each nation would form their own mission committee, from which a European committee would be organized (°Europäisches Mennonitisches Evangelisationskomitee, EMEK). This led to the founding of the DMMK in 1951 by the °°Conference of the Mennonites of South Germany (later Verband deutscher Mennonitengemeinden) and the cooperation of several congregations from North Germany. By 1986 all West German Mennonite congregations were participating in DMMK.

The first missionary was sent to Java in 1955 by EMEK. Following her return in 1968 another missionary was sent in 1971. In 1986 DMMK was carrying on a village mission in Neumühle, in the Palatinate, operated largely by American missionaries. One couple and a congregational assistant were working there. A missionary couple was also at work in Kaiserslautern together with the Arbeitsgemeinschaft Südwestdeutscher Mennonitengemeinden (Task Force of Southwest German Mennonite Congregations). A missionary from Stuttgart and a couple from Waldbröhl were working in the Chad under EMEK. DMMK thus strives to make its contribution to world mission.   FE

Leo Laurense, *25 Jahre Zusammenarbeit in der Mennonitischen Mission, 1947-1972* (EMEK, 1972); H. Penner, *Weltweite Brüderschaft*, 4th ed. (Weierhof: Mennonitische Forschungsstelle, 1985); Diether Götz Lichdi, *Über Zürich und Witmarsum nach Addis Abeba* (Maxdorf, 1983); S. H. Geiser, *Die Taufgesinnten Gemeinden* (Courgency 1971); *Menn. Jahrbuch* (1984), 114.

Development Work. The roots of development work by Mennonites are located in the willingness to help those in need. Such assistance, in the form of °relief work, was first extended across international boundaries as a part of missionary programs. Examples of organized international relief work are evident as early as 1897, when the °°Home and Foreign Relief Commission was established to provide assistance to the victims of a severe famine in India. It led eventually to mission work by Mennonites (MC, GCM) in India (1899, 1901).

A significant advance in °°relief work was the move to coordinate the relief efforts of the various Mennonite conferences. This occurred in the United States among those groups who sought to respond to the need for assistance for Mennonites in Russia after the 1917 °Russian Revolution. This act of coordination led to the creation of the Mennonite Central Committee (MCC) in 1920.

In addition to assisting Mennonites in the Soviet Union, MCC was involved with the emigration of Mennonites from the Soviet Union, including assistance to those who settled in Paraguay before and after World War II. The Dutch Mennonites provided similar assistance to the Mennonites who left the Soviet Union in 1929 and settled in Brazil. Subsequent to World War II, MCC became the primary institution for relief and development work by the Mennonite and Brethren in Christ churches in the United States and Canada.

During and after World War II, these churches

continued their relief work and their involvement with °refugees. At the same time, several new themes began to appear alongside these two forms of service. An important theme that informed the work of MCC was the World War II experience of °conscientious objectors who were organized into °°Civilian Public Service units (U.S.) and °°alternative service work camps (Canada). As a continuation of that idea, in part motivated by the military draft in the United States, a program called °°Pax (peace) was set up for young American men to serve abroad with specialized skills. Early programs included housing reconstruction in Europe and agricultural rehabilitation in Greece. Subsequently, the program expanded to include road construction, and development, and vocational training projects in a number of low-income countries in Latin America and Africa.

The °SELFHELP Crafts program within MCC also has its roots in the period immediately after World War II. The program provided a market in North America for the handcrafted products, initially for women's needlework. From these simple beginnings, MCC SELFHELP has grown into a significant international marketing venture, creating handicrafts employment projects for both men and women in more than 20 low-income countries.

A variety of forces, both local and global, shaped a general public interest in development work in the period after World War II. At the global level there were several significant forces: (1) the emergence of a "Cold War" between the United States and the Soviet Union; (2) the success of the Marshall Plan in the reconstruction of Europe; (3) a move in the 1970s by several Western countries to direct part of official overseas development assistance through nongovernmental organizations; and (4) the gradual realization of political independence by most of the low-income countries.

A primary force promoting general public interest in development work was the Cold War. This competition between the United States and the Soviet Union for international influence and control focused on the loyalties of the nations that began to emerge as °colonialism was dismantled. Development assistance was intended as an important means to capture the minds and the hearts of the newly emerging nations in Asia and Africa, as well as the existing countries in Latin America. This interest in development work, emerging within the general public, affected North American churches as well.

One of the first concrete influences on Mennonite churches of the development forces evident after World War II was the initiative by Mennonites involved in °business enterprises to create °Mennonite Economic Development Associates [MEDA] in 1954. This initiative drew on the general public acceptance of the Marshall Plan, which transferred capital from the United States for the reconstruction of Europe, as a model for development work. The members of MEDA identified a lack of capital and limited access to modern technology as the primary obstacles in the way of development. Given the poverty in low-income countries, it was assumed there would not be enough savings available to fund the necessary investment. Hence loans were made

by MEDA to organizations and individuals in low-income countries as a means to overcome this perceived shortage of savings.

The first programs were in Latin America, located in some of the Mennonite colonies in Paraguay. For example, a dairy was improved and a leather tanning factory was established. Subsequently, the program expanded to several African countries and to the Caribbean area.

The initiation of the Peace Corps by the United States government presented a new challenge: the international transfer of human skills. In 1961 Mennonites and Brethren in Christ concluded they could not support involvement in the Peace Corps. After an exploratory mission to Africa by Robert Kreider, it was decided in 1962 to establish a program within MCC to send teachers to Africa. The program was known as the Teachers Abroad Program (TAP).

The TAP focus on education was seen as a response to the importance the newly emerging African countries were placing on education. Teachers from developed countries, primarily from the United States and Canada, were placed in secondary schools and teacher training institutions in a number of African countries. In 1974 a shift began away from the formal school systems and toward providing assistance to nonformal education programs in low-income countries.

An independent, but similar, initiative is being carried out by Mennonite and Brethren in Christ medical personnel. Opportunities are created for medical students to receive part of their training in health institutions in low-income countries. In this way medical assistance is provided overseas and the experience of the medical personnel in such service opportunities is allowed to feed back to the churches in North America.

The emphasis in MCC programs has been changing gradually, away from relief to more explicit development work. The development theme has been evident, in some form, throughout MCC's history. For example, as early as 1921, the relief work among Mennonites in the Soviet Union included development work. An agreement with the Russian Socialist Federative Republic called for the transfer of tools and equipment for agricultural reconstruction in that area of the Soviet Union to prevent famines from occurring there in the future. Similarly, the Pax, SELFHELP Crafts, and TAP programs included development components. Gradually, development work was being grafted onto existing relief, education, and health programs.

The shift toward development work by many of the relief agencies in North America and Europe was accelerated with a decision in the early 1970s, by the governments of several developed countries, to enlist the involvement of non-governmental organizations (NGOs) in the delivery of development assistance. Switzerland, Canada, the United States, The Netherlands, Germany, and the Scandinavian countries have contributed overseas development assistance to NGOs. This new initiative by governments sought to establish a bridge between the peoples of the more developed countries and the peoples of low-income countries. The purpose of the bridge was to enable the two-way transfer of understanding and knowledge between the two sets of countries.

By the mid-1980s, the priorities of the MCC-related churches had shifted to development work. Financed in part by matching grants from Canadian International Development Agency (CIDA), plus other grants from several provincial governments, MCC has become primarily a development agency. A number of the °mission boards of the various Mennonite churches in Canada are also drawing assistance from CIDA to fund some development work alongside of their missionary programs.

The availability of government funds has also revitalized the development work of MEDA. Drawing on funds from both CIDA and the United States Agency for International Development, relatively large development projects have been initiated, primarily in several Caribbean and Latin American countries. MEDA is also involved in administering development projects for CIDA and is providing consulting services for development agencies such as CIDA.

For MCC the transition from relief to a greater emphasis on development work was formalized at the 1974 annual meeting in Hillsboro. The "Hillsboro Statement" expressed a concern about the deteriorating food situation in the world, and then identified family planning assistance and agricultural development assistance in combination with continued food donations, as the preferred solution. A commitment was made to strengthen both rural development and family planning programs, especially in those countries where churches related to Mennonite and Brethren in Christ mission efforts are located. This commitment included a resolve to make greater efforts to mobilize personnel, finances, and technical assistance to accomplish these development objectives. In 1984, this Hillsboro resolution was evaluated and reaffirmed. The role of war and North American agricultural policies were mentioned briefly as contributing causes to the ongoing food crisis in parts of the world, especially in Africa.

The increased emphasis on development work within MCC has been facilitated in part by MCC initiative to create a Canada-wide Food Bank. This institution has now evolved into a major relief organization, incorporating six denominations, in addition to MCC. It serves as a primary means of channeling grain directly from Canadian farmers, and Canadian government food aid to areas with pressing food needs. Such a food bank is able to respond quickly to food emergencies as they arise.

The shift from relief to development work within MCC was reversed, at least temporarily, with the major media focus in 1984 and 1985 on food shortages in several parts of Africa, especially Ethiopia. The response, in the form of donations and constituency interest, caused relief assistance once more to become a major MCC budget item. In addition, the Canada-wide Food Bank was moving large quantities of grain to these places in need. The result of this resurgence of relief assistance caused MCC to formulate an explicit food assistance policy.

The new food assistance policy, adopted in 1987, recognizes that North American and European food assistance can cause economic harm as well as provide a temporary means of feeding people. The new policy defines the conditions under which North American food assistance is appropriate. In addition, greater attempts will be made to monetize the donated food within the region to which the food aid is provided, and to use the money obtained in this manner to purchase local food and to promote increased local production of food. Finally, North American food is recognized as one of several resources—along with personnel, finances, and technology—that are available to MCC to facilitate and fund development work.

The emerging emphasis on development work by the various NGOs, as outlined above, has generated significant effects: on the donors, on those people who were sent overseas, and on the recipients in a number of low-income countries. There have also been shortcomings. NGOs do not spend much time defining what constitutes development work. They view whatever they are doing as development work. In most cases the NGOs are successful at what they are doing, so they see themselves as successful development agencies. This self-assessment does not always stand up when evaluated against an explicit, independent definition of development work. Second, the churches involved have formulated a theology of °service, as a basis for both relief and development work, but this theology does not encompass the need for change nor the means to promote needed change. Development requires change: in political, economic, and social institutions; in ways of life, beliefs, and attitudes. Without a theological basis for an understanding of changes required, development work has not been able to realize its full potential. Third, the development assistance provided has been primarily a one-way process, from North American and European donors to low-income country recipients. The intent of donor governments, to channel some development assistance through NGOs as a means to creating a bridge for the two-way transfer of understanding and knowledge between societies, thereby narrowing the distinction between donor and recipient, has not been realized. Again, there is some evidence that the design and delivery of MCC programs were shaped directly by the needs and priorities of the recipients (for example, TAP was based on the priority placed by African governments on education), but most of the development work initiatives were formulated primarily by the donors.

The place of the recipients in the development process is changing. In large part this is caused by the fourth force that shaped general public interest in development: the struggle by many societies for independence from their respective colonial masters. Their immediate concern has been liberation. The peoples involved have a deep longing for freedom, for the ability to shape and control their own political, economic and social destinies. They saw their own poverty as the product of their colonial status. It was assumed that with independence they would be able to share as equals in the prosperity evident in the more developed countries.

Political independence has not fulfilled the

dreams of the peoples in the newly emerging nations. Most of these nations remain mere providers of raw materials and importers of manufactured goods. The trade and aid relationships between the more developed countries and the low-income countries have generated significant economic benefits, but more than half of these benefits consistently flow to the more developed countries. As a result, international trade and foreign assistance are now recognized by the peoples of low-income countries as one of the means that increase the economic gap between the rich and the poor nations. Given this ongoing economic dependence on the more developed countries, the people in low-income countries still define development as liberation.

The deep longing for liberation among the recipients of development assistance is having an increasing impact on the nature of development work by Mennonite and Brethren in Christ churches. Numerous agencies have been created within the low-income countries either to receive some of the development assistance or to work with North American and European NGOs as partners in the design, implementation, and evaluation of development work. The place of women in the development process is gradually being recognized and the women are increasing their direct involvement. Low-income country governments are setting conditions that must be met before NGOs are free to provide assistance. Within the donor countries, there is an increased emphasis on education and on some recognition of the role of the more developed countries as contributors to the ongoing poverty and the lack of freedom in many parts of the world.

The increased involvement of the peoples in the low-income countries in the development process is a hopeful sign. As an effective two-way bridge is constructed between Mennonites and the peoples in a number of low-income countries, development work will mature. Development assistance will still flow and development workers will still be sent, but North Americans and Europeans will cease to be mere donors. Some members of the churches will be commissioned to go forth as development workers, they will be received as co-workers by the peoples in the host countries, and then they will be returned to their home churches by the peoples in the host countries. Together North Americans and Europeans will learn to receive as well as to give.

A partial listing of Mennonite and Mennonite-related development agencies follows: Associação Menonita de Asistência Social (AMAS, Brazil); Mennonite Colombian Foundation for Development (MENCOLDES); °International Mennonite Organization (IMO, Europe); The Economic Life and Relief Council (TELARC, India); Mennonite Agriculture, Development, and Relief Association, India (MADRA); °Mennonite Christian Service Fellowship of India; Rural Economic Development and Community Health Association (REACH) India; Yayasan Kerjasama Ekonomi Muria (YAKEM, Indonesia, °Gereja Injili di Tanah Jawa); Mennonite Economic Development Trust of Kenya (1978); Ogwedhi Sigawa Rural Development Center (Kenya); °Stichting voor Bijzondere Noden (The Nether-

lands); °Samenwerkingsverband van "de Vier Instellingen" in de Doopsgezinde Broederschap (The Netherlands); °Mennonite Central Committee (North America); °Mennonite Economic Development Associates (MEDA, North America); Asociación de Servicios de Cooperación Indigena-Menonita (Paraguay); Service for the Development of Agriculture (SEDA, Zaire). HRe

MCC Story, 5 vols. (1980-87); Merrill Ewert, *Humanization and Development*, Development Monograph Series, No. 2 (Akron, Pa.: MCC, n.d.); Donald R. Jacobs, *The Christian Stance in a Revolutionary Age*, Focal Pamphlet no. 14 (Scottdale, 1968); Carl Kreider, *Helping Developing Countries*, Focal Pamphlet no. 13 (Scottdale, 1968); Tim Lind, *Biblical Obedience and Development*, Development Monograph Series, no. 6 (Akron, Pa.: MCC, n.d.); Doris Janzen Longacre, *Nutrition and Development*, Development Monograph Series, no. 4 (Akron, Pa.: MCC, n.d.); Edgar Stoesz, *Thoughts on Development*, rev. ed., Development Monograph Series, no. 1 (Akron, Pa.: MCC, n.d.).

Devil. See Satan.

Devotional Literature (ME II:46). The chief devotional literature of the Mennonites over the centuries has been the Bible, especially the New Testament. Another major volume has been the °°*Martyrs Mirror* of T. J. van °°Braght, 1660. Previous °°martyr books included *Het Offer des Heern*, (1562) and several 17th-c. martyrologies, largely by Hans de °°Ries (1615, 1617, 1626, and 1631). The martyr books of the Dutch Mennonites were preceded by the Swiss Brethren hymnbook, the °°*Ausbund* (Selection) of 1564. Slightly earlier was the collection of eight of the best books of °Menno Simons, titled according to the first book, *The Foundation* (1562). The faith of the Anabaptists was strengthened by reading martyr stories over and over, and by reading meditations on Christian doctrine by Menno, °°Dirk Philips, and others. The *Martyrs Mirror* has gone through many editions. Yet one other category of devotional literature must be mentioned: the Anabaptists made much use of a prayer book, the °°*Ernsthafte Christenpflicht*. When Robert °Friedmann wrote the article on this prayer book for ME II, the earliest known edition was 1739. Since that time printings have been discovered of 1730, 1727, 1718, and 1708, and it is possible that the book appeared in the 17th c. It is certain that the Anabaptists and early Mennonites depended on prayer, the Bible, martyr stories, martyr ballads (as found in the *Ausbund*), and the prayer book—although some of the prayers seem to resemble those of °Pietists.

The end of all this effort is to be an enlightened child of God, to think of him much, to order one's life according to his will, to engage in fervent °prayer. Repentance must become a continuous attitude, one must become like Christ, one must be °nonconformed to the world. Pride must be kept far away (°humility). One must enjoy a life of submission and obedience, one must quietly enjoy the freedom of the Spirit and the sense of divine sonship, one must seek to walk as a humble and faithful child of God.

Much of the devotional literature of Christendom is Roman Catholic in origin, and indeed goes back to priests and monks, although some was written by devout nuns. Among this list are the works of

Augustine (354-430), especially his *Confessions*. Love for God and for his creation was especially strong in Francis of Assisi (1182-1226). One of the most influential pieces of literature is the anonymous *Theologie Deutsch* (German Theology) of the 14th c. Martin °°Luther was almost ecstatic when he discovered a portion of the manuscript about 1516, and he immediately had it published. Current editions follow the text of 1497—and they are numberless. Perhaps even more influential has been the *Imitation of Christ*, often ascribed to Thomas Hemerken of Kempen (1379-1471), a canon of the monastery of Mount St. Agnes near Zwolle in The Netherlands. Book One, on Christian life and character, is especially rich. The *Imitation* has been translated into a hundred languages and printed in 6,000 editions.

Much of the Roman Catholic devotional literature is tinged with mysticism, and some strongly so. This is not the case with the *Meditation on Psalm 25* (ca. 1537) by Menno Simons of Friesland—a book printed in Frisian as recently as 1930. Menno's *Meditation* is devotional literature at its best.   JCW

Robert Friedmann, *Mennonite Piety through the Centuries*, (1949); idem, "Devotional Literature of the Swiss Brethren 1600-1800," *MQR*, 16 (1942), 199-220; idem, "Mennonite Prayer Books," *MQR*, 17 (1943), 179-206; idem, "Devotional Literature . . . Danzig and East Prussia," *MQR*, 18 (1944), 162-173; idem, "Dutch Mennonite Devotional Literature from Peter Peters to Johannes Deknatel, 1625-1753," *MQR*, 25 (1941), 187-207. Devotional literature published by and for Mennonites includes the quarterly collection of daily meditations, *Rejoice!* (Scottdale and Newton).

See also Family Worship; Worship, Private.

Dhamtari, India (ME II:50), is situated 48 miles south of the district headquarters of the city of Raipur on the national highway No. 43 (which runs from Delhi to Madras) dividing the city into the eastern larger and older part with shopping center and the western newer section. In 1986 Dhamtari has a population of 60,000, reflecting considerable growth from the municipality (9,151 population in 1881) that existed when the Mennonite missionaries first arrived in 1899. Dhamtari has been a political nerve center since the days of the struggle for India's independence and Mahatma °Gandhi visited the town twice (Dec. 20, 1920, and Nov. 24, 1933).

The American Mennonite mission was a pioneer in education, medical, and vocational training institutions. In 1987 there were seven high schools, 25 primary schools, and one polytechnic institution, a government college of arts, commerce, and science. The religious affiliation of the population is: Hindu (76 percent); Muslim (12 percent); Sindhi (2 percent); Punjabi (1 percent); Christian (1.5 percent) and others (7.5 percent).

Dhamtari is the headquarters of the Mennonite Church in India, the location of its annual conference, and the site of such Christian institutions as the Dhamtari Christian Hospital, the Mennonite Higher Secondary (Hindi) School and the Mennonite English Medium Higher Secondary School. PJM

Dialect Literature and Speech, Low German (ME II:50; IV:186). The years 1955-85 have seen a marked decline in the use of Mennonite Low German (*Plautdietsch*) in the United States, Canada, Germany, and the Union of Soviet Socialist Republics. Only among Mennonites in Latin America is *Plautdietsch* holding firm. Even in the high-density Mennonite areas of southern Manitoba where the dialect is still spoken extensively in rural parts and towns like Steinbach, Winkler and Altona, it is losing ground steadily, especially in Winnipeg, which has the greatest urban concentration of Mennonites anywhere. In other Canadian communities where Low German is still common, as in the Niagara peninsula of Ontario, it is mostly recent immigrants from South America and Mexico who keep it alive. In North America generally the majority of Mennonites under the age of 40 no longer speak or understand *Plautdietsch*.

The decline in spoken Low German, however, has brought about an unexpected interest in it as a literary vehicle. Many culturally assimilated North American Mennonites now regard *Plautdietsch* nostalgically as an artistic repository for ethnic experience they can cherish only in memory. Interest in preserving the dialect as an artistic medium is especially strong in Winnipeg and Mennonite communities in southern Manitoba, although it can be found in other Canadian and American communities as well. The Low German "revival" has recently stimulated activities ranging from the compiling of literary anthologies and dictionaries to the writing of fiction and °poetry and the production of original and adapted stage plays, live readings, singing concerts and recordings.

That Manitoba should be the center of this Low German literary activity is not surprising, considering that it was there that Arnold °Dyck (1889-1970) wrote his masterful Low German comic novels, stories, and plays for an appreciative local and general Mennonite readership. Dyck was a major writer by any standard, and his *Collected Works* were published in four volumes by the Manitoba Mennonite Historical Society, 1985ff. His inimitable comic characters "Koop" and "Bua," the naive Manitoba "bush" farmers who embark on travels in three superb novels, can stand comparison with the great comic archetypes of world °literature. Had Arnold Dyck written as well in English as he did in *Plautdietsch* he would undoubtedly be ranked among Canada's finest humorists.

Other Low German writers have tried to follow Dyck's lead, starting with older writers like Fritz Senn (Gerhard Johann °Friesen, 1894-1983), whose rugged Low German poems about the lost Russian homeland are evocative and poignant, as are the poems and stories of Jakob Warkentin Goerzen of Edmonton and the poems and plays of Nicholas H. Unruh of Manitoba. Among the Low German writers active in the 1980s, most prolific and interesting are Jack Thiessen, Reuben Epp, and Elisabeth and Victor Peters. All four like to employ the sly, gently ironic tone that was Dyck's trademark. Thiessen, who can also be brash and abrasive, uses English loan words and trendy clichés to set up an ironic interplay between the simple old Mennonite rural ways and the more sophisticated, often more pretentious, new urban Mennonite style. Epp is well-versed in European Low German writing and is equally skilled at side-splitting comedy and serious fiction. Elisabeth and Victor Peters are essentially anecdotists with sharp eyes and ears for the idiosyncrasies and colorful behavior of rural Mennonite types. These and other writers are regular contributors to the Low German section of the *Mennonite Mirror*, a monthly magazine published in Winnipeg.

The promotion of *Plautdietsch* as a literary language has received added impetus from two Low German dictionaries compiled, respectively, by Jack Thiessen (1977) and by Herman Rempel (1979, revised 1984). In 1982 a group of Low German scholars and writers met in Winnipeg to devise a much-needed standardized spelling system. The new orthography closely resembles Arnold Dyck's mature system, although the new system is more phonetic and slightly anglicized. Most of the Low German writing now being published, including the two Low German volumes in the new edition of Dyck's works, employs the new spelling. A Low German translation of the New Testament by J. J. Neufeld was published under the auspices of the Wycliffe Bible Translators in 1988. *Plautdietsch* is also being mixed with English (Armin Wiebe, *The Salvation of Yasch Siemens*) and with High German (Jack Thiessen, *Predicht fier haite*) to produce hybrid languages for comic effect.

Radio Southern Manitoba still carries Low German church sermons, and a weekly secular program hosted by Gerhard Ens, another fine Low German writer. The Landmark Theatre Group in Manitoba, founded by Wilmer Penner, regularly presents original and adapted plays in *Plautdietsch*, and Low German singing groups like "Locusts and Wild Honey" perform widely in Mennonite communities and have made successful recordings.

How long these various artistic and cultural projects in *Plautdietsch* can thrive on an eroding base of Low German users remains to be seen, but the vitality and durability of this centuries-old Mennonite dialect should not be underestimated, both as an active language in the more remote Mennonite communities and as an artistic vehicle kept alive in assimilated Mennonite areas of North America. AR

John [Jack] Thiessen, *Studien zum Wortschatz der kanadischen Mennoniten* (Marburg: Elwart, 1963); idem, *Mennonite Low German Dictionary/Mennonitisches Wörterbuch* (Marburg: Elwart, 1977), limited to Low German words not cognate with High German words; J. W. Goerzen, *Low German in Canada: A Study of Plautditsch as Spoken by Mennonite Immigrants from Russia* (Edmonton, [Alta]: the author, 1970); Herman Rempel, *Kjenn Jie noch Plautdietsch? A Mennonite Low German Dictionary* (Winnipeg: Mennonite Literary Society, 1984); Harry Loewen and Al Reimer, "Origins and Literary Development of Canadian-Mennonite Low German, *MQR*, 49 (1985), 279-86; Al Reimer, Anne Reimer, and Jack Thiessen, eds., *A Sackful of Plautdietsch* (Winnipeg: Hyperion Press and Mennonite Literary Society, 1983); J. W. Goerzen, *Germanic Heritage: Canadian Lyrics in Three Languages* (Edmonton: the author, 1962; *Collected Works of Arnold Dyck*, vols. 1 and 2, ed. Al Reimer (Winnipeg: Manitoba Mennonite Historical Society, 1986, 1988); Al Reimer, "Innocents Abroad: The Comic Odyssey of *Koop enn Bua opp Reise*," *JMS* 4 (1986), 31-45; Rueben Epp, *Plautdietsche Schreftsteckja* (Steinbach: the author, 1972), poems and stories; Elisabeth Peters, *Dee Tjoaschenhatj—The Cherryhedge* (Steinbach: Derksen Printers, 1984), comic play; Jack Thiessen, *Predicht fier haite* (Hamburg: Helmut Buske Verlag, 1984), humorous collection of mock sermons; Armin Wiebe, *The Salvation of Yasch Siemens* (Winnipeg: Turnstone Press, 1984), comic novel; Al Reimer, "There's Now An 'Official' Way to Write Low German," *MM*, 11 (June 1982) 7-8.

See also Acculturation; Folklore; Humor; Mennonite Studies; Nicknames ("Offenbarungs Reima, Petikla Pitchy, and Hickerniss Hen" feature); Rhymes.

Dialect Literature and Speech, Pennsylvania German (ME II:50, IV:141, 671).

Pennsylvania German is popularly known as "Pennsylvania Dutch," even though it is a German dialect rather than Netherlands Dutch. It is well described by Melvin Gingerich in ME IV:141. Gingerich's prediction made in the late 1950s, was that the dialect would die out soon except where it is retained for religious reasons. This is now (1987) a reality.

Many areas in eastern Pennsylvania where people used the dialect at home, in community social events, and even in school-board meetings, have dropped it almost entirely. Older people may still enjoy using it when they get together. Younger people respond in English if addressed in the German dialect. In many homes only one parent knows the dialect, consequently the children do not learn it. The auctioneer at farm sales, and the public speaker at social events will often use some colorful Pennsylvania German words or expressions to arouse interest. Many of the so-called Pennylvania German events are conducted entirely in English. Many churches are still featuring an annual Pennsylvania German worship service; but it is becoming increasingly hard to find people who can conduct the service in Pennsylvania German with naturalness and spirituality. Lacking this it loses its appeal to the worshiper and becomes a cultural attraction.

The Amish and Old Order Mennonites try hard to retain Pennsylvania German in their homes and in their worship. They are likely to continue speaking it longer than the other speakers of the language described above. To Amish and Old Order Mennonites Pennsylvania German represents obedience to a principle of God and His holy Word: to remain separate in language and practice (°°nonconformity). Their zeal and dedication merit a lot of admiration. One young Amishman expressed it by the statement, "It is always best not to have too much to do with the English." But even with this serious intent they have their problems. Nobody has ever standardized the Pennsylvania German dialect. More and more English words are being accepted into day-to-day use of the dialect. This is the inevitable result of living in an English-speaking community and with constant pressures to accept English words, even if said with German prefixes and endings and in German sentences. Most of the Amish and Old Order Mennonites speak to each other in dialect, but if they write a letter to one of their own people it will be in English. Only a few of their more talented church leaders would write in German or Pennsylvania German today.

Gingerich mentioned the strong social pressure against the use of German during the wars with Germany. This pressure was so strong that many who spoke English poorly and with a very obvious "Dutch accent" denied knowing any German. Since then it has become popular to identify with the Pennsylvania German. Many who did not learn the dialect wish their parents had taught it at home. Adult classes in colleges, a few high schools, and historical societies are offered in Pennsylvania German. There is a widespread feeling that we have lost, or are about to lose, something that was too beautiful to lose so lightly. This nostalgia is illustrated by a recently published text for use in Pennsylvania German classes, in study groups who make tape recordings of conversation by people who speak the dialect at home, by local columnists who publish items written in the dialect and sent in by readers, and by several radio programs which invite listeners to call in items of interest relating to the dialect.   NG

Ellsworth M. Kyger, comp., *An English-Pennsylvania German Dictionary: A Working Manuscript*, Russell W. Gilbert Series of Pennsylvania German Dialect Publications, vols. 2-4 (Birdsboro, Pa.: Pennsylvania German Society, 1986); Earl C. Haag, *A Pennsylvania German Reader and Grammar* (University Park, Pa.: Pennsylvania State U. Press, 1982); Ernest G. Gehman, *Schwetz Deitsch*, tape recordings in Pennsylvania German, including poetry and stories (Harrisonburg, Va.: Eastern Mennonite College). Stories in Pennsylvania German appear in various newspapers and journals, including *PMH*.

See also Acculturation; Folklore; Humor; Mennonite Studies; Nicknames ("Offenbarungs Reima, Petikla Pitchy, and Hickerniss Hen" feature); Rhymes.

Dick, Amos Daniel Maurice (1894-1979), was born in Mechanicsburg, Pa. His father, John Dick, was a minister in the Brethren in Christ Church. In 1916 Amos Dick married Nellie Sider of Wainfleet, Ont., a daughter of Brethren in Christ bishop John Sider. After Amos was ordained a minister in 1918, the couple left for India where they served as missionaries for 45 years. Amos was superintendent of the Brethren in Christ Mission in Bihar. Under his leadership, men and women were trained for Christian service and developed evangelistic outreach to the villages. He was a self-taught man, very well read in the Bible, the Indian holy books, and the classics. His easy facility with languages (Hindi, Nepali, Bengali, Urdu, and Sanskrit) enabled him to communicate with well-educated Indians as well as with villagers. In 1952 the Dicks moved to Ulubaria, West Bengal, where Amos served as superintendent for 10 years with Churches of God Mission. He served on the faculty of the Calcutta Bible College, 1953-62.

The Dicks returned in 1962 to the Unites States, where Amos was pastor of the Silverdale Brethren in Christ Church, Silverdale, Pa., until 1970.   PSD

EV (Dec. 10, 1979), 5-7.

Dick, John R. (1906–November 1985), minister, educator and conference leader in the Evangelical Mennonite Brethren (EMB) Conference (°Fellowship of Evangelical Bible Churches). Born and raised in southern Manitoba, Dick was ordained in 1935 by the Steinbach, Man., EMB congregation, where he served as assistant pastor until 1936. He later pastored congregations in Henderson, Nebr. (1939-41), Luton, Iowa (1941-43), and Abbotsford, B.C. (1959-63). From 1943 to 1959 Dick was a faculty member and administrator at Grace Bible Institute in Omaha, Nebr. He served as either president or vice-president of the EMB Conference,

1945-64. His doctoral dissertation, "A Suggested Plan of Administration for the Evangelical Mennonite Brethren Conference," (Southwestern Baptist Theological Seminary, 1953) remains the basis for the conference's administrative structure in 1986.   KE-R

Obituary in *Gospel Tidings*, 25 (Dec. 1985), 7; Paul Kuhlmann, *The Story of Grace* (Omaha: Grace College of the Bible, 1980); O. J. Wall, *A Concise Record of Our Evangelical Mennonite Brethren Annual Conference Reports 1889-1979* (Freeman, S.D.: Pine Hill Press, 1980).

Dikes. See Water Technology.

Dirk Philipszoon (ME II:65).

Selected Bibliography: Willem Balke, *Calvin and the Anabaptist Radicals* (Grand Rapids: Eerdmans, 1981); Alvin J. Beachy, "The Concept of Grace in the Radical Reformation," *MQR*, 36 (1962), 91-93; idem, "The Grace of God in Christ as Understood by Five Major Anabaptist Writers," *MQR*, 37 (1963), 5-33: idem, *The Concept of Grace in the Radical Reformation* (Nieuwkoop: B. De Graaf, 1977); idem, "De herwaardering van Dirk Philips," *Doops. Bijdr.*, n.r. 7 (1981), 92-95; Cornelius J. Dyck, "The Christology of Dirk Philips," *MQR*, 31 (1957), 147-55; William E. Keeney, "Dirk Philips' Life," *MQR*, 32 (1958), 171-91; idem, "The Writings of Dirk Philips," *MQR*, 32 (1958), 298-306; idem, *Dutch Anabaptist Thought and Practice, 1539-1564* (Nieuwkoop: B. De Graaf, 1968); idem, "The Incarnation: A Central Theological Concept," in *A Legacy of Faith*, ed. Cornelius J. Dyck (Newton, 1962), 55-68; Marja Keyser, *Dirk Philips, 1504-1568* (Nieuwkoop: B. De Graaf, 1975); Dirk Philipsz, *Enchiridion, or Hand Book. . .*, trans. A. B. Kolb (Aylmer, Ont.: Pathway Publishing Corp., 1910); J. ten Doornkaat Koolman, "The First Edition of Dirk Philips' *Enchiridion*," *MQR*, 38 (1964), 357-60; idem, *Dirk Philips: Vriend en Medewerker van Menno Simons, 1504-1568* (Haarlem: H. D. Tjeenk Willink en Zoon, 1964); A. F. Mellink, *Documenta Anabaptistica Neerlandica, Eerste Deel: Friesland en Groningen (1530-1550)* (Leiden: E. J. Brill, 1975); Menno Simons, *Opera Omnia Theologica* (1681).

Disabilities. Between 1625 and 1900 there is virtually no known written record of Anabaptist or Mennonite response to people with disabilities. Therefore, we can only speculate, based on theological understandings, what attitudes and practices may have been prevalent.

Mennonites have always believed that life should be lived so as to reflect one's faith in Christ. This has typically meant serving those in need and showing love to one another through deeds of helpfulness and assistance in the practical affairs of life. The Dordrecht Confession of Faith of 1632 sets forth provisions for caring for the poor, feeble, sick, and needy of the church. This may have included people with disabilities who, according to prevailing attitudes, were probably viewed as children of innocence and people needing assistance.

Evidence from the late 19th and 20th c. indicates that most people with disabilities in Mennonite communities have been cared for at home by their families. The concept of caring for one's own runs especially deep among Amish, Hutterites, and the more conservative Mennonites. Until recently, it would appear, there was little actual involvement or assistance from local congregations.

In Amish communities differences in ability and intellect are seen as gifts from God. Those deficient in certain abilities are accepted as part of the family and community. Children with disabilities are sent to school because socialization is valued and adults are encouraged to perform useful tasks.

The earliest recorded work with deaf persons by Mennonites occurred in 1885 in South Russia where Mennonite churches opened and supported a boarding school for deaf children.

The first known community-wide response by Mennonites to people with mental retardation and mental illness occurred in 1910 with the establishment of the °°Bethania hospital. During its 16-year history this facility in the Chortitza settlement in southern Russia served 991 people of whom more than 50 percent were not Mennonites.

Mennonite immigrants fleeing Russia in the 1920s brought this concern and service model with them to Canada. In 1932 Bethesda was opened in Vineland, Ont.—the first Mennonite institution in North America to serve people with mental retardation and mental illness. Later this facility served exclusively people with developmental disabilities. In 1987 it is operated by the Ontario Mennonite Brethren Conference.

This concern for people with mental retardation and mental illness was carried by other Mennonite immigrants to the Paraguayan Chaco where Hoffnungsheim was established in 1945. This institution was located just outside Filadelfia and served the three Mennonite colonies of Menno, Fernheim, and Neuland. Hoffnungsheim has gained in expertise and provided leadership to Paraguay in the development of other disability and mental health services serving the general population.

Following World War II European Mennonites responded to the needs of children by opening °°orphanages. As this need diminished, French Mennonites were challenged to convert some of these homes to the care of persons with mental retardation. In 1951 this new mission was begun at Mont-des-Oiseaux (Vogelsberg), near Wissembourg in Alsace. Since that time, with the support of Mennonite Central Committee (MCC) and Mennonite Board of Missions, (MC) French Mennonites have developed other residential and sheltered workshop services across France from Wissembourg to Hautefeuille to Paris. These pioneering services to people with developmental disabilities have become models for all such service development in France.

In North America it was 25 years after Bethesda opened before any other similar services were initiated by Mennonites. The first was Adriel School of West Liberty, Ohio, which in 1957 became a residential and educational institution for mentally retarded children and later emotionally disturbed slow learners. It had been established in 1896 as West Liberty Orphans Home. Adriel School was operated by the Mennonite Board of Missions until the mid-1980s, when responsibility was transferred to local Mennonite congregations.

In the United States work with deaf people began in the 1950s in several Mennonite churches in Pennsylvania. Scottdale Mennonite Church and First Deaf Mennonite Church of Lancaster offered fellowship and interpreted worship services. The latter is the only deaf Mennonite congregation, and Raymond Rohrer, the pastor, is the only ordained deaf Mennonite pastor as of 1987.

Deaf Ministries, as an arm of Mennonite Board of Missions, was established in 1976 to provide consultation and advocacy to deaf people, families, and churches. Long-term goals in working with deaf people and churches include creating access to all congregational services, training for leadership, and fostering respect for deaf culture and language. *Signing*, a quarterly newsletter, is published by Deaf Ministries. Eli Savanick, Reuben Savanick, Pam Dintaman-Gingrich and Sheila Stopher Yoder have served as directors.

Developmental disabilities, which are defined as permanent substantial handicaps originating before age 18 and including mental retardation, cerebral palsy, epilepsy, autism, or neurological impairment, have received increasing attention from Mennonites in recent years. In 1963 Mennonite Mental Health Services, an agency of Mennonite Central Committee, established a Mental Retardation Study Committee under the leadership of John R. °Mumaw. This committee sought to determine what services should be developed by the church and worked to gain greater acceptance for people with disabilities. It was not until 10 years later that Mennonite Mental Health Services established Developmental Disability Services (then known as Mental Retardation Services) and employed a full-time staff person. Jack Fransen, Nancy Kerr Williams, Dean Preheim-Bartel, and Alonna Gautsche have served in this capacity.

Developmental Disability Services provides consultation and resources to families, churches, conferences, and Mennonite-related disability programs. This ministry also facilitates and assists in the development of new services and resource material and publishes a quarterly newsletter, *Dialogue on Disabilities*.

With the growing public awareness of the needs of people with disabilities in the 1970s, North American Mennonites through church conferences, local congregations, and Mennonite Central Committee initiated numerous direct-service disability organizations. Most active in development were the Mennonite Church (MC), Beachy Amish Mennonites, Conservative Mennonites and the General Conference Mennonite Church. By the mid-1980s there were as many as 10 annual retreats for families with a developmentally disabled member and at least 5 organized church sponsored parent support groups. In 1987 there are nearly 40 church-related Mennonite agencies providing residential, vocational, advocacy, and other support services to people with developmental disabilites in North America. Most of those being served are non-Mennonites.

Mennonite Central Committee Canada created the handicap Concerns Program under the leadership of Henry Enns in 1980. The purpose of this program was to sensitize the church constituency to the needs and potential of people with physical disabilities and to identify ways that the church could contribute towards their integration. The Handicap Concerns Program initiated the first Independent Living Centers in Canada. These are based on the philosophy of self-help, self-determination, community building, and the involvement of people with disabilities. In 1986 the national staff position was replaced with a representative committee which, together with provincial committees, continues to carry out the original purpose.

Some Mennonite churches are using the gifts of people with disabilities in such areas as ushering, music, teaching, worship leading, and pastoring. Many churches are making their buildings accessible for perons in wheelchairs. Congregations are discovering ways to support people with disabilities and to encourage and assist their families who have special needs. Caring for Mennonites and others with disabilites has become a congregational concern.

A list of Mennonite-related developmental disabilities facilities and organizations as of 1987 follows: Adriel School, West Liberty, Ohio; Casselman Valley Disabilities Support Group, Grantsville, Md.; Central California Mennonite Residential Services, Fresno, Cal.; Christian Residential Opportunities and Social Services, Chambersburg, Pa.; Cumberland Valley Parent Support Group for the Handicapped, Chambersburg, Pa.; Deaf Ministries, Mennonite Board of Missions, Elkhart, Ind.; East Coast MCC Developmental Disability Concerns Group, Akron, Pa.; Faith Mission Home, Mission Home, Va.; Franconia Conference Support Group; Friendship Community, Lititz, Pa.; Friendship Community Support Fellowship, Lititz, Pa.; Friendship Foundation for the Handicapped, Glendale, Ariz.; Glencroft Special Services, Glendale, Ariz.; Hartville Meadows, Hartville, Ohio; Hattie Larlham Foundation, Mantua, Ohio; Indian Creek Foundation, Harleysville, Pa.; Jubilee Association of Maryland, Silver Spring, Md.; Kansas Mennonite Disabilities Council/Central States MCC, North Newton, Ks.; Kings View Work Experience Center, Atwater, Cal.; Mennonite Association of Disability Programs, Mennonite Health Association, Elkhart, Ind.; Mennonite Developmental Disability Services of MCC US, Akron, Pa.; Mennonite Disabilities Committee, Goshen, Ind.; Mennonite Family Support Group, Lewis County, N.Y.; Mennonite Residential Homes, Elida, Ohio; Northview Development Services, Newton, Ks.; Oregon Mennonite Residential Services, Lebanon, Ore.; Pleasant View Home, Broadway, Va.; Salem Children's Home, Flanagan, Ill.; Shenandoah Parents Support Group, Harrisonburg, Va.; Southwest Community Services, Tinley Park, Ill.; Sunnyhaven Children's Home, Plain City, Ohio; Sunshine Children's Home, Maumee, Ohio; West Coast MCC Developmental Disability Program, Reedley, Cal.; Handicap Concerns Committee of MCC Canada, Winnipeg; Peace and Social Concerns Committee of MCC Alberta, Calgary; Clearbrook Achievement Centre, Clearbrook, B.C.; Community Living Program, Clearbrook, B.C.; Dohstrom House, Clearbrook, B.C.; Langley House, Langley, B.C.; Supportive Care Services, MCC British Columbia, Clearbrook, B.C.; The Cedars, Rosedale, B.C.; Twin Firs, Huntingdon, B.C.; Twin Firs Greenhouse, Huntingdon, B.C.; Vabich House, Abbotsford, B.C.; Association of Community Living, Altona, Man.; Eden Mental Health Service-Trainex Industries, Winkler, Man.; El'Dad Ranch, Randolph, Man.; Handicap Concerns Committee of MCC Manitoba, Winnipeg; Kindale Manor, Steinbach, Man.; Kindale Occupational Centre, Steinbach, Man.; Occupational Training Centre, Altona, Man.; Our Home, Winkler, Man.; Valley Rehabilitation Centre, Winkler, Man.; Opal

Inc., Petitcodiac, N.B.; Aldaview Residential Services, New Hamburg, Ont.; Bethesda Community Assessment Services, Vineland, Ont.; Bethesda Home for Mentally Handicapped, Vineland, Ont.; Handicap Ministries of MCC Ontario, Kitchener, Ont.; Independent Living Centre, Kitchener; St. Catharines Peer Support Group, St. Catharines, Ont.; Waterloo Regional Peer Support Group, Kitchener; Disability Concerns Committee of MCC Saskatchewan, Saskatoon; McKerracher House, Swift Current, Sask.; Menno Home of Saskatchewan, Waldheim, Sask.; Mont-des-Oiseaux, Wissembourg, France; Les Amis de l'Atelier, France; Domaine Emanuel, France; New Dawn Development Center, Taiwan; Servido Menonita de Salud Mental, Filadelfia, Chaco, Paraguay. Current listings for North America are published in *MC Yearbook*.   DAP-B

"Claggett Statement," in *Signing* (Oct. 1984); Ferne Pellman Glick, and Donald R. Pellman, *Breaking Silence—A Family Grows with Deafness* (Scottdale, 1982); Herbert J. Grossman, ed., *Classification in Mental Retardation* (Washington, D.C.: American Association on Mental Retardation, 1983); John A. Hostetler, *Amish Society* (1980), 322-24; Mitchell Kingsley, and Duane Ruth-Heffelbower, *After We're Gone: Estate and Life Planning for a Disabled Person's Family* (Akron, Pa.: MCC, 1987); Miriam S. Lind, *No Crying He Makes* (Scottdale, 1972); James A. Melton, "Old Order Amish Awareness and Understanding of Mental Retardation" (PhD diss., Ohio State U., 1970); Vernon H. Neufeld, ed., *If We Can Love* (Newton, 1984); Aldred H. Neufeldt, ed., *Celebrating Differences* (Newton, 1984); Robert Perske, *Hope for the Families* (Nashville: Abingdon, 1981); Dean A. Preheim-Bartel and Aldred H. Neufeldt, *Supportive Care in the Congregation* (Akron, Pa.: MCC, 1986); Edward Yoder, *Mennonites and Their Heritage*, no. 3 (Akron, Pa.: MCC, 1942). The following Mennonite offices serve as clearing houses for material on disabilities: Developmental Disability Services, 21 South 12th Street, Akron, Pa., 17501; Deaf Ministries, 500 South Main, Elkhart, Ind., 46516; Handicap Concerns Program, 134 Plaza Drive, Winnipeg, Man., R3T 5K9.

See also British Columbia; Fellowship of Mennonite Churches in Taiwan; Folk Art; Kake Elisabete; Mental Health Facilities and Services; Shidi Lazalo.

Disarmament. In the broadest sense *disarmament* means divesting of arms. The term is often used to refer to any effort to regulate, reduce, or eliminate armaments, though it sometimes has a narrower meaning focused on eliminating (rather than controlling) weapons, especially nuclear weapons.

The 20th c. has seen a renewed interest in disarmament. After World War I there was widespread public pressure for disarmament. It was often expressed in English-speaking countries in a liberal pacifism which was relatively hopeful about human nature and confident that war could be eliminated as its irrationality was demonstrated. Most Mennonites (here meaning North American unless otherwise specified) apparently had little to do with the disarmament movements of the time. They tended to be rather isolated, both geographically and psychologically. Many objected to the theological °liberalism of the wider pacifist movement and held to a church/world dualism which made them skeptical of disarmament schemes. Nevertheless, some U.S. Mennonites, mostly from the General Conference Mennonite Church, were involved at least on the edges of this movement. Perhaps the clearest Mennonite institutional expression of this involvement was the Kansas Institute of International Relations at Bethel College, 1936-40.

The experience of World War II and Reinhold Niebuhr's theological critique destroyed the liberal pacifist movement in North America and reinforced in Mennonites a sense of separation from the world and of the futility of pacifism or disarmament as public policy options. This perspective was expressed in a critique of °°"pacifism" by some Mennonite writers who defended °°"nonresistance" instead.

But after the war the atomic bomb provided a powerful impetus toward disarmament, particularly nuclear disarmament. Mennonites were rapidly becoming sociologically less separate from the wider society and were influenced by the general ups and downs of disarmament campaigns. After unsuccessful nuclear disarmament efforts following the war, by the 1950s disarmament had been rejected by most as idealistic. It was not widely discussed in Mennonite circles during this time. In the late 1950s and early 1960s pressure for nuclear disarmament mounted again in response to the dangers of atmospheric tests. With greater frequency writers and groups (e.g., Frank H. Epp, the Church Peace Mission and the General Conference Peace and Social Concerns Committee) called Mennonites to support disarmament. Concerns were also expressed by small groups of Mennonites in Japan and Europe, particularly among the Dutch Mennonites.

Public pressure and crises in Berlin and Cuba led in 1963 to the first major nuclear arms agreement. It confined tests to underground. It also marked a shift in thinking on nuclear disarmament from "disarmament" (seeking to eliminate nuclear weapons) to "arms control" (regulating them, dealing with more specific, negotiable problems). Although this new approach resulted in several other important agreements, after the test ban treaty pressure for nuclear disarmament declined dramatically both among Mennonites and more generally, particularly as the war in Vietnam took center stage.

In the late 1970s and the 1980s disillusionment with "arms control" set in on both ends of the political spectrum in the West. While right and left were bitterly opposed on many issues, both rejected the notion of managing nuclear arsenals in favor of drastically reducing them or eliminating them. Nuclear "disarmament" came back into public view and with it massive disarmament campaigns. Nuclear weapons became the central focus of American Mennonite peace concern in official circles, such as the Mennonite Central Committee (U.S.) Peace Section. Disarmament also had high visibility in Canadian Mennonite circles where Project Plowshares, with heavy Mennonite involvement and sponsorship, became one of the main private organizations devoted to disarmament research and education. In Europe some Mennonites participated in the efforts to prevent new deployments of North Atlantic Treaty Organization (NATO) missiles. But no consensus on disarmament activity was clear by the mid-1980s. Some argued that attention to disarmament distracted from the essential mission of the church (and that in a fallen world such weapons may be necessary for the state and could not be abolished). Others worked within political structures and in private groups seeking to influence policy through

legislation (often taking a gradualist, "realistic" perspective). Still others, for the first time on a significant (though still very small in overall Mennonite perspective) scale, engaged in prophetic acts of °civil disobedience against the idolatry of trusting nuclear weapons for security. The most visible protests in the Mennonite world took place at Rocky Flats, near Denver. In general one can say that some Mennonites in the 20th c. moved toward a more activist, pro-disarmament stance, although by the 1980s most remained largely uninvolved and the movement toward this posture had been somewhat sporadic. TJK

Mennonite (Nov. 6, 1962) 707-9; *GH* (May 19, 1959) 465; various articles by Frank H. Epp, Delton Franz, Alan Kreider, Carl Kreider, Ernie Regier, and John Stoner in *Bibl. on War and Peace* (1987) under Arms, Armament; Theodore W. Loewen, "Mennonite Pacifism: The Kansas Institute of International Relations" (unpubl. paper, Bethel College Library and Archives); Erwin W. Hiebert, *The Impact of Atomic Energy* (Newton, 1961), esp. 280-88 (Mennonite statements and activities on disarmament from World War II through 1960); Ted Koontz, "Has SALT II Lost Its Savor?" *Mennonite* (Dec. 4, 1979) 733; Donald B. Kraybill, *Facing Nuclear War: A Plea for Christian Witness* (Scottdale, 1982); *Canadian Mennonite* (May 23, 1958) 1; John R. Mumaw, "Nonresistance and Pacifism" (Scottdale, 1952); Ernie Regehr and Simon Rosenblum, *The Road to Peace: Canada and Disarmament* (James Lorrimer, 1988); *NATO Watch 1986-*, a small publication by European Mennonites and North American Mennonite workers in Europe seeking to make a peace witness to NATO; Reinhold Niebuhr, "Why the Christian Church Is Not Pacifist," in *Christianity and Power Politics* (New York: Scribner's, 1940); papers from the MCC Peace Section Assembly, 1982; Ronald J. Sider and Richard K. Taylor, *Nuclear Holocaust and Christian Hope* (Downers Grove, Ill: Intervarsity Press, 1982); Donovan E. Smucker, "A Mennonite Critique of the Pacifist Movement," *MQR*, 20 (1946) 81-88; John K. Stoner, Executive Secretary of MCC U.S. Peace Section from 1976-1988, strongly advocates active resistance to nuclear weapons in many articles and pamphlets; John K. Stoner, "SALT II: Opiate or Opportunity?" [MCC] *Peace Section Newsletter*, 9 (Feb.-Mar., 1979) 10-11.

See also Harshbarger, Eva; Peace.

Disaster Services (ME III:620). The Mennonite, Brethren in Christ, and related Anabaptist constituent churches respond through Mennonite Disaster Service (MDS) to help disaster victims. In keeping with their biblical and Christian °service theology, the Mennonite Disaster Service network provides volunteers to aid the victims of floods, tornadoes, hurricanes, earthquakes, and other disaster situations. This response to neighbors in crisis is an expansion of generations of °mutual aid practiced by Mennonites and Amish.

The organized response that led to the development of Mennonite Disaster Service began in 1950 in Hesston, Ks. By 1961 the national committee had hired an executive coordinator. In 1962 MDS became a section of Mennonite Central Committee.

The organization also developed in Canada and as of 1988 remains a binational organization. Representation on the Section (board) comes from the four regions in the United States and one in Canada, from nine participating conference bodies, and from the supporting Mennonite Central Committee Canada and Mennonite Central Committee U.S. organizations. Each of the more than 3,000 Mennonite, Amish, and Brethren in Christ churches and districts are encouraged to have representatives; these form the nearly 60 MDS units across the United States and Canada. The program is decentralized with local units springing into action as needs arise. In larger disasters, the regional and binational organizations provide support and personnel for the local units. The major thrust of MDS assistance is in the areas of postdisaster cleanup, repair, and rebuilding operations. Special emphasis is placed on helping those least able to help themselves i.e., single parents, the elderly, the handicapped, and widows. MDS workers serve without pay and request no fees for services provided.

Mennonite Disaster Service carries out its activities in a spirit of cooperation with the various agencies of the government and with other volunteer disaster service organizations. At the national level, MDS is a member of the National Voluntary Organizations Active in Disaster (NVOAD). MDS has a long history of cooperative efforts with the American °Red Cross. Local Red Cross operations, which primarily provide emergency food, shelter, and necessities, often refer cases for cleanup and repair to MDS. Many other church bodies also provide disaster response service, as do the federal governments (in the United States, through the Federal Emergency Management Agency [FEMA]).

While the thrust of Mennonite Disaster Service remains in the areas of response to natural disaster cleanup and repair, MDS personnel are willing to expand their areas of involvement where there is a need and volunteers are available. Among other tasks, MDS has assisted in repairing homes in urban or rural low income areas, participated in building or remodeling churches, and assisted Mennonite Central Committee in its °relief efforts. At the 25th anniversary observance of MDS at Hesston, Ks., in 1975, speaker Elmer Ediger said of MDS: "It has been as spontaneous a movement as we have had. It has shown that ordinary people, if they are dedicated and put in a place of need, can do great things."   LDet

Marketplace (July-Aug. 1986), 17-18; *MC Yearbook* (1988-89), 118, 134-35; Katie Funk Wiebe, *Day of Disaster* (Scottdale, 1976).

Discipleship (ME IV:1076) denotes a specific basis for Christian living. As such it is closely connected with the topic of Christian °ethics. Discipleship is seen by most scholars as the central framework for the Anabaptist and Mennonite understanding of ethics and the church. In the 1980s there are Christian ethicists from several other denominations advocating the use of this term to describe their ecclesiology. Also, Mennonite theologians, e.g. Gordon Kaufman and J. Lawrence Burkholder, have suggested that the term "responsibility" is an important component of discipleship and could serve as a corrective to a naive following of Jesus, because it can more readily deal with the ambiguities of contemporary society in relation to which a Mennonite ethic is to be constructed. The tension between discipleship and responsibility characterizes much of the current debate.

The discipleship understanding of Christian living sees the church as a body of believers (disciples) who together commit themselves to following Jesus

Christ (*Nachfolge Christi*). Hence it roots the identity of the church in the biblical story of faith. It suggests that Christians cannot be the church today, unless they understand and model their living after the Bible of yesterday.

This unique interpretation of the church had its roots in the Reformation. There the Anabaptists were in conscious opposition to both the Catholics and the Lutherans. For them Luther's strong emphasis and narrow interpretation of "justification by grace through faith" depreciated the importance of Christian living, while the Catholic foundation of "natural theology" ignored the centrality of Jesus as a model for the church. For the early Anabaptists, Christians were called to separate themselves from the world of sin and evil, and live a life of °love and °nonresistance as Jesus had taught.

Much of the current discussion on discipleship among Mennonite scholars today focuses on the moral agency of the church. In the 1940s and 1950s H. S. °Bender, and G. F. °Hershberger were the dominant Mennonite voices on the subject. In several articles Bender argued that being disciples implies nonresistance and a rejection of the use of force and power. Hershberger agreed and on this basis drew a sharp distinction between °°pacifism, which employs power, albeit nonviolently, and nonresistance, which refuses to employ power. The former he calls non-Christian. The latter follows from Christian discipleship.

With J. H. Yoder, who began writing on the subject in the late 1950s, the language changed only slightly. In his *The Politics of Jesus*, using as his foil the Niebuhr brothers, he articulated a Christian ethical framework based on discipleship which he defined as "imitation-participation." The central locus of discipleship is the Cross. "There is but one realm in which the concept of imitation holds . . . this is at the point of the concrete social meaning of the cross in its relation to enmity and power. . . . Thus—and only thus—are we bound by New Testament thought to 'be like Jesus' " (*Politics*, p. 134). Discipleship, as imitation-participation, is our moral linkage with the Cross. Here the question for the disciple is not how to change the world but how to be like Jesus; it is not how to be "responsible," but how to follow.

For Yoder as for Bender and Hershberger, being a disciple of Jesus means renouncing responsibility for and control over the world, just like it did for Jesus on the Cross. Christians cannot be disciples of Jesus unless they are willing to give up the desire to make history come out right; unless they resist the temptation to take responsibility for the world. This means that they must be willing to renounce all interest in effectiveness. Christians are not the ones to change history. God does that. Like Jesus, disciples also are willing to die rather than resist evil violently.

Ronald J. Sider, in his much discussed address at Mennonite World Conference (Strasbourg, 1984), emphasized the other pole of discipleship. He suggested that, for disciples of Jesus, the decade of the 1980s is a *Kairos* moment in history. The reality of nuclear arms has demonstrated the absurdity of war, and the heirs of those Christians who through the centuries have been a living testimony to this conviction, must rise up to use their influence to alter the course of history. He said: "The God of Shalom has been preparing us Anabaptists for a late 20th century rendezvous with history. . . . God's reconciling people will profoundly impact the course of world history." For Sider, discipleship implies taking responsibility for history and demonstrating the love of God through nonviolent direct action.

Sider's language is certainly closer to discipleship as "responsibility" than to discipleship as "imitation-participation." The two views of discipleship answer the question, "How ought disciples of Jesus relate to the world?" differently. Hershberger, Bender, and Yoder all held that discipleship implies that it is not our business to take responsibility for history. Sider, and earlier Kaufman and Burkholder, argued that it is our business, and moreover it is extremely urgent. This is the state of the current debate.

The current discussion raises the central issue of the Gospel message: the social and ethical meaning of the Cross event. Throughout Christian history the Cross has been understood as the Christian way of dealing with sin, even though there has not always been agreement on precisely how this happens. The discipleship view of the church has held that just as Jesus died nonviolently in response to the violence done to him, so his disciples are called to respond to sinners in love and forgiveness. The power inherent in this response can transform the lives of sinners. Yet can this power be used strategically to transform the world? On this Mennonites are not agreed.

It is important to note that the contemporary Mennonite discussion on discipleship has taken place in dialogue with other theologians and church denominations. Already when Bender and Hershberger were formulating their views of discipleship, in the 1940s, a German Lutheran theologian, Dieterich °Bonhoeffer, was articulating a very similar concept. German-speaking theologians, e.g., Karl Barth, and Jürgen Moltmann, have also been in considerable dialogue with Mennonite scholars on the topic. In North America, Stanley Hauerwas, a Methodist, and James McClendon, a Baptist, are two examples of theologians who are consciously developing ethical and ecclesiological models on the basis of an Anabaptist view of discipleship. In addition, there are several groups like the Sojourners community, Evangelicals for Social Action, the Shalom Institute (Vancouver, B.C.), and the Baptist Peace Fellowship of North America, which, in dialogue with Mennonites, have adopted the discipleship paradigm of being Christian.   HHue

Clarence Bauman, "The Meaning of Christian Discipleship," in *The Church in Mission*, ed. A. J. Klassen (Fresno: MB Board of Christian Literature, 1967), 50-67; Bender, "Vision"; Harold S. Bender, "The Anabaptist Theology of Discipleship," *MQR*, 24 (1950), 25-32; Dietrich Bonhoeffer, *Nachfolge* (Munich: Chr. Kaiser Verlag, 1937; Engl. trans. 1949); J. Lawrence Burkholder, "The Problem of Social Responsibility from the Perspective of the Mennonite Church," PhD diss., Princeton Theological Seminary, 1958; publ. by the author, 1988); idem, "The Anabaptist Vision of Discipleship," *Recovery*, 135-51; Stanley Hauerwas, *The Peaceable Kingdom: A Primer in Christian Ethics* (Notre Dame: U. of Notre Dame Press, 1983); Guy F. Hershberger, *War, Peace and Nonresistance* (Scottdale, 1944); Gordon Kaufman, "Nonresistance and Responsibility," *Concern* pamphlet no. 6 (1958); James W. McClendon, *Systematic Theology: Ethics* (Nashville: Abingdon Press, 1986); Jürgen Moltmann, *Following Jesus Christ in the World Today: Responsibility for the World and Christian Discipleship*, Occasional Papers, 4 (Elkhart: IMS, 1983; Winnipeg: CMBC, 1983; *Dialogue Sequel to Jürgen Moltmann's Following Jesus Christ in the World Today*, Occasional Papers, 8 (Elkhart: IMS, 1984; Winnipeg: CMBC, 1984); Ronald J. Sider, "God's Reconciling People," in *Proceedings of the Eleventh Assembly Mennonite World Conference*, Strasbourg, France, July, 1984; John Howard Yoder, *The Politics of Jesus* (Grand Rapids: Eerdman's, 1972).

See also Conversion; Legalism; Nonconformity; Salvation; Sanctification; Sermon on the Mount.

Discipline, Church (ME II:69). The doctrine and practice of church discipline have always been important in the Anabaptist and Mennonite tradition. The second article of the °Schleitheim Confession (1527) calls for the conscientious and faithful use of the °°ban to maintain a united and faithful church.

The subject of Anabaptist church discipline has received careful examination in two recent studies. Ervin Schlabach, "The Rule of Christ Among the Early Swiss Anabaptists" (1977) shows that the prevailing use of the term "ban" (*Meidung*) among the Anabaptists brought with it some of its prior connotations in the Catholic church, in that Anabaptist ban practice did not always make a clear distinction between the ban as admonition and the ban as punishment. "In spite of the repeated emphasis of the early Swiss leaders to practice the ban only in sincere Christian love, the potential punitive implications of the ban became increasingly problematic after Schleitheim." "After Schleitheim the Anabaptist church discipline took a variety of forms, including different degrees of punishment in dealing with offenses" (pp. 149-50). Schlabach states that concern for the ban may have taken precedence over concern for believers' baptism by the second decade of the Anabaptist movement.

The study by Jean Runzo, "Communal Discipline in the Early Anabaptist Communities of Switzerland, South and Central Germany, Austria, and Moravia, 1525-1550" (1978) is an essay upon "the actual operation of discipline, and the theory upon which it was based, within the Anabaptist communities in these regions. . . . Discipline among these groups was not a uniform phenomenon, as has often been thought" (p. 1). According to Runzo it was the Swiss Brethren who were most "rigorous" in the use of the ban. "In contrast . . . the early south German and Austrian Anabaptists . . . developed a more individual . . . less community-oriented" discipline. The Hutterites, thanks to the "relative stability" and "rich communal life" of their settlements in Moravia "afford our best example . . . of the actual operation of discipline."

The interested scholar will find an affirmation of church discipline in practically every Anabaptist and Mennonite confession of faith since Schleitheim, though there are few studies that explicitly review this theme in such confessions. One limited but useful study of the Swiss tradition (William R. McGrath, *Christlicher Ordnung, or Christian Discipline*, 1966) collects pertinent statements on discipline found in 10 confessions or regulations from Schleitheim (1527) to a Holmes Co., Ohio conference of 1865. The later examples of these regulations (*Ordnungen*) focus increasingly upon such matters as clothing and house decorations.

The 1963 Mennonite Church (MC) Confession of Faith contains a paragraph (art. 8: "The Church of Christ") on the "authority" given the church "to exercise discipline" in order "to restore . . . members who fall into sin, . . . to promote the purity of the church, . . . and to maintain the witness of the church before the world." The General Conference Mennonite (GCM) "Common Confession" of 1896, reprinted in the 1959, 1968, and 1984 General Conference constitutions, requires of congregations "the practice of a scriptural church discipline (Mt 18:15-17; Gal. 6:1)." The 1975 Mennonite Brethren Confession of Faith calls for a "constructive church discipline: under the standard of God's word to admonish, counsel, exclude (if necessary), and reinstate the repentant into fellowship."

A 1955 survey limited to the General Conference Mennonite Church (GCM) yielded 229 responses to a questionnaire mailed to 286 congregations (80 percent return). It shows that 74 percent of the responding congregations made provision for church discipline in their written constitutions. Forty-nine percent reported they *did* practice discipline; 51 percent reported they did *not*. Of the discipline actions reported, the highest proportion concerned immorality (27 percent), the next highest, beliefs (23 percent). Of the 376 persons dealt with, 49 percent were restored, 25 percent transferred, and 23 percent were lost to the church (*Studies in Church Discipline*, 1958, appendix).

The landmark sociological study by J. Howard Kauffman and Leland Harder of five North American Mennonite denominations (1975) found 60 percent of the respondents to its questionnaire agreeing that "Mennonite and Brethren in Christ churches should practice a thorough church discipline so that faltering or unfaithful members can be built up and restored or, in exceptional cases, excluded." It could be added that 24 percent were uncertain about this statement, and 13 percent disagreed. However, 35 percent agreed with the questionnaire statement, "The way to work with members in the church who have lapsed from the standards is never to exclude them from the church but rather to keep them on the membership roll, hoping they will mend their ways by heeding the advice of the minister or following the example of upright members." Again, it could be added that 24 percent were uncertain about the statement just mentioned, and 26 percent disagreed.

As a reliable social-scientific sampling, the Kauffman-Harder study, brief as it is on the subject of church discipline, is unquestionably important as the most recent and most reliable indicator of the position of five denominations of North American Mennonites in their *belief* or *profession* with respect to church discipline. Except for occasional student seminar studies of discipline in a local or district area, very few modern studies have been done on the actual practice of church discipline among Mennonites.

If the Anabaptist concept and practice of church discipline already showed diversity, contemporary Mennonite conceptions and practices show even more diversity in Mennonite churches from the Soviet Union to Western Europe, North and South

America, Africa, India, Indonesia, Taiwan, and Japan, not to mention Australia. A fairly traditional discipline, including "shunning" (°°avoidance) continues to be exercised among the Amish and Hutterites of North America and in the Church of God in Christ, Mennonite (often called the Holdeman Church). A much less traditional form of discipline is practiced in the Mennonite Church (MC), the General Conference Mennonite Church, and the Mennonite Brethren Church. For example, in many congregations of the Mennonite Church, remarriage after °divorce is no longer cause for indefinite excommunication as was generally the case until the 1960s.

In the 1980s the term *church discipline* is not used much among English-speaking Mennonite congregations of North America, but the reality is often there, practiced with most commendable Christian love and tact under other terms (e.g. "pastoral counseling"). Confidentiality determines that much of this Christian ministry does not become visible. In spiritually healthy congregations good teaching reduces the need for "corrective discipline." In many cases, however, the only course congregations take is periodic removal of the names of inactive members from the church's membership roster.

A recent theological study of church discipline by the present writer, *Discipling the Brother* (1972, 1979, 1988) urges a view of church discipline based upon the central Anabaptist and Mennonite doctrine of °discipleship. Church discipline is a ministry analogous to °evangelism and °mission. As evangelism and mission bring unbelievers into the way of Christ (discipleship), church discipline seeks to keep in the way of discipleship, or to restore to it, those believers who are in danger of abandoning the faith, whether through transgression, doctrinal error, coldness of heart, or any other cause. Like evangelism, the ministry of church discipline proposes to use only the power of the gospel and of the Spirit of God. Like evangelism, church discipline is not punitive, yet it brings erring believers to decision through the word of admonition, which is the presentation of the gospel. They must then be dealt with (again as in evangelism) according to their response. The goal of church discipline is thus the restoration of erring believers to the way of discipleship, the realization of a sanctified church, and the enhancement of the church's witness in the world.   MJ

Jean Ellen Goodban Runzo, "Communal Discipline in the Early Anabaptist Communities of Switzerland, South and Central Germany, Austria, and Moravia, 1525-1550" (PhD diss., U. of Michigan, 1978); Ervin A Schlabach, "The Rule of Christ Among the Early Swiss Anabaptists" (ThD diss., Chicago Theological Seminary, 1977); *Studies of Church Discipline* (Newton: MPO, 1958); Marlin Jeschke, *Discipling the Brother* (Scottdale, 1972, 1979, reissued in 1988 as *Discipling in the Church*); Kauffman/Harder *Anabaptists Four C. Later* (1975); *Concern* pamphlet no. 14 (1967); Loewen, *Confessions*.

See also Church Membership.

Dispensationalism has its roots in the teachings of John N. Darby (1800-1882), who left his law career in Dublin to become an Anglican clergyman. Dissatisfied with the established church he became a leader in the so-called Plymouth Brethren movement. A basic tenet in the dispensational system of interpretation is that God deals differently with men and women during the various eras of biblical history. According to C. I. Scofield who, among others (Lewis Sperry Chafer, Arno C. Gaebelein, and Harry A. Ironside), popularized dispensationalism in America, there are seven such dispensations: innocence—before the fall, conscience—from the fall to Noah, human government—from Noah to Abraham, promise—from Abraham to Moses, law—from Moses to Christ, grace—the church age, and the kingdom—the millennium.

In this scheme the church is seen as an "interruption," a parenthesis in God's plan with Israel. Based on an overly literal interpretation of Old Testament promises, it asserts that Jesus came to establish the kingdom of Israel. The gospel preached by Jesus was a gospel of an earthly Jewish kingdom. Because this offer of the kingdom was rejected by Israel, its establishment was postponed, and the church age has now intervened. Another implication is that the teachings of Jesus (Sermon on the Mount, parables, the ethical teachings of Jesus, etc.) are "kingdom truths," and therefore do not apply directly to the church.

Dispensationalists hold that the present age comes to an end with a pre-tribulation rapture of the church, including both the living and the dead in Christ. Once the church is gone, Satan through his emissary, the antichrist, will oppress Israel and the nations. After seven years of great tribulation the church returns with Christ, and that sets the stage for the conversion of Israel and the world-wide millennial reign of Christ from Jerusalem. At the end of the millennium, Satan and his followers rally for a final revolt against God, but they will be utterly defeated. In the end all the people of God will find their eternal home in the city of God, the New Jerusalem, whereas the ungodly suffer eternal punishment.

There is considerable diversity among dispensationalists on the details of this system of interpretation, but in spite of its exegetical and theological weaknesses, dispensationalism represents a popular hermeneutical approach to the Bible for many conservative Christians. A number of theological schools, both in the United States and other countries, are committed to the teaching of this system of reading the Bible.

The weakness of dispensational hermeneutics is that it does not take seriously the continuity of God's saving purposes in history. It fails to see the fulfillment of the hopes and promises of the Old Testament in the New. Its insistence on the cleavage between Israel and the church sets dispensationalism off from the historic faith of the church.

Dispensationalism was introduced into Mennonite communities in South Russia by some church leaders who had discovered the teachings of John Darby in Germany. Several outstanding preachers spread this system of interpretation not only in Russia but also, later, in North and South America. In North America dispensationalism made deep inroads on Mennonite churches through non-Mennonite literature and prophetic conferences, and through non-Mennonite

°Bible colleges and seminaries, leading to considerable dissension and controversy. Today relatively few Mennonite scholars espouse dispensationalism and it is advocated mainly by teachers and preachers who received their theological training in non-Mennonite schools.   DE

C. Norman Kraus, *Dispensationalism in America: Its Rise and Development* (Richmond: John Knox Press, 1958); Clarence B. Bass, *Backgrounds to Dispensationalism* (Grand Rapids: Eerdmans, 1960; reissued Baker Book House, 1977).

See also Fundamentalism.

Disputations. See Apologetics; Polemics, Anti-Anabaptist.

Divorce and Remarriage (ME II:74). The earliest Anabaptist tract on this subject, "Concerning Divorce", was written in 1527 and has been attributed by some to Michael °Sattler. It stressed the permanence of the °marriage bond, the priority of one's obligation to Christ over one's obligations to a marriage partner, adultery as the only grounds for divorce, taboos against marrying a fornicator, and sanctions against remarrying when divorced. °Menno Simons also called for faithfulness in marriage, allowing adultery as the only grounds for divorce, according to Mt 19:9 and 1 Cor 7:4. According to J. C. Wenger, the Swiss Brethren, the Moravian Hutterites and the Dutch Mennonites all had similar standards regarding divorce. With such a clear view among Anabaptists, what are Mennonite attitudes 450 years later?

Divorce rates in the United States have been among the highest in the world. The number of divorces peaked after World War II and declined to a low of under 200 per 100,000 population in 1960. However, since then divorce rates have been rising steadily, so that by 1980 they were well over 1,540 per 100,000. Divorce rates in Canada were in the vicinity of 40 per 100,000 population through the 1950s and until 1968, when divorces began to rise sharply with passage of the new Canada Divorce Act. Canadian divorce rates then escalated to 278 per 100,000 population in 1981. Thus, American rates were, at one time, more than six times as high as Canadian rates (260 compared to 40). By 1980 the ratio was about two to one.

°Industrialization and °urbanization tend to result in smaller nuclear °families which are more mobile, but also more vulnerable to breakdown. Although not yet as frequent as in North America, divorce is also increasing in Europe. One can also expect that divorce will also increase as Latin America, Asia and Africa, where divorce rates are still quite low, are increasingly influenced by industrialization.

Divorce rates do however vary considerably by religious orientation, as shown in Canadian religious comparisons in 1981. Non-Judeo-Christian groups have the highest rate of divorce (17 percent), followed by those who prefer no religion (12 percent). These two groups are significantly above the Canadian average of 7.7 percent in 1981. The Mennonites (3.3 percent) rank at the bottom with the Hutterites (.2 percent) and the Reformed bodies (1.9 percent). This suggests that ethnic, family, and small group ties, especially when combined with strong religious commitment, still inhibit divorce.

Kauffman and Harder, who surveyed most of the Mennonites in North America, found that 77 percent believed that marriage was a lifelong commitment never to be broken except by death; only one percent thought incompatibility was reason for divorce (data from 1972). Their study also indicated that only .3 percent of married couples were separated but not divorced, which was still a very low figure compared to national statistics.

Leland Harder, who surveyed General Conference Mennonites in North America in 1960, 1970, and 1980, found that divorce rates among Mennonites are rising (.6 percent of members reported breakdown in 1960 and 1.7 percent in 1980). Those who had ever been divorced rose to 4.8 percent in 1980. Eighty percent of the congregations reported that at least one or more members were either divorced or separated in 1980. One fourth reported 10 or more members separated or divorced; 4 churches reported over 40. While urbanization is a factor, other factors must be considered to explain these variations. Again, there were substantial national differences with .8 percent of General Conference Mennonite members having experienced marriage breakdown in the United States and .2 percent in Canada in 1960, a ratio of four to one. The same national differences remained in 1980 (2.4 percent and .6 percent) respectively.

Michael Yoder conducted a study of the Mennonite Church, the largest group of Mennonites in North America, in 1982. Yoder found that separation and divorce were lowest among active members (.5 and 1.0 percent) and highest among inactive members (2.0 and 4.2 percent). This may indicate that religious commitment is an important factor in marriage maintenance, although it may also indicate that those experiencing marriage breakdown tend to become inactive in congregations. While only 3.2 percent of the active members were ever separated or divorced, three times as many inactive members (9.3 percent) were in this category. Although the percentages were relatively low compared to national figures, about 5 percent, or almost 5,000 persons, in the Mennonite Church were or had been separated or divorced. This percentage was very similar to that of the General Conference Mennonite Church in 1980.

Yoder also found that one fourth (24.1 percent) of the blacks in his study had been separated or divorced at one time, while Asian Mennonites showed the lowest rate (1.8 percent) of marriage breakdown. Both groups are non-Caucasian and both were heavily urban (85 percent and 71 percent, respectively). The percentages seemed to be related to traditions of family stability within ethnic groups. While traditional white Mennonites appeared to be closer to the Asian type, Mennonites who were American Indians resembled more the pattern found among blacks, and Hispanic Mennonites were located in between.

Paul Lederach made an important study of youth in the Mennonite Church which compared the beliefs and attitudes of youth from broken homes with those of all youth. He found that youth from broken homes had weaker Christian convictions and

ethics, attended church activities less often, had more trouble getting along at home, and more often exhibited deviant behavior. The home is the primary place for socialization of children, and these data clearly show that broken families cannot compete with normal ones in the rearing of children. Much more research is required to determine to what extent these findings apply elsewhere in the world, and what are the many factors which cause family breakdown.   LDr

Leo Driedger, Michael Yoder, and Peter Sawatzky, "Divorce Among Mennonites: Evidence of Family Breakdown," *MQR*, 59 (1985), 367-382; Leland Harder, *General Conference Mennonite Church Fact Book of Congregational Membership* (Newton, 1971, 1980-81); John C. Wenger, "Concerning Divorce: A Swiss Brethren Tract on the Primacy of Loyalty to Christ and the Right to Divorce and Remarriage," *MQR*, 21 (1947), 114-119; Michael Yoder, "Findings from the 1982 Mennonite Census,"*MQR*, 59 (1985), 307-349; Kauffman/Harder, *Anabaptists Four C. Later* (1975), 122-23, 170-76; Wittlinger, *Piety and Obedience* (1978), 117-19, 525-27; *Menn. Bib. II,* index.

See also Childrearing; Eastern Pennsylvania Mennonite Church; Mennonite Church in India; Singleness.

Djakarta. See Jakarta.

Djimbo, Kubula (Timothée) (b. 1905), grew up as a slave of a chief. The chief gave him to missionaries Aaron and Ernestina Janzen as a student for their mission school at Kafumba. Kubala became one of the first converts, accepting Jesus Christ as Savior and Lord in 1927. After primary school he was sent to Kiandu to teach. He was called back to Kafumba and given more Bible teaching. In 1938 he was ordained and became the first African pastor of the Mennonite Brethren Church in Zaire. In addition he was also involved in reducing his language to writing and translating the Scriptures.

In 1960 he became vice-chairman of the Église du Christ au Zaire, Communauté des Églises de Frères Mennonites au Zaire, (Mennonite Brethren Church of Zaire) and a leader in the Reference and Counsel Committee. During the civil unrest of 1964-65 he and his wife had to hide in the forests, and he barely escaped execution. He has continued as pastor of the church at Kafumba and, even in 1987, although almost blind, he continues to give strength and encouragement to the church he helped found 60 years earlier.   ILF

Foreign Missions—Africa (Hillsboro, Ks.: MB Board of Foreign Missions, 1947, 28-30; B. Burkholder, ed., *They Saw His Glory* (Winnipeg and Hillsboro: Kindred Press, 1984), 39-43; J. B. Toews, *The Mennonite Brethren Church in Zaire,* (Fresno: MB Board of Christian Literature, 1978), 145-48, 225.

Djojodihardjo. See Sardjoe Djojodihardjo.

Djoko Punda. See Zaire.

Dlodlo, Ndabenduku (d. 1975), churchman, was the son of a Lindebele chief under the renowned Matabele King Lobengula. His first contact with Brethren in Christ work was at the Mapane outstation church and school. He became a Christian (1909) and was baptized in 1911 by Bishop Henry °Steigerwald. He began outstation work as an assistant in 1916 at Mapane and later at Suzana Mine.

He married Zihlatshana Magutshwa from Nsezi. The Lord blessed them with seven children. In 1919 Dlodlo moved to Nsezi where he ministered as pastor-teacher until 1930. Also in that year he was appointed an overseer. In this role he provided leadership for the Brethren in Christ Matopo District. He was ordained to the ministry in 1944. His work was characterized by integrity and total commitment; in his preaching he pointed out the dangers of sin and called for high standards of Christian living.   AMC/REP

Anna Engle, Leoda A. Buckwalter, and J. A. Climenhaga, *There Is No Difference* (Nappanee, 1950); "Introduction of African Natives Overseas," *EV* (June 28, 1948).

Doering, Alma (Apr. 18, 1878–July 12, 1959), an early leader in the °°Congo Inland Mission (later known as the Africa Inter-Mennonite Mission), was born in Chicago, Ill. Her parents were German Lutheran immigrants; her father's name was William. She attended Moody Bible Institute in Chicago and became a deaconess from the Bethany Deaconess Home in Brooklyn, N.Y. She began her missionary work 1898, as she later wrote, "in Chicago, the frontier back wood, mining districts and Indian reservations of the Lake Superior region."

Her foreign missionary career included service in the Belgian Congo (1900-1904) among the Bafioti people under the Swedish Missionary Society; in British East Africa among the Bantu (1906-10) under the Africa Inland Mission (which was supported by the °°Central Conference Mennonite Church and Defenseless Mennonites [Evangelical Mennonite Church]); and in the Belgian Congo under the Congo Inland Mission (1911-25) and the Unevangelized Tribes Mission (UTM), which she founded (1925-53). Her work for the Congo Inland Mission included fundraising and missionary recruitment in North America (1910-12, 1919-23) and in Europe (1912-19), as well as field work at the Mukedi station among the Bampendi people, 1923-25. Early in her career she received the Bantu name "Malembe," meaning "peace."

In 1905 Alma Doering addressed annual sessions of both the Central Conference Mennonite Church (which later became part of the Central District [GCM]) and the Defenseless Mennonite Church (later known as the Evangelical Mennonite Church), encouraging mission work under Mennonite sponsorship. In 1910 she began promoting independent Mennonite missions in Africa jointly sponsored by the Defenseless and Central Conference Mennonites. She resigned from the Congo Inland Mission after conflict with the governing board concerning the goals and identity of the mission. In 1955 she founded a vacation and retirement center for missionaries in St. Petersburg, Fla. Her writings include pamphlets and articles setting forth her missions philosophy. Central to her missions philosophy was the idea of a self-propagating church in the Congo.   SRE

Menn. Bib. II, p. 434; Alma E. Doering, *Leopard Spots or God's Masterpiece Which?* (Cleveland: "Malembe" Publisher, 1916), 3-14; Juhnke, *Mission* (1979), 67-70; William B. Weaver, *Thirty-Five Years in the Congo* (Chicago: Congo Inland Mission, 1945), 70-76, 79, 96-97, 103, 117-18, 171, 189, 207; idem, *History of the Central Conference Mennonite Church* (Danvers, Ill.: author, 1926), 163-66; Cecilia Irvine,

comp., *The Church of Christ in Zaire: A Handbook of Protestant Churches, Missions and Communities, 1878-1978* (Indianapolis: author, 1978), 70, 105-106, 107-108.

See also Africa Inter-Mennonite Mission; Congo Inland Mission.

Dominican Republic. See Conferencia de las Iglesias Evangélicas Menonitas, Dominican Republic (Evangelical Mennonite Church).

Doopsgezinde Vredesgroep (Mennonite Peace Association) (ME II:88). There is a significant increase in conscientious objection to military service in The Netherlands. This is correlated with the "church and peace" movement, a branch of the Dutch International Fellowship of Reconciliation (IFOR). Since 1980 the emphasis of the peace group has moved into the center of congregational life. This was caused, in part, by the increasing polarization of opinion surrounding the placing of atomic weapons in The Netherlands. The Algemene Doopsgezinde Sociëteit (ADS; Dutch Mennonite general conference) joined the Interkerkelijke Vredesberaad (IKV; Inter-Church Peace Council), which launched a campaign against placing of Cruise Missiles in The Netherlands in 1977. Literature to this end was also distributed by the ADS. *De Vredesbrief* (The Peace Letter), which had been published since 1967 by the peace group, was now placed as an insert in the Mennonite weekly paper (ADW), which enlarged the readership but also led to polarization and increasing polemics about the relationship of faith and politics.

Contacts are also maintained with those who refuse to pay °taxes for defense, as well as with other Mennonite and interconfessional groups both in Europe and elsewhere, e.g., Eirene and Church and Peace. In The Netherlands the peace group is part of the united committee to this end.   LLau

40 jaar Dopers en Dwars (published by Doopsgezinde Vredesgroep, 1986).

See also Peace Education; Peace Activism; Samenwerkingsverband van "de vier Instellingen" in de Doopsgezinde Broederschap.

Doopsgezinde Zendingsraad (Doopsgezinde Vereniging tot Evangelie-Verbreiding [Mennonite Mission Board (Mennonite Association for Evangelization)]) (ME II:113, IV:1024). The Doopsgezinde Vereniging tot Evangelie-Verbreiding joined the Algemene Doopsgezinde Sociëteit (ADS; Dutch Mennonite general conference) in 1957 to found the Doopsgezinde Zendingsraad (DZR). Members are named by the ADS, except one who represents the evangelism agency itself. Administrative reasons made the founding of this joint venture desirable.

Considerations influencing the forming of this mission agency were primarily the growing belief that mission is the calling of the entire brotherhood and every congregation, not simply that of certain individuals and friends of mission. The DZR is now the organ through which this concern can find expression. There was also increasing interest abroad, in Java, for broader contact between the Mennonite congregations there and in The Netherlands beyond that provided by mission personnel. A special publication was also requested. The issue was the desire for broader contacts of Dutch congregational members with mission congregation members. This has been realized in the fact that the ADS now supports this work financially rather than having the DZR find the necessary funds alone.

Nevertheless, while there is not one official mission organ the average congregation is still not really aware of the work being done and needing to be done. It is clear that mission also includes °peace and °development work as part of the total program.

The entire work of mission is coordinated by the inter-Mennonite European agency °Europäisches Mennonitisches Evangelisationskomitee (EMEK), in which DZR is responsible for contacts with Java. Special Dutch Mennonite projects have included the work of Roelf S. Kuitse in the ecumenical "Islam in Africa" project (1962-69), the sending of Frits °Kuiper as professor to the seminary in Montevideo, Uruguay (1964-67), and the moral support being given to the pioneer evangelism efforts in Australia. Still, in light of the mission needs on six continents, the DZR has increasingly seen the need for mission also in The Netherlands.

The publication of a separate paper *Evangelieverbreiding* (Spreading the Gospel) has been terminated and no annual mission reports have been published since 1969. In their place periodic general reports have been published in 1973, 1979, 1982, and 1985. LLau

Theodorus Erik Jensma, *Doopsgezinde Zending in Indonesië* ('s Gravenhage: Boekcentrum N.V., 1968); W. F. Golterman, *Tot alle volken* (DZR, 1959); L. Laurense, A. G. Hoekema, L. Koopmans, *Verder in het spoor van de Geest* (DZR, 1982); idem, *Doopsgezinde zending, toen, nu, straks* (DZR, 1983); L. Laurense, *Werven of sterven* (ADS, 1985), dealing with evangelization in Dutch Mennonite congregations.

Doornkaat Koolman, Jacobus ten (1889-1978). Born in Hamburg, Doornkaat-Koolman studied theology in Germany and, from 1911 to 1915, at the Amsterdam Mennonite Theological Seminary. Following graduation he served as a hospital chaplain in Solingen, Germany. Health reasons forced him to move to Davos, Switzerland, in 1919. In this, his second homeland, he served as pastor from 1920 in Schanfigg, Davos, and Otelfingen. From 1943 to 1954 he was the first full-time chaplain of the hospitals in the canton of Zürich.

He published numerous historical articles on Anabaptism in Amsterdam, East Friesland, and Zürich, and wrote the monograph, *Dirk Philips: Vriend en medewerker van Menno Simons, 1504-1568* (Haarlem: H. D. Tjeenk Willink, 1964). SV

C. F. Brüsewitz in *Doops. Bijdr.*, n.r. 5 (1979), 119-20 (includes bibliography).

Douglas, Maude Ethel (October 20, 1897–June 23, 1986), was born to George and Oda Dickerson at Coffeyville, Ks. Her first husband, John Brooke died of influenza during World War I. In 1922 she married Ed Buckingham. He died at the Mennonite Sanitorium, La Junta, Col., where Maude became acquainted with and joined the Mennonite Church (MC). She took her high school training at Hesston Academy, Hesston, Ks., and nurse's training at the Mennonite Hospital in La Junta, Col.

In 1932 Maude moved to Culp, Ark., with her third husband, John A. Douglas. There she pioneered in Sunday schools and practiced nursing and midwifery without physician support and in primitive conditions. Due to her efforts other Mennonites came to Culp and ministries in health care, education, and congregational life resulted. John A. Douglas died in 1956. After 1963 Maude served for 11 years at the Calico Rock, Ark., Medical Clinic and 3 years at White River Convalescent Home. She is buried in the Mennonite cemetery, Calico Rock, Ark. RSa

MWR (July 24, 1986), 11; Theron F. Schlabach, *Gospel Versus Gospel* (Scottdale, 1980), 122; Paul Erb, *South Central Frontiers* (Scottdale, 1974), 414-20; Linden M. Wenger, "A Study of Rural Missions in the Mennonite Church" (ThM thesis, Union Theological Seminary, Richmond, Va., 1955), 199-204.

Douglas-Moultrie Counties, IL, Old Order Amish Settlement. See Arthur, IL, Old Order Amish Settlement.

Dover, Del., Old Order Amish Settlement (ME III:166) was founded in 1915 by families from Virginia, Ohio, and Pennsylvania. Later migrations to the Dover area (Kent Co.) came from western Amish communities in Kansas, the Dakotas, and elsewhere. The Dover-Hartley community thus has many Amish who migrated west and then returned to the East Coast. Growth has been slow but steady. Many families moved away seeking "greener pastures" or affiliated with area Beachy Amish Mennonite and conservative Mennonite churches. Amish farms along the Hartley-Dover road are limited in growth opportunities because of industrial expansion. Farmers have grown primarily vegetables and produce for urban markets (truck farming). However, more recently, this community has moved into wheat and corn growing. Many heads of households, for economic reason, have established small shops or taken up furniture-making and -repair businesses. The Dover settlement was the first Amish community to establish a formal parochial school (°private Christian schools). Apple Grove School for grades one through eight was founded in 1925. By 1984 the community had grown to eight congregations with more than 1,300 people. SLY

Dozy, Jan Dionijs (Apr. 25, 1892 - July 30, 1965), married Henriette I. C. de Stoppelaar and served first as Mennonite pastor in West-Terschelling (1922-26), Leeuwarden (1926-33), and Amsterdam (1933-56). In 1933 he earned a doctor of theology degree. He became a member of the executive committee of the Algemene Doopsgezinde Sociëteit (Dutch Mennonite general conference), of which he was for a time vice-chairman. He was curator of the Amsterdam Mennonite Theological Seminary. His particular additional interest and service was in interchurch ecumenical relationships. RHof

J. D. Dozy, "Het feminisme als zedelijk vraagstuk" (diss., Amsterdam, 1933); *Naar de diepste werkelijkheid* (Amsterdam, 1938); *Wijsheid der dwazen* (Amsterdam, 1958); *Het ambt van Christus*, coauthored with E. L. Smelik en J. Koopmans (The Hague, 1942); articles *Woord en Daad* and in *Doops. Jaar.*; on Dozy see the memorial article in *Doops. Jaar.* (1966), 13-14.

Draft Resistance. See Conscientious Objection; Conscription; Peace; Sociopolitical Activism.

Dramatic Arts. After three centuries of near silence, dramatic works and theatrical enterprises among Mennonites have flourished in the 20th c. Mennonite playwrights have written on a diversity of subjects in a variety of dramatic styles. Commercially successful plays have been written about the Anabaptist and Mennonite experience, and Mennonites have ventured into theater education and theatrical professions. Prior to this century, Mennonites with an interest in drama would participate in folk dramas (recitations and games at weddings and holidays) or they might affiliate with and become advocates for other religious traditions (Joost van den °°Vondel).

The biblical play has been of recurring interest to Mennonite playwrights. In general, these scripts have offered reflections on the ethical questions presented in the biblical account. Some explore the biblical "commandment" motif vis-a-vis morals and °discipleship, while others investigate the ambiguities contained in the narratives and parables.

Peter N. Hiebert, *One and Two-Act Plays for Christmas* (1944), includes "Salvation is at Calvary" and "The Wise Men Seeking the Christ." Warren Kliewer has written "In the Beginning Was Eve" in *Azazel* (May 1966), "The Prodigal Son" in *Moralities and Miracles*, "Seventy Times Seven" in *Religion Theatre* (1977), and "The Wrestler." Urie Bender's *To Walk in the Way* (Scottdale, 1978) is a series of episodes based on the Gospel of Mark. Lauren Friesen has written "Abraham and Isaac" in *Faith and Art Magazine* (1972); *King David* (Pinchpenny Press, 1984, MA thesis); and "The Eagle and the Dove," a PhD dissertation on the writing of the fourth Gospel. Earl Reimer also focuses on Old Testament themes with *Ten Miles to Jericho* (Samuel French, 1978) and *Joseph* (Grand Rapids: Baker, 1987). John W. Miller authored *God's Search for Man* and *Judgment and Hope* (Newton, 1972) which contain short plays based on the Old Testament. *The Bible Speaks* (1974) is a one-act drama by William Gering that articulates a salvation history hermeneutic.

The earliest reference to an Anabaptist and Mennonite in drama is in Ben Jonson's *The Alchemist* (1610). The Anabaptist preacher in this play is a fiery orator with a strong moralistic and anti-intellectual flavor.

Mennonite history and other historical subjects have captured the attention of Mennonite playwrights. Plays have frequently been commissioned to celebrate historical events. Ruth Unrau wrote *Large Idea for a Small College* (1952) for Bethel College's 75th anniversary and for the 100th festival, Lauren Friesen penned *House of God* (1987). Urie Bender's *Tomorrow has Roots* (1974) was produced by Bethel College for the centennial of the coming of Mennonites to Kansas from Russia. Bender has also written historical dramas for the anniversary of Zürich Anabaptism (1525/1975), an untitled play about Conrad °Grebel, and *This Land Is Ours*, for the 150th anniversary of Amish immigration to Ontario. *Chasing the Wind* (1974), a musical by Lyle Preheim and Lauren Friesen was produced for General Conference Mennonite Church sessions.

Goshen College produced Caesar van Arx's play about the Swiss Anabaptist, *Brothers in Christ* (1962). The Mennonite World Conference commissioned Merle Good to write *These People Mine* (1972) and Robert Hostetter to write *Cheyenne Jesus Buffalo Dream* (1978). *We are Pilgrims* (1960) by Maynard Shelly reviewed Anabaptist history for the General Conference Mennonite Church sessions.

Historical plays have been written for purposes other than institutional festivals or anniversaries. Many of these plays are "thesis" plays in that they address an ecclesiastical, ethical, or theological problem and present a solution. Jack Braun's *The Anne Barkman Story* (1974) focuses on the Russian Mennonite migration in the 20th c. James Juhnke and J. Harold Moyer of Bethel College collaborated on *Blowing and Bending* (1975), a historical play on the crises of conscience among Mennonites in Kansas. John Ruth's *Twilight Auction* (1966) examines the issues which ensue when a Mennonite Harvard student brings home a friend who is uninformed about Mennonite practices. Lucille Kreider's *The Friendly Way* (1961) explores the theme of °peace. William Gering's *I Must Go* (1961) examines a young man's response to the draft. Cornelia Lehn's *The Bridge* (n.d.) also explores peace themes. Diana Brandt and Esther Wiebe's *The Bridge* (1974) portrayed a Mennonite community's response to a German Mennonite's decision to marry an Englishman. *Confessions of an Anabaptist Ringleader* (1975) by Leland Harder is a one-character play on Conrad Grebel. Esther Wiens has written *Sanctuary* (1986) about the plight of Latin American refugees.

Playwrights with little immediate experience with Mennonite heritage have written commercially successful plays, musicals, and an opera on Mennonite themes. Giacomo Meyerbeer composed *Le Prophete*, an opera in five acts (1880). The Swiss playwright, Frederich Dürrenmatt, wrote *Es Steht Geschrieben* (1943), then revised and retitled it as *Die Wiedertäufer* (1968). The play explores the °Münster Anabaptists' rebellion of the 1530s, and hints at that episode as a "foreshadowing analogy" to Germany of the Third Reich, namely, that which was anathema to German culture in the 1530s (Münster) became its national identity in the 1930s. Georges Rousseau's *Le Drama Anabaptists*, also about the Münsterites, was produced in the 1950s.

Comedies and farces by Mennonite playwrights have been produced with some regularity. Yet, the comedy form has been explored by very few Mennonite writers. Arnold Dyck's farces, *Dee Fria: Plattdeutsches Lustspiel, Onse Lied en ola Tiet,* and *De Opnaom* (1940s), continue to entertain Low German communities. Marie Regier's one-act *But Mother* (1940) was the first English-language comedy by a Mennonite. Other comedies include Warren Kliewer's *A Bird in the Bush* (1962), *Round the Cherry Tree* (1962), *A Trial Can be Fun if You're the Judge* (1967), *Half Horse, Half Cockeyed Alligator, How Can You Tell the Good Guys from the Bad Guys* (1975), and *Madame Cleo Here, at Your Service* (1970). I. Merle Good pursued the comic form with some of his plays: *Isaac Gets a Wife, A lot of Love, Sons Like Their Fathers,* and *Today Pop Comes Home* were produced by Good Enterprises.

Commercially successful comedies about Mennonites and Amish include: Patterson Green's *Papa is All* (1942) and John Rengier's, *By Hex* (1953), which makes the "hex" into a social ritual which determines the fate of many community members. Joseph Stein and William Glickman collaborated on the Broadway musical, *Plain and Fancy* (1954), which is a revelry in song and dance.

The tragic form has received even less attention. Warren Kliewer's *The Berserkers* (1975) and Anne Chislett's *Quiet in the Land* (1983) are the best examples of this form. The latter work, by a Canadian dramatist, portrays the personal and community pain in shunning a member for choosing military service and thereby threatening to compromise the °nonresistance principle. It received the Governor General's Literary Award in 1983 and was produced by the Manitoba Theatre Centre and the Blythe Festival (Ontario).

The form of dramatic realism—theater as reflection of life—is also nearly absent from Mennonite writing. This genre requires a trust in the ability of the story to contain meaning. Frequently, the attempts to write in this form have resulted in an emphasis on the rhetorical and didactic. The examples which overcome this tendency and stand as valid realistic dramas include: Warren Kliewer's *Sacrifice to Virtue* (1970) and *This Stubborn Soil* (1973); I. Merle Good's *Strangers at the Mill* (1969) and *Who Burned the Barn Down?* (1970); and Rudy Wiebe's *As Far as the Eye Can See* (1977). The last line of Wiebe's play illustrates the "slice of life" intent of realism plays, "We have listened to you, and we have understood you. Thank you."

Theatrical expression began on Mennonite college campuses shortly after their doors opened. At Bethel College (Kansas) there were recitations, skits, and pantomimes performed at the weekly °°literary society meetings in the 1890s. Theatrical productions began in the 1940s. At Goshen College, the literary societies sponsored play readings and performances shortly after the founding of the college, and full productions of plays, under the direction of Roy Umble, began in 1954 upon the completion of an auditorium in the Union Building. Fresno Pacific College has a unique outdoor amphitheater. All Mennonite colleges in North America now offer theater seasons.

The General Conference Mennonite Church and Mennonite Central Committee have both sponsored playwriting and producing "teams." A drama project in the 1970s produced nine one-act plays and skits for worship: *Thanksgiving; Twelve Becoming; Changing Faces, Say It, Amos; Peter's Denial; At Desert's Edge; Zacchaeus; The Prodigal Son;* and *Job*. A touring drama project in the 1980s, sponsored by MCC, developed skits which focused on Christian service and global awareness themes. They were published in one volume as *Learning as We Go*.

Professional theater artists with Mennonite roots emerged in the 1960s. Karl Eigsti, a set designer in New York, acknowledges his Mennonite heritage and its influence on his life (cf. Arnold Aronson, *American Set Design*. New York: Theatre Communications Group, 1985, p. 39). The 1987 Stratford Theatre

Festival season (Ontario) included the production of *Intimate Admiration* by Rick Epp. In Secaucus, N.J., Warren Kliewer has been director and playwright for the East Lynne Company, a residential and touring troupe. His recent productions include: *The Politician Outwitted* and *The Yellow Wallpaper*.

Professional theater companies have been founded in four geographical locations. In the early 1970s, I. Merle Good was the manager of Good Enterprises, Inc., which produced plays in summer stock near Lancaster, Pa. During the 1980s three companies emerged: The Mennonite Repertory Theatre in Winnipeg, Man.; a theater troupe in Brussels, Belgium, organized by Stephen Shenk, which produced, among other works, *Savonarola*; and in Goshen, Ind., Bridgework Theater, Inc. began to produce plays about sexual abuse, °drug abuse, and spouse abuse.

Two master theses on Mennonites and drama have been written: William Gering, "Mennonite Attitudes Toward Theatrical Enterprises" (Indiana U., 1961); and Jack Braun, "Mennonite Plays and Playwrights and the Mennonite Theme in Dramatic Literature in the United States" (U. of Kansas, 1968). 						LF

See also Literature; Literature, Mennonites in; Motion Pictures.

Dress (ME II:99). In the 1980s more than 120,000 people belong to Anabaptist- and Mennonite-related groups in North and South America who require a distinctive style of dress for their members. There are also about 7,000 members of Brethren (i.e., Church of the Brethren, or Dunker) groups and a small remnant of Friends (Quakers) who wear plain garb. The °°Apostolic Christian Church continues to observe definite dress requirements both in North America and Europe.

Two distinctive dress features shared by most plain groups of Swiss Mennonite background are the plain coat and the cape dress. The plain coat has a standing collar and no lapels. The frock version of this coat has a split tail and usually no outside pockets. The cape on women's dresses covers the front and back of the bodice. The older style comes to a point in the back. This item is derived from the three-cornered kerchief.

By far the largest and most conservative group that maintains plain is the Old Order Amish church. Amish distinctives for men include: beards, hair cut off straight in the back and banged in front, widebrimmed hats, suit coats and vest fastening with hooks and eyes, suspenders, and broadfall pants. Amish women customarily wear a headcovering with tie strings, uncut hair parted in the center and worn in a bun, a long dress with a pleated or gathered skirt, a cape, an apron, and black shoes and stockings. °°Bonnets and shawls are the approved outdoor garments. The Old Order Amish insist that all clothing be made of fabrics in solid colors and that there be no outside pockets on most clothing. Wrist watches are not allowed. There are many minor variations in dress among the different Amish communities. The "Nebraska" Amish of central Pennsylvania and the Swartzentruber Amish centered in Ohio are the most conservative.

The Beachy Amish Mennonite Fellowship continue to require beards for men and hooks and eyes for suit coats. Hats are seldom worn and broadfall pants and suspenders are no longer required in many congregations. Beachy Amish women wear tie strings on their head coverings and capes on their dresses but aprons are often omitted. The Kauffman Amish Mennonites (°°Sleeping Preacher Amish) are similar to the Beachy Amish in dress although in some respects more conservative (the men wear longer beards) but in others more liberal (lapel coats with buttons are worn).

The Old Order Mennonites (buggy groups) have dress standards similar to those of the Amish. In contrast to the Amish the men have very short hair and do not grow beards. Plain frock coats with buttons and vests with standing collars are standard for adult men in most churches. Women's dresses are typically made of printed fabric. The Pike or Stauffer Mennonite groups are the most conservative Old Order Mennonites. Men in these groups have longer hair and wider hat brims than other Old Order Mennonites.

Reformed Mennonite women traditionally dress in gray, including a large gray bonnet. The dress has a peplum on the bodice, a three-cornered cape, and an apron. Men are clean shaven, wear a plain frock coat, a plain hat, and a small black bow tie.

In reaction to the abandonment of plain dress in the Mennonite Church (MC) since the 1950s many groups have left the various Mennonite Church conferences to form independent groups and numerous unaffiliated churches. The Eastern Pennsylvania Mennonite Church, Fellowship Churches, Midwest Mennonite Fellowship, Mid-Atlantic Mennonite Fellowship, the Southeastern Mennonite Conference, and the Washington-Franklin Mennonite Conference are the largest groups in this °conservative Mennonite movement. The dress standards in these groups require plain coats for men and forbid neckties. Women are to wear cape dresses, headcoverings, uncut hair pinned up, and black stockings. Bonnets are frequently worn in some groups. Old Order Mennonites who permit automobiles dress similarly to the conservative Mennonites who recently withdrew from the Mennonite Church (MC).

Plain clothing has declined rapidly in the Mennonite Church (MC) since the 1950s. West of the Allegheny Mountains dress regulations were abandoned earlier than in the East. In many congregations few, if any, women wear head coverings and no other distinctive dress is practiced. In the East the majority of Mennonite Church (MC) congregations dropped most dress regulations in the 1960s and 1970s. Many people born before the 1940s continue to observe the old standards. Many ministers in the East still wear the plain coat although this is no longer mandatory.

A small minority of congregations in the Mennonite Church (MC) continue to prohibit women from cutting their hair and wearing slacks, shorts, and makeup. These churches also insist that the head covering (°prayer veil) be worn consistently in public and that no jewelry be worn, including wedding bands. Plain coats and cape dresses are numerous but not obligatory. Some of the conservative congregations belonging to the Lancaster Conference (MC), where conservative congregations are most numerous within the Mennonite Church, organized the Keystone Mennonite Fellowship in 1987.

There has always been a diversity of dress practices in the Conservative Mennonite Conference (MC). Since the 1950s nearly all the congregations that require the plain coat and cape dress have withdrawn from the Conservative Mennonite Conference. In the 1980s some churches that no longer require plain coats or cape dresses still do prohibit neckties and jewelry and do not allow women to cut their hair or go without a covering in public.

The Brethren in Christ had also emphasized plain dress for most of their history. During the first half of the 20th c. men typically wore plain coats and hats and often beards. Women appeared in headcoverings, bonnets, and cape dresses. Plain clothing became part of the written discipline of the group in the 1930s. Beginning in the 1950s pressure to enter the evangelical mainstream caused rapid abandonment of plain clothing. By the 1970s very few Brethren in Christ wore distinctive garb. The same is true of the related United Zion Church.

The Old Order River Brethren continue to wear traditional garb. Men wear long beards and cut their hair straight off in back. Plain frock coats and widebrimmed hats are part of the attire. Women wear opaque white headcoverings, capes, aprons, and a peplum on the dress bodice.   SES

Following World War II, but with increasing rapidity in the 1960s dress patterns changed in such groups as the Mennonite Church (MC) and Brethren in Christ which had had dress requirements. Many factors contributed to these developments: movement from rural to urban vocations; higher education; inroads of radio, television, and mass media, relaxing structures of traditional authority; and varied other forms of enveloping modernity.

In a time of transition and uneven resistance to change, dress regulations became a frequent and absorbing topic of discussion in family and congregational circles, evoking varying levels of concern and conflict. In the 1960s and 1970s a gradually increasing number of ministers and church leaders began appearing in public without the traditional ministerial garb.

The past generation of dress transition in the Mennonite (MC) and Brethren in Christ churches merits further study, particularly focusing on the following issues: (1) for groups with dress requirements comparison of rules for men and women; (2) women's perceptions on dress issues; (3) case studies in shifting dress patterns in particular congregations and church districts—including the role of open candid discussion and silent behavioral change; (4) case studies of individuals experiencing changing restrictions in dress; (5) comparative dress restrictions in other groups, e.g., Free Methodists, *Umsiedler* (emigrants) from Russia.   RK

Stephen Scott, *Why Do They Dress that Way?* (Intercourse, Pa.: Good Books, 1986); Melvin Gingerich, *Mennonite Attire Through Four Centuries* (Breinigsville, Pa.: Pennsylvania German Society, 1970); *Brethren Encyclopedia* (1983), 399-404; Wittlinger, *Piety and Obedience* (1978), 481-87.

See also Eastern Pennsylvania Mennonite Church; Folklore; Hutterian Brethren; Nonconformity; Old

Colony Mennonites; Simple Living; Luz y Esperanza Colony, Paraguay; Rio Verde Colony; Upper Barton Creek Colony, Belize.

Drug Dependency occurs with a great variety of drugs, including alcohol. The generic term is chemical dependency and includes all forms of addiction or dependency on any mood-changing substance.

What is drug dependency? It is any use, misuse or abuse of chemicals in such a way that it interferes with or causes problems in the person's social, family, personal, or spiritual life. The medical profession considers this form of dependency an illness which is characterized as follows: it is (1) chronic, i.e. it is lifelong; (2) progressive, i.e. it worsens over time; (3) insidious, i.e. the individual is frequently not aware of its occurrence; (4) incurable, i.e. abstinence is the only solution; and (5) it is ultimately fatal. Basic psychological effects are severe guilt, remorse, shame, isolation, anxiety, and panic.

Signs of dependency are many but two are outstanding: First, preoccupation with sedative effects, which is an emotional response to the drug-created effects within the individual. An initial euphoric response induces feelings of well-being and elation, which is subjective in nature and experienced as profound by the user. Recurrent preoccupation with future experience of elation or "getting high," is a first symptom and ultimate hallmark of drug dependence.

The second hallmark of drug dependence is loss of control which is present when someone uses sedative drugs against his own will, or when someone cannot entirely limit the amount she may consume once intake begins. The individual is frequently not aware of loss of control, which is identified over time as the user encounters an infinite variety of dependency complications. Sedative drugs and their effects become a refuge or a form of escape from the tensions created by drug use. An elaborate system of justification follows in which the individuals will rationalize, project, or deny drug use.

Drug dependence is cultural as well as personal. Social permissiveness and the availability of prescription drugs for medicinal purposes as well as recreational uses of alcohol and other nonprescription drugs are pervasive. Compounding these facts is the intensification of advertising about the medicinal and recreational uses of chemicals, upholding them as helpful or recreational and harmless. Understanding dependency requires understanding a cultural background from which such use arises. Drug use is a cultural and social problem and not just an individual matter.

Historically Mennonites displayed varied and mixed attitudes and practices towards the use of °°alcohol. Currently the use of alcohol and other sedatives is receiving renewed attention among Mennonites. An example is Daniel L. Haarer, *The Church's Attitudes toward Alcohol* (1984).

Biblical texts do not resolve the issue of drug and alcohol use. The Bible speaks clearly against drunkenness, while supporting moderate and culturally appropriate consumption or use. Drug and alcohol use at both the personal and cultural level raises issues to be debated and decided by con-

temporary Mennonites, who are indeed united in opposition to drunkenness and chemical dependency. The elusive and conflictual issue is that of moderate, controlled use of alcohol and of sedative, prescription, and nonprescription drugs.

Theologically, chemical dependency can be understood as a fundamental dislocation of the divine-human relationship. The essential ingredient in the theologically proper relationship between human beings and God is that humans understand and accept their dependence for creation and sustenance upon God alone. Chemical dependency, as other compulsive attachments, is a fundamental violation of the First Commandment: "Thou shalt have no other Gods before me." From this central sin and estrangement from God other multiple "sins" develop as relationships are violated and suffer. Addressing misdirected dependencies is the central and perennial mission of the church of Jesus Christ.

In addition to work with dependency, education, preventive measures, and standards of use also command the attention of the church. Christians have a moral obligation to provide an atmosphere and experience in which the fruits of the Holy Spirit are sufficiently evident to serve as effective alternatives to the fruit of the vine. Chemically dependent persons often describe in part their motivation to consume in terms of obtaining experiences that seem to parallel the apostle Paul's description of the "fruits of the Holy Spirit." Chemical dependency as a compulsive illness can be confronted by attractive alternatives. The choice to use or abstain must be made by individuals while retaining an awareness that drug use is a social and cultural matter that calls for the witness of the church.   FASchr/JKH

Daniel L. Haarer, *The Church's Attitudes toward Alcohol* (Newton and Scottdale, 1984); Kauffman/Harder, *Anabaptists Four C. Later* (1975), 123-29; F. H. Epp, *Mennonites in Canada 1*, pp. 86-87.

See also Friedensheim.

Dube, Nyamazana (d. 1957), churchman, was one of the earliest converts and outschool teachers in the African Brethren in Christ Church. He also was one of the first three African members to be chosen overseer (1921). He was baptized by Bishop Henry °Steigerwald in 1902 and in 1905 he began to serve as an outstation worker, teaching in a village a few miles from the Brethren in Christ Matopo center. In 1916 Dube worked with Manhlenhle Kukmalo in starting the church and school at Swazi. A few years later he was appointed overseer for the Mtshabezi District. In 1921 he married Siyanagi (Naka Danyeli) Nzima; after her death he married Jessie Ndhlovu from Mtshabezi. On July 23, 1944, he was ordained to the ministry of the African Brethren in Christ Church, and served faithfully until his death.   AMC/REP

Anna Engle, Leoda A. Buckwalter, and J. G. Climenhaga, *There is No Difference* (Nappanee, 1950); "Introduction of African Native Overseers," *EV* (June 28, 1948).

Dulaurin Bai (ca. 1888–ca. 1971), a first-generation Christian in the Mennonite Church (MC) in India, a nurse, and a longtime member of the Zion Mennonite Church at Sankra, was born into a Hindu family of the oil-crusher caste. While still a Hindu she married, but her home broke up in tragedy when, after two stillborn children, she was considered to be demon-possessed and was beaten and driven from home. She found shelter and work in the home of missionary physician Florence Cooprider [°Friesen], ca. 1920 at °Dhamtari. When Cooprider married Peter A. Friesen, Dulaurin Bai moved to Sankra to work in the Friesen home. In 1931 she began nurse-midwife training at a mission hospital in Katni. Returning in 1933 she worked with Friesen in the Sankra hospital and on the roadside leprosy clinics until 1941. Dulaurin Bai was a relentless worker. She was a humble woman with a strong will who never forgot the depth of desperation from which she had been lifted. In 1940 she adopted an orphaned baby and named him Lakhan. Her two grandchildren are graduate nurses (1987) and serve in the name of Christ. JAF

Durango (Nuevo Ideál) Colony, Mexico (ME II: 109). The first 90 families of the Durango Colony arrived from Saskatchewan, Canada, in 1924, because they had been deprived of their privileges in operating their private schools. They settled near the town of Patos, now called Nuevo Ideál. Bishop Jacob Wiens and ministers Johann Wall, Peter Wiens, Peter Klassen and Frank Harder, as well as *Vorsteher* (Chairman) Benjamin Goertzen, who had also been one of the delegates who looked for land, were the early leaders of the colony.

This colony was able to buy some land that was adjacent to the colony in the 1930s and 1940s on which more villages belonging to the Nuevo Ideál colony were established. After 1944 this colony began to look to other states for land for their rapidly growing colony. In 1987 Nuevo Ideál has daughter colonies in °Zacatecas State and °Campeche State.

In the 1950s Mennonite Brethren established a clinic in the town of Nuevo Ideál which served the Mennonites but made no attempt at church planting among the old Colonists. Mennonite Brethren did, however, conduct services in Spanish for the local people of Nuevo Ideál. This attracted some Mennonites eventually. By 1973 a group of Old Colony Mennonites invited the Mennonite Brethren to start a congregation using the German language. Thus a school and church were begun, which in 1985 became affiliated with the Evangelical Mennonite Mission Conference of Canada. Neither school nor church have drawn heavily from the Old Colonists for their membership.

The Durango colony has 25 schools with as many teachers. Worship services in High and Low German are held at 5 different meetinghouses. Approximately 800 people attend on Sunday mornings and on church holidays. In December 1986 the colony counted 5,503 inhabitants, with 1,838 being baptized members. Mixed farming is the main occupation. The 24 cheese factories in the colony receive ca. 60,000 liters (16,000 US gallons) of milk daily. The colony also has factories and shops where implements, buggies, windmills, etc. are built and repaired. HEns.

MWH (1978), 277-78; *MWR* (Mar. 14, 1985), 2.

See also Old Colony Mennonites; Mexico.

Durango Colony, Paraguay, was founded 1978 by German-speaking Mennonites from Mexico. On arrival they purchased 13,400 hectares (33,000 acres), only to discover that some of the land had been sold twice. This led to serious tensions and uncertainties which have not yet been resolved (1986). It appears, however, that the colony will continue. Nineteen villages have been established with 1,921 inhabitants, of whom 649 are members of the Old Colony Mennonite church.

The economic situation is very difficult. Soybeans and wheat are the primary crops, but dairy, poultry and hog farming are also included. A cooperative arrangement has been entered into by the settlers to provide a sounder economic base and the securing of loans.

The Mennonites in Durango are the most conservative Mennonites in Paraguay. Tractors with rubber tires are not permitted since they could facilitate contact with the "world." The settlement is located 310 km. (190 mi.) se. of Asunción. GR

MWH (1984), 101.

Durlach. See Karlsruhe.

Dürksen, Heinrich (b. May 31, 1910). Born in the °°Terek region of the Caucausus of Russia to Johann and Katharina Heinrichs Duerksen, Heinrich Dürksen spent his youth in the village of Menlertschik, Crimea, where in 1928 he was baptized upon confession of faith in 1928. In 1929 he and his family fled to Kiel, Germany. From there they emigrated to the °°Chaco of Paraguay, arriving in 1930. The family located in the village of Schonwiese, Fernheim Colony. Heinrich was elected a minister in the Mennonite church (GCM). On Oct. 25, 1932, he married Sara Kröker. They became the parents of 10 children.

From 1941 to 1944 Heinrich served as administrator of the mission station Yalve Sanga (°Licht den Indianern). In 1946 he was elected to the administrative council of Fernheim Colony; in 1949 he became °°Oberschulze (executive officer) for the colony. He served in the latter capacity for 20 years, 1949-57, 1962-70, and 1977-79. In 1953 Duerksen traveled to North America together with Kornelius Walde to secure credits for colony development, which led to the development of a creamery, other industrial developments, and the purchase of the first tractors for the Chaco. Heinrich Duerksen's interest was concentrated on the development and stabilizing of the economic life of the colony and the furthering of missionary activity (°Chaco mission). Following his retirement as administrator he served on the board of Licht den Indianern (Light to the Indians). PW

Dürrenmatt, Friedrich. See Literature, Mennonites in.

Dyck, Arnold (Abram Bernhard) (Jan. 19, 1889–July 10, 1970), writer, editor, publisher and cultural entrepreneur, was born in Hochfeld (Yazykovo), Ukraine. Having completed Kommerzchule (business-commercial studies) in Ekaterinoslav, he persuaded his reluctant father to let him study art in Germany (1909-10). After his term of forestry service (°*Forsteidienst*), Dyck studied art in St. Petersburg until World War I. During the war he served in a °Red Cross office, then returned to Yazykovo to teach art at Nikolaipol.

In 1923 Dyck emigrated to Canada with his family, settling in Steinbach, Manitoba. Unable to establish himself as an artist, he purchased the German weekly *Steinbach Post* in 1924 and began his remarkable career as editor, writer, and publisher. Not content with journalism, he optimistically launched *Mennonitische Volkswarte* (*Mennonite People's Sentry*, 1935), a monthly literary and cultural magazine. It became an important forum for a small but dedicated group of Russian Mennonite emigré writers. Lack of readers and financial means, however, forced him to discontinue the *Warte* after 1938.

Having sent his family to Germany in 1938, Dyck was prevented from joining them by the outbreak of World War II. In the meantime he had sold his newspaper to devote himself to a full-time literary and publishing career. With *Koop enn Bua opp Reise* (Koop and Bua on the Road, 1942-43) he began his popular series of Low German comic novels depicting the travel adventures of his two naive "bush" farmers from rural Manitoba. Two sequels—*Koop enn Bua faore no Toronto* (Koop and Bua Travel to Toronto, 1948-49) and *Koop enn Bua enn Dietschlaund* (Koop and Bua in Germany, 1960, 1961)— further established "Koop enn Bua" as comic characters with universal appeal.

Dyck's nostalgic autobiographical novel *Verloren in der Steppe*, (Lost in the Steppe) appeared in five parts between 1944 and 1948, a masterwork of its kind. Around this time he embarked on his one financially successful publishing project, the series of thirteen books on Russian-Mennonite history published by the "Echo-Verlag." He also wrote three well-received Low German plays—*Dee Fria* (The Suitor, 1948), *Wellkaom oppe Forstei* (Welcome to the Forestry Service, 1950) and *De Opnaom* (The Initiation, 1951)—and two collections of short fiction: *Dee Millionäa von Kosefeld* (The Millionaire of Goatfield, 1949) and *Onse Lied* (Our People, 1952). During his declining years Dyck lived with his daughter in Germany and died in Darlaten on July 10, 1970.

Arnold Dyck's stature as a major Mennonite writer remains secure, as evidenced by a handsome four-volume edition of his collected works (1985-89). Dyck forged his beloved *Plautdietsch* (Low German °dialect) into a superb literary language that makes his "Koop en Bua" works come alive as an authentic comic masterpiece, along with several of his short stories. His dry, gentle irony suffuses all his writing like an inner light. No other writer has surpassed Dyck in his wise and compassionate insights into the heart and soul of Mennonite ethnic experience.   AR

The Collected Works of Arnold Dyck, 4 vols., ed. Victor G. Doerksen, George K. Epp, Harry Loewen, Elisabeth Peters, Al Reimer (Winnipeg: Manitoba Mennonite Historical Society, 1985-86); Arnold Dyck, *Lost in the Steppe*, trans. Henry D. Dyck (Steinbach: Derksen Printers, 1974), gives some idea of the author's literary magic but falls well short of the original; idem, *Two Letters/The Millionaire of Goatfield/Runde Koake*, trans. Elisabeth Peters (Steinbach: Derk-

sen Printers, 1980), an accurate and lively translation of the author's three best short stories; Michael L. Hadley, "Education and Alienation in Dyck's *Verloren in der Steppe*: a Novel of Cultural Crisis," *German-Canadian Yearbook*, 3 (1976), 199-206; Al Reimer, "The Creation of Arnold Dyck's 'Koop enn Bua' Characters," *Mennonite Images*, ed. Harry Loewen (Winnipeg: Hyperion Press, 1980); idem, "'Derche Bloom Räde': Arnold Dyck and the Comic Irony of the Forstei," *JMS*, 2 (1984), 60-71; idem, "Innocents Abroad: The Comic Odyssey of *Koop enn Bua opp Reise*," *JMS*, 4 (1986) 31-45; Gerhard Wiens, "Arnold Dyck at Seventy," *Menn. Life*, 14 (Apr. 1959), 80-84; Elmer F. Suderman, "The Comic Spirit of Arnold Dyck," *Menn. Life*, 24 (Oct. 1969), 169-70; Warren Kliewer, "Arnold Dyck as a Literary Artist," *Menn. Life*, 14 (Apr. 1959), 85-87; Jack Thiessen, "Arnold Dyck—the Mennonite Artist," *Menn. Life*, 24 (April, 1969), 77-83; Elisabeth Peters, "A Tribute to Arnold Dyck," *Menn. Life*, 24 (Jan. 1969), 3-5; Mary Regehr Dueck, "Arnold Dyck: Non-Conformist," *Menn. Life*, (Dec. 1975), 20-24; *Menn. Bib. II*, p. 436.

See also Literature.

Dyck, Henry J. (May 31, 1880–July 26, 1970), was born in Laakendorf, °West Prussia, to Jacob and Sara Janzen Dyck. In 1893 he emigrated to Elbing, Ks., with his parents and was baptized there by C. H. Regier in 1895, joining the Zion Mennonite Church at Elbing. He earned a teaching certificate at Bethel Academy (1897-1900) and taught in Birmingham, Ohio (1904-08), at an orphanage under the direction of J. A. °°Sprunger of Light and Hope Publishing Co., Berne, Ind.

On Oct. 28, 1904, he married Katie Anna Regier (July 11, 1881 - Dec. 30, 1971) of Elbing. They had four children: Walter, Herbert (stillborn), Dorothea, and Gertrude.

Henry was ordained minister in 1909 and elder in 1914. For many years he served as itinerant minister in Kansas, Oklahoma, Colorado, and Texas, then as full-time minister of the Zion Church at Elbing, Ks. (1920-51). His preaching was irenic, Bible centered, and characterized by a warm spirituality. He was a charter member of Herald Publishing Co. (1920, Newton, Ks.), serving as board member for 50 years, and was a member of the board of Bethel Deaconess Hospital (Newton) for 35 years (1927-62). Henry and Katie Dyck undertook a spiritual ministry to °refugees in Europe under Mennonite Central Committee auspices, 1949-50. In later years he wrote ca. 150 "Messages for the Heart" in the *Mennonite Weekly Review* and remained in continuing demand as a supply preacher until the week of his death.   CJD

H. J. Dyck, *In Retrospect: The Story of My Life* (Elbing, Ks.: n.d.).

Dyck, John R. (July 19, 1913–May 14, 1988), churchman and farmer, was born to Johannes J. and Renate (Mathies) Dyck in Lysanderhoeh, Trakt Colony, Russia. In 1927 he moved to Canada with his parents and siblings, settling first in the Hanley district, Saskatchewan, and in 1933 in Tiefengrund (Laird) north of Saskatoon, Saskatchewan. In 1941 he married Paula Regier.

After taking a decade to establish a financial base they spent most of the rest of their lives in voluntary service. In 1947 he established the first General Conference bookstore in Canada at Rosthern. He also served as business manager and secretary of Rosthern Junior College for 17 years. In

1964 and 1965 he was one of three men who led in the building of the chapel at the Associated Mennonite Biblical Seminaries in Elkhart, Ind.

Recognizing his administrative skills Mennonite Central Committee (MCC) asked him to close out MCC work in Paraguay (1965-67), Korea (1969-71), and Jordan (1979-80). John and Paula Dyck also served under MCC in Calcutta (1974-75). From 1971 to 1973 they lived in Winnipeg, where John was instrumental in establishing the Mennonite Foundation for western Canada. They returned to Winnipeg (1975-77) to lay the groundwork for MCC Food Bank which soon expanded to the Canada-wide Food Bank (°development work). In the fiscal year ending Mar. 31, 1988, the food bank shipped 84,296 metric tons of grain worth $25,756,945. to starving people around the world. Of this amount 15,161 tons, valued at $8,255,478. came from Mennonites.

When they were not abroad John was usually involved in some conference committees and in fundraising activities for Swift Current Bible Institute, the General Conference Kingdom Commitments program, and others. He experienced considerable legal difficulty, and at times a lack of understanding among his own people, for his determined refusal to pay that portion of his °taxes which he considered war taxes. His active involvement in social concerns included a person-to-person prison ministry. CJD

A *Pilgrim People*, ed. by Cornelius J. and Wilma L. Dyck (Elkhart, Ind.: the editors, 1987), 74-76; Frank H. Epp, *Education with a Plus. The Story of Rosthern Junior College* (Waterloo, 1975), 451 index under Dick [sic] John R.

E

Eastern and Coptic Orthodox Churches. The churches of eastern Europe and the Middle East represent at least three tragic splinterings. The first is the non-Chalcedonian Orthodox family (Armenian, Syrian, Coptic [Egyptian], and Ethiopian) excommunicated at the Council of Chalcedon (451) over christological controversy—while the West and major orthodox bodies hold to two natures of Christ (the human and the divine), the non-Chalcedonian Orthodox hold to one nature, in which the divine and the human are one "without mingling, without amalgamation and without alteration." In 1054 other churches of the East split from the West; these 15 bodies (e.g., Greek, Serbian, Russian) are "orthodox" in that they accept the Chalcedonian christology (as do Western churches) but they acknowledge the patriarch of Constantinople as "ecumenical patriarch"—instead of recognizing the Roman pope's claims to be the jurisdictional head of the universal church. A third group, the Uniates (sometimes called Melkites), consists of five churches that have renewed ties with Rome after the 16th c., but retain their Eastern, non-Latin liturgies. (The Maronites of Lebanon claim never to have broken ties with Rome.)

Mennonite interaction with these churches, despite Mennonite presence in these areas, has been minimal. Mennonites in their two centuries in Russia had little to do with the Russian Orthodox, and recent North American Mennonite fraternal visits have concentrated on the °All-Union Council of Evangelical Christians - Baptists. The Eastern Mennonite Board of Missions and Charities (EMBMC) has had a vital interaction in Yugoslavia with Baptist and Pentecostal churches but not with the Serbian Orthodox. A student exchange between Mennonite Central Committee (MCC) and the Romanian Orthodox church resulted in Mennonites studying in Bucharest, and two priests, who later served Romanian parishes in Detroit and Vancouver, studying at Canadian Mennonite Bible College and Associated Mennonite Biblical Seminaries. In Jordan, there have been fraternal relationships between MCC and several Orthodox groups but no organizational or service ties. Some Mar Thoma (Eastern Syrian Orthodox—non-Chalcedonian) students from India have attended Mennonite schools in North America and there have been fraternal contacts with the Syrian Orthodox (Chalcedonian) in Lebanon. MCC has been an observer at the Orthodox-dominated Middle East Council of Churches, which was based in Cyprus in 1987, and an MCC health care worker has been made available to the council in its work in Lebanon. Close working and worshiping relations existed between MCC workers and Greek Orthodox bishop Ireneos in Crete (1962-77) when MCC cooperated in agricultural and vocational training projects; this was a reflection of close personal relationships rather than structural ecumenicity. Eastern Mennonite Board of Missions and Charities (MC) and MCC attention in Ethiopia has concentrated on the Meserete Kristos Church (Mennonite), and no relations with the Ethiopian Orthodox church exist. In Egypt, MCC involvement with the Coptic Orthodox began in 1970 with material aid shipments. Placement of a teacher of English in the Coptic Orthodox Institute followed in 1979. Since then, active MCC involvement with diocesan spiritual renewal movements has augmented such teacher placements. Several Coptic bishops have visited Mennonite centers in North America. In the Sudan's Atbara region MCC has helped sponsor events such as the World Day of Prayer that brings together Catholics, Evangelicals, and Coptic Orthodox. VR

Eastern District Conference (GCM) (ME II:131). The Frederick Home and Camp Men-O-Lan ministries have greatly expanded since the 1950s. The Home now includes enlarged nursing facilities, a number of residential cottages for older people, a community center, and more low-income apartments in the planning stage. The administrator in 1987 was Robert W. Miller. Camp Men-O-Lan, with Ray Linberger as administrator, has a year-round program of camping and retreats for all ages. The conference quarterly, *The Messenger,* under former editor Marjorie Geissinger, and current editor (1987) Curtis D. Bauman, has grown to include more news and articles from the congregations and people of the conference, the General Conference Mennonite Church, and Franconia Conference (MC).

A new effort toward coordination in the conference was made when a conference minister was appointed in 1982 in the person of David Hillegas. During recent decades church planting has been undertaken in lower Bucks Co., Germantown, and elsewhere. The conference began work among Hispanic people in 1958 in Lansdale. An important inner city outreach ministry called *Crossroads* has been active in North Philadelphia, including a community center, a food pantry, a prison ministry, 4-H clubs, and garden projects.

Perhaps most significant has been a growing cooperation with the sister Franconia Conference of the Mennonite Church, in such projects as the Germantown Church congregation and corporation, the Mennonite Heritage Center in Souderton, the Mennonite Historians of Eastern Pennsylvania, and the publication in 1984 of "a narrative account of life in the oldest Mennonite community in North America," a joint history of the Franconia Conference and the

Eastern District Conference (Ruth, *Maintaining*). Since the division of 1847 (°Oberholtzer) both conferences side-by-side had gone their separate ways, each continuing to meet in conference the first weekend in May. In recent years they began to meet together on the first Sunday evening in May at the end of their individual meetings to sing and pray together. On Friday evening, May 2, 1986, they finally met together in conference at the Deep Run (East) congregation to consider their several common projects—the first such session in 139 years! In 1986 the conference had 4,589 members in 27 congregations with 30 active ministers.   JHF

The Messenger of the Eastern District Conference, published quarterly, 1947- ; John L. Ruth, *Maintaining the Right Fellowship* (Scottdale, 1984); S. F. Pannabecker, *Open Doors* (Faith and Life Press, Newton, 1975).

Eastern Pennsylvania Mennonite Church was formed in 1968 when a group of bishops, ministers, and deacons were granted a release from the Lancaster Mennonite Conference. The separation was by mutual agreement and by official sanction of the conference.

The group adheres to the Mennonite Confession of Faith (1921, Garden City, Mo.; Loewen, *Confessions*, 71) and to many of the practices which had been upheld by the Lancaster Mennonite Conference, including the conference-type of church organization and government (°polity). The Eastern Pennsylvania Mennonite Church has a written statement of standards known as the *Rules and Discipline*, which is reviewed every three or four years and then ratified again by the congregations.

The purpose for seeking release from the Lancaster Mennonite Conference was to develop a church program that would help preserve biblical practice and the historic Mennonite values. The Eastern Pennsylvania Mennonite Church does not accept °divorce and remarriage. Women wear °headcoverings and have uncut hair. Men, as a rule, do not enter the °professions. They wear plain clothing (°dress), and their life is built around the church, schools, and religious activities. They do not engage in worldly °amusements, nor do they follow organized sports. The use of °radio and °television is not allowed. Their life-style reflects the old Mennonite traditions.

Regular worship services include Sunday school and preaching every Sunday morning, Sunday evening services, and midweek prayer meetings. The °singing is in four-part harmony without accompaniment with some emphasis on singing instruction and special song services. No special group singing is allowed in worship services. Ministers are unsalaried and chosen from the congregation by nomination and the use of the °°lot.

Life °insurance is not permitted and generally members do not use auto, health, fire, or other insurances, but rather employ a unique method of brotherhood assistance (°mutual aid) that is directed by the deacons of the congregations.

Children of members do not attend public schools. °Private schools are provided by the group so that all the member families have access to them. Teachers are not college trained. Many of the students continue in school through 10th grade.

The Mennonite Messianic Mission, Inc., is the official organization which directs the group's missions in British Columbia, Guatemala, the Bahamas, and Paraguay. The official monthly periodical is the *Eastern Mennonite Testimony* published by the Publication Board.

The group sponsors a 12-week winter Bible school (°Bible conferences) at Numidia, Pa. The school is especially provided for young people in their upper teens and early twenties, and offers a wide variety of Bible and practical studies. Each summer the school offers a two-week training course for school teachers, and in December a ministers' fellowship and seminar is provided. Service opportunities are provided in °relief work, literature evangelism, child care, and in elderly care.

The majority of the congregations are located in eastern Pennsylvania. Congregations are also located in New Jersey, New York, Maryland, Delaware, Florida, Georgia, Illinois, Missouri, Vermont, Texas, and in the countries mentioned above.

Statistics for 1988 taken from the *Church Directory* showed 55 congregations, 3,058 members; 12 bishops, 93 ministers, 59 deacons, 48 schools, 142 teachers, and 1,862 pupils.   JN

MC Yearbook (1986-87) 175-78; *PMH,* 7 (Oct. 1984), 2-10.

See also La Montana Colony, Paraguay.

Ebersole, Melinda Martin (Aug. 20, 1860–Mar. 6, 1933). The first long-term worker at the Mennonite Home Mission in Chicago, Melinda Ebersole was born near Elizabethtown, Pa., the third daughter of David D. and Anna Martin Ebersole. At the age of nine, she came to Sterling, Ill., with her parents. In 1891, she confessed Christ at a revival meeting led by John S. °°Coffman, and dedicated her life to serve others. In May 1894, she went to Chicago to enter nurse's training but instead joined the staff of the Home Mission, which had opened several months earlier. She was involved in visitation, Sunday school work, and teaching and also started a sewing class for girls. In 1896, the Home Mission closed due to lack of financial and spiritual support from the Mennonite Church (MC) as a whole. Melinda stayed on in Chicago with two other workers and did practical °nursing to support their continuing missionary efforts. The mission reopened in November 1897, sponsored by the Mennonite Evangelizing and Benevolent Board. Melinda served there until 1914, when she returned to Sterling, Ill., to take care of her aging mother. She later was elected president of the Illinois district of the Mennonite Women's Missionary Society (1919-21). Melinda continued her visits and contacts with the Home Mission until late in her life. She died in Sterling, Ill.   RAS

John Umble, *Mennonite Pioneers* (Scottdale: MPH, 1940), 41-53; Rich, *Mennonite Women* (1983), 147-49; Hist. Mss. 1-1-15, Box 119, folder 5, John F. Funk Collection, MC Archives (Goshen); Hist. Mss. 1-201, Box 8, folder 3, Clara Eby Steiner Collection, MC Archives (Goshen).

Ecclesiology. See Church, Doctrine of.

Ecology is the study of interacting biological

systems and their nonliving support. Ecologists study food chains, cooperation and competition between species, and special adaptations to environmental niches. Modern ecology is especially concerned with the impact of the human species on the rest of nature, both in relation to accelerating demands on the natural world by highly exploitive technology and in relation to the exponentially increasing number of humans who are making these demands. Human population ecology deals with problems of famine, pollution, disease, and even the violence associated with overpopulation pressures. This article deals primarily with North American Mennonites. The rise of a strong ecology movement in Europe, especially the "Greens Party" in Germany, and Mennonite responses to this and similar developments in The Netherlands, are not included here.

Rachel Carson established the case for the environmental movement in her 1962 bestseller, *Silent Spring.* She contended, among other things, that either we abandon the use of the new pest-killing technologies such as DDT and DDD, or we will lose a significant segment of the natural world, including the songbirds of spring. She concluded her book with the assertion that "control of nature" was an arrogant concept, "born of the Neanderthal age of biology and philosophy, when it was supposed that nature exists for the convenience of man" (Carson, p. 261).

The second major tract of the environmental movement was Paul Ehrlich's *The Population Bomb*, published first in 1968. The book contained dramatic and convincing warning on population growth.

The controversy over population control and limitations of world resources heated up considerably with the prescription of "triage" by William and Paul Paddock in their 1967 book, *Famine, 1975!* They proposed that only those countries which had a good chance of continued survival should be helped with food aid. Those countries, such as Haiti, which were beyond help, should be left to starve. Garrett Hardin contributed to the harshness of the debate with his observations on the "tragedy of the commons" and "lifeboat ethics." Hardin contended that greed and shortsightedness led to overgrazing the commons, that part of the ecosystem which is free and open for everyone's use but for which no one accepted responsibility for its protection. He used an analogy to express his view of the fortunate and unfortunate: the occupants of a lifeboat filled to capacity who fight off drowning people surrounding the boat out of fear that additional occupants would swamp the boat and doom those in it as well as outside it. The principle arose directly from ecology's concept of carrying capacity; if an ecosystem is taxed beyond its productive ability, the whole system may crash, often with little warning.

An important contribution to the ethical and religious debate was the article published in *Science* in 1967 by Lynn White, Jr., called "The Historical Roots of Our Ecological Crisis." White repeated Rachel Carson's contention that the Western Christian tradition fostered a "control of nature" philosophy.

Responses among Mennonites to the ecological crisis were varied. Many farmers resented the curbs on pesticides that were enacted following the warning by Rachel Carson; they disagreed strongly with her revered status among environmentalists. Mennonites reacted quickly and compassionately to urgent calls for food in the famine situations of the 1970s, rejecting the triage and lifeboat proposals. Hundreds of young agriculturists, nutritionists, and teachers responded to Mennonite Central Committee efforts at food °development projects throughout the world.

The Green Revolution rice and wheat varieties of the early 1970s helped prevent the great famine predicted by the Paddocks, but many farmers, especially in Africa, were unable to participate in the relatively high technology which accompanied the Green Revolution crops.

Mennonite colleges put more emphasis on ecological and world hunger topics. Eastern Mennonite College designed all-school seminars in 1972 and 1976 on ecologcal and hunger concerns. Courses such as "Food and Population" were introduced into the curriculum. Eastern Mennonite College, Bethel College, and Goshen College all began programs in agricultural development which graduated more than a dozen students a year in the 1980s.

Doris Janzen °Longacre's book, *Living More With Less*, was published in 1980, following the highly successful *More-With-Less* cookbook. Simple living was promoted as a way to "cherish the natural order" (Longacre, p. 42). Willard Swartley's "Biblical Sources of Stewardship," in *The Earth Is the Lord's* makes an eloquent plea to accept the world's resources as a common possession of all humanity (Jegen and Manno, 22-43).

Ron Sider's book *Rich Christians In An Age of Hunger*, continues its strong critique of injustice and complacency with its second edition. Most of these Mennonite and Brethren in Christ responses to the ecological crisis draw heavily from simple life positions advocated by E. F. Schumacher in his popular *Small Is Beautiful* treatise, first published in 1973.

Kansas farmers, with help from Mennonite Central Committee, organized a significant newsletter, *Swords Into Plowshares*, which dealt with ecological and justice concerns in relation to land and agriculture. Numerous conferences were held in Kansas, the Midwest, Ontario, and at Laurelville (Pa.) Church Center on agriculture and ecology, with concerns in the late 1970s and early 1980s dealing more directly with financial crisis among Mennonite farmers. Mennonites in Oregon and Pennsylvania were also active in preserving agricultural land through legal procedures, recognizing that the Amish were probably the leaders in protecting land from developers.

A profound ecological development in 1974 and 1977 was the dramatic rise in fuel costs. Mennonites responded in a way similar to that of the general public. Many households turned to wood for fuel; at least three Mennonite-owned wood stove factories flourished for several years in Harrisonburg, Va. (Riteway, Sierra, and Shenandoah). Mennonites in Kansas and Ontario organized solar collector manufacturing concerns. With the drop of fuel prices in the mid-1980s, these °businesses closed or greatly reduced their production. A recycling business, Earthkeepers, started in the mid-1970s at Eastern Mennonite College and continued uninterrupted by the erratic market cycle. The paper and glass recycling project is currently managed by a group of business students and enjoys excellent support in the community. Recycling has also been popular in other communities, often with the assistance and encouragement of local Mennonites.   KKB

Rachel Carson, *Silent Spring* (Greenwich, Conn.: Fawcett Publications, 1962); Paul Ehrlich, *The Population Bomb* (New York: Ballatine Books, 1968); William and Paul Paddock, *Famine, 1975!* (Boston: Little, Brown, 1967); Garrett Hardin, "Lifeboat Ethics: The Case Against Helping the Poor," *Psychology Today*, 8, no. 4 (Sept. 1974), 38-43; Lynn White, Jr., "The Historical Roots of Our Ecological Crisis," *Science*, 155 (Mar. 10, 1967), 1203-07); Doris Janzen Longacre, *Living More With Less* (Scottdale, 1980); Mary Evelyn Jegen and Bruce V. Manno, eds., *The Earth is the Lord's* (New York: Paulist Press, 1978); Ron Sider, *Rich Christians in an Age of Hunger: A Biblical Study* (Downers Grove, IL: Inter-Varsity Press, 1984); E. B. Schumacher, *Small Is Beautiful: Economics as if People Mattered* (New York: Harper and Row, 1973).

See also Creation; Land; Nuclear Energy; Simple Life.

Economics. While Mennonite economic activity varies widely over time and space, there are some common economic patterns, many of which follow from the centrality of °love, brotherhood, °nonresistance, °nonconformity, biblicism, and °discipleship. To narrow the focus, this article concentrates on the economics of the North American Mennonite Church (MC) and General Conference Mennonites (GCM) during the first half of the 20th c., yet makes reference to other regions and times. Emphasis is on attitudes toward private °property, °mutual aid, poverty, the "call" to a secular vocation, °work, saving money, °wealth, and achievement, as well as Mennonite economic characteristics: relative average income, poverty rates and income inequality, and representation in key economic sectors. One case, perhaps an aberration, shows Mennonite class conflict.

The birth of Anabaptism in the early 16th c. coincided with the breakup of feudalism and rise of °capitalism. But the nonresistant Anabaptists did not oppose capitalism. Even the Hutterite community, which held goods in common within a covenant community, never intended that their economic system be applied to society as a whole.

The 16th-c. Swiss Brethren believed owning private property was not for the selfish interest of the possessor but a sacred trust for the benefit of the church. The early Anabaptists practiced mutual aid, voluntarily sharing goods with needy members of the community, because the New Testament exhorted believers to bear the burdens of others (Gal 6:2,5). However, by the early 17th c. Dutch Mennonites had lost this emphasis, becoming individualistic, bourgeois, and wealthy.

Despite a history of mutual aid, and the worldwide Mennonite Central Committee effort in °relief, °development, and °service work for most of the 20th c., Mennonites have not generally regarded aid as the poor's right. The Anabaptist poor were not to expect or demand assistance. In 1526, according to Klassen, the Swiss Brethren rule was that anyone

able to work who refused to do so in the hope of drawing from the relief fund, was "put under the ban and regarded as a heathen." °Menno Simons stated that Christians ought to comfort the afflicted, assist the needy, clothe the naked, and feed the hungry, but not permit people to beg for a living.

Many North American Mennonites, influenced by the probusiness, individualistic culture around them, disapproved state attempts to redistribute income to the "undeserving poor." Kauffman and Harder found in 1972 that 30 percent of North American Mennonites agreed, 46 percent disagreed, and 25 percent were not certain that "for the most part, people are poor because they lack discipline and don't put forth the effort needed to rise above poverty." Less than a fifth favored increasing and more than half supported reducing welfare benefits. Raid (1947) even contended that Iowa Mennonites looked on a poor farmer as a poor church member. Moreover, relative income discrepancies increased within the North American church during the last half of the 20th c.

Mennonites have exemplified the asceticism in "worldly" activity that Max Weber (1864-1920) considered a part of the Protestant ethic shaping the spirit of capitalism. The ascetic Mennonite, for whom "all of life is for Christ," systematically regulates his whole conduct. For Mennonites, the highest expression of this self-control is not in the monastery, as in medieval Roman Catholicism, but in vigorous daily activity in a secular vocation.

The essence of the Mennonite's Christianity is discipleship, which stresses the place of good works (ethics). Mennonites believe the Bible admonishes them to be stewards of time and talent, work hard, and abstain from idleness and conspicuous consumption. Fretz points out: "The [Mennonite] with wealth or the one who longs to attain it has very few ways of displaying it without invoking upon himself the criticism of the entire group." Work and saving, if dedicated to God, are not just for the purpose of earning a living, but are also a sacred act.

Hard work contributed to prosperity, a dilemma for Mennonites who condemn the pride and materialism often associated with wealth, yet who also regard wealth as a sign of God's blessing. Additionally, the stress on °stewardship provided a spiritual motive to accumulate wealth and manage it prudently. J. S. Shoemaker wrote that "Christian stewardship is a divinely appointed office, the duties of which are sacred, because it means to be entrusted with the managing of affairs and disbursing of possessions which belong to the Lord." These attitudes restrict extravagance, leading to greater wealth accumulation (and perhaps giving).

Daniel °Kauffman, one of the most influential Mennonite Church (MC) leaders during the early 20th c., reflected the influence of Calvinism on Mennonite economic attitudes when he listed the reasons why "righteousness usually means prosperity": (1) "it is according to the plan of God, and therefore of unerring wisdom"; (2) "God has promised to care for His own, and never fails to keep His promises"; (3) "industry, economy, and the exercise of good common sense are part of the righteousness which God delights to see in His people. This of necessity promotes material prosperity. For these reasons a community of righteous people is usually a prosperous one."

Prussia's Duke Albert in the second quarter of the 16th c., Philip of Hesse in the middle of that century, Russia's Empress Catherine II in the 18th c., North American communities in the 18th c. and 19th c., and many others have tolerated, indeed welcomed, Mennonites, despite their refusal to bear arms, because of their honesty, diligence, and °°farming skills. Prosperity was often shortlived, however, as ruling officials shifted to °persecution, compelling Mennonites to seek refuge in friendlier lands. Yet Mennonites, when tolerated, have usually had average incomes at least as high as the society around them, and in some instances, such as Russia (before 1917) and Holland, substantially above average. Mennonites in the United States, according to Howard Kauffman's 1955 sample, had a much higher median family income than Americans in *both* farming and nonfarming occupations but, because of a disproportional representation in low-income agriculture, only a slightly higher median income overall. The Kauffman-Harder study indicates that U.S. Mennonites in 1971 had a median household income of $9,608 compared to $8,583 for the U.S. generally.

While income inequality and poverty rates have been lower among Mennonites than the population generally, Mennonites have experienced class discrepancies and conflict. For example, in the 1780s Catherine II invited Mennonites to immigrate from Prussia to the Ukrainian steppes to establish colonies, giving them substantial local autonomy. In the 19th c., according to Toews, a village or district ruling council governed and administered day-to-day affairs of each of the Mennonite colonies—Chortitza, Molotschna, and daughter colonies. The village commune held land title within the colonies, making the individual colonist vulnerable to the economic pressures applied by the Mennonite village elites. Although the village assembly and church congregation were separated organizationally, their interests tended to merge. Since the state granted legal privileges to the Mennonites corporately, church °discipline or excommunication could ultimately remove the offender from the protection of Russian colonial law. Those controlling the politics, religion, and economics of the colony created new class stratification within the Mennonite community.

By the mid-19th c., land distribution within the Molotschna community was highly unequal. When the large °°landless Mennonite proletariat united to exert pressure for reform, ministers, elected partly because they were economically self-supporting, joined other capitalists and landowners in opposing these demands. The landless who protested this inequality were disproportionally represented among the *Mennonitische Brüdergemeinde* (Mennonite Brethren) in 1860 who sought to replace the sterility and stratification of religious life with a brotherhood church. While Mennonite religious and political authorities cooperated to quell this threat, Russian authorities sided with the dissenters, who formed a new church within the Mennonite colony.

Psychological evidence indicates that a high need for (or inner concern with) achievement produces greater °business activity, which brings about faster economic growth. But while Mennonites tried for success in °occupations compatible with high Christian standards, their beliefs closed many avenues for achieving economic success. The high task orientation of Mennonites in small businesses and Mennonite farmers who "apply their best efforts to that which they are permitted to do," as Raid indicates, is a far cry from the drive of the dynamic, self-reliant business leader who seeks success for its own sake. The Mennonite emphasis on brotherhood and conformity to in-group values and lack of stress on individualism, innovation, and independent thinking contribute to a low need for achievement, a partial determinant of low Mennonite representation in the industrial corporate sector.

In the early 20th c., U.S. Mennonites pursued their secular occupations vigorously, but primarily within the rural Mennonite community (e.g., in farming and small business), because the Mennonite absolutist ethic was not compatible with the moral ambiguities of the large corporate sector. As the complexity of economic institutions increases, it is more difficult to unite individuals cohesively. Coercion is usually necessary to achieve social cooperation where secondary relations prevail, as within and between large °institutions. The Mennonite view on °love cannot cope with ethical dilemmas in the largest U.S. industrial corporations, which virtually correspond to the list of the top military contractors. Moreover, despite Horatio Alger stories of upward mobility to success in business, the parents of the U.S. corporate elite tend to have a high socioeconomic status, making it difficult for outsiders like Mennonites to enter. In the U.S., perfectionistic Mennonitism has contradictory effects on economic development: encouraging ascetic economic activity, but hindering it in key industrial sectors.   EWN

J. Winfield Fretz, "Mennonite Mutual Aid: A Contribution to the Development of Christian Community" (PhD Thesis, U. of Chicago, 1941); Daniel Kauffman, "Stewardship," *GH* (May 12, 1927), 738; J. Howard Kauffman, "A Comparative Study of Traditional and Emergent Family Types among Midwest Mennonites" (PhD thesis, U. of Chicago, 1960); Kauffman/Harder, *Anabaptists Four C. Later* (1975); Peter J. Klassen, *The Economics of Anabaptism, 1525-1560* (London: Mouton, 1964); E. Wayne Nafziger, "The Mennonite Ethic in the Weberian Framework," *Explorations in Entrepreneurial History/Second Series,* 2 (Spring/Summer, 1965), 187-204, reprinted in *Entrepreneurship, Equity, and Economic Development* (Greenwich, Conn.: JAI Press, 1986); Howard D. Raid, "Farm Succession Among the Mennonites of Zion Church, Donnellson, Iowa" (PhD thesis, Iowa State U., 1947); J. S. Shoemaker, "Christian Stewardship," *GH* (Apr. 6, 1922), 29-30; John B. Toews, *Czars, Soviets, and Mennonites* (Newton, 1982); Max Weber, *The Protestant Ethic and the Spirit of Capitalism,* trans. Talcott Parsons (New York: Charles Scribner's Sons, 1958).

Ecuador. Elam Stauffer, a former missionary in Nicaragua, started the Misión Evangélica Menonita en Ecuador in 1980 in the city of Guayaquil under the auspices of the Rosedale Mennonite Missions (Conservative Mennonite Board of Missions and Charities) of Ohio. In 1987 the Iglesia Evangélica Menonita Ecuatoriana was formed. The misson also has a ministry to drug addicts and students. The mission helped flood victims in the city of Manta in 1983. As a result a congregation was born. In 1987 it had 60 members and more than 125 people attending. A preventive health program and a student center are additional ministries· of the mission in Manta.

The German Language Service of Radio Station HCJB, also called *The Voice of the Andes,* in Quito was begun in 1953 by Canadian missionaries David and Anne Nightingale. They were sent out and supported by the Mennonite Brethren Board of Missions which staffed and supported the German service of HCJB for the first 30 years. In 1987 HCJB broadcast seven half-hour programs daily on shortwave in German to Europe and the southern part of South America. The content of the broadcasts is biblical, evangelistic, cultural and informative. More than 14,500 responses came from German-speaking listeners in 1986.   SSI

MWH (1984), 71; *Directorio de la Iglesia Evangélica del Ecuador* (Sept. 1985); material on the German HCJB Language Service is available in the Mennonite Brethren archives at the Center for MB Studies, Fresno, Cal.

Ecumenism. Arising in the 16th c. as protest movements against both the old and the new establishments, Mennonites have always had difficulty with ecumenical movements. That difficulty or tension does not take away the problem nor does it permit one to frame the issues of the 20th c. in terms identical with those of the 16th c. There is no death penalty for rebaptism, there are no dramatic public disputations, there is no absence of belief by the mainline churches in pluralism—at least not in North America and Western Europe. The major new development is the proliferation within the Mennonite households of faith, leading to two great expressions of Mennonite ecumenics: the Mennonite Central Committee (MCC) and the Mennonite World Conference.

The MCC is a coalition of Mennonites and Brethren in Christ who vary from Old Order groups to progressive Mennonites with their educated clergy and programs and institutions for outreach. The staff, the volunteers, and the supervisory committees display a great range in Mennonite cooperation. The most visible demonstration of this cooperation are the Mennonite °relief sales where the MCC constituency from the Amish to the progressives are present. Beyond this there are always relationships outside the Mennonite borders arranged by MCC as illustrated by the five-person delegation representing the °All-Union Council of Evangelical Christians - Baptists from the Soviet Union which visited North American Mennonites during the summer of 1987.

Mennonites utilize several strategies in relation to the ecumenical challenge. The first is to accept full membership in the mainline ecumenical bodies. In the case of the World Council of Churches (WCC) there are only two Mennonite conferences who are regular members: the Algemene Doopsgezinde Sociëteit of The Netherlands, and the Vereinigung der deutschen Mennonitengemeinden of West Germany. The Zaire Mennonites were members of the World Council starting in 1973. Five years later they withdrew.

The Zaire experience also illustrates the ecumenical coercion which can be inflicted on a Mennonite conference in the 20th c. In 1971 President Mobutu announced new laws recognizing the Roman Catholics, the Kimbanguist community and the Church of Christ in Zaire. All Protestant churches and mission agencies—including the Africa Inter-Mennonite Mission—were required to work through the Church of Christ in Zaire or close their work in the territory. The Disciples of Christ, Baptists, Community of Light, Presbyterians, the (Swedish) Evangelical Community, and Mennonites complied with this coerced ecumenical mechanism informing the Church of Christ in Zaire (CCZ)

In the Soviet Union there is another variant of coercion in the requirement for churches to be registered with the government. Most Mennonite congregations have complied with this request. But, the Christian radicals or purists refuse to register, risking imprisonment, fines, or both.

On the mission fields Mennonites have often joined the mainline councils of churches. They have accepted °comity agreements whereby territories are allotted to selected mission boards in order to avoid duplication. The children of missionaries have attended boarding schools like Woodstock School in India, and the Morrison secondary school in Taiwan, which were sponsored by interdenominational boards. The Union Biblical Seminary in Pune, Maharashtra State, India, is supported by a coalition of conservative denominations including three Mennonite conferences: Mennonite Brethren, General Conference and Mennonite Church. In Zaire the Institute Supérieur de Théologie de Kinshasa (Senior Institute of Theology of Kinshasa) includes three Baptist conferences, Presbyterians, Evangelicals, and two groups of Mennonites.

In North America there is another strategy in which Mennonites accept full membership in an evangelical interdenominational organization. A case in point are the Mennonite Brethren of Canada who have joined the Evangelical Fellowship of Canada. The Conference of Mennonites in Canada (GCM) indicated it would seek to join both the Evangelical Fellowship of Canada *and* the Canadian Council of Churches. In the United States the General Conference Mennonite Church was a charter member of the Federal (National) Council of Churches but withdrew during World War I because of the support of the war by the council.

The Vancouver meeting of the World Council of Churches in the summer of 1983 illustrated the strategy which may be the most frequently used pattern, namely attending the council as a delegated observer without a vote. Such an observer is sent by his or her conference, recognized by the WCC or a similar group with the privilege of attendance at all meetings large and small but without the right to speak or vote. At the side of the Vancouver sessions the °historic peace churches and peace organizations had a Ploughshares coffee house with lectures by Ronald Sider, John Howard Yoder, Ernie Regehr, and the former Paul Verghese, a Goshen College graduate, now known as Bishop Paulus Mar Gregorious of the Syrian Orthodox Church of India.

Another approach commonly used by North American Mennonite and Brethren in Christ churches is a selective membership in specialized ecumenical agencies: Project Ploughshares and Project North in Canada which bring together Christians of many backgrounds to deal with peace and native concerns, respectively. In both the United States and Canada there are programs concerned with community justice, victim-offender °reconciliation, mediation, refugees, and material aid in cooperation with both government and ecumenical bodies. Conrad Grebel College in Canada is a Mennonite academic subculture legally and functionally related to a secular provincial university and to three other church-related colleges: Catholic, Anglican, and United Church of Canada. There is also the Mennonite sponsorship of workshops on special issues to which Christians of many backgrounds are invited. For example, in Paraguay in 1986 the Mennonites sponsored a peace conference which was attended by German Lutherans, Methodists, and Baptists. In North America the progressive Mennonite conferences fully approve of ministers who join local ministerial associations or state or provincial councils of churches. Thus, 20th-c. Mennonites and Brethren in Christ have a pattern of cooperation among themselves in MCC and Mennonite World Conference. Throughout the world there are a variety of ecumenical strategies suggesting that Mennonite isolation is now rejected except among °conservative and Old Order Mennonites.   DES

Donovan E. Smucker, "Report from Vancouver: Faith Overcomes Ambivalence," and John Rempel, "A Postscript to the Sixth Assembly," *Conrad Grebel Review*, 2, no. 2 (Spring 1984), 117-37; *Proceedings of the Mennonite World Conference XI Assembly*, Strasbourg, 1984 (Lombard, Ill.: Mennonite World Conference, 1984), 90, 54-64, 360; Hans Georg vom Berg and others, eds., *Mennonites and Reformed in Dialogue* (Geneva: World Alliance of Reformed Churches, 1986.

See also Comity; Inter-Mennonite Cooperation; Inter-Mission Cooperation; Missions; Pietism; Zigler, M. R.

Ediger, Elmer M. (Apr. 4, 1917–Sept. 22, 1983). Born in Greensburg, Ks., the son of David J. and Anna Martens Ediger, Elmer Ediger grew up and attended public school near Buhler, Ks., Following his graduation from Bethel College in 1940, he taught high school at Ellis and Buhler, Ks, During World War II he entered °°Civilian Public Service (CPS) and eventually became educational secretary for the entire CPS program administered by Mennonite Central Committee (general director of MCC-CPS, 1946). He continued in MCC service from 1946 to 1951 as director of Mennonite Mental Health Services (MMHS) and executive secretary of the °voluntary service program. He is widely acknowledged as being the prime mover in launching both the MMHS program and MCC's postwar voluntary service program.

From 1949 to 1951 Ediger studied at Bethany Biblical Seminary and Mennonite Biblical Seminary in Chicago (MDiv, 1951). He became Executive Director of the newly established Board of Christian Service (GCM) in 1951. He is also recognized as the prime mover in establishing Prairie View Health Center, of which he was the chief executive officer from 1957 to 1983.

Ediger was a member of numerous national

professional organizations in the field of °mental health. Evidence of his leadership in this field may be found in Vernon H. Neufeld's *If We Can Love: The Mennonite Mental Health Story* (Newton, 1978). He was also a member and chairman of Paraguay-Kansas Partners and the Bethel College Board of Directors. He is credited as having been a highly creative and skilled administrator of church-related programs, one who had an unusual ability to assimilate ideas and to adapt and translate them into °institutional programs.

Ediger was married to Mildred Gerbrand, Oct. 6, 1943. They had three children. Mildred died June 11, 1974. On Sept. 14, 1975 Ediger married Tina Block, originally from Steinbach, Man. He and his family were members of the Bethel College Mennonite Church.   RK

Education (ME II:149). A few Mennonite groups still (1987) attempt to operate a sufficiently comprehensive school system to provide the basic education for all of their members. In Mexico, Paraguay, Belize, and Bolivia this is still largely the case, in part because public education is deemed inadequate, in part because certain Mennonite groups remain convinced that education is the responsibility of the church, not of the state. Many of the Old Order Mennonite and Amish groups in the United States and Canada who restrict formal education to the primary school level also seek to operate these schools for their own children. Hutterite communities accept public elementary schools, but supplement them with their own "German school" which all children attend.

The majority of Mennonite churches around the world are involved in some level of educational enterprise, but in most cases the schools they operate are not designed to enroll all of their children, nor are they intended to function at all levels and in all types of education deemed acceptable or necessary by the group. A survey of this variety of educational systems is best done by continent.

South and Central America. Mennonites in this region fall into three broad categories; those who left Canada in the 1920s and in 1948 to avoid government-imposed °public schools; refugees from the Soviet Union and eastern Europe, arriving 1929-30 and after the Second World War; and various mission agencies from North America and the churches resulting from their activity. These three major types of Mennonites are scattered in some 22 countries with a variety of national educational policies and school systems.

In Mexico, Paraguay, Belize, and Bolivia most of the Mennonites from North America and Europe continue to live in largely self-governing colonies. In each case a special agreement with government (°privileges) gives them full control over their own schools. Each village has an elementary school in which curriculum, teachers, and attendance are regulated by the church. The Reinlaänder (°Old Colony), °Sommerfeld Mennonites, °Bergthal Mennonites, and °°Kleine Gemeinde Mennonites discourage formal schooling beyond the elementary level and have no °secondary schools.

The European immigrant colonies in Brazil and

Paraguay, having established primary schools on arrival, began very soon thereafter with secondary schools on the model of the Russian Mennonite *Zentralschule* (ME II:155). Several of these have developed a teacher-training course or have expanded into junior colleges.

The °Chortitzer, Sommerfeld, and Bergthal Mennonites from Canada who founded °Menno Colony in Paraguay in 1927 began to plan for a post-elementary school in the early 1950s in a dramatic reversal of their firm opposition to higher education only two decades earlier. In 1957 they opened a secondary school in Loma Plata, built with financial assistance from the General Conference Mennonite Church and Mennonite Central Committee of North America.

Among the Reinländer Mennonites in Mexico the absence of any educational infusion from outside their own circles deliberately limited elementary schools and critically weakened the level of teaching. Gradually children from this community began attending the nearby school operated by a General Conference congregation made up of 1920s immigrants from Russia. In 1967 this conference school added a secondary level with the help of teachers from Canada, giving rise to considerable tension in the large Reinländer Church, which still firmly opposed all post-elementary education.

Mennonite missions active in Central and South America have not usually been involved in elementary or secondary schools. (Exceptions are Colombia [GCM], Honduras [MC], Panama [MB], and Puerto Rico [MC] for elementary, and Colombia [MB], Dominican Republic [EMCh], Honduras, and Puerto Rico for secondary.) The trend during the past 10 years has been toward closing existing schools rather than opening new ones.

EDUCATION
Compiler: Adolph Ens (author of article)

Table 1. Facilities for Pastoral Leadership Training in Central and South America, 1984

Country	Bible Institute	Seminary	TEE
Argentina			x
Belize	x		
Bolivia	x		
Brazil	x	x	x
Chile			x
Colombia		x	x
Costa Rica	x	x	x
Dominican Republic	x	x	x
El Salvador	x		
Guatemala	x	x	x
Haiti			x
Honduras	x		x
Mexico	x		x
Nicaragua			x
Panama			x
Paraguay	x	x	x
Puerto Rico	x		x
Uruguay	x	x	x
Venezuela	x		

Source: *MWH* (1984)

Bible institutes, offering biblical and pastoral training at various levels, were fairly common in 1984, with churches or missions supporting one or more of them in 13 countries as indicated in Table I. Of increasing importance in church leadership training however, is some form of °theological education by extension (TEE).

At the seminary level the Portuguese- and German-language °Bible institutes of the Mennonite Brethren in Brazil merged in 1975 to form the Instituto e Seminário Bíblico Irmãos Menonitas (Mennonite Brethren Bible Institute and Seminary). The seminary in Montevideo, serving the General Conference churches of Brazil, Paraguay, and Uruguay, closed in 1974, and was replaced in 1977 by the Centro Evangélico Menonita de Teología (Mennonite Theological Center) in Asunción. Cooperation between it and the Mennonite Brethren/Evangelical Mennonite Brethren Instituto Bíblico Asunción (Asunción Bible Institute) began in 1985.

A few vocational schools (Honduras, Paraguay) were in existence. The Teachers Abroad Program of Mennonite Central Committee (see below under Africa) operated in the Caribbean for some years.

North America. In the United States the number of °private Christian elementary schools has continued to increase steadily in the Amish and Mennonite Church (MC) constituencies, the latter opening an average of one school per year since 1970 for a total of 93 in 1986. The Amish had more than 200 such schools by 1967. The Association of Mennonite Elementary Schools (AMES) was founded in 1962 (replaced by the Mennonite Elementary Education Council in 1980) as a nonadministrative organization to enhance the schools' spiritual and academic effectiveness. The Church of God in Christ, Mennonite (CGC), paved the way for private elementary schools in its conference with a 1967 resolution allowing its congregations to open such schools provided that they could "operate without offense to civil governments and without violating any tenets of our Faith" (Hiebert 452).

In Canada Mennonite elementary schools ended when some 7,700 of their proponents emigrated to Latin America in the 1920s. Public school consolidation in Ontario during the 1960s led Old Order Mennonite and Amish groups to build their own schools. By 1981 there were 56 such schools, including some operated by Beachy Amish Mennonites and Conservative Mennonites. The Church of God in Christ, Mennonite, group opened several schools in western Canada during the 1970s, largely in response to declining local control of public schools through the consolidation of rural school districts into larger jurisdictions. In the 1980s a few urban elementary schools have been opened by Mennonite societies whose members come mainly from the large conference bodies. Other Mennonite congregations are supporting nondenominational Christian day schools.

The "decided trend" toward Mennonite private high schools discerned by Harder in the 1950s (ME II:152) was not sustained. Only two more have opened since then: Westgate (GCM - Winnipeg) in 1958 and Valley Christian Academy (Osler - Saskatchewan Bergthaler) in 1986. Three Mennonite high schools have closed. Most Canadian Mennonite schools are members of the Canadian Association of Mennonite Schools (CAMS).

In the United States high schools are operated primarily by Mennonite Church (MC) groups who now have 18 (1987) compared with 13 in the mid-1970s. The Church of God in Christ, Mennonite, gave guarded approval to high school education in 1959, and by 1970 several of their elementary schools either offered some high school grades or supervised students taking high school by correspondence (Hiebert 455). The Mennonite Church in 1968 initiated the High Aim program with the objective of making education in Mennonite high schools more accessible among minority groups.

Bible institutes have not been a very significant element among Mennonites in the United States. In Canada the movement has declined rapidly with only 3 of the 22 reported for 1947-48 (ME II) still operating, two of them as mergers. Two others have become Bible colleges with expanded curriculum: Steinbach (1978), and the Clearbrook school, a 1970 merger of Mennonite Brethren and General Conference Mennonite Bible institutes, which became Columbia Bible College in 1985. Meanwhile, in 1976 the Evangelical Mennonite Mission Conference opened a Bible institute in Ontario for Old Colony immigrants from Mexico and the Mennonite Brethren opened a French language Bible institute in Quebec. The Hispanic Mennonite Bible Institute opened in Pennsylvania in 1985.

Two Bible colleges founded in Canada in the 1940s developed university connections. Mennonite Brethren Bible College in Winnipeg established links with Waterloo Lutheran U. in 1961, switching to the U. of Winnipeg in 1970. Canadian Mennonite Bible College has been associated with the U. of Manitoba since 1964. A fifth college, Conrad Grebel, opened as a liberal arts institution on the campus of the U. of Waterloo in 1964. An endowed chair in Mennonite Studies was established at the U. of Winnipeg in 1978, followed in 1985 by the Mennonite Studies Centre at the same university. It was planned that the latter would develop into a liberal arts college to be called Menno Simons College.

In the United States the Mennonite Brethren colleges in Kansas and California were transferred from national to district conference control in 1979. Two other Mennonite colleges closed: Upland College (BIC - California) in 1965 and Freeman Junior College (GCM - South Dakota) in 1985. Other Mennonite colleges shifted their programs significantly in the direction of applied studies (e.g., nursing, teacher training, industrial arts, aviation) from their earlier liberal arts emphasis. Five Mennonite schools of °nursing operated in 1986. In 1987 there were four graduate-level Mennonite °seminaries in North America, two of which were located on a single campus (the GCM school moved from Chicago to Elkhart in 1958 to enter an association with the MC seminary in Goshen, which relocated its program to Elkhart in 1969). The Mennonite Church (MC) began a second seminary program at Eastern Mennonite College in Harrisonburg, Va., in 1961. The fourth school was Mennonite Brethren Biblical Seminary in Fresno. "Conference-Based Theological Education" received increasing emphasis in the

1980s, allowing pastors to enroll part-time in off-campus seminary courses sponsored by regional and district conferences and partly administered and entirely accredited through the graduate seminaries.

As a result of the "Overseas Churchmen Abroad Study-Service Programs" begun by the General Conference in 1972, some 15 Mennonite leaders from Africa, Asia, and Latin America were studying at the Associated Mennonite Biblical Seminaries in Elkhart in 1977, with others in Costa Rica and Japan.

As the enrollment of Mennonite students at state universities, colleges, and technical institutes rose sharply during the 1960s, the larger Mennonite denominations created Student [and Young Adult] Services committees to maintain contact with these geographically scattered young people. This trend also raised new questions about the role of Mennonite schools, especially at the postsecondary level.

Africa. Mennonite involvement in education in Africa began in the °mission context. Colonial governments for the most part allowed foreign missions a free hand in education, even providing financial support in some cases. Accordingly, the Mennonite and Brethren in Christ missions in Rhodesia (Zambia, Zimbabwe), Congo (Zaire), and Tanganyika (Tanzania) operated large numbers of primary schools and some middle or secondary ones (°mission schools).

The coming of political independence in the 1960s resulted in several shifts in Mennonite involvement in education. The emphasis of the governments of a number of newly independent countries on extending formal education oportunities to all children led Mennonite Central Committee to launch its Teachers Abroad Program in 1962. In cooperation with host governments in Nigeria, Malawi, Kenya, and Swaziland (in addition to the above) and with church or mission agencies, TAP placed hundreds of North American teachers in secondary and teacher training schools during the next decade. By that time the program was tentatively extending itself to the university level. By the later 1970s MCC felt some uneasiness about the elitist nature of formal education in the African context and began to emphasize greater support of non-formal education.

At the same time, control of schools begun by mission agencies was turned over to African personnel. Generally, these church schools had been integrated into the various national education systems by the early 1970s. In some cases this meant full governmental control and financing; in others (notably Zaire) the churches were allowed a large measure of continuing involvement.

Provisions for special training in Bible and pastoral leadership were developed in most countries in which a Mennonite church emerged. In the earlier years the emphasis was on residential Bible institutes (Ethiopia, Tanzania, Zaire, Zambia, Zimbabwe). By the 1980s these were replaced or supplemented by the Theological Education by Extension, Bible correspondence courses, and participation in ecumenical institutions of higher education, including the Institute Supérieur Théologique de Kinshasa and the (Protestant) Free University of Congo (which missionary Melvin

Loewen served as president for a term). A unique educational venture is the recent involvement of Mennonite mission agencies in providing Bible teachers for °African Independent Churches in southern Africa (Botswana, Lesotho, Transkei) and western Africa (Côte d'Ivoire [Ivory Coast], Benin).

Anomalies resulting from political circumstances included a 1963 decision to teach the Islamic faith in Mennonite mission schools in Somalia in order to receive governmental accreditation, and consideration (1979) of the Meserete Christos (Christ Foundation) church in Ethiopia to send pastors to the Baptist seminary in Moscow for training.

Asia. In Indonesia the very first missionary (1851) of the Dutch sending agency began work as a teacher. Ever since, the church has regarded education as a primary means of evangelism. An extensive network of mission-operated elementary schools was developed prior to local church autonomy and political independence in the 1940s. With financial assistance from European (Europäisches Mennonitisches Evangelisationskomitee) and North American Mennonites (MCC) the Indonesian churches expanded this school system and extended it to middle and secondary levels during the 1950s. By the 1980s there were more than 12 schools with some 3,000 students. A school for training pastors was opened in Pati in 1950, merging after five years with an ecumenical institution in Malang. In 1965 a new Mennonite Bible linstitute (Akademie Kristen Wiyata Wacana) was opened in Pati. At the same time the Mennonite churches also participate in an ecumenical seminary and a Christian university in central Java. A teacher training school for teachers of religion was opened in Pati in 1970. Through MCC's Education Assistance Program and the churches' scholarship fund, some 90 university and technical school students as well as hundreds of elementary and secondary pupils are supported.

In India political independence did not lead as immediately to church autonomy from the mission agencies. This gave rise to considerable tensions later on in the transfer of institutions, including quite extensive school systems, from mission agencies to national churches. Since schools were expensive to operate, efforts were made to have the government take them over. In the late 1970s the Mennonite churches were operating about 12 secondary schools with large enrollments. In 1986 education opportunities for the church were wide open, especially for English-language secondary schools. Several Bible institutes continued to operate in 1984, but with the rise in educational level of ministerial candidates, Union Biblical Seminary at Pune (in which most Mennonite churches in India cooperate) became more important.

In Japan a seminary was opened in Osaka in the 1960s as a cooperative venture of the Mennonite Brethren and some Baptist groups; in 1977 it became Mennonite Brethren property. The Eastern Hokkaido Bible Institute, established 1965 as a residential school, moved to a greater emphasis on shorter seminars and extension courses by the late 1970s. The Anabaptist Center in Tokyo does not offer a formal program of studies.

The Mennonite churches in Taiwan operate a nurses' training program at their hospital in Hwalien. A vocational school for boys begun by MCC in Korea in 1953 was transferred to a local board in 1969. Missions Now, a Mennonite church in the Philippines, operates a Bible institute. MCC and the Mennonite Mission agencies of North America began a China Education Exchange program in 1981.

Europe and Middle East. Direct involvement in educational institutions by European Mennonite churches has been very selective. The Mennonite seminary at the U. of Amsterdam, begun in 1735 continues to function with two faculty members. The secondary school founded at the Weierhof, Germany, in 1867, was reopened in 1959 (after being closed since early 1945) and enrolled some 700 students in 1982. In Switzerland the European Mennonite Bible school at Bienenberg serves the Swiss, French, and German churches. French Mennonites in 1984 joined in support of an Evangelical Theological Seminary in Vaux sur Seine. The Mennonite Brethren opened a Bible school in Traun near Linz, Austria, in 1975 (more recently, they have cooperated in an interdenominational Bible school at Ampflwang).

Mennonite Central Committee included extensive involvement in the Beit Jala secondary school and in elementary education in Hebron as part of its °refugee ministry in the Middle East during the 1960s and 1970s.   AE

AIMM Messenger (fall 1963); J. L. Brubaker, "A History of the Mennonite Elementary School Movement" (DEd diss., U. of Virginia, 1966); *MCC Story, 2: Responding to Worldwide Needs* (Scottdale, 1980); John W. Friesen, "Studies in Mennonite Education: The State of the Art," *JMS*, 1 (1983), 133-48; Nancy Heisey, *Integrating Education and Development* (Akron, Pa.: MCC, 1977); *GH* (Apr. 24, 1973); Daniel Hertzler, *Mennonite Education: Why and How?* (Scottdale, 1971); Clarence Hiebert, *The Holdeman People: The Church of God in Christ, Mennonite, 1859-1969* (Pasadena: William Carey, 1973); Kauffman/Harder, *Anabaptists Four C. Later* (1975); A. J. Klassen, *The Bible School Story: Fifty Years of Mennonite Brethren Bible Schools in Canada* (Clearbrook, B.C., 1963); P. G. Klassen, "A History of Mennonite Education in Canada, 1786-1960" (DEd diss., U. of Toronto, 1970); *Menn. Life,* 20 (Apr. 1965); Albert J. Meyer, *Study of Academic Sub-Communities or other Church-related Academic Resources on University Campuses* (Elkhart: Mennonite Board of Education, 1969); Rudy A. Regehr, "A Century of Private Schools," in *Call to Faithfulness,* ed. Henry Poettcker and Rudy A. Regehr (Winnipeg: CMBC, 1972), 103-15; Frederic W. Sprunger, *Theological Education by Extension in Japan* (Pasadena: William Carey Library, 1981); George G. Konrad, "Institutional Education and the Mission of the Church," in *The Church in Mission,* ed. A. J. Klassen (Fresno: MB Board of Christian Literature, 1967), 205-21; *MC Yearbook* (1988-89), 141-48, 190-92; *GCM Handbook* (1988), 130-33; John A. Hostetler, *Educational Achievement and Life Styles in a Traditional Society, the Old Order Amish* (Philadelphia: College of Liberal Arts Temple University, September 1969; U.S. Department of Health, Education, and Welfare, Office of Education, Bureau of Research).

See also Christian Education.

Église de Dieu en Christ Mennonite, Haiti (Church of God in Christ Mennonite. The Church of God in Christ Mennonite, had contact with the country of Haiti through °disaster relief work following Hurricane Flora in 1963. The first missionaries were sent to the Petionville area in 1966 to begin the work of establishing the Church of God in Christ Mennonite, of Haiti. Soon after this, efforts were made in Jacmel and the Bainet area which have led to the development of four congregations. Later, contacts were made in the area of Jeremie where continuing work has produced three churches. Meanwhile, through the years various congregations of believers have formed east and north of Port-au-Prince with more recent outreaches as far north as Thomassique, Hinche, and Desarmes. In 1987 there were 14 self-governing congregations scattered over central and southern Haiti with a membership of approximately 330.

Members are unified by annual fellowship meetings (general conferences) and leaders meetings hosted by various congregations upon approval by the conference body. Leaders, ministers, and deacons are chosen by the local congregations and are financially self-supporting.

The Church of God in Christ Mennonite in Canada and the United States has maintained a mission staff of five to seven families to assist the developing Haitian churches and to continue evangelizing. All work is undertaken with mutual cooperation between Mission Mennonite, which represents the Church in Canada and the United States, and the Church of God in Christ Mennonite of Haiti. One missionary serves as director of humanitarian aid projects. These include tuberculosis treatment clinics, nutrition centers for undernourished children and various community development work.   LN

MWH (1984) 77.

Église du Christ au Zaire, Communauté des Églises de Frères Mennonites au Zaire (CEFMZ; Community of Mennonite Brethren Churches of Zaire) (ME I:269). As early as 1893, Mennonite Brethren in North America considered mission work in Africa. The first mission ventures from North America in the Cameroons, by Peter and Margaret Wedel and Henry and Maria Enns, were terminated by illness and death within two years of their beginning in 1896. From 1912 to 1920, Aaron and Ernestina °Janzen laid the foundations of the Congo Inland Mission, now Africa Inter-Mennonite Mission (AIMM), at Kalamba in the Kasai district of Belgian Congo (Zaire) and at Nyanga among the Baluba people. In 1920 they independently began a new work for Mennonite Brethren at Kiandji in the °Kikwit area of what became Bandundu province, and in 1924 relocated to Kafumba, some 35 miles (56 km.) south of Kikwit. Covering an area some 50 miles square and including several hundred villages, Kafumba remained a major center of MB mission activity until the rebellion in 1964. Institutions included a primary school, a Bible school, a hospital, and a printing shop.

In the meantime, quite unrelated to the development of the present MB church in Zaire, Henry and Anna °Bartsch from Canada began a work among the Dengese people at Bololo some 450 miles (726 m.) to the nw. in the Deese territory of Kasai district. Begun in 1933, after the Bartsches assisted the Janzens in Kafumba for one year, this work was supported independently by the Africa Mission Society (consisting of Bartsches' acquaintants in Canada). In 1942, following much hardship and heroic endurance, the first baptism took place and a church was organized. Only after the Board of Missions assumed sponsorship in 1943 did the Africa Mission Society dissolve. Joining the Bartsches in their work at Bololo were Lydia Jantz and Katharine Harder in 1933, Margaret Siemens and Herman and Tina Lenzmann in 1937, and Carl and Maria Kraemer in 1938. Following a time of no missionaries from 1942 to 1946, William and Margaret Baerg and Susie Brucks were assigned to work among Dengese people, but relocated the mission center from Bololo to Djongo Sanga. This work continued until 1953, when it was transferred to nearby missions.

In 1946, Matende, 56 miles (90 km.) se. of Kikwit, became a new area of ministry some 35 miles square, serving 100 villages with an aggregate population of 50,000. Besides a church, Matende also had an elementary school, a teacher training school, a dispensary, and dormitories. A. F. and Mary Kroeker were the first missionaries at Matende.

In 1948, Kipungu, 60 miles (97 km.) sw. of Kikwit, was opened. Some 56 miles square and serving 200 villages and 40,000 people, Kipungu also had a church, an elementary school, a dispensary service, and dormitories. John and Ruth Kliewer began the work at Kipungu.

By 1950, the Kwango field with its three stations of Kafumba, Matende, and Kipungu had about 4000 baptized believers, one ordained minister, nine licensed preachers and evangelists, and up to 100 station and village teachers for its 100 village schools. In addition, medicines were dispensed as missionaries toured the villages for evangelism.

Further expansion to the south took place at Lusemvu in 1952 when an independent work begun in the 1930s, an institutional program centered on a school and dispensary, was purchased from Mrs. Near. Fran and Clara Buschman and Nettie Berg were placed there by Mennonite Brethren. Still farther south, the Unevangelized Tribes Mission (UTM) dissolved their two stations of Kajiji and Panzi in 1952 and offered them to the Mennonite Brethren with their missionary residences, schools, hospital, dormitories, and storage houses. At this time Clyde and Elizabeth Shannon and Rolfe and Edna Graves transferred from the UTM to the MB mission. The Kajiji church, first organized in 1942, had a membership of 100, and several hundred more joined after Mennonite Brethren began their work.

On June 30, 1960, Zaire became an independent nation and Belgian colonial rule (1884-1960) came to an end. With this birth of a new nation and the subsequent revolution until 1964, the indigenous church and the mission were severely tested. Missionaries were evacuated via Angola on July 12, 1960. Several returned within months. Others returned to provide relief in 1961, and by the summer of 1962 families were permitted to return. A number of new doctors responded to replace the colonial professionals. Also, extensive relief programs were channeled through Mennonite Central Committee. During this time of transition, the national church encountered harassment by revolutionary leaders, and many of its leaders went into hiding. Only in 1965 was the church regathered, the first post-rebellion conference being convened at Gungu.

In the interim, new forms of ministry emerged with a shift from rural to urban settings. The rebellion of 1964 under Pierre Mulele resulted in the destruction of Kafumba, Lusemvu, and Matende centers with very extensive property losses. Henceforth, missionaries concentrated their efforts at Kajiji, Kikwit, and °Kinshasa. The radio ministry, begun in Kikwit by Irwin Friesen, was begun again in Kinshasa in 1960, and later also aired via ELWA from Monrovia, Liberia (1961-71). At its height it beamed 146 broadcasts a month in four languages. This broadcasting was terminated because of Zaire government programming restrictions. A correspondence ministry, developed through radio broadcasts, offered 17 courses to 6,704 students in four languages in 1970. In the late 1980s this ministry continues in a somewhat reduced form under national leadership. The emphasis upon literature production continued. In 1949 the New Testament was printed in the Kituba language, utilizing a translation completed by Ernestina and Martha Hiebert Janzen with the assistance of Kathryn Willems. Since independence there has been close collaboration between missionaries and nationals in the production of hymnbook, Bible dictionary, Bible subject index, and most recently the Old Testament in Kituba, especially under the supervision of Hardy Schroeder.

Significant to the development of the Églises des Frères Mennonites au Congo (EFMC; Mennonite Brethren Churches in the Congo) was their official recognition as an independent denomination in 1971. As part of the authenticity policy of Zaire, the EFMC was subsumed under the Church of Christ in Zaire (ECZ) in 1973, Christian names were dropped in favor of authentic tribal names, and a new name was given to the MB churches, the Community of MB Churches in Zaire (CEFMZ). Until 1982 the executive committee included some missionaries. The first two national chairmen were Kilabi Bululu and Kusangila Kitondo. Church membership under national leadership grew rapidly from about 12,000 in 1973 to 35,000 in 1987, and numerous churches merged in the urban centers of Kinshasa and Kikwit. Missionaries have continued primarily as resource persons for evangelism, theological education, health and development ministries. In 1974 all Christian elementary and high schools were placed under government control. In 1977, the church again assumed control, but the Zairian Department of Education continued to pay teachers' salaries.

Theological education has developed both through formal institutions and informal programs. The Bible institute, earlier at Kafumba, was reopened in Kikwit in 1976 under national leadership. It continues under the leadership of Kilabi Bululu with some mission assistance both in personnel and finances. During the 1986-87 school year there were some 70 men and 66 women enrolled. At a more advanced level, the CEFMZ participates with several other denominations at the Institut Supérieur Théologique de Kinshasa (IST; Superior Institute of Theology of Kinshasa). Prior to joining IST, the MB mission and Congo Inland Mission (later known as Africa Inter-Mennonite Mission) jointly conducted a similar advanced school at Kajiji (1963-68). Annually, some 8

to 10 CEFMZ students attend IST, and both the CEFMZ and the mission have participating faculty. Several students also receive graduate training in theology at Bangui, Central African Republic, or Yaoundé, Cameroon. In recent years a new elementary lay leadership program was begun at Nzashi Mwadi, in sw. Bandundu province near the Angolan border, under the leadership of John Esau. Moreover, in 1973 Abe Esau began a theological extension program, centered at Kikwit. Led in 1988 by Rev. Kulupeta, it offers some 17 courses (in process of revision in 1987) serving some 900 students throughout Bandundu province.

The Mennonite Brethren were involved in agricultural development in the early stages of mission presence. In the 1960s they cooperated with other agencies in forming the Protestant Agricultural Program, a program designed to promote and assist the introduction of cattle and poultry and village extension agricultural training. In the 1970s they cooperated with Mennonite Economic Development Associates (MEDA) in promoting small business and animal husbandry. These programs have been discontinued. The agricultural promotion, fishpond extension, and community development are now carried on from small demonstration farms in cooperation with the village health program. In 1984 Mennonite Brethren Missions and Services with the assistance of Canadian International Development Agency began a vocational training school in Kinshasa. The first courses to be initiated were in carpentry and furniture making. The first students will be graduated in 1988.

A hospital begun in Kajiji in 1955 had 144 beds and a large maternity ward in 1966. More recently a tuberculosis treatment center was moved to the site, and both programs are enhanced by a nutritional center. The nurses' training school was also begun in 1955 with a three-year training program. In 1983 the program was revised with courses specifically geared to public health emphasis and extended to a four-year period. A major building program was completed in 1985.

A public health program was initiated in 1982. It was designed to provide initiative for the formation of village health committees and training village health workers. The goals of the project are that these village health workers with their committees will work towards better health by providing information on nutrition and sanitation and by encouraging vaccinations. Other areas of emphasis include family planning and under-five well-baby clinics. Regional dispensaries are provided for treatment of some of the more common ailments.   PMH

John B. Toews, *The Mennonite Brethren Church in Zaire* (Fresno: MB Board of Christian Literature, 1978); Phyllis Martens, *The Mustard Tree: The Story of Mennonite Brethren Missions* (Fresno: MB Board of Christian Education, 1971) 63-102; Gerhard W. Peters, *The Growth of Foreign Missions in the Mennonite Brethren Church* (Hillsboro: Board of Foreign Missions, 1952), 245-82; H. T. Esau, *First Sixty Years of MB Missions* (Hillsboro: MB Publishing House, 1954), 289-375; *MWH* (1978), 104-6; *MWH* (1984), 19.

Église du Christ au Zaire, Communauté Evangélique Mennonite (CEM; Church of Christ in Zaire, Evangelical Mennonite Communion). As has often been the case in Mennonite history, political upheaval, migration, and the suffering of refugees in Zaire resulted in the formation of a new and separate Mennonite Church.

The Tshiluba-speaking population of the Zaire provinces of West and East Kasai numbers more than 5 million people and comprises two major ethnic groups known as the Baluba and the Lulua. While there are slight dialect variations, they easily understand each other and trace their genealogy to a common and mutually acknowledged ancestor. But across the years, the Baluba came to consider the East Kasai as their homeland while the Lulua claimed the West Kasai as theirs.

With the advent of the Belgian colonial administration in the early 1900s and the discovery of diamonds along the Kasai River, which marked the western edge of Lulua territory, opportunities for training and employment soon began to attract people, notably the Baluba. By nature alert and aggressive, more and more of them migrated from the East Kasai to settle among the Lulua folk, their fellow Tshiluba-speaking kinsmen. In the meantime the local Lulua, deeply attached by nature to their agrarian way of life, were more inclined to remain in their rural villages to till their fields and tend their livestock.

In the meantime, Mennonite missionaries had also arrived. They eventually established three mission posts among the Tshiluba-speaking people along the Kasai River: Djoko Punda to the north, Kalamba (later moved and renamed Mutena) to the south, and Kalonda, situated between the two and adjacent to Tshikapa.

By the late 1950s, the ferment of political change was clearly detectable. All across black Africa there was agitation against colonial rule, and insistent calls for political autonomy were heard. The Belgian Congo was not excluded. After a hurried round of consultations in the early months of 1960, political independence was granted on June 30, 1960, and freedom came to a land and people who were ill prepared for it. Confusion and disorder quickly ensued and abruptly, as the public security became questionable, the Belgian administrators departed en masse.

When, along the Kasai River, it became clear to the Lulua people that they were in full transition to black government and that there were few members of their clans who were qualified to take government posts in their own region, they began to fear that they would soon come under the authority of government agents chosen from among the Baluba people. Resentful and fearful of such a possibility, the Lulua turned on the Baluba and soon conflict erupted along the river from village to village. After a series of violent encounters with much destruction of property and some loss of life, the Baluba people decided that they had but one choice: to return to the East Kasai, the land of their ancestors. This major migration of refugees took with it not only hundreds of Mennonite Christians but a number of the church's ablest pastors of that time.

While the early months of life as refugees brought hunger, sickness, and, for many, death, the resilient spirit of the Baluba people soon manifested itself. The Mennonite Christians immediately began to seek each other out and with the encouragement of their fellow refugee pastors, began to erect simple thatch-roofed shelters for prayer and worship. They gathered regularly to seek help and courage from one another and from God's word.

Separated as they were from their fellow believers of the Zaire Mennonite Church (CMZA) to the west both by geographical distance and by great political cleavage, they struggled for more than a year with the question of their future and identity. Who were they? Who would they be in the future? Meaningful continued fellowship with the Église du Christ au Zaire, Communauté Mennonite (CMZA) to the west was very problematic. What about schooling for their children? When appearing before local government authorities from whom they sought help, they were without identity or structure as a Christian group. Thus it was that they eventually made the decision to organize as an autonomous church independent of the CMZA and elected to call themselves The Evangelical Mennonite Church of the East Kasai, a name whose French equivalent has been shortened to the acronym CEM.

Critical during this period of pioneering and decisionmaking was the person and ability of their senior pastor, °Kazadi Matthew. Attracted as a lad by the opportunity of schooling at Djoko Punda, he early demonstrated his aptitudes as a student and his natural leadership qualities. Following his graduation from the station Bible school he was promptly recommended by the church as a pastoral candidate. After serving in the Djoko station church he and his wife became the first Zairian couple to open a new regional post in the Djoko church district. This took place at Basonga, a large Belgian palm oil center some 150 miles (240 m.) north on the Kasai River. In the late 1950s he returned to a leadership role on Djoko station. It was here that the tribal conflict of the early 1960s found him and this was eventually his point of departure for the East Kasai as a refugee.

Courageous, a man of vision and with a deep commitment to the church, Pastor Kazadi became something of a legend in his own time and clearly was the moving spirit behind the eventual establishment of the CEM. Under his leadership a legal charter was sought and obtained from the government which opened the door to subsidies for CEM schools and the launching of a modest medical service in the city of °Mbuji Mayi. A Bible institute was also started under his leadership. After graduating one class, the school closed following a period of disagreement between Pastor Kazadi and his staff over curriculum and policy questions. CEM pastoral candidates have since enrolled in training programs at Kalonda and °Kinshasa.

In cooperation with the Mennonite Central Committee, effort has been made in the Mbuji Mayi area in rural development, which has at different times featured the raising of poultry and rabbits.

The initiative to organize and promote a separate Mennonite Church in the East Kasai was for some time resisted and resented by the mother church, the CMZA. As a matter of fact, the Mennonite refugees of one clan chose not to identify with the new church preferring to wait until political conditions permitted them to be officially recognized as an eastern district of the CMZA. Fraternal relations, however, have long since been reestablished and there is now a mutual acceptance of each other as sister churches.

Since the early 1960s the CEM has planted in the East Kasai numerous congregations comprised both of former refugees and new people brought to faith in Christ. In recent years they too have sought out fellow believers who have gone elsewhere and established churches in such areas as Muena Ditu, °Kananga, and Kinshasa where they currently have four congregations. Total CEM membership in 1987 was approximately 8,200.   JEB

MWH (1978), 107-11, *MWH* (1984), 21.

Église du Christ au Zaire, Communauté Mennonite (CMZA; Church of Christ in Zaire, Mennonite Communion) (ME I:21, 690), has its origins in the ministry of the Africa Inter-Mennonite Mission (AIMM), which prior to 1971 was known as the °°Congo Inland Mission (CIM). Its first missionaries arrived in 1912 in the West Kasai region of the Belgian Congo (which became the Democratic Republic of the Congo in 1964 and the Republic of Zaire in 1971). They immediately established two stations along the banks of the Kasai River, one at Djoko Punda (renamed Charlesville during the Belgian colonial era) near the Wissman Falls and another near Kalamba, several days trek to the south. The placing of missionaries at Kalamba farther to the south was deliberate since it was the home village of Chief Kalamba known at the time as the king of the Lulua people. (This station was later moved and renamed Mutena.) At Djoko, ministry was started among a mix of Lulua and Baluba people.

Following World War I, two new stations were established among the Baphende people to the west whose villages were located on both sides of the Loange River. Nyanga station was built in the West Kasai Province and Mukedi in Bandundu Province, then known as the Kwilu. In both cases the stations were built adjacent to villages of the same name.

In the ferment following World War II, several smaller faith missions in the Kwilu (which later became the Bandundu Province) were dissolved. Congo Inland Mission acquired yet another station, Kandala, among the Baphende people to the south of Mukedi, plus a second post named Kamayala still farther to the south among the Chokwe people near the Angola border.

At the same time CIM was constructing two new posts in the Kasai. One was at Kalonda overlooking °Tshikapa, the Belgian diamond mining center on the Kasai River, where a mix of Lulua, Baluba, and Baphende had been drawn by opportunity for vocational training and employment. Yet another station was also under construction to the west of Djoko among the Bashilele people at a place called Banga. Thus by the early 1960s, CIM had missionary personnel situated at eight different stations scattered across an area roughly equivalent in size to Illinois, Czechoslovakia, or Bangladesh.

From the start, CIM philosophy of mission had been to prepare and enable African believers to be the evangelists of their own people. Thus it was that Baluba evangelists from Djoko were the first to reach out to the Baphende who in turn reached out

to the Banjembe, the Bawongo, and the Ambunda. Gradually, as clusters of believers began to emerge, all eight mission stations became major Mennonite church centers.

From earliest days the tradition of annual missionary conferences, to which African leaders were invited for fellowship, inspiration, and discussion with the missionaries, was established. With passing time, a system of dual church and missionary conferences was followed.

In 1959 a delegation from the CIM board came to Zaire for a meeting with the church leaders at Djoko and raised the issue of the future of their own church. They were invited to choose a name of their preference for their church and to consider the removal of missionary personnel from one or more of the established stations to allow national leaders to assume more responsibility. Some models of new relations between the mission and the church were also sketched and studied. The African leaders decided that their name was to be the Evangelical Mennonite Church of Congo, a name which would later be changed to the Mennonite Church of Zaire (CMZA). Before any of the envisioned structural changes could be implemented, political independence suddenly burst upon the scene. This occasioned the abrupt departure of Belgian administrators and civil servants, followed by a time of great turmoil and insecurity which saw, among other things, the temporary evacuation of the entire CIM missionary team and the migration of the Baluba people from the West Kasai to the land of their forebears in the East Kasai.

In 1965 Joseph Mobutu, with the backing of the army, took control of the government and a measure of stability was restored. Missionaries and African church leaders both realized that it was urgent to revive the discussions which had been opened at Djoko in 1959. A number of significant initiatives were taken: The church sought its own legal charter from the government; it was granted in 1964. This secured legal recognition for the church and its officers. Arrangements were made for the Zairian church officers to work with their missionary counterparts in a thoroughgoing orientation in the areas of administrative responsibility and pastoral care. At the same time a committee of missionaries and African leaders were working on a statement of faith and a constitution for the church. In 1971 at another major consultation in Zaire a plan of fusion was adopted in which the CIM was dismantled as a mission, its properties and equipment were turned over to the church and the church was recognized as an autonomous body.

With administrative headquarters at Tshikapa, the CMZA counts a total of 33 districts scattered from °Kinshasa in the west to °Mbuji Mayi in the east (1986). It administers a school program which has more than 50,000 primary school students and thousands more at secondary levels. It maintains a four-year Bible institute at Kalonda, secondary schools for both girls and boys at a number of church centers, a health service which includes four small bush hospitals and more than 40 rural dispensaries. CMZA also is a partner in a variety of interchurch projects. In Kananga it cooperates with the Presbyterian Church in a Tshiluba-language literature production and distribution program known as IMPROKA and LIPROKA, a recording studio for production of religious and public service programming known as STUDIPROKA for diffusion over the Kasai Provincial radio system, and a large reference hospital and nurses training school, called IMCK, at Kananga. CMZA is a shareholder in a large press and publishing house, CEDI, in Kinshasa, and a Protestant guest center known as CAP. CMZA also has representation on the board of a theological training school, Institut Supérieur Théologique de Kinshasa, in the city.

In the area of rural development, the CMZA works with Mennonite Central Committee (MCC) in sponsoring an experimental farm and rural development program, SEDA, near its center at Nyanga. A variety of agricultural experiments have been carried out primarily with soybeans and different strains of manioc. There have also been some successful pilot projects demonstrating the breeding and care of livestock.

CMZA also operates a portable saw mill in a forest area along the Kasai River north of Tshikapa. Originally funded by a loan from °Mennonite Economic Development Associates (MEDA), it was purchased and put into operation to provide lumber for various church building projects and for the local market, where it is always in great demand.

On the national church scene in Zaire, the Mennonite churches, like all others, find themselves in the presence of a national church, Église du Christ au Zaire (ECZ; the Church of Christ in Zaire). During the mission era, a strong and active inter-mission organization had been created called the Congo Protestant Council (CPC). With the transition from mission to church, the missionary delegates were gradually replaced in the annual assemblies by their Zairian colleagues who in due time elected a Zairian executive secretary. While there was little interest in maintaining the council as a consultative body, there was great interest in using it as a springboard for the creation of a national church of which all former CPC affiliates would automatically become members. As members, they would no longer be referred to as churches, but rather as "communities" which were members of a single Zairian Protestant Church, that is, the ECZ. This entire process created some stress and debate. With passing time, however, it has become clear that while officially there is but a single Protestant Church in Zaire, for all practical purposes each member group functions as, and is considered to be, a church in its own right in the area where it ministers. This is very much the case of the Mennonite churches in Zaire.

Church growth among Mennonite Churches in Zaire continues at a rapid rate as it does all across black Africa. Not sharing the Western predilection for the gathering and maintenance of precise statistics, exact membership figures are difficult to ascertain. The Mennonite World Conference membership figures released in October 1986 cite a total Mennonite membership for Zaire of 92,503. Of this figure, the CMZA would account for at least 50,000, a membership which is distributed across 33 districts in three provinces plus the city of Kinshasa. Part of the reason for this steady growth is the aggressive

way national leaders have followed rural Mennonites into the mushrooming urban centers and gathered them into prayer and fellowship cells which, in turn, frequently become the core groups for new congregations.

Another major factor is the active role which laymen and laywomen take in rallying believers and in witnessing to unbelievers in settings where no trained leaders are available. The active lay involvement is both a blessing and a problem. While the readiness and willingness to take initiative in the absence of church leaders is most laudable, it also means that the lack of biblical grounding at times makes such groups vulnerable to the teaching of sects which proliferate in black Africa. In effect, church growth in Africa is far outstripping the leadership training programs in place. This clearly constitutes one of the major problems of the African church at this juncture in its history.

CMZA has established its central headquarters at Tshikapa where the president, vice president, general treasurer, educational secretary, and medical coordinator are based. The task of administration and coordination, given the extent of CMZA's ministries, the spread of its membership, and the near total absence of surface transportation is a taxing assignment, to say the least. Regional and ethnic loyalties always lie close to the surface and are capable of exerting serious pressures on the unity of the church. Added to this is the sense of quest, on the part of a younger, better educated generation of believers and leaders, for their own identity and statement of purpose. A question frequently heard in the decade of the 1980s is: "What does it mean to be both African and Mennonite?" These are healthy kinds of issues, and it is in struggling with and resolving them that the future thrust, nature, distinctives, and ministry of the Zaire Mennonite Church will be determined.   JEB

MWH (1978), 112-16, MWH (1984), 20; Peter Falk, The Growth of the Church in Africa (Grand Rapids: Zondervan, 1979); Celia Irvine, The Church of Christ in Zaire (Indianapolis: Christian Church Press, 1978); Levi Keidel, Footsteps to Freedom (Chicago: Moody Press, 1969), idem, War to Be One (Grand Rapids: Zondervan, 1977), idem, Caught in the Crossfire (Scottdale, 1979); Melvin Loewen, Three Score (Elkhart, Ind.: Congo Inland Mission, 1972); William Weaver and Harry Bertsche, Twenty-Five Years in the Congo (Chicago: Congo Inland Mission, 1938); William Weaver, Thirty-Five Years in the Congo (Chicago: Congo Inland Mission, 1945); A.I.M.M. Messenger (and its antecedents), bound vols., 1929ff., at A.I.M.M. office, Elkhart, Ind., and at Bluffton College Historical Library, Bluffton, Ohio, and MHL (Goshen); Basil Davidson, Africa in History (New York: MacMillan, 1968); Guy Gran, The Political Economy of Underdevelopment (New York: Praeger, 1979); Alan Merriam, Background of Conflict (Evanston, Ill.: Northwestern U. Press, 1961); R. Slade, King Leopold's Congo (London: Oxford U. Press, 1962); Robert Smith and Dia Nseyila Siawau, Zaire: Perception and Perspective (Valley Forge, Pa., American Baptist Mission Society, 1982).

See also Église du Christ au Zaire, Communauté Evangélique Mennonite.

Église Mennonite Sonlight Mission (Mennonite Sonlight Mission Church) is a Haitian national church founded by Pastor Gabriel Georges in 1980. Since their organization, its four congregations have related to Mennonites mostly from Pennsylvania and Ohio who have constituted an independent organization called Sonlight Mission. The Mennonite Sonlight Mission Church had a total membership in 1987 of 300. Two primary schools are associated with these congregations with a total student enrollment of over 400. Besides the superintending pastor, the church has recognized four deacons and an evangelist as part of its leadership. This group is located in the southern peninsula of Haiti with its central church located in the village of La Colline.   ESto

MWH (1984), 78.

Egypt. Beginning in 1972 with the placement of teachers with the Coptic Evangelical (Presbyterian) church, Mennonites have become increasingly involved with the Egyptian churches. Emphasis is given to placement of health care workers (23 in 1985) and teachers of English, at both elementary and adult levels, in the medical and educational institutions of the Coptic Evangelical, Coptic Orthodox, Anglican, and Catholic churches. ("Coptic" simply means "Egyptian".) Mennonites, through Mennonite Central Committee, are also involved in promoting and funding °literacy programs, health clinics, and land reclamation projects, and in encouraging and assisting in the renewal movement within the Coptic Orthodox community. Mennonites are not interested in beginning yet another western church in a country where °Islam comprises 90 percent of the population, but in assisting the indigenous churches carry out their agenda.   VR

See also Eastern and Coptic Orthodox Churches.

Midwestern Midwife: Sara Block Eitzen

The sight of a shiny black-top buggy with a gentle brown mare skimming down country roads in a cloud of dust was familiar to residents of the Gnadenau and Ebenfeld area near Hillsboro, Ks., in the late 1880s. At a time when professional careers for married women were unknown in the Mennonite community, Sara Block Eitzen (1840-1917) dispensed medicines and practiced physiotherapy, homeopathy, and midwifery. Records show she delivered more than 1,800 babies. Her delivery fee was usually a modest $2.50 per baby.

In Russia she had apprenticed herself to a doctor as he made his rounds from village to village. After her parents, David and Sara Block, and their family migrated to Kansas, she married Abraham Eitzen, a widower with four children, on Nov. 20, 1866. She never regretted the way the lot turned out that she had used to determine her future.

In later years, she occupied herself with letter writing to missionaries and took a keen interest in the development of Tabor College. She faithfully attended °Bible conferences as well as some district and denominational conferences. She left her family a legacy of interest in health care. By 1979, 13 grandsons and great-grandsons had entered the medical profession. The furnishings in the obstetrics department of Salem Hospital, built in Hillsboro in 1918, memorialize her name.   KFW

Esther Loewen Vogt in *Women among the Brethren*, ed. Katie Funk Wiebe (1979) 71-80.

El Capulin Colony. See Casas Grandes Colonies, Mexico.

El Cuervo Colony. See Casas Grandes Colonies, Mexico.

El Salvador. Three Mennonite groups were active in El Salvador in 1986: the Iglesia Evangélica Menonita (Beachy Amish), the Iglesia Menonita de El Salvador (Metapán), and Mennonite Central Committee (MCC). The Iglesia Evangélica Menonita was begun in 1968 following six years of social service work in cooperation with the government. Seventy-five members meet in six locations in central and western El Salvador. In addition, the churches support a variety of social service projects including an orphanage, day schools, and refugee programs. The Iglesia Menonita del El Salvador (Metapán) is related to the Iglesia Evangélica Menonita Hondurena (Honduran Mennonite Church) begun by Eastern Mennonite Board of Missions and Charities workers. The congregation in Metapán began when Salvadorans living in Honduras were repatriated after the 1969 war between the two countries. The church has grown from a few members to more than 100 and erected a building in 1982. Now it is planting churches in nearby communities.

Mennonite Central Committee began its work in El Salvador early in 1981 in response to the tremendous refugee needs that were a result of the civil war which began the previous year. MCC supported the work of local churches that had already started assistance programs in several, primarily rural, areas of the country. The emphasis was on emergency assistance including housing, clothing, medical care, and food distributions. This aid was continuing in 1986 but it had become a lower priority. As some of the local churches began to recognize the long-term nature of the war, they began to see ways to address the root causes of the conflict in addition to providing emergency assistance. Over the years, MCC has cooperated with them in resettlement projects, advocacy of dialogue and negotiation, and attempts to provide aid to the most affected rural areas so that residents would not have to become refugees and further strain the services of the larger towns and cities. Increasing emphasis has been placed on education of North Americans in the hope that the United States policy based primarily on a military solution can be changed to one of encouragement of a negotiated solution. Another emphasis is to accompany the Salvadoran churches as they face persecution while ministering to the poor and seeking to be peacemakers.   RFl

MWH (1984) 73; MC Yrb (1984) 133, 169.

Elder (Ältester) (ME II:178). This article updates the use of the office of Ältester since the 1950s. The *Ältester* in the churches which continue to use the office is always a man, and is normally elected by the members of the congregation. In some churches in the Federal Republic of Germany, the *Ältester* is salaried. In Canada some *Ältester* were salaried during the transition to salaried ministry, however usually in the Soviet Union and in the Americas, the office is not salaried and is for life.

The *Ältester* keeps the church's records, ordains ministers and deacons, administers baptism, serves communion, presides over membership meetings and meetings of ministers and deacons, and provides general direction, °discipline, and pastoral care of the church.

The office of *Ältester* is used in the Mennonite churches in the Soviet Union and in the Federal Republic of Germany. Mennonite churches in the United States have generally discarded the office. The only exception is the Old Order Mennonite churches which refer to their deacon as *Ältester*. In Canada the Mennonite churches which have adopted conference structures have ceased using this office. The one exception is the Chortitzer Mennonite Church which has recently organized as a conference, and retains the office of *Ältester*. The other Canadian churches which continue to use the office of *Ältester* function as *Gemeinden* (congregations), and include the Old Colony, the Sommerfelder, the Saskatchewan Bergthaler, the Kleine Gemeinde, the Reinländer, and the Zion Mennonites.

In Mexico all churches use the office of *Ältester* including the General Conference, Old Colony, Sommerfelder, Kleine Gemeinde, and Reinländer. The Belize Old Colony and Kleine Gemeinde Mennonite churches continue to use the office as do the Old Colony, Reinländer, Bergthaler, and Sommerfelder Mennonites in Bolivia; the Bergthaler, Sommerfelder and Old Colony Mennonites in Paraguay; and the Old Colony Mennonites in Argentina.   JF

See also Bishop.

Electronic Church. The "electronic church," which is more accurately called the "electronic pulpit," since it gathers a clientele, not a church, has become a major parachurch phenomenon in American Christianity. The clientele is composed of listeners-viewers-contributors on the receiving end of religious radio and television empires who belong to "an invisible religion" which can be consumed privately without participation in a congregation.

The utilization of the electronic media by Mennonite agencies has varied from °broadcasts which replicated the worship traditions of the church on the public media (The °°*Mennonite Hour,* The °°*Calvary Hour, Abundant Life, Words of the Gospel* etc.) to non-worship-service broadcasts targeted at a broad audience as a witness of Christian faith. *Choice, Minute Spots, Your Time, Heart to Heart,* are radio productions with specific audiences and communication objectives, namely to serve as an educational ministry rather than an alternative to church.

The consumption of religious broadcasts by Mennonites has been high. Studies of listening and viewing habits indicate a strong following of radio and television evangelists. The amount of financial support given to the "electronic church" by Mennonite contributors is not known, but there is evidence in the reports of pastors that (1) the members of congregations often reflect the theology of °Fundamentalist or °Evangelical electronic church preachers more than the teaching and beliefs of their congregation; (2) the loyalty of listeners to their electronic heroes is evident in listeners' vocal defense against any criticism of these preachers; (3) the parachurch organizations do receive strong financial contributions from Mennonite church members; (4) the electronic church has become a significant rival to the doctrine, budgets, ministries, and regular participation in the life of the local church; (5) the common refusal to give candid accounting of financial resources by electronic church organizations has led to widespread abuses of the public trust and tragic failures in the lives of popular media preachers.

The popular image of radio and television programs as effective means of evangelism has not been supported by research. Studies show that more than 80 percent of people who have joined the church recently were influenced by a friend or relative. Fewer than one percent came as a result of electronic °evangelism.

The electronic media confer a false status on people; frequently communicate only opinion already "proper" to the listener; tend toward sensationalism, not authenticity of faith; value what is profit-producing, not what is prophetic and unpopular. It is in the local, gathered church that faithfulness, °discipleship and development of spirituality in responsible community occurs. The electronic media are not an alternative church, but a competitive and seductive substitute for faithful Christian worship and practice.   DWA

See also Mass Media.

Elementary Schools. See Education; Mission Schools; Private Christian Schools; Public Schools.

Elkhart Co., Ind., Old Order Amish Settlement. See Lagrange-Elkhart, Ind., Old Order Amish Settlement; Nappanee, Ind., Old Order Amish Settlement.

Emmental (ME II:205). It is important to distinguish between the valley of Emmental, the River Emme, and the Emmental as a distinct geographic region of the Canton Bern. Defining the boundaries of the Emmental is somewhat complex. Politically the administrative areas Trachselwald, Signau, and Konolfingen constitute "the Emmental." Some of the regions belonging to Konolfingen, e.g., the areas in the Aare Valley, are not part of the Emmental. Economically the Emmental belongs to the weakest areas of the Canton Bern, while the Oberaargau, which is not part of the Emmental (although the ME II article counted it as part of the Emmental), is among the wealthiest areas of the canton. Although the *Geographisches Lexikon der Schweiz* limits the Emmental to the administrative areas of Trachselwald and Signau, topographically several smaller regions bordering Burgdorf and Konolfingen should be included as part of the Emmental landscape. Tourist hiking maps also include a part of the Canton Luzern as part of the Emmental. It was precisely the Luzern area which became a place of refuge for persecuted Bernese Anabaptists in the 16th c.

Emmental is ethnically unique. The clothing, dialect, and character of people from the Emmental have historically been different from the rest of the canton, though they are gradually losing this distinctiveness. In other parts of the Canton Bern, people from the Emmental are considered backward and stubborn. This characteristic may also have been a root cause of their resistance to the introduction of the Protestant Reformation and their support of the peasant revolt in 1653. Since that time Anabaptism has unfortunately often been falsely identified with that revolt.

In summary, the boundaries of Emmental may be described as follows: in the east the canton boundary with Luzern, in the south the highlands Voralpen (Hohgant-Honegg), and in the west a line running through Krauchtal-Walkringen-Konolfingen-Oberdiessbach. In the north Burgdorf and Huttwil can be viewed as the gates to the Emmental. This description modifies that given in ME II, namely, the areas Aarwangen, Wangen, and Fraubrunnen are in no case part of Emmental (ME II:205); neither are Jegenstorf, Bipp (Niederbipp), Utzenstorf, Herzogenbuchsee, etc. (207). The family of Niklaus Haberli von Buchsee were citizens of Munchenbuchsee near Bern, not Herzogenbuchsee (208). In connection with the names listed on page 209, only Gerber and Schenk are Emmental families. Amsler, Baumann, Hofer and Born are not of Emmental origin.

A careful study of official records has shown the following: (1) Many people were identified as coming from Emmental because that was a temporary place of residence rather than their place of origin. (2) Opponents of Anabaptism identified as many people as possible as "Emmentaler," that is, they portrayed Anabaptists as people of little education and great stubbornness. In this way the region called Emmental was enlarged beyond historical and geographical justification. (3) In the 1960 registry of Swiss Mennonite names only 14 out of 70 were actually originally from the Emmental. Eleven additional names which are found throughout Switzerland, including Emmental, might be added. This would, nevertheless, indicate that in 1960 two-thirds of the Swiss Mennonites were not from Emmental. As more people of non-Mennonite background join Swiss Mennonite congregations, the percentage of Swiss Mennonites originating in the Emmental would be reduced to one-fourth. For the congregation in Bern itself, for example, the figure would be only 20 percent. An analysis of the state archives in Bern, beginning in 1527, indicates that only 24 percent of the Anabaptists were from the Emmental, while 20 percent were from the central part of the Bernese Canton, 16 percent were from Thun and the Highlands, 13 percent from other cantons, 26 percent carried general Swiss names found everywhere. Possibly 3 percent were foreigners.

It should be noted that the Anabaptists who emigrated to the °°Jura region from the Emmental area do not speak the Emmental dialect but the central Bernese Canton dialect. Nineteenth-century mandates, the last in 1847, requiring every Swiss citizen to be registered in a specific area of his ancestral origin, resulted in many Mennonites being registered in Emmental when they had, in fact, not originated there. This was true, for example, of the Zürcher family, whose roots go back to Zürich but had spent some time in the Emmental. IZ-G

Familien-Namenbuch der Schweiz, 6 vols. (Zurich 1969-1971); Ortsverzeichnis der Schweiz (Bern: ESTA-Ausgabe, 1920); Geographisches Lexikon der Schweiz, vol. 2 (Neuchatel, 1902); Hans Sommer, Volk und Dichtung des Emmentals (Bern, 1969); Delbert Gratz, Bernese Anabaptists and their Descendents (Scottdale, 1952); Ernst Müller, Geschichte der Bernischen Täufer (Frauenfeld, 1895); Isaac Zürcher, "Die 'Täufernamen' in der Schweiz," in Informationsblätter (Schweizerischer Verein Für Täufergeschichte; Bern, 1985); Täufer-Namens-Sammlung, in the Staats-Archiv at Bern; Statistische Quellenwerke der Schweiz Heft 488 (Bern 1972), maps with canton and township boundaries.

Engel, Jacob (1753-1833), the first River Brethren (Brethren in Christ) leader and overseer (°bishop), was born in Switzerland in November 1753. His family, along with other Mennonites fleeing persecution, arrived in Philadelphia in October 1754. The Mennonite group settled along the Susquehanna River (thus River Brethren) in Lancaster County, Pa. Township tax records indicate Jacob was a farmer, owner of a cloth processing mill, and a minister of average financial means. When a religious awakening swept through the German settlements, Jacob, assisted by his brother John, became the leader of the emerging River Brethren (ca. 1780). This new group brought together the crisis °conversion experience of the awakening with the Pennsylvania version of the Anabaptist view of the church. Little is known regarding the ministry of Jacob Engel. There is evidence that he was an evangelist. He was the shepherd of the newly formed River Brethren fellowships. Such leadership included a pastoral visit to the River Brethren in Canada. He may have written, but if so, such works are not extant.   MHS

Donegal Twp. Tax Lists, Lancaster Co. Historical Society Library, Lancaster, Pa., 1756-; Wittlinger, Piety and Obedience (1978), 15-36 passim, 129, 551-54; Martin H. Schrag, "BIC Attitude toward the 'World' " (PhD diss., Temple Univ., 1967) 14, 17-19, 22.

England. The Mennonite movement in modern English history can be traced to relief efforts by North American Mennonites during World War II. In 1940 Mennonite Central Committee (MCC) sent Ted Claassen to London, followed several months later by John E. Coffman. During the hostilities 24 MCC workers served in England.

After the war MCC's activities shifted to the European continent. But John Coffman, who had married Eileen Pells (the first 20th-c. English Mennonite), remained in London to do inner-city mission work. The Mennonite Board of Missions (MC) in 1952 sent Quintus and Miriam Leatherman to open the London Mennonite Centre, which until 1981, provided a ministry of caring and housing to international students of many races and national origins. In the centre, a °London Mennonite fellowship met regularly.

By the 1980s some English people, impelled by a world crisis of militarism and maldistribution of wealth and by an awareness that traditional forms of Christianity were disintegrating, began to show renewed interest in Anabaptist and Mennonite insights. In response, the London Mennonite Centre, led by Alan and Eleanor Kreider, began a Cross-Currents program to do discipleship training in the Anabaptist and Mennonite tradition for a wide variety of English people. A resource center, with library, book service, and conversation partners, was also developing. The Centre's workers made significant contributions to the Christian peace movement in England.

Simultaneously, a growing number of English Christians in the 1980s had claimed the Anabaptist heritage. Many of these were charismatic Baptists; others were members of networks of rapidly growihg charismatic °'"house churches." From 1936 onwards (with several interruptions), in a succession of communities in several parts of the English countryside, the Hutterian Society of Brothers (°Hutterian Brethren) had given its witness to communitarian Anabaptism. Either through affirmation or denunciation, thinkers in several English Christian traditions were beginning to pay tribute to the influence of Anabaptist and Mennonite positions.   AK

MWH (1984), 114.

Engle, Jesse M. (July 19, 1938 - Apr. 3, 1900), was among the first Brethren in Christ missionaries to southern Africa and was instrumental in establishing the first Brethren in Christ mission congregation at Bulawayo, Rhodesia (Zimbabwe). He was born in Bainbridge, Pa., the son of Henry Engle and Hanna Myers and the grandson of Jacob °Engel. He was the youngest of 12 children, and was orphaned by the age of 12. His education was limited to a rural school in Stackstown, Pa. He was converted at the age of 14, married at 19, ordained to the ministry at 22, and elected as elder at 38. He served the church in Cumberland Co., Pa., and later in Kansas, migrating with the first party of Brethren in Christ in 1879. He felt the call to the mission field and left Abilene, Ks., for Africa on Oct. 15, 1897. The mission party consisted of Jesse and his wife, Elizabeth, H. Frances °Davidson, Alice Heise, and Barbara Hershey. After meeting with Cecil Rhodes, they were granted a large tract of land for the mission among the Matabele people in the Motopo Hills near Bulawayo. Jesse Engle died of malaria after serving less than two years. His wife was Elizabeth B. Niesley; they had nine children: Jacob, Henry, John, Enos, Mary, Aaron, Elizabeth, Jesse, and Ezra.   EKE

Anna R. Engle, John A. Climenhaga, and Leola A. Buckwalter, *There Is No Difference* (Nappanee, Ind., 1950), 10-27, 361-62; H. Frances Davidson, *South and South Central Africa* (Elgin, Ill.: Brethren Publishing House, 1915), 19-44; Wittlinger, *Piety and Obedience* (1978), 183-87; Morris M. Engle, *History Of The Engle Family In America 1754-1927* (Mt. Joy, Pa.: The Bulletin Press, 1927), 137-38; Noreen Trautwein, *The Everywhere Missionary* (Nappanee, Ind., 1967), 1-32; E. Morris Sider, ed., "The Journal of Frances Davidson," *BIC Hist. Life*, vol. 8 (1985), 103-23, 181-204, vol. 9 (1986), 23-64.

Entertainment. See Amusements.

Environmental Movements. See Ecology.

Epp, Frank H. (May 25, 1929–Jan. 22, 1986), churchman, journalist, educator, and author. Born at Lena, Man., and educated in theology, mass communication, and history, Epp began his professional career as a public school teacher and was professor of history at Conrad Grebel College at the time of his death in Kitchener, Ont. He was president of Conrad Grebel College, 1973-79. An ordained minister, he was a part-time pastor in four Mennonite congregations in Canada and the United States.

His extensive public writing career began in 1951 as editor of the youth section of *Der Bote*, the *Jugendseite*, which served General Conference Mennonite youth in Canada. As founding editor of *The Canadian Mennonite* (1953-67) and *The Mennonite Reporter* (1971-73) he exercised a broad and sometimes controversial influence among Mennonites in Canada at a time when many of them were in a language transition from °German to English.

From 1957-1963 he was director and regular speaker for the Conference of Mennonites in Manitoba's "Abundant Life" radio program. During most of this time he also served the Board of Christian Service of the Conference of Mennonites in Canada in various capacities. He was a board member of Mennonite Central Committee Canada (MCCC) from its inception in 1963 until his death and was chairman of the international MCC Peace Section, 1979-86. From 1972 to 1978 he was on the presidium of °Mennonite World Conference.

Beyond the Mennonite churches, Epp served on four committees of the Canadian Council of Churches (1967-73) and was appointed to two advisory bodies by the federal government (Immigration, 1968-77, and Multiculturalism, 1980-85). For two years (1970-71) he served as Executive Director of the World Federalists of Canada, and since 1980 was active in the United Nations Association of Canada. In the 1979 and 1980 federal parliamentary elections he was a candidate for the Liberal Party in the Waterloo (Ontario) constituency.

Epp's research travels, related to °peace education and writing projects, included numerous trips to the Middle East (6), Southeast Asia (3), and the Union of Soviet Socialist Republics (3). Epp's twelve books include three on the Arab-Israeli conflict in the Middle East and three on Mennonites in Canada. Others deal with educational institutions and with peace and refugee concerns.

In 1953 Epp married Helen Dick of Leamington, Ont. They had three daughters and one son.   AE

Works by Frank Epp include the following: *Education with a Plus: The Story of Rosthern Junior College* (Waterloo: Conrad Press, 1975); *The Israelis: Portrait of a People in Conflict* (Toronto: McClelland and Stewart, 1980); *Mennonite Exodus: The Rescue and Resettlement of the Russian Mennonites Since the Communist Revolution* (Altona: D. W. Friesen and Sons, 1962); *Mennonite Peoplehood: A Plea for New Initiatives* (Waterloo: Conrad Press, 1977); *Mennonites in Canada, 1786-1920: The History of a Separate People* (Toronto: MacMillan of Canada, 1974); *The Mennonites in Canada, 1920-1940: A People's Struggle for Survival* (MacMillan of Canada, 1982); a third volume in the series was partially completed at the time of his death; *The Palestinians: Portrait of a People in Conflict* (Toronto: McClelland and Stewart, 1976); *Small College Set on a Hill: Reflections on Church College Education in the University Context* (Waterloo: the Author, 1979); *A Strategy for Peace: Reflections of a Christian Pacifist* (Grand Rapids: Wm. B. Eerdmans, 1973); *Whose Land is Palestine? The Middle East Problem in Historical Perspective* (Toronto: McClelland and Stewart, 1970); *Your Neighbour as Yourself: A Study on Responsibility in Immigration* (Winnipeg: MCCC, 1968); *I Would Like to Dodge the Draft-Dodgers, But . . .* (Waterloo: Conrad Press, 1970). See also *MWR* (Jan. 30, 1986), 2; Heinold Fast, "Nachrufe auf Grete Mecenseffy, Liesel Quiring-Unruh, Frank H. Epp," *Menn. Geschbl.*, Jg. 43-44 (1986-87), 234-40.

Epp, Katharina Ratzlaff (Aug. 16, 1902–Oct. 15,

1984), was born in Steinfeld, Sagradovka, South Russia, to Abram and Katharina Fast Ratzlaff. At age 14 she joined the Mennonite Brethren Church. In response to the needs of her community, she studied *Tracktmoaki* (chiropractic) and obstetrics. After three years of study at the medical school at Halbstadt, she realized that she could not receive a diploma because of her refusal to become a communist.

On Nov. 22, 1929, Katharina married Johann Epp. On Dec 17, 1930, they fled with all of the Mennonites of Shumanovka on 60 sleds across the °°Amur River and went on to Harbin, China. In May 1932 after over a year of harassment and poverty, the Epps sailed for Paraguay with 373 Mennonite refugees. The Harbin Mennonites settled in the Chaco in Karlsruhe 16. The Epps lived there for 33 years, building a farm, providing medical help, and helping to lead the Mennonite congregation (GCM) there. They raised six children.

Because of her experience and training, Katharina received many calls for midwifery, bonesetting, physical therapy, and counseling. She had a special concern for the Indians who lived near the village. She also helped start a *Frauenverein* (women's circle) in her congregation.

In 1965 the Epps moved from Karlsruhe to °Filadelfia. There Katharina was active in the mission society and spiritual counseling.   RU

Ruth Unrau, *Encircled,* (Newton, 1986), 275-83.

Epp, Theodore H. (Jan. 27, 1907–Oct. 13, 1985), was born at Oraibi, Ariz., to J. B. and Nettie Epp, missionaries to the Hopi people. Theodore was baptized on May 20, 1923, at First Mennonite Church, Newton, Ks., the congregation his grandfather (Johann Epp from West Prussia and Trakt Colony, Russia) had pastored. It was this congregation which had sponsored his parents' work in Arizona. Theodore Epp was converted at Flagstaff, Ariz., on Aug. 10, 1927 under the teaching of Norman B. Harrison.

Epp married Matilda Schmidt on Aug. 10, 1930, and was ordained at her home church (Zoar Mennonite, Goltry, Okla.), where he pastored, 1932-36. He was educated at Hesston College and the Bible Institute of Los Angeles (BIOLA). He received a ThM degree from Southwestern Baptist Seminary, Ft. Worth, Tex., in 1932. His thesis topic was: "Should God's People Partake in War?" In 1936 Epp joined the radio ministry of T. Myron Webb and, on May 1, 1939, launched the *Back to the Bible Broadcast* at Lincoln, Nebr. At the time of his death this program was aired on 800 stations. His funeral was held at the Rosemont Alliance Church of Lincoln, Nebr., where he and his family attended, but never became members.   AHE

Theodore H. Epp, *Forty-Five Years of Adventuring by Faith* (Lincoln: Back to the Bible, 1984); idem, *Should God's People Partake in War?*, 4th ed. (Steinbach: Evangel Book Shop, 1965); *Christianity Today* (Nov. 22, 1985), 57; John D. Thiesen, *Prussian Roots, Kansas Branches*, rev. by Menno Schrag (Newton: First Mennonite Church, 1986), 72-73, 128.

Erb, Alta Mae Eby (b. Feb. 23, 1891). Alta Mae Eby grew up at Kinzers (Lancaster Co.), Pa. She ob-

tained her final year of high school and her college education at Goshen College, graduating in 1912. From 1912 to 1940 she was on the staff of Hesston College. She taught mathematics and teacher education and was librarian from 1913 to 1928. In 1917 she married Paul Erb. They had two children: Winifred (Erb) Paul and Delbert.

From 1940 to 1945, she taught teacher education at Goshen College. In 1945 they moved to Scottdale, Pa., where Paul served as editor of the *Gospel Herald*. Her activities at Scottdale were principally in the area of the nurture of children. She served extensively in Christian education workshops and from 1954-58 was Home Life Editor of *Christian Living* magazine. Her book, *The Christian Nurture of Children*, was first published in 1944. A second edition followed in 1955. It sold a reported 12,000 copies. From 1944 to 1961 she wrote a weekly column on the Uniform Sunday School Lessons which appeared in the *Gospel Herald*.   DH

Who's Who Mennonites (1943), 60; *Menn. Bib. II*, p. 439; Mary Miller, *A Pillar of Cloud: The Story of Hesston College, 1909-1959* (North Newton: Mennonite Press, 1959), 128-30; Rich, *Mennonite Women* (1983), 121; Phyllis Good, *Paul and Alta* (Scottdale, 1978).

Erb, Paul (Apr. 26, 1894–May 7, 1984). Paul Erb was born near Newton, Ks., and died at Mount Pleasant, Pa. During his 90 years he provided a wide variety of services for the Mennonite Church (MC). His principal contributions were as educator and editor, but he also served as pastor and church administrator. His graduate training was in English.

He taught at Hesston College, 1913-41 (acting dean, 1924-28; and dean, 1932-41). Then he was called to be professor of English at Goshen College (1941-45). He completed course work for a doctorate at the U. of Chicago and was preparing at near the age of 50 to spend the rest of his professional life at Goshen.

Then he was summoned to Scottdale, Pa., to succeed the aged Daniel °Kauffman as editor of *Gospel Herald*. At first he resisted this call, but eventually he responded positively to the voice of the church even though it meant abandoning his graduate work in English. He was editor of *Gospel Herald* from 1944 to 1962 and book editor of Herald Press, 1959-64.

Paul married Alta Mae Eby in 1917; they had two children: Winifred (Erb) Paul and Delbert. Paul Erb was ordained to the ministry in 1919 and served as part-time pastor in addition to his teaching and editorial duties.

In addition to his inside work as teacher and dean, Paul had inadvertently prepared for the *Gospel Herald* work by extensive travel among Mennonite congregations on behalf of Hesston College. He was also a member of the Mennonite Commission for Christian Education and Young People's Work, 1937-51, and was a leader in the movement to organize Mennonite Youth Fellowship in 1948.

Although he raised editorial writing to a new height, he continued extensive activity outside the office. He became the first executive secretary of the Mennonite Church (MC) general conference (1958-61) and, after retirement, served as field worker for Allegheny Mennonite Conference, 1966-

69. Then he taught English at Eastern Mennonite College, 1969-71 and part-time in 1973.

His books include *The Alpha and the Omega* (1955); *Don't Park Here*, editorials reprinted from the *Gospel Herald* (1962); *We Believe* (1969); *Orie O. Miller* (1969); *South Central Frontiers* (1974); *Bible Prophecy: Questions and Answers* (1978). Among these the most important was *The Alpha and the Omega*, the Conrad Grebel lectures for 1955. This was an attempt to fashion a mediating position between premillennialism and amillennialism in an effort to overcome disagreement on this issue within the Mennonite Church.   DH

Who's Who Mennonites (1943), 60; *Menn. Bib. II*, p. 439; Phyllis Good, *Paul and Alta* (1978); Daniel Hertzler, *Not by Might* (1983) 87-91.

Esau, John J. (Feb. 12, 1900–Jan. 13, 1979). Born in Mountain Lake, Minn., Esau was the son of Dietrich and Katharina (Harder) Esau. He died in Mountain Lake, Minn.

He came to be known as "the blind evangelist," traveling throughout the General Conference Mennonite Church and other Mennonite groups for many years. John lost the sight of one eye through a childhood accident when a stick lodged in his eye. Then at the age of 27 he lost the sight of the second eye due to damage to the optic nerve in the original accident. This was the first year of his public ministry as well as his marriage to Elvina (Augsburger) of Bluffton, Ohio, on June 24, 1927.

Having graduated from Moody Bible Institute in Chicago, John sought for ministry opportunities within the Mennonite church. Failing to find such due to his impending blindness, he found three small Christian Union congregations near Lima, Ohio, willing to take the risk. Nevertheless, he sought ordination within the Mennonite church, first as a minister of the gospel in 1927 and then as an elder in 1935. He became the first pastor of First Mennonite Church of Omaha, Nebraska, an unaffiliated congregation related to Grace Bible Institute for whom he also worked as a traveling evangelist. He served several other congregations as an interim pastor, but most of the years of his ministry were as an itinerant evangelist, traveling throughout the United States and Canada. As a blind person he normally traveled by train and usually alone. During his final years of active ministry (1956-65), he traveled under the Board of Missions of the General Conference Mennonite Church. JAE

Esch, Christian David (Oct. 12, 1883–Feb. 21, 1931), missionary in India and physician. Born at Wellman, Iowa, Esch was the son of David and Fannie Kanagy Esch. He married Mina Ellen Brubaker (1887-1983) of Cherry Box, Mo., on Sept. 5, 1908. Together they raised a family of seven children. He died at °Dhamtari, Madyha Pradesh, India.

A graduate of Goshen College (BA) and Chicago Medical School (MD), he and Mina were appointed to mission service in India in 1910 by the Mennonite Board of Missions (MC). There he was responsible for the establishment and development of what became the Dhamtari Christian Hospital (ME IV:1076) in 1916. In recognition of his pioneering work in the modern treatment of °Hansen's Disease

(leprosy), the governor of the Madhya Pradesh (Central Provinces) presented him with the Kaiser I Hind Silver Medal in 1927.

Soon after arriving in India in 1911 he was ordained as minister and in 1924 as bishop. Widely known for his piety and versatility, Esch was a classic figure as a medical missionary, church leader, and hospital administrator.   JAL

John A. Lapp, *India* (1972), index; *Menn. Bib. II*, p. 439.

Eschatology. See Apocalypticism; Death and Dying; Dispensationalism; Eternity; Heaven.

Espelkamp (ME II:249), founded as a new city for German refugees from eastern areas of the former German empire, has become a center for Mennonites. On Nov. 21, 1952, the Espelkamp Mennonite congregation was established. Albert Bartel, the elder, selected the text for the celebration from Ps 133. A building in the munitions dump served as a meetingplace for 71 people (53 of them were baptized members). The church increased steadily by immigration. Return emigrants from South America started coming in 1965, and resettlers (°*Umsiedler*) from the Soviet Union in 1972. Membership in 1986 was 668, composed of about one-half resettlers, one-fourth return emigrants, and one-fourth °West Prussians. Further resettlers formed a Mennonite Brethren congregation on June 29, 1974 (670 members in 1986). Following a division, a second Mennonite Brethren congregation was formed in November 1980, numbering 245 members and led by the previous elder.   KKlaa

Estate Owners (Gutsbesitzer) were a landed elite who formed a distinct and privileged social group among Russian Mennonites. Although small in number they played an important part in the development of Mennonite life in Russia.

Many of the really wealthy landowners by 1914 were descended from a small group of entrepreneurs who had acquired land before 1860, usually the estates of impoverished Russian gentry. Land at this period was cheap and large acreages were needed to pasture the large flocks of sheep these entrepreneurs had acquired. Pastoral farming gave way to arable farming and by the end of the 19th c. cultivation was extensive, using modern machinery and peasant labor. In southern Russia cereal production provided estate owners with extremely large incomes.

By 1914 there were over 500 Mennonite private estates in the provinces of Ekaterinoslav, Taurida, Samara, Kherson, Kharkov and in the Don region. The largest concentration was in Taurida and Ekaterinoslav. Estates varied considerably in size from 100 desiatin to more than 100,000 desiatin (250-250,000 acres; 110-110,000 hectares), although 60 percent were under 500 desiatin (1,250 acres; 550 hectares) in area. An owner of more than 500 desiatin was considered a large landowner. Land purchased for a few rubles a desiatin was worth 400-500 rubles a desiatin by 1914.

Estate owners, particularly the large landowners, formed a separate social group. Considerable intermarriage occurred among the children of estate owners and marriage alliances were also made with the families of other wealthy Mennonites, particularly industrialists. Many industrialists and rich millers also purchased estates after 1860. Ownership of large estates was restricted to a few leading families whose life-style was very different from that of other Mennonite settlers. They lived in large houses, employed many °servants and traveled widely. Their children were often well educated and associated with the Russian and Mennonite intelligentsia. They were more integrated into Russian society than most Mennonites and were involved in local and national affairs. Two estate owners, Abraham Bergmann and Peter Schroeder, were members of the Imperial Duma (parliament).

Although a distinct social group, members of estate-owning families maintained close ties with the wider Mennonite community. Through payment of taxes and generous voluntary donations they supported major Mennonite social and welfare institutions before 1914 including the °Forsteidienst (forestry service), schools, hospitals, and various religious concerns.

In the 1917 °Russian Revolution and subsequent time of anarchy and civil war they lost most of their land and many were killed. Others fled to the colonies and many later emigrated, mostly to Canada.   JU

Adolf Ehrt, *Das Mennonitentum in Russland* (Langensalza, 1932); David G. Rempel, "The Mennonite Colonies in Russia" (PhD diss., Stanford U., 1933), 236-38, cf. *MQR*, 48 (1974), 15-32 passim; J. C. Toews, "Das mennonitische Gutsbesitzertum in Russland," series in *Der Bote* (June 30-Nov. 24, 1954); H. H. Klassen, "Mennonitische Gutsbesitzer in der Ukraine," *Der Bote* (Sep. 5, 1972); James Urry, "Through the Eye of a Needle: Wealth and the Mennonite Experience in Imperial Russia," *JMS*, 3 (1985), 7-35; Al Reimer, *My Harp Is Turned to Mourning* (Winnipeg: Hyperion, 1985).

See also Land Distribution.

Eternity is a concept understood and used differently within Mennonite and Amish circles. The literal interpretation of the Amish is quite different from the more sophisticated description by Mennonites with graduate school training. The conservative and orthodox Mennonites, as well as the Amish, are inclined to perceive of eternity as timelessness, acknowledging their inability to explain, but at the same time believing that God has given enough information to make life profitable on earth, with the assurance that the missing elements will be understood in the hereafter. The person with considerable formal education is more inclined to critical reflection, or poetic indulgence, such as "Dancing across the meadows of eternity," heard at Mennonite Church (MC) general assembly in 1987.

Eternity is generally understood in three main senses: (a) as an unending extent of time, (b) as that which is entirely timeless, and (c) as that which includes time, but somehow also transcends it. The majority of Mennonite and Amish who base their understanding on Rev 10:6 in the Luther German translation, or the King James Version, or both ("that there should be time no longer"), tend to conceive of eternity as entirely timeless, and from everlasting to everlasting, without end, but do not attempt a detailed explanation.

A study of word usage and origin, such as Gerald Studer in *After Death, What?* (Scottdale, 1976) brings to the surface issues which lead to a less precise view (pp. 122-28). Measures of °Fundamentalist orthodoxy in Kauffman and Harder, *Anabaptism Four C. Later* (pp. 112-13), show about 77 percent of respondents believing in the doctrine of eternal punishment. It is probably safe to assume that the percentage believing in heaven or the infinite continuation of a timeless timelessness, or both would undoubtedly be higher.

For some Mennonites, relationships take priority over considerations of time or timelessness. Embodied in that view, eternity is a continuation of a union, a relationship, begun on earth (Jn 15; the vine and branch). It is a transformation and completion of that relationship, in which time and space become irrelevant.   ESY

See also Death; God; Heaven; Hell (ME II); Salvation.

Ethics. See Development Work; Discipleship; Justice; Nonconformity; Mennonite Central Committee; Peace; Philosophy; Relief Work; Sectarianism; Sermon on the Mount; Service; Sociopolitical Activism.

Ethiopia. Located in eastern Africa, Ethiopia has an area of 460,000 sq. mi. (1,191,400 sq. km.) and an estimated population of 45 million. The people subscribe to Christianity, introduced in A.D. 335; Islam, begun in the 6th c.; and traditional (°animist) religions. Evangelicals began to evangelize in the 17th c. but did not prosper until the 20th c. Today (1987) 40 percent of the population belong to the Ethiopian Orthodox church and only 3 percent are evangelical.

The country has been independent except for the five-year domination by Italy in the early 1940s; consequently the people do not hold bitterness toward colonial powers as in some other parts of Africa.

Much of Ethiopia is a high plateau with a pleasant year-round climate. Early rains come in April; the heavy rains begin in July and last through September. The northeast is desert-like lowlands reaching from the inland mountains to the Red Sea. Here nomadic tribes live. In the mountains and deep river valleys people farm for a living, grow their grain and vegetables and raise cattle. Coffee and hides are important exports. The living standard is one of the lowest in Africa with an average income between $100 and $200. In 1974 a socialist government succeeded a monarchy of many centuries duration.

Mennonite Mission in Ethiopia. Mennonites first went to Ethiopia in 1945 as relief workers sponsored by the Relief Committee of Mennonite Board of Missions (MC). Samuel Yoder and Paul Hooley made initial contacts and found the country to be in need of medical and educational work because the Italian occupation left the country bereft of an educated class. Even so the government was reluctant to admit foreign missionaries. So the Mennonites tried to prove themselves as people of service and not as intruders in the nation's politics nor as proselytizers of Orthodox Christians.

Mennonites contracted with the government to renovate a cotton gin into a hospital at Nazareth, a town of 30,000 located at an elevation of 5,000 ft., 60 mi. (97 km.) se. of Addis Ababa. By 1947 renovation was complete for a 40-bed hospital, a training school for medical assistants (dressers), and an out-patient clinic. The place was named Haile Mariam Mamo Memorial Hospital in honor of a statesman killed during the war with Italy.

Eastern Mennonite (MC) Board of Missions and Charities, Salunga, Pa., sent Daniel and Blanch Sensenig in anticipation of being able to obtain permission to do mission work. Emperor Haile Selassie I invited Mennonites to function as a mission and do educational and medical work among Muslims in Hararge Province. A hospital and the first elementary school was built at Deder in Hararge Province, a school and clinic were opened at Bedeno, and an evening school was established in Dire Dawa. A School for the Blind, directed by Clayton and Martha Keener, was opened in Addis Ababa in 1952. In 1959 a Bible Academy was opened at Nazareth. A staff of 30 missionaries—doctors, nurses, teachers, pastors—were appointed by Eastern Board to maintain these institutions. Congregations were formed around these institutions. When the Meserete Kristos Church was organized in 1959 there were 400 attending worship at these places.

Meserete Kristos Church. Missionaries considered it a part of their work to establish churches. Complete freedom for this was given in Muslim areas such as Hararge Province, but restrictions were placed on such activity at Nazareth, a strong Orthodox area. The first believers were baptized in 1951; they were from Nazareth but were taken to Addis Ababa for the ceremony because of the government restrictions. The service programs set up by the mission opened doors and helped establish confidence with the people and the government. Jobs in teaching and medicine brought young people into contact with the missionaries. Doctors prayed before treating patients and national evangelists were hired to minister to patients.

The church officially began in 1959 when 11 Ethiopian lay leaders met with missionaries to set up a structure to coordinate the work of the five congregations which had formed on the mission stations. An annual Christian Life Conference helped make the church known to other evangelical groups. Under the direction of Daniel S. Sensenig and Chester L. Wenger a General Church Council was organized in 1959 with lay "counselors" chosen to each represent 20 members in the fellowship groups. By 1964 Ethiopians had replaced missionaries in the executive offices and missionaries then served as assistants. The council met semiannually to plan for nurture and evangelism and review institutional work. The name Meserete Kristos Bete Kristian (Christ Foundation Church) was chosen because the term "Mennonite" had no local meaning. The church took over the administration of the schools and hospitals begun by the mission in order to minister to the whole person. It organized a medical board, board of education, and evangelism board. These institutions helped the church become established. A number of leaders in

the 1980s came to the church from contacts made during medical and secondary training. On Sundays eager Christians went into the surrounding areas to witness to the gospel.

Congregations were established at Wonji, Shoa, and Meta Hara among people from other areas who moved to these places to work on sugar plantations along the Awash River. A church was built in the Bole area of Addis Ababa for the fellowship that met at the School for the Blind. By 1973 Meserete Kristos Church (MKC) had 8 congregations with 800 members, 11 elementary schools, 2 junior high schools, 1 boarding high school, 2 hospitals, 2 clinics, 2 guest houses, a bookstore with several branches and a literature program which produced a newsletter, *Zena*.

From 1966 to 1974 MKC joined with the Baptist General Conference Mission to form Globe Publishing House which published Sunday school materials and leadership training courses for evangelical churches.

In 1973 a spiritual awakening took place, after a long period of slow growth. It started in Nazareth where people started flocking to church and confessed their sins. Many zealous Christians gave their time to God's work. Each congregation has its own history of how God's spirit started to move among them. In the 1970s the number of congregations increased to 15. In 1973 the government closed the Pentecostal churches in Addis Ababa. The MKC Bole chapel tried to accommodate the influx of Pentecostals seeking a place to worship by building lean-to shelters and by conducting services in three shifts.

During this time choirs and the writing of music began to proliferate in evangelical churches. A new type of music—neither western nor Orthodox—was developed and spread throughout the country by cassette tapes.

With the coming of the new military rule in 1974 workers who felt oppressed under the monarchy began to demonstrate and demand more rights and better pay. The church, unable to meet the worker demands, transferred the hospitals to the government. The Menno Bookstore was nationalized in 1977; the Bible Academy in 1982. In 1982 also the government closed all 15 congregations of the Meserete Kristos Church and detained five of its leaders for four years. The church does not officially exist since that time. Mennonite Central Committee continues to carry on agricultural development work, reforestation, resettlement of refugees, and distribution of food in times of famine.   NH

MWH (1978), 76-81; *MWH* (1984), 11.

Ethnic Groups. See Hispanic Mennonites; Afro-American Mennonite Association; Indians, North American.

Ethnicity. Ethnic groups are those with a common cultural tradition and sense of identity which sets them off from the larger society around them. For most of their history Mennonites have been distinctive enough to qualify as an ethnic, as well as a religious, group. Whether this is still the case in the late 20th c. is more open to question than it was previously.

Several strands of Mennonite ethnicity developed

in Europe and were carried to the New World. The Swiss and South Germans, experiencing nearly 300 years of °persecution, fled to isolated rural areas and sought to stay physically and theologically separate from the hostile world around them. The Amish schism intensified already strict church °discipline which governed all of life. A strong teaching on °humility (*Demut*) was reinforced by their socially marginal position.

As the Swiss and South German Amish and Mennonites moved to the eastern United States and Canada in the 1700s and 1800s, they became known for their tightly-knit agricultural communities, their emphasis on plain °dress, and their separation from the "world," which included other religious groups. Those in Pennsylvania did share a "Pennsylvania Dutch" (Palatine German) tongue with their neighbors for a time, but were distinguished by their plainness of dress and severity of customs and church discipline from the "fancy Dutch" (German Reformed, Lutherans and others). Pennsylvania Dutch cooking, developed to its highest form by the Amish and Mennonites, includes such specialties as shoo-fly pie, snitz and knepp, a variety of sweet and sour pickles and condiments, custards, dumplings, soups, and a variety of dishes based on apples.

The Hutterites, who experienced the most severe and long-lasting persecution of all Anabaptist groups, also practiced plain dress, severity of church discipline, a strong two-world theology, and a German (Tyrolean) tongue. They alone developed the practice of New Testament sharing of resources (°mutual aid) into a formalized Christian communalism (Gütergemeinschaft) in which all property was held in common by the *Bruderhof*, at once a social, economic, and religious community. Those Hutterites who retained community of goods and the *Bruderhof* pattern after °migration to the western United States and Canada in the 1870s retain their distinctive language and culture. Those who gave up the communal pattern have been largely assimilated into the General Conference Mennonite Church in South Dakota.

The Dutch and North German Mennonites experienced less than a century of persecution, and mingled more freely with their non-Mennonite compatriots from whom they enjoyed a good deal of respect. They were the least isolated and least distinct of all European Mennonites. Whether they developed a separate Mennonite ethnicity in The Netherlands and North Germany is questionable.

However, some of these Mennonites moved east to take advantage of offers to settle and develop agricultural lands first in Prussia and then in Russia and the Ukraine. Here they developed their own distinctive low-German tongue (*Plattdeutsch*, or *Plautdietsch*), foods (e.g. *vereniki*, borscht, *pluma moos*), and eventually a subsociety virtually closed to outsiders. To be a Mennonite in the Russian colonies was perhaps even more a cultural than a religious phenomenon. As the Dutch/Russian Mennonites moved to western Canada and the United States and later to Mexico, Paraguay, and South Brazil, they retained their low-German culture, foods, and ethnic pride for several generations. It is still strongly in evidence among the more culturally and religiously conservative of them, the Old Colony Mennonites in

Mexico, and the colony Mennonites of Paraguay, Brazil, and Bolivia.

North American society, however, with its materialism, extreme individualism, °nationalism, °mass communication, modern transportation, and stress on °education and upward mobility, has taken its toll on the old style Swiss-German and Low-German ethnicity. Only the most °conservative groups, such as the Amish, Old Order Mennonites, Old Colony Mennonites, and the Hutterites, clearly retain the old ethnicity. For them separation from the world is of prime importance. Among the more progressive, °acculturated groups, those increasingly open to contact with the world and lacking strong collective discipline, the old ethnicity is gone or nearly so. New members, often of non-Mennonite and non-German background, have joined progressive Mennonite congregations and denominations (Mennonite Church [MC], General Conference Mennonite Church, Mennonite Brethren, Evangelical Mennonite Church) that at times find their ethnic heritage and customs an impediment to °evangelism and church growth. In fact, some new members may feel that their welcome is less than enthusiastic if they lack an easily recognized Mennonite surname. Some progressive Mennonites are also embarrassed by what they regard as ethnic provincialism. Increasing numbers of young Mennonites find non-Mennonite marriage partners, another significant departure from the fairly rigid endogamy of the past (°intermarriage).

Progressive Mennonites, however, strive to retain and build a less visible ethnicity of Mennonite ideals (e.g., °peace, °service, simplicity, mutual aid) fostered by °inter-Mennonite cooperation in Mennonite Central Committee, Mennonite Disaster Service, Mennonite mutual aid associations, and a growing number of inter-Mennonite business and professional organizations (e.g., °Mennonite Economic Development Associates, Mennonite Medical Association). The various North American Mennonite colleges and seminaries have been instrumental in establishing and fostering the new ethnicity of Mennonite ideals and inter-Mennonite cooperation.

The new Mennonite ethnicity, if one exists, is now portable, largely symbolic and ideological, rather than the old concrete, rooted rural ethnicity of language, food, dress, °family, customs, and land. Only time will tell whether a symbolic, portable ethnicity of values and ideals can endure once the ties of a distinct and common language, history, isolation, memory of persecution, and rural community have weakened or disappeared as they have for the progressive Mennonite groups of North America.　　　　　　　　　　　　　　　MLY

Cornelius J. Dyck, *An Introduction to Mennonite History* (Scottdale, 1967, 1981); James C. Juhnke, "Mennonite History and Self Understanding: North American Mennonitism As a Bipolar Mosaic," and Donald B. Kraybill, "Modernity and Identity: The Transformation of Mennonite Ethnicity," in *Mennonite Identity: Historical and Contemporary Perspectives*, ed. Sam Steiner and Calvin Redekop (Lanham, Md.: University Press of America, 1988); Paul J. Toews, "Dissolving the Boundaries and Strengthening the Nuclei," *Chr. Leader* (July 22, 1982), 6-8.

See also Folklore.

Ethridge, Tenn., Old Order Amish Settlement (ME

III:301) is located in Lawrence Co., 65 mi. (105 km.) south of Nashville. The Ethridge community began in 1944 with families moving from the now extinct Amish settlement at Lumberton, Miss. (Luthy, *Amish*, (1986), 234-37). The community has experienced steady growth. In 1986 it had five church districts (congregations) with a population of about 750. The Ethridge Amish are primarily farmers but they also engage in lumber-milling and furniture-making. Tennessee has four Amish settlements with the largest concentration at Ethridge. This community of over 40 years has served as the parent congregation for several new settlements in Kentucky and Tennessee.   SLY

Eucharist. See Communion.

Europäisches Mennonitisches Evangelisationskomitee (EMEK; European Mennonite Mission Committee) (ME II:202). This mission agency developed gradually through the cooperation of the Mennonites in West Germany, France, Switzerland, and The Netherlands. All missionaries from Mennonite groups in these countries are now (1987) sent out by EMEK.

Upon the request of the French Mennonites, responsibility for the work in Chad was assumed by EMEK in 1963. In 1986 a couple was sent to Burkina Faso jointly by EMEK and the Africa Inter-Mennonite Mission, Elkhart, Ind. When it appeared that the African doors for missions were being closed, EMEK began work with African students in Paris (Foyer Grébel), together with the Mennonite Board of Missions (MC), Elkhart.

Administrative responsibility is divided among the various members of EMEK. Thus Mennonites in The Netherlands are responsible for Java, Mennonites in Switzerland for Irian Jaya (Indonesia), and Mennonites in France for Chad. The 1986 budget equaled 730,000 West German marks, of which Mennonites in The Netherlands supplied 28 percent and those in the other member countries each 24 percent.

Important issues in 1986 were: the relationship between °mission and °relief work, the °peace witness as mission and the responsibility for mission in secularized Europe. The latter work is carried on together with American agencies.   LLau

Leo Laurense, *125 Jahre Zusammenarbeit in der Mennonitischen Mission, 1847-1972* (EMEK, 1972); *Menn. Jahrbuch* (1984), 115.

See also Deutsches Mennonitisches Missionskomitee; Doopsgezinde Zendingsraad; Mission Boards; Schweizerisches Mennonitisches Evangelisationskomitee.

Europäisches Mennonitisches Friedenskomitee (EMFK; European Mennonite Peace Committee) was reconstituted in 1981 as a result of discussing the need for a European representative to the °International Mennonite Peace Committee and the need to be affiliated with the Mennonite World Conference, and the Mennonite Central Committee. In 1984 the committee employed a secretary and appointed a treasurer and a chairperson. It is largely responsible for publishing the periodical titled *Natowatch.*

Discipleship is following Jesus to the cross, is daring steps toward °peace and °justice in a world of conflict. "Dialogue" has emerged as a major theme for the work of EMFK, in its associations with °relief work, the °International Mennonite Organization, the °Europäisches Mennonitisches Evangelisationskomitee, mediation services under MCC-Europe, the worldwide Mennonite Sunday for Peace, and European network of the organization, °Church and Peace.   HJW

See also Peace Education; Peace Activism.

Europe. See Association Mennonite Luxembourgeoise; Austria; Belgium; Bundesrepublik Deutschland; Deutsche Demokratische Republik; Greece; Hungary; Irish Mennonite Movement; Italy; London Mennonite Fellowship; Netherlands; Poland; Portugal; Spain; Sweden; Union of Soviet Socialist Republics; Yugoslavia.

Evangelical Church of Java. See Gereja Injili di Tanah Jawa (GITJ).

Evangelical Convention of Mennonite Brethren, Paraguay. See Convención Evangélica de los Hermanos Menonitas, Paraguay.

Evangelical Mennonite Association of Brazil. See Associação Evangélica Menonita, Brazil.

Evangelical Mennonite Brethren Conference. See Fellowship of Evangelical Bible Churches.

Evangelical Mennonite Brethren Conference of South America. See Konferenz der Evangelischen Mennonitischen Brüderschaft von Südamerika.

Evangelical Mennonite Church, Dominican Republic. See Conferencia de las Iglesias Evangélicas Menonitas, Dominican Republic.

Evangelical Mennonite Church, El Salvador. See Iglesia Evangélica Mennonita, El Salvador.

Evangelical Mennonite Church, United States (EMCh). (ME II:264) With 3,788 members (1986) in 25 congregations spread across Indiana, Illinois, Ohio, Michigan, and Kansas, the Evangelical Mennonite Church in the United States is a small but growing member of the Mennonite family. Since its origin in 1865 in Berne, Indiana, it has moved from its Amish roots through the middle of the Mennonite family and into the °Evangelical portion of the North American church spectrum. During the 30 years from 1955 to 1985, the denomination has continued its struggle to relate the "evangelical" and the "Mennonite" aspects of its name and heritage.

During the 1950s the Evangelical Mennonite Church took serious steps toward merger with the Evangelical Mennonite Brethren Conference (°Fellowship of Evangelical Bible Churches). In the 1960s merger was considered with the Missionary Church Association, an evangelical church with Mennonite roots that eventually merged with the °°United Missionary Church. Neither merger took place, and in 1974 the denomination officially tabled

EUROPE

LEGEND

MENNONITE CHURCHES IN EUROPE

- ■ Organized bodies
- ★ MCC involvement
- □ Other missions and programs (not incl. missions relating to organized bodies)
- • 500 members (approx. locations)

TABLE

Organized bodies	Membership (1986)
AUSTRIA	
Bund der Europäischen Mennonitischen Brüdergemeinden (European Menn. Br. Ch.)	638
BELGIUM	
Conseil Mennonite Belge (Belgian Menn. Council)	85
GERMANY, EAST (GERM. DEM. REP.)	
Mennonitengemeinden in der DDR (Mennonites in the G.D.R.)	244
GERMANY, WEST (FED. REP. OF GERM.)	
Bund der Europäischen Mennonitischen Brüdergemeinden (European Menn. Br. Ch.)	638
Mennoniten Brüdergemeinden (Ind. Umsiedler)	1292
Mennonitengemeinden (Ind. Umsiedler)	804
Verband deutscher Mennoniten-Gemeinden (Union of Menn. Churches in Germany)	1637
Vereinigung der Deutschen Mennonitengemeinden (United German Menn. Congs.)	7242
FRANCE	
Association des Eglises Evangéliques Mennonites de France (Assoc. of Menn. Churches of France)	2000
IRELAND	
Irish Mennonite Church	10
ITALY	
Chiesa Evangelica Mennonite (Menn. Ch. of Italy)	88
LUXEMBOURG	
Association Mennonite Luxembourgeoise (Menn. Comm. of Luxembourg)	105
NETHERLANDS	
Algemene Doopsgezinde Societeit (Dutch Menn. Brotherhood)	20000
SPAIN	
Communidad Cristiana (Chr. Comm.)	50
SWITZERLAND	
Konferenz der Mennoniten der Schweiz (Altaufer) (Conf. of Mennonites of Switzerland, Altaufer)	2750
U.S.S.R.	
Including members of the following groups: All Union Council of Evan. Christians-Baptists (AUCEB), Council of Churches of Evan. Chr. and Baptists (CCECB), Menn. Br. registered and unregistered congs., Menn. (Kirchliche) registered and unregistered congs.	55000
UNITED KINGDOM (ENGLAND)	
London Mennonite Fellowship	30

Other missions and programs (not incl. those relating to organized bodies)

FRANCE: Menn. Miss. Assoc. of Lorraine (EMBMC), French Menn. Miss.
GERMANY, WEST: Cons. Menn. B. of Miss. & Char., Evan. Menn. Conf. Board of Miss., Deutsche Heimatmission
PORTUGAL: Menn. Br. Miss./Services
SPAIN: Menn. B. of Miss.
SWEDEN: Menn. B. of Miss.

all merger discussion.

That decision indicated a deliberate shift in denominational thinking and policy. The new tendency was to work from the assumption that the group would continue to exist as an independent organization. A third executive staff member was added to headquarters staff at Fort Wayne, Ind. (1974); a new headquarters building was constructed (1977); a short denominational history was published (1979); denominational mission work *was established in other countries (Venezuela, 1980; Burkina Faso, 1983); and the denominational committee structure was overhauled (1986). These actions were seen as the kind of steps which an organization would probably not take while considering merger. Before 1974, merger was often proposed as a step toward more efficiency in denominational work and mission. Since then merger discussion has been seen more as a hindrance to mission, a waste of energy that should be channeled into direct ministry.

The form of ministry having most significance for the denomination's identity and future is the establishment of new congregations through church extension. Though there have been a few failures, on the whole, efforts have been so successful that over half of the present attenders worship in congregations which are less than thirty years old, e.g., Grace (Morton, Ill.), Brookside (Fort Wayne, Ind.), and Upland (Ind.). Other congregations are being formed in Illinois, Ohio, Indiana and Kansas. None of the new churches are in traditionally Mennonite communities; all of them have a heavy emphasis on personal conversion. The rapid growth of churches with such shallow Mennonite roots naturally affects the way the denomination as a whole sees itself. The trend is toward separating the concepts of °church planting and the Mennonite heritage, giving priority to church planting.

Overseas mission has continued as a high priority of the denomination with 43 percent of denominational funds in the 1986-87 budget being designated for overseas work. The position of Director of Overseas Missions was made full-time in 1982. A dwindling of career missionary personnel in the late 1970s had apparently been reversed by the mid-1980s. Missionary personnel were serving in Latin America (Dominican Republic and Venezuela) and, with the Africa Inter-Mennonite Mission, in Africa (Burkina Faso and Zaire).

Though mission giving has remained high and church extension has also received large contributions, there has been a trend toward spending an increasing percentage of congregational income locally. Major building projects usually in the interest of better Christian education facilities, have been undertaken since 1975 at Archbold (Ohio), Berne (Ind.), Brookside (Fort Wayne, Ind.), Grace (Morton, Ill.), Groveland (Pekin, Ill.), Lawton (Mich.), Pine Hills (Fort Wayne, Ind.), Sterling (Ks.), and Upland (Ind.). A second pastoral staff member has been added in numerous congregations, again usually for assistance with Christian education and youth work. In spite of these changes, the rate of denominational membership growth levelled off between 1981 and 1986, after showing an average gain of 8 percent every five years since 1960. This has caused serious reflection among current denominational leaders. There is a desire to see the Evangelical Mennonite Church become more effective in carrying out the Great Commission (Mt 28:19-20).

Doctrinally there have been no major debates or changes at the denominational level in recent years. Local and personal variations in theology are tolerated as long as they fall within the general position represented by such groups as the National Association of Evangelicals or those associated with the Lausanne Covenant.

Like other evangelical denominations, the Evangelical Mennonite Church has taken firm positions on issues controversial in the 1980s, including °divorce and remarriage, homosexuality, (°sexuality), and the ordination of °women. A woman staff member who was employed as a Christian Education director in the Archbold congregation in 1982 was given the status of "licensed Christian worker," analogous to that of women who were overseas missionaries. A part-time Director of Women's Ministries has been employed at the headquarters since 1986 to stimulate women's involvement throughout the denomination.

In a denomination as small as this one, generational changes can be observed. The past 30 years have largely borne the stamp of five men representing the denomination's first generation of seminary-trained leaders—Reuben Short, Andrew Rupp, Milo Nussbaum, Charles Zimmerman and Charles Rupp. All were raised in Mennonite homes and communities; all have served throughout the period in a variety of denominational leadership positions; and all were recently retired or near retirement in 1987. The three full-time executive members of the headquarters staff in 1987 were all under the age of 40, and none of them were raised in a Mennonite home or community. The years 1988-93 are likely to be especially significant ones as the outlook of a new generation of leaders and members is clarified and implemented.   SN

Stan Nussbaum, *You Must Be Born Again: A History of the Evangelical Mennonite Church* (Fort Wayne: Evangelical Mennonite Church, 1979), official history booklet intended for general readership, membership classes; Kauffman/Harder, *Anabaptists Four C. Later* (1975); *Annual Report and Directory* Fort Wayne: Evangelical Mennonite Church, see esp. 1986 Report, pp. 9-11; *EMC Today* replaced both the quarterly magazine *Build* and the monthly newssheet *Communique* in 1984 as the official denominational magazine; *MWH* (1984), 144; *MWH* (1978), 370-72.

See also Women's Auxiliary (EMCh).

Evangelical Mennonite Church, Vietnam. See Giáo Hội Tin Lành (Hệ-phái Mê-nô-nít), Vietnam (Evangelical Church [Mennonite Branch]).

Evangelical Mennonite Church of the Central Plateau of Mexico. See Iglesia Evangélica Menonita de la Mesa Central de Mexico (CIEMM).

Evangelical Mennonite Conference (Kleine Gemeinde) (ME III:196). The Kleine Gemeinde had its beginning in the Molotschna Colony of Russia in 1812. Its members emigrated to North America in the migration of 1874 as two separate churches; the larger group settled in Manitoba, and the smaller group of approximately 36 families settled in

Nebraska. The Manitoba Kleine Gemeinde changed its name to *Evangelical Mennonite Church* in 1952 and to *Evangelical Mennonite Conference* (EMCon) in 1960.

Recent research in Kleine Gemeinde history has provided additional information on certain aspects of the group's history while in Russia. Two areas of significance are Kleine Gemeinde migrations within Russia and the divisions of 1866, both of which are briefly mentioned in ME III.

The Kleine Gemeinde migrations from the Molotschna Colony began in the early 1860s as an attempt to provide farming opportunities for °°landless members and to avoid political and administrative involvement in the mother colony. In 1863 they rented a property known as Markusland in Ekaterinoslav province and established two villages, Friedrichsthal and Andreasfeld. About a year later a small number of Kleine Gemeinde members rented land in Gurshafka *vollest*, Kherson province and settled in the village of Nicolaithal. That same year, 1865, the Borsenko colony, 20 mi. nw. of Nikopol, was purchased and the villages of Blumenhof, Heuboden, Rosenfeld, Steinbach, and Anafeld were established. Two other villages situated near Borsenko, Friedensfeld (1866) and Gruenfeld (1867), were also bought and settled by Kleine Gemeinde families. As mentioned in ME III, there was also a Kleine Gemeinde presence in the Crimea. This settlement, however, was due to a renewal movement rather than a colonization effort by the Kleine Gemeinde.

The Kleine Gemeinde divisions of 1866 were precipitated by a disagreement on disciplining a member, Abraham Thiessen (1838-89). Abraham was one of the men in the Molotschna Colony who helped force colony administrators to divide colony land among the landless. This action produced sufficient opposition from the well-to-do farmers of the colony to force Russian government involvement. Evidently, the Kleine Gemeinde saw Thiessen's activity as being inconsistent with the church policy of non-involvement in administrative affairs, and so Thiessen was excommunicated.

It seems, however, that a technicality in excommunication procedure was the cause of disunity. Thiessen had been told that his case would be dealt with at a prearranged Sunday meeting when he could be present to defend himself, but because of the urgency of the matter his case was presented to the church a week prior to the arranged time and the church voted to excommunicate him immediately. Thiessen, as well as other family members, took exception to this lack of due process and sought reinstatement.

Elder Johan Friesen (1808-72) also had second thoughts about the hasty decision and proposed that Thiessen be restored to fellowship. About half the members, under the leadership of minister Heinrich Enns (1801-81), were opposed to this proposal and consequently left Friesen's church. This group ordained Enns as their elder in 1866. However, he served in this capacity for only a few years before he was asked to resign.

Stability returned to the church after Peter Toews (1841-1922) was elected as elder and reconciliation took place between Toews' group and a major part

of Johan Friesen's group under the direction of elder Jacob Wiebe (1837-1921) of the Crimea.

The members remaining with elder Johan Friesen were further divided in 1869 when Friesen excommunicated two ministers and two deacons. These excommunicated men formed the nucleus of another Kleine Gemeinde church which elected Abraham L. Friesen (1831-1917) as their elder. Most of this group emigrated to Jansen, Nebr., in 1874.

The Evangelical Mennonite Conference has undergone numerous changes since the 1950s. Numerically it has grown from 6 Manitoba churches with a membership of 1,870 in 1951 to 48 churches in five Canadian provinces (British Columbia to Ontario) and a membership of 5,800 in 1986. Not included in this total are mission churches in Germany, Mexico, Nicaragua, and Paraguay. Kleine Gemeinde members in Belize, who retained that name, have recently expanded to Nova Scotia.

The increase in membership in an expanding geographical area demanded new autonomy for the congregations. For a number of years after the congregations were given autonomy under Elder Peter Reimer in 1945, joint decisions were still made through regular ministerial meetings. However, greater laity involvement was soon reflected in the formation of Conference Council to help with administrative decisions. It was composed solely of men. The elected delegates from each congregation, together with ordained ministers and deacons, make up the council. In 1980 a revised administrative structure was accepted. The conference churches were divided into eight geographic regions. Each region elects one or more members to a General Board. The General Board, consisting of 15 members, is responsible for setting up an agenda for the semiannual Conference Council meeting. The Conference Council elects officers to conference and paraconference positions, evalutes and accepts an annual budget, and approves all administrative decisions. A conference pastor has been hired to maintain communication between the churches and regions, and an elected moderator chairs the General Board and Conference Council meetings. The EMCon, however, continues to call a number of ministerial meetings a year, the purpose of which is fellowship, sharing church information, and the presentation and discussion of theological and social issues.

While the ministerial meetings and the Conference Council continue to be open only to men, the women of the churches are increasingly involved in the support ministries of the conference. A special women's meeting is held concurrently with the Conference Council during the annual convention. A number of institutions, e.g., the Resthaven Home of Steinbach, Man.; Eventide Home of Rosenort, Man.; local hospitals; and Steinbach Bible College, are faithfully and practically supported by the women of the conference.

In practice the EMCon churches have changed significantly during three decades. Most notable is the transition from the °German to the English language in worship services. At the first annual convention in 1951 only the German language was used, but at the 1965 convention English had replaced German. °Communion services in most conference churches include °feetwashing, however, the common cup with wine has generally been replaced with grape juice and individual cups. Another significant change from tradition was made in 1973 when the Conference Council adopted a resolution that would allow churches to practice baptism by °immersion as well as the traditional pouring. While all of the older established churches continue to baptize by pouring, a few of the newer churches are also baptizing by immersion. In contrast to the 1950s, the majority of conference churches now support congregational °singing with musical instruments and encourage °choir and group participation. Many churches still practise a plural ministry with the leading minister placed on salary. Most of the younger ministers of the conference now have at least some formal theological training.

The Board of Missions was first organized in 1953 with five board members and a budget of $4,500. With an increase in expansion in home and foreign missions, the budget had risen to $1,088,000 in 1986. In 1987 81 missionaries were serving under the board in Canada, Germany, Mexico, Nicaragua, and Paraguay; four were serving under Africa Inter-Mennonite Mission and 58 under other associate missons. This work is presently administered by a nine-member board which is elected by the Conference Council.

The Missions Auxiliary, a paraconference fundraising organization, was instrumental in providing funds to construct radio station ZP-30 in west Paraguay in 1975. This station is jointly sponsored by the EMCon. and the Chaco Mennonite colonies (Fernheim, Neuland, Menno).

The Board of Education and Publication, consisting of nine members, is responsible for promoting Christian education in the conference and is the publishing agent and editorial board for all conference publications. It is also responsible for publishing the annual E.M.C. Yearbook, which records the yearly activities and records of the conference.

The Christlicher Familienfreund, a German language family paper containing church news, devotional articles, and personal letters, was first published in 1935. The paper was discontinued in 1984. The Messenger, an English biweekly publication of the EMCon., was begun in 1962. Its purpose is to inform readers about what is going on in the conference, to instruct in godliness and victorious living, and inspire readers to contend earnestly for the faith.

The conference archives are housed in the conference office in Steinbach, Man. The collection contains many early Kleine Gemeinde documents, as well as letters, sermons, diaries, and other records pertaining to the history of the Kleine Gemeinde.   HFa

Evangelical Mennonite Conference in Paraguay.
Evangelical Mennonite Conference missions first took interest in Paraguay in the late 1950s, when Henry Toews, a missionary from °Menno Colony in the °°Chaco region, attended Bible school in Manitoba. In 1962 he won support to purchase land adjacent to Menno Colony in order to settle a group of Sanapaná Indians. The settlement was called La Esperanza (Hope). The mission, supported in part by a Paraguay Missions Auxiliary (EMCon) in Canada, is

officially registered as the Misión Evangélica Menonita.

Mission workers from La Esperanza became involved in 1964 in East Paraguay, where members of a renewal movement in the °Bergthal Colony had established a new settlement called Buena Vista. Together they established Bible studies, a youth program (Christian Endeavor), schools, a new congregation, a clinic, and evangelization among the neighboring Guaraní Indians, 1964-65.

At the same time the La Esperanza settlement in the Chaco grew. In 1961 the Mennonite mission program in the Chaco was reorganized (°Chaco Mission), including the establishment of an Indian Settlement Board to supervise full-scale settlement and development work. Nurses were to be supplied by the EMCon, which also retained administration of the spiritual work. By 1973 there were approximately 350 Indians living at La Esperanza. A Bible institute for leadership training began in 1972 under the direction of Dietrich Lepp. It was later moved to Yalve Sanga. Other ministries included Radio ZP-30's program of cultural, educational, and religious broadcasts in eight languages.

In 1970 the families and mission workers of the EMCon church at Buena Vista moved to Tobatí; in 1973 the community organized as the °Tres Palmas Colony. Mission work which expanded to Paraguayan towns in the area around the colony included evangelism, Bible studies, correspondence courses, a film ministry, and a Christian bookstore in Caaguazú. Membership in the Tres Palmas congregation in 1984 was 200.   FK

Delbert Plett, The Golden Years: The Mennonite Kleine Gemeinde in Russia (1812-1849) (Steinbach: D.F.P. Publications, 1904), idem, Storm and Triumph: The Mennonite Kleine Gemeinde (1850-1875) (Steinbach: D.F.P. Publications, 1986), idem, History and Events (Steinbach: D. F. Plett Farms Ltd., 1982); S. Barkman, Ever-Widening Circles: E.M.C. Missions Silver Jubilee (1953-1978) (Steinbach, EMCon. 1978); EMCon Yearbooks, 1958-86; MWH (1978), 315-18; MWH (1984), 52, 132; Reimer, Quilt (1983), 46; Daniel Hertzler, From Germantown to Steinbach (Scottdale, 1981), 236-47.

See also Convención de las Iglesias Evangelicas Unidas, Paraguay; Conservative Mennonites (Dutch-Prussian-Russian); Kleine Gemeinde (Mexico); Reimer, Klaas.

Evangelical Mennonite Mission, Bolivia. See Misión Evangélica Menonita, Bolivia.

Evangelical Mennonite Mission Conference (EMMC) (ME IV:375) was formed on July 1, 1959, from the Rudnerweider Mennonite Church, which had been organized in 1937. There were a number of factors leading to this reorganization. While the centralized ministry had its strengths, many felt that a more localized leadership would be more effective. The growing diversity in the church made it difficult for all ministers functioning in the circuit to relate well to every community. Increasing urbanization, higher education, the shift to the English language, and new vocational interests among members all contributed to the call for change.

The new conference organization allowed for a greater degree of localization. Local congregations were now free to call their own ministers, function as autonomous groups, and more readily develop their own identities. However, the annual conventions tied these local congregations together in spirit and purpose as did the various conference boards made up of members from the various regions.

The change was difficult for some of the older ministers as well as some rural groups less affected by change in the larger society. The Board of Ministers and Deacons found itself quite occupied helping congregations move to the new system and in wrestling with ethical and theological issues brought on by the changing context.

The new Board of Missions continued sponsoring a large slate of missionaries serving under various faith missions. However, in the early 1960s it inherited three mission stations when the Western Gospel Mission dissolved, two in Manitoba and one in Saskatchewan. Then in the mid-1960s new mission opportunities arose farther afield.

In southern Ontario, conference evangelist John D. Friesen and others discovered a spiritual need among Mennonite immigrants returning to Canada from Mexico. By the mid-1980s EMMC efforts had resulted in at least six church centers in the Aylmer, Leamington and Kitchener areas. Also by this time the Aylmer Bible School, established to meet the unique needs of these congregations, had been in operation for about a decade.

In Central America, a new work was begun in Belize. By the early 1980s it had become largely autonomous. Developments here included ministries in the fields of education, medical care, and German and Spanish church ministries. In South America a German and Spanish ministry in the rural area of Chorovi, near Santa Cruz, Bolivia, was begun in the late 1960s. In later years the thrust of the work shifted to education and church planting concerns in Pedro Dias, a suburb of Santa Cruz. In other developments new ministries were opened in Seminole, Texas, and a few locations in Mexico, including Santa Rita and Nuevo Ideál.

The Board of Education and Publication was the most aggressive of the new conference boards in the early 1960s. It actively promoted (°summer) vacation Bible schools, Sunday schools, youth and music ministries and publication efforts. By 1964 the English paper, the *EMMC Recorder* had replaced *Der Leitestern* as the official conference paper. The most difficult issue the board faced was solidifying support for Bible school education. In 1972 this board gave up its responsibility for radio ministries when a new Board of Radio and Evangelism was formed. "The Gospel Message," a Low German radio broadcast was still receiving popular support in 1986.

The Board of Christian Service promoted Christian service ministries, including that of Mennonite Central Committee, until it was merged with the Mission Board in 1970 to create the Board of Missions and Service. The Board of Business and Administration was responsible for properties and financial transactions. In 1986 the membership of EMMC was 3,131 in 23 independent congregations and nine mission stations.   JH

MWH (1978), 319-20; MWH (1984), 50, 133; Reimer, *Quilt* (1983), 45; Jack Heppner, *Search for Renewal: The Story of* the *Rudnerweider/EMMC, 1937-1987* (Winnipeg: Evangelical Mennonite Mission Conference, 1987).

See also Conservative Mennonites (Dutch-Prussian-Russian.

Evangelicalism is a diverse, worldwide, Protestant movement which places strong emphasis on personal °salvation, the inspiration and authority of the Bible, and a life of personal piety and witness to non-believers. Some Mennonite groups and persons have strongly identified with evangelical thought and institutions, while others have attempted to clearly distinguish themselves from Evangelicalism. Between these two poles are those who have maintained a more complex relationship with this segment of Christianity.

The History and Nature of Evangelicalism.
Contemporary Evangelicalism can best be understood as a movement of denominations, persons, and institutions which emerged out of °Fundamentalism in the mid-20th c. Its adherents were attempting to recover and identify with an earlier evangelical spirit with roots in the Protestant °Reformation.

The word evangelical stems from the Greek *evangelismos*, meaning good news or the gospel. The term was used in denigrating fashion during the Reformation era to describe Protestants in general (including Anabaptists), because of their emphasis on salvation by faith through God's grace, in contrast to salvation by works. The first awakening, which appeared in England and the United States in the 18th c. under the leadership of John Wesley (1703-91), George Whitefield (1714-70), and Jonathan Edwards (1703-58), was often designated the "evangelical revival." Its counterpart on the continent of Europe was °Pietism, which affected German, Dutch, Swiss, and Scandinavian ethnic groups in North America in ways not easily distinguished from Anglo-American Evangelicalism. *Evangelical* was sometimes employed to describe the worldwide °mission movement beginning in the late 18th c. and continuing through the 19th c., the Second Awakening in America (early 1800s), low church Anglicanism in 19th-c. England, and the mainstream of 19th-c. Protestantism in the United States. These movements all shared an evangelical propensity for conservative theology and a life of piety reflected in prayer, Bible reading, and evangelism, as well as varying forms of social concern.

By the end of the 19th c. major evangelical tenets were being challenged by new social, intellectual, and religious forces. Notions of biological and social °evolution were casting doubt on the evangelical view of creation. Historical and higher critical methods of biblical studies were challenging long-held orthodox assumptions regarding the Bible and its historicity. The newly-emerging social sciences were probing into new ways of viewing the individual and society, so that structural transformation, as opposed to individual °conversion, was becoming the rallying cry in secular and in some religious quarters.

The confrontation between orthodox faith and the forces of °modernity led to major denominational divisions, personal attacks, and theological battles. One pole, the modernists (or theological °liberals), openly embraced the new understandings of science, psychology, and sociology in order to make the faith "meaningful" to a new kind of world. At the other end of the spectrum were those who, in reaction to the modernists, clung tenaciously to the fundamentals of orthodox Christianity. Eventually this group was labeled Fundamentalist, a term most adherents proudly defended.

The Fundamentalists did battle with the modernists over such issues as creation, the °inerrancy of the Bible, the virgin birth of Christ, and the substitutionary °atonement of Christ. Many also began to adopt a °dispensational theology, which was popularized by the Scofield Reference Bible (1909), and emphasized a rather pessimistic view of history and the imminent and premillenial return of Christ, as the only hope for a broken world. There were evangelical Christians who were essentially neither Fundamentalist nor modernists, but in numerous denominations and churches during the first four decades of the 20th c., the battle lines were so intensely drawn that few could clearly maintain that middle ground.

By the 1920s Fundamentalism was highly defensive, separatistic, and contentious. Over the years it developed its own denominations, Bible institutes (and eventually colleges), and publishing houses in isolation from other Christians. The militant spirit of this movement has often been strongly criticized, and rightly so, but it was in part a result of the treatment they received at the hands of the secular press and other church people.

By the 1940s there were growing numbers within Fundamentalism who were calling for changes—not so much in basic theology as in mood. Carl F. H. Henry (the first editor of *Christianity Today*), Harold Ockenga (a Boston pastor and first president of Fuller Theological Seminary), and evangelist Billy Graham were among the early leaders of what was to become essentially a new movement—Evangelicalism, or as some termed it Neo-evangelicalism. These and other leaders questioned the Fundamentalists' extreme ecclesiastical separatism, their failure to address social issues, and their antipathy to higher education (including both liberal arts education and graduate-level theological education). The new Evangelicals believed that the negativism and divisiveness of the past needed to be replaced by a cautiously positive and cooperative spirit. They emphasized their oneness with Fundamentalism in basic doctrines, but many Evangelicals tended to move away from dispensationalism or at least to modify it.

Evangelicals in the 1940s and 1950s developed numerous organizations, institutions, and magazines. They included: the National Association of Evangelicals (1942), Youth For Christ (1944), the Evangelical Foreign Missions Association (1945), Fuller Theological Seminary (1947), the Evangelical Theological Society (1949), World Vision (1950), Campus Crusade (1951), and *Christianity Today* magazine (1956). These institutions helped to give identity to denominations which were identifying more with Evangelicalism than with hard-line Fundamentalism. They also served as bridges for many in mainline denominations who over the years had been neither

truly Fundamentalist nor modernist but now found identity within Evangelicalism.

While there are numerous theological and polity differences among Evangelicals, most find general agreement with the seven major points of the National Association of Evangelicals' doctrinal statement. This statement includes: (1) the inspiration and infallibility of the Bible; (2) one God, eternally existing in three persons; (3) the deity of Jesus Christ as well as his miracles, atoning death, and resurrection; (4) the necessity of personal salvation through regeneration; (5) the indwelling of the Holy Spirit to enable godliness; (6) the future resurrection of believers to life and the lost to judgment; (7) the spiritual unity of believers in Christ.

The Relationship of Mennonites to Evangelicalism. The relationship of Mennonites to Evangelicals is quite complex and reflects the broad diversity among and within the Mennonite groups. The interaction can best be understood in terms of institutional relationships and theological relationships.

At a denominational level there are four Mennonite bodies with membership in the National Association of Evangelicals (NAE): the Brethren in Christ, the Evangelical Mennonite Brethren (°Fellowship of Evangelical Bible Churches), the Evangelical Mennonite Church, and the Mennonite Brethren Churches (USA). There are also a number of General Conference Mennonite congregations which have joined the NAE. The Canadian counterparts of these groups have tended to join the Evangelical Fellowship of Canada, as has the Canadian-based Evangelical Mennonite Conference. Although statistics are not available, it would appear that these Mennonite bodies also have more significant involvements in other Evangelical institutions and hence a greater evangelical identity.

The Mennonite Church (MC) and the General Conference Mennonite Church have had more selective institutional involvements, often more at a congregational or agency level than as a whole denomination, with Evangelicals. For example, these Mennonites have often participated in Evangelical events such as Billy Graham Crusades, Key 73, and the Lausanne Conference of 1974. Moreover, students from these two largest Mennonite groups can be found in most major mainline Evangelical institutions such as Wheaton College, Taylor University, and Fuller Theological Seminary. At the same time there are individuals and congregations from these two Mennonite denominations, who, for various reasons, avoid any Evangelical institutional involvement.

Theologically, Anabaptists and Mennonites have generally adhered to Evangelical tenets of the faith as outlined in the doctrinal statement of the National Association of Evangelicals. However, many Mennonites would wish to add to such a statement as well as place less emphasis on creed and more on action. A small minority would overtly reject the major theological emphases of Evangelicalism.

The Mennonite propensity towards evangelical or traditional orthodox Christian theology is evident in the study by J. Howard Kauffman and Leland Harder published in 1975. Using a general orthodox scale that focused on God, Christ, miracles, resurrection, Christ's return, a personal devil, and life beyond death, the authors found that among the five Mennonite groups studied 75 percent scored high on the orthodox scale, with another 14 percent in the next category, high middle. The groups with the greatest evangelical institutional identity scored the highest (Mennonite Brethren 87 percent; Brethren in Christ, 82 percent; and Evangelical Mennonite Church, 88 percent in the high category), while the General Conference Mennonite Church scored the lowest (65 percent were high in orthodoxy). The Mennonite Church was in the middle with 76 percent in the high category (Kauffman/Harder, 106).

The doctrinal statements and theological affirmations of the varied 20th-c. Mennonite bodies are in essential agreement with Evangelical theology. However, each of them would tend to move beyond Evangelicalism by including an affirmation of certain life-style and ethical issues, such as °nonresistance or °peace witness. Mennonite soteriology has also tended to add commitment to Christ or discipleship as an integral part of salvation by faith.

The Mennonite churches have been influenced by historic and contemporary Evangelicalism in numerous ways: °revivalism, °Sunday schools, °theology, and forms of piety. Some of these influences have at times been sources of contention within the Mennonite families. Mennonites have also made at least some impact upon Evangelicalism, especially in recent years. Numerous Evangelicals have found in the sons and daughters of Menno examples of Christian discipleship, peace concerns, and the balance of °justice and service concerns with personal piety.   DPH

James D. Hunter, *Evangelicals: The Coming Generation* (Chicago: U. of Chicago Press, 1987); Kauffman/Harder, *Anabaptists Four C. Later* (1975); C. Norman Kraus, ed., *Evangelicalism and Anabaptism* (Scottdale, 1979); Wittlinger, *Piety and Obedience* (1978), 479-81; George Marsden, *Reforming Fundamentalism* (Grand Rapids: Eerdmans, 1987); David Wells and John Woodbridge, eds., *The Evangelicals* (Nashville: Abingdon Press, 1975); David Zercher, "Opting for the Mainstream: The Brethren Join the National Association of Evangelicals," *Brethren in Christ History and Life* 10, no. 1 (Apr. 1987), 48-70.

See also Association of Evangelical Mennonites; Fellowship of Concerned Mennonites.

Evangelische Mennoniten Missions Gemeinde, Belize. See Evangelical Mennonite Mission Conference.

Evangelische Mennonitische Bruderschaft (Evangelical Mennonite Brethren Church), Argentina. See Alianza Evangélica Menonita de Argentina; Fellowship of Evangelical Bible Churches.

Evangelische Mennonitische Bruderschaft, Paraguay and Argentina. See Konferenz der Evangelischen Mennonitischen Brüderschaft von Südamerika; Fellowship of Evangelical Bible Churches.

Evangelism (ME II:269) is the presentation of the good news of Jesus Christ in the power of the Holy Spirit that people may come to place their trust in God through him, to serve him in the fellowship of the church and in the vocations of the common life.

This free quotation from the Commission on Evangelism under Archbishop William Temple (Anglican) expresses well a definition of evangelism quite acceptable to Mennonites. With an emphasis on discipleship of Christ, an understanding that ethics is related to Christ in the same way that salvation is related to Christ, Mennonites see evangelism in a wholistic manner. This is to say, evangelism is anything or everything that makes faith in Christ possible for the person. Deed is important as well as word; both the act of love and the work of love are reconciling.

As heirs of the 16th-c. Anabaptists, Mennonites recognize evangelism as basic to the existence of a °believers church. The 16th-c. Anabaptist church was developed by evangelism, by winning people to become disciples of Christ. A believers church, by its very nature, is evangelistic, and it calls for an adult, intelligent, voluntary commitment; whether from those who grow up within the Mennonite community or those who do not. Furthermore, evangelism is not just a call to change moral patterns but is a call to follow Jesus, to confess him as Lord and Savior, knowing that in him men and women are reconciled to God and are saved from becoming what they would be without him (2 Cor 5:17).

The presentation of the gospel, in an evangelistic sermon or a personal conversation, calls people to reconciliation in Christ (2 Cor 5:18-20). This means that commitment to follow Christ will change life's relationships, with God and with one's neighbor. The Anabaptist and Mennonite commitment to live by °peace and work for peace is grounded in the gospel (Eph 2:14-18). And the Mennonite emphasis on peace, freedom, °justice, and °community is to be heard in the context of the reconciling work of the cross (Eph 2:16).

Evangelism has taken on a new character since the 1950s with the awareness of the "global village." Mennonites have needed to find the Spirit's guidance in °contextualizing the gospel so that it is authentically understood in a particular culture; understood as the gospel and not as Western Messianic nationalism. As a consequence of contextualization, the world-wide Mennonite family, with a presence in some 70 countries, has seen new growth. While there is remarkable growth in Latin American and Asian countries (especially Indonesia), the greater numerical growth has been in Africa. By the year 2000, the majority of the one million Mennonites will not be of the Western world. And these countries of growth hold differing ideological and political positions. In the past decade, churches have also been opened in Australia and various Pacific Islands.

The new face of the world reflects °urbanization, the emergence of world cities with populations from one to twenty million, and the increased need for ministries of compassion in the face of injustice, inequity, poverty, and hunger. The awareness of new challenges led North American Mennonites to convene Probe '72, a Congress on Evangelism in Minneapolis; and Alive '85, a Congress on Evangelism sponsored by Mennonites and the Church of the Brethren in Denver. At the same time, different Mennonite denominations outlined goals for church growth, as seen in 1985 at Ames, Iowa, where the Mennonite Church (MC) adopted goals aimed to increase giving, plant 500 new churches, and double membership in 10 years. Also, Mennonite colleges and seminaries were developing courses for the training of leaders in evangelistic ministry.

Interchurch Evangelism, organized in the early 1960s for evangelistic crusades, has sponsored several hundred ecumenical city-wide evangelistic missions in the years since. From Salt Lake City to Schenectedy, these missions with Myron Augsburger and his team have helped the public to better understand the Mennonite Church and have brought many persons to the Christian faith. In 1981, Inter-Church, Inc. became the sponsoring agency for the planting of a new church on Capitol Hill in Washington, D.C.

The Mennonite Christian Leadership Foundation was organized in the early 1970s in the Eastern United States. Its primary role has been to enable Donald Jacobs to serve globally in leadership training seminars. In Henderson, Nebr., in the 1980s, Albert Epp developed the "Golden Stairways" Discipleship course to engage laity in Christian growth and evangelism. Arthur McPhee has written and conducted interdenominational seminars on "friendship evangelism." A special church planting emphasis has emerged among the Mennonite Brethren, as well as among other groups. These and other ventures are focusing attention on finding creative and contemporary ways to do evangelism in the urban context, especially in discipling young professionals.

Evangelism has called Mennonites to move beyond °ethnicity. This is true in global °missions, in strategies of contextualization, and in the North American churches where the pluralism now includes stronger Afro-American and Hispanic associations as well as developing Native American and Asian churches. °Mennonite World Conference helps churches give resources to each other in mission and helps Mennonite brothers and sisters in Christ become better acquainted.

Mennonites worldwide need a clear identity as disciples of Jesus and the ability to move beyond Mennonite ethnicity without surrendering basic Anabaptist principles. This includes conversion to walking with Jesus, community as a reconciled people, commitment to peace and nonviolence, and compassionate participation with the human family. Called by Christ to be harbingers of Christ's kingdom, believers are to model the good news that life in its fullness is known by identification with Christ as children of God.   MSA

Arthur McPhee, *Friendship Evangelism* (Grand Rapids: Zondervan, 1978); Lesslie Newbigin, *Foolishness to the Greeks* (Grand Rapids: Eerdmans, 1986); Wilbert R. Shenk, ed., *Anabaptism and Mission* (Scottdale, 1984); Paul Lederach, *A Third Way* (Scottdale, 1980); Myron Augsburger, *Evangelism as Discipling* (Scottdale, 1983); Joseph D. Graber, *The Church Apostolic* (Scottdale, 1960); John Perkins, *Justice for All* (Regal, 1982); David Claerbout, *Urban Ministry* (Grand Rapids: Zondervan, 1983); Allen Walker, *The Whole Gospel for the Whole World* (Nashville: Abingdon, 1957); Donald R. Jacobs, *Pilgrimage in Mission* (Scottdale, 1982); Orlando E. Costas, *The Integrity of Mission* (New York: Harper and Row, 1979); Peter Wagner, *On The Crest of the Wave* (Regal, 1983); F. H. Epp, *Mennonites in Canada II*, pp. 471-73; Kauffman/Harder, *Anabaptists Four C. Later* (1975), 80, 212, index.

See also Church Growth Movement; Lay Evangelists; Revivalism; Urban Church; Yamada Takashi.

Evangelization Board of the Mennonite Churches of Uruguay was organized in 1960 with officers representing the Mennonite Board of Missions (MC), the Commission on Overseas Mission (GCM) and the Konferenz der Mennonitengemeinden in Uruguay. In 1961 a Spanish-speaking representative was added.

In 1986 the Evangelization Board was made up of one delegate from each of the congregations of the Konferenz and the Convención de las Iglesias Menonitas del Uruguay. It dealt with administrative matters related principally to the life and mission of the Spanish-speaking groups. Although the North American mission boards continued to contribute to the budget of these churches through the Evangelization Board, they were no longer represented on the board. Both the Evangelization Board and the Convención had begun a process of self-study in order to determine their respective roles in their ongoing relationship.   MR

Evening Meetings. See Revivalism; Eastern Pennsylvania Mennonite Church.

Evil, Problem of. See Sin.

Evolution. Anabaptists did not develop their own theology of °creation during the Reformation, and Mennonites have not given the subject much attention since that time. As a result, theories of biological evolution have rarely been confronted and most Mennonites have assumed that evolution is in conflict with the Bible, especially when evolution teaches that human beings had animal ancestors. German-speaking Mennonites were introduced to evolution by Ernst Haeckel (1834-1919), who boldly attacked the veracity of the Bible. Christian °°Neff (1863-1946) reacted strongly to Haeckel but affirmed the work of other scientists of his day. He noted Charles Darwin's humility and suggested that the differences between evolution and the Bible might be of minor importance. P. J. Wedel (1871-1951), a science professor at Bethel College, also reacted to Haeckel and attempted a detailed scientific refutation of the theory of evolution in 1923.

The (Old) Mennonite Church (MC) in America became concerned about evolution through contact with the °revivalism of the 19th c., and, when this movement was followed by °Fundamentalism early in the 20th c., a large party within the church adopted the antievolution agenda. J. D. °°Charles (1878-1923) spoke for them when he condemned evolution as ". . . flatly in opposition to the teachings of the Bible and destructive of all Christian faith: . . ." (*GH*, 9 [1916], 115). Church colleges tolerated no "monkey business" and William Jennings Bryan's writings were welcomed in the *Gospel Herald* (MC) at the height of his antievolution activities. Antievolution convictions also played a significant part in the Modernist-Fundamentalist crisis at Goshen College (1918-1923). Similar crises have occurred in educational institutions of many North American Mennonite groups.

Although very little discussion of evolution has taken place in the Mennonite community since the 1920s, there has been a change of attitude among theological leaders. In 1954 John C. Wenger (b. 1910) rejected evolution using both scientific and theological arguments. This was to be the last attempt by a prominent Mennonite scholar to confront the scientific aspect of evolution. John Howard Yoder signaled the beginning of change in 1959 when he praised the usefulness of evolutionary thinking although he did not endorse any particular evolutionary view. Since that time, interpretation of Genesis, though often done, has been almost purely theological, with scant reference to science. This change occurred earlier in Europe than it did in America. Most Mennonite scientists of the 1970s and 1980s have accepted evolution and some have tried to show that it is not a threat to biblical faith.

The creation-science movement, an attempt to defend a literal reading of Genesis on the basis of empirical scientific data, which began in the United States in the 1970s has had a significant impact on most Mennonite groups. At least two groups (Evangelical Mennonite Conference of Canada and the Mennonite Brethren) have responded by publishing papers which affirm the necessity of believing in Adam and Eve as historical persons and which reject interpretations which teach that Genesis is myth or some other nonhistorical genre. No Mennonite has taken a prominent role in creation-science but Mennonites have been seen as prime targets for recruitment by creationist leaders. A survey of beliefs among Mennonite Brethren conducted in 1972 and repeated in 1982 indicates that about 90 percent believe in the flood of Noah as literally true, only about 50 percent believe that creation occurred in six days. This consensus remained unchanged over the 10-year period, indicating that even among theologically conservative Mennonites, the activities of creation-science have not resulted in a change of belief. Among Mennonites who accept creation literally, there is still a broad pluralism of opinion with respect to the age of the earth, the nature of the creation days, and the meaning of the biblical "kinds." Mennonite scientists (most notably the astronomer Owen Gingerich) have criticized creation-science strongly.

Mennonites in the Soviet Union have quietly resisted teaching of evolution in the schools by home instruction of their children. Upon immigration to the West, they are surprized to find evolution tolerated by Western European and by some American Mennonites and have been attracted strongly to creation-science. In Africa and Indonesia evolution has had no significant impact on the church because the people have not been secularized enough to give any importance to what they see as merely a human explanation of origins. Mennonites in Latin America are suspicious of evolution because they consider it to be either too theologically °liberal or too worldly. The latter opinion is also retained by large groups of culturally conservative Mennonites in North America.   GKla

John C. Wenger, *Introduction to Theology* (Scottdale, 1954), 73-80; Rodney J. Sawatsky, "The Influence of Fundamentalism on Mennonite Nonresistance 1908-1944" (MA thesis, U.

of Minnesota, 1973); Waldemar Janzen, *Still in the Image* (Newton, 1982), a modern theological interpretation of Genesis similar in approach to the writings of Perry Yoder, Allan Guenther, Marlin Jeschke, Helmut Harder, David Schroeder, and others; *MB Profile* in *Direction*, 24, no. 2 (1985), sp. issue; Owen Gingerich, "Let There be Light: Modern Cosmogony and Biblical Creation," in *Is God a Creationist?*, ed. R. M. Frye (New Yord: Scribner's, 1983), 119-37, support for conventional science together with an affirmation of faith, similar to Erwin Hiebert, H. Harold Hartzler, Carl Keener, Glen Klassen; Henry Hiebert, *Evolution: Its Collapse in View?* (Beaverlodge: Horizon House Publishers, 1979); Elmer Martens, "Perspectives on Creation," *MB Herald* (Aug. 15, 1986), 2-5, a statement endorsed by the MB Conference and by the faculty of the Mennonite Brethren Biblical Seminary in 1983; Evangelical Mennonite Conference, "Creation," *The Messenger*, 23, no. 15 (Aug. 9, 1985), 2-3, official statement by the EMCon.; David Ewert, "Difficult Bible Passages: the Creation Account," *Menn. Rep.* 6, no. 22 (1976), 5; no. 23, 5; no. 24, 5; John Howard Yoder, "The Impact of Evolutionary Thinking on Theology," paper read at the Mennonite Graduate Fellowship, Chicago, 1959; Christian Neff, "Die moderne Naturwissenschaft und unser Glaube," *Mennonitische Blätter*, 48 (Feb. 1, 1901), 13-15; (Mar. 1, 1901), 22-23, remarkably like Owen Gingerich's article cited above; Peter J. Wedel, "Evolution, die neue Religion der Wissenschaft," *Bethel College Monthly* (Feb. 1923), 9-14, (Mar. 1923), 8-12, (Apr. 1923), 13-16, (May 1923), 8-16, (June 1923), 14-18; John D. Charles, "Fallacies of Evolution," *GH* (May 18, 1916), 114-15; Chester K. Lehman, *The Inadequacy of Evolution as a World View* (Scottdale: MPH, 1933), similar to books or articles written in the 1920s and 1930s by J. D. Charles, John H. Moseman, Ralph D. Hostetter, Paul Bender, and others.

See also Sciences, Natural.

Excommunication. See Discipline.

Exile. See Russian Soviet Federated Socialist Republic (RSFSR); Spetskomandantura.

Exorcism (to drive out demons). While the Old Testament reports several cases of evil spirits afflicting humans (1 Sam 16:14; 18:10; Jgs 9:23), such is subsumed under God's sovereign judgement; the Old Testament reports no exorcism. In the New Testament, however, Jesus' driving out of demons was a prominent feature of Jesus' ministry and a key sign that the °kingdom of God had come and that God's Spirit was mightily at work through him (Mk 3:20-30; parallels in Mt 12:28; Lk 11:20). The world of Jesus' time, both Jewish and Greek, considered demon powers responsible for much ill fortune, especially sickness (see e.g., *The Testament of Solomon* in J. H. Charlesworth, *The OT Pseudepigrapha*, vol 1 [Garden City, N.Y.: Doubleday], 1983 or Tobit 6-8). While the synoptic gospels report that Jesus commissioned his disciples to drive out demons as part of the gospel's liberation of the oppressed (Mk 3:15; 6:7,13: Lk 10:17-20), and Acts shows them doing so (5:16; 10:38; 16:18; 19:12), neither the Pauline nor Johannine writings report exorcisms. During the next two centuries exorcism played an important role in the spread of Christianity, promising and bringing deliverance from demons (Ferguson, 129).

Early 3rd-c. documents describing baptismal rites include exorcistic abjurations as well as a period of several weeks before Easter when baptismal candidates participated in exorcistic liturgy daily to purify the person from the demonic power of past idolatrous worship (see Kelly and Webber). The Roman Catholic Church continued a rite of baptismal exorcism until the 1970s. Solemn exorcism apart from baptism is also practiced by authorized Roman Catholic priests. Lutherans, initially indifferent toward baptismal exorcism, later defended it against Calvinist opposition to it, opposition growing from a weakened sacramental theology (Martin in Swartley, *Bondage*, below). Exorcism apart from baptism never completely disappeared among Protestants but was rarely attempted in the face of Enlightenment rationalism and skepticism about the Devil. The Anabaptists never wrote about exorcism itself but opposed it in relation to infant baptism (Menno, *Writings*, 252, 570, 700; Marpeck in CRR 2: 219). Until quite recent years, however, Mennonite baptismal vows included a vow of renunciation of Satan and all his works. In Pentecostal and Evangelical circles where exorcism is practised the term *deliverance ministry* is preferred.

The relatively sparse Mennonite literature on the topic of *Satan* (Devil) gives almost no attention to exorcism or deliverance from evil spirits. Two articles by the Dutch °°Collegiant Frans °°Kuyper in the 17th c. argue the existence of demons, but primarily for the purpose of seeking to prove to atheists the truth of spiritual realities (some stories do show prayer as the only way to quiet the overcome sufferers, see °Satan). Likewise a lecture by Douwe Simon Gorter (1856) affirms belief in the existence of a personal devil and good and evil spirits but does not address exorcism.

Mennonite writings on Satan often use the word *devils* to refer to demons (Wenger as editor of Menno's *Writings*, both Lepp-Reesor and Hiebert, and Hostetter, as cited under °Satan). The German word *Dämonen* or the English term *demons* rarely occur. This is likely due to the influence of the KJV which translated the Greek *daimonia* as *devils*, rather than demons. The more common Mennonite use of the word demons after 1970 arose partly from use of newer Bible translations (RSV, NIV) as well as from worldwide missionary work, in which missionaries seeking to understand the culture of the people could not avoid the topics of demons, possession, and exorcism. Donald R. Jacobs' "Focal Pamphlet" entitled *Demons* (1972) arose from this context but also examined the need for and appropriate method of exorcism in the North American context. Jacobs said that great harm had been done to the gospel and missions by the Western assumption that belief in demons is superstition, making missionaries unwilling to attend to the topic. Because Western missionaries did not present Jesus Christ as the one who could defeat the demonic powers which the people experienced, the new believers accepted instead Western technology as the form of Christian power by which they were to order their lives. In contrast Pentecostal groups and growing °African independent churches announced "that Jesus Christ is Lord of all, even the powers of evil spirits" (34-36).

The rise of interest in the occult in American society, the influence of the °charismatic renewal movement, the turn toward inwardness and search for spiritual meaning, the continuing questions of missionaries about the gospel's deliverance from demons, the sensational movie *The Exorcist*, and the practice of exorcism by some Mennonites gave the topic new priority in the the 1970s and 1980s. Paul M. Miller's book, *The Devil Did Not Make Me Do It* (1977) sought to respond to the issues by giving basic biblical teaching on Satan and Christ's victory. He recognized Jesus' use of exorcism but resisted its use today on the basis of what he saw as a trend in the Pauline and Johannine writings to move away from exorcism and combat evil and Satan in other ways. He called instead for pastoral care of demonized persons. In a 1988 paper Miller takes the same position generally but recognizes some exceptions for those needing to be freed from bondage to occult practices and allegiances.

Two voices emerged in the 1960s to call Mennonites to consider exorcism as part of Christian ministry. In the French Mennonite setting Emile Kremer published "Les yeux ouverts" in the 1960s with the first English translation in 1969. An enlarged edition appeared in 1979 entitled *Eyes Opened to Satan's Subtlety*. The subtitle indicates the scope of treatment: *The Origin, Nature and Consequences of Superstition, Divination and Occultism, and the Full Redemption through the Cross*. He connected the authority to drive out demons both to the Lord's command to the disciples to do so and to the command "to bind and loose," which must be linked with honest and full confession of sins by the person in bondage (35-36). In North America Dean Hochstetler (Nappanee, Ind.) has ministered widely to people by employing exorcism when such was deemed necessary; he urged Mennonite colleges and seminaries to include training for this as part of Christian ministry. The Indiana-Michigan Conference (MC) appointed a consultation-evaluation committee for him in the late 1970s and after some years of evaluative reports from the committee ordained him for this ministry (see *GH*, 79 [Sept 30, 1986], 662-63).

The Associated Mennonite Biblical Seminaries, Mennonite Board of Missions (MC), Oaklawn Psychiatric Center (all in Elkhart, Ind.), and the Indiana-Michigan Mennonite Conference (MC) sponsored a consultation on "Bondage and Deliverance," July 30-Aug. 1, 1987. Major papers examined the issue from various points of view: biblical-theological, historical, Roman Catholic and Evangelical, anthropological, psychiatric, and pastoral care. The consultation included a case presentation by a person delivered 27 years before, with a paper of documentation and interpretation by a sociologist and clinical psychologist. As these papers and their bibliographies indicate, a growing body of literature worldwide, from biblical, historical, theological and psychiatric perspectives, has brought this agenda into the forefront of the church's theological reflection and evangelistic-pastoral practice (Swartley, ed., *Bondage*).

Two articles in *The Mennonite* present an overseas story of power encounter between Christ and the demons and a North American pastor's practical learnings (Entz, Winslow). Aware of the crucial need for exorism in a spiritist culture (Sicily), missionary Willard Eberly wrote an extensive research paper at Eastern Mennonite Seminary (Va.) on "A Biblical Theology of Exorcism." A recent social science study proposes some diagnostic distinctions between multiple personality disorders and demon possession (Isaacs, 1987); some recent psychiatric contributions discuss the topic in fresh ways (Pattison, 1977; Peck, 1983). **WMS**

David W. Augsburger, *Pastoral Counseling Across Cultures* (Philadelphia: Westminster Press, 1986), 273-312; *Churchman* (1980, no.3), sp. issue; Willard Eberly, "A Biblical Theology of Exorcism: Complete in Jesus and the Kingdom" (unpubl. paper Eastern Mennonite Seminary, 1987); Loren Entz, in *Mennonite*, 101 (Apr. 8, 1986), 164-65; Everett Ferguson, *Demonology of the Early Christian World* (New York and Toronto: Edwin Mellen Press, 1984); Craig T. Isaacs, "The Possessive States Disorder: The Diagnosis of Demon Possession," *Pastoral Psychology*, 34, no. 4 (1987), 263-73; Donald R. Jacobs, *Demons: An Examination of Demons at Work in the World Today* (Scottdale, 1972); Henry Ansgar Kelly, *The Devil at Baptism: Ritual, Theology, and Drama* (Ithaca and London: Cornell U. Press, 1985); Emile Kremer, *Eyes Open to Satan's Subtlety* (Stoke-on-Trent: M.O.V.E. Press, enlarged ed., 1979); Paul M. Miller, *The Devil Did Not Make Me Do It: A Study in Christian Deliverance* (Scottdale, 1977); Mansell Pattison, "Psychosocial Interpretations of Exorcism," *Journal of Operational Psychiatry*, 8 (1977), 5-19; M. Scott Peck, *People of the Lie: The Hope for Healing Human Evil* (New York: Simon and Schuster, 1983); Willard M. Swartley, ed., *Spiritual Bondage and Deliverance*, Occasional Papers, 11 (Elkhart, Ind.: IMS, 1988); Graham H. Twelftree, "The Place of Exorcism in Contemporary Ministry," *St Mark's Review* (Sept. 1986), 25-39; Robert E. Webber, *Celebrating Our Faith: Evangelism Through Worship* (San Francisco: Harper and Row, 1986); Mark Winslow, in *Mennonite*, 100 (Apr. 9, 1985), 153; Amzie Yoder, "Pastoral Care and Exorcism" (unpubl. paper, AMBS, ca. 1985).

F

Faith and Life Press. See Publishing.

Faith Healing. Mennonites generally have not identified with the faith healing movement of the 20th c. During the last half of the century, however, there was an observable shift on the subject. A few prominent leaders embraced and promoted the healing theology. In the late 1980s Mennonites participate in or even conduct healing services, sometimes in an ecumenical setting. More and more people are concluding that the gospel is for the whole person, including the body. Wide difference of opinion persists, however, on whether healing is for all or not, whether healing is in the atonement or not, and whether there should public healing services or not.

Articles have appeared from time to time in the Mennonite media reporting healing services of a moderate nature unlike those of the so-called professional divine healers whose beliefs and practices are unacceptable to many, if not most, Mennonites. This indicates a significant change of attitude and belief beyond the traditional view that the ordinance of the °°anointing with oil according to the Epistle of James should be done in private. Even this was so little taught and practiced in some quarters that some Mennonites felt driven to seek healing at the hands of a public divine healer. On this issue, Mennonites reflect the same changes which are visible in the larger Christian community where traditional views and practices no longer stand. Among Mennonites, the change of mood with regard to faith healing is more likely related to the growing °charismatic influence across the denominations which recognizes and emphasizes the person and work of the °Holy Spirit, including the gifts of the Spirit. Mennonite Renewal Services is a parachurch organization which promotes charismatic teaching, including glossalalia (speaking in tongues).

The official position of the Mennonite Church (MC) is stated in the 1963 Confession of Faith as follows: "We believe that the church should exercise a ministry of prayer for those who are in need. Prayer for the sick may be accompanied by a symbolic anointing with oil by the elders of the church. In response to the prayer of faith, and in accordance with His will, God heals in various ways, through the use of the healing arts, or by direct intervention. When healing does not occur, we believe that God's grace is sufficient. The full redemption of the body will come only at the return of Christ" (art. 8; Loewen, *Confessions*, 75). GeoRBrII

Empowered (published quarterly by Mennonite Renewal Services), esp. 5, no. 2 (1987); "Miracles, Signs and Wonders," *Christian Ministry* (Oct. - Dec. 1958); Gerald Studer, "The Revival of the Christian Ministry of Healing," *Canadian Mennonite* (Sept. 24, 1963); Nelson E. Kauffman, "An Impressive Healing Service," *GH* (July 5, 1962).

See also Brauche; Health Services; Medicine.

Family (ME II:293). The Mennonite family of the 1980s continues many of the same characteristics noted in the earlier ME article. However, some significant trends can be observed over the past three decades, due to the gradual °modernization and °acculturation of Mennonites under the impact of powerful secular forces of the late 20th c. Most notable are the continuing °urbanization of Mennonites and the fallout from two major social movements: the "sexual revolution" of the 1960s and the women's rights movement of the 1970s.

In past generations Mennonites maintained various social and cultural boundaries by which acculturation was resisted, but these appear to be weakening as Mennonites increasingly participate in social networks of the larger society. Only the most conservative groups (Hutterites, Old Order Amish, Old Order Mennonites, Old Colony Mennonites) maintain effective social barriers between themselves and the "outside world." Familism is still very strong among these groups, but among the more progressive Mennonite bodies family solidarity is increasingly eroded by patterns of geographic mobility and the individualistic ideologies of a "me first" generation. Not all is negative, however, as some social trends favor the family, such as increased economic resources and more favorable treatment of women in society.

The description and analysis of Mennonite family patterns has been enhanced by a number of empirical °sociological studies since the 1950s. Among these are (1) Kauffman's survey of 149 Midwest Mennonite (MC) families in the late 1950s; (2) the 1963 Mennonite family census conducted by the Mennonite Research Foundation; (3) Augsburger's investigation of the relation of family control patterns to the child's personality development; (4) Lederach's 1968 survey of Mennonite (MC) teenagers; (5) several surveys of the sexual attitudes and behavior of Mennonite college students; (6) the 1972 Kauffman-Harder survey of 3,691 members of five Mennonite denominations; (7) Harder's three censuses of General Conference Mennonite (GCM) congregations in 1960, 1970, and 1980; (8) Yoder's 1982 census of the Mennonite Church; and (9) studies on marriage and divorce among Canadian Mennonites by Driedger and others. In addition, some aspects of family life are included in Redekop's reports on Mennonites in Mexico and Paraguay, Hiebert's work on the Church of God in Christ Mennonite (Holdeman), and Hostetler's books on the Hutterites and Old Order Amish.

The Decline of Kinship. According to family

288

sociologists, a characteristic of modern society is the tendency of kinship structures and relationships to weaken in favor of the ascendency of the nuclear family unit. Interaction with, and a sense of duties and responsibilities toward, one's relatives beyond the nuclear family tend to diminish when adult children no longer live near their grandparents, uncles, aunts, and cousins and when community agencies, insurance, pension plans, and social security programs tend to displace the traditional obligations to care for the family's elderly relatives.

As long as Mennonites were primarily agricultural and married children continued to live in the community of their birth, kinship structures were dominant over individuals and nuclear family units. Choice of occupation, choice of spouse, aspects of personal behavior, obligations of °mutual aid, etc., were subject to the opinions, counsel, and informal sanctions of parents and other close kin.

With urbanization and its concomitant geographical mobility, Mennonites like others experience declining interaction with relatives despite increased phone calls and correspondence and the popularity of annual family reunions, sometimes poorly attended by the younger generation who live at a distance. "Familism" defined as a strong sense of relatedness and mutual obligations with one's kin, tends to give way to "individualism," a sense of detachment and resistance to family and kinship controls. Familism is still strong among the Old Orders and in the more conservative rural Mennonite communities, but among Mennonites who pursue higher education, urban occupations, and service assignments in distant places, nuclear families are often thrown upon their own resources and the resources of non-family friends, in meeting the exigencies of a fast-moving, competitive, urban way of life. As Bender (1982, p. 114) points out, modern society removes some of the supporting pillars of husband-wife units, and breakdowns are more likely to occur. Slowly increasing °divorce rates among Mennonites give testimony to this.

Trends in Family Demography. No trend among Mennonites is more striking than the recent shift from rural to urban residence and from farm to nonfarm occupations. Only the Hutterites continue to be wholly agricultural. Although they still avoid cities as a place of residence, an increasing proportion of Old Order families live on nonfarm plots and engage in nonfarm occupations. In northern Indiana it is estimated that at least half of Old Order Amish men are no longer farmers by primary occupation.

The trend among Mennonites is indicated by the 149 families surveyed by Kauffman in 1956 and 1979. Ninety-five percent of the husbands and wives were reared on farms, 68 percent were living on farms in 1956 (only 52 percent of the husbands were farmers), but only 18 percent of the children were living on farms in 1979, among whom only 12 percent were farmers by primary occupation. Yoder's 1982 census indicated that only about one-fifth of Mennonite Church (MC) adherents live on farms, although nearly two-thirds live in rural areas. The 1972 church member survey revealed that, of the five denominations included, the Mennonite Church was the most rural, followed in order by the Breth-

ren in Christ, Evangelical Mennonite Church, the General Conference Mennonites, and the Mennonite Brethren Church, the latter being most urbanized, with 56 percent living in urban areas.

Compared to the general American and Canadian populations, Mennonite households have somewhat higher average incomes. Home ownership rates are higher than the national populations, and the proportion of Mennonite family incomes below the poverty level is relatively low. Less than one percent of Mennonite church members, who in 1972 had not retired, reported themselves as unemployed. This compares to at least five or six percent unemployed in the national populations. Thus Mennonite families, on the average, enjoy a somewhat higher economic standard of living than other North American families. As Mennonites leave farming, the shift is more into professional, business, and other "white collar" occupations and less into "blue collar" trades and factory work which generally pay lower wages.

Apparently the movement of Mennonites away from farming does not result in less satisfaction, on the part of husbands or wives, with the husband's occupation, according to the 1956 survey.

Family demography also notes the marital status of a given population. Yoder's 1982 census of the Mennonite Church (MC) indicates the marital status of persons of marriage age, in this case all adults aged 20 and over, as follows: single (never married), 17.6 percent; married to original spouse, 70.2; widowed, 5.7; widowed and remarried, 1.6; divorced, 1.8; separated, 0.9; remarried after divorce, 2.2; (total = 100 percent). Harder's censuses of GCM congregations yielded the following distributions (the first percentage shown in each category is for 1970, the second for 1980): single, 19.4, 19.3; married, 72.4, 71.5; widowed, 7.3, 7.4; divorced, 1.0, 1.8. (Total percentage for 1970 = 100.1; for 1980, 100 percent.) His data did not distinguish between those married to their original spouses and those who had remarried after widowhood or divorce.

The tendency of many more women than men never to marry was reported elsewhere (°marriage); likewise the gradual increase in the small proportion who experience divorce. Compared to adult national populations, Mennonites are more married and less divorced.

Another significant trend among Mennonite families is the decline in the average size of families, defined as the number of °children ever born. The available data indicate that 30 years ago Mennonites (MC) had nearly 50 percent more children per family than was true in national populations. The families in the 1956 study ended up with an average of 3.9 children per family. Since then Mennonite fertility has declined more rapidly than fertility in the national populations, so that currently Mennonite fertility is no higher than national fertility, as indicated by the 1982 census. This reflects the lower birthrates associated with nonfarm residence and occupations, and with higher educational achievements. Contraception is widely practiced among Mennonites, reflecting changes from earlier generations (°birth control).

Hutterite and Amish birthrates are still much

higher than Mennonite rates, but there is some indication of very recent downward trends in the
number of children born to completed families, suggesting that birth control may be gradually entering
the thinking and practice of these conservative
groups.

Lastly, the employment of Mennonite wives has
witnessed a significant increase. Among Hutterites
and the Old Orders, gainful employment of married
women is very rare. Among Mennonites, however,
the data indicate that married women are employed
at rates at least equal to married women in comparable national populations. According to the 1972
church member survey of five denominations, 45
percent of all women, married and not married,
were employed at least part-time, compared to 40
percent for the population of the United States in
1970. Counting only housewives, 38 percent were
employed at least part-time. Only 14 percent were
employed full-time. The percentages of housewives
employed ranged from 23.5 for farm residents to
49.1 for those church members living in cities of
more than 25,000 people.

At the time of the 1956 survey 20 percent of the
Midwest Mennonite wives were employed at least
part-time; this was when they had children at home.
By 1979, 65 percent of these wives had been
employed at some time during their married years.
It is likely that even larger proportions of younger
Mennonite wives will have been employed during
their married years, perhaps for considerably longer
periods of time than the earlier generations. This is
certainly a significant outcome of the increased urbanization of Mennonite families. These trends are
related to declining birth rates and the desire of
wives to supplement the family income or to follow
career interests.

Family Relationships. Family interpersonal
relationships can be classified into at least four
categories; husband-wife, parent-child, sibling
relationships, and relationships of the members of a
nuclear family to other relatives. Are Mennonites
any different from other population segments with
respect to the quality of family relationships? For
example, does the strong Mennonite emphasis on
peace and harmony between peoples and nations
have any effect on peace and harmony within the
family?

Definitive answers to these questions are difficult
to obtain. The quality of personal relationships is not
easy to assess, and there have been very few attempts to apply empirical methods to the study of
relationships. With several exceptions, we are left
with chiefly inferential and speculative answers to
these intriguing questions.

At least four concerns have emerged as Mennonites have reflected in recent decades on the trends
occurring within their families: (1) What are the effects on the quality of family life resulting from urbanization? (2) Is the decline of patriarchy a gain or
a loss for Mennonite families? (3) How has the
°sexual revolution affected Mennonite families? (4)
How have Mennonite families been affected by the
°women's rights movement? Comments on these issues will be limited to Mennonites, since family life
among the Hutterites, Old Order Amish, Old Order

Mennonites, and Old Colony Mennonites appears to
be undergoing little, if any, change.

One can assume that urbanization and modernization affect Mennonite families in much the same
ways as non-Mennonite families. Family sociologists
note that some changes are positive. As a result of
improved medical care fewer families are broken by
the early death of a spouse or child. Family well-
being profits from improved material resources and
increased levels of living. There is more leisure time
for family members to share together, although there
is the question of how well that time is used.
Families have gradually become more "democratized" through more sharing of decisions between
spouses and between parents and children. There is
more overlapping of husband and wife roles, which
is believed to improve understanding and communication between spouses.

On the negative side, marital breakup rates have
soared and are about twice as high in urban areas as
among the rural farm population. The available data
indicate that this is true for Mennonites as well,
although the rates are comparatively low in both
rural and urban areas. For the general population,
crime and delinquency rates are higher in urban
areas. Data for Mennonites are lacking, but Mennonite cases seem to be very rare anywhere. Absence
of parents from the home, due primarily to their
employment, is greater in nonfarm areas, and this is
assumed to be a negative factor for family well-
being. It was noted above that urban mobility tends
to weaken kinship relationships. Urban children lack
the opportunity to learn many work skills that their
rural farm cousins regularly gain. Urban housing is
more crowded, with the result that space for family
members to work and play together is much more
limited. It has been generally assumed that greater
stresses in urban life are responsible for the higher
rates of mental disorders in cities. Data are lacking
to clarify how similarly Mennonite families share in
these aspects of urban society.

By the use of scales to assess the quality of
husband-wife and parent-child relationships,
Kauffman explored farm and nonfarm differences
among the families surveyed in 1956. Unfortunately
there were only 15 urban families in the nonfarm
category. No significant difference was found
between farm and nonfarm families with respect to
husband-wife and parent-child relationships.
However, further analysis indicated that rural
residence *per se* was favored, but the residence factor was overcome by the fact that farm families
tended to be more patriarchal, which factor was
detrimental to the quality of interpersonal relations.
In other words, if farm families were no more
patriarchal than nonfarm families, the interpersonal
relations scores would have averaged somewhat
higher among the farm families.

These findings speak to the question of the effect
of declining patriarchy on Mennonite families. Those
families in which the father was definitely or slightly
dominant were compared with those in which the
spouses shared responsibilities more equally. It was
found that the equalitarian families scored somewhat
higher on the husband-wife and parent-child relationships scales. Thus the decline of patriarchy

apears to be beneficial rather than detrimental for the quality of relationships between family members.

These findings tended to be corroborated a few years later by Augsburger in a survey of 293 students in Mennonite colleges. He compared respondents who had experienced "direct" family controls (administered more autocratically by an individual or individuals) with others who had experienced more "indirect" controls (administered more democratically through group processes). Direct control patterns were reported more frequently by students who were older, from farm backgrounds, and from eastern communities in the United States. Students who had experienced more indirect control patterns scored somewhat higher on scales measuring personal and social development, and on items indicating patterns of personal behavior such as church attendance and absence of disapproved behaviors such as smoking and drinking. Thus the movement away from traditional stricter control patterns, generally associated with patriarchy, appears beneficial.

Returning to the question of the impact of urbanization, it was found that children in farm families evidenced slightly fewer neurotic symptoms than the nonfarm children, and that farm children were somewhat more accepting of traditional Mennonite values. We conclude that rural residence is favorable in some ways, but not in others. The negative effects of greater patriarchy tend to offset the advantages of rural location, so that the overall effects of urbanization are not negative, insofar as the quality of personal relationships is concerned. Of course, this does not speak to other, possibly negative, aspects of the urban environment.

What has been the effect of the women's rights movement? Certainly Mennonite women, as others, have increasingly entered formerly exclusively male occupations, including the ministry. Doubtless the increasing rate of employment of Mennonite wives and the declining Mennonite birthrates have their connection to the achievement of more equality between women and men. It appears that the younger generation of Mennonite husbands is increasingly sharing with their wives in household tasks and °childrearing, and wives are sharing much more in providing family income. Does this greater overlapping of husband and wife roles enhance the quality of family interpersonal relationships and success in child rearing?

In the 1979 follow-up of families studied in 1956, data on 554 children were obtained and a measure of personal success was computed for each, based on educational and occupational achievement, church membership and attendance, involvement in service activity, community and church leadership, and the absence of social and emotional disorders. These "offspring success scores" did not differ significantly between those children reared in the more patriarchal families as compared to those reared in the more equalitarian ones. However, the success scores did average higher in those families where the husband-wife and parent-child relationships scores were higher in 1956. This suggests that the success of children is more closely related to the quality of the emotional relationships (particularly affection)

which the child experiences in the family than it is to the way authority is distributed between the parents.

Other findings with respect to offspring success scores indicate that children from rural families had slightly higher average success scores than the offspring of urban families. The success of children was found to be unrelated to family size or to whether or not the wife was employed outside the home while they were rearing their children.

Major changes have occurred in American and Canadian societies in connection with the so-called sexual revolution of the 1960s and 1970s. Most notable are the greater openness in the discussion of matters of sexuality, major increases in the rates of premarital and extramarital sexual relations, a major increase in illegitimate births, and greater public awareness and discussion of homosexuality.

With their concern for personal morality, Mennonites have sought to resist the inroads of loosening moral standards evident in the mass media and public behavior. During the early 1980s a major study on "Human Sexuality in the Christian Life" was undertaken by leaders and congregations in both the General Conference Mennonite Church and the Mennonite Church (MC). The resulting study report, accepted by both denominational assemblies, affirms the principle of limiting sexual relations to married couples. Although the report disapproves discriminatory attitudes and behavior towards persons of homosexual orientation, it does not approve the practice of homosexual acts.

The 1972 survey indicated that 85 percent of church members believe that a sexual relationship outside of marriage "is never justified." Seven percent were uncertain, and eight percent were ready to justify it under certain limited conditions. Those responding "is never justified" ranged from 66 percent of the 20-29 years age group to 95 percent of the members 50 years and over. Thus attitudes of the younger generation are clearly more permissive, probably affected by shifts in public attitudes. There are infrequent cases among Mennonites of extramarital intercourse, illegitimate children, and sexual abuse of children, but their occurrence has not been documented except as they are noted by family counseling agencies.

There have been several attempts to discover the rate of premarital intercourse among Mennonites—two surveys of Mennonite college students by Kauffman (in 1968 and 1978) and a master's thesis at Purdue University. The results of these studies indicated that there is an increase in recent years in the proportion of persons who have intercourse prior to marriage. The data indicated rates of about 20 percent in 1968 and 30 percent in 1978, both far below the prevailing rates in the national populations. Premarital intercourse occurred among Mennonites in the past as well as the present, but stricter standards in the past often required public confession of such behavior. The recent erosion of the standard is apparently accompanied by the assumption that the occurrence is not to be considered as a matter of public concern.

Family Life Education. Many programs have emerged in recent decades in the attempt to help individuals become better prepared to meet the increasing problems and risks of modern marriage and family living. These programs aim to help youth in their understanding and preparation for marriage and to help married people move successfully through the various stages of marriage adjustment and parenting and on into the retirement years. The church is only one of many institutions (schools, colleges, youth organizations, parent support groups, publishers of books and magazines, etc.) that attempt to influence youth in their steps toward marriage and to help married persons not only to save their marriages but to enrich them as well. Increases in the divorce rate and in attempts to save marriages have occurred over the same years. One can only hope that the tide of marriage and family problems and failures has been somewhat retarded by educational and counseling efforts.

Family life education courses have been included in Mennonite college curricula and in many church high schools. Some congregations have a committee that promotes family life education in the congregation, particularly among the youth. Some congregations promote marriage enrichment workshops. Seminary training has incorporated marriage counseling courses into the training of pastors and Christian educators. Denominational Christian education commissions have held workshops on family life education about every 10 years, for the purpose of developing and promoting family life education in the churches. The denominational publishing programs have produced a variety of books and articles designed to help Mennonites meet the problems of marriage and family living. Mennonite radio and television programming produces short messages emphasizing Christian values in marriage and family life. Traditional standards of sexual morality are periodically emphasized from the pulpit and in Sunday school classes. Recent emphases focus on improving the quality of parenting in the hope that the next generation will have better preparation for marriage because their parents were more successful in modeling parenthood and spousal relationships. If succeeding generations can stem the tide of family disorganization and disintegration, perhaps the current sense of urgency in working at the problems will be credited for some of their success. If the future of the church—not to speak of society in general—depends on what happens in families, as some stoutly claim, then the allocation of resources to family life education is timely indeed.   JHK

Kauffman/Harder, *Anabaptists Four C. Later* (1975), esp. ch. 3, 10; J. Howard Kauffman, "A Comparative Study of Traditional and Emergent Family Types among Midwest Mennonites" (PhD diss., U. of Chicago, 1960); idem, "Interpersonal Relations in Traditional and Emergent Families Among Midwest Mennonites," *Marriage and Family Living,* 23, no. 3 (August 1961), 247-52; Michael L. Yoder, Yoder, *MC Census* (1985), 307-49; Paul Redekop, "The Mennonite Family in Tradition and Transition," *JMS,* 4 (1986), 77-93; Leo Driedger, Michael Yoder, and Peter Sawatzky, "Divorce among Mennonites: Evidence of Family Breakdown," *MQR,* 19 (1985), 367-82; Alan Anderson and Leo Driedger, "The Mennonite Family: Culture and Kin in Rural Saskatchewan," in *Canadian Families: Ethnic Variations,* ed. K. Ishwaran (Toronto: McGraw-Hill Ryerson, Ltd., 1980), 161-80; A. Don Augsburger, "Control Patterns and the Behavior of Mennonite Youth," *MQR,* 39 (1965),192-203; Paul
M. Lederach, *Mennonite Youth* (Scottdale, 1971); Ross T. Bender, *Christians in Families* (Scottdale, 1982); Leland Harder, *Fact Book of Congregational Membership (GCM)* (the author, 1971), 7-19; idem, *Fact Book of Congregational Membership (GCM)* (the author, 1980-81); John A. Hostetler, *Amish Society,* (1980), 172-206; idem, *Hutterite Society* (1974), 234-51; Mennonite Church, General Conference Mennonite Church, *Human Sexuality in the Christian Life* (Newton, Ks.: GCM, 1985; Lombard, Ill.: MC, 1985); Calvin W. Redekop, *The Old Colony Mennonites* (Baltimore: Johns Hopkins U. Press, 1969), 68-73; idem, *Strangers Become Neighbors* (Scottdale, 1980), 107-12; Clarence Hiebert, *The Holdeman People* (South Pasadena, Cal.: William Carey Library, 1973), 459-69; J. Howard Kauffman, "Sexual Attitudes and Behavior of Mennonite College Youth," paper presented to Conference on Christianity and Sexuality, Aug. 5-9, 1968, copy at MHL (Goshen); Jean Huntington Phillips Hicks, "Premarital Sexual Intimacy: A Mennonite College Sample" (MS thesis, Purdue U., Jan. 1972); John Klassen, "Women and Family among Dutch Anabaptist Martyrs," *MQR* 60 (1986) 548-71.

Family of Love (ME II:293), was a movement founded by Hendrik Niclaes (1502-80) initially in Emden, East Friesland. The son of an orthodox Catholic merchant, Niclaes early showed interest in theological issues. On the basis of visions he received he believed himself to be called to a messianic ministry. In 1531 he moved to Amsterdam, which was beginning to become the center of Anabaptism, to begin his career as merchant. Following a brief arrest, presumably because of his religious activities, he moved to Emden in East Friesland to implement his sectarian vision. He lived there for 20 years, financing his work and the publication of his books through his commercial endeavors. The best known of his writings may have been the *Mirror of Righteousness*, published in Emden.

The structure of his "family (house) of love" was strictly hierarchical, headed by a bishop, who was Niclaes himself. The "family" was divided into seven orders strongly reminiscent of the hierarchy in Roman Catholicism. Movement up the ladder of orders was possible, except for women, who could only attain the lowest orders.

Niclaes recruited his membership particularly through business contacts. Thus Christoffel Plantijn, an Antwerp printer who published his books, became a member. Some intellectuals were also attracted to the movement—the geographer Abraham Ortelius and the orientalist Justus Lipsius. One of the enigmas of the movement is how Niclaes was able to attract persons of this caliber given the simplicity and lack of clarity or logic in his own writings. Ca. 1560 Niclaes was forced to leave Emden, the authorities having discovered that the successful merchant was, in fact, a dangerous heretic. He moved to Cologne where he lived until his death.

The ideas of Niclaes are strongly spiritualistic with neo-Stoic influence. He saw himself as sent by God to be a new mediator to continue the work of Christ. He believed that his followers should become one with Christ by imitating his life and spiritually experiencing his death on the cross. Being successful in this meant to become deified and perfect. The written Scriptures lost their significance since they were not inspired by the spirit which Niclaes believed he possessed. His emphasis on spiritualism and perfection led to a discarding of sacraments and other church practices. His followers were permitted to attend other churches to avoid persecution. Some of his teachings and practices coincided with those of the Anabaptist leader °David Joris of Delft.

The "Family of Love" received a serious blow when one of the oldest followers of Niclaes, Hendrik Jansen van Barrefeld (1520-1594) left the movement under the conviction he received in 1573 that he and not Niclaes was to be the direct link with God. Many of Niclaes' followers agreed with Jansen and the "witness" book he published in 1581. While his ideas were largely those of Niclaes, his spiritualism was even stronger and his messianic pretensions were more modest. He also lacked Niclaes' organizational ability.

Following the death of these leaders the movement slowly disappeared, except in England where Niclaes' books were available in English after 1570. Members of the movement were largely artisans until severe persecution forced their decline. By 1680 the "Familists" had largely merged with the Quakers.   SZ

J. van Dorsten, "Garter Knights and Familists," *Journal of European Studies*, 4 (1974, 178-88; H. de la Fontaine Verwey, "Trois hérésiarques dans les Pays Bas du XVIe siecle," *Bibliothèque d'Humanisme et Renaissance*, 16 (1954), 312-30; idem, "Het Huis der Liefde en zijn publicaties," *Uit de wereld van het boek I* (Amsterdam, 1975), 85-112; idem, "The Family of Love," *Quaerendo*, 6 (1976), 219-71; A. Hamilton, "Hiël and the Hiëlists: The Doctrines and Followers of Hendrik Jansen van Barrefelt,' *Quaerendo*, 7 (1977), 243-86; idem, *The Family of Love* (Cambridge, 1981); W. Kirsop, "The Family of Love in France,' *Journal of Religious History*, 3 (1962), 103-18; J. D. Moss, "Godded with God: Hendrik Niclaes and his Family of Love (Philadelphia, 1981); B. Rekers, *Benito Arias Montano (1527-1598)* (London and Leiden, 1972); I. Simon, "Hendrik Niclaes und das Huys der Liefde," *Gedenkschrift für William Foerste* (Cologne, 1970), 432-53.

Family Worship. Broadly conceived, family worship may refer to any type of religious activities occurring in the home. It may include prayer at meals and other times, singing, reading of the Bible or other devotional literature, meditation, listening to recordings of religious music, poetry, or prose, and other activities. It may occur on a regular schedule or irregularly. It may be observed by individuals alone, or in groups.

More narrowly defined, it would refer to group activities only (as distinguished from "private" worship), involving two or more household members and including something more than routine prayer at meals.

Broadly conceived, nearly all Mennonite families have family worship since almost all practice some form of grace at meals. According to information gathered in the 1972 survey of members of five Mennonite and Brethren in Christ denominations, 83 percent of households said grace at every meal and another 13 percent at most meals. However, only 45 percent reported having "a family or group worship, other than grace at meals."

Christian education publications uniformly encourage families to conduct worship in the home, and a variety of worship aids have been published throughout the centuries.

Worship in Mennonite homes had its beginnings in the small, hidden congregations of Anabaptists that gathered for worship from 1525 onward. Avoid-

ing worship in the state churches of Switzerland, Holland, and Germany, and suffering persecution at the hands of the civil authorities, worship gatherings were secretive and irregular, and took place in homes, barns, sheds, and even caves, wherever there was sufficient space to contain the worshipers.

Friedmann (1973, p. 147) reports that "sources on the conduct of worship among Anabaptists during the 16th c. are almost nonexistent." The "Congregational Order" that appears to have circulated with the °Schleitheim Confession mandated daily reading of the Psalter at home (CRR 1:44). To what degree families had worship within their own households in addition to their larger gatherings is not known. Early documents indicate that the Hutterites conducted a "worship hour" at about 6 p.m. which came to be known as *Das Gebet*, a daily practice that is still observed by Hutterites (Hostetler, 1974, p. 168). This, of course, is a colony gathering, not a household worship. Since other Anabaptists generally did not live in colonies, a daily worship service for the congregation would have been impractical.

Evidence that family worship was practiced in some homes in the 17th and 18th c. stems from the emergence of °°prayer books for use by families and individuals as well as in public worship. The most popular of these was the Swiss-Mennonite devotional book, *Güldene Äpffel in silbern Schalen* (Golden Apples in Silver Bowls), published anonymously at Basel in 1702 and 1742, with many later editions. Other works that served Mennonites in Switzerland and surrounding areas were *Send-Brieff* (published about 1720), *Die Ernsthafte Christenpflicht* (1739 with many later editions), and *Kleines Handbüchlein* (1786 and later editions). The development and use of °°devotional literature was probably related to the growth of Pietism in the 18th c., which emphasized the cultivation of a spiritual "inner life."

The Dutch Mennonites, enjoying an earlier and greater political tolerance than did the Swiss, produced religious literature earlier and in greater quantity than the Swiss and South German Mennonites. Notable among their productions were several widely-read literary works by Peter Petersz and Johann Philipp Schabalie, and, of course, van Braght's *Martyrs Mirror*. A few works by Dutch and Prussian Mennonites contained prayers and hymns for use in public as well as private worship, but the more pietistic, devotional prayer books were not generally produced (Friedmann, 1949, chap. II).

Bender reports that English-speaking American Mennonites have never produced nor used prayer books in public worship, and seldom, until recent times, in private or family worship (ME IV:211). However, a variety of short prayers are usually found in the worship guides and booklets that have been published for use in homes in the last half century.

Contemporary family and individual worship patterns were investigated in the 1972 church member survey. The proportion of respondents who reported that they experience family worship, whether daily or less often, was: Mennonite Brethren, 61 percent; Brethren in Christ, 51 percent; Evangelical Mennonite, 44 percent; General Conference Mennonite, 43 percent; and Mennonite Church (MC) 41 percent.

The practice of family worship appears to increase with age, with proportions ranging from about one-third among the 20-29 age group to nearly two-thirds among those over 70 years of age. The proportions having family worship did not vary significantly between educational levels, socioeconomic levels, or rural-urban residence categories. This seems to indicate that Mennonite household worship practices have not been curtailed under the impact of the secular forces of urbanization and educatiohal and economic advancement.

Ministers and non-ordained congregational leaders had higher rates of family worship than non-leaders. Family worship rates were highly associated with frequency of church attendance and other aspects of church participation. Higher rates were associated with higher scores on scales measuring orthodoxy of religious beliefs and adherence to Anabaptist principles. It is clear that church members in households conducting family worship, on the average, scored higher on all measures of religious attainment.

An important corollary of family worship is the practice of grace at meals. Only about four percent of Mennonites and Brethren in Christ households seldom or never have grace at meals. Four percent pray both before and after meals, a custom largely inherited from the Amish of bygone days. The remaining 92 percent have prayer *before* every meal or most meals.

Hostetler reports that prayer among the Amish is mostly silent. "Rarely is there a spontaneous audible prayer," although in some families the father may read a prayer from the prayer book when the family gathers before retiring (Hostetler, 1980, 165). Silent prayer was the custom also among Dutch Mennonites in the 16th and 17th c., and among some of the more conservative churches, on down into the 19th c. It is probable that °prayer customs (silent or audible; kneeling, standing, or sitting; memorized, read, or spontaneous) in the homes mirrored the custom followed in the congregation. Also it is likely that prayer customs, whether silent or audible, spontaneous or memorized, depend heavily on the skills and creativeness of the persons who lead the family worship.

Van der Zijpp reports that "family worship has never been very popular among the Dutch Mennonites, though it has been held occasionally" (ME IV: 211). He adds that formerly prayer was offered, usually silent, before and after meals, a custom still evidenced in many Dutch Mennonite homes.

The 1972 survey item, "Are prayers offered audibly or silently at meals?" elicited the following response pattern: "always audibly," 43 percent; "usually audibly, sometimes silently," 29 percent; "usually silently, sometimes audibly," 19 percent; "always silently," 9 percent. Silent prayer is more common among the Mennonite groups with strains of Amish in their backgrounds (particularly the Mennonite Church, MC) and is almost totally lacking among the Mennonite Brethren.

The use of memorized prayers is widespread among Mennonites, particularly for grace at meals. Parents often involve their children in family prayers at meals, bedtime, or other times, by having them learn and repeat memorized prayers ap-propriate for their age. Historically the Lord's Prayer has been widely used in both public and family worship.

Although the Dordrecht Confession of Faith does not refer to family or private worship, the 1963 Mennonite Confession of Faith (MC) includes a statement that "the Christian home ought regularly to have family worship." The denominational committees on Christian education include in their portfolios the promotion of family and private devotions, and have been instrumental in preparing worship aids for use in homes. For many decades the Sunday school lesson quarterlies included daily Scripture readings related to the International Sunday School lessons, intended for use at home.

The Women's Missionary and Service Association (MC) and its forerunners from 1925 onward published a °°*Prayer Guide* for home use until 1960. Denominational family worship periodicals in the United States and Canada have been published since the late 1950s. These included: *Light for the Day* and *Licht für den Tag*, 1959-71, published by the Conference of Mennonites in Canada; *Family Worship*, 1961-71 (MC); *Our Family Worships*, 1961-71 (GCM), and *Worship Together*, 1966-71, Mennonite Brethren. In 1972 these five publications were succeeded by *Rejoice!*, sponsored conjointly by the three denominations, a testimony to the increasing integration of Christian education programs by these major Mennonite bodies.

A rationale for conducting family worship is hardly required. A variety of pamphlets and articles have appeared promoting family and private worship in Mennonite homes during the past half century. Family life education programs have invariably emphasized the importance of family worship, reflecting the oft-quoted phrase, "the family that prays together, stays together." A 1984 publication authored by the Palmer and Ardys Becker, *Creative Family Worship*, inquires "Why Family Worship?" Their answers: To provide intimate Christian fellowship, give glory to God, learn biblical truths and values, prepare for witness and service, build parent-child relationships, and foster personal growth. The book includes suggestions for songs, readings, and other activities for conducting family worship.   JHK

Robert Friedmann, *Mennonite Piety Through the Centuries* (Goshen, Ind.: Mennonite Historical Society, 1949), 105-202; Kauffman/Harder, *Anabaptists Four C. Later* (1975), 96-99, 178-79; A. Donald Augsburger, "Parental Roles in the Development of Attitudinal Patterns in the Family Worship Experience" (MRE Thesis, Eastern Baptist Theological Seminary, 1956); Palmer and Ardys Becker, *Creative Family Worship* (Newton, 1984); Robert Friedmann, "Hutterite Worship and Preaching," *MQR*, 60 (1966), 5-26; *idem, The Theology of Anabaptism* (Scottdale, 1973), 147; John A. Hostetler, *Amish Society* (1980), 165-66; idem, *Hutterite Society* (1974), 168; Ernest Bohn, "Religion in the Home" in *Proceedings* of the 6th Annual Conference on Mennonite Cultural Patterns, held at Goshen College, August 1-2, 1947, pp. 87-94; *Christian Family Relationships*, Proceedings of the Study Conference on Home Interests . . . Held at Goshen College, . . . August 28-31, 1959 (Mennonite Commission for Christian Education, 1960), various articles; John R. Mumaw, *Worship in the Home* (Scottdale: Mennonite Publishing House, ca. 1941); Nelson E. Kauffman, ed., *For Family Worship: A Series of Doctrinal Meditations based on Scripture Selections for the Family Worship Hour. . .* (Scottdale, 1949); John R. Mumaw, "Vital Experiences at the Family Altar," in *Christian Ministry*, 5 (1952) 216-19.

See also Muganda Ezekiel Kaneja.

Fast, Aganetha Helen (July 31, 1888-Mar. 19, 1981). Born at Mountain Lake, Minn., Aganetha Fast was the daughter of Herman J. and Aganetha Becker Fast. She was baptized by H. H. Regier, Aug. 7, 1906. Her most admired Sunday school teacher was Elizabeth Dickman °Penner, pioneer missionary to India. She attended Bethel Academy, North Newton, Ks. (1912-14); Moody Bible Institute (1914-16); Witmarsum Theological Seminary (1924-26, ThB); Garrett Biblical Institute (summer, 1925); and Kennedy School of Missions (1934-36, MA). Ordained a General Conference Mennonite missionary to China, Aug. 8, 1917, she served in China, 1917-41, 1947-50.

Aganetha Fast supervised the Ching Lien Girls' Boarding School; directed city women's evangelistic and student work in Kai Chow [Puyang], Tsingfeng, Taming and Nanlo; founded and supervised Ling Shen Girls' Day School; supervised P'e Cheng boys' Day Schools; and was treasurer of the Kai Chow city evangelistic and educational work. Upon return to the United States she visited °°Civilian Public Service camps, congregations, and women's missionary societies, and served in Mexico in 1953.   MTS

H. C. Brown, *The General Conference China Mennonite Mission* (Taming-fu, China: the author, 1940), 126.

Fast, Henry A. (b. Oct. 12, 1894-Jan. 3, 1990), shaped the Mennonite witness as pastor, teacher, administrator, and relief worker, beginning in 1922 as professor of New Testament at Witmarsum Seminary (GCM), Bluffton, Ohio.

He was born in Mountain Lake, Minn., the son of Herman J. and Aganetha Becker Fast. A graduate of Bethel College and Witmarsum Seminary, he received his PhD degree from Hartford Theological Seminary in 1936, having done research on nonresistance in the synoptic gospels, a work later published as *Jesus and Human Conflict* (Scottdale, 1959).

In 1936, the General Conference Mennonite Church called him to visit its congregations, an assignment that covered Mexico, Paraguay, and Brazil, as well as the United States and Canada. In 1940, he was on the peace church team that worked with the United States government to develop °°Civilian Public Service (CPS), an alternative for World War II °conscientious objectors. He thus secured rights not available to him in 1918, when he was drafted into the army and endured abuse to secure work in the base hospital at Fort Riley, Ks. He directed the CPS camps assigned to the Mennonite Central Committee (MCC) until 1943 when he became professor of Bible at Bethel college, a post he held for 17 years.

After World War II, he promoted the movement that founded a number of Mennonite °mental health centers as well as Mennonite Mental Health Services. He was MCC's vice-chairman (1943-60) and, in 1951, led its relief work in Europe. He promoted °voluntary service and a ministry to the °aging both in MCC and as a member of the Commission on Home Ministries (GCM). From 1941 to 1968, he

helped the General Conference Mennonite Church rewrite its constitution and refine its organization.

He was pastor of the Bethel College Mennonite Church, North Newton, Ks. (1925-30), and the Eden Mennonite Church, Moundridge, Ks. (1965-71), and also taught in public schools in Whitewater, Ks., and Mountain Lake, Minn.   MSh

"Henry A. Fast" as told to Maynard Shelly, in *Something Meaningful for God: The Stories of Some Who served with MCC,* ed. Cornelius J. Dyck (Scottdale, 1981), 32-70; Barry C. Bartel, "Henry A. Fast: A Man with a Purpose," a research paper with bibliography of writings by Fast (1983, copy at MLA (North Newton); H. A. Fast, "C.P.S.—Past and Future," (n.d., a 4-page MS, MLA).

Federal Republic of Germany. See Bundesrepublik Deutschland.

Federation of European Mennonite Brethren Churches. See Bund Europäischer Mennonitischer Brüdergemeinden.

Feetwashing (ME II:347). Students of the New Testament are aware that the Lord's command to "wash one another's feet" (Jn 13:14) is one of the clearest in the New Testament sources. It is reinforced with the words: "I have set you an example: you are to do as I have done for you" (Jn 13:15). For this reason, it is not surprising that the practice made its way into the Anabaptist movement. At the same time, as Harold °Bender points out in ME II, largely based on research by Clarence Hiebert, it was not uniformly practiced among the Mennonites and this is still the case. Biblical scholars have done more research into the history of the practice and the meaning thereof. Indeed H. S. Bender's book on the church, while it does not speak about the practice as such, invokes it when he refers to the two great symbols of the church as the cross and the towel. For Bender the towel symbolizes service: "The Christ who took the towel to wash His disciple's feet is our example in service" (p. 96). With a renewal of physical contacts in church there has been some movement to institute or keep feetwashing, but by and large it seems to be suffering from neglect even as a deeper understanding of its symbolism is emerging. At least it is no longer practiced just because of historical reasons and greater efforts are being made to explain the action. There is little evidence that efforts are being made to keep the practice even as it is clear that views of service and models of service are much discussed.   WKla

H. S. Bender, *These are My People* (Scottdale, 1962), 96.

See also Communion; Evangelical Mennonite Conference; Old Order River Brethren; Ordinances.

Fellowship Churches. In the late 1950s and early 1960s, various scattered congregations of the Mennonite Church (MC) withdrew from the regional conferences and formed independent churches with a congregational church government. These congregations opposed the way the conferences were abandoning biblical principles and conservative practices. Though not homogenous, these congregations began fellowshiping together for mutual edification and encouragement. Other congregations left the conferences and joined them in subsequent years. In time these nonconference churches formed into groups called "Fellowships." One such became known as the Fellowship Churches.

The Fellowship Churches uphold seven Bible principles that they believed were being compromised or abandoned in the Mennonite Church: (1) The supreme authority of the Bible for life and doctrine. Cutting across time and cultures, Bible principles find a consistent practical application among God's people in every generation. (2) Believer's baptism. Only those who show evidence of real conversion and a change of life are fit candidates for baptism. (3) Scriptural church government. Not an ecclesiastical authority legislating to a carnal people, but Spirit-led men leading a body of committed disciples to confront sin and current issues. (4) Clean communion. Prompt dealing with sin and carnality to maintain the purity of the church and her communion table. (5) °Mutual aid. A commitment to meet each other's material needs, without depending on government aid or °insurance programs. (6) Scriptural separation from the world based on radical °discipleship (°nonconformity) and an uncompromisng stand against the pressures, trends, and fads of the world. (7) Every-member involvement in evangelism.

The Fellowship Churches do not maintain organizational ties but are bound together by common purposes and practices. The ordained brethren meet annually for inspiration and conferring. From small beginnings, the Fellowship Churches have grown to more than 2,100 members in 69 congregations in the United States, Canada, Mexico, the Dominican Republic, Paraguay, the Philippines, and Nigeria.

The Fellowship Churches actively support missions and the distribution of literature. Supported by the Fellowship Churches, Rod and Staff Publishers, Crockett, Ky., is developing a °private Christian school curriculum for grades one through ten. The Fellowship Churches consider providing a Christian education for children a scriptural requirement for the preservation of the faith.   EStr

Directory of the Fellowship Churches (Farmington, N.M.: Lamp and Light Publishers), published biennially; *MC Yearbook* (1988-89) 93-94; Reimer, *Quilt* (1983), 18.

See also Conservative Mennonite Church of Ontario; Conservative Mennonites; Ohio.

Fellowship of Concerned Mennonites had its beginning with a mass meeting held in connection with Mennonite Church (MC) general assembly at Bethlehem, Pa., 1983. It was formally organized under a constitution adopted at Landisville, Pa., Sept. 7, 1984, and is guided in its activity by a self-perpetuating board selected from the active membership of the group.

Formation of this organization was occasioned by the conviction of individuals throughout the church that some Mennonite scholars were either neglecting or rejecting such basic Anabaptist and Mennonite expressions of faith as biblical °inerrancy, the blood °atonement, and biblical °nonresistance. The purpose of the fellowship is to preserve and promote the true doctrine and practice of biblical faith

through: (1) open dialogue and conversation among Mennonite scholars and teachers, (2) promotion of sound teaching through area Bible conferences, (3) a vigorous campaign of literature as represented in the Biblical Heritage pamphlet series. Fellowship of Concerned Mennonites is pledged to work within the structures of the Mennonite Church (MC) rather than promote schismatic withdrawal.

While not organizationally identified with the fellowship, two independent Mennonite publications: °°*Sword and Trumpet,* published in Virginia since 1929, and *Guidelines for Today,* published at Johnstown, Pa., since 1965, have promoted the group's concerns.   LMW

MWR (Aug. 23, 1984), 4; Fred Kniss, *Ideological Conflict in an Intentional Peripheral Community: The Fellowship of Concerned Mennonites* (Chicago, Ill.: Kniss, 1986).

See also Fundamentalism; Evangelicalism; Association of Evangelical Mennonites.

Fellowship of Evangelical Bible Churches, formerly the Evangelical Mennonite Brethren Conference. The attempt to merge the conferences of the Evangelical Mennonite Brethren and the Evangelical Mennonite Church beginning in 1953 ended in 1962 without success. The reasons for this failure were largely administrative. The last issue of a joint paper, the *Evangelical Mennonite,* appeared in September 1962 and the *Gospel Tidings* was published again as the Evangelical Mennonite Brethren Conference journal. At the same time the conference was drawing closer to the Evangelische Mennonitische Bruderschaft von Südamerika (Evangelical Mennonite Brethren of South America) which had grown out of a renewal movement in the Molotschna Colony of South Russia. This movement was similar to that which led to the founding of the Evangelical Mennonite Brethren in North America. The South American group arrived in the Paraguayan Chaco in 1930 and on October 5 established a church of 44 members in the Fernheim Colony. Another church was established in Buenos Aires, Argentina, and a conference was formed.

In the 1950s the North and South American Evangelical Mennonite Brethren conferences developed an interest in each other. They were of similar background, country, language, faith, doctrine, and spirit. Communication and visits between the conference leaders led to a request by the South Americans to affiliate with the North Americans. This was accomplished at the annual conference of 1958. The South American Evangelical Mennonite Brethren Conference was made a district of the conference. It retained self-government with the North American part of the conference acting in an advisory capacity (see °Alianza Evangélica Menonita de Argentina and °Konferenz der Evangelischen Mennonitischen Bruderschaft von Südamerika).

The decade of the 1950s also brought a radical change in the organization of the conference. The constitutions of 1922 and 1941 provided for district superintendents to oversee the four districts of the conference. These districts were abolished by the constitution of 1960 and four commissions (Churches, Education and Publication, Missions, and

Trustees) were established to focus on different areas of conference concerns. The chairmen of the commissions together with the conference president, vice-president, administrative secretary, and editor of the the conference paper form the Conference Executive Committee which determines the direction of the conference. In 1956 the conference headquarters were moved from Mountain Lake, Minn., to Omaha, Nebr.

Several auxiliary organizations were planned. Plans were announced at the 1949 conference to organize a Young People's Society. Its purpose was to stimulate interest in the conference on the part of its young people. An organization meeting was held at the 1950 conference, and it was decided to call the organization "The Ember Youth Fellowship" because "this name implies youth aglow and it is our desire to be aglow for the Lord." The acrostic implication of the name was evident. The organization was an outgrowth of the Sowers of Seed Fellowship which had been organized in 1940. The Ember Youth Fellowship arranged a four-day program for its members at the annual conference. In 1962 a retirement plan for ministers and missionaries was developed. By 1983 it had 74 participants plus 16 retired persons receiving monthly payments for the rest of their lives. The Women's Missionary Society was established in 1943. In 1986 the name was changed to the "Evangelical Mennonite Brethren Women's Ministries." There were 164 members of the conference serving as °missionaries under 41 mission societies in 1986. With few exceptions these missionary organizations were non-Mennonite; the conference is represented on some of their boards. The constitution of 1960 held to the Anabaptist-Mennonite position on °nonresistance and warfare. The constitution of 1983 allows individuals to make their position on warfare a matter of personal conscience.

A 25-year debate on conference identity was settled on July 16, 1987, when the conference (by a 74-percent vote) changed its name to the *Fellowship of Evangelical Bible Churches.* In 1987 the conference consisted of 36 congregations with a total membership of 4,538, of which 3,539 were resident members. Of this total, membership in Canada (20 congregations) was 1,981; in Argentina, 62; and in Paraguay, 361. · ACS

Gospel Tidings (July/Aug. 1987), 7; *Evangelical Mennonite Brethren Annual Report* (1949), 50-51, (1951), 68-69, (1958), 60, (1986), 18-22; *MWH* (1978), 328; *MWH* (1984), 138; Reimer, *Quilt* (1983), 47.

Fellowship of Hope. See Shalom Covenant Communities.

Fellowship of Mennonite Churches in Taiwan (FOMCIT). Mennonite Central Committee (MCC) medical and relief programs for aboriginal peoples in Taiwan began in 1948. As the missionary medical program developed, an interest in church planting resulted. Since this was not part of its mandate, MCC turned to the Inter-Mennonite Council of Mission Board Secretaries, which gave the General Conference Mennonite Church the first option to start work in Taiwan. In Nov. 1954, Hugh and Janet

Sprunger arrived as the first missionaries under the General Conference. Worship services began the same year in a small bamboo chapel under the leadership of MCC worker, Glen Graber. The first Mennonite congregation in Taiwan, the Lin Shen Road Mennonite Church in Taichung was formally established on Mar. 12, 1955. A year later, the MCC program was officially turned over to the General Conference Mennonite mission in Taiwan. The result of MCC and mission work was the founding of Mennonite Christian Hospital and the Fellowship of Mennonite Churches in Taiwan.

Formed in 1962 as an autonomous church organization, FOMCIT has concentrated on church planting efforts in three urban centers. At the end of 1986 there were 17 congregations with a total membership of 1,200. The cities of °Taipei and Taichung each have seven churches, and three churches are located in Hualien. All property, whether used by the mission or FOMCIT is legally registered in the name of FOMCIT.

The ministry of evangelism, church planting, social service, theological education and publication is directed by an executive committee of 11 members, with working subcommittees for each area of ministry. Fellowship of Mennonite Churches in Taiwan invites and assigns missionaries of the Commission on Overseas Mission (GCM).

A monthly periodical, called *Manna* is published by the conference. Anabaptist/Mennonite materials are translated and published in Chinese. A theological training program on the pastoral and lay levels is being developed.

The Mennonite Christian Hospital (MCH) was founded in Hualien in 1954 to serve as a base for the mobile clinic work on the east coast of Taiwan. Under the leadership of Roland Brown, MCH continued to expand in size and services. When MCH came under joint FOMCIT-Mission control in 1986, it had 200 beds and a staff of 400. A board of trustees was established in 1961. M. J. Kao served as administrator (CEO) 1975-87, and Roland Brown continued as medical director until 1986. In addition to medical services, the hospital is classified as a teaching hospital. A six-member chaplaincy department ministers to patients and staff.

The New Dawn Development Center in Hualien, a day school for mentally handicapped children was begun by missionaries Otto and Elaine Dirks in 1977. The school is operated under the auspices of FOMCIT's Social Concerns Committee and is registered with the government. In 1986 the enrollment was 27 students, with a staff of nine.

An outgrowth of the New Dawn program was the founding of a Social Service Center in Hualien. The social programs include counseling, relief work, and the training of home care workers. An evangelist is appointed by FOMCIT to oversee the spiritual ministry of the center. SVS

MWH (1978), 183-87; Sheldon V. Sawatzky, "The Gateway of Promise: A Study of the Taiwan Mennonite Church and the Factors Affecting Its Growth," (MA thesis, Fuller Theological Seminary, 1970); idem, "Identity and Authority in the Taiwan Mennonite Church," *Miss. Focus,* 15, no 4 (1987), 54-56.

Feminist Movement. See Gender Roles; Women.

Bibliography: Gilbert Bilezikian, *Beyond Sex Roles: A Guide for the Study of Female Roles in the Bible* (Grand Rapids: Baker, 1985); Lois Gunden Clemens, *Woman Liberated* (Scottdale, 1971); Adela Yarbro Collins, ed., *Feminist Perspectives on Biblical Scholarship* (Scholars Press, 1985); Mary Lou Cummings, *Full Circle: Stories of Mennonite Women* (Newton, 1978); J. D. °Dozy, "Het feminisme als zedelijk vraagstuk" (diss., Amsterdam, 1933); Marlene Epp, "Women in Canadian Mennonite History: Uncovering the 'Underside,'" *JMS*, 5 (1987), 90-107; Mary Evans, *Woman in the Bible* (Downers Grove, Ill.: InterVarsity, 1983); Elisabeth Schussler Fiorenza, *In Memory of Her: A Feminist Theological Reconstruction of Christian Origins* (New York: Crossroad, 1983); idem, *Bread Not Stone: The Challenge of Feminist Biblical Interpretation* (Boston: Beacon Press, 1984); Melvin Gingerich, "The Mennonite Women's Missionary Society," *MQR,* 37 (1963), 113-25, 214-33; Gladys Goering, *Women in Search of Mission*; Nancy Hardesty, and Letha Scanzoni, *All We're Meant to Be* (Word, 1974); *Human Sexuality in the Christian Life* GCM and MC working document, 1985; James Juhnke, "The Role of Women in the Mennonite Transition from Traditionalism to Denominationalism," *Menn. Life*, 41 (Sept. 1986); Sharon Klingelsmith, "Women in the Mennonite Church, 1900-1930," *MQR,* 54 (1980); *Leadership and Authority in the Life of the Church* (Scottdale, 1982); Alverea Mickelsen, ed., *Women, Authority and the Bible* (Downers Grove, Ill.: InterVarsity, 1986; Dorothy Yoder Nyce, ed., *Which Way Women?* (Akron, Pa.: MCC Peace Section Task Force on Women, 1980); Rich, *Mennonite Women* (Scottdale, 1983); Sandra Schneiders, *Women and the Word* (New York: Paulist, 1986); Marla Selvidge, *Daughters of Jerusalem* (Scottdale, 1987); Veronica Strong-Boag and Anita Clair Fellman, eds. *Rethinking Canada: The Promise of Women's History* (Toronto: Copp Clark Pitman Ltd., 1986; Diane Tennis, *Is God the Only Reliable Father?* (Philadelphia: Westminster, 1985); Ruth Unrau, *Encircled: Stories of Mennonite Women* (Newton, 1986); Katie Funk Wiebe, *Women Among the Brethren*; Sheila Classen Wiebe, "The Influence of Feminist Consciousness upon the Mennonite Church from 1966-1986" (research paper, Associated Mennonite Biblical Seminaries, April 1987), 119 pp.; copy in AMBS Library; Don Williams, *Apostle Paul and Women in the Church* (Regal Books, 1987); Linda Raney Wright, *A Cord of Three Strands* (Revell, 1987); Elizabeth Yoder, ed., *Perspectives on Feminist Hermeneutics* (Occasional Papers no. 10: Elkhart, Ind.: IMS, 1987).

Fernheim Colony, Paraguay (ME II: 323). At the time of its founding, 1930-32, Fernheim Colony had ca. 2,000 inhabitants. Continuing emigration over the years, however, has slowed population growth. In 1986 the population was only 3,300. The most difficult crisis occurred in 1937 when approximately one-third of the inhabitants left to found Friesland Colony in East Paraguay. During the years 1950 to· 1970 the emigration to Germany and Canada was so strong that the very existence of the colony was jeopardized. However, since 1970 one can speak of stability and consolidation.

Political and economic stability throughout Paraguay also affected the Mennonite colonies. The building of the Trans-Chaco road facilitated communication and marketing. Long-term credits, the first of which was a million-dollar loan from the United States facilitated by Mennonite Central Committee, made a restructuring of agriculture and dairy production possible. Farms have gradually been mechanized. Through this colonists have been more able to cope with the climatic conditions of the °°Chaco. Food production and consumption improved and with it the general level of health in the colony. The hospital was improved, as were the schools, leading to better education for young people.

In 1984 the colony had three congregations affiliated with the Konferenz der Mennonitischen Brüdergemeinden (MB), totaling 715 members; one congregation belonging to the Vereinigung der Mennonitengemeinden (GCM), with 650 members; and one congregation of the Konferenz der Evangelischen Mennonitischen Brüderschaft von Südamerika (related to Fellowship of Evangelical Bible Churches, formerly EMB), with 308 members.

All social and economic arrangements are administered by the colony's producer-consumer °cooperative which has increasingly adapted itself to the Paraguayan situation. All of these factors have caused emigration to return to a normal level. The number of villages has increased from 17 to 25, with the town of °Filadelfia experiencing considerable growth.   PPK

Peter Wiens and Peter Klassen, *Jubiläumsschrift zum 25 jährigen Bestehen der Kolonie Fernheim* (Winnipeg, 1955); *50 Jahre Kolonie Fernheim* (Filadelfia, 1980); *MWH* (1978), 252; *MWH* (1984), 93-99 passim; *GCM Handbook* (1988), 39.

Filadelfia, Paraguay (ME II: 328). Filadelfia has been the administrative center of °Fernheim Colony since 1931. It is disproportionately large, with 1,700 Mennonite inhabitants out of a total population of 3,300 in the colony. An additional 200 non-Mennonites and more than 1,000 Indians also live there.

The reasons for the rapid growth of the town lie in the location of all necessary services there, e.g., schools, hospitals, cooperative store, industry. Many private enterprises have also located there. The teacher-training institute, the sanitarium Hoffnungsheim (Home of Hope), the office for the administration of Indian affairs, Radio ZP-30, and governmental organizations like SENALFA (an agricultural consulting office), and ANTELCO (the telephone and television service of the Paraguayan government), are also located in Filadelfia.

The spiritual life of the colony is also centered in Filadelfia and beyond. The three congregations in Fernheim Colony carry on their mission work °Licht den Indianern from this center. A major airport is located there. The location of Filadelfia between Menno and Neuland colonies has contributed substantially to its life and dynamic.   PPK

For bibliography see Fernheim Colony.

See also Loma Plata, Paraguay.

Filmmaking. Compared with °quilt-making, °publishing, or °preaching, filmmaking among Mennonites has not been widespread, nor particularly distinguished or distinctive.

Although films have been produced since the initial decade of the 20th c., Mennonites did not make their first films until the 1960s. Since then, the production has been limited, with relatively few producers, directors, writers, and cinematographers.

As of this writing, there is no known Mennonite-made film that has turned a profit for its producers, although some films have earned awards, some have been shown on national networks, and at least one has been syndicated by *Encyclopedia Britannica*. Films consequently have been heavily subsidized by individuals and reluctant institutions.

The most widely known genre in cinema literature is the feature film, but Mennonites have not made many features. (An example of a Mennonite-made feature is Merle Good's *Happy as the Grass Was Green*, by Good Productions, 1974; renamed *Hazel's People*.) The reasons may be tradition-oriented. Mennonites have maintained a long-standing remove from the "worldly" °motion picture industry, and a critical opposition to its products. In addition, Mennonites have been historically suspicious of public entertainment (°amusements), so that they are not highly literate in film history. Dramatic narratives have been no easier to accept. The vivid depiction of life—be it comic or tragic—has been somewhat problematic for Mennonites, both on stage and screen. But if Mennonites have not been comfortable with realistic cinema, abstract representations of life have not been considered useful either. Mennonites have been a practical, literal, down-to-earth people. (An example of a Mennonite-made dramatic narrative is *The Weight*, Sisters and Brothers Productions, 1983.) Film production has thus been limited largely to documentaries, drama-documentaries, instructional (and didactic) films, and promotional pieces.

Mennonites themselves were the initial focus of documentaries. Immediately available was the visually interesting subculture of Mennonites and Amish. (An example of a documentary film is John Ruth's *The Amish: A People of Preservation*, 1976.) While customs offered significant signs for the explication of faith, early critics of the documentaries mentioned that these films were more sociological than evangelistic.

Subsequent documentaries featured specific Mennonite communities, histories of immigrations, overseas mission and relief work, and Mennonite meetings and conferences. These projects allowed sociological formats "to tell the story" of the Mennonite experience. (An example of the institutionally produced documentary is Mennonite Central Committee's *Bangladesh Plowmen*, 1974, with the major work done by Burton Buller.) The drama-documentary has been used to recount historical events involving Mennonites (e.g, *And When They Shall Ask*, Dueck Productions, 1984.) Mennonites have not been reluctant to produce films to promote their own institutions and their programs. (For example, Goshen College's first of several promotional films was made in the early 1960s.)

The number of Mennonites who have earned a living by making films in production houses, church institutions, or private operations, has remained very low.

The emergence of less expensive video tape equipment is likely to give a more important role to filmmaking and filmmakers. Mennonites, however, will still have to think about what is a good film, and what a film is good for, before its filmmakers will enjoy the sense of a denominational commitment to their work. JDH

See also Interpretation and Information Centers; Journalism; Literature; Photography.

Fischer, Andreas (ca. 1480-1540). Evidence suggests that Andreas Fischer was born ca. 1480 in Bohemia and was educated at the University of Vienna. He was likely baptized by Hans °Hut or Oswald Glaidt, and appears with Glaidt in Silesia in 1528 as a leader and spokesperson for the °Sabbatarian Anabaptists there.

Between 1529 and 1532, Fischer worked as a missionary in Slovakia and had some success among the miners there. He narrowly escaped execution; his wife was drowned. He moved to the Nikolsburg area about 1532 and assumed the position of leadership among the °°*Schwertler* faction that had been left vacant by the exit to Prussia of Hans °°Spittelmayr. The Hutterite Chronicle reports that this group soon became known as "Sabbatarians."

After 1535, Fischer fled to the border region between Saxony and Bohemia to escape persecution. He returned to Moravia about 1537 and to Slovakia in 1540 where he was arrested and executed. DL

Daniel Liechty, *Andreas Fischer and the Sabbatarian Anabaptists: An Early Reformation Episode in East Central Europe* (Scottdale, 1988); cf. *MQR*, 58 (1984) 125-32.

Flag. Display of the national flag, a symbol that evokes powerful feelings of allegiance, is a controversial practice among some Mennonites. Congregational dissension over this emblem stems from debate regarding the separation of church and state, a principle embraced by 16th-c. Anabaptists.

In the United States, the refusal of a Mennonite pupil to salute the flag in 1918 in West Liberty, Ohio, led to civil prosecution. Similar incidents followed. In 1943 the U.S Supreme Court upheld the rights of persons conscientiously opposed to saluting the flag.

Flags began appearing in American church sanctuaries during the Spanish-American War and during the two World Wars. Wartime stresses led some °historic peace churches to display prominently their respect for country and gratitude for religious liberty. Certain congregations within the General Conference Mennonite Church, Mennonite Brethren Church, and Evangelical Mennonite Brethren Church displayed flags, although some congregations removed them during the postwar years.

American congregations of the Mennonite Church (MC) and those of smaller Mennonite groups which emphasize °nonconformity have never displayed flags. Moreover, Mennonites in most other countries do not exhibit their national flags. In recent years, international guests at Mennonite gatherings in the United States where flags are present have critiqued the practice. RWG

Bibl. on War and Peace (1987), 417-18; David R. Manwaring, *Render unto Caesar* (U. of Chicago Press, 1962); Rachel Waltner Goossen and Robert S. Kreider, *When Good People Quarrel: Studies of Conflict Resolution* (Scottdale, 1989), esp. ch. titled "That Our Flag Was Still There: The Flag in the Church" and "A Schoolboy Refuses to Salute the Flag"; R. L. Hartzler, "Time to Move Them Out," *Chr. Evangel*, 34 (May 1946), 99-100; J. N. Smucker, "Editorial," *Mennonite*, 68 (Dec. 1, 1953), 739.

See also Civil Religion; Delaware; Nationalism; Oath; Patriotism; Public Schools.

Florida (ME II:341). Lasting Mennonite presence in Florida began in the winter of 1926-27 when several

FLORIDA

LEGEND
MENNONITES IN FLORIDA
- − − State boundary
- ● Cities and towns
- ★ State capitol
- ▲ Church camps
- ~ Rivers
- <u>Old Order Amish settlements</u>
- **Church Membership**
  Includes BA, BIC, CGCM, EP, and MC
  congregations. Totals based on congregations'
  place of address and may not reflect their
  exact location of the actual distribution of
  members. O.O.Amish membership est. from
  number of church districts acc. to D. Luthy,
  Amish Settlements Across America (1985).

- ○ 0-250
- ○ 250-500
- ○ 500-1000
- ○ 1000-1500

Miles 0 10 20 30 40 50   100

Amish and Mennonite families arrived in Sarasota Co. from Ohio. Amish and Mennonites worshiped in both German and English in what they called a union service. Mennonite missionaries from Lancaster, Co., Pa., arrived in Tampa in 1927 and in February began holding meetings in a tent until a meeting place was built in 1928.

In 1987 there were 21 congregations in Florida affiliated with the Southeast Mennonite Conference (MC). Three other congregations are affiliated with the Lancaster Conference (MC), six with the Conservative Mennonite Conference, eight with the Brethren in Christ, one with the Beachy Amish Mennonite Fellowship, one with the New Order Amish, and one with the Eastern Pennsylvania Mennonite Church. There were two unaffiliated Mennonite congregations. Among these congregations four are Hispanic, three are Afro-American, and one is Haitian. Congregation size varies from only a few members to more than 600. The strongest center is in Sarasota Co.

The Mennonites of Sarasota have provided the core strength for the Sarasota Christian School (kindergarten through high school); a retirement village and nursing °home operated by Sunnyside Properties; a shelter for children (Agape Homes); a two-month °Bible institute (Southeast Bible Institute); a °camp and retreat center (Lakewood Retreat) operated by the Southern Mennonite Camp Association; a °mutual aid center (Southeast Mennonite Mutual Aid Board); a °SELFHELP Crafts store (World's Attic); a religious radio station, WKZM, operated by the Christian Fellowship Mission; and a church extension program in Dade Co. sponsored by the Association of Mennonite Ministries.

The Mennonite Central Committee sponsors °voluntary service units in Miami and Belle Glade, and the Eastern Mennonite Board of Missions (MC) sponsors a voluntary service unit at Homestead.   MWL

MC Yearbook (1988-89), 20-21; Luthy, *Amish Settlements* (1985), 7; Daniel Hertzler, *From Germantown to Steinbach* (Scottdale, 1981), 54-64.

Folk Arts (ME I:728). By "folk art" folklorists mean all of the aesthetically pleasing crafts that are produced within and for a particular folk community, meet community expectations and tastes, and feature techniques and designs that have been passed down through the years from artist to artist through customary example and imitation in face-to-face situations. By far the most important contributions of Mennonite-related groups to world folk arts are Habaner °°ceramics, Amish quilts, and Mennonite *Fraktur* and decorated furniture. °Ceramics, °*Fraktur*, °furniture, and °quilts are discussed in separate articles.

Excellent surveys of contemporary Mennonite household folk arts have been carried out in Canada by Bird, Brednich, Kobayashi, and Patterson, thanks to that country's recent emphasis on ethnic pluralism. In the absence of other such comprehensive surveys and fuller analyses, and with major genres discussed elsewhere, this article will mention some Mennonite achievements in miscellaneous folk art and conclude with some speculative comments on the role of the artist in conservative Mennonite folk culture and on the meanings that various scholars have found in some kinds of Mennonite folk arts.

All considerations of Mennonite achievements in folk art must be in the context of the ingrained Anabaptist, especially Swiss Anabaptist, suspicion of pictorial images. Those Swiss iconoclasts who eliminated all visual °symbols from the °worship service and the sacraments (°ordinances), and, in the Amish schism at least, forbade the depiction of the human form in strict obedience to the Second Commandment, nevertheless often produced striking examples of folk art. The form, design and function of this art need to be considered in the context of an inherent suspicion of the presumed luxury, pride, and idolatry that were associated with "art" by these people.

Paper Cutting. The art of cutting intricate designs with scissors in folded paper (*Scherenschnitt*) has been practiced by some known Mennonites, including Hans Hofer of Rufenacht, Switzerland (active 1950) and, of special note, Elizabeth Johns Stahley (1845-1930), Amish, of Lagrange Co., Ind. Mrs. Stahley produced hundreds of cuttings late in her life, primarily of flowers, leaves, and birds from her everyday experience. Most are symmetrical cuttings, done with single-folded paper. Patterson sees in her work everyday models executed in sufficient stylization to suggest spiritual symbols.

Carving and Sculpture. Three-dimensional representational art is particularly rare in Mennonite folk art, perhaps because of the fear of replicating the "idolatry" associated with the Catholics' use of statuary. One exception to this assumption are the doll-like nativity figures made among the Dutch-German Mennonites of Ontario, especially by Hella Braun (b. 1925), three of whose dolls appeared on Canadian postage stamps in 1982.

Many Mennonites, especially men, have become noted for their wood carvings, sometimes painted, of animals and other everyday subjects. Chief among recent ones is David B. Horst (1873-1965) of St. Jacobs, Ont., whose work Bird and Kobayashi regard as attaining "the highest level of Pennsylvania-German woodcarving found in Ontario." He is noted for the animals that he carved and watercolored (ca. 1935-45) after he was paralyzed by a stroke.

Other Ontario wood-carvers include Simeon Eby Martin (b. 1872), Daniel Kuepfer (active 1950), and Herman P. Lepp (active 1951). As of 1951 Isaac H. Funk was actively carving animals in Gretna, Man. Gerhard Esau (b. 1876) of Beatrice, Nebr., began carving animals when he was a 12-year-old boy in Russia. In the 1980s Christ L. Stoltzfus, Amish, of Narvon, Pa., was earning his living by selling painted farm animals cut out by bandsaw.

Some Mennonite and Amish families in the United States own intricate whittlings produced by Mennonite Daniel Rose (1871-1921) of Johnstown, Pa. Registered in Washington, D.C., in 1898 as "Champion Whittler of the United States," he is best remembered by the many intricate carvings—an entire village, Noah's ark, all the world's musical instruments—that he placed inside glass bottles.

Aaron Zook (b. 1921) of Kinzers, Lancaster Co., Pa., is a Beachy Amish Mennonite who makes three-dimensional carved paintings of Mennonite and Amish folklife, such as barn-raisings, auctions, quiltings, and feetwashing ceremonies. His twin brother, Abner, a Mennonite from Womelsdorf, Pa., makes very large genre paintings.

Gravestones. Nancy-Lou Patterson has studied the designs on several hundred gravestones in nine Waterloo, Ont., area cemeteries, especially the 110 slabs in the Eby Cemetery, the first one established by Mennonites there. Markers from 1804 to 1854 reflect Pennsylvania-Swiss-German designs, with vertical rectangular shape, architectural design tops, and (from 1833-1845) heart, tulip, willow, quatrefoil, eye, and six-point star decorations. Also working in Ontario, Bird and Kobayashi found a sun-like motif in the Vineland Mennonite Burial Ground and the Wideman Church cemetery, and a variety of designs—tulip, tree of life, heart, eye—in the East End Cemetery in Kitchener. Patterson speculates that the shape of the stone symbolically suggests the door (to heaven) and the arch (or heaven itself), and that the designs also carry the conventional symbolisms associated with heart, tulip, star, and eye in German folk art.

Painting. The most important Mennonite achievement in folk painting lies in *Fraktur* and furniture decoration, both of which often use interchangeable geometric and stylized designs from nature.

In addition, both European and American Mennonites and Amish have made wall-hung mottos, using the technique of reverse painting on glass backed with tinfoil, sometimes called "tinsel painting." Dutch-German Mennonites apparently brought the craft with them from the Ukraine to western Canada, where the art was produced by them well into the mid-20th c. Some (Old) Mennonites (MC), many Old Order Amish, and apparently also a few Hutterites still make such mottos. Since the Amish and (Old) Mennonites came from areas in Switzerland and Alsace that have nourished strong glass-painting traditions since the early Renaissance and Reformation, some Anabaptists in those areas must have practiced the art, too. The most famous Anabaptist glass painter, however, was from the Low

Countries—°David Joris learned the art in Antwerp and earned his living by it in England (briefly) and on the continent. Several other lesser known Dutch Anabaptists were involved in the trade (Waite, 65-68)

In the late 1980s the folk art of glass painting seems to derive from the early 1930s, influenced by the Art Deco revival of reverse painting on glass, by mass-produced wall decorations in reverse painting, and especially by elementary school art class instruction in that medium. In any event, Mennonites and Amish throughout the United States (although apparently not in Ontario) produced many home-made "mottos" featuring Scripture verses, moral sayings, and family records (birth, marriage, death, birthday, anniversary, etc.) from about 1930 to 1950, with interest tapering off then until the present, when the folk art barely survives.

Following the tradition of European Protestantism since the Reformation, the paintings almost always feature an inspiring or instructive text decorated by birds, flowers, or scenes from nature. The paintings are almost never wholly pictorial, nor do they often depict the human form—particularly those by the Old Order Amish. Nevertheless, even the Amish paintings verge heavily toward the pictorial and decorative, with the text sometimes minimized.

Designs come from needlework patterns, coloring books, other mottos—any easily available household source. Called "mottos" even if they contain no scriptural or moral reference, these paintings are sold informally to friends, neighbors, and relatives, or given as personal or commemorative gifts, much as was done with *Fraktur* by other Mennonite groups in earlier years. Sometimes they are also found for sale in country stores serving the Amish community. Women producing reverse glass mottoes in the 1980s in Elkhart and Lagrange Cos., Ind., include Jewel Miller (Mrs. Kenneth) Bontrager, Mary Yoder (Mrs. Merlin) Lehman, Martha Otto, and Katie (Mrs. Floyd) Miller (all Old Order Amish). The art is reported as still alive in Amish communities in Mississippi and Pennsylvania, as well.

The technique of painting mottoes on top of glass, with opaque paint applied to the backside, also has been popular among Mennonite and Amish groups since about 1930 and, in fact, has superseded tinsel painting in acceptance in the 1980s. Compared to the reverse glass mottos, these usually have minimal decoration and longer texts. The Willis Steiner family (Mennonite) of Dalton, Ohio, was a large supplier of mottos and materials for making them, until the death of Mrs. Steiner in 1985. Bertha Schrock (Amish) of Tempico, Ill., is now the main source of supplies. Since 1943 Virgie (Mrs. James) Lauver, Brethren in Christ, has been selling such mottoes wholesale to bookstores and other retailers through Friendly Sales of Quakertown, Pa.

Closely related to this motto tradition is the making of decorated family records especially by the Old Order Amish, sometimes (as noted above) using the tinsel technique. Ivan Hochstetler of Topeka, Ind., continues the art of Spencerian penmanship in making family records on paper for his Amish community. Members of the Abraham Z. Peachey family of Belleville, Pa., sell family records painted on top

of glass. John F. Glick of Gap, Pa., makes family records to be sold by mail order. His work comes closest to resembling older *Fraktur* techniques, since he decorates his pen-written records with painted flowers and flourishes.

As with almost all other folk groups, easel painting (oils or acrylics on canvas or board) is not a true folk art among Mennonite and Amish groups. That is, there is no easel painting tradition that has been used continuously over time by a community whose artists master the technique by the customary imitation of fellow artists.

There are, however, some "untaught" Mennonite and Amish "folk" artists whose works are widely known, even though they are not accepted, used, or commissioned by members of their own communities.

The most prominent one working today is probably Emma Schrock (b. 1924), of near Wakarusa, Ind., an Old Order Mennonite who paints genre scenes in acrylic. Although her church frowns upon representations of the human form, she often includes human beings in her paintings. Works by Emma Schrock are to be found in the Mathers Museum in Bloomington, Ind., and elsewhere.

Self-taught Amish painters likewise face the double dilemma of creating works that they themselves may not hang on their own walls and of painting human figures that are forbidden by the strict rulings of their congregations (church districts). Benuel King (b. 1925) of Cambridge, Pa., a farmer and horse dealer, does both, although most of his acrylics are of farmscapes and other local scenery. Abraham Z. Peachey paints Mennonite and Amish farmscapes of the Kishacoquillas Valley near Belleville, Pa., although he never paints the human figure.

Self-taught Mennonite painters in Waterloo Co., Ont., include Orvie Shantz of Lexington (active ca. 1930) and Benneval G. Martin (1876-1935) of St. Jacobs, makers of farmscapes; and Absalom Martin (1902-1977) of St. Jacobs, railroad scenes.

Although such artists do not fit the mold of the folk artist as well as do the tinsel painters, they are more "folk" than is the familiar Grandma Moses, with whom they are sometimes compared. Grandma Moses was a "memory painter"; that is, her scenes were naive, nostalgic renderings of a long-past era of American culture. All of the Mennonites and Amish named above, however, paint scenes from the life that surrounds them. That ties them and their work more intimately with the folk community and its meaning than is true of many other self-taught, sometimes called "folk," painters. With Emma Schrock they can say, "We live what I paint and I paint what I see."

One Mennonite memory painter is Leah Johnson, a Holdeman Mennonite (Church of God in Christ, Mennonite) from Montezuma, Ks., who since 1967 has painted sod houses set in various Kansas regional landscapes. She uses a self-developed, three-dimensional sand-painting technique that was revealed to her following the death of her husband when she was suddenly faced with earning her own living. She has also illustrated books with drawings of her favorite subjects, notably *True Sod*, written by Barbara Oringdeff.

Another memory painter from earlier Mennonite culture is Emil "Maler" Kym (1862-1918), of Buhler, Ks., who affiliated with the Mennonites following his immigration to Goessel, Ks., from Hoholen, Switzerland, in 1893. Between 1896 and 1915 he painted genre scenes of his Swiss homeland on the walls of his Mennonite neighbors' homes. His murals may be the latest and the farthest west of this genre of American folk art. Kym also did wood-graining and marbleizing and furniture-decorating. Other Mennonite wall decorators in the early Kansas settlements are Jacob Harms (active 1895-1920), a Holdeman Mennonite from near Moundridge; P. R. Doerksen (active 1913) from Inman; and John Wall from the Buhler-Inman area.

Folk Arts Revival. Mennonites have been active in the revival of traditional arts. In Switzerland, Hans Ramseier (b. 1909) of Eggiwil near Langnau gives woodworking lessons throughout Switzerland, having mastered the craft since attending a woodworking school in Brienz in 1930. He makes carved furniture, accessories, and ecclesiastical and commemorative items, and has passed the skill on to his daughter, Justina Zuercher, and his son-in-law, Fritz Rothlisberger.

In the United States, Carolyn Schultz of North Newton, Ks., is nationally known for her revival of wheat weaving, which she learned in England. In 1982 she conducted a workshop at the American Folklife Center in Washington, D.C. She has also published a book, *Wheat Weaving Made Easy.* Perhaps the greatest impact of Mennonites on the American revival movement, however, are the designs and colors of antique Amish quilts, described in several pattern books published for the mass market.

Artists. The status of the folk artist within Mennonite communities apparently differs from that of the practitioner of the "fine arts." Whereas the latter often feels estranged, the folk artist seems to enjoy respect and integration into the life of the folk group. That is particularly true of the folk artist who produces articles for the folk group, as opposed to the folk artist whose items are sold to outsiders. Yet there is often a more subtle social separation of the folk artist from the folk group. Except perhaps for furniture-makers who produce essential goods, other folk artists seem to play more marginal social roles.

For instance, a number of folk artists from the most conservative groups are physically disabled— Emma Schrock (Old Order Mennonite painter), Daniel Rose (Old Mennonite carver), Christ L. Stoltzfus (Old Order Amish carver). Leah Johnson (Holdeman Mennonite painter) and Sarah M. Weaver of Millersburg, Ohio (Amish poet and illustrator), are widows. Amish tinsel painters are often teenage girls or unmarried middle-aged women. The folk artist who produces things for pay, therefore, may be fully accepted by the community, but plays a secondary role in its economy, receiving special permission because of special employment needs. The matter deserves further study, particularly in comparison with the status of artists in other conservative religious folk groups.

Interpretation. Nancy-Lou Patterson has attempted the most interesting cultural and religious analyses of Mennonite folk art. In comparing Swiss-German and Dutch-German folk art in Waterloo Co., Ont., she finds that the former retains more of the stylization of earlier Germanic folk traditions and that the latter shows more acculturation to elite culture by being much more naturalistic. She accounts for this by claiming that the Swiss-Germans have always been more suspicious of academic art, have remained more rural and have long lived beside other Germanic folk groups. The Dutch-Germans, however, have always been more involved in the fine arts, were urban, educated, and industrialized even in Russia, and in Canada have tended to live beside people rather removed from peasant folk culture.

In examining the meaning of the content of Mennonite art, she joins such folk art historians as John Jacob Stoudt in finding religious symbolism in traditional German stylized designs as well as in landscapes and garden designs in contemporary Mennonite folk art. She is able to connect recently made rugs, paintings, and actual farm layouts with spiritualistic interpretations of gardens and dwellings, stemming, she claims, from books, e.g., Johann °°Arndt's *Das Paradiesgärtlein voller Christlicher Tugenden,* which have been part of Mennonite piety since the 17th c.

Although her conclusions are speculative and controversial, they nevertheless are correct in taking Mennonite folk arts seriously and probing them for cultural and spiritual meanings. Her work points the way to the more extensive study that remains to be done of historic and contemporary Mennonite folk arts.   EB

Ervin Beck, "Mennonite and Amish Painting on Glass," *MQR,* 63, no. 2 (April 1989); idem, "Glass Painting by Plain People," *Folklife Annual* (Washington, D.C.: American Folklife Center, 1988); Michael Bird and Terry Kobayashi, *A Splendid Harvest: Germanic Folk and Decorative Arts in Canada* (Toronto: Van Nostrand, 1981); Rolf Brednich, *Mennonite Folklife and Folklore: A Preliminary Report* (Ottawa: National Museums of Canada, 1977); Simon J. Bronner, "We Live What I Paint and I Paint What I See": A Mennonite Artist in Northern Indiana, *Indiana Folklore,* 12, no. 1 (1979), 5-17; "Daniel Rose—Champion Whittler," *Christian Monitor,* 18, no. 6 (June 1926), 163-64; Steve Friesen, "Emil 'Maler' Kym, Great Plains Folk Artist," *The Clarion* (Fall 1978), 34-39; Jan Gleysteen, "A Sampler of Swiss German-Pennsylvania Dutch Design," *FQ,* 8 (May-July 1981), 14-15; idem, "Emmental Folk Art Today: A Visit with Hans Ramseier," *FQ,* 8 (Feb.-April 1981), 38; idem, "The European Roots of Pennsylvania Dutch Art," *FQ,* 7 (Nov.-Jan. 1980-81), 33; Daniel and Kathryn McCauley, *Decorative Arts of the Amish of Lancaster County* (Intercourse, Pa.: Good Books, 1988); Barbara Oringdeff, *True Sod* illustrated by Leah Johnson, (N. Newton: MP, 1976); Nancy-Lou Patterson, "Death and Ethnicity: Swiss-German Mennonite Gravestones of the 'Pennsylvania Style' (1804-54) in the Waterloo Region, Ontario," *Menn. Life,* 37, no. 3 (Sept. 1982), 4-7; idem, "The Flowers in the Meadow: The Paper Cuttings of Elizabeth Johns Stahley," *Menn. Life,* 34, no. 1 (Mar. 1979), 16-20; idem, "'See the Vernal Landscape Glowing': The Symbolic Landscape of the Swiss-German Mennonite Settlers in Waterloo County," *Menn. Life,* 38, no. 4 (Dec. 1983), 8-16; Rachel T. Pellman, *Amish Quilt Patterns* (Intercourse, Pa.: Good Books, 1984); Carolyn Schultz and Adelia Stuckey, *Wheat Weaving Made Easy* (N. Newton: MP, 1977); John Joseph Stoudt, *Pennsylvania German Folk Art: An Interpretation* (Allentown, Pa.: Schlecter's, 1966); Gary K. Waite, "Spiritualizing the Crusade: David Joris in the Context of the Early Reform and Anabaptist Movements in the Netherlands, 1524-1543" (PhD diss., U. of Waterloo, 1986), 65-68, cf. *Sixteenth Century J.* 18 (1987).

Flowers in the Meadow: Elizabeth Johns Stahley's *Scherenschnitt*

She holds a many-leafed plant in her hands: not a conventional "rose" or "tulip" but a complexly articulated member of the *Compositae* family with every leaf elaborately contoured into dozens of thrusting points. Her hands are articulated too: deeply veined, well muscled, the tendons standing out as her fingers search and control the form. She looks intently at the plant, gazing into the intricacies of its leafy pattern while a gentle smile plays on her lips. These are the hands, and this is the contemplation, of an artist.

Elizabeth Johns Stahley turned her understanding of the structure of plants and flowers into a series of elegant, compelling paper cuttings which have been preserved by members of her family and their descendants, and which have recently inspired her great-niece, Phyllis Kramer, to turn her own hand to the art of paper cuttings. Paper-cut forms tend to be anonymous, floating out from between the pages of Bibles and old books, or namelessly framed and fading on walls or in attics, where nobody can identify them. The works of Elizabeth Johns Stahley afford a rare insight into the work of a single, identifiable practitioner of the art.

Born December 3, 1845, near Johnstown, Pa., she moved with her parents to Lagrange County, Indiana, in the spring of 1853. On December 20, 1868, she married John C. Stahley. She was the mother of nine children (five sons, four daughters), six of whom grew to adulthood.

The kind of life Elizabeth Stahley led is summarized by her nephew, Ira Miller, as follows:

"She was a farm homemaker and lived on the same farm all her life with the exception of her last days. Her schooling probably didn't go much beyond the sixth grade. (This is just a guess.) To my knowledge the cutouts she made for pastime in her later years. She made well over a hundred, no two alike. She had one son who cut out animals free hand."

These forms are not large: the biggest are not more than 10x25 cm. (4x10 inches), and the smallest are considerably smaller than that. Most of them were cut with the paper—always white—folded in half vertically. Her flowers include both round and pointed petals of composite form, and in like manner, her leaves are either slender and pointed or short and rounded. She favoured a sinuous line for her stems, and provided a groundline or vessel for the base in most cases. Tucked among her leafed and floral forms one sometimes spies out miniature birds—paired, of course, as a result of her technique. They are much out of scale for a floral bouquet, and their size and presence show us that these are really examples of the Paradise tree *Lebens-*

baum, i.e., Trees of Life out of the same primeval root from which the Bible—and her religion—sprang.

Some of the flower forms she used in her paper cuttings resemble a common Indiana wildflower, the Golden Aster (*Heterotheca camporum,*) a flower with numerous rays, on the end of long branches, all arising from a single base. Others resemble the genus *Centaurea* (Bachelor Buttons) which have a composite head including five or more individual florets (petals with a sharply serrated end) expanding from the rounded involucre. The leaves, both rounded and pointed, are known as "simple leaves." All of these elements are found in the physical reality of the artist though she has mixed and re-combined them with a fine disregard of nature. One single floral head shows especially sharp observation: the cutting includes both the ray florets (tiny central points) and surrounding disk florets (larger rounded petals) growing from the involucre. The *Compositae* family includes ragweed, wormwood, sunflower, and dandelion, as well as bachelor button, chicory, and golden aster; almost a survey of the "everyday flowers" in Elizabeth Stahley's environment. On the other hand these were also for her the very "grass of the field" of which Jesus spoke in the Sermon on the Mount (Mt 6:28-30).

The differing ways of using forms from the natural world—as subjects for observation and as images for spiritual contemplation—reflect a double trend in European history, which for modern culture has become a deep split into science on the one hand and religion on the other.

In the exquisite paper cuttings of Elizabeth Johns Stahley made early in the 20th c. both elements are present. Her flowers are based upon accurate observations of the "everyday flowers" of the natural world, just as Donald Shelley says. And she has used the images of "the flowers in the meadow" in the manner described by Stoudt, as "bridges to the spiritual world," changing them by the addition of tiny birds, from common field flowers into stately *Lebensbaums*. Both realities—the Indiana countryside, and the pastures of Paradise—were immediately present to her, and through her art she has left us a glimpse of her deeply spiritual vision.   NLP

Adapted from *Menn. Life*, 34 (Mar. 1979), 16-20. Photographs by John Cox. Used by permission. See also Donald A. Shelley, *The Fraktur Writings of Illuminated Manuscripts of the Pennsylvania Germans* (Allentown, Pa.: Pennsylvania German Folklore Society, 1961); John Joseph Stoudt, *Early Pennsylvania Arts and Crafts* (New York: A. S. Barnes, 1964).

Folk Medicine, Amish and Swiss-Pennsylvania German.

Mennonite and Amish emigrants from Europe in the 18th and 19th c. brought to America a storehouse of remedies for ailments. Before the days of modern medicine, folk remedies flourished, often bringing relief and even cures to the sick and ailing. The use of teas, ointments, tonics, salves, liniments, and poultices was common in the average household. Oral tradition as well as neatly penned recipes handed down from generation to generation have kept folk medicine alive in many Amish and Mennonite communities. Dozens of remedies are readily available for such ailments as rheumatism and arthritis as are brews and bitters for constipation and itch. Specially prepared health manuals, articles in farm almanacs, and notices on herbal medicines in *The Sugarcreek Budget* (a weekly newspaper for Amish and Mennonite readers) augment the information available.

While remedies are available for most common ailments, the literature also speaks to specialized problems such as sterility and impotence and to complications related to the change of life. A popular health manual among the Amish gives this remedy for prostate problems: After age 40, men often suffer from congestion of the prostate gland. To relieve this cut corn silk from the tip of the sheath surrounding the corn cob, of a half dozen ears of corn, cook it into a tea and drink three times daily for a week. Use fresh corn silk daily. If this does not help, try pumpkin seeds. These stimulate male hormone production and also act as a vermifuge or worm killer. Many health food stores carry pumpkin seed oil, which may be taken in small amounts, however, chewing fresh seeds is better.

In recent years, Amish and Mennonites have engaged in experimental cures for cancer. Laetril and the Hoxsey Cancer Clinic have had their effects on folk medicine. In search for better health, Amish have been known to travel great distances to visit "hot springs" and special quasi-chiropractic centers. Some Amish have spent a week sitting in old abandoned uranium mines to escape arthritic pains. Many communities maintain country stores stocked with natural health foods and vitamins along with juicers and vibrators, all as part of an effort to keep the body healthy. Herbal medicine has flourished, making use not only of the American and European practices, but also some exotic Oriental and South American jungle herbs.

Folk medicine, now as in ages past, brings a unique assortment of potions, generally prepared in the home, to afford healing to the mind and body of the believer.   SLY

William R. McGrath, *Amish Folk Remedies for Plain and Fancy Ailments* (1981); John A. Hostetler, *Amish* (1980), 313-32.

See also Brauche; Faith Healing; Medicine (for Dutch-Russian Mennonite folk medicine).

Folk Music. Mennonites use folk music in various ways. They borrow folk tunes for hymns, write religious music in the folk idiom, and use folk music as religious music, in addition to °singing and playing secular folk music.

In the 16th c., the poetic and musical styles of the *Volkslied* (folksong) were used for many martyr °ballads in the °°*Ausbund*. In contrast to the art music of the established church, this music of the common people was accessible to all and thus symbolic of the Anabaptist emphasis on the °priesthood of all believers.

Patterns of borrowing folk materials in more recent Mennonite hymnals reflect differing perceptions of Mennonite ethnic identity. Folk tunes were used for hymns and gospel songs in the *Gesangbuch der Mennoniten Brüdergemeinde* (1955). This contrasts with their use for children's songs in the *Gesangbuch der Mennoniten* (1965), where the chorale is the standard fare. Seven folk hymns from the *Harmonia Sacra*, representing the Swiss American Mennonite heritage, are found in the *Mennonite Hymnal* (1969, GCM, MC). This differs from the Anglo-Saxon folk tunes, taken from the general cultural milieu, found in the Mennonite Brethren *Worship Hymnal* (1971).

The best researched aspect of the traditional American Mennonite folk music is that of the folk hymns found in the °°*Harmonia Sacra*, the oldest shape-note book still in use. The book was first issued by Joseph °°Funk in Singer's Glen, Va., in 1832 as *Genuine Church Music*, and later became known as *The New Harmonia Sacra: a Compilation of Genuine Church Music*. Published in its 22nd edition in Dayton, Ohio in 1959, the book is central to the annual *Harmonia Sacra* hymn-sings still held in Virginia.

Contemporary folk hymns were introduced to Canadian Mennonites by groups such as the "Faith and Life Singers" on radio station CFAM in Altona, Man. The continuing influence of the 1960's North American folk music movement is evident in the publication of hymnbook supplements in the contemporary idiom. *Sing and Rejoice!* (1979) contains several international folkhymns, while *Sing Alleluia* (1985) includes several sacred folk songs.

The guitar and other folk instruments have become more acceptable in the church, especially in informal contexts. Mennonites such as Chuck Neufeld and Connie Isaac sing of their history and faith in folk and other contemporary idioms. Gordon Friesen, longtime editor of *Broadside*, a magazine of protest music, has also promoted the use of folk music to challenge traditional values and express compassion for the oppressed.

In the past few decades a new Mennonite folk genre, the folk opera, has emerged. *The Bridge* (1975) by Esther Wiebe and lyricist Di Brandt addresses such issues as intermarriage with non-Mennonites and contains traditional Russian Mennonite lullabies and "Schluesselbund Lieder" (singing circle games). Harold Moyer and James Juhnke's *The Blowing and the Bending*, also written in a folk idiom, voices reactions to participation in °°World War I.

Written and verbal references to singing secular folk songs often appear as criticisms of the one who sings *Putzenlieder*. Among Mennonites who have created sanctions against singing secular music, the contemporary religious music of the day has served that function. Where the chorale was used in church, the gospel song served as entertainment for the young people. °°Singings and barn dances among the Amish and folk and square dancing among Old Colony Mennonites, however, have provided a musical and social outlet for young people.

While Mennonites have traditionally borrowed secular folk music, even this process reflects Mennonite beliefs. The absence of *Marienlieder* (songs to the virgin Mary) and *Heldenlieder* (war hero songs) among 18th-c. Prussian Mennonites, but the increasing presence of *Soldatenlieder* (soldier songs) during the time of the early 20th-c. °Selbstschutz (see Heinrich Friesen collection), demonstrate changing

Mennonite values. Similarly, the singing of High German nature and homeland (*Heimatlieder*) songs by Mennonites in 19th- and early 20th-c. Russia, showed their essentially German orientation.

As in Russia, Canadian Mennonites have been introduced to folksinging in the home, in the school, and through such community °choirs as the internationally acclaimed Mennonite Children's Choir of Winnipeg.

In the wake of renewed Canadian ethnic consciousness, several Low German singing groups have been formed in southern Manitoba. "De Heischraitje en de Willa Honig" ("Locusts and Wild Honey," 1975) critique the foibles of Mennonite village life through songs accompanied by a jug band. "De Jereeschte Tweeback" ("Roasted Buns," 1981) have popularized the traditional Low German songs of Manitoba's Russian Mennonites found in Doreen Klassen's *Singing Mennonite* collection.

In the past few decades, Swiss and German Russian Mennonite traditions have been enriched by the introduction of Spanish, French, Afro-American, Chinese, and American and Canadian Indian musical idioms.   DoKla

Doreen Klassen, *Singing Mennonite: Low German Songs among the Mennonites* (Winnipeg: U. of Manitoba Press, 1988); Heinrich Friesen, untitled collection of folksongs, located in Conference of Mennonites of Canada archives, Mennonite Heritage Centre, Winnipeg, microfilm 69, n.d.); J. William Frey, "Amish Hymns as Folk Music," in *Pennsylvania Songs and Legends*, ed. George Korson (Philadelphia: U. of Pennsylvania Press, 1949); Richard H. Shaner, "The Amish Barn Dance," *Pennsylvania Folklife*, 13 (Winter 1962-63), 24-26; Allan Teichroew, "Gordon Friesen, Writer, Radical and Ex-Mennonite," in *Menn. Life*, 38 (June 1983), 4-17; Helen Martens, "The Music of some Religious Minorities in Canada," *Ethnomusicology*, 16, no. 3 (1972), 360-71; idem, "Hutterite Songs: The Origins and Aural Transmission of their Melodies from the Sixteenth Century (PhD diss., Columbia U., 1968); Kenneth Peacock, *Twenty Ethnic Songs from Western Canada* (Ottawa: National Museum of Canada, 1966); Harry Eskew, *Shape-note Hymnody in the Shenandoah Valley of Virginia, 1816-1860* (diss. Tulane U., 1966.

See also Folklore; Hymnology.

Folk Painting. See Folk Arts.

Folklore. Folklife in technologically-advanced societies is one of three constantly interacting spheres of culture—elite, popular, and folk—each of which is transmitted through a different medium.

Elite culture, for instance, is academic culture, transmitted through formal learning situations such as lecture halls, textbooks, and laboratories. Popular culture is mass culture, transmitted through °mass media such as newspapers, television, radio, and films. Both are consciously sponsored by "official" agencies—elite culture by the academy, popular culture by commercial interests. Folk culture, on the other hand, is transmitted by oral tradition (word of mouth) or customary imitation in face-to-face encounters. It is less official and less innovative than the other two spheres. Thus understood, folklore is not the quaint and curious ways of isolated, backward people. Everyone has folklore. In fact, it is made up of the most essential—because everyday and unselfconscious—elements of everyone's life.

Since folklore abounds especially in close-knit groups, particularly those separated somewhat from mainstream culture, the folklife of Mennonites, Amish, and Hutterites should be fuller, richer, more revealing than that of less culturally distinct groups. However, since the study of these groups' folklife has lagged behind the study of their history, sociology, and religion, this remains an attractive assumption that still needs to be proven. For instance, only one comprehensive survey of the folklore of a Mennonite community has been carried out by a professional folklorist—namely, Rolf Brednich among the Russian Mennonites of Saskatchewan (1977).

The various aspects of folklore and folklife mentioned in this article are dealt with briefly in related articles as indicated by asterisks. These brief articles survey the results of some completed studies, supply a modest amount of new information, and, perhaps most important, suggest areas for further research. In most areas of folklore, initial surveys of genres, items, and practitioners—both current and historical—still need to be done. Beyond that, many detailed case studies need to be carried out so that Mennonite folklife may be scrutinized in the same disciplined way that the traditions of other ethnoreligious groups—such as the Jews, Mormons, and (Russian Orthodox) Old Believers—have been studied.

In considering Mennonite lore, it soon becomes clear that most of the items and genres are probably not unique to these people, but, instead, are borrowed from surrounding culture. For instance, Melvin °Gingerich has shown that elements of presumably "distinctive" Mennonite folk costume (°°dress) early in the 20th c. were borrowed from dominant culture and then used by Mennonites for a longer time than their neighbors and, most important, for special purposes.

Many other such instances can be cited. Scott T. Swank has demonstrated that *all* German settlers—rich and poor, plain and fancy—in early Pennsylvania lived in sparsely furnished houses. In the late 20th c. the Amish are the Pennsylvania-German people who maintain that tradition most strictly, although for them it has assumed morally symbolic meanings.

Likewise, the typical church building for German Protestants in the rural American Midwest was the simple-gabled, clapboard-sided building, usually with multi-paned, clear glass windows. The Old Order Mennonites are the group that has maintained that folk building design most rigorously, with the result that their meetinghouses—refined through the years into a finely proportioned design—now seem unique in the rural landscape.

In more recent folklore, (Old) Mennonites (MC) in the early 1980s enthusiastically told the story of three Mennonite women on an elevator in New York City with baseball star Reggie Jackson. Although the story seemed to Mennonite tellers to be uniquely "Mennonite," it was actually an urban legend borrowed from mainstream American culture and adapted to the Mennonite experience, with special implications for the understanding of current Mennonite attitudes regarding °nonconformity, °urban life, °race relations and °gender roles.

Hence, the collection, description, and classification of Mennonite folklore is not enough, although it is a necessary first step in approaching the field. What is also needed are contextual studies that analyze the special meanings that the various folk traditions bear within these groups. Especially for current verbal folklore, analyses of performance situations that follow the "ethnography of speaking" approach are crucial in order to discover things about Mennonite °authority, °community, and personal interaction that are unavailable from other sources.

The encyclopedia's coverage of folklife will be by genres, derived from the typical threefold analysis of the field—oral, customary, and material traditions: (1) Oral Folklore: °ballads, °folk music, °humor, °nicknames, °rhymes, stories; (2) Customary Folklore: °brauche, °burial customs, °dance, °ethnicity, festivals, °folk medicine, °relief sales, °weddings; (3) Material Folk Traditions: °ceramics, °clocks, °folk arts, °Fraktur, °furniture and woodworking, °museums, °quilts.

Unfortunately, most discussions of folklife topics in ME V deal exclusively with Amish, Hutterites, and Mennonites in North America; little is said about Mennonite groups in Europe, South America, Asia, and Africa. This is because of the scarcity of information regarding those folk cultures, as well as the sheer impossibility of accounting for the many varied folk traditions present in worldwide Mennonitism.

The area of customary lore is particularly neglected in encyclopedia entries, because of the immense number of traditional practices that create denominational and community identity throughout the Mennonite world. In addition to the customary entries listed above, books below that survey Mennonite customs include the °sociological studies by Hostetler (Amish, Hutterites) and the novels by Reimer (Russian Mennonites), Stambaugh (early 20th-c. Lancaster Co. Mennonites), and Yoder (Amish). **EB**

Ervin Beck, "Reggie Jackson among the Mennonites," *MQR*, 58 (1984), 147-67; Rolf Brednich, *Mennonite Folklife and Folklore: A Preliminary Report* (Ottawa: National Museums of Canada, 1977); Jan Harold Brunvand, *The Study of American Folklore*, 3rd ed., (New York: Norton, 1986); Richard M. Dorson, *Folklore and Folklife: An Introduction* (Chicago: U. of Chicago Press, 1972); Melvin Gingerich, *Mennonite Attire Through Four Centuries* (Breinigsville, Pa.: Pennsylvania German Society, 1970); John A. Hostetler, *Amish Society* (1980); idem, *Hutterite Society* (Baltimore: Johns Hopkins U. Press, 1974); Al Reimer, *My Harp Is Turned to Mourning* (Winnipeg: Hyperion Press, 1986); Sara Stambaugh, *I Hear the Reaper's Song* (Intercourse, Pa.: Good Books, 1985); Scott T. Swank, "Proxemic Patterns" in *Arts of the Pennsylvania Germans*, ed. Swank and others (New York: Norton, 1983), 35-60; Barre Toelken, *The Dynamics of Folklore* (Boston: Houghton Mifflin, 1979); Joseph W. Yoder, *Rosanna of the Amish* (Huntington, Pa.: Yoder Publishing Co., 1940).

Following of Christ (Nachfolge Christi). See Discipleship.

FOMCIT. See Fellowship of Mennonite Churches in Taiwan.

Forced Labor. See Russian Soviet Federated Socialist Republic (RSFSR).

Forestation (Russia). Although not totally devoid of

trees, much of the steppe on which the first Mennonites settled lacked tree cover. The colonists were first encouraged to plant trees by Samuel °°Kontenius, who also established experimental gardens and tree nurseries. Trees were planted for shelter, fuel, and fruit production in household gardens, village plantations, and other areas. Mulberry trees were established to develop a silk industry; the leaves were fed to the caterpillars of the silk moth. By 1825 Mennonites had planted 217,684 trees in the Molotschna settlement, but the authorities encouraged them to intensify their efforts, sending agricultural experts to give advice. One of the aims of the °°Agricultural Association established in 1830 under the control of Johann °°Cornies, was to accelerate forestation of the colony. Between 1845 and Cornies' death in 1848, the number of trees planted increased by 40 percent to number almost three million. By 1854 almost six million trees had been planted in the colony.

Although many colonists resisted the dictatorial methods Cornies used to enforce his policies on forestation and other improvements, in time they came to appreciate the benefits of trees in their colonies. Owners of private estates and settlers in daughter colonies also took up three planting on a large scale. Mennonite expertise in this area was recognized by the establishment of the Forestry Service (°*Forsteidienst*) as an alternative to military service after 1881. Even so, some of the timber planted during the 19th c. was felled for profit by Mennonite entrepreneurs in the years before 1914. **JU**

David G. Rempel, "The Mennonite Commonwealth in Russia," *MQR*, 47 (1973), 259-308, vol. 48 (1974), 5-54.

Forgiveness is the central experience of faith for Western peoples—the forgiveness of God to resolve human guilt, the forgiveness of other persons to resolve alienation—but in other cultural settings the crucial issue varies. Instead of guilt and forgiveness the focus may be on alienation and inclusion, on shame and acceptance.

Forgiveness in Western theology is variously defined as benevolent generosity which sets the offender free again, as obedient acceptance of the wrongdoer not because of the nature of the forgiven but that of the one forgiving; as sacrificial acceptance of the cost of forgiving, of bearing one's own anger at the injury or injustice; as the restoration of love and the reconstruction of relationship between offender and offended. All forgiveness, whether divine or human is clearly by analogous processes (Col 3:13; Eph 4:32) and we are called to replicate the forgiveness of God in Christ in our relationships with those who sin against us. Forgiveness of others and the forgiveness of God are two aspects of the same reality (Mt 6:12ff; 18:23-35). They are indivisible and interdependent.

Forgiveness, in Anabaptist thought and practice, is "the mutual recognition that repentance is genuine and that right relationships have been restored or are now achieved." Forgiveness is thus seen as a reconciling, not an inner healing, event, as a relational process rather than an individualistic act, as reconstruction, not a private spirituality. By focusing on °reconciliation, Anabaptism sees forgiveness in communal context as defined in Mt 18:25ff. The goal is not personal release from guilt and responsibility but regaining the brother or the sister. In stressing relationship, Anabaptism moves forgiveness from the orientation toward individualism toward solidarity with the forgiven. By seeing repentance as integral to forgiveness rather than consequent (Lk 17:3-4) the negotiation of anger, alienation, and injustice becomes the work of forgiving in action. In stressing reconstruction of human relationships rather than a forgiveness of private spirituality, Anabaptism demands that sustaining the body of Christ and nurturing human community are the essence of a °discipleship that works for shalom. This perspective on forgiveness takes ethical integrity and °justice as central to forgiveness rather than seeing forgiveness as the °grace which transcends ethical failure, offers love instead of desiring justice, gives acceptance instead of working for renewed relationships. The Anabaptist tendency is to stress works more than grace, performance beyond intention, perfectionism rather than tolerance and a free pluralism. The balance of inner and relational forgiveness of acceptant grace and rigorous reconciliation, of individual release and communal integrity is valued in Anabaptism, but the balance is frequently as elusive as it is for American Evangelicalism which tends toward individualism, privatism, and benevolence without repentance in most writing about forgiveness.

In Mennonite churches in Asian, African and Latin American cultures forgiveness takes forms appropriate to the profound cultural values which shape alternate worldviews. Where modern Western assumptions of equality stress mutuality and reciprocity in horizontal forgiveness, traditional cultures tend toward more vertical patterns which see forgiveness as an undeserved gift in unchangeable situations or as earned acceptance in relationships requiring reparations. Repentance is seen as integral, but the processes follow cultural patterns which avoid confrontation and loss of face. In traditional or modern cultures, East or West, Anabaptism has stressed forgiveness as reconciliation whose prerequisite is love and whose work is the restoration of relationships.　　　　　　　　　　DWA

David W. Augsburger, *Caring Enough to Forgive* (Scottdale, 1981); William Klassen, *The Forgiving Community* (Philadelphia: Westminster, 1966).

See also Salvation.

Forsteidienst (Forestry Service) (ME II:353). From 1880 to 1917 Russian Mennonites were permitted by legislation to fulfill their military obligations by working in forestry camps under civilian administration. A total of nine main camps, and a mobile phyloxera unit in the Crimean peninsula were opened during these years.

The first two camps at Veliko Anadol and Azov were started up near the Bergthal Colony in the Ekaterinoslav government to admit the recruits of 1880. The next two camps, Ratzyn and Vladimirov began operating in the Kherson government during the following year, while the last two of the initial six, Neu and Alt Berdian, were established in the Taurian government, not far from the Molotschna

Colony, in 1883. The Crimean phyloxera unit came into existence not long afterwards.

After the Russo-Japanese war (1904-05), two more camps were set up at Ananiev (also known as Sherebkovo) and Snamenka (known as Chernoleskoi or Schwarzwald). Both were located north of Odessa. Early in 1914, the first year of the war, still another camp was pressed into service at Issyl Kul, a point on the Siberian railway, halfway between the cities of Omsk and Petropavlovsk.

During these four decades the total number of recruits rose from the initial group of 123 in the first two camps, to somewhat over 1,200 in the 10 sites managed by the Mennonites by 1914. David Klaassen and Henry B. Janz successively chaired IKSUMO, the organization which directed the forestry service program during the final years.

About 7,000 Mennonites served in forestry work during World War I. The majority of them were stationed outside the regular camps at other sites designated for °alternative service. By the summer of 1918, all the servicemen had been demobilized and the camps were then shut permanently. Lenin's decrees of Oct., 1918, and Jan., 1919, continued to make miliatry exemptions possible, but all service units were now run by the state. Some assignments to forest work, particularly in Siberia, continued right up to the time when alternative forms of service ended altogether around 1936.　　　　　LK

P. M. Friesen, *Brotherhood* (1980) / Friesen, *Brüderschaft* (1911); Waldemar Guenther, D. P. Heidebrecht, and Gerhard I. Peters, *Onsi Tjedils: Ersatzdienst der Mennoniten in Russland unter den Romanows* (Abbotsford, B.C.: the authors, 1966); Lawrence Klippenstein, "Mennonite Pacifism and State Service in Russia: A Case Study in Church-State Relations, 1789-1936" (PhD diss., U. of Minnesota, 1984); Walter Quiring, and Helen Bartel, eds., *In the Fullness of Time: 150 Years of Mennonite Sojourn in Russia*, trans. by Aaron Klassen (Kitchener, Ont.: Aaron Klassen, 1974); Hans Rempel, and George Epp, *Waffen der Wehrlosen: Ersatzdienst der Mennoniten in der UdSSR* (Winnipeg: CMBC Publications, 1980); John B. Toews, *Czars, Soviets and Mennonites* (Newton, 1982).

See also Alternative Service.

Fraktur (ME III:11-12). **Dutch-Prussian-Russian.** *Fraktur*, the art of beautiful penmanship and illuminated drawings on paper, flourished from 1760-1860 as a teaching tool in Mennonite Prussian and Russian schools. Teachers would also produce *Fraktur* to decorate house blessings and to inscribe title pages of books.

Most examples were written in German and can be grouped as: *Vorschriften* (copybooks), *Weihnachts* and *Neujahrswünsche* (Christmas and New Year's greetings), *Bücherzeichen* (bookplates), *Rechenbücher* (arithmetic books), *Belohnungen* (certificates of award), *Bilder* (drawings), *Haussegen* (house blessings), *Irrgarten* (labyrinths) and *Scherschnitte* (scissor or knife cuttings). The *Vorschrift* was used to teach children the alphabet; it was written in their best penmanship. The texts with illuminated letters and drawings were studies in Bible, nature, and geography. *Weihnachts- und Neujahrswünsche* were created by children as gifts to their parents. These reflected joys and hardships that the Mennonite people experienced. *Bücherzeichen* identified ownership of Bibles, catechism books, and hymnbooks, and would often include genealogical information. Among the illuminated books, *Rechenbücher* were the most common. These books included many handwritten pages of arithmetic problems, colorful designs, and illustrations. For excellent work and conduct, children were given a *Belohnung* (reward) drawing executed by the teacher. Texts for *Irrgarten* were penned in a verbal maze as a religious admonition, game, or love note. Delicately cut *Scherenschnitte* (papercuttings, see °folk arts) included narrations and colorful symbols similar to *Irrgarten*. Roses were the most common flower design; animals, angels, geometric patterns, and architectural settings were also used.

Rag paper and quills made from goose and turkey feathers were used prior to 1860. Pigments produced for water color drawings were derived from plants and trees.

Reference to *Vorschriften* first appear in a Dutch manuscript for the Mennonite church school in °°Altona, Germany; a later copy was translated into German about 1750. Some of the early Prussian educators adept in *Frakturmalen* (malen = painting, i.e., drawing) were Dirck Bergman (1789), Bernard Rempel (1831), and Peter Penner (1838). *Fraktur* instruction is noted in Russian Mennonite school manuals by Tobias Voth (1820), Jakob Braül (1830), and Heinrich Heese (1842). Many children and teachers continued *Frakturmalen* in later years. After 1870 some *Fraktur* works were written in Russian.   EEA

Swiss-Pennsylvania-German. Among German-speaking immigrants bringing the practice of "*Fraktur-Schriften*" to Pennsylvania were Mennonites with roots in Switzerland and southern Germany. Christopher °°Dock, a Colonial Mennonite schoolmaster who taught at Germantown, Skippack, and Salford, describes in his *Schul-ordnung* (1750) his way of encouraging his students by rewarding them with small drawings of a flower or a bird. At other times the reward might be a certificate (*Zeugniß*) or a writing-sample (*Vorschrift*). The earliest known examples of Pennsylvania *Fraktur* are attributed to Dock.

A number of students who were taught by Dock in the Salford and Skippack meetinghouses later became schoolmasters in this intensely Mennonite area. The result was an extensive local flowering of folk art in *Fraktur* form. Two of Dock's students were Huppert Cassel (b. 1751), who taught at Salford and Skippack, and Andreas Kolb (1749-1811), who taught at Salford and Saucon. Both became prolific and skilled artists in *Fraktur*.

Contemporary with these teachers was the Lutheran, Herman M. Ache (d. 1815), a resident of lower Salford. Of notable influence as a *Fraktur*-artist, he taught Mennonite children sporadically from 1756 to the 1770s at Franconia, Salford, and Skippack.

This tradition continued into the mid-19th c. in the Franconia Mennonite Conference, skillfully practiced by schoolmasters such as the following: Jacob Gottschall (1769-1845), a bishop at Franconia after 1813, who had been taught in a Bucks Co. Mennonite school by Lutheran *Fraktur* artist, Johan Adam Eyer (1755-1837); Jacob Hummel (d. 1822), a

Mennonite who taught at Lower Salford and Limerick; Durs Rudy, a Lutheran who taught Mennonite children at Skippack 1804-06; Isaac Z. Hunsicker (1803-70) of Skippack, a Mennonite teacher and itinerant *Fraktur*-writer whose work includes a reward for Susan Alderfer at Salford in 1831 and who soon thereafter moved to Canada where he continued his art; Henry Johnson (1806-79), a Mennonite teacher for decades at the Skippack school; and the three sons of Bishop Jacob and Barbara (Kindig) Gottschall, Martin K. (1797-1870), William K. (1801-76), and Samuel K. (1808-98), whose colorful and imaginative work grandly culminated a century of *Fraktur*-production in the Franconia-Salford-Skippack Mennonite community.

Mennonite *Fraktur* was almost completely school-related. The *Vorschriften* (writing samples) were used to teach the children penmanship and design, the Scriptures, hymns, and other spiritual truths. Other forms include small rewards, bookplates in manuscript singing school books and hymn books, and larger, illustrative "teaching pieces" used in the classroom to teach the alphabet and spiritual understandings.   MJLH

Appreciation for the aesthetic, moral, devotional, genealogical, and sentimental values associated with *Fraktur* art has increased markedly in recent decades in Pennsylvania, Maryland, and Virginia as is evident from the development of personal and church-related collections, from occasional courses devoted to the subject, and from a minimal revival of the art, most notably among Mennonites in Bucks and Montgomery Cos., Pa.

In Lancaster Co. and surrounding areas, the Lancaster Mennonite Conference Board of Congregational Resources sponsors occasional adult education courses on *Fraktur* and on calligraphic styles derived from *Fraktur*, but they are usually taught by non-Mennonite practitioners. At the People's Place Museum, Intercourse, Pa., Michael S. L. Kriebel, an Old Order River Brethren artist, was devoting the majority of his time to *Fraktur* art in the late 1980s. Few Mennonites in central and western Pennsylvania, Maryland, or Virginia have achieved distinction as serious practitioners of *Fraktur* art.

Institutions that have developed since 1950 and collected Mennonite-related *Fraktur* of the eastern United States include the following in Pennsylvania: Lancaster Mennonite Historical Society, Lancaster; Muddy Creek Farm Library, Denver; People's Place, Intercourse; Juniata District Mennonite Historical Society, Richfield; Germantown Mennonite Historical Library, Philadelphia; Mifflin County Mennonite Historical Society, Belleville; the Pequea Bruderschaft Library, Gordonville; Allegheny Conference Archives, Johnstown; and the Mennonite Historical Association of the Cumberland Valley, State Line. In Grantsville, Md., is the Casselman River Area Amish and Mennonite Historians group, and in Ontario, the Heritage Historical Library, Aylmer. Continuing, previously established centers with *Fraktur* collections, in addition to those mentioned in ME III, include Eastern Mennonite College, Harrisonburg, Va.; Messiah College, Grantham, Pa.; and the Mennonite Historical Library of Eastern Pennsylvania, Lansdale, Pa.   CCW

Ethel Ewert Abrahams, *Frakturmalen und Schönschreiben* (North Newton, Ks.: Mennonite Press, 1980); D. H. Epp, *Die Chortitzer Mennoniten* (Odessa: A. Schultze, 1899), 122-24; P. M. Friesen, *Brüderschaft* (1911), 633, idem, *Brotherhood* (1980), 780; Franz Isaac, *Die Molotschnaer Mennoniten* (Halbstadt, Taurien: H. J. Braun, 1908), 274-75; A Neufeld, *Die Chortizer Centralschule, 1842-1892* (Berdjansk: Druck von H. Ediger, 1893), 15; Ethel Ewert Abrahams, "Anna's Wünsche," *Menn. Life*, 34, no. 2 (June 1979), 21-25; idem, "Fraktur by Germans from Russia," *American Historical Society of Germans from Russia, Work Paper*, no. 21 (Fall 1976), 12-16; idem, "The Art of Fraktur-Schriften Among the Dutch-German Mennonites" (MA thesis, Wichita State U., 1975); Cornelius Duerksen, "Regeln der Rechtschreibung für Kleinkinderschulen, 1851," and "Rechtschreibunglehre, 1878," Alexanderthal village, S. Russia, handwritten in German, Raymond F. Wiebe collection (Hillsboro, Ks.); "Entwürfe und Aufzeichnungen über die Mennonitenschule in Altona-Hamburg" (n.d., possibly 1700-1750), handwritten in German, MLA (North Newton); Leonhard Froese, "Das Pädagogische Kultursystem der Mennonitischen Siedlungsgruppe in Russland" (diss., U. of Göttingen, 1949), 59-66; "Ontwerp om een Gemeenteluijke School in Altona" (n.d., possibly 1650-1700), handwritten in Dutch, MLA (North Newton); Gerald C. Studer, *Christopher Dock, Colonial Schoolmaster* (Scottdale, 1967; Christopher Dock, *Schul-ordnung* (Columbiana, Ohio: Jacob Nold, 1861); Frederick S. Weiser and Howell J. Heaney, comps., *The Pennsylvania German Fraktur of the Free Library of Philadelphia*, 2 vols. (Breinigsville, Pa.: The Pennsylvania German Society, 1976); Henry S. Bornemen, *Pennsylvania German Bookplates*, Publications of Pennsylvania German Society, 54 (Philadelphia: Pennsylvania German Society, 1953); idem, *Pennsylvania German Illuminated Manuscripts* (= vol. 46 of the Proceedings of the Pennsylvania German Society, 1937; rev. ed., New York: Dover Publications, 1973); Donald A. Shelly, *The Fraktur Writings or Illuminated Manuscripts of the Pennsylvania-Germans* (Allentown, Pa.: The Pennsylvania-German Folklore Society, 1958-59); E. Reginald Good, "Isaac Ziegler Hunsicker: Ontario Schoolmaster and Fraktur Artist," *Pennsylvania Folklife*, 26, no. 4 (1977); Mary Jane Lederach Hershey and others, "Andreas Kolb, 1749-1811," *MQR*, 61 (1987), 121-201; Frederick S. Weiser, "IAE SD: The Story of Johann Adam Eyer (1755-1837), Schoolmaster and Fraktur Artist with a Translation of His Roster Book, 1779-1787," in *Ebbes fer Alle-Ebber, Ebbes fer Dich (Something for Everyone, Something for You)*, ed Albert F. Buffington and others (Breinigsville, Pa.: The Pennsylvania German Society, 1980).

See also Folklore.

Franconia Mennonite Conference (MC) (ME II:368),

has the major portion of its congregations in the industrial and high technology area north of Philadelphia. The high per capita income of the 6,600 conference members (1988) is reflected in the highest per member giving of any of the 22 conferences of the Mennonite Church (MC). In 1988 Franconia Conference has 60 congregations, all located in Pennsylvania except two congregations in New Jersey, one in New York, and three in Vermont. Several congregations in Pennsylvania are located near the New York state line away from the conference center. One congregation (Germantown) is also affiliated with the Eastern District Conference (GCM); three with the Afro-American Mennonite Association and five with the New England Fellowship of Mennonite Churches. Franconia Conference officially affiliated fully with the Mennonite Church (MC) general assembly in 1971.

The conference meets semiannually and publishes the conference periodical *Franconia Conference News* 11 times per year. In 1987-88 it was involved in three new church planting efforts. Its camp association sponsors Spruce Lake Camp at Canadensis, Pa. The conference also participates in Indian Creek Foundation (Harleysville, Pa.) which furnishes community living and vocational training for develop mentally °disabled people. Dock Woods Community with five institutions at Lansdale and Hatfield, Pa., and Rockhill Mennonite Community, Sellersville, Pa., serve elderly people with personal care, skilled nursing care, and retirement living under conference sponsorship. The Mennonite Historical Library and Archives of Eastern Pennsylvania, founded in 1967, is sponsored jointly by the Franconia Conference and Eastern District (GCM). The conference high school (Christopher Dock) had 351 students in 1987.

In 1971 the conference reorganized into five commissions: Stewardship, Nurture, Mission, Leadership, and Brotherhood. The Conference Council oversees the work of the commissions on behalf of the conference. It employs the equivalent of 6.5 full-time staff members plus secretaries.   RSa

John Ruth, *Maintaining the Right Fellowship* (Scottdale, 1984); *MC Yearbook* (1988-89), 54-56, 122, 129, 132, 140, 149; Glenn Lehman, "Rich Heritage, New Life," *GH* (Jan. 19, 1988), 33-37.

Franklin Mennonite Conference (ME IV:892).

On Aug. 13, 1965, Washington-Franklin Mennonite Conference (MC) divided into two separate organizations. Senior Bishop Moses K. Horst stated in a regular conference meeting that Franklin Co. bishops and supporting ministers were no longer members of conference. It was known that Franklin Co. ministers were encouraging Washington Co. members in their efforts to start mission churches in surrounding areas. Two hundred adult members of Washington Co. congregations appealed to conference for change in methods for outreach and growth in mission work. When agreement could not be reached by the two bishop districts, appeals were made to Lancaster and Virginia conferences (MC).

An attempt by a tri-conference committee to work out solutions was unsuccessful. The Maryland bishops retained the name Washington-Franklin County Mennonite Conference, while the Pennsylvania bishops later chose to name their group Franklin Mennonite Conference. All agreed to disagree peaceably but pulpits are no longer exchanged.

A monthly conference newspaper (*Burning Bush*, June 1965) was started as a vehicle toward unity among congregations. Sixteen congregations receive the newspaper and report regularly in it. Both conferences have since then added other mission congregations to their membership.   BR

Records, including records of the separation process, are maintained by the conference secretary; *MC Yearbook* (1988-89), 56-57.

Franz, Leonard J. (1895-1972),

a Mennonite Brethren educator, administrator, and historian, was a native of Inman, Ks. In addition to serving as the sixth president of Tabor College, Hillsboro, Ks. (1956-62), he was academic dean (1947-57), during which time he also served as acting president for two one-year terms. He graduated from Tabor College (AB, 1922), McPherson College (AB, 1923), the U. of Kansas (MA, 1937), and the U. of Colorado (PhD, history, 1948).

Franz married Helen Reimer of Mountain Lake, Minn., in 1920. They had two children, Elfrieda (m. Erwin N. Hiebert) and Laura (m. T. G. Hiebert) both of whom also earned graduate degrees and became educators. Except for his early childhood years and during his graduate studies and travels in America and abroad, he was a life-long resident in Hillsboro. Prior to his appointment at Tabor, Franz was an administrator in the public schools in Hillsboro for 18 years. He was best known for his significant administrative qualities, his expertise as a historian and as a devout, reflective, and active Christian and churchman in the Mennonite Brethren constituency.

Franz's contributions as an educator included generating confidence in Tabor within the constituency, strengthening the academic program at the college through its faculty, curriculum, and facilities and progress toward academic accreditation.   CH

Fraser Valley, B.C. See British Columbia.

Fraternidad de Iglesias Evangélicas Menonitas de Nicaragua (Fraternity of Evangelical Mennonite Churches of Nicaragua). In 1966, after thorough investigation of mission needs in Central America, the Evangelical Mennonite Conference (EMCon) Board of Missions sent its first missionaries to Nicaragua. Bible colportage, Christian literature distribution, home visitations, and Bible studies in Morozan, a suburb of the capital city, Managua, resulted in people responding to the Good News. By 1969 there were eight baptized members in the emerging church and many other people were attending the regular church services. In 1970, with a membership of 18, the Morozan church, in partnership with personnel of the Board of Missions (EMCon), started congregations in Ciudad Sandino and La Paz.

The three local churches that had emerged by 1973 organized the Concilio Nacional (national council) for the purpose of evangelism and establishing churches in Nicaragua. This resulted in legally incorporating the national church, which was named La Fraternidad de las Iglesias Evangélicas Mennonitas. Before 1979, when the Sandinista revolution overthrew the Somoza government, missionaries served on the Concilio Nacional. The Fraternidad de las Iglesias Evangélicas Mennonitas de Nicaragua is an autonomous church, working in partnership with the Board of Missions. The conference is served by a monthly magazine, *El Mensajero* (The Messenger), published by Evangelical Mennonite Conference missionaries in El Paso, Tex.

The conference administers programs in community development, leadership training, and Christian education. It also operates bookstores. A camp and retreat center facilitates the church's training program. The public health program, which opened a number of communities to evangelism and church planting, was administered by the church and mission from 1974 to 1981. Theological training has been emphasized by the Fraternidad. Students have been and are receiving training in Bible schools in Managua and the United States, in °theological education by extension, and in SEMILLA, an inter-Mennonite seminary in Central America (°Consulta Anabautista Menonita Centroamericana). The conference was a founding member of SEMILLA.

According to the 1986 report of the Concilio Nacional, the conference had six locally organized congregations and eight unorganized preaching points, with an active baptized membership of 290. The church continues to seek to reach new areas and plant new churches.   HKla

MWH (1978), 233-35; *MWH* (1984), 89.

Free Church. See Believers Church.

Free Will. See Grace; Salvation.

Friedensfelder Mennoniten Gemeinde, Manitoba. In 1984, when the Altona branch of the Manitoba Reinländer Mennoniten Gemeinde decided to build a new meetinghouse which included a basement and was wired for electricity, some members, led by David Buhler, felt this was too modern and left. They were joined by a number of other families in Gnadenthal, Plum Coulee, Horndean, Austin, and Grunthal. They formed a new church and took the name *Friedensfelder Mennoniten Gemeinde*. They have a number of ministers and meet in three different locations, in Gnadenthal, Austin, and Grunthal. They have constructed a new meetinghouse in Gnadenthal. In the other two centers they meet in homes. The church has no *Ältester* (°elder), so for baptisms and communion they call upon an *Ältester* from a church near Swift Current, Sask. Total adult membership in the three centers is between 30 and 50.   JF

See also Reinländer Mennoniten Gemeinde.

Friedensheim (Home of Peace), Berlin, began in 1958 as a community center for assisting °refugees and displaced war victims. It was built on the site of a bombed building with help from the Beachy Amish Mennonites. Originally staffed by voluntary service workers from the Beachy Amish churches in the United States, the center cared for more than 1,000 children over the years. As a result of the strong evangelical ministry of the American missionaries a congregation of converted persons, mostly of people with no Mennonite background, was formed. In 1975 this congregation became an independent church. In 1971 a rehabilitation center for °drug and alcohol dependency was started and called *Friedenshafen* (Haven of Peace). This program was discontinued in 1985. A third center, *Friedensnest* (Peace Nest), was opened by the Friedensheim congregation to minister to the needs of Turkish immigrant families. Since 1982 the congregation has employed a German pastor as well as a matron for the community center.   LO/HN

Andrew Hershberger, *Into the Highways and Hedges (25 Years Amish Mennonite Aid)* (Abbeville, S.C.).

Friedmann, Robert (June 9, 1891-July 28, 1970), a major interpreter of Swiss-South German and Austrian Anabaptism from the 1920s to 1970. He also wrote a major work on the effect of classic Pietism upon South German and Swiss Mennonites up to the 19th c. (*Mennonite Piety Through the Centuries*, 1949).

Born in Vienna into a liberal Jewish family, Friedmann studied in various fields, including engineering and the various natural sciences. The disillusionment following the First World War deeply affected Friedmann, and he reentered the university (Vienna) in 1920 as a student of history and philosophy (DPhil, 1924). His scholarly work in Anabaptism began in 1923 when he prepared a seminar paper on the contents of three Hutterian codices, which "gripped [him] profoundly." Friedmann's first publications on Anabaptist themes came in 1927; his scholarly efforts led to a host of publications in Anabaptist studies over the next four decades. He was author of ca. 200 articles in ME I-IV, and a perennial contributor to *Mennonite Quarterly Review*.

In 1939 Friedmann was imprisoned in Vienna for 12 days along with Jews and others of Jewish background, then freed by friends who counseled him to emigrate immediately. He went, first to England, then to Yale Divinity School through the efforts of Roland Bainton, and then to Goshen Ind. through the efforts of Harold S. °Bender. For several years he helped organize the Goshen College Mennonite Historical Library. He became a baptized member of the Eighth Street Mennonite Church (GCM) during this time. In 1945 he accepted a position in history and philosophy at Western Michigan U. (Kalamazoo) which he held to the time of his retirement, working closely with the Goshen Anabaptist research center throughout this time.

Friedmann is perhaps best known for his view of Anabaptism as being "existential Christianity" (see his *Theology of Anabaptism*, 1973). His influence upon Harold Bender's classic synthesis of Anabaptism, "The Anabaptist Vision" (1944), has been documented (see Leonard Gross, "Recasting the Anabaptist Vision: the Longer View," *MQR*, 60 [1986], 352-63). He also published many articles on the Hutterites, appreciating this tradition deeply.

An important book-length manuscript that was never published is Friedmann's "Design for Living," which defines the nature of life in a manner that is at the same time to a great extent the sum and substance of the Anabaptist view of °discipleship, but described in philosophical terms (copy in the MC Archives [Goshen]), in the Robert Friedmann Papers).   LG

MQR, 47 (April 1974), sp. memorial issue including an extensive Friedmann bibliography, 1927-73.

Friesen, Florence Cooprider (Jan. 6, 1887-Sept. 12. 1985), was born in McPherson County, Ks., to John Albert and Henrietta (Brunk) Cooprider. In 1906, as a student at Goshen College Academy, she heard Mary °Burkhard, whose husband Jacob had died in India, emphasize the need for medical work among the women of India and felt an inner call to serve there. Florence graduated from the U. of Illinois College of Medicine in 1914. She served as a medical doctor in India under the Mennonite Board of Missions (MC) from 1916 to 1941. In 1922, on her first furlough from India, Florence married P. A. Friesen, whose first wife, Lena, had died in India, leaving him with four children: Peter H., William C.,

John A., and Edward H. The Friesens returned to Sankra, India, where Florence set up the first of many roadside clinics. Florence had two children, Grace (Slatter) and Paul A. From 1945 until 1953 she practiced medicine in Greensburg, Ks. where she delivered 66 babies. She continued her practice in Hesston, Ks., until 1959. A Hindu woman once said of Dr. Friesen, "Ah, your God must be a very good god, to send a doctor to women. None of our gods ever sends us a doctor."   ESR

Mary Lou Cummings, *Full Circle* (Newton, 1978), 82-86; Rich, *Mennonite Women* (1983), 175-77; *Who's Who Mennonites* (1943), 73-74; *GH* (Oct. 8, 1985), 708; Elsie D. Kaufman, *Monthly Letter* of Mennonite Women's Missionary Society, (Dec. 1, 1925); *WMSC Voice* (Apr. 1986), 7-8, 18; John A. Lapp, *India* (1972), 109, 113, 114.

Friesen, Gerhard Johann (Fritz Senn) (1894-1983). Born in Halbstadt, Molotschna Colony, Gerhard Friesen came to Canada in 1924 and lived near Stonewall, Man., and later in Kitchener, Ont., before he moved to Germany in 1938. Except for wartime service in the East and a stay in South Africa, he remained in Germany until his death. Educated as a teacher, he began writing °poetry in Russia, but only published poems and other writings after 1934. His poems appeared in *Der Bote*, the *Mennonitische Warte*, and a number of other Mennonite periodicals. An anthology of his poems edited by Elisabeth Peters appeared in 1974. His collected poetical works were published in 1987.

The poetry of Fritz Senn is primarily lyrical, celebrating the lost homeland of the Russian Mennonites, evoking the sights, sounds, and other sensory details of village and country life. His major work is a cycle of poems probing the Russian experience of his people and the catastrophic destruction of a world which his imagination could not release: "Hinterm Pflug/Stimmungen" ("Reflections, behind the Plow"), published 1935-36. His attempts to write longer prose works were not encouraged by his few literary advisors, Arnold °Dyck and Dietrich Epp, but surviving prose pieces are much like his lyrical verse—descriptive and evocative. Friesen is considered to be the best Mennonite poet writing in German. He was active as a poet for some 70 years, most of them hard and lonely. At the end he was also blind, but he never lost sight of the way of life symbolized by the Russian Mennonite village and what it had meant to him and many others.   VGD

Fritz Senn, *Gesammelt Gedichte und Prosa*, ed. Victor G. Doerksen (Winnipeg: CMBC Publications, 1987), contains all the known poetic writings of Friesen; Fritz Senn, *Das Dorf im Abendgrauen; Gedichte*, ed. Elisabeth Peters (Winnipeg: Verein zur Pflege der deutschen Sprache, 1974); Victor G. Doerksen, ed., "Fritz Senn: Hinterm Pflug/Stimmungen," in *Visions and Realities*, ed. H. Loewen and Al Reimer (Winnipeg: Hyperion, 1985), 149-73; Gerhard K. Friesen, ed., "Fritz Senn (1894-1983), Kurze Selbstbiographie (1975)," in *German-Canadian Yearbook*, 7 (Toronto, 1983), 89-92; Victor G. Doerksen, "The Divine Plowman and the Mennonite Clod: A Reading of *Hinterm Pflug/Stimmungen* by Fritz Senn" in *Annals 4 German-Canadian Studies* (Vancouver: Canadian Association of University Teachers of German, 1984), 208-29; *JMS*, 1 (1983), 122-23.

See also Literature.

Friesen, Maria Martens (June 15, 1861-Apr. 19,

1917). Born in Blumenort-Blumenau, Molotschna Colony, Russia, Maria and her husband Abraham Johann °°Friesen were the first Mennonite Brethren foreign missionaries. They served for 19 years in India. From 1885 to 1889 Maria studied "women's work" at Hamburg Baptist Seminary in Germany. Following a year of language training in Madras, the Friesens moved to Nalgonda, India, in Oct. 1890. They worked under the "American Baptist Missionary Union," though financially supported by the Russian Mennonite Brethren Churches. In 1891 they baptized 178 converts and founded an indigenous congregation. At the time of their first furlough, 1897-99, the Nalgonda congregation numbered 700 baptized members. Maria and Abraham returned to India in 1899 with additional missionaries. Maria's ill health forced them to return to Russia in 1908 by which time the Indian Mennonite Brethren churches numbered 3,000 baptized members. Both remained active in promoting mission work. Maria died in Spat, in the Crimea, Russia. She and her husband had two adopted children.   KR

P. M. Friesen, *Brotherhood* (1980), 674-87; G. W. Peters, *The Growth of Foreign Missions in the Mennonite Brethren Church* (Hillsboro: Board of Foreign Missions, 1952), 55-69; Abraham Kroeker, *Nachrichten des Volksfreund* (May 13, 1917), 4; Ken Reddig, "Trailblazers of Mennonite Brethren Missions," *Mennonite Brethren Herald*, 23 (July 27, 1984), 18-19.

Friesen, Martin Cornelius

Friesen, Martin Cornelius (Oct. 6, 1889-Apr. 7, 1968), was born on the east side of the Red River in the village of Osterwick (later renamed New Bothwell), southern Manitoba and died in the Menno Colony, Chaco, Paraguay. He was the son of Cornelius P. and Katharina Friesen who had emigrated from Bergthal Colony, Russia, to Manitoba in 1875. After his mother's death his father remarried, and Martin eventually married his stepsister Elizabeth Wiebe. They had four daughters and three sons.

Martin attended elementary school and later took initiative for study on his own, particularly in theology. In 1909 he was baptized and received into the Chortitzer Mennonite church, where he was elected minister in 1924 and elder in 1925.

In 1927 he led a large group of Mennonites from Manitoba to the Paraguayan °°Chaco, establishing what was to become Menno Colony. As leader of this group he was gradually able to institute significant reforms both within the congregation and the schools of the colony. This led to many changes, gradually however, in order that schisms might be avoided. Two weeks before his death he asked his children to pray that he might remain alive until a communion service on April 7, at which he wished to speak a word of farewell. This came about as he had wished. The afternoon after the service he died peacefully in bed. Thus a lifetime of kingdom work and experience came to an end.   MWF

Friesen, Peter Abraham (P. A.)

Friesen, Peter Abraham (P. A.) (May 22, 1879-Oct. 28, 1967), was a pioneer missionary in India and bishop in the Mennonite Church (MC) in India. He was born at Mountain Lake, Minn., the fourth of five children born to Johann and Marie (Bartsch) Friesen. P. A. attended local schools and early on became an active member in the Bruderthaler Mennonite (EMB, now Fellowship of Evangelical Bible Churches) congregation and an active participant in its mission program. He taught in the congregations's German school (1903-04) and worked as an evangelist and colporteur.

P. A. married Helena Hiebert in 1901 at Mountain Lake, and they applied for mission work with the Mennonite Evangelizing and Benevolent Board (MC), Elkhart, Ind. in 1903. On Dec. 23, 1906, P. A. was ordained to the ministry, and on Mar. 7, 1907, he and Helena arrived in India to work with the American Mennonite Mission in Dhamtari, C.P. (later Madhya Pradesh). They opened the Sankra station in 1911, and P. A. served as pastor of the Zion Mennonite congregation there for many years. He helped with drawing up the first constitution of the India Mennonite Conference (adopted 1912). He was ordained bishop in 1916. He personally favored an emphasis on evangelism over an emphasis on education and institutional ministries.

Two children, Mary and Rosa as well as his first wife, Helena (1921), died in India. In 1922 P. A. married fellow missionary Florence Cooprider, a physician. Working together at Sankra, they developed the Roadside Leprosy Clinics along with their district touring program. Throughout Durg District, "Burhwa Sahib" (the old gentleman) and "Sankra Daktarini" (the Sankra lady doctor) were household words spoken with reverence and respect.

In 1941 the Friesens retired from foreign service and accepted an assignment to administer a home for nursing students in Denver and to minister to the °conscientious objectors working in Civilian Public Service (CPS) in the city. Later they served in pastoral and medical work in Greensburg, Ks., and from 1955 until P. A.'s death they lived in Hesston, Ks. P. A. had eight children by his first marriage: Peter, Elizabeth, Mary, Ida, Rosa, William, John, and Edward. He had two children with Florence, Paul and Grace.   JAF

Ebenezer, 1889-1964, a history of the Evangelical Mennonite Brethren Church at Mt. Lake, Minn. (75th anniversary publication), 38-43, 62; M. S. Steiner, "Among Our Russian Brethren," *The Gospel Witness* (Dec. 27, 1905), 345; George J. Lapp, "Meeting New Missionaries," *The Gospel Witness* (Apr. 17, 1907) 36; "Report of the Nebraska Mennonite Conference," *The Gospel Witness* (Oct. 32, 1906), 490; Esther Rose Graber, comp., "MBM Missionary Directory (1984); Annual Reports of the American Mennonite Mission, India (1907) under Rudri Station, (1916), 64); "Facts and dates in the life of P. A. Friesen," compiled by Myrtle Friesen, 1980.

Friesland Colony, Paraguay

Friesland Colony, Paraguay (ME II:410), was the first Mennonite settlement in east Paraguay, established in 1937 by 144 families with a church membership of 748. The settlers had left the Fernheim Colony in the °°Chaco because they saw no economic future in the Chaco, the climate was too inhospitable for them (particularly the intense summer heat and severe sandstorms), the original villages had been located too closely together and more land was needed, and because of their opposition to the monopoly exercised by the producer-consumer °cooperative which regulated all commerce and prevented private enterprise.

In June 1937 6,911 hectares (17,000 acres) were purchased from Wilhelm and Arthur Strauch in

Montevideo at 10 Argentinian pesos per hectare, payable in seven years. This land is located ca. 50 km. (31 mi.) east of Puerto Rosario and 100 km. (62 mi.) by air ne of Asunción. By September 1937 nine villages had been established with a total of 146 farms. The colony was named *Friesland* in memory of the 16th-c. Frisian heritage of the settlers.

The pioneer years were very difficult, particularly because no cash products and market could be developed. Consequently, many settlers emigrated to Brazil, Canada, and Germany during the 1950s. In 1987 the inhabitants of the colony numbered 725. One of the early villages, Grünau number 4, has been completely eliminated, and another one, Grünau number 10 has only one family remaining. The colony has been able to acquire additional land: 755 hectares (1,864 acres) in 1946, 133 hectares (328 acres) in 1952, and 10,175 hectares (25,132 acres) in 1961 (the former Hutterite colony Primavera). Additional lands were acquired in 1984 and 1985, leading to a total acreage of 24,000 hectares (59,280 acres) in 1987.

Schools have been centralized with education possible through the ninth grade. A relatively well-equipped 24-bed hospital is in operation. Two congregations are active, the Mennonite Church (°°Kirchen-Gemeinden) and the Mennonite Brethren Church. Currently generators provide electricity in all the villages, but it is anticipated that the national electrification program will reach the colony in the near future.

Friesland Colony has the reputation of having introduced wheat to Paraguay. The process began with 30 hectares (74 acres) planted in 1959. These efforts soon received governmental support, with the colony being named the national center for wheat production, including providing seed grains to others. Since 1987 Paraguay no longer finds it necessary to import wheat flour and credits Friesland Colony with having made a significant contribution to this achievement. Two crops are harvested annually, wheat in winter and soybeans in summer. Considerable emphasis is placed on ranching and livestock, with ca. 28,000 head in the colony in 1987.

On Nov. 27, 1987, the colony celebrated its 50th anniversary, at which time the Paraguayan minister of agriculture, Hernando Bertoni, duly acknowledged the significant contribution of the colony. GR

Gerhard Ratzlaff, ed., *Auf den Spuren der Väter* (Filadelfia, Paraguay, 1987); idem, *Deutsches Jahrbuch für Paraguay* (1988).

Froese, Jacob J. (Nov. 13, 1885-Jan. 15, 1968). Born in the village of Reinland, Manitoba, Froese's education consisted of approximately seven years of study in a private Mennonite elementary school. About 1903 he moved to the village of Reinfeld with his mother and stepfather. Shortly after this he served as the village teacher for several years. He began farming after his marriage in 1906. In the early 1920s he served as the *Dorfsschulz* (village "mayor") for Reinfeld, until perhaps 1926. Most of the members of the Reinlaender Mennoniten Gemeinde (Old Colony Mennonite Church) migrated to Mexico in these years. Froese, however, decided to remain in Manitoba even though the church disbanded there

in the mid-1920s. When the Old Colony Mennonites emigrated they left their °°*Waisenamt* debt records with a law firm in Morden (for the purpose of collecting from non-emigrating debtors). It quickly became clear that people were unwilling to settle their accounts with outsiders. The law firm approached the debtors and asked them to elect someone to oversee the liquidation of outstanding debts. Jacob J. Froese was the person chosen.

By the 1930s many community leaders, including Froese, began to feel that a mistake had been made in disbanding the church. On June 25, 1936, a meeting was held at which the church was reorganized and Jacob J. Froese was elected as a minister. In 1937 the revived Old Colony Mennonite Church elected him as bishop (°elder).

In the 1940s he was active in the Manitoba *Ältestenkomitee* (elders' committee), which was concerned with matters related to military and °alternative service. In this connection he accompanied the committee's executive committee (bishops Peter A. Toews, David °Schulz, and J. F. Barkman, and minister David P. Reimer) on a trip to Ottawa to negotiate with governmental officials. Under his leadership the church was also strongly involved in the Canadian Menonite Relief Committee (until 1963) and after 1963, in Mennonite Central Committee Canada.

He served the church as bishop for more than 30 years (1937-68) and was a very successful farmer as well. During these years he delivered 1,700 sermons, presided at 200 funerals, conducted 94 marriages, and ordained 20 ministers, six deacons and two bishops, namely his successor in Manitoba and a Hutterite bishop at Pincher Creek, Alta.   JP

Frank Brown, *A History of Winkler 1892-1973* (Altona, Man.: D. W. Friesen, 1973); Gerhard Ens, *The Rural Municipality of Rhineland, 1884-1984* (Altona: Rural Municipality of Rhineland, 1984); E. K. Francis, *In Search of Utopia* (Altona: D. W. Friesen, 1955); Peter Petkau, and Irene Friesen-Petkau, *Blumenfeld: Where Land and People Meet* (Winkler, Man.: Blumenfeld Historical Committee, 1981); Calvin Redekop, *The Old Colony Mennonites: The Dilemma of Ethnic Minority Life* (Baltimore: John Hopkins U. Press, 1969); David P. Reimer, ed. *Experiences of the Mennonites of Canada during the Second World War* (Altona: D. W. Friesen, n.d.); Peter D. Zacharias, *Reinland: An Experience in Community* (Reinland, Man.: Reinland Centennial Committee, 1976).

Frontier. In 1920 Frederick Jackson Turner published *The Frontier in American History*, a book which became important for the understanding of America. It asserted that "the existence of an area of free land, its continuous recession, and the advance of American settlement westward, explain American development." And further, "The true point of view in the history of this nation is not the Atlantic coast, it is the Great West." Many historians do not agree with this thesis, but the "Great West" has been discussed much by scholars, has helped shape American myth (and possibly character), and remains a constant ingredient in novels, music, movies, and television.

For much of their history the Anabaptists and Mennonites have also been a frontier people. They have felt some of the same pressures to which Turner refers—the need for more land, desire for adventure, economic opportunity, "let's leave the past behind and start over"—but the single primary factor has usually been °persecution. During most of the 16th c. most of the Anabaptists fled simply to save their lives or were expelled upon threat of death if they returned. The impulse to survive drove them into the wilderness, to the frontiers of their day and, strange as it may seem, even some 20th-c. Mennonite °migrations have been what seemed to the migrants a search for survival, now not so much physically as culturally and, they would say, spiritually.

No fewer than 167 edicts or °°mandates were issued against the Anabaptists and Mennonites by various authorities from 1525 to 1599, demanding suppression, exile, or death, and an additional 55 from 1601 to 1761. Thus those who survived were truly forced to become the church in the wilderness (Ez 19:12-14, Heb 11, cf: *Martyrs Mirror*). Limited tolerance came first in the Netherlands, in the North in the 1570s and in the South in the 1590s, but various dukes, counts, and nobles gave them shelter earlier also, as did Countess °°Anna of Friesland in 1541. Moravia proved to be a particular haven of refuge for Anabaptists as early as 1526. It is estimated that from 20,000 to 30,000 found shelter there, including leaders like Balthasar °Hubmaier and Hans °Hut.

Eventually the Hutterian Brethren became the largest of the groups in Moravia, continuing their "Golden Period" until about 1600. The Hutterites were not only excellent agriculturists, but also excelled in many trades and crafts like °ceramics (pottery), cutlery, °clocks of all sizes, weavers, tailors, agricultural tools, milling, shoemaking. A total of 39 vocations were listed in their *Chronicle* (Gross). A few even became barber-surgeons serving the health needs of common people and nobility alike, being called to Prague and to various castles and monasteries (Friedmann). These skills obviously made the local authorities tolerant and eager to retain the Hutterites. Yet there was, since the 15th-c. Hussite wars, also a long tradition of religious tolerance in the region. Some nobles also found the faith of the Anabaptists attractive. It is believed that Johann of Liechtenstein, lord of Nikolsburg, received believers baptism.

Prussia, and Poland. Because of severe persecution, Anabaptists fled from the southern Netherlands, now Belgium, to the north and along the Baltic coastline to Bremen, Hamburg, and Danzig (Gdansk) beginning in the 1530s. Some of the refugees settled in Danzig, which was a part of West Prussia as was the Vistula Delta, including Marienburg (Marbork). Most of the Mennonites, however, initially located in East Prussia in the area around Koenigsberg (Kaliningrad).

Anabaptists (Schwenckfelders?) were found in Marienburg, as early as 1526 (Penner, *Ansiedlung mennonitischer Niederlaender*). It is likely that they came from Moravia. By 1530 the number of Anabaptists had increased, but the largest influx came from the Netherlands. In a letter dated May 2, 1534, the city council of Danzig asked the authorities in Emden, Amsterdam and Antwerp to certify the passenger lists of ships going to Danzig to prevent Anabaptists from going there, but they went anyway,

either as stowaways or overland or with the quiet connivance of ship captains.

No early evidence has been found to show that Prussian authorities seriously tried to prevent the Anabaptist immigration despite the warnings and edicts against them. The authorities of several Baltic-rim Hanseatic League cities, including Danzig, did plan to meet in Luneberg on July 1, 1535, to find ways of coping with the problem, but it is not clear whether the meeting took place. In any case, the substantial migration from the Netherlands was to continue for many years. In 1549 °Menno Simons visited the region and, a year later, °°Dirk Philips became permanent elder until his death on a trip to Emden in 1568.

Why were they tolerated? Not least, probably, because they were quiet and peace-loving citizens, but primarily because they proved to be a powerful economic asset. The Polish-Prussian War of 1519-1521 had devastated the region. The Anabaptists, in this case the Dutch Mennonites, were not only hard workers but also knew from life in their homeland how to drain the swamps of the Vistula River delta, build windmills, and restore or establish thriving new agricultural communities. Bringing the delta lands under control was to take the better part of a century and, in fact, became a constant challenge.

Royal Hapsburg pressure eventually did force authorities to ask the Mennonites to leave (East) Prussia, but they found a ready welcome nearby in West (Polish) Prussia. Other Mennonite refugees soon took their place again in the east. Even the Roman Catholic bishop of Lesslau refused to expel them, despite repeated urging by the authorities, because he needed their economic skills (Peter Klassen). Polish nobility maintained a considerable degree of autonomy in the 16th c. and were often open to new religious movements. Many "heretics" found shelter on their estates (Ratzlaff, Unruh).

We conclude from these accounts and those which follow that being an economic asset was to become a major, if not primary, reason for tolerating Mennonites in Moravia, The Netherlands, the °°Palatinate, Canada, the United States, and wherever they went, not least in Latin America, throughout their entire history to the late 20th c. They came to be known as self-sufficient, hardworking, frugal, and peaceful on the most difficult frontiers. There have also, however, been many examples of tolerance in principle, regardless of economics, as illustrated in Moravia and, notably in the 16th c., by Duke Philip of Hesse (Littell) and William of Orange of The Netherlands.

Russia. Social, agricultural, and economic pressures eventually caused many Prussian Mennonites to accept the invitation of Catherine II of Russia to migrate to the Ukraine beginning in 1789. The expulsion of the Tatars and Turks from that region made it necessary to occupy and restore the land. The earliest movements brought ca. 1,550 Prussian Mennonite families to the Ukraine. A barren new frontier awaited them. Migrations from Prussia continued into the 1860s but Mennonites in Russia also moved to new frontiers within Russia, particularly through the founding of daughter colonies. By 1914 there were ca. 120,000 Mennonites in Russia.

During World War II those Mennonites who survived the Stalin purges were again resettled on new frontiers in Asiatic Russia and Siberia.

While the Mennonites were only a small portion of European immigrants to Russia, they had become aware of their own unique economic power and used it as leverage to secure special °privileges, a practice which had already begun partially in Prussia. A 20-point petition requesting both limited and perpetual guarantees was submitted to the Russian authorities and largely granted, with the special consent of Catherine II (D. H. Epp). This was known as the *Privilegium* and set a precedent that has continued to the present in other contexts. Many of the articles applied to matters of faith and culture. If these were threatened or broken in the course of time, many Mennonites (often the more conservative?) packed up and left for a new frontier. This accounted for the 1870s migration from Russia to Canada and the United States.

Canada and the United States. A major reason for Mennonite success on hostile frontiers has been their cooperation among themselves, normally settling in colonies with a centralized economy and administration. This was particularly true in Russia. The degree of Mennonite cooperation was not as intense as that of Hutterian communalism which allowed no private property, but interdependence and °mutual aid often became the key to survival.

Thus the advance parties sent to investigate North America in 1873 looked for large tracts of land suitable for colony settlement. They were not disappointed in Canada, where the Secretary of Agriculture presented them with a 15-point *Privilegium* which included the two key guarantees of °block settlement and exemption from military service (F. H. Epp). A similar request in the U. S. Congress failed, despite powerful advocacy in the Senate based on the economic asset the new settlers would become (Smith). Land distribution seemed to be the prerogative of the railroads and military recruitment and °conscription were under the jurisdiction of the states. Mennonites were well-known in both countries, of course, since their settlement in Germantown in 1683, and in Upper Canada (Ontario), in 1786. The Dutch Mennonite °°Plockhoy had even earlier established a short-lived utopian communitarian colony at Horekill on the Delaware River, 1663-64.

Because of these developments the first Mennonite immigrants to Canada in the 1870s did settle on "reserves" provided especially for them, while the larger number immigrating to the United States settled in less compact communities in the Midwest. It may be that the Mennonite (sectarian) °work ethic played a role in securing special privileges both in Canada and the United States. Their history as successful pioneers on difficult frontiers was well known. Yet most religious groups were tolerated on the North American frontier. Mennonites were not above the laws of the land. They too went West until the frontier was gone (1890?).

When World War I came, tolerance became one of its casualties. In Canada it led to some Mennonite emigration to Mexico and Paraguay; in the United States to harassment and suffering. While Menno-

nites, along with many other groups, did seek lands where they might preserve their identity in isolation, and, where they did not emigrate, language temporarily replaced geography as a boundary marker. In time they inevitably became a part of the developing Canadian mosaic of peoples and of the U.S. melting pot.

Latin America. Because many Mennonites believed the Canadian government had not held to the terms of the *privilegium* large numbers of Old Colony and Sommerfeld Mennonites emigrated to Paraguay and to Mexico between 1922 and 1927. In Paraguay the requested privileges were guaranteed by *Decreto Ley* (law) 514 in 1921 and similar guarantees were secured by presidential decree in Mexico. Nowhere did the Mennonites encounter a more difficult frontier in their entire history than in the "green hell" of the Chaco, except perhaps in Siberian slave labor communities. But in time they made the desert bloom even in the °°Chaco (Friesen). Pioneering in Mexico was also difficult, but climate and roads were more manageable. Still, it was a barren, windswept frontier when they came (Fretz, Redekop, Sawatzky).

New groups of Mennonites entered the Chaco and Brazil in 1930, but in the latter without the privilege of exemption from military service. (Alternative service for conscientious objectors was written into the Brazilian constitution only in 1988.) Eventually new frontiers were found in Bolivia and Belize and, in the 1980s, in Argentina. During the 1980s new Mennonite immigrants have also come from Mexico to Texas as well as to Nova Scotia and other parts of Canada. Cheese and dairy products have become a major Mennonite contribution to the economies and human welfare of their new homelands, as have many other products and services. In Paraguay the development and production of wheat suitable to that climate turned the nation from complete reliance on imports to becoming a wheat-exporting country.

Summary. The era of special privilege in return for national economic gain may be over. Laws have changed, some because of Mennonite influence, but they are assumed to apply to all people, with some exceptions in Latin America. The movement has been from persecution to toleration to special privileges (*privilegium*) to integration or assimilation. First-generation Anabaptists did not ask for special privilege. What they claimed to be biblically right and true for themselves they claimed for all believers. The movement has come full circle.

Geographical frontiers have largely disappeared. The frontiers of faith and witness, but also occasional cultural distinctives, have taken their place as, for example, among the Amish, Old Order and Old Colony Mennonites. The absence of background literature about Mennonite frontiers in Asia and Africa made it seem prudent not to include them here though we do have some information on Indonesia and Australia.

In its time the frontier gave Mennonites the isolation they wanted, but not always for their good. Faith and culture atrophy in isolation, of which there are examples in the Mennonite experience, but the frontier also encourages faith, driving pioneers to their spiritual roots. The frontier fosters idealism, vision, self-reliance, and a certain individualism, yet invariably also interdependence and community. It provides opportunity for growth and experimentation. The frontier allows something new to emerge in all areas of human experience. Leadership emerges. Institutions flourish. The virtues of sharing and caring are nurtured on the frontier. Life and death take on new meaning. Persecution and frontiers have been primary motifs in shaping Mennonite identity.   CJD

General: Frederick Jackson Turner, *The Frontier in American History* (New York: H. Holt and Company, 1920); George Rogers Taylor, *The Turner Thesis* (Boston: Heath, 1956); John D. Unruh, Jr., *The Plains Across* (Urbana: U. of Illinois Press, 1979); Leland Harder, *The Sources of Swiss Anabaptism* (Scottdale, 1985); Peter James Klassen, *The Economics of Anabaptism, 1525-1560* (The Hague: Mouton and Co., 1964). *Moravia: The Chronicle of the Hutterian Brethren,* vol 1 (Rifton, N.Y.: Plough Publishing House, 1987); Donald F. Durnbaugh, ed., *Every Need Supplied* (Philadelphia: Temple U. Press, 1974); Robert Friedmann, *Hutterite Studies* (Scottdale, 1961); F. H. Littell, *Landgraf Philip und die Toleranz* (Bad Nauheim: Christian-Verlag, 1957); Leonard Gross, *The Golden Years of the Hutterites* (Scottdale, 1980). *Prussia:* Franziska Beck, *Vom Volksleben auf der Danziger Nehrung* (Marburg [Lahn]: Johann Gottfried Herder-Institut, 1962); Karl-Heinz Ludwig, *Zur Besiedlung des Weichseldeltas durch die Mennoniten* (Marburg [Lahn]: Johann Gottfried Herder-Institut, 1961); Walther Maas, *Zur Siedlungskunde des Warthe-Weichsellandes* (Marburg [Lahn]: Johann Gottfried Herder-Institut, 1961); Horst Penner, "The Anabaptists and Mennonites of East Prussia," *MQR,* 22 (1948), 212-25; idem, "West Prussian Mennonites Through Four Centuries," *MQR,* 23 (1949), 232-45; idem, *Ansiedlung Mennonitischer Niederländer im Weichselmündungsgebiet von der Mitte des 16. Jahrhunderts bis zum Beginn der Preussischen Zeit* (Weierhof [Pfalz]: Mennonitischer Geschichtsverein, 1963); idem, *Die ost- und westpreussischen Mennoniten,* vol 1: 1526 bis 1772 (Weierhof [Pfalz]: Mennonitischer Geschichtsverein e.V., 1978), esp. bibliography; Erich L. Ratzlaff, *Im Weichselbogen* (Winnipeg: "Christian Press," 1971); Abe J. Unruh, *The Helpless Poles* (Grabill, Ind.: Courier Printing Company, 1973). *Russia:* D. H. Epp, *Die Chortitzer Mennoniten* (Odessa: Selbstverlag, 1889); Franz Isaac, *Die Molotschnaer Mennoniten* (Halbstadt: H. J. Braun, 1908); J. J. Dyck, *Am Trakt* (North Kildonen, Man.: Echo Verlag, 1948); P. M. Friesen, *Brüderschaft* (1911); F. H. Epp, *Mennonites in Canada I*; John B. Toews, *Czars, Soviets and Mennonites* (Newton, 1982); William Schroeder, *The Bergthal Colony* (Winnipeg: CMBC Publications, 1974). *Canada and the United States:* Leland Harder and Marvin Harder, *Plockhoy from Zurik-zee* (Newton, 1952); C. Henry Smith, *The Coming of the Russian Mennonites* (Berne, Ind.: Mennonite Book Concern, 1927); Cornelius J. Dyck, ed., *An Introduction to Mennonite History* (Scottdale, 1981); Richard K. MacMaster and others, eds., *Conscience in Crisis* (Scottdale, 1979); MEA I; John L. Ruth, *Maintaining the Right Fellowship* (Scottdale, 1984). *Latin America:* J. Winfield Fretz, *Pilgrims in Paraguay* (Scottdale, 1953); idem, *Mennonite Colonization in Mexico* (Akron, Pa.: MCC, 1945); Annemarie E. Krause, "Mennonite Settlement in the Paraguayan Chaco," (PhD thesis, U. of Chicago, 1952); Martin W. Friesen, *Kanadische Mennoniten bezwingen eine Wildnis: 50 Jahre Kolonie Menno, 1927-1977* (Menno Colony: Verwaltung der Kolonie Menno, 1977); idem, *Neue Heimat in die Chaco Wildnis* (Altona, Man.: D. W. Friesen, 1986); Walter Regehr, *25 Jahre Kolonie Neuland Chaco Paraguay (1947-1972)* (Karlsruhe: Heinrich Schneider, 1972); idem, *Die lebensräumliche Situation der Indianer im paraguayischen Chaco* (Basel: Wepf, 1979); Calvin Redekop, *Strangers Become Neighbors* (Scottdale, 1980); Leonard Doell, *The Bergthaler Mennonite Church of Saskatchewan* (Winnipeg: CMBC Publications, 1987); G. S. Koop, *Pionier Jahre in British Honduras (Belize)* (Belize City: National Printers, n.d.); Calvin W. Redekop, *The Old Colony Mennonites* (Baltimore: Johns Hopkins Press, 1969); H. Leonard Sawatzky, *They Sought a Country: Mennonite Colonization in Mexico* (Berkeley: U. of California Press, 1971), cf. *Sie suchten eine Heimat* (Marburg: Elwert, 1986).

Courage and Conviction:
Verena Sprunger Lehman

Courage and determination, resourcefulness and ingenuity, conviction and dedication—these were the qualities which distinguished Verena Sprunger Lehman.

Verena was born November 2, 1828, into the devout Mennonite home of Abraham Sprunger in the Jura Mountains of Switzerland, an area where Mennonites had taken refuge. Their life was difficult because of unjust discrimination against Mennonites. When Verena was 15 her mother died, and, being the oldest daughter, Verena kept the household together.

At age 18 she was married to Peter S. Lehman, a young schoolteacher. He was chosen by lot for the ministry in July 1848. Four years later Father Abraham Sprunger, with his entire family, including Verena and Peter and their two little girls, migrated to America, coming to Adams County, Indiana. A congregation was formed with Peter S. Lehman as minister.

Peter Lehman has written, "Indiana was so wild—one has to see to believe it. . . . There were two tiny log cabins, very poor. One would have pitied chickens if they did not have a warmer house in the winter. I said we could not live long in such a hut, that I would soon make a better one—but we were in this house for several years." Two serious illnesses kept Peter from building a new cabin during the first two years. Later he suffered from a broken leg. With courage and determination Verena took over when her husband was laid up, doing a man's work as well as a mother's, and also being nurse to her husband. He wrote, "What a life in that miserable little hut. And what a winter for my dear wife caring for me night and day with the children. And on top of that she gave birth to little Rachel on November 10, 1853." Verena herself made a small crib from leftover handhewn shingles the day before the baby was born.

The growing family needed food. When the resourceful Verena found a deer caught in a thicket she killed it for meat. That provided many meals for the family. She walked 10 miles to a cane mill for a gallon of molasses. She was an excellent gardener, and, along with her vegetables, she also raised many herbs and teas to "doctor" her family when there was illness.

Conviction—Verena had that too. At a later time when almost every family had a wine barrel, she pounded a nail in the keg of wine in their own home. Not until the wine had seeped out did she tell her husband that the keg leaked. That took a lot of spunk!

Because of problems in the church the Lehman family moved to Missouri in 1868 to begin a new Mennonite church there. Once again they were pioneers, facing many of the same hardships which had marked their early experience in Indiana. By this time there were seven children. The two oldest had married and little Emma was only three months old. All of them, plus other relatives and friends, made the move. Verena gave birth to one more daughter in Missouri and became a grandmother many times.

For a while the church seemed to thrive. The Lehman family drew many English families to their home. The Lehman children were taught to sing harmony and many came to hear them sing. Verena was gifted in music and did some arranging. When their one son, Japhet, returned to Berne, Indiana, one of the girls learned to sing tenor. Much later, in 1913 at Verena's funeral, 40 of her grandchildren sang a hymn she had arranged.

The colony at Elkton, Missouri, did not thrive despite much hard work. There were crop failures due to severe drought and insect infestation. One after another the families moved away, many back to the Berne area. At last in 1893, Peter and Verena had no choice but to return to Berne. They purchased a home in town and retired there. Peter died suddenly in February 1899, following a severe stroke. Verena had never fully adjusted to retirement in town, and, after Peter's death, she moved to the country with one of her daughter's families—the Peter Gilliom family. Here she busied herself raising houseplants, reading the Bible or Spurgeon's sermons, and knitting socks for the Indian mission in Oklahoma. She knitted as many as 30 or 40 pairs a year, always bright red. She was sure the Indians liked that color best.

She suffered a broken hip, which was not set properly, and a special chair was made for her at home. But she attended every communion service in the church despite the pain caused by the church pews. Her commitment and dedication to Christ were evident.

After her death in 1913 one red sock was found in her knitting basket, its mate never having been completed. The sock was placed on display in the historical room at First Mennonite Church in Berne, a reminder of the indomitable spirit of Verena Sprunger Lehman.   NEL

Based on a chapter by Naomi Lehman in Ruth Unrau, *Encircled*, copyright 1986 by Faith and Life Press, Newton, Kansas, pp. 9-14. Used by permission.

Fundamentalism. The interpretation of American Fundamentalism has undergone considerable development during the past 20 years. A previous generation of scholarship understood it both theologically and culturally as a movement in the backwaters of American society that sought to deny the advances of modern culture in general and of science in particular. Academic interpreters recognized that it had something to do with religious faith but suggested it also reflected the sociological alterations in a society undergoing industrial and urban transformations. In the eyes of these historians the Fundamentalists were viewed primarily as opponents of °modernity who left their mark on denominational machinery of many Protestant bodies. Religiously, in this view, Fundamentalists expressed resistance to scientifically informed thought. Politically they expressed attitudes of alienation and distrust. Psychologically they tended toward authoritarianism and anti-intellectualism.

Historians in more recent analyses have suggested that these cultural explanations of Fundamentalism were caricatures of something that was also theological and stood in a legitimate intellectual and theological tradition. The work of Ernest Sandeen, *The Roots of Fundamentalism*, provided a corrective by noting the Fundamentalist rootage in 19th-c. theology, particularly a millenarian tradition and Princeton [Seminary] theology. He provided a theological definition of Fundamentalism by describing it as an alliance between °dispensational premillennialism and a doctrine of inspiration that guaranteed an °inerrant Scripture. This interpretation of Fundamentalism suggested not so much anti-intellectualism but rather intellectualism of a different sort.

The most recent scholarship, specifically the work of George Marsden, *Fundamentalism and American Culture* renders a much more complex interpretation that recognizes Fundamentalism as a variegated phenomenon that embraced many strands of the American religious past. It represented the confluence of lingering forms of 19th-c. °revivalism, °Pietism, °Evangelicalism, Presbyterian theology that was congealing at Princeton Seminary, historic Methodism as influenced by the °holiness movement and Pentecostalism, new millenarian interpretations, Common Sense or Baconian science, and many forms of denominational conservatism.

For Marsden the story of Fundamentalism centers on how people of diverse strands who commonly thought of themselves as evangelical Christians were influenced by and responded to the religious and intellectual crisis of the late 19th and early 20th c. These evangelicals were the heirs of the respectable Christians who had hoped to fashion a Christian society. They sensed that the culture in which they were located was clearly turning away from its religious past and from the shared assumptions that they and other Americans had long sustained.

The evangelical assumptions were fast corroding under the impact of modernity. Modernism comprised both a new theology and the cultural changes which that theology endorsed. It was the banning of God from the creation of the universe and thereby implicitly from his continuing role in the world, together with the social and cultural changes sustaining this new scientism. Fundamentalism was the militant opposition to modernism in both forms. These changes threatened the Puritan and early 19th-c. evangelical ideal of building a Christian civilization. The Fundamentalists alternatively wished to redeem America and restore the ideal or to abandon the social order even to the point of withdrawing from it. For Marsden it was a movement of both cultural and theological opposition to the drift of North American culture.

The Marsden interpretation suggests that while Fundamentalism was certainly a defense of the faith, it was also part of the larger search for the relationship between culture and Christianity within the American context. The agonizing reappraisal required by both the cultural and theological changes produced theological and cultural Fundamentalism.

For Mennonites Fundamentalism was also a way to reassess cultural and theological issues. The dialogue that Mennonite Fundamentalists engaged in paralleled the national discussion in various ways but was also modulated by historic Mennonite distinctives and concerns. With the exception of John °°Horsch, the Mennonite Church (MC) writer and historian, Mennonites were not participants in the larger Fundamentalist movement. Yet they were participants in their own way in both forms of Fundamental-ism—theological and cultural. The precise mixture of the two forms varied among Mennonite groups, depending upon the history of the particular group.

Mennonite scholarship of the 1970s and 1980s has suggested three conceptual frameworks for understanding Mennonite Fundamentalism. They reflect the impact of Sandeen and Marsden. The first interpretation assumes that ever since the mid-19th c. for General Conference Mennonites (GCM) and since the late 19th c. for Mennonite Church (MC) and Mennonite Brethren Mennonites the various groups had been in a process of developing the characteristics of American °denominationalism. Denominations are defined in various ways, but common to most definitions are the creation of purposive activities and a clearly articulated theology. The purposive activities are new forms of work and activity by which the group coheres and extends itself into the larger world (°evangelism, °mission, schools and other °institutions). The creation of an articulated theology is the necessary second stage in the creating of an identifiable denomination in the mosaic of American denominations. Theological Fundamentalism was part of the larger search for the distinctives of Mennonite theology. The American Fundamentalist movement coincided with this second stage of the denominationalizing process. Amidst the dividing of theology into two mutually exclusive and even hostile camps, Mennonites also had to define and distinguish a theology. In so doing, it was easy to borrow American formulations. The Mennonite Church (MC) adoption of the Eighteen Fundamentals at the 1921 general conference, as one example of this borrowing and systematizing, should be understood as part of the larger pattern of becoming a denomination in the American tradition.

The second framework suggests that the Mennonites who seem to be Fundamentalist were frequently denominational conservatives. Many of them distanced themselves from the highly structured and tightly guarded system of the Fundamentalist crusaders. Ambivalence about dispensational premillennialism characterized the major Mennonite groups. A softening of the constricted language of inspiration and the creedal quality of the "Fundamentalists" placed them in an older tradition of theological orthodoxy. They were the traditionalists who wished to conserve the distinctive traditions of the various Mennonite denominations. They meant to insure that the new issues of scriptural authority or millenarianism, did not overwhelm the older corpus of belief. These Mennonite conservatives frequently thought of themselves as more fundamental than the Fundamentalists in that they sought to preserve and even revitalize such historic fundamentals as °°nonconformity and °°nonresistance as well as the new issues in the "Fundamentalist party" agenda.

The third perspective suggests that Mennonite Church (MC) Fundamentalism was a response to the awakening or quickening (°renaissance) which had significantly transformed Mennonites' relationship to the larger world (°acculturation; °language problem); that General Conference Mennonite Church Fundamentalism was an initial way of responding to the cultural transition accompanying World War I and the subsequent adaptation of a substantially Germanic population to the psychic requirements of Americanization; and that Mennonite Brethren Fundamentalism emerged also with the transition from a largely closed Germanic culture and language to more open participation in American society. The awakening for the Mennonite Church (MC) and the cultural transitions for the Mennonite Brethren and General Conference Mennonite Church brought greater interaction with the larger Protestant and national culture. Among those who wandered more freely in these circles a few brought back hints of theological modernism. More brought back a refusal to utilize the categories of the strict Fundamentalists, and in a world of simple dichotomies they seemed to be °liberals. Even more brought back forms of cultural modernism: new fashions, new modes of conversation, new aspirations, new forms of church worship services, new educational degrees.

Fundamentalism came to differing parts of the North American Mennonite world at different times. But for all it was a way of responding to the groups' changed relationship to the dominant culture. Fundamentalism among Mennonites was as much an effort to redefine the relationship between culture and Christianity as a crusade to root out theological modernism. It was significantly a cultural movement because the theological modernism in the Mennonite world was only incipient and marginal. Cultural Fundamentalism was a way to codify doctrine, reassert churchly °authority and redefine cultural boundaries. More rigid forms of authority and order are antidotes to rapid social change.

As the Mennonite boundaries became more permeable, as the cultural shifts were navigated, and as newer theological formulations, largely rooted in the rediscovery of the historic tradition, emerged, the need for Fundamentalism diminished. Theologically Fundamentalism in the major Mennonite denominational bodies may be thought of as a transitional theology between an inherited 19th-c. theology, less doctrinal and precisely formulated, and the emergence of a theological biblicism rooted in a rediscovered Anabaptist hermeneutical tradition. After an initial stage in more formal theologizing when Fundamentalist categories seemed appropriate, they became increasingly less central to Mennonite theological reflection.   PT

George R. Marsden, *Fundamentalism and American Culture: The Shaping of Twentieth-Century Evangelicalism, 1870-1825* (New York: Oxford U. Press, 1980); Ernest R. Sandeen, *The Roots of Fundamentalism* (Chicago: U. of Chicago Press, 1970); Theron Schlabach, *Gospel Versus Gospel: Mission and the Mennonite Church, 1863-1944* (Scottdale, 1980); Rodney J. Sawatsky, "The Influence of Fundamentalism on American Nonresistance, 1908-1944" (MA thesis, U. of Minnesota, 1973); Guy F. Hershberger, "Comments on Sawatsky's Thesis, 'The Influence of Fundamentalism on Mennonite Nonresistance, 1908-1944,' " Guy F. Hershberger papers, MC Archives (Goshen); Rodney J. Sawatsky, "History and Ideology: American Mennonite Identity Definition Through History" (PhD diss., Princeton U., 1977); Beulah Hostetler, "Leadership Patterns and Fundamentalism in Franconia Mennonite Conference, 1890-1950," *PMH,* 5 (1982), 2-9; idem, *American Mennonites and Protestant Movements* (Scottdale, 1987); C. Norman Kraus, "American Mennonites and the Bible, 1750-1950," *MQR,* 41 (1967), 309-29; James

C. Juhnke, *Vision, Doctrine, War: Mennonite Identity and Organization in America, 1890-1930,* MEA 3 (Scottdale, 1989); Paul Toews, "Fundamentalist Conflict in Mennonite Colleges: A Response to Cultural Transitions?" *MQR,* 57 (1983), 241-56; Kauffman/Harder, *Anabaptists Four C. Later* (1975), index; Stan Nussbaum, *You Must Be Born Again* (Ft. Wayne: EMCh, 1980), 37-39.

See also Church Membership; Social Gospel.

Funerals (ME II:419). Sixteenth-century martyrdom scenes and moments of courageous witnessing to the faith in the presence of °death, may be said to be the first Anabaptist-Mennonite funerals. Narratives and songs have memorialized these events in the *Martyrs Mirror,* the °°*Ausbund,* and Mennonite hymnals. Mennonite funerals of later centuries, until the 19th c., are recalled only anecdotally, however °singing, rejoicing, and witnessing to the faith, in the home and at the cemetery, remained central features.

In the Dutch-Prussian-Russian Mennonite tradition, singing, meditations, and eulogizing the deceased were the core elements of the service. Special memorial songs for the deceased carried over into the *Grabschrift,* lengthy verses on the tombstones, a tradition continued on some North American gravestones. Services by congregation members and friends at the home and cemetery services appear to have been the most common features of Mennonite funerals in the European setting.

These funerary customs persisted in the North American setting, but took on Victorian trimmings. In a late 19th-c. Mennonite hymnal (°°*Gesangbuch mit Noten*), the section "Of Final Things" contained 74 hymns, many, in keeping with Victorian perspectives in British and American culture, glorifying death as a victory over this sinful life, and gilding the rewards of the afterlife.

The commercialization of the funeral, the sale of the coffin, and the practice of embalming the body, and all this under the direction of the professional mortician, have transformed Mennonite funeral customs in North America in the 20th c. Embalming, which was not practiced by Mennonites and most Western Europeans until the 20th c., reflected a growing this-worldliness. Embalming was later accompanied by the use of air-tight vaults, ostensibly to prevent decomposition of the body. With the exception of the Amish and Old Order Mennonites, who continued to practice plain funerals in the home and cemetery to the degree permitted by government health regulations, other Mennonites moved to the mortician-organized funeral, held in the mortician's chapel, the church, and the cemetery. This emphasis on the physical preservation and display of the deceased brought costs per funeral into the thousands of dollars, and made the funeral business very lucrative. By the mid-1970s, however, a reaction had set in against the alienation of death from the family and congregation. In some circles, there was a reemphasis on plain values: home-made coffins, services in the home or in church, memorial services, and a deemphasis on the material body in favor of the spiritual eternity of the believer.

Non-Western Mennonite funeral practices reflect an emphasis on the believers and family gathered for singing, pastoral meditations, and common grieving and rejoicing in faith. In India, Mennonites hold short funeral services in the home and the church. In the absence of undertakers and embalming, family and friends handle all aspects of the funeral. At the graveside service, each individual puts three handfuls of dirt onto the coffin before it is covered. In rural circles, there is sometimes a tendency for the cemetery portion of the funeral to be attended mostly by men, reminiscent of Hindu cremation, which is handled exclusively by men. In Central Africa, the all-night wake at the homes of the deceased's family, an important part of indigenous funerals, is also held by Mennonite and other Christians of the southern savanna (e.g., Zaire). However, the mourning and wailing that accompanies these funerals is replaced, in the Christian community, by hymn singing and pastoral meditations. Food is often brought by friends and church members.

In Indonesia, differing funerary patterns reflect the distinction between United Muria Synod (Persatuan Gereja-Gereja Kristen Muria) and the Javanese conference (Gereja Injili di Tanah Jawa). In the Muria Synod, after a short service with church members praying for the steadfastness of the family's faith, the deceased's body is washed and clothed (not embalmed), and kept in the hospital or home awaiting the final rites. When the family has gathered, often several days later, a service is again held preparatory to the procession to the cemetery. In families with strong adherence to Chinese custom, generational rank may be marked by the wearing of differing colored bands over white clothing. At the cemetery a more evangelical service is held, to witness to Muslims and Confucians present the Christian attitude toward death, before the coffin is let down and "dust is returned to dust" (Eccl 3:20). In the Javanese setting, °burial follows quickly after death, with a prayer meeting at the home of the deceased to offer courage to the family. Grieving and commemoration continues. The third day after burial there is a gathering at the home for prayer. Again, at intervals of 40, 100, and 1,000 days after the death, similar commemorative gatherings are held, reminiscent of the Javanese Slametan festival for this purpose.   JMJ

Descriptions of practices in India, Africa and Indonesia are based on information supplied by Lubin Jantzen, Fremont Regier, and Mesach Krisetiya.

Funk, Annie C. See Travel ("I Have No Fear" [feature]).

Furniture and Woodworking. Ever since the "discovery" of early American °folk and decorative arts in the 1920s, connoisseurs and historians of American decorative arts have placed a high value on furniture made by some Mennonite and Amish craftsmen. The distinctiveness of such furniture, however, usually lies in the decoration applied to it rather than in actual design and construction. Although Jan Gleysteen, for instance, suggests that the decorative designs originated in the Swiss homeland of the Mennonites, they probably result from more diffused origins and influences in Europe and America.

Colonial Swiss Mennonites are closely associated

with 22 surviving pieces of unpainted walnut furniture decorated with a distinctive sulphur inlay technique. Two of the most outstanding pieces are wardrobes made for Mennonite families in Lancaster Co., Pa. The one made for George Huber in 1779 is now in the Philadelphia Museum of Art; the one made in 1768 for Emmanuel (1745-1828) and Mary Herr is in the Winterthur Museum, near Wilmington, Del. The Huber piece, one of the finest pieces of furniture made in colonial America, is attributed to George's brother Christian (1758-1820) and Peter Holl III (d. 1825).

The sulphur inlay furniture is constructed in the heavy Swiss-German manner and the decorations—crowns, tulips, stars, urns, birds—are related to designs used at the °°Ephrata Cloisters. Such designs were sometimes applied to textiles, handkerchief borders, and ecclesiastical linens. Although the sulphur inlay technique may have been brought from Switzerland, it was more likely developed in Pennsylvania.

Johannes Spitler (1774-1837) of Shenandoah Co., Va., may have been a Mennonite from the community settled ca. 1733 by 51 Swiss and German pioneers from Lancaster Co., Pa. Spitler is famous for his softwood blanket chests and tall case clocks decorated boldly in white, red, and black designs on a blue ground. A tall case °clock made by him in 1800 is owned by the Abby Aldrich Rockefeller Folk Art Collection in Colonial Williamsburg, Va.

Spitler used geometric patterns and simple compass work as well as flowers, birds, and other representational motifs. Some designs are remarkably similar to the °*Fraktur* designs of Jacob Strickler (1770-1842), for whom Spitler also made and decorated a tall case clock in 1801. When that clock was sold for $203,500 at Sotheby's in New York in 1986, it established a record price for American folk-painted furniture. Strickler, a Mennonite preacher in Shenandoah Co., was Spitler's neighbor and relative by marriage. Spitler later moved to Fairfield Co., Ohio, where he died.

Christian Seltzer (1749-1831), a Mennonite, began the "Jonestown school" of decorated furniture in Lebanon Co., Pa. Others working with him include his son, John (1774-1845), and Lutheran brothers, Johannes Ranck (1763-1828) and Peter Ranck (1765-1851). They are known for their painted blanket chests, usually decorated with three panels depicting flowers in urns. A chest by Christian is to be found in the Smithsonian Institution, Washington, D.C.; one by John, in the Metropolitan Museum of Art, New York City.

Another distinctive school of Amish-Mennonite furniture developed in Somerset Co., Pa., in the little town of Soap Hollow (*Schmier Seife Durch*) in Conemaugh Twp. near Johnstown. The outstanding furniture-makers and decorators there were Jeremiah H. Stahl (1830-1907), Peter K. Thomas (1838-1907), Christian C. Blauch (1828-99), and Tobias Livingston (ca. 1822-91). Others include Joseph Sala (1848-1912) and John M. Sala (1852-1932), the sons of John Sala, Sr. (1819-82); and perhaps John Hershberger and a Reininger. Thomas and Stahl moved to Kent Co., Mich., in 1868 and 1880 respectively, and continued their craft there. Near Meyersdale, also in Somerset Co., worked Jacob Ganaegi (1796-1883), who made 1,123 bedsteads (according to family records) and also furniture resembling Soap Hollow work. He was succeeded by his son Elias (1832-1906). Soap Hollow furniture is often painted red with black and gold trim. Some pieces—especially those by Stahl—have a yellow ground and tan, brown, and bright green decoration. Designs, dates, and initials are usually stencilled. They are generally not applied free-hand.

Henry Lapp (1862-1904), an Amish joiner from Leacock Twp. in Lancaster Co., is noted for his painted furniture and household accessories done in an undecorated, plain style (although some of these pieces were painted to resemble wood grain). The coloring of his work is related to Welsh traditions; other aspects of his design derive from Philadelphia influences. His order book, now in the Philadelphia Museum of Art, contains watercolor paintings of the items he offered to his customers. Since Lapp was deaf and virtually mute, the order book may have served to communicate to his customers what he could do. Lapp and his sister Lizzie are also noted for their small watercolor paintings of animals, plants, and other everyday subjects.

John Bachman II (1746-1829), of Lampeter Twp. in Lancaster Co., is a good example of a Mennonite joiner who abandoned Germanic-style furniture for the English styles associated with Philadelphia furniture. He is noted for the "plain" Chippendale pieces he made, largely for Mennonite customers. After 1797 Bachman's son, John III (1775-1849), had established his own furniture-making business in McCartney's Corner, Pequea Twp., Lancaster Co. Jacob Bachman (1782-1849), another son of John II, and Jacob Bachman I (1798-1869), son of John III, were also cabinetmakers.

John Bachman II probably learned his craft from his father, John Bachman I, with whom he emigrated to Lancaster Co. from Switzerland in 1766. Later members of the Bachman family who were also cabinetmakers in Lancaster Co. include Jacob I's son, Christian (1827-1901), and Christian's son, Ellis (1856-1917?). Johan Bear (1745?-1803?) also made Chippendale-style furniture in Lancaster Co.

Between 1775 and 1810 John Bachman II trained 10 apprentices, among whom were Johannes Miller, Johan Rohrer, Valentine Meyer, Jacob Brand, Kitschli Miller, Heinrich Jung, Gottlieb Sener, and Jacob Sener. Although probably not all of these cabinetmakers were Mennonites, many have Mennonite family names. The Philadelphia-style furniture made in Lancaster by the Michael Linds (father and son) and Hans Jurig Burkhart was earlier attributed to John Bachman II.

In the Mennonite diaspora to Ontario and the Midwest, traditional furniture-making was often continued. The Ontario Mennonite tradition has been well surveyed; the Midwest achievement is less well documented.

In Ontario, John Grobb (1800-1885), Jacob Fry, J. H. Housser, Jacob Houser, and Israel Moyer worked in the Niagara Peninsula, but abandoned Germanic for English styles. Waterloo Co. Mennonite furniture retains a strongly Pennsylvania-German character. John Barkey, a Mennonite from Markham (York Co.), made fancifully painted cupboards and chests, ca. 1875. Moses Eby (1799-1854) is noted for a cherry slant-front desk of 1817, using inlaid designs. John Gerber (1809-89) and his son, Christian (1845-1928), were Amish cabinetmakers in Wellesley known for their painted furniture decorated with abstract motifs, ebonizing, and grained effects. As of 1981 Sidney Fry, an Old Order Mennonite of Conestogo, was still making furniture in traditional designs.

Early York Co., Ont., Mennonite furniture blends Germanic and English traditions. Abram Ramer, the first furniture-maker in Markham and eventually a manufacturer of chairs, is noted for his massive Germanic furniture in the Empire style. In the 1850s John and Jacob Barkey produced pine country furniture that sometimes incorporates a carved shell design or grain painting that suggests inlaid wood. Simon Reesor (1829-1909) made smaller, simpler furniture in Sheraton styles. The York Co. tradition ended with Samuel Burkholder, nephew of the Barkeys, who made Victorian-style furniture.

In Ohio, Moses K. Troyer (1838-1923) and David Hershberger (1813-87), both Amish Mennonites, made grained and decorated furniture in Holmes Co. Near Archbold, Jacob Werrey (1838-93), Mennonite, made painted and decorated furniture in the Germanic style, mainly blanket chests, one of which is in the Columbus, Ohio, Museum of Art.

Indiana furniture-makers in the Germanic tradition include Samuel M. Miller (1870-1943) of Lagrange Co., Ind., who made painted furniture in the style of Somerset Co., Pa., where many of the Amish in northern Indiana originated. M. H. Hochstetler made similar furniture ca. 1900 near Nappanee. Both were Amish. Old Order Mennonite John Weaver (1821-1907) of the Yellow Creek area made elaborately inlaid furniture after he retired from farming. One blanket chest used 11,800 pieces of inlay.

Little has been written about western American Mennonite furniture. However, Gerhard Esau (b. 1876), who learned cabinet-making from his father in Russia and emigrated to Beatrice, Nebr., in 1907, is noted for intricate inlaid tables, sometimes requiring as many as 8,500 separate pieces of wood. Also, museums and art historians have been attracted to European folk furniture forms that survive among western Mennonites, particularly the Hutterites and Russian Mennonites. Among them are the *Kiste*, or massive storage chest, and the *Schlafbank*, or sleeping bench. The latter is a kind of wooden sofa, usually painted, grained, or carved, and sometimes providing storage space as well as a place to rest.

Some (Old) Mennonites (MC) are known for the smaller household accessories—sugar buckets, saltboxes, eggcups, saffron boxes, etc.—that they made and decorated in a colorful, Germanic style. Chief among them is Joseph Lehn (1798-1892) of near Lititz in Lancaster Co. Another is Samuel Plank (1821-1900) of near Belleville, Pa., who made saltboxes decorated with *Fraktur* motifs.

The making of handcrafted furniture by Mennonites and Amish continues in the 1980s. Small woodworking shops flourish in most Amish communities, although the items produced there differ little from mainstream American designs. However, in some Ohio and Indiana Amish communities one still finds makers of bent hickory rockers in the Adirondack style as well as chair-makers who use older American designs. Among the Mennonites who produce custom-designed furniture in larger woodworking shops is Swartzendruber Hardwood Creations in Goshen, Ind., founded and owned by Larion Swartzendruber.

A few Mennonites now mass-produce furniture for national and international markets. Apparently the largest such manufacturer is Sauder's in Archbold, Ohio, founded by Erie J. Sauder, Mennonite (MC), in 1934. The various Sauder operations produce church and office furniture, as well as occasional furniture for the home. The DeFehr Manufacturing Co. of Winnipeg, Man., makes wooden and upholstered household furniture. It was founded in 1944 by A. A. DeFehr, Mennonite Brethren. Royal Creations of Upland, Cal., founded by Marlin Riegsecker, (Old) Mennonite, makes occasional furniture.

A cluster of furniture companies has arisen in the Swiss Amish Mennonite community of Berne, Ind. They include Dunbar (founded in 1919 by Homer Niederhauser and Aloysius Dunbar), Berne Furniture (founded in 1925 by L. Lawrence Yager) and Smith Brothers of Berne (founded in 1926 by Homer Niederhauser). Berne Furniture and Smith Brothers both manufacture upholstered furniture; Dunbar produces bedroom, dining room, and office furniture.

Although most such furniture conforms to the tastes of the general American consumer, it sometimes attains distinction of design, as for instance with the Body Form Chair produced by Sauder Designaire of Stryker, Ohio, one of which was purchased in 1986 for the permanent collection of the Museum of Modern Art in New York City.   EB

Gary P. Bell, "Joseph Lehn, Woodturner," *Community Historians Annual* (Schaff Library, Lancaster Theological Seminary), no. 6 (Dec. 1967), 28-50; Michael Bird and Terry Kobayashi, *A Splendid Harvest: Germanic Folk and Decorative Arts in Canada* (Toronto: Van Nostrand Reinhold, 1981); Samuel E. Dyke, "The Bachman Family of Cabinetmakers, 1766-1897," *Journal of the Lancaster County Historical Society*, 59 (1966), 168-80; Monroe H. Fabian, *The Pennsylvania German Decorated Chest* (New York: Universe, 1978); idem, "Sulfur Inlay in Pennsylvania German Furniture," *Pennsylvania Folklife*, 27, no. 1 (Fall 1977), 2-9; Beatrice Garvan and Charles F. Hummel, *The Pennsylvania Germans: A Celebration of Their Arts 1683-1850* (Philadelphia: Philadelphia Museum of Art, 1982); "Gerhard Esau, Artist in Wood," *Menn. Life*, 4, no. 1 (Jan. 1949), 12-13; Jan Gleysteen, "The European Roots of Pennsylvania Dutch Art," *FQ* (Nov.-Jan. 1980-81), 33; Stanley A. Kaufman and Ricky Clark, *Germanic Folk Culture in Eastern Ohio* (Walnut Creek, Ohio: German Culture Museum, 1986); Henry Lapp, *A Craftsman's Handbook*, introduction and notes by Beatrice Garvan (Philadelphia: Tindicum Press, 1975); Lynda Musson Nykor and P. D. Musson, *The Ontario Tradition in York County: Mennonite Furniture* (Toronto: James Lorimer, 1977); Benno M. Forman, "German Influences in Pennsylvania Furniture," in *Arts of the Pennsylvania Germans*, ed. Scott T. Swank and others (New York: Norton, 1983), 102-70; John J. Snyder, Jr., "The Bachman Attributions: A Reconsideration," *Antiques* (May 1974), 1056-65; idem, "New Discoveries in Documented Lancaster County Chippendale Furniture," *Antiques* (May 1984), 1150-55; Harley N. Trice, "Decorated Furniture of Soap Hollow, Somerset County, Pennsylvania," *Antiques*, 123 (May 1983), 1036-39; Donald R. Walters, "Johannes Spitler, Shenandoah County, Virginia, Furniture Decorator," *Antiques*, 108 (Oct. 1975), 730-35.

G

Gandhi, Mohandas Karamchand (Oct. 2, 1869-Jan. 30, 1948), was a social reformer and political leader of India who led his compatriots in "nonviolent resistance" to secure for India independent statehood from the British Empire. Professionally trained as a barrister in England, he began his career in South Africa (1893-1914) where he encountered the grim realities of racial injustice. Here the spirit of the reformer was awakened and the foundations of his philosophy of nonviolent resistance were formulated. The term *Satyagraha* emerged as the term to describe and identify the essence of the movement. Two words, *satya* (truth) and *graha* (grasp) were joined to form *Satyagraha* meaning "holding on to truth." Motivated by the conviction that "truth" was on the side of the Indian claim for self-rule (*Swaraj*) he returned to India and allied himself with the independence movement. The "War without Violence" that ensued included active resistance and culminated in independent statehood by 1946. Three basic principles—"truth," "nonviolence," and "self-suffering"—were to give direction to the forms of resistance and their implementation as the movement progressed. In his work, *War without Violence*, K. Shridharani classified the forms of resistance and graded them according to the level of coercion involved. These were identified as follows: "negotiation and arbitration," "agitation," "demonstration and ultimatum," "self-purification," "strike and general strike," "sit-down strike," "economic boycott," "civil disobedience," "assertive satyagraha," "parallel government," "fasting," and "national defense." Procedurally it was the intent to clarify the facts of a given situation of injustice, whether in personal, labor and management, or political situations, and then to employ whatever nonviolent forms of action seemed appropriate. To reduce the hatred and malice that otherwise might infect the negotiation process, fasting and self-imposed halting of action were instituted.

Mennonites in the search for alternatives to war and other forms of resistance to injustice have examined the Gandhian alternatives. Frequent references in Mennonite writings refer to and make comparison between "nonresistance" and "nonviolent resistance" or *Satyagraha*. Mennonite responses range all the way from rejection of the Gandhian forms of nonviolent resistance to at least some selective application in social and political situations. In *War, Peace and Nonresistance* Hershberger asserted "that non-resistant Christians cannot take part in a political °revolution for the overthrow of the government in power. But political revolution was Gandhi's primary objective. Gandhi's program was not one of nonresistance or peace. It was a new form of warfare" (pp 191-92). At the other end of the continuum would be the position expressed in the present writer's unpublished dissertation, "Some of the forms of *Satyagraha* which could conceivably be conducted in a manner consistent with the love-ethic are negotiations, arbitration, agitation, demonstration, strike, economic boycott, nonpayment of taxes, and noncooperation. Violence may enter into any one of these, but violence may enter into complete withdrawal in the form of hate. These modes of social action would represent love insofar as they retained emotional and physical discipline and were performed in the interest of a suffering minority (other than the one conducting the action), or in the interest of a principle of justice." (Groff, 212-13). As historically observed and documented the Gandhian movement did become violent and destructive at times. The course which he took by way of corrective was the self-purificatory fast and the cessation of *Satyagraha* activity. Inherent in both the principle of nonresistance and *Satyagraha* are self-regulatory criteria which test the rightness of the cause and the action employed. "*Satyagraha* is a principle of social action informing and controlling the conduct of social conflict, in which the end and the means thereto are consistent with the requirements of truth, nonviolence, and self-suffering. *Nonresistance* is the literal application to all relationships in society of the love-ethic of the New Testament. This is held to be the ethic of the spiritual kingdom to which the Christian owes prior loyalty. This loyalty in turn justifies abstention from those social and civil duties with which one cannot conscientiously comply; especially those that are not consistent with the divine moral law. The positive expression of the love-ethic (agape) is to 'overcome evil with good'." (ibid., 209).

Though Gandhi was known more popularly because of his involvement with the independence movement, his energies were also devoted to education and to economic and social betterment for the poor, especially the "outcastes," of India. He gave these persons the dignity of the name *Harijan* meaning children of God. This broader program of social service and experimentation came under the umbrella term *Sarvodaya* (welfare of all). Within this program was a scheme of basic education aimed at improving conditions for the masses of Indian people who lived in villages; particularly as it would enable them to be more self-sufficient by producing their own cloth, soap, etc.

Following independence and the partition of India and Pakistan, riots created turmoil and heavy loss of life for both Hindus and Muslims. Gandhi invested himself in an exhausting series of efforts to bring about reconciliation but was killed by an assassin's bullet.

In 1983 a highly-acclaimed commercial film, *Gandhi,* produced in Great Britain and directed by Richard Attenborough, brought the story of Gandhi to the attention of a later generation.   WWG

Weyburn W. Groff, "Nonviolence: A Comparative Study of Mohandas K. Gandhi and the Mennonite Church on the Subject of Nonviolence" (PhD diss., New York U., 1963); Guy F. Hershberger, *War, Peace and Nonresistance* (Scottdale, 1953); Ralph C. Kauffman, "Satyagraha and Christian Pacifism," *Mennonite* (Feb. 21, 1946), 3-6; Bal. R. Nanda, *Mahatma Gandhi* (Boston: Beacon Press, 1958); Krishnalal J. Shridharani, *War Without Violence* (New York: Harcourt, Brace and Company, 1939); Juhnke, *Mission* (1979), 43, 103, 165; John A. Lapp, *India* (1972), 82-83, 88-93; Griselda Gehman Shelly, "A Letter from Mahatma Gandhi," *Menn. Life,* 38 (June 1983), 25-27; *Menn. Life,* 25 (Oct. 1970), 155-59.

See also Nationalism.

Garber, Henry F. (1888-1968) was born in Lancaster Co., Pa., to Simon and Fannie Eby Garber. He graduated from Maytown High School and Millersville Normal School (1907). He was baptized at the Bossler Mennonite Church in 1907 and taught school for four years. After traveling through western United States he married Ada Nissley in 1913 and took up farming (he was recognized as a Pennsylvania "master farmer" in 1928). In 1932 he was ordained as minister at Mount Joy Mennonite Church, Pa., where he served for 36 years. Beginning in 1921 he served for 47 years as member of Eastern Mennonite Board of Missions and Charities (EMBMC). He served in various offices of EMBMC for short terms: as assistant treasurer (1927); treasurer and field worker (1932); and fifth member of the executive committee (1933). In 1934 he was elected president of EMBMC and served in this capacity for 22 years. In 1937 he became a member of Mennonite Central Committee executive board. In 1938 he visited the mission work in Tanganyika (Tanzania) begun by EMBMC in 1933. As a result of his trip to Central America in 1948 to investigate mission possibilities, work was begun in Honduras. After 1956 he served 12 years as an honorary member of the executive committee of EMBMC. His three children Catherine, Lois, and Robert served overseas as missionaries under EMBMC. Henry was buried at Kraybill Mennonite Cemetery.   HRC/RSa

Gardia, Surenda (b. Mar. 10, 1933), was born in a Christian home and was baptized as a third-generation Christian in his home village of Itchapur, India, in 1950. He earned an Intermediate in Arts degree; a diploma in teaching; BA and MA degrees in English Literature; a BEd degree; and a certifcate in Effective Modern Educational Administration.

He has been a teacher and administrator at Janzen Memorial Higher Secondary School, Jagdeeshpur (1950-62), the mission primary-middle-high school (headmaster, 1962-77), Beacon English School (principal, 1977-), all located in Korba. Although he has not married, he has taken in many of his relatives' sons and provided them with a Christian home environment and education. He has served the church in many different capacities including Secretary of the Bharatiya General Conference Mennonite Church. Many of the students of the Beacon English School have obtained highest honors in the All India

Higher Secondary examinations under Surendra's leadership. The school has (1987) four branch schools and a total enrollment of more than 2,000 students.   HR/RR

Garifuna People. See Belize Evangelical Mennonite Church; New York (state).

Garjan Bai (ca. 1889 - Nov. 9, 1918) was born to a humble Teli (oil-crusher caste) Hindu family, about 10 mi. (16 km.) from °Dhamtari, Madhya Pradesh (M.P.), India. She was brought by her uncle to the Mennonite mission orphanage in Dhamtari on Feb. 1, 1900, emaciated, covered with sores, and near death. The other members of her family died in the famine of 1900.

Garjan Bai's unusual gifts in leadership and spiritual maturity were recognized early. She was a persistent student and was recognized by both missionaries and fellow residents of the orphanage as a true spiritual leader. She had a very deep personal devotional life, and delighted to share Christ with all about her.

After she completed the 6th class in school in 1905, the American Mennonite Mission sponsored her for teacher training in the Female Normal School in Jabalpur, M.P. In 1907 she was appointed to teach in the mission girls school in Dhamtari. In 1910, while continuing some teaching, she became matron of the orphanage where she continued until her death. Her name means "thunder," or "thunderclap," hardly appropriate for a tiny baby girl, yet prophetically accurate for the brief life of one reclaimed from death's door and brought into the marvelous transforming light of the Gospel. Her Spirit-filled life touched all around her and remained a model for Christian discipleship for years after her death. The Garjan Memorial Middle School, Balodgahan, M.P., is named in her honor. JAF

American Mennonite (MC) Mission, Dhamtari, *Building on the Rock* (Scottdale: MPH, 1924, 1926), 79, 82; Annual Reports of American Mennonite Mission, 2nd (Apr.1-Dec. 31, 1901), pp. 4-5, and 5th, p. 11; M. C. Lehman, *Our Mission in India* (Scottdale: MPH, 1939), 39-40; James N. Kaufman, *Walks and Talks in Hindustan* (Goshen: the author, 1963) 138-40.

Geauga-Trumbull Counties, Ohio, Old Order Amish Settlement
(ME II:441) in ne. Ohio has pushed into Ashtabula and Trumbull Cos. since 1960 making this the second largest Amish settlement in Ohio, and the fourth largest in the United States. It was founded in 1886 by settlers moving in from °Holmes Co., Ohio, 80 mi. (130 km.) farther south. Early families found this area to be poor farming land, but through perseverance have built up the soil to make it a productive community. Dairy farming, cheese, and maple syrup have become the primary products of Geauga County farmers. This community has seen an unusual amount of moving in and out by Amish families. It has been the source of Amish moving to many other communities in Pennsylvania, as well as a number of settlements in the Midwest.

A unique problem for the Geauga community has been the encroaching industrial and urban development of the city of Cleveland. There has been a great exodus of city dwellers moving out of the city eastward to the hills of Geauga. Much farmland has been gobbled up for urban development, resulting in high land prices and high taxes. In the 1980s Cleveland Electric sought to enlarge its power lines across Amish farms to bring electricity from a nearby nuclear power plant to stations servicing area industry.

The Geauga settlement is a prime example of the ever growing conflict between rural farming communities and industrial complexes moving to escape the blight of the city. Many Amish farmers now work in factories, some are moving away. Even so, Geauga has 42 church districts (congregations) serving approximately 8,000 people.   SLY

Moses Burkholder and Mattie E. Burkholder, *History of Geauga County and History of the Amish* (n.p x 2, 1961).

Gehman, Ernest G. (Nov. 26, 1901-June 29, 1988), was for 50 years (1938-88) a minister of the gospel in the Northern District of the Virginia Mennonite Conference (MC); taught German and other subjects for 49 years (1924-73) at Eastern Mennonite College, and was associated with the periodical *Sword and Trumpet* for almost 60 years.

Born at Bally, Pa., Gehman was the son of Daniel and Elizabeth (Gehman) Gehman. He studied at Eastern Mennonite School, Goshen College, and took his baccalaureate and MA degrees from Franklin and Marshall College. In 1949 he received his doctorate from Heidelberg U. in Germany. In his teaching career he distinguished himself as a master of German and English composition which became his special fields.

On Mar. 26, 1938, he was ordained to the Christian ministry at Zion Mennonite Church near Broadway, Va. He was pastor of Pleasant Grove Mennonite Church, Fort Seybert, W. Va. (1939-45), and at Morning View Mennonite Church, Singers Glen, Va. (1946-75). He served in various offices and on numerous committees in the Virginia Conference and on the Publication Board of the Mennonite Church (MC).

Always of a conservative turn of mind he was associated with the *Sword and Trumpet* periodical from its beginning in 1929. He was office editor for many years and was a member of its corporate board. In the early years he illustrated the magazine with original gospel cartoons.

He was interested in the preservation of the Pennsylvania German °dialect. He frequently offered classes in the dialect at Eastern Mennonite College and gathered stories, poems, and anecdotes which he preserved in a tape collection.

He was married twice. He and Gertrude Nissley became the parents of three sons and two daughters. After her death, he married Margaret Martin, a fellow teacher at Eastern Mennonite College.   LMW

MWR (July 7, 1988), 7; *Sword and Trumpet,* vol 56, no. 10 (October 1988), and vol. 47, no. 3 (March 1979), 22.

Geiser, Samuel Henri (Dec. 24, 1884-May 28, 1973), was born near Corgémont, Jura. He received his early education in a German-speaking Mennonite school. Until his marriage to Marianne Gyger in 1911 he farmed with his father near Lajoux

(Freiberge). He next joined a farming partnership with others near St. Ursanne, but was able to rent his own farm eventually, located between Tavannes and Tramelan. Three daughters and four sons were born to Marianne and Samuel. Eventually the couple was able to purchase a farm in Châtelat where he was to spend the greater part of his life, and from where he also served as a minister and elder of the Kleintal congregation, one of the largest Mennonite congregations in Switzerland.

In due course Geiser became a self-educated scholar. His interest in church history was originally motivated by the reading of a copy of *Martyrs Mirror* which he found in an old Mennonite home. This interest led to the gathering of historically valuable documents, letters, lectures, Bibles, devotional literature and materials which are no longer available today. There is scarcely an old Anabaptist or Mennonite home in the Jura, Emmental, Basel, or Neuenburgergebiet which he did not search thoroughly for documents and books. The largest part of this collection is housed in the archives of the Conférence Mennonite Suisse/Konferenz der Mennoniten in der Schweiz (Swiss Mennonite Conference) in Jean Gui (Corgémont) and constitutes the core of a truly unique historical library.

It was this library which made possible the writing of his volume *Die Taufgesinnten Gemeinden* (1931), which is indeed the work of a scholar rather than that of a "mountain farmer." In 1971 he published an enlarged and revised edition, which places Anabaptism more into the context of general church history, under the title *Die Taufgesinnten Gemeinden im Rahmen der allgemeinen Kirchengeschichte* He also wrote significant articles for the °°*Mennonitisches Lexikon.* In 1972 the theological school of the University of Zürich conferred an honorary doctorate upon him.

In later years he sold his house in Brügg-Biel, where he spent the final years of his life, to the Swiss Mennonite conference as a retreat center and meeting place for the Mennonite congregation founded there in 1966.   IZ-G

Paul Schowalter, "Samuel Geiser," *Menn. Geschbl.,* Jg. 30, n.F. 25 (1973), 91-92.

Gemeenschap voor Doopsgezind Broederschapswerk (Society for Mennonite Brotherhood Work). See Algemene Doopsgezinde Sociëteit.

Gemeindekomitee—Asociacón Evangélica Menonita del Paraguay (Congregational Coordinating Committee) was organized in 1966 as the Komitee fur kirchliche Angelegenheiten für Paraguay (KfKfP, Committee for Church Affairs in Paraguay) but changed to the present name in 1968. It consists of the Konferenz der Mennonitisch Brüdergemeinden (Mennonite Brethren) congregations, the Vereinigung der Mennonitengemeinden (Mennonite Church, GCM) congregations, the Konferenz der Evangelischen Mennonitischen Brüderschaft von Südamerika (Evangelical Mennonite Brotherhood, °Fellowship of Evangelical Bible Churches), and the Evangelische Mennonitische Gemeinde (EMCon) of °Tres Palmas Colony. The Sommerfelder and Bergthaler and other immigrants from Mexico have not yet joined the organization. All congregational and conference leaders are members of the committee. Meetings are held semi-annually to review work in progress and give counsel on difficult situations. The executive committee meets more frequently. The committee is registered and has official legal status.

The following four areas are primary for the work of the committee: (1) Responsibility for the leper hospital (Centro de Salud Menonita, Kilometer 81). Ca. 1,600-1,700 patients with °Hansen's disease are seen annually at the hospital station, plus an additional 1,000 patients in outlying clinics. All treatment and medication is free of charge. In addition some 12,000-14,000 patients with a variety of other ailments are helped annually by the medical staff at this station. A full-time chaplain works diligently among all who come. Financially this work is supported by the Mennonite congregations in Paraguay, Mennonite Central Committee, the American Mission to Lepers, and other donors. (2) Christian (voluntary) service. This is promoted for the work at the leper hospital, the °mental health facility in °Filadelfia, retirement °homes, children's homes, °disaster service and other areas of need where the love of Jesus can find expression. (3) Peace. Through seminars, conferences, and special courses offered for youth and others in and through congregations the biblical doctrine of peace is taught and promoted. (4) Pastoral care of young people and others studying and working in Asunción.   DKla

Gemeinschaft and Gesellschaft. See Community; Institutions, Church; Sociological Studies.

Gender Roles can be identified as behavior or tasks done with some expectation or self-consciousness about being female or male. Influenced by societal factors, and linked to status, people's behavior may be inherent, imposed, or chosen. Culture determines what is "proper" and what to change.

People perform multiple and changing roles. °Women and men engage in both similar and different roles, depending on world view, established lines of authority, developed skills, or motivation. When roles are stereotyped or available to some but not others, influence can be detrimental. Sex roles, determined by basic biology, are performed by one sex or the other. But tradition, social hierarchy, technology, economy, and psychology control most gender roles.

Traditional and current stereotypes tend to assign women's roles to private spheres and men's to more public ones. Even though Christians may think this is based on Scripture, using the Bible to justify subordinate or superordinate roles diminishes the entire message. It fails to note, for example, how the original division of tasks by gender (in the Garden of Eden) came as a result of sin.

The first woman and man were given work to do. And it was good. They were to care responsibly for the rest of created life in exchange for the pleasure and food they received. Together they were to till and keep (serve and protect). To be human was to work. But when created goodness was marred by human desire to sin, or dominate, judgment followed. Instead of working together, human tasks

were separated; hierarchy displaced mutuality. Both woman and man came to experience pain through roles. Each was diminished because sexuality became perverted. For man to rule over his intended equal and for woman to be ruled by him indicated sin. Few Mennonite interpreters of Scripture have acknowledged that aspect of gender roles.

With 16th c. Anabaptists the "°priesthood of all believers" was a marked motif within patriarchal patterns. Women and men studied the Bible together, and each used it effectively in testimony. To stress silence for women would have been inconsistent. Loyalty to Christ was valued over that toward one's spouse. The role of missioning proved more important than bearing children.

But that stance has been reversed. Many churchmen condition women to believe that their prime duty is motherhood and household care. Headship for a husband, silence for women in the church, and primacy or normativeness of male experience characterize most Mennonite gender role teaching and practice. Based in androcentric (male-centered) interpretation of Scripture, both women and men neglected hearing Jesus' first call to all: "hear God's will and do it."

Some exceptions are noteworthy. Along with early Anabaptist men, Elizabeth Dirks was known as a *leeraresse* (teacher, minister). By 1823 women were noted for social work in Amsterdam; not until 1905 were there °°deaconess sisters among Mennonites in Kansas. In 1897 a *Herald of Truth* (MC) writer encouraged women missionaries to instruct, interpret, and exhort the way of salvation. Mennonite Brethren (MB) ambivalent practice emerged when women were ordained for missionary service but denied °ordination within the congregations that sponsored them. *Gospel Witness* writers, during the first decade of 1900, could not encourage Mennonite women to pattern themselves after 1st c. women apostles. However, following 1917 one-quarter of the ordained Mennonite ministers of The Netherlands were women. Presently, Mennonite women in North America are more likely than the average north American to be professionally employed.

The Mennonite Women's Calendar (1984-86) identifies more than 400 women who contributed to the church through significant home, church, community, and worldwide roles, often as volunteers. These inter-Mennonite, international exemplars were capable health workers, teachers, evangelists, writers, pastors, artists, administrators, pioneers, farmers, peace advocates, and providers of °hospitality. Because the story of our Mennonite heritage has not attended to women's experience, major books have recently appeared to clarify how some within General Conference Mennonite Church (GCM), Mennonite Brethren (MB), and Mennonite Church (MC) circles have countered the limits of traditional gender roles.

While church roles for women have been limited, men's "place" or options have been less confined. Only among some groups were unmarried men disqualified as church or social leaders. Otherwise, cultural norms opposed the idea of men caring for and teaching children or assisting in the kitchen. Fatherhood status has never equaled that of motherhood. Preachers and writers, mostly fathers, have exhorted women to be "keepers at home," often blind to their own absence as parent.

The Kauffman-Harder survey of five North American Mennonite groups (published 1975) showed that one quarter of employed males were farmers and that nearly one quarter of farm wives had "outside" jobs. On the item: "Should a large number of qualified women be appointed to church boards or committees at varied levels?" one third responded *Yes*, the rest declaring *No* or *Undecided*. Asking: "Should the policy on ordination in your denomination be changed to allow for the ordination of women to Christian ministry?" 16 percent affirmed while 23 percent declared they were uncertain and 61 percent said *No*. But 15 years have brought change. More GCM and MC women have joined men in the task of decision-making on boards; more are ordained for ministry; the MB group has named a task force to study some of these matters.

Hutterite women's roles are shifting too. Assertiveness in making wishes known, self-perception, extending the private sphere, and labor-saving machines affect this. At the same time, formal authority and power structures continue to reflect male dominance. While men are socialized for leadership, women are to be submissive and voiceless in church and colony policy.

Overall authority of fathers is prevalent also among Amish. Women are helpers. Men's roles include heavy farm duties, meat curing, and fruit tree spraying. Women are responsible for child care; food growing, preserving, and serving (to men and boys first); clothes; house and lawn care. While women are never church officials, both participate in the *Rat* (Council) of the church. Increasingly, men are taking temporary jobs in area factories while some women have become domestic workers employed by non-Amish.

Both Old Colony and Evangelical Mennonite Mission Conference Mennonites in Belize extend authority to the bishop. Although patriarchal patterns are being modified, most women think of themselves mainly as servants to their husbands. While they are permitted to be Sunday School teachers with women or children, women rarely make group decisions. Men conduct both church and public business.

Cultural factors affect Japanese Mennonites too. Girls and boys learn distinct roles. Pressure exists to give much effort to enroll sons in good schools. As churches become established, men assume leadership, but among the three largest Mennonite groups, a few women are active as pastors. Decisionmaking is done together.

As with general society, French Mennonite men lead in households. Among farm families, all join in doing chores; girls also complete indoor work. Young men pursue industrial jobs. That women are not also seminary students will affect church roles.

Food production becomes the fundamental role issue in Zaire. In some regions, women plant corn and food crops while men plant yams or crops for sale. Because of taxation, men turned to other employment for bringing in cash. Women fill secretarial roles. In Protestant groups like Brethren

in Christ, where expectations from men may be more orderly than for general society, women are also free to be leaders of strength.

Among Mennonites in India influence on gender roles of ancient culture and tradition remain. A wife often walks several steps behind her husband whom she is expected to always honor. A husband is to be "in control" whether with discipline or managing finances. A unique gender role is that of honor extended to the grandmother in households. Women supplement men as the primary providers. In rural areas, both may do field work; urban dwellers may earn as manual laborers. Many Mennonite young people are educated and prepared to bring useful change to church life.

Shifts also emerge among Swiss Mennonites, but focus on male headship remains. Most men either farm or operate a local business, but an increasing number of young people now attend university. Tension presents itself as women begin to serve churches as elders; only men teach catechism. Both serve as leaders of choirs and congregational singing.

Mennonite experience with gender roles is varied and in transition. From the first four years when only 22 of 269 Anabaptist leaders survived, to today's pattern of some being leaders for decades; from a 25-year-old Mennonite Church (MC) Confession of Faith suggesting gender roles that are outdated in 1987; from the imbalance when men alone determined roles for all to awareness that interdependence of woman and man in decisions is imperative; from patterns thought to be based in Scripture yet primarily formed by culture; from all of this, Mennonites enter a new century with new options for roles.   DYN

Perry and Elizabeth Yoder, *New Men New Roles* (Newton, 1977; John Klassen, "Women and the Family Among Dutch Anabaptist Martyrs," *MQR*, 60 (1986), 548-71; Judith Shapiro, "Anthropology and the Study of Gender," *Soundings*, 64 (1981), 446-65; Christine Kaufmann and Priscilla Stuckey Kauffman, project coordinators, *Mennonite Women's Calendar 1984-1986* (1983, available from Mennonite Historical Libraries); Karl Peter, "The Changing Roles of Hutterite Women," *Prairie Forum*, 7, no. 2 (1982), 267-76; Sharon Klingelsmith, "Women in the Mennonite Church, 1900-1930," *MQR*, 54 (1980), 163-207; James Juhnke, "The Role of Women in the Mennonite Transition from Traditionalism to Denominationalism," *Menn. Life*, 41 (Sept. 1986), 17-20; Steven Ozment, *When Fathers Ruled: Family Life in Reformation Europe* (Cambridge, Harvard U. Press, 1983); Lois Gunden Clemens, *Woman Liberated* (Scottdale, 1971); Ross T. Bender, *Christians in Families* (Scottdale, 1982); Ted Koontz, "Men/Women's Advocacy Positions on the Implications of Interdependence and Cooperation," *Persons Becoming*, ed. Dorothy Yoder Nyce (MCC Task Force on Women, 1974); Katie Funk Wiebe, "Mennonite Brethren Women: Images and Realities of the Early Years," *Menn. Life*, 36 (Sept. 1981), 22-28; John E. Lapp, "Woman's Work in the Church," *Christian Ministry* (Jan.-Mar., 1954), 4ff.; Frieda Shoenberg Rozen, "The Permanent First-Floor Tenant: Women and Gemeinschaft," *MQR*, 51 (1977), 319-28.

Genealogy (ME II:457). By genealogy we mean the cultivated study of ancestors, which includes preserving oral traditions in material form and discovering material sources for classification and preservation. The terminological distinction between family history, which encompasses the broad range of events in ancestors' lives, and genealogy, which has frequently been restricted to vital statistics of genetically connected generations, is less applicable to the approaches utilized in the late 20th c. As some genealogical research becomes more sophisticated, documented, and oriented toward the wider historical context, so have some academic historians embraced the field of local or nearby history, utilizing traditional genealogical methods and sources.

In order to begin genealogical research on one's family it is helpful to read an instructional booklet, enroll in a special course, or obtain advice from an expert. This saves much wasted effort and inaccurate record-keeping. Some basic guidelines follow: (1) One should begin at home, literally, with old letters, family Bibles, interviewing relatives, etc. The next steps involve visits to libraries, courthouses, and places where church records are kept. (2) One should not believe the first "facts" heard or read, but write them down accurately; the more sources which provide the same data, the higher possibility of truth. (3) One should not trust one's memory for all the details. Devise an understandable organizational system that can be expanded. (4) Goals and limits to one's projects are necessary so that their rewards can be enjoyed and communicated with others.

Increased genealogical activity among Mennonites has often coincided with similar interests among the general population. Among the factors awakening enthusiasm for genealogy are major group °migrations, rapid cultural changes within nuclear families, and increased °literary consciousness. However, it is helpful to examine how fundamental theological, historical, and cultural forces have proved fertile ground for thriving Mennonite and Amish genealogical activities in the 1980s.

Anabaptist theology strongly emphasizes face-to-face human interaction as the primary locus of God's grace, rather than mediation through a special ministerial hierarchy responsible for record-keeping. The norm of a °disciplined fellowship of adult believers in tension with secular society reinforced pressure for °marriage within the group. Above all, intense °persecution scattered groups far beyond their origins in Switzerland and The Netherlands,, so that the 17th, 18th, and early 19th c. saw few converts from different religious and ethnic backgrounds. In the midst of complex migration patterns, relatively stable marriage patterns within subgroups provided some security in a sea of often threatening events.

For the continuously harassed, insular, and rural communities in which European Mennonites and Amish of the Swiss stream lived in the 17th to 19th c., °family history provided a powerful, binding set of connections in the context of oral traditions, but church record-keeping was politically dangerous and theologically questionable. In the late 20th c. genealogical research on Mennonite and Amish Swiss background is hampered by the lack of church records, except in the case of Amish congregations in the region of Montbéliard and Belfort, France, where two mid-18th c. registers have been discovered.

The first permanent American Mennonite settlement at Germantown, Pa. (1683) was made up primarily of Mennonites of Dutch background. However, the major American immigration in the 18th c. (primarily to Pennsylvania) and the first half of the 19th c. (primarily to regions such as Ohio, Indiana, Illinois, and Ontario) ultimately stemmed from Switzerland, often via southern Germany. Though not politically dangerous in America, official church records among these groups were rare until the late 19th c. Diligent research in civil records, oral traditions, family Bible records, and other sources has nonetheless resulted in an impressive body of literature.

Mennonites of the Dutch stream, intensely persecuted for approximately fifty years in the 16th c., and then generously tolerated in their land of origin, became more urbanized, wealthy, and literate than their Swiss counterparts. They kept detailed church records, extant in The Netherlands from the early 17th c. and extant from the late 17th c. during their sojourn in Prussia. One of the earliest known European Mennonite genealogies, dealing with the influential van der °Smissen family of Hamburg, emerged from this stream in 1743. Beginning in 1788-89 some Mennonites left Prussia for Russia, where their separate economic and religious subculture was subject to mass emigration to North America in the 1870s and 1920s. Though church records were kept during these centuries, some have been destroyed or lost during the disruption of war, famine, and persecution.

Intermarriage between the Dutch and Swiss streams was rare before the 20th c. and within the many subgroups endogamy, communal migration, and mutual aid practices provided a degree of predictability for later genealogical research. Particular surnames can be associated with certain geographical areas, time periods, and national groups, thus providing possible research avenues where no clear direction otherwise exists.

Rapid change within nuclear families helped induce some people to embrace their Mennonite heritage genealogically when they could no longer do so religiously. The number of important early North American Amish and Mennonite genealogies compiled by people whose adult lives were spent outside the denominations is remarkable. Perhaps their distance, fueled by motivations of nostalgia, guilt, and respect, plus their organizational, financial and literary skills, enabled them to produce these valuable works. For example, Abraham J. Fretz (1849-1912), first a Presbyterian, then a Methodist minister, wrote approximately 13 genealogies on Mennonites in the region north of Philadelphia. Also, Hugh F. Gingerich has collaborated with Rachel W. Kreider, to produce an astonishingly comprehensive work, *Amish and Amish Mennonite Genealogies* (1986).

Genealogical activity varies among European Mennonites. Mennonite °historical societies in Switzerland and The Netherlands incorporate genealogy to a lesser degree, perhaps because the ancestors of contemporary Mennonites in these countries did not emigrate. Notwithstanding, many Dutch Mennonite families appear in the genealogical publication, *Nederlandsch Patriciaat*. The French Mennonite historical society, with considerable non-Mennonite participation, publishes a few family history articles in its annual periodical. The German Mennonite historical society encourages well-documented genealogy by providing a special section in its periodical. Immigration to Germany of Mennonites and Amish from Switzerland, France, and The Netherlands in the 16th and 17th c., plus the 20th c. influx of Prussian and Russian Mennonites has made Germany the crossroads of European Mennonite genealogy.

North American Mennonite organizations and periodicals emphasizing genealogy are expanding rapidly. Libraries belonging to the Swiss stream report that approximately one half of their genealogical researchers are non-Mennonites with Mennonite ancestors. Similar institutions from the Dutch stream report a much lower percentage of non-Mennonites, probably due to the later immigration of their constituencies and the consequently lower attrition rate out of the Mennonite churches.

Although genealogical research requests do overtax staff members at some Mennonite °historical libraries and organizations, the general thrust of increased genealogical activity has broadened the constituency support of Mennonite historical organizations, fostered cooperative research between Mennonites and non-Mennonites, and added to the fund of printed sources which historians, especially congregational historians, may use in the future.

While most written genealogies among Mennonites come from North America and Europe, family history is vitally important for many of the rapidly growing number of Mennonites on other continents. For example, in Africa the individual's identity is intimately tied with his or her clan membership and the generational links that define it. African Mennonites, too, possess this interest motivated by the whole culture rather than any sense of religious identity as a Mennonite. Tensions have arisen when first-generation Mennonites or Mennonites from Europe or North America perceive Asian or African concerns for clan ancestry as unbiblical °ancestor worship.

Genealogical research about Mennonites in the future will bring new challenges. Presently, Old Order Amish, Old Colony Mennonites, Old Order Mennonites and other traditionalist groups (°conservative Mennonites) exhibit stable genetic interaction. However, a growing Mennonite global community of many racial and ethnic strains, the shifting of previous conference boundaries, and the proliferation of inter-Mennonite agencies eventually will affect genealogies. The vast storehouses of computerized records of minute details about people in industrialized societies will provide much fodder for genealogists, but to future genealogical research on Mennonites, the familiar litany of names and places will never sound quite the same. **DJRS**

Genealogical research aids include the following: Bill R. Lindner, *How to Trace Your Family Tree* (New York: Everest House, 1978); Gilbert Doane and James Bell, *Searching for Your Ancestors: The How and Why of Genealogy* (Minneapolis: University of Minnesota Press, 1980); Val D. Greenwood, *The Researcher's Guide to American Genealogy* (Baltimore: Genealogical Publishing Company, 1973); Arlene Eakle and Johni Cerny, editors, *The Source: A Guidebook of American Genealogy* (Salt Lake City: Ancestry Publishing Company,

1984). Some of the European and North American periodical publications and sponsoring organizations which contain varying percentages of genealogical materials are *The Diary* (Old Order Amish); *Family Life* (Old Order Amish); *Mennonite Historian* (History-Archives Committee of the Conference of Mennonites in Canada and Centre for Mennonite Brethren Studies in Canada); *Mennonite Heritage* (Illinois Mennonite Historical and Genealogical Society); *Mennonite Historical Bulletin* (Historical Committee of the Mennonite Church); *Mennonite Family History* (privately published); *Mennogespräch* (Mennonite Historical Society of Ontario); *Pennsylvania Mennonite Heritage* (Lancaster Mennonite Historical Society); *Historical Center Echoes* (Juniata Historical Center, Pennsylvania); *Newsletter* (Mennonite Historians of Eastern Pennsylvania); *Mennonitische Geschichtsblätter* (Mennonitischen Geschichtsverein); *Souvenance Anabaptiste/Mennonitisches Gedächtnis* (L'Association Française d'histoire Anabaptiste-Mennonite); *Informations Blätter/Feuilles d'Information* (Schweizerischer Verein für Täufergeschichte/Société Suisse pour l'histoire Mennonite); *Bulletin* (Mennonite Brethren Historical Society of the West Coast); Mennonite Ancestry Research Service (a privately owned and operated center in Fresno, Cal.); Mennonite Genealogy, Inc./Mennonitische Familienforschung (a privately owned and operated research center in Winnipeg).

General studies include the following: David Luthy, "One Hundred Years of Amish Genealogies, 1885-1985," *PMH*, 8 (Oct. 1985), 28-31; Hugh F. Gingerich and Rachel W. Kreider, *Amish and Amish Mennonite Genealogies* (Gordonville, Pa.: Pequea Publishers, 1986); Adalbert Goertz, "Genealogical Sources of the Prussian Mennonites," *MQR*, 60 (1981), 372-80; Delbert L. Gratz, *Bernese Anabaptists and Their American Descendants* (Scottdale, 1953); John L. Ruth, *Maintaining the Right Fellowship* (Scottdale, 1984); Cornelius J. Dyck, ed., *Introduction to Mennonite History*, 2nd ed. (Scottdale, 1981); F. H. Epp, *Mennonites in Canada*, 2 vols (1974, 1982); "Mennonite Tricentennial Issue" *PMH*, (Oct. 6, 1983); Lawrence Klippenstein, "Canadian Sources for Mennonite Genealogists—The Mennonite Heritage Center," *Mennonite Family History*, 1 (April 1982), 11-13; David A. Haury, ed., *Index to Mennonite Immigrants on United States Passenger Lists, 1872-1904* (North Newton, Ks., Mennonite Library and Archives, 1986); Paul Roth, "Das Vergessene und Wiedergefundene Register der Gemeinde 'Lamā-Belfort' 1729-1843," *Souvenance Anabaptiste/Mennonitisches Gedächtnis*, 8 (1986), 53-54; Isaac Zürcher, "Die Täufernamen in der Schweiz" *Informations Blätter/Feuilles d'Information*, 8, (1985), 28-62; Jacob Gysbert de Hoop Scheffer, *Inventaris der Archiefstukken Berusten bij de Vereenigde Doopsgezinde Gemeente te Amsterdam* (Amsterdam: Amsterdam Mennonite Church, 1883-84). Important genealogies written by non-Mennonites: John Hertzler, Sr., *A Brief Biographic Memorial of Jacob Hertzler* (Elkhart, Ind.: Mennonite Publishing Company, 1885); Harvey Hostetler, *Descendants of Jacob Hochstetler: The Immigrant of 1736* (Elgin, Ill.: Brethren Publishing House, 1912); Theodore W. Herr, *Genealogical Records of Reverend Hans Herr* (Lancaster, Pennsylvania: the author, 1908); A. J. Fretz, *A Brief History of John and Christian Fretz* (Elkhart, Ind.: Mennonite Publishing Co., 1890).

See also Historical Libraries.

General Conference Mennonite Church (GCM)

(ME II:465). Elements of both continuity and discontinuity are evident in developments within the General Conference Mennonite Church since 1950. The constitutional revision in 1950, which saw the restructuring of the several boards, including administrative separations between home and foreign missions agencies, was itself revised in 1968. At that time the nomenclature was changed from boards to commissions, except for the General Board. A further basic change was that of representation. Whereas earlier all board members were elected by the general conference, after 1968 each regional or district conference in the United States and the Women in Mission placed one representative on each of the commissions and on the seminary board of trustees. The Conference of Mennonites in Canada placed two members on each.

The 1968 constitution delineated a change in the relationship to the South American churches (still listed annually in the *Handbook of Information*). These congregations subsequently established their primary relationships among themselves as regional or national conferences. Their tie to the General Conference became a fraternal one, fostered through the Commission on Overseas Missioh. During the last two decades there has been a gradual move to separate some of the issues into their national contexts. Canadian members thought it improper for the binational general conference to be dealing with issues that had to do primarily with the United States congregations. The result was the establishment of the US Assembly, a US Council and Commission on Home Ministries (US), 1981-83.

Growth. Growth of the General Conference Mennonite Church has continued at a slow pace, not for lack of focus on °evangelism, but for a lack of practical handles to bring people into the doors of the church. Periodically the conference has adopted statements on evangelism, with each conference session setting forth certain evangelistic and church growth goals. Thus the Commission on Home Ministries in 1983 presented its proposals for outreach, including one for the preparation of 300 church planters, and another for enriching evangelism with peace and justice witness, and expression of a strong desire to keep evangelism and the practical Christian life linked together.

In 1986, with the acceptance of 26 new congregations into the conference, the total stood at 364, with 65,321 members. This was an increase of 94 and 18,134 respectively from 1950. The most rapid growth has come in Canada. In the United States the increase in membership has been from 31,687 in 1950 to 35,356 in 1986. In Canada the increase has been from 15,500 in 1950 to 26,893 in 1986.

Commissions. The overall program of conference continues to be carried by the program commissions, the seminary, and several other agencies.

The Commission on Home Ministries, charged with ministry on the home front, has helped support church planting ventures among Hispanic, Mexican, Chinese, Laotian, Creole, Native or Indian, and Vietnamese peoples. It seeks to promote ministry to the poor and to law offenders, aid to °refugees, °peace education and peace activism (including assistance for draft-age youth), awareness of the danger of °nuclear weapons, aid to vocational shifts, ministry to the aged, and awareness of social changes and of possible Christian witness in response to such change.

At the 1986 triennial conference plans were presented to move more aggressively into ministry to ethnic and language minorities, in part because of the changed pattern of immigrants coming to the United States and Canada.

The mission thrust overseas, carried by the *Commission on Overseas Ministries* has seen both major expansions and radical adjustments. In the 1950s work was begun in Japan (1950) and Taiwan (1953). In both India and Zaire, where General Conference mission work had been underway much longer, the

process of turning over the work to Indians and Zairians was underway in the 1950s. In India this brought about considerable ferment. Attempts were made to develop a more peaceful partnership in the 1960s; the 1970s then culminated in the dismantling of the mission organization after some disturbing relationships. In Zaire, on the other hand, the political upheaval in the 1960s led to an accelerated move toward independence of the Zairian church. This was sparked first by what James Juhnke calls "organizing disintegration," followed by a split in the national church along tribal lines. Although the political scene did gradually stabilize, this was followed by severe economic deterioration. The Zaire Mennonite Church, nonetheless, matured in its independence, and then in turn invited the General Conference to send missionaries back as fraternal workers.

In the context of such changes the Commission on Overseas Ministries held a "Goals, Priorities and Strategies Conference" in 1972. Its purpose was to articulate for the commission its stated intent for the second century of witness, and to establish priorities for its task. The top five priorities were: evangelism and church planting, leadership training, transfer of the mission work to national leadership, strengthening of Anabaptist-Mennonite emphasis on °discipleship; °love; °peace, °nonresistance, and unity; and economic °development.

The *Commission on Education* (COE) continued its focus on preparing material to help the church in its educational task. Working with Faith and Life Press in partnership with Bethel College, it prepared °Sunday school literature and teaching aids and sponsored the publication of books and pamphlets, e.g. the Mennonite Historical Series. Jointly with the Congregational Literature Division of Mennonite Publishing House (MC), it prepared and published the Foundation Series (for children), the Adult Bible Study Guide for the International Uniform Lessons series, periodical (*Rejoice*), and, with other groups, published the Foundation Series for Adults. These joint ventures have resulted in some of the best teaching materials available for the local church.

Denominational periodicals continue to be published. *Der Bote* (The Messenger), published weekly in Winnipeg, continues to be a family paper bringing German-speaking Mennonites around the world into dialogue with one another. The number of subscribers continues to drop as the younger generation in Canada and the United States use less and less °German. *The Mennonite,* published biweekly, celebrated its centennial in 1985; that same year it commemorated the 125th anniversary of the founding of the General Conference Mennonite Church with a special issue.

Youth work continues as another of the portfolios of the COE. S. F. °Pannabecker wrote that by 1950 the youth work might be said to have come of age. Young people participated energetically in the work of the church with a program that emphasized particularly faith, fellowship, and °service. During the 1960s the focus shifted from overall conference planning to getting the local groups involved in their communities and districts. The result was the disbanding of the Young People's Union in 1969, with most of the regional conferences fostering strong youth programs. Annual statistical surveys by the COE have made it possible to remain in touch with youth studying at non-Mennonite institutions. A Student Services Committee was instituted in 1959 to minister to campus groups. *Arena*, a joint Mennonite graduate student periodical was begun in 1967 and *With*, a periodical for younger students saw a wide circulation. *Arena* changed to *Forum* in 1970, was discontinued in 1981, due in part to the controversial topics which were being discussed (°Student and Young Adult Services).

Theological Education. Mennonite Biblical Seminary, the theological training institution for the General Conference, was moved from Chicago (where it was associated with Bethany Theological Seminary (CBreth) for 13 years), to Elkhart, Ind. in 1958. It entered into an association with Goshen College Biblical Seminary (MC) to form the Associated Mennonite Biblical Seminaries (1958). Initially classes were taught on campuses at Goshen and Elkhart. The move to one campus at Elkhart, was made in 1969. The two seminaries operate with one academic program and one academic dean, but still maintain separate presidents to relate to their respective constituencies (1988). The association agreement allows for other Mennonite groups to join as well. With this joining of the two, the ministerial training program expanded to an enrollment of 244 in 1983. Offered are three degrees, the Master of Divinity, the Master of Arts in Peace Studies, and the Master of Arts in Theological Studies, the latter two being two-year programs.

Ministerial training has been expanded to conference-based centers in eastern Pennsylvania, Virginia, Kansas, and Ontario. In these centers courses are offered to pastors and laypersons affording them training while on the job. Recently the Committee on the Ministry has been charged with helping to determine and to plan for the type of pastoral training called for in the next decades. In Canada the Bible schools which have served a very strategic role in biblical training have fallen on hard times, and few continue to function. Canadian Mennonite Bible College, operated by the Conference of Mennonites in Canada in Winnipeg, on the other hand, has continued as a strong training school for church workers.

Auxiliaries. The Women's Missionary Association, which was organized in 1917, became °Women in Mission in 1974. Focusing on study and service, its 10,000 members drawn from churches throughout the conference interpret General Conference programs of the local church and support various local, regional, and national projects. Financially they assist each of the commissions and the seminary, preparing mission education materials, offering scholarships to women students, assisting Hispanic and overseas women in leadership training, sponsoring reciprocal cross-cultural visits with women overseas, aiding women in developing and sharing their gifts, strengthening family relationships, and fostering spiritual growth.

Organized in 1945, °Mennonite Men initially had two purposes: to assist financially with special projects and to help organize district Mennonite Men's groups for fellowship and service. After a decline during the 1970s, a new vitality has been born with the decision to assist financially in the establishment of new churches. The current project in the latter half of the 1980s, the Tenth Man program, solicits members to contribute annually for church planting.

Study Conferences. The General Conference has continued to emphasize an appropriate expression of the Christian faith. For some the verbal expression is very important; for others the practical life receives the focus.

Comprehensive doctrinal statements have not been drafted recently. However, doctrinal statements based on Scriptural teaching have formulated on many different, specific theological, ecclesiastical, and ethical issues. Unique have been the study conferences which have convened perodically since the 1950s. These have dealt with such issues as the Church, the Gospel and War (1953), the °Believers Church (1955), Evangelism (1958), Christian Unity in Faith and Witness (1960), and Church and Society (1961). These study conferences, together with a number of study commissions and various resolutions at triennial sessions, resulted in official statements, accepted by the conference, on the Believers Church, the Christian and Race, the Christian and °Nuclear Power, °Capital Punishment, °Inter-Mennonite Cooperation and Unity, Simultaneous Evangelism, Proclamation of the Gospel, °Nationalism, Poverty and Hunger, Church Renewal, °Authority of the Scriptures, Christian °Stewardship of Energy Resources, Offender Ministries, °Divorce and Remarriage, °Abortion, and Human °Sexuality. In 1979 a special conference session was convened to deal with the withholding of °taxes from the salaries of staff members at central offices in Newton. That session charged the General Board "to use all legal, legislative and administrative avenues for achieving a conscientious objector exemption from the legal requirement that the Conference withhold income taxes from the wages of its employees." A later triennial session approved this action. The wide divergence of viewpoints within the General Conference often led to statements adopted with as many as one-third of the delegates not in favor of the action. This resulted in unhappiness and criticism, and while there have never been major disruptive controversies, there was sufficient dissatisfaction to strain relationships. Periodically congregations have left the General Conference. Robert Kreider, speaking at the triennial session in 1971 stated: "We undoubtedly are a more frankly divided Conference than in 1953: [as is illustrated by] the Fundamentalist-non-Fundamentalist gulf, the generational gap, the peace-patriotism conflict, the distrust of institutions and structures, the new nationalism that separates the United States and Canada, the young churches overseas assertive of their new freedom. . ." (*Where are We Going?* p. 21).

To help to facilitate dialogue between those of differing viewpoints, and to speak specifically to the question of °biblical interpretation, two special conferences termed "Dialogue on Faith" were convened in the 1980s. Those who attended heard each other, and discovered an integrity which enabled them despite the differences to accept each other as brothers and sisters in Christ.

The distinctive features and characteristics of the General Conference Mennonite Church continue to be: readiness to cooperate in many inter-Mennonite activities, congregational independence, diversity of thought and life-style, a free borrowing from outside Mennonite tradition, laxness in applying Christian °discipline, a strong desire to remain biblical, yet recognizing that differences in hermeneutical approach to the Bible lead to differing interpretations of the Scriptures, a rediscovery and emphasis of a °peace position, a constant attempt to keep evangelism and °Christian education and nurture together, and a continued emphasis on church re newal. This renewal was given expression at the 1986 triennial session which adopted as a development plan a Call to Kingdom Commitments, calling for commitments of prayer, of time and service, and of financial support. Reaffirmed were four major goals: to evangelize, to teach and practice biblical principles, to train and develop church leaders, and to achieve Christian unity.   HP

Conference Reports and Minutes of Triennial Sessions (1953ff.); Commission and General Secretary's Reports (annually, 1953ff.); Handbook of Information (Newton: General Conference Mennonite Church, 1953ff.); reports of Women in Mission and the Women's Missionary Association (1953ff.); Lois Barrett, Vision (1983); Juhnke, Mission (Newton, 1979); Kauffman/Harder, Anabaptists Four C. Later (1975); Robert Kreider, Where Are We Going? Schowalter Memorial Lecture given at the 1971 triennial session in Fresno, California (Newton, 1971); S. F. Pannabecker, Open Doors (1975); S. F. Pannabecker, Faith in Ferment: A History of the Central District Conference (Newton, 1968); John L. Ruth, Maintaining the Right Fellowship [Eastern District] (Scottdale, 1984); David Haury, Prairie People [Western District] (Newton, 1981); Rodney J. Sawatzky, Authority and Identity: The Dynamics of the General Conference Church (Bethel College, 1987); MWH (1984), 145; MWH (1978), 344-51.

See also Central District Conference; Conference of Mennonites in Canada; General Conference Mennonite Church (United States); Conference of Mennonites in South America; Eastern District Conference; Northern District Conference; Pacific District Conference; Western District Conference.

General Conference Mennonite Church (United States). The General Conference Mennonite Church United States Assembly was organized on Aug. 1, 1983, and is made up of the General Conference Mennonite churches in the United States, totaling 35,961 members in 211 congregations in 26 states. The United States Assembly meets in conjunction with the General Conference Mennonite Church's triennial sessions. Business between sessions is transacted by the United States Council which is made up of United States members on the General Conference General Board Executive Committee, United States district presidents, and two persons elected to the Commission on Home Ministries (US).

Over the 10-year period preceeding its organization there was a growing awareness that there was no forum, apart from the binational triennial conference, to deal with questions pertaining exclusively to the General Conference Mennonites in the United States. The Conference of Mennonites in Canada serves this function in Canada. A consultation on May 14-16, 1981, was an important step in the process that led to the General Conference United States Assembly in 1983. The delegates from the United States churches to the General Conference triennial sessions constitute the voting members of the assembly. Concerns that clearly pertain to the United States include such items as: receiving reports from Mennonite Central Committee (U.S.) and Mennonite Mutual Aid, United States native ministries, °conscription concerns, and United States political issues.   JGing

See also General Conference Mennonite Church; Conference of Mennonites in Canada.

General Conference of Mennonite Brethren Churches. See Mennonite Brethren Church of North America.

Geography is a discipline that is not well understood in North American society. At the elementary school level, one thinks of geography as the subject matter that deals with countries, rivers, and mountains. Memorizing the names of these is seen as onerous and useless. Advanced studies in geography on the other hand frequently focus upon the relationship between human beings and their environment. This is known, in professional terminology, as the "man-land" tradition of geographic studies. Other approaches are the spatial and the behavioral traditions. All can be applied from a social, economic, political, or environmental perspective. Geographical studies of Mennonites have been done nearly exclusively within the man-land tradition. Consequently, it is not surprising that geographic scholars have analyzed all the major Mennonite settlement endeavors in the Americas. No major study has been done on the early settlements in Prussia and the Ukraine, nor of the African and Asian Mennonites.

The earliest major geographic settlement study in the Americas was done by Annemarie A. Krause. Her interest in Mennonites was stimulated when an article she read in the 1930s mentioned the migration of the Manitoba Mennonites to Paraguay. Her doctoral field work in the 1950s finally allowed her to observe their new agricultural and socioeconomic landscape. Although they had been forced to become subsistence farmers, they managed to survive. Geographic isolation required them to set up socioeconomic support systems ranging from schools to hospitals to local governments.

Probably the best known geographical studies of Mennonite settlements are those of John H. Warkentin and Harry L. Sawatzky. Warkentin's study of the beginnings of the °°East and °°West Reserves in Manitoba is a classic study and describes in great detail the difficulties of being the first settlers in the Canadian West. In the 1920s many Mennonites migrated to Mexico where they encountered an unfamiliar semi-arid tropical environment. This has been investigated by H. L. Sawatzky. Both studies strongly emphasize the relationship of the people to the land and explore in great detail the religious and traditional life in the new environments. In a recent article Sawatzky similarly examines the settlements of some of these Mexican Mennonites who migrated to Belize in the late 1950s. His analysis showed they still had not mastered the tropical environment, partly because they would not take any advice from indigenous agricultural practitioners. An earlier study by Jerry A. Hall had pointed out the same problem. In the late 1970s a major study by Walter Regehr linked the subsistence problem of the Indians in the Paraguayan Chaco in part to the Mennonite colonies there. The emphasis again was the man-land tradition. Other studies mentioned in the bibliography below have examined Mennonites from a behavioral perspective, but these have all focused on rural settings. Little geographical analysis has been done on the urban Mennonites, a void that should be corrected in the future.   AHcht

John Warkentin, "Canadian Geographers and their Contributions to Mennonite Studies," *JMS*, 1 (1983), 106-18; Annamarie A. Krause, "Mennonite Settlement in the Paraguayan Chaco" (PhD diss., U. of Chicago, 1952); John H. Warkentin, "The Mennonite Settlements of Manitoba" (PhD diss., U. of Toronto, 1960); Harry L. Sawatzky, "Mennonite Colonization in Mexico: A Study in Survival of a Traditional Society" (PhD diss., U. of Califormia, Berkeley, 1967); idem, "Deutsch-Mennonitische Kolonisierung in Belize, C.A., 1957-1985," *Jahrbuch für Ostdeutsche Volkskunde* (1986), 404-44; Jerry A. Hall, "Mennonite Agriculture in a Tropical Environment: An Analysis of the Development and Productivity of a Mid-Latitude Agricultural System in British Honduras" (PhD diss., Clark U., 1973); Walter Regehr, "Die Lebensräumliche Situation der Indianer im Paraguayischen Chaco," Basler Beiträge zur Geographie, Heft 25 (PhD diss., Basel, 1979); James E. Landing, "The Spatial Organization of an Old Order Amish-Beachy Amish Settlement: Nappanee, Indiana" (PhD diss., Pennsylvania State U., 1967; David De Lisle, "The Spatial Organization and Intensity of Agriculture in the Mennonite Villages of Southern Manitoba" (PhD diss., McGill U., 1975); Alfred Hecht, "The Agricultural Economy of the Mennonite Settlers in Paraguay: Impact of a Road," *Ekistics*, 42, no. 248 (1976), 42-48; Alfred Hecht and J. W. Fretz, "Food Production under Conditions of Increased Uncertainty: The Chaco (Mennonite) Example," in *Interpretations of Calamity*, ed. K. Hewitt (Allen and Unwin, 1983), 162-80; Robert A. Murdie, "Cultural Differences (Mennonite) in Consumer Travel," *Economic Geography*, 41 (1965), 211-33.

See also Anthropology; Sociological Studies.

Georgia. The first known Mennonite-related presence in Georgia began in 1953 when a half-dozen Beachy Amish Mennonite families, seeking to escape °urbanization, moved from Chesapeake, Va., to Macon Co. near Montezuma, Ga. They were followed shortly by a community of Church of God in Christ, Mennonite, people at Louisville in Jefferson Co. These two farm communities are generally credited with introducing to Georgia soil-building agricultural practices, which revolutionized an industry dying from repeated cotton-tobacco cropping.

In 1954 a Lancaster Mennonite Conference (MC) mission began at Colquitt (Miller Co.), followed by Virginia Mennonite Conference (MC) churches at Hephzibah (Richmond Co., 1959) and an outreach from there, Burkeland, at Waynesboro (Burke Co., 1970). In 1987 these three were part of Southeastern Mennonite Conference (unaffiliated), and reported memberships of 12, 35, and 38 respectively.

Lancaster Conference started a biracial mission in Atlanta during 1958 using a °voluntary ser ice (VS) unit. Although the unit was phased out in the mid-1970s, it had led to the founding of Berea Mennonite Church in 1962 (DeKalb Co., 52 members). In 1987 this congregation was affiliated with Southeast Mennonite Conference (MC). A Mennonite Central Committee VS unit opened in 1961 in conjunction with a regional racial-reconciliation ministry led by Vincent and Rosemarie Harding. The latter closed in 1967, but Mennonite Central Committee work, refocused to community development, has continued in several locations. Atlanta has had several Mennonite-related intentional communities and fellowships during these years, the earlier ones receiving nurture and vision from Reba Place in Evanston, Ill. The last such community, Adelphos, began meeting in 1974, but became inactive in the mid-1980s after efforts to obtain more formal leadership failed.

An Eastern Mennonite Board of Missions (MC, Lancaster Mennonite Conference) VS unit at Americus, providing personnel for Habitat for Humanity and community projects, has led to amicable contacts with former President and Mrs. Carter. Despite once ambitious visions for the state's larger cities, organized church planting, assumed by Southeast Conference in the 1970s halted following two unsuccessful ventures in Albany and on Atlanta's westside.

Other Mennonite churches include Dublin (Laurens Co., 1976; Eastern Pennsylvania Mennonite Church, 42 members), Cuthbert (Randolph Co., 1979; Conservative Mennonite Conference, 19), and an unaffiliated congregation in Mitchell Co. near Meigs (1979; 37). In addition to Montezuma, which has grown to some 90 families (220 members), there is a Beachy Amish Mennonite congregation near Cuthbert reporting a membership of 20. Recent articles (1987) in the *Sugar Creek Budget* indicate that there is now an Amish community near Jessup in Wayne Co.   DRY

MC Yearbook (1988-89), 21.

Gereja Injili di Tanah Jawa (GITJ; Evangelical Church of Java), the predominately Javanese Mennonite conference of the north central part of the island of Java, Indonesia, was formed on May 30, 1940, 81 years after the beginning of Dutch Mennonite mission work in the area around the Muria Mountain in the early 1850s. The new conference consisted of 10 congregations with their 30 branch congregations. It had 4,409 adult members. The original name of the conference was *Patunggilanipun para Pasamuan Kristen Tata Injil ing Wengkon Kabupatan Kudus, Pati lan Jepara* (current spelling; literally: Union of Gospel-Patterned Christian Churches in Kudus, Pati and Jepara Counties).

The Margorejo congregation had become independent of direct mission oversight in 1928 and in the 1930s some planning toward the formation of a conference body took place. However the actual formation of the conference in 1940 was a hurried response to the arrest and imprisonment of two of the four active men working with the Dutch Mennonite mission team, Hermann Schmitt and Otto Stauffer. Both were German citizens and both died when their prisoner transport was sunk. This imprisonment of German nationals by the Dutch colonial government was in response to the occupation of The Netherlands by the German army on May 10, 1940.

The board chosen to lead the new conference consisted of the two remaining missionaries, Daniel Amstutz and Dr. K. P. C. A. Gramberg, chairman and vice-chairman respectively; °Sardjoe Djojodihardjo, secretary; Wigeno Mororedjo, treasurer; and Soedjono Harsosoedirdjo and Samuel Saritruno as members. However, during the second assembly (May 1941) both of the missionaries resigned from their posts in the conference organization and were replaced in their roles by national leaders, Soedjono Harsosoedirdjo (pastor of the already independent Margorejo church) and Samuel Saritruno respectively.

Within a year these leaders were to be severely tested in a Muslim uprising at the time of the Japanese invasion in March 1942. The uprising resulted in the martyrdom of missionary Heusdens (on loan from another mission) at the Donorojo Leprosy Colony, and Leimena, the head of the plantation of the colony for the poor at Ngablak, and the attempted slaying of Dr. Ong, a Chinese Muslim staff doctor at the mission hospital in Tayu. It also resulted in the destruction of much property including the large, beautiful church building at Margorejo and the hospital in Tayu. The most serious damage, however, was spiritual—to the leaders and the members of the Margorejo, Tayu, and Ngeling congregations where the leaders, including Soedjono Harsosoedirdjo, Samuel Saritruno, Samuel Hadiwardojo, and Surat Timotius, were severely mistreated through efforts to try to force them to become Muslims. From that time to the present a series of capable leaders in addition to the above mentioned—including Sardjoe Djojodihardjo, Soehadiweko Djojodihardjo, Sastroadi and Pirenamoelja— have led the Evangelical Church of Java through military occupation, persecution, famine, revolution, and political, religious and economic upheaval.

The severe hardship suffered during the church's first decade is indicated in the sharp decline in membership from 4,409 in 1940 to ca. 2,400 by 1949. From the 1950s through the 1970s, despite continuing difficulties, a pattern of remarkable growth developed. By 1969 the 18 member congregations and ca. 125 branch congregations numbered 18,483 baptized members. In 1988 60 member congregations and 105 branch congregations reported a membership of 50,000. This latter figure is an estimate and should be taken to include both the children of Christian families and perhaps as many as 6,000 people who at one time or another registered interest in becoming Christians but have never been baptized. In 1969 the statistics showed 6,944 such persons in addition to the figure for baptized members given above.

Three Streams of Influence. The present-day Evangelical Church of Java represents the blending of three distinct streams of Christian influence. The first stream is that of the missionaries of the Doopsgezinde Zendingsvereeniging (Dutch Mennonite Mission Society) and the mission church they established in the area surrounding the Muria Mountain in the second half of the 19th c. The second stream is that of the indigenous Javanese Christian movement springing up during the same time period in the same area under the leadership of the Javanese Christian evangelist, Kyai Ibrahim °°Tunggul Wulung. A third stream of influence is that of Dutch Reformed Christianity.

The relationship between the first two of these streams was, in many respects, a contrapuntal one for several decades until after the death of Tunggul Wulung in 1885. Tunggul Wulung and his followers called themselves *Kristen Jowo* (Javanese Christians), while calling the Javanese followers of the Mennonite missionaries *Kristen Londo* (Dutch Christians). They viewed the Christianity of the Mennonite mission church as heavily compromised by its identification with the oppressive colonial regime and European culture in general. On the other hand, Jansz and his colleagues viewed Tunggul Wulung and his movement as a pathetic mixture of a few Christian ideas and practices with seemingly immoral Javanese cultural practices and superstitions. At one point Jansz confronted Tunggul Wulung with this question: "Why do you give the people mere pebbles of spiritual truth when you have the true pearls of the gospel to share?" Tunggul Wulung responded, "I'll just leave the sharing of the pearls to you." The fact was that 10 times as many people responded to Tungul Wulung's teaching and joined the Christian villages that he started than joined the mission churches. Could it be that Jansz just was not able to see pearls the Javanese people saw in Tunggul Wulung's teaching?

In the two decades following Tunggul Wulung's death the mission succeeded in drawing virtually all of the 1,000-member indigenous movement into the circle of the mission, whose congregations in 1879 had a mere 78 members. In the process the congregations of the movement were demoted to the status of being branches of the mission congregations as part of an effort to purify them and suppress their supposed syncretistic impulses. In the succeeding century many of the most capable leaders of the mission church would be drawn from the stream of the indigenous movement. However only with the formation of the Evangelical Church of Java as an independent body in 1940 and its rapid growth and development in more recent decades has the church been able to come to a more open appreciation of the part of its spiritual and cultural heritage that flows from the early indigenous movement. And only in the 1970s have the congregations that can be traced directly to the indigenous movement—Bondo, Banyutowo and Tegalombo—been recognized once more as mature, self-reliant full members of the conference.

The Mission Stream. More than any other person Pieter °°Jansz (1820-1904) shaped the character of the early Javanese Mennonite Mission church. As the first Mennonite missionary to be sent to a country of the non-Western world, Jansz went to Java in 1851 where he settled down to nearly 30 years of continuous mission work in the ancient port town of Jepara. He was joined for varying periods by other missionaries (H. °°Klinkert, Thomas °°Doyer, N. D. °°Schuurmans) and was finally succeeded by his son, Pieter Anthonie °°Jansz in 1881. The elder

Jansz was a teacher and a thoroughgoing pietist who expected his disciples to be able to testify to a clear experience of repentance from sin and conversion resulting in a distinctly new pattern of life. He also had a deep sense of the unjust and oppressive character of the Dutch colonial rule. This sensitivity came out in his various conflicts with government officials over his right to preach and teach the gospel, but was also very much present in his vision for a new and just agricultural community where Christian and non-Christian alike could live free from the grosser evils of colonial Javanese society.

Jansz was a gifted linguist who put forth a great deal of effort to (re)translate the Bible into Javanese and then revise his translation, creating dictionaries and grammars in the process. He was ultimately knighted by the queen of The Netherlands for his contribution to the knowledge of the Javanese language. But not unlike most of his missionary colleagues, Jansz had limited appreciation for the Javanese culture as a vehicle for the communication and expression of the Christian faith. Many Javanese customs and practices, in his view, had to be abandoned if Javanese people were to become truly Christian.

The church Jansz started grew slowly. He was frequently frustrated because members and even leaders of the young church failed to live up to his expectations. The gospel as he expressed it seems not to have engaged the Javanese in their situation as clearly and cogently as he hoped it would. He seems to have assumed that the Javanese, whose world was basically °animistic and pantheistic, should be able to apprehend and appropriate his (pietistic) expression of the gospel as readily as he himself and so many Europeans of his generation did. The pietistic interpretation of the gospel assumes on the part of the hearer a consciousness of a God who will hold humans accountable for their sins. The Javanese by-and-large live with a consciousness of a Deity that is something like the soul of the universe and permeates everything. They do not live in fear of punishment for moral infractions by a transcendent and holy God. Rather, their concern is with the myriad spiritual beings, forces, and ancestral spirits whom they might offend at any turn, and who might, therefore, retaliate by afflicting them with sickness or misfortune. As we shall see below Tunggul Wulung apparently had a better grasp of the situation of need in which the Javanese people lived and how the gospel of Jesus Christ could be appropriated to meet that need.

The mission team made initiatives in various areas. One of the most successful of the earlier initiatives was in response to inquiries coming from the village of Pulojati, located near the present-day town of Pecangaan about a third of the way between Jepara and the larger inland town of Kudus. The key leader in the fellowship that developed in Pulojati was °Pasrah Karso who later led his followers in the formation of what became the first permanent mission congregation, Kedungpenjalin (1869). Over the following two decades the Kedungpenjalin congregation developed nicely without direct mission tutelage, growing in 20 years to more than 150 adult members. That was in spite of the attraction of the developing mission colony of Margorejo founded in the early 1880s. Pasrah Karso remained the leader of that congregation until his death in 1895, at which time he was replaced by a missionary from Russia, Johann °°Hübert.

Perhaps the most characteristic feature of the Javanese Mennonite mission church was the development of several mission agricultural colonies. As it took shape under the leadership of Pieter Antonie Jansz, beginning in 1882, the first colony in Margorejo deviated in substantial degree from the original vision of the elder Jansz. The original idea developed in Pieter Jansz' mind in the 1850s and 1860s in interaction with indigenous evangelist, Tunggul Wulung. Already before coming to the Muria area Tunggul Wulung had experienced the Javanese Christian plantation village of Ngoro in East Java under the leadership of the Indo-European planter, Coolen. Now his impulse was to gather his converts together in remote areas away from the evil influences of the town and the colonial government and establish new Christian villages. Jansz liked the idea but preferred the new village be located in an area where he might be able to reside or at least visit readily to supervise the enterprise. Tunggul did not want such direct supervision by a European.

To the idea of creating a new Christian village, Jansz added the idea of obtaining a long-term lease from the government for the development of agricultural lands. In 1874 he described his full vision in a booklet titled, *Landontginning en Evangelisatie op Java* (Land Development and Evangelization on Java), and subtitled, "A Proposal to Friends of the Kingdom of God." The goal was to recruit Christian experts in agricultural enterprise who would lease a tract of land and set up a °development corporation. Both Muslims and Christians would be invited to live in a settlement located there and work portions of the land in return for a portion of their produce. Expert advice and resources would be provided in both agriculture and marketing. No one would be required to participate in the government's system of forced crop production. Health services and schools would be provided. Opium and traditional dances would not be allowed. Missionaries would minister among the Christians of the settlement. They would run the schools. But they would not be allowed to have any influence in the management of the corporation, nor would they be allowed to pressure anyone to become a Christian.

In the actual formation of the Margorejo agricultural colony it was missionary P. A. Jansz who worked out the lease agreement with the government and took the initiative in setting up and managing the colony. Residents were to live according to "Christian" standards of conduct which meant, among other things, not working on Sunday, attending church services, and participating in other church activities. They were also required to send their children to the mission school and raise their children in a Christian way. Obedience to the owner, that is, the missionary, was emphasized. The profit motive of the original vision was abandoned, the primary goal now being the evangelization of the residents.

It is not difficult to see that from the beginning the missionary in Margorejo was in a dominant position, a fact that inhibited later efforts to bring the whole enterprise under the direction of national leaders. However, the colony at Margorejo was, in many ways, successful. The whole Jepara congregation moved there as did many people from other areas, including the Reformed Church congregation in Kayu Apu that had been established by the Nederlandsch Zendelingengenootschaft (Netherlands Missionary Society, NZG).

The Indigenous Stream. Having participated in the war of rebellion against the Dutch in the 1820s, according to tradition, and later becoming a hermit mystic, Tunggul Wulung was about 50 years of age when he finally became a Christian in East Java (ca. 1852). Coming to Jepara after brief training as an evangelist by Reformed (NZG) missionary Jellesma in East Java, Tunggul Wulung sought acceptance as a coworker of Pieter Jansz in 1853. Jansz was not impressed with Tunggul Wulung's command of basic Christian teachings and proposed that he become Jansz' understudy for a time, living together with Jansz in his house, after which he might be able to become Jansz' assistant. To Tunggul Wulung this proposal from a Dutchman 20 years his junior was unacceptable. To Tunggul Wulung not only did Jansz assume too much right to dominate Javanese Christians, his way of expressing the gospel was less than appropriate to the Javanese situation.

Tunggul Wulung worked and taught in a way that was highly questionable to the missionaries but reflected a clear understanding of the life situation of Javanese people. He knew that one of their greatest needs was to be freed from the fear of the myriad spiritual powers and forces impinging on their daily lives. In the Christian conviction that Jesus is Lord, Tunggul Wulung saw as the center of his ministry the power encounter that would deliver Javanese people from the oppressive spiritual environment in which they lived. Further, he knew the debilitating effect of the oppressive colonial rule on the Javanese people. For Tunggul Wulung, Christian belief in the coming fulfillment of the Kingdom of God was a source of hope for eventual deliverance from that oppressive rule.

To relate the gospel directly to the issues of life the Javanese people faced, Tunggul Wulung developed teaching devices that marked Christian faith off clearly from Islamic belief. Whereas Muslims regularly confessed in Arabic that "there is no god but God, and Mohammed is the Prophet of God," Tunggul Wulung taught a confession of faith that began in the same way as the Muslim confession but continued into a second line in the vernacular Javanese affirming that "Jesus Christ is the Son of God." Instead of nonsensical magical formulas to ward off dangerous spiritual influences that the Javanese received from their shamans, Tunggul Wulung taught model prayers which fostered a sense of dependence on the power of God to free from the power of evil. Pieter Jansz wrote a tract urging people to "repent for the Kingdom of God is at hand," seeking thus to tie into the long-standing Javanese tradition of hope for the return of the Just Prince. In Tunggul Wulung's teaching there was a much closer correspondence between the traditional expectation of the return of the Just Prince to establish a just society and the Christian hope in the coming kingdom of the Prince of Peace.

Some of the beliefs, practices and reported activities of Tunggul Wulung and his followers were criticized by missionaries as entirely unacceptable for Christians. They thought Tunggul Wulung accepted too much honor from his followers, though it was customary for Javanese to kneel before Europeans in that day. But most galling was Tunggul Wulung's refusal to submit to the missionaries' direction and supervision.

On the other hand, Tunggul Wulung recognized that the mission was an important resource for him and his movement. He frequently went to Jansz' Bible lessons and was clearly one of his most inquisitive students. Later Tunggul Wulung sent his potential assistants to the mission schools for training. For a time he allowed the mission to establish a mission school in Bondo, until it became clear that the missionaries were using the school as a tool to draw the young people away from the indigenous movement and into the circle of the mission. Clearly Jansz and Tunggul Wulung learned much from each other. Hindsight suggests that greater openness on both sides might have made possible the development of a single united Christian movement in these early decades, a movement that would have been much more effective in evangelizing the surrounding society. In the final analysis, with later incorporation of the indigenous movement into the mission church Tunggul Wulung and his spiritual offspring have made an immeasurable contribution to the life and thought of the Evangelical Church of Java.

The Reformed Stream. The stream of Reformed influence is represented most concretely by the incorporation in 1898 of the Kayu Apu congregation near Kudus and its branch, Ngalapan, near Juana, into the circle of the Mennonite mission. These groups were formed beginning in the early 1850s under the care of missionaries of the Nederlandsch Zendelinggenootschap (Netherlands Missionary Society, NZG), but were finally turned over to the Mennonite Mission as part of NZG's strategy to concentrate its efforts and resources in East Java.

Since that time there has been much interaction and cooperation with other Indonesian churches many of which have a Dutch Reformed (or Rereformed) theological and ecclesiastical heritage, particularly in the area of ministerial training. There has been an especially close interaction with the other two larger Javanese churches, the Gereja Kristen Jawa (the Javanese Christian Church) of south central Java and the Gereja Kristen Jawi Wetan (the Christian Church of East Java). The first formal arrangement of this kind was the merging of the first theological school in Pati (1952-55) with the Bale Wiyoto Institute in Malang, East Java, which later merged with Duta Wacana Seminary in Yogyakarta. Mennonite missionaries from Europe (°Europäisches Mennonitisches Evangelisationskomitee, EMEK), and North America Mennonite Central Committee (MCC) workers taught at Bale Wiyoto. The Evangelical Church of Java has had a strong presence at both the board and student levels at Duta Wacana Seminary and at Satya Wacana Christian U. in Salatiga. The most obvious expression of Reformed influence in the Evangelical Church of Java to the visitor is the pattern of worship and church organization which bears strong resemblance to traditional Dutch Reformed patterns.

Present-day Theology and Ministry. *The Love Ethic.* Daniel Amstutz resigned from his position as chairman of the conference in 1941 because the conference wished to liberalize the initial conference constitution's position on the nonparticipation of Christians in armed conflict. The groundswell of Indonesian hope for freedom after four centuries of oppressive colonial rule was being felt in all segments of Indonesian society. Youthful Christians were especially sensitive to taunts from the Muslim majority that as followers of the Dutch religion they were surely supporters of continued Dutch rule. How could Christians prove to fellow Indonesians that, though they were Christians, they were nevertheless for a free Indonesia and against continued colonial rule? The church was torn between those who wished to hold on to the nonresistant position and those—mostly younger people—who saw no alternative to active participation in a struggle against the colonial regime.

The tension continues. During the revolution younger church leaders were involved in intelligence operations and other functions of the nationalist forces. In the intervening years some pastors have served as military chaplains. Though there is no military draft, some young men still join the armed forces. On the other hand, the response of Indonesian Christians to the needs of suffering people after the failed Communist coup in 1965 contrasted sharply with the radical Muslim declaration of Holy War against the assumed perpetrators of the coup. Many thousands of people were attracted to the Christian faith by the risk-taking love and care of Christians for the families of the people, who numbered ca. one million, who were killed or imprisoned in the aftermath of the coup attempt. This was a powerful demonstration of the compassion of the Suffering Servant.

Church Growth. It cannot be said that the reason for the remarkable growth of the Evangelical Church of Java has been the development of a highly organized program of evangelistic witness. The evangelistic ministry of the churches is generally in a low key and almost never involves anything like a public campaign. However there is a lively commitment among the leadership and membership to share their faith and respond to invitations to minister. Frequently this ministry will involve prayer for healing and deliverance from evil spiritual forces as well as encouragement to turn away from sin and commit oneself to Christ as Lord. Many Bible study groups and branch congregations have grown out of responses to such invitations.

During the late 1960s and the 1970s conference leaders expressed very live interest in fostering the formation and maturation of as many branch congregations as possible. Clear guidelines and procedures were set up for both the formation of branch congregations and the maturation of branch congregations into "adult" members of the conference no longer under the supervision of their mother congregations. Such rites of passage are carefully prepared for and celebrated publically in a grand fashion. Thirty-five congregations achieved "adulthood" during the 1970s. That represents a 200 percent increase in the number of congregations. Ten of them were offspring of the Pati congregation.

Service Ministries. The restoration of the churches' educational ministry was first priority after the decade of war and revolution. In the late 1980s the conference school board, BOPKRI, oversees the operation of about 12 elementary, junior and senior high schools.

Redevelopment of medical ministry, which had been a high priority during the mission era—with the hospitals in Kelet and Tayu with branches and clinics in various places and a large leprosarium in Donorojo—was also important to the conference leadership. Several clinics operated by Mennonite Central Committee (MCC) volunteers in the 1950s were finally superseded in stages by a medical ministry operated by a conference board, the *Yayasan Kesehatan Kristen Sekitar Muria* (Muria Area Christian Health Board), formed in 1959 and 1964. This board was not able to regain control of the Kelet hospital or the Donorojo facility from the government but finally regained control of the remains of the Tayu facilities where in the late 1960s and early 1970s a large hospital of more than 100 beds has been constructed. It operates now without outside personnel or financial support.

°Relief work was a major activity of MCC volunteers in the 1950s and 1960s. From the late 1960s to 1977 the Evangelical Church of Java, the Persatuan Gereja-Gereja Kristen Muria Indonesia (GKMI; Muria Christian Church of Indonesia), EMEK, and MCC worked cooperatively in economic development ministries through YAKEM, the Muria Cooperative Economic Development Foundation. Projects ranged from livestock production and fishing to irrigation and rice production. The venture was discontinued because of diversity of vision, management difficulties, and inadequate attention to internal controls. Other relief work has been carried out by PAKKRI for orphans with aid from Internationale Mennonitische Organization (IMO). A Commission for Development outside Java (KPLJ) has arranged for the migration of hundreds of landless Javanese peasant families to southern Sumatra, Kalimantan, and Sulewesi and followed up by sending mission pastors to form churches among them and encouraging MCC to develop an extensive agricultural development program in those areas. The churches collected and sent some relief supplies during the early troubles on the island of Timor.

A very significant service ministry carried on cooperatively with the Muria Christian Church of Indonesia with financial support from EMEK and MCC is that of the *Yayasan Beasiswa Mennonit* (the Mennonite Scholarship Foundation), which provides scholarships for dozens of technical school and university students each year. It also administers an MCC and IMO program for scholarships in the schools operated by the two Mennonite conferences in Java, the BOPKRI and Masehi schools.

Leadership Training. Besides the first theological school (1952-55) and the joint programs with other churches in theological education mentioned above, the Evangelical Church of Java, in cooperation with the Muria Christian Church of Indonesia, EMEK, and MCC, established another theology school in Pati in 1965, *Akademi Kristen Wiyata Wacana* (AKWW). The graduates of this college-level school have had a key role to play in the many new congregations formed over the last 20 years.

In response to the government's policy to require school students to study the religion of their choice—Islam, Christianity, or Hindu/Buddhism—and to train and hire people to teach these religion courses, the Evangelical Church of Java in 1970 formed PGAAK, a senior-high-school-level school for training teachers of Christian religion for elementary schools. This has been followed in 1980 with the formation of a similar program in conjunction with AKWW for the training of teachers of Christian religion for high schools.

Ecumenical Relations. From the beginning the Evangelical Church of Java has been a member of the *Dewan* (now *Persekutuan Gereja-Gereja di Indonesia* (Council [now Communion] of Churches in Indonesia). This means that they have a basic commitment to interact with other churches and to be concerned with what concerns them. It also means that they have close awareness of questions about the place and role of the Christian community in the wider Indonesian society. At many points members of the Evangelical Church of Java have made significant contributions to the theological, ecclesiastical, and policy discussions of this organization.

The primary links the Evangelical Church of Java has with churches overseas are through the °Doopsgezinde Zendingsraad (Dutch Mennonite Mission Board) and EMEK in Europe and through MCC in North America. The church has also participated in the Mennonite World Conference since 1952. Links with Mennonite churches in Asia have developed in limited degree through the reconciliation work camps and the Asian Mennonite Conference. One couple from the church has served for a period under Asian Mennonite Services and MCC in Bangladesh.   LMY

MWH (1978), 145-51; Philip van Akkeren, *Sri and Christ* (New York: Friendship Press, 1970); S. Coolsma, *De Zendingseeuw voor Nederlandsch Oost-Indie* (Utrecht: C. H. E. Breijer, 1901); Doopsgezinde Zendingsvereeniging, *Verslag van de Staat en de Verrigtingen der Doopsgezinde Vereeniging ter Bevordering der Evangelieverbreiding in di Nederlandsche Overzeesche Bezittingen* the annual reports of the Dutch Mennonite Mission Union published in Amsterdam beginning in 1848; A. G. Hoekema, "Kyai Ibrahim Tunggul Wulung (1800-1885), 'Apollos Jawa,'" *Peninjau*, 7, 3-23; idem, "Pieter Jansz (1820-1904), First Mennonite Missionary to Java," *MQR*, 52 (1978), 58-76; idem, "De Tijd is Vervuld," *Doops. Bijdr.*, n.r. 2 (1976), 144-59; P. Jansz, *Landonginning en Evangelisatie op Java* (Amsterdam: Hoveker and Zoon, 1874); idem, manuscripts of annual reports to the Doopsgezinde Zendingsvereeniging, in the archives of the Evangelical Church of Java in Pati, Indonesia; idem, personal correspondence and journal (Daagboek) in three handwritten vols. covering 1852-60, in archives of the Zoopsgezinde Zendingsraad in Amsterdam; Th. E. Jensma, *Doopsgezinde Zending in Indonesia* (The Hague: Boekcentrum N. V., 1968); *Jerih dan Juang* [National Survey on the Church in Indonesia] (Jakarta, Indonesia: Lembaga Penelitian dan Studi - DGI, 1979); Martati Ins. Kumaat, *Benih yang Tumbuh* [a survey of the Evangelical Church of Java], no. 5 in a series (Jakarta: Lembaga Penelitian dan Studi - DGI, 1973); Th. Muller-Kruger, *Sejarah Gereja di Indonesia* (Jakarta: Badan Penerbit Kristen, 1966); Wilbert R. Shenk, ed., "Mission and Politics in Nineteenth Century Java: Pieter Jansz's Tract on Dutch Colonial Policy," *MQR*, 54 (April 1980), 83-105; Lawrence M. Yoder, *Tunas Kecil, Sejarah Gereja Kristen Muria Indonesia* (Semarang, Indonesia: Komisi Literatur Sinode GKMI, 1985), also in English translation as "The Church of the Muria, A History of the Muria Christian of Indonesia (MTh thesis, Fuller Theological Seminary, 1981); J. D. Wolterbeek, *Babad Zending ing Tanah Jawi* (Purwokerto, Indonesia: De Boer, 1939); Lawrence M. Yoder, ed., *Bahan Sejarah Gereja Injili di Tanah Jawa* [Historical Resources on the History of the Evangelical Church of Java] (Pati, Indonesia: Komisi Sejarah Gereja GITD, 1977); idem, "The Introduction and Expression of Islam and Christianity in the Cultural Context of North Central Java" (PhD diss., Fuller Theological Seminary, 1987); Lawrence M. Yoder and Sigit Heru Soekotjo, "Sejarah Gereja Injili di Tanah Jawa" [History of the Evangelical Church of Java], unpublished manuscript; Lawrence M. Yoder, "Sejarah Margorejo," *Wiyata Wacana*, 7, no. 1 (1977), 18-25; idem, "Tunggul Wulung," *Wiyata Wacana*, 3, no. 2 (1974), 24-36.

Gereja Menonit Protestan Indonesia (Indonesian Protestant Mennonite Church). See Indonesia.

German Democratic Republic. See Deutsche Demokratische Republik.

German Language (ME II:50, III:290, IV:186). The German language is the original language of the Anabaptist-Mennonite tradition. Although formal use was made of Latin in some writings and disputations, almost all of the Anabaptist reformers and their followers were linguistically of German stock. The Swiss around Zürich and in other cantons, the Alsatians (Strasbourg), the Germans of Baden, Württemberg and the Palatinate (High German linguistically), those along the Rhine downstream to the Flemish and Dutch Low Countries and throughout the northern German territories (Low German linguistically), as well as in the upper (south) German areas of Bavaria, Austria and Bohemia—all of these shared a common linguistic bond, though their dialects were different. During the period of the Protestant Reformation the linguistic boundaries between Dutch, Low German, and the new High German coming from the Alps and neighboring regions were in a state of dynamic flux. The result of the changes was the ascendancy of High German and a separate literary Dutch language, while the Low German, which had been an important language of commerce, began its decline. Even the Dutch and Low German °dialects in which °Menno and others wrote (see °°Oosters) were little more than regional German dialects at that time, as was the Saxon dialect (East Middle German) that Luther fashioned into the forerunner of modern standard German (High German). For Mennonites the German Language in its various regional and historical forms is thus a "mother tongue" in an other than national sense. The variations of High and Low German which have been brought to the Union of Soviet Socialist Republics (USSR), the North and South American continents, and to various other Mennonite enclaves testify to the movements of different Mennonite groups in the intervening centuries, whether via the Palatinate and the Low Countries to Pennsylvania and Virginia, or from the Low

Countries to Prussia and from Russia to Canada, the United States, and Latin America.

Mennonite Low German (*Plautdietsch*) added words and expressions from the several cultures (Polish, Ukrainian, English) through which the Prussian-Russian Mennonites passed (Thiessen, *Studien Zum Wortschatz*), thus reflecting the historical experience of the group. The more formal "High German" used by these Prussian Mennonites also developed a peculiarity resting on a vocabulary limited by its narrow use in church and school and on borrowings from the *Plautdietsch*. "Pennsylvania Dutch" is the approximate "Swiss" American equivalent of the Russian Mennonite *Plautdietsch*, reflecting the origins and history in several upper German dialects (Swiss, Alsatian, Palatine, even Dutch) of the early Mennonite immigrants to the American colonies. In some situations Mennonites adapted more quickly than in others and some groups and "churches" shifted more rapidly than others, but in general it may be said that change has been slow and language retention has been high in Mennonite groups, relative to other ethnic and linguistic communities.

The classic texts peculiar to the Anabaptist-Mennonite tradition were written in German beginning with the letter of Conrad °Grebel and his friends to Thomas °Müntzer (1524), the °Schleitheim Confession (1527), the mystical writings of Hans °°Denck, the treatises of Pilgram °Marpeck and Menno Simons, and the texts collected in the °°*Ausbund* hymnal and the °°*Martyrs Mirror*. Dutch classics like *The* °°*Wandering Soul* by J. P. °°Schabaelje and *The Way to the City of Peace* by Pieter °°Pietersz (1574-1651) became popular in German editions, as did Menno's writings. The influence of °Pietism enters into the Mennonite vocabulary in the sermons and devotional literature of Jakob °°Denner and J. H. °°Jung-Stilling, *Das Heimweh*). Several of these standard Mennonite works were first published in America in the German language. Historically perceptive works of fiction, like Sara Stambaugh's *I Hear the Reaper's Song* (1985) preserve memories of a past in which formal "High German" as well as "Dutch" had a place in Mennonite social and religious communal life in Pennsylvania, Ontario, Virginia, and midwestern states. As in the case of the Russian Mennonites, formal "High German" was the church language, while the dialect, which unlike *Plautdietsch*, was of High German linguistic stock, was used in common parlance.

German Language since 1960. In Germany, due largely to the resettlement of the °*Umsiedler* from the Soviet Union and some returnees from South America, the number of Mennonites in Germany, who use standard German as a matter of course, has grown to ca. 11,000 as of 1986. These groups have their own German language publications, among them the traditional *Mennonitische Blätter* (founded 1854 in Danzig, merged with *Gemeinde Unterwegs* to create *Die Brücke* in 1986), but these do not project greatly into the non-German Mennonite world.

German-speaking Mennonites in the Soviet Union have made greater efforts to preserve their language—together with their faith—than their North American counterparts, since for many of them this is clearly seen as a key to preserving their identity as a group. After 1956, when a certain freedom of movement was again permitted, many "Germans," including Lutheran, Catholics, °Baptists, and Mennonites, moved to places where they could congregate as a linguistic and religious community (e.g., the German Mennonite Brethren Church in °Karaganda, which however dropped "German" from its name in 1967.) In recent decades a German subculture has developed in centers like Alma Ata, Khasakhstan, to which writers of Mennonite background have contributed along with others of German background. Their chief organ is *Neues Leben*, a literary paper published in Moscow and, since 1984, a literary journal called *Heimatliche Weiten*. Works by writers of varying ideological stripe but of Mennonite background are to be found in these periodicals.

In North America the generation of settlers to Canada and the USA in the 1920s produced an immigrant literature in German (Arnold °Dyck, Gerhard °Friesen), unlike their predecessors of the 1870s, who took an inward-looking stance linguistically. The importance of the later generation of pioneer writers, including also J. H. Janzen, Peter J. Klassen, Gerhard Loewen, and others, was only recognized later when German had been for the most part abandoned by the institutional church and for general use. German worship services have been continued for the older generation where appropriate, just as the German papers, *Mennonitische Rundschau* and *Der Bote* still supply a remnant of the Mennonite population with reading material. *Plautdietsch* continues to find some colloquial use and has been rediscovered for literary purposes, following the example of Arnold Dyck. The impetus for German language preservation has shifted from the churches to other institutions (societies for the preservation of "heritage languages" and °lobbyist groups, e.g., the German-Canadian Congress, and, specifically, Manitoba Parents for German Education, which are strongly supported by Mennonites. A 1986 study showed that about 50 percent of Canadian Mennonites retained High German and/or Low German skills, while the use of Pennsylvania Dutch in Ontario had almost been lost except among °Old Order Mennonites and °Amish (Driedger/Hengstenberg). In the eastern and midwestern United States traces of the older languages, both High German and dialects, are seen mainly in literature, art, and °folklore and in the continuing use of German hymnals and sermons by Old Order and Amish groups. More recent immigrants in Kansas and Nebraska and latterly in California also show proficiency in both High and Low German, but little is being done to counteract their erosion.

German is still used in the Mennonite settlements in Mexico and Central America, where a conservative orientation ensures language retention while it limits language use to utilitarian and religious purposes. W. Schmiedehaus paints a bleak picture of the present and future in respect of the Old Colony schools and language teaching in particular.

In South America German is still in active use,

although movement into Portuguese and Spanish urban areas is having the same effects as the °urbanization of North American Mennonites. The Paraguayan Mennonite colonies are able to ensure retention of both High and Low German within their communities. In both North and South America the German-speaking countries of Europe, especially the Federal Republic of Germany, have invested substantial resources to encourage and preserve the German language and Mennonites have not been reluctant to avail themselves of this help. Thus, while the earlier view seeing a necessary connection between faith and language has largely been overcome, the underlying attachment to the original "mother tongue," whether High or Low German, is still much in evidence.

For most Mennonites of the 1980s, who do not live in a viable German linguistic community, the German language has become a thing of the past. This has meant for some that High German is at best a literary language, learned at school and perhaps used for academic, artistic, or professional purposes. In the case of *Plautdietsch* attempts have been made to retard its loss by regularizing its individualistic orthography and publishing the Mennonite classics of Arnold Dyck and other authors. Some writers, like Rudy Wiebe (°literature) and Armin Wiebe, have made effective use of *Plautdietsch* in their English novels, the latter by inventive translations of the dialect idiom (referred to as "Flat German") into a comic context not too different from that created by Arnold Dyck in his *Koop en Bua* stories.   VGD

Leo Driedger, Peter Hengstenberg, "Non-official Multilingualism: Factors Affecting German Language Competence, Use and Maintainance in Canada," *Canadian Ethnic Studies*, 18 (1986), 90-109; Jacob A. Loewen, "The German Language, Culture and Faith" (unpubl. ms. 1986); John Thiessen, *Studien zum Wortschatz der kanadischen Mennoniten* (Marburg: Elwart, 1963); Walter Schmiedehaus, *Die Altkolonier-Mennoniten in Mexiko* (Winnipeg: CMBC Publications; Steinbach, Mennonitische Post, 1982); C. J. Wells, *German: A Linguistic History to 1945* (Oxford, 1985); Armin Wiebe, *The Salvation of Yasch Siemens* (Winnipeg: Turnstone Press, 1984).

See also Acculturation; Identity.

German Mennonite Mission Committee. See **Deutsches Mennonitisches Missionskomitee.**

German Mennonite Peace Committee. See **Deutsches Mennonitisches Friedenskomitee.**

Germany. See **Bundesrepublik Deutschland; Deutsche Demokratische Republik.**

Ghana. In addition to establishing a church in Ghana, Mennonites have served the wider church in several areas of the country. The biggest thrust of this activity began in 1969 when missionaries could no longer serve in Nigeria because of the Biafra War (1967-70). As a result some of them transferred to Ghana.

Larry Borntrager, worked in the northern part of Ghana in an agricultural project operated by the Christian Service Committee of the Ghana Christian Council and the Presbyterian Church. From 1969 to 1982 12 young men served two-year periods in this

program. The last one, Stanley Freyenberger, returned with his wife, Jane, and for six years managed one of the agricultural stations.

In another area Edwin and Irene Weaver began relating to the sister churches in Accra of the Spiritual Independent churches (°African Independent Churches) they had served in Nigeria. This resulted in the founding of a school called the Good News Training Institute (1971), a day school for training church leaders in these churches. The school is controlled by a board of governors composed of persons from the various denominations of the city and by the Sponsoring Churches Association. Over the years the following Mennonite missionaries served these churches and the school: Willard Roth, Stanley and Delores Friesen, and Erma Grove.

Several missionary doctors worked in hospitals operated by the Evangelical Presbyterian Church in the Volta Region. Assistance was also given to the following for short periods of time: Church World Service; Ghana Bible Society; *Christian Messenger,* a Christian newspaper; Christoffel-Blindenmission; Islam in Africa Project; Peace Corps; and in various teaching positions.

In 1987 there was one Mennonite missionary in Ghana, working with the Ghana Mennonite Church.   EGr

MWH (1984), 12.

Ghana Mennonite Church (ME IV: 1087). In 1955 George Thompson, a Ghanaian, became acquainted with Mennonites at a YMCA World Convention in Europe. This resulted in his spending some months with Quintus Leatherman, a Mennonite missionary, in London. On Jan. 4, 1956, he was baptized and at his request was commissioned to begin a Mennonite church in Ghana.

The Mennonite Board of Missions and Charities (MC) undertook the support of this program and in 1957 sent four missionaries to assist Thompson in the development of a church. They found small groups meeting for services in Accra, the capital, and in several nearby villages. Expansion came through the requests of the people for schools in their villages. If they agreed to allow the teacher to conduct church services on Sunday and if no other denomination seemed to be working in that village, their request was granted. George Thompson left the Mennonite church in 1958 and S. Jay Hostetler, one of the missionaries, assumed leadership. The church was received as a member of the Ghana Christian Council in June 1959. It continued to expand in more of the villages, but the group that met in Accra died out.

Before the missionaries came, Thompson had begun using the Home Bible Studies, a correspondence course of the Mennonite Church (MC) in the United States. Over the years this was carried on by missionaries and is handled today by a Ghanaian. The church leaders as well as people from all over Ghana have taken these courses. In recent years it has also been used in prisons.

In 1961 a missionary nurse, Anna Marie Kurtz, began operating a government clinic in Amasaman, a village 15 miles north of Accra in an area where there are several Mennonite congregations. She serves the churches as well as the sick of the community. In another area 150 miles northeast of Accra where there were other small congregations, Ellen Moyer, a Canadian missionary physician, with help of her husband, Carson, opened a clinic in 1961. Carson gave leadership to the church in the area.

As well as the local national teachers who served as church leaders, some missionaries who gave leadership were Donald Nofziger and Laurence Horst. A mimeographed, informal newsletter, *Mennonite News Herald*, was published between 1977 and 1984. The church for many years has been active in the movement for church unity.

Membership in 1986 was 800 in 17 congregations in five language groups. The church is autonomous with three ministers, four licensed ministers, 13 lay pastors and three catechists. It continues to relate to the Mennonite Board of Missions and receives a small monthly subsidy from it. One missionary, Anna Marie Kurtz is present on a supportive role.   EGr

MWH (1978, 82-84; S. Jay Hostetler, *The Mennonite Church in Ghana, 1957-1964: Memoirs of S. Jay Hostetler* (Elkhart: MBM, ca. 1979); *MWH* (1978), 82-84; *MWH* (1984), 12.

Giáo Hội Tin Lành (Hệ-phái Mê-nô-nít), Vietnam (Evangelical Church [Mennonite Branch]). The Vietnam Mennonite Mission began its witness in 1957 when James and Arlene Krupp Stauffer and Everett and Margaret Glick Metzler went to Saigon under the Eastern Mennonite Board of Missions and Charities (MC). The first baptism occurred in 1961. A large student center was developed in Saigon, and a fellowship group met there. As missionary personnel increased, witness was begun in Gia Dinh (1964) and Can Tho, (1970). A congregation emerged in 1965 in Gia Dinh, the provincial capital adjoining Saigon (which was incorporated with Saigon into Ho Chi Minh City in 1975). The Gia Dinh community center offered extensive educational, social, and medical services, supported partially by Mennonite Central Committee (MCC). After the destructive 1968 street fighting, several hundred families were helped in rebuilding their homes. *Tran* Xuan Quang was ordained pastor in March 1969 and a new church center dedicated in 1973. Many members were active in social ministries at the center and in the community.

The church became autonomous in 1973 with the formation of *Giáo-Hội Tin Lành (Hệ-phái Mê-nô-nít)* (Evangelical Church [Mennonite Branch]). Total church membership in 1975 was 152.

All the missionary personnel left Vietnam during the revolutionary military activity in April 1975. Pastor Quang had gone to Lancaster, Pa., to attend a mission conference in March, and stayed in the United States. James Klassen (MCC) encouraged the Saigon and Gia Dinh congregations until he left in Apr. 1976. All the Mennonite Church properties were confiscated. Some members left the country; others returned to the countryside. After the revolution the Mennonite congregation in Gia Dinh joined with other churches in *Tin Lành Thống Nhứt* (United Evangelicals), but little was heard about this movement after its leader died in 1976. In 1988 a Mennonite leader. *Nguyen* Quang Trung, reported 30 Mennonite families. They had been active in con-

gregations of the *Hội Thánh Tin Lành Việt-Nam* (Evangelical Church of Vietnam) and were planning to resume their own meetings for Bible study, fellowship, and worship.

Former members of the Mennonite church in Vietnam are (1987) giving leadership to Vietnamese churches in Philadelphia, Sacramento, and Honolulu.   LSM

James R. Klassen, *Jimshoes in Vietnam* (Scottdale, 1986); Luke S. Martin, "An Evaluation of a Generation of Mennonite Mission, Service, and Peacemaking in Vietnam, 1954-1976," a Vietnam Study Project commissioned by MCC, MCC Peace Section, and EMBMC, 1977; James E. Metzler, *From Saigon to Shalom* (Scottdale, 1985); Wilbert R. Shenk, ed., *Miss. Focus: Current Issues* (Scottdale, 1980), containing chapters by James Metzler, James Klassen, and Luke Martin commenting on the mission and service experience; *Miss. Mess.* (EMBMC), various articles, 1957-; *MWH* (1978), 188.

Giesbrecht, Gerhard Benjamin (Jan. 27, 1906-Nov. 25, 1977), was born in Steinfeld, Molotschna Colony, Russia, to Benjamin Giesbrecht and Maria von Niessen. In 1909 the family moved to Markovka in the Slavgorod Mennonite colony, Siberia.

Gerhard Giesbrecht experienced a conversion in 1922 and was baptized on Aug. 6 of that year, joining the Grishkov Mennonite Brethren church. He attended the Bible school in °°Davlekanovo, 1925-26, where he developed a strong sense of mission. He and Katharina Unrauh were married on Apr. 7, 1928 and emigrated to Paraguay with his parents in Nov. 1929.

In the °°Chaco the Giesbrechts settled in the village of Gnadenheim, °Fernheim Colony, where he served as elementary school teacher for six years. During this time, however, he was constantly thinking of working among the Indians, whom he called the "dear brown ones." In 1937 he and his family left the colony and settled at Yalve Sanga, the newly established mission station (Licht den Indianern). Except for minor interruptions their work continued at that place until 1960.

From 1964 he served the Mennonite Brethren church in °Filadelfia, but his heart remained with the work among the Indians. He died unexpectedly of a heart attack while preaching a sermon at the Mennonite Brethren Church in Filadelfia.   GR

Gingerich, Melvin (January 29, 1902-June 24, 1975), was managing editor of *Mennonite Encyclopedia*, vol. I-IV. This statement supplements the editor's biographical notice in *ME* IV:1149. Gingerich retired from major responsibilites as archivist of Mennonite Church Archives and managing editor of the *Mennonite Quarterly Review* and editor of the *Mennonite Historical Bulletin* in 1970, but continued his residence in Goshen and activities as researcher, writer, lecturer, and consultant to various church agencies at home and abroad until his death. A devoted member of the Mennonite Church (MC), his interest, concern, and service included the total Mennonite movement throughout the world. In 1969 he made a tour of Mennonite communities in Africa, Asia, and Latin America, discussing archival matters with leaders in these locations and helping them establish archival policies. In 1974 he became the first person to receive the Sister M. Claude Lane Memorial Award established by the Society of Southwest Archives and granted by the Society of American Archivists. He was a meticulous researcher, balanced writer, good organizer, and concerned counselor. Theologically he was conservative but not Fundamentalist, politically he was liberal but not leftist. His ability to communicate his strong convictions in patient compassion helped him to converse effectively with people of differing opinions inside and outside Mennonite circles. From Feb. 26, 1942, to July 19, 1973, the *Mennonite Weekly Review* published his book review column, "On My Desk." The books reviewed are evidence of the breadth of his interests, which enabled him to speak and write so effectively on many subjects. His special concerns were church history, social history, international relations, social problems, and theology. He wrote a book-length study of Mennonite °dress (1970).   NPS

Who's Who Mennonites (1943), 82-83; memorial notices in *GH* (July 15, 1975), 501, (Aug. 5, 1975), 554, and *MQR*, 52, no. 2 (Apr. 1978), special issue, including an extensive bibliography of Gingerich's writings; Melvin Gingerich, *Mennonite Attire Through Four Centuries* (Breinigsville, Pa.: Pennsylvania German Society, 1970).

Gingerich, Newton L. (Oct. 13, 1925-Aug. 1, 1979), an active and influential leader in Mennonite Church (MC) congregational, conference, and institutional work. He was born in the Drake-Guernsey area of Saskatchewan. He pastored three congregations in Ontario during his active ministry. He served on numerous conference, denominational, and inter-Mennonite committees and boards. He was chairman of Mennonite Central Committee (MCC), 1977-79, and a member of its executive committee, 1968-79; chairman of MCC (Canada) 1972-78; moderator of the Mennonite Church (MC), 1973-75 and half-time executive secretary for Mennonite Church, Region I, until his death. Gingerich served on the general council and the executive council of Mennonite World Conference. He was a strong advocate of °inter-Mennonite cooperation and one of the early supporters for the integration of various conferences in Ontario. He taught at the Ontario Mennonite Bible School and Institute; was its principal, 1958-59; and wrote the history of the school, *Mission Completed*. His formal training included work at Eastern Mennonite College, Harrisonburg, Va. He was married to Mary Sommers and had 3 sons and 1 daughter. He died in Kitchener and was buried in the cemetery at the East Zorra Mennonite Church.   RL

Gingrich, Arnold Elmer (1911-70) was born near Preston, Ont., and ordained a Mennonite minister in 1935. He was pastor of the Bothwell Mennonite Church, Kent Co., Ont., from 1935 to 1960, when he moved to London, Ont. He was president of the London Rescue Mission board from 1960 to 1964 and was field secretary for the Ontario Mennonite Mission Board, 1961-69. He was president of the London Council of Churches, later called the Inter-Church Council, in 1968 and 1969.

While at Bothwell, Gingrich conducted a weekly radio broadcast (World of Missions) on Chatham radio station CFCO. From 1969 until his death, he was executive secretary of the Ausable Springs Ranch, Ailsa Craig, Ont. Gingrich was president of

the London Folk Arts Council (1966-69) and member of the board of the Canadian Bible Society (1960-70). At his death he was survived by his wife Gladys (Shantz), a daughter Ruth Gingrich of Bella Coola, B.C., and a son, Paul, of Ann Arbor, Mich. DFl

Correspondence, radio transcripts, and other papers of Arnold Gingrich are held by the Mennonite Archives of Ontario, Conrad Grebel College, Waterloo.

Glaidt, Oswald (fl. 1520-46). See Sabbatarianism.

Glass, Esther Eby (Oct. 7, 1911-Oct. 11, 1972), was born in Denbigh, Va., and moved to Lancaster, Pa., when a teenager. She married Forrest Glass in 1934. They became the parents of two children. Her writing appeared in most of the Mennonite Publishing House periodicals, beginning with a 24-chapter serial in the *Youth's Christian Companion*, 1948-49. She wrote fiction (including several books for junior-age children), non-fiction, and curriculum (°Sunday School literature) pieces. Some of her writing was done on assignment but most of it came out of reflections on her observations, concerns, and interests. She was a gifted Sunday School teacher and speaker. She was employed in the book department at the Provident Bookstore in Lancaster and helped at the Mennonite Information Center. She was buried in Mellinger Mennonite Church Cemetery.   HA

Menn. Bib. II, p. 446; Rich, *Mennonite Women* (1983), 162.

God (Trinity), Doctrine of The doctrine of God is central to Christian °theology. In fact, the term *theology* in the broad sense means the study of God and is not restricted to Christianity. Usually Christian theology is understood more specifically to include reflection on the nature of God, on God's self-disclosure in creation and especially in Christ as witnessed to by the Scriptures, on God's ongoing interaction with the world through the °Holy Spirit, and on the consummation of God's purpose beyond time. It is quite appropriate therefore to say that Christian theology begins and ends with the doctrine of God.

A distinction needs to be drawn between a "doctrine" of God and a "concept" of God. The term *doctrine* denotes a "teaching" (Latin: *doctrina*) that is handed down by the church in accordance with the Scriptures. The term *concept* is more individualistic and has a more cognitive, philosophical connotation. It is noteworthy that as one moves into the °modern period one tends also to talk about God more in terms of concepts than doctrines. This shift is reflected in this article's concluding discussion of three theologians' notions of God.

For much of modern theology, characterized by the anthropocentric (human-centered) turn that came with the 18th-c. Enlightenment, the notion of God has become the primary issue or problem. In contemporary life and thought, be it psychological, sociological, political, philosophical, literary or theological, a recognition of the transcendent reality of God can no longer be taken for granted. This has led many Christian theologians, including some Mennonite thinkers, to find ways of reconceiving the concept of God in order to make it more comprehensible for modern people. We will come back to the modern view of God as a problem and various attempts at reinterpreting this doctrine for today.

Here we want merely to say that until the modern age there was no general agnosticism or rejection of the "existence" of God. The Bible itself simply assumed the reality of God (Ex 3:14: God says to Moses, "I am who I am") and the biblical authors were not *explicitly* preoccupied with metaphysical or philosophical speculation about the nature of God. Their primary concern was with God's self-revelation and historical action in the lives of people and the appropriate human response.

Implicitly, however, the Bible already raises theological and philosophical issues about who God is and how God can be known. These issues set the agenda for a development of a doctrine of God in the post-biblical period. In the Old Testament, for example, there is the problem of evil which confronts Job, and the fact that God allows the righteous to suffer. How can God be good if God brings about or tolerates such seeming injustice? Further, a variety of anthropomorphic images and metaphors, both masculine and feminine, used in Old Testament references to the divine stimulate the theological imagination to contemplate more fully the nature and attributes of God.

While both the Old and New Testaments are thoroughly monotheistic, new experiences of the acts of God in the New Testament era raise for early Jewish-Christians and Gentile-Christians much more sharply the issue of the nature of God. The early church's experience of salvation in Christ and divine power through the Holy Spirit poses for early believers the problem of how to reconcile these two phenomena with their unequivocal belief in the one God of the Old Testament.

During the first five centuries after Christ these issues were hotly debated by the Christian church around the question of the Trinity (Nicea, 325; and Constantinople, 380) and °Christology (Chalcedon, 451); the former dealing primarily with the relation of Christ to the Father, and the latter with the relation of the divine and the human in the person of Christ himself.

The trinitarian controversy is particularly important for us here and has ongoing relevance for any contemporary understanding of God. It revolved around two intrinsically related and archetypal concerns: the nature of God within himself and the nature of God for us. The first has been referred to as the *immanent trinity* (the threefold nature of God: Father, Son, and Spirit), the second as the *economic trinity* (God's threefold mode of being for us: as transcendent mystery above us, as historically disclosed to us in Jesus Christ, and as immanently present in us and the world through the Holy Spirit).

Unfortunately, we cannot here discuss at greater length the biblical concept of God nor these highly significant debates of the patristic period. It is important, however, to recognize that what occurred already within the Scriptures and continued during the post-biblical period was a *development of the doctrine of God* that has shaped all later Christian thinking in this regard, including our own.

Medieval theology contributed to this develop-ment in a number of important ways. Based particularly on such passages as Rom 1:18-21 and 2:14ff, which suggest that God in some sense reveals himself to believers and nonbelievers alike, a distinction was drawn between what is naturally knowable about God by everyone (sometimes referred to as natural revelation), and what can be known only by special revelation, e.g., the mystery of the Trinity and the incarnation.

Thus, in the Platonic-Augustinian tradition a pre-rational awareness of the reality of God is the condition for the very possibility of the moral and spiritual life. In the more Aristotelian-Thomistic tradition the natural knowledge of God takes a more rational form, reflected in the five arguments for the existence of God, although for Aquinas this rational knowledge was also closely linked to morality and spirituality (Rahner, ed., *Concise Sacramentum Mundi,* 564-66).

There was another stream of medieval theology concerning God which was especially important for certain segments of 16th-c. Anabaptism: the late medieval *unio mystica* traditions of Meister Eckhardt, John Tauler, and the *Theologia Deutsch.* While there were differences between the various mystical traditions on how the union between the divine and the human takes place, there was a common emphasis on the immanence of God, and the capacity of human beings for sharing a common nature with God (Packull, *Mysticism,* pp. 17-34).

Sixteenth-Century Anabaptists. The indebtedness of the Reformers to these various medieval streams concerning the doctrine of God is a highly complex and even controversial topic that cannot be summarized here without doing injustice to the thinkers involved. In general, however, it could be fairly said that the major Reformers, with their emphasis on human sinfulness and the need for a personal experience of justification through faith, tended to be suspicious of both the more rationalistic, scholastic natural theology tradition and the *unio mystica* theologies. Both Luther and Calvin stressed the transcendent sovereignty of God and the accompanying doctrines of grace and predestination, and tended to accentuate the gulf between the human and the divine. The Anabaptists, on the other hand, rejected predestination (although they did espouse a notion of election) in favor of free will and consequently were less inclined in their theology to emphasize the unbridgeable separation between God and humanity.

In our attempt to understand 16th-c. Anabaptist notions of God it is most important to note that what distinguished Anabaptism from its Reformation counterparts—the Catholic, Lutheran, Reformed and Anglican traditions—was the extent of its theological and sociological diversity. It was not one homogeneous mass but a collection of diverse movements spread throughout Europe, defined by local differences which affected each group's theology. Consequently, one cannot assume that there was one Anabaptist doctrine of God. Here as in other theological doctrines there was a dynamic plurality of views, cross-fertilizing each other and undergoing evolution especially during the early period.

Despite this heterogeneity, it is remarkable how

similar most of the early Anabaptists were in their concern for practical Christian living as an outgrowth of theological orthodoxy (orthodoxy defined here as fidelity to the traditional teachings of the church concerning Christology and the Trinity). It was not their formal acceptance of the church's historic creed in itself that is interesting but the way the formal confession of a triune God received content and functioned in their theology.

Both Robert °Friedmann and John C. Wenger have argued strongly that, while the weight of their concerns was not with doctrine but with discipleship, on the whole, 16th-c. Anabaptists were orthodox in their fundamental beliefs, accepting the Apostolic creed, Nicene trinitarianism, and Chalcedon Christology with few exceptions. Friedmann especially has taken care to defend the Anabaptists against the thesis that their theology tended toward Socinian rationalism and °°antitrinitarianism, and could thus be seen as a source of modern Unitarianism (Friedmann, 1973, pp. 53-57; Friedmann, 1948; Wenger, 1952, pp. 1ff).

Wenger's and Friedmann's claim that the Anabaptists were orthodox in their doctrine of God, but more faithful than other Protestant groups in their obedience to the ethical imperatives of Scripture, contains elements of truth. One needs, however, to guard against defining Anabaptism too narrowly and thus passing over the rich theological diversity that is part of the tradition. While it is true that on the whole the majority of early documents manifest a fidelity to the articles of the Apostles' Creed, for example, much of early Anabaptism exhibits a rather sophisticated reappropriation and reinterpretation of the theological tradition. Although there was a formal acceptance of the creedal affirmations, Anabaptists' preoccupation with the morally regenerated life was not simply an addition to the other doctrines but gave these doctrines, particularly the doctrine of God, a new flavor. The trinitarian nature of God was no abstract speculative doctrine of God but the necessary theological framework for ethics as we shall see. We need only turn to individual and corporate writings and confessions of the 16th c. to discover this close link between the primary Anabaptist concern for a regenerated life and the doctrine of God.

We look here at three varieties: (1) the South German-Austrian Anabaptism of Hans °°Denck and Hans °Hut; (2) the °Hutterian Anabaptism of Peter °°Riedemann; and (3) the North German-Dutch Anabaptism of °Menno Simons. (The Swiss Schleitheim Confession of 1527, with its seven articles—all concerned with practical matters of Christian life and distinctiveness—is perhaps the least doctrinally-oriented. Even here, however, the cover letter begins with a three-fold invocation of Father, Christ Jesus, and Spirit).

(1) While there were strong mystical elements in many early Anabaptists, it was the South German-Austrian stream, directly influenced by the cross-mysticism of the revolutionary Thomas °Müntzer, that most clearly reflected the themes of the *unio mystica* tradition alluded to above: no radical distinction between the natural and the supernatural, the immanence of God within the human soul, the

potential capacity of human beings to participate in divine nature, the close identification of °justification and °sanctification as a single process of gradual deification (Packull, pp. 25-27). There was in this branch of Anabaptism a strong link between the immanence of God (rebirth interpreted as the birth of the Son within the human soul), deification (participation of human nature in divine nature), and moral-ethical perfection (a gradual process of sanctification). This mystically-oriented doctrine of God was in its early phase not sectarian nor quietistic but, as illustrated by Müntzer himself, could be combined with an apocalyptic ideology directed at sociopolitical transformation (Packull, pp. 31ff).

(2) The Hutterian Anabaptism of Austria and Moravia was a later phase of South German-Austrian Anabaptism and reflects a more separatist and internally disciplined spirit, achieved primarily through an imposed communitarian uniformity. As in its earlier phase, the doctrine of God was explicated primarily in terms of its moral and ethical implications for human behavior, but was now more directly framed in terms of the concern for moral perfection within a separate community where all things were to be held in common.

The clearest example of this is Peter Riedemann's, *Account of Our Religion, Doctrine and Faith* (1545). The first part of the book is devoted to a theological commentary on the 12 essentials of the Apostolic Creed with the Anabaptist-Hutterite ethical concerns introduced right into the context of the various classical doctrines. What is remarkable is how each of these doctrines immediately receives practical application.

To confess the first article of the creed—that God is almighty father, creator of heaven and earth—is itself seen to be a moral act for "every sinner who remaineth and continueth in sin, and yet nameth God father, speaketh what is not true. . . ." Further, the whole purpose of confessing the second and third article of the creed—belief in Jesus Christ as the only begotten Son of God and the Holy Spirit as proceeding from the Father and the Son—is to acknowledge that through them we are "grafted. . . into the divine character and nature." This phrase, or versions of it, e.g., "participation in the nature of Christ (or God)," appears repeatedly in many of the Anabaptist writers and suggests, as we have already seen above, the deification of human nature in a way quite foreign to Luther and Calvin.

Concern for genuine moral regeneration is present in the *Account* from the start and the Hutterite commitment to Christian communalism is linked to the very immanent plurality within God himself: "Community, however, is naught else than that those who have fellowship have all things in common together, none having aught for himself, but each having all things with the others, even as the Father hath nothing for himself, but all that he hath he hath with the Son, and again, the Son hath nothing for himself, but all that he hath, he hath with the Father and all who have fellowship with him (Riedemann, *Account*, p. 43)."

(3) In our third representative Anabaptist group—North German-Dutch Anabaptism—we find one of the most explicit and straightforward treat-

ments of the doctrine of God in Menno's " Solemn Confession of the Triune, Eternal, and True God, Father, Son, and Holy Spirit" (1550), written in defense of the orthodoxy of his movement. It was a work intended to counteract the views of Adam Pastor, an Anabaptist bishop who had come to deny the full deity of Christ and was consequently excommunicated by Menno Simons and °°Dirk Philips, the very ones who had earlier ordained him.

While Menno remains simple, biblical, and nonphilosophical in his language, his expression of trinitarian orthodoxy is remarkably classic in outline (although his christology has sometimes been considered docetic—that is, it inadequately recognizes the human side of Christ). God (the Father) is Spirit, the "one and only eternal, omnipotent, incomprehensible, invisible, ineffable, and indescribable God . . . not physical and comprehensible but spiritual and incomprehensible." Jesus Christ is not a literal Word but "the eternal wise, Almighty, holy, true, living, and incomprehensible Word, which in the beginning was with God, and was God, by whom all things were made. . . ." This Christ "did in the fulness of time become, according to the unchangeable purpose and faithful promise of the Father, a true, visible, suffering, hungry, thirsty, and mortal man in Mary, the pure virgin, through the operation and overshadowing of the Holy Spirit, and so was born of her." In like fashion, Menno confesses the Holy Ghost to be "divine with His divine attributes, proceeding from the Father through the Son, although He ever remains with God and in God, and is never separate from the being of the Father and the Son" (Menno, *Writings*, 491-492, 496).

In the words of Menno, "these three names, activities, and powers, namely, the Father, the Son and the Holy Ghost (which the fathers called three persons, by which they meant the three, true, divine beings) are one incomprehensible, indescribable, Almighty, holy only, eternal, and sovereign God. . . . And although they are three, yet in deity, will, power, and works they are one, and can no more be separated from each other than the sun, brightness, and warmth. For the one cannot exist without the other" (Menno, *Writings*, 496).

What gives Menno's orthodox-sounding language its distinctive quality, as it does with the other Anabaptists, is his concern not so much for doctrinal orthodoxy in its own right as for the ethical function of the doctrine of God. John R. Loeschen gives a persuasive analysis of precisely this characteristic in his fine treatment of various Reformation views of the Trinity, church and ethics, in his *The Divine Community*.

Loeschen's thesis is "that the Christian understanding of the church, and hence of ethics, depends upon prior assumptions about God in his trinitarian functions" (p. 97). While all the Reformers were sensitive to the charge of doctrinal novelty, and argued that theirs was a genuine restoration of ancient views, what emerged were in fact new interpretations of Christ and the Trinity. The Holy Spirit received greater emphasis and the Trinity was valued more for its practical implications (the "economic" Trinity) than for its own sake (the "transcendent" or "immanent" Trinity).

This is particularly the case with Menno, who more than Luther or Calvin understood the classic doctrine of the Trinity christologically. His numerous references to the Holy Spirit, for instance, are directly associated with the "Spirit of Christ" (p. 73). His trinitarian theology is derived not from a "transcendental Trinity" but from the "immanent trinity of Christ's nature, Word, and Spirit" (p. 75).

While Menno's writings are full of biblical imagery pointing to the transcendence of God, his thought patterns are not explicitly ontological, metaphysical, or philosophical but historical and narrative. In the words of Loeschen, "Simons' effective trinity is an actual historical trinity of Christ's Word, Spirit and life, and not the transcendental, philosophical Trinity of Father, Logos, and Holy Spirit" (p. 80-81).

With Menno, as with the other Anabaptists, we see how doctrinal theological language, including trinitarian language, is linked to moral-ethical concerns. Trinitarian theology is important not for its own sake but as a necessary framework for the regenerated life. Christ, and more particularly, the Spirit of Christ, is that which unites the Christian with the nature and character of God. This participation in the character of Christ and through him in the very nature of God is one of Menno's most repeated themes; a form of sanctification (or even deification) which can occur only in the context of the visible believing community: the church. Menno's paradigm for this community is not a static one but the dynamic and evolving apostolic church which began at Pentecost and continued through the patristic period, receiving important theological definition in the early creeds, including that of Nicea (Loeschen, pp. 101-2).

Mennonites, Sixteenth to Twentieth Centuries. Hans-Jürgen Goertz has recently emphasized the discontinuity between 16th-c. Anabaptist confessions, which were primarily individual confessions of faith arising out of widely different situations, and later 17th-c. Mennonite confessions which had an ecclesiastical doctrinal character functioning more like mainline Reformation confessional statements. According to Goertz, the Anabaptists saw the whole of life as a confession and rejected what they perceived as the intellectualization and codification of faith by the other Reformers. For them verbal and lived confession was more important than fixed statements of belief. When they did come up with statements of orthodoxy it was usually in response to charges of heresy made against them.

This, maintains Goertz, changed during the 17th c. with the conservative reaction to the onset of modernity, and reflects a narrowing of the gap between Mennonites and the Reformed state church. In effect, what developed during this Protestant scholastic period was an authoritarian Mennonite orthodoxy, expressed in such doctrinal statements as the 1632 Dordrecht confession and the many subsequent confessions, for the purpose of uniting various factions around normative ecclesiastical formulations of belief and thereby guarding against freethinking subjectivism and nonconformity.

We cannot here trace the rather complex development of doctrine from early Anabaptist origins to later Mennonite confessions nor give a thorough analysis of the many individual church °confessions. What we want to do here is simply make a few observations about the doctrine of God as articulated in confessional statements between the 16th and 20th c.

First, what is remarkable is the multiplicity of confessions in a tradition that is supposedly non-creedal in orientation. Ironically, Mennonites have throughout their history probably produced more confessions and catechetical statements than ¹any other group. Noteworthy in this regard is the fact both of diversity (each confession arising out of a very particular social, historical and religious context) and unity, reflecting the heterogeneity and homogeneity of Mennonite origins. While there are significant differences between the General Conference Mennonite Church (GCM), Mennonite Church (MC), Mennonite Brethren, and other independent confessions, there are some remarkable common elements, in particular the four-fold axis around which most of the confessions are structured: creator, Christ, church, and consummation, with a particularly weighty emphasis on the life of the church and mission. Futher, virtually every confession begins with an article on God, often an extended article or series of articles on the Trinity and revelation.

Second, the Mennonite confessions of the 17th c. reflect a church that is beginning to consolidate its theology, christology, ecclesiology, and eschatology as a way of establishing a separate "sectarian" identity. With this comes a greater concern for spelling out in a *systematic* and *orderly* fashion the doctrine of a triune God and placing it in the proper sequence in a litany of doctrines. In most cases the chronology of these doctrines parallels the classical confessional and creedal tradition. While some of the confessions are more metaphysically oriented than others, there is a common concern to remain with biblical language as much as possible.

Third, the centrality of ethics and the Christian life (reflected in the weight given to ecclesiology and mission) is evident. The doctrine of God is carefully articulated not for its own sake but as the starting point for the more practically oriented articles that follow, including "free will, conversion, °feetwashing, church °discipline, Christian life and °nonconformity, integrity, and oaths, °nonresistance and revenge, the Christian and the state" (Loewen, 36). In this their ethical orientation the later Mennonites manifest a continuity with their early Anabaptist ancestry despite the discontinuities that historians (Goertz) legitimately point out. With the systematization of their various beliefs, including the doctrine of God, there is the increasing danger of intellectualizing faith, and separating ethics into sectarian dogmas held on to rigidly as a means of preserving static denominational purity.

One final observation may be in order before we leave this cursory summary of Mennonite theology prior to the 20th c. It would be erroneous to leave the impression that there was a uniform adherence to theological orthodoxy among Mennonites in the post-Reformation period. Friedmann, who takes great pains to point out the orthodox trinitarianism of early Anabaptists and later Swiss and Hutterian Mennonites, does allow that early on there was a softening of confessional orthodoxy among some European Mennonites particularly in The Netherlands, where certain "Dutch Mennonites became rather imbued with the spirit of Socinian [unitarian] rationalism" beginning in the second half of the 17th c. (Friedmann, 1948, 152-53).

Contemporary Mennonite Theology. Ever since the 18th-c. Enlightenment the concept of God has become a dominant preoccupation for much of Christian theology. As the relation of grace to nature (or revelation to reason) was a primary theological issue for medieval theology, justification and salvation for Reformation theology, and confessional orthodoxy for 17th-c. scholastic theology, so the very possibility of belief in a benevolent transcendent reality (God) has become *the* problem for 19th and 20th-c. theology.

Within modern theology itself there has been a shift. The earlier period, beginning with the Copernican revolution in philosophy associated with the name Immanuel Kant (1724-1804), saw the problem of God mostly in terms of epistemology: how can finite beings have any knowledge of reality that lies beyond sensory observation? Kant has been immensely influential for modern theology and his conclusion that we cannot have rational knowledge of God but that God remains a necessary postulate for ethics continues to surface in various ways in contemporary theology, including certain forms of political and liberation theology.

In the 20th c., marked by the novel experience of total wars, unimaginable atrocities, global environmental crises, growing disparity between the rich and the poor, the specter of a totally administered society, and the threat of the nuclear self-destruction of the human species, attention has shifted away from epistemological concerns to the question of transcendence and theodicy (the problem of good and evil). Is it possible to experience a transcendent reality in our technological age and, if so, how might that be expressed theologically and liturgically? Is it possible to believe in an all-loving and all-powerful God in the face of unmitigated evil and the suffering and annihilation of "innocent" victims throughout history? How might such a God be understood so as to preserve a belief both in God's providential sovereignty and control over the course of creation *and* the historical freedom of human beings actively to participate in the shaping of their own destiny?

One of the characteristics of contemporary theology is the diversity of answers given to these pressing questions concerning God. Whereas until recently, Mennonites did little explicit "systematic" theological thinking in general, let alone systematic reflection about the nature of God, in the late 20th c. they contribute significantly to and reflect the diversity of views in contemporary theological discourse. We can here offer only a brief sampling of this growing literature. We choose three systematic theologies to illustrate three diffferent 20th-c. approaches to thinking about God.

Early in the 20th c. there was the influential (that is, for Mennonites) systematic work of Daniel °Kauffman, who devoted much of his time articulating the fundamentals of the Christian faith, which he preferred to call *Bible doctrines.* Deeply concerned about the direction of the modern Mennonite church his theology reflects both the influence of °Fundamentalism in its fight against modernism (particularly the theory of evolution) and such historic Mennonite concerns as nonconformity to the world and nonresistance. In his major work, *Doctrines of the Bible,* his lengthy treatment of the doctrine of God resembles both in order and in content the scholastic method of 17th-c. Protestantism, so evident in the leading Fundamentalist theologians of his time. He even devotes considerable space to enumerating the various proofs for the existence of God. Daniel Kauffman sought clearly to present biblical doctrines as a bulwark against what he called the "critical age of liberalistic and modernistic tendencies" that he felt distorted modern theology. His theological orientation, while largely eclipsed by the so-called "Recovery of the °Anabaptist vision" school of thought, still attracts significant elements of the Mennonite population.

The more recent work of another systematic theologian, Gordon D. Kaufman, represents the other end of the 20th-c. theological spectrum. For Kaufman the issues raised by modern thought and life become the determinative factors in the theological enterprise. Gordon Kaufman has without a doubt given more attention to the "problem of God" (both in its epistemological and in moral-ethical dimensions) than any other Mennonite thinker. Demonstrating a broad understanding of contemporary philosophical and social thought, he has sought in his many writings to reinterpret traditional doctrines, especially the doctrine of God, from a post-Kantian historicist (nontranscendental) perspective.

His earlier writings, particularly his *Systematic Theology: A Historicist Perspective,* attempt to bridge traditional trinitarian language about God and biblical revelation with modern philosophical theories of knowledge and with historical and social-scientific views of human development. Becoming increasingly more radical in his dissatisfaction with the theological formulations of the past in his later writings, however, he argues that traditional concepts of God as unchanging and sovereign are no longer adequate to our nuclear age. It is imperative that we reconstruct imaginatively our doctrine of God to reflect our novel freedom as human beings to change fundamentally and even destroy totally our global environment, and to assume fully our responsibility not to do so (summary and critique by Froese, 1988).

The most recent attempt to write a full-length systematic theology from a "Believers Church" perspective but with a strong ecumenical orientation is Thomas Finger's two-volume *Christian Theology: An Eschatological Perspective.* Finger's theology can be seen as a middle position between Kauffman and Kaufman. It takes contemporary experience seriously while at the same time emphasizes the importance of God's sovereign initiative and the once-and-for-all nature of divine revelation. What is unique about Finger's approach is that he reverses the usual systematic order for presenting Christian doctrines. He begins not with the doctrine of God but concentrates in his first volume on the eschatological

themes of the New Testament proclamation, including the resurrection, judgment, heaven and hell, the nature and work of Christ. His system concludes with a consideration of the nature of God.

This method is consciously intended by Finger to highlight first God's activity in the world, and then to infer certain attributes about divine reality itself from the historical data of the church's experiences rather than from metaphysical speculation. Particularly significant is the weight Finger places on a doctrine that has, he admits, received little systematic treatment within the "believers church" tradition: the trinitarian nature of God. Here also, as with the other doctrines, Finger starts "from below;" that is, he develops a case for both the dynamic diversity and unity within the godhead from a consideration of the data of the human experience of divine reality and need for community. In this way he manages creatively to accentuate both the transcendence and immanence of God.

These are only three examples of contemporary Mennonites systematically thinking about God. One need only turn to the pages of *The Conrad Grebel Review* in its first six years of publication (1983-88) to discover the plethora of views concerning God within the Mennonite community. These positions range from a defense of classic creedal trinitarianism, to a God perceived in terms of modern process theology, to an Arian antitrinitarianism. A major new and creative impetus for reconceptualizing the doctrine of God has come from feminist theologians who challenge what they consider to be the almost exclusively male-dominated thinking of God as Father. A more comprehensive treatment of contemporary views concerning God would need also to deal with the theological movements arising among non-Western Christian churches.

Whether a synthesis of these various theological positions that are now vying with each other for prominence within the Mennonite communion is possible or even desirable remains to be seen. The theological diversity that is reflected in the historic Mennonite confessions and that is evident in the present is in line not only with the pluralism in contemporary Christian theology in general but is also consistent with the heterogeneity of the early Anabaptist movement itself. It seems clear, however, that historically Mennonites on the whole espoused a high, trinitarian doctrine of God, a doctrine that is in perpetual need of translation and interpretation but, nevertheless, continues to have relevance for every age. More important, however, is the urgency with which the modern challenges in the field of °technology, environmental concerns, °biomedical ethics, the °nuclear threat, and the growing concern for political and economic °justice call for a renewed sense of God as transcendent mystery and human beings as accountable stewards of the world. The common Anabaptist concern for a doctrine of God that is intrinsically related to a morally and ethically regenerated life in the context of the church in the world would appear to be a good theological starting point for facing the challenges of the postmodern age.

This heightened moral-ethical consciousness is the particular contribution that the Anabaptist and Mennonite traditions can make to the ecumenical discussion of the doctrine of God. Implicit in this our historic strength is, however, a danger: the danger of reducing the teaching concerning God to a notion of linear, ethical obedience to the historical Jesus alone. The challenge for Mennonites as a Mennonite communion will be to maintain a trinitarian framework for Mennonite ethical, historical, and communal concerns, a trinitarian framework which will guard both the transcendence and the immanence of God.　　　AJR

Mitchell Brown, "Jesus: Messiah not God," *CGR,* 5, no. 3 (Fall, 1987), 233-52; *Encyclopedia of Theology: The Concise Sacramentum Mundi,* ed., Karl Rahner (New York: Crossroad, 1986); Willard M. Swartley, ed., *Explorations of Systematic Theology: From Mennonite Perspectives,* Occasional Papers, 7 (Elkhart: IMS, 1984); Thomas N. Finger, *Christian Theology: An Eschatological Approach,* 2 vols. (Scottdale, 1985, 1989); idem, "The Way to Nicea: Reflections from a Mennonite Perspective," *CGR,* 3 (1985), 231-49; Robert Friedmann, "The Encounter of Anabaptists and Mennonites with Anti-Trinitarianism," *MQR,* 22 (1948), 139-62; idem, *Mennonite Piety Through the Centuries* (Scottdale, 1949, 1980); idem, *The Theology of Anabaptism* (Scottdale, 1973); H. Victor Froese, "Gordon D. Kaufman's Theology 'Within the Limits of Reason Alone': A Review," *CGR,* 6 (1988), 1-26; Hans-Jürgen Goertz, "Zwischen Zwietracht und Eintracht: Zur Zweideutigkeit täuferischer und mennonitischer Bekenntnisse," *Menn. Geschbl.,* Jg. 43/44 (1986-87), 16-46; Daniel Kauffman, *Doctrines of the Bible,* 2nd ed. (Scottdale: MPH, 1929); Gordon D. Kaufman, *God The Problem* (Cambridge: Harvard U. Press, 1972); idem, *Theology for a Nuclear Age* (Philadelphia: Westminster Press, 1985); idem, *The Theological Imagination: Constructing the Concept God* (Philadelphia: Westminster Press, 1981); Carl S. Keener, "The Darwinian Revolution and Its implications for a Modern Anabaptist Theology," *CGR,* 1, no. 1 (Winter, 1983), 13-32); Gayle Gerber Koontz, "The Trajectory of Scripture and Feminist Conviction," *CGR,* 5 (1987), 201-20; Loewen, *Confessions* (1985); John R. Loeschen, *The Divine Community: Trinity, Church, and Ethics in Reformation Theologies* (Kirksville, Mo.: The Sixteenth Century Journal Publishers, 1981); Werner O. Packull, *Mysticism and the Early South German-Austrian Anabaptist Movement 1525-1531* (Scottdale, 1977); A. James Reimer, "Mennonite Theological Self-Understanding, the Crisis of Modern Secularity, and the Challenge of the Mind Millennium," with response by J.Denny Weaver, in *Mennonite Identity: Historical and Contemporary Perspectives,* ed. Samuel Steiner and Calvin W. Redekop (Lanham, Md.: U. of America Press, 1988); A. James Reimer, "The Nature and Possibility of a Mennonite Theology," *CGR,* 1, no. 1 (Winter, 1983), 33-55; idem, "Theological Method, Modernity and the Role of Tradition," in *Prophetic Vision Applied to One's Academic Discipline,* Mennonite Graduate Seminar, (Elkhart, Ind.: Mennonite Board of Missions, 1978); Peter Riedemann, *Account of Our Religion, Doctrine and Faith* (London: Hodder and Stoughton, in conjunction with Plough Publishing House, 1938, 1950, 1970); Menno, *Writings;* J. Denny Weaver, "Perspectives on a Mennonite Theology," *CGR,* 2 (1984), 189-210; John C. Wenger, *The Doctrines of the Mennonites* (Scottdale, 1952).

Goertz, Elizabeth D. (1892-March 31, 1986), was born and raised in Marion Co., Ks. She graduated from the Bethel Deaconess School of Nursing, Newton, Ks., in 1918 and went to China as a missionary in 1921 under the General Conference Mennonite Church Mission Board. There she helped Abe M. Lohrentz in the dispensary at Kai Chow (later known as Puyang). She founded the successful Yu Jen School of Nursing there in 1930. When the Japanese occupied Kai Chow on Feb. 11, 1939, Goertz was interned in the notorious Shantung Compound.

After the mission work closed in China (1948) she worked as a nurse in mission work in India, China,

and the United States. She retired in 1976 to Hillsboro, Ks. where she remained until her death.　　　RSa

Juhnke, *Mission* (1979), 51, 59, 61; Henry J. Brown, *General Conference China Mission* (Taming-fu: the author, 1940), 126; *Menn. Rep* (Apr. 28, 1986), 23; *MWR* (Apr. 10, 1986), 12; *Menn. Bib. II,* nos. 14982, 18305.

Goertz, Peter S. (Oct. 3, 1886-1948), dean and professor of philosophy and religion at Bethel College, 1930-48. Born at Aulie-Ata, near Tashkent, in Asiatic Russia to Siebert Goertz and Helena Dalke-Goertz, Peter Goertz married Mathilda Harms in 1910. They had three children. After she died in 1931, he married Helene Riesen, 1933.

Goertz studied at McPherson College (AB, 1914), Yale Divinity School, (BD, 1917), and under Kenneth Scott Latourette at Yale U. (PhD, 1933). His thesis was "A History of the Development of the Indigenous Chinese Christian Church Under the American Board of Fukien Province."

Before coming to Bethel College as dean, Goertz was a school superintendent in Kansas, 1910-13 (Partridge and Hillsboro); missionary and seminary teacher for the American Board of Missions in China, 1918-26; and professor of philosophy and religious education, Tabor College, 1926-30. He was vice-chairman of the Mennonite Brethren peace committee, 1932-36.

Goertz is remembered as a gifted teacher who opened the door to the fascinating world of philosophy for his students. As a dean he was a gifted listener to students as well as faculty. He served Bethel College during its successful achievement of North Central Association accreditation. In his later years he moved from the Mennonite Brethren to membership in the General Conference Mennonite Church. He died suddenly in 1948 after returning from a sabbatical leave spent in °relief work in Europe.　　　JJE

Who's Who Mennonites (1943), 86-87; P. J. Wedel and E. G. Kaufman, *The Story of Bethel College* (North Newton: Bethel College, 1954), esp. 374.

Goerz, Martha Krehbiel (Apr. 18, 1876-Jan. 29, 1947), was born in Summerfield, Ill., to Christian and Susanna Ruth Krehbiel. The family moved to Kansas where Christian was involved in Kansas district and General Conference affairs. Surrounded by conference workers and guests, Martha developed a keen interest in the church.

She married Rudolph Goerz on Dec. 30, 1900. Their children were Harold, (b. 1902), and Frances (by adoption, b. 1911). The Goerz family had been influential in founding Bethel College and the Bethel Deaconess Hospital and Home in Newton, Ks. Rudolph and Martha retained an active lifelong interest in these institutions.

Martha's contribution to the General Conference Mennonite Church was her strong effort to establish the Women's Missionary Association (°Women in Mission). Elected to the first executive committee in 1917, she served as treasurer, Western District sewing supervisor (relief supples), secretary, vice-president, counselor, and editor of *Missionary News and Notes* in an almost unbroken span of 28 years.

She was an efficient organizer, tireless in her efforts to obtain official recognition for the association. She was determined to show that women could care for their families and homes and contribute to other projects as well. Her peers saw her as a courageous pioneer for women's work in missions. Martha was acknowledged as a cultured woman whose influence was felt in activities involving church, education and humanitarian service. GG

MLA (Newton), Women's Missionary Association files; Gladys Goering, *Women in Search of Mission* (Newton, 1980).

Golterman, Willem Frederik (b. June 14, 1898), following studies in Leiden and Amsterdam, was pastor in Makkum and Witmarsum (1933-36), then Amersfoort (1936-42), and Amsterdam (1942-47).

In 1942 he earned a doctorate in theology, and in 1946 he began lecturing at the Amsterdam Mennonite Theological Seminary and the U. of Amsterdam. From 1960 his lectures focused particularly on the history of 20th-c. Christianity, particularly relations among churches. He served in numerous additional capacities, as chairperson of the Algemene Doopsgezinde Sociëteit (Dutch Mennonite General Conference, 1946-51), secretary of the Doopsgezinde Zendingsraad (Mennonite mission board; 1951-53), and as research secretary of the ecumenical council of churches in The Netherlands (1953-60). RHof

Books, articles, and lectures by Golterman include the following: "De godsdienstwijsbegeerte van S. Hoekstra Bzn. (diss., Assen, 1942); "De liturgie van de eredienst" (public lecture, 1946); *Waar God ons aanspreekt* (Amsterdam, 1948); *Geloof en geschiedenis* (Amsterdam, 1948); *De kerkelijke situatie* (Amsterdam, 1951); *Liturgiek* (Haarlem, 1951); *Eén Heer, één kerk* (Nijkerk, 1956); *Tot alle volken* (Haarlem, 1959); "Karakter van de eenheid van Christus' kerk" (Nijkerk, 1960); Eenheid in de chaos der kerken (Haarlem, 1962); "Wat is oecumenische theologie?" (speech, Haarlem, 1965). Articles by Golterman appeared in the following books *Oecumene in 't vizier* (1960); *Spelregels* (1967); *Protestantse verkenningen na 'Vaticanum II,'* (1967). See also Golterman, A. Geense, and J.C. Groot on "Eenheid van doop en belijdenis," *Doops. Bijdr.* n.r. 4 (1978), 50-59. For information about Golterman see *Algemeen Doopsgezind Weekblad* (June 15, 1968).

Good, Mary Magdalene (July 23, 1890-Jan. 25, 1982), was born in Concord, Tenn., to Henry H. and Susan (Ressler) Good. She was the youngest of eleven children, nine of whom grew to maturity. She received a BA degree from Goshen College in 1919 and an MA degree from George Peabody College for Teachers in 1936. She served in India under the Mennonite Board of Missions and Charities (MC) from 1920 to 1952. She was principal of the Balodgahan Garjan Memorial School, which began in 1912 as a girls' school and became coeducational in 1936. Her master's thesis at Peabody set forth a program of study for the Balodgahan school, emphasizing the integration of learning and everyday life. Much emphasis was placed on individual growth, social relationships, and the Hindi language. During her last years she was a member of the Assembly Mennonite congregation at Goshen, Ind. She died at Greencroft Retirement Center, Goshen, Ind. ESR

Mary M. Good, "A Tentative Program of Study for the Garjan Memorial School" (MA thesis, George Peabody College, Nashville, 1936); Mary Neuhauser Royer, "Education of Vil-

lage Children in a Central Province, India" (MA thesis, George Peabody College, 1931); John Lapp, *India* (1972), 68, 71, 128-29, 255; Rich, *Mennonite Women* (1983), 142.

Government, Theory and Theology of. Menno Simons and the other 16th-c. radical reformers said relatively little about government. Since they lived in an absolutist autocratic society, as did Christians of the 1st c., they did not distinguish between the general state structure and the office-holders of the day. Their concerns did not focus on the origin of government nor did they stress its potential for good, although that aspect received some attention. Rather, accepting a biblical conception of two opposing kingdoms, the one characterized by peace and the other by strife, they saw the °political order as a lower order, the old order. They acknowledged that the state had a God-ordained responsibility to restrain evil, protect the good, punish transgressors, and do justice to the widows, the orphans, the poor, the despised stranger, and the pilgrim. Mainly, they saw the state as the restraining order in a society which had not accepted the lordship of Christ. Though they saw the political order as legitimate, they argued that, because it necessarily employed violence, which presumably included the shedding of blood, they could address political administrators and make policy recommendations but they could not personally participate. In fact, if chosen to serve as a magistrate, an Anabaptist should flee even as Christ did when his followers and admirers tried to make him king.

The early Anabaptists never adequately explained the apparent contradiction between their view that government was a God-ordained structure to keep order, and, if possible, peace, "outside the perfection of Christ," and their insistence that it was basically wrong for true Christians to participate in this God-ordained order. Since they lived in a society where the distinction between government and those who are governed was clearly marked, the inadequacy of their narrow, situation-determined, view of government was largely unnoticed. They emphasized living as model citizens, being supportive of government as much as possible, praying for the authorities, and insisting on religious freedom—which they were the first to champion.

For centuries this Mennonite view of °politics and government changed very little. Even in later generations, when Mennonites in several countries not only developed extensive interaction with governments as they negotiated °privileges and exemptions but also began participating in government administration, the official stance was hardly altered. Eventually, however, as Mennonites settled in free societies, a rethinking of the theory and theology of government became an urgent necessity. While a minority of Mennonites still tried to avoid any polit ical involvement—and some still do—most realized that in a complex °modern society political irrelevance is an impossibility. Given the blurring of the clear distinction between government and those who govern, the massive role and awesome pervasiveness of government, the fact that many governments now routinely do much of that which the faithful church pioneered, and the increasing participation by Mennonites in both elective and non-elective political offices, something needed to be done. In recent decades the problem has become even more urgent as Mennonites in various countries have tended to identify their Christian convictions with political ideologies ranging across the spectrum from °socialism and °"liberation theology" to °capitalist-conservatism and Christian-Americanism. A simplistic emphasis on withdrawal and avoidance has become obsolete.

At present several Mennonite theologians and social scientists are formulating revised interpretations concerning government. One significant analysis proceeds as follows. God's love has always extended even to people who reject him. Thus, after the fall, God did not abandon those who had abandoned him. When Cain killed Abel and feared anarchic retribution, God intervened. The evil of killing was to be restrained. That is how it came about that with the marking of Cain, Gn 4:15, God established civil °authority, civil government.

At various times, in both the Old Testament era and during the initiation of the church age, God reaffirmed the role of government and clarified its role. Romans 13, which must be read against the backdrop of Rom. 12, constitutes the fullest prescription. Government serves as an agent of God, has specific duties, and deserves conditional support. Importantly, as Jesus noted in Lk 3:14, government has no authorization to indulge in unrestrained violence.

Mennonites in the late 20th c. generally believe that God established and ordained civil authority because he knew that without some sort of overarching constraint, fallen mankind would sink into anarchy and lawlessness. Given his love even for disobedient and rebellious people, he would not permit that to happen. Besides, in God's great design society should remain sufficiently civil and orderly so that the church could go about its business. For it is the church, not government, which is the bearer of the meaning of history. However, as when Jehovah directed the people of Israel to crown Saul (1 Sm 8-10) even though the establishment of a monarchy was not God's preference, so also today God grants authority to sub-Christian governments to rule among the masses of people who have exercised their free will and have chosen not to be ruled by him directly.

In the late 20th c., partly because governments and church share an extensive common agenda, and partly because it is increasingly understood that opportunity plus ability creates accountability even in relation to governments, Mennonites are increasingly involved in politics. More than their ancestors, they see political involvement, especially in some countries, as having considerable potential for good. Presumably politically active Mennonites apply to governmental activity that ethical axiom which Anabaptists ought to apply to all other pursuits in life: no one becomes involved more than faithful servanthood permits. Participation in governmental affairs now ranges from mere voting to senior office-holding. A minority of Mennonites continue to abstain from voting.

In an Anabaptist theory of government several basic questions must be answered. First, are there guidelines for government? The following seem particularly noteworthy. Governments must resist the constant temptation to initiate policies and procedures which enhance the well-being of the ruling group or of some powerful pressure group at the expense of the general public. Further, the long-term interest takes precedence over the short-term. When governments consider only short-term popularity or the next election, future generations are loaded with a mountain of public debt, the physical world is polluted, proper planning is ignored, pressing crises may be shunted aside, and necessary but politically unpopular decisions postponed. Additional values should include procedural integrity, reasonable public disclosure, toleration of opposition, the development of a climate of freedom and proper decorum—dignity has always reinforced legitimacy and credibility.

Second, what public policy commitments should Christians be expecting from government? Governments have a major role in the responsible restraint of evil. Accordingly, they should be commended for establishing sensible agencies to restrain evil. Governments should specifically ensure freedom of religion and of unpopular minorities as much as possible. Governments have a God-given responsibility to rule, and ruling involves leading, assisting, educating, informing, regulating, persuading, enforcing, and, up to a point, providing. Given their ultimate control over society, governments, even though functioning at a sub-Christian level, have a broad mandate to ensure that society is made increasingly fair and humanitarian, that peace is promoted, that elemental needs are met for everyone, and that human dignity is protected and enhanced. In this mandate the church can cooperate extensively with government. Additionally, governments should themselves be subject to the laws they make and should address pressing issues such as racism, organized crime, appalling prison conditions, injustice, exploitation, bureaucratic bungling, waste, and the threat of nuclear disaster. Also, governments should actively seek counsel and criticisms from responsible societal groups, including the church.

Third, what should governments expect from Christians? They should expect Christians to be law-abiding, model citizens in all situations where laws do not conflict with God's requirements. Governments should expect Christian citizens to be informed, to be their most perceptive and reliable critics, and to be supportive in all morally sound undertakings. Christians should remember to be thankful and particularly to commend when they can so that they will be heard if they criticize when they must. Finally, governments should occasionally be reminded that they too, are accountable to God and should know that, following biblical instruction, Christians are constantly praying for them.   JHR

John Howard Yoder, *The Christian Witness to the State* (Newton, 1964); John H. Redekop, "Mennonites and Politics in Canada and the United States," *JMS*, 1 (1983), 79-105; idem, "The State and the Free Church," in *Kingdom, Cross and Community* (1976), 141-95; Elmer Neufeld, "Christian Responsibility in the Political Situation," *MQR*, 32 (1958), 141-62; John H. Redekop, *Two Sides; The Best of Personal Opinion, 1964-1984* (Winnipeg: Kindred Press, 1984), 179-296; John H. Yoder, *The Politics of Jesus* (Grand Rapids:

Eerdmans, 1972), 135-214; John H. Redekop, *Making Political Decisions: A Christian Perspective*, Focal Pamphlet, 23 (Scottdale, 1972); John A. Lapp, *A Dream for America: Christian Reflections for Bicentennial Reading* (Scottdale, 1976); Donald B. Kraybill, *Our Star-Spangled Faith* (Scottdale, 1976); James E. Wood, Jr., *The Problem of Nationalism in Church-State Relationships*, Focal Pamphlet, 18 (Scottdale, 1968); William Keeney, "Mennonite Cooperation with Government Agencies and Programs," paper read at the 15th Conference on Mennonite Educational Cultural Problems, (June, 1965), 62-74; Ed Correll, "The Mennonite Loan in the Canadian Parliament, 1875," *MQR*, 20 (1946), 255-75; Frank H. Epp, "Mennonites and the Civil Service," *Menn. Life*, 23 (October, 1968), 179-82; Adolf Ens, " Mennonite Relations with Governments: Western Canada 1870-1925" (PhD diss., U. of Ottawa, 1979).

See also Capital Punishment; Church-State Relations; Nationalism; Occupations; Revolution; Sectarianism and Cultural Mandate; Sociopolitical Activism.

Graber, Archie (b. 1901), born near Stryker, Ohio, Archie's spiritual nurture during childhood and youth centered in his home and the Lockport Mennonite Church. Convinced as a teenager that the Lord was calling him to missionary service, in 1927 he enrolled in Moody Bible Institute, where he met Evelyn Oyer. They married in 1930 after graduation and applied to the °°Congo Inland Mission. They left for the Belgian Congo (Zaire) in the same year.

Assigned to Djoko Punda for two terms, Archie constructed a variety of large buildings, including a beautiful chapel. He also gave time to extensive evangelism in the surrounding area. On furlough in 1947, Evelyn died of cancer. Archie returned to Congo alone in 1948 where he began developing a new station on the Kasai River at Tshikapa. He was joined in 1951 by Irma Beitler of Berne, Ind., a capable and enthusiastic nurse to whom Archie proposed marriage. At Tshikapa Archie also built a number of buildings.

In September 1960 refugee problems in the East Kasai assumed crisis proportions and Mennonite Central Committee (MCC) personnel turned to Archie for help. While his family remained in Ohio Archie provided administrative leadership to MCC and United Nations personnel in the southeast in a large refugee camp near Lubumbashi. In 1966, following the rebellion in Bandundu Province of 1964, the Grabers came out of retirement to undertake refugee rehabilitation ministries. In 1968 they moved on to Kinshasa to build a new mission hostel and to help finish a new inter-mission theological training institute. In 1974 the Grabers once again came out of retirement to build a church center at Tshikapa. They retired for the final time in Stryker, Ohio.   JEB

Graber, Christian L. (C. L.) (Dec. 20, 1895-Nov. 12, 1987), was born near Wayland, Iowa, to Daniel and Fanny Conrad Graber. He was baptized in 1909 and became a member of the Sugar Creek Mennonite Church. While a student at Hesston College (Kansas), he volunteered for °relief service in the Middle East (1919-20). On his return in 1920 he married Mina Amanda Roth (Oct. 13, 1895-Nov. 7, 1968) and was ordained to serve as associate pastor of his home congregation while farming to earn a living. They became the parents of six children. Fol-

lowing Mina Graber's death he and Phebe Ann King Erb (July 25, 1900-June 23, 1987) were married in 1969.

In 1924 C. L. was called to serve as business manager of Goshen College, Goshen, Ind., in which position he continued until 1949. During this time he also served as pastor of the Goshen College Mennonite Church from 1931 to 1942. Nevertheless he still found time to pursue a variety of business ventures. These included the reopening of the Wayland (Iowa) State Bank after the crash of 1929, the founding of Goshen Electric, Inc., a partnership in E. Z. Gas, Inc., and other successful ventures.

This business ability was also made available to the church at large. In 1945 he established the Mennonite Mutual Aid office in Goshen and served as its first executive officer until 1954. Mennonite Central Committee (MCC) frequently called upon him for help: as the first director of overseas relief after World War II, establishing the °°Pax reconstruction units in Europe, assessing the possibilities of relief and °development work in Puerto Rico, Morocco, the Philippines, and China. From 1954 to 1955 he served as MCC director for lower South America. He was the first director of Mennonite Disaster Service (MDS). He also served on numerous local church and civic boards, always known as a man of sound judgment and reliable character.   CJD

Who's Who Mennonites (1943), 89-90; C. L. Graber, *The Coming of the Moros* (Scottdale, 1964).

Graber, Joseph Daniel (Oct. 18, 1900-Jan. 25, 1978), was born at Noble, Iowa, to Daniel and Fanny Conrad Graber. He was educated at Hesston College and Goshen College. He received a BD degree from Princeton Theological Seminary (1943). He married Minnie Swartzendruber (June 28, 1925). They were appointed by the Mennonite Board of Missions (MC) to serve in India (1925-42). Graber served as general missionary, pastor, bishop, mission secretary, high school principal, and in other positions. He returned to the United States for furlough at the beginning of World War II and served as Mennonite Central Committee relief commissioner in China, 1943-44. While in China, he was elected as first full-time general secretary of the Mennonite Board of Missions, a position he held until retirement in 1967.

An effective public speaker, Graber exerted wide influence in the Mennonite Church (MC) in support of missions. He came into leadership at the beginning of a period of rapid growth both at home and overseas. He is credited with the slogan "Every church a mission outpost," which caught the imagination of many congregations across North America, resulting in a dispersion of motivated young people, primarily lay people. Alert to the issues being debated in °mission circles, he exerted strong influence on the mission philosophy and policies applied overseas. Keenly conscious of the implications of the movement for political independence sweeping across the non-Western world, he advocated the dismantling of colonial mission structures and adoption of an approach attuned to current sociopolitical realities (°indigenization). Graber was the most prolific Mennonite writer on missions prior to 1967. Graber's Conrad Grebel Lectures for 1959 (published as *The Church Apostolic,* 1960) present the essentials of his philosophy of missions. He was a part-time instructor in missions at Goshen Biblical Seminary, 1955-63. He died at Goshen, Ind.　　WRS

Who's Who Mennonites (1943), 90; Steven D. Reschly and Barbara Nelson, comps., *Bibliography of J. D. Graber's Printed Writings* (Elkhart: MBM, 1980); *Being God's Missionary Community: Essays in Honor of J. D. and Minnie Graber* (Elkhart: MBM, 1975).

Grabill-New Haven, Ind., Old Order Amish Settlement (ME I:55) in Allen Co., ne. of Ft. Wayne, Ind., was founded in 1853 by a number of families who migrated from Stark Co., Ohio. This is the only Indiana settlement made up primarily of 19th-c., Amish immigrants from °°Alsace. Until recently, the Allen Co. Amish, who came to America nearly 100 years after the 18th-c. groups in Pennsylvania, have had rather limited fellowship with the large °Lagrange Co. settlement 40 mi. (65 km.) farther north. Several families from Allen Co. have gone on to establish new Amish communities in southern Indiana. Allen Co. Amish maintain a strict church discipline, and operate several schools for the careful education of their children. In 1986 there were seven church districts (congregations) serving a population of around 1,000.　　SLY

Grace. The New Testament words for grace sometimes denote °forgiveness (Lk 7:42; 2 Cor 2:7, 10) or favor (Rom 11:5-6; 2 Tim 1:9; Heb 4:16) bestowed upon the undeserving. At other times, they indicate a living, transforming energy (Acts 4:33; Jn 1:14-17; 1 Cor 15:10; 1 Pet 4:10). Differences in theological understandings of grace often arise from regarding one or the other of these meanings as primary.

Eastern Orthodox and Roman Catholic Christians understand grace primarily as a sanctifying energy, which gradually bestows participation in the divine nature, or "divinization" (2 Pet 1:4). Grace is bestowed through sacraments, where individuals are sometimes fairly passive recipients, and (especially in Catholicism) through meritorious works, where individuals cooperate in some measure with God.

The Protestant Reformers, however, understood grace primarily as God's acceptance and forgiveness, granted through justification. Since °justification must occur before °sanctification can begin, grace, in this primary sense, could not be a transforming energy. Further, since no one can merit grace through works, one could not cooperate with it.

Among the Anabaptists, grace was primarily a transforming power. Many of them spoke of being renewed by, or participating in, the divine nature. Accordingly, some recent scholars have maintained that the Anabaptists regarded the primary work of grace as "divinization". This term is appropriate provided that it implies neither that humans actually become God, nor that grace absorbs one in °mystical contemplation removed from earthly concerns. On the contrary, the Anabaptists expected grace to produce a greater transformation of earthly character, activities and relationships than did either Protestants or Catholics. Because of this emphasis, the Reformers criticized them for minimizing °sin and overestimating human goodness. Yet the difference consisted chiefly in the Anabaptists' higher expectations for the transforming power of grace.

Like the Reformers, however, Anabaptists insisted that grace is God's freely initiated gift, and criticized the Catholic institutionalization of it through sacraments and other ecclesiastically approved channels. Yet the Reformers, who regarded grace primarily as forgiveness, generally limited its active power to the restoration of fallen human nature. Anabaptists, in contrast, regarded grace not merely as restorative, but also as creative. Through grace God had created the world from nothing, and could recreate people almost entirely anew. This understanding lay behind the Anabaptists' lofty behavioral standards. It also undergirded their rejection even of Protestant ecclesiastical structures, for Anabaptists believed that God could create new churches apart from established continuities. The same perspective underlay the sharp Anabaptist distinction between the church and the socio-political sphere; and among the Dutch, between Jesus' human nature and that which everyone else inherits from Adam.

If grace is a creative divine activity, and if it also transforms a person's daily actions, what relationship exists between the divine operation and the human response? Ever since the Synod of Orange (A.D. 529), Catholics officially held that no one could really begin turning towards God unless grace "came before" (prevenient grace) this turning. By the Reformation, however, many Catholics had adopted the view that even this first grace must be merited in some small measure by human effort. In reaction against this, the Protestant reformers denied that human merit could in any way earn God's pardoning grace. Accordingly, they insisted that faith, through which this justifying grace is appropriated, must arise wholly from God's work in one's heart. Faith, they argued, must precede repentance. In other words, before individuals can even begin regretting their sins and seeking forgiveness, God must have already enabled them, largely through subconscious processes, to begin believing in him.

Anabaptists were uneasy with the Reformers' teaching. It seemed, along with Protestant views on human depravity and predestination, to give people excuses for sinning, and for failing to seek and walk in Christ's transforming grace. Consequently, Anabaptists emphasized that earnest repentance belongs to the beginning of the saving process, and good works to its continuance. Some, particularly the Dutch Anabaptists, stressed this so strongly that repentance and works occasionally sounded like necessary means for meriting grace. Most Anabaptists, however, appear to have held that grace somehow "comes before" or prevenes even repentance. Among the °°Swiss Brethren, Michael °Sattler affirmed that "the willing and ability to turn to God are not of man but the gift of God through Jesus Christ our Lord" (CRR 1: 116).

Melchior °Hoffman, whose views often underlay those of Dirk Philipszoon and °Menno Simons, held that apart from Christ's atonement all humans are under °Satanic bondage and cannot even desire °salvation. Nevertheless, Hoffman argued that the atonement had universally restored to everyone a measure of free will. Through this first grace, everyone can now repent and receive the second, regenerating grace of the gospel. Dirk and Menno, who otherwise held extremely pessimistic views of human nature, probably could emphasize repentance only on the basis of such an assumption. In any case, all three affirmed that pardoning grace is universally imputed to infants by means of Christ's atonement. No one, that is, will be counted guilty of sin until they intentionally commit it. In at least this sense, Christ has placed all humanity in an initial state of grace.

South German Anabaptists grounded prevenient grace more in God's original creative activity than in Christ's atonement. Pilgram °Marpeck spoke not only of original sin, but also of original grace being passed on to all from Adam. Marpeck and Leonhard °°Schiemer mentioned a light of nature, or of conscience, as a first grace. Yet any such grace can only show people their sinfulness and need for Christ, and can never transform them. Balthasar °Hubmaier taught that the human spirit, in contrast to the flesh and the soul, was uncorrupted by the fall. Nonetheless, until the soul is converted, the spirit can do nothing but cry out like a prisoner in longing for God. Hubmaier also held that a common grace gives the soul a limited capacity to respond to God. This capacity, however, remained latent until awakened by the regenerating grace of the gospel.

In general, the Anabaptists, unlike the Reformers, spoke of a limited capacity to respond to God which preceded the specific work of regenerating grace. Usually, however, they sought to attribute this capacity not to any human ability but to some additional form of divine grace. In both what precedes and what follows conversion, they usually saw grace working more widely.   TNF

Alvin J. Beachy, *The Concept of Grace in the Radical Reformation* (Nieuwkoop: B. De Graaf, 1977); Kenneth R. Davis, *Anabaptism and Asceticism* (Scottdale, 1974); J. A. Oosterbaan, "Grace in Dutch Mennonite Theology," in *A Legacy of Faith*, ed. C. J. Dyck (Newton, 1962), 69-85; idem, "The Reformation of the Reformation: Fundamentals of Anabaptist Theology," *MQR*, 51 (1977), 171-95, cf. *Doops. Bijdr.*, n.r. 2 (1976), 36-61; Walter Klaassen, ed., *Anabaptism in Outline* (Waterloo, Ontario: Conrad Press, 1981), 23-100; C. Arnold Snyder, *The Life and Thought of Michael Sattler* (Scottdale, 1984), esp. 170-83; Michael Sattler, "On the Satisfaction of Christ" in CRR 1: 108-20; Menno Simons, "The Spiritual Resurrection", in Menno *Writings*, 53-62; idem, "The New Birth", 89-102; idem, "The True Christian Faith", esp. 324-43, 391-405; Balthasar Hubmaier, "On Free Will" in SAW, 114-35; John Calvin, *Institutes of the Christian Religion* Bk. III, ch. III, sect. 1-4.

See also Law; Love.

Graphic Design applies various forms to convey a visual and verbal message. Designers use typography, symbols, illustrations, photography, or combinations of these to reach an audience, trying for solutions that communicate well and are direct and inexpensive. Graphic design, a term coined in 1922, became a self-conscious discipline in the mid-20th c. when it was first taught in art schools.

Mennonite Press (North Newton, Ks.) and Mennonite Central Committee in the early 1950s were among the first Mennonite agencies to apply the problem-solving skills of designers to publications and other visual forms. Mennonite Publishing House and Herald Press (Scottdale, Pa.) and Faith and Life Press (Newton, Ks.) followed. This partial survey of the work of a number of graphic designers illustrates the value their special gifts have added to the life of the church.

In 1958, Kenneth Hiebert, an early designer for Mennonite Press, entered the graphic design class of Basel's Allgemeine Gewerbeschule. He later received the Swiss National Diploma in Design. On assignment from Mennonite Central Committee and Mennonite Publishing House (Herald Press), he was designer for Agape Verlag, a European Mennonite publisher, 1954-59. In 1964, he produced the Mennonite exhibit for the Protestant Pavilion at the New York World's Fair. For Mennonite Central Committee, he developed the dove and cross symbol adopted in the late 1960s, and designed annual reports and the More-with-Less books. For Fortress Press, he designed the Hermeneia Commentary Series which won an award from the American Institute of Graphic arts in 1971. He joined the staff of the Philadelphia College of Art as chairman of its graphic design department in 1966 and was named professor in 1973. His work is in the collections of the Museum of Modern Art, the Cooper-Hewitt Museum, and Gewerbemuseum-Basel and has also been noted in a major text (Meggs, p. 490).

The first graphic design course to be taught in a Mennonite school was introduced by Robert W. Regier in 1976 at Bethel College (Ks.) to provide skills for visual communication such as typography, layout, illustration, trademarks, and preparing of art for printing. He studied at the School of the Art Institute of Chicago and received his fine arts degree from the U. of Illinois. Chair of the Bethel College art department since 1965, Regier was staff designer for Mennonite Press, 1950-52, and for Mennonite Central Committee, 1953-55. He was art director for the General Conference Mennonite Church, 1957-63, where he developed the cross and orb symbol for the General Conference. Since 1984, he has been responsible for exhibition design at Kauffman Museum, North Newton, Ks.

Glenn Fretz, Toronto, from his own studio, offers specialties in signage, identity programs, corporate annual reports, and computer graphics. In 1978 he designed books, exhibits, signs, and symbols for the Mennonite World Conference, Wichita. He has developed symbols for the 1984 Strasburg and 1990 Winnipeg Mennonite World Conference assemblies and many other agencies including Associated Mennonite Biblical Seminaries; Mennonite Board of Missions (MC); Mennonite Bicenntenial Commission (Canada); °SELFHELP Crafts; Mennonite Credit Union (Ontario); Rockway Mennonite Collegiate, Kitchener, Ont.; and the Believers Church Bible Commentary series. He developed exhibits and interior design for the Meetingplace, St. Jacobs, Ont.

Gerald Loewen, Winnipeg, does graphic design for Canadian Mennonite Bible College and the Conference of Mennonites in Canada. He has also worked on design projects for Mennonite Central Committee Canada, °Mennonite Economic Development Associates, Manitoba Mennonite Historical Society, Mennonite Media Society, and Canada-wide Food Bank. He teaches graphics arts at Canadian Mennonite Bible College and graphic arts photography at Red River Community College.

Joseph Alderfer, formerly design director for Mennonite Publishing House, joined the U. of Chicago Press in 1967 to become manager of design with major involvement in books. In 1985, he designed a leaded glass window for the chapel at Philhaven Hospital, Mt. Gretna, Pa. He also designs *Sent,* a Mennonite Board of Missions (MC) magazine. His work has been recognized by the Society of Typographic Arts, the Chicago Book Clinic, the New York Art Director's Club, and the American Institute of Graphic Arts and has been published in *Graphis and Communications Arts.*

John M. Hiebert has been chief designer for Mennonite Press since 1954. Besides designing most of the books published by Faith and Life Press and other publications produced by the printery, he has been designer for Faith and Life Church Bulletin Service and, since 1963, art director for *The Mennonite,* which has been cited by the Associated Church Press for its visual quality.

Ann Graber Miller taught graphic design at Goshen College, 1986-88, and served as college designer. In her work for Mennonite Publishing House (Herald Press), 1982-85, her design for *The God of Sarah, Rebekah, and Rachel* by Barbara Keener Shenk received honorable mention from the Printing Industry of Western Pennsylvania.

Judith Rempel Smucker, designer for Mennonite Central Committee, 1979-85, was trained at U. of Manitoba, Bethel College, and Basel's Allgemeine Gewerbeschule. Her record jacket design for *I Can Make Peace* (Mennonite Central Committee, 1983) received special notice. She prepared the logo for the Lion and the Lamb Peace Arts Center, Bluffton College.

Christine Siemens Lautt, who served as designer for Mennonite Central Committee, 1973-1975, has designed publications for Southwestern College (Ks.), Bethel College, and for the General Conference Mennonite Church's Call to Kingdom Commitments. Scott Jost, Bethel College 1985, served as graphic artist for the Mennonite Central Committee, 1985-87, and for Bethel College.   MSh

Philip B. Meggs. *A History of Graphic Design* (New York: Van Nostrand Reinhold, 1983).

See also Painting and Printmaking; Photography; Publishing.

Great Britain. See England; Irish Mennonite Movement; London Mennonite Fellowship.

Grebel, Conrad (ME II: 566). For more than two decades Harold °Bender's biography of Grebel (1950) was read as the indisputable account. The following effort to update the Grebel °historiography in the light of more recent revisionist writings will be restricted to a cursory review of seven of Bender's interpretations.

Grebel's Role in the Anabaptist Movement. By portraying Grebel as the chief founder of Swiss and South German Anabaptism, Bender presented a heroic progenitor of what has become the traditional, normative, theological vision of Anabaptist origins. Through the work of later historians, e.g., James Stayer (1975), Martin Haas (1975), Hans-Jürgen Goertz (1980), it is less evident that Swiss-German Anabaptism had a single source. A movement is an aggregate of people with a common cause in a variegated sociopolitical context, and the younger students of the Anabaptist movement are giving more attention to its contextual developments than to its so-called normative vision. Although Grebel was asked to perform the first rebaptism in Zürich, it was °°Blaurock who made the request; and in any case °°Reublin had already put a halt to infant baptism in his parish in Witikon and °Castelberger had surely questioned the practice of infant baptism when he taught Paul's Epistle to the Romans in his pre-Anabaptist "school of the heretics" in Zürich. Before the Zürich baptismal event moreover, the writings of such German reformers as Karlstadt (°°Carlstadt) and °Müntzer had had a profound impact on the Zürich radicals. Grebel surely had an early role in certain aspects of mentorship, but the development of the movement resulted from interdependent roles.

Grebel's Prior Role in the Zwinglian Reformation. Bender's theses were valid as far as they went: that Grebel was won by the powerful evangelical preaching of Zwingli, as were many citizens of Zürich, and that for a year and a half he was a zealous advocate of the Zwinglian reformation. What Bender failed to understand sociologically was the contextual functions of radicalism which the Grebel group performed in the Zwinglian movement and the complexity of the sociopolitical factors involved in the subsequent schism.

From a behavioral perspective, Zwingli's attitude at this stage of his reformation was essentially radical in the sociological meaning of that term, i.e., favorable to fundamental change in the existing structures of one's social system. This need not imply that he was responsible for all of the actions of his most eager advocates, some of which caused problems for him as he steered the precarious course between °tradition and change. On one hand he moved cautiously and no faster than he felt the system could move with him. But on the other hand, he, together with his advocates, prepared the way for change and then allowed events to come to a crisis.

Heinold Fast portrays the Grebel group as Reformation storm-troopers, whose precipitous actions could advance Zwingli's cause at the same time that they could endanger it (Fast, 1975, 87). The nature of this precarious partnership can be observed in a sequence of demonstrations involving Grebel and other persons who were later participants in the Anabaptist separation. One was a preaching disturbance in the Dominican monastery by Grebel and three of his friends. In his attempt to play down Grebel's precipitous behavior, Bender wrote that "it is hardly possible that the four accused had been speaking against the monks [i.e. friars] from their pulpits, for they were laymen" (1950, 84-85). Following the review of these events by Goeters

(1969), Fast (1975), and others, it now appears less unlikely that Grebel and his friends were doing exactly what the chronicler said they were doing, what Fast calls "reformation through provocation"—acts of pulpit-storming in which the ambiguous partnership with Zwingli is surely evident.

The Humanist Background of Grebel's Theology and Ethics. Bender's claim that Grebel's °humanist education "made no evident contribution to his religious life or thinking" (ME II: 569) needs the corrective analyses found in articles by Robert Kreider (1952), Kenneth Davis (1974), and especially in Dale Schrag's dissertation (1984). With particular reference to Grebel's views of the °believers church, °discipline, ethical dualism, and °biblical authority, Davis documents the probable substantive influence of Erasmus (Davis, 1973, 170-71, 177). Bender's claim, moreover, that the pacifism of Grebel was fundamentally different than that of Erasmus deserves Schrag's criticism that Bender simply ignored most of the latter's writings on the subject. Erasmus was a thoroughgoing if not absolute pacifist; and his numerous writings on the subject are reflected not only in the teachings of Grebel's friend, Andreas Castelberger, leader of a pre-Anabaptist Bible study group, but in Grebel's letters to Vadian and Müntzer. To be sure, there were differences: Erasmus was a biblical realist and Grebel was a literalist. The theme of suffering nonresistance was not as dominant in Erasmus, although not absent either. Erasmus never left the Roman Catholic Church and preferred to work at reform from within and largely through renewal of biblical studies. In his ethical principles, however, Grebel was certainly closer to Erasmus than to Zwingli or Luther.

The Psychogenetic Nature of Grebel's Character. For Bender it was sufficient to explain Grebel's roles as Zwinglian advocate and Anabaptist leader in terms of a profound religious conversion during the spring of 1522. More recently, revisionists examining the letters and documents have questioned Bender's rationalizations concerning Grebel's character with particular focus on the chronic hostility he expressed toward his parents. There is no indication that Bender was aware of the question now being posed: Can Grebel's radical commitment be explained in psychogenetic terms, i.e., displacement of unresolved hostilities toward authority figures? There is now a substantial body of psychoanalytic literature to support the theory of a causal relationship between radical attitudes and social-psychological factors such as the pattern of family relationships and the quality of one's self-identity in the community. From this perspective we would expect to find that hostility toward one's parents, even though repressed, will continue to seek expression and will be displaced in later life against the substitute representations of the parent role in the community. There is little doubt that the evidence in the case of Grebel fits this pattern, although it does not warrant the conclusion that Grebel's leadership in the movement was not therefore motivated also by valid spiritual concerns about the depravity he felt within himself and his family and community networks, and about the fundamental wrongness of the existing socioreligious order. But on the other hand, as Fast admonishes, "acceptance of Grebel's view of Christian faith does not . . . require the rejection of the psychological and therefore thoroughly human substructure of the man" (Fast, 1982, 130).

The Socio-Economic Aspects of Grebel's Reformation Radicalism. On the issue of social ethics, Bender's portrait of Grebel was further tailored to fit another aspect of Bender's "Anabaptist vision": the Christian's separation from the ungodly world order and its institutions and the regeneration of the world order not by direct involvement but by converting individuals from the ungodly society of the world to the godly society of the church (ME II: 573). Thus Bender could allege that in the township of Grüningen, where the soil was well prepared for the movement of the common people who had long been agitating for self-government and economic autonomy from Zürich and where Grebel had his most successful mission, "Grebel delivered a purely religious message" (1950, 154), a claim not substantiated by the documents. On one occasion, for instance, while preaching at Hinwil, Grebel alleged that Zwingli welcomed the peasants' march on Zürich so that they could be massacred by the authorities and that Zwingli had said that the Zürich authorities should cut off the heads of several of the tithe-resisting leaders so that the rest of them would think twice before refusing to pay their °tithe (CRR 4: 415). These were assertions undoubtedly intended to appeal to the revolutionary mood of the people.

A more balanced review of the sources on this subject is found in Werner Packull's article on " the Origins of Swiss Anabaptism in the Context of the Reformation of the Common Man" with its conclusions that Swiss Anabaptism had its genesis in the converging interests of urban radicals (Castelberger, Grebel, °°Mantz, and others) and rural reformers (°°Stumpf, Reublin, °°Brötli, and others) and that Swiss Anabaptism was at least a partial sequel to the social revolution of the common man (Packull, 1985, 54-59). Surely, both in his pre-Anabaptist sympathies with the rural antitithe protestors and in his later mission in Grüningen, Grebel was a persistent witness to the social as well as "purely religious" concerns, for as late as Nov. 1525, during his prison interrogation, he was still proclaiming that Christians who were money-grabbers and usurers should, as taught in Scripture, be banned from the church (Harder, 1985, 439).

Anabaptist Civic Church or Free Church Congregationalism. Given the profound influence of Zwingli on the Grebel group in the pre-Anabaptist years, was the Grebel-Stumpf reform plan (Harder, 1985, 276-79) just another form of civic church based upon Zwingli's persistent vision of a *corpus Christianum?* While affirming that it was not a separatist sect-type vision, Bender interpreted the plan as the alternative to Zwingli's theocratic state-church: a free church congregationalism based on the separation of church and state. However, a number of scholars—Blanke (1961), Stayer (1975), Fast (1982), to name three—have drawn another conclusion about the plan, i.e., that it represented the very kind of civic church that Stumpf developed in his parish in Höngg, Reublin in Witikon, Brötli in Zollikon, Krüsi in Tablet, Reublin and Brötli in Hallau, and Hubmaier in Waldshut. Fast (1982, 126) writes that there were not two but three parts to the Swiss reformation: Zwinglian state churches, Anabaptist civic churches, and Anabaptist free churches. The third type cannot be dated prior to Grebel's letter to Müntzer, in which the free church principle was first enunciated. It was precipitated more by the growing °persecution than by a theologically mature solution to the problem of church reform. There were still inconsistencies within the movement and Bender was either not fully aware or not willing to admit how multifaceted the movement was and how much its leaders alternated among and within themselves.

The Schismatic Nature of the Anabaptist Movement. In his acute frustration with the Anabaptists, Zwingli came to believe that they "do everything for the sake of contention" and that "their activity is nothing but heresy, that is sectarianism and partisanship" (Harder, 1985, 363). While there is substantial evidence to support that conclusion, Bender preferred to celebrate the Anabaptists' faithful adherence to the first principles of the Zwinglian reformation. His portrayal had therefore to assert that it was Zwingli who abandoned the original vision, a theory now known as "the turning point in the Zwinglian reformation." A review of the evidence by Hillerbrand (1962), Walton (1968), Goeters (1969), and others, while perhaps exaggerated in the opposite direction, surely proves that Zwingli's disillusionment with the radicals came earlier than Bender thought and was precipitated by their incorrigible impatience. Packull concludes that "if there was a turning point it was in Grebel and not in Zwingli" (1985, 43).

Who then is to blame for the separation and violence that resulted from the dissension? This is Jean-Paul Sartre's question of good and bad faith, e.g., whether or not schismatics who rend the seamless coat of Christ as well as churchmen who kill their fellow Christians are held accountable for their actions. Most Zwingli scholars have absolved Zwingli of blame even though he used the instruments of violence to destroy his enemies. Mennonite scholars on their part have tended to overlook the provocations of the Anabaptists in order to lay the blame on the magisterial reformers. In the reassessment of the documents, would it be fair to say that neither side was without fault or blame?

If we are reviewing the breakdown in communication, the answer is surely "Yes". But if we are talking about equal responsibility for religious persecution, the answer is surely "no." In fairness to Zwingli it must be asked how it was possible that he, with such a high view of Biblical revelation, could have resorted to such violence of word and deed, a question that Bender never asked. A number of fair-minded scholars have arrived at a common answer. Blanke wrote that "if Zwingli had accepted or supported the free church movement, the entire Reformation would have been smothered by the magistrates, and Zürich would have returned to Catholicism" (Blanke, 1957, 64). Leo Schelbert wrote that "Zwingli experienced the cruel alternative which is so common in that deadly game of

rising ideologies. He either had to risk complete defeat of the truth as he saw it and to which his whole existence was committed, or he had to strike at . . . [his enemies] with ultimate force" (Schelbert, 1969, 63-64). This tragic dilemma was the main theme of the Zürich stage play, *Brueder in Christo*, written by the gifted Swiss playwright, Caesar von Arx (1947).

The other question that Bender failed to ask was how Grebel and his friends, with such a high view of love and Christian community, could have put the leader of the Reformation in Zürich into such a difficult position. Blanke concludes that "Zwingli's opponents, as well as Zwingli himself, would have sinned against their consciences if they had retreated" (Blanke, 1961, 19) and that "the collision between the Zwinglian and the Anabaptist views of the church was the tragic conflict of two significant syntheses, one of which was premature" (Blanke 1957, 64).   LDH

Caesar von Arx, *Brüder in Christo: A Drama in Three Acts* (Zürich: Verlag Oprecht, 1947); Harold S. Bender, *Conrad Grebel: The Founder of the Swiss Brethren Sometimes Called Anabaptists* (Scottdale, 1950); Fritz Blanke, *Brothers in Christ: The History of the Oldest Anabaptist Congregation* (Scottdale, 1961); idem, "Anabaptism and the Reformation," in *Recovery*, 57-68; Kenneth R. Davis, "Erasmus as Progenitor of Anabaptist Theology and Piety," *MQR*, 47 (1973), 163-78; Heinold Fast, "Reformation durch Provokation: Predigtstörungen in den ersten Jahren der Reformation in der Schweiz," in *Umstrittenes Täufertum*, 79-110; idem, "Conrad Grebel: The Covenant of the Cross," in *Profiles of Radical Reformers*, ed Walter Klaassen (Scottdale, 1982), 118-31; Hans-Jürgen Goertz, *Die Täufer: Geschichte und Deutung* (Munich: C. H. Beck, 1980); J. F. Gerhard Goeters, "Die Vorgeschichte des Täufertums in Zürich," in *Studien zur Geschichte und Theologie der Reformation*, ed. Luise Abramowski and J. F. G. Goeters (Neukirchen-Vluyn, 1969), 239-81; Martin Haas, "Der Weg der Täufer in die Absonderung," in *Umstrittenes Täufertum*, 50-78, published in English as "The Path of the Anabaptists into Separation," in *The Anabaptists and Thomas Müntzer*, ed J. M. Stayer and W. O. Packull (Dubuque: Kendall/Hunt Co., 1980), 72-84; CRR 4 (= Leland Harder, ed., *The Sources of Swiss Anabaptism: The Grebel Letters and Related Documents* (Scottdale, 1985); Hans J. Hillerbrand, "The Origin of Sixteenth-Century Anabaptism: Another Look," *ARG*, 53 (1962), 152-80; Peter I. Kaufman, "Social History, Psychohistory, and the Prehistory of Swiss Anabaptism," *Journal of Religion*, 68 (1988), 527-44; Robert Kreider, "Anabaptism and Humanism: An Inquiry into the Relationship of Humanism to the Evangelical Anabaptists," *MQR*, 26 (1952), 123-141; Werner O. Packull, "The Origins of Swiss Anabaptism in the Context of the Reformation of the Common Man," *JMS*, 3 (1985), 36-59; Leo Schelbert, "Jacob Grebel's Trial Revised," *ARG*, 60 (1969), 32-64; Dale R. Schrag, "Erasmian Origins of Anabaptist Pacifism: A Case Study in Humanism and the Radical Reformation," (MA thesis, Wichita State U., 1984); James M. Stayer, Werner O. Packull, and Klaus Deppermann, "From Monogenesis to Polygenesis: The Historical Discussion of Anabaptist Origins," *MQR*, 49 (1975), 83-121; James M. Stayer, "Die Anfänge des schweizerischen Täufertums in reformierten Kongregationalismus," in *Unstrittenes Täufertum*, 19-49; Robert C. Walton, "Was There a Turning Point in the Zwinglian Reformation?" *MQR*, 42 (1968), 45-56; John H. Yoder, "The Turning Point in the Zwinglian Reformation," *MQR*, 32 (1958), 128-40.

Greece. The Greek Orthodox Church invited Mennonite Central Committee (MCC) to help rebuild following the devastation of World War II and the guerrilla war which followed. °°Pax volunteers arrived in the village of Panayitsa, near the Yugoslav border, in 1952. Their objectives were to bring the land back into production through an extension program and the establishment of a dairy °cooperative.

In 1954 the project was expanded to the neighboring village of Tsakones, Olympia. By 1956 MCC had 13 Pax men in Greece at three project sites.

International interest in the postwar needs of Greece, especially after a serious earthquake in 1955, remained strong. In 1959, with the encouragement of the local Orthodox Church, a demonstration farm called *Protypon Agroktima Almopias* was established in the Aridea Valley. It became a government Ministry of Agriculture research substation in 1967. MCC involvement in the Greek mainland came to a close several years later.

Greek Orthodox Bishop Ireneos learned of the work done in Macedonia and invited MCC to open a program on the island of Crete. The bishop was concerned about the economic and spiritual hardship of the people, that was resulting in their migration to industrial Europe. MCC assisted in a vocational school in Kastelli and shipped in relief supplies in 1961.

In 1965 the Agricultural Development Center (ADC) was established in Kolymbari, Chania County, a cooperative effort between MCC and the bishop. Pax men, supplemented by several work camps, constructed the essential buildings. The main objectives of ADC were to provide food for orthodox youth hostels, and a demonstration and training center for local farmers, working with local rather than imported technology. The project focus was swine, dairy, poultry, and vegetable production, with a secondary focus on sheep and honey bees. ADC became a major supplier of animal feed in western Crete.

Greece's military government was, at points, a source of tension. Its antireligious stance made program adjustments necessary, including the closing of a children's Bible class which had been begun by MCC workers in 1966.

The relationship went beyond projects and included also Mennonite and Orthodox dialogue. This took place in informal, day-to-day settings as well as at official levels. An MCC couple spent three years in Orthodox academic institutions developing these relationships. Many years later leaders of the Orthodox Church still welcomed dialogue with Mennonites. The last MCC workers left Crete in 1977. Ten years later ADC is still functioning under Greek direction. It was estimated in 1977 that the ADC's influence had helped 90 percent of the local farmers. The Crete government adopted many of the ADC techniques. The Mennonite efforts in Crete helped to strengthen the bonds between the Christian brothers and sisters in Crete and around the world.   ES

Virgil Claassen, "The Agricultural Development Center: Its Inception and Growth (1965-1968)," Project Request Outline for Agricultural Development Center (Kolymbari, Chania, Crete, Oct. 1970); David Gerber, "Agricultural Development Center Progress Report" (1971); Roy S. Kaufman, "Orthodox-Mennonite Relations" (1972); Paul Longacre, "Report and Evaluation of MCC's Ten Years in Crete 1962-1972"; Roy S. Kaufman, MCC on Crete—An Evaluation After 24 years (1984), all items available in MCC files.

See also Eastern and Coptic Orthodox Churches.

Grosheide, Greta (May 20, 1880-May 27, 1959), was the descendent of a well known Reformed Church family. Because university study by women was not encouraged in her family she pursued teacher's training in Amsterdam. Nevertheless, while pursuing her teaching career in Leiden and Amsterdam she continued her preparation for university studies, particularly in history and geography, which she was eventually able to undertake under H. Brugmans at the U. of Amsterdam. She edited a collection of documents from court proceedings related to Anabaptists in Amsterdam (*Verhooren en Vonnissen der Wederdoopers, betrokken bij de aanslagen op Amsterdam in 1534 and 1535*, in *Bijdragen en Mededeelingen van het Historisch Genootschap* [1920], 1-197). This became the basis for her Amsterdam dissertation *Bijdrage tot de geschiedenis der Anabaptisten in Amsterdam* (published at Hilversum in 1938). Her many responsibilities as teacher prevented further publications in this area, with the exception of one article ("Altgen de Waal en Aeltgen Egberts," in *Nederlands Archief voor Kerkgeschiedenis* 34 [1943], 138-44. In her later years she published several articles on Dutch Reformed missions in Indonesia.   SBJZ

A. F. Mellink, *Amsterdam en de Wederdopers in de zestiende eeuw* (Nijmegen, 1978), 7ff.; F. Stoffels, "Tentoonstelling 'De lange en de korte weg'. Studeren als vrouw? Dat ging niet zomaar!" in *Vrije Universiteit*, 11 (1982), 83-87.

Grubb, Elmer F. (Aug. 12, 1872-Nov. 15, 1959). Born in Elkhart Co., Ind., to David B. and Elizabeth (Witters) Grubb, Elmer Grubb married Esther Eunice Johnston, (b. Mar. 17, 1877), the daughter of Jacob W. and Lydia (Nye) Johnston in 1896. On Oct. 15, 1897, they united with Silver Street Mennonite Church, Goshen Ind. Elmer Grubb was ordained in 1900 by his pastor, John C. Mehl. In May 1901 he became pastor of the Stevensville, Ont., congregation (GCM). In Nov. 1903 he began serving the Wadsworth Mennonite Church, Wadsworth, Ohio. He was called by the Home Mission Board (GCM) to begin the first °urban mission of the General Conference Mennonite Church—in Los Angeles. Arriving July 12, 1909, he started the River Street Mission at 1432 San Fernando St. (later North Spring St.). In 1912 the work was moved to Avenue 19 and Albion Street and named "Whosoever-Will Mission." His ministry was terminated July 1, 1917, when the board decided to develop a German-speaking Mennonite church.

Grubb became the assistant probation officer in Los Angeles Co., and retired in 1942. The family joined the Mount Washington Presbyterian Church of Los Angeles.

Elmer and Esther Grubb had three children: Ezra, (b. May 1, 1898), John C. (b. Jan. 13, 1901), and Ruth (b. Aug. 24, 1903). Elmer Grubb died at Los Angeles.   DHa

Lois Barrett, *Vision* (1983), 81-83, 106-8; H. D. Burkholder, *The Story of Our Conference and Church* (North Newton: Mennonite Press, 1951), 49-52; Reginald Good, "Stevensville: The First General Conference Mennonite Congregation in Canada, 1887-1917," *Mennonite Historian*, 12, no. 4 (1986); E. F. Grubb, "Sketch and History of the Mennonite City Mission of Los Angeles, Cal.," in *Mennonite Year Book and Almanac* (1914), 22-24; Willard Hunsberger, Rachel W. Kreider, and Russell Hart, "History of the First Mennonite Church, Wadsworth, Ohio, 1852-1952" (unpubl.); Minutes of the General Conference Mennonite Church Board of Missions, MLA (North Newton), I-la, folders 27-34; Anna G. Stauffer, "The Whosoever-Will Mission, Los Angeles, California," *Mennonite Year Book and Almanac* (1920), 29-32.

Grünthaler Mennonites. See Canadiense Colony, Bolivia; Migrations; Reinländer Mennoniten Gemeinde; Sommerfeld Mennonites. Guarituba Colony, Brazil. See Witmarsum Colony, Brazil. Guatemala. Mennonite involvement in this Central American republic began in 1964 when the Conservative Mennonite Fellowship began work among villagers in Chimaltenango, leading eventually to the Conservative Mennonite Fellowship, Guatemala. In 1968 the Eastern Mennonite Board of Missions and Charities (MC) and the Washington-Franklin Mennonite Conference (later continued by the Franklin Mennonite Conference) began work with Spanish-speaking (Iglesia Menonita de Guatemala) and Kekchi-speaking (Iglesia Nacional Evangélica Menonita Guatemalteca) people. The Eastern Pennsylvania Mennonite Church carries on mission work in Quetzaltenango. Mennonite Air Missions was organized in 1972. In 1977 the Church of God in Christ, Mennonite (CGC), began mission work in Guatemala, where they had participated in reconstruction following the 1976 earthquake. The first missionaries were Alvin and Mildred Koehn and Vada Unruh. In 1988 four couples and three single women serve the three congregations (Progreso, Sanarate and Jutialpa) and seven outposts located one to two hours north and east of Guatemala City. There are 19 baptized members and no ordained Guatemalan national leaders. A close relationship is maintained with the Church of God in Christ mission work in Mexico where the mission has published in Spanish the CGC hymnal and several booklets. Membership in the four Mennonite-related groups in Guatemala totaled ca. 3,100 in 1987.   AY

Gulf States Mennonite Fellowship (MC) in 1988 had 11 congregations with 517 members in Mississippi, Louisiana, and Alabama. Included were Native American (°Indian), Afro-American, Cajun, and Hispanic Mennonites. Early settlements of Mennonites (1920s) were made in Noxubee and Harrison Cos., Miss.; St. Charles Parish, La.; and Atmore, Ala. Although the primary goal of these settlements was inexpensive farm land, in the late 1980s the resulting congregations are increasingly becoming centers for mission outreach. Des Allemands Mennonite Church, St. Charles, La., is the largest of those congregations in southeastern United States that are not composed of people from Germanic Mennonite background. Amor Viviente congregation in New Orleans (a member of GSMF) is a mission work among Hispanic people from Central America begun by mission workers sent by their parent church, Amor Viviente, a Mennonite-affiliated church in Honduras.   ROZ

MC Yearbook (1988-89), 58; Paul Erb, *South Central Frontiers* (Scottdale, 1974).

Gutsbesitzer. See Estate Owners.

H

Habegger, Alfred (July 26, 1892-Jan. 17, 1956), was born at Berne, Ind., to David and Elisabeth (Lehman) Habegger. He married Barbara Hirschy in 1913. He attended Bethel College (Ks.), 1913-16, (BA); Mennonite Seminary, Bluffton, Ohio, 1916-17 (MA); and Witmarsum Seminary, Bluffton, Ohio (1927).

Alfred and Barbara were ordained Mar. 31, 1918, as missionaries to the Cheyenne Indians in Montana. He was the first man from the First Mennonite Church at Berne to be ordained as a missionary. Arriving at Busby, Mont., on May 31, 1918, he served until his death. He was one of a few non-Indians who learned to speak the Cheyenne language fluently. In 1942 he became the chairman of the mission work in Montana. Alfred labored diligently to lead people to faith, to train Indian leaders, and organize the church. He was buried at Busby.   DHa

Lois Barrett, *Vision* (1983), 34, 57; Alfred Habegger, "The Development of Missionary Interests Among the Members of the General Conference Mennonites of North America, 1917 (MA thesis, unpublished); idem, "Our Northern Cheyenne Mission Field," *Mennonite,* 36, no. 29 (July 28, 1921); idem, quarterly reports to the mission board (GCM) at MLA (North Newton), I-1, box 2, folders 15-17; box 3, folder 18; box 4, folder 53; box 57, folders 91, 92; Lois Habegger, *Cheyenne Trails: A History of Mennonites and Cheyennes in Montana* (Newton: MPO, 1959), 31-57; "Montana Mission Director Passes," *Mennonite,* 71, no. 6 (Feb. 7, 1956), 90; *Who's Who Mennonites* (1943), 92.

Habegger, Barbara Hirschy (July 8, 1892-Aug. 14, 1977). Born at Berne, Ind., to Samuel B. and Christina (Luginbill) Hirschy, Barbara Hirschy married Alfred Habegger in 1913.

The Habeggers had seven children: Marden (Feb. 21, 1917), Jeanne (Oct. 19, 1920), Helen (Apr. 19, 1922), Esther (Oct. 16, 1923), David (June 15, 1925), Lois (Sept. 16, 1926), and Bernard (b. Apr. 19, d. June 13, 1931).

Barbara Habegger graduated from Bethel College (Ks.) in 1916. She was ordained on Mar. 31, 1918, as a missionary to the Cheyenne Indians in Montana. She served 40 years in this ministry. Having learned the Cheyenne language, she taught Sunday school, Bible school and weekday classes; undertook counseling and pastoral visiting; served as a midwife and nurse; and instructed in sewing and cooking. The Cheyenne people early named her Manhova'e "Giver of water to drink." She died in Kansas and was buried at Busby, Mont.   DHa

Mrs. Alfred Habegger, "The Northern Cheyenne Camp Meetings," *Mennonite,* 36, no. 37 (Sept. 22, 1921), idem, "Cheyenne Missions," *Miss. News and Notes,* 37, no. 7 (Mar. 1958), 2, 3, 13, 14; Malcolm Wenger, "Witness of Faithful Service," *Mennonite,* (Apr. 25, 1978), 276-77; "Mrs. Alfred Habegger Retires from the Montana Mission Field," *Miss. News and Notes,* 36, no. 10 (June, 1957), 4-5.

Hackman, Walton N. (Dec. 18, 1937-Dec. 16, 1985), leader in peace and justice concerns, and a farmer. Hackman was born and died at his family's farm near Hatfield, Pa. He was the son of Arthur K. and Lizzie Nice Hackman, and he married Karin Erdmann (June 26, 1965). Together they raised a family of two sons. He was a member of the Plains Mennonite Church.

From 1960 to 1962 Hackman was in °voluntary service with the °Northern Light Gospel Mission, Red Lake, Ont. As a student at Eastern Mennonite College he was active in several campus organizations. He spent the summer of 1964 in Mississippi with the Student Non-violent Coordinating Committee (SNCC). From 1967 to 1971 he served as executive secretary of the Peace and Social Concerns Committee (MC) and associate executive secretary of Mennonite Central Committee (MCC) Peace Section. He represented Mennonite churches on the National Inter-Religious Service Board for Conscientious Objectors (°°National Service Board for Religious Objectors), 1965-69. He was executive secretary of MCC Peace Section, 1972-74, then returned to the family farm.

During the °Vietnam War epoch, Hackman played a critical role in helping the church grapple with the significance of draft resistance as a means of Christian witness. He was widely admired for his lawyer-like understanding of how to deal with the military draft. His concern for °peace and simplicity encouraged his close involvement with Doris Janzen °Longacre's *"More with Less"* books. He chaired the Franconia Conference (MC) and Eastern District (GCM) Hunger Concerns Committee and was instrumental in establishing the Souderton Thrift Shop. During the early 1980s he was active in state and local farm organizations and was a member of the MCC Farm Crisis Task Force.   JAL

Haidar, John (Feb. 22, 1890-Aug. 26, 1981), a minister of the Mennonite Church in India and a first-generation evangelistic worker with the American Mennonite Mission (MC) in °Dhamtari, Madhya Pradesh (M.P.), India, was born in Rajnandgaon, M.P. His parents were Muslims; his father being an imam (priest). His father died when John was very young and his mother, °Jebarbi Bai, worked as a domestic for American missionaries F. E. Ward and his wife. The Wards worked under the Missionary Bands of the World Mission. In 1899 John's mother became a Christian and an embittered John ran away from home. Love prevailed, and in 1900 John Haidar was baptized. He and his mother continued working for the Missionary Bands Mission until 1910. In 1911 John Haidar married a Christian woman from the mission orphanage in Rajnandgaon.

In 1910, he and his mother moved to Dhamtari where they found employment with the American Mennonite Mission, she as a Bible woman (°lay evangelist) and he as an office clerk under M. C. °Lehman. Haidar was soon assigned to teach Bible in the mission schools in Dhamtari and to work in village evangelism, also helping with pastoral work in the Sunderganj congregation. In 1920 he observed and studied mass movements with Mukut °Bhelwa in North India. In 1921 he was ordained deacon for the Sunderganj congregation, continuing also as a village evangelist until 1932, when he was ordained a minister. He was the first treasurer of the Home Mission program jointly sponsored by the mission and the church. Later, with the development of the Evangelistic Samaj (1931), he became a board member.

Until his retirement from active service in the mid-1950s, Haidar remained active in the conference and life of the American Mennonite Mission. He was a forceful and colorful speaker; fearless in the defense of the gospel before unbelievers and unhesitating his criticism of imperialism in missionaries. In addition to his work with the mission, he served pastorates in Sankra and Durg. In retirement he ministered to the Christian communities developing in the industrial area of Bailadila in Jagdalpur District.   JAF

Information from Lydia (Haidar) Thomas; American Mennonite (MC) Mission (AMM), *Building on the Rock* (Scottdale: MPH, 1926); *50th Anniversary of the American Mennonite Mission* (Scottdale: MPH, 1949); contribution register for Dhamtari Orphanage, AMM, 1914ff., at MC Archives (Goshen); minutes of the Evangelistic Committee, AMM, 1920-28, at MC Archives; minutes of the Evangelistic Samaj, 1934 MC Archives; AMM *Annual Report* (1923), 43-44, (1932), 137, 142; "History of the Rajnandgaon Mission Church," (from historical records of the Rajnandgaon Church, ca. 1979).

Haigh, Lawrence B. and Rose Boehning. Lawrence was born in Yorkshire, England, in 1882. He was a member of the Baptist Church of Holley, England. He eventually attended the Moody Bible Institute (Chicago). In Illinois he met and married Rose Boehning of Elgin, Ill. They became the first missionaries of the °°Central Conference Mennonite Church, leaving in 1906 for what was then known as British East Africa (Kenya, Uganda, and Tanzania).

It was in 1906 that the Defenseless Mennonite Conference also sent missionaries to East Africa. By 1910 the missionaries of both the Defenseless Mennonites and the Central Conference concluded it would be wisest to cede their work in East Africa to the Africa Inland Mission. The two Mennonite groups subsequently formed a new inter-Mennonite mission board (Congo Inland Mission, later known as Africa Inter-Mennonite Mission) in 1911. This board's first commissioned missionaries were Lawrence and Rose Haigh. After taking a brief course in tropical medicine in Britain in 1911 they explored for a field of service in Belgian Congo. They were joined the next year by Alvin Stevenson, and together they recommended opening stations along the Kasai River at Kalamba in the south and at Djoko Punda to the north.

The Haighs returned to the United States in 1915 for furlough. When they could not return to Africa because of World War I, they concluded their service with the Congo Inland Mission. Lawrence died in 1962.   JEB

Haiti. The first Mennonite missionaries, two couples from the Mennonite Brethren and Evangelical Mennonite Brethren churches in Saskatchewan (1948-49) came to southern Haiti under the West Indies Mission (later Worldteam). In 1979 Mennonite missionaries working with the group of national churches with which Worldteam was affiliated numbered 17.

Mennonite Central Committee (MCC) assistance began in 1958 with two °°Pax volunteers assigned to an agriculture project in Petit Goave with Haitian Methodist pastor Marco Depestre. Later MCC began sending nurses to Hospital Albert Schweitzer in Deschapelles. A program began in Grande Rivière du Nord in 1959 at the invitation of the Haitian government. Until 1979 MCC administered a hospital, assisted local schools, organized a cooperative of handicrafts producers, and carried out numerous activities in agriculture and community °development in Grande Rivière du Nord. Since 1979, MCC programs in the northeast and Artibonite Valley have focused on community development, food production, reforestation and community health.

Following hurricanes in 1963 and 1966, Mennonite Disaster Service (MDS) and MCC cooperated to construct houses in Côtes de Fer and Marigot. Various MDS team members continued to relate to several Haitian pastors they had met, particularly in Miragoane. Several independently constituted Mennonite organizations began visiting on a regular basis. Short-term workers came under the auspices of these organizations to work with the Haitian pastors in health clinics, agriculture, well-drilling, and construction of schools and churches.

In 1963 MCC introduced several representatives of the Church of God in Christ, Mennonite (Holdeman), to the government of Haiti and was instrumental in helping them get established. Registered in Haiti as "Mission Mennonite" (Égliese de Dieu en Christ, Mennonite), they are involved in church planting, nutrition, tuberculosis control, and water catchment for poor families. Goshen College established a Study Service Trimester program (SST) in Haiti in 1969, bringing college students to the island for short-term service and international education. Since early 1986, the SST unit is not operational. Eastern Mennonite Board of Missions and Charities (MC) has been involved since the mid-1960s in the Extension Bible School Program (EBEX) of the Council of Evangelical Churches of Haiti (CEEH). In 1986 an Eastern Board missionary couple was seconded to CEEH to work full-time in the EBEX leadership training program.

Among other Mennonite organizations with significant programs in Haiti are °Mennonite Economic Development Associates, Blue Ridge Christian Homes (Beachy Amish Mennonite Fellowship), Palm Grove Mission Board, Virginia Conference Mission Board, Christian Fellowship Mission, Gospel Mission to Haiti and Sonlight Mission ((Église Mennonite Sonlight Mission). A meeting of the proliferating Mennonite groups working in Haiti was organized in 1978 for the purpose of sharing concerns and common interests. This meeting, usually held in January, has continued almost annually since then.   ESto

Elaine Stoltzfus, *Tending the Vision, Planting the Seed* (Akron, Pa.: MCC, 1987); *MWH* (1984), 77-79.

See also Communion Mennonite d'Haiti.

Hansen's Disease (Leprosy). As with many other Christian missions, the Mennonite missions have directed much of their attention to people sick with Hansen's Disease (leprosy). No suffering of humankind has been greater than what leprosy patients have suffered. The stigma of the disease is related to the injustice in translation of the word *zarath* as found in Lev 13, unjust because it dealt with a moral question and not a disease caused by a bacillus. There are four peculiarities of leprosy which influence Christian mission to relate to it: it frequently affects the face; the bacillus that causes the disease was the first one seen under the microscope and is the only disease-causing bacillus that cannot be cultured after many, many trials; the incubation period is 3 to 15 years or more, much longer than for most diseases; no other bacillus selectively invades peripheral nerves. A simple definition that describes most cases of leprosy is, "a disease caused by a bacillus that invades the nerves and manifests itself in the skin." Though chemotherapy since 1941 has been of great benefit for the person with the disease, curing some, it has done nothing to prevent spreading the disease. With improved living standards and hygiene, leprosy would disappear. Demonstration of this is found in many places of the world. In Paraguay, the Mennonite refugees who came from the Soviet Union were very poor, and six of them contracted leprosy during their first 15 years in Paraguay. In contrast, none of the Canadian Mennonites, who came equipped to meet essential needs, got the disease. In the last 40 years, after Mennonites in Paraguay again acquired their accustomed standard of living and hygiene, no Mennonites have contracted leprosy. This is true despite the movement of Mennonites to other areas of the country, whereas in the first 15 years they were isolated in their colonies.

The disease draws a curtain that separates the leprosy patients from all plans they had in life. In rehabilitation, the social aspect is more important than the medical. There has been some change in this aspect but the special characteristics of this disease continues to make Christian love and Christian missions necessary for helping patients.

The Leprosy Mission and Medical Treatment Program in Paraguay started in 1951 where it pioneered in ambulatory treatment. Its main center is known as Centro de Salud Menonita (Mennonite Health Center), but also as "Kilometer 81," according to its location on the highway. A team consisting of a doctor, nurse, and chaplain go out to clinics and to homes to see the patients. Mennonite Central Committee and the American Leprosy Mission gave funds to start the work, and Mennonites in Paraguay provided the personnel. Good medical treatment has been the aim of the mission at all times, but a special concern has always been to treat the whole person. It takes time to bring all of these elements into the program, but extensive activities, including surgery, physical therapy, education, and evangelism, have been developed in this mission. Many mis-

sionaries in Paraguay report a widespread influence of the Mennonite Leprosy Mission throughout the country.   JRS

S.F. Pannabecker, *Open Doors* (1975), 311, 330, 331; Juhnke, *Mission* (1979), 30-32; John A. Lapp, *India* (1972), 107-11; *MCC Story*, 4, ch. 13.

See also Champa, India; Esch, Christian David; Gemeindekomitee, Paraguay; Mennonite Church of Trinidad and Tobago; Tanzania; India.

Pioneers of a Better Way

When Mennonites in Paraguay set out to build a leprosy treatment center as their gift to the nation that had given them a home, they had a vision of 250 victims of Hansen's disease being treated in an institution. John and Clara Schmidt, the medical team chosen to begin the program in 1951, wanted an ambulatory treatment program which would allow patients to live in their own homes. The Schmidts, a Kansas couple who had been in health work in Paraguay earlier, hoped to send workers into the countryside to find patients in their homes, examine them, and give them needed medicines. But the Mennonite Central Committee and the American Leprosy Mission, who had developed the plans for what later became Centro de Salud Menonita (Mennonite Health Center at Kilometer 81), said no. They were committed to the traditional colony approach.

The people of Itacurubi, the town nearest Kilometer 81, had dreams of turning their city into a tourist resort, and they became unwitting allies in the drive for more humane treatment. As soon as building began on the hospital site, townspeople came to protest with force and to say they would allow no further building. They were invited to have coffee and cake and told that the first buildings were for medical workers and not for leprosy patients and so they left with the rocks with which they had come to do battle still in their trucks.

This strong resistance to a leprosy colony made it seem desirable to modify the building program and test other ways of treatment. Instead of large pavilions to house many people, only a few smaller guest houses were built for the most seriously crippled, those needing intensive care, and the homeless. John Schmidt and his medical team combed the villages and farms, traveling often on horseback, to find the victims of the dreaded disease, many who had been deserted by their families and left to die. Within a few years, the dispersed clinics of Kilometer 81 were serving 500 patients, double the number that could have been served in the colony once planned.

In 1967, the American Leprosy Mission recognized the Schmidts as the first to try a venture that had become "the basis for leprosy-control work throughout the world." The mission also condemned the colony approach that "often caused as much crippling through long-term institutionalization as the disease itself" and called for an integrated medical program.   MSh

Maynard Shelly in *MCC Story* 4, pp. 310-45.

Harchand Master and Sugni Bai. Harchand Master, deacon and evangelist under the American Mennonite (MC) Mission (AMM) in Dhamtari, Madhya Pradesh (M.P.), India, was born in 1888 in the rural village of Amatola, Chauki Tahsil, District Rajnandgaon, M.P. He was orphaned in the 1898 famine and admitted to the orphanage of the Missionary Bands of the World Mission in Rajnandgaon where he completed his education through middle school.

In 1926 he married Sugni Bai, who was born in 1890 in Bhandara, Maharashtra State. During the famine of 1898 she was admitted to the same orphanage at Rajnandgaon. Here she learned to read through the middle school level and became a Christian. The mission sponsored her for teacher training in Jabalpur, M.P. She and her husband worked for the same mission, teaching in its primary schools for 10 years. When the Missionary Bands Mission had financial trouble in 1927, the Harchands were employed by the neighboring American Mennonite Mission as °lay evangelists. They served in this work in several stations including Sankra, Balod, Arjundah, Durg, Maradev, and Dondi until the paid evangelist and Bible woman program ended in 1952. In 1940 Harchand was ordained deacon to serve in the Durg congregation.

Harchand was not an eloquent speaker but led well by the quality of his deep spiritual life. Both he and Sugni Bai were of a quiet humble temperament that reflected an authenticity of commitment and made them effective witnesses of the gospel wherever they worked. They had four children: sons Joash and Sushil, and daughters Karuna and Angelina. They retired in 1952 in Balodgahan where Harchand died June 28, 1960. "Harchand" is a corrupted form of the Sanskrit "Harishchandra"; the next generation now uses the latter form as a surname. Sugni Bai died at Balodgahan on Feb. 22, 1970.   JAF

Information from Joash Harishchandra; Annual Report, AMM (1940), p. 91; American Mennonite Mission Committee minutes, MC Archives (Goshen).

Harder, Johannes (Hans) (Jan. 28, 1903-Mar. 7, 1987), writer, editor, publisher, minister, and Christian activist, was born in the Alexandertal settlement on the Volga. He emigrated to Germany as a young man and studied literature and philosophy at Königsberg. From 1928 to 1933 Harder pursued a career as editor and publisher, followed by active service in the dissident *Bekennende Kirche* (Confessing Church) to express his disapproval of the Nazis (°National Socialism). During those stormy years he wrote eight novels set in Russia, the earlier ones presenting recognizably Mennonite characters and settings, the later ones portraying ethnic German colonists in Russia.

After wartime service as a military translator in Russia, he began a new career as professor of sociology at the Pädagogische Hochschule (teacher's university) in Wuppertal. Retiring in 1968, he undertook yet another career as minister and elder of the Frankfurt Mennonite Church. Retired again, he remained active as a writer, editor, spokesman, and

political activist, and his home in Schlüchtern received frequent visits from former students, academic colleagues, and fellow writers. Chief among his awards and honors was the prestigious Federal Grand Cross for distinguished service to West Germany as the "father of socio-pedagogical method and practice in German universities."

As a man of letters and social philosopher Johannes Harder has had few peers among Mennonites of this century. His novels are authentic and powerful portrayals of life in Russia during the turbulent early Communist period, as well as nostalgic evocations of the era before the °Russian Revolution. Harder had a deep, abiding love for his Russian homeland and its people, including the Mennonites, and his realistic fiction is suffused with faith in the purgative effects of suffering and the presence of grace. His first novel, *In Wologdas weissen Wäldern* (In the White Forests of Vologda, 1934, translated into English as *No Strangers in Exile*, 1979), is a tragic but spiritually uplifting story about Russian-Mennonite families sent to Stalinist labor camps in the far north. *Das Dorf an der Volga* (The Village on the Volga, 1937) traces the history of a prosperous Mennonite colony to its destruction in the Soviet period. *Der deutsche Doktor von Moskau* (The German Doctor of Moscow, 1940), his most popular novel, deals with a German doctor in Russia during Napoleonic times who became a popular hero for his selfless service to his adopted people.

As a radical Christian Johannes Harder believed in the transforming power of Christ's love, but distrusted the institution of the church. He participated frequently in peace marches, even in advanced age. His profound understanding of the Anabaptist-Mennonite heritage and of literature and culture, made him a Mennonite spokesman and writer of rare eloquence and prophetic power who deserves to be more widely known among Mennonites in North America.   AR

Hans Harder, *No Strangers in Exile*, trans., ed. and expanded by Al Reimer (Winnipeg: Hyperion Press, 1979); idem, *Das Dorf an der Volga: Ein deutsches Leben in Russland* (Stuttgart: J. F. Steinkopf, 1937); idem, *Der deutsche Doktor von Moskau: Der Lebensroman des Dr. Friedrich Joseph Haas*, 5th ed. (Gießen: Wilhelm Schmitz Verlag, 1983); Johannes Harder, *Die Nacht am Jacotiner See* (Bielefeld: Ludwig Beschauf Verlag, 1960); idem, *Und der Himmel lacht mit: Heiteres von Theologen und Theolunken* (Freiburg: Herder, 1982); Al Reimer, "The Russian-Mennonite Experience in Fiction," in *Mennonite Images: Historical, Cultural and Literary Essays Dealing with Mennonite Issues*, ed. Harry Loewen (Winnipeg: Hyperion Press, 1980), 231-32; ME III: 370; *Brücke*, 2, no. 5 (1987), 68-69; *Menn. Mirror*, 16 (May 1987), 5-7; Al Reimer, "Johannes Harder (1903-1987): A Reflective Tribute to a Remarkable Mennonite," *JMS*, 5 (1987), 167-71; interview with Johannes Harder: "Ketterij als motor van de kerkgeschiedenis," *Doops. Bijdr.*, n.r. 8 (1982), 84-87; *Menn. Life*, 28 (June 1973), 54.

Harshbarger, Eva Geiger (Aug. 27, 1902 -), daughter of Calvin and Sarah Geiger, grew up in Bluffton, Ohio, where her father operated Noah's Ark, a general store. The Geiger family belonged to the Mennonite Church (MC).

Eva attended Bluffton College starting in 1920 and married Emmet Harshbarger after graduation. He taught high school and earned a PhD degree; she studied at Witmarsum Seminary one year and then became a mother of two. In 1933 they moved to North Newton, Ks., where Emmet taught history at Bethel College and started the Institute of International Relations (°disarmament). He died of spinal tuberculosis in 1942. Eva carried on efforts in international relations and became president of the branch of Women's International League for Peace and Freedom.

Bethel College offered Eva a job in the bookstore and snack shop. She worked summers on a master's degree in home economics from the University of Kansas in Manhattan and then taught English and home and family courses at Bethel College and also served as dean of women. She served with Mennonite Central Committee in Korea and Vietnam from 1953-56, taught at Goessel High School until 1967, and served in the World Friendship Center, Hiroshima, Japan, in 1976.   MKP

Mary Lou Cummings, *Full Circle* (Newton, 1978), 98-109; *Menn. Bib. II,* p. 452.

Hart, Homer (Dec. 3, 1896-Dec. 24, 1977), was one of the first Indian workers in the General Conference Mennonite (GCM) mission to the Southern Cheyenne in Oklahoma. As a young person he came in contact with Henry J. Kliewer, a Mennonite missionary under the Board of Foreign Missons (GCM). By age 12, he and Alfrich Heap of Birds assisted in a camp meeting service. In the fall of 1917 he became a paid worker (or "native helper") with the Red Moon Mission Church (later the Bethel Mennonite Church, Hammon, Okla.), assisting Kliewer. Hart continued in this work for more than 40 years. He was ordained as an elder in 1958. During the latter part of his ministry he served as an evangelist in other areas of Indian ministries in Montana and Arizona. Hart also served as a committeeman for the Southern Cheyenne and Arapaho. The committee was a forerunner of the Tribal Council. In 1936, he was selected as headsman of the Southern Cheyenne tribe. He was also a member of the Elk Soldier Society.   LB

Barrett, *Vision* (1983), 55, 70.

See also Indian Ministries.

Hartzler, John Ellsworth (1879-1963), was a Mennonite progressive, whose career as preacher, college administrator and theology professor exemplifies the informal continuum linking the early 20th c. Swiss-American Mennonite traditions, running from Old Order Amish on the traditionalist end through the Mennonite Church (MC) to the General Conference Mennonite Church on the progressive end. His several books and many articles reflect his changing outlook.

Born near Ligioner, Ind., to Old Order Amish parents, Joseph and Mary (Beyler) Hartzler, J. E. grew up in Cass Co., Mo. He attended the more progressive, Mennonite and English-speaking Bethel congregation. Revival meetings by John S. °°Coffman sparked a youthful ambition to preach. In 1895 Hartzler experienced conversion under revival preaching of A. D. °°Wenger. Hartzler was ordained in the Bethel congregation in 1904 by Bishop

Andrew Shenk, after Bishop Daniel °Kauffman had directed the election process. Hartzler quickly became a popular and colorful preacher throughout the Mennonite Church (MC). He remained a confidant of Daniel Kauffman until the relationship soured after 1918 due to financial mismanagement at Goshen College and Hartzler's development of a more liberal theology. Hartzler's chapters on the "Plan of Salvation" in Kauffman's *Bible Doctrine* (1914), was omitted from the revised edition (1929).

Hartzler studied at °°Elkhart Institute, Moody Bible Institute, Hamilton College of Law, McCormick Theological Seminary. He received BA (Goshen College), BD (Union Theological Seminary, New York, MA (U. of Chicago), law degree (Hamilton College), and PhD (Hartford Theological Seminary) degrees.

He served as pastor at Prairie Street Mennonite Church (Elkhart, Ind., 1910-13) and dean (1911-13) and president (1913-18) of Goshen College. He married Mamie M. Yoder in 1910. In 1918 he became a professor of Bible at Bethel College (Ks.) and served as president, 1920-21. As an early advocate of an all-Mennonite seminary, Hartzler became president of Witmarsum Theological Seminary when it opened in 1921 at Bluffton College (Ohio). At Witmarsum, Hartzler and others incurred frequent charges of modernism. Hartzler defended his loyalty to the essence of Mennonite faith, but a faith defined more in terms of individual rights than Anabaptist tradition.

After Witmarsum closed in 1931 Hartzler taught one year at American U. in Beirut and two years at Near East School of Religion. In 1936 he joined the faculty at Hartford Theological Seminary, serving 11 years. After his formal retirement, Hartzler continued a busy schedule of lecturing and preaching. Mamie Yoder Hartzler died in 1955. J. E. Hartzler's final years, spent at Goshen with his wife, Mrs. Myra H. Weaver, whom he married in 1957, proved to be a time of quiet reflection, a renewal of relationships with Goshen College, and a fruitful relationship with the younger generation of leaders within the church.   JDW

Hartzler Papers, MC Archives (Goshen); *Who's Who Mennonites* (1943), 99; *Menn. Bib. II,* p. 452; J. C. Juhnke, ed., "J. E. Hartzler: Autobiographical Notes," *MHB,* 42, no. 2 (Apr. 1981), 3-5; Janeen Bertsche [Johnson], "J. E. Hartzler: The Change in His Approach to Doctrine," student paper at Bluffton College, copies at Bethel, Bluffton, and Goshen college libraries; Paul Erb, *South Central Frontiers* (Scottdale, 1974); J. C. Juhnke, "Mennonite Progressives and World War I," *Menn. Life* 41 no. 4 (Dec. 1986), 14-16; E. G. Kaufman, comp., *General Conference Mennonite Pioneers* (North Newton: Bethel College, 1973); John Umble, *Goshen College* (Goshen, 1955); Peter J. Wedel, *The Story of Bethel College,* ed. E. G. Kaufman (North Newton: Bethel College, 1954).

Hartzler, Raymond Livingston (Nov. 28, 1893 - June 27, 1988). Born near Topeka, Ind., to Rufus and Nettie Byler Hartzler, R. L. Hartzler married Nora Burkholder, daughter of Simon and Emma Musser Burkholder of Wayne Co., Ohio, on Feb. 12, 1919. He had graduated from Topeka High School (1911) and Goshen College (BA, 1918). Hartzler taught school and farmed. Baptized on April 1, 1906, he comitted himself to Christian service at a YMCA retreat at Lake Geneva, Wis., in 1912. He was ordained as a minister (1916) and elder (1931). His pastorates included Maple Grove Mennonite Church (Topeka, Ind.), 1916-28; Carlock Mennonite Church (Ill.), 1928-41; and several interim pastorates.

Hartzler served the °°Central Conference Mennonite Church in a variety of capacities after 1927. He was conference secretary, 1928-37, and served on many boards (Mennonite Hospital Association, 1933-60; Central Conference Home and Foreign Missions, 1934-57; Publication Board, 1938-57; Congo Inland Mission, 1938-75; Mennonite Biblical Seminary, 1943-59). He edited the conference year book, 1937-57 and *The Christian Evangel*, 1938-57.

From 1941 to 1944 Hartzler served with °°Civilian Public Service as director of two camps and as area counselor for the central United States (1943). He was instrumental in the affiliation of the Central Conference Mennonite Church with the General Conference Mennonite Church (1946) and the merger of the Central Conference with the Middle District Conference in 1957 to form the Central District Conference of the General Conference Mennonite Church. He served the new district as conference minister, 1957-64. He was a member of the Committee on the Ministry (GCM), 1954-62.

He adapted the words for the hymn "Africa," which was published in 1940. The R. L. Hartzler Health Complex was dedicated in his honor in Bloomington, Ill., in 1977. He was awarded an honorary Doctorate of Humane Letters by Bluffton College (Ohio) in 1987. He died at Bloomington.   SRE

W. Richard Hassan, "R. L. Hartzler Reviews Central Conference Growth," *Mennonite Heritage*, 3 (1976), 1, 9-11.

Hatano Eichiro (b. Aug. 16, 1899), first moderator of the Nihon Menonaito Kirisuto Kyokai Kaigi (Hokkaido) (Japan Mennonite Christian Church Conference) and a lay pastor of the Shiroishi congregation, was born in Hokkaido. As a student he entered the medical department of Keio University in Tokyo, but left after studying for four years. On returning to Kushiro, his home town, he worked for a local newspaper as a reporter for eight years. When his father died in 1932, the hereditary system settled him as postmaster, and he stayed in that position until he retired at the age of 68.

In 1951 he and his wife, Katsuko, met Ralph and Genevieve °Buckwalter for the first time. They were baptized two years later. While managing the post office, he helped with the Buckwalter's missionary work in and around Kushiro.

In 1956 when the Japan Mennonite Christian Church Conference was established, he showed good leadership as chairman in coordinating the local churches for 12 years. After retiring from post office work in 1967, he attended Goshen Biblical Seminary, Elkhart, Ind., as an auditor. In 1968 he became lay pastor of the Shiroishi church in Sapporo and served faithfully for about 10 years.   KT

Hawaii, the 50th state of the United States, consisting of a group of eight major islands in the central Pacific ocean with a population of 965,000 in 1980 and an area of 6,450 sq. mi. (16,706 sq. km.). A Mennonite congregation began to emerge in Honolulu in 1986 under the leadership of Van Pham, a former Mennonite pastor in Vietnam, and his wife, Qui Thi Vu. The effort was supported by the Mennonite Board of Missions (MC) and the Lancaster and Franconia Conferences; the emerging congregation was linked to the Southwest Mennonite Conference.   Staff

GH (March 10, 1987) 172.

See also Urban Church.

Hazleton, Iowa, Old Order Amish Settlement (ME I:460) in Buchanan Co., 25 mi. (40 km.) east of Waterloo. Amish families settled here in 1914, coming from the °Kalona Amish community, seeking a more conservative church discipline. In the 1980s the Hazleton settlement is known for its conservatism and slowness to change in Amish customs. It is, therefore, a suitable location for families who are uneasy with change and who hold strong convictions about more traditional and stricter life-styles. In its 72-year history, it has grown to six church districts (congregations) with an estimated population of 1,200. Migration of several families to one of Iowa's other three small Amish communities has kept alive the zeal to develop and preserve an ideal, more perfectly nonconformed Amish tradition.   SLY

Headcovering (ME I:386, ME II:630, 678; ME IV:146, 212). Utilizing Richard Detweiler's Princeton study (1966), Kraybill (1987) summarizes Mennonite history of woman's veiling as: 1525-1865: symptom stage, with no distinctive religious significance given to women's headcoverings; 1866-1910: stabilized sign, with preachers appealing to 1 Cor 11:1-16; 1910-1950: veiling frozen as bonafide religious °symbol; 1950-present: disintegraing legitimacy of the veiling as a religious symbol.

This characterizes the Mennonite Church (MC), the largest North American group to retain the tradition during the first half of the 20th c. Amish, Beachy Amish Mennonites, Old Order Mennonites, Conservative Mennonite Conference, Hutterian Brethren and Old Colony Mennonite women continue to wear a headcovering (°prayer veil). Styles (color, material, strings) vary; other altering factors include age, public or home settings, single or married, or quantity of head actually covered.

Understandings about headcovering illustrate the historic headship pattern of men telling women what to do and why. As women become more disciplined students of Scripture and express insight from personal experience of role subordination, traditional bias will be exposed for what it is and has done.

For example, teaching about headcovering has relied on the premise of *created order* in Gen 2 and *headship* in 1 Cor 11. Interpretive bias suggests that women and men have distinct functions: men are leaders while women nurture and serve. Other careful translators of the texts understand such division to characterize what followed sin, rather than redemption. Their bias notes God's order to be genuine interdependence. Some point out that the Greek word *exousia*, often translated *veil* (1 Cor 11:10), is known to mean *authority*. Conviction will differ: when authority is identified as the woman's rather than as her husband's over her; when relationships in the body of Christ contrast rather than imitate those of the world.

Writers try to explain that role separation—symbolized through man's uncovered and woman's covered head—does not bless unequal value for woman and man. But research (Kraybill) conducted among more than 1,000 Lancaster Co., Pa., parents and youth shows how the veil has legitimated female subordination. It also verifies that decline in veil-wearing does not degrade ethnic identity or diminish support for ethnic institutions.

In addition to symbolic meanings of order and submission, women's headcovering traditionally fostered modesty, and opportunity for witness, particular identity, and connection to worship. It expressed °obedience and conformity, and both catered to and rejected broader cultural values.

Recent trends in MC practice (North America) include discontinuing the wearing of a headcovering, allowing diverse practice side-by-side, and reinforcing the expectation that women have their heads covered during worship. While more MC congregations (based on studies in Indiana and Ohio) support personal choice, which accommodates varied customs, other more conservative groups make even stronger appeals to conform to this expression of °°nonconformity. As more congregations call women to pastoral leadership, male power and one of its symbols is diminished. This, in turn, leads guardians of the tradition to buttress the claim that the prayer veil is of "Divine Order" and to remind MC membership of Article 14 ("Symbols of Christian Order") in the 1963 Confession of Faith (Loewen, *Confessions*, 76). For Brethren in Christ practice, see Wittlinger.

Mennonite churches worldwide also bring features of culture into patterns of headcovering. Whereas Swiss Mennonite women throughout the 20th c. have not used a prayer veiling, German Mennonite usage has diminished in the past 30 years. As a right of passage from girl to woman, a ritual part of Russian Mennonite marriage has included her donning a kerchief. This symbol of subordination to one's husband is worn by some Mennonite Brethren women at all times.

Mennonite women of India have naturally utilized the sari as headcovering for worship or expressing respect. Many African women see a head piece as part of their dressing. In contrast, to wear anything on the head while talking is improper in Japan. When headcovering expectations for MC women were first articulated in the late 19th c. they were problematic; further, an inconsistent message was given since General Conference Mennonite (GCM) groups did not expect the practice. For Mennonites worshiping in Israel, practice varies with the local church: with older churches of Christendom a veiling is worn while with mainline Protestant and Messianic Assemblies the custom is generally not followed.

Most Old Colony Mennonite women wear a headcovering all the time. Men wear hats except for worship and prayer. Associated with marital status rather than baptism, a single woman wears a white

covering while married women wear black ones. Couples are more interdependent when a husband grants his wife permission not to wear the covering; less conservative people may wear a smaller kerchief. **DYN**

Donald B. Kraybill, "Mennonite Woman's Veiling: The Rise and Fall of a Sacred Symbol," *MQR*, 61 (1987), 298-320; Melvin Gingerich, *Mennonite Attire Through Four Centuries* (Breinigsville, Pa.: Pennsylvania German Society, 1970); Sanford G. Shetler and J. Ward Shank, *Symbols of Divine Order in the Church, A Compendium on I Cor. 11:2-16* (Harrisonburg, Va.: Sword and Trumpet, 1983); J. C. Wenger, *The Prayer Veil in Scripture and History* (Scottdale, 1964), 29 pp.; Calvin W. Redekop, *The Old Colony Mennonites* (Baltimore: Johns Hopkins U. Press, 1969)sd, 131-32; Wittlinger, *Piety and Obedience* (1978), index under "prayer veiling." Congregation and conference studies include the following: Bill Detweiler, "Another Look at I Corinthians 11:2-16 (Kidron, Oh., 1970) 26 pp.; "We Consider I Corinthians 11:1-16,: prepared for the Mennonite Conference of Ontario under the direction of its executive committee (1965), 24 pp.; "Memorandum," Questionnaire Results, Committee on I Corinthians 11 (Goshen, In.: College Mennonite Church, 1968), 6 pp.; William McGrath, *A Biblical and Historical Review of the Christian Woman's Veiling* (East Rochester, Oh.: Amish Mennonite Publications, 1986), 33 pp.; Richard C. Detweiler, "The Historical Background, Development and Symbolism of the Woman's Headcovering as Practiced in the Mennonite Church" (unpublished paper; Princeton Theological Seminary, 1966); Melvin Gingerich, "The Virtue of Simple Dress," *Menn. Life* 26 (Dec. 1971), 150-54; Yorifumi Yaguchi, "The Covering Issue in the Mennonite Churches in Japan," (seminary course paper, Jan. 1964) copy at MHL (Goshen).

Healing. See Faith Healing; Health Services; Medicine.

Health Education. The home and school, both °public and °private, continue to be the primary agents for health education among Mennonites. Mennonite °secondary schools and colleges include in their curricula courses which promote health education and health care, not only in their physical education programs, but also in physiology and psychology. In North America several colleges include premedical training programs which qualify graduates to enter schools of medicine or dentistry. Several Mennonite colleges likewise have schools of °nursing, while other schools of nursing are hospital-related rather than college-related. In addition to Mennonite educational institutions, however, Mennonite °hospitals and clinics, and °mental health centers, carry on significant programs of health education for the benefit of the public and the church, including health forums, lectures, and seminars covering a wide variety of health issues. In addition, the Mennonite Mental Health Services (Mennonite Health Services since 1988) has a Committee on Awareness and Education which seeks to promote mental health awareness and programs in local congregations.

Mennonites around the world, as a dimension of medical missions, Mennonite Central Committee °relief and °development ministries or through the agencies of national churches, have made health education an integral part of compassionate ministry to the total needs of people, whether in Europe, North or South America, Asia, or Africa.

In North America, °Mennonite Mutual Aid of Goshen, Ind., in the 1970s began developing a special emphasis on the promotion of health awareness in local congregations. In 1975 it began distributing *The Tool Kit*, a newsletter which included many items promoting physical health. Then it published a series of brochures to promote "Wellness," a concept which sought to integrate the spiritual, mental, relational, vocational, physical, psychological, environmental, and social dimensions of health. In 1980 it sponsored a study program for local congregations entitled, "A Life of Wholeness." This was followed in 1983 by the appointment of a "wellness director" who gave initiative to the training of congregational leaders to promote health education in the local churches. By the end of 1987 more than 500 leaders had been trained and were being served by a regular newsletter called *Well Now,* begun in 1985. The "Wellness Program," which by the end of 1987, had affected several hundred local congregations, expanded to include children as well as adults. The larger program includes not only workshops and seminars, but also brochures, newsletters, and such publications as *Medical Ethics, Human Choices: A Christian Perspective* (Scottdale, 1988). One of the factors leading to this emphasis on wellness and health education has been the rising cost of health care and the involvement of Mennonite Mutual Aid in sharing health care financial aid (°mutual aid; °insurance).

The Mennonite Health Association (MHA) continues to promote health education through its various constituent agencies, e.g., the Mennonite Chaplains Association, the Mennonite Nurses Association, the Mennonite Medical Association, the Inter-Mennonite Council on Aging, the Mennonite Council for Hospitals, Mennonite Mental Health Services (Mennonite Health Services), Mennonite Developmental Disability Services, Mennonite Child Care Services, MHA's Inter-Mennonite Personnel Services, and particularly MHA's Council on Congregational Health Concerns. This council encourages every congregation to provide for its own health concerns council. It has published *Congregational Health Ministries Handbook: A Resource for Mennonite Congregations,* edited by Edwin F. Rempel (1987), which sketches a theology of health care, lists and describes the various constituent agencies represented in the Mennonite Health Association, and provides bibliographical information as well as a listing of Mennonite Health care agencies which can serve local congregations in their health care needs.

The *Mennonite Medical Messenger* is published quarterly by the Mennonite Medical Association and serves also the Mennonite Health Association as well as the Mennonite Nurses Association. It has a circulation of around 2,000. This organ serves primarily the members of these organizations, yet through them seeks to promote Christian understandings of illness and health and ethical standards in the practice of health care and delivery. Special attention is given to the promotion of transcultural experience in the practice of medicine. The Mennonite Medical Association for many years has placed medical students and supported them financially in settings which facilitate transcultural learning. In recent years it has cooperated in a medical component of the China Educational Exchange Program.

Together with the Institute of Mennonite Studies of the Associated Mennonite Biblical Seminaries, agencies of the Mennonite Health Association sponsored a major interdisciplinary seminar on shalom, health, and healing (June, 1988).

The Mennonite Medical Association, including more than 500 Mennonite physicians and dentists meet in convention annually, generally with the Mennonite Nurses Association, to study and discuss health care issues including °bioethical dilemmas, the costs of health care, wholistic approaches to medicine, and coping with conflict and change.

This association has also sponsored meetings of Mennonite physicians from around the world in conjunction with Mennonite World Conference sessions. One of its members, Sidney Kreider, has served with the World Health Organization (WHO) based in Geneva, Switzerland. It is also notable that Eric Ram, for several years the Director of the Christian Medical Commission (World Council of Churches) based in Geneva, Switzerland, is the product of Mennonite Medical Mission work in central India. EW

Health Services. A 1526 list of the Swiss Brethren includes a doctor and his wife. °Menno Simons is credited with the statement: "True evangelical faith cannot lie dormant. . . . It clothes the naked. It feeds the hungry. It comforts the sorrowful. It shelters the destitute. It serves those that harm it. It binds up that which is wounded. It has become all things to all men." Early Anabaptists believed in a whole gospel for the total person. They assumed that Christian people take care of people with needs. Health services had wide application among them from the start.

Among the Swiss and Dutch Anabaptists and Mennonites, midwifery was practiced (°midwives). Dr. Peter Dettweiler (d. 1904) is known for discovering a tuberculosis cure and also as the father of the sanatorium movement.

The Dutch Mennonites became socially and economically accepted sooner than Swiss Mennonites. They strongly emphasized community life that would care for its ill whenever possible; with the community assisting where families could not do it alone.

The Dordrecht Confession (1632), in article 9 refers to Jesus' concern for healing and restoration. This includes care for the poor, the aged, feeble, sick, sorrowing, and needy. °°Deacons and °°deaconesses were to provide many of these services.

In the migrations to the Palatinate and to Russia, health services continued to be integral parts of the communities. As late as 1880 only one trained physician is reported among the 60 Molotschna villages. But the bone-setters (Knochenärzte) and home remedies (see Klippenstein, Toews, 240-247) were common.

Chortitza Colony had a district hospital and added a 75-100-bed Red Cross emergency hospital during World War I. The first Molotschna hospital service at Muntau (1880) was soon followed by one in Waldheim, then Ohrloff and in the Neu-Samara (°Pleshanov) daughter colony. Bethania, a system consisting of a mental hospital, °°orphanages, a school for the deaf, and °homes for old people were also provided by Russian Mennonites. Occasionally, °°anointing services according to Js 5 were administered.

Anabaptists were pioneers in serving the poor and the orphans. Their opponents said this was proof that they considered good works above faith. In Augsburg it was argued that this undermined the role of the state.

The °°*Waisenamt* (Orphans' fund) was set up in Russia to administer estates of orphans. It was later used for services also to widows, elderly or anyone else needing help in financial matters (°mutual aid). Feeble-minded, the deaf, and epileptics inherited twice what was left to other siblings.

Early Mennonites in the United States and Canada continued to care for their own. Frank H. Epp, (*Mennonites in Canada I*) says, ". . . medical problems were abated by genuine neighborliness and community spirit. Every cluster of neighbors boasted a midwife and a bone-setter ready, willing and able to attend those medical needs which tea could not cure" (p. 87).

From the beginnng, some ministers also dispensed counsel for better health practices. As care for the ill became more specialized and health services more complex, mutual aid organizations sprang up to help where individuals, families and communities could not handle the needs. At first acting like a Christian version of °insurance agencies, the largest Mennonite mutual aid body (°Mennonite Mutual Aid) in 1987 is deeply involved in preventive training and in promoting wellness care.

The 20th c. saw a rapid rise in the number of Mennonites choosing the health services as acceptable °occupations. At first these people often either did not feel welcome in their home communities after graduation or else the graduates wanted to live in more progressive communities.

To strengthen the health services and to build bridges between them and the more traditional Mennonite communities, organizations were begun. The first were intended to promote homes for the aged (Germany, 1949), then to promote homes for the aged and hospitals (United States). This led to a new understanding of the need for health professionals. To work at this need and to develop greater acceptance, a Mennonite Nurses Association (1942, United States and Canada) and a Mennonite Medical Association (1946) were founded. There were also informal Mennonite Health "Assemblies" which convened annually. Mennonite Chaplains and Mennonite social workers (for a while) also organized.

In the meantime, World War II had put many Mennonites into °mental health institutions to do their °alternative service (°°Civilian Public Service) as °conscientious objectors. After the war these people wanted to continue providing new and better health services to the mentally ill. This led to rapid growth in Mennonite-related mental health centers in the United States and Canada. These became and continue to be model institutions for mental health services. It is likely also that the World War II experiences and the success in the mental health services contributed to the creative ways that other Mennonite health services began to develop. The

Mennonite hospital at Bloomington, Ill., for example, has become a multi-faceted institution providing a whole range of health services from acute care to self-care, at the central hospital, in various satellite service centers, and in homes.

When the latest Mennonite organization, the Mennonite Health Association (MHA), was formed in 1980, it began with a relatively fresh philosophy of health services that included agenda which earlier would likely not have been considered health services. Members include hospitals, aged and nursing homes, services to the aging, °chaplaincy services, °disability programs, administrative services, medical and °nursing services, volunteer services, and congregational health concern councils. While curative care is a large part of in its programs, the focus has been shifted from illness care to wellness care. Wellness care refers to the effort to encourage people to take care of their bodies, minds, emotions, and spirits as stewards of what God has given them. It urges people to practice a healthful expression with all of their being.

The wholistic model of health services which the MHA adopted as its goal still has some gaps. It does not yet include the human ecology (dietary and other homemaker services), and the abuse services (child, spouse, and °drugs).

The Mennonite model of health services as integral to all community living can also be seen in Mennonite °mission and °service endeavors. Wherever mission churches and °development services are found, health services are also found. This was so from the first Dutch-Mennonite mission work in Java (Indonesia) and remains characteristic of the development work in Bangladesh and elsewhere. Mennonite migration to Mexico, Paraguay, Brazil, Bolivia, Belize, and other places has also included continuing emphasis on health services.

While basic health services among Mennonites began as the work of the church, Mennonites, like other people in the Western world of the 20th c., gave much of the health care responsibility to governments and to health professionals. This served to make such care less a part of the wholistic goal which was envisioned. But it seemed to work when combined with relatively good insurance or government support.

However, in the 1980s health technologies were developed that were able to sustain life artificially and to change life artificially. Scientists and physicians learned to splice genes, °abort pregnancies, create life outside of the uterus, replace vital organs with mechanical or donor organs and to sustain "brain dead" people with life support systems. Along with these potential new services came enormous costs and complex °bioethical issues. Who decides when an abortion is therapeutic? Should the professionals decide when to end life or should the patient and family decide whether heroic measures are proper? Who are the parents when embryos are started in test tubes and then implanted in surrogate wombs? Where is the money to come from and what is a fair proportion of taxes to go for health services? These questions are never far from the surface in the Western world when health services are discussed in the late 20th c.

Mennonite health institutions feel the pressure directly. Fifty representatives of 145 Mennonite and Brethren in Christ health service institutions met in Denver, Col., Mar. 4, 1986, to discuss their survival. To make it past the current crises, it was agreed that essential adjustments would have to be made. One would be to work more cooperatively. Mennonite churches, like other churches, have left the resolution of much of this dilemma to health professionals. The latter feel more and more uneasy and keep calling for greater involvement by church leaders, theologians, and all those who receive health services. There is a growing mood in the late 1980s that health services must once again be guided by the total church community. And as much responsibility as possible for each person's healthfulness needs to be taken by each person.   BW

Frank H. Epp, *Mennonites in Canada 1,* 87, 295; Steven R. Estes, *Christian Concern for Health: The Sixtieth Anniversary History of the Mennonite Hospital Association* (Bloomington, Ill., 1979), 1-4; John A. Hostetler, *Amish Society* (1980), 313-32; Lawrence Klippenstein and Julius G. Toews, eds., *Mennonite Memories* (Winnipeg: Centennial Publications, 1977); Vernon H. Neufeld, ed., *If We Can Love: The Mennonite Mental Health Story* (Newton, 1983); Martin E. Marty, and Kenneth L. Vaux, eds., *Health/Medicine and the Faith Traditions* (Philadelphia: Fortress, 1982); *MC Yearbook* (1988-89), 124-30.

See also Community Health Work; Medicine.

Heaven. Because of symbolic language and interpretation problems, the biblical doctrine of heaven is somewhat elusive. However, it may be said that the Bible presents heaven in three specific ways: as the abode of God and of angels (Is 63:15; Mt 5:16; Mt 24:36), as the place of the saints' future inheritance (1 Pet 1:4), and as the dynamic spiritual invasion of earth by Jesus and His ministry. "Jesus began to preach, saying, 'Repent, for the °kingdom of heaven is at hand'" (Mt 4:17, RSV).

In addition, and apart from the actual word "heaven," many concepts and images appear in the Bible in regard to the final destiny of God's people. It will be in the house of the Father (Jn 14:2), and there his servants shall see his face (Rev 22:4). It will involve glory (1 Pet 5:1, 4, 10), paradise (Rev 2:7), and rejoicing (Rev 19:7). It is spoken of as a future city (Heb 13:14), a prepared kingdom (Mt 25:34), and an eternal reign (Rev 22:5).

Revelation 21:1-4 is a special case. While it is often cited as symbolic of the eternal home of God's people, it is also interpreted as the present church (Kepler), and as the temporary location of deceased saints prior to the resurrection (Ladd). The "new heaven and . . . new earth" (RSV) language of 21:1 may indicate that heaven will be established at least partially in a newly created or renewed earth.

The 16th c. Anabaptists referred many times in their testimonies and writings to three New Testament passages that seem to deal with heaven. Portions of Rev 6:9-11 are cited in *Martyrs Mirror* no fewer than 23 times; 1 Cor 2:9 is quoted 21 times, and Rev 21:1-4 is cited, in whole or in part, 19 times. °Menno Simons declared, "We shall . . . sit down in the kingdom of God with Abraham, Isaac, and Jacob possessing that noble and pleasant land of endless eternal joy" (Menno, *Writings,* 348). Felix

°°Manz, George °°Blaurock, °°Dirk Philips, Balthasar °Hubmaier, Peter °Riedemann, and Jacob °°Hutter all wrote in simple biblical language about the reality of heaven. For example, Felix Manz, in an admonition to the brethren, referred to "the heaven of eternal joys. . . ." (*Martyrs Mirror,* 415), and Dirk Philips wrote of "the eternal kingdom with God in heaven (Heb 4:9) to which the Lord Jesus Christ ascended, to prepare us a place . . ." (Dirk, *Enchiridion,* trans. Kolb, p. 336).

By contrast, Hans °°Denck quite possibly held that heaven is not to be considered as the literal eternal home of God's people, but as a present spiritual reality for the committed Christian.

The Mennonite confessions of faith consistently depict heaven as the literal future state of the redeemed. The °°Dordrecht Confession of 1632, recognized by the Mennonite Church (MC) as one of its official confessions, declares, "the good or pious shall . . . be received by Christ into eternal life, where they shall receive that joy which 'eye hath not seen . . .' [and] where they shall reign and triumph with Christ forever and ever" (art. 18; Loewen, *Confessions,* 69). The MC Confession of Faith of 1963 speaks of "the eternal bliss of the world to come" art. 20; Loewen, 77).

The Cornelis Ris confession, a recognized confession of the General Conference Mennonite Church, describes heaven as "a life of eternal and heavenly bliss (Lk 15:7; Rev 19:7), imperishable and unfading, which will be enjoyed under conditions of perfect delight . . ." (art. 35; Loewen, 104/102). The General Conference Articles of Faith (1933) says that "the state of the blessed will be one of perfect joy and happiness and glory . . ." (art 14; Loewen, 111/109). And the Mennonite Brethren Confession of Faith (1975) states that "At death the righteous enter a state of rest in the presence of God, in fellowship with Christ. . . ." and that they will be "with Him forever" (art. 16; Loewen, 178).

The Christian Fundamentals Articles of Faith (MC, 1921) asserts that "heaven is the final abode of the righteous, where they will dwell in the fulness of joy forever and ever" (art. 18; Loewen, 72). The 18 articles of this 1921 "Fundamentals" declaration obviously came into being as a positive response to the 12 volumes of *Fundamentals* published between 1910 and 1915. However, in regard to the doctrine of heaven, there was no direct connection between the 1910-15 volumes and the 1921 articles, for the simple reason that the *Fundamentals* did not contain a treatise on heaven.

A number of 20th c. Mennonite scholars have written on heaven. Gordon Kaufman refers to heaven as a symbol of the divine consummation of history. Paul °Erb, David Ewert, Chester K. °Lehman, Gerald Studer, and John C. Wenger use more literal or conventional language. A simple and beautiful statement is made by Paul Erb on the final page of *The Alpha and the Omega:* "The Christian has something beyond. He has Someone there, Someone he knows. He has a Lord and Saviour in heaven, who has given him life and hope. . . . This Saviour has promised . . . that where He is we may be also" (p. 153).   SCS

Eldon T. Yoder and Monroe D. Hochstetler, *Biblical References in Anabaptist Writings* (Aylmer, Ont.: Pathway, 1969), 252, 390, 397; Menno, *Writings*, 348, 1054, 1058-59, 1065-67; Dietrich Philip (Dirk Philips), *Enchiridion,* trans. A. B. Kolb (1910), 336-38, 351, 400-402; James Lafayette Gurley, "The Eschatology of the Sixteenth Century Anabaptists" (thesis, Northern Baptist Theological Seminary, 1958), 88-94; Gerald C. Studer, *After Death, What?* (Scottdale, 1976, 131-46; Paul Erb, *The Alpha and the Omega* (Scottdale, 1955), 152-53; John C. Wenger, *Introduction to Theology* (Scottdale, 1954), 333-34; Gordon D. Kaufman, *Systematic Theology: A Historicist Perspective* (New York, 1968), 323, 471-72; David Ewert, *And Then Comes the End* (Kitchener, 1980), 147-71; Chester K. Lehman, *Biblical Theology: The New Testament* (Scottdale, 1971), 531-32.

See also Eternity; Fundamentalism; Salvation.

Hell. See Eternity; Heaven; Salvation.

Herald Press. See Publishing.

Herald Publishing Company, Inc. See Publishing

Hermeneutics. See Biblical Interpretation.

Hershberger, Guy F. (b. Dec. 3, 1896), was born in Johnson Co., Iowa, the first of nine children of Ephraim D. and Dorinda Kempf Hershberger. He was baptized in 1909 at the East Union Amish Mennonite Church. After graduating from high school in 1915, he taught in rural schools until his marriage to Clara Hooley, of Goshen, Ind., on Aug. 1, 1920. Their two children are Elizabeth (Bauman), born in 1924, and Paul, born 1934.

Guy and Clara both enrolled at Hesston College in the fall of 1920 and graduated in 1923. He taught in the Hesston Academy, 1923-24, while Clara served as dean of women. After Sanford C. °Yoder, formerly the pastor at East Union, invited him to join the faculty of the reopened Goshen College, Hershberger earned an MA degree at the U. of Iowa in 1925. Further graduate study at the U. of Chicago and Iowa led to the PhD degree (Iowa, 1935), with a dissertation on Quaker politics in colonial Pennsylvania. Hershberger's long career at Goshen, teaching history, sociology, and ethics, began in 1925. He helped found *The Mennonite Quarterly Review* (1927) and continued on its editorial staff throughout his life, serving as editor in 1963-65.

In 1925, Orie O. °Miller, secretary of the Mennonite Church's Peace Problems Committee, enlisted Hershberger as an ally in the cause of °peace education and activity, although Hershberger was not a member of the committee until 1959. Hershberger's life-long interest in broader peace circles began in 1927 at the St. Louis conference of the World Alliance for International Friendship Through the Churches.

The need for peace literature for Mennonites led to a series of articles in the °°*Youth's Christian Companion* that were later published as a book, *Can Christians Fight?* (1940). Hershberger introduced peace concerns into the college program by building up a peace library, launching the Peace Society, and teaching his basic course "War, Peace, and Nonresistance" to hundreds of students. At a Mennonite peace conference in 1935, Hershberger presented a paper that became the foundation for the alternative service program of World War II. His major work

War, Peace, and Nonresistance appeared in 1944, with revisions in 1953 and 1969. He published *The Mennonite Church in the Second World War* in 1951.

In 1939, a second career focus emerged with the forming of the Committee on Industrial Relations (MC), later the Committee on Economic and Social Relations. As its executive secretary from 1939 to 1965, Hershberger led the way in shaping a Mennonite social ethic which was spelled out in *The Way of the Cross in Human Relations* (1958). Along with many significant writings, Hershberger also expressed his vision through his role in the founding of Mennonite Mutual Aid (1945) and the Mennonite Community Association (1946). In the 1960s, he gave guidance to the church's response to the civil rights movement.

After retirement from Goshen College in 1966, the Hershbergers moved to Phoenix, Ariz., where he remained active in writing and speaking on the ethical issues facing a changing church. In 1985, they returned to the Goshen area, residing at Greencroft.   JRB

See *Kingdom, Cross, and Community* (Scottdale, 1976), an 80th-birthday tribute to Hershberger, edited by J. R. Burkholder and Calvin Redekop, especially the essays by Theron Schlabach, Leonard Gross, and Robert Kreider, and the bibliography of Hershberger's writings (1922-1976); see also interviews with Hershberger by Melvin Gingerich, 1975, transcript in MC Archives (Goshen) and excerpts in *MHB,* 48 (Jan. 1987); *Who's Who Mennonites* (1943), 103-4; *GH* (March 3, 1987) 146-48; *Sharing* (Winter 1987), 6-11.

Hershey, Mae Elizabeth (Dec. 22, 1877-Feb. 22, 1974). Mae Elizabeth Hertzler was born near Concord, Tenn., to Levi B. and Katherine Stoltzfus Hertzler. As a child she felt a definite call to be a missionary. Converted at age 17, she was baptized by her great-grandfather, John Stoltzfus, in a creek near the local Mennonite church.

Mae earned a BS degree in education from the Ewing-Jefferson Cumberland Presbyterian Junior College, Marysville, Tenn. (1898), and took summer teachers' courses at the U. of Tennessee, Knoxville. She taught school for six years.

She married Tobias Kreider Hershey (Dec. 27, 1904) at Concord, Tenn., and moved with her husband to a small farm near Gap, Pa. The Hersheys worked in °urban mission and pastorates in Youngstown, Ohio; La Junta, Col.; and Bluffton, Ohio. On Aug. 16, 1917, the Hersheys, with their two children, Beatrice and Lester, sailed with J. W. and Emma °Shank and family, to Argentina to serve as missionaries under the Mennonite Board of Missions (MC).

Mae made at least three major contributions to the mission work in Argentina: with Emma Shank she set up kindergarten and primary schools; with the aid of Albano Luayza (pastor) and his wife, Dona Querubina, she established The Evangelical Chain of Mennonite Women of Argentina. She also helped set up a training program for Sunday School teachers, and encouraged a Bible reading program in church members' homes.

At the time of her death at age 96 in Chicago, Ill., where she lived with her daughter, Beatrice, Mae was still a keen Bible student and intercessory prayer warrior. She was buried in Hershey Mennonite Cemetery near Kinzers, Pa.   BHH

J. W. Shank, *Southern Cross* (1943), 173-74; Rich, *Mennonite Women* (1983), 143-44; T. K. Hershey as told to Daniel Hertzler, *I'd Do It Again* (Elkhart: MBM, 1961).

Hershey, Tobias Kreider (Mar. 14, 1879-Oct. 31, 1956), was born near Intercourse, Pa. He was the sixth son of Tobias Kreider Hershey, Sr., and Lydia Hartman Hershey. At eight years of age he felt the desire to become a missionary. He was converted at age 17 and the next year was appointed superintendent of a nearby mission Sunday School. He married Mae Elizabeth Hertzler (Dec. 27, 1904) at Concord, Tenn. He graduated from Goshen College in 1911.

"T. K.," as he was known, took charge of the Youngstown, Ohio, Mission in 1911 and was ordained a Mennonite minister in 1913 at the Mid-way congregation, Columbiana, Ohio. When he suddenly lost his voice in 1914, his physician advised a change of climate, so he went to La Junta, Col., and six months later was joined there by his wife and children. In 1916 he pastored the Zion congregation at Bluffton, Ohio. On Aug. 16, 1917, he and his family, together with the J. W. °Shank family, left for mission work in Argentina under the Mennonite Board of Missions (MC). T. K. served in central Argentina as a pastor, bishop (ordained in 1925 at Columbiana, Ohio), evangelist, superintendent of the Argentine Mission, financial agent, and printer. The Hersheys retired from the Argentine mission service in April 1948. In 1949 they served one year as church workers in Puerto Rico.

After returning to the United States, T. K. and Mae Elizabeth were active in missions, evangelism, discipling, church planting, and Bible teaching in the United States and Canada. He died at Goshen, Ind., and was buried in the Hershey Mennonite Cemetery near Kinzers, Pa.   BHH

T. K. Hershey as told to Daniel Hertzler, *I'd Do It Again* (Elkhart: MBM, 1961); T. K. Hershey, *Old Time Revival* (Scottdale, 1937); idem, *Old Time Revival Again* (Scottdale, 1953); *Menn. Bib* II: 455 (index); J. W. Shank, *Southern Cross* (1943), 173; *Who's Who Mennonites* (1943), 105.

Hiebert, John Nicholas Christian (1904-56), and his wife, Anna Jungas Hiebert, served as missionaries in India with the Mennonite Brethren Mission, 1929-42, 1947-52. Born in Mountain Lake, Minn., to Mennonite Brethren pastor Nicholas N. Hiebert and Susie Wiebe Hiebert, John studied at the St. Paul Bible Institute, Christian Missionary and Alliance Bible School at Nyack, N.Y., Tabor College (BA), Willamette U., and the U. of Southern California (MA degree in South Asian history).

In his early years, J. N. C., as he was known, gave himself to evangelism in both North America and India. In his later life he felt the call to develop leaders for the church. Under his leadership the Mahbubnagar High School was the first of the Mennonite Brethren schools in India to gain government accreditation. During the war years (1943-47), he served as the principal of Immanuel Academy, Reedley, Cal., and guided it to accreditation and relocation. In 1952, he returned to the United States to serve as the president of Tabor College (1952-53).   PGH

Mrs. H. T. Esau, *First Sixty Years of M.B. Missions* (Hillsboro: M.B. Pub. House, 1954) 116-17; *Zionsbote* (Feb.

20, 1941), 2, (Apr. 9, 1941), 2, (May 20, 1941), 2, (July 29, 1942), 3, (Aug. 5, 1942), 2, (Aug. 3, 1949), 3, (Aug. 10, 1949), 3, (June 21, 1950), 2, (Dec. 5, 1951), 4; *Chr. Leader* (June 1937), 7-9, (March 1939), 7-8, (June 1939), 39, (October 1940), 8-10, (Sept. 15, 1956), 21 [obituary]; G. W. Peters, *The Growth of Foreign Missions in the M.B. Church* (1949); A. E. Janzen, ed., *Foreign Missions, India: The American M.B. Mission in India* (Hillsboro, 1948); idem, *Missionary Album* ed. (Hillsboro, 1951), 26; J. H. Lorenz, *The M.B. Church* (Hillsboro, 1950), 229ff.; correspondence in the Center for MB Studies, Fresno, Cal.

Hiebert, Mary J. Regier (Sept. 4, 1884-Jan. 31, 1970). Following the destruction by fire of the administration building at Tabor College, Hillsboro, Ks., in 1918, Mary J. Regier, Tabor alumna (BA, 1924), sold 80 acres of land inherited from her father valued at $20,000, and gave $15,000 to the college as an annuity to build a women's dormitory. Her gift covered approximately one-half the cost of construction of the "Ladies Home," providing living quarters for women students' dining facilities for both men and women. Several years after the fire, while a student at the Bible Institute of Los Angeles, she accepted the invitation to become the first matron of this home, a position with a large and varied job description. She continued in this position for 20 years, receiving only free board and room and the interest on her annuity gift. She left Tabor in 1940 to establish a rooming house for female students at Emporia, Ks. In 1955 she donated $5,000 for the purchase of books for the new library to enable Tabor to comply with accreditation standards. At the age of 76 she married J. J. Hiebert.   KFW

Wanda Frye Horn in *Women Among the Brethren* (1959), 185-95.

Hiebert, Peter C. (Apr. 5, 1870-May 27, 1963), Mennonite Brethren educator, minister, and relief agency leader. He was the son of Kornelius and Katherine Wiens Hiebert, who came to Kansas in 1876 from South Russia. Kornelius served as farmer-minister in the Ebenfeld Mennonite Brethren congregation, the first organized Mennonite Brethren congregation in North America (1876).

After completing country school, Peter attended Hillsboro High School. He studied at McPherson College (AB, 1906), the Baptist seminary in Rochester, N.Y., and the U. of Kansas (MA). He married Katherine Nikkel in 1907. Hiebert taught in rural schools in Kansas for five years and then, together with H. W. °°Lohrenz, helped establish Tabor College in Hillsboro, Ks., 1908. Here he served as teacher, dean, vice president, and president (1932-34) for 25 years. Then he taught at Sterling College for 13 additional years. He was a strong advocate for Christian liberal arts education.

Ordained as minister by the Ebenfeld Church, he served his conference as secretary or chairman of the Board of Home Missions for 18 years; moderator of Pacific District, Southern District, and the Mennonite Brethren general conference; chairman of the Relief Committee (MB) for 40 years; chairman of the committee which compiled the 1953 hymnal; and as traveling minister for over 60 years in United States, Canada, Europe, Russia, and South America. He represented the North American Mennonite

Brethren conference at the Mennonite World Conference three times.

P. C. Hiebert helped organize the Mennonite Central Committee (MCC) and served as its chairman for the first 33 years. He first met Orie Miller at an organizational meeting in the Prairie Street Church, Elkhart, Ind., 1920. Here a friendship and partnership developed that enriched the lives of thousands with whom they worked through the MCC around the world. P. C's work with the MCC began with a trip to South Russia in 1922 to aid Mennonites in the colonies suffering from famine, drought, and revolution. Between the wars Hiebert worked hard to keep the MCC alive through projects related to colonization, °refugees, and °relief. He was the first chairman of the MCC Peace Committee (Peace Section) and helped develop, in collaboration with the Church of the Brethren and Friends, "A Plan for Action for the Mennonites in Case of War." He helped organize the °°National Service Board for Religious Objectors (NSBRO), an agency through which the °historic peace churches could together deal with Selective Service (US). This, in turn, led to the establishment of the °°Civilian Public Service Camps.

Hiebert's leadership touched the lives of people around the world through service "in the name of Christ." His life was deeply colored by the Anabaptist vision of Christian discipleship. His witness was focused by two crosses—the cross of Christ's atonement and the disciple's cross. These two crosses gave unity and purpose to his life. WP

Who's Who Mennonites (1943), 110; *Menn. Bib. II*, p. 455; P. C. Hiebert and Orie O. Miller, *Feeding the Hungry* (Scottdale: MCC, 1927); idem, *Mitteilungen von der Reise nach Süd-Amerika* (Hillsboro: MB Publishing House, 1937); *Menn. Life*, 14 (July 1959), 105-9.

High, Norman (June 15, 1913-Dec. 4, 1974), educator. Born in Lincoln Co., Ontario, Norman High was the son of Alfred and Alda Culp High and the great-grandson of Daniel °°Hoch. He studied at Ontario Agricultural College (BSA, 1940) and Cornell U. (MS, 1941; PhD, 1950) in the fields of education, rural sociology, and agricultural economics. He was said to be the first member of the Mennonite Conference of Ontario and Quebec to obtain a PhD degree. High married Eleanor H. Young in 1945. High was a professor and administrator at Ontario Agricultural College (1946-61), the first Dean of Arts at the U. of Waterloo (1961-67), professor of adult education at Ontario Institute for Studies in Education, and Professor of Sociology at the U. of Waterloo (1971-74). He served on the Conrad Grebel College board of directors from its inception (1961) to his death, and was acting president of the college in 1972. He was on founding committees for both Conrad Grebel College (1960) and Rockway Mennonite School (1944). SSt

Obituaries in *Kitchener-Waterloo Record* (Dec. 5, 1974), 39; and *GH* (Dec. 31, 1974); J. Hampton High, *Hoch-High Family in America: A Record of Some Hoch Immigrants and Their Descendents* (n.p.: Hoch-High Family Reunion, 1962), B-11 - B-15; Norman H. High Papers and other records in Mennonite Archives of Ontario, Conrad Grebel College.

Hinduism. Mennonites have encountered Hinduism,

the major religion of India, primarily in India where they were involved in the mission of bringing the gospel of Jesus Christ. However, in the 20th c., as Hinduism became more agressive and its devotees moved into Europe and North America, there was encounter, either directly with Hinduism or with religious movements having Hindu components. Departments of religion in colleges and universities offered courses in Hinduism or at least dealt with Hinduism in courses on world religions. With the immigration of Indians to North America in recent years, Hindus have become next-door neighbors for some Mennonites.

A scholarly exponent of Hinduism, Shri Sarvepalli Radhakrishnan, who also served as president of the Republic of India (1962-67), describes Hinduism as "not a definite dogmatic creed, but a vast, complex, but subtly unified mass of spiritual thought and realization." The expression of this religion manifests itself in philosophical exposition by learned teachers, religious festivals, °caste regulations, household rituals, visual representation of gods (icons), sculpture, drama, and literature.

As western missionaries, including Mennonite missionaries, encountered Hinduism they tried to understand what it was they were confronting. Superficially it appeared to be a religion of superstition, enslavement, and oppression (caste, subjugation of women, fatalism, appeasement of the gods, etc.) Missionary libraries included books about Hinduism and Indian culture. There are numerous accounts in reports of mission activity which include observations of Hindu faith and practice, experience of dialogue and confrontation. However, there are no records of formal group-interaction with representatives of Hinduism and no documents which could be identified as Mennonite-Hindu statements of understanding. Mennonite missionaries and Indian Christians worked at separating from the Hindu cultural fabric the strands that would compose an Indian Christian fabric that had integrity. Some of this occurred informally, and some of it occurred in conferences of the denominations and in interdenominational settings, such as conferences and consultations of the National Christian Council of India and its subsidiary organizations. Publications of these events were available to Mennonite readers even though they may not have participated directly in the conferences or dialogues.

Peter Hamm, a missionary of the Mennonite Brethren Church, has identified typical approaches which Christians have taken toward other religions, including Hinduism. Individual Mennonites would find themselves, no doubt, taking one of these approaches: (a) "Radical displacement" or "conflictual," i.e., viewing "non-Christian religions as enemies of the gospel, adherents of this approach find little or nothing that is commendable in another faith and militantly seek to destroy it and displace it by Christianity. And although called an attitude of hostility and 'religious imperialism,' this is not usually accompanied by hatred on the part of the missionary." (b) "Fulfillment," i.e., "Christianity fulfills all that is good and true in non-Christian faiths. Stressing resemblance rather than contrast, this attitude sees the gospel as the completion of those truths anticipated in non-Christian religions." (c) "Co-operation," i.e., "the way of synthesis," "based on the premise that each religion has something of value to contribute and to receive . . . this view stresses inter-religious communion or 'dialogue' but fails to emphasize Christianity's unique contribution." (d) "Discontinuity," i.e., insisting on "a fundamental discontinuity 'between God's self-revelation in Jesus Christ and the whole range of human religion.' Therefore, the task of the missionary is not to attempt to find points of contact, or even of contrast with other religions, but simply to confront them with the message of God's 'act of redemption' in Christ Jesus and summon them to respond in faith."

Two doctoral dissertations represent inquiry by Mennonite scholars into Hindu thought, namely, "The Religious Significance of the Writings of Harischandra" submitted by Martin C. °Lehman at Yale University in 1933, and "Nonviolence: A Comparative Study of Mohandas K. Gandhi and the Mennonite Church on the Subject of Nonviolence," submitted by Weyburn W. Groff at New York University in 1963.   WWG

Peter M. Hamm, "A Reappraisal of Christianity's Confrontation with Other Religions," and Paul G. Hiebert, "Mission and the Understanding of Culture," in A. J. Klassen, ed., *The Church in Mission* (Fresno: MB Board of Christian Literature, 1967), 222-50; John A. Lapp, *India* (1972), 81-82; George J. Lapp, "Strengths and Weaknesses of Hinduism," (unpubl. manuscript, Lapp papers, MC Archives [Goshen]).

See also Contextualization; Gandhi, Mohandas K.

Hiroshima, Japan, in southern Honshu, pop. 1,045,856, is on a delta bisected by six branches of the Ohta River. It was a castle town ruled by the Asano family for 250 years before emerging as a leading military city. Population was estimated at 350,000 when on Aug. 6, 1945, it became the first city destroyed by an atomic bomb. Fatalities to date (1986) are estimated at 200,000. In 1949 government support began for rebuilding the city as a symbol of peace.

Peace Memorial Park, with the Peace Memorial Museum and Peace Memorial Hall, preserves the memories of A-bomb realities. It hosts 2 million visitors annually. Religious, political, and educational peace organizations abound. Every August 6 a joint memorial service is held. Mennonites, the Society of Friends, and the Church of the Brethren help support World Friendship Center, an agency promoting peace and service to A-bomb survivors.

Mennonite churches in Hiroshima: are the Kita Christian Church (Nihon Menonaito Burezeren Kyodan, MB) founded in 1976; and the Hiroshima Mennonite Christian Church (Nihon Menonaito Kirisuto Kyokai Kaigi, GCM) founded in 1979. Mission efforts continue, but to date there is no Mennonite work in the sister city of Nagasaki.   OJG

The Committee for the Compilation of Materials on Damage Caused by the Atomic Bombs in Hiroshima and Nagasaki, *Hiroshima and Nagasaki*, trans. Eisei Ishikawa and David L. Swain (Tokyo: Iwanami Shoten, 1981).

Hispanic Mennonites. During the last decades, Hispanics (i.e. speakers of Spanish in the Western Hemisphere) have been the most rapidly growing minority group in North America. The United States, with more than 23 million Spanish-speaking people, is the fifth country in the world in Spanish-speaking population, outnumbered only by Mexico, Spain, Argentina, and Colombia. It is believed that by the year 2000, the United States will rank second in Spanish-speaking world population.

With awareness of the challenge in their midst, Mennonites began work among the Spanish-speaking people in the United States during the first half of the 20th c. Of the Mennonite groups, the three largest ones especially directed their efforts to the Hispanic agenda: The Mennonite Church (1932), the Mennonite Brethren (1937), and the General Conference Mennonite Church (1958).

The *Mennonite Church (MC)* initiated contacts with the Hispanic community in North America in 1932 in the city of Chicago. By 1934 the first Hispanic Mennonite congregation, which became known as the Lawndale Mennonite Church, had been established. In its beginning J. W. °Shank, David Castillo (the first Hispanic Mennonite pastor), and Nelson °Litwiller played very important roles.

Even though the formal beginning of the church dates from 1932, an even earlier connection had occurred in 1916 when Simón del Bosque, from Mexican background, participated in the English-speaking Mennonite congregation in Tuleta, Tex. In addition to this, Hispanics were also contacted sporadically in La Junta, Col., during the 1920s.

After these beginnings, the Hispanic work began to spread, and during the decades of the 1940s to the 1960s, congregations were established in six other states. This growth, however, was slow and decentralized. It was not until the end of the 1960s that a thrust was realized, and during the 1970s that formal organization took place. It was in these years of growth that the church developed the elements that would counteract existing lethargy: solidarity, self-identity, and organization. During this period the first Hispanic Mennonite Conference was held (1973), women's activities were initiated (1973), an office on Latin affairs was established (1974), the National Council of Hispanic Mennonite Churches was formed (°Concilio Nacional, 1975), and programs of literature and congregational education (1976) and theological training (1979) in Spanish were started.

In 1986, the Hispanic Mennonite Church has an approximate total of 70 congregations and 2,450 members. As a whole, the congregations are small; they average around 35 members. They are located in Washington, D.C., 16 states, two provinces of Canada, and Mexico. The majority are in the ne. part of the United States, especially in Pennsylvania and New York.

The Hispanic Mennonite congregations have emerged due to several principle factors: the Mennonite missionary commitment to develop °urban missions, the immigration of Latin American Mennonites to North America, the relocation of missionary personnel who have returned from Latin America, the establishment of °voluntary service units in Hispanic communities, and the evangelistic and missionary vision of Hispanic leaders and workers.

Though the Mexicans and Puerto Ricans dominate,

the Hispanic Mennonite conglomerate is made up of a great variety of national backgrounds from practically all the Spanish-speaking countries. This heterogeneous factor in the church is manifested in a cultural, idiomatic, educational, religious, and social diversity that converts the Hispanic North American ministry into a significant challenge.

The Hispanic Mennonite Church has experienced remarkable numerical growth. From 185 members in 1955, it grew to 490 in 1970 and 2,450 in 1986. In the first five years of the 1980s, the growth of membership was 33 percent. In 1955 there were 4 congregations, while in 1986 there were approximately 70. The growth of congregations between 1981 and 1986 was 34 percent. These statistics are more significant when compared with the less than one percent annual growth rate of the North American Mennonite Church (MC) in general. The formal organization of the church, the obedience to the Great Commission, the extroversion of the Hispanic believers, the vision of the Hispanic Mennonite pastors, the awakening of self-identity and self-dependence, and a spirit of renewal are reasons for this rapid growth.

In spite of this growth, Hispanics as a minority group face challenges: language, culture, prejudice, and adjustment to the environment. In addition, internal problems also exist, some of which are experienced by Mennonites in Latin America, while others result from the socio-cultural situation of North America. Among these can be mentioned the lack of trained leadership, generational gaps, economic dependence, and the diversity of national backgrounds.

Mennonite Brethren have centered their Spanish-language work in two states with large Hispanic populations: Texas and California. In Texas the work began in the town of Mission (1937), and by 1982 there were 284 members and seven congregations near the Mexican border. In California the work was initated in 1956, and in 1982 there were 291 members and eight congregations, located mainly in the area of Fresno and Reedley. Generally the congregations are in small towns with the ministry directed to Mexicans and Mexican Americans. The Mennonite Brethren Church has its own program for the training of Hispanic leaders at Mennonite Brethren Biblical Seminary in Fresno.

The *General Conference Mennonite Church* began its work among Hispanics in Lansdale, Pa., in 1958. After a period of little activity, a spirit of revival has occurred during the 1980s and churches have been established in several states and in Toronto, Canada. By 1986, this group had grown to nearly 100 members and seven congregations.   RFal

Rafael A. Falcón, *La Iglesia Menonita Hispana en Norte América, 1932-1982* (Scottdale, 1985); Eng. trans. by Ronald Collins as *The Hispanic Mennonite Church in North America, 1932-1982* (Scottdale, 1986); José M. Ortiz, "Church Growth Among Spanish-Speaking North Americans," in *Miss. Focus,* 9 (1980), 442-52; Emma Oyer, *What God Hath Wrought* (Elkhart, Ind.: MBM, 1949), 23, 130-38; Willard H. Smith, *Mennonites in Illinois* (Scottdale, 1983), 420-27; Mrs. H. T. Esau, *First Sixty Years of M.B. Missions* (Hillsboro: Mennonite Brethren Publishing House, 1954), 481-95.

Historic Peace Churches (ME IV:1092) is a label that refers collectively to the Mennonites, the °°Society of Friends (Quakers), and the Church of the °°Brethren. The term first appeared in the title of a meeting of representatives of the three communities held at Newton, Ks., in 1935. Though the three groups, which originated separately in the 16th, 17th, and 18th c. respectively, were in occasional contact over the centuries, modern joint endeavors were triggered by challenges growing from World Wars I and II—support for °conscientious objectors and alternatives to military service, war sufferers °relief, °peace witness and the like.

While American Mennonites joined neither the National Council of Churches in the United States, nor the World Council of Churches (WCC), the other two groups did, thereby facilitating an ecumenical peace witness by the peace churches, particularly in relation to the WCC (°Puidoux Conferences). In the United States, the historic peace churches joined the peace societies of the major Protestant denominations in the Church Peace Mission (1950-67), a mission of °peace education directed to the churches. That conversation continued thereafter through the 1980s in a group of pacifist-just war ethicists called the War-Nation-Church Study Group.

Joint historic peace church endeavors began in "continuation committees," first in the United States, then in Europe, composed of representatives of the three groups, relief and service agencies. Later occasional meetings brought representatives of other agencies in these denominations together. °Peace studies programs in peace church colleges and seminaries, notably at Earlham (Friends) and Manchester (Brethren) Colleges and Associated Mennonite Biblical Seninaries, all in Indiana, stimulated further joint thought and endeavor. By the late 1970s, as the result of increasing shared experiences, particularly during the war in °Vietnam, an effort was launched to involve local and regional bodies of the three denominations in common reflection, leading in 1978 to an ongoing program of actions called "The New Call to Peacemaking."

Though effectiveness of such efforts is not readily assessed, the presence of the "historic peace churches" has become a constructive point of reference ecumenically. Representatives of these churches have interacted variously with World Council of Churches actions in international relations and peace. The fifth WCC Assembly, meeting in Nairobi, Kenya, in 1975, instructed its new Central Committee to launch a consultation on disarmament. Resources to be drawn on were to include, among others, "the experience of the historic peace churches." New convictions concerning the peacemaking implications of the gospel in major church bodies in Europe and North America led several of these, by the early 1980s, to embrace "peace church" language.   PPea

Historic Sites. See Bern; Interpretation and Information Centers; Museums.

Historical Libraries (ME II:749). During the last three decades many older libraries have been strengthened greatly in terms of housing, staffing, growth, and professional control. The number of institutional and private Mennonite historical libraries continues to increase. Some institutions combine library, °archival, and °museum collections. Others maintain sharper distinctions. There is a great deal of confusion in the minds of patrons between archival and library collections.

In Europe, the Amsterdam Mennonite Library has been moved from Singel Mennonite Church across the canal to the University of Amsterdam where it is maintained as a special collection within the university library. With the deaths of Ernst and Rose °Crous the Mennonitische Forschungsstelle has been relocated to the °Weierhof near Bolanden, West Germany. The Schweizerischer Verein für Täufergeschichte has established a library and archives housed at the European Mennonite Bible School, Bienenberg-Liestal. Another Swiss collection, the Archiv der Schweizer Mennonitengemeinden (begun by Samuel °Geiser), is located in Jean-Gui, Sonnenberg, Corgémont. The Mennonites of France have recently organized and begun a collection under the direction of the Association Française d'Histoire Anabaptiste-Mennonite.

North American Mennonite librarians and archivists meet occasionally to share information and discuss mutual problems. They produce a newsletter for reporting between sessions. The two largest collections, Mennonite Historical Library, Goshen, Ind., and Mennonite Library and Archives, North Newton, Ks., have improved the professional quality of their card catalogs with funding from the United States National Endowment for the Humanities. They and several other Mennonite libraries are entering cataloging records into an international data base to which approximately 7,000 libraries have access by computer. The North Newton library has published catalogs of its holdings of archival materials, art objects, and photographs. Mennonite Brethren have vigorous programs in three Centers for Mennonite Brethren Studies on the campuses of their colleges at Fresno, Cal.; Hillsboro, Ks.; and Winnipeg, Man. The Menno Simons Library and Archives, Harrisonburg, Va., has strengthened its holdings, particularly of Dutch Mennonitica. Other historical collections are to be found at Associated Mennonite Biblical Seminaries, Elkhart, Ind.; Bluffton College, Ohio; Conrad Grebel College, Waterloo, Ont.; Freeman Academy, S.D.; and Messiah College, Grantham, Pa.

Amos B. Hoover's private collection of °Old Order Mennonite materials in his Muddy Creek Farm Library, Denver, Pa., includes archival, library, and museum materials. Amish materials are being collected at the Heritage Historical Library, Aylmer, Ont., and, more recently, in the collections of Leroy Beachy, Millersburg, Ohio; Abner Beiler's Pequea Bruderschaft Library, Gordonville, Pa.; and others. The late Martin E. Ressler, Lancaster, Pa., had a collection of Mennonite hymnals numbering 4,000 volumes.

The Lancaster Mennonite Historical Society, Pa., is recataloging its collection. Perhaps no other Mennonite library has been affected as much by the heavily increased demand for °genealogical services. Mennonite Genealogy, Winnipeg, specializes in genealogical materials relating to descendants of Russian Mennonites. The regional collections of the Eastern District (GCM) and Franconia Conference (MC) have been combined at Lansdale, Pa., in the Mennonite Historical Library and Archives of Eastern Pennsylvania. Other regional collections include those of the Juniata Mennonite district, Pa. (MC), and libraries operated by British Columbia, Illinois, Iowa and several local Mennonite °historical societies.

In South America, there are some beginning collections, particularly that of the Geschichtsarchiv der Mennonitischen Brüdergemeinde Paraguay in Asunción. The collection begun by Gan °Sakakibara at the Japan Anabaptist Center in Tokyo has played a role in the publication of more than a dozen Anabaptist books in Japanese, both new studies and translations.

A current list of historical libraries and archives is published bienially in the *MC Yearbook*.   NPS

Directory of Mennonite Archives and Historical Libraries (Winnipeg: Mennonite Heritage Centre, 1984).

Historical Societies (ME II:751). The number of explicitly Mennonite historical societies has dramatically increased since Harold S. °Bender reported a total of four in 1956. In 1988 there were at least 25 in North America and Europe alone.

Some of the societies are national in scope— Schweizerischer Verein für Täufergeschichte (Switzerland); Mennonite Historical Society of Canada; L'Association Françoise d'Histoire Anabaptiste-Mennonite (France); Doopsgezinde Historische Kring (The Netherlands); and Mennonitischer Geschichtsverein (Germany).

Many of the remaining societies are statewide, provincial, or regional in scope. These include societies in each Canadian province west of Quebec and in the states of Oregon, Iowa, and Illinois. Mennonites in Pennsylvania support several large societies—Lancaster Mennonite Historical Society; Mennonite Historians of Eastern Pennsylvania; and the Juniata Mennonite District Historical Society. The Lancaster society is the largest of the Mennonite historical societies, with a membership in 1986 of 1,918. Local societies include the Mennonite Historical Society at Goshen, Ind. (the oldest continuing Mennonite historical society in North America, see below); the Essex-Kent Mennonite Historical Organization (Ontario); the Casselman River Area Amish and Mennonite Historians (Grantsville, Md.), and the Mennonite Historical Association of the Cumberland Valley (Md.).

A third type of historical society maintains loose affiliation with denominational bodies. This category includes the Brethren in Christ Historical Society and the Mennonite Brethren Historical Society of Canada. The Mennonite Historical Association is a membership group loosely affiliated with the Historical Committee of the Mennonite Church (MC) an official program committee supervised by the denomination's general board. There are also several regional Mennonite Brethren societies.

The Mennonite Historical Society, which publishes the *Mennonite Quarterly Review* and the monograph series "Studies in Anabaptist and Mennonite History" for Goshen College [Ind.] and the Associated Mennonite Biblical Seminaries, Elkhart,

Ind., is perhaps unique in its institutional connection.

The lack of societies in major Mennonite communities does not imply lack of historical activity. Many district and regional conference historical committees would parallel the role of an independent society in one-denominational Mennonite communities. "Secular" local history groups in communities with high Mennonite populations serve a similar purpose, for example in areas of Manitoba, Kansas, and Ohio.

Activities of the societies are varied. Many publish a newsletter, but some publish substantial journals, usually annually or quarterly. Contents range from community histories, biography, and family genealogies to scholarly articles on doctrinal influence upon or changes within the Mennonite community. The most important society journals include *Informations-Blätter (Switzerland*; *Pennsylvania Mennonite Heritage* (Lancaster); *Souvenance anabaptiste* (France); *Doopsgezinde Bijdragen* (The Netherlands); *Mennonitische Geschichtsblätter* (Germany); and *Brethren in Christ History and Life*.

Another activity that has fueled the rapid growth of Mennonite historical societies is the increasing interest in Mennonite family °genealogy. This is not limited to active members of Mennonite churches; many of the North American societies include a substantial number of non-Mennonites researching their families' roots. Many of the society periodicals include genealogy sections that publish family trees, genealogy book reviews, lists of names currently being researched, and results of cemetery tombstone transcriptions.

Sponsorship of °historical libraries and °archives in support of research and genealogical study is a third phase of society activity. Some of these are operated solely by a particular society (e.g., Lancaster and Illinois), but most support a library in conjunction with a Mennonite educational institution or conference.

Publication or sponsorship of books or audio-visual materials is a fourth common area of activity. The European societies and the larger North American societies have been particularly active in this field. In addition to Mennonite Historical Society at Goshen (see above), the Doopsgezinde Historische Kring, Mennonitischer Geschichtsverein, and the Lancaster Mennonite Historical Society publish monograph series.

°Museums and oversight of historic Mennonite sites is a fifth area of activity for a number of societies. The Hans Herr House (Lancaster), Mennonite Heritage Centers (Eastern Pennsylvania and Illinois), Mennonite Village Museum (Manitoba), Historical Center (Juniata) and Brubacher House (Ontario) are among museums that are or have been associated with Mennonite historical societies.

Other activities by some of the societies include sponsorship of academic conferences; book auctions; dramas; bus tours; °tourist °interpretation and information centers; lecture series; workshops for local, congregational, and family historians; and ethnic festivals featuring typical Mennonite foods and crafts.

The grassroots historical interest necessary to develop these societies is not restricted to Europe and North America. Gathering of source documents is beginning in Latin America and perhaps elsewhere, but usually within the organizational structure of local conferences or communities. Independent societies may be more a feature of a "middle-aged" church.

A current list of Mennonite historical societies that maintain some form of library or archives is maintained in the *MC Yearbook*, published biennially. SSt

Informations-Blätter (Schweizerischer Verein für Täufergeschichte); *Newsletter* (Manitoba Mennonite Historical Society); *Mennogespräch* (Mennonite Historical Society of Ontario); *Mennonite Historian* (Mennonite Brethren Historical Society of Canada in cooperation with History-Archives Committee of the Conference of Mennonites in Canada); *Mennonite Quarterly Review* (Mennonite Historical Society, Goshen); *Mennonite Historical Society of Alberta*; *Pennsylvania Mennonite Heritage* and *The Mirror* (Lancaster-Mennonite Historical Society); *Souvenance Anabaptiste* (L'Association Francoise d'Histoire Anabaptiste-Mennonite); *Doopsgezinde Bijdragen* (Doopsgezinde Historische Kring); *Mennonitische Geschichtsblätter* (Mennonitischer Geschichtsverein); *Brethren in Christ History and Life* (Brethren in Christ Historical Society); *Newsletter* (Mennonite Historians of Eastern Pennsylvania); *Historical Center Echoes* (Juniata Mennonite District Historical Society); *Mennonite Heritage* and *Illinois Mennonite Heritage Newsletter* (Illinois Mennonite Historical and Genealogical Society); *Mennonite Historical Bulletin* (Historical Committee, MC); *Bulletin* (Mennonite Brethren Historical Society of the West Coast).

Historical Writing (ME II:751). Mennonites have developed a new interest in things historical since World War II. This interest has ranged from the writing of personal memoirs, genealogies, and family histories, to biographies and congregational and conference histories. Volumes on special themes and regions, e.g., the role of women among Mennonites, peace issues past and present, the experiences of Mennonites in Canada, the United States, Asia, Africa, and Latin America, and even a handbook of essays and statistics for Mennonite World Conference (*MWH* [1978]) have also appeared. Historical novels are also making a significant contribution.

This explosion of literature has made it almost impossible, even for a library, to remain fully informed and supplied. Many writers do their own publishing and have no clear channels for distribution and promotion of their books. While oral history and other projects are also in process, Mennonites seem to be quite print-oriented. Total sales of any given volume are normally not large.

Considerable impetus is given to historical interest through the work of historical committees. In Canada and the United States most major national conferences, as well as most regional, district, state, and provincial conferences have active historical committees (°historical societies). These arrange conferences, sponsor libraries and museums, commission manuscripts, and facilitate book distribution. Random illustrations of these would be the Mennonite Historical Committee of Canada which sponsored the two volumes on *Mennonites in Canada* by Frank H. Epp (1974, 1982) and is continuing with a third volume; the Illinois Mennonite Historical and Genealogical Society which commissioned Willard H. Smith's *Mennonites in Illinois* (1983); the Histori-

cal Committee of the General Conference Mennonite Church (GCM) which sponsored S. F. Pannabecker's *Open Doors: The History of the General
Conference Mennonite Church* (1975).

Conference educational institutions also play a
major role in encouraging historical studies through
the development and support of libraries, archives,
and research ventures. This is true of most Mennonite colleges and seminaries. Goshen College, for
example, later joined by the Associated Mennonite
Biblical Seminaries (AMBS), founded the Mennonite
Historical Society in 1924, which became the
sponsor of *Mennonite Quarterly Review* (1927-) and
of the monograph series, "Studies in Anabaptist and
Mennonite History" (30 volumes, 1929-89). A similar
"Mennonite Historical Series," with fewer volumes
thus far, is being carried on by the General Conference Mennonite Church. An *Anabaptist Mennonite
Time Line* has been prepared by Robert S. Kreider
of Bethel College (1986).

Several regional and private library collections
have also been established. An illustration of the
former would be the Lancaster Mennonite Historical
Society, which has built up a significant library, and
publishes the *Pennsylvania Mennonite Heritage*
journal. An illustration of a major private library
would be that of Amos B. Hoover of Denver, Pa.,
who published the 1536 *Froschauer Bibel* (1975)
among other items. Some publishers concentrate on
production and distribution but usually also maintain
a research collection. Plough Publishing House,
Rifton, N.Y., and its journal *The Plough* would be an
example of this, as would Pathway Publishers, Inc.,
of Aylmer, Ont., and *Festival Quarterly* published by
Good Books, Lancaster, Pa., which also serves as distributor of other Mennonites writings.

The Institute of Mennonite Studies (IMS), Elkhart,
Ind., has published and is facilitating publication of
a number of series, both theological and historical,
since 1962. These include the Mennonite Missionary
Study Fellowship, in which no. 11 appeared in 1985;
MCC Story, 5 vols., 1980-88; the "Classics Of The
Radical Reformation" (CRR), a series of English
translations of 16th c. Anabaptist writings, 5 vols.,
1973-89; "Mennonite Experience in America"
(MEA), 3 vols., 1985-89, a fourth projected for
1990; Text-Reader series designed for graduate
classroom use, begun in 1984; "IMS Occasional
Papers," 12 vols., 1981-88; the IMS "Faith and Life"
series begun in 1961, and other serial and single
volume publications.

Similar series are being sponsored by the Center
for Mennonite Brethren Studies in Fresno, Cal.,
beginning with "Perspectives On Mennonite Life
And Thought" in 1977. In 1987 Bethel College
(Kansas) published the first two volumes in a new
"Cornelius H. Wedel Historical Series." *Mennonite
Life* (1946-), published by Bethel College, normally
publishes an annual report of historical research in
progress. The *Mennonite Historical Bulletin* (1939-),
published by the Historical Committee of the Mennonite Church, and the *Mennonite Historian* (1976-),
published by the History-Archives Committee of the
Conference of Mennonites in Canada and the
Centre for Mennonite Brethren Studies in Winnipeg,
are both quarterlies filled with articles, book notes,

and reviews. A similar service is rendered by the
Journal of Mennonite Studies, an annual publication
(1983-) of the Chair in Mennonite Studies at the
University of Winnipeg, and by *Brethren in Christ
History and Life*, published by the Brethren in
Christ Historical Society.

Many privately published books, and others, are
announced in a small catalog by Mennonite Books of
Winnipeg, and by CMBC Publications (Canadian
Mennonite Bible College), Winnipeg. *Der Bote*, a
German weekly of the General Conference Menno-
nite Church, normally prints a column "Das neue
Buch," where such titles as *Storm Tossed* and *Mia* by
Gerhard °Lohrenz; *Waffen der Wehrlosen*, by Hans
Rempel; *Immer Weiter Nach Osten*, by A. J. Loewen;
The Diary Of Anna Baerg, 1916-1924, ed. by Gerald
Peters, are found. The list seems endless.

Interest in family histories and °genealogy con-
tinues strong among Mennonites. The most ambitious
recent publication in this field may well be Amos B.
Hoover's monumental 1,128-page *The Jonas Martin
Era* (1982). There are many others: Willis Herr, ed.,
*The Sprunger Family: The Descendents of the Peter
Sprunger Family, born 1757* (1975); *The House Of
Heinrich*, edited by Anna Epp Ens (1980); *Klassen:
A Family Heritage* (J. J. Klassen), edited by P. D.
Zacharias, 528 pages (1980); *A Pilgrim People*,
edited by Cornelius J. and Wilma L. Dyck (1987).
The *Mennonite Family History* journal is one of
numerous resources for this kind of writing. Closely
related to these are biographies: Cornelius J. Dyck,
Twelve Becoming (1973); J. C. Wenger, *Faithfully,
Geo. R.: The Life and Thought of George R. Brunk I
(1871-1938)* (1978); Mary Lou Cummings, ed., *Full
Circle* (1978); Katie Funk Wiebe, ed., *Women Among
The Brethren* (1979); Elaine S. Rich, *Mennonite
Women* (1983); Ruth Unrau, ed., *Encircled* (1986);
H.-J. Goertz, ed., *Profiles Of Radical Reformers*,
edited in English by Walter Klaassen (1982). These
again are a few among many.

Novels have become another form of historical
writing among Mennonites. A story still in print in
1988 is *Henry's Red Sea* by Barbara Claassen Smucker (1955). Ernst °Behrend's six volumes are only
available in German. Herta Funk has written a dissertation analyzing them ("Die religioese Weltanschauung in Ernst Behrend's Romanreihe 'Das Volk
der Wanderschaft' [1981]). Rudy Wiebe's *The Blue
Mountain Of China* (1970) and other volumes by
him have become well known. Al Reimer's *My Harp
Has Turned To Mourning* (1985) reflects on the
demise of the golden age among Mennonites in Russia.

Non-North American writings are less voluminous,
but no less significant. Gan °Sakakibara of Japan has
written *A Historical Study of the Classical Age of the
Anabaptist Church* (in Japanese [1972]) and also
translated many volumes on Anabaptism from
English into Japanese. An Anabaptist Center in
Tokyo includes major library holdings.

Sheldon Sawatzky has written *The Body of Christ
Metaphor: An Interpretation to Stimulate Taiwanese
Reflection on the Nature and Task of the Church
Within Chinese Society* (1980). "The Church of the
Muria: A History of the Muria Christian Church of
Indonesia" (ThM thesis, Fuller Theological Semi-

nary, 1981; published in Javanese in 1985) has been written by Lawrence M. Yoder. Peter Falk wrote *A History of the Church in Africa* (1979). David W. Shenk wrote "A Study of Missionary Presence and Church Development in Somalia From 1950-1970" (diss., 1972), and later *Mennonite Safari*, describing the work of the Eastern Mennonite Board of Missions (MC) in East Africa. Anni Dyck described the Mennonite pastors' response to violence in *Ils n'ont pas resisté* (1977). David A. Shank wrote "A Prophet of Modern Times: The Thought of William W. Harris" (diss., 1980).

In South America historical libraries have been established in Paraguay at °Filadelfia and °Loma Plata and in Brazil at Witmarsum Colony. Monthly periodicals carry historical items. *Kaputi Mennonita* is a discussion of the 1930s Chaco War by Peter P. Klassen (1976), while Walter Regehr discusses the agricultural situation among Chaco Indians in *Die lebensräumliche Situation der Indianer im paraguayischen Chaco* (1979). Martin W. Friesen wrote *Kanadische Mennoniten bezwingen eine Wildnis* for the 50th anniversary celebrations of Menno Colony in 1977, and later *Neue Heimat in der Chaco Wildnis* (1987). Hans Duerksen and Jacob Harder edited *Fernheim, 1930-1980* (1980). Similarly Peter Pauls, Jr., edited *Mennoniten in Brasilien, 1930-1980* (1980). Gerhard S. Koop wrote *Pionier Jahre in British Honduras (Belize)* (n.d.). Materials in Spanish and Portuguese are becoming more numerous, including translations of Anabaptist writings.

In Europe historical societies are active in Switzerland, France, Germany, and The Netherlands. In Germany the *Mennonitische Geschichtsblätter* are in their 42nd year, and the *Mennonitisches Jahrbuch*, which also carries historical articles, is in its 88th year in 1988. A major library and research center is located at the °Weierhof in the Palatinate. The second volume on Prussian Mennonite history, *Die ost-und westpreussischen Mennoniten* was published by Horst Penner in 1987. H.-J. Goertz has published a series of volumes on Anabaptism, including *Die Taufer* (1980) and edited *Umstrittenes Taufertum: 1525-1975* (1975). Diether Goetz Lichdi has published a general Mennonite history (1983) as well as *Mennoniten im Dritten Reich* (1977).

Two major volumes on Anabaptists and Mennonites were published in France; Jean Séguy, *Les Assemblées Anabaptistes-Mennonites de France* (1970), and Neal Blough, *Christologie Anabaptiste* (1984). Marc Lienhard of the Protestant faculty at the University of Strasbourg encourages Anabaptist studies, as did the late Richard Stauffer at the Sorbonne.

Dutch Mennonites have long had an active historical society, the Doopsgezinde Historische Kring (DHK). An annual journal, the *Doopsgezinde Bijdragen*, published from 1861-1919, was revived in 1975. Numerous monographs appear under the society's sponsorship in the series "Doperse Stemmen" (no. 6 appeared in 1986). The preparation of a critical edition of the writings of Menno Simons is being undertaken. The DHK is also responsible for the publication of primary documents through its Commissie tot de Uitgave van de Documenta Anabaptistica Neerlandica (CUDAN) agency. A chair in Anabaptist-Mennonite studies has long been an established part of the Amsterdam Mennonite Theological Seminary program in Amsterdam.

This brief overview is intended to be more illustrative than exhaustive. While it offers guidance to major areas of writing it is not a definitive bibliography. It does, however, point up the variety of historical writings available and coming. Poetry and fiction, as well as writings on the arts and other fields might have been added. For post-16th-c. Mennonite writings in general see *Menn. Bib.* Since 1977 a bibliography of Anabaptist, Mennonite, and Radical Reformation publications has appeared annually in *Mennonite Life*. The indexes and book reviews of *MQR, Sixteenth Century Journal, JMS, CGR*, and other relevant publications, including publishers' catalogs, especially those of Herald Press and Faith and Life Press, are also helpful. For peace issues see *Bibl. on War and Peace* (1987). Many of the writers and editors identified in the present article are not professional historians, but there is also a clear trend to increasing professionalization. The number of "freelance" writers has grown substantially since the 1950s. The wide global interest in Anabaptist and Mennonite historical issues by Mennonites themselves is amazing, not to speak of the many non-Mennonite participants who are not listed here. CJD

Frank H. Epp, *Stories with Meaning: A Guide for the Writing of Congregational Histories* (Winnipeg: Mennonite Historical Society of Canada, 1978) 32 pp.; Melvin Gingerich, *The Work of the Local Church Historian* (Goshen, Ind.: Mennonite Historical and Research Committee, 1962); Dale Schrag, John D. Thiesen, David A. Haury, *The Mennonites: A Brief Guide to Information* (Newton 1967).

See also Historiography (Anabaptist, 16th c.); Mennonite Studies; Publishing.

Joe Walks Along

I have been asked to tell you the story of my life. I am glad to do it. It will be an Indian story because I am an Indian American. The history books you use in school say very little about Indians or about America when it belonged to them, and what they say is often wrong.

I am an American of the Cheyenne nation, which calls itself *Wohehiv*, and means "The Morning Star People." We are not really Indians like everybody calls us. The name "Indian" was given to us by mistake. When Columbus landed on our shores he was lost. He thought he had discovered India, and so we were called Indians. By the time people found out that America was not India, it was too late to change the name.

I will never forget the stories my father told me about life among the Cheyenne nation long ago. Many, many ages ago our people used to live in the woodland country around the Great Lakes. Then they began moving westward until they came to the Red River in what is now Minnesota and the Dakotas. They did some hunting, but game was scarce. Most of their food came from gardens. Their houses, made of earth, were partly underground.

There had never been horses in America until the Spaniards brought them along from Europe. Some of these ran away and multiplied on the prairies until large troops of wild and free mustangs galloped across the plains. Our fathers found that they could ride them, and that changed everything. Now they could hunt for food many miles away from home. They could run down and kill all the buffalo they wanted. The buffalo skins made good tepees which were cool in summer and warm in winter and could be moved easily. Soon the earth houses were forgotten, and my fathers moved wherever there was good hunting and fresh water.

White Americans often think of Indians as having been cruel and blood-thirsty. That is not true. The Cheyennes were a particularly peaceful nation, but they were not cowards. When the white man took more and more of their land and destroyed village after village, the Indians finally fought back in order to survive. White men did not know one tribe from another. "The only good Indian is a dead one," they used to say.

One day Cheyenne hunters found 20 steers which had wandered away from the white settlers' herd and chased them many miles back to their owners. But the owners said the Indians had stolen them, and called soldiers to hunt them down. The soldiers came upon Chief Lean Bear with a party of braves on the hunt. He had been in Washington the year before and met President Lincoln, who had given him a medal. Chief Lean Bear held up his medal and identification papers and rode out to meet them, but the soldiers opened fire and killed him, together with 26 of his men.

That same year the territorial governor of Colorado called on all citizens to "kill and destroy" the Indians. When our fathers heard this they sent a friend to Colonel Chivington, the commander of the area, to assure him of our desire for peace.

But the colonel, who incidentally had once been a minister, said, "Scalps are what we are after; kill and scalp all Indians—big ones and little ones."

A short time later his troops stormed over the village and killed over 300 of our people. Two women, five children, and Chief Black Kettle escaped. All the rest perished. But they had done no wrong. After that our people planned revenge. They called the colonel "Squaw Killer."

No one hated us more than did Colonel George A. Custer, who made a name for himself killing Indians. Early on the morning of November 27, 1868, for example, he and his men quietly surrounded a Cheyenne village near the Washita River and then attacked. Chief Black Kettle and 103 of his people perished. The whites then found out that it had been a friendly Cheyenne village, but Custer said the massacre was "a great and gallant victory for our beloved country."

Revenge came eight years later, on June 25, 1876, when Custer rode into a trap he had planned for our people. He and every one of his soldiers was killed, 265 in all. But many Indian braves also perished. The battlefield is now a tourist attraction 40 miles west of my home in Lame Deer.

These are the stories my father and my uncles and the wise men of our Cheyenne nation told us when I was young. I have not forgotten them. Today I tell them to my own children.   CJD

Adapted from Cornelius J. Dyck, *Twelve Becoming*, copyright 1973 by Faith and Life Press, Newton, Kansas, pp. 111-18. Used by permission.

Historiography, Anabaptist (ME II:751). More than half a century ago American historian Carl Becker observed that every generation must rewrite its own history. His dictum is illustrated nowhere more amply than in Anabaptist historiography of the past 25-30 years. A body of ardent revisionists has staked out claims to fresh, stimulating interpretations. Other scholars, both non-Mennonite and Mennonite, have poked about in the nooks and crannies of Anabaptist life and thought, publishing a large number of dissertations, monographs, and articles, with non-Mennonites regaining the initiative that Bender and others had seized earlier for Mennonites.

The primary, but not exclusive, object of the revisionists has been the so-called "Bender school"—Harold S. °Bender, Robert °Friedmann, J. C. Wenger, to a lesser extent Cornelius °Krahn, and some of their Mennonite students writing in the 1950s. The revisionists also challenged the work of Methodist Franklin Littell, some Baptist scholars (Davis, Estep), Swiss Reformed Fritz °Blanke and Congregationalist-Unitarian George H. Williams. All of these latter authors themselves revised or extended the work of Bender and others, but were at one with him in the larger task of rescuing Anabaptists theologically from the dogmatic misinterpretations of traditionalist historiography. To Bender and his colleagues, Anabaptists were voluntaristic in religious choice (and therefore insisted upon °believers' baptism for adults), advocates of a church completely free from state influence, biblical literalists, nonparticipants in any government activity to avoid moral compromise, °suffering servant disciples of Jesus who emphasized moral living and who were °persecuted and °martyred as Jesus had been, and °restitutionists who tried to restore pre-Constantinian Christian primitivism, etc.

Bender and Friedmann themselves had been self-conscious revisionists, using theology and a normative mode of inquiry to justify the Anabaptist movement in the light of four centuries of defamation in the name of confessional rectitude (Kurtz, for example). Lutherans Karl Müller and Karl Holl, among others, revived confessionalism within Reformation scholarship, Holl as it applied to the *Schwärmer* including the Anabaptists. Apparently Bender and his colleagues thought the obvious retort needed to be couched in confessional terms in order to find acceptance in the scholarly world, or even to make both Anabaptists and later Mennonites theologically respectable. This nascent Mennonite historiography created in effect a free church confessionalism with orthopraxis replacing orthodoxy, ironical in that the Anabaptists detested confessionalism, and "free church confessionalism" is a contradiction in terms. The "Bender school" used contemporary historical methodology, pioneered for Anabaptism by Carl °°Cornelius and others, utilizing primary sources based on views of the Anabaptists directly expressed instead of 16th-c. polemics composed by their bitter enemies. That methodology received the approbation of secular scholars. The Bender school's search for essence, for that *mentalité* that somehow characterized all Anabaptists worthy of the name, coincided with Western historians' then-current passion for finding essence and emphasizing synthesis as against describing diversity and analyzing particularity. (Renaissance scholars were wrestling with the essence of that movement when Bender put forward his singular °Anabaptist Vision; he suited the historiographical mood of his times.) But Bender's fresh synthesis of Anabaptism was too idealistic, too nice, almost too sweet despite its cross theology and bitter Christ; it invited revision.

What was revised, by whom? Here follow some of the more significant areas of revision:

(1) Scholars rehabilitated Melchior °Hoffman as a bonafide Anabaptist, one whose influence was paramount for Dutch Anabaptists and widely pervasive in other regions (Deppermann; Deppermann, Packull, Stayer; Krahn, 1964; Voolstra). Hoffman's reappearance coincided with a broader return to a vital Anabaptist spirituality (Klaassen 1960, 1963; Seebaß 1972; Packull, 1977; Oosterbaan, 1977; Ozment; Erb) as against a narrow biblicism-only interpretation used by Bender to counter Holl. More recently scholars have rescued Hoffman's disciple °David Joris from near oblivion, casting his movement as a viable option to that of Menno's followers and interpreting his spiritualism as a gradual development (Zijlstra; Stayer, 1984, 1985; Waite). Scholars have also tended to see more clearly the Hoffman legacy in the life and work of °Menno (Voolstra; Bornhäuser).

(2) Some revisionists reexamined the Anabaptism of °Münster, viewing it as theologically viable under Bernhard °Rothmann with adherents from middle and artisan classes joining voluntarily not because of intolerable pressure, and established deliberately as the regnant religious pattern by a duly elected city council of its own free will—not under duress (Kirchhoff 1970, 1973; *Jb. für Westfälische KG,* 78 [Oct. 1985], entire issue; Stayer 1986; many others). Kirchhoff's discovery of indigenous upper- and lower-middle class origins, coupled with Peachey's earlier work on social class origins of Swiss Anabaptists, provided impetus for a growing rejection of the older theory that Anabaptists were initially entirely of lower class origin.

(3) Gottfried Seebaß (1972) restored Hans °Hut and his strain of mystical-apocalyptical thought to the fold of legitimate Anabaptists. South German Anabaptism became more unique and varied, drawing from Hut as well as °°Denck, distinctly different from the Swiss Brethren variety (Packull, 1977).

(4) Small wonder that Anabaptist particularity, especially in origins (Deppermann, Stayer, Packull, 1975) but also in character, began to dominate historiography. Some scholars thought that Williams (1962) had not demarcated his three Anabaptist hearths (Zürich, Nürnberg, Amsterdam) sharply enough, though as an independent scholar Williams' position on three distinct places of Anabaptist origins seemed clear.

(5) Led by Clasen (1972) and paralleling broader 16th-c. studies, scholars began to examine more carefully the broadest possible social conditions of Anabaptists. They probed especially the radical social and economic, as against exclusively theological or eccelesial, roots of Anabaptism, and laid bare a movement built upon a vigorous protest against lower class living conditions, taking issue with Clasen on this point (Goeters; Seebaß, 1972, 1974; Stayer, 1975; Haas; Mellink, 1978, 1979; Goertz, 1979, 1980, 1985, 1987).

(6) Marxist historians, especially those from the German Democratic Republic, while retaining their interest in and affection for social revolutionary Thomas °Müntzer, have increasingly seen Anabaptists and other radical reformers as motivated essentially by religion. And they have helped Western historians to recognize the significance of economic and social class struggles in these movements (Zschäbitz; Hoyer; Laube; Looss; Vogler).

(7) With regard to Anabaptist nonresistance, Stayer (1972) wrote one of the most thoroughly researched studies of Anabaptists in the past 25 years, focusing on the Anabaptist biblically defenseless position (Bauman) but also on those who used the sword or defended its use by Christians. He solidified and greatly expanded the earlier, geographically more narrowly restricted, studies of nonpacifist Anabaptists by Yoder (1959, 1962-68), Klaassen (1960), and Oyer (1964).

(8) When did Anabaptism begin: Jan. 21, 1525, in Zürich with the first believers' baptisms, or late in February 1527 at Schleitheim? The latter has been proposed as the time and place of origin because the "Brotherly Union" (°Schleitheim Confession) established the separatist—or °sectarian—character of Anabaptism (Yoder, 1972; Deppermann, Packull, Stayer; Snyder, 1984-I).

(9) Some interpreters focused on several Anabaptist leaders who projected a commanding personal charisma, especially when they preached the imminent return of Christ—preeminently Hut and Hoffman. This emphasis was all the more necessary to offset an exclusive moderate biblicism of the earlier scholars (Seebaß, 1972; Packull, 1977; Deppermann; Davis, 1979).

(10) Medieval antecedents of Anabaptism, if not medieval forerunners, came into vogue again. Influence may well have emanated from the Brethren of the Common Life, perhaps the Hussites, some forms of °monasticism—but no one quite repeated Ritschl's theory of Franciscan Tertiaries as forerunners (Davis, 1974; Zeman, 1976; Packull, 1977; Snyder, 1984-I, 1987; Erb; Martin, 1986, 1988).

(11) Hubmaier again entered center stage, based upon his obvious commanding theological influence even on those who disliked him (perhaps Sattler; certainly the Hutterites): theology of baptism, soteriology, free will among others (Yoder, 1959; Armour; Bergsten; Windhorst; Liland).

(12) Scholars have reasserted the subtle but vital influence of °°Erasmus and other °humanists on Anabaptists, refuting primarily Bender (Friedmann always thought there was a connection, but out of respect for Bender he never declared himself in public on the point; see works by Robert Kreider; Horst, 1967; Burger; Augustijn, 1986; Schrag).

(13) Most recently scholars have raised basic questions about the role and significance of women among the Anabaptists, challenging scholarly

negligence as well as prior assertions about Anabaptist egalitarianism. More recent students have suggested that the Anabaptists did not raise the status or widen the range of permissible activities of women, especially in religious affairs, beyond the subordinate role established by Protestants (Bainton, 1971; Irwin, 1979, 1982; John Klassen; Marr; Umble; Kobelt-Groch).

Although revisionism aroused the livelier interest and debate among students of Anabaptism, scholars published many other studies of high merit that were not revisionist either in intent or influence. Some can be clustered around significant themes or persons; others are less amenable to organizational patterns. Here follow some observations about a selected few.

(1) Two studies deserve special mention because of their authors' mastery of massive amounts of sources: Williams (1962) and Clasen (1972, 1978 for data). Each author in his own way compelled all scholars of Anabaptism to wrestle with either his synthesis or his nuanced theses and interpretations, Williams on theology and morphology, Clasen on social history. Williams' work was brilliant. So also was Clasen's, despite Mennonite scholars' neglect of him; scholars will find themselves returning repeatedly to mine its richer lodes.

(2) A spate of studies probed Anabaptism in person or region or by topic, a few of them spawned by Bender's own enthusiasm for farming out topics for "definitive" treatment (Armour; Balke; Bauman; Beachy; Bergsten; Bornhäuser; Dalzell; Davis, 1974; Gingerich; Gismann-Fiel; Gross; Hillerbrand, 1962; Horst, 1972; Jecker; Keeney; Peter Klassen; William Klassen; Oyer, 1964; Packull, 1977; Pater; Plümper; Rempel; Schäufele; Schlabach; Snyder, 1984-I; Voolstra; de Vries; Windhorst; Yoder, 1962-68; Zeman, 1969).

(3) Some scholars returned to the role of martyrs and their influence on survivors and on the temperament of the entire movement. For instances, was there a discernable martyr theology as Stauffer had claimed (Alan Kreider; Doerksen; Dyck; John Klassen; Umble)?

(4) Students of °Marpeck have come into their own, elevating him to his proper formative role because of the wide influence of his mature theological synthesis (William Klassen; Blough, 1984, 1987; Boyd).

(5) Fresh research on Menno led many scholars to reevaluate his views on the incarnation (°Christology), the church, soteriology (°salvation), hermeneutics (°biblical interpretation), the °°ban, the quality and sophistication of his theology, as well as his ability to handle several languages including Latin (Oosterbaan, 1961; Meihuizen; Poettcker; Keeney; Bornhäuser; Irwin, 1978; Voolstra; Klaassen, 1986; Augustijn, 1987).

(6) Scores of scholars treated Anabaptist hermeneutics at least tangentially, then directly in several studies of significance (Klaassen, William Klassen, and Poettcker, entire issue of MQR, 41 [April 1966], in addition to the dissertations of Klassen and Poettcker; Yoder, 1967; Dyck, 1978).

(7) Italian scholars reassessed Italian Anabaptism, reaffirmed the °°antitrinitarian core but fitted it more securely within general Anabaptism than earlier scholars had done. Stella utilized fresh archival sources, tied the movement more closely to Neapolitan spiritualism, especially Juan de Valdès, but also to the Marranos (Stella, 1967, 1969; Williams, 1972; Rotondò).

(8) What differences existed, conscious or not, between North German and South German Anabaptists? (Deppermann; Oyer, 1984).

(9) Liberation theology. Scholars and churchmen alike have applied Anabaptist protests to present-day conditions of oppression against the lower class, especially outside Europe and North America (Rutschman; MQR, (Aug 1984), entire issue; Arnold Snyder, 1984-II).

One might suppose that after the alterations of many revisionists, and under the influence of dozens of additional scholars changing earlier views of Anabaptism, no synthesis remains, nor is it possible to shape one. If the scholar concentrates on differences among Anabaptists, the multifaceted nature of the movement emerges most clearly, so that the word Anabaptism is in some sense a misnomer. But if she asks how the Anabaptists differed from particular Protestant Reformers or from Catholics, a discernible core of Anabaptist thought and practice does indeed emerge, or remain. Within the sweep of church history it is more remarkable that a large majority of Anabaptists espoused and practiced biblical nonresistance than that a minority did not; Christianity has been a religion that glorified warriors. Or, Bender's (and Kühn's before him) °discipleship motif, based largely on the study of Swiss Brethren, describes surprisingly well the first-generation Anabaptists in Central Germany or the Netherlands or Austria, even those whose dominant early religiosities were more mystical than biblicist. Why? Not because Anabaptists from different geographical regions regularly conferred with each other and hammered out agreements. Morphology and broad synthesis are in ill repute at the moment, but they may well return to some prominence when scholars tire of fragmentation in our present mood of examining particularity and again crave the kind of meaning found only in generality or synthesis more broadly cast (Packull, 1979; Williams, 1984; Dyck, 1984; Weaver, 1985, 1987).

The historiography of Anabaptism is an inexhaustible topic. Only a few of the many strands of historiography of the past 25 years can be touched in one article, and only a few representative samples of significant scholarly works can be included in the bibliography. In fact the latter has been shaped consciously to fit the former. By design this study has not covered the publication of sources or of collective works—essays from symposia, festschriften—omissions of material so important that the article suffers in its usefulness to many readers. But some limitations had to be set.　　　　　JSO

Rollin S. Armour, Anabaptist Baptism (Scottdale, 1966); Cornelis Augustijn, "Erasmus and Menno Simons," MQR, 60 (1986), 497-508; idem, "Der Epilog von Menno Simons' 'Meditation,' 1539," in Anabaptistes et dissidents au XVIe siècle, Jean-Georges Rott and Simon L. Verheus (Baden-Baden: Koerner, 1987), 175-88; Roland H. Bainton, Women of the Reformation in Germany and Italy (Minneapolis: Augsburg Publ. House, 1971), 145-58; Willem Balke, Calvijn *en de Doperse radikalen* (Amsterdam: Ton Bolland, 1973); Clarence Bauman, *Gewaltlosigkeit im Täufertum* (Leiden: Brill, 1968); Alvin J. Beachy, *The Concept of Grace in the Radical Reformation* (Nieuwkoop: De Graaf, 1977); Harold S. Bender, "The Anabaptist Vision," *Church History*, 13 (1944), 3-24, reprinted in *MQR*, 18 (1944), 67-88; idem, *Conrad Grebel, 1498-1526* (Goshen, Ind.: Menn. Historical Society, 1950); Torsten Bergsten, *Balthasar Hubmaier—Seine Stellung zu Reformation und Täufertum* (Kassel: Oncken, 1961); Fritz Blanke, *Brüder in Christo* (Zürich: Zwingli Verlag, [1955]; English trans. 1961); Neal Blough, *Christologie Anabaptiste: Pilgram Marpeck et l'humanité du Christ* ([Geneva]: Labor et Fides, 1984); idem, "Pilgram Marpeck, Martin Luther and the Humanity of Christ," *MQR*, 61 (1987), 203-12; Christoph Bornhäuser, *Leben und Lehre Menno Simons'* (Neukirchen/Vluyn: Neukirchener Verlag, 1973); Stephen B. Boyd, "Pilgram Marpeck and the Justice of Christ" (PhD diss., Harvard Divinity School, 1984); Edward K. Burger, *Erasmus and the Anabaptists* (PhD diss., U. of California at Santa Barbara, 1977); Claus-Peter Clasen, *Anabaptism: A Social History, 1525-1618* (Ithaca: Cornell U. Press, 1972); idem, *The Anabaptists in South and Central Germany, Switzerland and Austria* (Goshen: *MQR*, 1978); Carl A. Cornelius, *Geschichte des Münsterischen Aufruhrs*, 2 vols. (Leipzig: Weigel, 1855-1860); Timothy Dalzell, "The Anabaptist Purity of Life Ethic" (PhD diss., North Texas State U., 1985); Kenneth R. Davis, *Anabaptism and Asceticism: A Study in Intellectual Origins* (Scottdale, 1974); idem, "Anabaptism as a Charismatic Movement," *MQR*, 53 (1979), 219-34; Klaus Deppermann, *Melchior Hoffman: Soziale Unruhen und apokalyptische Visionen im Zeitalter der Reformation* (Göttingen: Vandenhoeck und Ruprecht, 1979; Engl. transl., Edinburgh: T. and T. Clark, 1987); Klaus Deppermann, Werner O. Packull, James M. Stayer, "From Monogenesis to Polygenesis: The Historical Discussion of Anabaptist Origins," *MQR*, 49 (1975), 83-121; Victor G. Doerksen, "The Anabaptist Martyr Ballad," *MQR*, 51 (1977), 5-21; Cornelius J. Dyck, "Hans de Ries, Theologian and Churchman: A Study in Second Generation Anabaptism" (PhD diss., U. of Chicago, 1962); idem, "Hermeneutics and Discipleship," in *De Geest in het geding*, ed. I. B. Horst and others (Alphen: Rjeenk Willink, 1978), 57-72; idem, "The Anabaptist Understanding of the Good News," in *Anabaptism and Mission*, ed. Wilbert R. Shenk (Scottdale, 1984), 24-39; idem, "The Suffering Church in Anabaptism," *MQR*, 59 (1985), 5-23; Peter C. Erb, "Anabaptist Spirituality," in *Protestant Spiritual Traditions*, ed. Frank C. Senn (New York: Paulist, 1986), 80-124; William R. Estep, *The Anabaptist Story* (Nashville: Broadman Press, 1963; rev. ed. Grand Rapids: Eerdmans, 1975); Heinold Fast, "Die Sonderstellung der Täufer in St. Gallen und Appenzell," *Zwingliana*, 11 (1960), 223-40; idem, "Europäische Forschungen auf dem Gebiet der Täufer—und Mennonitengeschichte (1962-1967)," *Menn. Geschbl*, 24 (1967), 19-30; Robert Friedmann, *Hutterite Studies*, ed. Harold S. Bender (Goshen, Ind.: Menn. Hist. Soc., 1961); idem, *The Theology of Anabaptism* (Scottdale, 1973); Ugo Gastaldi, *Storia dell'anabattismo*, 2 vols. (Torino: Claudiana, 1972, 1981); Ray C. Gingerich, "The Mission Impulse of Early Swiss and South-German-Austrian Anabaptism" (PhD diss., Vanderbilt U., 1980); Hildegund Gismann-Fiel, *Das Täufertum in Vorarlberg* (Dornbirn: Vorarlberger Verlagsanstalt, 1982); Hans-Jürgen Goertz, ed., *Umstrittenes Täufertum, 1525-1975: Neue Forschungen* (Göttingen: Vandenhoeck und Ruprecht, 1975, 1977); idem, ed., *Radikale Reformatoren: 21 Biographische Skizzen von Thomas Müntzer bis Paracelsus* (Munich: Beck, 1978); idem, "History and Theology: A Major Problem of Anabaptist Research Today," part of "Problems of Anabaptist History: A Symposium," with replies of six scholars: Carter Lindberg, John S. Oyer, William Klassen, Kenneth R. Davis, Werner O. Packull, and James M. Stayer, in *MQR*, 53 (1979), 175-218; idem, *Die Täufer: Geschichte und Deutung* (Munich: Beck, 1980); idem, "Das Täufertum—ein Weg in die Moderne?," in *Zwingli und Europa: Referate und Protokoll des Internationalen Kongresses aus AnlaB des 500. Geburtstages von Huldrych Zwingli*, ed. Peter Blickle and others (Zürich: Vandenhoeck und Ruprecht, 1985), 165-81; idem, "Aufständische Bauern und Täufer in der Schweiz," in *Bauern und Reformation*, ed. Peter Blickle and Peter Bierbrauer (Hamburg: Chronos, 1987), 1, 267-89; J. F. Gerhard Goeters, "Die Vorgeschichte des Täufertums in Zürich," in *Studien zur Geschichte und Theologie der Reformation: Festschrift für Ernst Bizer*, ed. Luise Abramowski and J. F. G. Goeters (Neukirchen/Vluyn: Neukirchener Verlag, 1969), 239-81; Leonard Gross, *The Golden Years of the Hutterites*

(Scottdale, 1980); Martin Haas, "Der Weg der Täufer in die Absonderung: Zur Interdependenz von Theologie und sozialem Verhalten," in *Umstrittenes Täufertum* [see Goertz] (1975), 50-78; Hans J. Hillerbrand, *Die politische Ethik des oberdeutschen Täufertums: eine Untersuchung zur Religions- und Geistesgeschichte des Reformationszeitalters* (Leiden: Brill, 1962); idem, *A Bibliography of Anabaptism, 1525-1620* (Elkhart, Ind.: IMS, 1962); idem, "Die neuere Täuferforschung," *Evangelische Theologie*, 13 (1968), 95-110; idem, ed., *The Radical Reformation: Divergent Interpretations* (St. Louis: Sixteenth-Century Studies Conference, 1988); Karl Holl, "Luther und die Schwärmer," in Holl, *Gesammelte Aufsätze zur Kirchengeschichte, I: Luther* (Tübingen: Mohr, 1923), 420-67; Irvin B. Horst, *Erasmus, the Anabaptists and the Problem of Religious Unity* (Haarlem: Tjeenk Willink, 1967); idem, *The Radical Brethren: Anabaptism and the English Reformation to 1558* (Nieuwkoop: de Graaf, 1972); Siegfried Hoyer, "Lay Preaching and Radicalism in the Early Reformation," in Hillerbrand (1988); Joyce L. Irwin, "Embryology and the Incarnation: A Sixteenth Century Debate," *Sixteenth Century Journal*, 9, no. 3 (1978), 93-104; idem, *Womanhood in Radical Protestantism, 1525-1675* (New York: Mellen, 1979); idem, "Society and the Sexes," in *Reformation Europe: A Guide to Research*, ed. Steven Ozment (St. Louis: Center for Reformation Research, 1982), 343-60; Hanspeter Jecker, *Die. Basler Täufer: Studien zur Vor—und Frühgeschichte* (Basel: Historische Gesellschaft, 1980); William E. Keeney, *Dutch Anabaptist Thought and Practice 1539-1564* (Nieuwkoop: De Graaf, 1968); Karl-Heinz Kirchhoff, "Was There a Peaceful Anabaptist Congregation in Münster in 1534?" *MQR*, 44 (1970), 357-70; idem, *Die Täufer in Münster 1534-1535: Untersuchungen zum Umfang und zur Sozialstruktur der Bewegung* (Münster: Aschendorff, 1973); Walter Klaassen, "Word, Spirit and Scripture in Early Anabaptist Thought" (D Phil diss., Oxford U., 1960); idem, "Spiritualization in the Reformation," *MQR*, 37 (1963), 67-77; idem, *Anabaptism: Neither Catholic nor Protestant* (Waterloo: Conrad Press, 1973); idem, "Menno Simons Research, 1937-1986," *MQR*, 60 (1986), 483-96; John Klassen, "Women and the Family Among Dutch Anabaptist Martyrs," *MQR*, 60 (1986), 548-71; Peter J. Klassen, *The Economics of Anabaptism, 1525-1560* (London: Mouton, 1964); William Klassen, *Covenant and Community* (Grand Rapids: Eerdmans, 1968); Marion Kobelt-Groch, "Why Did Petronella Leave Her Husband," *MQR*, 62 (1988), 26-41; Cornelius Krahn, *Menno Simons Lebenswerk* (Amsterdam: Gleijsteen, 1937); idem, *Dutch Anabaptism: Origin, Spread, Life and Thought, 1450-1600* (The Hague: Nijhoff, 1964); Alan F. Kreider, "'The Servant is Not Greater Than His Master': Anabaptists and the Suffering Church," *MQR*, 58 (1984), 5-29; Robert S. Kreider, "Anabaptism and Humanism: An Inquiry into the Relationship of Humanism to the Evangelical Anabaptists," *MQR*, 26 (1952), 123-41; Johann Kurtz, *Lehrbuch der Kirchengeschichte für Studierende*, 9th ed., (Leipzig: Neumann, 1885), esp. 148-56; Adolf Laube, "Radicalism in the Reformation: A Research Problem for Scholarship," in Hillerbrand (1988); Daniel C. Liechty, *Andreas Fischer and the Sabbatarian Anabaptists* (Scottdale, 1988); Peder M. I. Liland, "Anabaptist Separatism: A Historical and Theological Study of the Contribution of Balthasar Hubmaier" (PhD diss., Boston College, 1983); Franklin H. Littell, *The Anabaptist View of the Church* (Hartford: Amer. Society of Church History, 1952), reprinted as *The Origins of Sectarian Protestantism* (New York: Macmillan, 1964); Siegrid Looss, "Andreas Carlstadt," in Hillerbrand (1988); M. Lucille Marr, "Anabaptist Women of the North: Peers in the Faith, Subordinates in Marriage," *MQR*, 61 (1987), 347-62; Dennis D. Martin, "Monks, Mendicants and Anabaptists: Michael Sattler and the Benedictines Reconsidered," *MQR* 60 (1986), 139-64; idem, "Catholic Spirituality and Anabaptist and Mennonite Discipleship," *MQR* 62 (1988), 5-25; Albert F. Mellink, *Amsterdam en de Wederdopers in de zestiende Eeuw* (Nijmegen: Socialistiese Uitgeverij, 1978); idem, *De radikale Reformatie als Thema van social-religieuze Geschiedenis* (Nijmegen: Socialistiese Uitgeverij, 1979); H. W. Meihuizen, *Menno Simons: Ijveraar voor het Herstel van de nieuwtestamentische Gemeente* (Haarlem: Tjeenk Willink, 1961); Karl Müller, *Kirchengeschichte*, 2 vols. (Tübingen: Mohr, 1905- 1919); idem, *Luther u. Karlstadt* (Tübingen: Mohr, 1907); J. A. Oosterbaan, "The Theology of Menno Simons," *MQR*, 35 (1961), 187-96; idem, "The Reformation of the Reformation: Fundamentals of Anabaptist Theology," *MQR*, 51 (1977), 171-95, cf. *Doops. Bijdr.*, n.r. 2 (1976), 36-61; John S. Oyer, *Lutheran Reformers against Anabaptists:*

Luther, Melanchthon and Menius and the Anabaptists of Central Germany (The Hague: Nijhoff, 1964); idem, "The Strasbourg Conferences of the Anabaptists, 1554-1607," MQR, 58 (1984), 218-29; Steven Ozment, Mysticism and Dissent: Religious Ideology and Social Protest in the Sixteenth Century (New Haven: Yale U. Press, 1973); Werner O. Packull, Mysticism and the Early South German-Austrian Anabaptist Movement, 1525-1531 (Scottdale, 1977); idem, "Some Reflections on the State of Anabaptist History: the Demise of a Normative Vision," Studies in Religion, 8 (1979), 313-23; Calvin A. Pater, Karlstadt as the Father of the Baptist Movements (Toronto: U. of Toronto Press, 1984); Paul Peachey, Die soziale Herkunft der Schweizer Täufer in der Reformationszeit, 1525-1540 (Karlsruhe: Schneider, 1954); Hans-Dieter Plümper, Die Gütergemeinschaft bei den Täufern des 16. Jahrhunderts (Göppingen: Kümmerle, 1972); Henry Poettcker, "The Hermeneutics of Menno Simons," (ThD diss., Princeton Theological Seminary, 1961); John D. Rempel, "Christology and the Lord's Supper in Anabaptism: A Study in the Theology of Balthasar Hubmaier, Pilgram Marpeck, and Dirk Philips" (ThD diss., U. of Toronto, 1986); Antonio Rotondò, Studi e ricerche di storia ereticale italiana del Cinquecento (Torino: Giappichelli, 1974); LaVerne Rutschman, "Anabaptism and Liberation Theology," MQR, 55 (1981), 255-70; Wolfgang Schäufele, Das missionarische Bewußtsein und Wirken der Täufer (Neukirchen/Vluyn: Neukirchener Verlag, 1966); Ervin Schlabach, "The Rule of Christ Among the Early Swiss Anabaptists" (ThD diss., Chicago Theological Seminary, 1977); Dale Schrag, "Erasmian Origins of Anabaptist Pacifism: A Case Study in Humanism and the Radical Reformation" (MA thesis, Wichita State U., 1984); Gottfried Seebaß, "Müntzers Erbe: Werk, Leben und Theologie des Hans Hut," (unpublished Habilitations dissertation, Erlangen, 1972); idem, "Bauernkrieg und Täufertum in Franken," Z. für KG, 85 (1974), 284-300; C. Arnold Snyder, The Life and Thought of Michael Sattler (Scottdale, 1984-I); idem, "The Relevance of Anabaptist Nonviolence for Nicaragua Today," GR, 2 (1984-II), 123-38; idem, "Michael Sattler, Benedictine: Dennis Martin's Objections Reconsidered," MQR, 61 (1987), 262-79; James M. Stayer, Anabaptists and the Sword (Lawrence, Kans.: Coronado Press, 1972, 1976); idem, "Die Anfänge des schweizerischen Täufertums im reformierten Kongregationalismus," in Goertz, Umstrittenes Täufertum [see Goertz] (1975), 19-49; idem, "The Anabaptists," in Reformation Europe [see Ozment, 1982]), 135-59; idem, "Davidite vs. Mennonite," MQR, 58 (1984), 459-76; idem, "David Joris: A Prolegomenon to Further Research," MQR, 59 (1985), 350-61; idem, "Was Dr. Kuehler's Conception of Early Dutch Anabaptism Historically Sound? The Historical Discussion of Münster 450 Years Later," MQR, 60 (1986), 261-88; Aldo Stella, Dall'anabattismo al socinianesimo nel Cinquecento veneto: Ricerche storiche (Padua: Livania, 1967); idem, Anabattismo e antitrinitarismo in Italia nel XVI secolo: Nuove ricerche storiche (Padua: Livania, 1969); Friedwart Uhland, "Täufertum u. Obrigkeit in Augsburg im 16. Jahrhundert" (PhD diss., U. of Tübingen, 1972); Jenifer Hiett Umble, "Women and Choice: An Examination of the Martyrs Mirror," (master's thesis, Southern Methodist U., 1987); Günther Vogler, "The Anabaptist Kingdom of Münster in the Setting of Imperial Politics," in Hillerbrand (1988); Sjouke Voolstra, Het Woord is Vlees Geworden: De Melchioritisch-Menniste Incarnatieleer (Kampen: Kok, [1982]); O. H. de Vries, Leer en Praxis van de vroege Dopers (Leeuwarden: Dykstra, 1982); Gary K. Waite, "Spiritualizing the Crusade: David Joris in the Context of the Early Reform and Anabaptist Movements in the Netherlands" (PhD diss., U. of Waterloo, 1986); J. Denny Weaver, "The Work of Christ: On the Difficulty of Identifying an Anabaptist Perspective," MQR, 59 (1985), 107-29; idem, Becoming Anabaptist: The Origin and Significance of Sixteenth-Century Anabaptism (Scottdale, 1987); J. C. Wenger, Even Unto Death (Richmond, Va.: John Knox Press, 1961); idem, "Doctrinal Position of the Swiss Brethren as Revealed in Their Polemical Tracts," MQR, 24 (1950), 65-72; George H. Williams, The Radical Reformation (Philadelphia: Fortress Press, 1962), revised substantially with responses to specific revisionist critiques, as La Reforma Radical, trans. Antonio Alatorre (Naucalpan, Mexico: Fondo de Cultura Economica, 1984); idem,, "Two Social Strands in Italian Anabaptism, ca. 1550," in The Social History of the Reformation, ed. Lawrence P. Buck and Jonathan W. Zophy (Columbus: Ohio State U. Press, 1972), 156-207; idem, "The Radical Reformation Revisited," Union Seminary Quarterly Review, 39 (1984), 1-24; Christoph Windhorst, Täuferisches Taufverständnis: Balthasar Hubmaiers Lehre zwischen traditioneller und reformatorischer Theologie (Leiden: Brill, 1976); John H. Yoder, "The Turning Point in the Zwinglian Reformation," MQR, 32 (1958), 128-40; idem, "Balthasar Hubmaier and the Beginnings of Swiss Anabaptism," MQR, 33 (1959), 5-17; idem, Täufertum und Reformation im Gespräch: Dogmengeschichtliche Untersuchung der frühen Gespräche zwischen Schweizerischen Täufer und Reformatoren, 2 vols., (Weierhof: Menn. Geschichtsverein, and Zurich: EVZ Verlag, 1962, 1968); idem, "The Hermeneutics of the Anabaptists," MQR, 41 (1967), 291-308; idem, "Der Kristallisationspunkt des Täufertums," Menn. Geschbl., Jg. 29, n.F. 24 (1972), 35-47; idem, trans. and ed., The Legacy of Michael Sattler (Scottdale, 1973) (= CRR 1); Jarold K. Zeman, The Anabaptists and the Czech Brethren in Moravia 1526-1628: A Study of Origins and Contacts (The Hague: Nijhoff, 1969); idem, "Anabaptism: A Replay of Medieval Themes or a Prelude to the Modern Age?" MQR, 50 (1976), 259-71; S. Zijlstra, Nicolaas Meyndertsz van Blesdijk: Een Bijdrage tot de Geschiedenis van het Davidjorisme (Assen: Van Gorcum, 1983); Gerhard Zschäbitz, Zur mitteldeutschen Wiedertäuferbewegung nach dem grossen Bauernkrieg (Berlin: Rütten and Loening, 1958).

History, Theology of. Discussion of Anabaptist theologies of history typically focus on the themes of "primitivism" or "°restitutionism"—the quest to restore, or reinstitute, the primitive purity of the church. Restitutionism, however, is only one element in much broader Anabaptist understandings of history and as such must be placed into context. Post-Anabaptist Mennonites, in contrast to the Anabaptists, tended to value historical continuity and tradition rather than novelty. However, periodically renewal movements arose to reemphasize restitutionism (temporarily) in support of their cause. The Brüdergemeinde (Mennonite Brethren) in Russia and the "recovery of the Anabaptist vision" school in America were two such examples. Especially but not exclusively, for this latter school, certain moments in history became theologically so important, that theology and history became almost indistinguishable. The degree to which this theology of history accordingly distorted the history of theology continues to be debated.

Central to many Anabaptist and most Mennonite understandings of history is the incarnation of God in Jesus Christ (°Christology). (1) The incarnation confirmed unequivocally the Old Testament truism that God acts within space and time to effect his will. (2) God's agenda from creation to consummation is uniquely revealed in the incarnation—in the composite of Jesus' teachings, life, death, and resurrection. (3) Jesus Christ in his life and teaching, his °love and °suffering, is the norm for all human activity within the present dispensation. Adult human beings are free moral agents, who (4) can and must decide as individuals how they will respond to the incarnational revelation. Those who respond in °obedience to God's grace through faith are not only saved from sin but also are empowered by the resurrection of Christ through the Holy Spirit to become disciples of Christ within history. (5) The primary mediating agency of God's grace and incarnational expression of Christ's presence in history is the church—the voluntary and °disciplined °community of °believers. And lastly, the full realization of the kingdom of God on earth, when good triumphs over evil and the faithful remnant vanquishes the principalities and powers, awaits God's divine intervention in a second coming of Christ. History is thus an

°eschatological drama beginning and ending with God, given definitive direction in Jesus the incarnate Christ, yet shaped in its detail by human beings and their insitutions, the accountable actors on stage of history.

Within this larger drama, restitutionism is a response to the perceived failure of the church to be the church and a quest to reverse the proceses of history. Three historical stages are critical to this reading. First is the normative stage, that Edenic era of the primitive church which defined the church's identity for all times and places. Accepting the assumption that the stream flows purest at its source, normativity is defined by the charismatic origins, not by the routinization over time.

The fall of the church follows as the second stage. At some historical moment or with some historical movement the normative church is compromised to the degree that the essence is a least grossly obscured if not completely vitiated. The precise location of the fall varied somewhat among Anabaptists, as it does among all restitutionists, depending on the details of the normative essence deemed lost. Most commonly Anabaptists located the fall in the Constantinian-Theodosian revolution (A.D. 312-95) when the church shifted from being an exclusive, intentional community defined by personal decision, ethical rigor, and consequent °persecution to becoming an inclusive, compulsory imperial organization with the resultant ethical and ecclesiastical compromises necessary to be the official and only tolerated religion of the Roman empire.

The restitution of the normative church of converted and disciplined believers follows as stage three. As indicated, for those Anabaptists whom Mennonites consider exemplary, the incarnation and the early church provided the restitution norm in both beliefs and practise. Voluntarism and adult °baptism, ethical rigor including °nonresistant love, church discipline and the °°ban, suffering from persecution were identified as marks of the true church. The more °apocalyptically-oriented Anabaptists, such as those at Münster, pushed the normative era back into the Old Testament and sought the restoration of the kingdom of David, while the more spiritualist-oriented, such as Sebastian °°Franck, deemphasized the institutional dimensions of restoration in favor of a spiritual essence beyond the historical.

Differentiation of the mainline or magisterial from the sectarian or radical reformation movements in the 16th c. in terms of their contrasting views of history—reformation versus restitution respectively—has been championed especially by Franklin H. Littell. Before him Roland Bainton followed several European scholars in noting the contrast and after him Frank Wray devoted a dissertation to the distinction. But Hans Hillerbrand responded that all reformers considered themselves restitutionists and H. W. Meihuzen demonstrated that not nearly all Anabaptists referred to themselves as restitutionists and when they did varied considerably in their useage. John Howard Yoder, in defense of Littell, argued for the utility of the differentiation of reformation and restitution if each is viewed ideal-typically.

Yoder, however, disagreed with Littell and others who considered the restitutionist perspective as essentially ahistorical. The attempt to radically reverse the course of history by erasing centuries of fallen church history to recapture a lost innocence can be viewed as "historyless," or as naive with regard to the shaping influence on their own understanding of the history they rejected. Yet Yoder argued the opposite. The restitutionists were profoundly historical, said Yoder, in that they did not simply accept the judgment of history but rather judged history according to a historical norm (the Incarnation), analyzed what went wrong in history, and set about to rectify the situation on the premise of human freedom rather than historical determinism. Drawing similar conclusions, C. J. Dyck maintained that Anabaptist restitution was not so much a rejection of history as a restoration in the present by the power of the Spirit, of the faithfulness of the first Christians. This was possible, they believed, through personal conversion, biblical literalism and church discipline.

But restitutionism has its detractors even among Mennonites. Recently Dennis Martin countered Yoder and Dyck by both reiterating the view that restitutionism is ahistorical and critiquing Anabaptist and Mennonite restitutionism from a reformist perspective. Martin's critique is basically twofold. For one, that Mennonites are both creators and victims of °modernity and its limitations, insofar as the modern ethos is premised on the rejection of continuity in history as implied by restitutionism. Secondly, says Martin, restitutionists do not take the second generation seriously and hence are ill at ease with the inevitable °institutionalization that develops—because institutionalization seems to compromise their perfectionist vision.

That tradition is inevitable for the second generation Dyck acknowledged. While Dyck found this reality discomforting in that the Spirit was thereby limited, for Martin it confirmed the wisdom of the reformist approach to history. In fact the reformist emphasis on continuity and tradition became the dominant Mennonite paradigm early on. At least from the *Martyrs Mirror* to the 20th-c. renaissance of Mennonite °historiography, Mennonites defined their identity primarily through a recitation of their sectarian history. Indeed for the most traditional—the °Old Orders and °Old Colony—continuity with the past became the primary mark of faithfulness. For some continuity need go back only to the 16th-c. founders and then leap over the fallen centuries to the primitive church. For others, some influenced by the 19th-c. Münster archivist Ludwig °Keller, continuity was also sought in the "old evangelical brotherhoods," such as the °Waldenses, down through the Middle Ages to the time of Christ.

History as the story of the sectarian tradition had many uses. It not only provided the necessary collective memory for a minority movement, frequently challenged by a hostile environment, it also legitimated conservativism and traditionalism and even religious lethargy. But the counterpoint of restitutionism also remained readily available in the cause of revitalization. Repeatedly a restitutionist mode was invoked to leap across decades and even millennia to the 16th and 1st c. in the cause of church reform. Thus, for example, the Mennonite Brethren in Russia (1860s) rejected the established Mennonite community in the name of Menno Simons and the New Testament and called upon the faithful to restitute the true church. Similarly in mid-20th-c. America "the °Anabaptist Vision" movement sought at least a recovery of the vision if not a restitution of its ecclesiology. Indeed, the younger visionaries writing in a series of °*Concern* pamphlets (1954-71) challenged Harold S. Bender, the father of the movement, to go beyond recovery to restitution. John H. Yoder's "Anabaptist Vision and Mennonite Reality" is perhaps the most sustained historical explication of these younger restitutionists. Mennonite history is thus critiqued from the vantage of a normative Anabaptism.

The question recent historiography has asked is: how close is this Anabaptist vision to Anabaptist reality? Undoubtedly the Mennonite theology of history has contributed significantly to the extensive study and renewed appreciation, especially in this century, of the previously much maligned Anabaptists. But the study thus encouraged is a two-edged sword. While it can define a vision of "evangelical Anabaptism" particularly relevant as a norm for 20th-c. Mennonites, it can also question the historical reality of that vision. If historical scholarship successfully questions the historicity of significant elements of the Anabaptist vision, the role of Anabaptism will need to be redefined in Mennonite restitutionism. Restitutionism *per se* may require redefinition, in turn. Whatever redefinitions are necessary, the larger theology of history will remain as a centerpiece in Mennonite theology.   RJS

Cornelius J. Dyck, "The Place of Tradition in Dutch Anabaptism" *Church History,* 43 (1974), 34-49; Hans-Jürgen Goertz, "History and Theology: A Major Problem of Anabaptist Research Today" *MQR,* 53 (1979), 177-88, plus six responses to Goertz in the same issue of the *MQR*; Franklin H. Littell, *The Origins of Sectarian Protestantism: A Study of the Anabaptist View of the Church* (New York: The Macmillan Company, 1964; originally published as *The Anabaptist View of the Church,* 1952); Dennis D. Martin, "Nothing New Under the Sun? Mennonites and History," *CGR,* 5 (1987), 1-27, responses 147-53, 260-62; H. W. Meihuizen, "The Concept of Restitution in the Anabaptism of Northwestern Europe," *MQR,* 44 (1970), 141-58; Rodney J. Sawatsky, "History and Ideology: American Mennonite Identity Definition through History" (PhD diss., Princeton U., 1977); Frank J. Wray "The Anabaptist Doctrine of the Restitution," *MQR,* 28 (1954), 186-96; John Howard Yoder "Anabaptism and History," in *Umstrittenes Täufertum* (1975), 244-58; reprinted in Yoder, *Priestly Kingdom* (Notre Dame U. Press, 1984), 123-34; idem, "Anabaptist Vision and Mennonite Reality," in *Consultation on Anabaptist-Mennonite Theology,* ed. A. J. Klassen (Fresno: MBBS for Council of Mennonite Seminaries, 1970), 1-46.

Hoffman (Hofman), Melchior (ca. 1495-1544?) (ME II:778), was the most significant early propagator of Anabaptism in northern Germany. Christian Neff's excellent article based on the thorough scholarship of Leendertz, zur Linden, and Kawerau needs only minor revisions.

Biography. Hoffman came from a family of middle artisan status in Schwäbisch-Hall. He arrived in Livonia sometime during 1521 or 1522, earlier than previously thought. During his four- to five-year stay he mastered the Low German language spoken there. It was in Livonia that he experienced the coming of the Reformation, sided with Reformers and became involved in iconoclastic disturbances. Although Hoffman considered himself a Lutheran, Pater has suggested an early influence by Karlstadt (°°Carlstadt). Hoffman's views on the Eucharist and on the church as a charismatic community of equal brothers and sisters thus differed from the view held by Luther. Hoffman's expulsion from Livonia, his ministry in Sweden and Schleswig-Holstein, and his break with Luther need no reiteration. Hoffman's conversion to Anabaptism presumably took place during his first stay at Strasbourg. Deppermann has suggested contact with the branch of Anabaptism that stood in continuity with a °°Denck-°°Kautz-°Hut line. Given Hoffman's strong sense of prophetic calling, Depperman speculates that he initiated adult baptism on his own, and that it would be wrong therefore to place him into any *successio Anabaptistica,* certainly not one originating in Zürich. In need of correction is the notion of a second visit by Hoffman to Strasbourg in the fall of 1530. His first stay extended from June 1529 to April 1530. The wrong dating of a document by Röhrich had led to the postulation of a return visit in the fall of 1530 (*TA Elsaß I,* 309-10).

Hoffman's so-called "recantation" remains controversial. The document, discovered by Hulshof, had been solicited from Hoffman by Peter °°Tasch in conjunction with the little known "second synod" of Strasbourg, May 26-28, 1539. According to this document and statements made later by °°Blesdijk, Hoffman eventually retracted all the positions for which he had been condemned at the first synod (1533). Needless to say this made him no less a martyr—a martyr of conscience, who suffered more than ten years imprisonment. Curiously, records indicate that shortly after the assumed death of Melchior Hoffman in Strasbourg (late 1543 or early 1544), an Anabaptist, also named Melchior Hoffman, appeared in Hoffman's home area of Schwäbisch-Hall (Packull, 1983).

Teaching. It is now recognized that Hoffman's pre-Anabaptist views were not simply derived from °°Luther or Karlstadt. It appears that his visionary °apocalyptic spiritualism had roots reaching back to the Spiritual Franciscan tradition. His insistence on the superiority of the spirit over the letter was supported by a medieval allegorical hermeneutic, while the visions of Johns's Revelation served as the keyhole through which he scanned the rest of Scripture. In his "mature" phase, Hoffman combined these elements with a form of Anabaptism stamped by Denck and Hut. Although the resulting synthesis was Hoffman's own, it would be anachronistic to accuse him of "arbitrary interpretation of Scripture' and of "unbridled fantasy" as Neff, following others, had done. To be sure, Hoffman's ministry remained unique. Perhaps the strong anticlericalism of his message provides a partial explanation for his popularity. Even as an Anabaptist leader he attempted consistently to win the authorities for his reform program. His suspension of baptism for two years was equally unique. Unusual for an uneducated artisan were Hoffman's lengthy biblical commentaries as well as the many other publications.

Significance. It has been argued that Hoffman's

ministry proved counterproductive (Depperman). The social disorders that followed his preaching in Livonia helped frighten the landed nobility back into the old church, and hastened the triumph of conservative forms of Lutheranism in the cities. A similar case can be made for Schleswig-Holstein. The apocalyptic excitement aroused in Strasbourg led to reactionary measures that proved detrimental to all nonconformists. The disaster of Münster had far-reachng consequences for Anabaptists everywhere. Münster itself was recatholicized. However, assessments of Hoffman's historical significance must take account of the fact that his labors in the various territories coincided with the introduction of the Reformation in them. That his influence waxed and waned with popular initiative helps to explain why for a brief period the Melchiorite movement took on mass dimensions in The Netherlands. If Münster constituted an expression of that movement, so did the peaceful remnant gathered by °Menno Simons. Hoffman remains of historical significance precisely because he introduced Anabaptism to the North.

Sources. To the 18 writings of Hoffman cited by Neff, 9 others originating with Hoffman or his closest collaborators can be added. Deppermann has listed all these documents as well as their present location. We provide in an abridged form only the titles not mentioned in Neff's article.   WOP

(1) *Dat Nikolaus Amsdorff der Meydeborger Pastor/ nicht weth/ wat he setten/ schriuen edder swetzen schal/ darmede he syne logen bestedigen moge/ unde synen gruweliken anlop* (Kiel: Hoffman, 1528), reproduced by Gerhard Ficker under the title, "Melchior Hoffman gegen Nikolaus Amsdorff," in *Schriften des Vereins für Schleswig-Holsteinische KG.*, 5 (1928); (2) *Das Niclas Amsdorff der Magdeburger Pastor ein lugenhafftiger falscher nasen geist sey/ offentlich bewiesen durch Melchior Hoffman* (Kiel: Hoffman, 1828), reproduced by Gerhard Ficker in *Schriften des Vereins für Schleswig-Holsteinische KG,* 4 (1926); (3) *[Das] Erste Capitel des Evangelisten St. Mattheus* (1528), *Vorrede,* reprinted by Johannes Melchior Krafft in *Ein Zweyfaches Zwey-hundert-Jähriges Jubel-Gedächtnis* (Hamburg, 1723), 440-45; (4) *Dat Boeck Cantica Canticorum odder dat hoge leedt Salomonis uthgelecht dorch Melchior Hoffman* (Kiel: Hoffman, 1529); (5) M. H. [Melchior Hoffman], *Das ware trostliche unnd freudenreiche Euangelion* (Straßburg: Jakob Cammerlandere, 1531); (6) M. H. [Melchior Hoffman], *Een waraftyghe tuchenisse under gruntlyke verclarynge wo die worden tho den Ro. IX. Ca. van dem Esau und Jacob soldeen verstaen worden* (Deventer: Albert Paffraet, 1532); (7) [Hoffman, published by Poldermann], *Die Epistel des Apostell Sanct Judas erklert unnd . . . außgelegt* (Hagenau: Valentin Kobian, 1534), reproduced in *TA Elsaß II,* no. 479, pp. 241-45; (8) Johannes Eisenburgk [presumably with Hoffman], *Die Epistel deß Apostels S. Jacobs erklart/ und . . außgelegt/* (Straßburg: Jakob Cammerlander, 1534), reproduced in part in *TA Elsaß II,* no. 480, pp. 245-48; (9) Caspar Beck [pseudonym], *Eyn sendbrieff an den achtbaren Michel wachter/ in welchem eroffnet würt/ die uberauß greuwliche mißhandlung/ die in vergangnen zeyten zu Jerusalem wider dye ewige worheit und der selbigen zeugen gehandlet ist/* (Hagenau: Valentin Kobian, 1534), reproduced in "Ein Sendbrief Melchior Hofmanns aus dem Jahre 1534," ed. by E. W. Kohls, *Theologische Z.,* 17 (1961), 356-65; (10) "Bekenntnus des Melchior Hofmanns vom kindertauf," published by Hulshof in *Geschiednis van de Doopsgezinden te Straatburg,* pp. 180-1; (11) "Summarium dess was Melchior Hoffman im Thurm uff 24 Tücher geschriben hat (1537)," ed. by T. W. Röhrich, *Z. für die historische Theologie,* 30 (1860), 104-6.

It should be noted that Pater and others believe that the *Dialogus* (ME II:780) was really Karlstadt's work based on Hoffman's account. Neff was mistaken when he believed that pamphlets written

under the pseudonyms of Caspar Becker and Michael Wächter had been lost (see item 9 above). The name Caspar Beck, if it hides the same author as the pseudonym Caspar Becker, refers to Peter Tasch (Packull, "Peter Tasch," *MQR,* 1988). It should also be noted that Hoffman's *Auslegung* described by Neff as a pamphlet was Hoffman's major treatise consisting of more than 150 pages. Hutterite copyists transcribed and rewrote this commentary, in the process losing the author's name. "The Ordinance of God," was in part translated by G. Williams in SAW (1957), 182-203.

Important primary sources related to Hoffman's life and theology include: Nikolous Amsdorf, "Eine Vermanung an die von Magdeburg, das sie sich fur falsch propheten zu hüten wissen" (Magdeburg, 1527); idem, "Das Melchior Hoffman ein falscher Prophet und sein leer vom jüngsten Tag unrecht, falsch und wider Gott ist; an alle Heilige und Gläubige an J. Chr. zu Kiel und in ganzen Holstein" (Magdeburg, 1528); idem, "Das Melchior Hoffman nicht ein wort auff mein Büchlein geantwort hat" (Magdeburg, 1528); Nikolaas Blesdijk, *Historia vitae, doctrinae, ac rerum gestarum Davidis Georgii haeresiarchae* (Deventer, 1642); idem, "Van den Oorspronck ende anvanck des sectes welck men wederdoper noomt," a manuscript rediscovered by S. Zilstra in the Joris Lade at the University Library of Basel (described by Zilstra, see below); J. Bugenhagen, *Acta der Disputation zu Flensburg/ die sache des Hochwirdigen Sacraments betreffend, im 1529. Jar* (Wittenberg, 1529); idem, *Eynne rede vam sacramente. Dorch Joannem Bugenhagen Pomeren tho Flensborch nah Melchior Hoffmans dysputatien geredet* (Hamburg, 1529); Martin Bucer, *Handlung inn dem offentlichen gesprech zu Strassburg jüngst im Synodo gehalten/ gegen Melchior Hoffman/ durch die Prediger daselbst* (Strasbourg, 1533); M. Schuldorp, *Breef an alle Glövigen der Stadt Kyll weder eeren Prediger Melchior Hoffman* (Hamburg, 1528), the title as reconstructed by Pater; E. Wydenszehe [Weidensee], *Eyn underricht uth der hilligen schryfft/ Melchior Hoffmans sendebreff/ darynne he schryfft/ dat he nycht bekennen kone dat eyn stucke liiflikes brodes syn Godt sy/ belangende* (1529).

Secondary accounts related to Hoffman included the following: Ernst Crous, "Von Melchior Hofmann zu Menno Simons" in *Menn. Geschbl.,* 19, N.F. 15 (1962), 2-14; Klaus Deppermann, "Hoffmans letzte Schriften aus dem Jahre 1534," *ARG,* 63 (1972), 72-93; idem, "Die Strassburger Reformatoren und die Krise des oberdeutschen Täufertums im Jahre 1527," *Menn. Geschbl.,* 30, N.F. 25 (1973), 24-41; idem, "Melchior Hoffmans Weg von Luther zu den Täufern" in *Umstrittenes Täufertum* (1975), 173-205; idem, "Melchior Hoffman and Strasbourg Anabaptism," in *The Origins and Characteristics of Anabaptism,* ed. by Marc Lienhard (Hague: Nishoff, 1977), 216-19; idem, "Melchior Hoffman: Widersprüche zwischen Lutherischer Obrigkeitstreue und apokalyptischen Traum," in *Radikale Reformatoren,* ed. H.-J. Goertz (Munich, 1978), 155-66; Engl. tranls. in *Profiles of Radical Reformers* (Scottdale, 1982), 178-90; idem, *Melchior Hoffman: Soziale Unruhe und apokalyptische Visionen im Zeitalter der Reformation* (Göttingen: Vandenhoeck and Ruprecht, 1979; Engl. transl. Edinburgh: T. and T. Clark, 1986); Walter Klaassen, "Eschatological Themes in Early Dutch Anabaptism," in *The Dutch Dissenters,* ed. by I. B. Horst (Leiden, 1986), 15-21; Mark A. Noll, "Luther Defends Melchior Hofmann," *Sixteenth Century J.,* 4 (1973), 47-60; Werner O. Packull, "A Hutterite Book of Medieval Origin Revisited. An Examination of the Hutterite Commentaries on the Book of Revelation and their Anabaptist Origin," *MQR,* 56 (1982), 147-68; idem, "Melchior Hoffman—A Recanted Anabaptist in Schwäbisch Hall?" *MQR,* 57 (1983), 83-111; idem, "Der Hutterische Kommentar der Offenbarung des Johannes: Eine Untersuchung seines Täuferischen Ursprungs," in *Die Hutterischen Täufer Geschichtlicher Hintergrund und handwerkliche Leistung* (Munich, 1985), 29-37; idem, "Melchior Hoffman's Experience in the Livonian Reformation: The Dynamics of Sect Formation" *MQR,* 59 (1985), 130-46; idem, "A Reinterpretation of Melchior Hoffman's *Exposition* Against the Background of Spiritual Franciscan Eschatology with Special Reference to Peter John Olivi," in *The Dutch Dissenters,* ed. by I. B. Horst (Leiden, 1986), 32-61; idem, "Peter Tasch: From Melchiorite to Bankrupt Wine Merchant," *MQR,* 62 (1988),

276-95; idem, "Sylvester Tegetmeier, Father of the Livonian Reformation: A Fragment of His Diary," *J. of Baltic Studies*, 16 (1986), 343-56; Calvin A. Pater, *Karlstadt as the Father of the Baptist Movements: The Emergence of Lay Protestantism* (U. of Toronto Press, 1984); idem, "Melchior Hoffman's Explication of the Songs[!] of Songs," *ARG*, 67 (1977), 173-91; idem, "A Study of Selected Doctrines in Melchior Hoffman" (ThD diss., New Orleans Baptist Theological Seminary, 1978); James M. Stayer, *Anabaptists and the Sword* (1972, 1976); Sjoue Voolstra, *Het woord is vlees geworden: De melchioritisch-menniste incarnatieleer* (Kampen, 1982); G. Wunder, "Über die Verwandtschaft des Wiedertäufers Melchior Hoffman," *Der Hallquell: Blätter für Heimatkunde des Haller Landes*, 23 (1971), 21-23; S. Zijlstra, *Nicolaas Meyndertsz van Blesdijk* (Assen, 1983).

Hokkaido, Japan ("north-sea way"), the northernmost and second largest of Japan's four main islands. Although once a new frontier, it has become the largest prefecture in Japan, and ranks fifth in population. The capital is Sapporo (pop. 1,500,000). A snow festival featuring huge snow sculptures is observed in that city every February. Several mountain ranges cross Hokkaido. Its total area is 83,513 sq. km. (32,236 sq. mi.), and its population is about 5,576,000 (1980). The island has long winters and heavy snowfall, especially in the western portion. By contrast, summer in Hokkaido is warm and beautiful. The main agricultural crop is rice; grain, vegetables, and dairy farming flourish on broad plains. Fishing, forestry, and mining have long been an important part of Hokkaido's economy. Hokkaido is noted for its scenic national parks. They include hot springs, active volcanos, deep lakes, and vast virgin forest. Black bears can be found. The island was originally inhabited by the *Ainu* (aborigines), but the majority of them were exploited and displaced by Japanese settlers in the latter half of the 19th c. The *Ainu* still exist in Hokkaido, but their language and culture are rapidly disappearing.

Many Americans feel the climate of Hokkaido resembles that of Minnesota. Winter sports abound, and the Winter Olympic Games have been held there.

There are 17 Mennonite churches (MC) on the island, organized into the Nihon Menonaito Kirisuto Kyokai Kyogikai (Japan Mennonite Church Conference). The work began in 1951. Except for Sapporo, the churches are all located in central and eastern Hokkaido. Besides Catholic (69) and Orthodox (8) churches, there are 34 Protestant denominations (302 churches) involved in mission on Hokkaido. HT

"Hokkaido" in *Kodansha Encyclopedia of Japan*, vol. 3, (Tokyo: Kodansha, 1983), 212-213; *MWH* (1978), 174.

Holdeman, John (ME II:789), founder of the °Church of God in Christ Mennonite, married Elizabeth (Shriner) Ritter, Nov. 18, 1852. He became a member of the Eight Square (Chester Mennonite) Church in Wayne Co., Ohio, at age 21. During the first year of his marriage he experienced spiritual tribulation followed by "joyful light and quiet conscience" and a series of dreams and visions that convinced him of a call to ministry.

Study of the Bible and Anbaptist writings led him to assert that the (Old) Mennonite Church (later MC) could no longer be considered "the true church." There was little significant response to Holdeman's °restitutionist agenda. He was not even among those who were nominated to be considered as a candidate for the ministry for election by °°lot. On Jan. 24, 1858, he began to preach. In April 1859 a new congregation of four was formed in his father's home. His father joined; his mother did not. Between 1862 and 1879 he traveled widely, preached, and wrote earnestly while eking out an existence as a farmer. The cost of publishing his own writings and his frequent absences from farming operations resulted in severe financial crises. In 1883 he, his family, and the entire Wayne Co. Church of God in Christ congregation, moved to Jasper Co., Mo.; in 1897 he moved to McPherson Co., Ks., where he had gained his largest following. He died at age 68; his wife outlived him by 32 years, reaching 98 years of age.

Holdeman's significance can be assessed from various perspectives. For the immigrants from °°Volhynia and the °°Kleine Gemeinde members who joined the Church of God in Christ Mennonite at a crucial juncture, his emphases and style were a Godsend in their frustrations and needs. He enabled them to rise above their own history of rejection, confusion, and feeling of lostness. His historic fellow (Old) Mennonites, however, regarded him as a disillusioned, church-rejecting, church-splitter who had been frustrated at not being called to the ministry among them. Other historians identify him as a son of his times, authenticated for the impact he made by his typical 19th-c. characterizations with his revelations, dreams, and visions, and his °revival meeting tactics, millennial views, °°nonconformity emphasis, and authoritarian leadership in the midst of America's democratization and the idealogical upheavals of the times. His was one of many similar renewal movements of the 19th c.—a number of them from America's (Old) Mennonite Church (°renaissance, Mennonite). In his own eyes, his chief concern was the restoration of the "true church of God."

Because he was bilingual (German and English), an avid reader, well-traveled and more broadly informed than many fellow Mennonites; because he came from Mennonite moorings, sympathetic to the feelings which the rejected felt, and appropriately accepting of some of the "new ways" (e.g., revivalism, publishing, etc.) he was uniquely suited to make his impact.   CH

Menn. Bib., II:457.

See also Church of God in Christ Mennonite.

Holdeman Mennonite Church. See Church of God in Christ Mennonite.

Holidays. See Christian Calendar.

Holiness Camps. The camp meeting is a North American contribution to church history. Begun as frontier wilderness evangelistic meetings, they were not the original invention of the Methodists, who were among the leaders in the "holiness" movement. However, they fit so well with the Wesleyan message and itinerant methods of ministry that holiness groups came to play a prominent role in the camp meeting phenomena across America. Attempts to introduce camp meetings to the settled church life in Europe had only short-lived and modest success, though they did lead to the establishment of the Primitive Methodist denomination in England. They had greater success in the countries outside Europe and North America where Wesleyan groups established missionary work.

The rise of holiness denominations in the last half of the 19th c. was significantly tied to the camp meeting tradition. It was felt that the older Methodist churches were neglecting John Wesley's doctrine of entire °sanctification. Holiness advocates in the Methodist churches joined hands with the newer Wesleyan denominations to make the camp meetings the major platform for holiness teaching. Thus, the National Camp-Meeting Association for the Promotion of Holiness, the parent body of what became the Christian Holiness Association, was born in 1867. The number of camp meetings held annually in North America has reached ca. 1,000 in the late 1980s, indicating the continuing strength of the movement.

Holiness camp meetings became a part of the two Anabaptist-Mennonite churches which espoused Wesleyan views in regard to the doctrine of sanctification: the Missionary Church (one branch of which was formerly called the Mennonite Brethren in Christ) and the Brethren in Christ Church.

Less than a decade after several Mennonite groups came together to form the Mennonite Brethren in Christ Church, the first camp meeting was held in 1880 at Fetter's Grove near Wakarusa, Ind. Within a matter of a few years, meetings were being held in all districts of the church. In time property was purchased and permanent camps established. In 1986 Missionary Church camp meetings were located in James River, Alta.; Fetters Grove, Ind.; Ludlow Falls, Ohio; Stayner and Kitchener, Ont.; Brown City and Mancelona, Mich.; Weeping Water, Nebr.; and Mountain View, Wash.

The Brethren in Christ Church did not hold its first camp meeting until 1936 at Roxbury, Pa. It was an outgrowth of evangelistic meetings held annually at Roxbury from 1933 onward by area Brethren congregations. When it became apparent that the ten-day camp meeting for the promotion of holiness had become an annual event, land was purchased in 1941 and buildings constructed to assure the permanence of the camp and enhance its ministry. It holds the distinction of being not only the first, but also the largest of the Brethren in Christ camp meetings.

Soon, however, other districts of the church established camp meetings in their areas. Niagara Holiness Camp began at Fort Erie, Ont., in 1941. Memorial Holiness Camp near West Milton, Ohio, was launched in 1944. Other camp meetings were conducted for a time in Iowa, Kansas, and California. In 1963 Camp Freedom was begun in Florida to minister to those who frequented Florida. The °United Zion Church, closely related to the Brethren in Christ, also operates a camp meeting grove.

The central purpose of the camp meetings was to promote the doctrine and the experience of entire sanctification. No other structure of these churches,

except possibly the annual congregational revival meetings, has proved as effective as camp meetings in leading church members to experience the more extensive work of the Holy Spirit in their lives.

Initially the camps enjoyed extensive evangelistic influence in the communities where they were held. While the evening evangelistic service is a regular feature of most camps, it now ministers more to the church constituency than it does the community. Home and foreign °missions have been enthusiastically supported by the camp meetings, with special emphasis days devoted to missions promotion. Along the way, the special needs of children and youth have given rise to separate facilities and programming for them.

The camp meetings through the years have been a unique °family experience, both in terms of the nuclear family and the church family. They have brought together more members of the churches in something of a family union atmosphere than any other church structure. Consequently, they have helped to shape a denominational identity through intimate association and focused teaching regarding the distinctive doctrinal emphases of the respective denominations. While some aspects of the camp meeting histories are difficult to appreciate today, this positive benefit can not be overlooked. It is one reason why the camp meetings remain a vital force today though different in style than they were in past generations. LLK

Eileen Lageer, *Merging Streams: Story of the Missionary Church* (Elkhart: Bethel Pub. Co., 1979), 65-70; E. Morris Sider, *Holiness Unto the Lord: The Story of Roxbury Holiness Camp* (Nappanee: Evangel Press, 1985); Everek Richard Storms, *History of the Missionary Church* (Elkhart: Bethel Pub. Co., 1959), 171-80; Wittlinger, *Piety and Obedience* (1978) 331-38.

Holiness Movement (ME II:790). The holiness movement comprises those groups which have perpetuated and popularized the Wesleyan message of °sanctification in the 19th and 20th c. It is significant that both the Missionary Church (ME III: 603; II: 710, formed by a merger in 1969) and the Brethren in Christ were influenced by the holiness movment in the latter half of the 19th c., for that was when the movement reached its greatest strength in North America and Europe. The Missionary Church was born at this time, and the Brethren in Christ endorsed the Wesleyan view of sanctification as they entered the second century of their existence. Holiness theology has also had a slight impact on the Evangelical Mennonite Church and other Mennonite groups.

The emergence of a holiness theology in the Mennonite Brethren in Christ (Missionary Church) was a rather uneventful development, growing out of the religious experience of their early ministerial leadership and through their almost immediate use of the camp meeting (°holiness camps), popularized by the holiness movement. For the Brethren in Christ, the transition to a Wesleyan theology of holiness was a slow development, critiqued, modified, and at times resisted, by the "growth view" of sanctification entrenched by a century of denominational heritage. From 1887 to 1910 there was a trend toward a cautious Wesleyan view of sanctification. The holi-

ness message spread, mainly through annual evangelistic meetings and later the camp meetings, until it
climaxed in the 1940s with an unqualified stance on
Christian perfection in the mold of the American
holiness tradition.

Since the 1950s, both denominations have modified their Wesleyan stance somewhat, though with
different dynamics in each case. Both denominations
have entered into the larger °Evangelical movement
and have been affected by its non-Wesleyan atmosphere. This has been particularly noticeable in
some areas of the Missionary Church which have
shifted to a Calvinistic understanding on sanctification. For the Brethren in Christ, historical studies,
both in Brethren in Christ roots and in the theology
of John Wesley (1703-91), which is more complex
and less radical than the American camp meeting
theology, have modified Brethren in Christ doctrinal
expression regarding "entire sanctification." In
general, more attention has been given in the last
two decades to the process of sanctification as the
necessary complement to the crisis aspect of the
holiness message. Near the end of the 20th c., the
Brethren in Christ have more fully integrated their
Wesleyan and Anabaptist traditions and thus are
more comfortable with Anabaptist thought and activities than is the Missionary Church.

Since the holiness tradition gave both churches a
strong teaching emphasis upon the °Holy Spirit's
work in the life of the believer and in the congregation's worship and ministry, the °charismatic movement has not had the impact upon them that it has
had upon other segments of the Mennonite community. The traditional teaching has tended to insu-
late them from the charismatic emphasis. While not
as hostile to charismatics as they were a generation
ago, the emotional need for the charismatic experience is not widespread in the groups touched by
Wesleyan theology.   LLK

Articles in *Brethren in Christ History and Life* (December,
1983); Owen H. Alderfer, "The Mind of the Brethren in
Christ" (PhD diss., Claremont Graduate School, 1963); Mel-
vin Dieter, "The Holiness Movement," *Beacon Dictionary of
Theology*, ed. Richard Taylor, J. Kenneth Grider, and Willard
Taylor (Kansas City: Beacon Hill Press, 1983) 260-61; Luke
L. Keefer, Jr., *Everything Necessary* (Nappanee, Ind., 1984);
Timothy Smith, "A Historical and Contemporary Appraisal of
Wesleyan Theology," in *A Contemporary Wesleyan Theology*,
ed. Carter, R. Thompson, and Wilson (Grand Rapids: Zon-
dervan [Francis Asbury Press], 1983), 77-101; Everek R.
Storms, *History of the United Missionary Church* (Elkhart:
Bethel Publishing Company, 1958) 30-59, 171-180, 220-26;
Wittlinger, *Piety and Obedience* (1978), 227-57, 321-41;
Stan Nussbaum, *You Must Be Born Again: A History of the
Evangelical Mennonite Church* (Fort Wayne, Ind.: EMCh,
1980), 40-41.

See also Grace; Pietism; Zook, John R.; Zook, Noah.

**Holmes-Wayne-Tuscarawas Counties, Ohio, Old
Order Amish Settlement** (ME II:793), the world's
largest Amish settlement, is located 35 mi. (55 km.)
sw. of Canton, Ohio. Its first settlers arrived in 1807
from Somerset and Mifflin Cos. in Pennsylvania;
however, the community began developing when
Jonas Stutzmen built a log cabin near Walnut Creek
in 1809. In 1986 this hilly, picturesque community
has over 110 church districts (congregations) serving a total population of about 30,000 people. Amish

population has doubled in the last 25 years, due
mainly to large family size.

The state of Ohio has 23 separate Amish settlements which support more than 150 parochial
schools. The majority of these schools are found in
the Holmes County area. Amish schooling reflects
the seriousness given to childrearing, not only in the
development of the basic skills, but more importantly, the moral content and cultural standards to be in-
stilled in the °socialization process.

The Holmes Co. community has experienced a
greater amount of factionalism than is found in most
Amish settlements. More than 20 distinct groups of
Amish and Mennonites can be identified by their
variations of dress, modes of transportation, or
degrees of °modernity. Groups are often identified
by the names of their leaders, usually a minister or
bishop. Some groups avoid full fellowship with each
other because of differences in church °discipline.
Such cultural and religious differences create a
certain curiosity that attracts tourists. Holmes Co.
has become one of the major tourist areas in the
state, although not fully sanctioned by the Amish.
°Tourism has invited craft shops, restaurants
specializing in Amish cooking, and other commercial
endeavors to an otherwise quiet, tranquil community. Amish nonfarmers are increasingly involved
in the tourist business. The area is nationally known
for its Swiss cheese and homemade Trail Bologna.
Sugarcreek, a small town in Tuscarawas Co., is well
known for it publication of *The Budget*, a popular
weekly newspaper that serves hundreds of Amish
and Mennonite communities in the United States,
Canada, and several other countries.   SLY

**Holocaust. See Judaism and Jews; National
Socialism.**

Holy Spirit (ME II:795). The reality of the Holy
Spirit was central to Anabaptist theology. The Anabaptists were in harmony with the orthodox Christian statements regarding the Holy Spirit. Some disagreed with the *filioque* clause in the western versions of the Nicene Creed, i.e., the assertion that
the Holy Spirit proceeds from the Son as well as
from the Father. In his *Confession of the Triune God*,
Menno Simons writes that the Holy Spirit proceeds
"from the Father through the Son, although he ever
remains with God and in God, and is never
separated from the being of the Father and the Son"
(Menno, *Writings*, 496). In other places Menno asserts that the Spirit proceeds from the Father
through the Son or the Word.

For the most part, the Anabaptists made no abstract theological statements about the Holy Spirit
and whenever they did write about him, they usually
used biblical language. The important thing for them
was how the Holy Spirit worked in the life of the
believer and the church. Much is said in Anabaptist
writings about the *work* of the Holy Spirit (Klaassen,
1961, 130-132).

Considering the disparate origins of the movement
it is not surprising to note that there is not only one
Anabaptist view of the Holy Spirit. However, on the
main points there was remarkable agreement.
Throughout Anabaptism there was a profound con-

viction that the Spirit was at the center of Christian experience enabling the follower of Christ to rise above °legalism to the transforming life of joyful obedience (Peter Klassen, in *Witness of the Holy Spirit*, 242).

The centrality of the Holy Spirit and his work in Anabaptist leaders arises out of their covenant theology. The new covenant in Christ is marked by the gift of the Holy Spirit to every believer. Already in the September 1524 letter of Conrad Grebel and the Brethren in Zürich to Thomas °Müntzer, we are informed that in the Old Testament the Word of God was written on tablets of stone, but in the New Covenant it is written in the fleshy tablets of the heart. The biblical references given were 2 Cor 3:3, Jer. 31:33, and Jl 2:28 (CRR 4: 289; Klaassen, 1961, 132).

Early Anabaptist writers develop the theme of the new covenant. In 1526 Hans °°Denck noted: "Whoever has received God's new covenant, that is whoever has had the law written into his heart by the Holy Spirit, is truly righteous. Whoever thinks that he can observe the law by means of the Book ascribes to the dead letter what belongs to the living Spirit" (CRR 3: 73).

In 1538 at the Bern Disputation the Swiss Brethren again affirmed that the possession of the Spirit was the chief mark of the new covenant: "Thus the essence and the usage in the old and new covenants is not the same. . . . That the ancients had the Gospel preached to them as with us today we cannot admit. . . . Thus the old obedience of the Law is not to be compared with the new obedience of the Spirit. . . . (They) are not against each other, but each in its own place" (Klaassen, 1961, 132).

Hans °Hut and Peter °°Riedemann also indicate how the old covenant, one of servitude, is superseded by the new covenant of liberty, which comes by the indwelling Spirit. The strongest proponent of this position was Pilgram °Marpeck who taught that there was a radical discontinuity between the old covenant and the new. There was no resemblance between the Spirits working in the old covenant and the new. The Spirit did not operate giving his gifts, comfort, and insight into truth in the old covenant, taught Marpeck. This work only began after Pentecost. "Only with the Holy Spirit of Christ did the law of love make its appearance, for only through this Spirit can it be fulfilled" (Klaassen, 1961, 133).

All Anabaptists believed that the Holy Spirit is the agent of the new birth. Furthermore, the Spirit, wrote Menno "adorns us with his heavenly and divine gifts . . . frees us from sin, gives us boldness, and makes us cheerful, peaceful, pious, and holy" (Menno, *Writings*, 496). The reception of the Holy Spirit follows upon hearing the Word, which produces faith, and upon water baptism. As they understood the words of Paul, the Anabaptists believed that the Holy Spirit takes control of the life of the person who believes and is baptized.

Anabaptists have often been labeled spiritualists, i.e., people who believe in the direct inspiration of the Spirit apart from Scripture. It is true that Anabaptists believed they were living in the age of the Spirit and that they often spoke about being led by the Spirit and being given divine illumination. There even were some cases of rejecting the Word in favor of the Spirit. But most Anabaptists managed to maintain the tension between Word and Spirit, holding firmly to both. The overriding view, affirmed even by men like Denck, °°Kautz, and Hut, who had spiritualist tendencies, was that Spirit and Scripture could never be in opposition. The Scripture always served as the norm to prevent claims of extrabiblical revelation.

For the Anabaptists, the work of the Spirit in the individual believer is at the same time the Spirit at work gathering and building the church. The individual was subordinate to the group and Anabaptists believed that the Holy Spirit expressed himself through the consensus of the believing community.

In Anabaptist and Mennonite confessions of faith, the Holy Spirit has a transforming function, with his work in regeneration and °sanctification being highlighted. The doctrine of the Spirit does not receive pronounced attention in the confessions. There is, however, a uniform emphasis on the nature (deity, personality, trinity, and procession from the Father) and the function (office and characteristics) of the Spirit (Loewen, *Confessions*, 39-40).

Mennonite catechisms affirm faith in the Trinity and in the Holy Spirit. The popular Waldeck Catechism, patterned after the Cornelis Ris Confession (1766), has appeared in at least seven German reprints among American Mennonites and in many English reprint editions. The Waldeck Catechism notes that the Holy Spirit testifies of Jesus; he comforts believers, he sanctifies them, and leads them into all truth; and through the Holy Ghost, the love of God is shed abroad in the hearts of believers" (Wenger, 106).

American Mennonite groups accept the historic position regarding the nature of the Holy Spirit but they reflect some differences in their teachings regarding the work of the Holy Spirit in Christian experience. The Brethren in Christ, while not unanimous in their interpretation of sanctification (°holiness movement), agree on the importance of sanctification as a separate work of the Spirit. The 1961 *Manual of Doctrine and Government*, states: "As a Christian experience, sanctification embodies the setting apart of the believer in entire consecration and the cleansing of the believer's heart from carnality, accompanied by the baptism of the Holy Spirit. . . . The work of holiness which was begun in regeneration is perfected, and the believer is 'sanctified wholly'" (Loewen, *Confessions*, 234). In its *Discipline*, the Evangelical Mennonite Church affirms that the baptism with the Holy Spirit is a distinct experience subsequent to regeneration. "It is necessary for holiness and fruitfulness of life and endowment with power for service" (Loewen, *Confessions*, 218).

Mennonites by and large seek to be a faithful model of the community of the Spirit based on a personal knowledge of Christ. At the Eighth Mennonite World Conference (1967), gathered around the theme "The Witness of the Holy Spirit," J. B. °Toews stated that correct theology, even Anabaptist theology, without experiential knowledge of Christ through the Holy Spirit leaves the Church impotent. "The life of a dynamic church is in Christ through the Holy Spirit" (*Witness of the Holy Spirit*, 59). WU

Cornelius J. Dyck, ed., *The Witness of the Holy Spirit: Proceedings of the Eighth Mennonite World Conference* (Elkhart, Ind.: Mennonite World Conference, 1967), esp. J. A. Oosterbaan, "Word and Spirit," 9-16; J. B. Toews, "Spiritual Renewal," 56-63; Peter Klassen, "The Anabaptist View of the Holy Spirit," 242-48, reprinted in *Menn. Life*, 23, no. 1 (Jan. 1968), 27-31; Walter Klaassen, "Some Anabaptist Views on the Doctrine of the Holy Spirit," *MQR*, 35 (1961), 130-39; idem, "Spiritualization in the Reformation," *MQR*, 37 (1963), 67-77; CRR 3, ch. 3: "The Holy Spirit"; John C. Wenger, *The Doctrines of the Mennonites* (Scottdale: MPH, 1952); William Klassen, *Covenant and Community: The Life, Writings, and Hermeneutics of Pilgram Marpeck* (Grand Rapids: Eerdmans, 1968), esp. 67-77; Dale W. Brown, *Led by Word and Spirit*, Foundation Series adult curriculum (Nappanee, Newton, Scottdale, Elgin, copublished by Mennonite, Brethren in Christ, and Church of the Brethren publishing houses, 1983); George R. Brunk, ed., *Encounter with the Holy Spirit* (Scottdale, 1972).

See also Charismatic Movement; Ordinances; Worship.

Homes, Retirement and Nursing (ME II:797). The philosophy and the procedures of Mennonites in providing retirement programs have undergone drastic change in Canada and the United States, particularly during the last four decades. It was historically Anabaptist and Mennonite for the church to be concerned about the welfare of the whole body. In Europe the care for the aged, the indigent, the ill and the orphans had always been an integral part of the religious and social life of the total Mennonite body. In North America to provide for aging parents and even other relatives who needed help had been considered largely a local responsibility carried primarily by the family and secondarily by the local congregation. In this statement we do not include the Old Order Amish and Old Order Mennonites who follow a time-honored and, for them, a very successful program, for retiring parents and grandparents who live in an independent unit or a house called the "grossdoddy house" next to an adult child or children who can help meet nearly every need.

The first Mennonite homes for the aged were established between 1894 and 1899. While county or other government agencies had provided emergency care, the feeling has been that the church has the responsibility of Christian sharing. For instance, the first residents of the Mennonite Home at Eureka, Ill., established in 1922, were largely indigent Mennonites from the Midwest who had no responsible relatives or other persons willing to take care of them. In 1987 this home is called Maple Lawn Homes and emphasizes retirement living in all its stages and ignoring the idea that everybody over 65 is an old person with special needs.

Frequently homes for older persons operated by Mennonites are sponsored by community organizations. They are often located in larger Mennonite communities, where Mennonites have taken part in organizing and then have been asked to operate the institutions. The Christian motivation is still a very important factor but now it goes far beyond serving members of the Mennonite churches; in most of these institutions non-Mennonites outnumber Mennonites. For instance, 62 percent of the 850 residents at Greencroft, Inc., at Goshen and Elkhart, Ind., (the largest institution of its type in the state) are not Mennonites. Retirement institutions are no longer thought of as places to serve only the indigent, those who do not have caring families, or those who cannot live independently. Currently the number of homes for older persons in Canada and the United States under Mennonite auspices is more than 100, a growth of more than 800 percent over the 12 institutions operating in 1940. One-fourth of these homes are in Canada.

The greater change in philosophy comes with the purposes behind these communities or institutions. These are full-service retirement communities ranging from complete independent living facilities to full-scale nursing service and services between. These homes are living centers and not places to wait for death. Even the names have changed from "Old People's Home," "Beulahland," or Sunset Home," to "Green Hills Center," "Pleasant Manor," "Swiss Village," or "Parkview."

There are numerous reasons why people by choice or through necessity spend their later years in retirement communities and in cases of severe physical or mental impairment or both, may need a nursing home:

(1) While in 1900 and for some years after, most North American Mennonites were rural, in 1985 only about 15 percent were. The large farm residence built for large families which sometimes served three generations at one time, is gone.

(2) Mennonite families no longer average six or seven children, as in the early 1900s or even three or four as did the families of the late 1950s, but are about the same as the national average of fewer than two children. Rural children, with little education, lived close to their parents, much as the Amish continue to do, and these children cared for remaining parents in the home community.

(3) The population has many more older persons. In 1900 an infant could expect to live 47 years. In 1987 the expectancy is 75 years, 71 for males and 79 for females. Sixty percent of people over 65 are women. The most rapidly growing group, is women beyond 85. In 1900 four percent of the population was over the age of 65; in 1987, 12 percent is.

(4) In 1900 with short life expectancy and large families, it was typical for one parent to die while there were still one or two children in the home who took care of the parent. The home in this sense was unbroken and did not call for the parent to change residence.

(5) With small families and expanded longevity, in the late 20th c. the average couple can expect to live together 15-20 years after the last child leaves home. Fifty-year marriages are no longer a novelty. These longer marriages call for quite a different type of housing and living accommodation than earlier met the needs of rural people.

(6) Older persons who reach 65 today are in better condition financially, educationally, and physically than were their elders. Before government programs like Social Security in the United States, if people retired or came to poor health and could no longer work, they were likely do be dependent on others. Two-thirds of the people who reached retire-

ment were dependent upon others, chiefly children or other relatives before 1935. They had little choice regarding a retirement community or facility. The generation retiring in the 1970s and 1980s also benefited from rapid economic expansion and considerable prosperity in North America after World War II, a marked contrast with those retiring between 1900 and 1950, whose prime earning years were characterized by the agricultural depression of the 1920s and the general economic depressions of the 1890s and 1930s.

(7) With small demand, earlier church institutions for older persons had somewhat the same appeal as the "County Farm," or the "Poor Farm" that society provided for the indigent. In the 1980s many older persons can afford to enter a retirement community of their choice and many others can do so because of the good graces of the government which subsidizes facilities for those less financially viable.

(8) The demand for housing facilities in the future seems staggering. In the United States there are 29,000,000 persons older than 65 years. In Canada there are slightly less than one-tenth that number. In 40 years the figure is projected to have grown to 65,000,000 for the United States and a comparable increase for Canada. Should Mennonites attempt to double the number of retirement centers for older citizens or should they look to alternate means, such as increased home services? In recent years Mennonites have put little money into brick and mortar, and have instead left this burden to the governments of Canada and the United States. It looks as though, because of the staggering increases of hospital, medical and nursing home costs, that some rationing of services will be required. Which ones are ethical and expedient? What are the alternatives?

(9) A new trend has developed in facilities for older persons, largely in the last two decades. This is the retirement community for those who can now live independently and wish to prolong this independence by moving to facilities such as courts or apartments free from snow removal, grass mowing, home maintenance, and other obligations. However, they do want close like-minded neighbors in a friendly Christian community which provides activities and programs in which they are free to participate or not. Also, these persons want to be part of a community in which they are eligible for further health services as the ensuing years may dictate—food services, home health care, smaller living quarters with more supervision and, if need be, a nursing home. This more recent retirement dimension has been a very important factor in the tremendous growth of retirement communities under Mennonite auspices since the 1960s.

(10) The church and the community are beginning to see that in the growth concept of wholeness the physical and biological aspects of the aging process are only a small part of growth and we must give more attention to the intellectual, social, and spiritual resources of our elders and not become complacent because we have made them more comfortable physically and extended the days of their years.

Mennonites in Germany operate retirement-nursing homes at Thomashof near Karlsruhe, Burg-weinting, Enkenbach, and Bad Oldesloe; Mennonites in The Netherlands have 19 such homes offering a wide range of care (1985). French Mennonites operate Résidence Rosemontoise at Valdoie near Dijon. Lar Betesda, near Curitiba, Brazil, opened in 1978. Mennonites in other countries use a variety of public and private institutions, including families, to care for aging members. Traditionalist Mennonite groups in Latin America (°Old Colony Mennonites, °Sommerfeld Mennonites) depend on family care of the elderly in a manner similar to that described for the Amish in North America. The communal life of the Hutterian Brethren makes possible integrated care for the elderly without establishing independent homes or apartment complexes. TRS

Lists of North American retirement and nursing homes are published in *MC Yearbook* (annually to 1986; biennially since 1986), *Doops. Jaar.*, and *Menn. Jahrbuch*. Not completely listed in these directories are the Church of God in Christ Mennonite retirement and nursing homes: Linden Nursing Home, Linden Alta.; Greenland Home, Sainte Anne, Man.; Bethel Home, Montezuma, Ks.; Valhaven Home, Lehman, B.C.. For further reading see *The Church and Its Older People*, a report of the conference at Goshen College, Goshen, Ind., Oct. 31-Nov. 2, 1961; David Hockett Fischer, *Growing Old in America* (New York: Oxford U. Press, 1977); Yoder, *MC Census* (1985); Tilman R. Smith, *In Favor of Growing Older* (Scottdale, 1981); Edwin F. Rempel, ed., *Congregational Health Ministries Handbook* (Elkhart, Ind.: Mennonite Health Association, 1987); American Association of Retired Persons, *A Profile of Older Americans, 1985*; John A. Hostetler, *Amish Society* (1980), 168-71; idem, *Hutterite Society* (1974), 247-49.

See also Aged, Care for; Iglesia Evangélica Menonita, Colombia; Mennoniten Gemeinde zu Mexico; Spain; United Zion Church.

Homosexuality. See Sexuality.

Honda Colony, La. See Zacatecas Colonies.

Honduran Mennonite Church. See Iglesia Evangélica Menonita Honduras.

Honduras (ME IV:1093). Eastern Mennonite Board of Missions and Charities (Lancaster Conference, MC) was the first Mennonite group to come to Honduras. It began work in 1950 in the coastal town of Trujillo, and from there moved inland to rural, then urban areas. Evangelism was priority but went hand-in-hand with medical, educational, agricultural, and community-based programs. Voluntary service workers first came in 1959 and later worked with Honduran youth in community and church programs.

The growing national church gradually assumed leadership and became autonomous as the Iglesia Evangélica Menonita Hondureña (Honduras Mennonite Church) in 1969. Membership in 1987 reached 2,600 in 55 congregations subdivided into six geographical regions. Oversight is provided by a national president and executive committee, regional councils and coordinators, and an annual national council comprised of pastors and congregational representatives. Church offices are in La Ceiba.

From the early 1970s onward a °charismatic emphasis, typical also in other denominations, has influenced many congregations; and in the early 1980s, beginning particularly with the work with Salvadoran refugees, came a new emphasis on how

Anabaptism is contextualized in the Honduras setting. The two movements have brought moments of conflict and confusion to the church.

Education and leadership training has continuously received focus. From the start in Trujillo a Bible Institute helped prepare new leaders, and in following years it continued in various forms; in 1987 both residence and °theological education by extension programs helped train new and continuing pastors and lay leaders. A grade school was operated several of the early years in Tocoa. Pine Grove Academy in Tegucigalpa was founded in 1964 as a boarding school for missionary children, and from 1977 on has been operated by an independent board of various evangelical churches, serving both nationals and expatriates. The Mennonite Vocational Institute in La Ceiba opened in 1975 to offer vocational preparation to national students and is operated by the Ministry of Education since 1979. In 1987 some 20 Honduran pastors were studying with SEMILLA, a seminary based in Guatemala City that offers extension education (°Consulta Anabautista Menonita Centroamericana). These pastors in turn share learnings through the national Bible Institute programs.

In 1980 Mennonite Central Committee (MCC) began a supportive role with the Honduras Mennonite Church as Honduras Mennonites in the border regions encountered Salvadoran °refugees fleeing civil war in their homeland. The needs of the refugees for shelter, safety, and food were great, and the Honduras Mennonite Church responded out of a commitment to a gospel they believed needed to be lived out. The Honduras Mennonite Church and MCC worked together along with other national and international churches and agencies under the umbrella of the United Nations High Commissioner for Refugees. The refugees were gathered into camps in the border regions and the Mennonites were given various assignments including oversight of construction of semi-permanent housing, infrastructure, and agricultural projects. With the formation of the church's Social Action Commission, MCC cooperated with the Honduras Mennonite Church in working out a vision and theology of social activism and expanding activity into Honduran communities with programs for preventive health education, sewing workshops, °appropriate technology, and agricultural development.

Amor Viviente (Living Love) was founded in 1974 in Tegucigalpa, also by Eastern Mennonite Board workers, although the intent at the start was not to form a new group, but to provide a Christian witness and alternative to urban youth caught in the power of drugs, alcohol, prostitution and abandonment. The charismatic ministry grew rapidly as youth saw a practical Christianity that brought healing and liberation. From Tegucigalpa, Amor Viviente extended into other urban centers, and became a missionary church sending workers to New Orleans in 1985, and to San José, Costa Rica, in early 1988. By 1987 Amor Viviente in Honduras included 17 congregations in primarily urban areas, with a total membership of 2,800. Its members' growth strategy is through cell groups, where evangelism and discipleship occurs. Other ministry areas include a drug and alcohol rehabilitation center, counseling, children's clubs and nutrition program, Bible Institute, and music ministry.

The Guaimaca Mennonite Church is located in Guaimaca, Olancho, inland from Tegucigalpa, and has a unique history, beginning from 1968, when an Old Order Amish family from Aylmer, Ontario, settled there as part of Amish interest in evangelization by colonization. From 1968 through 1970 at least 10 families from Canada and Indiana moved to the settlement. By 1974 there were 16 Amish families living in the colony.

Several of the original families bought two large farms which were divided and sold off to other families. Each family established its separate home and occupation, with the latter including vegetable and dairy farming, mechanic and furniture shops, a general store, feed mill, and farm supply.

In the early years traditional Amish practices were upheld, with the exception that some Spanish, rather than exclusively German, was used during church services. A plane-load of draft horses was brought from Canada with the hope of promoting, among Honduran neighbors, better means for working the soil. The group was intent on sharing the gospel of Jesus Christ, as well as care and cultivation of the soil, dairy methods, etc. They soon established an orphanage, a school for local children, and an English school for Amish children.

With time there were changes. Intermarriage with Honduran church members was on the horizon; a promising outreach in another community required hiring a truck because mountainous terrain was unsuitable for horse and wagon transportation. More conservative families gradually returned to the United States and Canada. As this happened, and as Amish customs were being abandoned, the group decided on a major change. Because the draft horses did not do well in the Honduran climate, and other equipment and transportation needs were not easily met, the group decided to permit tractors for farming and to permit the use of other motorized vehicles. Those families not in agreement with this decision sold their properties and left, leaving North American families as a minority within the settlement. The Honduran group then affiliated with Beachy Amish Mennonites in North America. (They had been known as "Mennonites" from their first days in Honduras, not as "Amish.") A further division within the group took place in 1986 over issues of appropriate dress. Slightly more than half of the members separated, built another meetinghouse, and affiliated with a less conservative Beachy Amish group, receiving bishop oversight from Indiana. It has three established congregations. The more conservative group, meeting in two congregations, is affiliated with the °Fellowship Churches.

Both groups continue to be active and are well known for their various forms of work and ministry, including their care of the land, dairying, feed mill, bake shop, sale of produce in local markets, schools for local children, children's home, and homes for older youth. Approximate total membership in January 1988 was 200. Their distinctive dress and disciplined life-style set them apart as a well-respected group in the Guaimaca community. JMBren

Linda Shelly and Grace Weber, "The Development of 'Word and Deed Ministry' in the History of the Honduran Mennonite Church" (unpublished paper, San Marcos, Honduras, 1985) available at MCC, Akron, Pa.; "Historia de la Iglesia Amor Viviente, Honduras," (unpublished report, Tegucigalpa, Honduras: Amor Viviente); Luis Cesar Flores, "Una Historia Breve de la Proyección de la Iglesia Evangélica Menonita Hondureña en el Programa Social," (unpublished paper, San Marcos, Honduras, July 2, 1983) available at MCC, Akron, Pa.; "SEMILLA, Seminario Anabautista Latinoamericano, Memoria 1984-1987," (Guatemala: SEMILLA, 1987); *MWH* (1978), 220-24; *MWH* (1984), 80-81; Luthy, *Amish Settlements* (1985), 2.

Hong Kong. The Mennonite presence in Hong Kong in 1988 was the Conference of Mennonite Churches in Hong Kong. It was related to the Eastern Mennonite Board of Missions and Charities (MC) and the Commission on Overseas Mission (GCM). It was founded in 1976 and had 3 congregations with a membership of 54 in 1988. Eight North American workers were serving in this work.   RSa

MWH (1984), 26; *GCM Handbook* (1988), 91.

Hoover, Christian (1793-1867), was born near Pleasant Hall in Franklin Co., Pa. He was ordained a bishop in the River Brethren Church in 1834. About 1857 Christian separated from the main body of River Brethren (Brethren in Christ) and helped organize the Lower District Old Order River Brethren congregation in Franklin Co. He was the son of Heinrich and Maria (Wenger) Hoover. He married Christena Oberholser (1798-1840) and had ten children. One of Christian's sons, John (1819-1886), became a bishop in the Upper District Old Order River Brethren congregation in Franklin Co. A large percentage of members among the Franklin County Old Order River Brethren are descended from Christian Hoover.   SES

Laban T. Brechkbill, *History Old Order River Brethren* (n.p.: Brechbill and Strickler, 1972), 156-59; Barbara H. and Anna Mary Burkholder, *The Genealogy of Henrich Huber* (Pleasant Hall, Pa., 1965), 60.

Hope Rescue Mission, South Bend, Ind. See Rescue Missions.

Hopi People. See Indians, North America.

Horch, Ben (b. Nov. 19, 1907). Benjamin Horch was born in Freidorf, Russia, of Lutheran Pietist parents. The Horch family moved to Winnipeg, Canada, in 1909. They worshiped in the North End Mennonite Brethren Church where Benjamin became a member in 1926. The Horch family was a musical family and two of his brothers became professional musicians in Winnipeg. In 1932 he married Esther Hiebert. They had one daughter.

He began his teaching career as choral director and teacher of music theory at Winnipeg Bible Institute (7 years). In 1934 he began a long career as "Kurseleiter" (choral clinician) for Mennonite churches in Canada. He became well known for introducing new music to choirs and encouraging young musicians. For four years he studied at the Bible Institute of Los Angeles (BIOLA). He returned to Manitoba where he directed music departments at Winkler Bible Institute (1943-44) and Mennonite Brethren Bible College (1944-55).

During this time he founded and conducted the Mennonite Symphony Orchestra, and was an editor of the Mennonite Brethren *Gesangbuch* (1952). In the mid-1950s he began working as a broadcaster in California and Manitoba, before becoming a music producer and consultant for the Canadian Broadcasting Corporation in Winnipeg. During this time he commissioned the "Mennonite Piano Concerto."   KR

Lloyd Siemens, "Ben Horch: Dean of Mennonite Conductors," *MM*, 4 (Oct. 1974), 12-14, (Nov 1974), 9-10; Peter Klassen, "The Many Contributions of Ben and Esther Horch," *Mennonite Brethren Historical Society Newsletter*, 3 (1982) 1-4; Wesley Berg, *From Russia With Music* (Winipeg: Hyperion, 1985); F. H. Epp, *Mennonites in Canada II*, p. 462.

"Horning Group." See Old Order Mennonites.

Horton, Rhondo D. (1895-June 23, 1986), was born to parents who had been slaves to the Horton family in Caldwell Co., N.C. He received his high school education in the Elk Park High School begun by the Krimmer Mennonite Brethren conference and Peter Siemens in 1927. Horton was ordained in the Krimmer Mennonite Brethren church in 1933. He continued as part-time minister and business man until his retirement in 1972. He was known for his well prepared sermons, his leadership of the conference and his wise advice. In the Boone, N.C., community he served as a major leader in peaceful change in race relations.   ADue

W. Kroeker, "Reverend Rhondo - Elderstatesman," *Chr. Leader* (June 1977), 8-9; K. Siemens, *Go Tell it on the Mountain* (privately printed, 1984, copy at Center for Mennonite Brethren Studies, Fresno).

Hospice Movement. Hospices, places of rest and entertainment, began almost 2,000 years ago with hospitality to pilgrims. When Dr. Cicely Saunders, founder of St. Christopher's Hospice in London, in the 1960s expanded and developed the idea of rest at the close of life's journey, the modern hospice movement was born. More recently this hospice movement, with emphasis on offering presence during the dying part of life's journey, began in North America. Mennonites have become involved in community needs assessments and planning and organizing of local hospice programs (e.g., in Virginia, California, Iowa, and Indiana.)

There are a large number of Mennonites from all walks of life involved as hospice volunteers. They are available to meet the needs of people facing °death. Nurses are involved in hospital-based hospice centers, community-based organizations, home health care agencies, and as volunteers. Ministers have become involved also in this team approach to care. There is no registry of Mennonite people involved in hospice ministries. Each is involved primarily on the local level.

Mennonites interviewed about their involvement have ready responses. One said, "It's natural because we've been doing it all along, but are now pushing it out to an organized thing." Another reported not being able to say good-bye to a parent. "Death deserved careful attention since it is as much a part of life as is birth."

Because people focus more on life as they are

given guidance in the dying process, involvement in hospice is a tremendous growth experience in communion with God our Maker.   LS

See also Death and Dying.

Hospitality is defined as the reception and entertainment of guests or strangers with liberality and kindness. Paul exhorted Christians at Rome to "contribute to the needs of the saints, practice hospitality" (Rom 12:13, RSV). Abraham received three angels and earnestly invited them and served them himself while Sarah, his wife took care to make ready provisions for his guests. (Gn 18:2-8). Peter and Paul with great care recommended hospitality to the faithful: "Use hospitality one to another without grudging" (1 Pet 4:9). Christ said, "I was a stranger and ye took me not in. Inasmuch as ye did it not to the least of these ye did it not to me" (Mt 25:41-45). Mary's humble receptivity in welcoming God's Spirit contrasts sharply with the lack of hospitality she and Joseph received at Bethlehem (Lk 1-2).

In Christian history hospitality and love of enemy (from the Latin, *hospes*, meaning "stranger") were considered an important virtue, above all in the medieval Catholic °monastic tradition. It is a basic practice and highly valued virtue in all traditional societies (°modernity). Affluent Mennonites from Mennonite Central Committee or mission boards have frequently remarked upon people in non-Western countries who receive guests generously and share meager food and lodging freely. Hospitality is becoming an important concept in °mission theology as well.

Mennonites have valued hospitality from their beginnings, having known exile and persecution themselves. °Menno Simons 1552, said "It is not customary that an intelligent person clothes and cares for one part of his body and leaves the rest naked. The intelligent person is solicitous for all his members. Thus it should be with those who are the Lord's church and body. All those born of God are called into one body and are prepared by love to serve their neighbors."

It was customary, and continues in the late 20th c. to a certain extent among the more °acculturated Mennonites groups in North America, and to a large extent among Amish and Old Order families to have their families and relatives as guests on Sunday for °visiting and eating together. Strangers and relatives from outside the community were invited, fed, and bedded. Tramps and hoboes generally received some food and at times a place to sleep at night. Mennonite hospitality in comparison with that of the general population remains a subject for careful research. Wives of ministers, °bishops, and °elders, were expected to carry a large responsibility for hosting visitors; some viewed this as a particular calling and ministry. Because it was not formally recognized as such, although frequently informally praised, some have criticized the greater attention given to the pastoral work of men when compared with lack of attention to this ministry by women.

Among some of the Dutch and northern German Mennonite groups it was customary to have *Vaspa* (light lunch) on Sunday afternoons for friends and visitors. This consisted of *Zwiebach* (a special bread roll), butter or preserves, possibly pieces of cheese or ham, and a torte or pie and coffee.

In the 1970s and 1980s the *Mennonite Your Way* directory has appeared, a listing of Mennonite families across the United States, Canada, and other countries who are willing to provide overnight lodging for Mennonites and other travelers. This to a certain extent expresses hospitality, even though hosts are often paid modestly for their services. People who have entertained or have been entertained have found "Mennonite Your Way" a very hospitable and rewarding experience.   ERK/DDM

John A. Hostetler, *Amish Society* (1980), 217-22; *Rule of St. Benedict*, ch. 53, 66; John Koenig, *New Testament Hospitality: Partnership with Strangers as Promise and Mission*, Overtures to Biblical Theology, 17 (Philadelphia: Fortress Press, ca. 1985); Mortimer Arias, "Centripetal Mission or Evangelization by Hospitality," *Missiology*, 10, no. 1 (Jan. 1982), 69-81.

Hospitals, Clinics, and Dispensaries (ME I:82; II:817). The years since the 1960s have witnessed a radical shift in what for almost 100 years had been a reasonably clear ministry of health care of the Mennonite churches through hospitals, clinics, and dispensaries. During this time most of the non-Western health care systems wrestled with issues of how to bring limited resources to meet overwhelming needs and how church and state resources could work together without exercising too much control over each other. Western countries were caught up much more in regulation, legislation, and technology. These and other radical influences changed markedly the shape and substance of health-related facilities in the United States and Canada.

Increase in technology and professionalism turned fairly simple health care structures into well paid, highly departmentalized, multispecialized systems. This increased the demand for additional layers of management as well as complicating the communication process necessary for efficiency. As the systems became more complicated, the composition of church ownership and operating boards changed from predominately clergy to a more complex mix of business, professional, and community leaders.

Policies and procedures once developed simply on the basis of a hospital's mission statement began to be shaped by government legislation, joint commission standards, and demands of third party payers (e.g., insurance companies). Religious health care facilities were not exempted from an increasing wave of suspicion and attack by consumer groups on high cost and fading creditability in health care systems. An increase in lawsuits and liability for hospitals and health professionals forced hospitals to join the wave of defensive medicine practices which perpetuated the vicious cycle.

Increased technology and improved techniques have made many long hospital stays unecessary and cut the average length of stay in hospitals in half, leaving many hospital beds unoccupied. Again, Mennonite hospitals fell prey to the same problems as other community health systems by having built for the demands of the 1960s only to find empty beds and serious financial problems in the late 1970s and early 1980s.

Some Mennonite health care systems became part of the creative thrust to innovate and pioneer in new health-related services such as outpatient and home care, adult day care, outpatient wellness programs, and creative pastoral care and counseling programs. However innovative and mission-minded these new services were, they did not produce large enough revenues to avoid financial crises. Some Mennonite hospitals were forced to close or sell out. Others consolidated with other Mennonite hospitals or with other church-related hospitals. The most significant of these consolidations occurred in 1981 when the Health and Welfare Committee of the Mennonite Board of Missions (MC) which had oversight of nine hospitals in addition to numerous nursing homes and facilities for the developmentally disabled and children, founded Mennonite Health Resources, Inc. A majority of the nine hospitals joined the new corporation which was to provide management resources and various other services to strengthen the financial, operational, and spiritual base for Mennonite hospitals.

Other factors for which Mennonite health systems were not always well equipped affected the shape and substance of hospital and health care ministries. Outside competition became aggressive and marketing of hospitals and health services led Mennonites to ask whether services that were initiated as a ministry and mission of the church should be advertised. As commercial health care systems became more common, they challenged church-related health care institutions to identify their distinctiveness. What had formerly been given to communities as a "gift" of ministry was now demanded by consumers as a "right."

One other factor made the Mennonite churches' efforts minister through health care systems more difficult. That was the onset of super technology creating difficult ethical issues. A variety of life and death issues and concerns about the quality of life arose (°bioethics). The high cost of service and decreasing availability of service to the poor became a serious moral issue. Very often institutions were called upon to make ethical decisions being pushed from one direction by physicians and consumers groups while being counseled in another direction by the church. Issues of °abortion and numerous situations surrounding the right to die, organ transplants, quality of life, etc. threatened relationships with supporting churches and often caused stress within congregations and conferences.

Those health care systems that survived the financial and other numerous threats of the 1960s and 1970s often did so through consolidation with other systems or by diversifying into areas such as nursing °homes and outpatient services. Some Mennonite health care systems saw as much as a hundredfold increase in budget during the 30 years between 1956 and 1986.

During that 30-year period there was a slight decrease in the number of Mennonite hospitals in the United States but a major increase in United States and Canada in Mennonite nursing homes, retirement centers, and programs for the °aging and disadvantaged. By 1987 the Congregational Health Ministries Handbook published by the Mennonite

Health Association listed some 167 Mennonite-related health and human services agencies, institutions, and programs in the United States and Canada.

During this time Mennonite Central Committee (MCC) and Mennonite-related °mission programs made great efforts to avoid ownership of any institutions or health systems in most countries being served by MCC workers or missionaries. It was their policy instead to send trained professionals to operate and function within facilities owned by governments or other agencies. In countries where the Mennonite Church had sufficient strength and identified hospital work as part of its mission (e.g., India, Taiwan) such hospitals continued not without struggle around similar issues of those in the United States and Canada.

One other effect of the crisis in institutional-based health care among Mennonites was an increase in the number of Mennonites training to go into health-related professions. In 1987 it was estimated that ca. 2,000-3,000 Mennonites served in the United States and Canada in some health-related system or profession. It is estimated that ca. 10 percent of all Mennonites in the United States work in fields related to health and human services.

Some historians have reflected upon the fact that the church has throughout its history responded to human needs in a spontaneous way that often becomes institutionalized only to be taken over later by governments or those who in some way are responsible for the maintenance of social systems and order. These historians have implied that the role of the church has been most effective in creating ministries of healing in response to the mandate of Christ. However once institutionalized these ministries fall prey to organizational hazards and lose their dynamic. This thesis may well be born out in observing the Mennonite health care efforts in United States and Canada during the 1980s. In this view, as hospitals and health care facilities became more dependent upon third party payers, government regulations, and legislation, they became less dependent upon the church, which, in turn withdrew its interest and support. This did not, however, alienate Mennonites from their original mandate to "preach, teach, and heal in the name of Christ." The Mennonite Health Association has become one such evidence of this effort on the part of Mennonite health professionals to nurture and encourage one another in their health-related calling and to speak to and with the church about its role and mission in health care.

By 1988 an umbrella corporation to aid and support hospitals and other health-related institutions was developed. This was a unified effort through MCC's work with Mennonite Mental Health Services and the Mennonite churches which owned a number of health-related facilities. In 1987 Mennonite Health Association, in cooperation with °Mennonite Mutual Aid, gave impetus to developing congregation health resources promoting various models by which congregations can become more active in the role of healers through preventive health care programs and other secondary ministries in local congregations (°health education). The congregation where people find meaning in relationship to God and their fellow human beings, is once again being seen as the place where health and healing begin. RRo

Current listings of Mennonite-related hospitals in North America are published in *MC Yearbook*. A partial listing of Mennonite-related hospitals and clinics outside North America follows (additional information on some of them is found in articles on these countries and the Mennonite conferences in these countries): *India*: Dhamtari Christian Hospital; Mennonite Brethren Medical Center, Jadcherla; Madhipura Christian Hospital; NavJivan Hospital, Satbarwa, Bihar State; Prendra Road Sanitarium; Sankra Christian Hospital; *Indonesia*: Kelet Christian Hospital; Tayu Christian Hospital; Mardi Rahayu Christian Hospital; *Paraguay*: Centro de Salud (Kilometer 81); *Taiwan*: Mennonite Christian Hospital; *Tanzania*: Bukiroba Dispensary; Bumangi Dispensary and Maternity Unit; Kisaka Bedded Dispensary; Mugumu Hospital; Mugango Dispensary and Maternity Unit; Nyabasi Dispensary and Maternity Unit; Shirati Hospital; *Zambia*: Macha Hospital; Sikalongo Hospital; *Zimbabwe*: Matopo Clinic; Wanezi Clinic; Phumula Hospital; Mtshabezi Hospital.

See also Mental Health Facilities.

Hostetler, Ida (Miller) and Sylvan Jay, can duly be called explorers. They began church work in settings in India and Ghana; they pastored Mennonite Church (MC) congregations in Illinois, Indiana, and Michigan. Not daunted by the unknown or difficult, they approached assignments intent to learn, with a spirit of adventure, with warmth toward people.

Born Sept. 16, 1900, Ida died on Jan. 5, 1972. S. J. lived from Mar. 7, 1901, until Oct. 7, 1978. Both were from Indiana; they married Aug. 22, 1924. Parents of one son and two daughters, Ida and S. J. were missionaries in India, 1928-49, and in Ghana, 1957-64, during which time they also explored mission possibilities in Nigeria. During S. J's last five years, he was married to Leona Yoder, who earlier served in Ethiopia and Jordan.

Whether at work with different idioms in language study; meeting needs of boarding school boys, of whom one-third were orphans; on preaching tour to scattered villages; fact-finding with missionaries of other denominations; attending to obstacles or hostility that new Christians met; deciding about schools for non-Christian girls; or reporting to North American churches, Jay and Ida believed in sharing the Good News. They believed in prayer, practiced humor, adapted with grace, and modeled teamwork.

After work in °Madhya Pradesh (Central Provinces), India, the decade of the 1940s was given by Hostetlers to establish a mission in °Bihar State. Working with tribal people who were primarily basket weavers, S. J. and Ida rejoiced when ten were baptized in 1941. Twelve years later there were 10 missionaries, 15 full-time Indian workers effective in gaining the confidence of people, and 92 church members.

Ida proved to be systematic in checking Home Bible Studies materials in Ghana; she created a course on the Gospel of Mark for new Christians. S. J. gathered 25 topics into a resource for baptism candidates. During 1958 and 1959 he made five trips to explore the Nigeria field. Convinced of the future in mission, both wrote informative articles, rich with anecdotes, for North American readers. DYN

S. J. Hostetler, *We Enter Bihar* (Elkhart, Ind.: MBM, India Mission Study Kit, 1951), also titled "History of Bihar Mennonite Mission 1940-1950," 45 pp.; idem, "Supplement to We Enter Bihar 1950-53" (1954), 14 pp.; idem, "The Mennonite Church in Ghana 1957-1964," (Elkhart: MBM, 1979?), 53 pp.; idem, "Beginning in Bihar," *Chr. Monitor* (Jan. 1946), 14-18; idem, "Lessons in Discipleship" (1956, 1958 editions), 64 pp.; frequent articles in *GH* by both S. J. and Ida Hostetler (*Menn. Bib. II*, p. 459).

Hostetter, Christian N., Jr. (1899-1980), was born in Lancaster Co., Pa. His father, Christian Hostetter, was bishop of the Manor District of the Brethren in Christ Church and president of Messiah Bible College (later Messiah College) from 1916 to 1921. C. N. Hostetter, Jr., attended the college. After graduation in 1922, he served as pastor of the Refton congregation near the city of Lancaster. At the same time he earned a living by selling peanut butter for Mennonite minister and businessman John Moseman.

In 1934 Hostetter became president of Messiah Bible College. He served in that role until 1960, and continued to teach on a part-time basis until 1963. Following his resignation as president, he pastored the Brethren in Christ congregation at Palmyra, Pa., until 1970.

Hostetter was active in numerous other ways in the denomination. For nearly 50 years he was a much requested evangelist. From 1924 to 1953 he was a member of the Home Mission Board, for most of those years as secretary, the remainder as chairman. Through the 1950s he sat on the Church Review and Study Committee, a body that led the denomination in a significant transition in its life and thought. From 1959 onward he was a member of the Publication Board. He was moderator of General Conference four times, and delivered the General Conference sermon a record three times. From 1936 to 1957 he was bishop of the Grantham district (3 congregations).

In time, Hostetter became active outside the Brethren in Christ Church. He sat for two terms on the Board of Administration of the National Association of Evangelicals (NAE). In 1953 he was appointed to the World Relief Commission (NAE), and from 1959 to 1967 was its chairman. Hostetter brought a strong peace position to the NAE, on several occasions helping to organize sessions to facilitate dialogue between those holding opposing views on peace.

Outside his own denomination, Hostetter's most significant work was done with the Mennonite Central Committee (MCC). During World War II he was active in °°Civilian Public Service ministry. In 1948 he became the Brethren in Christ representative on MCC. From 1953 to 1967 he served as MCC chairman. Thus he was chairman of two world relief agencies,—MCC and the World Relief Commission, at the same time. He made several trips abroad for MCC as an administrator and in pastoral ministry. EMS

E. Morris Sider, *Messenger of Grace: A Biography of C. N. Hostetter, Jr.* (Nappanee, Ind., 1982); C. J. Dyck, *Something Meaningful for God* (Scottdale, 1981), 170-93; *EV* (Aug. 25, 1980), 5.

House Churches, in 20th-c. Mennonite experience, are groups of people small enough to meet face-to-face, who have covenanted with God and with each other to be the church under the authority of Christ and the guidance of the Spirit. House churches often meet in homes, but may sometimes meet in public buildings or church meetinghouses. More important than the place of meeting is the closeness of relationships implied by the word "house."

While house churches are known by a variety of terms ("small groups," "K-groups," "Koinonia groups," "care groups," "base communities"), house churches differ from groups organized only for fellowship or only for Bible study in that they are free to take on all or almost all the functions of the church, including °worship, pastoral care, accountability, teaching, gift discernment, °decision-making, and °mission and °service.

Some congregations are made up of one house church of 7 to 20 people. Other congregations are clusters of several house churches that may meet jointly as often as once a week or as infrequently as once every seven weeks. House churches tend to be found more often in cities, where people may not have close extended family or other networks of relationship with other Christians. They are looking for more caring and accountability than they might get from simply attending worship on Sunday morning in a large congregation.

Among Mennonites, house churches have been part of the neo-Anabaptist renewal movement, seeking to embody the values of Anabaptism in a 20th-c. environment (°restitutionism).

Churches have met in houses since New Testament times (see Acts 2:41-27; 12:12; 16:15, 40; 17:7ff.; Rom 16:5; 1 Cor 16:15, 19; Col 4:15; Phlm 2). The early churches' move from house to sanctuary or basilica generally coincided with the Constantinian change from independent church to government-endorsed church in the Roman empire. As the center of worship moved from the house church to the altar, the Lord's Supper became not a fellowship meal, but a rite of the altar.

Throughout the centuries, renewal movements within Christianity have rediscovered the house church in the New Testament. Monastic movements often worshiped in small groups and emphasized discipline and accountability. The Anabaptists in 16th-c. Europe often met in homes, not only to hide from heresy-hunting authorities, but as a symbol of a community of covenanted believers who cared for each other, admonished each other, and both gave and received in their meetings for worship. Early Quakers and Methodists in England and Pietists on the continent also met in homes.

Modern interest in the house church arose from the writings of Ernest Southcott, an Anglican parish priest, published in the United States in 1956. Hans-Ruedi Weber, then chairman of the Department of Laity of the World Council of Churches, also published an article on house churches, which was reprinted by Mennonites in *Concern,* No. 5 (June 1958). Some Mennonites within this °*Concern* movement in 1957 began Reba Place Fellowship, Evanston, Ill., an intentional community following the house-church concept. Many Mennonite house churches have also gained inspiration from the Church of the Saviour, Washington, D.C.

There is no accurate estimate of the number of house churches currently among Mennonites in North America. The 1986 *Mennonite Yearbook* listed 46 "church communities" in the United States and Canada, but some congregations were included that were not communities or house churches and other house churches were not listed. In addition to the congregations that are made up strictly of one or more house churches, many larger Mennonite congregations have several "house churches" or "small groups" performing many of the functions of house churches.

Mennonite churches in Taiwan and Japan are generally small and have often functioned as house churches. Among other Christian groups, house churches are numerous. Mainline Protestant, Catholic, evangelical, and nondenominational house churches are found around the world and are serving as a means of church renewal. An estimated 20,000 Catholic base communities are meeting in Brazil alone.   LB

Robert and Julia Banks, *The Home Church: Regrouping the People of God for Community and Mission* (Sutherland, Australia: Albatross Books Pty. Ltd., 1986); Robert Banks, *Paul's Idea of Community: The Early House Churches in Their Historical Setting* (Grand Rapids: Eerdmans, 1980); Lois Barrett, *Building the House Church* (Scottdale, 1986); Del Birkey, *The House Church: Model for Renewing the Church* (Scottdale, 1988); *Christianity and Crisis,* 41 (Sept. 21, 1981), sp. issue; *The House Church,* published by the Commission on Home Ministries (GCM) (Newton, 1978-85); Dave Jackson, *Coming Together: All Those Communities and What They're Up To* (Minneapolis: Bethany Fellowship, 1978); Bernard J. Lee and Michael A. Cowan, *Dangerous Memories: House Churches and Our American Story* (Kansas City, Mo.: Sheed and Ward, 1986); Elizabeth O'Connor, *Call to Commitment: The Story of the Church of the Saviour, Washington, D.C.* (New York: Harper and Row, 1963); Charles M. Olsen,*The Base Church: Creating Community Through Multiple Forms* (Atlanta: Forum House Publishers, 1973); *The Other Side,* vol. 13, no. 2 (April, 1977), sp. issue; Ernest Southcott, *The Parish Comes Alive* (New York: Morehouse-Gorham Co., 1956); Virgil Vogt, "Small Congregations," *Concern,* no. 5 (June 1958), 52-67; Hans-Ruedi Weber, "The Church in the House," *Concern,* no. 5 (June 1958), 7-28.

See also Meetinghouses; Restitutionism; Iglesia Hermanos en Cristo, Nicaragua.

House of Friendship of Kitchener, Kitchener, Ont. See Rescue Missions.

Hübert, Jakob Fr. (June 14, 1873 - Sept. 25, 1964). Born at Margenau, Molotschna, he was converted and baptized in the Mennonite Brethren Church at age 17. He married Helene Kasdorf 1903 and moved to the Omsk, Siberia, region where he was ordained minister (1907) and elder (1913).

He was arrested in 1929 but escaped to Germany, from where he emigrated to Brazil in 1930. He was elected to organize and lead the new Mennonite Brethren church, which required wisdom and love to shape a congregation whose members had come from many different parts of Russia. In 1936 he was called to serve as leader of the Mennonite Brethren church in Curitiba. With the coming of World War II use of the German language was prohibited, forcing him to preach and lead worship in Low German (closely related to Dutch). He was known particularly for his pastoral concern and the irenic spirit in which he worked with others including elder David °Koop of the [°kirchliche] Mennonite congregation (GCM). He was one of the last to serve in the office of °elder in the Mennonite Brethren church.   HlnaEns

Hubmaier, (Huebmör), Balthasar (ME II:826), an Anabaptist theologian and martyr. Educated at the universities of Freiburg (im Breisgau) and Ingolstadt. In the latter university he was both the prorector and lecturer in theology before becoming cathedral preacher at Regensburg. In 1521, Hubmaier became pastor at Waldshut. While here he began to embrace certain Reformation concepts. By the October Disputation in Zürich (1523), after a brief second stay at Regensburg, he openly championed the Swiss Reformation. Upon his return to Waldshut he began to reform the faith and order of his church and those of his fellow priests. His reformatory efforts were accompanied by a vigorous writing campaign in which he set forth a form of Reformation teaching that was neither Lutheran nor Zwinglian but had an affinity with the emerging Anabaptism of Zürich. By Easter, 1525, Hubmaier was baptized by Wilhelm °Reublin along with 60 of his parishioners and he, in turn baptized some 300 others. The Anabaptist movement in Waldshut was short-lived since a threatened invasion by Austria drove Hubmaier and his wife from the city. After imprisonment and torture in Zürich, he managed to escape, a chastened and subdued man. Hubmaier next became the leading pastor in Nikolsburg, Moravia, in 1526 where he won local preachers for Anabaptism and the Lichtenstein barons, as well. It was here that Anabaptism enjoyed in greatest numerical success. After 16 or 17 months, Hubmaier and his wife (Elizabeth Hugeline) were arrested by King Ferdinand of Austria, who had recently acquired jurisdiction of Moravia. After a time of imprisonment in Vienna and the Kreuzenstein Castle, where he was tortured, Hubmaier was taken to Vienna and burned to death on Mar. 10, 1528. His wife was drowned in the Danube three days later.

Controversial in life, Hubmaier was no less so in death. Although he was not a thorough-going pacifist, neither was he the militant advocate of war he has at times been represented. He did hold the possibility of a Christian magistrate and argued further that a Christian would make a better magistrate than a non-Christian. In all other major doctrines he was in step with the majority of Anabaptists. In fact, he was the most eloquent spokesman and profound theologian of 16th-c. Anabaptism. His writings on religious freedom, baptism, and freedom of the will became foundational. He can be considered the theologian of the "new birth" for he was the first to articulate clearly the concept that became basic in Anabaptist and Mennonite self-understanding and an essential ingredient in evangelical soteriology. Hubmaier's lasting significance is evident more in his writings than in personal influence. Even the Hutterites, whose leader he had opposed in Nikolsburg, were greatly indebted to him for much of their faith and practice. His published works in German and in English still stimulate and challenge those who like Hubmaier hold to believers' baptism.   WRE, Jr.

Torsten Bergsten, *Balthasar Hubmaier: Seine Stellung zu Reformation und Täufertum, 1521-1518* (Kassel, 1961; abridged Engl. transl. Valley Forge: Judson Press, 1978); W. R. Estep, Jr., "Von Ketzern und iren Verbrennern: A Sixteenth Century Tract on Religious Liberty," in *MQR*, 43 (1969), 271-282; idem, "Balthasar Hubmaier: Martyr without Honor," in *Baptist History and Heritage*, 13, no. 2 (1978), 5-10, 27; idem, "The Anabaptist View of Salvation," *Southwestern Journal of Theology* 20, no. 2 (1978), 32-49; Walter Klaassen, "Speaking in Simplicity: Balthasar Hubmaier," *MQR*, 40 (1966), 139-47, examines Hubmaier's hermeneutics; Gunnar Westin and Torsten Bergsten, eds., *Balthasar Hubmaier Schriften*, vol. 29 in *Quellen zur Geschichte der Täufer IX* (Karlsruhe, 1962), critical edition; an English translation of Hubmaier's writings trans. and ed. by John Howard Yoder and Wayne Pipkin will appear as CRR 5 (Scottdale, 1989); John D. Rempel, "Christology and Lord's Supper in Anabaptism: A Study in the Theology of Balthasar Hubmaier, Pilgram Marpeck, and Dirk Philips" (ThD diss., St. Michael's College, Toronto School of Theology, 1986); Christoph Windhorst, *Täuferisches Taufverständnis: Balthasar Hubmaiers Lehre Zwischen traditioneller und reformatorischer Theologie* (Leiden: Brill, 1976); David C. Steinmetz, "Scholasticism and Radical Reform: Nominalist Motifs in the Theology of Balthasar Hubmaier," *MQR*, 45 (1971), 123-44; James M. Stayer, *Sword* (1972, 1976), esp. 104-7, 141-45.

Huisinga-Bakker, Pieter. See Bakker, Pieter Huisinga.

Human Rights are those basic rights which, when afforded by one person to another, indicate a belief in the other's full humanity. Where a person or group denies these basic rights to others, that denial indicates a belief that the others are less than human.

The most basic human rights are the rights to life, self-determination, and personal security. Self-determination means deciding, within reasonable limits, where one will live, how one will support oneself, and with whom one will associate. Personal security means physical safety from violence. Oppression is the taking away of any of these rights. Oppression becomes slavery where it includes taking from others the fruit of their labors. In industrialized capitalist societies individual liberty is the key criterion of human rights. In industrialized socialist societies the key is the right to social participation. For poor, nonindustrialized societies the key is a right to survival and liberation from oppression by industrialized societies.

When Anabaptists claimed the right to religious self-determination it led to brutal oppression. As toleration for Anabaptists increased, they began to lead lives of quiet prosperity. Concern for individual poor people, rather than concern for oppressive structures which created poverty, was an interest of Anabaptists. Separation of church and state, which would give Anabaptists religious freedom, was the only systemic human rights issue which they addressed with any concentration.

Anabaptist groups began to work for privileges for themselves, and have been successful in many places. Special °privileges were granted to Mennonites by Catherine the Great of Russia to induce them to migrate to the Ukraine. Mennonites have also obtained special privileges in the United States, Canada, Mexico, Bolivia, Paraguay, Belize (British Honduras), and other places. Ethnic European Mennonites have colonized lands freshly taken from native peoples. Concern for displaced native peoples has been real among these Mennonites, but has not extended to giving up special privileges.

Mennonites participated to some extent in the effort to abolish slavery in the United States, and have, since World War II, been active in helping to reclaim human rights for native peoples and mentally and physically handicapped persons (°disabilities). Mennonites have been active in working for °peace in many ways, and have begun to focus more on restoration of °justice as a way to peace. Victim-Offender °Reconciliation Program is a method by which Mennonites have worked to bring peace between individuals by showing victims and offenders how to recognize each other's full humanity.

Mennonites have, along with the rest of the world, discovered the issue of human rights on a broad scale only since World War II. The advent of mass communications has allowed all to understand more clearly how oppression breeds war, and how the denial of human rights leads to violence as the poor and powerless seek to be heard by the rich and powerful. Mennonite efforts on behalf of the oppressed around the world recognize increasingly that restoration of human rights is part of the ministry of reconciliation given by God to those who believe the message of salvation.   DR-H

Margaret E. Crahan, ed., *Human Rights and Basic Needs in the Americas* (Washington, D.C.: Georgetown U. Press, 1982); Frank H. Epp, *Human Rights and Christian Responsibility* (Winnipeg: MCC [Canada], n.d.); Robert A. Evans, and Alice Frazer Evans, *Human Rights; A Dialogue Between the First and Third Worlds* (Maryknoll: Orbis Books, 1983); Alfred Hennelly, S.J., and John Langan, S.J., eds., *Human Rights in the Americas: The Struggle for Consensus* (Washington, D.C.: Georgetown U. Press, 1982); Urbane Peachey, ed., *Mennonite Statements on Peace and Social Concerns, 1900-1978* (Akron, Pa.: MCC, 1980).

Human Nature. See Grace; Sexuality; Sin.

Humanism (ME II:841). To consider the term *humanism* in an Anabaptist and Mennonite context is to confront at the very outset a significant definitional problem. In the 20th c. the term has come to imply a world view that is uncompromisingly and exclusively secular and nonreligious, a view that has been reinforced both by the self-proclaimed "humanists" and their °Fundamentalist Christian detractors. The *Humanist Manifesto II* (1973) openly denies the existence or significance of a supernatural power; the Fundamentalists have equated humanism, often with the modifier *secular* added, with atheism and reduced the term to a kind of catchword for all manner of evil in the modern world. If this radically secular definition of humanism is accepted, then *Christian Humanism* is a self-contradictory term and then humanism can only be seen as antithetical to the most fundamental tenets of the Mennonite faith.

Even a cursory review of the origins of the term, however, reveals the inadequacies of this oversimplified 20th c. definition. When applied to the 16th c., for example, the term humanism carries a markedly different connotation. Paul Oskar Kristeller, perhaps the greatest contemporary scholar of Renaissance humanism, defines the term very narrowly as deriving from the *humanista*, the professional teachers of the *studia humanitatis* (the

"studies befitting a human being" or the "study of the humanities"). Since the Renaissance humanists were unquestionably more enamored of the excellence and dignity of mankind than had generally been the case during the Middle Ages, early historians of the Renaissance, for example, Jacob Burckhardt (1818-97), emphasized, indeed overemphasized, the secular nature of Renaissance humanism. More recent historical scholarship, however, has demonstrated that such an image of an irreligious, or even nonreligious, Renaissance humanism is simply not supported by the evidence. Lewis Spitz, *The Religious Renaissance of the German Humanists* (1963), established without question the religious—even devout—nature of humanism in the north of Europe. Charles Trinkaus, *In Our Image and Likeness; Humanity and Divinity in Italian Humanist Thought* (1970), similarly shattered the myth of a pagan Italian Renaissance humanism. The best historical evidence, therefore, suggests that the Renaissance humanists were, in virtually all cases, Christian; indeed, in many of the most outstanding cases, they were deeply Christian. This is especially true with the "Prince of the Humanists," Desiderius °°Erasmus of Rotterdam (1466?-1536). Though early 20th-c. historians emphasized a highly rational, largely secular Erasmus, the overwhelming consensus of modern scholarship portrays a profoundly Christian Erasmus. In the 16th c., then, the term *Christian humanist* is more self-evident than paradoxical.

This distinction is critical, because it has long been recognized that a good number (e.g., Conrad °Grebel, Hans °Denck) of the 16th-c. Anabaptists received "humanistic" educations and moved in humanist circles. They clearly read (and in a few cases may even have visited) Erasmus. Moreover, there are a number of apparent similarities between the agenda of 16th-c. humanism and the theology of the Anabaptists. The humanists were committed to returning to the pure sources of classical and Christian civilization; their rallying cry was *ad fontes* ("to the sources"); they looked to those sources for models of behavior, exemplars after whom to pattern their own lives. Anabaptists likewise sought to restore primitive Christianity: their commitment was to the °restitution of 1st-c. Christianity, not to the reformation of 16th-c. Christianity; and they found their exemplar in the person of Jesus Christ. The humanists emphasized human freedom and dignity; the Anabaptists, in contrast to all the major Protestant movements in the 16th c., denied the doctrine of predestination and insisted on an anthropology of free will. And, for the humanists, behavior—not belief—was the measure of a man; similarly, for the Anabaptists, discipleship (i.e., behavior)—not belief—was the key to °salvation.

An earlier generation of Mennonite historians, seeing the similarities but convinced that humanism and Christianity were mutually exclusive categories, simply denied the possibility of influence. Thus Harold S. °Bender, for example, could claim that Conrad Grebel's humanist period "made no evident contribution to his religious life or thinking" (*ME* II: 569). But in light of the research of Kristeller, Spitz, Trinkaus, and others, we can acknowledge the reality of Christian humanism and affirm its role as one of the formative influences which shaped 16th-c. Anabaptism.   DRS

For the *Humanist Manifesto II*, see *The Humanist*, 33 (Sept.-Oct. 1973), 4-9. For a thorough and precise discussion of the term "humanism," see Vito R. Giustiniani, "Homo, Humanus, and the Meanings of 'Humanism,'" *J. of the History of Ideas*, 46 (Apr.-June 1985), 167-95. For discussions of the nature of Renaissance humanism, see Paul Oskar Kristeller, *Renaissance Thought: The Classic, Scholastic, and Humanistic Strains* (New York: Harper and Row, 1961), esp. 110-12, and other works by Kristeller; Lewis Spitz, *The Religious Renaissance of The German Humanists* (Cambridge, Mass.: Harvard, 1963); and Charles Trinkaus, *In Our Image and Likeness: Humanity and Divinity in Italian Humanist Thought*, 2 vols. (U. of Chicago Press, 1970), and *The Scope of Renaissance Humanism* (Ann Arbor, Mich.: U. of Michigan Press, 1983). On Anabaptism and humanism generally, see Robert Kreider, "Anabaptism and Humanism; An Inquiry into the Relationship of Humanism to the Evangelical Anabaptists," *MQR*, 26 (1952), 123-41. For discussions of Erasmian influence on the Anabaptists, see Cornelis Augustijn, "Erasmus and Menno Simons," *MQR*, 60 (1986), 197-508; Kenneth R. Davis, "Erasmus as a Progenitor of Anabaptist Theology and Piety," *MQR*, 47 (1973), 163-78; Thor Hall, "Possibilities of Erasmian Influence on Denck and Hubmaier in Their Views of Freedom of the Will," *MQR*, 35 (1961), 149-70; CRR 4; Dale R. Schrag, "Erasmian and Grebelian Pacifism: Consistency or Contradiction?" *MQR* (forthcoming).

Humanitarianism, a broad term that generally denotes thinking and action centered in humans and for the benefit of the human species. Like humanism, it distinguishes itself on the one hand from the bestial and on the other from the divine. In a strict sense, humanitarian is one who promotes human welfare and social reform without reference to God or Jesus Christ. To examine humanitarianism is to take a closer look at philanthropy, the effort of promoting good will and human welfare by the will and action of humans alone.

Thus seen, humanitarianism is for some Mennonites a pejorative term when applied to °relief and °service efforts of the church. Other Mennonites regard any act of love as a witness to God. To reject the humanitarian component in the complex matrix of service is not without its pitfalls. All service is of necessity performed by people for people, even when the motivation is to glorify God. To negate the human element in the churches' relief and °development work is to deny that "love, joy, peace, patience, kindness, goodness, faithfulness, gentleness and self-control" (Gal. 5:22) need flesh and blood to make them useful and real. When John says that "the Word became flesh and dwelt among us," (Jn 1:14) he is affirming the humanness of Jesus Christ. Recognizing the extent of inhuman behavior in society, the mischief done by ruthless dictators, the senseless battles fought over ideologies, the shameful enslaving and exploitation of the many by the few, one gains a new appreciation for the milk of human kindness. Perhaps this is what Jesus had in mind when He said that what was done "to one of the least of these my brethren, [was done] to Me" (Mt 25:40).

On the other hand it is well to remember that men and women are not the measure of all things, that there is more to life than easing the lot for others, and that ultimately all our good works are meaningless unless they point to Him who is the source of all life.   PJD

Humanities. See Historical Writing; Historiography; Literature; Philosophy; Theology.

Humility. Christians have traditionally considered pride to be the most basic of human sins, and humility a most necessary attitude for persons to come into proper relationship with God. Teachers and preachers from John Cassian (ca. 360-ca. 435), Pope Gregory I (ca. 540-604), and Thomas Aquinas (ca. 1225-74) to William F. "Billy" Graham (b. 1918) have put pride on the list of the seven or eight chief sins. In the 16th century, the Protestant reformers Martin °°Luther and John °°Calvin considered pride, or *hubris*, the very essence of fallen humans' rebellion against God.

For 16th-c. Anabaptists, if one attitude underlay all sin, it was disobedience. And when they defined obedience they did not make humility the central or organizing idea. Instead, borrowing apparently from medieval °monastics and °mystics, they emphasized *Gelassenheit* (yieldedness), self-denial, readiness to suffer, and *Nachfolge* (°discipleship—imitation and following after Christ). Of course those were self-denying concepts in the same family with humility. And as Anabaptist writers elaborated, they mentioned humility as characteristic of a truly Christian life and walk. Moreover, before the 16th c. ended, some Anabaptists developed very explicit rules for expressing humility. For instance a discipline drawn up at Strasbourg in 1568 enjoined tailors and seamstresses to make and members to wear only simple and plain clothing, to wear "nothing for pride's sake." Nonetheless, in Anabaptist thought and teaching, the ideas of pride and humility were not as central as they were for the Protestant reformers—or as they would become about 1800, in a quite different way, for Mennonites in North America.

In North America, in the first three-quarters of the 19th c., humility assumed its most important and comprehensive role ever in Anabaptist-Mennonite understanding of Christian faithfulness. In 1763 in a posthumous book, *Eine Restitution. . . .*, a very influential eastern-Pennsylvania elder named Heinrich °°Funck asked why Jesus' nonresistant followers were no longer suffering. His remarks were only a small part of his book, but the most practical part. Funck's answer: °Suffering had ended because nonresistant Christians had sought political power, °wealth, and other marks of status to the point that the world no longer saw them as a rebuke to its proud ways. Suffering would return if Jesus' followers would be more humble.

To Funck, the test of whether one stood against the ways of the world, the mark of the true Christian, was suffering. However, within three or four decades a shift occurred. The mark came to be humility itself. The shift was especially clear in a small book by Christian °°Burkholder, a pastor and elder in Lancaster Co., Pa.: *Nützliche und Erbauliche Anrede an die Jugend* (*Helpful and Edifying Address to Youth*), penned in 1792, published in 1804. Through Burkholder's *Address* ran a central motif: Jesus' peaceable followers were humble. They studiously avoided all impulses and marks of pride and self-promotion, whether spiritual or outward.

Burkholder did not call on youth to follow a grand and conquering Christ. He taught new birth and °atonement through Jesus' shed blood, yet his call was not even primarily for sinners to come and repent beneath the Savior's cross. Instead it was for the earnest seeker to follow the "meek and lowly" Jesus—in practical life and walk. To Jesus' manger, Burkholder wrote, "we are to direct our course." The Christ in the manger was "an example to us of true humility."

For six or seven decades after the first printings of Burkholder's *Address* its humility theology dominated North American Mennonite (and Amish) thought. The second edition, published the same year as the first, carried an endorsement from 27 ministers and deacons of the influential Lancaster Mennonite community. Before the 19th c. ended, the booklet appeared in a dozen German or English editions. More editions came in the 20th c., mainly for Old Order groups.

As yet no scholar has adequately explained the shift to humility theology. Possible explanations include: (1) In America, Mennonites were getting on so well economically and socially that the suffering idea grew too distant from their experience; so they sought another motif for self-denial. In this view, Heinrich Funck's desire for suffering was ironic, for he himself was a wealthy miller, landowner, and bishop with ample prestige in his own circles. (2) Mennonites borrowed humility language from °Pietists. To find phrasing that became the code-language of 19th-c. Mennonite humility theology one has only to read key passages from an early Pietist, Johann °°Arndt. Book two, chapter eleven of Arndt's *Wahres Christenthum*, for instance, continually pits the *Demut* (humility), *Armut* (weakness, poverty), and *Sanftmut* (meekness) of the pious against the *Hofart* (pride, arrogance) and *Weltliebe* (love of the world) of ungodly neighbors. (3) Mennonites were reacting against aggressive self-assertion which they found particularly in the newly formed United States, some of it expressed in revivalism. It is clear in Burkholder's *Address* that its author rejected both the slogans of liberty so common in the new nation and a tendency of revivalists to speak much of their personal religious experience. To him the test of genuine new birth was objective fruits, not such testimonies. And his list of fruits began with humility.

Whatever hypotheses are correct, humility theology provided Mennonites with a message very relevant to Americans. It was not a complete message, for it contained almost nothing of the triumphant, conquering tone also to be found in the Bible. Moreover, it carried a built-in dilemma: the very humility that Mennonites might have offered as a prophetic message to the proud "world" held them back from asserting the message clearly and forthrightly. But whatever its problems, humility theology stood in sharp contrast to the public mood of the United States just when that nation was acting on boasts of "manifest destiny" and other arrogant slogans. Hardly any message could have been more relevant to the time and place.

Compared to Burkholder's *Address* other Mennonite writings did not state the humility paradigm quite so prominently. Some of these other writings include *A Description of the New Creature* (1838, in English and German) by eastern-Pennsylvania minister Abraham °°Godshalk and commentaries which Virginia elder Peter °°Burkholder added to an 1837 edition of an old Dutch Mennonite confession. Yet the theme was there, by then taken more or less for granted. Humility theology had taken deep root. That fact is evident for instance throughout early volumes of the *Herald of Truth*, the paper John F. °°Funk began publishing in 1864 primarily for "old Mennonites" (MC) and Amish Mennonites. In 1866 and 1867 there came a fresh and more self-conscious statement of humility theology: *Pride and Humility*, a small booklet in English and in German by the Ohio "old Mennonite" elder and church-wide leader John M. °°Brenneman. Brenneman recounted salvation history essentially as God's efforts to deal with human pride and spelled out how humility should express itself objectively: in plainness of furniture or buildings or attire, in accepting a modest position at table, and in other very particular, visible, practical, day-to-day ways.

Such emphasis on the practical and visible was a strong feature of that early 19th-c. humility theology. While not ignoring the inner quality, Mennonites insisted that humility show itself explicitly and objectively rather than remain essentially spiritual and subjective. The theology of humility reinforced pacifism and vice versa: the meek and humble were also those who let themselves be vulnerable rather than seeking vengeance or doing violence, and vice versa. Moreover, from the Protestant Reformation onward, Protestants had put greater emphasis than had Anabaptists on the steps of repentance and yielding which prepared the way for initial °justification; Anabaptists and Mennonites put somewhat greater emphasis on the self-denial and yielding which would make possible a Christian walk and a genuine discipleship after initial, forensic justification. In the 19th c. the same difference reappeared in the way Mennonites and Protestants treated humility. Careful investigation would probably show that while Mennonites borrowed humility language from Pietism, they used the words differently, referring less to the yielding and submission of self in the *Bußkampf* (repentance-struggle—a favorite concept of Pietists) and more to the lifestyle and outer marks of faithfulness of Christians, both individually and as church. Something similar may have accompanied the Mennonite encounter with °revivalism: Lewis O. Saum has demonstrated that there was a strong theme of humility also in the faith and outlook of many everyday Americans in contrast to bombastic rhetoric of their nation and its leaders. But again, a careful reading of Saum suggests an emphasis more subjective than that of the Mennonites, an emphasis focused more on spiritual submission and repentant yielding.

Humility theology took root primarily among "old Mennonites" (MC) and Amish in America, and even more deeply among old-order groups as they emerged during or at the close of humility theology's era. "Progressives" such as the constitutional reformer John H. °Oberholtzer in 1847 and the founders of the °°General Conference (GCM) in

1860, or revivalists such as Daniel °°Hoch in Ontario or Daniel °°Brenneman in Indiana, chose other principles. Indeed, to a large extent they reacted against humility theology as not activist enough, or not sufficiently modern, or not enough oriented to inner religious experience. As for "Russian" Mennonites who settled in North America in the 1870s, few of them made humility their main paradigm. To be sure, some small "Russian" Mennonite groups had something which resembled humility theology. For instance in 1833 in the Ukraine an articulate *Kleine Gemeinde* (°Evangelical Mennonite Conference) minister named Heinrich °°Balzer published a pamphlet which among other points lamented Mennonites' preoccupation with business and their "pride, ostentation, vanity, greed for money, lust for wealth, avarice," and other signs of degeneracy. And although °°Krimmer Mennonite Brethren who left the Crimea and settled near Hillsboro, Kans., in 1874, emphasized inner experience more than did North American Mennonite humility theology, their rules called for plain carriages and dress and other objective signs of humility much as John M. Brenneman did in his booklet. But for the larger groups coming from the Tsarist Russia, humility was not the central concept. Of course, like virtually all Christians, they and progressive Mennonites with longer histories in America taught that humility was a key Christian virtue. But teaching it as a virtue, even a key one, was not the same as using it to define the very self-identity of the followers of Jesus. It was not the same as making it the central test of faithfulness.

Among "old" and Amish Mennonites, John M. Brenneman's booklets of 1867 marked a climax; soon thereafter, humility theology rapidly waned. Within 15 years younger leaders led especially by evangelist John S. °°Coffman were creating a Mennonite quickening (called by partisans a "great awakening" [°renaissance, Mennonite]) which brought revivalism, churchwide programs and institutions, and a general spirit of activism. The main code words of the quickening era were not "humility" and "the meek and lowly Jesus" but rather "active" and "aggressive work." The test of faithfulness became not a life-style eschewing pride so much as vigorous Christian service. Coffman and such leaders as Menno S. °°Steiner and Daniel °Kauffman still taught plainness and sometimes spoke of meekness or humility. But now plainness was not always the mark of a meek and quiet spirit. It could just as well be an aggressive °nonconformity—a way (as a young activist put it in 1894) for God's army to appear in uniform.

No doubt a great deal of the self-perception of humility survived in the folk-Mennonite soul long after the public discourse of "old" Mennonites and Amish Mennonites had become more assertive and aggressive. But the era of making humility the central, organizing ideal of objective Mennonite faithfulness had ended. The time of making it the central difference between God's peaceful children and a status-seeking and vengeful world, had passed. By about 1885 or 1890 the era of humility theology was history.   TFS

Joseph C. Liechty, "Humility: The Foundation of Mennonite Religious Outlook in the 1860s," *MQR*, 54 (1980), 5-31; [Christian Burkholder], *Nützliche und Erbauliche Anrede an die Jugend* ([Ephrata, Pa.?], 1804); or *Useful and Edifying Address to the Young. . . .*, bound as pp. 179-257 with [Gerrit Roosen], *Christian Spiritual Conversation on Saving Faith, for the Young, in Questions and Answers. . . .* (Lancaster, Pa.: John Baer and Sons, 1857) esp. 183-84, 187-89, 194-95, 206, 211, 218-24, 227-28, 239-44 (1857 ed.); John M. Brenneman, *Pride and Humility: A Discourse, Setting Forth the Characteristics of the Proud and the Humble*, first published as a series of articles in *Herald of Truth* in 1866; or as a separate pamphlet, *Hoffart und Demuth: Einander gegenüber gestellt* (Elkhart, Ind.: John F. Funk, 1867); MEA 1: 176-82; MEA 2: ch. 1, 4; Theron F. Schlabach, "The Humble Become Aggressive Workers," *MQR*, 52 (1978), 113-26; Lewis O. Saum, *The Popular Mood of Pre-Civil War America* (Westport, Conn.: Greenwood Press, 1980); Kenneth R. Davis, *Anabaptism and Asceticism* (Scottdale, 1974), esp. ch. 4; Robert Friedmann, *The Theology of Anabaptism* (Scottdale, 1973), esp. pp. 65-70; Johann Arndt, *Sechs Bücher vom Wahren Christenthum. . .* (Philadelphia: J. Kohler, 1866), esp. pp. 506-08, trans. and abridged by Peter C. Erb as *True Christianity* (New York: Paulist, 1979); Heinrich Balzer, *Verstand und Vernunft*, trans. and ed. in Robert Friedmann, "Faith and Reason: The Principles of Mennonitism Reconsidered, in a Treatise of 1833," *MQR*, 22 (1948), 75-93; H[arold] S. Bender, "The Discipline Adopted by the Strasburg Conference of 1568," *MQR*, 1 (1927), 58-66; David V. Wiebe, *Grace Meadow: The Story of Gnadenau* (Hillsboro, Kans.: Mennonite Brethren Publishing House, 1967), esp. 56-69; Peter Burkholder, *The Confession of Faith of the Christians Known by the Name of Mennonites. . . .* (Winchester, Va.: Robinson and Hollis, 1837); Abraham Godshalk, *A Description of the New Creature* (Doylestown, Pa.: W. M. Large, 1838), published in German as *Eine Beschriebung der neuen Creatur* (Doylestown, Pa.: J. Jung, 1838); William F. (Billy) Graham, *The Seven Deadly Sins* (Grand Rapids, Mich.: Zondervan, 1955); *MQR* (Jan. 1950), sp. issue on Anabaptist Theology; Werner O. Packull, *Mysticism and the Early South German-Austrian Anabaptist Movement, 1525-1531* (Scottdale, 1977); Menno, *Writings*, esp. pp. 82-227, 1046-49; J[acob]. St[auffer]., *Eine Chronik, oder, Geschicht-Büchlein von der sogenannten Mennonisten Gemeinde. . .* (Lancaster, Pa.: Johann Bär und Sohnen, 1855); Lester K. Little, "Pride Goes before Avarice: Social Changes and the Vices in Western Christendom," *American Historical Review* 76 (1971) 16-49.

Humor. The word *humor* does not appear in Mennonite bibliographies until recent times. Early Mennonite teaching on °holiness or °nonconformity to the world, taught that in their general demeanor Mennonites were to be restrained and quiet, rather than loud, talkative, or boastful, traits that reflected the spirit of the world. Their interpretation of the New Testament, especially Ephesians 5:4, did not allow for jesting or joking. The Christian was expected to prune the heart and mouth of all unbecoming thoughts, words, and actions. Unseemly lighthearted behavior was often summed up in the word "levity." In addition, the Mennonites were concerned that houses of prayer and worship not be turned into houses of entertainment and mirth through humorous allusions and stories.

This serious mien was reinforced by the long period of intense °persecution in the early development of Anabaptism. As the radical left wing of the Reformation movement, Mennonites took their stand against the state church, a stance which often resulted in loss of life, livelihood, and family, situations hardly conducive to humor. At other periods in their history, Mennonites, in their search for purity of life, also protested one another, particularly with regard to church practices and ethics, dividing in the process into splinter groups. When that schismatic activity slowed, Mennonites in the 20th c.

renewed their protest against war, the draft, and nuclear rearmament, none of which encourages a humorous self-critical approach to life, but is, in truth, a form of judgment of others.

Another factor inhibiting humor is conviction that the Christian would always speak only the truth (Mt 5:34-37), thereby discouraging the telling of tall stories, the use of hyperbole and understatement, or any madeup story told as being true. Some conservative evangelical groups prefer true stories to fiction.

Although early Mennonites in The Netherlands were humorously portrayed in poetry, fiction, and drama with digs at their conservative dress, their supposed weakness for rich food and drink, their "tricks and dodges," and their sanctimoniousness (°°literature), Mennonites themselves did not use humor in faith-related activities until much later.

Although opposition to levity in speech is evident in most Mennonite traditions, some of the Russian Mennonite groups, especially those who seceded from larger bodies to protest the lack of spiritual and moral life, spoke against it corporately. John °Holdeman, founder of the Church of God in Christ, Mennonite, wrote that "All . . . jesting and joking . . . are works of the flesh, and if we live therein we lack of that holiness which is taught in the Scriptures." Historian Clarence Hiebert states that Holdeman contributors to *Messenger of Truth* admonished against jokes, jesting, and laughing 21 times between 1903 and 1960.

The Kleine Gemeinde (Evangelical Mennonite Conference) taught its children to take life seriously, and therefore, laughing and joking were frowned upon. Other small schismatic groups such as Krimmer Mennonite Brethren and Evangelical Mennonite Brethren (Fellowship of Evangelical Bible Churches) also taught nonconformity in speech.

Mennonite Brethren in America in a formal recommendation at their General Conference sessions in 1900 asked members to desist from jesting and joking, whether verbal or in writing, in conversation or in published periodicals.

The Mennonite Church likewise taught nonconformity in speech. In Daniel °Kauffman's *One Thousand Questions and Answers on Points of Christian Doctrine* (1908), question 529, "What forms of worldly amusement are specified in the Bible?" was answered with "Church entertainments, banquetings, revelings, foolish talking and jesting (Eph 5:4)." By 1952 J. C. Wenger interpreted Eph 5:4 as meaning that Christians should be able to enjoy clean humor. It is not forbidden to laugh. "He who lacks a sense of humor has neither the flexibility of good mental health nor the normal winsomeness of a child of God." Jesting, on the other hand, is "worldly and sensual wit, exhibition of mental wit, lightmindedness."

In the late 20th c., Mennonite use of humor as an approach to life is slowly moving beyond these restrictions, out of the understanding that Old Testament writers as well as Jesus used humor to communicate an idea in a more easily comprehended way. Though coarse jesting is still frowned upon, humor is accepted freely in informal social situations, occasionally in church publications if restraint is used, and less often in worship services.

North American Mennonite humor emphasizes the distinctive characteristics of the Mennonites, reflecting their struggles with the traditional traits of an overt honesty, frugality, dedication to °work, close-knit communities, traditional °occupations, foods, language, and life-style customs, as well as travel experiences which highlight the "innocents abroad" theme.

New expressions of humor emerge constantly in relation to Mennonite-sponsored group events, such as assemblies, conferences, °institutions, Mennonite Central Committee service, °relief sales, and Mennonite Disaster Service. Humor as an attitude of joy toward °suffering is emerging from experiences with Mennonite Disaster Service with people going through natural disaster, but there is less evidence of it as related to Mennonites' own suffering in the Jewish tradition, as a compensation for suffering. Like other humor, Mennonite humor springs up at the edge of change, when cherished values are challenged; for example, the patriarchial nature of the family and the role of °women in the church.

Insider humor includes social criticism of established traditions and of persons in power. Mennonite humor focuses on men, especially on influential men in public positions in local, national, and worldwide situations, caught in weak moments. Mennonite anecdotes include any aspect of beliefs Mennonites have difficulty holding to fully, such as °nonresistance, or in which there is some variance with another branch of the church, such as forms of °baptism. °Inter-Mennonite rivalries are also the frequent butts of humor.

Satire as a comment on the human condition has not been used successfully in Mennonite periodicals, even if clearly labeled satire, indicating that the point of view expressed is likely to be the opposite of what is expressed. The *Gospel Herald* (MC) has experimented with "The Prayers of Luke Warm," "Seth's Corner," "Wit and Wisdom," and "Sisters and Brothers," the last-mentioned being a cartoon series by Joel Kauffmann beginning in the fall of 1978. Negative reader response to the cartoons caused the editor to cut the cartoons back although a later series, "Pontius Puddle" has gained acceptance in other Mennonite and non-Mennonite publications since 1982. Other editors have had similar experiences with satire.

Certain subjects are still taboo for Mennonite humorists. The fine line dividing the sacred from the secular is tenuously drawn. Jokes about some ethnic groups occasionally take place in hell; jokes about Mennonites are more likely to take place in heaven. Stories about Mennonites engaged in adultery, drinking and drunkenness or acts of violence are not freely told. Tall tales are usually absent, except in the °folklore tradition of some branches of the Mennonites. Immigration hardships are acceptable as subjects for humor, and more recently the passing from °rural life to the new more sophisticated °urban life.

Iconoclastic Mennonite humor has had difficulty being accepted in essay, cartoon, or °poetry form. However, with the passing of ministers, preachers, and elders (bishops) as models of the ideal Mennonite Christian, the common Mennonite is more readily being accepted as the focus of humor, bringing with it the introduction of a frame of mind toward life that is humble and playful.

Within Mennonite groups who use some °German or Dutch °dialect, a body of humor exists which developed naturally and spontaneously out of a world view comfortable to its users. The Russian Mennonites, and their North American descendants, lived in two language worlds, and therefore in two related cultures, for decades. The Low German dialect was spoken where life was lived warmly, comfortably and intimately—in the home, on the barnyard, in the store, at social gatherings. People ate and digested, courted and loved, fought and made peace, bought and sold, argued and "neighbored" in the dialect. On the other hand, standard or High German, was the language of seriousness, scholarliness, sophistication, and to some Low German dialect speakers, the language of pretense and pomposity. Although the Low German dialect is often considered funny in itself, a concept reinforced by modern playwrights and song writers who choose humorous material to work with, some scholars argue the language is not funny but is capable of expressing humor because of its immense resourcefulness in distinguishing between nuances with great precision. Like Yiddish, it has a large variety of terms to distinguish between shades of connotations. The humor present in proverbs, sayings, and anecdotes is an expression of the ways things are and an invitation to the listener to see the world in a new way, that of the speaker. Low German humor is frequently a dry type of irony, seldom derisive and cruel, as in black humor, although it is readily recognized for its attempts to cut down class pretensions or dissimulations. Arnold °Dyck's comic characters Koop and Bua have been termed the Mennonite Laurel and Hardy team. Because of its restricted subject matter and because the humor lies in the idioms and culture, rather than in plot and action, Low German humor does not usually appeal to an outside audience.   KFW

Katie Funk Wiebe, "How to Start a Civil War," *Chr. Leader* (Feb. 23, 1982), 19; idem, "The Humble Approach," *Mennonite* (Feb. 15, 1972) 104; idem, "Why Mennonites Can't Laugh at Themselves," *FQ*, 1 (Summer, 1974), 522; idem, "How Do Mennonites Spell Relief?" *With* (July-August, 1985) 17ff.; Daniel Hertzler, "Humor and the Human Condition," *GH* (Jan. 12, 1982), 32; idem, "Can Laughter Save the Country?" *GH* (Mar. 32, 1981) 256; idem, "Laughing at Karl Barth," *GH* (July 19, 1983), 512; idem, "What's So Funny," *GH* (May 31, 1978), 444; "Reclassified," column of Mennonite humor in *FQ* (1975-); "The Serious Side of Life," *GH* (Aug. 5, 1926), 405; *Mennonite Distorter* (Ottawa, 1986-), mixes church politics (gay rights, feminism) with humor, cf. columns by Ivan Emke in *Menn. Rep.*, 1988-; A. E. Janzen and Herbert Giesbrecht, *We Recommend. . .: Recommendations and Resolutions of the General Conference of the Mennonite Brethren Churches* (Fresno: MB Board of Christian Literature, 1978), 81; Clarence Hiebert, *The Holdeman People* (South Pasadena, Cal.: William Carey Library, 1973) 131, 590-94; *Profanity: Swearing, Jesting and Joking* (Moundridge, Ks.: Gospel Tract and Bible Society of the Church of God in Christ, Mennonite, n.d.); John Holdeman, *A History of the Church of God* (Hesston, Ks.: Church of God in Christ, Mennonite, Publication Board, 1959) 162; Wittlinger, *Piety and Obedience* (1978), 120-23; Ervin Beck, "Reggie Jackson Among the Mennonites," *MQR*, 58 (1984), 147-67, idem, "Mennonite Trickster Tales: True to Be Good," *MQR*, 61 (1987), 58-74; John C. Wenger, *Separated Unto God* (Scottdale: MPH, 1952) 97; E. Bachman, "Laugh with the Children," *Mennonite* (Sept. 14, 1982) 441; Emerson L. Lesher, *The Muppie Manual* (Intercourse,

Pa.: Good Books, 1985). On Low German humor, see, in addition to the bibliography following the articles on Arnold Dyck and literature, the essay by Harry Loewen and Al Reimer, "Canadian Mennonite Low German," *MQR*, (1985), 279-86; Al Reimer, Anne Reimer, and Jack Thiessen, eds., *A Sackful of Plautdietsch: A Collection of Mennonite Low German Stories and Poems* (Winnipeg: Hyperion, 1983); Katie Funk Wiebe, "The Style of Low German Folklore," *J. of Amer. Historical Society of Germans from Russia*, 5 (Fall 1982), 45-52; idem, "Low German: The Language of the True Believer," *FQ*, 10 (August-October 1983) 12-13; Victor Peters, "With 'Koop enn Bua' on a Journey," *Menn. Life*, 14 (Apr. 1959), 89; Reuben Epp, *Plautdietsche Schreftsteckja* (Steinbach, Man.: Derksen Printers, 1972); Armin Wiebe, *The Salvation of Yasch Siemens* (Winnipeg: Turnstone Press, 1984); Agnetha Duerksen, *Low German Folklore* (Hesston, Kans: Agnetha Duerksen, n.d.); Don Ratzlaff, "Mennonite Brethren Game," *Chr. Leader*, (May 4, 1982), 12-13; Warren Kliewer, "Collecting Folklore Among Mennonites," *Menn. Life*, 24 (Oct. 1969), 169; Gordon Nickel, "Laughter with a Hollow Ring," *MB Herald* (Feb. 15, 1980), 6-9; Melanie Zuercher, "Mennonites, Heroes, and Humor," *FQ*, 13 (Spring 1986), 10-11; J. G. de Hoop Scheffer, "Mennisten-Streken," *Doops. Bijdr.* (Leeuwarden, 1868), 23-48; Al Reimer, "Innocents Abroad: The Comic Odyssey of *Koop enn Bua opp Reise*," *JMS*, 4 (1986) 31-45.

Hungary (ME II:843), has since World War II been a socialist republic, but the religious life of its people has been conditioned by a turbulent history that antedates the establishment of communist rule by many centuries. The gradual reforms of its economic life, which followed the restrictions imposed after the dramatic uprising of 1956, were not until the 1970s matched by moves to normalize relations between the state and the large religious communities, especially the Catholic church. Mennonite involvement has centered chiefly on the small Protestant groups in the free-church tradition, particularly the °Nazarene movement. Mennonite Central Committee since 1979 has sponsored several young North Americans for studies (history, music, theology) and fraternal relations to specific communities of faith.   NGS

Trevor Beeson, *Discretion and Valour: Religious Conditions in Russia and Eastern Europe*, 2nd ed. (London and Philadelphia: Fount Paperbacks, and Fortress Press, 1982), 256-87.

Hut, Hans (ME II:846), was by far the most significant early apostle of Anabaptism in the region extending from Thuringia to the Tirol and from Württemberg to Moravia. Scholarship of the last two decades has drastically revised the impression left by Hutterite sources that Hut belonged to those who "valiantly suffered for the non-resistance attitude of true discipleship" (ME II:849). The revisions affect conclusions about Hut's indebtedness to Thomas °Müntzer, the significance of his baptism by Hans °°Denck, his clash with Balthasar °Hubmaier and the related °°Nikolsburg Articles.

It is now clear that Hut's contact with Müntzer was more than casual. A "Hans of Bibra" appears among the signatories of the "eternal league" formed by Müntzer and Heinrich Pfeifer on Sept. 19, 1524, at Mühlhausen. In October 1524 Müntzer and Pfeifer, expelled from Mühlhausen, visited Hut in Bibra. Accompanied by Pfeifer, Hut took Müntzer's manuscript of the *Special Exposé* to the press of Hans Hergot in Nürnberg. Hut was present at the batttle of Frankenhausen until the "shooting became too thick," and he defended the peasants' cause after that in Bibra, supporting the efforts of the local leader, Jörg Haug. He fled the area only when troops of the Swabian League approached.

That his baptism at the hands of Denck on May 26, 1526, did not constitute a sudden break with his past becomes clear from Hut's first converts at Uetzing and Königsberg in Franconia. These new Anabaptists, recruited primarily from veterans of the °Peasants' War of 1525, expected an invasion by the Turks to succeed where the peasants had failed—in the punishment of the godless. It seems that Hut had translated the revolutionary hope of 1525 into °apocalyptic language.

Hutterite chroniclers subsequently confused Hut's conviction that Anabaptists should not resist the invading Turks with their own principled position of °nonresistance. The fact that the ideal of community of goods inspired some of Hut's followers may have contributed to his retroactive rehabilitation into a proto-Hutterite. Contrary to the chronicles, the clash with Hubmaier at Nikolsburg did not center on Hut's nonresistance. As for the controversial Nikolsburg Articles, Gottfried Seebaß has shown that claims by Friedmann and Williams that these had been "forged by enemies of the Anabaptists" were premised on wrongly dated documents. What are now known as the Nikolsburg Articles were, in fact, a tendentious selection, presumably made by a Catholic opponent, from 52 articles drawn up by Hubmaier against Hut and others. It appears that unfavorable news of his clash with Hubmaier preceded Hut to the "Martyrs' Synod" at Augsburg in the fall of 1527. Here, too, his apocalyptic teachings created discontent. Arrested around September 15, Hut was put on trial along with Jacob °°Gross, Jacob °°Dachser, and Sigmund °°Salminger. While the other three recanted and survived, Hut's fate was sealed when evidence of his earlier connections to Müntzer came to light.

Because of their problematic textual transmission, the two treatises attributed to Hut must be read in the context of the other sources. These include four letters by Hut, his Scripture concordances, the records of his interrogations, and the many statements made by his converts. The oldest statement by Hut appears to be the "seven judgments" or "decrees." The first two of these dealt with baptism, the Eucharist, and ecclesiology: the last five dealt with apocalyptic concerns. Hut's treatise Of the Mystery of Baptism elaborated on the first judgment. The notion of the "gospel of all creatures" found there became a distinguishing mark of Hut's influence. Müntzer's impact on Hut's understanding of the birth of faith as an inner experience of the bitter Christ is apparent. Water baptism became a sign of a painful inner process of death to the creaturely. The larger context suggests that Hut saw baptism as the sealing of the 144,000 end-time elect. Statements by his followers make it clear that they perceived themselves to be a persecuted apocalyptic remnant. A shift in fortunes was expected around Easter, 1528. Pestilence, famine and an invasion by the Turks were expected to shake the established order. Not the end of the world but a new order based on justice and peace lay in the immediate future. James Stayer has rightly described Hut's political ethic as one of suspended vengeance or "sheathed sword."

Mecenseffy has underlined Hut's significance for the spread of Anabaptism. Although his followers did not constitute a homogenous group it is possible to speak of them as generically distinct from other Anabaptists. Hut's apocalyptic orientation and indebtedness to Müntzer justifies the rejection of the older monogenesis explanation of Anabaptist origins which emphasized his conversion to a normative Swiss Anabaptism. WOP

(1) Hut's *Missionsbüchlein*, described in earlier scholarship as the *Taschenbüchlein*, probably predates Hut's baptism. It contained the Ten Commandments, a song by Luther, a catechism and a number of apocalyptic statements. See Friedrich Roth in Z. *des historischen Vereins für Schwaben und Neuburg (ZdhVfSuN)*, 27 (1900), p. 38, note 1.

(2) The *Rote Büchlin*. It contained a catechism, a prayer of thanksgiving for meals, and a scriptural concordance. It seems to be a manuscript left by Hut with Hans °°Langenmantel. Augsburg Stadtarchiv, Literaliensammlung, Jan. 9, 1528, f.25v-28r. (a) Seebaß arranged "Hut's Katechismus" of the *Rote Büchlin* into 32 items in the appendix to "Müntzers Erbe," pp. 2-3. (b) The "Konkordanz" found in the *Rote Büchlin* consisted of 81 topics with Scripture references. Roth had published only the topics in *ZdhVfSuN*, 27 (1900, 38-40. (Seebaß, "Müntzers Erbe", app., pp. 3-9. (3) The "Konkordanz zu den 'sieben Urteilen" seems to be a copy made by Ambrosius °°Spittelmaier of Hut's so-called "seven judgments." Nürnberg Stadtarchiv, Ansb. Rel. Akten Bd 39, f. 219r - 219v; Seebaß, "Müntzers Erbe", app., pp. 10-12.

(4) Four letters by Hut: (a) "Den christlichen bruedern N. Gnad und frid von Got dem vater . . ." alludes to the clash between Hubmaier and Hut at Nikolsburg. It must have originated in Augsburg in Aug. or Sept. 1527. Nürnberg Stadtarchiv, Ansb. Rel. Akten Bd. 39, f.216r-218v; Seebaß, "Müntzers Erbe", app., pp. 9-10. (b) "Die rain forcht Gottes wünsch ich zum anfang götlicher weysheit" contains a passage concerning the "gospel of all creatures," Hut's identification badge. Nürnberg Stadtarchiv Ansb. Rel. Akten Bd 39, f. 220r-220v; Seebaß, "Müntzers Erbe," app., pp. 12-14. (c) Seebaß followed Gordon Rupp in identifying Hut as the author of the anonymous letter in *Zwen wunderseltzsam sendbrieff zweyer Widertauffer . . . durch Urbanum Rhegium* [Augsburg: A. Weyssenhorn, 1528]. (d) *Ein Sendbrief Hans huthen . . . ains furnemen Vorsteers. . .* had also been published by Urbanus Rhegius [Augsburg: A. Weyssenhorn, 1528] and was partly reproduced by Lydia Müller in *TA Oberdtsch I*, p. 12n.

(5) (a) Seebaß accepted the authenticity of *Von dem geheimnus der tauf* but suggested that a manuscript submitted by Jörg Schöferl of Freistadt during his trial in August 1527 comes closest to Hut's original draft (*TA Osterreich I*, pp. 21-24). Schiemer and Schlaffer must have possessed similar copies. Müller's edition was taken from an expanded Hutterite source (*TA Oberdtsch I*, p. 12ff. Gordon Rupp's English translation utilized both a Hutterite codex and *Das Kunstbuch* (Patterns of Reformation [1969], pp. 379ff.). (b) *Ein christlicher underricht* [n.p., 1527] was changed in at least 20 places when it was published by Landsperger. Müller's edition, taken from a later Hutterite codex, is probably even less reliable. See *TA Oberdtsch I*, pp. 28ff.

(6) The authenticity of the four or five songs attributed to Hut remains disputed.

(7) Additional archival material regarding Hut's trial has come to light: (a) the official record of the interrogation of Jacob Gross and Hans Hut (before Sept. 16, 1527), consisting of 87 questions; (b) a note written by Augsburg's secretary, Peutinger, defending pedobaptism against Hut, Gross, Dachser and Salminger; (c) the record of Hut's interrogation of Nov. 4, 1527, consisting of 31 questions; (d) preliminary questionnaires for Hut's interrogations of Nov. 14 and 26 respectively. The added information puts previously undated documents into proper perspective (Meyer, *ZdhVfSuN*, (1874), 207-256). See Seebaß, "Müntzers Erbe", app. pp. 31ff.

G. Bauer, *Anfänge täuferischer Gemeindebildung in Franken* (Nürnberg, 1966); G. Berbig, "Die Wiedertäufer im Amt Königsberg i. Fr., 1527/1528," *Deutsche Z. für Kirchenrecht (DZK)*, 35 (1903), 309-16; idem, "Die Wiedertäuferei im Ortslande zu Franken, im Zusammenhang mit dem Bauernkrieg," *DZK*, 44 (1912); U. Friedwart, "Täufertum und Obrigkeit in Augsburg im 16. Jahrhundert" (diss. U. of Tübingen, 1972); Ray C. Gingerich, "The Mission Impulse of Early Swiss and South German-Austrian Anabaptism" (PhD diss., Vanderbilt Univ., 1980); T. Hansen, "Reformation, Revolution und Täufertum - Eine Einführung," *Mühlhäuser Beiträge zu Geschichte und Kulturgeschichte*, 3 (1980), 3-20; Walter Klaassen, "Hans Hut and Thomas Müntzer," *Baptist Quarterly*, 29 (1962), 209-27; H. Klassen, "The Life and Teachings of Hans Hut," *MQR*, 32 (1958), 171-205; 267-304; Grete Mecenseffy, "Die Herkunft des oberösterreichischen Täufertums," *ARG*, 47 (1956), 252-58; Werner Packull, "Denck's Alleged Baptism by Hubmaier: Its Significance for the Origin of South German-Austrian Anabaptism," *MQR*, 47 (1973), 327-38; idem, "Gottfried Seebaß on Hans Hut: A Discussion," *MQR*, 49 (1975), 57-67; idem, *Mysticism and the Early South German-Austrian Anabaptist Movement, 1525-1531* (Scottdale, 1977); Gordon Rupp, "Thomas Müntzer, Hans Huth and the 'Gospel of all Creatures'," *Bulletin of the John Rylands Library*, 43 (1960/61), 492-519; idem, *Patterns of Reformation* (London, 1969), 325-53, with a translation of Hut's "Of the Mystery of Baptism," 379ff.; H-D. Schmid, " Das Hutsche Täufertum: Ein Beitrag zur Charakterisierung einer täuferischen Richtung aus der Frühzeit der Täuferbewegung," *Historisches Jahrbuch der Görres Gesellschaft*, 91 (1971), 328-44, idem,, *Täufertum und Obrigkeit in Nürnberg* (Nürnberg, 1972); Gottfried Seebaß, "Müntzers Erbe: Werk, Leben und Theologie Hans Hut" (Habilitationsschrift, U. of Erlangen, 1972), with an appendix containing 22 items or primary sources relating to Hut; idem, "Bauernkrieg und Täufertum in Franken," *Z. für KG*, 85 (1974), 284-300, partial English translation in *Anabaptists and Thomas Müntzer*, ed. by J. Stayer and W. Packull (Dubuque, Iowa: Kendall-Hunt, 1980), 138-64; idem, "Hans Hut" in *Profiles of Radical Reformers*, ed. by H-J. Goertz, W. Klaassen (Scottdale, 1982), 54-61; James M. Stayer, " Hans Hut's Doctrine on the Sword: An Attempted Solution," *MQR*, 39 (1965), 181-91; idem, *Anabaptists and the Sword* (Lawrence Ks.: Coronado Press, 1972; rev. ed. 1976); W. Stoesz, "At the Foundation of Anabaptism: A Study of Thomas Müntzer, Hans Denck and Huns Hut" (PhD diss., Union Theological Seminary and Columbia University, 1964); P. Wappler, *Die Täuferbewegung in Thüringen von 1526-1584* (Jena, 1913), 228-44; W. Packull and G. Seebaß in *Umstrittenes Täufertum, 1525-1975*, ed. by Hans-Jürgen Goertz (Göttingen: Vandenhoeck und Reprecht, 1975), 138-64, 165-72.

Hutterian Brethren (Hutterische Brüder)

Hutterian Brethren (Hutterische Brüder) (ME II:854, IV:1126), practice community of goods, as first established in Moravia in 1529 and re-established by Jakob Hutter in 1533 according to the example of the first church in Jerusalem (Acts 2:44), "And all that believed were together, and had all things in common." The basic beliefs and way of life, including community of goods, are the same today as when the movement began.

In 1987 there were about 350 Hutterite colonies with a population of more than 32,000. They were situated in British Columbia (1), Alberta (119), Saskatchewan (39), Manitoba (76), Washington (4), Montana (41), North Dakota (7), South Dakota (48), Minnesota (2), Pennsylvania (1), New York (2), Connecticut (1), England (1), and Japan (1).

The Hutterians in Japan began as a small group of Japanese Christians in 1969. They had all things in common and in a worldwide search for other groups living according to the gospel and Acts 2 and 4, their leader, Izeki, visited the Hutterian Brethren. He was baptized at Wilson Siding Bruderhof in 1975 and confirmed as Servant of the Word two years later.

The Hutterians who fled to the United States from Russia in the 1870s and moved to Canada after World War I because of hostility and mistreatment on account of their °conscientious objection against military participation, encountered fresh discrimination following the outbreak of World War II and in subsequent years. The Hutterians refused to join any branch of the military forces, but accepted °alternative service under civilian jurisdiction.

In 1942 the Alberta legislature passed an act preventing the Hutterites from buying land if the site was closer than 40 miles (65 km.) from an existing colony and the amount of land was limited to not more than 6,400 acres (2600 hectares). In 1960 the law was amended. New colonies were formed in Montana in 1948 and in Saskatchewan in 1952.

In Manitoba attempts were made to introduce restrictive legislation. Fearing restrictions like those in Alberta, a "gentleman's agreement" with the Union of Manitoba Municipalities stipulated the location of no more than one or two colonies per municipality and at least 10 mi. (16 km.) apart. In 1971 this agreement was terminated.

The °°*Schmiedeleut* (Manitoba and Dakota colonies) set up their own mutual °insurance in 1980. The other two groups do not insure, but depend upon intercolony °mutual aid when a fire or disaster strikes. Sizable donations are given every year to local funds and to the disaster fund of the Mennonite Central Committee. The Dakota colonies formed a health or hospital insurance fund while the Canadian colonies participate in provincial health plans.

Hutterian children attend kindergarten (age 2-5), and elementary school (age 6-16). Normally the colony supplies the building, heating, and the maintenance costs. The local school division and board selects and pays the salary of the teachers, administers the school and, in most cases, pays a small rent for the building. In the past 10 years a number of colonies which have experienced difficulties in acquiring teacher grants have educated their own members as qualified teachers. It is also felt that a colony's own teacher will offset the worldly influence of the outside teacher. In Manitoba the Hutterite English teachers formed an association which provides inservice training sessions geared to the colony teacher's needs.

The children also receive two hours of German instruction daily from their own German teacher. The °°*Dariusleut* and *Schmiedeleut* have German school from October to May, while the °°*Lehrerleut* have it from September to June. Training sessions of two to three days per year for German teachers have been held for 10 years in Manitoba and South Dakota. Many of the teachers have replaced the Tyrolean dialect with the use of standard (high) German as the language of instruction.

The Hutterite Education Committee, along with other German teachers, has developed a history course for use in English and German schools. Other materials and new books have been introduced on hymnology, grammar, literature, etc. Many schools have copying and printing machines. A bookstore at James Valley Bruderhof in Manitoba stocks most school and church materials as well as books in English and German. All German schools in Manitoba colonies receive sizable cultural grants from both federal and provincial governments for the retention of language, printing of cultural or historical books, and training sessions.

As of 1970, mission work is practiced to a small extent. Delegates have been sent to seeking people in Germany, England, Paraguay, Japan, and, together with Hutterian Brethren from New York and England, to Israel, Czechoslovakia, and New Zealand.

The five Hutterian Brethren communities located in New York State, Pennsylvania, Connecticut, and England had their origins in the Bruderhof founded in Germany in 1920 through Eberhard °°Arnold and Emmy °Arnold, which united in 1930 with the Hutterian Brethren in North America. Because of persecution in °National Socialist Germany, the Cotswold Bruderhof was established in England in 1936. The name °°*Society of Brothers* (known as Hutterians) was adopted. The members were largely English and German, living in harmony and giving a witness for peace. When World War II began in 1939, irrational suspicions grew in the surrounding English population, and hostile actions, provoked by the war atmosphere, took place. To prevent the division of the community through the possible internment of the German members, the Bruderhof's members decided to emigrate. The British government was sympathetic to the dilemma of the community and consented. In spite of affidavits of support by the Hutterian Brethren in Canada and the United States, immigration into these countries proved impossible for the time being.

The Bruderhof emigrated to Paraguay with the help of the Mennonite Central Committee and with the same privileges as the Mennonites. A branch colony was established in Uruguay. In South America the communities were named *Sociedad Fraternal Hutteriana* until the break with the Hutterians in North America (1955-56, see below) from which date their name was *Sociedad de Hermanos* (1956-61). Daughter communities founded in England and North America were known as *Society of Brothers* until the time of reuniting with the Hutterians in 1974. From then on the name *Hutterian Society of Brothers* was used until 1985, when it was decided to be identified simply as *Hutterian Brethren*, reflecting their unity with the older Hutterian Bruderhofs in the western United States, Canada, and Japan.

For earlier history of the eastern Bruderhofs see: °°Alm Bruderhof, °°Community of Goods, °°Cotswold Bruderhof, °°Liechtenstein, °°Paraguay, °°Primavera, °°Rhönbruderhof, °°Sinntal Bruderhof, and °°Woodcrest.

During the time of departure from England to Paraguay in 1940-41 and afterwards, new people wished to join the community but the government would not permit them to leave England. For this reason the *Wheathill* Bruderhof (1942-62) was started in Shropshire. To extend the outreach, the *Bulstrode* Bruderhof (1958-66) was founded near London.

After the war the Bruderhof communities felt a longing to start again in Germany and sent several members to make a beginning on the Hohenstein (1955) near Nürnberg, and later in the *Sinntal* Bruderhof (1955-61) near Bad Brückenau.

Members of the Bruderhofs in South America were sent on a number of journeys to North America, beginning in 1949, to ask for financial help, mainly for the medical services to their Paraguayan neighbors, the majority of whom lived in poverty. On these journeys they met many friends who were also seeking for a life of brotherhood. This eventually led to the beginning of the *Woodcrest* Bruderhof (1954-) near Rifton, N.Y. New people joining and the members moving from the other Bruderhofs made it necessary to start two new places: *Oak Lake* (1957), later renamed *New Meadow Run* (1965-) in Farmington, Pa., and *Evergreen* (1958), later renamed *Deer Spring* (1975-) in Norfolk, Conn. For the outreach in Europe the communities in North America started the *Darvell* Bruderhof (1971-) in Robertsbridge, England, south of London. Because many newcomers and most of the grown-up children of the Bruderhof families joined the community it became necessary to start the *Pleasant View* Bruderhof (1985-) in Ulster Park, N.Y.

The basis of all relationships between the individual members and between the different communities in all spheres of life is: Love God above everything, and love your fellow human beings as yourself; set your mind and heart on God's kingdom and his justice before anything else, and all the rest will come to you as well. This love and justice led to complete economic sharing, as it was with the early Christians in Jerusalem (Acts 2 and 4).

The example of the early church shows that true °community is a fruit of the spirit of God alone, and not of human ideas and planning. This truth was experienced by the Bruderhofs in a series of crises which started after the death of Eberhard Arnold in 1935 and came to a head in the 1960s, when their unity collapsed like a house built on sand. The cause of these crises lay in the shift of the spiritual center from the personal relationship with the living Christ to human ideals of community. The ensuing situation should be seen in the light of Paul's warning to the Ephesians (6:12): our fight is not against flesh and blood, but against spiritual powers. God does not quarrel with people (Gn 6:3), but withdraws his Spirit when men and women tolerate the rule of other spiritual powers. Any such rulership causes disunity, a fact that Christendom has experienced many times and often confused with true plurality.

In its crises the Bruderhofs experienced disunity not only within and between communities in Paraguay, Europe, and the United States, but also between them and the older Hutterian communities in western North America (1955-56). The whole crisis brought about the loss of many members, and it became necessary to dissolve the Bruderhofs in South America and Europe and to gather in the North American communities to seek and find unity again.

Through God's grace, unity was given after serious searching of hearts and repentance, under the eldership of Johann Heinrich (Heini) Arnold. It opened the door for the return of former members and for the reuniting in 1974 with the older Hutterian communities in the West. This new unity has been deepened and strengthened by many visits between the western and eastern Bruderhofs. It also found expression in joint baptism meetings, weddings, and other mutual support, including the exchange of workers for the building up of new Bruderhofs (e.g.,

Darvell, Pleasant View, Concord), teachers for Bruderhof schools, and practical help in other communal work departments.

The Hutterian Brethren have felt the urge to share this newly given unity with others. Since Christ's message is only believable when its messengers are themselves united (Jn 17:21), they sought this unity in the Spirit of Christ with other movements and individuals who seek it too. With this intention, brothers and sisters from both eastern and western Bruderhofs participated jointly in various meetings and conferences, sometimes together with Mennonites, with other Christian and Jewish (Kibbutz) community movements, and with seeking people in Germany, Switzerland (1984), Canada and Israel (1985), Pennsylvania (at a Mennonite Historical Society meeting in Lancaster, 1986), South Tirol (at the *Täufertagung* in the Puster Valley, 1986), and New Zealand (1987). In this spirit they also took part in a historic, first consultation of the following Radical Reformation movements: Waldensians, Hussites, Czech Brethren and Moravians, Anabaptists (including Mennonites and Hutterians), Quakers, and Church of the Brethren. This took place in Prague in 1986. Its purpose was to learn from the groups' respective histories what the radical message of Jesus means in the late 20th c.

Other journeys were undertaken to India, Sweden, Germany, the Dominican Republic, and Nicaragua. In addition, the Bruderhofs were able to increase their outreach through visiting prisoners and helping the hungry and poor in their neighborhoods, and through such agencies as the Mennonite Central Committee and Oxfam International in the wider world. The Plough Publishing House contributes to the outreach with its publications. Of special importance is the publication in 1987 of the first English edition of *The Chronicle of the Hutterian Brethren*, written in German by the brothers in the 16th and 17th c., recounting in detail the material and spiritual struggles and tribulations, the imprisonment and °martyrdom, and also the wonderful protection of God that the communities experienced up to the year 1665.

The care for and education of children is seen by the Hutterian Brethren as a primary mission task. Here also the atmosphere of unity in the whole environment, especially between parents and teachers, is decisive.

Every member of the Bruderhof is willing to do any work as a service for the whole body (1 Cor 12:12-27). The brotherly atmosphere within and between the different work departments is more important than economic considerations. There is no differentiation in value between income-producing work departments, such as farming and industries (educational play equipment, furniture for schools and day care centers, equipment for the handicapped), and the many services needed for the daily life of all the members of the community and its guests, such as kitchen, laundry, sewing room, school, clerical work, historical archives, publishing, medical work. The brothers and sisters who are responsible for the different departments are appointed unanimously by the community, as are the

overall services of the Elder, Servants of the Word, stewards, work distributors, and housemothers.

Anyone who is interested is invited to write and visit at the following address or at the other community addresses: Hutterian Brethren, Woodcrest, Rifton, NY 12471.   JHo/HMei/JVH

Eberhard Arnold, *Inner Land: A Guide into the Heart and Soul of the Bible*, 5 vols. (Rifton, N.Y.: Plough Publishing House, 1975); idem, *God's Revolution: The Witness of Eberhard Arnold*, ed. by the Hutterian Brethren and John Howard Yoder (Ramsey, N. J.: Paulist Press, 1984); idem, *Salt and Light: Talks and Writings on the Sermon on the Mount*, 3rd ed. (Rifton, 1986); idem, *The Early Anabaptists* (Rifton, N.Y.: Plough, 1984); Eberhard Arnold, Emmy Arnold, Christoph Blumhardt, and Alfred Delp, *When the Time was Fulfilled: On Advent and Christmas*, introd. by Dwight Blough (Rifton, 1965); Eberhard Arnold and Emmy Arnold, *Seeking for the Kingdom of God: Origins of the Bruderhof Communities* (Rifton, 1974); Emmy Arnold, *Torches Together: The Beginning and Early Years of the Bruderhof Communities*, 2nd. ed., (Rifton, 1971); Hardy Arnold, Hans Meier, Winifred Hildel, and others, "In Pursuit of Jesus: An Oral History of the Bruderhof," *Sojourners*, 13 (May 1984) 16-20; John W. Bennett, *Hutterian Brethren: The Agricultural Economy and Social Organization of a Communal People* (Stanford U. Press, 1967); *The Chronicle of the Hutterian Brethren [Große Geschichtbuch]*, trans. and ed. by the Hutterian Brethren (Rifton: Plough, 1987); Ulrich Eggers, *Gemeinschaft-lebenslänglich: Deutsche Hutterer in den USA* (Witten: Bundes Verlag, 1985), English transl. *Community for Life* (Scottdale, 1988); Andreas Ehrenpreis and Claus Felbinger, *Brotherly Community, the Highest Command of Love* (Rifton, 1978), two important Anabaptist documents of 1650 and 1560, with introd. by Robert Friedmann; Robert Friedmann, ed., *TA Oberdtsch.* II (1967); idem, *Hutterite Studies: Essays by Robert Friedmann, Collected and Published in Honor of His Seventieth Anniversary*, ed. Harold S. Bender (Goshen: Mennonite Historical Society, 1961); idem, *Die Schriften der Hutterischen Täufergemeinschaften: Gesamtkatalog ihrer Manuskriptbücher, ihrer Schreiber und ihrer Literatur, 1529-1667* (Vienna: Hermann Böhlaus Nachfolger, 1965); idem, "Fifty Years Society of Brothers, (1920-1970): Their Story and their Books," *Menn. Life*, 25 (Oct. 1970), 159-64; Leonard Gross, *The Golden Years of the Hutterites: The Witness and Thought of the Communal Moravian Anabaptists During the Walpot Era, 1565-1578* (Scottdale, 1980); Paul Gross, *The Hutterite Way: The Inside Story of the Life, Customs, Religion and Traditions of the Hutterites* (Saskatoon: Freeman Pub. Co., 1965); John Hofer, *The History of the Hutterites* (Elie, Man.: The Hutterian Educational Committee, James Valley Bruderhof, 1982); Joshua Hofer, *Japanische Hutterer: Ein Besuch bei der Owa Gemeinde* (Elie, Man.: James Valley Book Centre, 1985); Peter Hofer, *The Hutterian Brethren and Their Beliefs* (Starbuck, Man.: The Hutterian Brethren of Manitoba, 1955); Michael Holzach, *Das Vergessene Volk: Ein Jahr bei den deutschen Hutterer in Kanada* (Munich: Deutscher Taschenbuch Verlag, 1982); John A. Hostetler, *Hutterite Life*, 3rd ed. (Scottdale, 1983); idem, *Hutterite Society* (Baltimore: Johns Hopkins U. Press, 1974); idem, *Source Materials on the Hutterites in the Mennonite Encyclopedia* (U. of Alberta, 1962); *Die Hutterischen Epistel: 1527 bis 1767*, 3 vols. (Elie, Man.: Hutterischen Brüder in Amerika, James Valley Book Centre, 1986); *Die Lieder der Hutterischen Brüder. . . .* (Scottdale, 1914; reprints: Winnipeg, 1953; Cayley, Alta., 1962); Jakob Hutter, *Brotherly Faithfulness: Epistles from a Time of Persecution* (Rifton, N.Y.: Plough, 1979); Jacob Kleinsasser, Hardy Arnold, Jakob Hofer, and Daniel Moody, *For the Sake of Divine Truth* (Rifton, 1974), a report on a journey to Europe in the summer of 1974; Bernd Längin, *Die Hutterer: Gefangene der Vergangenheit, Pilger der Gegenwart, Propheten der Zukunft* (Hamburg and Zürich: Rasch und Roehring, 1986); Hans Meier, "The Dissolution of the Rhön Bruderhof in Germany," *MHB*, 41 (July 1980), 1-6; Merrill Mow, "Community Living in our Time. An Account of the Bruderhof Communities," in *Brethren Life and Thought*, 1, no. 5 (Autumn 1956), 43-52; Victor Peters, *All Things Common: The Hutterian Way of Life* (Minneapolis: U. of Minnesota Press, 1965); Peter Riedemann, *Account of Our Religion, Doctrine, and Faith*, trans. Kathleen E. Hasenberg (London: Hodder and Stoughton, and Plough Publishing

House, 1938, 1950, 1970) Barbara R. Thomson, "The Challenge of True Brotherhood," *Christianity Today* (Mar. 25, 1985), 22-28; Gary J. Waltner, "The Educational System of the Hutterian Anabaptists and their *Schulordnung* of the 16th and 17th Centuries," (MA thesis, History Dept., U. of South Dakota, 1975); *MWH*, (1978), 352-56; *MWH*, (1984), 141.

Hyderabad, India, the capital of °Andhra Pradesh state, is the fifth largest city in India. It was for the love of Bhagmati that the fifth king of Golkonda, Mohd, Quli Qutbh Shah, founded the city of Bhagyanagar in 1589. Later when Bhagmati joined the royal house and received the title "Hyder Mahal," the king renamed the city Hyderabad. The metropolitan area is 259 sq. km. (100 sq. mi.), the altitude is 536 m. (1,758 ft.), and consists of twin cities (Hyderabad and Secunderabad) with a population of 2.2 million. The languages spoken inlude, Telugu, Urdu, Hindi, and English. The city has great natural beauty which together with medieval Indian, Saracenic, Mughal and British colonial architecture creates an exuberance and richness rarely found in other cities of India.

The India Mennonite Brethren church in Hyderabad developed from the American Mennonite Brethren Mission (1899-). The mission and church has expanded (1987) to nine congregations, a high school with ca. 2,000 students, and a Bible institute in Shamshabad near Hyderabad. The socioeconomic impact of Christian relief agencies (Mennonite Central Committee, Mennonite Christian Service Fellowship of India, Mennonite Brethren Development Organization) is felt and appreciated much in and around the city of Hyderabad. RSA

R. S. Aseervadam, "Mennonite Brethren Church and Social Action in Andhra Pradesh," *Ithihas, Journal of Andhra Pradesh Archives*, vol. 5, no. 1 (Hyderabad: State Archives, Govt. of A.P., 1977); idem, "The Mennonite Brethren in Andhra Pradesh" (PhD thesis, Osmania U., Hyderabad, 1980); idem, "A Study of the Growth of the Mennonite Brethren Church in Mahbubnagar, India" (MA thesis, Mennonite Brethren Biblical Seminary, Fresno, 1973); *Manorama, Year Book, 1986* (Kottayam, India: Manorama Publishing House); *Hyderabad-Tourist Guide, 1986* (Hyderabad: Government Central Press).

Hylkema, Teerd Oeds Ma Hylke (June 16, 1888-Sept. 13, 1968), had great influence among Dutch Mennonites. As pastor he served the Mennonite congregations in Giethoorn (1912-29), Amersfoort (1929-36), and Amsterdam (1936-49). He was the founder of the Vereniging voor Gemeentedagen (Union for Retreats), serving as chairperson, 1917-27. It was during these years that the building at Elspeet was erected (°camps and retreat centers). Upon his initiative retreat centers were also erected in the Giethoorn congregation. Hylkema was the primary inspiration for the building of the well-known brotherhood house, *Fredeshiem* in 1929 and gave new life to the center at Bilthoven.

In his longing for witnessing, serving, and peace-loving congregations he did much for the cause of peace. He was chairman of the Doopsgezinde Vredesgroep (Dutch Mennonite Peace Society), a member of the executive committee of the Dutch peace center *Heerenwegen* at Zeist, an adviser to the government commission on °conscientious objectors, and an active participant in the national peace bureau.

Hylkema was already active in behalf of °refugees before World War II. With his help hundreds of Russian Mennonite refugees emigrated to North and South America. He arranged for the transport of Jewish children to London. During World War II (1940-45) he gave much help to a variety of refugee camps and other camps. He was the primary leader for Dutch help to Mennonite refugees. RHof

Doops. Jaar. (1963), 17-20.

Hymnology (ME II:869; ME IV:1096). The following Mennonite denominational hymnals have been published since the mid-1950s. *The Hymn Book* (1960, Winnipeg) is an English version of the earlier *Gesangbuch der Mennoniten Brüdergemeinde* (1955, Winnipeg) published by the Canadian Conference of the Mennonite Brethren church. All 555 hymns were translated and numbered exactly as in the *Gesangbuch*, a unique arrangement making it possible for bilingual congregations to sing in both languages at the same time.

Gesangbuch der Mennoniten (1965, Newton) is a collection of 599 German hymns produced by the Conference of Mennonites in Canada to serve German-speaking congregations. A committee of 10 led by H. H. Epp, chairman; George D. Wiebe, vice-chairman; and Walter Thiessen, secretary, compiled this hymnal. The table of contents reflects a very clear and useful organization of hymns (19 sections with subheadings). A distinct feature is the inclusion of one or more Scripture verses for each hymn, reflected in an index which is helpful for planning worship services. Another unique feature is a historical survey of 8 different periods, from pre-Reformation to hymns of England and North America, including a brief description of each period. The hymns for each period are listed as such.

The Mennonite Hymnal (1969, Newton and Scottdale) is the culmination of many years of work by committees of the General Conference Mennonite Church (GCM) and the Mennonite Church (MC) which began working jointly in 1961. The resulting hymnal replaced *The Church Hymnal* (MC, 1927) and *The Mennonite Hymnary* (GCM, 1940). The organizational structure included a Joint Hymnal Committee of 10 people, two denominational music committees (9 in each), a Text Committee (7), a Tune Committee (6), and a Worship Aids Committee (4). Vernon Neufeld served as chairman of the Joint Hymnal Committee; Mary Oyer as the executive secretary. The project benefited greatly by Mary Oyer's research, especially during a sabbatical year in Great Britain under the tutelage of Erik Routley.

The Text Committee made an effort to maintain the integrity of original versions; some alterations were made for theological, linguistic, or traditional reasons. The Tune Committee also examined original settings of the music, preserving 12 out of 653 as unison melodies. All other music was arranged for 4-part singing. The original rhythmic structure of several German chorales was restored. The collection was published both in round note and shaped note editions. The collection is somewhat innovative for including 3 *Ausbund* texts, 6 Genevan psalm tunes, 6 non-Western hymns, 4 plainsong chants, 2 Gelineau psalm chants, and 5 four-part Anglican chants. The committees made a conscious effort to include contemporary materials. Seven of 58 20th-c. texts and 11 of 52 20th-c. tunes were written after 1950. Several new tunes were commissioned to be composed for specific texts. From the earlier end of the historical spectrum the collection includes 8 Greek and early church texts. Thirty texts are translations of original Latin hymns. Ninety-one of the texts (14 percent) were originally written in German, 30 of them translated by Catherine Winkworth. Fifteen of the original German texts are included. By far the greatest number of texts are British (340 [52 percent]), 37 by Isaac Watts, 24 by Charles Wesley, 171 from the 19th c., and 23 from the 20th c. North American writers contributed more than 100 texts. Almost 10 percent (60) of the hymnal consists of 19th- and 20th-c. gospel songs.

The Tune Committee chose 63 folk tunes, including 20 American, 7 English, 2 Negro spirituals, 4 Welsh, 3 Chinese, and others (German, French, Bohemian, Danish, Dutch, Finnish, Hebrew, Indian, Irish, Japanese, Scottish, and Swedish).

Forty-seven pages of the hymnal are devoted to additional worship resources, including 65 Scripture readings (making use of 5 translations, mostly RSV) to be read in unison, responsively, or antiphonally. Four affirmations of faith, 10 congregational responses for various occasions, and 18 prayers are all intended for corporate usage.

Hymnal Companions. Several supplementary resources were published some years after the *The Mennonite Hymnal*. The Worship and Arts Committee (GCM) initiated *Exploring the Mennonite Hymnal*, which consists of two volumes. The first, *Essays* (1980, Newton and Scottdale) by Mary Oyer, is an extended discussion of 34 hymns with "tangential material." The second, *Handbook* (1983, Newton and Scottdale), by Alice Loewen, Harold Moyer, and Mary Oyer, contains brief comments on all the hymns in the collection, much in the style of the *Handbook to the Mennonite Hymnary* (1949) by Lester Hostetler.

Assembly Songs, A Hymnal Supplement—Hymns Both New and Old (1983, Scottdale and Newton) is a collection of 161 hymns prepared for "Bethlehem '83", the first joint meeting of the General Conference Mennonite Church and the Mennonite Church (MC). Eighty-three hymns selected from *The Mennonite Hymnal* together with 44 contemporary and crosscultural, 14 historical hymns, and 20 new hymns written for Bethlehem '83 made up the volume. Language in about 20 hymns was altered in response to concern about the issue of inclusive language.

Worship Hymnal (1971, Hillsboro) was compiled and edited by the Hymnal Committee of the General Conference of the the Mennonite Brethren church. It was the first "fruitful, cooperative effort in hymnal production between Canadian and United States churches." It is the successor to two Mennonite Brethren hymnals, *The Hymn Book* (Canadian, 1960) and the *Mennonite Brethren Church Hymnal* (United States, 1953). A Hymnal Committee of two church musicians and one theologian from each area conference developed the hymnal. Paul Wohlgemuth served as chairman and editor. The denominational

tone is evident in the selection of hymns—the evangelical emphasis given to various sections, and the original contributions by members of the Mennonite Brethren Church through translations, poems, and musical settings. The most innovative feature of this collection is a group of 23 hymns in the "Children" and "Youth" sections. These include several rounds, folk hymns, hymns in the style of contemporary popular music, Scripture songs, and Negro spirituals, all presented with only the melodic line and chord indications for guitar or keyboard. Aids to worship make up 52 pages, including 82 Scripture readings, 3 affirmations of faith, 13 congregational responses, and 11 prayers.

In 1983 the Center for Mennonite Brethren Studies (Hillsboro, Ks.) published *Worship Hymnal Concordance*, compiled by Paul W. Wohlgemuth and Steven P. Wohlgemuth with the help of a computer. It is an alphabetical arrangement of 4,324 key words of the hymn texts, intended for ease in finding appropriate hymns for varied uses.

Hymns for Children and Youth. *The Youth Hymnary* (1956, Newton), edited by Lester Hostetler, was intended for use by children of ages 9 to 15. In addition to 100 standard hymns, 14 of them with a descant, the book includes 24 spirituals, 32 carols, 76 part songs (40 SSA, 14 SAB or SSAB, 22 SS or SA), 5 responses, 3 choruses, and 24 canons.

Our Hymns of Praise (1958, Scottdale), edited by J. Mark Stauffer and illustrated by Esther Rose Graber, "represents the generous labors of the Music Committee of Mennonite General Conference" (MC). It is a collection of 200 hymns for "primary and junior children of grades one to six to eleven," intended for a cappella singing, arranged for one or two or three parts.

The Children's Hymnary (1968, Newton), edited by Arlene Hartzler and John Gaeddert and illustrated by Ruth Eitzen, was planned for use with kindergarten-, primary-, and junior-age children (each hymn classified according to appropriate age groups). The collection includes "carols, folk tunes, and great hymns of the church" as well as table graces, offertories, and prayers. All hymns have simple accompaniments. Thirteen German texts are included.

Songs to be Sung (1969) and *More Songs to be Sung* (1971), originally appeared as a part of *With* magazine (Scottdale), each including 20 songs with unison melody line and chord indications for and by Mennonite young people.

Contemporary Hymnody. During the 1960s and 1970s there was a gradual influx of hymns in styles that traditionally were considered to be secular: folk, pop, jazz, etc. Originally these appealed mostly to young people, but some were used by congregations. The guitar became a popular instrument within the church, together with other °instruments. Contributing to new and different ways of singing was the °charismatic movement with Scripture songs, often sung to simple memorized melodies from texts projected on a screen.

Goshen College (Ind.) was the site of large gatherings in three successive years (1972-74), the Festival of the Holy Spirit for the first two years, then the Festival of the Word in 1974. For each of these gatherings, planned and sponsored by Goshen College, Associated Mennonite Biblical Seminaries (Elkhart, Ind.), the Central District Conference (GCM) and Indiana-Michigan Conference (MC), songbooks of contemporary hymns were compiled, to be used along with *The Mennonite Hymnal. Festival of the Holy Spirit Song Book* (1972 and 73), and *Festival of the Word Song Book* (1974, Goshen), include hymns by several Mennonites as well as hymns from other renewal movements of the time.

In 1975 Herald Press (Scottdale, Pa.) asked Orlando Schmidt to compile and edit a songbook, which would reflect recent developments, for congregational use. Titled *Sing and Rejoice* (1979, Scottdale), this collection reflected not only the developments in North America, but drew on the worldwide resources represented by *Cantate Domine,* the hymnal for the gathering of the World Council of Churches in Kenya (1975), as well as *International Songbook* (Lombard, Ill., 1978) used at the Mennonite World Conference assembly in Wichita, Ks., 1978.

Private Publications. Two titles, not published by church agencies, were planned by Mennonites for the Mennonite community. *The Christian Hymnary* (Uniontown, Ohio, and Sarasota, Fla., 1972), compiled by John J. Overholt, includes 1,002 hymns. The compiler has included 12 hymns from the *Ausbund,* two by °Menno Simons, and two by °Dirk Philips, with Overholt's own translations and musical settings. *Anabaptist Hymnal* (Hagerstown, Md., 1987), edited by Clarence Y. Fretz, is the largest collection of Anabaptist hymns translated, versified, and set to music for English-speaking Mennonites. Anabaptist texts include: 45 from the *Ausbund,* 18 from *Die Lieder der Hutterischen Brüder,* and four others. The *Unpartheyisches Gesangbuch* (1804, Lancaster), an early American Mennonite hymnal (German) is the source of 24 texts. These and 28 other texts are included, since "among American Mennonites [they] show typical Anabaptist moral and spiritual earnestness."

Hymnal for the Twenty-First Century. In 1983 the General Conference Mennonite Church and the Mennonite Church (MC) agreed to work with the Church of the °Brethren and the Churches of God General Conference (who have been using the *Brethren Hymnal*) in planning for a hymnal to be published in 1992. Text, music and worship committees, as well as publishers have been working jointly, meeting at least twice a year.   OS

See also Cheyenne (Julia Yellow Horse Shoulderblade [feature]); Choirs; Old Order River Brethren; Poetry; Singing; Whiteshield, Harvey.

Teaching the Songs of Heaven: The Legacy of William Wade Harris

Many Western missionaries have throughout the years set off for the mission field with a strong sense of superiority regarding their own cultural and religious traditions. "Evangelizing" was often perceived as only half of their divine mandate. "Civilizing" was the other.

To become a Christian consequently meant far more than merely accepting a new faith. For many young believers it also implied adopting new cultural patterns as modeled by the missionary. Not surprising then is the response of a young African chap when asked whether or not he was a Christian. "No," he replied, "I don't boil my drinking water."

One area in which Western influence has remained particularly noticeable is that of worship. Only rarely have African traditional music sources been successfully tapped and brought over into the developing liturgical patterns of the newly emerging church. "Again and again," complains one Nigerian observer, "our choirs have been made to sing or screech out complicated anthems in English while they barely or do not all appreciate what they are singing."

An important exception to this rule was the insightful approach of the Liberian-born prophet William Wade Harris during his remarkable evangelistic ministry from 1913 to 1915 throughout southern Côte d'Ivoire [Ivory Coast]. New converts responding to his call pled with the prophet, "Teach us the songs of heaven so that we can truly bring glory to God." But Harris—though himself a lover of Western hymns learned since early childhood—refused easy answers. "God has no personal, favorite songs," the prophet told the crowds. "He hears all that we say in whatever language. It is sufficient for us to compose hymns of praise to Him with our own music and in our own language for Him to understand."

Encouraged by these words of counsel, the new believers set to work writing hymns of praise to God.

> It was the Lord who first gave birth to us
>   and placed us here
> How were we to know
> That the Lord would give birth to us a second time!

Thanks to Him, we can live in peace on this earth. An impressive repertory of several thousand songs composed by Harrist men and women through the years is sung by Harrist believers in the 1980s. Some of these hymns fill a liturgical function as entrance, exit, or offertory songs. Others tell Bible stories or relate events from Harrist history. This body of hymnody includes prayers, mini-sermons, and confessions of faith—all set to music and all composed by Africans, for Africans, in a language that Africans can well understand. The opening lines of the Apostles' Creed, when adapted by one Harrist hymn writer, take the following form:

> My God, our Father, Almighty, Almighty,
> Creator of the heavens and the earth.
> It is He who is Truth, our Father alone.
> And it is Jesus who is our Defender.
> As for the Holy Spirit sent by Jesus,
> He is Life and Healing for us all.

Mennonite Board of Missions personnel, serving with Harrists among the Dida people since 1979, have worked with local church leaders at preserving several hundred of the oldest of these hymns for future generations. Four hymnbooks with accompanying cassette recordings have resulted from this common venture.   JRK

I

Ibandla Labazalwane Kukristu e-Zimbabwe (Brethren in Christ Church in Zimbabwe). Although from its beginning (ca. 1780) the Brethren in Christ Church (BIC) has placed emphasis on sharing the Good News, it was not until 1898 that the church launched foreign mission work. In 1898 the church sent a party of five, led by Bishop Jesse °Engle, to southern Africa and in particular to the area that was the home of the Ndebele people. The missionaries were confirmed in their choice when Cecil Rhodes granted them 3,000 acres of land in the Matopo Hills in what is now Matabeleland, South Province, Zimbabwe. (Zimbabwe will be used throughout this article, even though the area was known as [southern] Rhodesia for most of the period under discussion.) Two of the first missionaries left in 1906 to begin a new work in what is now Zambia.

Outreach was based in mission stations from which evangelism was carried on in the surrounding villages. In addition to Matopo, stations were established at Mtshabezi (1904), Wanezi (1924), and Pumula (1959). Training and advanced educational schools, as well as major medical facilities, were located at the mission stations. Outstations, centered on a primary school and a church, also developed at an early stage. The religion of the Ndebele people was mainly °animistic with a strong accent on ancestor worship.

As soon as they learned something of the language, missionaries engaged in village evangelism. Gifted converts aided the missionaries in these visits and in other forms of evangelism. In 1915 a school was begun at Matopo to train African leaders who would teach and preach at the outstations and pastor churches as they were planted. This school became known as the Matopo Teacher Training Institute. By 1930 national evangelists moved from outstation to outstation (there were ca. 78 outstations in 1948), holding annual evangelistic meetings. The evangelists also gave energy to developing preaching points. The evangelistic mandate was also operative in mission station schools, medical work, and literature outreach. Since the 1960s °Church Growth movement methods have been successful in the conversion of people, especially in urban areas. Another recent means of evangelism has been the Brethren radio ministry, "Amagugu Evangeli," begun in 1974. A new church planting effort (1985) in Binga among some Tonga-speaking people has developed into a church of 64 members at four preaching points.

In summary, Brethren in Christ church evangelistic work in Zimbabwe has shown steady growth, with rapid gains in more recent years. In 1930 there were almost 700 members, in 1950 a few over 2,000, and in 1986, 9,255. To the 148 churches brought into being must be added 27 preaching points. In 1987 approximately 3,000 people were in catechetical (inquirers) classes.

The Brethren in Christ church of Zimbabwe has also worked to spread the gospel beyond the Zimbabwean borders. In 1979 the Brethren in Christ churches in Zimbabwe, Zambia, and North America began a cooperative work in London, ministering to expatriate African Brethren in Christ members there. In 1985 some 200 Christians (13 congregations) in Malawi asked to become part of the Brethren in Christ church, giving rise to the Brethren in Christ church in Malawi.

From the beginning of the work in Zimbabwe, Christ-centered education was given high priority. A primary school was opened at Matopo within three months of the missionaries' arrival. Soon a boy's boarding school was built at Matopo and then a school for girls at Mtshabezi. All pupils were given instruction in basic subjects (reading, arithmetic, etc.) and health and hygiene. In addition, the boys were taught brickmaking, gardening, carpentry, etc., and the girls were taught home economics, gardening, sewing, etc. Above all, the Bible was central to the educational endeavor.

Gradually the missionaries developed a large primary school system. With financial aid and supervision from the government, the system was staffed by graduates of the Matopo Teacher Training Institute. In the 1950s secondary schools were established at the main mission stations. By 1970 these schools had a student body of 17,116 and a teaching staff of 464. In 1971 the government took over the schools, and from that time the mission has limited education efforts to the primary and secondary schools located at the major mission stations. These schools in recent years have enrolled an increasing number of students.

Medical missions became important with the arrival of two professionally trained nurses in 1924. Clinics were opened at Matopo, Mtshabezi, and Wanezi. In 1951 the first medical doctor arrived to take charge of the newly constructed hospital at Mtshabezi. A second hospital was built in 1959 at the Pumula Mission Station. In 1987 two clinics at Wanezi and Matopo were also in operation.

In order to build a self-sustaining national church the first African Conference was held in 1919, the first three African overseers were appointed in 1921, and the first deacons were elected in 1922. In addition to the Matopo Training Institute, the Wanezi Bible School was opened in 1948. When it was moved to Mtshabezi, it was upgraded to a Bible institute (Ekuphileni Bible Institute). It provides pastoral training at the secondary and postsecondary levels. Pastors who could not become full-time students have received further training through °theological education by extension. Some African church leaders have studied in non-Brethren in Christ Bible colleges and seminaries, and some have studied at Messiah College, Grantham, Pa.

Until the 1960s the North American Brethren in Christ Mission Board administered the work in Northern Rhodesia (Zambia) and Southern Rhodesia (Zimbabwe) as one church body. Since then the churches in each area have become independent self-governing bodies. Philemon M. Khumalo was the first African elected as bishop of the Ibandla Labazalwane Kukristu e-Zimbabwe (1970-79). He was succeeded by Stephen N. Ndlovu. These two men ably guided the church in Zimbabwe through the period of guerrilla warfare, 1970-80. Under their leadership membership has increased from 3,726 to 9,255.

The war for independence against the white minority government had a catastrophic effect, disrupting the normal flow of life. Schools, hospitals, and many churches were closed. Some church members met in homes; others fled to °Bulawayo. Several church leaders were killed. Most white missionaries left the country. The end of the war did not bring final peace to Matebeleland because the government was largely in the hands of the Shona people, giving rise to tension in relation to the Ndebele and other ethnic groups. Zimbabwean government troops swept through Matebeleland in search of "dissidents." Acts of cruelty and oppression were perpetrated. Gradually tensions eased and life returned to more normal levels.

The Brethren in Christ church had the task of renewing, restoring, and restructuring the church. Hospitals, schools, and church buildings were repaired or rebuilt. Staffing was developed, and the church returned to the task of evangelism and church planting—with success. In 1986 2,225 members were added to the church. The social dislocation and personal insecurity of the war made many receptive to the gospel. A new district, the Urban District, was added to the existing districts of Matopo, Mtshabezi, Gwaai, and Wanezi. Theological education by extension was reinstituted. The Matopo Book Center was moved to Bulawayo in 1963 and has since added five branch stores. The church in Zimbabwe affiliates with the °Africa Mennonite and Brethren in Christ Fellowship, the Christian Council of Zimbabwe, the Evangelical Fellowship of Zambia, and the °Mennonite World Conference. NNK/MHS

Brethren in Christ Handbook of Missions (1950-1970), copies at Messiah College, Grantham, Pa.; *Brethren in Christ Church 75th Anniversary Celebration* (Bulawayo: Rhodesian Christian Press, 1973); Francis H. Davidson, *South and South Central Africa* (Elgin, Ill.: Brethren Publishing House, 1915); Anna R. Engle, John A. Climenhaga, and Leoda A. Buckwalter, *There Is No Difference* (Nappanee, 1950); Bruce M. Khumalo, "Communicating the Gospel and the Establishment of the Zimbabwean Brethren in Christ" (M.A. thesis, Ashland Theological Seminary, 1986); Jake Shenk, "White Unto Harvest," *Therefore* (April-June, 1984); Harvey Sider, *The Church in Mission* (Nappanee, 1975); *Therefore* (July-Sept. 1984); Don Zook, "Prayer and Growth," *Therefore* (March 1984); *MWH* (1978), 93-96; *MWH* (1984), 23.

See also Mbungano Yabunyina Muli Kristo.

Ichikawa Uno was a resident of Hagi in Japan's Yamaguchi Prefecture. She was already in her 60s when she responded to the first Brethren in Christ evangelistic effort in August of 1953. Her commitment both to missionaries Peter and Mary Willms and to the beginning church was unswerving. She was a quiet person, but joined enthusiastically in the second campaign in Hagi in July 1954, announcing the street meetings from the van's loudspeaker and sometimes singing in her quavering voice. She was one of the first three converts baptized in Oct. 1954. Her quality of faith and dedication was recognized by the missionaries and by the church, which chose her as one of the leaders of the new group of believers. She cared for the tiny church when the missionaries were absent for language study and illness. She and her aging husband gave up their home to serve as caretakers of a building rented for church meetings, then without complaint moved into a tiny apartment when the church purchased a property two years later. Childless, the Ichikawas were taken by their nephew in 1975 to a retirement home in Tokyo where they lived into their 90s. DCB

Idaho F(ME III:3) had 819 Mennonites in 1985, located at: Aberdeen (GCM), 317; Nampa, Filer and Boise (MC), 232; Bonners Ferry (CGC), 225; Hammett (unaffiliated), 33; Cataldo (°Western Conservative Mennonite Fellowship), 12. Congregations that disbanded after 1955 were: Caldwell (GCM), 1947-1962; Faith (GCM) at Filer, a division of Filer (MC), 1955-1968; Highland (unaffiliated at Twin Falls, also a division of Filer [MC]), 1960-1964; City Acres (MC) at Nampa, 1963-1974. Disbanding and decreases in membership occurred due to limited irrigated farmland and employment opportunities, young people not returning after college, the influence of sects, changing neighborhoods, and divisive leadership. Hyde Park at Boise (1977) began as a mission outreach of Nampa, and Cataldo (1981) was a mission station of Porter (Western Conservative Mennonite Fellowship) at Estacada, Ore. Aberdeen Mennonites dedicated Palisades Camp in 1963. Southern Idaho congregations began a Thrift and MCC °SELFHELP Crafts shop in Nampa in 1980. HKL

Hope Kauffman Lind, "Mennonites in Oregon and Related Congregations in Neighboring States (1876-1976)," (unpubl. manuscript); Lee Price Campbell, "Seventy-Five Years on the Shore of the Peaceful Sea: A History of the Pacific District Conference of the General Conference Mennonite Church of North America" (M.Div. thesis, Western Evangelical Seminary, Portland, Ore., 1973), 17-24, 73-78; H. D. Burkholder, *The Story of Our Conference and Churches* (North Newton: Mennonite Press, 1951), 58-64; *MC Yearbook* (1988-89), 21; Pacific District Conference (GCM), Annual Report (1986), 12; Pacific Coast Conference (MC), Annual Report (1986), 9; *GCM Handbook* (1988), 6.

Identity. See Acculturation; Apologetics; Conservative Mennonites; German Language; Institutions; Mennonite; Mennonite Studies; Modernity; Sociological Studies; Tradition; Union of Soviet Socialist Republics.

Bibliography: Harry Loewen, ed., *Why I Am a Mennonite: Essays on Mennonite Identity* (Scottdale, 1988); Rodney J. Sawatzky, *Authority and Identity: The Dynamics of the General Conference Mennonite Church* (North Newton: Bethel College, 1987); Calvin Redekop and Sam Steiner, eds. *Mennonite Identity: Historical and Contemporary Perspectives*

(Lanham, Md.: U. Press of America, 1988); Leo Driedger, *Mennonite Identity in Conflict* (Lewiston, N.Y.: Edwin Mellen Press, 1988).

Idleness. The English word "idleness" means habitual avoidance of work or indolence. The root meaning of "idle" or *eitel* (German) is "empty," "worthless," or "vain." The ancient term *acedia* (Greek) connoted sloth or apathy and originally referred to spiritual neglect.

Paul's admonition "if any would not work, neither should he eat" (2 Thes 3:10, KJV) was interpreted by Thomas Aquinas (d. 1274) to mean that labor was necessary only for the maintenance of the individual and community. Contemplation within God's kingdom took precedence over mere labor. In western traditional society out of which Anabaptists emerged, the idleness of the aristocratic classes was not viewed as evil—their work was to govern and fight wars. Yet sloth (*acedia*) was considered as one of the "Seven Deadly Sins" and was characterized as "the Governor of all vice" and idlers as the "the nurse of sin." Ernst °°Troeltsch assumed that the Anabaptist movement emerged, for the most part, from the laboring classes under trained pastoral leaders and that their concerns about idleness were less class oriented. Menno Simons reproved those magistrates "who are after fat salaries and a lazy life" and preachers who live "a sensuous, vain and lazy life" and condemned their "pomp, luxury and carousing" (Menno, *Writings*, 195, 259).

The °Puritan emphasis was on work within one's "calling" outside of which a person's accomplishments were insignificant. Troeltsch asserted that in The Netherlands the Mennonites, though oppressed by orthodox °°Calvinism, were strongly influenced by its concept of the "calling" and merged into public life to a degree that they became bourgeois and prosperous. Mennonites elsewhere in Europe also related their work and °business to their religious calling as illustrated by Max Weber's (1864-1920) mention of the Prussian ruler Frederick William I's toleration of Mennonite refusal to perform military service because he considered them indispensable to industry in East Prussia.

Nineteenth-century American (U.S.) Mennonites imbibed the °work ethic that was so prominent in the burgeoning °capitalistic American economy. This is evident in the rhetoric used in the occasional periodical articles and editorials on idleness, work, or diligence which were usually bolstered by the familiar Pauline admonition. Later Mennonite °recreation leaders would frown on the assertion of one writer that anything that "amuses serves to kill time, lull the faculties and banish reflection." Most important, however, there was the inference and often the exhortation to exert spiritual effort to work out one's own salvation or to help and encourage those in need, a different emphasis than the Calvinist concept of the "calling."

It would seem that the ancient idea of idleness or sloth (*acedia*) which connoted spiritual lethargy is most appropriate for Mennonites in an industrial and post industrial age with its accompanying rise of absorption in consumerism and with the society's felt need for °amusement or relaxation. For idleness disqualifies one for leisure which is, most authentically, a mental and spiritual attitude which brings one into the whole of °creation.   SLH

Ernst Troeltsch, *The Social Teachings of the Christian Churches*, vol. 2: 691-706, 781-82; Max Weber, *The Protestant Ethic and the Spirit of Capitalism* (London, 1930, 44, 144-45, 148, 157-59, 163; Edmund Spenser, *The First Book of the Faerie Queen Contayning the Legend of the Knight of the Red Crosse or of Holinesse*, Canto IV, in Edmund Spenser, *Selected Poetry* (New York, 1958), 58-9; Morton W. Bloomfield, *The Seven Deadly Sins* (East Lansing, Mich., 1952), 193, 210, 242; Josef Pieper, *Leisure the Basis of Culture* (New York, 1952), 16-18, 24-8, 78-9; Kauffman/Harder, *Anabaptists Four C. Later* (1975), 141-43; Richard Henry Tawney, *Religion and the Rise of Capitalism* (New York, 1926); Harold Lehman, *In Praise of Leisure* (Scottdale, 1974); G. Brenneman, "Apply Your Hearts unto Wisdom," *Herald of Truth*, 1, no. 7 (July, 1864), 42-3; idem, "Idleness," *Herald of Truth*, 4, no. 1 (Jan., 1867), 1-2; idem, "Be Diligent," *Herald of Truth*, 10, no. 7 (July, 1873), 119; Laura Suter, "Work, Recreation and Pleasure," *GH*, 1, no. 39 (Dec. 26, 1908); "Duty," *Mennonite*, 3, no. 1 (Oct. 1887), 6; Henry Fairlie, "The Seven Deadly Sins Today, Sloth or Acedia," *The New Republic*, 177, no. 18 (Oct. 29, 1977); *Young People's Paper* (Jan. 6, 1894), 2, 7, (Mar. 3, 1894), 34-35, (Apr. 14, 1894), 59, (Apr. 28, 1894), 71.

Iglesia de Los Hermanos in Cristo, Cuba (Brethren in Christ Church, Cuba). Serious consideration of Cuba as a Brethren in Christ mission field began in 1953 when several Brethren in Christ ministers found the Cubans receptive to the gospel. Their successful tent ministry caused them to repair an unused church building located in the town of Cuatro Caminos. A congregation was now in the making. The Brethren evangelists asked the brotherhood to assume responsibility for the work and the foreign misson board (BIC) did so in 1954. The first missionaries sent out by the Board were Howard and Pearl Wolgemuth.

Additional missionaries were sent out as the work grew. Methods used were Sunday schools, preaching, home visitation, and youth work. Workers also began a Christian elementary school. A second congregation was formed at Nazareno. In 1958 the mission had two congregations, three additional places of worship, four Sunday schools (attendance, 180), and 27 church members. Membership in 1986 was 46; attendance was often significantly higher.

The Cuban revolution (1959) resulted in the missionaries leaving in 1960. Fortunately an able member of the church with Bible Institute training, Juana Garcia, assumed leadership responsibilities. Under her guidance the church has weathered the difficulties, grown, and remained spiritually alive.

Fifteen years of separation between the Cuban and North American Brethren in Christ Churches ended when Canadian brother Ross Nigh visited Cuba in 1976. Some additional visits have taken place since then. In this way the Cuban and Nicaraguan Brethren in Christ Churches have developed a fraternal relationship.   DRZ/MHS

Wittlinger, *Piety and Obedience* (1978), 516-18; *EV* (May 23, 1955), 9, (April 25, 1976), 8-9, (Nov. 1984), 17-18; *MWH* (1984), 68.

Iglesia Evangélica Menonita, Argentina (Argentine Mennonite Church) (ME I:154). All properties and institutions of the Argentine Mennonite Mission described in ME I have been transferred to the Iglesia Evangélica Menonita, Argentina. Membership, reported at 650 in 1953, had reached 2,000 by 1988, with regular attendance at services totaling more than 3,000. Approximately 30 congregations are served by Argentine pastors, most of whom earn their own support. A few are paid salaries by their congregations. In 1988 one couple supported by Mennonite Board of Missions (MC) was working in leadership training. The Argentine Mennonite Church is growing toward maturity and responsibility. Several congregations are located in °Buenos Aires.

The Mennonite Bible School at Bragado, Buenos Aires, closed when the Seminario Evangélico Menonita de Teología (Mennonite Theological Seminary, ME IV: 1106) opened at Montevideo, Uruguay in 1955 (closed 1974). Argentine Mennonite Church leaders study at seminaries of several different denominations in Buenos Aires. Many are trained in their own congregations through a program affiliated with the Facultad Latinoamericana de Estudios Teológicos. The church owns a campground in Bragado, where general conferences are held annually. The official periodical of the conference, *La Voz Menonita* (The Mennonite Voice, 1932-) became first *El Discipulo Cristiano* (The Christian Disciple), and then *Perspectiva* (Outlook).   ROG

See also Evangelische Mennonitische Bruderschaft; Remeco-Guatrache Colony.

Iglesia Evangélica Menonita, Chile (Evangelical Mennonite Church, Chile).

The Mennonite presence in °Chile came about as a result of contacts in Canada among Chileans. Keith and Nancy Kyjuk Hostetler were instrumental in relating a group of Chileans to the Mennonite church in Edmonton, Alta. Subsequently Mennonite Board of Missions (MC) commissioned the Hostetler family to serve in Chile, responding to an invitation of a small group of independent congregations in Chile who were associated with some of the Chileans in Edmonton. The vision was to provide Bible teaching and leadership training and to do church planting. The Hostetlers arrived in March 1983. Don and Marilyn Brenneman joined them in September 1984. In March 1985 it was decided to discontinue the relationship between these congregations and the mission board because of irreconcilable differences. In March 1985 the Mennonite Christian Center was opened in Santiago to serve as a meeting place, office, and literature resource location.   DB

Iglesia Evangélica Menonita, Colombia (General Conference Mennonite Evangelical Church) (ME I: 643),

began in 1945 with the coming of four missionaries from the United States: Gerald and Mary Hope Stucky, Mary Becker, and Janet Soldner. After studying Spanish for a year at the Presbyterian Spanish Language School in Medellín, Colombia, they moved to an eight-acre (three-hectare) farm, owned by a German, close to the small town of Cachipay on the western slope of the eastern range of the Colombian Andes. Later they found Ruth Birckholtz-Bestvater and her mother Anna, two Mennonites from Danzig (Gdansk) who had been brought over by Kurt Birckholtz-Bestvater a few years earlier, instead of going to Paraguay with other Mennonite emigrants. These two were not active in church work until they moved near Cachipay. Ruth taught for some time in the boarding school.

The group founded an elementary boarding school for healthy children of parents suffering from Hansen's disease (leprosy) and for children from other Protestant families. The school began classes late in Febrary 1947, with 19 children, 3 preschoolers, and 2 older girls who helped. This was the beginning of the Colombian Mennonite Mission which, in 1988, is in the hands of the Colombian nationals and legally incorporated as the Iglesia Evangélica Menonita de Colombia. It still relates to the Commission on Overseas Mission (GCM).

After 40 years of active work there are 10 organized congregations and several preaching points, 9 ordained pastors, and about 700 active members. The total attendance of all congregations exceeds 1,000.

In addition to evangelism and church planting the church has developed other ministries. There is a home for the elderly, two elementary schools, a retreat center, four bookstores, a foundation for development (MENCOLDES) in cooperation with the Mennonite Brethren church, and an attractive and functional Mennonite Center in Bogotá. The church publishes *Menoticias* (Menno-News).

Iglesia Evangélica Menonita, Colombia, is active in inter-church cooperation. It is a member of the Colombian Confederation of Protestant Churches (CEDEC), and of the National Anabaptist Committee. It also cooperates with the Presbyterian Seminary in Bogotá and participates with other Christian groups in joint seminars dealing with topics of common interest, and in some service projects.

The emphases of the church in the last few years have been evangelism and church planting, leadership training, Anabaptist identity, peace witness, and service to the needy.   HGVV

MWH (1978), 213-15; Juhnke, *Mission* (1979), 147-61.

Iglesia Evangélica Menonita, Ecuador (Ecuadoran Evangelical Mennonite Church).

The Conservative Mennonite Board of Missions and Charities (also known as Rosedale Mennonite Missions), Irwin, Ohio, first sent workers to Ecuador in November 1980. The arrival of Elam and Doris Stauffer in Guayaquil, the country's largest city, represented the first efforts of a Mennonite mission agency in that country. The first believers were baptized in 1982 and a congregation was organized in 1983. A second missionary family, Robert and Myreya Miller, began work in the coastal city of Manta in 1983. In response to widespread flooding, the Millers directed a major housing project that provided shelter for 340 families. In 1984 a church was organized and a chapel was built.

An expanded missionary team has since developed additional ministries in health, rehabilitation counseling and youth ministry. Membership in 1987 was 80. The Misión Evangélica Menonita en Ecuador became the Iglesia Evangélica Menonita Ecuatoriana as a result of a reorganization in 1986.   HM

MWH, (1984), 71.

Iglesia Evangélica Menonita, El Salvador (Evangelical Mennonite Church), is an outgrowth of a community development project begun in 1962 when Amish Mennonite Aid (BAM) was invited to provide workers as part of a Salvadoran government land reform program. Under the initial agreement, volunteers were not allowed to do evangelistic work and church planting but Amish Mennonite Aid (AMA) officials hoped that permission to do that would be granted once they were recognized by the government. In 1968, the first ordained minister was sent to El Salvador and began preaching services in the capital. Evangelism has been the main thrust of the AMA work since then.

In 1986 there were six regular meeting places in central and western El Salvador with 75 members and a total attendance of about 300. In 1979, a Salvadoran member, Saul Pacheco, was ordained as a minister. He was serving as bishop in 1986. North American Beachy Amish missionaries and Voluntary Service workers continue to live and work in three different locations.

The church has been involved in a variety of social service projects. Perhaps the most significant is an orphanage located 30 km. (19 mi.) north of the capital, opened in 1972. More than 70 children have been adopted by families in North America. The orphanage was moved into the capital in 1984 because of the increasing threat of violence resulting from the civil war. A refugee assistance program is administered with Mennonite Central Committee. Clinics and day schools are operated in several areas.   RFl

Andrew Hershberger, comp. *Into the Highways and Hedges: AMA Mission Report* (Plain City, OH: Amish Mennonite Aid, 1980); *MWH* (1984), 72.

Iglesia Evangélica Menonita, Honduras (Evangelical Mennonite Church), had its beginnings in Trujillo in 1950 with the arrival of the first Mennonite missionaries, George and Grace Miller, from Eastern Mennonite Board of Missions and Charities (MC), Lancaster, Pa. Trujillo was a small isolated coastal town where the United Fruit Company had been active, but left when disease struck the banana trees.

From the start missionaries proclaimed a gospel that responded to people's physical needs, including work in the areas of agriculture, health, education, and community °development. By 1951 a clinic was established, operated by a missionary nurse, Dora Taylor, and a new believer, Tilda Imbott, who also accompanied the Millers on Sunday morning visits to give Bible lessons in Spanish.

By late 1952 the first church building was completed in Trujillo, services were being held, and there were six members. The work was already spreading inland, through the fertile Aguan Valley to Olancho, then following the major traffic routes through the three largest cities and their outlying areas. A voluntary service program began in 1959. North American volunteers, and later, Honduran youth, worked in community programs alongside church planters.

The 1960s marked the transition from missionary to national leadership. Growth was gradual, from 65 members in 1960 to 292 in 1970. In 1961 local councils were formed, and in 1962 the general church council was organized, with four missionaries and four national elders. By 1964 the general council elected an executive committee. A leadership training program was begun at Trujillo in 1965. By 1969 a church constitution and statement of faith was drawn up, accepted by the Eastern Mennonite Board of Missions, and adopted in Trujillo.

Iglesia Evangélica Menonita, Honduras (Honduras Mennonite Church), thus became an autonomous conference. Its first president was Manuel Medina (1973-75), followed by Damian Rodríguez (1975-83), Bladimiro Cano (1983-85), and Isaías Flores (1985-). Church administration is facilitated by division into six regional areas: Colón, Olancho, Atlántida, San Pedro Sula, Ocotepeque and Tegucigalpa, all of which are coordinated by local councils and overseers. National church offices are in La Ceiba.

Growth in membership and program was rapid during the 1970s and into the 1980s. Membership in 1987 included 55 congregations and nearly 2,600 members in 9 provinces. The church in San Pedro Sula, an industrial city, was started in 1970, grew quickly among middle class professional people, and soon had numerous churches in surrounding areas, a discipleship program, several youth teams that worked in service projects, and a choir that traveled to the United States.

In La Ceiba the Mennonite Vocational Institute was begun in 1975 to provide vocational and biblical training. In 1979 the Bible institute was separated and the vocational institute turned over to the Honduran government's Ministry of Education.

In 1980 the church, primarily rural, typically conservative, and heavily influenced by charismatic renewal, entered a new phase of awareness when it began work with Salvadoran war refugees in camps in the border areas. Leaders saw this involvement as a natural Christian response to human suffering, something they had seen demonstrated since the church's beginning. Praying was important, but was not the only solution; they had to take of what they had, and help. It was not a pondered political move, but it has had serious implication for the church coming to grips with its Anabaptist heritage and struggling to be faithful to the gospel in a country touched by war on all sides, and itself an obvious puppet of the United States. Mennonite Central Committee has supported the Honduran Mennonites in this work, where they have worked together with other agencies under the United Nations High Commissioner for Refugees.

In 1982 when military service was made obligatory, the church was one of several Mennonite and Friends groups who united to send a statement to the Honduran Congress making known their historic °nonresistant position and asking for alternative service opportunities. In 1986 the Mennonite church formally denounced the Nicaraguan Contra presence in the country, noting particularly that it had displaced the Moriah Mennonite congregation and taken over the church building. They asked for the government's protection of its people. Frank letters to the newspapers about current situations, and interactions with officials are quite common; several church workers have been detained for questioning.

Other priorities include work in community development and leadership training, which led to the creation of two new church commissions in 1984. The Commission on Social Action, along with the support of Mennonite Central Committee, attempts to develop vision and theology, and the practice of social activism among Honduran communities. It coordinates the work with the refugees and rural development. The Commission on Theological Education coordinates the efforts of various leadership training programs, including the Bible Institute residence program which trains new pastors; the extension program, which serves active pastors and lay leaders; and SEMILLA, seminary-level program of practical °theological education by extension, which is based in Guatemala and involves 10 Anabaptist conventions in Central America, including the Honduran Mennonite Church (°Consulta Anabautista Menonita Centroamericana). An additional particular focus is that of forming a broader base for peace and justice concerns. Mennonite Central Committee is also supporting this program.   JMBren

MWH (1984), 81; A. Grace Wenger, unpubl. manuscript on EMBMC work, ch. 2: "Overseas Missions—Latin America" (Salunga, Pa.: EMBMC, Aug. 1983), 1-57; Ovidio Flores, "Brief Historical Summary of the Mennonite Church in Honduras" (Goshen College, 1982), unpubl. paper available through Honduras Mennonite Church, La Ceiba, Honduras; Linda Shelly and Grace Weber, "The Development of 'Word and Deed Ministry' in the History of the Honduran Mennonite Church" (San Marcos, Honduras, 1985), unpubl. paper available through MCC, Akron, Pa.; Eastern Mennonite Board, executive committee minutes, 1948ff.; Mennonite Central Committee, monthly and annual reports; Luis Cesar Flores, "Una Historia Breve de la Proyección de la Iglesia Evangélica Menonita Hondureña en la Programa Social" (San Marcos, Honduras, July 2, 1983), unpubl. available through MCC, Akron, Pa.; MWH (1978), 221-24; Damian Rodriguez, and others, petition to National Congress concerning obligatory military service (March 17, 1982), available through Honduras Mennonite Church, La Ceiba, Honduras; Honduras Mennonite Church, statement to Honduras President and Congress concerning Contra activity (May 15, 1986), translation available through Eastern Mennonite Board, Salunga, Pa.; GH (June 3, 1986), 390.

Iglesia Evangélica Menonita, Mesa Central de Mexico (Evangelical Mennonite Church of the Central Plateau of Mexico). The first congregation was formed in 1959 through efforts of workers sent to the environs of Mexico City by the Franconia Mennonite Conference (MC) in 1958. The conference was organized in 1964. In 1988 there were 150 members worshiping in six centers. The church was under national leadership according to Mexican law. Training of church leaders and general Bible training for lay members has been done through an extension Bible institute giving Bible teaching in the local congregational centers and in homes. In 1988 four Americans were giving support to the local leadership.

In 1960 work was begun among the Trique Indians in the state of Oaxaca, 300 mi. (480 km.) se. of Mexico City, including the translation of the New Testament into the Trique dialect. From slow beginnings the Trique church as grown to a membership of 200 in 1988.   RSa

MC Yearbook (1988-89), 159; MWH (1978), 227-29; MWH (1984), 84.

Iglesia Evangélica Menonita, Noroeste de Mexico (Northwest Mexican Evangelical Mennonite Church). In 1960 the Pacific Coast Conference (MC) began work in Ciudad Obregon, Sonora, Mexico. The James Roth family were the first Mennonite missionaries in this area. In 1962 a permanent building was erected in Ciudad Obregon for services. An outreach was also started in a village outside of the city at Campo 77. Also in 1962 Francisco Urias was converted and baptized. He came from the State of Sinaloa. When he returned home he invited the missionaries to his home village where the work in Sinaloa began. The first baptisms in Sinaloa, were celebrated in 1963. In 1966 the Mexico Church Conference was formed and a Mexican pastor, Raul Vazquez, was ordained in 1967. By 1969 there were six missionary families in northwest Mexico. Two families worked in the state of Sonora and the remainder in Sinaloa. By 1977 only the Tadeo family remained on the field; they were still involved in 1986, when there were six organized congregations with eight mission stations in Sinaloa led by three ordained pastors and eight lay leaders. In Sonora there were two organized congregations with two mission stations, served by one lay leader, two licensed pastors, and one ordained pastor. Rufino Gaxiola was the only full-time supported worker. He was the conference president. Raul and Vanita Tadeo made their home a resource center where the church leaders and others could obtain Sunday School materials, cassettes for learning at home, and filmstrips for teaching and evangelism. The total membership of the conference was approximately 200.   RT

MWH (1984), 85.

Iglesia Evangélica Unida: Hermanos Menonitas, Panama (United Evangelical Church: Mennonite Brethren). The indigenous people known as the Choco Indians live along the rivers of the dense tropical rain forest on both sides of the border between Colombia and Panama. They are composed of two distinct language groups, the majority being Embera and the minority, Wounaan. The Wounaan were first contacted by Mennonite Brethren missionaries in the Colombian Choco in the late 1940s. Then in 1956, anthropologist Jacob Loewen began work among the Embera-speaking group in Panama. °Literacy work was the principal approach in those early years, and soon many Wounaan, recently arrived from Colombia, were included in the work as well.

These first Christians gathered into villages, and congregations with indigenous leadership were formed. Some of the adults completed their primary education and became °literacy promoters as well as church leaders. This led to a request for schools for their children, and these were provided in time by the government of Panama in most villages. In 1971, the first five congregations were officially organized into the United Evangelical Church. In 1985, the church board requested official recognition as a Mennonite Brethren conference.

Since 1971, with assistance from Mennonite Brethren Board of Missions and Services, the work has spread to some 25 of the 60 Embera and Wounaan villages in the eastern jungles of Panama. More than 1,000 have been baptized over the years but, being a highly mobile people, only some 600 Choco people are active members today in 15 congregations. Ambitious outreach plans by indigenous evangelists, agriculturalists, and health workers call for reaching all 60 villages through United Campaigns by 1990.

With its beginnings in a literacy program, the United Evangelical Church has always had a concern for an integral presentation of the gospel. Since 1978, Mennonite Brethren Board of Missions and Services has assisted the national church with a comprehensive °development project. This included the construction of two cultural centers for students, one in the capital, Panama City, and the other in the jungle town of Yaviza. These centers, combined with scholarship assistance, have allowed many young Embera and Wounaan people to complete secondary school. More than 130 have also completed teacher training and some are now enrolled in university studies. A program of agricultural demonstration farms and village public health promotion has also been part of the project.

Church leadership has always been in the hands of the Indians themselves, while Mennonite Brethren missionaries have served as advisors and resource persons. Five men have graduated from the Baptist seminary in Panama City. But with the church growing, many more village congregational leaders are needed. Two village Bible schools, one for each language group, were begun in the village of Canaan and Caleta in 1985. These should provide the needed church leaders for the future.   HE

Phyllis Martens, *The Mustard Tree* (Fresno: MB Board of Christian Education, 1971), 190-97; John A. Toews, *History MB* (1975), 431-32; *Witness: Mennonite Brethren in World Mission*, 1, no. 1 (Jan./Feb., 1987), 2; *MWH* (1978), 239-41; *MWH* (1984), 92.

Iglesia Hermanos en Cristo, Nicaragua (Brethren in Christ Church). With the closing of Cuba to North American missionaries and a growing interest in mission work in Latin America, the Brethren in Christ began work in Nicaragua in 1964. First efforts were in the Managua (national capital) area; within a few years the work expanded so that by 1985 Brethren churches were established in 9 of the 16 provinces (departments) of the country. After a slow beginning, growth gained momentum in the mid-1970s and then accelerated rapidly (1969: 19 members in 1 congregation; 1976: 50 members in 8 congregations; 1985: 1,794 members in 54 congregations). The church is strongly committed to evangelism and church planting.

This growth took place despite of and because of some crisis events. These were the Managua earthquake (1972), the overthrow of the Somoza government by the Sandinista movement (1978-79), and the United States-Nicaragua confrontation (since 1982). These crises have sharply focused such social problems as poverty, illiteracy, and disease. They also have opened many hearts to the gospel.

The nature of the developing Brethren in Christ Church has also been shaped by the method of evangelism. Instead of churches pastored by mis-

sionaries, emphasis has been placed on church planting, on °house churches (with subsequent construction of church buildings), and, most important, on using Nicaraguans as pastors. This has meant identifying and training pastors. There has been much on-the-job training and there have been many local and national seminars. Some pastors have attended Central American seminaries and Bible institutes. Such training has involved both men and women. Only one missionary couple has been on the field since 1981, and they have given much of their time to °pastoral education.

In 1980 Enrique Palacios was elected executive minister of the Brethren in Christ Church in Nicaragua. The church organized on a national level as the Iglesia Hermanos en Cristo, Nicaragua. Palacios has stated that the growth of the church has been due to the Brethren distinctives of the new birth, dependence on the °Holy Spirit, °peace witness, and ministry to the whole person.

Social activities, undertaken sometimes by the Brethren themselves, sometimes with the Mennonite Central Committee, and sometimes with the government, have included organizing adult °literacy programs, operating °health clinics, providing safe water, securing electricity, building latrines, feeding the hungry, providing food supplements, improving agricultural productivity, meeting housing needs, and helping refugees. The Brethren in Christ have worked with other evangelicals in meeting emergency needs.

The prominent role played by °women in the Brethren in Christ church is indicated by the organization in 1980 of the National Women's Union, and has manifested itself as they, beyond preaching and teaching the gospel, have dealt with such matters as proper child care, managing the household, sewing clothing, and preparing nutritional food. In these and other ways the women are making an important contribution.   DRZ/MHS

Wittlinger, *Piety and Obediance* (1978), 518-21; BIC Missions, *Annual Reports* (1979ff.); BIC Missions, *Therefore* (1972ff.); Bert Sider in *EV* (Feb. 10, 1976), 3-4; *MWH* (1978), 236-38; *MWH* (1984), 100.

Iglesia Menonita de Bolivia (Mennonite Church in Bolivia, since the late 1980s officially known as Iglesia Evangélica Menonita Boliviana). Mennonite mission presence in Bolivia grew directly out of Mennonite Central Committee (MCC) involvement in Sunday schools and other spiritual ministries and MCC's request for specialized help. Prior to 1971 special visits by Nelson °Litwiller, Frank Byler, and Argentine Mennonite youth workers augmented the MCC contribution. Those involved concurred in the MCC request for longer term mission personnel.

In 1971 Jose and Soledad Godoy arrived. They were supported conjointly by the Argentine Mennonite Conference (Iglesia Evangélica Menonita), Mennonite Board of Missions (MC) and the Commission on Overseas Mission (GCM). Between 1971 and 1975 they worked primarily in evangelization in eight different rural communities from their base in Tres Palmas Mennonite colony: Itapaque, Los Tajibos, Cosorió, El Vi, Las Gamas, Zafranilla, La Cruceña, and Don Lorenzo. All of these communities had had MCC workers living in them previously.

From 1975 to 1982 the work of the mission focused primarily on discipleship. In five of the communities in which Godoys worked, leaders were identified and discipleship courses were offered to help them grow in their spiritual understandings. Groundwork for several congregations in the greater Santa Cruz area (500,000 population) also began.

From 1982 to 1987 the work consolidated more and moved more specifically to leadership training in four established congregations. The other communities in which contacts had been made earlier were dropped due to disinterest or the work was assumed by other groups or consolidation. Leadership teams became the backbones for the following congregations: Las Gamas, Los Tajibos, San Julian/Don Lorenzo, and Santa Cruz. Training efforts included °theological education by extension and much counseling during weekly visits. Special weekend seminars were held three to four times per year on selected topics. Approximately one-third of the leaders have been women. Young people are beginning to complete high school and several have attended seminaries of other denominations.

In 1986 Leonidas Saucedo, a leader in the Santa Cruz congregation, was elected chairperson of the Administative Board—a position held by North Americans until that time. Las Gamas has had a church building since 1976. The other three congregations were involved in meetinghouse construction during 1986.

A joint church planting and development project was started in 1984 by MCC and the two North American mission boards. It is located in semirural outskirts of Santa Cruz in the neighborhood known as Heroes del Chaco. In 1986 approximately 40-50 people attended services regularly.   GM

MWH (1984), 56.

Iglesia Menonita de El Salvador [Metapán] (Mennonite Church in El Salvador [Metapán]). The Centro de Discipulado Cristiano, Misión Menonita (Center for Christian Discipleship, Mennonite Mission) began in 1969 when more than 100,000 Salvadorans were expelled from Honduras during the war between El Salvador and Honduras. Among those were two or three families who had been active in the Iglesia Evangélica Menonita of Honduras (Honduran Mennonite Church). The group met in homes in the town of Metapán in northwest El Salvador for several years until a building was constructed in 1982 with some assistance from the Eastern Mennonite Board of Missions (MC). The church grew rapidly, numbering 110 baptized members in two congregations in 1986. Leadership was initially shared by a team of lay preachers, and that pattern has continued since the ordination of Adelso Landaverde as pastor in May 1984. The congregation is active in regional Mennonite meetings and training seminars.   RFl

Iglesia Menonita de Guatemala (Guatemala Mennonite Church) is the result of mission work cosponsored by the Eastern Mennonite Board of Missions and Charities (MC) and the Franklin-

Washington Mennonite Conference (later continued by the Franklin Mennonite Conference) of Chambersburg, Pa. In 1968 Richard and Lois Landis began church planting work in Guatemala City. By 1971 the first congregation was formed in a low-income colony, La Brigada, where a few years later the first meeting house was built. This congregation on the western side of the city had 10 different pastors, 3 of them missionaries, during its first 12 years. A similar pattern followed for the four other congregations that were formed in these same years. Nearly all of the first decade's pastors came into the Mennonite church, many temporarily, from other denominations with little or no understanding of Mennonite history and theology. Congregations experienced sporadic growth and instability. A resident Bible institute functioned from 1980 to 1984 to offer training for pastors and prospective leaders. In 1984 a large, centrally located property was purchased to provide a meetinghouse for Casa Horeb, the new 200-member middle-class congregation and a center of operations for the conference that had been organized in 1975. This Mennonite Center includes the conference administrative offices, DESEC (Department of Christian Education), CPSS (Permanent Social Service Committee), and the central clinic and pharmacy. Mennonite Central Committee's °appropriate technology program also has a subcenter with an experimental herb garden on the back part of the lot. The health program under CPSS operates five health and nutrition clinics in the five low-income congregations. Since 1986 DESEC offers Saturday Bible institute studies, and, in 1987, it sponsored a primary school using the Mennonite chapel in one of the poorest suburbs until the government school is built there. The two congregations formed by Mennonite- and Anabaptist-oriented leaders in the central part of the city in the early 1980s include people with secondary school and university training. Many of these are participating in the SEMILLA (Seminario Ministerial de Liderazgo Anabautista, see °Consulta Anabautista Menonita Centroamericana) program of °theological education by extension and carry various conference leadership responsiblities capably. The total membership of 900 in eight congregations is led by four ordained and four licensed ministers.   AY

MWH (1978), 219; *MWH* (1984), 74.

See also Iglesia Nacional Evangélica Menonita Guatemalteca.

Iglesia Nacional Evangélica Menonita Guatemalteca (Guatemalan National Evangelical Mennonite Church), is the name of one of the church conferences which emerged from the joint effort in Guatemala of Eastern Mennonite Board of Missions and Charities (MC) and the Mission Board of the Washington-Franklin Mennonite Conference (later known as Franklin Mennonite Conference). The mission to Kekchi-speaking people began in 1968. The first three members were baptized in 1972. The conference was formally organized in 1980 with offices in San Pedro Carcha, Alta Verapaz.

Conference membership is made up primarily of Kekchi living in two northern departments of

Guatemala—Alta Verapaz and Peten. The total Kekchi population, which extends into Southern Belize, numbers about 400,000. In 1987 there were 51 congregations in the Iglesia Nacional Evangélica Menonita Guatemalteca, with a Christian community of about 5,000.

Each congregation has a pastor and several deacons. Leaders are usually chosen from within the congregation. The conference is divided into five districts. Each district is represented on an executive committee which is responsible for the overall work of the conference. Other major committees include (1) the education committee responsible for the Bible institute, adult literacy, women's training, Sunday school and pastoral education programs; (2) the evangelism committee responsible for outreach to communities at a distance from existing churches; and (3) the service committee which gives leadership to the programs of health, agriculture, °appropriate technology, and adult education.

The conference has close fraternal ties to the Iglesia Menonita de Guatemala, the conference of Spanish-speaking Mennonites in Guatemala. Representatives of the conference participate in the annual sessions of the °Consulta Anabautista Menonita Centroamericana (CAMCA). The church is a member of Mennonite World Conference. It has international partnership relationships with Eastern Mennonite Board of Missions and Charities, the Franklin Mennonite Conference mission board, and Mennonite Central Committee.   MG

MWH (1984), 75.

Iglesia Nacional Evangélica Menonita Kekchi. See Iglesia Nacional Evangélica Menonita Guatemalteca.

Igreja Evangélica dos Irmãos Menonitas em Angola (IEIMA; Evangelical Mennonite Brethren Church of Angola). The Mennonite Brethren Church in Angola began when Angolan refugees of diverse church backgrounds, who had joined the Mennonite Brethren Church in Kinshasa, Zaire, were led by Pastor Makanimpovi S. Sikonda of the Njili 13 church to return to Angola in October, 1980. Initially joining an independent, charismatic "Church of Christ," they soon applied to the Ministry of Justice for separate registration and were provisionally granted this in in October 1983, with the help of the Angolan Council of Churches (CAIE). The IEIMA is also affiliated with the Association of Evangelicals in Angola (AEA).

At the time of the first visit by North American representatives of the Mennonite Brethren Board of Missions and Services in February 1984, there were some 154 baptized believers in four congregations in the capital city of Lukanda and an undisclosed number in another seven congregations in the province of Uige. At the time of the second visit in February 1986, the CAIE reported some 1,200 members in a total of 13 congregations. Since its recognition of the Angolan Mennonite Brethren church, the board has assisted the church with church roofing material, one jeep, and a small quantity of clothes. As a result of the last visit, the church is now negotiating with Brazil for permission to send students there for theological studies and with Zaire for permission to send students for training in agriculture and primary health care.

By 1988 Angolan refugees remaining in Zaire had organized four Portuguese-speaking congregations, affiliated with the Église du Christ au Zaire (MB). Membership was 407.   PMH

Courier 1, no. 2 (1986), 16; *MWH* (1984), 10; *MWR* (May 3, 1984), 7, (May 19, 1988), 1; *Menn. Rep.* (July 8, 1985), 2.

Illinois (ME III:6). Mennonites and Amish started coming to the Peoria-Bloomington area of Illinois in the 1830s—the Amish arrived in 1830 (not 1829 as stated in ME III:6) and the Mennonites in 1833.

In 1986 there were the following conferences and other groups of Mennonites and Amish represented in Illinois: Illinois Conference (MC, 4,436 members); General Conference Mennonite Church (GCM, 2,394); Evangelical Mennonite Church (1,042); Old Order Amish (1980 data, 1,014); Conservative Mennonite Conference (174); Beachy Amish Mennonite Fellowship (156); Eastern Pennsylvania Mennonite Church (104); Reformed Mennonite Church (40); Mennonite Brethren (including former Krimmer Mennonite Brethren, 16); unaffiliated Mennonite (310). Since a few congregations have dual membership (MC, GCM) their members are counted twice. The total number of Mennonites and Amish groups in Illinois in 1986 would be not less than 9,320.

It should be explained that the Eastern Pennsylvania Mennonite Church resulted from a division within the Lancaster Mennonite Conference (MC) in 1969. Three congregations affiliated with the Eastern Pennsylvania Mennonite Conference are located in southern Illinois; a fourth small congregation has recently separated from this group and in 1987 was listed as unaffiliated.

More important than growth in numbers since the 1950s have been the changes that have come to the Illinois Mennonites in religious practices and customs, and the growth toward cooperation and unity, especially between the Mennonite Church (MC) and the General Conference Mennonite Church (GCM) congregations. Another change is the attitude toward °"nonconformity." Some groups have changed more than others. The Reformed Mennonites and the Old Order Amish have changed very little. Probably no group has changed more than the Mennonite Church (MC). Changes in a variety of nonconformity issues are outlined in the Illinois Mennonite Conference article.

Other changes that indicate the new interpretation of nonconformity among the major Mennonite bodies in recent decades include the use of life °insurance, acceptance of °motion pictures and °drama, and a wider use of the °political process—voting and office-holding.

Reaching out to groups outside the German and Swiss Mennonite °ethnic heritage has also gone much further than before. Two small °Hispanic congregations in Rock Island and Moline, are under the Iowa-Nebraska Mennonite Conference (MC). A small congregation in a Milwaukee, Wis., suburb and three Hispanic congregations in Chicago are a part of the Illinois Mennonite Conference (MC): (Lawndale (founded 1934) with 54 members; Iglesia Menonita Hispana (1979) with 42 members; and Iglesia Menonita Cristiana (1979) with 25 members.

The Mennonite outreach in Illinois has also included Afro-Americans. Those churches affiliated with the Mennonite Church (MC) are Bethel Mennonite Community in Chicago (1944), 64 members; Rehoboth at St. Anne (1949), 58 members; and Englewood in Chicago which is a continuation of the °°Mennonite Home Mission congregation (1893). Englewood is a good example of a church that became black, or largely so, through shifting population rather than by design as in the case of Bethel. Other predominantly Afro-American congregations are: Community Mennonite in Markham (1957), 53 members (GCM/MC); and Joy Fellowship in Peoria (1984), 83 members (GCM/MC); and First Mennonite Church in Chicago (GCM).

Though the more progressive branches have used the talents of women in church for many years, progress toward their greater use has been marked in recent decades. Emma Richards of the Lombard Mennonite Church was not the first Mennonite woman licensed to preach in Illinois, but her ordination in 1973 constituted an important milestone.

Significant, finally, is the change among Illinois Mennonites toward cooperation and unity. This is especially true among the more progressive bodies, but in such things as the annual Mennonite relief sale even the more conservative groups—the Old Order Amish and others—participate increasingly. Only one Old Order Amish settlement—at °Arthur— remains in the state. The Illinois Mennonite Historical and Genealogical Library and Archives was established at Metamora in 1969. Its sponsoring society publishes two periodicals. Retirement facilities and nursing homes are located at Tinley Park, Eureka, and Chenoa. Camp Menno Haven is at Tiskilwa (1957), and Camp Rehoboth is at St. Anne (1949). Four elementary schools (at Arthur, Chicago, Ewing, and Anna) and the Mennonite School of Nursing at Bloomington are among Mennonite institutions in the state. WHS

Willard H. Smith, *Mennonites in Illinois* (Scottdale, 1983); H. F. Weber, *Centennial History of the Mennonites of Illinois* (Goshen, Ind., 1931); *MC Yearbook* (1988-89), 21-22; Wittlinger, *Piety and Obedience* (1978), 131-32.

Illinois Mennonite Conference (MC) (ME III:9).

After the organization of the Illinois Mennonite Conference (1920-21) by the merger of the (Old) Mennonites (MC) and the Illinois Amish Mennonite congregations that had been members of the the the Western District Amish Mennonite Conference, conservatism continued to dominate the new organization. But later constitutions, especially from the 1940s on, show a moderating trend toward a less rigid belief in the Mennonite Church (MC) policy of °nonconformity to the world. Though basically still emphasizing simplicity and the simple life, the Mennonite Church (MC) has become less restrictive in patterns of °dress, wearing of jewelry, use of °musical instruments in °worship, and the use of the °prayer veil. While never emphasizing "plain clothes" to the extent that the eastern conferences did, the Illinois Conference (MC) urged and at

times required its ministers to wear what was often called the "plain coat." Giving up this requirement was a churchwide trend, but from the 1950s on Illinois led the way having dropped the requirement in 1949.

Since 1949 the conference has also dropped the prohibition on the use of musical instruments in worship, though still continuing to emphasize unaccompanied congregational °singing. Since there has also been a shift in recent decades from conference to congregational control, the amount of change varies from congregation to congregation. Use of the prayer covering, for example, while decreasing in general, is still more widespread in some congregations than in others. This is also the case with the wearing of jewelry, and other practices. Included here would be the use of more ornate architecture in the building of homes and meetinghouses.

Handling the °divorce problem has also become more flexible than formerly. Instead of having a rigid conference position that no divorced person under any circumstances, except when the cause of divorce was adultery, could be a Mennonite, in 1987 the major bodies have statements that continue to emphasize the high view and permanency of marriage, but which under carefully restricted guidelines do permit membership for divorced people.

Since there also has been a shifting in recent decades from conference to congregational control, the amount of change on the above practices varies from congregation to congregation. As to the ordination of °women to the ministry, the conference reached a milestone in 1973 when it permitted the Lombard congregation to ordain Emma Richards to serve with her husband. The conference operates Camp Menno Haven. Its publication is *The Missionary Guide.* WHS

Willard H. Smith, *Mennonites in Illinois* (Scottdale, 1983); *MC Yearbook* (Scottdale, 1988-89), 58-60.

Illuminated Manuscripts. See *Fraktur*.

Imitation of Christ. See Discipleship.

Immersion (ME III:14). The largest Mennonite immersionist conference (Mennonite Brethren in the United States and Canada) declared officially in 1963 that local churches be permitted "to accept into fellowship believers who have been baptized upon an experiential and confessed faith with a mode other than immersion." Such members were not to be transferred by letter from one church to another, but in 1972 the issue reappeared and a resolution was passed allowing transfers of nonimmersed members among churches.

In each of the instances stated above it was made clear that immersion continues to be the one form of baptism practiced. In 1987 the Mennonite Brethren Conference (United States and Canada) for the first time stated that candidates for ordination to the pastoral ministry who have been baptized upon confession of faith by some other mode of baptism be accepted. The rationale stated that pouring (or affusion) signifies the reception of the Holy Spirit and therefore is "biblically tenable."

Conferences still practicing immersion exclusively include the Brethren in Christ, Missionary Church, Evangelical Mennonite Church, and the Mennonite Brethren Church.

Immersion has been used on mission fields by those conferences generally using other modes where it appeared to prevent confusion when working in areas where immersionist bodies were also active. Immersion is an option in some General Conference Mennonite and Mennonite Church (MC) congregations in North America. One General Conference congregation in central Kansas (Hebron) has provided such an option since its founding. That option still remains and a majority of baptismal candidates choose immersion. While little has been said in non-immersionist churches about immersion as an option, some young people in North American Mennonites churches have requested immersion.   MHein

Minutes (MB) (1963), 38-39, (1972), 14-15, (1987).

See also Evangelical Mennonite Conference.

Incarnation. See Christology.

Independent Churches. See African Independent Churches.

India is the seventh largest country in the world. It is a union of 22 states and nine territories combined into a socialist secular democratic republic with a parliamentary form of government.

India's population in 1981 was 685 million people living in 2,949 towns and 557,138 villages. This is an increase of 25 percent over the 1971 census. Rural population makes up 77 percent of the total. In 1981 the °literacy rate was 36 percent. From the numerous languages and dialects spoken, 15 have been specified in the eighth schedule of the constitution. India is one of the 10 major book-producing countries of the world and ranks third in production of English titles. India expects to achieve available health facilities for all of the people by A.D. 2000. The birth rate is expected to fall to 21 per 1000 and the death rate to 9 per 1000 population by the year 2000.

In 1981 the following major religious groups were registered: Hindus, 550 million (83 percent); Muslims, 75.5 million (11 percent); Christians, 14.3 million (2.4 percent); Sikhs, 13 million (2 percent); Buddhists, 4.7 million (.71 percent); Jains, 3.2 million (.5 percent); others, 2.7 million (.4 percent).

Mennonite and Mennonite-related institutions in India include the following: Nav Jivan Hospital; Dhamtari Christian Hospital; Dhamtari Christian Hospital School of Nursing; Sankra Christian Hospital; Shantipur Leprosy Hospital; Bihar Mennonite Hostel; Mennonite Service Agency, Bihar; Mennonite Higher Secondary School, Dhamtari; Garjan Memorial School, Balodgahan; Mennonite Primary School, Dhamtari; Mennonite English Primary School, Dhamtari; Calcutta Bible Institute; Jadcherla Christian Hospital; Mennonite Brethren Development Association; Union Biblical Seminary, Pune (formerly Yeotmal). God Has Spoken Ministries; Mennonite Brethren Property Association; Mennonite Brethren Development Association.

Historical Background. In the late 19th c., Mennonite Brethren in Russia were interested in foreign missionary work, but they did not have their own mission board. They were sending their mission offerings to the Dutch Mennonite missionary organization for the support of the work of Peter °°Jansz in Java. They also were supporting the work of the American Baptist Missionary Society in India. The Mennonite Brethren sent their first missionary couple to India (Abraham and Miriam Friesen) from the Ukraine under the auspices of the American Baptist Missionary Society. The Friesens worked in the Nalgonda district of what was then Nizam's State (later part of Andhra Pradesh State). The Friesens were in India until the beginning of World War I (1914) when it became impossible to receive support from Russia. This work was transferred to the American Mennonite Brethren Mission in 1898.

From the beginning the various Mennonite and Brethren in Christ missions focused on planting Indian churches which would ultimately become self-governing and self-supporting. The influx of North American missionaries lasted until World War II (1942). The phasing out of foreign missionaries became inevitable then due to the Indian struggle for freedom and the problem of missionary visas after independence in 1947.

Almost all of the Mennonite and Brethren in Christ missions began their work with °°orphanages and other institutions, and they all established mission compounds in which these institutions were located. This created a liability of dependence of the Indian Christians on the foreigners and their boards. The first generation of Indian Mennonite and Brethren in Christ were the founding fathers of the present churches. Without their utter dedication and sacrifices there would not have been any churches.

Socially and culturally Indian Mennonites come from the low °caste and *harijans* ("children of God"). For instance the Malas and Madigas in the Mennonite Brethren Church in India are leather-workers, weavers, and entirely landless farm laborers. In the Bihar region the Brethren in Christ Church Society congregations are composed largely of *adivasies* (aboriginal) marginal farmers. The Bihar Mennonite Mandli membership is drawn from a similar background. There is a closer affinity between Santalies, Oraans, Mundas, and other °animist groups who have become Christians in North and South Bihar and the United Missionary Society (Bharatiya Jukta Christa Prachar Mandali) in the Purulia district of West Bengal and the Surguja District of Madhya Pradesh with the General Conference Mennonites (Bharatiya General Conference Mennonite Kalisiya). Caste Hindus were converted in the Mennonite Church in India and the Champa-Korba area of the General Conference Mennonite churches, with a tiny sprinkling of high caste Brahmin.

Linguistically the Mennonite and Brethren in Christ churches are a heterogenous group speaking more than a half-dozen languages and able to communicate with each other only in the English language or limited Hindustani. Geographically they are at great distances, being spread out in four large states of India, namely, °Andhra Pradesh, °Madhya Pradesh, North and South °Bihar and the West

INDIA

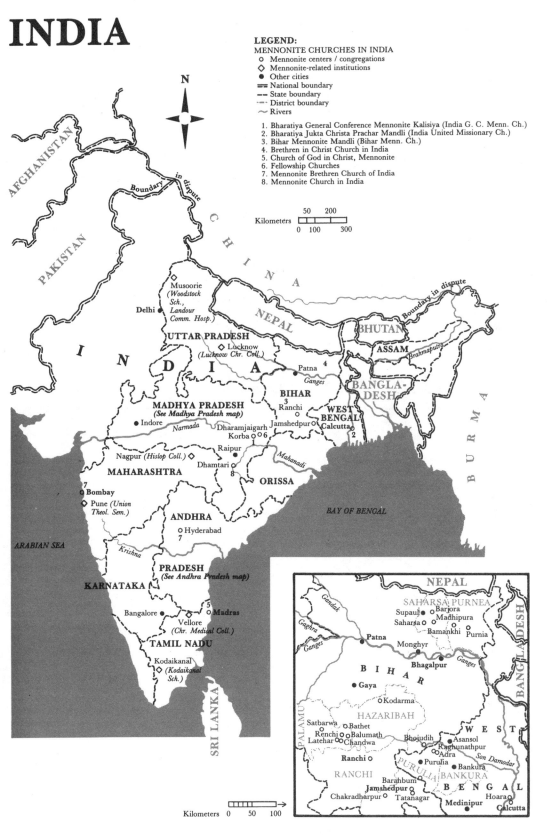

LEGEND:
MENNONITE CHURCHES IN INDIA
○ Mennonite centers / congregations
◇ Mennonite-related institutions
● Other cities
══ National boundary
-- State boundary
-·- District boundary
∼ Rivers

1. Bharatiya General Conference Mennonite Kalisiya (India G. C. Menn. Ch.)
2. Bharatiya Jukta Christa Prachar Mandli (India United Missionary Ch.)
3. Bihar Mennonite Mandli (Bihar Menn. Ch.)
4. Brethren in Christ Church in India
5. Church of God in Christ, Mennonite
6. Fellowship Churches
7. Mennonite Brethren Church of India
8. Mennonite Church in India

Kilometers 50 200
            0 100 300

Bengal. From the site of the Brethren in Christ worshiping center at the Koshi Barrage at the Indo-Nepalese border to the Mennonite Brethren churches in the Nalgonda district at the Nagarjun Sagar Dam on the River Krishna is a distance of more than 3,500 km. (2,170 mi.). Nearest in respect to location are the Mennonite Church in India and the Bharatiya General Conference Mennonite Kalisiya in Madhya Pradesh at a distance of 150 mi. (240 km.).

Description of Mennonite and Brethren in Churches in India. *Mennonite Brethren Church in India,* with a total of 40,000 members in 1987, is spread out in 10 field associations covering over 2,000 villages. Each field association is further divided into circuits of five to six villages where the local ministers and elders are stationed. Each circuit preacher is responsible for evangelistic and pastoral work. New work in the city of Bombay with the migrant Telegu-speaking people has begun. The Telegu Mennonite Brethren are strongly motivated to field evangelism, and they baptize annually some 300 to 400 non-Christians. The church growth rate is much higher than any other Mennonite group in India. The governing council of the Mennonite Brethren churches is made up of five members from each of the ten field associations who elect the five-member executive committee. The governing council meets annually.

Mennonite Churches in Madhya Pradesh (Central Provinces) resulted from the Mennonite Church (MC) mission in °Dhamtari (1899) and the General Conference Mennonite Church (GCM) mission in °Champa (1900). From the beginning the two missions and their missionaries cooperated well. For example, the General Conference missionaries lived in Dhamtari for a year until they could learn the language and locate their own field of service. While the missionaries themselves met more frequently, their Indian counterparts seldom met in a conference or retreats before 1950.

The *Mennonite Church in India* is the official title of the church in the Dhamtari area. It functions under the annual conference established in 1912. It has 17 congregations spread out in four districts of se. Madhya Pradesh, namely, south of the Raipur district, and in the Durg, Rajanandgaon, and North Bastar districts. But its members are very widely scattered throughout India. The hub of its work is located in the town of Dhamtari, and most of the village churches have become depleted in numbers due to the migration of the second generation of Christians seeking employment in industrial centers. The growth of the church has been sporadic and disappointing. Membership of the church has remained at ca. 2,500 since 1950. The American Mennonite Mission ceased to exist in 1952, and all

ANDHRA PRADESH

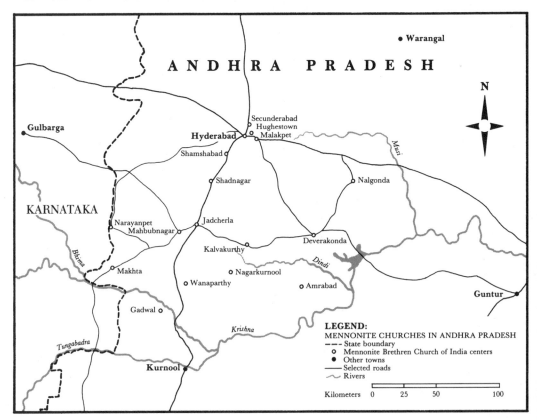

MADHYA PRADESH

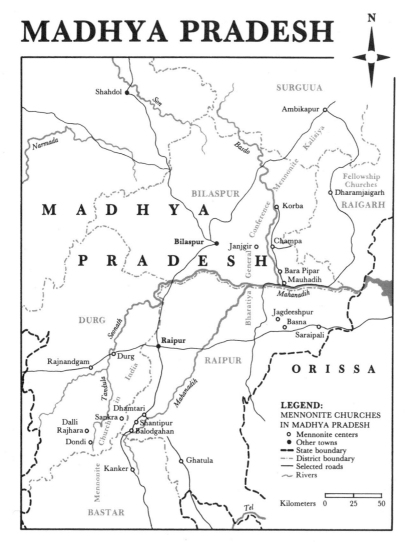

administrative responsibilities were transferred to the Mennonite Church in India. The Mennonite Board of Missions (MC) continued to provide personnel and funds (regular monthly budget payments ended in 1975). However, there are new openings where members have moved to other places for work and have established themselves well financially.

The *Bharatiya General Conference Mennonite Church* can be broadly divided into three regions: the Surguja field in the north among the *adivasies*, the older work in the Champa-Korba and Janjgir-Mahhadih area, and the work in the southern area largely in the Jagdeeshpur-Saraipaalli area. Divisions along regional lines have on occasion been sharp. Those in the south are mostly from the Oriya-speaking group from the older field of the British Baptists and they form a numerical majority. The most encouraging feature of General Conference Church is that it is a growing church. What seemed to be a barren field in the 1940s in the Korba-Champa area is now exhibiting growth both in the

establishing of new worshiping centers developing into permanent congregations, but also in the expansion of educational institutions. Recently all of the educational work of the church has been registered under a new educational society called Menno Christian Educational Society (Jan. 1986). Under this function three Mennonite high schools (Jantzen School at Jagdeeshpur, 1939; Jyothy School at Korba, 1970; and the Beacon English Medium School at Korba, 1962). Indigenous leadership provides spiritual care and shepherding of the flock in the Korba industrial complex at 8 places of worship. Membership in 1987 was approximately 7,500.

While the Mennonite Church in India is a member of the National Council of Churches in India and works very closely with Churches Auxiliary for Social Action, the General Conference church is a member of the Evangelical Fellowship of India and works with the Federation of Evangelical Churches of India and Evangelical Fellowship of India Committee on Relief.

Both churches have been cooperating in several

areas, especially in the translation, publication, and distribution of Vacation Bible School materials published by Herald Press in Scottdale, Pa. From time to time the two churches have cooperated in the area of peace literature and education. The Union Bible School at Janjgir was a union institution in which the Dhamtari and Champa groups cooperated. It played a vital role in preparing village preachers. It has become the Union Biblical Seminary at Bibwewadi Pune, Maharashtra State (formerly at Yavatmal). Conference properties for both churches are held by the Evangelical Trust Association of North India. The churches were charter members of the Mennonite Literature and Radio Council (MELARC).

At special meetings during conventions and retreats pastors and church leaders from both churches exchange pulpits. Yet there are many unexplored areas for cooperation and the differences are also unique. While the Mennonite Church in India receives no grants or personnel from the Mennonite Board of Missions and Charities, the General Conference church receives regular funds from the Unites States for nurture and women's work and it still has one foreign missionary family in residence. Both churches are deeply motivated to remain Mennonite and Anabaptist in outlook and witness.

The Brethren in Christ Churches in North Bihar were founded in 1914-16 by Brethren in Christ missionaries in the upper regions of North Bihar. The Koshi River flows down the entire length of the BIC mission field. The Koshi is well known as "the river of sorrow" because it keeps changing its course every 10 years. This affected the establishment of mission stations. Small groups of believers are found in Saharsa, Begusrai, Supaul, Madhipura, and Banmankhi. This is largely a Hindi-speaking church with low-caste Hindu background. Rice and jute are the main crops of this area.

A new advance was made by the Brethren in Christ churches with the extensive evangelistic work among the Santali people. The advance was so distinctive that the number of Brethren in Christ members in India almost quadrupled to around 1,200 members. The churches are growing in the Banmankhi and Purnea districts among the Santali people through a people's movement and "each-one-win-one" approach of personal contact among friends and relatives. This Santali group finds close affinity with those in South Bihar and, in the Purulia district of West Bengal, with the Bharatiya Jukta Christo Prachar Mandli (United Missionary Church).

Bharatiya Jukta Christo Prachar Mandli is the official and registered title of the United Missionary Church in India. The vernacular name literally can be translated as "Indian United Christ Evangelistic Church." The work of this church is under three conferences and in five language areas, namely Hindi, Santali, Telegu, Bengali, and English. It is spread out in Bihar, West Bengal, and borders of Orissa and Assam. It has strong evangelistic outreach in rural areas through Bengal Bible Institute in the Purulia district and Calcutta Bible Institute with its Bible Correspondence School since 1956 reaching out to 150,000 persons. It has made a strong impact on the lives of many people in different stations of

life. Total membership is ca. 2,500 in 28 congregations (1987). Denominational headquarters are in °Calcutta. The church is affiliated with Mennonite World Conference, although its parent body in North America, the Missionary Church, is not (ME III:603; IV:774), and is therefore not included in this encyclopedia.

Bihar Mennonite Mandli is the registered name of the Bihar Mennonite Churches. Mennonite (MC) missionaries moved from the Dhamtari area in search of a new field in 1939-41. The work started by S. J. and Ida °Hostetler in the Kodarma area where the Roman Catholics and Lutherans were already working. Later the missionaries decided to move to the Palamau district of South Bihar. The work was mostly in the rural areas and was established with four mission stations, Chandwa, Bethet, Latehar and Satbarwa. With the opening of the *Good Books* program in Banchi a missionary family (Paul and Esther Kniss) are located in this large city. Mostly the churches are in the rural area and agrarian in nature. A total of 16 small congregations with 800 members exist today. This is a homogenous group comprising two tribes (Araon, Munda), and the members' animist cultural background is evident in many social events, e.g., weddings. In partnership with the Mennonite Central Committee the church operates two hostels, (for girls at Latehar and for boys at Chandwa with 30 students). These students attend public schools.

Culturally and linguistically this church has more affinity with congregations in the Banmankhi and Purneas districts of the Brethren in Christ Church Society and with those in the Purulia District of the United Missionary Society.

Relief and Service Programs. The Mennonite Relief Committee of India (MRCI), a precursor to the Mennonite Central Committee (MCC) of India, was organized on April 9, 1942. Mennonite and Brethren in Christ missionaries of the India field met whenever the MCC administrator (Orie O. °Miller) came on his India visit. The committee was formed by representatives of each of the five Mennonite and Brethren in Christ missions in India. S. M. King was the first president and P. W. °°Penner served as secretary-treasurer. They allocated 30 percent of the field remittance to relief and 70 percent for war sufferers. Most of the relief work was carried on by the missionaries.

The Bengal famine of 1942 presented the MRCI with a major effort at organized relief work. Milton C. °Vogt and A. K. °Biswas served as the first relief workers, confronted by the needs of more than 6 million people. Calcutta became the hub of relief activities and the work was carried out by the MRCI until 1944.

During the partition of India into Pakistan and India (1947-48) millions of refugees crossed the borders from the Punjab and West Bengal to find new homes. This was accompanied by much violence. More than a million refugees were temporarily settled in tents on the Ramlilla grounds in New Delhi. At the call of Prime Minister Jawahrlal Nehru a massive relief operation was organized by the National Christian Council of India (NCCI) bringing personnel and supplies from overseas. Mennonite

Central Committee flew several million units of penicillin to New Delhi.

The Mennonite Relief Committee of India was terminated in 1950 and MCC took its place, with headquarters in Calcutta. E. C. Benedict, a missionary for the °°Mennonite Brethren in Christ (°°United Missionary Church) at Balarampur, was the first MCC representative and also served as liaison with the Committee on Relief and Gift Supplies of the National Christian Council of India. For sometime MCC's work was confined to Calcutta and its suburbs giving medical aid and establishing poultry projects.

In 1962 a regional office was set up in Calcutta to administer MCC programs in India, East Pakistan (later Bangladesh) and West Pakistan, Afghanistan, Nepal, and Ceylon (Sri Lanka). In 1963 the °Mennonite Christian Service Fellowship of India was organized (P. J. °Malagar director) to assist MCC in °disaster relief, °voluntary service, °peace education, and inter-Mennonite fellowship. Together these organizations assisted in Chittagong in East Pakistan in 1964, flood relief in the Midanpur District of West Bengal, refugee work in Bangladesh together with Bengal Relief Service (World Council of Churches), and other relief agencies. The MCC office was active in organizing the Evangelical Fellowship of India and helped this agency in refugee relief in the Dum Dum area. When Bengal Relief Service was active in Shyamnagar in a refugee housing project MCC volunteers lived in the housing çolony and engaged in community health, fisheries, and poultry work. The medical programs of Bengal Relief Service were eventually turned over to MCC and MCSFI. Together they formed a board to administer the Shyamnagar Christian Hospital.

Mennonite Central Committee was also heavily involved in the development of °water resources and with Action for Food Production to counteract the recurring drought and monsoon flooding. Well-drilling machines were imported and small dams were built. Drought relief was also intensive in the MCSFI constituency. Other regular MCC programs include the °SELFHELP artisan program, educational aid, vocational training, and cooperation with the following development agencies in the MCSFI constituency: REACH (Rural Economic Development and Community Health Association) at Jagdeeshpur, Madhya Pradesh; MADRA (Mennonite Agricultural and Development and Relief Association) at Dhamtari, Madhya Pradesh; MBDO (Mennonite Brethren Development Organization in Jadcherla and Mahhubnagar in Andhra Pradesh; MSA (Mennonite Service Agency) in Chandwa, South Bihar; BICDS (Brethren in Christ Development Society) at the Bammankhi-Purnea area of North Bihar; and CHERRADA (Community Health Employment Relief Relief Development and Agriculture) at Ambikapur, Madhya Pradesh. Both cash and grain for Food for Work projects (building roads and dams and digging wells) are supplied by MCC.

Mennonite Central Committee in India relates to India Mennonite and Brethren in Christ churches and takes an active part in these churches' annual conferences and their church-wide programs for youth, women, and pastors. The MCC staff is now entirely indigenous except for overseas representatives.   PJM

Gerhard Wilhelm Peters, *The Growth of Foreign Missions in the Mennonite Brethren Church* (MB Board of Foreign Missions, 1947), 27-88; *India Mennonite Brethren Church at Cross Roads* (Governing Council of the Conference of the MB Church of India, March 1972); John A. Lapp, *India* (1972); P. J. Malagar, *MC India* (1981); Juhnke, *Mission* (1979); Anna R. Engle, John A. Climenhaga, and Leoda A. Buckwalter, *There Is No Difference* (1950); Everek Richard Storms, *History of the United Missionary Church* (Elkhart, Ind.: Bethel Publishing Company,. 1958), 233-49; Pronoy Sarkar, "A Memorandum prepared for the Missionary Church International Conference of Presidents, Family Life Center, La Vega" (Sept. 5-12, 1986); Sushil Khaka, unpub. manuscript on Bihar Mennonite Mandli; *MWH* (1978), 122-44; *MWH* (1984) 27-32; Leoda Buckwalter, *Silhouette: Colonial India as We Lived It* (Nappanee, 1988).

See also All-India Mennonite Women's Conference; Bharatiya General Conference Mennonite Kalisiya; Bihar Mennonite Mandli; Brethren in Christ Church Society, India; Mennonite Church in India.

India General Conference Mennonite Church. See Bharatiya General Conference Mennonite Kalisiya.

India Mennonite Conference. See Mennonite Church in India.

India United Missionary Church. See Calcutta; India.

Indian Ministries, North America (ME III:22). From the late 1940s to the 1980s Mennonites and Brethren in Christ added 20 or more new mission efforts among the Native peoples of North America to the work started by the Mennonite Brethren and the General Conference in the late 1800s. In 1986 these new efforts budgeted over $2.5 million and had more than 300 staff members including many volunteers. In addition local churches and individuals were involved in advocacy, foster and adoptive care, and participation in education, medical, social work, and administration for Indian peoples. For example, Widow Netha Boschman and her seven children began a reception home for up to 120 native people a month brought to Carrot River, Sask. for medical care. The Croghan, N.Y., Conservative Mennonite congregation helped defuse a potentially violent situation when traditional Mohawks laid claim to an abandoned camp in their area.

Alongside the expansion there has been attrition even in the newer work. The General Conference Mennonite Church closed churches at Thomas, Longdale, and Fonda, Okla., and at Birney, Mont. The Mennonite Brethren gave up a church planting effort in Saskatoon, as did the Evangelical Mennonite Mission Conference at Rosseau River, Man. The hospital and school of the Brethren in Christ Navajo mission were closed as the government took over these functions. Other boards are looking at possible cutbacks.

There has been a growing realization that injustices to Indian people have a bearing on the response to the Christian gospel. Most Mennonite work has included a concern for the educational, medical, and economic areas of life as well as the spiritual. For David Weaver, support of Choctaw Indian rights resulted in death threats and three bombings of the Nanih Wayia church. Interdenominational Project North, with the participation of Mennonite Central Committee (Canada), influenced the pace and direction of development in Canada's North. The Houma people, once thought to be extinct, were found by Mennonite Central Committee (U.S.) in Louisiana and helped, along with other unrecognized Indian groups, to establish their identity and gain government recognition.

Mennonites have become increasingly aware that they brought the Good News to the Indian people in a white man's cup, thus fostering Indian alternatives such as the Peyote religion. To help express the message in Indian languages Mennonites have been involved in translations in the Hopi and Ojibway languages and revisions in Cheyenne-language resources. Indigenous gospel songs have been collected in Comanche and Cheyenne hymnals and work is progressing on Crow hymnbook. Some mission leaders are asking if the growing Indian spirituality provides common ground with the Christian faith in the manner of Paul at Athens.

Indian self-determination in the political realm has sometimes been ahead of that in the church, but Indian control of, and responsibility for, their churches is growing. A Native Mennonite Conference has been formed in northwestern Ontario with participation by three missions. Through the Mennonite Indian Leaders Council (GCM), Cheyenne, Arapaho, and Hopi Christians have gained some control over Indian ministries in the General Conference.

Theological and geographical distance have made it difficult for Mennonite Indian Christians and mission workers to meet for fellowship and sharing, but several attempts were made in the last 25 years. For example, an inter-Mennonite group gathered at the Brethren in Christ Navajo mission in 1973. Interdenominational gatherings, some of them sparked by Mennonites, have provided a forum for fellowship and learning.

In addition to traditional Bible schools, extension leadership training efforts drawing on the experience of missions in Africa and Latin America are being used (°theological education by extension). A few Indian Christian leaders want to plan their own patterns of training. Special training in recovery from and avoiding alcoholism is beginning to be seen as important. With most Indian churches congregations numbering fewer than 50 active members, alternatives to the dependency-fostering salaried ministry are being sought. The following paragraphs summarize the various programs as of 1986-88:

Beachy Amish Mennonites, through the Mission Interests Committee, work with Ojibway people (also Cree people, at Bearskin Lake and Fort Severn, Ont.) at Sioux Lookout, Red Lake, Hudson, Lac Seul, Sioux Narrows, Bearskin Lake, Fort Severn, and Kenora, Ont. Church planting and education work began at Red Lake in 1956. Private Christian day schools were established at Red Lake (1975) and Sioux Narrows (1976). A boarding school (1956-64) and a short-term Bible school (1965-74) operated at Red Lake. A bookstore (1964-) at Hudson, and prison ministry at Kenora and organized congregations at Bearskin Lake and Red Lake have been part

of the work. Committee members, workers and pastors have included Mahlon Wagler, Ben F. Lapp, Ezra T. Peachy, David Hersberger, Loren Kipfer, David and Greta Mosquito, Elijah and Emma Stoney, Lazarus Stoney, and Sylvanus Schrock. Total budget was $155,000 ($40,000 received for services). *Mission Interests Committe Newsletter*, published at Abbyville, S.C. contains current information. *Brethren in Christ* ministries are related to the Navajo people at Bloomfield, N.M. (boarding school, 1947-81; hospital, 1952-76; community center, 1978-, leadership education, fellowship) and Chaco, N.M. (organized congregation), and to the Cree people at Timber Bay, Sask. (Timber Bay Children's Home, a dormitory for public school children, operated by Northern Canada Evangelical Mission, 1950-68, by Brethren in Christ, 1969-) and La Ronge, Sask. (Girl's Home). Workers and pastors in New Mexico have included Lynn and Eleanor Nicholson, Rose Eyster, Wilmer Heisy, George Bundy, John Peter Yazzie. The budget in 1987 was $92,000; five staff members were employed. The Timber Bay home's budget was $300,000, two-thirds of which was supplied by the government. *Navajo News,* (Bloomfield, N.M.), *EV,* and *Therefore* (Mt. Joy, Pa.) contain current information.

Since 1965 the *Conservative Mennonite Church of Ontario* sponsors programs in church planting and community development among Ojibway people near Emo (Manitou, Sabaskong and Mines Center Reserves), Ont. The *Ontario Informer* and *The Messenger,* a four-page paper circulated on the reserves, carry current information. The budget was $4,000. Workers have included William Kurtz, Fred Nighswander, and Gleason Martin.

The *Church of God in Christ, Mennonite (Holdeman),* through USA Missions (formerly Central District Mission Board), has sponsored work among Navajo people at Greasewod, Wide Ruins (later moved to Kalegetoh, Salina Springs, and Jeddito (and Keams Canyon), Ariz., since 1951. Programs have included a boarding school (1951-64), children's home (1951-62, moved to Window Rock, see below), a clinic (1951-65), prison ministry, and church planting (organized congregation at Wide Ruins). Pastors and workers have included Carrie and Herman Frank, Inez Unruh, Irvy and Imogene Goossen, Vernon and Opal Giesbrecht, James and Emma Joe, and Lloyd and Elizabeth Koehn. The budget was $100,000. The Christian Public Service Board (CGC) established children's homes at Window Rock and Gallup, N.M. (Navajo), from 1962 onward, and the Canadian CGC Christian Public Service Board has an outpatient home among the Cree people at Carrot River, Sask., since 1984. Total staff for all these programs numbered 22.

Evangelical Mennonite Conference programs include church planting efforts at Virden, Man. (Sioux Valley Reserve), Kamsack, Sask. (Cote and Keeseekoose [Ojibway] reserves), and Swan River, Man. (Ojibway). Pastors and workers have included Farnk and Mary Braun, Dave Plett, John and Brenda Cosens. A staff of four full-time workers was supported by a $45,000 budget. Information is found in *The Messenger* (Steinbach, Man.).

Evangelical Mennonite Mission Conference sponsored church planting work with Ojibway people through the Western Gospel Mission at Roseau River, Man. (1952-61) and has placed workers with the Northern Canada Evangelical Mission in York Factory, God's Lake, Thompson, and Shamattawa, Man.; Lac la Biche, Alta. (Bible school, extension education); and Round Lake, Ont. In 1960 The Board of Missions (EMMC) took over the work of the Western Gospel Mission at Roseau River, Man. (1961-71) and started work with a congregation (Lakeside Gospel Chapel) at St. Laurent, Man. (Métis). Workers and pastors have included Ben D. Reimer (EMCon.), Jake and Dora Hoeppner, Sara Gerbrand, Nettie Penner, and Arnold and Elvira Heppner. The budget was ca. $25,000 and staff members numbered five. Information is found in the *EMMC Recorder* (Winnipeg).

The *Fellowship of Evangelical Bible Churches* (Evangelical Mennonite Brethren) is involved with Ojibway and Cree people in the Dallas Bible Church and the Fisher Bay Bible Camp at Dallas, Man., since 1976 (two staff members; budget of $15,000-18,000). Information is available from *Gospel Tidings* (Omaha, Nebr.).

The Mennonite Indian Leaders Council of the *General Conference Mennonite Church* coordinates programs and congregations in Oklahoma (Southern Cheyenne and Southern Arapaho), Montana (Northern Cheyenne), and Arizona (Hopi). Three half-time staff members administered a budget of $140,000. Oklahoma congregations are located at Clinton, Hammon, Seiling, and Canton (Arapaho). Pastors and leaders have included Betty E. Hart, and Bob and Nancy Koehn. Northern Cheyenne congregations are located at Ashland, Busby, and Lame Deer, Mont.; workers and pastors have included Ted Risingsun, Rick and Linda Cullen, Willis and Nadine Busenitz, and Joe and Victoria Walks Along. In Arizona congregations are located at Kykotsmovi, Hotevilla, and Tuba City (Moencopi), with church planting efforts underway in Phoenix. Pastors and workers have included Rhoda Lomahoema, Karl and Louise Nasewytewa, Lorenzo Yoyokie, Fred Johnson, Daniel and Uberta Quimayousie, Elmer and Nadenia Myron. Information is found in *The Mennonite* and Lois Barrett, *Vision and Reality* (1983).

In Canada the Native Ministries program of the *Conference of Mennonites in Canada [GCM]* (formerly known as Mennonite Pioneer Mission [Bergthal Mennonites of Manitoba]) has worked since 1948 from offices in Winnipeg (reception home, community development, leadership training, advocacy, camping programs) and with Ojibway, Cree, and Métis peoples in Winnipeg (2 congregations), Wanipagow (resident ministries), Bloodvein River (resident ministries), Paungassi (congregation since 1955), Little Grand Rapids (itinerant ministries, 1956-), and Cross Lake (Elim congregation since 1956; Cree), Man. In addition the Native Ministries organization has been involved with Métis people at Matheson Island (itinerant ministries, 1948-), Anama Bay (1953-54), Pine Dock (itinerant ministries, 1949-), Loon Straits (itinerant ministries, 1955), Riverton, and Selkirk (Selkirk Christian Fellowship), Man. Other programs include work with Blackfoot (Blood) people at Cardston, Alta. (1964), and with Métis and Cree at Saskatoon (1986-). These programs were carried out by a staff of 8 (plus 4

volunteers) with a budget of $437,400. Workers and pastors have included David Schulz, J. N. Pauls, J. N. Hoeppner, J. W. Schmidt (at Winnipeg offices); Annie Janzen, Willie and Maria Guenther, Genny and Neil Funk-Unrau, Elijah and Jeanette McKay, Jake and Trudy Unrau, Neill and Edith Von Gunten, Jake and Martha Bergman (Métis); Oliver and Hulda Heppner, Evan and Arlie Schultz, Jacob Owen, St. John °Owen, Spoat Owen, David Owen, Henry and Elna Neufeld (Ojibway); Jeremiah and Fannie Ross (Cree); Margaret and Ernie Sawatzky (Blackfoot); Ray and Arlene Dumais (Métis and Cree at Saskatoon). Information is found in *Intotemak "Our Friends"* (Winnipeg), *Mennonite Reporter*, and in Lois Barrett, *Vision and Reality* (1983).

The Conference of Mennonites in Alberta (CGM) has sustained ministries with Blackfoot (Blood) people at Glenwood (church planting, 1944-66), Standoff (Bible studies, 1984-86), and Gleichen, Alta. Workers and pastors have included Henry Klassen, John H. Dyck, Henry Kopp, and Alvin Lepp. The Conference of Mennonites in Saskatchewan has sponsored work with Cree and Métis at Rosthern (childrens' camp, 1980-) and Saskatoon (in cooperation with Native Ministries of Winnipeg). Workers include Henry W. Friesen and Ray and Arlene Dumais.

Mennonite Brethren work has been carried on by several district conferences. Building on work begun in 1894, the Southern District sponsored programs in church planting among Comanche people at Indiahoma (Post Oak congregation, 1958-) and Cache (independent congregation, 1979-), Okla. Herb and Pauline Schroeder have served in pastoral roles. The Crestview congregation at Lawton, Okla., no longer has Comanche involvement. The Central District Conference worked with Sioux people at Pine Ridge and Porcupine, S.D., since 1948 (2 congregations). Leaders have included Arthur and Isabelle Unrau and Ted and Mamie Standing Elk. The Alberta Provincial Conference has placed workers through the Northern Canada Evangelical Mission, working with Cree people at Hobbema, Alta., in church planting since 1973 (Reinhold and Helen Fast). In British Columbia, the Harbour of Hope congregation at Port Edward (Anne Neufeld) has merged with the Prince Rupert Mennonite Brethren church and the provincial conference has placed workers through the North American Indian Mission at Seabird Island Reserve (1973-85; Ed and Dianne Cooper). The Saskatchewan Provincial MB Conference has supported church planting efforts among the Cree people and others in Saskatoon, 1974-85 (Reuben and Edith Block). Information on Mennonite Brethren work is found in *Chr. Leader* and *MB Herald*.

Mennonite Central Committee (Canada) has supported a variety of voluntary service programs (teachers, nurses, researchers, community development, resource development, justice witness) among Cree, Ojibway, Dene, Kwakiutl, Stoney, Métis, Inuit, and Innu peoples in all provinces (except Quebec), the Arctic Coast, and the Northwest Territories. Menno Wiebe has given leadership. The budget for the MCCC Native Concerns programs was $150,000 with a staff of 3 members (ca. 200 volunteers, 1974-87). *Mennonite Central Committee (U.S.)* has carried out specialized ministries to Indian communities since 1974, including assistance to unrecognized tribes in the process of gaining government recognition (Houma and Clifton Choctaw in Louisiana, Penobscot in Maine), summer volunteers (Hoopa, Tunica in California, 1975-76), and Indian rights advocacy and urban ministries in Minneapolis-St. Paul, Minn., and Philadelphia (1979-). MCC (US) involvement with Native Americans began when Lawrence Hart (Cheyenne) was named to the executive committee. The budget was $77,734 (one third from recipients of services). Forty-one workers served in 33 locations, 1982-87. *Mennonite Disaster Service* has repaired houses damaged by floods in Moencopi, Ariz. (Hopi), Wounded Knee, S.D. (Sioux), and Winisk, Ont. (Cree).

The Gulf States Conference of the *Mennonite Church* (MC) has sponsored church planting work among Creek people in Alabama (Atmore, 1953) and Choctaw people in Mississippi (Mashulaville, later moved to Louisville, 1959-; Preston, 1960-; Philadelphia, 1973-). Four congregations are organized. Leadership has come from David Weaver, Rudy Detweiler, Will Wallace, Ethan Good, and D. Glenn Meyers as self-supporting workers. In the North Central Conference church planting among Ojibway people at Morson, Ont. (1952-), has been led by Irvin and Helen Grabill and Willie Longenecker. Information is found in the *North Central Conference Bulletin* and the *Gospel Herald*. The Northwest Conference has sponsored voluntary service (1972-85) and congregational development among Blackfeet people at Browning, Mont., led by Terry and Rhonda Longenecker. Information is found in the conference newsletter. The Southwest Mennonite Conference has carried out congregational work among Navajo people at Chinle (2 congregations, 1954, 1964; radio ministry 1955-) and Phoenix (1986-), Ariz. Leaders have included Stanley and Arlie Weaver, Henry and Eleanor Smiley, Peter and Lita Rose Burbank, Larry and Esther Haskie, Naswood and Peter Burbank. Information is found in the *Southwest Messenger* and the *Gospel Herald*.

Northern Light Gospel Missions, since 1953, with a center in Red Lake, Ont., has carried out church planting, translation work, and teaching among Ojibway people in Ontario at Pikangikum (1953-), Poplar Hill (1953-; development school since 1962), Deer Lake (1955-), Sandy Lake (1956-), North Spirit Lake (1957-), Slate Falls (1957-), Grassy Narrows, MacDowell Lake (1960-), Cat Lake (1961-), Osnaburg House (1963), Pickle Lake (1967-), Savant Lake (1969-), Armstrong (1972-), Ear Falls, Stormer Lake (1973-; fellowship center, retreats, Bible school), and Thunder Bay (youth ministry). Leaders have included Irwin and Susan Schantz, Llewelyn and Edith Groff, Elizabeth Peake, Sam Quill, Patric Owen, Albert Strang, Moose Strang, John Strang, Cello Meekis, Gordon Meekis, Daniel Meekis, Saggius Rae, John Mamageesic, Frederick Kakagamic, Jacob Kakagamic, Johnny Rae, Enos Miller, Magnus James, Ralph Halteman, Jess King, Wayne Watson, and Lee Martin. Information is found in the *Northern Light Gospel Missions Newsletter* (Red Lake, Ont., and Loman, Minn.). The budget was $100,000 for a staff of 100. (See also Northern Light Gospel Mission Conference.)

Clair and Clara Schnupp have worked with Northern Youth Programs among Ojibway people in Dryden (ministry to high school students and families, 1967-; Beaver Lake Camp, 1971-), Stirland Lake (Wahbon Bay Academy, a high school for boys, 1971-86; coeducational since 1986)s, Cristal Lake (school for girls, 1976-86; family resource center, 1988-), Beaver Lake (Debwewin Bible Institute, 1980-), and Thunder Bay (urban ministry, 1986-) in Ontario, and with tribes from Florida to Alaska in marriage and family education. Information is found in the organization's newsletter (Dryden, Ont.). Its budget was $312,000 with a staff of 100.   MWe

Menno Wiebe, *Miss. Focus*, 15 (Sept. 1987), 33-39.

Indiana (ME III:23). This article will summarize the progress and status of the Mennonite-related churches in the state of Indiana since 1954.

Old Order Amish. It is estimated that there are about 24,000 Amish people in Indiana, living in 3,630 households. This includes 10,500 baptized members in 116 church districts (congregations) located as follows (numbers in parentheses refer in each case to the number of districts and households): Elkhart-Lagrange Co. (50 districts, 1,696 households); Nappanee, Marshall, Kosciusko Co. (20, 600); Kokomo, Howard Co. (2, 51); Milroy, Rush Co. (2, 49); Adams Co. (19, 460); South Whitley, Whitley Co. (1, 13); Allen Co. (9, 350); Hamilton, Steuben Co. (1, 20); Daviess Co. (11, 374); Salem, Washington Co. (1, 15).

The life-style of the Amish has changed little in the past 30 years. While they do not own automobiles, they do travel in autos, buses, and trains. They often use telephones located in phone booths near their homes. They farm with horses, with which they sometimes pull gasoline-powered hay balers. They live in rural areas but because of land shortages are being forced to work in construction and other industry. Some Indiana Amish have moved to Wisconsin and Michigan in search of land. Small shops in which stoves, furniture, and horse-drawn equipment are built are springing up. Some Amish people have opened roadside markets and stores to sell fabrics, bulk foods, and farm produce.

Worship services are held in the homes rather than in meeting houses. The German language is used. The service is simple. There are no musical instruments or Sunday School classes. The families are large. The Amish population is growing.

Mennonite Church. There are 68 congregations related to the Mennonite Church in Indiana, with a membership of 10,188 (1985). Twenty-seven of these congregations were started since 1954: *Elkhart Co.* Walnut Hill (1956), Waterford (1959), Tri Lakes Chapel (1961), Bonneyville (1962), South Side Fellowship (1965), Iglesia Del Buen Pastor (1970) Assembly (1974), Fellowship of Hope (1975), Berkey Ave. (1979), East End Covenant (1981). *Lagrange Co.*: Lake Bethel (1956). *St. Joseph Co.*: Kern Road (1960), Community (1961), Iglesia Anabautista Emanuel (1986). *Marshall Co.*: Bourbon Mennonite Chapel (1962). *Kosciusko Co.*: Maranatha Chapel (1979). *Allen Co.*: Fairhaven (1954), North Leo (1966), Central (1969). *Marion Co.*: First Mennonite in Indianapolis (1954). *Miami Co.*: Santa Fe (1960).

Grant Co.: Iglesia Menonita Emanuel (1977). *Orange Co.*: Paoli Mennonite Fellowship (1974). *Porter Co.*: Valparaiso (1966). *Daviess Co.*: Bethel (1964), First Mennonite in Montgomery (1980). *Tippecanoe Co.*: Lafayette Mennonite Fellowship (1983). Assembly, Paoli, South Side Fellowship, Iglesia Anabautista Emanuel, and Lafayette Mennonite Fellowship hold dual memberships with the Mennonite Church (MC) and General Conference Mennonite Church (GCM). South Side Fellowship and Iglesia Anabautista Emanuel also hold memberships with the Church of the Brethren.

By 1987 there were three licensed and three ordained women serving Indiana congregations. During the past number of years several °charismatic, less traditional, and intentional groups have sprung up in northern Indiana. They have often attracted members from the established congregations. Some of these new groups have been received into the Indiana-Michigan Conference (MC) and the General Conference (GCM) as congregations. *Mennonite Renewal Services*, with headquarters in Goshen, is attempting to bring charismatic renewal into the various Mennonite denominations, especially the Mennonite Church (MC).

General Conference Mennonite Churches (GCM). The General Conference Mennonite Church had 13 congregations in Indiana with a combined membership of 2,649 (1985). Of this total 310 members were also counted with the Mennonite Church (MC) membership. New congregations since 1954 are: *Elkhart Co.*: Hively Ave. (1958), South Side Fellowship (1965), Assembly (1974). *Orange Co.*: Paoli Mennonite Fellowship (1974). *Allen Co.*: Maplewood Mennonite Church (1960). *Tippecanoe Co.*: Lafayette Mennonite Fellowship (1983). The First Mennonite Church at Berne had 1,163 members, thus making it the largest Mennonite congregation in Indiana. In 1984 the Silver Street congregation moved from five miles east of Goshen to west Goshen, and was renamed Silverwood Mennonite Church. The Indiana (GC) churches have ordained and licensed women as pastors.

Old Order Mennonites. In 1987 there were about 340 Wisler Mennonites who worship in two meetinghouses west of Goshen: Yellow Creek Frame and Fairview. In 1872 Bishop Jacob °°Wisler separated from the Indiana Conference Mennonites over the issues related to the use of the German language, four-part singing, Sunday Schools, and evening services (ME IV:47). In 1907 a group led by John W. Martin, left the Wisler church and formed the Old Order Mennonite Church. Forty years later, in 1947, Joseph F. Martin, John's son, returned to the Wislers with about one-third of the Old Order Mennonites. The Wislers are less strict than the Old Order Mennonites.

In 1981 there was a further schism among the Old Order Mennonites over the issue of rubber-tired tractors. William G. Weaver, who had been the bishop of the Old Order Mennonites, a more lenient leader, was left with 25 families. The more conservative group of about 80 families has identified with Pennsylvania Old Order Mennonites and has ordained Elvin Martin as its bishop.

Both Old Order groups °dress simply and travel by horse and buggy. They have used meetinghouses from the beginning. The Wisler Mennonites drive automobiles.

Beachy Amish. A number of the more progressive Amish groups have joined what are called the (Beachy) Amish Mennonites. They, like the Amish, are conservative in their dress but use electricity, tractors, automobiles, and meetinghouses. They have a membership of 750 in Indiana in 10 congregations: Berea Fellowship (Kosciusko Co.), Bethany Fellowship (Howard Co.), Christian Mission Fellowship (Adams Co.), Fairhaven (Elkhart Co.), Fellowship Haven (Allen Co.), Hebron Christian Fellowship (Lagrange Co.), Maple Lawn (Elkhart Co.), Mt. Olive Church (Daviess Co.), South Haven and Woodlawn Amish Mennonite (both Elkhart Co.).

Conservative Mennonites. The oldest Conservative Mennonite Conference congregation in Indiana is Townline congregation, east of Goshen (1876). The Conservative Mennonite Conference developed out of the 19th c. Amish-Mennonites (ME I:700). They were much like the Mennonites of the area but preferred baptism in streams. In 1987 they are more conservative in dress than the Mennonite Church (MC).

There are 11 congregations in Indiana, with a membership in 1985 of 1,017. The churches (with nearest town in parentheses) are: Austin; Cuba (Grabill); Griner (Middlebury); Maple City Chapel (Goshen); Mt Joy (Goshen); Oak Grove (Campbellsburg); Pine Ridge (Middlebury); Pleasant Grove (Goshen); Roselawn (Shipshewana); Townline (Shipshewana); and Sunrise Chapel, founded in 1982 (Grabill).

Unaffiliated Mennonite Churches. There are 12 Mennonite congregations in Indiana which are not part of any Mennonite conference. They have no official organization but conduct a "Sharing Concerns Bible Conference" in July and Dec. of each year. This meeting attracts Mennonites of like concern from various parts of the United States and Canada. They are concerned with retaining traditional values and practices of the Mennonite Church. These congregations, of which Salem is the largest (247 members), had a total membership of 617 (1985): Butlerville (Butlerville); Grace Fellowship (Goshen); Pleasant View Conservative, and Rich Valley (Kokomo); Believer's Fellowship (Loogootee); Milford Chapel (Milford); Pleasant View Conservative (Montgomery); Fairview Amish Mennonite and South Union Fellowship (Nappanee); Ridgeview Amish (New Haven); Salem (New Paris); and Toto (North Judson).

Brethren in Christ. Four Brethren in Christ congregations are located in Indiana: Christian Union (Garrett); Mt. Zion (Marengo); Nappanee (Nappanee); and Union Grove (New Paris). Total membership was 205 in 1985. Since 1950 there has been a revival of social and missionary concern in the Brethren in Christ Church. The first woman delegate to conference was elected in 1964 and by the late 1970s women were members of the major boards. The headquarters of the General Conference of the Brethren in Christ and Evangel Press are located at 301 Elm St., Nappanee, Ind.

Evangelical Mennonite Church. In 1985 the 10

Evangelical Mennonite Church congregations in Indiana had a combined membership of 1,120. The churches are: Berne (Berne); Brookside, Highland Bethel, and Pine Hills (Ft. Wayne); Evangelical Mennonite (Grabill); Hope Fellowship (Wabash); Evangelical Mennonite (Lafayette); Evangelical Mennonite (Union City); Evangelical Mennonite (Upland); and Evangelical Mennonite (Woodburn).

In 1875 the General Administrative Board (EMCh) restricted its regular involvement to four Mennonite organizations: Mennonite Central Committee, Mennonite Disaster Service, Council of Overseas Mission Board Secretaries (later renamed the Council of International Ministries); and Africa Inter-Mennonite Mission. The Evangelical Mennonite Church is a member of the National Association of Evangelicals.

Missionary Church. The Missionary Church (ME III:603; IV:774) in the United States and Canada, is divided into 12 districts with a membership of 27,000. Indiana churches are located in the Central and North Central districts. In 1979 the North Central District (north of U.S. Highways 6 and 24) had 39 Indiana churches and the Central District had 31 Indiana churches. The Indiana churches therefore made up 70 of the 359 congregations in the denomination.

The North Central District has developed large congregations such as Zion and Beulah (Elkhart); Gospel Center (South Bend); and Brenneman Memorial (Goshen). In 1977 a $2,500,000 retirement community, south of Elkhart, called Hubbard Hill Estates, was completed and dedicated. Bethel College in Mishawaka was founded in 1947. The Missionary Church denominational press for the United States is Bethel Publishing Company, located in Elkhart.

The Central District of Indiana is at the hub of the activity. Denominational offices and Ft. Wayne Bible College are located in Ft. Wayne, in the Central District.

From 1883 until 1947 the Missionary Church was called Mennonite Brethren in Christ. In 1947 the name was changed to United Missionary Church. In 1952 the Pennsylvania District, unhappy with the name change and certain doctrines and purposes, withdrew with about 4,500 members. In 1959 congregations of the Pennsylvania District named themselves Bible Fellowship Church. In 1969, after many years of negotiation, the United Missionary Church and the °°Missionary Church Association, with headquarters in Ft. Wayne, merged to form the Missionary Church.

Other Mennonite offices and institutions in Indiana include the following: *In Elkhart*: Mennonite Board of Congregational Ministries(MC); Mennonite Board of Education (MC); Mennonite Board of Missions (MC); Africa Inter-Mennonite Mission (GCM, EMB, EMCh, MB, EMMC); Oaklawn Psychiatric Center, Associated Mennonite Biblical Seminaries (GCM, MC). *In Goshen*: Mennonite Mutual Aid, Goshen College (MC); Greencroft Incorporated (Retirement Home). *In Kokomo*: Friendship Haven (Retirement Home, 1979, MC). *In Berne*: Swiss Village (Retirement Home, 1968, GCM). **RRK**

J. C. Wenger, *The Mennonites in Indiana and Michigan*

(Scottdale, 1961); idem, *The Yellow Creek Mennonites* (Goshen: Yellow Creek Mennonite Church, 1985); Eileen Lageer, *Merging Streams* (Elkhart: Bethel Publishing Co., 1979); *MC Yearbook* (1988-89), 22-24; Stan Nussbaum, *Ye Must Be Born Again: A History of the Evangelical Mennonite Church* (Ft. Wayne: EMCh, 1980); Eli E. Gingerich, *Indiana Amish Directory of Elkhart and Lagrange Counties* (Middlebury: the author, 1980).

See also articles on each Mennonite-related group mentioned in this article; Nappanee, Ind., Old Order Amish Settlement; Lagrange-Elkhart, Ind., Old Order Amish Settlement; Berne, Ind., Old Order Amish Settlement; Grabill-New Haven, Ind., Old Order Amish Settlement; Montgomery, Ind., Old Order Amish Settlement.

Indiana Co., Pa., Old Order Amish Settlement. See Smicksburg, Pa., Old Order Amish Settlement.

Indiana-Michigan Mennonite Conference (MC) (ME III:29). From 1954 to 1986 the Indiana-Michigan Mennonite Conference (MC) grew from 66 congregations to 106, and from 8,076 members to 12,498.

Several organizational changes have taken place. Before 1964 three separate organizations carried on work in the conference district (all of them had forerunners): the Indiana-Michigan Mennonite Mission Board, organized in 1913; the Indiana-Michigan Mennonite Conference (1916); and the Indiana-Michigan Mennonite Christian Worker's Conference (1943). These three had separate governing groups, constitutions, and meetings. In 1964 the Christian Worker's Conference voted to become a Christian Education Cabinet under the conference, and in 1970 the Mission Board also came under the conference as its Mission Commission.

In 1970, when a new constitution was adopted, the role of the executive committee changed from that of supervising the conference and congregations to that of coordinating the work of five commissions: Church Life, Mission, Nurture, Peace and Service, and Finance. The new executive committee was made up of the conference president and the five commission chairpersons. The 1978 constitution enlarged the executive committee by two members to be elected at large. Representatives of the Indiana-Michigan °Women's Missionary and Service Commission were invited to be on the executive committee as affiliated members.

There was yet another change in 1986. The executive committee was to consist of the conference president, the conference representative to the Mennonite Church (MC) General Board, a representative from an ethnic or racial minority group, plus seven representatives from the area councils. The conference is organized into 16 geographic area councils. This change was made to make the work of the executive committee more objective. Commission chairpersons were no longer on the executive committee.

The 1956 constitution had declared only officially recognized bishops, ministers, and deacons as members of conference. Each congregation however, was entitled to elect one lay *brother* as a delegate. In the 1970 constitution lay delegates were designated as *persons* thus allowing for women delegates. In 1987 women serve on the commissions and several have been ordained to the ministry. The 1978 constitution states that members of the congregations of conference, as well as the ordained persons, are members of conference.

Bethany Christian High School, Goshen, Ind. (1954), and Camp Amigo, Sturgis, Mich. (1957) are both owned and operated by the conference. The Indiana-Michigan Conference offices are located in Elkhart, Ind., until 1987, when they were moved to Goshen. Officers and staff members in 1987 were the president, executive secretary, administrative assistant, office secretary and bookkeeper, conference minister, conference youth minister, minister of missions, and treasurer. The conference publishes the *Gospel Evangel* 10 times a year as a source of information and inspiration.

In 1987 the Indiana-Michigan Mennonite Conference (MC) met jointly with the Central District Mennonite Conference (GCM) at Goshen in the first of such fraternal meetings. RRK

MC Yearbook (1988-89), 60-63; J. C. Wenger, *Mennonite Handbook* (Indiana-Michigan Conference, 1956); idem, *The Mennonites of Indiana and Michigan* (Scottdale, 1961); idem, *The Yellow Creek Mennonites* (Goshen: Yellow Creek Mennonite Church, 1985). Minutes of the Annual Meetings were published in booklet form through 1972. Beginning in 1973 they wre published as an insert in the *Gospel Evangel*.

Indians, North America. Mennonites have been involved with the following Native peoples in North America:

Arapaho. An Algonkian people who in the 19th c. lived along the Platte and Arkansas rivers and were closely allied with the Cheyenne. The treaty of Medicine Lodge in 1867 placed the tribe on reservations in Wyoming and Oklahoma. In 1892 part of the land was allotted in individual holdings and the "surplus" land opened for white settlement. In 1880 the General Conference Mennonites began their first mission with a school for Arapaho children at Darlington, Olka. Maggie Leonard (Caddo/Arapaho), was the first convert (baptized in 1888). Zion Mennonite Church at Canton, Okla., has had as leaders Walter Fire, Willie Meeks, Ralph Little Raven, and Arthur Sutton. Mary Meeks and Rose Birdshead currently (1988) give leadership.

Blackfeet. A group of three closely related peoples, the Blood, Piegan, and Siksika or Blackfeet proper, roamed the plains from the Saskatchewan River to the headwaters of the Missouri in the 19th c. The near extinction of the buffalo brought death by starvation to some 600 Piegan and ended their military prowess. In the 1980s they live on reservations in Montana and Alberta. General Conference Mennonites worked on the Blood and Blackfoot reserves in Alberta in the late 1940s. The Mennonite Church (MC), after 13 years of °voluntary service programs began church planting at Browning, Mont., in 1984.

Cheyenne. A Plains people of the Algonkian family who lived between the Platte and the Arkansas rivers in the 19th c., the Cheyenne were noted both as warriors and for their peace chiefs. Traditional ceremonies included the "Lodge of Purification" (Sun Dance) and the "Renewal of the Arrows." Separate groups were formalized by the Treaty of Fort Laramie in 1851. The Southern Cheyenne now live in nw. Oklahoma and the Northern Cheyenne,

after a heroic exodus from Oklahoama, live in Montana. The General Conference began work with the Southern Cheyenne in 1880 and with the Northern Cheyenne in 1904. Mennonite leaders have included Milton °Whiteman, John Stands In Timber, William Fighting Bear, Eugene Standing Elk, James Atwood, James and Julia Yellow Horse Shoulderblade (°Cheyenne [feature]), Joe Walks Along, Sr. (°historical writing [feature]), and Ted Risingsun among the Northern Cheyenne, and Homer Hart, Guy Heap of Birds, John Heap of Birds, Harvey °Whiteshield, and Lawrence Hart among the Southern Cheyennes.

Choctaw. Outstanding agriculturists of the Southeast the Mushkogean people lived in what is now Mississippi. Pressure for land to raise cotton took 15 million acres of their land. Indian removal in 1830 forced 14,000 to what became Oklahoma, many dying en route while 15,000 remained behind as "citizens." The Mennonite Church (MC) began church planting in 1958 at Mashulaville, Miss. Mennonite Central Committee helped a community in Louisiana to regain its Indian identity and gain government recognition.

Comanche. This once mighty tribe roaming hunting grounds from the Republican River (Kansas) to the Rio Grande was decimated by disease, hunger, and warfare and placed on a reservation in southern Oklahoma. Forced from the hunt and warfare they "despised the pale face but learned his vices." The Mennonite Brethren began work at Post Oak in 1894-95.

Cree. An Algonkian people living in what is now Canada, sharing both woodland and plains culture, the Cree are now spread form Ontario to Alberta with one group living in Montana. The Mennonite Pioneer Mission (Bergthal Mennonites), now Native Ministries of the Conference of Mennonites in Canada, contacted the Cree at Cross Lake. Jeremiah °Ross pastors the Elim Mennonite Church at Cross Lake. The Beachy Amish Mennonites, Brethren in Christ, and Mennonite Brethren have also worked with the Cree.

Creek. The largest division of the Muskhogean peoples once lived in what is now Georgia and Alabama. Their economy was based on corn, beans, and squash. An important annual religious festival, the Busk or Green Corn Ceremony, was a time when every wrongdoing, grievance, or crime short of murder was forgiven. Involvement in the quarrels of the white people deprived them of most of their land until in the 1830s they were forced to move to Indian Territory (Oklahoma). A remnant stayed in Alabama and the Mennonite Church (MC) began a ministry to some of these people in 1951.

Hopi. The westernmost of the Pueblo Indians, the Hopi have lived for hundreds of years in villages on or near three mesas in what became northern Arizona, skillfully raising corn, beans, squash, peaches, apricots, and grapes with very little rainfall. They speak a Uto-Aztekan language and have very elaborate relgious ceremonies. Known as "the Peaceful Ones," encroachment of the Navajo people has caused years of tension. General Conference Mennonite mission work began in 1890. Christian leaders have included Fred Johnson, Daniel °Schirmer, Daniel Quimayousie, Karl Naseyetewa, and Elmer and Nadenia Myron.

Métis. Decendants of Indian women and French or other European men, Métis developed a distinct culture in the prairie provinces of what became Canada and established the first government of Manitoba. The intrusion of Lord Selkirk's English settlement on the Red River led eventually to the "rebellion" led by Louis Riel (1869-70). Mennonite Pioneer Mission (Native Ministries), began work with the Métis of Manitoba in 1948. Norman Meade has served on the Native Ministries board. Evangelical Mennonite Mission Conference also works with the Métis.

Navajo. The largest Indian group in the United States, with a reservation in Arizona, Utah, and New Mexico, the Navajo are an Athabaskan people, who may have arrived in the Southwest portion of North America between A.D. 900 and 1200. They came under strong influence of the Pueblo people in agriculture and the arts. A four-year captivity of 8,000 of the people in New Mexico under the United States military in the mid-1860s left a legacy of bitterness and distrust that has not entirely disappeared. The Brethren in Christ began mission work with the Navajo in 1945, the Church of God in Christ, Mennonite (Holdeman) in 1951, and the Mennonite Church (MC) in 1954. Mennonite leaders include Naswood and Bertha Burbank, Peter and Lita Rose Burbank, John Peter and Esther Yazzie, Henry and Eleanor Smiley, Larry and Esther Haskie and James and Emma Joe.

Ojibway (Saulteaux, Chippewa). An Algonkian people living around the western Great Lakes to the prairies, the Ojibway traditionally lived on wild rice, maple sugar, berries, fish, and game. Though they believed in a sky-god who ruled the universe, witchcraft was a constant dread. Mennonite groups working with the Ojibway include Native Ministries, Northern Light Gospel Missions, the Mennonite Church (MC), the Beachy Amish Mennonites, Northern Youth Programs, the Evangelical Mennonite Mission Conference, the Conservative Mennonite Church of Ontario, and the Fellowship of Evangelical Bible Churches. Christian leaders include: Jacob Owen, David Owen, Spoat Owen, St. John °Owen, Patric Owen, Sam Quill, Albert Moose, John Strang, Cello Meekis, Gordon Meekis, Daniel Meekis, Saggius Ray, David and Greta Mosquito, Elijah and Emma Stoney, Lazarus Stoney, John Mamakeesic, Frederick and Jacob Kakagamic, Johnie Rae, Magnus James, Elijah McKay, and Clara Major.

Sioux. An Indian people who lived on the northern plains, the Sioux called themselves *Dakota* or *Lakota,* meaning "allies." After the encroachment of the whites the Ghost Dance religion, which promised the coming of a messiah, a return to the old life, and a reunion with the dead took a strong hold on the Sioux. Jittery soldiers fired on a dance resulting in the massacre of Wounded Knee. The Mennonite Brethren began work in 1948. Mennonite leaders include pastor Ted and Mamie Standing Elk, Clifford and Angela Monroe, and Martha Red Hawk. The Evangelical Mennonite Conference works with the Canadian Sioux.

Other Native Peoples. The Mennonite Central Committee, besides working with national Indian organizations, has had special contact also with Innu, Dene, Kwakiutl, and Stoney in Canada, and Hoopa, Houma, Tunica, Mohawk, Passamoquoddy, and Penobscot in the United States.   MWe

Virginia Cole Trenholm, *The Arapahoes Our People* (Norman: U. of Oklahoma Press, 1970); Althea Bass, *The Arapaho Way* (New York: C. N. Potter, 1966); John C. Ewers, *The Blackfeet* (Norman: U. of Oklahoma Press, 1970); John Standsintimber, and Margot Liberty, *Cheyenne Memories* (Lincoln: U. of Nebraska Press, 1967); Donald J. Berthrong, *The Southern Cheyennes* (Norman: U. of Oklahoma Press, 1963); *Cheyenne Spiritual Songs, Tsese-Ma'heone-Nemeototse* (Busby, Mont.: Northern Cheyenne Mennonite Churches, 1977); Ashbranner, *Morning Star, Black Sun: The Northern Cheyenne and America's Energy Crisis* (New York: Dodd Mead, 1982); Stan Hoig, *The Peace Chiefs of the Cheyenne* (Norman: U. of Oklahoma Press, 1980; Arthur H. De Rozier, *The Removal of the Choctaw Indians* (Knoxville: U. of Tennessee Press, 1970); Angie Debo, *Rise and Fall of the Choctaw Republic* (Norman: U. of Oklahoma Press, 1934); idem, *And Still the Waters Ran: The Betrayal of the Five Civilized Tribes* (Norman: U. of Oklahoma Press, 1984); Grant Foreman, *Five Civilized Tribes* (Norman: U. of Oklahoma Press, 1931); T. R. Ferenbach, *Comanches: The Destruction of a People* (1974); Ernest Wallace, and Adamson E. Hobel, *The Comanches: Lords of the Southern Plains* (Norman: U. of Oklahoma Press, 1952); Diamond Jenness, *The Indians of Canada,* National Museum of Canada Bulletin 65 (Ottawa, 1960); Rudy Wiebe, *The Temptations of Big Bear* (Toronto: McClelland and Stewart, 1973); Harry C. James, *Pages from Hopi History* (Tucson: U. of Arizona Press, 1974); Polingaysi Quyawayma, *No Turning Back* (U. of New Mexico Press, 1964); Laura Thompson, *Culture in Crisis* (New York: Harper, 1950); D. Bruce Sealey, and Verna J. Kirkness, *Indians Without Tipis* (William Clare, 1973); Emma LaRoque, *Defeathering the Indian* (Agincourt: The Book Society of Canada, 1975); Ruth Underhill, *The Navajos* (Norman: U. of Oklahoma Press, 1971); Ethelou Yazzie, ed., *Navajo Histories,* rev. ed. (Navajo Curriculum Center Press, 1974); Jules Loh, *Lords of the Earth: A History of the Navajo Indians* (Crowell-Collier Press, 1971); George Hyde, *Red Cloud's People* (Norman: U. of Oklahoma Press, 1947, 1976); John G. Niehardt, *Black Elk Speaks* (Lincoln: U. of Nebraska Press, 1932, 1974).

Indigenization. The adjective "indigenous" is derived from the Latin compound *in* + *de* + *gena* (within + from + to beget) and means "produced, growing, or living naturally in a particular region or environment." It refers to that which is native or born from within, in contrast to that which is foreign or alien. The term *indigenization* is widely used in Christian °missions where it refers to making the Gospel understood in the language and thought forms of the local people and to efforts to make the church autonomous in its organization.

The idea that Christianity must, in some sense, adapt to the culture in which it finds itself is not new. Leaders in the early church disagreed over the extent to which the church should adopt Hellenistic practices. Some argued that the gospel challenges existing cultures because they are the creations of sinful humans, others believed that Christianity must accommodate to cultures in order to win people to the church. The picture changed radically when Christianity became the official religion of the Roman Empire late in the 4th c. Church leaders acquired sociopolitical power, and often turned to the sword rather than to the cross to spread Christianity. The result was often a superficial conversion of the tribes on the frontiers of the empire. The Eastern Orthodox churches translated the liturgy into local vernacular languages in its extensive missionary outreach in Eastern Europe so that the people could worship in their own languages. In contrast, in western Europe the vernacular language initially was Latin and the liturgy needed no translating; eventually Latin developed into various Romance languages and the languages of worship, ecclesiastical Latin, slowly became largely unintelligible to the uneducated. This was even more true when Christianity spread outside the old borders of the Roman Empire to Germanic peoples of northern Europe.

In the 16th c. the modern Roman Catholic missionary movement was born. The Jesuits spoke of the need for accommodating Christianity to the Chinese and Indian cultures, while the Franciscans and Dominicans called for the total rejection of customs such as °caste, °ancestor veneration, and polygamy.

The Protestant Reformation came at a time of rising levels of literacy, which stimulated the translation of the Bible into western European languages by Wycliffe, Tyndale, and Luther. Protestants proclaimed the right of all Christians to read and interpret the gospel in their own cultural settings. Luther went further and insisted on the Germanization of Christianity. The reformers felt, however, the need for an ongoing partnership of sacred and secular powers.

The Anabaptists were more radical. They taught the priesthood of all believers within hermeneutical communities, thereby opening the door for local congregations to choose appropriate ways to express their faith. They also called for the separation of church and state, and held that the °kingdom of God, not earthly norms, is the standard by which all human orders, including the church, must be judged. The gospel must be proclaimed in ways the people understand; but it remains prophetic, judging some parts of their culture to be good (for as humans they are created in the image of God), and some to be bad (for as sinners they create sinful cultures).

The early Protestant missionaries emphasized the need for establishing indigenous churches. In the 19th c., however, Protestant missionaries, including Mennonites, became increasingly identified with European °colonialism, and a Western sense of superiority justified by the theory of cultural evolution. The result was young churches that were dependent on missions, and estranged from their cultural surroundings. Disturbed by the foreignness of the young churches, and their prolonged dependence on mission agencies, two mission leaders, Rufus Anderson and Henry Venn, urged missionaries to turn control of new churches over to native leadership as soon as possible. The goal of missions, they said, is the planting of self-supporting, self-governing, and self-propagating churches. When this is achieved the missionaries should disband or move on.

Despite this plea, the transfer of power from missions agencies to the newly planted churches was slow. Few national leaders were ordained as pastors and bishops, and finances for the Western-styled educational and medical institutions came largely from outside. This was true of most Mennonite missions, which were deeply influenced by the dominant missionary practices of the day. In the end, the emergence of °nationalism and the collapse of colonialism led to the autonomy of most churches around the world.

The call for indigenization of the church raised another question: how should churches in other lands be organized and what types of leadership did they need? Most missionaries introduced the °polity of their sending churches. Anglicans appointed priests and bishops, Mennonites introduced elections and paid ministers. In most cases, however, these organizational forms were foreign to the new Christians. Few attempts were made to use local patterns of organization based on kinship, elders, and lay ministries.

In recent years, there has been a growing awareness of the need not only to indigenize the church as an organization, but also the gospel and its message. Mennonite missionaries have played important roles in Bible translation. However, influenced by other protestant missions, and fearful of syncretism (mixing of Christian and non-Christian practices and beliefs) they often resisted the use of local worship forms and practices. Western hymns of were translated and sung to Western tunes and little emphasis was placed on the development of local hymnologies. Western styles of prayer, preaching, dress, and church architecture were introduced, and drums, dramas, dances, and bardic orations were generally rejected as pagan. Traditional wedding and funeral rites were replaced with ceremonies patterned after Western customs. Polygamy, initiation rites, ancestor veneration, and other customs were condemned, often with little understanding of the social problems created by their elimination. Only in recent years have non-Western Mennonite churches begun to reevaluate their rites and practices in the light of Scriptures and their own cultures.

In the late 1980s there is a growing concern with culturally appropriate methods of evangelism. in the past, most missions, including those sponsored by Mennonites, placed great emphasis on °literacy as a means of church planting. Consequently extensive school systems were built. While recognizing the need for a literate church, many are beginning to use other, more indigenous methods for proclaiming the gospel such as oral communication in rural areas, and rallies and media in the cities.

The question of theological autonomy is also becoming more critical. Do young churches have the right to interpret the Scriptures within their own historical and cultural contexts (°theologies from impoverished peoples)? Does not a positive response to this question open the door to theological relativism and syncretism? Many Protestant churches have opposed the development of indigenous theologies because they view theology as a fixed creed. They have tended to equate their own theology with biblical truth, and to hold it above culture and history. Consequently, to change it is threatening. Non-Western churches, however, face questions that Western theologies do not answer, and Western theologies are molded not only by the Bible, but also by the worldviews of Western cultures.

Given their radical view of the priesthood of all believers, and of discipleship as living daily in obedience to Scripture, Mennonites view theologies as confessions—as human understandings of the Bible within different cultural contexts. They hold their theologies with deep conviction, but do not equate these with the whole of biblical truth itself. They also recognize the need for theologies to change as new questions arise, and as each generation discovers what God is saying to it. They believe, however, that the theological task ultimately belongs to the church, not individuals.

Because of their view of theology as confession, not creed, and of the church as a hermaneutical community, Mennonite missionaries have been more open to, and, in some cases, have encouraged, the development of indigenous theologies. They have also been more willing to work with native churches that have sprung up on the edges of the Western missionary movement. An example of this is the pioneering work of Edwin and Irene Weaver, and the work of the African Inter-Mennonite Mission and other Mennonite missions. with °African Independent Churches.

The concept of indigenization itself was the product of a particular period in mission history when missionaries went from the West to other lands. Now the church exists around the world, and the usefulness of the term is in question because it is tied to a unidirectional view of missions, and to the goal of independent churches.

Since 1972 missionary leaders have begun to use the term °*contextualization* to move beyond the concept of indigenization. The new term carries the basic meanings of the old, but recognizes that the goal for churches, young and old, is interdependence and partnership, and that the gospel belongs to no one culture but judges them all in the light of the kingdom of God. Indigenization is achieved when every society has a church native to its cultural setting. Contextualization is the ongoing process of a church seeking to live as Christ's body within its own cultural and historical setting.   PGH

P. J. Malagar, *MC India* (1981), 40-52.

Indonesia (ME III: 31). Only China, India, the Soviet Union, and the United States have more people than Indonesia, an island nation of 166,070,000 people (1985). This population is made up of 300 distinct ethnic groups speaking 250 distinct languages. They inhabit 3,000 of the country's 13,000 islands strung along the equator in a cluster stretching 5,400 km. (3,086 mi.) east to west and 1,600 km. (987 mi.) north to south. This largest of the world's archipelagoes is bordered on the north by Singapore, Malaysia, the South China Sea, the Philippines, and the Pacific Ocean; by Papua New Guinea on the east; by Australia on the south; and by the Indian Ocean on the south and west.

More than half of the people of Indonesia live on the island of Java where, as on neighboring Bali, the population density approaches 800 per sq. km. In contrast, the vast expanses of the tropical rain forests of Kalimantan and other islands have hardly one person per sq. km.

The Nation State. Indonesia declared itself an independent nation in 1945 after 450 years of increasingly pervasive colonial rule under first the Portuguese and then the Dutch. During its first quarter century of independence, Indonesia was plagued with several immense problems. First was five years of armed struggle to resist Dutch efforts to reassert control after the Japanese occupation during World War II. Second was the effort to establish a democratic form of government that would function in that context. Third was the struggle to gain control of the divergent forces impinging on the development of the economy of the young republic. Fourth was the struggle to forge some kind of national unity in the face of immense diversity and forces that threatened to tear the young republic apart.

The fifth challenge was the struggle to prevent the displacement of a government based on the *Pancasila*, the five foundational principles of the republic—belief in one God, humanity, sovereignty for the people, social justice, and democracy—by either a Marxist or an Islamic government. The most traumatic event in this long struggle was the failed coup d'état of Sept. 30, 1965, and its violent aftermath in which an estimated half million suspected communists were killed and another half million were imprisoned, many for a decade or more without due legal process. This crisis precipitated the displacement of a weakened President Sukarno (who had guided the republic since its inception) by General Soeharto who continues as president in 1988. The failure of the early experiment with liberal democracy precipitated the development of a pattern of government called "guided democracy" in which the president, with the backing of the military, seeks to guide the political and economic development of the country and ward off threats to the established order.

Before Europeans arrived in the archipelago at the end of the 15th c., a whole succession of Indonesian kingdoms based in Java and Sumatra ruled areas that sometimes extended as far as the expanse of the modern nation state of Indonesia. The most notable of these were Sriwijaya, a maritime power based not far from present-day Palembang in central eastern Sumatra, and Mojopahit, the agriculturally based kingdom of Java which succeeded in becoming a great maritime power as well. Some of these Indonesian kingdoms have left a heritage of monumental architecture treasured among the architectural and artistic wonders of the world.

Religion in Indonesia. The vast majority of Indonesia's people are identified formally as Muslims. Muslim traders began to appear in the port towns of the archipelago by the 7th c. after Christ. They established a series of petty kingdoms along the coasts of Sumatra and the Malay peninsula. But Islam was not able to penetrate into Javanese society and displace the powerful Shiva-Buddhist Mojopahit kingdom until the 14th c., when a series of Islamic kingdoms began.

Under Dutch colonial rule it was assumed that the people of Java were Muslims, and government regulations required the people to marry by Islamic law and rites. However, Islam in much of Indonesia has been described as a "thin and flaking glaze" overlaying not only older Hindu and Buddhist religious traditions, but, more importantly, the aboriginal religions of the Indonesian peoples. The world religions (Buddhism, Hinduism, Islam, Christianity) that have been introduced into Indonesia have in many respects undergone a process which, in the case of Java, scholars call "javanization." In a large measure this can be described as the adaptation of the external forms of the world religions to the expression of the aboriginal religious impulses of the Javanese people. However Islam in Indonesia is undergoing significant revitalization with the result that there is continuing interest in converting the religiously pluralistic republic of Indonesia into an Islamic republic.

Christianity, according to some ancient sources, was already present in Indonesia by the 7th c. Whatever Christian presence may have been established there—ostensibly by missionaries of the ancient Nestorian Church of the East—Indonesian Christian communities in the 20th c. can be traced only as far back as the the the coming of Portuguese Roman Catholics at the end of the 15th c.

At the time of the displacement of the Portuguese by the Dutch at the turn of the 17th c., most of the Roman Catholic communities in the archipelago were transformed into Protestant communities. During the first 100 years of rule by the Dutch East India Company, Christian ministry in the archipelago was limited largely to the pastoral care of European Christians present there. Significant mission activity in the archipelago did not begin until the 19th c. Furthermore, because the Dutch colonial administration did not want to disturb business operations among Muslims, it prohibited evangelization in certain areas.

Mennonites in Indonesia. Indonesia is a place of historical importance in the story of Mennonite overseas mission. The first Mennonite mission society was established in The Netherlands in 1847 specifically to send missionaries to The Netherlands East Indies. This society sent its first missionary, Pieter °°Jansz (1820-1904), to Indonesia in 1851. He, together with colleagues Thomas °°Doyer, N. D. °Schuurmans, and Hildebrand °Klinkert, brought about the formation of a mission church among the Javanese in the area near the Muria mountain along the coast of north central Java. Jansz and Klinkert made extraordinary contributions to the translation of the Bible into the Javanese and Malay languages, respectively.

Beginning in the 1880s the development of that mission church was characterized by (1) the formation of Christian agricultural colonies, a special approach to mission; (2) the incorporation of a large indigenous Christian movement that had arisen under the leadership of Javanese evangelist Kyai Ibrahim °Tunggul Wulung (d. 1885); and (3) the recruitment of most mission personnel from the °°Kirchen-Gemeinden Mennonites in south Russia.

Before any of the Mennonite missionaries from Russia began to work in Java, the Dutch Mennonite Mission Society opened an entirely new field for them in Mandailing, the southernmost part of the province of North Sumatra. The church that developed in Mandailing was turned over to the larger Protestant mission church in that province in the 1930s as a result of the cutoff of the support base for that enterprise after the Russian Revolution. Several of those congregations regrouped in the 1950s to form the Gereja Mennonit Protestan Indonesia (Indonesian Protestant Mennonite Church), which interacted with the Mennonite churches in Java and Mennonite Central Committee. However,

in the mid-1970s, at the time of the formation of the Angkola-Mandailing-speaking Angkola Christian Batak Protestant Church, the Gereja Mennonit Protestan Indonesia, because of its small size, was incorporated into the new body. Special provision was made for the continuation of Mennonite practices in congregations of Mennonite origin.

Very early in his work Pieter Jansz showed interest in Indonesians of Chinese descent. He worked with them himself. He invited Chinese evangelists to come and minister among them. By the turn of this century, the mission began recruiting people to work especially among the Chinese. However little headway was achieved, partly because converts of this group were expected to be incorporated into Javanese congregations. In 1920 a new Chinese Christian fellowship was formed at the instigation of a businessman who became Christian in the town of Kudus (°Tee Siem Tat). This group became identified with the Mennonite mission, although it quickly moved toward independence in 1926. Today this group is called the °Persatuan Gereja-Gereja Kristen Muria Indonesia (Muria Christian Church of Indonesia).

The main body of the (predominantly Javanese) Mennonite mission church in Java was organized in 1940 into a conference whose original Javanese language name was Patunggilanipun para Pasamuan Kristen Tata Injil ing wengkon Kabupaten Kudus, Pati, Jepara (Union of Gospel-patterned Christian Congregations in Kudus, Pati, and Jepara Counties). In 1988 it is called the °Gereja Injili di Tanah Jawa (Evangelical Church of Java). It has some 60 mature congregations with 105 branches and numbers ca. 50,000 adherents, including children.

Mennonites in Indonesia have a history of ecumenical involvement that can be traced back to Pieter Jansz's role as "Elder Missionary" leader of the ecumenical missions conference during his lengthy retirement from active mission work. Both Mennonite churches in Java have from early on been involved as members of the Indonesian Council (later Communion) of Churches. Both of them are involved deeply in various ecumenical enterprises most notably in a university and seminary. Mennonites have for decades played lead roles in the development of both Satya Wacana Christian University in Salatiga and Duta Wacana Theological Seminary (now also a university) in Yogyakarta.

The °Doopsgezinde Zendingsraad (Dutch Mennonite Mission Board), as part of the °Europäisches Mennonitisches Evangelisationskomitee (European Mennonite Mission Board), returned to Indonesia after the war and revolution of the 1940s placing personnel to work primarily with the Evangelical Church of Java and with a new ecumenical work being started in Irian Jaya (West New Guinea). In 1947 the North American Mennonite Central Committee (MCC) began to make contact with and assist the Mennonite churches in Java who were cut off from the outside world by war and revolution. Working for the most part in very close partnership with those churches, MCC has also placed personnel in North and southern Sumatra, Halmahera, Timor, Sulawesi, and West Kalimantan.

Pekabaran Injil dan Pelayana Kasih (PIPKA), the mission board of the Muria Christian Church of Indonesia, began in the mid-1970s to invite the participation of Mennonite Brethren Mission and Services, MCC, and Eastern Mennonite Board of Missions (MC) in its strong thrust to establish new churches in Sumatra, Java, and Kalimantan.   LMY

Th. Jensma, *Doopsgezinde Zending in Indonesia* (The Hague: Boekcentrum, 1968); Ruth McVey, ed., *Indonesia* (New Haven, Conn.: HRAF Press, 1967); Lawrence M. Yoder, *Tunas Kecil: Sejarah Gereja Kristen Muria Indonesia* [Little Shoot: History of the Muria Christian Church of Indonesia] (Semarang: Komisi Literatur Sinode GKMI, n.d. [1985]), also available in English translation under the the title "The Church of the Muria: A History of the Muria Christian Church of Indonesia" (Th.M. thesis, Fuller Theological Seminary, 1981); Lawrence M. Yoder, and Sigit Heru Soekotjo, "Sejarah Gereja Injili di Tanah Jawa" [History of the Evangelical Church of Java], unpub. manuscript; *MWH* (1978), 145-56; *MWH* (1984), 33-34.

See also Jakarta; Java, Island of; Kudus; Pati; Salatiga; Semarang; Yogyakarta.

Inductive Bible Study. See Biblical Theology Movement; New York Theological Seminary.

Industrial and Vocational Education. See Disabilities; Education; Mission Schools.

Industrialization. By industrialization we mean the increasing use of machines to replace human skills in the production of goods and services. Human and animal energy were increasingly replaced by inanimate sources of power first in northern Europe and later in North America and Japan. Workers left their agrarian communities to work in centers where these machines were located, establishing new communities which greatly accelerated °urbanization and also altered °community and °family patterns. The division of labor also greatly changed work roles, and new structures were created to coordinate and control workers which led to increased bureaucratization.

The expansion of science and technology increased the need for better trained workers, specialized scientists, and technologists so that more advanced °educational systems were required. These increasingly involved the state. Work and labor institutions grew in size and with this growth came an increase in these institutions' power over individuals, so that in the 20th c., multinational corporations are on the rise. For industrialized nations the standard of living and health services have been raised, and it has freed many from spending most of their time eking out a life of subsistence. However, it has also greatly differentiated the income, education and occupations of the population so that social class and socio-economic status now vary enormously. There is now less dependence upon the changes of nature because nature can be controlled more, but this has also made humans more dependent upon the production system. Proponents and opponents of industrialization argue as to which of the two dependencies (nature or machines) contributes more to the advance of humanity.

While industrialization increased in western Europe and North America, the °capitalist system of economics emerged with its laissez-faire (a French phrase meaning "let people do as they choose") emphases on free enterprise, individual initiative,

competition, the profit motive, and inheritance which encouraged °the accumulation of capital which was again invested in more machines and industry. The capitalist system encourages higher levels of consumption so that maintaining production and jobs often becomes a more important goal, than meeting the needs of people. Regulation of production is a problem when periods of rapid economic growth alternate with periods of economic depression. Times of profit-taking and economic depression put laborers in disadvantageous situations of losing their jobs and means of livelihood. Stratification increases where the rich become richer and the poor poorer, so that governmental welfare organization increasingly becomes a necessity. While raw materials and resources seemed endless in newfound lands, we now see that the toll upon the natural environment is growing asd resources become depleted, as water and air pollution rise, and as farmers try to get more out of their land by increased use of fertilizers and chemicals.

These imbalances and problems of the industrial revolution became increasingly evident in the 19th c. so that sociologists such as Karl Marx and Max Weber began to probe the contradiction inherent in industrial capitalism. The aftermath of the French Revolution and the discontent of workers prompted Marx to investigate the causes of problems related to the factory system, breakdown of traditional family patterns, and the suffering of a transient population. Workers seemed to be alienated from their work as they spent long hours in tedious repetitive work behind machines where their movement and freedom were greatly restricted. Marx concluded that workers were not getting a sufficient return for their labor, and that the arrangements of power must be reordered. Masters monopolized economic power too much and often reneged on their social responsibilities in the interests of profit.

Max Weber, like Marx, was also concerned with the industrialization process but thought Marx oversimplified the polarity between *bourgeoisie* (those who have capital) and proletariat (the workers) and based his understanding of the dialectical process of history too much on materialistic grounds. Weber thought that industrialization has to do with rational processes working toward efficient and effective means of attaining economic goals and that these means became ends in themselves. He believed also that ideology (especially Calvinist doctrine) was an important factor. He spent much of his life trying to show that there were religious or ideological reasons for the capitalist system and he expounded on these in *The Protestant Ethic and the Spirit of Capitalism.* The possibility of connections between the rise of industrialization and religious beliefs has implications for Mennonites as well.

Anabaptists emerged in the 16th c. in Europe, in a commercial, but not yet industrialized society. The old rural feudal structures had begun to give way to leadership from an urban merchant class. Some new technologies, e.g., the the printing press, were emerging and led to reformulations of beliefs and religion as more began to read and write for themselves. Anabaptists were heavily involved in this commercial culture. Especially in The Netherlands many were involved in trades and artisan crafts, e.g., baking, weaving, brewing, carpentry, shipbuilding, butchering and other crafts to make a living. In Switzerland and Germany many Anabaptists were likewise from artisan circles. However, soon after their beginnings, most Mennonites outside The Netherlands retreated into agricultural areas because of severe persecution.

In the late 20th c. although the majority of Mennonites still live in the most industrialized countries of the world (the United States, Canada, Germany, Japan and the Soviet Union), they have only recently moved from agriculture into various urban °professions and industrial jobs.

In the late 20th c. Mennonites live in at least 57 countries on all continents of the world. Thus they are located in industrially developed, developing, and undeveloped areas. In 1984 well over half of all Mennonites (426,072 or 58.8 percent) lived in 16 industrialized countries in North America and Europe; 10.7 percent lived in 23 countries of Latin America, many which were considered developing countries, including Mexico (4.3 percent) and Paraguay (1.9 percent); and the remaining 30.3 percent lived in 18 countries of Asia and Africa, most of which are industrially undeveloped, including Zaire (9.2 percent), Indonesia (8.7 percent), India (6.1 percent) and Tanzania (1.9 percent).

Industrialization has greatly influenced rural Mennonites who engage in agriculture, especially those living in the industrially developed areas of North America and Europe. John B. Toews and others have shown that farm industry developed greatly in Russia between 1861 and 1934, a process which also changed the work of Mennonite craftsmen, factory working conditions, salaries, and job security. Blacksmith shops developed into wagon factories, cleaning mills, farm machinery factories, and the like. The milling industry mushroomed so that when the elder Niebuhr died he had 20 mills in 16 villages and one city. Surprisingly, little research has been done on agricultural industry in North America, but we know that there are many large Mennonite farms using the latest machinery and conveniences. Agriculture has become a highly technical enterprise.

As Mennonites move to cities, they also enter all the jobs and vocations which industrialized societies have to offer. Melvin Gingerich reports that a 1950 Mennonite Church Family Census in North America showed that out of a sample of 14,253 income earners, fewer than half (44.1 percent) were occupationally engaged in farming or related °businesses. Interestingly Gingerich found that of the hundreds of church statements made over 25 years, very few addressed issues related to technology. Mennonites have usually been drawn to the opportunities of the entrepreneural enterprise as Carl Kreider's volume *The Christian Entrepreneur* with its emphasis on land, labor, and capital, illustrates. Kauffman and Harder, in a 1972 study published in 1975, found that most Mennonites also favor joining °labor unions so laborers can pressure management to offer better ways and working conditions. The periodical *Marketplace*, published by the °Mennonite Economic Development Associates, illustrates the extent to which Mennonites have entered business and the professions.

In his lecture *The Promise of Work*, Calvin Redekop illustrates how industrial technology is changing human work and the workplace, showing that job satisfaction tends to decline and machines increasingly enter the scene. As work is spatially separated from the family, work satisfaction declines and status and security become greatly dependent on "the job" where labor is sold to the highest bidder, rather than enjoyed as a way of life. Multinational corporations tend to focus on profit so that the integration of work with the family, neighborhood, and community are neglected.

Technology and industrialization tend to differentiate work into extremes. Professionals gain more and more control and status in their work, while bluecollar workers become more tied to technology sacrificing much of their flexibility and control over work. Thus, physicians, professors and other professionals identify themselves with their work, while machinists and laborers are often left with meaningless jobs. Donald Kraybill and Phyllis Pellman Good warn against the perils of professionals who acquire much power by gaining respect and a monopoly over supervising and controlling °occupations; who set their own fees and rules, and titles; who enjoy special and secure incomes. Mennonites have entered the service °professions of teaching and °medicine extensively in industrialized countries.

Very little has been written on the leisure patterns of Mennonites (°recreation; °amusements). With the rise of °technology, the need to get away from it all also increases, indicating yet another result of industrialization. Melvin Gingerich surveyed changes in leisure patterns among Mennonites in 1945, and found many changes, first centering around the family and church, followed later by more participation in spectator sports and travel and greater interest in the entertainment and information media. Thus, Mennonites in urban industrial places also follow the trends, because relief from machines and industry are needed by all humans, while farming in the past included more integration of both work and play. LDr

Joseph Smucker, *Industrialization in Canada* (Scarborough, Ontario: Prentice-Hall, 1980), 1-41; John B. Toews, "The Emergence of German Industry in the South Russian Colonies," *MQR*, 55 (1981), 289-371; Calvin Redekop, *The Promise of Work* [Eby Lecture, Conrad Grebel College], (Waterloo: Conrad Grebel College, 1983), 1-19; Donald B. Kraybill and Phyllis Pellman Good, *Perils of Professionalism* (Scottdale, 1982); Carl Kreider, *The Christian Entrepreneur* (Scottdale, 1980); Melvin Gingerich, "Mennonite Attitudes to Wealth: Past and Present," *Proceedings of the Conference on Educational and Cultural Problems* (Hesston College, 1953), 89-98; Kauffman/Harder, *Anabaptists Four C. Later* (1975).

See also Demography; Modernity.

Inerrancy of Scripture. Since the 16th c., Mennonites have emphasized the °authority of Scripture for faith, life, and church °polity. Minimally this has meant that the Bible is the *supreme* rule for faith and life, maximally it has meant that it is the *only* rule for faith and life. Because Mennonites have seen commitment and practice as the decisive test for Christian faithfulness, they have given less attention to precise doctrinal formulations. Doctrinal and moral truth is that which corresponds to Christ and the Bible; error is that which deviates in practice or doctrine from Scripture, especially from the teaching, example, and spirit of Jesus Christ.

In the 17th c., Protestant theology developed a doctrine of biblical authority which maintained that the entire Bible is infallibly true and wholly free from errors of any kind. North American °Fundamentalism and neo-Fundamentalism (°Evangelicalism) have made a similar doctrine of inerrancy the decisive test for orthodoxy in the early and recent decades of the 20th c.

Before the 20th c., Mennonite confessional statements rarely include a specific treatment of Scripture. The °Schleitheim (1527) and °°Dordrecht (1632) confessions do not. Only the Cornelis Ris Confession (1766) does: the Bible is the "only infallible and sufficient rule of faith and conduct" (Loewen, *Confessions*, 63-70, 79-105/103).

Under the influence of °Fundamentalism, the Mennonite Church (MC) adopted an inerrantist position in the "Christian Fundamentals: Articles of Faith" (1921, Loewen, 71-72). Influenced by neo-Fundamentalism, Mennonites later struggled again with the concept of inerrancy. In a series of conference discussions, position statements, and confessions of faith, they have used the terms *inspiration* and *infallibility* within a general doctrine of revelation rather than the concept *inerrancy* as the basis for the authority, trustworthiness, and reliability of Scripture. These statements include the Brethren in Christ "Manual of Doctrine and Government" (1961; Loewen, 231-40), the General Conference Mennonite Church statement "The Authority of Scriptures," (1962), the Mennonite Church (MC) "Mennonite Confession of Faith," (1963; Loewen, 73-77), and the Mennonite Brethren Church "Mennonite Brethren Confession of Faith" (1975; Loewen, 175-78).

Infallibility usually means that the Bible will not fail to accomplish its purpose of revealing God's will and salvation, and is based on passages such as Jn 10:35, which says that Scripture cannot be broken. *Inspiration* is affirmed on the basis of 2 Tim 3:16 and 2 Pet 3:21. Because Scripture does not explain the mystery of inspiration, so the argument runs in most accounts and discussions since the 1950s, it is inappropriate to elaborate a particular doctrine of inspiration and infallibility.

Simultaneously Mennonites generally have given increasing attention to methods of °biblical interpretation, as represented by the Mennonite Church (MC) statement on "Biblical Interpretation in the Life of the Church" (1977) rather than to a doctrine about the Bible. Mennonites associated with the independent periodical *Sword and Trumpet* and the °Fellowship of Concerned Mennonites (1984), and many other Mennonites consider a doctrine of inerrancy the decisive and foundational issue for biblical interpretation and authority.   MEM

Willard M. Swartley, ed., *Essays on Biblical Interpretation: Anabaptist-Mennonite Perspectives* (Elkhart: IMS, 1984), collection of articles, includes bibliography; J. C. Wenger, *God's Word Written; Essays on the Nature of Biblical Revelation, Inspiration and Authority* (Scottdale, 1966, reprinted 1968), an exposition of the position represented in and around the 1963 Mennonite Church (MC) Confession of Faith; "The Authority of the Scriptures," *The Mennonite* (May 22, 1962), 338-343, reprinted in pamphlet form entitled *A Christian Declaration on the Authority of Scripture* by the General Conference Mennonite Church (Newton, n.d.); "Biblical Interpretation in the Life of the Church, A Summary Statement," adopted by Mennonite Church (MC) General Assembly, June, 1977 (Scottdale: MPH, 1977); Willard M. Swartley, *Slavery, Sabbath, War and Women: Case Issues in Biblical Interpretation* (Scottdale, 1983), summarizes and compares different interpretations of the Scripture on each of the four issues, proposes guidelines for personal and scholarly Bible study; Perry Yoder, *From Word to Life: A Guide to the Art of Bible Study* (Scottdale, 1982); Paul Zehr, *Biblical Criticism in the Life of the Church* (Scottdale, 1986); "The Berea Declaration," *The Sword and Trumpet* (May 1984), 8-10, a declaration of understanding and intent adopted by the Fellowship of Concerned Mennonites.

See also Biblical Interpretation; Fundamentalism.

Infant Dedication. See Dedication of Infants.

Information Centers. See Interpretation and Information Centers.

Inheritance (United States and Canada) (ME III: 39). In the 1980s North American Mennonites are changing the way they view and leave their property at death. (The following paragraphs reflect primarily patterns in the United States and Canada.) Providing for a spouse, if married, and for children remains a major goal. Passing on the family farm or °business, while still desired and possible for some, is facing difficulties: a distressed farm economy, how to be fair to non-farm heirs and children choosing other careers.

Many parents choose to help their children, if they can, when they need it most—acquiring an education, starting a business or building a home, rather than making them wait until the parents die. They are considering family needs during life and at death, rather than merely accumulating assets to leave to survivors.

This approach recognizes also that needs of survivors differ as age levels and circumstances change. Appropriate planning, therefore, takes these differences into account. For example, leaving a life interest in property to a surviving parent with young children provides income to the survivor and safeguards the interest of the children. If neither parent survives, young children will likely need all that their parents leave. Grown children who are financially established will have fewer needs. Children or adults with disabilities may have special needs. Adults surviving to retirement age will need income and possibly special care.

Another part of this approach is planning for charitable bequests or remainders for church institutions or other charities as a final "thank you" to God and an extension of lifetime giving. Mennonites, like others, are living longer. They are more prosperous. They have benefited from hard work and industriousness. The North American and European economic systems have been good to them. Their children may be financially well off. Unmarried individuals and childless couples may have no dependents. So "adopting" church institutions as "heir" to a tenth, a child's share, one-half or more of one's estate is appealing and practicable, even for people with modest means.

Provision for charitable bequests or remainders must be made in a will, trust, or other legal instrument. If an individual dies without a will, no charitable gift is allowed and the deceased person's property will be divided according to the state's formula which may not reflect the individual's wishes or values.

°Mennonite Foundation offers consultation for wills, planned giving, and estate planning. °Mennonite Mutual Aid does the same for health and life insurance and retirement benefits.

The church, primarily through its teaching ministry and, in particular, through the Mennonite Foundation in Canada and the United States is attempting to inform and guide the attitude toward inheritance with the biblical understanding that the Lord is the source and real owner of material wealth (Ps 24:1) and, as God's trustees (Gn 1:28), all we have is a trust to use responsibly and joyously for our needs and others (2 Cor 8-9).   PLG

See also Wealth; Aged, Care for; Land Distribution; Stewardship; Investments; Property; Prosperity; Mennonite Foundation.

Institute of Mennonite Studies (IMS). See Bible Study; Historical Writing; Mennonite Studies; Scholarship.

Institutions, Church. Given their collective size, the Mennonite churches are among the most institutionalized of churches. Their institutions represent various dimensions of Mennonite life in their corporate forms. Proliferation of Mennonite institutions during the 20th c. reflects the vitality of Mennonite life and the breadth of Mennonite concern.

That Mennonites should organize institutions on a per-capita-member basis in excess of the major denominations is ironic in light of Mennonite history and theology. Mennonite theology is anti-institutional. Mennonites have defined the church strictly in communal terms. The church consists of congregations organized for personal communion; not institutions organized for mission. Mennonites focus upon what happens when "two or three ar gathered together" for (usually non-liturgical) °worship, fellowship, mutual support and °discipline. Anabaptists reacted against the "institutional" church as an establishment with its objective (sacramental and liturgical) means of grace, its hierarchical organizations and its massive structures. The Anabaptists attempted to strip down the church to its New Testament proportions. Since they believed that primitive Christianity had no institutions, Anabaptists and Mennonites resisted institutionalization for some 300 years and to this day Mennonites have no theology of °institutions. The anti-institutional tendencies of °sectarian Christianity are well documented and interpreted by °sociologists, e.g., Max Weber and Ernst °°Troeltsch. They made the classic distinction between the *Gemeinschaft* (community) and the *Gesellschaft* (society, or association).

That Mennonites would sometime come to terms with institutionalization could have been predicted on the basis of the history of the Christian church as well as the rudimentary principle that continuous, corporate, goal-oriented activity will require organization, bureaucracy, routinization, °authority, and defined responsibilities. The establishment of Mennonite institutions was to place on a permanent basis activities which could not be carried out personally and intermittently. Church institutions grow out of the universal implications of the gospel as a source of knowledge and as a healing and reconciling power: hence °mission boards, elementary and °secondary church schools, °Bible schools, colleges, °seminaries, °relief organizations, °hospitals, church °camps, retirement °homes and °mutual aid societies. Even patterns of worship and respect for °tradition are forms of institutionalization. These followed periods when the vitality and the vision of the church were renewed and broadened. Ironically interpretations of Christianity during times of renewal are distinctly personal, often reactionist. But with few exceptions the Spirit settles into permanent structures as the church seeks to conserve its gains and transmit its experience to succeeding generations.

Two historical developments account in particular for institutional developments in United States and Canada: extension of fairly advanced institutional life among Russian Mennonites in the 19th c. and influences stemming from the revivalistic movement among Mennonites at the beginning of the 20th c.—the so-called Mennonite °"Renaissance," "Awakening," or "Quickening." The earliest American Mennonite institutions were founded by General Conference Mennonites (GCM)—the Wadsworth School in Ohio (1868) and Bethel College in Kansas (1893). Goshen College was founded in 1903 and thereafter colleges and seminaries followed in response to theological and regional needs.

Mennonites, as representatives of the free church (°Believers' Church) tradition, espoused accepted principles of institutional authorization and legitimation. Mennonite institutions have come into existence here and there at the initiative of concerned individuals or as a result of regional conference action. Sometimes institutions have been started as private "enterprises" and later turned over to the church. Some Mennonite institutions are legally independent of any conference or denomination even though they are well integrated into Mennonite life. Sometimes Mennonite institutions have been organized in direct oppositon to other Mennonite institutions.

Mennonites also founded schools, hospitals, and leper asylums in China and India at the beginning of the 20th c. In India institutions preceded congregations because famines left a legacy of need that could be met only by organizations of a permanent sort. To be sure, mission policies changed after World War II in the face of high costs and political problems. Nevertheless, Mennonites planted in foreign countries a considerable number of institutions, some of which were nationalized but continue to serve human needs.

One of the values of Mennonite institutions is their cohesive role within Mennonite communities. Beyond their evident purposes such as educational, medical, retirement, relief services, Mennonite institutions serve as centers where Mennonites of various groups meet. Institutions assist in identity formation. Sometimes they serve as catalysts, as preservers of the tradition, and as places where Mennonites interact with the world. Mennonite hospitals, mental institutions, colleges and seminaries accommodate people of all kinds and sorts. "Where there are no institutions the people perish" (cf. Prv 29:18, KJV) may be too strong a statement, but is one which is sometimes pressed to counter anti-institutional sentiments frequently manifest by Mennonites, particularly those of the Swiss-German ethnic origins.

It would appear that Mennonites are good managers of institutions. Administrations are usually efficient, honest, and responsible. Were it not for good administration, many Mennonite institutions would not survive since they are as a rule inadequately funded. Most college histories include chapters telling about underpaid, if not unpaid, faculty. Buildings are generally simple and functional with little regard for aesthetics. Endowments are small. Some Mennonite leaders go out of their way to insist that institutions are not the church. Rather they are "agencies" or "arms" of the church. At best they are "servants" of the church. Mennonites frequently fail to understand that institutions represent a "permanent" commitment to the church and to the world. The chief executive officer (CEO) of a Mennonite institution sometimes faces a dilemma representative of conflicting interpretation of Christian ethics. On the one hand, Mennonites sometime expect the institutions to "take no thought for the morrow," to shun endowments and large gifts, while the other hand they demand balanced budgets based upon aggressive financial campaigns, slick advertising, wise investment, and prudent hiring and firing (°personnel management). In general, it may be said that Mennonites have not faced the sociological and theological implications of institutional life. Were they to do so, they would come to terms theologically with reasonable capital investments, at least moderate wealth, long-term commitments and· structures for which °justice is the operative principle. Ironically they sometimes expect Mennonite institutions to be run according to *Gemeinschaft* and *Gesellschaft* principles at the same time.

Having said that, however, Mennonite institutions quite properly seek ways by which some of the principles of the *Gemeinschaft* may ameliorate the structures of the *Gesellschaft*. Mennonite institutions frequently seek to provide an atmosphere of care, generosity, warmth, and imagination reflecting some of the better aspects of Mennonite life. Also vertical authority structures are qualified by cross-departmental communication, by thoughtful administration and by distributing power as far as efficiency and order will permit. What cannot be accomplished structurally is sometimes accomplished by fostering an ethos of concern and affection.

In the °modern world it has been generally assumed by sociologists and political reformers that institutions are so conservative that they cannot be prophetic. Historically institutions have been the object of prophetic criticism rather than the sources of prophecy. Prophets according to the stereotype are lonely individuals after the image of Amos and Hosea who, as outsiders and therefore uncorrupted

by power, lay their message on the king. In this connection, some have assumed that the withdrawn community is in a stronger position to be nonconformed and therefore prophetically authentic than the socially involved institution. But that is not how it has worked out for Mennonites during the 20th c. Almost invariably Mennonite institutions have led the church in the prophetic ministry. Mennonite colleges, seminaries, and mental health institutions have generally been more conscious of the need for social change than the general Mennonite constituency.

Furthermore, Mennonite institutions have been the principle carriers of Mennonite historical consciousness in many sections of the church. Congregations have not been a significant source of new and creative ideas. Almost all creative changes in 20th c. Mennonite life may be attributed to the thinking of people in the institutional situation. Many institutions, such as colleges and seminaries, have as many of the "marks" of the °church as most congregations, even though, according to Mennonite doctrine ecclesiology, they are not given the dignity of being the church. The theological status of church institutions within congregational order is a classical issue yet to be considered by Mennonites.

One of the problems facing Mennonites is what some would consider an inordinate demand of institutions upon Mennonite leadership potential. Institutions must be administered; hence many able leaders who may otherwise serve the church as pastors, scholars, teachers, and missionaries are drawn into administrative positions. They may make fine contributions as administrators but some of their more creative energies are squelched. Some pastors are drawn to institutional careers because the expectations of Mennonite institutions offer greater job security, albeit low salaries. Sometimes church administration offers professional identity over against the undefined character of the Mennonite "lay" °°ministry.

One of the most significant contributions of institutions and church agencies is their impact upon Mennonite consciousness of the world. Experience as relief workers, missionaries, and volunteers in °disaster situations in many continents enables Mennonites to break out of ethnic boundaries. Through Mennonite agencies such as Mennonite Central Committee, and Disaster Service organizations, Mennonites have become "world citizens" transcending to a significant degree national and cultural differences.

It should also be pointed out that many institutions founded by Mennonites have become controlled by boards representing communities at large. They may be said to be quasi-Mennonite. Oak Lawn Psychiatric Center and Hospital at Elkhart and Goshen, Ind.; Mennonite Hospital at Bloomington, Ill.; and Kings View at Reedley, Cal., are examples of institutions founded by Mennonites but which are viewed by most people as community institutions even though Mennonites as individuals may continue to occupy administrative positions and serve as members of the board.

The future of Mennonite institutions is ambiguous. Some are struggling for survival while others are being enlarged or created anew. Since the Mennonite churches have no effective central control (°polity), it may be presumed that economic factors may be more significant in determining the future of Mennonite institutions than consideration of the mission of Mennonites as a whole. JLB

Calvin Redekop, "Institutions, Power, and the Gospel," in *Kingdom, Cross, and Community*, ed. J. R. Burkholder and C. Redekop (Scottdale, 1976), 138-50; research in progress by Albert J. Meyer, Mennonite Board of Education (MC); John Tonkin, *The Church and the Secular Order in Reformation Thought* (New York: Columbia U. Press, 1971).

See also Business; Conservative Mennonites; Inter-Mennonite Cooperation; Public Relations.

Instituto e Seminário Biblico Irmãos Menonitas, Curitiba, Brazil (Mennonite Brethren Bible Institute). See Associação das Igrejas Irmãos Menonitas do Brasil.

Insurance (ME III:42; 343). From the earliest days of the insurance business, insurance has been seen as a way to bear one another's losses. It began as a simple system of cooperation in which "each contributes a small sum to a fund to indemnify in part or in whole against a loss by any other individual of the group similarly situated" (Troyer, p. 16).

The basis for insurance is risk—the uncertainty of not gaining or losing something of value. Financial loss is the major concern about risk. Insurance transfers, or reduces, risk already in existence. The presence of an existing condition separates insurance from gambling. The risks covered by insurance usually fall into three categories: (1) risks that involve the person (life, health), (2) risks that involve loss of or damage to property (fire, windstorm, loss of income), and (3) risks that involve loss or injury to other persons or to the property of others (liability).

Though the concept of insurance is closely akin to Christian concepts of sharing (°mutual aid), attitudes against buying insurance or participating in insurance plans developed among Mennonites in the last century for a number of reasons.

In those days companies were inadequately controlled by government. Consequently, insurance companies maintained insufficient financial reserves, resulting in many company failures. Companies were unscrupulous in sales methods, capitalizing on fear and on the need to provide for survivors. Often policies were written with conditions for the payment of claims so limited that policy holders were unable to collect. In addition, the purchase of insurance, especially life insurance, was seen as a poor investment because a lapse in paying premium resulted in the loss of all money paid. Further, Mennonites for the most part opposed buying on credit (°debts). Insurance was seen as encouraging persons to overextend themselves financially and thus to foster greed.

With misgivings like these it was not hard to find Bible texts to support a position against insurance. In the main, insurance (especially life insurance) was seen as out of harmony with God's way to support the needy, since God was able to take care of his people (Acts 6:1-6, Jn 19:25-27). Insurance also appealed to wrong motives—fostering selfishness (Lk

6:33, 34) on one hand, and undermining thrift, an essential to the God-honoring life, on the other. To have insurance seemed to many Mennonites to be evidence of unbelief, a lack of faith in God and his promises (Ps 118:8, 37:25, 1 Pet 5:7, Mt 6:25, 26). It was also an "unequal yoke" (2 Cor 6:14-18) since both believers and unbelievers were policy holders.

Jacob °°Stauffer (1812-55), a Mennonite minister in Lancaster Co., listed 10 articles that could not be tolerated or permitted in the °nonresistant church according to God's Word. The fourth article noted . . . "it is not permitted to be a member of an insurance company" (Horst, p. 37).

In *Bible Doctrine*, edited by Daniel °Kauffman and published in 1914 under the auspices of the Mennonite Church (MC) general conference, an entire chapter was devoted to the evils of life insurance from both a religious and a social viewpoint. Life insurance was presented as a poor investment and an encouragement to crime and greed (Kauffman, 1914, pp. 575-587). By 1929 a revision appeared as *Doctrines of the Bible*. This made a distinction between life insurance and property insurance, giving approval to property insurance. In this view the two had much in common, but on one point they differed widely: it was right to deal in property, it was not right to traffic in human life. Property insurance made merchandise of property; while life insurance made merchandise of human life (Kauffman, 1929, pp. 542, 543).

In the late 19th c. many small fire and windstorm insurance companies emerged in Mennonite communities to share the costs of these types of property losses. The 20th c., however, brought the °automobile. A Lancaster Conference (MC) teacher-minister, I. B. Good, saw the importance of church members working together to maintain the biblical principle of reimbursing for bodily injury or for damage to property for which Mennonites became liable through operating automobiles. Good encouraged the formation of an automobile insurance company. This was realized in 1926 by establishing the Goodville Mutual Casualty Company, with George C. Souder, president; H. S. Witmer, vice-president; Wayne S. Martin, secretary; and Horace K. Martin, treasurer.

In 1950 leaders of the Virginia Mennonite Conference (MC) invited the Goodville Company to serve beyond the state of Pennsylvania by providing liability coverages in connection with the Virginia Mutual Aid Plan, which wrote property and automobile physical damage insurance.

Seeing what was done in Virginia and Pennsylvania representatives of Mennonite Church (MC) general conference soon appealed to Goodville Mutual Casualty Company to write liability insurance in other states where Mennonites lived. In response to this, Goodville expanded and became licensed in 17 states. During the 1950s and 1960s (until the reorganization of the Mennonite Church [MC] in 1971), Mennonite Mutual Aid (MMA) reports to the Mennonite Church general conference regularly recommended that Mennonites use the auto physical damage coverage provided through the MMA program and that liability coverage be secured through Goodville Mutual Casualty Company.

Mennonite Mutual Aid mentioned above was

founded in 1945 to provide help for returning °°Civilian Public Service men following World War II. It soon put in place insurance programs to cover health needs, and also provided a life insurance program. At the outset, because of opposition to the term "life insurance," "burial aid" was used to label its early life insurance products. In the mid-1950s Mennonite Mutual Aid began Mennonite Automobile Aid to share auto physical damage losses. By that time the climate of opinion had shifted. Mennonite church members were willing to buy not only insurance to cover losses caused to another person (liability coverage); they were also ready to cover their own losses (collision and comprehensive coverage).

With the growth in numbers of insurance companies in the Mennonite context the need for coordination became evident. This led to the founding of the Association of Mennonite Aid Societies, which met in Chicago for the first time, July 14-15, 1955.

In 1987 there are at least 35 insurance companies within the Mennonite constituency (including Brethren in Christ and related groups, i.e., portions of the Church of the Brethren). They provide a wide range of contracts in personal insurance (life, health), liability (personal, auto), and fire and windstorm. In addition many forms of commercial coverages (products, workers' compensation) are available. These insurance companies seriously take into account Christian principles of mutual aid. They practice careful yet considerate underwriting, are prompt and fair in settlement of claims, avoid litigation in favor of arbitration, and many share profits with church causes.

The insurance industry within the Mennonite and Mennonite-related groups is perhaps the least visible and least understood aspect of church life. All of the companies intend to serve the Mennonite constituency. All are zealous to promote mutual aid concepts. Yet at times the concepts of mutual aid tend to get lost among the companies themselves when, for example, one company views another as a competitor rather than a part of the church with which cooperation is necessary, so that all resources may be available to provide the best coverages possible.

Questioning whether Mennonites should purchase insurance has ceased. The nature of society in the latter part of the 20th c. requires people to have insurance coverage on home, car, farm, business, health, and life. The new question is, how can the Mennonite constituency be encouraged to meet insurance needs with coverages purchased from church-related insurance companies rather than from commercial organizations? Too often the purchase of coverages is made solely on the basis of price, without taking into account the provider's commitment to the biblical principles and practice of mutual aid.   PML

Isaac R. Horst, *Close Ups of the Great Awakening* (Mt. Forest, Ont.: the author, 1985); Kauffman, ed., *Bible Doctrine* (1914); Kauffman, ed., *Doctrines of the Bible* (1929); H. N. Troyer, *Life Insurance* (Scottdale: MPH, 1932).

For a list of mutual aid and insurance companies, see the article on Mutual Aid; current lists are published in *MC Yearbook*, biennially since 1986; annually to 1986.

Intentional Communities. See Shalom Covenant Communities.

Interchurch Evangelism. See Evangelism.

Intermarriage (ME III:720). In sociological parlance, intermarriage (alternately, "mixed" marriage or exogamy) refers to the marriage of persons of differing race, religion, or nationality. Among Mennonites, interracial marriages are rare, although their small number has been increasing in recent decades. North American Mennonites mostly share a common Germanic origin, but current nationality (Canada or the United States) appears to be of little concern in the choice of spouses. National or ethnic (tribal) differences may be of some significance among Mennonites in non-Western countries, or even in Europe, but the matter has not been formally investigated.

Among Mennonites, religion appears to be the salient factor in considering intermarriage. They have been very cautious, even quite resistant, to the marriage of their offspring to someone of another faith. Even the marriage of persons from different Mennonite groups has been discouraged at times and places, usually by those of a more °conservative stance in respect to those of a more open, less sectarian, identity. Until the 20th c., intermarriage rates apparently were very low, due to a combination of rural isolation and strong attitudes opposing intermarriage (°°mixed marriage).

Hostetler studied membership gains and losses in the Mennonite Church (MC) in the period from 1942 to 1951 but did not include data on the proportion of all marriages that were mixed. However, he found that intermarriage rates were higher among exmembers than among converts.

The 1972 Kauffman-Harder church member survey (in the United States and Canada) probed rates of intermarriage defined as marriage between persons of differing Mennonite denominations as well as between Mennonites and non-Mennonites. Twenty-seven percent of the married church members did not belong to the same denomination *at the time of their wedding.* The proportions varied by denomination: Mennonite Church, 18.5 percent; Mennonite Brethren, 24.6 percent; General Conference Mennonite Church, 35 percent; Brethren in Christ, 40.8 percent; and Evangelical Mennonite Church, 64.5 percent. However, only six percent of the married couples were still members of different denominations *at the time of the survey,* indicating that sometime subsequent to the wedding, in most cases, one spouse joined the other's church. The rate of intermarriage between Mennonites of any branch and non-Mennonites was not determined in this survey.

Reflecting chronological trends, younger persons had higher rates of intermarriage than older members. Slightly higher intermarriage rates were observed among urban than rural residents, among women than men, and among lay people than ministers. Farmers had lower rates of intermarriage than other occupational groups.

Substantially higher intermarriage rates were found among those who do not attend church regularly, and among those who are nonresident members of their local congregations. Those of mixed marriage background scored somewhat lower on scales measuring doctrinal orthodoxy, adherence to Anabaptist principles, religious practices, and moral attitudes. Thus intermarriage appears to be associated with weaker support of church doctrines and practices.

Driedger, Vogt, and Reimer (1983) investigated intermarriage among Mennonites in Canada, defining intermarriage more broadly as the marriage of a Mennonite (of any branch) to a non-Mennonite. Among 13 religious groups reported in the 1981 Canadian census, only Jews had lower rates of intermarriage than Mennonites. The rate of endogamy (Mennonites marrying Mennonites) declined from 93 percent in 1921 to 61 percent in 1981. The reported rate may be too low, however, since the census definition of Mennonite includes some persons who are not actually members of a Mennonite church.

Several surveys by Driedger and his associates support several generalizations. (1) In general, the more conservative the Mennonite body, the lower the rate of intermarriage. Hutterites have virtually none. (2) Intermarriage rates· were considerably lower in rural than in urban areas. (3) The younger generation is much more accepting of intermarriage than older generations. (4) Whereas Mennonite intermarriage in Manitoba was almost nonexistent prior to the 1950s, by the 1970s one-fourth married outsiders. (5) Although in the past intermarried couples often left the Mennonite church, intermarriage is increasingly a form of recruitment and possible revitalization.

Although there may be some positive aspects associated with the marriage of Mennonites to those of other backgrounds, in terms of recruitment and stimulation, most of the indicators are negative. In the larger society, higher divorce rates are associated with mixed marriage. There is some evidence that this is true among Mennonites, but the question needs further investigation. In general, the empirical evidence assembled thus far tends to support the traditional view that endogamy is best. JHK

Leo Driedger, Roy Vogt and Mavis Reimer, "Mennonite Intermarriage: National, Regional and Intergenerational Trends," *MQR*, 41 (1983), 132-44; Kauffman/Harder, *Anabaptists Four C. Later* (1975), 172-77; Leo Driedger and Jacob Peters, "Ethnic Identity: A Comparison of Mennonite and Other Students," *MQR*, 47 (1973), 225-44; John A. Hostetler, *The Sociology of Mennonite Evangelism* (Scottdale, 1954), 195-97.

See also Kirchliche Mennoniten; Marriage.

Intermenno Trainee Program. See International Exchanges.

Inter-Mennonite Conference (Ontario). See Inter-Mennonite Cooperation; Mennonite Conference of Eastern Canada.

Inter-Mennonite Cooperation (ME III:44). Mennonites have an exceptional history of scattering on account of °migration and °mission. Consequently, various elements of tradition, geography, and language have created distinct movements and considerable separatism (°schisms). While the separat-

istic tendency never was fully overcome, movements toward unity and reconciliation began to appear, beginning notably in the early 20th c. This article summarizes developments since the 1950s.

Africa and Asia. On these two continents the Mennonite and Brethren in Christ conferences are wholly indigenous, for the most part the result of the European or North American mission activity. The denominational divisions of North America and the geographical and theological identity of Europe are reflected in a certain measure in many of these conferences, which consciously assume an identity related to the founding denomination. Others have chosen to be Mennonite but without such specific identity, and still others have no Mennonite mission background but are nonetheless by choice related to the Mennonite community.

There are certain countries where multiple North American mission agency activity has resulted in multiple Mennonite denominations (India, Zaire, Japan). However, in many cases "inter-Mennonite relations" is simply a euphemism for transcultural, transnational fraternal relationships.

Significant efforts at cooperation have been initiated in India. The °Mennonite Christian Service Fellowship of India (MCSFI), organized in 1963, brings together six conferences in a cooperative agency for mission, service, and peace activity. In Japan, the Nihon Menonaito Senkyokai (Japan Mennonite Fellowship) fulfills a similar function for at least some of the Mennonite bodies.

Of special significance are the continental organizations: °Africa Mennonite and Brethren in Christ Fellowship, Asia Mennonite Conference (°regional Mennonite conferences).

The earliest Mennonite foreign mission activity was initiated by a Dutch missionary in Indonesia in 1851. Members of two synods, one resulting from the Dutch Mennonite mission work, the other fully indigenous in its origins, live in a common area. Informal working relationshps are common, but the Mennonite Scholarship Commission is the only joint project of the two synods. The Akademi Kristen Wiyata Wacana (AKWW; Mennonite Bible Academy) is the Bible academy of the Gereja Injili di Tanah Jawa (GITJ; "Javenese Mennonite Synod"), also serves students from the Persatuan Gereja-Gereja Kristen Muria (GKMI; "Muria Mennonite Synod").

The two synods in this nation have recently pointed to a new dimension of international, inter-Mennonite activity by a 1985 GITJ document calling for "conference-to-conference" relationships. This refers especially to a desire for a fraternal contact with the Algemene Doopsgezinde Sociëteit (ADS; "Dutch Mennonite Conference") and with Mennonite conferences in North America, rather than limiting overseas contacts to mission and service organizations as has been the story of the past.

Central, South America. Mission activities in this area have been extensive, as have been migrations of Mennonite from Europe and Canada. There is considerable diversity of conference affiliation and a variety of language and ethnic groupings, often in the same country. The differences among Mennonites of Spanish, Portuguese, German, English, and Indian cultures are surmounted with some difficuilty if at all.

On the other hand, cooperation among various denominations within the language groups has been significant. The German emigrant groups, including three major conferences, Mennonite General Conference (°Kirchliche Mennoniten), Mennonite Brethren, and Evangelical Mennonite Brethren, worked together closely in the difficult pioneer days in Paraguay. These habits persist.

A °Gemeindekomitee (church committee) brings together conference leaders from all German-speaking groups in Paraguay. The Komitee für Kirchliche Angelegenheiten (committee for church affairs) in °Neuland and °Fernheim colonies brings together the leaders of the three conferences locally. Likewise, these conferences have formed a united mission, °Licht den Indianern, which has successfully planted new churches among the neighboring Indian population.

A second mission committee known as °Mennonitisches Missionskomitee für Paraguay (Mennonite Missions Committee for Paraguay) has been formed by General Conference Mennonites and Evangelical Mennonite Brethren for work in Menno Colony and eastern Paraguay. Four conferences comprised of Indian and Spanish speaking congregations have resulted from these inter-Mennonite mission activities.

The development of the Indianern Beratungsbehörde (Indian Counsel Agency), more recently known as Asociación de Servicios de Cooperación Indigena-Menonita (ASCIM; Mennonite-Indian Cooperative Service Association) in 1961, has been an all-colony effort of considerable magnitude. Through this agency, education, health, and resettlement services have been provided to the Indian peoples.

Smaller Mennonite populations in Brazil and Uruguay have worked together informally with less structure. Among the Old Colony Mennonites of Bolivia, Belize, and Mexico, inter-Mennonite cooperation is very limited.

Only a few countries have multiple conferences, but throughout Latin America there are numerous nations with Spanish, Portuguese, or English-speaking Mennonite communities, many of them quite small. Except for Central America, distances prevent extensive cooperation. The °Congreso Latino Americano (Latin American Congress) has met occasionally. Other area-wide Spanish activities include the newly formed (1984) Agrupación Menonita Latino-Americana de Comunicaciones (AMLAC; Latin American Mennonite Communications Group) with a mandate to unify the churches by enhancing communication and suppporting mass media activities among the Spanish-speaking conferences. The Curriculo Anabautista de Educación Biblica Congregacional (CAEBC) is a cooperative inter-Mennonite group formed to prepare Spanish-language curricula for conferences both in North America and Latin America.

Another approach to cooperation has been the development of regional organizations within the larger continental area. The °Consulta Anabautista Menonita Centroamericana (Central American Anabaptist and Mennonite Consultation) meets annually with representation from seven or eight nations. By 1986 it had had its 13th meeting. A mission consultation, sponsored by the Latin American Congress in 1986, drew representatives from the entire area including representatives of the various language groups. Also sponsored by churches in eight nations of Central America is the Seminario Ministerial de Liderazgo Anabautista (SEMILLA; Seminary for Anabaptist Ministerial Leadership), a program of °theological training by extension (°Consulta).

Another group, Congreso Menonita del Cono Sur (Mennonite Congress of the Southern Cone), representing Mennonites in Paraguay, Uruguay, Brazil, Bolivia, and Argentina, meets less often but is also a vigorous and effective gathering of leaders and conference representatives.

Latin America became the first continent other than Europe or North America to host a Mennonite World Conference assembly—the ninth assembly held in Curitiba, Brazil, in 1972.

Europe. Development after World War II, including the emergence of the European Economic Community, have facilitated cooperation among European Mennonites in the postwar period. Within France a major move was the merger in 1980 of the Groupe des Églises Mennonites de Langue Française (French-language Mennonite Church Group) with the Association des Églises Evangéliques Mennonites de France (AEEMF); Association of Evangelical Mennonite Churches of France) under the latter name.

A similar movement developed in Germany as the two German Mennonite conferences known as the Verband deutscher Mennonitengemeinden (Federation of German Mennonite Congregations) and the Vereinigung der deutschen Mennonitengemeinden (Union of German Mennonite Congregations) began discussions in 1982 by sponsoring a fellowship meeting for members of both conferences. In 1983 the Arbeitsgemeinschaft deutscher Mennoniten (AdM; German Mennonite Task Force) was formed. The task force is led jointly by the presiding leaders of both "Vereinigung" and the "Verband." In 1983 an annual Gemeindetag (church fellowship day) was begun.

A very concrete expression of this growing unity was the merger of the official periodicals sponsored by the two German conferences. The *Mennonitische Blätter* of the "Vereinigung" and the *Gemeinde Unterwegs* of the "Verband" were combined into a new periodical named *Brücke* as of January 1986.

The most inclusive agency of Mennonites in Europe continues to be the °Europäisches Mennonitisches Evangelisationskomitee (EMEK; Europe Mennonite Evangelism Committee). In 1967 Europe's own °relief and °service agency was formed, patterned after the example of the North American Mennonite Central Committee (MCC). This new agency, named °International Mennonite Organization (IMO), represents joint relief committee activity of the Dutch and German churches together with the Mennonite Brethren of Europe. While France and Switzerland have separate relief committees, the Mennonitische Tschad Hilfe (Mennonite Chad Aid) unites the broader European community in a common cause.

The older European-based °°International Mennonite Peace Committee), not to be confused with the

°International Mennonite Peace Committee that has emerged under Mennonite World Conference auspices, has been reactivated as the °Europäische Mennonitische Friedenskomite (EMFK; European Mennonite Peace Committee) with broad representation from the major European Mennonite groups.

The invitation to °Mennonite World Conference (MWC) to hold the 11th assembly in France (Strasbourg, 1984) became the first occasion for a Mennonite World Conference assembly to be sponsored by the five major conferences of Europe rather than the churches of a single country.

Other activities include the Inter-Menno trainee program (°international exchanges) and the Europäische Mennonitische Bibelschule/Ecôle Biblique Mennonite Européene (European Mennonite Bible School) at Bienenberg, Liestal, Switzerland, governed by a broadly based board of Mennonite representatives from most of the European Mennonite conferences.

Mennonites of Europe and North America have long maintained fraternal relationships, most frequently via exchange of students and visits by mission and service administrators and conference leaders. North American mission work in Europe has on occasion been reviewed with European leaders. EMEK and IMO periodically send representatives to counterpart MCC and Council of International Ministries (CIM) sessions in North America. Canadian leaders have worked closely with the German and Dutch churches in their ministry to Mennonite resettlers (°Umsiedler) from the Soviet Union to Germany. For many years a North American has been serving on the faculty of the Bienenburg Bible School.

A consultation regarding common concerns in relief work administration in Europe was held in 1979 attended by North American and European representatives. Of special significance was a subsequent meeting held at the Bibelheim der Mennoniten Thomashof, near °Karlsruhe, Germany, on Nov. 13, 1986. This brought together a broader group representing both relief and mission agencies such as IMO, EMEK, and EFMK, together with representatives of MCC and four North American mission agencies. Also present were representatives of three younger churches in Spain, Portugal, and Ireland. This three-way working session was cast in the context of looking at Europe as a mission field—a concept stimulated by the message of Leo Laurenz on the occasion of his retirement as chairman of EMEK. It is notable that inter-Mennonite cooperation in this remarkable consultation was occasioned by a concern for mission.

North America. Inter-Mennonite cooperation in North America, which did not begin in any substantial way until 1911 and only came to fruition after 1940 (ME III: 44ff.), did indeed escalate rapidly in the postwar years. The organization of the °°Congo Inland Mission in 1912 and the MCC in 1920 were the harbingers of a movement toward proliferation of cooperative organizations that reached a peak in the decade of 1961-70. During that period, 23 new inter-Mennonite projects were initiated. By 1974 a cumulative total of 72 such projects could be recorded. While no subsequent annotated list is available, the trend has continued but probably not at the same rate of increase.

A North American consultation on inter-Mennonite Relations in 1974, a subsequent gathering in 1982, and several consultations in Canada and other events continue to probe the frontiers of organizational cooperation.

The inevitable question of merger continues to appear periodically. After many years of discussion, the merger of the °°Krimmer Mennonite Brethren with the Mennonite Brethren Church in North America was consummated in 1960. Also merged were the °°Missionary Church Association and the °°United Missionary Church in 1969, creating the Missionary Church (not included in ME V).

In the mid-1960s both the Mennonite Church (MC) general conference and the General Conference Mennonite Church appointed interchurch relations committees to study the broad area of developing interdenominational and, specifically, inter-Mennonite relationships. This study included meetings between the two committees in 1966 and in 1969. The possibility of merger between the two bodies did not receive support from either of the two conferences. In effect, the need to wait for broader local congregational initiative, the hesitancy to impose a bureaucratic decision and the desire for broader inter-Mennonite relationships with other Mennonite bodies led to a negative decision regarding merger at that point.

However, the emergence of dually affiliated congregations, a phenomenon limited largely to congregations related to the General Conference Mennonite Church and the Mennonite Church, opened a new, if not altogether satisfactory, level of congregational activity. In 1974 a study reported 15 congregations with dual or triple affiliation. That pattern has continued with the *Mennonite Yearbook (1986-87)* listing more than 60 congregations that were affiliated with at least one other Mennonite or Brethren in Christ denomination.

Meanwhile, the broad variety of organizational relationships continued. MCC (Canada) was formed in 1963, replacing several °historic peace church organizations and other inter-Mennonite agencies, thus becoming the national body with the broadest involvement of Mennonite and Brethren in Christ groups. Subsequently, MCC (United States) was also formed, while MCC itself continued as a joint, binational North American body. The other earlier group, Congo Inland Mission, became the Africa Inter-Mennonite Mission (AIMM) in 1972 and broadened its representaiton, continuing as the only inter-Mennonite mission agency in North America.

The range of organizational activity continued to expand as additional projects of mutual interest were shaped into new structural patterns. The Columbia Bible Institute, a joint project of the Mennonite Brethren and the Conference of Mennonites in British Columbia (GCM) and the Associated Mennonite Biblical Seminaries, a joint seminary for the Mennonite Church and the General Conference Mennonite Church in Elkhart, Ind., are two illustrations of a long line of activities in the area of history, scholarship, missions, literature and peacemaking.

The Mennonite Church biennial assembly and the General Conference Mennonite Church triennial sessions were held jointly at Bethlehem, Pa., in 1983. The joint conferences issued a statement on inter-Mennonite relationships. Continued references to merger were heard, but the recurrent theme was caution—cultivating broader Mennonite relationships in North America was viewed by many as a prior consideration.

In more recent years, inter-Mennonite activities have tended to move beyond cooperation among existing projects and programs of the various major groups. There has been notable expansion into the development of common projects of major significance. These include such projects as the Believers' Church Bible Commentary Series, the Mennonite Experience in America history project, two hymnal projects (*Mennonite Hymnal*, 1969 [GCM and MC]; a new hymnal in process in the late 1980s), and the formation in 1987 of an inter-Mennonite group assigned to work on a new Mennonite confession of faith. Each of these involves the major North American Mennonite groups in various ways.

In 1976 the Council of Mission Board Secretaries (COMBS) was enlarged and renamed Council of International Ministries (CIM). From the time of its inception in 1958, the Council of Mission Board Secretaries (COMBS) has opened up a new pattern of inter-Mennonite fellowship and discussion. In addition to the value of this interaction, the COMBS group was instrumental in dealing with broad issues of mission and service strategy and philosophy, which left a considerable impact on the growing overseas missionary and relief activity of the North American churches. The cooperation among administrators also resulted in a series of consultations on "Hunger and Population pressures" in 1968, "The Christian Worker in Revolutionary Situations" in 1971, and "Relief, Service and Missions Relationships Overseas" in 1964.

In addition, discussions in this context were influential in the development of several notable projects such as MCC's Teachers Abroad Program (TAP), the Council of Mennonite Colleges (CMC) and International Education Services (IES).

Perhaps the most creative and radical development was the formation of China Educational Exchange (CEE) in 1983. This became the joint administrative arm of the °mission boards, MCC, MCCC, and the Mennonite colleges as a new style of service evolved when China opened its doors to the West.

It was in the context of COMBS in its earlier years that North American assistance and relationships to growing churches in other continents were initiated and coordinated. The organization of what came to be known as the Africa Mennonite and Brethren in Christ Fellowship (AMBCF) and the Asia Mennonite Conference (AMC) as well as the Mennonite Christian Service Fellowship of India (MCSFI) received encouragement and support through this group. In its revised format, the CIM continues as a context for consultation, a vehicle for joint action and a setting for missiological study.

The emergence of the Council of Moderators and Secretaries (CMS) in 1972 brought a new focal point to North American inter-Mennonite efforts. For the first time, the heads of the four largest North American denominations (BIC, GCMC, MB, and MC) began to meet regularly, although there had been an earlier series of North American all-Mennonite conferences which set the stage for broader inter-Mennonite cooperation (°regional Mennonite conferences). The group claimed no administrative authority but served as a forum for exchange, discussion, mutual information, and acquaintance. Emerging issues of North American inter-Mennonite activity came under its purview. Of special note was the initiation of regular reporting to North American inter-Mennonite agencies to the leadership of various conferences through this channel. Increasingly, concerns of mutual interest to the churches came to the agenda of the CMS, such as the proposal for a Christian Peacemaker Team (CPT), first suggested at the MWC Assembly in Strasbourg in 1984. This proposal was picked up and studied in an inter-Mennonite context, culminating in a broadly representative consultation in December 1986.

Of special note is the fact that in addition to working together in MCCC, the leaders of Canadian conferences began to meet as a council of Mennonite and Brethren in Christ moderators. A series of annual meetings held in connection with the annual MCCC meetings culminated in a theological consultation in Jan. 1987. Eight groups sent official representatives; five more sent observers. The meeting concluded with a brief but dramatic announcement that "The Canadian Council of Mennonite and Brethren in Christ Moderators" had just held its inaugural meeting.

The influence of developing projects more closely related to the congregation produced a growing openness in receptivity by churches to interaction with other Mennonites. Such activities as Mennonite Disaster Service (MDS), °Mennonite Economic Development Associates (MEDA), °relief sales, and MCC °SELFHELP Crafts project involve more and more people in local congregations. Even the books that were published and became best sellers, such as *Mennonite Community Cookbook* (Herald Press, 1950), *More-with-Less* (Herald Press, 1975), facilitated growing awareness and sensitivity. Such inter-Mennonite periodicals as the *Mennonite Reporter* (Waterloo, Ontario), and the *Mennonite Weekly Review* (Newton, Ks.) added their influence.

A remarkable and creative new initiative emerged in Ontario, Canada, as the two district conferences of the Mennonite Church (MC), the Western Ontario Mennonite Conference and the Mennonite Conference of Ontario and Quebec, and the Conference of United Mennonite Churches of Ontario (GCM) began a process of integration that approached completion in 1987. The decision to achieve final integration in 1988 resulted in the first truly inter-Mennonite district conference with dual denominational affiliation, the Mennonite Conference of Eastern Canada.

The planners of the Mennonite Church and the General Conference Mennonite Church assemblies agreed to meet jointly at Normal, Ill., in 1989. A major new step is the invitation to the Mennonite Brethren and the Brethren in Christ to share with these two bodies in planning a joint study conference in connection with that event, thus broadening the base of inter-Mennonite discussion and contact. This, together with the confession of faith study and the work of the Council of Moderators and Secretaries, elevates inter-Mennonite reality to the highest level of denominational leadership on the part of the four major North American bodies.

The plans for the 12th Mennonite World Conference Assembly in Winnipeg, Manitoba (1990), promise to be the most inclusive base yet established for any MWC assembly. Three years prior, the hosting committee is organized with representation from at least ten Canadian conference bodies.

The implicit, if not explicit, goal of inter-Mennonite relationships and cooperation may be deemed to be greater unity or perhaps eventual merger. The theological, cultural, social, and geographical diversity of Mennonites brings into tension several elements of Mennonite polity and tradition. On the one hand, there is the question of faithfulness to one's conscience, biblical understanding and tradition. In the non-creedal pattern of Mennonite ecclesiology, the congregation is essentially autonomous, and the authority of the district or conference is limited. On the other hand a strong sense of °community and interdependence, also arising out of the Anabaptist heritage, requires a commitment to one another as individuals, congregations, and districts, and indeed at all levels of church life with a semblance of unity and well-defined identity.

The tension between autonomy and community, between individual freedom and mutual responsibility will continue to influence the relationships among Mennonites. C. J. Dyck, in a paper read to the 1982 Consultation on Inter-Mennonite Relations, declared that Mennonites were more united than the list of inter-Mennonite activities would indicate. Paul Toews wrote in 1983 that the events that have been and are most effective in eroding the boundaries between and among Mennonites are theological renewal after World War I, the development of °institutions that generated common work activities, and the growing °ecumenical trend after World War II.

It is clear that a younger generation in North America and Europe is less concerned with historic separations. The issues that prevailed and divided Mennonites a generation or two ago are no longer as relevant as they seemed then. In the younger churches around the world, the impact of a multiplicity of mission and service agencies representing a series of North American conferences, each with their individual overseas activity, is often confusing and intimidating. In any event, the emergence of a worldwide Mennonite community puts the question of unity in new perspective (°Mennonite World Conference).

Not only overseas, but also in North America, the issue of inter-Mennonite cooperation becomes critical on the frontier of mission witness and church planting. New congregations are emerging in urban areas, or among the rapidly growing émigré communities. In such "foreign" communities close to traditional North American Mennonite communities, the term "Mennonite" is much more easily understood than the various terms that modify the name and signify specific traditions within the larger Mennonite community.

It is not surprising that growing interest in the Mennonite faith, the presence of several Mennonite groups in our larger urban centers and the development of cooperative evangelistic efforts raise questions about the identities of new churches. This problem was a significant issue in the development of the Mennonite Conference of Eastern Canada and will most likely have a strong influence in future considerations of new frontiers in inter-Mennonite cooperation.

The proliferation of Mennonite structures may seem out of proportion to the size of a small denomination. The instincts that gave priority to spiritual unity and fraternal cooperation ahead of structural change seem right. Yet, it is clear that structures will also need to be altered when the mood of the church calls for organizational changes that reflect the true character of growing Mennonite spiritual unity and common commitment to one another. PNK

For current listings of inter-Mennonite organizations, see *MC Yearbook*, published biennially since 1986, annually to 1986. Additional inter-Mennonite agencies are listed in *Menn. Jahrbuch*. See also C. J. Dyck, ed., *An Introduction to Mennonite History*, 2nd ed. (Scottdale, 1981); idem, "Where Have We Come From? A Review of the Past 25 Years of Inter-Mennonite Agency Developments," Proceedings of Consultation on Inter-Mennonite relationships October 21-23, 1982; Paul N. Kraybill, "North American Inter-Mennonite Relationship," *Proceedings of Inter-Mennonite Consultation* (Rosemont, Ill., Oct. 28-30, 1974), copy at MHL, Goshen; *MWH* (1978); *MWH* (1984), new edition projected for 1990; James M. Lapp, ed., *Principles and Guidelines for Interchurch Relations* (Scottdale: Interchurch Relations Committee of Mennonite General Conference [MC], 1971); Diether Götz Lichdi, *Über Zürich und Witmarsum nach Addis Abeba* (Maxdorf: Agape-Verlag, 1983); Peter Retzlaff, *Research in Inter-Mennonite Relations* (Elkhart: IMS, 1967); Calvin Redekop, *Strangers Become Neighbors* (Scottdale, 1980); Wilbert R. Shenk, *An Experiment in Interagency Coordination*, (Elkhart: Council of International Ministries, 1986); John A. Toews, *History MB* (1975); Paul Toews, "Dissolving the Boundaries and Strengthening the Centers," *GH* (Jan. 25, 1983), 49-52; Kauffman/Harder, *Anabaptists Four C. Later* (1975), 252-60.

See also Bender, Harold S.; Epp, Frank; Gingerich, Newton L.; Graber, J. D.; Hiebert, P. C.; Hostetter, Christian N., Jr.; Miller, Orie O.

Inter-Mission Cooperation. Examples of collaboration and partnership between mission and church groups around the world provide a veritable patchwork quilt of varieties and styles both inter-Mennonite and interdenominational in nature. Diverse as they are, however, some basic underlying dynamics are often to be found which contribute appreciably to °ecumenical cooperation. Among the most common are: the need for a united voice and concerted action in the presence of powerful political and religious adversaries; the sheer size of an area and population which Christian missions hope to reach, a size which often far exceeds the capability and resources of any one mission alone; the possibility of maintaining joint programs which profit all groups but which would otherwise be impossible; a concern for the portrayal of the unity of the body of Christ; a hunger for fellowship and opportunity to take counsel together with people of like mind and faith.

Unique circumstances and mixes of common objectives often give rise to ecumenical groupings and initiatives which would seem strange in Europe and North America. Removed from the Western setting of sharply drawn lines of policy, tradition and bias, however, Christians of many persuasions have often found sufficient ground and reason for cooperation in Christian mission.

°Ecumenism, however, has on occasion been less helpful overseas when it has generated different groups within a country which adopted an adversarial stance with regard to each other and competed for a following among the Christians and churches within the country. The tendency to export and impose western theological perspectives and divisions upon the overseas churches, even if with the sincerest of motivations, has often been confusing to and little appreciated by national leaders.

In many areas where Mennonite missions are at work, missionaries find themselves in the presence of competing Christian councils or associations which reflect the theological preoccupations which are familiar to Western Christians. Mennonite response to such situations has not been uniform. Some Mennonite °mission boards have felt that if they must relate to one or the other, they will affiliate with the group of evangelical persuasion as opposed to those of conciliar orientation (World Council of Churches; various national and local councils of churches etc.). Other Mennonite boards, however, have hesitated to identify exclusively with any single cluster but have preferred to seek ways of relating to all groups within a given context with the hope of sharing Anabaptist perspectives and convictions with all.

As for the relationship between mission work and the rise of ecumenism overseas, it can certainly be said that mission work has favored a spirit of ecumenism in many areas. However such ecumenism has rarely been born directly of idealism. Christian councils and associations have tended first to take shape because of urgent need and the pressures of common problems and aspirations. Once in place, such groups then became the framework within which the benefits of ecumenical relations and fellowship were experienced and increasingly appreciated.

Ecumenical activity will certainly remain a feature of the world of the younger churches in the future. As nationals increasingly assert leadership, their own agendas and perspectives will heavily influence the nature and scope of the interchurch affiliations to come.

A sample listing of programs featuring (1) inter-Mennonite and Brethren in Christ collaboration on the part of mission boards or conferences and (2) Mennonite and Brethren in Christ collaboration with interdenominational agencies follows (AIMM = Africa Inter-Mennonite Mission; EMBMC = Eastern Mennonite Board of Missions and Charities [MC]; MBM = Mennonite Board of Missions [MC]; COM =

Commission on Overseas Mission [GCM]); the list is subject to continual change and is offered solely as an illustration of the variety of such involvements at one point in time:

(1) Inter-Mennonite and Brethren in Christ programs: °Africa Mennonite and Brethren in Christ Fellowship; Mennonite Ministries, a joint program of AIMM and Mennonite Central Committee (MCC) in Botswana; SEDA, a rural development program based at Nyanga, Zaire, jointly sponsored by Communauté Mennonite au Zaire (CMZA; Mennonite Church of Zaire) and MCC; Asia Mennonite Conference; Hong Mennonite Ministries (GCM and MC mission boards); °Mennonite Christian Service Fellowship of India; Japan Mennonite Fellowship, Anabaptist Center in Tokyo, and °Tokyo Chiku Menonaito Kyokai Rengo (Tokyo Area Fellowship of Mennonite Churches); Hwalien Mennonite Christian Hospital in Taiwan; SEMILLA, an Anabaptist-Mennonite program of °theological education by extension based in Guatemala City (°Consulta Anabautista Menonita Centroamericana); joint ministry by EMBMC and MBM in Israel; Iglesia Menonita de Bolivia (Mennonite Church of Bolivia), related to COM, MBM, and MCC; Associação Evangelica Menonita and Associação Menonita de Assistêcia Social in °Brazil; the Comité Nacional Anabautista, which coordinates Mennonite mission agencies in Colombia; MENCOLDES (Fundacion Menonita Colombiana para el Desarollo), an inter-Mennonite relief and development agency in Colombia; Seminario Anabautista Andino, a training program serving Anabaptist churches in Colombia and Venezuela; Centro Evangélico Menonita de Teología Asunción (CEMTA, Mennonite Evangelical Center for Theology) and Comité Menonita de Acción Evangélica y Social en el Paraguay, both in Paraguay.

(2) Interdenominational programs (the cooperating Mennonite or Brethren in Christ agency is given in parenthesis): Association of Evangelicals of Africa and Madagascar (BIC); Inter-Confessional Protestant Council, Benin (MBM); Federation of Evangelical Missions and Churchs, Burkina Faso (AIMM); United Evangelical Mission, Chad (Europäische Mennonitische Evangelisations-Komitee); Evangelical Seminary of Bangui, Central African Republic (Mennonite Brethren); The Christian Council, Ghana (MBM); Centre d'Editions et de Distribution, an inter-Protestant press and publishing house in Zaire (CMZA and Communauté des Frères Mennonites au Zaire [CFMZA, Mennonite Brethren Church of Zaire]); Église du Christ au Zaire, in which most Protestant groups in Zaire have become members by government ruling (CMZA, CFMZA, and Commmunauté Evangélique Mennonite [CEM, Mennonite Evangelical Church]); Christian Medical Institute of Kasai, a reference hospital and training center sponsored jointly by the Presbyterian church and the CMZA; Institute Supérieur de Théologie de Kinshasa, an inter-Protestant training program for pastors (CMZA and CFMZA); the Protestant Book Store of the Kasai (Presbyterian, CMZA, CFMZA, CEM); Programme Agricole Protestant, based in °Kikwit, sponsored by the Église du Christ au Zaire, MCC, the local government, and the CFMZA; International Assistance Mission, Afghanistan (MBM);

Christian Council of Hong Kong (COM): Evangelical Fellowship of India (COM, MB); National Council of Churches in India (COM); Union Biblical Seminary at Pune, India (COM, MBM, MB); Woodstock School for missionary children (most Protestant missions in India have had ties with this school); Japan Evangelical Mission Association (COM, MB); Taiwan Missionary Fellowship (COM); Taiwan Mission Center in Taipei (COM); United Mission to Nepal (MBM); San Jose Biblical Seminary, Costa Rica (COM); The Evangelical Committee for Development of Nicaragua [CEPAD] (Conservative Mennonite Board of Missions and Charities); Evangelical Alliance of England (BIC); Consortium of European Missions [EKUMINDO] (related to Mennonite work in Indonesia); Persekutan Geraja Indonesia [Community of Churches in Indonesia], to which the Gereja Injili di Tanah Jawa (Evangelical Church of Java [GITJ]) and the Persatuan Gereja-Gereja Kristen Muria Indonesia (United Muria Synod [GKMI]) belong; Edinburgh Medical Missionary Society Hospital at Nazareth, Israel (MBM); Immanuel House Fellowship and Student Center at Tel Aviv, Israel (MBM); United Christian Council in Israel (MBM); Asociación Nacional de Evangélicos Bolivianos [National Assocation of Bolivian Evangelicals] (Evangelical Mennonite Missions Conference); Confederación Evangélical de Colombia (Iglesia Evangélica Menonita [IEM] and Asociación de Iglesias Hermanos Menonitas); Futuro Juvenal, an interdenominational program for children and orphans (IEM Colombia); Seminario Teologica Presbiteriano de Bogota (IEM Colombia); Venezuela Evangelical Fellowship of Churches (BIC).   JEB

See also Comity.

International Exchanges. The International Visitor Exchange Program (IVEP) began when Mennonite Central Committee (MCC) workers in Europe, who since 1946 had helped selected students from Europe for the Council of Mennonite and Affiliated Colleges, proposed a nonacademic exchange program for worthy young people to live and work for one year in North America. The goal of the program was to further international understanding, broaden horizons, and advance Christian unity.

After approval from the United States Department of State (1948), farmers from Europe arrived in New York in 1950. The program expanded to include nonagricultural fields in 1952; the first non-European came from Japan in 1955. From 1950 to 1986, a total of 1,758 young people aged 19-30 participated from 53 different countries in Africa, Asia, Europe, Latin America and the Caribbean.

The 12-month program usually consists of two 6-month placements. Sponsors in the North American Mennonite constituency provide work experience, a home away from home, and pocket money to the exchangees and send a monthly donation to MCC in exchange for the vocational participation of the overseas visitors. Participants are selected by national Mennonite and Brethren in Christ leaders, missionaries, or MCC personnel in the sending country. All participants must return home at the end of the one year. Placements are made both in the United States and Canada (since 1960). Administering the overall program have been Doreen Harms, Elma Esau, Katherine Penner Hostetler, Pauline Jahnke Bauman, and Emma Schlichting.

The Polish Agricultural Visitor Exchange (PAVE) was born in April 1971 to facilitate contact with people in Eastern European countries. Up to 35 people participated annually. Placement and funding were similar to those of the IVEP. Martial law in Poland brought on termination of the program in March 1983. During its 12-year existence, 246 Polish agriculturists participated. The program was conducted in cooperation with Stowarzyszeniem Inzynierow i Technikow Rolnictwa, a Polish umbrella agricultural agency.

The Intermenno Trainee Program (ITP) is a one-year cultural exchange in Europe for North American young people 19-27 years of age. It was initiated in 1963 by the Diakoniewerk der Mennoniten the forerunner of the °International Mennonite Organization. After Dutch Mennonites joined the program in 1965, placements were made in The Netherlands, West Germany, Switzerland, France, and Belgium. Similar in purposes and operations to IVEP, the ITP is administered by the European Mennonite Committees in The Netherlands and West Germany with ties to Mennonite conferences and relief and service agencies in each of these countries. From 1963 to 1986, 847 North American young people were sponsored by ITP.

The China Educational Exchange (CEE) was created in December 1981 as an offspring of an exchange between Goshen College and the Sichuan Bureau of Higher Education. It is made up of representatives from Mennonite °mission boards, MCC, the Mennonite Medical Association, Mennonite Mental Health Associates, and interested Mennonite colleges. North American teachers of English are sent to China for two-year terms. Chinese teachers of language, history, and culture are placed in North American colleges; visits of medical doctors, nurses, and agricultural people are also administered. Exchanges of engineers and mental health personnel were under negotiation in 1986. A total of 38 professional people came from China and 85 North Americans went to China through CEE, 1981-86.   DFH

International Mennonite Organization (IMO) was organized in 1967 by the Mennonite relief organizations of The Netherlands and Germany as well as the Mennonite Brethren Church in Europe to carry out social welfare and °development aid. The relief organizations of the Mennonites of France and Switzerland were not yet members in 1986. Projects such as the Trainee Exchange Program and cooperation in sending relief and development volunteers are carried out together with Mennonite Central Committee. Projects especially supported by IMO are Indian settlement in the Chaco in Paraguay; food aid and social construction programs (medicinal care, school education, child sponsorship, economic development) in Brazil, Uruguay, Nicaragua, Guatemala, India, Chad; and care of refugees and resettlers (°Umsiedler) in Europe. The annual budget of IMO amounts to 1.3 million West German marks.

IMO wants to engage itself in Asia, Africa, and Latin America, preferably in long-term social development projects ("help towards self-help"). But again and again it sees itself called also to give short-term food and °refugee aid. Wherever possible IMO also sends volunteers to the above-named projects, usually for a minimum of three years. PJFo

Menn. Jahrbuch.

See also Inter-Mennonite Cooperation; Neuwied; Stichting voor Bijzondere Noden.

International Relations. Mennonite global awareness and involvement has been shaped by several activities of which the first is °migration. Mennonites have moved around considerably in this century and that has had a broadening influence. The major 20th c. Mennonite movements have been from the Soviet Union to Canada (1920s and 1940s), South America (1930s and 1940s), and Germany (1970s and 1980s); from Canada to Mexico (1920s), Paraguay (1920s and 1950s), and Bolivia (1970s); and from Mexico to Belize and Bolivia (1970s) and back to Canada. In the 1980s Mennonites helped a significant number of Asian refugees to immigrate to Canada and the United States. This activity has diversified the cultural exposure of North American Mennonites.

Mennonite world awareness and involvement has also been broadened through participation in °mission and °service activities. From 1852 to 1935 Mennonites and Brethren in Christ went as missionaries to the East Indies (Indonesia), India, China, the Congo (Zaire), South Africa, East Africa, and Argentina. Mission work expanded to Japan, Taiwan, and other countries of Latin America, Europe, and Africa in the 1950s and following decades. In 1920 the Mennonite Central Committee (MCC) was established to minister to Mennonites starving in Russia. Following World War II MCC engaged in sizable °relief and reconstruction projects in Europe and helped relocate war °refugees in Paraguay, Uruguay, and Argentina. This experience helped to establish a partner relationship between Mennonites in North America, South America and Europe.

By the 1950s the Mennonite world awareness had reached a point where Mennonite agencies were expected to respond to major needs wherever they occurred. Major development and relief programs have been undertaken in Bangladesh, Bolivia, Brazil, Central America, Greece, Haiti, India, Indonesia, Jordan, Korea, and Vietnam. In Africa the emphasis was on education through the Teachers Abroad Program initiated in the early 1960s. Literally hundreds of teachers have served in a variety of schools under church and government administration with a special concentration in such countries as Malawi, Nigeria, Zaire and Zambia. Teaching assignments in China and Japan have been common in the 1970s and 1980s (°international exchanges).

As of 1984 Mennonite and Brethren in Christ mission and service boards had 1,397 appointed workers in overseas assignments with a combined budget of $27 million. In 1986 the Mennonite World Conference listed Mennonite or Mennonite-related groups with a combined membership of 774,000 in 57 countries. Representatives of these churches meet every 6 years in the Mennonite World Conference which provides a truly global experience of international sisterhood and brotherhood.

Through participation in these activities Mennonites have gone beyond studying the global scene theoretically. Mennonites have become involved, not only by sending money but through sending their sons and daughters, and in following them with their support.

The practice of addressing world need through the medium of workers who come out of the membership ranks has resulted in many congregations having one or more members who have served overseas. Most of the faculty members of Mennonite colleges have served or studied overseas. Most Mennonite colleges have programs which permit or in some cases, require students to study abroad. Mennonite business persons have created their own organization (Mennonite Economic Development Associates) to support and partner with entrepreneurs in other countries. In the 1930s the Kansas Institute for International Relations at Bethel College (Kansas) was an early effort to raise consciousness about issues of international politics, economics, and °disarmament.

Mennonites, because of their history, have felt a special concern for suffering which results from political disruption. Mennonites have experience and skills which permit them to participate in develoment and °disaster relief programs. Mennonite understanding of Scripture calls for a readiness to help persons in need. Mission and service organizations have been brought into existence to give practical expression to these concerns.

Through this multifaceted global exposure Mennonites are coming to a new understanding of Christian responsibility which transcends national borders, of the missionary character of the church, and of the enrichment which results from exposure to other cultures and other Christians. ES

In addition to *Menn Bib.* nos. 7731, 8057, 25172, 27131, see *Bibl. on War and Peace* (1987), 230-37; Urbane Peachey, ed., *The Role of the Church in Society: An International Perspective* (Menn. World Conference, 1988).

Interpretation and Information Centers. The national attention given Amish and Mennonite communities has brought an influx of °tourists to see first hand people in a living museum on their own turf. This is a recent phenomenon as more and more city dwellers seek to escape the fast pace of urban life in search for the quiet and peaceful environment of rural America. With increased attention from the media of mass communication to their unique way of life, Amish communities have become prime tourist spots. In the last two decades every major Amish community in America has established an information center. In most cases, Mennonites have taken the initiative in establishing information centers as a response to the thousands of inquiries about a people who chose not to be modern, inquiries that frequently have received ambiguous or erroneous answers when addressed to the people in nearby towns. There is a strong cultural wall between the Amish and the tourist; a wall the Amish hope to maintain. Amish see their religion and culture as a private matter and therefore have great reluctance to share their life-style with the outside world. Preaching in Amish church services dwells heavily on °nonconformity to the ways of the world. This throws a cloud of secrecy over church functions and creates a reticence to open their society to the outsider, especially the tourist.

In contrast, many information centers operate with all the latest technologies, e.g., video cassettes, film, and audio tapes to tell the Anabaptist story as comprehensively as possible. Most of the information centers have animated visual effects to depict with all the drama of an epic movie aspects of the Protestant Reformation and Anabaptist °persecution, °migrations, and modern-day faith in action. A recent trend at many centers is the preparation of full-color pamphlets giving a strong Anabaptist message with the intent of low-key evangelism. Professionally prepared literature is widely distributed in order to compete for the tourist's time and attention.

Information centers have many times helped the Amish by giving correct information while encouraging the tourist to respect the Amish desire for privacy and peace and quiet in their daily lives. Information centers in large tourist areas have contributed much to the economic climate of the area. Special Amish cooking is a favorite of tourists. Bed-and-breakfast lodging, sometimes in Amish homes, is a delight to the vistor. A variety of craft shops and °quilt barns have all brought a degree of prosperity to some Amish and Mennonite communities. Most information centers operate without admission charge, although there is ample opportunity for visitor donations. Other centers operate as profit-making business enterprises.

While most of the interest in Amish and Mennonite religion and culture seems to be in the United States and Canada, there are several similar centers of note in other countries. The Menno Simons Center in Witmarsum in The Netherlands receives many visitors from all parts of the world. Located in the heart of early Anabaptist history in the 16th c., the center becomes an appropriate stop for Mennonite tourists making the trek to Witmarsum to visit the Menno Simons Monument. A second information center is located in Tokyo, Japan. The Anabaptist Center serves Mennonites as a home while in Tokyo, however, its primary function is to disseminate Anabaptist information to the Japanese. Additional information and study centers can be found in London, Paris, and Brussels.

Some of the most notable visitor and information centers in North America are:

Mennonite Information Center, Lancaster, Pa., one of the first and most complete information centers, is located in the heart of one of the top ten tourist centers in the United States.

Mennonite Heritage Center, Souderton, Pa., displays three centuries of Mennonite life.

People's Place, Intercourse, Pa., exhibits Amish and Mennonite heritage and culture through art and film and provides one of the largest collections of books on Amish, Mennonites, and Hutterites.

Mennonite Information Center, Berlin, Ohio, provides information on the history, religion, and customs of the Amish and Mennonites who farm, run businesses, and raise their families in this rural, quiet, rolling countryside in Holmes Co.

Menno-Hof, Mennonite and Amish Visitor Center, Shipshewana, Ind., tells the story of the Anabaptist origins, persecution, migrations, and faith in action in an early meetinghouse setting.

Brubacher House, Waterloo, Ont., is a restoration of a 19th c. Mennonite house.

The Meeting Place, St. Jacobs, Ont., offers information on early Anabaptists and contemporary Mennonites in Ontario.

Heritage Historical Library, Aylmer, Ont., is a collection of resources for researchers in Amish history and genealogy.

Mennonite Heritage Center, Metamora, Ill,. portrays honestly and in depth the characteristics and the pilgrimages of the various Mennonite groups in Illinois.

Warkentin House, Newton, Ks., a 19th c. Mennonite house featuring Turkey Red wheat brought to America by the Russian Mennonites.

In addition to the major information centers listed above, there are a number of similar centers featuring Amish farms, amusement parks, Pennsylvania Dutch restaurants, and craft shops. Most notable of these are: Dutch Wonderland, Route 30 East, Lancaster, Pa.; Amish Farm and House, Lincoln Highway East, Lancaster, Pa.; Amish Heritage Village, Berlin, Ohio; Amishville, Berne, Ind.; Amish Acres, Nappanee, Ind.; Rockome Gardens, Arcola, Ill.

Other attempts at bringing the Mennonite, Amish, and Hutterite story to a wider audience make use of °filmmaking. In the last decade, several full-length films were produced, some achieving national acclaim. A major commercial feature film entitled "Witness" was filmed in Pennsylvania using the Amish countryside in Lancaster Co. as a setting for this murder mystery. Its portrayal of Amish life was not authentic. Some of the most successful films produced and available today are *The Amish: People of Preservation*, an excellent presentation of the Lancaster Co. Amish with good historical content; *Hazel's People*, which combines professional excellence with faithfulness to the spirit of the Mennonite community; *And When They Shall Ask*, which presents the story of the Russian Mennonites, their life in the rich farmlands of South Russia, persecution, and finally, emigration; *Menno's Reins*, a dramatic documentary on the Russian Mennonites in Canada; *The Hutterites*, a classic on the Hutterite colonies in nw. United States and western Canada, with strong emphasis on the religious community, faith, and way of life; *Beyond the Buggy*, a documentary on the Amish community in northern Indiana, the third largest in North America; *Choosing Not to Be Modern*, a documentary filmed in Holmes Co., Ohio, by two New Yorkers who lived in the community and won the confidence of some Amish; *Wichita '78*, a film that explores the themes of international Christian community through a world conference of Mennonites from 42 countries; *Pilgrim Aflame*, the story of Pilgram Marpeck, an early Anabaptist leader in South Germany.

Additionally, numerous slide programs on the Amish and Mennonites have been developed and have contributed significantly to dissemination of information at the established information centers as well as at hundreds of meetings responding to the renewed interest by church and civic groups.   SLY

Current lists of interpretation and information centers are published biennially in *MC Yearbook*; Gordon Hunsberger, "The Mission of the Meetingplace," *WMSC Voice*, 60 (Oct. 1986), 6-7.

See also Identity; Mennonite Studies.

In Search of a Better Beehive: Mennonite Inventions

According to John J. Brown an invention is an idea embodied in a piece of physical equipment which provides some goods or services that formerly were not available. According to that definition, he further states, there are very few inventions that can be attributed to one person or to a team of reseachers. Most inventions are really the result of a process where one idea builds on another and each step brings an improvement in the goods or services which are provided.

Most Mennonite ingenuity would fall into the same category. Their major area of contribution would be agricultural machinery. However, it is often difficult to discern at what point in the process Mennonites made their contribution. The history of agricultural machinery development, like any other area of invention, is colored by nationalistic interests. Therefore there are often conflicting claims to the development. Canadians and Americans claim one thing or another and many European nationalities will make similar claim. One example would be the steel plow. The idea of a plow was not new. To make it out of steel was a new idea. This, in turn opened up the possibility of making it in a better shape and with a smoother finish so that mud would not stick to it. Who first made a better steel plow, though, did not depend on the ideas of shape and surface as much as on the availability of good quality steel that could be shaped and smoothed accordingly. The whole process of im proved steel production involved many people on different continents. So one idea built on another. Methods of production, supply of materials, and distribution of the finished product all had a part in bringing the idea to embodiment in a steel plow. Somewhere in this process the Russian Mennonite firm of Wallman and Lepp made their contribution to the production of a better quality steel plow in the 19th c.

Of course, the development of better quality steel had implications for much farm machinery development. One type of farm machinery was wagons. The quality of steel for the axles and wheels was a factor in the quality and efficiency of the wagon. The quality of workmanship of Russian Mennonite wagonmakers was well known in the part of Russia where Mennonites resided. An innovation which they contributed to the wagon was an efficient handbrake made by Klaas Reimer.

Mennonites also made contributions in other areas. Isaac B. Plett from Steinbach, Manitoba, Canada, produced a self-feeder for a threshing machine in 1886. In 1937 his son, Isaac D. Plett, also of Steinbach, produced a machine for reinforcing the wax foundation used in a beehive by a process of imbedding wire into the wax. In 1928, Henry Plett, also of Steinbach, patented a door latch which would not catch the harness of a horse passing through the doorway. More examples could be given, including the work of a number of Mennonite Central Committee volunteers in the area of °appropriate technology.

One could conclude that there was a general contribution made by many individuals in many parts of the world to the improvement of a piece of physical equipment. It is difficult, if not impossible, to attibute any one of these to a single individual. In this milieu Mennonites had their part. They were attempting, like many others, to improve the physical equipment which they were regularly using so that their lives would be better.   BF

J. J. Brown, *Ideas in Exile: A History of Canadian Invention* (Toronto: McClelland and Stewart, 1967); W. H. G. Armytage, *A Social History of Engineering* (London: Faber and Faber, 1961); W. G. Broehl, Jr., *John Deere's Company: A History of Deere and Company and Its Times* (New York: Doubleday, Inc., 1984); A. Warkentin, *Reflections on our Heritage: A History of Steinbach and the Rural Municipality of Hanover from 1874* (Steinbach, Man.: Derksen Printers, 1971); James Urry, "The Closed and the Open: Social and Religious Change Amongst the Mennonites in Russia, 1789-1889" (PhD thesis, Oxford U., 1978); *Unterhaltungsblatt für die deutschen Ansiedler im suedlichen Russland*, a periodical which contains a series of articles which mention Mennonite contributions from 1849 to 1861, available in the Centre for Mennonite Brethren Studies, Winnipeg, Man., Canada; *Odessaer Zeitung* (from 1876 to 1888); *MWR* (July 7, 1988), 6.

Investments involve time, energy, and resources, that is, a Christian is required to be sensitive to God's will in these three areas. The Christian church also needs the investments of its members in the same three areas. A °tithe of 10 percent is a common measurement used in Scripture to designate what the Lord requires as a minimum. Various scenarios can be developed about this figure depending on one's life-style, conviction and sense of responsibility for mission.

For the sake of brevity, this article is limited to the last of the three: resources. How time and energy are used often reflects one's resources. What is a safe investment policy for our resources?

Old Order Mennonites advocate that members with excess resources beyond family needs be encouraged to loan some to the deacons fund at 2 percent interest. The deacons in turn loan out to more needy families these resources at the same rate of interest.

Modern society in both urban and rural areas has become complex. Christians' funds need to be invested somewhere. Conventional advice cautions against investing all surplus resources in one place. Further, a balance should be kept between government, municipal or utility bonds, debentures and stocks. Bonds and debentures are usually low risk bonds and relatively low interest securities. Growth stocks in respectable companies not involved in practices or products harmful to people or society are also a good form of investment. Companies with proven management and a loyal and competent work force with a consistent history are known as "blue chip" stocks and are usually a preferred investment. Loaning money to church agencies or congregations can also be termed a "blue chip" investment for the Christian.

Many Mennonites are farmers and invest heavily in land. Land has proven a solid investment over the years but, unless located near an urban area, land values have fallen in the mid-1980s in the wake of depressed world agricultural markets.

Wise employment of resources given by God can immensely increase one's ability to tithe in an even greater percentage. In business there is a factor known as "hedging," "forward selling," "bulk purchase," "commodity handling," dealing in "futures,"—all of which may prove beneficial. The only investment in which the writer has full confidence, the only investment yielding no known losses, offering constant dividends, and granting preferred stock as sons and daughters of God, is in salvation and grace offered by Jesus our Lord! Such an investor has a bright future.   HJS

Mennonites have traditionally looked with disfavor on investment in war bonds. In the United States this issue was especially prominent during World War I. In more recent decades a variety of social and political issues have been raised, including the Christian morality of investments in companies doing business in or with the Republic of South Africa (because of that country's policy of °racial discrimination, or *apartheid*). The appropriateness of investments in companies supplying weapons or other military equipment has also been debated among Mennonites. Some Mennonite °sociopolitical activists have advocated an alternative policy: purchasing stock in companies supplying questionable products or engaged in questionable practices and then seeking as shareholders to influence company policies. These issues become especially significant for Mennonite °institutions, °pension funds, and °mutual aid and °insurance companies. The °credit union movement, international °development programs (°Mennonite Economic Development Associates), the °°*Waisenamt* (orphans' bureau) among Russian-Canadian Mennonites, and various escrow accounts for war °tax resisters are further examples of Mennonite involvement with the investment of money.   DDM

Association of Mennonite Aid Societies, proceedings of the Second Conference on Mennonite Mutual Aid, Chicago, 1956, copy at MHL (Goshen); Carl Kreider in *GH*, 37 (Feb. 9, 1945), 900-901; see also bibliography under Business.

See also Bankruptcy (feature: "A Letter from a Small-Town Banker"); Business; Inheritance; Jacob Engle Foundation (BIC); Mennonite Foundation.

Iowa (ME III:49) had 37 Mennonite and Brethren in Christ congregations in 1987, with a combined membership of approximately 4,500, representing Mennonite Church, General Conference Mennonite Church, Conservative Mennonites, and Beachy Amish Mennonites. Amish and other churches not affiliated with any conference add another 23 congregations.

New areas where congregations were founded by the Mennonite Church (MC) since 1955 are in Des Moines (1956), Fort Dodge (1956), Davenport Spanish (1963), Muscatine Spanish (1969), Ames (1977), and Cedar Falls (1981). Ames and Cedar Falls are also affiliated with the General Conference Mennonite Church. Kalona Mennonite Church began in 1956 as a second place of worship for the East Union Church and was organized as a separate congregation in 1958. What had begun at Eureka as an outreach of Wayland area churches became the Washington Mennonite congregation in 1958.

New settlements were established by the Old Order Amish in Van Buren Co. near Milton in 1969; in Davis Co. at Bloomfield in 1971; and in Mitchell Co. at McIntire in 1975. Beachy Amish Mennonites established a congregation at Leon in Decatur Co. in 1958.

Since 1960 the Amish have established their own elementary schools in all of their settlements. In 1978 interested Conservative Mennonites started the Pathway Christian School near Kalona. Using an A.C.E. (individualized instruction) curriculum, the 1987 enrollment in grades kindergarten through twelve was 53.

In 1985 Brethren in Christ congregations were located at Dallas Center and Des Moines (combined membership, 39).

Pleasantview (1958) and Parkview (1963) are Mennonite retirement homes located in Kalona and Wayland, respectively. Crooked Creek Christian Camp (1980) is sponsored by the Southeast Iowa Mennonite Camp Association and is located about three mi. (five km.) south of Washington. Iowa City and Pulaski have Mennonite Central Committee (MCC) °SELFHELP Crafts and thrift shops. Since 1980, an annual MCC °relief sale has been a project of Iowa Mennonites.   GT

MC Yearbook (1988-89), 24; 1986 Annual Reports, Iowa-Nebraska Conference (MC); Luthy, *Amish Settlements* (1985), 8; Jonas Beachy, *Districts of Johnson and Washington Counties, Iowa* (1986).

See also Kalona, Iowa, Old Order Amish Settlement; Hazleton, Iowa, Old Order Amish Settlement.

Iowa-Nebraska Mennonite Conference (MC) (ME III:52), formed in 1920 by a merger of the Western Amish Mennonite Conference and the Mennonite Conference west of Indiana, in 1987 had 1 congregation in Colorado, 1 in South Dakota, 2 in Minnesota, 2 in Illinois, 13 in Nebraska and 21 in Iowa. These 40 congregations had a total membership in 1986 of 4,707. Eight of these congregations were started within the preceding eight years, the most recent being a church planting effort in Burlington, Iowa, begun in the spring of 1987.

Congregations, not individuals, can become members of conference by subscribing to four criteria as stated in the bylaws adopted Aug. 1, 1980. The delegate body is comprised of one delegate per 75 members of a congregation or fraction thereof plus all active licensed and ordained leaders of member congregations. In addition all members of Conference Council, the mission board executive committee, conference boards, and the executive committee of the Women's Missionary and Service Commission are members. There are four clusters of congregations in geographical proximity that meet together periodically for mutual upbuilding.

A "Congregation In Partnership" program, which pairs larger and smaller congregations together for mutual caring, sharing, and fellowship, was established in 1985. The Iowa-Nebraska Mission Board is an incorporated entity comprising the entire delegate body of the conference. Its purpose is to promote and assist in establishing, supporting, and directing new church planting ventures. *The Challenge*, the official conference paper is published 10 times each year.   EH

MC Yearbook (1988-89), 63-64.

Irish Mennonite Movement (IMM) began in 1978 when Mike Garde was sent to Dublin by the °London Mennonite Fellowship. He was joined by two families from North America and later by Irish members.

The goal of the team was to address Irish Christians with Anabaptist and Mennonite insights in the area of peace and biblical ethics. The project was jointly supported by Mennonite Central Committee and the Mennonite Board of Missions (MC).

The first few years were spent in renovating a house purchased in 1979 to serve as a focus of ministry. An intentional community was established to incarnate members' beliefs, but they chose not to form a Mennonite denomination. The Dublin Mennonite Community had eleven members in 1986, A °peace church is essential in a country where Catholic and Protestants are not reconciled.   MGa

Mike Garde, "Irish Theology," in *Mission Focus: Current Issues* (Scottdale: Herald Press, 1980), 200; *MWH* (1984), 120.

Irrigation. See Water Technology.

Isaac, Anna Penner (June 18, 1890-June 5, 1971), daughter of Abraham Penner and Maria Buhler Penner, was born in Mountain Lake, Minn. Her early education, including German Preparatory school, was in Mountain Lake. In 1911 she went to Bethel College, Ks. On Oct. 14, 1914, she married Ferdinand Isaac in Moundridge, Ks. Anna and Ferdinand worked for seven years in California under the Home Missions Board of the General Conference Mennonite Church. In 1920 a call from the Foreign Mission Board took them to India where they served for three terms (26 years). They had four children, three of whom died before maturity. Ferdinand died in India in 1946. Anna returned to the United States. She worked as a visitor at Bethel Hospital in Newton, Ks., and promoted missions. Later she moved to Mountain Lake, Minn., to become superintendent of Eventide Home. Anna was the first treasurer and one of the organizers of the General Conference Women's Missionary Society (°Women in Mission) which was formed in 1917.   LDe

Gladys Goering, *Women in Search of Mission* (Newton, 1980), 3, 4, 5; obituary filed in MLA (North Newton).

Isaak, Jakob (Oct. 8, 1900-Oct. 12, 1981), was born in Lindenau, Molotschna Colony, Russia, to Gerhard Isaak and Maria Mantler. He was baptized May 17, 1920, and joined the Mennonite church (°°Kirchen-Gemeinden). He married Elisabeth Hildebrandt,

whose parents were Gerhard Hildebrandt and Elisabeth Goossen, on Sept. 5, 1924. Jakob and Elisabeth became the parents of 12 children, including Kornelius °Isaak. The Isaak family was able to leave Russia in 1929 and settled in the village of Auhagen in Fernheim Colony, Paraguay. Jakob Isaak was ordained a minister on Oct. 28, 1934, assumed responsibility for the congregation in 1944, and served as elder, 1948-70.

Elder Isaak's two great concerns were the strengthening of spiritual life among the congregations and the evangelizing of the Chaco Indians (°Chaco mission). Youth work was formally organized in 1940 and a choir in 1945. A new church building was dedicated in Filadelfia in 1950. Once a month the entire congregation met for Bible study, to give testimony, and to receive instruction. The relationship of the Mennonite church (CGM) to other congregations and conferences (Mennonite Brethren, Evangelische Mennonitische Brüderschaft) was particularly cordial because of Jakob Isaak's work. He was chairman of the °°Kommission für Kirchenangelegenheiten (Commission for Church Affairs) for 16 years, of °Licht den Indianern (Light to the Indians), the °Vermittlungskomitee, and the Conference of Mennonites in South America.   PW

Isaak, Kornelius (June 13, 1928-Sept. 11, 1958), was the son of Jakob and Elisabeth Isaak. He was born in Karpovka in the °°Memrik settlement of the Ukraine and migrated with his family to Paraguay in 1930. He experienced a spiritual conversion in 1943 and was baptized on Oct. 1, 1944, becoming a member of the Mennonite church (°kirchliche Mennoniten/GCM) in the Fernheim Colony. He served as Sunday school teacher for several years in his home village of Blumenort. In 1949 he declared his interest in missionary work among the Indians (°Chaco Mission) and attended the Bible school in °Filadelfia for two years. On Apr. 9, 1954, he married Mary Born, who shared his vision for mission. Their mission field was the Chulupí station in Neuland Colony. It was there that he felt the call to attempt contacting the Moro (Ayoreo) people in the northern °°Chaco. During his first contact with them he was fatally wounded by a spear. His death was as a grain of wheat which falls into the ground and bears much fruit (Jn 12:24). His wife Mary was expecting their fourth child at the time of his death.   GR

Christian L. Graber, *The Coming of the Moros: From Spears to Pruning Hooks* (Scottdale, 1964); A. E. Janzen, *The Moro's Spear* (Hillsboro, Ks., 1962).

Islam is the only post-Christian religion of worldwide scope. The number of Muslims is estimated at about 800 million. The countries with the largest groups of Muslims are Indonesia, Pakistan, India, Bangladesh, and the Soviet Union. As a post-Christian world religion, Islam accepts Jesus as one of the prophets preceding the last prophet, Muhammad. Through Muhammad, Allah has, according to Islamic belief, spoken his final word to the world. This word has been preserved in the *Qur'an*, the holy book of Islam. The word of Allah has become book. Christians have gone astray by deifying their prophet Jesus and by a trinitarian concept of God. The crucifixion of Jesus is rejected as contrary to the power and the will of God. Islam emphasizes the freedom and sovereignty of Allah, who requires submission and obedience to his will, expressed in the laws. These laws cover human life in all of its different aspects. The Islamic community, a religious-political community, is regarded as the best of all the communities in the world. It is intended to be a victorious community. One of the reasons of the crisis in modern Islam is the discrepancy between divine intention and historic reality.

Christian missions have not made a deep impact in the Islamic world. Muslims resist Christian missions firmly and change of religion is seen as betrayal of the community to which a Muslim belongs.

Mennonites have also worked among Muslims in different parts of the world. Mennonites in °°Asiatic Russia settled among Muslim peoples. In Indonesia (on the island of Java) European Mennonites have done mission work. The churches which resulted from this mission effort were exposed to °persecution by Muslims in 1942. The Eastern Mennonite Board of Missions and Charities (MC) works among Muslims in East Africa. The Mennonite Brethren have made contact with Muslims in Europe and Pakistan. Africa Inter-Mennonite Mission has planted small churches among Muslims in Burkina Fasso. Mennonite Board of Missions (MC) and the Europäisches Mennonitisches Evangelisationskomitee (European Mennonite Evangelization Committee) have contributed to the "Islam in Africa" project, a project to assist churches and missions in their encounter with Islam. In different parts of the Islamic world Mennonite Central Committee has carried out relief and development work (Middle East, Bangladesh, Indonesia, and Africa).   RSK

Badu D. Kateregga and David W. Shenk, *Islam and Christianity* (Grand Rapids: Eerdmans, 1980); Frans Husken, "Islam and Collective Action: Rural Violence in North Central Java in 1942," in *Conversion, Competition, and Conflict* (Amsterdam: Free University Press, 1984).

See also Animism; Hinduism; Judaism; Shintoism.

I Cannot Follow Two Paths

Salah lived in Algeria where nearly everyone is Muslim. In Koranic school he learned to read the Muslim holy book and heard his teachers criticize Christians, telling how they had fought and killed many Muslims in the Crusades in order to claim the Bible lands for the Christians. His teachers said, "Christians believe there are three Gods! They believe that Jesus is God's son! How can God have a son? The Koran tells us that Jesus is only a great prophet."

This made Salah curious, and he wanted to find out more about Christianity. After he became a Christian he began to work for the Bible Society as a traveling Bible salesman. Sometimes he would set up a little stand at the weekly markets. This sometimes brought him into conflict with the local authorities. But his real troubles with the police began after the war in 1967 between Israel and its Arab neighbors. Algeria is an Arab country too, and didn't trust any foreigners who might be friends of

Israel. Salah, of course, was an Arab, but people suspected him because they thought that his religion, Christianity, was a foreign religion which had no place in a Muslim land. Many times the police questioned and arrested him. Often he used those times to talk about his faith. Once the police asked if he sold his books to Jews, Christians, or Muslims. Salah answered, "I am introducing you to the Bible as something for everyone, not a Jewish book or a book on politics. I sell it to all who feel their need of one."

Another time when he was arrested they asked him, "If Israel attacked us, would you fight with us or with the Jews?"

Salah replied, "I'm not for either side. I'm for Christ. War comes from Satan."

Then the Algerian police inspector sent for some Muslim religious leaders to try to persuade him to give up his Christian faith and become a Muslim. Salah told these leaders, "If I wanted to lie to you, it wouldn't be hard for me to say that I am a Muslim. But I am a Christian, and I can't be both at the same time. I can't follow two paths. There is only one path to God."

The police inspector then asked Salah to repeat the Muslim creed, "There is no God but God, and Muhammad is his prophet." These words would turn him into a Muslim. Salah refused.

The inspector told one of his officers, "Place your machine gun at his head and fire if he will not say the creed." The man placed his gun at Salah's head. Salah answered, "I am not afraid. I will be happy to leave this world and be with God."

Instead of commanding the officer to fire, the inspector asked Salah if Christians prayed. When Salah said yes, the inspector asked to pray so that he could listen. Salah prayed for the poor and the sick, for the Algerian government, and for God's help in his own difficulties.

After that the police made it impossible for him to work in Algeria and impossible for him to leave the country, so he fled by a secret route and went to France, knowing he would never be able to return. He now lives in a city in the south of France, and God is using him again among the thousands of North Africans who live there. He spends his time selling books and visiting North Africans in their homes or at the university or in the residences for immigrant families, but most come alone, leaving their families back in North Africa. Many of these men cannot read or write, and Salah helps them to write letters back to their families.

Through the North Africans that he can reach while they are in France he may be doing more for the church than he could do if he were still in North Africa—some of the 60 North Africans whom he helped lead to Christ have returned to their homes and families, thus becoming missionaries to their own people.

Salah has also been able to share his faith with members of the Muslim Brotherhood, fanatical Muslims who are also trying to influence the North Africans. He has also been able to give Bibles to some *imams*, the religious teachers in the mosques, who have not accepted the Bibles, but promised to read them.

(Salah had contact with Mennonite missionaries

while he was in Algeria, and in France has received support from Mennonite Board of Missions, MC). MH

Adapted from "The Fearless Messenger," a story appearing in Marian Hostetler and Ruth Liechty, *God's Messengers* (Scottdale, copyright Mennonite Publishing House, 1985), 45-48; cf. *They Loved Their Enemies* (Scottdale: Herald, 1988). Used by permission.

Israel. Mennonites have been serving in Israel since the early 1950s. The Mennonite Board of Missions (MC) sent the first workers to the young state in 1953, complementing the presence of Mennonite Central Committee (MCC) personnel already beginning to work in the °West Bank of Jordan. The early relief work of MCC among Palestinian °refugees gradually evolved in the direction of °self-help and development projects as well as °peace education and advocacy work. With headquarters in East Jerusalem, MCC has also been involved in education. Hope Secondary School in Beit Jala is still partially supported by MCC as is Bethlehem Bible College, (1979-). Mennonite Board of Missions workers in Israel proper, scattered around the country and not exceeding five families, have served in a variety of contexts including the Nazareth Hospital, the United Christian Council in Israel, Sharon Tours, university student ministries, and Immanuel House, a congregation in Tel Aviv for Messianic Jews. The mission stance of Mennonites in Israel has been to be supportive of local expressions of the church rather than establish Mennonite churches.

Since 1967 when the Six Days War brought the West Bank under Israeli control, Mennonites in both Israel and the West Bank have enjoyed fellowship and mutual support. Joint retreats are held periodically and information is shared. Aware that the Mennonite constituencies in North America represent a variety of viewpoints on the theological significance of modern Israel, Mennonite workers seek to be sensitive to the painful historical experience of both Jews and Palestinian Arabs. Dispensationalism, which views modern Israel as the fulfillment of prophecy, and the church as God's interim arrangement, has gained some support among Mennonites. However, such a perspective, if understood at all, is looked upon with suspicion by both Jews and Arabs and is neither appropriate nor helpful. Rather, Anabaptist insights into the radical newness of the °believers church, the importance of °reconciliation, and the loving response to human need should address the tensions and problems of the Middle East. Thus, while continuing to relate to needs within their respective spheres of service among Israelis and Palestinians, Mennonites are attempting to present the case for peaceful resolution of the conflict and the claims of Jesus as Messiah and Lord.   JMH

Italian Mennonite Church. See Chiesa Evangelica Mennonita Italiana.

J

Jacob Engle Foundation (BIC). The Jacob Engle Foundation, Inc., was proposed and approved at the 1972 general conference of the Brethren in Christ and incorporated in the State of Indiana on Sept. 29, 1972. The foundation is legally qualified to care for gifts to the church, and to any charitable agency, including local congregations. The foundation's board of directors reports annually to the general conference's Board of Administration, which composes the membership of the foundation. °Investments are to be consistent with Brethren in Christ belief and the wishes of donors.

A division of the foundation, the Brotherhood Loan Fund, receives investments at reasonable rates from individuals and church groups. The funds are then loaned to build church-related facilities.

At the end of 1985 the combined assets of the foundation were $21,200,000. The office is in Upland, California, with a branch office at Mechanicsburg, Pennsylvania. DPM

Minutes (BIC) (1984) 66-67, 167-68; (1982) 237-39.

See also Inheritance; Investments; Mennonite Foundation; Stewardship.

Jacobszoon, Jacob Pieter (1925-83), was pastor of the Mennonite congregations in Oldeboorn (1951), IJmuiden (1956), and Haarlem (1959). From 1966 to 1967 he was visiting lecturer at Eastern Mennonite College, Harrisonburg, Va. From 1981 until his death he was professor at the Amsterdam Mennonite Theological Seminary, being particularly responsible for the studies of students admitted to the "Second Way" established in 1979 (°Algemene Doopsgezinde Sociëteit). He was particularly well informed in the area of °Pietism, having written his thesis on the Amsterdam pastor Joannes °°Deknatel, a friend of °°Zinzendorf. SV

Jakarta is the capital city of the Republic of Indonesia. Its 6.7 million people make it almost three times larger than any other city in the archipelago. Included among its inhabitants are groups of people from most of the country's 300 ethnic groups, each group maintaining ties with its community of origin.

Beginning in the early 1960s, leaders of the °Persatuan Gereja-Gereja Kristen Muria Indonesia (The Muria Christian Church of Indonesia) had a growing vision of establishing a cluster of churches in the Jakarta area to serve as a base for launching mission efforts to far-flung parts of the archipelago. By the 1970s several churches had already been established and Pekabaran Injil dan Pelayana Kasih (PIPKA), the mission board of the conference, had set up its headquarters and Mission Training Center in the adjacent port city of Tanjung Priok.

Among the important Christian institutions in the city are Sekolah Tinggi Teologia Jakarta, an interdenominational seminary; Badan Penerbit Kristen Gunung Mulia, a major Christian publishing house; and Persekutuan Gereja-Gereja Kristen di Indonesia (the Communion of Christian Churches in Indonesia). LMY

Jamaica (ME III:69). Since 1955 the Jamaica Mennonite Church has continued to develop. In 1957 the first church building was erected and named the Good Tidings Mennonite Church. The first annual conference convened and the church was organized with an executive committee. By 1971 the conference dispensed with the office of bishop and appointed an administrator to work for the executive committee. Pastors are appointed by the executive committee annually prior to conference meetings. Individual congregations take care of their own outreach. Pastors are receiving training at local Bible schools and colleges and refresher seminars conducted by visiting teachers from the United States. Lay leader seminars are also conducted by national people. Its official publication is *The Quest*. The Virginia Mennonite Conference (MC) mission board reduced its presence in the late 1970s. In 1988 there is one North American worker relating to the conference.

Jamaica Mennonite Central Committee, founded in 1970, is related to Mennonite Central Committee (international), which sponsored Teachers Abroad Program in the 1970s and continues a presence in the country in 1988 working with other agencies in urban settings in education, social work, and medical service (nursing). °Mennonite Economic Development Associates (MEDA), together with MCC, founded "Mennonite Ventures" (ca. 1986), which works to create employment by finding outlets for farm produce and the processing and sale of locally grown spices (1988). MCC is working closely with the Jamaica Mennonite Church and does not operate any independent projects in 1988. RSa

MWH (1978), 225-26; *MWH* (1984), 82; *MC Yearbook* (1988-89), 158.

Jamaica Mennonite Church (ME III:69). The Jamaica Mennonite Church began in 1955 when the Virginia Mennonite Conference (MC) mission board assumed supervision of a program begun by D. H. and Annie Loewen. The Alpine congregation was an outreach of the initial congregation, Good Tidings Mennonite church. In addition to these two congregations, Temple Hall and Waterloo congregations are located in the Kingston area. The Ocho Rios and Calvary congregations are found in the northern part of the island. Bethel congregation is located east of Mandeville on the higher elevation of Jamaica's interior. Joyland and Abrams congregations developed on the Santa Cruz mountain. In 1977 the Salter's Hill church was established close to Montego Bay. Thus from one end of the island to the other, churches have emerged as a result of people being obedient to the Holy Spirit. In 1988 these 10 congregations have a membership of approximately 450. Five congregations operate elementary-level schools for their communities.

The Maranatha School for the Deaf and the Way to Life Ministries are two programs of the Jamaican Mennonite churches. The school is operated by an elected board consisting of members of Jamaica Mennonite churches, Mennonite Central Committee workers, and community leaders. Way to Life provides correspondence Bible study courses, counseling, Christian literature, and a radio ministry.   MJH

See Jamaica for additional information and bibliography.

Jamesport, Mo., Old Order Amish Settlement is located 75 mi. (140 km.) ne. of Kansas City. This Daviess Co. community was established in 1953 and was the first of the newer Missouri settlements. Cheap land and greater freedom in the education of their children have attracted the Amish to this area. The Jamesport community has become the largest of the 12 Missouri settlements. Six church districts (congregations) serve approximately 1,200 Amish in this community.   SLY

Practical Missionary: Hermann Jantzen

Hermann Jantzen was a farmer, civil servant, and self-appointed missionary among the asiatic ethnic groups in Turkestan, the Caucausus, and Bulgaria— and a gifted lay preacher, musician, mission strategist, and missionary statesman. "I am not a trained theologian and not even an ordained preacher," he would tell the Muslim Kirgsten people who lived on the Russian steppes, adding, "I am only a witness to Jesus Christ."

Born May 28, 1866 in the Trakt Mennonite settlement on the Volga in south Russia, as a 12-year-old he accompanied his parents and other Mennonite families on the 1880-81 migration to Russian-controlled central Asia, including Turkestan, a region between Iran and Siberia. The move was prompted both by the government's repeal (1874, effective 1880) of the Mennonites' exemption from military service and the stirring among some in the Mennonite colonies about the millennial rule of Christ that they expected to originate in the East. Claasz °°Epp, Jr., Jantzen's uncle, became the emigrants' main prophetic leader.

Enroute on the wagon train journey, Hermann, with a number of other youth, was converted. He had earlier promised minister Johannes Penner—one who did not go along with Epp's ideas but did go along on the trek—to spend a few minutes in prayer each day, asking, "Lord, show me my heart." One night Hermann prayed those words repeatedly. The Lord revealed his heart to him and he jumped from the wagon and ran into the low hills to agonize in prayer until dawn. "At that instant a miracle happened, which I cannot describe. In my heart it was as though a voice spoke: 'Arise, your sins are forgiven; for they have been paid long ago on Calvary by Jesus Christ.'"

Hermann spent eight years in language study, also studying the Koran, and the Schariatt, the Muslim statement of faith and the five prayer forms. By 1885, having become fluent in the Uzbek-Turkish language, he was appointed an interpreter by Khan Seit-Muhametsha-Sim Bagadur in the city of Chiwa, located only about seven kilometers (four miles) from the Mennonite villages. New schisms in the church (which included the ouster of Epp and about 10 families including Hermann's parents) and "the glamorous and loose life at the court" injured his spiritual life. As a consequence, he and his young wife and infant son and three other families in 1890 moved to Aulie-ata near the city of Tashkent where the group had first settled after leaving south Russia. Here, because of his fluency in the country's four languages, Hermann was asked to become a forest ranger; eventually he became chief forester of the area.

The appointment as a state official meant that the congregation "promptly put me off the membership roll." He and his 10 subordinates had to superintend the forests and assign the grazing rights among the nomadic Kirghiz, Kasaken, Kuraminsan, and other tent dwellers in the surrounding hills of the Tjanschen mountains.

Political unrest among the Muslim people, occasioned by the "nationalities question," placed forester Jantzen in a precarious position. Straightforward and truthful toward all, he was falsely accused of conspiracy against the area leader, was arrested, and imprisoned. He was eventually exonerated and made chief forester of the whole Aulie-ata region of Turkestan.

In spite of growing status and wealth he wrestled with the inner knowledge that he was going against the voice of the Holy Spirit. A number of spiritual leaders, including E. G. Broadbent, from England, were influential during this time of search. Finally, the seeming judgment of God shown in the loss through illness of cattle and horses and the illness of one of his sons with typhus brought chief forester Jantzen, acclaimed in various government circles, to his knees before God. He struggled with "all my sins and the injustice that I, in my pride, had committed against many people, especially the Mohammedans of my district." His prayer was answered, and peace replaced hate and bitterness. "Even at that time I could have embraced those Kirghiz that had become so loathsome to me and tell them: 'Come with me to the Lord Jesus; he loves you and wants to save you and give you joy.'"

After these experiences he said farewell to public service and sought out a spiritual vocation. His first step was to be a witness for Christ among the Muslims with whom he had dealt as government official for 18 years. About 12 years later (1911-12), he studied at the Alliance Bible School in Berlin (later moved to Wiedenest in the Rhineland of Germany). He thereafter returned to Turkestan and continued missionary work among Muslims and Russians, including evangelistic services among the Mennonites remaining in Ak-Mechet.

Political revolts in 1916 and the Bolshevik Revolution of 1917 created new difficulties for Jantzen, as they did for the entire Mennonite community. In the required local elections he was elected, with no right of declining, to be assistant district commissar. As a representative of the people, he was asked to sign the expropriation edict from Moscow. He refused, citing the government's duty to protect as well as provide for the proletariat. He was eventually imprisoned, again escaping death.

Marked as a counterrevolutionary by the Bolshevists in 1923, he and his wife nonetheless miraculously secured permission and passage to leave Turkestan for Germany, where they established a new home in Berghausen, close to the Wiedenest Bible School. They had to leave their children and their familes behind. One son was killed in prison and the other three sent to Siberia. His wife died in 1928.

As a Wiedenest Bible School staff member he served as a lay preacher and evangelist in Austria, Switzerland, Germany, and The Netherlands. In 1929 he undertook a missionary journey to Bulgaria at the invitation of young missionaries who had gone out from Wiedenest. Having lived among Muslims for 45 years, he advised new missionaries to "win their confidence, be a Turk to the Turks, learn to feel with them. Once they open up you will find that the Turks also have homesickness of the soul, and one can talk to them." In 1931 Jantzen married Mrs. Abram Janzen, a widow with three children, who had also fled from Turkestan.

Neither prison, nor political, economic, social, and religious adversity could daunt Hermann. His was a simple and confident faith in the sufficiency of God in every circumstance. He said, "God often makes use of political upheaval to open doors for His Word." He saw himself as a "practical missionary," one schooled in the Scriptures and daily communion with God. He seized the moment to witness for Jesus Christ, whether before state officials, Muslims in the tea parlors, university students, pastors and congregations of numerous denominations, or with individuals who sought him out. He was burdened by divisiveness in the church, where dogma and doctrine seemed to stand above the Bible.

His ministry during the 1930s, the Second World War, and following was characterized by his usual full-hearted and capable response of combining word and deed to bring the joy of the gospel to those in every walk of life who were yet without the joy and peace of Christ. Hermann Jantzen, age 93, died November 13, 1959, at his rural home near Hilversum, The Netherlands. JMB

Hermann Jantzen, *Im Wilden Turkestan: Ein Leben unter Moslems* (Gießen and Basel: Brunnen, 1988), transcribed from handwritten German by Ernest Kuhlman and translated into English by Joseph A. Kleinsasser as "Memoirs of Hermann Jantzen" (typescript, n.p., n.d. [ca. 1975]).

Janz, Benjamin B. (1877-1964), Mennonite Brethren minister, was an influential leader in the Mennonite world, particularly during World War I and during the large Mennonite migration from Russia to Canada from 1923 to 1926. His entire life, noted for its integrity and tenacity, was dedicated to the support and guidance of Mennonites by his active involvement in their institutions, boards, and agencies. He was known as a "conference man," who promoted a strong church and a belief in nonresistance.

Janz was born in the Gnadenfeld district in Russia to Benjamin and Helena (Penner) Janz. After a lengthy spiritual crisis, he was baptized by immersion, joining the Mennonite Brethren Church in 1897. As a consequence of his own long experience, he frequently spoke of being "in conversion." He remained faithful to the Mennonite Brethren throughout his life, for he saw in them a voluntary body of believers, practicing radical ethics and strong church °discipline and promoting thorough Bible study.

In 1905 he married Maria Rogalsky, and they became the parents of six children. Maria's "quiet, patient, praying, concerned, active support" (Toews, *Courage,*, 142) of his ministry made difficult decisions and circumstances bearable for him. He was ordained in his early teaching years (1909), and soon moved into church work as leader and preacher. During World War I he served in the forestry service (°*Forsteidienst*).

In 1921 he began the first of many tasks which would bring him into contact with government officials as negotiator and diplomat on behalf of the Mennonites. He was asked to negotiate the release of Mennonite young men who had been conscripted into the Red Army. This was followed by a request that he assist in negotiating with American Mennonites for help for the famine-stricken colonies in the Ukraine. He was among the first to seriously explore emigration as a possibility for the Mennonites, rejecting the possibility that reconstruction was possible in the Ukraine.

In 1926 as an immigrant farmer in the Coaldale, Alta., area, he was soon elected Mennonite Brethren Church leader. Before long he was again involved in the larger church constituency, serving with the °°Canadian Mennonite Board of Colonization in an appeal to American Mennonites to help the sick among the Canadian Mennonite immigrants. He helped the board liquidate the travel debt accumulated with the Canadian Pacific Railways by the immigrants.

When he saw that Mennonite young people needed better preparation to enter secular society, he devoted his energies to developing institutions, becoming instrumental in founding the Coaldale Bible School and the Coaldale Mennonite High School.

During the years after World War II, he spent time in South America in a ministry of reconciliation and resettlement for displaced persons becoming known for his oft-repeated phrase, "Ich suche meine Brüder" (I am looking for my brethren).

Throughout his life he maintained a wide-ranging correspondence, admonishing, correcting, and encouraging. As a man caught between the Russian and Canadian cultures his ministry, seen as being traditionalist, gradually became obsolete. Yet around his personality developed a mythology that indicated his voice was one that could not be disregarded lightly.

Almost until his death he continued active in various boards and committees, e.g., the Board of Reference and Counsel and the Board of Welfare and Public Relations of the Mennonite Brethren General Conference, Board of Reference and Counsel of the Canadian Mennonite Brethren Conference, Board of Mennonite Brethren Bible College, Mennonite Central Committee, Mennonite Central Relief Committee, Board of Christian Press Limited, Committee on Nonresistance (conducting an extensive pastoral ministry to young men in °alternative service), and a member of *Dienst am Evangelium.*   KFW

John B. Toews, *With Courage to Spare: The Life of B. B. Janz (1877-1964)* (Winnipeg: General Conference MB Churches, 1978); idem, *Lost Fatherland: Mennonite Emigration from Soviet Russia, 1921-1927* (Scottdale, 1967); Frank H. Epp, *Mennonite Exodus* (Altona, Man.: Canadian Mennonite Relief and Immigration Council, 1962); J. A. Toews, *History MB* (1975), index. The Mennonite Brethren Archives at Mennonite Brethren Bible College in Winnipeg houses the B. B. Janz Collection.

Janz, Willy (Nov. 7, 1926-May 28, 1986), was a major leader among the Mennonite Brethren congregations in Paraguay and Brazil. He was born in Grossweide, Molotschna Colony, Russia and emigrated to Paraguay in 1930 with his parents. He was converted at a young age and joined the Mennonite Brethren congregation in Filadelfia.

From 1945 to 1950 he studied in Canada and the United States. Following his return he married Elsie Lenzmann, who had accompanied him from Canada. They worked together in Paraguay for 12 years, then moved to Brazil. During this time they also studied at Tabor College and the Mennonite Brethren Biblical Seminary in Fresno, Cal. (1957-59).

Brother Janz loved his congregation and his conference. He gave to this work everything he had to give. He was able to absorb and overcome many difficulties because of his love for the cause of Christ. He was not a popular preacher, but his sermons were organized systematically and rich in content. His vision was broad, including the entire Mennonite fellowship. He introduced triennial South American Bible retreats, for all German-speaking congregations from Paraguay, Brazil, and Uruguay. He actively promoted the translation of the *Foundation Series* °Sunday school material, and edited books, booklets, and other resources for church workers. He wrote a drama "Ich sende Euch" (So Send I You) for the 50th anniversary of the coming of the Mennonites to Paraguay. He took the initiative in many areas including youth work, marriage enrichment seminars, the building of a Bible camp as well as a retirement center in Brazil, and the establishing of an archival center. From 1973 to 1979 he was chairman of the South American Conference of Mennonite Brethren. He and his wife were killed in a car accident.   GR

Willy Janz and Gerhard Ratzlaff, eds., *Gemeinde unter dem Kreuz des Südens: Die Mennoniten Brüder Gemeinden in Brasilien, Paraguay und Uruguay, 1930-1980.*

Janzen, Aaron A. and Janzen, Ernestina Strauss. Pioneer missionaries in Zaire (Belgian Congo) for a combined total of 70 years, the Janzens worked in evangelism, medicine, education and agriculture. Aaron (1882-1957) was born and raised on a farm near Mountain Lake, Minn., where he attended grammar school and Bible school. Later he studied at Moody Bible Institute and the German Baptist Seminary in Rochester, N.Y. At age 24, he experienced a radical conversion, was baptized, and joined the Mennonite Brethren Church. Ernestina (1879-1937) studied nursing in preparation for mission.

Upon marriage in 1911, they left for the Belgian Congo, serving with the Congo Inland Mission (CIM) at Nyanga (1912-20). They encountered untold hardships: hostility of the Bapende people, inadequate diet, tropical disease, and death of their only two children. In anticipation of establishing a Mennonite Brethren mission, the Janzens found Kikandji near the commercial center of Kikwit. They made the 480 km. (300 mi.) trek in 1922. The people were receptive to the gospel, but physical conditions proved intolerable. Two years later they relocated to Kafumba, the "elephants' nest," 10 km. (6 mi.) away and built a mission center on a 120-acre land grant from the government. In 1926, they baptized 37 people and founded the Mennonite Brethren Church of Zaire without official support from either the Mennonite Brethern Mission Board or the CIM. During their first furlough (1927-28), the Janzens renewed contact with home churches, stimulated interest in Africa, and received financial support.

Ernestina died Sept. 24, 1937. Africans mourned the death of "Mama Nkende," mother of mercy. A man of prayer and faith in God, Janzen wrote, "Thou art more to me than all earth's brimming cups could be." After six years, Janzen married Martha Hiebert, missionary at Kafumba since 1929. The Janzens experienced two highlights: a growing national church, and the acceptance of the work by the Mennonite Brethren Board of Missions in 1943. They stayed at Kafumba until 1956. Aaron Janzen has left a wealth of written material on mission both theological and cultural, but none has been published. He died in Mountain Lake where Martha lives in retirement (1988).   HK

J. B. Toews, *Mennonite Brethren Church in Zaire* (Fresno: MB Board of Christian Literature, 1978), 39-55.

Janzen, Abraham Ewell (b. Nov. 22, 1892). The parents of A. E. Janzen were Abraham H. and Eva Neufeld Janzen, who came to Kansas from the Ukraine in the 1870s. They settled on a farm in the Springfield community south of Lehigh, Ks. Abraham attended country schools in Marion Co., Tabor College Academy, Salt City Business College, and Tabor College, and he earned his BA degree at Kansas U. in 1924 (MA, 1927). He completed his course work requirements for a doctorate in economics at the U. of California, Berkeley. He married Zola Lantz on Dec. 24, 1917.

Janzen taught country school in Marion Co. for two years and then started teaching at Tabor College in 1916. From 1931 to 1935 he taught at Friends U. He served as president of Tabor College (1935-42) during the Great Depression, helping develop a plan for the survival of the college after it had been closed for a year in 1934. After he left the administrative post at Tabor College he accepted a one-year assignment to work for the Mennonite Central Committee in the Mennonite colonies of South America. The purpose of the assignment was to deal with the economic crisis caused by inflation, to provide spiritual leadership in the churches, and to strengthen ties with the North American Mennonites.

In 1945 Janzen was appointed executive secretary of the North American Mennonite Brethren mission board. He served in this capacity for 15 years. Prior to 1945 Mennonite Brethren missionaries served six fields in the United States (Oklahoma), India, Africa (Congo/Zaire), China, Paraguay, and Canada. With the great expansion of missions after World War II, 10 new fields were added: Colombia, Brazil, Peru, Japan, Mexico, Ethiopia, Ecuador, Germany, Austria, and Panama. The number of missionaries rose by 241 to a total of 279. During the Janzen era there was a trend toward °indigenization—a shift from a mission-dominated administration to a "sister church" relationship, and a shift from country villages to urban areas.

Janzen was an active writer. His publications include the following: *Glimpses of South America* (1944); *Survey of Five Mission Fields* (1950); *A History of Tabor College, Part One* (1958); *Mennonite Brethren Distinctives* (1966); *Moro's Spear* (1962). He helped edit and translate Jacob Becker, *Origin of the Mennonite Brethren Church* (1973), and served on the editorial board of *Marion County Kansas, Past and Present* (Van Meter, 1972). Janzen's autobiography, *Memoirs: Each Step of the Way,* published in 1988.

During his retirement years Janzen continued to serve the church and his community. He served as archivist for the Tabor College Historical Library, director of the Mennonite Brethren Historical Society, and president of the Marion County Historical Society. He was involved in local history projects and the Golden Years Club and was active as lay leader in the Hillsboro Mennonite Brethren Church. He reached the age of 95 years in Nov. 1987, at Parkside Homes, Hillsboro.   WP

Menn. Bib. II, p. 461; *Who's Who Mennonites* (1943), 127; John A. Toews, *History MB* (1975), index.

Janzen, Henry H. (1901-1975), was a Bible expositor. He was born, educated, and married in the Molotschna settlement in Russia. He migrated to Canada in 1925 and began his public ministry in 1927.

Janzen's pastoral ministry included the following Mennonite Brethren (MB) congregations: Kitchener (Ont.), 1932-46; South End (Winnipeg), 1947-49; North End (Winnipeg), 1953; and Clearbrook (B.C.), 1962-64. He was moderator of the Ontario Mennonite Brethren Conference, 1932-46, and was on the executive committee of the Canadian Mennonite Brethren Conference, 1946-49, 1951-52, 1963. He was the moderator of the North America Mennonite Brethren Conference, 1954-57.

In addition to short-term teaching in congregations and at °Bible conferences, he taught at the: Russian Bible Institute, Toronto, Ont. (1943-46);

Mennonite Brethren Collegiate Institute, Winnipeg (1946-47); Mennonite Brethren Bible College, Winnipeg, where he was dean (1946-48), and president (1948-56); and in Europe, primarily at the European Mennonite Bible School at Bienenberg and St. Chrischona Bible School, both in Switzerland, 1950-51, 1957-62, 1965-66, 1969-71, 1974.

In Europe, as in North America, Janzen was involved in an itinerant preaching ministry among refugees, Mennonite churches, Baptist churches, Russian-speaking people, and others under Mennonite Central Committee and the Mennonite Brethren mission agency between 1947 and 1974. He was the president of the Africa Mission Society from about 1935 to 1944. He was also involved in a radio preaching ministry in Europe and North America both in the German and Russian languages, 1959-74.

Janzen was a man who was able to have influence in many differing groups. He was an articulate Bible expositor who could make himself understood widely. He had an aura about him that could appeal equally to the individual and a large audience. Therefore, he was a leader for many groups and causes.   BF

Books and pamphlets by H. H. Janzen include *Der Römerbrief* (Winnipeg: Christian Press, 1975); *Und Ich Sah: eine Auslegung des Buches der Offenbarung* (Darmstadt: Radiomission Quelle des Lebens, 1963); *Jesu Rede über die letzte Zeit* (Basel: Verlag Christliche Radiomission, Janz Team, 1959); *A Brief Outline Study of the Seven Churches* (Winnipeg: Christian Press, 1949), also published in German as *Die heutige Weltlage in biblischer Sicht* (Basel: Buchdruckerei Haupt, 1957); *Von der Herrschaft des Geistes* (Basel: Brunnen-Verlag, 1968); *Die Mennonitische Brüdergemeinde* (Neuwied/Rhein: Mennonitischen Brüdergemeinde in Europa, 1957); *Wie Er uns erwählt hat* (Winnipeg: Christian Press, 1962); *Glaube und Heiligung: Eine schlichte Auslegung von 1. Petrus Kapitel 4, vers 7* (Karlsruhe: Buchdruckerei Heinrich Schneider, 1951); *Seventy-five Years in Minnesota: 1874-1949* (Mountain Lake: Mennonite Churches in Mountain Lake, 1950); with A. H. Unruh he wrote *Der ewige Sohn Gottes* (Winnipeg: Verlag-Mennonite Brethren Bible College, 1948). H. H. Janzen, Mrs. K. Janzen, and E. Ratzlaff, compiled "Lebensgeschichte," *Mennonitische Rundschau,* vol. 99, no. 40, (Oct. 6, 1976) to vol. 100, no. 43 (Nov. 23, 1977), 53 segments. The minutes, correspondence of the General Conference of Mennonite Brethren Churches (containing Africa Mission Society material) Box 18 A255.1-13 to A256 (material to 1937) and Box 19 A256.1 (material from 1938), are held in the Centre for Mennonite Brethren Studies, Winnipeg. See also John A. Toews, *History MB* (1975), 172, 210-211, 277, 295, 316, 433.

Janzen, Marie J. Regier (Franz) (b. May 25, 1897). Born near Whitewater, Ks., to John and Emilie Wiebe Regier, Marie Regier attended Bethel Academy and Bethel College (Kansas), graduating in 1926. She was a missionary to China, 1926-40, 1948-55. She received a masters degree from the U. of Chicago Divinity School in 1936. During World War II she was interned by the Japanese in a camp at Weihsien, Shantung, China (1943-45). Further mission work included Bible teaching in the Mennonite colonies in Paraguay (1950-53), and in Taiwan (1954-62). She helped at the Woodlawn Mennonite Church in Chicago, 1962-65. She received the Outstanding Alumni Award from Bethel College in 1967. Later in life she married R. E. Franz (1969-73) and B. H. Janzen (1976-). In 1988 she resides in Newton, Ks., and is a member of the Bethel College Mennonite Church.

For a woman of her time Marie was exceptional

for her theological training, social activism, and her exuberant love of life. With pencil sketches and as a writer she documented her mission and concentration camp experiences. She wrote insightful analyses of mission policy and church life. In later life after her involvement in the United States civil rights movement of the 1960s she intensified her efforts for justice by writing letters to newspapers, church periodicals, and government leaders.   SR

Mary Lou Cummings, *Full Circle* (Newton, 1978); Langdon Brown Gilkey, *Shantung Compound* (New York: Harper and Row, 1966), includes sketches of concentration camp activities drawn by Marie J. Regier; Juhnke, *Mission* (1979), 59, 61, 131; Marie J. Regier, *But Mother* (New York: Samuel French, 1940), a one-act play about Marie's youth and home life; idem, "The Cloud That Hung over my Second Term in China," unpubl. MS, at MLA (North Newton), MS-54, box 2, folder 29; idem, "Cultural Interpretation in a Local Community in China" (MA thesis, U. of Chicago Divinity School, 1936), copy at MLA, MS-54, box 3, folder 30; idem, "Mennonite Teaching and Practice in a Chinese Community" (BC thesis, Chicago Theological Seminary, 1950).

Japan (ME III:97) is an island country located just off the continent of Asia. Four main islands make up the archipelago: Honshu, Hokkaido, Kyushu, and Shikoku. Land area totals 377,708 sq. km. (145,800 sq. mi.). It is slightly smaller than California, extending about 2,500 km. (1500 mi.), approximately the distance from s. Italy to Denmark or from Buenos Aires to Cape Horn.

The population is 121,000,000 (1986 est.). Density is 320 persons per sq. km. (830 per sq. mi.), and, since Japan's land surface is four-fifths mountainous, this is probably the highest population density in the world.

For administrative purposes the country is divided into 47 prefectures (counties). Government is a constitutional democracy, with the emperor but a figurehead. The Diet (Parliament) is in Tokyo.

The ancient history of Japan, also known as "*Nihon*" or "*Nippon*" ("origin of the sun"), is shrouded in mythology. But competing clans were unified under the Yamato Dynasty (3rd-8th c. A.D.), centering in the emperor. Imperial courts then flourished in succession to the end of the 12th c. After that a feudal system of military rule prevailed until the Meiji Restoration in 1868.

By the early 20th c., Japan had shifted from an agrarian to an industrial society. In spite of wars between China and Japan (1930s) and Russia and Japan (1904-5), and despite the devastation of World War II, the country reconstructed itself and became once more a major economic power.

Japanese culture is largely based on °Buddhism and Confucianism, brought in from China and Korea during the 6th c. °Shintoism, native, and at one time the state religion, also has had a pervasive influence.

Christianity did not arrive until 1549, via Francis Xavier, a Roman Catholic missionary. By the early 1600s there were about 300,000 Christians in Japan. But feeling threatened, the Japanese feudal government decided to close itself off to western countries. Thus Christianity was also banned. Japan remained isolated from the rest of the world for over 200 years, until forced open by U.S. military pressure (1853) to trade with the West. The policy then became, "from Asian to Western."

From 1858, Protestants also began evangelistic efforts. Progress was not rapid. Although, in 1986, freedom of religion is guaranteed by the constitution, membership in both Catholic and Protestant churches exceeds no more than about 1.1 percent of the entire population. The impact of Christians however far outweighs mere numbers. Kanzo *Uchimura* and Toyohiko *Kagawa* are names from the past familiar to most, and *Miura* Ayako and Shusaku *Endo* from the present. Many educators and even some prime ministers have been Christian.

For several reasons Christianity's progress has been slow. First, wanting to be independent of western colonialism Japanese had great interest in modern technology, but not in western religion. Second, Japan had a long history of Shintoism, Confucianism, and Buddhism before Christianity came. Third, having been forbidden at one time, Christianity still carries a stigma of "foreignness." Fourth, many Japanese misunderstood this new religion as western cultural ethics, rather than "good news," and as individualistic in nature, making it hard to build community, a prime value in Japanese culture.

In modern times prosperity and materialism are obstacles. The image of the church has been tarnished in other ways as well. Most Japanese churches gave in to nationalism and the war and had little vision afterwards.

Mennonites have been working in Japan since about 1950, in the Tokyo (GMC, MC), Hokkaido (MC), Osaka (MB), Yamaguchi (BIC) and Miyazaki (GCM) areas. Unlike other Protestant and Catholic groups, they had no experience of suppression as in the closed Edo Period (17th- to mid-19th c.) and during World War II. It is difficult for so-called "peace churches" to make a "peace witness" during a peaceful era, although Mennonite Central Committee did have a Peace Section representative in Japan during the 1960s.

Article nine of the Japanese Constitution forbids Japan from having military forces. This has been interpreted so as to permit a Self-Defense Force. Nationalism has also been gaining strength in the 1980s. The government, for instance, wants to nationalize Yasukuni Shrine (Shinto) for the war dead. Military expenditures are rising. There is danger that the country might alter its stance against nuclear weapons.

There are a few military °tax resisters. Almost none of the churches, Protestant or Catholic, have a peace theology. Mennonites need to reflect on their course, past and future, if they are to be faithful in the present, and fulfill the vision of being "neither Catholic nor Protestant."   TTo

"Japan" in *Kodansha Encyclopedia of Japan*, vol. 4, (Tokyo: Kodansha, 1983), 2-9; *MWH* (1978, 157-77; *MWH* (1984), 35-39.

See also Nihon Kirisutokyo Keiteidan; Nihon Menonaito Burezaren Kyodan; Nihon Menonaito Kirisutokyo Kyokai Kaigi; Nihon Menonaito Kirisuto Kyokai Kyogikai (Hokkaido); Nihon Menonaito Senkyokai; Tokyo Chiku Menonaito Kyokai Rengo; Osaka Prefecture; Miyazaki Prefecture; Hokkaido; Yamaguchi Prefecture; Work Camps.

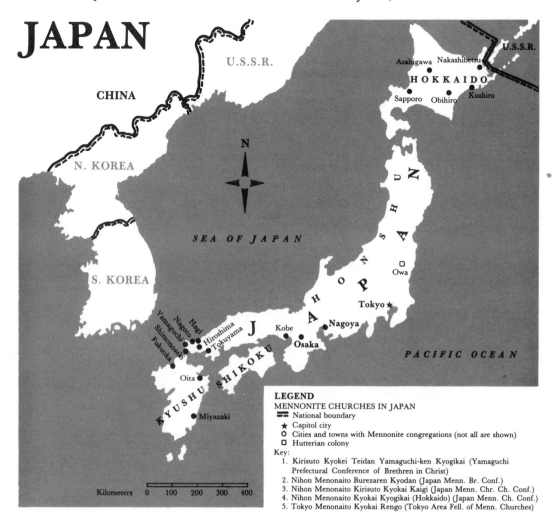

JAPAN

U.S.S.R.

CHINA

N. KOREA

S. KOREA

SEA OF JAPAN

HOKKAIDO

Asahigawa Nakashibetsu

Sapporo Obihiro Kushiro

U.S.S.R.

N

H O N S H U

Owa

Tokyo ★

Nagoya

Kobe

Osaka

PACIFIC OCEAN

J

Yamaguchi
Nagoto
Hagi
Hiroshima
Tokuyama
Shimonoseki
Fukuoka

S H I K O K U

K Y U S H U

Oita

Miyazaki

LEGEND
MENNONITE CHURCHES IN JAPAN
▬▬ National boundary
★ Capitol city
○ Cities and towns with Mennonite congregations (not all are shown)
□ Hutterian colony
Key:
1. Kirisuto Kyokei Teidan Yamaguchi-ken Kyogikai (Yamaguchi Prefectural Conference of Brethren in Christ)
2. Nihon Menonaito Burezaren Kyodan (Japan Menn. Br. Conf.)
3. Nihon Menonaito Kirisuto Kyokai Kaigi (Japan Menn. Chr. Ch. Conf.)
4. Nihon Menonaito Kyokai Kyogikai (Hokkaido) (Japan Menn. Ch. Conf.)
5. Tokyo Menonaito Kyokai Rengo (Tokyo Area Fell. of Menn. Churches)

Kilometers 0 100 200 300 400

Japan Brethren in Christ Church. See Nihon Kirisuto Kyo Keiteidan.

Japan Mennonite Fellowship. See Nihon Menonaito Senkyokai.

Java, Island of (ME III:99). Politically, economically and culturally Java is the most important island of the island nation of Indonesia. Having 96,892,900 people with a land area the size of England or New York State gives Java a population density of about 2,000 people per sq. mi. The majority of the work force is involved in agriculture.

The Javanese people comprise about 60 percent of the population of Java and inhabit roughly the eastern two-thirds of the island. The Sundanese are the dominant ethnic group on the western third of the island, with a large mixed population from all parts of the archipelago living in the metropolitan area of °Jakarta, the nation's capital.

Java's religious, cultural, and political history goes back more than a millennium, with unwritten traditions reaching back much further. Java has been the seat of a series of kingdoms and empires, the most expansive one, Mojopahit, exercising hegemony over a broad sweep of southeast Asia in the 14th c. The aboriginal religion of Java, various forms of Hinduism, Buddhism, Hinduism and Buddhism together, and Islam have been the official religions of successive Javanese kingdoms. Islam became the religion of the majority of the Javanese people under the 350-year rule of The Netherland East India Company and the Dutch Colonial government.

Christianity was introduced among the Javanese little more than 100 years before the end of Dutch colonial rule in 1942. The first Javanese Christian communities took shape in East Java in the second quarter of the 19th c. They were the outgrowth of the work of lay people, e.g., the Indo-European planter Coolen, in the Christian plantation community he established in Ngoro, and the Dutch watchmaker Emde, who worked in Surabaya.

The first Mennonite to be sent overseas as a missionary was sent to the island of Java in 1851. Pieter Jansz was sent out from The Netherlands by the newly formed Dutch Mennonite Missionary Society (the °°Doopsgezinde Zendingsvereeniging . . .) and began to work among the Javanese in the ancient coastal town of Jepara in 1852.

This Mennonite mission work resulted, directly or indirectly, in the formation of the two Mennonite-related conferences on Java. The °Gereja Injili di Tanah Jawa (Evangelical Church of Java), has a distinctly Javanese ethnic identity and uses the Javanese language as its primary language of worship. Its city congregations also have Indonesian language services, and most of its conference and organizational activity is conducted in the Indonesian language. The °Persatuan Gereja-Gereja Kristen Muria Indonesia (Muria Christian Church of Indonesia), sprang up as an indigenous movement under the leadership of °Tee Siem Tat in the midst of the Chinese communities of the towns of the Muria area beginning in the 1920s. The Muria church deliberately branched beyond the Chinese community beginning about 1960 and today has established mission churches in southern Sumatra, West Kalimantan, and in various areas of Java among several other ethnic groups.   LMY

Th. Jensma, *Doopsgezinde Zending in Indonesia* (The Hague: Boekcentrum, 1968); Lawrence M. Yoder, and Sigit Heru Soekotjo, "Sejarah Gereja Injili di Tanah Jawa" [History of the Evangelical Church of Java], unpublished manuscript; Lawrence M. Yoder, *Tunas Kecil: Sejarah Gereja Kristen Muria Indonesia* [Little Shoot: History of the Muria Christian Church of Indonesia] (Semarang: Komisi Literatur Sinode GKMI, n.d. [1985]) also available in English translation under the the title "The Church of the Muria: A History of the Muria Christian Church of Indonesia" (ThM thesis, Fuller Theological Seminary, 1981).

See also Indonesia.

Jebarbi Bai ("Ma") (ca. 1864-1932). Mystery and legend surround the colorful life of Jebarbi Bai, an early Bible woman (°lay evangelist) of the American Mennonite (MC) Mission (AMM), °Dhamtari, Madhya Pradesh, India. She was born into a Muslim home, received a minimal education, and married a Muslim imam (priest) who died a few years later in an accident.

Her first contact with Christianity came when she began domestic work in 1895 for Rev. and Mrs. F. E. Ward, American missionaries in Rajnandgaon under the Missionary Bands of the World Mission. She accepted Christianity in 1899 and continued with the Wards until they returned to the United States in 1910. She moved to Dhamtari in 1914 with her son, John (°Haider), and began working for AMM. From then until her death she served as a lay evangelist in and about the villages of Dhamtari. She was a woman of rare spiritual stature, dressing simply, always in white and without ornamentation. Her eyes flashed authority and her voice was compelling. Old age was reflected in her face early, earning her the title "Ma" (Mother). She related well to all non-Christians, especially Muslims. Legend had it that she was 101 years old when she died; more probably she was in her middle or late sixties. She was an authentic witness to the redeeming and transforming love of Christ.   JAF

Information supplied by grandchildren; AMM *Annual Reports* (1915-32); AMM Evangelism Committee file for 1922, MC Archives (Goshen), IV-5-4.

Jesus Christ. See Christology.

Jews. See Judaism and Jews.

Jivanlal, Kiyaram (Mar. 27, 1925-Aug. 15, 1987), a teacher, minister, and church leader of the Mennonite Church (MC) in India was born in Durg, Madhya Pradesh (M.P.). He was the second of three sons born to Birjhuram Sahu, a Hindu cultivator family living in Kundani village, Durg District. The parents were socially and economically well-positioned and followers of the Kabir Pant sect.

Kiyaram received his primary education through the fourth class with private tutors. In 1936 he was enrolled in the American Mennonite Mission middle school at Balodgahan, where he was deeply influenced by Christ's teachings. In 1943 he completed high school in the Mennonite Higher Secondary school in °Dhamtari, and was baptized. At this time he adopted a new name "Jivanlal" (Beloved Son of Life) and thereafter was always known by this name. From 1945 to 1948 he attended South India Bible Institute in Kolar, South India and later earned an MA degree at Ravishankar U. in Raipur.

From 1948 until his retirement in 1985 Jivanlal served on the staff of the Mennonite Higher Secondary School in Dhamtari, teaching political science and also serving as warden of the boys hostel for a number of years. In 1968 he was ordained deacon for the Sundarganj congregation in Dhamtari and in 1978 was ordained to the Christian ministry. From 1963 until his death he was conference treasurer. From 1984 to 1987 he served as India delegate to Mennonite World Conference.

In 1953 he married Lena Nathan, a Christian woman from Dhamtari. They had two sons, Sharad and Madhu, and two daughters, Jyoti and Mamta. Jivanlal's courageous step out of Hinduism into Christianity was always a clear testimony of the high cost of discipleship. He died of a sudden heart attack.   JAF

Information from Sharad Jivanlal (Wichita, Ks.); Mary M. Good, *American Mennonite Mission Report* (1936), 108; *Garjan Memorial School Report of the Christian Missionary Activities,* Enquiry Committee, M.P., vol. 2, part B (Nagpur: Govt. Printing Press, 1956), 72-73.

Joe Walks Along (feature). See Historical Writing [feature].

Johns, Otis N. (1889-1975). An able bishop and leader among Ohio and Pennsylvania Mennonites (MC), O. N. Johns was born at Goshen, Ind., the son of Bishop Daniel J. °°Johns. He married Margaret Rickert of Columbiana, Ohio in 1910. He farmed until he was ordained a minister to serve the Canton, [Ohio] Mennonite mission in 1923. On July 19, 1925, Johns was ordained bishop of the Beech congregation near Louisville, Ohio. He moved to a farm, as a means of self-support, in the spring of 1926 and served the Beech congregation for 35 years—years of activity and progress. Being an energetic bishop, he served the church at large in a variety of ways: on the constitution and by-laws committee for merging the Ohio Mennonite Conference and the Eastern Amish Mennonite Conferences

(1927); as secretary of the merged conference for its first 22 years; on the conference ministerial committee for years; as bishop with oversight, at one time or another, of 28 congregations in Ohio and Pennsylvania (Pennsylvania congregations that later became the Atlantic Coast Conference); as secretary of the Mennonite Publication Board (1927-49); as teacher or principal of winter Bible schools; on the executive committee of the Ohio Christian Workers Conference (1924-38); as counselor to Ohio °conscientious objectors during World War II; and as chaplain at Hartville Manor Nursing Home. He retired from church responsibilities in 1960. The children of O. N. and Margaret Johns were Gladys Krabill, Velma Miller, Lois Yoder, and David Johns.   JAS

Who's Who Mennonites (1943), 131; *Menn. Bib. II,* p. 462.

Johnson, K. T. (Tuwaletstewa), was one of the early converts of the General Conference Mennonite (GCM) mission among the Hopi in Arizona. He later served as a paid worker ("native helper") with the mission. His conversion to Christianity meant, for him, rejection of all aspects of traditional Hopi religion.

Johnson had been head of the Bow Clan, which controlled the One-Horn and Two-Horn societies, which had important and exclusive roles to play in the seasonal cycle of Hopi religion. When Johnson became a Christian, he rejected attendance at the Hopi ceremonial dances as well as rejecting tobacco, white dances, and movies. In Aug. 1922, Johnson consulted with other Hopi Christians in Oraibi and decided to burn the Bow Clan altar and other paraphernalia connected with it. Johnson, as head of the Bow Clan, had possession of the altar, which was used in one of the most secret Hopi ceremonies.

On the next Sunday afternoon, when many white tourists as well as Hopis were gathered to watch the Snake Dance, the Hopi Christians gathered in the center of New Oraibi for prayer and singing. Johnson set up the secret altar in the public square, spoke to the crowd about the evils of idol worship, poured gasoline over the altar, and set fire to it while the Christian group sang the hymn "When the Roll Is Called Up Yonder" in Hopi. "Thus passed away the most important Hopi religious ceremony," commented Otto Lomavitu, another Hopi Christian.   LB

John P. Suderman, *A Hopi Indian Finds Christ: The Experience of Mr. K. T. Johnson and His Judgment on Idolatry* (Oraibi, Ariz.: the author, n.d.); Frank Waters, *Book of the Hopi* (New York: Ballentine Books, 1962), 381-82.

Jokes. See Humor.

Jones, Rufus Matthew (Jan. 25, 1863-June 16, 1948), was the leading worldwide Quaker spirit within the Society of Friends in his time. He wrote more than 50 books and 600 articles. In 1917 he founded with others, the °°Americn Friends Service Committee, whose °relief work in Europe attracted Mennonite cooperation. This in turn helped give birth to the °Mennonite Central Committee in 1920. In the 1930s Jones helped shape the °historic peace church movement and °°Civilian Public Service. Harold S. °Bender, in his "Anabaptist Vision" article

(1944), accepted Jones' interpretation of Anabaptism at several points: Jones' typology, introducing his essay on Hans °°Denck (*Spiritual Reformers in the 16th and 17th Centuries,* 1914), and Jones' assessment of Anabaptism as a movement, in his chapter, "The Anabaptists" (*Studies in Mystical Religion,* 1909). Jones' emphasis on the mystical dimension of the Quaker faith has drawn some scholarly criticism. (For an interpretation of this, see Douglas Gwyn, *Apocalypse of the Word: The Life and Message of George Fox* [Richmond, Ind.: Friends United Press, 1986], xiii-xxiii.)   LG

David, Hinshaw, *Rufus Jones: Master Quaker* (New York: G. P. Putnam's Sons, 1951; reprint, Arno Press, 1974); Elizabeth (Gray) Vining, *Friend of Life: The Biography of Rufus M. Jones* (Philadelphia: Lippincott, 1958).

Joris, David. See David Joris.

Journalism. Within 100 years of Johann Gutenberg's advances with movable type, early Anabaptist leaders recognized the power of the pen and the press to advance the movement. In the first 325 years of Anabaptism, journalistic efforts were limited largely to pamphlets and books written by leaders. Some Anabaptist were itinerant booksellers and °pamphleteers, in many ways the occupation closest to modern journalism in the 16th c. (Hans °Hut; Andreas °Castelberger). Beginning in the 19th c., however, Mennonite involvements in journalism became multifaceted and far-reaching, first within the church and later in secular media. Nonjournalistic types of publishing are dealt with under °°publishers and °publishing.

In Kitchener (then Berlin), Ont., in 1835, pioneer Mennonite bishop Benjamin °°Eby was a shareholder in a printing business which also published a newspaper, *Das kanadische Museum* (Canada Museum). In 1840 ownership was transferred to Heinrich °Eby, Benjamin's son. Benjamin used this connection to publish some primers and, in 1841, *Kurzgefasste Kirchen-Geschichte und Glaubenslehre* (A Brief Church History and Primer of Belief), a successful book on Mennonite history and doctrine.

In the Franconia area of eastern Pennsylvania in 1836, Henry Bertolet, probably an ordained minister, published a 16-page paper, *Der evangelische Botschafter* (The Evangelical Messenger), a short-lived attempt to establish a Mennonite periodical. More successful in establishing a periodical was minister John F. °Oberholtzer, whose *Religiöser Botschafter* made its apearance in 1852 to support the progressive changes he advocated among his followers in eastern Pennsylvania. Another Franconia native, Joseph °°Funk, left a permanent mark on the Mennonite church as a printer in Virginia. Funk, who was a translator, compiler, and teacher of church music, established a business near Harrisonburg in 1847, primarily to meet a growing demand for a songbook known, after the fourth edition, as the °°*Harmonia Sacra.* Funk's works were printed mostly in English, marking him as an innovator among Mennonites.

During the U.S. Civil War, still another Franconia native emerged as a publisher. John F. °°Funk, Joseph's distant cousin, dominated Mennonite journalism for almost half a century. He began his career in Chicago in 1863 by writing a 16-page booklet titled "Warfare: Its Evil, Our Duty." With encouragement from ministers, Funk determined to launch a periodical "devoted to the interests of the Denomination of Christians known as 'The Mennonites'" and in 1864 issued the *Herald of Truth* in English and its German equivalent, *Herold der Wahrheit*. These periodicals steadily gained subscribers, and beginning in 1866 Funk devoted himself full-time to publishing and other church work. One year later, he moved to Elkhart, Ind., where he added a printing plant to his editorial enterprises.

Funk's reputation as a publisher and leader attracted John F. °°Harms, a German-speaking Russian Mennonite immigrant, to Elkhart in 1880 to edit the *Mennonitische Rundschau* and to assist with the *Herald*. (Since 1940 the *Rundschau* has been published by the Christian Press of Winnipeg, Man., making it the oldest Mennonite periodical to appear without interruption under one name.)

In central Kansas in the 1870s, Mennonite immigrants depended on community newspapers published by fellow believers to orient them to their new surroundings. These included David Goerz' *Zur Heimath*, which was folded into the *Christlicher Bundesbote* in 1882 to become General Conference Mennonites' official German-language paper. Others, including J. F. Harms, published at least five German-language newspapers in Kansas towns in the late 1880s. At the turn of the century, German-language newspapers with no official ties to the church, especially the Hillsboro *Vorwaerts* and the Newton *Der Herold*, were nevertheless vital to Kansas Mennonites. Mennonite editors of these papers interpreted news of the outside political world in a way that shaped viewpoints while respecting their readers' sectarian values.

After World War I, Mennonites established numerous publications with a journalistic orientation with the goal of reaching readers within the various groups. One such periodical has been the *Mennonite Weekly Review* with headquarters in Newton, Ks., where it was first published in English in 1923.

Thirty years later, *The Canadian Mennonite* was begun in Winnipeg to serve as the first English-language newspaper for Mennonites across Canada. Founding editor Frank H. °Epp envisioned a paper that would connect the various groups to each other and promote inter-Mennonite cooperation through Mennonite Central Committee. *The Canadian Mennonite* ceased publication in 1971, but many of its functions were assumed by *Mennonite Reporter*, established at Kitchener-Waterloo, Ont., in 1971, with Epp again at the editorial helm.

Cooperation among journalists of various Mennonite publications increased with the formation of Meetinghouse in 1972. Editors from nine different periodicals meet annually to plan cooperative projects. In addition, one reporter frequently represents all the association's members to cover stories with broad appeal.

In the late 1980s hundreds of periodicals align themselves with the Mennonite denominations, many officially and some privately. They have developed out of the need to interpret church-related programs and issues to a more highly educated laity combined with the ready availability of printing and other communication technologies. Springer and Klassen's *Mennonite Bibliography* lists 671 periodicals in North America alone and dozens in other countries for the 1631-1961 period.

Also in the 20th c., individual Mennonites have increasingly entered secular journalism as a business or profession. One unusual community newspaper, *The Sugarcreek Budget,* was launched in Ohio in 1890 by an Amish-Mennonite, John C. Miller. This weekly, with a mostly Amish readership, emphasizes correspondence from far-flung settlements, a practice which had attracted more than 16,500 subscribers by 1987.

Mennonite publishers of community newspapers after mid-century have included David K. Friesen, who founded *The Altona Echo* (now the *Red River Valley Echo* in Manitoba in 1941; H. Ralph Hernley, who launched the Laurel Group of five weekly newspapers and a magazine in western Pennsylvania in 1965; and Richard and Marlene Benner, who owned newspapers in central Pennsylvania, 1973-84.

Mennonite reporters have worked for daily newspapers in many cities, including Toronto, Winnipeg, and Vancouver in Canada and Lancaster, Pa.; Harrisonburg, Va.; Elkhart, Ind.; and Wichita, Ks., in the United States. Mennonite broadcast journalists have worked with radio and television stations in several cities and with the Canadian Broadcasting Company and American Public Radio. Journalists with Mennonite backgrounds hold senior positions with the Associated Press and *Newsweek*.   SWS

Frank H. Epp, "D. W. Friesen and His Life Work," *Menn. Life,* 11 (July 1956), 118-19; idem, "Death of a Church Paper and Resurrection," *Mennonite* (Apr. 6, 1971), 226-29; idem, Mennonites in Canada I; idem, "On Mennonite Journalism," *The Canadian Mennonite* (Aug. 8, 1967), 4; Orlando Harms, *Pioneer Publisher: The Life and Times of J. F. Harms* (Winnipeg and Hillsboro: Kindred Press, 1984); Daniel Hertzler, "Meetinghouse," *GH* (Jan. 5, 1988), 16; Irvin B. Horst, "Joseph Funk, Early Mennonite Printer and Publisher," *MQR,* 31 (1957), 260-77; John A. Hostetler, *God Uses Ink* (Scottdale, 1958); James C. Juhnke, *A People of Two Kingdoms* (Newton, 1975); MEA 1; John Ruth, *Maintaining the Right Fellowship* (Scottdale, 1984); C. Henry Smith, *The Story of the Mennonites,* 4th ed. (Newton: MPO, 1957); Nelson P. Springer, and A. J. Klassen, compilers, *Mennonite Bibliography 1631-1961,* 2 vols. (Scottdale, 1977); John A Toews, *History MB* (1975); Harvey Yoder, "The Budget of Sugarcreek, Ohio, 1890-1920," *MQR,* 40 (1966), 27-47.

See also Broadcasting, Radio and Television; Filmmaking; Mass Media.

Jubilee observances are part of the economic legislation of the Old Testament (Lv 25; Dt 15:1-18). Related themes include the cycles of sabbath days (Ex 20:8-11) and years (Lv 25:1-7). The jubilee year capped seven cycles of sabbatical years. On Yom Kippur (The Day of Atonement) of the jubilee year a ram's horn was sounded as a fourfold call to: (a) liberation of slaves; (b) cancellation of debts; (c) cessation of agriculture for one year; and (d) education for a spiritual democracy through study of the Scriptures (Torah).

Biblical scholars disagree whether the jubilee was actually practiced. Evidence of this observance is found in Neh 5:1-13, Jer 34:8-22, and Ez 46:16-18. A key prophetic text with jubilee themes is Is 61:1-2. This text Jesus of Nazareth applied to himself in his home synagogue (Lk 4:16-19) in A.D. 26-27, which, according to calculations by Andre Trocmé, was a sabbatical year. Some scholars also view the "all things in common" texts (Acts 2:43-47 and 4:32-37) as jubilee-inspired observances of the early church. Paul's concept of "mutual aid" (2 Cor 8:13-14) may also reflect jubilee influences.

The jubilee was not a major observance in the Western (Roman) church, with the hierarchy of church leaders (excepting the monastic orders) accumulating worldly power and wealth. The Roman Catholic church did maintain the prohibition against usury (requiring excessive interest on loans).

Protestant Reformation leaders (Martin °°Luther, John °°Calvin, Martin °°Bucer, and Huldrych °°Zwingli) all abandoned the usury prohibitions. They were maintained only by the Anabaptists. The Swiss Brethren and South German Anabaptists practiced mutual aid, while the Hutterian Brethren practiced having all things in common. Among 20th c. Mennonites, only the Church of God in Christ Mennonite (Holdeman), group rejects giving and taking interest (°business, °economics, °investments).

The 1970s and 1980s saw a resurgence of attention by North American Mennonite scholars to the jubilee themes. The General Conference Mennonite Church declared 1975 to be the ninth jubilee since the origin of Anabaptism in 1525. Observances occurred at Bethel College (Ks.), and in a number of congregations. In 1987 the Sabbatical Voluntary Service theme was a current jubilee-inspired application sponsored by the Mennonite Central Committee Canada.   RHul

Robert North, *The Sociology of the Biblical Jubilee*, Analecta Biblica: Investigationes Scientificae in Res Biblicas, 4 (Rome: Pontifical Biblical Institute, 1954); Andre Trocmé, *Jesus and the Nonviolent Revolution*, trans. Michael H. Shank and Marlin E. Miller (Scottdale, 1973; originally published in French, 1961); John Howard Yoder, *The Politics of Jesus* (Grand Rapids: Eerdmans, 1972), 34-41, 64-77; Peter James Klassen, *The Economics of Anabaptism 1525-1560* (The Hague: Mouton and Co., 1964), 29-49, 66-67, 90, 105; Clarence Hiebert, *The Holdeman People: The Church of God in Christ, Mennonite, 1859-1969* (South Pasadena, Cal.: William Carey Library, 1973), 472-79; Don Blosser, "Jesus and the Jubilee - Luke 4: 16-30; The Year of Jubilee and Its Significance in the Gospel of Luke" (PhD diss., St. Andrews U., Scotland, 1979); John Driver, "The Jubilee Legislation of Moses and the Historical/Political Situation of Jesus," *Church and Peace Quarterly Report* (Schoeffengrund, West Germany), vol. 2, no. 1 (Jan. 1980), 13-21; David Habegger, "The Year of Jubilee," *Mennonite* (Feb. 11, 1975), 81-83; Robert Hull, "Sabbatical Service," *Mennonite* (Jan. 27, 1981), 49-51, (Feb. 3, 1981), 68-69.

Judaism and Jews. *Judaism* is the name first given by Christians to Jews in the 3rd c. (Tertullian). *Jew(s)* is a term used in late Old Testament times (e.g., 2 Kings and Esther) based on "Judah." Judaism is the Scriptures, oral traditions, the faith, practice, and polity of the people of Israel from the time of Moses to the present.

Judaism is "an evolving religious civilization as well as a religion and a way of life" (*About Judaism*). Characterized by deep spirituality, a moral life that gives more stress to deeds than words, Judaism is concerned "to make all of life holy." Holidays, rituals, and symbols are the means of letting every generation participate in the foundational events in the Jewish Bible.

One of the oldest of all religions, beginning with Abraham and Moses, the Jewish faith is centered on covenant. Through four millennia of persecution, trials, and renewal, Judaism has held fast to the gospel of uncompromising monotheism. The sanctity of relationships toward family, neighbor, time, property, and the inner life is carefully prescribed in a brief set of "ten words" (Ex 34:28). Creeds or dogmas are few. Yet certain basic beliefs in addition to the above are the belief that men and women are created in the image of God and should imitate God, faith in atonement and forgiveness, and the belief that God works through human agency (the Messiah) to bring *shalom.*

Roughly the counterpart to the New Testament in Christianity is the Talmud in Judaism. It is a commentary on the Jewish Bible based on oral tradition. The 1st c. church did not have the New Testament. A living testament was the church. Jew and Gentile Christian together became 'our epistles known and read by all," according to Paul (2 Cor 3:2). Furthermore, even when written down, the New Testament was intended only for the eyes of Jews and Gentiles who had become disciples of Jesus of Nazareth, the rabbi from Galilee. Since they expected the immediate return of Christ, the urgent order of the day was that flesh and blood witnesses, both Jews and Gentiles would go to synagogues scattered over the world.

Two ways of dealing with anti-Semitism in the New Testament are: substituting "establishment" for "Jews" (J. H. Yoder) or "'some of' the Jews" (Baehr) whenever the term is used in a negative way. All the disciples, Paul, and, of course, Jesus Himself were Jews.

Some Mennonites whose careers have involved long-term exposure to Jews are: Karl H. Baehr of Garden City, N.Y.; O'Ray Graber, St. Louis, Mo., John Kampen, Dayton, Ohio; Frits °Kuiper, The Netherlands; Roy Kreider, Israel (Harrisonburg, Va., 1988); Paul Swarr, Israel (Powhatan, Va., 1988); and John H. Yoder, Elkhart, Ind. These have been engaged in depth dialogue with Jews.

Millard Lind, on behalf of Associated Mennonite Biblical Seminaries (AMBS), Elkhart, Ind., led the first full-credit graduate-level semester program in Israel in 1985. Jacob Elias (dean, AMBS), William Klassen, John H. Yoder (U. of Notre Dame, Ind.), and John W. Miller (Conrad Grebel College) have participated in the life of Tantur, an inter-faith study center near Bethlehem, West Bank, Jordan.

Through courses in Hebrew language and culture Mennonite colleges and seminaries have encouraged participation in Passover and Feast of Tabernacles as well as visits to temples and synagogues. Some Mennonite congregations have come to celebrate these as well. *Nes Ammim* (from Isa 11:10, "ensign to/for the peoples") is the name of a Christian kibbutz in Galilee. Frits Kuiper, a Mennonite theologian in The Netherlands who was very sympathetic with the Jewish cause during World War II, was instrumental in starting the kibbutz as a Christian witness and expression of repentance. Since American Mennonites wanted the kibbutz to become a basis for establishing congregations this came to be seen as proselytizing by the Dutch Mennonites. The kibbutz was taken over by the Dutch Reformed and the Christian Reformed groups of The Netherlands.

"Dutch Mennonites Wrestling With Attitudes To

Jews," was the front-page headline of the *Mennonite Reporter* (Canada) on Sept. 14, 1987. An independent evangelistic team had insisted that the "his blood be upon us" passage from Matt 27:25 speaks clearly of Jewish "collective guilt" in the crucifixion of Jesus. General secretary of the Dutch Mennonite conference, Ed van Straten, in a statement accepted by at least one third of the Mennonite congregations, wrote: "In the 1930s when it was of paramount importance to protest against anti-Semitism and abhor it as evil, our community was silent." Such was their confession of guilt in the face of Nazi Germany's death camps which destroyed millions of Jews. Their position was strongly supported by Paul's Epistle to the Romans (chaps. 9-11) in which he expressly says in the strongest terms that God has not rejected his chosen people: ". . . I could wish that I myself were accursed and cut off from Christ for the sake of my brethren, my kinsmen by race."

A *Shofar* (ram's horn) Committee under the Eastern Mennonite Board of Missions (MC) has encouraged Mennonites to observe the Feast of the Tabernacles. Paul and Bertha Swarr, who have worked in Israel since 1957, and Joe and Elaine Haines, with 20 years of work there, were on the same program with Rabbi Rich Nichol of *Ruach* (Spirit) Israel Messianic congregation in Boston.

Annual institutes on the Holocaust sponsored by the National Conference of Christians and Jews are held in Philadelphia. Both academic and religious education dimensions as well as fine arts have been part of the programs. AMBS has been represented at the institutes by John Howard Yoder and Jacob J. Enz. Franklin H. Littell, a Methodist scholar who has written on Anabaptist and °believers' church history, is very active in the Holocaust movement phase of the National Conference of Christians and Jews. Repentance, Littell pleads, will not come until Christian liturgy includes ". . . prayers and hymns and antiphonies" of the holocaust.

"Comprehending," as Christians, our profound identity with our Jewish brothers and sisters even on the plane of Holy History is indeed difficult. The dialogue, sometimes very intense, goes on between those who affirm Christians' Jewishness and those who emphasize the need for Jews to become Christians (conversionists). Roy Kreider and Paul Swarr have stressed affirmation of Jewishness first. Immanuel Study Center in Jaffa, a suburb of Tel Aviv, serves about 150 participants. Kreider, director of studies, and Swarr, pastor, have recently turned over the leadership to local personnel, including Salim Munayer, an Arab Christian. Several Jews have become Mennonites, including one Mennonite minister in 1988.

It comes as a great surprise to Christians that the Jewish philosopher Maimonides [1135-1204] "affirms a special Jewish theology for Christianity (and Islam). He taught that Christianity and Islam are missionary arms of Judaism created by God to bring the 'pagans and heathens of the world under the Lord's canopy.'" These words come from L. C. Yaseen's *The Jesus Connection: To Triumph Over Anti-Semitism*, a book carrying introductions by Billy Graham (Protestant), Theodore Hesburgh (Roman Catholic), and Marc Tananbaum (Jewish).   JJE

About Judaism (South Deerfield, Mass.: Channing L. Bete Co.), a leaflet that uses drawings to clarify Judaism's beliefs and three main "denominations"; Karl H. Baehr, "The Churches Confounded by Israel Reborn: A Mennonite's Journey to Zion" (unpublished); Clarence Bauman, "The Quest for the Real Jesus," transcript of a lecture given Dec. 8, 1968, at Society of Friends in Edinburgh, Scotland; David Berger and Michael Wyschograd, *Jews and "Jewish Christianity"* (New York: KTAB, 1978), 71 pp., a Jewish response to Christian "conversionists"; Robert L. Brawley, *Luke-Acts and the Jews: Conflict, Apology, and Conciliation* (Atlanta: Scholars Press, 1987); Alice L. Eckardt, "The Reformation and the Jews," unpublished paper, ca. 1986, includes references to Anabaptists; Jacob J. Enz, "Where Are Messiah's People?" *Mennonite* (Dec. 8, 1981), 702-3; E. J. Fisher, A. J. Rudin, and M. H. Tannenbaum, eds., *Twenty Years of Jewish-Catholic Relations* (New York: Paulist Press, 1986); Waldemar Janzen, *Still in the Image: Essays in Biblical Theology and Anthropology* (Newton, 1982; Winnipeg: CMBC, 1982); Kauffman/Harder, *Anabaptists Four C. Later* (1975), 248ff; Franklin H. Littell, *The Crucifixion of the Jews* (New York: Harper and Row, 1975); *Mennonite Witness as it Relates to Jewish People* (Salunga, Pa.: Home Ministries Dept. Eastern Mennonite Board of Missions and Charities, 1985); *The Plough* (Rifton, N.Y.), no. 16 (Sept. 1986); N. Gerald Shenk, "A Poet, a Linguist, and a Synagogue: Symbols of Hope and Renewal," *Menn. Rep.* (Dec. 21, 1987), on Jewish-Protestant cooperation in Yugoslavia; Leonard Yaseen, *The Jesus Connection: To Triumph over Anti-Semitism* (New York: Crossroad, 1985).

See also Christology; Israel, State of; National Socialism.

Julia Yellow Horse Shoulderblade. See Cheyenne People [feature].

Just War. Never promulgated as formal church teaching, the "Just War Tradition" developed in early medieval thought as a substitute for the rejection of warfare by the dominant teaching of the pre-Constantinian church.

There is no official statement of the just war criteria, but the growth of the tradition has come to include most of the following: (*a*) The *jus ad bellum* or "the right to fight," which includes the existence of legitimate authority, a just cause, and a right "intention" (both objective and subjective). (*b*) Following due form and process, including recourse to war as a last resort; maintaining respect for international law, customs, and treaties; the presence of probability of victory, and maintaining proportionality of the values at stake. (*c*) The *jus in bello* or "fighting rightly," i.e., that the conduct of war be indispensable, proportional, discriminating and controllable; that it respect the immunity of the noncombatant and respect the humanity of the adversary.

Recognizing that war is a material evil, needing moral justification, the just war tradition states that by meeting such specifiable criteria war may be, exceptionally, justified. The tradition evolved gradually through the centuries after the age of Constantine (d. 337), was never given prominence, but was supported by a consensus of official theologians. The "magisterial" Protestant Reformation wrote the tradition into its creeds (the Lutheran Augsburg Confession of 1530, article XVI; the Anglican Thirty-Nine Articles of 1563 [Latin 1571], article 37; the Presbyterian Westminster Confession of 1647, article 23) as a response to the challenge of the Anabaptists, thereby decreasing the doctrine's capacity to be a means of restraint. Roman Catholic moralists sought to use it to critique 16th-century Spanish and Portugese colonial wars, and jurists (e.g.

Hugo Grotius, 1583-1645) transposed it into the language of international law, but political "realism" largely left it behind in the age of national sovereignty and "total" war.

In modern times the resources of the just war tradition have begun to be drawn upon in criticisms of nuclear war as disregarding the criteria of discrimination and noncombatant immunity. They were implicitly operating in the phenomenon of selective °conscientious objection which for the first time became important during the United States' war in °Vietnam 1965-75.

Just war tradition has in common with Christian pacifism its rejection of the cynical or "realistic" notion that there can be no moral restraint in the realm of war, and the rejection of the "crusading" notion that war may be a holy cause. Most real and likely wars since the age of Grotius, if honestly measured by the just war criteria, would stand condemned. "Just War" thinkers and pacifists may make common cause in their rejection of modern militarism.

The pacifist critique of just war tradition (a) doubts that churches and governments intend or are able seriously to apply the just war restraints in real political or strategic decisions, either on the level of states' making costly decisions against their selfish interest, or on the level of citizens' refusal to support the illegitimate actions of their rulers and (b) finds in the teachings or example of Jesus no warrant for war, even for just causes, even in the hands of legitimate authority. Another kind of pacifist critique further (c) finds the just war tradition unrealistic in its estimating too optimistically the cost/benefit consequences of the spiral of violence and estimating too pessimistically the potential of nonviolent means. (d) The appearance of logical clarity and rigor is deceptive; each of the criteria is debatable and culturally conditioned. "Legitimate authority," for example, may stretch all the way from monarchical conservatism to °revolution.

Some suggest that strategy thinking about nonviolent direct action, which without taking life may be said to "coerce" or to "manipulate" an adversary for good social ends, might also be fruitfully illuminated by using criteria of authority, cause, means, last resort, etc., in a way analogous to those of the just war tradition (°sociopolitical activism; °peace). JHY

James Childress, *Moral Responsibility in Conflicts* (Baton Rouge: Louisiana State University Press, 1982); James Turner Johnson, *Can Modern War Be Just?* (New Haven: Yale U. Press, 1984); idem, "Historical Tradition and Moral Judgment: The Case of Just War Tradition," *J. of Religion,* 64 (1984) 299-317; idem, *Ideology, Reason, and the Limitation of War* (Princeton U. Press, 1975); idem, *Just War Tradition and the Restraint of War* (Princeton U. Press, 1981); Michael Walzer, *Just and Unjust Wars* (New York: Basic Books, 1977); John H. Yoder, *When War Is Unjust* (Minneapolis: Augsburg, 1984); idem, *Christian Attitudes to War, Peace, and Revolution* (Elkhart: Goshen Biblical Seminary, 1983), 55-112, 455-86.

See also Church-State Relations; Conscription; Military Participation Nonresistance; Patriotism.

Justice has been on the Christian agenda since the 4th c. During the Middle Ages the Catholic Church accepted justice as the principle that makes civilization possible. It was thought to be reflected in nature and it was formulated as natural law. With the help of Aristotle, medieval philosophers and theologians made distinctions between punitive, attributive, and distributative justice.

At the same time, the Christian church upheld what it considered an even higher principle, namely °love. Love (*agape*) was thought to be grounded in eternity, reflecting God's nature and will as revealed in Jesus Christ. Love was seen to be non-resistant, uncalculating, non-prudential, infinitely forgiving and completely self-giving.

Throughout Christian history, the Catholic church and mainline Protestant denominations upheld both love and justice. While refusing to confuse them, as if they were identical, the church accepted both in a complementary but dialectical manner. Theoretical and practical relationships between love and justice became a perennial issue of Christian ethics.

The Anabaptist attitude toward justice was unique in the history of Christendom though it may have been typical of the New Testament church. It is sometimes referred to as the °"sectarian" view.

The Anabaptists agreed with their contemporaries that justice is grounded in the will of God and is reflected in nature. But they refused to accept justice as a category of Christian ethics. Love alone is Christian. Justice is essential to civilization but the establishment and maintenance of civilization is the responsibility of the world. By contrast the task of Christians is to create a new community structured by love alone.

The root of the problem lay in the use of force and in preferential decision-making in multilateral situations. For justice by its very nature defines "rights," makes love preferential, and may allow reasonable defenses of the self and the neighbor against untoward demands of others. The Anabaptists were so taken by the Sermon on the Mount and their perception of Jesus as a non-resistant suffering servant that they saw the struggle for justice with its restraints on love and its imposition of power as compromise.

The initial attitude of the Anabaptists toward justice appeared in the °Schleitheim articles (1527) in connection with the magistracy. The Anabaptists rejected the magistracy, declaring that that office and presumably the world which it represented lie "outside the perfection of Christ." Even the rational definition and orderly dispensation of justice through law was rejected since conflict between claimants presupposes selfishness. "Christ did not wish to decide or pass judgment between brother and brother in the case of the inheritance, but refused to do so. Therefore we should do likewise." For most of Mennonite history, Mennonite ethics with respect to justice reflected the Schleitheim articles.

Of course if one were to follow Mennonite life since Schleitheim, one would find few groups that practice love alone even within the church. For when love is structured it takes the form of justice. Mennonites in their most withdrawn circumstances incorporated both love and justice in their own communities. Even the °Hutterites in their attempt to set up a system of "love communism" (i.e., a structure of love), incorporated, however unconsciously, the principle of justice as they up-held what is fair, honest, and right. One may be sure that Mennonite merchants in Amsterdam used correct weights, paid just wages, and joined fair competition. Within Mennonite life the principle of justice was taken for granted, at least in its distributive forms. Although justice was practiced and injustice was suffered, Mennonites did not provide a theological basis for those dimensions of life. In the spirit of *Gelassenheit* (yieldedness) they would not insist upon justice for their own sakes but they would practice it quite unconsiously in ordinary life.

In the writings of Guy F. °Hershberger, justice comes off poorly. To be sure, Hershberger is conscious of the need for justice in human relations. But as with Schleitheim, he contrasts justice and the means by which it is achieved with love as "Biblical °nonresistance." Since Christians should not resist evil, they may not pursue justice in the manner in which it is sought even by Christian "pacifists" and nonviolent reformers such as °Gandhi: by insisting upon rights, by competition, by political pressures, by organized nonviolent resistance, by sit-ins and political demonstrations (°sociopolitical activism).

In *War, Peace and Non-Resistance* (1944) and in *The Way of the Cross in Human Relations* (1958), Hershberger upheld "doing justice." However, he uncompromisingly rejected the pursuit of justice by the use of nonviolent resistance. In his critique of °labor unions he wrote "The relentless pursuit of justice for oneself or one's own group is always inimical to the way of Christian love and it is difficult to see how the right to strike . . . can be reconciled with the way of the cross, however effective it may be as a way of bringing about a more just social order" (Way of the Cross, 269). It is probable that Hershberger began to think more positively about justice following the nonviolent racial revolution in America led by Martin Luther King.

Although Mennonites traditionally have refused to accept responsibility for society as a whole, they have responded from time to time to unjust conditions. For example, in 1688 the Mennonite congregation of Germantown, Pa., formulated what some would consider the first written protest by a church against slavery in American history.

Also Canadian Mennonites have been known to protest unjust treatment of Indians. Furthermore °conscientious objectors in °°Civilian Public Service during World War II called for reform of °mental health hospitals.

Significant differences in attitudes toward justice began to appear, however, in the 1970s and 1980s. Mennonites began to speak about both love and justice as Christian ideals. Love and justice were frequently uttered in tandem. In written form they were hyphenated, as if to signal that they are somehow different but compatible.

Reasons for the entry of justice into Mennonite vocabulary are diverse but interrelated. For one thing, as noted above, certain Mennonite leaders were attracted to Martin Luther King and challenged by the evil of °racial segregation. Martin Luther King's nonviolent approach to social change was admired and, the ring of his prophetic voice, his pulpit eloquence, and his piety appealed to many Mennonite theologians. Some Mennonites even participated in sit-ins and at least one Mennonite pro-

fessor was jailed in 1963 for direct nonviolent action. Some Mennonites expressed their preference for nonviolence over nonresistance since by comparison nonresistance seemed entirely too passive for the times.

Furthermore °liberation theology, in which salvation was described as deliverance from injustice, emerged in the 1970s. Liberation theology was discussed in Mennonite seminaries and missionaries were introduced to its various forms in Latin America. At issue were questions of means and ends, since some non-Mennonte proponents of liberation theology advocated the use of violence to change oppressive structures.

In addition certain groups within the Mennonite churches became so bold as to insist upon their "rights." Minorities sought just representation on church boards. As feminist theologies upheld just treatment for women, Mennonite °women appealed for just recognition as human beings and as church leaders. Clearly Mennonites of the 1970s and 1980s reflected the cause of °human rights as a worldwide movement.

At the same time, christological interpretations began to shift in directions that would allow one to appeal to the life of Jesus as a basis for social action. Jesus was interpreted increasingly as a reformer in the prophetic tradition (Yoder, *Politics*, 90-93). Provocative criticism of Jewish power structures in behalf of the poor led Jesus, so it was claimed, to His crucifixion. Studies of the historical Jesus rendered problematic the possibility of reducing Jesus' teachings to an abstract principle such as nonresistance. Furthermore scholars tended to emphasize the Old Testament prophetic call for justice for the "widow and orphan."

Interest in justice also followed °economic and social shifts as Mennonites moved from °rural to °urban contexts. °Professional and business involvements placed justice, both in its theoretical and practical forms, within Mennonite experience. Furthermore concern for justice in its many forms and applications followed church °institutionalization.

In 1960 J. Lawrence Burkholder presented a series of lectures at a conference of the Association of Mennonite Aid Societies in Chicago on "Love and Justice in Mennonite Mutual Aid." In "The Generosity of Love" he attempted to set forth a conception of love as "limitless generosity" only to be followed by a lecture on "Justice—The Arithmetic of Love" in which he sought to show how love takes the form of justice in complex, structured, corporate, situations defined by law and administered by duly appointed officials. The relation of pure love and prudent justice was examined at some length (*Compassionate Community*, 51-78).

In the 1980s Mennonite leaders came to realize that justice must be addressed officially. This led to a statement entitled "Justice and the Christian Witness" which was approved at the meeting of the Mennonite Church and General Conference Mennonite Church at Bethlehem, Pa., in Aug. 1983. The statement attempts to place justice within the context of Biblical faith and a covenant people. The statement consciously rejects classical conceptions of justice. What Bethlehem meant by justice was left somewhat ambiguous. Nevertheless, it tended to legitimize justice as as goal for Christian mission. Increasingly Mennonite utterances seemed to suggest that Christian love is for the sake of justice. Furthermore, Mennonites began to acknowledge a connection between justice and peace. Peace without justice is less than Shalom.

While it is clear that Mennonites became increasingly concerned about justice in the 1970s and 1980s very little was done of a theoretical nature. Mennonites had not clearly articulated a theology within which basic elements such as love, power, and justice were defined and related to one another. Possibly this could be done only by ontological analysis for which Mennonites have had no inclination. Nevertheless Mennonites, on the level of church life and witness, began to take justice seriously as part of the Christian life and witness. JLB

Emil Brunner, *Justice and the Social Order* (New York: Harper and Brothers, 1945); J. Lawrence Burkholder, *"The Problem of Social Responsibility from the Perspective of the Mennonite Church,"* (ThD diss., Princeton Theological Seminary, 1958; published Elkhart, Ind.: IMS, 1988); John Rawls, *A Theory of Justice* (Cambridge, Mass.: Harvard, 1971; Paul Tillich, *Love, Power and Justice* (Oxford University Press, 1960); Ernst Troeltsch, *The Social Teachings of the Christian Churches,* trans. Olive Wyon, 2 vols. (New York: Macmillan, 1931); John Howard Yoder, *The Politics of Jesus* (Grand Rapids: Eerdmans, 1972); Ralph H. Hernley, ed., *The Compassionate Community: A Collection of Lectures Presented at the Conference of the Association of Mennonite Aid Societies* (Scottdale: Assoc. of Menn. Aid Soc., 1970).

See also Civil Disobedience; Institutions; Law; Peace.

Justification. The Bible speaks of both God and humans as being justified. God is justified when his acts of judgment and salvation are openly displayed, and recognized and praised as just (Is 45:22-25, Rom 3:3-5). Humans are justified when God declares them to be righteous in his judgment (Rom 8:33-34, 1 Cor 4:4). The early Anabaptists eagerly anticipated God's eschatological deliverance of the righteous and condemnation of the wicked. In this sense, they emphasized the coming justification of God. Nevertheless, when Anabaptists and Mennonites used "justification" terminology they were usually referring to a major dispute between Roman Catholics and Protestants that began in the Reformation: to the question of how a man or woman can be considered righteous by God and thus be freed from fear of condemnation.

Catholics argue that justification is a comprehensive act in which God not only declares persons to be righteous, but also makes them so. Justification, then, cannot be sharply distinguished from the process of °sanctification. Sanctification is attained as humans co-operate with divine °grace, which is imparted largely through sacraments and other ecclesiastical channels. Protestants counter that in order to truly begin sanctification, individuals must first be justified. For unless they are first freed from fear of condemnation, simply by faith in Christ's °atonement, individuals can never perform those selfless acts of love which produce true sanctification.

Anabaptists seldom used "justification" to describe their own views, for they approached the issues involved from a different angle. Like Protestants, they emphasized that God initiates the °salvation process, and that individuals enter it through faith. Yet they often complained that Protestants, by emphasizing "faith alone", minimized sanctification and encouraged sub-Christian behavior. Like Catholics, Anabaptists insisted that sanctification, or actually becoming righteous, is the goal of God's saving work. Yet they argued that this occurs not within Catholicism's ecclesiastical framework, but primarily through acts of love in daily life. And although human co-operation is involved in the process, most Anabaptists maintained, as did Michael °Sattler, that the works involved "are not the work of man, but of God and Christ, through whose power a man does such works . . . because God through them wishes to give to man something of his own." (CRR 1:113)

Today there is probably little value in seeking to identify the Mennonite perspective with either traditional Protestantism or Catholicism. Since Anabaptists viewed the issues from a different angle, Mennonite contributions to the often stalemated discussion can best be made by seeking to recover this perspective. Perhaps consideration of the eschatological justification of God, as an overarching (though formally unarticulated) horizon for Mennonite theologizing, can provide helpful insights for rediscovering that perspective. TNF

Council of Trent, "Decree on Justification" in *The Sources of Catholic Dogma,* ed. Henry Denziger (St. Louis: B. Herder, 1957), 248-61; John Calvin, *Institutes of the Christian Religion* (Philadelphia: Westminster, 1960), Bk III, ch. XI-XIV, pp. 725-88; Heinrich Heppe, ed., *Reformed Dogmatics* (Grand Rapids: Baker, 1978), 543-64, CRR 3: 85-100; Robert Friedmann, *The Theology of Anabaptism* (Scottdale, 1973), 78-101; Kenneth R. Davis, *Anabaptism and Asceticism* (Scottdale, 1974), 129-217; Michael Sattler in CRR 1: 108-20; Hans Denck, "Recantation" in *Selected Writings,* ed. Walter Fellmann (Pittsburgh: Pickwick, 1975), 122-31; Thomas N. Finger, *Christian Theology,* vol. 2, ch. 7; Balthasar Hubmaier, "On the Christian Baptism of Believers" in *Anabaptist Beginnings,* ed. William Estep (Nieuwkoop: B. De Graaf, 1976), esp. 94-98; Menno Simons, "Confession of the Distressed Christians" in *Writings,* esp. 503-8, and "True Christian Faith in *Writings,* 324-405.

K

Kabangy Moise (d. 1979) was born in the eastern part of Kwilu Province in the Belgian Congo (Zaire) near Kandala, a mission station pioneered in 1926 by an independent Canadian Baptist couple, Percy and Rosalind Near. In the early 1940s Kabangy enrolled in the mission school, where he responded to the story of Jesus and became a Christian. After further training at Mukedi, a station of the °°Congo Inland Mission 100 mi. (160 km.) to the north, he returned to Kandala, where he served for a number of years as a teacher and lay church leader.

In 1963 Kabangy was chosen to enter a new post-primary pastoral training program sponsored by the Congo Inland Mission (Africa Inter-Mennonite Mission) and the Mennonite Brethren Mission at Kajiji near the Angolan border. The student body incorporated people from a broad variety of tribes, leading at times to frictions and misunderstandings. More and more Kabangy was drawn into such situations because of his gift for counseling and achieving reconciliation.

Upon graduation he returned to Kandala and served as pastor for a time at the station church. In 1971 he was elected president of the Église du Christ au Zaire, Communauté Mennonite (CMZA; Zaire Mennonite Church). He was noted for his strong pastoral gifts, traveled much, and assured the broad mix of major clans within the church that they were all important to him, to the church, and to the Lord. Perhaps his crowning achievement was to help bring about a reconciliation between the Zaire Mennonite Church and the Église du Christ au Zaire, Communauté Evangélique Mennonite (CEM; Evangelical Mennonite Church) of East Kasai, which had begun in the troubled days of the early 1960s.

When, in 1979, bone cancer placed him on his deathbed, he convened a cluster of church leaders and made two statements: first, referring to the African worldview which typically attributes death to sorcery, he clearly stated that he held no one accountable for his impending death and he forbade anyone else to do so. He then turned to those assembled around his bed and charged them to guard and care for the Mennonite church as he had sought to do. He was buried at the Kandala churchyard, the place where he began his pilgrimage of faith and service.   JEB

Kaddar (Kadar), Mrs. P. See Parimala Bai.

Kafutshi Kakesa. The daughter of Christian parents, Kafutshi is a second-generation Christian of the Église du Christ au Zaire, Communauté Mennonite (CMZA; Zaire Mennonite Church). She was educated in the 1950s in the schools of Mukedi Station of the °°Congo Inland Mission (Africa Inter-

Mennonite Mission). She was married in her teens to Kakesa Khakha, the son of Christian parents from the same station. In the late 1960s she moved with her family to the Tshikapa church headquarters where her husband served as the first legal representative of the Zaire Mennonite Church. At the end of his term the family moved to Kikwit in Kwilu Province and became active in the local Mennonite congregation.

When asked to join a special traveling teaching team which was to hold seminars in a variety of Mennonite regional church centers, she at first declined. While she was eager to speak on the topic of Christian marriage and family life in the African context, she was concerned about disapproving reactions she would encounter. Strongly encouraged by other members of the team to accept the invitation, she finally agreed. Kafutshi is an excellent speaker and her presentations to groups made up mostly of men had a sharp impact and, as expected, stirred agitated response. Kafutshi, however, was quietly affirmed and encouraged by both the team members and her husband. Convinced of the justice of her call for a larger role and voice for women in the Zaire home and church, she did not yield ground.

In 1982 Kafutshi, almost single-handedly, convinced the General Assembly of the Zaire Mennonite Church delegates to recognize the women's organization as a department of the church in its own right.   JEB

Kake Elizabete came as a girl to Nyanga, a station of the °°Congo Inland Mission (Africa Inter-Mennonite Mission) in the West Kasai of the Belgian Congo (Zaire), to continue her grade school education. She married in her teens and soon bore a son. After some years her husband left her. Meanwhile, her son in early adulthood showed signs of mental instability. To support herself and her disabled son she took the opportunity offered by medical missionaries at Nyanga for training in midwifery.

From the beginning it became clear that quiet, self-effacing Kake wanted to learn the skills of midwifery well and that she brought to her work a concern and compassion for the women who came under her care. No hour was too early or too late for her to be roused from her bed if a prospective mother needed her. The tribe or social status of the woman made no difference to Kake; they were all her sisters, and they all received her sacrificial and loving care.

Unless prevented by her work at the maternity clinic, she was always in church for services and meetings of the women's group. For the annual women's harvest festival offering Kake always had her own woven hamper full of hand-threshed millet to give as an offering, millet she somehow found time to plant, cultivate, and harvest in the midst of her busy life. To learn to know her was to admire her, to be inspired by her, and to love her as a dear sister in the Lord. JEB

Kalona, Iowa, Old Order Amish Settlement (ME III:117) in Johnson and Washington Cos. in eastern Iowa. The first Amish settlers arrived in 1846, migrating from settlements in Maryland, Pennsylvania, and Ohio. Amish families who chose to push on west beyond the developing northern Indiana settlement located in this Iowa community because of its rich farming potential. The Kalona community is the largest Amish-Mennonite settlement west of the Mississippi River. The population is stable with seven church districts (congregations) serving more than 1,200 people. The Kalona settlement is known for its contribution of many persons who have gone on to become leaders in the Mennonite Church or who have distinguished themselves in the scholarly professions. A number of Amish families in 1914 left the Kalona area to establish a new community (°Hazelton) in Buchanan Co. 75 mi. (140 km.) to the north, in order to regain more traditional and conservative church discipline. SLY

Kamayala, Zaire. See Zaire.

Kampuchea (Cambodia) is a country in southeast Asia that was devastated by war and internal revolution in the 1970s. Mennonite Central Committee (MCC) placed its first representatives in the capital city of Phnom Penh in 1981 and became involved in health, agriculture, education, technical assistance, and emergency aid. The two MCC representatives are primarily aid administrators, since the Kampuchean government requires that all assistance be negotiated with appropriate ministries of the central government. Assistance has been concentrated in Svay Rieng and Prey Veng provinces. Short-term technical experts frequently lend their professional skills through MCC channels. Two Mennonite medical teams from India served in the MCC health program in Kampuchea, 1984-86. BS

Kanadier. The term *Kanadier* developed in Canada. It identified the Mennonites who immigrated from Russia in the 1870s, and distinguished them from those who immigrated during the 1920s (°Rußländer). The Kanadier Mennonites were shaped by difficult pioneer experiences, and by conflicts with provincial governments over control of schools and municipal organizations. Before World War I a number of divisions were created within Kanadier Mennonite churches by the activity of Mennonite missionaries from the United States.

Differences between Kanadier and Rußländer sometimes resulted in tensions. The most visible tension occured during World War II when Kanadier and Rußländer disagreed on how to relate to the Canadian government over the issue of exemption from military service. The two groups organized separate committees to relate to the government. The Kanadier committee, called the Ältesten Komitee (Committee of Elders) wanted complete exemption from military service for all men of military age. The

Rußländer committee, called the Military Problems Committee of Western Canada, was willing to offer to the government that their young men would do some form of alternative service, or even serve in the noncombatant medical corps of the army.

Since the 1970s the meaning of the term *Kanadier* has shifted, especially within MCC Canada. It is now used to refer to only a portion of the descendents of the 1870s immigration, namely those who are "conservers" (e.g., °Old Colony Mennonites and °Sommerfeld Mennonites). It includes the "conserver" Kanadier descendants in Canada, and also those who have emigrated to Mexico, Belize, Bolivia, Paraguay, and Argentina. Mennonite Central Committee (Canada) has formed a Kanadier Mennonite Colonization Committee to provide services for these groups. One of the services is the paper, *Die Mennonitische Post.* JF

F. H. Epp, *Mennonites in Canada II*, 242-45, 416-17.

See also Conservative Mennonites (Dutch-Prussian-Russian).

Kananga, Zaire. Situated approximately 790 air miles (1,250 km.) east of Kinshasa and 150 mi. (250 km.) east of °Tshikapa, Kananga is the second largest urban center of Zaire (its population exceeds 1,000,000) and serves as the provincial capital of the West Kasai Province. Situated astride a major rail line which runs from the copper mines of se. Zaire to the river port Ilebo in central Zaire, it is an important commercial center and features an airport which accommodates jet passenger and freight service to other major cities of the country.

Known as Luluabourg during the Belgian colonial era, Kananga has historically been the administrative and ministry center of the Southern Presbyterian Mission, whose area of work bordered that of the °°Congo Inland Mission (CIM; later Africa Inter-Mennonite Mission) to the east. Early Presbyterian missionaries played a key role in influencing Mennonites to enter a large unevangelized area to their west along the Kasai River in south central Congo. Across the years Mennonite Christians migrated to this growing city from the rural CIM stations at Djoko, Kalonda, and Mutena and became the core groups of Mennonite congregations which were to follow. Given the fact that both the Presbyterians and the Mennonites have long worked in an area of several million Tshiluba speaking people, joint ministry projects which served the needs and interests of both missions and related church groups developed early in the histories of these groups. These projects include a book store (LIPROKA), a press (IMPROKA), a recording studio for the preparation of Tshiluba language programs aired over the provincial government radio (STUDIPROKA), and a large hospital and nurses' training school (IMCK).

The Mennonite Church of Zaire (Église du Christ au Zaire, Communauté Mennonite; CMZA) has five congregations in the Kananga area and several primary schools (1986). The Evangelical Mennonite Church (Église du Christ au Zaire, Communauté Evangélique Mennonite; CEM) has one congregation in the city. JEB

Kandala, Zaire. See Zaire.

**Kanisa la Mennonite Tanzania (Tanzania Menno-
nite Church) (ME I:21).** In ME I Elam °Stauffer
summarized the establishment of Mennonite mission
work in various parts of Tanganyika, initially in an
area east of Lake Victoria (1934-40), later in other
parts of the territory (1940-50). From 1950 to 1954
the church experienced local expansion. Workers
were placed in Ikoma-Mugumu, and stations were
established at Kisaka, Tarime, and Musoma. Only in
1963 were workers were placed in Dar es Salaam.
Thus, for 30 years Mennonite efforts focused on a
two-county area, in part because applications to the
colonial government and respect for °comity with
other missions were obstacles to expansion.

Since 1970 the church has planted congregations
in Mwanza, Biharamulo, Arusha, Tabora, Dodoma,
and Sumbawanga. The church had 200 members in
1944, 1,000 in 1954, 4,000 in 1964, 10,000 in 1974,
13,000 in 1984, and 23,000 in 280 congregations by
1988. The accelerated rate of growth after 1964
resulted from ongoing revival, programs of special
training for leaders, and the transfer of leadership to
national leadership (first Tanzanian bishop in 1974).

Congregational Life and Relationships. Elam
Stauffer led the missionaries in efforts to establish a
"self-supporting, self-propagating, and self-governing
church," the classic marks of °indigenization in the
missionary tradition. Human efforts were fruitless
and God intervened through revival. In 1942 he
hovered over clusters of Christians at Mugango, at
Nyabasi, and at Shirati, calling them to repent of
their sins and to rely upon the indwelling Christ. In
1946 he reawakened them with concern for the
body of Christ; he called them to remove barriers
and walk in fellowship, to help and encourage one
another. In both awakenings Stauffer led the people
in responding to the Spirit. Sometimes he, sometimes they, came short and made mistakes. But God
faithfully called them back, creating a quality of fellowship in which black and white, tribe and tribe,
worked together in building the church.

Self-Propagation. Walking with Jesus, believers
give witness in whatever they do. In the 1930s and
1940s home visitation was common. Annual spiritual
life conferences provided nurture and fellowship.
Each district established worship centers in new
places; they recruited potential workers into
Bukiroba Bible School.

The calling of national pastors and deacons added
impetus to evangelistic outreach. Many of those baptized during the 1950s and 1960s had been won
through weekly Bible classes in schools. Congregational youth groups and Christian groups in boarding
schools provided mutual pastoral care, a springboard
for evangelism. Since the 1970s, youth choirs have
sung in weekly worship, in special conferences, and
in marketplaces.

Self-Government. At the beginning all members
shared in congregational decisions. As numbers increased, elders were chosen to assist in pastoral
care. They also served in congregational and district
councils; they chose representatives to General
Church Council (GCC). In 1946 the council began
to write a church polity. A committee was chosen to
help with difficult marriage problems and another to
give counsel in matters of evangelism. Other committees are formed as needed.

In 1947 the church had to choose whether to participate in the developing national education system.
Recognizing that the decision should be made by
Tanganyikans, the mission called a joint session with
the GCC, promising to support the council in its
choice. The first Tanganyikan pastors and deacons
were called by their respective districts—in 1950
Ezekiel °Muganda and Andrea Mabeba were ordained at Mugango and Zedekia °Kisare and Nashon
Nyambok at Shirati. During the decade that followed, 17 more pastors and deacons were ordained.
During this period consensus developed for the
name, Tanganyika Mennonite Church (TMC). As
need arose, the bishop called meetings of the ordained leaders to handle matters of doctrine, church
°polity and the °discipline of ordained persons. The
first bishop was chosen in a meeting of this type,
and since then, all candidates for ordination have
been chosen in these sessions. Overall administration continued to be handled by GCC. In preparation for autonomy, the GCC officers served with the
mission officers.

The constitution drafted by a GCC committee did
not satisfy bishops of the Lancaster Mennonite Conference (MC), the sponsoring North American conference for the Tanganyikan Mennonite mission. At
issue were matters of separation from the world and
refusal of military service. The bishops offered suggested revisions through fraternal delegates to a
special meeting of the GCC. The council offered its
own revisions and adopted its constitution on Aug.
25, 1960. The church now became a church conference (*mkutano mkuu*) with an executive committee
(*komiti kuu* to handle matters between annual meetings. After the church received government registration, properties were transferred and the mission
dissolved. In 1961 the church sent Ezekiel Muganda
and Zedekia Kisare on a three-month fraternal visit
to North America. This helped develop stronger ties
between the conferences and congregations.

The Mennonite Theological College, established in
1962, provided special training for key leaders. This
group assisted Stauffer and his assistant, Simeon
Hurst, in developing a simple °worship liturgy. The
bishops also spent two weeks in each district training congregational leaders. The church participated
in the formation of the °Africa Mennonite and
Brethren in Christ Fellowship and began developing
relationships with the Anabaptist churches across
Africa.

In 1966 Zedekia Kisare was chosen as first national bishop. This was a time of celebration; prayer and
waiting had brought reconciliation and agreement.
In 1972 the church revised its constitution and
adopted a Swahili name, *Kanisa la Mennonite Tanzania* (KMT), although "Tanzania Mennonite Church
(TMC)" is also used. The ordination of a second
bishop, Hezekiah °Sarya, in 1979 was followed by
the formation of two dioceses. Bishop Kisare was
given oversight of the areas with large Luo populations, North Mara Diocese and Kenya, and Bishop
Sarya of the Southern Diocese.

Self-Support. To help establish a self-supporting
church, each catechumen and Christian was given a
card on which weekly offerings were recorded. Tithing was taught and special offerings were received

at harvest, at Easter communion, and at Christmas. Each bush school pupil paid fees. Missionaries contributed from their tithes. Each district treasury supported evangelist-teachers, helped needy people, and maintained church buildings. Special funds were raised for erecting new buildings.

The move toward total self-support followed some debate between the missionaries and national leaders. In 1950 the newly ordained leaders thought they would be absorbed into the mission, whereas the missionaries were speaking of withdrawal. The missionaries opened the mission accounts to their national colleagues, and directed some overseas funds to the church's evangelistic efforts. The Tanganyikan church responded by working to do its part, for example giving a week of free labor to make possible the church's first boarding school at Bumangi. In the euphoria of national independence, the church was influenced by the political slogan, "aid without strings." Against advice, overseas funds were used to subsidize the wages of pastors. To overcome such dependency the church adopted a five-year development plan proposed by interim bishop Donald Jacobs. One goal was that each district support its own leaders. In the first year, despite droughts, floods, and cattle disease, offerings increased 50 percent. But continuing drought, the worldwide oil crisis, and war against Amin of Uganda contributed to long-term economic decline. A few pastors began to teach stewardship; in those congregations offerings doubled. By calling as pastors those who had sources of income other than church funds, the team of pastors was enlarged. As of 1988, the church leadership is not dependent on overseas subsidy.

Service Ministries. *Ministries to Women and Girls.* Each station held weekly sewing and Bible classes to attract women to the church. Women's conferences enlarged their circle of friendship and gave help on spiritual issues. In time the women's groups were structured to develop leadership skills. In many places church women, Mennonites included, gave leadership to the women's progress groups promoted by the political party.

In the first two decades each station provided a home where girls from pagan environments could grow up in a Christian setting; the homes at Shirati and Mugango gave some training in homemaking. Since 1964, domestic science courses at Bukiroba have been popular.

Whereas in the 1940s one-third of those attending church were women, by the 1970s they numbered two-thirds. A few women have been called as congregational elders or lay leaders in worship centers.

Medical Ministries. Mennonites in Tanzania have been diligent in ministry to the sick. Within a year Shirati had a dispensary staffed by a doctor and nurse and within 20 years a full-fledged hospital and leprosarium. After 18 years the leprosarium could be closed because new patients with leprosy (Hansen's Disease) received medication in local dispensaries and the enlarged hospital provided treatment for the advanced cases. Since 1964 Shirati Hospital has been the base for significant research and since 1974 has been conducting maternal child health clinics, part of a nationwide preventive ministry.

From the beginning there was training for medical aides. A nurses' training school was launched in 1960; midwifery was added in 1970. Each of the other five stations also moved beyond the dispensing of pills and established dispensaries. Bedded dispensaries were developed at Nyabasi, Mugango, and Kisaka. For a time some remote churches were served by a medical van or flying doctor service. For the past 50 years health ministries in Mara Region have contributed to population growth, the decline in incidence of Hansen's Disease, and some control of malaria. The Christian witness during medical assistance has brought some to the faith.

Educational Ministries. The Mennonites operated a network of bush schools in which first-generation church and community leaders got their start. Successful bush schools developed into primary schools. The first two registered primary schools were established in 1947. Through the participation of the churches, in 10 years the nation had half of its children in primary school. After the nationalization of education in 1970 the Tanzania Mennonite Church turned over 44 primary schools. Mennonites shared in developing two graded Bible courses used throughout the nation. Teacher training was perhaps the church's most important educational ministry. Across the nation Christian schools, primary and secondary, set the pace in character, academics, and sports. The Mennonites participated in the alliance that managed Katoke Teacher Training College and Kahororo Secondary School, Bukoba; they became a managing partner in Musoma Alliance Secondary School. The church sponsored students in Mennonite colleges and in vocational trainee programs.

Mutual involvement in service ministries, particularly education, helped the churches grow in unity. They began to learn from one another's heritage, a cross-fertilization which included the Roman Catholics. Together the churches trained many of the nation's leaders.

Literature Ministries. Mjumbe wa Kristo (Messenger of Christ, 1938-) featured testimonies and Bible expositions. After the 1946 reawakening *Mjumbe* became a channel of communication for the revival fellowship with wide circulation. In the mid-1960s *Sauti ya TMC* (Voice of TMC) was launched with a major focus on TMC news. The economic hardships of the 1970s brought the demise of both.

Mennonite missionaries gave a hand in Bible translation, in compiling hymnals, and in preparing °literacy primers—in the Jita, Zanaki, and Kurya languages. They helped with a Swahili primer for use nationwide and assisted in training literacy teachers in Mara Region. Two hymnals and three primers were printed on the hand-fed press at Bukiroba. The Mennonite catechism and supplement were produced in both Swahili and Luo. *Tenzi za Rohoni* (Spiritual Songs), released in 1950, was quickly picked up by revival fellowships; most denominations use it as a supplementary hymnal. A colportage effort in the cotton markets of Majita developed into a fruitful ministry. Musoma Bookshop was established in 1960.

Community Development. Tanzanian Mennonites learned some modern agricultural practices from missionary gardens and government extension service. A number gave leadership in community cooperatives. When Tanzania began moving rural peoples into village settlements, church youth launched a small farm which developed into a settlement. Ten miles (16 km.) away a Bumangi group functioned within another settlement. While small voluntary settlements had prospered, compulsory settlement did not work and the policy was withdrawn. Traditional agricultural methods are being taken more seriously.

By the later 1950s fewer than half of primary school graduates could find opportunity for further study. The Mennonites in Majita and Shirati experimented with establishing community schools, but failed. In the early 1980s a small vocational school was launched by Nyabasi Mennonites. °Mennonite Economic Development Associates (MEDA) made resources available for a score of projects in the mid-1960s. While this gesture of brotherhood was welcomed, only a few caught the MEDA vision and succeeded.

North Mara Diocese (Dayosisi Ya Mara Kaskazini). Established in 1980, the North Mara Diocese comprised only the political district of Tarime, plus responsibility for the churches in sw. Kenya and in the city of Nairobi, Kenya. As of August 1988 Kisumu and Migori, Kenya, will become autonomous dioceses, so North Mara is projecting expansion into new areas. North Mara Diocese's membership in Tanzania was 7,000 in 1987. Each of the 85 congregations has a lay leader plus congregational counselors. General oversight is provided by 6 deacons, 9 ministers, and Bishop Zedekia Kisare. Steps are underway for additional ordinations in 1988.

A three-year program of training for lay leaders has just been completed; it took the form of °theological education by extension (TEE), in which each person studied at home and participated in monthly seminars in his district. In the next phase, the classes will be open to all interested people, with the pastors giving leadership. Training on higher levels will be arranged for those who did well in the basic courses. The women's auxiliary is also taking its seminars to the rural areas.

Evangelism happens through person-to-person encounters, through weekend conferences (youth choirs attract crowds to evening services), and through Bible classes in the public schools. Occasionally an evangelistic team will spend several days in a community; such teams include someone qualified to dispense medicines.

Medical ministries stem from the 150-bed Shirati Hospital, with its medical, surgical, maternity, pediatrics, and leprosy departments plus out-patient and maternal child health clinics. The hospital supervises the Nyabasi bedded dispensary and maternity unit and several rural dispensaries. Shirati participates in medical research, particularly on control of malaria and causes of cancer. Currently being launched is the training of village health promoters, a link in the government's effort to make primary health care available to all communities. These "barefoot doctors" will promote health and hygiene, dispense simple medicines, and refer the seriously-ill to a medical institution.

The hospital has spearheaded such community development projects as the bringing of public electricity to Shirati and extending the water supply to surrounding villages. Irrigation by solar power has proved feasible and additional agricultural projects are being developed. The next focus will be on small projects using local resources (°appropriate technology). A community center is being established at Shirati to provide facilities for women's activities, preschool classes, and youth groups, a conference center, library, and diocesan offices.

Overall planning for the diocese and coordination of activities takes place through an annual conference, its executive committee, several standing committees, and an occasional meeting of the ordained leaders. Participation in the Christian Council of Tanzania (CCT) provides fellowship, vision, resources, and opportunity for joint action and for dialog with political leaders. The diocese is enriched by fellowship and brotherly address in the Council of East African Mennonite Churches, African Mennonite and Brethren in Christ Fellowship, and Mennonite World Conference.

Southern Diocese (Dayosisi Ya Kusini). As defined in 1980, the Southern Diocese includes the political districts of Musoma, Bunda, and Serengeti, plus a number of urban congregations. Membership in 126 congregations was 13,000 in 1987. Pastoral care is provided by 126 lay leaders, plus congregational counselors, and general oversight by 14 deacons, 21 ministers, and Bishop Hezekiah Sarya. This diocese has strengthened its leadership by enlisting self-supporting people as part-time pastors. Thought is being given to dividing into smaller dioceses.

Theological education by extension Bible studies and monthly seminars are being provided for lay leaders of the congregations located within normal driving distances. It is hoped to assign one pastor to establish the program in each of the scattered districts. For those who excel in TEE, Bukiroba Bible School is to be reopened on an inter-diocesan basis. The school of domestic science at Bukiroba continues to attract many.

There is person-to-person evangelism. Three-day spiritual life conferences, with youth choirs participating, are held at harvest time, at baptisms and communions, at Christmas and Easter. Bible teachers go to the public schools, primary and higher, and to hospitals and prisons. Efforts are made to follow up Mennonites in towns across the nation, encouraging them to meet in worship and to reach out to others. The Dar es Salaam congregation is undertaking ministries among Muslims and youth. Some districts work with Tanzania Bible Society in distribution of the Scriptures.

As another contribution to nation-building, the church supervised the building of government's Mugumu Designated District Hospital and provided a doctor. Opened in 1980, this modern 90-bed institution provides medical, surgical, maternity, and pediatric services and a daily out-patient clinic. Supervision is given to the church's dispensaries at Bukiroba, Mugango, Bumangi, and Kisaka. The hospital will share in the training of village promoters of primary health care. Church leaders have been active in pastoral ministry to staff and patients.

The diocese operates a press, a bookshop, and a hostel-conference center. Diocesan personnel supervised the building of Bunda Teacher Training College; a Mennonite chaplain-teacher serves on the staff. Some congregations, and the women's auxiliary, have launched small projects using local resources and appropriate technology: pottery, agriculture, cabinet-making, masonry and carpentry, grinding of grain, selling staple foods, fishing, water supply, etc. Mennonite Central Committee volunteers who live in the church communities provide help and encouragement.

An annual conference, its executive committee, standing committees, and an occasional meeting of the ordained leaders provide overall planning and coordination of activities for the diocese. This diocese, like North Mara, contributes to and receives from the interchurch activities of Christian Council of Tanzania and in the inter-Mennonite bodies: the Council of East African Mennonite Churches, Africa Mennonite and Brethren in Christ Fellowship, and Mennonite World Conference.   MMH

MWH (1978), 85-90, 100-103; MWH (1984), 16-17; George R. Anchak, "Experience in the Paradox of Indigenous Church Building: History of the Eastern Mennonite Mission in Tanganyika, 1934-1961" (PhD thesis, Michigan State U., 1975); Eastern Mennonite Board of Missions and Charities files at Salunga, Pa., and Miss. Mess.; Merle W. Eshleman, Africa Answers (Scottdale, 1951); Marwa Z. Kisare, and Joseph C. Shenk, Kisare, A Mennonite of Kiseru (Salunga, Pa.: EMBMC, 1984; Mahlon Hess, Pilgrimage of Faith: The Tanzania Mennonite Church, 1934-1983 (Salunga: EMBMC, 1984); originally appeared in Swahili as Safari Ya Imani); Paul N. Kraybill, ed. Called to Be Sent (Scottdale, 1964), 55-65, 115-22, 162-67, 172-81; Catharine Leatherman, Ye Are God's Building (Salunga, Pa.: EMBMC, 1959); Josiah Muganda, "The Impact of the Mennonite Mission on Mara Region, Tanzania, 1934-67" (MA diss., Howard U., 1978); David W. Shenk, Mennonite Safari (Scottdale, 1974); Dorothy Smoker, and Merle W. Eshleman, God Led Us to Tanganyika (Salunga, Pa.: EMBMC, 1956); Elam W. Stauffer, "Account of God's Working at Shirati, August 1942," unpublished manuscript, copy at EMBMC; Ada M. Zimmerman, and Catharine Leatherman, Africa Calls (Scottdale, 1937); Grace Wenger, "Eastern Mennonite Board of Missions and Charities, 1894-1980," unpublished manuscript available at Lancaster Mennonite Historical Society.

See also Kenya Mennonite Church.

Kansas (ME III:143). The Mennonite population and institutions of Kansas have exhibited many continuities over the past 30 years. The Mennonite church membership in Kansas was 21,417 in 1985, compared with a total of 18,294 in 1955. Mennonites constitute roughly one percent of the population of Kansas.

Kansas has 109 Mennonite congregations (including 5 Old Order Amish congregations or "districts") representing 10 Mennonite groups, compared with 108 congregations and 9 groups in 1955. The Western District Conference is the largest district of the General Conference Mennonite Church with 70 congregations and 14,000 members. Of this total, 47 congregations with 11,776 members are in Kansas (53 — 11,118). (The number of congregations and membership from 1954 or 1955 are given in parentheses). The Mennonite Brethren have 16 congregations in Kansas with 3,600 members (13 — 2,449, including 3 Krimmer Mennonite Brethren congregations); Church of God in Christ, Mennonite 19 and

3,145 (14 — 1,917); Evangelical Mennonite Brethren, 1 and 133 (2 — 297; Evangelical Mennonite Church, 1 and 222 (1 — 143); Conservative Mennonites, 3 and 188 (1 — 113); Brethren in Christ, 4 and 280 (5 — 240); Mennonite Church, 18 and 2,358 (13 — 1,575); Beachy Amish, 2 and 298 (no listing); and Old Order Amish, 5 districts and about 400 members (6 districts — 386).

These statistics do not reveal several significant changes. Nearly one-third of the Mennonite congregations existing in 1955 were extinct in 1985, and an almost equal number of new congregations have been established since that date. The rural Mennonite communities have generally experienced declining population with many of the smaller congregations, especially those in western Kansas, closing or moving to nearby urban centers. The congregations established during the past 30 years tend to be in urban centers such as Kansas City, Topeka, Wichita, Manhattan, Lawrence, and Newton. Included in this number are several °"house" churches and university fellowships with different patterns of organization, leadership and commitment. Also of special interest are several congregations affiliated with two or more of the Mennonite groups. Six congregations belong to both the South Central Conference (MC) and the Western District Conference (GCM). One congregation, the Manhattan Mennonite Fellowship, maintains this dual affiliation and also a third membership in the Southern District (MB). The dual-conference congregations represent growing cooperation on various projects and levels between the General Conference Mennonite Church and the Mennonite Church.

Central Kansas remains a major Mennonite educational and organizational center. Bethel, Tabor and Hesston Colleges not only educate the youth of the General Conference, Mennonite Brethren, and Mennonite Church respectively, but also provide a vast array of cultural programs and continuing education activities for their constituencies. The General Conference headquarters in Newton have expanded several times since the 1950s, and the Western District of the General Conference now maintains its offices in North Newton. The Mennonite Press (also Faith and Life Press) operated by Bethel College and the General Conference, has recently moved from North Newton to facilities at the Newton airport. The Mennonite Library and Archives, sponsored by Bethel College and the General Conference, has moved into expanded facilities within the Mantz Library (dedicated October 5, 1986) on the Bethel College campus. The Center for Mennonite Brethren Studies at Tabor College, organized in 1974, serves as the archival center for Mennonite Brethren congregations in the United States, excluding the Pacific District. Mennonite Brethren Bible and seminary education has shifted from Hillsboro to Fresno, Cal., and in 1979 Tabor College became an area college operated by a Senate with representatives from the Southern, Central, North Carolina, and Latin American (South Texas) Mennonite Brethren districts. The Mennonite Brethren Publishing House in Hillsboro was sold in 1982, but The Christian Leader office remains in Hillsboro. The national offices of the Mennonite Brethren Board of Missions are in

Hillsboro and Winnipeg. Mennonite Central Committee (MCC) operates a regional office with a clothing distribution center in North Newton.

The ethnic and religious distinctiveness of the Kansas Mennonites has continued to erode since the 1950s. Only a few conservative groups maintain their own schools, °plain dress, or °German language. The manifestations of °nonconformity have nearly all disappeared. Kansas Mennonites have entered the various modern °professions and experienced virtually every °modern social problem. While many Mennonites are distinguished from the general population by their strong social consciousness and °service ethic, the Mennonite emphasis on °nonresistance has dwindled within most groups. A variety of celebrations promote Mennonite culture and ethnic food.

Nevertheless, Kansas Mennonites are leaders in promoting °peace education and social involvement. A vast array of °hospitals, retirement °homes, and other institutions in central Kansas operate with direct or indirect ties to Mennonite congregations or conferences. Mennonites minister to inmates in prisons and provide assistance to those afflicted by natural disasters through Mennonite Disaster Service. Prairie View, a mental hospital founded by MCC east of Newton, continues its leadership in °mental health care. A few Mennonite institutions have closed, such as Bethesda Hospital in Goessel, creating a deep sense of loss within communities. New institutions, e.g., the Kidron retirement community in North Newton, have continued the impact of Mennonite institutions on the quality of life in central Kansas.   DAH

Dennis D. Engbrecht, "The Americanization of a Rural Immigrant Church: The General Conference Mennonites in Central Kansas, 1874-1939" (PhD diss., U. of Nebraska, 1985); Paul Erb, South Central Frontiers: A History of the South Central Mennonite Conference (Scottdale, 1974); David A. Haury, Prairie People: A History of the Western District Conference (Newton, 1981); James C. Juhnke, A People of Two Kingdoms: The Political Acculturation of the Kansas Mennonites (Newton, 1975); David V. Wiebe, They Seek a Country: A Survey of Mennonite Migrations (Freeman: Pine Hill Press, 1974 ed.); Edward A. Dyck, Riesen and Dyck: Hardware and Implements (Hutchinson: Edward A. Dyck, 1984); Jacob D. Goering and Robert Williams, "Generational Drift on Four Variables Among the Swiss-Volhynian Mennonites in Kansas," MQR, 50 (1976), 290-97; Leland Harder, A Joint Study of Four Hillsboro-Lehigh Area Churches in Kansas (typescript, 1964); Orlando Harms, Pioneer Publisher: The Life and Times of J. F. Harms (Winnipeg: Kindred Press, 1984); David A Haury, "Bernhard Warkentin: a Mennonite Benefactor," MQR, 49 (1975), 179-202; idem, A People of the City: A History of the Lorraine Avenue Mennonite Church, 1932-82 (Wichita: Lorraine Avenue Mennonite Church, 1982); Clarence Hiebert, ed., Brothers in Deed to Brothers in Need: A Scrapbook about Mennonite Immigrants from Russia 1870-1885 (Newton, 1974); A Hstory of the First Mennonite Church: Pretty Prairie, Kansas (Pretty Prairie: Prairie Publications, 1983; Justus G. Holsinger, Upon this Rock: Remembering Together the Seventy-five Year Story of Hesston Mennonite Church (Hesston: Hesston Mennonite Church, 1984); "Kansas Mennonite Settlements, Part II: Illustrations," Menn. Life, 25 (April 1970), 65-80; Cornelius Krahn, "A Centennial Chronology, Part One and Part Two," Menn. Life, 28 (May-June, 1973), 3-9, 40-45; idem, "Mennonite Centennial Publications," Menn. Life, 29 (May-June 1974), 47; idem, "Views of the 1870s Migrations by Contemporaries," MQR, 48 (1974), 447-59; Christian Krehbiel, Prairie Pioneer: The Christian Krehbiel story (Newton, 1961); David Aldan McQuillan, "Adaptation of Three Immigrant Groups to Farming in Central Kansas, 1875-1925" (PhD diss., U. of Wisconsin, 1975); Joseph S. Miller, Beyond the Mystic Border: the Pennsylvania Mennonite Congregation near Zimmeredale, Kansas (MA thesis, Villanova University, 1984); Peace, Progress, Promise: A 75th Anniversary History of Tabor Mennonite Church (Newton: Tabor Mennonite Church, 1983); "Pioneers, Wheat, and Faith. Centennial Photo Section." Menn. Life, 29 (May-June 1974), 24-29; Marion Keeney Preheim, The Story of Faith: Twenty-five Years, 1958-1983 (Newton: Faith Mennonite Church, 1983); Abraham Ratzlaff, Diary of the Reverend Abraham Ratzlaff (North Newton: Bethel College, 1983); Abraham Ratzlaff, Memoirs of the Reverend Abraham Ratzlaff (North Newton: Bethel College, 1983); Laurine A. Rogers, "Phylogenetic Identification of a Religious Isolate and the Measurement of Inbreeding" (PhD diss., U. of Kansas, 1984); C. B. Schmidt, "Kansas Mennonite Settlements, 1877 Part I: Text," 25, Menn. Life, (April 1970), 51-58; Lester D. Schrag, "Elementary and Secondary Education as Practiced by Kansas Mennonites," (PhD diss., U. of Wyoming, 1970); Gail Niles Stucky, A Guide to Congregational Records in the Western District Conference (North Newton: Bethel College, 1983); Phillip P. Stucky, Heritage and Memories of Phillip P. Stucky (Seattle: Phillip P. Stucky, 1984); Frieda Pankratz Suderman, Commitment and Reaffirmation: the First Mennonite Church, Hillsboro, Kansas (Hillsboro: First Mennonite Church, 1983); Swiss-German Cultural and Historical Association,. A Study Guide of the Swiss Mennonites Who Came to Kansas in 1874 (Kansas: Swiss-German Cultural and Historical Association, 1974); for additional congregational histories (to 1981), see Haury, Prairie People.

See also Acculturation; Politics; Publishing.

Karaganda, a city of ca. 650,000 inhabitants, is located in the heart of the steppes of the °Kazakhstan Soviet Socialist Republic in the U.S.S.R. The city was founded in the 1930s and has become the coal mining center of the Soviet Union. From its beginning Mennonites, especially ministers, were exiled there as criminals. In 1941 the entire °°Alexandertal (Alt-Samara) settlement was exiled to this area.

A small Baptist congregation was founded in the city immediately following World War II. This also served the spiritual needs of many homeless Mennonites. After 1956, when Germans were allowed to move more freely, a steady stream of Mennonites who had been scattered throughout the land came to Karaganda. The first Mennonite Brethren congregation was founded here in December 1956 and grew to a membership of 900 by 1958. A Mennonite church (°kirchliche Mennoniten) was also established, both congregations working cordially with each other. In 1967 both congregations were registered with the Ministry of Cults. The Mennonite Brethren congregation was permitted to build its own house of worship, which the Mennonite church also used. Since 1986 the latter have their own meetinghouse. Preaching and singing is done exclusively in German in both congregations, but exceptions are made at weddings and funerals since Russian-speaking visitors also participate. The probability of increasing use of the Russian language is clear.

Membership in the Mennonite Brethren congregation exceeded 1,000 in 1986. Choirs, Sunday school activities for children, and youth work are carried out. The Mennonite church congregation is not as large. A second Mennonite Brethren congregation, unregistered, meets in private homes throughout the city. Circa 20,000 of the 70-80,000 German inhabitants of the city are of Mennonite background.   HWö

Heinrich Wölk and Gerhard Wölk, Die Mennoniten Brüdergemeinde in Rußland, 1925-1980 (Fresno: Center for

MB Studies, 1981), Engl. transl. as A *Wilderness Journey* (Fresno, 1982).

Karlsruhe, Germany. Founded 1715 as the administrative residence of the Duke of Baden-Durlach and Baden-Baden (after 1771); after 1806 capital of the Grand-Duchy; and, from 1918-45, capital of the State of Baden, Karlsruhe is the administrative, scientific, educational, and economic center of the Upper Rhine. In it are located a number of significant buildings, including the baroque Palace and the Schwarzwaldhalle (Black Forest Hall), in which the sixth Mennonite World Conference was held (1957). The state archives contain significant Anabaptist and Mennonite documents.

Anabaptist groups were present in the Karlsruhe area from 1527 to 1604, with Mennonite refugees from Switzerland settling there after 1722. From 1790 to 1890 Mennonite families from the °Kraichgau began renting and settling on estates in the area, e.g., Hohenwettersbach, Batzenhof, Lamprechtshof and Rittnerthof. By 1900 they were also locating in Karlsruhe and Durlach itself.

Since 1960 the Durlach Mennonite congregation (°ME II:111) has met in the retreat center *Thomashof* near Karlsruhe and is known as the Mennonite congregation of Karlsruhe-Thomashof. Since 1975 two elders carry responsibility for the congregation (Adolf Schnebele, preaching; Heini Bachmann, congregational leader) together with an elected advisory committee and a volunteer committee. Membership in 1986 was 136.

The *Thomashof* (ME IV:716) is a retreat and Bible study center, supported since 1962 by the 22 congregations of the Verband der deutschen Mennonitengemeinden (Federation of the German Mennonite Congregations). Additions to the buildings in 1956, 1966, and 1985 made possible an enlarged ministry to Mennonites in the form of church retreats, a vacation center, and since 1960, a meeting place for the Mennonite congregation Karlsruhe-Thomashof. The retreat center has 55 beds, the retirement home 40 beds. Since 1904 the Thomashof has also served as the center for °°deaconesses, of whom only one was still living in 1986.   TGlü

TA Baden/Pfalz; *MM* (Oct. 1984), 5-8; Adolf Schnebele, "Geschichte des Bibelheims der Mennoniten," *Gemeinde Unterwegs* (May, 1984).

Karlstadt, Andreas Rudolff-Bodenstein von (1486-1541), a scion of Franconian nobility, became the first Reformer to develop a baptist theology. He wielded a seminal influence, especially among nonresistant Anabaptists. Upon leaving Franconia, he took on the name "Karlstadt," after his native town. He studied at the modernist University of Erfurt (BA 1502), the Thomist University of Cologne, and the newly founded University of Wittenberg (MA 1505). He earned a doctorate in theology from Wittenberg (1510) and a doctorate in canon and civil law (*utriusque juris*) from the Sapienza in Rome (1515-16).

During his teaching career at Wittenberg (1505-22) Karlstadt at first blended Thomism and Scotism and absorbed medieval mysticism when he annotated the Sermons then attributed solely to Tauler (Augsburg: 1508). Luther's publication of the

Theologia Deutsch in 1516 was also influential. Karlstadt's *Gelassen* (1520), *Gelassenheyt* (1522), *Sabbat* (1524), and *Axiomata* (1535) demonstrate the persistence of mystical ideas.

Prodded by Luther to purchase Augustine's writings in 1517, Karlstadt proclaimed the reformation of his thought on 26 April 1517, when he nailed his *151 Theses* to the door of the Church of All Saints (the "Castle Church"). Although Luther influenced Karlstadt, their paths never fully converged.

Karlstadt's first major contribution came from his preoccupation with hermeneutics. As a result of his long-term study of Hebrew, he declared the Apocrypha to be non-binding (*Scripturis*: 1518-20). The first sign of his social concerns came in his public attack on mendicancy. He publicly denounced papal supremacy in 1520 (a year after Luther). However, he attacked conciliarism well before Luther (1515-16). He gradually moved from the thirteenth to the sixth century in dating the Fall of the Roman church. He saw the alternative as the *heuflein gottes*, the true church of the sainted few—a believers' church, congregationally led and governed. In *Gewaldt* (1521), Karlstadt denounced the use of force on behalf of the church, since it is in the nature of the church to endure violence.

Crucial was Karlstadt's lifelong dissent from predestinarianism. Karlstadt held that human inability is met by God's enabling power. This freely grants to all the power to choose, during the moment of discernment between good and evil—whether in this life or in a flameless purgatory in the afterlife. Also seeing human choice and divine enabling power as preceding baptism, Karlstadt had to reject infant baptism.

In May and June 1521, Karlstadt was in Denmark, advising King Christian II. He stimulated the enactment of legislation curbing the power of bishops, exempting only *married* clergy from taxation, reforming the monasteries, and disallowing appeals to Rome. This established the Danish national church.

Later in 1521, Karlstadt demanded that all clergy be married. He abrogated all his own monastic vows and become the first professor at Wittenberg to marry (January, 1522). He recognized that his reasons for opposing monastic vows voided all vows and the swearing of all oaths.

Karlstadt also opposed churchly images as prohibited by Moses and Paul, because they imbue the people with superstition and fear. He advocated their legal removal. However, when a new town council reneged on promises made by its predecessor, and students broke some images, Karlstadt neither participated with nor condemned the students. His *Bylder* (1522) was to be used as the basis of Ludwig Hätzer's *Ein urteil gottes* (1523). By January 1522, Karlstadt was also promoting social reform, including opposition to compulsory greater and lesser tithes.

His involvement as Archdeacon of the Church of All Saints kept Karlstadt from being a merely academic theologian. On Christmas 1521, without vestments, he conducted the first publicly reformed communion. He omitted the elevation of the bread and wine, expunged the canon and all sacrificial references from the Mass, and shouted in German (rather than whispering in Latin) the words of institution.

These reforms led to friction with Frederick the Elector and Luther, who now returned from the Wartburg and temporarily restored Roman practice. No longer being allowed to publish freely, and having been made the butt of Luther's *Invocavit Sermons*, Karlstadt withdrew to Orlamünde to establish his own reformation. The organ was removed from the church. Psalm singing by the congregation in the vernacular was substituted. Infant baptism was no longer practiced. Up to three members of the congregation were allowed to prophesy in the service. Karlstadt, meanwhile, took to farming, though he still led the little flock as "Brother Andrew," the minister whose congregational call had been divinely confirmed by the casting of lots.

In 1523, Karlstadt fully repudiated the intercession of the saints, even of the Virgin Mary. Until his expulsion in August 1524, Karlstadt composed six treatises on the Lord's Supper and one on baptism. Karlstadt and his brother-in-law, Gerhard Westerburg, then visited Conrad Grebel and Felix Mantz and their followers in Zurich, who raised the necessary financial support to have the treatises printed. From late October till early November 1524 (while Karlstadt was secretly lodged at the house of Lorenz Hochrütiner) Westerburg, Mantz, and probably Andreas Castelberger had the six works dealing with the Lord's Supper printed. This permanently rended the unity of Protestantism.

Karlstadt left Basel, entrusting the manuscript of *Dialogus Vom Tauff* to Mantz, who tried to have it printed. However, both Johannes Bebel and Thomas Wolf, who had printed the other tracts, rebuffed him. On the basis of historical, theological, and philological evidence, Mantz's *Protestation* on baptism to the Zurich council appears to have been based on the manuscript of Karlstadt's dialogue. Frustrated by the loss of the first manuscript, Karlstadt composed another dialogue, which he published anonymously in 1527. He felt grateful for Mantz's earlier efforts, so a major participant in the new dialogue was named "Felix."

Karlstadt had already in 1523 demanded that baptism be administered only upon repentance and amendment of life as signs of dying and rising with Christ. Thus he no longer baptized infants during his final year (1523-24) in Orlamünde. He was, however, a baptist, not an Anabaptist, for he did not baptize adults who had been baptized as infants. In that he resembled the mainline reformers, who also accepted Roman baptism as valid, despite its errors. Karlstadt was a transitional figure, but where he prevailed, his spiritual children became (Ana)baptists.

During the Peasant Revolt, Karlstadt found refuge in Rothenburg on the Tauber, but in the summer of 1525 he fled to Wittenberg. Forced to make his peace with Luther, his creativity as a theologian came to a halt. In 1529 he sought refuge with Melchior Hoffman in Holstein and composed with him the *Dialogus* on the trial of Hoffman in Flensburg. Karlstadt's writings, especially his doctrine of the church, had already left a remarkable imprint on Hoffman's theology.

Being driven out of Holstein, and unwelcome in Strassburg and Basel, Karlstadt, for the sake of his starving family, made his peace with Huldrych Zwingli. In June 1534 he was called to Basel, where he spent the last seven years of his life as Professor of Old Testament, rector of the university, and pastor of the University Church of Saint Peter.

To what extent did Karlstadt compromise his baptist insights during his final years in Switzerland? Obviously he had not capitulated to Luther from 1525-29. However, he was received kindly in the Swiss confederacy, and the Reformed churches stood closer to him than did Luther. One way to gauge Karlstadt's influence in Basel is to compare the First Confession of Basel (1534), before his arrival with the Second Confessin of Basel (1536), also known as the First Helvetic Confession. Although the Anabaptists were still reproached for secessionism and unspecified heretical teachings in the Second Confession, no special section was devoted to them anymore. Neither were their views on infant baptism described as an "abomination" and a "blasphemy."

The outright rejection of the Anabaptist position on oaths of 1534 was now (1536) replaced with an affirmation of oaths "where they are manifestly not opposed to Christ." This accommodated Karlstadt perfectly. Finally, in the Second Confession the section on predestination was worded so ambiguously that it could embrace both a Reformed and a Karlstadtian interpretation. Double predestination was opposed by implication with Karlstadt's favorite text: "Our salvation is from God, but from ourselves is nothing but sin and damnation."

While in Basel, Karlstadt promoted a compromise with the Lutherans on the Lord's Supper. He was accused of knowingly harboring unreconstructed Roman Catholics and Anabaptists in his congregation. He ministered to all during the plague of 1541, to which he himself on Christmas eve fell victim.

For over three centuries, Karlstadt's reputation fell prey to his opponents, but he has been rehabilitated in the twentieth century, first by Hermann Barge, then by Ronald Sider (who refuted the traditional polemic against Karlstadt). Others aiding the rehabilitation include Ulrich Bubenheimer (who has filled in old lacunae in respect of Karlstadt's life and his concerns with jurisprudence) as well as Calvin Pater (who dealt with Karlstadt's views of Scripture, ecclesiology, baptism and his impact on the Swiss and northern Dutch and German Anabaptists). The popular sketch of Gordon Rupp in *Patterns of Reformation* (Philadelphia: 1969) is now obsolete. Only Denis Janz has recently accused Karlstadt of knowingly falsifying Thomism, but his whole argument assumes that Karlstadt wrote the annotations added to his *151 Theses* in 1520 by the censors of the Sorbonne University in Paris.
CAP

Calvin A. Pater, *Karlstadt as the Father of the Baptist Movements: The Emergence of Lay Protestantism*, pp. 303-27 and Ulrich Bubenheimer, 'Karlstadt,' *Theologische Realenzyklopaedie* vol. XVII (1988), pp. 655-57.

Kasai Kapata (Bernard) was the son of a doctor diviner in Belgian Congo (Zaire). He received his education at Kafumba, the first Mennonite Brethren mission station in Zaire. He accepted Christianity early in life and began his Christian ministry as church secretary and assistant to Pastor °Djimbo Kubala at Kafumba, and, later, as a pastor-evangelist in a village 30 mi. (50 km.) away.

During the Mulele rebellion (1964-65) Kasai and his family fled. Later, when he was on his way back to Kafumba to see how the Christians were faring, he was apprehended and forced to dig his own grave with a hoe. Some of the captors felt more kindly and he was buried only up to his neck. Three days later he was dug out. He often said after that that Jesus Christ was with him in the grave. He came away from the experience with a renewed commitment to Christ and his service.

Kasai's greatest contribution was at Pai-Kongila and its surrounding area where the Mennonite Brethren mission contracted with the government to supply staff for the government hospital. Kasai was asked to serve as hospital chaplain and pastor of the local congregation. Through his ministry 10 congregations and 10 extension churches have sprung up with a total membership of 2,300.   ILF

B. Burkholder, ed., *They Saw His Glory* (Winnipeg and Hillsboro, Ks.: Kindred Press, 1984), 44-48; J. B. Toews, *The Mennonite Brethren Church in Zaire*, ed. Paul G. Hiebert (Hillsboro, Ks.: MB Publishing House, 1978), 145-46, 227.

Kauffman, Christmas Carol (Dec. 25, 1901-Jan. 30, 1969), a writer of inspirational fiction, was born in Elkhart, Ind., the second of four daughters of Abraham R. and Selena Bell (Wade) Miller. She graduated from Elkhart High School and attended Goshen College and Hesston College. She began writing at Hesston and for years she wrote a short story a month for a weekly youth magazine published by Herald Press, completing more than 100 stories. In 1924 she married Norman Hostetler, who was accidentally electrocuted in 1926. In 1929 she married Nelson E. °Kauffman, a Mennonite pastor. She was the mother of four children.

She worked with her husband as a missionary in Hannibal, Mo., for 22 years. In Hannibal she began writing her popular novels, which were published by Herald Press and include *Lucy Winchester*, 1945; *Life within Life*, 1952; *Not Regina*, 1954; *Hidden Rainbow*, 1957; *For One Moment*, 1960; *Light from Heaven*, 1961; and *Search to Belong*, 1963. She died from hepatitis in Elkhart.   EBM

Menn. Bib. II, p. 463; Robert J. Baker, in *Chr. Living* (Nov. 1969), 3-5; Paul Erb, *South Central Frontiers* (Scottdale, 1974), 117.

Kauffman, Daniel (ME III:156), was the leading spirit within the Mennonite Church (MC) from 1898 to ca. 1930 and continued as a strong leader up to the time of his death in 1944. He made his mark, theologically, with his *Manual of Bible Doctrines* (1898), a new less historical approach to defining faith and life for the Mennonite Church. He made his mark as a churchwide leader, in the creation of Mennonite Church (MC) general conference (1898), again, a new approach to denominational structures for (Old) Mennonites, including the idea of a central authority which would in effect transcend the authority of the area conferences already established. (Four area conferences, in part because of this central authority from without, decided not to join formally the new denominational structures.) Thirdly, he made his mark within the church structures by becoming editor of *Gospel Witness* in 1905, and its successor in 1908, the official denominational paper, *Gospel Herald*, remaining in this position through 1943.

In each of these attempts, Kauffman emerged successful, at least over the short term, in introducing and then maintaining a well-defined concept of doctrine. The term "doctrine" was hardly known within Mennonite circles before 1894, when Kauffman introduced the idea into the pages of the *Herald of Truth*. His *Bible Doctrines* volume, published four years later, set programmatically the concept in a manner still felt among some Mennonites in the 1980s. Kauffman's doctrinal approach emphasized a "true orthodox evangelical faith," to be expressed in modest, indeed, uniform °dress for all church members, along with proper Christian demeanor and conduct in all areas of life. Kauffman's *Bible Doctrines* of 1898 spelled all this out carefully and categorically.

From 1898 to the 1920s Kauffman helped fill a void that was caused by a shift from German to English as the mother tongue of most Mennonite Church (MC) members. The English language rekindled the sense of witness and mission as given by Christ in his Great Commission (Mt 28:18-20). Many youth longed to serve the church as "Christian workers," both at home and abroad. Kauffman's doctrinal approach was seen as useful within this context. Indeed, new and expanded versions of *Bible Doctrines* came out in 1914, and again in 1928, with Kauffman serving as editor. This suggests a broad, accepting response on the part of the church at that time to Kauffman's approach to doctrine.

With the coming of the Second World War, new forces were on the horizon that brought Kauffman's doctrinal era to an end for most of the Mennonite Church (MC). By 1944, a new configuration was in place which began to replace the doctrinal approach of Kauffman with an era defined by the Anabaptist Vision of Harold S. °Bender and many others (°Concern movement). The ahistorical era of Kauffman was transformed into a more traditonal Mennonite approach to Christianity, including both faith and history as being of the essence of the Anabaptist-Mennonite faith.   LG

Leonard Gross, "The Doctrinal Era of the Mennonite Church," *MQR*, 60 (1986), 83-103; Beulah Stauffer Hostetler, *American Mennonites and Protestant Movements* (Scottdale, 1987); Theron F. Schlabach, *Gospel Versus Gospel* (Scottdale, 1980).

See also Renaissance, Mennonite.

Kauffman, Milo Franklin (Feb. 13, 1898-Apr. 19, 1988), was born near Harrisonville, Mo. He spent his boyhood on a farm in North Dakota. He received the BA degree from Hesston College, the BD degree from Northern Baptist Theological Seminary, the MA degree from McCormick Theological Seminary and the STD degree from Pikes Peak Seminary. He married Clara Fricke in 1931; they were parents of nine children.

From 1932 to 1951 Kauffman served as president of Hesston College (Ks.). His optimistic, positive leadership was instrumental in leading the school through difficulties caused by the Great Depression into a period of growth and vitality.

Following Kauffman's ordination to the ministry Dec. 7, 1924, he served the church as pastor, evangelist, overseer of Mennonite Church (MC) congregations in Kansas, Bible instructor, assistant in church relations for Hesston College, moderator of conferences, and writer. He wrote *Personal Works* (1940), *The Challenge of Christian Stewardship* (1955), and *The Stewards of God* (1975).

In 1953 he prepared the Conrad Grebel Lectures on the subject of Christian °stewardship. The lectures were given in more than 250 churches in the United States, Canada, India, and Japan.   MKM

Who's Who Mennonites (1943), 133; *Menn. Bib. II*, p. 464; *GH* (Jan. 28, 1986), 54-55; *MWR* (Feb. 19, 1987) 8.

Kauffman, Nelson E. (Oct. 5, 1904-June 18, 1981), a Mennonite Church (MC) bishop and conference leader, was born in Garden City, Mo., and grew up at Minot, N.D. He graduated from Hesston College in 1929. He was ordained a minister (1934) and bishop (1940) and served 22 years (1934-56) as a missionary and pastor in Hannibal, Mo. Kauffman was secretary for home missions of the Mennonite Board of Missions and Charities (MC), 1955-70. As president of Mennonite Board of Education (1950-70) he was one of the architects of cooperation in formation of Associated Mennonite Biblical Seminaries and one of the founders of the Conrad Grebel Projects Committee. As bishop he served congregations in Missouri, Indiana, and Michigan. Kauffman's study and writing resulted in many articles in Mennonite periodicals. He wrote three pamphlets on personal and congregational witness (Menn. Bib. 2: 464).

Kauffman was married June 10, 1929, to Christmas Carol (Miller Hostetler) °Kauffman. She died in 1969. Their children are Stanlee, James, Marcia (Miller), and Madonna (Eberly). Kauffman married Lois (Gerber Keener) in 1970.   SGG

Paul Erb, *South Central Frontiers* (Scottdale, 1974), index.

Kauffman, Edmund G. (1891-1980), was a General Conference Mennonite missionary to China (1917-25) and president of Bethel College, Ks. (1932-52). He was the son of John P. and Carolina Schrag Kaufman and grew up in the Swiss-Volhynian Mennonite community near Moundridge, Ks. He earned degrees at Bethel College (AB, 1916); Witmarsum Seminary, Bluffton, Ohio (AM, 1917); Garrett Biblical Institute, Evanston, Ill. (BD, 1927); and the U. of Chicago (PhD, 1929). He was a vigorous teacher, administrator, churchman, and intellectual leader.

Kaufman was a progressive. He endeavored to lead Mennonites out of sectarian isolation and dogmatic narrowness into wider arenas of service and mission. In China where he served as superintendent of the Mennonite Mission School at Kai Chow (Puyang), he pioneered in blending Chinese cultural elements with the Western-style Christian marriage ceremony. By training leaders and responding to their need for cultural authenticity, he helped pave the way for independence for the national church. He arranged for two Chinese Mennonite leaders,

James °Liu and Stephen °Wang, to study at Bluffton College and Bethel College in the United States.

Kaufman became president of Bethel College during the economic depression of the 1930s. He strengthened the school through faculty recruitment, a building program, financial drives, and a revised curriculum. In 1938 the North Central Association granted accreditation to Bethel. Kaufman enhanced the Mennonite identity of the college through development of the Mennonite Library and Archives and the Kaufman Museum. His commanding presence on campus was expressed in chapel services, in his required senior course in Basic Christian Convictions, and in his rigorous attention to the details of college activities.

Mennonite °Fundamentalists and traditionalists criticized Kaufman's liberal ideas, his studies at the U. of Chicago, and the assumptions of human progress in his publications, such as his PhD dissertation, *The Development of the Missionary and Philanthropic Interest among the Mennonites of North America* (1932). After resigning from the presidency at Bethel, he wrote or edited six additional books, including *Living Creatively* (1966), *Basic Christian Convictions* (1972), and *General Conference Mennonite Pioneers* (1973).   JCJ

Edmund G. Kaufman collection in MLA (Newton); oral interviews with Edmund G. Kaufman by Fred Zerger, 1970-71, including the tapes of 10 interviews and 310-page transcript, MLA (Newton); Robert S. Kreider, ed., "Edmund George Kaufman: Autobiographical Reflections at Seventy-nine," *Menn. Life*, 42 (March 1987), 39-45 and 42 (June, 1987), 17-18; *Who's Who Mennonites* (1943), 133.

See also Liberalism.

Kaufman, Elsie Drange (July 2, 1886-Nov. 13, 1939), the oldest of four children, was born to John and Amelia Sonderhoff Drange in Chicago, Ill. Here she grew up and with other members of her family became Christians and members of the Mennonite church in 1898 through the ministry of Amos H. Leaman and Melinda °Ebersole at the Chicago Home Mission (MC).

Elsie enrolled in the Goshen (Ind.) Academy to prepare for Christian service and was appointed in 1908 by the Mennonite Board of Missions and Charities (MC) for service in India. In 1909 Elsie married James Norman Kaufman who had gone to India in 1905. Together they served until 1934 in °Dhamtari, where Elsie helped in the management of the orphanage for boys and working with the Bible women (°lay evangelists). The Kaufmans had three children: Russel, Paul, and Kathryn.

In 1934 Elsie and her husband returned to the United States and lived in East Peoria, Ill., where Norman was pastor of the Pleasant Hill Mennonite Church.   JAF

Building on the Rock (Scottdale: MPH, 1926) 178; Esther Rose Graber, comp., "MBM Missionary Directory" (1984); J. N. Kaufman, *Walks and Talks in Hindistan* (Goshen: The Author, 1963); interviews with Mary Royer, Lois Shertz, and Minnie Graber.

Kaufman, James Norman (Oct. 20, 1880-July 31, 1966), the fourth of seven children of Jacob and Catherine Blough Kaufman, was born in Davidsville, Pa. He grew up in the Johnstown, Pa., area and taught in the public schools. He was ordained to the ministry in 1902 and served the Rockton Mennonite Church for three years. He married Elsie Drange in 1909.

As a pioneer Mennonite missionary in °Dhamtari, India (1905-34), Norman did much to develop the institutional ministries. He had a good command of the Hindi language and was an able administrator. He also served as field secretary and treasurer 1917-34.

After returning to the United States in 1934 Norman served as pastor of the Pleasant Hill Mennonite Church in East Peoria, Ill., until 1945 (bishop, 1941-45). He served as president of the Mennonite Board of Missions and Charities (MC), 1937-44, and continued as a member of the board until 1949.

After the death of Elsie Drange °Kaufman in 1939, Norman married Lillie Shenk °Kaufman in 1941 and returned to India for a short term (1945-48). In 1963 the Kaufmans moved to Goshen where Norman died.   JAF

Esther Rose Graber, comp., "MBM Missionary Directory" (1984); J. N. Kaufman *Walks and Talks in Hindustan* (Goshen: the author 1963); *Building on the Rock* (Scottdale: MPH, 1926); John A. Lapp, *India* (1972); *Menn. Bib.*, author index.

Kaufman, Lillie Shenk (June 13, 1899-Feb. 13, 1971), was born to Abram J. and Malinda Good Shenk in Elida, Ohio. She grew up in Elida attending the public schools there through her third year of high school. She received her diploma from Goshen Academy in 1920.

She committed herself at an early age for missionary service and attended Goshen College, 1920-21; U. of Virginia, 1921-22; and Bridgewater College, 1922-23. She graduated from Womens' Medical College, Philadelphia, in 1930. Lillie worked as a physician at the Laurelton State Village for girls, near Allentown, Pa., and then went to East Africa under the Eastern Mennonite Board of Missions and Charities (MC) in 1934 to pioneer the medical work at Shirati, Tanganyika (°Tanzania).

After four years in Africa, Lillie returned to the United States and practiced medicine for eighteen years in Fisher and East Peoria, Ill. In 1941 she married J. Norman °Kaufman and together they served in India (1945-48) in medical work at the Dhamtari Christian Hospital. The Kaufmans retired at Goshen where Lillie died.   JAF

Rich, *Mennonite Women* (1983), 183; Elma Hershberger and Lydia Shank in *Miss. Evangel* (July 1971); *Menn Bib.*, nos. 26330, 27656; Esther Graber, comp., "MBM Missionary Directory" (1983); interview with John H. and Ruth Mosemann.

Kazadi Matthew was born to Baluba parents in the village of Katanda in the East Kasai of the Belgian Congo (Zaire) in the first decade of the 20th c. As a boy he joined other family members in a move to West Kasai to find work. There Kazadi enrolled in the school of the Djoko Punda station of the °°Congo Inland Mission (Africa Inter-Mennonite Mission). After finishing five years of elementary education he enrolled in the station Bible school and upon graduation began a teaching and preaching ministry as a lifelong vocation.

He was one of the first Africans to be ordained in what later became the Église du Christ au Zaire, Communauté Mennonite (CMZA; Zaire Mennonite Church) and the first African to open a major regional church center away from the station without resident missionary help. He became the first president of the Zaire Mennonite Church and was the first African Mennonite church leader to make fraternal visits to North America.

During the turmoil following the political independence of Zaire in 1960, Kazadi accompanied the migration of his people to East Kasai. There, a refugee among refugees, he rallied and organized his fellow Mennonites into small congregations for mutual encouragement and support and gave leadership to founding a new church, which became known as Église du Christ au Zaire, Communauté Évangélique Mennonite (CEM; Evangelical Mennonite Communion). Kazadi was its first president.   HGra

Kazakhstan Soviet Socialist Republic. Founded in 1936, the Kazakhstan SSR is the second largest republic of the Soviet Union in size (2,049,000 sq. mi./2,715,000 sq. km., about the size of Argentina) and the fourth largest by population (16,000,000). Commonly viewed as a part of °Soviet Central Asia (°°Asiatic Russia), it lies east of the Caspian Sea, sharing a border with China for nearly 3,000 km. (1,860 mi.) farther east and, to the north, with the °Russian Soviet Federated Socialist Republic (RSFSR), to which it once belonged.

Mennonites first traveled through desert sections of this area during the 1880s when they trekked from the Am Trakt villages to Khiva and Ak Metchet under the leadership of Claas °°Epp. Settlement in large numbers had its beginnings during World War II when hundreds of thousands of Germans and people of other ethnic backgrounds in western parts of the Soviet Union were forcibly relocated to work camps at °Karaganda and other cities of the Kazakhstan republic. After the restricted regime regulations of this period were relaxed around 1955 (°Spetskomandantura), many families were reunited. Others moved in from regions further north and east to which they had been scattered by exile and imprisonment during the 1940s.

Many church communities, Mennonite and also others (e.g., Lutherans and Catholics), had their beginnings in Kazakhstan during these years. As internal migration continued, some of these were dissolved while several of the major cities became centers of permanent congregational life. For Germans generally, now numbering over 900,000 in the republic, Tselinograd became a kind of "capital," while Karaganda, Alma Ata (the actual capital of Kazakhstan), and Dzhambul attracted several thousand Mennonites who live there at present (1987).

A Baptist church began to function in Karaganda right after the close of the war, and many Mennonites simply joined this congregation, as they did in various other locations. In 1957 many Mennonites left the Karaganda Baptist Church to form a Mennonite Brethren congregation. The group wanted to conduct services in German and felt that the leader of the Baptist congregation was too strict in forbidding any services to be held outside the church building. The group gained much strength from the leadership of Heinrich Wölk and Wilhelm Mathies who came to Karaganda in 1960 and 1961 respectively.

This congregation was registered with the government in 1967 as an autonomous Mennonite Brethren Church, i.e., not belonging to the °All-Union Council of Evangelical Christians - Baptists (AUCECB). Several years later the congregation put up a building to seat the 900 members who had joined by then. Mathies and Wölk emigrated to West Germany in the 1970s. Others left as well but the congregation now (1987) has more than 1,000 members with Heinrich Goerzen and Alexander Becker serving as leading ministers in recent years.

Other Mennonites, commonly referred to as °Kirchliche Mennonites, began to meet separately also in 1957. They ordained four ministers in 1959, but there were disturbances in the early 1960s, so the group did not really get underway until later in the decade. In 1968 they obtained permission to meet in the Mennonite Brethren church, and continued the joint use of the premises until 1985. At this time they were able to erect and dedicate their own house of worship. Membership had reached about 400 by then, with Julius Siebert acting as leading minister (Ältester [°elder]) in the congregation.

The Kirchliche Mennonite congregation at Alma Ata began with a group who met together for a while at Nitva. It began to meet in Alma Ata in 1960, but was often disrupted for the first six years. In 1966 Cornelius Wiebe led a move to obtain registration of the church. The group received permission to obtain a building in 1973. Registration came later. Many have emigrated to West Germany since then, but the church continues with a membership under 200. A smaller Kirchliche Mennonite congregation exists as well in Dzhambul, where several unregistered Mennonite Brethren groups have also been very active in recent years.   LK

Peter Epp, on the Dzhambul congregation in *Der Bote* (Sept. 24, 1986), 4-5, (Oct. 1, 1986), 4-5, (Oct. 8, 1986), 4-5; Walter Sawatsky, "Mennonite Congregations in the Soviet Union Today," *Menn. Life*, 33 (March, 1978), 12-26; Heinrich Wölk, and Gerhard Wölk, *Wilderness Journey: Glimpses of the Mennonite Brethren Church in Russia, 1925-1980* (Fresno: Center for MB Studies, 1982), a German edition was published in 1981; Aloish Keklabaev, *Kazakhstan* (Moscow: Novosti Press Agency Publishing House, 1987).

Keihin (Menonaito) Dendo Kyoryoku-Kai. See Tokyo Menonaito Kyokai Rengo.

Kent Co., Del., Old Order Amish Settlement. See Dover, Del., Old Order Amish Settlement

Kentucky (ME III:166). By 1988 Mennonite influence had expanded to 28 congregations sponsored by 10 conferences or denominations with total membership of more than 700. The number of congregations and membership (in parentheses) for the various groups was: Beachy Amish Mennonite Fellowship (5 congregations, 252 members); Brethren in Christ ([1986] 5, 143), an additional congregation had been established by 1988; Conservative Mennonite

Conference (7, 128); Evangelical Mennonite Church (EMCh, 2 congregations); Fellowship Churches (2, 76); Indiana-Michigan Mennonite Conference (2, 43); Ohio Conference of the Mennonite Church (1, 25); Virginia Mennonite Conference (1, 10); Washington-Franklin Mennonite Conference (1, 13). One other congregation was sponsored jointly by the General Conference Mennonite Church and the General Board of the Mennonite Church (MC).

Other Mennonite-sponsored institutions in the state were: one church camp at Clayhole owned by the Rosedale Mennonite Missions; one elementary school at Crockett (grades 1-8) with 3 teachers and 40 students (1987-88), sponsored by the Faith Hills Fellowship congregation; and 5 voluntary service units (3 sponsored by Mennonite Central Committee, 1 by the Evangelical Mennonite Church Board of Missions, and one by the Conservative Mennonite Board of Missions). There were two church planting efforts at Lexington and Louisville by the Conservative Mennonite Conference (MC) and one by the Virginia Mennonite Conference (MC) at West Liberty.

As of 1985 there were seven Old Order Amish settlements in Kentucky with a total of nine congregations. The oldest settlement was founded in 1958 in Todd Co. Other settlements with single congregations were located in Casey, Christian Crittenden, Barren, and Harrison Cos.   RSa

MC Yearbook (1988-89), 25-26, 50-52, 60-63, 74-76, 82-84, 93-94, 100, 120, 122, 143, 151, 164-168, 247; Luthy, *Amish Settlements* (1985), 8; *GCM Handbook* (1988), 8, 149; *Minutes* (BIC, 1986), 247; Wittlinger, *Piety and Obedience* (1978), 419, 448, 452, 534.

Kenya. The Republic of Kenya lies astride the equator in eastern Africa and is bounded by Uganda to the west, Tanzania to the south, the Indian Ocean and Somalia to the east, and Ethiopia and Sudan to the north. The name is derived from the Gikuyu word for Mt. Kenya (*Kere-Nyaga*). Much of the north and eastern part of the country is semiarid. Most of the country's 16 million people live on the sw. highlands (3,700-10,000 ft. [1,100-3,000 m.] altitude) with ideal temperatures and rainfall. The Great Rift Valley pierces Kenya from north to south, west of °Nairobi.

In the mid-19th c. the British entered East Africa to protect their shipping routes to India. A railroad was built from Mombasa to Lake Victoria to create a link with Uganda, over which they had claimed a protectorate. Nairobi, begun as a railroad supply station, soon became the capital of Kenya. The British government then encouraged settlers to farm the highlands in the area north and west of Nairobi. The Gikuyu were forced onto reservations.

The Gikuyu resented this taking of their land, so they organized politically to better their situation. After World War II, a secret society known as the Mau Mau was formed. Its members pledged to reduce the influence and presence of the Europeans. Violence in the early 1950s led to the declaration of a state of emergency. The Mau Mau leader Jomo Kenyatta was arrested and sent into detention to the barren northwest. In 1963 the British granted Kenya its independence with Kenyatta as president. He made the Swahili work

KENYA

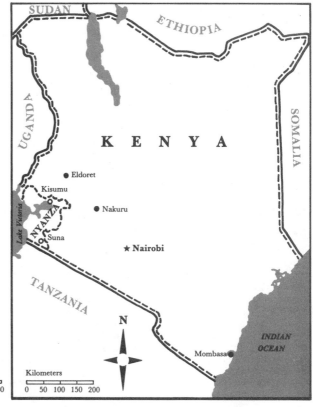

Kilometers
0   20   40   60   80

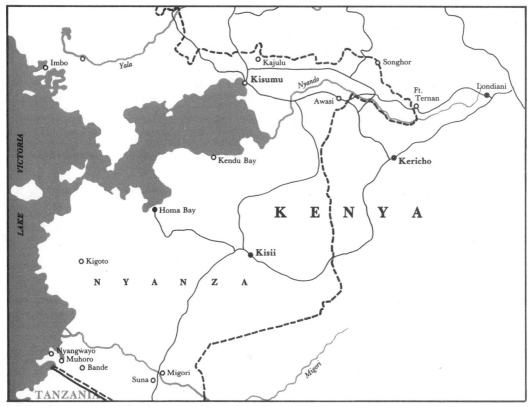

Harambee (pull together) a national slogan. He was succeeded in 1978 by Daniel arap Moi.

When the Mennonite Church entered Kenya, °Nairobi became the center for Mennonite Central Committee (MCC) and Eastern Mennonite Board of Missions and Charities programs. The Mennonite Guesthouse established in the 1960s provides a valuable service to missionaries of all denominations who come to Nairobi for business and rest. Rosslyn Academy was founded in 1967 to serve the elementary education needs of missionary children in Tanzania and Somalia. The Baptist mission joined with the Mennonites in the operation of the school in 1976. Beginning in 1988 a high school will be added to further its ministry. MCC involvement began with a Teacher's Abroad Program and has moved toward °development work in the drier areas of the country, particularly among several nomadic tribes.   DLW

MWH (1978), 85-90l; *MWH* (1984), 13.

See also Kenya Mennonite Church; Kanisa la Mennonite Tanzania (North Mara Diocese).

Kenya Mennonite Church is an outgrowth of the Kanisa la Mennonite Tanzania (Tanzania Mennonite Church, TMC), formerly the Tanganyika Mennonite Church. Youth from Suna attended school at Shirati in Tanganyika (Tanzania) from the mid-1930s onward. Scarcely aware of the political boundary, families traditionally moved back and forth within the tribal area. Before long some Shirati members were living in Kenya.

Following the revival at Shirati in 1942, Nikanor Dhaje and Wilson Ogwada, a Kenyan schoolboy, spent 22 days witnessing in the Suna area. In subsequent years, Zephenia Migire, Dishon Ngoya, Zedekia °Kisare and others made regular visits to Kenya to witness. Groups of believers emerged at Bande, Nyangwayo and other places.

In 1945 Suna residents, 60 in number, requested a Mennonite station, but the government refused permission. Steady follow-up continued, led by Jonathan Mabeche and Clyde Shenk. Not until 1965 were the Mennonites recognized as a church body.

In 1965 many Luo people from Kisaka, Tanzania, returned to Kenya to take up some of the rich farmland available for resettlement. Groups led by Naaman Agola and Elifaz Odundo went to Songhar and Kigoto. To lead the emerging churches, TMC set Hellon and Joyce Amolo to Suna in 1966, and in 1968 Clyde Shenk and Alta Barge °Shenk were transferred to Migori. The Shenks found 125 members to shepherd. Alta Shenk died in 1969. By the time Clyde and Miriam Shenk retired in 1976 there were 900 members in 40 worship centers.

The local congregation is the basic unit of the Kenyan Mennonite church life. When there is a nucleus of committed members at a worship center, congregational life begins. District clusters of congregations come together in annual spiritual life conferences featuring guest speakers. Each worship center (congregation) is led by an evangelist or catechist. These leaders, a few of them women, are appointed by the church planter or church council. Elders chosen by the congregation assist the leader. Leaders and elders in an area constitute a district church council. Leaders come together for occasional refresher courses. In response to persistent calls for a Bible school, Eastern Mennonite (MC) Board of Missions and Charities (EMBMC) provides Bible and leadership classes in each district. An ordained pastor oversees the district and officiates at baptisms and communions. Women's activities depend on local initiative.

In preparation for the Shenks' retirement in 1976, Bishop Kisare ordained the first national pastors, Musa Adongo and Nashon Arwa. In 1977 he also organized a central committee as the interim administrative body of the church. This enabled EMBMC to begin relating directly to Kenya leaders. With 50 congregations and 2,400 members, additional pastors were ordained in 1983: Naaman Agola, Elifaz Odundo, Hellon Amolo, and Joshua Okello (leader of the °Nairobi congregation established in 1966).

In preparation for organizing a church conference and calling a Kenyan bishop, a committee was chosen to draft a constitution. The handling of this document precipitated misunderstandings and division. In February 1988 the leaders were reconciled. Two dioceses are being formed, with steps toward ordination of bishops and a new emphasis on leadership training. There are 3,000 members in 70 congregations.

To reach large numbers of Somali Muslims in Nairobi, a community center was established at Eastleigh in 1977. It provides a study center, classes and other ministries, including a correspondence course for people of Islamic background. The center also spearheads ministry to Muslims in other towns, part of the interchurch "Islam in Africa" project.

As latecomers to Kenya, Mennonites did not establish primary and secondary schools. Instead they provided teachers for secondary schools and teacher training colleges. David Shenk, a lecturer at Kenyatta University, trained teachers in the use of the religious instruction syllabus for Kenya. He helped write some of the textbooks.

Missionaries and their national colleagues ministered to physical and social needs. In sw. Kenya they taught carpentry and building skills in the Migori Village Polytechnic. A nurse helped establish a community medical center on Rusinga Island; another served in Ombo Hospital, Migori. A demonstration farm was established at Ogwedhi Sigawa. Deliberately located on the tribal boundary, it helped build relationships and trust between the Masai, the Kurya and the Luo peoples.

In ne. Kenya missionaries responding to a government request following a famine, helped settle nomadic Somalis, establishing an agricultural community near Garissa. Nurses served in government hospitals at Garissa and Rhamu. Missionaries taught in the secondary schools at Mandera and Garba Tula. Another produced three primers for a literacy program. Mennonite Central Committee Teachers Abroad Program (TAP) served across the nation.

Missionary Harold Miller served the national Christian council as a development officer, first in bleak Turkana and then nationwide. Serving for all the churches, he will be remembered for helping people to recall traditional ways of surviving natural disasters. For example, traditional farmers planted three or four varieties of rice seed in each plot. If rains were plentiful, one kind flourished; if they were short, another kind took over.

Across Kenya the churches continue to grow; in 1987 the Christian population exceeded 80 percent. With rapid population growth; the nation faces serious social and economic problems. Many Kenyans and others, are praying for healing of relationships in the Kenya Mennonite Church so that it can share more fully in the harvest and grow in contributing to nation-building.   MMH

Clinton M. Ferster in *GH* (Mar. 16, 1948), 238; Elam W. Stauffer in *GH* (Jan. 17, 1950), 65; EMBMC staff in *GH* (May 7, 1968), 403-404; Daniel Hertzler in *GH* (Mar. 16, 1976, 216; Grace Wenger, "Eastern Mennonite Board of Missions and Charities, 1894-1980," unpublished manuscript available at Lancaster Mennonite Historical Society; Mahlon M. Hess, *The Pilgrimage of Faith of Tanzania Mennonite Church, 1934-83* (Salunga, Pa.: EMBMC, 1985), 81, 122, 170; *MWH* (1978), 85-90; *MWH* (1984), 13.

See also Kanisa la Mennonite Tanzania.

Kibuza Joseph was already an adult and the husband of two wives when the pioneer missionaries of the °°Congo Inland Mission (Africa Inter-Mennonite Mission) arrived in 1923 to establish a new mission post adjacent to Mukedi, Kibuza's village in Kwilu Province of the Belgian Congo (Zaire). In time Kibuza confessed faith in Christ and, finding forgiveness, peace and joy, embraced his newfound faith with an enthusiasm which was to characterize his entire life. Unable to read, he memorized key passages of Scripture. With these passages and many memorized hymns, he began evangelizing fellow villagers. He visited and prayed with new converts and encouraged them in the faith. Later, when medical services were developed at Mukedi, Kibuza became the hospital evangelist. Untrained and uneducated though he was, his vibrant faith and testimony was blessed in a remarkable manner. When he died members of the Mukedi church lost a rich spiritual resource, but was left with the memory of a life which had been uniquely blessed and used of the Lord among them.   JEB

Kikwit, Zaire. A river port on the farthest navigable point inland on the Kwilu River, Kikwit early became a center of commercial activity in Zaire during the colonial period, when the area was known as the Belgian Congo. Its location some 390 air miles (625 km.) east of Kinshasa amidst a productive agricultural area has greatly enhanced its growth. Its population in 1986 exceeded 350,000 people.

Mennonite missionary presence and work in the area dates to the 1920s when, after serving two terms with the Congo Inland Mission, Aaron and Ernestina Janzen, a Mennonite Brethren missionary couple, began an independent work in the Kafumba area some 35 mi. (56 km.) south of Kikwit along the Kwilu River. It was after World War II that the Mennonite Brethren Board of Missions officially picked up sponsorship of the Janzens' work.

Both the Mennonite Brethren Church (Église du Christ au Zaire, Communauté des Églises de Frères Mennonites, CFMZA) and the Mennonite Church in Zaire (Église du Christ au Zaire, Communauté Mennonite, CMZA) are now active in Kikwit. In 1986

the CFMZA had seven congregations in the city and the CMZA three. Both sponsor grade and high schools in the rapidly growing center. In addition, the CFMZA operates a three-year Bible School which had some hundred students enrolled in 1986.

Since the 1960s, the Mennonite Central Committee has provided funding and occasional expatriate personnel for a development program which has at different times featured cattle, poultry, a feed mill, and a peanut oil processing plant. It is also at Kikwit that a Habitat for Humanity housing project, for which the Africa Inter-Mennonite Mission has provided expatriate administrative personnel, was begun in 1984.   JEB

Kilabi Bululu (b. 1932) was born in the village of Kilembe, Kwenge, and became one of the most prominent leaders and ministers of the Église du Christ au Zaire, Communauté des Églises de Frères Mennonites au Zaire, (Mennonite Brethren Church of Zaire) in Africa. He heard the Christian message first in 1948 and accepted Christ. He graduated from Bible institute in Kafumba. From 1967 to 1971 he studied at the Faculté de Théologie, Vaux-sur-Seine, France, receiving both BA and MA degrees (the first Zairian Mennonite Brethren to receive an MA degree in theology).

Kilabi held the positions of chairman of the Administrative Council of the Institut Supérieur Théologique de Kinshasa (Superior Institute of Theology in Kinshasa) and chairman of the National Theological Committee. For 10 years he served as vice-president within Bandundu Province for the Church of Christ in Zaire, the national unitary Protestant church. For years he was also a member of the Kikwit city council. He served as the first Zairian chairman and legal representative of the Mennonite Brethren Church of Zaire (1974-84) During these years the church membership grew from 12,000 to ca. 30,000. Since 1985 Kilabi is director and professor of the Mennonite Bible Institute in Kikwit. In 1987 he also accepted the position of assistant pastor in Kimpwanza church, which he had previously pastored for three years.   MDyck

King, Emma (Hasseoveo), was a mission worker in the General Conference Mennonite mission in Lame Deer, Mont. In 1919 she was the first person who gave testimony against the sexual practices connected with the Cheyenne Sun Dance. Her testimony led to the U.S. Bureau of Indian Affairs banning the Sun Dance for a time. Later she became one of the few women hired by the mission as a "native helper." She was not only a translator, but a preacher who gave messages from the pulpit "when emergency called." Missionary Bertha Kinsinger °Petter reported that one Cheyenne had asked her, "Why not ordain Hasseoveo for the ministry? . . . Although a woman, she is capable as the men. Her life is consistent. She knows the Word and speaks well. We all love her." In spite of King's acceptance in a leadership role, she was never ordained to the ministry.   LB

Mrs. Rodolphe (Bertha) Petter, "Hasseoveo, a Beloved Christian," *Mennonite* (Nov. 25, 1947), 3-4.

Kingdom of God. According to many scholars, the kingdom of God is the most central and comprehensive theme in the entire Bible. The main features of this theme are present, at least implicitly, in Yahweh's establishing of the Sinai covenant with Israel (see esp. Ex 19:4-6). The kingdom of God is rooted, first, in the divine initiative and consists in God's unhindered rule. Yahweh delivered the people of Israel from Egypt in order to govern them directly. Second, God's kingdom rule is to be actualized among a particular people (in this case, Israel) called especially to that task.

Third, God's kingdom will be actualized where this people is obedient. Obedience consists, on one hand, of keeping commandments which regulate unique forms of social relationship; on the other hand, obedience must spring from inner allegiance to Yahweh. Fourth, God's kingdom has a missionary thrust. Through Israel's obedience it is to spread to all nations. Finally, God's kingdom will be fully established only in the future. The kingdom of God is a dynamic movement which stretches forward in time.

During Old Testament times God's kingdom was actualized only in small measure. This was largely due to Israel's tendency to identify its present national existence with the kingdom of God. Instead of continually responding to Yahweh's initiative, Israel often regarded its kingdom status as guaranteed. Instead of keeping Yahweh's social commandments, Israelite society increasingly split into groups of rich and poor; rather than remaining inwardly loyal to Yahweh, Israelites increasingly turned towards foreign gods. Overestimating its own superiority, Israel often neglected its mission and despised Gentiles. Finally, being overly satisfied with its present situation, the nation frequently forgot God's forward call. As a result of all this, Israel came under Yahweh's judgment, and by Jesus' time the kingdom of God still seemed a largely unfulfilled hope.

Jesus' main message was: "the kingdom of God is at hand!" (Mk 1:15) The divine initiative was present in his healings, exorcisms, and teachings. While his messsge went out to everyone, it was directed especially towards a "little flock" willing to follow a "narrow way." Jesus called for obedience: for keeping his commands as well as for inner allegiance of heart. He especially stressed the life of self-giving, servant-like love which, among other things, could heal destructive social relationships between rich and poor, and between men and women. Jesus also called for the reversal of attitudes towards Gentiles, opening the way for the kingdom's missionary thrust. Finally, Jesus looked towards the future actualization of God's rule over all.

Scholars agree that Jesus emphasizes the initiative and reign of God in general, and called for different attitudes by Jews toward Gentiles. They disagree, however, over other features of his message. Most scholars contend that Jesus called mainly for conversion of the heart, and that his specific commands regarding social behavior were not as central to his message. In this way they interpret his efforts to be directed primarily towards individual hearers, and not as much towards the formation of a committed group of disciples or towards their social impact. Scholars also disagree over the extent to which Jesus understood God's kingdom to be present ("realized"), future, or both. Most of them agree, however, that Jesus saw the kingdom, paradoxically, as in some way "already" present and "not yet" fully consummated.

The earliest Christians retained this paradoxical tension, understanding God's kingdom to be already among them, but expecting it to be fully established in the near future when Jesus returned—that is, in an earthly and therefore social manner. Over the next few centuries, however, this expectation dimmed, and the consummation was pushed further into the future and into a heavenly, or spiritual realm. Subsequent interpretations differed primarily in the way they emphasized the present vs. the future, and also the social (or earthly) vs. the spiritual (or heavenly) dimensions of God's Kingdom.

While medieval piety focused on a future, spiritual and heavenly hope, Catholicism, at least since Augustine (354-430), could also regard God's kingdom as present in a secondary way through the establishment of the church, and in society insofar as the church influenced it. This led to a sacralization of Catholicism and of medieval society which the Protestant reformers sought to challenge.

Martin Luther spoke of two kingdoms, both of which were largely present. God was most directly active in the kingdom of Christ. This consisted in the spiritual relationships between justified individuals and God, and among such individuals in the church; here affairs were regulated by Jesus' teachings about radical self-giving love. God was indirectly present in social affairs, however, through the kingdom of this world; here God maintained order through traditional social structures and the violence exercised by the temporal rulers. Although Luther intended to identify the political government less directly with God's kingdom than did Catholicism, his insistence on conformity to established structures and rulers led to similar practical results.

One of the leaders of the Reformed tradition, John Calvin, spoke primarily of God's kingdom as spiritual, heavenly, and future. Yet he acknowledged that certain beginnings of it are present on earth. Reformed Christians, unlike most Lutherans, increasingly regarded the kingdom of God as a dynamic force transforming political and economic life. At times this led to social criticism and transformation. Often, however, it also led to a sacralization of violent means of change (as in the English Civil War, 1642-48) and of new social arrangements (as among American Puritans).

In the 19th c. Protestant °liberalism stressed the social and earthly aspects of God's kingdom so strongly that its heavenly and spiritual dimensions sometimes disappeared. They emphasized Jesus' radical social commands, confident that these were becoming more practicable because humanity was becoming more moral. They often equated this supposed moral evolution with the future dimension of God's kingdom. But insofar as they identified it with such movements as °socialism and °democracy, liberals sacralized them and underestimated the radicality of Jesus' call for spiritual conversion.

Liberalism's optimistic alignment of social movements with God's kingdom aroused two very different protests in the 19th and 20th c. °Dispensationalists argued that Jesus' social teachings were to be followed literally in God's kingdom—but that this kingdom was wholly future and would be established only at his return. In the present "Church Age" only the spiritual emphasis of Jesus was relevant. Quite differently, existential theologians, e.g., Rudolf Bultmann (1884-1976), claimed that Jesus' teachings really had no social import, but that God's kingdom was present whenever individuals responded to God. Despite their differences, both theologies located the essence of Christian life not in social and historical movement, but in a present, inward realm.

Mennonites have strongly affirmed that the kingdom of God has future and heavenly dimensions. Yet what distinguishes their perspective most sharply from others is the way they find the kingdom taking root in present earthly life. Although God's kingdom transforms hearts, Mennonites cannot assign it to this spiritual realm as many Lutherans, existentialists, and modern biblical scholars have. Along with Catholics, liberals, and the Reformed, they find it also being actualized in social relationships. Nevertheless, these relationships cannot be identified, even indirectly, with those prevailing in any earthly society. For to do this is to sacralize behaviors, structures and special interests quite different from those of God's kingdom.

Instead, Mennonites find God's kingdom most fully present wherever groups are committed to living out Jesus' teachings about self-giving, servant-like love, and are doing so by means of God's initiating °grace, whether their actions seem in tune with their larger sociocultural context or not. Mennonites stress not only the role of spiritual and social obedience in general, but also that of the called-out community, or "little flock," through which these take concrete, social shape.

In extreme cases, Mennonites may have virtually identified the church with God's kingdom and may have relegated the rest of society and culture to the devil's rule. Sometimes they have separated themselves socially and geographically and, like ancient Israel, minimized the kingdom's forward movement and its missionary thrust. Today, however, Mennonites are increasingly aware that society can be most deeply affected by the radical examples set by deeply committed minorities. Some are also asking whether God might be initiating the kingdom, or at least opportunities for its actualization, in some way in other social or cultural movements. Yet however they grapple with this, Mennonites will be extremely unlikely to identify any such movement with the kingdom of God, for they will expect the kingdom's reality to be focused and actualized primarily through communities committed to Jesus' radical way. TNF

Paul Althaus, *The Ethics of Martin Luther* (Philadelphia: Fortress, 1972), 43-82; Augustine, *The City of God*, Bks. 16-18; John Bright, *The Kingdom of God* (Nashville: Abingdon, 1953); Rudolf Bultmann, *Jesus and the Word* (New York: Scribner's, 1934); C. H. Dodd, *Parables of the Kingdom* (New York: Scribner's, 1961); Thomas N. Finger, *Christian Theology*, vol. 2, ch. 15; George Ladd, *The Presence of the Future* (Grand Rapids: Eerdmans, 1974); ide[...] *Questions about the Kingdom of God* (Grand Rap[...] mans, 1952); Alva J. McClain, *The Greatness of th[...] (Grand Rapids: Zondervan, 1959); H. R. Niebuhr, [...] dom of God in America* (New York: Harper, 1935[...] Perrin, *The Kingdom of God in the Teaching[...] (Philadelphia: Westminster, 1963); Walter Rausche[...] *Theology for the Social Gospel* (New York: Abingd[...] Herman Ridderbos, *The Coming of the Kingdom* [...] phia: Presbyterian and Reformed, 1962); Rudolf Sc[...] berg, *God's Rule and Kingdom*, rev. ed. (New York[...] and Herder, 1963); Juan Segundo, *The Historical* [...] *the Synoptics* (Maryknoll, N. Y.: Orbis, 1985); [...] Snyder, *The Community of the King* (Downer's Gr[...] InterVarsity, 1977); Amos Wilder, *Eschatology and* [...] *the Teaching of Jesus* (New York: Harper, 1950); [...] Yoder, *The Politics of Jesus* (Grand Rapids: Ee[...] 1972); *Menn. Bib.*, subject index contains referenc[...] large number of articles and pamphlets on the subjec[...]

See also °°Chiliasm; Sectarianism; Sermon o[...] Mount; Sociopolitical Activism.

Kinshasa, Zaire. Located at the site of what [...] was a small fishing village on the banks of the [...] River, Kinshasa has known phenomenal gr[...] Named Leopoldville by colonial rulers in hon[...] the Belgian king, its traditional African name [...] restored after political independence was gaine[...] 1960. The city's population of some 300,000 pe[...] in 1960 has grown to more than 3 million in 1[...] and continues to mushroom, reflecting the powe[...] °urban drift which characterizes many other area[...] the underdeveloped world.

As long as church program and policy making s[...] lay in missionary hands, inter-mission °comity [...] rangements were respected. This limited Mennon[...] church planting to the three rural provinces [...] original assignment. Once such issues became t[...] agenda of national church leaders, however, the[...] former agreements were dismissed as no long[...] relevant and determined effort was made to locat[...] Mennonites who had migrated to the capital and t[...] bring them together for purposes of nurture and th[...] formation of organized churches. In 1987 Kinshas[...] has 20 congregations of the Église du Christ a[...] Zaire, Communauté des Frères Mennonites (CFMZA[...] Zaire Mennonite Brethren Church), 11 congrega-tions of the Église du Christ au Zaire, Communauté [...] Mennonite (CMZA; Zaire Mennonite Church), and 4 [...] congregations affiliated with the Église du Christ au [...] Zaire, Communauté Evangélique Mennonite (CEM; [...] Evangelical Mennonite Church).

Both the Africa Inter-Mennonite Mission (AIMM) and the Mennonite Brethren Board of Missions and Services (BOMAS) maintain missionary personnel in Kinshasa who provide support services for their church and expatriate personnel located in the interior regions of Zaire. AIMM also maintains a missionary children's hostel in the city.

There is a three-year pastoral institute in Kinshasa (Institut Supérieur Théologique de Kinshasa [Superior Institute of Theology in Kinshasa]) to which AIMM and BOMAS have contributed heavily in the past. Originally launched by a group of 12 missions, the participating groups have gradually been reduced to 5, among which AIMM and BOMAS are numbered. Both Mennonite Boards continue to provide missionary teaching staff for the school. All three Mennonite Churches of Zaire send students

n, *Crucial*
ids: Eerd-
e Kingdom
The King-
); Norman
of Jesus
nbusch, *A*
n, 1917);
Philadel-
hnacken-
: Herder
Jesus of
Howard
ve, Ill.:
thics in
ohn H.
rdmans,
es to a
.

n the

once
Zaire
owth.
or of
was
d in
pple
986
rful
s of

till
ar-
ite
of
he
se
er
e
o
e

has also across the years
rsonnel to the staff needs
press and publishing house
e Mennonite Central Com-
rovided staff people for the
u Christ au Zaire (Church of
ational church federation to
nonite groups belong, which
the capital.   JEB

en (ME III:179), a term that
Russian Mennonites, except for
breakaway Brethren, but now
in the Soviet Union. In English
mes translated as "Mennonites"
hurch" in contradistinction to
en," in Latin America and else-
"Church Mennonites." The latter
and theologically awkward con-
he best translation of "Tserkovnyi
official designation for them in the
till another designation in some
literature is "Old" Mennonites in
"New" Mennonites, i.e., the Menno-
ovement that began in the 1860s.

nting a fusion of former Flemish and
ts and no longer showing distinctions
nonites from various of the Russian
olonies—since virtually all *Kirchliche*
ive in new regions far from the old
distinctive features of the *Kirchliche*
uted to memories of the common expe-
lony life. Noticeable is the stronger role
der (as bishop) when compared to the
Brethren practice in the Soviet Union,
ore concern for a common pattern of wor-
g with other free churches, they shared a
experience of religious °persecution, spiri-
val after World War II, and sustained re-
on access to religious literature or educa-
a result, their theological emphases have be-
entical to those of other Soviet evangelicals,
h they remain separate for cultural reasons
cause of a different mode of baptism.

ticing baptism of adult believers by pouring,
irchliche continue to be discriminated against
mersionist Mennonite Brethren and Baptists.
includes denying them communion rights, even
gh the leadership of the °All-Union Council of
ngelical Christians - Baptists (AUCECB) issued a
ective to its member churches in 1964 urging
ternal relations. Several *Kirchliche* congregations
gistered with this government-approved council
ecided within the past decade to perform baptism
y immersion so that their young people would be
ecognized by neighboring Baptist and Mennonite
Brethren congregations, thus avoiding complications
in case of °intermarriage.

An effort to form a union of *Kirchliche* congrega-tions in 1957 was blocked by the authorities, who imprisoned the leaders. Since the mid-1980s, elders and ministers of congregations in °Kirgizia and °Kazakhstan have been meeting informally each month to share concerns. The first *Kirchliche* Men-nonite congregation to be registered was Novosibirsk (1967). Others are gradually moving through stages

of unofficial acknowledgement of their existence, to registration as a filial group of a Baptist church, to full registration as an individual local Mennonite "society." Leaders submitted to the government a constitution, based on the confession of faith used in the Russian Mennonite colonies, but minus the non-resistance clause which would have resulted in out-right and immediate rejection of their application. They have borne the brunt of the stigma from the Mennonite Self-Defense league (°*Selbstschutz*), which operated during the °Russian Revolution and Civil War.

Of the approximately 12,000 to 15,000 *Kirchliche* Mennonites in the Soviet Union in 1988, about 2,800 can be accounted for in the following registered congregations:

In Kirgizia Soviet Socialist Republic (SSR): Tok-mak, Elder Johann D. Schellenberg, 230 members; Krasnaia Rechka, Peter K. Braun, minister, 100 members; Romanovka, Abram P. Abrams, minister, 90 members; Stantsia Ivanovka, not registered, Dietrich Penner minister, 20 members.

In Kazakh SSR: Alma Ata, leadership in flux, 145 members; Dzhambul, Elder Viktor Schmidt, 135 members; Politotdel, Elder Peter Klassen, 60 mem-bers; Karaganda, Elder Julius Siebert, 375 members; Martuk, Elder Jakob Peters, 143 members. Else-where in °*Central Asia*: Dushanbe, Tadzhikistan, 20 persons led by Peters; Kumsangir, Tadzhikistan, Elder Franz Pauls, 80 members; Dzhetisai, Uzbeki-stan, Dietrich Neufeld minister, 40 members.

In Western Siberia: Novosibirsk, Elder Bernhard Sawadsky (deceased May 1988), Jakob Wiebe minis-ter, 180 members; Neudachino, Novosibirskaia Oblast, Gerhard Neufeld minister, 100 members; Grishovka, Altai, Abram Isaak, minister, 30 members; Nikolaifeld (5 villages near Omsk), Abram Adrian minister, 200 members; Protassovo, Altai, Heinrich Dyck, minister, 50 members; Tomsk, Derksen, minis-ter, 30 members.

In °Orenburg region: Chortitza No. 1, Andrei J. Rempel, minister, 100 members; Petrovka No. 2, Ivan A. Bal'mann, minister, 104 members; Kant-serovka No. 3, Jakov J. Dik, minister, 23 members; Zhdanovka Nos. 5 and 8, Peter P. Bartel, minister, 120 members; Nikolaevka No. 6, B. B. Rempel, min-ister, 60 members; Feodorovka No. 7, Andrei (Hein-rich) J. Wiebe, minister, 50 members; Dolinovka No. 9, recognized for meeting, 20 members; Kitchkas No. 12, Elder Dietrich Ivanovich Thiessen, 96 mem-bers; Pretoria No. 14, 35 persons meeting; Sol' Iletsk, Ivan A. Friesen, minister, 51 members; Stepanovka (Perevolozhski r-on), Ivan I. Martens, minister, 96 members.

Since immigration to West Germany was resumed in February 1987 (°*Umsiedler*), there has been a marked attrition of leaders and stalwart members that is putting the ongoing viability of the *Kirchliche* Mennonites in doubt. Changes under the new *Perestroika* policy of the late 1980s seem too un-certain for this ethnic and religious minority, and the pull of family members in West Germany is strong.

People of *Kirchliche* origin established churches in Brazil and Paraguay following emigration in 1929 and after World War II. These *Kirchliche* conferences developed close ties to the General Conference Mennonites of North America, in which other *Kirchliche* Mennonites had become a major force, especially in Canada. *Umsiedler* from *Kirchliche* backgrounds have usually joined existing Mennonite churches in Germany, but at least 3 have formed congregations independently. All churches with significant *Umsiedler* contingents formed the Arbeitsgemeinschaft zur geistliche Betreuung der Umsiedler Mennoniten (AGUM) in 1978, and had almost become a distinct conference by 1988.   WWS

MWH (1978), 310; *MWH* (1984), 126.

Kirgizian Soviet Socialist Republic. Located in the ne. sector of °Soviet Central Asia, the borders of the Kirgizian SSR touch the Kazakhstan SSR to the north, the Uzbekistan SSR to the west, the Tadjikistan SSR to the south, and the People's Republic of China to the east. Its size, just under 200,000 sq. km. (76,880 sq. mi.), makes it one of the smaller Soviet Socialist republics but equal nevertheless to the territory of Portugal, Belgium, The Netherlands, and Switzerland combined. The Kirgizian republic has a population of 4,000,000 people. Its capital city is Frunze.

The major ethnic group is Kirgizian; the major religion is Islam. Besides other Central Asian ethnic groups, the population includes sizable numbers of Russians, Ukrainians, and Germans. Most of the Germans appeared in this region during and after World War II, when the Soviet government undertook to resettle all Germans then living in the European part of the country.

The warm climate and better living conditions brought Mennonites to this region after Mennonites and ethnic Germans confined to labor camps farther north were released beginning in 1955 and 1956 (°Spetskomandantura). Among the leaders at that time were *Ältester* (°elders) Heinrich Voth and Peter Heese of Tokmak, not far from Frunze. Heese and Hans Penner traveled to Moscow ca. 1966 with registration requests from a number of °*Kirchliche* Mennonite congregations around Alma Ata and Frunze. Voth served as *Ältester* for all *Kirchliche* Mennonites in the Soviet Union until his death in 1973. He was succeeded for a time by the aging *Ältester* Johann Penner. A vital role was also played by *Ältester* Hans Penner of Frunze, who translated the Mennonite confession of faith into Russian.

There are presently (1987) four active *Kirchliche* congregations in several outlying villages and towns not far from Frunze. There is also one Mennonite Brethren congregation in Novopavlovka, a suburb of the capital. The latter, a group of about 150 persons, is served by *Ältester* Martin Balzer. It was registered as an autonomous congregation in 1977.

The groups at Romanovka and Krasnaja Rechka, with about 140 and 165 members respectively, were registered in 1967. They are led by *Ältester* Abram Abrams and Peter Braun. The largest of these groups, at Tokmak, has about 200 members under the leadership of *Ältester* Johann Schellenberg. A small, 20-member congregation, still unregistered, also meets regularly near the railway town of Ivanovka.

The Mennonites of this region, like those elsewhere in Central Asia, continue to stress their German identity. This means that Low German is fostered as a language in the homes, even though Russian and other local languages are spoken everywhere else. High German is the language of the congregation in worship although some singing in Russian is included occasionally, and special services, e.g., funerals, may include Russian sermons. Young people often speak Russian best and prefer its use in the services of the church.

Many Mennonites in the Kirgizian SSR have found their way into other congregations, mostly Baptist congregations, but sometimes Lutheran ones. Quite a few belong to unregistered groups of one kind or another. The emigration of the 1970s and more recently, also of the late 1980s (°*Umsiedler*) has affected these communities significantly. Here too, many church members have emigrated to West Germany, including a number of ministers and other church leaders who were active in their home congregations at Tokmak or elsewhere.

Tourists have found it possible recently to visit in these congregations, although they were closed to outsiders before. People from these areas do visit relatives in the West and it is possible for Soviet emigrants, now living in the West to stay with their relatives in Kirgizia for weeks and sometimes several months at a time. Frunze, like Alma Ata and other capitals of republics, is highlighted on routes for tourists and various kinds of delegations.   LK

Walter Sawatsky, "Mennonite Congregations in the Soviet Union Today," *Menn. Life*, 33 (March, 1978), 12-26; idem, *Soviet Evangelicals Since World War II* (Scottdale, 1981); Gerd Stricker, with Walter Sawatsky, "Mennonites in Russia and the Soviet Union: An Aspect of the Church History of the Germans in Russia," *Religion in Communist Lands*, 12, (Winter, 1984), 295-314; Kadyr Omurkulov, *Kirgisien* (Moskau: APN Verlag, 1987).

Kirisuto Kyokei Teidan Yamaguchi-Ken Kyogikai. See Nihon Kirisuto Kyo Keiteidan (Japan Brethren in Christ Church).

Kisare, Susana Nyaeri (1915-83), a sister in the Tanzanian Mennonite Church (Kanisa la Mennonite Tanzania) and wife of Bishop Zedekia Kisare. Her commitment to Christ advanced the cause of the church as did the love and gifts she extended to husband, immediate and extended family, and church fellowship.

Born in the Luo village of Rwang'enyi, Nyaeri (Susana was her later adopted Christian name) met her future husband when he came to her village to operate a cream separating business. The business failed, though the relationship flourished. Nyaeri at their first acquaintance, found Zedekia to be gentle and soft-spoken, though, being a careful and thoughtful person, she did not entertain thoughts of marriage until she had had friends inquire whether he acted the same way in his home village of Shirati. They were married in 1933.

Susana Kisare managed the meager family income, astonishing her husband and other missionaries in her ability not only to make the money reach, but to save enough to pay for such purchases as a kerosene lantern and the major part of the air ticket for their son's travel to school overseas.

During three years at the Bukiroba Bible School, Zedekia, in reading the Bible carefully, began to see that in Christ he and Susana were equal before God. "During the first years of our marriage I insisted on having the last word in our home. . . . I struggled to make her an obedient wife. Then I saw from my study of the New Testament that a husband and wife are to work together. All our quarreling ceased."

Susana was a take-charge kind of person, graced by insight and gentleness. From her "office" in the kitchen she skillfully taught girls how to cook. All was well in her "office" if the water barrel was full, if she had a sack of ground grain, and if her woodbox was full. One missionary observed that everybody felt they had a special relationship with her; somehow she made all feel special. She saw herself as a mother to all peoples represented in the church—Luo, Bantu, Canadian, and American. She treated everyone with respect and common sense, noticing people's strengths and refusing to have any part in gossip.

She and her husband had four sons and ten daughters; three of the four sons died in infancy.

The funeral of Sister Susana on August 8, 1983, was a moving testimony to her wide influence and the love with which she was regarded by all. Her death was reported on Radio Tanzania. The Mennonite community, and government representatives, including the Regional Commissioner as personal representative of President Nyerere, were among the some 2,000 people who came for the extended days of remembering Susana's life. Susana Kisare was buried outside the Shirati church, that symbol on earth of God's new village, to which her adult life had given witness.   JMB

Kisare, Zedekia Marwa (b. 1912), first national bishop of the Tanzania Mennonite Church (Kanisa la Mennonite Tanzania, founded 1934). He and his wife Susana studied in the Bukiroba Bible School (1936-39); he taught at the school during the 1950s, and in 1965 graduated from Mennonite Theological College, Bukiroba. The couple served in evangelism and church planting in the Shirati area and in the newly-established Luo settlement at Kisaka, some 80 mi. (130 km.) from Shirati.

Bishop Kisare grew up in Shirati, a Luo people's village in an area called Kiseru, in Mara Region between Lake Victoria and the Serengeti Plain. Following Luo custom, he was a goatherd as a boy and a cattleherder as a youth. His first contact with Christians was with Seventh-day Adventist African evangelists.

As a five- or six-year-old, Kisare recalls musing on the question, "How did I, Marwa, come to be a human being?" Though not much is said about God in traditional Luo worship, the answer that came to him in that moment was, "If God would not have been, then I, Marwa, would not have been. God is both the purpose (why) and manner (how) of my existence."

When he was 14 years old he began attending the Adventist church in a nearby village in Kenya. Wanting to walk pleasing to God, he was baptized and became a member of that church in 1933. He chose a new name, Zedekia, though years later, with

perspective on the meaning of names, began using his given name, Marwa, in addition to his Christian name.

In 1933 he married Nyaeri Akello from a Luo village 12 mi. (20 km.) away. He eventually sought work with the new mission station of the Eastern Mennonite Board of Missions and Charities (MC) at Shirati. His first contacts were Elam °Stauffer and John °Mosemann.

The dramatic story of Bishop Kisare's life reveals a person dedicated to the mission of Christ. The story includes leadership roles in the Tanzania Mennonite Church as evangelist, minister (ordained Dec. 10, 1950), and the first African bishop (ordained Jan. 15, 1967), spanning the very beginning of that church through the missionary era to independence and beyond, well into the era of the indigenous church. Basic to his leadership was experiencing and preaching a revival that frees from fleshly sins, jealousy, pride, and self-righteousness, giving place to reconciliation; learning the Bible so that a concordance was not needed; making do with meager financial resources; seeing the church grow to more than 30,000 members; observing and serving the church on six visits to North America; seeing his beloved wife and coworker die in 1983; and remarriage in 1984 to Margaret Awiti.

In one of his sermons on a preaching safari Bishop Kisare said, "Confession of our sin is not something we do once and then forget about. It is a way of life practiced by God's people."   JMB

Zedekiah Kisare and Joseph C. Shenk, *Kisare: A Mennonite of Kiseru* (Salunga, PA: EMBMC, 1984).

Kishacoquillas Valley, Pa., Old Order Amish Settlement. See Belleville, Pa., Old Order Amish Settlement.

Kiwoma Agalunga (Jean) (b. 1921), was born at Kisupain the vicinity of the Kafumba station of the Mennonite Brethren mission in Belgian Congo (Zaire). His uncle, who was attending Bible school, took Kiwoma to Kafumba to look after his children. Kiwoma entered the primary school and became a Christian while attending school. He attended Bible school after his primary education, finishing in 1940. He served as head teacher in the primary school and worked at the printshop in the afternoons. He also became the assistant pastor. Summer holidays were spent in village evangelism.

After nine years of service at Kafumba, Kiwoma was sent to establish a church and start a school at an outpost on one of the Lever Brothers plantations. At that time the colonial government agreed to accredit and subsidize mission schools. In 1951 Kiwoma was sent to an accredited pedagogical school to qualify for teaching under the new government program. He then was sent to Gungu, a government post 50 mi. (80 km.) south of Kafumba to start a church and a school there. He was there for nine years and was then transferred to the Kajiji station where he taught for three years. After this he was transferred to Kikwit, the political and commercial center for the whole region, to teach in the primary school there.

He was ordained in 1968 and established the

second Mennonite Brethren church in Kikwit. He became president of the church district council for the Kikwit district. He is still (1987) pastoring the church he established.   ILF

J. B. Toews, *The Mennonite Brethren Church in Zaire* (Fresno: MB Board of Christian Literature, 1978), 226.

Klassen, David D. (Feb. 5, 1902-Sept. 4, 1985). Born in Halbstadt, Man., to David and Anna Klassen, David Klassen attended a private elementary school up to the age of 12 and a public school for a few years after that. He was baptized at the age of 18 and joined the Bergthaler Mennonite Church. In 1920 he married Susanna Heinrichs, daughter of Wilhelm and Maria Heinrichs of Halbstadt, Man.

On July 13, 1930, David D. Klassen was ordained as a minister in the Bergthaler Mennonite Church. He and his family were pioneers in the Mennonite settlement in Homewood, Man., where he helped to found the Homewood Bergthaler Church. For 25 years he was a member of the board of directors of the Mennonite Collegiate Institute, Gretna, Man., and for 18 years of the board of Canadian Mennonite Bible College, Winnipeg. In 1961 he was ordained an °elder of the Bergthaler Mennonite Church. He also served at various times on boards and committees of the Conference of Mennonites in Canada and the Conference of Mennonites in Manitoba.

For many years Klassen was in some demand as a popular speaker on biblical themes. His favorite ones were eschatology and biblical °nonresistance. In 1957 he accepted an invitation from the Radio Committee of the Conference of Mennonites in Manitoba to be the regular speaker on its weekly broadcast "Word of Life." Klassen made the messages largely expository. On occasion he would sing an unaccompanied solo on the air. These songs became so popular that a number of recordings were made and sold.

David and Susanna Klassen were married for almost 65 years and had a family of six daughters and nine sons, all of whom survived the father when he died at the age of 83 in Carman, Man.   GE

Henry J. Gerbrandt, *Adventure in Faith* (Altona: Bergthaler Mennonite Church, 1970), index; *Menn. Rep.* (Sept. 16, 1985), 1.

Kleine Gemeinde. See Atlantic Provinces; Blue Creek Colony, Belize; Evangelical Mennonite Conference; Mexico; Spanish Lookout Colony, Belize.

Koejemans, Anthoon Johan ("Koej") (1903-82), communist and later Mennonite commentator on public affairs, whose idealism led him to become a member of the Communist Party in The Netherlands at age 17. In 1929 he became editor of the Dutch Communist daily paper, *De Tribune*, and during World War II editor-in-chief of the illegal paper *De Waarheid* (1943; The Truth). As a member of the party executive (1944) he was responsible also for dialogue between communists and Christians. A change in party organization at the beginning of the "Cold War" (December 1947-January 1948), led to his being relieved of all responsibilities including membership in the party "senate."

In 1955 he renounced his membership in the Communist Party. In 1958 he was baptized in the Mennonite church in Amsterdam by Frits °Kuiper. In a statement requesting his reception as a member of the Amsterdam congregation he wrote, "I know that especially the Mennonites in the Soviet Union have been subjected to extreme persecution. I cannot separate myself from that fact by saying 'I did not know about it. I am guilty of the suffering and death of untold numbers there. I feel that my request to join your congregation will help mitigate a small fraction of my guilt. . . .'"

He continued the communist-Christian dialogue in his books, searching and evaluating. His book *God in Berlin*, however, is not critical enough about the German Democratic Republic (East Germany). He served as a member of the Amsterdam Mennonite church council (1960-66) and, together with others, founded the paper *In dit Amsterdam*, serving as co-editor from 1961 to 1968. Koejemans was a warm Christian brother whose concerns centered particularly in truth and justice. He was convinced that we are living in revolutionary times, but that victory will ultimately come through Jesus Christ himself.   JMW

Books and articles by A. J. Koejemans after 1955: *Van "ja" tot 'Amen'* (Amsterdam, 1963, 2nd ed.), an autobiography; *Jezus in Magnitogorsk* (Amsterdam, 1964); *Doperse ketterijen* (Amsterdam, 1965), collected speeches and articles; *David Wijnkoop* (Amsterdam, 1967); *God in Berlijn* (Amsterdam, 1973); *Mennist . . . Merkwaardig* (Kollum, 1977); "Een Doopsgezinde patriot in West-Brabant en de eerste Nederlandse grondwet," in *Doops. Jaar.* (1983), published posthumously. See also A. Oosterbaan, "Anthon Johan Koejemans," *Doops. Jaar.* (1983).

Kohm (Kohn?), Mathilde. In 1896 Mathilde Kohm became the first overseas missionary sent from the Evangelical Mennonite Church, United States, 10 years before the first male missionary of that denomination. From 1896 through 1910 she did pioneer evangelistic work in the Belgian Congo (Zaire) under the auspices of the Christian and Missionary Alliance. This period included four years of teamwork with Alma °Doering, marriage to a missionary widower Alvin Stevenson (1904), the birth of four children and the burial of one, and the deaths of two close missionary colleagues.

From 1910 through 1912 she and her husband, who joined her church, were influential in the founding of the Mennonite mission board later known as Africa Inter-Mennonite Mission (°°Congo Inland Mission). She stayed with her children in Illinois while Alvin Stevenson went back to the Congo in 1912 to identify a field of work for the new agency. He died there in February 1913; she remained a strong promoter of missions throughout the denomination.   SN

"Alvin James Stevenson," two-page published obituary including picture of the family in 1911, no publication details, copy in Evangelical Mennonite Church historical files, Fort Wayne, Ind.; Melvin J. Loewen, *Three-Score* (Elkhart: Congo Inland Mission, 1972), 31-41, the origins of Africa Inter-Mennonite Mission, including references to Mathilde Kohm and Alvin Stevenson.

Komitee für kirchliche Angelegenheiten für Paraguay. See Gemeindekomitee, Paraguay.

Konferenz der Evangelischen Mennonitischen Bruderschaft von Südamerika (Evangelical Mennonite Brethren Conference of South America). Founded in 1963 by four congregations in Paraguay and Argentina, this group's roots go back to Russia where the °°Allianz Gemeinde was formed in 1889. Although not directly related when first established, since the mid-20th c. the conference has worked in close cooperation with the similarly-named Evangelical Mennonite Brethren Conference (since 1987, °Fellowship of Evangelical Bible Churches) in North America.

Following the migration from Russia to Paraguay, 1929-1930, 23 Allianz members gathered to form a congregation in the °Fernheim Colony under the direction of Nikolai Wiebe, their first minister. They called themselves the Evangelische Mennonitische Bruderschaft. The church has experienced steady growth since its founding, numbering 380 members in 1986. In its mission outreach to Indians and Paraguayan nationals it works closely with the Mennonite Brethren and General Conference Mennonites. It publishes the *Informations Blatt* (Information Paper).

During the migration to Paraguay following World War II, a number of Mennonites chose to remain in Buenos Aires in 1947. Others came to the city for employment. With Mennonite Central Committee encouragement Martin Duerksen gathered these families for worship and gave spiritual leadership to their needs. A congregation soon formed in the city. The cultural and language transition from German to English was more rapid in the Argentine congregation than in Paraguay. The mission outreach of the congregation into a suburb of Buenos Aires has led to the founding of another congregation in 1986, the Iglesia Evangelical Menonita de Delviso (°Alianze Evangélica Menonita de Argentina). PW/ABos

MWH (1978), 247-48; *MWH* (1984), 97; *Minutes (EMB)* (1984), 55-56.

Konferenz der Mennonitengemeinden in Uruguay (Conference of Mennonites in Uruguay). This conference includes the German-speaking Mennonite (GCM) congregations of Uruguay, consisting of those Mennonites who fled °°Danzig and °°West Prussia in 1945. The first group of 750 immigrants arrived Oct. 27, 1948. Of these more than 500 were from Danzig and West Prussia, more than 100 from Lemberg, in °°Galicia, and 82 from Poland. They founded the El Ombú congregation in 1950. The second group of immigrants, comprising 429 persons, arrived Oct. 19, 1951. These founded the Gartental Colony in 1952. A congregation was also organized in Montevideo the same year. The congregation at Delta was founded in 1955.

These three settlements (Delta, El Ombú, and Gartental) are primarily agricultural, have organized separate producer-consumer °cooperatives. Each settlement has a school, retirement center, and a hospital-nursing home. While the congregation in each settlement is autonomous, there is much cooperation. The conference meets in session annually for discussion of mutual interests and work.

In 1956 the Seminario Evangélico Mennonita de Teología (Evangelical Mennonite Theological Seminary) began its work in Montevideo. Students and church workers from other countries in Latin America also participated in the program until it was moved to Asunción, Paraguay, in 1974. A home for students studying in Montevideo was established in 1960.

The conference coordinates the service and social welfare work of the congregations, including the mission congregations among Spanish-speaking Uruguayans (°Convención de las Iglesias Menonitas en Uruguay). A bookstore has been established to provide literature to the German-speaking congregations. A monthly periodical, *Konferenznachrichten* (Conference News), helps to maintain contact among the congregations. In 1986 the four German-speaking congregations had a membership of 525. JBe

ML, 4: 396-97; *Menn. Jahrbuch* (1978), 48-52, (1979), 44-46; Klaus Dück, "Neue Heimat in Uruguay," *Mennonitischer Gemeinde-Kalender* (1957), 30-35; Richard Rupp, "Die 'Lemberger Gruppe' in Uruguay," *Jb. der Mennoniten in Südamerika* (1961), 83-87; *GCM Handbook* (1988), 40; *MWH* 1978), 270-71; *MWH* (1984), 106.

Konferenz der Mennonitischen Brüdergemeinden, Paraguay (Conference of Mennonite Brethren Churches). Five Mennonite Brethren congregations were founded during the initial immigration into Paraguay, two in Fernheim Colony in 1930, one in Friesland Colony in 1937, and one each in Neuland and Volendam colonies in 1947. These congregations joined their sister congregations in Brazil in 1948, and somewhat later those in Uruguay, to form the South American district conference of the Mennonite Brethren. At the ninth conference meeting in Curitiba, Brazil, in 1960, it was agreed that Mennonite Brethren in each country should organize their own conference in order to pursue mission and educational activities which varied from land to land according to language and culture. Consequently the Mennonite Brethren Conference of Paraguay was founded in Filadelfia in July 1961, with Willy °Janz as chairman, Albert Enns as vice-chairman, and Peter K. Neufeld as secretary-treasurer. Conference membership at that time was 1,098. In 1964 the congregations in Blumental, Fernheim, and Asunción were received, and in 1982 the Nuevo Toledo congregation of East Paraguay joined.

The conference promotes: (1) a sense of unity and the preparation of workers for the congregations; (2) mission work among the Indian peoples of the °°Chaco region (°Chaco Mission) and among native Paraguayans in cooperation with the Spanish-speaking Convención Evangélica de Iglesias Paraguayas Hermanos Menonitas; (3) Bible schools in Fernheim and Friesland colonies and, since 1971, the Instituto Bíblico Asunción (Bible Institute of Asunción) which was founded in 1966. The work of this school is under the direction of a committee of representatives from both the German-speaking and Spanish-speaking Mennonite Brethren conference in Paraguay.

An educational center has been established in Asunción to accommodate the offices of the two conferences; the Colégio Alberto Schweitzer (elementary and high school), which is the responsibility of the conference since 1983; the Instituto

Bíblico Asunción; and the studio and offices for the radio work in East Paraguay which is carried on jointly by the two conferences. The Konferenz publishes a *Konferenzblatt der Mennonitischen Brüdergemeinden.*

Membership in the German-speaking conference in 1985 was 1,272. The reason for this low membership in Paraguay is the continuing emigration to Canada and Germany. Two Mennonite Brethren congregations in Germany and five in Canada are made up largely of Mennonites from Paraguay.   HW

Willy Janz and Gerhard Ratzlaff, eds., *Gemeinde unter dem Kreuz des Sudens: Die Mennonitischen Brüdergemeinden in Brasilien, Paraguay und Uruguay 1930-1980* (Curitiba, 1980); minutes of the Konferenz der Mennonitischen Brüdergemeinden in Paraguay; *MWH* (1978), 251-57; *MWH* (1984), 98; *Menn. Jahrbuch* (1984), 156-58.

Konferenz der nordwestdeutschen Mennonitengemeinden (Conference of Northwest German Mennonite Churches). This union of the Mennonite congregations in Emden, Gronau, Leer-Oldenburg, and Norden was formed to facilitate the services of a single pastor. When the congregation in Leer was unable to support a minister financially in 1920 and the Norden congregation faced a similar situation in 1931, Abraham Fast (1886-1962), who had been pastor of the Emden congregation since 1918 and of the Gronau congregation since 1922, was invited to serve these congregations also. The union occurred in 1942 and was integrated into the °Vereinigung der deutschen Mennonitengemeinden in 1953. Legal incorporation of the union followed in 1973.   HFas

Menn. Jahrbuch (1984), 141.

See also Niedersachsen.

Konferenz süddeutscher Mennonitengemeinden (Conference of South German Mennonite Churches) (ME I:675). The "Konferenz," since November 1967 known as the *Konferenz Süddeutscher Mennonitengemeinden,* celebrated its centenary in 1986. It is still the place where the currently 36 Mennonite congregations, all located in the southern part of Germany, can meet in conferences, by exchanging their preachers and by visiting each other, particularly at the meeting taking place in September every year.

The Konferenz has developed since 1951, especially in the field of youth work. Other programs have been taken up by the recently established °Arbeitsgemeinschaft deutscher Mennonitengemeinden der Bundesrepublik und West Berlin which is responsible now for the °Deutsches Mennonitisches Evangelisationskomitee, the *Mennonitisches Jahrbuch* (°yearbooks), and the *Mennonitisches Gesangbuch* (hymnbook). The Konferenz has accepted new activities in the field of group-oriented work for adults and women and in cooperation with the °Deutsches Mennonitisches Friedenskomitee it arranges for employment for volunteers in peace work. The Konferenz supports the European Mennonite Bible School at Bienenberg in Switzerland.

Christian Neff and Abraham Braun were presidents of the Konferenz until 1965, followed by Heinrich Funck of Unterbiegelhof (1965-66), Adolf Schnebele of Karlsruhe (1968-77, 1980-81), and Hans-Werner Janzen of Weierhof (1977-80). Since 1981 the Konferenz has been chaired by Klaus Hübert of Ingolstadt.   ASchn

Menn. Jahrbuch (1951-).

Koolman. See Doornkaat Koolman, J. ten.

Koop, David (Aug. 18, 1900-Jan. 28, 1982), was born in °°Orloff, Russia. He was ordained a minister in the Mennonite church (°Kirchliche Mennoniten) in 1925. He was with the group that was able to leave Russia in 1929, emigrating via Germany to Brazil. The first settlement in Stolzplateau, Santa Catarina, was not successful and he moved, together with others, to Curitiba, ca. 1935. He was ordained °elder in 1948, serving in this capacity until 1970. David Koop was known for his biblical and doctrinal preaching and his irenic relationships to other groups, including the Mennonite Brethren churches and the Mennonites in North America. He was active in both the Associação das Igrejas Menonitas do Brasil (Association of Mennonite Churches of Brazil) and the Conference of Mennonites in South America.   HenEns

Proceedings of the Fourth Mennonite World Conference, 1948 (Akron, Pa.: MCC, 1950), 226-27.

Korea, Republic of. Mennonite Central Committee (MCC) became involved in South Korea in 1950 with war relief programs. This included a variety of material aid programs, widows' self-help, medical assistance, inservice training for orphanage staffs, the first family-child assistance program in Korea, and a vocational school for orphan boys. While there were no Mennonite-sponsored programs in Korea in 1986, the Commission on Overseas Mission (GCM) and MCC representatives regularly visited South Korea on mission and peace concerns. The Commission on Overseas Mission has placed one short-term teacher in the country, and Koreans have been host to several Mennonite °work camps for Asian youth.   EM/HRT

GCM Handbook (1983-84), 58.

Kosciusko Co., Ind., Old Order Amish Settlement. See Nappanee, Ind., Old Order Amish Settlement.

Krahn, Cornelius (b. Aug. 3, 1902, d. Aug. 3, 1990), noted 20th c. Mennonite historian, writer, editor and teacher, has contributed significantly to scholarship about Dutch Anabaptism and to the preservation and dissemination of Mennonite history.

Born to Mennonite parents in Chortitza, the Ukraine, Krahn left the Soviet Union in 1926. He studied church history and theology in Bonn, Berlin, and Amsterdam. In 1936, at the U. of Heidelberg, he completed a dissertation on the life of °Menno Simons. The following year, Krahn entered the United States, where he studied languages at Bethel College in North Newton, Ks., and at the U. of Wisconsin. From 1939-44 he taught at Tabor College in Hillsboro, Ks. In 1940 he married Hilda Wiebe of Beatrice, Nebr.

A member of the Bethel College faculty from 1944 to 1974, Krahn taught church history and Russian history as well as German. He served as director of the Bethel College Historical Library (Mennonite Library and Archives). Working from a small collection begun by Abraham °°Warkentin, Krahn developed a major historical library emphasizing Dutch, Prussian, and Russian Mennonite materials. In 1946 he founded the quarterly magazine *Mennonite Life*, and for the next 25 years served as its editor.

In 1953 he received a Fulbright Fellowship to pursue research in The Netherlands on religious life during the Reformation; his book, *Dutch Anabaptism: Origin, Spread, Life, and Thought (1450-1600)*, appeared in 1968. In addition, Krahn wrote or edited more than 18 books and leaflets and published articles in Mennonite periodicals and scholarly journals. As assistant editor of the four-volume *Mennonite Encyclopedia* (published 1955-59), he contributed 686 articles. In the late 1960s he edited, assisted by Melvin °Gingerich and Orlando Harms, a slightly revised reprint of the *Mennonite Encyclopedia*.

Krahn helped to shape several historical projects, including the North American Committee for Documentation of Free Church Origins, which formed in 1963. He served for many years on the Historical Committee (GCM) and the Western District (GCM) Historical Committee. After his retirement from Bethel College in 1974, he traveled and lectured widely, and continued to collect rare books and other materials pertaining to Mennonite life and thought.   RWG

"Cornelius Krahn — Pelgrim in Europa en Amerika," *Doops. Bijdr.*, n.r. 5 (1979), 114-18; H. Quiring, "Cornelius Krahn zum 80 Geburtstag," *Menn. Geschbl.*, Jg. 39, n.F. 34 (1982), 93-95; Marion Keeney Preheim, "A Rare Mennonite Historian," *Mennonite* (Apr. 9, 1985) 166; biography and bibliography in *Menn. Life*, 32 (Sept. 1977) sp. issue; the files of Cornelius Krahn are located at the MLA (North Newton).

Krahn, Henry George (July 7, 1923-Dec. 9, 1985). Born as his family was enroute from the Soviet Union to Canada, Henry spent his early years in Saskatchewan. Later, his family moved to Abbotsford, B.C., where he completed his high school education.

As teacher, historian, and administrator Henry served God within Mennonite Brethren institutions. After graduation from Mennonite Brethren Bible College and Tabor College he worked with Hispanic people and the Comanche people under the Board of Foreign Missions (MB). Following further studies in Fresno and the U. of Washington he, together with his wife Alice (nee Bauman) and their three children, served for six years coordinating the Mennonite Brethren missions schools in India.

Upon completing graduate studies in Reformation history at the U. of Washington, he taught at Fresno Pacific College (1967-74). In 1974 he accepted the invitation to become president of the Mennonite Brethren Bible College in Winnipeg. During his eight years as president (he continued teaching at the college until his death) the college grew in enrollment and faculty. Henry was a popular teacher. No student could sit through his courses without being caught up with his infectious zeal for truth. Narrow sectarianism and dogmatic assumptions were foreign to him. He constantly exhibited a rare combination of biblical piety with a fearless openness to new theological concepts.   KR

Harry Loewen, in *MM* 5 (1986), 26; Ken Reddig, in *JMS*, 4 (1986), 268-69.

Kraichgau (ME III:231). Comprising the rolling land areas between the Odenwald and the Black Forest, the Kraichgau has belonged to the state of Baden since 1803-1806. Before 1806 parts of the Kraichgau belonged to the Elector Palatine, the Bishiop of Speyer, the Margrave of Baden, the Duke of Württemberg, and various imperial knights.

Research still in progress shows the first Swiss Anabaptist settlers from the Zürich area arrived in 1648 in the villages of Dühren, Eichtersheim, and Elsenz. In 1650 the nobleman von Venningen reached a settlement and protection agreement with them. From 1650 to 1679 settlements were established in the Electoral Palatinate area near Sinsheim. In 1671 Anabaptist refugees from Bern settled in no fewer than 30 villages of the Electoral Platinate region.   TGlü

See also Baden-Württemberg Federal State.

Kreider, Amos E. (Oct. 19, 1889-Feb. 11, 1976), pastor, Bible teacher, influential conference and missions leader, was born to John H. Kreider and Magdalene. Ebersole-Kreider, at Sterling, Ill. He married Stella R. Shoemaker, Freeport, Ill., on Sept. 5, 1917; they were the parents of Robert S. and Gerald R. Kreider. Educated at Goshen College and Garrett Biblical Institute, A. E. Kreider returned to teach at Goshen College, 1917-18, 1921-23. He also taught at Bluffton College and Witmarsum Theological Seminary between 1923 and 1931 and at Bethel College (Ks.), 1935-43. Ordained at Maplewood Mennonite Church, Topeka, Ind., on May 5, 1915, he served also as pastor at Science Ridge, Sterling, Ill., (1918-21); College Church, Goshen (1921-23); First Mennonite, Bluffton, Ohio (1931-35); and Eighth Street, Goshen (1943 until retirement). Significant church board memberships include: Mennonite Board of Education (MC, 1920-23); Board of Missions (GCM, 1935-53); Board of Mennonite Biblical Seminary (GCM, 1945-62), in which he became a significant bridge in MC-GCM relationships.   EW

Krimmer Mennonite Brethren. See **Mennonite Brethren Church of North America.**

Kroeker, Susanna Schowalter (b. ca. 1879), a pioneer missionary (GCM) at Janjgir, India, was born in Mühlhausen, Alsace (then part of the German empire). She lived with an aunt at the castle Geisberg in Alsace, part of which was maintained as a resort or vacation home, part of which was home for six families who farmed the surrounding land for the landowners.

Susanna met her future husband, Johann F. °°Kroeker, when he visited the Geisberg and Schafbush while a student in the mid-1890s at St. Chrischona Bible School near Basel, Switzerland. J. F. Kroeker, born in Gnadenfeld in the Molotschna colony, was one of several Mennonites from Russia to study at this °Bible school. Kroeker thereafter studied at Bethel College, North Newton, Ks., graduating from the academy in 1899.

Susanna and Johann Kroeker and P. A. and Elizabeth °°Penner, were the first General Conference Mennonite missionaries to India, arriving at Bombay on Dec. 9, 1900. The Kroekers opened a mission among the outcaste Chamar and Ghasia people located on the west side of the Hasdeo River on the central part of the northern plain known historically as Hindustan.

The couple first lived in a small one-room hut in the midst of the people. As with every other home in Bhatapara, they had no well or toilet facilities. Later when they had secured land for a mission station they moved into a tent. While living in the tent Susana became very ill and the government doctor who came to attend her said, "I can give you no hope." Yet God restored her. The station eventually included a four-room bungalow, a row of houses for the Indian workers, a boys' boarding school, and later a girls' boarding school.

Suffering sicknesses repeatedly, the couple resigned in 1908 but were persuaded to stay on until the spring of 1909, completing eight and one-half years of service. The family now included three sons and two daughters. They returned to Germany with plans to move to the United States to assume a pastorate. The move was prevented because J. F. had lost his citizenship, whereupon they returned to the place of his birth to serve the church in itinerant evangelism. During the °Russian Revolution they were taken by Red Army officers and separated. Susanna and the children never saw J. F. again. They kept in touch by sending letters by proxy and finally he was sent to Siberia where he died of typhus fever.   JMB

Samuel T. Moyer, *They Heard the Call* (Newton, 1970), 34-40; Harold Ratzlaff, "Planting a Church in India" (MTh thesis, Mennonite Biblical Seminary and Bethany Biblical Seminary, 1950), 7-43.

Kuamba Charles was born of Lulua parentage along the Kasai River in south central Belgian Congo (Zaire). The opportunity for education attracted him to the °°Congo Inland Mission (Africa Inter-Mennonite Mission) at Djoko Punda, where he came to a personal faith in Christ. Although by nature a quiet person, he had strong musical gifts and soon became an active layman in the station church. He taught in the Bible institute and directed a variety of choirs. His patience and sensitivity equipped him well to serve as a language tutor for missionaries for many years.

Kuamba's faith commitments were deep. These were never more severely tested than during his first marriage. Although he and his bride greatly desired children, they lived with deepening disappointment. Furthermore, his wife became ill at an early age and experienced steadily declining health. Childless and burdened with a wife who eventually became an invalid, Kuamba resolutely resisted the pressure from fellow clansmen to return his wife to her people and take another wife. He cared for her until her death. His second marriage was blessed with a total of 11 children, the first of which were twins. During the political upheaval of the early 1960s the Baluba and Lulua people in the Kasai found themselves in conflict. When asked which tribe he belonged to, Kuamba responded by saying he belonged to neither because he had joined a new tribe, "the tribe of Jesus."

After moving south to °Tshikapa with his family Kuamba was proposed for ordination and continues (1987) as a pastor of a Mennonite congregation in that urban center.   HGra

Kudus, an important industrial city in Indonesia with an estimated population of 133,000, is located at the southern foot of Mount Muria 50 km. (30 mi.) e./ne. of °Semarang, the capital of the province of Central °Java. The economy of the city is dominated by the manufacture of clove-flavored cigarettes. Other major industries include printing and the manufacture of bus and van bodies. Mennonites play important roles in these industries.

Kudus is an important center of Islamic influence. It is the site of a famous ancient mosque whose architectural form is obviously influenced by pre-Islamic Hindu architectural style. It is also the burial place and shrine of Sunan Kudus, one of the *wali songo,* the nine Muslim missionaries who according to tradition are responsible for the conversion of Java to Islam. The burial place and shrine of a second of those nine Muslim missionaries, Sunan Muria, is located near Kudus on the slopes of Mount Muria. These shrines are the objects of pilgrimage for innumerable Javanese Muslims. Significant Islamic educational and publishing institutions are located in Kudus.

But this town is also the birthplace of the Persatuan Gereja-Gereja Kristen Muria Indonesia (Muria Christian Church of Indonesia), one of the two Mennonite conferences of Indonesia. It was in this town that °Tee Siem Tat, an anxious and infirm businessman of Chinese descent, found Jesus Christ to be the healer of his disease and immediately proceeded to gather around a group of new believers. This gave birth to what was originally called the Chineesche Doopsgezinde Christengemeente (Chinese Mennonite Christian Church).

In 1988 there are at least three Mennonite congregations of that conference in Kudus. There are also two congregations of the Gereja Injili di Tanah Jawa (Evangelical Church of Java), the Javanese Mennonite conference. Each of these congregations has a number of branches in and around the city of Kudus.

Two major service institutions of the Muria church are located in Kudus, both of them under the direct auspices of the original congregation. First is the Masehi (Christian) Educational Foundation with schools from kindergarten to senior high school. Second is the more than 100-bed Mardi Rahayu Christian Hospital.

Some of the earliest effective mission work to take place in Java was carried on at Kayu Apu, just a few kilometers north of Kudus. Beginning in 1853 Netherlands Missionary Fellowship missionary Hoezoo formed a congregation here. This mission work was turned over to the Dutch Mennonite Mission in 1898. Pieter °Jansz (1820-1904), the first Mennonite missionary sent by a Mennonite mission agency to a non-European people, was buried in Kayu upon his death in 1906. It was later Mennonite missionaries Johann °Fast (1861-1941) and Hermann °°Schmitt who, though assigned to the village of Kayu Apu, shifted the focus of their attention, in contrast to the general policy of the mission, from rural communities to the towns and cities of the Muria area.   LMY

Th. Jensma, *Doopsgezinde Zending in Indonesia* (The Hague: Boekcentrum, 1968); Lawrence M. Yoder, *Tunas Kecil: Sejarah Gereja Kristen Muria Indonesia* [Little Shoot: History of the Muria Christian Church of Indonesia] (Semarang: Komisi Literatur Sinode GKMI, n.d. [1985]), also available in English translation under the title "The Church of the Muria: A History of the Muria Christian Church of Indonesia" (ThM thesis Fuller Theological Seminary, 1981); Lawrence M. Yoder, and Sigit Heru Soekotjo, "Sejarah Gereja Injili di Tanah Jawa" [History of the Evangelical Church of Java] (unpubl. manuscript).

Kuiper, Frits (Dec. 7, 1898-Mar. 7, 1974), was the son of Abraham Kornelis Kuiper and Henriëtte Sophie Muller. His father and grandfather were Mennonite ministers in Amsterdam. He married Maaike Anna Heuvelink in 1927. He interrupted his studies at the U. of Amsterdam and the Amsterdam Mennonite Theological Seminary (1918-23), with an 18-month stay in the Soviet Union (1922-24), sent by the European student relief organization. He was a member of the Dutch Christian student movement executive committee. In 1923 he submitted his graduation thesis on the subject "The Lot of the Russian Church under the Soviets."

He began his pastoral work in Amersfoort in 1925, followed by work in Krommenie-Wormer-Jisp, 1928-32, and Alkmaar, 1932-45. From 1945 to 1947 he served as director of the study center *Vrij Nederland* after which he served as minister in Amsterdam to 1963. At that time he accepted the invitation of the Dutch Reformed mission board to serve as professor of theology at the Mennonite seminary in Montevideo, Uruguay. He returned in 1965 and retired in Krommenie.

Kuiper was an unusual person, a hard worker with great sensitivity to events surrounding him and an ability to develop and defend his own convictions. He did not avoid confrontations. He continued his studies and became particularly interested in the work of Karl Barth. In 1924 he became a member of the Mennonite Task Force against War which affiliated with the annual congregational retreat movement.

Kuiper was conservative and Anabaptist in his faith, but radical in politics. In 1925 he joined the Social Democratic Workers Party (SDAP) and attended the International Socialist Youth Festival in 1929, which was antimilitaristic. While the pastors belonging to the SDAP were largely liberal, Kuiper founded the "Committee for Socialism and Church" with a Christian orthodox emphasis.

During World War II (1940-45), he continued contacts with the illegal *Vrij Nederland* (*Free Netherlands*) paper and published some issues of *De vrije Alkmaarder* in 1944-45. Following his call to serve in Amsterdam in 1945 he became involved with a Roman Catholic leader and a Jewish rabbi in the publication of *De Stem van Israël* (*The Voice of Israel*). From 1961 on he brought new life into the

Mennonite publication *in dit Amsterdam* (*In this Amsterdam*) together with A. J. °Koejemans and A. Oosterbaan.

Kuiper was above all a theologian who struggled for meaning and clarity about Anabaptism, socialism and Zionism. This led him to the publication of three volumes: *De Gemeente in de Wereld* (*The Church in the World*, 1941), *Leven uit de hoop* (*Living in Hope*, 1958), and *Een klein drieluik van onze bevrijding* (Baarn, 1974 [posthumously], translated into English as *A Small Tryptych of Our Liberation*, 1980). By liberation he did not mean freedom from the wartime German occupation but the liberation of all people to which, according to Kuiper, Karl °Barth, Franz Rosensweig, and Lenin were primary contributors. Kuiper was a Zionist, not only because of Israel but as a Christian with Messianic expectation of the new kingdom. Kuiper was also particularly concerned for the renewal of worship among Mennonites and the rediscovery of spiritual freedom and depth. He understood his calling as pastor to proclaim the message of the Old and New Testament within the context of Messianic expectations. In this connection he meant much to many, both within and beyond the Mennonite boundaries.   JMW

Writings by Frits Kuiper: *De Russische kerk en haar lot onder de Sovjets* (Amsterdam, 1923); *De opstanding,* Barth on 1 Cor 15 (Assen, 1928); *Sovjet Rusland en het christendom* (Amsterdam, 1937); *Karl Barth's veroordeling van de kinderdoop* (Amsterdam, 1939); *De Gemeente in de Wereld* (Haarlem, 1941); *Gelooft het evangelie* (Alkmaar, 1944), sermons, 1940-44; *De ware vrijheid* (Haarlem, 1947), on Galatians; *Ontmoeting met het Oude Testament* (Haarlem, 1950); *Israël en de Gojiem* (Haarlem, 1951); *Het Amsterdams gesprek over Israël* (Amsterdam, 1952); *Leven uit de hoóp* (Amsterdam, 1958); *Twee dienaars van één Heer* (Amsterdam, 1961), Samuel Muller and Jan de Liefde; "Communism and Our Christian Faith," in The Lordship of Christ (Elkhart, Ind., 1962); *El designo de Dios para Israël y la iglesia* (Montevideo, 1965); *Der Vorrang der Bibel in der Geschichte der Mennoniten* (Montevideo, 1966); *Met de gemeente de wereld, 1914-1969: Herinneringen van een theoloog* (Amsterdam: Algemene Doopsgezinde Sociëteit, 1969); *Dorst naar recht* (Bussum, 1970); *Christen en socialist Frits Kuiper 1933* (NCSV Zeist [posthumously], 1979).
Kuiper published articles in *De Zondagsbode, Algemeen Doopsgezind Weekblad, Stemmen, In dit Amsterdam, Brieven, Doops. Jaar., Eltheto, Theologie en praktijk, Nederlands Theologisch Tijdschrift, In de Waagschaal, Wending.* He translated Franz Rosenzweig, *Das Büchlein vom gesunden und kranken Menschenverstand* as *Gebruik je verstand* (Rotterdam, 1967). Many printed and duplicated lectures for congregations, ministerial associations, and seminary classes cover topics ranging from the history of grace to messianic Judaism and Mennonite history to Karl Barth and Ernst Bloch.
Memorials to Kuiper appeared in *in dit Amsterdam,* 12, no. 3, (December 1963); *Doops. Jaar.* (1975), 7-12 and articles about him are found in *Doops. Bijdr.,* n.r. 3 (1977), 21-32; *In de Waagschaal,* 17 (Nov. 14, 1981), 391-96. See also E. I. T. Brussee-van der Zee, "De Doopsgezinde Broederschap en het nationaal-socialisme 1933-1940," *Doops. Bijdr.* n.R 11 (1985), 118-29; Marc Jansen, "Frits Kuiper in Kazan: Hulp aan hongerende studenten, 1922-1924," in *Rusland in Nederlandse ogen* (Amsterdam, 1986), 187-212. An incomplete bibliography can be found in the English version of Kuiper, *Klein Drieluik* (Fritz Kuiper foundation, 1980), 145-46.

Kulopeta Madizanga (b. 1933), teacher and pastor of Église du Christ au Zaire, Communauté des Églises de Frères Mennonites au Zaire (Mennonite Brethren Church of Zaire), was born to the Muhenia family in Kavuya Kambolo locality, Mukoso. His non-Christian parents never sent him to school, but hoped he would become their chief. At age 13 he heard a teacher in the Protestant School read about two houses. He wanted to learn more so he secretly attended school, receiving severe punishment at the return of his father, a palm-nut cutter. After two years of harassment, his parents approved his schooling. At age 16 he accepted Christ and was baptized in 1951. At Gungu in 1961 he married Bambenu Kafutshi, who bore him ten children.

Kulopeta studied at the Mennonite Brethren Bible Institute, Kafumba, and the Teachers' Training School, Nyanga. From 1960 to 1964 he taught in Mennonite Brethren Primary and Secondary Schools at Gungu and Kajiji. Because of political unrest the Bible Institute was moved and reopened in Kikwit with Kulopeta as its first Zairian director (1965-67). From 1967 to 1969 Kulopeta studied at the Institute Biblique de Nogent-sur-Marne, France. When he returned to Zaire he began mission work in Kitabi among the Bakwese people, who had a reputation as resistant to the gospel. Through many difficulties Kulopeta and his family persisted there from 1970 to 1980, leaving a church of 145 members and two primary schools. In 1977 Kulopeta was ordained to the ministry.

In 1980 directorship of the °theological education by extension program was given to Kulopeta. In 1987 he reported an enrollment of 1,080 students in 78 centers.   MDyck

Kushal, Sim (ca. 1907 - Apr. 20, 1973), a deacon in the Mennonite Church in India and longtime staff member of the Dhamtari Christian Hospital, was born in the village of Tansi, Charama Police Station, District Bastar, Madhya Pradesh (M.P.), India, to Kushal and Dularin Bai. He was one of three brothers brought to °Dhamtari by his mother and admitted into the American Mennonite Mission boys orphanage.

Sim received an education through the tenth class in the mission schools in Dhamtari. During these years he became a baptized member of the Mennonite Church in India. In 1929 he was selected for compoundry (pharmacy) training by Dhamtari Christian Hospital. From 1932 to 1970 he was head compounder and anesthetist at the hospital. In 1938 he was ordained deacon to assist with the pastoral needs of the Sundarganj congregation members living in and about Baithena. He was also interested in singing and village evangelism.

Sim's first wife died, and he then married her sister Jona Bai. They had two sons and four daughters. After his retirement, Sim opened a small dispensary in Lataborh village, close to Balod. He died while leading singing for the Good Friday service in Dhamtari.   JAF

Biographical data supplied by P. J. Malagar; American Mennonite Mission *Annual Report* (1929).

Kuyf, Wilhelmina (1901-67), missionary and mission administrator, was born in Antwerp, Belgium, of Dutch parents who emigrated to Pennsylvania. At age 12 she joined the First Mennonite Church (GCM) at Philadelphia. She studied at Bluffton College (AB, 1935), and Hartford Theological Seminary. Her career in mission spanned the era of change in the China mission program from before to after World War II. In her career she participated in the full range of opportunities available for service among Mennonites.

Kuyf was sent to China in 1936 by the Board of Foreign Missions (GCM). There she served in Daming (Taming), Hebei (Hopei) Province, in evangelism and public health. She was interned by the Japanese in Taming on Dec. 8, 1941, and repatriated on the *Gripsholm* in June 1942. From 1944 to 1948 she worked for the Mennonite Central Committee, serving temporarily in Akron, Pa., and Calcutta, India, finally reaching China, where she worked in the relief program in Henan (Honan) Province. From 1948 to 1951 Kuyf again served as a missionary, this time working with students in Sichuan Province. She was administrative assistant in the office of the Board of Foreign Missions (GCM) at Newton, Ks., 1951-63.   ARR

Ruth Unrau, *Encircled* (Newton, 1986), 261-73.

L

La Batea. See Zacatecas Colonies, Mexico.

La Honda Colony. See Zacatecas Colonies, Mexico.

La Montaña Colony, Paraguay. See Montaña Colony, La, Paraguay.

Labor Unions (ME III:266). The growth of labor unions in the 20th c. has created difficulties for Mennonites. A 1941 statement on industrial relations, adopted by both the Brethren in Christ and the Mennonite Church (MC), describes the problem. The document states that it is "our conviction that industrial organization in its present form involves a class struggle and conflict which is ultimately due to an absence of the Christian principle of love." Significantly, the document criticizes "unfair and unjust" practices by both employees and employers, rejecting the "coercive methods" of both "labor and capital." Acknowledging the propriety of some kinds of union activity, the conferences affirmed that "As employers we can have no part in manufacturers' or employers' associations in so far as they are organized for the purpose of fighting the labor movement." Extending the Christian love ethic to the rural sector they added, "As agriculturalists we can have no part in farmers' organizations in so far as they are organized for monopolistic or coercive purposes, ultimately employing such methods as the boycott and the strike."

In 1954 the Committee on Economic/Social Relations of the Mennonite Church (MC) modified the earlier stance. "In a manner analogous to that of the state, labor organizations as we know them serve a useful purpose for the maintenance of justice and a balance of power in a sub-Christian society." Conditional involvement would thus be permitted. "For this reason the Christian may cooperate with the union (as he does with the state) in so far as doing so does not conflict with his Christian testimony."

Since 1954 most other North American Mennonite conferences have adopted a similar stance. For example, in 1969 the General Conference of the Mennonite Brethren Churches decided, "That we ought not to forbid union membership," but counseled its members "to join no union which demands primary allegiance from its members over all other commitments. . . ." Employees were urged "To seek to exert a Christian influence where such influence is possible." The Old Order Mennonites, the Amish, and other socially conservative groups still hold, generally, to noninvolvement.

That the issue of labor union membership presents a great dilemma for Mennonites is substantiated in the Kauffmann-Harder data found in the 1975 volume, *Anabaptists Four Centuries Later*. On the one hand the labor union efforts to counteract the dehumanizing and exploitative aspects of certain kinds of industrial production are seen by some as compatible with the Anabaptist ethic. Doubtless the union emphasis on better wages and improved working conditions also played a part. On the other hand, Mennonites could not endorse the inherent reliance on coercion. The conflicting pressures that many thousands of Mennonites experienced as they found themselves pressured to join unions and tightly controlled professional associations seem evident in the responses.

Only 18 percent agreed with the statement that "a church member should not join a labor union if getting or holding a job depends on union membership." Percentages varied from a low of 18 for the Evangelical Mennonite Church to a high of 25 for the Mennonite Church (MC). The statement, "A church member who owns or manages a shop should refuse to recognize or bargain with a labor union" was supported by 22 percent of all five Mennonite groups surveyed. Further, only 17 percent disagreed with the statement that "the best attitude of a Christian laborer toward a union is to join and exert a Christian influence within the union's program and activities." The data cross-tabulation indicates that in labor relations as in other matters, the more °urbanized Mennonites become, the less they adhere to the more traditional conference positions. For better or worse, most Mennonites who encounter labor unions seem to have found at least the minimal requirements of union membership compatible with their profession of faith.

Another expression of North American Mennonite views concerning labor unions can be found in the 1979 "Report on Management/Labor Relations" produced by an inter-Mennonite study committee appointed by the influential and broadly based Mennonite Industry and Business Associates. Published in *The Marketplace* in March 1980, following unanimous acceptance at a MIBA convention, the report, claiming to be neither "pro- or anti-management or labor," stressed that "the Christian's primary allegiance is to God, not to management, union or profession." It rejected "coercion, violence, militancy, threats, misrepresentation" and other similar tactics and added that "each Christian, in the context of the Christian community, must determine his or her response to management/union operation under given circumstances."

While developing an inclusive, biblically argued and analytically advanced document, the MIBA group has clearly modified as well as extended most of the earlier conference views. The report addressed the labor union question in the context of larger issues related to theology of work and theology of relationships. The MIBA report, enhanced by its broadly based inter-Mennonite authorship, identifies the complex issues and presents creative alternatives. It stands as arguably the best Mennonite treatment of the subject.

By the late 1980s the question of what constitutes the best Mennonite stance towards labor unions had become a major issue in many countries. A strike by primary school teachers in Mennonite Church (MC) °mission schools in India, the 1958 confrontation with unions during the construction of buildings for the Mennonite Biblical Seminary in Indiana, and the fact of Mennonite leadership of strikes by school teachers and by professors in various regions of Canada, illustrate the dimensions and scope of the problem. As unionization gradually extends to the service sector, the °professions, the civil service, and even agriculture, Mennonite congregations in North America and abroad find themselves grappling with a pressing set of questions. Many leaders and congregations have not known what advice to give striking teachers, nurses, physicians, factory workers, and, especially in Canada, postal workers and other government employees. The situation becomes even more difficult when Mennonites belonging to the same congregation find themselves involved on opposite sides during a crisis situation or when church members find themselves caught up in illegal strikes or lockouts.

As Mennonites leave closed communities and increasingly merge economically and socially with a society largely governed by adversarial and self-serving norms, they experience much difficulty holding to an alternate love ethic. Some seek to resolve the problem by consciously avoiding certain vocations or work situations. Others manage to negotiate exemption arrangements, some avoid the union aspects of their work, and still others compromise their ethics. Some, both employees and employers, have experienced major losses or severe penalties for holding consistently to their love ethic.

On balance, Mennonites have had major difficulty successfully relating the °peace position to their interaction with labor unions. In the years ahead ethical issues dealing with labor unions will be one of the most important practical testing grounds of Christians committed to the way of peace and reconciliation. JHR

Bibl. on War and Peace (1987), 282-86; Kauffman/Harder, *Anabaptists Four C. Later* (1975), esp. 144-48; John A. Lapp, *India* (1972), 124; Wittlinger, *Piety and Obedience* (1978), 401-4.

See also Industrialization; Ulery, Orville Benjamin.

Lagrange-Elkhart, Ind., Old Order Amish Settlement (ME II:187) in northern Indiana was founded in 1841 when four Amish families from Somerset Co., Pa., moved onto newly acquired farms se. the village of Goshen. The Lagrange-Elkhart community was populated almost exclusively by Amish migrations from Holmes (Ohio) and Somerset Cos. Settlement of this large community resulted in an interesting pattern of grouping with Pennsylvania families locating in the Lagrange County area while Ohio Amish were concentrated in Elkhart County. The two communities differ in degrees of "progressive-

ness" but remain in full fellowship. Even so, differences persist after 140 years in areas such as rubber-tire °buggies, English Bible study and the general degree of °modernity.

Nearly one-third of Amish youth leave the community and generally affiliate with Mennonite and related church groups. All Mennonite churches east of Goshen are heavily populated by first- or second-generation former Amish. Additionally, most members of the seven Conservative Mennonite and four Beachy Amish Mennonite congregations in the area are former Old Order Amish. Even with this attrition rate, the Lagrange-Elkhart community continues to grow. In 1986 it had 65 church districts (congregations) with an overall population of about 10,000. Growth of the community is mainly to the east and north, reaching into Michigan. Latest census figures show that more than one-fourth of Lagrange Co. population is Amish.

Shipshewana, located in the heart of the Amish settlement, with its weekly auctions and 30-acre flea market draws over a million visitors each year. With the influx of tourists, have come craft shops and roadside fruit and vegetable stands to accommodate the busloads of visitors. Menno-Hof, a large visitor center, provides the °tourist a leisurely step back through the centuries of Anabaptist history and tells the story of Amish and Mennonite faith in action. Other towns serving this large Amish population are: Middlebury, Millersburg, Topeka, Emma, Honeyville, and Lagrange. Honeyville boasts the only area public school with nearly 100 percent Amish enrollment. The Amish community supports about 30 private elementary schools.

The recent increase in factory work and building trades have affected this community stimulating greater mechanization on the farm and in the workplace. SLY

Lall, Obdiah Paul (b. Dec. 16, 1913), the second Indian bishop of the Mennonite Church in India, was born in °Dhamtari, Madhya Pradesh (M.P.). His parents, Nandlal and Nohri Bai, were evangelistic workers with the American Mennonite Mission (MC). When Obdiah was age seven his mother died, and because his father was blind, Obdiah was admitted to the Boys Boarding School in Dhamtari. He attended the mission schools through high school level in Dhamtari. In 1940 he graduated from Leonard Theological Seminary, Jabalpur, M.P., with a GTh degree. He was the second national Christian in the Mennonite Church in India to receive formal theological training. In 1940 he married Rhoda Bhagwani, a Christian school teacher.

Lall began his ministry as a language tutor for new missionaries and also served as a village evangelist at Balodgahan. In 1945 he was ordained to the ministry by the church conference. In 1965 he was ordained bishop. Though officially retiring in 1978, he continued to be active in leadership roles. He worked in church planting in Bailadila, Jagdalpur District, an iron mining community, for several years. In 1987 he continued to serve as conference moderator. He served many terms as chairman of the Jalsa Committee (the Mennonite Church in India's annual convention committee), chairman of the

Chattisgarh Christian Mela Committee (an annual interchurch convention in Madhya Pradesh), member of the conference evangelistic committee, editor of the conference paper, *Mennonait Mandli Samachar Patrika*, moderator of the Mennonite Church in India, and chairman of its executive committee for many years.

O. P. Lall is a gifted communicator. His evangelistic messages were free of Western phraseology and he brought dignity and freshness to the worship service. He was also an excellent Bible teacher. His main pastoral assignments were in Sankra, Balodgahan, and Sundarganj (Dhamtari). JAF

Information supplied by Obdiah P. Lall, J. M. Bhelwa, and E. P. Bachan; *Annual Report* Mennonite (MC) Board of Missions (1946), 112-13; "50th Anniversary Brochure" (Mennonite Board of Missions and Charities, 1946), 22.

Lancaster Mennonite Conference (MC) (ME III: 275), the largest conference of the Mennonite Church (MC), has shifted from the relative uniformity of religious thought and expression of the 1950s and has extended borders geographically, ethnically, and numerically. Membership in 1950 numbered 14,061 in 18 bishop districts, all but one in Pennsylvania. Membership in 1986 was 17,033 in 30 districts with approximately one-third outside Pennsylvania, from Maine to Florida.

Increased involvement in foreign and home missions and in higher education led to formation of more bishop districts, which decentralized the authority of the Bishop Board. Congregations developed greater autonomy and formal organization, dropped specific membership requirements, and tolerated more diverse patterns of religious thought and expression, such as instrumental music, open rather than close communion, °charismatic influences, increased employment of professional staff members in greater divisions of labor, and the appropriation of prevailing cultural values (°acculturation). Preference still exists for team ministry.

Several schisms developed in response to these compromises. In 1960 nine ordained men withdrew to form the Mennonite Christian Brotherhood; some of them eventually associated with the °Fellowship Churches. In 1969 the Eastern Pennsylvania Mennonite Church was organized in the wake of differences over general trends and specific issues related to °divorce and remarriage, °television, and relaxed °dress requirements. In 1975 approximately 200 members formed the °Conservative Mennonite Churches of York and Adams Counties.

Despite repeated invitations and limited fraternal ties, Lancaster Conference did not officially join the Mennonite Church (MC) general conference (general assembly) until 1971. In 1977 it reorganized in a structure parallel to the Mennonite Church (MC). Instead of all committees and boards responsible to the Bishop Board as previously, the Bishop Board still serves as the executive board of the conference but is assisted by a Conference Coordinating Council, which coordinates four program boards: Eastern Mennonite Board of Missions and Charities, Board of Education, Board of Brotherhood Ministries, and Board of Congregational Resources. Four other agencies serve the conference: Leadership Council,

Lancaster Mennonite Historical Society, Women's Missionary and Service Commission, and Finance Committee. *Lancaster Conference News* began in 1981 as the semimonthly successor to *Pastoral Messenger* and *Newsletter*. It provides news and interpretation of conference programs and needs. CCW

Robert Bates Graber, "An Amiable Mennonite Schism: The Origin of the Eastern Pennsylvania Mennonite Church," *PMH*, 7 (Oct. 1984), 2-10; Donald B. Kraybill, "Amish, Mennonites, and Brethren in the Modern Era," *PMH*, 10 (April 1987), 2-20.

Lancaster-Chester Counties, Pa., Old Order Amish Settlement (ME III:274) is nestled in the gently rolling countryside of eastern Pennsylvania. The first Amish family migrated to this area in 1752, but the actual settlement developed in 1760. The Lancaster community, which spills over into Berks and Chester Cos., is considered to be the first and oldest Amish settlement in America. In 1988, there were 90 church districts serving a population of more than 15,000 (children and adults), representing the second largest Amish community in the United States. Pennsylvania has 40 Amish settlements and many of these originated from the Lancaster community.

More than 20 distinct groups of Amish and Mennonites are found in the Lancaster settlement. These often represent the perennial "search for purity" groups who choose to differ on such issues as church architecture, plain °dress, horse and °buggy, hooks and eyes and buttons. Each fall and spring Amish ministers and bishops meet for consultation and clarification of issues that may infringe on Amish church discipline.

Amidst the fertility and beauty of Lancaster County, the Amish have lived for almost 250 years. This has given communal stability, °tradition, and heritage. Family names have become prominent, suggesting a certain ethnic purity. Forty-eight percent of the Amish population in this area claim Fisher, Stoltzfus, or King as a surname. Against this rural backdrop flourishes a busy, hectic, tourism industry. In fact, Lancaster has become one of the top ten tourist centers in the United States. The Old Philadelphia Pike from Lancaster City to the town of Intercourse and US Highway 30 east have become important °tourist pathways, often to the dismay of the Amish. Tourists from large industrial cities come primarily to see the plain people in their picturesque agricultural community. The People's Place and the Mennonite Information Center are key information stops for the dozens of busloads of visitors each week. These, coupled with farmer's market and roadside stands, nourish the tourist industry. In this setting, the movie *Witness* was filmed and produced, despite the disapproval of the Amish.

Expensive land prices ($5,000 per acre and higher) and the pressure to modernize have spurred Amish migration to other areas into the 1970s. Since 1978 the trend to nonfarm occupations has replaced migraion as a way to cope with these pressures. In 1987 more than one-third of the Amish in the Lancaster settlement are employed in nonfarm Amish-owned and operated cottage industries and small businesses. With all the changes, Lancaster is still considered by most Amish as the "mother" settlement for all 18th c. immigrants.   SLY

Land, Attitudes toward. See Ecology; °°Farming; Forestation; Occupations; Old Colony Mennonites; Rural Life; Sociological Studies; Work Ethic.

Bibliography: In addition to literature cited under the aforementioned topics, see John A. Hostetler, "The Cultivation of the Soil as a Moral Directive: Population Growth, Family Ties, and the Maintenance of Community Among the Old Order Amish," *Rural Sociology,* 45 (1980), 49-68; Vicky Schreiber Dill, "Land Relatedness in the Mennonite Novels of Rudy Wiebe," *MQR,* 58 (1984), 50-69; Sandra L. Cronk, "Gelassenheit: The Rites of the Redemptive Process in the Old Order Amish and Old Order Mennonite Communities" (PhD diss., U. of Chicago, 1977), cf. *MQR,* 55 (1981), 5-44.

Land Distribution (Russia).
Mennonites settled in colonies in Russia in principle were subject to regulations covering land ownership and land distribution outlined in a law of March 1765 which imposed a system of hereditary household tenure on all foreign colonists. All land was placed in the perpetual and incontestable possession of the colony as a corporate group, and could not be sold or mortgaged to outsiders. Each Mennonite colonist received a separate allotment of 65 desiatin (160 acres; 70 hectares) which they and their descendants could use in perpetuity. This allotment could not be subdivided, but, while the 1764 law specified that only the youngest son could inherit the property, Mennonites, through provisions granted in their 1800 °Privilegium, could follow their own inheritance customs. Usually the eldest Mennonite son inherited the land and homestead, but he had to compensate his siblings for their portion of the estate.

Each allotment included areas of arable, meadow, pasture, and, if available, woodland. Also included was the house and garden plot of 1.5 desiatin. The colony retained rights over wasteland, rivers and lakes; the rest of the land was divided into village areas. At the time of settlement one sixth of the village land was set aside for future population increase (the surplus land) and a further area in the colony to establish new villages (the reserve land) once the surplus land was exhausted. A smaller area was reserved in the villages for the households of those who did not require farm land but who wished to pursue a craft or trade.

Although the colonists lived in compact villages, the land was divided among individual farmers, and their pasture portions were usually consolidated. Sometimes the farmer's land was further divided and shared out by the village assembly so that each received a similar portion where land quality varied. Land-use was also organized and rationalized by common agreement.

During the first half of the 19th c. few farmers cultivated their full allotment. Large areas were given over to pasture for sheep and much of the reserve and surplus land was rented out for the same purpose. As the population of the colonies increased, as arable farming replaced sheep rearing in terms of profitability, demand for land increased. The problem of land shortage and the need to respond to the growing number of landless was recognized as early as 1840 but the crisis really emerged after 1860. Following the °Crimean War (1853-56)

inflation increased and many artisans wished to take up agriculture.

A period of bitter dispute erupted (°°landless) until the government ordered the remaining surplus and reserve land to be distributed. After 1866 the colonists could hold allotments of 32 desiatin (half-farms of 80 acres or 35 hectares) and 12 desiatin (quarter- or small-farms). The colony was made responsible for the settlement of future landless, a poll-tax was instituted, and areas were set aside for rent to raise capital to purchase land for new colonies. A number of these daughter colonies were founded after 1860 by the mother colonies of Molotschna and Chortitza and the system of land distribution in the new settlements usually followed that of the mother colony. Both landless and landowners who wished to better their position had access to land in daughter colonies although it is unclear exactly who was selected or rejected.

As colonies were founded outside European Russia after 1890, Mennonites who settled in Central Asia and east of the Ural Mountains in Siberia adapted to local conditions. Siberian colonists in the first decade of the 20th c. received individual grants of 15 desiatin (37 acres, 16 hectares), but Mennonites still attempted to settle in compact, closed communities.

The problem of landlessness, was never entirely settled. Arguments persisted in the colonies over access to pasture, the division of land, and the selection of settlers for new colonies.

After 1860 many Mennonites rented land from gentry outside the colonies on long-term leases, or they purchased land. Private land purchases had begun before 1860 by entrepreneurs who formed the vanguard of a new social group of °estate owners. But individuals and particularly small groups who purchased land after 1860 often formed compact communities. Unlike in the colonies they were free to farm as they liked, to subdivide their land, and to buy and sell property.

All privately owned land was seized by the Soviet government and redistributed after 1921, although most private landholders had abandoned their land during the Civil War. In the colonies land was redistributed, each family receiving 12 desiatin (30 acres, 13 hectares). This system prevailed throughout the years of New Economic Policy (1921-28), after which land was collectivized.   JU

David G. Rempel, "The Mennonite Colonies in New Russia" (PhD diss., Stanford U., 1933), 102-112, 179-211, cf. *MQR,* 47 (1973), 259-308, and 48 (1974), 5-54. Extensive correspondence on problems of land distribution can be found in the newspaper *Odessaer Zeitung* after 1862.

See also Block Settlement; Wealth.

Land Distribution (Canada and Latin America).
After the American Revolution some Mennonites of Swiss origin in Pennsylvania moved to Ontario, which at that time was known as the Canadian West. One of the reasons for migrating was the availability of land, since inexpensive land in Pennsylvania had become scarce. Some of the land in Ontario was free, other land was available for an inexpensive price.

The first Mennonite settlement in Ontario was

founded in 1786 in the Niagara Penninsula about 20 mi. (32 km.) west of the Niagara River. The second settlement was established about the same time in what became Waterloo County In both of these settlements land was purchased by individuals. When it was discovered that the Mennonites who had purchased the land in the Waterloo Twp. area had been defrauded and were about to lose their land, a stock company was formed by a group of Pennsylvania Mennonites. This stock company collected money in Pennsylvania, bought 60,000 acres (two-thirds of Waterloo Twp.), paid off the mortgage, and made the land available to Mennonites. A number of years later another similar stock company was formed to purchase 45,000 acres in Woolwich Twp. immediately west of Waterloo Twp. This land was in turn sold to individual Mennonites. The land near Markham, Ont., was purchased directly by individuals.

The first Amish settlement in Ontario was inspired by Christian °°Nafziger, from Bavaria, who took out an option on a large tract of land in Wilmot Twp. west of the Mennonite settlements. Amish began to settle on this land in 1824, with individuals taking out title to their own land.

Russian Mennonites who moved to Manitoba in the 1870s also were looking for large tracts of land (°block settlement) sufficient for their expanding populations. Many of the people who immigrated had been °°landless in Russia. In the Bergthal Colony in Russia in 1874, for example, there were 350 landless families. This included about half of the colony. When the Bergthal Colony decided to move, they devised a financial system whereby even the poorest could afford to migrate. The colony decided that all members who had money invested in the local financial institution (°°*Waisenamt*) would contribute 10 percent of their account toward the travel costs of the landless. This allowed everyone to move without a travel debt.

In addition to desiring land adequate for their population, Russian Mennonites who moved to Manitoba, i.e., 3,000 Bergthaler, 690 Kleine Gemeinde, and about 3,240 Reinländer, desired to establish the traditional Russian Mennonite institutions. They established the civil administration of village and *Gebietsamt* (municipality) which was responsible for schools, roads, land distribution, and financial organizations. They also established church organizations (*Gemeinden*), each of which was led by an *Ältester* (°elder) and ministers. The churches provided the religious rationale and basis for the institutions and patterns of living.

All three churches, the Bergthaler, Kleine Gemeinde and Reinländer, decided that in Manitoba they would establish the Russian Mennonite village pattern. Even though villages contravened the Canadian homestead provision which required each homesteader to live on the land to which he claimed title, the Canadian government acceded to the Mennonites' request and allowed them to settle in hamlets. Because the government decided that a hamlet had to have a minimum of 20 householders, original villages normally contained 20 farmyards, 10 on each side of a central street, with 20 quarter-sections (160 acres [65 hectares] per quarter-section) of land surrounding the village. Each quarter-section was legally registered in the name of one of the householders, but the village and the land within the 20 quarter-sections was divided according to the traditional pattern of a street village (*Straßendorf*), a large common pasture, and long narrow strips of land (kögel) upon which crops were grown. This redistribution of land generally had no basis in law, but was undergirded by the authority of the church. In those areas where church authority broke down or where churches split, the villages frequently disbanded. In Manitoba a tension was thus established between the wishes and the legal rights of the individual on one hand, and the good of the community on the other.

Some of the Bergthal villages in both the East and West Reserve in Manitoba fell apart fairly early. When the young people needed more land, land acquisition became an individual or family matter. This tended to cause economic differences to increase with the rich becoming richer and the poor becoming poorer.

The Reinländer Mennonite Church on the West Reserve in Manitoba retained the village pattern, and land acquisition for its growing population was a community concern. The Reinländer church attempted to negotiate for larger tracts of land upon which villages could be established in the traditional pattern, and in which people could apply for homesteads or purchase land. Consequently the Reinländer church negotiated with the Canadian government for a large tract of land in the Hague-Osler area in 1895, and in the Swift Current area in 1905. Both regions were part of the Northwest Territories during the time of negotiation, and within the province of Saskastchewan since 1905. The terms of the reserve were that the land was set aside for exclusive Mennonite settlement, but all the land was purchased or taken up in homestead individually. The wealthier people were consequently able to purchase more land for themselves and their children than were the poor families.

The major reason for the Mennonite emigrations to Mexico and Paraguay from western Canada in the 1920s was the resolve by a number of churches to prevent the Saskatchewan and Manitoba governments from assuming control of their schools. In addition to this principal reason, the leadership of the churches had begun to view with some unease the growing general °wealth, and the increasing disparity between the wealthy and the poor. Some leaders felt that a difficult pioneer experience in a new land might help to level the economic ability of the members, and create a more united church.

The groups which emigrated in the 1920s, namely the Reinländer (°Old Colony) and °Sommerfelder to Mexico, and the Sommerfelder, Saskatchewan Bergthaler, and °Chortitzer to the Menno Colony in Paraguay, all decided to establish the village system in their new settlements. They laid out their villages in the tradtional Russian Mennonite *Straßendorf* pattern.

When the Sommerfelder Church settled in Mexico it decided to allow its members to decide whether they wanted to acquire legal title to their land communally through a corporation from which the land would be purchased by individuals, or whether they wanted to own their land by individual title.

The Old Colony Church in Mexico, in contrast, decided that each colony, namely Manitoba, Swift, and Durango colonies, would each be owned communally in the name of a corporation consisting of men selected by the church in each of the colonies. The land was subsequently divided into villages, and the people, even before they left Canada, were able to select which land in which village they wanted to purchase. Those in Canada who were wealthier, could purchase more land. All purchases were, however, made from the corporation and not from the government. In this way the church could control who initially bought land and to whom land could subsequently be sold. It is also evident the vexatious problem of economic disparity was built right into the initial Old Colony settlements in Mexico. Since the 1950s in the Old Colony settlements in Mexico, the economic disparities between rich and poor, landowners and landless, have become ever greater.

The Old Colonists who emigrated from Mexico to Belize, Bolivia, Paraguay, and Argentina retained the Mexico pattern of land ownership. They settled in villages. The land on which the villages were laid out was owned by a corporation established by the church. The church was thus able to control the purchase and sale of land. This was considered an important protective device because nearly without exception, Mennonite churches from Canada or the United States carried on missions directed at the Old Colonists. If the land was not controlled by the church, the church feared that members who converted to these mission churches could break up the village communities as had happened in Manitoba before the emigration to Mexico in the 1920s.

Colonies in Paraguay which were founded by Mennonites who moved from Canada (Menno Colony, 1926; Bergthal and Sommerfeld, 1948) and from Europe (Fernheim, 1930; Friesland, 1935; Vollendam, 1948; Neuland, 1948) have also followed the pattern in which the land comprising the colony is legally owned collectively by the colony. The colony controls who can sell and purchase land. In some colonies, e.g., Menno Colony, the colony's producer-consumer °cooperative handles the transactions of land. In the Fernheim colony the principal town, Filadelphia, has been opened up to permit non-Mennonites to reside in it. Generally, though, control of land purchase allows colonies to prevent non-Mennonite Paraguayans from moving into colony communities.

Mennonite missions in Paraguay have converted numerous people of two nomadic peoples, the Lengua and Chulub (Chulup), to the Mennonite faith. From their Mennonite mentors these nomadic people have learned the practice of settled agriculture. During the past number of years, Paraguayan Mennonites, with help from West German Mennonites, have helped these people purchase their own land.   JF

Isaak M. Dyck, *Auswanderung der Reinlaender Mennoniten Gemeinde von Canada nach Mexiko* (Cuauhtemoc, Mexico, 1971); Adolf Ens, "Mennonite Relations with Governments—Western Canada 1870-1925" (PhD diss., U. of Ottawa, 1978); F. H. Epp, *Mennonites in Canada, I*; E. K. Francis, *In Search of Utopia* (Altona, Man.: D. W. Friesen, 1955); Martin Friesen, *Neue Heimat in der Chacowildnis*

(Loma Plata: Menno Colonie, 1987; Altona: D. W. Friesen, 1987); Harry Leonard Sawatzky, *They Sought a Country: Mennonite Colonization in Mexico* (Berkeley, Cal.: U. of California Press, 1971); idem, *Sie Suchten eine Heimat: Deutsch-Mennonitische Kolonisierung in Mexico 1922-1984* (Marburg, Germany: N.G. Elwert Verlag, 1986); Walter Schmiedehaus, *Die altkolonier Mennoniten in Mexiko* (Winnipeg, CMBC, 1982); William Schroeder, *The Bergthal Colony*, rev. ed. (Winnipeg, CMBC, 1986).

Laos, a small, landlocked country in Southeast Asia. Mennonite Central Committee (MCC) placed its first representatives in the capital city of Vientiane in 1975. This was a time of uncertainty and transition, since Laos had just been through a major war and had suffered intense bombing by the United States. Early MCC assistance to Laos focused on increasing food production and helping displaced families resettle in their home villages. In 1981 MCC shifted its focus to village level, locally sustainable education and health programs. MCC also began working with officials of the heavily bombed province of Xieng Khouang to clear fields and villages of unexploded ordinance. In 1987 MCC had two volunteers involved in projects in 11 of 16 provinces.   BS

Lapa Colony (Núcleo Leiteiro). See Witmarsum Colony, Brazil.

Lapp, Esther Ebersole (June 26, 1880-May 7, 1917). Born at Sterling, Ill., Esther was the daughter of Elias R. and Barbara Stauffer Ebersole. She lived most of her early life in Adams Co., Nebr. After graduation from the nurse's training course at the Passavant Memorial Hospital, Chicago, she married Nebraskan George J. °°Lapp on June 25, 1905. Along with her husband, she sensed a call to missionary work in India. Appointed by the Mennonite Board of Missions and Charities (MC) they served at several locations in the Chhattisgarh region of the Central Provinces, later known as Madhya Pradesh. They were involved in educational and medical programs as well as the establishment of several congregations. She pioneered in developing a small group of women teachers called Bible women (°lay evangelists). Mother of three daughters, she was a significant representative of a group of early 20th c. Mennonite women who used their professional training in a church vocation. She died at Darjeeling, India, at the age of 36.   JAL

American Mennonite MC Mission, Dhamtari, India, *Building on the Rock* (Scottdale: MPH, 1926), esp. 179-80; John A. Lapp, *India* (1972), index.

Lapp, Fannie Hershey (Dec. 9, 1882-Oct. 14, 1963), was the daughter of Amos H. and Lavina Hershey of Manheim, Pa., where she grew up and graduated from high school (1898). She felt led to prepare for Christian service and received a certificate from Bethany Bible School, Chicago, Ill., in 1911, and a BSL degree in 1930 She also trained to become a practical nurse.

Before coming to India in 1913 under the Mennonite Board of Missions and Charities (MC), she served as a teacher in a winter Bible school at Canton, Ohio (°urban churches). While on her first furlough, on Apr. 14, 1920, she married George J.

°°Lapp, a widowed fellow missionary. Together she and George developed the work at the Ghatula evangelistic station and other stations, where Fannie distinguished herself as an able Bible teacher and worker with the Bible women (°lay evangelists). She was a constant support to her husband in his pastoral and conference responsibilities.

The Lapps retired in 1945 to Goshen, Ind., where she edited the *Daily Prayer Calendar* and related °mission education materials. George Lapp died in 1951, Fannie died in Arlington, Mass., but is buried in the Elkhart Prairie cemetery, Goshen, Ind.   JAF

Building on the Rock (Scottdale: MPH, 1926) 180; Esther Rose Graber, comp., "MBM Missionary Directory" (1984); *GH* (Nov. 26, 1963) 1062; Rich, *Mennonite Women* (1983) 97, 144, 215; John A. Lapp, *India*, 68, 72, 255; MC Archives (Goshen), Hist. MSS 1-143; interview with Harriet (Lapp) Burkholder.

Lapp, John Edwin (Sept. 11, 1905-Sept. 1, 1988), Mennonite Church (MC) pastor, bishop, and church leader, was born in Lansdale, Pa., the son of Isaiah L. and Kate Krupp Clemmer Lapp. In 1920, he joined the Plains Mennonite congregation, where on June 22, 1933, he was ordained by lot to the ministry. Previously he had worked at many types of work after his graduation from high school in 1923, and had finally settled on the ownership of a small family-run grocery store and delicatessen in Lansdale. On Sept. 15, 1926, he had married Edith Nyce, daughter of Allen and Emma Nyce. Their children are: John A., Mary Lapp Swartley, James, Daniel, Samuel, Joseph, Sarah Lapp Kolb, Ruth Lapp Guengerich, and Rhoda Lapp Greenlee. Edith died on May 27, 1984.

On June 1, 1937, John was ordained bishop in the middle district of Franconia Conference. That same year he was appointed to the newly organized Peace Problems Committee of Franconia Conference (member, 1937-62; chairman most of that time).

During John's tenure as a bishop and moderator (1953-69) of Franconia Conference, the conference passed actions to permit Bible studies, young people's meetings, and young people's institutes, and eventually permitted presentations by special music groups during congregational worship (°singing)—all actions that John helped to promote.

In the wider church John has written articles for numerous Mennonite publications since the late 1930s. In 1941 he was elected to the Peace Problems Committee of the Mennonite Church (MC) general conference (later Committee of Peace and Social Concerns; chairman, 1962-71). He was also a member of Mennonite Central Committee (MCC) Peace Section, and the consultative council of the °°National Service Board for Religious Objectors (1940-). On two occasions in 1967 he presented testimony before the House Armed Services Committee in response to a new bill that would have inducted °conscientious objectors into the armed services before their applications for alternate service could be considered. A strong advocate of conscientious objection to military service, John and other members of the Committee on Peace and Social Concerns in 1969 supported denominational recognition of nonregistrants.

In retirement John took up the folk art of

°*Fraktur* and made nearly 500 decorative pieces.
                                                                    JCM

Tape-recorded interviews with John E. Lapp, March 4 and 18, 1987, Souderton, Pa., in possession of J. C. Munro, Harleysville, Pa.; Beulah Stauffer Hostetler, *American Mennonites and Protestant Movements* (Scottdale, 1987); *MWR* (Oct. 27, 1988), 15.

Lapp, Sarah Hahn (July 9, 1869-Oct. 25, 1943), was born in Clarence Center, N.Y. She was the eldest of five children born to Jacob and Anna Eyman Hahn. When Sarah was 30 years old she took nurse's training in Chicago and there became acquainted with Mahlon Lapp a worker at the Mennonite Home Mission (MC). They were married on June 10, 1901. That same year the couple were appointed by the Mennonite Evangelizing and Benevolent Board (later Mennonite Board of Missions and Charities, MC) for service in India where Mahlon served as superintendent of the American Mennonite Mission (MC) and bishop of the emerging °Mennonite Church in India.

After her husband's death in 1923, Sarah continued her service in India in village evangelism, touring with her team of evangelists and Bible women (°lay evangelists) in and around the area south of her Balodgahan station. She was a hardy woman who seldom became sick and had a quiet disposition and deeply devotional spirit. She was not a gifted speaker, but her relentless passion to share the Good News and to minister to the sick and suffering endeared her to Christians and non-Christians.

She retired from the mission field in 1942 and died at New Watergate, Ohio, after a scant year at home visiting her friends.   JAF

GH (Nov. 25, 1943), 735; *Building on the Rock* (Scottdale: MPH, 1926), 177-78; *Chr. Monitor* 36 (Jan. 1944), 14-15; Esther Rose Graber, comp., "MBM Missionary Directory" (1984); Rich, *Mennonite Women* (1983), 144; John A. Lapp, *India* (1972), 70, 161, 254.

See also Urban Churches.

Lark, James and Rowena. James Lark was born May 4, 1888 in Savannah, Ga., the only child of Lela and James Lark. Orphaned at six years of age, with the help of relatives and friends he graduated from Quaker Institute for College Youth (which later became Cheney State College) in Pennsylvania in 1916. He taught for a time at Florida Baptist Academy at Jacksonville. He was baptized in a Baptist church at age 16.

James and Rowena were married in 1918. They had six children: James, Juanita, Essie, Rowena, Emma, and Alexander. In 1927 the family moved to a farm near Quakertown, Pa. There they eventually became members of the Rocky Ridge Mennonite mission. The Larks were invited to surrounding communities to help conduct summer Bible school programs. In the summer of 1944 they were called to lead the summer Bible school program in Chicago. On Feb. 18, 1945, James and Rowena entered full-time service as superintendents of the Mennonite mission work among the Afro-Americans of the Chicago area. They began a number of activities for children such a boys' club, girls' chorus, camping program, and summer Bible schools. James was ordained a minister in October 1946. Their Sunday school work led eventually to the establishment of the Dearborn St. Mennonite Church. In 1949 they started a camp near Hopkins Park, Ill. (later called Camp Rehoboth) and the St. Anne Congregation in Rehoboth. Later the Larks engaged in summer Bible school ministries in Saginaw, Mich.; St. Louis; and Los Angeles.

In the mid-1960s the Larks moved to Fresno, Cal., where they started a church which did not have Mennonite affiliation. They also started a number of programs aimed at strengthening the black community both educationally and economically. After Rowena died in March 1970, James continued with urban church planting. In Wichita, Ks., he started an ambitious project aimed at presenting a wholistic ministry including day care, nursery, a recreational program, Bible studies, a clinic, and a community garden. He helped revitalize a dying church there (renamed Zion, his last pastorate). He died on Jan. 10, 1978, after a long illness.   MT HB

Adapted from *MC Yearbook* (1981), 8-9; John Ruth, *Maintaining the Right Fellowship* (Scottdale, 1984), 484, 485, 522.

Las Pavas Colony. See Reinland Colony, Bolivia.

Las Piedras Colony, Bolivia. See Piedras Colony, Bolivia.

Las Virginias Colony. See Casas Grandes Colonies, Mexico.

Latin America District Conference (MB) began in 1937 as a mission effort of the Southern District Conference (MB). Harry and Sarah Neufeld were the first missionaries to work with the Hispanic Americans living in a valley at the southern tip of Texas, separated from Mexico by the Rio Grande River. Other workers during the early years included Henry and Anna Esau, Henry and Ruth Thomas, Ruben and Eva Wedel, Daniel and Elsie Wirsche, Alvin and Ruth Neufeld, Ruth Loewen, and A. W. Epp.

A Christian day school built in El Faro, Tex., in 1948 reached a peak of 120 students in 12 grades. It was closed after 21 years of service.

In the early 1960s the mission was organized as the Latin American Mennonite Brethren District Conference (LAMB) with seven churches in the United States (Casita-Garciasville, La Grulla, La Joya, Mission, Lull, Donna, and Pharr) and three churches in Mexico (Reynosa, Diaz Ordaz, and Magneyes). The LAMB conference, consisting of 300 members in 1984, conducts work in youth activities, missions, Christian education, general welfare and Mennonite Disaster Service, and administration. Among the leaders of the conference are Alfredo Tagle, Ricardo Pena, Inocencia Garcia, and Roland Mireles.   WP

Anna Hiebert Esau, *What God Has Done: The Story of the Latin American Mennonite Brethren Conference* (Scottdale, 1988); *MB Yearbook* (1981), 195.

Latin American Mennonite Congress. See Congresos Menonitas Latinoamericanos.

Law, Attitudes toward Civil and Criminal. Mennonite attitudes toward criminal and civil law can best be understood against the background of the "Two Kingdoms" doctrine in the theology of Martin °°Luther. While the Anabaptists departed significantly from the views of Luther and °°Zwingli on matters regarding the relationship between the church and the state and Christian participation in law and °government, they nevertheless accepted the way in which Luther defined these institutions and structured the problem in his "Two Kingdoms" theology.

There are several elements of this theology that are significant for the understanding of law. First, it holds that there are two realms in which God is active, each governed by different norms. The "spiritual kingdom" is the realm governed by the gospel norms of °love and °grace, revealed in Jesus Christ. The "earthly kingdom" is the realm of the sinful human nature, which necessarily must be governed by the norms of law, force, and justice. Second, the state is an institution "ordained by God" (Rom 13) in the earthly kingdom to restrain evil and do °justice in the sinful world. Law is understood as the means by which the state accomplishes this purpose. It is the command of a state, backed up by the coercive threat of force or even violence. For this reason both Luther and the Anabaptists almost always referred to the state and its laws as "the sword."

Luther recognized that, because law is essentially coercive, it is inconsistent with the standards of Christian love and grace that ought to guide the conduct of Christians in the "private sphere" of their individual relations with each other. The major disagreement the Anabaptists had with Luther was not over this point, but over the nature of the Christian's proper relationship to the two kingdoms. While Luther believed that Christians necessarily lived in both kingdoms and assumed obligations in both, the Anabaptists for the most part believed that the whole of the Christian life should be lived within the spiritual °kingdom of love and grace and should be governed by its norms. For them, the church was a community of believers set apart from the earthly kingdom, which should live completely according to the norms of the gospel.

While the Anabaptists did not have a uniform view of the specific implications of this general principle in matters relating to the participation in government and legal activities, in general they viewed such participation with extreme skepticism, if not totally rejecting it. Most held that a Christian ought not to serve as a magistrate in either criminal or civil procedures, nor should a Christian use the civil courts to bring action against others.

With Luther, the Anabaptists viewed both civil and criminal law as the product of the °°state, and the state they both agreed, was ordained by God. Thus, law was not founded upon some "natural" or social moral order, as the scholastic tradition of "natural law" jurisprudence held. In this latter tradition law received its authority over the consciences of citizens from the fact that it embodied fundamental norms of morality and justice. A law that violated the moral law of God or of "nature" was not, strictly speaking, a law at all. It did not "bind in conscience;" that is, it had no moral authority, and hence did not require the obedience of its subjects.

As part of their rejection of Roman Catholicism, Luther and the Anabaptists rejected all forms of natural law thinking. For both Luther and the Anabaptists, the law receives its authority from the coercive power of the state. This distinction is important for several reasons. First, it makes force and will (e.g., the will of the sovereign) the source of the law's authority rather than some independent standard of justice and moral virtue (natural law). And second, it creates a gap between the authority law exercises over its subjects and the authority of the state to promulgate law. In other words, for Luther and the Anabaptists, the state is divinely ordained by God to govern its citizens by its laws, but those laws exercise authority over citizens because they are the enforceable demands of the state, not because they reflect the will of God for the society. For Luther the validity of law does not depend upon its content but upon its source in a divinely ordained state having the power to enforce it.

In the terminology of modern jurisprudence, the Lutheran and Anabaptist view of law closely resembles the doctrine known as "legal positivism." It attempts to define law in purely descriptive rather than normative terms. Laws are simply those commands issued by states which they are able to enforce through threat or use of force. The validity of the law depends solely upon its being recognized as law and followed by the bulk of the citizens. It has nothing to do with its conformity to any particular standards of morality or justice. In the "natural law" view, the authority of any given state depends upon the moral validity of its laws. For the legal positivists it is the other way around. The authority of the state is primary, and the validity of law consists solely its being the enforceable commands of that state.

It is easy to see why both Luther and the Anabaptists viewed law as the antithesis of Christian love and grace, for its primary nature is the coercive force which backs it up. They did not distinguish civil law from the criminal law, since both were in the final analysis instruments of this coercive force. Whether the function of law was execution, imprisonment, fine, or the awarding of claims, it was still the coercive extension of the "sword."

It is also not surprising that the Anabaptist and Mennonite tradition generally does not make a clear distinction between the state as an institution and the phenomenon of law. Both are lumped together under the rubric of "the sword." Consequently, the questions of Christian participation in the government offices, of the relationship of church and state, of participation in war, of the enforcement of law, and the use of law and courts, also tend to be treated as one. In all of these the primary issue is the Christian use of, or participation in, actions or institutions of coercion and force. This tendency continues into the 20th c. It is clearly evident in the most influential 20th c. discussion of these issues among North American Mennonites, Guy F. °Hershberger's War, Peace, and Nonresistance (1944).

This attitude is reinforced by the belief that all of these institutions and activities are a part of the "earthly kingdom" and are "outside the perfection of Christ." It is also reinforced by the fact that the phenomena of coercion, force, and violence tend to be treated as morally equivalent. This is because, as Hershberger's title suggests, the fundamental moral concept for Mennonites has been "nonresistance," which is usually understood to require the rejection of all forms of coercive and forceful, as well as violent, means of resisting evil. Again, all distinctions usually drawn among these concepts are blurred by the tendency to treat all of them under the term "the sword." Thus, the "nonresistance" principle makes the moral question of Christian participation in °politics, government, and law essentially the same as that of participation in war.

Thus, throughout Mennonite history there has been among them a general reluctance to use the courts for the enforcement of personal rights against others. But as Mennonites became more °urbanized and entrepreneurial they found it more difficult to conduct affairs without recourse to litigation and their reluctance to use litigation tended to wane. In Russia and South America, where Mennonites developed almost completely autonomous communities, they even established among themselves quasi-legal mechanisms for the control of both civil disputes and criminal offenses as well (Kreider, 1951). A supportive theology for such activities, however, was not developed in those contexts.

As late-20th c. Mennonites became more urbanized and integrated into the social and economic institutions of their society, there also emerged new interpretations of the doctrine of nonresistance. These attempted to draw moral distinctions between the uses of coercive and even forceful resistance on the one hand, and the use of violence on the other, admitting the appropriateness of the former while continuing to reject the latter (Sider, 1979; Friesen, 1986). This reinterpretation of the traditional doctrine permitted as well a different approach to the use of law as a coercive, though not necessarily violent, instrument for the pursuit of °justice.

This changing position is reflected in the *Summary Statement on the Use of the Law* officially adopted by the Mennonite Church (MC) General Assembly in 1981. It went beyond the prevailing traditional Mennonite view of law by affirming the "positive role of law in human society," and "encouragement for the professional practice of law." It advocated that "Christians should use the positive provisions of the civil law . . . in order to fulfill the intention of law," including especially the bringing of justice to the poor and the oppressed. However, the *Summary Statement* affirmed the view that use of the law must always be governed by the basic Christian goals of peace and reconciliation, beyond those of justice, and never by the aim to "satisfy selfish desires."   CGB

Bibl. on *War and Peace* (1987), 287-302; Guy F. Hershberger, *War, Peace, and Nonresistance* (Scottdale, 1944); Willard M. Swartley, ed., *The Bible and Law*, Occasional Papers, 3 (Elkhart: IMS, 1982); CRR 3, ch. 12-13; Mennonite Church (MC) General Assembly, *The Use of the Law* (Scottdale, 1982); Ronald J. Sider, *Christ and Violence* (Scottdale, 1979); Duane K. Friesen, *Christian Peacemaking and International Conflict: A Realist Pacifist Perspective* (Scottdale, 1986); Robert S. Kreider, "The Anabaptist Conception of the Church in the Russian Mennonite Experience, 1789-1870," *MQR*, 25 (1951), 17-33.

See also Authority; Church-State Relations; Lawsuits; Occupations; Persecution.

Law, Theology of. Law may be defined as "the order of justice and right to which individuals and groups should conform and which judicial authority should enforce" (Patrick, 4). Moral law is what a person or groups are obligated to do regardless of legal consequences; judicial law is what sovereign authority is obligated to enforce. Both are part of a legal system. "Theology of law" is then the relation of God to "the order of justice and right," a relationship which profoundly affects the definition of law itself.

Harold Berman maintains that modern western law began in the 11th and 12th c. A.D., under church guidance. Motivated by a struggle for supremacy between pope and emperor, it resulted in a counterbalancing between secular and religious authorities, the codification of canon (church) and civil law, and the establishment of both church and civil courts. Both authorities shared in a common "integration of law with religion, of order and justice with faith and morals, in an integrated community which transcended both" (Hawke, 98). An advantage of this system was that law and "state" were not synonymous, since there were both church and civil courts. The integration meant, however, that the laws of both were backed by coercive force.

Early Lutheranism accepted this Constantinian solution, but rejected the church's jurisdiction of law, making law the exclusive domain of the state. Lutheran doctrine of the two kingdoms maintained that the Christian, citizen of both, was to follow the Sermon on the Mount in private life, but in public life was to uphold law by engaging in vocations such as executioner and soldier.

Though Calvinists agreed with many of Luther's teachings, they modified his doctrine of two kingdoms. For them the church consisted of congregations, each with its own elected leadership and legal authority. This legal authority, like the older Catholic vision, was balanced against the civil polity and might dominate it. Congregations had their own laws regulating worship, theological doctrine, and morals, including aspects of economic and political life.

Most English Calvinists (°Puritans) did not challenge the king's authority over the church as Calvin would have done, but attempted to reform the English church from within. They took over leadership of Parliament in the 17th c., believing that God had destined England an elect nation to incarnate the divine purpose for humanity. In England and America they believed that the principle use of moral and judicial law was to teach humanity the way of God, a way for individual and corporate life.

Varied in their beliefs, Anabaptists like °Hubmaier held that the Christian may be a judge, and "bear the sword in God's stead against the evil doer"; others such as the apocalyptic °Münster Anabaptists maintained that God had established the final kingdom at Münster and that the elect were to execute vengeance on oppressors of the poor.

This essay will deal with those southern Anabaptists represented by the °Schleitheim Confession (1527); Hans Schnell's statement on law (ca. 1575), which breathes the spirit of Schleitheim; the view of the Hutterite leader, Peter °°Riedemann; and the writings of °Menno Simons, leader of the northern wing of Anabaptism.

The Anabaptist theology of law should be understood against the background of the legal revolution begun in the 11th-12th c. and the 16th c. reformers. It was based upon a doctrine of two kingdoms which, unlike that of Luther, defined the congregation as voluntarily baptized adults, and argued for a strict separation of church and state. Accepting Christ's demand to love the enemy, Anabaptists rejected Luther's concept that the prince was (emergency) head of the church, maintaining that Christians should not be magistrates since magistrates were expected to enforce law by use of arms against the principality's internal and external enemies. They insisted that Christians were to serve neither as executioners or soldiers, and that the state on the other hand was not to interfere with or persecute the church.

Hans Schnell, naming three types of law, argued that government is based upon the Noahic law of vengeance (Gen 9:6), i.e., the "natural law" which he identified with Paul's admonition in Rom 13. A positive institution in a fallen world, government's power is limited to punishing the evil and protecting the good, for which Christians pay taxes. Although Paul called government a "minister of God," Schnell pointed out that he thus spoke of Nero, persecutor of Christians; of Pharaoh, a "vessel of wrath fitted for destruction"; of the Babylonian king who was God's rod to punish Israel; and of Pilate, who crucified Jesus. Whether it performs well or badly, government performs as a slave rather than as an heir, and will be rewarded or punished according to its performance.

Schnell's second type of law, which God gave through Moses that Israel might know sin until Christ comes, is equated with the Old Testament. It includes a physical kingdom with a ruler, power of the sword, a priesthood, and literal law. Though this law included the law of vengeance (body for body), the Hebraic law differed from Gentile law in that it "foreshadowed the true essence in Christ and his kingdom."

Schnell's third type of law, the law of Christ, annuls the law of vengeance: "For Christ is the end of the law. We become dead to the law through the body of Christ, so that we have another law. There it is no longer a matter of body for body but only love and mercy, repentance, and forgiveness of sins, loving the foe and praying for him."

Schnell tends to equate the Old Testament law of vengeance with state law which, in the new order represented by the church, is annulled in Christ. He maintains that the law of vengeance and the law of Christ should not be mixed as when Constantine assumed the name Christian, "which is indeed itself a cause for lamenting. . . ." Schnell cites Mk 10:42 to contend that if any ruler wishes to be a Christian he must be born again by the Spirit, dare no longer execute vengeance with the sword, "but must love his enemy and in suffering with Christ must pray" for him, bearing the cross of Christ.

The Hutterite leader, Peter Riedemann, admonished Christians not to go to law with their own case nor to be judges (1 Cor 6).

Menno Simons, taking on the task of transforming the remnants of the Münsterite Anabaptists into the peaceable kingdom, had a more positive attitude toward government than did the Schleitheim Confession though he says little about law. Addressing princes, he admonished them to: ". . . believe Christ's word, fear God's wrath, love righteousness, do justice to widow and orphans, judge rightly between a man and his neighbor, fear no man's highness, despise no man's littleness, hate all avarice, punish with reason. . . ." He condemned rulers who accept bribes, pervert justice, and who persecute Christians.

Ernst °°Troeltsch assessed that the Protestant reformers added nothing new to medieval jurisprudence: "The Protestant theory of the state is in both [Lutheranism and Calvinism] based on that very same Christian 'Law of Nature' which, in the Middle Ages, was compounded out of Stoicism, Aristotle, and the Bible. . . ." (Troeltsch, 107). He maintained that the parent of modern human rights was not church Protestantism but Anabaptism and Spiritualism which the Reformation hated and drove forth into the new world. It is generally recognized that in this area Anabaptism has made a major contribution to modern jurisprudence.

Because of persecution the strategy of nonresistant Mennonites since the Reformation has been largely one of withdrawal, by which they maintained the Anabaptist attitude toward state law. Communities in Russia accepted some state characteristics, but never lost the tension between coercion and biblical pacifism. Communities in Colonial America became somewhat more positive to state law because of William Penn's "Holy Experiment." Canadian communities are more active in a government sympathetic to minorities, though not without some tensions of faith.

Influenced by Great Awakening, °revivalism, two °world wars, °urbanization, °education, world °mission, °relief service, °health work, and reconciliation and prisoner rehabilitation programs, North American Mennonites have largely ended their strategy of withdrawal, reviving an interest in justice and law.

Writing in the mid-20th c., Guy °Hershberger attempted to apply the Schleitheim position to the modern world. He maintained that Christians may use state law for purposes of justice, may defend themselves in court but should work for a just and peaceful settlement outside the courts, and should settle their own disputes among themselves. He recognized a need for Christian attorneys who walk in the way of the cross, whose services do not include aggressive litigation, and who assist fellow Christians in this way. More recently there is renewed interest in victim-offender °reconciliation programs for justice alongside of and outside of state legal structures.

Theology of law is being clarified further among Mennonites by modern biblical studies. Modern study of Old Testament law began with the discovery of an extensive body of Near Eastern law, dramatized especially by the Hammurabi Code. Old Testament law deals with secular concerns comparable to Near Eastern law, but is oriented away from violent kingship power to the structures of covenant and worship. Its dominant characteristic is not vengeance but the motive/model clause, especially Yahweh's liberation of Israel from Egypt. Though Old Testament law codes provide for capital punishment, some Old Testament texts emphasize forgiveness and reconciliation even for capital crimes (Gn 4; Hos 1-3; 11; Jer 3). Old Testament law is especially concerned for the slave, the poor, and politically weak. Its goal is an egalitarian society, each household an economic unit free from tyranny. From a Near Eastern perspective, Old Testament law represents a major break from state law, a turning toward Jesus and the New Testament.

New Testament studies reveal that Jesus affirms covenant law in the synoptic Gospels. In the Sermon on the Mount, household laws, and Apostolic admonitions, Jesus and early church deepened and widened covenant law for all nations by orienting it about the authority and example of Christ's person.

In summary then, biblical theology of law represents a new "order of justice and right," which annuls state law, brings believers into tension with it or both.   ML

Harold J. Berman, *Law and Revolution, The Formation of the Western Legal Tradition* (Harvard U. Press, 1983); Leonard Gross, "Jurisprudential Perspectives in the Light of Anabaptist-Mennonite Tradition: Bibliography with an Interpretive Introduction," *Christian Legal Society Quarterly*, 5, no. 2 (1984); idem, "The Anabaptists and Law" (unpublished paper, 1986); Guy Franklin Hershberger, *The Way of the Cross in Human Relations* (Scottdale, 1958); James C. Juhnke, "Mennonites in Militarist America: Some Consequences of World War I," in *Kingdom, Cross and Community*, ed. J. R. Burkholder and Calvin Redekop (Scottdale, 1976), 171-78; CRR 3; William J. Hawke, Millard C. Lind, and John E. Toews, in *The Bible and Law*, Occasional Papers no. 3 (Elkhart: IMS, 1982); Millard C. Lind, *Transformation of Justice: From Moses to Jesus*, New Perspectives on Crime and Justice: Occasional Papers of the MCC Canada Victim Offender Ministries Program and the MCC U.S. Office of Criminal Justice, no. 5 (Dec. 1986); Dale Patrick, *Old Testament Law* (Atlanta: John Knox Press, 1985); Peter Rideman, *Account of Our Religion, Doctrine and Faith*, trans. Kathleen E. Hasenberg (London: Hodder and Stoughton, and Plough Publishing House, 1950, 1970); Hans Schnell, "Thorough Account from God's Word, How to Distinguish Between the Temporal and Spiritual Regimes. . .," ed. Leonard Gross, trans. Elizabeth Bender (unpublished); Ernst Troeltsch, *Protestantism and Progress, A Historical Study of the Relation of Protestantism to the Modern World*, trans. by W. Montgomery (Boston: Beacon Press, 1958).

Lawrence Co., Tenn., Old Order Amish Settlement. See Ethridge, Tenn., Old Order Amish Settlement.

Lawsuits (ME III:375). The traditional position of Mennonites has been to avoid lawsuits almost at any cost. This position was in part based on Biblical interpretation (particularly on the doctrine of °nonresistance), but also resulted from the cultural milieu in which Mennonites found themselves. As long as Mennonites lived in insular rural communities they could settle disputes among themselves and avoid contact with the law except that necessary to carry out transfers of property.

Though many Mennonites continue to hold this view of the law, the changed environment in which North American Mennonites find themselves in the late 20th c. has made it increasingly difficult for them to avoid contact with the law. Mennonites have continued to move from agriculture into °businesses and the °professions; from rural communities to °urban and suburban settings; from dealing primarily among themselves to dealing primarily with non-Mennonites. Mennonites now commonly purchase automobile or health °insurance policies that include subrogation clauses requiring the insured to authorize the insurance company to sue if liability disputes arise. Mennonites now frequently direct institutions and corporations that own property, and thus must think of the institutional as well as the personal consequences of a "no litigation" policy.

This has led to a continual reexamination of the Mennonite theological position on litigation. Mennonite Auto Aid sponsored a study of the problem from 1959 until 1965, including a 1961 conference, "Consultation on Problems of Litigation Facing Mennonites Today." The Peace Problems Committee reported to the Mennonite General Conference (MC) on the topic in 1961 and again in 1963. In 1976 a task force was appointed by the Mennonite Church (MC) General Board which reported to the church's general assembly in 1977 and 1979. Finally the 1981 Mennonite Church General Assembly adopted a statement on *The Use of the Law*, which is the latest theological articulation on this subject.

The statement continues to urge Mennonites to go the second mile in avoiding litigation and to settle disputes quickly and amicably. It recognizes, however, that legal problems can be quite complex, and that litigation may sometimes be appropriate for Christians. It affirms the positive role that °law plays in society and the role Christians can play in using the law to bring about °justice. It urges Christians to seek out alternatives to litigation, such as mediation and conciliation (°reconciliation) services, which can resolve conflict with less animosity than adversarial litigation. It finally urges that the discernment of the church be brought to bear on determining in what situations litigation may be appropriate.

Mennonites are increasingly involved in the practice of law. Whereas the *Mennonite Encyclopedia* could note in 1957 (III: 376) that there was only one lawyer in the Mennonite Church (MC), compared to a larger number in the General Conference Mennonite Church, in 1986 there were dozens of lawyers in the Mennonite Church (MC). Mennonite lawyers met for a symposium in 1980 and many were present the following year when the Associated Mennonite Biblical Seminaries held a conference on law and the Bible. Some Mennonite lawyers have been active in legal aid programs assisting the poor, others have been active with mediation and victim-offender programs, such as the Mennonite Conciliation Service, seeking to offer an alternative to litigation. TSJ

Bibl. on War and Peace (1987), 287-90; Mennonite Church General Assembly, *The Use of the Law* (Scottdale, 1981); J. R. Burkholder, "Litigation: Mennonite Church Teaching and Its Scriptural Background" (unpublished essay, 1978); Marlin E. Miller, "Witnesses to the Law of Christ," a paper read at the Mennonite Lawyers Symposium (Mennonite Student and Young Adult Services, 1980); Carl Kreider, in *GH* (July 3, 1979); Samuel S. Wenger, in *Chr. Living* (Feb. 1958), 6-8, 33.

See also Peace.

Lay Evangelists, as related to overseas missions, refers to the ministry of lay national workers, men and women, employed by missionaries or mission organizations, in the task of evangelism. The men were variously referred to as "evangelists," "catechists," or "colporteurs." The women were known as "Bible women." In north India they were called "zenana workers" (workers with women). These workers were the foot soldiers of the modern missionary movement through the 19th- and up to the mid-20th c. As much as anyone, they were the ones who introduced the Gospel in terms the masses could understand.

Lay evangelists were used in missions in the Middle East, Africa, and throughout Asia. At the end of the last century a survey among major mission societies in India showed that more than 2,000 workers were employed by missions. The largest employer was the British and Foreign Bible Society, which employed 552 Bible women in 1899. The American Marathi Mission (India) reported a team of 109 Bible women and 84 evangelists in 1902. During a peak year in 1918, the American Mennonite (MC) Mission (Dhamtari, Madhya Pradesh) had an evangelistic task force of 23 evangelists and 41 Bible women. Other missions in areas of rapid church growth employed relatively larger numbers of lay evangelists.

Lay evangelists generally had only a modest education (primary or middle school) with a year or two of Bible training in a mission school or by a missionary supervisor. Over the years missions in India, China, and Japan developed many excellent training centers for lay workers, particularly for the women. Both the American Mennonite Mission (Dhamtari) and the General Conference Mennonite Mission (Champa) operated schools for training workers.

The lay evangelist's work was to share the Good News in the spirit of Mt 10:5-15. They usually worked in pairs, moving out into surrounding villages and confronting people with the claims of Christ, holding meetings in village squares, market places, and country bazaars. Much of their preaching was simple and conversational, explaining the great missionary texts of the Bible. Women met separately with women and children, perhaps in a private courtyard. The workers sold Gospel portions and other Christian literature. They prayed for the sick and offered counsel in health and hygiene. They were generally held in high esteem.

Lay workers had to keep careful records of where they went, what they talked about, and the number of listeners and inquirers. They reported regularly to the missionaries.

During the cool season and dry months in India missionaries engaged in "touring" (extended evangelistic campaigns in the villages beyond the normal reach of the lay workers). Together with a team of evangelists and Bible women, a missionary would live in tents and carry out an intensive evangelistic effort.

Where many people were coming into the church, lay workers were indispensable as catechists and disciplers of prospective converts. Many workers went on to become pastors and church leaders. Of the first five ordained ministers in the Mennonite Church in India (Dhamtari) four had served many years as village evangelists. Undoubtedly, one of the most gifted spokesmen of the gospel in this century was Simon Patras, or "Blind Simon," the singing bard of Chattisgarh. India will be forever indebted to the saintly ministry of Pandita Ramabai (1858-1922; see "Woman of the Bible: Bundi Bai Chauhan Walters" below).

Paid lay evangelism had run its course by the end of World War II. In Japan and China the war had drastically altered the course of missions. In India, independence and the resurgence of Hinduism and Islam forced the Christian church to voice its mission in less arrogant tones than had been characteristic of much open-air preaching. The Mennonite Church in India, taking over the evangelistic ministry from the American Mennonite Mission (Dhamtari), phased out its workers in 1955. Some conservative groups and independent missions attempted to carry on as before but by the mid-1960s paid evangelism was no longer considered a valid model.   JAF

The Encyclopedia of Missions, 2nd ed. (N.Y.: Funk and Wagnalls Co., 1904), 89-91; John Murdoch, *The Indian Missionary Manual*, 4th ed. (London: James Nisbet and Co., 1895), 450-59; Eddy Asirvatham, *Christianity in the Indian Crucible* (Calcutta: YMCA Publishing House, 1955); American Mennonite Mission, *Annual Reports* (1918, 1955); P. J. Malagar, *MC India* (1981), 40-52.

See also Li Ching Fen; Nsongamadi Joseph and Baba Naomi.

A Woman of the Bible:
Bundi Bai Chauhan Walters

Bundi Bai, oldest of two children born to a wealthy Kshatriya family named Chauhan, near Bhopal, Madhya Pradesh, came from a Marathi ethnic group which dates back several millennia to the Scythian invasion of the western coast of India. When she was about eight years old, she and her brother, Hiralal, two years younger, became orphans in the Great Famine of 1898-1900. The children wandered from home to home and village to village to beg for a life-sustaining morsel of food, or, when this wasn't forthcoming, to search for berries, roots, and leaves in the jungle.

The famine was particularly severe in western India. Thousands of orphans' lives were saved when missionaries gathered them up and placed them in mission orphanages. Frightened, but assured of food and care, Bundi Bai and her brother climbed confidently into one of several freight cars rapidly being filled with famine orphans. Some children jumped out and ran away when the train stopped, but not Bundi Bai and Hiralal. Bundi Bai found a home in Pandita Ramabai Mukti Mission in Pune, her brother in the Methodist Boys' Boarding Home in Bombay. Bundi Bai received a new name, the vernacular name *Karuna* (Mercy) and the English name *Rachel*, but she was most affectionately known by her given name of Bundi Bai.

At age 12 Bundi Bai became gravely ill. All despaired of her life except Pandita Ramabai who spent 24 hours a day, days on end by the sick girl's bed, praying for her recovery, whispering the assuring words into her ear that God had a great ministry for her and would surely make her well. When Bundi Bai recovered, she set her heart on serving the Lord in "zenana" work, mission work among women in Bombay.

The handsome young headmaster of the Methodist Middle School for boys in Raipur, Madhya Pradesh, John °Walters, himself a mission protégé, changed Bundi Bai's plans when he asked for her hand in marriage. Bundi Bai and John Walters were married in the Methodist church in Pune and then made their home in Raipur where John continued his teaching profession. As John's wife, she was appointed housemother for the boys in the boardinghouse. Nevertheless, "zenana" work received a high priority from her. In later years, as "Bible woman" and pastor's wife, she was able to fulfill her youthful dream to her heart's content.

Her husband, she quickly discovered, had an insatiable thirst for knowledge. He was already well educated by the mission, in business college and in biblical and theological studies. As a teacher he had recurring opportunity to improve his teaching on a self-study basis. This was not enough. He had a special interest in church history, which he studied privately and in which he passed an examination with success. He could read, write, and speak fluently in three different languages with three different scripts—English, Hindi and Urdu. He also enjoyed preaching and would walk miles on Sundays in surrounding villages to preach and to teach. Seeing his interest in preaching, the mission assigned him to preach in Gondia, Dongargarh, Dondi Lohara, and Durg, totaling a period of 16 years.

Bundi Bai and her husband were blessed with five sons and five daughters. Three died while they served in Gondia; one died upon their return to Raipur. Sensing their need of change for their own spiritual growth, the couple requested a transfer to Narsingpur. The mission did not approve. John resigned his position. P. W. °°Penner, of the General Conference Mennonite Mission heard of John Walters' resignation and the couple's availability as church workers, and invited them to join the Mennonite mission. John served for many years as pastor of the Janjgir church, became a teacher in the Janjgir Bible School, served as conference treasurer, edited the conference periodical *Mennonite Bandhu*, and later pastored the Jagdeeshpur church for several years.

Plague, known as black fever, took their beloved six-year-old Yonathan soon after they settled in Janjgir. Two years later another son, Wilfred, was born. Once again the family was as complete as it had been when they came to Janjgir: three boys, Joel, David, and Wilfred, and three girls, Taramani, Martha, and Ashalata. One more, Taramani, was to die during their stay in Janjgir. At age 38 Taramani had come with her two children from Delhi to be nursed by her parents. After her death, the children returned to their father in Delhi, only to die soon thereafter.

Bundi Bai, with only a fourth-grade formal education, was a remarkably self-taught person, especially knowledgeable in the Bible. The loss of her children one by one drove her to find comfort in God's Word. Her faith in God's love despite all the sorrow that had come to her, made her a Christian of unusual and strong character. Also, coming from a sturdy race of invaders as she did, a race with warlike characteristics, she brought to bear upon her ministry, especially to women, that same unwavering determination and steel-like discipline that she had inherited and exercised in her own life. She was a forceful speaker in the Hindi language even though she had grown up with the Marathi tongue.

She was considered an "aggressive" Bible woman. In group preparatory meetings with her women she demanded modesty, courage, boldness, and, no less, discipline. If any younger women would sit with head uncovered, she would chide them to pull their *saris* over their heads. If she and others would start off on an afternoon of teaching in a village and any failed to bring her Bible, she would say that no soldier starts out without full equipment. The Christian workers must always bring their Bibles.

In dress, too, she was exact. No frills, fashions, or perfume were tolerated. Sleeves must be three-quarter length, blouses and *saris* worn so as not to draw attention to the wearer. The only jewelry she allowed herself was what her husband had given her on her wedding day. But in matters of compassion and kindness, there was no limit. She knew from experience the loneliness and deprivation of being an orphan and her loving heart and generous hands reached out to the needy, especially to widows and orphans.

Bundi Bai shared her husband's ministry for about 40 years, but she also left her own mark on the church by a life that was deeply committed to the Lord and by her individual traits of character and purpose. She died on May 2, 1969, eleven years after her husband's death. HKor

Leadership. See Authority; Decisionmaking; Education; Ordination; Polity.

Leaman, Amanda Eby (Jan. 10, 1876-Jan. 15, 1938), a long-time worker at the Chicago Mennonite Home Mission (MC), was born in Creston, Ohio, to Tobias and Susanna Eby. In 1891, through the preaching of John S. °°Coffman, she accepted Christ. By request of C. K. Hostetler, she went to work at the Chicago Mennonite Home Mission, arriving there on Oct. 13, 1898. She worked there until mid-1900, when she became engaged to Amos Hershey °°Leaman who had been superintendent of the mission since 1898. From 1900 to 1902, she lived with her family in Ohio, returning to Chicago Home Mission in Sept. 1902 after her marriage to A. H. Leaman on June 22, 1902. Amanda carried various missionary roles. She worked in the mission Sunday school, did home visitation, led home Bible studies and women's meetings, gave sewing classes, helped with a children's fresh air program and distributed clothes. She did editing and copy editing for the mission newsletter. She served as hostess to guests and church leaders.

In 1909, she wrote the notes for the primary Teachers Sunday School Quarterly, published in Scottdale, Pa. She also frequently spoke at Mennonite Sunday school conferences and was involved in the Mennonite Women's Missionary Society, started by her sister, Clara Eby °Steiner. In 1920, Amanda and Hershey moved out of the Chicago Home Mission but her missionary outreach in Chicago continued until her death. RAS

Rich, *Mennonite Women* (1983), 165.

See also Urban Church.

Lebanon. Mennonite Central Committee (MCC) assisted Armenian refugees in the 1920s and World War II victims in 1948-49. From 1958 to 1962 MCC opened and maintained a Menno Travel Service office, and then returned in 1976 following the outbreak of civil war to aid the victims of the Lebanese conflict in cooperation with the Middle East Council of Churches. Rural development and emergency assistance in South Lebanon has been the focus for the past 11 years, with MCC volunteers living in Sidon and Nabatiyeh. MCC personnel were frequently in very serious physical danger. Since the June 1982 Israeli invasion MCC has also assisted Palestinians in the Tyre and Sidon camps. In 1987 MCC directors located in Jordan, a nurse resident in Lebanon, and several Lebanese staff workers in Lebanon carry out the work of rural development and health and vocational training. PM

Lederach, Mary Mensch (Jan. 24, 1898-July 16, 1980), a shepherdess in the Mennonite Church (MC) was born in Skippack, Pa., to Jennie D. Heckler and Abraham B. Mensch. Graduating in 1914 from tenth grade, she entered Millersville State Normal School, completing her studies there in 1918. She taught five grades at the Iron Bridge Public School in Rahns, Pa., then in 1919-20 taught at Hesston College in Kansas. Returning in 1921 to nurse her mother and grandmother, Mary married Willis K. Lederach. That year, the Lederachs moved to Norristown, Pa., to assist the Franconia Mennonite Conference Board of Missions (MC) in its first mission, where they served until 1928. Throughout se. Pennsylvania Mary became known as an excellent public speaker, making over 200 appearances to church and civic groups, giving family-life talks in a manner that was both commanding and engaging. She embraced plain dress and modesty, and for over three decades gave talks on human °sexuality. Secretly she donated all her income as a post office worker and real estate agent to assisting needy people. Her children are Paul Mensch Lederach, Ruth Mensch Lederach Rittgers, Mary Jane Lederach Hershey, and John Mensch Lederach. JCM

Rich, *Mennonite Women* (1983), 98-100.

Lee, Rhoda (April 26, 1857-Nov. 19, 1899), mission advocate. The daughter of L. C. and Laura Noble, Rhoda Noble was born in West Union, Iowa. She moved to Kansas at age 20 and married James H. Lee of Abilene, Ks. They had five children. She wrote many articles for the *Evangelical Visitor*

(BIC). Influenced by the World's Gospel Union, she labored with her husband in gospel work among coal miners in Scranton, Ks. She died at age 42 in Abilene.

Rhoda Lee is best known for her appearance at the Brethren in Christ General Conference, held near Abilene in 1894. There she made an impassioned plea for a foreign mission fund, and later in an unprecedented move, grabbed a hat and passed it through the spellbound audience to collect an offering.

At the 1895 conference, held in Ontario, she chided the church for taking no action. This time a foreign mission board was appointed and the church began a vital foreign mission program.   WIM

Wittlinger, *Piety and Obedience* (1978), 111, 179-81, 523; Wilma I. Musser, "Rhoda E. Lee," *BIC Hist. Life*, 2 (June 1979), 3-20; Carlton Wittlinger, "Rhoda E. Lee, Missionary Enthusiast," *Notes and Querries* (July 1961), 11-19.

Leendertz, Johannes Matthias (1885-1977), was pastor of Mennonite congregations in Wieringen (1910), Koog-Zaandijk (1923), and Haarlem (1927-50). He was strongly influenced by Rendel Harris of the Quaker center at Woodbrooke (England), leading him to a search for the deepening of evangelical faith among the Dutch Mennonite congregations. This led him to the establishment of the "Gemeentedagbeweging" in 1917 (congregational retreat movement), later known as the "Elspeetse Vereniging" and still later as the "Fellowship of Mennonite Brotherhood Work, (Gemeenschap voor Doopsgezind Broederschapswerk). From 1947 on he took the initiative for the regular organization of retreats. Leendertz visited the Mennonites in the United States after World War I and became a consistent advocate of increased contacts between Dutch and American Mennonites.   SV

Leendertz, Willem (1883-1970) studied theology at the universities of Amsterdam and Groningen, completing doctoral work in 1913. After serving as Mennonite pastor in Nes (Ameland), he became assistant librarian at the Dutch School for Economics in Rotterdam in 1922 and full librarian in 1924. In 1933 he became lecturer and in 1944 professor of theology and ethics at the Amsterdam Mennonite Theological Seminary. In 1946 he was appointed professor of the philosophy of religion at the U. of Amsterdam, a position he held until his retirement in 1954. His field of specialization was philosophical ethics. He was particularly knowledgeable about Søren Kierkegaard.   SV

Legalism may be defined as the position which sees religion or morality consisting of strict obedience to a prescribed set of laws. Otherwise stated, it is the theory that by doing good works or by obeying the °law, a person earns and merits salvation. It can also be defined as the strictness by which one conforms to a code of action as a means of being justified.

For the early Anabaptists, strict faithfulness to a code of action was called for by their understanding of Scriptures, not because this was a means to being justified, but because this was a demonstration of the changed life. The changed life gave evidence of one's regeneration. To this way of life the Christian committed herself voluntarily.

But the "new life" did not just happen. It was encouraged by exhortation, and it was aided by church °discipline. Church discipline was the practice by which the faithful were seen to be in good standing, and by which the unfaithful were separated from the believing fellowship. The Anabaptists very soon received the reputation of living exemplary lives. They differed from the Lutherans, e.g., in believing that God's grace did not only offer forgiveness, it also enabled victorious daily living.

The good repute which the Anabaptists enjoyed, even from their enemies, on the basis of their Christian walk carried both a price tag and a danger with it. The price lay in the task of ascertaining what characteristics marked the Christian's everyday walk. They asked, "What is the biblical, especially the New Testament, mandate?" The danger lay in the application of that biblical mandate through an unloving use of church discipline to keep church members in line. Here legalism lay close at hand.

The history of the Anabaptists pictures the tension which existed. The Dutch Anabaptists in the time of Menno Simons were very strict with the use of the °°ban and °°avoidance of the disciplined person. Menno counseled less rigorous application of avoidance in such instances as between marriage partners. His fellow elders made the application too extreme, causing disruption in the fellowship. Menno, however, was himself accused of legalism when the Lutherans, believing that they had just moved out of the deadly grip of Roman Catholic works righteousness, saw the Anabaptist call for holy living as backsliding into a very similar perversion of the Gospel. This, of course, was not true.

Menno's understanding of grace was pristine. No one could earn salvation. God's grace alone accomplished it. One reason for Menno's writing the booklet *The True Christian Faith* was to answer the charge of legalism. It was here that he dealt with such themes as law and gospel, letter versus spirit, and how one deals with commandments. His writing flows with the spontaneity of the fruits of the life of faith, and for him obedience to Christ's commandments is not legalism, but the loving response of the believer who has recognized God's Son as Redeemer and as Lord.

Notwithstanding, the legalistic tendency was there, and this became evident when the Dutch Anabaptists, adapting more and more to their culture, sought to spell out in detail what the church could not tolerate. Thus when Mennonite merchants acquired stock in sailing vessels which were armed, the church stipulated that, because this was contrary to the biblical teaching, to have more than a small percentage of the stock could not be tolerated. The Swiss Brethren similarly had their lists of permissible and nonpermissible practices.

Through the centuries the issue of legalism has continued to raise its head. Kauffman and Harder in their Anabaptist profile, *Anabaptists Four Centuries Later* (1975), point out that at given times and places Mennonites have clearly been caught in the problem of a legalistic moralism. For some Mennonite groups this has been more marked than with others. Adaptation to the surrounding culture has always occurred to some extent. However, the Mennonite Church (MC), the Mennonite Brethren, and the Brethren in Christ undertook more rigid enforcement of prescriptions and proscriptions than the General Conference Mennonite Church and the Evangelical Mennonite Church. The lists of proscriptions have varied with the groups and varied with the time, covering a broad range of items such as the use of communication media, °dress, °recreation, use of alcoholic beverges, membership in lodges, etc.

More recently church conferences have been asked to deal with the application of biblical teachings to the practices of °divorce and homosexuality (°sexuality). Those who believe that the Scriptures clearly designate these practices as wrong, and therefore to be condemned, are considered by others as applying law separate from the love and forgiveness of God. Commendable is the continued openness to consider life-style and ethical issues, to receive such new light as the Spirit of God may grant to those who take their Christian walk seriously.   HP

Alvin J. Beachy *The Concept of Grace in the Radical Reformation* (Nieuwkoop: B. DeGraaf, 1977); General Conference Mennonite Church, *Study Conference on the Believers' Church* (Chicago, 1955); idem, *Studies in Church Discipline* (Newton: MPO, 1958); John A. Hostetler, *Amish Society* (1980); Kauffman/Harder, *Anabaptists Four C. Later* (1975); CRR 3; Menno, *Writings*; J. A. Oosterbaan, "Grace in Dutch Mennonite Theology," in *A Legacy of Faith*, ed. C. J. Dyck (Newton, 1962), 69-85; Frank C. Peters, "The Ban in the Writings of Menno Simons," *MQR*, 29 (1955), 16-33; Peter Rideman (Riedemann), *Account of Our Religion, Doctrine and Faith*, trans. Kathleen E. Hasenberg (London: Hodder and Stoughton, and Rifton, N.Y.: Plough Publishing House, 1938, 1950, 1970); J. C. Wenger, *Basic Issues in Non-conformity* (Scottdale, MPH, 1951); idem, *Christianity and Dress* (Scottdale, 1943); idem, "Grace and Discipleship in Anabaptism," *MQR*, 35 (1961), 50-69; idem, *Historical and Biblical Position of the Mennonite Church on Attire* (Scottdale, 1944); Wittlinger, *Piety and Obedience* (1978), esp. 475ff.

See also Apologetics; Discipleship; Nonconformity.

Lehman, Chester Kindig (1895-1980), first dean of Eastern Mennonite College and Seminary, 1923-56, exerted significant influence in building its academic strength. He set an example of intellectual pursuit in the context of full-orbed faith with his professional credentials and successful teaching for 50 years in biblical studies, systematic and biblical theology, Greek, and ethics. He led in development of the advanced Bible curriculum and the founding of the seminary. His leadership also bore fruit in state accreditation of EMC as a four-year college in 1947. He fostered positive relationships between eastern and western regions of the United States in Mennonite higher education. His writings include *The Inadequacy of Evolution as a World View, The Holy Spirit and the Holy Life, Theology of the Old Testament,* and *Theology of the New Testament.* A vigorous promoter of music, he directed choruses and helped compile four Mennonite hymnals and song books. Over a period of about 60 years he pastored four congregations near Harrisonburg, Va.

He married Myra Kendig. They were parents of three daughters and a son.   HRP

Who's Who Mennonites (1943), 155; *Menn. Bib. II*, p. 472.

Lehman, Lydia (Leichty) (Sept. 28, 1884-Dec. 16, 1969), was active in the Mennonite Church (MC) as a missionary, editor, and Mennonite Central Committee worker. She married M. C. Lehman in August 1905. They were parents of two daughters and one son.

A missionary in India from 1906-1930, Lydia wrote *Gospel Herald* articles to inform people of Indian widows, victims of leprosy (°Hansen's disease), and Bible women (°lay evangelists); to express the pain of boarding school parent-child separation; to request prayer and workers.

Writer of the *Booklet of Prayer* and a *Handbook of Information for Missions and Institutions* (MC), Lydia also edited the *Missionary Sewing Circle Letter*, 1932-46. As literature secretary of the General °°Sewing Circle Committee, she wished women to be informed about church work and world conditions and to do systematic Bible study.

With Christian motivation to assist the needy, Lydia both packed clothing at U.S. Mennonite relief centers and distributed it to suffering Europeans during World War II.   DYN

Missionary Sewing Circle Letter, ed. by Lydia Lehman from early 1930s through mid-1940s, writings by her in each issue; idem, many articles in Mennonite periodicals, e.g., "The Home Life of Our Indian Sisters," *GH* (Dec. 4, 1930), 778-79; idem, "Naked—and Ye Clothed Me," *GH* (Mar. 5, 1942), 1056, 1059; idem, "The Education of Missionaries' Children," *Chr. Monitor* (Oct. 1921), 301-2; John A. Lapp, *India* (1972), 86, 254-55; Sharon Klingelsmith, "Women in the Mennonite Church, 1900-1930," *MQR*, 54 (1980), 163-207, at 184.

Lehman, Martin Clifford (Mar. 16, 1883-Dec. 22, 1963), was a gifted, respected Mennonite Church (MC) leader. One year after he and Lydia Leichty were married (1905), they began a 25-year missionary career in India, 1906-30.

With insight M.C. Lehman wrote about the relationship between the Indian and American Mennonite church, world conditions and their impact on missions, rural education in India, the realities of °caste in family life, and theologians like Barth. From 1912-1924 he was associate editor of *Christian Schayah*. His PhD dissertation (Yale, 1933) examined the religious significance of 19th c. author Harishchandra; his Mission Study Course (1939) clarified Mennonite Church work in India.

For a year following November 1939 and again after the spring of 1941, M. C. was with MCC in Europe for relief work. His pen again informed Mennonites of the history and principles of relief work—in the spirit of Christ; offered a bibliography of resources; described the misery of uprootedness and disease and the suffering caused by inadequate food, shelter, and clothing; and called on North American Christians to respond to these needs with prayer and materials.   DYN

Who's Who Mennonites (1943), 156; *Menn. Bib. II*, p. 472; M. C. Lehman, "Indian Life at Close Range," *Gospel Witness*, 2 (Jan. 16-Feb. 27, 1907), 667, 682, 699, 730-31, 762; "A Trip to the American Mennonite Mission," *Gospel Witness*, 3 (Sept. 25-Oct. 30, 1907), 405, 421, 436, 452, 468, 484; idem, "Present World Conditions and Mennonite Mission," *GH* (July 16, 1931), 381-84, (Sept. 3, 1931), 518-20; idem, "The Religious Significance of Writings of Harishchandra" (PhD diss., Yale U., 1933), copy at MC Archives (Goshen); idem, *Our Mission Work in India*, Mission Study Course (Elkhart, Ind.: MBM, 1939); idem, *Mennonite Relief Work*, an annotated bibliography, (Goshen College: Mennonite Relief Training School, 1943); idem, "Needs and Conditions in Europe," *Chr. Monitor*, (series: July-Dec., 1945), 175, 205, 233, 240, 256, 288, 323; idem, *History and Principles of Mennonite Relief Work: An Introduction* (Akron, Pa.: MCC, 1945), 44 pp.; John A. Lapp, *India* (1972), index; *Edward: Pilgrimage of a Mind*, ed. Ida Yoder (Wadsworth, Ohio, and Irwin, Pa.: Ida and Virgil Yoder, 1985), 29, 282, 308, 398; *PMH*, 11 (Apr. 1988), 18-19; Theron F. Schlabach, *Gospel Versus Gospel* (Scottdale, 1980), e.g., 133-35.

Lehman, Verena Sprunger. See Frontier ("Courage and Conviction" [feature]).

Leisure. See Recreation; Work Ethic.

Lengua Evangelical Convention. See Convención de las Iglesias Evangélicas de los Hermanos Lenguas.

Leprosy. See Hansen's Disease.

Lesher, Christian (1775-1856), River Brethren (BIC) bishop, churchman, and writer, was born in Lancaster, Pa. He moved to Franklin, Pa., about 1810, serving as bishop for River Brethren in that county from 1825 to 1856. His unique contribution was in his writings. His first work, *Zeugniß der Wahrheit* (Testimony of Truth) written in 1841 (no copies extant) and outlining discipline as found in Mt 18, was printed in English translation in 1904 issues of the *Evangelical Visitor*. Several copies of his second book, *Das kleine Geistliche Magazin* (The Small Spiritual Storehouse, 1849), have survived. Theologically oriented, the book deals with such issues as the incarnation of Christ, predestination and free will, and the spiritual status of children. His third work, "Das Geistliche Uhrenwerck" (The Spiritual Clockwork, 1850) a °devotional writing, is in manuscript form and may not have been printed. Bishop Lesher's writings are in the Brethren in Christ tradition of stressing the inner life and outer obedience.   MHS

Christian Lescher, *Zeugniß der Wahrheit: eine klare Anweisung nach dem Wort Gottes, wie Kinder Gottes in der Gemeinde Jesu Christi haushalten Sollen, oder Ordnung halten untereinander* (1841), idem, *Das kleine Geistliche Magazin, als ein Zeugniß der Wahrheit: bestehend in unterschiedlichen Stücken des Christlichen Erkenntnisses* (Chambersburg, Pa.: M. Kieffer and Company, 1849); idem, "Das Geistliche Uhrenwerck als ein Zeugnisz Der Wahrheit welches bestehet in Zwelf Betrachtingen," original in Christian Lescher papers, Kittochtinny Historical Society Museum, Chambersburg, Pa., English trans. by Noah Good in Brethren in Christ Historical Library, Messiah College, Grantham, Pa.; idem, *Christian Magazine*, trans. by Laban T. Bechbill (published by translator, 1971); idem, "How to Keep Order in God's House," *EV* (June 1, 1904, June 15, 1904, July 1, 1904); Martin H. Schrag, "The Brethren in Christ Attitude Toward the 'World' " (PhD diss., Temple U., 1967).

Lesotho, Kingdom of, is a small (11,720 sq. mi.; 30,354 sq. km.) mountainous, independent nation in southern Africa, surrounded by the Republic of South Africa. Its population of ca. 1.4 million lives from an economy based on livestock, subsistence agriculture, small industry, and migrant labor in the Republic of South Africa.

Mennonite Central Committee (MCC) first began work in Lesotho in early 1973, placing teachers and development workers in various assignments. As of November 1986, MCC had 17 workers involved in teaching, community development, health and social services.

Africa Inter-Mennonite Mission (AIMM) also began working in Lesotho in 1973. Its staff has numbered from four to ten persons since that time. The primary ministry of AIMM is among the °African Independent Churches through Bible teaching and leadership training. Other assignments have included university chaplaincy and pastoral leadership in a multiracial international context.   VMG

MC Yearbook (1988-89), 159; *GCM Handbook* (1988), 88.

Li Ching Fen. Li Ching Fen was a native of Taming city and a graduate of the Mennonite (GCM) mission Girl's Boarding School. Her parents had engaged her to marry a young man. She knew very little about the life and character of the young man except by hearsay. She hoped he would become a Christian. They were married but they did not live together very long after their little daughter was born.

Li remained faithful to the church and to her Christian faith. She was a member of different committees of the Taming church and served as its moderator for several years. She also served on several committees of the Mennonite mission as she worked hard for the work of the Lord. She was especially interested in country work and gave much time to taking out the gospel to the countryside (°lay evangelists). Her gifts of speech, good humor and discernment found expression in women's meetings and visitation work with other Christians.   JCL

Juhnke, *Mission* (1979), 59-60.

Liberalism (ME III:332), is a product of the Enlightenment and of Deism. In America it "came of age" ca. 1750-1820. Both the Enlightenment and Deism correlated with the American Revolution and the rise of the new nation. Benjamin Franklin (1706-90) and Thomas Jefferson (1743-1826) were "free thinkers," as were Ethan Allan (1738-98), Thomas Paine (1737-1809; "that dirty little atheist"), and many others. All believed that there is *one* God, not three, that sin derives from human choices, that reason is "my church" and the Bible is largely the product of "priestcraft" which has corrupted the simple message of Jesus with metaphysical speculations (Jefferson). The Sermon on the Mount is the heart of the Bible. Works lead to salvation, Christ's death is a moral example, and there will be a judgment at some future time but everyone will enjoy blessedness (universalism).

Several movements grew out of, or against, this background, including theological liberalism, evangelical liberalism (or progressive orthodoxy), Transcendentalism, and scientific modernism. Such evangelical liberals as Walter Rauschenbusch (1861-1918), Washington Gladden (1836-1918), and Horace Bushnell (1802-1876) condemned Deism as terrible infidelity. They defended revelation and miracles. Bushnell's book, *Christian Nurture* (1847), for example, stressed the importance of Christian education and, thereby the work of the church. He stressed the deity of Christ more than his humanity, but in interpreting the °atonement he gave greater emphasis to the moral influence theory than to substitutionary salvation. Rauschenbusch placed great emphasis on a personal °conversion experience and on °discipleship. The goal of evangelical liberals was to realize the °kingdom of God on earth through preaching, teaching, and nonviolent social action.

Theological liberalism included Charles W. Eliot (1834-1926), William Newton Clarke (1840-1912), Harry Emerson Fosdick (1878-1969) and others. In their view Christianity was truth and reason combined, the Bible should be read like any other book, the effects of sin are more important than its origin, and revelation affirms the mystery and miracle of the incarnation, Christ's death and resurrection, and other eternal truths. They tended to affirm historicism, that is, the interrelatedness of all events past and present.

This historicism led to a variety of liberal emphases, chief among which was probably the affirming of evolution, thereby undercutting belief in a literal understanding of the Genesis account of creation. In this they took their cue from Darwin's *Origin of Species* (1859). While liberals insisted that evolution was simply "God's way of doing things," this position became a major challenge to biblical authority. It marked the beginning of biblical criticism as method. Beyond this liberals also applied evolution to society and became firmly optimistic about the progressive future of the human race. This meant a weakened doctrine of personal and corporate sin. Then too, a new interest in the history of religions led to considerable liberal interest in the truths of other religions and, thus, to questions about the uniqueness of Christianity. This, in turn, had a negative impact on missions.

Interest in comparative religions was also strong among Transcendentalists like William Ellery Channing (1810-1884), Ralph Waldo Emerson (1803-1882) in America, and, of course, F. D. E. Schleiermacher (1768-1834) in Germany. In this view oriental religions have many truths to teach. Transcendentalists stressed taking feelings, intuitions, and nature seriously. There is little difference between the natural and revealed order. Jesus was divine because of how he lived. He was the world's best teacher. Religious consciousness is primary. Christology in this theology was generally weak, mystical, almost pantheistic. Elements of Romanticism were embodied in the movement.

Finally there was also scientific modernism, represented best by the "Chicago School" of the early 20th c.—Shailer Mathews (1863-1941), S. J. Case (1872-1947), and Henry N. Wieman (1884-1975). That "era" had run its course in Chicago by the end of World War II. All whom we have identified as scientific modernists were committed to applying the scientific method to biblical, theological, and historical studies. God became an objective, verifiable reality. Religion, to them, was a human phenomenon to be found world-wide in a variety of forms, including Christianity. While scientific modernism shared many assumptions with liberalism, and

liberals used higher criticism, the rigor and presuppositions of scientific modernism's methodology made it a different movement in its time. Thus it becomes confusing to use the terms modernism and liberalism synonymously without specific explanation of what is meant in a given context.

The Mennonite response to these issues cannot be understood without a parallel reading of the impact of °Fundamentalism upon them. The 25 years from 1920 to 1945 were probably the most crucial for Mennonites in relation to this controversy, though some point to articles in church papers as early as the late 1890s warning against the dangers of higher criticism (Schlabach, 113). A primary continuing difficulty is to distinguish between classic Fundamentalism (cf: *The Fundamentals*, 12 vols, 1910-1914) and simple Mennonite conservatism—the former being post-critical, the latter pre-critical. It is difficult to measure scattered Mennonite theology against propositional Fundamentalism, to sort out the cultural variables, and to remain objectively irenic.

Two prominent leaders who identified themselves as Fundamentalists were John °°Horsch and Daniel °Kauffman. Both published numerous articles in church papers and wrote books in defense of the true faith, Horsch with *Modern Religious Liberalism* in 1920, and Kauffman with *The Two Standards* in 1924, as well as editing the widely used *Doctrines of the Bible* (1914). Horsch's first volume was not directed against Mennonites *per se*, but a second volume in 1924 was *The Mennonite Church and Modernism*. Schools and leaders with advanced degrees were particularly suspect, and not without reason since, for example, some had taken advanced degrees at the U. of Chicago or at universities in Europe. No one directly identified themselves as liberals or modernists, but the °°*Christian Exponent* took up the defense against elements of Fundamentalism in a 16-page biweekly publication (1924-28).

The tensions are a matter of historical record and can be traced in the appended bibliography. Some Goshen College faculty moved to Bluffton College, which increased Mennonite Church (MC) suspicion of the General Conference Mennonite Church. Goshen College closed its doors for a year (1923-24). The founding of Grace Bible Institute in 1943, now Grace College of the Bible (Omaha, Nebr.), was at least partly the result of criticism of Bethel College (Kansas). Other realignments occurred, but peace did prevail and a new generation of Mennonites was hardly aware of this history unless they were working specifically on related issues. In 1958 the Mennonite Church and the General Conference Mennonite Church began joint seminary training and by the late 1980s many joint projects were in process, including the drafting of a new confession of faith.

A parallel flow of events occurred in Canada, primarily in Ontario, as part of the debate in the United States. It may be that there was greater awareness in Canada of how accepting Fundamentalist language and thought distanced Mennonites from historic Anabaptism. "Historic Anabaptism and North American fundamentalism nonetheless represented two different 'forms of faith,' which, according to J. B. °Toews, clashed with each other" (Epp, 56).

Quoting Paul Martin in another context, Epp says ". . . Mennonites showed their greatest interest in the Fundamentalists. I believe it was at this stage that we learned to use the Bible in very legalistic and prescriptive ways." But healing also came to the Canadian scene, though a small committee of "Concerned Mennonites" (pastors) continued to meet on these issues from time to time.

The issues of liberalism and modernism were not dead in the late 1980s, but they were not interconference issues. *The Sword and Trumpet* periodical continued to alert readers to issues of unorthodoxy among Mennonites. Some church leaders complained of the inroads of "secular humanism" into schools and pulpits, but the meaning of that term had not yet been clearly defined. Was the rapid increase of pastoral counseling training drawing on humanistic roots? Did the vast network of Mennonite mental health centers across North America violate biblical truths in their therapy? Or was secular humanism a commentary on a perceived increasing secularization of North American Mennonite faith and culture? As part of the total North American scene Mennonites too had moved from earlier left and right theological polarities to a broad middle ground which most people simply preferred to call Evangelical. This broad coalition, of course, itself tended to make that term hard to define.   CJD

Sidney E. Ahlstrom, *A Religious History of the American People* (New Haven, 1972), ch. 46; Lloyd J. Averill, *American Theology in the Liberal Tradition* (Philadelphia, 1967); Edward J. Carnell, *The Case for Orthodox Theology* (Philadelphia, 1959); L. Harold DeWolf, *The Case for Theology in Liberal Perspective* (Philadelphia, 1959); F. H. Epp, *Mennonites in Canada II* (1982), ch. 2; *GH*, various issues 1922-25; Robert T. Handy, *A History of the Churches in the United States and Canada* (New York, 1977), ch. 9; David A. Haury, *Prairie People: A History of the Western District Conference* (Newton, 1981), ch. 9; John Horsch, *Modern Religious Liberalism* (Scottdale, 1920); idem, *The Mennonite Church and Modernism* (Scottdale, 1924); MEA 3; E. G. Kaufman, comp., *Mennonite Pioneers* (North Newton, Ks., 1973); Daniel Kaufman, ed., *Doctrines of the Bible* (Scottdale, 1914); idem, The Two Standards (Scottdale, 1924); Kauffman/Harder, *Anabaptists Four C. Later* (1975); C. Norman Kraus, "American Mennonites and the Bible, 1750-1950," *MQR*, 41 (1967), 309-29; Martin E. Marty, *Modern American Religion*, vol. 1, *The Irony of It All, 1893-1919* (Chicago, 1986); George M. Marsden, *Fundamentalism and American Culture. The Shaping of Twentieth-Century Evangelicalism: 1870-1925* (New York, 1980); idem, ed., *Evangelicalism and Modern America* (Grand Rapids, 1984); S. F. Pannabecker, *Faith in Ferment* (Newton, 1967); idem, *Open Doors. A History of the General Conference Mennonite Church* (Newton, 1975); Theron F. Schlabach, *Gospel Versus Gospel* (Scottdale, 1980); *Mennonite*, various issues, 1923; Paul Toews, "Fundamentalist Conflict in Mennonite Colleges: A Response to Cultural Transitions?" *MQR*, 57 (1983), 241-56.

See also Evangelicalism; Fundamentalism; Modernity; Neo-Orthodoxy; Social Gospel.

Liberation Theologies constitute a movement which integrates theology with sociopolitical concerns emerging from historical contexts of injustice, oppression, and massive human suffering. Among the Afro-American, feminist, Hispanic, native North American, Asian, and African liberation theologies, Latin American liberation theology has offered the most systematically articulated and developed theological reflection. Theological themes highlighted in the Latin American context have influenced theologies of liberation elsewhere. The Latin American contribution is particularly significant from the standpoint of the Anabaptist-Believers Church tradition for historical and theological reasons.

Some parallels between liberation theology and the 16th c. Reformation movement are noteworthy, including the liberationist base ecclesial communities' emphasis on creative protest (the so-called "Protestant principle"), the °priesthood of all believers motif, and the central place of the Bible in the life and mission of the church. Indeed, some striking analogies between socioeconomic conditions at the close of the Middle Ages and conditons in 20th c. Latin America (e.g., feudalism and unequal land distribution; rudimentary forms of national and international capitalism; urbanization; the ravages of war; a growing popular self-assurance; and newer means of communication) have been suggested as supporting the idea of a certain new Reformation— or even a *Radical Reformation*—in the making. in this light, the contributions of the liberationist movement can then be seen as consistent with the legacy of the Radical Reformation of the 16th c. at some key points. Further parallels may be seen in the emergence of grassroots Christian ecclesial communities as "free churches" that assert the importance of voluntary association rather than culturally transmitted faith and that reject the marriage of "altar and throne." In addition liberation theologies' prophetic critique of the social order, ecclesial as well as °political and cultural, their openness to ecumenical cooperation and their defense of religious freedom; and their view of biblical faith as the existential and historical following of Jesus Christ (i.e., discipleship understood as "orthopraxis" or obedient, faithful living) have much in common with Anabaptist beliefs.

Liberation theology defines the method of theology as "critical reflection on Christian praxis (practice) in the light of the Word." It criticizes traditional theologies as too intellectual and academic. Liberation theology advocates active solidarity with the oppressed, and costly discipleship in terms of the practical social and political implications of following Jesus. Five major tenets merit special attention.

Conscientization. The method of liberation theology is inspired in the program and philosophy of popular education originally implemented in Brazil in the early 1960s. An integrated process of learning and personal and societal transformation combined literacy with political awareness, including concrete involvement and participation in communal change. "Conscientization" names the process of emerging critical consciousness whereby people become aware of the historical forces that shape their lives as well as of their God-given potential for freedom and creativity; the term also connotes the actual movement towards liberation and human emergence in persons, communities and societies. Analogous views of conscientization can be found in all forms and versions of liberation theology.

Utopian and Prophetic Vision. Liberation theologies underscore the political and eschatological dimensions of the gospel by focusing on the teaching, ministry, and redeeming work of Jesus Christ in the light of the biblical symbol of the reign of God. Liberationists move beyond the progressive contributions of European political theology in that their methodological approach to theologizing is more grounded on concrete experience and praxis, more specific in analyzing socio-economic realities, and more committed to action and transformation. Liberation theologies are interested not only in critically interpreting the world but also in transforming that world.

Praxis Epistemology. Liberationists contend that *orthopraxis*, rather than orthodoxy, becomes the truth criterion for theology—obeying the gospel rather than defining, prescribing, or even defending it. By asserting that the faithful following of Jesus is the precondition for knowing Jesus, they in fact restate a kind of epistemology of obedience. Further, according to this view, Christian faith can be seen as committed participation in God's liberating and re-creating work for the sake of the world. Liberationists thus combine a biblical understanding of knowing and faith with Marxist-inspired notion of praxis as the dialectic of action and critical reflection.

Hermeneutical Circulation. "Critical reflection on Christian praxis *in the light of the Word*" calls for a hermeneutical process involving the "pretext" of the current historical situation, the biblical text, and the context of the Christian ecclesial community. At the heart of the theological method, then, is hermeneutical circulation seen as the interplay between the Scriptures in their historical context and the interpreting community which reads the text in its own socio-historical context. The final aim of this process is not to interpret the Bible better, but to see reality more clearly and to transform it more faithfully.

Base Ecclesial Communities. In the Latin American setting, the purported "new way of doing theology" on the part of liberation theologians has correlated with the proliferation of base (or basic) ecclesial communities as a "new way" of being and viewing the church. The term *base* primarily refers to the poor and oppressed Christians and to those who live in solidarity with them in worship and Bible study, mutual aid and service, and education and social action. This phenomenon of the base communities was facilitated in part by the ecclesial and theological renewal promoted by Vatican II as well as by the reality of poverty and oppression of millions of people in need of material, spiritual, and political support.

It is obvious that, on the one hand, a number of critical concerns must be raised regarding liberation theologies, such as the risks of reducing the gospel to a °revolutionary ideology; the pitfalls of a simplistic interpretation of historical developments; the risk of being dominated by the present social situation interpreted through particular explanations of social struggle and change (e.g., the limitations of °Marxism); and the danger of situational pragmatism in the emphasis on praxis and truth. On the other hand, the witness of liberation theologies converges at crucial points with that of the Anabaptist-Believers Church tradition and it also challenges present-day heirs of this tradition to restate their views of faith as discipleship, the church as God's alternative community and beachhead of the coming

kingdom, and Jesus' ethics of love, °justice, and peace. DS

MQR, supplement to vol. 58 (Aug. 1984), sp. issue on Latin America and Anabaptism; Daniel S. Schipani, ed., *Freedom and Discipleship: Liberation Theology in Anabaptist Perspective* (Maryknoll, N.Y.: Orbis, 1989); Leonardo Boff, *Church, Charism, and Power: Liberation Theology and the Institutional Church*, trans. John W. Dierksmeier (New York: Crossroads, 1985); idem, *Jesus Christ Liberator: A Critical Christology for Our Time*, trans. Patrick Hughes (Maryknoll, N. Y.: Orbis, 1978); Robert McAfee Brown, *Theology in a New Key: Responding to Liberation Themes* (Philadelphia: Westminster, 1978); Rebecca Chopp, *The Praxis of Suffering: An Interpretation of Liberation and Political Theologies* (Maryknoll, N.Y.: Orbis, 1986); James H. Cone, *God of the Oppressed* (New York: Seabury, 1975); idem, *For My People: Black Theology and The Black Church* (Maryknoll, N.Y.: Orbis, 1984); Guillermo Cook, *The Expectation of the Poor: Latin American Basic Ecclesial Communities in Protestant Perspective* (Maryknoll, N.Y.: Orbis, 1985); J. Severino Croatto, *Exodus: A Hermeneutics of Freedom*, trans. Salvator Attanasio (Maryknoll, N.Y.: Orbis, 1981); Dean William Ferm, *Third World Liberation Theologies: An Introductory Survey/A Reader* (Maryknoll, N.Y.: Orbis, 1986); Paulo Freire, *Pedagogy of the Oppressed*, trans. Myra Bergman Ramos (New York: Herder, 1970); Gustavo Gutiérrez, *A Theology of Liberation*, trans. Caridad Inda and John Eagleson (Maryknoll, N.Y.: Orbis, 1973); idem, *The Power of the Poor in History*, trans. Robert R. Barr (Maryknoll, N.Y.: Orbis, 1983); José Porfirio Miranda, *Marx and the Bible: A Critique of the Philosophy of Oppression*, trans. John Eagleson (Maryknoll, N.Y.: Orbis, 1974); José Miguez Bonino, *Doing Theology in a Revolutionary Situation* (Philadelphia: Fortress, 1975); idem, *Christians and Marxists: The Mutual Challenge to Revolution* (Grand Rapids: Eerdmans, 1976); Letty M. Russell, *Human Liberation in a Feminist Perspective* (Philadelphia: Westminster, 1974); Daniel S. Schipani, *Religious Education Encounters Liberation Theology* (Birmingham, Ala.: Religious Education Press, 1988); Juan Luis Segundo, *The Liberation of Theology*, trans. John Drury (Maryknoll, N.Y.: Orbis, 1976); idem, *The Historical Jesus of the Synoptics*, trans. John Drury (Maryknoll, N.Y.: Orbis, 1985); Jon Sobrino, *Jesus in Latin America*, trans. Robert R. Barr (Maryknoll, N.Y.: Orbis, 1987); idem, *The True Church and the Poor*, trans. Matthew J. O'Connell (Maryknoll, N.Y.: Orbis, 1984).

Licht den Indianern (Light to the Indians) (ME III: 334; IV:119), a missionary association organized at a special meeting on Sept. 17, 1935, in the °Fernheim Colony of Paraguay. Forty-eight of the 97 mission supporters, representing all three Mennonite denominations (MB, GCM, and Konferenz der Evangelischen Mennonitischen Brüderschaft) in Fernheim, were present for the founding and setting forth of the purpose of Licht den Indianern. Russian immigrants responded in mission out of thankfulness for having been led out of Russia into a challenging new situation, bringing them into contact with the Lengua Indian people in the °°Chaco of Paraguay.

With limited resources but wholistic goals in mind, mission work was begun among the Lengua people, with the dedication of the first mission workers, the Abram Ratzlaff family and Abram Unger in Oct. 1935. It was necessary in the winter of 1936 to move to a more suitable "campo" (grassland), known to the Lengua people as "Yalve Sanga" (waterhole of the armadillo).

The first missionary to begin learning the Lengua language was the well-known Gerhard B. °Giesbrecht, who began working among the Lengua people in 1937. The Giesbrecht family was joined in this difficult task in 1938 by a young missionary, Bernhard Epp, from Canada. Very slowly the Lengua Indian people responded to the Mennonite mission effort. After 11 years of dedication, proclaiming the Good News more and more clearly in Lengua, 7 young Lengua men turned their lives over to Christ. They were baptized on Feb. 24, 1946, thus forming the first Lengua congregation.

The presence of Mennonite colonies in the central Chaco region attracted more and more migrating Indian peoples. Since 1936 Chulupí People from the south (Pilcomayo region) began moving into the area. In 1946, as a result of an official cooperation with the North American Mennonite Brethren Conference it became possible, to invite a missionary couple, Jakob Franz, from Canada, to begin mission work among the Chulupí People. In 1949 they were joined in the difficult task of learning the Chulupí language by two other young local missionaries, Kornelius °Isaak and Gerhard Hein. After a sudden exodus in 1951-52 the Chulupí returned with the fervor of having come into contact with the Pentecostal movement. Using this as a starting point the missionaries were able to give more biblical teaching to these people, resulting in the formation of the first Chulupí congregation in 1958 when 22 new members were baptized.

The work of Licht den Indianern extended also among other Lengua and Toba groups where new contacts were made. Thus it became possible in 1952 for Dietrich Lepp and Jakob A. Klassen to begin work among a group of approximately 500 Indians (mainly Toba people) who had settled on land belonging to the Fernheim Colony. Also near Waldrode in Neuland Colony, a young missionary named Alex Bartel began work among a Lengua group in 1952. Kornelius Isaak and David Hein, where also ordained to make contact with the warlike Ayoreo (Moro) people from the north. This became possible in 1958, but the death of Kornelius °Isaak caused Licht den Indianern to pull back from this frontier which was later taken up by New Tribes Mission, who continue to work among the Ayoreo Indian people. Work was also begun among the Guaraní Indian people resulting in the formation of a Guaraní congregation in 1975.

One of the greatest challenges to which Licht den Indianern responded from the beginning was to translate biblical texts into the Indian languages. Two missionaries, Dietrich Lepp (Lengua) and Gerhard Hein (Chulupí), were assigned to this important task. After 10 years of pioneering work, the New Testament in Lengua and Chulupí was ready for publication in the early 1970s. These New Testaments, along with translated portions of the Old Testament, have provided the basis and guiding force in Indian congregational life. The same two missionaries continue the work of translating the complete Old Testament.

The Indian congregations which are accompanied by Licht den Indianern have grown rapidly: the 5 Lengua congregations have a total membership of ca. 1,300 (1987) and are joined together under the conference °Convención de las Iglesias Evangélicas de los Hermanos Lengua. The 7 Chulupí congregations have a total membership of ca. 1,400, and are joined together under the conference °Convención de las Iglesias Evangélicas Chulupí. The 2 Guaraní congregations have a membership of ca. 300. These congregations exist among a total population of approximately 7,000 Indian people.

The work of Licht den Indianern in the 1980s has changed from the early years of pioneer work. It has become the joint mission work of the Mennonite congregations of Fernheim and Neuland. The priorities of Licht den Indianern lie in the areas of accompanying the Indian congregations and conferences in an advisory role, especially focusing on teaching and equipping Indian people for the many ministries within their congregations. The challenge in the mission work today is stronger than ever in that it needs to find a way to build more bridges of trust, fellowship, and Christian community between two peoples, German and Indian, who live side-by-side in the Chaco of Paraguay, a unique mission situation.   EG

Wilmar Stahl, "Mission und Indianersiedlung," in *50 Jahre Kolonie Fernheim* (Filadelfia, 1980), 132-69; Sieghard Schartner, and Wilmar Stahl, *Wer ist mein Naechster? Indianermission im zentralen Chaco von Paraguay* (Asunción, Paraguay: Imprenta Cromos S.R.C., 1986); *Licht den Indianern*, brochure, 1987.

Literacy (Campaigns). As Mennonite involvement in the cause of Christian mission steadily expanded in the 20th c., there has been growing encounter with and concern about the pervasive human problem of illiteracy. Basic reasons contributing to this situation worldwide may be summarized as follows: rapid population growth, which frequently outpaces a government's capacity to educate the people it governs; poverty and the inequitable distribution of resources and opportunity; geographical isolation of segments of the population; indifference on the part of the government or perhaps, in some cases, even a deliberate political strategy to keep literacy rates low as a means of avoiding pressures for improvement and change from a better informed populace.

Modern Christian missions historically have devoted very significant amounts of resources and personnel to the cause of literacy and this basically for two reasons. First, since knowledge is power, literacy is seen as an effective means of validating human beings and enabling them to take charge of their own lives in a more effective manner. Furthermore it has been the conviction of modern missionaries that for believers of whatever race or culture to endure and thrive in the Christian faith, they must have direct access to the Scriptures.

Sharing these convictions, Mennonite and Brethren in Christ missions have across the years engaged in language analysis and the translation of Scripture and associated Christian literature in many areas around the world. At the same time, much effort was devoted to teaching people how to read. During an earlier pioneering era in Africa, India, and China, full-blown educational systems were launched with the conviction that education, evangelism, church planting, leadership training, and spiritual nurture could all be integrated parts of the same process. The great impact of °mission schools as Christian training centers for both church and community leaders has been richly documented.

Later, as national governments began to take over school systems and to launch their own literacy campaigns, Mennonite missions and churches have frequently offered personnel, services, and resources to help promote such campaigns in their areas. Whatever the involvement, the underlying rationale has always remained the same, namely, to equip individuals to lead better informed and more productive lives within their society and to enable Christians to nurture their faith and blossom within their community of believers because of their ability to draw spiritual strength and guidance from the printed page. JEB

P. J. Malagar, *MC India* (1981), 40-52; Bill Shouse, *The Blind Mule and Other Stories,* comp. Melanie Zuercher (Akron, Pa.: MCC, 1988), 28 pp., stories told to a literacy worker in Kentucky.

See also Brethren in Christ Society of India; Egypt; Iglesia Evangélica Unida: Hermanos Menonitas, Panama; Kanisa la Mennonite Tanzania; Mbungano Yabunyina Muli Kristo.

Literature (ME III:352). This article on Mennonite literature (fiction or creative writing) will focus on Canadian and American writers, ca. 1950-85, as Mennonites in these countries have been leading in this endeavor since the articles on literature appeared in *Mennonite Encyclopedia,* vol. 3. Only the most important authors will be mentioned by name and only representative titles of their works will be included. For a more complete list of references the reader is referred to the bibliography at the end of this article.

Canadian-Mennonite creative writing owes much to the storytellers and poets who came to Canada from Russia in the 1920s. These writers prepared the literary soil among Mennonites by writing and publishing—often at their own expense—their novels, plays, and poems, and by educating the Mennonite reading public through the year books and journals edited by Arnold °Dyck (1889-1970) of Manitoba. These writers wrote in High (standard) °German and in the Low German °dialect about the tragic experiences of Mennonites and the loss of their Russian homeland after World War I.

Arnold Dyck, arguably the greatest Mennonite literary figure writing in German in Canada, established the basis for Canadian-Mennonite writing by encouraging other writers and by helping them to publish their works. His own most ambitious novel, written in High German, is the five-part *Verloren in der Steppe* (*Lost in the Steppe,* 1944-48), and his most successful literary creation is no doubt the *Koop enn Bua* series, written in Low German, the language closest to Dyck's heart. The Manitoba Mennonite Historical Society began publishing the collected works of Arnold Dyck in 1985.

The finest lyrical poet to emerge from among the Russian Mennonites was Fritz Senn (Gerhard °Friesen) (1894-1983). Publishing his poems in such periodicals as *Mennonitische Warte* and *Der Bote,* Fritz Senn more than any other Mennonite writer of the older generation expressed his love and longing for the forever-lost Mennonite world in Russia. His °poetry, however, is not just nostalgia for the past but deals with timeless human issues and values as well as with the Mennonite experience. Thus the plowman motif in his "Hinterm Pflug/Stimmungen" ("Behind the Plow/Moods") cycle, written in the 1930s, not only describes the faith and life of Mennonite farmers but also symbolizes Mennonite °suffering throughout history. Publication of Fritz Senn's collected poems and prose is projected for 1987.

There are other Canadian-Mennonite writers who continue writing in the Mennonite-German tradition. Valentin Sawatzky of Ontario has published several volumes of poems both in Canada and in Austria. Jacob Warkentin Goerzen of Alberta has published poems in German, Low German, and English. Continuing the Low German literary tradition are such storytellers and poets as Elisabeth Peters, Reuben Epp, Gerhard Ens, and Jack Thiessen. Much of their work has appeared in such magazines as *Mennonite Mirror* and *Der Bote* and in anthologies such as *Harvest* (1974), *Unter dem Nordlicht* (*Under the Northern Lights,* 1977), both edited by George K. Epp and others, and *A Sackful of Plautdietsch* (1983), edited by Al Reimer, Anne Reimer, and Jack Thiessen.

Surprisingly flexible and adaptable, Low German shows a close affinity with such near relatives as High German and English and can be combined with either of them to produce a hybrid style that works well for both serious and comic writing. Two recent works of fiction, one in English and the other in German, brilliantly exploit this kind of stylistic and linguistic mixture for comic purposes. Armin Wiebe's comic novel *The Salvation of Yasch Siemens* (1984) mixes Low German with English, and Jack Thiessen's *Predicht fier haite* (1984) (*Sermon for Today*) mixes Low with High German to good effect. Both works have been highly popular with readers, including non-Mennonites. One of the most distinguished Canadian novelists, Rudy Wiebe, explores issues related to Mennonite faith and life, but also extends his concerns to those in Canadian society—mostly Indians and Métis—who have suffered (and continue to suffer) at the hands of white society. For his novel *Temptations of Big Bear* (1973) Wiebe won the national Governor-General's Award for fiction in 1974. Wiebe's specifically "Mennonite" novels include *Peace Shall Destroy Many* (1962), *The Blue Mountains of China* (1970), and *My Lovely Enemy* (1983), for which latter novel the author was severely criticized by some Mennonite leaders because of its unorthodox treatment of adultery and reinterpretation of Christian sexuality. Another Western Canadian writer, Andreas Schroeder, has received critical acclaim especially for his novel *Dustship Glory* (1986) which is based on the life of a legendary Canadian eccentric.

Barbara Smucker of Ontario is a reputable writer of juvenile fiction. She writes with a compassion and understanding about the problems of young Indians and black children and with a desire to give Mennonite children a sense of their heritage. *Days of Terror* (1979), for which Smucker received the Canada Council Award for children's literature, tells the story of a pacifist Mennonite family leaving their Russian village during the upheavals after 1917. Her reputation was first established while living in the United States with the appearance of *Henry's Red Sea* (1955), the story of the exodus of Mennonite °refugees from Berlin. Some of Smucker's stories have been translated into other languages, including Japanese.

There are several promising young poets who are publishing their work with such reputable publishers as Turnstone Press in Winnipeg. With four published collections of poems to his name, Patrick Friesen has firmly established his reputation as a Canadian poet. His narrative poem *The Shunning* (1980), which deals with the traditional Mennonite practice of °°avoidance was adapted into a successful stage play in Winnipeg. Similarly, David Waltner-Toews of Ontario has several published collection of poems to his credit, including *The Earth is One Body* (1979) and *Good Housekeeping* (1983). Waltner-Toews addresses issues that concern Mennonites and other Western societies as they wrestle with problems related to °wealth and poverty and questions of social °justice.

The Chair in Mennonite Studies at the University of Winnipeg and the Mennonite Literary Society of Winnipeg sponsor translations and publications of Mennonite literature. With their support Al Reimer has translated and published Dietrich Neufeld's *A Russian Dance of Death* (1977) and Hans Harder's *No Strangers in Exile* (1979), both dealing with Russian-Mennonite suffering after World War I. Reimer has also written a successful Mennonite historical novel, *My Harp is Turned to Mourning* (1985), which deals with the same turbulent period. Other publications sponsored by the above-mentioned institutions include *Mennonite Images* (1980), edited by Harry Loewen, and *Visions and Realities* (1985), edited by Harry Loewen and Al Reimer. Both collections include poems and literary prose written by Mennonite authors.

Mennonite writers in the United States have also made notable contributions to creative literature within the last half century. Peter G. Epp (1888-1954), who emigrated from Russia to the United States in 1924 taught Russian and German at Bluffton College and at Ohio State University and in his leisure time wrote novels and short stories about life in the Russian colonies, including a fine novel *Eine Mutter* (*A Mother*, 1932). Gordon Friesen, another Russian-Mennonite, wrote *Flamethrowers* (1936), set in Kansas. It is a powerful novel in the psychological realism tradition, but it seems to suffer from exaggeration and improbable characters and situations.

Writing out of the Swiss Mennonite tradition, Merle Good of Pennsylvania portrays in his novel *Happy as the Grass was Green* (1971) the clash between old Mennonite values and the modern American world. The novel was also made into a successful film, *Hazel's People*. Merle and Phyllis Good edit a literary and cultural magazine, *Festival Quarterly*, which carries poems and prose by Mennonite writers. Joseph W. Yoder in his novel *Rosanna of the Amish* (1973) has painted an idyllic picture of Amish life. Historian, writer, and °filmmaker John L. Ruth has written among other things a fictionalized biography of the Anabaptist leader, *Conrad Grebel, Son of Zurich* (1975), and promotes creative writing among Mennonites through lectures and articles, e.g., *Mennonite Identity and Literary Art* (1978). Kenneth Reed, in his novel, *Mennonite Soldier* (1974), tells the story of two brothers, one who joins the army during World War I and the other who refuses to join and consequently has to suffer for his pacifist stance. Sara Stambaugh's novel, *I Hear the Reaper's Song* (1984), tells the story of a Lancaster County community so well that the reader can "almost smell the arbutus and feel the crackle of ice underfoot," in the words of one reviewer.

Born in the Soviet Union, Ingrid Rimland came to the United States after World War II via Germany, Paraguay, and Canada. Her first novel, *The Wanderers: A Saga of Three Women Who Survived* (1977), caused a sensation among Mennonites when it first appeared. Drawn from vivid personal experiences and historical research, the novel takes the reader into the grinding jaws of a modern struggle between those who want only to live in peace and those who will not let them. Rimland continues to write, her latest story being *The Furies and the Flame* (1984), a moving account of her handicapped son's educational progress and her own development from a stifling background to personal identity and freedom. Another writer from the Russian Mennonite tradition is Wilfred Martens of California whose first novel *River of Glass* (1980) tells the story of how fleeing Mennonites from the Soviet Union crossed the Amur River into China in the early 1930s. Warren Kliewer's *The Violaters* (1964), a novel set in Manitoba, shows what happens when a body of people concerned only with purity of self allows no new thinking to infiltrate its midst. Kliewer has also published his poems in such periodicals as *Mennonite Life*.

Of the more established American Mennonite poets is Elmer F. Suderman who is well-known for his poetry published in Mennonite magazines and journals, notably in *Mennonite Life*. In his poems Suderman wrestles with issues and problems related to Mennonite identity in modern society. He has also translated poems and stories from German into English. Of the younger American Mennonite poets the following have had their poems published in various Mennonite and non-Mennonite publications: Keith Ratzlaff, Eric Rensberger, and Jeff Gundy. All three have done graduate work at Indiana University. Other Mennonite poets and dramatists in the United States include David Rensberger in Georgia, Lauren Friesen at Goshen College, Shari Miller Wagner at Indiana University, Anne Ruth Ediger Boehr, whose poem "I am Dancing With My Mennonite Father" appeared in 1985, and Jean Janzen of California who published a slender volume of poems, *Words for the Silence* (1984).

Mennonites have produced a wealth of devotional verse and stories in a popular vein. Outstanding among the popularizers of Mennonite life and history was Gerhard °Lohrenz (1899-1986) of Winnipeg, whose many publications, while not of great literary value, are much appreciated by young and older readers alike. Some of this popular literature, especially that which comes from prisons and exile, not only carries much emotional intensity but comes close to being literary art. Mennonite poets and storytellers in the Soviet Union continue to publish their work in such publications as *Neues Leben* (*New Life*), a Communist paper, and in anthologies.

A well-known Mennonite author in Germany, Johannes °Harder, who wrote several novels before World War II, also published short stories and articles of a historical, sociological, and theological nature after the war. His short story *Die Nacht am Jakotiner See* (A Night at the Jakotin Lake, 1960) deals with the Nazi past and issues related to the post-1945 period. Harder has also translated stories of Russian authors into German. His projected series of novels about Mennonites throughout history never materialized. Art historian Abram Enns of Lübeck, Germany, who wrote and published poems and at least one short story, *Der Tod der Turteltauben* (Death of the Turtledoves, 1924) before World War II, continues to write poems, although not many of them have been published.

Much could be said about the reception of Mennonite creative writing by Mennonites and non-Mennonites. Space limitations do not allow for elaboration in this regard. It suffices to say that Mennonite authors such as Rudy Wiebe and Patrick Friesen are increasingly taken seriously by literary critics, as the bibliography at the end of this article indicates. Mennonite poetry and creative prose—but not °dramatic arts—is coming of age, making significant contributions to the literary arts, especially in Canada and the United States.   HaL

For lists of the published works of Arnold Dyck, Gerhard Friesen [Fritz Senn], Johannes [Hans] Harder, see the biographical entries under their names. In addition, see the following works: Stanley C. Shenk, "American Mennonite Fiction" [a bibliography], *Menn. Life*, 23 (July 1968), 119-20; Elmer Suderman, "American Mennonite Fiction: A Contribution Toward a Bibliography" *Menn. Life*, 22 (July 1967), 131-33; George K. Epp and Heinrich Wiebe, eds., *Unter dem Nordlicht: Anthology of German-Canadian Writing in Canada* (Winnipeg: Mennonite German Society of Canada, 1977); George K. Epp, Heinrich Wiebe, and others, eds., *Harvest: Anthology of Mennonite Writing in Canada* (Winnipeg: Mennonite Historical Society of Manitoba, 1974); Peter G. Epp, *Eine Mutter*, excerpts transl. by Peter Pauls in *JMS*, 4 (1966), 208-17; complete transl. forthcoming; Anna Friesen, *The Mulberry Tree* (Winnipeg: Queenstone House Pub., 1985); Patrick Friesen, *bluebottle* (Winnipeg: Turnstone Press, 1978); idem, *the lands i am* (1976); idem, *The Shunning* (1980); idem, *Unearthly Horses* (1984); Merle Good, *Happy as the Grass Was Green* (Scottdale, 1971); Jean Janzen, David Waltner-Toews, Yorifumi Yaguchi, *Three Mennonite Poets* (Intercourse, Pa.: Good Books, 1986); Anne Konrad, *The Blue Jar* (Winnipeg: Queenstone House Pub., 1985); Wilfred Martens, *River of Glass* (Scottdale, 1980); Dietrich Neufeld, *A Russian Dance of Death*, transl. by Al Reimer (Winnipeg: Hyperion Press, 1977; Elisabeth Peters, *Dee Tjoaschenhatj—The Cherryhedge* (Steinbach, Man.: Derksen Printers, 1984); Keith Ratzlaff, *Out Here* (Pitchford, N.Y.: State St. Press, 1984); Kenneth Reed, *Mennonite Soldier* (Scottdale, 1974); Eric Rensberger, *Standing Where Something Did* (Bloomington, Ind: Ink Press, 1984); Ingrid Rimland, *The Wanderers: A Saga of Three Women Who Survived* (St. Louis: Concordia, 1977); idem, *The Fury and the Flame* (Novato, Cal.: Arena Press, 1984); John L. Ruth, *Conrad Grebel, Son of Zurich* (Scottdale, 1975); idem, *Mennonite Identity and Literary Art* (Scottdale, 1983); Al Reimer, Anne Reimer, and Jack Thiessen, eds., *A Sackful of Plautdietsch: A Collection of Mennonite Low German Stories and Poems* (Winnipeg: Hyperion Press, 1983); Al Reimer, *My Harp is Turned to Mourning* (Winnipeg: Hyperion Press, 1985); Valentin Sawatzky, *Glockenläuten* (St. Michael: Gläschke Verlag, 1983); Barbara Schmucker, *Amish Adventure* (Toronto: Clarke, Irwin and Co., 1983); idem, *Cherokee Run* (Scottdale, 1957); idem, *Days of Terror* (Penguin, 1979; idem, *Henry's Red Sea* (Scottdale, 1955); idem, *Underground to Canada* (Penguin, 1977); idem, *White Mist* (Richmond Hill, Ont.: Irwin, 1985); Andreas Schroeder, *Dust-Ship Glory* (Toronto: Doubleday, 1986); Sara Stambaugh, *I Hear the Reaper's Song* (Intercourse, Pa.: Good Books, 1984); David Waltner-Toews, *The Earth is One Body* (Winnipeg: Turnstone Press, 1979); idem, *Good Housekeeping* (Winnipeg: Turnstone Press, 1983); Jakob Warkentin Goerzen, *Germanic Heritage: Canadian Lyrics in Three Languages* (Edmonton: the author, 1962); Armin Wiebe, *The Salvation of*

Yasch Siemens (Winnipeg: Turnstone Press, 1984); Rudy Wiebe, *The Blue Mountains of China* (1970); idem, *First and Vital Candle* (1966); idem, *My Lovely Enemy* (1983); idem, *Peace Shall Destroy Many* (1962); idem, *The Scorched-Wood People* (1977); idem, *The Temptations of Big Bear* (1973); idem, *Where is the Voice Coming From?* (1974), all published in Toronto by McClelland and Stewart, and "Chinook Christmas," in *Alberta: A Celebration* (Edmonton: Hurtig Publishers, 1979).

Critical studies of Mennonite literature include Karin G. Gürtler and Friedhelm Lach, eds., *Annals 4 German Canadian Studies* (Vancouver: Canadian Association of University Teachers of German, 1983); Harry Loewen, ed., *Mennonite Images: Historical, Cultural and Literary Essay Dealing With Mennonite Issues* (Winnipeg: Hyperion Press, 1980); Harry Loewen and Al Reimer, eds., *Visions and Realities: Essays, Poems and Fiction Dealing with Mennonite Issues* (Winnipeg: Hyperion Press, 1985); and numerous articles in *JMS*. See also Mary E. Bender, "Truth in Fiction," *Menn. Life* (Oct. 1963), 184-87; Victor G. Doerksen, "The Anabaptist Martyr Ballad," *MQR* 51 (1977) 5-21; Katie Funk Wiebe, review of Rudy Wiebe's *My Lovely Enemy* in *CGR*, 2 (1984), 752-80; Michael Hadley, "Education and Alienation in Dyck's *Verloren in der Steppe*: A Novel of Cultural Crisis," *German Canadian Yearbook*, 3 (1976); Maxine Hancock, "Wiebe: A Voice Crying in the Wilderness," *Christianity Today*, (Feb. 16, 1979); Jim Juhnke, review of Robert Hostetter. *Cheyenne Jesus Buffalo Dream* (Mennonite World Conference Drama, 1978) in *Menn. Life*, 33 (Sept. 1978), 239-31; W. J. Keith, ed., *A Voice in the Land: Essays by and About Rudy Wiebe* (Edmonton: NeWest Press, 1981), and "Sex and the Dead," *Canadian Forum* (May 1983); Cornelius Krahn, "Hans Harder—A Mennonite Novelist," *Menn. Life*, 8 (Apr. 1953), 78-79; Daniel Lenoski, "The Sandbox Holds Civilization: Pat Friesen and the Mennonite Past," *Essays on Canadian Writing*, Prairie Poetry issue, ed. by Jack David, pp. 131-42; Harry Loewen, "Canadian Mennonite Literature: Longing for a Lost Homeland," *The Old and the New World: Literary Perspectives of German-Speaking Canadians*, ed. by Walter Riedel (Toronto: University of Toronto Press, 1984); Harry Loewen and Al Reimer, "Origins and Literary Development of Canadian-Mennonite Low German," *MQR*, 59 (1985), 279-86; Miriam Maust, review of Barbara Smucker's *White Mist* in *CGR*, 4 (1986), 177-78; Magdalene Redekop, "For the Love of God," *Books in Canada* (June-July 1983), 11-132; Al Reimer, review of *My Lovely Enemy* in *Mennonite Mirror*, (June 1983); John L. Ruth, *Mennonite Identity and Literary Art*, Focal Pamphlet 29, (Scottdale, 1978); Vicky Schreiber Dill, "Land Relatedness in the Mennonite Novels of Rudy Wiebe," *MQR*, 58 (1984) 50-69; Stephen Scobie, "Rudy Wiebe: Where the Voice is Coming From," *Books in Canada*, 9, no. 2 (Feb. 1980) 3-5; Sam Solecki, "Giant Fiction and Large Meanings: The Novels of Rudy Wiebe," *The Canadian Forum*, 60 (March 1981), no. 707; Elmer Suderman, "Universal Values in Rudy Wiebe's *Peace Shall Destroy Many*," *Menn. Life*, 24 (Oct. 1969), 172-76, "The Comic Spirit of Arnold Dyck," *Menn. Life*, 24 (Oct. 1969), 169-70, and "A Study of the Mennonite Character in American Fiction," *Menn. Life*, 22 (July 1967), 123-30.

See also Ballads; Hymnology; Mennonite Studies; Suffering; Yaguchi, Yorifumi.

Literature, Mennonites in (German, Canadian, American) (ME III:353). In the 1920s and 1930s Josef Ponten, a German writer, traveled to many countries, including the Soviet Union and the Americas, in search of material for his planned series of novels about Germans throughout the world, *Volk auf dem Wege* (People Underway). Ponten also visited the Mennonites in the Volga region of the Union of Soviet Socialist Republics and included them in his Russo-German cycle of novels written between 1930 and 1940. Ponten did not know the Russian Mennonites well. He portrayed them as rather simple, pious people who had little to do with politics and who tried to live according to their understanding of the Bible. Ponten's proposed American cycle of novels did not materialize.

The most ambitious series of novels about the Mennonites comes from the pen of a North German writer, Ernst °Behrends (1891-1982). Under the general title of *Das Volk der Wanderschaft* (Wandering People), Behrends wrote six novels between 1966 and 1977 about the Mennonites from the 16th c. to the end of World War II.

In *Der Ketzerbischof* (The Heretic Bishop, 1966), Behrends focuses on the story of Menno Simons, faithfully adhering to the known biographical and historical facts relating to this leader. *Die Rose von Wüstenfelde* (The Rose of Wüstenfelde, 1973) takes the reader to northern Germany and the period of the Thirty-Years' War, during which a young Mennonite woman experiences many hardships and the joys and sorrows connected with love. The novel *Der rote Tulipan* (The Red Tulip, 1977) takes place against the background of the Great Northern War between Sweden and Russia, Saxony-Poland, and Denmark-Norway (1700-1721). It is a love story in which the protagonists, a brother and a sister, are severely tried. *Stromaufwärts* (Upstream, 1970) deals with the world of the West-Prussian Daniel Willms who travels to the Netherlands, Hamburg, and in the end to the Ukraine in search of himself and his Mennonite tradition. *Der Steppenhengst* (Prairie Stallion, 1969), in structure and theme similar to *Stromaufwärts* takes the reader to the Mennonite settlements in Russia. The last novel in the series, *Wir trotzen dem Irrlicht* (We Spite the False Light, 1976), tells the tragic yet heroic tale of the Mennonite refugees during World War II and their emigration to the Americas.

Behrends' Mennonite novels are not "great" literature. As one critic (Mary E. Bender) wrote of *Der Ketzerbischof*: The book's world "is a flat world, reported, not experienced, discussed, not felt." This applies in large part to most of Behrends' prose, although in some of his works the author rises at times to epic heights. Perhaps the most successful novel in the series is *Die Rose von Wüstenfelde* in which the author succeeds in telling a most touching story—a story that has universal appeal—about the hopes, faith, and love of a Mennonite woman.

While Mennonite readers will not identify readily with Behrends' characters and world because the "outsider" author, Behrends, fails to understand fully the Mennonite world from within, they can appreciate his monumental life's work and his sympathetic treatment of Mennonites. His characters are more German than Mennonite and his settings, while resembling the environments in which Mennonites lived, are not the well-known homes of Mennonite readers.

The German novelist Günter Grass has included West-Prussian Mennonites marginally in his novel *Hundejahre* (Dog Years, 1963). The author satirizes the "coarse" Mennonites who wear clothes with hooks and eyes and the "fine" Mennonites who wear clothes with buttons and pockets. The religious fanaticism of Simon Beister, a "coarse" Mennonite, leads to his setting fire to the windmill belonging to a Catholic.

A play by Dieter Forte, *Martin Luther und Thomas Münzer oder Die Einführung der Buchhandlung* (Martin Luther and Thomas Müntzer, Or, The Intro-

duction of Bookkeeping, 1971), deals also only marginally with Anabaptism. The dramatist shows how rising capitalism during the Reformation period contributed to the plight of the lower classes in Germany. While Luther is portrayed as a pawn in the hands of the princes, who in turn are controlled by the mighty Fugger banking family, °Müntzer pleads the cause of the peasants and the working people, urging them to trust no one but themselves and their weapons.

Another German play, *Das Sauspiel, Szenen aus dem 16. Jahrhundert* (Pig's Game, Scenes from the 16th Century, 1975) by Martin Walser deals with Anabaptism as a major theme. The main characters are divided into two opposing groups: the Renaissance figures such as the artist Albrecht Dürer and the reformer Philipp °°Melanchthon and the imprisoned Anabaptists, including Hans °°Denck, awaiting sentencing. The problem the authorities face is how to punish the Anabaptists while retaining a good conscience. Luther in the end comes up with a solution: The Anabaptists must not be punished for their faith—this would make them martyrs—but as rebels against the state. With the removal of the Anabaptists the world is made safe for intellectual, cultural and technological development.

In the United States, Leigh Brackett wrote a science fiction novel about the aftermath of an atomic holocaust, *The Long Tomorrow* (1955). The conservative and skillful Mennonite farmers are among the survivors of the Great Destruction, virtually controlling the government. They seek to maintain a simple agrarian civilization, resisting any return to a technological and urban society. But human nature has not changed. Two young Mennonites, Len and Esau Coulter, are not satisfied with the drab and anti-intellectual life of their community. They discover the secret place where a large computer is hidden and the information necessary to rebuild the old technological world. Having developed a sense of curiosity, Len repeats the Fall into sin, as it were, and is unable to return to the simple community from which he came. The novel ends with the suggestion that technology will again lead to disaster.

In James Michener's novel *Centennial* (1974) Mennonites play a major role. One wonders what sources the author used for his Mennonites. While they are good farmers and generally thrifty, honest, and good people, the Mennonites in this novel seem to be preoccupied with their sexual and marital norms. Moreover, there is no suggestion that Mennonites are peace-loving, non-violent people. As in earlier novels about Mennonites (e.g., H. Martin, *Tilly: A Mennonite Maid*, 1904), there is in this novel the suggestion that in order to become free and self-fulfilled, Mennonites have to shed their past and leave their backward community.

In Canada, Anne Chislett has written a successful drama about a rural Ontario Amish community during World War I. *Quiet in the Land* (1983) recreates accurately the denominational distinctives of the Amish, portraying the diversity of human conflict within a particular milieu. Like Rudy Wiebe's *Peace Shall Destroy Many* (1962), Chislett shows that, while it is possible to hold on outwardly to traditional regulations with regard to peace and non-violence, it is more difficult to love real persons, including members of one's family and church. The play has been staged successfully before appreciative audiences.   HaL

For bibliographic details on the writings of Ernst Behrends see his biography. Writings by other writers mentioned above follow: Leigh Brackett, *The Long Tomorrow* (New York: Ballantine Books, 1974); Anne Chislett, *Quiet in the Land* (Toronto: Coach House Press, 1983); Dieter Forte, *Martin Luther and Thomas Münzer oder Die Einführung der Buchhandlung* (Berlin: Verlag Klaus Wagenbach, 1974); James Michener, *Centennial* (New York: Random House, 1974); Martin Walser, *Das Sauspiel: Szenen aus dem 16. Jahrhundert* (Frankfurt am Main: Suhrkamp Verlag, 1975); review of Caesar von Arx, *Brüder in Christo,* in *Menn. Life,* 3, no. 1 (Jan. 1948), 21; Mary Eleanor Bender, "The Sixteenth Century Anabaptists in Literature," in *The Recovery of the Anabaptist Vision,* ed. Guy F. Hereshberger. (Scottdale, 1957), 275-90; review of Eva Caskel, *Marguerite Valmore* (Hamburg: Maria Honeit Verlag, 1948) in *Menn. Life,* 6, no. 1 (Jan. 1951), 48; review of Friedrich Dürrenmatt, *Es steht geschrieben* in *Menn. Life,* 3, no. 1 (Jan. 1948), 21; J. W. Dyck, "The Image of the Mennonites in Josef Ponten's *Volk auf dem Wege,*" in *Mennonite Images,* ed. Harry Loewen (Winnipeg: Hyperion Press, 1980d), 237-45; Heinold Fast, "Ernst Behrends, 1891-1982," *Menn. Geschbl.* 39, n.s. 34 (1982), 96-105; Herta Maria Funk, "Die religiöse Weltanschauung in Ernst Behrends Romanreihe, *Das Volk der Wanderschaft.*" (PhD diss., U. of Kansas, 1982); Susan Rempel Letkemann, review of Anne Chislett's *Quiet in the Land,* in *Mennonite Historian* (Winnipeg), 11, no. 4 (Dec. 1985); Harry Loewen, review of Martin Walser's *Das Sauspiel,* in *MQR,* 52 (1978), 347-49; idem, review of Dieter Forte's *Martin Luther and Thomas Münzer,* in *MQR,* 50 (1976), 144-45, idem, "Anabaptists in Gottfried Keller's Novellas," in *Mennonite Images,* ed. Harry Loewen (Winnipeg: Hyperion Press, 1980) 209-19; idem, "Anabaptists and Utopia in Grimmelshausen's *The Adventurous Simplicissimus,*" in *Visions and Realities,* ed. Harry Loewen and Al Reimer (Winnipeg: Hyperion Press, 1985), 61-74; idem, "Grimmelshausens Wiedertäufer und der Utopiegedanke im 'Simplicissimus;,*" *Menn. Geschbl.* Jg. 39, n.s. Bd. 34 (1982), 11-23; idem, "Theses and Symbols in the 'Mennonite' Novels of Ernst Behrends," *Menn. Life,* 37, no. 1 (March 1982), 14-18; Levi Miller, review of James Michener's *Centennial* in *GH* (Sept. 22, 1981), 717-19; Horst Quiring and Cornelius Krahn, "Mennonites in German Literature 1940-1950," *Menn. Life* 7, no. 2 (April 1952), 85-87; Elmer F. Sudermann, "The Mennonite Community and the Pacifist Character in American Literature," *Menn. Life,* 34, no. 1 (March 1979), 8-15, and "Mennonite Culture in a Science Fiction Novel [Brackett, *Long Tomorrow*]," *MQR,* 49 (1975), 53-56.

See also Dramatic Arts.

Litwiller, Ada Ramseyer (b. 1900), a pioneer missionary in Argentina, 1925-67, with the Mennonite Board of Missions (MC), Elkhart, Ind., grew up near New Hamburg, Ont., and attended the Steinmann (Amish) Mennonite Church. Although baptized at age 12, Ada had a "real conversion experience" two years later in evangelistic meetings at the Baden Mennonite Mission. As a new Christian, she felt called to serve God on the mission field. She completed seventh grade, then worked at home on the farm and took two years of Winter Bible School taught by S. F. °°Coffman. Shortly after she and Nelson Litwiller were married (Apr. 23, 1919), they left for study at Bethany Bible Training School (CBreth) in Chicago, Ill. They were the parents of four daughters and one son, four of whom served in overseas mission. Though her Amish Mennonite conference had had little to say in favor of missions, she and Nelson found family, and soon conference support for their endeavor. Sister-in-law Edna (Litwil-

ler) and Amos °Swartzentruber preceded Ada and Nelson in mission work in Argentina by one year. While Ada's family and support role overshadowed her public role (helping in visitation, as hostess at the Mennonite seminary in Montevideo, Uruguay, and some speaking), her own clear sense of call to mission permeated her life work.   JMB

John Bender, ed., *Pilgerleben, Pilgrims, Perangrinos* (Western Ontario Mennonite Conference, 1984).

Litwiller, Nelson (Feb. 16, 1898-Nov. 18, 1986), a leader in Mennonite mission in Latin America (1925-67), in retirement was active in itinerant ministries in North America and overseas, later especially within the Mennonite renewal and ecumenical °charismatic movements. Born at St. Agatha, Ont., he and his wife, Ada Ramseyer, studied at Bethany Bible Training School (CBreth) in Chicago (1919-24), followed by a year at Goshen College where Nelson received the BA and BD degrees. He was ordained in 1925 at College Mennonite Church in Goshen by Bishop David A. Yoder. He and Ada served with Mennonite Board of Missions (MC), Elkhart, Ind., in Argentina for 31 years (1925-56). He was named bishop in 1947. In Montevideo, Uruguay, he became founding president of Seminario Evangélico Menonita de Teología (1956-67), serving additionally as mission field secretary for all of Latin America. In 1968 the Litwillers moved to Goshen, Ind. In 1970, at a point of deep searching, Nelson experienced the baptism of the Holy Spirit in a Roman Catholic °charismatic prayer meeting at nearby South Bend, Ind. For the rest of his lifetime, expressed as "revitalized retirement," he promoted unity within the body of Christ, serving as a bridge between traditional church leaders and those in charismatic circles. In 1975 he helped start Mennonite Renewal Services (MRS), the charismatic arm of the Mennonite church. He died of cancer, Nov. 18, 1986, in Goshen and was buried at the St. Agatha Mennonite Church. The couple had five children, Lois (m. Albert Buckwalter), Beulah (Gonzales), Eunice (m. Daniel Miller), John (d. 1971), and Esther (m. James Shertz).   JMB

Menn. Bib. II, p. 474.

Liu, James (Chung-Fu) (b. June 19, 1904) was born in the city of Puyang (formerly Kai Chow) in Henan (Honan) Province, China. His Buddhist parents converted to Christianity at the General Conference Mennonite Church mission station. James was baptized in 1920. His education, begun in a Confucian school, continued in the Mennonite mission school and Yenching University. From 1930 to 1932 James studied at Bluffton College (Ohio) and Bethel College (Ks.). Returning to China, James was principal of the Mennonite mission high school at Kai Chow until 1946, when he and his wife fled for their lives. They worked with the Mennonite Central Committee, 1946-52. James then taught in a government school, but during the Cultural Revolution (1966-69) he was imprisoned for three years and tortured. In 1985, at age 82, James with his son Timothy visited in the United States and Canada as a guest of Mennonite friends.   JWF

Juhnke, *Mission* (1979), 59, 61-62; *MWR* (Sept. 5, 1985), 7; *Courier* 1, no. 1 (Jan. 1986), 12-13; *Mennonite* (Apr. 21, 1936), 19-20, (Feb. 25, 1986), 80-81; *MWR* (Apr.27, 1987), 1.

Living Love Movement. See Amor Viviente Movement.

Lobbying. Bringing citizen perspectives to bear on governmental policy may be motivated by either altruistic (concern for the welfare of others) or self-seeking interests. The means of seeking to influence government decisions may take the form of letter-writing, appointments with people in congressional offices, testifying in congressional hearings, etc. Mennonites, as individuals and as denominational or agency representatives, have utilized all of these options in varying degrees.

Since 1525 Mennonites have appeared before high government officials to present their petitions. In the course of the four centuries delegations representing Mennonite bodies have traveled to such capitals as St. Petersburg (Leningrad), Moscow, Berlin, Jerusalem, Saigon, Asunción, Djakarta, Winnipeg, Ottawa, and Washington, to present their requests, traditionally in defense of conscience on issues of °peace and war.

As early as 1775, Mennonites wrote a petition to the Pennsylvania Assembly regarding the bearing of arms. In 1916, the editor of the *Gospel Herald* (MC) wrote United States President Woodrow Wilson, requesting assistance for beleaguered Mennonites suffering in Russia. In 1917 the Eastern Amish Mennonite Church wrote President Woodrow Wilson petitioning him to exempt their members from military service. More than 20,000 Mennonites signed petitions sent to Washington in 1920 to forestall the renewal of conscription. Since 1940 Mennonites in America have testified periodically before congressional committees, especially on the matter of conscription which directly affected their families and faith perspective.

Only in more recent times have Mennonites established an ongoing presence near the seat of government. In 1968 the Mennonite Central Committee (MCC) Peace Section opened an office in Washington and in 1975, MCC Canada established an office in Ottawa. These offices serve as "listening posts" for constituents. Staff members monitor legislation and policy developments that affect the life and work of the Mennonite and Brethren in Christ churches at home and abroad. °Refugee concerns, world hunger, °human rights, the environment (°ecology), °criminal justice and °nuclear arms are among the issues added to conscription as legitimate areas of concern by the churches. Information is published for interested constituents, contacts with government are facilitated, and seminars are conducted.

The expanding global Mennonite presence in places of poverty, injustice, and warfare has increasingly resulted in requesting meetings with government officials to enable MCC and mission workers and interested church members to communicate observations and concerns that might helpfully enlighten governmental perspective and policy.

As education, travel, and communication media expand Mennonite awareness of the connection between governmental policy, the alleviation of human suffering, and threats to the planet's survival, so to the interest of church members in influencing those policy decisions has expanded. Some 6,000 Mennonites receive the *Washington Memo* of the MCC Washington office, and the "Ottawa Notebook" appears regularly in the *Mennonite Reporter*. Both publications are designed to inform and equip readers for communication with appropriate people in government. Mennonites are of diverse perspectives on whether or not to influence government policy. "Lobbying" may be viewed in either a positive or negative light, depending on how and for what purposes it is done.   DF

Wittlinger, *Piety and Obedience* (1978), 367, 377; *GH* (July 20, 1916), 301.

See also Sociopolitical Activism; Church-State Relations; Civilian Public Service (ME I).

Lohrenz, Gerhard (Dec. 13, 1899-Feb. 6, 1986), was born in the village of Neu-Schönsee in the Zagradovka colony in the Ukraine, Russia. After completing elementary school and some classes in the colony's *Zentralschule* (ME II: 155-57), he graduated from the Business School (*Handelsschule*) in Alexanderkrone, Molotschna colony, in 1918. From 1918 to 1922 Lohrenz served first in the White Army as a volunteer in the °Red Cross, and then in the Red Army as a conscript. In 1923 he was elected secretary of the local soviet, and shortly thereafter as district chairman responsible for five villages. He resigned his positions in November 1924. In January 1925 the members of his church elected him to represent them at the All-Mennonite Conference in Moscow.

In September 1922 Lohrenz married Anni Harder. They had four children: Mary, John, Hilda, and Sophie. In March 1925 he and his family migrated to Canada.

After a three-year attempt at farming in Saskatchewan he attended the Mennonite Collegiate Institute in Gretna, Man. (1928-30), and the Normal School in Manitou, Man. (1930-31). He completed a BA degree at the U. of Manitoba through the summer school program. He taught at an elementary school in Lydiatt, Man. (1931-38); continued teaching at Springstein, Man. (1938-47); and at the Mennonite Brethren Collegiate Institute, Winnipeg as (teacher and principal, 1947-52) and Canadian Mennonite Bible College, Winnipeg, (1952-65).

Lohrenz was a dedicated churchman. He was baptized in 1921 in the Nikolaifelder Mennonite Church in Zagradovka, Russia. He was ordained minister of the Sargent Avenue Mennonite Church, Winnipeg, in 1954, as *Ältester* (°elder) in 1959 and served in the latter office until 1971. He also served on numerous provincial and Canadian conference committees.

He had a strong interest in history, especially in Russian Mennonite history. He was instrumental in developing the Mennonite Historical Library and Archives at Canadian Mennonite Bible College. Of the 33 tours he led, 17 visited the Soviet Union. In his retirement he authored 13 books, all of which dealt with Russian Mennonite life. He chaired the committee which planned the Manitoba Mennonite Centennial celebrations in 1974. In October 1974 the U. of Winnipeg bestowed upon Lohrenz an honorary DD for his numerous contributions. He led an active life up to his sudden death in Winnipeg.   JF

Gerhard Lohrenz, *Storm Tossed* (Winnipeg: the author, 1976), an autobiography; idem, *Sagradowka* (Rosthern, Sask.: Echo-Verlag, 1947); Gerhard Ens and George K. Epp in *Der Bote* (Feb. 19, 1986), 4, 6.

Lohrenz, John H. (Nov. 2, 1893-Mar. 5, 1971). Born to Henry and Elizabeth Wiens Lohrenz, John H. Lohrenz was a missionary educator and writer in India for 37 years (1920-57). A graduate of Tabor College, with postgraduate studies at Bluffton College and Kansas City Baptist Theological Seminary, he married Maria Klaassen of Hillsboro, Ks., on June 6, 1918, and was ordained for missionary service under Mennonite Brethren on May 9, 1920. His missionary activities at Nagarkurnool, Kalvakurthy, Shamshabad, and Hughstown in °Hyderabad State consisted of administration, evangelism, and particularly Bible school instruction and production of Telugu literature. Besides writing short biographies of Mrs. Maria Lohrenz, John H. Voth, John H. Pankratz, Daniel F. Bergthold, John A. Wiebe, and his brother H. W. Lohrenz, in 1950 he published *The Mennonite Brethren Church*, a history and handbook covering 1860 to 1948. In 1964 a series of Bible lessons titled *The Doctrinal Teachings of the Bible*, was published in India and translated into Telugu and Marathi. Following the death of his wife in 1962, he married Susie Richert of Dinuba, Cal., in 1963. Lohrenz died at Fresno, Cal.   PMH

S. T. Moyer, *They Heard*, 113.

Lohrenz, Marie Klaassen (Nov. 28, 1892-July 19, 1962). Born at Hillsboro, Ks., to Peter A. and Maria Jantzen Klaassen, Maria Klaassen Lohrenz was a missionary in India for 37 years (1920-1957). A graduate of Tabor College, she taught for four years in Kansas rural schools. In preparation for missionary service, she completed one year of training at °°Bethel Deaconess Hospital, and, after her marriage on June 6, 1918, attended Bluffton College. During a furlough she graduated with honors from Kansas City Baptist Theological Seminary. Her missionary activities at Nagarkurnool, Kalvakurthy, Shamshabad, and Hughestown included extensive touring of villages with her husband and the training of Bible women (°lay evangelists). Her longest stint of service was at Shamshabad where she taught in the Bible school and served as principal of the middle school for a number of years. She published in Telugu a book of gospel songs and a *Guide to the Study of the Old Testament*. Following a final term in urban ministries in Hyderabad, she retired with her husband to Fresno, Cal., continuing her extensive correspondence and hosting guests until her death at Fresno.   PMH

S. T. Moyer, *They Heard*, 113.

Loma Plata, Paraguay, is the administrative, economic, and social center of Menno Colony. Located on nonarable land, in 1937 it became the center of such cooperative enterprises as trade and industry, as well as the offices of the colony administration. It received its name from the Mennonite expedition which explored the Chaco for settlement possibilities in 1921. When the first settlers came in 1927-28 a large preliminary camp of settlers was located at this place.

In 1988 ca. 2,000 people (550 families) live in Loma Plata. Originally the central school served as worship center also, but in 1988 three large church buildings serve as meeting places for the Menno Colony's multicongregation church (Mennonitengemeinde) of ca. 1,500 members. The three congregations have choirs, music groups, women's organizations, youth clubs and youth work, and volleyball and football clubs, etc. A large elementary school and a high school with full national accreditation is also located here, as is a Bible school, agricultural school and a school for special purposes. The offices of the colony administration, security services, and agricultural bureau as well as a number of private enterprises including general stores, furniture establishments, an agricultural machinery factory, and various other enterprises are found in Loma Plata.

The producer-consumer °cooperative of the colony is headquartered here. This includes a cotton processing plant, an oil press, a power station, a plant converting wood to gas, a meat market, and a creamery processing ca. 70,000-80,000 liters (ca. 20,000 gallons) of milk daily. Loma Plata is also the location of a hotel, telephone and radio services, and a 45-bed hospital, including five doctors and a nursing school. Daily bus service to Asunción is maintained as is occasional air service. The colony museum and historical °archives are also in Loma Plata. In 1988 ca. 430 Mennonites and 80 Indians are employed by the colony in these enterprises.   MWF

See also Filadelfia.

London Mennonite Fellowship began in 1952 as a ministry to students in the newly-opened London Mennonite Centre (°England). Mennonites scattered by the effects of World War II also participated. The growth of the fellowship as an English congregation began in 1975 when Stephen Longley, later a Mennonite missionary to Nepal joined. In the following year the tiny fellowship adopted its covenant which, after a crisis, was revised and reaffirmed in 1982. In 1983 the church, which had begun to grow, moved its worship out of the London Mennonite Centre, and in 1988 the church began to take root in another part of North London, Wood Green. Its growing maturity was indicated by its calling in 1986 of English elders to lead the church and in 1987 by its hiring of its first paid worker. In 1987 the fellowship, together with the Evangelical Mennonite Association (the legal trust for London Mennonite Centre), formed the United Kingdom Conference of Mennonites. Membership in 1987 was 33. AK

Longacre, Doris Janzen (Feb. 15, 1940-Nov. 10, 1979), was born in Newton, Ks. She received her BA degree in home economics from Goshen College and did graduate studies at Goshen Biblical Seminary and Kansas State U. With her husband, Paul Longacre, and two daughters, Cara Sue and Marta Joy, she worked with Mennonite Central Committee in Vietnam (1964-67) and in Indonesia (1971-72). She served as chairperson of the Akron Mennonite Church, as a member of the Board of Overseers of Goshen Biblical Seminary, and as a frequent speaker on world hunger.

"More-with-Less" came to be associated with Doris through two books she compiled as part of a Mennonite Central Committee assignment. *The More-with-Less Cookbook*, a collection of recipes and suggestions on how to enjoy more while consuming less of the world's resources, was published in 1976 (Scottdale). It was sold widely, both within and outside Mennonite circles and was translated and adapted for publication in German. Doris died of cancer just months before the completion of her second book, *Living More with Less* (Scottdale, 1980). This book, filled with personal testimonies of people searching for ways to simplify their living, is a tribute to Doris' lifelong quest for ways to live responsibly and joyfully in a world neighborhood. PHM

Lord's Supper. See Communion.

Louisiana (ME III:403). In 1988 the Gulf States Fellowship (MC) had started planting a congregation in New Orleans with a membership of 35. The other two congregations of this conference in the state (at Des Allemands and Venice) had a total membership of 156. In addition there were two congregations belonging to the Church of God in Christ, Mennonite (Holdeman), at De Ridder and Transylvania. Mennonite Central Committee operated a voluntary service unit in New Orleans.   RSa

MC Yearbook, (1988-89), 26, 58, 151; Daniel Hertzler, *From Germantown to Steinbach* (Scottdale, 1981), 65-75; *GH* (Aug. 9, 1988), 537-39.

See also Indian Ministries, North America.

Love (ME III:404) is central to the Christian faith. The universal Christian affirmation is that because God loved men and women he provided °salvation for them through Jesus Christ. Despite this universal affirmation, the theological understanding of love has been the subject of intense debate. Love has been defined as *eros, philos,* and *agape.* The Protestant Reformation revolved around competing interpretations of love with Luther defining God's love as °grace, namely, as wholly undeserving love. In contrast, the Catholic Church argued that in addition to loving men and women even when they did not deserve to be loved, God also showed love to those who, in a certain limited sense, earned it.

The Anabaptist-Mennonite understanding of love was shaped within the context of the Reformation debates. Anabaptists questioned Luther's interpretation of love, because it tended not to transform human relationships. The Catholic option was also unsatisfactory because although it challenged people to love, the expectations for ordinary people were very low.

The various Anabaptist-Mennonite groups thus developed interpretations of love which affirmed both divine initiative and the necessity of human response. God's love to humanity was freely initiated by God himself, and yet people were also called to love God and their fellow human beings. Anabaptists and Mennonites also addressed the question of the quality of character of love among humans. The quality of this love they said should be characterized by °nonresistant or peaceful love, namely love which forgives rather than retaliates, a love which is willing to suffer rather than inflict °suffering. This understanding of the quality of love they believed was not only based on isolated Bible passages, but was modeled on the quality of love shown by God to humanity in the salvation God provides through Christ Jesus.

Nonresistant or peaceful love became the model or paradigm through which Anabaptist and Mennonite groups, including the Swiss, Dutch, Hutterite, and German groups perceived relationships among people. All the groups believed that broken fellowship should be dealt with on the basis of the "The Rule of Christ," [Mt 18], the °°ban was to be used instead of capital punishment, the sword was to be rejected for personal defense, and participation in °military service was rejected when European states began to form citizens' armies.

This quality of peaceful love was expressed not only in the narrowly religious dimensions of their lives, but was also allowed to shape their °economic and social relationships. The Hutterites expressed their love to each other in practicing °°community of goods, Dutch Mennonites organized a °relief agency which aided the Swiss, Hutterites and Polish Mennonites. Polish Mennonites organized a fire insurance organization, and negotiated exemption from service in Polish armies. Russian Mennonites developed the organization of a °°*Waisenamt* which cared for the estates of widows and orphans. Swiss Mennonites and Amish developed numerous informal communal support relationships like barn-raisings.

At least two areas can be identified in which Mennonite communities historically fell short in their expressions of love. One, because of the belief that the church must be pure and spotless, Mennonites frequently exercised church °discipline, "The Rule of Christ," for the sake of ridding the church of sinners rather than restoring the sinner to fellowship. Love became judgmental and punitive instead of redemptive. Second, the various expressions of love in the economic and social areas of life were expressed almost exclusively among fellow Mennonites. There was not the vision that love ought to be expressed within the wider social setting. There were good historical reasons why this rather narrow and limited view of love developed, and yet the fact remains that his view of love was restricted.

Since the 1950s at least four major Mennonite views of love can be differentiated. One view of love is that expressed by the conservers, namely the various groups of Mennonites, Hutterites, and Amish who are frequently identified as °conservative or Old Order. These groups have been concerned to maintain or conserve the values and practices which have stood the test of time. The conservers rarely theologize about love, but rather express their theology of live in maintaining local communal patterns of mutual support and interrelationships. These patterns include barn-raisings, village organizations, fire insurance associations, the *Waisenamt*, and numerous more informal patterns of relationship within the church community. Rarely do these relationships extend beyond the church's boundaries. Love among the conservers also usually includes an attitude of °humility and °service, and a rejection of dominance and lordship. In times of war conservers have usually rejected military service.

The more °acculturated Mennonites in North America have revised the traditional understanding of love in a number of ways. One view of love has been shaped by the influence of the °Evangelical and °Fundamentalist movements upon Mennonites. The Evangelical movement influenced Mennonite communities strongly already in the 19th c., and the influence has continued throughout the 20th c. The Evangelical movement emphasized individual experience of salvation, portrayed evangelism as the primary concern of the church, and characterized denominational emphases as traditional and unbiblical. The Evangelical movement tended to reject the historic Mennonite emphases of Christian love as lived in economic, social, and political relationships. Because the Evangelical movement was thoroughly Anglo-American and usually nationalistic, the peace theology of Mennonites was threatened.

Fundamentalism injected into this movement a concern for theologically correct belief as defined by Fundamentalists. This belief included among others, belief in Scripture as verbally °inerrant, in the deity of Christ, in the virgin birth of Jesus, and in the substitutionary atonement by Christ. Nonresistance as the interpretation of God's love to humanity, was rejected.

Rather than broadening the historic Mennonite understanding of love, this influence has restricted love even more. God's love is seen primarily as providing salvation for the soul in preparation for heaven. This love is stated primarily in substitutionary rather than in relational terminology. Human love is seen primarily as responding to God by accepting salvation. Expressing love to people is not seen as integral to salvation. The historic Mennonite relationship between God's love, and human life in all its dimensions, is broken.

A further interpretation of love, in this discussion the third view, is that view inspired by Harold °Bender, and summarized in his article "The Anabaptist Vision." The characteristics of Mennonite love are described as nonresistance, expressing love within the community of people, and living out this love in a life of °discipleship. In this movement there was the attempt to state the historic Mennonite view of love in such a manner that the historic emphases would b retained, and also so that the Evangelical-Fundamentalist attacks on these emphases would be blunted.

Because of Bender's fear of attack from Fundamentalism, he reshaped the historical Mennonite emphases on love in such a manner that he could not be accused of being a modernist (°liberalism) or a proponent of the °social gospel. Consequently he eschewed a definition of love which would aim at transforming the social and economic order of society. Love toward society ought to be expressed in religious forms such as charity, relief, and missions. The more radical aspects of love which deal with changes in the social and economic structures he largely rejected. At most such social and economic concerns ought to be expressed within the community of believers.

This interpretation of love has played a powerful role in most Mennonite church groups in North America and Europe since the 1950s. This perspective has become a powerful force for church renewal and a platform for maintaining an Anabaptist-Mennonite identity.

The most recent interpretation of the theology of love, in this discussion the fourth view, was developed since the 1960s and is based largely on the methodology of the social sciences. Social science methodology interpreted Mennonite life and theology, including the theology of love, within the context of social relationships and changes within society as a whole. The view of "The Anabaptist Vision" approach which perceived the Mennonite community as largely a separated religious community which was bombarded by new ideas from the outside, was rejected. Rather, the Mennonite community was seen as extricably interwoven with society on a continual basis. Because of this interwoven nature, the social science view of love was that love could and should be expressed within the whole social order. The agenda as to what issues love should address, it was believed, should arise from the society, and the response to that agenda should be addressed to the whole society not only to the church community. The result of this emphasis has been that Mennonite churches have addressed issues of °divorce and remarriage, homosexuality (°sexuality), spouse abuse, as well as other forms of family violence. The final result has, however, usually been that most of the attention is given to how the church will deal with these issues, rather than having the church attempt to change laws or conditions within society.

Another major new issue from the perspective of social sciences is °justice. The proponents of the social science approach argued that Mennonites cannot separate themselves from the social and political order, especially within °democratic political societies, and therefore Mennonites must take some responsibility for changing unjust social and economic structures which are oppressing people. This view was argued both in relation to conditions in North America and in other countries.

This approach provides a much broader intrepretation of love than did the historical view, the Mennonite view shaped by Evangelical-Fundamentalism, or Bender's revision of the historical view. However, this reinterpretation of love also disturbs many people. The social science approach to attaining justice, when it is argued on the basis of rights which are demanded and when it advocates using political or social power to attain these rights, seems to contradict the very essence of love as historically understood by Mennonites. Because of this difficulty, others have worked at developing a theology of love which includes justice for people in the larger society, and which is based not on rights, but rather on the emphases of nonresistance and a willingness to suffer.

These four theologies of love are strongly represented among Mennonites in the United States and Canada today. They coexist with each other, sometimes in tension, at other times in conflict.   JF

H. S. Bender, "The Anabaptist Vision," *Church History,* 13 (Mar. 1944), 3-24, reprinted *MQR,* 18 (1944), 67-88, reprinted in *Recovery,* 29-54; John Drescher, "The Language of Love," *MB Herald* (Mar. 27, 1981), 2-4; David Ewert, "The Greatest of These Is Love," *MB Herald* (June 25, 1982), 7-8; Aubrey B. Haines, "Let's Turn Our Other Cheek," *Mennonite* (Oct. 12, 1982), 500; Gordon Houser, "The Twin Sins and the Twin Commands," *Mennonite* (June 25, 1985), 332; Gordon D. Kaufman, *Non-resistance and Responsibility and other Mennonite Essays* (Newton, 1979); idem, "What Is Our Unique Mission?" *Menn. Life* (July 1961), 9; William Klassen, "Love Your Enemy: A Study of New Testament Teaching in Coping with the Enemy," *MQR,* 37 (1963), 147-71; Norman C. Kraus, ed., *Evangelicalism and Anabaptism* (Scottdale, 1979); Willard S. Krabill, "To Be Sexual and Be Intimate," *Mennonite* (Aug. 13, 1985) 384-86; Maurice Martin, "The Pure Church: the Burden of Anabaptism," *CGR,* no. 2 (Spring 1983), 29-41; Dick McSorley, "The Gospel of Peace," *Mennonite* (Aug. 11, 1981), 453-45; Anders Nygren, *Agape and Eros,* trans. Philip S. Watson (New York: Harper Torchbooks, 1969); Theron F. Schlabach, *Gospel Versus Gospel. Mission and the Mennonite Church, 1863-1944* (Scottdale, 1980); Keith G. Schrag, "Let's Add More Compassion," *Mennonite* (May 22, 1984), 263; Irving Singer, *The Nature of Love,* 3 vols., 2nd ed. (Chicago: U. of Chicago Press, 1984-87); James Waltner, "Bound by Love," *Mennonite,* (May 10, 1977), 308.

See also Ordinances.

Lumeya Nzashi (b. ca. 1928), an influential teacher and preacher of the Église du Christ au Zaire, Communauté des Églises de Frères Mennonites au Zaire (Mennonite Brethren Church of Zaire), was born in the village of Kimbengi near the Kafumba mission station. While in primary school he accepted Christ and was baptized. In 1944 he graduated from the four-year course of the Mennonite Brethren Bible Institute at Kafumba.

From 1945 to 1965 Lumeya taught at the Kafumba Primary School, where his teaching ability became apparent. Together with the head-pastor, °Djimbo Kibala, Lumeya was also active in Bible teaching in schools and churches, and in village evangelization. He was a Bible teacher in official schools in the city of Kikwit from 1962 to 1968. In 1968 he was ordained for church ministry and became pastor of the Kikwit, Kimpwanza congregation. He held this position for four years.

Since 1973 Lumeya is coordinator of evangelism in the entire northern district of the Mennonite Brethren Church of Zaire, which includes a population of ca. 350,000. He spends much time in the villages giving seminars for pastors and other church workers and counseling members and others in need. He has long been known as an ardent Bible student and a sincere and powerful preacher. His oldest son is completing his doctoral studies at Fuller Theological Seminary and his second son is a lawyer in °Kinshasa (1988).   MDyck

Lusangu Kapenda (b. 1918) was born in Panzi, Belgian Congo (Zaire). After primary school he became a teacher at Panzi. In 1952 he became president of the central office of the Mennonite Brethren (MB) at Kikwit and pastor of the Kimpwanza congregation in Kikwit. Since 1968 he has served as an evangelist at Panzi and is responsible for evangelism in the entire Southern Region of the Mennonite Brethren conference (Église du Christ au Zaire, Communauté des Église de Frères Mennonites).   AP

Luxembourg. See Association Mennonite Luxembourgeoise.

Luz y Esperanza Colony, Paraguay, was founded in East Paraguay by Beachy Amish Mennonites from the United States in 1967. Some of these had earlier settled in the °°Chaco region. A total of 2,147 hectares (5,300 acres) of land were purchased. The colony's name means "Light and Hope." The settlement maintains fellowship with the °Augua Azul and °Rio Corrientes colonies. The churches in the three colonies make up the Mennonite Christian Brotherhood.

Separation from the world is stressed and is visible in the wearing of plain °dress, °headcoverings, and beards. The major emphasis, however, is not on form but on practical Christian living, love for neighbors, friendliness, and missionary zeal. The latter is truly significant. Worship services are conducted both in English and Spanish.

The economic struggle is severe. A number of members have emigrated and some have died. A small clinic serves emergency needs. There were 15 families in the settlement in 1986, of whom 31 were members of the congregation, with 24 speaking English and 7 Spanish.   GR

MWH (1978), 252; *MWH* (1984), 100.

M

Madhya Pradesh State (Central Provinces State), India. Area: 443,446 sq. km., population: 52,178,844; capital: Bhopal; Principal language: Hindi. The economy of Madhya Pradesh is primarily agricultural with nearly 80 percent of the population living in villages. Over 42.5 percent of the land is arable and 14 percent is irrigated. Forests cover nearly 32 percent of the state. The state is divided into 45 districts. There are seven major river systems. Mennonite churches are scattered in the five southeastern districts, viz., Rajandgaon, Durg, Raipur, Bilaspur, and Surguja. PJM

India 1985, comp. and ed. by Research and Reference Division, Ministry of Information and Broadcasting, Government of India (New Delhi: Allied Printers, 1986) 579-81; Juhnke, *Mission* (1979), 17-43 passim; John A. Lapp, *India* (1972).

See also India; Mennonite Church in India; Bharatiya General Conference Mennonite Kalisiya.

Maine. See New England.

Malagar, Pyarelal Joel (b. 1920), the first India national ordained to the office of bishop in the Mennonite Church in India. His parents, Joel and Janki, residents of Balodgahan via °Dhamtari, were village evangelistic workers (°lay evangelists) employed by the Mennonite Board of Missions (MC). Pyarelal received elementary education in Balodgahan, and secondary education in Dhamtari. After graduation from the Mennonite high school he joined the evangelistic program of the mission. He was sent to the Bangalore Bible Institute in south India to train for evangelism. In 1948-50 he studied in Goshen College and Goshen Biblical Seminary, Goshen, Ind., receiving the BA and ThB degrees. Later he received the BD degree from Serampore Theological College in West Bengal.

He married Satyavati Prabhudas, a teacher in the English Primary School in Dhamtari. They have two sons and one daughter.

Pyarelal was ordained a minister (1945) and bishop (1955) in the Mennonite Church. He has served for various periods in the following positions: editor of *Shanti Sandesh*, a peace magazine; director of Mennonite Central Committee of India; director of °Mennonite Christian Service Fellowship of India; president of Fellowship of Reconciliation in India; moderator of the annual conference of the Mennonite Church in India.

Pyarelal's second visit to North America was in 1975. He and Satyavati attended the biennial meeting of Mennonite Church (MC) General Assembly in Eureka, Ill., and the meetings of the Mennonite World Conference presidium, of which he was a member. WH

John A. Lapp, *India* (1972), 180, 191; P. J. Malagar, *MC India* (1981).

Malawi. See Ibandla Labazalwane Kukristu e-Zimbabwe.

Mandli (mun'-dah-lee), an abstract noun derived from the Sanskrit word Mandal, meaning circle, orbit, enclosure, or area within. *Mandli* has social implications, referring to persons, or people "within the enclosure" of a particular social, political, economic, or religious community.

Mandli has been widely used by the church in the Hindi and Hindi-related language areas, (Hindi, Marathi, Gujarati, Bengali, and Nepali) to denote congregation, fellowship, brotherhood, or community, e.g., "Mennonite Mandli" or "Methodist Mandli," etc. However, Christians addressing non-Christians do not speak of themselves as the "Christian Mandli," but rather as the Christian *Samaj* (also meaning community or society). The Persian word *Majhab* is also frequently used. It is a word denoting a religious sect.

Since the 1950s *Mandli* is rapidly being dropped in favor of *Kalisiya*, a word coined from the Greek "ekklesia." All newer translations of the New Testament have consistently used the latter word. While *Mandli* is not an inaccurate translation, the use of *Kalisiya* probably reflects a concern to be identified more closely with the original biblical concept. JAF

Hindi Dictionaries: *Brihat Hindi Kosh* (Varanasi U.P.: Gyanmandal Ltd.); *Pramarnik Hindi Kosh* (Varanasi, U.P.: Sahitya Ratnamala Karyalay).

See also Bihar Mennonite Mandli; Bharatiya Jukto Christa Prachar Mandli; India (for groups using Kalisiya).

Manitoba (ME III:457) is a province in central Canada in which Mennonites have lived since 1874. The 1981 census reported 63,980 Mennonite and Brethren in Christ living in Manitoba, a 43 percent increase since 1951. Part of this increase is due to continued immigration of German speaking Mennonites from Paraguay and Mexico, and from the Union of Societ Socialist Republics via Germany.

Most (70 percent) of the increase is in the major city of Winnipeg, which, with 19,105 Mennonites, is now the city with the largest Mennonite population in the world. The 43 congregations in the city include congregations made up primarily of the following ethnic groups: Chinese (2), Hispanic (2), Vietnamese (1), and French (1).

Church Developments. In the Conference of Mennonites in Manitoba a transition took place from multicongregation churches under the leadership of an elder to more or less autonomous congregations,

533

MANITOBA

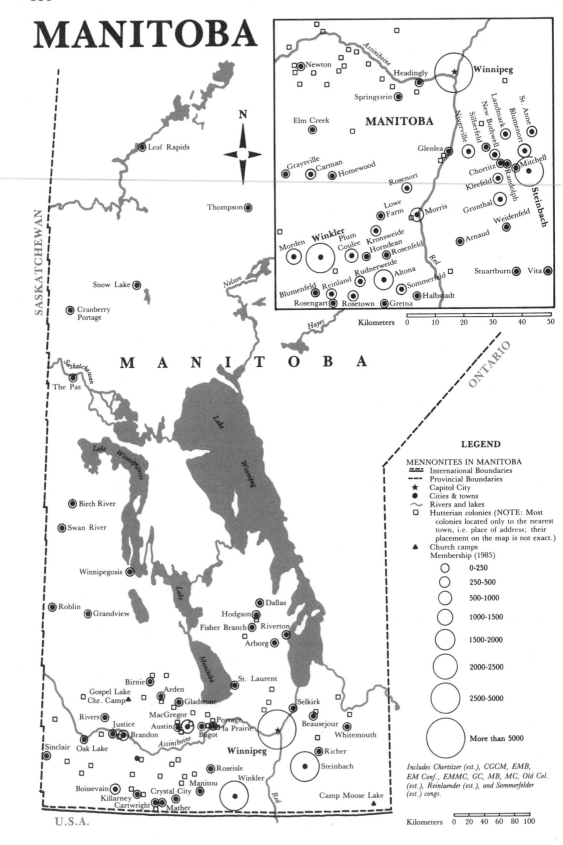

MANITOBA

N

Assiniboine

Newton
Headingly
Springstein
★ Winnipeg

Elm Creek
MANITOBA

Leaf Rapids

Graysville Carman
Homewood

Glenlea
Niverville
New Bothwell Landmark
Silberfeld St. Anne
Blumenort

Rosenort
Chortitz
Mitchell
Kleefeld Randolph
Steinbach

Thompson
Lowe
Farm Morris
Grunthal
Weidenfeld

Morden **Winkler** Plum
Coulee Kronsweide
Horndean
Arnaud

Blumenfeld Reinland Rudnerweide Altona
Rosengart Rosetown Gretna
Sommerfeld
Halbstadt

Stuartburn Vita

Rosenfeld

Snow Lake
Cranberry
Portage

Nelson

Hayes

Kilometers   0   10   20   30   40   50

Saskatchewan

The Pas

M A N I T O B A

ONTARIO

Birch River

Swan River

Lake

Lake Winnipegosis

Lake Winnipeg

LEGEND

MENNONITES IN MANITOBA
▬▬ International Boundaries
--- Provincial Boundaries
★ Capitol City
● Cities & towns
∼ Rivers and lakes
▢ Hutterian colonies (NOTE: Most
    colonies located only to the nearest
    town, i.e. place of address; their
    placement on the map is not exact.)
▲ Church camps
Membership (1985)

○   0-250

○   250-500

○   500-1000

○   1000-1500

○   1500-2000

○   2000-2500

○   2500-5000

○   More than 5000

Winnipegosis

Roblin Grandview

Lake Manitoba

Dallas
Hodgson
Fisher Branch Riverton
Arborg

Birnie
Gospel Lake
Chr. Camp ▲
Arden
Gladstone
St. Laurent

Rivers
Justice
MacGregor
Austin Portage
la Prairie
Selkirk
Beausejour
Whitemouth

Brandon Bagot
Assiniboine
Sinclair Oak Lake
Winnipeg ★
Richer

Roseisle
Steinbach

Boissevain
Manitou
Killarney Crystal City
Cartwright Mather
Winkler
Red
Camp Moose Lake ▲

Includes Chortitzer (est.), CGCM, EMB,
EM Conf., EMMC, GC, MB, MC, Old Col.
(est.), Reinlaender (est.), and Sommerfelder
(est.) congs.

U.S.A.

Kilometers   0   20   40   60   80   100

each under the leadership of its own pastor. The Bergthal Mennonites, the largest of the multi-congregation churches, with 20 places of worship in 1955, completed its dissolution in 1972. The resulting congregational units for the most part remained in the Conference of Mennonites in Manitoba. Since 1968 many of them have also joined the General Conference Mennonite Church (GCM). Several rural congregations of the Manitoba Conference of Mennonite Brethren Churches have closed since the 1950s, while a number of new ones have been begun in urban centers.

The Kleine Gemeinde, Rudnerweider, and Chortitzer Churches developed conference structures, with the first-named body becoming the Evangelical Mennonite Church in 1952, then adopting the name "Evangelical Mennonite Conference" (EMCon) in 1960. The Rudnerweider church became the Evangelical Mennonite Mission Conference (EMMC, 1959), and the Chortitzer church became the Chortitzer Mennonite Conference (1972). The latter, however, has retained the elder as central leader.

Both the Sommerfelder Mennonites and Old Colony Mennonites experienced further divisions in the difficult process of trying to adjust to modern society without compromising essential aspects of the faith. This resulted in the formation of the Reinländer Mennonite Church (1958) and Zion Mennonite Church (1980). The Reinländer group in turn experienced a division in 1986, giving rise to the Friedensfelder Church.

Mission outreach has resulted in a number of Cree and Saulteaux congregations relating to the Conference of Mennonites in Canada (CMC).

Since its founding in 1963, the Mennonite Central Committee (Canada) office has been located in Winnipeg.

Education, Publication, and Broadcasting. The Mennonite conferences actively promote higher education. Mennonite Brethren Bible College and Canadian Mennonite Bible College, founded in Winnipeg in the 1940s, have established formal relations with the two provincial universities in the city. In addition, the University of Winnipeg has an endowed Chair in Mennonite Studies and a Mennonite Studies Centre. Steinbach Bible Institute moved to college status in 1978, sponsored jointly by the EMC, EMMC, Chortitzer Mennonite Conference and two other congregations in Steinbach. Some of the other Mennonite groups, on the other hand, continue to have reservations about any formal education beyond the minimum required by law. The result, according to the 1981 census, is that 36 percent of Mennonites age 15 and older have less than grade nine education, while 12 percent have at least some university studies.

Manitoba is also an important Mennonite publishing center. The *Mennonitische Rundschau*, published in Winnipeg since 1923, was purchased by the Christian Press in 1945 and continues to serve German-speaking Mennonite Brethren. Its English companion, the *Mennonite Observer*, founded in 1955, became the *Mennonite Brethren Herald* in 1961. *Der Bote* moved its publishing site from Rosthern, Sask., to Winnipeg in 1977 and continues to serve the General Conference Mennonite Church. The official paper of the Evangelical Mennonite Mission Conference, *Der Leitstern* (founded 1944), became the *The EMMC Recorder* in 1967 and was being published in Winnipeg in 1986. *The Messenger*, published biweekly in Steinbach, has been the English language organ of the EMCon since 1962. The *Mennonite Mirror*, published ten times a year in Winnipeg by the Mennonite Literary Society, was begun in 1970. *Die Mennonitische Post*, founded in 1977 by MCC Canada, is published biweekly in Steinbach and serves German-speaking Mennonites with Canadian connections in Mexico, Bolivia, Belize, and other countries. Since 1982 the *Journal of Mennonite Studies* has been published annually by the Chair in Mennonite Studies.

Among Mennonite book publishers the most active

STATISTICS OF MANITOBA MENNONITE CHURCHES, 1985

Compiler: Aldolf Ens (author of article)

Name	Number of Congregations	Baptized 1985	Members 1950	% Increase
Chortitzer Mennonite Conference	9	1,800	1,648	9
Church of God in Christ, Mennonite	12	1,406	773	82
Conference of Mennonites in Manitoba	47	11,021	6,547	71
Evangelical Mennonite Brethren	11	810	400	103
Evangelical Mennonite Conference	30	4,445	1,920	132
Evangelical Mennonites Mission Conference	14	2,213	1,760	29
Mennonite Brethren	32	5,721	3,512	63
Northwest Mennonite Conference	1	15	-	-
Old Colony Mennonite Church	4	941	638	47
Reinländer Mennonite Church	6	683	-	-
Sommerfelder Mennonite Church	13	3,981	4,120	-3*
Unaffiliated Mennonite	5	?	-	-
Hutterian Brethren	18	5,940**	1,990**	198

*includes loss of Reinländer
**total population

are Kindred Press (Mennonite Brethren), CMBC Publications (Conference of Mennonites in Canada), the Mennonite Literary Society, and Derksen Printers in Steinbach. Centennial celebrations beginning in 1974 gave rise to a large number of local histories of Mennonite communities.

Mennonite church-produced radio programs date back to 1947. The founding of Radio Southern Manitoba by a group of Mennonite businessmen in 1957 greatly stimulated this activity. It broadcasts from transmitters in Altona, Steinbach, and Boissevain. In 1987 the CMM had weekly broadcasts in English, German, and Low German, and MB Communications in Winnipeg aired programs in German, Low German, and Russian, while other groups had one weekly program. Participation in television broadcasting was more occasional, with only the MB "Third Story" a regular program.

Cultural Activities and Political Involvement.
The combined Oratorio choir of the two Mennonite Bible colleges in Winnipeg performs annually in the main concert hall of the city. The Winnipeg Mennonite Children's Choir has gained international recognition, as have several Mennonite soloists. A Mennonite Theatre Society is active since 1972 and a Mennonite Orchestra since the 1940s. A few novelists, poets, artists, and filmmakers are receiving widespread recognition. The Mennonite Village Museum in Steinbach seeks to preserve artifacts of the pioneer years. The Mennonite Historical Society promotes research, writing, publication, and the collection of archival material.

From an earlier stance of aloofness, Manitoba Mennonites have become increasingly active in political affairs. Between 1969 and 1977 there was a 70 percent increase in the number of Mennonites voting in elections. Mennonites have regularly been elected to the provincial legislature since 1959, representing four different political parties. They have been represented in the provincial cabinet since 1966, some in senior portfolios. In the electoral district of Rhineland virtually all candidates in Provincial elections since 1962 have been Mennonite. Several Manitoba Mennonites have been elected to the national Parliament and one has been appointed to a cabinet minister's position.

Urbanization and Demographic Trends. Only 22 percent of Manitoba Mennonites were part of the rural farm population in 1981. The shift to °urban centers and to rural nonfarm occupations does not reflect a decrease in total acreage farmed by Mennonites; rather it is an indication of the rapid mechanization that has taken place in the agriculture. This mechanization released a large pool of workers, making possible a very significant growth in industry in such predominantly Mennonite towns as Winkler, Steinbach, and Altona. By 1981, about 53 percent of the province's Mennonites lived in "urban" centers (population over 1,000).

The 5,940 Hutterian Brethren in Manitoba, an almost three-fold increase since 1950, continue to be almost exclusively (98 percent) a rural farming people. The few in urban settings are all below age 35. Hutterites as a group are considerably younger than Mennonites according to the 1981 census. Over half (52 percent) of the Canadian Hutterite popula-

tion was below the age of 20, compared to 37 percent for Mennonites. On the other hand, only about 13 percent of Hutterites were over 45 years compared to 27 percent among Mennonites.   AE

Statistical data taken from the 1981 Decennial Census of Canada and from the annual yearbooks of the various Mennonite conferences. Additional information is available in periodicals, especially the *Canadian Mennonite, Mennonite Reporter,* and *Mennonite Mirror.* No comprehensive new study comparable to E. K. Francis, *In Search of Utopia,* (1955) has appeared. Helpful studies of the former °°East Reserve area are Abe Warkentin, *Reflections on Our Heritage* (Steinbach: Derksen Printers, 1971); Royden Loewen, *Blumenort* (Blumenort: Blumenort Mennonite Historical Society, 1982); Lydia Penner, *Hanover: One Hundred Years* (Steinbach: R. M. of Hanover, 1982). For the former °°West Reserve area see Gerhard J. Ens, *The Rural Municipality of Rhineland, 1884-1984* (Altona: of Rhineland, 1984); Henry J. Gerbrandt, *Adventure in Faith* (Altona: D. W. Friesen and Sons, 1970); and Peter D. Zacharias, *Reinland: An Experience in Community* (Reinland: Reinland Centennial Committee, 1976). Margaret Loewen Reimer, *One Quilt, Many Pieces* (Waterloo: Mennonite Publishing Service, 1983) is a concise reference guide to Mennonite groups in Canada, including Manitoba.

See also Archives; Camps; Historical Libraries; Homes, Retirement and Nursing; Literature.

Manitoba Colony, Mexico (ME III:466). In March of 1922 the first Old Colony Mennonites, then known as Reinländer Mennonitengemeinde, arrived at the railroad station San Antonio de los Arenales, later known as °Cuauhtémoc, in the State of Chihuahua. They established 47 villages to the north and south of the railroad station on a tract of land (*plan*) located on a plateau well over 2,000 meters (6,500 ft.) above sea level. The region has a semiarid climate and an interior drainage system, draining into Lake Bustillos, east of the settlement. They bought 60,000 hectares (150,000 acres) of land from Don Carlos Zuloaga in 1921 at $8.25 (U.S.) an acre.

By December 1922 more than 2,000 Mennonites peopled the plains where ranch cattle had roamed before. By 1926 well over 16,000 colonists were settled on the Manitoba Plan (Tract). The land titles were made out to Klaas Heide, Peter Neufeld, Johann W. Rempel, Kornelius Wall, and the Reinländer Weisenamt. The villages were similar in plan and settlement to the Mennonite villages in the Uraine (Russia) a century earlier. The *Privilegium* (°privileges) assured the colonists of self-government, and their own educational system. Although lack of roads and modern communication technology isolated them from the rest of the world at first, in the course of the years these isolation barriers crumbled.

In 1924 several families from Meade, Ks., settled on 2,000 hectares (5,000 acres) of land, also in the Bustillos valley. They were of °°Kleine Gemeinde background and left the United States for reasons similar to those that convinced the Old Colonists to leave Canada. Eventually they lost their Kleine Gemeinde identity and became part of the larger Reinländer or Old Colony group of the Manitoba colony. After the °Russian Revolution some Mennonites from the Soviet Union found their way to the Mennonite colonies in Durango and later in Chihuahua. Instead of settling on the Manitoba Tract they located in the small town of Cuauhtémoc, where they established businesses. They remained in close comunication with other Mennonites, especially with those of the Manitoba Colony.

The severe drought in the early 1950s caused the Old Colonists to look for material aid. Upon suggestion and invitation of the °Rußländer Mennonites, Mennonite Central Committee (MCC) came to the rescue. This eventually resulted in the formation of a General Conference Mennonite congregation and school.

During the late 1970s and early 1980s the influence from the Kleine Gemeinde colony at Los Jagüeyes, some 100 km. (60 mi.) north of the Manitoba Tract Colony, became very noticeable. By 1987 they had established three schools and one church on the Manitoba Tract drawing their membership from the Old Colony.

The Paul Landis fellowship group (Conservative Mennonite) from the United States came in the early 1980s and several of their families settled on the Manitoba Tract ca. 6 km. north of Cuauhtémoc. They built a school, printery, and bookstore, but until 1987 failed to gain an appreciable number of church members from the Old Colony. A German Pentecostal group, also from the United States, built a church and school at Lowe Farm (Campo 6.5) in the early 1980s. The German Seventh Day Adventists built a meeting house in Cuauhtémoc, trying to attract the Mennonites. Their effort to establish themselves on the Manitoba Tract had been unsuccessful until 1987. The German Church of God, with headquarters in the Swift Current settlement, met with more success, since many members of the Swift Current settlement had migrated to Belize, Bolivia, and Paraguay, leaving the colony without strong leadership. The Church of God also drew members from Manitoba and Nord colonies. The new Reinländer Mennonite Church (a division from the Sommerfeld Mennonites in Manitoba) also came to Mexico and helped to speed the process of a changeover to motor vehicles.

A highway built in the early 1960s, passing through the Manitoba Tract, a power line in the 1980s, the constant interchange with Old Colony Mennonites in Canada and Texas, the motor vehicles, the apple industry, the proximity of the rapidly growing city of Cuauhtémoc, and rapid industrialization have helped to break down isolation barriers.

The organization of the *Hilfskomitee* in 1983 has been a unifying factor. This committee draws its members from the various colonies and churches. They have helped with refugees in Chiapas, reconstruction work in Jalisco after the September 1985 earthquake, and with housing and feeding illegal transients in Juárez. The senior citizens home at Kilometer 14 was built and is run by this inter-Mennonite *Hilfskomitee*.

Because of the different church groups present in the Manitoba Tract Colony, exact population figures are hard to come by. The Old Colony Mennonites numbered 11,854 at the beginning of 1987. Together with all the groups the total population of the Manitoba Tract Colony could be 12,500.   HEns

MWH (1978), 277.

See also Nord Colony, Mexico; Old Colony Mennonites.

Manitoba Colony, Paraguay, was founded in 1982 by Old Colony Mennonite settlers from Chihuahua, Mexico, because of a shortage of arable land in the latter country. The settlement consists of 11,900 hectares (29,400 acres) located 15 km. (9 mi.) from the °Rio Verde Colony. Four villages had been established by 1986, with a population of 320 (57 families) and a congregational membership of 126. Further emigrants from Mexico are expected.   GR

See also Manitoba Colony, Mexico.

Manitoba Conference of Mennonite Brethren Churches (ME III:466). In 1929 the Mennonite Brethren congregations in Manitoba united to form a conference, which was incorporated in 1940 and amended its organization in 1982. Total membership in 1986 was 5,606 distributed among 35 congregations, with a heavy concentration of members in Winnipeg. A vigorous and active conference program concentrates on building the Kingdom of God. The 1986 budget was $3,380,900. The Board of Missions and Church Extension supervises and supports 112 churches planted in the last 10 years. MBCommunications oversees television programs and English-, German-, Low-German-, and Russian-language radio releases. The German and Russian releases are broadcast all over the world. The Board of Educational Institutions directs the 60-year-old Winkler Bible School, and the Mennonite Brethren Collegiate Institute with 431 students. The conference is also very active in °inter-Mennonite projects, including Mennonite Central Committee, Mennonite Disaster Service, and Eden Mental Hospital in Winkler.   WIN

Winkler MB Church minutes; Manitoba MB Conference yearbooks.

Mankes-Zernike, Anna (ME IV:1139). Born Apr. 30, 1887, Anna Zernike studied theology at the U. of Amsterdam and the Amsterdam Mennonite Theological Seminary (1905-1911). In 1911 she became the first woman pastor in The Netherlands when she accepted the invitation of the Mennonite congregation in Bovenknijpe. In 1915 she married the artist-painter Jan Mankes. Following his death in 1920 she became the leader of the Dutch Protestant organization "Linker-Maasoever" in Rotterdam, continuing in that work until her retirement in 1948. It was disappointing to her not to receive further invitations from Mennonite congregations after that. She spent her last years in the retirement center at Amersfoort. She died Mar. 6, 1972.

Theologically she was attracted to the freethinking Protestantism represented also by her teacher G. A. van den Berg van Eysinga. While she fulfilled her pastoral tasks with thoroughness and care, she also became a frequent commentator on social and international issues. In 1918 she wrote her doctoral dissertation on historical materialism and the social democratic ethic. Together with R. N. Roland Holst she wrote the biography *Jan Mankes* (Utrecht, 1923, 1928). Other publications included *Opvoedingsproblemen* (Amsterdam, 1924), *Rainer Maria Rilke: Een benadering* (Rotterdam, 1925), and *Historische godsdiensten en universeele religie* (Assen, 1938). She also published her memoirs in *Een vrouw in het wondere ambt: Herinneringen van een predikante* (Amsterdam, n.d.).   SBJZ

Doops. Jaar. (1973), 13-17, (1986), 34ff.; R. Boeke, "Dr. A. Mankes-Zernike 1887-1972," *Rotterdams Jaarboekje* (1973), 189-193.

Marandi, Benjamin (ca. 1890-1979), was born in a tribal village in Santal Parganas, South Bihar, India. Like his parents, he grew up practicing °animism. By age 25, he was initiated into the Santal priesthood and became a charismatic leader of his people. However, 13 years later he converted to Christianity after animistic rituals failed to prevent the death of his first four children.

In 1948, soon after the Brethren in Christ Church had begun a ministry among the Santal people of Purnea, North Bihar, Benjamin accepted an invitation to become an itinerant preacher to his own tribe. Adapting a cultural custom, he walked from village to village, preaching the Gospel and giving himself unstintingly to evangelism. A good voice combined with his violin, quick wit, and dynamic and fearless preaching, attracted an audience wherever he went. His evangelistic fervor was complemented with a sincere concern for the physical needs of people. Out of his own poverty, he often shared his food and clothing with those less fortunate.

Benjamin's wife remained in their home village because she felt life in the north was too harsh, but his daughter, Dina, one of two children born after he became a Christian, accompanied him and became an evangelist in her own right.

Marandi served as the district superintendent of the growing Santal church until the baptized membership reached nearly 1,000. Although he retired in 1973, he continued to preach until his death.   HRS

See also Lay Evangelists.

Marpeck, Pilgram (ME III:491). Recent archival research has shed more light on Marpeck's background and activity. Having moved from the Bavarian town of Rosenheim, Marpeck's father, Heinrich, served Rattenberg, Austria, as a councilman, mayor, and district magistrate. After the death of his first wife, Sophia, with whom he had one daughter, Margareth, Pilgram Marpeck married Anna and adopted three foster children. Professionally, he worked in the city hospital, organized the city's crossbow competition, and acted as purchasing agent for the mining guild's infirmary before entering office as mining magistrate in 1525. Politically, he served on the outer and inner city councils and as mayor (1522), taking an active role in regulating the city's craftsmen; negotiating the release of the reform-minded preacher, Stephan Castenbaur (Agricola); and hiring a priest to fill the pastoral office in the city's parish church. As mining magistrate, Marpeck was required by Archduke Ferdinand to hand over miners who, like he, were sympathetic to the Anabaptist preachers Leonhard °°Schiemer and Hans °°Schlaffer. After initial consent, Marpeck resigned his office a few days after Schiemer's execution. From Rattenberg he traveled to Bohemia and Moravia, where he most likely received baptism and a commission as an Anabaptist elder.

After joining the Strasbourg gardener-wagoner guild and buying citizenship in 1528, Marpeck led a communal group of Anabaptists and social radicals, for which he was arrested and released sometime before 1530. From 1530 to his expulsion in 1532, he served the city as lumbering supervisor, overseeing the cutting and delivery of wood from the city forest near Hausach on the Kinzig river. During this time he led a group of Anabaptists, most closely associated with the Swiss Brethren, and contributed to the differentiation among the city's Anabaptist groups by criticizing the spiritualistic tendencies of Hans °°Bünderlin and Christian °°Entfelder and the apocalyptic speculations of Melchior °Hoffman.

From 1532 to 1544, Marpeck resided in Switzerland and traveled to Tirol, Moravia, South Germany, and Alsace where he established congregations and had contact with the Hutterites and Swiss Brethren. This was the period of his major controversy with Caspar °Schwenckfeld.

By 1544 he was working in Augsburg's city forest near Füßen. Later, as city engineer in Augsburg, Marpeck supervised this lumbering activity and contributed to the renovation and extension of the city's water works. Although warned three times to desist from Anabaptist activity, he participated in the leadership of a group which met in his home on public property. He continued significant correspondence with Anabaptist groups in Switzerland, Alsace, South Germany, and Moravia.

In recent years, four anonymous works have been attributed to Marpeck. William Klassen argues that he wrote two booklets, *Clare verantwurtung . . .* (1531; "Clear Response") and *Ain Klarer/vast nützlicher unterricht . . .* (1531; "Clear and Useful Instruction"), contributing to the differentiation of Marpeck's group from Strasbourg's spiritualistic radicals, the apocalyptic Melchiorites, and an extremely separatist Swiss group. Walter Klaassen believes that, during the same period, Marpeck authored *Aufdeckung der babylonischen hürn . . .* ("The Exposure of the Babylonian Whore"), a provocative tract in which he criticizes the Protestant reformers and Schwenckfeld for justifying the use of the civil sword in the cause of Christ as a disguise for the advancement of their own economic interests. Fast argues that Marpeck also produced a *Bekenntis* (ca. 1535-39; "Confession") that was submitted to Jan von Pernstain, a Moravian governor, on behalf of an Anabaptist congregation that had been accused of denying Christ's divinity.

Recent research has focused on the importance and implications of the incarnation for Marpeck's °christology, soteriology (°salvation), ecclesiology, ethics, sacramental theology (°communion), and hermeneutics (°biblical interpretation). (Influences on Marpeck's theology are suggested in parentheses.) In his arguments with Schwenckfeld, Entfelder, and Bünderlin, Marpeck affirmed the divinity of Christ, but stressed Christ's historical, physical humanity. The "unconstraining Spirit," poured out in Christ's death, gathered those who willingly received it into the "unglorified body" of Christ on earth, which awaited union with his "glorified body" in heaven. The reception of the Spirit, justification, which is sealed by baptism, the "covenant of good conscience" (Sebastian °°Franck, Bernhard °Rothmann, Schiemer and Schlaffer), progressively reordered one's life (Schwenckfeld, °°Theologia Deutsch), affected sanctification, and led to a commitment to justice, not only internally before God, but also externally before humanity. Because of the unconstraining nature of Christ's Spirit, Marpeck criticized the pursuit of that justice by means of either the civil sword (e.g., his arguments against Protestant and Catholic theologians) or coercive legalism (e.g., his objection to these tendencies among the Hutterites and Swiss Brethren). Due to the decisive character of the incarnation, he insists that the Old and New Covenants must be distinguished (Schwenckfeld) and that the Bible is properly understood only in the context of and by the whole community of believers.   SBB

There is only one known copy of the *Clare verantwurtung* . . . (Württembergische Landesbibliothek, Stuttgart, R16 ver. 2, formerly Theol. oct. 18515) and of the *Ain klarer/vast nützlicher unterricht* . . . in the British Museum (no. 3906 a 77); translations of both are found in CRR 2:43-106; see also W. Klassen, "Pilgram Marpeck's Two Books of 1531," *MQR*, 33 (1959), 18-30. There are extant copies of two editions of the *Aufdeckung der babylonischen hürn* . . . . The only copy of one edition is bound with the copy of the *Clare verantwurtung* found in Württembergische Landesbibliothek (see above); the two copies of another edition are in the Bayerische Staatsbibiliothek, Munich (4o Polem. 3342 [21]) and the Augsburg Stadtbibliothek (4o ThH 190); also the photostatic reproduction of the Augsburg copy in Hans J. Hillerbrand, "An Early Anabaptist Treatise on the Christian and the State," *MQR*, 32 (1958), 29-47. W. R. Estep, ed., *Anabaptist Beginnings (1523-1533)* (Nieuwkoop: B.d. Graaf, 1976), 156-63, translates part of this work and Klaassen is preparing a full English translation; see also Walter Klaassen, "Investigation into the Authorship and Historical Background of the Anabaptist Tract *Aufdeckung der Babylonischen Hürn*," *MQR*, 61 (1987), 251-61. The only known copy of the "Bekenntnis für Jan von Pernstain" is found in manuscript in the Regensburg Stadtarchiv (Eccl. I, 52, 74), published by Hans Hillerbrand, "Ein Täufer Bekenntnis aus dem 16. Jahrhundert," *ARG*, 50 (1959), 40-50, it will also be included in Heinold Fast's critical edition of the *Kunstbuch*, the book of devotional writings from Marpeck's circle. Secondary sources on Marpeck include Harold C. Bender, "Pilgram Marpeck: Anabaptist Theologian and Civil Engineer," *MQR*, 38 (1964), 231-65; Neal Blough, *Christologie Anabaptiste: Pilgram Marpeck et l'humanité de Christ* (Geneva: Labor et Fides, 1984); Stephen B. Boyd, "Pilgram Marpeck and the Justice of Christ" (ThD diss., Harvard U., 1984); Jan J. Kiwiet, *Pilgram Marbeck: Ein Führer in der Täuferbewegung der Reformationszeit* (Kassel: Oncken, 1958); William Klassen, *Covenant and Community: The Life, Writings, and Hermeneutics of Pilgram Marpeck* (Grand Rapids: Eerdmans, 1968); idem, "The Limits of Political Authority as Seen by Pilgram Marpeck," *MQR*, 58 (1982), 342-64; idem, "Pilgram Marpeck: Freiheit ohne Gewalt," in *Radikale Reformatoren*, ed. H.-J. Goertz; C. H. Beck, 1978] trans. in *Profiles of Radical Reformers*, ed. Goertz and Walter Klaassen (Scottdale, 1982), 168-77; William Klassen, "The Relation of the Old and New Covenants in Pilgram Marpeck's Theology," *MQR*, 40 (1966), 97-111; Torsten Bergsten, "Pilgram Marpeck und seine Auseinandersetzung mit Caspar Schwenckfeld," *Kyrkohistorik Arsskrift* (1957 and 1958), 39-100, 53-87; Heinold Fast, "Bemerkungen zur Taufanschauung der Täufer," *ARG*, 57 (1966), 131-51; idem, "Nicht was, sondern das'. Marpeckhs Motto wider den Spiritualismus," in *Evangelischer Glaube und Geschichte: Grete Mecenseffy zum 85. Geburtstag*, ed. A. Raddatz and K. Lüthi (Vienna: Evangelischer Oberkirchenrat, 1984), 66-74); idem, "Variationen des Kirchenbegriffs bei den Täufern," *Menn. Geschbl.*, Jg. 27. n.f. 22 (1970), 5-18; Walter Klaassen, "Church Discipline and the Spirit in Pilgram Marpeck," in *De Geest in het Geding*, ed. Irvin B. Horst, A Jong, D. Tjeenk (Willink: Tjeenk, 1978), 169-80; John D. Rempel, "Christology and the Lord's Supper in Anabaptism: A Study in the Theology of Balthasar Hubmaier, Pilgram Marpeck, and Dirk Philips" (ThD dissertation, St. Michael's College, Toronto School of Theology, U. of Toronto, 1986); D. J. Ziegler, "Marpeck versus Butzer: a Sixteenth Century Debate over the Uses and Limits of Political Authority," *Sixteenth Century J.*, 2 (1971), 95-107.

Marriage (ME III:502). In order to discuss contemporary Mennonite marriage beliefs and customs it is important to recognize the considerable variations among the 20 separate Mennonite, Amish, Hutterite and Brethren in Christ denominational bodies. These variations stem from the degree of °modernization that has transpired. The most conservative groups still hold to traditional norms of belief and behavior, while the more liberal groups conform to much of the prevailing culture of the larger societies within which they are located.

It is helpful to conceptualize a conservative-liberal continuum along which the separate bodies can be arranged, with Hutterite, Old Order Mennonite, and Old Order Amish groups at the conservative end and such groups as the General Conference Mennonites, the Mennonite Brethren Church, and the Evangelical Mennonite Church at or near the more liberal end. In between are the Beachy Amish Mennonites, Old Colony Mennonites, Conservative Mennonite Conference, Sommerfeld Mennonite Church, Mennonite Church, Brethren in Christ, Church of God in Christ (Holdeman Mennonite), and the several additional small groups.

In North America, customs originating in the 19th c. and earlier (e.g., parental approval of choice of spouse and publishing the banns) are still found among the most conservative groups, while most of these customs have been lost among the liberal groups.

It is also necessary to recognize variations in beliefs and practices *within* each Mennonite, Amish, or Hutterite group, primarily among the more liberal groups which tolerate wide variations. For example, recent empirical studies reveal a lack of uniformity among church members as to the meaning and permanence of marriage. Whereas conservative members tend to reject °divorce completely, the more liberal members and groups accept divorce for reasonable cause and, in some cases, accept remarriage by a divorced person while the former spouse is still living.

As reported in ME III, the Anabaptists rejected the sacramental view of marriage but held the marriage covenant in high esteem, basing their views on New Testament passages which compare marriage to the mystical union of Christ and the church (Eph 5). The marriage covenant was seen as second only to the spiritual covenant between the person and God. Even today, the practice of the °°ban among the Old Order Amish still includes, in the case of a wayward or unbelieving spouse, the marital °°avoidance rule, which signifies that the marital covenant is subservient to the person-God relationship as interpreted by the church authorities. In a Hutterite wedding ceremony the young man must promise that in case he should lose his faith and leave the colony, he will not cause his wife to follow him.

Among less conservative groups, however, marriage of a Mennonite to a non-Mennonite, although formally or informally discouraged, does not invalidate the Mennonite spouse's church membership. Indeed, among the most liberal groups, the spouse's commitment to the Christian faith is viewed as more important than membership in the same denomination, reflecting recent greater openness to ecumenical views.

In the Mennonite Church (MC) in the first half of the 20th c. the writings of Daniel °Kauffman attempted to elevate marriage to one of the "ordinances" of the church. However, the 1963 Mennonite Confession of Faith (MC) does not refer to marriage as an ordinance, but states simply that God instituted marriage, and that "It is God's will that marriage be a holy state, monogamous, and for life" (Loewen, *Confessions*, 78).

In all Mennonite denominations marriage is celebrated as a religious event and as a spiritual covenant, performed by an ordained minister, bishop, or elder, and viewed as coming under the aegis of the church. The degree of control over marriage varies with the degree of conservativeness of the specific Mennonite denomination. Among Mennonites in North America a civil marriage ceremony is almost unheard of; if it occurred it would generally be assumed that the principals were not in good standing with the church, as in the case where the remarriage of a divorced person was not approved. In northwest Europe typically the state requires a civil ceremony. Mennonites comply with this requirement, but normally follow with a religious ceremony under the auspices of the church.

Where churches have been established as a result of Mennonite missions in Africa, India, and southeast Asia, the church has struggled to bring marriage under its auspices and control. Traditional marriage is controlled by the °family and kinship group, and western ideals of Christian, church-sponsored marriage ceremonies have been accepted only gradually, to a greater extent in some areas (e.g., East Africa) than in others. Western missionaries, including Mennonite missionaries, rejected polygamy, and African church leaders have generally accepted this, although not always wholeheartedly. Western missionaries were less united in opposition to the African custom of giving bride price, often tending rather to work toward reducing and standardizing the price in order to eliminate or minimize the more commercial aspects of traditional marriage negotiations between the families of the bride and groom. Parental control over mate selection has been gradually reduced under church influence, although this, as well as the giving of bride price, still continues to some extent.

North American Mennonite views on the permanence of marriage were revealed in the results of the 1972 survey of members in five Mennonite and Brethren in Christ denominations (Kauffman and Harder, 1975). Seventy-seven percent of the respondents viewed marriage as "a lifelong commitment never to be broken except by death." Another 22 percent checked "a lifetime commitment, but may be broken only if every attempt to reconcile disharmony has failed." Only 1.3 percent took a more liberal view, holding that marriage may be terminated if the couple is not compatible or one partner wished to break the marriage.

Mennonite marriages are exogamous with respect to close kinship as required by law. No state or province in North America permits first cousins to obtain a marriage license; some states deny a license to "first cousins once removed." Cousins of more distant relationships occasionally marry, especially in communities (such as the Old Order Amish and Old Order Mennonites) where kin groups are large and lines of descent are more intertwined. Hutterites actually prefer to marry one of their distant relatives rather than a person who is unrelated.

Among Hutterites and the Old Orders, marriage to a person who has not joined their group is not permitted. Less conservative Mennonite and Amish groups discourage °°intermarriage with persons of other faiths, but the more liberal Mennonites are less likely to make this a serious issue. All groups urge their members to "marry in the Lord," meaning a person of similar faith.

The more liberal Mennonite bodies have declared themselves as accepting interracial and interethnic marriages, so long as the parties are of similar faith. Nevertheless, such marriages often have rough traveling, due to the informal prejudices that exist in local churches and communities and to the cultural differences that exist between the spouses themselves. When asked about marriage between Christians of different races in the 1972 five-denomination survey, 16 percent responded that it is "always wrong," and 44 percent considered it "sometimes wrong." With respect to the "marriage of a Christian to a non-Christian" the responses were 42 percent "always wrong" and 45 percent "sometimes wrong."

Marriage Rates. Data on marriage rates among North American Mennonites is limited, but support the following conclusions: (1) Mennonite men marry in *larger* proportions than men in comparable national populations, (2) Mennonite women marry in somewhat *lower* proportions than women in national populations, and (3) the proportion of Mennonite women who never marry is high but declining in recent decades. Of the responding 1972 church members over the age of 45, 1.6 percent of the men and 9.3 percent of the women had never married. A 1982 census of Mennonite Church (MC) congregations yielded proportions never married, for person 45 years and older, of 2.5 percent for men and 12.5 percent for women. Apparently more men than women leave their Mennonite backgrounds, by marriage outside or otherwise. Among the Hutterites few persons remain unmarried. For the population aged 30 years and over as of 1950, only 1.9 percent of the men and 5.4 percent of the women had never married.

Age at Marriage. The median age at first marriage of the 1972 American Mennonite church members was 23.1 years for men and 21.6 years for women; for Canadian Mennonites it was 24.3 and 22.7 years. The national medians in 1971 were 23.1 and 20.9 for the population of United States, and 24.9 and 22.1 for Canadians. Hostetler reports that the median age at first marriage among the Old Order Amish is just under 22 years for women and just over 23 years for men. Thus the Amish marry at average ages very similar to American Mennonites. The median age at marriage for Hutterites who married prior to 1950 was reported as 23.5 for men and 22.0 for women, only a few months older than for the Amish and Mennonites. In all three groups, the average age difference between husbands and their wives is 1.5 years.

Weddings. As in most societies, Mennonite, Hutterite, and Amish °weddings are high ocasions—high in religious meaning and in social celebration. Among the Hutterites the marriage ceremony is appended to the Sunday morning worship service, following the preaching. The couple is called to the front of the congregation where they respond to several questions put by the bishop or preacher, receive the blessing, and are pronounced husband and wife. The wedding meal follows and the congregation continues to visit throughout the afternoon. The wedding is simple, in that no special clothing or formalities are required, no money is spent for decorations, special musicians, or photography. The social interaction, however, is elaborate, as it includes relatives from a distance, and it is a great time for the young people to interact, even to court. It is significant that the wedding ceremony always conforms to the traditional pattern and the couple has little to do with the arrangements or the content of the proceedings. Tradition and group prerogatives leave no place for individualistic preferences.

Old Order Amish weddings are all-day celebrations, occurring normally on a weekday, often Thursday, which allows more time for elaborate meal preparations. The marriage vows follow a long forenoon worship service, and the remainder of the day and evening is spent in informal festivities, visiting, and playing of games by the youth.

Among the more modernized Mennonite groups, weddings tend to take on the special features of typical Protestant church weddings. The wedding is a ceremony unto itself, often on Saturday, and requires much preparation and some practice, so that all the proceedings may be executed with precision. The couple tends to carry the major responsibility for planning the wedding, with the counsel and assistance of the bride's parents, friends of the couple, and the officiating minister. Elaborate preparations will be made with respect to the attire of the couple and their attendants, flowers and decorations, arrangements for photography, special music during the wedding and reception, and all the food service preparation that accompanies the reception. The couple in some cases may even write and deliver their marriage vows, so as to seemingly control the content of the pledges they make to each other. This is a matter of concern in some churches, lest the marriage ceremony avoid a pledge to be faithful "until death do us part."

Among the more traditional groups the marriage officiant will be the bishop or other head minister. In the more modernized groups, the couple is permitted the choice of the officiating minister, who may be a relative or friend of the couple, and not necessarily the pastor of the congregation in which the marriage takes place. Most weddings are performed in the church building, although occasionally in a home or special chapel. Traditional weddings highlight the sermon, which often emphasizes the pitfalls and problems of marriage and the need of divine help to sustain a faithful marriage until death terminates the union. More modern weddings tend to shift the sermon to a short meditation, with emphasis on the themes of love and communication in marriage, enabled by the love of God and his indwelling spirit.

Marital Relationships. It is generally agreed that modernization (°urbanization, industrial and °technological development, and rationalization) has made a significant impact upon Western family systems. The gradual extension of the principles of °democracy and social equality has affected the family in many ways, notably in the decline of patriarchy and the advocacy of sexual equality in marriage. Urbanization and the extensive employment of married women have promoted greater overlapping of husband and wife roles. The immediate rewards of career development outside the home have, for many women, supplanted traditional status achievement through homemaking and °childrearing.

Farming societies tend to be patriarchal, since farming is a family enterprise headed by the husband-father whose leadership, if not domination, tends to permeate family affairs both on and off the farm. Until the middle of the 20th c., Mennonites were largely farmers, and patriarchy naturally prevailed, supported by many societal customs and laws that circumscribed the roles which women were allowed to fill. Urbanization, the decline of patriarchy, and the increased employment of wives have affected the quality of husband-wife relationships.

Over the past 50 years family sociologists and psychologists have made many empirical studies of the quality of marital relationships. Burgess and Wallin (1953) pioneered in developing models for the investigation of husband-wife relationships. Following their lead, Kauffman (1960) studied the quality of husband-wife and parent-child relationships in 149 midwest Mennonite (MC) families. A principal objective was to determine the extent of patriarchy among Mennonite families and to discover whether the trend to equality in marriage was beneficial or detrimental to family interpersonal relations.

Kauffman's survey data revealed that about one-third of the Mennonite families were *definitely* patriarchal (husband-led or husband-dominated), almost a third were *slightly* patriarchal, and in another third the husbands and wives claimed equal sharing of authority. A few families may be described as mildly matriarchal, in that the wife tended to make more of the decisions than the husband. On the average, farm families were more patriarchal, while nonfarm families evidenced somewhat more democratic and equalitarian characteristics. Decisionmaking patterns varied widely within both residence categories, indicating that factors other than residence were important also in determining the distribution of authority. It can be concluded that Mennonite marriages are gradually becoming more equalitarian, particularly under the influence of recent societal emphases on sexual equality both within and outside marriage.

A principal finding of the survey was that scores

on the husband-wife relationship scale tended to average somewhat higher for equalitarian marriages than for patriarchal ones. Similarly, scores on a child-parent relationships scale averaged somewhat higher in the more equalitarian families. Thus it was concluded that, insofar as family interpersonal relationships are concerned, the trend away from patriarchy is beneficial. Other findings indicated that the child's perception of parental love was more important in the child's positive development and success in life than the level of parental control (whether strict or lenient) which the child experienced.

Mennonite marriages appear to be more successful than marriages generally in the national populations. At current divorce rates, approximately 40 percent of all first marriages in the United States will end in divorce. Canadian rates are substantially lower. Data on Mennonite families is very limited, and completely lacking outside North America. The 1972 church member survey indicated that fewer than two percent of all married church members had experienced divorce. Probably some persons who divorced have left Mennonite churches. The 149 midwest Mennonite marriages studied in 1956 were revisited in 1979. Only one couple had divorced, and another had separated, in the intervening 23 years. As of 1979 these families had 554 living children, aged 15 to 41. Of those who had married, 11 percent had divorced or separated from their first spouses. Of those married children who were members of Mennonite churches, 7 percent had divorced. Of those ever married children who were not members of any church in 1979, 39 percent had divorced, about equal to the national rate. It is clear that divorce rates among Mennonites are increasing and that the rates are inversely related to church-relatedness.

From the responses of the 149 Mennonite couples in 1956, it appeared that about 10 percent were less than happy in their marriages. This is substantially less than the percentages (around one-third) indicating unhappiness in studies of married couples by Burgess, Locke, and other investigators in the United States. Areas of disagreement between husbands and wives were probed in the 1956 study; the most frequently mentioned were "wife's working outside the home," "disciplining the children," and "ways of dealing with relatives."

Another area of frequent disagreement was "sharing household tasks." This adds to the evidence that, as in marriages generally, Mennonite spouses are caught up in the prevailing debates over sex role identities and °gender equality, both within and outside of marriage. Two views can be posited as to how the goals of sex equality might be ultimately achieved. The prevailing view among North American activists is that gender equality in marriage can only be achieved when wives share equally with husbands in career development outside the home. For wives to achieve this, husbands need to share heavily in household tasks and in child care (if there are children). It may be that full gender equality can never be achieved in this manner, due to a combination of gender differences in biological functions (childbearing in particular) and gender prejudices and preferences, particularly on the part of tradition-minded husbands.

Another alternative would be to continue traditional division of labor between the sexes while contending that homemaking and childrearing are equally praiseworthy, rewarding, and status-conferring with career development outside the home. This traditional view holds that motherhood and childrearing are a high calling to be preferred to "having to work outside the home." In view of current widespread sentiments, this traditional view would be regarded by many as curious, if not ridiculous, particularly by parents who have concluded that childrearing is troublesome at best and more likely annoying or frustrating.

Have Mennonite sentiments been swept along with these currents of thinking in the larger society? Unfortunately we do not have solid evidence to answer this question definitively. There are signs that traditional values are still preferred, particularly by the Amish and other conservative groups. Familism is still strong in those quarters, but the social forces of urbanism, individualism, and secularism appear to be molding the sentiments of more liberal Mennonites, particularly in educated circles, in favor of career development and self-enhancement of both husbands and wives over the traditional sentiments of "family first."

What conclusions can be reached in regards to the relationship between sex role identity and marital success? If permanence of the marriage bond is the highest virtue, then traditional patriarchal societies rate best. If the quality of husband-wife relationships is of greatest importance, then the more modern equalitarian type of marriage rates highest. Permanence of marriage in traditional societies appears to be bought at the price of circumscribing the role and authority of women in marriage. Equality of sex roles appears to be purchased at the price of ever-rising divorce rates. Already ultraconservative religious voices want to preserve marriage solidarity by restoring more patriarchal and, as they see it, more biblical norms of husband-wife relationships. At the other extreme are the voices of Christian humanism who emphasize self-development and sex equality in marriage without looking seriously at their possible effects on marital stability. Like others, Mennonites are caught up in the dilemmas of these often contradictory viewpoints. The debates are likely to increase rather than diminish.

Is there a middle way—a Jesus way? Can somehow the best elements of both views be brought together? If God is love, the infilling of his spirit should enable all persons of spiritual commitment to permanently maintain their marriages. Even if a marriage is threatened by some wrongdoing, the invocation of divine and human forgiveness should prevent the disintegration of a marriage among those who claim to be God's children. Mennonites have sought to be peacemakers and finders of middle ways. The challenge is to find marital permanence through spiritual means—the practice of love, tenderness, and service as modeled by Jesus, avoiding the self-seeking, power-seeking human inclinations to dominate others.   JHK

J. Howard Kauffman, "A Comparative Study of Traditional and Emergent Family Types Among Midwest Mennonites" (PhD diss., Department of Sociology, U. of Chicago, 1960), copy at MHL (Goshen); Kauffman/Harder, *Anabaptists Four C. Later* (1975), ch. 10; Yoder, *MC Census* (1985); John A. Hostetler, *Amish Society* (1980), 172-206; idem, *Hutterite Society* (1974), 234-51; Johann Heinrich (Heini) Arnold, *In the Image of God: Marriage and Chastity in Christian Life* (Rifton, N.Y.: Plough, 1977); Paul Redekop, "The Mennonite Family in Tradition and Transition," *JMS,* 4 (1986), 77-93; Aaron Martin, "Courtship and Marriage Practices of Lancaster Mennonites," *Menn. Life,* 17, no. 1 (Jan. 1962), 31-35; George H. Williams, *The Radical Reformation* (Philadelphia: Westminster, 1962), ch. 20; Ernest W. Burgess and Paul Wallin, *Engagement and Marriage* (Chicago: J. B. Lippincott Company, 1953), 470-506.

See also Children; Courtship; Family; Singleness.

Marshall Co., Ind., Old Order Amish Settlement. See Nappanee, Ind., Old Order Amish Settlement.

Martin, Jesse Bauman (1897-1974), son of Daniel E. and Blandina (Bauman) Martin, members of Martins Old Order Mennonite congregation, north of Waterloo, Ont. With the permission of his parents, Jessie joined the St. Jacobs Mennonite congregation of the Mennonite Conference of Ontario (MC) in his late teens. His attendance at Hesston College and Bible School, 1919-23, and a short term at Goshen College in 1924, prepared Jesse for a life of service to the Mennonite Church (MC). He married Naomi Collier in 1926.

Ordained in 1925 as pastor of the Weber congregation at Strasburg, Ont., he was transferred to the Erb St. Mennonite congregation, Waterloo, in 1929, where he served until 1964. Ordained bishop in 1947, he served in the Central District, in the Niagara District, and at Clarence Centre, N.Y. His activities in the Mennonite Conference of Ontario included: home evangelist, 1929-34, 1937; Ontario Mennonite Bible School faculty, 1932-65 (principal, 1958-65); assistant moderator of the conference, 1936-45; moderator of the conference 1946-60.

He served the larger Mennonite Church (MC) on a wide variety of committees dealing with peace and conscientious objection, youth work, conference administration, and publications. Martin also worked with several committees and programs of the Mennonite Board of Missions and Charities (MC), including time spent establishing a Mennonite presence in Israel, 1953-54. He was in charge of local arrangements for the Mennonite World Conference (MWC) assembly at Kitchener, 1962, and a member of the MWC presidium, 1964-66. He served the Conference of Historic Peace Churches of Canada as a member of the Peace Problems Committee, 1941-58, and of the Military Problems Committee 1941-64. He served on several Mennonite Central Committee committees, 1944-68, including a term as chairman of the board, 1955-61.   LBe

Urie A. Bender, *Four Earthen Vessels* (Kitchener and Scottdale, 1982); *Who's Who Mennonites* (1943), 164; *Menn. Bib. II,* p. 477; various records of committees and agencies in the Conrad Grebel College Archives (Waterloo).

Martin, Jonas H. (Jan. 15, 1839 - July 3, 1925), was one of seven children born to Jonas S. and Nancy (Hershey) Martin. He spent most of his life as a farmer in East Earl Twp., Lancaster Co., Pa., as did his ancestors for several generations. In 1865 Jonas Martin married Sarah Witwer (1845-89), and after her death he married Annie Wenger (1852-1927).

Eleven children grew to maturity.

Martin embraced the Mennonite faith of his forebears and was baptized at 20 years of age. On Dec. 7, 1875, his home church called him to the ministry, and six years later, on May 3, 1881, he was chosen as bishop of nine congregations. He served in the ministerial capacity for nearly 50 years until he passed away at the age of 86.

Jonas Martin is best remembered for his conservative position in his work as bishop. He opposed modern church practices, especially the introduction of °°Sunday schools. In the fall of 1893 he led his conservative followers out of the Lancaster Conference to found his own Weaverland Conference (often called the Martinites). Most of his followers were from ne. Lancaster Co., although ripples of that division were felt over many counties as well as in all the major settlements of other states. His group merged with the °°Wisler groups of Ohio, Indiana, and Ontario. The Weaverland Conference, the Groffdale Conference, and the Reidenbach Mennonites all originate from the Martinites. The 1987 estimated total membership of these groups is 8,700. They are often known collectively as °Old Order Mennonites.   ABH

Amos B. Hoover, *The Jonas Martin Era* (Denver, Pa.: the author, 1982); idem, in *Pennsylvania Folklife* (Winter 1983-84), 90-94; Raymond S. Martin and Elizabeth S. Martin, *Bishop Jonas H. Martin, His Life and Genealogy* (1985).

Martyrdom, Theology of (ME III:519). See Apocalypticism; Crossbearing; Liberation Theologies; Nonconformity; Nonresistance; Persecution; Recantations; Suffering.

Bibliography: Menno Simons, "The Cross of the Saints" (1554), in Menno, *Writings; Het Offer des Heeren* (1562), in BRN 2; *Ausbund* (1564); Dirk Philips, *Enchiridion* or *Handbook* (1564), trans. Kolb (1910); *The Chronicle of the Hutterian Brethren,* vol. 1 (Rifton, N. Y.: Plough, 1987); Hans de Ries, ed., *Historie der Martelare ofte waerachtighe Getuygen Jesu Christi* (Haarlem, 1615); Thieleman J. van Braght, *The Bloody Theater or Martyrs Mirror of the Defenseless Christians. . . .1660* (Scottdale, 1950); Lydia Mueller, *Glaubenszeugnisse oberdeutscher Taufgesinnter* (Leipzig, 1938).
David W. Augsburger, *Why, My God, Why?* (Harrisonburg, 1967); Elizabeth Bauman, *Coals of Fire* (Scottdale, 1954); James E. Bertsche, "The Shadow of Suffering," in *A Kingdom of Priests,* ed. Wilbert R. Shenk (Newton, 1967); J. Lawrence Burkholder, "The Theology of Suffering," in "The Problem of Social Responsibility from the Perspective of the Mennonite Church," (PhD diss., 1958; published Elkhart, Ind.: IMS, 1989); John M. Drescher, *Strength for Suffering* (Scottdale, 1969); Cornelius J. Dyck, "The Suffering Church in Anabaptism," *MQR,* 59 (1985), 5-23; Robert Friedmann, *The Theology of Anabaptism* (Scottdale, 1973); Alan F. Kreider, "'The Servant Is Not Greater than His Master': The Anabaptists and the Suffering Church," *MQR,* 58 (1984), 5-29; Henry H. Winter, *Ein Hirte der Bedraengten* (Wheatley, Ont., 1988); T. Alberda-Van der Zijpp, "'Het Offer des Heeren': Geloof en getuigenis van de martelaren," in *Wederdopers-Menisten-Doopsgezinden in Nederland, 1530-1980* (Zutphen, 1980), 46-61; James and Marti Hefley, *By Their Blood: Christian Martyrs of the 20th Century* (Milford, Mich., 1979).

Marxism. The standard Mennonite approach to Marxism has been to take note of the special interest that Friedrich Engels (1820-95), later also Karl Kautsky (1854-1938), and Ernst Bloch (1885-1977), paid to the Anabaptists, but to point out that this was based on a misreading of the historical data. (°°Communism and Mennonites). Abraham Friesen sought to show in his dissertation and subsequent writings that these writers' image of the Anabaptists was based on Wilhelm Zimmermann's history (1843) of the Peasants' Wars, a romantic reading back into 1525 of ideas that were in the air before the European revolutions of 1848. Further, the Engels-Kautsky interpretation depended on including under Anabaptism persons such as Thomas °Müntzer who were not part of Evangelical Anabaptism, and it deemphasized Müntzer's religious motives in favor of political ones.

But subsequent Anabaptist research by Goertz, Stayer, and others that began to take social history and social theory more seriously (°historiography), has produced a new synthesis of Anabaptism as a more diverse movement with different persons and streams offering alternative solutions to a common concern for society. This also includes a renewed examination of the °°chiliast (°apocalyptic) strain in Anabaptism, lessening the conventional sharp distinction between Dutch Anabaptists and the °Münster Anabaptists. Political change in Eastern Europe in the late 1980s—the atmosphere of *perestroika*—and the anniversary celebrations of Luther (1983) and Müntzer (1988-89) have prompted Marxist shifts in historiography to the point where the religious motivations of Müntzer are again seen as central. Hence there may be fruitful dialogue between Mennonite scholars and Marxists in the future.

Mennonites have shown little interest in the study of Marxism. There are no major philosophical critiques. Mennonite writings in theology have focused on articulating differences over against main-line Protestantism and have generally ignored Marxist writings. Miranda's *Marx and the Bible* occasioned some serious reflection since it showed a shalom justice theme pervading the Old Testament, and emphasized the radical nature of the biblical thrust, but the references to Marx were seen as incidental. Even in the more recent examination of °liberation theologies, Anabaptist thinkers have tended to warn against a readiness to commit violence which they see implied in some of that literature, tending to set a purist 16th c. Evangelical Anabaptist ethic against it. The use of Marxist means of analysis as well as the assumption of a °socialist vision for society by liberation theologians have not been points of dialogue.

In a more indirect and subtle way, the Marxist impact on scholarship also affected Mennonite scholars. This is beginning to include the use of social history methods in writing religious history, more so when writing modern Mennonite history than in Anabaptist research, but the impact goes further. Mennonites as small, interesting sect, quantifiable and measureable, prompted many sociologists to make them a subject for research and the subsequent social theorizing. Mennonites have developed an extensive and competent network of sociologists who draw on the theories of the competing schools, once again sensing an affinity for the more critical °sociological schools inspired or challenged by Marxism, than for the status quo orientation of structural functionalism, for example. Given the fundamental impact of Marxism on the rise of the social sciences and in causing the latter to take a position vis-à-vis Marxism as a political ideology, this beneficial impact of Marxism on Mennonite and other academics is an acknowledged fact. That is not to say, however, that Marxism and Mennonites (or other Christians for that matter) are compatible, even with Western or Critical Marxists, as long as the latter continue to reject divine transcendence.

Several Mennonites, encouraged also by Mennonite Central Committee Peace Section, have participated actively in Christian-Marxist dialogue efforts. The most experienced is no doubt Paul Peachey, through his involvement in the °Christian Peace Conference, °Christians Associated for Relations with Eastern Europe, and, more recently, through the Institute for Peace and Understanding as cohost for seminars between Marxists (including Soviets) and Christian scholars. Numerous others have developed individual contacts and friendships, while MCC encouraged a student and service program in Eastern Europe (since 1976) that included dialogue with Marxists as a goal. Only one conference to reflect on these experiences as Anabaptist/Mennonites has been held (1979), scarcely enough to clarify even the diversity of learnings that conference participants reported on.   WWS

MQR, 55 (July 1981), sp. issue on Anabaptism and Marxism; *JMS*, 1 (1983), sp. issue on Mennonite studies in North America, especially pp. 33-63, 79-105; Martin Jay, *Marxism and Totality* (Los Angeles: UCLA Press, 1984); unpublished papers from the Mennonite peace Theology Colloquium (Winnipeg, June 1988) on liberation theology; Abraham Friesen, *Reformation and Utopia: The Marxist Interpretation of the Reformation and Its Antecedents* (Wiesbaden: Steiner, 1974); José Porfirio Miranda, *Marx and the Bible*, trans. John Eagleson (Maryknoll, N.Y.: Orbis, 1974).

Maryland (ME III:532). Some 50 Mennonite congregations are scattered across the state in 1988 with heaviest concentration in Garrett and Washington Cos. The following groups are represented with the number of congregations and membership (1986) respectively in parentheses: Allegheny Conference [MC] (5, 599; the Hyattsville congregation is also affiliated with the General Conference Mennonite Church); Atlantic Coast Conference [MC] (5, 231); Lancaster Conference [MC] (14, 431); Conservative Mennonite Conference [MC] (4, 205); Beachy Amish Mennonite Fellowship (2, 86); Cumberland Valley Mennonite Church (3, 154); Eastern Pennsylvania Mennonite Church (2, 72); Washington-Franklin Conference (8, 796); unaffiliated Mennonites and fellowship churches (3, 150). Settlements of Old Order Amish are located in Garrett and St. Mary's Cos. with sizable congregations.

While a number of mission stations of the Mennonite Church (MC) have been closed, the Highland Association, a cooperative ministry of the Mennonite Church (MC) and Beachy Amish Mennonite Fellowship has a strong witness in Garrett Co., including regular visitation in some 50 homes, providing both a social and spiritual ministry and material aid in a low-income area. At Gortner in southern Garrett Co., Conservative Mennonites and the Church of the Brethren worship together in a union church. At Menadier Ridge near Grantsville, Harvest Baptist Church has a significant ministry in a one-room school owned by Highland Association.

Since 1957 Mennonites have established 10 private schools with enrollment in 1988 numbering 636. The Paradise school near Hagerstown combines special education with a ministry to the hearing impaired. Mennonite services and institutions include Brooklane Psychiatric Center, Hagerstown (1945), sponsored jointly by Mennonites and Church of the Brethren; two nursing homes at Grantsville and Maugansville; one group home for retarded adults at Silver Spring; student and young adult services in Baltimore; an MCC SELFHELP Crafts Shop in Hagerstown; and a private self-help shop in Grantsville. Highland Association also opened a thrift shop in Grantsville in 1987 and operated a community center in Jennings, with services for preschool children and senior citizens and other community programs.

Mennonite archives were established at the Casselman Hotel in Grantsville (1987) by a group including Mennonite Church (MC), Conservative Mennonite, Beachy Amish Mennonite Fellowship, and Old Order Amish members. Also in 1987 an Anabaptist Peace Center was initiated by Penn Alps, Inc., in a restored log house on its campus just east of Grantsville. It is closely associated with a craft village complex in which 8 to 10 artisans work during the summer months, attracting thousands of guests who will be exposed to the Anabaptist love and peace ethic.   AES

MC Yearbook (1988)89), 26-27; Luthy, *Amish Settlements* (1985), 8; Wittlinger, *Piety and Obedience* (1978), 129-32.

Mass Media. Reading popular novels, attending moving picture shows, and owning °radio and °television sets have been either discouraged or forbidden by some Mennonite conferences in North America during the 20th c. In 1918, the Franconia Conference (MC) Ordinances stated that church members were not allowed to attend picture shows (Hostetler, 1987). During the 1930s, many Mennonite leaders warned against the dangers of radio. A tract printed in Virginia in the late 1930s concluded that radio "wastes time and hinders religious study and meditation. . ." ("The Radio Problem"). The writer argued that radio brought into the home messages that Christians could otherwise avoid; prize fights, sporting events, music from movies, dances and theater. Radio mixed business and religion on the Lord's Day for "worldly gain," cultivating irreverence for sacred things.

Later similar arguments were made against television. In 1949, the Lancaster Conference (MC) reiterated its rejection of television, amending the conference position to state that "Brethren or sisters who are responsible for the sale and or use of television forfeit their membership" (Bishop Board Minutes, Sept. 13-15, 1949). Not until the late 1960s was the Lancaster Conference prohibition dropped from their discipline. Old Order Mennonite groups today continue the prohibition.

In the midst of these warnings, tract writers often recognized that some good might come from the mass media. While church leaders were cautious, a number of individuals with strong vision demonstrated how the media might be used for religious purposes (see °Broadcasting).

One such visionary was Eugene Graber of Kalona, Iowa. He dreamed of putting Christian reading materials in public places; waiting rooms, hotel lobbies, airports, and laundromats. With assistance from Urie Bender, then Secretary for Literature at Mennonite (MC) Board of Missions (MBM), he began to develop district-based, bookrack evangelism programs. In 1965, MBM transferred oversight of the work, called "Life Line Books," to the media Division. The program was renamed "Choice Books" in 1973, and its mandate expanded to include both the distribution and the publication of "wholesome and inspirational reading material to the general reading public," to assist persons in developing a better understanding of the gospel (Pellman, 1979). By 1988, Choice Books had sold its 10 millionth book through 18 locally owned and operated district organizations. MBM provides centralized ordering and distribution. Many of the local organizations are °inter-Mennonite, i.e., involve more than one Mennonite denomination.

Filmmaking. Mennonite perceptions of °filmmaking early in the century were shaped by the worldly and decadent images of Hollywood. Religious leaders across many denominations of the day deplored the sex and violence of early motion pictures. Several Mennonite pioneers, however, imagined a different kind of motion picture. William Zehr, a General Conference Mennonite, developed his filmmaking skills as the Director of Audio Visual Services for a school district, and produced documentary films for the United States Government Housing Authority in the mid-1940s in Oregon. In 1946, he organized Better Films Library and Productions to provide evangelistic films and filmstrips, slides, and records to congregations. Later he worked with Evangel Films to produce several dramatic films with evangelistic messages. In 1953, he was appointed to a Film Committee of the General Conference Mennonite Church to help them produce films about their mission activities among the Northern Cheyenne. In the late 1950s, films on Japanese missions were jointly sponsored by Mennonite Brethren, Mennonite Church (MC), and General Conference Mennonites. The film library was turned over to the General Conference Mennonite Church in 1962 when Zehr's health failed, after he had completed nearly 30 films (Zehr, 1971). Zehr, by his conviction and his filmmaking, demonstrated the value of both documentary and dramatic audiovisual aids for teaching and inspiration in the congregational setting.

Two other pioneers demonstrated the ability of film to communicate compelling stories and to record events as they unfolded. Working for Mennonite Central Committee (MCC), both Norman Wingert and Peter Dyck carried eight-millimeter film cameras with them on their travels to the Mennonite colonies in South America and to Europe during World War II. They did so out of personal interest, but their footage triggered the imaginations of missions administrators, ushering in two decades of institutional filmmaking during the 1960s and 1970s. Peter Dyck was an eloquent advocate for the power of storytelling. In 1968, MCC hired Burton Buller to begin an audiovisual department. Under his guidance, MCC became a leader among Mennonite institutions in the production of documentary films that interpreted MCC program activities around the world. The Mennonite Church (MC) and the General Conference Mission Boards sometimes joined MCC to produce films overseas. During these years, MBM retained a three-person team, headed by Harold Weaver, to produce missions films. Most of these films were produced for distribution in congregations and were documentary in style. Other films produced at this time captured special events. For example, Robert Hostetter produced *Beyond this Land*, a film about the sesquicentennial celebration of the coming of the Amish to Ontario (1972). Several films recorded the sessions of Mennonite World Conference in the 1970s and 1980s. Later Burton Buller and John Ruth teamed to produce two award winning documentaries; one on the Amish, *The Amish: A People of Preservation*, and another on the Hutterites, *To Care and Not to Care*. Both of these films have received wide distribution in educational settings and on public television.

Mennonites, however, have produced fewer dramatic films for the general public. In 1973, I. Merle and Phyllis Good broke new ground with the production of a dramatic film for theatrical distribution. *Hazel's People* attempted to dramatize and interpret how Mennonites experience life and faith for audiences beyond Mennonite circles.

The production of dramatic films continued in the early 1980s when Sisters and Brothers, Inc. (SBI) was formed by a group of Mennonite filmmakers for the purpose of producing and distributing films and videos that examined the world through the eyes of faith from an Anabaptist perspective. Their first major project, *The Weight*, was the story of a young man turning 18 in the shadow of the Vietnam draft. The film dramatizes his struggle with questions of conscience and faith. SBI has also produced, among others, several children's films, a series of videos by J. C. Wenger on Anabaptist faith, and a full-length feature film on the life of Michael Sattler for theatrical distribution. Since 1986, SBI has operated a film and video library in Goshen, Ind., on behalf of the Mennonite Church, for the distribution of quality Christian film and video materials to congregations.

Television. While Old Order Mennonite and Amish groups held to prohibitions against the ownership of radio and television sets, 87 percent of the members of other Mennonite groups owned at least one television set by 1972 (Kauffman/Harder, 1975). By 1987, over 93 percent of the Mennonite Church (MC) members owned at least one set (Elliott, 1987). Nevertheless, Mennonites had an ongoing concern about the impact on Anabaptist faith and values of mass mediated messages. In the 1970s Mennonite agencies formed several organized responses.

High levels of violence and sexual activity on American commercial television were one catalyst of concern. Another was concern about the potential erosion of Anabaptist theology in the face of exposure to religious ministries, first through radio and later television. Dubbed "the °electronic church," religious television ministries flowered in the 1970s and 1980s, first with the introduction of UHF television channels, and later with the growth and diffusion of cable television systems. Both developments provided outlets for a growing number of television evangelists who purchased broadcast time or provided cable programming at a time when the appetite for programming expanded.

One response to concerns about erosion of values was to train leaders and promote media education across the church. Television Awareness Training (TAT), a program initially developed by the Church of the Brethren, United Methodists, and American Lutherans, consisted of workshops designed to help participants become aware of the values presented on television, to articulate their own values, and to become more critical and selective consumers of programming in their homes. TAT workshops and regular articles in denominational periodicals continued to be a part of media education efforts in the 1980s.

One tangible response to concerns about the electronic church came in 1980 when the Media Division (GCM) and Media Ministries (MC) participated in an Ad Hoc Committee on Religious Television Research, a broad-based coalition with representation ranging from the Old Time Gospel Hour (Jerry Falwell) and the Christian Broadcasting Network to the U.S. Catholic Conference and the Episcopal Church. The committee was formed to conduct research on who is reached, how many are reached, and how the electronic church affects local church participation. Among other things, the study concluded that the estimated audience for religious television is smaller than previously assumed (around 13.3 million compared to previous estimates ranging from 25 to 71 million). Furthermore, the electronic church reached highly religious people and served to confirm their points of view, rather than evangelizing the unchurched (Fore, 1984 and 1988; Umble, 1985). Heavy viewing of general television programming was seen as the greater threat to local church participation.

MBM Media Ministries responded to concerns about impact by becoming a member of the sponsoring group for *Media and Values*, a quarterly magazine designed as a resource for congregations in the areas of media awareness and education. *Media and Values* also maintains a center for speakers and resource materials.

Little research has been conducted to assess the actual impact of the media on Mennonite values and theology. Two studies completed in the late 1980s from contrasting theoretical and methodological orientations claim different findings. One argues that heavy viewing among Mennonites is associated with greater identification with the values of the cultural mainstream than with traditional Mennonite values (Umble, 1986). The other argues that Mennonite viewers are highly critical of television. They use viewing to test and reinforce their uniquely Mennonite conceptions of the world (Hague, 1988). Each perspective probably represents an aspect of the total picture. While research on effects remains inconclusive, a study of Mennonite Church (MC) members showed that Mennonites appear to consume television at levels comparable to members of the general population. Less than 13 percent were regular viewers of religious television programs. They tended to be moderate to light viewers, watching one to two hours daily. News programs were watched most regularly (Elliott, 1987).

Computers and Video Cassette Recorders. The 1980s were hailed as the Information Age. Old boundaries separating the various media were blurred as broadcasting was supplemented with cable television services, providing not only entertainment but also informational and instructional services. Televisions, computers, and telephones were linked, creating new communications possibilities with specialized, rather than mass audiences. With the introduction of home video cassette recorders (VCRs), consumers had more control over what programs they watched and when they watched them at home.

Rather than rejecting these technologies, most Mennonite groups appear to have embraced them, but not without awareness of ethical concerns. Computers can be found in denominational headquarters as well as on the desk of the local pastor. They handle tasks ranging from sophisticated financial analysis to the maintenance of membership records to word processing. Church leaders grappled with questions about the proper role of computers: who has access to which data? what information is important or necessary? what is the appropriate level of investment in computer equipment at various levels of the denomination?

In 1985, the Council of Mennonite Computer Users (CMCU) was founded "to find ways to share information about computers among conferences, churches, and church agencies" (GH [Apr. 12, 1988]). CMCU meets twice yearly and represents more than 15 church °institutions as well as individuals. CMCU has promoted better communication in the church through "Mennonet" (a telecommunications system that connects church agencies, providing electronic mail and conferencing services) and ."Mennonews" (an electronic service for the distribution of news releases among church organizations and church publications). CMCU has several advisory committees: a Congregational Software Committee, and Ethics Committee and a Data Dictionary Committee. All three committees provide information and guidelines on computer usage.

Like computers, VCRs presented Mennonites with new challenges and possibilities. Like computers, use of video crossed the traditional agency boundaries. While media ministries in the past focused on broadcast production in support of mission efforts, video had applications both within and beyond the church. Cable and broadcast distribution were options, as was distribution to congregations, Sunday school teachers, youth leaders, and to individual Mennonite homes. Video technology presented Mennonite °publishers, °educators, and °public relations staffs with new ways of communication with their respective constituencies.

In 1984, the Inter-Mennonite Media Group (IMMG) hosted a two-day conference, Video-Com '84, to study the possibilities and problems presented by video in relation to the church. The consensus of the participants was that more education and advocacy in the area of new communications was needed. Media literacy was a priority both to cultivate Mennonite understanding of how new technologies can be used by local congregations and to educate Mennonites about the effects new technologies can have on societies in North America and around the world. (The Council on Church and Media [CCM] replaced IMMG in 1985. See °Broadcasting.)

By the late 1980s, Mennonite agencies were producing a variety of video materials for a variety of purposes. And Mennonite congregations were using video in a variety of ways. For example, MBM Deaf Ministries initiated the production of a series of video tapes for deaf persons, involving deaf teachers demonstrating how they relate the teachings of Jesus to the every-day realities of deaf persons. Another video produced by MBM was distributed to every MC congregation in an effort to describe and interpret evangelism goals established for the period 1985-95. MBM, the General Conference Mennonite Youth Office, and MCC worked together to produce a video, *Youth Serve,* to present opportunities for service to youth across the church.

MBM Media Ministries produced its first video program, *All God's People,* in 1985. Designed for use in both congregations and on cable television or broadcast television, this magazine format program focuses on three or four Mennonites who share their personal stories of faith in action. The ninth edition of *All God's People* was produced in the fall of 1988. In 1988, captioned editions for the hearing-impaired were produced.

In late fall, 1988, *All God's People* became one of the Mennonite-produced programs to be featured weekly on a satellite network serving cable television systems. Vision Interfaith Satellite Network (VISN) was organized by a coalition of 20 religious denominations, including Mennonites, to provide alternative religious programming in the wake of the failures of several televangelists in the 1980s. VISN has a potential viewing audience of 18 million households.

Demand for video resources across the Mennonite church has increased. In 1988, a survey of Hispanic congregations showed that 90 percent were using video and wanted more resources. The topics of interest included family, youth, children, and Christian education. A 1987 survey of Mennonite Church (MC) congregations showed that one quarter of the members owned VCRs and another 10 percent were planning to buy one, a level slightly under averages for North Americans in general. Sisters and Brothers, Inc., has acted as a clearing house for video and film resources produced by Mennonite agencies. In 1986, MBM, the Mennonite Board of Congregational Ministries and the Mennonite Publishing House developed and published *Preview,* a newsletter for congregational leaders that reviews video and film materials.

Ken Weaver, director of Media Ministries, sees video as the shape of the future and the challenge of the 1980s and 1990s. As access to both secular and religious video materials increases, Mennonites will continue to need to exercise selective judgment with respect to the types of video resources brought into their homes and their congregations. Furthermore, more and more congregations around the world will be able to create their own video resources as video equipment becomes increasingly portable and less expensive.

By 1970, a generation of North Americans has grown up with television. They were increasingly visually-oriented and decreasingly print-oriented. In order to maintain communication among Mennonites themselves, denominational agencies will need to pursue visual forms of communication, not only print forms. In order to reach out into their communities, Mennonite lay people will also need to develop a repertoire of communications skills, both interpersonal and mediated. While most Mennonite colleges offer speech and journalism courses, audio and video production courses are limited. Only one Mennonite college, Goshen College, offers a communications major, while communications minors are offered on some other Mennonite campuses. Apart from an occasional seminar, Mennonite seminaries in the 1980s were not offering media training. Though training opportunities are limited at Mennonite colleges and seminaries, Mennonites have produced °journalists, broadcasters and film and video makers. Some Mennonites work in denominational settings, and others work in commercial and public broadcasting or as independent producers.

In the future, educating Mennonites to be both producers and critical consumers of media materials will be a challenge, both in North America and around the world. Mennonites in developing countries will likely call for increased media education for their members. During the 1970s and 1980s, developing nations were concerned about the survival of indigenous culture in the face of massive doses of imported Western programming. They struggled to create their own media forms and structures, as well as programs and materials. As communications technologies become less expensive and increasingly portable and durable (e.g., audio cassettes and video recorders), local persons can begin to create their own communications messages, using their own voices instead of being an audience for someone else.   DZU

"Bishop Board Minutes." Meeting at Mellinger Meeting House, Sept. 13-15, 1949, Lancaster Mennonite Historical Society; *MWR* (Aug. 11, 1988), 4; Cheryl J. Elliott, MBM Media Ministries Summary Report on Research and Consultations," (Harrisonburg, Va.: Media Ministries, 1987); William F. Fore, "Religion and Television: Report on the Research," *Christian Century* (July 18-25, 1984), 710-13; idem, *Television and Religion* (Minneapolis, Minn.: Augsburg Publishing House, 1987); Barth Hague, "The Impact of Mediated Popular Discourse on a Subculture: The Meaning of Television Among Mennonites" (MA thesis, U. of Texas at Austin, 1988); Stewart M. Hoover, *The Electronic Giant* (Elgin, Ill.: Brethren Press, 1982); Beulah S. Hostetler, *American Mennonites and Protestant Movements* (Scottdale, 1987); Ben Logan, ed., *Television Awareness Training: The Viewer's Guide for Family and Community* (New York: Media Action Research Center, Inc., 1979); *GH* (Aug. 27, 1985), 602, (Aug. 16, 1988), 564; Ernest E. Miller, "The Use of the Radio Among the Mennonites of the Indiana-Michigan Conference," *MQR* 14 (1940), 131-48; *MWR* (Sept. 15, 1988), 1; *GH* (Feb. 21, 1984), 134-135; Hubert R. Pellman, *Mennonite Broadcasts: The First Twenty-five Years* (Harrisonburg, Va.: Mennonite Broadcasts, Inc., 1979); "The Radio Problem," (Harrisonburg, Va.: Tract Press), undated copy in the Muddy Creek Farm Library, Denver, Pa.; *GH* (Apr. 12, 1988), 257; Diane Zimmerman Umble, "The Consequences of Television Viewing for a Subculture: A Study of Mennonite Orientations" (MA thesis, U. of Pennsylvania, 1986); idem, "What We Know About Religious Television: Analysis of Annenberg/Gallup Research on Religious Television Report Commissioned by the Council on Church and Media, 1985; *GH* (June 5, 1985), 409-10; William and Edith Zehr, "Better Film Productions," *Menn. Life*, 26 (April 1971), 65-69.

Massachusetts. See New England.

Materialism. See Modernity; Transcendance; Community.

Matsitsa Matsi was born at the village of Mwini-Kenge, (Belgian Congo) Zaire. He received Christ and was baptized at Panzi (1942). In 1955 he married Tandu; they have eight living children. Matsitsa attended primary school (1945-48), taught primary school at Panzi (1949-50), and attended the pastors' school at the Baptist Mission Kimpese (1950-54). From 1954 to 1960 he taught at the Baptist Mission Moanza and during the next three years directed the primary school at Panzi. Matsitsa then served as assistant legal representative for the Mennonite Brethren conference (Église du Christ au Zaire, Communauté des Églises de Frères Mennonites), 1961-78. He was inspector of the Mennonite Brethren schools (1963-75) and accountant for government schools (1975-77). Since 1976 he has been a counselor for Mennonite Brethren conference schoolteachers (1977-87), part-time treasurer of the Mennonite Brethren conference (1982-84), and assistant pastor of the Basonde and Kimwanga church in Kikwit (1985-).   AP

Matthijssen, Johannes Petrus (1924-78), studied at the missionary high school in Oegstgeest (The Netherlands) and at Goshen Biblical Seminary (United States). He married Mary Berkman. From 1951 to 1958 they worked under the Dutch Mennonite mission board (later known as the °Doopsgezinde Zendingsraad) in °Java (Indonesia). Following their return in 1958 he served as executive secretary of the mission board, and from 1960 he was pastor of the Mennonite congregations in Meppel and Hoogeveen. From 1964 until the time of his death he served as pastor of the Mennonite congregation in Amsterdam. He assumed primary responsibility for local arrangements for the Mennonite World Conference held in Amsterdam in 1967.   SV

Mazemba Pierre was a teenager in Kipoko village on the banks of the Kasai River in the Belgian Congo (Zaire) when he first heard about Jesus from °°Congo Inland Mission (Africa Inter-Mennonite Mission) missionaries from Djoko Punda. Later a mission station was established near Nyanga ca. 10 mi. (16 km.) west of Mazemba's village. Mazemba was among the first boys to enroll in a school at the new station. There he confessed Christ as his Savior and was baptized, becoming one of the first three members of the Nyanga church. When he graduated from the school he married and began a lifelong commitment to Christian service.

Recognizing early that the young African church would be able to provide only modest support for its leaders, Mazemba became a farmer-pastor. All through his life he had large fields, fruit groves, and plots of coffee trees which provided an abundance of food for his growing family as well as a modest cash income. His most notable characteristic was a blend of wisdom and courage. He had a gift for listening to lengthy debates regarding local church life, then, when others had all spoken, would quietly summarize the issues and express his point of view.

He frequently incorporated both the wisdom of the tribal forefathers and the teaching of Scripture. When, on occasion, his position was not a popular one, he demonstrated the courage of his convictions and stood alone, if necessary, for what he believed was right. Mazemba Pierre typifies a first generation of Zaire Mennonite leaders who with minimal formal training shouldered major responsibility for evangelization of their own people.   JEB

Mbuji Mayi, Zaire. Taking its name, *Goat Water,* from the folklore of the Baluba people for whom it is a center, Mbuji Mayi has known a stormy history. Lying approximately 940 air miles (1500 km.) to the east of °Kinshasa, the city serves as the provincial capital of the East Kasai and has become a major Zairian commercial center. One reason for its development is the rich diamond pipe which was originally discovered and exploited by the Belgian colonial authorities and which continues to yield a rich flow of quality stones under the Zairian national administration. The aggressive and enterprising nature of the Baluba people is also a major contributing factor to the growth of the surrounding area which in 1986 numbered some 5,000,000 people.

Mennonite presence in Mbuji Mayi has its roots in the migration of Baluba Mennonite refugees, who fled the tribal conflict which erupted along the Kasai River 300 mi. (500 km.) to the west in the months following the political independence of the Congo in June 1960. During this time of great political insecurity, the Baluba people along the Kasai River trekked across the countryside to their traditional homeland in the East Kasai, a migration which took with it hundreds of Mennonite Christians and their pastors. It was at the height of this refugee period that the Mennonite Central Committee provided funds and desperately needed emergency supplies, and °°Congo Inland Mission missionaries, Archie Graber and Glenn Rocke, supervised the distribution of these materials.

Out of these circumstances two Mennonite groups have emerged in the area, namely, the Église du Christ au Zaire, Communauté Mennonite (CMZA; Mennonite Church of Zaire) and the Église du Christ au Zaire, Communauté Evangélique Mennonite (CEM; Evangelical Mennonite Church). Both churches count a number of congregations in the city and surrounding area.   JEB

Mbungano Yabunyina Muli Kristo, Zambia (Brethren in Christ Church in Zambia), one of two Brethren in Christ churches in Africa. Claiming 4,395 members in 1985, the church operated through 15 organized congregations and 110 additional preaching points along the rail line from Livingstone in the south to Kitwe in the north. Theological training, church planting, Christian education, literature sales, literacy, radio and television ministry, and medical and educational institutions are all part of the life and work of the church. The Brethren in Christ Church in Zambia is affiliated with the °Africa Mennonite and Brethren in Christ Fellowship, the Christian Council of Zambia (CCZ), the Evangelical Fellowship of Zambia, and the °Mennonite World Conference.

Beginnings. Brethren in Christ missionaries from North America arrived in southern Africa in 1898. Having felt a call to the African continent, a group of five people decided during their boat travel to Cape Town, now in the Republic of South Africa, to focus on the area that was home to the Matabele people. A tract of land in this area was obtained through the British Charter Company. The work of building, learning the Ndebele language, and teaching school begn shortly afterward.

One member of the group, however, was not satisfied. Having joined the missionary endeavor with a concern for "Interior Africa," H. Frances °Davidson eventually began discussing with her colleagues the idea of moving farther north for a new mission effort. After a furlough to North America in order to discuss her idea with the mission board, Davidson returned to Africa. In 1904 a railroad designed to stretch eventually from the Cape in South Africa to Cairo in Egypt had reached Victoria Falls. While Davidson claimed that this fact had no effect on the final decision to begin the move north, it certainly provided the means. In July 1906 she and Adda Engle with two Matabele Christian young men left their colleagues in Southern Rhodesia to begin the trek into the interior, then known as Northwestern Rhodesia.

Following negotiation with the British land commissioner, the group from the south settled in the territory of Chief Macha, for whom their first station was named. Their site was chosen for its agricultural potential, its access to water, the distance from mosquito- and malaria-producing swamps, and its proximity to the Tonga people. The task of building a house came first, quickly followed with some visiting in nearby villages, and initial efforts at Tonga language, for which no written grammars or dictionaries were then available.

The missionaries noted a difference in the response of their new neighbors as compared to their earlier experience in Southern Rhodesia. When they announced the opening of school in January 1907, no one came to begin classes. However, a special week of prayer in February during which Chief Macha arrived, bringing his son to study, marked a change. By the end of that year 17 boys were studying and living on the mission station. In 1909 10 boys were baptized and received into the church. By 1910 girls had joined the ranks as day students at Macha, and both girls and boys were studying at schools opened in several neighboring villages. Their teachers, young men among the first converts, lived at the mission and went to their daily work from there, since it was feared that their position as Christians would be too lonely and threatened if they lived in the villages.

Myron Taylor, a third member of the missionary team, arrived in 1907, and two years later he and Adda Engle were married. With an active interest in village work, the Taylors began to think of another mission station. It was not until 1920, however, that land was obtained at Sikalongo. The Taylor family moved to begin their new work early the next year, starting once more with a school.

Missions and Institutions. The desire to teach the Tonga people to read, and especially to read the

Bible, was central to the missionaries' motivation for starting their work with schools. Quickly, however, pressure was felt to make education relevant to the world introduced into Africa by the colonial presence. Schools which at first were totally organized by missionary teachers soon became part of the expanding colonial administration. In 1931 the station school at Macha closed, and later that year it reopened as a district girls school. It was 17 more years before anyone completed primary school work at Macha. At Sikalongo the day school quickly developed to a boarding school and in 1938 it became an upper level primary school, with earlier primary teaching taking place in the village outstation schools.

In 1952 a teacher training program was begun at Macha. A year later there were 2,443 pupils at mission-run village day schools, and 327 students in boarding schools at Sikalongo and Macha. Before the end of the decade the teacher training program had moved to Livingstone, in a cooperative effort through the Northern Rhodesian Christian Council (later known as the Christian Council of Zambia). A Brethren in Christ church member trained at Messiah College in the United States was among the first instructors there. The Brethren in Christ joined with the Pilgrim Holiness Mission to begin a secondary school at Choma in 1962, and the junior secondary level was added to the girls school at Macha in the 1960s as well.

The need for medical work was obvious to the first missionaries, who observed many basic health problems among their neighbors when they arrived. Even untrained missionaries found themselves treating wounds and fevers, but they were clearly relieved when the first trained nurse arrived in Northern Rhodesia in 1924. In the 1930s a hospital with maternity facilities was developed at Macha and clinic work grew at Sikalongo. In 1954 a missionary doctor moved from one of the Brethren in Christ hospitals in Southern Rhodesia to begin work at Macha. Training Zambian health care workers was central to the medical effort. Macha Hospital School of Nursing graduated its first class in 1969.

The Growth of the Church. While a great deal of missionary effort went into building and maintaining institutions, the task of evangelism and church development was always at the forefront of the missionaries' thinking. The schools themselves, first on the stations and then in surrounding villages as well, were thought of as "lighthouses" for evangelism. As clinics and the Macha hospital developed, these institutions also served as centers for preaching. The church grew slowly from this witness, with 140 baptized members in 1921, 141 members in 1936, and 240 members 10 years later.

Developing leadership among the Tonga Christians was also at issue, although missionary understandings of whether and when to entrust leadership functions were not always clear. Early converts were directed toward the tasks of village evangelism (°lay evangelists) and teaching. Later, Christians were elected to functions such as that of deacon. During the 1950s students training as pastors and evangelists began to travel to a Brethren in Christ school in Southern Rhodesia. A Bible institute was founded at Sikalongo in 1967, graduating its first class of three in 1969. Pastors who needed a higher level of training continued to travel to the south until the 1970s. In the 1980s Sikalongo Bible Institute developed from a two to a four-year program, with an internship for third-year students. A major effort to provide Bible training more broadly began in the mid-1970s under the °theological education by extension program (TEE), and in 1985 there were more than 15 active TEE centers, awarding 200 certificates each year.

From the beginning the church in Northern Rhodesia, which became Zambia after independence, and in Southern Rhodesia, which eventually became Zimbabwe, was conceived of and administered as one entity by the North American mission board. During the 1950s an administrative structure was formed which made missionaries responsible for the institutional system and a board composed of Africans and missionaries responsible for the work of the church. Beginning in 1962, two missionaries functioning as °bishops, directed the work of the church through northern and southern regional conferences. In 1964, as Britain granted independence to Zambia, the mission board gave full authority to the African church. At that point Zambian and (Southern) Rhodesian overseers were brought onto the executive board which dealt with all aspects of church, mission and institutional life. Political realities forced the hand of the African Brethren in Christ Church, as a minority white government in Rhodesia declared unilateral independence in 1965, and closed its borders with Zambia in the early 1970s. Travel became so difficult that the last joint general conference was held in 1973, after which the Zambian church assumed its own separate identity (for Zimbabwe, see °Ibandla Labazalwane Kukristu e-Zimbabwe).

William T. Silungwe was elected the first Zambian bishop in 1976. Under his leadership the church has grown from slightly more than 1,200 members to more than 4,000 in 1985. Bible conferences and evangelistic meetings are a major focus of church work. An effort to plant new churches had led to the placement of a Zambian pastor in the "Copperbelt" in Zambia's industrial north. In 1985 the church was organized into four districts: Choma, in the area of the mission's original work; Livingstone in the south; Lusaka, Zambia's capital; and the Copperbelt.

A missionary group, numbering 35 in 1986, continues to work under Zambian church administration. Many of them staff the schools and hospitals at the historic mission stations. Others are part of the church's recent outreach movement. Missionaries and Zambian church leaders continue to search for the best ways to witness to the good news in modern Zambia.   NRH

MWH (1978), 117-20; MWH (1984), 22; [MYMK] Annual Report (1985); Frances H. Davidson, South and South Central Africa (Elgin, Ill.: Brethren Publishing House, 1915); Anna R. Engle, J. A. Climenhaga, and Leoda A. Buckwalter, There Is No Difference (Nappanee, Ind., 1950); EV (esp. 1950, 1955, 1960); J. Earl Musser, "Zambia," in the report of the Africa Mennonite Fellowship meeting, Bulawayo, Rhodesia, March 1965, pp. 45-47 (copy at MHL [Goshen]); Robert I. Rotberg, Christian Missionaries and the Creation of Northern Rhodesia, 1889-1924 (Princeton,

1965); Glenn J. Schwartz, "Critical Issues of the Brethren in Christ in Zambia" (masters degree thesis, Fuller School of World Mission, 1974); Carlton O. Wittlinger, *Piety and Obedience* (1978), esp. 178-85, 456-61.

McCammon, Don (July 7, 1920-Oct. 11, 1988), was born at Ames, Iowa, to Benjamin and Wilma McCammon. He graduated from Goshen College in 1945 and married Dorothy Snapp on Sept. 1 of that year. The McCammons served as missionaries in China under the Mennonite Board of Missions (MC, 1947-51). In January 1951 Don, who had been arrested a few days previously, was tried by a "people's" court, threatened with execution, and then expelled. Six months later Dorothy and their newborn daughter, Julia, were also allowed to leave the People's Republic of China.

From 1952 to 1958 the McCammons served as missionaries to Japan, and then Don worked as an administrator at the Mennonite Board of Missions headquarters in Elkhart, Ind. (1960-66). In 1966 Don began working as administrator of the Goshen College bookstore where he remained until his retirement in 1986. During his abbreviated retirement Don devoted much of his time to Mennonite °voluntary service and disaster relief assignments.

Don and Dorothy also had a son Michael who preceded Don in death, and a grandson Michael who died earlier. Don died in Omaha, Nebr.   RSa

Dorothy S. McCammon, *We Tried to Stay* (Scottdale, 1953); *GH* (Nov. 8, Nov. 15, 1988).

Mecenseffy, Grete (Aug. 9, 1899-Sept. 11, 1985). Born in Vienna and resident there her entire life, Mecenseffy taught history and German in secondary school and also in the *Volkshochschule* (continuing education for adults). Her research field was 17th c. Hapsburg political history, especially relations between Spain and Austria. In 1947 she returned to the U. of Vienna for a second doctor's degree, this one in theology, and then taught church history and history of dogma at the Protestant Faculty of the U. of Vienna, the first woman to hold a chair in the faculty, and one of the earlist Austrian women to be ordained to the ministry (in the Austrian Reformed Church). In 1952 she narrowed her studies from Protestants in Austria to Austrian Anabaptists. She wrote at least 128 significant scholarly works (including three major books) on various aspects of Austrian or Moravian Anabaptism. During the last 33 years of her life she gathered and edited 1,740 printed pages of Anabaptist documents in three volumes of Austrian *Täuferakten* (Anabaptist documentary sources; °ME IV:237).   JSO

Heinold Fast, "Nachrufe auf Grete Mecenseffy, Liesel Quiring-Unruh, Frank H. Epp," *Menn. Geschbl.,* Jg. 43-44 (1986-87), 234-40; John S. Oyer, "Grete Mecenseffy, 1898-1985," *MQR,* 60 (1986), 104; Alfred Raddatz and Kurth Lüthi, eds., *Evangelischer Glaube und Geschichte: Grete Mecenseffy zum 85. Geburtstag* (Vienna: Evangelischer Oberkirchenrat, 1984), espec. the bibliography of her publications, pp. 11-20; G. Mecenseffy, "In Memoriam: Robert Friedmann," *MQR,* 48 (1974), 187-92; *Reformiertes Kirchenblatt für Österreich* (Vienna, esp. several years in the 1950s when she was coeditor); her own writings, some 138 items, especially *Geschichte des Protestantismus in Österreich* (Graz: Böhlau, 1956), her most important study beyond Anabaptism; *TA Österreich I, II, III.*

Medford, Wis., Old Order Amish Settlement is located in Taylor Co. in north central Wisconsin. This Amish community is unique in that it was founded in 1925, 45 years before the other 13 settlements in the state. The size of the Medford community is sustained, primarily, by families moving in from other Wisconsin settlements that appear to be phasing out. Medford is one of two Amish communities in Wisconsin with at least four church districts (congregations) serving about 600 people. Medford lies in rich farming and dairying country. Its cold winters have had an effect on the slow growth in the settlement's 65 years of existence.   SLY

Medical Missions. See Health Services; Hospitals, Clinics, and Dispensaries; Medical Services; Medicine.

Medical Service. See Alternative Service; Conscientious Objection.

Medicine (ME III:550). Frank H. °Epp writes of Mennonites in Canada, "Every cluster of neighbors boasted a °midwife and a bone-setter ready, willing, and able to attend to those medical needs which tea could not cure" (*Mennonites in Canada,* I, 87). While Epp speaks here of the early Canadian Mennonites, it is a picture that was quite generally relevant to the more conservative Mennonites of Europe and the Americas until the mid-20th c.

H. Clair Amstutz, Nanne van der Zijpp, Robert Friedmann, and Cornelius Krahn (*ME III*) admirably portray the general development of Mennonite involvement with medicine. There were exceptional medical people among Mennonites from the beginning. This was so in Holland, Switzerland, Prussia, and Russia. Some made outstanding leadership contributions. The Hutterites were well ahead of how others might have regarded them in medicine, particularly dentistry. Dutch Mennonites moved rapidly in deaconess services and training. In Russia the medical concern led quickly to institutions for the mentally ill, the aged, the orphaned, etc.

The movement toward more professionalized medicine did find much opposition among many dedicated Anabaptists and Mennonites from the outset. One can only speculate why there is evidence of seemingly spectacular advances and leadership from the beginning in Europe, yet parallel evidence of a strong commitment to natural healing with herbal treatments, chiropractic manipulation, and the occasional "anointing" according to the Bible. It may be that Anabaptists became a persecuted group, it became difficult to train further professionals and their reliance on cures closer to "nature" became natural. It can also be argued that a few professionals did remain among Mennonites.

Perhaps because the early Mennonite immigrants to America from the less-educated and more conservative groups, medicine had to begin over again. Even when in Russia it became clear that not all students wanted to study for education or agriculture careers, the next step was to set up a business college (Kommerzschule, ME III:156). Mennonites had become a people of the land who believed in strong, fairly "closed" communities. To keep these going, young people were encouraged to train for service to maintain these.

Medicine became one of the built-in features in North American Mennonite communities: "From what we've been told by our mothers and grandmothers, we are convinced that there were few ailments that they did not try to remedy in one way or another. . . . The remedies. . . included items such as salt, vinegar, goose grease, sour cream, bran, and even the lowly onion, to mention only a few. . . . After the village store became an established part of the community, such items as apodoldac, wonder oil, 'russisches Schlagwasser', electric oil and a few other patent medicines soon became an integral part of the stock of medicines that were stored in the corner cupboard" (Tina H. Peters, in *Mennonite Memories*, 240). Frank H. Epp also reminds us that, even in North America, some of the °°*Reiseprediger* (itinerant ministers) would dispense medicine (*Mennonites in Canada*, I, 295).

But it did not take long for Mennonites in North America to start pursuing medicine as a field of study. At first they usually did not come back to their home communities to practice. They often found their broadened thinking unacceptable to some of the closed thinking about healing and other "worldly" matters. So they initially were largely lost to the Mennonite churches.

The major turnaround came with World War II. Through Mennonite Central Committee (MCC) involvements in world relief work, doctors and °nurses suddenly were in demand. Anybody in medicine was welcomed to help and often these people were asked to provide models for new endeavors. Especially significant was the government's willingness to let °mental health services be an acceptable °alternative service for °conscientious objectors. Suddenly the Mennonite people in medicine were even in demand to help develop more humane ways to deal with mental illness.

When the war ended, this impact on Mennonite medicine did not end. To provide for bridge-building so that Mennonite physicians would no longer feel a need to leave Mennonite communities, the Mennonite Medical Association was formed in 1944. Already in 1942 the Mennonite Nurses Association had been founded.

There was, as usual, a mix of reasons for both groups. Not only the new mental health frontier, but also the longstanding involvement in medical missions on foreign field, were beckoning for the services of dedicated physicians and nurses. Once mission executives and missionaries saw the plight of millions in the underdeveloped countries, the old Mennonite vision for wholistic care came to the fore. Medicine, education and conversion needed to serve together. At the same time, the newly identified challenges in mental health care made profound impressions on Mennonite medicine. Many Mennonites entered specialized fields of medical practice and research related to mental health. Others became teachers in the field.

In the 1980s, in North America, like almost everywhere that Mennonites live in the world (there are exceptions in isolated places to which Mennonites have recently emigrated), medicine is a highly respected and even a sought-after °profession and vocation.

In 1986 the Mennonite Medical Association (MMA) had a membership of well over 500 physicians from the United States and Canada. These people voluntarily contribute funds annually to give financial aid to medical students interested in a student elective term in a cross-cultural setting. This is done to broaden medical training and is usually carried out in conjunction with mission agencies and MCC so that these students may also get a feel for missionary medicine. in addition, the MMA sponsors the *Mennonite Medical Messenger* (into which *The Christian Nurse* has been integrated) since 1949, a quarterly publication to promote Christian health care. It has a subscriber list of nearly 2,000 names. The MMA has also initiated and participated in special research consortiums on special medical issues, and has initiated medical exchanges with Mennonites from other countries.

While the MMA has been strongest among Mennonites in eastern North America (largely MC) and has been quite strong across the United States, many Canadian Mennonite physicians identify more with the Christian Medical Association (CMA) than the MMA.

The Mennonite Nurses Association (MNA) has about 500 members in 1987 and has aggressively encouraged nurses to serve overseas and in other need settings. Divided into chapters, they provide scholarships for urgent research and for students coming from needy settings, and they make supplies available for °nursing education in developing countries. The MMA and MNA jointly hold an annual Mennonite Medical Convention that usually draws 200-300 practicing health care professional people. At the March 1987, Mennonite Health Association annual convention, it was estimated that about 6,000 Mennonites in North America were, at that time, directly involved in medicine as physicians and nurses.

In 1987 Mennonites were found on all the fronts of medicine: genetic research, surgeries of all kinds, textbook writing, teaching, administration, and °bioethics. Their emphasis is frequently seen as a refreshing foray into the current emphasis on preventive medicine rather than total immersion in curative medicine. They were also found at the front lines with those who wanted to emphasize total wellness of people where body, soul, mind and emotions were regarded as one whole being.

When a special section at the 1984 Mennonite World Conference in Strasbourg, France, was given over to health care, about 40 people assembled from a variety of countries. All spoke enthusiastically about Mennonite involvement in this broader area, and also identified deep commitments to encouraging future Mennonite participation in all the critical areas related to medicine.   BW

Mennonite Medical Messenger (1949-); F. H. Epp, *Mennonites in Canada*, II, index under "medicine"; Lawrence Klippenstein and Julius G. Toews, eds., *Mennonite Memories: Settling in Western Canada* (Winnipeg: Centennial Publications, 1977), esp. 235-47. Walter Klaassen, *The Anabaptist Tradition*, in R. L. Numbers and D. W. Amundsen, *Caring and Curing* (Macmillan 1986), 271-287.

See also Brauche; Folk Medicine; Healing; Health Services.

Meihuizen, Hendrik Wiebes (Aug. 29, 1906-Nov. 26, 1983), was pastor of the Mennonite congregations at Wieringen (1933) Veendam-Pekela (1936), and The Hague (1938). From 1965 to 1976 he was lecturer in the history of Anabaptists and Mennonites at the °°Amsterdam Mennonite Theological Seminary. He published the following volumes: *Galenus Abrahams 1622-1706: Strijder voor een onbeperkte verdraagzaamheid en verdediger van het Doperse Spiritualisme* (Haarlem, 1954); *Menno Simons: IJveraar voor het herstel van de nieuwtestamentische gemeente, 1496-1561* (Haarlem, 1961); and *Van Mantz tot Menno: de verbreiding van de doperse beginselen* (Amsterdam, 1975). He also published the first critical edition of Menno Simons *Foundation Book* (*Menno Simons, Dat Fundament Des Christelycken Leers* [The Hague, 1967]. He was working on an edition of the complete theological works of Menno Simons at the time of his death. SV

Doops. Jaar (1985), 13-14.

Mellinger, Lydia Stauffer Sauder (Apr. 30, 1878 - June 27, 1952), served the Mennonite Church (MC) full-time for more than half a century. During 29 years as matron of the Millersville, Pa., Mennonite Children's Home she became "Mama Sauder" to 800 and to her church and community as well. Born in Farmersville, Pa., the daughter of Samuel and Maria Stauffer, she moved to the Welsh Mountain Industrial Mission in 1899 to work among impoverished blacks. In 1906 she married coworker Levi Sauder and became second mother to his son, J. Paul. The Sauders supervised the mission from the spring of 1910 until March 1911, when they opened the Children's Home. They had two sons, John L. and H. Richard. During Levi's ten-week illness and after his death (Oct. 1940) Lydia managed the office. In December 1941 she married Jacob D. Mellinger and with him served for four years in a CPS camp near Hagerstown, Md. They left the camp one morning in February 1946 and before noon began work as steward and matron of the Mennonite Home near Lancaster, Pa., where Lydia died in 1952. AGW

GH (July 29, 1952), 758 (Dec. 5, 1940), 767, (Jan. 8, 1942), 870, (Aug. 14, 1979), 662; *Miss. Mess.* (Sept. 1947), 2, 3; *MRJ*, 2 (Apr. 7, 1961), 16; Martin G. Weaver, *Mennonites of Lancaster Conference* (Scottdale: MPH, 1931), 298-302, 334-36); Leroy Bechler, *Black Mennonite Church in North America, 1886-1986* (Scottdale, 1986).

Melville, John (1802-86), a Scottish evangelist active in southern Russia between 1837 and ca. 1875. An unofficial agent of the British and Foreign Bible Society, he also distributed religious tracts and held secret meetings with Ukrainian peasants, many of whom later joined the Shtundo Baptists. A frequent visitor to the Mennonite colonies of Chortitza and Molotschna, Melville was acquainted with a number of religious leaders interested in evangelical work, including Jacob Martens (1802-70) of Molotschna. Through these contacts and the dissemination of foreign religious literature he was one of the many influences on Mennonite life before 1860 which contributed to a growing interest in religious ideas and activities beyond the Mennonite tradition. JU

James Urry, "John Melville and the Mennonites: A British Evangelist in South Russia, 1837-ca. 1875," *MQR*, 54 (1980) 305-22.

Membership, Church. See Church Membership.

Men's Fellowship (EMCh) founded simultaneously in 1950 in several congregations, by 1953 was organized on the conference level. The original intent was fellowship, mutual encouragement, personal evangelism, and service involvement. The first major joint service project was a plan to provide housing for missionaries on furlough. In 1959 an "Adventurer" program was organized, the purpose of which was to underwrite financially the EMCh church extension program. The Christian Service Foundation, a subsidiary corporation of the denomination, sold $42,000 in debentures, designating the proceeds for church extension projects. The men's "Adventurer" program paid the interest and retired the debentures over a ten-year period. New churches that benefited, upon becoming financially capable, paid back the principal amount of the benefit to the Christian Service Foundation which converted the money into a revolving fund, interest-free, to other newly founded churches. Charitable estate money was added to the interest-free money, which thus became a permanent resource fund for beginning churches. Additional projects of Men's Fellowship include sending short-term work teams to the mission fields of the Dominican Republic and Burkina Faso. There is now an annual retreat during the winter months for reporting, seminars, and specialized learning. Other special projects include purchasing pews for extension churches, work days at Miracle Camp, Lawton, Mich., and responding to specific requests for involvement on the conference level. RS

Regular reports in *Minutes (EMCh)*.

Men's Work. Church men's groups in most denominations declined in North America in the 1960s and 1970s. Men's groups in some Mennonite denominations followed the same pattern of decline in this period. Television developed rapidly at this time and may have been part of the competition for men's time. Also the increase of two-career families that demanded more sharing of housekeeping chores, the increase of single-parent families, night classes or a second job eliminated for many men the leisure time available for church men's groups. Lyle Schaller also lists civic, professional, social, political, and other church groups (for Mennonites these might have been Mennonite Disaster Service, MCC relief sales, the small group movement and other developments) competing for time that once was used by church men's groups. Further reason for the decline may have been the drop in church attendance and membership in the 1960s and 1970s and the wider acceptance of secular service clubs by Mennonites that meet at the more convenient times of lunch or breakfast hours.

In the late 1970s and 1980s church men's groups have been increasing in number in a variety of denominations. Lyle Schaller has isolated six possible reasons. (1) A religious "revival" in North America reflected in the many men's Bible study and prayer groups that have replaced the more formally organized and elected officer-led groups. (2) A clear purpose: currently church planting for Mennonite, Lutheran, Southern Baptist, and other denominations, is the distinctive purpose of the revitalized men's organization. (3) A sense of belonging for adult males who need a group just as much as participants in the church women's group, youth group, choir, children's clubs and classes, young couples' groups and ministers' organizations. (4) As congregations grow larger, small groups providing a face-to-face experience are needed. Men's groups help to fill that need. (5) Among all the groups for couples there is also a need for groups that could accept °single men. (6) As female church leadership became more widely accepted, men who were displaced needed a place to use their gifts. Men's groups 'helped slow down a tendency for a male exodus and the "feminization" of the church. In addition longevity has increased and more men with leisure time are seeking a significant place for service and fellowship. Among Mennonites the clearest example of decline and renewed interest in men's groups is found in the °Mennonite Men (GCM) organization. ESB

Lyle Schaller, "Don't 'Vrite Off the Men's Groups," *Leadership*, 6, no. 1, p. 94.

See also Men's Fellowship (EMCh).

Menno Colony, Paraguay (ME III:575). The 1927 emigrants to Paraguay from Canada came from three different °Bergthal Mennonite groups: 70 percent from the Chortitz congregation (Manitoba °°East Reserve), 20 percent from the Sommerfeld congregation (Manitoba °°West Reserve), and 10 percent from the Saskatchewan Bergthal congregation (Rosthern area, closely related to Sommerfeld Mennonites). Ca. 1950 the joint name "Chortitzer Mennonite Church of Menno" was changed to "Mennonite Church of Menno." While the original settlement comprised 550 sq. km. (211 sq. mi.), in 1986 the settlement comprised 4,350 sq. km. (1672 sq. mi.) with a population of ca. 6,600 persons (1,450 families) in 80 villages. The birthrate rose to 60 per 1,000 inhabitants, then sank to 25 births per thousand (1986). Deaths were 10 per 1,000 until 1950, but have fallen to an average of 5 per 1,000. During the pioneer years this latter figure was 100 per 1,000.

Colony administration is based on Paraguayan law number 514 of July 1921 and is known as the "Sociedad Civil Chortitzer Komitee." This administration is responsible for all economic and social affairs of the colony and is the legal agency for colony issues. The chairman of the colony administration is the "Administrador General" (°°*Oberschulze*). The Chortitzer Committee is the legal owner of all lands, making them available to individual families as needed.

The colony administration is responsible for schools, the hospital, road maintenance, insurance, and the operation of the colony's producer-consumer cooperative. This cooperative is in turn responsible for the industrial and agricultural development of the colony. It secures credits and arranges for exports, imports, and all nonprivate business enterprises. It employs more than 500 people, including more than 100 Indians. Offices and marketing facilities for colony produce are maintained in Asunción. The primary sources of income for the settlers is from cotton, peanuts, milk products, and cattle.

Eleven schools are in operation with ca. 1,100 students and 50 teachers. An accredited secondary school is operated in Loma Plata, with six branch schools in other areas. Fernheim and Menno Colonies together maintain a teacher training school (located in Fernheim) and an agriculture school (located in Menno).

Development of the colony has been southward until ca. 30 percent of the colony population is located in South Menno. In 1980 the large North Menno congregation was divided into six local units and the South Menno congregation into three units. North and South have formed separate "conferences" and together make up a joint "conference," or congregation—all nine local groups are considered part of the Mennonitengemeinde (Mennonite congregation) of Menno Colony. This conference is a member of the General Conference Mennonite Church of North America, as well as of the Conference of Mennonites in South America, the Vereinigung der Mennonitengemeinden in Paraguay, and the Chaco Mennonite Conference (the latter consists of all Mennonite congregations in Neuland, Menno, and Fernheim colonies).

Mennonite Church (GCM) activities in Menno Colony take place in eleven large church buildings. Total membership is ca. 3,000, including 55 ministers and 40 deacons. The entire *Gemeinde* is divided into nine regions as described above, with a leading minister responsible in each. Several local churches have organs. Each local church has a °choir and musical instrument groups which serve on Sunday mornings and on other occasions. °Singing in harmony rather than unison has been practiced for some years already. Martin C. °Friesen served as leading elder of the entire *Gemeinde* for many years until 1966 and was responsible for many of the changes in congregational practice, as well as in the introduction of higher levels of education. Oberschulze Jacob B. °Reimer was a significant partner in these changes. Jacob A. Braun (1893-1979) was particularly responsible for the introduction of cooperative economic efforts. Jacob N. Giesbrecht has been particularly responsible for the industrial development in the colony. Abraham W. Hiebert and Bernhard W. Toews (1909-74) deserve much credit for the mission program among the Lengua Indians (Chaco Mission).

Menno Colony has long cooperated with the other two Chaco colonies (Neuland, Fernheim), as well as with Friesland and Volendam in every possible way. It is also a member of the Asociación de Servicios de Cooperación Indigena Menonita (Council for Indian Concerns). The colony also has its own relief organization, the Comité de Asistencia Social, which seeks to help poor Paraguayans in a special way. It is helped in this by the °International Mennonite Organization of Europe. MWF

MWH (1978), 252; *Menn. Jahrbuch* (1984), 157; *Atlas der Menno Kolonie* (Menno Colony: School Administration of the Menno Colony, 1987); Martin W. Friesen *Neue Heimat in der Chacowildnis* (Altona, Man.: D. W. Friesen Printers, 1987; Menno Colony: Chortitzer Komitee, 1987).

See also Bergthal Mennonites; Evangelical Mennonite Conference (Kleine Gemeinde) Paraguay.

Menno Simonszoon (ME III:577). Research in the

20th c. on Menno Simons is summarized in three basic articles: the article by Cornelius Krahn in ME III, the 1962 article "Menno Simons Research (1910-1960)," also by Krahn, in *No Other Foundation* (North Newton, 1962), 65-76, and in an article by Walter Klaassen, "Menno Simons Research, 1937-1986," *MQR,* 60 (1986), 483-96. To these should be added the papers read in Amsterdam at the Menno Simons Colloquium in 1986, published in Dutch in *Doopsgezinde Bijdragen,* n.r. 12-13 (1986-1987), and in English in *MQR,* 62 (July 1988).

Scholars have long agreed that Menno was not the founder but the organizer of Dutch Mennonitism; beyond that almost every question about him has been a matter of debate from his own time to the late 20th c. His contemporaries, both supporters and opponents, debated vigorously with him. Only a small group, which soon died out, used his name, though it came into broader, and eventually global use. In the 1980s his writings are being studied with new respect, also by non-Mennonites, perhaps because the real Menno is emerging in place of the hero Mennonites wanted and needed.

It is now generally agreed that Menno initially was a Melchiorite, that is, a follower of Melchior °Hoffman, and that he called the °Münster Anabaptists "brothers" but broke decisively with them over the use of force to bring in the kingdom of God. Studies continue on his educational background and intellectual ability. On the former G. K. Epp reports Praemonstratensian roots in *Mennonite Images* (1980), ed. Harry Loewen. Cornelis Augustijn is convinced that Menno had a "fair" education influenced by the spirit and thought of Erasmus, that he was a very formidable debater and that "the essential features of his theology may be traced to Erasmus" (*MQR,* 60 [1986], 497-508). Irvin B. Horst had traced this influence earlier and came to a similar conclusion, but stated it less emphatically in *Erasmus, the Anabaptists and the Problem of Religious Unity* (Haarlem, 1967). S. Voolstra and W. Bergsma, eds., and trans., *Uyt Babel ghevloden, in Jeruzalem ghetogen: Menno Simons' verlichting, bekering en beroeping,* Doperse Stemmen, 6 (Amsterdam: Doopsgezinde Historische Kring, 1986), and Voolstra in *MQR,* 62 (July 1988) offer additional interpretation of Menno's biographical background and motivation. Older images of the simple Menno who was "slow moving. . . not easily stirred and changed. . . even his small corpus of writings is often boringly repetitious" are reaffirmed by John R. Loeschen in *The Divine Community* (1981), 67, even though the volume is a comparison of Luther, Menno, and Calvin on the doctrine of the Trinity and Menno received fair treatment.

No single organizing center of Menno's thought has been identified but there is general agreement that he moved from a stress upon conversion early in his career to a gradually increasing emphasis on the church which, in turn, led to greater emphasis on discipline. The vision of a pure church also led Menno to stress the heavenly origin of the human Christ, a doctrine which caused much controversy already in his time, but has more recently been affirmed as a vital part of Menno's understanding of salvation and the possibility of believers becoming Christlike (S. Voolstra, *Het Woord Is Vlees Geworden*

[1982]). Menno may, at times, sound like a docetist, but he was not one. So also Menno's stress upon a return to the spirit and norm of the church in the Bible (restitutionism) as a way to achieve a pure church has often been identified (Jaroslav Pelikan, *The Christian Tradition,* 4 [1984], 313-22). In an earlier attempt to refute works-righteousness J. A. Oosterbaan identified Menno's understanding of grace with the doctrine of creation itself ("Grace in Dutch Mennonite Theology," *A Legacy of Faith,* ed. C. J. Dyck [1962], 69-85). Work continues on Menno's political theory. As Menno grew older he came to reject °capital punishment, but continued to defend the possibility of a Christian magistrate. Some scholars find a strong anticlericalism in his writings (e.g., H.-J. Goertz, "Der Fremde Menno Simons: Antiklerikale Argumentation im Werk eines melchioritischen Täufers," *Menn. Geschbl.,* 42 [1985], 24-42).

Menno's original works are now available on microfiche. In 1988 work had begun in Amsterdam on a text-critical edition of all of Menno's writings. CJD

Menno Simons and the White Lie

On one of his many journeys Menno Simons traveled by stage coach and, because all the inside seats were taken, sat outside next to the driver. Suddenly a group of armed riders approached, stopped the coach and asked, "Is Menno Simons in there?" Whereupon Menno reached back to open the door and said, "They want to know whether a Menno Simons is in there." After a short pause he was told "no," whereupon he turned to the riders with the words, "They say he is not in there." The riders continued on their way and Menno's life was saved.

This story was told in 1868 by the venerable Dutch Mennonite church historian, J. G. de °°Hoop Scheffer, but he did not believe it to be true. An earlier researcher had investigated it in 1676 and thought it might have happened to Hans °°Busschaert (Busscher), a Mennonite preacher in Antwerp. In that account, however, it was the local count (margrave) who was hunting for Busschaert.

De Hoop Scheffer doubted that the event ever happened at all. He thought rather that it was attributed to Menno through folklore tradition to justify, through the high authority of their venerable leader Menno, the possibility of Mennonites speaking the truth in such a way as to allow for a double meaning. This may have served a useful purpose during interrogations or trials (as some accounts in the *Martyrs Mirror* illustrate) and eventually became a Mennonite characteristic, just as Calvinists were known to be authoritarian and Lutherans stubborn. When de Hoop Scheffer wrote this in 1868 he was not certain that Mennonites had overcome this practice, though they firmly believed in Christ's injunction to "Let what you say be simply 'yes' or 'no'" (Mt 5:37).   CJD

J. G. de Hoop Scheffer, "Mennisten-streken," *Doops. Bijdr.* (1868), 23-48, at p. 26; Karel Vos, *Menno Simons* (1914), 261.

Mennonite (ME III:586) is the most common designation since the mid-17th c. for the largest continuing Christian tradition rooted in 16th c. °Anabaptism. *Mennonite* and its earlier versions, *Menist* or *Mennonist*, is derived from °Menno Simons, the major leader and organizer of North European Anabaptism following the aborted °Münster revolution. The use of "leader" here is deliberate for Menno was not a founder of Anabaptism even in the North. Rather he was above all else an organizer and thus represented the more intitutionalized, second generation of Anabaptism. *Mennonite*, in turn, referred to the less charismatic and more quietist offspring of their frequently villified Anabaptist parents.

Not nearly all the children of Anabaptism were prepared to be identified with Menno Simons. The °°Batenburgers, °David Jorists, and similar northern Anabaptist subgroups neither accepted Menno's post-Münster theology nor, for that matter, became ongoing communities as did the Mennonites. Much closer to Menno were the °°Waterlanders in the Netherlands who became known as the *Doopsgezinden* (Baptism-minded, i.e., baptists). While sharing much with Menno, they considered him too strict and too conservative, particularly in the area of church °discipline, to accept his name. Farther south, the communalist Anabaptists became known as °Hutterites, and thereby were differentiated from the more individualistic °°Swiss Brethren. The Swiss along with other south German and central German Anabaptists, despite a series of conferences through which they sought to gain unity with the North German and Dutch Mennonites, were unable to accept either Menno's strict discipline, especially shunning (°°avoidance), nor his celestial flesh Christology (°°incarnation). They remained "Brethren," were renamed *Taufgesinnte* (baptism-minded) or, especially in the °°Alsace, became °Amish, when they sided with Jacob °°Ammann in a dispute primarily over discipline. (Actually Ammann accepted Menno's strict view on discipline but rejected his Christology.) Ironically, in Germany, Switzerland, and France the label *Mennonite* gained increasing currency by the mid-17th c., despite earlier resistance, while in Holland, the *Doopsgezinden* designation remains in the late 20th c. although this community simultaneously identifies with international Mennonitism.

Why did the term *Mennonite* replace *Anabaptist?* Apparently because in the larger society *Mennonite* did not have the negative theological and political connotations of *Anabaptist*. The designation *Mennonite* was thus increasingly used by insiders and friendly outsiders alike to avoid the sanctions associated with *Anabaptist*. At the same time by the mid-17th c. sufficient theological commonality was attained to weaken earlier resistance to the name. Even the northern Mennonites (*Doopsgezinden*) dropped Menno's celestial flesh Christology and with time deemphasized Menno's strict discipline. The °°Dordrecht Confession of 1632 written by the northern Mennonites and soon accepted as normative by the more southern Mennonites is a symbol of this developing commonality. Significantly all the Swiss and south Germans of Anabaptist persuasion who arrived in America in the early 18th c., usually by way of the Rhine River, the °°Palatinate, and Dutch *Doopsgezind* communities, identified themselves as Mennonites. They thus in name were the same as all those Mennonites who migrated from the low countries and northern Germany to Prussia and Poland, and from there to Russia and the Americas.

While perhaps the label *Mennonite* avoided the negative connotations of *Anabaptist, Mennonite* was not without ambiguity. At various times and places the term was considered too negatively loaded and hence unacceptable as a label. While earlier the *Doopsgezinden* in Europe did not wish to be identified with Menno's separatism and legalism, more recently in North America the Mennonite Brethren in Christ became the (°°United) Missionary Church, so to emphasize separation as well as to enhance its missionary image. Other smaller Mennonite groups and numerous congregations in recent decades have similarly deemphasized or even dropped the Mennonite label for similar reasons. Leaders of the Mennonite Brethren church, the third largest North American Mennonite denomination, also ask themselves periodically if the name *Mennonite* compromises their evangelical message. Some have suggested that they should once again identify themselves as *Anabaptists* now that this term has been largely rehabilitated by recent scholarship. Perhaps the Mennonite label could also be rehabilitated but the ambiquities of the term will not readily disappear.

Mennonite is ambiguous in definition for several basic reasons. In the first place, the Mennonite tradition embraces an inherent tension between °sectarian separation from the world and missionary responsibility to the world. Some of the many Mennonite subdivisions emphasize one or the other of these two, while other Mennonite groups seek a synthesis of them. Accordingly, *Mennonite* identifies those strictly separatist groups known for their rejection of °modern culture including, for some, modern technology. These are the most visible Mennonites, and hence they influence the public reading of Mennonite out of all proportion to their numbers. In fact, sociologists frequently look to them as archtypical sectarians. By contrast *Mennonite* also identifies adjectively a number of denominations identified less by their separatism than their active involvement worldwide alongside many other Christian denominations in °education, °publishing, °mission, and °service. Almost innumerable institutions and organizations labeled *Mennonite* pursue this denominational agenda. The vast majority of Mennonites are of this less separatist and more activist persuasion, yet the former create the more identifiable public image.

Mennonite is ambiguous, secondly, because it has both ethnic and religious connotations. The quest to nurture their vision of the true church in peace and quiet and to separate themselves from a hostile and evil world, encouraged Mennonites over the centuries to pursue a strategy of relative ideological and geographical withdrawal. Assisted by endogamy (marriage within the group) and other mechanisms of boundary maintenance, the Mennonites over time developed a sense of being a unique people—even an ethnic group. Indeed, the °sociologist E. K. Francis developed his seminal definition of ethnicity on the basis of a study of the Mennonites in Russia and southern Manitoba. The fact that frequent migrations, undertaken either voluntarily or under pressure, had robbed them of a national identity further assisted this process of creating a Mennonite ethnicity. Although their ethnicity is premised not on racial or national but on religious distinctives, that Mennonite has both religious and ethnic meanings cannot be gainsaid.

Mennonite ethnicity is, however, not uniform. In the past Mennonites divided essentially into two ethnic groupings—the Swiss/South German/Pennsylvania and the Dutch/North German/Russian—each with various sub-groupings. Prior to the 20th c. accordingly, at least two ethnic traditions of Mennonite language, customs, dress, food, art, etc. are identifiable. For various historical reasons, however, the Dutch tradition became the more ethnic while the Swiss remained the more sectarian. But the processes of °acculturation, especially in the 20th c., are rapidly transforming both traditional Mennonite ethnicities and sectarianism. Furthermore as a product of Mennonite missions numerous other ethnicities now also share the name *Mennonite*, with the result that *Mennonite* is becoming heterogeneously ethnic while acculturation processes simultaneously result in new homogenization.

If *Mennonite*, at least in some areas, refers to an ethnic group entered by birth as well as a religious community entered by adult decision, who is a Mennonite? The confusion is related to the rite of becoming a member in a Mennonite church. While it is clear that one becomes a Mennonite upon baptism into a Mennonite church as an adult, the children born into Mennonite homes tend also to be considered Mennonite until they are baptized. Frequently even if they do not choose to be baptized they continue to be considered or to consider themselves to be Mennonite. Emphasis upon the Christian family and on Christian nurture encourages a more inclusive definition of Mennonite than the strong emphasis on adult voluntarism might imply. This same issue arises in those countries where Mennonites have missionized and added numerous other ethnicities to the Mennonite household. Is a child or grandchild of a Mennonite community in India, who is herself only nominally Christian, considered to be a Mennonite, particularly if this person has been acculturated into the uniquenesses of the Indian Mennonite subculture and become distanced from other Indian cultures in the process? This so-called "second generation" reality is the third factor complicating the meaning of Mennonite, even though it is hardly unique to Mennonites.

Further reasons could be cited for the ambiguity of the term *Mennonite*, e.g., the variety of theological, political, and cultural perspectives found under the Mennonite banner. The Mennonite community worldwide embraces the entire spectrum from liberal to conservative, left to right, iconoclasts to iconodules. Furthermore, as already noted, the word *Mennonite* is used in so many different ways: as a adjective, as a noun, as an adverb, and even as a verb—it is seemingly possible to "Mennonite your way," i.e., staying with other Mennonites while traveling.

What then does *Mennonite* mean? *Mennonite* clearly refers to an identifiable Christian tradition which embraces a variety of Christian communities around the world. Greater specificity however, is difficult because the term has changed over time and continues to change. *Mennonite* is becoming more inclusive than exclusive, and more dynamic than static. The one commonality providing definition is history (°tradition). To be Mennonite is not so much to share a creed or a liturgy but a story—the story of the Mennonite experience over nearly five centuries of history. This story is premised upon an incarnational theology, upon the quest to become a people, the body of Christ by God's grace rooted in the life and teachings, death and resurrection of Jesus, in a world frequently alien or even hostile to this Way. It is frequently a story of failure, yet also of faithfulness. To be a Mennonite then means to identify with a particular Christian community with a particular story, remembering what has been in the beginning and over time, and shaping what might yet be to the glory of God.   RJS

Heinold Fast, "Wie sind die oberdeutschen Täufer 'Mennoniten' geworden?" *Menn. Geschbl.*, 43/44, (1986/87), 80-103; E. K. Francis, "The Russian Mennonites: From Religious to Ethnic Group," *American J. of Sociology*, 54 (Sept., 1948), 101-7; Calvin Redekop and Sam Steiner, eds. *Mennonite Identity: Historical and Contemporary Perspectives* (Lanham, Md.: U. Press of America, 1988); John H. Redekop, *A People Apart: Ethnicity and the Mennonite Brethren* (Winnipeg and Hillsboro: Kindred Press, 1987); Harry Loewen, ed., *Why I Am A Mennonite: Essays on Mennonite Identity* (Scottdale, 1988).

See also Anabaptism; Conservative Mennonites.

Mennonite Air Missions, Guatemala, was envisioned by Harold Kauffman while serving as a missionary with the Conservative Mennonite Fellowship in Guatemala. Its purpose is to establish churches in the unevangelized areas in the interior of Guatemala which have no access roads. The mission was organized in 1972 and has a board of directors in the United Sates and an Official Board incorporated in Guatemala with all national members reelected annually under the name Misiones Aereas Menonita. A plane and pilot were hired initially until Harold acquired his own plane and flying license. In addition to the congregation at the base on the western side of Guatemala City, 10 other congregations and established missions are located in seven departments of Guatemala. Harold Kauffman serves as bishop along with 14 leaders. Five Guatemalan ministers and one deacon are ordained and the other nine are commissioned lay leaders. Missionary nurses and teachers in church schools are a part of the congregational witness. A Bible institute was begun in 1983. The total baptized membership was about 180 in 1987.   AY

MWH (1984), 76; *MC Yearbook* (1988-89) 156, 164.

Mennonite Brethren Church of India. See India.

Mennonite Brethren Church of North America (MB) (ME III:242, 595). A number of significant developments have taken place with respect to the Mennonite Brethren Church in North America since the middle of the 20th c. One of these was the merger with the °°Krimmer Mennonite Brethren Conference (KMB) in 1960. This marked the culmination of a series of contacts and cooperative activities almost since the beginning of both groups' North American experience. The earliest merger proposals were already discussed in the 1870s, and there had been cooperative efforts especially in education. Between 1949 and 1960 the merger issue was a constant agenda item. Problems that had to be resolved were particularly the nature of the KMB missions program, which was carried on under the auspices of a number of mission boards. Other concerns such as the relatively small size of the KMB conference, no doubt, were also factors. Nevertheless, in 1957, the churches of the KMB conference decided by a two-thirds majority to merge with the MB conference and the formal merger ceremony took place in Reedley, Cal., on Nov. 14, 1960, at the occasion of the centennial general conference sessions of the MB church. The KMB membership at the time was 1,648 and the conference was supporting 31 missionaries in nine countries. The merger also brought six black congregations from North Carolina into the new MB conference. It should also be noted that the article on the KMB in ME III (pp. 242-45) did not mention the significant influx of members from the Hutterite communities in KMB churches in earlier decades, especially in South Dakota.

With the rapid growth in membership of the Canadian MB churches in the years after World War II there followed an increasing trend toward a greater degree of independence on the part of the Canadian churches. Indeed by 1951 the membership of the Canadian District had already exceeded that of the other three districts combined. At the general conference sessions in Hillsboro, Ks., in 1954 the issue of independence came to a head and it resulted in the emergence of the concept of "area conferences." Each area (United States and Canada) took on major responsibility in such matters as higher education, church schools, youth work and home missions. The Canadian conference withdrew its support of Tabor College. In 1981 further significant constitutional changes were effected. In 1987 the work of the general conference is carried on by seven boards, including the Board of Reference and Counsel, Board of Mass Media, Board of Missions and Services, Board of the Mennonite Brethren Biblical Seminary, and Board of Trustees.

One of the most significant changes has taken place in the area of °education and the training of church leaders. Whereas various undergraduate theological programs largely met the needs for the training of church leaders in earlier years, the demand for graduate training increased at the same time that most churches moved to full-time pastoral ministries, and in many cases to the employment of two or more salaried full-time staff in leadership positions. Seminary education had begun at Tabor College, Hillsboro, Ks. (1944) and was moved to Fresno, Cal. (1955), where the Mennonite Brethren Biblical Seminary was begun, but without the support of the Canadian constituency. In Canada, where ministerial preparation had largely been done at the Mennonite Brethren Bible College, a Bachelor of Divinity program was begun in 1961. This program was phased out in 1971 and a study commission was appointed to study the alternatives for higher theological education in Canada. This resulted in the decision for a seminary sponsored jointly by United States and Canadian Mennonite Brethren, to be located at Fresno. This became a reality in 1975. Since that time many pastors and church workers have been trained at MBBS in Fresno, although undergraduate schools also continue the training of church leaders, especially in Canada, where the lay ministry and multiple ministry is still operative in many churches. The seminary, together with the Mennonite Brethren Bible College, Tabor College, Fresno Pacific College, and the Board of Christian Literature now jointly publish the journal *Direction*, a successor to the *Voice* and the *Journal of Church and Society*. The Center for Mennonite Brethren Studies in Fresno houses the archives for the North American conference, whereas the main archives for the Canadian and United States conferences, are housed at Winnipeg and Hillsboro, respectively. A Historical Commission appointed by the seminary board directs the work of the center in Fresno and works cooperatively with the other two centers.

The work of the Board of Missions and Services has continued to expand. At the general conference sessions in Reedley in 1984 one hundred years of foreign missions was celebrated. At that time the conference was supporting 137 missionaries in 23 countries with a budget of over five million dollars. Whereas earlier most of the administrative work was centered in Hillsboro, various factors made it desirable to create two national offices, one of which is located in Winnipeg. The offices of the general secretary of the mission board as well as a number of other offices are also located in Winnipeg.

In the area of publications, much of the work is done independently by the two national conferences, each having its own periodicals. However, the Board of Christian Literature has published quite a number of significant books and pamphlets of special interest and value for Mennonite Brethren. Included among these are John A. Toews, *A History of the Mennonite Brethren Church* (1975), and Peter M. Friesen, *The Mennonite Brotherhood in Russia* (1978), translated from German (1911). Kindred Press is now the official Mennonite Brethren publishing agency.

Important changes have also taken place in the area of church music. In 1963 the compilation of a new hymnal for the use of both the Unites States and Canadian conferences was authorized and the result was the publication in 1971 of the *Worship Hymnal* (Board of Christian Literature). This hymnal has been used very extensively, although some churches have also made extensive use of other hymnals and song books. As rapid changes continued to take place in music in subsequent decades, a further step was taken with the publication of *Sing Alleluia*, a supplement to the earlier hymnal, in 1985.

The Board of Christian Education has been particularly involved with the production and use of °Sunday School literature for the churches. This is an issue on which unanimity has been impossible to achieve. Full participation with other Mennonite conferences in the production of materials such as the Foundation Series has not been possible, although there has been some cooperation in that venture. There has also been some cooperation with other publishers, such as Scripture Press, but in general there is wide divergence in the type of material that is used by the MB congregations.

The Mennonite Brethren Church has continued to struggle over the years with the issues of nationalism, regionalism, and fragmentation. Although a cooperative seminary program has helped to counteract some of the tendencies, there have been many forces which have threatened the unity of the conference. Theological diversity has developed not only because of the continued training of young people and church workers in a variety of North American institutions but also because of the influence of the °mass media and the forces of general °acculturation. Mennonite Brethren are no longer primarily a people of the land but are largely °urbanized, are represented in virtually every °profession and are scattered geographically throughout North America. Consensus on many issues, whether related to ethics, °theology, or °worship style, is difficult or impossible to achieve. A revision of the Mennonite Brethren confession of faith was completed in 1976, but the long process demonstrated an increasing divergence on many issues.

In 1982 a profile of church members was conducted in an effort to update the findings of the Kauffman and Harder study of 1972 (*Anabaptists Four Centuries Later*, 1975). The findings, which were published in *Direction* (Fall, 1984), revealed a number of trends, some of which are quite disconcerting. Although Mennonite Brethren in North America are strong in their affirmation of the Christian faith, there is a great disparity between faith and practice. The °discipleship and °peace emphases appear to be eroding and the study revealed that this was particularly true among leaders. Fewer than half of the respondents agreed that Christians should actively promote the peace position. Loyalty to the local congregation appeared to be weakening affirmations of denominational identity. There was an increasing trend toward an individualistic and pietistic view of Christianity and an erosion of the corporate and sectarian views.

While many have felt that the Mennonite Brethren Church faces a crisis in terms of its own identity, significant steps have been taken to reaffirm the church's historic identity and awaken a new sense of °mission in the world today. The Board of Reference and Counsel in particular faces the serious challenge of seeking to create a vision for the church's task. More positive indicators are the strong evangelistic emphases evident in many churches; these have resulted in significant growth. Old ethnic and cultural barriers have been broken in many places and the influx of members from many different backgrounds, including Chinese, French Canadian, Spanish, and Vietnamese, portend a bright future for the church if it can realize a new sense of its distinctive mission within the North American environment. The total church membership in 1984 was 40,248, 16,942 of whom were in the United States and 23,306 of whom were in Canada.　　　　　　　　　　AJD

John A. Toews, *History MB* (1975); idem, *Perilous Journey: The Mennonite Brethren in Russia, 1860-1910* (Scottdale, Kindren, 1988); Janzen/Giesbrecht, *Recommend* (1978); *Yearbook of the General Conference of the Mennonite Brethren Churches*; Katie Funk Wiebe, *Who Are the Mennonite Brethren?* (Winnipeg and Hillsboro: Kindred Press, 1984); *Direction*, 14, no. 2 (Fall, 1985), a profile of MB church members; Herbert Giesbrecht, *The Mennonite Brethren Church: A Bibliographic Guide* (Scottdale: Kindred, 1983); Richard G. Kyle, *From Sect to Denomination* (1985); Peter Penner, *No Longer at Arm's Length: A History of Mennonite Brethren Home Missions in Canada* (Scottdale: Kindred, 1986); C. F. Plett, *The Story of the Krimmer Mennonite Church* (Scottdale: Kindred Press, 1985); *MWH* (1978), 337-43; *MWH* (1984), 140.

See also Associação das Igrejas Irmãos Menonitas do Brasil; Associacion de Iglesias Hermanos Menonitas, Colombia; Bund Europäischer Mennonitischer Brüdergemeinde, Austria and Germany; Communauté des Églises des Frères Mennonites au Zaire; Comunidad Christiana de los Hermanos Menonitas de España, Spain; Igreja Evangélica dos Irmãos Menonitas em Angola; Konferenz der Mennonitischen Brüdergemeinden, Paraguay; Nihon Menonaito Burezaren Kyodan, Japan; Canadian Conference of Mennonite Brethren Churches; Alberta, British Columbia, Manitoba, Ontario, Quebec, Saskatchewan provincial conferences; Central, Latin American, North Carolina, Pacific, and Southern district conferences; Mexico; Afghanistan; Austria; Bangladesh; Botswana; Brazil; Colombia; Ecuador; India; Bundesrepublik Deutschland; Japan; Nepal; Nigeria; Pakistan; Panama; Paraguay; Peru; Spain; Uruguay; Union of Soviet Socialist Republics; Zaire; Polity.

Mennonite Central Committee Canada (MCCC) is the °peace, °relief, and °service agency of Canadian Mennonites and Brethren in Christ. It was founded in 1963 through the merger of a number of regional °inter-Mennonite service organizations, the main ones being the °°Non-resistant Relief Organization, the Canadian Mennonite Relief Committee, the Canadian Mennonite Relief and Immigration Council, the Conference of Historic Peace Churches, and the Historic Peace Church Council of Canada.

In April 1963 the Historic Peace Church Council of Canada, a Canada-wide inter-Mennonite peace organization, called a meeting of all existing inter-Mennonite peace, relief, and service agencies, as well as representatives of all Mennonite and Brethren in Christ conferences. Out of this meeting came the decision to form a national inter-Mennonite body that would unite all Canadian Mennonite groups in all the activities they wished to do together. MCCC was born in Dec. 1963 in Winnipeg.

MCCC became the most comprehensive of Canadian Mennonite and Brethren in Christ organizations. The MCCC board included representatives from 11 Mennonite and Brethren in Christ groups. The organization was given a broad mandate to work in the areas of °peace education, relief and °development, °voluntary service, immigration, government contacts (°lobbying), and other areas of mutual concern. Provincial MCCC offices were established from Ontario to British Columbia.

From the start its founders agreed that MCCC would work closely with MCC (international). Relations between the two organizations have generally been good, but there have been tensions from time to time. Some Canadian Mennonites have felt that MCC operated like an American rather than a binational institution. Several adjustments in MCC structures have been made in response to this criticism.

MCCC carries out most of its overseas relief and development work through MCC. Its own overseas programs include a ministry to the *Kanadier* Mennonites (those who migrated to Central and South America in the 1920s and 1940s, some of whom have since returned to Canada), relating to Mennonites in the Soviet Union, sponsoring °refugees, gathering commodities such as grain, milk powder, cooking oil, etc., for shipment overseas, and administering its own SELFHELP Crafts program.

Since 1963 there has been tremendous expansion in MCCC's activities in Canada. A voluntary service program places 150 volunteers in communities across the country. A Peace and Social Concerns Committee raises awareness on peace and current social issues. A Native Concerns program promotes economic development in Native communities and engages in advocacy on behalf of Native people (°Indian ministries). An Ottawa office, established in 1974 after nine years of discussion, facilitates relations with government. A victim-offender ministry supports groups pursuing mediation and °reconciliation as an alternative to the secular justice system. Since 1980, MCCC has also begun programs to address the needs of women, disabled persons, the unemployed, and the mentally ill.

In 1976 MCCC created the Mennonite Food Bank as a means of channeling surplus grains grown by Mennonite farmers into overseas use. In 1982 MCCC invited other Canadian churches to participate in this venture. The following year the Canadian Foodgrains Bank was formed, with MCCC taking its place as one of seven member church organizations.

Since 1963 MCCC has grown from a staff of two and a budget of $300,000 to a staff of 50 and a budget of $17 million. Since 1969 MCCC has received matching grants from the Canadian International Development Agency (CIDA) of the Canadian government. In 1986 CIDA grants accounted for nearly half of MCCC's revenues.   EE-T

Esther Epp, "The Origins of Mennonite Central Committee (Canada)" (MA thesis, U. of Manitoba, 1980); Frank H. Epp, ed., *Partners in Service: The Story of Mennonite Central Committee Canada* (Winnipeg: Mennonite Central Committee Canada, 1983); *MCC Canada Report 1986*.

See also Relief Sales.

Mennonite Central Committee Canada, Peace and Social Concerns Committee. When Mennonite Central Committee Canada (MCCC) was formed in December 1963, the need for °peace education was already part of the thinking, and in October 1964 a temporary Peace and Social Concerns (PSC) Committee (briefly known as "The Peace Committee") was appointed. The areas of responsibility included: peace witness (within the Mennonite and Brethren in Christ constituency, and also to government, other churches, and the world at large), labor relations, social concerns, government contact and alternatives to military service. In 1967, Daniel Zehr was appointed as part-time staff person for the PSC Committee. A full-time staff person was first appointed in 1976.

Since its inception, the "social concerns" have varied and have frequently given rise to new programs, e.g., Native concerns (°Indian ministries), the Ottawa office (°lobbying), and women's concerns. Peace education has, however, remained central to the mandate of the PSC Committee.

Staff members write and speak about peace and °justice issues within the Canadian context, and work cooperatively with MCC (international) Peace Section in planning events such as meetings of the Intercollegiate Peace Fellowship and several "peace theology colloquia." They also act as consulting editors for the *MCC Peace Section Newsletter* and cooperate with other MCC departments and provincial MCCC offices and peace committees.

The committee sometimes commissions people to work at projects such as *Where We Stand*, a collection of peace and social concerns statements made by Canadian Mennonites and Brethren in Christ, 1787-1982, compiled by Bert Friesen; *Responses to Militarism*, a study packet on militarism in Canada; and *The Warman Story*, a story of a Mennonite community's response to a proposed uranium refinery. The Peace and Social Concerns Committee continues to have a broad mandate for education and other activities on peace and social concerns with the long-term objective of helping to identify, understand, and assess current issues of peace and justice.   PPe

Mennonite Central Committee [international] (ME III:605). In August 1985 Robert Burkholder, who was living and working with his wife Jill and their four boys in southern Lebanon, was picked up one morning at their home in Nabatiya by a group of armed men. He was taken to Beirut for interrogation —to find out what he was doing as a foreigner in war-torn southern Lebanon. Late that same evening he was released, too late to return home. When he did return to his wife and children in Nabatiya the next day, representatives from all the local fighting factions were there to greet him and welcome him back.

At the annual MCC meeting in January 1985, there was intense discussion about MCC personnel in El Salvador who worked in contested areas as well as in areas controlled by the government. In May of that year Blake Ortman and Susan Klassen, along with a Salvadoran Catholic health worker, were picked up by the military in Cacaopera, a town in the northern transitional area periodically visited by both the army and the "guerrillas." They were taken to the regional army headquarters and eventually to the capital city, San Salvador, for interrogation. They were accused of teaching Marxism and of associating with the "guerrillas." Eventually they were released.

In July 1987 residents of the coastal town of Homoine in ne. Mozambique were massacred by antigovernment bandits who killed 424 people in their attack and took another 298 persons, including some infants, as captives. The massacre was witnessed by MCC worker Mark Van Koevering, an agronomist working with the Christian Council of Mozambique, who was in Homoine during the attack. Van Koevering reported that the farmers he worked with were often too terrorized to sleep in their homes, but rather took refuge in fields and irrigation ditches. The massacre created uncertainties about

Van Koevering's own return to Homoine, but after consultation and prayer with his African and MCC colleagues, it was decided to support Mark in his return to Homoine. "As a member of the Christian Council of Mozambique," he said, "I represent the Christian church of Mozambique, and in a very concrete way the Christian church worldwide. I am returning to Homoine for only one reason, because we are Christians called by God to serve him and his people. Our action in Homoine is being watched by the government and I believe it will be a powerful witness in the community."

The Mennonite Central Committee is known as the cooperative °relief, °service, and °development agency of North American Mennonite and Brethren in Christ churches. The MCC is a Christian resource for meeting human need.

In his article on the MCC in ME III, Harold S. Bender, longtime MCC assistant secretary, traced the development of the Mennonite Central Committee from its origins in 1920, noting the following nine program developments: (1) the original joint Mennonite Famine Relief Program in Russia; (2) the resettlement of Russian Mennonite °refugees from Europe to Paraguay in 1930; (3) the War Sufferer's Relief Program during and following World War II in Europe beginning in 1939; (4) the operation of the °°Civilian Public Service Program in the United States, 1941ff.; (5) the resettlement of Russian and Danzig Mennonite refugees after World War II in Paraguay and Uruguay; (6) development of the °Voluntary Service program for young Mennonites in North America beginning in 1945; (7) development of the Mennonite °Mental Health Services Program with establishment of the first mental hospital at Brooklane Farm in Maryland; (8) aid to the Old Colony Mennonites in Mexico from 1950 to 1956; and (9) development of the I-W °alternative service program (ME III:56) as a military service alternative beginning in 1952.

Since those earlier beginnings the Mennonite Central Committee has grown into the largest °inter-Mennonite organization in the world with a vast variety of organizational relationships and program involvements, from shipping grain provided by the Canadian Food Bank to famine areas in Ethiopia to assistance with the translation and production of Bible commentaries for Christians in the Soviet Union. For many persons in the Mennonite constituencies the worldwide programs of the Mennonite Central Committee have come to symbolize what it means to be an Anabaptist Christian in today's world.

In 1987 the Mennonite Central Committee had more than 1,000 workers serving two- to three-year assignments in some 50 countries, including volunteers and staff in North America. Many times that number serve as short or long-term local volunteers —an estimated 5,000 serve as volunteers in the 130 MCC SELFHELP Crafts and Thrift Shops in Canada and the United States. Roughly three-fourths of the long-term staff and two- to three-year volunteers are from MCC constituent groups (Mennonite and Brethren in Christ), and the other one-fourth from a variety of non-Mennonite groups. The largest number of volunteers are in the developing countries of Asia, Africa, and Latin America, and in Canada and

the United States. Assignments include agricultural development, water conservation, health education, participation in village health teams, formal and informal education, economic and technical projects, church-related programs, social services, East-West dialogue, and peacemaking. The majority of MCCers work in long-range development activities. Strengthening the work of local churches and community groups is a priority. Wherever possible volunteers work closely with local churches as well as with Mennonite and other mission agencies.

Volunteers also provide food and other emergency services to people caught in drought, famine, and warfare. The supporting churches in North America provide the MCC with material aid to help meet the immediate needs of people throughout the world. Mennonites and Brethren in Christ, along with those from other church families, contribute meat (canned in MCC's portable canner), corn, wheat, and beans. They also contribute other gifts in kind, e.g., bedding, clothing, soap, bandages, and school supplies.

The MCC (international) budget in the 1980s totaled nearly 30 million dollars annually, roughly 20 million dollars in cash and 10 million dollars in material aid. Of the cash budget, approximately two-thirds comes from the constituency. Other sources of support include the contributed earnings of volunteers, °SELFHELP crafts, grants from private or Canadian government agencies, and contributions from Mennonite churches abroad.

MCC programs include SELFHELP crafts, a job creation program that enables approximately 30,000 artisans in many developing countries to earn at least part of their own living; the International Visitor Exchange program, which brings °international young people to North America for a year to promote better understanding; the Child Sponsorship program wh:ch makes it possible for North Americans to pro de assistance for students to attend schools in various locations around the world; and the MCC Peace Office which serves as a resource to the international ministries of the MCC.

The Mennonite Central Committee, though involved in a worldwide program, is essentially a North American or binational organization of Mennonite and Brethren in Christ groups in Canada and the United States. In the United States the MCC representatives are for the most part appointed by the respective Mennonite conferences—Beachy Amish Mennonite, Brethren in Christ, Conservative Mennonite Conference, Emmanuel Mennonite Church (Meade, Ks.), Evangelical Mennonite Conference, General Conference Mennonite Church, Lancaster Conference (MC), Mennonite Brethren, and Mennonite Church (MC). MCC (International) representatives from Canada are selected from the MCC provincial and MCC Canada organizations. The MCC board, which meets annually in January for program review and policy decisions, has 39 members. The executive committee, which meets four times a year, has six members from Canada and six from the United States. The overseas program administration is centered in the international headquarters offices in Akron, Pa., supplemented by overseas services of the MCC Canada. The °Mennonite Central Committee Canada offices in Winnipeg, Man., and the °Mennonite Central Committee

United States offices in Akron, Pa., administer North American programs and represent the MCC to its respective constituencies. The provincial and regional offices also serve as links from the constituency to the MCC.

As the Mennonite Central Committee has grown in scope and complexity, so have the questions and issues related to its identity, its organization, and its programs in the world. As a binational organization that does not presume to represent Mennonites and Brethren in Christ from all parts of the world, the MCC nevertheless seeks in a variety of ways to internationalize its staff and program. Examples are the cooperation with the °International Mennonite Organization of European Mennonites, cooperation with the mission and service organizations of the Paraguayan Mennonites, and cooperation with various service and development organizations of Mennonites in countries such as India, Zaire, and Colombia.

As the introductory stories from Lebanon, El Salvador, and Mozambique suggest, the workers of the Menonite Central Committee, seeking faithfulness in meeting human need, have also become more involved in complex issues of war and peace, and of international economics and politics. Throughout its history the MCC has had programs in 84 countries. The development from war sufferers' relief, to a variety of service ministries, to long-range agricultural and economic development, has involved the MCC in issues of oppression and injustice. This has also led to considerable disagreement within the constituency and to some groups distancing themselves from especially those program activities which seem to have political entanglements.

Further is the larger and broader °mission issue of how Christians, especially Christians from wealthy and politically dominant countries in North America and Europe, should best be present in the world today—in relationships with the poorer peoples of the world and especially also peoples of other cultures, religions, and political commitments. Economic development programs in many parts of the world, especially when unilaterally administered, have fallen into considerable disrepute. Even the traditional Mennonite service stance, when suggesting a paternalistic relationship, is being seriously questioned. In many parts of the world, MCC workers have been emphasizing a "Christian presence" relationship with a strong emphasis on a listening and learning stance, out of which a mutual giving and receiving relationship may develop.

The executive secretaries of the Mennonite Central Committee have been Levi Mumaw, 1920-35; Orie O. °Miller, 1935-57; William T. Snyder, 1958-81; Reg Toews, 1982-84; and John A. Lapp, 1985-. The MCC board has been chaired by P. C. °Hiebert, 1920-54; C. N. °Hostetter, 1954-68; Ernest Bennett, 1968-77; Newton °Gingrich, 1977-79; and Elmer Neufeld, 1979-. EN

The major MCC newsletters are Contact, Intercom, Peace Section Newsletter, Washington Memo, and Food and Hunger Notes. Publications providing additional MCC information are Mennonite Central Committee Workbook, prepared each year for the annual meeting. See also P. C. Hiebert and Orie O. Miller, Feeding the Hungry: Russian Famine, 1919-1925 (Scottdale, 1929); John D. Unruh, In the Name of Christ: A History of the Mennonite Central Committee and Its Services 1920-1951 (Scottdale, 1951); Irvin B. Horst, A Ministry of Goodwill—A Short Account of Mennonite Relief, 1939-1949 (Akron: MCC, 1950); Paul Erb, Orie O. Miller: The Story of a Man and an Era (Scottdale, 1969); MQR, 44, no. 3 (July 1970), sp. issue; MCC Story, vols. 1-5 (1980-88).

See also Disaster Services; Indian Ministries; Mennonite Christian Service Fellowship of India; Relief Sales; Stichting voor Bijzondere Noden.

In the Name of Christ

Mennonite Central Committee (MCC) was involved early in healing the wounds of World War II (1939-45). By 1940 work had been undertaken with needy children in France and England. This included the providing of food, shelter, and clothing. One of the first MCC workers in England in 1940 was John E. Coffman of Ontario, Canada. Soon he was receiving and distributing large bales of clothing from North America. This led him and his helpers to an idea which is still being followed. In a letter of April 14, 1941, to Orie O. Miller of MCC, Akron, Pa., Coffman wrote: "May we present a suggestion which has come to us which might be useful in promoting the cause of Christ, as we administer the clothing which is made and donated by our people. This is to have suitable labels prepared which could be attached to the garments as they are made or packed. The labels might be of paper or cloth, and bear the name of the Mennonite Central Committee. A little slogan, such as: 'In the Name of Christ' should be included on the label and a place left or designated for marking the size of the garment or the age of person for whom it was made. There are brethren or sisters at home who could work out a suitable design for such a label and they could be printed and distributed to the various individuals who are making the clothing, and sewn on the garment. . ." Sincerely yours, John E. Coffman.

The idea was well received, the label was designed with the words "In the Name of Christ" prominent on it, and it has appeared on just about every item of material aid distributed by MCC around the world since that time. CJD

Mennonite Central Committee Peace Section (ME IV:131, 1106). The scope of Peace Section interest was global from its inception in 1946 and included war and preparation for war, industrial relations, °church-state relations, "class strife," racial strife, litigation, °capital punishment, war °taxes, conciliation ministries (°reconciliation), and °women's concerns.

The Peace Section provided counsel and assistance for °conscientious objectors from 1951 to 1975, secured project approval for °alternative service (1-W) projects, and arranged for U.S. Selective Service clearance for their work assignments.

The Peace Section in its several divisions has played a major role in North American Mennonite °peace and °justice education throughout the agency's history. Justice terminology became increasingly prominent in the 1960s when the Peace Section witnessed against racial discrimination, through the 1980s when the Peace Section supported the °human rights struggles of various church groups living under oppressive governments.

Peace education through literature preparation and study conferences in North America and abroad was always a priority for the Peace Section, in consultation with the peace committees of various Mennonite Conferences. The Peace Section sponsored church-state study conferences (1964-65), annual peace assemblies, a series of peace theology colloquia (papers published in *MQR*, [July 1981 and Aug. 1984] and in the Institute of Mennonite Studies, Occasional Papers series 1988]), and congregational peace education. A document that was influential in winning improved status for conscientious objectors internationally was, "International Provisions for Conscientious Objectors" (1981). Regular publications included *Report* (in the 1960s) *Peace Section Newsletter, Washington Memo, Report* of the MCC Committee on Women's Concerns, and the Mennonite Conciliation Service's, *Conciliation Quarterly.*

The Peace Section was reorganized in 1974 on the pattern of MCC's reorganization (distinct boards for United States and Canada [Peace and Social Concerns Committee in Canada]). After 1987 the Peace Section was reorganized into the MCC Peace Committee; the structure of the two national bodies continued as before. The Peace Section also played a role in the reorganization of the °International Mennonite Peace Committee, affiliated with Mennonite World Conference since 1986.

The protracted °Vietnam conflict deepened North American Mennonite concern over the role of the United States in international conflict. This contributed to the appointment in 1968 of Frank H. °Epp to a two-year term as director of studies in international conflict. This appointment stimulated interest in East-West and Middle East study tours and in publications seeking to interpret the Middle East conflict. The Peace Section established the Washington Office in 1968 to serve as observer and interpreter and to monitor legislation. From 1954 to 1973 the Peace Section and other MCC representatives in Europe participated in a series of ecumenical study conferences, known as the °Puidoux Peace Conferences. The Peace Section had a resident representative in Europe nearly continuously, 1946-85. The Peace Section worked in close cooperation with other MCC departments in promoting peace efforts in southern and eastern Africa, Latin America, Asia, and Europe.   UP

John A. Lapp, "The Peace Mission of the Mennonite Central Committee," *MQR,* 44 (1970), 281-97; Melvin Gingerich, *Service for Peace: A History of Mennonite Civilian Public Service* (Akron, Pa.: MCC, 1949); John D. Unruh, *In The Name of Christ* (Scottdale, 1952); Peace Section Annual Report in *Mennonite Central Committee Workbook 1966*; Urbane Peachey, comp., *Mennonite Statements on Peace and Social Concerns, 1900-1978* (Akron, Pa.: MCC US Peace Section, 1980).

Mennonite Central Committee United States is an agency of the Mennonite and Brethren in Christ churches in the United States. Mennonite Central Committee U.S. is closely related to the Mennonite Central Committee, the parent body sometimes referred to as MCC binational or MCC international. Mennonite Central Committee U.S. is essentially parallel in function to Mennonite Central Committee

Canada. All three of these organizations have as their basic purposes °relief, °service, °development, and °peace-related activities. The United States MCC organization was formed at a meeting in Reedley, Cal., in 1979, by the U.S. representatives to MCC international, for the purpose of assuming program responsibilities in the United States and to address domestic concerns. Those initial board members were primarily appointees of the Mennonite and Brethren in Christ groups with headquarters in the United States. To this initial board membership have been added representatives of four regions and five members at large.

Prior to the establishment of MCC U.S., domestic U.S. concerns were handled by the Mennonite Central Committee staff, MCC executive committee, and the MCC board, thus creating problems in the U.S./Canadian relationships, especially since MCC Canada, with its provincial organizations, had already assumed responsibility for Canadian program and Canadian concerns.

Two MCC regional centers were in a sense predecessors to the MCC U.S. organization—MCC Central States and West Coast MCC. At the present MCC U.S. has four regional organizations—MCC Central States with offices in Newton, Ks.; West Coast MCC with offices in Reedley, Cal.; MCC Great Lakes with offices in Kidron, Ohio; and MCC East Coast with offices in Akron, Pa.

The MCC U.S. offices are housed in Akron, Pa, together with MCC international offices. The organizational and financial structures of MCC U.S. continue in a process of development. To date (1987) MCC U.S. operates under the corporate or legal structure of MCC international. Likewise MCC U.S. has not developed its own fundraising structures, but develops a budget in consultation with MCC international, a budget which represents a certain percentage of the MCC constituency contributions originating in the United States. This leaves continuing uncertainties about the extent of authority and responsibility lodged in MCC U.S. as a national organization and in the regional organizations for development of programs to meet needs in the respective areas. There is also continuing discussion about the appropriate role of MCC U.S. as a national organization in the respective regions. The regions see their interests and responsibilities as relating not only to domestic programming, but also in a strong relationship to the MCC international program—as resources for the international program and as channels of communication back to the U.S. constituency.

MCC U.S. has a four-fold statement of purpose: (1) to carry overall responsibility for MCC domestic programs in the United States; (2) to generate constituency support for the worldwide ministries and programs of MCC; (3) to work at constituency relations in cooperation with MCC; and (4) to encourage °inter-Mennonite cooperation in local and regional MCC groupings in the United States and to provide the MCC administrative linkage and counsel for established regions.

The MCC U.S. programs include °voluntary service, °urban ministries, immigration and °refugee concerns, criminal justice, Mennonite conciliation service (°reconciliation), and °SELFHELP crafts. Other inter-Mennonite organizations with relationship to MCC U.S. are MCC Peace Section (U.S.), Mennonite °Disaster Service, and Mennonite °Mental Health Services, including the developmental °disabilities program. MCC U.S. has an annual budget of over $3 million (1987) and a total of approximately 200 workers under its assignment. The chairpersons of MCC U.S. have been Paul G. Landis of Salunga, Pa., Anna Juhnke of Newton, Ks., and Phil Rich of Archbold, Ohio. The first MCC U.S. executive secretary was Reg Toews, and the secretary in 1987 was Wilmer Heisey.   EN

Mennonite Chaplains' Association. See Chaplaincy.

Mennonite Christian Service Fellowship of India (MCSFI) is a service and fellowship organization of the six Mennonite and Brethren in Christ churches in India. It was organized at the two-day consultation at the Lee Memorial Centre, °Calcutta, Feb. 1-2, 1963. This consultation was called together by Orie O. °Miller together with the Mennonite Central Committee, India office. P. J. °Malagar was the first director (1963-1981) of MCSFI; R. S. Lemuel has been director since 1981.

In 1968 MCSFI was registered as a service society with the following objectives: (1) to encourage and promote Christian service in the Spirit of Christ in educational, social, medical, philanthropic and religious fields; (2) to assist all or any of the activities of such societies and other charities now existing or hereafter to exist in connection with the work of the society in caring for relief of orphans, aged, sick, helpless, and indigent persons, particularly in times of war, famine, and (3) to seek ways and means to strengthen the fellowship of Christian churches.

In line with these objectives MCSFI has worked incessantly relieving suffering from cyclone, flood, drought, or other natural calamities. It has engaged the services of no fewer than 100 volunteers at the Mana Camp (1964) and at the Devi Taluk in Coastal °Andhra Pradesh (1974). Since 1963 it has arranged many retreats, youth conferences, and other meetings. It arranged for the first all-India Mennonite peace conference at °Dhamtari (1966). This conference included representatives of other historic peace churches in India and representatives from the Fellowship of Reconciliation in India.

The constituency of MCSFI responded to appeals for funds and volunteers (two couples were sent) to Vietnam and Kampuchea. In 1987 4,000 school kits were sent to Kampuchea from the Dhamtari Christian Hospital.   PJM

See also Development Work; Relief Work.

Mennonite Church (MC) (ME III:610), is that branch of the world Mennonite communion composed largely of congregations growing out of early Swiss-South German Mennonite and Amish immigration, to North America, sometimes referred to as "Old Mennonites." Alongside the General Conference Mennonite Church (GCM) and the Mennonite Brethren, it is one of the three main Mennonite groups in North America. Membership in the Mennonite Church (MC) in North America in 1985 stood at 100,567; with 9,400 members in 85 congregations located in Canada, and 91,167 members in 989 con-

gregations in the United States. Additionally there were 39,743 members in non-North American churches and programs related, in some instances loosely related, to the Mennonite Church (MC). From the mid-1950s to the mid-1980s, North American (MC) membership increased by approximately 20 percent; overseas membership increased almost 1,000 percent.

The Mennonite Church (MC) in the United States and Canada is organized into conferences, the majority of which participate in Mennonite General Assembly. The assembly is an agency designed to corporately carry forward the ministry and mission of the church. Participating conferences are: Allegheny, Atlantic Coast, Conservative, Franconia, Franklin, Gulf States, Illinois, Indiana-Michigan, Iowa-Nebraska, Lancaster, Mennonite Conference of Ontario and Quebec (after 1988, part of the Mennonite Conference of Eastern Canada), NYS (New York State) Fellowship, North Central, Northwest, Ohio, Pacific Coast, Rocky Mountain, South Central, Southeast, Southwest, Virginia, and Western Ontario. For additional information see the pertinent article on each conference.

Mennonite Church (MC) conferences not participating in Mennonite General Assembly include: Conservative Mennonite Fellowship, Cumberland Valley, Fellowship Churches, Mid-Atlantic, Mid-West Mennonite Fellowship, Northern Light, Southeastern, Washington-Franklin, Western Conservative, Conservative Mennonite Churches of York, and Adams Cos, and a large group of unaffiliated Mennonite churches.

Overseas Mennonite churches include the following (most of these are outgrowths of North American MC mission and service programs; few have independent origins but have established relationships with MC agencies): °Iglesia Evangélica Menonita, Argentina (1,350 members in 1985); °Australian Conference of Evangelical Mennonites (12); °Conseil Mennonite Belge (45); °Caribbean Light and Truth in Belize (100); °Belize Evangelical Mennonite Church (275); °Iglesia Menonita de Bolivia (100); °Associação Evangélica Menonita Brazil (812); °Convención Evangélica Menonita de Costa Rica (858); °Conferencia de las Iglesias Evangélicas Menonitas, Dominican Republic (975), °Misión Evangélica Menonita, Ecuador (61); °Iglesia Evangélica Menonita, El Salvador (75); United Kingdom Conference of Mennonites [°London Mennonite Fellowship] (24); °Ghana Mennonite Church (800); °Conservative Mennonite Fellowship, Guatemala (126); °Mennonite Air Missions, Guatemala (167); °Iglesia Nacional Evangélica Menonita Guatemalteca (1,068); °Iglesia Menonita de Guatemala (537); °Iglesia Evangélica Menonita, Honduras (1,800); °Amor Viviente Movement, Honduras (1,500); °Hong Kong Mennonite Ministries (32); °Bihar Mennonite Mandli, India (621); °Mennonite Church in India (2,127); °Irish Mennonite Movement (10); °Chiesa Evangelica Mennonita, Italy (72); °Jamaica Mennonite Church (351); °Nihon Menonaito Kirisuto Kyokai Kyogikai (Hokkaido), Japan (400); °Kenya Mennonite Church (2,700); °Iglesia Evangélica Menonita, Noroeste de Mexico (178); °Iglesia Evangélica Menonita, Mesa Central de Mexico (150); °Convención de las Iglesias

Evangélicas de Nicaragua (457); °Nigeria Mennonite Church (3,000); °Convención de las Iglesias Menonitas de Puerto Rico (900); °Kanisa la Mennonite Tanzania (15,600); °Mennonite Church of Trinidad and Tobago (52); °Convención de las Iglesias Menonitas en Uruguay (247); °Concilio de las Iglesias Evangélicas Menonitas, Venezuela (121); °Giáo Hôi Tin Lành, Vietnam (32). This response to Mennonite mission, relief, and service programs around the world has been one of the most notable developments in the Mennonite Church (MC) in the decades since World War II. Some of the above groups also grew out of Mennonite Central Committee involvements, some have fraternal relationships with General Conference Mennonite agencies or other Mennonite organizations.

By the mid-1950s the vast expansion of mission and service programs in the Mennonite Church (MC) presented a major challenge to existing program structures and patterns of religious life. North American Mennonites were also becoming highly trained and educated, full participants in °business and the °professions. Those who remained in agriculture similarly found their situation transformed by pressures to specialize and mechanize. In the coming decades °institutionalization, professionalism, and internationalism would increasingly characterize the American Mennonite Church (MC). The °Mennonite Mutual Aid organization, initially begun to aid returning conscientious objectors, who were not eligible for national veterans' benefits, expanded to provide structured aid for multiple needs of members including health, automobile, and survivors' °insurance. Regional mental hospitals (°mental health facilities and services) were established to serve both Mennonites and the wider community. Volunteer opportunities of short duration such as Mennonite °Disaster Service supplemented longer .term relief and service projects, greatly increasing the number of people able to participate. (Most of the above-mentioned organizations involve other Mennonite groups in addition to the Mennonite Church [MC].) Limitations on associations with non-Mennonite organizations and activities relaxed. Simultaneously multiple congregational, conference, and churchwide activities were being organized, generally under the leadership of lay persons.

The 1960s were a time of reinterpretation, characterized by leadership and organizational adjustments to a changed reality. A new *Mennonite Confession of Faith* was adopted in 1963 in the context of discussions saturated with the theme of change. At the Mennonite Church (MC) general conference sessions (the forerunner of the Mennonite General Assembly) held in Lansdale, Pa., in 1961, °communion was served for the first time at such a gathering. The event signaled the waning of close communion, which allowed only members in full fellowship to participate in congregationally-based communion services. It also heralded the relaxation of °discipline, which had been closely tied to the preparatory meeting which preceded close communion. °Dress restrictions were eased, making the plain coat no longer mandatory for ministers and church workers and easing the recommended wearing of bonnets by women members. The use of °musical instruments in worship became widespread, although many congregations retained unaccompanied °singing. Cut hair and the wearing of slacks by women members became commonplace, as did the wearing of jewelry. Participation in competitive °sports became a structured part of school programs, and theater (°dramatic arts) and °motion picture attendance became acceptable. Following careful study processes the °prayer veil for women became optional in many conferences. °Divorce and remarriage was also studied on a conference and a congregational level and restrictions were eased.

The increasing face-to-face contacts in °service projects at home and abroad challenged a °nonresistance expressed primarily by passive withdrawal. In 1961 a new statement, "The Christian Witness to the State," was adopted by general conference and appended to the 1951 statment, "A Declaration of Christian Faith and Commitment with Respect to War, Peace, and Nonresistance." Although the position outlined in the new statement remained controversial, it supported a much more active °peace witness than had previously been affirmed (°sociopolitical activism, °church-state relations).

A change in church °polity on the congregational and conference level accompanied a church-wide reorganization study which was initiated in the mid-1960s. There was a general return to congregational autonomy, with conferences being advisory. Some of the conferences continued to administer programs such as missions and °voluntary service. On the congregational level the °bishop, °°preacher, °°deacon pattern was altered in many areas to that of pastor or pastoral team, together with a church council or a board of elders or both. Increasingly ministers were salaried, in some cases also seminary trained, although part-time ministry, with or without special training, continued. In some instances a conference minister performed many of the functions earlier carried out by the bishop. In other areas overseers performed these functions. Conference training programs which supplemented seminary training programs were initiated. °Women began serving in ministry: some were ordained, serving as pastors or co-pastors; many more served as part of a team ministry.

Following an extensive study process, the various regional conferences in the Mennonite Church (MC) in the United States and Canada became organized in a Mennonite General Assembly, a structure formally approved at a Constitutional and General Assembly held at Kitchener, Ont., Aug. 16-19, 1971. The assembly is made up of delegates proportionately representing the participating conferences. It meets biennially. A moderator is selected to serve one biennium as assistant moderator and the following biennium as moderator. The work of the general assembly is carried forward by an executive secretary and board and agency secretaries who, together with regional conference representatives, make up a general board.

A nominating committee develops a constituency-wide slate of nominees from which individuals are elected or affirmed to the various committees and boards by vote of the delegates to the general assembly. Women participate on the boards and committees, and in administrative positions. A Council of

Faith, Life, and Strategy discerns issues needing consideration and reports directly to the general board and the general assembly.

The general board of the general assembly coordinates the work of five program boards: Mennonite Board of Congregational Ministries, Mennonite Board of Education, Mennonite Mutual Aid Board, Mennonite Publication Board, and Mennonite Board of Missions. Each program board is represented at the general board level through its executive secretary, and in turn is advised by its own board composed of representatives from constituent congregations and conferences. The five boards have independent budgets which are reviewed by the general board and presented to the general assembly for approval.

The Mennonite Board of Congregational Ministries has departments responsible for services to congregational education, evangelism, family life, and leadership. Each department is directed by a staff secretary, who is advised by a commission representing the constituency. Additional departments deal with peace and service concerns, congregational program planning, °stewardship, °worship and the arts, and youth ministries. The board maintains a Ministerial Information Center to assist with pastoral placement. Approximately 50 church °camps, campgrounds, retreat, and conference centers relate to the board through the Mennonite Camping Association.

The Mennonite Board of Education gives guidance to the operation of three colleges and two °seminaries. It also works in a coordinating and consulting relationship with 11 Mennonite high schools (coordinated by the Mennonite °Secondary Education Council) and 23 elementary schools.

The Mennonite Board of Missions (°mission boards) is headquartered in Elkhart, Ind., with a regional office in Harrisonburg, Va. Its work is carried on through a Home Ministries Division, an Overseas Ministries Division, and an Administrative Resources Division. (The Eastern Mennonite Board of Missions [Lancaster Conference], the Virginia Mennonite Board of Missions, and the Conservative Mennonite [Conference] Board of Missions and Charities [Rosedale Mennonite Missions] are individual conference mission boards with extensive programs, including work outside North America.)

The fourth program board, Mennonite Mutual Aid, has experienced vast growth, and serves General Conference Mennonite Church, Mennonite Brethren, and other members of the Mennonite Central Committee constituency.

The Mennonite Publication Board, through the Mennonite Publishing House and Herald Press, publishes books, congregational literature, and periodicals, including the denominational organ, the *Gospel Herald.* Seven bookstores serve the constituency. °Christian education publications have included far reaching inter-Mennonite publishing projects such as the Foundation Series for °Sunday schools.

The *Mennonite Yearbook,* published annually until 1985 and biennially thereafter by Mennonite Publishing House, contains listings of conferences and congregations, their membership, and designated leaders. Sections detail the staff and programs of the

five boards and provide information on inter-Mennonite projects and overseas programs. The directory gives a listing of Mennonite-sponsored °health and human services, including child welfare services; °hospitals; mental health centers; and retirement °homes and nursing homes. The numerous regional Mennonite archives and °historical libraries are also listed. The directory also supplies information on overseas Mennonite churches and programs, including a world Mennonite directory and information on other Mennonite bodies including the Beachy Amish Mennonite Fellowship and the Eastern Pennsylvania Mennonite Church. The *Yearbook's* listings of Mennonite congregations by states and provinces include all the Mennonite and Brethren in Christ bodies in North America (Amish and Hutterites are not included).

The Historical Committee of the Mennonite Church is directly responsible to the general board through the committee's executive secretary. The executive secretary is responsible for the Archives of the Mennonite Church located at Goshen, Ind. Also directly relating to the general board are the °Afro-American Mennonite Association, the °Concilio Nacional de Iglesias Menonitas Hispanas, and the °Women's Missionary and Services Commission.

Task forces have been regularly appointed by the general assembly to prepare study documents on issues of concern to the church. These include *The °Holy Spirit in the Life of the Church* (1977); *°Biblical Interpretation in the Life of the Church* (1977); *Affirming Our Faith in Word and Deed* (1979); *Leadership and °Authority in the Life of the Church* (1979); and *°Justice and the Christian Witness* (1981). General assembly study committees active in 1987 were dealing with human °sexuality, women in leadership, revision of the °confession of faith (jointly with General Conference Mennonite Church), spirituality, war °taxes, and homosexuality.

Not all Mennonites endorsed the pervasive changes of the 1960s and 1970s (°conservative Mennonites). A conservative "breaking away" took place in the Pacific Coast Conference ca. 1966-67. Segments withdrew from the Lancaster and Franconia conferences in 1969-70, forming the Eastern Pennsylvania Mennonite Church. Many of the groups listed above as not participating in the Mennonite Church (MC) General Assembly also opposed aspects of change and chose not to join the general assembly when it was formed. Others within the assembly membership formed a °Fellowship of Concerned Mennonites in 1983. Several conferences designed to address their concerns were held at Laurelville, Pa., in 1984, 1985, and 1986.

In the 1970s the °charismatic movement, which was international in scope, permeated both leadership and laity in the Mennonite Church (MC). While some charismatic congregations were formed, both charismatics and noncharismatics endeavored to create an atmosphere of mutual cooperation and acceptance. Mennonite Renewal Services, founded in 1975, serves selected needs of Mennonites involved in the charismatic movement and functions as a liaison between Mennonite charismatics and denominational leaders.

The two Mennonite Church (MC) conferences in

Ontario, together with the Conference of United Mennonite Churches in Ontario (GCM), formed the °Mennonite Conference of Eastern Canada in 1988. The General Assembly of the Mennonite Church met jointly with the triennial session of the General Conference Mennonite Church at Bethlehem, Pa., in 1983, and in a second joint meeting at Normal, Ill., in 1988. Numerous local congregations are affiliated with both MC and GCM bodies. BSH

MWH (1978), 357-62; *MWH* (1984), 142; *MC Yearbook*; *Proceedings of Mennonite General Conference, 1955-1969*; *Proceedings of Mennonite General Assembly, 1971-1985*; *MEA* 1-4; Beulah Stauffer Hostetler, "Midcentury Change in the Mennonite Church," *MQR*, 60 (1986), 58-82; idem, *American Mennonites and Protestant Movements* (Scottdale, 1987), esp. 279-329; Theron F. Schlabach, *Gospel versus Gospel: Mission and the Mennonite Church, 1863-1944* (Scottdale, 1980); J. C. Wenger, *The Mennonite Church in America* (Scottdale, 1966); F. H. Epp, *Mennonites in Canada, I* and *II*; Urbane Peachey, comp., *Mennonite Statements on Peace and Social Concerns, 1900-1978* (Akron, Pa.: MCC, 1980); Richard C. Detweiler, *Mennonite Statements on Peace, 1915-1966* (Scottdale, 1968); H. Ralph Hernley, *The Compassionate Community* (Scottdale: Assoc. of Menn. Aid Societies, 1970); Wilbert R. Shenk and others, *The Challenge of Church Growth* (Scottdale, 1973); J. R. Burkholder and Calvin Redekop, eds., *Kingdom, Cross, and Community* (Scottdale, 1976); Rich, *Mennonite Women* (1983); Guy F. Hershberger, *The Way of the Cross in Human Relations* (Scottdale, 1958); Kauffman/Harder, *Anabaptism Four C. Later* (1975); Melvin Gingerich, *Mennonite Attire Through Four Centuries* (Breinigsville, Pa.: The Pennsylvania German Society, 1970); Edward Yoder, *Edward: Pilgrimage of a Mind*, ed. by Ida Yoder (Irwin, Pa.: Ida Yoder and Virgil E. Yoder, 1985); Paul Erb, *Orie O. Miller: The Story of a Man and an Era* (Scottdale, 1969); John L. Ruth, *Maintaining the Right Fellowship* (Scottdale, 1984); Willard H. Smith, *Mennonites in Illinois* (Scottdale, 1983); Grant Stoltzfus, *Mennonites of Ohio and Eastern Conference* (Scottdale, 1969); Paul Erb, *South Central Frontiers: A History of the South Central Mennonite Conference* (Scottdale, 1974); J. C. Wenger, *Mennonites in Indiana and Michigan* (Scottdale, 1961); John A. Lapp, *India* (1972); James O. Lehman, *Creative Congregationalism* (Smithville, Ohio: Oak Grove Mennonite Church, 1978); J. C. Wenger, *The Yellow Creek Mennonites: The Original Congregations of Western Elkhart County* (Goshen, Indiana: Yellow Creek Mennonite Church, 1985); John M. Drescher, "The World Today, A Threat and a Challenge," *GH*, 56, no. 45 (Nov. 12, 1963) 1001, 1004, 1021; Paul Mininger, "Limitations on Nonconformity," *MQR*, 24 (1950), 163-69; idem, "Our World, Our Church, and Our College," *MQR*, 37 (1963), 279-309.

Mennonite Church in India (ME III:20), is the official title of the Mennonite congregations in the Dhamtari area of Madhya Pradesh. Its antecedents lie in the efforts of the American Mennonite Mission of the Mennonite [MC] Board of Missions and Charities (MBMC). The Mennonite churches in what later became °Madhya Pradesh State came into existence with the nucleus of unclaimed boys and girls after the Mennonite (MC) famine relief work at °Dhamtari closed in 1901. An elementary school was started to educate the boys and girls, which developed into an English medium high school with the first class of boys graduating in 1912. The orphanage and middle school for girls were moved to °°Balodgahan in 1906. Gradually several primary schools were opened in different villages where mission stations were started.

The Mennonite Church Conference was organized at the Bethel Church in Balodgahan on the first Tuesday in January 1912 according to a constitution drawn up by two visiting representatives of the MBMC together with the pioneering missionaries. There were four congregations at that time, all pastored by missionaries. Total membership of the church was 488 with 36 delegates (12 missionaries and 24 nationals).

At the conference session in 1929 the constitution was revised. Attending as voting members of the conference were 7 ordained missionaries and 9 ordained national delegates together with 53 lay representatives from 7 congregations. At that time there were 1,279 church members with an additional 735 unbaptized persons participating in congregations.

By 1947 a number of trained members were available for leadership in administrative, educational, evangelistic, medical, and pastoral services so that the national members expected responsibilities and treatment on an equal basis. With national independence, the government instructed the foreign agencies to hand over responsibilities to the nationals as soon and as far as possible. The MBMC showed good faith by calling a national delegate to the fourth Mennonite World Conference held in the United States in 1948. The church was ready for participation and sharing in responsibilities. The MBMC agreed and formed a unification commission in 1950 comprising six missionaries and 6 nationals to work on a constitution with the secretary of the board. According to this new constitution, which took effect on July 1, 1952, mission and church were merged into one. After independence Christians took their original °caste and tribal names for their surnames. The "Mennonite Church" name was changed to "Mennonite Church in India" in the new constitution.

In 1952 the executive committee was enlarged from 10 to 14 members. It administered on behalf of MBMC and the church through councils for the areas of education, institutions, evangelism, pastoral care, and medical work. At that time there were 10 congregations with a membership of 1,470 plus 1,205 unbaptized children and youth. There were 67 voting representatives at the 1952 conference session (5 ordained missionaries, 8 ordained nationals, 6 deacons, 1 deaconess, and 47 lay delegates). The provisions for lay delegates are still in force in 1987.

The government strongly objected to evangelism with the use of foreign funds. As a result, the church retired a number of °lay evangelists in 1956 with financial aid to these people offered by MBMC. Since then evangelism has been the responsibility of every church member, which has been quite ineffective. In another change, which was introduced on July 1, 1960, independent autonomous boards for education, medical and literature services were registered and the church became fully responsible for congregational and evangelistic services in accordance with the constitution registered with the government. Thus the church became self-witnessing, self-propagating, self-supporting, self-governing, independent, and indigenous. MBMC cooperates in some new projects on a partnership basis.

With education now chiefly the responsibility of the Indian government, church-sponsored village schools were closed. At present (1987) there are primary, higher secondary schools at Dhamtari, and primary and middle schools at Balodgahan. An English medium school started in 1974 has developed into a full high school and is maintained by the education board at Dhamtari.

Of the 16 congregations in 1986, 5 are large, 5 medium-size, and 6 are small; with membership ranging between 810 and 17. Four congregations are served by full-time fully paid pastors, five by resident ordained part-time ministers, four by locally ordained deacons and three by appointed local lay leaders. Three second-generation Mennonite youths, sons of lay evangelists, graduated from Jabalpur Methodist Seminary (1932-40) and four young men graduated from Bangarpet Bible School in south India. Two of these persons taught in secular school while others served or are serving as evangelists and pastors. Since 1960 MBMC has offered free seminary training on the ThB and BD levels at Union Biblical Seminary (Yavatmal; later at Pune in

Maharashtra State). By 1986 nine young men have graduated from the seminary at Pune, of whom 6 are working for non-Mennonite institutions after serving the church for bond periods, but maintaining their church membership, while the other 3 are serving as Mennonite pastors.

The first deacons (4) were ordained in 1913, the first deaconess in 1947, and the first Indian pastor in 1927. The first Indian bishop was ordained on May 8, 1955; the second bishop in 1965. In 1986 there were 13 deacons, 1 deaconess, 14 ministers, and 2 bishops working in 16 congregations.

Original membership was formed by conversion and baptisms of the orphan boys and girls, and the converted families brought from other areas for labor and help. There have been few conversions

DEACONS, MINISTERS, AND BISHOPS OF THE MENNONITE CHURCH IN INDIA, DHAMTARI, MADHYA PRADESH, 1900-1980
Compiler: John A. Friesen

Name	Date of Birth	Deacon	Minister	Bishop	Died
Manohar Sukhlal	1888?	1913	1931		1960
Elisha Munshi	1880?	1913			1960?
Kuarman	1890?	1913			1915
Pershadi B. Panchayat	1885?	1913	1938		1978
Mukut Bhelwa	1884	1913	1936		1959
Sadhuram	1890	1916			1965
Daniel B. Peter	1894	1916			1973
John Haidar	1890	1921	1932		1981
Budhbal	1895	1923			1930?
Shivraj Singh	1890?	1926			1979?
Isa Baksh	1890?		1927		1970?
Malwa Kalib	1898	1931			1970?
Obed P. Ram	1908	1933	1945		1977?
Sim Kushal	1907	1938			1973
Harchand	1908	1940			1960
Daniel A. Sonwani	1911		1945		
Pyarelal J. Malagar	1920		1945	1955	
Obdiah P. Lall	1913		1945	1965	
Stephen S. Solomon	1914	1947	1970		
Phoebe Solomon	1917	1947			
Eli Tatu	1919	1952			
Irenius Joseph	1923		1953		
Joseph Bhelwa	1924	1968	1978		
Chandra Kumar Jebiar	1928		1957		
Kiyaram Jivanlal	1925	1968	1978	1987	
Puran Chand	1922?	1970	1977		
Theophilus P. Singh	1932		1970		
Itwari S. Rawat	1928?	1976			
G. S. Paul	1930?	1976	1978		
Daniel Dasru	1916		1977		
Shant Kumar Kunjam	1950?		1977		
Madhukar Das	1955?		1977		
Christopher Nath	1947?		1978		

Italic   = Ordination revoked by MC India
boldface = Former evangelists for Am. Menn. Miss. or MC India
?   = Estimated date

Sources: MBM Annual Reports; *Mennonite Yearbook*, 1979; family members.

since and most of the membership today comes from children of the original members.

In 1946 a Hindu boy studying in a church school acknowledged Jesus Christ as personal Savior a year before his graduation from high school. On Sept. 26-27, 1972, from 60 families belonging to the Satnami caste, 79 men and women took baptism in Jhara, their own village, about 200 km. (125 mi.) from Dhamtari. Then 10 young men from the same village and community were baptized in Zion church, Sankra, during the conference session on Oct. 23, 1972. A resident evangelist was appointed there for almost a decade to teach, preach, and strengthen the people in the faith. Land was purchased for building a chapel and parsonage. Almost all of these people reverted in 1981 except three or four, of whom one graduated from seminary and worked in village church areas for a few years. He is now working among non-Christian students with his converted brother-in-law in Haridwar, a pilgrimage center for Hindus.

There have been two divisions in the church for different reasons. On Nov. 10, 1977, 34 families with 68 baptized members and some 60 unbaptized individuals formed a new Mennonite group in Balodgahan. The other division took place on Oct. 2, 1984, because of disagreements about administrative actions by church leaders. The protesting group separated as the "Ad Hoc Mennonite Church in India." Efforts at reunion are underway. In 1968 a few families joined two Pentecostal groups in Dhamtari.

Sunday school, worship, and women's meetings are normally weekly on Sunday morning. Sunday school is limited to children. The children are absent from worship services which have singing, responsive reading, Bible reading, sermon, offering and announcements. The sanctuaries are full when there are special services with outside speakers and music programs, or competitions, and healing activities.

Traditonally communion services were held three times a year (spring, fall, winter). The rule that those who do not partake at least once a year should be excommunicated has not been enforced. Communion services are led by a bishop or a minister after regular worship, and emblems are distributed by ordained members. Feetwashing customarily comes after taking the emblems. Weddings are performed mostly in a simple way without recordings, band bugles, dancing, and dowry demands. Electric light decorations are now becoming common as well as suits in place of the dhoti (shirt) for the groom. Brides dress in a white sari. Only the affluent wear jewelry. Song, Bible reading, and a sermon precede the exchange of vows and joining of hands. Marriage is not sealed with a ring, but in the holy name of the Lord God for life. Marriage is a lifelong bond and there is no °divorce under any circumstances, neither is there any question of homosexual marriage. When marriages break up divorce is not granted, nor is civil marriage or civil divorce accepted by the church. A feast follows wedding ceremonies and gifts are given to the couple at dinner.

The Mennonite Church in India believes the Scriptures to be the very Word of God, inspired by God and the Holy Spirit and written by his chosen and appointed persons. As the Word appeared in flesh in the form of Jesus Christ, it is with us in the form of the Bible. We believe in what it actually says, its literal and spiritual meanings, not human interpretations.   SNS

P. J. Malagar, *MC India* (1981); John A. Lapp, *India* (1972), 168; *MWH* (1978), 142-44, (1984), 32.

Mennonite Church of Guatemala. See Iglesia Menonita de Guatemala.

Mennonite Church of Trinidad and Tobago. Virginia Mennonite Board of Mission (MC) work in Trinidad began in June 1969 with a weekly *Way to Life* radio broadcast. This was followed by medical work with victims of Hansen's disease (leprosy). The first public worship service was held in Diego Martin on June 23, 1974. This group became the first established congregation. On Dec. 4, 1983, a second congregation formed in Cunupia. Additional outreach occurred in Charlieville, Las Lomas no. 1, and Brother's Road. People of African, Chinese, and Indian ancestry have been joined in a common bond in Christ. There has been a strong emphasis on local leadership with Trinidadian teaching, preaching, leading worship, guiding youth groups, and involved in decision making. Membership in 1987 was 77.   RFK

MWH (1984), 103.

Mennonite Community of Zaire. See Église du Christ au Zaire, Communauté Mennonite.

Mennonite Conference of Eastern Canada is the result of an integration of three Ontario Mennonite groups: the °Mennonite Conference of Ontario and Quebec (5,110 members, 1987), °Western Ontario Mennonite Conference (3,195 members, 1987), and the °Conference of United Mennonite Churches in Ontario (5,192 members, 1987). The first two groups are conferences of the Mennonite Church (MC). The last is a provincial conference related to the Conference of Mennonites in Canada, which is one of the districts of the General Conference Mennonite Church.

The Mennonite Conference of Eastern Canada is rooted in a long history of cooperation including the formation of the Nonresistant Relief Organization (1917), Conference of Historic Peace Churches (1940s), a joint Mennonite Mission and Service Board (1950s), and Conrad Grebel College (1960s). In 1973 the three conferences formed an Inter-Mennonite Conference (Ontario) to direct the growing cooperative work in mission, education, and congregational resources. The separate conference structures remained intact, and they reserved the right to make final decisions on policy and budgets.

A 1979 proposal to amalgamate all three groups was defeated. In 1986, however, the conferences decided to "integrate" (this term, it was felt, implied less of a melting pot than "merger" or "amalgamation") by 1988.

In March 1987 delegates from the three conferences approved a structural model for the proposed integration. They also decided to become associate members of each others' North American general conferences for a six-year get-acquainted period rather than leave wider affiliations up to each individual congregation. The Mennonite Conference of Eastern Canada was officially inaugurated on Mar. 1, 1988. RRe

Inter-Mennonite Cooperation.

Menn. Rep. (Nov. 9, 1987), 5; *MC Yearbook* (1988-89), 52-54.

Mennonite Conference of Ontario and Quebec (MC) (ME IV:67) was formerly known as the Mennonite Conference of Ontario. The rediscovery in 1985 of annotations in the Bishop Jacob Moyer Bible indicated that annual meetings of Ontario Mennonite ministers began in 1810, placing the conference's formation earlier than indicated in ME IV.

Conference missions work expanded into Quebec in 1956 when Harold and Pauline Reesor and Tilman and Janet Martin began study and outreach in that province. In 1987 there were ca. 140 members in five congregations in Quebec. The growth of this work led to a change in the conference name in 1982. In 1987 the Hmong and Spanish languages, in addition to the French language used by Quebec congregations, were spoken in congregations affiliated with the conference.

Leadership style changed dramatically in the 1970s as ordained men took a less dominant role in conference organization. The first lay moderator of conference was elected in 1976; by 1983 only two ministers were part of the executive committee. In 1973 Doris Gascho became the first woman to serve as congregational chairperson. In 1987 there were 12 licensed or ordained women ministers in the conference.

Formal cooperation with the Western Ontario Mennonite Conference and the Conference of United Mennonite Churches in Ontario increased through the formation of the Inter-Mennonite Conference (Ontario) in 1973. Merger of these conferences into the °Mennonite Conference of Eastern Canada was approved in 1987 and implemented in 1988.

In 1960 six ordained men, led by Bishops Curtis Cressman and Moses Roth, withdrew from conference and together with some members of Wilmot Township area congregations, formed the °Conservative Mennonite Church of Ontario.

In 1986 the Mennonite Conference of Ontario and Quebec had 47 congregations with 5,110 members. SSt

E. Reginald Good, "Jacob Moyer's Mennonite Church Records: An interpretive sketch," *Mennogespräch*, 3 (1985), 1-3; *Yearbook* (Inter-Mennonite Conference [Ontario]), 13 (1986); Mennonite Conference of Ontario and Quebec Collection and Inter-Mennonite Conference (Ontario) Collection, both in the Mennonite Archives of Ontario, Conrad Grebel College, Waterloo, Ontario; *MC Yearbook* (1986-87), 80-82, (1988-89), 52-54.

Mennonite Disaster Service (MDS). See Disaster Services.

Mennonite Economic Development Associates (MEDA). The emergence and metamorphosis of MEDA is highly instructive of the changes that have taken place in the Mennonite society and begs for deeper analysis. The original MEDA emerged in 1952 as a response to requests from Mennonites in Paraguay for assistance by North American Mennonite entrepreneurs, since Mennonite Central Committee (MCC) was not in a position to respond directly. Among MEDA's primary objectives and procedures were to help people to help themselves by entering into partnership agreements, with initiative from local people for economically viable business ventures.

Because the Paraguayan experiment was successful, the program was expanded to projects in Tanzania, Somalia, Zaire, Ethiopia, Kenya, Nigeria, Ghana, Sicily, Indonesia, Vietnam, India, Philippines, Colombia, Belize, Costa Rica, Guatemala, Honduras, Mexico, and Bolivia. Many of the projects were only moderately successful for a variety of reasons, including cultural discontinuities.

In the meantime, the °°Mennonite Community Association (MCA) movement seemed no longer to serve the needs of non-farming Menonites entering the broad commercial and industrial world. Together with Mennonite colleges, the MCA formed Church, Industry and Business Associates (CIBA) in 1969 to make church and community resources available to Mennonites in business and industry. CIBA's objectives were basically the education, counsel, inspiration, and mutual sharing which were missing in the institutional church setting. Regional seminars on ethics in °business, annual conventions, a journal called *Marketplace*, and relations with college business departments and their students were some of the main activities. In 1973 Mennonite Business Associates (MBA) emerged in the eastern United States. CIBA and MBA merged to produce MIBA (Mennonite Industry and Business Associates) in November 1976 (*Marketplace*, Jan. 1977).

After several joint meetings, MEDA and MIBA were officially merged in November 1981. The "new" MEDA is a pronounced synthesis of the old MEDA interests and the newer MBA and CIBA concerns. There is a domestic section (with offices in Akron, Pa.) which has an educational, inspirational, and discernment mission expressed in annual conventions, regional chapters and programs, MEDAnet, (an employment service for Mennonite College students in business), and other activities. The international section, headquartered in Winnipeg, carries forward the economic °development objectives, mainly in underdeveloped nations where Mennonite missions have operated. It is supporting extensive small business development and °cooperatives. A cocoa-producing cooperative in Haiti and woodworking business in Jamaica are recent thriving examples. There is considerable government support for MEDA international programs, especially from the Canadian International Development Agency (CIDA).

The "new" MEDA is an expression of lay concern regarding the interplay of faith and economics with surprisingly little official church support and recognition. Clearly the traditional rural church knew how to integrate the farming occupation into its ecclesiology and faith, but the Mennonite church community has yet to learn how to relate to the burgeoning commercial and business membership. CWR

J. Winfield Fretz, *The MEDA Experiment* (Waterloo: Conrad Press, 1978); idem. *Immigrant Group Settlements in Paraguay* (North Newton: Bethel College, 1962); *Marketplace: A Journal for Christians in Business* (Winnipeg: MEDA, 1971-).

Mennonite Encyclopedia, The, published in four volumes from 1955 to 1959, is the most accessible and authoritative reference work available on a host of Anabaptist and Mennonite topics. Published jointly by the Mennonite Church, the General Conference Mennonite Church, and the Mennonite Brethren Church, the set contains maps, illustrations, and 13,688 articles contributed by more than 2,700 writers.

In 1945, at a meeting of the Mennonite Research Fellowship in Bluffton, Ohio, historian C. Henry °°Smith proposed that American Mennonites translate and expand the °°*Mennonitisches Lexikon,* a German project that had been nearly halted during World War II. Smith and his colleagues formed a "*Lexikon* Committee." Three years later, the scholarly effort had grown to include a network of editors and a 50-member council representing 13 Mennonite groups and 6 non-Mennonite denominations. Smith's death in 1948, however, was a blow to the project.

The *Encyclopedia's* continuing editor, Harold S. °Bender, and associate editor, Cornelius °Krahn, wanted to stimulate young adults to pursue Anabaptist and Mennonite studies and sought to share contemporary research with a wide circle of non-Mennonite church historians and theologians. They included articles of the following types: doctrinal, denominational, institutional, ecclesiastical, biographical, and cultural. They also included articles on publications and on family and place names. Less than one-sixth of the completed work contained translated *Lexikon* material.

Editors Bender and Krahn researched and wrote many of the major articles. The historical perspectives of the two men differed markedly; however, they retained their cooperative partnership. Bender supervised scholarship pertaining to the South German and Swiss Anabaptists and Mennonites, while Krahn assumed responsibility for topics related to the Dutch, Prussian, and Russian streams of Mennonite history. Nanne van der °Zijpp of The Netherlands also contributed substantially. Managing editor Melvin °Gingerich and translator Elizabeth Horsch Bender provided valuable editorial assistance.

During the past 30 years, researchers have noted various weaknesses of the *Encyclopedia*. Some point to unevenness in the quality of writing and lament the dominance of European and North American subjects. Others cite the dated quality of some articles. Still others emphasize the inadequate coverage of theological issues. In 1978, Mennonite scholars from around the world laid plans for a supplemental fifth volume.

An enduring legacy of the *Mennonite Encyclopedia* is the sense of denominational pride which guided its editors. Some contemporary scholars suggest that the *Encyclopedia* enabled Mennonites to establish themselves as a mainline Protestant church body during the post World War II years. Indeed, the publication of this inter-Mennonite reference work became a celebrated moment in the denomination's history.   RWG

Rachel Waltner, "From Anabaptism to Mennonitism: *The Mennonite Encyclopedia* as a Historical Document," *Menn. Life,* 37 (Dec. 1982), 13-19; Harold S. Bender, "*The Mennonite Encyclopedia:* Report of the Editor to the Publishing Committee," *MQR,* 38 (1964), 361-67; Melvin Gingerich, "Harold S. Bender and *The Mennonite Encyclopedia,*" *MQR,* 38 (1964), 172-74; files of the *Mennonite Encyclopedia* are located at the MC Archives, (Goshen), and at the MLA, (North Newton).

Mennonite [Evangelical] Church of Colombia. See Iglesia Evangélica Menonita de Colombia.

Mennonite Evangelical Community of Zaire. See Église du Christ au Zaire, Communauté Evangélique Mennonite.

Mennonite Foundation, Canada. The formation of Mennonite Foundation of Canada was the outgrowth of a previously chartered Mennonite Mutual Foundation, a venture of the Mennonite Conference of Ontario and Quebec, and Mennonite Foundation, an unchartered venture of the Conference of Mennonites in Canada. Conversations between the two groups began as early as 1970. A federal charter under the name of *Mennonite Foundation of Canada* was granted in December 1973. On July 1, 1974, a head office in Winnipeg managed by J. K. Klassen, and a regional office in Kitchener managed by Rufus Jutzi opened.

The purpose of the foundation was to provide °stewardship teaching and responsible use and disposition of accumulated possessions. A central thrust was counseling about wills and estate planning. Administration of various endowment funds plus a variety of charitable investment objectives became part of the program. Investments included commercial bonds and mortgages to congregations and other church-related institutions.

Initially the participating conferences were: the Conference of Mennonites in Canada (GCM), the Mennonite Conference of Ontario and Quebec (MC), the Northwest Conference of the Mennonite Church (MC), and the Western Ontario Mennonite Conference (MC). The Evangelical Mennonite Conference (1984) and the Evangelical Mennonite Mission Conference (1987) joined later.

In 1986 MFC served a constituency across Canada from offices in Calgary, Winnipeg, and Kitchener. The assets under administration were $7,250,000. RJ

MC Yearbook (1988-89), 136.

See also Inheritance; Jacob Engle Foundation; Stewardship.

Mennonite Foundation, United States (ME IV:1107), is a °stewardship service agency of the Mennonite churches. It was organized as a not-for-profit, charitable corporation by °Mennonite Mutual Aid in 1952. Tax-exempt status was granted by the Internal Revenue Service. The foundation offers estate planning and planned giving services for individuals and investment management services for congregations and church institutions. All gifts distributed by the foundation are donor directed. The foundation has no projects of its own and issues no grants. Major staff time was not used until 1965 when gift assets totaled $152,000. Since then gift assets have grown to over $68,000,000 in 1987. The foundation attempts to be self-supporting and operate on a break-even basis. Operating funds come from service charges, investments, and contributions from institutions and individuals.   PLG

MC Yearbook (1988-89), 112, 136; annual reports of the foundation are available from its office at Goshen, Ind.

See also Inheritance; Jacob Engle Foundation; Stewardship.

Mennonite Health Association (MHA). See Health Education.

Mennonite Medical Association. See Health Education; Health Services; Medicine.

Mennonite Men (GCM) (ME III:631). In the General Conference Mennonite Church, the need for help in church planting had the most to do with the revival of the Mennonite Men's organization. The district conference men's groups often had some challenging projects but the General Conference Mennonite men had completed theirs and had not adopted new ones.

In 1983 at the Bethlehem, Pa., General Conference sessions, representatives from the Commission on Home ministries and Mennonite Men presented a plan to help new congregations handle the burden of buying a new meeting place. The concern was that new congregations were so burdened with debts and payments that little energy was left for evangelism, welcoming new members, and caring for the present ones. The General Conference Mennonite Men decided to sponsor the plan for three years. In 1988, this Tenth Men Church Building Plan is continuing to assist new churches and has to date contributed 171,000 in grants.

Mennonite Men are also active on the district conference level. A number of local congregations have active men's groups participating in projects. Mennonite Men organizations in the Eastern District, Central District, Northern District, Pacific District, and Western District meet at least annually and assist a variety of projects from leadership training and seminary education to camps, youth work, and disaster relief.

There appears to be strong support for a revitalized program for men throughout the General Conference as shown by a survey completed in 1986. In 1986 a task force approved by the General Conference at Saskatoon, Sask., began efforts to continue development of the various levels of the program, and to coordinate it with the work of °Women in Mission (GCM). The General Conference Mennonite Men employed Randall Kaufman as a part-time administrator on Feb. 1, 1987.   ESB/IDV

GCM Handbook (1988), 97.

Mennonite Mission in Ecuador. See Misión Evangélica Menonita en Ecuador.

Mennonite Missionary Study Fellowship. See Mission; Missionary Education.

Mennonite Mutual Aid (MMA) (ME III:632) was incorporated in 1945 as an Indiana nonprofit corporation sponsored by the Mennonite Church (MC). Its purpose was to provide a means for members, congregations, and church communities in the United States to carry out the historic Anabaptist and New Testament practice of stewardship of material and financial resources, and to share in times of crisis and hardship.

In the two decades following 1945 additional corporations were formed to accomplish the purpose of °mutual aid and °stewardship ministries. In 1967 these corporations were consolidated under one board. In 1988 MMA consisted of eight corporations.

Mennonite Mutual Aid, Inc. (1945), administers salaries and office services for 210 employees and coordinates the administration of other MMA entities. °*Mennonite Foundation* (1952) is a tax exempt stewardship service agency. *Mennonite Automobile Aid* (ME IV:1106), organized in 1954, provides comprehensive and collision coverage, and avoids °lawsuits. Approximately 25,000 vehicles are enrolled. °°*Mennonite Church Buildings* (1956) formerly provided investment opportunities and financing for institutions and congregations. This program is being phased out. MCB is the tax exempt corporate entity that holds title to MMA buildings and equipment. *Menno Insurance Service* (1957) enables MMA to broker °insurance products to members and church institutions. This includes employee benefit management, casualty, and property products. Approximately 2,500 policies are in force. *Mennonite Retirement Trust* a tax exempt corporation formed in 1963, provides °pension plans for church workers and employees of church institutions. There are approximately 4,500 participants. *Mennonite Mutual Aid Association* is a tax exempt fraternal benefit society organized in 1965. It provides health insurance, life insurance, and retirement annuities. Fraternal benefits provide beyond-contract assistance and grants to members and participating churches. Educational programs include wellness, health ethics, safe driving, stewardship, and mutual aid. There are approximately 53,500 adult participants in health plans, 6,400 persons covered by life insurance, and 3,800 annuity certificates. *ShareNet Insurance, Inc.* (1987), provides group health, life, and disability insurance plans for congregations, institutions, and businesses.

These eight corporations, known as Mennonite Mutual Aid (MMA) are governed by a 17-person board appointed or elected by Mennonite Church (10 members); General Conference Mennonite Church (5 members); and Mennonite Brethren (2 members). The board appoints a president who is responsible for administration through vice presidents appropriate to meet the needs of the organization.

MMA is inter-Mennonite in its board and membership. It is also a program board of the Mennonite Church (MC), with a formal relationship to the Mennonite Church General Board. MMA is also accountable to the broader Anabaptist constituency through its inter-Mennonite board and through its members.

The Mennonite Mutual Aid Association states that "Mennonite and related Anabaptists" qualify for membership. It serves the broad spectrum of Mennonites, Brethren in Christ, the Church of the Brethren, and others whose roots and history grow out of the Anabaptist and °Believers' Church movements.

In the mid-1980s MMA decentralized its distribution activities, working with regional advisory committees and placing representatives in many church communities. The network of congregational representatives was given new focus in an effort to promote mutual aid in local communities and in congregations. MMA cooperates with other mutual aid organizations of the Associated Mennonite Aid Societies (AMAS) so that congregations can use the rich resources of organized societies to meet needs in the congregation.

Sharing is published quarterly for members. It is a popular interest way for members to share their experiences in giving and receiving help in times of unusual need. *Tool Kit* is a simple two-page leaflet, published bimonthly. It offers information and advice for building health, safety, and life-style (°health education).

The combined assets managed by MMA on behalf of institutions and members in 1987 were $175 million (US). This includes gift investment accounts of the Mennonite Foundation, life insurance, Mennonite Retirement Trust, Annuity programs, and reserves for the various health plans.   LP

Sharing, 14, no. 2 (Summer 1980), 21, no. 4 (Winter 1987); *MHB* (July 1978); *MC Yearbook* contains statistical, organizational, and personnel information biennially.

Mennonite Nurses Association. See Nursing.

Mennonite Press. See Publishing.

Mennonite Publishing House. See Publishing.

Mennonite Renewal Services (MRS). See Charismatic Movement.

Mennonite Secondary Education Council. See Secondary Schools.

Mennonite Service Agency, Bihar, India, is a registered service agency with headquarters at P. O. Chandwa, Dist. Palamau, Bihar, India. It was established in 1967 as a result of the famine of 1966-67 in the whole of Palamau district in South Bihar. It serves the relief and development needs of the area. It is funded by the Mennonite Central Committee and the Church's Auxiliary for Social Action (CASA) a relief and development wing of the National Council of Churches in India. The director in 1987 is M. Bhengra who has served in this position since 1977. Among the immediate beneficiaries of the work of MSA have been the members of the °Bihar Mennonite Kalisiya who are mostly rural marginal farmers.   PJM

Mennonite Sonlight Mission, Haiti. See Église Mennonite Sonlight Mission.

Mennonite Studies. Mennonite studies is a relatively new discipline, combining research, teaching and publication in the area of Mennonite °history, °theology, °culture, and °literature.

The impetus for Mennonite studies came from the older Mennonite colleges in the United States, notably Goshen College in Indiana and Bethel College in North Newton, Kansas, where such scholars as Harold S. °Bender, John °°Horsch, Cornelius °Krahn, and Robert Kreider established and promoted vigorous programs of teaching, research and publication. The fruit of their academic and scholarly activity led to the founding of two journals: *The Mennonite Quarterly Review*, published at Goshen College since 1927, and *Mennonite Life*, published at Bethel College since 1946.

The groundwork done by these institutions, especially their research into Anabaptist sources, resulted among Mennonite institutions in North America in a greater interest in the life and faith of Anabaptists and Mennonites. Whereas in the first half of the 20th c. Mennonite courses were hardly ever included in the curricula of some Mennonite institutions, in the second half of this century Mennonite colleges in the United States and Canada began to devote more time and effort to Mennonite studies.

One of the most successful Mennonite studies programs is the Institute of Mennonite Studies of Associated Mennonite Biblical Seminaries of Elkhart, Ind. Led by C. J. Dyck for many years, the institute's list of scholarly publications and conferences is impressive. Conrad Grebel College in Waterloo, Ont., under the leadership of Walter Klaassen, Calvin Redekop, Rodney Sawatsky, J. Winfield Fretz, and Frank H. °Epp, has also advanced Anabaptist-Mennonite studies in its teaching and research programs. In 1983 Conrad Grebel College launched its *Conrad Grebel Review*, a "journal of Christian inquiry."

In 1978 the U. of Winnipeg established a Chair in Mennonite Studies. Endowed by the government of Canada through its program of multiculturalism and by David Friesen, a Winnipeg businessman, this first and only such chair in a university was designed to teach and conduct research in the areas of Mennonite history and literature. Since 1983 the *Journal of Mennonite Studies*, edited by Harry Loewen, and various books have been published by the Chair in Mennonite Studies in cooperation with the Mennonite Literary Society and other Mennonite institutions. Encouraged by the success of the Chair in Mennonite Studies, the U. of Winnipeg established in 1985 the Mennonite Studies Centre (funded by the David Friesen family) which is to develop into an affiliated Menno Simons College by 1990. G. K. Epp was appointed the first director of the centre. The two Mennonite colleges in Winnipeg, Mennonite Brethren Bible College and Canadian Mennonite Bible College, also teach courses in Mennonite history, and the latter has a successful publications program (CMBC Publications).

Other Mennonite institutions in which Mennonite history and theology are taught and researched are: Eastern Mennonite Seminary, Harrisonburg, Va.; Bluffton College, Ohio; Tabor College, Hillsboro, Ks.; Fresno Pacific College and Mennonite Brethren Biblical Seminary at Fresno, Cal., and Columbia Bible College, Clearbrook, B.C. The journal *Direction* is published by a variety of Mennonite Brethren schools and program boards. Centers for Mennonite

Brethren Studies were established at Fresno, Hillsboro, and Winnipeg in 1974. The center at Fresno was preceded by a Mennonite Bethren historical library affiliated with Mennonite Brethren Biblical Seminary and its predecessors, beginning in the early 1960s. A large number of °historical libraries, °museums, °archives, and °interpretation centers have been established in recent years. *Festival Quarterly* (1972-) is a leading journal for Mennonite art and °folklore; *Pennsylvania Mennonite Heritage* (1978) is one of the larger °periodicals published by historical libraries and societies.

In Europe research and scholarship in Mennonite studies have a long and honorable tradition. The Amsterdam Mennonite Theological Seminary was the first Mennonite theological training centre in the world and its scholarship in Anabaptist studies has been considerable, including the journal published by the Dutch Mennonite historical society (Doopsgezinde Historische Kring), *Doopsgezinde Bijdragen*. In Germany the Mennonitische Geschichtsverein publishes a fine journal, *Mennonitische Geschichtsblätter*. The European Mennonite Bible School on the Bienenberg near Basel also teaches courses in Mennonite history.

Mennonite studies are not confined to Europe and North America. The Japan Anabaptist Center in Tokyo sponsors research and lectures on Anabaptist and Mennonite themes. Mennonites in Central America have established a theological journal, *Esperanza en Camino*.   HaL

JMS, (1983) special issue on Mennonite studies; Paul Schowalter, "The Mennonitische Forschungsstelle: Twentyfive Years," *MQR*, 47 (1973), 358-61.

See also Acculturation; Historical Writing; *Mennonite Encyclopedia*; Sociological Studies.

Mennonite Voluntary Service. See Voluntary Service.

Mennonite World Conference (ME III:640). The fifth Mennonite World Conference (MWC) meeting in Basel in 1952 focused on "The Church of Christ and Her Commission." This signaled a new focus in MWC assemblies. The succeeding conferences moved from a focus on historical celebration and concern for the Mennonite family to a series of deliberate themes focusing on theological issues. A list of conferences and themes follows: (6) Karlsruhe, Germany, 1957: "The Gospel of Jesus Christ in the World"; (7) Kitchener, Ont., Canada, 1962: The Lordship of Christ"; (8) Amsterdam, The Netherlands, 1967: "The Witness of the Holy Spirit"; (9) Curitiba, Brazil, 1972: Jesus Christ Reconciles"; (10) Wichita, Ks., U.S.A., 1978: "The Kingdom of God in a Changing World"; (11) Strasbourg, France, 1984: "God's People Serve in Hope"; (12) Winnipeg, Canada, 1990: "Witnessing to Christ in Today's World." The sixth conference in 1957 was notable for growing interest and attendance and an increase in the number of nations represented (12). This trend increased steadily until Mennonites from 70 countries attended the Strasbourg assembly in 1984.

The 8th assembly, held in Amsterdam, came at a historic moment when the impact of the changing character of the Mennonite world community became more dramatically visible. Growing non-Western attendance and a Sunday morning sermon by an Afro-American Mennonite civil rights activist, Vincent Harding, gave clear evidence that the dominance of German ethnic communities in the MWC sessions was already in transition. For the first time a constitution was adopted, and a conference message was issued.

This trend continued when, in contrast to the first eight conferences held in North America and Europe, the ninth was planned in another continent for the first time (Curitiba, Brazil 1972). This conference quickly became the focus of controversy as Mennonites from various regions expressed reluctance to meet in a country whose political situation generated strong protests and controversy. After careful discussion, the conference venue remained unchanged, although some persons and groups chose not to participate. The attendance, while not as large as previous conferences, was notable for a much broader balance from five continents (33 nations represented).

The question of MWC's future came to the floor in Curitiba as a major issue in light of the controversy surrounding the venue for the conference and the growing question whether MWC could survive in the face of shifts in the ethnic balance of the worldwide membership. While some were predicting the demise of MWC, its continuation was confirmed by a delegate body action that called for another conference, for strengthening the organization, and for an even greater equalization of international representation. A conference message was also adopted.

Following the ninth assembly in 1972, Erland Waltner, who had succeeded Harold S. Bender as president of MWC, resigned, and C. J. Dyck, who had served as executive secretary during the term of these two presidents, asked not to be reelected. In 1973 the presidium for the tenth assembly met in Basel and chose Million Belete of Ethiopia as its new president, the first non-Western president of MWC. Action was also taken to appoint a new executive secretary, Paul N. Kraybill. For the first time authorization was given to provide a part-time salary for a staff officer. The headquarters office was moved from Elkhart, Ind., to Rosemont, Ill. (later relocated in Lombard, Ill.).

A major task of the new presidium and its staff was to build up a stronger financial base for MWC and to develop a new model for a more equalized, international representation. The presidium gave direction to an extensive study of membership and developed a new model. The presidium was replaced by a new general council with representation from each conference which chose to affiliate with MWC. An executive committee of nine persons was planned. The general council was designed as a policy-making group. Meetings were scheduled in connection with the general assembly (now meeting every six years) and once in the midterm between assemblies. The executive committee, as a smaller group, was understood to be meeting more frequently as the group responsible for administering the work of the general council.

These new changes were incorporated in a constitutional revision which was circulated to the member conferences and then adopted at Wichita in 1978 during the tenth assembly. The initial membership of the general council totalled 86 representing 70 groups in 38 nations. The delegates were chosen on a pattern of one for the first 10,000 members, two for 10,000-25,000 and three for those groups with membership over 25,000.

The tenth assembly in Wichita in 1978 was marked by large attendance representing 48 nations. The development of a travel fund was a significant factor in enabling much broader attendance from Asia, Africa, and Central and South America. At least 100 delegates and participants from those areas were enabled to attend directly as as result of the travel subsidies made available through this fund.

A broad program involving speeches, Bible study, discussion groups, interest groups, and a wide range of musical events created a celebratory mood and a new sense of a global community in which Mennonites of widely diverse backgrounds could come together in joyous fellowship and worship.

A delegation from the Soviet Union was able to attend and was received by the audience with thunderous applause and tears of joy. For the first time in its history, MWC experienced the presence of Russian representatives, and in a real sense the East-West division created by World War II was symbolically closed. This together with the broader representation on the general council from five continents, made this the most unifying and broadening experience in Mennonite history.

Following the conference, the general council in its first meeting asked that a permanent office be established and a full-time executive secretary be employed. Paul Kraybill, who had been appointed first in 1973, was appointed to this new position. Succeeding Million Belete was a second president from a non-Western nation, Charles Christano, a pastor and conference leader from the Persatuan Gereja-Gereja Kristen Muria (Muria Synod, GKMI), of Indonesia.

In 1981 the executive office was moved to Strasbourg, France, at the request of the European Mennonite conferences to facilitate the first MWC assembly to be held in France. This event, the 11th assembly, took place in 1984 as a cooperative venture sponsored by the five Mennonite conferences in France, Switzerland, Germany, and The Netherlands. A program committee and an organizing committee were appointed representing the five conferences. Attendance and interest exceeded all expectations reaching a peak of 8,000 on Sunday morning and embracing representatives from 70 nations.

At the conclusion of the 11th assembly in Strasbourg in 1984, Ross T. Bender of Lakewood, Col., was elected to succeed Charles Christano as president for a six-year term. Following the assembly the executive office was returned to Lombard, Ill. Later in 1986 the office was moved to a nearby Chicago suburb, Carol Stream. In 1987 a branch office was opened in Winnipeg in preparation for Assembly 12 planned for July 1990.

Growing expectations and interest throughout the world call for development in the program and activities of MWC. The International Mennonite Peace Committee, an ad hoc group, was formed at Curitiba in 1972 and organized more formally at Wichita in 1978. This committee had operated independently as a gathering of persons representing international peace groups. In 1985 the committee requested and in 1986 the executive committee of MWC accepted the proposal that this become a committee under the direction of MWC. Hansulrich Gerber of Bern, Switzerland, was the first executive secretary to be appointed to this position by MWC with his office located in Bern, Switzerland. He began his service June 1, 1987.

In 1986 MWC began the publication of *Courier*, a quarterly periodical with an international staff of corresponding editors. A Spanish edition was also launched under the name of *Correo*. These two periodicals together with a biweekly news service distributed worldwide greatly enhanced the communication role of MWC.

The purpose of MWC as outlined in the new 1978 Constitution is "Fellowship, Communication, and Facilitation." The MWC as an international body represents a diverse constituency of Mennonites throughout the world. It seeks to find ways to bring into focus the common concerns of this far-flung group of people. While they seek to express their Anabaptist heritage in many different forms, they do have in common a basic understanding of Scripture and faith. Structurally, logistically, and financially many issues remain unsolved, but there is clearly an emerging awareness of global community.   PNK

MC Yearbook (1988), 163-165; *MWH* (1978); *MWH* (1984).

See also Inter-Mennonite Cooperation; Regional Mennonite Conferences.

Siaka Traoré

I am from Burkina Faso, from a Muslim family. I was trained in this religion by my parents and followed the practices of Islam to please them. But in my teen years some conflict with my father developed. I felt I should be able to worship God freely, and not be forced to do so.

After I got my school diploma I got a job in a sugar manufacturing plant. My work there was so satisfactory to the management that in eight months I had moved up four positions. This was good for me but created many difficulties with the other workers. The men who had been working there longer saw that I advanced past them, and they resented it. The ones above me in the system resented me also, fearing I would continue upward and take their places. Both groups began to work together to make life miserable for me. I was caught in the middle. This was in 1979.

I needed help from somewhere and was tempted to seek it by the ways we Africans often use—by sacrifice or by consulting those who practice magic. Instead I prayed to God to find an answer, not really sure who I was praying to. I asked God, "Who is right?" God said to me, "You must quit your job." I was puzzled and didn't want to accept this answer. But each time I prayed, the same answer came, and each time I said "No."

This struggle continued for several months until I

finally said, "God, I put my confidence in you. I'll leave my work." Everyone thought I was crazy when I left my work in the city and went back to my home village.

There I found a booklet for teaching catechism, and in reading it, I first heard of Jesus. I learned the Lord's Prayer and repeated it every day. I had not yet met any Christians.

Later I asked, "Are there any Christians or any missionaries anywhere around here?" I found out that in a town 18 km. (11 mi.) away there were some missionaries and a small church. It was the work of Africa Inter-Mennonite Mission, although that meant nothing to me then. I presented myself to them and said I wanted to go to school to learn more about the Bible. Some were not sure what to think of me, arriving like that, but when James Bertsche, the mission secretary, visited there, he said, "Maybe the Lord has sent him," and encouraged them to help me.

I went to the nearest Bible school, then to a Bible institute in Côte d'Ivoire (Ivory Coast), and then to a seminary in Bangui, Central African Republic, where I am in a five-year program.

My life now is certain—it has been prepared for me. I only need to humbly find it and follow it. It's different from the struggles I went through before. There is still struggle, but it's a positive one.

[In 1984 Siaka attended Mennonite World Conference at Strasbourg, France, as the first delegate from Burkina Faso to participate in a Mennonite World Conference general assembly.]   MH

Adapted from *Purpose* (July 27, 1986), copyright Mennonite Publishing House, Scottdale, Pa. Used by permission.

Mennonite-Your-Way-Travel Directory. See Hospitality.

Mennonitenbrüdergemeinden (Independent Umsiedler). See Umsiedler.

Mennonitengemeinde zu Mexico (Mennonite Church in Mexico) (GCM). During the late 1920s some 124 Mennonite families came to Mexico from the Soviet Union, partly as a result of efforts made by the Mennonite Colonization Board (ME III:617) to settle these Mennonites, partly because it seemed to be the only alternative for them. They came from varied church, family and geographical backgrounds in Russia, and they encountered many difficulties in trying to become established in their new homeland. Many of them used Mexico only as a stopover to Canada or the United States, but by 1927 a small group of these families had found their way to Cuauhtémoc in Chihuahua. This town was the trading center for the young Old Colony Mennonite settlement, that had begun in 1922.

Since the Old Colony Mennonite Church, then known as "Reinländer", would not accept the "Rußländer" group into its church body, these families organized their own fellowship and for some time worshiped together with the German Lutherans, who also had settled in this area. Late in 1938 these "Russian Mennonites" formally organized under the name of Hoffnungsau Gemeinde (congregation) with a Jakob Janzen, one of the immigrants, as minister and H. P. Krehbiel (GCM) from Kansas,

as elder (*Ältester*). In October 1939 the Hoffnungsau church formally joined the Western District Conference (GCM), with H. P. Krehbiel serving as their delegate. In April 1940 Jakob Janzen was authorized to officiate as elder of the newly organized church.

During the 29th General Conference (GCM) in 1941, the Hoffnungsau congregation became a member of the General Conference Mennonite Church. It was now entitled to solicit help from the Home Mission Board (ME II:800). During the next decade several German-speaking ministers from the United States and Canada served this small congregation. The Home Mission Board also provided teachers, often a preacher-teacher, for the two small schools, one in Cuauhtémoc and one in Santa Clara, where two "Rußländer" families had settled near the °Sommerfeld Mennonite colony. When, in 1968, all GCM work in foreign countries was assigned to the Commission on Overseas Mission (COM), Mexico was regarded as a foreign mission field.

During the late 1940s and early 1950s a severe drought brought hardship and even famine to the Old Colony and Sommerfeld colonies in Chihuahua. Upon the suggestion of the Hoffnungsau congregation Mennonite Central Committee (MCC) came to help with a relief program. This was the beginning of an agricultural and medical program initiated by MCC, but after August 1957 administered by the Board of Christian Service of the General Conference Mennonite Church. The agricultural program was later discontinued when the federal Instituto Nacional de Investigaciones Agricolas (INIA) opened a research center in Cuauhtémoc and hired the General Conference board's agriculturist, Philip Dyck. The Board of Christian Service and later COM also supplied the local government hospital in Cuauhtémoc with three registered nurses and one administrator until 1963. Then a clinic was established in an isolated ranch, Nuevo Namiquipa, ca. 45 km. (75 mi.) north of Cuauhtémoc, with two registered nurses and an administrator. The new federal hospital, Centro de Salud, employed one COM-sponsored worker, Tina Fehr, as hospital matron until 1979. A training school for auxiliary nurses was initiated by COM personnel both in Cuauhtémoc and Nuevo Namiquipa. In 1985 the clinic became local property with administration by a civic association composed of Mennonites from the Santa Clara and Santa Rita colonies. The Commission on Overseas Mission continued to supply two nurses.

The Hoffnungsau congregation's schools had eventually attracted students from the Old Colony and Sommerfeld Mennonite settlements. The parents of these students also began to attend the Hoffnungsau church. By 1963 these facilities had become inadequate, and the parents from the Old Colony Mennonites, together with the teacher from the Hoffnungsau school planned to build a larger school outside of the city of Cuauhtémoc, but not on Old Colony land, since the Old Colony Mennonites were opposed to the advanced school. The site chosen was Quinta Lupita, a farming area about three km. (two mi.) north of town. This school eventually came to be the first incorporated Mennonite school in Mexico that offered government-prescribed courses at elementary and °secondary levels and was administered by another local civic association called Comite pro Mejoramiento Educacional Menonita. Also during the 1960s elementary schools were established at Steinreich, ca. 25 km. (40 mi.) north of Cuauhtémoc and in the Swift Current colony.

Old Colony parents who sent their children to a "Konferenz" (GMC) school were excommunicated from the Old Colony church. Debates among Hoffnungsau church members over how best to relate to Old Colony Mennonites eventually led to a rift within the Hoffnungsau congregation. In June 1963 they severed their relations with COM workers, with the General Conference Mennonite Church and with the ostracized Old Colony families. The latter, together with COM workers, established a fellowship at Quinta Lupita, constructing a church building that could seat ca. 400 people. By 1981 the congregation had outgrown the building and a new meetingplace with capacity for ca. 800 and ample educational facilities was erected at Km. 11, Blumenau. The school continued at Quinta Lupita.

The small Santa Clara school and church fellowship disbanded due to emigration and lack of continuing growth. The remaining members joined the Steinreich school and church group, where church building, school and a school dormitory were built. In the 1970s a GCM-affiliated fellowship was also formed in the Swift Current colony and a church and school building were constructed in Burwalde.

A Christian bookstore was initiated by the Quinta Lupita congregation and later administered by *Die Mennonitische Post*. It serves all the different Mennonite and Mexican Evangelical groups in and beyond the Cuauhtémoc area. The Sunday School Teacher Conferences, started by the General Conference Leadership Training Center, are well attended by Sunday school teachers from the Los Jagüeyes colony (Kleine Gemeinde). Foundation Series material is used in the different Sunday schools (°Sunday School literature).

Members from GMC congregations are active in the newly created inter-Mennonite *Hilfskomitee*. Peter Rempel from the Blumenau congregation was the founding president. This organization has built a home for the aged, collaborated with MCC in the refugee and reconstruction work in Chiapas and Jalisco respectively, and is helping with relief work among the Tarahumara Indians.

Total membership in GCM-related congregations in Mexico in 1984 was 360. Many members have left for Canada or the United States (Seminole, Tex.) where they have joined General Conference, Evangelical Mennonite Missions Conference, or Evangelical Mennonite Conference congregations.   HEns

Harry L. Sawatzky, *They Sought a Country* (Berkeley: U. of California Press, 1971); *MWH* (1978), 230-32; *MWH* (1984), 87; information from J. Rempenning; letters by P. H. Krebiel to J. Janzen; conversations with B. H. Janzen and A. Redekopp; Barrett, *Vision* (1983), 124-26, 190; Juhnke, *Mission* (1979), 196-97; S. F. Pannabecker, *Open Doors* (1975) 234-38.

Mennonitengemeinden in der Deutschen Demokratischen Republik. See Deutsche Demokratische Republik. Mennonitengemeinden (Umsiedler). See Umsiedler.

Mennonitische Europäische Regionale Konferenz

(MERK; (European Mennonite Regional Conference) originated when several leaders attending the Mennonite World Conference (MWC) at Curitiba, Brazil, in 1972 suggested the planning of an assembly in 1975 to commemorate the 450th anniversary of the beginnings of the Anabaptist movement. The meeting's purpose was to strengthen and renew Mennonite congregations in Europe. Although intended initially as a one-time event, at the end of the meeting participants decided to create a lasting structure with meetings to be held once or twice between sessions of MWC assemblies. In this way European Mennonites formed a regional conference similar to those on other continents: the Asia Mennonite Conference, the °Africa Mennonite and Brethren in Christ Fellowship; and the °Congreso Menonita Latinamericano. MERK has become an instrument for reflection and reorientation of Mennonites in Europe. Meetings were held as follows: July 8-13, 1975, at Bienenberg, near Liestal, Switzerland; May 19-22, 1977, at Elspeet, Holland; May 28-31, 1981, at Enkenbach, Germany; May 12-15, 1988, at Tramelan, Switzerland.   SGer

See also Inter-Mennonite Cooperation.

Mennonitische Heimatmission (MHM; Mennonite Home Mission) is an independent association to support evangelization and the establishing of congregations. It was founded on May 18, 1969 by members of German Mennonite churches. Its first president was Wolfgang Schmutz of Fränking. Church planting work was done first in Freising (1969), later in Dachau (1970), Munich (1971), Neuburg (1974), Siegsdorf, (later at Prien; 1979), Heidelberg (1980), Moosburg (1980), Neustadt on the Weinstraße (1980), Brixen (Bressanone, Italy; 1981), Mannheim (1983), Aichach (1984), and Dillingen (1985). Work was also undertaken at Blumberg in the Black Forest (1977-80), Neufahrn (1977-80), Beverungen (1979-84), and Bad Pyrmont (1982-83). The Bad Pyrmont effort began under Rosedale Mennonite Mission Board (Conservative Mennonite Conference) auspices before 1982 and was resumed by that board after 1983. Heimatmission workers also ministered to workers from Turkey in Munich and Augsburg (1972-80) and since 1981 in Wiesbaden in cooperation with the *Orientdienst* (Eastern Service) agency. Mennonite Central Committee volunteers augmented Heimatmission work with refugees from East European, African, and Asian countries seeking political asylum in the camp of Neuburg on the Danube (since 1983) and in Munich (1986). The Proclama-Buchmission was founded in 1976 to publish evangelistic literature. Located in Freising since 1978, it also operated a bookstore, 1980-84 (since 1983 located in Fränking/Weichs. Proclama merged with the Membra publishers in Neuwied in 1981, purchased another publishing house in 1983, and then Proclama formed an enterprise independent of Membra in 1984. Besides the Mennonite churches themselves, the Mennonitische Heimatmission is also supported by friends at home and abroad. Circular letters are distributed bimonthly to inform about Heimatmission activities.   HeFu

Menn. Jahrbuch (1972-); *Der Mennonit* (1970), nos. 1 and 8

(1971), no 8, (1972), no. 11, (1973), nos. 2 and 7; *Gemeinde Unterwegs* (1975), no. 9, (1979), no. 10, (1980), no. 1, (1982), no. 6, (1984), no. 11; *Mennonitische Blätter* (1985), no. 2; *Brücke* (1986), no. 12.

Mennonitische Umsiedlerbetreuung (Mennonite Resettlers' Service). See Umsiedler.

Mennonitisches Missionskomitee für Paraguay (MMKfP; Mennonite Missions Committee for Paraguay). This committee, also known as the Comité Menonita de Acción Evangélica y Social en el Paraguay (Mennonite Committee for Social and Evangelical Action in Paraguay), was founded in 1963 by Mennonite congregations (GCM) of the following colonies, Volendam, Friesland, Neuland, Fernheim, and Menno and by the Asunción congregation. Also participating were the Evangelische Mennonitische Brüderschaft (EMB-related; Fellowship of Evangelical Bible Churches) of Fernhem and the Mennonite Church (MC) of North America.

The original committee consisted of the following members: Gerhard Schartner (Fernheim), Kornelius Dyck (Neuland), Bernhard Toews (Menno), and Bruno Epp as field secretary. The MMKfP assumed responsibility for the Indian mission in Menno Colony (°Chaco mission) and missionary activity in Villa Hayes as well as in East Paraguay. It also related to the Centro de Salud Menonita, Kilometer 81, a hospital for victims of Hansen's disease (leprosy).

By 1987 14 congregations had been established, each with their own place of worship (Convención de las Iglesias Evangélicas Unidas). Membership was ca. 500. Four of these congregations have missionary leadership, the other ten are being served by national workers. Mission schools have been established by the MMKfP at two of these congregational centers.

MWF/KB

S. F. Pannabecker, *Open Doors,* (1975), 242; Juhnke, *Mission* (1979), 193.

See also Gemeindekomitee.

Mental Health Facilities and Services, North America (ME III:653). Mennonite Mental Health Services (MMHS), Akron Pa., was incorporated in December 1952 and replaced the Homes-for-Mentally Ill Planning and Advisory Committee founded in 1947. MMHS is a health agency sponsored by the Mennonite Central Committee on behalf of the Mennonite and Brethren in Christ churches in North America. MMHS assists churches in their mission of responding to human need by providing resources and promoting wholeness of people in supportive, advisory, and collaborative services including: mental health centers (1949), developmentally disabled (1971), law offenders (1971), Mennonite Disaster Service workers (1977), international psychiatric programs (1972), and Mental Health Awareness and Education Committee (1982).

Mennonite Mental Health Services initially operated member mental health centers, but in 1969 recognized the quasi-independence of the centers. By 1971 Mennonite Central Committee appointed to the agency representatives from the centers and sponsoring churches at large, in order to support a partnership in mental health services.

The mental health centers focused increasingly on professionalism and the contribution science offered in the field of prevention and treatment of mental illness. Principles and motivation of the church coupled with a high level of professionalism soon won recognition and approval of accrediting agencies, professional associations, and federal, state, and local agencies who provided grants and contracts to those centers which applied. The following mental health centers are part of Mennonite Mental Health Services as of 1987:

Brook Lane Psychiatric Center, Md., began as Brook Lane Farm in 1947, was incorporated as Brook Lane Farm Hospital in 1959, and was named Brook Lane Psychiatric Center in 1965. It expanded from a 23-bed facility in 1949 to a 48-bed facility by 1987. Brook Lane Psychiatric Center includes both in-patient and out-patient treatment, community consultation, education, diagnostic evaluation, and full-time pastoral services.

Eden Mental Health Centre, Winkler, Man., dedicated June 3, 1967, is a venture sponsored by eight Manitoba Mennonite conferences and churches and the government of Manitoba. Eden Mental Health Centre affiliated with Mennonite Mental Health Services in 1968. The facility is a 40-bed hospital providing acute and chronic care for in-patients. It also offers out-patient services, psychogeriatric services, family and marital counseling, desensitization, relaxation therapy, marriage enrichment, and rehabilitation in terms of independent living and employment.

Kern View Community Mental Health Center and Hospital, Bakersfield, Cal., was established in 1966 through joint efforts of Kings View, Mennonite Mental Health Services, and Greater Bakersfield Community Hospital. Originally it was part of the Kings View system, then was incorporated in 1967 as a separate organization with its own board of directors. The hospital has 24 beds, offers in-patient and out-patient services, has a 20-bed chemical dependency program, operates the Phoenix Learning Center (a program designed to aid teenagers experiencing both emotional and academic problems), and offers pastoral counseling. In 1975 the Kern View Foundation was incorporated to provide fundraising services.

Kings View, Fresno, Cal., is a nonprofit corporation named in 1981 to direct all Kings View programs. Kings View Homes, Reedley, Cal., was founded in 1951 became Kings View Hospital in 1960, and Kings View Center in 1979. It consists of a 92-bed in-patient psychiatric hospital, and Rio Vista (1979), an open door 16-bed residential treatment facility offering interdependent group living on the hospital grounds. Kings View Work Experience Center, Atwater, Cal., is a privately operated program (1975) that provides work activity and evaluation services to developmentally disabled people. Kings View Corporation contracts with three central California counties to provide comprehensive mental health services.

Kings View Foundation, organized in 1972, develops resources to supplement funding of ongoing and new programs. MennoCare, founded in 1987, is funded by Kings View Foundation to offer homes with Christian modeling to psychiatric patients needing independent living experience. Birch Tree

Home, Dinuba, Cal. (1987), is licensed for five residents and operates as an independent living situation.

Oaklawn Psychiatric Center, Elkhart, Ind., began in 1963 as a day hospital and an out-patient clinic, including a Recovery of Hope program, that serves the churches and local community. The facility expanded to include a 78-bed hospital located in Goshen, Ind., in 1987 and offers treatment for psychiatric and addictive illnesses.

Penn Foundation for Mental Health, Sellersville, Pa., was dedicated Nov. 1956 and joined Mennonite Mental Health Service in 1981. It is a mental health center providing intensive, day-long treatment, including group therapy and individual counseling. It reaches out to the community through family life education and consultation services to schools, police, and businesses. In-patient services are provided at two local hospitals closely associated with Penn Foundation.

Philhaven, Gretna, Pa., is owned and operated by the Lancaster Mennonite Conference since 1952. It joined Mennonite Mental Health Services in 1972. The facility provides mental health services including a 96-bed in-patient hospital, out-patient care, and a day care program called FOCUS. Other programs are Family Care, which places clients in supportive substitute family settings; Stepping Stone, a halfway house; and the Recovery of Hope program.

Prairie View, Newton, Ks., was established in 1954. It is a mental health center that includes a 43-bed in-patient hospital and out-patient services available throughout several states. Prairie View offers consultation services to other agencies, an extensive family life education program, clinical experiences for students in medicine, psyichiatric nursing, °clinical pastoral education, and social work. Recovery of Hope, founded in 1982 by Prairie View, is a program offering a guided plan of reconciliation for troubled marriages. Growth Associates, established in 1971, a division of Prairie View, serves organizations and individuals throughout the Midwest with education and consultation services.

Mennonite Developmental Disabilities Services, Akron, Pa., is an outreach program sponsored by Mennonite Central Committee that was assumed by Mennonite Mental Health Services in 1971. The service is a ministry working with churches in educational and development programs fostering awareness, acceptance, and supportive care of people with disabilities. The agency provides consultation and resource materials to families, churches, conferences, and Mennonite-related direct service disability programs. The following institutions and agencies offer developmental °disabilities services:

Aldaview Residential Services, New Hamburg, Ont., is an agency serving mentally handicapped children, long-term to age 18 and short-term (parent relief) to age 17. Adriel School, West Liberty, Ohio, replaced Mennonite Orphanage in 1957. It is a treatment center for persons 10-15 years old whose intelligence quotients fall between 55 and 80. Bethesda Mental Hospital and Bethesda Home for the Mentally Handicapped Inc., Vineland, Ont., serves mentally handicapped persons 18 years and older. Craigwood Youth Services, Ailsa Craig, Ont., was founded in 1954. It is a children's mental health

center for girls and boys between the ages of 12 and 16. Faith Mission Home, Inc., Star Route 1, Mission Home, Va. (founded 1965), is a training center for brain injured children. Friendship Community, Lititz, Pa. (founded 1972), is a group home for mentally retarded adults. The agency offers crisis care facilities for any age, counseling and in-home services to Mennonites with handicapped children, foster homes, and supervised apartments. Indian Creek Foundation, Harleysville, Pa., was founded in 1975. It offers community living arrangements, congregational services, and vocational training for developmentally disabled persons ages 21 and older. Jubilee Association of Maryland, Inc., Silver Springs, Md. (founded 1978), provides group home and apartment living arrangements for mentally retarded adults. Kansas Mennonite Disabilities Council, North Newton, Ks. (founded 1982), consists of a group of south central Kansas Mennonites who are interested in helping local congregations serve as a Christian resource care for persons and their families with developmental or other disabilities. Meadowlark Homestead, Inc., Newton, Ks., is a 35-bed facility founded in 1951. It offers care for adults ages 18-60 who experience chronic mental illness. Three facilities provide a continuum of care designed for transitional living. MCC British Columbia Mental Health Services Program, Clearbrook B.C., was founded in 1974. It provides adult care for mentally retarded persons. The facility has two group homes, community care facilities and an achievement center. Menno Home of Saskatchewan, Waldheim, Sask., serves developmentally disabled persons ages 18-60.

Other facilities for the developmentally disabled are the following: Mental Disabilities Committee, Goshen, Ind., serves all ages including church awareness and respite care. Pleasant View Home for the Handicapped, Inc., Broadway, Va. (founded 1970), has four residences for adult mentally handicapped and a one-day training center for severe, profound, and adults with multiple handicaps. Sunnyhaven Children's Home, Plain City, Ohio (founded 1970), is a residential facility and group home for trainable and retarded children and adults. Sunshine Children's Home, Maumee, Ohio (founded 1949), is a residential and developmental facility including community homes for people with developmental disabilities, especially retardation. Wellspring Wholistic Care Center, Freeman, S.D., is a Christian counseling agency providing individual, marriage, and family counseling (founded 1979). West Coast MCC Developmental Disabilities Program, Reedley, Cal., began May 1981. It is an advocacy and supportive services program for families and developmentally disabled persons of all ages. The following homes are affiliated with the program: Huntington House, Fresno, Cal.; Eight Street Mennoheim, Albany Ore.; Sweethome, Sweet Home, Ore.; Twenty-First Mennoheim, McMinnville, Ore.   EJ

Current listings of institutions are published biennially in MC Yearbook, e.g., (1988-89), 125-27. For historical accounts see Vernon H. Neufeld, If We Can Love (Newton, 1983), cf. MQR, 56, no. 1 (Jan. 1982), sp. issue. See also Edwin F. Rempel, Congregational Health Ministries Handbook (Elkhart, Ind.: Council for Congregational Health Ministries of the Mennonite Health Association, 1987), 41-46; Mennonite Mental Health Services minutes, Oct. 1985, Oct. 1986, Apr. 1987.

Mercy of God. See Forgiveness; Grace; Salvation.

Mergers. See Inter-Mennonite Cooperation.

Meserete Kristos Bete-Kristian (Christ Foundation Church). See Ethiopia.

Métis. See Indians, North America.

Metzler, Abram Jacob (b. Dec. 4, 1902), was born at Martinsburg, Pa., the son of Abram and Katherine (Kreider) Metzler. While working as superintendent at the Musselman canning plant at Inwood, W.Va., he was ordained by his home church at Martinsburg in 1924 and became its minister in 1925. In 1926 he was called to lead the Mennonite church at Masontown (Fayette Co.), Pa. He was ordained bishop in the Southwestern Pennsylvania (later Allegheny) Mennonite Conference in 1928, later chairing its Sunday school conference, young people's institute, and ministerial committees, and serving as the conference's moderator.

From 1935 to 1961 he was general manager of Mennonite Publishing House, Scottdale, Pa. He completed terms as vice president and president of the Protestant Church-Owned Publishers Association. He played a leading role in the process leading to the establishing of Laurelville Mennonite Church Center in 1943. From 1953-55 he was moderator of the Mennonite Church (MC) and served on many churchwide committees. He sat at various times on the governing boards of Eastern Mennonite College, Goshen College, and Hesston College. He was a member of the Mennonite Board of Education (MC) 1942-52, 1956-1960 (president in 1960).

With his wife, Alta (Maust), he moved to Elkhart, Ind., in 1974 and to Greencroft Center in Goshen, Ind., in 1985. He helped establish the Elkhart Community °Hospice program.   PMS

Who's Who Mennonites (1943), 166; *Menn. Bib. II*, p. 481.

Mexico (ME III:663) attained its independence from Spain in 1821, and, with the exception of the French Intervention (1862-67), has been a federal republic largely modeled after the United States. Through the Texas and Mexican Wars (1836 and 1846-48), and the Gadsden Purchase (1853) Mexico ceded approximately one-half of its original territory to the United States. Its 30 states plus a federal district extend from its frontiers with the United States to Guatemala and Belize, covering an area one-third larger than Quebec or Alaska, twice the size of Egypt. The population is expected to reach 85 million in 1988. The northern two-thirds of the country, with the exception of Baja California, is a plateau ranging in elevation from 2,700 m. (8,800 ft.) in the south, to 1,000 m. (3,300 ft.) in the north, characterized by a semi-arid to arid climate and a basin-and-range topography, descending to narrow coastal plains on the Gulf of Mexico and Pacific sides, and to the Isthmus of Tehuantepec in the south.

Mexico's agricultural potential, as a consequence of its latitudinal span from the lower middle latitudes to the tropics and its highly varied topography, covers a broad range. However, only 12 percent of the national area is classed as arable and, due to a shortage of precipitation or water for irrigation, or both, only about 60 percent of the arable land regularly produces crops. Erosion on unirrigated land, and salt contamination on land under irrigation, are major problems.

Since 1929 Mexico has been governed without interruption by the Institutional [formerly National] Revolutionary Party (PRI). By Latin American standards, Mexico has had relatively stable political conditions. The PRI has exercised a highly interventionist (but non-Marxist) policy in economic affairs and social development, styling Mexico under its rule as a "guided democracy." The president, whose term of office is six years, and who may not succeed himself, is invested with very great powers.

Mennonite settlement in Mexico began in 1922, following the granting of a *Privilegium* (°privileges) by the Mexican government under the leadership of President Alvaro Obregóon. The *Privilegium* was similar to those extended to the Mennonites in Russia and elsewhere in Latin America. By 1927 some 7,000 Old Colony and Sommerfeld Mennonites from Manitoba and Saskatchewan were living in the Manitoba Colony (1922), Swift Current Colony (1922), and Santa Clara Colony (1922) in Chihuahua State; and at Patos (1924), also known as the Hague Colony, in Durango State. These groups had emigrated from Russia to Canada in the 1870s in response to offers of reserved homestead lands and privileges and immunities equivalent to those inherent in the *Privilegium* held in Russia. When they perceived developments in Canada, especially the anglicization and secularization of the school system from 1916 onward, as an invasion of these privileges and immunities, and as a threat to influence and authority by community leaders, they left Canada. Following a concerted search throughout North and South America, Mexico proved to be the only country besides Paraguay willing to accept them on their terms, and Mexico became the choice of all of the Old Colony Mennonites and a minority of Sommerfeld Mennonites.

The pioneer years were very difficult. Civil order was generally in disarray in the first decades after the revolution of 1910-20. The crops and land management practices to which the Mennonites were accustomed were only marginally applicable to the semi-arid highland environment.

By 1940, despite the return to Canada of approximately 20 percent of the colonists, and despite many deaths, especially of infants, the colonies needed more land. Since that time the Mennonites of Mexico have been continuously in search of land. While their numbers have increased almost 500 percent from 1940 to the late 1980s, to an estimated 45,000-50,000, their land holdings have increased by only slightly more than 100 percent. From 1948 to 1952, some 150 families (595 persons) of °°Kleine Gemeinde (Evangelical Mennonite Conference) affiliation from Manitoba established the Quellenkolonie (Quellen Colony) on 142 sq. km. at Los Jagueyes in Chihuaua, 40 km. north of the Swift Current Colony, after obtaining inclusion in the *Privilegium* covering the Old Colony and Sommerfelder.

Other, smaller groups of Mennonites, from Russia, the United States, and Canada, have made attempts at colonization in Mexico. In 1924 three families of

MEXICO

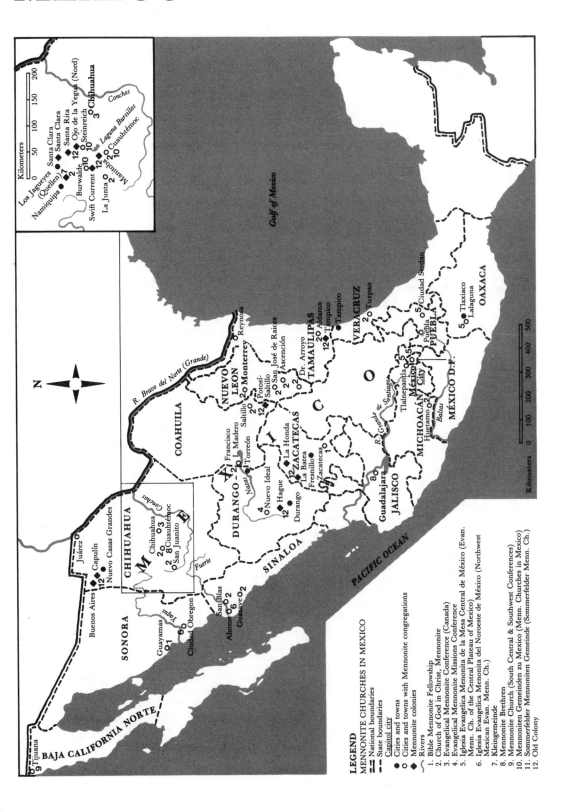

Conchos

Gulf of Mexico

Inset map (Chihuahua area):

Kilometers

Los Jagueyes (Quellen)
Namiquipa
Santa Clara
Santa Clara
Santa Rita
Ojo de la Yegua (Nord)
Steinreich
Chihuahua
Burwalde
Swift Current
La Junta
Mamibos
Laguna Burtillos
Cuauhtémoc

R. Bravo del Norte (Grande)

N

PACIFIC OCEAN

BAJA CALIFORNIA NORTE

Tijuana

SONORA

Buenos Aires
Juárez
Capulín
Nuevo Casas Grandes
Guayamas
Ciudad Obregon
San Blas
Ahome
Guaaave

CHIHUAHUA
Chihuahua
Cuauhtémoc
San Juanito

DURANGO
Francisco I. Madero
Torreón
Nuevo Ideal
Hague
Durango
La Honda
La Batea
Fresnillo
Zacatecas

ZACATECAS

COAHUILA

NUEVO LEON
Monterrey
Saltillo
Potosí-Saltillo

SINALOA

Fuerte

Nazas

Reynosa
San José de Raíces
Ascención
Dr. Arroyo
Aldama
Tampico

TAMAULIPAS

VERACRUZ
Tuxpan
Ciudad Serdán
Tlaxiaco
Lalaguna

OAXACA

PUEBLA
Puebla
MÉXICO City
MÉXICO D.F.
Tlalnepantla
Tlatamo
MICHOACÁN
Balsas

JALISCO
Guadalajara

R. Grande de Santiago

Kilometers

LEGEND

MENNONITE CHURCHES IN MEXICO

National boundaries

--- State boundaries

Capitol city

● Cities and towns

●○ Cities and towns with Mennonite congregations

◆ Mennonite colonies

Rivers

1. Bible Mennonite Fellowship
2. Church of God in Christ, Mennonite
3. Evangelical Mennonite Conference (Canada)
4. Evangelical Mennonite Missions Conference
5. Iglesia Evangelica Menonita de la Mesa Central de México (Evan. Menn. Ch. of the Central Plateau of Mexico)
6. Iglesia Evangelica Menonita del Noroeste de México (Northwest Mexican Evan. Menn. Ch.)
7. Kleingemeinde
8. Mennonite Brethren
9. Mennonite Church (South Central & Southwest Conferences)
10. Mennoniten Gemeinden zu Mexico (Menn. Churches in Mexico)
11. Sommerfelder Mennoniten Gemeinde (Sommerfelder Menn. Ch.)
12. Old Colony

Kleine Gemeinde affiliation from Kansas established a small settlement north of the Manitoba Colony. Most of them soon returned to the United States; the rest were absorbed by the Old Colony. Beginning in 1924 various attempts by the Kansas-based Mennonite Board of Colonization to resettle in Mexico several groups of refugees from the Soviet Union failed as opportunities to enter the United State or Canada opened up. Those attempted settlements were, in the States of Coahuila, Chihuahua, Guanajuato, Durango, and Baja California. Ultimately only about 6 out of 200 *Rußländer* families remained in Mexico (°Mennonitengemeinde zu Mexico).

In 1927 four related families of Church of God in Christ Mennonite (Holdeman) affiliation from Oklahoma established a small settlement at Cordovana, north of the Swift Current Colony. This became a Church of God in Christ mission settlement in 1945. In 1943 six families of Mennonite Church (MC) and Amish background came first to Chihuahua, then attempted to settle at Rascón, and later at Rayóon, in San Luís Potosí. The survivors returned to the United States in 1946.

In 1948, 38 families (246 persons) of Old Colony affiliation from Manitoba and Saskatchewan participated as a separate group in the Quellenkolonie venture of the Kleine Gemeinde. Most of them shortly returned to Canada; of those remaining all but a few left the colony.

Agriculture as the economic basis of the colonies and an agrarian ethic relating status to property ownership remain dominant. Nevertheless, food processing and services related to agriculture have achieved wide representation. Dominant in the secondary sector is cheese production, which has become the economic mainstay in all but a few of the colonies. Dairying helps maximize returns from agriculture because it makes use of crop residues. Since the 1960s wheat production has increased substantially while corn, oats, and bean production have decreased proportionately, especially in Chihuahua. Production of tree crops, particularly apples, has also grown. Since about 1955 Mennonite crop production has been fully mechanized.

Non-colonizing Mennonite and non-Mennonite groups have increasingly established a presence in and near the Mennonite colonies. In 1947 the Mennonite Central Committee established a center in the town of Cuauhtémoc to help Old Colony Mennonites in Chihuahua who were suffering after widespread crop failure. This center expanded to include medical services and, ultimately, under the auspices of the General Conference Mennonite Church (GCM), state-accredited primary schools, a secondary school, and the Blumenau congregation (GCM). During the 1950s the Mennonite Brethren established a clinic at Nuevo Ideál (Patos), in Durango State, which offered services to the Old Colonists on the same basis as the Mexican populace. Gradually, a Mennonite Brethren congregation, supporting an elementary school, since 1973 located within the Patos colony, emerged.

Divergent opinions about innovation in economic and technological areas have stimulated tensions within Old Colony congregations. A number of other religious groups have established a proselytizing, evangelizing presence (°Manitoba Colony) that attracts marginalized Old Colonists. Among these groups are the Church of God, the Seventh Day Adventists, Pentecostals, and the Evangelical Mennonite Mission Conference (EMMC).

In Mexico conservative Mennonites encountered a social and political environment more like that of the Russian Empire than that of Canada. In Mexico, within the provisions of the *Privilegium*, it proved once more possible to establish and maintain aloofness, if not isolation. The host society is very different in language, culture, and religion, and is so structured politically that ultimate recourse may be had to a final arbiter in the person of the president. After more than six decades the Mennonites have been significantly influenced by the host society, but not in ways that have made great inroads on the traditional aloofness between the Mennonites and Mexican society. Social contacts are still minimal, and intermarriage is rare. The government has adhered to the terms of the *Privilegium* to a very high degree, although in dealing with occasional tensions between Mexicans and Mennonites it may find itself in the political and moral dilemma of adjudicating between citizens with rights, and aliens with privileges. Nevertheless, perceived threats to their status have provided considerable basis for emigration, most notably to Belize in the late 1950s, and to Bolivia and Paraguay in the 1960s and 1970s. Examples of points of tension with the government include the proposed universal implementation of a social security system in the 1950s, and several subsequent cases in which Mennonites had to forfeit lands with defective title to ownership. More profound appears to have been the gradual dissolution of internal solidarity due to increasing divergence of opinion in sectarian and secular matters. This has stimulated some migration within Mexico, and a great deal to new frontiers in Bolivia and Paraguay. Also, there has been a persistent flow, mostly to Canada, some to the United States, and, since 1986, to Argentina, primarily for economic reasons. The majority of Mennonites still in Mexico in the late 1980s, however, entertain little thought of emigration, and their continuing presence and the associated economic impact upon the regions in which they have settled, appears to be assured.　　　　HLS

Abe Warkentin, compiler, *Strangers and Pilgrims* (Steinbach, Man.: Die Mennonitische Post, 1987); H. Leonard Sawatzky, *Sie Suchten eine Heimat* (Marburg, 1986); idem, *They Sought a Country* (Berkeley, 1971); W. Schmiedehaus, *Ein feste Burg ist unser Gott* (Cuauhtémoc, 1948; Winnipeg, 1982); Calvin W. Redekop, *The Old Colony Mennonites* (Baltimore, 1969); W. Quiring, *Im Schweisse deines Angesichts* (Steinbach, 1953); *MB Yearbook* (1981), 115-16; *MWH* (1978), 227-32; *MWH* (1984), 83-88; *MWR* (June 23, 1988), 8; (June 30, 1988), 6, (July 7, 1988), 6.

See also Old Colony Mennonites (chart of various colonies); Iglesia Evangélica Menonita de la Mesa Central de Mexico; Iglesia Evangélica Menonita del Noroeste de Mexico; Evangelical Mennonite Conference; Kleine Gemeinde (Latin America); Mennoniten Gemeinde zu Mexico; Evangelical Mennonite Church; Sommerfeld Mennonites; Casas Grandes Colonies (Buenos Aires, El Capulin, Buena Vista, Las Virginias, El Cuervo); Cuauhtemoc; Durango Colony (Nuevo Ideál); Manitoba Colony; Swift Current Colony; Nord Colony; Potosi-Saltillo Colony; Zacatecas Colonies (La Batea, La Honda, Campeche).

Meyersdale-Springs, Pa., Old Order Amish Settlement (ME IV:572) is located in Somerset Co. The first Amish settlers migrated to this area at the height of the Methodist revival movement in Lancaster and Berks Cos. Amish young people were leaving the church and marrying non-Amish, which spurred several devout church leaders to move to a new location. Three settlements sprang up in Somerset Co. in 1767. Only the Meyersdale-Springs community remains Amish. Other groups have since affiliated with related Amish-Mennonite and Mennonite churches. In 1927, a major split resulted in the formation of the °Beachy Amish Mennonite Fellowship.

Somerset Co. was the source of many Amish settlers who chose to form new settlements in Ohio, Indiana, Iowa, and Illinois. In 1986 the Meyersdale-Springs community, rich in Amish history and culture, had four church districts (congregations) serving approximately 700 people spread over an area reaching south into Garrett Co., Maryland.   SLY

Michigan. The Mennonite Church (MC) has begun 12 new congregations in this state since 1956. Two of these 12, both in Kalamazoo, did not survive. The 10 new congregations that continue include four dual-conference fellowships (two in Ann Arbor, one in Detroit and one in East Lansing). The dual-conference relationships are all with the General Conference Mennonite Church (GCM). Other new congregations are Stutsmanville Chapel in Emmet Co. with a membership of more than 100, North Park in Grand Rapids; Wasepi near Sturgis; West Odessa in Ionia Co.; Templo Menonita de la Hermosa in Kalamazoo; and Christian Fellowship Center in Sturgis.

Of the Mennonite Church congregations already existing in 1956, five closed and four left the Indiana-Michigan Conference, Bowne in Kent Co. joined the Conservative Mennonite Conference, Seney in Michigan's Upper Peninsula joined the Mid-West Mennonite Fellowship, and White Cloud and Pleasantview (both in west-central Michigan) are unaffiliated in 1986. The Detroit Mission, begun in 1926, has changed its name to Peace Mennonite Church and, like both congregations in Saginaw, is interracial but largely Afro-American. Camp Amigo, near Sturgis, is owned by the Indiana-Michigan Conference and has offered a strong camping and retreat program since opening in 1957. Little Eden Camp at, Onekema has been an association-operated camp since 1945. The number of MC congregations increased from 35 to 36, 1956-86. Membership grew from 1,700 to about 2,400 in those years.

Several small fellowships have begun at Fairview. Conservative Mennonite Fellowship began as a small group from the Fairview (MC) congregation in 1967. Since that time two other small groups have emerged from that one—Fairview Conservative (1977) and Pilgrim Fellowship (1984).

General Conference Mennonites (GCM) grew by way of the dual-conference fellowships noted above. Camp Friedenswald in Cass Co. has a full schedule of camps or retreats. It was founded in 1950.

The Conservative Mennonite Conference (CM) has grown by two congregations since 1956. Bowne joined the conference after being unaffiliated for a

time and North Wayne in Dewagiac, Cass Co., was organized in 1974. This began as a mission in 1958 with Floyd Brenneman as superintendent. When the congregation was organized, he was ordained to be pastor. His son Robert was pastor in 1987. The membership of the conference has increased from 428 to 659 in 10 congregations during the past 30 years.

The Brethren in Christ (BIC) continue to have seven small churches in Michigan. The Lakeview Community Church in Goodrich, is a new congregation but the Dearborn congregation was closed. The Oak Grove congregation at Gladwin continues as a BIC church but leadership is provided by the Fairview Mennonite (MC) congregation. In 1965 Camp Lakeview near Goodrich was opened. Two years later a half-interest was sold to the Missionary Church. It is now operated jointly.

The Evangelical Mennonite Church (EMCh) has three congregations, having added Lawton Church in 1974. They also purchased a camp near Lawton and offer a full camping and retreat program. Michigan membership is 188.

The Church of God in Christ Mennonite (Holdeman) closed the Harrison church (except for Sunday school and summer Bible school) and established Mt. Calm Mennonite Church at Carson City. Membership in two congregations, Mt. Calm and Newark (near Ithica) totals 350. They have their own school with 85 students (1987).

Amish districts in Oscoda Co. that died out were replaced in 1968 by an influx from Ohio and Indiana forming two church districts (congregations). Around °Centreville, near the Indiana border, they have grown from three to six districts with 140 families. Hillsdale Co. has two districts (established 1956). Branch Co. has two districts (established 1960), and Calhoun Co. has two districts (established 1960). Residents in Branch and Calhoun Cos. came mostly from the Grabill, Ind., settlement. One district began near Greenville in 1970, another in Eaton Co. in 1975, and one in Iosco Co. in 1978. Two districts were formed in Gladwin Co. in 1981 by immigrants from Kenton, Ohio, and one by folks from Wayne Co., Ohio. Close by, near Clare, one district was begun (1981) by people from °Holmes Co., Ohio. In addition, a small group came from Mifflin Co., Pa. (°Belleville) to Rosebush (1981); a group from °Arthur, Ill., to Ludington (1983). A group of Amish is located near Reed City (1985). In 1982 and 1984 two small groups also moved near Stanwood and in 1986 a group began near Athens. Nine of the 17 settlements in Michigan began since 1980.

About five families from the Old Order Mennonites (Wisler Mennonites) of Elkhart Co., Ind., moved to Snover in the "Thumb" area of Michigan in 1981. Joined later by five more families from the same community and a family from Wisconsin, they still remain a part of the Elkhart Co. congregation. On Dec. 24, 1986, David Miller was ordained by Leonard Martin, bishop of the congregation to lead the Michigan part of the congregation.

Some families from St. Joseph Co., Mich., were driving to the Fair Haven Amish Mennonite Church (Beachy Amish) near Middlebury, Ind., in the early 1950s. The Fair Haven congregation helped them form a new congregation. Thus the Oak Grove

Church was begun near Nottawa. Later this church dissolved under some stress but out of this the Pilgrim Fellowship was formed in 1969 and Sharon Bethel became a renamed remnant of the original group. These two continue to be Beachy Amish churches. In addition, the Shiloh Fellowship (1970) of Constantine came largely from the Oak Grove church and is now part of the Mid-West Mennonite Fellowship.

The Missionary Church (formerly °°United Missionary Church) continues to have the largest Michigan membership of any Mennonite-related group. In 1969 their membership was increased by a merger with the Missionary Church Association. About 16 congregations were added by the merger. Others were added by active evangelism and church planting. In 1987 there were 67 Missionary Church congregations; total membership was ca. 3,800. Forty-eight of the congregations are in the Michigan District and 19 are part of the North Central District, which also reaches into Indiana. Camping is an important part of the program with three camps at Mancelona, Brown City, and Goodrich.   GJ

MC Yearbook (1956, 1986-87); Luthy, *Amish* (1986); Wittlinger, *Piety and Obedience* (1978), 132; Clarence Troyer, *The Mennonite Church in the Upper Penninsula of Michigan* (Engadine: the author, 1986).

Mid-Atlantic Mennonite Fellowship was founded in 1978. It consists of 13 congregations located in south central Pennsylvania (9), central Pennsylvania (2), northern Pennsylvania, (1), and southern New York (1). The fellowship was organized by a number of ordained brethren from various independent congregations and congregations affiliated with regional Mennonite Church (MC) conferences who felt the need for a broader church organization to give cohesion for missions, Christian education, and fellowship in the historic Anabaptist vein of life and practice.

In 1987 the fellowship consists of 985 members with 6 bishops, 23 ministers, and 15 deacons providing leadership. There is a strong emphasis on Christian education for the youth. Mission emphasis, in addition to local evangelism by individual congregations, consists of full-time prison ministry, a street and tract evangelism ministry, and support of foreign missions, with workers in Guatemala, Haiti, and Canada (1987).

Mid-Atlantic Mennonite Fellowship does not sponsor or send delegates to the Mennonite Church (MC) General Assembly or to regional conference meetings. The fellowship's members enjoy fraternal relationship with the Mid-West Fellowship, Southeastern Mennonite Conference, Cumberland Valley Mennonite Church, and various other independent churches of like precious faith.   RKH

MC Yearbook (1988-89),95.

Midwest Mennonite Fellowship grew out of a number of ministers' desire for fellowship for themselves and their congregations along with seeing the need of a winter Bible School for their young people. Most of these ministers were from the midwestern United States. A few were from eastern Ontario.

On Oct. 1, 1976, 15 of these interested ministers gathered at Fairview, Mich., for a day of fellowship and sharing of concerns. Out of this meeting grew an interest in including others unaffiliated with a conference. At this meeting a committee of three were elected to plan the next meeting. The three brethren chosen were Samuel Yoder (Minn.), Leighton Martin (Ont.), and Roman Schlabach (Mich.).

The second meeting was held on Feb. 8-10, 1977, at Stone Lake, Wis. This meeting was well attended, with 50 ministers present, along with the representation from the local congregation. A third meeting was held at the Salem Mennonite Church near Kinross, Iowa, July 1-3, 1977. About 500 people attended these services. Interest in a winter Bible school was the main topic of the ministers business session. There was strong support for the school and an association to support it. The latter was organized by 23 ministers gathered at Nappanee, Ind., on Sept. 21, 1977. The first program committee was made up of Leon King (Ohio), Homer Miller (Ind.), and Alvin Mast (Wis.). A five-member school board was chosen as follows: Leighton Martin (Ont.), Victor Miller (Mich.), Arnie Skrivseth (Minn.), Olen Miller (Ind.), and Samuel Yoder (Minn.). Thirteen churches joined the Midwest Fellowship as charter members. In 1987 the fellowship had 24 congregations with a total membership of 1,250.

A former elementary school building at Lansing, Minn., was chosen as the site for the winter Bible School. The building, leased at first and later purchased, is also used to hold the annual winter ministers' meetings early in December. Bible School begins the first Monday of January and runs for 12 weeks. Approximately 200 different students attend each year.   DSchr

MC Yearbook (1988-89), 95-96.

See also Conservative Mennonites.

Midwives. The 16th c. was a period of many profound changes. Among other things the events of the time precipitated changes in the practice of midwifery and also in the standards applied to that vocation. The Anabaptists influenced some of these changes, for in certain areas there appear to have been a large number of midwives among the Anabaptists. This was no doubt occasioned by the fact that some Anabaptist midwives were willing to say they had conducted an emergency baptism of an infant ostensibly in danger of dying, when in fact the child may have been healthy and the midwife had not baptized it at all. In such a way the child could be recorded as having been baptized when it was not. Furthermore, Anabaptist women needed to be able to trust their midwives in order to be sure the midwife would not baptize in the case of a sickly newborn child, and it may be that this was another reason why they took up the calling themselves. Another area in which Anabaptists were a factor is that they argued that if unlettered midwives, never formally ordained to do so could conduct a valid baptism, why should not Anabaptist leaders be authorized to baptize adults?

The time of baptism had always been something of a problem in the church. Codifying the traditional practice of the 1st- and 2nd c. church, 6th c. church councils decreed that Easter and Pentecost were the proper days for baptism; only when there was danger of death were exceptions to be made. By the 11th c. this rule had been relaxed in some areas to permit baptism on any day of the year.

Although some theologians held that unbaptized infants would go to heaven, or to an intermediary state (limbo), others feared otherwise, and, especially anxious parents, pushed baptism to an ever earlier age.

Laypeople were permitted to baptize in an emergency (when the child was near death). There is a pamphlet from the 16th c. which clearly indicates the Anabaptist involvement in the issue of emergency baptism. It is anonymous, entitled, *An Instruction for Midwives, How they are to baptize in an emergency*. It is undated and is available as far as is known only in the British Museum Library. On the basis of style and contents it should be dated around 1570.

It was provoked by the Anabaptists who made fun of emergency baptism (the author calls it *Jachtauff* [a joke baptism]) and ridiculed it in order to promote their "heresy" more strongly and to ridicule the true, correct baptism. The tract's author then sets out to establish that a baptism is valid no matter who performs it, if it meets three conditions: (1) A normal child has to be born; no severely disfigured child or any unborn child is to be baptized, "for one has to be born before one can be reborn." If the child dies before birth we can commend it to God for he is able, by his grace, to give the rebirth without water. The author rejects intrauterine baptism because that is given mainly for the comfort of the mother. (2) Water is necessary for real baptism. At every birth water for baptism should be available so that substitutes are not used, e.g., snow, wine, or whatever. Babies should not need to be carried away for baptism because of the absence of water. (3) The trinitarian formula, which the midwives should know and when demanded, "speak in considered courage, forthrightly, and so that it is clearly understood, so that other wives can also hear it and bear witness to it later." Similar instructions to laypeople about emergency baptism were included in standard medieval catechisms and manuals for parish priests.

Midwives had been receiving more recognition soon after they became a more visible and more socially acceptable group and their performance was monitored. The first name of a midwife, Frau Aleyt, appears in Koblenz in 1298, from where we also have our first oath taken by all midwives which already included the line: "I promise . . . to care for the children in order that they may come to baptism, and to be faithful in the house. Also not to keep any gifts given to the child at baptism but to hand them faithfully on to the mother." By 1460 major efforts were made to control the quality of midwives. In Regensburg in 1452 the oldest order for midwives placed them under the authority of the doctor (Franken).

Among the Anabaptists there is considerable evidence that women practiced this profession. Thus the court records reveal that a certain Elizabeth Salmen, the wife of Jerg, was ordered to Stuttgart for the second time but did not come because she was very pregnant ("gross Schwanger"). The court continues: "The suspicion exists in this market town that the midwife takes money and says that she car-

ried out emergency baptism on the children of the Anabaptists so that they will remain unbaptized. The pastor and other trustworthy people say that when the child was brought to church it had a quite lively color and healthy scream. Since no one attended the emergency baptism except two wives, one of whom is related to Elizabeth, the observer in the presence of the bailiff and the pastor of Fellbach asked the midwives under oath if they had baptized the child, which they affirmed, "for the child was weak at that time" (Bossert, 380). Another directive instructs the official "to insist that the midwives cease baptizing infants without specific authorization, and not in the presence of people who are suspected of being Anabaptists. If they violate this rule they will be punished seriously."

Evidence also is given of a certain Martha, the wife of Michl Rielin, from Miedelsbach, also a midwife. She had not been coming to church and repeated orders have been given to her to desist her midwifery and she was even punished with fines. In the spring of 1574 the record reads: "Martha is still a midwife, even though she is no longer authorized. We have dealt with her often, but to no avail." Again in 1577 and as late as the fall of 1578, this "evil Anabaptist" is often seen, continues her work but does not come to baptism (Bossert, 390, 505, 516). In May 1598 a certain Anne Mayer is accused of taking communion only once in nine years, never coming to church. She affirmed that she "will not sponsor a child at baptism, rejects emergency baptism by midwives because Christ commended baptism to his disciples" (*TA Württemberg*, 725) and, on these grounds, was suspected of being an Anabaptist.

Research deserves to be conducted on the subject of Anabaptist midwives. Did they perhaps see in the deeds of the Hebrew midwives, Shiphrah and Puah (Ex 1:15-22) a precedent, perhaps even a justification for their deviousness? At any rate their deeds will always stand as part of the record of dissent against practices and a system that violated values which we today take for granted.

In the rural Mennonite communities of the 18th, 19th, and early 20th centuries, midwives were common, as they were in non-Mennonite communities (Rich). In the late 20th c., as part of the ecology movement some Mennonites have gone back to midwives and natural birth techniques as a protest against the "clinical" removal of the process of birth from the home. In St. Jacobs, Ont., one midwife, Elsie Cressman, has attracted international respect and also the respect of her colleagues in the medical community for the way in which she had brought the birthing process back into the family. Her birthing clinic has served many Old Order Mennonites and others and has taken a vigorous lead in making midwives socially and legally acceptable.   WKla

Anonymous, *Eyn vnterricht für die Hebammen wie sie in der not täuffen sollen* (n.p.: n.d.), copy in the British Library; M. Franken, "Hebammenausbildung in alter und neuer Zeit," *Deutsche Hebammen Zeitschrift*, 5 (1953), 76-79; Albert Schmidt, "Von der alten Hebammenkunst, Die Hamburger Bademoder," *DHZ*, 7 (1955), 103-4; R. Mey, "Zur Geschichte des Hebammenwesens in Baden," *DHZ*, 17 (1965), 4-8; K. Adler, "Die Entwicklung des Hebammenwesens in Westfalen," *DHZ*, 9 (1957), 40-44; Rich, *Mennonite Women* (1983), 168-70; Walter Conway, *The Time and Place of Baptism* (Washington: Catholic U. of America Press, 1954); A. Mingana, "Synopsis of Christian Doctrine in the Fourth

Century according to Theodore of Mopsuestia," *Bulletin of the John Rylands Library*, 5 (1918), 296-316, esp. 311-312; Claus-Peter Clasen, *Anabaptism, A Social History, 1525-1618* (Ithaca: Cornell U. Press, 1972), 148-49; David Ayerst and A. S. T. Fisher, eds., *Records of Christianity*, vol. 2: *Christendom* (Oxford: Blackwell, 1977), 213-16 (excerpts from John Myrc, *Instructions for Parish Priests*, ca. 1400).

See also Kake Elisabete.

Mifflin Co., Pa., Old Order Amish Settlement. See Belleville, Pa., Old Order Amish Settlement.

Migrations

Migrations (ME III:684). This article will discuss the migrations of Mennonites of European origin since the 1950s. The reasons for the migrations varied. Mennonites have migrated to maintain an agrarian way of life, to escape the pressures of governments, to escape the influence of Mennonites conforming to the world (°°nonconformity), to improve economic opportunities, and to carry on mission and evangelism.

In North America one of the most significant migrations has been °urbanization, a continent-wide phenomenon, largely due to the mechanization of agriculture. Even though Mennonites were historically agriculturalists, since the 1950s many Mennonites have been forced to relocate to urban settings in order to find jobs and °professions. The increased individualism, mobility, and freedom present in urban settings has forced a restructuring of organizations and patterns of interdependence.

An indication of the rapid urbanization of Canadian Mennonites is that in the 1951 census 20 percent of Canadian Mennonites were identified as urban, 16 percent as rural-nonfarm, and 64 percent as rural-farm. In 1981 the corresponding figures were 51 percent urban, 26 percent rural-nonfarm, and only 23 percent rural-farm.

Canadian Mennonites have responded to urbanization by establishing churches in cities across Canada. For example, in 1987 Winnipeg had 40 Mennonite churches with a combined urban membership of about 10,000. Canadian Mennonites have also built a plethora of other °institutions as a means of creating new community structures. The institutions include elementary and °secondary schools, colleges, °credit unions, and nursing and retirement °homes. In Canada, Mennonites of Russian/Prussian descent have urbanized more rapidly than have those of Swiss background. In both groups, however, large numbers of adherents have chosen not to identify with Mennonite churches when they migrate to the cities.

In the United States Mennonites who have moved into towns and small cities have frequently established Mennonite churches. Mennonites who have moved into the larger urban centers have had greater difficulty founding Mennonite churches, and thus have often joined non-Mennonite churches.

In contrast to the urbanization of many Mennonites, in both Canada and the United States, other Mennonites have migrated in order to maintain a rural lifestyle. Attracted by the availability of good quality land and relative isolation from political and cultural pressures, the surplus populations of Old Colony, Reinländer, Sommerfelder, Chortitzer, and Saskatchewan Bergthaler churches have migrated to the Peace River and other northern areas of Alberta and British Columbia.

In the United States, Old Order Amish and Mennonites, as well as some Conservative Mennonites, have migrated to acquire sufficient land for their people. They have been buying land in the states of Alabama, Arkansas, Florida, Kentucky, Minnesota, Missouri, Montana, New York, Oklahoma, Tennessee, Texas, and Wisconsin as well as in those areas of Pennsylvania, Ohio, Indiana, and Michigan that previously had no Amish or Old Order communities.

A few groups in the Unites States and Canada have also used rural migration as a mission strategy. Through group relocation in various parts of North America, they have attempted to form nuclei of churches which were expected to grow by drawing in people from the surrounding population. The Church of God in Christ Mennonite (Holdeman), Beachy Amish, and Conservative Mennonite churches have migrated not only within North America, but also into Latin America, for this reason.

Some Mennonites in Canada found migration to °frontier lands inadequate to meet the threat of urbanization and acculturation. Beginning in the early 1960s, a few hundred Mennonites migrated to Bolivia. A number have since returned to Canada.

Numerous migrations have been carried on since the 1950s by Old Colony Mennonites in Mexico. Old Colonists, who had migrated to Mexico in the 1920s, were committed to an agrarian way of life. To protect their agrarian community life they also reject most forms of modern technology, especially technology which made them dependent on the larger society.

Since the 1950s, a dramatic growth in population due to a decline in infant mortality has forced Mexico Old Colony Mennonites to found numerous new settlements. Some new settlements were established in Mexico, but Mexico's restrictive land purchase laws made expansion difficult. In 1958 a new settlement was established in Belize (British Honduras). In 1966 the Old Colony settlements in Belize totaled about 2,800 people. These settlements alleviated the population problem in Mexico only slightly, and in 1967 Old Colonists in Mexico began new settlements in Bolivia. By 1986 nine settlements had been founded in Bolivia by Old Colonists with an adult population of about 5,200. In 1969 the first Old Colony settlement was established in East Paraguay to meet the needs of surplus populations in Mexico. Some Old Colony Mennonites from Belize and Bolivia have joined the Mexico Mennonites in East Paraguay. In 1987 the total number of Old Colonists in Paraguay was about 5,000. In the mid-1980s a new settlement by Old Colonists was founded in Argentina, and by 1987 numbered about 1,000.

In these various migrations a selection process which frequently developed was that those Old Colonists who migrated were the conservers, namely those who felt that the others had left too many of the old ways and had compromised the true faith (°Conservative Mennonites [Dutch-Prussian-Russian]). In addition, those who migrated had to have the financial means to pay for migration and resettlement.

The Old Colonists in Mexico who were landless

and too poor to follow the migrants south, had to look to other options. Many of them trekked north as individuals and as families to the Aylmer region of southern Ontario to work as seasonal laborers. (A return to Canada was possible because many of them had retained Canadian citizenship). This migration resulted in a large Old Colony settlement of about 10,000 to 12,000 people. Part of the group has become settled in Ontario, but a large portion migrates back and forth to Mexico on a seasonal basis. Other Old Colonists have been migrating back to Manitoba from Mexico since the 1950s. In both Ontario and Manitoba they rarely have the opportunity to become landowners and thus become tenant farmers, laborers, or seasonal workers.

A group of about 500 Old Colonists established a settlement at Seminole, Tex., in 1977. Restrictive United States immigration laws have made further settlement in that country impossible. Despite all these emigrations, the Mexico Old Colony population has remained large. In 1984 it numbered about 29,000 adult members.

°°Kleine Gemeinde Mennonites who moved to Mexico in 1948 have also been forced to found new settlements. In 1958 they founded the Spanish Lookout settlement in Belize. In 1983 the Belize Kleine Gemeinde founded a new settlement in Nova Scotia. In 1968 a group of Sommerfeld Mennonites from Mexico founded a settlement in Bolivia. This church was named the Sommerfelder Mennonite Church.

Since the 1950s, hundreds of Paraguayan Mennonites from the Menno Colony have migrated. Some migrated to Bolivia in 1956 and founded the Gruenthal Mennonite Church. Others moved back to Manitoba because the Canadian economic opportunities were attractive. Mennonites in those colonies in Paraguay founded by refugees from the Soviet Union in 1930 and in the late 1940s, namely Fernheim, Friesland, Neuland, and Volendam, have migrated in even larger numbers to Canada. Some Mennonites from these later four colonies have moved to the Federal Republic of Germany. A few Mennonites from Brazil and Uruguay have also migrated to Germany.

One of the larger migrations of Mennonites in the 1970s and 1980s has been the migration from the Soviet Union to the Federal Republic of Germany, and to a lesser extent to Canada. This migration began in 1972 and continued strongly for about a decade. The migration became possible because of an agreement between the Federal Republic of Germany and the Soviet Union to allow family reunification. According to lists published in Sept. 1987, 12,849 Mennonite immigrants from the Soviet Union have landed in the Federal Republic since 1972. JF

Leonard Doell, The Bergthaler Mennonite Church of Saskatchewan 1892-1975 (Winnipeg: CMBC, 1987); Martin W. Friesen, Neue Heimat in der Chacowildnis (Altona, Man.: D. W. Friesen, 1987; Menno Colony: Chortitzer Komitee, 1987); 50 Jahre Kolonie Fernheim (Paraguay: Kolonie Fernheim, 1980); MWH (1984); MC Yearbook (1986-87); Peter Penner, "Kleinegemeinde Settlers Make a Mark in Nova Scotia," Menn. Rep., (Feb. 18, 1985), 9; Calvin W. Redekop, Strangers Become Neighbors: Mennonite and Indigenous Relations in the Paraguayan Chaco (Scottdale, 1980); Harry Leonard Sawatzky, Sie Suchten Eine Heimat: Deutsch-Mennonitische Kolonisierung in Mexiko, 1922-1984 (Marburg, Germany: N. H. Elwert, 1986); earlier version in English:

They Sought a Country (Berkeley: U. of California Press, 1971); Walter Schmiedehaus, Die Altkolonier-Menoniten in Mexiko (Winnipeg: CMBC, 1982); "Troubles Continue for Seminole Settlers," Menn. Rep. (Mar. 19, 1979), 1; David V. Wiebe, They Seek a Country: A Survey of Mennonite Migrations (Freeman: Pine Hill Press, 1974); Peter Wiens, Mennonites in Paraguay (Filadelphia, Paraguay: Fernheim Colony, 1987); James O. Lehman, "A Grand Migration Scheme," MQR, 59 (1985), 383-97.

See also Refugees.

Military Participation. During 20th c. wars, Mennonites in the United States and Canada represented the vast majority of °conscientious objectors. But many Mennonite young men opted for military service in each war. One of the unsettling discoveries in World War II was to find that despite the excellent °alternative service opportunities available to Mennonites in the °°Civilian Public Service (CPS) program in the United States and alternative service work camps in Canada, more Mennonite young men chose military service than alternative service.

During the period 1940 to 1947 in the United States 9,809 Mennonites were drafted. Of those 4,536 chose CPS and 5,273 joined the military. That is, 53.8 percent chose military service. This article concentrates on data from United States Mennonites.

In reflecting on these figures Guy F. Hershberger (Mennonite Church in the Second World War, Ch. 4) suggested peer pressure as a major factor in many decisions for military service. From an analysis of the data it is clear that a much higher percentage of men who attended high school entered military service than did those with grade school or Mennonite college educations.

Military participation was also affected by the degree of °acculturation and Americanization; for example almost no men went into the military from the Old Order Amish and Old Order Mennonite groups. They were simply not as aware of and subject to the wartime patriotic blandishments as their compatriots who attended high schools, or were in other ways more closely knit into their local communities.

Data on Mennonite military participation during the Korean and °Vietnam wars is not readily available, but the percentage of military participation seems to have declined substantially. The 1-W program with its attractive features of pay-for-service and easy entry, and the considerably less popular enthusiasm for the the wars all helped reduce the lure of military service for Mennonite young men.

How did Mennonite congregations deal with members in military service? In 1944 the editor of the Gospel Herald concluded that the plain teaching of the Scriptures and the stated position of the Mennonite Church (MC) made it impossible to retain in good standing in the church someone who was part of the military. The editor observed that some congregations expel members in the military while others leave the issue open until the return of the young man to the community.

The Mennonite Church (MC) Peace Problems Committee in World War II recommended to district conferences that young men in the military be treated as out of fellowship with the church, but that efforts be made to restore the men to fellowship. Most district conferences took action on the matter along lines outlined by the Peace Problems Committee. In most cases congregations required public confession of error and repentance before reinstatement was carried out (°discipline).

One of the tragedies of military participation has been the fact that as many as two-thirds of the military participators did not return to the church after military service. This represents a heavy loss to the church which can never be replaced.   ANK

Guy F. Hershberger, *The Mennonite Church in the Second World War* (Scottdale, 1951); Kauffman/Harder, *Anabaptists Four C. Later* (1975), 130-35; *Bibl. on War and Peace* (1987), 350-405, 651-716.

See also Conscription.

Millennialism. See Apocalypticism; Dispensationalism.

Miller, Ernest E. (1893-1975), was born to Daniel D. and Nettie Hostetler Miller at Middlebury, Ind. In 1918 he married Ruth Blosser, from Ada, Ohio. Two children, Thelma Miller Groff and Donald, were born to this union.

Miller was an educator throughout his active life. He earned a BA degree from Goshen College, Goshen, Ind. (1917) and MA (1929) and PhD (1939) degrees from New York U. After serving as principal and superintendent of schools in Shipshewana, Ind., (1914-18), he and his wife became missionaries in India under the Mennonite Board of Missions (MC) (1921-37). Here also he engaged largely in educational work, serving as principal of what became the Dhamtari Christian Academy.

In 1939 Miller became personnel director at Goshen College, and then served as president of the college, 1940-54. His administration brought the college into the North Central Association, increased the student body, greatly enlarged the international student program, erected new buildings, and established the Goshen College Biblical Seminary and the Collegiate School of Nursing.   WHS

John A. Lapp, *India* (Scottdale, 1972); Historical Committee of the American Mennonite Mission, Dhamtari, India, *The Love of Christ Hath Constrained Us* (Scottdale: MPH, 1949); John S. Umble, *Goshen College, 1894-1954* (Goshen College, 1955); *Goshen College Bulletin* (Apr., 1975); *Who's Who Mennonites* (1943), 169.

Miller, Mary Martha (1897-Sept. 21, 1963), professor of English at Hesston College, 1926-58, was born in Champaign Co., Ohio, in 1897. She moved frequently with her parents as they pioneered in Oklahoma, Texas, and Kansas. She graduated from Hesston College (BA, 1926) and the U. of Kansas (MA, 1928). Mary Miller was a teacher who lit the "lights" for hundreds of students—beginning in the elementary grades in both rural and city systems. At Hesston College in addition to classroom teaching of literature and composition, Mary served as dean of women.

She motivated students to write because she herself was a writer. For a period of 30 years, Mary wrote articles and short stories for various church periodicals. She helped to write the first Mennonite °summer Bible school materials. As a Sunday school teacher, she was in demand. A scholar and lover of the Scriptures, she made the Bible applicable to contemporary living. For a number of years she wrote a biblical drama to be given during the Christmas season. These were published in the *Builder*, 1956-59. From 1945 to 1947 she served in France under MCC. She wrote *A Pillar of Cloud* (North Newton: Mennonite Press, 1959, the story of Hesston College. Hesston College's Mary Miller Library, named in her honor, was dedicated in 1965.   MK

Menn. Bib. II, 482; Rich, *Mennonite Women* (1983), 123.

Miller, Orie O. (1892-Jan. 1977), a Mennonite (MC) layman, administrator who bridged the worlds of °business and church. The eldest in the family of Bishop D. D. and Jeanette Hostetler Miller, Middlebury, Ind., O. O., directed the farm work when his father traveled as an evangelist. Orie wanted to serve the church full-time as a school teacher, minister, or missionary. Before college he taught public school, and after his freshman year at Goshen College he directed Goshen's school of business.

Orie graduated from Goshen College in 1915, and that August married classmate Elta Wolf. The couple moved to Akron, Pa., where Orie soon became a part-owner in the shoe company headed by his father-in-law. Despite the growing success of the shoe business, Orie still felt called to church work, particularly the ministry. Three times he was a ministerial candidate at Ephrata Mennonite Church but the °°lot failed to fall on him. Speaking of his first experience in the lot, he said, "I just couldn't understand it. God didn't confirm my call. These were the most difficult days of my life." The church, however, did call Orie, asking him to help in °relief work in Syria and Armenia after World War I. As church leaders met in Lancaster, Pa., to discuss a request for Mennonite workers for overseas relief, "Father Miller leaned over to me [and said], 'Orie, shouldn't you volunteer for this?'" With his wife's assent and a leave from the business for several months, Orie sailed for Beirut on the the the USS *Pensacola* on Jan. 25, 1919.

Three months after his return to the United States, at a meeting regarding Mennonite needs in Russia, Orie again said yes when asked to go. But, how could he represent all of the committees? The idea for a Mennonite Central Committee (MCC) was born and became a reality on July 21, 1920. Orie was chosen to direct the first unit of volunteers. However, Orie's father-in-law, heading a business adversely affected by the postwar economic slump, was not ready to release him again. "You can't mix business and the church," he said. "You must give full time to the business or leave it." Orie went to Russia.

Orie and Clayton Kratz got into Russia and made arrangements to do relief work, however, the overthrow of the Wrangel Government prevented plans from being carried out. Orie returned to Constantinople and organized relief activities among the Russian refugees pouring into that city. He returned to Akron in spring 1921. He and his father-in-law eventually arrived at an arrangement whereby Orie gave about two-thirds time to the business and one-third to the church. Church work centered in world relief, °missions, and education. He was executive secretary of MCC, 1935-58.

In 1940, at age 48, Orie was ready to devote even more time to the church. He turned over the sales work to others he had trained and continued as director and secretary-treasurer of Miller Hess and Company, president of Highland Shoe Company, also in Akron, and treasurer of A. N. Wolf Shoe Company, Denver, Pa. In the church, his influence was felt in the vast program of Mennonite relief and °refugee resettlement, the °°Civilian Public Service Program, the organization and growth of °Mennonite Economic Development Associates (MEDA), the organization of Menno Travel Service and °Mennonite Mutual Aid, and numerous other Mennonite and inter-church causes.

Orie spelled out his philosophy of administration in three words: freedom, responsibility, and structure. "The administrator's job is to build a structure so everyone knows what his job is and to whom he is responsible. The capable administrator helps people work together without wasting time, fighting, or stepping on each other's toes. He helps people become a team. When a person accurately senses the structure, and fulfills his responsibility, he is free."

Orie and Elta had five children. Elta died in 1958. In 1960 Orie married Elta Sensenig. Orie died at the Landis Retirement Home near Lancaster, Pa.   JMB

Paul Erb, *Orie O. Miller* (Scottdale, 1969); J. Daniel Hess, Series of articles in *Chr. Living* (Feb., Mar., Apr., 1963); *Who's Who Mennonites* (1943), 172.

French Fries and World Missions

Orie O. Miller felt called to the ministry, was three times rejected by the °°lot, yet became one of the most remarkable, innovative, and courageous Mennonite leaders of his generation. He keenly sensed the interrelatedness of the score or more of agencies, both Mennonite and nondenominational, on whose boards of directors he sat—all of these agencies were part of the church and its mission. His vision and utter self-discipline made all this possible. Annually he read his Bible through from cover to cover, which enabled him to quote Scripture as others quoted the newspapers.

Orie Miller was not without a sense of humor. He claimed that he could travel around the world, which he did about 17 times, and order his meals anywhere with the three words: omelette, cocoa (or chocolate), and french fries. When he did just that in Paris, the annoyed French waiter snapped back: "We don't fry the French" and refused to take the order. Orie's philosophic response was characteristic: "That's how you get when you lose an empire," he said. France had just "lost" Morocco and Algeria. Someone said that Orie Miller saw more of the world than Marco Polo, opened more mission fields than David Livingstone, and was as innovative in church ministries as Thomas Edison was in technology. He was God's gift to the church.   PJD

Milverton, Ont., Old Order Amish Settlement in Perth Co., 20 mi. (35 km. west of Kitchener-Waterloo), is the oldest and largest of seven Amish settlements in Ontario, and is the only remaining Canadian Old Order Amish community. Settlements established since World War II are usually seen as the Canadian New Amish. New settlements are largely made up of Amish who migrated to Canada from the United States to avoid post-war military conscription or alternate service. Later Canadian restrictions have, however, caused some Amish to return to the United States. This has caused most Ontario settlements to remain at one to two church districts (congregations). Amish in the Milverton area hold to older traditions in dress and °buggy styles, e.g., open buggies without tops. Interaction between the old and new communities is minimal. In a sense, the Milverton community is the last of a much larger group (°°East Zorra, Wilmot; ME IV:62, 64), many of whom are now affiliated with Beachy Amish Mennonites and Conservative Mennonites.   SLY

Ministry, Pastoral. See Ordination; Pastoral Counseling; Pastoral Education; Pastoral Visiting; Relief Work.

Minnesota (ME III:707). The largest concentration of Mennonites in Minnesota is in the Mountain Lake area in the sw. part of the state. Congregations are also found in northern Minnesota and one congregation is located in se. Minnesota. Mennonite groups in Minnesota include the General Conference Mennonite Church (GCM; 7 congregations), Mennonite Church (MC; (5 congregations), Mennonite Brethren (3 congregations), Conservative Mennonite Conference (3 congregations) Evangelical Mennonite Brethren (°Fellowship of Evangelical Bible Churches; 2 congregations), and Midwest Mennonite Fellowship (2 congregations). Faith Church in Minneapolis is affiliated with both the General Conference Mennonite Church and the Mennonite Church (MC). Total membership in 1986 was 2,693 of which 1,610 belong to General Conference congregations.

Approximately 50 Amish families from Ohio moved to Fillmore Co. in se. Minnesota in 1974. Beachy Amish Mennonites also came in the 1970s, settling in two communities in central Minnesota.

In 1954 the Mennonite Brethren began a church in Minneapolis, moving in 1964 to the suburb of New Hope. General Conference (GCM) people in Minneapolis, who had been worshiping with the Mennonite Brethren, began their own fellowship in 1960 (Faith Church). A General Conference congregation begun in Mankato in 1979 was disbanded in 1985. Another church planting effort began in Duluth in 1984 (sponsored by the Northern District of the General Conference Mennonite Church). General Conference Mennonites and the Mennonite Church (MC) have combined to plant churches in St. Paul (1984) and Moorhead (1986). The Mennonite Church (MC) began church work in International Falls in 1969.

Minneapolis has been the site of several large Mennonite gatherings including Probe '72 the General Conference special sessions on civil responsibility in 1979, and the United States Conference of the Mennonite Brethren in 1980.

In the late 1960s and early 1970s a General Conference voluntary service unit was assigned to the Minneapolis Workhouse. In 1979 the Mennonite Central Committee began a voluntary service unit in Minneapolis-St. Paul working primarily with Native American agencies.   MDS

MC Yearbook (1986-87), 30, 99; *Minutes and Reports*, Northern District (GCM; 1986), 45-46; *MB Yearbook* (1984); congregational anniversary program; Wittlinger, *Piety and Obedience* (1978), 147.

Misión Evangélica Menonita, Bolivia (Evangelical Mennonite Mission Conference in Bolivia). From 1965 to 1968 radio programs in Low German and High German for Mennonite colonies were the start of what led to Evangelical Mennonite Mission Conference (EMMC) involvement in Bolivia. David and Tina Wiebe, New Tribes missionaries at the time, later became the founding missionary couple (with EMMC 1969-77) at Chorovi—an area halfway between the Tres Palmas and Bergthal colonies, on the eastern edge of the Canadiense colony (°Sommerfeld Mennonites; °Bolivia). While some individuals from different colonies have been spiritually enriched by the EMMC ministry, colony leadership has usually felt threatened and been concerned about EMMC presence. (The °Evangelical Mennonite Mission Conference in Canada originated in a division within the °Sommerfeld Mennonites in Canada.)

A five-bed clinic, built in 1973-74, has provided health treatment for a 25-mi. (40-km.) radius—to both colony and Bolivian populations. Its services have included staff nurses, a preventive health program in surrounding communities (1983-), and regular visits from an evangelical Bolivian doctor (1985-) .

Two Bolivian congregations have resulted from EMMC ministry. Zafranilla, located near the clinic, began in 1974 (50 members, 1986). Pedro Dias, located in a semi-urban squatter community of the same name on the outskirts of Santa Cruz, is the second effort. It began in 1983. Drilling safe water wells, providing public health services, a dynamic congregation of 75 members, and a 200-student private school (kindergarten to third grade) are features of this effort.   GM

MWH (1984), 57.

Misión Evangélica Menonita en Ecuador (Mennonite Mission in Ecuador). See Iglesia Evangélica Menonita, Ecuador.

Missiology. See Mission.

Mission (ME III:712; IV:1093). The study of Christian mission is a relatively recent addition to the theological curriculum. Formal attempts to write theologies of mission only began toward the end of the 19th c. Specialist mission training schools emphasized the practical aspects of Christian mission and offered instruction in methods of °evangelism and church development along with the biblical basis of missions. Graduate seminaries and universities were concerned that the study of missions was not academically respectable. When courses in missions were finally allowed in such institutions, they were placed under the rubric *practical theology*.

Critics have argued that the academic world has fundamentally misunderstood both the nature of mission and the function of theology. Mission is not an addendum to the church or one of several marks of the church. In the well-known aphorism of Emil Brunner, "The church exists by mission as fire exists by burning." By the same token, theology ought to focus on the nature and execution of the church's witness to the world.

Missiology. Whereas the term *missiology* is a rather recent import into the Anglo-American world, it has been used much longer in Europe. However, whether one speaks of mission studies or missiology, the subject is the same. Missiology is the discipline of studying the Christian mission in terms of its biblical and theological foundations, the history of the spread of the Christian movement, and appropriate methods and strategies in light of the goal of mission. Missiologists employ tools of various academic disciplines in carrying out their work: °history, °theology, °biblical studies, °anthropology, and other social sciences. Thus *missiology* is a more comprehensive term than *theology of mission*. It includes theology as well as all other aspects of the study of Christian mission.

Developments since 1950. Two major streams of thought have dominated Protestant missions in the 20th c. Churches and mission agencies that identified with the World Missionary Conference held at Edinburgh in 1910 and the International Missionary Council comprise the conciliar movement. Especially since the Fundamentalist-Modernist controversies that crested in the 1920s, more conservative Protestants began developing alternative channels for association (Interdenominational Foreign Mission Association, 1917; Evangelical Foreign Missions Association, 1945). Some Mennonite groups affiliated with the Foreign Missions Conference of North America (founded 1893). When FMC merged with the National Council of Churches (NCC) in the United States in 1950, Mennonite agencies retained only an associate relationship to the FMC and its successor, the NCC's Division of Overseas Ministries. Other Mennonite and Brethren in Christ mission agencies joined the National Association of Evangelicals' Evangelical Foreign Missions Association. Within the Mennonite family there has always been this range of views. Each of these two wings of Protestantism developed agencies and mechanisms for defining characteristic positions on the theology of Christian mission. The conciliar wing has been marked by considerable innovation while the conservative movement has attempted to maintain what it considered to be its historic position.

The theology of mission has been in considerable ferment since the 1950s. Under the impact of the °Biblical Theology movement the importance of ecclesiology for theology of mission was stressed. Especially in Europe there was a call to give eschatology greater prominence in mission thought. In the 1950s a consensus began to emerge among theologians of Christian mission that the source of true missionary witness is in the very nature of God rather than ecclesiology, eschatology, pneumatology, anthropology, or practical theology. To speak of the *missio dei* is to recognize that God has acted in a missionary way in sending Jesus Christ into the world. We therefore properly speak of *mission* as that overarching divine purpose and *missions* as those specific efforts which groups of Christians organize in particular times and places in response to God's own sending. That consensus came under attack from those who insisted that the impulse for missionary witness resulted when the church responded to the agenda set for it by the world. In more recent years the assertion has been made that the °kingdom of God is the central theme in mission. But is is generally felt that with the emergence of local or indigenous theologies, including °liberation theology, attention shifted away from the theology of mission over the past decade.

Conservative Protestants have experienced growing tension and debate concerning a theology of mission. Dispensational eschatology, which played an important role in conservative theology of mission earlier, has lost influence. Conservative Protestants have increasingly been challenged to face the social implications of the gospel. This challenge has produced widespread debate over the relationship between proclamation of the gospel and Christian social ministry (°social gospel).

A series of international conferences sponsored by various groups of Conservative Protestants have helped shift the terms of debate: Wheaton (1966), Berlin (1966), Lausanne (1974), Pattaya (1980), Grand Rapids (1982), and Wheaton (1983). Leaders of the non-Western churches are increasingly entering into these debates, bringing other than the Western worldview to bear on the terms of discussion.

Mennonites have participated actively in most of these conferences. In their own practice and understanding of mission they did not separate proclamation from demonstration. This has made them uneasy with the conservative Protestant prescription. But Mennonites have appreciated the conservative concern to maintain fidelity to the Bible and continued engagement in the world.

Following publication of his book, *The Bridges of God* in 1955, Donald McGavran organized an Institute of Church Growth. The °church growth movement has subjected mission strategy to a vigorous critique using growth of the church as the key criterion. Especially conservative Protestants have welcomed this approach. Some Mennonites have raised questions about the church growth concept, in particular its early stress on the homogeneous unit principle (HUP) and group identity. Others have enthusiastically adopted the methodology worked out by church growth leaders.

An important development for all mission thought and practice is the emergence in 1972 of the concept of °contextualization. Initially, this was developed as successor to °"indigenization" and was applied to theological education. Increasingly it has come to be seen as a shift in understanding which involves all aspects of the life of a church. Mission theory is still struggling to work out its implications.

Mennonites and Theology of Mission. Notwithstanding the important precedent set by their Anabaptist forebears in the 16th c., Mennonites and Brethren in Christ late in the 20th c. were still struggling to apprehend a missionary vision which would serve as as basis for motivating their people

for witness to the world. For the Anabaptists the church was mission; for 20th c. Mennonites mission is but one aspect of church life, not its integrating dynamic.

The modern missionary movement, which emerged around 1800 as a product of the 18th c. evangelical revival, and various subsequent renewal movements spurred Mennonites in the late 19th c. to engage in missionary work. Mennonites invested little effort in developing a theological understanding of mission out of their own tradition. Rather they relied on what other traditions produced.

For example, J. D. °Graber, the most prolific Mennonite writer on mission up to 1965, canvassed the entire range of Protestant missiological writings and interpreted key insights for the Mennonite public. He did not attempt to develop a Mennonite position. In his influential statement of "The Anabaptist Vision" (1945), Harold S. °Bender made no reference to the missionary character of the 16th c. Anabaptists. But in 1946 Franklin H. Littell wrote of "The Anabaptist Theology of Mission" which, he argued, was of the essence of the movement. No immediate attempt was made to follow this with a contemporary Mennonite theology of mission.

By the 1960s a number of people were asking whether it was possible to draw insights and inspiration from the 16th c. Anabaptist experience that would help Mennonites develop a missiology that was more consistent with their convictions than that offered by either conciliar or conservative Protestants. A number of essays have appeared which contribute to this development, but to date no sustained and systematic treatment has been offered.

The Mennonite Missionary Study Fellowship, which began as a project of the Institute of Mennonite Studies (Elkhart, Ind.) in 1971, has been a forum for promoting explorations into various missiological themes. The "Mission Studies Series," published by Herald Press and initially a byproduct of MMSF, has promoted research and writing which contributes to development of a Mennonite missiology. Since 1972 the quarterly journal, *Mission Focus*, has cultivated Mennonite reflection and writing on missiological themes. In addition, various histories of Mennonite missions and books dealing with aspects of the mission task have been published since the 1950s.

Developments in Mennonite Missions Since 1950. The period since the end of World War II must be divided into several stages. The first (1945-59) was a time of sustained growth. Immediately following the end of the war a major °relief program was mounted in Europe and elsewhere to assist those suffering the effects of war. At the same time steps began to be taken to send missionaries to found new missions. The following tabulation of the number of Mennonite and Brethren in Christ mission programs established in each decade since 1850 puts the period in perspective. 1850-59 - 1; 1860-69 - 0; 1870-79 - 1; 1880-89 - 0; 1890-99 - 5; 1900-1908 - 7; 1910-19 - 5; 1920-29 - 1; 1930-39 - 4; 1940-49 - 18; 1950-59 - 42; 1960-69 - 17; 1970-79 - 28; 1980-86 - 15. These figures do not include relief and °development projects administered by Mennonite Central Committee. The 60 mission projects established in 20 years (1940-60) were more than twice the number established during 90 years from 1850 to 1940.

The second post-war period (1960-69), by contrast, was a time of consolidation for Mennonite missions. This perioid coincided with the end of colonial rule for many countries which had been under the control of European powers. The climate changed as tensions between missions and the churches they founded began to mount. Civil wars in Nigeria and Zaire, and the protracted war in °Vietnam marked this period as one of profound unrest.

A third period (1970-75) brought about retrenchment and adjustment. Some of the tensions which surfaced in the previous decade were not resolved until the early 1970s. The world economy which boomed during the period after World War II began to stagnate. Resources for missions and development contracted and consequently fewer new projects were launched.

The next period (1976-86) marked a partial recovery from the sluggishness of the early 1970s but there has been nothing approaching the scale of development during the 1945-60 period. Although new programs have been established these typically have been smaller in scale and frequently in association with established churches or other groups.

In summary, the missionary movement has been undergoing important structural change during the past two decades, parallel to the world economy and political order. Centers of initiative are emerging in the non-Western world which will take their place alongside, or even supplant, those in the West. The most outstanding example of this development is the church in China. Following the closing of China to outside influences in 1949 until the opening of China to such contact in 1979, it was difficult to obtain reliable assessments of the condition of the church in China. Many observers concluded that the church had suffered irreparable harm under the communist government and thus had been wiped out. Since 1979 it has become clear that the church in China, in spite of great persecution and suffering, has survived and now has a sense of identity as the church in China rather than being a foreign implant. This is representative of a worldwide development among mission-founded churches.   WRS

"Bibliography of Mennonite Missions," *Mission Focus*, 12 no. 4 (Dec. 1984); J. D. Graber, *The Church Apostolic* (Scottdale, 1960); Donald R. Jacobs, *Pilgrimage in Mission* (Scottdale, 1983); A. J. Klassen, ed., *The Church in Mission* (Fresno: MB Board of Christian Literature, 1967); G. W. Peters, *Foundations of Mennonite Brethren Missions* (Hillsboro and Winnipeg: Kindred Press, 1984); Wilbert R. Shenk, ed., *Anabaptism and Mission* (Scottdale, 1984); idem, ed., *Mission Focus: Current Issues* (Scottdale, 1980); Wittlinger, *Piety and Obedience* (1978), ch. 9; Peter Penner, *No Longer at Arm's Length: A History of Mennonite Brethren Home Missions in Canada* (Scottdale: Kindred, 1986); Eric Hege, "The Development of Mission Interest Among French Mennonites," *MQR*, 58 (1984), 258-71; Lois Barrett, *Vision* (1983); James C. Juhnke, *Mission* (1979); Theron Schlabach, *Gospel Versus Gospel* (Scottdale, 1980).

See also Moratorium; Service; Urban Church.

A Young Church Leads the Way

A new congregation, started at the request of a newly converted young Japanese businessmen, met in the garage of a house used by a mission agency in Kobe. Around 20 people, most young, gathered on Sundays and weekdays. A spirit of freedom, warmth, joy and expectation always prevailed. Yet it was a development that had not been anticipated by the newly arrived General Conference Mennonite missionaries. They were still in language school. They were not supposed to "really start" church planting until they reached their intended destination: the island Kyushu. Kobe is located on Honshu.

Three young men were baptized a year later, in October 1952. But soon after, the mission decided, in light of informal °comity agreements with other Mennonite mission agencies, not to be responsible for the group any more. When told of this unexpected change, these people took courage and immediately decided to continue on their own, willingly assuming all the responsibilities of preaching, pastoral care, and witnessing, asking the mission only to lend them the garage and give some spiritual assistance when necessary. This lively fellowship continued for several years until the early leaders of the group left for Christian training and ministry in other places. Two of them were serving as Mennonite pastors in 1986.

By necessity the group learned together and disciplined one another. Having a keen interest in the Anabaptist-Mennonite faith and history, they studied spontaneously, trying to re-interpret Anabaptism in their own situation. Viewing critically the existing churches following after a western pattern, they struggled to be an °indigenous Christian fellowship, putting primary emphasis on "relation" (koinonia) rather than "function" (institutionalized church life). The Kobe group may have been a naive indigenous expression of an Anabaptist congregation, the °voluntary association of believers.   TY

Juhnke, *Mission* (1979), 110.

See also Yamada Takashi; Yanada Hiroshi.

Mission Boards. The first mission board to be organized by North American Mennonites was established by members of the General Conference Mennonite Church in 1872. The Mennonite Brethren followed in 1878, Mennonite Church (MC) in 1882, and Brethren in Christ in 1895. Most groups formed these boards with a mandate to conduct missionary work both in North America and internationally. Since World War II several groups have reorganized the domestic and foreign programs under separate boards. The Mennonite Brethren look to their districts to administer domestic church extension.

Lack of a clear or uniform polity among Mennonites is reflected in the way mission agencies have been formed. Since most groups did not have strong denominational organizations prior to 1945, the mission, health and welfare, and educational programs enjoyed considerable autonomy. The Mennonite Church (MC) developed mission structures at the district conference level. Each district mission board, in turn, appointed members to the Mennonite Board of Missions. After the early 1930s several of these district conferences, most notably Lancaster Mennonite Conference, developed substantial programs, including international projects. Since the

NORTH AMERICAN
MENNONITE/BRETHREN IN CHRIST MISSION BOARDS
Wilbert Shenk, compiler and author

Name	Address	Founded	No. of Countries(1987)	No. Workers Abroad (1987)
°Africa Inter-Mennonite Mission	Elkhart, Ind.	1911	5	80
#°Brethren in Christ Missions	Mount Joy, Pa.	1895	8	38
	Stevensville, Ont.			
Church of God in Christ, Mennonite	Moundridge, Ks.	1933	10	152
Evangelical Mennonite Brethren	Omaha, Nebr.	1936	28	87
°Evangelical Mennonite Church, Commission on Overseas Missions	Fort Wayne, Ind.	1943	5	20
°Evangelical Mennonite Conference Board of Missions	Steinbach, Man.	1953	4	95
°Evangelical Mennonite Mission Conference	Winnipeg, Man.	1939	4	19
General Conference Mennonite Church	Newton, Ks.	1872		
°Commission on Overseas Mission			15	162
#Commission on Home Ministries				
#°Mennonite Brethren Board of Missions and Services	Hillsboro, Ks. Winnipeg, Man.	1878	23	149
Mennonite Church				
#°Conservative Mennonite Board of Mission and Charities/Rosedale Mennonite Missions	Irwin, Ohio	1919	4	21
#°Eastern Mennonite Board of Missions and Charities	Salunga, Pa.	1914	21	132
#°Franconia Mennonite Conference Mission Commission	Souderton, Pa.	1917	1	6
Franklin Mennonite Conference	Chambersburg, Pa.		1	12
#°Mennonite Board of Missions	Elkhart, Ind.	1882	26	130
Mennonite Mission Board of Pacific Coast Conference	Salem, Ore.	1906	1	2
°Virginia Mennonite Board of Missions	Harrisonburg, Va.	1919	3	8
#°Mennonite Central Committee	Akron, Pa.	1920	48	527
Other Mennonite Bodies:				
Bible Mennonite Fellowship Missions Committee	Albany, Ore.		1	
Caribbean Light and Truth	Keota, Iowa	1976	1	2
Conservative Mennonite Fellowship Mission Board, Inc./Guatemala	Logan, Ohio	1964	1	11
Eastern Pennsylvania Mennonite Church/ Mennonite Messianic Mission Board	Lititz, Pa.	1968	2	
Fellowship Churches Mission Programs:				
Open Door Ministries (Mexico)	West Liberty, Ky.			
West Indies Witness (Dominican Republic)	Farmington, N.M.			
Conservative Mennonite New Life Endeavor (India)	Hensall, Ont.			
Philippine Witness (Philippine Islands)	Tilley, Alta.			
Light of Life Mission (Nigeria)	Columbiana, Ohio			
Mennonite Air Missions Board	Guatemala	1972	1	7
Mid-Atlantic Mennonite Fellowship Mission Board	Bethel, Pa.	1978		
Northern Light Gospel Mission Conference	Red Lake, Ont.			
Southeastern Mennonite Conference Mission Board	Dayton, Va.	1972		
Washington-Franklin Mennonite Conference Home Missions Committee	Greencastle, Pa.			
Mission Interests Committee of Beachy Amish Church	Christiana, Pa.	1953	4	

°Denotes members of Council of International Ministries.
#Denotes members of Inter-Mennonite Home Ministries Council.

1950s a number of new agencies have been formed by groups which either were never formally a part of a Mennonite conference or deliberately separated themselves from such a body.

The Evangelical Mennonite Brethren (since 1987 known as the Fellowship of Evangelical Bible Churches) have never created their own mission program overseas. Rather they pursued the policy of recruiting workers and providing support to various interdenominational and faith missions. The Mennonite Brethren Board of Missions and Services has given support to members of their constituency serving with interdenominational agencies while administering Mennonite Brethren mission program as well.

The Northern Light Gospel Mission was founded by Irvin Schantz in Minnesota in the late 1930s and then relocated to Red Lake, Ont., about 1953. Schantz raised his support from interested individuals and congregations. In 1965 the churches of the Red Lake region were organized into an independent conference (°Northern Light Gospel Mission Conference) without ties to other church bodies or agencies.

Early in the 20th c. mission interest among Mennonites had the effect of fostering °inter-Mennonite cooperation. Such cooperation was generally focused on a specific mission and did not lead to a union movement in North America. Thus the China Mennonite Mission Society was formed out of initiatives by the Bartel family, Krimmer Mennonite Brethren, Mennonite Brethren, Evangelical Mennonite Brethren, and Missionary Church Association. The Evangelical Mennonite Brethren supported a couple for service in India in association with the Mennonite Church (MC) in 1907. This arrangement lasted several years only. The most enduring cooperative effort has been the Africa Inter-Mennonite Mission, formerly the Congo Inland Mission, founded in 1911. Six Mennonite groups were participating in AIMM in 1987.

Formation of the Mennonite Central Committee (MCC) in 1920 as a cooperative relief effort, eventually involving all Mennonite and Brethren in Christ groups, has become the major united effort. MCC has had a variety of programmatic relationships with the constituent mission agencies. In 1958 the Council of Mission Board Secretaries, known since 1976 as the Council of International Ministries (CIM), was formed as a vehicle for better coordination between MCC and the mission agencies. CIM meets semi-annually. CIM has been a means of contact and consultation with the Europäische Mennonitische Evangelisationskomitee (EMEK; European Mennonite Mission Committee).

The Inter-Mennonite Home Ministries Council was organized in 1968. It meets annually as as forum for exchange between administrators of mission and service programs in Canada and the United States.

Some Mennonite mission agencies publish mission magazines to promote their work: *Missionary Messenger* (Eastern Mennonite Board of Missions and Charities [MC]), *AIMM Messenger* (Africa Inter-Mennonite Mission), and *Therefore* (Brethren in Christ Missions). Others rely on their denominational periodicals or women's missionary association magazines to promote their work. WRS

Lois Barrett, *Vision* (1983); Juhnke, *Mission* (1979); Melvin J. Loewen, *Threescore: The Story of an Emerging Mennonite Church in Central Africa* (Elkhart, Ind.: Congo Inland Mission, 1972); Theron F. Schlabach, *Gospel Versus Gospel* (Scottdale, 1979); Wilbert R. Shenk in *MWH* (1978), 20-31; idem, *An Experiment in Interagency Cooperation* (Elkhart, Ind.: Council of International Ministries, 1986); J. B. Toews, *The Mennonite Brethren Church in Zaire* (Fresno, Cal.: MB Board of Christian Literature, 1978); J. J. Toews, *The Mennonite Brethren Mission in Latin America* (Winnipeg: MB Board of Christian Literature, 1975).

See also Chaco Mission; Doopsgezinde Zendingsraad; Licht den Indianern; Mennonitisches Missionskomitee für Paraguay; Persatuan Gereja-Gereja Kristen Muria Indonesia (for the PIPKA mission board).

Mission Education. During the late 1950s Mennonites in North America identified and isolated mission education (sometimes called education for mission) as a focus within congregational Christian education. A seminar at Laurelville Mennonite Center near Scottdale, Pa., in July 1959 emphasized, in line with Anabaptist concepts of °discipleship and witness, that missions are at the center of church life with mission education an integral part of °Christian education.

Mission education, the seminar findings suggested, lays groundwork for understanding and undertaking the world outreach of the church. It develops attitudes, convictions, ideals, and commitment. It involves a long-range effort to bring individuals face to face, in an orderly sequence, with mission philosophy, needs, and work throughout the world. It provides historical and other backgrounds necessary for adequate interpretation of what is going on in the mission work of the church.

Convened by the Mennonite publishers, an inter-Mennonite Mission Education Council functioned from 1960 to 1977. Active partners were the General Conference Mennonite Church and Mennonite Church (MC), with Mennonite Brethren and Brethren in Christ less active. Mennonite Central Committee staff participated fully in both planning and financing. The council produced a series of congregational study materials for adults and for children, including occasional films.

In October 1974 at Rosemont, Ill., the council extended its regular meeting to consider theological and cultural understandings which undergirded Mennonite mission and service in the mid-1970s and to discuss how these understandings related to mission education. Findings of the full-day's deliberation recorded seven consensus points: (1) Mennonites have a common framework—a need for proclamation, the universality of the gospel, the lordship of Christ, the church as community, the believer's servanthood stance. (2) Mennonites are all experiencing change in their mission with the subsequent opportunity to help people understand these changes. (3) They are aware of and concerned about the economic contrasts among Mennonites from poverty to affluence—with related life-style implications. (4) Mennonites recognize the relationship between culture and the proclamation of the gospel, noting areas related to North American affluence. (5) The consultation agreed that Mennonites carry concern for shared decision-making and seek ways to close the economic gaps. (6) They affirm that Christian mission is multidirectional and that third world churches have something to teach North Americans. (7) The consultation underscored the realization that the call to Christian mission is not primarily to individuals but to a people.

By May 1977 at Hillsboro, Ks., the council agreed to dissolve with the anticipation that mission education agenda be considered through other continuing °inter-Mennonite associations such as the Council on International Ministries, Home Ministries Council, and Mennonite Publishers Fellowship.

In so doing, the council reiterated that mission education is a significant ongoing task in Mennonite congregations. The council observed that mission education is integral to overall educational agenda and not to be relegated to a narrow slot so labeled. Evolving patterns of congregational life call for increasingly creative ways of providing resources for mission education, with those resources including different ingredients at different times.

Mennonite Board of Missions (MC) organized a Mennonite Church consultation on education for mission in April 1983. Thirty-nine participants worked intensely for three days identifying steps toward a comprehensive denominational design of education for mission. The consultation recognized four resource areas for the task: the Holy Spirit who renews vision and motivates; people in congregations gifted by God for mission; gifted and trained leaders who can model mission and enable members in the mission; communication technology to create global awareness and dispense information.

The 1983 consultation made seven summary declarations: (1) The Mennonite Church (MC) is at a point of transition in mission philosophy and practice. (2) The mission of the church must be carried out both by the local congregation and the broader church. (3) The congregation, in partnership with related congregations and church agencies, is the primary instrument of God's mission and must be significantly involved in mission in its own context. (4) The future of the world mission rests in congregations being aware of and relating to congregations around the world in an experience of global interdependence. (5) Effective education for mission demands congregational vision and follow-through as well as collective cooperation in developing and formulating vision and in sharing vision and resources throughout the Christian world community. (6) Mission education strategies will be varied in light of the many and varying types of congregations present in our peoplehood. (7) Leadership training is of crucial significance for education for mission.
WER

Minutes of respective meetings are filed in MC Archives (Goshen).

See also Missionary Education and Training; Women in Mission; Women's Missionary and Service Commission.

Mission et l'Église Mennonite en Burkina Faso (Mennonite Mission and Church in Burkina Faso). The first missionaries from Africa Inter-Mennonite Mission (AIMM) arrived in Burkina Faso (Upper Volta) during the latter part of 1978. After having had formal French studies in France these four missionaries and one child had to learn the local trade language of Dioula (Jula). Orodara, the capital city of the Province of Kenedougou, was chosen as their base.

The goal of the work was to establish churches throughout the province where both the spiritual and the physical needs of the people would be ministered to. In 1980 the first congregation was organized, and since then three more have begun.

In 1984 the mission (church) was officially recognized by the government. Within the church organization there is equal representation of both national and foreign people on the board (1988). There were more than 40 members in the four congregations (1988). Along with local discipleship training, two of the members have gone to Bible school and one attended seminary in Bangui, Central African Republic.
DLR

MWH (1984), 18.

Mission Schools. When early missionaries arrived in their respective locations they found that educational opportunities, even on the elementary level were not available to large segments of the population. This was especially true in rural areas and among the economically and socially marginal people. In some cultures formal educational opportunities (schools) were for boys and young men only. The notion of universal educational opportunity, which Western missionaries brought with them, thus motivated the establishment of schools. Records show that as educational efforts showed up on the agenda of the mission agencies, there was also considerable questioning and resistance on the part of certain constituencies in the supporting sending churches. Not fully understanding the needs in the respective fields, there were those who were critical of the attention and resources devoted to schools. These people thought that missionaries and their resources should be devoted to the preaching of the gospel and the salvation of souls.

Missionaries perceived that °literacy was important to overcome social and economic exploitation and to enable people, whether Christian or non-Christian, to experience fuller lives. For Christians, literacy was necessary to enable individual and corporate reading of the Scriptures, hymns, and other religious literature. A literate and enlightened body of Christians was essential to the growth and development of the national church and its ministries. Leadership training for men and women would provide indigenous leadership for the churches as well as for the communication of the gospel to non-Christian neighbors. The whole spectrum of educational institutions (elementary, middle, secondary, and Bible schools; colleges and °seminaries) emerged on the mission scene. On the collegiate and seminary level involvement was cooperative with other mission groups.

Vocational education of various kinds (e.g., carpentry) as well as professional training, (°nursing schools, normal schools for teachers) were responses to the human and institutional needs encountered in most fields where Mennonite missions operated. Such training and resultant economic opportunity provided income-producing employment for people who were then better able to support themselves, their dependents, and the program of the indigenous church. This was especially true in those settings where it was common for converts to be ostracized or boycotted (Hindu caste discipline) or otherwise alienated from the social and economic security of their respective communities. Orphan children who came to the mission orphanages needed more than elementary schooling if they were to become homemakers and self-supporting responsible community and church members.

Religious instruction was included in the curriculum of the mission-maintained institutions. Sometimes this was limited by the social and political climate of the country. Prescribed state curricula and standards needed to be respected. Generally nationals who had the qualifications required by government standards were employed. Although preference was given to Christian candidates because of the objectives of the school, they were not always available in specific subject areas.

Bible schools and pastors' training schools prepared evangelists, teachers, and pastors. In some cases these schools were cooperative ventures supported by several mission agencies. On the seminary level three Mennonite groups (Mennonite Church, General Conference Mennonite Church, and Mennonite Brethren Church) have participated in the interdenominational Union Biblical Seminary at Pune, India (formerly at Yavatmal). In Colombia the Mennonite Brethren mission participated in the United Biblical Seminary of Colombia, which was unique in its efforts to provide °theological education by extension. In Indonesia the Dutch Mennonite efforts in theological education were also cooperative in structure.

Schools established by the missions have in some settings continued under the auspices of the national churches. Others have been closed as respective governments have made provision for educational needs. Others were transferred to government control as part of emerging national educational systems. It can be said that the pioneering in and modeling of education for boys and girls, and young men and women have been significant factors in social change, as well as contributing to the indigenization of the churches. The schools have made a lasting contribution to many individuals and to the enrichment of the communities where they brought the good news of Jesus Christ and the gospel's concern for the whole person. The records will show, furthermore, that many persons trained in mission schools have risen to significant places of leadership, not only in the church, but in educational work, commerce, industry, and national governments.   WWG

Lois Barrett, *Vision* (1983), 19-23; Martha R. Burkhalter, "Higher Education of Women in India under Christian Auspices" (MRE thesis, Biblical Seminary in New York, 1934); Ernest P. Dyck, "An Analysis of American In-Service Education as a Basis for the Improvement of In-Service Teachers in the American Mennonite Brethren Mission in the Belgian Congo," (MA thesis, U. of Washington, Seattle, 1959); Juhnke, *Mission* (1979), 35-37; John A Lapp, *India* (1972), 117-35; Martin C. Lehman, "Experiments in Rural Education Work at Dhamtari C. P. India" in *Fourteen Experiments in Rural Education*, ed., A. B. Van Doren (Calcutta: Association Press, 1928), 26-39; Phyllis Martens, *The Mustard Seed: Story of Mennonite Brethren Missions* (Fresno,

Cal.: Mennonite Brethren Board of Christian Education, 1971); Ernest E. Miller, "The Problem of National Education in India" (MA thesis, Biblical Seminary in New York, 1929); Josiah M. Muganda, "The Impact of the Mennonite Missions on Mara Region, Tanzania 1934-1967" (MA thesis, Howard U., 1978); Samuel F. Pannabecker, *The Christian Mission of the General Conference Mennonite Church* (Newton, 1961); Theron F. Schlabach, *Gospel Versus Gospel* (Scottdale, 1980), 132-43; John J. Thiessen, "The Synagogue and the Mission School: How the Synagogue in St. Paul's Time Prepared the Mindset of the People for the Gospel" (MA thesis, Bluffton College, 1931); Lawrence M. Yoder, "The Church of the Muria: A History of the Muria Christian Church of Indonesia (MTh diss., Fuller Theological Seminary, 1981); Mary M. Good, "A Tentative Program of Study for the Garjan Memorial School" (M.A. thesis, George Peabody College for Teachers, Nashville, 1936); Mary Neuhauser Royer, "Education of Village Children in a Central Province, India" (M.A. thesis, George Peabody College for Teachers, Nashville, 1931).

See also Sprunger, Lilly Bachman and Vernon.

Missionary Education and Training. When Pieter Jansz was sent to Java by the Mennonite Society for the Spread of the Gospel in The Netherlands Overseas Possession in 1851 as the first modern Mennonite missionary, he received biblical and theological training at the Mennonite seminary in Amsterdam and training in the language, geography, and ethnology of Java at the Royal Academy in Delft.

Later in North America in the 1860s, Mennonites opened the Wadsworth Institute with training for missions as a primary goal. This was also part of the motivation for the opening of later educational institutions. In the 1980s all four graduate-level Mennonite °seminaries in North America have specialized centers for training in °evangelism and °mission.

Since Pieter Jansz went to Java in 1851, Mennonites have used a wide variety of Bible schools, colleges, universities, and seminaries and have also studied at specialized institutes set up to train for mission service. Most of these institutions have been in Europe or North America. Mission candidates have usually studied language in institutions in their country of service and a very few have also done formal study in Bible and theology in those countries.

Mennonites have never been of one mind on the need for specialized training for mission. Many have gone into service with no training at all, others with many years of specialized graduate-level preparation. However Mennonites have probably emphasized specialized mission preparation more than most conservative groups of similar size. Mennonite missionaries have been particularly known for their work with the languages of the people among whom they serve.

A new chapter in preparation for mission was opened in 1971 when the Commission on Overseas Mission (GCM), the Mennonite Board of Missions (MC), Goshen Biblical Seminary (MC), and Mennonite Biblical Seminary (GCM) jointly set up the [Overseas] Mission Training Center in Elkhart, Ind. This marked the first time that Mennonite sending agencies and schools together established an institution for the training of workers and the first time that both schools and agencies participated directly in such training. The Mission Training Center is selfconsciously a place which brings together agency and school perspectives on the missionary task.

The Mennonite Missionary Study Fellowship, sponsored by the Mission Training Center in Elkhart, is open to all Mennonites and others interested in missiological study and research from a believers church perspective. The fellowship sponsors lectures by noted missiologists and its sessions have resulted in a series of books, the Missionary Study series, published by Herald Press.   RLR

Missions Now, Inc. (Mennonite) began as an independent missionary work in rural areas and tribal places of the Philippine Islands. It is evangelical in doctrine and practice, with a Mennonite persuasion, organized under the laws of the Republic of the Philippines.

Early in 1950 a home Bible study was started in Paete, Laguna Province. A few months later another preaching center was opened in Lumban, which became the center of the ministry to other places throughout Luzon. By 1978 this gospel undertaking brought into existence seven congregations with their own chapels and 15 house churches and preaching points.

Eight of these groups were composed of impoverished members of the Filipino society. Most of the church members and worshipers were members of the mountain tribes. Their subsistence-level economy was precariously dependent on "slash and burn" agriculture and the sale of some handwoven articles.

The 1st c. church is described in Acts 2:42 as the body where believers in Christ "met constantly to hear the apostles preach, to share the common life, to break bread, and to pray." The local Mennonite churches in the Philippines meet constantly to hear the pastors teach and to pray. Each group in different places meets regularly, especially Sunday morning, to study God's word, and to attend the worship service. Sunday evenings are for sharing testimonies among members and invited friends.

The membership in the other 14 congregations was composed of people from the lowlands; with 75 percent coming from farming areas.

Members seek to live out the gospel by sharing with one another. Through the help of loans from the Mennonite Economic Development Associates, Missions Now has opened economic projects to increase the resources available to local congregations and pastors. Many handicrafts have been marketed through °SELFHELP Crafts in North America.

In 1972 Missions Now began associating with the Eastern Mennonite Board of Missions. The primary focus of the assistance provided by Eastern Board personnel has been in leadership training. The Philippine Mennonite Biblical Institute, established south of Manila in Lumban has been the center of this training program.   FAS

Portions of the above were adapted from the article by Santiago Bulfa, Sr., in *MWH* (1978), 178-82.

Mississippi (ME III:717). In 1988 there were 18 Mennonite congregations in Mississippi. Six of these congregations belonged to the Church of God in Christ Mennonite (Holdeman), and four, with a total membership of 227 were not affiliated with any conference. The remaining eight congregations belonged to the Gulf States Mennonite Fellowship (MC) and had a total membership of 287. Pine Lake Fellowship Camp (MC) was located at Meridian, and the Mennonite Board of Missions (MC) operated three voluntary service units at Macon and Philadelphia. The Conservative Mennonite Board of Missions (Rosedale) administered voluntary service units at Jackson and Prairie.   RSa

MC Yearbook (1988-89), 28-29, 58, 98-99, 120, 151.

Missouri (ME III:717). Mennonite Church (MC) membership in Missouri increased from 514 in 1956 to 791 in 1987. Three congregations have become extinct, Gospel Center, Lick Creek, and Walker. Three of four new churches are in St. Louis: Bethesda, founded 1958, membership 62; St. Louis Mennonite Fellowship, 1975, membership 40; Word of Joy Fellowship, 1985, membership 22. The fourth, Harrisonville Mennonite Church, 1968 (membership in 1987 of 142), started with 54 charter members mostly from the nearby Sycamore Grove congregation. There are 10 Mennonite Church (MC) congregations in the state.

General Conference Mennonite Church (GCM) congregations are: Bethel at Fortuna; Brookside Christian Fellowship (1983), Kansas City; and St. Louis Mennonite Fellowship which has dual MC and GCM affiliation.

Mennonite institutions are the Beth-Haven Nursing Home, at Hannibal, established 1958, with 66 residential care units, and 102 retirement apartments in two separate units; Harrisonville Christian School (MC), established 1974; and the Home for Mentally Retarded Children located north of Linn.

°°Horning Mennonites (OOM) first came to Missouri in 1972. There are five congregations, one at Versailles and four in ne. Missouri, with a total membership of 343. The Eastern Pennsylvania Mennonite church has one congregation at Versailles since 1982 with 22 members. Other Mennonite groups include: °°Wenger Mennonites (OOM), two congregations at Versailles; Church of God in Christ Mennonites (Holdeman) at Versailles; and two unaffiliated Amish Mennonite (CM) congregations (Buffalo and Otterville), whose members came from Tampico, Ill.

In 1984 there were 12 Old Order Amish settlements in Missouri. The following list gives the name of the settlement (the county it is located in), year of founding, and number of church districts (congregations) as of 1984: °Bowling Green (Pike), 1947, 4; °Jamesport (Daviess), 1953, 6; °Clark (Randolf), 1954, 5; Anabel (Macon), 1957, 1; Seymour (Webster), 1968, 3; Dogwood (Douglas), 1969, 1; Marshfield (Webster), 1970, 1; Windsor (Henry), 1975, 1; LaPlata (Macon), 1976, 1; Dixon (Pulaski), 1980, 1; Prairie Home (Cooper), 1980, 1; Maywood (Marion), 1980, 1. The settlement at Fortuna established in 1967, disbanded in 1975.   DK

MC Yearbook (1988-89), 29; Luthy, *Amish Settlements* (1984), 2, 9; Wittlinger, *Piety and Obedience* (1978), 147, 149-50.

Miyazaki Prefecture, Kyushu, Japan, is located on the se. side of Kyushu Island, in sw. Japan. The prefecture is roughly 900 miles from Tokyo. It has a land area of 17,734 sq. km. (2,985 sq. mi.). About 76 percent is forested and 11 percent is farmland. The northern, western, and southern parts are surrounded by mountains, and the east faces the Pacific Ocean.

There are four distinct seasons. Summer is hot with a rainy season early, important for rice growing. There are occasional typhoons. In winter cold winds come from the west. Some places, such as the tiny island of Aoshima, are almost semi-tropical. The average low temperature in January is about 2 degrees C. (36 degrees F.); the average high in Aug. is 31 degrees C. (88 degrees F.). Annual precipitation is approximately 2,500 mm (98 in.). The latitude is similar to the U.S. state of Georgia.

Since the prefecture was established (1873) the population has increased threefold. As of 1980 it was 1,151,000. Miyazaki City, the capital, has about 250,000 inhabitants. But many towns and villages exist too. Being largely rural, agriculture, forestry, and fishing are some of the main industries. There is also some manufacturing, and development is expected in electronics. Around 60 percent of the population lives along the coast.

Miyazaki is widely known as a sightseeing area because of its beautiful scenery, like that along the Nichinan Coast. Palm trees and wild horses can be seen. Many historical sites are also associated with early Japanese legend. For example, Jimmu Tenno, supposedly the first emperor (660 B.C.), is said to be a descendant of the Sun Goddess, whose grandson came down on the top of Mt. Takachiho in Kirishima National Park. The emperor is said to have later moved to the Kyoto region. Every fall traditional dances re-enacting some of the mythology are staged. Old burial mounds remain. The General Conference Mennonite Church (GCM) began working in Miyazaki in 1952, and today 10 congregations and the Japanese conference offices of the Nihon Menonaito Kirisuto Kyokai Kaigi (Japan Mennonite Christian Church Conference) are situated there.   SS

"Miyazaki Prefecture" in *Kodansha Encyclopedia of Japan*, vol. 5 (Tokyo: Kodansha, 1983), 221; *MWH* (1978), 168-72.

Modernism. See Liberalism; Fundamentalism.

Modernity.
One of the dominant themes of the past 500 years in Western society (and increasingly in non-Western societies) has been modernness. The modern period coincides with Anabaptist and Mennonite history. Yet the relationship of Anabaptists and Mennonites to the modern experiment is difficult to describe and define. The roots of the modern worldview appear to lie in social and intellectual changes of the 12th and 13th c., as the rural-centered, feudal society gave way to renewed urban and commercial growth. ("Urban" is used here in a relative sense—most of the *population* of Europe and North America remained rural until the 19th c., and urban centers were dominated by artisans, not by industrial factories. Yet the *cultural* center of gravity shifted from the countryside to the towns during the 13th and 14th centuries.) Intellectually this shift to an urban culture included the rise of universities and growing exploration of rational, empirical, "scientific" knowledge. In the church, scholastic-rational theology and religiosity grew as sacramental,

monastic, and mystical religiosity declined. A literate laity developed. Other developments contributing to the modern world included the emergence of territorial nation-states with powerful, absolute monarchs (15th-17th c.) and the growth of modern science in the "Age of Reason" (17th c.).

All of these developments, however, constitute in a certain sense only the threshold of the modern era. Strictly speaking, the modern world arrived in the 18th and 19th c. with the transfer of power from the aristocracy and the absolutist kings (Louis XIV in France and James I in England) to the middle classes, or bourgeoisie. The middle classes were represented by constitutional assemblies, legislatures, and parliaments which took power from the kings and aristocrats by violent revolutions or reform legislation: England (1688, 1830s), the United States (1776), France (1789, 1830, 1848, 1870), Canada (1840s and 1850s); Germany (1848, 1918). Japan embarked on a deliberate program of modernization in the late 19th c. and early 20th c.

The shift of power was accompanied by the Industrial Revolution and liberal, or free enterprise, economic theory (laissez faire), the economic counterpart of the middle class political revolutions. Critique of this modern, middle-class, democratic, and laissez-faire industrial system emerged at various points in the 19th c., most notably in the °Marxist and °socialist movements. Although these movements of the working people were critical of the middle class entrepreneurs who led the 18th and early 19th c. modern revolutions, Marxists and socialists remained modern in most of their assumptions. Thorough-going critique of the modern worldview and its rational-scientific outlook, its rationally organized economic factory system, and its rationally centralized bureaucratic politics did not emerge until the late 19th c. and early 20th c. Such critique came at first only from philosophers (e.g., Friedrich Nietzsche [1844-1900]), scientists (Albert Einstein [1879-1955], Sigmund Freud [1856-1939]), and artists. Only in the late 20th c. has such postmodern critique become widespread. For most people in the 1980s, in Europe and North America and increasingly around the world, modern ways of life dominate, although intellectuals have been attacking or reinterpreting modern views for some time.

One of the best ways to understand modernity is to look at countervailing social, political, and religious manifestations. As anthropologists, sociologists, and historians have studied the "traditional village societies" that survived in a few remote areas of Europe and in non-Western cultures, they have learned much about the nature of the modern Western worldview (Berger). The very name *traditional society* focuses on what is perhaps the most important single aspect. *Modern* means "now"—a worldview focusing on the now, on the latest, on the newest. A *traditional* society takes "handed down" things (Latin: *tradita*) as its starting point and modifies them slowly even as it tries to be faithful to the inherited ideas and customs. A modern worldview implicitly assumes the superiority of the latest and newest as liberating and expansive, and almost invariably scorns the old-fashioned as constrictive and oppressive.

The relationship of Christianity to the modern

world has been very complicated. Often °Roman Catholic and Eastern Orthodox leaders and people have resisted the modern emphasis on individualism, rationalism, and democracy. They have insisted on the °authority of traditional structures, liturgies, and beliefs. The major Protestant groups emerged in an atmosphere in which "tradition" was blamed for many abuses in the church. Although in this sense they opened the way for modern ideas in the church, Luther, Calvin, and others were socially conservative. The most radical wings of the major Protestant groups (Zwingli, the Puritans) were the most critical of the authority of °tradition, of traditional liturgy, sacramental theology, and ecclesiastical institutions (e.g., bishops). The relationship of the Puritans to the middle class political and social revolutions of the 17th-19th c. has been much debated but that some relationship existed between them is undeniable.

Anabaptists, Mennonites, and Modernity. The Anabaptist and Mennonite relationship to modernity is likewise complicated. Historians involved in the "recovery of the °Anabaptist vision" (ca. 1925-55) stressed the Anabaptist contribution to modernity in the Anabaptist emphasis on the voluntary nature of the church and religious liberty (see the bibliography under °Anabaptism). More recently, scholars have studied the ways in which the Anabaptists continued medieval theologies and piety (°historiography). Yet, whatever content Anabaptists retained from late-medieval Catholic asceticism or mysticism, they resolutely rejected the church's traditional °worship patterns and ecclesiastical organization. Students of Anabaptist history are increasingly recognizing the powerful role played by anticlericalism and iconoclasm (antisacramentalism) in giving the Anabaptist movement its dynamic thrust.

Anabaptists became °Mennonites and developed their own traditionalism, liturgies, customs, and cultures. For much of the 17th-19th c., Mennonites perceived themselves and were perceived by outsiders as nonmodern, old-fashioned traditionalists. As European and North American societies were modernizing, and as the middle class political system and industrial economic system came to power, Mennonites remained °rural and agricultural. Traditionalism remains characteristic of the "conserving" Mennonite groups: Amish, Hutterian Brethren, Old Colony Mennonites, Old Order Mennonites, and others. These groups have made a transition from a first generation of radical religious sectarianism to a second generation of structured, custom-based authority, patterns of worship (liturgy), and "rites of redemptive process" that parallel in many ways traditional Eastern Orthodox or medieval Catholic Christianity (Cronk, Martin, 1988).

At the same time, implicit in the "believers' church" vision is an emphasis on individual, adult faith and voluntary commitment that is at odds with traditional religion and societies. Traditional societies assume that religion, like the rest of culture, is handed down and mediated from one generation to another, and that it is no less genuine for having been handed down than if it were discovered for the first time. The implicit questioning of tradition resulting from the Believers' Church understanding of faith has made Mennonites uneasy even during their traditional periods and it is one factor that led to the embracing of °revivalism as a means to ensure that faith is genuine and individually appropriated rather than acquired second-hand. Yet even where revivalism was embraced it was embraced with misgivings about its effect on °community. The debates over °Sunday schools, °missions, °°revival meetings, life-style (°dress, household furnishings, °automobiles, electricity, °radio), the organization of conferences with written constitutions (°Oberholtzer), and many other issues are manifestations of this same tension within Mennonite circles. An illustration of this is found in the use of °democracy within Mennonite °polity. As heirs to an anticlerical protest tradition, the more °acculturated Mennonite groups have often insisted on democratic °decisionmaking by consensus or vote, rather than permitting a small circle of leaders to make decisions. Yet traditionalist Mennonites were suspicious of the thoroughgoing democratic constitutionalism of the early 19th c. Oberholtzer controversy (in Pennsylvania, with parallels elsewhere). Most °conservative Mennonites have thus retained some form of clerical authority, with aspects of "priestly" holiness attached to their bishops and °elders (°bishop, "My Good Bishop" feature).

Most Mennonites, however, relinquished traditionalism and embraced modernity in differing degrees and at differing pace in Europe and North America. The Dutch and North German Mennonites were among the first to become acculturated to many aspects of modern Western culture (17th-19th c.). Mennonites in Russia, because of their autonomy and self-government, in many ways lived in traditional village societies. Once they left those villages, however, they have embraced modern North American culture more readily than their Swiss-Pennsylvania cousins who, given the religious liberty of their modern North American surroundings, held on to a traditionalist religious subculture longer. Both groups have experienced rapid acculturation in the 20th c., although the debate over these trends has given rise to numerous Old Order and conservative Mennonite divisions.

Further research comparing developments in Canada and the United States would be quite illuminating in this regard. In some ways Canadian society as a whole resisted the modern, middle class, laissez-faire, liberal, democratic political and economic system more than the United States, embracing it fully only after World War II (George Grant). Yet Mennonite acculturation and modernization has proceeded more rapidly in Canada, in many ways, than in the United States. In part this may be the result of the emigration of large groups of Canadian Mennonite traditionalists to Mexico and South America, in part it may be the consequence of more recent immigration of Mennonites displaced from Europe in the 20th c. These immigrants arrived in Canadian cities as Canada began to embrace the modern industrial-urban culture that already dominated the United States in the 19th c. The Mennonite story in Europe is also complex. Research comparing modernization among North German, Prussian, and Dutch Mennonites on the one hand, and South German, Swiss, and Alsatian Mennonites on the other hand, could be extremely illuminating.

Modernity in Asia, Africa, and Latin America. Modernization is a crucial development in non-Western countries where the number of Mennonites has grown rapidly since World War II. Mennonite Central Committee (MCC) workers and Mennonite missionaries have encountered many of the modernization issues in a variety of ways. Protestant missionaries often imported modern Western culture along with their Christian faith. (Protestants often criticized Roman Catholics for "syncretism"—the blending of indigenous cultures with Christianity. One reason Catholics were more likely to proceed this way is that Catholicism never fully embraced modern European culture, thus Catholic faith and culture was closer to traditional, non-Western cultures than was modern Protestant faith and culture.) Strong reactions against this Western cultural imperialism in 20th c. has not stopped rapid global modernization. Efforts to preserve traditional non-Western societies are underway but powerful economic and political forces make this very difficult. Mennonite °development workers have frequently been sympathetic to these efforts, as, for example, in MCC work with °appropriate technology. Few intact traditional village societies are left in the late 20th c. non-Western world, just as television and the automobile have virtually eliminated traditional rural society in North America and Europe. Yet aspects of traditional society remain in both urban and rural areas and "modernization" proceeds in varied ways around the world.

Assessment. The virtues and failures of modernity are beginning to come into focus for social scientists, philosophers, and theologians in a postmodern era. "Advances" in medicine, science, transportation, and political relationships are coupled with serious ecological, social, and religious problems: pollution, alienation, medical costs, care for elderly people, crises of religious belief and overt paganization of society. What is liberating for one person or group is a tragedy for another. Within the church, democratization of leadership may constitute an advance over the tyranny of bishops or elders for some, yet lead to weak leadership and confusion for others. For four centuries Protestants perceived their rejection of images, liturgy, and sacraments as a liberation from superstition and idolatry, yet this rejection of sacrament and liturgy is perceived by many in the 20th c. as having left worship devoid of °symbols, pale, lifeless, and alienating.

Both °Fundamentalism and °Liberalism (modernism) have accepted modernity, The very term "liberal" referred to modern (19th c.) constitutional democracy and laissez-faire economics long before it became a designation for a kind of theology. Fundamentalism also emerged out of circles that accepted modern Enlightenment rationalism, if only in the moderate "common sense" way absorbed by the Princeton theology (Marsden). Liberal, Fundamentalist, and °Evangelical theologies alike are products of the Protestant Reformation and modern society. Ideologically Anabaptists and Mennonites are part of this broad stream, although, to the degree that they settled into traditionalist subcultures, they are not.

Thus some Mennonites tried to walk a middle line and critique both Fundamentalism and Liberalism out of their traditional community theology, even while they remained committed to a certain kind of modern individualism and voluntaryism, rooted in their insistence on individual faith prior to adult baptism rather than infant baptism based on the presence of faith mediated through family and church. For centuries, the major resistance to modernity came from Catholic sacramentalism and clericalism, both of which were off limits to Mennonites officially, although in practice they developed their own forms of sacraments, tradition, and hierarchy. To some degree this Mennonite traditionalism informed Mennonite critique of both Liberalism and Fundamentalism.

Virtually every sociological, ethical, theological, or cultural theme covered in this encyclopedia relates to some aspect of modernity. The body of writings, films, and other commentary on the subject is immense, yet Mennonites are only beginning to analyze the subject. A conference of scholars from Mennonite, Church of Brethren, and related groups at Elizabethtown College dealt with the subject in 1987 (papers published in *Brethren Life and Thought*, 33 [1988], 148-249) and another conference is planned for 1989 at Fresno, Cal. A conference on Mennonite self-understanding and identity, held at Conrad Grebel College in May, 1986, also addressed many of these issues (Steiner/Redekop).

DDM

Donald B. Kraybill, *The Riddle of Amish Culture* (Baltimore: Johns Hopkins U. Press, 1988); idem, "At the Crossroads of Modernity: Amish, Mennonites, and Brethren in Lancaster County in 1880," *PMH*, 10 (Jan. 1987), 2-12; idem and Donald R. Fitzkee, "Amish, Mennonites and Brethren in the Modern Era," *PMH*, 10 (Apr. 1987), 2-11; Donald R. Kraybill, "The Face of Modernity," Ted Koontz, "Mennonites and 'Postmodernity'," and Rod J. Sawatsky, "Beyond Modernity: A Vision for Believers' Churches," papers for the Council of Mennonite Seminaries consultation on "The Believers' Church Vision in the Postmodern World" (Fresno, Cal., Apr. 1989); Samuel Steiner and Calvin Redekop, eds., *Mennonite Identity: Historical and Contemporary Perspectives* (Lanham, Md.: University Press of America, 1988); Alvin Dueck, "North American Psychology: Gospel of Modernity?" *CGR*, 3 (1985), 165-78, with responses in *CGR*, 4 (1986), 63-69, 166-67; A. James Reimer, "The Nature and Possibility of a Mennonite Theology," *CGR*, 1 (1983), 33-55; Dennis D. Martin, "Nothing New Under the Sun? Mennonites and History," *CGR*, 5 (1987), 1-27, with responses pp. 147-53, 260-62; idem, "Catholic Spirituality and Anabaptist and Mennonite Discipleship," *MQR*, 62 (1988), 5-25; Hans-Jürgen Goertz, "Das Konfessionelle Erbe in neuer Gestalt: Die Frage nach dem mennonitischen Selbstverständnis heute," *Menn. Geschbl.*, Jg. 43-44 (1986-87), 157-70; idem, "Das Täufertum—ein Weg in die Moderne?" in *Zwingli und Europa*, ed. Peter Blickle and others (Zürich: Vandenhoeck und Ruprecht, 1985), 165-81; Jarold K. Zeman, "Anabaptism: A Replay of Medieval Themes or a Prelude to the Modern Age," *MQR*, 50 (1976), 259-71; John A. Hostetler, *Amish Society* (1980); Beulah Stauffer Hostetler, *American Mennonites and Protestant Movements* (Scottdale, 1987); Sandra Cronk, "Gelassenheit: The Rites of the Redemptive Process in the Old Order Amish and Old Order Mennonite Communities: (PhD diss., U. of Chicago, 1977), cf. *MQR*, 55 (1981), 5-44; Theron F. Schlabach, "Mennonites, Revivalism, Modernity—1683-1850," *Church History*, 48 (1979), 398-415; Michel Durrive, Juan Matas, Freddy Raphael, "The Mennonites of Alsace Facing Modernity," *MQR*, 58 (1984), 272-88; Donald R. Jacobs, *The Christian Stance in a Revolutionary Age*, Focal Pamphlet, 14 (Scottdale, 1968). For general studies of modernization, see Ferdinand Tönnies, *Community and Society* (New York: Harper and Row, 1957); Peter Berger, with Brigitte Berger, *The Homeless Mind* (New

York: Basic Books, 1973); Peter Berger, *Pyramids of Sacrifice* (New York: Doubleday, 1974); idem, *Facing Up to Modernity: Excursions in Society, Politics, and Religion* (New York: Basic Books, 1977); James Davison Hunter and Stephen C. Ainly, eds., *Making Sense of Modern Times* (New York: Routledge and Kegan Paul, 1986); James Turner, *Without God, Without Creed: The Origins of Unbelief in America* (Baltimore: Johns Hopkins U. Press, 1985); T. Jackson Lears, *No Place of Grace: Antimodernism and the Transformation of American Culture, 1880-1920* (New York: Pantheon, 1981); Larry Schmidt, ed., *George Grant in Process: Essays and Conversations* (Toronto: Anansi Press, 1978); George Grant, *Technology and Empire: Perspectives on North America* (Toronto, 1969); Lester K. Little, *Religious Poverty and the Profit Economy in Medieval Europe* (Ithaca: Cornell U. Press, 1978); George Marsden, *Fundamentalism and American Culture* (New York: Oxford, 1980).

Anthropology; Ethnicity; Geography (esp. the bibliography); Prayer Veil.

Moldavian Soviet Socialist Republic. Moldavia, on the extreme sw. edge of the Soviet Union, is one of the smallest republics with an area of only about 13,000 sq. mi. (33,600 sq. km.), about the size of Taiwan. Its population of more than four million people nevertheless makes it one of the most heavily populated regions of the country. Most of what is Moldavia in the 1980s, was once known as Bessarabia, and the rest, incorporated into the Soviet Union during World War II, belonged formerly to Romania. Kishenev is the capital city of this region.

Baptist congregations in Moldavia came to join the °All-Union Council of Evangelical Christians—Baptists after World War II. Germans in the area had been evacuated eastward during the war. Moldavia became an area of interest to Mennonites in Central Asia when for a time it seemed easier to emigrate to West Germany from this republic, as had been true of the °Baltic republics for some years. A number of families came to Moldavia from the Estonian and Latvian republics when the authorities there sought to stop the German influx by refusing to offer residence permits.

In Moldavia it was difficult to obtain housing so the German families often settled as isolated families in local villages. For a time a cluster developed around the city of Tiraspol where a certain Pauls served as minister in a Baptist congregation. One Gennadi Dyck led a Mennonite Brethren church for a while in Grigoropol, where some Mennonites sought registration under Baptist sponsorship.

These groups remained relatively insignificant, and, in time, most have emigrated to other areas, or abroad. The story of Mennonites in Moldavia was, therefore, as brief as it had been in the Baltic region. Those Mennonites who stayed have either found their way into other churches or remained in scattered isolation. There has been no recent move to the Moldavian SSR although church life in other groups continues in many places.   LK

Walter Sawatsky, "Mennonite Congregations in the Soviet Union Today," *Menn. Life*, 33 (March, 1978), 12-26; idem, *Soviet Evangelicals Since World War II* (Scottdale, 1981).

Monasticism. Catholic and Protestant reformers in the 16th c. occasionally spoke scornfully of Anabaptists as "new monks," referring to Anabaptist insistence on holy living and intense spiritual life (e.g., *TA Elsaß I*, 110-13). Anabaptists occasionally accepted the comparison (CRR 2: 217) but more frequently rejected it (CRR 2: 215-16; Menno, *Writings*, 369, 401), in part because monks often came from the socially privileged classes. Several scholars have used monastic history as an aid to interpret Anabaptism (Troeltsch, Ritschl, Davis, Snyder, Martin). Many Anabaptists and Mennonites, beginning with the Hutterite chronicle, pointed to quasi-monastic sectarian medieval movements, especially °°Waldenses, as forerunners of Anabaptism (these theories are promulgated or discussed by Keller, Gratz, Verduin, Durnbaugh). One of the most extensive efforts to relate monasticism and Anabaptism drew on both monastic and quasi-monastic traditions (Davis). Most scholars have carefully limited their interpretations to pointing out "intellectual parallels" or general similarities; some have argued for direct continuity and influence.

The crucial interpretive question revolves around the nature of monasticism: is it a nonconforming sectarian development critical of the institutional church (Workman) or an intensified institutional core of the ecclesiastical establishment? Or, did monasticism begin as a charismatic, lay, "sectarian" movement in the 4th c. but become fully integrated into the sacramental, ecclesial, institutional church by the early Middle Ages (Rousseau, Martin)? How central the critical, separatist aspect of early monasticism is to monastic identity is disputed, even by those within the monastic community (Eoin de Bhaldraithe). Particularly significant in this regard is the distinction between contemplative monastic orders (Benedictine, Cistercian, Carthusian) and more lay-oriented, urban mendicant orders and houses of regular canons of the late Middle Ages (°°Franciscans, Dominicans, Augustinian Friars, Praemonstratensians, Augustinian Canons). The latter orders were associated with the middle class and were visibly and pastorally active; the former were often but not always associated with the nobility and lived in secluded and rural areas. Most Anabaptist links to "monks" appear to have been with the mendicants and canons regular. Michael °Sattler is the main exception to this generalization.

Most interpreters agree that Anabaptists rejected the sacramental and institutional "culture-church" of the Middle Ages in favor of a voluntary, non-institutionalized, even anti-clerical church of the faithful few, in effect, reducing the church to a devout "monastic" core. At issue among scholars is whether the label "monastic" should properly be applied to a sectarian, pure church vision such as that held by Anabaptists, since most monks did not believe that the church was made up solely of monastics, rather, they believed that monks and nuns were part, perhaps the most important part, of the church. The qualities and virtues prized by Anabaptists and Mennonites (°hospitality, °humility, °community, °°*Gelassenheit*, obedience, repentance, °nonresistance, etc.) were also prime monastic virtues, although all medieval Catholics were exhorted to practice these same virtues.

Significant parallels to monastic spirituality are found in the Mennonite period of post-Anabaptist history in which Anabaptist first-generation identity was transformed into a sacramental, ecclesial, institutional, cultural (ethnic) faith, even though Mennonites, Amish, and Hutterites avoided the language of sacramental and institutional Christianity (Cronk, Martin). During the 1980s growing Mennonite concern about the role of single adults in the church has not yet taken account of the traditional Christian monastic theology, with its implications for both °marriage and °singleness. Recent scholarship on monasticism emphasizes the social role of celibate communities, which enhanced the role of marriage while creating a sphere of activity for those remaining unmarried (Brown, Leclercq). Further research is needed in all these areas of Anabaptist and Mennonite history and culture.   DDM

Ernst Troeltsch, *The Social Teachings of the Christian Churches*; trans. Olive Wyon (New York: Harper and Row, 1960), esp. 239-46, 332-33; for Ritschl, Gratz, Verduin, Keller, and others see Kenneth R. Davis, *Anabaptism and Asceticism: A Study in Intellectual Origins* (Scottdale, 1974), 27-31; Donald F. Durnbaugh, "Theories of Free Church Origins," *MQR*, 41 (1968), 83-95; C. Arnold Snyder, "The Monastic Origins of Swiss Anabaptist Sectarianism," *MQR*, 57 (1983), 5-26; idem, *The Life and Thought of Michael Sattler* (Scottdale, 1984); Eoin de Bhaldraithe, "Michael Sattler, Benedictine and Anabaptist," *Downside Review*, 105 (April 1987), 111-31; Dennis D. Martin, "Monks, Mendicants and Anabaptists: Michael Sattler and the Benedictines Reconsidered," *MQR*, 60 (1986), 139-64; reply by Snyder, "Michael Sattler, Benedictine: Dennis Martin's Objections Reconsidered," *MQR*, 61 (1987), 251-79; Dennis D. Martin, "Catholic Spirituality and Mennonite Discipleship," *MQR*, 62 (1988), 5-25; idem, "Nothing New under the Sun? Mennonites and History," *CGR*, 5 (1987), 1-27; Sandra Cronk, "Gelassenheit: The Rites of the Redemptive Process in the Old Order Amish and Old Order Mennonite Communities: (PhD diss., U. of Chicago, 1977), cf. *MQR*, 65 (1981), 5-44. For general information on monastic history, see David Knowles, *Christian Monasticism* (New York: McGraw-Hill, 1969); Otto Gründler, "Devotio Moderna" in *Christian Spirituality: High Middle Ages and Reformation*, ed. Jill Raitt (New York: Crossroad, 1987), 176-93; Herbert B. Workman, *The Evolution of the Monastic Ideal from the Earliest Times to the Coming of the Friars*, 2nd ed. (London, 1927), reprinted with introd. by Knowles (Boston: Beacon, 1962); Philip Rousseau, *Ascetics, Authority, and the Church in the Age of Jerome and Cassian* (New York; Oxford, 1980); Peter R. L. Brown, "The Notion of Virginity in the Early Church," in *Christian Spirituality: Origins to the 12th C.*, ed. Bernard McGinn and John Meyendorff (New York: Crossroad, 1985), 427-43; Jean Leclercq, *Monks and Love in 12th-C. France* (Oxford: Clarendon, 1979); Michael Novak, "The Free Churches and the Roman Church," *J. of Ecumenical Studies*, 2 (1965), 426-47.

See also Historiography; Sociological Studies.

Montana (ME III:742). Since 1955 two congregations (Bethel, at Wolf Point, and First Mennonite in Glendive) have withdrawn from the General Conference Mennonite Church (GCM) and become community Bible churches. The Bethel congregation at Lustre disbanded on Oct. 13, 1974. The Northern District Conference (GCM) began planting a congregation in Billings in 1983. The White Chapel Church (MC) in Glendive assumed GCM and MC dual affiliation in 1987. The Red Top (MC) and Bethlehem (GCM) congregations near Bloomfield have been served by the same pastor during part of the 1980s. The Mennonite Brethren (MB) have three congregations in the Wolf Point-Lustre-Larslan area in 1987. The Evangelical Mennonite Brethren (°Fellowship of Evangelical Bible Churches) continued with one congregation (Lustre) in 1987. Total Mennonite membership in Montana has declined to slightly more than 750 members in 1987.

The Lustre Bible School begun in 1928 with 25 students, has been known as Lustre Christian High School since 1978. It had 45 students, 1986-87. The Beacon Bible Camp near Frazer and the Eastern Montana Bible Camp ne. of Bloomfield are supported and used by area Mennonite churches.

The only Amish settlement in the state, is located at Rexford (one church district, or congregation). In 1982 the number of Hutterian colonies in Montana had increased to 31. They were still located mostly north, south, and west of Great Falls.   OJW/RSa

MC Yearbook (1988-89), 29; Luthy, *Amish Settlements* (1985), 9; Daniel Hertzler, *From Germantown to Steinbach* (Herald, 1981), 198-210.

Montaña Colony, La, Paraguay, is a small Mennonite settlement 140 km. (87 mi.) ne. of Encarnación in southern Paraguay. Its name means "The Mountain." It was founded in 1980 by settlers from °Agua Azul who left partly because of differences within the colony and partly to find new mission opportunities. One thousand hectares (2,470 acres) of land have been purchased. The congregation is called Faith Mennonite Church and is affiliated with the °Eastern Pennsylvania Mennonite Church. In 1986 the congregation consisted of 44 members in 17 families of whom 6 were Americans, 10 Paraguayans and one Paraguayan-American. Stephen M. Stoltzfus is pastor of the congregation and leader of the settlement.   GR

Montgomery, Ind., Old Order Amish Settlement (ME II:19) is located in Daviess Co. in southern Indiana. First settlers came from the Allen Co. Amish community near Ft. Wayne in 1868. Dominant names such as Graber, Stoll, Wagler, and Wittmer identify this community as settlers from °°Alsace who immigrated to America in the middle of the 19th c. The Berea Mennonite Church (MC) was established in 1921 by Amish families in Daviess Co. Another group of Amish founded the Odon Beachy Amish Mennonite congregation in 1948. The settlement near Montgomery has experienced slow but steady growth so that in 1984 there were 10 church districts (congregations) serving approximately 1,500 people.   SLY

Moratorium. The word "moratorium" was used for the first time in relation to °mission at the conference of the All African Council of Churches in Lusaka (1974). In an effort to come to more mature relations between churches in Africa and churches in Europe and North America the proposal was made to suspend for a certain time all financial and personal assistance coming from churches outside Africa. The desire for independence and self-reliance, the emphasis on the necessity to respond directly to the challenges of the African context and a strong reaction against paternalistic structures formed the background of this call for a moratorium. The call has not found general acceptance and it has not directly influenced the relations between Mennonite churches in Africa and other continents.   RSK

International Review of Mission, 64, no. 254 (Geneva, Apr. 1975), sp. issue on Moratorium.

Morgenland Colony. See Canadiense Colony, Bolivia.

Mosemann, John H. (b. Aug. 6, 1907), Mennonite missionary, administrator, teacher, and pastor, was born at Lancaster, Pa., the fifth child of Bishop John and Lillie S. Forry Mosemann.

In 1932 he graduated from Elizabethtown College and married (Nov. 20) Ruth Landis Histand, of Doylestown, Pa. On April 19, 1933, he was ordained to the ministry at Mellinger Mennonite Church by Bishop Noah H. Mack, and in 1934 he and Ruth (along with Elam and Elizabeth Stauffer) arrived in Tanganyika Territory (later Tanzania) as the first missionaries sent to Africa by the Eastern Mennonite Board of Missions and Charities (MC). The Mosemanns served at Shirati, 1934-39. Due to health problems they were unable to return to the field after their furlough.

Mosemann worked in °°Civilian Public Service administration (1941-43) at Grottoes, Va., and Akron, Pa. He graduated from Eastern Baptist Theological Seminary (BD, 1945) and from Princeton Theological Seminary (ThM, 1948). From 1946 to 1955 he taught at Goshen College Biblical Seminary.

Mosemann served as pastor (1947-50) of Yellow Creek Mennonite Church near Goshen, Ind., and of the College Mennonite Church in Goshen (1950-75). In 1945 he became a member of the Mennonite Board of Missions, and from 1948 to 1971 was its president. He was also president (1976-79) of the Indiana-Michigan Mennonite Conference (MC). SCS

John H. and Ruth H. Mosemann, *The Descendants of Jacob and Magdalena Frey Mosemann* (1978), 79; *Who's Who Mennonites* (1943), 174-75; John C. Wenger, *The Mennonites in Indiana and Michigan* (Scottdale, 1961), 312-13; Anabelle Troyer, "The History of the African Mennonite Church," pp. 6-17, Mennonite History term paper, copy at MHL (Goshen); George R. Anchak, *An Experience in the Paradox of Indigenous Church Building: A History of the Eastern Mennonite Mission in Tanganyika, 1934-1961* (thesis, 1975; available from University Microfilms, Ann Arbor, Mich.), 57-116, 311-12; Mahlon Hess, *Pilgrimage of Faith: Tanzania Mennonite Church, 1934-83* (Salunga, Pa.: EMBMC, 1985), 30-35.

Moser, Henry and Emma. Henry Moser was born in 1894 in Adams Co., Ind., and Emma Bixler was born in 1893 in the same county. They both became members of the Evangelical Mennonite Church, applied for service with the °°Congo Inland Mission (Africa Inter-Mennonite Mission), and were commissioned as missionaries in the Evangelical Mennonite Church of Grabill, Ind., early in 1923. They arrived in the Belgian Congo (Zaire) in April of that year.

They pioneered a new station among the Baphende people west of the Loange River in Kwilu Province. Accompanied by Agnes °Sprunger (1885-1973) of Berne, Ind., and Erma Birky (1894-1979) from Hudson, Ill., they trekked overland with native porters to the large village of Mukedi, the home of a major chief. A few months later lightening struck their thatch and stick station shelter and destroyed it. In the process of rebuilding with more permanent materials they developed a construction technique that was later widely copied by others. The Mosers are remembered for their enthusiasm for evangelism and a high degree of self-discipline. Their mission-

ary careers ended prematurely when Henry died of a heart attack in 1946 at Grabill, Ind., while they were on furlough. Emma died in 1978.   JEB

Motion Pictures. In the first half of the 20th c. many, but not all, Mennonite groups considered motion pictures and stage theater as "Hell's Playground"—to use the title of a 1921 booklet circulating among Mennonites. An author writing in the *Gospel Herald* (MC) in 1930 called the opera, theater, and movies a "trio of soul seductive institutions." A widely circulated Mennonite booklet, "The Menace of the Movies," printed in 1940 (reprinted 1943) argued that motion pictures overemphasize crime and sex and portray love as "animalism." Honest toil, the booklet claimed, is depreciated while immorality is glorified in movies. Moreover, the author contended that motion pictures produce "nervous and emotional debauchery, provide schooling in crime and contribute to moral delinquency."

The strong Mennonite opposition to motion pictures was rooted in several factors. In the 19th c. some Mennonite groups had opposed °photography believing it violated the biblical commandment against making graven images. Moving pictures were an embellished form of photography that accentuated sex, violence, crime, pleasure, and greed. Motion pictures produced by non-Christian screenwriters and actors threatened the innocence and isolation of rural Mennonites. The content and medium of the motion picture were simply incongruous with a religious subculture that valued simplicity, modesty, °nonresistance, integrity, and separation from an evil world (°°nonconformity). Hollywood in the eyes of many Mennonites symbolized a den of worldly iniquity. The Brethren in Christ expressed a similar disdain and condemnation of motion pictures in the first half of the 20th c. In the 1980s Old Order Mennonite and Amish groups continue to forbid attendance at theaters and movie houses, although some of their youth may attend on the sly before baptism.

By the middle of the 20th c. motion pictures were gradually becoming acceptable among many Mennonite groups. Even congregations affiliated with the Mennonite Church (MC), which had vigorously castigated the evils of motion pictures before World War II, gradually relaxed their objections in the last third of the century. In fact by 1972 a survey of five Mennonite groups conducted by Kauffman and Harder revealed that only 18 percent of the respondents thought it was always wrong to attend movies rated for children and adults while 48 percent thought it was always wrong to watch adult-rated movies. For some Mennonites the *Sound of Music* became their rite of passage to the movie theater during the 1960s. The production and distribution of religious films by such evangelists as Billy Graham further eroded the resistance to films. In 1973 a feature-length film on Mennonite life, *Hazel's People*, was produced by Good Enterprises, an independent Mennonite production company. *Festival Quarterly*, an independent Mennonite magazine, began offering reviews of commercial films in 1973 and in the 1980s some Mennonite colleges were offering courses in film criticism. Film strips, 16mm films, and video tapes were widely used by all types of Mennonite organizations—including colleges, mission boards, and historical societies—to communicate their stories in the last quarter of the 20th c. The acceptance of motion pictures, in short, followed the trail of acculturation as Mennonites were transformed from a rural sectarian group to a modern religious denomination.   DBK

I. E. Burkhart, *The Menace of the Movies* (Scottdale: MPH, 1940), 31 pp.; Clayton F. Derstine, *Hell's Playground: Theaters and Movies* (Eureka, Ill.: the author, 1921); Kauffman/Harder, *Anabaptists Four C. Later* (1975), 122-23; J. S. Schoemaker, "The Opera, Theatre and Movie," *GH* (July 3, 1930), 298-99; Donovan E. Smucker, "The Menace of Modern Movies," *Chr. Monitor* (Mar. 1947), 95; Ella May Miller, "Sick Movies and Dancing," *GH* (May 21, 1968), 454-55; J. Daniel Hess, "Why I am Teaching a Course about Movies," *GH* (Aug. 23, 1983), 580-82; Wittlinger, *Piety and Obedience* (1978), 344-45; "Theaters: Indoor, Outdoor," (Salunga, Pa.: The Bishop Board of Lancaster Mennonite Conference, 1961); Amos W. Weaver, "Shall I Attend 'Good Movies' at the Theater?" *Youth Messenger* (Apr. 4, 1967), 2.

See also Amusements and Entertainment; Dramatic Arts; Filmmaking.

Moyer, Metta Habegger (July 10, 1891-May 11, 1970), was born near Berne, Ind. She married Samuel T. Moyer on June 20, 1920. Later that year they left for India as missionaries of the General Conference Mennonite Church.

In November 1921, the Moyers were assigned to open the fifth mission station in a new area that was later (1924) called Jagdeeshpur. With meager medical training, Metta opened a dispensary and treated many sick. She also cared for and found homes for many small unwanted children. During a term in Janjgir, Metta taught in the Bible school and served as principal for one year. She mastered the Hindi language and supervised the Hindi section of the Landour Language School for several years.

The Moyers had one adopted son, Theodore. They retired from India in 1956.   HR/RR

See bibliography for S. T. Moyer.

Moyer, Samuel Tyson (Apr. 10, 1893-Jan. 9, 1972), was reared on the farm of his parents, Samuel Clymer and Emma Tyson Moyer of Lansdale, Pa. He earned a BS degree in agronomy from Pennsylvania State College (1914) and after a few years attended Witmarsum Seminary (1917-19). He married Metta Habegger on Apr. 20, 1920, and they left for India Oct. 25, 1920.

In India the Moyers were assigned to open a new mission station (the fifth General Conference station) in the Deovri-Phuljhar area ca. 65 mi. south of the original General Conference Mennonite mission field. For the next three years the Moyers lived in tents and other temporary housing surrounded by wild animals and opposed by some of the local people. By 1927 Moyer had baptized 400 people and established what was later called the Jagdeeshpur station. At home on furlough the Moyers adopted an infant boy, Theodore.

During their second term Moyer continued to develop an innovative method of evangelism, planting an indigenous church. He prepared a series of Bible stories and Indian gospel songs designed to fit into the life situation of the villagers. Volunteer workers and paid evangelists memorized these stories and songs and divided into groups to spend at least a month teaching in chosen villages. During this time Moyer wrote, "The Self Supporting Church at Basna, C.P." published in the *Indian Witness*. This gave him recognition in missions throughout northern India. By the end of the second term more than 1,000 members had been added to the church in that area.

Moyers spent their third term at Janjgir. During S. T. Moyer's tenure as principal of the Janjgir Bible School it became the Union Bible School under a "board" which had representatives from nearby missions. During their fourth term, Moyer was principal of the Janzen Memorial Higher Secondary School in Jagdeeshpur.

The Moyers left India in 1956 after which they pastored the Bethel Mennonite Church, Pekin, Ill., until retirement in 1967.   HR/RR

Who's Who Mennonites (1943), 176; Samuel T. Moyer, *With Christ on the Edge of the Jungles* (Jubbulpore, C. P. India, 1941); *Twenty-Five Years with God in India* (Berne, Ind.: Mennonite Book Concern, 1929), 195; Samuel T. Moyer, *They Heard the Call* (Newton, 1970), 106-57; Ruth Ratzlaff, ed., *Fellowship in the Gospel India: 1900-1950* (Newton, Ks.: MPO, 1950), 91-95, 129, 151-57; Juhnke, *Mission* (1979), 37-43, 234.

Moyo Mapendla (ca. 1913-69), was an outstanding educator in the school system of the Brethren in Christ Church in what is now Zimbabwe. As a student, he prepared to become a teacher in the Brethren in Christ Matopo school system. He continued his education through the extension program of the U. of South Africa and at Messiah College, Grantham, Pa. (1963-66; BA 1966). He served as a teacher of the Standard III class at the Matopo Training Institute (1938-39), became Head Teacher at the Matopo Teacher Training Institute (1944), and was the headmaster of the Wanezi Central Primary School (1945-63). He is also remembered for his ability as an interpreter for visiting Brethren in Christ leaders, as well as for such noted Christian leaders as Billy Graham.   REP/AMC

EV (Aug. 7, 1961), (Jan. 10, 1973).

Mozambique. Mennonite involvement in Mozambique grew out of assistance given by MCC and Eastern Mennonite Board of Missians and Charities (MC) to Mozambican refugees in Tanzania during Mozambique's independence struggle of the 1960s. Occasional visits by MCC personnel, 1974-75, led to the shipment of medicines in 1976 via the °American Friends Service Committee. Representatives of the Kanisa la Mennonite Tanzania and MCC established a relationship with Christian Council of Mozambique and local churches in 1978. Regular shipments of material aid were made to Rhodesian refugees in Mozambique before 1982, and 18,000 tons of cereals were shipped by MCC and distributed under the auspices of the Christian Council to flood, war, and drought victims in Mozambique, 1982-86. Harold Wenger (Eastern Board missionary) in Swaziland developed contacts with °African Independent Churches, 1978-80.   JWS

Muatende Pierre (b. 1914) was the son of a Lulua

chief in the Belgian Congo (Zaire). As a teenager, Muatende found his way to Kalamaba, a station of the °°Congo Inland Mission (Africa Inter-Mennonite Mission) in the West Kasai of Belgian Congo. His study in primary school was interrupted by his father, who insisted that he return to his village and accept a wife in traditional fashion. With missionary assistance Muatende was able to return (with his wife, Luanganyi) to the mission station where he finished studies in the station Bible school in 1937.

In 1938 he was appointed a village teacher and catechist. He first worked among the Badinga people. a neighboring tribe with different language and customs. He was eventually able to win acceptance in the village for both himself and his message. Later he served in a variety of areas, including a refugee camp of some 10,000 people during the political turmoil of the early 1960s in the West Kasai. Muatende was officially ordained a pastor in 1971 and soon was named regional evangelist of the Mennonite church (Église du Christ au Zaire, Communauté Mennonite). He often was called to resolve conflicts and call people to repentance. He had a remarkable ability to memorize Scripture which he quoted throughout his sermons.   JEB

Mubaybulu Ekaka (1930-July 23, 1978) was born at Mikungu in Bandundu, Belgian Congo (Zaire). He was married to Mossese Berenise; they had no children. Mubaybulu was baptized at the Baptist Tshene Mission (1938) and attended the primary school at Tshene (1938-48). He taught school from 1948 to 1953 and then attended the Mennonite Brethren Bible Institute at Kafumba (1953). From 1961 to 1963 he studied at the Mennonite Brethren Theology School at Kajiji. In 1964 he became an evangelist working in Kikwit. He then served as the Kituba radio pastor for the Mennonite Brethren radio broadcasts (1965-70). When the radio work closed, he became the supervising pastor responsible for the Mennonite Brethren churches in °Kinshasa where he served until his death.   AP

Mudenda Samson (1916-1984), educator and churchman, was one of the national leaders in the Brethren in Christ Church in Zambia during the years from 1965 to 1984. He and his wife, Anna Muleya, were blessed with five children.

Mudenda attended the Union Bible Institute in South Africa (1955), Wanezi Bible Institute in Zimbabwe (1956), and Ekuphileni Bible Institute in Zimbabwe (3 years). He also studied at Messiah College, Grantham, Pa. (1962-63, and 1975-76), majoring in biblical studies, and at the International Institute of Communications, Harare, Zimbabwe. He served in the Brethren in Christ educational program as pastor and teacher in Zambia until his election as overseer for the Macha Circuit. He was ordained in 1956. After returning from Messiah College with a BA degree in 1976, he served as the principal of the Sikalongo Bible Institute until his death.   REP/AMC

Muganda Ezekiel Kaneja (Dec. 1910-Jan. 4, 1974). While serving as evangelist at Mugango Mission, Muganda completed upper primary grades with his oldest son. In 1938 and 1939 he studied at Bukiroba Bible School and in 1962 to 1965 at Mennonite Theological College. He first tried Islam while working in Mombasa, Kenya; then he identified with the Salvation Army. Back home he was baptized in the Africa Inland Church in 1933. After making a full commitment in the 1942 revival that moved through the emerging Tanganyika Mennonite Church, he began to experience victory over sin. A diligent Bible reader, Ezekiel became a popular preacher. Even during the ferment of national independence, he was faithful to his calling. The chief of Majita relaxed, knowing that this cousin was no threat to his throne.

Muganda had two children, Josiah and Nyabise, from a preconversion marriage. In 1930 he married (Raheri) Nyaburuma Machumu, mother of Mukama, Rhoda, Bernard, Esther, Perucy, Samuel, Alexander, Emmanuel, Anna, Nellie, and Elam. Ezekiel and Raheri made their family their first responsibility; each day began and ended with °family worship. The children remember answered prayers, e.g., milk for a sick child, the birth of another son (Samuel), and receiving each year sufficient funds to pay the fees for secondary and college education. They experienced judgment for wrongdoing and forgiveness because of Jesus' death. These children now serve in responsible positions in Tanzania and internationally.

As a churchman Muganda served in Mennonite congregations for 15 years as an evangelist and elder and 23 years as pastor. Besides ministering in his congregation, he taught the Scriptures in the schools, the hospital, and the prison. Churches called him to preach in Bible conferences. When Tanganyika Mennonite Church first built a boarding school, he walked 18 miles (30 km.) with his parishioners to help for a week. In 1960 he participated in bringing the Tanzania Mennonite Church (TWC; Kanisa la Mennonite Tanzania) to autonomy. With Zedekia °Kisare he was invited to North America in 1961. When asked to speak he responded: "Frequently I saw your wealth. Sometimes my attention was distracted by the disunity of your church. Occasionally I was troubled by your too busyness. I needed to confess wrong attitudes to the Lord, and again he would show me only Jesus at work among you." When Kisare was chosen bishop of TWC in 1966, Muganda was designated vice-chairman. The close fellowship between these brothers helped their congregations overcome traditional tribal rivalries.   MMH

Mahlon M. Hess, *The Pilgrimage of Faith of Tanzania Mennonite Church, 1934-83* (Salunga, Pa.: Eastern Mennonite Board, 1985), 36-37, 44, 47, 57-58, 91, 93-95, 97, 98, 104-5, 111-12, 119, 127-28, 141; Zedekia M. Kisare, Elam W. Stauffer, and Josiah M. Muganda, "In Memoriam: Ezekiel Kaneja Muganda, " *Miss. Mess.* (June 1974), 6; *GH* (Oct. 17, 1961), 916-17, (Feb. 19, 1974), 152, (July 17, 1951), 686-87; Ezekiel K. Muganda, "Evangelism," *GH* (July 26, 1949), 748; idem, "The Witness in Musoma," *GH* (July 17, 1956), 686-87; W. Ray Wenger letter in *Miss. Mess.* (May 11, 1941), 11-12.

Mukebai Ambroise. Born to Baluba parents, Mukebai's parents eventually found their way to Tshikapa, a growing urban center on the banks of the Kasai River in south central Belgian Congo (Zaire). As a child Mukebai enrolled in primary school of the °°Congo Inland Mission (Africa Inter-Mennonite Mission). Post-primary formal Bible training was limited, so Mukebai spent much time in personal study of his Tshiluba Bible. He was proposed by his church district as a pastoral candidate and upon ordination was asked to start a new congregation in Kele, a growing suburb of Tshikapa. In this setting his ability as a pastor and preacher soon became evident.

Quiet in demeanor but with a direct gaze and a quick smile, he initially held meetings in a school building which soon became overcrowded. Instead of looking to the mission for help he introduced an extra Sunday morning offering for a building fund, which he insisted be placed in the hands of a lay committee. In due time a large chapel was constructed completely by local efforts.

Mukebai has incorporated much of African flavor into his preaching and worship services, while consistently insisting upon the preeminence of Scripture over cultural patterns. He has also successfully encouraged members to participate in the life of the church. In a land where pastoral roles are frequently confused with those of a traditional chief, Mukebai's low profile has been remarkably effective.   JEB

Mukoso Mbavu (b. 1930) was born at the village of Tshenda, Belgian Congo (Zaire). He converted to Jesus Christ (1943) and was baptized. He received a certificate from primary school (1950), attended the Kikwit high school, and received a certificate from the Mennonite Brethren Bible Institute in Kikwit (1962). In 1952 he married and subsequently became the father of seven living children. Mukoso was a teacher and Sunday school and congregational secretary (1950-60), then served as secretary of the Mennonite Brethren conference (Église du Christ au Zaire, Communauté des Églises de Frères Mennonites), 1961-74. In the latter capacity he traveled to visit churches in all Mennonite Brethren conference districts. At the same time he was deacon in charge of local church finances and a Sunday school teacher. From 1974 to 1979 Mukoso was assistant treasurer and accountant for the Mennonite Brethren conference and then served as head of the conference personnel department, while continuing as local deacon and prayer group leader. Since 1984 Mukoso has served as a garage and carpenter shop foreman, but has continued his position as deacon and effective prayer group leader.   AP

Mumaw, John Rudy (b. 1904), has devoted his life to leadership in Mennonite (MC) education. Collegiate and graduate studies prepared him for more than 40 years of teaching, mostly at Eastern Mennonite College and Seminary, in Bible, English, and practical theology, with a specialty in °marriage and °family life. From 1948 to 1965 he was president of the college and seminary. His tenure saw a doubling of enrollment, erection of major buildings, enlargement of curriculum, professional growth of faculty, progress toward a separate high school and a full seminary program, and membership in the regional accrediting association. He led in articulating a philosophy of education, with aims and objectives for the college. He directed the first long-range professional planning for the college and seminary and brought it into closer involvement with the larger Mennonite Church (MC) and into the wider educational world. He helped found and lead the Council for Advancement of Small Colleges.

Mumaw was also an evangelist, pastor, and leader in Virginia Mennonite Conference (MC) and in churchwide missions and service work. He edited the missions section of *Gospel Herald, Program Builder,* and *Christian Ministry,* and wrote *Assurance of Salvation* and *The Resurrected Life.*

He married Esther Moseman, with whom he had five daughters; after her death in 1964, he married Evelyn King, former Eastern Mennonite College dean of women.   HRP

Who's Who Mennonites (1943), 177; *Menn. Bib. II,* p. 484; *GH* (Aug. 7, 1984), 548-51.

Münster Anabaptists (ME III:777). Anabaptist governments ruled Münster, the major city of Westphalia, (Germany) for 16 months from February 1534 to June 1535, under continuous siege by the bishop of Münster, who received military assistance from both Catholic and Lutheran rulers. During the siege the Anabaptists instituted a harsh internal regime based on °°community of goods and polygamy, and attempted with some limited success to win military assistance from Anabaptists in Westphalia and the Netherlands.

Recent research on Münster Anabaptism has focused on the preconditions for the Anabaptists' coming to power in Münster and on the social composition of the fraction of the Münster citizenry that rallied to Anabaptism.

The Reformer of Münster, Bernhard °Rothmann, was an independent, eclectic theologian who borrowed heavily from Swiss and South German sources. He would have preferred a non-Lutheran magisterial Reformation similar to those in the Swiss cities. But Münster's Reformation, ratified by the Treaty of Dülmen, February 1533, obligated it to the Lutheran Augsburg confession. Rothmann responded to the attempts of Lutheran theologians at Wittenberg and Marburg to force him and Münster into Lutheran orthodoxy by opening the city to the influence of the sect of Melchior °Hoffman, the major leader of Anabaptism in North Germany and The Netherlands. Melchiorite Anabaptism was distinguished by an idiosyncratic °Christology focused on the divinity of Christ and by the charismatic authority of °apocalyptic prophets. Hoffman had begun to administer believers' baptism in 1530, but suspended it again in 1531 in response to the execution of some of his Dutch followers. The leading early Melchiorite influence in Münster was that of the °°Wassenberg preachers, led by Heinrich Roll. By summer 1533 they won Rothmann to open advocacy of adult baptism. Rothmann and the Wassenberg preachers authored the *Confession of the Two Sacraments* in November 1533. Roll brought it to The Netherlands, where the aspiring Melchiorite prophet, °°Jan Matthijs of Haarlem, used it to justify his reinstitution of adult baptism at the end of 1533. Jan Matthijs' emissaries came to Münster in January 1534 and baptized Rothmann, the Wassenberg preachers, and their followers. The *Confession of the*

Two Sacraments was a classic peaceful Anabaptist statement, recognized as such by Pilgram °Marpeck when he made it the basis of his *Vermahnung* of 1542, the most fundamental expression of the Marpeck congregations.

Fateful for the course of the Münster Reformation was Rothmann's success in winning about half of the town's elite of notables, the leaders of the guilds, to support his radical theology. The Münster council supported Lutheranism, but Lutheranism in Münster was shallowly rooted, based on little more than the political necessity for the town to maintain the support of the powerful Schmalkaldic League. The authority of the council collapsed dramatically on Feb. 9-11, 1534, when, accompanied by the vision of three suns in the sky, the previously nonviolent Anabaptists took arms at the instruction of their prophets. This rescue from their enemies was for the Münster Anabaptists an experience of God's intervention in history, an otherwise inexplicable deliverance like that of the Israelites crossing through the Red Sea.

Responding to the events in Münster, apocalyptic excitement swept over all estates in Westphalia and The Netherlands. The Anabaptist assumption of power temporarily lent Jan Matthijs uncontested charismatic authority. His call for Netherlanders to hurry to Münster in March 1534, if they wanted to escape God's vengeance, provoked a mass response. Socially, Münster Anabaptism does not seem to have exercised a disproportionate attraction for the poor. Reinforcing literary evidence about rich participants in the trek of March 1534, is Karl-Heinz Kirchhoff's study of Anabaptist property-holders native to Münster. They appear to have had a distribution of wealth very similar to that of the Münster citizens who opposed Anabaptism. And, despite the introduction of community of goods, the Anabaptist leaders tended to be people who had been well-to-do in the old order.

The Dutch Melchiorites began to doubt the militant prophets of Münster with the failure of Jan Matthijs' prediction that the world would end at Easter 1534. Instead, he was slain in battle that day. The rule of °°Jan of Leyden from Jan Matthijs' death to the fall of Münster was a desperate struggle for survival. Although Jan of Leyden claimed universal kingship, his authority among Melchiorites was in decline, as indicated by the rise of Jan van °°Batenburg, a new "promised David," to oppose him.

Reality and appearances were at odds in Münster Anabaptism. Behind the appearance of community of goods was the continuing privileged status of an elite. Behind the polygamous reordering of marriage was the officering of the female majority by men. A few small uprisings in The Netherlands, concluded by an utter fiasco in Amsterdam, were the only fruit of Rothmann's grand proclamation of a worldwide crusade for vengeance on the godless. Münster's authority was already waning after Easter 1534 and, after Münster fell, the majority of Melchiorite Anabaptists turned away from polygamy and a physical kingdom towards the peaceful leadership first of °David Joris and then of °Menno Simons.   JMS

Willem de Bakker, "Civic Reformer in Anabaptist Münster. Bernhard Rothmann, 1495-1535" (PhD diss., U. of Chicago, 1987); Martin Brecht, "Die Theologie Bernhard Rothmanns," *Jb. für westfälische KG*, 78 (1985), 49-82; Karl-Heinz Kirchhoff, *Die Täufer in Münster 1534/35* (Münster: Aschendorff, 1973); idem, "Was There a Peaceful Anabaptist Congregation in Münster in 1534?," *MQR*, 44 (1970), 357-70; Taira Kuratsuka, "Gesamtgilde und Täufer: Der Radikalisierungsprozess in der Reformation Münsters: Von der reformatorischen Bewegung zum Täuferreich 1533/34," *ARG*, 76 (1985), 231-70; Otthein Rammstedt, *Sekte und soziale Bewegung: Soziologische Analyse der Täufer in Münster* (Cologne and Opladen: Westdeutscher Verlag, 1966); Heinz Schilling, "Aufstandsbewegungen in der Stadtbürgerlichen Gesellschaft des Alten Reiches: Die Vorgeschichte des Münsteraner Täuferreiches, 1525-1534," *Der Deutsche Bauernkrieg 1524-1526*, ed. H.-U. Wehler (Göttingen, 1975), 193-238; James M. Stayer, "Was Dr. Kuehler's Conception of Early Dutch Anabaptism Historically Sound? The Historical Discussion of Münster 450 Years Later," *MQR*, 60 (1986), 261-88; Günther Vogler, "Das Täuferreich zu Münster als Problem der Politik im Reich," *Menn. Geschbl.*, 42 (1985), 7-23.

Müntzer, Thomas (ME III:785), remains one of the most controversial and important radical reformers. The article in ME III refuted any connection between Müntzer and Anabaptism. It contrasted an image of Müntzer created by a historical tradition dependent on Luther with an ideal type of Anabaptism shaped by studies of the Swiss and Hutterian Brethern. Müntzer, the unbalanced *Schwärmer* (fanatic) and inconsistent conspirator given to inspirationism or prophetic fantasies, could have little in common with sober disciples of Jesus. It became a rhetorical rather than a historical question whether Müntzer could even be considered a Christian! The impressions left by Friedmann are in obvious need of revision. Unfortunately, space permits only a correction of the more glaring misrepresentations and an updating of biographical details.

Biography. Of artisan stock, Müntzer received a humanist education that included knowledge of Latin, Hebrew, and Greek. At Leipzig and Frankfurt [Oder] he earned the MA degree and completed the *Baccalareus Biblicus* stage of theological studies, the latter earmarking him for an academic career in theology. After ordination in 1513, he accepted an appointment as priest at St. Michael's in Braunschweig (May 1514). He apparently drew a stipend from this position until 1521. Between 1516 and 1517 he also served as provost of a convent in Frohse. In late 1518 or at the beginning of 1519, he seems to have visited Wittenberg. Early in 1519 he defended the need of reforms against Franciscans at Jüterbog (Jüterborgk). It seems likely that he witnessed the debate between Luther and Eck at Leipzig later that year. On his way he appears to have stopped at Orlamünde. The first Catholic polemic using the label "Lutheran" included him under the designation. From 1519 to 1520, Müntzer served as confessor to Cistercian nuns near Weissenfels. During this period he studied the writings of Johann Tauler (ca. 1300-1360), Heinrich Suso (ca. 1295-1366), and the °°*Theologia Deutsch*. A book order dating from 1520 provides evidence of his keen reading habits. The 74 items include works of the church fathers, mystical literature, canon law, church history and publications by °°Erasmus, °°Luther, and Karlstadt (°°Carlstadt). Still in 1520 and with the support of Luther, Müntzer obtained the preachership at Zwickau. His polemical style and popularity among the economically hard-pressed weavers contributed to iconoclastic disturbances and a polarization of the community. This in turn led to his dismissal on Apr. 16, 1521. The better known events that followed need no reiteration here.

Teaching. Although shaped by the turbulent conditions of the early Reformation, Müntzer's ideas reveal a remarkable coherence and consistency. Scholars have disagreed on what constitutes the core of his theology. Spiritualism, °mysticism, °apocalypticism, and perfectionism have been variously identified as chief traits. Related issues concern (1) Müntzer's indebtedness to the mystics; (2) his dependence on Luther; (3) the influence of the °°Zwickau prophets, or Karlstadt (°°Carlstadt) or both; (4) his break with Luther, i.e., the turning point from would-be reformer to revolutionary; (5) the consistency or inconsistency between his political radicalism and his theology; (6) his connection to the Anabaptist movement. Each of the above issues has received attention in recent research and needs no detailed discussion here. It suffices to state that an emerging consensus suggests that Müntzer brought his own assumptions to the Reformation agenda. These were shaped by late medieval "realism," (i.e., the belief that particular things are manifestations of unseen universal, realities), a mystical inwardness, popular anticlericalism, his reading of church history, and certain apocalyptic expectations. His key theological premises were formed well before meeting the Zwickau prophets. His indebtedness to Luther was at best qualified. An astute observer, Müntzer was one of the first to fault Lutheran preaching for its lack of power to change both individual and collective life. Accusing Luther of emphasizing only the "sweet Christ," Müntzer insisted on the experience of the "bitter Christ." The cross as the mortification of the flesh had to be experienced by every believer in surrender to the will of God. In his view the debate about works righteousness versus justification by faith alone seemed misplaced. Salvation concerned not a question of meritorious works, but whether humans were prepared to suffer God's work, a work that began in fear of judgment and in death to self and to the lusts of the flesh, but also was grounded in an experience of cleansing, spiritual regeneration, and newness of life. The spiritualist and perfectionist tendencies were rooted in an existential participation in Christ's death and resurrection. The movement of the Spirit involved in the sanitive process of death and rebirth became exchangeable with the redemptive activity of Christ, the eternal Word. When given an epistemological twist, the living Word heard in the soul could be directed against too close an identification of Word with Scripture. Behind the Lutheran emphasis on the written and preached word, Müntzer came to suspect the self-interested bibliolatry of the preacher-exegete, who hoped to replace the priest as the privileged officeholder in the church. Against the emergence of the learned elite, Müntzer emphasized the °priesthood of all believers. He believed that the division of the church into laity and clergy had led to corruption immediately after the apostles. The free movement of the Spirit and the possibility of regeneration of all believers permitted no such distinction. Justifica-

tion through regeneration meant a being made righteous. The tensions between the implied perfectionism and Müntzer's populism were overcome by the conviction that the apocalyptic harvest was at hand. The church, about to be restored to its pristine purity, would inherit the earth.

Much of the scholarly debate has been concerned with the consistency of Müntzer's theology and his political-social activism. How could an emphasis on cross mysticism and regeneration lead to an attempt at advancing the kingdom through the °Peasants' War? H.-J. Goertz has suggested an answer in Müntzer's unique integration of the "inner and outer order." Müntzer astutely surmised a reciprocal relationship between individual and collective well-being. The salvation of the community depended on the regeneration of its individual members, but sociopolitical structures that reinforced fear of man or were preoccupied with creaturely matters could hinder the proper spiritual orientation toward God. Rulers who set themselves against the second coming in its individual and collective expression forfeited divine approval. The right to resist them devolved upon the people. Seeing the events of 1525 as resistance to godless tyranny and God's instrument to purify Christendom, Müntzer placed his considerable talents at the disposal of the great uprising of the peasants and "common man." Although not its instigator, he became one of its theologically most articulate defenders.

Significance. Müntzer's influence on his contemporaries was considerable. His involvement on the side of the commoners brought notoriety and fame while his critique of Luther fell on receptive ears. A number of Anabaptists later considered him their spiritual father. Factions of the movement in Thuringia, Hesse, Franconia, Bavaria, Swabia, Upper Austria, Salzburg and Northern Tirol unmistakably carried his ideological traits. Melchior °°Rinck, Hans °Hut, Hans °°Denck, Balthasar Reif, Hans °°Römer and Heinz °°Kraut were some of the Anabaptists compromised in one form or other by contact with him. The founding members of Swiss Anabaptism drafted a controversial letter to him (CRR 4: 284-94), and Hutterian chroniclers nurtured his memory. Generally, most Anabaptists shared with him a strong anticlericalism (social animosity toward priests), a corresponding anti-sacerdotalism (rejection of the idea of priestly mediation), and a radical application of the priesthood of all believers. Related to these views was the Anabaptist tendency toward a subjective interpretation of the sacraments (°ordinances); their critique of the theology of °justification by faith alone and of Reformation preaching that produced no change in life; and their advocacy of apostolic °restitutionism and zeal for a pure church. Needless to say, none of this made Müntzer the founder of Anabaptism. Anabaptism, a heterogeneous, decentralized movement that defies easy generalizations, went beyond Müntzer by making believers' baptism normative, rejecting violence, and establishing separated brotherhoods. Even those factions strongly influenced by his cross-mysticism eventually shed the spiritualizing tendencies.

Modern scholarship has been fascinated by Müntzer's theological integration of individual and collective salvation. His engagement on the side of the commoners makes it tempting to see in him a forerunner of °liberation theologies. His intuition about the interconnection between institutional structures and ideological legitimation appears provocatively modern. However, Müntzer's modernity should not be exaggerated. Nor should less attractive aspects of his ministry be ignored. He was not the atheist-socialist that Friedrich Engels thought he was. His egalitarianism was qualified by the advocacy of charismatic leadership, above all his own. The radical priesthood of all believers was mitigated by an elitism of the regenerate elect whose identification defied empirical verification. Müntzer misread the signs of the times. He failed to see that an armed defense of the future kingdom inevitably led to new coercive structures in the present. But despite these delinquencies or perhaps because of them, Müntzer deserves a fair hearing and a rightful place in the all-too-human story of the Reformation and of Anabaptist beginnings. WOP

Until the planned new critical edition appears the key source remains G. Franz,ed., *Thomas Müntzer Schriften und Briefe: Kritische Gesamtausgabe* (Gütersloh, 1968); cf. S. Bräuer, and W. Ullmann, eds., *Thomas Müntzers theologische Schriften aus dem Jahr 1523*, 2nd ed. (Berlin, 1982); M. Schaub, *Müntzer contre Luther: Le droit divin contre l'absolutisme princier* (Paris, 1984), contains translations into French of Müntzer's three major pamphlets of 1524; P. Mathison of John Knox College, Dunedin, Otago, New Zealand, and E. J. Furcha of McGill U., Montreal, have both promised English editions of Müntzer's works. Regarding secondary sources, for literature to 1976 students should consult: Hans J. Hillerbrand, *Thomas Müntzer: A Bibliography* (St. Louis, 1976); Werner O. Packull, "Thomas Müntzer Between Marxist-Christian Diatribe and Dialogue," *Historical Reflections*, 4 (1977), 67-90; S. Bräuer, "Müntzerforschung von 1965 bis 1975," *Luther Jb.*, vol. 44 (1977), 127-41, vol. 45 (1978), 102-39; Abraham Friesen and Hans-Jürgen Goertz, eds., *Thomas Müntzer: Wege der Forschung* (Darmstadt, 1978), with a comprehensive survey of the history of Müntzer research; James M. Stayer, and Werner O. Packull, eds., *The Anabaptists and Thomas Müntzer* (Dubuque, Iowa and Toronto, 1980). Selected monographs and articles include M., Baylor, "Thomas Müntzer's First Publication," *Sixteenth Century J.*, 17 (1986), 451-58; M. Bensing, *Thomas Müntzer und der Thüringer Aufstand 1525* (Berlin, 1966); Peter Blickle, "Thomas Müntzer und der Bauernkrieg in Südwestdeutschland," *Z. für Agrargeschichte und Agrarsoziologie*, 24 (1976); S. Bräuer, "Thomas Müntzer und der Allstedter Bund," and Siegfried Hoyer, "Die Zwickauer Storchianer - Vorläufer der Täufer?" in *Anabaptistes et dissidents au XVIe siècle: Bibliotheca Dissidentium scripta et studia*, ed. by J. Rott and S. Verheus (Baden-Baden, 1987), 65-83, 85-101; Ulrich Bubenheimer, "Thomas Müntzer in Braunschweig," *Braunschweigisches Jb.*, vol. 65 (1984), 37-76, vol. 66 (1985), 79-114; idem, "Thomas Müntzer und der Anfang der Reformation in Braunschweig," *Nederlands Archief voor Kerkgeschiednis*, 65 (1985), 1-30; idem, "Thomas Müntzer," in *Protestantische Profile: Lebensbilder aus fünf Jahrhunderte* (Frankfurt, 1983), 33-46; C. Demke, ed., *Thomas Müntzer: Anfragen an Theologie und Kirche* (Berlin, 1977); A. W. Drummond, "Thomas Müntzer and the Fear of Man," *Sixteenth Century J.*, 10, no. 2 (1979), 63-71; Richard van Dülmen, "Müntzers Anhänger im oberdeutschen Täufertum," *Z. für bayerische Landesgeschichte*, 39 (1976), 883-91; Klaus Ebert, *Thomas Müntzer: Von Eigensinn und Widerspruch* (Frankfurt a. M., 1987); W. Elliger, *Thomas Müntzer: Leben und Werk*, 3rd ed. (Göttingen, 1976); Abraham Friesen, "Thomas Müntzer and the Anabaptists," *JMS*, 4 (1986), 143-61; W. Gericke, "Thomas Müntzer als Theologe des Geistes und seine Sicht von der Erziehung der Menschheit," *Herbergen der Christenheit* (1977/78), 47-63; Hans-Jürgen Goertz, *Innere und äussere Ordnung in de Theologie Thomas Müntzers* (Leiden, 1967); idem, "The Mystic with the Hammer: Thomas Müntzer's Theological

Basis for Revolution," *MQR*, 50 (1976), 83-113; idem, "'Lebendiges Wort' und 'totes Ding': Zum Schriftverständnis Thomas Müntzers im Prager Manifest," *ARG*, 67 (1976), 153-78; idem, "Thomas Müntzer," in *Profiles of Radical Reformers*, ed. by H.-J.Goertz and Walter Klaassen (Scottdale, 1982), 29-44; Eric W. Gritsch, *Reformer Without a Church: The Life and Thought of Thomas Müntzer* (Philadelphia, 1967); Hans J. Hillerbrand, *A Fellowship of Discontent* (New York, 1967); C. Hinrichs, *Luther und Müntzer: Ihre Auseinandersetzung über Obrigkeit und Widerstandsrecht*, 2nd ed. (Berlin, 1962; Carter Lindberg, "Conflicting Models of Ministry: Luther, Karlstadt and Muentzer," *Concordia Theological Quarterly*, 41 (1977), 35-50; A. James Reimer, "Bloch's Interpretation of Muentzer: History, Theology, and Social Change," *CLIO*, 9, no. 2 (1980), 253-67; H. P. Rüger, "Thomas Müntzers Erklärung hebräischer Eigennamen und der liber de interpretatione hebraicorum nominum des Hieronymus," *Z. für Kg.*, 94 (1983), 83-87; Reinhold Schwarz, *Die apokalyptische Theologie Thomas Müntzers und der Taboriten* (Tübingen, 1977); Tom Scott, "The 'Volksreformation' of Thomas Müntzer in Allstedt and Mühlhausen," *J. of Ecclesiastical History*, 34 (1983), 194-213; idem, "Thomas Müntzer - Bemerkungen zu Herkunft und Charakter seiner Ideologie," *Mühlhäuser Beitdräge*, 4 (1983), 3-16.

Murthy, Rayasam Radha Krishna (b. Feb. 29, 1928). Born in Govindapuram, a small village in Andhra Pradesh State, India, Murthy was a Brahmin by birth. He began his career as a Telugu language teacher in the Mennonite Brethren mission schools (20 years). As he used the Gospel of John as a text in teaching, the Telugu language to missionaries, he accepted its message and was baptized by Henry G. Krahn on Sept. 16, 1957. He was ordained a minister by Calvary MB congregation, Mahbubnagar on Feb. 4, 1968 and worked with Mennonite Brethren radio broadcasts until 1969; then with *God Has Spoken* ministries and *Trans World Radio* for 10 years prior to 1987. He is well known throughout Andhra Pradesh and neighboring states as a successful Bible teacher and revival speaker. He is also a gifted writer and journalist. He edited *Suvarthamani*, the official organ of the Mennonite Brethren churches, for more than a decade; translated some books into Telugu; authored two books, one a commentary on Revelation; and founded and edited *Spandana*, a monthly magazine with a circulation of 10,000. Murthy is in great demand as a speaker at conventions and conferences. MAS

Museums portraying Anabaptist and Mennonite history and peoplehood have become immensely popular. In 1987, more than 20 museums in Canada and the United States interpret the Amish or Mennonite heritage; in future years, museums with Mennonite or Anabaptist connections will likely appear in other countries.

The late 19th c. witnessed a surge of museum founding in North American society. Many early museums celebrated the legacies of wealthy and civic-minded leaders. Mennonites, however, valuing humility, founded museums only after establishing other types of °institutions. Newly founded colleges sparked interest among Mennonite scholars for preserving historical materials, and the colleges eventually opened specialized °historical libraries and °archives. In 1987 the historical libraries of several colleges maintain cultural artifacts for their church constituencies.

Some museums began through the interest of individuals. Notable Mennonite collectors include

Charles Kauffman, who founded the Kauffman Museum at Bethel College (Ks.); John C. Reimer, a teacher whose collection of pioneer artifacts formed the nucleus of Mennonite Village Museum at Steinbach, Man.; and Erie Sauder, whose living history museum celebrates the industrial heritage of the Black Swamp region in nw. Ohio.

Community pride lends local color to many Mennonite-related museums. In the 1950s and 1960s, °historical societies formed museum boards and solicited contributions for fledgling museums. Today these museums, often relying on volunteers, make distinctive contributions to their communities. By focusing on regional history, they reinforce a sense of rootedness and identity.

In recent years, Mennonite entrepreneurs have embraced new concepts for sharing Anabaptist faith and heritage. Three main °interpretation and information centers (The People's Place in Intercourse, Pa.; The Meetingplace in St. Jacob's, Ont.; and Menno-Hof in Shipshewana, Ind.) offer films, exhibits, and educational programs. One trend reflected in these visitor centers is inter-Mennonite participation. Located in a popular tourist area, Menno-Hof, for example, is sponsored by churches of several Mennonite and Amish conferences.

Museum professionals are exploring other ways of attracting tourists. In Berlin, Ohio, and Intercourse, Pa., art galleries exhibit the works of contemporary Mennonite artists. Annual festivals are also popular: Threshing Days in Goessel, Ks.; Heritage Festival in Metamora, Ill.; and Apple Butter Frolic in Harleysville, Pa.; are but a few of the events that draw thousands of visitors to Mennonite communities.

For at least some museums, professional accreditation and higher technology beckon. The American Association of Museums aids nonprofit museums in achieving standards in exhibit design, educational programming, publications and fund-raising. Some Mennonite museums use computers to aid in research and collections management. Others pursue ever widening constituencies. The Hans Herr House in Lancaster County, Pa., for example, advertises its events in more than 60 newspapers in the ne. United States.

For Mennonite-related museums, a mobile society interested in the values that Anabaptist groups represent has serious ramifications. Many of the museums serve a primarily non-Mennonite public. Some museum professionals critique traditional Mennonite exhibits as "cabinets of curiosities" that foster negative stereotypes. Museum personnel agree that, in general, ethnic Mennonites tend to take their heritage for granted, while persons from other traditions seek to understand and appreciate unique aspects of Amish and Mennonite culture.

The best museums compel visitors, of whatever background, to clarify values of faith. In the coming years, as these museums gain stature, they will undoubtedly emphasize values of religious heritage that transcend ethnicity. A list of museums, their locations, dates of founding, and sponsoring agencies follows: The People's Place, Intercourse, Pa. (1976; Good Enterprises, Ltd.); Springs Museum, Springs, Pa. (1957; Springs Historical Society); Heritage Hall Museum, Freeman, S.D. (1976; Freeman Academy);

Germantown Mennonite Museum, Philadelphia, Pa. (1953; Germantown Mennonite Church Corporation); Hans Herr House, Willow Street, Pa. (1969; Lancaster Mennonite Historical Society); Lancaster Mennonite Historical Society, Lancaster, Pa. (1958; Lancaster Mennonite Historical Society); Mennonite Heritage Center, Souderton, Pa. (1973; Mennonite Historians of Eastern Pennsylvanis); German Culture Museum, Walnut Creek, Ohio (1980; Heritage Preservation Committee, Inc.); Sauder Farm and Craft Village, Archbold, Ohio (1971; nonprofit organization founded by Erie J. Sauder); Kauffman Museum, North Newton, Ks. (1910; Bethel College/Kauffman Museum Association); Mennonite Heritage Museum, Goessel, Ks. (1971; Mennonite Heritage Museum Association); Pioneer Adobe House Museum, Hillsboro, Ks. (1958; town of Hillsboro); Warkentin House, Newton, Ks. (1971; Warkentin House Association); Iowa Mennonite Museum and Archives, Kalona, Iowa (1948; Mennonite Historical Society of Iowa); Mennonite Village Museum, Steinbach, Man. (1964; Mennonite Village Museum [Canada] Inc.); Menno Simons Historical Library/Archives, Harrisonburg, Va. (1950; Virginia Mennonite Conference); Historical Center, Richfield, Pa. (1978; Juniata District Mennonite Historical Society); Penn Alps, Grantsville, Md. (1967; Penn Alps, Inc.); Archives of the Brethren in Christ Church, Grantham, Pa. (1952; Brethren in Christ Church and Messiah College); Mennonite Historical Library, Goshen, Ind. (1906; Board of Education [MC]); The Meetingplace, St. Jacobs, Ont. (1979; St. Jacobs Mennonite Church); Mennonite Heritage Center, Metamora, Ill. (1975; Illinois Mennonite Historical and Genealogical Society); Menno-Hof, Shipshewana, Ind. (1987; collaborative effort of several Mennonite conferences and agencies); Doopsgezinde Bibliothek, Amsterdam, The Netherlands (Algemene Doopsgezinde Sociëteit, since 1960 with the U. Amsterdam); Mennonite Heritage Centre, Winnipeg, Man. (1978; Conference of Mennonites in Canada); Heritage Historical Library, Aylmer, Ont. (1972; Pathway publishers).   RWG

Lists of Mennonite-related museums and galleries are published in *Festival Quarterly*,. See also *Museums for a New Century* (Washington, D.C.: American Association of Museums, 1984), 17-21, 46-47, 75-79. Questionnaire responses received by Rachel Waltner Goossen from 24 Mennonite, Amish, or related museums and historical libraries, during January and February 1987, have been deposited in the Mennonite Library and Archives, North Newton, Ks.

See also Folklore.

Music, North America (ME III:791). The musical scene among Mennonites of North America during the last three decades has been one of vigorous activity, new experiences, and high levels of achievement. This development can be explained by several factors that have emerged during the last 30 or 40 years: (1) an increasing cooperation among Mennonite groups, (2) more intense musical activity in the churches' educational institutions, (3) a growing interest in the fine arts in general, and (4) a stronger financial support for the making of music.

The locus for the most impressive activity is likely that of the largest metropolitan concentration of

Mennonites—in Winnipeg, where educational institutions at several levels have produced an unusual amount of musical achievement, where local congregations have created numerous musical groups and a high standard for worship music, and where community organizations have produced music in every conceivable form and style, from children's choirs to Mennonite opera. Other centers of vigorous activity also are located mostly in areas where church schools are active: Waterloo-Kitchener, Ont.; central Kansas; Goshen, Ind.; Harrisonburg, Va., and others, such as central Ohio, central California, and eastern Pennsylvania.

Congregational Singing. The heart of music for worship among Mennonites has always been and still is the °singing of hymns by the congregation. This is a worldwide phenomenon, as demonstrated in gatherings of Mennonites in Wichita (1978) and Strasbourg (1984).

Mennonite Church (MC) congregations of North America, as well as some of the more conservative groups, have continued to promote four-part a cappella singing, which, according to Walter E. Yoder, began "about 1875 in the more progressive congregations and was gradually adopted by all of our churches during the 1890s. The church really came into four-part singing after they had been taught in singing classes and the church adopted the English language and the Gospel songs." Four-part singing of German chorales in congregations of Mennonites in Russia began in the mid-19th c., when the practice was introduced with "ziphern" (numbers) on the musical staves, similar to the North American method of shaped notes.

During the 1960s and 1980s the *Gospel Herald* published numerous articles with suggestions for song leaders, encouraging people to attend church music conferences (late 1950s and early 1960s), giving information on specific hymns (often with a devotional emphasis), and addressing many other concerns that relate to effective congregational singing. Alice Parker, who composed several musicals based on the Mennonite community. stated in an interview that she "sees nothing wrong with having a organ in church," but she quickly adds "I think it's a shame if the a cappella tradition is let go."

More congregations have introduced instruments in recent decades. One church leader estimated that in 1988 about 50 percent of Mennonite Church (MC) congregations have pianos or organs in their churches. Some of these may be in the basement, and not all of them are used for congregational singing. Organs are mostly electronic. Glenn M. Lehman stated in 1986 that "Music buffs tell me there are about 14 pipe organs which have been deliberately purchased."

Church °choirs have not become a part of regular worship in the Mennonite Church (MC). Many congregations have established choirs and smaller musical groups, but "almost no Mennonite Church congregations have choirs that sing every Sunday."

With the publication of the *Mennonite Hymnal* in 1969, a new era emerged for the larger Mennonite community. More and more Mennonites gradually used the same hymnal, creating a greater commonality in worship experiences. Some congregations in both conferences that produced the hymnal, however were not unanimous in accepting the hymnal, some clinging to the older collections, others preferring to sing from hymnals that included more gospel songs and music of the °charismatic movement.

The General Conference Mennonite Church and the Mennonite Church (MC) have been working together with the Church of the Brethren since 1984 on a hymnal project that is scheduled to be completed in 1992. A fourth group, the Churches of God General Conference, is also involved in this project, since they have been using the *Brethren Hymnal*. This is the most ecumenical venture that North American Mennonites have attempted in the area of °hymnody.

Planning a new hymnal presents the unique opportunities and challenges of this particular time, influenced strongly by events and movements of the last three decades, a time of unusual creativity, with the fervent movements of the 1960s and 1970s and the new hymns that these movements produced. At the same time several great hymn writers have emerged, both in Britain and in North America. Since the church is gradually developing a global outlook, there is also the opportunity to accept hymns from non-Western sources.

The most difficult challenge is that of language. During the last four decades there has been a church-wide trend to move away from archaic words to a more contemporary, conversational style. Can this be done with traditional hymn texts? Another aspect of the language challenge is that of inclusiveness, brought about largely by the feminist movement the last few decades.

Mass Choirs. The tradition of many church choirs gathering together for a *Sängerfest*, first established in Russia and continued for many decades in both Canada and the United States, still continues in some areas. A more recent development has been the organization of large choirs in concentrated areas. It was in 1955 that Abner Martin became the first director of the Menno Singers in Ontario, continuing until 1987, when Leonard Enns became the director. The Ontario musical scene reached a high point with the performance of Benjamin Britten's *War Requiem* in celebration of the Mennonite Bicentennial in 1986. This work requires an unusually large group of musical resources, both instrumental and choral, including a children's choir.

In Pennsylvania Hiram Hershey has directed community choirs for a number of years, both in Lancaster and Franconia. In 1987 he conducted a choir traveling to the Soviet Union for the fourth time. Other choirs have traveled to the Soviet Union, particularly from Canada.

In 1966 the choirs of Canadian Mennonite Bible College (CMBC) and Mennonite Brethren Bible College (MBBC) joined for the first time, performing J. S. Bach's *Christmas Oratorio*. This was the beginning of an annual tradition by the combined choirs of singing major works.

Another Winnipeg tradition is that of the Church Music Seminar. The sixth seminar was held in January 1985 with Robert Shaw as conductor. The Centennial Concert Hall was the setting for a performance of Bach's Cantata No. 4 (70 voices) and Brahms' *German Requiem* (250 voices), sung with the Winnipeg Symphony Orchestra. Before the concert, Shaw told a press conference that he had never worked with a finer-sounding group of amateur singers anywhere, that there voices blended so homogenously, as though they were all cousins. The next Church Music Seminar was planned for January, 1989, with Helmuth Rilling from Germany.

Another large choir is the Kansas Mennonite Men's Chorus, directed by Paul Wohlgemuth until his death in 1987. This choir has been large, with a membership as high as 300. Concerts have often been sung at Bethany College (Kansas), where there is space to accommodate such a large choir.

Children's Choirs. In 1949, Ruth Krehbiel Jacobs, daughter of First Mennonite Church in Reedley, California, founded the Choristers Guild, the national organization for directors of children's choirs. Since her death in the early 1960s (on her way to a children's choir festival in North Newton, Ks.), there has been a steady growth of junior choirs in Mennonite congregations. The Western District Conference (GCM) has sponsored workshops and festivals for children's choirs. The biennial Church Music Seminar in Winnipeg (cosponsored by CMBC and MBBC) has featured resource people for children's choirs. Romaine Sala has traveled through many states for the Mennonite Church (MC) to encourage children's choirs. Helen Litz organized the Winnipeg Mennonite Children's Choir in 1957. This group was the first Mennonite choir to perform for a national convention of the American Choral Directors Association, meeting in Nashville in 1983.

Composers. During the last decades there has been considerable interest in musical drama. Church conferences have asked Mennonite composers to prepare these for their gatherings. This is particularly true of denominational conference meetings and Mennonite World Conference assemblies. Harold Moyer, Esther Wiebe, Carol Ann Weaver, and Carol Dyck are some who have composed for such events. Other composers having received commissions to compose include Leonard Enns, Harris Loewen, James W. Bixel, and Philip K. Clemens.

Organ Builders. *Jacob Hallman,* Kitchener-Waterloo, Ont., inventor, completed his first electronic organ in 1949. Production began in 1951. Five hundred electronic organs were produced in just over a decade. In 1953 he began to "assemble" pipe organs. About 75 of his pipe organs are in use across Canada.

In 1976 those attending the Organ Historical Society's national convention visited and listened to an organ in Lancaster Co., completed in 1835 by early American Mennonite John Ziegler, who built four pipe organs, a fact which was not generally known among Mennonites of today. Rudolf von Beckerath, (1907-76) born in Munich, Germany, was a member of the well-known Mennonite °°Beckerath family. He was known throughout the organ world, having installed many organs in North America, as a leading figure in the organ revival after World War II.   OS

Walter E. Yoder, "Our Great Heritage—Congregational Singing," *GH* (Sept. 2, 1958); Jim Bishop, "Alice Parker Church Music Apologist," *GH* (June 28, 1983); Glenn M

Lehman, "The Pipe Organ's Second Wind", *GH* (Sept. 9, 1986); idem, "Church Choirs: Established or Permitted?" *GH* (Sept. 16, 1986); *Menn. Rep.* (June 22, 1987); Orlando Schmidt, "Mennonite Organ Builders You May Not Know," *FQ* (Nov., Dec., 1978; Jan. 1979).

Music, Instrumental (ME III:794). Almost 200 years after musical instruments were first introduced into Mennonite worship in Germany and The Netherlands, North American congregations of the Mennonite Church (MC) began using instruments during worship services. In the 1700s, in European Mennonite churches, organs were installed to improve congregational °singing. During the 1960s, they were introduced for preservice music and the offertory. It was often assumed that the instruments would not be used to accompany singing. Preceding this development was the increased introduction of keyboard instruments and other instruments into Mennonite homes and church schools, as well as exposure to instrumental programs in public schools.

During the last decades there has been a pronounced change in organ building; on the one hand the development of electronic organs, on the other hand, the emergence of the Neo-Baroque organ. The latter is the result of the *Orgelbewegung* (organ movement or revival), a return to earlier principles of organ structure: mechanical action, encased pipes, organs placed within the worshiping space, etc. These new/old instruments are often called *tracker organs.*

Almost all congregations that have installed organs for the first time in recent decades have purchased electronic instruments, usually because of low cost and convenience of installation. The first North American Mennonite congregation to install a tracker organ was Zion Mennonite, Souderton, Pa. (Fisk organ, 1968), followed by West Zion, Moundridge, Ks., and Kern Road Chapel, South Bend, Ind. The first educational institution to introduce a tracker organ was Bluffton College (Flentrop, built in The Netherlands, installed 1964), followed by Associated Mennonite Biblical Seminaries, Elkhart, Ind.; Goshen College, Goshen, Ind.; Canadian Mennonite Bible College, Winnipeg; Bethel College, North Newton, Ks., and Conrad Grebel College, Waterloo, Ont.

The bell choir is a fairly recent phenomenon in the musical life of some Mennonite communities, both for young people and adults. This form of musical expression seems to be limited to congregational life; it is not associated with church schools.

The introduction of °folk music and other popular styles of music in the 1960s and 1970s brought with it the introduction of guitars, drums, and other instruments into church life.

Several Mennonite musicians have been successful in pursuing a career in instrumental music, usually in areas of teaching but also, to a lesser degree, in performance.   OS

J. W. Bixel, Cornelius Krahn, Esko Loewen, and Phyllis Bixel in *Menn. Life,* 13 (July 1958), sp issue; O. Schmidt in *FQ* (1978-79); P. Jenkins and George Taylor, "Rudolf von Beckerath," *The Diapason,* 68, no. 3 (Feb. 1977), 1, 3, 10-11; A. Carkeek in *Music/The AGO-RCCO Magazine* (Apr. 1977); O. Schmidt, *Church Music and Worship among the Mennonites* (Newton, 1981); Wittlinger, *Piety and Obedience* (1978), 361-62.

See also Bert, Sarah Hoover; Evangelical Mennonite Conference; Menno Colony.

Musoma, Tanzania. Located on the eastern shore of Lake Victoria, this lake-port city of 56,000, was founded by the Germans in the late 19th c. It serves as the governmental headquarters and commercial center for the Mara Region of Tanzania. The area produces cotton and textiles, corn (maize), hides, dairy products, and sisal fiber. Subsistence farmers raise cassava, millet, and some rice. Fishing is an important local industry.

Tanzania Mennonite Church (Kanisa la Mennonite Tanzania) had its beginnings in this region in 1934. The congregation in the town was started in 1937. Mennonite ministries based in the town are a bookshop and a conference center and hostel. Prior to nationalization of educational institutions, the church also operated a primary school, a girls' middle school, and was an owner partner in operating an alliance secondary school.   DLW

Musselman, Amanda (Oct. 17, 1869-June 17, 1940), spent 25 years in pioneer missionary service in Philadelphia, Pa. Born near New Holland, Pa., the daughter of Jacob and Mary Stoner Musselman, she was converted in 1896, after two friends died in an accident returning from a party. Amanda was baptized into the Groffdale Mennonite Church and became involved in the newly organized Sunday school. In 1899, after spending a winter to gain experience at the Chicago Home Mission, she moved with Mary °Denlinger to Philadelphia and began work under the direction of the Mennonite Sunday School Mission. Building strong community ties, the two women carried responsibility for the mission (later the Norris Square Mennonite Church) until J. Paul Graybill was appointed full-time pastor in 1922. Amanda and Mary left Philadelphia in 1924, spent the sumemr of 1925 at Mummasburg, Pa., and in the autumn moved to Lancaster, where Amanda became active in the East Chestnut Street congregation. She was buried at Groffdale.   AGW

PMH, 5 (Oct. 1982), 2-18; Rich, *Mennonite Women* (1983), 131, 150, 165.

Mutena. See Zaire.

Mutual Aid (ME III:796). Caring and sharing is a practice as old as the human family. When God spoke to his people, as recorded in the Old Testament, a major focus was the welfare of others. The Ten Commandments (Ex 20) are concerned with relation to God and relationships to other people. In a list of laws for living we read, ". . . love your neighbor as yourself. I am the Lord" (Lv 19:18). In speaking of the greatest commandment, Jesus said, "Love the Lord your God, . . . Love your neighbor as yourself: All the Law and the Prophets hang on these two commandments" (Mt. 22: 34-40).

Immediately after Pentecost the new church drew heavily from the Old Testament background and the teaching of Christ in shaping the life of the faith °community. The simple practice of sharing material resources to meet each other's needs was a natural and spontaneous expression of faith (Acts 2:42-47; 4:32-37).

When there was discontent among believers because of inequity in "the daily distribution of food," the apostles arranged for simple assignment of responsibilities so everyone's needs could be addressed. This was important so the ". . . attention to prayer and the ministry of the word" could be effective. The result was growth among the disciples in Jerusalem (Acts 6:1-7).

Over the centuries the vitality and fervor of the early church was often diminished. Out of the 16th c. Reformation came a rediscovery of practical expression of Jesus' teaching: love of God and love of neighbors. The Anabaptists in particular tried to understand the essence of Jesus' teaching and to recreate the practices of the early church.

The harsh conditions resulting from persecution, famine, and political upheavals motivated the believers to gather into communities where they depended on each other for physical and spiritual survival. Sharing material goods and caring for each other's needs were major elements of the Anabaptist movement. When persecution subsided and when community life became stable, mutual caring was often formalized and was built into ongoing community life.

Anabaptists who settled in Moravia in relative peace developed a °°community of goods. American Hutterites are their spiritual descendants. Early records show that mutual insurance was practiced by some Mennonites in Europe in the beginning of the 17th c. In 1663 a group living in West Prussia organized the *Tiegenhöfer Privat Brandordnung* (Tiegenhof Private Fire Insurance Association). This association continued until 1945 when the Russian invasion wiped out these communities (ME III:199).

In the 18th c. Dutch Mennonites grew to be among the wealthiest in the country. They were liberal contributors to worthy causes, especially to those in distress. They often assisted Swiss and South German Mennonites who were driven from their homeland, or who were enroute to America. They sent money to their oppressed brothers and sisters in Prussia, Moravia, Switzerland, and Palatinate. They had a reputation of taking care of the needs of their own people, a practice deeply rooted in their historical faith tradition (Smith).

Russian Mennonite communities were stable, successful, and often well organized. Typically they grouped themselves into small farm villages of 15-30 families. Each family had its own farm land and large garden. Common grazing land was sometimes shared by village residents. They undertook various municipal enterprises for the common good.

These communities had a large degree of local autonomy, and established such political institutions as best suited their needs. They provided for their own schools, roads, and poor relief. They made their own fire regulations and had an °insurance fund to care for their own delinquents, their sick, and people with mental illness or °disability, as well as widows and orphans (°°*Waisenamt*). They established their own °hospitals, orphan homes, insurance companies, old people's °homes, a school for the deaf, and in 1911 a sanitarium for epileptics and those with nervous diseases.

As in Europe, Russia, and in many countries and

cultures where Anabaptist communities thrive, there is much variety and local adaptation of mutual aid practice across North America. The prevailing culture and theological pluralism are making strong imprints on today's North American Mennonites and related Anabaptist churches; yet an important expression of faith is the quest to make practical Jesus' and New Testament church's teaching and example. This happens spontaneously in congregatinal life. But Mutual Aid and sharing are often formalized through elders, boards of deacons, and appointed person or committee, and ordained deacons or deaconnesses.

Formal and organized community structures in North America borrowed heavily from European and Russian communities in the early years. While the political environment were different in Canada and the United States, basic community patterns and congregational life developed out of the heritage and faith that immigrants brought. Mutual insurance companies and associations were organized in Steinbach and Altona, Man., and in Mountain Lake, Minn., in 1874. A similar organization formed in Freeman, S.D., in 1882 (ME III:799).

ME III, published in 1956, has entries for 36 property insurance societies, 7 auto aid insurance companies, 14 burial aid plans, and 6 loan aid organizations. The founding dates for the two oldest are: 1858 (Amish Mennonite Storm and Fire Aid Union, Wellesley, Ont.) and 1866 (Mennonite Mutual Aid Society, Bluffton, Ohio).

Since the mid-1950s Mennonite population has shifted increasingly to °urban areas. In many places such as eastern Pennsylvania and se. Virginia, the metropolitan area moved out to absorb what formerly were small towns and Mennonite farms.

In the late 1980s fewer than 20 percent of Mennonites receive their primary income from farming. Most Mennonites work in °professions, °business, construction, industry, °teaching, social services, or medical services. Some are self-employed or small entrepreneurs. Most work for organizations or corporations that provide a paycheck in return for time, skills, and effort.

Whether Mennonites live in the country, the village, or the city, the financial base of church and community is a money economy, rather than the agricultural economy of earlier decades. It is more difficult to live as a people apart when daily employment requires involvement in the business and economic life of the secular community. Mennonites increasingly use tools of money management and insurance to reduce risk, to carry responsibility against excessive loss of property, or to provide security against crisis or income loss in the event of a wage earner's death.

The Mennonite-owned property aid companies have grown strong during these years. There has been increased cooperation with several consolidating into one organization. In the mid-1950s people active in mutual aid organizations called several meetings for fellowship and exchange of ideas. In 1956 the Association of Mennonite Aid Societies (AMAS) was organized. They have met annually since, with an attendance of 150-200 persons.

As the AMAS companies met they discovered they had in common the need for greater "per-risk" capacity. Some were overextended and unable to meet the needs of their members. By February 1957, a stock company called Mennonite Indemnity, Inc. (MII) was formed. Control was vested in the Mennonite Central Committee. The founders and stockholders were concerned that MII should be under control of the church and serve the risk sharing needs of church-related institutions. Through MII reinsurance, participating companies have the capacity to cover individual risks as high as a million dollars or more. The policyholder deals only with the local mutual aid company. Through commercial reinsurance the practice of mutual aid is greatly strengthened and a high level of professional expertise and security is available to members through their local companies (Raid, *Twenty-Five Years*, 23-27).

Goodville Mutual Casualty Company, New Holland, Pa. (organized in 1924), is unique among Mennonite insurers. The company covers liability and property damage. It provides the liability coverage needed by the property companies, who then reinsure through Mennonite Indemnity, (MII). This is a good example of combining resources and agencies to accomplish more with less.

Old Order Amish; Church of God in Christ, Mennonites; and some of the unaffiliated or non-conference Mennonite groups continue strong patterns of caring for their own people in times of hardship or special need. These are similar to Amish and Mennonite practices in Europe, Russia, and North America over four centuries.

In the United States, since the era of President Roosevelt, in the 1930s, and the Great Society of the Johnson administration, in the 1960s many state and federal welfare programs addressed needs in the American society. The effectiveness of these programs is mixed. The federal welfare system is a collection of more than 100 programs that evolved in a haphazard way over half a century. A large share of people in poverty receive no welfare benefits. While government spending on social programs has grown substantially from 1965 to 1985, much of the growth has benefited the elderly regardless of their economic status. Many government welfare programs are geared to sustain people in poverty rather than teach them to get out of poverty.

As government welfare programs diminish there is new opportunity for the church to provide for the needs of each other in the same spirit of mutual aid that sustained the Anabaptist faith communities for more than 450 years. Congregations engaged in outreach and church planting often find that mutual aid, formal or informal, is a ministry that speaks of love and caring, drawing people into the fellowship of faith. There is again emerging a quest for the meaning of community and caring in the new urban churches and among young professional adults. Topics listed for conferences, retreats, and topics in the church press will verify this observation. In Acts 4:32-37 unity, sharing, and the testimony of Christ's resurrection were elements that empowered the fledgling church to spread to the ends of the earth.   LP

Current lists of Mennonite mutual aid and insurance organizations are published in *MC Yearbook*, biennially since 1986; C. Henry Smith, *The Story of the Mennonites* (Newton, MPO, 1950), 216-28; Howard D. Raid, *Twenty-five Years: A Brief History* (Mennonite Indemnity, Inc., 1982); *MC Yearbook* (1986-87), 114-15, 137-39; H. Ralph Hernley, ed., *The Compssionate Community* (Scottdale, Association of Mennonite Aid Societies, 1970); June A. Gibble and Fred W. Swartz, ed., *Called to Caregiving* (Elgin, IL: Brethren Press, 1987); Howard Raid, "Living the Mutual Aid Way," *Sharing*, 19 (Fall 1985), 4-7; *MHB* (July 1978); F. H. Epp, *Mennonites in Canada II*, pp. 370-76; *Marketplace* (Jan.-Feb. 1986); Peter J. Klassen, "The Anabaptist-Mennonite Witness Through Mutual Aid," in *The Church in Mission*, ed. A. J. Klassen (Fresno: MB Board of Christian Literature, 1967), 101-14.

See also Bankruptcy ("A Letter from a Small-Town Banker" [feature]); Cooperatives; Mennonite Mutual Aid.

Mysticism is a generic term used to describe a wide variety of experiences in which individuals understand themselves to be united with the divine. Mystical experiences are most often recorded by adherents of one of the major world religions, but similar experiences are documented by individuals who have felt themselves united with the 'spirit' of nature and by those who have undergone a drug-induced altered state of consciousness.

Classic descriptions of the mystical experience in Christianity occur in 2 Cor. 12:2-3, in Augustine [354-430] (*Confessions* Bk. 7, ch. 17; Bk. 9, ch. 10) and Bernard of Clairvaux (1090-1153). The great age of Christian mysticism occurs between the time of Bernard and the 16th c. Mysticism of this period is often divided into two types. The first (*Brautmystik*) described the mystical union primarily in terms of the union between bride and bridegroom, the second (*Wesensmystik*) as a union of essences. In the 14th c. mystical literature was particularly abundant in the Rhineland (Meister Eckhart, Johan Tauler) and in England. The 16th c. in Spain marked the golden age of Catholic mysticism in John of the Cross and Teresa of Avila.

In its 'classic' Christian form the mystical experience proper was understood as the final phase of a three-fold path. In the first (the purgative) the believer practiced the purgation of sin, in the second (the illuminative) the development of a virtuous life, and in the third (the unitive) she experienced union itself. The unitive experience was generally understood as a union of essences in which the believer retained his individuality (in distinction to essential union described in much Eastern mysticism in which the believer is lost in the divine) and as open to only a few. By the 15th c. this threefold path was democratized and mystical vocabulary was often used to describe every Christian's union with Christ in faith and particularly when receiving the Eucharistic sacrament. This tendency is especially evident in two late medieval spiritual treatises which were popular among later Protestants, the °°*Theologia deutsch* and the *Imitation of Christi*.

As the term is generally understood, "mysticism" ought not to be used in describing either Anabaptist or Mennonite spirituality. Mystical themes and images can be found in Anabaptist writings, but neither the Anabaptists nor the Mennonites made wide use of mystical manuals such as the *Theologia deutsch* (as did the Lutherans, for example.) The term °°*Gelassenheit*, current in mystical literature of the 13th to 15th c. does appear in Anabaptist literature but by the 16th c. it was a common spiritual term and its presence does not indicate a direct influence of mysticism, although it and other terms and themes in Anabaptist writing may indicate that some mystical literature of the period was read by the Anabaptists.   PCE

Peter C. Erb, "Anabaptist Spirituality," in Frank C. Senn, ed., *Protestant Spiritual Traditions* (New York: Paulist, 1986), 80-124; Werner O. Packull, *Mysticism and the Early South German-Austrian Anabaptist Movement, 1525-1531* (Scottdale, 1977); Stephen B. Boyd, "Pilgram Marpeck and the Justice of Christ" (ThD diss., Harvard U., 1984); Dennis D. Martin, "Catholic Spirituality and Anabaptist and Mennonite Discipleship," *MQR*, 62 (1988), 5-25; Bernard of Clairvaux, *Selected Writings*, Classics of Western Spirituality (New York: Paulist Press, 1988); Lando Eitzen, "The Mennonites and Mysticism" (MA thesis, U. of Minnesota, 1948).

N

Nairobi, Kenya. The capital city of Kenya was founded in 1905 as a railway supply center for the Uganda railroad. It has since blossomed into East Africa's largest metropolis with a population exceeding 1 million. The city serves as industrial, economic, political, and religious center for the nation. Nairobi is also a center for a number of international agencies and multinational corporations and hosts many international conventions. A booming tourist trade adds to its cosmopolitan setting.

The Mennonite Church founded in neighboring Tanganyika (°Tanzania) in 1934, soon began to use the city as a supply center. As members of the church moved into Nairobi from newly independent Tanzania (1964), it became clear that the church should follow its members. In 1965 land and buildings were purchased and the Mennonite Guest House came into being. A coffee plantation became available for purchase and the missionary children's school moved to Nairobi to better serve children from Somalia and Tanzania. The Nairobi congregation was founded in 1966 and continues to minister to people of several ethnic backgrounds. Mennonite Central Committee and Menno Travel Service have offices in Nairobi, and the Eastern Mennonite Board of Missions and Charities (MC) has had personnel in the city since 1965.   DLW

Nappanee, Ind., Old Order Amish Settlement (ME III:228) is located in Elkhart, Marshall, and Kosciusko Cos. in northern Indiana. This community was first settled about 1848 by Amish families from °Holmes and Wayne Cos., Ohio, and later joined by a number of settlers from the larger °Lagrange-Elkhart settlement 25 miles (40 km.) away. These two northern Indiana settlements were parallel from the beginning. Even though families were related and acquainted, they have not yet today (1986) filled in the 10-mile (16 km.) gap that separates the communities. Amish in these areas are in full fellowship with each other facilitating the frequent interaction between the two groups.

The Nappanee settlement has seen several divisions resulting in the establishment of the First Mennonite Church (GCM) and a large part of the North Main Street Mennonite Church (MC). In 1940 the Burkholder Amish congregation (later affiliated with the Beachy Amish Mennonite) was the result of a minor division. Amish families also established the Conservative Mennonite congregation (Bethel) in 1954. In 1986 there were 19 Old Order Amish church districts (congregations) serving approximately 3,000 people.

Amish Acres, a restored Amish farm one-half mile (1 km.) west of Nappanee has become a large °tourist attraction.   SLY

National Evangelical Mennonite Church of Guatemala. See Iglesia Nacional Evangélica Menonita Guatemalteca.

National Socialism [Nazism] (Germany). At the beginning of the 19th c. German Mennonites finally gained full citizenship. This shift in status—along with the growing nationalist sentiment, the economic success of the German Mennonites, and their respect of their neighbors—encouraged social integration. The traditional Anabaptist detachment from state and society was being lost. By the beginning of the 20th c., government was often being understood as belonging to "God's order," thereby meriting far-reaching obedience. Another outside influence was 18th and 19th c. °Pietism, for which personal °sanctification had a higher priority than centering one's life around the congregation. In addition, Luther's teaching on heavenly and earthly authorities was gaining acceptance. As religion became privatized, °nonconformity was deprived of its significance. Assimilation into a more prevalent religiosity was also accompanied by the abandonment of °nonresistance and a readiness to take on public office. In National Socialism (NS), the growing willingness to bear arms was based on the commandment to "love thy neighbor," with "neighbor" understood here as a term of *proximity* rather than universality. Mennonites were politically inexperienced—as were most Germans. With the loss of World War I behind them, they were not in a position to resist the growing national resentment or the vengeful slogans; in many cases, National Socialist propaganda fell on fertile soil.

Mennonites in °°West Prussia were particularly affected by the results of World War I. Their "home" was divided between three states, so that if they wished to come together as a whole they were faced with the borders of Germany, Poland, and the Free State of Danzig (Gdansk). Anticommunism—a basic tenet of National Socialism—was strengthened among German Mennonites through awareness of nearly 30,000 Mennonite refugees from Russia, as the Bolshevik Revolution had led to the destruction of many blossoming Russian Mennonite communities. Also, Mennonites were like many Germans in not accepting the Weimar Republic with its cumbersome democratic-parliamentary procedures, even though the Weimar constitution had fulfilled their longstanding desire for the separation of church and state. But party maneuvers, libertarianism in the press, and frequent public and political scandals left Mennonites open to Hitler's promise to create a "strong new order." His appeal to idealism and community, and his emphasis on "positive Christianity" also met with approval. The burning of the *Reich-*

stag, the Enabling Act (*Ermächtigungsgesetz*), the boycott of Jewish businesses, or the construction of concentration camps could have been "danger signals," but either they were not perceived as such or Mennonites repressed such uneasiness as did arise. And while the Weimar Republic's economic policies had led toward the demise of German agriculture, Hitler's plan for "national self-sufficiency" opened the way for economic recovery in the farmlands; the Law on Entailed Estates (*Erbhofgesetz*) and governmental regulation of debts ("breaking the bonds of capitalist usury") were also important in this regard. As farmers, most Mennonites profited from these policies.

Mennonites also differed little from their fellow Germans in their endorsement of Hitler's "seizure of power" on Jan. 30, 1933. Many of them were swept along with the prevailing enthusiasm, this trend continuing until 1940. The persuasiveness of Hitler's manifold successes was so penetrating that the apathetic and the skeptical were pulled into the mass intoxication. On Sept. 10, 1933, the Konferenz der ost- und westpreußischen Mennoniten sent Hitler their salutations: "It is with profound thankfulness that our Conference senses the vast ascendancy which God has granted our *Volk* through your endeavors; for our part, we pledge our joyful collaboration in the reconstruction of our fatherland from the power of the Gospel." By that time, the board of trustees of the Vereinigung der Mennonitengemeinden im Deutschen Reich (Vereinigung) had already waived any claim to conscientious objection—voluntarily and without any provocation. The board explained that "in case compulsory military service is reintroduced, German Mennonites no longer wish to lay claim to any special privileges." This official position was widely endorsed, and was mentioned in many articles in various Mennonite periodicals. Contrary to their custom, a politicizing process was encroaching upon many Mennonites.

The *Deutsche Christen* (DC)—who advocated "the Gospel and *Volksverbundenheit* [national solidarity] of National Socialism"—started recruiting among Mennonite congregations in 1933, impressing many. The Konferenz der ost- und westpreußischen Mennoniten twice called upon its members to exercise restraint in regard to the *DC*. Originally, the regime had wanted to see all denominations enrolled in one "confessional front" as a vehicle for carrying through its *Führerprinzip* (authoritarian principle) and *Gleichschaltung* (coordination of public, private, and legislative corporate bodies). With this policy in mind, representatives of the Vereinigung and the Verband badisch-württembergisch-bayischer Mennonitengemeinden (Verband) met during the winter of 1933-34 to work out a unification of German Mennonites based on a common confession. These efforts remained unsuccessful, and Mennonites evaded the regime's intention to introduce the *Führerprinzip* and *Gleichschaltung*. However, this did not have any consequences, since the government had already lost interest in the *Gleichschaltung* of the numerous smaller groups in German society, and the DC—the protagonist in this matter—had fallen into disfavor.

In the following period, youth work was intensified. A full-time youth worker (*Jugendwart*) was employed in 1935 by the Konferenz süddeutscher Mennoniten (KSM) and the Konferenz der ost- und westpreußischen Mennoniten. In bringing the youth in the congregations together, the Judgendwart's role was to counter the influence of various National Socialist youth organizations. A number of retreats and youth conferences were organized, and a periodical, *Die Mennonitsche Jugendwarte*, was published regularly. Also, five nationwide Mennonite gatherings (*Deutsche Mennonitentage*) took place between 1935 and the outbreak of the war; these were intended to strengthen the sense of community among Mennonites. In addition, both conferences attempted to emphasize a specific Mennonite identity in appealing to the Party and to government bureaucracy to accept a "pledge" in place of an oath, although, admittedly, these efforts had more to do with an exchange of terms ("I solemnly promise" as opposed to "I swear") than with an uprising of conscience.

Once the initial excitement had subsided and the ideological claims of the National Socialist regime were becoming clearer and clearer, some Mennonites started to withdraw and a small number criticized certain government policies. A circle of young adults had formed a *Rundbrief-Gemeinschaft* ("circular letter society"), and used these circulars to discuss questions about faith, nonresistance, and the National Socialist ideology. Comments critical of the regime surfaced in the process; not surprisingly, the *Rundbrief* was discontinued in 1937 through indirect pressure by the Party. *Gemeindeblatt*, the periodical of the Verband, was closed down in 1941 after a Christmas meditation by Christian °°Neff described the war as a sin, as treading upon God's honor. Shortly thereafter all periodicals were discontinued because of a shortage of paper.

Despite anti-church propaganda, in operation since 1935, congregational life continued in its accustomed manner: worship services were held (although attendance went down in some congregations); communion was celebrated; younger sisters and brothers were taken into the congregation through baptism; and deacons, preachers, and elders were selected and consecrated for their respective tasks.

During the Third Reich, German Mennonites safeguarded the existence of their denomination, yet in that process they defended neither the gospel nor their Anabaptist heritage. They were tested by National Socialism and succumbed to its temptations because their theology was not based on solid ground. As a result, the Bible was interpreted to suit the demands of the times. Through a reorientation of their values—which was unconscious and certainly unconsidered—the gospel came to be understood as in line with the "system." As a consequence, rather than the world being Christianized, the gospel was secularized.   DGL

H. Fast, "Die Eidesverweigerung bei den Mennoniten," *Menn. Geschbl.*, Jg. 22, n.F. 17 (1965), 18; Hans-Jürgen Goertz, "Nationale Erhebung und religiöser Niedergang: Missglückte Aneignung des täuferischen Leitbildes im Dritten Reich," in *Umstrittenes Täufertum* (1975), 259-89; Diether Götz Lichdi, *Mennoniten im Dritten Reich*, Dokumentation und Deutung, no. 9 (Korntal-Münchingen: Schriftenreihe des Mennonitischen Geschichtsvereins,

1977); idem, "The Story of Nazism and Its Reception by German Mennonites," *Menn. Life*, 3 (1981); idem, *Über Zürich und Witmarsum nach Addis Abeba: Die Mennoniten in Geschichte und Gegenwart* (Maxdorf, 1983); idem, "Erinnerung und Auftrag - zum 8. Mai 1945," *Gemeinde Unterwegs* (May 1985); idem, "Römer 13 und das Staatsverständnis der Mennoniten um 1933," *Menn. Geschbl.*, Jg. 37, n.F. 32 (1980), 74; Horst Penner, Walter Quiring, Horst Gerlach, *Weltweite Bruderschaft* (Weierhof, 1985).

National Socialism [Nazism] (The Netherlands). Already with the rise to power of Adolf Hitler in 1933 Dutch Mennonites began to struggle with the issue of which position they should take on National Socialism. During the years 1933-45 Dutch Mennonites were characterized by particular unity under the Algemene Doopsgezinde Sociëteit (ADS), which had represented the congregations since 1923. Consequently these years, especially after 1936, saw increasing contacts between the ADS and the congregational retreat movement (*Gemeentedag* movement, see °°Broederschapswerk), which often entailed considerable difficulty, but which increasingly accented the unity among the brothers and sisters of the fellowship. Help also came from the latter movement, especially following the German occupation in July 1940. Under the leadership of its chairman Frits °Kuiper, who had been strongly influenced by Karl Barth, adherents of the congregational retreat movement had already worked towards a deepening of faith and owning of their heritage before the war. Within this unity movement the task force against military service was the first to point to the dangers of National Socialism for the freedom of the gospel.

The ADS had already been at work before the war identifying the unique tradition of the Mennonite congregations, stressing particularly their apolitical stance. This attitude could be seen, for example, in its attempt to prevent political issues from being discussed at the Mennonite World Conference in 1936. Similarly the ADS withheld affirmation of the statement on "Christian Attitudes to State and Society" prepared by the Centrale Commissie voor het Vrijzinnig Protestantisme (Central Committee for Liberal Protestantism).

The congregational retreat movement was likewise nonpolitical and undogmatic, permitting membership of some who were clearly of National Socialist orientation and very active. Nevertheless, discussion about the nature of National Socialism was facilitated within the congregational retreat movement. Both the congregational retreat movement and the ADS worked to promote unity with Mennonites in Germany. These contacts declined after 1937, however, when the Hutterite communities were forced to leave Germany, without the German Mennonites speaking up in their behalf. This led to considerable protest among Dutch Mennonites.

The traditional Mennonite emphasis upon practical Christianity became more visible in 1938 and 1939 through the work of the Algemene Commissie voor Buitenlandse Noden (°Stichting voor Bijzondere Noden, the Dutch Mennonite relief work commission) and the task force "Quakers and Mennonites," both being activated through the initiative of the work group against military service. The fellowship "Quakers and Mennonites" was changed into "Task Force of Mennonites and Like-Minded Groups" during the war years.

While warnings against the dangers of National Socialism emanated from the congregational retreat movement, the ADS kept a relatively low profile until 1939, though it also warned about the dangers of the movement. Differences of opinion about how one should relate to the occupation forces became apparent in due course. The decision of the ADS to be nonpolitical determined its actions, though it did issue circulars and messages clarifying how congregations in the Anabaptist tradition should conduct themselves in this situation. During the early years of the war, therefore, the attitude of the brotherhood might be characterized as one of "neutrality," being careful of its actions and possibly fearful of the regulations of the occupation forces. On the initiative of the congregational retreat movement a "shadow cabinet" of the ADS, in the form of a commission for spiritual concerns, was created in 1941 to help coordinate unity in the face of the occupation. However, this commission could also not prevent the ADS from remaining neutral in April 1942 when a union of churches prepared to announce from all pulpits a condemnation of the way Jews were being treated by the National Socialists. Still, this commission for spiritual concerns, did help congregations and the ADS to a clearer understanding of the dangers of National Socialism, including its antisemitic aspects. It was because of this commission that the ADS increasingly opposed the occupation. We might say that the ADS abandoned its neutrality during the second half of the war.

At the same time the brotherhood was occupied with its own future, both organizational and spiritual. During the second half of the war the focus of the congregations within the ADS rested on surviving the storm intact. This meant a continuation of the centralization begun in 1923, which had been terminated in July 1940. As a whole this also meant that in addition to the organizational aspects, the ADS was occupied with work and reflection upon the spiritual foundations of the brotherhood. H. W. °Meihuizen declared that a spiritual gain of war was that "the unity and solidarity of the brotherhood was greater than before." EITB

Archival materials are found in the ADS Gemeente Archief, Amsterdam; in the Rijksinstituut voor Oorlogsdocumentatie, Amsterdam (doc. 1-1128 [J. ter Meulen], doc. 1-988 [R. Kuipers], and doc. 1-1290 [F. J. Overbeek]); and in private collections by G. van Room (located in the Archief der Nederlands Hervormde Kerk, Leidschendam) and C. Inja. Published materials include F. B. Bakels, *Nacht und Nebel: Mijn verhaal uit Duitse gevangenissen en concentratiekampen* (Amsterdam, 1977); "De Huterschen in Nederland en Engeland," *Doops. Jaar.* (1938), 51-60; E. I. T. Brussee-van der Zee, "De Doopsgezinde Broederschap en het nationaalsocialisme, 1933-1940," *Doops. Bijdr.*, n.r. 11 (1985), 118-29; H. Dam, *De NSB en de Kerken* (Kampen, 1986); F. Dijkema, "De oecumenische beweging en de Doopsgezinden," in *Oecumenisch Christendom: Organ van de Nederlandsche Afdeeling van den Wereldbond voor internationale vriendschap door de Kerken*, 24, no. 3 (Rotterdam, 1940), 134-40; G. Fopma, "De volkstelling 1930," *Doops. Jaar.* (1934), 64-73; S. H. N. Gorter, "Internationale Doopsgezinde Opbouw," *Doops. Jaar.* (1931), 64-71; L. de Jong, *Het Koninkrijk der Nederlanden in de Tweede wereldoorlog, deel 5, eerste helft. Het laatste jaar II* (The Hague, 1981); L. D. G. Knipscheer, Sr., "Een halve eeuw doopsgezinde vredesaktie," *Doops. Jaar.* (1973), 18-37; J. Koekebakker, "De organisatie onzer Broederschap," *Doops. Jaar.* (1938), 32-50; H. C. Leignes-Bakhoven, "Het Algemeen Congres," *Doops. Jaar.* (1937), 58-65; H. W. Meihuizen, "De Nederlandse Doopsgezinden van 1938 tot 1948," *Doops. Jaar.* (1949), 19-31; Christian Neff, ed., *Der Allgemeine Kongress der Mennoniten gehalten in Amsterdam, Elspeet, Witmarsum (Holland) 29 Juni bis 3 Juli 1936* (Karlsruhe, n.d.); F. H. Pasma, "A.D.S. voorzitter in oorlogstijd," *Stemmen uit de Doopsgezinde Broederschap,* 12, no. 1 (Assen: 1963), 1-39; G. van Roon, *Protestants Nederland en Duitsland 1933-1941* (Utrecht, 1973); H. C. Touw, *Het verzet der Hervormde Kerk* (The Hague, 1946); A. P. van de Water, "Het Protestants-Joodse vluchtelingenwerk," *Doops. Jaar.* (1940), 50-56; H. Wethmar, "Gemeenteleven en instellingen: Ontwikkelingen in de 20ste eeuw," in *Wederdopers Menisten Doopsgezinden in Nederland 1530-1980* (Zutphen, 1980), 240-75; J. IJntema, *Wij Doopsgezinden,* no. 61, 2nd ed. (Amsterdam: de Verstrooiing, 1941); idem, "De Doopsgezinden in verleden en heden," *Doops. Jaar.* (1937), 46-57; N. van der Zjpp, *Geschiedenis der Doopsgezinden in Nederland* (Arnhem, 1952).

See also Judaism and Jews; Bonhoeffer, Dietrich.

Nationalism is the ideological component of loyalty to the entity known as nation. Each nation thus has its own "ism" or as one scholar has put it, "Nationalism is what nationalists have made it." A comprehensive notion of nationalism will be based on the study of how it is expressed in each individual national movement and how this doctrine changes in the course of time.

In the past nationalism was often seen as a cultural and psychological phenomenon. Hans Kohn called it "first and foremost a state of mind, an act of consciousness . . . the individual's identification of himself with the 'we-group' to which he gives supreme loyalty." More recently scholars, e.g., John Breuilly, emphasize that "nationalism should be seen as a political movement seeking or exercising state power and justifying such actions with nationalist arguments."

Whether French, Canadian, Brazilian, Kenyan, Indian, Russian, or American, the national idea includes a number of common components. There is first of all the notion that humanity is divided into nations, that each nation has its own peculiar character, that the source of political power is this collectivity, that its interests and values take priority over all other interests and values, and that nations find fulfillment in their own state organization. Nationalism is the ideology of the "nation as state."

Not all nations become states. There is such a phenomenon as cultural nationalism which may or may not include a home territory. There will surely be common cultural characteristics. Nationalism is not the product of nature but of history. At most we can talk about nationalism since the 15th c. There is some evidence that "its day has largely passed" given the increasing global character of contemporary politics and culture.

Nationalism as defined here emerged clearly in 17th and 18th c. Europe. This set of beliefs developed as governments assumed a more dynamic relationship with the peoples within the borders of the state. Monarchs cultivated the support of the people. People within a given area began to think of themselves in political terms, as participatory citizens. Modern technology made possible more rapid forms of communication and transportation, making larger political entities possible. The church, which was in many ways the primary institution for most Europeans, lost its prestige during the course of the religious conflicts and in the face of the growing attraction of scientific and secular ideas. The nation rather than the church increasingly became "a collective personality, a true mystical body" which supplied the emotion to complement the abstractions of Enlightenment political ideas. The American and French Revolutions were important movements when nationality and nationalism were harnessed in the formation of new or renewed political units.

In the course of time nationalism has changed its character. From the 17th to the 20th c. nationalism moved from being essentially an aristocratic and elite concept to one involving the entire public. Local and regional loyalties tended to diminish in favor of larger entities as the Germanies became one state, Italy was united, and, after World War I, the Eastern European nations arose out of fallen Austrian and Turkish empires.

Nationalism can be categorized as "liberal" (from *liberal* in its 19th c. meaning: *free*) or constitutional in contrast to "integral" or authoritarian. The tendencies are present in all nationalisms and that which prevails is determined to a great degree by historical experience. The nationalism which strongly espouses personal freedoms, an open political structure, and representative government, has predominated in Western Europe and North America. But the cult of the nation which is belligerent, expansive, intolerant, racist, and militaristic prevailed in the Axis powers of World War II. Groups driven with similar values exist in almost every national state and become the essential ingredients of Fascism and what Latin Americans call the "National Security State."

A significant change in the history of nationalism has been the movement of this ideology from Europe to the world. Instead of 10 or 20 nationalisms, in the late 20th c. there are 160 or more. Sometimes this post-World-War-II phenomenon is called the "new" nationalism. What is new is primarily the location of these movements outside Europe and North America.

This nationalism has been intrinsically anti-imperial, anticolonial, and, to a considerable degree, anti-Western. Egyptian President Nasser in 1965 stated it sharply. "Whenever we look behind, we do so to destroy the traces of the past, the traces of slavery, exploitation, and domination." These nationalisms are not necessarily spontaneous or self-generating movements. Rather, they focus on getting rid of the alien intruder and asserting a rediscovered or newly created identity.

A second essential of the new nationalism is its revolutionary character. The older nationalism grew slowly along with and frequently after a unified state was created. The new nationalism, an idea largely picked up under imperial tutelage, has to develop the very stuff of nationhood itself and assume power quickly. A whole new set of relationships needs to be established and older ones diminished or destroyed. The loyalties of a traditional society (°modernity), which are religious, racial, familial, tribal, or °caste, now have to be reoriented to follow territorial boundaries. But the first priority is to develop a sense of nationality and the structures of nationhood.

The impact of the West on the new nationalism

has been enormous. This has included the idea of the nation and more than that the territorial entities themselves. It was the imperialists who created an Algeria where there was once the Barbary Coast. As recently as 1947, Chief Awolowo pled with the British to abandon their idea of unitary state. "Nigeria," he said, "is not a nation. It is a mere political expression. There are no 'Nigerians' in the same sense that there are 'English,' 'Welsh' or 'French'."

It is worth noting that much of the hostility to the West expressed by the new nationalism resulted from a revulsion at Europe's failure to live up to its own ideals. The notion of human equality was crushed in the racism of the conquerors. The notion of political freedom was drowned in the repression of the freedom movements. The notion of humanity and fraternity were overwhelmed by the brutality of war.

Nationalism in the Two-Thirds World has had to deal in a special way with the plural or communal quality of many societies. Linguistic and religious differences have been especially difficult obstacles in the way of establishing a national state. While the anticolonial movement was led by liberal nationalists, increasingly a more narrow, intolerant mentality has emerged. The drive for religious states—Islamic, Jewish, Buddhist, Christian—reflects a push for a strong national identity but has also given rise to profound internal and external tensions. Wherever one explores the religious situation today one important ingredient will be the power and style of the nationalism present.

Nationalism has to be an important concern for the Christian church which is committed to a world created by God and a redeemed humanity which transcends national, racial, and cultural divisions. A beginning place for exploring the Christian task in a nationalistic world is to recognize the Christian source of many nationalistic ideas—certain beliefs about humans, the chosen people, equality, justice, freedom and the vision of a brighter future. In addition, the importance Christians placed on history is the root of much national historical consciousness. Many of these ideas, particularly in the Third World, were nurtured in Christian schools, as any roll call of nationalist leaders can attest.

Nationalism is not merely an interpretation of reality, or an explanation of nationality, or even a lust for power. It represents a deeply felt need on the part of modern men and women to belong, to be affiliated. It offers hope of a meaningful life and relief from frustration and fear.

More than this it is also necesssary to recognize the interesting role of nations in the biblical record. Nations appear to be part of the natural order (Gn 10) as well as a punishment for human pride and self-sufficiency (Gn 11). The nations are judged but they are also pictured as bringing their glory and honor into the city of God (Rev 21:24-26). There are legitimate aspirations for a people to control their own lives in freedom, with justice and equality. The church in Canada, Tanzania, and India among other places, is properly concerned for national well-being. Indian Christians in 1960 said that "Christians, if loyal to their faith, should be fully involved in the nation's concern to be truly a nation,

exercising its vocation as a nation among nations, and safeguarding its integrity against disruptive forces from within or without." Others feel a certain national consciousness is necessary for the church to be aware of its local identity in order to be responsibly missionary.

Mennonites have experienced nationalism and its effects wherever they have lived in the modern world. Americanization, Prussianism, Russiafication have helped to stimulate outward °migrations and a thorough evaluation of how a self-conscious church relates to nationalizing forces. Missionaries and service workers in China, India, Zaire, and Tanzania, among other places, have had to cope with nationalist movements.

Nationalism has many of the characteristics of a religion. In many cases traditional faiths merge with national faiths in what has been called in recent times a °"civil religion." Then the tension with the political order becomes conflict over the essentials of the faith itself.

Nationalism as a political phenomenon needs to be constantly evaluated and critiqued first by its own standards but also by the values of the Christian church. Does it promote peace, harmony, justice, mutual respect, fraternity, and well-being, or does it contribute to alienation, discrimination, conflict, and violence? Within the universal church itself every effort must be made to build connections to overcome the boundaries of national identities.   JAL

John Breuilly, *Nationalism and the State* (1985); Frank H. Epp, *Mennonite Peoplehood* (1977); Charles W. Forman, *The Nation and the Kingdom* (1964); Harold R. Isaacs, *The Idols of the Tribe* (1975); Boyd C. Shafer, *Faces of Nationalism* (1972); Anthony D. Smith, *Theories of Nationalism* (1971).

See also Church-State Relations; Gandhi, M. K.; Japan; Patriotism; Japan.

Native Mennonite Conference of nw. Ontario had its beginnings in the early 1960s. Several missionaries under Northern Light Gospel Mission (ME IV:1112) organized a gathering of Native Christian men. At that time a "conference" was not the purpose for gathering, but fellowship and teaching was. This gathering became an annual event and subsequently the Native men helped to plan this meeting. In 1987 they are totally responsible for the meeting and are involved in planning outreach programs and other ministries as a part of their church. The Native pastors and their executive committee seek to minister to and nurture their members, guiding them in the way of the Lord. Through this kind of involvement they have come to feel a greater responsibility for each other and a greater sense of spiritual kinship, and they perceive better how they all fit together as a body in Christ.

Since travel in the past was difficult and continues to be expensive this may be the only time of the year (early July) that some of the Native Christians see each other. They have found this gathering to be an important time in the life of the church.   HH

See also Northern Light Gospel Mission Conference; Indians, North America.

Natural Sciences. See Sciences, Natural.

Navajo People. See Indians, North America.

Nazarenes (ME III:815). Following World War II many Nazarenes left Eastern Europe for Germany, Austria, North America, Brazil, Argentina, and Australia. Military service continued to be required in all European lands. Those who refused military service served long prison sentences. During the past several years the Nazarenes in Hungary have been given the possibility of civilian °alternative service. In Romania worship services are discouraged by the authorities. In 1986 there were ca. 7,000 Nazarene members in Romania, Hungary, and Yugoslavia. Of these ca. 3,000 were in Hungary, ca. 3,000 in Yugoslavia and ca. 800-1,000 members in Romania. BO/AM

Peter Brock in *MQR,* vol. 54 (1980), 53-63, vol. 57 (1983), 64-72 (19th c. Nazarenes in Hungary).

See also °°Apostolic Christian Church.

Nazism. See National Socialism.

Nebraska (ME III:815). There have been several changes in the Mennonite Churches in Nebraska since 1950. Churches that have closed their doors for various reasons are Salem, at Wisner (1957), and Roseland, at Roseland (1959). The Mennonite Church at Chapell merged with the Julesburg, Colo., Mennonite Church in 1974. An Old Order Amish settlement established in 1978 at Pawnee City was dissolved in 1982 because of a conflict with authorities over certified teachers for the settlement's school. The Sunset Home for the Aged at Geneva closed its doors in 1981 after 30 years of service.

Mennonite Church (MC) congregations established in Nebraska (membership in parentheses) in the last three decades are First Mennonite at Lincoln (56), which is also affiliated with the General Conference Mennonite Church; Beth-El, at Milford (118); Bellwood, at Milford (215); and Omaha Mennonite Fellowship (13). Mennonite Church (MC) membership in the state was 1,300 in 12 congregations (1985), including one congregation affiliated with the Afro-American Mennonite Association. Four General Conference Mennonite Church congregations (in addition to the dually affiliated Lincoln congregation) had 1,600 members. Faith Mennonite Church at Geneva was established in 1963 (60 members). Four Mennonite Brethren congregations have been established since 1950. One disassociated itself from the conference in 1977, another closed in 1977, leaving a total of four congregations active in 1987. Five Evangelical Mennonite Brethren (°Fellowship of Evangelical Bible Churches) congregations (583 members in 1984) and one unaffiliated Mennonite congregation, complete the roster of the state's 26 Mennonite congregations (ca. 3,700 members).

The Nebraska Mennonite Central Committee °relief sale has become a major event in the life of the Mennonite churches in Nebraska. Established in 1980, it is held annually on the last weekend of March or the first weekend of April as a joint venture of all the churches in Nebraska.   IET

MC Yearbook (1988-89), 29.

Neo-Orthodoxy, a stream of 20th c. Protestant theology which attempted to recover some essential elements of Reformation theology, notably emphasis on the sovereignty and grace of God, human sinfulness, and the primacy of revelation through Scripture.

Karl Barth (1886-1968), Reinhold Niebuhr (1892-1971), Helmut Richard °Niebuhr (1894-1962), and Emil Brunner (1889-1965), while differing from one another in some important respects, are influential voices in this stream. Neo-orthodox theology, forged in the crucible of post-World-War-I Europe and refined there and in the United States during the World War II years, strongly criticized aspects of 19th- and early 20th c. °liberal theology: liberalism's emphasis on the immanence of the divine in the human spirit, its tendency to view sin as a result of ignorance or natural impulse rather than willful wrong, and its optimistic view of history as a progressive overcoming of evil and gradual building of the °kingdom of God.

The publication of Karl Barth's book on the *Epistle to the Romans* in 1918 (English trans., 1922) marked the beginning of neo-orthodox theology. Concerned about theology's turn to the human subject, a direction set by Friederich Schleiermacher (1768-1834) early in the 19th c., Barth asserted in *Romans* that the starting point for theology is not humankind or human thoughts about God, but God and God's Word. Revelation, not religious experience, is the foundation of theology.

During the development of his multi-volume *Church Dogmatics* (1936-69) Barth shifted away from his early "dialectical theology" which had been stimulated by Kierkegaard (1813-55) and characterized by an appreciation for paradox. However, he continued to press the primacy of the Word of God preached, written in Scripture, and revealed in Jesus Christ. Barth's commitments led him to greater exegetical sophistication in his later work, to a strongly christocentric systematic framework, and to insistence on the "objective" reality, not simply the subjective effect, of God's reconciling activity in history.

Barth's work has influenced both directly and indirectly several generations of Mennonite scholars, educators, and pastors. His influence helped prepare the way for the emergence of the so-called °biblical theology movement (ca. 1950-70) in North America and the continuing interest in "biblical realism" which characterizes the writing of Mennonite scholars John Howard Yoder, Willard Swartley, Millard Lind, and David Schroeder, among others. Barth's legacy has affected Mennonites through their graduate study at various institutions, notably Basel University and Princeton Seminary, through the resurgence of interest in Barth among evangelical scholars, and through the work of Jürgen Moltmann.

The attraction of some Mennonites to Barth may be partially explained by J. A. Oosterbaan, a Dutch Mennonite theologian, who argues that Barth and °Menno Simons share a christocentric method of interpreting Scripture, disagree with Calvin's view of °predestination, elevate the humanity of Jesus, and reject infant baptism and sacraments as a means of grace. J. H. Yoder further finds traces of an implicit free church theology in Barth, and suggests that this developing ecclesiology helps explain his movement toward a position close to pacifism and his distinction between the church community and the civil community. Barth's christocentric and revelation-centered approach to theology has been criticized by Gordon Kaufman, a Mennonite theologian who has helped shape some emerging Mennonite theological work.

While Barth is the most prominent of the theologians referred to as neo-orthodox, Reinhold Niebuhr and H. Richard Niebuhr have also had import for Mennonites. Less exegetically oriented than Barth and somewhat more appreciative of human religious experience, the Niebuhr brothers' writings in theological ethics stimulated a flurry of responses by Mennonites on issues of pacifism, distinctions between church and world, and Christian social responsibility. John H. Yoder formulated his basic Christian pacifist position in debate with Reinhold Niebuhr. Other Mennonite leaders active in the 1980s whose teaching and work have been shaped by or in response to issues posed by Reinhold include, among others, Donovan Smucker, J. Lawrence Burkholder, J. Richard Burkholder, Theodore Koontz and Duane Friesen.   GGK

Karl Barth, *Church Dogmatics*, 4 vols., tr. G. T. Thomson (Edinburgh: T. and T. Clark, 1936-62); idem, *The Epistle to the Romans*, tr. Edwyn C. Hoskyns (London: Oxford U. Press, 1963); Emil Brunner, *Dogmatics*, 3 vols., tr. Olive Wyon (Philadelphia: Westminster, 1950-62); Tom Finger, *Christian Theology: An Eschatological Approach*, 2 vols. (Nashville: Thomas Nelson, 1985; Scottdale, 1987), a work from a Mennonite perspective that shows the influence of Barth and Moltmann; William Hordern, *A Layman's Guide to Protestant Theology*, rev. ed. (New York: Macmillan, 1968); Gordon Kaufman, *Systematic Theology: A Historicist Perspective*, 2nd ed. (New York: Scribner's, 1978); preface; James C. Livingston, *Modern Christian Thought: From the Enlightenment to Vatican II* (New York: Macmillan, 1971); H. Richard Niebuhr, *Christ and Culture* (New York: Harper and Row, 1951); idem, *The Meaning of Revelation* (New York: Macmillan, 1941); Reinhold Niebuhr, *The Nature and Destiny of Man*, 2 vols. (New York: Scribner's, 1941, 1943); idem, "Why the Christian Church is Not Pacifist," in *Christianity and Power Politics* (New York: Scribner's, 1940); J. A. Oosterbaan, "The Theology of Menno Simons," *MQR*, 35 (1961), 187-96; John Howard Yoder, "The Basis of Barth's Social Ethics," extempore lecture at the Midwestern Section of the Karl Barth Society at Elmhurst, Ill., Sept. 29-30, 1978; located in Yoder personal files, Elkhart, Ind.; Yoder's comments about Barth's distinction between the church and the civil communities refer to Karl Barth, *Church and State*, tr. G. Ronald Howe (London: SCM Press, 1939); John Howard Yoder, "Reinhold Niebuhr and Christian Pacifism," *MQR*, 29 (1955), 101-17, also published as Church Peace Mission Pamphlet, no. 6 (Scottdale, 1968).

Nepal. Through much of its history Nepal was virtually closed to outsiders. Political changes in 1950 led to a more open stance. In 1951, Christian missionaries were permitted to enter Nepal. The United Mission to Nepal (UMN) was founded in 1954. It is an ecumenical agency through which various mission groups work together. By 1987 the UMN numbered about 400 missionaries from more than 20 countries. They are sponsored by 39 mission boards. Assignments include medical, educational, and economic development work. In 1956, Rudolf Friesen was sent by the Mennonite Central Committee (MCC) to work in Nepal. Later that year two

°°Pax volunteers joined him. In 1957 Lena Graber became the first worker under the Mennonite [MC] Board of Missions (MBM). Since then numerous MCC and MBM workers have served under UMN in professional, administrative, and clerical roles. Maynard and Dorothy Seamons have been supported by the Mennonite Brethren Board of Missions and Services since 1960. They are engaged in medical work under The Evangelical Alliance Mission (TEAM) in western Nepal. The Christian church in Nepal numbers about 20,000 in 1986 and is experiencing steady growth despite persecution.   RAL

MC Yearbook (1986-87), 159-60; *MB Yearbook* (1981).

Netherlands, The (ME III:824). In reporting on developments among Dutch Mennonites (°Algemene Doopsgezinde Socëteit, ADS) during the past 30 years we cannot report a triumphant song of the great deeds God has done among us. Nevertheless we are convinced that despite the decline in membership and obvious failures in our work, particularly also among the younger generation, the Lord is telling us through the fact that he has brought us thus far, that he still has work for us to do. Congregational membership declined from 38,446 in 1956 to 18,358 in 1986. It should be noted that a similar decline in membership has occurred during this period in all of the denominations in The Netherlands and throughout Europe. This phenomenon is not limited to the Mennonites only, but heightened among them through the fact that families have grown smaller, consisting normally of one or two children, and that families in which both parents are Mennonite are now in the minority.

It is clear, however, that the percentage of active members participating in the work of the church is greater in 1986 than it was in 1956. This is apparent in the sacrificial spirit with which members support their local congregations and, beyond that, in mission work and international °relief and °development programs. It is also important to note that international relationships with Mennonites have increased. This is evident, for example, in the convening of the Mennonite World Conference in Amsterdam in 1967. The impact of that conference upon the congregations was great. This desire for international contact was also evident in 1984 when some 500 Dutch Mennonites, of whom 30 percent were youth, participated in the Mennonite World Conference in Strasbourg. The significance of this interest is also indicated by 1,000 people who came to the Mennonite congregational retreat on Oct. 6, 1985, at Leiden to encourage and strengthen themselves and each other in the faith.

During the past several decades the Dutch Mennonites have been greatly concerned about their identity. This became evident in the establishing of the Doopsgezinde Historische Kring (Mennonite Historical Society) in 1974. In 1986 its membership stood at 600. The concern of this society is not only with the past, but also with assessing and promoting the Mennonite heritage of faith in the present and for the future. It is clear that a spiritual change is taking place and that new interest in the Anabaptist founders has replaced the earlier liberal indifference. This is also apparent in the unmistakable interest in the constitutive elements of Mennonite unity.

Further signs of this search were the two study conferences sponsored by the ADS. The 1980 session centered on the search for a peace church. This was the period of international discussion over the implications of nuclear weapons, particularly the neutron bomb. The conference was inspired by one brother who called out during a meeting of Mennonite leaders, "but we are a peace church." In 1984 the theme of the conference was "The Courage of Hope." This theme arose from Mennonite participation in the Interchurch Peace Council (Interkerkelijk Vredesberaad), beginning in 1967. Numerous members did not participate in this discussion, feeling that political considerations had no place in the congregation. Nevertheless participation at the conference equaled the number of persons active at the congregational level. The results of both conferences were a clear decision to continue in the direction of peace activities.

Meanwhile there was movement within the brotherhood. New congregations have arisen in Noord-Oostpolder (1953), Haren (1957), 's Hertogenbosch (1964), Gouda (1966), Zoetermeer (1969), Noord-Oost Veluwe (1973), Stiens (1975), and Hoogevven (1978). New church buildings have been erected in Buitenpost, Eenrum, and Warga (1957), Franeker (1959), Hengelo (1960), Witmarsum and Emmen (1961), Breda (1966), Stadskanaal (1967), Haren and Veendam (1968), and Schagen (1976).

Youth work is coordinated through a central youth office (Doopsgezinde Jeugd Centrale) established in 1952. Five regional youth councils cooperate closely with this central office. A youth worker is active in each of these regions, helping congregations in their youth work and unifying total activities. The Doopsgezinde Jongerenbond, a task force uniting the various youth groups, thus representing ca. 800 young people, likewise cooperates with this central office. The Commission for Children and Congregations (Commissie Kind en Gemeente) is responsible for materials needed for the nearly 2,000 children participating in local Sunday schools regularly; it too works with the Jeugd Centrale. The monthly Jongerenbond publication De Hoeksteen (The Cornerstone) has been replaced with a quarterly publication.

Education in the congregations is carried on through the Gemeenschap voor Doopsgezind Broederschapswerk (Society for Doopsgezind Brotherhood Work), which has appointed an advisor for this purpose. Educational and other learning programs are established in the local congregations. Regional and national agencies help in the training of resource people for various areas of this work, which includes conferences for church council members (Conferenties voor Kerkraadsleden, also organized by the Broederschapswerk). These conferences are held annually in three different places throughout the land.

Dutch Mennonite retreat centers (Broederschapshuizen) have survived a difficult period brought on by changing vacation patterns of Mennonite participants. Restoration work and new buildings have helped revive their activities (°camps and retreat centers). The center in Bilthoven was no longer needed and was closed. A new building in Aardenburg, founded in 1964, functions primarily as a general education center. The houses in Elspeet (250 beds) and in Fredeshiem and Schoorl (each with 100 beds) are functioning well. The "Bloem en Bos" center on the island of Texel, as well as the "Samen Een" center founded in Giethoorn in 1984, each have 60 beds. Both of these latter centers are used primarily by young people. "Bloem en Bos" is owned by the Dutch Mennonite peace group (°Doopsgezinde Vredesgroep).

New retirement °homes have been built in Amsterdam, Bolsward, 's Graveland, The Hague, Deventer, Purmerend, Zaandam, Zwaagwesteinde, and Zwolle. In all of this Dutch Mennonites reflect an awareness of the limitations of their resources. In relation to evangelism the veteran former missionary Leo Laurense published a booklet with the title Werven of Sterven (Evangelize or Perish) in 1986. Despite limited resources Dutch Mennonites are striving with considerable energy and conviction to retain an invaluable heritage expressing what it means to be a Christian in today's world. CFB

S. Groenveld and others, eds., Wederdopers, menisten, doopsgezinden in Nederland, 1530-1980 (Zutphen, 1980); MWH (1978), 303-6; MWH (1984) 123.

Neufeld, David P. (Apr. 24, 1919-Apr. 7, 1982), was born at Kitchkas, Orenburg, Russia. His family immigrated to Canada in 1926. A graduate of Bethel College, North Newton, Ks., "D. P." was a farmer-preacher in Rosemary, Alta.; taught at the °°Menno Bible Institute in Didsbury, Alta., for five winters; and became a significant conference and inter-Mennonite leader in Canada.

On May 31, 1942, he married Helen Neufeld, and later that year he was ordained to the ministry. In 1961 the Neufelds moved to Winnipeg where he became the first full-time executive secretary of the Conference of Mennonites in Canada (1961-67). In that position he worked for the strong national base for General Conference Mennonites and resisted any provincialism which would erode national unity. He had other nationwide dreams. He was instrumental in the formation of Mennonite Central Committee, Canada, projecting a vision for its being, and serving as its chairman from its founding in 1963 until 1972. In this capacity he worked for a simple, flexible yet large structure, and for a unified voice when speaking to government and society. He was also deeply involved in the formation of °Mennonite Foundation, Canada, and acted as its first chairman (1971). He pastored two churches, Bethany Mennonite, Virgil, Ont. (1967-77), and Olivet Mennonite, Clearbrook, B.C. (1977-82). He died of cancer.

He was recognized as an excellent preacher and communicator, a good pastor, an able administrator, and a leader and organizer who could bring vision into reality. He considered himself an Anabaptist evangelical. GH

Frank H. Epp, ed., Partners in Service: The Story of Mennonite Central Committee Canada (1963-1982) (Winnipeg: MCC Canada, 1983), 20-28; David P. Neufeld, "My Dream About Canadian Mennonite Council," unpublished paper available from MCC Canada; Conference of Mennonites in Canada, Yearbook (1962), 48-49, (1967), 24-26.

Neufeld, Kornelius H. (Dec. 10, 1892-Jan. 12, 1957). Born in Nikolayevka, Ukraine, K. H. Neufeld emigrated to Canada in 1923 and in 1924 established a printing business in Winkler, Man. His passion for choral music soon became evident. He organized a choir of immigrants in 1924, became conductor of the Winkler Bergthaler Choir in 1928 and the Altona Bergthaler Choir in 1933. In 1935 he organized the Winkler Male Voice Choir. In the beginning he worked within his own Mennonite Brethren Church but was accepted more readily by groups like the Bergthaler Church in Manitoba and the Rosenorter Church in Saskatchewan.

He was especially well known for his choral festivals, which he organized first in Manitoba and, after 1935, in provinces from Ontario to British Columbia and in a number of states in the United States. He was also instrumental in establishing the Southern Manitoba Music Festival in 1932. Beginning in 1944 and continuing until 1956, Neufeld was engaged by the Manitoba Mennonite Youth Organization to undertake systematic work in music in Manitoba General Conference Mennonite churches during the summers. He taught at the Swift Current Bible Institute during the winters of 1953 and 1954. Neufeld composed four cantatas for his own use at choral festivals in the 1950s and assembled collections of choral music he entitled "Singet dem Herrn."

Known as the "Wandering Conductor from Winkler," K. H. Neufeld had a profound influence on the development of church choirs and choral music in the prairie provinces, especially in congregations and communities established by immigrants in the 1870s (°*Rußländer*) fostering a love for choral music in thousands of Mennonite young people.   WB

Wesley Berg, *From Russia With Music: A Study of the Mennonite Choral Singing Tradition in Canada* (Winnipeg, Manitoba: Hyperion Press, 1985); F. H. Epp, *Mennonites in Canada II*, pp. 462, 463-64; J. A. Toews, *History MB* (1975), 252.

Neuland Colony, Paraguay (ME III:852). Originally 2,474 persons arrived in this Chaco area of Paraguay with the help of Mennonite Central Committee in 1947-48 and settled in 27 villages. Due to many serious pioneering difficulties many immigrants went on to Canada or returned to Germany. Better years followed eventually. The mechanization of agriculture added considerably to the stability of the colony. In 1987 there were 21 villages with a total population of 1,325 persons.

The administration of the colony is carried out by an elected committee, of which one member is chosen to serve as mayor (°°*Oberschulze*). This committee is responsible for the sale of colony products as well as the purchase of supplies needed by the settlers. It is also responsible for operating the hospital and school system. Most families belong to the producer-consumer cooperative which is the economic center of the colony.

The original small village schools have been replaced by one central elementary school, with 150 pupils in grades 1-6, and a high school, with 55 students in grades 7-12. The former is conducted in the German language, but the latter is fully integrated with the national Paraguayan plan of instruction. The colony also has its own 30-bed hospital, a doctor, several nurses and a pharmacist.

Agricultural activities consist in dairy and cattle herds as well as the cultivation of 7,500 hectares (18,525 acres) of land. Most of this acreage is used to plant peanuts, but cotton, corn, and other crops are also produced. The non-dairy cattle herd consists of some 36,500 head, grazing on 32,400 hectares (80,028 acres).

Meetinghouses have been built by both the Mennonite congregation (GCM), which had 500 members in 1984, and the Mennonite Brethren congregation, which had 110 members in 1984. After 40 years Neuland Colony has become home to its inhabitants.   HBr

MWH (1978), 252; *Menn. Jahrbuch* (1984), 157; *GCM Handbook* (1988), 40.

Neuwied (ME III:859), a city of more than 30,000 people, favorably located in central West Germany, frequently hosts Mennonite meetings and conventions. In 1986 there were four flourishing Mennonite churches in Neuwied. (1) The Evangelische Mennonitengemeinde (431 members) dates back to 1680. The congregation almost became extinct after World War II, but attracted °°West Prussian Mennonite refugees when a settlement on the "Torney" hill was erected with the assistance of the Mennonite Central Committee and °°Pax volunteers (1950-54). The historic meetinghouse in the old city, built in 1768, has been sold because most of the members are living near the new center at the "Torney." (The old rococo-style meetinghouse was gutted by fire and will be reconstructed as a cultural center for the city of Neuwied.) (2) The Mennoniten-Brüdergemeinde - Evangelische Freikirche (300 members) was established in the 1950s by the missionary efforts of the North American Mennonite Brethren mission board. The members are predominantly not of Mennonite background. (3) The Mennonitengemeinde (90 members) was established in 1977 by °"kirchliche" Mennonites resettling from the Soviet Union (°*Umsiedler*). (4) The Neue Mennoniten-Brüdergemeinde Neuwied (230 members) was established in 1979 by resettlers with a Mennonite Brethren background. Both resettler churches chose not to join the established churches; they do not belong to a conference. Mennonite Central Committee European offices and offices of the °International Mennonite Organization are also located in Neuwied.   DGL

Menn. Jahrbuch (1984), 106-7, 111-12.

New Amish. See New Order Amish.

New Brunswick. See Atlantic Provinces, Canada.

New Call to Peacemaking. See Peace Activism; Peace Education.

New England. The 14 Mennonite congregations in New England are small, scattered, and diverse. Though largely the result of mission efforts by groups from Pennsylvania, only a few of the congregations have membership reflecting the Germanic background of sponsoring conferences. Significant groups responding to Mennonite church planting efforts include blacks, whites, hispanics, Chinese, and

Laotians. In 1987 the total number of people active in all 14 congregations was about 750.

The first structured Mennonite presence in New England appeared in 1947, when Franconia Conference (MC) began °summer (vacation) Bible school missions in Vermont. The Bible school program helped establish three enduring congregations in the state: Andover (1947), Bridgewater Corners (1952), and Taftsville (1960).

While teaching at Harvard Divinity School in 1962, J. Lawrence Burkholder gave leadership at Boston to the first Mennonite fellowship elsewhere in New England (this congregation later affiliated with the Atlantic Coast Conference [MC] and the General Conference Mennonite Church [GCM]). Lancaster Conference (MC) came to the region with a mission church at New Haven, Conn., in 1968.

After a period of dormancy in outreach, the 1980s saw a major thrust of church planting. Lancaster Conference added two churches in Maine, two in Connecticut and four in Massachusetts. Franconia Conference began a new congregation in Vermont. Most of these groups started as house fellowships under the leadership of a "church planter" sponsored by conference mission boards.

The New England Fellowship of Mennonite Churches was formally organized in 1985. It has two objectives: to promote fellowship and communication among leaders of all congregations, and to foster vision for °evangelism and church planting. All congregations continue to receive oversight from conferences outside the region. The New England Fellowship supplements this by circulating a newsletter, sponsoring a variety of leadership seminars, and encouraging interaction among the scattered churches. JNKr

MC Yearbook (1988-89), 20-42 passim, 88-89.

New Jersey. Contemporary Mennonite presence in New Jersey began with a church planting venture led by Henry and Ida Swartley at Oxford in Warren County in 1956. In 1988 there were nine Mennonite congregations in the state affiliated with four different conferences as follows: Atlantic Coast Conference (MC), 1 congregation, 46 members; Franconia Mennonite Conference (MC), 2, 105; Lancaster Mennonite Conference (MC), 5, 300; Eastern Pennsylvania Mennonite Church, (1, 30). The Puerto de Sion congregation in Trenton participated in °Concilio Nacional de Iglesias Menonitas Hispañas. Friendship Mennonite Chapel at Carneys Point was affiliated with the Afro-American Mennonite Association. Lancaster Mennonite Conference had three church planting centers at Atlantic City, Camden, and Mizpah. The Vineland Mennonite congregation sponsored an elementary school with 21 students (1988). RSa

MC Yearbook (1988-89), 30, 60-70, 105, 122, 173.

New Mexico (ME III:863). Mennonites and Brethren in Christ began to move into the state after World War II. Brethren in Christ missionaries to the Navajo people entered New Mexico, Sept. 1, 1945. A Brethren in Christ work began in Albuquerque in 1950. Mennonite families in Albuquerque started a home Sunday School in 1948; a pastor (MC) was assigned in 1950. Mennonite Voluntary Service units in Grants, Albuquerque, and Carlsbad supported developing congregations in the latter two places. Voluntary service workers shared in the Navajo Mission programs in Bloomfield from 1950 through the 1970s. A Church of God in Christ Mennonite (Holdeman Mennonite) Christian service program in Albuquerque led to a congregation in the 1980s. A Conservative Mennonite Conference church planting ministry was started there in the 1980s. A nonconference Mennonite ministry began in Farmington in the 1970s. JWH

MC Yearbook (1988-89), 30; Daniel Hertzler, *From Germantown to Steinbach* (Scottdale, 1981), 91-101.

"New Order" Amish (New Amish) is an informal name used to describe groups that emerged out of the Old Order Amish in the mid-1960s. Their settlements are found almost exclusively in Pennsylvania and Ohio. Although in doctrine and practice they are very similar to the Old Order Amish (some Old Order settlements allow "New Order" ministers to preach in Old Order congregations), "New Order" distinctives include: the use of electricity and telephones in homes; utilization of modern farming implements, in particular the tractor; minor differences in their pattern of dress and appearance (including a unique head covering for women); and an emphasis, in some communities, on young peoples' meetings and assurance of salvation. The New Order have not adopted the °Beachy Amish Mennonite practices of driving automobiles and using meetinghouses for worship services. TJM

John A. Hostetler, *Amish Society* (1980), 97, 277, 286.

See also Amish; Ohio.

New Reinland Mennonite Church of Ontario is composed of congregations in Leamington and Aylmer and was formed from a division among Old Colony Mennonites in 1984. The elder of the new group, Cornelius Quiring, was formerly elder in the Old Colony. Total membership in 1988 was ca. 300. This body has not affiliated with any other conference, but maintains fraternal relations with conservative groups in Manitoba (Old Colony Mennonite Church, Sommerfeld Mennonite Church and Reinland Mennonite Church). The New Reinland group continues to use the Old Colony catechism, and follows similar practice and discipline. Exceptions include greater use of the English language in worship and limited openness to cut hair for women. There is no formal connection between this group and other conferences that use variations of the "Reinland" (Reinländer) name. SSt

MWR (Mar. 7, 1985), 5.

See also Zion Mennonite Church.

New Testament. The New Testament is that collection of 27 writings which the Christian church added to the Hebrew Scriptures to make up the Christian Scriptures. The New Testament is unified by the conviction that in Jesus of Nazareth the fulfillment of the messianic hopes of the Hebrew Scriptures has taken place. Christians therefore refer to the earlier Scriptures as the Old Testament and to their own sacred writings as the New Testament— the old has been superseded, but not completely replaced, by a new covenantal relationship between God and people.

The word *testament* is from the Latin translation of the biblical term for covenant. "New Testament" and "new covenant" are synonyms in Christian usage even though "testament" does not adequately express the meaning of covenant in biblical writings. Although the specific usage of "Old Testament" and "New Testament" dates only to the latter half of the 2nd c., the concept of new covenant is found in New Testament writings themselves. Paul cites Christ, at the Last Supper, as saying, "This cup is the new covenant in my blood" (1 Cor 11:25 [RSV]). The idea of "old covenant" is expressed in 2 Cor 3:14 and Heb 8:13. Indeed, the earliest reference to a new covenant is made by the prophet Jeremiah (31:31ff.). The first Christians saw this as a prophecy fulfilled in Jesus Christ.

By the end of the 2nd c. the form of the New Testament canon was largely determined. However, the final fixation of the canon took place near the end of the 4th c. At the time of the Reformation the shape of the New Teatament was beyond serious debate. Martin Luther had questioned the inclusion of the book of James, calling it "a strawy epistle," because of its alleged "works righteousness" theology. His viewpoint did not affect the content of the canon; however, Luther's opinion does illustrate that his central focus on justification by faith became a guideline of interpretation by which to judge and relate the various parts of the New Testament. This hermeneutical assumption, or principle of °biblical interpretation, in effect created a canon within the canon. Such a feature is not unique to Luther. All theological traditions demonstrate to one degree or another a hermeneutical frame of reference by which the New Testament, and the Old, are explained and proclaimed.

The Anabaptists approached the New Testament with certain clear assumptions which correlated with their theological views and distinguished them from other reformers. With other Christians they held to the centrality of Christ in understanding the Bible. However, a Christ-centered approach meant something different since they stressed the teaching and example of Jesus as much as his saving death and resurrection. Their emphasis on obedient following of Christ, i.e., °discipleship, led them to uphold an ethical standard that superseded the standards of the Old Testament. The writings of the Anabaptists speak often of the greater status of the New Testament in relation to the Old. The two testaments were not on the same level of authority even though all Scripture is the Word of God. This principle became a key defense of their absolute nonviolence against the appeal of others to the practice of warfare described in the Old Testament.

Along with a hermeneutic of discipleship, the Anabaptists practiced a hermeneutic of restoration (°restitutionism). This refers to the conviction that the church, as depicted in the New Testament, is the norm for all time. This biblicism, as it has been called, brought the Anabaptists in conflict with the established church. The church which they found in the New Testament was a church of true believers who stood over against a society outside the perfect will of Christ. This stance again could not accept any appeal to the Old Testament to limit or modify the direct application of New Testament teaching. Their hermeneutic rejected, for example, the support of infant baptism by analogy to circumcision in Israel. Anabaptists also found an appeal to the theocratic character of Israel as a nation to justify the union of church and state to be unconvincing.

Within the New Testament itself, the Anabaptists made no apparent distinction in terms of one part having more weight than another. It is true that the teaching of Jesus (especially the °Sermon on the Mount) has an especially crucial role in the definition of discipleship. The assumption is made, however, that the rest of the New Testament is consistent with that teaching and is an elaboration of it. The typical expression for the final norm in interpretation is "the life and doctrine of Christ and the apostles." Statistical information on citations from different books in the New Testament seems to indicate such a balance in their practice.

In recent years, Old Testament scholars in Mennonite circles have called for a corrective in Mennonite thinking about the Old Testament. The christocentric hermeneutic is affirmed but the critique is made that Mennonites are prone to miss the spiritual and theological contribution of the Old Testament on its own terms. Interestingly, the Old Testament has become important in the greater emphasis among Mennonites on issues of peace and justice and on the relevance of faith to the political and social questions of the present age. An important area of future work is to clarify the christocentric implications for the church's response to these issues. GeoRBrIII

Willard Swartley, ed., *Essays on Biblical Interpretation: Anabaptist-Mennonite Perspectives* (Elkhart, Ind.: IMS, 1984); Myron S. Augsburger, *Principles of Biblical Interpretation in Mennonite Theology* (Scottdale, 1967); John C. Wenger, *God's Word Written* (Scottdale, 1966); William Klassen, *Covenant and Community: The Life and Writings of Pilgram Marpeck* (Grand Rapids: Eerdmans, 1968); CRR 3:140-61.

See also Biblical Interpretation.

New Wilmington, Pa., Old Order Amish Settlement (ME III:300) in Lawrence Co. in western Pennsylvania about 30 mi. (50 km.) east of Youngstown, Ohio, was first settled in 1849 by families from Mifflin Co., Pa. Later migrations from Holmes Co., Ohio made the New Wilmington Amish community one of the largest in Pennsylvania. Amish in New Wilmington demonstrate strong identification with some of the more conservative groups in Mifflin Co. in matters of °dress and °buggy style. Buggy tops are uniformly burnt orange in color and brown is the dominant color in apparel. In spite of several divisions in this Amish community resulting in the formation of related Beachy Amish Mennonite congregations, there has been slow growth in its 140 years of existence with 11 church districts (congregations) serving approximately 2,000 people. SLY

New York (ME III:863). Since World War II the Mennonite population in New York State (not including the Old Order Amish) has nearly tripled to more than 2,700 distributed among 45 congregations and 10 different conferences, most of which have their conference base outside the state. However, in the last 15 years a number of congregations have relinquished their relationships to outside Mennonite conferences and formed their own °NYS Fellowship of Mennonite Churches (NYSF). Since the founding of this conference in 1973, 23 congregations with 2,033 members relate to it. The Northeast cluster around Lowville has 10 Mennonite congregations (8 in NYSF) with 1,405 members and more than half of all Mennonites in the state. Smaller clusters of the NYSF are Western Tier (near Buffalo: 4 congregations, 306 members); Southern Tier (near Corning-Elmira: 6, 284); Central Tier (Rochester-Syracuse: 5, 127). There are seven additional congregations scattered throughout the state, each belonging to a different out-of-state conference. These 7 have a total of 171 members. Most of the 30 Mennonite churches outside New York City were started since World War II. Only four originated earlier (Crogan, 1833; Lowville, 1913; Alden, 1924; and Clarence Center, 1923).

The other large cluster of Mennonite churches is in the se. end of the state, in the New York City metropolitan area. Seventeen congregations (including 2 Brethren in Christ churches in the Bronx and Brooklyn), with about 550 members scattered throughout the five boroughs of New York City, were founded since 1949. Since 1980 these churches (except the Brethren in Christ) have formed a New York City Council of Mennonite Churches which is developing into a separate district conference. The NYC Council of Mennonite Churches grew out of a ministers' fellowship that began in 1960. The council has had cooperative programs. Camp Deerpark (85 mi./136 km. nw. of the city) at Westbrookville, has been owned and operated by the New York City Mennonite churches since 1969.

In 1988 NYC congregations belong to district conferences other than the NYSF (Atlantic Coast Conference, 5; Lancaster Conference, 8; Brethren in Christ, 2); Conservative Mennonite Conference, 1. Three congregations were in the process of formation. Members of seven of these congregations are Spanish-speaking. Four congregations have an integrated but predominantly Afro-American membership. Five are integrated congregations with several ethnic groups present. Most NYC Mennonite congregations have many ethnic groups represented, some as many as 15. These 16 Mennonite congregations have other national Mennonite affiliations. Most of the seven Spanish-speaking congregations affiliate with the °Concilio Nacional de Iglesias Mennonitas Hispañas. At least four congregations affiliate with the °Afro-American Mennonite Association.

The Mennonite population in New York City is very diverse and multi-ethnic. For example the present pastors of these NYC congregations are from the following ethnic backgrounds: Afro-American, Swiss-

German, Garifuna (decendants of black slaves and indigenous Carib peoples in Belize), and various Hispanic groups (Puerto Rican, Colombian, Dominican Republic). These different ethnic groups are all represented on the executive committee of the New York City Council of Mennonite churches and at its bimonthly meetings.

The New York City Mennonite churches are developing a vision that will make them completely indigenous (self-governing, self-supporting, self-propagating) and integrated. They have a positive partner relationship with the founding mission boards and conferences which spawned them (Eastern Mennonite Board of Missions and Charities, and Mennonite Board of Missions, Lancaster Conference, and Atlantic Coast Conference). They are developing a mission strategy that calls for planting new churches and developing older ones to be strong and less dependent. They are developing their own urban leadership training program that will pave the way for stronger and more effective °urban churches. In the next decade the Council of Mennonite Churches may become the first district Mennonite Conference that is totally urban. With NYC Mennonite Churches becoming a conference and the NYS Fellowship already one, Mennonites in New York State represent some of the most diverse, most integrated and most aggressively mission-minded in the country.

As of 1985 the 10 Mennonite and Brethren in Christ conferences and their congregations in New York State were: (1) Conservative Mennonite Conference: 7 congregations, 1,026 members, mostly around Lowville; (2) NYS Fellowship, 17, 1,007 (most of the Conservative churches also were affiliated with NYSF, making a total of 23 congregations and 2,033 members); (3) Lancaster Mennonite Conference (MC): 9, 267 (8 in New York City, 250 members: 1 in Bolivar, N.Y., 17 members); (4) Atlantic Coast Conference (MC): 5, 200 (all in New York City); (5) °Eastern Pennsylvania Mennonite Church (EP): 2, 50; (6) °Fellowship Churches: 1, 41; (7) Beachy Amish Mennonites: 1, 26; (8) Mid-Atlantic Mennonite Fellowship: 1, 20; (9) Franconia Mennonite Conference (MC): 1, 17; (10) Brethren in Christ: 2, 153.   JIS

MC Yearbook (1988-89), 30, 89-90; Luth, Amish Settlements (1985), 9-10.

See also Conewango Valley, N.Y., Old Order Amish Settlement; Urbanization; Urban Churches ("A Seventeenth-Century Mennonite Pioneer in the Bronx").

New York State Fellowship. See NYS Fellowship of the Mennonite Church.

New York Theological Seminary was known as W. W. White's Bible Teachers Training School from 1900 until 1921. Most Mennonites until 1961 knew it as The Biblical Seminary in New York (hereafter BSNY).

"Professor of English Bible" is the academic title Erland Waltner chose as the first president of Mennonite Biblical Seminary in the newly organized Associated Mennonite Biblical Seminaries in Elkhart,

Ind. (1958). This mirrors accurately the essential objective of the New York model. Travel to the world's mission fields by Wilbert W. White (1863-1944) and close association with the enthusiasm of William Rainey Harper (1856-1906), the founding president of the U. of Chicago, who had studied with White at Yale U., furnished the vision for graduate-level study of Scripture in the student's vernacular language. One half of each semester's study was in the Bible on a book-study basis. Either Greek or Hebrew was required for graduation. Mastery of the biblical text under study is assumed before turning to exegetical opinion.

In White's view the other disciplines—historical, theological, pedagogical, psychological, homiletical, and pastoral—must always be legitimated by the Scriptures, and he believed one must bring the contributions and insights of those disciplines to bear on the full understanding of the Scriptures. For example, a book by long-term faculty member Louis Matthew Sweet, *To Christ Through Evolution*, related philosophy and the natural sciences to the Scriptures; similarly Albert Clark Wyckoff's course, "The Bible and Modern Psychology," helped Gerald Stucky, pioneer Mennonite missionary to Colombia (GCM), become a participant in the first-ever offering of a °clinical pastoral education program at the University of Michigan (summer of 1942). Teaching courses in Bible as well as in their major discipline also helped professsors bring about such integration, e.g., Ralph Key, the teacher in philosophy taught the Book of Jeremiah. The third dimension, community service, brought the Scriptures to bear on the needs of the larger New York City setting.

The substantial representation of Mennonites in the student body led to an invitation to Orie O. °Miller to join the BSNY board of trustees. Miller served in this capacity for 20 years and two of his sons, Daniel and John, attended the seminary. Some 22 Mennonite students were enrolled at one point during Miller's service on the board. Miller's time on the board, as he observed to someone, overlapped with the planning for the beginning of the Associated Mennonite Biblical Seminaries (AMBS).

One might conclude that the school's stress on the study of individual books and the whole Bible in the form in which we now have them anticipated redaction criticism, canon criticism, and the °Biblical Theology movement; that the careful observation of literary form taught by BSNY professors anticipated the emphasis of Hermann Gunkel on *Gattungen* (genre criticism) and anticipated the present stress on story or narrative theology and on the Bible as literature; and that the prominence given to women in major roles in instruction at BSNY also anticipated later developments in seminary and °pastoral education.

A number of Mennonite college and seminary teachers have been exposed to the inductive Bible study method, either directly through study at BSNY (Stanley C. Shenk, Jacob J. Enz, Erland Waltner, Erna Fast, Gertrude Roten, Orlando Schmidt, Marcus G. Smucker), or indirectly through study under BSNY graduates at Union Theological Seminary in Richmond, Princeton Seminary, and Bethany Biblical Seminary (Howard Charles, Willard Swartley, Donovan Smucker and others). (Bethany Biblical Seminary [CBrethr], established by A. C. Wieand in direct imitation of W. W. White's school, was closely associated with Mennonite Biblical Seminary, 1945-58.) Two presidents of °seminaries outside North America were Mennonites who studied at BSNY: Peter Buller (Kinshasa, Zaire) and Kenneth Bauman (Union Biblical Seminary, Yavatmal, later Pune, India). Other BSNY Mennonite graduates have served in various Mennonite agencies and organizations.   JJE

Charles R. Eberhardt, *The Bible in the Making of Ministers, The Scriptural Basis of Theological Education: The Life Work of Wilbert Webster White* (New York: Association Press, 1949); Jacob J. Enz, "Living Bibliocentrism," *The Bulletin: Mennonite Biblical Seminary*, 23, no. 4 (Oct. 1960), 4-5; David Schroeder, *Faith Refined by Fire* (Newton, 1985), the first volume in the Faith and Life Bible Studies series—most authors in the series have been exposed to the inductive Bible study approach; Howard T. Kuist, "Scripture and the Common Man," *Theology Today*, 3, no. 2 (July 1946), 205-20; idem, *These Words upon Thy Heart: Scripture and the Christian Response* (Richmond, Va.: John Knox, 1947); Willard M. Swartley, *Mark: The Way for All Nations* (Scottdale, 1979), dedicated to Howard H. Charles as a teacher in the inductive approach who in turn was taught by Kuist at Union Theological Seminary, Richmond; George A. Turner, *Portals to Bible Books* (Wilmore, Ky.: Asbury Theological Seminary, 1957); Erland Waltner, "Drenched in the Word," *The Mennonite Biblical Seminary and Bible School Bulletin*, 20, no. 3 (July 1957); Perry Yoder, *From Word to Life* (Scottdale, 1982); idem, *Toward Understanding the Bible* (Newton, 1978).

See also Burkhalter, Martha.

Newfoundland. See Atlantic Provinces, Canada.

Nganga Diyoyo (Paul) (b. 1921), was six months old when he was adopted by missionaries Aaron and Ernestina Janzen at Kafumba in Zaire. He received Christ at a very early age. Nganga attended primary school and graduated from the Bible school in 1939. He was useful in many ways on the mission station. He helped translate educational and Christian literature into the local language and also helped operate the printing press. In 1958 he moved to Kikwit and became the secretary of the legal representative of the mission. He was sent to Brussels, Belgium, to improve his French, typing, and mathematics and to take further theological studies. In 1962, after the church had received its autonomy, he became its first Zairian legal representative. In 1970 the mission and the church fused into one organization, the Église du Christ au Zaire, Communauté des Églises de Frères Mennonites au Zaire (Mennonite Brethren Church of Zaire), with Nganga continuing as legal representative. In 1975 he became treasurer of the church.

In 1980 he left church administration to establish a farm of his own, where he started a church and became its pastor. He commented, "I was happy to . . . minister . . . in the field of administration. . . . I realized that I had spent much time in administration, but had had little time to preach. . . . I see people give themselves to Jesus here at the farm and receive baptism. This gives me greater joy than I had known previously. Before, I worked to make a living for myself, but now I am serving the Lord for the life that has no end."   ILF

Foreign Missions - Africa (Hillsboro, Ks.: MB Board of Missions, 1947), 31-32; J. B. Toews, *The Mennonite Brethren Church in Zaire* (Fresno: MB Board of Christian Literature, 1978), 116, 118, 165, 226.

Ngongo David. See Zaire ("Ngongo David's Strong Heart [feature]).

Nicaragua is a country in Central America (49,579 sq. mi./128,410 sq. km.; about the size of the state of New York) located between Honduras and Costa Rica. The populace of three million is about 80 percent Roman Catholic and 9 percent Protestant. Active in the land are three Anabaptist-rooted denominations and the Mennonite Central Committee.

The work of the three denominations has followed a similar pattern. All three, the Brethren in Christ, the Conservative Mennonite Conference and the Evangelical Mennonite Conference (Kleine Gemeinde, Manitoba), began work in the 1960s. As the work grew, more missionaries were sent out. Three extraordinary events influenced their work: the 1972 earthquake that destroyed much of Managua (the capital city), the Sandinista overthrow of the Somoza government (1978-79), and the Unites States-Nicaragua clash (1982ff.).

The results of the revolution and clash were that most of the missionaries returned to North America and those remaining have given themselves almost exclusively to pastoral and leadership training. Actual leadership and administration of the churches has been given over to Nicaraguans. In addition, although life is subject to disruption by the strife, the events have made and are making many Nicaraguans receptive to the gospel. Because of religious motivation and political factors, churches are giving attention to social and economic problems.

War and militarization have focused the matter of °conscientious objection to war. Discussions with the government have resulted in draft exemption for pastors and seminary students but not for lay people. Mennonite and Brethren in Christ men have responded in different ways. Some are serving in the army, some have on the local level secured noncombatant work within the army through arrangements with their superiors, some have hidden, and some have fled.

The Iglesia Hermanos en Cristo (Brethren in Christ Church) began its work in 1964 in the Managua area. After a few years the work gained momentum so that by 1985 there were 54 congregations located in 9 of the 16 provinces (departments) with a total membership of 1,794. From the beginning the Brethren in Christ approach has been to train and use national leaders. The church has been organized on a national level as the Iglesia Hermanos en Cristo, Nicaragua.

The Conservative Mennonite Conference (MC) began in 1968 with a large °voluntary service program. The first missionaries arrived in 1973 and within a few years a national conference of the congregations was organized under the name Convención de las Iglesia Evangélicas Menonitas de Nicaragua (Conference of Evangelical Mennonite Churches in Nicaragua). In 1986 the conference consisted of 30 congregations and mission locations with 780 members. Some 80 members were in refugee camps in Costa Rica because of the fighting.

The missionary work of the Evangelical Mennonite Conference began in 1966. In 1986 the outgrowth of this work was known as Fraternidad de las Iglesias Evangelicas Menonitas de Nicaragua (Brotherhood of Evangelical Mennonite Churches, Nicaragua). It was active in seven provinces, had organized six congregations and established eight preaching points. Membership in these congregations was 300.

The Mennonite Central Committee (MCC) responded to the acute needs following the 1972 Managua earthquake. In that context the Evangelical Committee for Aid and Development (CEPAD) was formed and MCC worked with it in relief and housing construction programs. All three Mennonite-related conferences mentioned above belong to CEPAD. MCC returned in 1979 following the deposing of Somoza and again assisted in reconstruction work, largely through CEPAD. In 1986 MCC had five workers in the country engaged in three types of work: supplying large amounts of food for people displaced by war, working with the three Mennonite-related conferences in rural development activities, and lending two people to the Ministry of Agrarian Reform to help in designing and constructing irrigation systems. MCC is also concerned to encourage peace, and is seeking to help North American Mennonites and Brethren in Christ to better understand developments in Nicaragua.   DRZ/MHS

Wittlinger, *Piety and Obedience* (1978), 518-21; MCC *Workbook* (1986); *MWH* (1978), 233-38; *MWH* (1984), 89-91.

Offenbarungs Reima, Petikla Pitchy, and Hickerniss Hen: Mennonite Nicknames

Eatjenomes, or nicknames, were used among the Mennonites, as among other groups, to identify or describe more exactly a person or a family, or to differentiate one family from another. The Mennonite Low German *Eatjenome* does not stem from *Eajennome* (*Eigenname*), but finds its origin in *ekename*, which means a "name added" to a given name. In earliest times an *ekename* was a surname, and even in the word "surname" we have the same meaning in the French *sur*, which means "over" or "above," a name "over and above" the first name.

Occupations were and are a common source for nicknames: e.g., "Schusta-Schallenboajch" (Shoemaker Schellenberg); "Stoa" or "Lauftje" Jaunze ("Stoa" from the English "store," and "Lauftje" from the Russian "lavka"); "Tjnibla-Wiebe" (Chiropracter Wiebe). "Schriewa Ditj" or "Dichta Ditj" were names frequently applied to the writer Arnold Dyck.

Physical or other descriptive attributes were another source: "Lange Jeat Wiebe" (Long Gerhard Wiebe); "Fromme Petasch" (Pious Peters, member of the Mennonite Brethren church); "Turksche Thiesse" (Rough as a Turk Thiessen); "Fülle (Lazy) Wiens"; etc.

Place of residence also provided a variety of nicknames: "Kaumpsche Kloassen" (Klassen, a former resident of an island known as "Kaump" in the Dnieper River); "Mexikaunsche Friesen" (a Canadian Mennonite who had returned from Mexico); "Atj" (Corner) Siemen (a Siemens who lived at the intersection of two village streets).

Numerous other associations provided an unlimited source for nicknames. In Steinbach, Man., there was an "Offenbarungs Reima" (a minister whose favorite scriptural text came from the book of Revelation, the "Offenbarung" in German). In Paraguay there was a "Foagel Unga," a man by the name of Unger who held and tamed wild birds (*Vögel* in German). "Eftje Panna" and Sauntje Panna" referred to a situation where one Penner had a wife named "Eva" and the other one named "Susanna." "Schrugge Hiebat" was a man named Hiebert who took great pride in his horses, while "Hunjsche Hiebat" (Hound-dog Hiebert) was known for his rough and ready ways. "Kose Kloosse" (Goat Klassen) was known for his pointed beard (goatee). "Klocke Tjreaja" (Clock Kroeger) manufactured large and durable clocks in Russia, and his descendants in Canada are still known by that name. "Schlopbeintje" (Sleeping Benches) Wiebe reputedly had nine bunks ("sleep-benches", each one providing sleeping accommodation for one or two children. JTh

In an Amish community in which almost all the people are Stoltzfus, Güngrich, Yoder, Beiler, and Kanagy, and nearly all of them are rather closely related and using English in the broader public, but Pennsylvania German at home and in worship, nicknames become a practical necessity. The Old Order Mennonites also live in rural communities like the Amish, with many of them closely related. The surnames will be Martin, Witmer, Musser, Good, Bauman, Leinbach and usually a few given names prevail. The mail carrier may well have five Abner Yoders to deliver mail to. In the past this was a puzzling problem. Postal regulations have recently required box numbers to meet this problem; but businesses need to know which John Yoder gets the bill. Nicknames and abbreviations often help.

In a group that is bilingual it is not unusual to hear slightly different pronunciations of the same name. The English Jake sounds like Tscheck among the German-speaking people; Dave is Dafe, Pete is often Pitt, and Joe is often Yoss. When fond mothers and family and schoolmates of small children say it we often hear Sollie for Sol, Abie for Abe, Maggie for Margaret, and Danny for Dan or Daniel.

Among people who make use of a few Bible names, who usually pick a name of a close relative, and who have a theology that insists on simplicity, the use of a simple nickname becomes important and practical. There are surely going to be many people with identical names. A good nickname should be for one person only if it is to be really helpful.

Benjamin Gehman was known among his close relatives with identical names as Haase Bentsch because he raised so many rabbits for sale as pets and for table meat. Jacob Gehman went to Michigan as a young man and in middle age came home to Pennsylvania to live among his many Jacob Gehman relatives. They called him Michigan Tscheck. When Solomon Good was a little boy his mother called him Solly. When he was an old man, a carpenter with a serious hearing problem and a hearing aid he was still Solly Guth. An Amishman by the name of Peachey had a strong desire to keep his farm clean,

so much so that the non-Amish people called him Particular Peachey. His German-speaking friends liked it and called him Petikla Pitchy. Naturally the non-Amish adopted that quickly. Henry had a small farm with dozens of hickory nut trees from which he harvested and sold a good crop each year. He was known as Hickerniss (Hickory Nut) Hen.

Nicknames are often used jokingly as as token of familiarity; or they may express scorn or ridicule. Among the Amish and Old Order Mennonites nicknames have an added dimension. They are a part of the simple life-style which they hold so important. Because so many who live in close contact have identical names the nickname is a practical necessity. NG

Victor Peters and Jack Thiessen, *Mennonitische Namen/Mennonite Names* (Marburg: N. G. Elwert, 1987); Eleanor Yoder, "Nicknaming in an Amish-Mennonite Community," *Pennsylvania Folklife*, 24 (Spring 1974), 30-37; Kathleen Miller Wenger, "Posey Sam Miller," *The Casselman Chronicle*, (Summer-Autumn 1962), 12; Werner Enninger, "Amish By-Names," *Names*, 33, no. 4 (Dec. 1985), 243-58; Mrs. Herbert R. Schmidt, "Nicknames among the Mennonites from Russia," *Menn. Life*, 16 (July 1961, 132; Lester O. Troyer, "Amish Nicknames from Holmes County, Ohio," *Pennsylvania Folklife*, 18 (Summer 1968), 24; Alta Schrock, "Axie Yoder of Yetter Stadt," *The Casselman Chronicle* (Winter 1962), 9; Don Yoder, ed., "Nicknames from a Mennonite Family," *Pennsylvania Folklife*, 16, no 3 (Spring 1967), 42-43; Maurice A. Mook, "Nicknames Among the Amish," *Pennsylvania Folklife*, 18 (Summer 1968), 20-23; Elmer Smith, "Amish Nicknames," *J. of the American Names Society*, 16, no. 2, 105; Naomi Preheim, "Schweizer Mennonite Nicknames," *Menn. Life*, 29 (Dec. 1974), 85.

See also Dialect Literature and Speech; Folklore.

Niclaes, Hendrik. See Family of Love.

Niebuhr, H. Richard (1894-1962), younger brother of theologian Reinhold Niebuhr, is usually associated, as is Reinhold, with the development of °neo-orthodox theology in America. In contrast to the optimistic humanism of °liberal Christian theology, H. Richard had a profound sense of the tragedy of human sinfulness, a sense sharpened by the human and political realities of the world wars. His theological work is also characterized and undergirded by an enduring faith in the sovereignty of God.

A "teacher of the church" most of his life and a scholar who helped introduce sociological analysis into North American theological and ethical reflection (*The Social Sources of Denominationalism*, 1929; *The Kingdom of God in America*, 1937; *The Responsible Self*, 1963), Niebuhr has had particular import for Mennonites through publication of *Christ and Culture* (1951). There he outlines a typology of five ways Christians relate to culture and illustrates the "Christ against culture" type with reference to Mennonites. Many contemporary scholars accept Niebuhr's types rather uncritically, categorizing and dismissing Mennonites as "irresponsible" in relation to transformation of culture. Written material criticizing and responding to Niebuhr's typology as it relates to Mennonites is currently (1987) in manuscript or prepublication form. GGK

James Fowler, *To See the Kingdom: The Theological Vision of H. Richard Niebuhr* (Nashville: Abingdon Press, 1974), comprehensive bibliography; Beverly Wildung Harrison, "H. Richard Niebuhr: Towards a Christian Moral Philosophy" (diss., Union Theological Seminary, 1974), comprehensive bibliography; Lonnie Kliever, *H. Richard Niebuhr* (Waco, Texas: Word Books, 1977); Gayle Gerber Koontz, "Confessional Theology in a Pluralistic Context: A Study of the Theological Ethics of H. Richard Niebuhr and John H. Yoder" (PhD diss., Boston U., 1985); Paul Ramsey, ed., *Faith and Ethics: The Theology of H. Richard Niebuhr* (New York: Harper and Row, 1965); John Howard Yoder, "'Christ and Culture': A Critique of H. Richard Niebuhr" (manuscript, Yoder personal files, Elkhart, Ind., · 1964); Charles Scriven, *The Transformation of Culture: Christian Social Ethics after H. Richard Niebuhr* (Scottdale, 1988).

Niedersachsen (Lower Saxony) Federal State, Germany. In 1949 there were 2,800 Mennonites registered in Lower Saxony, most of them refugees from °°East and °°West Prussia. The unity among them was strengthened through their common origin, family relationships, and working together in receiving help from Mennonite Central Committee (MCC). In the years following, those who wanted to be members of a congregation for personal faith reasons organized congregational groups as possible. Thus the groups in Luneburg and Celle belong to the Hannover congregation. Oldenburg belongs to

the congregation at Leer. There are no Mennonite settlements in Lower Saxony.

The congregations are small: Oldenburg with 110 members, Göttingen with 125 members, Hannover with 115 members. They meet in facilities rented from other denominations. Not all ministers have received theological training. The congregations are members of the °Vereinigung der Deutschen Mennonitengemeinden (Union of the German Mennonite Congregations) and work together with them in relief and the °International Mennonite Organization. A youth worker, whose activities extend beyond the boundaries of the congregation, is being supported. New congregations are organized as immigrants arrive from Russia, for example, Wolfsburg with 50 members and Hannover with 38 members.   OW

Menn. Jahrbuch (1982, 1985); *Unser Blatt* (published by MCC for refugees in Germany), 1947-49.

Nigeria. Mennonite Central Committee (MCC) began its program in Nigeria in 1963. Its Teachers Abroad Program (TAP) had nine teachers scattered in Nigeria in 1964. By 1970 that number had increased to 48. They were placed in government

NIGERIA

LEGEND

MENNONITE CHURCHES IN NIGERIA
== National boundary
-- Selected state boundaries
O Mennonite centers (not all towns with congs. are shown)
★ Capitol city
● Other towns & cities
— Selected roads
~ Rivers

Nigeria Menn. Church
1 Church of God in Christ, Mennonite
2 Fellowship Churches
3 Nigeria Mennonite Church

schools as well as church-operated ones. Not all the teachers were Mennonites. At one time only 6 of 17 arriving teachers were Mennonites.

After the Biafra War (1967-70) MCC carried out relief work in the East Central State. In addition, they worked with Save the Children Fund. Three °°Pax volunteers worked with the Christian Council of Nigeria, the Faith and Farm program of the Church of Christ in Nigeria, and Sudan United Mission. As the relief needs declined they began a comprehensive rural health program.

In 1975 the goals of the MCC program were to (a) be a Christian witness in an over-missioned country; (b) provide quality education by supplying adequately trained teachers who are Christian; (c) supplement the teaching force of Nigeria in areas where insufficient numbers of Nigerian teachers were available; (d) assist agricultural and community development programs under Nigerian and long-term mission leadership; (e) provide an opportunity for cultural exchange within a Christian framework. After a program of universal primary education was achieved by the Nigerian government in 1975, MCC decided to strengthen its program because of the great need for teachers. A board of Nigerians was appointed to consult with MCC on its future directions in Nigeria.

By 1980 MCC work had shifted to the Muslim area of the North with Jos as the headquarters. Greater emphasis was put on learning the languages of the area so as to become more deeply involved with local churches and communities. In 1986 the number of personnel had dropped to 13, because of fewer applicants, and also because of the shift from a mainly educational program to a rural community work program. Eleven years after first applying, MCC was registered in 1987 as an official organization with the Federal Government.

Stanley and Delores Friesen, MBM, worked in the "Islam in Africa Project" in Ibadan, 1969-70. Mennonite Brethren Board of Missions and Services has placed workers with the Sudan Interior Mission in Nigeria.   EGr

MCC Workbook (1963, 18970, 1975, 1980, 1986); *MB Yearbook,,* (1981), 110.

Nigeria Mennonite Church (ME IV:1112).

In 1958 S. Jay and Ida Hostetler, who were serving in Ghana under Mennonite Board of Missions (MC), received a letter from Paul Peachey, a Mennonite working in Japan, stating that a Nigerian church of about 3,000 members wanted to become Mennonite. After consulting with Mennonite Board of Missions (MBM) the Hostetlers made their first of ten visits to these congregations located in Calabar Province of southeastern Nigeria. It was decided, eventually, that Edwin and Irene Weaver would go to assist these churches. They arrived in November 1959.

The Weavers faced opposition from the leaders of the many missions and churches already operating there. After a time they gained favor of the Presbyterian Church who took the responsibility of sponsoring the Mennonites to the government.

After working some time with these 50 or 60 congregations of independent churches who originally wanted to be Mennonite, there were 10 who finally decided they would like to form a New Testament

church under the name *Mennonite.* The Weavers worked hard to bring about better relationships between all these many churches. They formed a United Independent Church Fellowship of more than 200 congregations, including those calling themselves Mennonite. The initial project of UICF was a Bible school for the purpose of training leaders. Named the United Church Bible School, it opened in Feb. 1964 with Stanley Friesen of MBM as principal. By 1964 the Mennonite Church had grown to 25 congregations with 1,000 members. It ordained its first Nigerian minister, O. E. Essiet, on Easter Sunday, 1967.

Cooperation grew with the Presbyterian Church in education, medical service and in the Presbyterian Church itself. A new hospital was built in Abiriba by the community and the government. It replaced a smaller one, formerly operated by the Presbyterians, which closed for lack of personnel. The Mennonites were asked to operate the new one. In addition to staffing the hospital, teachers were sent to secondary schools, universities, and vocational training schools. In the period from 1959 to 1967, 47 people served in the MBM program in Nigeria.

The Biafra War (1967-70), made it necessary for most of the MBM persons to leave the country in 1967. As the Weavers could not return to Nigeria they began working with similar churches in Ghana. The Mennonite church in Nigeria operated mostly on its own from then on. In August of 1979 Darrel and Sherill Hostetler came to the church to help in what they understood was the Nigeria Mennonite Seminary. Upon arrival they were asked by the church leaders to teach in a church-run secondary school instead. The difficulty of this assignment made it necessary for MBM to recall them.

The 1986 *Mennonite Yearbook* gave the membership of the Nigeria Mennonite Church as 2,000 in 20 congregations in four districts with two ministers, three evangelists, 17 elders, 14 deacons and 12 deaconesses. Mennonite World Conference figures were 5,000 members in 37 congregations, located in Cross River State.   EGr

S. Jay Hostetler, *The Mennonite Church in Ghana 1957-1964: Memoirs by S. Jay Hostetler* (Elkhart: MBM, ca. 1979); Edwin Weaver and Irene Weaver *The Uyo Story* (Elkhart: MBM, 1970); MBM Annual Reports; *MWH* (1978) 91-92; *MWH* (1984), 14.

Nihon Kirisutokyo Keiteidan (Japan Brethren in Christ Church)

began with an evangelistic campaign on street corners in Hagi City, °Yamaguchi Prefecture, in August 1953. Seekers' meetings were begun in the home of the missionaries, Peter and Mary Willms. The first three converts were baptized in October 1954. Lay leaders emerged out of the newly formed church (Omotomachi Church). From an emphasis on cell groups and home meetings, other Yamaguchi area churches were formed in Nagato (Fukawa Church, 1960), and Shimonoseki (Yamanota Evangelical Church, 1970). Meetings were also held in Nishiichi, and Takibe is still a preaching point.

In 1963 the Brethren in Christ (BIC) mission planted a church in the western Tokyo suburb of Koganei (Nukui Minami-cho Church). Small church groups followed in Kodaira, Fuchu, and Tachikawa. A voluntary service program of teaching English was established by the mission to aid the Japan churches in their outreach. Twenty-three volunteers have taught during short term assignments, 1960-85. Only one long-term missionary couple is left, so almost all pastoral work and evangelism too is conducted by Japanese leaders, who are mostly self-supporting.

The mission encouraged the churches to remain as a loose fellowship of independent churches and to avoid the formation of another denomination. However, with an increasing number of seminary-trained pastors and the desire of the national leadership to be more clearly identified with the Brethren in Christ in North America, the Yamaguchi Brethren in Christ Conference was inaugurated in September 1971.

In November 1983 a combined conference of the Yamaguchi and Tokyo churches was effected. A Pioneer Evangelism Committee was established by the conference, and partnership teams consisting of a missionary and a national pastor were designated for existing churches and new outreach. Under the "partnership" concept, churches were begun in Shin-Shimonoseki in 1982 and Nagoya (Midori Evangelical Church) in 1983. At the Second General Conference in 1984, the Brethren in Christ Church in Japan observed its 30th anniversary celebration. Total membership is around 200. An occasional publication is *Ochibo* (Gleanings).   DCB/AN

Doyle C. Book, *The Threshhold Is High: The Brethren in Christ in Japan* (Nappanee, 1986); *MWH* (1978), 161-63.

Nihon Menonaito Burezaren Kyodan (Japan Mennonite Brethren Conference). In 1949 Mennonite Central Committee (MCC) pioneered relief work in the °Osaka area headed up by H. G. Thielman. From 1950 to 1953, 12 Mennonite Brethren missionaries arrived on the field. Of these pioneers, 9 have continued to serve for 30 or more years, giving stability to development.

The early strategy of concentrating church planting efforts in the metropolitan Osaka area and its suburbs promoted fellowship between the congregations and a conference spirit. In 1958 the Japan Field Council, in which Japanese leaders joined with the expatriate missionaries, was set up to promote the work of the Japan Conference.

From the beginning, there was concern that the work become °indigenous. Training national leaders was seriously considered. In 1957, the mission established the Japan Mennonite Brethren Bible Institute in the former MCC center. Four years later, the first three pastors were licensed. Ca. 1965-75 the school (renamed Osaka Biblical Seminary) entered into a cooperative arrangement with two Baptist groups and was largely operated by the respective missions. While that was being phased out, the Japan Mennonite Brethren Conference in 1971 assumed complete responsibility for the school and named it the Evangelical Bible Seminary. This leadership training program, from which all the Mennonite Brethren pastors have graduated, has been a key factor in promoting doctrinal unity and maintaining evangelistic fervor among the churches.

The Japan Mennonite Brethren mission has from the beginning enjoyed a very amicable relationship with the Japan Mennonite Brethren Conference (*Nihon Menonaito Burezaren Kyodan,* organized 1964).

As leadership matured, the cooperative Field Council was replaced by the Japan Conference Council. Japanese leaders assumed complete responsibility for the work of the conference, though missionaries could attend as observers or serve on committees. A regular conference publication is called *Yokiotozure* (Good News).

Monthly conference prayer meetings and a bimonthly pastor-missionary fellowship have been a real source of maintaining mutual understanding and fellowship. A committee made up of both Japanese and expatriate leaders expedites missionary assignments. The early recognition of the mission as a "partner" in working with the Japan conference has made for a healthy relationship between equals.

As of 1986 the Japan Mennonite Brethren Conference has grown steadily and is in its second 10-year evangelism program. The work has spread from the Osaka base to include eight prefectures. (Osaka, Hyogo, Nara, Mie, Aiichi, Yamaguchi, Hiroshima, and Yokohama). There are over 1,600 members. Twenty-three local churches have their own land and buildings, and three newer outreaches use other facilities. In addition, the conference operates a year-round camp facility. In 1986 there were 25 Japanese pastors, 9 of whom are ordained. Two missionary families serve in church planting ministries. One missionary couple and a single worker assist in the seminary training program, and four American young people serve one-year terms in church-centered English classes. One Japanese couple is serving in Papua New Guinea as Bible translators, and a single worker is being sent to Pakistan.   HaFr

MWH (1978), 164-67.

Nihon Menonaito Kirisutokyo Kyokai Kaigi (Japan Mennonite Christian Church Conference). In the spring of 1950, William C. °Voth, former missionary to China, stopped in Japan to investigate mission opportunities. A decision to open work in Japan was made at the General Conference Mennnonite Church (GCM) sessions held in Freeman, S.D., in August 1950.

In 1951 ten missionaries arrived in °Kobe, Hyogo Prefecture, for language study. The same year William Voth and Verney Unruh made a survey of southern Kyushu Island and recommended °Miyazaki Prefecture as the place to establish churches. Missionaries engaged in various types of evangelism, e.g., English Bible classes, radio, tent meetings, hospital visitation, literature, prayer meetings, Sunday worship, and Sunday School. A bookstore was opened in Miyiazaki City in 1955, a kindergarten in Nichinan in 1955, camp work at Aoidake in 1962, and a university student center in 1963 (this developed into a congregation). From 1959 on, a number of °°Pax workers arrived in Japan, mainly to teach English. As a result of these various efforts seven congregations were established.

When the missionaries first came to Japan, they made all the decisions and carried out the work. The only organization was the General Conference Mennonite mission. As the church grew and leaders matured, an agreement was reached to become one body and form a conference. In October 1964 the Japan Mennonite Christian Church Conference (*Nihon Menonaito Kirisutokyo Kyokai Kaigi*) was officially started with seven congregations and the mission cooperating.

The conference plays an important role in helping the different congregations. Its structure does not control congregations from the top. rather all the member congregations are independent and self-governing. Key decisions are made at the annual meeting of the church conference in February, by delegates representing all the churches, pastors, and missionaries. Between annual conferences the conference's executive committee or other committees transact necessary business. A small paper *Menonaito* ("The Mennonite") is published bimonthly.

From 1952 to 1967 Miyazaki Prefecture was the main area of evangelistic work. Outreach was then extended to Oita Prefecture, Fukuoka City (1976), and °Hiroshima (1979).

In 1986 the conference had a total of about 730 baptized members. Sixteen churches have been established, twelve of which have Japanese pastors, three of which are pastored by missionaries. One church has lay leadership. Six of the churches are outside Miyazaki Prefecture. A few members have served abroad in England, Africa, and Vietnam.   HI

MWH (1978), 168-72; W. Frederic Sprunger, *Theological Education by Extension in Japan* (Pasadena: William Carey Library, 1981).

See also Mission ("A Young Church Leads the Way" [feature]).

Nihon Menonaito Kirisuto Kyokai Kyogikai [Hokkaido] (Japan Mennonite Church Conference, Hokkaido) began in November 1948, when Dr. Takuo *Matsumoto* (1888-1986) of Hiroshima Girls College gave a chapel talk at Goshen College. Some students who heard him describe the havoc caused by the atomic bomb felt they should go to Japan as missionaries. Carl and Esther Beck and Ralph and Genevieve °Buckwalter landed in Yokohama, in December 1949.

After language study they started working at Obihiro and Kushiro, central cities in the cold eastern part of Hokkaido in June 1951. The Gospel found a ready response, and the testimony of conscientious objector experience helped Japanese realize the authenticity of the Bible's teaching. Eleven were baptized on Nov. 25, 1951, at Obihiro.

New missionaries from the Mennonite Board of Missions and Charities came to more rural towns. By 1956 there were six congregations—four in the Tokachi (Obihiro) area, and two in the Konsen (Kushiro) area. Winter Bible schools and summer camps were held. It seemed desirable to work closer together on projects requiring cooperation, but at the same time respect the autonomy of each congregation. The Japan Mennonite Christian Church Conference (*Nihon Menonaito Kirisuto Kyokai Kyogikai*) was thus established in May 1956.

A "Mennonite Hour" radio program and correspondence course begun in 1956 broadened contacts. Some members moved to Sapporo, the capital city of Hokkaido, and became the core of new groups in a new area. As of 1986, there were 17 congregations: 5 in Konsen, 7 in Tokachi, and 5 in Do-o (Sapporo). Total membership was about 450.

A decrease of population in rural villages is of concern. Three churches run kindergartens; some conduct English classes or evangelistic meetings. Recent emphasis is on strengthening the koinonia character of each group. Rather than large churches, the goal is to increase the number of small, close-knit congregations. At first graduates of seminaries or Bible schools in Tokyo were invited to lead churches, but only a few stayed. The conference concluded that leaders should emerge from the congregations themselves and be given training. So the Eastern Hokkaido Bible School (*Doto Seisho Gakuin*) was founded in 1965 in Kushiro (later in Obihiro). The stated purpose was to train workers in the Hokkaido context, and to do this with Anabaptist and Mennonite emphases (fellowship of believers, discipleship, peace witness). The school has no building. It goes where the students are. In Sapporo is the Fukuzumi hostel and study center. Many leaders are lay men and women. Some have received theological training abroad also.

One special project has been publication of Anabaptist-oriented literature through the Japan Mennonite Literature Association. A conference paper called *Michi* ("The Way") is published bimonthly. Two families have served abroad, one in radio work in Ecuador, the other in agricultural work in Bangladesh. A few individuals have served elsewhere.   TTan

MWH (1978), 173-77.

Nihon Menonaito Senkyokai (Japan Mennonite Fellowship, JMF) was organized on May 4, 1971. Its purposes are (a) to strengthen the common bonds of fellowship of all Mennonite and Brethren in Christ churches in Japan and (b) to promote the study of the Anabaptist and Mennonite heritage and define the identity of Mennonites in Japan in the light of the present Asian situation.

Participation by Mennonite groups in Japan is voluntary. But JMF also assumes a liaison role with overseas organizations such as the Mennonite Central Committee (MCC) International Visitor Exchange program, and seeks to inform churches of Asia Mennonite Conference and Mennonite World Conference activities.

The predecessor of JMF was the Japan MCC Consulting Committee, sponsored by the MCC Peace Section. A change of policy by MCC and the maturing of Japanese churches brought about the birth of JMF.

The main task of JMF is to take a leadership role in development of a peace witness and theological education in the Japanese context. A peace seminar is becoming an annual event, and an Anabaptist seminar is held every other year.   TN

MWH (1984), 44.

Niswander, Catherine (Jan. 10, 1884-1979), was a General Conference Mennonite (GCM) missionary in Chicago; Portland, Ore.; and Philadelphia for 53 years. Born in Bluffton, Ohio, Niswander graduated in 1911 from Fort Wayne (Ind.) Bible Institute and attended Bluffton College. At the urging of William S. °°Gottschall, her minister at First Mennonite Church, in Bluffton and member of the General Conference Home Mission Board, she began serving as city missionary in Chicago, together with W. W. Miller, superintendent. The mission began as a °rescue mission, but the following year moved to a neighborhood of homeowners in West Englewood. Niswander surveyed the area door-to-door (making as many as 581 calls in one year), invited children to Sunday school, taught Sunday school, and managed mission finances through seven ministerial changes at First Mennonite Church as it was later named.

In 1928 she was transferred to the Alberta Community Church, Portland, Ore., to help start a new congregation. Niswander was the only full-time worker in Portland during her nine years there. An anniversary booklet from the First Mennonite Church in Philadelphia, where she later served, listed her as "superintendent" in Portland. She did all the pastoral functions there except preaching. Most of the preaching was done by visiting ministers or seminary students. When the Home Mission Board decided to send two men to Portland as ministers, Niswander was transferred to Philadelphia in 1937.

During almost 13 years at First Mennonite Church in Philadelphia, Niswander did visitation and organized children's classes and Bible schools. On occasion, when pastor J. J. Plenert was absent, she also preached on Sunday morning. Then until her retirement in 1967, Niswander served the Germantown Mennonite Church in Philadelphia.

When she began her work, Niswander was one of a number of single women serving as °urban missionaries. However, by 1942, she was the only such missionary for the General Conference Home Mission Board.   LB

Barrett, "City Mission Worker: Catherine Niswander," in *Full Circle,* ed. Mary Lou Cummings, (Newton, 1978), 176-83; Barrett, *Vision* (1983), 86-89, 109, 136-37.

Nonconformity (ME III:890) to the world is the historic Christian emphasis on Godly living and being in secular and often pagan society. Many Christian groups in the history of the church have stressed total obedience to the teachings and example of Jesus Christ, some to the point of complete perfection. The Anabaptists of the 16th c. took this divine calling with unusual seriousness and many of their descendants among the Mennonites, Amish, and Hutterian Brethren still do in late 20th c. Theory and practice, however, have never been easily held together.

The relevant biblical texts and secondary literature to the mid-1950s are cited in ME III. A key volume in that literature is J. C. Wenger's *Separated Unto God* (1951) which also included major bibliographical listings with each chapter. Yet the book marked the end of an era for Mennonites and Brethren in Christ. A generation of Mennonites came on the scene after World War II with new experiences in °°Civilian Public Service, global Mennonite Central Committee (MCC) involvements and more college graduates in an increasingly °urbanized society. The civil rights movement of the 1960s and the peace marches of the early 1970s gave many young Mennonites causes in which they could legitimately participate both as believers and as citizens. A new social respectability seemed to have been achieved.

These kinds of developments, in turn, led to new questions, new ideas and a new image of themselves as Mennonites and their place in society. Mennonite Mutual Aid was born. It became a symbol of fresh involvements as a church in such °businesses as °insurance and °investments. A new level of prosperity was being achieved by Mennonites in rapidly urbanizing societies in North America and Europe. Mission outreach expanded rapidly. The Amish, Hutterian Brethren, and Old Colony Mennonites were obviously also aware of change, but not to the degree of the new generation of Mennonites.

Gradually "Plain People" came to refer not to Mennonites but to Amish (Lancaster Co., Pa., Holmes Co., Ohio, Lagrange Co., Ind., and Waterloo Co., Ont.), together with a few Old Order Mennonites here and there, the Hutterian Brethren in the Northeast, the Hutterian Brethren in the Canadian and American Midwest, and the Old Colony Mennonites in Canada, Mexico, and other parts of Latin America. Tourists loved to visit Amish and Hutterian communities. Soon Mennonites were busy setting up °interpretation centers to tell visitors what the simple life was all about. Despite occasional losses, the Hutterian Brethren and the Amish were growing rapidly. Though the demise of the latter had been predicted by some scholars, they grew from ca. 8,000 in 1900 to ca. 75,000 in 1977 (Hostetler, 1977). And they largely maintained their nonconformity in most areas of life and faith.

Meanwhile it became increasingly difficult for most Mennonites to maintain or define just what nonconformity meant, not so much historically, but in the present. For them geographical separation had largely disappeared and was not an option in any case. Earlier "boundaries" were also no longer acceptable to the °acculturated new generation. There was gradual or full conformity to social customs in regard to °dress, wedding bands, °recreation, °automobiles, farming equipment, houses, and other externals.

Nevertheless, many did succeed significantly, against great odds, in finding new, relevant forms of nonconformity even in an urbanized, highly secular environment. Not all of the following responses to the call of Christ would be acceptable to all, but the momentum was broad and, for the most part, encouraging. It was based both on biblical and historic Anabaptist premises.

(a) With MCC encouragement Doris Janzen Longacre (1940-79) published the *More-with-Less Cookbook* (1976) supplying nourishing, healthy but cost efficient recipes, with commentary, for a simple life style. Over 520,000 copies had been sold by 1988. Her sequal, *Living More with Less* (1980) was also well received. (b) From 1975-77 basic steps were taken by MCC in Canada to establish a "Food Bank" of donated grain for the hungry of the world. In the fiscal year ending Mar. 31, 1988, some 84,296 metric tons worth $25,756,945 were shipped abroad. Approximately one-third of the grain came from Mennonites.

(c) Mennonites have normally identified °nonresistance closely with nonconformity. Here the evidence was less encouraging. The Kauffman-Harder study in 1975 found that 71 percent of respondents to the study affirmed a preference for °alternative service, while 11 percent chose noncombatant service and five percent regular military service (Kauffman/Harder, 133). A more recent study of the Vietnam era by James Amstutz showed 42.8 percent affirming °conscientious objection, 26.4 percent received deferments, 6.8 percent choosing noncombatant service, and 14 percent choosing regular military service. Thus, even without knowing how the 26.4 percent would have chosen, nonresistant convictions seemed to have declined between 1975 and 1986 among the major groups of Mennonites studied. Conformity to social expectations had increased.

(d) On the other hand some Mennonites took a much more serious step by not paying that portion of their federal taxes which they believed went for war purposes, remitting that amount to MCC, the World Peace Tax Fund, or similar causes. They did this knowing that their bank accounts would be confiscated for that amount and that official harassment might follow. (e) Some took steps to limit their income to where they would have little or no tax liability. (f) Some took direct nonviolent action through demonstrations at weapons facilities or other forms of protest against war which did end with prison sentences or fines or both. Other Mennonites, however, felt these actions were not in keeping with biblical nonresistance. (g) The refusal to swear a formal oath in civic or legal situations remained an article of faith for most Mennonites in Europe and North America.

(h) °Peace and °service programs were developed, in addition to those already available through MCC, as alternative ways of expressing °love. Businessmen united to form °Mennonite Economic Development Associates (MEDA) in 1953 to facilitate economic development in North America and globally as resources permitted. Mennonite Disaster Service (MDS) had already been organized in 1950 to assist victims of natural °disasters. (i) Under the direction of Mennonite Mutual Aid, congregations were encouraged to contribute to a "Fraternal Fund" which provided help to needy individuals and causes.

(j) The earlier emphases on personal nonconformity were not neglected. The biblical virtues of modesty, °humility, peace, sobriety, compassion, love, and the integrity of business, social and personal ethics, were stressed in sermons and treatises and remained a significant part of Mennonite identity. Some of the biggest changes came in the areas of dress regulations, which were largely given up, as were restrictions on recreation and entertainment (°amusements), though this varied from region to region.

(k) Though the Mennonite °family remained strong, °divorce did occur even as congregations struggled to find ways of redemptive help and healing in these situations. There were occasional cases of litigation. A Victim Offender Reconciliation Program worked effectively with the judicial system in many cities to mediate disputes in society at large. New interest in spiritual disciplines, stimulated in part by Roman Catholic, Quaker, and other writings, led to the training of resource persons and the founding of numerous small retreat centers across the United States and Canada.

In all of these trends and activities the historic conviction remained that nonconformity is not first the adherence to codes governing external behavior but an attitude of heart and mind, a commitment to discipleship and the simplification of life style precisely in the midst of a complex society with all of its advertising and seductiveness. That the expression of this attitude, and these values, would also find visible exprssion was assumed and expected.

If there was indeed a Mennonite "identity crisis" in the late 20th c., as some scholars believed, it would be safe to assume that it was related, at least in part, to the loss of earlier codes of nonconformity and the search for new ethical, theological, and personal boundaries. For centuries the church-world dualism of Romans 12:2 "Do not be conformed to this world" had been the ideal, albeit imperfectly achieved even in legalism.

Early Anabaptist confessions confirmed this ideal, particularly article 4 of the "Brotherly Union of °Schleitheim" (1527) when it stated: "We have been united concerning the separation that shall take place from the evil and the wickedness which the devil has planted in the world. . . . Now there is nothing else in the world and all creation than good or evil, believing and unbelieving, darkness and light . . . Christ and Belial, and none will have part with the other."

In the late 1980s have Mennonites become a part of the social mainstream or are there still signs of a counterculture intention and, if so, where could these signs be found—in economics, politics, family life, personal values, worship, or service motivation? The signs are mixed in North America, and certainly globally. Yet, except for the Amish and Old Order groups, the sectarian black and white world seemed to have almost disappeared. Only time would tell whether this is spiritual gain or loss.   CJD

James Amstutz, "Sources of Mennonite Draft Statistics," and "MCC Vietnam Draft Pilot Study," unpublished student papers at AMBS, 1986; J. R. Burkholder, "What's Wrong with Nonconformity?" GH (Sept. 5, 1950), 879; Marvin Dueck, "Old Colony Mennonites in Mexico: Defensive Structures to Preserve a Way of Life," unpublished student paper at AMBS, 1987; Michel Durrive and others, "The Mennonites of Alsace Facing Modernity," MQR, 58 (1984), 272-88; Frank H. Epp, Education with a Plus: The Story of Rosthern Junior College (Waterloo, 1975), ch. 9; J. Winfield Fretz, The MEDA Experiment, 1953-1978 (Waterloo, 1978); Melvin Gingerich, "Change And Uniformity in Mennonite Attire," MQR, 40 (October 1966), 243-59; idem, Mennonite Attire Through Four Centuries (Scottdale, 1970); Allen R. Guenther, "Unmasking the Self-Love Lie," Chr. Leader (Sept. 2, 1980), 6-8; Beulah Stauffer Hostetler, "Midcentury Change in the Mennonite Church," MQR, 60 (1986), 58-82; idem, "Defensive Structuring and Codification of Practice: Franconia Mennonite Conference," MQR, 60 (July 1986), 429-44; idem, American Mennonites and Protestant Movements: A Community Paradigm (Scottdale, 1987); John A. Hostetler, "Old Order Amish Survival," MQR, 51 (1977), 352-61, the entire issue is given to articles on "The Plain People"; Kauffman/Harder, Anabaptists Four C. Later (1975); "Christian Nonconformity to the World," in Proceedings of the Fourth Mennonite World Conference (August 3-10, 1948), 41-62; J. C. Wenger, How to Live a Dynamic Christian Life (Scottdale, 1955); CRR 1.

See also Dancing; Dramatic Arts; Education; Motion Pictures; Plain People; Prayer Veil; Political Participation; Political Attitudes; Private Christian Schools; Sociological Studies; Sociopolitical Activism; Television.

Nonresistance (ME III:897). The simple command of Jesus in Mt 5:39, "resist not evil," is the source for a foundational category in Mennonite ethical thought—nonresistance. The 16th c. European Anabaptists spoke of *Gewaltlosigkeit* (literally, the abstaining from the use of force), meaning the refusal of violent self-defense and the rejection of °military service.

In early 19th c. America, "nonresistance" became for a time the label used by pacifist abolitionists such as Adin Ballou and W. L. Garrison (of the New England Non-Resistance Society), but their politically aggressive movement had little in common with the quietist rural Mennonites.

American Mennonites first faced military °conscription during the °Civil War. The church was poorly prepared to deal with this challenge and many young men accepted military service. This experience evoked a revival of nonresistance teaching. Booklets by John F. °°Funk and John M. °°Brenneman appeared in 1863. The 1864 tract by Reformed Mennonite Daniel Musser, "Non-Resistance Asserted," later came to the attention of Leo Tolstoy.

°World War I again tested the nonresistant convictions of American Mennonites and became the occasion for renewed emphasis on the doctrine. Significant exponents of nonresistant teaching from the first part of the 20th c. include John °°Horsch, Daniel °Kauffman, H. P. °°Krehbiel, C. Henry °°Smith, and Edward °°Yoder.

Guy F. °Hershberger, at midcentury the chief interpreter of the theme, described nonresistance as "the term which in Anabaptist-Mennonite history has come to denote the faith and life of those who believe that the will of God requires the renunciation of warfare and other compulsive means for the furtherance of personal or social ends" (ME III:897). Nonresistance means "pouring out one's love without reserve, even as Christ poured out His life completely on the cross for His enemies" (*Way of the Cross*, 41). Thus the word became synonymous with the way of °suffering °love as exemplified in Jesus.

In Hershberger's formulation, nonresistance had implications for every area of life. Beyond personal relations in the Christian community, it was also the guideline for industrial, legal, political, and economic relations, as denominational statements on these issues, especially from the 1940s and 1950s, testify. Its normative expression included refusal to sue at °law or to join °labor unions. Always more than a merely negative stance, nonresistance was extended to include positive activities of Christian service, grounded in a community of faith.

Nonresistance was taught as the only authentic biblical and Anabaptist norm, consistent with the nonpolitical "two kingdom" theology of the °Schleitheim confession. In its practical implications, however, this ethic also enabled a prophetic witness that helped move the church into more active forms of social service and witness in the wider world, even into areas of °political activism.

Up to the 1950s, practically all Mennonites saw their nonresistant stance as distinct from both °°pacifism and nonviolence. Nonviolence was viewed as a tool of the liberal religious pacifist movement, derived from the efforts of °Gandhi in his struggle for Indian self-determination. Nonviolence was a human strategy of coercion used to obtain a specific social goal, though without the use of physical force.

Critics have labeled classic Mennonite nonresistance as psychological asceticism, resulting in an unhealthy stance of withdrawal and self-denial. Moreover, it is an inadequate social ethic, unable to respond to competing neighbor claims or to the need for the protection of third parties. The larger questions of °justice and social responsiblity are bypassed in order to preserve personal purity, it is alleged.

In the generation since 1955, these challenges have been addressed by Mennonite scholars. J. Lawrence Burkholder and Gordon Kaufman led the way in questioning the adequacy of the traditional ethic for responding to the changing social context of Mennonite communities, no longer isolated from °modern society, and to the urgent needs of the postwar world. They along with others argued that the traditional stance was too narrow and simplistic to cope with such problems as the threat of nuclear weapons and third-world revolutions.

With the growth of civil rights activism and the 1955 Montgomery, Ala., bus boycott, Mennonites became aware of a new form of nonviolent action for social justice. This emerging movement, nurtured in the black churches and led by Martin Luther King, Jr., was cautiously appraised by Hershberger as more of "a strategy of appeal and less one of compulsion, and thus would seem more nearly to approach New Testament nonresistance."

New developments in biblical scholarship also enabled change. Hershberger (and others such as H. A. °Fast) depicted the purpose of Jesus in purely nonpolitical terms. But the newer studies uncovered the political dimensions of Jesus' ministry in its historical setting. Although never approving physical violence to people, the Jesus of the gospels agressively engages the sociopolitical issues of his time. He is the leader of a movement rooted in the faith of Israel and directed to concrete needs and expectations, modeling a strategy for social action that is neither escapist nor violent.

John H. Yoder's *The Politics of Jesus*, solidly grounded in current biblical exegesis, became the landmark study on this theme, gaining recognition far beyond Mennonite circles. Lawrence Burkholder in his writing demonstrates that both nonresistance and nonviolent resistance are to be found in the ministry of Jesus.

The basic ethical criterion of this emerging position is the rejection of violence. Nonviolent resistance in a just cause, particularly for the sake of others rather than self, can be an expression of Christian love. But a faithful follower of Jesus will always accept suffering, even death, rather than do injury to others.

Thus, contemporary Mennonite ethics has responded to the times with a renewed appropriation of the resources of biblical faith, moving beyond the tradition of nonresistance. More and more, the language of nonviolence is replacing that of nonresistance. A more comprehensive social ethic, biblically grounded but also indebted to Gandhi, King, and others, is being created by the present generation of Mennonites. JRB

Bibl. on War and Peace (1987); Guy F.Hershberger, *War, Peace, and Nonresistance* (Scottdale, 1944, 1953, 1969); J. Lawrence Burkholder, "The Problem of Social Responsibility from the Perspective of the Mennonite Church" (ThD diss., Princeton Theological Seminary, 1958; published Elkhart; IMS, 1988); idem, "Nonresistance, Nonviolent Resistance, and Power," and John Richard Burkholder, "A Perspective on Mennonite Ethics," in *Kingdom, Cross, and Community*, ed. by J. R. Burkholder and Calvin Redekop (Scottdale, 1976), 131-137, 151-66; Gordon Kaufman, *Nonresistance and Responsibility, and Other Mennonite Essays* (Newton, 1979); John Howard Yoder, *The Politics of Jesus* (Grand Rapids: Eerdmans, 1972); Paul Toews, "The Long Weekend or the Short Week: Mennonite Peace Theology, 1925-1944" *MQR*, 60 (1986), 38-57; Henry A. Fast, *Jesus and Human Conflict* (Scottdale, 1959); Martin Luther King, Jr., *Stride Toward Freedom* (New York: Harper and Row, 1958); J. C. Wenger, *Pacifism and Biblical Nonresistance* (Scottdale, 1968); Guy F. Hershberger, *The Way of the Cross in Human Relations* (Scottdale, 1958); John Richard Burkholder, *Continuity and Change: A Search for a Mennonite Social Ethic* (Akron Pa.: MCC, 1977); Richard C. Detweiler, *Mennonite Statements on Peace, 1915-1966* (Scottdale, 1968); John Howard Yoder, *The Original Revolution* (Scottdale, 1972); General Conference Mennonite Church, "The Way of Peace," an official statement in 1971.

See also Conscientious Objection; Peace; Revolution; Taxes.

Nonviolence. See Nonresistance; Peace.

Nord Colony, Mexico, also commonly known as the "Ojo de la Yegua" colony, is the result of a series of land purchases by °Manitoba Colony. As early as 1933 the Manitoba Colony bought the Mexican ranch "Saucito," now Campo No. 35 and renamed it Altenau. By 1962 all of the land as far north as the °°Santa Clara Colony had been acquired by the Manitoba Colony. After the land of the Ojo de la Yegua ranch was bought in 1948 people in the new area became an independent colony, electing their own °elder (bishop) and *Vorsteher* (chairman). In 1962 the northern section of the Nord Colony, the Santa Rita Colony, became a separate entity as well. In the early 1960s a small group of farmers from Campo 38.5 (Steinreich farm) requested help from the General Conference Mennonites in North America to establish a school. This eventually resulted in a General Conference school and church. The boarding home for elementary school children functioned for several years. In 1987 these facilities were made available to the adult education center, also part of the General Conference church work, which was then transferred from Kilometer 17 to Steinreich. Both the German Church of God and the Evangelical Mennonite Conference from Canada established schools in Campo No. 67.

Many of the conservative Old Colonists of the Nord Colony emigrated to Bolivia and Paraguay. The Old Colony population of Ojo de la Yegua Colony on Jan. 1, 1987 stood at 11,854. Of these 4,390 were baptized church members. HEns

MWH (1978), 277-78.

Norte Colony, Del, Bolivia. The Del Norte Colony was founded in 1980 by settlers from the Santa Rita and Nord colonies in Mexico. It is located approximately 150 km. (95 mi.) ne. of Santa Cruz, east of the Rio Grande river, and adjacent to Valle Esperanza colony. Its people belong to an Old Colony Mennonite congregation led by bishop Ben Wieler

(1986). The population of this colony in 1986 was 400 inhabitants, of whom 143 were church members. IHie

North Carolina (ME III:915). The small groups resulting from the °°Krimmer Mennonite Brethren conference mission work were transferred to the General Conference of the Mennonite Brethren (North Carolina District Conference [MB]) when the two conferences merged in 1960. In 1987 the membership of the six congregations was 189. Since 1955 other Mennonite conferences have established congregations in North Carolina with the number of congregations and membership in 1988 as follows: Virginia Conference (MC; 7 congregations, 261 members); Atlantic Coast Conference (MC; 2, 74); Fellowship Churches (1, 51). One of the Virginia Conference congregations, Durham, also belonged to the Eastern District Conference (GCM). RSa

MC Yearbook (1988), 30, 48-49, 82-84, 93-94; Wittlinger, *Piety and Obedience* 146; Elizabeth Wiebe, "The Founding and Pioneer Work of the Krimmer Mennonite Brethren Mountain Mission in North Carolina," *Christian Witness*, 10 (Mar. 15, 1950), 5-7.

See also Wiebe, Elizabeth Pauls and Henry V.

North Carolina District Conference (MB). In 1956 Peter and Katherine Siemens left the North Carolina °°Krimmer Mennonite Brethren churches. At that time there were congregations in Boone, Bushill, Lenoir, Laytown, Beech Bottom, Darby, Cove Creek, Shell Creek, Heaton, Cranberry, and Elk Park. The last five congregations no longer exist. Since 1956 the remaining congregations have moved toward greater independence under the leadership of Rondo °Horton. Pastoral leadership in 1987 included seven part-time pastors; total membership was 189. A critical need reported by conference leaders is the retention of young people and the training of leaders. There has been a significant ministry to university students in Boone in the 1980s. The North Carolina Conference joined the General Conference of the Mennonite Brethren Churches of North America when the Mennonite Brethren and the Krimmer Mennonite Brethren merged in 1960. ADue

MB Yearbook (1981), 195.

North Central Mennonite Conference (MC) includes 14 congregations of the Mennonite Church (MC) in the United States and Canada (13 congregations in Minnesota, Montana, North Dakota, and Wisconsin, and 1 congregation in Rainy River, Ont.). Two congregations (in Casselton, N.D. and Glendive, Mont.) belong to both the North Central Conference and the Northern District Conference (GCM). Total membership in 1988 was 491. The conference publication is the *North Central Conference Bulletin*. RSa

MC Yearbook (1988-89), 72, 140.

North Dakota (ME III:916). In 1988 three congregations of the Northern District (GCM) with 289 members, six Mennonite Brethren congregations, and three congregations of the North Central Mennonite Conference (MC) with 197 members were located in North Dakota. One of the congregations listed had membership jointly with the Northern District and North Central Mennonite Conferences. In addition there was one unaffiliated congregation and one congregation of the Church of God in Christ Mennonite. An emerging fellowship in the Fargo, N.D., and Moorehead, Minn., had members belonging to the Northern District and North Central Conference. An MCC Thrift Shop was located in Minot.   RSa

MC Yearbook (1988-89), 31, 72, 99, 149; *GCM Handbook* (1988), 10, 31, 141.

Northern District Conference (GCM) (ME III:923) had its beginning in Mountain Lake, Minn., at the First Mennonite Church, in 1891. After almost 100 years, the conference's 5,500 members still emphasize a program of encouragement, Christian education, and evangelism. The district has churches in five states and the number of congregations has varied from 35 to 45. The largest congregation, Bethesda Mennonite of Henderson, Nebr., had more than 1,000 members in 1987 and the smallest congregation, Sermon on the Mount in Sioux Falls, S.D., had 22 members.

Since 1950 most of the new congregations have joined as a result of mission and outreach. Another characteristic of the congregations joining in recent years is that many belong to two conferences. Among these are Faith Mennonite, Minneapolis, Minn. (1956), Sermon on the Mount (1977), First Mennonite, Lincoln, Nebr. (1986), Casselton Mennonite, Casselton, N.D. (1980), and White Chapel Mennonite, Glendive, Mont. (1987). The first three are members of the Iowa-Nebraska Conference (MC) and the last two are members of the North Central Conference (MC) in addition to their membership in the Northern District Conference (GCM). This will result in a number of joint district conference sessions beginning in 1988.

There has been a real attempt to unite the churches through Swan Lake °Camp in South Dakota and the camping programs of the Cheyenne churches in Montana. Conference members are also united through the ministry of "Choice Books," the monthly conference publication, *Northern Light,* a district youth minister, and a conference minister.

In 1987 missionaries and pastors are being called from the new urban churches as well as those established for many years.

From its founding, Freeman Junior College has proved to be a vital witness linking district churches through Christian education. The junior college graduated its last class in 1986. Freeman Academy continues to offer classes for grades 7-12. In 1987 the 94th session of the Northern District Conference recognized Bethel College, Kansas, as the district's institution of higher learning.

Future plans include new congregations at Billings, Mont., St. Paul, Minn., and Fargo, N.D. "New Call to Commitment" program of the General Conference Mennonite Church (1987) includes plans for a building to house a district center for peace and district offices, in addition to a continued vision for °church planting.   ENe

GCM Handbook (1988), 114, 141-42, 149-50.

Northern Light Gospel Mission Conference (NLGMC), based in Red Lake, Ont., was originally formed in 1965. The purpose of this conference was to serve Northern Light Gospel missions, (ME IV:1112). With 19 mission outposts under the mission agency and a growing staff of more than 100 people, along with outside pressures, the need was felt to form a local conference. The conference was intended to provide ordinations of both staff members and Native brethren, to be the official organ for recognition with government offices etc., and to provide an annual gathering of missionaries in a conference setting.

With the emergence of the °Native Mennonite Conference and the reorganization of the mission, the original mandate of NLGMC is nearly met. In 1987 leaders were evaluating what the future of the conference should be, since most of the Native congregations are being placed under the Native Mennonite Conference. A change in the conference's name and a reorientation toward an association of "white" churches is anticipated.   HH

MC Yearbook (1988-89), 96.

See also Indian Ministries, North America.

Northern Rhodesia. See Zimbabwe.

Northwest Conference of the Mennonite Church (MC) (ME I:34). The Northwest Conference replaced the Alberta-Saskatchewan Mennonite Conference by delegate action in 1971. A new constitution patterned after the Mennonite Church (MC) General Assembly model (conference board and leadership, missions, nurture, and stewardship commissions) was adopted. Edgar Boettger became the first conference president who was not a minister. The conference convenes its sessions in July and October and a renewal conference, *Reach Out To Jesus,* has been endorsed annually since 1980. The first salaried employee was hired in 1984 (executive secretary, Timothy Burkholder).

The congregational Winter Bible School begun in the 1940s was terminated in 1956 as a definite shift toward higher education in the 1950s and 1960s absorbed prospective students. The majority of students obtain their higher education in Alberta's colleges and universities with Bible school training taken in schools outside the constituency.

Congregational leadership shifted from plural, self-supported ministry to single fully-supported pastors working with church councils. Early leaders were selected from within the congregation whereas in 1987 trained persons from without the congregation are hired including an influx of leaders from other conferences. In 1987 Harold Boettger was the only remaining bishop (retired). The bishop function has been replaced by a conference ministers (in 1987, Samuel V. Martin and Paul Voegtlin), working as pastor to the pastors.

Northern Alberta mission posts begun at Bluesky, Eaglesham, and Smith in 1948 developed into congregations under church planters Paul and Doris Burkholder, Loyal and Ruth Roth, and Willis and Florence Yoder and their families. The period from 1955 to 1973 was characterized by many °voluntary service projects beginning with Ike and Lillie Glick at Calling Lake, Alta. Many families moved to Alberta from the United States, including most voluntary service personnel, who chose to stay in Canada when their term was completed. This was followed by a shift to urban projects beginning with Edmonton and Calgary. In 1981, a house church at Anchorage, Alaska, joined the conference. Hispanic churches in Edmonton and Calgary (1981) have since expanded to three other locations. Two congregations hold dual membership (MC/GCM) and one has formed a community church with the evangelical churches in the community. Recent church planting locations include Browning, Mont., among the Blackfoot people; and Grande Prairie, Sherwood Park, and a Hispanic group at Medicine Hat, Alta.

Total membership in the conference in 1987 was 1,030. The conference publishes a *Newsletter of the Northwest Conference of the Mennonite Church.*
TBurk/PV

MC Yearbook (1988-89), 73; *GH* (May 24, 1988), 353-56.

Northwest Mexican Evangelical Mennonite Church. See Iglesia Evangélica Menonita del Noroeste de Mexico.

Nova Colony (Bagé), Brazil. Located near °°Bagé, the Nova Colony experienced serious difficulties since its founding 1949-51, particularly crop failures during the early 1950s and large scale emigration to the °Curitiba area of Brazil as well as to Canada. Early dependence on wheat as primary crop has been replaced by diversified agriculture including cattle and a dairy industry. In 1987 the colony is well established and progressive in cultural, social, economic educational and church affairs. A total of 143 families live in the colony, with an additional 14 families in the Medici colony, a new settlement nearby.

In 1987 the Mennonite Brethren church had a membership of 324 in German-speaking congregations and two Portuguese-speaking congregations with 140 members. Three missionaries work full-time with four mission stations and six places of witness. A philanthropic community society was founded in 1962 to promote cultural and educational activities, the hospital, and centers for physical and spiritual renewal. The society is also responsible for emergency assistance and other °mutual aid as needed, and it supports a museum and a library. In 1987 the Menno Simons school had 188 pupils enrolled in grades kindergarten-eight.

Economic life centers in the °cooperative founded in 1959, which includes farmers in the surrounding area. It had a membership of 1,700 in 1987. Up to 100,000 liters of milk can be produced daily. A pasteurization plant located in Bagé can handle 50,000 liters. In 1986 9,700 metric tons (10,670 U.S. tons) of wheat, 9,000 tons of rice, 6,600 tons of sorghum, and 700 tons of other grain were produced. The services of veterinarians, agriculturists, and other specialized personnel are arranged through the cooperative. The total 1986 volume was 11 million dollars (U.S.). At government request the cooperative is also assisting in the development of a new colony of some 125 Indian families which have been displaced

from a reservation and are being relocated near the colony on a tract of ca. 2,500 hectares (6,000 acres).
PP,Jr.

Nova Scotia. See Atlantic Provinces, Canada.

Novosibirsk. See Russian Soviet Federated Socialist Republic (RSFSR).

Nsongamadi Joseph and Baba Naomi are names that will always be associated with pioneering, first-generation evangelism and church planting in the Église du Christ au Zaire, Communauté Mennonite au Zaire (CMZA; Zaire Mennonite Church). During his life-long ministry as an evangelist Nsongamadi Joseph took the gospel to three tribal groups other than his own.

Born to Baluba parents, after attending school at the °°Congo Inland Mission (Africa Inter-Mennonite Mission) station at Djoko Punda, he and his wife Baba Naomi were first placed among the Bashilele people to the west. There they experienced genuine persecution by the suspicious and resistant village folk. Finally, after an attempt was made to poison their children, Joseph and Naomi were moved by the mission to a village of the Lulua people. Later when the mission decided to open a new work among the Baphende people to the southwest, Nsongamadi accompanied the missionaries on an exploratory trip and was later placed near Mukedi village in Kwilu Province to the west. He and Naomi worked alone until resident missionaries were placed there in 1923.

As more Baphende people accepted the gospel, Nsongamadi and his family eventually returned to Djoko where he served as the chaplain at the station hospital until his death. Baba Naomi went to Kananga, the capital of the West Kasai, to serve as a visiting Bible woman (°lay evangelist) in the large city hospital. In her ministry there she brought cheer and hope to many patients and distributed large quantities of New Testaments and Gospels.   JEB

Ntambue Paul (b. 1912) was born into the Baluba tribe in the area of Djoko Punda, one of the early stations founded by the Congo Inland Mission (Africa Inter-Mennonite Mission) in the West Kasai of Belgian Congo (Zaire). He enrolled as a student in the station school and accepted Christ early.

Ntambue served as a deacon in Djoko for many years as well as Bible instructor in the station schools. He was a gifted teacher with an unusual ability to study on his own with very limited resource materials. He played a major role in the station church and gave many hours to the local council. A large man with a resonant bass voice, he spoke slowly and deliberately in a manner which underscored insight into local tribal customs and his effort to apply scriptural principles as he understood them. He gained the respect and appreciation of Africans and missionaries alike with his unbiased approach to issues and his firmness in dealing with problems.

In the political turmoil after Belgian officials left in 1960, Ntambue migrated with many others to their traditional homeland in the East Kasai. There he was ordained a pastor by the Église du Christ au Zaire, Communauté Evangélique Mennonite (CEM,

Zaire Evangelical Mennonite Church), which recognized and welcomed his rich teaching and pastoral experience.   HGra

Nuclear Weapons, United States. An atomic bomb, nicknamed "Little Boy," inaugurated the age of nuclear weapons when the United States exploded it over Hiroshima in 1945 at the close of World War II. Apart from several brief editorials in church papers, Mennonites said little about nuclear weapons in the first two decades of the nuclear age. In the 1950s several leaders in the General Conference Mennonite Church (GCM) and one of their official resolutions (1959) called for a ban on atomic bomb tests. Mennonites began to speak forthrightly about the threat of nuclear weapons in the late 1970s some 30 years after Hiroshima, as a spiraling arms race between the United States and the Soviet Union defied control. A resolution on the nuclear arms race, issued by the Mennonite Central Committee (U.S.) Peace Section in 1978 called upon all "peoples and nations to renounce the research, development, testing, production, deployment and actual use of nuclear weapons." The statement also contended that nuclear deterrence, based on trust in nuclear weapons, is "a form of idolatry." In 1978, Mennonites joined with the Society of Friends and the Church of the Brethren in a New Call to Peacemaking effort which urged the "Worldwide abolition of nuclear weapons." In the late 1970s and 1980s the Peace Section of the Mennonite Central Committee (U.S.) produced and distributed some 8,000 copies of a poster declaring, "It's a sin to build a nuclear weapon." This bold announcement underscored the theological and moral issues entwined in nuclear weaponry.

Mennonite concern about nuclear weapons escalated as a rising tide of public opinion called for a nuclear freeze in the early 1980s in response to a massive American military buildup initiated by U.S. President Ronald Reagan. In short order, several books by Mennonite authors appeared condemning the nuclear arms race and exposing the inadequacy of the "just war" logic for the nuclear age: *Nuclear Holocaust and Christian Hope* (1982), *Facing Nuclear War* (1982), and *Faith in a Nuclear Age* (1983). Mainstream Protestants as well as Catholics joined Mennonites in advocating a nuclear pacifism that considered any use of nuclear weapons immoral. In the 1970s and 1980s a small but persistent number of Mennonites deliberately trespassed on facilities involved in the production of nuclear weapons. These people were arrested and served time in prison because of their opposition to U.S. nuclear arms policies. Mennonites, however, have not acted collectively as denominations in a concerted response to the nuclear threat. They have not engaged in sustained political action comparable to the Mennonite response to °conscription. The Mennonite witness against the terror and spiritual idolatry of nuclear arms has been largely carried by the Peace Section of Mennonite Central Committee along with selected individuals and academic leaders.   DBK

Bibl. on War and Peace (1987), 634-39; Ronald J. Sider and Richard K. Taylor, *Nuclear Holocaust and Christian Hope* (Downers Grove, Ill.: InterVarsity Press, 1982); Donald B. Kraybill, *Facing Nuclear War* (Scottdale, 1982); idem, "Tam-

ing the Nuclear Threat," *Chr. Living* (Dec. 1982), 12-16; idem, "Hearing the Laughter of God," *The Other Side* (Oct. 1982), 11-14; idem, "The Cloud, the Rainbow and the Dove," *GH* (Aug. 6, 1985), 541-43; Duane Beachey, *Faith in a Nuclear Age* (Scottdale, 1983); John K. Stoner, "Take the Message to Jerusalem," *Sojourners* (Aug. 1980), 91-93; idem, "Conscientious Objection to Nuclear Deterrence," *GH* (Oct. 2, 1979), 782; Gordon D. Kaufman, *Theology for a Nuclear Age* (Philadelphia: Westminster Press, 1985); Urbane Peachey, ed. *Mennonite Statements on Peace and Social Concerns, 1900-1978* (Akron Pa.: MCC, 1980), 164-65, 217-18, 232-35; Donald B. Kraybill and John P. Ranck, *Nuclear War and Lancaster County* (Elizabethtown, Pa.: The Star Co., 1981), a 105-p. monograph available from the authors.

See also Disarmament; Nonresistance; Peace.

Nueva Holanda Colony, Bolivia, located about 90 km. (56 mi.) ne. of Santa Cruz. It was established in 1983 by settlers from the Reinland colony, mostly those Reinland residents who had come originally from the Menno Colony in Paraguay. The reasons for leaving the Reinland Colony were growing problems with thieves, disunity in the church, and proximity to the city.

The church is oriented to the °Sommerfeld Mennonites, with bishop Peter Giesbrecht as their leader. In 1985 there were 157 baptized church members in Nueva Holanda with a total population of 394.

The group purchased 10,000 hectares (24,700 acres) of land and has established four villages. Several village schools and a church had been established by 1987. Farms in Nueva Holanda are mechanized, but motorized vehicles (cars, pickup trucks, other trucks, and motorcycles) are not used. There is a flour mill in Nueva Holanda, the only one in the Mennonite colonies in Bolivia.   IHie

See also Bergthal Mennonites.

Nuevo Ideál Settlement. See Durango Colony, Mexico.

Nursing. As one of the most dynamic professions, nursing is a natural vocation for people in a church committed to communicating Christ through caring ministries. Both in North America and around the world, nursing gives form to a theology of °discipleship. Nursing is a humanistic and scientific discipline which focuses on caring behaviors and skills in assisting individuals, families, and communities to attain and maintain a health status congruent with their cultural values and life patterns, and their physiological, psychosocial, and spiritual needs. "Humanistic" refers to attributes which denote a person's abilities to express compassion, empathy, respect, and reverence for life. The scope of nursing practice involves the nursing process, observation and counseling, use of resources, managing ancillary staff, peer review and setting standards, professional growth, and research. The nursing process includes assessment, nursing diagnosis, planning, intervention, and evaluation. Nursing diagnosis is the description of a condition or problem which the nurse is able and licensed to treat.

There has been a slow increase in the number of men and non-white nurses. Initially Mennonite nurses were educated in diploma (hospital) schools. With the national goal of having two levels of entry into nursing from degree programs, and the development of one Associate Degree (AD) and five Bachelor of Science in Nursing (BSN) programs in Mennonite institutions (°nursing education), more Mennonite murses have collegiate degrees. The number of Mennonite nurses with master's and doctoral degrees is increasing.

Many Mennonite nurses are employed in hospitals, but increasing numbers are employed in °community health settings, schools, clinics, and in nursing education. Mennonite nurses tend to be at home or be employed part-time during childrearing years, and then return to employment in nursing. Many Mennonite nurses are involved in church service including missions, Mennonite Central Committee, °voluntary service, Mennonite institutions, teaching, and local congregations.

Mennonite Nurses' Association (MNA) was formed in 1942. It is a national organization promoting and supporting Christian nursing in North America and other countries. Along with the Mennonite Medical Association, MNA publishes "The Christian Nurse" in the *Mennonite Medical Messenger*. NJW

See also Medicine.

Nursing Education (ME III:928). In the 1960s approximately three times as many Mennonite students as non-Mennonite students chose nursing as an area of study. By 1987, in North America, the Mennonite Church (MC) had one Associate Degree (AD) program, four Bachelor of Science in Nursing (BSN) programs, and one Registered Nurse (RN) completion program (RNs only). These schools all have voluntary National League for Nursing accreditation indicating excellence in standards.

Hesston College has a two-year AD program, including general education as well as nursing courses. The AD graduate is prepared to plan, provide, and evaluate nursing care for individuals and small groups of patients in hospitals or long-term care facilities, offices, or clinics.

The schools with BSN programs include: Goshen College, Eastern Mennonite College, Bethel College, and Mennonite College of Nursing at Bloomington, Ill. The BSN is a four-year program which includes general education and nursing courses, nursing theory and practice, community health, and leadership. A BSN graduate is prepared to provide preventive, therapeutic, and rehabilitative health care and to direct care given by the nursing team to patients in a variety of settings. The BSN is required for school nursing and °community health work and is recommended for work overseas. It is the basis for graduate study at the master's level, for teaching, for administative positions, and for research.

Bluffton College admits only RNs to a nursing program providing upper-level nursing courses together with supporting and general education courses required for a BSN. Each of the other BSN programs admit RNs as well as beginning students.

During the 1970s and early 1980s nursing enrollments were high. In the later 1980s declining enrollment became a major national problem with enrollments decreasing 23 percent from 1983 to 1987. During the same years, there was a decline in en-

rollment of 40.5 percent in Mennonite nursing programs. In 1988 the Bluffton nursing program was being phased out with the last class having been admitted in the fall of 1988.

In other countries, Mennonite nursing programs include: Dhamtari Christian Hospital School of Nursing, India (MC); Shirati Nurses Training Unit, Tanzania (MC); Zambia Enrolled Nurses Training School (BIC); and a program at the Kajiji hospital (MB) in Zaire. The schools in Dhamtari and Shirati are three-year hospital programs with an optional additional midwifery course. The Kajiji program is a four-year program. The hospital at Filadelfia, Fernheim Colony, Paraguay, has had a nursing education program for 40 years; in 1988 it graduated 15 "tecnicas de enfermeria" (nursing technicians) from a three-year, government-recognized course in 1987. The Mennonite Christian Hospital in Taiwan also has a nursing school program. NJW

Current listings of nursing programs are found in *MC Yearbook*, e.g., (1988-89) 130; *Courier*, 3, no. 2 (1988), 15.

See also Education; Medicine; Professions; Zaire.

Nyanga. See Zaire.

NYS Fellowship of the Mennonite Church (MC). In the late 1960s and early 1970s lay and pastoral leaders with intense desire to mobilize human resources for mission efforts formed a fellowship of 16 congregations from four different conferences, Indiana-Michigan Mennonite Conference (1), Lancaster Mennonite Conference (4), Mennonite Conference of Ontario [and Quebec] (1) Conservative Mennonite Conference (8), and two emerging house fellowships. Organizational structures established in 1973, were to facilitate fellowship and local mission projects while all other church polity questions remained with the established conferences.

The resources needed by newly emerging churches eventually encouraged the NYS Fellowship to undertake all conference functions. (The State of New York prohibits the use of "New York State" in titles of nongovernment organizations; hence the name *NYS Fellowship* rather than *New York State Fellowship*.) In 1987 17 congregations with 1,007 members look to the fellowship for all conference functions, and 6 conservative Mennonite congregations, (1,026 members), maintain dual affiliation. A delegate assembly with an executive committee is responsible for policies and direction. A ministerial committee is responsible for the credentials and nurture of pastoral leaders. An executive secretary carries out administrative tasks and serves as as resource for affiliated congregations. MHei

MC Yearbook (1986-87), 75-76.

Nzelenga Mulehu (Philip) (1900-1983), a Zairian Mennonite Brethren pastor, evangelist, and overseer of village work, was born at Matshitshi in the vicinity of the Mennonite Brethren mission station of Kafumba. He was one of the early converts to Christianity. He finished primary school at Kafumba and graduated in the first graduating class of the Bible school.

Nzelenga then established a church at Mbutu. He

was ordained and became an overseer of 40 village evangelistic posts with schools teaching the first and second grades. He walked for miles to bring people the gospel.

During the Mulele rebellion Nzelenga and his family hid in the forest. His wife and daughter were caught and underwent indescribable experiences in a distant rebel camp. Nzelenga gave himself up to the soldiers, but was not reunited with his family for more than a year. After the rebellion he returned to the church at Mbutu where he continued to serve until his death.   ILF

J. B. Toews, *The Mennonite Brethren Church in Zaire* (Fresno: MB Board of Christian Literature, 1978), 146, 226.

O

Oberholtzer, John H. (ME IV:13). In the earlier decades of the 20th c. the work of historians C. Henry °°Smith, H. P. °°Krehbiel, J. C. Wenger, and others described the prominent role John H. Oberholtzer played in the founding in 1847 of what became known as the °°Eastern District Conference and in 1860, of the General Conference Mennonite Church. More recently scholars have more thoroughly evaluated Oberholtzer and his contributions to North American Mennonite church life from a historical and theological viewpoint.

Robert °Friedmann took a rather negative view of Oberholtzer's contributions, maintaining that he and his group followed "the way of adjustment and greater conformity to the general pattern of American Protestantism which proved to be a way toward full secularization and loss of substance" (Friedmann, 1949, p. 260). An article by Leland Harder used the tools of a sociologist and theologian and cogently affirmed that "the concepts of organizational disequilibrium, which are not apparent in Friedmann's interpretation, are also needed in order to appreciate the degree to which Oberholtzer's ideas do represent consistent and authentic renewal" (Harder, 1963, p. 330).

In 1972, John S. Oyer, editor of *Mennonite Quarterly Review*, brought together for the first time in translation an important and balanced collection of primary sources on the *Oberholtzer Division of 1847*, namely the recently discovered Mensch papers from the Old Mennonite perspective, as well as fresh translations of Oberholtzer's own documents from the new Mennonite position. Oyer offers them "as an invitation to scholars to reexamine and possibly to reinterpret" what he suggests may be "psychological dynamics of the Division" and "personality frictions," and finally asks whether "they reveal a peculiar Anabaptist-Mennonite psychology of strife?" (p. 328).

S. F. °Pannabecker's comprehensive history of the General Conference Mennonite Church, *Open Doors* (1975), calls Oberholtzer "a man of considerable ability and initiative" and delineates his major contributions as (1) the authorship of the *Ordnung*, the first known Mennonite church constitution (1847). (2) The practice of *Kinderlehre*, or children's classes: by 1847 Oberholtzer had begun children's instruction classes on Sunday afternoons, which consisted of singing, praying, memorization of Scripture, and explaining the catechism. These led in 1858 to the establishment of one of the first Mennonite Sunday schools. (3) Oberholtzer also edited, printed, and published *Der Religiöser Botschafter* (The Religious Messenger), the first Mennonite church paper to last beyond one issue, (1852ff.). This paper, and its successor, *Das Christliche Volksblatt* (The Chris-

tian People's Paper), did much to establish the Mennonite General Conference in the 1860s, to promote the founding of °°Wadsworth Institute, to publicize mission work among the Indian peoples in Oklahoma, and ultimately to bring about the amalgamation into the General Conference the large numbers of Mennonite immigrants from Russia, who arrived in the 1870s.

John L. Ruth's narrative history of the Franconia Conference and Eastern District Conference, *Maintaining the Right Fellowship* (1984), has added some fascinating, colorful lore to our knowledge of Oberholtzer and his contributions. Ruth gently chides scholars when referring to Oberholtzer's carefully written but unfinished 73-page manuscript of 1884 residing in the Grubb Collection at Bluffton College, stating "Surely, the pathos of this old man's feeling has deserved a closer look than the fellowship he founded has felt motivated to give."

John Oberholtzer's most lasting contribution to Mennonite life in North America was not his polemical positions or writings, perhaps not even his important *Ordnung*, which occasioned the unfortunate 1847 schism, but rather his role as editor, printer, and publisher of the first Mennonite periodical in the New World, the lineal ancestor of General Conference German periodicals down to the present day *Der* °°*Bote*. Likewise this man with the same press, alone among Mennonites in his day, and often till late into the night, translated, set type, printed, and disseminated catechisms, confessions, children's hymns, and devotional books, the effects of which are still felt in the spiritual formation of Mennonite lives. JHF

Robert Friedmann, *Mennonite Piety Through the Centuries* (Goshen: Menn. Hist. Soc., 1949); Leland Harder, "The Oberholtzer Division: 'Reformation' or 'Secularization'?" *MQR*, 37 (1963), 310-31; H. P. Krehbiel, *History of the General Conference* (publ. by the author, 1898); *MQR*, 4 (1972), sp. issue; S. F. Pannabecker, *Open Doors* (Newton, 1975); John L. Ruth, *Maintaining the Right Fellowship* (Scottdale, 1984); C. Henry Smith, *Story of the Mennonites* (Newton, 1941).

Occupations. For much of Mennonite history, to be a Mennonite was to be engaged in farming or a closely related occupation. It was not true in the beginning, and it is no longer true, but agricultural occupations were the norm for centuries for most Mennonites of European origin. The homogeneity and solidarity of Mennonite communities was strengthened by the nearly universal Mennonite dedication to agriculture, at which Mennonites have excelled and for which they are widely recognized.

Early Mennonites, however, were rarely farmers. They were city folk in Switzerland, North Germany, and Holland. As such they dedicated themselves to

°urban occupations. Many early Mennonite leaders were well educated and some were from prominent families. In Switzerland and South Germany, Michael °Sattler had been a monk and Balthasar °Hubmaier a theologian and pastor. Pilgram °Marpeck was a civil engineer. °Menno Simons of Friesland was a former priest. Less prominent and less educated Mennonites were generally artisans such as smiths, hatmakers, basket makers, and weavers, as the names in *Martyrs Mirror* reveal.

Following the relatively short-lived persecution among the 16th c. Dutch Mennonites which ended in 1579, many Mennonites rose to positions of prominence. Dutch and North German Mennonites were often medical doctors, some of whom also led the church as pastors. Others were shipbuilders, owners of fishing and whaling fleets, or lumber and textile merchants. Dutch Mennonites distinguished themselves in the fine arts, also. Carel van Mander was a Haarlem poet and painter. Jan Luyken, a poet, painter, and etcher, did engravings for van Braght's *Martyrs Mirror.* Joost van den Vondel, the Dutch Shakespeare, was a deacon in the church before reverting to Catholicism. A number of Mennonites were personal friends of Rembrandt van Rijn, and may have influenced his painting.

The rise of the Dutch Mennonites to prominence in °medicine, °business, and the arts, however, was made possible only by the relative religious freedom in The Netherlands from the late 16th c. on. In other areas Mennonites experienced more severe and long-lasting persecution which prevented success in prominent urban occupations.

Isolated rural areas in Switzerland and South Germany afforded greater freedom from three centuries of Swiss-German Mennonite persecution than did Zürich and other cities. Mennonites quickly developed skills in both crop production and animal husbandry even when they were employed only as tenants and farmhands. This was frequently the case, since they were usually not allowed to own land.

Wealthy nobles were sometimes willing to offer both limited sanctuary and work for farmers and artisans on their private estates. The Hutterites in particular might not have survived had they not been sheltered on various occasions by sympathetic nobles and princes. In addition to agriculture, they developed notable skills in pottery making (°ceramics), smithing, shoemaking, carpentry, and bookbinding.

The Dutch and North German Mennonites who were invited to Prussia and later to Russia included both farmers and artisans. Those in Prussia distinguished themselves by draining and then making productive the lowlands of the Vistula River (°water technology). The greatest accomplishments in agriculture and related industries, however, were made by those who accepted Catherine the Great's invitation to form nearly autonomous settlements on formerly unproductive land in the Ukraine and Russia. After initial hardships, they transformed the steppes into productive land, growing grain, introducing adapted varieties of fruit, and raising livestock. Johann °°Cornies (1789-1848) distinguished himself in upgrading agriculture and education in the Molotschna and Chortitza colonies, as well as serving as something of a Mennonite ambassador to the Russian authorities. Cornies also helped the Hutterites reestablish communal agriculture and industry after they had reached the Ukraine following terrible persecution in areas of what later became Czechoslovakia and Romania.

As their farms prospered and population grew, some Russian Mennonites began agriculturally-related industries, managing prosperous flour mills, creameries, and farm implement factories. The majority, however, remained farmers and farmhands. Some attained fabulous wealth and bought the private °estates of impoverished Russian nobles. Some, unable to buy land themselves, worked as day laborers or craftsmen, usually for fellow Mennonites (°°landless).

Due to their reputation as productive and industrious farmers in Europe, countries such as Canada, the United States, and later Mexico, Paraguay, Brazil, Bolivia, and Belize welcomed various Mennonite groups in the 18th-20th c. Virtually all new Mennonite immigrant settlements in the New World were agricultural, so that the first generations of Mennonites in the New World were predominantly farmers or engaged in providing goods and services for fellow Mennonites who were farmers. This was true both for the culturally and religiously °conservative groups (Amish, Hutterites, Old Colony, Sommerfeld, and Old Order Mennonites) and initially for the larger and eventually more culturally and religiously progressive groups. (Mennonite Church [MC], General Conference Mennonites, and Mennonite Brethren).

Since the mid-20th c., however, economic and social forces in North America have resulted in marked transformations in the occupations of members of the more progressive Mennonite groups. The mechanization of agriculture, the cost-price squeeze, and the pressure for large-scale agriculture to maximize profits have driven many progressive Mennonites out of agriculture. More notably, their sons and daughters have been attracted to a variety of managerial and professional occupations offering higher and more regular income and higher status than farming. In many cases higher education, often obtained at Mennonite colleges, has facilitated and perhaps even accelerated the transition to nonagricultural occupations.

Recent empirical °sociological studies document the North American Mennonite exodus from farming into the °professions and °business. Comparable studies in both the General Conference Mennonite Church and the Mennonite Church (MC) have revealed that the percentage of farmers has been cut in half in 20 years. In General Conference congregations, the percentage of men in farming declined from 32 to 16 percent from 1960 to 1980. In Mennonite Church congregations the percentage declined from 39 to 19 percent from 1963 to 1982.

The exodus from farming was countered by a near doubling in the percentages of Mennonites employed in professional and technical occupations in both groups in the same period. Among General Conference Mennonites of Canada and the United States the percentage of men and women employed in professional occupations increased from 16 to 28.

In the Mennonite Church the percentage for men doubled from 8 to 16, and for employed women and men combined it doubled from 10 to 20 percent. The percentages of persons employed as managers, officials, and proprietors increased from 5 to 8 percent in the General Conference from 1960 to 1980, and from 5 to 11 percent in the Mennonite Church from 1963 to 1982. A recent study of Mennonite Brethren congregations in Canada and the United States revealed 25 percent of all employed members to be in the professions, 20 percent in business, and only 18 percent in farming, as of 1982.

The trend is clear for North American progressive Mennonites. They are rapidly leaving farming as a livelihood, and taking up business and professional occupations. North American Mennonite women of the progressive groups are now just as likely to be employed outside the home as are their non-Mennonite neighbors. Those employed outside the home are even more likely than Mennonite men to have professional occupations, although many Mennonite women are employed in relatively low-paying service professions such as teaching, °nursing, and social work.

While the transformation out of agriculture is clearly evident for the progressive Mennonite groups of North America, the culturally conservative groups (Hutterites, Amish) are not leaving farming as rapidly. Their preference for agriculture is more deeply rooted and often given religious significance. Choice of occupation is less likely to be a matter of individual choice, and is much more heavily influenced by group sanction. Hutterites will permit young men to leave the *Bruderhof* for a short time to try life in the surrounding "world," but to remain a Hutterite necessitates return to the colony and work in agriculture or a related area. Work choices are not made by the individual, but by the colony boss.

The Amish exercise greater individual freedom than the Hutterites, but farming is still strongly preferred. Yet the high cost and shortage of land and Amish proximity to urban areas and suburban development have forced many Amish, particularly the young, to take off-farm jobs, even if the eventual goal is to get a farm. In some communities less than half the Amish are now engaged in farming. If non-farm work is necessitated, carpentry and factory jobs, preferably among other Amish workmen, are preferred.

Intermediate between the conservative and progressive groups are the Church of God in Christ Mennonite (Holdeman), Old Order Mennonites, and others. They retain a preference for farming and related occupations, but have also had to adapt to economic forces in North American society by taking a variety of off-farm jobs. Preferred are those which allow one to stay in the rural community.

Ethnic Mennonites in Latin America have been able to stay in agriculture somewhat more easily than their North American cousins, due to lower land costs and in some cases greater tolerance of Latin American governments for the nearly autonomous Mennonite colonies. (Colonies are no longer acceptable or possible in North America, except among the Hutterites.) Countries which have permitted Low-German (Dutch-Russian) Mennonite and Amish (Swiss-German) agricultural colonies include Mexico, Paraguay, Brazil, Bolivia, and Belize. These colonies have not prospered to the degree of the earlier colonies in Russia.

Assimilation into the larger North American society among the progressive Mennonite groups has caused a weakening of earlier prohibitions against previously forbidden occupations. Business, legal, medical, and other professional positions requiring extensive interaction with non-Mennonites and even non-Christians, often in urban areas, are now generally socially approved rather than discouraged or forbidden. Whereas a career in °law would have been highly suspect among even most progressive Mennonites until at least the mid-20th c., 1987 witnessed a symbolically important event in Mennonite circles, when a practicing attorney, Joseph Lapp, was installed as president of Eastern Mennonite College in Virginia.

Conversely, involvement in the brewing of °°alcoholic beverages or production or sale of tobacco products is probably more suspect among progressive Mennonites in the 1980s than it was previously, partly due to the early 20th c. temperance movement in North America and partly due to modern health concerns.

Military employment or service and careers in °government and public service have traditionally been discouraged or forbidden in most Mennonite groups, since they were thought to conflict with the °peace position and to necessitate moral compromise. However, toleration of these occupations became somewhat common in The Netherlands as early as 1700 and is growing in recent years in North America. Mennonites of Dutch/Russian origin have been more accepting of government posts than has been true for Swiss-origin Mennonites. Involvement of Mennonites in government in North America has been most visible in Canada.

Firm data about occupations of non-ethnic Mennonites are lacking, but it would appear that they are less likely than ethnic Mennonites to be employed in agriculture, especially in North America, Latin America, and Europe. Given the rural residence of considerable numbers of Mennonites in Africa, Indonesia, and India, it is likely that there are appreciable numbers employed in agriculture there, but with a variety of other occupations also present. MLY

Cornelius J. Dyck, *An Introduction to Mennonite History* (Scottdale, 1967, 1981); F. H. Epp, *Mennonites in Canada I*; Leland Harder, *Fact Book of Congregational Membership, 1980/81* (Newton: General Conference Mennonite Church, 1982); John A. Hostetler, *Hutterite Society* (1974); idem, *Amish Society* (1980); Yoder, *MC Census* (1985); *MB Profile, 1972-82* in *Direction*, 14, no. 2 (1985), sp. issue.

See also Acculturation; Conservative Mennonites; Industrialization; Work Ethic.

Ohio (ME IV:24) is the home of 350 congregations of various Mennonites and Amish and 13 Brethren in Christ churches, totalling about 32,000 baptized members. Since many families have unbaptized children the total number of people would exceed 50,000. Of the 215 congregations that are some variant of Amish or Beachy Amish, about 83 percent

N

LEGEND
MENNONITES IN OHIO
== International boundary
-- State boundary
-·-· Counties
★ State capitol
● Cities and towns
▲ Church camps
~ Rivers
----- Approx. border of O.O. Amish settlement (1985)
O.O. Amish settlements (est. membership)

Church Membership
○ 0-250
○ 250-500
○ 500-1000
○ 1000-1500
○ 1500-2000
○ 2000-2500
○ 2500-5000
○ More than 5000

Membership includes BA, BIC, CGCM, EMC, GC, MC, and OOM (est.) congregations. Totals are based on congregations' place of address and may not reflect their exact location or the actual distribution of members.

OHIO

are Old Order Amish. "New Order Amish," a recent development, and Beachy Amish make up the other congregations. Amish baptized members total about 14,500, while Mennonites and Brethren in Christ number about 17,500.

Amish congregations seldom exceed 100 baptized members, but among major Mennonite groups many congregations are larger. Among the nearly 150 Mennonite and Brethren in Christ congregations, two-thirds are affiliated with the Mennonite Church (MC). Of the 11 General Conference Mennonite (GCM) congregations, three hold membership also with the Ohio Conference of the Mennonite Church (MC). Eleven congregations are not affiliated with a conference. The Evangelical Mennonite Church (EMCh) has four congregations in Ohio. Four churches belong to the Mid-West Mennonite Fellowship; an equal number consider themselves Fellowship Churches (also known as Nationwide Fellowship). Some half-dozen other Mennonite varieties each have one or two congregations.

Mennonites and Amish are often heavily intermingled, particularly in Ohio's densest Mennonite-Amish area centered on Wayne and °Holmes Cos. In the roughly rectangular area from the Wooster, Smithville, Orrville, Dalton area, and southward to Wilmot, Dundee, Sugarcreek, and Baltic, and from there westward to Clark, then northward through Millersburg, Holmesville, and back to Wooster, lies one of the largest combined settlements of Amish and Mennonites in North America. It covers a span of about 35 miles north and south and 20 miles east and west. In that locale are found virtually every variety of Amish and Mennonite in the state and about half of the congregations.

Surrounding this concentration, which also touches the counties of Stark, Tuscarawas, and Coshocton, are many more scattered churches and communities. There are pockets of Mennonites and a few Amish in the Hartville and Louisville area of Stark Co., several congregations in the Wadsworth area of Medina Co., and some in °Ashland and Richland Cos. To the south, in Morrow, Knox, and Licking Cos. are found more than a dozen Amish congregations. Ohio's second heaviest concentration of Amish, almost all Old Order Amish, lies in °Geauga, Trumbull, Lake, and Ashtabula Cos. (45 congregations).

Historic concentrations of Mennonites continue in eastern Ohio in Mahoning and Columbiana Cos., in west-central Ohio in the regions of Plain City and West Liberty, and northward around Elida and Bluffton. The nw. corner of the state has numerous Mennonite congregations in the area surrounding West Unity, Archbold, and Wauseon. Brethren in Christ congregations are found primarily in the Dayton-Springfield area west of Columbus and in the Massillon-Canton area of Stark Co.

Significant cultural changes and considerable shifting across boundary lines of some groups have occurred in the last several decades. Hundreds of young men spent two years in °alternative service, either °voluntary service or I-W service in the 1950s and 1960s. Most of them worked in large metropolitan areas. Mass evangelism in the 1950s brought ferment and renewal with the Brunk tent meetings and the Christian Laymen's Tent Evangelism Association, which was based at Orrville, Ohio (°revivalism). Numerous Amish families moved into the rapidly growing Beachy Amish Mennonite congregations (often known as Beachy Amish Fellowship churches) and the Conservative Mennonite Conference (MC). A few Amish joined the Church of God in Christ Mennonite (Holdeman). Some Conservative Mennonite Conference congregations in the 1950s and 1960s withdrew in protest against the changes occurring in that conference. They sometimes became known as "non-conference conservatives." In 1987 some are still unaffiliated but increasing numbers are moving toward or have joined the Fellowship Churches movement. Several Old Order Mennonite (Wisler) churches in the 1970s added Bible conferences and Bible study meetings to their program and began to move toward the Fellowship Churches affiliation, and away from their former "Wisler" ties. There are now three kinds of "Fellowship Churches" in the state—those sometimes known as "Nationwide" Fellowship, the Mid-West Mennonite Fellowship, and the Conservative Mennonite Fellowship. These congregations tend to emphasize similar patterns of plain °dress, often have Christian day schools for their children, and operate with considerable independence.

Among the Beachy Amish there are several groups, the more traditional ones still using some German and not having Sunday schools. Among the Old Order Amish are a number of groups who have minor differences in dress, the application of the °°ban, and in their outlook on what constitutes "worldliness." In the last decade the "New Order Amish" have developed. To the outsider they appear similar to the Old Order but they permit hard rubber tires on buggies and rubber-tired tractors for field use, and they make more serious attempts to keep young people in line with standards. They are considered a renewal movement. The "Schwartzentruber Amish," comprising eight congregations, are the most conservative and withdrawn of the Amish. Except where someone is under the ban, many of the various types of Amish will generally speak to each other readily in the familiar "Pennsylvania Dutch" and intermingle freely in weekday or neighborly activities, even if they will not worship or engage in the rite of communion together.

The Mennonite Church (MC) with more than 90 congregations in Ohio, has experienced rapid °acculturation and general loss of plain dress in recent decades. With it has come more emphasis upon trained and salaried ministers; a general rise in the level of °education; more involvement in the °professions; more participation in °urban ministries, social issues, and voting; more involvement in public high school activities; much greater diversification in °worship patterns; some influence from the more °charismatically oriented groups, and other changes. This is particularly true of the Ohio Conference congregations and to a somewhat lesser extent among Conservative Mennonite Conference churches. The former Ohio and Eastern Conference had developed historically into a large conglomerate that included 130 congregations in 15 states by 1972, and nearly 16,000 members by 1978. The following year the eastern wing peacefully organized into the fully autonomous Atlantic Coast Conference. In 1987 the Ohio Conference of the Mennonite Church has 80 congregations with a membership of 11,135. All but seven of its congregations are in Ohio. A number of congregations have other affiliations—General Conference Mennonite Church (GCM), °Afro-American Mennonite Association, the loosely identified group of intentional "church communities" (*MC Yearbook* (1988-89), 31-33, and °Concilio Nacional de Iglesias Menonitas Hispañas (National Council of Hispanic Mennonite Churches).

For many years the slogan "a mission outpost for every congregation" was popular in the Ohio Conference. Fifteen new mission churches were begun in Ohio in the 1950s, 12 in the 1960s, and 3 in the 1970s. Two more have begun in the 1980s.

Major changes have occurred in Ohio in the last several decades in regards to Mennonite and Amish institutions. When consolidation of public schools brought the loss of one- or two-room country schools, the Amish began establishing their own °private schools. The first few began in Wayne Co. in the 1940s and had non-Amish teachers who were trained. Nearly all now have Amish teachers. One person who has been a long-time member of the Amish School Committee, who has done more than anyone else, and who is well-known in the state capital, Columbus, for assisting new schools is Henry J. Hershberger of Kidron. A recent history of the Amish school movement, *A Struggle To Be Separate* indicates that in 1985 there were 145 such schools in Ohio, 91 of which were in the general Wayne-Holmes area. When curriculum became a problem, the Amish began writing their own textbooks or reprinting favored texts. About 75 percent of the curriculum is thus Amish-produced.

A few Mennonite private Christian schools began also in the late 1940s, e.g., Crown Hill near Smithville and Sonnenberg near Kidron. The former closed after 10 years and the latter by 1964. More conservatively oriented congregations began building schools in the 1960s and 1970s; in 1987 many such congregations operate parochial elementary schools. Meanwhile, after years of preparation, the Ohio Conference (MC) established Central Christian High School at Kidron in 1961 with grades 9-12. In 1987 it had an enrollment of 210 in grades 7-12. From the beginning emphasis has been placed upon broad-based support and quality education, a goal it has successfully maintained despite the support many Mennonites give to public schools by providing students and teachers. Central Christian has made a significant contribution to Ohio Mennonites.

Ohio has the only Mennonite °Bible institute in the United States. Rosedale Bible Institute at Irwin, near Columbus, is operated by the Conservative Mennonite Conference. It began with the Berlin Bible School, first held in January 1952 at the Pleasant View Conservative Mennonite Church with 136 students. In 1964 it moved to Irwin and two years later college-level courses were added. After purchasing the Ontario Mennonite Bible Institute library, adding buildings, and sending Gospel teams and a chorale out frequently, Rosedale Bible Institute began to have wide appeal. Enrollment

reached 393 students from 26 states and three foreign countries in 1987. Rosedale Mennonite Missions, the missions agency for the Conservative Mennonite Conference is also located at Irwin. Overseeing a number of voluntary service and church planting endeavors in the United States, it has 106 assigned field workers in nine states and four foreign countries. Its annual budget is $1,160,000.

Messiah Bible School at Carbon Hill, Ohio is operated by the Conservative Mennonite Fellowship. It is a winter Bible school with four short terms and a summer teacher's institute. Board members are from Ontario, Maryland, Indiana, and Ohio. A variety of short courses in biblical studies, church history and missions, and practical Christian living are taught usually by ministers. Rigorous social standards and plain dress requirements are outlined in the school's catalog.

Bluffton College, affiliated with the General Conference Mennonite Church, continues its strong program of providing a liberal arts education in a Christian college context. Enrollment is above 600. Its Mennonite Historical Library includes special emphasis on Swiss Mennonites, the archives of the Africa Inter-Mennonite Mission, and the records of Central District Conference of the General Conference Mennonite Church. Smaller attempts at preservation of °historical materials have begun at the German Culture Museum at Walnut Creek, and with the formation of the Kidron Community Historical Society and the Stark County Mennonite and Amish Historical Society. A large and strong °museum program, not exclusively Mennonite-focused, is found near Archbold with the Sauder Museum.

Ohio has a half-dozen °voluntary service units and nine Mennonite Central Committee °SELFHELP and thrift shops. In 1987 °church planting efforts were underway at Bellefontaine, Canton, Columbus, Fremont, and Grafton. Increasingly, Mennonites are involved in °health and human service facilities. Ironically, the pioneer Mennonite °°Home for the Aged at Rittman closed its doors in 1974, the victim of rising standards in building codes. However, whether it be private or community-based health facilities and retirement centers, such as Bluffton Community Hospital, Mennonite Memorial Home at Bluffton, Green Hills at West Liberty, OrrVilla at Orrville, Walnut Hills at Walnut Creek, or Fairlawn Haven at Archbold, Mennonites are involved at many levels. Adriel School (in earlier days the Orphan's Home or Children's Home) at West Liberty has changed focus several times. In the late 1980s, it features residential and day treatment programs for children with learning, behavioral, or emotional problems. Other institutions are the Hattie Larlham Foundation at Mantua for children with developmental °disabilities and the Sunshine Children's Home at Maumee. The Sunnyhaven Children's Home at Plain City is for trainable retarded children and adults.

The village of Kidron has become a central meeting place for several major activities involving Mennonites and Amish. The annual Ohio Mennonite °Relief Sale is held on the grounds of Central Christian High School and raises $200,000 per year for Mennonite Central Committee. Several huge auctions of horse-drawn implements each year draw thousands of Amish and others, some from out of state, to the village. Kidron also has conference headquarters for the Ohio Conference of the Mennonite Church.

The Holmes-Wayne Co. area has in recent decades seen a tremendous mushrooming of cottage industries and small businesses and entrepreneurs. The annual *Down Home Shoppers Guide: Ohio's Complete Amish Country Tour Guide* documents several hundred businesses that are operated by Amish or Mennonites or that cater to the "Dutch" or Amish theme. With Berlin, Walnut Creek, and Sugarcreek as hubs, °tourism has become big business. Many Amish and some Mennonites are farmers or engage in agriculturally related vocations, but increasing numbers are driving to cities or are being transported there for work. °Urbanization and commercialism are encroaching upon the peaceful rural Amish and Mennonite communities in Ohio.   JOLe

Conference Organs: *Ohio Evangel,* Ohio Conference of the Mennonite Church, bimonthly; *Brotherhood Beacon,* Conservative Mennonite Conference, monthly. Directories and Annual Reports: *MC Yearbook* (1988-89), 31-33; *GCM Handbook*; *The New American Almanac* (Baltic, Ohio: Ben J. Raber), an annual list of Amish congregations; *Minutes (EMCh)* (1986); *Ohio Beachy Fellowship Family Directory* (Sugarcreek: Schlabach Printers, 1985); *Ohio Amish Directory: Holmes County and Vicinity* (Sugarcreek: Schlabach Printers, 1981); *Ohio Amish Directory: Geauga County and Vicinity* (Sugarcreek: Schlabach Printers, 1982); *Directory of the Fellowship Churches, 1986-87* (Farmington, N.M.: Lamp and Light Publishers, 1986); *Down Home Shoppers Guide: Ohio's Complete Amish Country Tour* (Millersburg, Ohio: Down Home Publications, 1987); *Minutes (BIC)* (1986); Annual Reports, Ohio Mennonite Conference of the Mennonite Church, various years. See also Grant M. Stoltzfus, *Mennonites of the Ohio and Eastern Conference* (Scottdale, 1969); Ivan J. Miller, *History of the Conservative Mennonite Conference* (Grantsville, Md.: Ivan J. and Della Miller, 1985); Levi Miller, *Our People: The Amish and Mennonites of Ohio* (Scottdale, 1983); Stan Nussbaum, *You Must Be Born Again: A History of the Evangelical Mennonite Church* (Fort Wayne, Ind.: Evangelical Mennonite Church, 1979); *Histories of the Congregations of the Church of God in Christ, Mennonite,* (Moundridge, Ks.: Gospel Publishers, 1975); Elmer S. Yoder, *The Beachy Amish Mennonite Fellowship Churches* (Hartville, Ohio: Diakonia Ministries, 1987); *Mennonites of Northwestern Ohio 1834-1984* (Archbold: Published privately, 1984); Noah Hershberger, *A Struggle To Be Separate: A History of the Ohio Amish Parochial School Movement* (Orrville, Ohio: published privately, 1985); Elmer S. Yoder and Paton Yoder, *The Hartville Amish and Mennonite Story 1905-1980* (Hartville: Stark County Mennonite and Amish Historical Society, 1980); Luthy, *Amish Settlements* (1985), 2, 10.

Ohio Conference of the Mennonite Church (MC) (ME IV:31), had its origins in the °°Ohio Mennonite Conference (1843; some accounts trace the origins of the conference to 1834) and the °°Eastern Amish Mennonite Conference (1893). These two conferences merged in 1927 to form the Ohio Mennonite and Eastern Amish Mennonite Joint Conference, later shortened to °°Ohio and Eastern Mennonite Conference. In 1978 another realignment occurred when the eastern congregations, located largely in Pennsylvania, New York, Maryland, and New Jersey, formed the Atlantic Coast Conference of the Mennonite Church. The remaining Ohio congregations then formed the Ohio Conference by the present name.

In 1986 the conference had 11,136 members (80 congregations) and 164 ministers. The congregations are located in Ohio except for four in western Penn-

sylvania, one in Michigan, and one in Kentucky. The main settlements of these congregations are in Holmes Co., Wayne Co., the area around the town of Archbold, Stark Co., the area around the town of West Liberty, Logan Co., and Columbiana Co. Some small, rather isolated, rural churches were established in the late 1940s and 1950s. Since then greater effort has gone into beginning new congregations in urban and suburban areas. In 1987 there were four congregations in Cleveland.

The Kidron community in Wayne Co. serves as a base for many of the conference's programs. Here are located the conference offices with staff serving in administration, youth ministries and nurture, and peace and service work. In the late 1960s a full-time conference minister along with overseers replaced the traditional Mennonite °bishop system of pastoral oversight to congregations. Camp Luz, a Mennonite-affiliated youth camp, is located near Kidron, as is Central Christian High School (founded 1961). The latter is a 200-student °secondary school. The bimonthly periodical of the conference is *The Ohio Evangel.*

When strong leaders have emerged in the Ohio Conference in the post-World War II period, they have tended to move outside of the conference to where the churchwide institutions are located. For example, the Elida community (Allen Co.) produced the Augsburger family of leaders (A. Don, Myron, David), and the Oak Grove congregation in Wayne Co. produced outstanding educational and theological leaders in the Meyer (Albert J.) and Yoder (John H.; Mary Ellen Yoder Meyer) families.

The conference has had theological and social interaction with the three other main Mennonite bodies within the state including joint meetings with the Central District (GCM) in 1984. Four congregations have affiliations with both conferences. Church planting and mission efforts are increasingly coordinated between these two conferences. Various informal contacts with the Conservative Mennonite Conference and the large Ohio Amish population continue.   LM

Grant M. Stoltzfus, *Mennonites of the Ohio and Eastern Conference* (Scottdale, 1969); Levi Miller, *Our People, The Amish and Mennonites of Ohio* (Scottdale, 1983); *GH* (April 5, 1988), 234-36; *MC Yearbook* (1988-89), 74-76.

Ojo de la Yegua Colony, Mexico. See Nord Colony, Mexico.

Oklahoma (ME IV:33). In 1988 there were 42 Mennonite congregations in Oklahoma. They were affiliated with six conferences as follows: The South Central Conference (MC), 4 congregations, 353 members; Western District Conference (GCM), 17 congregations, 1,517 members; Beachy Amish Mennonite Fellowship, 1 congregation, 42 members; Church of God in Christ Mennonite (Holdeman), 4 congregations; Mennonite Brethren, 15 congregations; Fellowship of Evangelical Bible Churches (formerly Evangelical Mennonite Brethren), 1 congregation. The Brethren in Christ had 3 congregations with 206 members (1986). The Old Order Amish had two settlements with three congregations (1985). Clarita (Coal Co.) with one congregation was founded in 1978. The older settlement (°°Chouteau, Mayes Co.) was started in 1910. Three other settlements existing in 1956 (Weatherford, Thomas, and Mazie) had disbanded by 1985.

There were two retirement homes: Fairview Fellowship Homes (100-bed intermediate care and 20 retirement apartments) at Fairview, and Maple Lawn Manor (60-bed intensive care facility) at Hydro. The Oklahoma Convention, a subgroup of the Western District Conference (GCM), appoints two members to the °°Oklahoma Bible Academy Board.   RSa

MC Yearbook (1988-89) 33-34, 78-79, 129, 168; Luthy, *Amish Settlements* (1985), 10; *GCM Handbook* (1988) 10, 143-144; *Minutes (BIC)* (1986), 251.

Old Colony Mennonites (ME IV:38, ME I:76) have their primary roots in those elements of the "Flemish" congregations of Danzig and West Prussia which, in 1789, founded the Chortitza (Chortitza) "Old" Colony in South Russia. In 1875 the first of some 3,200 persons from Chortitza, and its daughter settlement of Fürstenland (established 1864), settled along the Canada-United States boundary in Manitoba, west of the Red River. In 1876 the government of the Dominion of Canada accommodated them by establishing on their behalf, the Mennonite °°West Reserve of 17 townships (612 sq. mi./1,620 sq. km.). In Manitoba they proclaimed themselves the Reinländer Mennonitengemeinde, and set about recreating a cultural landscape characterized by a *Straßendorf/Gewannflur* (ME IV:821-822) pattern of occupance, an internal self-administration in which ecclesiastical authority dominated, and an economy based upon grain crops and livestock. They persisted in viewing themselves, and continued to be viewed by others, as "Altkolonisten," (Old Colonists).

By 1880 the self-imposed, preferred state of isolation of the Old Colony Mennonites in Manitoba was beginning to be breached on two fronts. Historically related but separate and less conservative elements of the °Bergthal Mennonites, who had commenced settlement on the Mennonite East Reserve in 1874, began to relocate to the still vacant portion of the more fertile, open grassland of the West Reserve. In 1880 also, the Manitoba Municipal Act made provision for secular local government. Moreover, the provisions in respect to homesteading under the Dominion Lands Act were individualistic, rendering the continuation of the communal aspects of "colony" life, as dictated by Old Colony philosophy, possible now only with universal voluntary participation. The communal life thus was becoming an anachronism that was increasingly difficult to sustain.

By 1890 "progressive" Bergthaler had created a teacher-training facility featuring instruction in the English language and secular curriculum provided for in the newly proclaimed but not yet universally imposed Manitoba Schools Act. The Mennonite Brethren had also established an evangelizing presence in the West Reserve. In sum, these internal and external factors in a major way prompted the withdrawal of substantial numbers of Old Colonists to as yet unorganized parts of the Northwest Territories (Hague, [Sask.] 1890ff.; Swift Current, [Sask.] 1900ff.).

The universal enforcement from 1916 onward, of compulsory attendance of all children ages 7-14 in provincially accredited schools, uncertainties engendered by a universal manpower registration (°conscription) during World War I, together with increasing difficulty in enforcing °discipline and conformity within Old Colony ranks, prompted a determination to emigrate. Beginning in 1922, the majority of Old Colony adherents emigrated, and established the Manitoba Colony in the Bustillos Valley of west-central Chihuahua State in Mexico, leaving behind in the West Reserve an excommunicated and leaderless rump. The Canadian daughter settlements in Saskatchewan established the Swift Current Colony in Chihuahua State, and the Patos (Hague) Colony in Durango State.

Among those who chose to remain in Canada there were, nevertheless, many who wished somehow to avoid what they considered to be the threat of °acculturation and secularization inherent in the imposition of the secular school curriculum and English as the language of instruction. Until the early 1960s it was possible to avoid this threat by homesteading beyond the fringes of built-up settlement, on the agricultural frontiers of northern Saskatchewan and in the Peace River region of Alberta and British Columbia, (Carrot River, La Crete, Fort Vermilion, Worsley, Ft. St. John, Burns Lake, Dawson Creek, etc.) When the secular world, and particularly the public schools, penetrated their settlements, the more conservative would move on. Upon the consolidation of the schools and raising of school-leaving age to 16 years in the late 1950s and early 1960s, this strategy was no longer workable, and a substantial number emigrated to new frontiers of settlement in British Honduras [Belize] and the Santa Cruz region of Bolivia.

Mexico. The Old Colony Mennonites obtained in 1921 from President Alvaro Obregón and his government, documented °privileges and immunities "in perpetuity" equivalent to those granted to their forebears by Catherine the Great of Russia.

The debt incurred by the Manitoba and Swift Current Colonies in purchasing contiguous tracts of 600 sq. km. (150,000 acres) and 300 sq. km. (75,000 acres) from the Carlos Zuloaga estates at the unrealistic price of $20.50 per hectare ($8.25 per acre) in gold, when equivalent land could have been had for $4.00 or less per hectare, proved so burdensome that the Swift Current Colony eventually relinquished some 20 percent of its area, while the Manitoba Colony struggled for 35 years before finally discharging its obligations. The Patos (Hague) Colony (1924ff.) escaped a similar dilemma because initial land purchases were restricted to immediate need.

Since 1944, the Old Colonists in Mexico have initiated or participated in 17 colonization ventures in 5 states, of which 13 have been at least a qualified success.

Of the approximately 7,000 Old Colony Mennonites who emigrated from Canada in the 1920s, some 5,500 remained in Mexico. Their net reproduction rate has consistently been one of the highest documented for any group, averaging over 4 percent, and occasionally exceeding 5 percent per year. Despite emigration to Belize (1958ff.), Bolivia (1966ff.), Paraguay (1972ff.), Argentina (1986ff.)

OLD COLONY MENNONITES
Compiled by H. L. Sawatzky (author of the article)

Daughter Colony	Mother Colony	Date/s	Population, 1988
Agua Nueva, Coahuila	Manitoba	1944 (abandoned)	
Ojo de la Yegua, Chih.	Manitoba	1948-	5012
Yermo, Durango	Manitoba	1949-1974 (abandoned)	
Conejos, Durango	Patos (Hague)	1950-1952 (abandoned)	
Cerro Gordo, Durango	Patos (Hague)	1952-1954 (abandoned)	
Manuél, Tamaulipas	Santa Clara (Sommerfelder)	1951-	1400 (est.)
Buenos Aires, Chihuahua	Manitoba	1958-	1579
La Batea, Zacatecas	Patos (Hague)	1961-	814
Capulín, Chihuahua	Manitoba	1962-	1656
Santa Rita, Chihuahua	Manitoba	1962-	500
La Honda, Zacatecas	Patos (Hague)	1964-	3834
Monclova, Coahuila	(mixed background)	1974-	40
El Cuervo, Chihuahua	Buenos Aires	1979-	600 (est.)
Las Virgenias, Chihuahua	Manitoba	1981-	1,379
Nueva Padilla, Tamaulipas	Manuél	1983-	600 (est.)
Yalnon, Campeche	Patos (Hague)	1983-	761
Hopelchen, Campeche	La Batea	1984-	200
Hecelchakan, Campeche	La Honda	1986-	164
	Manitoba (incl. GCM)	1922-	13,200
	Swift Current	1922-	2,300
	Patos (Hague)	1924-	5,675

and the United States and Canada (totalling at least 10,000), by 1988 the Old Colony population in Mexico had grown to some 40,000, representing a doubling time of approximately 16 years.

Belize. In 1958 Old Colony settlers from Mexico founded the Blue Creek (465 sq. km./176 sq. mi.) and Shipyard (70 sq. km./27 sq. mi.) colonies, in the nw. and north-central part of the Crown Colony of British Honduras. Internal tensions developed almost immediately over the level of technical innovation permissible in the development of a mixed farming economy under tropical conditions. About 40 percent abandoned the colonization effort in the first few years. Shipyard attracted the conservative majority of those who remained. The result was overcrowding at Shipyard, expressed in poverty, instability, and further emigration. The small population at Blue Creek eventually (1973) forfeited half the colony's lands in lieu of accumulated unpaid taxes. The ca. 400 colonists remaining in 1988 were affiliated in approximately equal numbers with the Kleine Gemeinde (EMCon) and the Evangelical Mennonite Mission Conference (EMMC).

In 1978 Old Colonists from Shipyard, together with a few from Blue Creek, acquired Little Belize (155 sq. km./60 sq. mi.) in ne. Belize. A small number of ultra-conservatives, desiring a total retreat from modern technology and other "worldly" influences, have affiliated themselves with like-minded people of Kleine Gemeinde, Amish, and Old Mennonite backgroumd in small settlements under primitive conditions on Upper and Lower Barton Creek in west-central Belize. In the meantime, a quit-rent settlement at Richmond Hill occupied by Old Colonists from the Peace River region of Canada, had disbanded.

The economies of all Old Colony-derived settle-ments are based on field crops (primarily corn and beans), fruit and vegetables, timber extraction, livestock and poultry, small manufacturing and service enterprise, in varying combinations. Since 1970 substantial numbers of Old Colonists have emigrated, primarily to Bolivia (Nueva Esperanza, Tres Cruces, and other colonies), where they affiliated themselves with Old Colonists from Mexico; and, since 1983, to the optimistically viewed settlements in the nearby Mexican state of Campeche, located in the Yucatan Peninsula.

Bolivia. Commencing in 1967, Old Colonists from Mexico began emigrating to Bolivia. Mennonite colonization in the Santa Cruz region of the Bolivian Oriente, below the eastern foothills of the Andes, had begun from the settlements in the Paraguayan Chaco (1954), and from Canada (1968). Though these settlers were not of Old Colony affiliation, the generally positive reports emanating from them drew Old Colonists from Mexico, where land scarcity was acute. In 1962 the President of Bolivia, Paz Estenssoro, personally committed himself to gain for Mennonites in Bolivia a status equivalent to that enjoyed by Mennonites in Mexico. By 1975, of the 13 Mennonite settlements and colonies in Bolivia, 6 were of Old Colony derivation (from Canada, Mexico and Belize). On Dec. 30, 1975, President Hugo Banzer declared Paz Estenssoro's commitment to the Mennonites null and void, and proclaimed them subject to the rights and duties applying to Bolivian citizens generally. On Mar. 27, 1985, President Hernan Siles Suazo reinstated Mennonite special status. During this 10-year interval, during which the foreign-born could, as aliens, continue to claim exemption from military service and other civic duties, the oldest of the Bolivian-born Old Colonists came of age. In practice, nothing of consequence had changed from 1975 to 1985, but confidence was undermined. Paraguay, where the "Privilegium" is enshrined in law, was by the late 1960s coming into focus as a destination for Old Colony migration, and increasingly supplanted Bolivia. Since 1975, only two groups of Old Colonists, one from Mexico, and the other partly local, partly from Canada have established new settlements in Bolivia.

The following colonies are located in Bolivia (date of founding, country[ies] of origin, and total population [1987] in parentheses): Riva Palacio (1967, Mexico, 5,690); Swift Current (1967, Mexico, 2,510); Santa Rita (1967, Mexico, 1,500); Las Piedras (1968, Canada, 780); San José (1974, Mexico/Belize, 1,670); Hoffnungsthal (1974, Mexico, 1,400); Colonia del Norte (1980, Mexico, 400); Tres Cruces (1982, Bolivia, 785); Las Piedras II (1984, Bolivia/Canada, 380).

Paraguay. Old Colony Mennonite settlement commenced in 1969, and has been drawn exclusively to northern East Paraguay from colonies and settlements in Mexico, Belize, and Bolivia. The region has generally adequate (and occasionally superabundant) precipitation and was heavily forested. Development of an open-field system adapted to mechanical tillage has been expensive, but to some degree offset by the salvaging of timber during clearing. Old Colony economic focus shows little change from that in the countries of origin. Some wheat is grown, and soybeans have largely replaced table beans as a legume cash crop. Corn and grain sorghum are the main commercial crops. The animal sector focuses on dairying, with cheese the primary product. As in Mexico, Belize, and Bolivia, new colonies tend to have their origins in a single mother colony. Economic progress in all East Paraguay Old Colony settlements has been generally sastisfactory. Ideologically rigid restrictions on the adoption of modern technology may, as has been the case elsewhere, diminish economic viability in some aspects of both the field crop and livestock sectors.

Old Colony settlements in Paraguay are as follows (1987): Rio Verde (1969, from Mexico) and Mexico Colony (1975, from Mexico, combined population of Rio Verde and Mexico colonies 2,480); Durango (1978, Mexico, 2,050); Campo Alto (1980, Belize, 125); Manitoba (1983, Mexico, 335).

Argentina. In 1986 Old Colony Mennonites from Bolivia and Mexico founded the settlement of Remeco, some 700 km. (430 mi.) sw. of Buenos Aires and 120 km. (75 mi.) from the Atlantic Ocean, in the province of La Pampa. The region is suited to grain, stone fruits and other relatively hardy fruits, and livestock; hence the prior agricultural experience of the colonists is generally appropriate to the venture. Although the leaders continue to express confidence that a "Privilegium" will yet be issued, no such concession has been forthcoming and, judging by official Argentinian response to repeated formal inquiries from 1919 onward, the realization of such a deviation from policy must be considered highly unlikely. By mid-1987 the Ministry of Education had taken the initial steps to establish accredited schools. The settlers, who represent the ultraconservative element among the Old Colonists, viewed this prospective intervention with great concern, since it must be expected to cause many to depart and dis-

courage others who had intended to come, thus potentially disrupting the entire venture. Until some formal arrangement in respect to schools and national service is arrived at, this re-entry of Mennonites into a mid-latitude prairie setting must be regarded as tentative. In mid-1987 the Remeco settlement had a population of about 600, in 100 families.

United States. In 1977 some 100 Old Colony families and 20 families of General Conference Mennonite Church (GCM) affiliation but Old Colony background, from Mexico and Canada, undertook separate settlement ventures at Seminole, Tex. Great difficulties were experienced in meeting United States immigration requirements, despite active intervention by Senator Lloyd Bentsen and Representative George Mahon. Precipitation proved inadequate to sustain the intended dry farming. Excluded groundwater rights, however, precluded irrigation on 4,160 of the Old Colony's 6,420 acres (1,685 out of 2,600 hectares). In 1979 the venture was liquidated in default of arrears of principal and interest. The General Conference Mennonite group had fared somewhat better, managing to hold on to its land (1,172 acres). Those of both groups who had their immigrant status confirmed through ratification of a private bill by Senators Bentsen and Boren (Oct. 1980) have maintained a presence in the Seminole area, some as farmers, a few in business, the majority as laborers.

Canada. Despite majority emigration including that of their spiritual leaders, Old Colony Mennonites reorganized and have maintained a presence in all their original areas of settlement in western Canada. Since colonization in Latin America began in the 1920s, there has been a persistent flow of people of Old Colony background to Canada, capitalizing on retained Canadian citizenship or that of immediate forebears. In the 1930s returnees from Mexico tended to relocate in their former home communities, or on the frontiers of settlement, especially in the Peace River country of nw. Alberta. In the late 1950s and mid-1960s small numbers of people of Old Colony background from Chihuahua participated in settlement ventures in the Clay Belt of northern Ontario (Matheson), soon abandoned, and in the Rainy River area (Stratton) of Ontario. Since that time no group agricultural settlements have been attempted in Canada by Old Colony Mennonites. Old Colonists from Mexico began arriving in southern Ontario in 1954. Since the late 1960s the dominant destination in Canada has been the intensive farming and industrial region focusing on the Ontario counties of Norfolk, Essex and Niagara, where many have become affiliated with the Evangelical Mennonite Mission Conference (EMMC).HLS

Abe Warkentin, ed., *Strangers and Pilgrims* (Steinbach, Man.: *Mennonitische Post*, 1987); H. L. Sawatzky, *Sie Suchten eine Heimat* (Marburg: N. G. Elwert Verlag, 1986), cf. idem, *They Sought a Country* (Berkeley: U. of California Press, 1971); W. Schmiedehaus, *Ein Feste Burg Ist Unser Gott* (Cuauhtemoc, 1948; Winnipeg, 1982); Calvin W. Redekop, *The Old Colony Mennonites* (Baltimore: Johns Hopkins U. Press, 1969); W. Quiring, *Im Schweiße Deines Angesichts* (Steinbach, Man., 1953); *Mennonitische Post*, vol. 6, no. 5; vol. 10, no. 14, and vol. 11, no. 9; G. S. Koop, *Pionier Jahre in British Honduras (Belize)* (Belize City, n.d.); Gary S. Elbow and Simone Gordon, "Mennonite Colonization Efforts at Seminole, Texas, 1977-79," *West Texas Historical Association Yearbook*, 57 (Lubbock, 1981); Hildegard M. Martens, *Mennonites from Mexico: Their Immigration and Settlement in Canada* (Waterloo, 1975); John Everitt, "Mennonites and Migration: The Belizean Case" (unpubl. paper Brandon, Man., 1981); J. H. Warkentin, "Mennonite Agricultural Settlement in Southern Manitoba," *Geographical Review*, vol. 49, pp. 342-68; idem, "The Mennonite Settlements of Southern Manitoba" (PhD diss., U. of Toronto, 1960); *MWH* (1978), 313; *MWH* (1984), 134, 135; Reimer, *Quilt* (1983), 41-42.

See also Amish; Chortitzer Mennonite Conference; Conservative Mennonites; Elder; New Reinland Mennonite Church; Sommerfeld Mennonites; Schisms; Zion Mennonite Church; various colonies mentioned above.

Old Order Amish. See Amish.

Old Order Mennonites, Pennsylvania (ME IV:47). The °°Stauffer Mennonites began in 1845 under the leadership of Jacob Stauffer (1811-1855) in the congregation at Pike, Earl Twp., Lancaster Co. Since its reorganization in 1916, the largest branch of this church is known as the Jacob Stauffer Church. The group is named after Jacob S. Stauffer (1889-1987), a leader for more than 60 years and grandson of the Jacob Stauffer mentioned above. This group is located in Lancaster and Snyder Cos. Pa.; St. Mary's Co., Md.; and Dallas Co., Mo. In 1987 a settlement began in Kentucky. This group has about 500 members.

If the name *Stauffer Mennonite* is used in the broad sense of the word, it can refer to at least nine different groups, each of which have in a measure descended from the original 1845 Jacob Stauffer group. The groups usually are named after their founding bishops. These groups are the Jacob Stauffer, Phares Stauffer, Joseph Brubaker, Noah Hoover, Titus Hoover, Aaron Martin, Allen Martin, Martin Weaver, and Jonas Weaver groups.

Stauffer Mennonites in general hold to orthodox Mennonite beliefs, adhere to the 18 articles of the °°Dordrecht Confession of 1632, hold to rigid homemade dress patterns, and forbid the use of automobiles and modern farm machinery. Perhaps the most noticeable difference between them and other Old Order Mennonite groups is their more rigid view on shunning (°°avoidance).

Next to the Jacob S. Stauffer group in numerical strength is the young and growing Noah Hoover group. It is located in Snyder Co., Pa.; Allen Co., Ky.; and Belize, Central America. They have an associated group in Huron Co., Ont. This group may total about 150 members, having its largest settlement in Kentucky. This group in some ways is also the most conservative, as, for example, they permit no engine power at all.

Although there are no summary census figures available, the 1987 total of baptized members among the various Stauffer Mennonite groups is estimated at 800 (2,000 counting unbaptized children).

°°*Weaverland Conference Mennonites* are an Old Order Mennonite group that began in Weaverland, in East Earl Twp., Lancaster Co., Pa. This group is also called the °°*Horning Mennonites*, after Bishop Moses Horning (1871-1955). It was founded on Oct. 6, 1893, when Bishop Jonas H. °Martin and Deacon Daniel Burkholder, with several hundred followers, withdrew from the Lancaster Mennonite Conference (MC). It was founded as a measure of protest against the innovations that came into the Mennonite

Church at that time, especially °°Sunday schools, solemnizing marriages of nonmembers, church charters, and modern church furnishings and buildings. In 1987 the Weaverland conference still adheres to its founding principles. This group has made some concessions in favor of worship in the English language, modern farm machinery and black automobiles. Its members do, however, hold to the usual Old Order Mennonite principles of °°nonresistance and °°nonconformity and use the Dordrecht Confession. This conference works closely with the (Old Order) Mennonite conference of Ohio and Indiana (°°Wisler-Ramer group) and the Markham-Waterloo conference of Ontario. The Weaverland conference has daughter congregations in numerous counties in Pennsylvania, and also in the states of Virginia, Missouri, New York, and Wisconsin. In 1987 the Weaverland conference had 4,200 members, 69 ordained leaders, and 28 meetinghouses.

°°*Groffdale Conference Mennonites* are a body of Old Order Mennonites also known as °°*Wenger Mennonites*, so named after the group's first bishop, Joseph O. Wenger. The Groffdale Conference is often thought of as a sister conference to the Weaverland Conference. Both of these conferences share a common legacy, and many of the meetinghouses of both conferences are used in common. The Groffdale conference was founded on Apr. 8, 1927, by the withdrawal of the conservative element of the Weaverland conference from the more progressive portion which had accepted °automobiles. The Groffdale conference prefers horse and °buggy for conveyance, and excludes ownership of rubber-tire tractors and automobiles. They tenaciously adhere to the German language in worship and home life (°dialect literature and speech).

The membership of this conference was estimated to be 4,200 in 1987. It has 32 meetinghouses and 65 ordained men. This conference has daughter settlements and is affiliated with similar groups of independent origins in numerous Pennsylvania counties and in the states of Missouri, Ohio, New York, Wisconsin, Kentucky and Indiana (°°Wisler-Martin group). Associate conferences exist in Virginia and Ontario.

For Old Order Mennonites in Ontario, Indiana, and elsewhere, including details on history, worship, and church life, see *Mennonite World Handbook* (1978), 374-81, and Cronk and Horst, below. The total number of Old Order Mennonites in the Weaverland, Groffdale, Reidenbach, and related groups is estimated at 8,700 in 1987.   ABH

Eine Chronik oder Geschichtbüchlein . . . Durch J.(Jacob) St.(Stauffer) (1855); Joseph E. Schwartzberg, "A Geographic Analysis of Old Order Amish and Stauffer Mennonite Communities in Southern Maryland" (thesis, U. of Maryland, 1951); *Directory of the Weaverland Conference Mennonite Churches* (1985); *Mennonite Calendar of Weaverland Conference* (1985); records of ordinations of the Mennonites leading to and including the Weaverland Conference, 1750-1981; *Calendar of Meetings of the Groffdale Conference* (1987); records of ordinations of the Old Order Mennonites, Groffdale Conference Churches, 1750-1980; *MWH* (1978), 374-81; *MWH* (1984), 135, 146; Reimer, *Quilt* (1983), 10-13; Amos B. Hoover, ed., *The Jonas Martin Era* (Denver, Pa.: the author, 1982); Sandra L. Cronk, "Gelassenheit: The Rites of Redemptive Process in the Old Order Amish and Old Order Mennonite Communities" (PhD diss., U. of Chicago, 1977), cf *MQR*, 55 (1981), 5-44; Isaac R. Horst, *Separate and Peculiar* (Mt. Forest, Ont.: the author, 1979).

See also Conservative Mennonites; Ohio.

Old Order River Brethren. The River Brethren in eastern Pennsylvania experienced a three-way division in the 1850s. According to tradition, the conservative element (The Old Order River Brethren) felt that the moderate majority (the °°Brethren in Christ) did not properly discipline Bishop Matthias Brinser and his followers for constructing an unauthorized meetinghouse (Brinser founded the °United Zion Church). The exact date the Old Orders withdrew from the larger body is unknown but an official letter sent to Matthias Brinser in 1853 lists the names of ministers who later identified with either the Old Order or the Brethren in Christ. This would indicate the split had not yet taken place.

The majority of the River Brethren in York County, Pa., sided with the Old Order. Thus the Old Order River Brethren have often been referred to as *Yorker Brethren.* Jacob °Strickler, Jr. (1788-1859), was the first Old Order bishop in York County. Bishop Joseph °Strickler (1797-1879) was sent from York Co. to shepherd the flock in Lancaster Co. that was organized soon after the group's formation. An Old Order church had emerged by 1857 in Franklin County, Pa., under the leadership of Bishop Christian °Hoover (1793-1867).

Other Old Order River Brethren congregations were established in Montgomery County, Pa. (in 1987 a few members remained); Bedford Co., Pa. (extinct 1902); Stark Co., Ohio (extinct ca. 1920); Darke Co., Ohio (extinct 1984); Noble Co., Ind. (one member was living at Winona Lake in 1987); and in the Waterloo and Markham areas in Ontario (extinct 1961). A settlement started in Dallas Co., Iowa, in 1876 still exists. The York Co. Church gradually dwindled to a few members and ceased to be an independent congregation.

In 1919 the Old Order River Brethren made the nonuse of automobiles a test of membership. When some bishops refused to enforce this decision Bishop Simon Musser (1878-1978) of Lancaster Co. withdrew to form a separate group in 1921. The larger Old Order River Brethren Church continued to discourage automobile use, and when Bishop Jacob Keller (1862-1934) in Dallas Co., Iowa, openly allowed cars he was expelled in 1930. All the Iowa church sided with Keller as well as half the Ohio church and a few members from Franklin and Lancaster Cos. in Pennsylvania. Tension between Bishop Simon Musser and Minister John Strickler (1885-1976) resulted in a division in 1948. Bishop Jacob Horst (1885-1975) of the "Old" church in Lancaster Co. felt that automobiles should be allowed. This resulted in a gradual division about 1960-63. Most of the Franklin Co. Church sided with Horst; Seth Meyers became the bishop there in 1962.

Many members and leaders began to see the divided condition of the Old Order River Brethren Church as detrimental to the cause of Christ. In 1969 the Keller group and the Strickler group merged. In 1977 the Musser group joined this union. The combined group (often referred to as the Strickler group) in 1986 had 94 members in Lancaster Co., Pa., 44 members in Franklin Co., Pa., and 34 members in Dallas Co., Iowa. The Horst group had 109 members in Franklin Co. and 12 in the Lancaster district. Nearly all of the 34 members of the "Old" church or horse-and-buggy group reside in Franklin Co.

The three groups of Old Order River Brethren are very similar in most respects. Meetings for worship have traditionally been held in the homes of the members. This practice continued, but meetinghouses and public buildings are also used for church services. The ministry is unsalaried and preachers receive no formal training. A bishop, two ministers, and one or two deacons have been the traditional body of ordained men for each congregation. The English language has been used exclusively in Old Order River Brethren services since about the 1940s. In the 1980s few members could speak Pennsylvania °German. °Singing is from small books without musical notation (*Spiritual Hymns,* originally used by the Brethren in Christ from 1874 to 1902; a revised version was published by the "Strickler" group in 1980). Traditional slow tunes designated by meters are usually used. The experience or testimony meeting is an integral part of every worship service. There is no Sunday School. The two-day love feast observance of °communion is practiced which includes °feetwashing. Baptism is by trine immersion. Very conservative plain clothing (°dress) has been a distinctive of the Old Order River Brethren. All brethren wear full beards, sometimes with a mustache. Opaque white °headcoverings are peculiar to the sisters. Children do not wear the traditional garb until conversion. In the "Old" church the use of horse-drawn vehicles is maintained. The Musser group permitted car ownership in 1951 and the Strickler group in 1954. Electricity and telephones have been accepted in all the groups for many years, but °television is forbidden. A newsletter called *The Golden Chain* is published monthly. Sonlight River Brethren School was started in Lancaster Co. in 1984.   SES

Laban T. Brechbill, *History Old Order River Brethren* (Brechbill and Strickler, 1972); Myron Dietz, "The Old Order River Brethren," *BIC Hist. Life,* 6, no. 1 (June 1983), 4-34; Beulah S. Hostetler, "An Old Order River Brethren Love Feast," *Pennsylvania Folklife,* 24, no. 2 (Winter 1974-75), 8-20; Stephen Scott, "The Old Order River Brethren," *PMH,* 1, no. 3 (July 1978), 13-22; Stephen and Harriet Scott, *Directory of the Keller-Strickler Group of Old Order River Brethren* (1974, 1978; Lancaster: Sauder Printing, 1984); Dwight W. Thomas, "Old Order River Brethren Hymn Tunes," *BIC Hist. Life,* 5, no. 1 (June, 1982), 65-95; Wittlinger, *Piety and Obedience* (1978); *MWH* (1984) 146.

See also Conservative Mennonites.

Omsk. See Russian Soviet Federated Socialist Republic (RSFSR).

Oncken, Johann Gerhard (ME IV:60), born Jan. 26, 1800 in Varel, Germany and died on Jan. 2, 1884 in Zürich. He came to personal faith in a Methodist congregation in London in 1820. Following this radical conversion experience he began missionary activity in North Germany in 1823 as a representative of the British Continental Society. After his baptism by immersion in 1834 he led in the founding of the first °Baptist congregation in continental Europe. During his time in Hamburg Oncken maintained intensive contact with the Mennonite congregation there. His understanding of church order indicates Mennonite influence. The Baptist historian Hans Lukey has discovered that Oncken was in possession of a volume of select writings of Menno Simons, compiled by the Mennonite preacher Jan

Decknatel, at least 10 years prior to his baptism. Other contacts with Mennonites before and after his baptism have also been documented. This may have influenced Oncken's choice of the name "Evangelical Baptism Minded" as the name for his congregation in 1837.

Oncken undertook numerous missionary journeys in Germany, Denmark and Switzerland. In 1841 he undertook his first trip to East Prussia where he founded a congregation in Memel. It was through this congregation that contacts with the Mennonites in Russia developed. In 1864 Oncken traveled to St. Petersburg to intercede with the Tsar on behalf of the Mennonites. This trip also facilitated contact with the Mennonites in South Russia, where one of his missionaries, W. Pritzkau of Hamburg, was active. In the fall of 1869 he traveled to Old Danzig in South Russia where he ordained Pritzkau as elder of the German Baptist congregation and Abraham Unger as elder of the Mennonite Brethren congregation in Einlage. Later Oncken sent August Liebig to give further assistance to the young Mennonite Brethren movement. This in turn led to a long and fruitful relationship with the Mennonite Brethren in Russia. While this relationship did not lead to organizational unity between the two movements, many contacts between the Mennonite Brethren and the German and Russian Baptists have continued to the present time.

Changes in German Baptist congregational structure diminished these contacts eventually and led to Oncken's own loss of influence among Baptists. He eventually settled in Switzerland and died a lonely man.　　　　　　　　　　　　　　　　　JR

Otto Ekelmann, *Gnadenwunder: Geschichte der ersten Ostpreußischen Baptistengemeinde in Memel und ihrer Missionfelder in Ostpreußen und Rußland 1841-1928*; Hans Luckey, *Johann Gerhard Oncken* (Kassel, 1958); G. Balders, *Treuer Bruder Oncken* (Kassel, 1978); P. M. Friesen, *Brüderschaft* (Halbstadt, 1914); A. H. Unruh, *Die Geschichte der Mennoniten Brüdergemeinde* (Winnipeg, 1954).

Ontario (ME IV:61). The first Mennonites in Canada (1786) emigrated to Ontario from the United States after the American Revolution (1776). They came from Pennsylvania, home to Mennonite immigrants since 1683.

Beginning in 1824, Amish settlers from Europe came to Waterloo, Oxford, and Perth Cos. From 1953 to 1969 a wave of Amish migration from Ohio resulted in settlements at Aylmer, Chesley, and other parts of the province. The Amish publishing house, Pathway Publishers based in Aylmer, publishes three periodicals, prints textbooks for Amish schools, and issues German and English books for Old Order Amish readers in and beyond Ontario. In 1988 Old Order Amish have about 725 membes in 14 congregations; they sponsor 18 °private elementary schools.

There were 181 (1988) congregations of the various Mennonite and Brethren in Christ bodies in Ontario. The groups cooperate closely in Mennonite Central Committee, Ontario. Three bodies, Conference of United Mennonites in Ontario (GCM), Mennonite Conference of Ontario and Quebec (MC), and Western Ontario Mennonite Conference (MC), united in 1988 to form the Mennonite Conference of Eastern Canada. The group sponsors Rockway

Mennonite Collegiate in Kitchener, United Mennonite Educational Institute in Leamington, and Conrad Grebel College in Waterloo as well as homes for seniors and handicapped, camps, and a wide variety of urban ministries.

Another major group is the Ontario Conference of Mennonite Brethren Churches with 3,553 members in 21 congregations. It operates Eden Christian College and Camp Crossroads.

Old Order Mennonites in Ontario stem from an 1889 division in the Mennonite congregations in Waterloo Co. The group's faith is based on the Dordrecht Confession of Faith (1632) and worship is held in plain white meetinghouses. Three additional divisions have occurred, resulting in slight variations in worship and °discipline. The group has 1,387 members in about 10 congregations; they sponsor 28 private elementary schools.

Waterloo-Markham Conference, stemming from the Old Order Mennonites, has 935 members in seven congregations and is largely found in the Waterloo area. Some of the children attend the Old Order schools. Modern influences such as radio and television are resisted but many things are left to individual discretion.

The Beachy Amish Mennonite Fellowship has five loosely affiliated congregations in Ontario, located in Mornington and Wellesley Townships of Waterloo Co. and in Red Lake.

Conservative churches of Swiss Pennsylvania Mennonite origin in Ontario include the Conservative Mennonite Fellowship (1956), 95 members in two congregations (1956); Conservative Mennonite Church of Ontario (1959), 325 members in 8 congregations and 7 schools up to grade 10; Fellowship Churches (1978), a loose grouping of 14 congregations in Canada and the United States that includes the Conservative Mennonite Church of Ontario; and Midwest Mennonite Fellowship whose four churches in Ontario are part of a 16-congregation fellowship in North America. The Ontario congregations resulted from divisions in the Conservative Mennonite Church and the Old Order Amish.

Northern Light Gospel Missions has about 287 members in 21 congregations in nw. Ontario. The programs are primarily a mission to Ojibway Indians. Northern Youth Programs, an independent outreach program to Indian youth, began in the mid-1970s. With headquarters in Dryden, the program includes camping, a Bible Institute, a high school for girls, a high school for boys, and family life and native youth seminars. Reformed Mennonites have a congregation at New Hamburg and Stevensville with a membership of 162 (1988).

Southern Ontario is home to various other groups of Russian Mennonite origin, including a congregation of Sommerfelder Mennonite immigrants from Mexico. A major movement of Old Colony Mennonites to Canada from Mexico has occurred in the 1970s and 1980s; Ontario is home to four congregations of 1,122 members, as well as the New Reinland Mennonite Church of Ontario, formed out of a division within the Old Colony Mennonites in 1984. Other churches represented in Ontario include the Evangelical Mennonite Mission Conference (4 congregations), Evangelical Mennonite Conference (2), and Church of God in Christ Mennonite (1).　　JMB

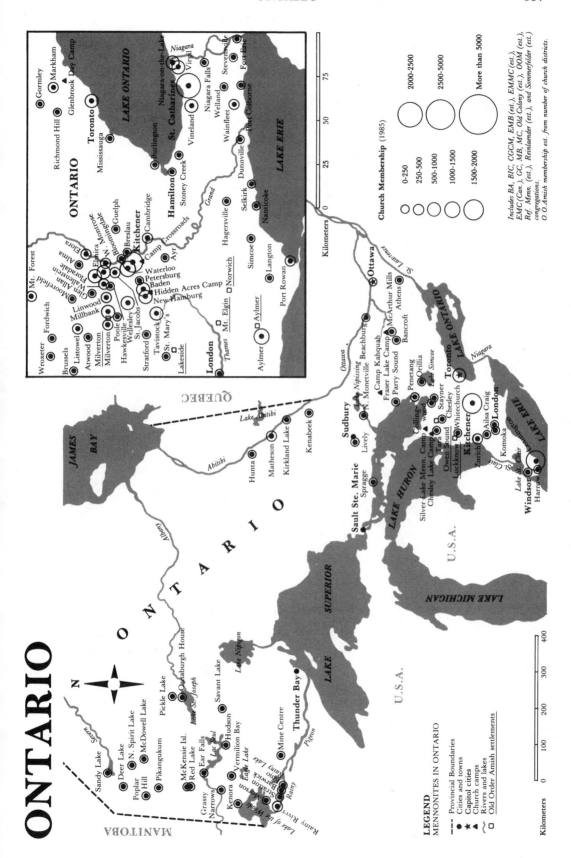

ONTARIO

Church Membership (1985)

2000-2500
2500-5000
More than 5000

0-250
250-500
500-1000
1000-1500
1500-2000

LEGEND
MENNONITES IN ONTARIO
- - - Provincial Boundaries
● ★ ▲ Cities and towns
★ Capitol cities
▲ Church camps
〰 Rivers and lakes
□ Old Order Amish settlements

Reimer, *Quilt* (1983, 1984); Luthy, *Amish Settlements* (1985), 2, 10-11; *MC Yearbook* (1988-89), 14-16; *GCM Handbook* (1989), 10-11; Miriam Maust, *Mennonites in Ontario: A Mennonite Bicentennial Portrait, 1786-1986,* (n.p.: Mennonite Bicentennial Commission, 1986), 176.

Ontario Conference of Mennonite Brethren Churches

(ME IV:65). The conference was founded Nov. 20, 1932, by five Ontario Mennonite Brethren congregations, with a membership of 287. In 1987 there were 20 congregations with a membership of just under 4,000 and a budget of $539,000 to support conference ventures. The conference has been a member of the North American and Canadian conferences of Mennonite Brethren churches since 1939 and 1945 respectively. The conference supports a denominational high school and Eden Christian College (founded in 1945). The Ontario MB Bible School (founded 1944) was discontinued in 1964. Ontario students attending MB Bible schools in western Canada are subsidized by the conference. An active church extension program has resulted in the formation of five new congregations. One senior °home (Tabor Manor) has operated since 1969, and The Bethesda Home for the mentally handicapped has been open since 1944.   EBo

Ed Boldt, "The Baptism Issue: An Episode in the History of the Ontario Mennonite Brethren Churches," *Mennonite Historian,* (Winnipeg), 13, no. 2 (1987), 1-2; John A. Toews, *History MB* (1975), 171-74, 205, 208, 211, 238, 265-68; "He Leadeth: History of the Mennonite Brethren Churches of Ontario 1924-57," *Jubilee Booklet,* ed. Henry H. Dueck (Kitchener, 1957); "When Your Children Shall Ask: A History of the Ontario Conference of Mennonite Brethren Churches 1957-82," *Jubilee Booklet* (Kitchener, 1982); *Year Book* (Ontario Conference of M.B. Churches, 1987).

Ontario Mennonite Conference (MC). See Mennonite Conference of Ontario and Quebec.

Orange Walk, Belize. See Belize Evangelical Mennonite Church.

Ordinances

(ME IV:72, 397). From the time of Jesus onward the church has used outward and visible actions to represent inward, invisible power at work. Jesus anointed a man's eyes with clay to restore his sight (Jn 9:6ff.). In the early church anointing with oil was a way of claiming the blessing of God for a sick person (Jas 5:14ff.). By the 12th c. the long evolution of Christian sacramental life in the western church was formalized when definitive rituals were specified by which saving °grace was given. They were: °communion (Eucharist, °°Lord's Supper), °baptism, °°confirmation, °marriage, °ordination, penance (°discipline), and °°anointing with oil. In these sacraments the grace which was signified was also effected in the person. For example, the bread of the Lord's Supper represented the body of Christ but, through the mediatorial role of the priest, it also became the body of Christ.

To the Protestant reformers of the 16th c. the medieval preoccupation with priestly and sacramental power obscured the personal access each believer has to the grace of God through faith in Christ. The Reformation rejected the necessity of the mediation of salvation by a priest and by the definitive seven sacraments. The principle of *sola Scriptura* (by Scripture alone) led Protestants to retain as sacraments only communion and baptism, claiming

that Jesus had ordained only these two (Mt 26:26ff. and parallels, Mt 28:19). At the same time individual reformers included, for example, preaching and °love of neighbor '(Luther) and church discipline (Calvin) as marks of the church.

Those Anabaptists who retained the term "sacrament" to describe the Lord's Supper and baptism or other marks of the church generally redefined it because of negative associations carried by the term. Pilgram °Marpeck was typical. He resorted to the term's ancient meaning as an oath of loyalty, thereby shifting the emphasis from exclusive preoccupation with the divine to focus also on the human action (CRR 2:169-72). By means of the function of cowitness, Marpeck described a sacrament as a dynamic event in which bread and wine or water testify to the person of faith that Christ is savingly present (CRR 2:88; Marpeck, *Vermanung* in *Gedenkschrift,* ed. C. F. Neff [1925], 207; Marpeck *Verantwortung* in *Marbeck-Schwenkfeld,* ed. J. Loserth [1929], 109). At the same time, Marpeck showed a strong preference for the term "ceremony" which he defined as any external ritual given by Christ to proclaim the Gospel (CRR 2:44). His list of ceremonies included not only baptism and the Lord's Supper but feetwashing, preaching, the ban, and acts of neighbor love. While not including infant dedication in this list, he did provide a theological rationale for its practice (CRR 2:140, 147, 242, 247).

Balthasar °Hubmaier and most Swiss Brethren shared Marpeck's preference for the term "ceremony," generally limiting its scope to baptism and the Lord's Supper. They understood ceremonies as human responses to previously received grace. This response, however, comes not only from the individual but also from the church. In the act of baptism, for instance, the believer confesses faith in Christ; at the same time the church gathers the believer into the community. In communion believers promise each other that they will love and discipline each other and suffer for Christ in the world (Hubmaier, *Schriften,* 346, 104, 317-18).

In the Dutch-North German communities the marks of the church were most often called "ordinances," from the fact that Christ had ordained them. Dirk Philips stipulates seven ordinances (ordination, sacraments, feetwashing, discipline, neighbor love, crossbearing, suffering) (Dirk *Enchiridion,* trans. A. Kolb, 383-400). The term "sacraments" in this list refers to communion and baptism; it is used to indicate their primacy in the life of the church. All the ordinances make the church's life of obedience visible. On the other hand, the two sacraments are signs of obedience but also of the grace which makes obedience possible.

Even though Anabaptists were anti-clerical in the sense described above, most of them including Hubmaier (*Schriften,* 355ff.) Dirk (Kolb, 67ff., 77ff.) and the °Schleitheim Confession (art. V), emphasize the role of an ordained leader in presiding over those ordinances which are part of worship.

Without formally designating them as ordinances, the formative Mennonite confessions of faith all include marriage, ordination, feetwashing, discipline, and neighbor love (often under the category of °nonresistance) as essential signs of how God orders the life of the church (Dordrecht in Loewen, *Con-*

fessions, 66-69; Flemish-Frisian-High German, *ibid.*, 117-27/115-25; Ris, *ibid.*, 96-102/94-100). The Mennonite Brethren (MB) confession of 1902 adds preaching to baptism and the Lord's Supper as "means of grace" (Loewen, *Confessions*, 166).

Though they are not listed in confessional or °worship documents prior to the 1890s, oral tradition in some Mennonite circles has preserved the practices of infant °dedication and anointing of the sick. The Gnadenfeld rite of the main Mennonite group in Russia (°"Kirchen-Gemeinden") includes an infant dedication service clearly adapted from the ritual of infant baptism, no doubt because the Gnadenfeld congregation was originally Lutheran (*Handbuch für Prediger*, 64-65). Although other marks of the church have receded in use, infant dedication has become an almost universal practice among the main Mennonite conferences in North America. The greater attention to children as people in their own right has contributed to the desire of parents to have their children included in the care of God and of the church by means of a specific event. Attention has been given to make the difference between infant presentation and baptism clear (e.g., *Minister's Manual*, [EMConf], 52). In some circles, however, infant dedication is increasingly seen as the inclusion of children in all aspects of the church's life. This has both stemmed from and led to less emphasis on conversion, catechism, and baptism as the necessary prerequisites for full participation in the life of the church.

The renewal of extraordinary healing as practiced in the °charismatic movement has encouraged the more regular use of the practice of anointing the sick. The 1983 Mennonite Church (MC)-General Conference Mennonite Church (GCM) minister's manual includes a healing service (Janzen and Janzen, *Minister's Manual*, 106-10).

Only two Mennonite confessions speak to the question of celibacy; the Ris and the 1930 General Conference Mennonite statements give it the same status as marriage (Loewen, *Confessions*, 102, 307). Among the Mennonites in Russia the celibate life was given structure in the form of communities of sisters, most of whom became nurses. The last of these to survive are the °°deaconesses who managed a hospital in Newton, Ks., until the early 1980s.

About 1900 Daniel °Kauffman tried to counter the assimilation of his community into its North American environment by developing a strong and specific teaching on ordinances (*Bible Doctrines* (1914), pt. VI, pp. 353-458). He sought not only to strengthen doctrine and practice concerning baptism, communion, feetwashing, anointing, and marriage, but to elevate the °°kiss of peace and the devotional covering or °prayer veil to the status of ordinances. Both of the latter originate in the New Testament (2 Cor 13:12; 1 Cor 11:2ff.) and have been practiced throughout the centuries but have never been seen as fundamental marks of the church.

Kauffman's goal was to use these outward signs to distinguish visibly the life-style of the Mennonite Church (MC) from that of the world around it. His understanding one-sidedly emphasized ordinances as tests of obedience to church teaching so that no room was left for them also to be evidences of grace. Kauffman's list of ordinances was never given

formal sanction in a confession of faith except for the 1952 Statement of Doctrine of the Church of God in Christ Mennonite (Holdeman) (Loewen, *Confessions*, 205).

Mennonites universally celebrate baptism and communion as essential marks of the church, and as Marpeck said, as ways of proclaiming the Gospel. The term sacrament is often used as Dirk used it, to describe the primacy of these two rituals above the other ceremonies of the church. But an unwritten theology has developed around the other traditional ordinances as well. Preaching is commonly understood as the decisive event in the life of the church in which the word of God comes to life. The wedding service is widely perceived as the event in which God makes a marriage out of two people's love. Except in very liberal circles, the act of ordination is thought of as the setting aside of a minister for life-long service. Where ministers are chosen by casting °°lots, it is believed that God's choice is revealed through a process culminating in the selecting of a book. In many congregations, especially those with membership from a predominantly Pennsylvania-German background, feetwashing is practiced in conjunction with the Lord's Supper. In the smaller, conservative bodies excommunication and readmission to the church come about through ritual public acts believed to embody the will and grace of God.

There has never been complete clarity in the Mennonite mind as to what status and meaning to give to the various ceremonies by which the church expresses its life. A surprising variation exists not only in the number of ordinances practiced, but in their form. For example, immersion, sprinkling, and pouring have all been practiced as modes of baptism since the 16th c. The liturgical ordering of all church rituals has varied since the beginning but even more since the movement of worship renewal and experimentation which began in the 1960s. Oral tradition and minister's manuals are considered as guides rather than rules of observance.

Historically, as Mennonites have °acculturated into their religious and cultural surroundings, the status and number of their ordinances has diminished. The extreme of this tendency took place in 19th c. Holland. By then feetwashing and church discipline had vanished. But for a short time several urban congregations did away even with baptism and communion! Recent Mennonite teaching, as evidenced by instruction in theology schools and texts (e.g., Kaufman, Finger, the °Worship series published jointly by the Mennonite Church and General Conference Mennonites) concentrates almost exclusively on baptism and communion as marks of church.

By way of brief theological commentary on the development of Mennonite teaching on ordinances the following may be said. There has been an enduring ambivalence concerning the role of ceremonies in the life of the church. With other Protestants Mennonites have taught that each believer has unmediated access to the grace of God through faith in Christ. Because of their conviction that salvation is given through an existential relationship with Christ, Mennonites believe that baptism may be offered to believers only. At the same time they have claimed that the church is the bearer of grace. It is through the church's mediation of the gospel across time that the individual comes to faith and is sustained in faith. That is, each person comes to Christ through the witness of the church and, upon confession of faith, is baptized and brought into its community. One might say that in Mennonite theology the church itself is the sacrament of Christ's presence. Its individual ceremonies particularize both his grace and the believers' faith.

Several factors have complicated this double conviction about the church's mediation of grace and the unmediated access of each believer to grace. From the beginning theologians have found it difficult to describe how this reality is present in individual ordinances. Marpeck was the only Anabaptist who worked out a systematic position. Dirk's writings mirror the ambivalence of his community. Hubmaier's resolution was radical but also one-sided. He described a ceremony as only a response to grace rather than also a means of grace. The Spirit, without external mediation, was the means of grace. But the response to grace was both an individual and communal act. For example in baptism, the individual externalized her faith. At the same time, by baptising someone and bringing him into its community the church confirmed the individual's faith. Hubmaier and, to a lesser extent, Dirk represent the dominant historic Mennonite interpretations of ordinances.

In time, especially with the rise of individualism, the role of the church receded. Baptism, communion, and other marks of the church were increasingly understood as individual acts of confession, thanksgiving, etc. Gradually, what was believed concerning baptism was carried over to what was believed concerning salvation: it was a humanly willed decision to live as Christ had commanded. Correctives to this overly simplified view went in two directions. One was the pietistic or revivalistic emphasis on an individual relationship with Christ in which the church and sacraments had no essential role. The other was the objective use of ceremonies, as illustrated by the example of baptism, to bring people into the church without a response of personal faith. This was the tendency of Mennonites of North German background in the 19th c. and led to protests, one of which resulted in the formation of the Mennonite Brethren Church (MB) in Russia. Daniel Kauffman's attempt at a renewal of the ordinances, on the other hand, challenged individualism and reemphasized the church but made ceremonies signs of ethical achievement, further separating them from the work of grace.

Revivalistic individualism, mechanical sacramentalism, and ceremonies as signs of nonconformity all continue to be practices in the Mennonite churches and to remove them from the Anabaptist "double conviction" about the inseparability of the individual's and church's role in salvation. At the same time, the recovery of the Anabaptist vision in the past generation has led to a strengthened theology of the church. The implications of this eccesiology for sacraments has not yet been widely realized. In large part this is a result of a lack of attention to °Christology throughout most of Mennonite history. That is, if Christ is present in the church today his presence must be taken into account in practicing the ordinances, which whatever else they be, are signs of his work in the church. The recent systematic theologies of Gordon Kaufman and Thomas Finger work toward a broader theology of baptism and communion, though without an anchor in Mennonite tradition. The popular clamor for a fuller theology and practice of worship, exemplified in a festival of worship held at Goshen, Ind., in 1986, has led to considering sacramental life as part of its search.

In 1982 the World Council of Churches issued the fruit of 50 years of ecumenical debate and research under the title, *Baptism, Eucharist and Ministry*. It attempted to move beyond the traditional Orthodox, Catholic, and Protestant formulations. Responses to this statement from °Believers Church perspectives, including Mennonite views, were published in 1986 (Strege, ed.)..

No one has shown concern to rehabilitate neighbor love or °suffering as ordinances, i.e., as concrete events in which Christ is present and in which the church takes form. To do so might strengthen their place in the life and mission of the church, demonstrate the inseparability of grace and faith, and show how ethically relevant it really is to concern ourselves with the ceremonies Christ left us.   JDR

Thomas Finger, *Christian Theology: An Eschatological Approach*; Heinz and Dorothea Janzen, eds., *Minister's Manual* (Newton, 1983); Daniel Kauffman, ed., *Doctrines of the Bible*, 2nd ed. (Scottdale, 1929); Gordon Kaufman, *Systematic Theology: A Historicist Perspective* (New York: Charles Scribner's Sons, 1968); ed. Balthasar Hubmaier, *Schriften*, G. Weston, T. Bergsten (Gütersloh: Gerd Mohn, 1962); Marpeck, *Vermanung* in *Gedenkschrift*, ed. C. F. Neff (1925); idem, Verantwortung in *Marbeck-Schwenkfeld*, ed. J. Loserth (1929); *Baptism, Eucharist, and Ministry* Faith and Order Paper no. 111, (Geneva: World Council of Churches, 1982); *Handbuch für Prediger* (Berdyansk: n.p., 1911); *Ministers Manual* (Steinbach, Man.: EMConference, 1983); Rollin S. Armour, *Anabaptist Baptism* (Scottdale, 1966); Karl Barth, *Church Dogmatics* vol. 4, Fragment 1, Baptism (Edinburgh: T and T. Clark, 1969); Alvin Beachy, *The Concept of Grace in the Radical Reformation* (Nieuwkoop: B. de Graf, 1977); idem, *Worship as Incarnation* (Newton, 1966); N. Clarke, *A Theology of Sacraments* (London: SCM, 1960); Sandra Cronk, "Gelassenheit: The Rites of the Redemptive Process in the Old Order Amish and Old Order Mennonite Communities: (PhD diss., U. of Chicago, 1977), cf. *MQR*, 65 (1981), 5-44; Vernard Eller, *In Place of Sacraments* (Grand Rapids: Eerdmans, 1972); Hans-Jürgen Goertz, *Die Täufer* (Munich: C. H. Beck, 1980); W. Goltermann, "Eens Consens over de doop," in *De Geest in het Geding* (n.p: H. D. Tjeenck Willink, 1978); Walter Klaassen, *Biblical and Theological Basis for Worship in the Believers' Church* Worship Series no. 1, (Newton, 1978) cf. related titles in this series; J. Martos, *The Catholic Sacraments*, (Wilmington: Michael Glazier, 1983); Russell Mast, *Preach the Word*, (Newton, 1968); John D. Rempel, "Christology and the Lord's Supper in Anabaptism: A Study in the Theology of Balthasar Hubmaier, Pilgram Marpeck, and Dirk Philips" (ThD diss., St. Michael's College, Toronto School of Theology, U. of Toronto, 1986); idem, "Christian Worship: Surely the Lord Is in this Place," *CGR*, 6 (1988), 101-17; Merle D. Strege, ed., *Baptism and Church*, papers from the 7th Believers Church Conference, 1984 (Grand Rapids: Sagamore Books, 1986); Christoph Windhorst, *Täuferisches Taufverständnis*, (Leiden: E. J. Brill, 1976); D. D. Martin, "Menno and Augustine on the Body of Christ," *Fides et Historia*, 20, no. 3 (Fall 1988), 41-64; John Howard Yoder, *Täufertum und Reformation im Gespräch*, (Zurich: EVZ Verlag, 1968).

See also Apocalypticism; Baptismal Theology; Bishop ("My Good Bishop" feature); Folk Art; Symbols; Tradition.

Ordination (ME IV:73) is an act by which the

church, after appropriate personal and corporate discernment, calls and appoints a person to a leadership ministry in the life and mission of the church. The service of ordination normally includes the laying on of hands, prayer, and other appropriate rituals of commitment and celebration. The church ordains with a sense that it has been so led by God's Spirit and is acting to express God's leading to confirm this gifted person for a particular public and representative ministry in and for the church.

Mennonite nonsacramental assumptions have often created problems for understanding ordination. Mennonites have resisted setting some persons over and above others. They have failed to find in Scripture any explicit teaching or example which could rightly be called ordination, though there are numerous examples of the church affirming persons for ministry and mission. However, Mennonites have chosen leaders for the church and in doing so they have followed a variety of patterns which they have called ordination, often following the examples of other Christians.

One view of leadership in the New Testament is based on 1 Timothy where three terms are used: °°deacons, °elders, and °bishops. While the terminology has often changed, the larger Christian community ·has affirmed over and over again this basic threefold ministry. In Anabaptist and Mennonite history this same threefold ministry has emerged repeatedly at various times and in diverse ways as the pattern for the church's leadership.

Broadly conceived, the bishop ministry is that of oversight covering a group of churches in a given geographical area; the elder ministry is that of a leader-preacher within a congregation; the deacon ministry is a lay ministry of service within the congregation and to the community.

In North America, the Mennonite Church (MC) has called for an ordination for each type of ministry: deacon, preacher, bishop, and hence it was possible for one person to be ordained three times in that sequence. The General Conference Mennonite Church often followed a similar pattern, though not in the same order. Persons giving pastoral leadership and preaching were first ordained as ministers and only later as full elders which then included the right to lead in administering the sacraments (°ordinances). Deacons were sometimes ordained though not always. Generally the General Conference Mennonite Church did not have bishops, though in parts of the church the elders (Ältester) functioned in a similar capacity of oversight. The Mennonite Brethren Church brought to North America a pattern of ordaining elders, ministers, and deacons as a part of a multiple lay ministry. With the transition to a trained and paid pastor, the elder system of leadership declined both in the United States and Canada. The Mennonite Brethren Church continues to ordain people for the ministry of the gospel calling for a lifelong commitment.

The latter half of the 20th c. has seen considerable change in understanding ministry and ordination among North American Mennonites. In the Mennonite Church there has been a gradual decline in the ordination of bishops, vesting the responsibility of oversight in conference ministers and overseers. In the General Conference Mennonite Church

there was a major process in each decade extending over five decades responding to changing understandings. Perhaps most significant was the change to a single ordination as elder during the 1950s and 1960s. Out of concern for the increasing diversity among Mennonite Brethren ministers, there was a proposal in 1951 to establish a Board of Elders to unify the calling and training of ministers, but it failed to gain adequate support.

Among Canadian Mennonites particularly and to a lesser degree in the United States, there has been and continues to be a strong commitment to lay ministry. Such persons who earn their living in other vocations are ordained for ministry and often have given lifelong leadership in congregations. At present there is a strong reaffirmation of this lay ministry heritage, but more often such persons serve alongside of the professional pastor. In some groups there is discussion of changing ordination to commissioning for lay ministry, especially where such leadership may be limited by time, place, or a particular ministry position.

A major change among North American Mennonites has been the growing openness to the ordination of women within the General Conference Mennonite Church and the Mennonite Church; the Mennonite Brethren Church at the present time (1987) does not accept women for ordination, though the issue continues to be discussed. In 1974 the General Conference Mennonite Church passed a resolution on ordination which committed the church to "Affirming that in Christ there is neither male nor female and that God is no respector of persons, neither race nor class, nor sex should be considered barriers in calling a minister." In 1987 44 women were in licensed or ordained ministry positions in the General Conference Mennonite Church, either as pastors or as chaplains. In the Mennonite Church the issue is being debated on an area conference basis. Half of the conferences are ready to ordain women, and 34 women are serving in licensed or ordained ministerial leadership positions in the Mennonite Church. Included in the above numbers are 14 women who serve in dual-affiliated congregations.

The 1980s saw again much discussion concerning the understanding of ordination among North American Mennonites. Among Mennonite Brethren the discussion centered in their seminary community, Mennonite Brethren Biblical Seminary of Fresno, Cal. In the Mennonite Church there were a series of consultations and documents: "Leadership and Authority in the Life of the Church" (1981) and "Consultation on Ordination" (1986). The General Conference Committee on the Ministry gave leadership also in 1986 to a consultation to evaluate a document "Ordinal: Ministry and Ordination in the General Conference Mennonite Church." As a result of the two consultations in 1986, there was a strong sense of convergence in understanding ordination and a process begun for these two groups to develop a common polity statement on ministry and ordination. In addition to the consensus around the overarching threefold ministry tradition (oversight, pastor-special ministries, and lay ministry), there is an agreement in the use of terminology (licensing, ordination and commissioning). *Licensing* is an initial approval for ministry, given to a candidate for ordination. The short time of one or two years of licensed ministry is understood as a period for testing and discernment by the candidate and the church as to whether or not ministry can be confirmed in ordination. *Ordination* is a rite of the church giving approval for ministry within and for the church; it is understood as a long-term ongoing commitment to ministerial leadership. *Commissioning* is an approval for ministry which is limited to a particular time or term, or limited to a particular place or task. It may be the appropriate approval for those serving the church as lay ministers.

Discussion continues in several Mennonite denominations around other issues related to ordination. (1) Should ordination be seen in a strongly functional manner—for persons assigned specific tasks or because of their special gifts, or should ordination invest in the person a representational quality of the position of leadership for the church? Related to this question is the issue of whether ordination has to do with "being" or only with "doing." (2) What is the place of ordination for those in so-called special ministries: chaplains, pastoral counselors, administrators of church institutions, etc.? There is generally a strong sense that chaplains should be viewed as the church's ministry in the world and that they are therefore appropriately considered a part of ordained ministry. But there is less clarity about others. (3) Is ordination for life or is it limited by actual functioning in a ministry role? In a time of changing vocations, should ordination at least be voluntarily laid aside when one no longer serves in the church's ministry? (4) Is ordination tied to professional ministry (training, vocational commitment, and accountability) or should ordination be granted to a broader group of leadership persons in congregations? (5) Is ordination the responsibility of each separate congregation, or should the church carry out ordination in a more connectional system of congregations, area conferences and denomination? Issues of authority and accountability are being widely discussed. (6) What is the authority for the termination of ordination in cases of moral failure or substantial theological digression?

In the ferment around ordination there continues to be a strong commitment among Anabaptist-Mennonites of the need for effective leadership within the church. Thus ordination continues to be used (1) in recognizing the personal gifts of leadership, (2) by offering the privilege and the responsibility to exercise that leadership in a representative position for the church, and (3) for providing boundary clarity for the respective roles and functions of clergy and laity.   JAE

A. E. Janzen and Herbert Giesbrecht, *We Recommend: Recommendations and Resolutions of the General Conference of the Mennonite Brethren Churches* (Fresno: MB Board of Christian Literature, 1978); *Leadership and Authority in the Life of the Church: A Summary Statement* (Scottdale, 1982); *Ordinal: Ministry and Ordination in the General Conference Mennonite Church* (Newton: Committee on the Ministry, 1987); Samuel Floyd Pannabecker, *Open Doors: A History of the General Conference Mennonite Church* (Newton, 1975); *Statement of Convergence: Consultation on Ordination in the Mennonite Church* (Elkhart, Ind.: MC Board of Congregational Ministries, 1986); John A. Toews, *History MB* (1975).

See also Ordinances.

Ordnung (Order). The *Ordnungen* comprise the rules and regulations of the church community. The word is used in Mennonite, Amish, and Hutterite tradition to cover both the written and oral compendia of modes of behavior and organizational structure which give form and meaning to daily life. The *Ordnung* may contain broad principles of faith, e.g., °nonresistance and common ownership of goods (in the case of Hutterites), as well as very specific applications of principles, e.g., permissible styles of clothing, (°dress) or home furnishings.

The purpose of the *Ordnung* is not only to provide a list of individually acceptable or proscribed ethical behaviors but to structure a whole way of life, lived according to God's will, as expressed in the gospels. The *Ordnung* reflects God's order as opposed to the order of the world.

The use of the *Ordnung* has significant implications for the way participating communities understand both the content and structure of God's order. The *Ordnungen* in the Anabaptist heritage reflect some common understandings of the content of God's order. These common themes come from commitment to Jesus as the °suffering servant, redeemer of humankind. Through Jesus' life, teachings, and death on the cross believers receive God's saving love and the call to °discipleship. Discipleship requires °nonconformity to the self-centered, power-seeking values of the world.

Structurally, commitment to the *Ordnung* puts the °disciplined church °community, rather than individual religious experience, at the center of Christian faith. It is in daily life with one's religious brothers and sisters that Christ's redemptive work is manifested.

The *Ordnung* provides a path of discipleship by outlining a pattern of Christian ritual, i.e., a set of °symbolic acts which expresses an obedient relationship with God. The symbolic acts of the *Ordnung* structure a life of yieldedness, suffering °servanthood, °humility, defenselessness, and nonconformity with the world. These ritual acts are a way for the community to participate in and embody the reality of Christ's redemptive work in the world. The *Ordnung* thus becomes an expression of faithful community life.

It is also an expression of the community's process of spiritual formation. For example, it is by living in and through a community that lives by defenselessness that one learns to love one's enemies and to trust in God's power for protection. Both the community and its individual members grow into the fullness of Christian life by living within this framework. On this level the *Ordnung* has close parallels with the use of the Benedictine Rule as a mode of communal spiritual formation within °monasticism.

Implicit within the concept of the *Ordnung* is a strong prophetic and eschatological critique of the world (i.e., that part of the social order not obedient to God's will). This prophetic critique has taken the form of active mission work and confrontation with the world in some eras of history and silent separation and nonconformity in others. The *Ordnung* also reflects an eschatological belief in God's coming °kingdom and a corporate decision to live in the end time of Christ's reign here and now.   SC

William R. McGrath, *Christlicher Ordnung, or Christian Discipline, Being a Collection and Translation of Anabaptist and Amish-Mennonite Church Discipline* (Aylmer, Ont.: Pathway Publishing Corp., 1966); John A Hostetler, *Amish Society*, 3rd. ed. (Baltimore: John Hopkins, 1980), 75-92; John B. Mast, *Letters of the Amish Division, 1693-1711* (Oregon City, Ore.: Christian J. Schlabach, 1950); Harvey J. Miller, "Proceedings of Amish Ministers' Conferences, 1826-1831," *MQR*, 33 (1959), 132-42; *The Chronicle of the Hutterian Brethren*, Vol. 1, trans. and ed. by the Hutterian Brethren (Rifton, N.Y.: Plough Publishing Co., 1987), see esp. the *Ordnung* of 1529 on pp. 77-79 and the articles of faith on pp. 235-38, 251-94, and 333-38; John S. Hostetler, Leonard Gross, and Elizabeth Bender, eds., *Selected Hutterian Documents in Translation, 1542-1654* (Philadelphia: Communal Studies Center of Temple U., 1975); Ira S. Johns, J.S. Hartzler, and Amos O. Hostetler, comp., *Minutes of the Indiana-Michigan Mennonite Conference, 1864-1929* (Scottdale: n.d.).

See also Authority; Humility; Obedience; Polity; Tradition.

Oregon (ME IV:74) had approximately 4,545 Mennonites in 1986. Most of Oregon's people, including Mennonites, live in the Willamette Valley, which extends a distance of 100 mi. (160 km.) south of Portland and has a breadth of 40 mi. (65 km.) west to east. Oregon's first Mennonites traveled by train to California, then by boat to Oregon, until transcontinental rail service reached Oregon in 1883. Some settled on government homestead land; many purchased or rented already cleared farmland. The first Mennonites settled in Oregon in 1876, and by 1880 ministers served congregations of Old Order Amish near Hubbard and Swiss Mennonites near Silverton. Temporary Amish Mennonite congregations organized in the next decade. In 1890 the Waldo Hills/Emmanuel (GCM) congregation organized at

OREGON

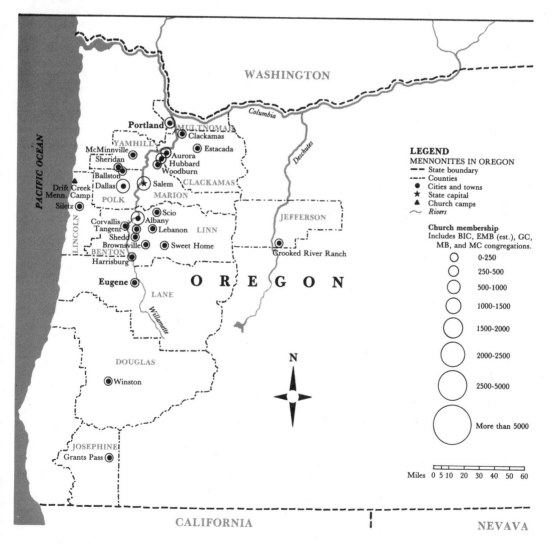

LEGEND

MENNONITES IN OREGON

- – State boundary
---- Counties
● Cities and towns
★ State capital
▲ Church camps
~ Rivers

Church membership
Includes BIC, EMB (est.), GC, MB, and MC congregations.

○ 0-250
○ 250-500
○ 500-1000
○ 1000-1500
○ 1500-2000
○ 2000-2500
○ 2500-5000
○ More than 5000

Miles 0 5 10 20 30 40 50 60

Pratum, east of Salem, but in 1984 it withdrew from Mennonite affiliation. In 1986 Oregon's oldest existing Mennonite congregation was Zion (MC) at Hubbard, organized in 1893.

Many Mennonites moved to Oregon between 1920 and 1950. In 1986 the largest group, the Mennonite Church (MC) had 19 congregations and 1,958 members. Other Mennonite groups, with numbers of congregations and total membership, included: six unaffiliated Mennonite congregations, 631; four General Conference Mennonite (GCM), 543 (about 56 members in GCM-MC congregations); three Mennonite Brethren, 431; three Western Conservative Mennonite Fellowship, 172; two Evangelical Mennonite Brethren (EMB, Fellowship of Evangelical Bible Churches), 633; one Church of God in Christ Mennonite (Holdeman; CGC), 77. Oregon's small Old Order Amish group divided in 1961, after some members bought cars. The other families left Oregon, and the remaining congregation disbanded about 1978. Two Brethren in Christ congregations, with approximately 100 members, function as community churches but remain affiliated with the denomination.

Western Mennonite High School (MC) north of Salem is a boarding school. Seven congregations (unaffiliated, EMB, and CGC) operate day schools. A voluntary service unit (MC) serves the Albany area. Mennonites administer the Lebanon Community Hospital and own and operate Drift Creek Camp near Lincoln City and three nursing °homes and retirement communities. They also operate four group homes for °mentally retarded or developmentally °disabled persons and three Mennonite Central Committee °SELFHELP and thrift shops. They began an annual MCC fund-raising festival in 1984 (°relief sales). HKL

Hope Kauffman Lind, "Mennonites in Oregon and Related Congregations in Neighboring States (1876-1976)" (unpublished manuscript); Pacific Coast Conference (MC), Annual Report, 1986, 9; Pacific District Conference (GCM), Annual Report, 1986, 12-13; MC Yearbook (1986-87), 36, 82-83, 101-104, 120, 124, 125, 129, 131, 141, 144, 146, 150, 152; Lee Price Campbell, "Seventy-Five Years on the Shore of the Peaceful Sea; A History of the Pacific District Conference of the General Conference Mennonite Church of North America," MDiv thesis, Western Evangelical Seminary, Portland, Ore., 1973, 31-36, 55-73; H. D. Burkholder, The Story of Our Conference and Churches (North Newton: Mennonite Press, 1951), 22-36; MC Yearbook (1988-89), 34; Wittlinger, Piety and Obedience (1978), 147, 149; Daniel Hertzler, From Germantown to Steinbach (Herald, 1981), 161-172.

Orenburg Region (ME IV:75). The Mennonites of the Orenburg (Kitchkass) and the old Neu Samara (Pleshanov) settlements were not dislodged and permanently relocated as had been the case with most other Mennonites who lived west of the Volga River before World War II. All the farming communities had been collectivized, of course, and sovietization was carried forward in other aspects of community life as well. The churches were all closed in the Stalin era, and the majority of adults and young people had to join the Trud Armia (labor army) during the war.

The repressions of the late 1940s and early 1950s gave way temporarily to a period of recovery and reconstruction after the death of Stalin in 1953. The end of the special regime (°Spetskomandantura) restrictions for all Germans came two years later. Most of those who left the Orenburg communities during the preceding decade, if they had survived, were able to return to their home villages in this region.

Revivals, which had begun here as early as the late 1940s, were renewed about this time when the arrested church leaders were released. Small groups were able to meet for worship and fellowship once more. There were, however, more arrests in 1958-62. In 1965 those from the Pleshanov region of the former Neu Samara settlements were freed and church life could be organized here once again.

In April 1972, the Donskoi congregation requested registration, but was not granted the privilege until four years later. Construction of a house of worship began immediately, and in the ensuing years this group has become the largest congregation of the area. Daniel Janzen has been the leading minister (Ältester [elder]) for most of this period. The congregation numbers about 400 members (1987).

Among the dozen or more older Mennonite villages of this area there are now registered Mennonite Brethren congregations not only in Donskoi, but also in Podolsk and Ischalka, with unregistered groups active in Klinok, Kaltan, Kuterlja, Krassikova, Lugovsk, and Totz Koe. The total Mennonite Brethren membership of this area is around 1,000 baptized members. Some °Kirchliche Mennonites live in these villages also.

Most of the Kirchliche Mennonite congregations in the Orenburg settlements are located in villages once established by Chortitza families from Ukraine. The Ältester of the total body, Diedrich Thiessen, led his own registered congregation at Kitchkass (No. 12) until his recent emigration to West Germany. This group has about 100 members. Registered congregations are also found in the villages of Chortitza (No. 1), Petrovka (No. 2), Kanzerovka (NO. 3), Zhdanovka (earlier Deyevko) (No. 5), Nikolaevka (No. 6), Fejodorovka (No. 7), Sol-Iletzk (south of Orenburg), and Stepanovka. Unregistered congregations are active in Dolinovka and Pretoria. Seven of these congregations have their own church buildings, and the total membership is around 700 (1987).

A dozen or more Mennonite Brethren congregations are located in these villages also. At least eight of them have built new meetinghouses during the past decade. Each congregation has its own Ältester, and the total membership is more than 1,500. Groups have been registered in the following locations: Chortitza, Petrovka, Kanzerovka, Kamenka, Zhdanovka, Fejodorovka, Suvorovka, Pretoria, Kubanka, Stepanovka, Alisovo, and Susanovo. Hundreds of former Mennonites have found their way into nearby Baptist congregations, notably those in the city of Orenburg itself.

Emigration has not affected the Orenburg communities as it has the Mennonites of western Siberia and °Soviet Central Asia, e.g., °Kazakhstan and °Kirgizia. The whole area was recently opened to tourists and other travelers, so that east-west exchanges have increased significantly during the past five years (1983-88). LK

J. H. Brucks, and H. Hooge, *Neu Samara am Tock* (Clearbrook, B.C., 1964); Wilma Derksen in *Menn. Rep.* (Nov. 11, 1985), 2; Abram Hamm, and Maria Hamm, *Die Wege des Herrn sind lauter Güte* (Gummersbach: Verlag Friedensstimme, 1985); Olga Hildebrand, "Die Orenburger Ansiedlung, 1920-1970," *Der Bote* (Jan. 8, 1986), 5, 8; Lawrence Klippenstein, "An Unforgotten Past: Recent Writings by Soviet Emigré Baptists," *Religion in Communist Lands,* 14, no. 1 (Spring, 1986), 17-32; David E. Redekop, "Gemeindeleben in Russland 1985," *Mennonitische Rundschau* (Nov. 27, 1985), 18-22; Walter Sawatsky, "Mennonite Congregations in the Soviet Union Today," *Menn. LIfe,* 33 (March, 1978), 12-26; *Courier,* 2, no. 1 (1987) 1-3.

Organs. See Music; Music, Instrumental.

Orthodox Churches. See Eastern and Coptic Orthodox Churches.

Osaka Prefecture is located in central Japan, on the main island of Honshu. To the west is Osaka Bay and the Inland Sea. On the other three sides are mountains encircling a broad plain. It is a commercial, financial, and industrial center, and home of the large Hanshin (Osaka-Kobe) Industrial Zone. That complex includes textile, chemical, steel, and other heavy industries. The total area is 1,858 sq. km. (717 sq. mi.), making it the smallest prefecture in Japan, but the population is 8,473,000 (1980) and in that it ranks second.

The prefectural capital is Osaka City. In population (2,648,000) it ranks third among Japanese cities, next to Tokyo and Yokohama. It is known as the "city of merchants"—wholesaling is big business. Its location has always made it a strategic hub for land and marine transportation. Many goods go in and out of the port. But in the same way, much art, science, and philosophy have also flowed into the country (especially from China) and have had a tremendous influence on the development of Japanese culture.

Old tombs and archeological finds suggest the area was settled early. Some of the feudal warlords established their strongholds there, and the magnificent Osaka Castle (built 1586), a major attraction, attests to the city's importance historically. Osaka is also proud of its canals and cultural traditions such as *bunraku* puppets and *kabuki* drama. Nearby are the ancient capitals of Nara and Kyoto (794-1868).

As for climate, the average low temperature in January is about 2 degrees C. (36 degrees F); the average high temperature in August is about 32 degrees C. (90 degrees F). Annual precipitation is approximately 1400 mm. (55 in.). There is some farming in rural districts.

The World Exposition was held at Osaka in 1970. A huge artificial island is being constructed in the bay as the site of the New Kansai International Airport. A high speed train connects Osaka and Tokyo in three hours.

The Mennonite Brethren mission began working in Osaka in 1950. In 1986 ca. 15 congregations were concentrated there, forming the core of the Nihon Menonaito Burezaren Kyodan (Japan Mennonite Brethren Conference). YS

"Osaka Prefecture" in *Kodansha Encyclopedia of Japan,* vol. 6, (Tokyo: Kodansha, 1983), 122.

Overseer. See Bishop.

Owen, St. John, the leading Ojibway Indian pastor of the Pauingassi Mennonite Church in Manitoba. Together with his brother Jacob and cousin Spoot Owen, he was ordained to the ministry in 1972. When the sponsoring mission board, Mennonite Pioneer Mission, indicated their interest in having a local indigenous pastor ordained, the local congregation responded by nominating first the above three, then adding a fourth, David Owen, a brother to Spoot Owen. In 1987, all four are serving as pastors with St. John giving the overall leadership and officiating at baptisms, weddings, and funerals.

St. John Owen came to the faith following a series of Bible studies conducted by a Mennonite missionary, Dave Burkholder of the Northern Light Gospel Mission, (ME IV:1112) and an Ojibway local leader, Sam Quill of Pikangikum, Ont. Although St. John did not make his commitment overtly at the meetings, he did so when he entered the workshop of missionary Henry Neufeld on Oct. 14, 1964. His longstanding trust in Henry Neufeld was enough for St. John to share his quest for the faith, his willingness to abandon those aspects of "Indian medicine" which were harmful. In the words of Henry Neufeld "after St. John's confession and after our discussion, we knelt right there in the workshop, prayed and St. John came to the faith."

As a means of nurturing his faith, St. John meets with his colleague pastors and other Christians of Pauingassi to read the Scriptures from the Cree Bible (the Ojibway New Testament was first printed in July 1988), deliberate on the meanings, and pray for strength. As part of their itinerant ministry among Native communities of northern Canada, Henry Neufeld and his wife Elna regularly return to Pauingassi to assist the local leaders and the congregation with Bible studies.

St. John Owen and his wife Mary continue to make their living in the traditional way by hunting, fishing, and gathering wild rice. MW

Oyer, Emma (Aug. 6, 1886 - May 10, 1951), worked at the Mennonite Home Mission in Chicago from 1907 to 1946. She was born near Metamora, Ill., to John P., and Mary (Smith) Oyer and died at St. Johns, Mich. At age 14 she became a member of the Metamora Mennonite Church (MC). During the 39 years she worked at the Mennonite Home Mission in Chicago she taught Sunday school, summer Bible school, and a women's Bible class; did counseling and visitation; and was in charge of a "Fresh Air" program which sent Chicago children to live with rural Illinois Mennonite families during the summer months. For 30 years her co-worker was Anna °Yordy. Emma wrote a history of the Home Mission entitled *What God Hath Wrought: In a Half Century at the Home Mission* (Elkhart: MBM, 1949), which contains additional information about her ministry. In 1946 failing health caused her to retire to the home of her parents and sisters in St. Johns, Mich., where she spent the rest of her life. ESR

Missionary Sewing Circle Monthly (July, 1951); Rich, *Mennonite Women* (1983), 149.

See also Urban Church.

P

Pacific Coast Conference (MC) (ME IV:103) included 24 congregations in Oregon, Idaho, and Washington in 1986. The membership of these congregations was 2,284. The South Seattle and (Portland) Peace congregations had joint Mennonite Church (MC) and General Conference Mennonite (GCM) affiliation, and Ranch Chapel near Culver included members affiliated with other denominations. Sixteen congregations, including four Hispanic ones, were organized after 1955; two of these disbanded. Eleven congregations have withdrawn from the conference since 1960. One soon disbanded, one has no Mennonite relationships, two function as community churches but relate to the conference, and two relate to Western Conservative Mennonite Fellowship. Several also relate to Bible Mennonite Fellowship.

The Pacific Coast Mennonite Mission Board began mission work in Mexico in 1955. In 1970 a committee representing conference and unaffiliated congregations assumed oversight of the work. The board also encouraged church planting in the United States in the early 1980s. In 1981, Logsden began the Toledo Mennonite Fellowship; New Covenant at Portland organized in 1981 and withdrew in 1985; Emmaus at Portland organized in 1982 and disbanded a year later. *Missionary Evangel* is the quarterly conference publication. The official conference archives is located in a vault at Western Mennonite High School, with additional holdings in Eugene and elsewhere; holdings are not indexed or catalogued. The conference owns and operates Western Mennonite High School at Salem and the Mennonite Home at Albany, which provides nursing and residential care and independent living apartments for the elderly. HKL

Hope Kauffman Lind, "Mennonites in Oregon and Related Congregations in Neighboring States (1876-1976)" (unpublished manuscript); Pacific Coast Conference (MC), Annual Report, 1986, 9, 13; *MC Yearbook* (1986-87), 82-83, 124-26, 129, 131, 133, 159.

Pacific District Conference (GCM) (ME IV:103), with its 26 churches and 2,611 members, has become increasingly urban and ethnically diverse in recent years. Eleven new churches planted between 1960 and 1987 have become part of the district. All are in large urban areas in Arizona (4), California (4), Washington (2), and Oregon (1). Congregations include people of Hispanic, Chinese, Hopi Indian, Dutch, and Swiss ethnic backgrounds. Currently (1983-85) 62 percent of those baptized in the conference's congregations do not have parents who are Mennonites. In 1985, the conference set the goal of more than doubling the number of congregations within seven years.

Despite the new congregations, total membership is about 800 less than in 1959. Some older congregations have declined, while three congregations left the conference in the 1980s because of the lack of sympathy with Anabaptist teachings. In response, the conference is giving more emphasis to °church planting and growth as well as more guidance in the calling of pastors.

Increased cooperation with the two Mennonite Church (MC) district conferences in the five-state area has occurred. Joint annual conferences and a pastor-and-spouse retreat have been held with both Pacific Coast and Southwest Conferences. Four new congregations have been started in joint ventures with Southwest Conference. Discussion is underway to promote further cooperation and possible future integration. JRW

Henry Esch, ed. *The Mennonites in Arizona* (Phoenix: the author, 1985); Stephen Intagaliata, "An Accurate Picture of the Pacific District Conference of the General Conference Mennonite Church: 1975-1985" (unpublished manuscript, Fuller Theological Seminary, 1986); Hope Kauffman Lind, "Mennonites in Oregon and Related Congregations in Neighboring States (1876-1976)" (unpublished manuscript); *GCM Handbook* (1988), 115-16, 142, 150; *Pacific District Messenger*, is published six times a year.

Pacific District Conference (MB) (ME IV:104), established in 1912 at Reedley, Cal., consisted of 43 congregations with an approximate membership in 1986 of 7,350. Two congregations are located in Washington, three in Oregon, thirty-seven in California, and one in Arizona. Nineteen other congregations have existed at various times but have since closed. During its first few decades, the Pacific District received new members primarily through migration from midwestern Mennonite Brethren congregations, especially during 1915-20 and 1935-40, when the conference experienced its most significant growth. The conference supports Fresno Pacific College, a liberal arts college founded in 1944 as Pacific Bible Institute. A high school and five retirement °homes are supported by various congregations within the conference, although they are not formally affiliated with the conference as a whole. Since the mid-1950s the conference has engaged in significant ministry among °Hispanics in California's San Joaquin Valley; eight Pacific District congregations are primarily Hispanic in membership (1986). A Bible school, Instituto Biblico del Pacifico (Bible Institute of the Pacific) was founded in 1984. The archives of the Pacific District Conference are housed in the Center for Mennonite Brethren Studies at Fresno, Cal. KE-R

Year book of the Pacific District Conference of Mennonite Brethren Churches (1912ff.); John A. Toews, *History MB* (1975) 146-49, 202, 205, 209.

Page, Alice Thut and William B., physician and missionaries to India. Born at Oakland Mills, Pa., Jan. 5, 1871, William B. Page died at Goshen, Ind., June 14, 1945. He was the son of Tobias and Anna Brubaker Page. He and Alice Thut (1872-1951) of New Stark, Ohio were married on July 3, 1895. Together they parented five children.

While William was a student at Chicago Medical School, he and Alice were among the founders of the Chicago Home Mission (MC). After several years of medical practice they volunteered to accompany J. A. °°Ressler as missionaries to India in 1899. William Page and Ressler traveled throughout Central India before locating a field in the Chhattisgarh region of the Central Provinces (°Madhya Pradesh). William Page was quickly involved in a medical ministry but due to ill health had to return to North America in 1900. He continued his medical practice in Middlebury and Goshen, Ind., where he and his wife were founding members of Eighth Street Mennonite Church.   JAL

Who's Who Mennonites (1943), 185; Rich, *Mennonite Women* (1983), 132, 148, 227; John A. Lapp, *India* (1972), 37.

Painting and Printmaking (ME I:165). During the mid-20th c. a new awakening in the visual arts occurred among North American Mennonites. This article focuses primarily on developments in the United States. The awakening happened, in part, due to the establishment of visual art programs at several Mennonite colleges and because of the need for artists at Mennonite publishing houses. An exhibition of visual art organized by the Goshen College art department staff in 1975, celebrating the 450th anniversary year of the Anabaptist Mennonite movement, attracted 54 professional Mennonite artists. A subsequent exhibition of Mennonite artists' work at Goshen College was held in 1980. A catalog of these artists' work was published for each exhibition. A visual arts exhibition was held at the Tenth Mennonite World Conference, Wichita, Ks., in 1978. This exhibition and its catalog, the latter edited by Ethel Abrahams, identified an additional 74 Mennonite artists. Thus these three exhibitions identified 128 artists who were professionally active in making art in North America.

While many Mennonite artists of Canada and United States received their education at art institutes, state universities, and private colleges, the majority of the documented North American Mennonite artists received their undergraduate art education in Mennonite colleges. J. P. Klassen (1888-1975), a potter-sculptor, directed an art program at Bluffton College, Ohio from 1924 to 1958. He was followed by Darvin Luginbuhl (b. 1921), a potter, who chaired the department from 1958 to 1984. He was joined by Jay Baumbaugh (b. 1966). Gregg J. Luginbuhl (b. 1949), a potter, began chairing the department in 1984. A similar program was begun in 1926 at Goshen College, (Ind.) by John F. Slabaugh. He was followed in 1927 by Arthur L. Sprunger (1897-1972), a painter-sculptor who developed eight courses in art offered in alternate years. He worked part-time at the college while teaching full-time at Goshen High School. He was followed by Ezra S. Hershberger (b. 1904), a painter, who expanded the

program to 16 courses in 1955, establishing a full major in art. He retired from teaching in 1970. Abner H. Hershberger (b. 1934), a painter-printmaker, began teaching at Goshen in 1965, chairing the department from 1970. He was joined by Marvin P. Bartel (b. 1937), a potter, in 1970; Alta Hertzler (1937-1983), a fiber artist; and Judy Wenig-Horswell. Two hundred art majors had graduated from Goshen College by 1987. Art courses at Bethel College (Ks.) began as early as 1895. Lena Waltner (b. 1895), a painter, taught art from 1934 to 1960 during which time a minor in art was begun. Robert W. Regier (b. 1930), a printmaker-painter, has chaired the department since 1966 and has developed an art major along with Paul A. Friesen (b. 1923), a potter-sculptor and part-time instructor at Bethel (late 1950s to 1987). To this staff was added Miguel Almanza who taught from 1968 to 1981, and Gail Lutsch, 1981ff. By 1987 more than 110 students have graduated from Bethel with art majors. Friesen began an art program at Hesston College (Ks.) in 1956 and was followed by John R. Blosser (b. 1944), a painter, in 1978. Katherine Bartel (b. 1953), a fiber artist, joined the art staff at Bethel College in 1985. An art major was begun at Eastern Mennonite College, Harrisonburg, Va., in 1970 by Stanley A. Kaufman (b. 1939), a painter, and joined in 1975 by Jerry Lapp (b. 1945), a potter. This program was discontinued in 1985 due to budget cuts. The art gallery program along with a few art courses were retained. On the West Coast Rod Harder (b. 1950), a painter, taught art courses at Pacific College, Fresno, Cal., from 1972 to 1985 and then moved to New York City to continue painting there.

At each of the Mennonite colleges offering a major in art, gallery programs were developed during the 1960s. These monthly exhibits provided a rich source of original works of art for the students and communities they serve. The above mentioned artist-teachers involved in the development of Mennonite college art programs have been dedicated not only to teaching art, but also in the production of art. All have shown their work regularly in local, regional, and in many cases, national exhibitions. Their art works are included in numerous art collections. In response to the "Mennonite Artists Contemporary" art exhibition held at Goshen College, Dennis Adrian, a Chicago art historian and critic, wrote the following:

"What this fascinating effort demonstrates conclusively is that modern Mennonite artists have come to feel (and have felt for some time) that any art, if it be understood as the revelation of the positive activity of the human awareness, is an enhancement of and contribution to the spiritual basis and purpose of both the artist and his public. This does not mean that Mennonite artists concern themselves with exclusively "spiritual" doctrinal or religious subject matter, but that the contemporary Mennonite community has for some time now regarded the visual arts as being as naturally and as properly integrated within Mennonite identity as music has been for more than four centuries."

Painters and printmakers are highlighted in the paragraphs that follow. For information about Mennonite artists in related visual media see °Ceramics,

°Graphic Design, °Folk Art, and °Photography; also see an additional list of painters and printmakers at the end of this article and the following catalogs: Abner H. Hershberger, *Mennonite Artists Contemporary* (Goshen College Press, 1975, 1980); Ethel Ewert Abrams, *Mennonite World Conference: Tenth Assembly* (Hillsboro, Ks.: Mennonite Brethren Publishing House, 1978).

Albert Henry Krehbiel (1873-1945) was an early American Impressionist painter and for almost four decades a member of the faculty of the School of the Art Institute of Chicago. He was the son of Anna and John Jacob Krehbiel of Denmark, Iowa. (His father later became a carriagemaker and a cofounder of Bethel College, Ks.) In the 1890s A. H. Krehbiel studied at the Art Institute of Chicago and was awarded the school's American Traveling Scholarship, which enabled him to study for several years under European artists, including Jean Paul Laurens at the Academie Julian in Paris. Krehbiel received four gold prizes of the Academie and also the Prix de Rome. Returning to the Chicago area he became known as a landscape painter. In 1907 he was commissioned to paint the murals for the Illinois Supreme Court in Springfield.

Oliver Wendell Schenk, (b. 1903), a painter from Gomer, Ohio, lives and works at Southwest Harbor, Maine. He attended Goshen College and the Art Students League of New York City. His artwork appeared with some regularity in the *Saturday Evening Post, Colliers Magazine,* and *Ford Times,* 1949-60. His work includes portraits of Mennonite and Anabaptist leaders, including Christopher °°Dock, George °°Blaurock, Conrad °Grebel, and Felix °°Mantz. The latter three paintings were commissioned by Laurelville Mennonite Center in Pennsylvania.

Ezra S. Hershberger (1904-) painter, was born at Milford, Nebr. He graduated from Goshen College in 1934. He studied at the Art Institute of Chicago and U. of Iowa and received an MA degree in 1956 at the U. of Northern Colorado. He taught at Mount Herman School, Darjeeling, India (1938-42); McPherson College, Kansas (1945-55); and at Goshen College (1955-70). His paintings, mostly of the landscape, are representational in style, have been shown at the U. of Northern Colorado, South Bend Art Center, Wabash College, and Fort Wayne Art Center. He is represented in the collections of McPherson College and Goshen College.

Woldemar Neufeld (b. 1909), was born in the Ukraine and immigrated with his family to Waterloo, Ont. After graduating from the Cleveland Art Institute he moved to New York City in 1945, and four years later settled at New Milford, Conn., where he established a permanent studio. His watercolors, oils and relief paints depict such themes as New England landscapes, New York City East River scenes, and Lancaster Co. Pa., scenes. Neufeld's work is found in the permanent collections of the Metropolitan Museum of Art, the Cleveland Museum of Art, the Library of Congress, and the Boston Public Library.

Margaret Balzer Cantieni (b. 1914), from Northfield, Minn., is a painter who studied at Carleton College and the School of the Art Institute of Chicago. Additionally, she received instruction from Josef Albers, W. S. Hayter's Atelier 17 in Paris, and Black Mountain College. She taught at Berea College, 1937-46, and at the Baum School of the Allentown Art Museum 1965-70. Her work has been shown at the Brooklyn Museum, the Art Institute of Chicago, and Lehigh U., and is found in the collections of Berea College, the U. of Louisville, Lehigh U. and Carleton College.

Naomi Nissley Limont (b. 1927), a printmaker-painter in Philadelphia was born in Chester Co. Pa. She received her art education at the Pennsylvania Academy of Fine Arts and studied at Tyler School of Art completing a graduate level degree there in 1965. Her work has been exhibited nationally and is represented in collections at Harvard U., the Philadelphia Museum of Art and the U. of Pennsylvania. Her illustrations were featured in the *Mennonite Community Cookbook,* edited by Mary Emma Showalter.

Warren Rohrer (b. 1927), a painter born in Lancaster, Pa., attended Eastern Mennonite College and studied art at the Pennsylvania Academy of Fine Arts. He taught at the Academy of Fine Arts, then, in 1978, at the Philadelphia College of Art. He has shown his work throughout the United States and is represented in the permanent collections of the Philadelphia Museum of Art, the Pennsylvania Academy of Fine Arts, the U. of Delaware, and the Metropolitan Museum of Art in New York City. Best known of his works among Mennonites is a woodcut of Menno Simons located at the Goshen College Mennonite Historical Library.

Robert W. Regier (1930-) painter-printmaker, was born at Mountain Lake, Minn. He graduated from Bethel College, Kansas (BA, 1952), studied at the Art Institute of Chicago, Wichita State U., and the U. of Illinois (MFA, 1965). He was art director for Mennonite Central Committee and the General Conference Mennonite Church (1957-63). He taught art at Bethel College, 1965-. Exhibitions of his paintings and prints, usually abstract images derived from nature, have been shown at Northwest Printmakers, Seattle; 7th Midwest Biennial, Omaha; Annual Boston Printmakers, Tulsa; and Regional and Mid-America Exhibit, Kansas City. His work is represented in the collections of DeCordova Museum of Contemporary Art, Lincoln, Mass.; Wichita Art Museum; Kansas State College, Fort Hays, Ks., and at Hesston (Kansas), Goshen and Bethel colleges.

Abner H. Hershberger (1934-) painter-printmaker, was born at Milford, Nebr., moved to Casselton, N.D. in 1937. He studied art at Goshen College (BA, 1960), and until 1964 taught art in Indiana public schools. He studied at the U. of Notre Dame, Indiana U. (MAT, 1965), and at the U. of Michigan (MFA, 1970). He taught art at Goshen College since 1965. His work, generally abstract and based on themes from nature, has been shown at Avanti Gallery, New York City; U. of Michigan; Indianapolis Museum of Art; Gruen Gallery, Chicago; and Adamson Gallery, Washington, D.C. He is represented in the collections of Wesley Theological Seminary, Washington, D.C.; Jackson, Mississippi Art Center; Kala Institute, Berkeley, Cal.; and at Eastern Mennonite, Goshen, Hesston, Bluffton, Bethel, and Messiah colleges.

Gathie Falk (b. 1940), of Vancouver, B.C., works in two- and three-dimensional art media. She has shown widely in North America including shows at the U. of California, Santa Barbara; the New York Cultural Center; and the Montreal Art Museum. She is represented in collections at the U. of British Columbia, the Vancouver Art Gallery, the federal Department of External Affairs in Ottawa, and many private collections. She has been featured numerous times in *Arts Canada* since Dec. 1969, and in *Studio International* (Winter 1970) and *Art in America* (May 1972).

John R. Blosser (1944-) painter, lived at North Canton, Ohio. He attended Bluffton College and graduated from Goshen College in 1970 with a BA in art. He also studied at Bowling Green State U. (MA, 1979), and at Arizona State U. (MFA, 1987). He taught at Garden Valley Collegiate, Winkler, Manitoba (1975-78), and at Hesston College since 1978. His drawings and paintings are usually integrated abstract and representational compositions. He has shown at Bowling Green State U., Arizona State U., U. of Kansas, and at Wichita State U., Eastern Mennonite, Hesston, Bluffton, Goshen, and Bethel colleges.

Elizabeth Wenger of Goshen (b. 1946), creates two-dimensional art works in the medium of *petit point* needlework. Images in her work are figurative, are presented in rich colors, and are usually based on themes taken from biblical texts. She has shown her works at Conrad Grebel College, Goshen College, and the South Bend [Ind.] Art Center. A major collection of her work resides at Associated Mennonite Biblical Seminaries, Elkhart, Ind.

Erma Martin Yost (b. 1947), a painter from Goshen, studied at James Madison U. (BA, 1969; MA, 1975). She has shown her work at the NOHO Gallery in New York City Rockland Center, Nyack, N.Y.; Jersey City Museum; World Trade Center, New York City; and the Bargen Community Museum, Paramus, N.J.. She is represented in collections at Pace U., the Virginia Art Institute, James Madison U., Harrisonburg, Va., and Goshen College. Her paintings are composed of landscape motifs and quilt images.

Wanda Koop (b. 1951), a painter from Vancouver, B.C., graduated in 1973 from the U. of Manitoba with a fine arts degree. Born to a Russian Mennonite family, she was featured in a special cover article in *Canadian Art* (Fall, 1984). Her paintings are representational, billboard size, and have been shown throughout Canada including the Winnipeg Art Gallery, Toronto's Art Gallery and the Glenbow Museum in Calgary. In 1981 she did a 52-foot (16-meter) environmental piece entitled "Wall" for the Manitoba Legislature Building.

Additional painters and printmakers worthy of mention are the following: Ethel Abrahams, James D. Ashcraft, Jerry L. Bontrager, Stanley Paul Book, Mary Lou Brubaker, Sylvia Gross Bubalo, Vladimir L. Bubalo, Jon Cutrell, August R. Ebel, Susan Elaine Ebersole, Allen Eitzen, Ruth Eitzen, Philip Epp, Geneva Flickner, John L. Fretz, Victor Friesen, Anna Emerson Friesen, Clayton Funk, Patricia Galinski, Jena-Pierre Gerber, Ernest Goertzen, Mary Lou Rich Goertzen, Philip Hershberger, Dorcas B. Kraybill, Julie Longacre, Stan Miller, Verna Oyer, Maryls Penner, Randy Penner, Gwen Entz Peterson, John Redekop, Daniel Wade Rupe, James L. Stauffer, Brian Stucky, Paul J. Wolber, Edith L. Yoder, Martha Becker Yoder, Ray Yoder, David Zeizet. AH

Paul Friesen, Gordon D. Kaufman, Warren Kliewer, V. Gerald Musselman, Robert W. Regier, Elaine Sommers Rich, Orlando Schmidt, and David H. Suderman in *Menn. Life,* 20 (Jan. 1965), sp. issue; Ardis Grosjean, "New York City Seminar Focuses on the State of the Arts," *Mennonite* (May 1981), 318; Larry Kehler, "The Artistic Pilgrimage of John P. Klassen," *Menn. Life,* 28 (Dec. 1973), 114-18, 125-27; "John P. Klassen—Artist and Teacher," *Menn. life,* 24 (Oct. 1969), 147-50; Walter Klaassen, "A Christian View of the Fine Arts," *Menn. Life,* 21 (July 1966), 99-106; Rebecca F. Krehbiel, "Albert Henry Krehbiel, 1873-1945: Early American Impressionist," *Menn. Life,* 40 (Mar. 1985), 4-8; John W. Miller, "Creativity and Discipline," *Menn. Life,* 21 (July 1966), 111-14; Randy Penner, "Commercial Art," *Menn. Life,* 21 (July 1966), 115-17; Marion Keeney Preheim, "Robert Regier: Searching for the Essence," *Mennonite* (Nov. 1981), 658; Robert W. Regier, "Art as Process," *Bethel College Bulletin* (Mar. 1968); idem, "The Anabaptists and Art: The Dutch Golden Age of Painting," *Menn. Life,* 23 (Jan. 1968), 16-21; idem, "Art and Environment," *Menn. Life,* 22 (July 1967), 105; idem, "Recent Protest Art," *Menn. Life,* 23 (Apr. 1968), 70-75.

Pakistan. Mennonite Central Committee undertook °refugee work in Lahore, 1948-49, just after the partition of India; participated in a land-leveling project, 1960-76; distributed °relief supplies in East Pakistan, 1963-71; and was briefly involved with Afghan refugees, 1981-82.

The Mennonite Brethren Board of Missions and Services sent Gertrude Klassen, RN (Canada) to the Mission Hospital, Tank, to work with World Mission Prayer League in a village health program, Nov. 1981-May 1985. Ophthalmologist Herb Friesen and his family worked at the Christian Hospital, Taxila, Feb. 1982-Aug. 1983, and with the SERVE relief agency in Peshawar (Afghan Eye Hospital, Aug. 1983-. The Gordon Nickel family (Canada) and Keiko Hamano (Japan) began a church planting ministry in Karachi in 1987. HF

MB Yearbook (1981), 109.

Palmeira, Brazil. See Witmarsum Colony.

Pamphleteering. The early Reformation pamphlets could serve as reminders that the broad public debate of the 1520s does not permit Luther studies, Anabaptist studies, urban studies, peasant studies, etc., to be neatly distinguished. The pamphlets addressed a variety of issues and presented a plethora of views. Illustrated broadsheets appealed beyond the literate to the common people, thus foreshadowing the function of the modern °mass media. Colporteurs read pamphlets aloud in the marketplace while literate laypeople read to friends and relatives at home. Even herdsmen on Alpine pastures were caught up in the trend. They sent for capable readers. The word had become print, reading a social event, and the study of Scripture a passionate pastime. Without pamphlets there would have been no Reformation, and this despite the fact that only about 10 percent of the people could read.

Many of the earliest Anabaptist leaders (e.g., °°Bünderlin, °°Dachser, °°Denck, °°Entfelder, Freisleben [°°Eleutherobios], °°Hätzer, °Hoffman, °Hubmaier, °Marpeck °°Salminger) were themselves pamphleteers. Two colporteurs, Andreas °Castelberger and Hans °Hut, played significant roles in the beginnings of Swiss and (south) German-Austrian Anabaptism respectively. A number of printers such as Balthasar Beck of Strasbourg, Valentin Kobian of Hagenau, Hans Hergot of Nürnberg, Philip Ulhart of Augsburg, and Simprecht Sorg-Froschauer of Nikolsburg appear to have been sympathetic to the radical cause. While some of these times have been noted in marginal comments, Anabaptist scholarship has paid little attention to the pamphlet phenomenon as a whole. As a consequence, scholars lost sight of the public debate within which the early Anabaptist protest was born. Too much ink has been spilled judging the religious content of the lay movement in the light of scholastically honed theologies of the magisterial reformers.

A broad survey of the pamphlet literature suggests that many of the original issues agitating the Anabaptists were aired by the pamphleteers prior to 1525. Not surprisingly, artisans-turned-authors brought a practical agenda to the discussion of reform. Anticlerical feelings nourished by economic, social, or moral grievances provided the leitmotif for much of the pamphlet literature. Clergy, it must be remembered, functioned as landlords and as wardens over bondsmen and collected °tithes, rent, and interest while claiming immunity from the laws and duties that bound ordinary lay people. The pamphleteers denounced clerics as usurious, parasitic manipulators, alcoholics, adulterous fornicators, and hypocrites; they decried *Gelehrten* (the learned) as the *Verkehrten* (the perverted). In contrast the pamphleteers featured the commoner, whether artisan or peasant, as a devotee of the simple gospel, thereby articulating and encouraging lay people to throw off clerical tutelage. They demanded the right for the local community to appoint God-fearing pastors. Some sang the praises of lay preachers who supported themselves by the labor of their hands. Obviously such views had implications for the payment of church taxes (tithe), the taking of interest (usury) on church endowment investments, and the welfare of the poor (common chest), issues inextricably interwoven with early Anabaptist concerns. Calls for a return to the apostolic practice of community of goods (Acts 2) or °mutual aid, the strong moral-ethical teaching on °discipleship (*Nachfolge*), and the °apocalyptic mood could be singled out as other pamphlet themes pertinent to Anabaptist piety. While the identification of such themes does little to explain Anabaptist beginnings or peculiarities, it does delineate the broader climate of opinion out of which the Anabaptist vision emerged.

Modern classifications of the pamphlets are largely irrelevant to Anabaptist studies. Marxists (H. Entner and W. Lenk) distinguished three groups: (1) catholic-feudal, (2) bourgeoisie-reformed and (3) peasant-plebeian. A. Laube and W. Seiffert distinguished further between a moderate orientation and a radical orientation in pamphlets relating to the "revolutionary peoples' movement" of 1525. Non-Marxist classifications seem hardly more imaginative. H. Scheible classified the pamphlets under (1) re-

form, (2) reformation and (3) revolution. At best, such designations help classify authors and content; but contemporary readers did not make such distinctions. The known facts about Anabaptists in Zürich and about Hans Hut's circle may illustrate the point.

Evidence suggests that the founding members of Zürich Anabaptism were familiar with a wide spectrum of pamphlet literature cutting diagonally across modern classifications from moderate to radical. They read °°Erasmus, °°Luther, °°Zwingli, and some of the other reformers (e.g., °°Oecolampadius). In a letter to Vadian, dated July 15, 1523, Grebel cited a pamphlet by Jacob Strauss of the same year, a tract by Erasmus which appeared one month previously and a work by Ulrich von Hutten which had appeared in Augsburg only two weeks previously. He also cited "Balaam's Ass" with the revealing subtitle "Concerning the Ban That It Dare Not Be Imposed in Payment of Money Debts and Similar Slight Matters and That the Clergy Are Responsible to Obey the Worldly Authorities If They Desire to be Christian" by Mathis Wurm of Geydertheim. As tension between the radicals and Zwingli increased, the reading menu shifted to Karlstadt (°°Carlstadt), °°Westerburg, °Müntzer, Stiefel, Ziegler and Hätzer. The pamphlets of these authors ranged from discussions of usury to images, purgatory, mass for the dead, the nature of the sacraments including baptism, and questions of tarrying for the weak in matters of reform. The radicals were interested in content with a direct application to their situation. In his Bible school for commoners, Castelberger functioned as both a supplier and interpreter of the literature as well as a guide to Scriptural study. We learn that within a week of the appearance of Zwingli's "Little Book on Baptism" (*Taufbüchlin*) in 1525, Castelberger read and refuted the same before peasant visitors. Without question then, the original Anabaptists were not closeted readers of the Bible, but avid students of current affairs who kept abreast of the latest press releases. Further research may identify other reading materials pertinent to understanding their development.

The literature read by Hans Hut and his inner circle is more difficult to determine. Evidence suggests that from 1521 on he bought, bound, and sold books and pamphlets in an area that stretched from Wittenberg to Salzburg and from Würzburg to Nikolsburg. He dealt in works by Luther, Karlstadt, Müntzer, and others. He brought one of Müntzer's invectives against Luther to the press of Hans Hergot in Nürnberg and must have known Heinrich Pfeiffer's manuscripts. He had dealings with three other pamphleteers, Jorg Haug, Johannes Landsperger, and Wolfgang Vogel, and was probably familiar with the pamphlets of Hans Greiffenberger. Hut knew the Anabaptist pamphleteers Hubmaier, Denck, °°Langenmantel, Dachser, Salminger, and possibly the Freisleben brothers. Future studies of the literature circulating in the geographic area of Hut's activity may shed further light on the religious-social concerns of his followers.

The above examples illustrate that the first generation of Anabaptists heartily embraced a relatively new form of communication to inform themselves and others. They were anything but disinterested bystanders in a broad public debate.   WOP

"Sixteenth-Century Pamphlets in German and Latin, 1501-1530," ed. by Hans-Joachim Köhler et al. (microform edition by the Interdocumentation Company, Zug, Switzerland). The best biography is still Arnold Kuczynskis, *Thesaurus Libellorum Historiam Reformationis Illustrantium. Verzeichniß einer Sammlung von nahe zu 3000 Flugschriften Luthers und seiner Zeitgenossen* (reprint, Nieuwkoop, 1969). Among useful published editions are the following: Arnold E. Berger, ed., *Die Sturmtruppen der Reformation. Ausgewählte Flugschriften der Jahre 1520-1525*, 3 vols. (Leipzig, 1935-36); Otto Clemen, ed., *Flugschriften aus den ersten Jahren der Reformation*, 4 vols. (reprint, Nieuwkoop, 1967); Oskar Schade, ed., *Satiren und Pasquillen aus der Reformationszeit*, 3 vols. (reprint, Hildesheim, 1966); Adolf Laube and Hans-Werner Seiffert, eds., *Flugschriften der Bauernkriegszeit* (Cologne, 1978); A. Götze and L. E. Smitt, eds., *Flugschriften der Reformationszeit: Aus dem sozialischen und politischen Kampf* (Cologne, 1953). Secondary publications on the pamphleteers, presses, printers, and pamphlets are voluminous. A sampling follows: Karl Schottenloher, *Philip Ulhart: Ein Augsburger Winkeldrucker und Helfershelfer der 'Schwärmer' und 'Wiedertäufer' (1523-1529)* (reprint, Nieuwkoop, 1967); H. Entner and W. Lenk, "Literatur und Revolution im 16. Jahrhundert," *Weimarer Beiträge*, 16 (1970), 139-62; Heinz Scheible, "Reform, Reformation, Revolution: Grundsätze zur Beurteilung der Flugschriften," *ARG*, 65 (1974), 108-43; Werner Lenk, "Frühbürgerliche Revolution und Literatur," *Weimarer Beiträge*, 21 (1975); John S. Oyer, "The Influence of Jacob Strauss on the Anabaptists: A Problem in Historical Methodology," in *The Origins and Characteristics of Anabaptism*, ed. Marc Lienhard (The Hague, 1977), 62-82; Hans-Joachim Köhler, ed., *Flugschriften als Massenmedium der Reformationszeit* (Stuttgart, 1981); Ferdinand Seibt, "Johannes Hergot: The Reformation of the Poor Man," in *Profiles of Radical Reformers*, ed. by Hans-Jürgen Goertz (Scottdale, 1982) 97-106; Werner Packull, "The Image of the 'Common Man'" in the Early Pamphlets of the Reformation (1520-1525)," *Historical Reflections*, 12 (1985), 253-77; Paul Russell, *Lay Theology in the Reformation: Popular Pamphleteers in Southwest Germany, 1521-1525* (Cambridge U. Press, 1986).

See also Peasants' War.

Panama. Mennonite presence in Panama is represented by the Iglesia Evangélica Unida (Evangelical United Church), which was founded among the Choco people in Darien Province of southern Panama in 1961. The congregations of this conference originated through a literacy and adult education program aided by the Mennonite Brethren Board of Missions and Services. This was an outgrowth of Mennonite Brethren mission work in Colombia. The conference has been mainly indigenous from the beginning and is fully autonomous. It was officially incorporated in 1971 with a board of directors.

Leaders of the conference are trained through an extension Bible school, and some of the leaders have training in health services and teaching education from national schools. The conference takes an active part not only in evangelizing, but also in health care and training in hygienic practices and in basic education, which is partially supported by the national government. The conference is confronted with some resistance to the implementation of modern health practices and education and must work to help the people with their economic and social problems while also insuring that their cultural identity is maintained. Loss of church membership through scattering of people seeking economic improvement is also a problem. In 1984 the conference had 400 members worshiping in 15 centers.   RSa

MWH (1978), 239-41; *MWH* (1984), 92; *Chr. Leader* (Aug. 21, 1984), 39.

Pannabecker, Charles Lloyd (Apr. 15, 1896-Jan. 18, 1987), medical missionary and superintendent of the mission hospital in Puyang [formerly Kai Chow], Hebei [Hopei] Province, China, 1926-41. (In 1987 Puyang is located in Henan [Honan] Province.) He and his wife, Lelia E. Roth (1898-1956), served under the Board of Foreign Missions (GCM). He guided the hospital during years in which military encounters and natural disasters occurred frequently in that area. The hospital grew from 35 to 80 beds during that time and maintained outstation clinic work and a school of nursing. It was the only recognized hospital within a six-county area (pop. 2,200,000).

Pannabecker was born in Petoskey, Mich., the son of Jacob Nelson and Luna May (Plowman) Pannabecker. His father was a minister in the Mennonite Brethren in Christ church [Missionary Church]. Pannabecker was baptized and joined that church in his youth. He studied at Bluffton College (AB, 1917), the U. of Michigan (MD, 1925), and completed residency training in ophthalmology at the U. of Michigan (1944). He and his twin brother Floyd served together in China; younger brothers were Karl and Ray (minister and educator in the [United] Missionary Church).

After returning from China, C. L. Pannabecker practiced ophthalmology in Peoria, Ill. (1944-1974), where he was active in the Presbyterian church. Children of Lloyd and Lelia were Betty Jean, Anita (Bohn), Donald L., and Daniel N. In 1961 he married Clara Neumann.   ARR

Who's Who Mennonites (1943), 187; *Mission Quarterly*, 4, no. 3 (Newton, May, 1928), 2-8; "Kai Chow General Hospital," *Mennonite* (Apr. 21, 1936), 11-13; *MWR* (Jan. 22, 1987) 3.

Pannabecker, Samuel Floyd (Apr. 15, 1896-Sept. 14, 1977). Born at Petoskey Mich., to Jacob Nelson Pannabecker and Luna May Plowman-Pannabecker, S. F. Pannabecker married Sylvia Lydia Tschantz, of Dalton, Ohio, on Aug. 3, 1921. Their children were Richard, Robert, Alice Ruth (m. Robert Ramseyer). Reared in a Mennonite Brethren in Christ (Missionary Church) home, S. F. Pannabecker graduated from Bluffton College (AB, 1917), Witmarsum Theological Seminary (MA, 1918), Garrett Biblical Institute, (BD, 1933), and Yale U. (PhD, 1944) and was awarded honorary doctorates by Bethel College, Bluffton College, and Bethany Biblical Seminary (Chicago).

After teaching science for five years at Bluffton College, he went to China as a missionary and educator under the General Conference Mennonite Church (1923-41). Proficient and well-trained in the Chinese language as well as in biblical and historical studies, from 1935 to 1941 he was chairperson of the China mission of the General Conference of Mennonites at Puyang [formerly Kai Chow], Hebei [Hopei] Province, China. (In 1987, Puyang is located in Henan [Honan] Province.) After completing doctoral studies at Yale and teaching one year at Bluffton College, he returned to China, 1945-46, he opened the Mennonite Central Committee relief unit in Kaifeng.

Unable to continue missionary service in China because of the Sino-Japanese War and later the People's Revolution, he served Mennonite Biblical

Seminary, first as dean and professor of missions, then as president in Chicago (1947-58), and then, in Elkhart, as dean (1958-64), registrar (1964-69) and archivist (1969-77). Highly appreciated and respected as missionary mentor, seminary administrator, and church historian, he authored three major publications, *Faith in Ferment* (Newton, 1968), a history of the Central District Conference (GCM); *Ventures of Faith* (Elkhart: Mennonite Biblical Seminary, 1975); and *Open Doors* (Newton, 1975), the history of the General Conference Mennonite Church based on his Yale doctoral dissertation. Skilled also in photography and fascinated by his status as a twin of Charles Lloyd °Pannabecker, a medical missionary and ophthalmologist, he also wrote for his grandchildren *We Two, Twice Twinned: Story of the Pannabecker Twins from Cradle to College*, published posthumously by his family (1977).   EW

Who's Who Mennonites (1943); *Menn. Bib. II*, p. 489.

Pannabecker, Sylvia Tschantz (Jan. 29, 1893-June 2, 1974). Born at Dalton, Ohio, to John H. and Elizabeth (Geiger) Tschantz; Sylvia Tschantz married Samuel Floyd Pannabecker on Aug. 13, 1921. She was the mother of Richard (Bluffton, Ohio), Robert (Kailua, Hawaii), and Alice Ruth (m. Robert Ramseyer), a missionary to Japan.

While attending the academy and the college at Bluffton, Ohio, she developed a strong sense of a missionary call, was active in the Student Volunteer Movement as well as the YWCA, and graduated in 1917. She then went to China as a missionary in 1923. Together she and her husband studied the Chinese language at Beijing and Tamingfu and then served many years at Puyang [formerly Kai Chow]. As social and political conditions in China deteriorated after 1937 and the Sino-Japanese War got under way, she experienced wartime dangers and hard-

ships and in 1941 on advice of the American consul returned to the United States with the children while her husband remained in China for a few additional months. From 1944 to 1946 she taught religious education in the Bluffton, Ohio, public schools.

When her husband was called to administrative leadership in Mennonite Biblical Seminary in Chicago, Ill., Sylvia soon gained stature as a beloved and admired "seminary hostess," recognized especially for her deep spirituality and her personal interest in and helpfulness to many generations of seminary students. This ministry continued also into the years after Mennonite Biblical Seminary relocated to Elkhart, Ind., in 1958. A biographer has characterized her ministry with the caption "Prayer—Her Most Important Work" (Unrau). Manifestly, the partnership of Samuel Floyd and Sylvia Tschantz Pannabecker as a kingdom team in missions and in theological education has made a significant impact on Mennonite Biblical Seminary and the General Conference Mennonite Church.   EW

Ruth Unrau, *Encircled* (Newton, 1986), 177-84.

Paper-Cutting. See Folk Arts; Folk Arts ("Flowers in the Meadow" [feature]).

Paraguay (ME IV:117). The time after the Paraguayan war against Brazil, Uruguay, and Argentina (1864-70), in which most of the men of Paraguay were killed and in which it suffered great territorial losses, was a time of political chaos. From 1860-1954, a period of 94 years, Paraguay had 40 different presidents, many of whom were removed by strikes or revolution. The result was a very slow national recovery, hindered also by the bloodletting of the °Chaco War (1932-35).

In 1954 General Alfredo Stroessner, son of a Ger-

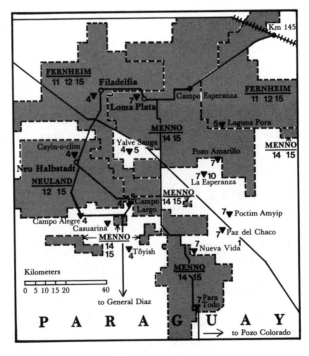

PARAGUAY

LEGEND

MENNONITE CHURCHES IN PARAGUAY

- ▦ International boundary
- ○ Towns & cities with Mennonite congregations
- ● Other towns & cities
- <u>Capitol city</u>
- ◆ Mennonite colonies
- --- Colony boundaries
- ▼ Indian settlements with Mennonite congregations
- — Selected roads
- ╫╫╫ Selected railroads
- ? Indicates the location is only approximate
  (Not all colonies, towns, & settlements with congregations are shown.)

KEY TO GROUPS

Groups	Members
1. Altkolonier Mennoniten Gemeinden (Old Colony)	1100 (1)
2. Beachy Amish Church	59 (2)
3. Bergthaler Mennoniten Gemeinde (Berg. Menn. Ch.)	780
4. Convención de las Iglesias Evangélicas Chulupí (Chulupi Evangelical Convention)	1400
5. Convención de las Iglesias Evangélicas de los Hermanos Lenguas (Lengua Evangelical Convention)	1186
6. Convención Evangélica de los Hermanos Menonitas (Evangelical Convention of Mennonite Brethren)	800
7. Convención de las Iglesias Evangélicas de las Indígenas (United Evangelical Convention)	1450
8. Convención de las Iglesias Evangélicas Unidas Menonitas (United Evangelical Mennonite Churches)	300
9. Eastern Pennsylvania Mennonite Church	38 (2)
10. Evangelical Mennonite Conference Missions/Evangelische Mennonitische Gemeinde	200 +
11. Konferenz der Evangelischen Mennonitischen Bruderschaft von Südamerika (Evan. Menn. Br. Conf. of S. A.)	ca. 200
12. Konferenz der Mennonitischen Brudergemeinde von Paraguay (Conf. of the Menn. Br. Churches of Paraguay)	1200
13. Mennonite Christian Brotherhood	118 (2)
14. Sommerfelder Mennoniten Gemeinde (Sommerfelder Menn. Ch.)	600 (3)
15. Vereinigung der Mennonitengemeinden von Paraguay (Assoc. of Menn. Churches of Paraguay)	4500

Membership figures according to Mennonite World Handbook Supplement (1984).
(1) Membership of 2 colonies.
(2) According to Mennonite Yearbook (1986-87).
(3) Sommerfelder Colony only.

<u>Detail Map</u>

Groups designated by colony only, not by individual congregation.

Colony boundaries as of 1975, acc. to Walter Regehr, Die lebensräumliche Situation der Indianer in paraguayischen Chaco.

man immigrant father and Paraguayan mother, became president. With the support of the Colorado party he has governed Paraguay to the present day (1987). Paraguay's recovery during this time was rapid, not only in its infrastructure, but also in its external political relationships. This also affected the Chaco region, which was won for Paraguay through the Chaco War and which was increasingly integrated into the Paraguayan economy.

While the population of Paraguay grew from 1 million (1930) to 3.5 million, this still is only eight inhabitants per square kilometer. Immigration remains low though the immigration laws are very favorable. The °privileges granted to the Mennonites in 1921, confirmed in law No. 514, remain intact. This has led to further immigration of Mennonites, especially from Mexico since 1969. Total Mennonite membership in Paraguay was estimated in 1987 at 14,000. Though they enjoy special privileges, Mennonites are still well received in Paraguay, particularly by the government, due in large part to the strength of their economic contribution, particularly their °cooperative approach to economics.

Several North American Mennonite-related groups have attempted migrations to Paraguay during the last 30 years, including Old Order Amish (1967-78) at Fernheim Colony and °Beachy Amish Mennonites (1967-) at Luz y Esperanza Colony.   PPK

Herbert Krier, *Tapferes Paraguay*, 4th ed. (Tübingen, (1982); Martin W. Friesen, *Neue Heimat in der Chacowildnis* (Altona, Man.: D. W. Friesen, and Menno Colony: Chortitzer Komitee, 1987); Hans Duerksen, *Fernheim, 1930-1980* (Filadelfia, 1980); Peter P. Klassen, *Immer kreisen die Geier* (Filadelfia, 1983); P. J. Kroeker, "Lenguas and Mennonites: A Study of Cultural Change in the Paraguayan Chaco, 1928-1970" (thesis, Wichita State U., 1970); Wilmar Stahl, *Guided Social Change in the Paraguayan Chaco* (Filadelfia, 1973); Annemarie E. Krause, "Mennonite Settlement in the Paraguayan Chaco" (PhD diss., U. of Chicago, 1952); *Mennoblatt* (1930-); Rudolf Plett, *Presencia menonita en el Paraguay* (Asunción: Instituto Bíblico Asunción, 1979); H. Hack, *Die Kolonisation der Mennoniten im Paraguayischen Chaco* (Amsterdam: Kon. Tropeninstitut); David Dueck, *To Build a Homeland: Home in a Strange Land* (Winnipeg: Mennonite Historical Society of Canada, 1981); Walter Quiring, *Rußlanddeutsche suchen eine Heimat* (Karlsruhe: Heinrich Schneider Verlag, 1938); Walter Regehr, "Die lebensräumliche Situation der Indianer im paraguayischen Chaco" (diss., U. of Basel, 1979); *MWH* (1978), 242-60; *MWH* (1984), 93-101; *MC Yearbook* (1986-87), 160; *GCM Handbook* (1988), 39-40, 92; Luthy, *Amish Settlements* (1985), 2; *MB Yearbook* (1981), 117-18; *Menn. Jahrbuch* (1984), 156-58; Abe Warkentin, comp., *Strangers and Pilgrims* (Steinbach, Man.: Mennonitische Post, 1987); J. W. Fretz, *Immigrant Group Settlements in Paraguay* (North Newton, 1962); H. G. Warren, *Paraguay and the Triple Alliance* (Austin: U. of Texas Press, 1978); Paul H. Lewis, *Paraguay under Stroessner* (Chapel Hill, N.C.: U. of N. Carolina, 1980); Gerhard Ratzlaff, *Deutsches Jahrbuch für 1988: Geschichte, Kultur, Unterhaltung* (Asunción, Paraguay, 1988).

See also Agua Azul Colony; Bergthal Colony; Bergthal Mennonites; Convención Evangélica de Iglesias Paraguayas Hermanos Menonitas; Convención de las Iglesias Evangélicas Chulupi; Convención de las Iglesias Evangélicas de los Hermanos Lenguas; Convención de las Iglesias Evangélicas Unidas; Convención Evangélica Menonita Indiginista; Evangelical Mennonite Conference (Kleine Gemeinde); Fernheim Colony; Friesland Colony; Konferenz der Evangelischen Mennonitischen Brüderschaft von Südamerika (Paraguay and Argentina); Konferenz der Mennonitischen Brüdergemeinden von Paraguay; Licht den Indianern; Luz y Esperanza Colony; Manitoba Colony, Paraguay; Menno Colony; Mennonitisches Missionskomitee für Paraguay; [La] Montaña Colony; Neuland Colony; Old Colony Mennonites; Reinfeld Colony; Rio Corrientes Colony; Rio Verde Colony; Santa Clara Colony; Sommerfeld Colony, Paraguay; Sommerfeld Mennonites; Tres Palmas Colony; Vereinigung der Mennonitengemeinden von Paraguay; Vermittlungs-Komitee; Volendam Colony.

Parimala Bai (b. May 17, 1904), more often addressed in Christian circles as Mrs. Kadar, was born in Hyderabad, Andrha Pradesh, to Narsaya and Sundra Bai. When she was still quite young the family moved to Raipur, Madhya Pradesh, where her father became a minister of the Evangelical Reformed Mission church. Parimala completed her school through the eighth class in the mission schools. She married Kadar Master, a Christian school teacher, ca. 1922, and they moved to Ghatula (an outstation 45 mi. [70 km.] se. of Dhamtari) when he was offered employment with the American Mennonite Mission (MC).

In 1930 Parimala began serving as a Bible woman (°lay evangelist) and continued as a paid evangelist, Bible teacher, and Sunday school worker with the Ghatula evangelist team until 1957. She was an effective communicator of the gospel. At age 83 (1987) she was the oldest living evangelist in the Mennonite Church in India.   JAF

Biographical data supplied by Parimala Bai and J. M. Bhelwa, Ghatula Mennonite Church; 50th Anniversary publication of American Mennonite Mission (1949), 43.

Part Singing. See Singing.

Pasrah Karso (d. 1895). Kedungpenjalin, the first permanent congregation of the Mennonite mission church in Java, Indonesia, was founded (1869) and pastored for 25 years by Pasrah Karso. He was perhaps the most effective of that church's first-generation national leaders. Pasrah (originally Serwo) was born in the village of Sintru near Pati into the family of a nominally Muslim construction worker. His literacy and the respect he was able to command as a leader suggest that traditions about family connections to people of the ruling class may have some credence.

In his youth Pasrah's family moved to the new village of Pulojati near the present-day town of Pecangaan about 7 mi. (11 km.) se. of Jepara. As a young man he, not unlike many Javanese in that time, was on the lookout for new spiritual insight. Frequent dreams and even a mysterious scrap of writing about a God who was the creator of the heavens and earth figures into this search. A new dimension to his search began in 1855, when an acquaintance by the name of Kimah came from Kayu Apu near Kudus to tell him about the new religion being taught there by Nederlandsch Zendelingengenootschap missionary Hoezoo and his assistant, Filemon. Pasrah became very interested and went to Kayu Apu to learn more. Some time later, having agreed to baptism, he failed to appear at the appointed time. Soon thereafter he learned about a missionary working in Jepara, much closer to his home. This was Mennonite missionary Pieter °°Jansz. Karso was attracted by the teaching of Jansz and his assistants, Klinkert and Andreas Ngariman, but he was confused by the fact that they restricted baptism to adults and gave no baptismal certificate. After much hesitation he was finally baptized on Christmas Day, 1865, by Pieter Jansz. He changed his name to Pasrah Karso which means "Surrendered Will."

In sharp contrast to °Tunggul Wulung, the well-known leader of the indigenous Javanese Christian movement in the area, Pasrah Karso willingly served and learned under the guidance of the European missionaries. Soon he was appointed full-time gospel teacher.

Opposition, including arson, in Pulojati caused Pasrah Karso and his associates to seek another location. After several failed attempts, including placement by Jansz in Bondo, a village of the indigenous Christian movement, in order to gain mission influence there, Pasrah Karso finally led his group to form a new hamlet, Kedungpenjalin, in the area of Karanggondang, in 1869. The settlement and the congregation prospered under Pasrah Karso's able leadership without a resident missionary. This took place in spite of Tunggul Wulung's ministry in nearby Bondo and the launching by the mission of the attractive mission agricultural colony project in Margorejo. At the time of Pasrah Karso's death the mission saw it necessary to take firmer action in response to Roman Catholic and Irvingite Apostolic activities in the area and placed Johann °°Hübert, a new missionary from Russia, in Kedungpenjalin. A negative effect of this move, however, was the effective dissolution of the fabric of national congregational leadership that had developed so effectively over the previous quarter century. The youthful national leaders, Yahuda Limbundan and Yohanan Semadin, whom Pasrah had trained to take over leadership now took a back seat. LMY

S. Coolsma, *De Zendingseeuw voor Nederlandsch Oost-Indie* (Utrecht: C. H. E. Breijer, 1901); Doopsgezinde Zendingsvereeniging, *Verslag van de Staat en de Verrigtingen der Doopsgezinde Vereeniging te Bevordering der Evangeliever-breiding in de Nederlandsche Overzeesche Bezittingen* the annual reports of the Dutch Mennonite Mission Union published in Amsterdam beginning in 1848; A. G. Hoekema, "Pieter Jansz (1820-1904), First Mennonite Missionary to Java," *MQR*, 52 (1978), 58-76; P. Jansz, manuscripts of annual reports to the Doopsgezinde Zendingsvereeniging, in the archives of the Evangelical Church of Java in Pati, Indonesia; idem, personal correspondence and journal (Daagboek) in three handwritten vols. covering 1852-1860 in archives of the Doopsgezinde Zendingsraad in Amsterdam; Th. E. Jensma, *Doopsgezinde Zending in Indonesia* ('s Gravenhage: Boekcentrum N. V., 1968); Sigit Heru Soekotjo and Lawrence M. Yoder, "Sejarah Gereja Injili di Tanah Jawa (History of the Evangelical Church of Java), unpublished manuscript; J. D. Wolterbeek, *Babad Zending ing Tanah Jawi* (Purwokerto, Indonesia: De Boer, 1939); Lawrence M. Yoder, ed., *Bahan Serjarah Gereja Injili di Tanah Jawa* [Historical Resources on the History of the Evangelical Church of Java] (Pati, Indonesia: Komisi Sejarah Gereja GITD, 1977); Lawrence M. Yoder, "The Introduction and Expression of Islam and Christianity in the Cultural Context of North Central Java" (PhD diss., Fuller Theological Seminary, 1987).

See also Gereja Injili di Tanah Jawa (Evangelical Church of Java).

Pastoral Counseling is a healing, supporting, guiding, liberating ministry of the faith °community that is based on a relationship between a pastor or a pastoring team with counseling skills and a person or family who come together to engage in conversation and interaction. The relationship is a dynamic process of caring and exploration with a definite structure, and mutually contracted goals. It occurs within the tradition, beliefs and resources of the faith community which surrounds and supports the participants.

Pastoral counseling grounded in an °Anabaptist theology stresses (1) embeddedness in the faith community, which is the context of pastoral care; (2) the integration of both the therapeutic and the ethical dynamics of intrapersonal and interpersonal conflicts; (3) the unity of personal, familial, social, national, and global aspects of °peacemaking and the creation of shalom. Thus, the pastoral counselor in the Mennonite context seeks to nurture healing relationships within the healing community; to clarify health and wholeness as well as °justice and ethically right relationships; to invite reconciliation with oneself, one's significant others and the larger community and world.

A History of Pastoral Care. Pastoral care and counseling have taken different forms throughout the centuries of the Christian faith. In primitive Christianity the focus was on supported care and the endurance of persecution in view of the imminent end of the age. In the period of Roman persecution (ca. 180-324) reconciliation of those who broke down under pressure, and disciplining those who erred was central. Under Constantinian Christianity (after 324) the central motif was guidance and unification of values. Medieval Christendom stressed healing through sacramental rituals as means of grace. In the Protestant Reformation individual reconciliation, particularly of men and women to God, received most attention. During the 18th-c. Enlightenment supportive care which sustained people with moralistic guiding, experiential rigor, and conversionist change was prominent. In the 20th c., individual guidance for self-realization and self-fulfillment have followed the trend toward individualism in the midst of Christian pluralism and private religion.

Anabaptism in its first centuries followed patterns parallel to early Christianity. The first period focused on supportive care for those °suffering persecution. Menno's letters to spouses of martyred pastoral leaders exemplify excellent pastoral care in written communications. In the second period, °discipline and moral guidance were practiced with concern for the sanctity of the group frequently surpassing the welfare of the person. The concern for the integrity and solidarity of community continued the moral approach to the care of souls into the 20th c. Multiple influences contributed to change in pastoral care and the emergence of pastoral counseling as a discipline in training and a contractual relationship of intensified pastoral care. Among these influences were (1) the involvement of Mennonites in °mental health care during °alternative service in World War II; (2) the establishment of mental health centers by Mennonite bodies; (3) the movement from a spirituality of self-sacrifice and self-denial to a spirituality of self-realization; (4) the acceptance of the social sciences and such disciplines as °education, °history, and °sociology; (5) the experience of °clinical pastoral education by pastors; (6) training of pastors in depth counseling for individual, marital, and familial problems; (7) Mennonite pastoral counselors' involvement with their peers in such ecumenical organizations as the Canadian or American Association of Pastoral Counselors. As the pastoral counseling movement has become the fourth major group of persons offering mental health care (psychiatry, °psychology, social work, pastoral counseling), Mennonite pastors and other recognized ministering people in congregation and community have also developed gifts and claimed certification in the practice of psychotherapy from a theological-ethical grounding.

Pastoral Care Across Cultures. Pastoral care and counseling takes varied forms across cultures. The modern Western culture's fascination with introspection is less attractive in much of the Two-Thirds World because (1) there is a preference in non-Western cultures for action-oriented therapies which result in more immediate behavioral change; (2) the deference given to the pastor places more emphasis on guiding, directing, suppporting rather than interpretation and inner exploration; (3) the reliance on the joint family (India), the three-tiered family (China, Japan, Indonesia), and on tribal-communal-familial relations (Africa, Latin America) results in resolving more difficulties within the group. The focus is much more on pastoral care than counseling, more on the relational than the intrapersonal, more on the familial than the individual. Since the resolution of conflict in traditional cultures is preferably done by third-party negotiation rather than direct confrontation, the pastor frequently functions as mediator-facilitator in healing strained relationships.

Pastoral counseling, as a function of intensive pastoral care, takes forms varying from short-term crisis intervention to long-term reconstructive therapy, from individual contract to family therapy, from personal change to communal and social transformation.   DWA

David Augsburger, *Pastoral Counseling Across Cultures* (Philadelphia: Westminster, 1986); P. M. Miller, *Peer Counseling in the Church* (Scottdale, 1975).

See also Spiritual Direction and Formation.

Pastoral Education. Before 1900 the training of Mennonite church leaders was mainly informal in North America and Europe, although a Mennonite theological seminary existed in Amsterdam as early as 1735. With the exception of the Dutch Mennonites there is no Mennonite theological seminary in Europe or the Soviet Union in 1988.

In North America Bible schools, °Bible institutes, colleges and °seminaries have been established for the training of ministers particularly among the General Conference Mennonite Church, Mennonite Brethren, and the Mennonite Church (MC) denominations.

Among the North German and Dutch stream of Mennonites a high priority was placed on trained church leaders. The first North American school among the General Conference Mennonite Church to train young men for Christian work operated from 1868 to 1878 in °°Wadsworth, Ohio. °°Witmarsum Theological Seminary (1921-31) was another early venture which eventually closed its doors. In the 1980s the General Conference Mennonite Church

operates one seminary (Mennonite Biblical) in Elkhart, Ind. The Mennonite Brethren Church has a seminary in Fresno, Calif.

Among Mennonites from the Swiss and South German stream, the Elkhart Institute, forerunner of Goshen College, was established by Mennonite Church (MC) leaders in 1894 to provide "higher education for our young people." There is no explicit reference to the training of church leaders although the result was that some of these students became leaders in the denomination. As with the other Mennonite groups the Mennonite church has experienced the rapid development of educational institutions for the training of pastoral leaders. In 1988 there are two Mennonite Church seminaries. Goshen Biblical Seminary, Elkhart, Ind., which, together with Mennonite Biblical Seminary (GCM), is part of the Associated Mennonite Biblical Seminaries (AMBS). Eastern Mennonite Seminary (EMS) is located at Harrisonburg, Va. Amish Mennonites were slower to accept educated leaders and maintained the uneducated lay ministry as the norm. In 1988 most Amish and conservative Mennonite groups avoid higher education although Bible schools are emerging in some sectors.

The Brethren in Christ have not developed their own seminary-level schools. Messiah College is the major institution providing undergraduate training for the church's ministry. Until the 20th c., ministerial training was informal. It consisted of the heritage one derived from prolonged association with the church and the personal efforts one exerted to improve his knowledge of the Bible, after being chosen by the congregation for ministry among them. Key elements of this informal training were observation of the more experienced ministers and insight gained from one's own involvements in ministry.

As college training gained acceptability among Brethren in Christ, formal training became a significant part of the education for pastoral ministry. In 1988 64 credits of post-secondary courses in Bible and related subjects are required of those seeking ordination. Included in these credits are four required courses in Brethren in Christ history, doctrine (2), and polity. The educational requirements for ordination can be fulfilled through correspondence courses (administered by the denomination's Board for Ministry and Doctrine) or through study at a Bible college, Christian liberal arts college (preferably Messiah College), or seminary. Since younger candidates frequently desire a seminary education, the denomination has made available scholarship aid to assist them, and has recommended their study at schools within the Anabaptist, Wesleyan, or Pietist heritage. Ministers transferring into the church from another denomination are required to meet the same standards noted above for ministerial credentials, including the mandatory Brethren in Christ courses.

The larger Mennonite groups in North America have followed mainline Protestant churches in opting for a professionally trained ministry with the three-year Master of Divinity (MDiv) degree as the primary professional degree. The Bachelor of Theology degree, a forerunner of the MDiv degree, continues to be the primary pastoral training degree for various Bible colleges particularly in Canada.

Pastoral education in Canada has taken a specific shape reflecting the needs of various Mennonite groups. In the 1930s, 1940s, and 1950s °Bible colleges, Bible institutes, and Bible schools offered leadership education for most Mennonite denominations. In Winnipeg Mennonite Brethren Bible College (1944) and Canadian Mennonite Bible College (Conference of Mennonites in Canada [GCM], 1947) emerged in response to growing educational expectations. These schools, alongside the Bible colleges developed more recently, e.g., Columbia Bible College (a joint MB and CMC [GCM] institution in Clearbrook, B.C.) and Steinbach Bible College (EMCon and EMMC; Steinbach, Man.) provide basic training for ministry at the baccalaureate level (BTh). As Mennonites have moved to a more professional view of ministry, educational expectations, have risen as well. In 1988 educational patterns remain mixed in the smaller Mennonite groups, where many leaders serve with the basic BTh degree or less.

Regent College (Vancouver) and a variety of nondenominational Bible colleges have become attractive options to an increasing number of Mennonites preparing for service as pastoral leaders. Conrad Grebel College (CMC [GCM], MC; Waterloo, Ont.) developed a Master of Theological Studies program in 1987 to offer a graduate academic degree for lay people interested in the study of Christianity and the mission of the Christian church in the world.

The continuing recognition of lay ministry as a viable model particularly in segments of the Mennonite Church (MC) has necessitated the development of in-service training programs. The mentor-trainee teaching model has spawned Paul-Timothy programs which combine reading and reflection with the experience of ministry. The Conference-Based Theological Education program initiated by AMBS and EMS is another response to district conference interest in training leaders on location. These programs have not only been designed to train lay leaders as well as providing continuing education for those leaders with previous training but some conferences have also designed programs with academic courses leading to the basic MDiv degree. Students can take up to two years of credit in this manner and finish their final year at one of the Mennonite seminaries.

No other movement has affected pastoral training as significantly as has °clinical pastoral education (CPE). Using the ministry context as a learning base this movement has incorporated the teaching elements of experience, reflection, supervision, case studies, peer support groups, action-reflection research papers, and relevant literature to provide another model to educate pastors. Seminaries have recognized the value of this form of education and have adjusted their programs in order to incorporate CPE into the curriculum. CPE has had a strong institutional bias in that training usually occurs in hospitals and prisons. Some efforts have been made to offer this training in congregational settings as well. Training for °urban ministries and for ministry to socially disadvantaged groups has followed similar models of action-reflection learning.

°Theological education by extension is another form of decentralized pastoral education more common in Central and South America. Church educators in North America are exploring the possibilities of training pastoral leaders in this way particularly for those people coming from other cultures or for those people who live in areas isolated from educational institutions or without high concentrations of Mennonite churches. Hesston College has developed (1980) the Pastoral Studies Independent Learning program as one response to this educational need.

The various Mennonite groups continue to struggle with the tension between the professional ministry and the ministry of the whole people of God. A common view is that all Christians participate in sharing the good news of the gospel and their ministries are varied both in the gathered community of faith and in the world. Leadership ministries are exercised by pastoral leaders who are called by God and the congregation to "shepherd the flock." Pastoral education focuses on the training of these leaders primarily for ministry in congregations although graduates serve as chaplains in institutions or in other church leadership roles, e.g., conference ministers.

With the professionalization of ministry has come a series of °polity and procedural questions. Such issues as determining the length of tenure, calling and dismissal, leadership evaluations, rights and privileges, and ministerial ethics are some of the more crucial matters faced by those who oversee pastors as well as by congregations and pastors themselves. Mennonite groups have given increasing attention to the development of guidelines and standards both for those who serve and for congregations who employ pastoral leaders.

In the last three decades major attention has been given to the nature of pastoral education in the °believers church tradition. The publication of The People of God by Ross T. Bender (1971) is one major attempt at outlining a theology of the church and spelling out implications for training leaders. Two recent efforts at interpretation are reflected in the Mennonite (MC) Board of Education's document "Pastoral Education in the Mennonite Church" (1987), and Paul Zehr's doctoral project "The Development of a Curriculum Guide for Mennonite Conference-Based Education" (1987).

Pastoral education can be viewed as a combination of training elements and modalities. It embodies elements of theological education, professional training, °spiritual formation and an emphasis on personal development. Modeled after the theological schools of Europe, American seminaries often emphasize the cognitive dimensions of learning, namely the acquisition of a relevant body of knowledge, the ability to think critically, and the development of an understanding of Scripture. Professional education has focused on the development of skills needed in the practice of ministry—healthy interpersonal relationships and leadership skills (e.g., problem solving and conflict management). In recent years there has been a renewed interest in developing a disciplined and systematic pattern of spiritual growth. Attention to personal growth and a healthy personal and pastoral identity are increasingly seen as necessasry for effective ministry in the church. The four training elements receive varying degrees of attention in

Mennonite seminaries. There are major attempts at incorporating all four elements into the seminary training experience. It is also clear that there needs to be collaboration with related program and community resources (e.g., CPE, congregations) in order to meet the broader goals in the training of pastoral leaders.

Pastoral education is viewed as a life-long experience. For an increasing number of leaders basic training for ministry includes the acquisition of a professional degree i.e., Master of Divinity. For others it will mean a comparable level of training and experience with some in-service education. Given the demands on the pastoral leader continuing education is assumed as a norm. The growing and effective leader will want to upgrade knowledge and work at improving professional competence. In order to nurture the spiritual and personal dimensions of one's person the pastoral leader will be involved in enrichment experiences in an ongoing way.

The models and expectations related to the training for ministry continue to change. The Mennonite and Brethren in Christ churches continue to wrestle with the varied and sometimes divergent needs and expectations of its constituent congregations. It is clear from current experience that pastoral education will continue to be both diversified in terms of models and dispersed geographically beyond the boundaries of the established training institutions.   RL/LLK

Ross T. Bender, *The People of God: A Mennonite Interpretation of the Free Church Tradition* (Scottdale, 1971); Paul Zehr, "The Development of a Curriculum Guide for Mennonite Conference-Based Pastoral Education" (DMin thesis, Eastern Baptist Theological Seminary, 1987); "Pastoral Education In The Mennonite Church," a statement developed by the Theological Education Committee of the Mennonite Board of Education (MC), Elkhart, Ind.; J. Lawrence Burkholder, "Theological Education For the Believer's Church," *Concern* (1969), 10-32; Ralph Lebold, *Learning and Growing in Ministry* (Scottdale: MPH, 1986); Menno H. Epp, *The Pastor's Exit: A Study of the Dynamics of Involuntary Termination of Pastors in the Mennonite Church* (Winnipeg: CMBC Publication, 1984); Leland Harder, *The Pastor-People Partnership: The Call and Recall of Pastors in a Believer's Church Perspective*, Occasional Papers, No. 5 (Elkhart, Ind.: IMS, 1983); *Ordinal: Ministry and Ordination in the General Conference Mennonite Church* (Newton: Committe on the Ministry, 1987); Wittlinger, *Piety and Obedience* (1978), 284-312, 433-40; Herman Enns and Rudy Regehr in *Call to Faithfulness: Essays in Canadian Mennonite Studies*, ed. Henry Poettcker and Rudy A. Regehr (Winnipeg: CMBC, 1972), 93-102, 103-15; Alle G. Hoekema, "Developments in the Education of Preachers in the Indonesian Mennonite Churches," *MQR*, 59 (1985) 398-409; Nanne van der Zijpp, "Die Ausbildung der Mennonitenprediger in den Niederlanden," *Menn. Geschbl.*, Jg. 21, n.F. 16 (1964), 11-15; J. Brüsewitz, "'Tot de aankweek van leeraren: Der predikantsopleidingen van de Doopsgezinden, ca. 1680-1811," *Doops. Bijdr.*, n.r. 11 (1985), 11-43

See also Christian Education; Education (chart for Latin American Mennonite programs); Missionary Education and Training; New York Theological Seminary; Ordination; Self-Education.

Pastoral Placement. See Personnel Management.

Pastoral Visiting. Expectations and experiences surrounding the visitation of families within the congregation had its own uniqueness prior to the time of salaried pastoral leadership. The care of the church was understood to be the task and privilege of extended families. Many factors contributed to making this a satisfactory and supportive arrangement. Most Mennonite congregations were located in rural settings and in close geographic proximity. Most Mennonites lived and worked on farms. They not only worshiped together, but also assisted each other with harvesting, building, and other tasks that required the resources of the larger community. Mennonite children usually attended the same school and in some settings were actually in the majority. Young people normally assisted on the farm of their parents or were hired by relatives or other church friends.

Open communication surrounding family needs and congregational concerns were shared in natural and informal ways, over the line fence and around the dinner table. °Visiting each other was the natural extension of good church community relationships. Everyone expected it to happen. There was no need to make appointments or to wait for invitations. Within this informal arrangement, most of the people were informed about and interested in the spiritual welfare, joys, and sorrows of the larger church family. Appointed congregational leaders were the recipients of such visits in the same manner as others within the church setting.

When individuals or families experienced illness, the visitation program already in operation became the primary focus of the laity and designated congregational leaders. Offering and providing assistance with farm or household duties were concrete ways in which care and concern were demonstrated. In addition to this good support network, the deacon would normally be the first of the ministerial leadership to contact the family. The added dimension of the deacon's presence would have been to ascertain the mutual aid concerns. It was his duty to be a good steward of the charities of the church and to facilitate their distribution to members, especially the sick, widows, and orphans as may be appropriate. When people had spritual needs, or if strife was evident, the deacon may also have been the first ministerial leader to make the contact.

Among other tasks, a minister's primary function was to preach. The bishop or elder preached and officiated at special ceremonies of the church. In addition to the deacon, they also became involved in visitation, depending on their gifts, interests, or according to the customs of the local community.

In the days of an unsalaried ministry, pastoral visitation was the function of the total community of faith. As leadership shifted to salaried and professional pastors, some aspects of visiting were transformed into pastoral and psychological counseling often by referral to professional counselors. Some congregations have formalized and organized pastoral care through lay elders who relate to clusters or small groups within the congregation. Other congregations have organized pastoral care committees to assist ministers in pastoral care. The role of deacons has declined or disappeared in most congregations of the more acculturated Mennonite groups. The Old Order Mennonites, Amish and similar conserving groups retain the informal patterns described above.   HES

Pathway Publishers was founded in 1964 by two °Amish farmers, David Wagler and Joseph Stoll, out of a thirst for more printed materials pertaining to Anabaptist literature. With an earnest desire to reprint old books, the business opened in a farm home in Canada. Neighbors became interested in the new venture and several people, all Amish, with a variety of technical aptitudes, joined the printing enterprise. The Pathway Publishers office is located near Aylmer, Ont., with equipment and presses powered by diesel generators since no commercial electricity is allowed. The business publishes books by Amish authors, some classic Anabaptist literature, and an assortment of pamphlets for the plain people. Biggest sellers are the Pathway Readers, a complete set of stories compiled by Amish scholars for grades one through eight, including workbooks and teacher's guide. They are used in Amish °private schools.

Pathway Publishers also publish three monthly periodicals, each with a circulation of more than 14,000. *The Blackboard Bulletin* focuses on the needs of Amish teachers, parents, and school board members. *Young Companion* aims at Amish youth. *Family Life* is a popular publication for the promotion of Christian living. Readers of the last-mentioned paper are given information on new Amish settlements, history, and human interest stories as well as recipes, household hints, and health tips.

The main thrust in Amish publishing is to articulate many of the assumptions of Amish culture that have never been recorded. Older beliefs are being reexamined. New interpretations are given for changing circumstances. Amish readers respond in a variety of ways to this new literature. New ideas cause objections. The thrust toward greater literacy and articulation may meet the needs of some readers; others fear that such movements of enlightenment may tend to undermine the nonverbal character of the Amish. Pathway Publishers is thriving today with record sales on such major works as *The Amish in America: Settlements That Failed, 1840-1960* (1986) by David Luthy.

Pathway Publishers have developed a comprehensive Amish Historical Library at Aylmer under the direction of David Luthy. Visitors are welcome by appointment. SLY

John A. Hostetler, *Amish Society* (1980), 366-68.

See also Historical Libraries; Publishing.

Pati is an Indonesian city of some 70,000 inhabitants located 75 km. (46 mi.) east/ne. of °Semarang, the capital of the province of Central Java. Pati is the administrative center for both the *kabupaten* (county) and the residency (comprising several counties) of Pati. Though Pati is the largest city in the *kabupaten* of Pati, and the next largest town, Juana, has only some 20,000 inhabitants, the remaining small towns and several hundred agricultural villages have a total population of about one million.

The synod offices of the Gereja Injili di Tanah Jawa (GITJ; Evangelical Church of Java or Javanese Mennonite Church) are located on Rogowongso Street in Pati, making use of the church building the Pati congregation has long outgrown. The synod's Wiyata Wacana Theological College, originally operated jointly with the synod of the Persatuan Gereja-Gereja Kristen Muria Indonesia (GKMI; Muria Christian Church in Indonesia) is located in Pati. So are its two (government-supported) schools for training teachers of Christian faith in the public schools, 3 of the 10 schools in its Christian (BOPKRI) school system, and three of the synod's congregations. The offices of the inter-Mennonite Scholarship Foundation and Development Commission for Outside Java are located in the building on Penjawi Street that for about 20 years served as Mennonite Central Committee headquarters for Indonesia. The inter-Mennonite economic development foundation, YAKEM, was headquartered in Pati before its demise in the late 1970s.

The Pati congregation of the GITJ led the way in fostering the formation of new congregations during the late 1960s and 1970s. Ten of its branch congregations came to maturity during that period.

The Pati congregation of the GKMI was formed about 1940. This congregation has also been instrumental in the formation of several congregations in the surrounding area. LMY

Patos Colony, Mexico. See Durango Colonies, Mexico.

Patriotism is love and loyal or zealous support for one's own country. At its best patriotism is an affirmation of neighbor and a sense of joy in a particular land, shared memory, and sense of peoplehood. For Mennonites, dogged by persecution in many generations and countries, patriotism is a relatively new sentiment. Those who have been liberated from a status as persecuted outcasts may react with lavish gratitude to the country which grants them toleration. Mennonites have observed how patriotism is often associated with freedom and independence.

Patriotism as loyal support for one's country was not a sentiment of the 16th-c. Anabaptist forebears of today's Mennonites. Walter Klaassen, in an article titled, "The Nature of the Anabaptist Protest," says that the political protest of the Anabaptists consisted in their refusal to bear the sword to protect the state. This was viewed as treason. The punishment was death, and thousands of Anabaptists paid with their lives. Such was the meaning for them of giving their lives for their country. Many Anabaptists ignored territorial boundaries in pursuit of their sense of calling. When apprehended for crossing a state's border, they declared, "The earth is the Lord's."

Perhaps the persecution of one generation may seed the patriotism of the next. What compromises with the state will Christians make to avoid the sufferings of the past? Genuine appreciation for religious toleration can merge into uncritical obedience to the political powers which grant it. Mennonite immigrants who established colonies under benevolent dictators have illustrated this process over the centuries. The comfortable status of Mennonites in Canada and the United States today may also be an example of this.

For Christians, whose membership is in the church as a global community, patriotism poses inherent problems because it competes with loyalty to Christ and the church (°nationalism). The Mennonite understanding of the biblical view of nation is best expressed in verses like Ps 10:16: "The LORD is King for ever and ever; the nations will perish from his land." The nations are viewed as temporary structures, passing away. Ps 2:1-2 reflects the characteristic opposition of nations to God's sovereignty: "Why do the nations conspire and the people plot in vain? The kings of the earth take their stand and the rulers gather together against the LORD and against his Anointed One" (NIV).

Jesus expressed doubt about the actual status, or authority of heads of state when he said of them: "You know that those *who are regarded as* rulers of the Gentiles lord it over them," (Mk 10:42). These Scriptures strike the major biblical chord regarding country or nation, a chord which puts distance between God's people and the nations. Paul's call for submission to the authorities in Rom 13 is a minor chord in the total witness of Scripture.

The meaning of patriotism is severely tested in times of revolution. Which country (government, people) shall one love? In the American Revolution of the 1770s, most Mennonites asked a larger question: "How could they remain faithful to their pacifist understanding of the Christian gospel amid the emotionalism of wartime?" (MEA 1; Ruth, *Seeding Time*).

But the subsequent wars of America found Mennonites divided over loyalty to government and loyalty to their pacifist (°°nonresistant) understanding of the gospel. In the late 1980s the Cold War against °communism still feeds on uncritical patriotism. °Civil religion, prayer in school and in public ceremonies, the national °flag in church buildings, the pledge of allegiance to the flag, and the celebration of the military fit the patriot's dream. Yet words of caution are issued by prophetic Mennonite and Brethren in Christ voices from time to time.

Mennonites in Canada during World War I found provincial governments seeking to use the schools to instill patriotic sentiments and foster Canadian nationalism. Later, as Hitler rose to power in Germany, some German Mennonite immigrants in Canada voiced support for his social reforms (Epp, *Mennonites in Canada II*, 548-56). Military °conscription during wartime tested Mennonite loyalties. In recent years as Mennonites have gained recognition in all sectors of Canadian life, Canadian Mennonite patriotism has increased.

Among prosperous people the causes of patriotism are similar: reaction to persecution and avoidance of suffering, appreciation for comfortable circumstances and the desire for social acceptance. It may be argued that the great Mennonite outpouring of °relief activity after World War II was in part an effort to demonstrate that Mennonites were good citizens and patriots. The consequences too are similar: muting the call for °justice for the poor and oppressed, negating the °peace witness and ignoring that the church is an international body.

The poignant cry of Hubert Brown, a black American Mennonite, may sum up the global challenge which patriotism poses for Mennonites and all Christians: ". . . somewhere along the way from Anabaptism to Mennonitism something drastic has taken place. In my estimation, it is our Mennonite incompatibility with the Anabaptist Christ. As a black

Mennonite living in these times of painful oppression and exploitation, I have to wonder what kind of Christ we are serving. I want nothing to do with an American Christ, a blue-eyed white dude that affirms the values of a sick and fallen society. I don't trust the American Christ" (*Black and Mennonite*, 80).   JKS/RK

Urbane Peachey, ed., *Mennonite Statements on Peace and Social Concerns, 1900-1978* (Akron, Pa.: MCC, 1980), esp. 5-9; Donald B. Kraybill, *Our Star-Spangled Faith* (Scottdale, 1976); John H. Redekop, "Mennonites and Politics in Canada and the United States," *JMS*, 1 (1983), 79-105; Walter Klaassen, "The Nature of the Anabaptist Protest," *MQR*, 45 (1971), 291-311; MEA 1: 229-80; John L. Ruth, *Twas Seeding Time* (Scottdale, 1976); Frank H. Epp, *Mennonites in Canada II*, 543-92; Hubert Brown, *Black and Mennonite: A Search for Identity* (Scottdale, 1976); Menno Wiebe, "Mennonite Adaptation and Identity," in *Call to Faithfulness: Essays in Canadian Mennonite Studies*, ed. Henry Poettcker and Rudy Regehr (Winnipeg: CMBC, 1972), 117-88; James C. Juhnke, *A People of Two Kingdoms* (Newton, 1975); John A. Lapp, *A Dream for America* (Scottdale, 1976); "Citizens and Disciples: Christian Essays on Nationalism" (Akron: Mennonite Central Committee, 1974), 31pp; John B. Toews, *Czars, Soviets, and Mennonites* (Newton, 1982), 63ff.

See also Shintoism.

Paul, Tranonidhi N. (July 3, 1904-Nov. 14, 1987), was the fourth of five sons and a daughter born to Shyamsundar Haripal, a weaver, and Champa Bai. His parents had to flee from their wealthy family to Arda, in Orissa, after accepting Christianity. Tranonidhi Paul was born in Arda, but moved with his parents to Phuljhar state where the English Baptist Mission sent them. Later he attended the boys' school in Mauhadih where two of his brothers died.

Paul married Dukhi Bai, the daughter of Chaitan and Bhalkundi Kumar on May 10, 1922. They had one daughter, Esther, and later took four more girls and a boy into their home. Tranonidhi Paul was a weaver-farmer, but he was sent to Koksa village to teach school in 1927. The next year he was assigned to evangelistic work. He completed his middle school education at Mauhadih in 1930. He returned to Phuljhar to evangelism work. From 1934 to 1936 he and his wife studied at the Bible School in Janjgir and following graduation he served full-time in the pastoral ministry until 1957 at the isolated Antioch congregation. He was ordained elder in 1945. He transferred to the Salem congregation in 1957 and served the Ephesus congregation from 1962 until his retirement in 1968. He was a very effective and beloved pastor. Upon the death of his son-in-law, he and his wife moved to Jagdeeshpur to stay with their daughter. His prayerful interest in church and conference continued until his death.   HKor

Juhnke, *Mission* (1979), 42.

Paurito Colony, Bolivia. See Santa Rita Colony, Bolivia.

Payne, Ernest Alexander (1902-80), was a faithful British Baptist and a dedicated ecumenist, an outstanding administrator and a learned scholar, a "private" person and a public figure. He served the British Baptist Union with distinction as pastor, teacher, and writer before becoming its general secretary and president. In the ecumenical field he held high office in the Free Churches, the British Council of Churches, and the World Council of Churches where he was elected president. In recognition of his ecumenical work the Queen was pleased to make him a Companion of Honour.

A man of broad sympathies and wise judgment, he demonstrated his indebtedness to his Baptist and Anabaptist forebears and his dedication to the church's ongoing task. In the controversy over Baptist origins, his writings supported the view that argued for significant Mennonite and Anabaptist influence on °Baptists. With Kierkegaard he could say that although "life can only be understood backwards, it must be lived forwards."   DSR

Peace. Mennonites are known for their "peace position" and are often referred to as one of the °"historic peace churches" (along with the Church of the °°Brethren and the °°Society of Friends). Their witness against violence and warfare is demonstrated in °conscientious objection to °military service and a quest for alternatives to violence.

Traditionally Mennonites have expressed their beliefs about the way of peace in the language of °"nonresistance," derived from literal obedience to the teaching of Jesus in Mt 5:38ff.: "resist not evil, turn the other cheek, love your enemies." Thus ME I-IV had no article on *peace*, but the topic of °°*nonresistance* was developed at length, in both biblical and historical perspectives (see also °°pacifism).

This approach reflects the fact that in the earlier part of the 20th c., many Mennonites hesitated to be identified as "pacifists." They made a point of distinguishing between their own commitment to biblical "nonresistance" and the "pacifism" of other religious and political groups whose position was considered to be based more on humanistic or philosophical views than on biblical authority. This view remains central for many Mennonites. Other Mennonites have refocused the peace testimony during the last generation as a primary theme in the identity of the Mennonite churches. As Mennonites have responded to the events of the times, their thinkers have created a comprehensive peace theology; denominational agencies have developed extensive programs of °peace education and °sociopolitical and °peace activism. Mennonite church life has thus continually been challenged with opportunities to demonstrate the meaning of Mennonites' professed adherence to the way of peace.

The Foundation of Nonresistance. Nonresistance was for several generations the key concept in Mennonite ethics. The term included a number of social implications: costly °discipleship, °relief and °service efforts, attitudes on industrial (°labor unions) and race relations—in short, the way of the cross embodied in a faithful church community.

The major work of Guy F. °Hershberger, *War, Peace, and Nonresistance* (1944, with new editions in l953 and 1969) set forth a Mennonite peace position more fully than ever before. The book included both Old and New Testament exegesis, the history of peace thought in the Christian church with particular attention to Anabaptist and Mennonite experience, and discussion of the contemporary implications of the peace position. This landmark study functioned as a foundational peace theology for all

the major Mennonite bodies in North America; the numerous denominational resolutions and position statements from the 1940s to the 1960s reflect a consensus based on Hershberger's views, with no significant deviations.

Hershberger's work enabled Mennonites to move beyond more than two decades of debate (especially in the Mennonite Church [MC]) over the proper political posture of the church. One wing of Mennonitism, influenced by °Fundamentalism and °dispensationalism, was critical of efforts to influence governments toward more peaceful policies. These critics claimed that Christians were not called to prevent wars, but only to maintain their own nonresistant stance. Proponents of this view, fearful of what they termed modernist social gospel tendencies, also denounced Mennonite fraternization with other religious pacifists, including efforts to join in public matters with Quakers (Friends) and the Church of the Brethren as "historic peace churches."

On the other hand, the leadership of the Peace Problems Committee (MC) and the parallel agencies of the General Conference Mennonite Church, beginning in the decade after World War I, had taken a more active posture, ready to challenge the state to practice more explicitly Christian policies, both internationally and domestically.

What Hershberger offered was a centrist way, a view of biblical nonresistance that was in essence nonpolitical, yet provided a platform for prophetic witness that had relevance for the political and social order. This enabled the mainstream of Mennonitism to move from a largely withdrawn, self-protective posture into more active forms of service and reconciling ministries (see Beulah Hostetler and Paul Toews essays in bibliography below).

Biblical Sources for Mennonite Peace Theology. Throughout Anabaptist and Mennonite history, the nonresistance doctrine was grounded in simple faithful obedience to the teaching of Jesus, especially the °Sermon on the Mount (Mt 5-7). In Mt 5.38-48, Jesus admonished his disciples, "Do not resist one who is evil," and illustrated this principle with the examples of turning the other cheek and going the second mile. The following command to "love your enemies" extended beyond the negative "defenseless" posture to call for positive reconciling action, in harmony with Mt 5.9: "Blessed are the peacemakers."

In addition to the teaching of Jesus, traditional Mennonite thought also emphasized the exemplary "way of the cross," in which the Messiah accomplishes his mission as a °suffering servant-savior. Nonresistance was found in the numerous teachings on peaceful discipleship in the New Testament epistles. It was practiced by the apostles, and further attested in the consistent witness of the early church against the taking of life.

The present generation of Mennonite biblical scholars has expanded and deepened the scriptural base of peace theology, with significant work on such themes as shalom, holy war, the politics of Jesus, and °salvation and °atonement theology.

Unfolding the rich "shalom" vocabulary in the Old Testament has granted new insight into God's purposes for the community of the faithful. This Hebrew word, occurring hundreds of times, is often translated as "peace," but also includes a range of other meanings: health, wholeness, °justice, righteousness, harmony, and well-being. Closely related to covenant and salvation, shalom in the Old Testament is both present reality and future hope, a harbinger of the °"kingdom of God" theme in the New Testament.

But the Old Testament, with its long history of the wars of Israel, also raises the troublesome issue of God's apparent approval of violence and bloodshed. Mennonite thinkers have taken at least three approaches in responding to this problem. (1) The simplest is based on the words of Jesus that divide history into two epochs: "You have heard . . . but I say to you." Whatever may have been commanded by Yahweh in the old dispensation is now superseded by the new way of Jesus. (2) G. F. Hershberger, concerned to find a more consistent understanding of the divine will, wrote of God's "concession to disobedience." Because the people of Israel were not faithful to God's high calling, they were consigned to live on the lower level of warfare and bloodshed. (3) More careful attention to the unique characteristics of biblical "holy war," at first glance a troublesome issue for peace theology, has revealed a theological model that minimizes human engagement in warfare as it calls for total trust and obedience to Yahweh, the transcendent warrior-king.

The earlier Mennonite studies viewed Jesus as a primarily religious figure, whose words and deeds were largely independent of their historical setting. But John H. Yoder's landmark study, *The Politics of Jesus,* challenged this consensus. Building on the results of a generation of biblical exegesis, Yoder set forth the total historical career of Jesus as one who proclaimed the kingdom of God in terms relevant to the actual sociopolitical context of oppression and revolution. The ethic and example of Jesus is in fact a social strategy that creates a distinct community through which the gospel works to change other structures. Central to the convictions of this new order is the way of suffering °love.

Recent biblical theology has also emphasized the basic links between the cross of Christ, salvation, and ethics. In outline, this comprehensive view of atonement states that the God who made peace at the cross (Col 1) overcomes and defeats human enmity through this reconciling act ("peace with God," Rom. 5), which serves as both example and power for peacemaking activity (Eph 2) by those who experience salvation and security ("the peace of God," Phil 4) through their response to the gospel. For sources of this theological development, see the following: *traditional views*: Daniel Kauffman, Hershberger, Henry Fast, Edward Yoder; *shalom and holy war*: Millard Lind, J. H. Yoder, Perry Yoder; *politics of Jesus*: Ronald Sider, J. H. Yoder; *atonement*: J. R. Burkholder and John Bender (ch. 4), John Driver, C. Norman Kraus, Perry Yoder.

Theological Trends. Mennonite peace theology has matured significantly since the 1950s, as a result both of digging deeper into biblical and historical foundations and of creative interaction with the issues of the times.

This theological development was especially enhanced through opportunities for dialogue with other Christian traditions, as American peace church representatives, serving in Europe after World War II, engaged in sustained discussion with the mainstream churches. The series of °Puidoux conferences (1955-62) provided a unique opportunity for testing peace church convictions in a larger arena. The innovative work of these younger scholars, such as Paul Peachey and John Howard Yoder, came back to America first through informal publications such as the °"Concern" series of pamphlets.

According to Duane Friesen, "In 1950 the Mennonites had essentially no theology of witness to economic and political structures." That is, the main thrust of the nonresistant ethic, while refusing warfare, focused on interpersonal relations within the Christian community and social service to individuals beyond the community. Actual practice, however, may well have been ahead of the theology. Some public statements against °conscription, for example, dared to challenge the whole conscription system itself as contrary to the purposes for which the state is ordained by God. But only in the 1960s was a rationale developed that legitimated such efforts to change the structures of the world by direct appeal to authorities.

Ever since the °Schleitheim confession (1527), Mennonite thought has wrestled with the doctrine of "two kingdoms." On one hand, the disciple lives out the love ethic in direct obedience to Jesus. On the other hand, God, who is sovereign over all, orders history through human authorities, and thus use of force by the state is legitimate. This view has sometimes led to a rigorous dualism that offers no critique of the state. Some Mennonites have believed that God wills a particular aggressive military action (to halt the advance of °communism, for example) even though nonresistant Christians should have no part in it.

The emerging Mennonite position of recent decades affirms the lordship of Christ over all the "powers" of the cosmos as a basic theological premise. If Christ is indeed lord over both church and world, then prophetic witness to the state is an integral part of the gospel message proclaiming the new age. Governmental authorities, however, cannot be expected to understand gospel language, but presumably can be addressed through secular norms ("middle axioms"), ideals of equality and justice that are ultimately grounded in the redemptive plan of God.

Thus there is only one moral standard for both church and world; the crucial difference is in the response to that standard. This conviction enables Christians to call all of society, including the state, to account for its conduct in response to the will of God as made known through Christ. This more contemporary theology, while assuming a basic separation of church and state, enables the church to carry out a ministry of reconciliation and witness to both world and state.

A second development has been the shift away from a narrow understanding of nonresistance toward recognition of the appropriateness of some forms of nonviolent resistance. The 1944 Hershberger view, characteristic of prevailing Mennonite thought, ruled out all forms of coercion and resistance, even nonviolent resistance. The movement led by Mohandas °Gandhi was criticized as a human strategy for achieving political goals, rather than the biblical way of peace.

The appearance of Martin Luther King, Jr., and the American civil rights movement presented a new form of nonviolent activity that challenged Mennonites who shared the concern for racial justice and peaceful social change. Observing that the King movement was rooted in the Afro-American churches, and noting its readiness to endure suffering, even unjustly, Hershberger and others were ready to consider both the legitimacy of the cause and the method.

As Mennonites became involved with interfaith peace movements and joined demonstrations against nuclear weapons, the °Vietnam war, and the draft, Mennonite thinkers turned to the current issues of °civil disobedience and nonviolent action. They projected new directions for Mennonite thinking and action that accepted nonviolent direct action as a proper mode, given the motive of neighbor love and the limits of noninjury to people. (See the work of J. Lawrence Burkholder, Frank Epp, Duane Friesen, Donald Kaufman, Gordon Kaufman, John A. Lapp, and Ronald Sider; also the articles on °nonresistance and sociopolitical activism in this volume and pacifism in ME IV)

The growing involvement of Mennonite individuals in public nonviolent actions and the more frequent official church appeals to government were not approved by all segments of the church. A conservative reaction appeared in such publications as *The Sword and Trumpet* and *Guidelines for Today*, as well as the readers' pages in other Mennonite periodicals. Some voices urged a return to the traditional stance of withdrawal; others rebuked the perceived "leftist" slant of the new activism.

In his 1958 doctoral dissertation, J. Lawrence Burkholder analyzed the tensions facing the Mennonite ethic as Mennonites moved from cultural isolation into the mainstream of American life. He predicted that the basic Mennonite concern to do good for the neighbor in need would inevitably bring about change in the traditional peace theology. By the 1980s, his views were recognized as prophetic.

The Mennonite Central Committee (MCC) Peace Section sponsored a series of "Peace Theology Colloquia," beginning in October 1976, when the topic was Yoder's *Politics of Jesus*. Since then other issues of peace and justice ethics have been examined in these gatherings of scholars and church workers.

The Peace Witness in the Life of the Churches. Historians have observed that during the first half of the 20th c., American Mennonites were most in danger of losing their normative Anabaptist roots, in part because of the influence of °Fundamentalism and in part due to the lack of a creative theological effort to deal with the massive pressure of social change. Moving from the withdrawal stance of the 1920s to almost total social and cultural participation in the 1980s has put heavy strains on the inherited theological and ethical formulations, or at least on the ways in which they have often been understood.

The churches did produce leaders and resources to address the issues. The World War I experience demanded dealings with government, resulting in conference peace committees and the Mennonite Central Committee. From 1919 to 1971, the Peace Problems Committee of the Mennonite Church (MC; later called the Committee on Peace and Social Concerns) served as the chief source of authoritative statements on peace and °church-state issues for the Mennonite Church (MC). Among its leaders for five decades were Orie °Miller, Harold °Bender, Guy Hershberger, and John E. °Lapp. Parallel efforts in the General Conference Mennonite Church were led by such men as A. J. °°Neuenschwander, H. P. °°Krehbiel, H. A. °Fast, C. Henry °°Smith, and Ernest Bohn. Prominent in peace witness among the Mennonite Brethren were B. B. °Janz, C. F. °Klassen, and P. C. °Hiebert.

These leaders played important roles in shaping both thought and action in the sociopolitical arena, as the church learned from its experience and made a better showing in the 1930s, both internally through educational efforts on nonresistance, and politically by sending delegations to Washington and Ottawa. The creation of the °°Civilian Public Service program of World War II, through cooperation with other peace churches and the government, represented a major new institutional effort.

The experience of Mennonite conscientious objectors during two world wars undoubtedly shaped the planning for a new draft situation in the early 1950s. This time the church was ahead of the government, by preparing, through MCC Peace Section, plans for °alternative service which were then presented to government officials. During this period Mennonite spokesmen regularly presented statements in appropriate governmental settings, opposing °universal military training and speaking to other aspects of conscription.

In the 1950s Mennonites entered Vietnam, first in MCC service, then in mission work supported by the Eastern Mennonite Board of Missions and Charities. Within a few years the American military presence in Vietnam had turned into an undeclared war. Soon, Mennonites were speaking out against that war, based on the historic position of the church and grounded in the °mission and service experience of Mennonite personnel in Vietnam. An official statement of Mennonite Church (MC) in 1965 included a telegram to President Lyndon Johnson, questioning "the moral basis of the American involvement in Vietnam" (Peachey, ed., *Mennonite Statements* [1980], 237).

American Mennonites responded in various ways to the social turmoil of the 1960s—civil rights activities, antiwar protests, resistance to the draft and to war °taxes. Social activism on college campuses spilled over into communities and congregations. As the whole society debated vital questions of pacifism, politics, and resistance, some Mennonites joined in civil disobedience and a few were arrested. Mennonites worked with organizations such as the Fellowship of Reconciliation and SANE; some joined intentional communities dedicated to resistance. Canadian Mennonites offered their resources to young men from the United States escaping the draft.

During these turbulent times, Mennonites were pushed to re-examine and extend the traditional teachings as they sought to respond to events in light of biblical understandings. Delegates to church conferences passed numerous resolutions on demonstrations, draft resistance, war tax refusal, nuclear weapons, and war itself. Attitudes and positions on these controversies ignored denominational boundaries, with both progressive and conservative voices to be found in every grouping.

At the level of actual practice, attitudes toward pacifism were analyzed in a sociological study of five Anabaptist denominations in the United States and Canada (Kauffman/Harder, *Anabaptists Four C. Later* [1975]). Overall, 73 percent of respondents agreed that Christians should take no part in warfare. But their views on related church programs and political activity varied much more widely. More recent analysis by sociologist Donald Kraybill documents the diversity of Mennonite understanding and behavior in relation to the peace position. While most Mennonites profess some kind of adherence to pacifist beliefs, many have no hesitation in voting for militarist politicians or working in defense-related industries.

In 1976, American Mennonites joined with Brethren and Quakers to explore their common commitment under the banner of "New Call to Peacemaking." This initiative had been launched by evangelical Friends seeking to recover and extend the biblical peace testimony of early Quakers. Numerous regional meetings between the three "historic peace churches" culminated in a national conference at Green Lake, Wis., in 1978. Two more national conferences followed in 1980 and 1982. With part-time staff and occasional steering committee meetings, "New Call" continues to sponsor publications and gatherings that seek both to meet needs within the peace church constituency and to promote peace activity among other Christians.

Such efforts at interchurch cooperation in peacemaking are one of the significant developments of the 1980s. As local peace centers were formed in scores of cities, Mennonites were involved in staffing and funding for at least 40 such projects. The typical program for such centers includes furnishing educational resources, planning public events, and organizing networks for peace and justice activists.

Other recent local ecumenical efforts have brought together representatives from other denominational groups for interfaith dialogue on peace theology and peacemaking. Mennonites have joined with Baptist, Roman Catholic, and Reformed groups in consultations and specific activities. There are growing opportunities for Mennonites to share their peace concerns with other Christians.

Two other recent projects demonstrate interest in active peacemaking that goes beyond the basic rejection of violence. Mennonite Conciliation Service (affiliated with MCC Peace Section) is the organizational base for training and practice in the skills of mediation. Christian Peacemaker Teams are the outgrowth of the call to costly nonviolent action brought to the 1984 Mennonite World Conference by Ronald Sider. In December 1986, major Mennonite agencies approved the concept and moved toward training programs. The intent is to prepare teams of persons to intervene in conflict situations, attempting to reduce violence and foster justice through nonviolent action.

Global Peacemaking. The renewal of a peace testimony among the Mennonites of Europe (see ME III:903-6) has continued in the last decades. Dutch, German, and Swiss Mennonites have active peace committees (°Doopsgezinde Vredesgroep; °Deutsches Mennonitisches Friedenskomitee; °Europäisches Mennonitisches Friedenskomitee; °Schweizerisches Mennonitisches Friedenskomitee/Comité Mennonite Suisse pour la paix). These groups advise conscientious objectors, sponsor occasional conferences and seminars, engage in occasional publishing, and carry on conversation with other church groups. There has been significant growth of conscientious objection in Germany, among both Mennonites and other groups. Mennonites have been active in public peace and disarmament movements.

European Mennonites have cooperated in "Eirene," an organization providing opportunities for international °voluntary service which also sponsored various efforts at peace education. A newer ecumenical network, "Church and Peace," has contributed greatly to the renewal of the peace testimony in Europe, with major involvement from Mennonites and MCC. A series of study tours and delegations to eastern Europe and the Soviet Union have been a significant part of Mennonite peace activity.

From its beginning in 1942, the MCC Peace Section (see also Mennonite Central Committee Canada Peace and Social Concerns Committee) has been involved in international efforts to strengthen and expand the peace witness of the church, increasingly in cooperation with mission boards and national churches. In the 1940s peace missioners were assigned to Europe and South America, followed by similar efforts in Japan, India, and other parts of Asia and Africa. Missioners to Japan have included Melvin °Gingerich, Paul Peachey, Ferd Ediger, and Carl Beck. Japanese Mennonites have been involved in significant peace education and antiwar projects.

Peace themes have been part of the agenda at the three meetings of the Asia Mennonite Conference (Dhamtari, India, 1972, Osaka, Japan, 1980, Taipei, Taiwan, 1986), especially at the third conference in Taiwan which sent a message of concern about nuclear issues to more than 30 governments around the world. The formation of the °Mennonite Christian Service Fellowship of India in the early 1960s was in part an expression of growing interest in peace education under the leadership of P. J. °Malagar. At the invitation of this group, peace teaching missions were conducted in the churches of India by Edgar Metzler in 1964 and Norman Kraus in 1978.

In the 1960s, Elmer Neufeld and Henry Hostetter carried out special assignments in Africa. More recently, Mennonites have been engaged in efforts to bring reconciliation themes and skills to the troubled situation in southern Africa.

Conflict situations in Vietnam and the Middle East provided opportunity for special peacemaking ministries, often not directly related to Mennonite constituencies, but concerned with understanding conflict and working at reconciliation. Atlee Beechy, Frank H. °Epp, John A. Lapp, and others have carried out assignments in these areas. Frank Epp served MCC Peace Section for a time as Director of Studies in International Conflict.

Early Mennonite mission efforts in Latin America lacked a consistent peace teaching and the peace witness record of the Mennonite immigrant communities in Brazil, Paraguay, and Uruguay is uneven. But more recently, Latin America Mennonites have strengthened their efforts at developing peace convictions among the churches, as well as engaging in ecumenical conversations on the role of the church in a violent society.

Although official recognition for conscientious objection has been virtually nonexistent in Latin America, Mennonite youth have occasionally been granted noncombatant options. Mennonites in Argentina and Brazil have worked on models for alternatives to military service. Nicaraguan Mennonites, faced with widespread compulsory service, have engaged government officials in an endeavor to find alternatives for their young people. Honduran Mennonites have begun on their own to create alternative service structures that might meet government approval.

In the midst of a revolutionary political situation in Central America, the small Mennonite bodies in five countries have been singularly alert to peace and justice concerns. Plans for special personnel assignments and publications have been supported by the churches with MCC cooperation. A broadly based Latin American "missions consultation" in Guatemala in 1986 included significant presentations on peace and justice issues.

The °International Mennonite Peace Committee (not to be confused with the °°International Mennonite Peace Committee in Europe, since renamed Europäisches Mennonitisches Friedenskomitee), which had met informally at Mennonite World Conference (MWC) assemblies for many years, was restructured at the 1972 Curitiba, Brazil, conference. Since 1986 it has been integrated into the MWC structure, and is committed to serve churches around the world as a resource for peace witness.

At the end of the 1980s, it is difficult to assess the Mennonite peace position. On one hand, there has been impressive growth in church agency activity, in educational programs, and in theological sophistication. In the wider Christian world, the cogency and relevance of Mennonite pacifism has made a significant impact. At the same time, the rapid assimilation of Mennonites into the mainstream of society (particularly in the Western world) threatens to erode the traditional commitment to stand over against the world in faithful obedience to the love of Christ.   JRB

Bibl. on War and Peace (1987); Clarence Bauman, *Gewaltlosigkeit im Täufertum*; J. Lawrence Burkholder, "The Problem of Social Responsibility from the Perspective of the Mennonite Church," (ThD diss., Princeton Theological Seminary, 1958; published Elkhart, Ind.: IMS, 1988); J. R. Burkholder and John Bender, *Children of Peace* (Elgin Ill.: Brethren Press, 1982), esp. ch. 4 on salvation and peace; John Richard Burkholder, *Continuity and Change: A Search for a Mennonite Social Ethic* (Akron Pa.: MCC, 1977); John Richard Burkholder and Calvin Redekop, eds, *Kingdom, Cross, and Community* (Scottdale, 1976); *Concern*, a series of pamphlets published beginning in 1954; Richard C. Detweiler, *Mennonite Statements on Peace, 1915-1966* (Scottdale, 1968); John Driver, *Understanding the Atonement* (Scottdale, 1986); Donald F. Durnbaugh, ed., *On Earth Peace: Discussions on War/Peace Issues between Friends, Mennonites, Brethren, and European Churches, 1935-75* (Elgin Ill.: Brethren Press, 1978); Frank H. Epp, *A Strategy for Peace: Reflections of a Christian Pacifist* (Grand Rapids: Eerdmans, 1973); Frank H. Epp and Marlene G. Epp, *The Progressions of the Mennonite Central Committee Peace Section* (Akron Pa.: MCC, 1984); Henry A. Fast, *Jesus and Human Conflict* (Scottdale, 1959); Duane K. Friesen, *Christian Peacemaking and International Conflict* (Scottdale, 1986); idem, *Mennonite Witness on Peace and Social Concerns: 1900-1980* (Akron Pa.: MCC, 1982); General Conference Mennonite Church, "The Way of Peace" an official statement in 1971; General Conference Mennonite Church, "Christian Declaration on Amnesty" (1974); articles in *Guidelines for Today*; Helmut Harder, *The Way of Peace*; Guy F. Hershberger, *War, Peace, and Nonresistance* (Scottdale, 1944, 1953, 1969); idem, *The Way of the Cross in Human Relations* (Scottdale, 1958); idem, "Nonresistance," in ME III:897-907; idem, *The Mennonite Church in the Second World War* (Scottdale, 1951; Beulah S. Hostetler, "Irrelevant Outsider or Almost Insider?: Mennonites and Mainline Peace Emphases" (unpublished); Juhnke. *Mission*, 120-23, on Japanese Mennonites; Daniel Kauffman, ed., *Doctrines of the Bible* (Scottdale, 1929) esp. part VII, ch. VII, for the traditional Mennonite view of nonresistance; Kauffman/Harder, *Anabaptists Four C. Later* (1975); Donald Kaufman, *What Belongs to Caesar?* (Scottdale, 1969); Gordon Kaufman, *Nonresistance and Responsibility* (Newton, 1979); idem, *Theology for a Nuclear Age* (Philadelphia: Westminster, 1985); William Keeney, *Lordship as Servanthood* (Newton, 1975); William Klassen, *Love of Enemies* (Philadelphia: Fortress, 1984); C. Norman Kraus, *Jesus Christ Our Lord: Christology from a Disciple's Perspective* (Scottdale, 1987); Donald Kraybill, "C. Henry Smith Peace Lecture" (March 1987), unpublished; Ronald Kraybill, *Repairing the Breach* (Scottdale, 1981); John A. Lapp, *India* (1972), 91-93; idem, "The Peace Mission of the Mennonite Central Committee," *MQR*, 44 (1970), 281-97; John A. Lapp, ed., *Peacemakers in a Broken World* (Scottdale, 1969); Millard C. Lind, *Yahweh Is a Warrior: The Theology of Warfare in Ancient Israel* (Scottdale, 1981); James E. Metzler, *From Saigon to Shalom* (Scottdale, 1985); MCC Peace Section, Reports and Publications, especially *Peace Section Newsletter*; Mennonite Church (MC) General Assembly, *Justice and the Christian Witness*, statement adopted by both the General Conference Mennonite Church and the Mennonite Church (MC) General Assembly (1985); Mennonite Church (MC) General Conference, "The Christian Witness to the State" (1961); Urbane Peachey ed., *Mennonite Statements on Peace and Social Concerns, 1900-1978* (Akron Pa.: MCC, 1980); Robert L. Ramseyer ed., *Mission and the Peace Witness* (Scottdale, 1979); LaVerne Rutschman, "Anabaptism and Liberation Theology," *MQR*, 55 (1981), 255-70; Maynard Shelly, *New Call to Peacemakers*; Ken Johnson Shenk, "The Japanese Church Faces Militarism and Violence—A Historical Perspective," *Miss. Focus* 14, no. 1 (March 1986), 5-9; Ronald J. Sider, *Christ and Violence* (Scottdale, 1979); Mark Siemens, "Waging Peace: What Four Mennonite churches Are Doing," *Chr. Leader* (Oct. 18, 1983), 2-5: various articles in *Sword and Trumpet*; John E. Toews and Gordon Nickel eds, *The Power of the Lamb* (Hillsboro, Ks.: Kindred Press, 1986); Paul Toews, "The Long Weekend or the Short Week: Mennonite Peace Theology, 1925-1944," *MQR*, 60 (1986), 38-57; J. C. Wenger, *Pacifism and Biblical Nonresistance* (Scottdale, 1968); John H. Yoder, *Christian Attitudes to War, Peace and Revolution* (Elkhart: Menn. Cooperative Bookstore, 1983); idem, *The Politics of Jesus* (Grand Rapids: Eerdmans, 1972); idem, *The Original Revolution* (Scottdale, 1972); idem, *Nevertheless: The Varieties of Christian Pacifism* (Scottdale, 1971); idem, *The Christian Witness to the State* (Newton, 1964); Perry B. Yoder, *Shalom: the Bible's Word for Salvation, Justice, and Peace* (Newton, 1987).

Peace Activism. For several centuries Mennonites were not activists in the sense of directly pressuring for political and social change. Their main witness was against war and resulted in °conscientious objection. Otherwise they tried to live a peaceful life and engaged in acts of Christian compassion toward victims of war and other °disasters. Mennonites have often made a distinction between °°nonresistance and nonviolence. Peace Activists who use "nonviolent direct action" engage in political, economic, and social action even when it may involve coercion of an adversary. Mennonites have often hesitated to use coercive actions such as strikes and boycotts, whereas nonviolent activists permit themselves to use such tactics as long as they do not cause harm to people. In recent decades, organized nonviolent direct action has been proposed by some theorists as an alternative national defense strategy (e.g., Sharp, summarized in Friesen, 149-57).

In the period between World War I and World War II some Mennonites became involved in some of the larger peace movements. World War II did not produce a great deal of active opposition. Nevertheless, °°Civilian Public Service brought many American Mennonites into contact with pacifists who were inclined to activism. Some Mennonites became more involved in such issues as race relations, improving conditions in °mental hospitals, and opposition to °conscription.

The period after World War II gave rise to an increase in Mennonite peace activism, both in Europe and in North America. The particular issue was the concern about °nuclear weapons. In the late 1950s and early 1960s, members of the °Doopsgezinde Vredesgroep (Dutch Mennonite Peace Association) participated in marches against nuclear weapons. The Vredesgroep has had a continuing debate between those who would hold to the more traditional Mennonite position on °nonresistance and those who would be more politically and publicly active on behalf of °peace.

In the United States and Canada some were influenced by Catholic activists such as Daniel and Philip Berrigan. Others participated in demonstrations against nuclear weapons and even in °civil disobedience by trespassing at nuclear weapons installations or production facilities. The emergence of the civil rights movement in the United States, particularly beginning with the Montgomery, Ala., bus boycott in 1956 and later activities such as the Freedom Ride, the sit-ins, the marches, drew attention to nonviolent direct action. Already in the early 1960s Mennonites were participating in such activities. The next major development was the anti-war movement during the °Vietnam War. Many Mennonites, particularly Mennonite students, became involved in peace activism during that period.

An evidence of Mennonite growing awareness that making peace is more than just refusing to participate in war or to bind up wounds of the victims of war is found in the establishment of offices of the Mennonite Central Committee (MCC) in the national capitals of Washington and Ottawa. The constituent members of MCC have not come to full agreement on whether or not Mennonites should be involved in influencing legislation and government programs except when it directly affects the rights of Mennonites to practice their religious convictions. Issues on which they are ready to seek redress from the government include the right to refuse military service, to establish °private Christian schools, and not to participate in the United States social security program.

MCC experiences have brought more active involvement and have raised awareness of injustices in places such as the Middle East, South Africa, the Philippines, and Central America. Mennonites have struggled with the issue of uses of power for °justice in relation to their traditional views on nonresistance.

More recent issues have included the question of refusal to pay military °taxes. This began in the United States but, after Vincent Harding raised the issue at the Mennonite World Conference in 1967, Dutch and Japanese Mennonites also have acted on the issue. In the 1970s and 1980s broader issues of °sociopolitical activism include °women's rights, refusal to register for future military conscription, and °abortion. WK

Bibl. on War and Peace (1987); *God and Caesar* (War Tax Resistance Newsletter, Commission on Home Ministries, Newton, Ks.); *Op zoek naar een vredesgemeente* (Amsterdam: Algemene Doopsgezinde Sociëteit, 1980); Phil Shenk and Melissa Miller, *The Path of Most Resistance* (Scottdale, 1982); Vincent Harding, "The Peace Witness and Modern Revolutionary Movements," in *The Witness of the Holy Spirit*, ed. C. J. Dyck (Elkhart: Mennonite World Conference, n.d. [ca. 1967]), 337-44; Simon L. Verheus, "Beleden vrede—omstreden vrede," and Sjouke Voolstra, "De roerige jaren dertig," in *Wederdoopers, menisten, doopsgezinden in Nederland 1530-1980*, ed. by S. Groenveld, J. P. Jacobszoon and L. L. Verheus (Zutphen: De Walburg Pers, 1980); "Vredeskerk of geen Kerk," *Doops. Jaar.* (1979), 72-79; Gene Sharp, *The Politics of Nonviolent Action* (Boston: Porter Sargent, 1973); Duane K. Friesen, *Christian Peacemaking and International Conflict* (Scottdale, 1986).

See also Reconciliation; Sociopolitical Activism.

Peace Education. During the 19th c. and early 20th c. Mennonites in the United States became somewhat complacent about °nonresistance. World War I shocked many out of their complacency regarding the issue. During the period between the two world wars, certain leaders determined they would not be caught unprepared again, so they began to promote peace education. Books were written and conferences were held, especially with the °°Society of Friends (Quakers) and the Church of the °°Brethren.

The Dutch Mennonites also had a renewal after World War I. Only one Dutch Mennonite declared himself a conscientious objector in World War I. Leaders who went to a Quaker center in England started a movement to recover traditional Mennonite positions, including more than just the peace position. The Werkgroep tegen Krijgsdienst (Taskforce against Military Service) was formed.

After World War II, American and European Mennonites continued to expand their peace education efforts. Already during the war, the American Mennonites had produced the so-called "Core Course" booklets to help those in °°Civilian Public Service camps understand more about their Mennonite heritage, including the peace position.

Since World War II, the efforts at peace education have been intensified and extended. In Europe, Mennonites have founded peace groups and many joint conferences have been held, including meetings of the °historic peace churches and the series of °Puidoux Conferences. In the latter series theological discussions were held between churches not holding the peace position and European and American pacifist theologians. Other intellectual conferences were held, including study conferences, MCC peace assemblies, and new, vigorous attempts to relate °service, °relief, °mission, and °development programs to the peace witness. In the United States and Canada the efforts have been expanded, in part through an initiative taken by the Society of

Friends (Quakers). The New Call to Peacemaking first engaged Mennonite, Brethren, and Friends in renewing their understanding of peace on the basis of the Scriptures, and later others were invited to participate.

Other areas in which Mennonites have become concerned about peace education include its relation to the °family, to conflict resolution, and to criminal justice. The interest in relating nonresistance to missions has resulted in the translation and preparation of materials in several languages. For example, materials have been produced in Spanish to be used in Latin America, Puerto Rico, and among Spanish-speaking Mennonites in the United States.

Beginning in 1973 and 1974 a program of congregational education was undertaken. It has resulted in the peace and social concerns committees of some of the American conferences becoming more responsive to concerns from the congregations. At the same time a series called "Lordship as Servanthood" was developed and put on tapes and distributed to congregations. The scripts were later published in English and Spanish, and recently they are being published in Portuguese.

Mennonite colleges have not only introduced °peace studies degree programs, they have also had peace lectures series for all students and the general public. Bethel College recently had a Kansas Peace Institute endowed to serve both the College and the state as a whole.

The MCC Peace Section has developed an "overseas peace library" available on request by institutions overseas who want resources to help educate others about the issues. The various writings of John Howard Yoder have reached a wide audience, especially beginning with his book *The Politics of Jesus* (Eerdmans, 1972). WK

Bibl. on War and Peace (1987), esp. 69-95, 564-71; Duane Friesen, *Christian Peacemaking and International Conflict: A Realist Pacifist Perspective* (Scottdale, 1986); William Keeney, *Lordship as Servanthood* (Newton, 1975); Robert L. Ramseyer, ed., *Mission and the Peace Witness*, IMS Missionary Studies Series, no. 7 (Scottdale, 1979); J. Lorne Peachey, *How to Teach Peace to Children* (Scottdale, 1982); Susan Clemmer Steiner, *Joining the Army that Sheds No Blood* (Scottdale, 1982).

See also Christian Education; Sociopolitical Activism.

Peace Studies

Peace Studies is a relatively new field of study. The first degree programs offered in peace studies were at Manchester College (1948), and Manhattan College (1970). By 1986 Bethel College (Ks.), Goshen College, Conrad Grebel College, and the Associated Mennonite Biblical Seminaries had established programs in peace studies. Other Mennonite colleges and schools operated by other °historic peace churches offer courses in peace studies. The programs generally study the resolution of conflicts of all types, from the interpersonal to global levels. They also include courses on nonviolent direct action. A significant aspect of the programs usually is an internship where students engage in a participant-observer relationship with an organization or agency engaged in peacemaking at some level.

The Consortium on Peace Research, Education, and Development (COPRED) is the organization which seeks to promote peace studies. Its national office was at Bethel College from 1978 to 1980. The U.S. Institute of Peace and Conflict Resolution came into existence in 1985. WK

William Keeney, "New Perspectives on Peacemaking," *Menn. Life*, 35 (March, 1980), 4-7; Duane K. Friesen, "Peace Studies: Mennonite Colleges in the North American Context," *Menn. Life*, 35 (March, 1980), 13-18; Barbara J. Wien, ed., *Peace and World Order Studies: A Curriculum Guide* 4th ed., (New York: World Policy Institute, 1984); *To Establish the United States Academy of Peace*, Report of the Commission on Proposals for the National Academy of Peace and Conflict Resolution to the President of the United States and the Senate and House of Representatives of the United States Congress (Washington DC: U.S. Government Printing Office, 1981); "Directory of Peace Studies Programs" (COPRED, 911 West High St., Room 100 Urbana, IL 61801), updated frequently.

Peasants' War

Peasants' War (ME IV:1114), the traditional label for a social upheaval early in 1525 in wide areas of southern and central Germany and Austria. Called a "peasants' war" by its aristocratic enemies, it involved various estates of commoners in the regions it affected (peasants, rural artisans, miners and unprivileged townspeople) and it was led most often by non-peasants. In its time it was also, more accurately, referred to as "the rebellion of the common man in town and countryside," although contemporary illustrations show women among the participants. Although it was anticipated by a preliminary uprising in the Black Forest in the summer of 1524 and had a militant aftermath in the Tirol and the bishopric of Salzburg stretching into 1526, the commoners' resistance extended mainly from late January to early June, 1525. It affected Upper Swabia, the Upper Rhine, Franconia, Württemberg, Alsace, Thüringia, and the Tirol. It can be divided into two ten-week periods. In the first period, until the end of March, the commoners' resistance was essentially an armed mass movement of protest aimed at achieving binding negotiations or legal redress or both. Only with the beginning of April is the label "war" at all appropriate, and then it was a war by princes and their mercenary armies, led mainly by the Swabian League, to disperse or destroy the large bands of commoners. Even in this last period the commoners' military actions were hesitant and defensive, and most of the battles were one-sided slaughters. Only in the summer in the Austrian Alps were there some rebel victories. The rebel groups numbered 300,000 at their high point and 100,000 persons lost their lives.

In the first, relatively nonviolent, period of the commoners' resistance, the grievances were directed more against the clergy, particularly monasteries and cathedral chapters, than against the aristocracy. Economic anticlericalism protesting against serfdom, labor services, and landlords' exploitation of forests, waters, and common meadows was linked with demands by villagers to administer their own °tithes and to choose pastors who would preach the Word of God "without human adulteration." The overwhelming majority of commoners in the movement of 1525 thought of it as part of the Reformation and took for granted that it was appropriate to apply God's law to economic, political, and social abuses. Despite Luther's well-known disavowal of the rebels, they were, by intention, part of the Reformation. Their political programs sought to remove the clergy, but not the aristocracy, from positions of worldly authority. They sought greater autonomy for village self-government and greater power for all urban and rural commoners in the representative assemblies of the territorial states. There were also attempts among resisters in southwestern Germany to copy the model of the neighboring Swiss Confederation. Such programs were modeled on contemporary working political institutions (e.g. peasant estates in Scandinavian representative assemblies) and were practicable and realizable, not "utopian."

Early Anabaptism intersected with the commoners' movement of 1525 in many instances, although deficient source materials prevent us from knowing the extent of the connection of the two movements. Early Anabaptist preachers of 1525, Hans °°Krüsi in the rural environs of St. Gall, Johannes °°Brötli and Wilhelm °Reublin in Hallau, and Balthasar °Hubmaier in Waldshut, were involved, as Anabaptists, with the rebels. It is probable that Hubmaier authored or edited two Black Forest peasant programs, the "Letter of Articles" and the "Draft of a Constitution." Major Anabaptist leaders in south and central Germany, Hans °Hut and Melchior °°Rinck, not only were themselves involved in the uprising before becoming Anabaptists but turned to fellow rebels to make their first Anabaptist converts. Hans Hut assigned the rebellion of 1525 °apocalyptic significance as the starting point of the three-and-a-half year period immediately preceding the second coming of Christ. The Christian idealism that the commoners of 1525 turned against social inequality and property continued in another form in the Moravian Hutterites' community of life and goods.   JMS

Peter Blickle, *The Revolution of 1525: The German Peasants War from a New Perspective* (Baltimore and London: Johns Hopkins, 1981); Horst Buszello, *Der deutsche Bauernkrieg als politische Bewegung* (Berlin: Colloquium, 1969); Henry J. Cohn, "Anticlericalism in the German Peasants' War 1525," *Past and Present*, 83 (1979), 3-31; Günther Franz, *Der deutsche Bauernkrieg,* 9th ed., (Darmstadt, 1969); Tom Scott, "The Peasants' War: A Historiographical Review," *Historical Journal*, 22 (1979), 693-720, 953-74; Robert W. Scribner and Gerhard Benecke, eds., *The German Peasant War 1525: New Viewpoints* (London: Allen and Unwin, 1979); Gottfried Seebaß, "Bauernkrieg und Täufertum in Franken," *Z. für KG*, 85 (1974), 284-300; James M. Stayer, "Radikaler Frühzwinglianismus: Balthasar Hubmaier, Fabers 'Ursach' und die Programme der Bauern," *Menn. Geschbl.*, Jg. 42, n.F. 37 (1985), 43-59; Günther Vogler, *Die Gewalt soll gegeben werden dem gemeinen Volk: Der deutsche Bauernkrieg 1525* (Berlin: Dietz, 1983).

See also Historiography; Müntzer, Thomas; Pamphleteering.

Pekabaran Injil dan Pelayana Kasih (PIPKA). See Indonesia; Persatuan Gereja-Gereja Kristen Muria Indonesia.

Penner, Elizabeth Dickman (Oct. 29, 1875 - Jan. 3, 1906), came to America at the age of a few months when her parents migrated from South Russia to Mountain Lake, Minn. Elizabeth's education was limited; she attended Bethel College for one year. She married Peter A. °°Penner in 1900. Together with her husband and J. F. and Susanna °Kroeker, she was one of the four missionaries sent to India to pioneer the first overseas mission work of the General Conference Mennonite Church. She helped in the establishing of the Bethesda Leprosy home and endured the often depressing loneliness of those early years. She bore two daughters, Miriam and Linda. Linda lived less than two years. Elizabeth died from a thrombosis and is buried in the Lower Circular Road Cemetery in Calcutta, India.   RR

Mennonite (Feb. 15, 1906), 4-5.

Penner, Martha Richert (Feb. 15, 1881 - Oct. 1957), was born in Goessel, Ks. She received her deaconess training at the German Deaconess Hospital in Cincinnati, Ohio. On Aug. 24, 1909, she married Peter A. Penner, and later that year went to India as missionaries for the General Conference Mennonite Church. Her husband had founded the Bethesda Leprosy Home in Champa, India, in 1902.

Martha served a widespread community with her medical skills, until other medical personnel arrived in November 1925. Martha was known as a gracious hostess to the lowly as well as to high officials who visited in her home. Although she had no children of her own, she was a loving mother to many healthy children of parents who had leprosy (°Hansen's Disease), and to her stepdaughter Miriam. She and her husband retired from the mission field in 1941.   RR

Samuel T. Moyer, *They Heard the Call* (Newton, 1970), 29-33; Miriam Penner Schmidt, "My Stepmother—Personal Data" unpublished located with Ruth Ratzlaff, Newton, Ks.; India Missionaries, *Twenty-Five years With God in India* (Berne, Ind.: Mennonite Book Concern, 1929), 45, 187-88; Juhnke, *Mission* (1979), 28, 32, 33, 91.

Penner, Mathilde Ensz (Apr. 27, 1879 - Nov. 3, 1961). Born at Halstead, Ks., Mathilde Ensz grew up on a farm and attended country schools. She became a member of the Brudertal Mennonite Church near Hillsboro, Ks. After her marriage to childhood sweetheart, Peter W. °°Penner, Aug. 7, 1902, she and her husband attended German Wallace Seminary, Berea, Ohio, 1904-08. They were ordained missionaries (GCM) to India on Sept. 20, 1908, and arrived in India a few weeks later to begin evangelistic work at °°Janjgir. On their first furlough, 1916-21, they took along Nellie Asna, a motherless invalid Indian child; later they adopted and educated her. She became a teacher and a high school principal. The Penners worked at the Mennonite °°city mission in Los Angeles, 1919-21 (E. F. °Grubb). They returned to Janjgir, 1921-38. Their zeal for the Lord took them to hundreds of villages with the gospel, where Mathilde also used her medical skills. From 1940 to 1949 they worked at Bethesda Leprosy Hospital and Homes, Champa, and then in evangelistic work in the Champa-Mauhadih area. After 40 years of service in India, they retired to Hillsboro, Ks., in 1949.   KLJ

Twenty-Five Years with God in India (Berne: Mennonite Book Concern, 1929), 188, 213-14; 217, 221, 227, 229, 232; Ruth R. Ratzlaff, ed., *Fellowship in the Gospel, India: 1900-1950* (Newton: MPO, 1950), 13-23, 143; Samuel T. Moyer, *They Heard the Call* (Newton, 1970), 63-72; P. W. and Mathilde Penner, "Around Mauhadih," *India Calling*, 4, no. 3 (Autumn, Aug. 15, 1943); Mathilde Penner, "High Peaks of Late," *India Calling*, 4, no. 4 (Christmas issue, Nov. 15, 1943); Martha Burkhalter and others, "Forty Years in the Vineyard," *India Calling*, 12, no. 3 (Autumn 1949), 1, 2-4.

Pennsylvania. See Belleville, Pa., Old Order Amish Settlement; Dialect Literature and Speech; Folk Arts; Lancaster-Chester Counties, Pa., Old Order Amish Settlement; Meyersdale-Springs, Pa., Old Order Amish Settlement; New Wilmington, Pa., Old Order Amish Settlement; Nicknames; Smicksburg, Pa., Old Order Amish Settlement; Spartansburg, Pa., Old Order Amish Settlement.

Pension Plans. The development of pension or retirement funds must be understood in the context of the changing patterns of ministerial leadership among North Americn Mennonites over the course of the 20th c. Equally important are the changing societal and demographic patterns during the same period. Another factor has been the dramatic growth of Mennonite-related °institutions and the need to provide for staff members not only during years of active service but also during retirement. Thus the retirement concerns for the church have become much larger than pastors and missionaries.

In an earlier period of unsalaried lay ministry, there was no need for the church to concern itself with pension plans. Pastors made their living by other vocations, usually farming; and they were responsible for and had resources available for their own retirement years. Included of course was the home in which they had lived throughout their years of ministry.

During the course of the 20th c. several significant changes occurred which brought crises to some who gave themselves to the service and ministry of the church. After several decades of foreign mission work, missionaries who had served for years began to return to North America with no accumulated assets for housing or for retirement living. In North America the change to trained and salaried ministry had the same effect. Pastors who served with minimum salaries, and who moved from one parsonage to another came to retirement with the dilemma—what to do about housing and retirement income. There were those who survived well, either because of inheritance or independent income. But many faced retirement with bleak prospects.

Another major factor during the 20th c. was the dramatic increase in life expectancy. According to data from *Statistical Abstracts of the United States 1986*, the life expectancy at birth of men went from 53.6 years in 1920 to 71.1 years in 1984 and women from 54.6 years in 1920 to 78.3 years in 1984. Furthermore, in 1982 men who survived to age 65 could expect to live to 79.5 years and women to 83.9. What this often meant, of course, was that the surviving spouse faced several additional years of financial uncertainty.

The concern for retirement security is not only an issue for the church but also one for the whole society. National pension programs have become common in most industrialized countries. In the 1930s, in the United States, the response came in the form of the Social Security System to provide a base for retirement, though it was never intended to be a full retirement income. For pastors this was not an adequate answer since they were still considered self-employed, though eventually they were permitted to choose to·enter the Social Security program. To add to the confusion, a change was again made in

1968, according to which pastors were automatically in the Social Security program unless they chose not to be for reasons of conscience, an interesting exception made largely to accommodate the Amish. Still pastors were considered self-employed, were subject to much higher tax rates for social security than were other employees, and they received no additional benefits.

In Canada there has been government assistance available to all persons of retirement age through a program called "The Old Age Security Pension;" this is a non-contributory program based on age, residence and legal status in Canada. In the same program is a guaranteed income supplement for persons with little or no income. In addition the Canada Pension Plan, similar to U.S. Social Security, is a contributory social insurance program which provides retirement benefits and other benefits as well.

Despite these gains in retirement benefits in North American society, they have been far from adequate to meet the needs of church workers in retirement. The church has responded in several ways. (1) Several Mennonite denominational bodies have provided a missionary and pastor's aid fund to supplement those with the very lowest income who did not benefit from more recent pension programs. (2) They have developed more systematic forms of retirement income through pension plans provided for pastors, missionaries, and workers in the institutions of the church.

In 1947 the General Conference Mennonite Church authorized the development of a pension program for ministers, missionaries, and church workers under the leadership of a "Committee on Pensions" (later under the Division of Administration). With this plan it was the intention of the church that congregations or employing institutions would set aside 10 percent of income (cash salary plus housing) to be invested for retirement and other needed benefits. These funds paid to the General Conference Mennonite Church have then been invested with the Presbyterian Minister's Fund as a group flexible premium-deferred annuity. Various changes have been negotiated over the years, all with the goal of increasing the eventual benefits to the persons enrolled. In 1987 approximtely 47 percent of the General Conference pastors in the United States were participating in the conference pension plan. The Conference of Mennonites in Canada developed a similar group retirement plan with contributed funds being invested with the Excelsior Life Insurance Company. Overall the goal has been to provide a reasonable retirement income when the combined resources of personal savings, church pension plans, and government programs were available for pastor, missionaries, and church workers.

In 1963 °Mennonite Mutual Aid of Goshen, Ind., began a pension plan called Mennonite Retirement Trust. This inter-Mennonite agency thus made available to the larger Mennonite community in North America another retirement plan option, since those previously described were limited to the General Conference Mennonite Church personnel. Included on the Mennonite Mutual Aid Board were persons representing the Mennonite Church (MC), the Mennonite Brethren, and the General Conference Mennonite Church. Again a certain percentage of salary was to be placed with Mennonite Retirement Trust each year, with the accumulated investments and earnings to be made available upon retirement or total disability.

Operating on a somewhat different investment philosophy than the General Conference program, Mennonite Retirement Trust used the funds entrusted to it to invest in stocks and bonds, etc. with the goal of 8 percent annual growth. Over the most recent 10-year period the actual returns have been 10.1 percent with a high in 1985 of 15.86 percent.

Over 4,300 people are presently enrolled in Mennonite Retirement Trust and the total assets at the end of 1986 were 34.4 million dollars. Mennonite Retirement Trust became the primary retirement plan for the Mennonite Church (MC). However, as an inter-Mennonite agency, Mennonite Retirement Trust had persons enrolled representing many different Mennonite groups.

In 1974 the Mennonite Brethren church made the Mennonite Retirement Trust the recommended plan for pastors in the United States. Several districts put in an annual minimum amount for all pastors in order to assure maximum participation. In addition, each congregation is encouraged to contribute six percent of salary and each pastor is encouraged to give an additional three percent of salary as annual contributions to Mennonite Retirement Trust. The Mennonite Brethren church in Canada has its own pension program for church leaders.

By 1987 many pastors, missionaries, and church workers were enrolled in one of these plans. These together with Social Security and Canada Pension Plan and personal savings were seen as providing the essential, though certainly not extravagant, income for the retirement years. For pastors an additional factor has changed the picture regarding housing. The 1970s saw a major shift from church-owned parsonages to pastors purchasing their own homes and thus gaining enough equity to provide housing during retirement years. In 1985, 83 percent of the General Conference and Mennonite Church pastors who responded to a salary survey reported that they owned or rented their own homes rather than living in a parsonage.   JAE

People's Republic of China (ME I: 560). With the defeat of the Kuomintung movement and the establishment of the People's Republic of China in 1950, Chinese Mennonite churches found themselves in a totally new situation. Virtually all Mennonite missionaries and relief personnel left China by 1951. Chinese authorities permitted the churches to meet according to established customs but not for long. Church properties were confiscated and with the coming of the Cultural Revolution in 1965 virtually all traces of the churches were erased, even though some Mennonites remained Christian in conviction and personal piety. Virtually no direct communication between North American mission boards and Chinese Christians was possible until the Cultural Revolution came to a close in 1978.

However a new and exciting chapter in Mennonite-Chinese relations began in 1979. In that year, Goshen College negotiated an educational exchange with the Sichuan Provincial Bureau of Higher Education. It was the first exchange between a Chinese

university and an American undergraduate college since Liberation. Accordingly, 20 Goshen College students spent 16 weeks at the Sichuan Provincial Teacher's College in 1980 while 10 Chinese teachers of English from Sichuan Province spent the 1980-81 academic year at Goshen College studying English pedagogy. Exchanges continued on an annual basis. By 1987, 160 Goshen students had spent a Study-Service-Trimester in Chengdu while some 70 Chinese teachers of English had studied at Goshen College. Since China had been virtually closed to American visitors before 1978, a book entitled *The New China* (1982) by Winifred Beechy, helped the Mennonite Church as well as the broader reading public to understand China's life and culture under socialism. (Winifred and Atlee Beechy led the 1978 Goshen College contingent.) Goshen College also provided teachers of English for the North-East Institute of Science and Technology at Shenyang in Laoning Province. Chinese officials and American Mennonite medical doctors, agricultural experts, and educators exchanged visits annually.

The initial success of the Goshen College program led in 1980 to a general invitation for the Mennonite churches to supply China with as many qualified teachers of English as possible. In order to meet this unusual challenge, various branches of the Mennonites organized in 1980 the China Educational Committee, with Bert Lobe of Mennonite Central Committee as director. In 1981 two North American teachers were sent to Sichuan Province. The numbers increased gradually. By 1986 a total of 52 North Americans had participated in the exchange. Eastern Mennonite College and Bethel College (Ks.), hosted Chinese teachers.

Relationships between the Mennonite churches and China became unusually respectful and trusting. Probably no American denomination entered into such intimate and friendly relationshps with Chinese authorities as did the Mennonites. Since cultural, religious, and philosophical differences were obvious, cordial working relations between American Mennonites and Chinese Communists gave rise to considerable reflection. What is there in the Chinese experience and Mennonite attitudes that would foster such positive relationships? Does the Mennonite China experience speak to questions about the shape of Christian witness in China? On an even deeper level, how may one think theologically about the Chinese Communist revolution?   JLB

MWR (Aug. 23, 1984), 6, (Aug. 30, 1984) 6; Robert and Alice Ramseyer, *Mennonites in China* (China Educational Exchange, 1988).

Committed to China: The Loyal Bartel Story

Loyal Bartel (1901-71) was the first child of H. C. and Nellie °Bartel, born on the high seas as his parents were enroute to China for their first term of missionary service.

He was converted at an early age and dedicated his life to Christian service. At age 17 he began preaching and working with orphan boys. When he was 19 he went to the United States to study at Moody Bible Institute in Chicago, Fort Wayne (Ind.) Bible College, and Northern Baptist Seminary in

Chicago. After graduation, he worked with the Chicago Hebrew Mission. On June 4, 1926, he was married to Susan Schultz. Five children were born to their union.

The couple went to China as missionaries in 1927, serving in Caoxian (Tsaohsien), Shandong Province, in the Bible school, the publishing house, and in preaching as requested. The only time Loyal returned to the United States was for a furlough in the winter of 1936-37.

When the Bible school was closed in the early 1940s, the couple continued to try to help the Chinese church. During the time of the Japanese occupation of North China, Loyal's youngest brother, Jonathan Bartel, who had spent some years teaching in Shanghai and later served as a missionary in Japan, came to Caoxian to teach Loyal and Susan's three daughters. All other missionaries had left or were detained by the occupation force. During this time the Bartels went through many experiences, including detention and trying to make ends meet by farming.

On Loyal's birthday on November 23, 1941, just before the outbreak of war between the United States and Japan, the family and Jonathan drew Bible verses from a promise box for Loyal. One verse was Job 23:0, "But he knoweth the way that I take: When he hath tried me, I shall come forth as gold." The verse foreshadowed Loyal's experience in the years to come.

Close to the end of World War II, Loyal and his family and Jonathan were taken by the military police to Heze (Tsao Cho Fu), located about 30 mi. (48 km.) north of Caoxian, where Loyal was accused of being a spy on behalf of the guerrillas roaming the villages. From Heze he was taken to higher military authorities in another city, where daily torture of other prisoners was taking place. Here the Lord gave him a promise from Ps 27:5, "For in the day of trouble he will conceal me in his tabernacle. In the secret place of his tent he will hide me; he will lift me up on a rock." Shortly thereafter, unharmed, Loyal was released.

Finally, in October 1948 Susan and the children and Jonathan left China to return to the United States. Loyal felt constrained to stay. Although during subsequent years under the communist rule, family members tried to encourage him to leave, he insisted that he had no such leading, even though he could not be directly involved in any church work. He moved to the village where he farmed a small plot of land that had not been collectivized. Here he was able to grow enough to support himself for about 10 months of the year. His modest home, with a small coal-burning stove, was a gathering place for local farmers during the winter. He was not free to preach, but he could respond to their questions. Almost all of his books, Bibles, photo albums, and other effects had been either confiscated or burned in front of his house. One leaf of his Bible blew out of the flames. It contained chapter 16 of Matthew, verse eight, "Upon this rock I will build my church and the gates of hell shall not prevail against it."

After China again began to open up, brothers Jonathan and Paul Bartel traveled there to gather further details about Loyal's death. They were told he had been imprisoned during the Great Cultural Revolution (1966-69), had been accused as a spy of imperialist America, and that he had died a natural death as a prisoner. Their Christian informants, however, did not know the exact date of his death or place of burial.

In May 1987 Jonathan again went to China with the sole purpose of getting to his hometown of Caoxian. Although the city was still closed to travelers from abroad, he was given a travel permit by the Shandong provincial police. In Caoxian he asked the chief of police for a statement of exoneration for his brother. The chief informed him that Loyal had never been accused of being a spy and therefore he would not be able to give him a statement of exoneration. He did, however, suggest that Jonathan could take Loyal's remains back with him. According to the police, Loyal died on March 16, 1971. A memorial and burial service was held in Mountain Lake, Minnesota, on August 22, 1987.

In 1949 there were approximtely one million Christians in China. In the late 1980s there are at least 50 million. When Jonathan visited Caoxian in 1987, the Caoxian church had just completed a new church building. The church has some 1,000 believers attending on Sundays. He also learned that there are an estimated 20,000 believers in that county alone.   JMB

Adapted from an address by Jonathan Bartel at the memorial service for Loyal Bartel, Mountain Lake, Aug. 22, 1987.

Perfectionism. See Forgiveness; Grace; Holiness Movement; Sectarianism; Work Ethic.

Periodicals. The first four volumes of the *Mennonite Encyclopedia* contain articles on specific types of periodicals, e.g. "Almanacs," and specific periodicals, e.g. "Christlicher Bundesbote," but no general article on "Periodicals." These four volumes included approximately 200 entries on periodicals. *Mennonite Bibliography, 1631-1961* (published in 1977), lists slightly more than 830 periodicals. This does not include publications of very limited audience. A complete count of Mennonite periodicals in 1988 would probably total more than 3,000, some ephemeral, others passing the century mark in duration of publication.

The earliest known Mennonite periodical is °°*Naamlijst der Tegenwoordige in Dienst Zijnde Predikanten der Mennoniten in de Vereenigde Nederlanden*, published irregularly under variant titles, 1731-1829. The title with longest continuous publication seems to be the annual *Meeting Calendar of All the Mennonite Churches in Eastern Pennsylvania*, 1854-. The earliest known European journal published more frequently than annually is *De Philosooph* (weekly), 1766-69. In North America it was °°*Religiöser Botschafter*, 1852-55, superseded by *Das* °°*Christliche Volksblatt*, 1856-88; (title later changed to *Der* °°*Mennonitische Friedensbote*. The journal with longest continuous publication in Europe is the Swiss °°*Zionspilger*, 1882-; in North America, °°*Mennonitische Rundschau*, 1880-, which superseded °°*Nebraska Ansiedler*, 1878-80. The Dutch Mennonite *De* °°*Zondagsbode*, 1887-1942, North German °°*Mennonitische Blätter*, 1854-1941, and South German °°*Gemeindeblatt der Mennoniten,* 1870-1941, were casualties of World War II. Dutch Mennonites have published °°*Algemeen Doopsgezind Weekblad,* since 1946. Both German periodicals resumed publication, but were replaced by *Brücke* in 1985. In North America the °°*Evangelical Visitor* (BIC, 1887-), the German-language organ °°*Zionsbote* (MB, 1884-), and *The Mennonite* (GCM, 1885-) have passed the century mark. The *Gospel Herald* (MC, 1908-), was preceded by the privately published °°*Herald of Truth* (1864-1908), °°*Herold der Wahrheit* (1864-1901), and °°*Gospel Witness* (1905-08). Official organs of other Mennonite groups will be found under their own titles or under the relevant denominational historical sketches.

The 20th c. has seen an ever-increasing expansion in the number of Mennonite journals, differing widely in content, intended audience, level of scholarship, frequency of publication, and length of life. The shift from letterpress and other more cumbersome methods of printing to printing from photomechanical plates and masters has stimulated professional and amateur printing alike. This has been accompanied by a tendency in major Mennonite organs, both in Europe and North America, to a more journalistic style, briefer articles, more informal institutional news, more illustrations, and less personalia, except for formalized birth, marriage, and death notices. For younger Mennonite churches outside Europe and North America for and by whom there had been very little literature produced, the newer methods of printing have facilitated production of journals. The older major denominational and a few inter-Mennonite journals, including scholarly journals, now compete with a burgeoning flood of periodical literature from departments and committees of an increasing number of church °institutions, °minority and special interest groups, local congregations, regional °historical societies and family °genealogists. Unfortunately, the obscurity and complex nature of this body of literature so important to researchers is such that there is little hope of exhaustive listing or preservation except or even through combined efforts of Mennonite °historical libraries.   NPS

Nelson P. Springer and A. J. Klassen, *Mennonite Bibliography, 1631-1961* (Scottdale, 1977).

See also Publishing.

Persatuan Gereja-Gereja Kristen Muria Indonesia (GKMI; Union of Muria Christian Churches of Indonesia). The conference of the Gereja-Gereja Kristen Muria Indonesia (Muria Christian Churches of Indonesia), commonly called the Muria Synod or simply GKMI, was formed at the time of its first assembly on April 18 to 22, 1948. Originally called the *Gereja-Gereja Doopsgezind/Tiong Hwa Kie Tok Kauw Hwee/Classis Muria* (Muria Conference of the Chinese Mennonite Church) the conference consisted of eight Malay-speaking Chinese congregations in the towns of Kudus, Jepara, Pati, Welahan, Mayong, Tanjung, Bangsri, and Demak. These churches are all located in the area surrounding the Muria Mountain on the north coast of central Java, and at that time had a total of about 500 baptized members.

The first church of this conference was organized in the town of Kudus on Sept. 27, 1925, as the *Chineesche Doopsgezinde Christengemeente* (Chinese Mennonite Christian Congregation) with about 100 baptized members including small branch congregations in Mayong and Tanjung. Six months later the new church made application to the government and on Feb. 3, 1927, was granted official recognition as a church by the Governor-General of the Netherlands Indies (though still dependent on the mission for services of baptism and communion). As such the Chinese Mennonite Church in Kudus was the first Chinese church to be recognized by the government of Netherlands East Indies and the first independent non-Teutonic Mennonite church in the world.

The Chinese Christian group in Kudus began in about 1918 as a largely indigenous movement under the leadership of the newly converted Chinese businessman, °Tee Siem Tat ("He Drove a Ford" [feature]). Tee, a follower of the traditional Chinese religions—Confucianism, Buddhism, and Taoism flowing together in a single stream—fell ill in about 1917 with an ailment that neither traditional healers nor western medical doctors were able to cure. Faced with her husband's recalcitrant ailment Sie Djoen Nio began to tell Tee of the many accounts of Jesus healing the sick that she had been secretly reading in a Bible a relative had given their daughter. Could it be that Jesus would heal Tee too?

Tee went to several Christian meetings in a relative's house in Rembang to learn more about Christianity and then invited the leader, the Ambonese Salvation Army Lieutenant Tanuhatu, to come to Kudus and teach his family and friends. Tee's gradual acceptance of the gospel was accompanied by his gradual healing. His growing faith was then confirmed in the sudden healing of his wife's niece. Tee's conversion precipitated a dramatic reorientation of his priorities. He turned most of the daily operations of his printing business and other commercial activities over to his children, and began to give increasing amounts of time to sharing his new-found faith with friends and relatives. Though there was sharp opposition from the supporters of the traditional religions, soon several dozen people were attending meetings in Tee's house.

The question of baptism eventually caused a reluctant disengagement between Tee's group and the Salvation Army (though they continued to use the Salvation Army songbook for more than 20 years). The group found itself unable to reconcile the Salvation Army's military-style induction ceremony with the practice of baptism they found in the Bible. Thus they began to seek out a relationship with some other established Christian body to give them teaching and guidance, to provide services of baptism and communion, and give a certain social and legal legitimacy to their group.

Tee contacted a Seventh Day Adventist missionary from Salib Putih near Salatiga who came to Kudus to share that church's teachings. Another group, the Salatiga Mission (of the New Church movement in Germany), was party to the inter-mission territorial °comity agreements and was therefore unwilling to come to work with Tee in Kudus without at least contacting the Mennonite missionaries in whose area Kudus was located. The response of the Mennonite missionaries was to contact Tee and his group themselves. Whatever all of the factors entering into the consideration, the teachings of the Mennonite missionaries seemed to Tee very close to what he saw in the Bible and he finally asked for baptism from Russian Mennonite missionary Nicolai Thiessen. The first group of 25 persons was baptized in Kudus on Dec. 6, 1920. Within a year another 24 people were baptized.

The energetic and independent character of the new group was demonstrated in their dynamic outreach activity and their moves to organize themselves and seek recognition from the government. Before long they began to feel restricted by mission policies. They expected more support from the mission but the mission was suffering the loss of its primary support base in the Mennonite colonies of the Ukraine caused by the °Russian Revolution and Civil War. They also did not understand the mission's continuing reluctance to credential Tee or any of the groups' leaders as ministers in spite of the fact that it was Tee who had evangelized the group. Finally in 1927, without knowledge of the missionaries, the group applied directly to the government and received recognition for Tee and his associate, Oei Tjien Gie, as ministers for a church the government had officially recognized only that year. They also sought and received government license to evangelize the Chinese populace in the Muria area. When the Mission Conference was faced with these developments in its November 1927 meeting, it had little choice but to grant the group's request that they be acknowledged as an independent congregation.

Mennonite missionaries had been working in the Muria area since the 1850s. Though their efforts were primarily directed toward the majority Javanese population, there was recurrent missionary interest in the small populations of Chinese people in the smaller towns of the area. This interest extended at one point to the appointment of a Chinese evangelist from China to work among Muria-area Chinese. And they recruited other evangelists especially to work among the Chinese in the small towns of the area. The missionaries, however, expected the resulting small number of Chinese converts to become integrated into the Javanese congregations. They did not give adequate attention to the linguistic and cultural barriers inhibiting such integration. Nor did they recognize that the Chinese communities of the area were made up predominantly of people "of Chinese descent" (Kiauwseng) who had abandoned Chinese language and ties with China in favor of the language and land where they had settled. "Overseas Chinese" (hoakiao) evangelists who preferred to speak Chinese and had a strong orientation toward China found limited acceptance in the Malay-speaking Kiauwseng communities of the Muria area. By the second decade of the century the mission, with its rural orientation, had only a handful of Chinese Christians in its care and had made virtually no effort to minister in Kudus, the largest town of the Muria area, much less to evangelize the Chinese population of that town. It was this situation which provided the setting for the rise of a strong indigenous Chinese Christian movement in the Muria area centering in Kudus.

After gaining recognition as an independent

church the Chinese Mennonite Christian Church faced some new challenges. Working out a new kind of working relationship with the mission became a source of considerable misunderstanding. On the one hand since the government had granted the new Chinese church the license to evangelize the Chinese population in the whole Muria area, the mission wanted to turn all responsibility for the work it was doing among the Chinese in the other towns of the area over to the church.

On the other hand, Tee felt the mission wanted to leave him in the lurch with no support for evangelization among the Chinese. His feelings were exacerbated when the mission proceeded to place a missionary in Kudus to work among the Javanese people there. This seemed to Tee to be an effort to compete with his group. If the mission had money to place a missionary in Kudus, why was there no money for the evangelistic work of the new Chinese church. The final result of these misunderstandings was that Tee wrote a letter to the mission announcing the decision that he and the members of the church had made to separate the church completely from the mission, that is abandon its Doopsgezind (Mennonite) name and stop sending reports to the Mennonite Mission Board. While Tee did not follow through with a legal change of name, this action illustrates the difficulty of the transition from mission to independent and indigenous church.

Soon there were efforts to iron out these misunderstandings, but this crisis was the trigger that precipitated a major departure in ministry activity for the church. Now there were more deliberate efforts to evangelize the Chinese populations of neighboring towns and to form new congregations. During the 1930s new Chinese congregations were established in Jepara, Bangsri, Pati, and Welahan. Work begun in several other towns did not yet produce permanent results. The vigor of the Jepara group soon began to rival that of the Kudus group. One of the leaders of the Jepara group, Sie Giok Gian (later called Gombak Sugung), had converted to Christian faith from a position of leadership in the traditional Chinese religious and social organization, the Tiong Hwa Hwie Kwan. He was thus well-positioned to introduce the Christian gospel into the heart of the Chinese community and pursuade many people to become Christians. The Jepara people also soon became active in outreach to other towns in the area.

As these new congregations developed the question of their relationship to the Kudus congregation arose. From the perspective of Kudus it seemed that the new groups were branches of Kudus. This concept seemed appropriate to the small groups in Mayong and Tanjung, but it seemed less appropriate to large, growing congregations like Jepara. During the 1930s the Chinese churches in other parts of Java with the encouragement of the various mission agencies were organized into conferences or synods. Because of the early independence of the Chinese church in Kudus and because of the weakness of the vision of the Mennonite missionaries for development of a national church organization, there was less mission guidance in this area. Further, the activity of the charismatic figure of Tee Siem Tat, traveling and ministering frequently among the churches in the Muria area, seemed to obviate the need for an intercongregational organization, although the articles of incorporation of the Jepara church (1935) seem to reach in that direction.

The 1940s brought a whole new set of challenges to the church. They began (May 1940) with the imprisonment and later death of Herman Schmitt, the young (German) Mennonite missionary most closely involved with the Chinese Mennonite churches. This was followed on Oct. 2, 1940, by the death of the charismatic founder of the movement, Tee Siem Tat. Then came the anti-Chinese, anti-Christian Muslim uprising in March 1942, the Japanese occupation (1942-45) and the revolutionary struggle (1945-50). These represented a great challenge to the new leadership of the Muria Church.

Now there was a strong motivation for Chinese people to break off their longstanding sense of identity with the Dutch under whose colonial administration they had enjoyed certain (though not unmixed) benefits and advantages. But should they identify fully with the Indonesian nationalist movement? Only certain members of the younger generation took that option. Many of the Chinese population sought a new sense of identity in their Chineseness, though only a few of them could use much Chinese language. These crosscurrents and changes are represented in the several revisions of the church order prepared during the 1940s. Early versions used many Dutch words. By the late 1940s these were replaced with many Chinese-language terms. Later only Indonesian (Malay)-language terms came to be used.

The key leader in this period was Tan King Ien, the son-in-law of Tee Siem Tat. It was finally through his leadership that the Muria Church conference was organized in 1948. Though a conference constitution was not created at this time patterns were set which served the conference reasonably well during its first decade. Tan king Ien remained conference chairman until 1956.

The appearance of Mennonite Central Committee workers in Central Java in the late 1940s made possible the sending of Tan Hao An (Herman Tann), the son of Tan King Ien, and his wife, Jo Nio, to study theology at several Mennonite colleges in the United States. When they returned they were quickly placed into positions of synod leadership. Expectations were high. On the one hand the Tans were now supposed to be able to teach what Mennonite theology and practice was really about since none of the earlier leaders had received any specific training from the Mennonite mission. They were expected to know how Mennonites organize things. On the other hand, Tan King Ien left a legacy of dissatisfaction for his apparently somewhat dominant style of leadership both in the Kudus congregation and in the conference. For his son to take over conference leadership seemed—in a time of exploding interest in democratic ideals—like nepotism to some. Further, there was a vocal minority that was opposed to sharpening the church's Mennonite identity at the expense of ecumenical relations with other Chinese churches.

The late 1950s were a period of growing social, economic and political turmoil in Indonesia. Conference assemblies were not held according to the established schedule. The government was pressuring people of Chinese descent to identify themselves clearly as Indonesians. The church had to deal with government pressure requiring that foreign language organizational names be replaced with Indonesian language names. They abandoned the Dutch language name of the conference and the Chinese language names they had started to use—Tiong Hwa Kie Tok Kauw Hwee (Chinese Christian Church) and Khu Hwee (conference)—and adopted the Indonesian (Malay) language name Persatuan Gereja-Gereja Kristen Muria Indonesia. The ecumenists in the group wanted to use the name Gereja Kristen Indonesia (Christian Church of Indonesia) that other Chinese churches had adopted, but others insisted on using the place name Muria to replace the Dutch language term Doopsgezinde (Mennonite) asserting that for more than 100 years the name of the area had been associated with the Mennonite mission. To them "Muria" means "Mennonite." For a time, however, local congregations were called simply Kudus (or Jepara or Pati) Christian Church.

In 1958 an emergency meeting of the synod was called to take action on a Mennonite confession of faith that Herman Tann had prepared and modeled on an American Mennonite confession. Small booklets about Menno Simons and basic Mennonite beliefs were published and circulated in cooperation with the Javanese Mennonite Church (Gereja Injili di Tanah Jawa) and the Dutch Mennonite Mission.

Herman Tann had two major influences on the Muria Church. First was his conviction that specifically Mennonite beliefs and practices were important enough to challenge the previously held position that the Mennonite churches should limit their work to the historically agreed upon Mennonite area, the area around the Muria mountain. In his opinion the Muria churches should follow their increasingly mobile members to other cities, gathering them together to become the nuclei of new congregations. But more than this the Tanns believed that the Muria churches had a responsibility to evangelize people beyond the Muria area and beyond the circles of Chinese community. In proclaiming his vision Tann faced substantial opposition from ecumenists in the churches who insisted that the Muria church should not compete with other churches outside the Muria. But in the late 1950s a new congregation was launched in the provincial capital city of Semarang where now several additional congregations and the synod headquarters are located. Soon the vision extended to Jakarta, the nation's capital and to the other cities of Java. Tann's mission convictions were stronger than his commitment to synod leadership. Soon he moved to Jakarta to set up a Christian radio station and worked toward the formation of churches there. He also nurtured a vision of involving American Mennonites in his vision for mission.

In 1965 under the leadership of Herman Tann and Thio Tjien Swie (Theopilus Muryadi Hadipraesetyo) a number of new departures in outreach began to develop. A mission board was formed. Its name, PIPKA, is an acronym for Pekabaran Injil dan Pelayanan Kasih (evangelization and service). However support for this mission board was not forthcoming either from the Muria churches or from overseas Mennonite agencies to the degree that the initiators had hoped for.

In the early 1970s the Mennonite Brethren Board for Missions and Services responded to overtures from Muria Church leadership to enter into a cooperative mission enterprise with PIPKA. Through this arrangement both personnel and funds from North America were administered by the national organization. Well over 50 new mission posts have been started; by the late 1980s some were moving steadily toward maturity. This initiative spurred Mennonite Central Committee (MCC), which up to this time had been hesitant to support PIPKA, to become involved in a wholistic church planting ministry in Kalimantan. There they placed both MCC personnel and personnel seconded from Eastern Mennonite Board of Missions and Charities (MC) on a mission team under Indonesian supervision with support levels identical to the Indonesian members of the team.

In the early 1960s a strong spiritual awakening among the youth of the Muria churches, facilitated in part by annual Bible camps, produced a substantial crop of new leaders for the church. Many of these people received theological education at a variety of schools, a few of them attending the new theological college in Pati, Akademi Kristen Wiyata Wacana, operated jointly with the Gereja Injili di Tanah Jawa, Europäisches Mennonitisches Evangelisationskomitee (EMEK; European Mennonite Mission Board), and MCC. Though Herman Tann and his wife finally withdrew from the circle of the Muria church to launch a personal mission to the United States, they did not do so without making a profound impact on this new generation of leaders. Thus was the stage set for a major transition from a predominantly untrained lay leadership to the predominantly trained professional (paid) leadership characteristic of the Muria churches in the 1980s.

From the beginning in Kudus there was interest in providing Christian elementary and secondary schools for children of Christian and non-Christian families. These schools were clearly evangelistic in intent. Military occupation and revolution disrupted some of these schools. Today, however, several of the churches—Kudus and Jepara in particular—have extensive educational programs. The Muria churches are also involved at the student, faculty, administration, and board level with the interdenominational Satya Wacana Christian University in Salatiga and Duta Wacana Christian University in Yogyakarta. They also participate with the Javanese Mennonite Churches in the cooperative Mennonite Scholarship Foundation which administers MCC and °International Mennonite Organization scholarship programs for children attending the churches' schools and also provides scholarships for university and technical school students open to future service in church ministries.

In the 1950s interest arose in Kudus to begin a medical ministry. That vision has today produced the more than 100-bed Mardi Rahayu Christian Hospital. Interest in economic development work precipitated the formation in the late 1960s of the Mennonite (later Muria) Economic Development Foundation in cooperation with the Javanese Mennonite Church, MCC, and EMEK. After functioning for about a dec-

ade this agency was disbanded because of differences of vision and management philosophy.

Already in the 1930s the Muria church experimented with a special church-run business to support church ministries. In the 1970s a local endowment and funds from °Mennonite Economic Development Associates (MEDA) made possible a bus project operated by the conference's Dorcas Foundation. Herman Tann's early vision for a radio ministry in Jakarta has grown into the well-established ICHTHUS Radio Station in Semarang.

The most substantial ministry program of the Muria conference remains PIPKA, the mission board. The work of the mission among several different ethnic groups in Java, Sumatra, and Kalimantan will in the future result in a clearly multicultural conference, a change that will require considerable sensitivity and adjustment both in practice and organization.

The Muria conference in 1983 had 18 congregations, some 50 branch congregations mostly under PIPKA auspices, with a total baptized membership of 4,583.   LMY

Th. Jensma, *Doopsgezinde Zending in Indonesia* ('s-Gravenhage: Boekcentrum, 1968); Lawrence M. Yoder, *Tunas Kecil: Sejarah Gereja Kristen Muria Indonesia* [Little Shoot: History of the Mura Christian Church of Indonesia] (Semarang: Komisi Literatur Sinode GKMI, n.d. [1985]), also available in English translation under the title *The Church of the Muria: A History of the Muria Christian Church of Indonesia* (ThM thesis, Fuller Theological Seminary, 1981); idem, "Onstaan en Groei van de Christelijke Kerk Rond de Muria in Indoinesië,"; *Doops. Jaar.* (1984), 61-78; *MWH* (1978), 152-56.

Persecution. In this article persecution will be defined as coercion for religion's sake. It is often thought of as primarily physical torture and extremely cruel forms of execution such as crucifixion by the Romans. But mental forms of persecution have always existed and have been revived with sadistic twists in the 20th c. In Anabaptist and Mennonite history discrimination for the sake of religion has been a common if less severe form of persecution.

Religious people have frequently persecuted those of other religious persuasions. Pagan Romans persecuted early Christians. Fifth-century Christians triumphantly persecuted pagans; early in the sixth century a pagan Roman senator wrote one of the most eloquent pleas for religious liberty that any civilization has produced. Seventeenth-century Japanese persecuted Roman Catholics in support of official Buddhism. New secularists, worshippers of the Goddess of Reason, persecuted staunch Roman Catholics, especially clergy, during the French Revolution (1790s). In the 19th c., Russian Orthodox Christians persecuted Roman Catholics in Poland and Moslems in Turkey. For many centuries Christians have persecuted Jews systematically and capriciously. Many Mennonites think that some forms of excommunication, applied rigorously with the °°ban, constitute persecution of Mennonites by other Mennonites (Bear; P. Friesen). In short, religious conviction easily turns to righteous indignation against religious nonconformists or dissidents and breeds a malice that has produced some of the most cruel forms of persecution humans have ever devised.

Traditionally Mennonites viewed early Christians and the Anabaptists as focal points of the most severe persecutions in church history. Van Braght shaped his *Martyrs Mirror* around those two periods. Early Christians were harassed, imprisoned, and executed in barbarous ways, commonly on the charge of atheism since they did not believe in the socially accepted divinities. Or they were accused of sedition because they refused to regard the emperor as *deus et dominus*, god and lord; Romans believed absolute allegiance to an absolute god-emperor to be a necessity for holding together in one society many people of diverse ethnicities and religious cults. Romans displayed their predilection for terror as a means of cowing conquered tribespeople into submission in the form of uncommon cruelty in torture and over-eager execution. But they had a penchant for the rule of law, and they created a body of law and juridical thought of the highest order. Generally they intended to grant free exercise of religion to the diverse cults of their heterogenous subjects. Indeed, one of the major reasons for Christianity's success was the Roman Empire's relative freedom of worship, interrupted by some vicious but usually local outbreaks of persecution. Systematic, empire-wide persecutions under Decius and Valerian (250-59) and Diocletian and Galerius (303-11) were the exception to the rule.

Anabaptists were persecuted severely. It makes little difference whether one counts several hundred or many thousand martyrs: the psychological impact was terrifying, persuading many to recant and frightening away many more prospective converts. Catholics imprisoned and burned Anabaptists as apostates. Lutherans exiled or beheaded them for blasphemy and sedition. Reformed leaders (Calvinists) imprisoned and drowned them for sectarianism and breaking the body politic. (It should not be forgotten that Lutherans were also persecuted by Catholics in Austria or that Protestants routinely executed Roman Catholic priests when they were discovered while ministering to the underground Catholic church in England well into the 1600s.)

Almost everyone used torture to compel these religious deviants to return to the true church. Societies have always used torture, both to punish but also to extract confessions, in some places and times more than others. In the West juridical torture derived largely from the rediscovery of Roman law. Used largely by the church in its Inquisition (early 13th c. and following), it was adopted increasingly by civil courts because it was thought to be effective. By the 16th c. its use was common, in many Germanic lands routine, in numerous types of court cases but especially where heresy was presumed. It was used to induce confession, secondarily to extract information about Anabaptist leaders, places of meeting, etc. Physical forms of torture included primarily the rack—stretching the body until the joints separated; often the thumbscrew; sometimes the suspension of the body from arms tied behind the back or from the thumb of one hand, with weights attached to the feet. Today many European museums display standard instruments for late medieval torture.

By the beginning of the 20th c. the West thought that it had decisively rejected juridical torture, beginning generally in the 18th c. But the 20th c. has introduced newer forms, quasi-legal or sanctioned by law, gravitating more toward mental forms, although some new physical forms have been invented—electric shocks to sensitive parts of the body, for instance. Brainwashing is the term invented in our times to describe mental torture. In the 16th c. interrogators tortured victims mentally by questionings so lengthy that they exhausted the prisoners, promising reunion with spouse and children if one recanted, giving filthy quarters and insufficient food for weeks on end to reduce resistance, etc.

Anabaptists sometimes remonstrated against persecution. One of the best illustrations is Menno's moving tract, "A Pathetic Supplication to All Magistrates" (*Writings*, 523-31). He knew that governments used the edicts of Theodosius II (emperor, 401-50) against rebaptizers (418ff.) to persecute Anabaptists, and complained that those proscriptions had been wrung from Theodosius by bloodthirsty bishops. He pleaded for mercy, but also for that kind of justice in which magistrates would compare the moral lives of Anabaptists with those of other Christians.

Europe's wars of religion bred a new class of *politiques*, leaders who preached religious indifference as a necessary way to end the bloodshed in which one religious group fought another in the name of God. In the spirit of the *politiques* the more severe forms of persecution gradually were replaced by discrimination, sharp in southern Germanic regions until the French Revolution granted citizenship to every human including Mennonites and Jews, mild but still painful in the North.

What forms did it take in the South? In the Swiss Confederation Mennonites could not inherit land, and their children were technically illegitimate because the state had not legally approved their marriages. Or they were imprisoned for longer periods of time on bread and water only. In 1710-11 the Bernese government devised an elaborate deportation scheme, working with a land agent to send them to the Carolinas. Some were sent on their way by barge down the Rhine, then released through the political intervention of their Dutch co-religionists when their boat reached the Netherlands. (The Old Order Amish of North America still keep alive oral tradition in the tales of that ordeal.) Some were sold as galley slaves to the Italian city-states. Swiss democracy emphasized equal participation of all, especially in times of war, more than the rights of the individual before the law.

In southern German states, including °°Alsace, Mennonites and Amish paid a special tax merely because they were religious dissidents. Or they were forbidden to buy more land when their population increased. Or they were harried into court, for example, when they baptized two young girls, born Amish but forcibly raised Catholic, contrary to the express prohibition to proselytize. Or, if they developed good pasture on mountainsides too steep to till, jealous villagers drove their own livestock into those pastures and forcibly excluded cattle of the Mennonites.

In northern regions Mennonites were often forbidden to enter the standard craft and trade guilds (in Danzig, for example). Some therefore became innkeepers. Or they were excluded from the universities and therefore from certain professions such as law, a prohibition that was galling to the Dutch Mennonites who were bursting with creative energy. There were other forms of discrimination; but on the whole, northern Teutonic Mennonites were less discriminated against than were the southerners.

Other times and places of special persecution or discrimination against descendants of the Anabaptist family include the Hutterian Brethren in late 18th-c. Hapsburg lands of eastern and central Europe; Russian Mennonites in the 1920s and since World War II; some African, Asian, and Latin American Mennonites, especially since World War II; and finally, some North American Mennonites during wartime.

Hapsburg Empress Maria Theresa (ruled 1740-80), true to a sincere but dogmatic Hapsburg family Catholicism, finally exiled those few Hutterian Brethren who refused to recant. The recanters were subjected to rigorous religious supervision, required to attend mass or special Catholic homilies and prayers, or both, more frequently than were their native Slavic neighbors—well into the 20th c. according to the memory of some of their surviving so-called °°Habaner descendants (Velke Levaré, Czechoslovakia, for instance). The exiles wandered in misery from one region to another before finding refuge in the Ukraine.

Twentieth-century Mennonites in Russia were driven from their villages and sent to slave labor camps where many perished. Some of their most severe tribulations occurred during and immediately after wars—World War I, the Civil War, World War II—and cannot be separated easily from the normal but intense suffering caused by modern warfare. (All ethnic Germans were subjected to mistreatment under the °Spetskommandatura [deportation regime], 1941-55.) There is no doubt that Mennonites were persecuted for their religious faith; other Christians and Jews suffered similar persecution from a self-proclaimed atheist government determined to impose absolute conformity on everyone for the benefit of all. There is some dispute among Russian Mennonite historians on the issue of whether or not Mennonites were singled out especially for persecution. The Bolsheviks reproached them for their use of weapons in self-defense against bands of anarchists (°Selbstschutz).

Mennonites in Asia, Africa, and Latin America have been persecuted, more commonly as Christians than specifically as Mennonites. In the 1960s in Zaire Mennonites were caught in the cross-fire between rebels and the central government, and were suspect in both camps. Some suffered the destruction of houses and goods, others were threatened with death, still others were impressed into forced labor. In each known instance the Mennonite was presumed to be a spy, or at least a partisan, of the other side. The church learned that Christianity means persecution. In Indonesia in the late 1940s Mennonites were suspected, sometimes accused, of being partisans of either Dutch colonialists because of their contact with missionaries, or of native freedom fighters. And during the anti-Communist upheaval in the mid-1960s Mennonites, together with other Christians, were falsely accused of Communist affiliation. No one seems to have been killed, but many were threatened; and the church learned the painful lesson of persecution for the sake of Christ.

In the 1980s Central American Mennonites are persecuted together with other Christians.

In the 19th c. Pieter °°Jansz, the first Mennonite missionary in modern times, was harassed by the Dutch colonial government in Java (later part of Indonesia), in part because he criticized colonial policies in tracts that he published in The Netherlands. His friends in the Dutch Estates General supported him. But the Javanese Dutch government treated him much more harshly than Reformed missionaries.

Warfare has been the occasion for persecution or discrimination. All people suffer during war, especially those who are caught in the theaters of battle. But Mennonites have often been especially singled out for accusation or threatened violence or outright attack because of their °nonresistance: Palatines during the French Revolution, Virginians during the Civil War in America, Alsatians in 1870, American draftees during °World War I (two Hutterian Brethren died as a result of maltreatment), in addition to instances mentioned earlier.

European and North American Mennonites often think of the *Martyrs Mirror* when they reflect upon persecution. They have not kept careful records of discrimination or outright persecution in the 20th c.; nor have they tried to learn much about persecution of their brothers and sisters in the non-Western countries. Often public inquiry by Westerners puts indigenous Christians under jeopardy of property destruction and even death. But an urgent desideratum for our times is a serious study of contemporary persecutions and martyrdoms.   JSO

For the Anabaptists see among others: Thieleman J. van Braght, *The Bloody Theatre, or Martyrs Mirror of the Defenseless Christians. . .* (see ME II:527 for various editions); *The Chronicle of the Hutterian Brethren,* vol. 1 (Rifton, N.Y.: Plough, 1987), cf. A. J. F. Zieglschmid, ed., *Die älteste Chronik der Hutterischen Brüder* (Evanston, 1943), and Rudolf Wolkan, ed., *Geschicht-Buch der Hutterischen Brüder* (Vienna, 1923); Claus-Peter Clasen, *Anabaptism: A Social History, 1525-1618* (Ithaca: Cornell, 1972), esp. 358-422; Horst W. Schraepler, *Die rechtliche Behandlung der Täufer in der deutschen Schweiz* (Tübingen: [Fabian Verlag], 1957); Hans H. Th. Stiasny, *Die strafrechtliche Verfolgung der Täufer in der freien Reichsstadt Köln, 1529 bis 1618* (Münster: Aschendorff, 1962). On Mennonites in Russia, a few selected examples: Johann Epp, *Von Gottes Gnade getragen* (Gummersbach: Verlag Friedensstimme, 1984); Gerhard Hamm, *Du hast uns nie verlassen: Erfahrungen christlicher Familien in der Sowjetunion* (Wuppertal: Brockhaus, 1978); John B. Toews, "The Origins and Activities of the Mennonite Selbstschutz in the Ukraine (1918-1919)," *MQR,* 46 (1972), 5-40; idem, *Czars, Soviets and Mennonites* (North Newton, Kans: Mennonite Press, 1982); Heinrich Wölk and Gerhard Wölk, *Die Mennoniten Brüdergemeinden in Russland, 1925-1980* (Fresno: Center for Mennonite Brethren Studies, 1981), Engl. trans. as *Wilderness Journey* (Fresno, 1982). On Mennonites in Africa and Asia, see James E. Bertsche, "The Shadow of Suffering," and Wilbert R. Shenk, "Who Is This Christ?" in *A Kingdom of Priests: The Church in the New Nations,* ed. Wilbert R. Shenk (Newton, 1967), 126-39, 10-22; Ben Eidse, *Pastor Emmanuel in the Fiery Trial* (n.p.: Congo Inland Mission, n.d.); Alle Hoekema, "Pieter Jansz (1820-1904): First Mennonite Missionary to Java," *MQR,* 52 (1978), 58-76; Juhnke, *Mission* (1979), 142, for Taiwan. See also Elizabeth Bauman, *Coals of Fire* (Scottdale, 1954); Robert Bear, *Delivered Unto Satan* (Carlisle, Pa.: the author, 1974); Patrick Friesen, *The Shunning* (Winnipeg: Turnstone Press, 1980); John A. Hostetler, *Hutterite Society* (1974); *Das Kleingeschichtsbuch der hutterischen Brüder,* ed. A. J. F. Zieglschmid (Philadelphia: Carl Schurz Foundation, 1947), 287ff; J. C. Wenger, "The Voice of Mennonite History, *CH,* 42 (1949), 730-33; and numerous articles in Mennonite periodicals, some of which can be located by using the *Bibl. on War and Peace* (1987), or *Menn. Bib. II,* p. 609.

See also Church-State Relations; Civil Disobedience; Concentration Camps; Taxes.

Pershadi, Guru Panchayat (ca. 1885-Dec. 18, 1978), was born to a family of the oil-crusher caste. He was received by W. B. °Page into the American Mennonite Mission orphanage in 1899 during the great famine and received his education in the mission schools in Dhamtari, completing the 7th class of the Vernacular Middle School. He also took a normal course and later was sent to the Mission Bible School in Ghatula. Until the late 1920s he served as teacher, headmaster, and evangelist at the Mission Primary School in Maradev.

"Pastor Pershadi" served as secretary of the conference in 1912. In 1913 he was ordained a deacon for the Maradev congregation and in 1938 was ordained as a minister. He served as pastor for 4 years at Sankra, 4 years at Shantipur, and ca. 20 years at Maradev. He was highly respected for his deep commitment, shrewd judgment, and farming acumen.

Pershadi was married twice. He had five sons and a daughter from his first wife Sewanti Bai and one son and two daughters from his second wife Ramsir, a widow with three children from her first marriage.　　JAF

American Mennonite Mission Annual Report (1900-1901), (1914), p. 8; biographical data supplied by E. P. Bachan and Ruth Pershadi.

Personnel Management. The nature of personnel services is influenced by one's theological understanding of men and women, organizations, and the church.

The church is people. The work of the church is done by people, for people, and with people. Everyone is important. With the rise of schools and mission and service agencies, it became necessary to give more attention to the welfare of agency staff members. The number and expectations of people employed by congregations have also significantly increased.

Personnel administration is concerned to help people maximize their potential for life and service. This involves helping individuals find a place to use their gifts in compatible service opportunities. It also involves counseling individuals to develop their gifts more fully.

In 1962 an °inter-Mennonite Committee on Personnel Service (COPS) was founded. This is the main forum for the discussion of personnel matters related to Mennonite church agencies and °institutions. COPS has participants from all of the major Mennonite church agencies and institutions: schools, mission boards, Mennonite Central Committee, Mennonite Mutual Aid, Mennonite homes for the aged, and psychiatric centers.

Each of the major Mennonite groups in North America as well as the Dutch Algemene Doopsgezinde Sociëteit have a congregational leadership office or committee that serves as a ministerial clearing house or placement service. The Dutch Mennonite committee is called Commissie ter Begeleiding van Gemeenten en Predikanten in hun Onderlinge Relatie. These offices and committees serve the district and conference ministers in their work of being pastors to pastors and congregational consultants in leadership matters. These offices suggest salary levels and other benefits for ministers and guide congregational evaluations and leadership style and practice. Mennonite seminaries have field education directors to arrange for and supervise ministerial internships. Mennonite °business leaders and teachers in Mennonite college business departments also address issues of personnel management.

Terms used in addition to those mentioned above for persons responsible for personnel services in the Mennonite church are "secretary of personnel," "director of personnel," and "personnel counselor." The term "director" refers more to directing the personnel services than to directing personnel. The director is a consultant to program administrators rather than the one who evaluates performance or dismisses employees. The conference ministers also function in a similar manner in relation to congregational ministers and congregations.　　DHS

Peru. As a result of the merger between Mennonite Brethren (MB) and Krimmer Mennonite Brethren (KMB) in 1960, the Mennonite Brethren Board of Missions and Services (BOMAS) assumed responsibility for the work in the eastern jungles of Peru begun by KMB missionaries some 10 years earlier. In 1987 this work continued in association with Wycliffe Bible Translators, Swiss Indian Mission, and the South America Mission.

Mennonite Brethren missionaries work in the areas of Bible teaching, literature, agriculture, community development, and public health. They live in Pucallpa, Mazamari, and Satipo. About 25-30 village congregations have resulted from this ministry among the Campa Ashaninca people. In 1986 the independent Association of Ashaninca Evangelical Churches was organized.

In 1983, Mennonite Brethren Missions and Services responded to a flood disaster in northern Peru by sending food, medicines, and mission workers. This led to the formation of several Bible study groups and in 1986, the Mennonite Brethren Church of Peru was officially recognized by the government of Peru. Two congregations with total membership of about 60 have been organized in Sullana and Vichayal. More missionaries are preparing to join this work.

In 1985 Eastern Mennonite Board of Missions and Charities (MC) sent an investigative team to Peru. As a result of their visit and support from new churches of the Lancaster Mennonite Conference (MC), a missionary couple was sent to Peru in January 1987 to study the Quechua language in Lima in anticipation of a church planting effort among the Quechua people.　　HE

John A. Toews, *History MB* (1975), 429-31; *Mennonite Brethren in World Mission*, 2, no. 4 (July/Aug., 1986), 3; Phyllis Martens, *The Mustard Tree* (Fresno: MB Board of Christian Education, 1971), 198-203; *Miss. Mess.*, 62, no. 12 (Apr., 1986), 1-3, and 63, no. 9 (Jan. 1987), 21.

Peter, Daniel B. (Aug. 15, 1894-Apr. 22, 1973), was born into a Hindu family. His father's name was Deonath. He was one of 16 orphans from Raipur that W. B. °Page received into the American Mennonite mission orphanage in 1900 during the great famine.

Daniel was sent to Allahabad for his high school training and was the first student from the American Mennonite Mission to complete high school. He later earned an IA (intermediate arts) degree from the Benares Hindu U., Varanasi, Uttar Pradesh, and served as a teacher in the Mission Middle School in Dhamtari until his retirement in 1957. He was ordained deacon for the Sunderganj Mennonite congregation in Dhamtari in 1916 and served in this capacity until his death. He married Grace Das, a Christian woman from Dhamtari, and had three children.   JAF

Building On the Rock (Scottdale: MPH, 1926), 190; American Mennonite Mission Annual Report (1916-17), 52; biographical data from E. P. Bachan, Dhamtari Madhya Pradesh, India.

Peters, Frank Cornelius (July 5, 1920 - Oct. 7, 1987), was a person of vigorous enthusiasm and humor. Peters was a popular preacher, teacher, and public speaker within Mennonite and Evangelical circles around the world. Born in a Mennonite village in South Russia, he migrated to Canada with his family as a child. He lived in Herbert, Sask., and later in Yarrow, B.C., leaving school at the age of 15 during the economic depression of the 1930s to earn money for his family. Following two years of °°alternative service in Campbell River, B.C., during World War II, he pursued further education and earned a BA degree from Tabor College (Ks.) and a MSc from Kansas State Teachers College (Emporia). He went on to earn a ThD degree from Central Baptist Seminary (Kansas City), and a PhD degree in psychology from the U. of Kansas.

As an educator Peters served as president of Tabor College (1954-56), professor and academic dean at Mennonite Brethren Bible College (Winnipeg, 1957-65), and president of Wilfrid Laurier University (Waterloo, Ont, 1968-78). It was his politically astute leadership that helped guide this school from a church-supported university (Lutheran) to one receiving full provincial status and financial support.

As a servant of the church Peters was moderator of the General Conference of Mennonite Brethren Churches (MB), 1965-69, and moderator of Canadian Conference of MB Churches (1975-77). He pastored the Kitchener, Ont. MB church (1949-54, 1965-73), and the Portage Avenue MB church in Winnipeg (1980-83). He was married to Melita Krause. They had five children.   KR

Menn. Rep. (Oct. 26, 1987); *Menn. Bib.II*, p. 490.

Peters, Jacob (Oct. 17, 1813 - May 7, 1884), was born and married in the Frisian village of Kronsweide, Chortitza settlement in Russia. He joined 28 other families in 1839 to establish the village of Heuboden, Bergthal settlement.

He served first as *Beisitzer* (assistant), was elected °°*Oberschulze* of Bergthal Colony in 1851 or earlier and re-elected until his emigration to Canada. Peters' leadership abilities were recognized by the Tsar who awarded him a gold watch for exercising diligence in providing care for soldiers in the area during the °Crimean War. In response to the impending loss of °privileges, Peters, as *Oberschulze* and as delegate to America in 1873, worked tirelessly for the emigration to which, with Aeltester Ger-

hard Wiebe, he gave leadership.

When Jacob Peters, successful farmer and compassionate community leader, joined the last Bergthal emigrants in 1876, almost the entire colony of 525 families had been transplanted to Manitoba's °°East Reserve, where Peters continued to provide leadership. He played a statesmanlike role when he was chosen to address the Governor-General of Canada who visited the Mennonites in 1877.   JD

William Schroeder, *The Bergthal Colony* (Winnipeg: CMBC Publications, 1986); Gerhard Wiebe, *Causes and History of the Emigration of the Mennonites from Russia to America*, trans. Helen Janzen (Winnipeg: Manitoba Mennonite Historical Society, 1981); Abe Warkentin, *Reflections on our Heritage: A History of Steinbach and the Rural Municipality of Hanover* (Steinbach: Rural Municipality of Hanover); Klaas Peters, *Die Bergthaler Mennoniten* (reprinted Steinbach: Mennonitische Post, 1983); Lydia Penner, *Hanover: One Hundred Years* (Steinbach: Rural Municipality of Hanover); William Enns, *Das Verstossene Kind* (Steinbach: Derksen Printers); a biography of Jacob Peters by John Dyck is forthcoming (Winnipeg: Manitoba Mennonite Historical Society, 1987).

Petter, Bertha Elise Kinsinger (1872-1967), was a General Conference Mennonite (GCM) missionary among the Southern Cheyenne and Arapaho in Oklahoma (Indian Territory) and among the Northern Cheyenne in Montana. She served from 1896 to 1963.

Born near Trenton, Ohio, she earned a BA degree from Wittenberg College, Springfield, Ohio, in 1896 (MA, 1910). Possibly the first Mennonite woman to earn a college degree, she had studied Latin, Greek, German, philosophy, calculus, and logic. She came to Indian Territory in 1896 as a teacher in the Cantonment school under the General Conference Foreign Mission Board (GCM). She was the first General Conference single woman to make a career as a missionary. Along with Agnes Williams, she was in charge of the Clinton mission field from 1907 to 1909. They conducted funerals, preached sermons, led worship services, and visited in Cheyenne camps.

In 1911, Kinsinger married fellow missionary Rodolphe °°Petter, whose first wife, Marie Gerber Petter, had died in 1910. The collaboration on linguistics and the Cheyenne language, which they had already begun, continued after their marriage. The 1,226-page *Cheyenne-English Dictionary* published under Rodolphe's name was the result of their joint efforts.

The Petters moved in 1916 to Montana, where they continued mission work among the Northern Cheyenne. A complete new Testament in Cheyenne, translated from the Greek, was finished in 1935.

After Rodolphe's death in 1947, Bertha remained on the Northern Cheyenne reservation until 1963, when she moved to a retirement home in Billings, Mont.   LB

Barrett, *Vision* (1983), index; Rodolphe Petter, "Some Reminiscences of Past Years in My Mission Service Among the Cheyenne," *Mennonite*, 51, no. 44 (Nov. 10, 1936), p. 16 (also printed as a separate pamphlet).

Petter, Marie Gerber (Oct. 24, 1869-July 31, 1910), was a General Conference Mennonite (GCM) missionary among the Southern Cheyenne and Arapaho in Oklahoma (Indian Territory) from 1891 to 1910.

She was born to Christian Gerber and Elisabeth

Geiser, Mennonites living on the Les Veaux Farm in the Jura Mountains of Switzerland. In 1890 she married Rodolphe °°Petter, of Reformed Church background, whom she had met while he was visiting her brother. When she and Rodolphe married, he joined her church.

When S. F. °°Sprunger from Berne, Indiana, visited Switzerland, he persuaded the Petters to come to the United States as the first Swiss Mennonite missionaries. The Petters toured Mennonite congregations in North America and spent a year in English language study before beginning their missionary assignment in Indian Territory. They were the first missionary couple there to be assigned exclusively to reaching adults and to learning the language. Two children were born to the Petters: Olga and Valdo. Marie Gerber Petter died of tuberculosis. She is buried in the Cantonment, Okla.   LB

Barrett, *Vision* (1983); Rodolphe Petter, "Some Reminiscences of Past Years in My Mission Service Among the Cheyenne," *Mennonite*, 51, no. 44 (Nov. 10, 1936), also printed as a separate pamphlet.

Pfeddersheim Disputation (ME IV:158). On Aug. 25-26, 1557, at Pfeddersheim in the Palatinate, some 40 Anabaptists held a disputation with Lutheran leaders, the only known disputation between members of those two groups. In July 1983 the protocol (minutes) of the disputation was rediscovered in the *Forschungsbibliothek* at Gotha, German Democratic Republic, under the signature Cod. Chart. A94, folios 96v-113v. Both Palatine Elector °°Otto Henry and the Anabaptists had requested the disputation, the former to induce the Anabaptists to return to the state church, and the latter to clear their good name against slanders. Neither the elector nor the Anabaptists succeeded in their objectives.

Johannes °°Brenz, the major Lutheran leader who never consented to the death penalty for religious dissidents, was the principal Lutheran spokesman. Jacob °°Andreae, Johannes °°Marbach and Michael °°Diller, also participated for the Lutherans. Diebold °°Winter was the spokesman selected by the Anabaptists. Occasionally unnamed Anabaptists entered the conversation briefly. Only five topics were discussed, inadequately at that: baptism, Christians' relation to government, the oath, the Lord's Supper as sacrament, and attendance at the state church (including the use of the °°ban).

The officials of the electoral court declared the Lutherans to be winners, and demanded that the Anabaptists either recant or accept exile; evidence indicates no °recantations, and only some left the Palatinate; Diebold Winter remained to participate 14 years later in the much more thorough disputation at Frankenthal. A 20th c. reader of the minutes might find the Lutherans vastly superior in use of logic, and the Anabaptists generally holding their own with arguments from Scripture.

The disputation bears no relation to the *Contra Anabaptistarum opinionem* (TA *Württemberg*, 148-61) as Bossert surmised; the latter is a much more thorough refutation of Anabaptist "errors" and does not use the arguments employed at Pfeddersheim. Nor does Pfeddersheim bear any relation to the °°*Prozess wie es soll gehalten werden mit den wiedertäufern* . . . (Worms: Köpflein, 1557), which is an-

other detailed refutation of Anabaptist "errors" drawn almost exclusively from °°Melanchthon's earlier °polemics.   JSO

The minutes were edited and translated by John S. Oyer in *MQR*, 60 (1986), 304-51. See also Oyer, "The Pfeddersheim Disputation, 1557," in *Bibliotheca Dissidentium, Scripta et Studia* (Baden: Koerner, 1987); Christian Hege, *Die Täufer in der Kurpfalz* (Frankfurt: Minjon, 1908); Heinold Fast, "Die Täuferbewegung im Lichte des Frankenthaler Gespräches," *Menn. Geschbl.*, Ig. 30, n.F. 25 (1973), 7-23; Iohn S. Oyer, *Lutheran Reformers against Anabaptists* (The Hague: Nijhoff, 1964).

Philippines, an archipelago of 7,000 islands in Southeast Asia. The people were colonized by the Spanish following Magellan's exploration in 1521 and ruled by them until the Filipino revolution in 1896. The United States then subdued the Filipinos after much bloodshed and controlled the nation until the Japanese invasion in 1942. Filipinos were granted political independence following World War II.

At that point Mennonites first began working officially in the Philippines. By the end of 1946 the Mennonite Central Committee (MCC) had placed 17 workers in °relief assistance to war victims. Their program soon focused on the province of Abra in north-central Luzon, whose capital (Bangued) had been destroyed by bombing. When MCC staff left in 1950, they had established a hospital in Bangued and a high school in the isolated mountain village of Lamau. Both have been operated and expanded by local Christians in the years since then.

Twenty years later Eastern Mennonite [MC] Board of Missions and Charities (EMBMC) responded to an invitation of a small independent group by transferring a family from their Vietnam staff. Mennonite Ministries was based in Quezon City with the objective of working in supportive roles to assist Filipino church groups. By 1972 substantial relationships had been formed with Missions Now, Inc. Through the years 1970-87 EMBMC has maintained a small staff to assist in leadership training through a Bible school opened in Lumban, and in economic development which has included some Mennonite Economic Development Associates (MEDA), MCC, and °SELFHELP projects.

After visits by MCC leaders in 1975-76, a decision was made to open a new work in the Philippines. This action responded to requests for personnel; it also allowed MCC to build on the learnings from Vietnam with a program shaped around peacemaking and justice concerns. In the past 10 years (1977-87) a select team of experienced workers have engaged in community and agricultural development, research, and writing. Their goal has been to articulate and live out a theology of the cross in the midst of economic inequities and injustice.

This time the major effort has been geared to the conflict with the Muslim populations in the southern island of Mindanao. From their basic stance of a ministry of presence, which emphasizes a listening and reconciling role among oppressed peoples, the MCC staff have worked with and channeled small amounts of resources through various Filipino groups with similar concerns. Other smaller programs have related to political detainees and their families and to the "hospitality women" (prostitutes) who live near the huge United States military bases.

In 1985 MCC reported having an ideal level of 10 persons for its program in the Philippines. The staff continued to be firmly committed to the way of nonviolent love in the midst of an increasingly polarized and bloody conflict. A significant part of the ministry is seen in the witness MCC workers and their Filipino co-workers are giving across North America through writing, speaking tours, and contacts with political leaders.

The approach taken in their work has had its problems. Not all supporters and church leaders in North America have understood or affirmed the stance of the team. And working *with* the people rather than *for* them can be quite frustrating, with results that are more difficult to measure or report. Yet the dramatic rise of "People Power," enabling the nonviolent replacement of the Marcos government with that of Corazon Aquino in 1986, suggests that MCC's objective has been well-tailored for the situation. JEM

Winifred Nelson Beechy, "Review of Mennonite Central Committee Work in the Philippines," unpublished paper, May 1986; MCC staff, *Spirit in Struggle* (MCC, 1985); *Miss. Mess.* (EMBMC), various articles and letters; *MWH* (1978), 178-82; *MWH* (1984), 40.

Philipszoon, Dirk. See Dirk Philipszoon.

Philosophy. If by philosophy we mean the tradition of critical reflection with roots in the Greek classical tradition and its development in Western civilization of which such philosophers as Aquinas, Kant, Descartes, Hegel, and Dewey are representatives, it may be observed that Mennonite participation has been at best marginal.

Mennonite participation has been marginal in part for historical reasons. For most of their history, Mennonites, a persecuted minority, have had neither the opportunity nor the inclination to reflect upon universal themes. Rather, they have concentrated upon practical necessities of life intent upon survival within a hostile world.

Furthermore Mennonites have neglected philosophy for theological reasons. Insofar as philosophy seeks to understand the meaning of life based upon human experience, Mennonites have been distrustful, since the world is thought to be sinful and corrupt. Philosophy has been considered a diversion from the single and undivided task of preaching the gospel and of promoting the kingdom of God and the church. Also while believing in °creation, Mennonites have seldom been convinced that creation is a source of meaning, at least to the extent of developing a natural theology. Mennonites have had no interest in ontology, the study of what "is." Rather they have concentrated upon what is "to be" in the future (°apocalypticism) or what ought to be (ethics) as revealed in a particular Person and history. Hence Mennonites have cut off philosophy in principle, not simply by accident.

Such considerations may account for the fact that at most Mennonite colleges, philosophy commands only a minor place in curricula. Teachers of philosophy are frequently theologians by training. Many have led professional lives of short duration (Wiens, 1987). They have no clear relationship as philosophers to the reflective councils of the Mennonite Church. There are no Mennonite associations from which to gain a sense of identity. While Mennonites build historical libraries and collect theological volumes by the thousands, few shelves are devoted to philosophical literature.

Furthermore, Mennonite theology, besides neglecting nature and human experience as sources of meaning, has discouraged systematic formulations. The tendency of theology to move beyond biblical studies is suspect since to order Christian thought "systematically" is to introduce principles of organization and presuppostions (prolegomena) that are philosophical in nature. Hence even "post-sectarian" or °acculturated Mennonites have done little in systematic theology and philosophical theology is held at bay. In this respect one may note the powerful influences of Karl Barth and Oscar Cullmann upon Mennonite theologians after World War II. In effect, Karl Barth encouraged Mennonites to remain within the "theological circle" and Oscar Cullmann would have Mennonites confine their thoughts to "Heilsgeschichte" (salvation history) and to "de-Platonized" conceptions of God, "Christ" and "Time." Furthermore Mennonite scholars have had a tendency to de-emphasize the influence of Hellenistic thought in the New Testament.

Nevertheless, Mennonites have been influenced by philosophy however indirectly. After all, no person or group within the stream of western society can escape its influence completely. For one thing the language of theology is to a considerable extent philosophical in origin. Futhermore orthodox theology, in its classic as well as fundamentalist forms is rooted in philosophical speculation. Such orthodox doctrines as God, Christ, Holy Spirit, sin, and creation contain elements derived in part from universal human experience and were formulated by such philosopher theologians as Athanasius, Gregory of Nyssa, Augustine, Aquinas and others. Until recent years philosophy has been, for the most part, a support to theology by making it understandable and therefore believable for successive generations. Indeed even the Bible reflects philosophical thought, not to speak of the wisdom literature of the Old Testament that shows direct borrowing.

It should be noted also that while the Mennonites have been relatively successful in their rejection of traditional philosophy, when philosophy generally provided support for theology, they have been surprisingly open to its 19th and 20th c. positivist ("secular" or "scientific") offspring. That is to say, while rejecting that great philosophical stream of thought rooted in idealism, Mennonites have opened their arms to empirically grounded sociology, psychology, historical criticism, and even language analysis as if these disciplines were less speculative and less threatening to faith. Somehow to speak about God "in history" and of the Christ as a "historical being," of the church as a "visible" reality, of communion as memorial, of sin as misused freedom, however true and necessary, but without the supporting glue of an idealistic vision of reality, cannot but expose Christian faith to the rocks and shoals of secular positivism. For it is one thing to come to the Bible and the Christian community naively as unsophisticated people do and another thing to come to the Bible and the community with relativistic tools of criticism sharpened by empirical presuppositions devoid of philosophically perceived views of transcendence, mystery, soul, sacrament, and spiritual reality.

There have been times, of course, when Mennonites have sought to understand themselves philosophically. In 1943 R. C. Kauffman wrote an article entitled, "The Philosophical Aspects of Mennonitism" in which he claimed that "There is a certain antithesis between being philosophical and being Mennonite." However, he went on to say that Mennonite °authority implies the use of reason as it appeals to sources beyond itself. Critical analysis tends to expose implicit and possibly unconscious principles that are philosophical in nature.

On another level Robert °Friedmann attempted to interpret Anabaptism as a kind of "existentialism," since Anabaptists resisted "system building" and focused on voluntary rather than "ontic" reality. His extensive manuscript "Design for Living" (1954), a rather reflective overview of life and values, was never published.

On still another level, Mennonites like any other self-conscious community have reflected upon human life in general on the basis of their experience. Such reflection takes the form of persistent themes in their °literature, their interpretation of °history and their °folklore. Certainly the *Martyrs Mirror* is more than a chronicle of °persecution. It speaks by implication about the life of God's people as heroic °suffering. Suffering functions as a philosophical principle when it is universalized in the renowned hymn of the Martyr George Grünwald, "Kommt her Zu mir, Spricht Gottes Sohn" (Come to me, says the Son of God). "Alle Creatur bezeugen das/ Was lebt in Wasser, luft und Gras,/ Durch Leiden muss es enden." (All creatures testify that all that lives in water, air, and grass must end by suffering.)

Speak to any convinced Hutterite about "community of goods" and the apology will be philosophical in nature. Thus it may be claimed that Mennonites, while having resisted formal philosophy, have in fact upheld values, made choices, maintained chronicles, interpreted histories, and perpetuated life-styles which, when reflected upon against a universal background, constitute implicitly a philosophy. In many communities, including Israel, such common thought would be named "wisdom."

Wisdom is rarely made explicit, however, except when challenged from the outside. Historically the challenge in Western culture took the form of metaphysics. Today with the virtual death of metaphysics the challenge is positivism. (Positivism rejects transcendent, "spiritual," or "trans-physical" [metaphysical] explanations of reality, concentrating instead on "scientifically" observable, experimental explanations.) Mennonites may ponder whether, having participated in the demise of metaphysics by rejecting medieval culture at foundational levels, during the Reformation they may have contributed unwittingly to the rise of modern positivism with its insidious power to destroy what it claims only to explain (°modernity).

That Mennonites have failed to identify with the philosophical tradition is of course due not only to the internal dynamics of Mennonite life and thought. It is also due to the misfortunes of philosophy itself. As stated earlier, classical philosophy came upon hard times during the first half of the 20th c. as metaphysics surrendered to logical positivism with its emphasis upon language analysis. Concurrently philosophy lost ground within academic communities as university departments of philosophy declined in numbers and influence in deference to science and technology. Hence the pressure on small denominational colleges to offer courses in philosophy diminished. Also philosophy simply could not offer its practitioners a way to earn a living.

Nevertheless a case for philosophy could be made, since philosophy, both in its classical and analytical forms, could function within the Mennonite community as a source of clarification and meaning. For it is through critical analysis that the meaning of theological language, particularly biblical language, may be translated into the modern idiom and it is by comparison with classical thought that the significance of theological language may be discerned. JLB

Delbert Wiens, "Philosophy and Mennonite Understanding" (unpublished, 1987); Ralph C. Kauffman, "The Philosophical Aspects of Mennonitism," in *The Curricula of Mennonite Colleges: Proceedings of the Second Conference on Mennonite Cultural Problems, Goshen, Ind., July 22-23, 1942,* ed. P. S. Goertz (n.p.: Council of Mennonite and Affiliated Colleges, 1943), 113-26.

Photography, during the 150 years since its discovery, has become not only a means of recording images but also a medium of expression and a powerful new art form. Among Mennonites and related groups it was not immediately accepted by all. For example, in the 1880s, the Brethren in Christ feared that photos would nourish pride (°°nonconformity; °humility). Later, they banned the showing of slides in churches because such use might encourage attendance at °motion picture theaters. By the 1940s, the pressures of missionaries wanting to report on their work with slides and motion pictures opened the way to the use of projected images in churches (Wittlinger, *Piety and Obedience* [1978], 345-46). In the late 20th c. Amish and some other conservative and Old Order Mennonites continue to consider photographs a form of graven image (Ex 20:4).

Most Mennonites have used cameras to document life and culture as well as the work and witness of the church for more than 100 years. Some photographers have moved beyond record-making into photojournalism, using pictures to tell a story. Still others have made their photography an art. This survey can only provide a small sample of what is being done in this field.

Leon C. Yost, Jersey City, N.J., a graduate of Eastern Mennonite College, has used his camera both to document and to interpret the cave and rock wall pictographs and petroglyphs of the Southwestern Indians, the ancestors of the Navajo, Hopi, and Zuni. As subjects for his photographic art he has also used the deserts and canyons of the sw. United States as well as the glaciers and mountains of the Yukon and Alaska.

Mark S. Wiens, Wichita, Ks., specializes in Kansas small towns and landscapes such as the Flint Hills. His Cibachrome prints of Kansas architecture are part of the collection of the Paraguayan-American Cultural Centre, Asunción.

Blair Seitz lived in Kenya and the Philippines for nine years between 1972 and 1982 and completed photo assignments in 14 African and 7 Asian countries. He received a silver medal in New York's International Film and Television Festival for a series of sound filmstrips on the life of four ethnic groups in Kenya. He supplied the photographs for *Amish Country* (Crescent, 1987).

Suzanne Harnish Bishop of Goshen, Ind., combines documentation and art. A series called "Mennonites in Service" showing people at work in Haiti was exhibited at the Purdue convention of the Mennonite Church in 1987.

In his photographs in *Meditations on a Place and a Way of Life* (Winnipeg: Hyperion Press, 1983), Ken Loewen captured in his southern Manitoba community a reflection of the kind of life which Mennonite pioneers brought from their homes in southern Russia. MSh

See also Filmmaking; Graphic Design; Journalism; Motion Pictures; Mass Media; Painting and Printmaking.

Piedras Colony, Las, Bolivia. The Las Piedras (I) colony was established in 1968 by Old Colony Mennonites from the Peace River area in Alberta, Canada. Approximately 90-100 families have moved to Las Piedras directly from Canada. This colony is located 123 km. (75 mi.) nw. of Santa Cruz. There are no direct relationships between the church of this colony and the rest of the Old Colony Mennonites in Bolivia. In 1986 Las Piedras had a population of 594 people with about 200 church members. The bishop of this group in 1987 was Isaac Goertzen.

Las Piedras II was started in 1983 as a branch colony of Las Piedras. It is located north of Tres Cruces. It is also under the leadership of bishop Isaac Goertzen. In 1986 the population of this young colony consisted of 382 people with 115 church members. IHie

MWH (1978), 279.

Pietism (ME IV:176), as a historical movement began in the 17th c.; as an element in Christian life and thought it has always been present. It arose in the 17th c. out of (1) the moral, and spiritual chaos attending the °°Thirty Years' War; (2) the sterility of Lutheran and Reformed orthodoxy with its neoscholasticism, emphasis on pure doctrine and sacraments at the expense of warm, personal and lay piety; and (3) the continuing mystical-evangelical milieu represented in part in Puritanism, Quakerism, Johann °°Arndt and his book *True Christianity,* (Lutheran), as also Lewis Bayly's (d. 1631) *The Practice Of Pietie* (Puritan).

It is difficult to compare Anabaptism and Pietism, particularly since both movements claim the Bible and the early church as a common source and norm. Both movements have many similar core values. Friedmann's thesis that Pietism represented a weakened Anabaptism which survived the era of persecution through quietism and withdrawal from society, cannot really be sustained. A methodology beyond intellectual history is needed. Yet his *Mennonite Piety Through The Centuries* (Goshen College 1949) was an early and most helpful pioneering effort at describing key similarities and differences in the movements. Pietism and Anabaptism both had a variety of groups (branches) with unique emphases in each.

Late 20th c. Mennonites reflect genuine Anabaptist roots at numerous points, as well as influence from a broad spectrum of Pietism *and* fidelity to the Bible. Thus, for example, to stress the importance of conversion is good Anabaptism and Pietism (especially the Spener-Halle variety), but it is also simply biblical though, in North America, °revivalism may have unduly shaped its meaning. So also the desire for a deeper, more genuine spirituality (*Vertiefung*) reflects a clear Herrnhut (Moravian) concern, but is also biblical and Anabaptist. The "blood and wounds" theology and the "dark night of the soul" (*Bußkampf*) motifs are clearly from Gerhardt °°Tersteegen and Rhineland Pietism, but are not unbiblical. There are traces of these in Anabaptism. South German (Württemberg) Pietism, which particularly influenced the Mennonites in Russia, revived the Anabaptist tradition of Bible study and an open, ecumenical spirit toward others. This became a dynamic source for mission activity, which the Mennonites had lost.

When Pietism arose ca. 1675 many Mennonites had lost their first love, though some Dutch Mennonites had a vision for church renewal which preceded that of Philipp Jakob Spener. This vision is seen, for example, in the *Martyrs Mirror* (1660), the writings of Jan Philipsz °°Schabaelje, Jean de Labadie (1610-1677; °°Labadists) and others, later especially the influential Joannes °°Deknatel. Part of this impulse for renewal came to the Dutch Mennonites through Quakerism, the left wing of Puritanism.

°Tradition and relative tolerance had institutionalized Mennonite church life. Pietism stressed small group meetings and prayer, Mennonites stressed the church. Pietism actively taught °sanctification, Mennonites stressed °discipleship, especially °nonresistance and the nonswearing of oaths. Dutch Mennonites were more permissive about smoking, drinking, dancing, and °dress codes than Pietists, but less mission-minded. In the 18th and 19th c. both Pietism and Mennonitism, the latter especially in Russia, were strongly committed to institution building —schools, hospitals, orphanages, but Pietism placed greater emphasis on "home missions." In North America some emphases of °Fundamentalism and °dispensationalism reinforced negative Pietistic tendencies among Mennonites, e.g., a datable conversion experience, a tendency to biblical prooftexting, premillennialism, a negative attitude towards group social action but a tendency to nationalism. Much further study is needed on the interrelationship of Pietism, Anabaptism, and Mennonitism and their respective impact on Mennonite life and thought.

Most research on Pietism has and is being done in Germany. The recognized leader in this field was Martin Schmidt, one of whose major contributions was *Wiedergeburt und neuer Mensch* (Witten, 1969). *Der Pietismus in Gestalten und Wirkungen,* by Heinrich Bornkamm and others (Bielefeld, 1975) was dedicated to Schmidt. A commission for the study of Pietism was founded in West Germany in 1965 with a publication series entitled *Arbeiten zur Geschichte des Pietismus* (Bielefeld, 1967-), and a journal called *Pietismus und Neuzeit,* with the first volume published in 1974. See, for example, Martin Brecht, *Pietismus und Neuzeit* (Göttingen, 1979). Note also Martin Greschat, *Zur Neueren Pietismus-forschung* (Darmstadt, 1977). These are only select samples of many recent titles. The strong interest in Pietism in Germany began after World War II, motivated in part by a search to seek where, how and why the church had failed under Hitler.

An interest in Pietism is also gradually emerging in North America, promoted especially by three persons: F. Ernest Stoeffler, Donald G. Bloesch and Dale W. Brown. In Stoeffler's article "Pietism" in *The Encyclopedia of Religion,* vol. 11 (New York, 1987) some credit for Pietist origins is given to Anabaptism. A major positive analysis of the movement is made by Bloesch in *The Evangelical Renaissance* (Grand Rapids, 1973). Brown has done most to vindicate the movement against its detractors and correlates some of its history and emphasis with that of Anabaptism in *Understanding Pietism* (Grand Rapids, 1978). The most extensive comparison of Pietism, Anabaptism, and Mennonitism has been done by Martin H. Schrag in *Continental Pietism and Early American Christianity,* ed. F. E. Stoeffler (Grand Rapids, 1976). Pietism is no longer the stepchild of church historians, nor of Mennonite scholars, and new major studies may be anticipated.   CJD

Dale W. Brown, "The Bogey of Pietism," *The Covenant Quarterly,* 25 (Feb. 1967), 12-17, cf. idem, *Understanding Pietism* (Grand Rapids: Eerdmans, 1978); Peter C. Erb, ed., *Pietists: Selected Writings* (New York, 1983); idem, "Pietist Spirituality: Some Aspects of Present Research," and "The Medieval Sources of Pietism: A Case Study," in *The Roots of the Modern Christian Tradition* (The Spirituality of Western Christendom II), ed. E. Rozanne Elder (Kalamazoo: Cistercian Publications, 1985), 249-70, 271-92; August Langen, *Der Wortschatz des deutschen Pietismus* (Tübingen, 1968); Carter Lindberg, *The Third Reformation?* Charismatic Movements and the Lutheran Tradition (Macon, Ga., 1983), 131-79; Werner Mahrholz, ed., *Der Deutsche Pietismus: Eine Auswahl von Zeugnissen, Urkunden und Bekenntnissen aus dem 17., 18., und 19. Jahrhundert* (Berlin, 1921); K. S. Pinson, *Pietism as a Factor in the Rise of German Nationalism* (London, 1934); Philipp Jakob Spener, *Pia Desideria* (Philadelphia, 1974); F. Ernest Stoeffler, *The Rise Of Evangelical Pietism* (Leiden, 1965); James Tanis, *Dutch Calvinistic Pietism in the Middle Colonies* (The Hague, 1967); Orlando H. Wiebe, "The Missionary Emphasis of Pietism," in *The Church in Mission,* ed. A. J. Klassen (Fresno: MB Board of Christian Literature, 1967), 115-33.

See also Evangelicalism; Holiness Movement.

Piety. See Spiritual Life.

Pike Co., Mo., Old Order Amish Settlement. See Bowling Green, Mo., Old Order Amish Settlement.

Pilgrim Fellowship Missions (Mennonite), Belize, is the name of the local corporation through which Amish Mennonite Aid (°Beachy Amish Mennonites), Plain City, Ohio, channels its mission efforts in Belize. The obvious material need created by Hurricane Hattie in 1962 provided the open door for a mission program which over the years has grown to include 25 adult volunteers at 6 locations. The main emphasis is church planting with an effort toward indigenous churches. Each location has a church; three have mission-sponsored schools and one has a clinic.
                                                                    JSN

MWH (1984), 53.

PIPKA. See Persatuan Gereja-Gereja Kristen Muria Indonesia.

Place Names

Place name studies relating to Anabaptists and Mennonites hold interest for folklorists, ethnologists, and historians. Some names such as *Anabaptist bridge, cave, ditch,* etc., in Switzerland recall the persecution that compelled Anabaptists to seek secluded places for worship. Some reflect markedly different social conditions, e.g. *Menniste Hemel* (Mennonite Heaven), a rural area between Amsterdam and Utrecht where wealthy 18th-c. Mennonite merchants built villas. In North America places bearing Mennonite names may recall early settlers: °°*Weaverland* and °°*Johnstown,* Pa.; *Jansen,* Neb.; and *Erb Street,* in Waterloo, Ont. Some may have been very short-lived, e.g. *Camp Evart* and *Buller, Funk, Schrag, Sudermann,* and *Unruh Stations* on a map published by an 1873 committee exploring settlement possibilities in Dakota Territory for Russian Mennonite immigrants. *Amish,* Iowa, once a postal address, became a crossroad settlement known locally as Joetown. *Lelystad,* The Netherlands, memorializes Mennonite engineer, Cornelis °°*Lely,* who planned the reclamation of the Zuiderzee. Even such insignificant places as North American rural railroad crossings have varied names of former owners of land sold or given as right of way to railway companies.

Mennonite migrations have carried place names from country to country, e.g. °°*Gnadenthal,* a Mennonite village name transplanted within the Soviet Union and carried to Kansas, Manitoba, Mexico, Paraguay, and Saskatchewan. Some place names are widely known among Mennonites out of proportion to their relative importance nationwide. *Akron* to many Mennonites means Akron, Pa., with the Mennonite Central Committee headquarters, not Akron, Ohio, much better known by most Americans. The °*Weierhof* in the Palatinate, a hamlet unknown by the average German, is visited by dozens of American Mennonite °tourists each year. The Swiss may have heard of the *Bienenberg* as a former spa. To Mennonites it is synonymous with European Mennonite Bible School.

Some names seem to be flukes. According to legend *Menno,* S.D., adjacent to but outside a Mennonite community, received its name as a result of a railway employee's mistake in distributing station signs.

Name changes pose special problems for Mennonite scholars, particularly 20th c. changes in Eastern Europe. J. K. Zeman provides assistance for those studying Moravian Anabaptists. For other guides to name changes as well as for histories of place names, researchers should consult "Names, Geographical" in library subject catalogs.

A companion study to Mennonite place names is a study of surnames and °nicknames derived from places, e.g. Augsburger (someone from Augsburg), or Tennessee John Stoltzfus, leader of Amish Mennonites from Pennsylvania who moved to Tennessee in the 19th c.   NPS

J. K. Zeman, *Historical Topography of Moravian Anabaptism.* (Goshen, Ind.: Mennonite Historical Society, [1967]); Isaac Zürcher, "Täufer auf und in Orts-, Flur- und Strassennamen," *Informationsblätter,* 1 (1977/78), 13-15.

Plain Dress. See Dress.

Plain People. In the mid-19th c. most Mennonites, Amish, Brethren in Christ, and °°Brethren (Dunkers, Church of the Brethren) could be considered "Plain People." The °°Society of Friends (Quakers), who probably coined the term, were rapidly losing their plainness by this time. Separation and °°nonconformity to the surrounding world are essential to the plain life. Plainness mainly refers to the use of simple, modest °dress. Clothing is plain because it is free of ornaments and stylish appendages. To "dress plain" means to wear a distinctive, traditional garb which is not in fashion with the world. By the late 20th c. the majority of the groups once considered plain have been outwardly assimilated into the larger society. Some of those who are visibly conformed to the world still identify themselves as plain people by virtue of their inner values and simple life-style.

The Old Order Amish are the largest group of Plain People. The Old Order Mennonites, Reformed Mennonites, Beachy Amish Mennonites, and various °conservative Mennonites who withdrew from the large Mennonite Church (MC) since the 1950s are also plain. The °Old Colony Mennonites and other groups of Russian-Manitoba background (°Sommerfeld Mennonites, °Chortitzer Mennonite Conference, Saskatchewan °Bergthal Mennonites, °Kleine Gemeinde in Latin America) adhere to principles and practices similar to those of the Pennsylvania German Plain People. Hutterites also have some distinctive features in their dress. The Old German Baptist Brethren and the Dunkard Brethren as well as several smaller Brethren groups and a minority within the Church of the Brethren carry on the plain traditions of their Dunker forebears. The Old Order River Brethren have retained the plain ways that have largely been lost by their Brethren in Christ cousins.　　　　　　　　　　　　SES

"The Plain People," *MQR,* 51 (1977), 261-394, a special issue.

See also Conservative Mennonites.

Plattdeutsch/Plautdietsch. See Dialect Literature and Speech (Low German); German Language.

Pleshanov Settlement (ME IV:193). Unlike most other Mennonite settlements in European Russia, the Pleshanov community was not forcibly relocated in 1941. Of the original 14 villages, 12 remain.

During the 1920s, about 700 persons (of a total population of about 3,300) had emigrated, mostly to Canada. Collectivization of agriculture, loss of traditional privileges, and the implementation of antireligious policies ended traditional patterns. Church buildings were transformed into schools, as in °°Lugovsk, or clubhouses, as in Pleshanov.

In 1986 the villages of the settlement are organized into collectives, with most of the villages forming part of the Karl Marx or Lenin collective farms. The former has been honored as an exemplary *kolkhoz.* The village of Pleshanov serves as the administrative center of the local area, which in turn is situated in the °Orenburg *Oblast* (administrative region).

In the 1980s, a substantial part of the Pleshanov population is Russian, although the Low German dialect is still commonly heard on village streets. Agriculture continues to dominate the local economy, with a wide variety of grains being raised. Dairy, poultry, and hog products are also important. Most families have their own garden plot and a few animals for personal use.

Both °"kirchliche" Mennonites and Mennonite Brethren have active congregations. In 1978 the latter built a new church in °°Donskoye seating at least 500 persons. The local membership is about 400 and is registered as Mennonite Brethren. Another church has been built in the village of Podolsk. In addition, a number of village congregations meet in private homes. Close ties are maintained with Orenburg Mennonites, some 150 km. (95 miles) to the east. Another large church has been built at Susanova, situated between Pleshanov and Orenburg.　　PJK

J. H. Brucks and H. Hooge, eds., *Neu-Samara am Tock* (Clearbrook, B.C., 1964); *Menn. Rund.* (Nov., 27, 1985), 18-22; K. Stumpp, "Die deutschen Siedlungen im Raum Alt-Samara, Neu-Samara . . .," *Heimatbuch der Deutschen aus Russland* (Stuttgart, 1964), 23-30; Heinrich Wölk and Gerhard Wölk,, *A Wilderness Journey,* trans. Victor G. Doerksen (Fresno: Center for MB Studies, 1982), 127-129 (originally published in German at Fresno, 1981); Peter J. Klassen, "Die Brücke zur Herkunft," *Heimatbuch der Deutschen aus Russland, 1973-1981* (Stuttgart, 1981), 97-99.

Poetry. A survey of Mennonite poetry should begin with a reference to articles on °°hymnology in ME II that trace the history of Anabaptist hymn-writing from its beginnings in the 16th c. Even though the early hymns of the Anabaptists were, as H. S. °Bender observes, not primarily "literary vehicles," many of the early hymnaries were explicitly intended to be read for the "edification of souls," and so can legitimately be regarded as the forerunners of the religious verse that dominated the earliest manifestations of modern Mennonite poetic expression.

Mennonite poetic writing even in the early years was restricted neither to the kind of verse that found its way into the early hymnals, nor to the martyr stories, as the several articles on °°literature reveal. For even as the martyr poems and hymns were being composed, the first of the Dutch Mennonite poets *qua* poets emerged as significant national literary figures. They included the great Dutch master Joost van den °°Vondel (b. 1587) and Karel von °°Mander (b. 1548).

N. van der °Zijpp draws attention to later Dutch Mennonite poets active in the 17th and early 18th c.: the gifted lyricist Jan Luyken (b. 1649), for example, and Elisabeth Koolaert-Hoofman (b. 1664), one of the first Dutch women poets to publish her work.

There are significant gaps in Mennonite literary history between the early 18th and late 19th c. Whether these gaps reflect a radical disruption in literary productivity, the lack of access to publication, or simply a hiatus in scholarship remains to be fully explored. (Given the evidence for a tradition of informal literary activity among the Mennonites throughout the centuries, one would assume that those with poetic temperaments would have continued to compose, even under adverse circumstances.)

What one could speak of as the modern tradition of Mennonite poetry began in the late 19th c. when a palpable interest in things literary, access to a receptive audience, some sense of leisure, and the means of publication developed among the German-speaking Mennonite colonists in the Ukraine. Among the poets of this period were Bernhard °°Harder (whose work *Geistliche Lieder und Gelegenheitsgedichte* was published in 1880), Heinrich Johann °°Janzen, Johannes Heinrich °°Janzen, Martin Fast, and Gerhard °°Loewen (°°literature). All, of course, wrote in German.

Of the Russian Mennonite emigrants who settled in Germany after World War I, A. B. Enns published a book of poems entitled *Die Hütte* (Emden, 1924) and Hans °Harder, best known for his prose, wrote poems as well (a few examples of which have appeared in the *Mennonite Mirror*).

Among the German-speaking Russian Mennonite colonists who settled in Canada, Isaac P. °°Friesen published two volumes of verse, *Im Dienste des Meisters* (Constance, Germany, ca. 1910) and J. H. Janzen a collection called *Durch Wind und Wellen* (Waterloo, 1928). G. A. Peters published *Gedichte* I, II (Winnipeg, 1923) and G. H. Peters *Blumen am Wegrand* (North Kildonan [Winnipeg], 1946). The several volumes of poetry by Johann P. Klassen are listed in the article on °°literature. Heinrich Görz published *Gedichte* (n.d.) in North Kildonan, and J. W. Goerzen published *Germanic Heritage* in Edmonton in 1962. Valentin Sawatsky published several volumes of poems in the tradition of these German-Canadian Mennonite poets between 1958 and 1983: *Lindenblätter* (1958), *Heimatglocken* (1962), *Friedensklänge* (1971), *Abendlicht* (Waterloo, 1977), *Eichenlaub* (Waterloo, 1981), *Glockenläuten* (Waterloo, 1982), *Einkehr* (Steinbach, 1983). Many of these poets published their own work, which was never widely distributed. Little of it is remarkable from a purely literary perspective.

Most highly respected of the emigré poets for the literary quality of his work is Gerhard Johann °Friesen (pseud. Fritz Senn, b. 1894), whose poems (characteristically laments for the poet's lost idyllic world of the Russian steppe) were collected in *Das Dorf im Abendgrauen*, edited by Elisabeth Peters, and in *Gesammelte Gedichte und Prosa*, edited by Victor G. Doerksen (CMBC Publications, 1987).

Most of these German-speaking poets wrote conventional verse in a style predominantly influenced by German Romanticism. Their themes, as the titles of the volumes suggest, most often reflect the authors' concerns about religious devotion or their deep sense of nostalgia for a lost homeland; subject matter tends to range from religion and nature to less prominent concerns about Mennonite history and matters of daily living.

Among American Mennonites writing in English and German in the early part of this century, Harold S. Bender, in *Two Centuries of American Mennonite Literature; A Bibliography of Mennonitica Americana 1727-1928* (Goshen, 1929), lists William Gross who published several poetical works in Pennsylvania between 1890 and 1910; Simon P. Yoder, *Poetical Meditations and Thoughtful Paragraphs* (Denbigh, Va., 1916); Susan Good Hostetler, *Memories: A Collection of Poems* (1919); J. P. Klassen, *Krümlein, Gedichte* and *Wegeblumen, Gedichte* (1927); and H. D. Friesen, *Blumen und Blüten* (1927).

The transition from German to English Mennonite poetry in North America stretches over several decades. It is readily discernible in the various Mennonite newspapers and magazines that publish verse. Among those that publish English poetry with some regularity are *The Mennonite Mirror, The Christian Leader, Christian Living, The Gospel Herald, The Mennonite,* and *Mennonite Life*. Poets whose work appears in the English serials include, most often, Jean Janzen, Elmer Suderman, Wilfred Martens, Tim Wiebe, Sarah Klassen, Clint Toews, Elaine Sommers Rich, and Menno Wiebe—only a few of whom have published collections of their work. There is no want of poetry in the Mennonite periodicals of North America; much of it falls into the categories of inspirational or occasional verse, its publication usually (apparently) based on extra-literary considerations.

The most sophisticated poetry by Mennonites (and most satisfying from a literary perspective) is that which has been published in Mennonite and secular literary journals, as well as in poetry chapbooks, during the 1970s and 1980s. This is work that ranges in subject matter from the profane to the mystical; it tends to be contemporary in style. Noteworthy among these strong modern Mennonite voices are Japanese professor and lay minister Yorifumi °Yaguchi (b. 1932), who has published two collections of poems in English, as well as five in Japanese; and Americans Lauren Friesen, Jeff Gundy (b. 1952), and [Canadian-born] Jean Janzen (b. 1933). In Canada, where a strong literary tradition developed among the Mennonites, especially in Manitoba, in the 1960s, 1970s, and 1980s, the best poets are highly respected outside, as well as inside, the Mennonite community. Particularly significant are the works of Patrick Friesen (b. 1946), Di Brandt (b. 1952), and David Waltner-Toews (b. 1948). Others who have published volumes of verse include Sarah Klassen (1932), Audrey Poetker (b. 1962), E. F. Dyck, and Victor Jarrett Enns (b. 1955).

Contemporary Mennonite poetry begs a question raised as early as the 17th c., when the Dutch Mennonite poet Joost van den Vondel converted in mid-career to Roman Catholicism: "how can one define Mennonite poetry?" (Can the poetry of van den Vondel's "Catholic period" be considered "Mennonite poetry," for example? Does the category "Mennonite poets" include converts who were reared and learned to write in another cultural or religious context; does it include those who have left the church and the community but were reared within the Mennonite tradition?) Can one speak of particular Mennonite themes?

Much of what the new Mennonite poets compose is, broadly speaking, secular. Yet the Mennonite ethos remains as a palpable force in much of their work: as something to rebel bitterly against (in Victor Jarrett-Enns and the early Patrick Friesen); in the use of High German and Low German words and phrases; in the persistent evocation of the loss of a sense of community; and in the moral and theological questioning. Perhaps this most recent (and most literarily sophisticated) poetry is, despite its secular posture and form, the most "Mennonite" of all. HFT

[All Goshen publications are by Pinchpenny Press.] Dale Bowman and Mary Jo Frederick, *From Under the Bed a Moo* (Goshen, 1981); Di Brandt, *Questions I Asked My Mother* (Winnipeg: Turnstone Press, 1987); Hubert Brown, *Black Coffee* (Goshen, 1970); idem, *Through the Smoke Holes* (Goshen, 1971); Paul Conrad, *My Adventures with James and the Curry Kid* (Goshen, 1967); William De Fehr, et al., eds., *Harvest: Anthology of Mennonite Writing in Canada* (Altona: D. W. Friesen and Sons, 1974); Charity R. Denlinger, *A Time to Speak* (Goshen, 1988); E. F. Dyck, *The Mossbank Canon* (Winnipeg: Turnstone, 1982); idem, *Pisscat Songs* (Coldstream, Ont.: Brick Books, 1983); Victor Enns, *Jimmy Bang Poems* (Winnipeg: Turnstone, 1979); Victor Jerrett Enns, *Correct in This Culture* (Saskatoon: Fifth House, 1985); Amanda Friesen, *Verse From Twisted Fingers* (Freeman, S. D.: Pine Hill, 1982); Lauren Friesen, *The Fallow Field* (Goshen, 1971); idem, *Prairie Songs* (Goshen, 1987); Patrick Friesen, *Bluebottle* (Winnipeg: Turnstone, 1978); idem, *Flicker and Hawk* (Winnipeg: Turnstone, 1987); idem, *The Lands I Am* (Winnipeg: Turnstone, 1976); idem, *The Shunning* (Winnipeg: Turnstone, 1980); idem, *Unearthly Horses* (Winnipeg: Turnstone, 1984); Willard Gingerich, *Tamoanchan* (Goshen, 1976); J. W. Goerzen, *Germanic Heritage: English, Low German, German: Canadian Lyrics in Three Languages* (Edmonton: the author, 1962, 1967); Carl Good, *Cave Paintings* (Goshen, 1987); Jeff Gundy, *Johnny America Takes on Mother Nature* (Goshen, 1975); idem, *Surrendering To the Real Things. The Archetypal Experience of C. Wordsworth Crockett* (Normal, Ill.: The Pikestaff Press, 1986); idem, *Back Home in Babylon* (Goshen, 1974) Cynthia Habegger, *Eating the Buds* (Goshen, 1978); Elta Harnish, *Throughout the Years* (Gordonville, Pa.: Print Shop, 1979); Dan Herr, *Like a Fish* (Goshen, 1970); idem, *Listen to the Worm* (Goshen: Pinchpenny, 1972); Elaine Strite Hess, *Eighth Street Apocalypse* (Goshen, 1972); Dennis Huffman, *Poems* (Goshen, 1980); Jean Janzen, Yorifumi Yaguchi, David Waltner-Toews, *Three Mennonite Poets* (Intercourse, Pa.: Good Books, 1986); Jean Janzen, *Words for the Silence* (Fresno: Center for Mennonite Brethren Studies, 1984); Steven Ray Johns, *Kissing the Sky* (Goshen, 1981); Barbara Keener, *Rimes for Our Times* (Lancaster, Pa.: Barkeesh, 1979); Sarah Klassen, *Journey to Yalta* (Winnipeg: Turnstone, 1988); Warren Kliewer, *Liturgies, Games, Farewells* (Francestown, N. H.: The Golden Quill, 1974); idem, *Moralities and Miracles* (Francestown, N. H.: The Golden Quill, 1962); idem, *Red Rose and Gray Cowl* (Washington, D.C.: Omega, 1960); Christopher Laur, *No Said the Bird* (Goshen, 1982); John L. Liechty, *West of Ohio* (Goshen, 1984); Sam Manickam, *Seeds and Seasons* (Goshen, 1986); Shari Miller, *When the Walls Crumble* (Goshen, 1979); Barb Mosemann, *Fishbowl* (Goshen, 1972); idem, *Sojourn of a Beggar* (Goshen, 1971); idem, *To Heidi's House* (Goshen, 1972); Jeffrey S. Peachey, *Stone Styrofoam* (Goshen, 1988); Audrey Poetker, *I Sing For My Dead in German* (Winnipeg: Turnstone, 1986); Keith Ratzlaff, *Out Here* (New York: State Street Press Chapbooks, 1984); Fred Redekop, *Cornucopia* (Goshen, 1986); Al Reimer, et al., eds. *A Sackful of Plautdietsch* (Winnipeg: Hyperion Press, 1983); Pauline Ressler, *Poems for Praise and Power* (Crockett, Ky.: Rod and Staff, 1978); Elaine Sommers Rich, *Am I This Countryside?* (Goshen, 1980); Philip Ruth, *This Lit Brow* (Goshen, 1981); Barbara Keener Shenk, *The God of Sarah, Rebekah and Rachel* (Scottdale, 1985); Andreas Schroeder, *File of Uncertainties* (Surrey, B.C.: Sono Nis, 1971); Barbara Esch Shisler, *Reprieve* (Goshen, 1970); idem, *This Way to Exile* (Goshen, 1976); Julia Spicher, *Moss Lotus* (Goshen, 1983); Elmer F. Suderman, *We Must Try Words* (St. Peter, Minn: Daguerreotype, 1980); idem, *What Can We Do Here?* (St. Peter, Minn.: Daguerreotype, 1974); David Waltner-Toews, *The Earth is One Body* (Winnipeg: Turnstone, 1979); idem, *Endangered Species* (Winnipeg: Turnstone, 1988); idem, *Good Housekeeping* (Winnipeg: Turnstone, 1983); idem, *That Inescapable Animal* (Goshen, 1974); Elizabeth Wenger, *Foretaste* (Goshen, 1972); idem, *Hail to the Brightness* (Goshen, 1970); idem, *Heal on Monday* (Goshen, 1974); Dallas Wiebe, *The Kansas Poems* (Cincinnati: Cincinnati Poetry Review, 1987); Norman A. Wingert, *Mosaics in Verse* (Nappanee, 1968); Samuel W. Witmer, *Green Squirrel and Other Rhymes*

for Children (Goshen, 1978); Yorifumi Yaguchi, *Resurrection* (Goshen, 1972); Donald C. Yost, *Milo* (Goshen, 1970); idem, *Powr-kraft 34-37203-1/2 lb.* (Goshen, 1972); Jeff Gundy, "Separation and Transformation: Tradition and Audience for Three Mennonite Poets," *JMS*, 4 (1986), 53-69.

See also the features at Allebach, Harvey G., and Hymnology.

Poland (ME IV:199, 920). Mennonite mission and service in Poland, a socialist yet predominantly Roman Catholic country, have developed in the period since the mid-1950s despite various obstacles. Decades of Polish-German antagonism have affected the views of Poles and Mennonites toward each other. The difficult course of East-West relations and Polish domestic turmoil has also hampered the forming of stronger Mennonite ties to Poland. Nevertheless, a variety of formal and informal contacts have developed, providing an ever-broadening framework for future activity.

The détente years of the 1970s ushered in the most intense period of program development by Mennonite institutions. In the field of educational and cultural exchange, Mennonite Central Committee (MCC) brought Polish farmers and young people to North America under the International Visitors' Exchange Program, while Goshen College sent and received students and faculty as part of the Study-Service Trimester (SST) program. MCC has also sponsored full-term volunteers who, through their capacities as teachers and students, have worshiped with Polish Christians, talked with representatives of various sectors of Polish society, and, on occasion, helped administer °relief aid. Peter Foth has actively promoted broader European Mennonite contacts with Poland. In the years 1979 to 1983 MCC provided relief aid during the Polish economic crisis as well as disaster relief after flooding in the Plock region, where Mennonite colonies formerly existed.

The generally neglected story of the four centuries of Mennonite experience in Poland has drawn increasing attention from a small body of Polish historians as well as a new generation of Mennonite scholars. There is a growing Mennonite conviction of the need for a symbolic gesture of gratitude for the tolerance, refuge, and decades of privileges offered by successive Polish kings to the early Mennonites. In addition, the long shadow cast by the hostilities of the last two centuries seems to be giving way to a more sympathetic understanding from both sides.   SM

John Friesen, "Mennonites in Poland: An Expanded Historical View," *JMS*, 4 (1986), 94-108; Peter Klassen, "Faith and Culture in Conflict: Mennonites in the Vistula Delta," *MQR*, 57 (1983), 194-205; Horst Penner, *Die ost- und west-preussischen Mennoniten* (Weierhof: Mennonitischer Geschichtsverein, 1978); Kazimierz Mezyński, *From the History of Mennonites in Poland* (Warsaw: Akademia Rolnicza w Warszawie, 1975); idem, "Über die Mennoniten in Polen," *Menn. Geschbl.*, Jg. 25, n.F. 20 (1968), 49-66; Wojciech Marchlewski, "The 'Hollander' Settlements in Mazovia," *Menn. Life*, 41 (1986), 5-9; Erich L. Ratzlaff, *Im Weichselbogen* (Winnipeg, 1971); Janusz Tazbir, *A State Without Stakes: Polish Religious Toleration in the 16th and 17th Centuries*, trans. A. T. Jordan (New York: Kosciuszko Foundation, Twayne Publishers, 1973).

Polemics, Anti-Anabaptist. Polemics constitute a

branch of theology traditionally following dogmatics and °apologetics. The theologian identifies and refutes theological and ecclesiological error as necessary defense of truth. Polemicists of the 16th c. reflected late medieval attitudes of mind about religious error as metaphysically dangerous. Error not only misled simple folk and damned them eternally; it also countered the purposes of God in the universe. Refuting it therefore was an urgent necessity.

The 16th c. overflowed with polemical controversy of rich variety: Lutherans against Sacramentarians (°°Sacramentists), Catholics against different groups of Protestants, Catholics against Catholics, etc. In this common form of religious discourse Anabaptists probably were treated no worse than other Christians, except for that special note of alarm that colored the first-generation anti-Anabaptist polemics. Europeans were anxious about the prospect of renewed °Peasants' Wars or a recrudescent °Münster at some fresh location, and they linked all Anabaptists to both.

Generally the Anabaptists did not write polemics, strictly interpreted. They wrote theological defenses of themselves and even intemperate attacks—against Protestants and Catholics, but also against each other. Polemics belong to religious argumentation that shapes its thought by traditional categories of logic. Most Anabaptist and Mennonite authors did not think that truth itself was enhanced, or even made clearer, by the use of formal logic; indeed, if anything they thought that logic obscured truth. Clarity of religious thought and expression was necessary for Christians, but was enhanced by simpler forms of thinking, especially by direct scriptural exegesis.

Lutheran Polemics. Beginning with °°Luther himself, the Lutheran critique of the Anabaptists centered on the means by which God had chosen to mediate his grace to humans: the Word *and* the sacraments (°ordinances). To deny the efficacy of sacramental grace was blasphemy, a denial of the power of God in those means of grace that God himself had selected. In theological consequence Luther and °°Melanchthon, and °°Menius and °°Rhegius to only a slightly lesser extent, found the Anabaptists insufferably spiritualistic; they had spiritualized away that special union of matter and Spirit that God had bound into the form of the sacrament, for which the Incarnation was the most prized model. °Baptism was the sacrament most frequently discussed. Luther and his co-workers were literally horrified at the radicality of Anabaptist rejection of infant baptism, believing that Anabaptists thereby damned infants, the most innocent of all humans.

But baptism of adult believers was also wrong because it broke the body of Christendom. Thereby the Anabaptists shattered an entire set of delicately shaped relations between church and state, insisting on a complete separation of the "two swords." That was sedition in Lutheran eyes. Although observers from later centuries, or Roman Catholics of the times, accused Luther of the same mistake, he and other Reformers of the first generation thought that they were restoring true faith to a singular body of Christ, which the Romans stubbornly rejected. Hence the monotony of the Lutheran detailed polemical attacks on "rebaptism." Therefore also the casual Lutheran expectation that Anabaptists would be spiritualists; all of them rejected the most essential work of God in the human by appropriating grace in extra scriptural forms, in the Lutherans' view.

In their polemics against the Anabaptists Menius and Rhegius elevated the issue of faith vs. works to a high level of significance. Both of them had met bona fide Anabaptists much more frequently than had either Luther or Melanchthon, and they had heard the Anabaptist complaint about Lutheran faith as dead because it produced no fruit in the form of good works.

Sacraments per se, baptism, civic order, good works vs. faith—on all of these points the Anabaptists developed a position so radical that the Lutherans expected the most extreme forms of social disruption. The events at Münster in the early 1530s rather than coming as a surprise, offered the supreme illustration of the diabolical fury of the Anabaptists, and therefore became a constant reference point in post-1535 Lutheran polemics.

Reformed Polemics. In the eyes of Reformed theologians in southern Germany and Switzerland Anabaptist errors regarding baptism, the Lord's Supper, excommunication and the ban, and the search for the creation of a pure church were all attacks on the newly established church and on its supporting governments. Adult believers' baptism was the first act of Anabaptist separation. Baptism became therefore the most frequently discussed issue in Reformed polemics. The Reformed preferred parallels between Old and New Covenants: circumcision in Old and baptism in New both brought infants under watch and ward of God's people. To deny that connection between the covenants was both a rejection of God's promise and a cruel denial to infants of God's love mediated through his people. Neither Reformed nor Anabaptist laid sacramental value on either baptism or the Lord's Supper (°communion), even when a few Reformed wanted more of the Real Presence as spiritual food in the elements than did the Anabaptists. The Reformed found Anabaptists insufferably sectarian.

In this latter connection they attacked Anabaptists' claims about the perfectibility of their church. Anabaptist close communion and their exercise of the ban with excommunication gave added focus to the issue of pure church.

The Reformed were disturbed by the sharp distinction drawn by Anabaptists between the two kingdoms, between the church and the world. In some sense the Reformed theologians could never quite understand the Anabaptists' rejection of the notion that civic office was Christian because of the forms of force used by the magistrate. Nor could they understand Anabaptist objections to selection of preachers by the state. In their eyes the Anabaptist rejection of the sword was an intolerable concession to either anarchy or Turkish hegemony.

The final subsuming issue was hermeneutics. The Reformed found Anabaptist biblicism too legalistic, and their preference for the New Testament an unbalanced interpretation of God's complete Word. Although hermeneutics underlay much of the Reformed polemics, it did not always rise to become a conscious issue for comment and refutation.

°°Zwingli, °°Bucer, °°Bullinger, and °°Calvin, in that chronological order, were the most widely read anti-Anabaptist polemicists among the Reformed theologians.

Catholic Polemics. Catholic polemics against Anabaptists is a large, diffuse topic that is inadequately researched. No scholar has yet waded through the routine Roman condemnatory catalogs of heretics including Anabaptists, and certainly not the published and unpublished reports of papal nuncios or of Jesuits within their own order. Probably no scholar has found the topic intriguing enough to undertake because, with a few exceptions, Catholic authors tended to group the Anabaptists either with other Protestant Reformers, who seemed more dangerous to the Catholics, or grouped them with that long historical line of heretics going back to the early church: Hussites, Brethren of the Free Spirit, Cathari (°°Albigenses), °°Waldenses, and °°Donatists. Most Catholic polemicists did not bother to learn much about the 16th c. Anabaptists' "heresies," which they described indifferently and inaccurately (Domenico Gravina, Georg °°Cassander, Johannes °°Corbachius, even Dickus on baptism, and others).

Relative indifference to the details of Anabaptist errors could be attributed to the events at Münster, which disqualified Anabaptist thought and all Anabaptists with it. Or, after the imperial edict of 1529 mandating death for Anabaptists, the nerve for refuting them in order to justify capital punishment already had been cut. Indeed, there is evidence to suggest that some Catholic jurists were aware of Roman imperial edicts against both "rebaptized" and "rebaptizers," going back to the early 5th c., and that those edicts may have influenced 16th c. enemies of the Anabaptists to give them the opprobrious nickname "Anabaptist" (rebaptizers) in order to bring them under the capital-crime penalities of Roman law. Catholic polemicists saw the Anabaptists either as the natural fruit of the Reformers' rebellion or the expected continuation of earlier heretics. Their accounts lacked the crispness of description and tinge of anger that characterized Lutheran and Reformed polemics.

There were exceptions, primarily in places and times where Anabaptists acquired some regional prominence. Hermann von °°Kerssenbroick, describing the Anabaptists of Münster; Christoph °°Erhard and Christoph Andreas °°Fischer, excoriating the Hutterian Brethren; earlier Johann °Faber (Heigerlin), depicting the errors of his erstwhile academic colleague and friend Balthasar °Hubmaier—all of these Catholics and a few more wrote with emotion, both to persuade political lords to be more resolute and to extirpate the Anabaptists, or to dissuade potential converts from joining.

Seventeenth-Century Polemics. Several distinctive features of these polemics marked them as substantially different from their 16th-c. predecessors.

(1) These polemics against Mennonites were fewer in number and less virulent. Composed by theological lightweights, often pastors instead of the most able theologians, they were directed more toward instructing common folk on how to avoid succumbing to erroneous Mennonite teaching and life, and less toward purifying an otherwise sullied truth of God.

(2) Anabaptist-Mennonite righteous living, compared with the moral lives of other Christians, had made far too strong an impression on rank and file Christians to permit Protestant leaders to characterize Mennonites as lustful Münsterites. Reformed polemicist Georg °°Thormann reported that his Bernese parishioners believed that because of virtuous living Mennonites stood in better salvific relations with a righteous God than did their Reformed neighbors.

(3) A century of religious wars, including the most gruesomely destructive of all, the °°Thirty Years' War (1618-1648), had blunted the edge of the search for an absolute theological rectitude. Surely a policy of adjusting to each others' religious differences in the interest of ending or avoiding civil war, the position of the so-called *politiques* of the late 16th c., was superior to the wanton destructiveness of the wars of religion.

(4) Authors writing against Mennonites reverted to critical history or unadorned disputation on confessional issues, rather than the more traditional polemics, writing in tones much less harsh than a century earlier. Johann °°Ottius wrote the former. In 1645 Johannes °Müller, writing for his Hamburg parishioners, refuted the errors of Syvaert °°Pietersz's Confession of 1620. Ottius was informative and even erudite. Müller was theologically weak. That he, rather than some more astute theologian, should write against the Mennonites reflected perhaps a relatively lesser interest in the errors of those erstwhile archheretics.

Although Mennonites could not yet be justified in the thought-world of the religious, they were no longer excoriated as viciously as their Anabaptist forebears had been. JSO

This bibliography includes books or articles that treat polemics, not those that deal more broadly with religious differences. Heinold Fast, *Heinrich Bullinger und die Täufer* (Weierhof: Menn. Geschichtsverein, 1959); John S. Oyer, *Lutheran Reformers against Anabaptists* (The Hague: Nijhoff, 1964); Winfried Eisenblätter, "Die katholische Auseinandersetzung mit dem Täufertum," *Menn. Geschbl.*, 22 (1965), 47-53; Willem Balke, *Calvijn en die doperse Radikalen* (Amsterdam: Ton Bolland, 1973; Engl. trans., Grand Rapids, Mich.: Eerdmans, 1981); Harry Loewen, *Luther and the Radicals: Another Look* (Waterloo, Ont.: Wilfrid Laurier U., 1974); Leland Harder, "Zwingli's Relation to the Schleitheim Confession of Faith," *16th C. Journal*, 11 (Winter 1980), 51-66. See P. J. A. Nisen, "De anti-doperse Geschriften van Petrus van Blommeveen, Cornelius Crocus, Joannes Bunderius en Georgius Cassander," *Doops. Bijdr.*, n.r. 11 (1985), 171-84, for fresh work in prospect on Catholic polemicists. For bibliographical information on polemical books and tracts, see the biographical articles in *ME* I-IV on the polemicists mentioned above, plus Nicolaus von Amsdorf, Johann Bugenhagen, Johann Gast, Nikolaus Gerbel, and Lambertus Hortensius; see also citations in Walter Köhler, "Catholicism and Anabaptism," *ME* I: 532-35. Some routine Catholic polemics, most of which were not included in *ME* I-IV, include Georg Cassander, *Opera quae reperiri potuerunt omnia* (Paris: Pacard, 1616); Scipione Calandrini, *Trattato dell' origine delle heresie et delle schisme* (Poschiavo: Landolphi, 1572); Gabriel Dupreau, *De vitis, sectis, et dogmatibus omnivm haereticorum...* (Cologne: Quentel, 1569); Domenico Gravina, *Catholicae praescriptiones adversvs omnes veteres et nostri temporis haereticos* (Naples: Roncalioli, 1619). For the 17th c., beyond Thormann and Müller, see Menno Hanneken, *Sylloge quaestionum theologicarum, qvas orthodoxis movent, Photiniani, Anabaptistae, Suenckfeldiani,*

Weigeliani (Marburg: Chemlin, 1637). Finally [Syvaert Pietersz], *Bekentenisse des Gheloofs* (Hoorn, 1620); and Petrus Bontemps, *Kort Bewijs van de menigh-vuldighe Doolingen der Wederdoopers ofte Mennisten: Met Wederlegginghe van hare Uytvluchten ende Bevestiginge der Christelijker Waerheydt* (Amsterdam: Ravesteyn, 1653).

See also Apologetics; Pfeddersheim Disputation.

Political Attitudes. Mennonite attitudes toward political parties and authorities have differed widely among the many groups in the Mennonite mosaic and within the more than 50 countries to which Mennonites have scattered. Mennonite attitudes have reflected both the Anabaptist teaching that governments are ordained by God to maintain order and the teaching that government authority is limited and not to be obeyed when it contradicts the will of God (°civil disobedience). Modern warfare and the Mennonite refusal of °military service have provided the focus for the shaping of Mennonite attitudes in the modern era of nationalism and militarism.

Mennonites generally have not shown a preference for either liberal or authoritarian systems, but have honored any government which offered them toleration and autonomy. Thus Mennonites gave their deference and appreciation to the tsars of Russia, to the dictator Alfredo Stroessner of Paraguay, but also to the liberal °democracies of the United States and Canada and to the "secular state" program of the Congress Party in India. The severe suffering of Mennonites under Russian °Communism produced a strong anti-Communist sentiment, especially among emigrés from Russia. In the 1930s some Mennonites in Canada and Paraguay expressed sympathies for the anti-Communist stance of °National Socialism in Germany.

Modern democratic theory and practice have changed the context of Mennonite political attitudes and behavior. In the 17th and 19th c. in Europe, Mennonites had the status of subjects with personal obligations to rulers or princes. In this relationship Mennonites often traded special taxes for toleration. In modern democratic states which claim to derive authority from the people, Mennonites have had the status of citizens who are responsible for the civic order. The earliest Mennonite experience with democratic pluralism was in America. Historian Richard MacMaster has shown (MEA 1), contrary to earlier opinions, that Mennonites in colonial Pennsylvania voted in elections and gave support to the ruling pacifist Quaker party which protected their interests. The American War for Independence (1775-83), in which the willingness to bear arms and swear a loyalty oath became tests of citizenship, removed Mennonites from political participation and made them "more than ever a people apart." American Mennonite immigrants of Swiss background maintained a stricter two-kingdom dualism and separation from politics than did the Dutch-Russian immigrants of the 1870s and 1880s in America. Some American Mennonites became active in state and national politics, but they needed to drift away from their Mennonite connections. Old Order Mennonites, Old Order Amish, and other traditionalist groups have attempted a strict separation from political participation.

Mennonites who have an official or unofficial stance of political noninvolvement often do have political preferences. Some theologically conservative Mennonites influenced by °dispensationalist teachings have been keenly interested in contemporary events, often relating to the State of Israel, which are said to reveal God's plan for the fulfillment of history. A study of the political socialization of "Old" Mennonite (MC) secondary school students (Leatherman, 1960) showed that Mennonites, compared to an American norm, were distinctively noninvolved in partisan political activity but that they also reported unusually high identification with the Republican Party (70 percent). According to this study, historical factors which fostered the Republican preference included Mennonite opposition to slavery and to the Democrat South's Civil War rebellion against the national government (°American Civil War), a positive response to generous Republican land policies on the frontier, and the concentration of Mennonite settlements in strongly Republican states.

In a sociological study of five Mennonite and Brethren in Christ groups in the United States and Canada in 1972 (Kaufman/Harder, 1975), 76 percent of the respondents said that church members should vote in public elections. Of those who expressed a party preference, three-fourths of the American Mennonites identified with the Republican Party. In Canada the party preferences were more evenly divided: 40 percent Conservative, 32 percent Liberal, 20 percent Social Credit.

A historical study of the political acculturation of Kansas Mennonites (Juhnke, 1975) showed that the distinctiveness of Mennonite party preferences changed over time. Until 1940 Kansas Mennonites (mostly General Conference and of Dutch-Russian background) scattered their votes among the political parties in about the same percentages as their non-Mennonite neighbors. There was substantial variation among congregations, however. The Swiss-Volyhnians were less strongly Republican than were the Dutch-Russian Alexanderwohlers. In the 1940 election, when it was clear that President Franklin D. Roosevelt was leading the country into war, the Kansas Mennonites voted in Republican majorities which were distinctively larger than their non-Mennonite neighbors. The Democrat party was identified with war, as it had been in the Civil War and again in °World War I. Issues of war and peace affected American Mennonite political attitudes and behavior more than did issues of social welfare, although Mennonites voted in especially large numbers in which "moral issues" such as °Prohibition or °capital punishment were at stake.

Since World War II Mennonites in the five western provinces of Canada became more extensively involved as voters and as officeholders in provincial and national politics than Mennonites have ever been anywhere. In recent elections from 3-10 Mennonites have stood for provincial offices while 15 or more have been nominated for national offices. In 1979-80 Jake Epp of Manitoba, a member of the Progressive-Conservative party, served as national Minister of Indian Affairs and Northern Development, more recently as Minister for Health. Canadian Mennonite politicians have belonged to many different political parties and have expressed widely varying political views, including positions on military defense which are in tension with Mennonite pacifist teachings. In recent years North American Mennonite scholars and church leaders have addressed °church-state issues in numerous conferences and publications. The issues of war °taxes and of registration for the military °draft surfaced during and after the Vietnam War. Two Mennonite theologians who gained wider prominence for their writings were Gordon Kaufman of Harvard Divinity School and John Howard Yoder of Associated Mennonite Biblical Seminaries and Notre Dame University. Anabaptist-Mennonite thinking has been particularly influential in the °liberation theology of some Latin American theologians.

Mennonite churches which are the product of mission work in Asia, Africa, and Latin America have expressed varying political attitudes in their different circumstances. Anabaptist-Mennonite teachings have often combined with minority religious status to place Mennonites in a situation of dissent. Japanese Mennonites have joined other Christians in that country in resisting the remilitarization of Japan and the revival of Shintoism as a state religion. Taiwanese Mennonite political attitudes have been shaped by their status as ethnic Taiwanese who have been politically dominated by Mandarin-speaking Nationalists from the Chinese mainland. The political attitudes of African Mennonites have been shaped by intertribal relationships. The Brethren in Christ in Zimbabwe, for example, were mainly from the Ndebele tribe which took second place to the majority Shona tribe in the violent struggle for national independence. In Ethiopia in 1982 a Marxist government suppressed the Mennonite Church (Meserete Christos Church), expropriated church property, and detained Mennonite church leaders without charges and without trial for more than four years. In Latin America, Spanish-speaking Mennonite churches are generally small in size and part of a Protestant minority in the context of a historic Catholic church-state alliance.

As Mennonites across the world are scattered into nearly 150 organized bodies on the five continents and Australia, generalizations about political attitudes are difficult to make. In recent years the Mennonite World Conference has become an increasingly significant forum for inter-Mennonite sharing of religious and political concerns.   JCJ

Frank H. Epp, "An Analysis of National Socialism in the Mennonite Press in the 1930's (PhD diss. U. of Minnesota, 1965); James C. Juhnke, *A People of Two Kingdoms* (Newton, 1974); Kauffman/Harder, *Anabaptists Four C. Later* (1975), 150-69; Gordon D. Kaufman, *Theology for a Nuclear Age* (Manchester, England: Manchester, U. Press, 1985); Daniel R. Leatherman, "The Political Socialization of Students in the Mennonite Secondary Schools" (MA thesis, U. of Chicago, 1960); John H. Redekop, "Mennonites and Politics in Canada and the United States" (paper for Conference on Mennonite Studies in North America, 1982); John Howard Yoder, *The Politics of Jesus* (Grand Rapids: Eerdmans, 1972); F. H. Epp, *Mennonites in Canada II*, pp. 543ff.; Wittlinger, *Piety and Obedience* (1978), 405ff.

See also Capitalism; Communism; Liberation Theologies; Revolution.

Political Science. See Politics.

Politics. Concerning politics the traditional Mennonite stance, despite some deviation and exceptions, may be described as separationist or apolitical. The earliest major comments are found in the °Schleitheim Confession (1527) which spoke of two orders, one inside the "perfection of Christ" and the other outside. Among those items which the separated believers "should shun and flee" the authors included "civic affairs." Because Jesus did not accept any political office, his faithful followers should likewise refuse to be "a magistrate if one should be chosen as such." "The worldly princes lord it over others by use of the sword," by the use of force, "but not so shall it be with you."

By the middle of the 16th c. a significant segment of the Dutch Anabaptists were permitting their members to hold local political offices not involving °capital punishment. In his later writings °Menno Simons himself seemed less certain about nonparticipation in the magistracy. Perhaps he thought that local office holding could be justified in the same manner as he justified calling "emperor, kings, lords and princes" to recognize their "spiritual King" and to govern wisely.

In Switzerland, and later in North America, nonparticipation in °government became the official norm, at least until the late 19th c. In northern Europe some, mainly local, political participation persisted. In Russia, meanwhile, Mennonite migrants from northern Europe developed substantial settlements and by the early 19th c. were fully involved in the political administration of their own "Mennonite Commonwealth." Their activism flourished. By the early 1900s these Mennonites were electing their own representatives to the Duma, the Russian national parliament. The entire Mennonite experience in Russia, from the late 18th c. until after the 1917 Bolshevik Revolution (°Russian Revolution), is rife with political activism locally as well as with national authorities.

While the principle of avoiding politics persisted among Mennonite groups in Canada and the United States, the reality hardly reflected the theory. In Pennsylvania, Ohio, and Ontario Mennonite leaders, perhaps unconsciously at first, became important political activists. For example, in what is now Ontario, Mennonite leaders petitioned for military exemption as early as 1793. Abraham Erb, leader of the first Waterloo, Ont., settlement in 1806, probably did not consider himself to be a political leader, though he surely was one. Similarly Moses Springer, the first mayor following Waterloo's incorporation in 1857, probably would not have wished to be called a Mennonite politician, at least not until he was elected to the provincial legislature a few years later. Analogous accounts can be cited for most of the other early Mennonite settlements as well. We should note, in passing, that sometimes the role of these Mennonite political leaders had more to do with the Mennonite ethnic community than with the Mennonite church.

The coming of the politically experienced, often astute, Mennonites from Russia in the 1870s widened Mennonite political involvement, especially in

Canada. For example, in the spring of 1873 a Mennonite delegation from Russia drove a hard bargain for settlement lands in western Canada. Hesitantly the delegation's spokesman agreed to "accept" eight townships in southern Manitoba. They thanked the Canadian government for its extensive assistance but then added, "Should we after the arrival of the first of our immigrants, think that another location than the present one which you have reserved for us would suit us better, then we hope that you will exchange the reserve to such parts as we should find preferable, . . ." On July 25, 1873, their amended requests were granted. Such clever, not always subtle, "pressure" politics, or at least self-serving interaction with politicians, has been widespread ever since.

Even though their leaders were deeply involved in group politics, and occasionally held individual elected offices, most Mennonite conferences in North America continued to endorse the traditional stance of noninvolvement. For example, in 1878 the Mennonite Brethren organized as a conference only in the United States passed a resolution which stated "That members are not permitted to hold government offices or take any part at the polls. However, we appreciate the protection we enjoy under our Government."

By 1890 the MB stance had changed somewhat. The delegates that year decided "That members of the Church refrain from participation or involvement in the contentions of political parties, but are permitted to vote quietly at elections, and may also vote for prohibition." In 1893 their position was modified further, perhaps by a developing influence from the newly founded, more politically activist, Canadian sector. The conference agreed "That our brethren shall not hold the offices of justice of the peace or constable. A member may be a 'notary public'." This position was not officially modified for more than a half century. Parallel developments can be traced for the other major Mennonite groups, roughly at the same time for the General Conference Mennonite Church (GCM) but substantially later for the largest group, the Mennonite Church (MC) also known as "Old Mennonites."

The awareness of political relevance and involvement developed slowly. A major article by Edward Yoder in 1939, "The Obligation of the Christian to the State and Community — 'Render to Caesar'," still relied on more traditional Mennonite categories (*MQR*, 13 [1939], 104-22). Increased °urbanization, socioeconomic advancement, rising levels of °education and of affluence, greater participation in the °professions and the broad impact of World War II forced Mennonite groups to rethink their political pronouncements. Guy F. Hershberger's 1944 volume, *War, Peace and Nonresistance*, while still advocating substantial nonparticipation, broadened both sociopolitical awareness and sociopolitical concerns.

Simultaneously most North American Mennonite groups, having initiated or completed a language transition, found themselves compelled to rethink the social implications of the gospel. An important study conference held at Winona Lake, Ind., in 1950 attempted to set forth a Mennonite position distinct from both the evangelical (°Fundamentalism) and

°liberal °social gospel positions. The ethical stance spelled out at that time was invoked frequently in subsequent decades to justify an increasingly activist, though mainly nonpartisan, political stance in the United States.

The decade of the 1950s witnessed some major shifts. In 1951 the Mennonite Church (MC) passed a policy statement which still focused mainly on °peace, war, and °nonresistance, while also recognizing some positive roles for the state (°church-state relations). Importantly, however, the document stressed "witness to the state" and "claims" of the state, not participation in politics.

The years 1956 and 1957 produced several key publications. In 1956, while contributors to the volume edited by Guy F. Hershberger, *The Recovery of the Anabaptist Vision*, raised mainly historical questions, Elmer Ediger, in a short piece in *Mennonite Life*, recast the issue in his essay, "A Christian's Political Responsibility." Simultaneously J. Winfield Fretz, also in *Mennonite Life*, asked, "Should Mennonites Participate in Politics?" In 1958 Guy F. Hershberger probed new practicalities with his study, *The Way of the Cross in Human Relations*, and Elmer Neufeld advanced the discussion substantially with his widely noted *MQR* article, "Christian Responsibility in the Political Situation." In new settings new options gradually gained a hearing. By 1959 the question was put clearly by Harley Stucky in *Mennonite Life*, "Should Mennonites Participate in Government?"

Thereafter the theological and also socio-political reassessment of church-state affairs, particularly in political terms, progressed quickly. John Howard Yoder's 1964 analysis, *The Christian Witness to the State*, broke new ground. The 1965 Chicago Consultation of 46 Mennonite scholars in theology and notably, the social sciences provided *A New Look at the Church and State Issue*. With the 1972 release of John Howard Yoder's pivotal *The Politics of Jesus* and the appearance in the same year of John H. Redekop's pamphlet, *Making Political Decisions: A Christian Perspective*, the theoretical underpinnings of selective Mennonite °sociopolitical activism were taking shape.

But the broader Mennonite constituency had not waited. In Canada early political activism included, at the provincial level, the election of Cornelius Hiebert in Alberta (Didsbury-Conservative), 1906-9, and Gerhard Enns in Saskatchewan (Rosthern-Liberal), 1905-14.

In the 1950s and thereafter, many Canadian Mennonites, virtually all from the General Conference Mennonite Church (Conference of Mennonites in Canada) or Mennonite Brethren conferences, and almost all with roots in Russia, won election to provincial parliaments. In Alberta Ray Ratzlaff (Three Hills-Social Credit [SC]), was elected in 1967 and went on to serve as minister of tourism, etc., and Robert H. Wiebe (Peace River-SC), was also elected in 1967. Werner Schmidt was elected as provincial Social Credit Party leader but was not elected to the legislature in 1971 and in subsequent attempts.

In British Columbia Harvey Schroeder, though not a Mennonite church member, was widely viewed as a Mennonite legislator when first elected in 1972

(Chilliwack-SC). He served as minister in several departments and eventually was elected Speaker of the legislature. In 1984 Peter A. Dueck (Fraser Valley-SC) was elected for the first time and promptly became minister of health.

In Manitoba Robert Banman (La Verendrye-Progressive Conservative [PC]) won election in 1973 and eventually served in six different ministries. Jake M. Froese (Rhineland-SC) served in the legislature from 1959-73. Harry J. Enns (Rockwood-Iberville-PC) was elected in 1966 and served successively as minister of three departments. Arnold Brown (Rhineland-PC) gained election in 1973. Albert Driedger (Emerson-PC) became an elected representative in 1977. In the same year Victor Schroeder (Rossmere-New Democratic Party [NDP]) began a lengthy stint as an elected Mennonite democratic °socialist, serving in various capacities, including minister of finance.

Saskatchewan similarly produced many Mennonite provincial legislators. David Boldt (Rosthern-Liberal [L]) served in various ministerial portfolios following his election in 1960. Isaak Elias (Rosthern-SC) was elected in 1956. Allen Engel, another democratic socialist (Assiniboia-Gravelbourg-NDP), first gained office in 1971. Harold Martens (Morse-PC) won in 1982. In 1978 Herbert Swan (Rosetown-Elrose-PC) began a stint which included a time as Speaker. One of the early Mennonite democratic socialists, John Thiessen (Shellbrook-Cooperative Commonwealth Federation [CCF]), won in 1956.

Numerous other Mennonites ran for provincial office, representing all of the major and some of the minor political parties. Such Mennonite political activism is now firmly entrenched. In any provincial election in the five western provinces Mennonites can now be found as candidates and as activists

At the national level parallel trends developed. Erhart Regier (New Westminster, B.C.-CCF/NDP), not formally a churchman, was elected a Member of Parliament (MP) in 1953 and served until 1962. Other MPs included Siegfried J. Enns (Portage la Prairie, Man.-PC), 1962-68; Dean Whiteway (Selkirk, Man.-PC), 1974-79; and Jake Epp (Provencher, Man.-PC), 1972-. A member of the Mennonite Brethren church, Epp has served in various cabinet portfolios and is the only Mennonite to be appointed to the Canadian federal government's cabinet. Other Mennonite MPs have included Benno Friesen, not now (1987) a Mennonite church member (Whiterock-Surrey-Delta, B.C.-PC), 1974-; Jake Froese (Niagara Falls, Ont.-L), 1979-80; and John Reimer (Kitchener, Ont.-PC), 1979-80, 1984-.

There has been no shortage of Mennonite candidates at the national level, at least since the 1950s. If we include all who identify with the Mennonite ethnic community or the Mennonite church, or both, then the total number reached 16 in the 1974 election and 11 in 1980.

Canadian Mennonites have also attained high offices as nonelected appointees. In Manitoba Peter Thiessen served as assistant to the province's premier, Edward Schreyer (NDP), in the 1970s, and William Regehr served as principal secretary and chief-of-staff to Premier Howard Pawley (NDP) in the 1980s. At the national level Peter Harder served as executive assistant to Progressive Conservative Party Leader Joe Clark, who was Prime Minister of Canada, 1979-80.

Throughout the national, provincial, and local civil servant sector, Mennonites are commonplace. Not surprisingly a 1965 Conference of Mennonites in Canada (GCM) survey revealed that about one percent of conference membership was in "Government service." As a percentage of income earners the figure would have been substantially higher.

The magistracy, more narrowly defined, has also been penetrated by Mennonites in Canada. Several Mennonites, mostly lawyers, are gaining judicial experience. In Manitoba John Enns has served as crown prosecutor of the provincial government.

In the United States, relatively speaking, Mennonites have been less involved in partisan politics, at least in running for public office at the state and national level. Doubtless the dominance of the more conservative Mennonite Church (MC) and the smaller percentage of Mennonites in the total population of a very large country have been relevant factors. But there were activists, even in earlier years: Christian William Ramseyer, Republican (R) from Iowa (1915-33); Benjamin F. Welty, from Lima, Ohio (1917-21, Democrat [D]); and Edward Clayton Eicher, from Washington Co., Iowa, (1932-38, D) all were members of Congress. Eicher became a commissioner on the Securities and Exchange Commission in Washington, D.C. (1938-42) and chief justice of the US District Court for the District of Columbia (1942 ff.). More recently, in 1970, James Juhnke ran unsuccessfully as a Democrat in Kansas' fourth congressional district, and, in 1980 and 1982 Leroy Kennel, a member of the Lombard, Ill., Mennonite church (MC) ran as an unsuccessful Democrat candidate for the United States Congress.

At the local level Mennonites in the United States, but not particularly those with Russian roots, have undertaken some successful ventures. In Kansas several Mennonites have served in the state legislature. Ferdinand J. Funk was elected state representative for one term in 1984. Peter J. Galle was elected in 1902. Walter W. Graber, a Democrat, won a seat in the 1960s. H. P. Krehbiel served one term, 1908-10. J. A. Schowalter served three terms beginning in 1934 and Harold P. Dyck served nine terms, 1970-88. In Nebraska Maurice A. Kremer, a Mennonite from Aurora, was first elected as a nonpartisan senator in 1962. He served several terms. In South Dakota Harvey Wollman served for several years as Democratic lieutenant-governor and in 1978 served briefly as acting governor. Interestingly, Lieutenant-Governor Wollman was "sworn in" as acting governor by his brother, Roger, a Republican member of the State Supreme Court since 1970 and subsequently chief justice of that court. In 1984 South Dakota had two Mennonite state legislators, Terry Miller (Freeman-R) and Benny Gross (Onida-R). Several other Mennonites have served in state legislatures.

In the United States, as in Canada, Mennonites have become very active in a wide range of political party activity. For many the distinction between two kingdoms has become obscure.

The establishment of a Washington Office by the

MCC Peace Section, in 1968, marked a major milestone in Mennonite political activism (°lobbying). Delton Franz has developed it into a significant national political voice. In 1975 MCC Canada established a similar office in Ottawa. William Janzen, who had an uncle who was excommunicated by a Mennonite church for voting, has served as director.

The Mennonite political presence in Ottawa, and also to a large degree in Washington, builds on a long tradition of political activism, albeit mainly to further self-serving causes dealing primarily with °migration, settlement, °conscription, °education, and assorted exemptions. Importantly, from the 1920s until the 1980s a Canadian Mennonite delegation has met with every Canadian prime minister. In the United States, Mennonite leaders have often met with senators and congressmen.

In light of the growth of Mennonite political activism, it is hardly surprising that the 1972 Kauffman-Harder study found extensive constituency support for political activism. Seventy percent felt it "proper for congregations to urge citizens to vote." For Mennonite Brethren and the Evangelical Mennonite Church the figure rose to 94 percent. An average of 32 percent considered it "proper for congregations to encourage groups within the church to engage in political action."

In the United States where much political activism in recent decades has been rooted in ventures related to Mennonite Central Committee, such activism has been more theologically informed than in Canada. It has also, however, been much more controversial. In Canada, where political activism has been more pragmatic and partisan it has generally been less rooted in any form of Anabaptist theology. While in the United States Mennonite political activism, at least its high profile component, has since the 1960s consisted mainly of information campaigns and lobbying, in Canada it has consisted mainly of partisan organizational activity, campaigning, and public office-holding, although lobbying has developed in Canada also, sometimes in cooperation with non-Mennonites. Project Ploughshares is a notable example.

In both countries the spiritual descendents of Menno are well on the way to becoming part of the general political establishment. Increasingly, in these free and prosperous lands, as they move up the socioeconomic scale, Mennonites are learning, for better or worse, to take political activism seriously.   JHR

John Howard Yoder, *The Christian Witness to the State* (Newton, 1964); Kauffman/Harder, *Anabaptists Four C. Later* (1975), 150ff.; John H. Redekop, "Mennonites and Politics in Canada and the United States," *JMS*, 1 (1983), 79-105; John Howard Yoder, *The Politics of Jesus* (Grand Rapids: Eerdmans, 1972), 135-214; Elmer Neufeld, "Christian Responsibility in the Political Situation," *MQR*, 32 (1958), 141-62; John H. Redekop, "The State and the Free Church," in *Kingdom Cross, and Community* (1976), 179-95; idem, *Making Political Decisions: A Christian Perspective*, Focal Pamphlet no. 23 (Scottdale, 1972); Donald B. Kraybill, *Our Star-Spangled Faith* (Scottdale, 1976); William Keeney, "Mennonite Cooperation with Government Agencies and Programs," *Proceedings of the 15th Conference on Mennonite Educational and Cultural Problems* (June, 1965), 62-74; Frank H. Epp, "Mennonites and the Civil Service," *Menn. Life*, 23 (Oct. 1968), 179-82; James C. Juhnke, *A People of Two Kingdoms: The Political Acculturation of the Kansas*

Mennonites (Newton, 1975); Delton Franz, "The Washington Office: Reflections After Ten Years," *Washington Memo* (July-August, 1978); John H. Redekop, "Involvement in the Political Order," *Chr. Leader* (Sept. 27, 1977), 10-14.

See also Government; Sociopolitical Activism.

Polity (ME I:199) is the term used to describe the way in which the church is governed. Mennonites, while looking to the example of the church in the New Testament as normative, exercise considerable freedom and flexibility in working out their patterns of church government. In the past several decades there has been a considerable shift in patterns of congregational oversight in the North American churches, for example, with some conferences eliminating the office of °bishop in favor of conference ministers and area overseers. The Brethren in Christ, meanwhile, have strengthened the office of bishop with a bishop responsible for the administrative and spiritual oversight of each district conference.

The Mennonite churches of the Two-Thirds World during their formative years by and large took on the organizational and leadership patterns of the founding churches of North America and Europe as mediated and interpreted to them by the pioneer missionaries. Other factors over the years have also been significant in shaping their governing structures, notably the theological influences of the °seminaries and °Bible schools where the pastors have studied. The °indigenizing process has also affected the way in which the younger churches have modified their organizational life. Yet an additional factor has been the way in which a growing number of these churches are reading the Anabaptist sources, not simply adopting 16th-c. European models but adapting basic Anabaptist principles to their own situation in life.

There is considerable diversity in forms of governance among the several groups of Mennonites and Brethren in Christ and even within a given group. Some congregations have a plural ministry with the historic threefold pattern of °elder or bishop, °°preachers, and °°deacons; some have lay ministers; and an increasing number have professionally trained and salaried ministers. Some have boards of elders and others have boards of deacons who, along with the pastors, provide spiritual °leadership within the congregation.

Mennonites tend more toward the congregational pattern than episcopal, or presbyterian forms (°congregationalism). That is, they emphasize the central importance of the local fellowship of believers though they vary on the relative degree of congregational °°autonomy. Each congregation is responsible for church °discipline, for maintaining standards of faith and life. Each has a voice in the selection of its pastoral leadership. Each is free to plan its own order for °worship services. The lay members participate in the governance of the congregation and of the wider church organizations as well.

However, Mennonites are not pure congregationalists and have at some points in their history drawn certain elements (bishops, elders) from both the episcopal and presbyterial traditions. General Conference Mennonites lean closest to a congregational model while the Brethren in Christ would be least congregational. The Mennonite Church (MC) in its reorganization of 1971 emphasized the centrality of the local congregation. At the same time in the decade following, its 21 district conferences took on new strength and vitality in their roles.

Mennonites have historically recognized their need for mutual support and counsel from beyond the single congregation and their patterns of organization have reflected this. All of the several Mennonite, Mennonite Brethren, and Brethren in Christ bodies have organized themselves into general (churchwide) conferences coordinated by a general board. All have also organized themselves into district conferences. In addition they have provided some form of congregational oversight ranging from consultation only to direct administrative and spiritual supervision.

In many parts of the church in North America, conference ministers or area overseers serve functions similar to those of the bishops at an earlier time with somewhat less authority and a more narrowly focused range of responsibilities. In some cases, administrative and spiritual guidance responsibilities have been separated with administrative guidance given by an executive secretary for the conference. This pattern is still in process of being refined as the district conferences gain more experience with it.

On the local level, many congregations have set up (1) church councils for administrative oversight and program coordination and (2) boards of elders or deacons for the spiritual oversight of the congregation and counsel to the pastor(s). The trend on congregational, district and church-wide levels seems to be that of separating administrative and spiritual direction rather than keeping them integrated.

The historic Mennonite pattern of ordaining bishops or elders for pastoral oversight continues in many places in the church, notably among the Brethren in Christ and in several conferences of the Mennonite church (MC) in the eastern United States (e.g., Lancaster, Virginia, and Franklin) which have bishop districts. Midwestern and western Mennonite church conferences have overseer "districts," "clusters." and "councils" with oversight provided by "overseers," "coordinators," and those bishops ordained for life who are still active in the conference.

The historic Mennonite office of bishop should not be confused with the classic episcopacy. "Bishop" in Mennonite practice has its roots not in the Anglican or Catholic tradition but in the tradition of Titus 1:5. It has simply been a term meaning senior minister or pastor. The ministers were normally chosen from among the brethren in the congregation and the bishop was selected from among the ministers. There was no sacramental distinction, only a functional one, between the ministers and the people and between the bishops and the ministers. Nor was there any thought of apostolic succession through ordination.

One of the most significant developments of the past decade is the ordination of °women in the Mennonite Church (MC) and General Conference Men-

nonite Church (GCM). There have been strong differences of interpretation and opinion as these denominations and their constituent district conferences and congregations have taken up this issue. Proponents of the ordination of women have emphasized spiritual gifts, asserting that gifts of leadership, preaching, and pastoral care are sovereignly bestowed by the Spirit of God and given to various women and men alike without regard to gender. Opponents have emphasized office and the spiritual authority that goes with the pastoral office holding that the Scriptures are clear that women are not to exercise authority over men. Here again the considerable diversity of interpretation and practice on this issue has not for the most part caused the churches to break fellowship with each other. This is further testimony to the belief that freedom and flexibility with their attendant diversity are appropriate when it comes to church polity.

The following paragraphs are a description of the organizational patterns of four of the larger groups of Mennonites in North America.   RTB

Mennonite Church (MC). The Mennonite Church (MC) maintained its principal office in Lombard, Ill., until 1988, when it was moved to Elkhart, Ind. Its organization includes a (1) General Assembly which meets every two years with delegates from the 2 district conferences in Canada and the United States and a (2) General Board which serves as the church's board of directors. Each district conference is represented on the General Board; there are also a number of members at large.

Each district conference is composed of local congregations. The delegates from the local congregations normally meet at least once each year both for spiritual inspiration and for conducting the business of conference. Their agenda has to do with the mission of the church in evangelism, nurture, church planting, stewardship, youth work, congregational leadership and oversight, and being a liaison between the programs of the larger denomination and the local congregations. The determination of ministerial credentials is a district conference responsibility.

The bylaws of the Mennonite Church (MC) state that "the congregation is God's people with a common confession of Christ uniting in worship, nurture, fellowship, proclamation, service, discernment, reconciliation, mutual care and discipline. It is a local group of believers whose commitment to Christ and to each other and whose proximity to each other makes it possible to experience these activities on a regular and continuing basis."

There are five church-wide program boards whose work is coordinated and reviewed by the General Assembly and the General Board. They are Congregational Ministries, Publication, Missions, Education and Mutual Aid. The Mennonite Mutual Aid Board has become an inter-Mennonite board serving also the General Conference Mennonites and the Mennonite Brethren. Some program board members are elected by the General Assembly delegates and some are appointed by the General Board.

The General Assembly, in addition to receiving reports from program boards, standing committees, and associate groups (e.g. the °Women's Missionary and Service Commission, the °Afro-American Mennonite Association, and the °Concilio Nacional [National Council of Hispanic Mennonite Churches]) deals with issues of faith and life identified by the district conferences. This usually involves a process of study and discernment covering several biennia and involving local congregations. It may result in policy statements referred to in the bylaws as "interpretive guidelines for congregations and conferences in biblical and practical doctrine." One important issue before the General Assembly in 1987 was the development and adoption of a contemporary confession of faith.   WN

General Conference Mennonite Church (GCM).
The General Conference Mennonite church has central offices in Newton, Ks. Every three years delegates from its member congregations meet. The °Conference of Mennonites in Canada, the conferences in various regions and provinces of Canada, and the conferences of the five districts in the United States, meet annually. They are a part of the General Conference.

Each conference is composed of autonomous local congregations. Decisions and actions of conferences are not binding on their member congregations. The General Conference constitution states: "The congregations have every responsibility to support the conference and, therefore, the conference has a right to lay claim to the support of the local congregations. However, in fulfilling its mission, the conference seeks to serve and strengthen the local congregations and regional conferences, not to control them."

The three commissions—on education, on home ministries, and on overseas mission—carry out the programs of the conference under the overall coordination of the General Board which sets the annual budgets and reviews the work of the commissions. The Conference of Mennonites in Canada and the district conferences in the United States have representation on these commissions.

Each conference seeks to serve the congregations. Conferences cooperate to reduce duplication and competition. General Conference is a resource to regional conferences and to congregations.

In each district and each province a conference minister assists congregations who are seeking pastors and support the pastors. A regional conference committee processes candidates for ordination who are ordained in and by the local congregation with some involvement of that conference.

General Conference has no national conference in the states. Annually the district presidents and the U.S. members of the conference executive committee meet as a U.S. council to handle unique agenda. A U.S. delegate assembly gathers each time General Conference meets.

Women in Mission serves a vital role in mission education, service projects, and fund raising for their own and General Conference projects. Mennonite Men also are organized but less active.

Resolutions can be brought to a triennial session by the General Board, one of the commissions or a resolutions committee. A study process is used for major issues which may or may not result in a statement voted upon by the delegates at a triennial ses-

sion.

General Conference has consistently sought to be open to inter-Mennonite cooperation. The Africa overseas mission work is carried out through the Africa Inter-Mennonite Mission.   VP

Mennonite Brethren Church (MB). The General Conference of the Mennonite Brethren Churches (which became the Mennonite Brethren Church of North America in 1987) is registered as a corporation in the state of Kansas. The head office of the conference shall be in the town of Hillsboro, Ks., or at such place as the conference may from time to time determine.

The conference includes all churches founded on the confession of faith adopted by its members at a regular convention. The conference in session has the right to make the final decisions in all matters that relate to the united activities and the common welfare of the churches. Each church is autonomous in the government and administration of its own local affairs. However, churches are to accept as binding decisions made by the conference in accordance with the provisions of its constitution.

The churches that comprise the General Conference come from two national conferences: Canada and the United States. These in turn are divided into six provincial conferences and five district conferences respectively.

The General Conference convenes once in a period of three years. This convention is called for the purpose of hearing reports, projections, and recommendations of the conference boards. There are seven General Conference boards: Reference and Counsel, Christian Education, Christian Literature, Mass Media, Missions and Services, Mennonite Brethren Biblical Seminary, and Trustees. In addition, there are three committees: Executive, Nominating, and Program. The Executive Committee, made up of a moderator, assistant moderator and secretary, is responsible for those affairs of the conference not within the jurisdiction of any board or committee. These three officers are members of the Board of Reference and Counsel. This Board is to watch over the spiritual life of the General Conference and its churches and give guidance in matter of faith, doctrine and Christian life. It also convenes study and faith conferences for the purpose of examining faith and discipleship.   HJB

Brethren in Christ (BIC). The Brethren in Christ is a General Conference comprised of six regional conferences in Canada and the United States and over 200 congregations.

Each local congregation represents a self-governing unit, functioning with the oversight of the bishop and under the direction of the pastor and the church board. When a pastor is being chosen, the bishop serves as chairman of the local church board. Each congregation holds its own business meeting and is responsible for its life and practice, but with ties to its regional conference and the General Conference.

The bishops each reside in their own regional conference, but are chosen by the General Conference. The bishops are responsible for the administration of their respective regional conferences in cooperation with the General Conference. There is an annual meeting of each regional conference.

The General Conference has a biennial meeting as a representative body of all regions and congregations. It is served by a Board of Administration that includes representatives of the regions, the six General Conference boards, and administrative personnel. The general secretary of the General Conference is accountable to the moderator of the General Conference (one of the six regional bishops), and the six bishops are accountable to the general secretary. The six General Conference boards are: Board for Brotherhood Concerns, Board for Congregational Life, Board for Evangelism and Church Planting, Board for Media Ministry, Board for Ministry and Doctrine, and Board for World Missions. The Board of Administration also has within its structure the Board of Bishops, the Board for Stewardship and the Jacob Engle Foundation. The Board for Ministry and Doctrine with the Board of Bishops care for the credentialing of ministers.

The decisions of the General and Regional Conference are considered guidelines for all congregations. The *Manual of Doctrine and Government* includes the denominational statements of faith (under revision in 1987), bylaws and conference rulings, conditions for membership, and guidance in Christian living. These are given to local churches to be received for unity, to promote spirituality, and increase efficiency in program. Some congregations are more oriented to General Conference ties; others tend toward independence. North American culture accents the latter, but as a conference, Brethren in Christ call for a focus on the concept of the larger church family, including other evangelical groups in such associations as Mennonite Central Committee, the National Association of Evangelicals, and the Christian Holiness Association, with which they have official representation. RDSh

See also Authority; Church, Doctrine of; Congregationalism; Democracy; Institutions; *Ordnung*; Priesthood of All Believers.

Portugal. Mennonite presence in Portugal began spontaneously when a young Mozambican student in Lisbon, Miguel Anelo Jardim, happened upon David Augsburger's book, *Free to Forgive*. This book gripped Jardim to the point that he sought more information about Mennonites. He began corresponding with the London Mennonite Centre and Mennonites in Brazil. Jardim visited the Mennonites in Brazil and was baptized by Theo Penner in 1985.

Back in Portugal, Jardim began gathering a small group of like-minded people and this became the core of the new Mennonite church. The first official worship service was held on Aug. 31, 1986, and a short time later the first three people were baptized.

There were over a million refugees in Portugal (1986) from former Portuguese colonies in Africa. In November 1985 Greet Lodder from The Netherlands (sponsored by Mennonite Central Committee and the °International Mennonite Organization [IMO]) began working with African refugees at Amadora near Lisbon. Her work receives spiritual assistance from the new Mennonite church. In July 1986 IMO and MCC began making plans to expand the project at Amadora to include small agricultural developments for the refugees. A West German television program telling the story of the church and the refugee work of Greet Lodder aired April 4, 1987.

The Mennonite Brethren decided in January 1986 to begin church planting in Loures, a suburb of Lisbon. The Mennonite Board of Missions (MC), in the spring of 1987, investigated the possibility of mission work in the country. Efforts by IMO to coordinate the work of various conferences and agencies began in 1986. RSa

Brücke (Oct. 1986), 151; *Menn. Rep.* (May 11, 1987), 2.

Possessions. See Property.

Potosí-Saltillo Colonies, Mexico (ME IV:409). In 1943 six Amish and Old Mennonite (MC) families tried to settle in the State of San Luis Potosí, first at Rascón in a tropical region, then at Rayón, in central San Luis Potosí, in a semidesert region. Climatic, cultural, and economic difficulties proved to be too much. When, after three unsuccessful years, their minister died in 1946 the group returned to the United States, where they settled in Tennessee and Alabama. On Mar. 4, 1944, some 20 Old Colony Mennonite families from the Chihuahua colonies (°Manitoba Colony) left by train for Agua Nueva, near Saltillo, in Coahuila State, to found the first daughter colony in Mexico. Good reports of the land had been circulated, yet when the colonists began to cultivate it, they discovered that the soil was too calcified to be productive. By June of the same year after the *Vorsteher* (chairman) had declared farming to be futile on that land, and after the sudden death of their minister Franz Loewen, the group disbanded and returned to Chihuahua. Fortunately they were able to sell the land for a fair price, so that this effort at colonization was not a complete loss. HEns

MWH (1978), 277.

Pottery. See Ceramics.

Prayer (ME IV:210). Mennonite experience of prayer has been shaped by the ethical imperative to follow Jesus at all costs. Prayer sustained the persecuted Anabaptists who cried out to God in praise and triumph as they lingered in prison or were led to execution. As they yielded themselves to God in humble trust (°°*Gelassenheit*) they prayed for strength to remain faithful rather than to be delivered from their fate.

Although Mennonites became known as the "quiet in the land" when they sought ways to avoid the sword of the state, their prayers continued to be an expression of their concern to remain faithful to God as they continued to be accountable to one another in covenant community. In their search for a faithful life-style, Mennonites rejected elaborate liturgy and dogmatic theology in favor of practices that were more simple and quiet. Initially Mennonites (Dutch) prayed silently during worship. They knelt to send up their prayers to the Almighty God as "everyone called upon the Lord without confusion or indecent noise" (Friedmann, *Piety*, 177). In time they prayed silently twice during each service, a practice some maintained until the end of the 18th c. At home also their prayers were in silence before and after meals.

Their silent prayer was enhanced by kneeling during worship, a custom many Mennonites continued into the 20th c. From Switzerland and South Germany the custom was brought to Pennsylvania. Mennonites in Russia practiced the kneeling posture as did their descendents in Canada and the United States until recent times. Kneeling is still practiced by such groups as the Amish and the Old Colony Mennonites.

As the religious life of the Mennonites became more settled they began to experience some changes. Late in the 16th c. Hans de °°Ries, a Dutch pastor, initiated audible prayers during worship. Soon others also began praying audibly and no longer kneeling in worship, a change that brought some discord. In time some also began to embrace °pietistic elements and attend primarily to the salvation of the soul (*Gottseligkeit*) rather than also to following Jesus faithfully even to the cross.

Soon there were collections of prayers written by Mennonite authors for use by Mennonite preachers in public worship or in private devotions. By the late 16th c. and the 17th c. the works of Dutch authors such as Leenaerdt °°Clock were being collected; some of these were made part of the Swiss Brethren devotional literature. The outstanding German Mennonite prayer book, *Die ernsthafte Christenpflicht* (The Committed Christian Life), published in 1739, was followed by at least 10 more editions in Europe to 1852, and at least 24 editions (to 1940) in America, where it became the prayer book of the Amish. A Swiss prayer book, *Kleines Handbüchlein* (Little Manual) had six European editions from 1786 to 1867 and two American imprints, 1835 and 1872. Dutch and German prayer collections have never been translated into English, except for excerpts from *Die ernsthafte Christenpflicht* (1982). English-speaking American Mennonites did not produce or use prayer books in public °worship and seldom in private and °family worship until recent times. Since 1925 daily prayer guides have been printed primarily to undergird °mission and °relief activities of the church.

Mennonite practice of prayer has been shaped by Mennonite understandings of the gospel which includes obedience (faithful following) and *Gelassenheit* (yieldedness, °humility). Prayer is the grateful expression of a trusting heart to the One who enables right living in the Christian community and in the world. Mennonites have reflected an "alternate understanding of the gospel—one that was more lived than spoken, more relational than dogmatic, one seeking peace rather than conquest" (Hostetler, 327). Mennonite prayer has been rooted in Mennonite life-style, a prayer of simple trust in the presence and care of God in all things.

Without the inherent formative power and continuity provided by liturgy and dogmatics, Mennonite practice of prayer has been both vulnerable and flexible as Mennonites have encountered different times and cultures. The ethical imperative to follow Jesus in simple faith has remained in Mennonite thought throughout Mennonite history. However

Mennonite understanding of this ethic and its outworking in their practice of prayer has been influenced by rationalism and pietism in 17th c. Europe, pietism in 18th c. North America, various strands of °revivalism in 19th c. Russia and North America, missions and revivalism in 20th c. North America, and more recently in a variety of expressions of Christianity among Mennonites throughout the world.

Although these changes often brought tension and sometimes °schism in the Mennonite churches, on the whole Mennonites have been able to absorb different expressions of worship and prayer based upon their sense of need at the time. Today there is no uniform practice in prayer among Mennonites but rather a kaleidoscope of expressions of members in a vast array of cultures and circumstances seeking to follow Jesus faithfully in their own setting.

In the Western world some Mennonites remain more quiet and private in their expressions; some have embraced the more emotionally expressive patterns of °charismatic renewal; some are turning to more liturgical forms of prayer and worship and to more use of °symbolic expressions to aid in their prayers. Currently there is a renewed interest among North American Mennonites in the practice of meditation and reflection as part of prayer.

The practice of prayer among Mennonites in Asia, Africa, and South America has developed into some unique forms and expressions which have emerged from cross fertilization of the gospel, as brought by the missionaries, with non-Western cultures and experience. On the whole non-Western Mennonite experience of prayer is much more spontaneous and rigorous than that of their western brothers and sisters.   MGS

Robert Friedmann, *Mennonite Piety Through the Centuries* (Goshen, Ind.: Mennonite Historical Society, 1949); Beulah S. Hostetler, *American Mennonites and Protestant Movements* (Scottdale, 1987); Theron F. Schlabach, *Gospel Versus Gospel: Mission and the Mennonite Church, 1963-1944* (Scottdale, 1980); MEA 1.

Prayer Meetings (ME IV:212). Corporate prayer was practiced by the early church (Acts 1:12-14; 2:42; 12:12). The °°Swiss Brethren movement was born in a prayer meeting in Zürich, on Jan. 21, 1525, at which time those present "bowed their knees to the most High God in heaven, and called upon Him to enable them to do His divine will and to manifest His mercy to them." Anabaptists and Mennonites have always believed in prayer and practiced it. The Mennonite Brethren, who organized in Russia in 1860, following the preaching of Edward Wüst, a German pietist, established Bible study groups and prayer cells.

It is ironic that there have been times when prayer meetings were discouraged and even forbidden by Mennonites. In 1872 the Indiana-Michigan Mennonite Conference (MC) took a position against scheduled prayer meetings because they threatened the peace, unity, and prosperity of the church. As late as 1911 the Franconia Mennonite Conference (MC) took action stating that regular prayer meetings were not approved. This regulation was apparently adopted to check the tendency toward worldliness. The "worldly" Protestant churches had prayer meetings. The Mennonites continued to practice prayer in their worship services even though there were controversies regarding audible and silent prayers, the use of prayer books, and posture in prayer.

The early 20th c. saw prayer meetings become firmly accepted and established in the churches. The meetings were often attended, however, by a minority of the membership. The gatherings were usually designed for adults and were held in church buildings or private homes on a weekday evening. Features of the meetings were Bible study, sharing of concerns, and prayer.

In recent years there has been a trend toward making the midweek meeting a family night with separate classes for age groups. The meetings are more instructional with a minimum of prayer. In other congregations the single midweek meeting has been replaced by small groups which meet in various homes, on different nights of the week, and which follow something of the regular prayer meeting pattern. In some cases religious study guides and books other than the Bible are used. Many small congregations still maintain the traditional midweek meeting with a separate meeting for children. Some congregations and church institutions issue prayer lists to be used by congregations, families and individuals. Public school programs, television, and increased community activities have militated against the midweek prayer meeting and a number of congregations have abandoned it altogether.

Corporate prayer has sometimes moved out of the meeting house to the market place, courthouse lawns, or munition plants. Prayer vigils and protests have been conducted to protest nuclear bombs and the arms race.   RRK

Prayer Veil (ME IV:212). The wearing of a °headcovering was a nearly universal practice by women in Europe and North America before the middle of the 19th c. As long as it was a general practice, especially by the Lutherans, Reformed, and Quakers, Mennonites practiced it, but wrote very little about it as a biblical teaching. For instance, the Dordrecht Confession (1632) made no reference to it. It was accepted, however, as the teaching of the Scriptures and as the long-established custom of the people and the church. But when Protestant women ceased wearing it during religious services, Mennonites, especially those within what became the Mennonite Church (MC) and closely related groups, began to write more about it and stressed the biblical basis for the practice of the veiled head. This article focuses on the Mennonite Church (MC). (For Brethren in Christ, see Wittlinger.)

Before 1900, the practice was looked upon as the practical application of Paul's teaching that the woman's head should be covered (1 Cor 11). It was not until the turn of the century that it began to be referred to as an °ordinance. Furthermore, as explained by Gingerich, when it was considered as more than a simple application of a covering, and was raised to the level of an ordinance, the names used were also gradually changed from "cap," or covering, to prayer headcovering or devotional covering. This thesis, of its elevation and name change,

is supported by Beyler, Schlabach, and others. Shetler and Shank do not address it specifically, but emphasize instead "the perennial and universal qualities of the entire passage and the need for the observance of all Christ's 'commands.'" They also suggest even broader names such as "prayer-and-prophesy veiling" and "headship veiling" as more accurate than prayer veiling or devotional covering.

In the *Manual of Bible Doctrines* (1898) Daniel °Kauffman referred to the practice of wearing the veiling as an ordinance. The designation may not have originated with him but his employment of it in an influential book was picked up and used by some of the Mennonite Church (MC) district conferences, and was shared by a majority at the adoption in 1921 of the *Christian Fundamentals* by Mennonite Church (MC) general conference at Garden City, Mo. Article 14 is entitled, "Ordinances," and states among other things, "that Christian women praying or prophesying should have their heads covered." Forty years later, in 1963, the Mennonite *Confession of Faith* (MC) was adopted at Kalona, Iowa. Article 8 includes the veiling of Christian women and identifies it as an ordinance.

It is significant that within 20 years of adopting the 1963 confession, there was a call (1983) by the moderator of the Mennonite Church (MC) general assembly for a new and "less culture-specific confession." Among the specifics mentioned was the veiling. The two decades from 1963 to 1983 were regarded, by him, as representing the equivalent of time, in terms of the rapidity of cultural change, to the 40 years from 1921 to 1963.

Based on articles in *Herald of Truth* and *Gospel Herald*, there were three surges in number of contributions devoted to the veil. The first was a minor surge at the turn of the century, at the time the concept of the veiling as an ordinance was introduced. The second was just prior to and following the adoption of the *Christian Fundamentals* in 1921. The third occurred in the two decades prior to the adoption of the 1963 confession, apparently in an attempt to "stay the trend." The number of articles in *Gospel Herald* and the numerous booklets, leaflets, and official statement papers indicate that most leaders in the 1950s still held to the practice of the veiling, but at the same time, the conviction and practice had already been seriously eroded among the laity. In the last two decades only a few articles appeared in *Gospel Herald* on the veiling. The question for the majority of Mennonites in the middle 1980s is no longer whether the veiling should be worn. Mennonites are now debating whether and in what ways women should exercise leadership, including the question of ordination.

The generation from 1955 to 1985 witnessed greater changes within the Mennonite Church (MC), in respect to the veiling, than any previous one. The 1921 *Fundamentals* and the 1963 *Confession* did not stem the trend. It appears that the conferences and fellowships which most staunchly maintain the position of the women wearing the veiling are the ones still subscribing to the Dordrecht Confession (1632), which has no reference to the veiling, either by name or Scripture reference (1 Cor 11:2-16).

There were many local variations in the style of

the veiling. Gingerich states that nearly 100 different styles were handled by the plain clothes department of the Hager and Brother store in Lancaster, Pa. The adaptations, such as the Latin American mantilla transferred to North America, and the later use of doilies and other styles, did not stem the trend toward non-wearing. The most frequent wearing in the Mennonite Church (MC) in the 1980s is found in some localities east of the Allegheny Mountains.

It also appears that in most congregations and conferences, the change in practice took place by default, rather than by some deliberate course of action. Some individuals have openly acknowledged their change of understanding and position. Among them is Paul M. Miller, whose 1956 booklet is still used by conservative groups in support of the veiling. At the conference "Conversations on Faith" (Laurelville Conference Center, Pennsylvania, 1986), while relating his "pilgrimage with the Bible," he openly shared his change of understanding. The change represented by this leader is even more accelerated and broad among the laity.

On the other hand, some conservative Mennonites not affiliated with the Mennonite Church (MC) General Assembly, and still using the Dordrecht Confession, view the veiling as an ordinance, and as a keystone in the whole structure of °nonconformity. A Rod and Staff publication maintains that once this practice falls by the way, it is only a matter of time until all clear distinctions of nonconformity will disappear.

The change of the past generation was largely a response to societal trends and pressures, two of which deserve mention. One was the impact of the feminist movement, which was partially responsible for the ending in 1969 of the nearly 1900-year-old practice of the Roman Catholic Church, which had required women to cover their heads in church. Another factor was the shift in the interpretation of 1 Cor 11:2-16. From being understood and taught as an ordinance to be practiced literally by Christian women, the passage is viewed as teaching a principle, but having been a cultural accommodation to the Corinthian church, and not a binding practice for all times.   ESY

Ross T. Bender, in *MC Yearbook* (1983), 6-8; Clayton Beyler, "Meaning and Relevance of the Devotional Covering: A Study in the Interpretation of I Corinthians 11:2-16" (ThM thesis, Southern Baptist Theological Seminary, 1954); Richard C. Detweiler, *The Christian Woman's Head-Veiling* (Scottdale, 1964); 29 pp.; Paul Erb, *South Central Frontiers* (Scottdale, 1974), 282, 312, 323, 352, 441, 467; Melvin Gingerich, *Mennonite Attire Through Four Centuries*, Publications of the Pennsylvania German Society, 4 (Breinigsville, Pa.: PGS, 1970), 109-38; C. Norman Kraus, "American Mennonites and the Bible, 1750-1950," *MQR*, 41 (1967), 309-29, reprinted in *Essays on Biblical Interpretation* (1984), 131-50; Donald B. Kraybill, "Mennonite Woman's Prayer Veiling: The Rise and Fall of a Sacred Symbol," *MQR*, 61 (1987), 298-320; J. Irvin Lehman, *A Study of the Ordinance of the Christian Woman's Veiling* (Bishop Board of Lancaster Mennonite Conference, 1956), 12 pp.; Loewen, *Confessions*; William R. McGrath, *Christian Woman's Veiling: A Biblical and Historical Review* (East Rochester, Ohio: Amish Mennonite Pub., 1986), 33; Paul M. Miller, *The Prayer Veiling* (Scottdale, 1956), 24 pp.; Merle Ruth, *The Significance of the Christian Woman's Veiling* (Rod and Staff Publishers, 1980), 23 pp.; Sanford G. Shetler, and J. Ward Shank, *Symbols of Divine Order in the Church* (Sword and Trumpet and Guidelines for Today, 1983), 109 pp.; *The Christian Woman's Veiling* (Conservative Mennonite Conference, 1979), 20 pp.; *The Devotional Covering: The Biblical Basis for This Ordinance and Ten Reasons for Its Observance*, prepared and distributed by the General Problems Committee of the Mennonite General Conference (MC) (1946), 6 pp.; *We Consider I Corinthians 11:2-16* (Executive Committee of Mennonite Conference of Ontario, 1965), 24 pp.; John C. Wenger, *The Prayer Veil in Scripture and History* (Scottdale, 1964), 29 pp.; Wittlinger, *Piety and Obedience* (1978), index.

See also Dress.

Preaching. Mennonite preaching has traditionally been characterized as hortatory, with emphasis on admonition. That concern to foster °discipleship and provide encouragement for the Christian walk continues. However, increasing attention is being given to telling the story, teaching the Bible, and equipping for mission. The prophetic character of preaching, the ways that the sermon can undergird the church's concern for social justice, is also recognized. In most Mennonite congregations, the act of preaching continues to be at the center or climax of the worship service, and is given major time. However, other forms of "sermon" are also utilized, such as readings, dialogue, drama, and use of other arts as vehicle for proclamation.

Mennonite preachers are not generally orators, but tend to be more modest in style. The pastoral care function of preaching is recognized. Forms of biblical preaching predominate, strengthened in recent years by the training in Bible school, college, or seminary for increasing numbers of pastors. Here attention is given to better hermeneutical and communication skills. The existing Mennonite seminaries provide supervised experience in preaching.

There is a growing use of *The Common Lectionary* by Mennonite pastors, as well as preaching in relationship to the church year and series of sermons. Lay participation in preaching and the issue of inclusiveness in language and gender are receiving attention.

Mennonites have, however, published very little regarding preaching or sermons in written form. In a 1987 review of the catalogued holdings of the Associated Mennonite Biblical Seminaries library at Elkhart, Ind., of 684 listings in the card file on preaching, only 10 were by Mennonite writers, and only 5 were published works.

Several studies have examined Mennonite preaching. "Mennonite Preaching, 1864-1944" a 1949 dissertation by Roy H. Umble, was a study of sermons of 11 representative ministers from 1864-1944, which included the initial transition from lay to trained ministry.

Paul M. Miller's study (1961) of the relationship between Mennonite theology and worship included a study of 21 sample congregations in the Indiana-Michigan Conference (MC). His findings indicated that the sermon was obviously regarded as the central and most essential experience in worship, that 16 of 21 sermons were expositions of Scripture, and that the majority of the sermons attempted to admonish worshipers how to live.

In 1965 Paul Erb edited a collection of 26 contemporary sermons, *From the Mennonite Pulpit* (Scottdale). The sermons submitted showed a special emphasis in the area of mission and Christian living, indicating also the desire to propogate and not only preserve faith.

A 1971 study by James Waltner on "The Authentication of Preaching in the Anabaptist-Mennonite Tradition" included a survey of preaching of the ministers in the General Conference Mennonite Church. Observations included: (1) the Scriptures are still seen as the primary source and authority for preaching, (2) the theme of discipleship in Christian living is strong, (3) in spite of the move toward a trained professional ministry there is interest to utilize aspects of lay preaching as members of the congregation share the task of proclamation, and (4) on the question of authentication, the Scriptures and the Holy Spirit are seen as central, though a sense of call confirmed by the church, and the preacher's example of following Christ in life are also factors that give authenticity to the preaching for the people.

John H. Neufeld's study in 1982 on "Preaching as Equipping for Ministry" takes seriously the understanding of the whole people of God as called to ministry in the world, and preaching as a crucial element in this equipping. This study also relates preaching to insights regarding the dynamics of adult life and faith development for adults.   JHW

Cornelius J. Dyck, "The Role of Preaching in the Anabaptist Tradition," *Menn. Life*, 17 (Jan. 1962), 21-25; Russell L. Mast, *Preach the Word* (Newton, 1968); John H. Neufeld, "Preaching as Equipping Believers for Ministry" (DMin thesis, Bethany Theological Seminary, 1982); James H. Waltner, "The Authentication of Preaching in the Anabaptist-Mennonite Tradition" (DMin diss., Claremont School of Theology, 1971); Paul M. Miller, "An Investigation of the Relationship Between Mennonite Theology and Mennonite Worship" (ThD diss., Southern Baptist Theological Seminary, 1961); LeRoy E. Kennel, *Preaching as Shared Story* (Dubuque: Kendal/Hunt, 1987); Erland Waltner, "Preaching the Bible in the Church," paper for the April, 1977, Council of Mennonite Seminaries hermeneutics consultation, available in the AMBS library, Elkhart, Ind.; Roy Umble, "Characteristics of Mennonite Preaching," *MQR*, 27 (1953), 137-42.

See also Worship, Public.

Premillennialism. See Apocalypticism; Dispensationalism.

Pride. See Humility.

Priesthood of All Believers (ME IV:1116). In contrast to the Old Testament, the New Testament does not use the term *priest* for a particular ministry among the people of God. "Priest" or "priesthood" is reserved either for the unique priesthood of Jesus Christ or for the priesthood of all Christians. The first epistle of Peter and the book of Revelation refer to the believers corporately as priests of God, as a kingdom of priests or as a royal priesthood (1 Pet 2:5, 9; Rev 1:6; 5:10; 20:6).

This imagery builds on references in the Old Testament. According to Ex 19:6 God has set the people of Israel apart, among the peoples of the world, to serve as priests. Is 61:6 envisions the day when the other peoples will recognize Israel as God's priests and ministers as well as tend their flocks and cultivate their fields. First Peter specifies the believers' priestly functions: Christians offer spiritual sacrifices and declare God's wondrous deeds among the nations. According to the book of Revelation, the Christian community has been gathered from all the peoples of the earth, purified by Christ, and made a kingdom of priests to serve God and rule on earth with Christ.

During the early centuries of Christianity, the churches reverted to having a priesthood as a mediatorial class set apart from and over the laity. The Protestant Reformers reacted against this pattern and tried to correct it. Particularly Martin Luther articulated a doctrine of the priesthood of all believers and made it a popular Protestant motto by his early essays *An Open Letter to the Christian Nobility of the German Nation, The Babylonian Captivity of the Church*, and *A Treatise on Christian Liberty*, all written in 1520.

According to Luther the priesthood of all believers has spiritual, ecclesiastical, and social implications. Socially, he accepted the context of western Christianity, where temporal rulers belong to the body of Christendom. Within the Christian social order, the rulers are ordained of God to punish evildoers and protect those who do good. Luther argues against the medieval division between the temporal and the church authorities and their separate jurisdictions in all matters. Because the German nobles too are baptized and therefore belong to the priesthood of all believers, they should exercise their vocation by correcting wrong-doing and reforming specific practices in the church without respect to pope, bishops, and priests.

Ecclesiastically, Luther rejects the clergy's monopoly on interpreting Scripture, determining correct doctrine, forgiving sins, and exercising °discipline. Because all believers are priests, all are to participate in these functions of the Christian community. Properly understood, "priests" should be ministers of the Word, who are called by the congregation to preach the Word and administer the sacraments with the consent of and in the service of the congregation.

Finally, Luther applies the term "kingdom of priests" to all believers in a spiritual sense. As many as believe on Christ are kings and priests with him. All are kings because by faith all are exalted above all things which seek to harm them and because all things are compelled to work together for their salvation. And by faith, all are priests, worthy to approach God in prayer for others and to teach one another the things of God.

Anabaptist writers in the 16th c. rarely refer to the priesthood of all believers, although they have much to say in opposition to clericalism ("anticlericalism," see °Anabaptism). °Menno Simons does use the concept in *The Christian Faith* (1541). According to Menno, believers have been made kings and priests in order to be a chosen and holy people which serves God in love. As such, believers are to publish God's power and show by their life that God has called them out of darkness into light. As kings, Christians already reign, but with the sword of God's holy Word rather than with worldly weapons. And God's Word is more powerful than wealth, armies, persecution, death, or the devil.

All believers are also priests because they have

been sanctified and are called to live as those sanctified by God. They are to sacrifice their own unrighteousness and evil lusts as well as admonish others to do the same. They are not priests who sacrifice bread and wine for the sins of the people or sing masses. Instead, they purify their own bodies daily, are willing to sacrifice themselves and to suffer for the Lord's truth, pray fervently, and give thanks joyfully (Menno, *Writings*, 326-27).

In Menno's interpretation of the church as a royal priesthood, he thus emphasizes the spiritual and moral quality of its life, its missionary witness, the self-discipline and mutual discipline of its members, its dependance on the power of God's Word, and its willingness to suffer for the gospel. He does not apply the priesthood of all believers to the temporal authorities as did Luther. And apparently neither Menno nor other Anabaptists and Mennonites of that time related the question of Christian °ministry or the appointment and °ordination of ministers in the church to the priesthood of all believers.

Since then Mennonites have usually agreed in theory, if not always in practice, that the church should be a community of believers rather than a combination of lay and clerical classes. They have usually agreed in theory, if not always in practice, that all believers are called to participate in the life and witness of the church, to share in mutual discipline and forgiveness, and to test the interpretation of Scripture and doctrine. And they have usually agreed in theory, if not always in practice, that ministers are to be appointed by the community of believers and to serve for its welfare. But these understandings have been based on other New Testament teachings and examples rather than linked with a doctrine of the priesthood of all believers.

In the 20th c. some Mennonites and non-Mennonites have made passing references to "the priesthood of all believers" to characterize some aspect of an Anabaptist (or presumably Anabaptist) view of the church or Christian life. For some, it means that every Christian is a minister (Kauffman/Harder, Yoder). For some, it signifies a process of making decisions in the church (Littell, Yoder). For one, it refers to the believer's access to God without the mediation of a priest and to being a channel of grace for other Christians (Bender). For another, it represents the Radical Reformation's rejection of dividing the church into clergy and laity (Williams). So far, Mennonites have neither developed a common understanding nor elaborated a particular view of "the priesthood of all believers."   MEM

Franklin H. Littell, *The Origins of Sectarian Protestantism* (New York: Macmillan, 1964; originally published as *The Anabaptist View of the Church*, 1952), 94; Kauffman/Harder, *Anabaptists Four C. Later* (1975), 184-85; Wim Kuipers, "Het priesterschap aller gelovigen," *Doops. Bijd.*, n.r. 6 (1980), 65-77; John Howard Yoder, *The Priestly Kingdom* (Notre Dame, Ind.: U. of Notre Dame Press, 1984) 22-23; idem, *Fullness of Christ: Paul's Revolutionary Vision of Universal Ministry* (Elgin, Ill.: Brethren Press, 1987), cf. °*Concern* pamphlet no. 17 (1969), 33-93; George H. Williams, *The Radical Reformation* (Philadelphia: Westminster, 1962); *Luther's Works*, vols. 31, 36, 44 (Philadelphia: Fortress Press, 1955-); Cyril Eastwood, *The Priesthood of All Believers: An Examination of the Doctrine From the Reformation to the Present Day* (London: Epworth Press, 1960), summarizes the doctrine according to various Protestant theologians and denominations, does not refer to Anabap-tists or Mennonites.

See also Authority; Democracy; Ordination; Polity; Worship.

Primavara Colony, Palmeira near Curitiba, Brazil. See Witmarsum Colony.

Primitive Christianity. See Restitutionism.

Prince Edward Island. See Atlantic Provinces, Canada.

Private Christian Schools, United States. From the beginning of settlements in America, Mennonites have been involved in private schooling. The earliest schools were elementary level. °Secondary schools, often referred to as academies, began to appear in Mennonite communities in the late 19th c. Some were affiliated with a developing Mennonite college. Examples were the school developed at °°Freeman, S.D. (1900); °°Hesston, Ks. (1909); and Harrisonburg, Va. (°°Eastern Mennonite School, 1917). This early growth period for Mennonite private schools was parallel to the movement into missions and external service activities.

Two themes, in juxtaposition, provided the purposes for Mennonite elementary and secondary schools from the late 19th c. through the early 1960s: emergence from isolation and preservation of a way of life. The former developed from a felt need to be better prepared for serving in the church's expanding °missions and °service efforts. The latter took shape in response to increasing threats to the church's accepted life-style (°nonconformity). By 1900 American youth were attending the nation's growing number of high schools and Mennonite youth were entering °public schools in increasing numbers. Of those Mennonites who completed high school, a few were entering colleges and universities, mostly other than Mennonite institutions. In these public school environments, Mennonite youth were being exposed to the mores and life-styles of the dominant youth culture which provided significant threat to the longstanding traditions of the church. Both themes took further shape during World Wars I and II and the years immediately following. These events were significant influences in bringing Mennonites from isolation into contact with the outside world.

How was the church to respond? From the early 1940s through the early 1960s the above developments provided the impetus for Mennonites to establish significantly more elementary and secondary schools. High schools emerged in most population concentrations of Old Mennonites (MC). Of the 10 current members of the Mennonite Secondary Education Council (MSEC), all but one were established during these two decades. Most of the current members of the Mennonite Elementary Education Council (MEEC) were also established during this period, but they were heavily concentrated in the Mennonite population centers of the eastern United States.

The differing regional and denominational patterns for establishing Mennonite schools are interesting. Whereas both elementary and secondary schools developed side-by-side in the eastern centers, west of the Allegheny Mountains the new schools were predominately high schools. Moreover, most of the schools developed after 1940 were among the Mennonite Church (MC) and Amish populations. Why these differing patterns?

Several explanations are worth considering. First, the decades of the 1940s and 50s marked the beginning of the end of nearly a century of major emphasis on Mennonite conformity in external matters, such as °dress, hairstyles, participation in athletics and school °dances, and attendance at °motion picture theaters. Moreover, militarism was running rampant in the public schools. That public schools in America have served as the most dominant influence in developing conformity among middle and late adolescents is well documented in the educational literature. By 1950 many Mennonite youth were attending and graduating from high school. Mennonite schools as an alternative to the public schools were envisioned as a vehicle for assisting congregations to combat the enormous pressure for conformity to the world the young people were experiencing. The emphasis on the Mennonite high schools over the elementary schools emerged because the most apparent breaches of life-style patterns were occurring during middle and late adolescence. Almost all of the statements of purposes of the Mennonite high schools refer in one way or another to the concern for preserving the accepted life-style patterns. Those Mennonite groups less threatened by life-style changes also had less reason for establishing private schools. This explains the significantly less interest among the General Conference Mennonites in developing high schools during this period.

Second, in each region Mennonites were influenced by the local public schooling patterns. In the East, for example, the private school system predates the public school system at all levels. The latter half of the 19th c. was a period of rapid growth of public high schools, which coincided with the settlement of many communities in the Northwest and the Plains States by Mennonites and others. Mennonites became deeply involved in these local public schools. Many held positions on school boards or became teachers and administrators. These rural communities were settled largely by Protestants and the Mennonites did not experience the alienation that resulted from the religious diversity of eastern population centers a century earlier. The newcomers west of the Alleghenies were comfortable with and committed to public education. When the retreat from participation in public high schools came about in the 1940s over the threat to traditional life-styles, church leaders and parents apparently did not perceive the public elementary schools to pose the same level of threat. Even today, in Mennonite communities east of the Alleghenys a larger percentage of the Mennonite population participates in Mennonite high schools than is true of the rest of the country. Several eastern high schools enroll over 50 percent of the local Mennonite population whereas elsewhere the range is from 20 to 30 percent.

Since 1961 only a few Mennonite schools have been established. Attendance continued to increase in the Mennonite schools as the postwar "baby boom" generation moved through the school years. Enrollment entered a period of decline in the late 1960s and early 1970s, and since then has gradually increased.

Among the Amish, however, the private school movement followed a different pattern. Not until the emergence of the movement to consolidate small rural public schools in the late 1950s and early 1960s did the Amish establish many independent schools. So long as the public schools were primarily small rural schools, the Amish were generally content to send their children to these community-based schools where frequently the population consisted largely of Amish children. As consolidation brought together students from many sectors of the community, the Amish no longer felt comfortable in these settings. In the larger Amish settlements of Holmes Co., Ohio; LaGrange Co., Ind.; and Lancaster Co., Pa., only a small minority of the Amish children attend the public schools (1987).

The governance patterns for Mennonite schools are primarily of two types: conference schools and patron schools. Unlike the colleges and seminaries, the Mennonite Board of Education (MC) does not govern any of the high school and elementary schools. The majority of the high schools are owned by regional conference bodies, whereas the elementary schools are predominantly patron schools. In both governance types, school boards of 6 to 12 members direct the work of the staff.

The Mennonite Secondary Education Council (MSEC) and the Mennonite Elementary Education Council (MEEC), both with precursors dating to the 1940s, evolved into their present (1987) forms in the 1970s. The programs of MSEC are more developed than those of the MEEC, although the programs of the MEEC are expanding while those of the MSEC have stabilized. Both councils have focused on in-service education for administrators. The MSEC also includes in-service activities for board members and teachers. The Mennonite Church's Board of Education (MBE) and the MSEC have cooperated in identifying joint priorities and in providing staff assistance for achieving these common goals. In 1987, the MBE held a similar planning session to identify joint goals with the MEEC. Whether these planning initiatives will lead to employment of staff members sufficient to meet the joint priorities remains to be seen. Both councils are beginning to develop curriculum for Bible teaching.

Mennonite schools secure their teaching materials from a variety of publishing sources, including nonsectarian, mainline denominational, evangelical, and fundamentalist. Although several Mennonite-related private publishing groups are preparing materials focused on the Mennonite private school market, none has been successful in making a major inroad on the market. Rod and Staff and Christian Light publishers are two examples. In staff development materials, the *Blackboard Bulletin* has had significant impact on teaching in the Amish schools (°Pathway Publishers). Neither the efforts of the publishing houses in Scottdale, Pa. (MC), or Newton, Ks. (GCM), has been successful in developing sufficient interest in Mennonite schools to warrant publishing comprehensive curriculum materials, although Mennonite

Publishing House at Scottdale is discussing involvement in the elementary school Bible curriculum described above.

From meager beginnings, Mennonite schools have developed into first-class operations. Their students are among those best prepared in the church for further study in high schools and colleges. Providing adequate funding for the Mennonite schools continues to be a struggle. School facilities are generally not as elaborate as are those of the public schools in the same communities, but are in most cases adequate. Although the Mennonite schools struggled in their earlier years to attract competent teachers, in the late 1980s the teachers are equally prepared and on the whole probably more competent than the public school teachers. Most teach with credentials issued by the states in which the Mennonite schools operate. The same is true of the school administrators.   OY

Noah Hershberger, *A Struggle To Be Separate: A History of the Ohio Amish Parochial School Movement* (Orrville, Ohio: published privately, 1985).

See also Amish; Bergthal Mennonites; Church of God in Christ Mennonite (Holdeman); Eastern Pennsylvania Mennonite Church; Fellowship Churches; Socialization. See articles on most groups listed in Conservative Mennonites article and articles on individual Amish settlements.

Private Worship. See Worship, Private.

Privileges (Privilegia) (ME IV:220). Since the late 16th c. Mennonites in various countries have received official documents from rulers or governments defining their rights or privileges with respect to specific issues, usually including release from military service and from the swearing of oaths. Since the late 19th c., schools, language, °mutual (aid) insurance, and the Mennonite °°inheritance system have been added to the contents of a requested *Privilegium*. The following specific documents should be added to the list provided in ME IV:

(l) Russia, Mar. 3, 1788, Tsarina °°Catherine II; printed in D. H. Epp, *Die Chortitzer Mennoniten* (Odessa, 1889), 24ff.

(m) Canada, Aug. 13, 1873, Order-in-Council P.C. 959; printed in William Schroeder, *The Bergthal Colony* (Winnipeg, 1974, 1986), appendix C.

(n) British Honduras (Belize), Dec. 18, 1957, Governor Sir Colin H. Thornley; printed in H. Leonard Sawatzky, *They Sought A Country: Mennonite Colonization in Mexico* (Berkeley: U. of California Press, 1971), appendix.

(o) Bolivia, 1930; renewed and slightly revised on Mar. 16, 1962, Decree no. 6030, President Victor Paz Estensoro; English translation printed in James Walter Lanning, "The Old Colony Mennonites of Bolivia: A Case Study" (MSc thesis, Texas A. and M. University., 1971), appendix B. The Bolivian privileges were abolished on Dec. 30, 1975, and almost totally reinstated Mar. 27, 1985.

Swiss and German Mennonite immigrants to British North America in the 17th and 18th c., and Mennonites coming from Russia to the United States in the 19th c., did not obtain special privileges.

Refugees from the Soviet Union settling in Brazil in 1930 failed to obtain a *Privilegium*. The Mennonite request for alternatives to military service, presented to the Brazilian government, Mar. 28, 1979, was again unsuccessful. Mennonites settling in Argentina beginning in 1986 also did not have a *Privilegium.*

Descendants of the Mennonites who arrived in Russia between 1788 and 1820 came to consider a *Privilegium* almost as an essential condition of settlement. Thus they had a strong tendency to consider emigration whenever key elements of privileges granted appeared to be threatened. The 1873 delegates sent by the Molotschna colony to explore settlement possibilities in North America were explicitly instructed on four points to be assured in an agreement with the host country. Although the 11,000 Russian Mennonites who emigrated to the United States in the 1870s were unable to obtain a *Privilegium* from the American government, the 7,000 going to Canada received the desired guarantees in a Cabinet order (see *m* above). Descendants of the latter made the successful negotiation of a *Privilegium* a necessary prerequisite in their migrations to Mexico, Paraguay, Bolivia, and Belize.

Many of the *Privilegia*, especially in recent times, are more a defining of mutual rights and obligations than the granting of special privileges. Generally they facilitate the maintenance of compact group settlement, thereby making it possible for local self-government to perpetuate effectively a number of peculiarly Mennonite °communal arrangements. These, however, were just as effectively maintained by other groups, such as Old Order Amish and Old Order Mennonites in the United States and eastern Canada, who have no *Privilegium.*

Special privileges were not an unmixed blessing. While they fostered a stance of separation from the world by the defined separation from the host society (°nonconformity), they also discouraged the developing of a sense of responsibility towards those outside the privileged community. The granting of special privileges to select groups was sometimes resented by members of the host society, especially in times of national crisis. Since similar resentment was directed also at immigrant groups who did not have a *Privilegium*, but who stood out from the rest of society through differences in customs, language, and culture, it is difficult to determine to what extent these negative feelings were caused by the special privileges.   AE

J. Winfield Fretz, "A Visit to the Mennonites in Bolivia," *Menn. Life*, 15 (Jan. 1960), 13-17, at 15; Leonhard Sudermann, *Eine Deputationsreise von Russland nach Amerika* (Elkhart: Mennonitische Verlagshandlung, 1897), 10; Peter Pauls, Jr., *Mennoniten in Brasilien: Gedenkschriften zum 50 Jahr=Jubilaeum ihrer Einwanderung* (Witmarsum, 1980), 78-80; John B. Toews, *Czars, Soviets, and Mennonites* (Newton, 1982), esp. 51ff; Peter P. Klassen, *Die Mennoniten in Paraguay* (Bolanden-Weierhof: Menn. Geschichtsverein, 1988), 40-62; W. Mannhardt, *Die Wehrfreiheit der Altpreußischen Mennoniten* (Marienburg, 1863).

See also Church-State Relations; Migration.

Professions. Lawyers, professors, doctors, and ministers have traditionally been considered professionals. In recent years, however, a multitude of other °occupations have vied for professional status. The unique traits of a profession are typically used to differentiate professions from other occupations. Factors such as extensive training, specialized knowledge, rigorous standards for admission and practice, a high degree of internalized self-control, an orientation to serving the public good, legal recognition through licensure and certification, as well as membership in and control by a professional organization were deemed the distinguishing characteristics that set professions off from other occupations. The proliferation in recent years of occupations that in one way or another fit these characteristics has shifted the definition from a trait approach to one that emphasizes the social power of a profession. Occupations, according to the power perspective, cannot be neatly sorted into professional and nonprofessional categories but can be viewed on a continuum ranging from low to high power. Professions lie at the high power end of the spectrum since they exhibit two distinguishing characteristics: monopoly and dominance.

The power approach focuses on the extent to which an occupation controls the nature of its own work and that of other occupations. A profession, in short, tries to gain a monopoly on a segment of the labor market for its members and then controls who gets into the profession, how they are trained, the conditions of their work, who they work for, under what type of regulations they work, and how much they are paid. In addition, a profession tries to free itself from the control of other occupations and indeed attempts to dominate the work of other work groups. Physicians for example rank high on the professional spectrum since they control the nature and conditions of their work and dominate related occupations—medical technicians, nurses, physical therapists, and pharmacists. Although the power perspective is widely used in analyzing professions it does not provide discrete categories for labeling occupations as professions.

Prior to World War II Mennonites were conspicuously absent from many of the professions. A variety of reasons accounted for their aversion to the professions. Anticlerical attitudes and a scathing critique of professional pastors at the outset of the Anabaptist movement in the 16th c. became embedded in Mennonite thinking for several centuries. The intense persecution in Europe created a sectarian mentality of suspicion and caution toward the dominant culture, a mentality that was reinforced by a separatist and rural social life in many Mennonite congregations throughout the 19th c. (°°nonconformity). Professions were viewed as worldly pursuits of power, prestige, and status—at the very center of the worldly social system—and thus incongruent with the quiet values of °humility and separation that were the hallmark of Mennonite life. Vigorous teaching of the church against the use of °law for resolving conflicts resulted in a particularly stern rejection of the practice of °law as an acceptable Mennonite occupation.

Thus, well into the 20th c. the rural, and separatist subculture that undergirded Mennonite life was not oriented toward the professions. Teaching and °medicine with their emphasis on humanitarian ser-

vice were the first professions to become widely accepted among Mennonites. Since World War II Mennonites have moved into virtually the full spectrum of professional life propelled by a variety of factors. Involvement in °alternative service during World War II (°°Civilian Public Service) and in the following years of military draft placed many Mennonites into urban areas and exposed them to professional life, especially to medical occupations. The decline in farming (agriculture), the spread of °urbanization, the rise in education and the cultural assimilation (°acculturation) of many Mennonite groups in the last half of the 20th c. nudged many members into professions. Amish and Old Order Mennonite groups that continue to reject higher education and embrace an agrarian life-style have little if any involvement in the professions.

In a national study of five Mennonite groups in 1972 Kauffman and Harder discovered that 27 percent of the employed men and 38 percent of the employed women were involved in professional and technical occupations. This compared to 14 and 15 percent respectively for males and females in the United States at large. Thus by 1972 Mennonites had not only entered the professions but had penetrated them more heavily than the population at large. In some communities the transition from plow to profession was rapid. In 1974 Hostetler and his colleagues reported a study of Mennonite high school students in the Lancaster community where 2 percent of their grandfathers and 9 percent of their fathers were involved in professions, but 47 percent of the students aspired to a professional job—identical to the responses of non-Mennonite students in the same community. Thus in a matter of two generations Mennonites were matching the level of professionalism in the larger society. Yoder, in a study of the Mennonite Church (MC) in 1982, reported that 16 percent of the employed men and 27 percent of the employed women were working in professional and technical occupations compared to 15 and 16 percent respectively for the United States labor force (Yoder, MC Census). The high number of employed Mennonite women working as professionals likely results from their employment as teachers, nurses, and social workers, occupations congruent with the Mennonite °service ethic. In the last third of the 20th c. Mennonites were entering virtually all types of professions. The 1976 Mennonite Business and Professional Directory reported the following number of persons in selected professions: lawyers (33), physicians and surgeons (145), professors (120), psychiatrists (5), and psychologists (12). Entertainment, °politics, and the ministry were not listed as occupations in the directory. Mennonite congregations in recent years have increasingly employed professional, seminary-trained pastors in a complete turnabout from the anticlericalism of the early days of the Anabaptist movement (°pastoral education). There are two notable trends in the Mennonite exodus from the farm. Many Mennonites have gone directly from plow to profession thus bypassing a whole array of blue collar occupations. The service orientation of the professions as well as the independence and autonomy of the farmer likely contributed to this frequent mobility from farm to profession. As they moved into the professional world, Mennonites have organized specialized professional groups to provide fellowship, community and identity. Mennonite professional associations have been organized by physicians, lawyers, and °mental health professionals, to name just a few.

DBK

Donald B. Kraybill and Phyllis Pellman Good, eds., *Perils of Professionalism* (Scottdale, 1982); Eliot Freidson, *The Professions and their Prospects* (Beverly Hills, Cal.: Sage Publication, 1973); *Doctoring Together* (NY: Elsevier, 1975); Student and Young Adult Services, *Professionalism: Faith, Ethics, and Christian Identity* (Elkhart, Ind.: Mennonite Board of Missions, 1978); *Conflict in the World of Professions* (Elkhart, Ind.: Mennonite Board of Missions, 1979); Kauffman/Harder, *Anabaptists Four C. Later* (1975), 60-61; Yoder, *MC Census* (1985); *Mennonite Business and Professional People's Directory 1976* (Mt. Pleasant, Pa.: Mennonite Business Associates, 1976); John A. Hostetler, Gertrude Enders Huntington, and Donald B. Kraybill, *Cultural Transmission and Instrumental Adaptation to Social Change: Lancaster Mennonite High School in Transition,* Final Report (Washington, D.C.: U.S. Department of Health, Education and Welfare, 1974), 110-111; E. E. Miller, "Opportunities in the Professions," *Chr. Living* (Sept. 1956), 16-17; Harry Lowen, ed., *Mennonite Images: Historical, Cultural, and Literary Essays* (Winnipeg: Hyperion, 1980), 137ff.

See also Eastern Pennsylvania Mennonite Church; Education; Industrialization; Nursing; Work Ethic.

Property is a right or a complex of rights, of the person or social units involved, to possess, use, and dispose of economic goods of scarce value. The object involved may be tangible, such as food, clothing, and shelter required for life; a productive resource, such as land; or the creation of law, such as a patent or a copyright. Property rights are defined by social practice; these practices are recognized or established by government.

Social practices vary among societies and over time. As a result, the concepts of property and property rights have evolved. The Anabaptist and subsequent Mennonite concepts of property are rooted firmly in a particular understanding of the Bible, but they are also products of the °social, °economic, and °political systems in which the Anabaptists and Mennonites have found themselves.

The biblical basis for the Anabaptist concept of property is primarily the Old Testament. There, private ownership of property, including the passage of heritage, was accepted; but such ownership was in the nature of a trust from God. This stewardship concept modified property rights with specific responsibilities and duties in the use of property when in relationship with other persons. Also, the Year of the °Jubilee placed limits on the transfer and concentration of property, assuring each family some access to the most important productive resource, land.

The New Testament did not change this concept of property. Jesus did not see property per se as evil; property was judged on the basis of its effect on people. Jesus placed more emphasis on duties and responsibilities associated with property than on the rights associated with ownership of property. There are several expressions of communism in the New Testament, but the members stressed love more than equality.

A strong challenge to the biblical view of property was Roman law which has become the basis for a number of legal systems, including the modern British property law tradition. The Roman jurists set law free from religious imperatives of what ought-to-be, placing it on a more impersonal basis, which enabled the scientific development of law. They moved away from either the clan or the family as the basic social unit, and defined individual rights. With reference to property, individual rights of ownership replaced existing communal rights. Contract law was developed as a corollary, which included the freedom to dispose of property owned by the individual. These property rights were rather absolute and rigid, favoring particular classes within Roman society.

During the first several centuries the church attempted to maintain the biblical position, especially against the excesses of Roman law as applied to the ownership of land. The obligation of the wealthy land owners to the poor and the landless was stressed. By the time of Ambrose (339-97), charity had been elevated from a mere gift by the wealthy to a right to be claimed by the poor. The emergence of a monastic movement was inspired, in part, by the abuses of private ownership of property, especially land.

A positive, Christian view of property was formulated by Thomas Aquinas (1225-74). Combining Aristotle's ideas on property with the biblical tradition, Aquinas justified private property on the grounds of increased productivity (people take better care of that which is their own); social peace (people will work more and fight less if individual property rights are defined), and philanthropy. These property rights were not absolute—the owners had a duty to share the use of their possessions with others and they might be regulated by government. Capital goods had not become important productive assets, so the charging of interest (usury) was condemned. Communal property represented an ideal, reserved for those who desired to live a life of perfection.

Roman law and the church provide the larger context for the Reformation. The immediate origins of the Anabaptist position was the unique Germanic views of property. The primary social and economic unit was the village community (*Genossenschaft*), a virtually self-sufficient group of households with a strong sense of community, in which the welfare of the larger social unit took priority over the individual. Property rights were relative and changing, with different levels of rights applying to different objects, e.g., consumer goods versus productive assets. The laws tended to show a greater concern for personal rights than for property rights. Temporary possession of a good, solely for the purpose of exchanging it for private gain, was hardly tolerated within the community.

Many aspects of the Anabaptist concepts of property reflected this immediate and larger social environment. A high priority was placed on the welfare of the members of the immediate community; property rights were not absolute, stewardship in the use of property was advocated; and both the charging of usury and mere trading for personal gain were condemned. Some of the unique contributions of Anabaptists to the existing Germanic and Catholic traditions included: (1) effective constraints on consumption, as shown in their critiques of the life-styles of the Protestant clergy; (2) the practice of °mutual aid, so that no one had to beg; (3) voluntary membership and participation in the religious community; and (4) defining normative practices for the members of their religious community only, versus the more universal ethic of both the Catholic and Protestant churches.

The attitude and expression of yieldedness (*Gelassenheit*), featured prominently in the spiritual life of the Anabaptists and, subsequently, the Mennonites. A dependence on God and on the Christian community for all aspects of security in the face of illness, imprisonment, death, or natural disasters, served to foster °spiritual life. Accumulation of °wealth or the expression of self through conspicuous consumption served to reduce the dependency on God and each other and was disruptive to the well-being of the church community. Such expressions of pride could be punished with a ban. The Hutterites were the one exception; they took the concept of *Gelassenheit* further, by extending the practice of communism beyond consumption to productive assets as well.

In large part because of extensive persecution, Mennonites became essentially a rural people, involved in farming and village crafts. The concept of *Gelassenheit* remained important, expressing itself in a rural way of life. A simple life-style, with effective constraints on personal consumption, remained characteristic of Mennonites until °urbanization became important: during the early part of the 20th c. in parts of Europe and after World War II in North America. On these two continents, effective constraints on consumption are now evident only among such minorities as the Amish, the Old Order Mennonites, the Old Colony Mennonites, the Church of God in Christ Mennonite (Holdeman), and some intentional communities. Similarly, the various Mennonite settlements in Latin America continue to reflect the rural way of life, including some constraints on consumption and °cooperative (*Genossenschaft*) economic organization.

Even though Mennonites were primarily a rural people, ownership of °land does not appear to have been a significant property issue within the community. Because of rapid population growth, various Mennonite groups experienced overall land constraints and had significant numbers of °°landless within their midst. This problem was addressed through community efforts to obtain more land, e.g., establishing daughter colonies in Russia or various migrations to countries with available land. The problem of landlessness within the community does not appear to have been attributed to a wealthy few having taken private control of the available land.

The emigration of Mennonites to North America brought them under the British view of property, which was based on Roman Law as modified by the unique contribution of John Locke (1632-1704). Locke identified property as inherent to the output of one's labor (people have property in their own life), and the other resources utilized (mixed with one's own labor) to produce with one's labor. Locke then derived political rights from these personal rights to one's own property, i.e., government may

not touch private property (e.g., levy taxes), without the consent of the property owners through their representatives. As Locke's concern was the definition of political limits, he had an absolute view of property, without effective constraints, which allows for vast differences in wealth.

The combination of the British view of property and the productive effects of the Industrial Revolution eventually eroded the ability of the Mennonite churches to constrain individual consumption. With this breakdown, *Gelassenheit* proved unacceptable as well. The majority of the North American and European Mennonites combined private °insurance, °pensions, and savings with emerging public programs to provide protection for their families against natural °disasters, unemployment, ill health, and old age. Those who could not afford private protection had to be content with available public programs. Poverty, especially for the chronically ill, the unemployed and some of the elderly, has become evident among Mennonites. Some mutual aid is still practiced at the local level and some mutual aid has been institutionalized within the larger Mennonite church. These supplement existing private and public programs and are run on a commercial but nonprofit basis.

The contemporary high standard of living is the product of both extensive use of capital as a productive asset and the role of knowledge as a source of technology. Given the role of both physical and human capital, borrowing money has become productive and the condemnation of charging interest has ceased to be relevant. Associated with these important roles of capital and technology has been the evolution of corporations as the primary institution which holds ownership of vast quantities of both natural resources and productive capital assets. The corporation, as if it were an individual person, can use the combined Roman and Lockean view of property to its advantage. Within the large corporation, the individual shareholder is effectively divorced from either managing the corporation's property or from exercising stewardship over how the corporation's property is used. The church's justification for individual ownership of property on productivity grounds as well as the individual's responsibility to exercise stewardship over how the property is used are both lost.

The extensive involvement of Mennonites in all aspects of society—as successful farmers and business persons, as corporation shareholders, as professionals, as holders of knowledge, and as consumers—has largely eroded the fundamental Anabaptist concept of a unique pattern of life that is intended to be normative for the members of the community only. Rather, the majority of the Mennonites have been caught up in the Protestant ethic that is now normative in the larger society.

Mennonite scholars are distinctly critical of the ethos of wealth, competition, and consumerism that characterizes the pattern of life in developed countries. Along with other Protestant and Catholic scholars, as well as °socialists and °Marxists, there is a call for justice. Mutual aid is advocated, but profit-sharing or other modes of organizing production are the distinct exception in Mennonite practice.

Charity is widely practiced, especially through institutions such as Mennonite Central Committee, °Mennonite Economic Development Associates and the various °mission boards, but the underlying causes of persistent poverty are rarely addressed in a creative manner.

The ready acceptance of the standards of consumption of the larger society limits the Mennonite church's ability to critique either the concentration of power in corporations, including the misuse of that power, or the significant disparities in income and wealth within our countries and among countries. Indeed, the Mennonite churches have not been able to address significant disparities in income and wealth among members within a congregation or among the different Mennonite churches.

HRe

Charles Avila, *Ownership: Early Christian Teaching* (Maryknoll: Orbis Books, 1983); Ernst Correll, "The Sociological and Economic Significance of the Mennonites as a Culture Group in History," *MQR*, 16 (1942), 161-66; Donald F. Durnbaugh, ed., *Every Need Supplied: Mutual Aid and Christian Community in the Free Churches, 1525-1675* (Philadelphia: Temple U. Press, 1974); J. Winfield Fretz, "Brotherhood and the Economic Ethic of the Anabaptists," in *Recovery*, 194-201; idem, "Mennonites and their Economic Problems," *MQR*, 14 (1940), 195-213; Jane C. Getz, "The Economic Organization and Practices of the Old Order Amish of Lancaster, Pennsylvania," *MQR*, 20 (1946), 53-80, 98-127; Frank Grace, *The Concept of Property in Modern Christian Thought* (Urbana: U. of Illinois Press, 1953); Lewis H. Haney, *History of Economic Thought*, 4th ed. (New York: Macmillan Co., 1949); Guy F. Hershberger, *The Way of the Cross in Human Relations* (Scottdale, 1958); Walter Klaassen, "The Nature of the Anabaptist Protest," *MQR*, 45 (1971), 291-311; Peter J. Klassen, *The Economics of Anabaptism: 1525-1560* (The Hague: Mouton and Co., 1964); Carl Kreider, "Economic Program for the Mennonite Community of Tomorrow," *MQR*, 19 (1945), 143-55: idem, *The Christian Entrepreneur* (Scottdale, 1980); Joseph C. Liechty, "Humility: The Foundation of Mennonite Religious Outlook in the 1860s," *MQR*, 54 (1980), 5-31; Doris Janzen Longacre, *Living More with Less* (Scottdale, 1980); Calvin Redekop, "The Old Colony: An Analysis of Group Survival," *MQR*, 40 (1966), 190-211; Ronald J. Sider, *Rich Christians in an Age of Hunger: A Biblical Study* (New York: Paulist Press, 1977), ch. 5; Donald Sommer, "Peter Rideman and Menno Simons on Economics," *MQR*, 28 (1954), 205-23; Roy Vogt, "Economic Questions and the Mennonite Conscience," in *Call to Faithfulness: Essays in Canadian Mennonite Studies*, ed. Henry Poettcker and Rudy A. Regehr (Winnipeg: CMBC, 1972), 157-66; idem, "Mennonite Studies in Economics," *JMS*, 1 (1983), 64-78.

See also Capitalism; Nonconformity.

Prophecy. The prophetic tradition in Israel stretches all the way from Genesis (20:7) to Malachi (4:5). The Hebrew word for prophet (*nabi'*) appears more than 300 times in the Old Testament and is applied to a wide range of characters. Etymologically *nabi'* means "one who is called," but by usage it came to mean a spokesman or proclaimer. In earlier days the prophet was also called a seer (*hozeh* or *ro'eh*) (1 Sm 9:9), although all three terms continued to be used interchangeably (1 Chr 29:29).

Because the prophet had a special relationship with God, in the Bible he is called "a man of God" (1 Kgs 12:22; 13:1, 26). As God's messengers the prophets are also known as "God's servants" (Jer 7:25; 44:4). Sometimes the prophet is called "the man of the Spirit" (Hos 9:7:), because he was inspired by the Spirit of God. Prophets are also known as "God's messengers" (Hg 1:13; Mal 3:1).

The Old Testament reveals great diversity in the personality and function of the prophet. All true prophets, however, had the conviction that they were called of God to proclaim his word, although relatively few described their private encounters with God.

Of the hundreds of prophets in ancient Israel (including prophetesses such as Miriam, Deborah, Huldah) only a few recorded their oracles (or had them recorded). Most of them, such as Elijah and Elisha, were "oral" prophets. We know more about what these prophets did than what they said.

Many of the prophets were related to Israel's cult (worship practices). Samuel, for example, but also the later prophets Ezekiel and Jeremiah and others, were associated with the priesthood (Ez 1:1; Jer 1:1). The temple provided a natural center for prophets to exercise their prophetic gifts.

Some prophets could be viewed as court prophets because they conveyed messages from Yahweh to the reigning monarchs. Sometimes rulers even sought out prophets to hear a word from the Lord. However, with the threat of Assyria, which conquered Israel in 721 B.C., and of Babylonia, which conquered Judah in 586 B.C., there appears to have been a shift to the "free prophets," who were not necessarily related to cult or court. From the 8th c. on we have prophets like Amos and Hosea in Israel, and Micah and Isaiah in Judah, who acted quite independently of existing authority structures. As with cult and court prophets, these "free prophets" were often consulted by those desiring a word from God, even though the inquirers did not always appreciate the response they received. Some of these "troublers of Israel" (1 Kgs 18:17) were severely persecuted by those who objected to their messages.

God's prophets often found themselves in opposition not only to the ruling powers, but also to the "false prophets." The mark of a true prophet was that his word was fulfilled (Dt 18:22; 1 Kgs 22:28; Is 30:8). False prophets sometimes promised salvation because that was the message their audiences wanted to hear (Jer 28:8; 1 Kgs 22). They were accused of proclaiming their own dreams and not God's word (Jer 14:14; 23:25-28). Instead, the true prophet was described as one who had been given a divine commission and lived in keeping with the covenant stipulations laid down by Moses (Dt 13:1-3).

As portrayed in Scripture the prophets received their messages directly from Yahweh. "The word of the Lord came to me," was a standard introduction to prophetic utterances. Sometimes they received their messages in the form of "visions" (Is 1:1). At other times they simply felt the hand of the Lord upon them (Ez 3:14; 8:1; Is 8:11). Revelatory trances were at times attended by ecstatic elements which strike modern readers as strange. Prophetic ecstasy as such, however, was nowhere condemned (1 Sam 10:5; 19:24; 1 Kgs 18:21; Nm 11:24-30).

Although the prophets received their messages from God, they put their own stamp on these messages. The form of their oracles reflects not only the personalities of the various prophets, but also the times in which they spoke, the issues to which they spoke, and the audiences they addressed.

A great variety of literary forms are found in the

prophetic writings. The most common type of prophetic oracle is the announcement of judgment on Israel or on the surrounding nations. Less common, but also very prominent, is the promise of salvation to those who repent and return to the covenant. Blessings or curses are contingent on how the hearers respond to the warnings, the exhortations, and the promises of God given by the prophets.

At times the prophet would carry out a symbolic act in order to attract the attention of the people. He might wear a yoke or break a flask or make iron horns to symbolize his message. Some prophets even gave their own children symbolic names in order to get their message across to Israel.

A number of prophets who spoke oracles of doom on a wicked nation looked beyond judgment to a brighter day. They looked forward to the time when God would establish a new covenant with a cleansed people of God (Jer 31). This hope was seen by New Testament writers as having been fulfilled in Christ.

The prophets addressed the needs of the people in their own generation. They sought to enforce the requirements of the Mosaic covenant, promising blessing for faithfulness and curses for disobedience. They were not simply radical social reformers or avant-garde thinkers, for they called people back to the Mosaic covenant, which always remains normative for the prophets.

In the Bible the prophets firmly believed that God is the Lord of history and so their messages embraced not only the present but also the future. The predictive element, however, usually concerned the immediate future of the nation rather than the distant. Modern readers, therefore, should not look for a timetable of future events in the prophetic books.

In the light of the Christ event, however, the writers of the New Testament often saw deeper meanings in what the Old Testament prophets said (Heb 1:1,2). But even the so-called messianic passages (such as Is 7:14) had relevance for the original audience.

During the intertestamental period, when it was believed that authentic prophecy had ceased, a new form of literature appeared, known as °apocalyptic. Although it grew out of prophecy and has many resemblances with prophecy, it was a distinct genre. The prophets were concerned about the present; the apocalypticists about the future. The apocalyptic writers (and they were writers not speakers) saw no hope within history. The world had gone completely bad and there was hope only beyond history. Apocalyptic is basically pessimistic as far as life in this world is concerned.

Apocalyptic, in contrast to prophecy, is also quite esoteric. Only a select few can understand what the writer is saying. The messages are not addressed to the people as a whole, calling them to repentance, but only to the wise. Also, much of the imagery of apocalyptic literature is different from that of prophecy. There is a heavy emphasis on symbols and numbers. One might call it "cartoon" language. Moreover, the apocalyptic books are pseudonymous. They are written in the name of some great worthy of Israel's sacred past.

Apocalyptic literature is crisis literature. It is born out of despair. One simply hopes for God's intervention in the end. It lacks the ethical emphasis found in the prophets, where obedience to the message of the prophet holds the promise of God's favor and of hope.

New Testament. With the coming of the forerunner, John the Baptist, authentic prophecy was reborn (Lk 1:76). Jesus, however, is portrayed in Scripture as the prophet par excellence—the prophet like Moses (Mt 21:11; Acts 3:22). Like the prophets of old he has received a divine commission and speaks God's word with authority, calling Israel to repentance. That he is more than a Prophet goes without saying. In contrast to Old Testament prophets, Jesus introduces the age of fulfillment. In him many of the hopes and dreams of the Old Testament prophets were fulfilled. The prophetic message of Jesus focuses on the inbreaking of the °kingdom of God and the formation of a new people of God in continuity with the saving purposes of God proclaimed by the Old Testament prophets.

Jesus expects the continuation of the prophetic ministry among his followers (Mt 10:41; Lk 11:49). Through the gift of the Spirit of the risen and exalted Lord, the gift of prophecy has been given to the Christian community (Acts 2:18). This gift, however, is an endowment (charism) given only to certain men and women. Men such as Agabus (Acts 11:28), Judas, and Silas are prophets (Acts 15:32), as are the four daughters of Philip (21:9). Luke also mentions prophets among the leaders of the Antiochian church (13:1).

For Paul prophecy is a highly valued gift because by it (in contrast to tongues) the church could be encouraged, comforted and built up (1 Cor 14:3). Prophecy plays an important role in the worship of the early church (1 Cor 11:4, 5), and because of its spontaneous character it has to be kept in check (1 Cor 14:29-33). At other times it has to be encouraged (1 Thes 5:20). The exact content of these prophetic utterances, however, is difficult to determine. Evidently they are utterances given by sudden impulse to exhort, instruct, warn, and encourage the Christian community. Prophecy could also take the form of prediction, as in the case of Agabus who predicts a famine. From its close connection with insight and knowledge (1 Cor 13:2) one might infer that it combines spiritual perception with the gift of communicating insights into spiritual truths.

Several times Paul lists the prophets with the apostles and teachers (1 Cor 12:28; Eph 4:11). Moreover, he speaks of apostles and prophets as founders of the church (Eph 2:20) and as agents of divine revelation (Eph 3:5). However, Christian prophecy seems to be a rather unstructured institution within early Christianity. By contrast, the role of the apostle (at least in the primary sense of that word) is more clearly defined.

Since prophetic utterances in the congregation need to be tested by others (1 Thes 5:20, 21; 1 Cor 14:29), one should probably not put the prophets in the early church on the same level as the apostles, whose teachings remain the authoritative guide for the church. Some prophets appear to be itinerant, like apostles, whereas others function within established churches. That there are also false prophets can be seen from the many warnings of Jesus and the apostles against such pretenders (Mt 7:15; Acts 20:29; 1 Jn 4:1; Rev 2:20, 24).

With the death of the apostles (who were not replaced) the gift of prophecy seems to disappear as well. Increasingly the teacher takes the place of the prophet. There is, however, no indication in the New Testament that this is to be expected or that the gift of prophecy is given to the apostolic church only.

In Mennonite circles apart from the °charismatic movement, it is still widely held that the predictive element is at the heart of Old Testament prophecy. And since the messages of the prophets are usually cast in national categories, the restoration of the modern state of Israel is seen by many as a fulfillment of Old Testament hopes. In this approach an important Anabaptist principle of interpretation is overlooked, namely, that the Old Testament is to be interpreted in the light of the New. The New Testament denationalizes Old Testament prophecies and sees them fulfilled in the Christ event or in the Day of the Lord at the end of the age. By taking their cues from Jesus and the apostles, Mennonite scholars are coming to a deeper appreciation of the prophetic messages of the Old Testament.   DE

C. E. Armerding, "Prophecy in the Old Testament," in *Dreams, Visions, and Oracles* ed. C. E. Armerding and W. W. Gasque (Grand Rapids: Baker, 1977); David E. Aune, *Prophecy in Early Christianity and the Ancient Mediterranean World,* (Grand Rapids: Eerdmans, 1983); J. Blenkinsopp, *A History of Prophecy in Israel* (Philadelphia: Westminster, 1983); F. F. Bruce, *The New Testament Development of Old Testament Themes* (Grand Rapids: Eerdmans, 1968); Walter Brueggemann, *The Prophetic Imagination* (Philadelphia: Fortress, 1978); Philip E. Hughes, *Interpreting Prophecy* (Grand Rapids: Eerdmans, 1976); R. R. Wilson, "Prophet," in *Harper's Bible Dictionary,* ed., Paul J. Achtemeier (San Francisco: Harper and Row, 1985), 826-830; Werner Schmauch, "The Prophetic Office in the Church," *Concern* pamphlet No. 5 (June 1958), 68-76.

See also Biblical Interpretation; Civil Disobedience; David Joris; Dispensationalism; °°Sleeping Preacher Churches; Sociopolitical Activism; °°Zwickau Prophets.

Proverbs. See Dialect Literature and Speech; Folklore.

Psychology and Psychiatry. The field of psychological investigation and treatment of mental disorders was not something that was of specific concern to Mennonites until the early 20th c. Nevertheless there is evidence of concern about psychological principles in °education and °childrearing even though we can only call it that in retrospect. Christopher °°Dock's "School Management," written in 1750, gives such documentation. In the next century, Johann °°Cornies, the Russian Mennonite economic and educational reformer, introduced a set of "General Rules Concerning Instruction and Treatment of School Children," which is sensitive to psychological issues. There is good evidence that the first generation of Russian Mennonite immigrants to the United States carried with them the same concern about good educational psychology. The °°German Teachers Institute of Kansas formed in 1894 conducted an annual two-week course of studies with a three-year curriculum that had a heavy em-

phasis on psychology. It is reported that Johann Cornies also set up a program of special education for mentally retarded children. He sent teachers to be trained in Germany, so that they could establish such programs in the Mennonite colonies in the Ukraine.

In 1910 the first Mennonite residential facility for the mentally ill, Bethania, was built by the Chortiza colony in Russia. Bethania was modeled after Bethel at Bielefeld in Germany, and the first staff members were trained there. Doctor I. Thiessen, who joined the staff soon after its opening, stayed with Bethania until it was closed in 1925.

When Mennonite young people entered higher education in greater numbers in the 20th c., they also became interested in psychology as a field of scientific investigation and as an academic discipline. Some returned to teach in Mennonite colleges. They were objects of particular scrutiny by those who upheld traditional Anabaptist beliefs because of the widespread assumption that the Christian worldview was at odds with the scientific disciplines, especially in the areas of the origin of life and the nature of human mental functioning. Rational explanations of behavior were sometimes considered to be in conflict with the understanding that Mennonites shared with orthodox, and in North America, fundamentalist Christian thinking which considered all humankind to be fallen since the Garden of Eden experience. The only manner in which this nature could be changed was by a confession of faith in Jesus Christ who redeems humans, thereby allowing them to cast off their old sinful nature. To raise questions of causation beyond this theological answer could be interpreted as questioning the doctrinal assertion that the Scriptures were the sole °authority on matters of faith.

Psychological investigators of the 19th c. were looking into the determinants of intelligence as well as the behaviors exhibited by the mentally ill. Questions asked by scientific investigators did not take at face value the assumptions made by biblical literalists about human nature and instead looked for other, natural determinants of behavior. Studying the works of those who openly challenged the traditional view that behavior is the result of the individual's choice to follow either Christ or Satan was of itself a challenge to the religious establishment and marked the questioner as being at odds with Christian thinking.

Some of the first Mennonite scholars entering the field of psychology left the Mennonite church, thus reenforcing the concern about the fundamental incompatibility of being a Christian and scholar in a secular field. Others worked at integrating the information gathered about human behavior in a scientific manner into a Christian frame of reference, and returned to teach psychology at Mennonite schools.

With the advent of World War II and alternative service for °conscientious objectors (°°Civilian Public Service, °°I-W Service) a fortuitous decision was made to place thousands of young men in state mental hospitals in the United States and Canada. They learned first-hand about mental illness and about the deplorable conditions in the hospitals for the mentally ill. Some of these men returned home to go into careers related to caring for the mentally ill and helped to create the Mennonite Mental Health Services network of hospitals across the United States and Canada.

Others entered the fields of psychiatry and clinical psychology because these disciplines were taking on new visibility and respectability in society. Many saw in these fields an opportunity to address the call to Christian service in a new way. Usually they worked alongside °professionals of different persuasions and did not necessarily see a uniquely Christian dimension to their work. Some who did work in avowedly Christian settings had difficulty in establishing their credentials as Christians and left. Overall, Mennonites working in the °mental health care field have found ways of being true to the traditions derived from their heritage, namely to provide help to those who are needy and unloved.   GD

P. M. Friesen, *Brotherhood* (1911, 1980); Menno S. Harder, "The Origin, Philosophy and Development of Education Among the Mennonites (PhD diss. U. of Southern California, 1949), copy at Tabor College Library; Vernon H. Neufeld, ed., *If We Can Love: The Mennonite Mental Health Story* (Newton, Mennonite Press, 1983); Bill W. Dick, "Psychology and Mennonite Studies," *JMS*, 1 (1983), 149-60.

See also Disabilities; Pastoral Counseling.

Public Relations. Mennonites began to use the term "public relations" during the late 1940s and early 1950s. As the public and secular °mass media popularized the term, many people within Mennonite circles began to mistrust the meaning and the motivations behind the words. Some Mennonites feared being manipulated by the use of "public relations" techniques. However, as conferences (denominations), boards, and institutions became increasingly complex, Mennonites were forced to work at "public relations" for survival. By 1975 most boards and agencies of the Mennonite churches had a "public relations" department of some sort.

In theory "public relations," for a Mennonite agency, should grow out of the agency's reason for being and should meet the specific wants and needs of the people it serves. Good "public relations" develop in an exchange of wants and needs between people. For example, a church agency wants and needs advocates, prayers, and support (both financial and personal services support). On the other hand, the people supporting or being served by the church agency must have their wants and needs met also, or they will not respond in supporting the church agency. This exchange notion can be diagrammed as follows:

In planning a public relations program it is important that the church agency takes the first move in this exchange equation, otherwise the supporters will not respond and meet the needs of the agency. This process of responding to each others' needs is certainly Christian and within the Mennonite concern for brotherhood and for community.

During planning sessions it is customary for a church agency to divide its audiences into smaller segments in order to serve each section better. For instance, a school will need to respond to the needs of parents, students, donors, church conferences, congregations, etc. Each of these publics require different forms of reporting. Being sensitive to these needs is certainly a responsible Christian approach.

"Public relations" done well will be unnoticed. If an agency is crude and manipulative, "public relations" are repulsive. The apostle Paul is a good model to follow. Each of his epistles is an example of good "public relations." For instance, Paul reported on work being done, thanked people for their gifts, shared opportunities for new avenues of services, asked for continued support, managed a mission board for 14 persons, compared one congregation's response to another congregation's (Philippi with Corinth), and held forth a model of Christian living and expression. This is "public relations" at its best.   DEK

PUBLIC RELATIONS CHART
Compiler: Daniel E. Kauffman (author of article)

Church Agency's Wants and Needs	First Action → ← Exchange of Services	Wants and Needs of the People Serviced by the Agency
• Advocacy • Prayer • Financial and service • support	(responding action)	• Assurance the agency's mission is being fulfilled • Careful management of resources • Effective results for services rendered • Carefully reporting the results of the services rendered • Expressions of appreciation from agency for the gift or service given by the supporter • Meaningful opportunities for involvement of the church member

Public Schools. In western European countries Mennonites generally resided in heterogeneous communities. They accepted state schools for their children and established few °private schools. Mennonite migrants to Russia were located in homogeneous settlements in which they established and conducted their own schools where instruction was given in the German language. All early migrants to North America, including Mennonites, established schools before state governments introduced universal public education. As in Russia, so in Canada and the United States, and later in Latin American countries, most early Mennonite immigrants settled as homogeneous communities in which they conducted their own schools.

Separated from the cultures of its origin and removed from institutions of higher learning, Mennonite schooling gradually declined in quality and comprehensiveness. In Russia a major move for the improvement of schooling occurred under the leadership of Johann °°Cornies about 1843. Mennonite teachers and students were encouraged to obtain professional education in Germany and Switzerland, some qualified teachers were imported from the same countries, and Mennonite teacher training institutions were established in the Mennonite colonies. Though the standard of schooling improved, Mennonite schools remained aloof from the culture of the host country until the government enforced instruction in Russian in the 1860s. This, along with a subsequent policy of deliberate "russification," caused the more conservative Mennonites who were unwilling to accept such accommodation to emigrate to North America.

The first Mennonite immigrants to Manitoba assumed that they had received for all time a promise of complete autonomy with respect to the schooling of their children—a promise extended by federal officials in contradiction to terms inherent in the Canadian constitution (°privileges). They suffered a rude awakening during World War I when compulsory school attendance was legislated, English mandated as the only language of instruction, the °flag ordered to be flown at every school, and all teachers required to receive preparation and certification as directed by the Manitoba Department of Education. Also, children were not authorized to attend any private school which did not meet these same conditions. Where deemed necessary, public schools were located by the department in Mennonite communities, and in some cases private school buildings were requisitioned for public school purposes. Parents refusing to comply with the new laws were fined and some served jail terms. The more conservative members who feared and resented government intrusion in the education of their children migrated during the 1920s, some farther west in Canada where for a time they were beyond the reach of public education authorities, and in larger numbers, to Mexico.

However, prior to public enforcement, the Manitoba government in 1891 had invited H. H. °°Ewert from Kansas to direct a teacher training program in the newly established private high school in Gretna (°°Mennonite Collegiate Institute), and also to act as its inspector of Mennonite schools, most of which were private and much in need of improvement. Ewert's endeavors were welcomed by the liberal elements while at the same time resented by the conservatives (°Sommerfeld Mennonites). At the turn of the century state-approved teacher training was also introduced at Bethel College and other Mennonite colleges.

The Mennonite schools in Mexico deteriorated further because of the absence of any formal teacher preparation. Attempts by Canadian and American Mennonites to assist in the improvement of these schools were at first resisted and in part boycotted upon the insistence of the local ministers. The Canadian experience was replicated in the 1930s when the Mexican government insisted upon higher standards in the instructional program and mandated that instruction be given in Spanish. Similar events and developments took place in other Latin American countries to which Mennonites migrated from Mexico and Canada (Belize, Bolivia, Brazil, Paraguay) at various times from the 1930s to the 1960s. Impoverished and disillusioned, some of the migrants returned to Canada for a new start. The Mennonites of Brazil seem to have accepted the reality of cultural pluralism more readily.

Mennonites have desired to conduct their own schools so that their children would be nurtured in the "faith of the fathers" and preserve their ethnic traditions and customs. To this end private schools and instruction in a language different from that of the host country served to build in-group cohesiveness and boundaries against the assimilative forces of the surrounding culture (°acculturation, °°nonconformity). On the other hand, public authorities were not motivated by educational standards alone, but desired the assimilation of the immigrants and the building of a spirit of national patriotism. Therefore they mandated instruction in the national language by teachers who had been trained in public institutions and certificated by state authorities. In some public schools the use of any language other than the dominant national language even on the playground, was expressly forbidden. Particularly during the world wars Mennonites feared the militaristic attitudes which public schools were expected to implant in their students. Both world wars caused consternation among Mennonites as public education authorities looked upon private schools with suspicion, particularly so where German was used as a major language of instruction. In response to the ill-feeling of the surrounding community, for example, Bethel College closed its German Department during World War I. On the other hand, in some communities increased parochialism was engendered by such public resentment. Such has been the case for Mennonites in Russia, Canada, the United States, and Brazil.

Separation from the national public education systems has not necessarily assured the preservation of Mennonite intellectual and spiritual integrity. Of this Paraguay serves as an example, where during the 1930s German nationals persuaded many, including some of the ministerial leadership, to accept the ideas of German °National Socialism.

When a community is closed to cross-fertilization with major cultures, generally intellectual impoverishment sets in. Yet some groups have managed to thrive under such conditions as have the Old Order Amish, the Old Order Mennonites, the Church of

God in Christ Mennonite (Holdeman), and the Hutterites. Nevertheless, no community in North America is totally isolated and public education authorities have managed to impose minimal educational standards for children in most schools whether these be private or public.

Some post-World-War-II attempts to revive the maintenance of German cultural manifestations were made in Manitoba along with lesser support in some other provinces. These included the introduction of a short-lived Mennonite German educational periodical, the establishiment of a Mennonite society for the preservation of German as a mother-tongue, and in Manitoba the employment by Mennonite school boards of a Mennonite "school inspector" to assist teachers in the instruction of religion in the German language, as well as instruction in German itself, both of which occurred mainly after regular school hours in public schools in Mennonite communities. However, such efforts did not stem the tide towards acculturation, and the acceptance of English not only as the language of instruction in Sunday school, but also of worship in the churches.

Beginning in the 1970s, a North American movement for freedom of choice in schooling gained momentum among public educators. Associated with this has been an increasing tolerance for and an acceptance of private schools. Examples of this are the Amish school question in Iowa in the 1960s (regarding compulsory school attendance beyond age 15) and the Alberta Holdeman private school question in the 1970s (regarding the right of the community to employ its own noncertificated school instructors). In both cases the courts found for the defendants (Amish, Holdeman Mennonites). Also, in both cases part of the problem was brought about by the consolidation of school districts and busing of students to centralized larger schools. Public school districts, at one time comprising fairly homogeneous Amish or Holdeman rural communities, had disappeared, thus forcing the children to be part of a diverse school population and raising the fears of their parents regarding the consequences of such education for their children and for their children's loyalty to the parent communities. Also, the secularization of public schools serving an increasingly pluralistic constituency militated against explicit Christian teaching. An arrangement permitting an alternative Christian school to operate under the direction of the public school board in Calgary, Alta., during the 1980s was terminated. However, in Edmonton, Alta., a Jewish alternative school continued to enjoy relative autonomy under the direction of the public school board.

Whereas private schools had been judged by the extent to which they met public school standards, in the 1980s public schools in several countries have been judged, in part, by their comparison to the best standards found in outstanding private schools. An example of such recognition is the fact that private schools which satisfy certain public education criteria also receive a measure of government funding in five of Canada's ten provinces. Whereas about 1960 the controversial question of whether to accept such funding was left unresolved at a provincial meeting of Mennonites in Winnipeg, in the 1980s such assistance is readily accepted as a equitable accommodation because all citizens through taxes support public schools. In the 1980s the Manitoba government also employed a Mennonite educator as its inspector of private schools, only a few of which were Mennonite. In British Columbia, the inspector of private schools, an Anglican, found Mennonite private schools equal to the best public schools in the province in 1986.

In 1985 the commissioner for the study of private schools in Ontario recommended the public funding of private schools which met standards equal to those held for public schools, a privilege enjoyed only by Catholic schools operated separately as public schools. The privileged position of Catholic schools prompted the commissioner's recommendation, which had not yet been considered by the Ontario government by 1987. A specific private schools statute in Quebec gives parents the right to choose private schooling for their children. British Columbia also has specific private school legislation since 1977. In some of the provinces conditions for private schools are stipulated in the context of public school legislation, and some provinces make no reference at all to private schools in legislation.

The constitution of the Federal Republic of Germany provides for the right of parents to choose private schools for their children. Moreover, such private schools are largely supported through government funding. Such is also true in The Netherlands and Australia. So far the United States has been somewhat unique in that its courts have ruled that private schools shall not receive any public funding.

Though the work of Christopher °°Dock is recorded in some American histories of education, it is doubtful that his influence extended beyond the early Mennonite private schools in Pennsylvania. Modern equivalents of Dock are scholars whose works are published in academic journals, whose papers are read at learned conferences, and whose ideas infuse both public and private education. Likewise, most modern Mennonite leaders—both laypersons and ministers—are people educated in both public and private institutions, who, like Cornies and Ewert, bridge the gaps between Mennonite orthodoxy and world cultures. Furthermore, modern communication and transportation enable Mennonites of diverse world cultures to meet and develop understandings without trivializing any one particular tradition.

During the latter half of the 20th c. several Mennonite private colleges have sought and obtained public accreditation and some also affiliation with public institutions of higher learning. Some private college instructors also teach in their public affiliates. Most Mennonite college instructors have obtained their advanced degrees from public universities. Others have chosen their professional careers in public educational institutions, some as senior civil servants in government. Mennonite teachers, including those trained in Mennonite schools, also teach in public schools.

Some Mennonite educators have chosen to work in public institutions in order to enjoy greater academic freedom and intellectual autonomy. At times public institutions serve as models of intellectual freedom for some Mennonite schools which severely constrain their instructors in questions of their conformity to orthodoxy.

The U. of Winnipeg in 1977 accepted funds to establish a Chair in Mennonite Studies under the direction of Harry Loewen, and in 1984 a Mennonite Studies Centre under the direction of George K. Epp (former president of the Canadian Mennonite Bible College, Winnipeg). Both of these have been funded by the David Friesen Family Corporation. Other Mennonite professors at the university provide assistance in the instructional programs of the two units.

Another example of the bridging between the public and the private education sectors is that of former president of the Mennonite Brethren Bible College (Winnipeg), Frank C. °Peters, who subsequently served as president of Wilfrid Laurier U. (Waterloo), 1968-78, where he led the school as it shifted from a private to a public university.

Researchers have found it difficult to establish indisputable cause and effect relationships between public education and Mennonite values and beliefs when they must also account for many noneducational variables. However, it is not difficult to ascertain a trend towards an acculturation in which the benefits of public education are accepted while at the same time specific Mennonite teachings, such as those on matters of religious faith and peace and service education, are best promoted within Mennonite institutions. JJB

Frank H. Epp, *Mennonites in Canada I*, 334-58; John E. Hartzler, *Education Among the Mennonites of America* (Danvers, Ill.: Central Mennonite Publishing Board, 1925); John B. Toews, "Cultural and Intellectual Aspects of the Mennonite Experience in Russia," *MQR*, 53 (1979), 137-59; E. K. Francis, "The Mennonite School Problem in Manitoba, 1874-1919," *MQR*, 27 (1953), 204-37; Harry Leonard Sawatzky, *Mennonite Settlements in British Honduras* (Winnipeg: U. of Manitoba, 1959), 56-59; idem, *They Sought a Country—Mennonite Colonization in Mexico* (Berkeley: U. of California Press, 1971), 14-30, 305-15, 365-67; Johann S. Postma, *Fernheim, fernes Heim* (Newton: Mennonite Library and Archives, 1946); Reynolds H. Minnich, *The Mennonite Immigrant Communities in Paraná, Brazil* (Cuernavaca, Mexico: Centro Intercultural de Documentacion, 1970), 8/14-26; J. T. M. Anderson, *The Education of the New Canadian* (Toronto: J. M. Dent and Sons, 1918); John W. Friesen, "Studies in Mennonite Education: The State of the Art," *JMS*, 1 (1983), 133-48; John J. Bergen, "Freedom of Education in a Religious Context: The Alberta Holdeman Private School Case," *MQR*, 55 (1981), 75-85; idem, "Choice in Schooling," *J. of Educational Administration and Foundations* (U. of Manitoba), 1 (1986), 37-48; Donald B. Kraybill, "Religious and Ethnic Socialization in a Mennonite High School," *MQR*, 51 (1977), 329-51; Charles E. Finn, "Why Public and Private Schools Matter," *Harvard Educational Review*, 51 (1981), 510-14; John A. Hostetler and Calvin Redekop, "Education and Assimilation in Three Ethnic Groups," *The Alberta J. of Educational Research*, 8 (1962), 189-203; Robert Kreider, "Anabaptism and Humanism: An Inquiry into the Relationship of Humanism to the Evangelical Anabaptists," *MQR*, 26 (1952), 123-41; Adolf Ens, "The Public School Crisis Among Mennonites in Saskatchewan 1916-25," and Don Wiebe, "Philosophical Reflections on Twentieth-Century Mennonite Thought," in *Mennonite Images*, ed., Harry Loewen (Winnipeg: Hyperion Press, 1980), 73-81, 149-64; Theodore W. Jentsch, "Change and the School in an Old Order Mennonite Community," *MQR*, 50 (1976), 132-35; Harrell R. Rodgers, *Community Conflict, Public Opinion and the Law—The Amish Dispute in Iowa* (Columbus, Ohio: Charles E. Merrill Publishing Co., 1969); William T. Vandever, "The Education of Teachers at Bethel College in Kansas, 1893-1927," *Menn. Life*, 42 (Mar. 1987), 4-9; John A. Hostetler, *Children in Amish Society* (Toronto: Holt, Rinehart and Winston, 1971), 97-116; Walter Quiring, "Die Witmarsumer von Morgen," *Der Bote* (July 21, 1937), 2; Leo Driedger and Peter Hengstenberg, "Non-Official Multilingualism: Factors Affecting German Language Competence, Use and Maintenance in Canada," *Canadian Ethnic Studies*, 18, no. 3 (1986), 90-109.

See also Bergthal Mennonites: Education; Old Colony Mennonites; Private Christian Schools; Socialization.

Publishing (ME IV:228) is a complex enterprise and "of making many books there is no end" (Eccl 12:12). Publishing requires authors, editors, and printers as well as capital for investment and marketing of the product. Throughout their history, Mennonite and Brethren in Christ conferences have prepared printed materials for transmitting the faith to their young, interpreting the tradition for other people, and for strengthening the faith of the community of adherents.

In recent decades many new publishers have appeared on the Mennonite roster. New periodicals and the annual production of major trade books by the main Mennonite publishers in North America have more than doubled from ca. 20 per year in the 1950s to more than 40 in the mid-1980s. Mennonite publishers frequently operate their own bookstores. These too have grown in number, but equally significant is the variety of books and other materials on their shelves.

Mennonite publishing takes place in many countries, but Mennonites in Canada and the United States publish the most. The largest publishers are Mennonite Publishing House and Herald Press (MC), Scottdale, Pa.; Faith and Life Press (GCM), Newton, Ks.; Kindred Press (MB), Winnipeg, Man. and Hillsboro, Ks.; and Evangel Press (BIC), Nappanee, Ind. These publishers sometimes work together in common ventures. For example, Meetinghouse Publications is a functional association begun in 1972 in which the articles and news reports of inter-Mennonite activities produced by one periodical are made available to editors of other member publications. Initially only *Gospel Herald* and *The Mennonite* were involved, later *Evangelical Visitor*, *Mennonite Reporter*, *The Messenger*, the *Christian Leader*, *The Mennonite Brethren Herald*, and *The Mennonite Weekly Review* joined.

A significant publication and joint effort of the Mennonite Church, General Conference Mennonite Church, Brethren in Christ, and Church of the Brethren since 1955 is "The Foundation Series," a Mennonite and Believers' church Sunday School curriculum which is an alternative to the International Sunday School lessons. It emphasizes the Believer's church heritage from a biblical perspective for children, youth, and adults. Other major series published in the last three decades include Classics of the Radical Reformation (CRR), Studies in Anabaptist and Mennonite History, Believer's Church Bible Commentary, the Caring Enough series by David Augsburger, the Christian Peace Shelf, and a Mennonite Missionary Study series. Some significant individual titles of recent years by Mennonite publishers include Guy °Hershberger, ed. *The Recovery of The Anabaptist Vision* (1957); Frank H. °Epp, *Mennonite Exodus* (1962); C. J. Dyck, *An Introduction to Mennonite History* (1967, 1981); *The Mennonite Hymnal* (1969); John H. Yoder, *The Original Revolution* (1971); Marlin Jeschke, *Discipling the Brother* (1973, 1979; retitled *Discipling in the Church*, 1988); Doris Janzen °Longacre, *The More With Less Cookbook* (1976); Nelson Springer and A.

J. Klassen, comp. *Mennonite Bibliography* (1977); Mary Lou Cummings, ed., *Full Circle* (1978); Donald Kraybill, *The Upside Down Kingdom* (1978); Katie Funk Wiebe, *Women Among the Brethren* (1979); Walter Sawatsky, *Soviet Evangelicals Since World War II* (1981); Willard Swartley, *Slavery, Sabbath, War, and Women* (1983); and Ruth Unrau, *Encircled* (1986).

Most of the Mennonite churches issue periodicals to keep their constituents informed. The Mennonite Publishing House, Scottdale, Pa., publishes *Gospel Herald* (MC) weekly. Faith and Life Press publishes *The Mennonite* (GCM) biweekly. The Mennonite Brethren Church of Canada through Christian Press in Winnipeg, publishes *The Mennonite Brethren Herald* and *Das Mennonitische Rundschau*. The Mennonite Brethren Board of Communications publishes the *Christian Leader* at Hillsboro, Ks., for readers in the United States, biweekly. Inter-Mennonite Herald Publishing Co., Newton, Ks., publishes the *Mennonite Weekly Review* (1920). Another inter-Mennonite tabloid of news and opinion is *Mennonite Reporter* (1971) from Mennonite Publishing Service, Inc., Waterloo, Ont. (biweekly). The Brethren in Christ Board for Media Ministries publishes books and *Evangelical Visitor*, a monthly magazine, at Nappanee, Ind.

Christian Light Publications (MC) at Harrisonburg, Va., publishes Sunday school quarterlies, books, and grade one-to-twelve Christian Day School curriculum since 1969. Rod and Staff Publishers of Crockett, Ky., serves Conservative Mennonites with periodicals, books, and tracts since 1958. Evangelical Mennonite Conference Board of Education and Publications (1962) of Steinbach, Man. publishes *The Messenger* (biweekly). Church of God in Christ, Mennonite (Holdeman), Moundridge, Ks., publishes *Messenger of Truth* (biweekly) since 1965. Mennonite Board of Missions and Mennonite Central Committee (MCC), Akron, Pa., and Winnipeg, also publish a variety of materials. MCC issues *MCC Contact* (1977) and *Jottings* (1979), which offer information for constituent churches, and releases several quarterly newsletters. Mennonite World Conference publishes *Courier* (quarterly). Most district conferences, especially in North America, publish periodic newssheets or magazines to keep their local membership informed. Many other Mennonite agencies publish periodicals, most of which are listed in *MC Yearbook* under "Publications."

Amish publishers and publications have increased conspicuously in recent years. Amish Mennonite Publications (1981) of Minerva, Ohio serves the Beachy Amish Mennonites with devotional and theological books. The Beachy Amish also read the *Calvary Messenger* (1970). °Pathway Publishing Corp. (1964), Aylmer, Ont., provides religious and educational books and periodicals for Old Order Amish and Old Order Mennonites. *The Sugarcreek Budget* (Schlabach Printers, Sugarcreek, Ohio) serves the Amish and others all over America. Amish Brotherhood Publishers (1984) of Millersburg, Ohio, publishes doctrinal books and tracts of practical Biblicism. Pequea Publishers (1970) of Gordonville, Pa., produces devotional books and Amish genealogies.

The Golden Chain is published by the Old Order River Brethren at Colombia, Pa. The Hutterian Brethren publish many religious and family educational books in both German and English through the Plough Publishing House, Rifton, N.Y., and E. Sussex, England.

Several privately owned printing companies such as D. W. Friesen and Sons, Ltd. of Altona, Man.; Hyperion Press Ltd., Winnipeg, Man.; or individual publishers such as Good Books of Intercourse, Pa., or Sand Hill Books, Inc., St. Jacobs, Ont., publish religious or regional and ethnic interest books and papers. A growing proportion of Mennonite historical genealogical and cultural writings are privately printed and distributed by the writers themselves.

The Mennonite colleges also publish alumni bulletins, newsletters, yearbooks, and literary or historical research journals. Some have their own presses (Canadian Mennonite Bible College—CMBC Publications; Goshen College—Pinch Penny Press; Conrad Grebel College—Conrad Press; Associated Mennonite Biblical Seminaries in conjunction with the Council of Mennonite Seminaries—Institute of Mennonite Studies). Mennonite historical societies in Lancaster, Pa.; Goshen, Ind.; Winnipeg, Man.; Fresno, Cal., and elsewhere all publish researched information about the Mennonite past.

In Africa many of the Mennonite and Brethren in Christ conferences publish a °yearbook or directory. Some have an official publication such as a newsletter or calendar but we are unaware of any publishing houses. Tanzania formerly had a publishing agency but it is currently (1987) not active. Mennonite groups in France, Germany, Switzerland, and The Netherlands also publish yearbooks and directories and official periodicals but have no official publishing houses. Historical societies, such as *Mennonitischer Geschichtsverein* or *Doopsgezinde Historische Kring*, publish occasional books of church history and regular historical journals. Since 1969 Mennonitische Heimatmission (Mennonite Home Mission) in West Germany through Proclama publishes a bimonthly bulletin as well as books for the protection of the environment. The Proclama book ministry (1976) as part of the Mennonite Home Mission and the Memra Publishing House, Neuwied, a private initiative with partnership in Proclama, separated from Home Mission in 1985. Agape Verlag in West Germany publishes items on Anabaptist-Mennonite theology and experience (°church-state relations). A summary of European publishers is found annually in *Mennonitisches Jahrbuch*. Since 1986, *Brücke* (Bridge), a combined official periodical of the two main German Mennonite groups, continues the work of *Gemeinde Unterwegs* (Church Underway) and *Mennonitische Blätter* (Mennonite Pages).

In India the Mennonite Brethren Church issues an official paper. The Gereja Injili di Tanah Jawa (Evangelical Church of Java) publishes a yearbook and the Persatuan Gereja-Gereja Kristen Muria Indonesia (Indonesian United Muria Christian Church Conference) produces an official paper as well. In Japan official publications are issued by the Nihon Menonaito Kirisuto Kyokai Kaigi (Japan Mennonite Christian Church Conference), Nihon Menonaito Burezaren Kyadan (Japan Mennonite Brethren Conference), and Tokyo Chiku Menonaito Kyokai Rengo

(Tokyo Area Fellowship of Mennonite Churches). The Fellowship of Mennonite Churches in Taiwan produces both an annual conference report and a monthly publication. The Australian Conference of Evangelical Mennonites—Church of Hope officially publishes *De Mennist.*

The Iglesia Evangélica Menonita, Argentina (Argentine Mennonite Church), publishes *Perspectiva,* the Belize Evangelical Mennonite Mission Conference publishes *Recorder,* and Belize's Caribbean Light and Truth issues a newsletter. The °°Kleine Gemeinde in Belize publishes both *Der Leserfreund* and a yearbook. The Associação das Igrejas Irmãos Menonitas do Brasil (Association of the Mennonite Brethren Churches of Brazil) produces a paper and a yearbook. The Associação das Igrejas Menonitas do Brasil (Association of Mennonite Churches in Brazil) publishes *Bibel und Pflug.* The Associação Evangélica Menonita (Evangelical Mennonite Association) and the Convenção Brasileira das Igrejas Irmãos Menonitas (Brazilian Conference of the MB Church) both have official publications. So does the Iglesia Evangélica Menonita de Colombia (Colombian Mennonite Church) and the Conferencia de las Iglesias Evangélicas Menonitas, Dominican Republic (Evangelical Mennonite Church). In Guatamala three Mennonite groups publish official papers. One of the Mennonite churches in Honduras produces a

yearbook. The Jamaican Mennonite Church publishes *The Quest.* The Old Colony Mennonites of Mexico read *Die Mennonitische Post,* published in Steinbach, Man., by a committee of MCC (Canada), and the Iglesia Evangélica Menonita de la Mesa Central de Mexico (Evangelical Mennonite Church of the Central Plateau of Mexico) publishes *Gaceta Menonita.* The Fraternidad de Iglesias Evangélicas Menonitas de Nicaragua (Fraternity of Evangelical Mennonite Churches of Nicaragua) publishes *El Mensajero.* Paraguay's Convención Evangélica de los Hermanos Menonitas (Evangelical Convention of Mennonite Brethren) publishes *La Voz del Rebano,* and Konferenz der Evangelischen Mennonitischen Bruderschaft von Südamerika (Evangelical Mennonite Brethren Conference of South America) publishes *Informationsblatt.* The Konferenz der Mennonitischen Brüdergemeinden von Paraguay (Conference of MB churches) issues *Konferenzblatt.* Puerto Rico's Convención de las Iglesias Evangélicas Menonitas (Mennonite Conventions) publishes both a paper and a yearbook. In Uruguay both the Consejo del las Congregaciónes de los Hermanos Menonitas (Council of MB Congregations) and the Konferenz der Mennonitengemeinden in Uruguay (Conference of Mennonites) publish newspapers as does Venezuela's Concilio de las Iglesias Evangélicas Menonitas (Council of Mennonite Churches).

WEST INDIES

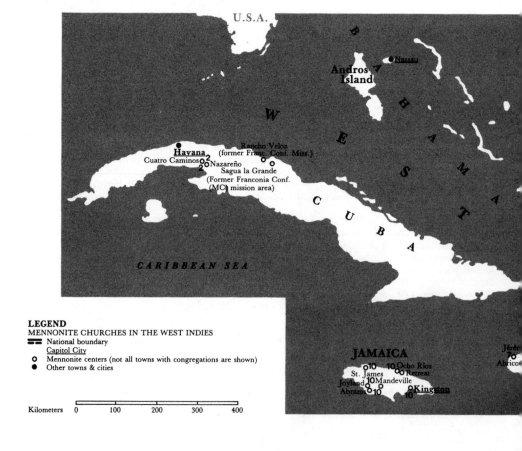

LEGEND
MENNONITE CHURCHES IN THE WEST INDIES
National boundary
Capitol City
○ Mennonite centers (not all towns with congregations are shown)
● Other towns & cities

Kilometers   0   100   200   300   400

The Mennonite Board of Missions(MC), with Arnoldo J. Casas as editor, has translated and published a Mennonite Faith series of books by J. C. Wenger, Myron S. Augsburger and others for use by Hispanic Mennonites. A Sunday school curriculum in Spanish for both adults and children is now available. A. Rafael Falcon also wrote *Iglesia Menonita Hispaña en Norte America* (the Hispanic Mennonite Church in North America, Scottdale, 1985, 1986) for both Spanish- and English-speaking audiences. SEMILLA is a publication arm of the Seminario Ministerial de Liderazgo Anabautista, a °theological education by extension program, which is a joint effort of Central American Mennonites, Mennonite Brethren, and Brethren in Christ. It also produces and distributes biblical literature with an Anabaptist perspective in Latin America. The MCC Latin American Peace Portfolio and Mennonites in Honduras initiated *Esperanza en Camino*, a grass-roots journal which publishes reflective articles by Latin Americans on current issues. The Currículo Anabautista de Educación Biblica Congregaciónal (Anabaptist Sunday school curriculum in Spanish) is an emerging cooperative Anabaptist entity hoping to develop publications for the Latin American continent and Hispanics in North America.

Some publication companies (e.g., EMB Publications, Omaha, Nebr., or Choice Books of Mennonite Board of Missions Media Ministries in Harrisonburg, Va.) are simply suppliers of printed matter but do not actually publish anything. Many Mennonite writers are published by non-Mennonite publishers such as Augsburg, Abingdon, Crown, B. De Graaf, Editions "Le Phare," Eerdmans, Martinus Nijhoff, McClellan and Stewart, Ltd., MacMillan, Methopress, Word, Westminster. Mennonite writers also appear in non-Mennonite religious journals, e.g., *Christian Century, Christianity Today, Christianity and Crisis, Sojourners,* and secular journals.

Because of the diversity of modern publishing, it is almost impossible to include all publishers because they appear and disappear with some regularity. Publications of Mennonite groups, especially the newer churches in Africa, Asia, and Latin America, vary widely in degree of "official" status and in regularity of publication. Specific titles of periodical publications of the various conferences can be found in *The Mennonite World Handbook* (1978, 1984) published by the Mennonite World Conference.AWL

See also Mass Media; Periodicals.

Puerto Rico (ME IV:230). The Convención Iglesias Evangélicas Menonitas de Puerto Rico (Puerto Rican Mennonite Conference) was organized in 1955 for fellowship, unity, evangelization, and service. It

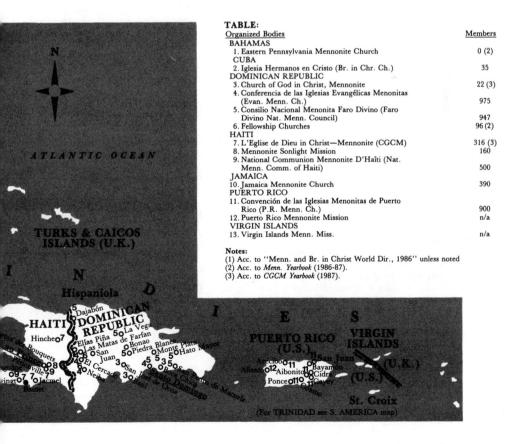

TABLE:

Organized Bodies	Members
BAHAMAS	
1. Eastern Pennsylvania Mennonite Church	0 (2)
CUBA	
2. Iglesia Hermanos en Cristo (Br. in Chr. Ch.)	35
DOMINICAN REPUBLIC	
3. Church of God in Christ, Mennonite	22 (3)
4. Conferencia de las Iglesias Evangélicas Menonitas (Evan. Menn. Ch.)	975
5. Consilio Nacional Menonita Faro Divino (Faro Divino Nat. Menn. Council)	947
6. Fellowship Churches	96 (2)
HAITI	
7. L'Eglise de Dieu in Christ—Mennonite (CGCM)	316 (3)
8. Mennonite Sonlight Mission	160
9. National Communion Mennonite D'Haïti (Nat. Menn. Comm. of Haiti)	500
JAMAICA	
10. Jamaica Mennonite Church	390
PUERTO RICO	
11. Convención de las Iglesias Menonitas de Puerto Rico (P.R. Menn. Ch.)	900
12. Puerto Rico Mennonite Mission	n/a
VIRGIN ISLANDS	
13. Virgin Islands Menn. Miss.	n/a

Notes:
(1) Acc. to "Menn. and Br. in Christ World Dir., 1986" unless noted
(2) Acc. to *Menn. Yearbook* (1986-87).
(3) Acc. to *CGCM Yearbook* (1987).

originated in the work of °°Civilian Public Service (1943) and of the Mennonite Board of Missions (MC) starting in 1945. Most churches are located between San Juan in the north and Ponce in the south. An executive committee, served by the executive secretary, carries out the decisions of conference delegates to an annual assembly.

During the 1950s Mennonite Board of Missions (MBM) sponsored 55 persons in Puerto Rico to support and plant churches and institutions. Most were from rural backgrounds, but in the 1950s workers planted most churches in towns. The Mennonite Bible Institute trained young Christians who later became leaders. Institutions established in the 1940s— the Mennonite Hospital at Aibonito, the Betania Mennonite Academy, and Luz y Verdad (Light and Truth) radio program—were rooted more firmly in the church, and Mennonite Voluntary Service provided personnel, 1950-84. The conference grew to 425 members by 1960.

In the 1960s the church planted its first urban churches (San Juan and Bayamon). The Bible Institute, now an extension program (°theological education by extension), provided training of pastors and other members. Puerto Rican leaders tentatively began to shape the life of the church, although missionary models still dominated. By 1970 the conference had 660 members and 13 congregations.

In the 1970s the church continued to move toward coastal cities while experiencing disconcerting situations: social-political changes and an economic depression; the emigration of some church leaders; increasing varieties of church piety and practice; the exit of most missionaries and voluntary service personnel; and adjustment to new leadership styles. By 1980 the conference had about 950 members in 17 congregations.

Since then the church has worked to forge a common identity; evaluate its relation with MBM and the Mennonite Church (MC); train current and potential leaders effectively; relate wisely with Mennonites in the Caribbean and Central America, and with other denominations; reshape its peace witness; affirm national leadership and assimilate leaders trained in other Christian traditions; and disciple new members and retain current members.

In 1986 the conference had 893 members in 16 congregations, ranging from 9 to 137 members. The average age of the congregations is 23 years. Half of the members are in rural churches, the rest in towns and cities.

Literature: *Alcance Menonita*, the monthly conference newspaper; annual pre-Assembly congregational studies; a *Ministerial Manual*; participation in Latin American Anabaptist Curriculum; *Desde la oficina*, a bulletin from the executive office. Institutions: Luz y Verdad radio ministries at Aibonito (ceased its affiliation with the conference in 1972, when it became part of Junta Ejecutiva Latinoamericana de Audiciones Menonitas [JELAM], a Latin American Mennonite board to promote mass communications, 1972-84); Mennonite Bible Institute, Aibonito; Mennonite Hospital, Aibonito (directed by community, MBM, and church representatives on board of directors, not a conference-sponsored institution); Mennonite Voluntary Service (1950-84); Libería Cristiana Unida (United Christian

(Bookstore) at Ponce; Mennonite Credit and Saving Cooperative, Aibonito; Betania Mennonite Academy at Pulguillas, Coamo; Mennonite Academy in Summit Hills, San Juan (sponsored by the Summit Hills Mennonite Church); Mennonite Audiovisual Center, Aibonito. Organizations: Mennonite Disaster Service Committee, Mennonite Youth Group (JEMP), Mennonite Women's Group (DEMP), Pastor's Committee. DWP

Manual Ministerial, Una Guía de Doctrinas, Prácticas y Recursos (Concilio de la Convencón de las Iglesias Evangélicas Menonitas de P. R. (1986); Justus G. Holsinger, *The Mennonite Work in Puerto Rico, 1941-1981* (Elkhart: MBM, 1981); idem, *Serving Rural Puerto Rico: A History of Eight Years of Service by the Mennonite Church* (Scottdale, 1952); Raul Rosado, "Las congregaciónes evangélicas Menonitas," and Luis Elier Rodrigues, "Las Iglesias Menonitas Unidas para servir," in *Unidos para que el mundo crea*, ed. David W. Powell (Aibonito, PR: Iglesias Evangelicas Menonitas de Puerto Rico, 1982), 37-44, 45-48; *MWH* (1978), 261-63.

See also Broadcasting, Radio and Television.

Puerto Rico Mennonite Conference. See Convención de las Iglesias Evangélicas Menonitas de Puerto Rico.

Puidoux Conferences were a series of theological consultations held in Europe between 1955 and 1962 under the general theme, "The Lordship of Christ over Church and State." Scholars from the continental Lutheran and Reformed theological faculties and scholars from the °"historic peace churches" participated. The initiating meeting was held in the Swiss village of Puidoux, hence the name.

These conferences were an unanticipated by-product of conversations initiated on behalf of the peace churches by the late M. R. °Zigler (Church of the Brethren) with officials of the World Council of Churches (WCC), soon after that body's establishment in 1948. Those conversations eventuated in a document submitted to the WCC by the peace churches' committee and published under the title, "Peace is the Will of God." The Puidoux Conferences were triggered by discussion surrounding that document, though not related to the WCC. They developed rather as perhaps the first serious theological conversation since the Reformation era between the original Protestant traditions in Europe and the "radical Reformation".

Three major consultations were held (Iserlohn, 1957; Bievres, 1960; and Oud Poelgeest, 1962), with detailed recording of the procedures. These were supplemented by a number of smaller encounters. The Puidoux papers are important, both as way-station in the development of theological reflection on °peace and war, and as the overture to a broadening dialogue that has fanned out in a variety of ways meanwhile. Mennonites played a key role in the Puidoux series, especially given their direct roots in the radical reformation of the 16th c. Donald F. Durnbaugh edited a volume of documents related to the conferences under the title, *On Earth Peace*. (Brethren Press, 1978). PPea

Pulesar Bai (ca. 1915-Aug. 18, 1976) was a Bible woman (°lay evangelist) with the American Mennonite Mission and the Mennonite Church (MC) in India. Her parents were Baganath and Tulsi Bai, a

Hindu family who lived at Umaradah near °Dhamtari. She received a primary education in Dhamtari at a Hindu school and later completed the seventh class at the Balodgahan Girls' Boarding where she became a Christian. She was sent to the Disciples of Christ Female Training School in Bilaspur for Bible training.

In 1930 she married Israel Bhelwa and from 1932 until 1957 served as a Bible woman in the evangelistic program at Ghatula. Her husband died in 1940. They had four sons and one daughter. Pulesar's deep devotion to Christ made her a respected saint and ambassador of the Gospel.   JAF

American Mennonite Mission Annual Report (1913), 19; E. P. Bachan, "Changing attitudes and Developments within the MCI" (Mennonite Board of Missions Report, 1957); idem, "In India to Stay" (MBM Report, 1958), 40; biographical data from J. M. Bhelwa and Mennonite Board of Missions (MC) missionaries.

Puritanism was the English Calvinistic dissenting movement against established Anglican religion of the 16th and 17th c. Ardent Protestants who worked to purify and reform the church along Reformed lines were called "Puritans." Their early leaders included Thomas Cartwright (1535-1603) and William Perkins (1558-1602). Puritanism spread beyond England into America and among immigrant English people in Holland.

Up to the time of the English Revolution (1640-60), most Puritans tried to work from within the Church of England. A small Separatist movement of the most extreme Puritans led by Robert Browne (ca. 1550-1633), refused all compromise and withdrew into separate churches. The "Pilgrim Fathers" of Plymouth Colony in Massachusetts were of this sort. The Separatist and non-Separatist Puritans eventually fragmented further into various orthodox denominations, e.g., Presbyterians, Congregationalists, and Baptists; moreover, Puritanism was also parent to many still more radical groups, including the Levellers, Diggers, Quakers, and Fifth Monarchists. During the English Revolution, many Puritans supported the revolutionary political and religious programs of Oliver Cromwell (1599-1658).

In another sense, Puritanism can also be viewed as a universal type of Christianity, which has recurred many times and places, not only in England. The "Puritan" is the intense, pietistic, purifying Christian, exemplified by aspects of St. Augustine (354-430), Tertullian (ca. 160-220), or the °°Donatists (ca. 311-412ff.) as much as by Cartwright, Perkins, and Browne. Anabaptism in the 16th c. is one of the main examples of this universal type of Christianity. Many of these groups favored a restoration of primitive Christian purity (°restitutionism).

The essence of English Puritanism was a balanced combination of doctrinal Calvinism and intense personal piety. Puritans stressed (1) the purified church (2) personal righteousness, and (3) the absolute authority of the Bible. They wanted to purify the Church of England of its more "Catholic elements," notably aspects of the bishop's role and liturgical worship.

Puritanism and Anabaptism intersected at various places in England, Holland, and America. One English Separatist congregation at Amsterdam, led by John °Smyth (ca. 1570-1612), decided on rebaptism, and eventually joined the Dutch Waterlander Mennonites (1615). Another part of Smyth's congregation, led by Thomas Helwys (ca. 1575-1616), returned to England and founded the General Baptists. Thus, the Baptists can claim both an Anabaptist and a Puritan origin.

In theology and practice, Puritanism and Anabaptism had certain similarities in their common desire for purifying the church, simplicity of worship, and personal piety. However, Puritanism, in the main, followed a Calvinist, predestinarian theology and also allied itself with the political state, hoping thereby to purify the political order as well as the ecclesiastical.   KLS

William Haller, *The Rise of Puritanism* (New York: Columbia U. Press, 1938); Patrick Collinson, *The Elizabethan Puritan Movement* (Berkeley: U. of California Press, 1967); B. R. White, *The Separatist Tradition from the Marian Martyrs to the Pilgrim Fathers* (Oxford: Oxford U. Press, 1971), 76-90, 457-61; Larzer Ziff, *Puritanism in America* (New York: Viking Press, 1973).

See also Pietism.

Q

Quebec. Although some 36,000 Mennonite immigrants have passed through the province of Quebec on their way to new homes in Ontario and western Canada, none remained in Quebec.

In 1956 the Mennonite Board of Missions and Charities (MC) and the Mennonite Conference of Ontario sent two Ontario couples, Tilman and Janet Mills Martin and Harold and Pauline Short Reesor, to Quebec. They were to begin a Mennonite mission outreach in this solidly French and Roman Catholic province.

In 1957 and 1958 church planting efforts began in the cities of Montreal North and Joliette. Two other French congregations have since been established in Rawdon and Rouyn-Noranda; also an English and a Spanish congregation in Montreal. Membership of the present five congregations numbers approximately 140.

In 1982 the supporting Ontario conference changed its name to Mennonite Coference of Ontario and Quebec (MCOQ) in recognition of the Quebec churches. These congregations all became part of the inter-Mennonite Mennonite Conference of Eastern Canada in 1988.

The Mennonite Brethren Church, through its Canada Inland Mission, began work in Quebec in 1963. They sent Ernest Dyck and Lydia Krahn Dyck, former missionaries in the Belgian Congo (Zaire), to the city of St. Jérome. Ten other French congregations followed in Ste. Anne-des-Plaines, St. Donat, St. Eustache, St. Laurent, Montreal, New Richmond, Quebec City, Ste. Rose, and Ste. Thérèse. An English congregation emerged in Waterloo. The French congregations were recognized as a provincial conference by the Canadian Mennonite Brethren Conference in 1984. Membership in the province totaled 850 in 1987.

A third group, the Brethren in Christ, sent David Miller and Patti Gillis Miller to Quebec City in 1981. A congregation of 30 people has been established.

In addition to church planting, the Mennonite churches have also begun Institut Biblique Laval (MB), Camp Peniel (MB), Camp le Sablier (MCOQ), and the Montreal House of Friendship (Mennonite Central Committee Canada and MCOQ).

The Montreal House of Friendship, a community center located in a low-income neighborhood of downtown Montreal, was established in 1973. Its activities include daytime care for children, family services, refugee assistance, children's clubs, camping, language classes, and offender ministries. Some 50 Mennonite Central Committee volunteers have served in these programs. It is also the meeting place for English and Spanish Mennonite congregations. RM-K

MC Yearbook (1984), 17; *GCM Handbook* (1983-84), 8; microfilms of Mennonite Brethren archival records are found in the Centre for MB Studies, Winnipeg.

Quebec Conference of Mennonite Brethren Churches. Between 1949 and 1959 many Mennonite Brethren missionaries on their way to the Belgian Congo (Zaire) lived briefly in Quebec to learn the French language. Some of them brought Quebec to the attention of the Canadian Mennonite Brethren Conference and its mission board (1957). In 1961 the Ernest Dycks, back from the Congo, settled in St-Jérôme about 25 miles nw. of Montreal to begin a church planting ministry. The first baptismal service was held in 1964; in October of the same year the first congregation was organized with 16 members.

In July 1984 the Quebec Mennonite Brethren congregations joined the Canadian Conference as a fully recognized provincial conference. It is the only French-speaking Mennonite Brethren conference in North America. It is composed of nine congregations with a membership of 642 in January 1986. With the support of the Canadian Conference, the Quebec Conference administers its church-planting program, a camp and a Bible school, the Institut Biblique Laval in the Montreal suburb of Saint-Laurent. J-RT

MM (May 1986), 11-13.

Quilts. Although quilted bedcovers were being made in Europe when America was being settled, it was in North America that quiltmaking flourished. Amish and Mennonite women collectively represent a group whose quiltmaking tradition claims a significant contribution to the current worldwide craft, a contribution ranging from collecting to documenting, design, and construction.

American quiltmaking traditions, a rural life-style, and a religious view of women as householder imposed upon Amish and Mennonite women placed them dutifully alone or together around the quilt frame. As Mennonite churches became less rural and as the role of women changed, quiltmaking changed. Amish women have experienced fewer changes so the social structure of quiltmaking has remained the same over the past 100 years.

For Mennonite women the coming of the °°sewing circle concept as permitted by the church fathers after World War I has been significant in their continuing quiltmaking tradition. The ongoing householder role and the Amish preference for "plain style" has contributed to the popularity of the Amish woman's quilt.

Together the women of both groups were positioned in their religious and socioeconomic cultures to receive, from the 1960s onward, the attention of Americans pursuing ways to balance their lives in response to problems of technology and warfare. During this time two factors popularized Amish and Mennonite women and their quilts. First, the interest in quiltmaking stemming out of the "grass roots," "back to our roots," and "back to nature" encouraged many women to seek out quiltmakers and to learn quiltmaking. Amish and Mennonite women were among these quiltmakers. A quiltmaking revival then flourished and continues in the late 1980s. The success of quilt sales at Mennonite °relief auctions has been due largely to the momentum of this revival. A second factor involved the outcome of the Mennonite sewing circle movement. The average age of the sewing circle quilter had been increasing at this time and fewer younger women were quilting. The quilt revival drew some younger Mennonite women to quiltmaking. The quilts made by these sewing circles represent the majority of quilts donated to Mennonite relief auctions. These sewing circles were often asked to do custom quilting and many have done so, donating the money to the church. The demand for custom quilters inspired many Amish and Mennonite cottage quilt industries.

However, it was the declaration of quilts as art that popularized them, especially Amish quilts. In 1971 antique Amish quilts were included in an exhibit at the Whitney Museum in New York City. This exhibit titled "Abstract Design in American Quilts" drew thousands of people and helped to change the course of the Amish quilt.

The antique Amish quilt pattern most focused on, admired and collected was the "Center Diamond." A minimal pattern, allowing the interchange of colors to create a bold centering mandala-type design also facilitates an optimum plain field for displaying stitches. The Amish Center Diamond pattern, unique to the Amish of eastern Pennsylvania, rarely appeared in other Amish communities. Its regional existence may be related to the early American whole cloth, "linsey-woolsey" quilt. Also, center medallion designs appeared in quilts of early Americans as well as Europeans. The Amish application of the design, however, is unique.

From the interest in the Amish center diamond quilt and others displaying bold design such as "Bars," and "Sunshine and Shadow" interest expanded to include all Amish quiltmaking traditions. It was the use of solid color fabrics rather than printed fabrics that distinguished Amish quilts from others. The pieced design of Amish quilts of midwestern United States were the same as "English" quilts.

In the 1980s there are fewer older examples of Mennonite and Amish quilts held by Mennonite and Amish people. When quilts became popular they were actively sought after and many quilts left their family owners and are now found in museums and corporate or private collections in the United States, Europe, and Asia. That these quilts have left the culture has surprised some, but can be explained by the practical view (especially of the Amish) that places value on the process rather than the product; on the fact that grandmother quilted and so does mother and so do I, rather than focusing on grandmother's quilt.

Even with the strong interest in quilting in the 1980s there is little interest among Amish and Mennonites to document and collect this form of woman's art. A major exception has been the work done both through publication and exhibition by *The Peoples Place*—a Mennonite and Amish educational °interpretation and information center in Intercourse, Pa. Documentation of decorative arts by Mennonite museums or other institutions has concentrated on items such as °*Fraktur* and °furniture, both done primarily by men. Serious documentation of quilts has been carried out instead by larger state or national institutions. For instance the Indiana State Museum in Indianapolis made a major purchase of 277 Indiana Amish quilts from a private collector in 1988. The Museum of American Folk Art in New York owns another significant collection of Amish quilts.

The popularity of Amish and Mennonite quilts has had an influence on quilt design and construction done currently (1987) by women from these groups. Because of the popularity of the eastern Pennsylvania Amish quilt designs mentioned, many quilters including these from midwestern United States have reproduced them. It is not unusual, therefore, to find today the Amish Center Diamond quilt design in Indiana or Iowa.

As quilts have been viewed as art and have moved from use on the bed to art on the wall a new smaller size of quilt has emerged, uniquely different in function—the quilted "wall hanging." This trend developed in the early 1970s and its popularity is visible at Mennonite relief sales and quilt shops in Amish country.

While the demand for art quilts such as the "wall hanging" has aided the custom-quilting business and has influenced the increase in earnings it has been suggested that generally the quality of quilting has declined. Those women who first turned to Amish and Mennonite quiltmakers as their teachers now often can claim superior execution of the craft. Another concern commonly voiced by potential buyers at Mennonite relief sales is the lack of more traditional-looking Mennonite and Amish quilts. This is a response to the fact that contemporary Mennonite and Amish women have been influenced by the designs done for custom-quilt buyers, prefer to try new designs and fabrics and have less time to quilt.

Quiltmaking trends of Amish and Mennonite women will most likely continue to be influenced by the delicate balance of values of their religion and the larger world in which they live out their religious values. RH

For more detailed information on Amish and Mennonite quilt patterns, fabric, and quilting motifs see: *Mennonite Quilts and Pieces* (Intercourse, Pa.: Good Books); Rachel T. Pellman and Kenneth Pellman, *The World of Amish Quilts* (Intercourse, Pa.: Good Books, 1984); David Duttinger, *Quilts from the Indiana Amish* (New York: E. P. Dutton, 1983); *Quilting Designs from the Amish* (C. and T. Publishers).

See also Folk Arts.

R

Radio. Regularly scheduled radio programming began to fill the air waves in North America in 1920. The radio provided a direct link to the larger culture for Mennonites who were a largely rural people at the time. The initial Mennonite reaction to the advent of the radio varied widely by conference and regional groups. Acceptance of the radio fluctuated directly with the degree of °acculturation of the various Mennonite groups. The more acculturated groups, e.g., the General Conference Mennonite Church, accepted the radio in stride. The editor of *The Christian Exponent*, writing in 1924, described his newly purchased radio with delight and noted that it along with other recent inventions was bringing Mennonites "into direct contact with the world about us." Mennonites and Amish groups which stressed separation from the world rejected the radio outright. Old Order Mennonite and Amish groups in the 1980s continue to forbid use of the radio. In many conferences of the Mennonite Church (MC), the radio stirred controversy between 1920 and 1950. A survey by Ernest E. Miller of radio use in the Indiana-Michigan Conference in 1939 identified some 600 homes with radios, most of which were purchased in the previous two years. Respondents to the survey were sharply divided on their attitude toward the radio.

As early as 1924 the Virginia Conference (MC) said, "We deem it wrong to have the radio in our homes," and by 1931 the same group made ownership of the radio a test of membership. Widespread use of the radio by lay members forced the Virginia Conference to relax its position in 1944 although it continued to protest the "evils of radio." Owning a radio was discouraged in the Lancaster Conference (MC) until the late 1950s. In some conferences members left the church or were excommunicated when they began using the radio for gospel broadcasts. Although many members of the more conservative conferences owned radios, sometimes surreptitiously, ministers would often sell their radios upon ordination. Although perceived to be less of a threat than °television, the radio was seen as a source of worldly influence that could corrupt the minds of members and weaken their separation from the world. Indeed, as conference groups became acculturated they invariably dropped their resistance to the radio. The sanctioning of *The Mennonite Hour* as the official radio voice of the Mennonite Church in 1951 and the proliferation of religious radio stations after 1960 effectively ended resistance to the radio among mainstream Mennonite groups (°broadcasting). No longer subject to the vices of worldly programming, many Mennonites now enjoyed religious programs throughout the day while other Mennonites tuned their radio dials to secular stations. DBK

See also Amusements; Conservative Mennonite Church of Ontario; Eastern Pennsylvania Mennonite Church; Mass Media.

Vernon Smucker, "The Editor Listens In," *Christian Exponent* (Jan. 18, 1924), 19; William G. Detweiler, "Proper Use of the Radio," *GH* (Feb. 18, 1937), 994; J. L. Stauffer, "The Radio Problem," *GH* (Oct. 18, 1934), 639-40; Ernest E. Miller, "The Use of the Radio Among the Mennonites of the Indiana-Michigan Conference," *MQR*, 14 (1940), 131-48; "Dangers in the Radio," *GH* (Sept. 14, 1948), 853-54; Hubert R. Pellman, *Mennonite Broadcasts: The First 25 Years* (Harrisonburg, Va.: Mennonite Broadcasts Inc., 1979), 9-19; "Radio Dangers to Your Spiritual Life," (Salunga, Pa.: Lancaster Mennonite Conference, 1961); Wittlinger, *Piety and Obedience* (1978), 344, 509-12; James O. Lehman, *Sonnenberg: A Haven and a Heritage* (Kidron, Ohio: Kidron Community Council, 1969), 292-93, 306; Frank H. Epp, *Mennonites in Canada II*, p. 436; John L. Ruth, *Maintaining the Right Fellowship* (Scottdale, 1984), 468, 482, 496; Beulah Stauffer Hostetler, *American Mennonites and Protestant Movements* (Scottdale, 1987), 212, 244.

Railroads and Mennonites have had an ambivalent relationship. For the older, isolated, and relatively prosperous Mennonite settlements in Europe and eastern North America the railroads were a troublesome intrusion which brought Mennonites into closer contact with the outside world and its many problems, but also with its lucrative markets for agricultural products. For others, the railroads opened up new °frontiers which offered an escape to new and relatively isolated settlements.

The railroads, almost invariably coupled with protective trade tariffs, were seen by governments everywhere as one of the most effective means to enforce policies of economic °nationalism. In Germany, after the unification of 1871, railroads were used by the government to reorient old trading patterns, forcing the newly confederated territories to trade through Berlin and the north German port cities. Danzig, along with Berlin, Hamburg, Koenigsberg, Bremen, Kiel, and their surrounding areas, all obtained rail facilities before unification, but these railways and the 1878 tariff facilitated their commercialization and industrialization. For the many Mennonites living in those centers this also marked the end of isolation.

In Russia wagon roads fairly close to the Chortitza and Molotschna regions were built to reinforce military supply lines from Moscow to the south after the °Crimean War. Railroad development, however, was seriously delayed in all of the Ukraine, largely because of conflicting policies by state agencies and private railroad promoters. The Russian government, supported by influential Moscow and Petersburg merchants and industrialists, were determined to redirect northward much of the Ukrainian agricultural trade that had formerly made its way to international markets through southern Black Sea ports. Foreign capitalists, however, were more interested in building railroads northward and eastward from Odessa and other Black Sea ports.

Limited financial resources of the Russian state treasury and failures by private interests delayed construction of any Ukrainian railroads until 1869. In that year a line from Moscow to Kharkov and Taganrog was completed. This line ran a considerable distance from the Mennonite settlements, but six years later a new railway from Kharkov to Sevastopol in the Crimea provided the Chortitza and Molotschna colonies with rail service. Local branch lines in the 1890s brought the railroad right into Chortitza and Halbstadt. Access to northern markets was thus provided, and certainly helped the economy of the Mennonite colonies. But the policy of economic russification of the Ukraine was soon followed by other russification reforms that were not appreciated in the Mennonite colonies.

The Mennonites on the Atlantic seaboard of the United States first encountered the railroads in the 1840s and 1850s. The canals, particularly the Erie Canal (which established New York's dominance in the western trade), had taught businessmen in all the eastern cities the importance of competitive transportation links to the "West" (Midwest). The advent of the railroad age led to intense intercity rivalry for the traffic of the interior. This was matched by a keen awareness on the part of traders and speculators in the interior that, without rail connections, their particular towns would be quickly overtaken by others with such connections. Thus big city promoters and hinterland boosters and speculators urged westward railroad extensions.

The Mennonites in Pennsylvania and Virginia regarded all this frantic boosterism with understandable skepticism. There was certainly much to encourage them to support the railroads and to buy railroad bonds and stocks. But this involved a yoking of believers with unbelievers in decidedly dubious and often scandalous ventures. Since many of the eastern Mennonite settlements were relatively close to large market centers especially Philadelphia, they tended to see the railroads as a convenience rather than as an absolute economic necessity. Some quickly realized that the railroads would not only provide an economic service. They also brought the outside world very much closer.

Further west, in the Ohio, Mississippi and Missouri valleys, the railroads were urgently needed if pioneer farmers were to be able to transport their produce to market. There was consequently stronger initial support among the Mennonites in those states, and correspondingly greater disillusionment when the railroads failed to provide all the services promised at reasonable rates.

The entire railroad network in the northern states underwent major changes during the °Civil War. The former east-west orientation of the railroads was forcibly altered as military leaders sought to establish reliable military supply lines from northern manufacturing and trading centers to the battlefronts farther south, including a new line down the Shenandoah Valley. This brought the railroads much closer to many of the Mennonite settlements and facilitated increased trade after the conflict. During the Civil War some Mennonite men who refused active military service were compelled to do railroad construction work.

Mennonites in Ontario in the 1850s and 1860s largely shared the attitudes of their American coreligionists. Geographically the Niagara and Waterloo settlements were closer to the Ohio Valley than the Atlantic seaboard, but transportation patterns in Canada were different than in the United States. The best and cheapest natural transportation route on the continent was the Great Lakes and St. Lawrence River water navigation system. This route was still open to Canadian farmers, but was closed after the Civil War to their American neighbors by high American tariffs which were designed to force traffic from the interior through American cities on the Atlantic seaboard. In addition, the financing of the early Canadian railroads came mostly from England.

After 1870 Mennonites had new and different experiences with the railroads, particularly with those railroads that opened up important new agricultural frontiers. Disgruntled Russian Mennonites seeking new and remote settlement opportunities found North Americn land-grant railroads very eager to do business with them. These railroads had been given large tracts of land to subsidize construction costs. But these lands were of very little value to the railroads unless they could be sold to *bona fide* settlers who would generate traffic for the railroads. In the United States the Mennonites entered into negotiations with at least half a dozen western land grant railroads, but ultimately gave most of their business in Kansas to the Atcheson, Topeka, and Santa Fe Railroad (ME IV:417), and in Nebraska to the Burlington and Missouri Railroad (ME I:478) and the Chicago, Burlington, and Quincy Railroad. The railroads sold their lands on generous credit terms, extended transportation credits to prospective settlers, and provided other necessary assistance for those immigrants who actually occupied the land. The settlers generated desperately needed rail traffic, and gave assurances that the entire indebtedness would eventually be repaid.

In Canada there was, in 1873, only the promise of a future railroad when the Russian Mennonites approached the Canadian government for a land grant and other concessions (°privileges) in Manitoba. The Mennonites received their land from the government, which was at that time busily at work on a government railroad project. The first Mennonite settlers that came to Manitoba, however, had to take American railroads to Minnesota and then move by riverboat to Manitoba. The government did complete a railroad from Winnipeg to Pembina on the American border in 1878, thus providing Manitobans with their first rail service.

In 1881 the Canadian government signed a contract with a private syndicate to build a proposed transcontinental Canadian railroad. The new Canadian Pacific Railway (CPR; ME I:509), like many western American railroads, was given a huge western land grant. Canadian Pacific officials quickly realized that the Mennonites were excellent settlers and thus were eager to attract new Mennonite immigrants to its lands, or to facilitate the relocation of any who expressed a desire to leave the original

Manitoba reserves and settle farther west on company lands.

The CPR proved a particular benefactor in the 1920s when thousands of Russian Mennonites desperately sought to escape Soviet Russia. The CPR and Canadian National Railways exerted decisive influence on the government to have restrictions against Mennonite immigration removed, and then offered the Mennonite immigrants credit, transportation, land, and advice, much of it on unusually easy terms. The Mennonites had longer and closer links with the CPR and chose to deal mainly, though not exclusively, with that company. Without the assistance of the CPR the 22,000 Mennonites who came to Canada from the Soviet Union in the 1920s would not have been able to emigrate.

Russia also had an agricultural frontier, but east and north of the established Mennonite colonies. Construction of the Trans-Siberian Railroad, begun in 1891 and completed in 1906, opened up vast new tracts of virgin lands at a time when severe overcrowding threatened the older colonies. The Mennonites established a number of daughter colonies near that railroad. Most of these were established after 1907, and had not yet surmounted early pioneering difficulties when World War I and the ensuing °Russian Revolution and Civil War engulfed them.

Railroads in Latin America were usually somewhat more remote from the Mennonite colonies. Many of those who decided to migrate from Canada to Mexico, Paraguay, Brazil, Belize, Honduras, and other Latin American countries did so to reestablish a separation and isolation that had been disrupted. The railroads had been one of the principle instruments of such disruptions. Mennonites arriving later in Latin America did not necessarily share the original colonists' insistence on isolation, but by that time roads provided an alternative and superior means of transport by truck.

The railroads were, for approximately 100 years, the most important link between isolated Mennonite agricultural communities and the metropolitan centers which provided the markets for their agricultural produce and the source of materials and supplies that could not be produced in the Mennonite settlements. Parodoxically, the railroads destroyed the isolation of many Mennonite settlements, facilitating economic integration into larger national and international trading systems, at the same time that they took many Mennonites to new and relatively isolated areas. TDR

Friederich Jungnickel, Staatsminister Albert von Maybach. Ein Beitrag zur Geschichte des preussischen und deutschen Eisenbahnwesens (Stuttgart und Berlin: J. G. Cotta'sche Buchhandlung, 1910); Hajo Holborn, A History of Modern Germany vol. 3 (New York: Knopf, 1969); Hira Jagtiani, The Role of the State in the Provision of Railways (London, 1924); George Rogers Taylor, The Transportation Revolution, 1815-1860 (New York: Harper Torchbooks, 1951); Charles Francis Adams, Railroads: Their Origin and Problems (New York: G. P. Putnam and Co. 1878); Samuel Horst, Mennonites in the Confederacy (Scottdale, 1967); C. Henry Smith, The Coming of the Russian Mennonites (Berne, Ind.: Mennonite Book Concern, 1927); G. P. deT. Glazebrook, A History of Transportation in Canada (Toronto: Ryerson, 1938); F. H. Epp, Mennonites in Canada, I and II; Konstantyn Kononenko, Ukraine and Russia: A History of the Economic Relations Between Ukraine and Russia (1654-1917) (Milwaukee: Marquette U. Press, 1958); J. N. Westwood, A History of Russian Railways (London, 1964); John B. Toews, "The Mennonites and the Siberian Frontier (1907-1930): Some Observations," MQR, 47 (1973), 83-101; Martin W. Friesen, Neue Heimat in der Chaco Wildnis (Asuncion, Paraguay: Chortitzer Komittee, 1987); Hans Duerksen and Jacob Harder, Fernheim, 1930-1980 (Fernheim, Paraguay: Administracion de la Colonia Fernheim, 1980); Harry L. Sawatzky, They Sought a Country. Mennonite Colonization in Mexico (Berkeley, CA.: U. of California Press, 1971).

See also Business; Land Distribution; Migration.

Ramer, Clarence J. (May 30, 1905-Aug. 22, 1987), prairie pioneer and church statesman, was born in Martinsburg, Pa., but accompanied his family to the prairie town of Duchess, Alta., in 1917. He spent 1926 to 1929 studying at Eastern Mennonite School in Harrisonburg, Va. to which he returned from time to time for continuing education. He was ordained in 1930 and married Ethel Martin of Duchess in 1931.

Despite the depression of the 1930s they began the operation of a dairy farm which eventually won a trophy for the best improved dairy herd in Alberta (1965). He soon became involved in many church activities. In 1934 he was instrumental in starting the Alberta-Saskatchewan winter Bible school, and took a leading role in establishing Sunday schools in the Mennonite Church (MC) in his home province. In 1946 he taught at the Hesston, Ks., winter Bible school. He served as principal of Western Mennonite School in Oregon (1956-58). He traveled extensively as an evangelist.

Ramer was particularly interested in biblical symbolism and the Jewish tabernacle. This interest led to his teaching on Jewish forms of worship and the tabernacle at Rosedale Bible Institute, Irwin, Ohio, annually from 1970 to 1979. It also led to his writing of the book God's Unfolding Plan (1984). He was a strong peace advocate and worked closely with Mennonite Central Committee in promoting peace issues. CJD

Menn. Rep. (Sept. 14, 1987), 4.

Ramseyer, Lloyd Louis (Nov. 5, 1899-June 24, 1977), was born near Hudson, McLean Co., Ill., a son of Michael and Anna (Stahly) Ramseyer. He married Ferne Yoder of Middlebury, Ind., June 4, 1927. Their children are Robert, Mary Jean (Wells), and William. Lloyd Ramseyer studied at Bluffton College (AB, biology) and Ohio State U. (MA, PhD in audio-visual education, 1938). He was a high school teacher, coach, and principal in Heyworth, Ill., 1924-36, and summer school faculty member at Bowling Green State U. and in Ohio State U., 1938-41. He co-authored with his major professor at Ohio State U. a standard textbook on the use of motion pictures in teaching (1937).

During his long tenure as president of Bluffton College, 1938-65, the school received North Central Association accreditation (1953), added several significant instructional departments and a number of new buildings, gained financial stability, and grew from fewer than 100 students to more then 500. After 1965 Lloyd and Ferne Ramseyer directed the Mennonite Central Committee relief program in Korea. Lloyd Ramseyer was also an interim pastor of three congregations in Ohio and Kansas; served on several conference and institutional boards, including Mennonite Biblical Seminary (1962-77) and the Board of Education and Publication (GCM; chairman, 1950-62); and was active in college administrators' professional associations, 1950-57.

Some of Ramseyer's weekly chapel talks at Bluffton College were published as *The More Excellent Way* (1965). During his presidency at Bluffton College he was a valiant proponent of truth, forthrightness and practicality in all phases of life and a strong supporter of the Mennonite peace position at a time when such a firm stand was not popular.   DG

The Bluffton News (June 30, 1977);*Scope, The Bluffton College Bulletin* (Sept. 1977); *Who's Who Mennonites* (1943), 195-96.

Recantation. Under the pressure of interrogation with or without torture, many 16th-c. Anabaptists were induced to recant and rejoin the dominant regional church. In some regions, especially where capital punishment for religious error prevailed (Hapsburg lands, central Germany), recanters numbered well over 50 percent of the Anabaptists who appeared in court. In other regions, often where exile was the unofficial but ultimate form of punishment (Strasbourg, some other south German cities, Hesse), the percentage of recanters was much lower.

Why try to induce recantation? Church and court authorities were traditional: recanting was morally advantageous to the soul because the recanters could be received back into the church (Catholic or Protestant) to their salvific benefit. Both Catholics and Protestants, especially the latter, saw the advantage in obtaining recantations from prominent leaders in order to use them to persuade other Anabaptists to recant. From 1538 through about 1560 Strasbourg used recanted Anabaptist Peter Tasch to induce perhaps 200 Anabaptists to recant.

Why did Anabaptists recant? Most of them were pressured intolerably to abjure their faith. Torture, threat of torture, separation for life from spouse and/or children, appeals of relatives and friends, threat of death or at least exile—any of these could be decisive. Furthermore, many Anabaptists (like many Protestants) were troubled in conscience by separation from the church, even a church they thought was an abomination in the sight of God. Therefore some were persuaded to recant by pastors or theologians who themselves continued to exercise a critique against the church (e.g., Michael Schneider at Passau, 1538). Such recanters often retained a substantial element of Anabaptist thought and ethic. One such recanter administered the poor relief program in Strasbourg for many years.

Some, probably most, recanted because they were Spiritualists (°°Obbe Philips) and relied more on the intervening Spirit and less upon the gathered church of believers. Some Anabaptists recanted several times, rejoining the Anabaptist fellowship between recantations. A few of these appear to have been Nicodemites who maintained some active underground fellowship with like-minded Anabaptists but who outwardly led lives of religious conformity to the dominant church.

Many recanters were fresh converts, immature in Anabaptist thought and life; some had been Anabap-

tists for only a few months or even weeks. The standard pressures overwhelmed them and they displayed an awesome ignorance of their new faith in court or under interrogation. But major leaders also recanted: Balthasar °Hubmaier (who recanted and retracted twice), Jacob °°Dachser, Jacob °°Kautz (recanted feebly while seriously ill), Obbe Philips, Hans °°Pfistermeyer, Eitelhans °°Langenmantel, Georg (Jörg) °°Rothenfelder (who retracted and would not recant again) are only a few examples.

It is impossible to find an absolutely clear relation between recantation and torture. Torture was used too frequently as a routine form of interrogation in religious cases to be thought worth recording, even in regions such as South Tirol where it had only recently been introduced into legal practice. Routine torture derived from Roman law, and thus also was standard practice in canon law. There are instances of Anabaptists recanting only after the excruciating pain of torture.

Some authorities used formulae for recantation; these disguised the individual's convictions but also made relative adherence to Anabaptist thought and practice after recantation less apparent.

Protestant churchmen and political leaders tried instruction to persuade Anabaptists to recant, all the more as executions for religious reasons decreased. Many leaders spent many hours with imprisoned Anabaptists. In some Protestant regions church leaders instructed recanting Anabaptists in detail, covering much more than the normally disputed issues of baptism, nature of the church, oath, and government.

°Menno Simons and other Anabaptist leaders of his kind generally disapproved of recantation, associating it in the North at least with extravagant Spiritualism. Some Anabaptist groups were reluctant to receive back into fellowship a retracting recanter. But because of intolerable pressure to recant including torture, Anabaptists usually were reluctant to visit too harsh a penalty on recanters who wanted to return to the fellowship.

Recantation did not necessarily bring release from punishment. Some recanters were flogged, others fined, still others branded on the forehead, a few even killed. In many regions, both Protestant and Catholic, recanters underwent public penance—for example, standing bare-headed with lighted candle, clothed in special coarse cloth, in front of the church or beside the altar at the end of mass or worship for a designated number of Sundays (*Schamstrafe*). In some regions recanters were required to wear a particular cloak, one that set them apart, for a year and a day. Many were required to swear a special oath (ME IV:2), the *Urfehde*, to remain faithful to the church under penalty of death if they relapsed.   JSO

The best material is the largely unworked raw data in the court records, especially in the *Täuferakten* (ME IV:237), which forms the basis for the present article. Occasional brief references to recantation are found in biographies of some Anabaptists in *ME* I-IV. For one brief account see Claus-Peter Clasen, *Anabaptism: A Social History, 1525-1618* (Ithaca, N.Y.: Cornell U. Press, 1972), 366-70. For parallels in early church history related to the readmission of lapsed believers and public penance similar to the *Schamstrafe* described above, see W. H. C. Frend, *Rise of Christianity* (Philadelphia: Fortress, 1985), 318-24, 409-11.

See also Persecution.

Reconciliation is a classic New Testament concept. Though Jesus only used the term once, and Paul used it rarely, it is qualitatively the heart of the message and theology of the New Testament. It is not without antecedents in the Old Testament and Judaism, but in its full development is distinctively Christian.

Its central meaning is the overcoming of an enmity. This enmity is towards humanity from God's side (i.e., his wrath), and towards God on the part of humanity (sin, rebellion, indifference, disobedience, etc.). Both parties therefore need reconciliation, but in the God-human relationship, God is the initiator.

Paul is the only New Testament writer to use the actual terminology of reconciliation, specifically in Rom 5:10-12; Rom 11:15; 1 Cor 7:11; 2 Cor 5:18-20; Eph 2:16; and Col 1:20-23. Related concepts are °forgiveness, °justification, fellowship, °sanctification, °atonement, °peace, freedom, "sonship" (i.e., filial relationship). These terms are employed by a variety of authors.

Reconciliation with God (theological) through Christ becomes in Jesus and Paul the essential paradigm for all other relationships: to oneself (psychological); to one's neighbor (sociological); to the entire creation (ecological, cosmological). Reconciliation is the operative antidote to all consequences of the Fall, which may be described always as breakdown of relationship—or enmity and conflict.

"As the concept of *shalom*-peace is a harmonic of *tesdeka*-justice, peace is a harmonic of reconciliation" (Allard, 110). Christ's sacrifice on the cross epitomizes the understanding that God's justice vis à vis human conflict has reconciliation as its goal. Punishment and retribution as ends in themselves in response to human conflict (for example crime) have no legitimate place in Christian vocabulary, action, or call to the state. Alternatively: "law is in the service of reconciliation and °peace," a statement that is the conclusion and title of a major exegetical study of the New Testament on law (Meurer, *Das Recht im Dienst der Versöhnung und des Friedens*). "Remove the concept of peacemaking from proclaiming the Gospel and the very meaning of Gospel changes. . . . Reconciliation among humans is the identifying mark of God's new creation" (Kraybill, 8, 12). That God's forgiveness is God's law is the breathtaking teaching of the New Testament. As in the Old Testament, law is quintessentially mercy. Old and New Testament texts point to this conclusion (see Lind, *Transformation of Justice: From Moses to Jesus*; Meurer).

Vengeance too is definitively at God's initiative (Rom 12:19)—and is never the Christian's prerogative personally. Neither is the Christian to call for or desire vengeance by the state. But even from God's perspective, if he ". . . has willed the dire consequences that ensue on sin, it does not necessarily follow that he has willed them retributively, punitively. It may be that he has willed them as the only way of doing justice to the freedom and responsibility of the human personality, as he has created it" (Moule, 23). Vengeance is self-consciously omitted from Jesus' agenda—even when he quotes Scripture with such themes in it (Jeremias).

Against a centuries-long tradition of near universal acceptance by Christians, after the 3rd c., of vengeance and violence in response to human conflict, and in spite of the contemporary magisterial Reformers' renewed baptism of the "sword," with minor exceptions 16th c. Anabaptists consistently rejected this traditional means of conflict resolution, conceiving it to be "outside the perfection of Christ" (°Schleitheim Confession, 1527). Peter Riedemann's words of 1545 are representatively adamant: "Now if vengeance is God's and not ours, it ought to be left to Him and not practiced or exercised by ourselves. . . . There is therefore no need for many words, for it is clear that Christians can neither go to war nor practice vengeance. Whosoever doeth this hath forsaken Christ and denied Christ's nature" (Bender, 12, 13).

One of the period's poignant stories illustrating this is of Dirk Willems of Asperen, Holland, an Anabaptist who was being pursued because of his faith by a thief-catcher across the ice. When the thief-catcher fell through the ice Willems turned back to rescue him. Then, against the thief-catcher's will, Willems was arrested at the insistence of the burgomeister, and subsequently put to an agonizing death at the stake (*Martyr's Mirror*, 741-42).

Anabaptist history is replete with similar stories. One 20th c. example is the murder of an Amish baby, Adeline Schwartz, on Aug. 31, 1979. An object thrown out of a passing pickup truck at a buggy killed the infant. In the subsequent investigation, four boys (occupants of the truck) were found to have been guilty of numerous previous attacks on Amish targets. The Amish community and the parents however steadfastly refused to seek vengeance or retaliation (Siegel).

Programs reflecting this theology have recently emerged in North America, drawing as well from a wider renaissance of an "Alternative Dispute Resolution" approach to conflict, but adding their own biblical distinctives. In Canada, Community Justice Initiatives in Kitchener, Ont. is an umbrella organization for several programs with reconciliation the goal. The Victim Offender Reconciliation program was the first, starting in 1975. It deals with a variety of crimes at a post-trial level by bringing victim and offender together through a third-party mediator. The Community Mediation Service followed, offering a means of dispute settlement before cases go to trial. Victim Services ensued, assisting victims and offenders in sexual abuse cases. Most recently, the Network for Community Justice and Conflict Resolution has been initiated to coordinate disparate groups interested in conflict resoluton and new justice models and systems. The network extends across Canada. In the United States, the Mennonite Conciliation Service began in 1975, emphasizing regulation over avoidance in a variety of conflict situations. It has cooperated with the wider network of Christian Conciliation Service chapters. In Elkhart, Ind., a Victim Offender Reconciliation program was begun in 1978. In both Canada and the United States, and wider afield, these programs continue to develop apace.   WNo

Bibl. on War and Peace (1987), esp. 302-11; Vincent Taylor, *Forgiveness and Reconciliation: A Study in New Testament Theology* (London: Macmillan, 1941); Ralph P. Martin, *Reconciliation: A Study of Paul's Theology* (Atlanta: John Knox, 1981); Leon Morris, *The Apostolic Preaching of the Cross* (Grand Rapids: Eerdmans, 1965), 214-50; Henry A. Fast, *Jesus and Human Conflict* (Scottdale, 1959); Siegfried Meurer, *Das Recht im Dienst der Versöhnung und des Friedens* (Zürich: Theologischer Verlag, 1972); C. F. D. Moule, "Punishment and Retribution: An Attempt to Delimit their Scope in New Testament Thought," *Svensk Exegetisk Arssbok*, 30 (1966), 21-36; Pierre Allard, "The Statement of the Correctional Service of Canada Values and a Biblical Perspective for the Role of Chaplain," (DMin thesis, Northern Baptist Theological Seminary, 1986), 70-131; Gerald Austin McHugh, *Christian Faith and Criminal Justice: Toward a Christian Response to Crime and Punishment* (New York: Paulist, 1978); Millard Lind, *Transformation of Justice: From Moses to Jesus*, New Perspectives on Crime and Justice: Occasional Papers of the MCC U.S. Office of Criminal Justice, and MCC Canada Victim Offender Ministries, issue no. 5 (1986); Willard M. Swartley, ed., *The Bible and Law*, Occasional Papers no. 3, (Elkhart, Ind.: IMS, 1982); William Klassen, *Release to Those in Prison* (Scottdale, 1977); Ronald S. Kraybill, *Repairing the Breach: Ministering in Community Conflict* (Scottdale, 1981), 7-14; Joachim Jeremias, *New Testament Theology*, pt. 1: *The Proclamation of Jesus*, trans. John Bowden (London: S.C.M., 1971), 204-8; Harold S. Bender, "The Pacifism of the Sixteenth Century Anabaptists," *MQR*, 30 (1956), 5-18; Barry Siegel, "A Quiet Killing in Adams County," *FQ*, (May-June-July, 1981), 19-26; Norma Rudy, "Community Justice Initiatives: A Major Study of Nonviolence" (unpublished paper Conrad Grebel College, 1984), available from C.J.I. office, Kitchener, Ont.; MCC Peace Section *Newsletter*, 16, no 1 (1986), sp. issue; "Mennonite Conciliation Service Historical Summary," excerpts from Document Files of MCS, 1975-86, prepared by Dave Brubaker, MCS staff associate, presented to the MCS Review Committee of MCC U.S. Peace Section, Oct. 28, 1986; John Driver, *Understanding the Atonement for the Mission of the Church* (Scottdale, 1986).

See also Peace.

Recreation is usually defined as the voluntary participation in an activity during leisure time by an individual because of immediate satisfactions or pleasure. One has a choice of the activities to be participated in because it occurs during that time period not required by the individual to earn a living or perform tasks essential to the sustenance of life. Some argue that the term *recreation* implies that the activity be re-creative in nature and socially acceptable. For the purposes of this article we will assume that recreation is participation in a leisure-time activity without making a moral evaluation of the specific activity. Historically the Christian church has struggled to determine which activities are acceptable and which ones should be shunned (°amusements). This article deals with Mennonite recreation in the United States.

Anabaptists found themselves in difficult times immediately upon their formation in Holland and Switzerland where they were persecuted and frequently were forced to migrate from one area to another. Life was not easy and demanded all of one's time and resources to maintain life. Coming to North America did not ease the demands on time as the work establishing homes in the new land demanded all of their time and energies.

Mennonites satisfied their recreational needs through their participation in church activities, visiting neighbors and relatives, working together in productive social events (husking bees, barn raisings, butcherings, quiltings). Times spent in these activities provided for social needs as well as being productive. (Even in the late 20th c. many prefer to participate in combination service and social activities, e.g., Mennonite °Disaster Service, canning meat for Mennonite Central Committee, or spending hours in preparation for a °relief sale.) Hunting and fishing were acceptable activities that also produced food for the table. Sunday afternoons and evenings were spent reading, writing letters, visiting friends and relatives, or in other edifying activities, e.g., Bible study. Participation in arts and crafts (°folk arts) again was primarily determined by utilitarian factors. °Singing and music were seen as important components of °worship. Women gave creative expression through needlework such as crocheting, knitting, and in the making of °quilts.

There were three major forces that played vital roles in the determination of Mennonite recreation. These were Scriptures, separatism (°°nonconformity), and °economics.

Mennonites have always looked to the Scriptures as their primary source of guidance and have placed a high value on searching the Scriptures, particularly the New Testament, for guidance in making decisions in all aspects of life. Therefore, much of the free time of people was used to read the Bible and in the attendance of church and Bible study nights. The use of leisure time and leisure activities needed to be in accord with their interpretation of the Scriptures.

Acceptance of Jesus Christ as saviour and Lord implies that one becomes a new creature who is now interested in spiritual things and removes herself from participation in "worldly" activities. Traditionally, this has meant that Christians should not participate in socially accepted "worldly" activities such as °dancing, drinking (°°alcohol), card-playing, and pool (billiards) playing (°amusements).

As long as the Mennonites were able to maintain their identity by living in agricultural communities separate from the "world" they were able to reduce, if not eliminate, the pressures from the outside world. Considering the industriousness of the Mennonites and the hardships that they endured as pioneers one can surmise that play was thought of as suitable for children but not for adults. If adults had leisure time it should be spent in a more productive manner. Mennonite concern about participation in questionable amusements is evident from the more than 120 conference resolutions defining and condemning worldly amusements passed by the various Mennonite district conferences after 1865 (ME I:112).

Before 1900 survival made such demands on Mennonites' time and energy that there was very little time for recreational activities. Work on the farms started early in the morning and was continued on into the dark of night. Sundays were taken up with church activities and was a time for visiting relatives and friends. Families were large, and each child was an asset to the family labor force.

Probably because of the many °migrations and the difficulties of pioneer life, the owning of good farmland became increasingly important. So, even though the family needs were met, there was this continuous drive to earn more so that one could buy more land. It has been said that Mennonite recreation was focused on making money and purchasing farmland.

The growth of population and the industrial revolution made a major impact on the Mennonites and their attitudes toward recreational activities. °Farm machinery made larger farms possible. Mennonite families were large, and it was soon evident that there was not enough land available for all of the children to stay on the farm. Compulsory education also brought the Mennonites into contact with others and soon the walls that once protected the Mennonites in their rural colonies began to evaporate.

Mennonites began to accept jobs in the factories and in the cities. The industrial revolution brought with it leisure time as they now worked a 40-hour week and had free time evenings and weekends. Contact with people of other backgrounds presented them with many different views of and opportunities for recreation. The °automobile made it possible to go into a neighboring city to see a movie or to participate in some other questionable form of recreation without fear that someone in the home church would know about it. Thus a new freedom came quickly upon Mennonites. With this freedom came a defensive posture about leisure time with strong feelings that it was no one's business as to how they spent their leisure time because they had earned it (°discipline).

Just as the industrial revolution transformed the agricultural society into an urban factory production society the communication revolution described by John Naisbitt in his book *Megatrends* (1982) is again changing society. Through the use of communicaiton satellites we now are able to witness almost any event anywhere in the world as it is occurring. Just as the industrial revolution moved people from the rural farm life into urban factory life, so the communication revolution is moving people from factory jobs into communication and information jobs. In 1790 98 percent of the population lived in rural areas and only 3 percent in the cities. "Farmers, who as recently as the turn of the century constituted more than one-third of the total labor force, now are about 3 percent of the work force. In fact, today there are more people employed full-time in our universities than in agriculture" (Naisbitt, *Megatrends*, 14). In the 1980s only 13 percent of the labor force is employed in manufacturing.

The challenge facing Mennonites is how they will be able to adapt to these rapid changes. Television brings violence and corruption into our homes as well as religious programs. Computers bring knowledge into our homes and give us access to information that was only dreamed of a few years ago. Our children are exposed to the ways of the world as never before. Toys, games, and cereals are brought to their attention in graphic and appealing ways. Living a life separate or apart from the world is becoming increasingly difficult.

The future will bring increased amounts of leisure time. Not only is the work week getting shorter but we are retiring at an earlier age. This together with an increasing life expectancy will provide us with large blocks of leisure time. With better salaries,

faster transportation, increased marriages to non-Mennonites, and greater availability of recreation opportunities it remains to be seen if the Mennonites will take advantage of these opportunities to become creative Christians or if they will be absorbed and bcome one with the "world" that they once rejected so vigorously.   OHG

John A. Hostetler, *Amish Society* (1980), 166-67, 218-20; Harold D. Lehman, *In Praise of Leisure* (Scottdale, 1974); Charles Evan Oswald, "A History of Sports in the Mennonite Church of North America Since 1900" (master's thesis, U. of Illinois, 1956); Frances Clemens, Robert Tully, and Edward Crill, *Recreation and the Local Church* (Elgin: Brethren Publishing House, 1956); Richard Kraus, *Recreation Leader's Handbook* (New York: McGraw-Hill, 1955); Harold D. Meyer, and Charles K. Brightbill, *Community Recreation* (Englewood Cliffs, N.J.: Prentice-Hall, 1956); John Naisbitt, *Megatrends* (New York: Warner Books, 1982).

See also Idleness; Sports; Urbanization; Work Ethic.

Red Cross. The International Red Cross, a humanitarian agency with national affiliates, was established in 1864 to care for war victims. Later it was broadened to relieve other forms of human suffering.

During World War I in Russia more than 6,000 young Mennonite conscientious objectors served in hospital service in lieu of military service. They served with the All-Russian Union of Zemstvos which was a civilian organization, parallel to but associated with the Russian Red Cross. Some North American Mennonites also served in Red Cross ambulance units during World War I.

In 1921 the young Mennonite Central Committee organization was seeking ways of opening relief programs in the Soviet Union; MCC workers conferred with and were aided by the Red Cross affiliated agency of *Fridtof Nansen*, the International Russian Relief Executive. In World War II (1946-47) the Dutch Red Cross provided the MCC with a supply line for food supplies for the 1,200 Russian Mennonite refugees isolated in West Berlin.

The American (U.S.) Red Cross Disaster Services Division and Mennonite Disaster Service (MDS) have cooperated and supported each other in responding to natural °disasters since the 1950s. The liaison was a somewhat spontaneous process.

American Red Cross often provided food service and lodging for the Mennonite Disaster Service workers. Survey and damage assessment personnel, canteen and fixed food service cooks and workers, shelter managers, caseworkers, staff secretarial and record keeping, and building advisors were often provided by MDS to augment American Red Cross disaster response teams. In the 1960s, American Red Cross frequently supplied the building materials and MDS supplied the skills and voluntary labor to rebuild many homes.

After declared government programs of benefits and funding were introduced in the 1970s, the two agencies continued to work together. American Red Cross caseworkers referred at an earlier stage in the recovery process the most needy families to Mennonite Disaster Service for cleanup and temporary repairs. The two agencies also supported each other in permanent repairs and reconstruction for families in the nondeclared areas.

Because the various national Red Cross (Red

Crescent in Muslim countries) are often funded by and linked to national governments, Mennonites have often been cautious in their collaboration with the Red Cross. CNH

Katie Funk Wiebe, *Day of Disaster* (Scottdale, 1976); John B. Toews, *Czars, Soviets, and Mennonites* (Newton, 1983) 63ff.; Al Reimer, *My Harp Is Turned to Mourning* (Winnipeg: Hyperion, 1985), e.g., 209ff.; Lawrence Klippenstein, "Mennonite Pacifism and State Service in Russia, . . . 1789-1936" (PhD diss., U. of Minnesota, 1984), 131, 160-66, 198.

See also Lohrenz, Gerhard; Reformed Mennonites; Refugees.

Reformation, Catholic. Like other reform movements in the 16th c., Anabaptism owed much to the Catholic tradition. Some early Anabaptist leaders were members of the Catholic clergy, both regular (monastic) and secular (parish clergy); others had been educated in a variety of Catholic schools. All of them were products of a society powerfully influenced by Catholic thought and practice. The Reformation was an age when church and state were intertwined in the fabric of society. Most people did not question the view that God's kingdom should be built through the close collaboration of the two comprehensive institutions. As the Reformation gained ground, most reformers did not question this established belief. Yet, as change came in the religious arena, many who had hailed reformers such as Luther and Zwingli became unhappy with the speed and extent of reform; they demanded more radical change, usually a more deliberate return to what they believed to be New Testament beliefs and practices. Anabaptism was satisfied neither with the new movements nor with the traditional faith.

In its rejection of much Catholic doctrine and practice, and in its expressed discontent with Protestant reform, Anabaptism quickly gained the censure of the Catholic hierarchy, Protestant leaders, and secular authorities. Official pronouncements by ecclesiastical and political rulers denounced Anabaptists as heretics, to be punished by death. The edict issued by the imperial diet in 1529, prescribing the death penalty for Anabaptists, was supported by Catholics and Protestants alike. Records such as the *Martyrs Mirror*, court documents, and contemporary chronicles bear witness to Anabaptist °suffering. In this respect, actions taken by Catholic and Protestant authorities were very similar.

In some areas, Anabaptists stood closer to Catholicism than did many other reform movements. For example, Anabaptists expressed dissatisfaction with Luther's emphasis upon salvation by faith alone. While they rejected what they regarded as the Catholic teaching of a "works righteousness," they insisted that good works were a necessary corollary to living faith. Anabaptists such as °Menno Simons did not share Luther's uneasiness about the Epistle of James; instead, they welcomed its emphasis upon good works.

A number of Anabaptists also retained something of the Catholic °monastic legacy. A de-emphasis upon acquisition of temporal possessions and a recognition of the biblical pattern of °community were at least in part derived from Catholic patterns and nurtured by those who for a time had pursued the ideals of monasticism. In some Anabaptist groups, these views led to a repudiation of private property. Hutterites insisted on sharing economic possessions and on living in a closely-knit community. Anabaptist pursuit of the ideal of the congregation as a community of brothers and sisters in Christ could not be reconciled with the usual patterns of °authority. It should, however, be noted that before long Anabaptists developed their own authority figures; in many instances, °°"elders" or °°"bishops" emerged to provide strong leadership that often weakened egalitarian community practices. Indeed, struggles for °leadership are a prominent part of fractious tendencies noticeable in Anabaptism.

Early Anabaptism was also characterized by an emphasis upon active expressions of piety and devotion. Here too the monastic and °mystic traditions made an impact. It is not accidental that devotional literature, similar to that characteristic of the *devotio moderna,* formed an important part of Anabaptist spiritual nurture. Late medieval Catholic mysticism and piety helped to shape Anabaptism. Anabaptists, however, insisted that devotion and piety should be characteristic of all believers; there should be no special "holy" calling as in monasticism. Thus, bearing arms was forbidden to all, not just the clergy.

Anabaptist insistence on believer's baptism provided the most obvious difference between the traditional faith and Anabaptism. When the Council of Trent (Session VII, canon 13) condemned Anabaptist teaching on baptism, it was echoing a sentiment that had been expressed frequently in temporal statute and ecclesiastical pronouncement. Similarly, Anabaptists rejected the Catholic view that sacraments (°ordinances) were a means of grace; rather, baptism and communion were regarded as acts in which the individual, in the midst of the believing congregation, confessed a living faith, and expressed fellowship with Christ and the church.

Anabaptism, in common with most other reform movements, emphasized scriptural authority. Many Anabaptists taught, however, that the meaning of biblical teachings could best be discerned, not in isolation and not through the *magisterium* (official church teaching), but rather in the community of faithful believers. At the same time, other Anabaptists placed so much emphasis upon direct illumination by the Holy Spirit that some of them were accused of subordinating biblical authority to subjective experience. Most Anabaptists, however, held to a very high view of the Scriptures, and rejected the Catholic position that insisted on a recognition of both Scripture and °tradition as authoritative. A number of Anabaptists, however, reflected contemporary acceptance of the Apocrypha as a significant witness to faith and practice. In this respect Anabaptists such as Hans °°Denck stood closer to traditional Catholic views than did reformers such as Luther and Calvin. Menno Simons, °Dirk Philips and other Anabaptist leaders often quoted from the Apocrypha; at the same time, Menno and others specifically rejected doctrines such as those of purgatory, which had been based in substantial measure upon readings of certain texts in the Apocrypha.

In their rejection of the papacy and the entire Catholic hierarchical system, Anabaptists tended to be less strident than many Protestant leaders. Anabaptists often expressed discomfort with diatribes that denounced the pope as Antichrist. Many Anabaptists readily admitted that they believed many Catholics were part of the family of God. The distinction between the church of Christ and what Menno Simons called the "church of Antichrist" was to be found in matters of belief and practice, not in specific leaders or offices.

Unlike the Anabaptists, most Protestants of the Reformation era retained Catholic views of church and state. The state was presumed to be God's instrument for implementing divine ideals; coercion in the arena of faith, buttressed by theological writing was accepted by Catholic and Protestant for centuries. Most Anabaptists rejected the view that physical force should be used to defend or compel faith, although °Münster provided a notable exception. For the Anabaptist, the believer's role in society was thus radically different from what Catholic tradition held. For most people of the Reformation era, the Anabaptist notion of separation of church and state, and the insistence on religious toleration seemed dangerous and contrary to traditional views of how God's kingdom should be built upon earth. Catholics based their views of church and society upon their understanding of the Scriptures and their centuries-old traditions. Anabaptists contended that the life and teachings of Christ as portrayed in the New Testament provided the authoritative model and guide.　　　　PJK

Kenneth R. Davis, *Anabaptism and Asceticism* (Scottdale, 1974); A. G. Dickens, *The Counter Reformation* (New York: Harcourt, Brace and World, 1969); H. O. Evennett, *The Spirit of the Counter-Reformation*, ed. John Bossy (London: Cambridge U. Press, 1968); Robert Friedmann, *The Theology of Anabaptism. An Interpretation* (Scottdale, 1973); Hubert Jedin, *A History of the Council of Trent*, 2 vols., trans. E. Graf (St. Louis: Herder, 1957, 1961); Walter Klaassen, *Anabaptism: Neither Catholic Nor Protestant* (Waterloo: Conrad Grebel Press, 1973); Marvin R. O'Connell, *The Counter Reformation* (New York: Harper and Row, 1974); J. C. Olin, ed., *The Catholic Reformation: Savonarola to Ignatius* (Loyola, New York: Harper and Row, 1969); Werner O. Packull, *Mysticism and the Early South German-Austrian Anabaptist Movement 1525-1531* (Scottdale, 1977); C. Arnold Snyder, *The Life and Thought of Michael Sattler* (Scottdale, 1974); George H. Williams, *The Radical Reformation* (Philadelphia: Westminster Press, 1962).

See also Roman Catholic Church.

Reformation, Protestant. The religious renewal movements of the 16th c. took many forms; some remained within the traditional ecclesiastical structures, others broke away to form different religious communities. Gradually the term "Protestant" (from the "protesting" estates at the Diet [parliament] of the Holy Roman Empire in Speyer in 1529) came to be applied to most of the new religious bodies, although it was originally designed primarily for the followers of Martin °°Luther.

In the decades following Luther's protest against what he regarded as corrupted belief and practice in the traditional ecclesiastical system, reform movements gained a strong following in most of Europe.

Often, they were successful in becoming the new "official" religion of a state or area, and so Lutheran, Reformed (Calvinist), and Anglican churches came to be the established religion in various countries, and continued the traditional close interaction of church and state. Loosely categorized as Protestant, they shared a large body of doctrine and traditional practice; all regarded themselves as bearers of the legacy of the early church. At the same time, each of the new movements developed its own distinctives. These differences proved strong enough to prevent the development of a united church body, although many Reformation leaders, such as Martin °°Bucer and Philipp °°Melanchthon, tried repeatedly to bring about closer cooperation.

One of the expressions of the quest for church renewal came to be known as °Anabaptism, an epithet that reflected a rejection of the validity of infant baptism and an insistence on baptizing only believers. In their call for a church independent of the state (hence, a "free" church), Anabaptists rejected traditional views of the society as a body of Christians (*corpus Christianum*). Catholic and Protestant opponents alike denounced them as a threat to religious and political order, a threat that should be suppressed. Very few states were tolerant enough to permit Anabaptists to live in peace; they stood outside the boundary of accepted religious and social deviation. Hundreds of court records attest to the zeal with which Catholic and Protestant authorities pursued these nonconformists and often subjected them to torture and to sentences of death, imprisonment, exile, or confiscation of property. Such incessant pressure eventually broke the dynamism of many Anabaptist groups so that they often tried to escape by withdrawing from society.

Although Anabaptists were perceived as an unacceptable threat to the religious and social order, they constituted a rather diverse movement, with differing theological and social emphases. Anabaptism drew its inspiration from many sources; reformation impulses such as those of °°Zwingli in Zürich; medieval Catholic traditions of asceticism and piety; social revolutionary movements such as the Peasants' War; anticlerical expressions rampant in the early 16th c.; dissatisfaction with the nature and extent of church renewal as advocated by such reformers as Luther and Zwingli. At the same time, Anabaptists shared the widely held view that reformation was necessary, and that the Scriptures must be recognized as the source of °authority and direction in any spiritual renewal. Like other reform movements, Anabaptism viewed itself as a recovery of the life of the early church (°restitutionism).

The Scriptures. Luther's insistence on the unique authority of Scripture (*sola scriptura*) was echoed by other Protestant leaders. Religious belief and practice were to be determined by appeals to the Bible. The role of tradition in shaping current practices remained a matter of dispute; Anglicanism in particular, in statements such as the *Laws of Ecclesiastical Polity* by Richard Hooker (ca. 1554-1600), argued for a greater emphasis on historical precedents in the church than continental reformers generally accepted. Anglicans and continental reformers agreed, however, that over the centuries the ecclesiastical system had acquired a form and substance at variance with biblical principles. A reformation in "head and members" (a phrase used since the late medieval era) had become necessary.

Most Anabaptists agreed that the Bible should be regarded as the expression of God's will for the church. Yet not all parts of Scripture were equally authoritative. Anabaptists tended to place special emphasis upon the life and teachings of Christ. Beyond that, many of them insisted that the New Testament, rather than the Old Testament should be regarded as normative. Thus, when Luther, Zwingli, Calvin, and other reformers appealed to the Old Testament to justify their views of church-state relations as well as other beliefs, the Anabaptists appealed to the model of the New Testament church.

On other occasions, some Anabaptists warned that the Bible should not be viewed as a self-sufficient agent of spiritual renewal; rather, it could be effective only when illuminated by the Holy Spirit and received by the "pious heart," as Hans °°Denck said.

Another characteristic of many Anabaptists was an insistence on an almost wooden literalism in applying biblical statements. Only that which was enjoined by Scripture was to be accepted and retained. In this matter they stood much closer to Zwingli than to Luther and many other reformers.

The Nature of the Church. For Luther and for many of his contemporaries, the distinguishing marks of the church were that the Word of God be rightly preached and the sacraments rightly administered. The essence of the church was to be found in the objective work of Christ, not in the subjective experience of the believer. For many, this also meant that the efficacy of a sacrament did not depend ultimately upon the state of the recipient; rather, it represented a work of grace, quite apart from human merit. Membership in the body of Christ was dependent upon divine grace alone, and reflected divine election.

Most Anabaptists were uneasy with Luther's doctrine of salvation "by faith alone" (*sola fide*). Nor could they accept the view that subscribing to propositional truth was enough to make a person a believer and a member of the church. Rather, belief must be accompanied by a determination to follow "in the footsteps of Christ," as Hans °Hut stated. The church was the company of the committed, not simply those who had once been baptized. It is thus not surprising that Anabaptists tended to take church °discipline very seriously, indeed some developed rigidly legalistic standards. In this respect they shared some of Calvin's insistence on strict adherence to external forms of piety.

Early in the Reformation Anabaptists adopted the practice of expelling from their fellowship those regarded as insufficiently committed to a life of discipleship. The pronouncement of the °°"ban" became a very controversial issue, and it demonstrated a determination to go beyond many other reformers, such as Luther, who held that a person should be barred from the life of the church only if guilty of flagrant sin. It is not surprising that Anabaptists, with their insistence that faith must be combined with works, were sometimes accused of holding to belief in salvation by works, to a doctrine of "works righteousness."

Baptism and the Lord's Supper. When Luther published his treatise, *On the Babylonian Captivity of the Church* (1520), he alienated many who had earlier supported him. To reject many of the traditional sacraments was enough, as Erasmus said, "to rend the seamless robe of Christ." Luther's retention of only °baptism and °communion provided the model for Protestantism, but at the same time, the meaning of these sacraments (°ordinances) became very controversial within the reformation movements. Some reformers insisted that baptism was essential to salvation; others were content to describe it as a covenant sign. Luther and many Protestant contemporaries regarded the teaching of the real presence in the Lord's Supper so important that they refused to recognize as fellow-believers those who, like Zwingli, regarded the elements as symbolic. On the other hand, some movements of reform, such as Anglicanism, eventually accepted creedal statements designed to be elastic enough to permit broadly divergent views on the sacraments.

In their practice of baptism, Anabaptists most visibly and sharply differed from other Reformation movements. Baptism symbolized conscious identification with Christ and his church; only an adult believer was capable of taking such action. When reformers such as Luther insisted that baptism was essential to salvation and should be administered to infants, Anabaptists responded that baptism had meaning only when it was the expression of personal and deliberate choice. Again, when Calvin and Zwingli stressed baptism as a covenant symbol, similar to Old Testament circumcision, Anabaptists, while affirming the covenantal nature of the church, insisted that the New Testament covenant of faith required faith on the part of the individual participant. They rejected any notion about the adequacy of "dormant" or "vicarious" faith. At the same time, Anabaptists did not accept the widely held Catholic and Protestant view that infants were born condemned because of °°original sin.

Since most reformers, as well as the traditional church, still adhered to the view that members of society should constitute the *corpus Christianum* and be initiated into it by baptism, the Anabaptist rejection of °°infant baptism quickly brought confrontation. Protestants and Catholics alike contended that this revolutionary view would be destructive of both church and society and could not be tolerated. Numerous edicts condemned Anabaptists and prescribed the death penalty for them.

Differences between Anabaptists and other Reformation movements on the doctrine of the Lord's Supper were less pronounced, for the reformers differed sharply in their views. Very few Anabaptists agreed with Luther's insistence on the real presence of Christ in the Eucharist; rather, they stressed that the elements were to be viewed as mere symbols and thus largely shared Zwingli's interpretation of communion. In addition, many of them viewed the Supper as an expression of identification with Christ in his °suffering and as an expression of fellowship among the participants, as a demonstration of their unity.

Political and Religious Structures. In their hope to create God's kingdom on earth, or at least a society that would be patterned on biblical principles, most Protestant reformers held that the state was the divinely-ordained institution to assure adherence to these principles. Coercion, even inflicting the death penalty, was viewed as appropriate for the sake of achieving this lofty goal. In Luther's two-kingdom theory, the arena of faith functioned in accordance with laws quite different from those that regulated society at large. The one should be guided by principles of love and faith; the individual believer should emulate the life of Christ. The state, however, was dedicated to the maintenance of peace and order; it was to be guided by ideals of justice as enunciated (especially for Luther) by the apostle Paul in his letter to the Romans. Other reformers appealed to the Old Testament to justify their views on how societies should function. For most reformers, the belief that the power of the state should be used to preserve truth was axiomatic. Evil made the use of force necessary. The coercive suppression of nonconformity was the result.

In their earliest comments about church-state relations, Anabaptists were somewhat ambiguous about how the rule of Christ on earth might be effected. Clearly, many leaders hoped that their message of renewal would be widely accepted, and thus form the basis for a changed society. When it became apparent that these expectations would not be realized, they adopted a radically different approach. They called instead for a separation of church and state structures so that a church "free" of political and secular entanglements might be formed. This revolutionary proposal struck most reformers as dangerous and divisive; a centuries-old tradition would have to be abandoned. Many Anabaptists responded by withdrawing from any participation in political institutions. They would not be part of a system that used coercion in matters of faith, and that rejected the view that the ethics of Christ should be normative in society. In part their repudiation of the citizen's °°oath reflected this view, although they also insisted that Christ's prohibition about oath-taking should be taken literally. Similarly, many Anabaptists rejected participation in war, contending that it was contrary to the rule of Christ and usually a means of aggrandizement of states and rulers. Some Anabaptists, e.g., Balthasar °Hubmaier, supported the right of military self-defense, and argued that the believer owed such service to society. Other Anabaptists, such as those at °Münster, were prepared to use violence to achieve their goals. Most Anabaptists, however, followed the position taken by the °°Swiss Brethren and °Menno Simons: Christ's call to a life of love and service was incompatible with participation in war. It was better to suffer than to kill.

Most reformers held to the °just war theory, and regarded the resort to war as an appropriate response by the state to certain kinds of problems. It should be noted, however, that they usually (with the possible exception of Zwingli) did not condone aggressive war, or attempts to use the military crusade to gain religious goals. Both Luther and Calvin regarded the state as God's gracious gift to a world torn by evil; law and order must be maintained so that the work of the gospel might not be impaired. In the pursuit of that goal, the use of force, including warfare, was a valid option.

The Role of Clergy and Laity. Luther's emphasis on the °priesthood of all believers came to be shared by most of Protestantism. Thus, the priest was no longer viewed as an essential intermediary between God and members of the church. Most Protestant reformers, however, continued to stress the necessity of maintaining a separate clergy, empowered to carry out the functions of the church. Some movements, such as Anglicanism, retained a rigidly hierarchical form of episcopal church government. The bishop (*episcopos*) ruled the church, and was also very closely tied to political structures. Calvin, on the other hand, stressed the necessity of sharing authority between clergy and laity. His "consistory," however, as a form of representative government, still fell short of the Anabaptist °polity of congregational autonomy.

Protestants, such as Luther and Calvin, stressed the role of the preacher in spreading the new teachings. Anabaptists urged all members to become advocates of their beliefs.

For the Anabaptists, the difference between clergy and laity was de-emphasized, often obliterated. Some of the insistence on this equality may have stemmed from an anticlericalism that grew out of perceived abuses of the priestly office; on the other hand, Anabaptists tended to reject sacerdotalism, that is, an emphasis on the sanctity of the priesthood (from *sacerdos*, Latin for priest). Everyone should participate in the same way in the life of the church; a professional clergy was viewed with suspicion.

Anabaptists generally held that ministers should be selected by the members of the congregation, and that policies within the body should be decided by the entire membership. They thus rejected episcopal structures. It should be noted, however, that many Anabaptist congregations later chose authority figures, such as °°elders, or °°bishops and vested them with considerable power in the congregation.

The Church and Social Responsibility. Most reformers agreed that society bore a significant measure of responsibility for the well-being of those unable to care for themselves. At the same time, no one should presume on the generosity of someone else. Luther stressed the dignity of labor and the importance of one's calling, or vocation, to "secular" occupations. Similarly, Calvin held that each person's work should be viewed as a means of glorifying God. Many of the reformers also stressed the necessity of implementing popular education. Here the church played a major role; indeed, in the Europe of the Reformation, education continued to be the province of the church.

For the Anabaptists, however, the church held center stage both in social welfare and education. Anabaptists generally insisted that religious belief must find social expression. Members of the congregation were expected to help those in need (°°mutual aid). Failure to do so could bring expulsion from the congregation.

Some Anabaptists, most notably in Moravia, felt

that there could not be a true community of spirit unless there was also a °°community of goods. Thus, they rejected private property. Economic possessions were given to the entire community, to be dispersed by stewards as needed. Court records of Anabaptists being prosecuted demonstrate that most reformers and political leaders regarded the practice of having community ownership of property as revolutionary and dangerous. It was not to be tolerated.

Anabaptists also stressed education in the home and in the congregation. Learning was often tied to religious goals. In this, Anabaptists shared a widespread characteristic of the Protestant Reformation.   PJK

Rollin S. Amour, *Anabaptist Baptism: A Representative Study* (Scottdale, 1966); James Atkinson, *Martin Luther and the Birth of Protestantism* (Baltimore, Md.: Penguin, 1968); Roland Bainton, *Here I Stand* (New York: Mentor Books, 1956); idem, *Women of the Reformation,* 3 vols. (Minneapolis, 1971-73); Harold S. Bender, *The Life and Letters of Conrad Grebel* (Goshen, Ind.: Mennonite Historical Society, 1950); Neal Blough, *Christologie Anabaptiste: Pilgram Marpeck et l'humanité du Christ* (Paris: Labor et Fides, 1984); Heinrich Bornkamm, *Luther's Doctrine of the Two Kingdoms in the Context of his Theology,* trans. by K. H. Hertz (Philadelphia: Fortress Press, 1966); Geoffrey W. Bromiley, *Thomas Cranmer, Theologian* (London: Oxford U. Press, 1956); Miriam Usher Chrisman, *Strasbourg and the Reform* (New Haven: Yale U. Press, 1967); Claus-Peter Clasen, *Anabaptism: A Social History, 1525-1618* (Ithaca: Cornell U. Press, 1972); Kenneth R. Davis, *Anabaptism and Asceticism* (Scottdale, 1974); A. G. Dickens, *The English Reformation* (London: Batsford, 1964); John Dillenberger, ed., *John Calvin: Selections from His Writings* (Garden City, N.Y.: Doubleday, 1971); idem, ed. *Martin Luther: Selections* (Garden City, N.Y.: Doubleday-Anchor Books, 1956); Jane Dempsey Douglas, *Women, Freedom, and Calvin* (Philadelphia: Westminster, 1985); Cornelius J. Dyck, ed., *A Legacy of Faith: The Heritage of Menno Simons* (Newton, 1962); Mark U. Edwards, *Luther and the False Brethren* (Stanford, Calif.: Stanford U. Press, 1974); Geoffrey R. Elton, ed., *The Reformation, 1520-1559* (vol. 2 of) *The New Cambridge Modern History* (Cambridge U. Press, 1958); Erik H. Erikson, *Young Man Luther: A Study in Psychoanalysis and History* (New York: Norton, 1958); William R. Estep, *The Anabaptist Story* (Grand Rapids: Eerdmans, 1975); Heinold Fast, *Heinrich Bullinger und die Täufer: Ein Beitrag zur Historiographie und Theologie im 16. Jahrhundert* (Weierhof: Mennonitischer Geschichtsverein, 1959); Robert Friedmann, *The Theology of Anabaptism: An Interpretation* (Scottdale, 1973); Abraham Friesen, *Reformation and Utopia: The Marxist Interpretation of the Reformation and its Antecedents* (Wiesbaden: Steiner, 1974); Hans-Jürgen Goertz, ed., *Umstrittenes Täufertum 1525-1575* (Göttingen: Vandenhoeck und Ruprecht, 1975); Harold J. Grimm, *The Reformation Era, 1500-1650,* rev. ed. (New York: Macmillan, 1973); Hans J. Hillerbrand, *The Reformation: A Narrative History Related by Contemporary Observers and Participants* (New York: Harper and Row, 1964); Irvin B. Horst, *The Radical Brethren: Anabaptists and the English Reformation to 1558* (Nieuwkoop, 1972); Walter Klaassen, *Anabaptism: Neither Catholic Nor Protestant* (Waterloo: Conrad Grebel Press, 1973); Cornelius Krahn, *Dutch Anabaptism: Origin, Spread, Life, and Thought, 1450-1600* (The Hague: Nijhoff, 1968); Franklin Littell, *The Anabaptist View of the Church,* 2nd ed., rev. (Boston: Starr King Press, 1957); John S. Oyer, *Lutheran Reformers against Anabaptists* (The Hague: Nijhoff, 1964); Steven E. Ozment, *Mysticism and Dissent: Religious Ideology and Social Protest in the Sixteenth Century* (New Haven: Yale U. Press, 1973); idem, *The Reformation in the Cities* (New Haven: Yale U. Press, 1975); Werner O. Packull, *Mysticism and the Early South German and Austrian Anabaptist Movement, 1525-1531* (Scottdale, 1977); T. H. L. Parker, *John Calvin: A Biography* (Philadelphia: Westminster, 1975); G. R. Potter, *Zwingli* (Cambridge: Cambridge U. Press, 1977); W. S. Reid, *Trumpeter of God: A Biography of John Knox* (New York: Scribner's 1985); John D. Rempel, "Christology and the Lord's Supper in Anabaptism: A Study in the Theology of Balthasar Hubmaier, Pil-

gram Marpeck, and Dirk Philips" (ThD diss., St. Michael's College, Toronto Toronto School of Theology, U. of Toronto, 1986); Robert W. Scribner, *For the Sake of Simple Folk: Popular Propaganda for the German Reformation* (New York: Cambridge U. Press, 1966); Ronald J. Sider, *Andreas Bodenstein von Karlstadt* (Leiden: Brill, 1974); Lacey Baldwin Smith, *Tudor Prelates and Politics* (Princeton: Princeton U. Press, 1953); Lewis W. Spitz, *The Protestant Reformation, 1517-1559* (New York: Harper and Row, 1985); James M. Stayer, *Anabaptists and the Sword* (Lawrence, Kansas: Coronado Press, 1972, 1976); Leonard Verduin, *The Reformers and Their Stepchildren* (Grand Rapids: Eerdmans, 1964); Robert C. Walton, *Zwingli's Theocracy* Toronto: U. of Toronto Press, 1967); George H. Williams, *The Radical Reformation* (Philadelphia: Westminster Press, 1962); John H. Yoder, *Täufertum und Reformation im Gespräch* (Zürich: EVZ-Verlag, 1968); Lowell P. Zuck, *Christianity and Revolution: Radical Christian Testimonies, 1520-1650* (Philadelphia: Temple U. Press, 1975).

See also Atonement; Biblical Interpretation; Grace; Justification; Roman Catholic Church; Salvation.

Reformed Mennonites (ME IV:267). The membership of this denomination as of June 1, 1987 was 412. Congregations were located at North Easthope (92 members) and Stevensville (63) in Ontario; Sterling, Ill. (44); Shelby, Mich. (24); Bluffton (30), Marshallville (9), and Wauseon (32) in Ohio; Memphis, Tenn. (9); Waynesboro (14), Longeneckers (68), and Middlesex (19) in Pennsylvania; and 8 members in other areas.

A division took place in 1917 under the leadership of John Miller, minister of the Reformed Mennonite Church in Huron Co., Ohio, in disagreement over conducting funerals in cooperation with non-Reformed Mennonite ministers and over the support of the American °Red Cross during World War I. Three congregations formed the New Reformed Mennonite Church. They were located in Huron, Richland, and Lucas Cos., Ohio. There were also several members in Ontario. The last service was held in their church near Willard, Ohio, in August 1967. The last member, a minister named Harry Pittenger, died in 1985 at Willard, Ohio.

In 1975 Minister Willis Weaver and several Reformed Mennonite families withdrew from their church in Lancaster Co., Pa., over personal differences with the other ministers. There were 17 members in this group in 1987. The Reformed Mennonite Church no longer operates a home in Lancaster, Pa.   DG

Reimer, *Quilt* (1983), 24; *MWH* (1978). 373.

Refugees (ME IV:270), victims of wars, revolutions, and ideologies, are far more numerous in the 20th c. than are victims of natural °disasters. To escape °persecution, torture, or death because of race, religion, or political views, refugees flee the country of their origin in search of asylum. According to the United Nations (UN) High Commissioner of Refugees there were 10,304,400 refugees in 1985, with almost half of them crowded into camps—those inhuman institutions with their characteristic atmosphere of despair, hopelessness, and the curse of enforced idleness. The UN listed the number of refugees in the world (1985) as follows: Asia - 2,974,500; Africa - 2,930,200; Middle East - 1,902,900; North America - 1,528,000; Europe - 677,000; Central America - 165,200; Australasia - 104,400; South America - 22,200.

Millions more are "displaced persons" in their own countries who have been forced to flee their home communities for much the same reasons that refugees flee across national boundaries. Until 1987 West Germany claimed to be the only country that constitutionally guaranteed asylum to political refugees.

One of the most dramatic refugee movements in all history was the exodus of the Israelites from Egypt, their 40 years of wilderness wanderings, and their ultimate settlement in Canaan. For 3,000 years the Jews have been refugees. One of them wrote: "By the waters of Babylon, there we sat down and wept, when we remembered Zion" (Ps 137:1). Joseph and Mary were refugees, caught in a political web not of their own making and fleeing out of fear for the safety of the infant Jesus (Mt 2: 13).

Persecution of those who dissented from official church law or doctrine, or both, produced some refugees during the Middle Ages: Jews (12th c. ff.), the Cathari or Albigenses (12th-13th c. ff.), the Waldenses (12th c. ff.), the Lollards and Hussites (15th c.). The wholesale religious wars and persecutions of the Reformation era produced even more refugees during the 16th and 17th c. Among those who most frequently found themselves fleeing for their lives were the Huguenots (French Calvinists) and Anabaptists.

The main records of Anabaptist persecution, torture, and death are *Het Offer des Heeren* (1562-63), *The Martyr's Mirror* by Thieleman J. van Braght (1660), and the great *Chronicle of the Hutterites* ("Geschicht-Buch") about 1665. In the 16th and 17th c. Anabaptists were driven from their homes and communities in Switzerland, Austria, Holland, France, Moravia and elsewhere. In the Swiss canton of Berne a special police called "Anabaptist-Hunters" (Täuferjäger) was employed to ferret them out and arrest them.

Mennonites also have a long history of aiding refugees. In 1553 North German Mennonites gave asylum to English Calvinists fleeing for safety from their Catholic queen. In the 1660s Dutch Mennonites sent large contributions to the Hutterian Brethren persecuted in Hungary, and likewise to the Swiss Brethren in 1672. In 1710 they organized the Foundation for Foreign Relief (Fonds voor Buitenlandsche Nooden) which helped 400 refugees from Switzerland settle in the Netherlands and contributed large sums of money to aid in the migration of Swiss Brethren from the Palatinate to Pennsylvania.

North American Mennonite assistance to people of their faith who came to Canada and the United States in large °migrations in the 1870s (more than 18,000) and the 1920s (more than 20,000) might not be regarded as assistance to refugees because, although these people left Russia for a variety of reasons including lack of religious freedom, they would not all qualify as refugees under the current UN definition of a refugee. Theirs was a typical push-and-pull situation resulting in more or less normal immigration. The line between refugee and voluntary emigrant is still difficult to draw.

The Mennonites who left the Soviet Union in 1929 should probably be regarded as people whose journey began as emigrants but ended in a nightmare as refugees. About 14,000 made it to Germany. The rest were dispersed by force either to Siberia or sent home. The best account of this tragic event is *Vor den Toren Moskaus* (At the Gates of Moscow, 1960). Mennonite Central Committee (MCC) raised about $100,000 (US) for their resettlement in South America. Ultimately 5,769 did find new homes in the following countries: Brazil - 2,533; Paraguay - 1,572; Canada - 1,344; Argentina - 6; Mexico - 4; USA - 4; Germany - 306.

About the time of the Moscow disaster another group managed to escape over the frozen Amur River into Harbin, China. MCC assisted about 200 to settle in the United States, 373 in Paraguay, and 180 in Brazil. *River of Glass* by Wilfred Martens (Scottdale, 1980) tells this dramatic story.

World War II made many refugees, including more than 12 million in Germany alone. The first contact with Mennonite refugees from the Soviet Union was in mid-1945 when 33 showed up in Holland. With the assistance of T. O. °Hylkema, pastor of the Mennonite church in Amsterdam, MCC negotiated an agreement with the Dutch government to provide asylum for more of these people. MCC and the Dutch Mennonites guaranteed full maintenance and onward movement at the earliest opportunity. To formalize and facilitate this arrangement a "Menno Pass" was issued to each refugee admitted into the country. All but one, who because of mental illness had to be institutionalized, left Holland within a year or two.

The open door to Holland and fear of being kidnapped by Soviets in Germany and forcedly returned to the Soviet Union made hundreds of Mennonites flee to the town of Gronau in Westphalia on the German-Dutch border. As the city became innundated with refugees and the news became public it attracted the attention of the Soviet authorities. Consequently under pressure from the USSR, Holland closed its borders but adamantly refused to return to the Soviet Union those Mennonites that had already been admitted.

The consequence of the refugee influx to Gronau was that MCC opened a major camp, with hospital, in that city. Meanwhile, a refugee camp was opened in Berlin starting with 125 persons and closing nine months later, on January 31, 1947, with over 1,200 refugees. This group was joined by 300 from Holland and over 1,000 from Munich in South Germany and was the first major refugee transport and resettlement effort, of any group—Mennonite or non-Mennonite—to leave Europe after World War II.

Ultimately four transports left Bremerhaven, Germany, for South America with a total of 5,616 persons as follows: Jan. 31, 1947 on the *Volendam*, 2,303; Feb. 25, 1948 on the *Heinzelman*, 860; May 16, 1948 on the *Charlton Monarch*, 758; Oct. 7, 1948 on the *Volendam*, 1,695.

The International Refugee Organization (IRO), the first international agency created by the UN in 1947, provided considerable funding for those refugees that were eligible according to the UN definition; the rest of the money needed to come from the Mennonite churches. The last *Volendam* transport included 751 Prussian and Danzig Mennonite refugees who settled in Uruguay and 115 non-Mennonites selected by the Hutterian Brethren (Society of Brothers) for settlement in their Primavera colony in Paraguay. In addition to the temporary nine-month camp in Berlin and the Gronau camp, MCC also maintained camps at Backnang near Stuttgart and had special staff members at Falingbostel assisting those going to Canada and the United States as well as at Oxboel, Denmark, assisting the Danzig and Prussian refugees.

Many of the refugees from Russia and Prussia chose to stay in West Germany. To help them get established and also to prevent scattering, MCC provided funding and manpower for the construction of settlements (*Siedlungen*). °°Pax volunteers began in 1951 to build houses for them at Torney, Espelkamp, Backnang, Wedel, Enkenbach, and Bechterdissen, as well as for the *Gemeinschaft der Evangelisch Taufgesinnter* (°Nazarenes) refugees in Taxach near Salzburg, Austria. No settlement was considered complete until a church building had been erected. A total of 486 Pax volunteers served for two years in Germany (76 in Austria). In 1948 MCC established *Der Mennonit*, a 16-page German monthly paper primarily for the benefit of the scattered refugees. In 1953 C. F. Klassen, special commissioner for MCC, initiated a systematic tracing service (*Suchdienst*) to facilitate the finding of scattered refugees in Europe and their relatives in Canada and elsewhere.

A new concern for refugees emerged in the Mennonite churches of Canada and the United States in the 1970s. Earlier efforts had concentrated mainly, though not exclusively, on helping Mennonites, but with the end of the °Vietnam War in 1975 and the emergence of the "boat people" refugees, MCC turned to helping non-Mennonite refugees, primarily from southeast Asia but, after 1980, also from Central America. There were at least three reasons for this: first, Mennonites, rooted in Scripture, read often the words of Jesus, "I was hungry and you gave me food . . . I was a stranger and you welcomed me." (Mt 25: 35) Secondly, there was a realization that the 20th c. had brought with it an entirely new phenomenon not known before, the difficulty of fleeing one country and the problem of entering another. With the emergence of passports and visas, the tightening of securities at borders and the ideological tensions there emerged the "stateless person," the unwanted refugee who often could not get out, yet could not get in. Thirdly, there was the deep involvement of the United States in the unpopular Vietnam war, and the long service of MCC and the Eastern Mennonite Board of Missions and Charities (MC) in Vietnam, providing much awareness of the post-war plight of these people, and perhaps also a sense of guilt.

At its annual meeting in 1980 MCC adopted a resolution on refugees resolving to "give special attention during the next three years to the needs of refugees in Africa, Southeast Asia, the Middle East and other regions." Assistance was to be in personnel, money, and material aid, helping refugees to return to the countries of their origin or resettling them elsewhere. Always there was to be a strong concern for the social and spiritual needs of these people.

As the linkages between revolutions and refugees, ideologies and homeless people, injustice and poverty became increasingly obvious, MCC attempted to work also at solving root causes. °Peace and °reconciliation efforts attained new meaning and urgency. Concern also shifted from non-Western countries, where refugees walked the lonely roads, to Canada, the United States, and Europe, where the weapons were made that drove these people from their homes and countries. In books like *Making a Killing* by Ernie Regehr the linkage was documented.

Concern was also directed to active involvement in nonviolent action, to shifting from traditional peacekeeping to active peacemaking (°peace activism). Evidence of this shift and a greater readiness to engage in challenging the civil authorities was also seen in a refugee program called Overground Railroad (ORR). The ORR was started in 1983 as a service for Central American refugees by Jubilee Partners of Georgia; Reba Place in Evanston, Ill.; and MCC. It shuttles refugees from south Texas to host congregations in various parts of the United States and ultimately to Canada, where congregations often act as official sponsors providing housing, food and clothing, orientation, and the necessary care and moral support. The ORR program, in addition to helping individual refugees and families, is a direct and bold challenge to unjust United States refugee policy. During 1985 ORR assisted 200 refugees from Central America to reach haven in Canada, via Mennonites and other churches.

Canada has a long history of helping refugees. Since World War II more than a half-million refugees settled in Canada. MCC Canada on June 3, 1981, signed an "Extension of Agreement with Regard to the Sponsorship and Joint Assistance of Refugees" with the Canadian government, primarily at that time for the sake of helping refugees from Indochina. During a six-year period (1980-85) nearly 3,000 refugees were sponsored by Canadian Mennonites. From 1975 through 1986 4,216 refugees were sponsored to resettle in the United States through MCC US.

MCC's response to refugees has been to help them return to the country of origin if possible, to assist in resettling them in the country of their first asylum, or to resettle them in a third country. Assistance consists in food and clothing, medical and educational services, employment, training, and meeting agricultural, housing, social, and spiritual needs.

While the refugee problem is complex it can be said that wars and revolutions, ideologies, and intolerance are the chief culprits. Massive indifference is the major obstacle to solving the refugee problem.   PJD

Bibl. on War and Peace (1987), 596-611; Frederick A. Norwood, *Strangers and Exiles*, 2 vols. (Nashville: Abingdon Press, 1969); Peter J. Rose, *Working with Refugees*, Proceedings of the Simon S. Shargo Memorial Conference (New York: Center for Migration Studies, 1986); Frank H. Epp, *Mennonite Exodus* (Alton, Man.: D. W. Friesen and Sons Ltd., 1962); Komitee der Flüchtlinge, ed., *Vor den Toren Moskaus* (Yarrow, B.C: Columbia Press, 1960); John D. Unruh, *In the Name of Christ* (Scottdale, 1952); John B. Toews, *Lost Fatherland* (Scottdale, 1967); J. Winfield Fretz, *Pilgrims in Paraguay* (Scottdale, 1953); Walter Regehr, ed.,

25 Jahre Kolonie Neuland Chaco-Paraguay (1947-1972)
(Karlsruhe: Heinrich Schneider, 1972); Martin W. Friesen,
ed., *Kanadische Mennoniten Bezwingen eine Wildnis* (Kolonie
Menno, Paraguay, 1977); Peter Pauls, Jr., ed., *Mennoniten in
Brasilien* (Witmarsum, Brazil, 1980).

See also Relief Work; *Umsiedler* (resettlers).

Overland Exodus: Henry's Red Sea

The homes and villages of many Mennonite
farmers in the Russian Ukraine were burned to the
ground at the end of World War II. The inhabitants
fled to escape prison or death. Hundreds started
west looking for homes in some land of freedom.
When they finally reached Berlin, Germany, they
were near starvation. Peter and Elfrieda Dyck of the
Mennonite Central Committee (MCC) found them in
an empty, half-bombed warehouse. Through the efforts of the Dycks and the MCC, a temporary
refugee center was provided in the American sector
of Berlin. After many months, transportation was
scheduled on the Dutch ship *Volendam* to take these
1,000 homeless people to Paraguay.

The story of the *Volendam* was a modern miracle,
likened to the Israelites crossing the Red Sea. The
ship was waiting in the dock in Bremerhaven, ready
to sail. But Bremerhaven was located in the British
occupation zone of Germany, separated from Berlin
by part of the Russian occupation zone of Germany.
Other Mennonite refugees from Munich and Holland
were already on board the ship. The Soviet government refused to give permission for the Berlin
refugees to cross the Soviet Zone. The ship could
wait no longer. Peter Dyck left to bid the other
refugees goodbye. Elfrieda remained with the
stranded people in Berlin.

Then the miracle took place. Suddenly the Russian
officers gave permission for the Mennonite people
to go through their territory. They had one hour to
get ready. American army trucks took them to a
waiting freight train. It was winter and bitterly cold
and the rows of cars had only straw-covered floors
and flimsy woodburning stoves. Everyone got on
board with Elfrieda in charge. As it started, word
came that Peter Dyck had returned to join them.

A version of this story was written for children in
a novel called *Henry's Red Sea* by Barbara Claassen
Smucker and published by Herald Press in 1955.
Thirty-two years later it is still in print. The main
character in the story is an 11-year-old boy, Henry
Bergen. Following is an excerpt from the book:

The train began slowing down. The rhythm of the
wheels grew slower and slower and then it stopped!

"We are in the Russian Zone," whispered old Mr.
Harder, "Lie on the floor or bend down as much as
possible. Do not make a sound. Perhaps the soldiers
outside do not know we are aboard. We must not
risk being discovered."

Henry turned his head slowly toward the freight
car door. If it were going to open he might as well
see it happen. Then he saw Grandma with her head
bowed in prayer. He, too, closed his eyes and began
to pray. The train creaked slowly. Then the wheels
began to roll and the train started.

"Praise the Lord!" cried old Mr. Harder.

The train moved on but soon the noise of the
turning wheels sounded slower and slower again. It
stopped. With a jar the freight car door swung open.
Peter Dyck stood before the people in Henry's car.
His face was joyous with relief.

"We have crossed the Russian Zone," he cried
with open emotion. "You are safe! You are free!
Praise God!"

He closed the door to shut out the snow and wind
that blew in bitter gusts. Behind the closed door of
their train car Henry and the others could hear
Peter and Elfrieda Dyck calling the glad words of
safety and freedom to others down the long railroad
track, and following their words came the melodious
swell of voices singing, "Now thank we all our God /
With heart and hands and voices; / Who wondrous
things hath done, / In whom His world rejoices."

The train began to move, but the singing did not
stop. At the end of one chorus, Henry looked at
Grandma. He thought he had never seen her face so
radiant.

"We crossed the Red Sea, Grandma," he called to
the old woman.

She answered him quietly still smiling, "Yes,
Henry, I knew we would."   BCS

[Selections from *Henry's Red Sea*, copyright 1955 by
Herald Press, Scottdale, Pa.; used by permission].

Regeneration is the theological term applied to the
idea of new birth in the gospels and signifies the recreation of fallen human nature by the action of the
°Holy Spirit (Jn 3:5-8). This spiritual necessity
stated by Jesus is restated and reenforced in the
epistles under such concepts as transformation, new
creation, and "new man" (Rom 12:1-2; Eph 4:23-24;
Col 3:10; Ti 3:5). The regenerate are radically
renewed; the old life is over and a new life is begun
(Rom 6:3-11; 2 Cor 5:17; Col 3:9-11).

Christian writers of the 2nd-4th c. developed
their understanding of regeneration around the
cleansing and rebirth experienced in °baptism, the
Eucharist, and for some, a rebirth into heaven—in
martyrdom. They most commonly used the phrase
"restoration of the image of God," which had been
disfigured by sin, to describe the process. The 16th-
c. Protestant reformers produced a more systematic
outline of the "order of °salvation" in which they
emphasized the concept of justification and incorporated regeneration as an aspect of the whole.
Focusing on the forensic aspects of salvation, they
saw men and women as reckoned righteous through
Christ. However, they taught that the old nature
remained and the bondage of the sinful human nature continued to plague Christians so that they
repeatedly sin.

For Anabaptists regeneration held a place of
priority in the °conversion process. The °Schleit-
heim Confession (1527), the earliest corporate Anabaptist statement, reflects this emphasis on regeneration in its first article, declaring that baptism shall
be given only to those who know true repentance
and amendment of life—that their sins are taken
away and they walk in the resurrection (CRR 1:36).
This implies a relation to the living Christ and a life

reflecting that relation in the here and now.

The thrust of Anabaptism generally was to assert that divine grace and human faith quicken new life in the individual so that a life of holiness may be produced. True repentance is made evident by new life, which is the sign of regeneration, the activity of the Holy Spirit in the believer. This is a corollary to Anabaptist emphasis on the visible church, holy living, and the way of peace. Walter Klaassen summarizes the position as follows: "We find . . . the conviction that once God works in human life by his Spirit an ontological change takes place. They are changed into divine beings after the image of Jesus. There is, therefore, also a rejection of Luther's view that even a Christian is at the same time a sinner and justified." (CRR 3:42).

Differences in emphasis upon the way in which regeneration occurs have led to tensions among Mennonite and Brethren groups in modern times. Some groups, influenced by °Pietism and °revivalism, emphasize regeneration or new birth as an immediate experience when the faith of the believer takes hold in a moment of quickening. Others maintain that regeneration is a quiet process which occurs as as result of growing faith. Still others associate it with baptism as the culminating act in a process of faith.   OHA

Harold S. Bender, "Walking in the Resurrection: The Anabaptist Doctrine of Regeneration and Discipleship," *MQR*, 35 (1961), 96-110; Cornelius J. Dyck, "The Life of the Spirit in Anabaptism," *MQR*, 47 (1973), 309-326; CRR 3: 41-117 passim; Paul M. Lederach. *A Third Way* (Scottdale, 1981).

See also Discipleship; Salvation; Sanctification.

Regional Mennonite Conferences. Regional organizations or conferences are relatively new in the Mennonite worldwide community. As with many cooperative and ecumenical movements, the origins can largely be traced to mission and the development of younger churches.

Out of the cooperative work of the Council of Mission Board Secretaries (COMBS) in North America came efforts to facilitate regional meetings or associations of churches in Africa, Asia, and Latin America. Discussion between COMBS and the Mennonite Central Committee (MCC) Peace Section led to planning for an Africa peace mission in 1959-60. The report of this assignment called for a conference of leaders of African Mennonite and Brethren in Christ churches. This meeting convened in Limuru, Kenya, Mar. 28-Apr. 1, 1962 with the theme, "The Christian in Modern Africa." A follow-up meeting took place in March 1965 in °Bulawayo, Rhodesia (Zimbabwe). There the group founded the Africa Mennonite Fellowship later renamed °Africa Mennonite and Brethren in Christ Fellowship.

Asian leaders, with considerable initiative on the part of veteran churchman, P. J. °Malagar, of °Dhamtari, India, visualized the formation of an Asia Mennonite conference. This came into being in October 1971 with the assistance of representatives of the COMBS group. The first Asia Mennonite conference was held in Dhamtari, India, in 1971. A second meeting was held in Osaka, Japan (1980), and a third in Taipei, Taiwan (May 1986).

The literature ministry of the Mennonite Board of Missions (MC) led to a call for a study of literature needs in Spanish-speaking Latin America. A consultation was organized in Bogotá, Colombia, in February 1968. Several subsequent assemblies were held under the designation °Congreso Latino Americano (Latin American Congress).

In Europe a °Mennonitische Europäische Regional Konferenz (MERK) was formed. A meeting was scheduled for May 1988.

In 1970 an all-Mennonite North American Bible Congress was held, but this event did not develop any formal continuity of structure. It was followed by °inter-Mennonite events centered on °evangelism, e.g., "Probe 72" in 1972, in Minneapolis; and "Alive 85," in Denver, 1985.

Regional all-Mennonite conferences in North America trace their origins to the all-Mennonite convention, a triennial gathering in the period 1913-36 (°°Inter-Mennonite relations). While that movement did not continue, new initiatives arose in the 1960s. Although Mennonites had worked together for many decades, there were fewer occasions when they worshiped together.

A remarkable development was the emergence of an all-Mennonite ministers' meeting, held first in 1963 in Chicago, with subsequent sessions in 1965 and again in 1968. In the 1968 sessions, 70 ministers from 11 North American Mennonite groups attended.

These meetings led to a larger event, an all-Mennonite Bible Congress held in Winnipeg in July 1970 with an attendance of more than 250 people representing at least eight Mennonite groups.

The Council of Moderators and Secretaries (CMS) comes closest to a regional organization in North America and serves officially as the most representative, continuing, cooperative group. This group represents the four major North American bodies: Mennonite Church (MC), the General Conference Mennonite Church (GCM), the Mennonite Brethren (MB), and the Brethren in Christ (BIC). The organization had its origin in consultations arising out of the planning for "Probe 72."

Subsequent consultations on inter-Mennonite relationships in 1974 and 1982, and especially meetings of the CMS group in 1985 and 1986, have confirmed the intention of this group to function as an oversight body for North American inter-Mennonite organizations, who have no counterpart inter-Mennonite group to whom they are accountable.

Also of special significance was the emergence of the "Canadian Council of Mennonite and Brethren in Christ Moderators" in 1987.

Regional activities and organizations have faltered for many reasons. Mennonite °polity is based on congregational autonomy, except where modified by varying degrees of regional and denominational conference authority. In any event there is no authority beyond the individual conferences (denominations) that validates any regional associations. Globally the Mennonite World Conference has functioned with considerable influence and worldwide interest, but it is clearly defined as a fellowship organization with no hierarchical status.

Mennonites are a small group, extremely diverse

and widely scattered. They live in more than 50 nations, and many of the national bodies are quite small. Distance, culture, language, and tribal barriers inhibit regional associations, particularly in the two-thirds world. These limitations make regional groupings extremely difficult.

The history of the regional organizations in Africa, Asia, and Latin America has been influenced by the urge toward cooperation initiated by mission agencies. But much of that influence was external, especially that deriving from organizational and financial assistance. The absence of that assistance as churches achieve autonomy removes one of the major facilitating factors.

Among the three continents of the two-thirds world, Mennonites in Asia have best succeeded in maintaining continuity of meeting. Latin American Mennonites, however, have developed an effective alternative to continent-wide gatherings, in the form of smaller, limited-area groupings. Initiative has been taken in the Southern Cone of South America and in Central America (°Consulta Anabautista Menonita Centroamericana) for gatherings of this type. PNK

Wilbert Shenk, *An Experiment in Interagency Coordination* (Elkhart: Council of International Ministries, 1986); John A Toews, *A History of the Mennonite Brethren Church* (Fresno: MB Board of Christian Literature, 1975).

Reimer, Jacob Braun (Sept. 13, 1916-Feb. 4, 1985), was born in the Altona area of Manitoba, died in the Menno Colony, Chaco, Paraguay. In Manitoba he attended elementary school until age 10, then accompanied his parents Jacob F. and Katharina Reimer to Paraguay in 1927. There he continued in school until age 14. In many ways he became a self-educated man. He was baptized in 1949 and married Neta Wiebe that same year. They had three daughters and one son, also adopting another son.

Reimer served as business manager of the Menno Colony cooperative and was elected mayor (*Oberschulze*) in 1950, a position he held until 1967 and again, 1974-75. Later he served on the advisory committee for Indian settlements. He died while returning home from work one day. As *Oberschulze* he worked in close cooperation with elder Martin C. °Friesen and helped bring about many reforms in the colony. MWF

Reimer, Klaas (ME IV:278), church reformer and founding elder of the Kleine Gemeinde (now Evangelical Mennonite Conference), was characterized by earlier historians as narrow, uneducated and ultra-conservative. Recent scholars, notably Delbert Plett, assess Reimer's role in Russian-Mennonite church history more favorably. They see him not as an intractable, fanatical religious legalist who established an obscure splinter group in the Molotschna colony, but as a dynamic, far-sighted leader who envisioned a "pure" church stressing Anabaptist tenets such as active discipleship, the use of the °°ban for offenders, and a simple, humble way of life away from others.

Already an ordained minister when he emigrated to the Molotschna settlement in 1805, Reimer was soon feuding with Elder Jakob Enns over such issues

as contributions to government war funds and church authority versus civil authority. Reimer was well-versed in Anabaptist-Mennonite writings and saw himself as upholding that tradition. By 1812 he and his few followers were holding their own services, and after all appeals and even threats of banishment to Siberia had failed, Enns excommunicated Reimer and his group. Leaving the parent church caused Reimer much agony and soul-searching, but he persevered in the face of prolonged harassment and persecution from his co-religionists backed by government officials. Reimer also had to overcome the internal strife fomented by over-zealous supporters who considered him too moderate. Klaas Reimer's "descendants and brethren," according to Plett, "regarded him as a giant man of God," who deserves to be remembered as one of the most important Russian-Mennonite church leaders of the 19th c. AR

The main source for Klaas Reimer's life and career is the brief autobiography he wrote shortly before his death: "Ein kleines Aufsatz," unpublished ms in the Evangelical Mennonite Conference Archives, Steinbach, Manitoba. Reimer's account has been translated and annotated by Delbert Plett in *The Golden Years: The Mennonite Kleine Gemeinde in Russia (1812-1849)* (Steinbach: D.F.P Publications, 1985), 149-97; idem, *ibid.*, 148-213 et passim, gives a detailed although polemical account of Reimer's career and achievements; Al Reimer, "Klaas Reimer: Rebel Conservative, Radical Traditionalist," *JMS*, 3 (1985), 108-17, another favorable but more balanced view; James Urry, *None But Saints: The Transformation of Mennonite Life in Russia 1789-1889* (Winnipeg: Hyperion Press, 1988). See also David P. Reimer, "The History and Character of Our Great Grandfather Klaas Reimer," and Peter J. B. Reimer, "Klaas Reimer and His Times," in *Familienregister der Nachkommen von Klaas und Helena Reimer mit Biographien der ersten drei Generationen* (Winnipeg: Regehr's Printing, 1958), 16-21, 24-27. For the less favorable, conventional view of Klaas Reimer see P. M. Friesen, *Brotherhood* (1911) and ME IV:278.

Reinfeld Colony, Paraguay, was founded in 1965 on 500 hectares (1,235 acres) of land near San Ignacio, 238 km. (147 mi.) se. of Asunción. These families left the Sommerfeld and Bergthal settlements in south Paraguay because they feared an erosion of their faith and tradition. Horse-drawn conveyances are used instead of tractors and cars. In 1986 120 persons in 20 families were in the settlement, of whom 64 were members of the congregation. GR

MWH (1978), 252.

See also Sommerfeld Mennonites.

Reinland Colony, Bolivia, is located 24 km. (15 mi.) east of Santa Cruz, or 8 km. (5 mi.) south of the town of Cotoca. It was founded in 1963 by approximately 15 families from the Menno colony in Paraguay and from the Canadiense colony in Bolivia. From 1966 to 1968 some 80 families from Manitoba, Canada, settled alongside the Paraguayan Mennonites and the two groups became one structure under the leadership of the Reinländer Mennonite church.

In 1975 a group from the Reinland colony, composed mainly of those who had come from Canada, started the Rosenort colony on the east side of the Rio Grande river, and in 1983 yet another group, mainly from Paraguay, started the Nueva Holanda colony, also across the Rio Grande.

In 1987 only a few families remained in the once well-established colony after their church leader, the bishop Corny Nickel, also moved to Rosenort. These families then became part of the Canadiense colony. Among the reasons for moving across the river were an increasing number of attacks and thefts by bandits, the disunity between the two groups within the colony, and the proximity to the city. IHie

See also Bergthal Mennonites; Bolivia.

Reinländer Mennonite Church (Manitoba) (ME IV:1117) grew out of the Sommerfelder Mennoniten Gemeinde (°Sommerfeld Mennonite Church) in 1958. The new body was the second church named *Reinländer* in Manitoba - the first, popularly known as the Old Colony Church, emigrated to Mexico, 1922-25. The immediate issue in the 1958 division was the introduction of electricity into Sommerfelder meetinghouses, but underlying causes were complex. There was an uneasiness, more felt than defined, that the values of the faith community were in danger of gradual erosion. Some 800 baptized members (about a fifth of the official Sommerfelder membership), including 12 ministers, joined the new church. Cornelius C. Nickel was chosen as the first elder (bishop). Groups forming the new church first met for worship on Sunday, Apr. 13, 1958. Services were held in a vacant house in Blumenfeld, a machine shed south of Plum Coulee, in private homes near Rosenfeld, Roseau River, and elsewhere. The construction of new meetinghouses with separate Sunday school buildings began within months. New facilities were dedicated at Blumenfeld, Altona, Winkler, and Austin in 1958; at Stuartburn in 1960; and at Inwood in 1963 (the latter group eventually discontinued).

Other Reinländer groups emerged. In 1960 some families of °Chortitzer Mennonite Church origin formed a congregation at Grunthal, Man. Mennonite immigrants from Mexico formed another at Rainy River, Ont. in 1966. In 1968 a number of families, led by Elder Nickel, emigrated to Bolivia. Additional settlers from Saskatchewan and the Paraguayan Chaco joined them to establish a Reinländer congregation.

In 1969 Peter A. Rempel was chosen as the new Manitoba elder. He was active in the founding of a sister church at Swift Current Colony, Cuauhtémoc, Chihuahua, Mexico, in 1979. This group soon grew to include over 3,200 people (including children) meeting in five locations. Gerhard Neufeld became the elder. Other groups were organized at Santa Rita, Chihuahua, and at Seminole, Tex., with Johann Krahn and Heinrich Reimer serving as elders respectively. As Elder Rempel's health declined, he urged the election of a co-elder. William H. Friesen was chosen in 1982. The spiritual nurture of the church was enhanced by a harmonious relationship between the two elders. They sought to incorporate the rising generation into the church community. Sunday schools and youth groups flourished

When electricity was installed in new meetinghouses at Winkler and Altona in the mid-1980s, some families left the church and formed the Friedensfeld Mennonite congregation.

In 1987 the northern Reinländer body counted 660 baptized members and 734 unbaptized children meeting at six locations in Manitoba and one in nw. Ontario. PDZ

MWH (1978), 195, 273, 278, 314, 322; *MWH* (1984), 134; Reimer, *Quilt* (1983), 40.

See also Bergthal Mennonites (chart); Conservative Mennonites (Dutch-Prussian-Russian); Friedensfelder Mennoniten Gemeinde, Manitoba; Old Colony Mennonites.

Reinländer Mennoniten Gemeinden. See Old Colony Mennonites.

Relief Sales are a unique way to raise funds for aiding needy people around the world. These sales, which numbered 35 in 1987 in the United States and Canada, raised $3.5 million to support the programs of Mennonite Central Committee in more than 50 countries.

From the first publicized relief sale held in a barnyard near Morgantown, Pa., in 1957, this people's movement has grown to an annual festival in each region and province of the Mennonite constituency. New Hamburg, Ont., was the site, in 1967, of the first relief sale in Canada. Relief sales are popular because people can serve in a worldwide ministry at home in a way reminiscent of earlier community efforts such as barn raisings, butcherings, and threshings.

Relief sales occur wherever North American Mennonite communities are clustered, whether rural or urban. Words such as "fund raising, fellowship, fixin's, festivity, far-reaching, fun, faithfulness, and food" were used in a 1978 folder to describe a relief sale.

Although the idea of relief sales did not originate with MCC, its material aid director, John Hostetler, has been the liaison with the sale committees for information and advice for the past quarter-century. He also assists such cooperative ventures as the meeting of relief sale organizers held annually at one of the relief sale sites.

Local committees and autonomous organizations have bonded people in a grassroots movement inspired with a desire to help others. Preparations and committee meetings are generally a year-round operation. Items are sold at auction or offered at a set price. Always there are food specialties: dried fruit and New Year's cookies, borscht and zwieback, shoofly and strawberry pies, funnel cakes and Russian pancakes, applebutter and peanuts, sausage and cheese. Setting the date for a relief sale is usually determined by agricultural seasons, providing a time when it is most convenient for rural dwellers to participate. In urban areas, the school and church calendar determine whether to hold the sale in spring, summer, or fall.

Spring sales are held at Lancaster and Harrisburg, Pa.; Peoria, Ill.; Aurora, Nebr.; Minot, N.D.; Fresno, Cal.; Hutchinson, Ks.; Guelph and New Hamburg, Ont.; Black Creek, B.C.; and Iowa City, Iowa. Summer sales are scheduled for Swift Current and Saskatoon, Sask.; Montgomery, Ind.; Coaldale, Alta.; Fairview, Mich.; Kidron, Ohio; and Bath, N.Y. Sales in the fall are held at Arthur, Ill.; Brandon and Morris, Man.; Chilliwack and Prince George, B.C.; Black Creek and Waterloo, Ont.; Goshen, Ind.; Fisherville, Va.; Sioux Falls, S.D.; Ritzville, Wash.; Rickreall, Ore.; Harrisonville, Mo.; Rocky Ford, Col.; Johnstown and Gap, Pa.; Fairview, Okla.; and Warman, Sask.

The seed idea of a relief sale may have been planted in Lancaster Co., Pa., in 1948, when a group of Mennonite farmers gathered harvest produce, quilts, and farm items for auction at a sale in the town of Gap and gave the income to MCC. Following the 1957 Morgantown sale on the Ralph Hertzler farm, also promoted by Ford Berg and Milford Hertzler, the idea of relief sales spread rapidly. Giving to MCC rose as relief sales spread across the continent. During the 1970s, relief sales contributed about one-fourth of MCC's total income from its constituency. Through 1987, 435 relief sale events in the United States and Canada netted $32 million for the °relief, °service, and °development work of MCC.

Lively participation of men, women, young people, and children has created networks and friendships across Mennonite, Amish, and Brethren in Christ denominational lines. Special talents and interests are nurtured as people serve on planning committees and contribute their skills in quilting, hog butchering, public relations, food service, arts and crafts, gardening, woodcraft, and home baking.

Sale promoters have sought to cover all costs in advance so that on sale day they can say, "Each dollar raised goes directly to MCC for helping needy people." Kickoff dinners or banquets are held prior to the sale in some areas to promote the sale and raise funds for sale expenses. In Kansas fellowship dinners have become popular since the first event in 1981. Families volunteer to be guests or hosts. On a designated Sunday, host families serve a meal to guests from other congregations assigned to them by a sale committee. In return for the dinner, the guests make a contribution to the relief sale budget. In 1988, 832 people went as guests to 160 host homes in 54 churches raising more than $12,000 for the Mid-Kansas MCC Relief Sale. Additional money was raised through pledges from churches and Sunday school classes. In Manitoba, one person has raised substantial funds for sale expenses by taking pledges for his marathon run.

Promoters interested in encouraging the wider public to attend the sales have turned to media coverage, including television public service announcements and radio talk shows. At some sales, buses bring people from long distances for the event. Products advertising the sale come in the form of custom-designed belt buckles, yardsticks, T-shirts, caps, and mugs.

Efforts have been made at some relief sales to interpret to visitors what their contributed dollars will do. Special projects are promoted which not only raise money but also educate about the way aid is given as through the demonstration of °appropriate technology like the Bangladesh rower pump used for irrigation. Needs of a distressed country are emphasized and contributions received to aid that country. Since the beginning of the Nebraska relief sale in 1980, a peace booth has sought to connect the militarism of rich nations with the injustices and poverty experienced by poorer nations.

During the late 1960s, when relief sales were spreading rapidly to new states and provinces, questions were raised about the validity of sales as fundraisers. Some felt that the church was tending toward commercialism and undercutting voluntary giving. However, others felt that relief sales were a creative way to allow people to give of themselves, to raise money that would not be given in traditional ways, to foster cooperation between denominations, and to be a positive witness in the community. Controversy over the philosophy of °stewardship has not hindered the interest in and the growth of relief sales.

When patterns of North American consumption came under scrutiny in the 1970s, some argued that relief sales did little to promote a responsible Christian life-style. After publication of the *More-with-Less Cookbook* and *Living More with Less,* by Doris Janzen °Longacre, a number of sales featured ways that North Americans might limit consumption and develop new eating patterns. In 1977, at the Kansas relief sale, a More-with-Less kitchen featured sample foods and sold cookbooks autographed by the author. Some relief sales have booths promoting natural foods and offer fresh fruits, juices, nuts, and dried fruit as in alternative to less nutritious foods.

Overseas crafts (°SELFHELP) in the decade of the 1970s began to appear at relief sales. The wide range of useful and decorative items coming from skilled artisans in many developing countries found a new marketing outlet. Foreign crafts add an international flavor to an otherwise local event. Often volunteers from SELFHELP/thrift shops in the area handle the sale of these crafts at a relief sale.

Nearly all Mennonite congregations in the area of an MCC relief sale find some way to take part in this festival and benefit auction event. A relief sale is people sharing their skills and gifts to help the hungry at home and abroad.   GS

Rachel Waltner Goossen and Robert S. Kreider, "Organizing Festivals for MCC: Relief Sales," in *MCC Story,* 5 (Scottdale, 1988); current listings of relief sales are found in *MC Yearbook.*

Relief Work (ME IV:284). Early Mennonite baptismal vows emphasized the duty of Christians to help those in need. For the purposes of this article "relief work" is defined as the sharing of material and other assistance with those in need in a spirit of love and mutual respect. Many factors have influenced where and how Mennonites have carried out relief during the 30 years, 1956-86. One factor, involvement in World War II, brought new awareness of the degree of human suffering caused by war. It also deepened convictions that relief sharing is a response to God's °grace and his call to be °reconciling, compassionate servants. Some North American Mennonites saw relief work as a way to prove to the nation that they were not indifferent to the problems of the world and that their °peace witness was more than a refusal of military service. The communications media have had a strong impact on relief efforts by bringing the suffering of war to the attention of Mennonites. Relief aid became an opportunity to relate to Mennonite churches around the world, though Mennonites stressed that relief should go to those in greatest need irrespective of race, religion, nationality, or political ideology. These factors stimulated support for a continuing relief effort in many different settings.

Mennonite relief involves a large network of local, regional, national, and international individuals and groups. Thousands of people contribute goods and money, organize fund-raising projects, work in Thrift and °SELFHELP shops, make up school kits for children, manage food banks, help resettle °refugees, and organize distributions in consultation with national and church partners. Wherever relief work takes place, citizens of the country in which it is carried out play a very important role.

Relief Work, 1956-1965. In this decade the focus of Mennonite relief work shifted from Europe to Asia, Africa, Central America, and South America. Some refugee housing and migration assistance continued in Europe as did some development programs in Greece and Crete. German, Dutch, and North American Mennonites cooperated in the Internationales Mennonitisches Hilfswerk, which supported the Menno Heim in Berlin. East-West concerns and European-North American Mennonite relationships grew in importance. The °Europäisches Mennonitisches Evangelisations Komitee (EMEK) and Mennonite Central Committee (MCC) cooperated in relief projects in Chad and Indonesia. Many patterns of cooperation developed among various Mennonite groups in Europe, as International Mennonite Organization (IMO). In India MCC cooperated closely with °Mennonite Christian Fellowship of India (MCSFI) and the Mennonite Service Agency in Bihar which used a Food for Work approach to provide labor for agricultural development.

In this period North American Mennonites were involved with refugee needs in the Middle East, Africa, Hong Kong, and South Vietnam. Earthquake tragedies in Morocco and Chile and a tidal wave in Honduras brought Mennonite assistance to these countries. Zaire (the Congo) with its Mennonite population, its conflicts and emergency and development needs became an important area of Mennonite work. Independence and tribal struggles in Africa and Asia made relief work difficult and sometimes dangerous for nationals and foreign workers. In May 1962 MCC worker Daniel Gerber was taken by a military group from a medical clinic in °Vietnam and has not been heard from since then. North American Mennonites helped Paraguayan Mennonites secure a much needed development loan in 1957, assisted in the trans-Chaco road project completed in 1961, and cooperated with Paraguayan Mennonites in a ministry to Indians. They also participated in a major forestry project in Algeria in the early 1960s. SELFHELP crafts under Edna °Byler's leadership, continued to grow. The Teachers Abroad Program (TAP) became an important form of educational assistance, particularly in Africa. In 1962 there were 23 TAP teachers in Africa and in 1965 there were 64, including a number from Europe.

Mennonite Relief, 1966-1975. Mennonite relief during this decade continued to expand in the quantity of relief materials, in long-term °development projects, in geographic areas, and in the number of workers. °°Pax, a program utilizing young single men with a variety of skills, remained an important program until the early 1970s. Many were loaned to other agencies in Africa. For some, Pax service was performed instead of military service.

By 1974 there were 480 persons serving with MCC in 39 countries, including 152 TAP teachers in Africa. In that year material assistance valued at 3.5 million dollars (US) was sent to developing nations. The first SELFHELP Crafts shop was established in Bluffton, Ohio, in 1974. Work with refugees continued or was initiated in the Middle East, Burundi, Sudan, India, Bangladesh, and Vietnam in this period. Power struggles, ethnic rivalries, political and economic oppression, racism, wars and natural °disasters helped create over 14 million refugees and displaced persons. Mennonites responded to earthquakes in Peru and Nicaragua and a cyclone along with droughts and floods in India. Nine million East Pakistan refugees streamed into India in 1971 during the Pakistan-Bangladesh war. Mennonites responded with food shipments and initiated long-range development plans to increase food production. Food, medical supplies, and services were contributed to both sides during the Nigeria-Biafra conflict in 1968 and 1969.

North American Mennonites first went to Vietnam in 1954 at the time of the division of the country. They contributed material aid, provided community and agricultural development assistance, and medical services. In 1965 the situation escalated into a more violent and costly war as the major powers became more deeply involved. American Christians, some of whom felt a measure of responsibility for the destruction, wished to respond. In January 1966 Vietnam Christian Service, a cooperative Protestant relief agency made up of Church World Service, Lutheran World Relief and MCC, was formed. Mennonites furnished 40 percent of the eventual 200 field personnel. MCC, because of its experience in Vietnam and its long peace tradition, was asked to take leadership and did so for the first five years.

Mennonites withdrew from VNCS at the end of 1972 but continued a ministry of reconciling service. After the change in governments in April 1975 four MCC workers remained in Vietnam to demonstrate concern for all of the people of Vietnam. The last worker, a Japanese Mennonite, left Saigon in September 1976. The events in Vietnam raised questions of church and state and of how to respond to those designated as enemies and illustrated the complexities, ambiguities, and challenges of doing relief work when a country is at war. Mennonites believe that Christians and the church belong where there is oppression and suffering.

Beginning in 1965 Mennonites had periodical contacts with representatives of the Provisional Revolutionary Government and the Democratic Republic of Vietnam to interpret peace concerns and express interest in helping the Vietnamese under their governments. Some limited medical supplies were sent, but no regular channels were possible until 1974 when Mennonites began to send substantial material aid, including food, medicines, and school supplies. Agricultural development, including irrigation projects, was the central focus of later assistance.

In this decade Mennonite involvement in Bolivia grew substantially with a focus on agricultural development. New patterns of cooperation between local churches, mission boards, and MCC emerged. Mennonites joined Roman Catholics and others in the fight against poverty and injustice in ne. Brazil. Conflicts resulting from long-term unmet needs in Central America, along with natural disasters, brought visibility to this area. MCC and other Mennonite agencies became increasingly involved, mostly in cooperative efforts with local Mennonite groups and other churches. Relief efforts in southern Africa were affected by apartheid and liberation struggles. Mennonites participated in the United Mission to Nepal, supplying personnel with educational, community development, °appropriate technology, and medical skills. In the Middle East Mennonites continued to work on both sides of that region's conflict in services to refugees and in development programs.

In 1974 MCC annual meeting approved the historic Hillsboro Resolution on world hunger. This resolution informed Mennonites of the nature and scope of the food crises, called MCC to give priority in the coming decade to helping developing countries increase their food production, and called Mennonites to find a way to collect food grains for distribution to famine areas when needed. This led to the establishment of the Canadian Food Bank in 1976, to a strengthened food and hunger education program, and to the appointment of an MCC Food Aid Coordinator in 1979. Representatives of North American mission boards and the MCC met together periodically for some years to share information and planning. In a December 1976 meeting the group's name was changed from Council of Mission Board Secretaries to Council of International Ministries. The council, which meets twice each year, is the vehicle through which planning and coordination of Mennonite overseas work is done and reflects increased cooperation between North Americn mission boards and MCC.

Relief Work 1976-1986. Emergency relief, food production, forestry and water projects, nonformal and formal education, agricultural and community development, appropriate technology, skill training and job creation, SELF-HELP crafts, nutrition and health, church relations, and peace and justice issues dominated this decade. There was some shift toward greater participation of nationals. The aim, though never fully realized, was to achieve a more genuine partnership in which mutual respect, listening and learning were integral to sharing and serving. The awareness that war and violence were primary causes of hunger came into clear focus as a result of Mennonite experience in eastern and southern Africa, Central America, the Middle East, the Philippines, and Southern Asia. As a result MCC overseas secretaries and field representatives moved toward greater integration of peacemaking and °justice into all aspects of MCC program. In 1984 a full-time Food and Reconciliation resource person was appointed for Africa.

Relief needs continued to expand in Africa, Asia, and Central America because of wars, natural disasters, economic and trade policies, political oppression, and power manipulations. More and more refugees and displaced persons were created. In a 1979 resolution on the growing refugee problem (then 16 million), MCC called on Mennonites to work on various levels—services in camps and assistance to those returning to their homes or being resettled in other areas. Mennonites expressed concern to governments about policies and military actions that created refugees and displaced persons and about unfair immigration policies.

Canadian Mennonites have a long history of assisting refugees to resettle in Canada. Between March 1979, when Canada signed a new agreement for the private sponsorship of refugees, until December 1980, 3,300 Southeast Asian refugees were sponsored by Canadian Mennonite and Brethren in Christ congregations. Since that time the focus of Canadian Mennonite sponsorship has broadened to include Central American and East African refugees. MCC, the Conference of Mennonites in Canada, the Mennonite Brethren Conference of Canada, and European Mennonites cooperated in church building and in providing resources for a spiritual ministry to the 13,000 Mennonite *Umsiedler* (resettlers) who migrated from the Soviet Union to Germany between 1972 and 1985.

Mennonite and Brethren in Christ congregations in the United States sponsored 4,000 refugees from Southeast Asia, Central America, East Africa and Eastern Europe in this decade. Seventy-five Mennonite congregations declared themselves sanctuaries for Central American undocumented aliens (to 1986). This included physical, emotional, and spiritual assistance and a readiness to risk government prosecution.

Mennonites responded to the food crisis in Ethiopia with relief shipments in 1985 and 1986 totaling 31.4 million pounds (14.1 million kilograms) valued at approximately 5.5 million dollars (US). In Ethiopia, MCC and the Eastern Mennonite Board of Missions have cooperated with the Ethiopian Mennonite Church in relief and development within governmental structures and policies. In 1985 and 1986 Mennonites also sent relief supplies to the provinces of Eritrea and Tigray, two provinces which were engaged in armed resistance to the Ethiopian government, again reaching across political and ideological lines to serve those in greatest need.

In Uganda, Sudan, the Middle East, Central America, Southern Africa, and Kampuchea, war and injustices have created suffering, dislocation, fear, hate, and despair. Mennonites, through MCC, have tried to be the reconciling presence as they have carried out relief and development in the midst of turmoil. In this period Mennonites assisted Bangladesh to expand its food production, increase self-help crafts, and create jobs. Relief continues in the socialist countries of Laos, Vietnam, and Kampuchea, whose people suffer from natural disasters and the effects of a long war. Food, medical assistance, and agricultural development are important components of the Mennonite response to these nations that continue to be labeled "enemy" by the United States. Improving international understanding and reconciliation suffuses Mennonite motivation for such efforts. This same spirit energizes the °international exchange program and other contacts with the Soviet Union, Eastern Europe, and China. In 1981 North American Mennonites established China Educational Exchange, composed of Mennonite °mission boards, MCC, Mennonite Medical Association, and Mennonite colleges.

The primary administrative channel for relief work of North American Mennonites is MCC International, though MCC Canada administers selective programs overseas within the binational umbrella of MCC. Mennonites in various parts of the world administer relief in different ways—through their own agencies; through participation in cooperative patterns with MCC, mission boards and national churches; or through other ecumenical channels such as national councils of churches or the World Council of Churches. German Mennonite agencies (Hilfswerk der Vereinigung der deutschen Mennonitengemeinden and Christenpflict) participate in and support IMO programs and also carry out relief projects of their own. This is also true of °Stichting voor Bijzondere Noden, the Dutch Mennonite relief organization. Swiss and French Mennonites have their own relief committees, Schweizerische Mennonitische Organization für Hilfswerke and Caisse de Secours. They support a variety of relief projects, some of which are related to their overseas mission interests. Amish Mennonite Relief, organized in 1955 by Beachy Amish Mennonites in the United States, work in Germany, El Salvador, Belize, and Paraguay. The Brethren in Christ Board of World Missions regularly contributed relief funds to MCC, raised above-budget support for meeting overseas and domestic hunger needs, and organized agricultural projects in some overseas missions. MCC, the largest Mennonite relief agency, contributed 364.5 million pounds (164 million kilograms) of relief materials valued at more than 106 million dollars (US) from 1956 through 1986 to people in 93 countries. Overseas volunteers initially serve two- or three-year terms. Approximately 40 percent of MCC volunteers return for a second or third term. In 1986 there were 510 MCC workers active outside North America, including 19 from non-North American countries.

Summary. In summary we note the following trends in Mennonite relief work since 1956: (1) Response to emergency needs remains a central part of Mennonite relief activity. (2) Long-term °development needs such as food production, nutrition, health, education, housing, jobs, ecology, reconciliation, and justice have become increasingly important in Mennonite response to human need. (3) There is a trend toward greater involvement of nationals in need assessment and in planning, administering, and evaluating relief work. This grows out of greater awareness that genuine partnership involves compassion, listening, learning, and mutual respect (°service). (4) There is increased cooperation of Mennonite relief agencies with local churches, other church-related groups and non-governmental agencies. (5) There has been significant growth in the

purchase of SELFHELP crafts, °relief sales income, informal and adult education, development and use of appropriate technology, integration of peace and justice into relief and development efforts, and education of church constituencies and the public on the broader issues of relief, development and justice. (6) Mennonite relief involvement in socialist countries and Islamic areas has increased. (7) Mennonite personnel now work in many contested and militarized areas. This presents complexities, risks and opportunities. AB

Mennonite Central Committee Annual Workbook, 1956-86, prepared under supervision of the executive secretary of MCC; *Proceedings of Mennonite World Conference*, esp. Orie O. Miller in *1957 Proceedings*, 77-82; C. N Hostetter in *1962 Proceedings*, 245-52; R. W. Kylstra in *1967 Proceedings*, 194-98; William T. Snyder in *1967 Proceedings*, 179-86; Yorifumi Yaguchi in *1972 Proceedings*, 122-26; Albert Widjaja in *1978 Proceedings*, 81-91; Gilberto Flores in *1984 Proceedings*, 154-72; Georgine Boiten-du-Rieu, Elke Hubert, Willi Wiedemann in *1984 Proceedings*, 188-208; *MCC Story*, vol. 1-5 (Scottdale, 1980-87); *Vietnam Christian Service: Witness in Anguish*, a report of an evaluation conference of Vietnam Christian Service, published by Church World Service, 475, Riverside Drive, New York, NY 10115; Luke S. Martin, *An Evaluation of a Generation of Mennonite Mission, Service and Peacemaking in Vietnam, 1954-1976* (Akron, Pa.: MCC, MCC Peace Section, Eastern Mennonite Board of Missions and Charities); Andrew Hershberger, comp., by Ervin Hershberger, ed., *Amish Mennonite Aid* (Plain City, Ohio: Amish Mennonite Aid, 1980); Frank H. Epp, ed., *Partners in Service: The Story of Mennonite Central Committee Canada* (Winnipeg: MCCC, 1982); Tim Lind, "Inquiry Into MCC Africa Purpose and Presence, an unpublished study and evaluation paper of MCC, Africa" (Akron, Pa.: MCC, 1986); Helen Glick, *Spiritsong: MCC Twenty-five Years in Boliva* (Akron, Pa.: MCC, 1983); James C. Juhnke, "Mennonite Benevolence and Civic Identity," *Menn. Life*, 25 (Jan. 1970), 34-37; "Proceedings of the Consultation on Relief, Service and Missions Relationships, May 7-8, 1964" (Akron, Pa.: MCC, 1964).

See also articles on most countries mentioned above.

Religious Studies. For the first half of the 20th c., Mennonite religious studies centered on Swiss Anabaptist and Mennonite history (°°historiography), written both to strengthen Mennonite identity and as a witness for such key Mennonite emphases as °discipleship, °peace, and °believers church ecclesiology. Most of these contributions to religious studies were done from a base in the Mennonite colleges and °seminaries.

In the 1980s, Mennonite religious studies have a different look. First, while the Mennonite schools continue to provide the locus of much Mennonite scholarship, increasingly Mennonite scholars belong to faculties in major universities, where they deal with aspects of Anabaptist and Mennonite history and °sociology, and teach such subjects as °theology and ethics from Mennonite-informed positions. This trend is most pronounced in Canada, where Mennonites have benefited from Canada's support of °ethnic studies. In addition to the several Mennonite °Bible colleges, Mennonites are integrally involved in the Canadian university system. The U. of Winnipeg has a chair of °Mennonite studies, a number of universities have courses in Mennonite studies, Conrad Grebel College functions as a Mennonite college within the U. of Waterloo, and individual Mennonite scholars appear across the entire university system. Canadian Mennonite historians such as Frank °Epp have stressed the Mennonite experience in Russia and Canada. They also produce several periodicals, including two academic journals founded in 1983: *Conrad Grebel Review,* which focuses on theology, ethics and biblical studies from an Anabaptist and Mennonite perspective, and *Journal of Mennonite Studies,* oriented by °literature and the arts but providing significant sections for theology and history.

Second, the content of Mennonite religious studies has changed. Going beyond Mennonite history and apologia, contemporary Mennonite religious studies has gone much farther in understanding Anabaptist and Mennonite thought as a comprehensive stance from which to address all aspects of theology and the modern world. On that basis, Mennonite scholarship has made several contributions to religious studies per se. For example, Millard Lind's work on war in the Old Testament is not a defense of pacifism but a comprehensive analysis of the Old Testament from a peace perspective. The *shalom* biblical theological project from the Institute of Mennonite Studies (Elkhart, Ind.) exhibits a similar comprehensive outlook. Mennonites have made seminal contributions to the series of believers church conferences, which have given visibility to that ecclesiology. The sixth such conference (Bluffton College, 1980) applied the believers church idea to °Christology. Mennonite scholars have major roles in the writing of a believers church Bible commentary series. John H. Yoder's writings have established believers church ecclesiology and the normativeness of Jesus in such a way that a prominent ethicist—Stanley Hauerwas—lists Yoder as one of the foundations for his own view of ethics. Gordon D. Kaufman's ethical and theological writings project Mennonite emphases from the perspective of ecumenical Protestantism. Mennonite peace theology is certainly one of the impulses which has contributed to the reawakening of a peace witness in °Roman Catholicism, portions of °Evangelicalism, and in ecumenical Protestantism.   JDW

William Klassen, "Mennonite Studies as a Part of Religious Studies," *JMS,* 1 (1983), 161-74; John H. Yoder, *Politics of Jesus* (Grand Rapids: Eerdmans, 1972); idem, *Priestly Kingdom* (Notre Dame: Notre Dame, 1984); Stanley Hauerwas, *Peaceable Kingdom* (Notre Dame: Notre Dame, 1983); J. Denny Weaver, "Believers' Church Christology," *MQR,* 57 (1983), 112-31; idem, *Becoming Anabaptist* (Scottdale, 1987), 113-41; Gordon D. Kaufman, *Context of Decision* (New York: Abingdon, 1961); idem, *Systematic Theology* (New York: Scribner's, 1968, 1978); Millard Lind, *Yahweh is a Warrior* (Scottdale, 1980).

See also Theology.

Remecó-Guatrache Colony was the first Mennonite agricultural colony in Argentina, established in March 1986 by Old Colony Mennonites from Mexico and Bolivia. It is located in La Pampa Province on a ranch of ca. 10,000 hectares (25,000 acres), ca. 700 km. (435 mi.) west of Buenos Aires, halfway between Santa Rosa and Bahia Blanca. By April 1987 100 families (600 persons) had already located on this land. An additional 50 families (300 persons) were still expected.

Villages have been established, but as of September 1986, had not been named, except Reinfeld,

which was the first village established. The land is well-suited for mixed agriculture. Crops being produced and planned are wheat and other grains, vegetables, citrus fruits, apples, peaches and apricots. Chicken and animal husbandry is also being initiated. New arrivals live in the ranch's main buildings until single dwelling units can be built. When asked about the settlement, a businessman with whom they had dealt in Guatrache commented that on meeting them he knew immediately that these were honest people whom he could trust fully, but they also reminded him of how things must have been in the 19th c.   MD

MWR (Dec. 11, 1986) 2, (Jan. 8, 1987) 3.

See also Casas Grandes Colonies, Mexico.

Renaissance, Mennonite, a period of awakening, or quickening, within the Mennonite Church (MC), that had its beginnings during the American Civil War (1861-65), came into its own by the 1890s, with definite second and third stages extending from the 1890s to the present time.

John F. °°Funk, and later, John S. °°Coffman, were at the center of the beginning stage (1860-1908), commencing formally in 1863 with publications on the Mennonite position on war, and in 1864 with the founding of Funk's °°*Herald of Truth* and °°*Herold der Wahrheit,* and ending in 1908 when the *Herald of Truth* ceased publication. During this period, renewal efforts for the church centered in the innovation of the °°Sunday school (ca. 1863ff), and later, °°revival meetings. This latter development is where John S. Coffman made his significant contribution as the first churchwide evangelist (ca. 1881-99).

Through these efforts a new generation of English-speaking young Mennonites developed, many of whom were eager to serve the church as Christian workers in mission and °°relief work, and who also felt the need for further °°education in way of preparation for service. Partly as cause, partly as effect, not only °publishing (1860s onward) but also °°home and foreign °°missions (1880s and 1890s onward), education (1894ff), °°mutual aid (1860s onward), and relief efforts (1890s onward), took on a formal and °institutional character within the church at this time.

Important for an understanding of this first stage is the language transformation: after the Civil War, English slowly evolved as the mother tongue displacing German for many in the Mennonite church, so that by 1901 the *Herold der Wahrheit* ceased publication for lack of readership. Up to 1908, however, John Funk attempted consciously to maintain the Mennonite tradition which combined faith and history—the *Martyrs Mirror* tradition, where the church looked to its own roots, and to its own historic ways of interpreting the Bible.

With the publication of Daniel Kauffman's *Manual of Bible Doctrines,* and the creation of Mennonite [Church] General Conference (MC), both in 1898, a second stage came into being, strengthened in 1908 by the new church organ, the *Gospel Herald.* From 1898 to 1944, a new doctrinal approach which tended to minimize the historical dimension of the

Mennonite faith took many of its cues for definitions of truth from sources outside Mennonite circles. By now, the German-language tradition with its whole corpus of literature had all but disappeared in the Mennonite approach to defining faith and life. Formal rules and °discipline in matters of uniform dress and deportment also came into being. This era has at times been called the Daniel °Kauffman era, due to the central role Kauffman played throughout these 40 and more years.

The third stage has as its center a conscious effort on the part of Harold S. °Bender and many others to recover "the °Anabaptist vision." This quest began ca. 1924, took on a formal dimension with the establishment of the *Mennonite Quarterly Review* in 1927, and found its synthesis with Bender's "Anabaptist Vision," first published in 1944 (*MQR*, April 1944).

The triad of ideas found in Bender's "Anabaptist Vision,"—°discipleship, the gathered, disciplined church, and the spirit of °peace and °love—found wide resonance among many Mennonite groups, in a manner that could still be felt into the last years of the 20th c. Continuing affirmation of the doctrinal approach could also be found among a few Mennonite groups during these same decades after 1944, even though the "Anabaptist Vision" was the prevailing center for articulating the Christian faith for most Mennonites at this time.   LG

Leonard Gross, "The Doctrinal Era of the Mennonite Church," *MQR*, (1986), 83-103; Theron F. Schlabach, *Gospel Versus Gospel* (Scottdale, 1980); Guy F. Hershberger, ed., *The Recovery of the Anabaptist Vision* (Scottdale, 1957); Beulah Stauffer Hostetler, *American Mennonites and Protestant Movements* (Scottdale, 1987); Guy F. Hershberger, *The Way of the Cross in Human Relations* (Scottdale, 1958); J. R. Burkholder and Calvin W. Redekop, eds., *Kingdom, Cross and Community* (Scottdale, 1976); John H. Yoder, "Anabaptist Vision and Mennonite Reality," in *Consultation on Anabaptist-Mennonite Theology*, ed. A. J. Klassen (n.p.: Council of Mennonite Seminaries, 1970), 1-46.

See also Holdeman, John.

Republic of China. See Taiwan.

Republic of Korea. See Korea, Republic of.

Republic of South Africa. The region where the Republic of South Africa is located—the southern tip of Africa, has a long history of European settlement. Dutch settlers first arrived in the 17th c., and were followed in the 19th c. by large numbers of English colonists. In 1987 the population of 27 million included 5 million white people. The country has a history of conflict between Dutch (Afrikaner) and English; between Afrikaner and black natives and among black nations. Since 1948 *apartheid* (separateness), has been in place. This form of discrimination assigned the majority black population to ten "homelands," i.e., rural reserves, which make up 13 percent of the land. The blacks are citizens of these areas only, and their access to the rest of South Africa, including industrial centers, is restricted.

Mennonite Central Committee (MCC) contacts within South Africa began in the mid-1960s. They grew out of interest sparked by the black passive resistance campaigns against *apartheid*. Difficulty in obtaining work permits stymied personnel placements in South Africa at that time, and instead MCC opened programs in neighboring countries. Some relationships with groups in South Africa continued from these neighboring programs.

In 1976 a request for assistance and personnel came to MCC from the Transkei Council of Churches (TCC), a regional body of the South African Council of Churches based in the black "homeland" area of the Transkei. Between 1978 and 1987, four couples served as MCC workers under the TCC, two in administrative support and staff training and two as rural development workers. In addition, three workers were sent to the TCC by Africa Inter-Mennonite Mission to work in the Council's program of Bible training for leaders of independent churches. In 1986 MCC also placed a couple in the Ciskei, another of South Africa's black homelands.

Mennonites are committed to supporting the church in South Africa as it struggles with issues of justice and violence. Important relationships continue with the Conscientious Objectors' movement, which has grown since 1979; with the South African Council of Churches; and with other, smaller groups who seek to address the violence of that society. Mennonite workers struggle with what reconciliation means in South Africa, where most of the people are oppressed by the government.

In 1987 a regional office was set up in Gaborone, Botswana, to administer the MCC South Africa program and to serve as a resource base for Mennonite programs and workers throughout the Southern Africa region (Zambia, Zimbabwe, Botswana, Lesotho, Swaziland, South Africa). Events in South Africa impinge on these neighboring countries, which are part of the same economic sphere.   JZH

Information about current programs is published in *MC Yearbook* and *GCM Handbook*, in addition to MCC publications.

Rescue Missions (ME IV:1117). Ministry to the poor and homeless has long been part of the church's witness and reached a new level of development in 18th-c. °Pietism (Halle orphanages and schools) and in the response of 19th-c. German, English, and North American Christians (e.g., the Salvation Army in London, 1865-78) to the new poverty of the Industrial Revolution. The first North American rescue mission was founded by Jerry McAuley in October 1872 at 316 Water Street, New York City. Five years later on Sept. 15, 1877, Colonel Clarke's Mission (later Pacific Garden Mission) opened its doors at 386 South Clark Street in Chicago. These missions were evangelistic in nature but also provided food and lodging for street people and transients.

Since Mennonites were rural people they did not begin °urban missions until the turn of the 20th c. In fact they were slow in starting missions anywhere. Between 1893 and 1910 a number of city missions were begun. While these missions were not rescue missions in the conventional sense, most of them did some social work. For example, the constitution of the Mennonite Gospel Mission (MC) in Kansas City, Ks., founded in 1905, called for workers to provide clothing and food for the worthy poor, provide free medical aid for the afflicted poor, and put homeless children in Christian homes.

Many years before the General Conference Mennonites began city missions some members from Pennsylvania helped in New York City missions sponsored by other churches. Others were more aggressive in starting missions. The Fort Wayne, Ind., Rescue Mission was actually founded and organized in 1903, by two Mennonites (Witmer and Stuckey) from the Berne Mennonite Church (GMC). During the early years the Berne congregation largely supported this work financially. Later support for the Fort Wayne Mission was taken over by others.

In 1910, E. F. °Grubb (GMC) of Wadsworth, Ohio, opened a mission in Los Angeles, which, in addition to conducting meetings, classes, and visitation, gave food and clothing to the poor.

In 1914 a General Conference work headed by W. W. Miller of Pulaski, Iowa, was opened in a hall in Chicago. After some time it was felt that the Mennonite people "were better adapted to take up a suburban district and build a church there and do real organizing and permanent work, instead of doing the so-called rescue work among the transients." The General Conference people were also suspicious of the °revivalistic methods used in rescue mission work.

One of the more inclusive and active Mennonite rescue missions is the House of Friendship on Charles Street in Kitchener, Ont. It was founded in 1939. This mission offers more than 16 different services and ministers to 18,000 persons annually. In 1987 the House of Friendship approved a $3.5 million project to purchase a half acre of inner city property, on Erb Street, to "provide permanent housing for those left out." The mission is sponsored by congregations belonging to the Ontario Mennonite Brethren Conference and the Mennonite Conference of Eastern Canada (MC, GCM).

The Maison de l'Amitié (House of Friendship) in Montreal, Quebec, was opened in 1973 and is sponsored by Mennonite Central Committee Canada and the Mennonite Conference of Eastern Canada. It gives aid to refugees, holds workshops, visits prisoners, and operates camps and a day care center. It is not a rescue mission in the traditional sense.

The Hope Rescue Mission in South Bend, Ind., was begun by the Mennonite Board of Missions (MC) in 1954 but is now (1987) governed by a community board of directors, including a number of Mennonites. The Rock of Ages Mission, Portland, Ore. (MC), which operated from 1952 to 1982, was sponsored by the Pacific Coast Mennonite Conference. The Brethren in Christ have a rescue mission in San Francisco, Cal. Recently (by 1987) they discontinued the feeding and housing of transients and began focusing on abused women and unwed mothers.

A number of rescue missions, such as Faith Mission, Elkhart, Ind.; Little Lighthouse, Moncton, N.B.; Haven of Rest Rescue Mission, Battle Creek, Mich.; and Water Street Rescue Mission, Lancaster, Pa., are not owned by Mennonite organizations but have heavy Mennonite support.

The ministry of most rescue missions has changed in the 1980s. They assist not only men who come off the streets but women and children as well. The missions have added services in suicide prevention, drug and alcohol control, psychiatric and emotioal treatment, nutritional awareness, and recreational activities. RRK

Wittlinger, *Piety and Obedience* (1978), 177, 454, 456, 503, 528; *MC Yearbook* (1986-87), 131.

See also Voluntary Service.

Come, See a Man

Can a shy Amish boy carve out a separate niche for himself in the frightening English world about him? Can a youth who threatened his own father with death, grow up and assume a position where he ministers to the man who would take his own life through suicide? Can a young man who ran the sin gamut from "A" to "Z" change from a life of evil to one where he leads the vilest of men and women to a saving knowledge of Jesus Christ? Can one who experienced Satan's complete domination help others to find release from demon-possession? Can one who despised the cross, lift up that same cross to fallen men? Can a man with an eighth-grade education successfully manage a large business complex in a tough, inflationary economy? Can a farm boy from the Nappanee, Indiana, area make it on "Main Street" South Bend, Indiana? Can a man who fled the Mennonite Church two weeks before he was to be baptized, who abandoned the Amish Church just two weeks after he was baptized, have the stability and common sense to talk three hours to a woman contemplating suicide, persuading her to lay down a loaded .38 caliber revolver?

The answer to each of the above questions is "Yes." I sat in the office of Tobe E. Schmucker, "Mr. Hope Rescue Mission," South Bend, Indiana, and listened to this man uncover his past, much of it unpleasant, talk calmly about the present, look forward unperturbed to the future.

Born on September 29, 1918, at Nappanee, Indiana, the twelfth of fourteen children, Tobe Schmucker was raised Amish. In 1941 he went to Ohio to live with an older brother to try to find himself spiritually. Asking at a grocery store in Middlefield, Ohio, where he could find a church in which to worship, James Hostetler directed him to the Aurora Mennonite Church some 30 miles away. And there the confused young man began instruction class, still unsettled, hoping to find in these sessions that for which he was seeking.

Two weeks before his baptism was to take place, Tobe's grieving Amish parents came to Ohio and persuaded him to return to Nappanee and declare his intention to enter the Amish church. So Tobe did. But two weeks after that baptism, extremely shaken by the immorality of a lifelong friend whom he had admired from boyhood days, Tobe said good-bye to the Amish church. He moved to Elkhart, Indiana, a young man of twenty-two, perplexed, bewildered, unsaved. But finally at the North Main St. Mennonite Church in Nappanee Tobe Schmucker met Jesus Christ and his spiritual pilgrimage took on a new direction.

From 1942 to 1946 Tobe served in Civilian Public Service, much of that time on the violent ward in the Norristown (Pa.) State Hospital. There he worked among the wretched, the castoffs of society, sometimes wondering if he himself would not crack under the pressure of such an environment. But he survived both ward and war, remaining open, waiting for the Lord's leading in his life.

From 1946 to 1954 Tobe managed a successful insurance business in Goshen, Indiana. Active with the Ambassadors for Christ, a layman's organization of that area, he became involved at South Bend, Indiana, in holding street meetings. There he sought to rent the basement of a business house, not quite sure why, only feeling that the Lord was calling him to some sort of a more permanent witness to the down-and-outer of South Bend. At this time he came to the attention of the General Mission Board at Elkhart, Indiana. J. D. °Graber invited Tobe to consider the operation of a rescue mission at South Bend under the board.

Brother Schmucker has been deeply involved in the Hope Rescue Mission at South Bend, Indiana, since its beginning in 1954. The work at first was primarily for the transient, to provide him with a bed for the night, a meal for the day, a change of clothes for on his way. In 1957 they added a rehabilitation program for alcoholics. In the early 1960s they worked toward the establishment of a withdrawal center for alcoholics and drug addicts, and by 1967 the withdrawal center was in operation.

While I was in Tobe Schmucker's office the phone often rang. If it was a routine call Tobe sent it to another office in the building or asked for the party to call back. But sometimes the call could not be diverted. Once "Mary" called. She had spent a week in the withdrawal center. She was an alcoholic. She had left, dried out, only to fall again and gulp down a half-pint of whiskey at one sitting. Now she was "cold turkeying" it again at her South Bend home and suffering the torments of hell as she was sweating it out. Every tissue in her 110-pound body was screaming to be sopped in alcohol again. And that wasn't all that was screaming. She told Tobe on the phone how her husband, his nerves on edge, added to the turmoil. "Mary" turned to Tobe. She needed help. Tobe took that call, forgot about me. His office chair swiveled around, feet went up on the bookcase as he verbally wrestled with her. She must do nothing desperate, she must take one of the pills they had given her, she must fix a good lunch for her husband, she must not miss her appointment at the listening service offered by the mission, she must call one of the three women from Alcoholics Anonymous who were at her disposal. I listened to Tobe calmly advise, warn, cajole, demand. He listened, he spoke, he belonged to "Mary," divorcing himself entirely from our conference. And finally he was able to calm her, gently replacing the phone on the hook. He took a call later from Notre Dame University, setting up a meeting with a doctoral student doing his dissertation in an area of alcoholism, then advised a church pastor who called that the mission would care for a transient who had wandered to their doorstep. A former resident of this mission, a man of the streets whom the Lord picked up and

saved, now operating a rescue mission in Illinos, called for counsel and comfort from Tobe, and he gave it. And once one of Tobe's sons stuck his head in the door to whisper that he had brought a used Ford Galaxie to the mission for Dad to give an OK on before he sank his "life savings" into it.

Tobe by his own admission is operating way above his own level. The Amish farm boy with the mini-education, however, seems to rise to the occasion. Perhaps when God takes a man, he doesn't worry as much as we do about the number and quality of degrees pigtailing after that man's name.

Tobe reads widely, attends Rescue Mission Institutes, soaking up information where he can to make up for that lack of formal education. And in some areas of this work there is no precedent. So you pioneer. And you can get discouraged. The years 1954 to 1958 were tougher years than the rest. When his insurance business savings were used up and his car and furniture were falling apart, he gave his resignation to the board of directors. They handed it back and gave him an increase in salary. Offers have come from Detroit, from Washington, D. C., for Tobe to serve in rescue mission activity, but so far the Amish boy has stayed at South Bend.

I asked Tobe, "And what about the future?" Tobe shrugged. How could he tell me where God would lead? God kept adding new responsibilities, new activities, new sidelines. The mission was now operating a Clothing Resale Shop to supplement its income. When I pressed Tobe about what new activity was in the books, he only shook his head and said, "I know of none. We just 'dop' along." Ah, spoken like a true Pennsylvania Dutchman!

Hope Rescue Mission is meeting the need of the transient, the person seeking to withdraw from alcohol or drugs, the person seeking rehabilitation after withdrawal, and potential suicides, with a listening service being a catchall provision for the first four. At Hope, someone will listen.   RB

Adapted from *Christian Living* (May 1970), pp. 20-22.

Ressler, Lina Zook (1869-1948), editor, city mission worker, teacher, missionary in India, wife and mother, was a remarkable Mennonite woman. She was born in 1869, the oldest of the seven children of David and Magdalena (Blough) Zook and was nurtured in the Oak Grove Mennonite congregation near Smithville, Ohio. She worked at the Gospel Mission (Home Mission, MC) in Chicago, 1896-1900, and attended church meetings as a speaker. She taught at Elkhart Institute, 1901-03. In 1903 she married Jacob A. Ressler, and they served as Mennonite missionaries in India for five years. Due to her poor health, they returned to the United States in 1908. By 1911, they were in Scottdale, Pa., where Lina assisted her husband, who was editor of the *Words of Cheer*. Lina also edited *Beams of Light* from 1937 to 1946. She wrote many articles, co-edited a book, and compiled four volumes of poems and stories for children. She is lovingly remembered as "Aunt Lina" to a generation of Mennonite readers.   EmSR

John A. Hostetler, *God Uses Ink* (Scottdale, 1958), 142; John

A. Lapp, *India* (1972), 69, 134; Emma Oyer, *What God Hath Wrought in a Half Century at the Mennonite Home Mission* (Elkhart: MBM, 1949), 10, 14; Rich, *Mennonite Women* (1983), 130-36; Theron F. Schlabach, *Gospel Versus Gospel* (Scottdale, 1980), 65-68; Sharon Klingelsmith, "Women in the Mennonite Church, 1900-1930," *MQR,* 54 (1980), 163-207, at 172, 179-80 et passim.

Restitutionism (ME IV:302) was not only an important category in Anabaptist self-understanding, but has remained so throughout Mennonite history. Mennonite renewal movements from the °°Kleine Gemeinde through the °°Mennonite Brethren and the Church of God in Christ Mennonite, to the °house church movement, the intentional communities, and the °Concern Pamphlets movement after World War II all bear the mark of a search for a pristine church before it "fell" into apostasy or error. °Menno Simons recognized that the introduction of infant baptism and some of the other aspects of Catholicism he rejected had occurred long before Constantine (306-37), and that the "fall of the church" would need to be placed soon after the deaths of the apostles, if not during their lifetimes (Menno, *Writings,* 279-80). In more recent decades the "Constantinian Fall" of the church has been the most common rallying point for Mennonite restitutionism. This is evident in much contemporary Mennonite °peace and °sociopolitical activism as well as Old Testament studies of kingship and prophets, Mennonite feminism, and the Mennonite °charismatic renewal. In contrast, the neo-°Hutterian movement led by Eberhard °°Arnold, which bore many of the marks of classic restitutionism throughout much of its history, has in the last two decades begun to establish a traditional theology and culture similar to much of Hutterite, Amish, and Mennonite history. It thus appears to be making the transition from restitutionism to second-generation institutional and traditional Christianity. Additional aspects of the Anabaptist and Mennonite understanding of °history and °tradition are covered in articles on those subjects.   DDM

In addition to suggestions for further reading listed under °history and other articles designated above, see Alan Kreider, *Journey toward Holiness* (Scottdale, 1987); Paul Peachey, "The Challenge of Europe," *Mennonite* (Apr. 10, 1951), 236-51, 253; Robert L. Ramseyer, "The Revitalization Theory applied to Anabaptists," *MQR,* 44 (1970), 159-80; John H. Yoder, "The Recovery of the Anabaptist Vision," *Concern,* pamphlet no. 18 (July 1971); J. C. Wenger, *Glimpses of Mennonite History and Doctrine,* 2nd ed. (Scottdale, 1947), 1-11; Johannes Harder (interview), "Ketterij als motor van de kerkgeschiedenis," *Doops. Bijdr.,* n.r. 8 (1982), 84-87; J. A. Oosterbaan, "De reformatie der Reformatie: Grondslagen van de doperse theologie," *Doops. Bijdr.,* n.r. 2 (1976), 36-61, translated in *MQR,* 51 (1977), 171-95; Richard T. Hughes, "A Comparison of the Restitution Motifs of the Campbells (1809-1830) and the Anabaptists (1524-1560)," *MQR,* 45 (1971), 312-29; Wolfgang Eggers, *Community for Life* (Scottdale, 1988), esp. 252-65; Dennis D. Martin, "Nothing New under the Sun?: Mennonites and History," *CGR,* 5 (1987), 1-27; John S. Oyer, transcriber and translator, "The Pfeddersheim Disputation of 1557," *MQR* 60 (1986) 304-51.

See also Holdeman, John; Revolution; Sabbatarianism; Sectarianism.

Resurrection. The Anabaptists of the 16th c. referred to the resurrection in four basic ways. (1) They acknowledged that Jesus had been crucified,

that he died and rose again on the third day (Hubmaier, *Schriften,* 134, 254, 289, 296-97, 350, 368-69; Riedemann, *Confession,* 30; *CRR* 2:59). (2) In their view the resurrection of Christ signified that there would also be a resurrection for those who believed in Christ. This hope gave them confidence and strength in °suffering, knowing that Christ would be victor over sin and death (Menno. *Writings,* 53; Hubmaier, *Schriften,* 217, 371, 325; Riedemann, *Confession,* 23, 32, 46, 214; *CRR* 2:408; Klassen in *MQR,* 32: 271). (3) Most often the resurrection was referred to in relation to the new birth, a central point of discussion in the disputes and in the teachings of the Anabaptists. Baptism was viewed in analogy to the death and resurrection of Christ—"In baptism [the regenerate] bury their sins in the Lord's death and rise with him to a new life" (Menno *Writings,* 93). Frequent references were made to Paul's concept of being buried and raised with Christ in baptism (Col 2:12; Rom 6:4-5). Baptism was seen as a sign of the new birth, of being raised to a new life in Christ. This new birth, however, was the entrance into the body of Christ, the church, and was signified by baptism (Wenger, *Glimpses,* 141, 149; Hubmaier, *Schriften,* 180, 181, 188, 194, 217, 230, 244, 338, 487; Riedemann, *Confession,* 18, 30, 57, 77; *CRR* 2:83; Menno, *Writings,* 93, 122). (4) A unique and theologically significant use of the resurrection appears in article one of the °Schleitheim Confession (1527). "Baptism shall be given to all those who have been taught repentance and . . . who desire to walk in the resurrection of Jesus Christ." The concept of "walking in the resurrection" was arrived at by putting together the oft-quoted passages of 1 Pet 1:3 (resurrection and new birth), 1 Pet 3:21 (resurrection and a good conscience) and the references of Paul "to walk in newness of life' (Rom 6:4) and to be buried and raised with Christ (Col 2:12).

H. S. °Bender sees this reference to walking in the resurrection as central to the Anabaptist ethic and emphasis (1961). It catches well their emphasis on the new birth, the new life in Christ, °discipleship, "walking in the will of the spirit" (Felix Manz, *TA Schweiz I [Zürich],* 237-38), the empowerment of the spirit, and their willingness to suffer for the sake of Christ. In contrast to others who thought that Christians could never really break the bondage of sin and live in holiness, the Anabaptists lived in the resurrection, i.e. in the power of the resurrected Lord, who now lived in them. To walk in the resurrection meant putting away the old person of sin and putting on the new person of holiness; it meant living the life of love toward all people.

This emphasis on discipleship, obedience, love and self-sacrifice earned the Anabaptists the accusation of work-righteousness, but unjustifiably so, as J. C. Wenger has pointed out (1961). They believed that, under the power of the Holy Spirit, it was possible to live a life in good conscience to God (1 Pet 3:21); that it was possible to do the will of God; and that it was possible to live a Christ-like life. Before the resurrection people were powerless against sin, but after the resurrection people could live in the power of the resurrected Lord; before people were not free; now God's people were free to do God's will (Humbaier, *Schriften,* 321). Everywhere in their writings, the Anabaptists linked the resurrection with a new and °sanctified life (Menno, *Writings,* 265; Hubmaier, *Schriften,* 188, 230, 244, 338, 487, 150, 136, 312, 112, 122, 134; Riedemann, *Confession,* 30, 69, 77, 79, 224; *CRR* 2: 112, 187, 193).

In several instances the Anabaptists were accused of not believing in the bodily resurrection of Christ. (Marpeck *Verantwortung,* ed. Loserth, 1929, pp. 331, 238, 403, 510; Wenger in *MQR,* 1938, p. 255; Krahn, *MQR,* 1955, pp. 256-58; Neff in *ML,* I:90; Hubmaier, *Schriften,* 312; Riedemann, *Confession,* 30, 40-45, 52; Dyck in *MQR,* 1962, pp. 147-54, 165). This was not the case however, for Hubmaier makes an explicit attempt to refute such rumors (*Scriften,* 312) and Riedemann makes it explicit as well (*Confession,* 40-45). Several items, however, contributed to this misunderstanding. Calvin referred to the resurrection as a resuscitation to which the Anabaptists replied that of such a fleshly or physical event they knew nothing (Farley, 113). The other contributing factor was Menno Simons' view of the birth of Jesus as simply passing through the body of Mary, taking none of her flesh. This then had implications for the heavenly body in terms of heavenly flesh (*Writings,* 432-33).

Another point of contention was the frequent reference to the life after death in terms of °°"sleep" (Williams, *Radical Reformation,* xxvi; *ML* I:90; Hubmaier, *Schriften,* 312; Riedemann, *Confession,* 30, 52, 40-45; Farley). Anabaptists were seen by their opponents as holding to the death of the soul after physical death and the resurrection of the soul at the last day. Williams, using Calvin's words, refers to their position as psychopannychism. The Anabaptists did not so much advocate the death of the soul after death, but they were insisting that the teachings on purgatory were not biblical.

It is clear that in the early years of the Anabaptist movement eschatology was a strong motivating force. The hope of the resurrection gave them the power to live by the Gospel and signaled that the time was short, time that must be spent in the service of Christ, and in vigorous °missionary work. The decline of the eschatological fervor in the Anabaptist movement caused it to lose some of its missionary zeal and some of its radicalism, but the view of the resurrection and its ethical importance remained.

The time of °liberalism and the time of radical, critical historicism had its impact on some of the Mennonite leaders and scholars such as Sytse °°Hoekstra Benedictuszoon (d. 1898) in Holland and Gordon Kaufman in America. The °Fundamentalist-Modernist controversy in North America shaped the way such leaders as Daniel °Kauffman spoke of the resurrection. But the basic theological position sketched above remained representive for the Mennonites. This can be seen in the more recent °confessions of faith, in written articles, and in the lack of controversy over the question of the resurrection. DSchroed

John Calvin, *Treatises against the Anabaptists and against the Libertines* ed. and trans. Benjamin W. Farley (Grand Rapids: Baker, 1982); Robert Friedmann, *The Theology of Anabaptism* (Scottdale, 1973); Helmut Harder, *Guide to Faith* (Newton, 1979); John Horsch, *The Failure of Modernism* (Chicago: The Bible Institute Colportage Association, 1925); Edmund G. Kaufman, *Basic Christian Convictions* (North Newton: Mennonite Press, 1972); Walter Klaassen, ed., *Sixteenth Century Anabaptism* (Waterloo: Conrad Grebel Press, 1982); Cornelius Krahn, *Dutch Anabaptism* (Scottdale, 1981); *CRR* 2 (Marpeck); *CRR* 1 (Sattler) and *TA Baden/Pfalz*; *TA Elsass I-II*; Marpeck, *Verantwortung in Marbeck-Schwenckfeld,* ed. Loserth (1929); *SAW;* John R. Mumaw, *The Resurrected Life* (Scottdale, 1965); John S. Oyer, *Lutheran Reformers against Anabaptists* (The Hague: Martinus Nijhoff, 1964); Dietrich (Dirk) Philips, *Regeneration and the New Creature Spiritual Restitution and the Church of God* (Elmira, Ontario, Menno Sauder, 1958); *Prophecy Conference* (Scottdale: MPH, 1953); Peter Riedemann, *Account of Our Religion, Doctrine and Faith,* trans. Kathleen E. Hasenberg (London: Hodder and Stoughton, and Plough Publishing House, 1938, 1950, 1970); Cornelis Ris *Confession* in Loewen, *Confessions,* 87-105/85-103; Arnold C. Snyder, *The Life and Thought of Michael Sattler* (Scottdale, 1984); Robert Stupperich, ed., *Die Schriften Bernhard Rothmanns* (Münster, Westfalen: Aschendorff, 1970); James H. Waltner, *This We Believe* (Newton, 1968); John C. Wenger, *Glimpses of Mennonite History and Doctrine* (Scottdale, 1947); idem, *Introduction to Theology* (Scottdale, 1954); George H. Williams, *The Radical Reformation* (Philadelphia, 1975); Christian Neff in *ML* I:90; *ME* IV:543; H. S. Bender, "Walking in the Resurrection," *MQR,* 35 (1961), 96-110; John C. Wenger, "The Theology of Pilgram Marpeck," *MQR,* 12 (1938), 205-56; idem, "Schleitheim Confesson of Faith" *MQR,* 19 (1945), 243-253; idem, "Grace and Discipleship in Anabaptism," *MQR,* 35 (1961), 50-59; Herbert C. Klassen, "Ambrosius Spittelmayr: His Life and Teachings," *MQR,* 32 (1958), 251-71; idem, "The Life and Teachings of Hans Hut," *MQR,* 33 (1959), 267-304; Cornelius J. Dyck, "The Middelburg Confession of Hans de Ries, 1578," *MQR,* 36 (1962), 147-54; Ekkehard Krajewski, "The Theology of Felix Manz," *MQR,* 36 (1962), 67-87; Vincent G. Harding, "Menno Simons and the Role of Baptism in the Christian Life," *MQR,* 33 (1959), 323-34; Willis M. Stoesz, "The New Creature: Menno Simons," *MQR,* 39 (1965), 5-24; George H. Williams, "Sanctification in the Testimony of Several So-called Schwärmer," *MQR,* 42 (1968), 5-25; Ronald J. Sider, "Karlstadt's Orlamünde Theology: A Theoloy of Regeneration," *MQR,* 45 (1971), 191-218; 352-76; Leonard Verduin, "Menno Simon's Theology Reviewed," *MQR,* 24 (1950), 53-64; Cornelius Krahn, "The Emden Disputation of 1578," *MQR,* 1956), 256-58; Kauffman/Harder, *Anabaptists Four C. Later* (1975), 106.

See also Death and Dying; Theology.

Retreats (ME III:699). A retreat, in the strict sense, focuses on communion with God. Mennonites, along with countless other Christian groups, however, have tended to gather to look at a particular need, task, issue, or problem in the light of Scripture and with prayer and to call the event a retreat. Sometimes, for example, Mennonite retreats focus on the needs of ministers, or singles, or the elderly, or on the tasks of church planting, working with immigrants, or making a peace witness. Mennonites also lead and attend Marriage Encounter, Marriage Enrichment, and Progoff Journal Writing retreats as well as retreats for people experiencing grief, loss, the particular challenges of living with handicapped family members, or people wanting emotional healing.

The story of the development of the retreat movement among Mennonites is an inspiring one because so many people donated tools, money, time, expertise and energy to provide both places and program for retreats.

According to Jess Kauffman, "holding °camps and retreats within the Mennonite and Brethren in Christ churches of North America was not an isolated movement with a defined beginning all its own. It was closely related to and influenced by other events both within the church and in society at large." (*A Vision and a Legacy* [1984].) Pastors and teachers in urban areas, for example, started taking children from the cities out into the country for several weeks in the summer. Between 1910 and 1940 this led to organized camping which became an established institution within the church. Further, the "awakening" or °"renaissance" among North American Mennonites between 1880 and 1910, World War I, the Russian Mennonite immigrations to western North America, the acceptance of the °Sunday School movement, and, in later decades, World War II and the movements to and involvements in both higher °education and the cities (°urban church) called for thinking together about new ideas, plans, and programs. Conferences, Christian worker's institutes and youth fellowships emerged. A Christian Worker's Conference in Bluffton, Ohio, in January 1925, with a focus on "Our Young People" led to a nine-day retreat for youth, Aug. 9-16, 1925, on the Bluffton College campus. The campus was the scene of such retreats for five years.

Retreats came to be recognized as a spiritual force in the church and as an accepted means for nurture and for evangelism. Many of the early retreats were held in the interests of youth. S. F. °Pannabecker commented that in the retreat setting youth were no longer represented *by* their elders, but rather came into their own as they reacted *with* church leaders. He saw this to be a significant contribution of the retreat movement. Four characteristics came to be prized in the early retreats: new thinking, actual religious experience, physical recreation, and social development. The closing commitment service of retreats "introduced a whole generation of church youth to serious decisions as to their relation to Christ and Christian vocation." Retreats in the last half of the 20th c. in some sense did what the °revival movement did in an earlier period.

There has been an ongoing expansion of the phenomenon of retreats in the Mennonite and Brethren in Christ churches. The decades of the 1940s, 1950s, and 1960s were decades of growth, building, and expansion. From the early days the vision perceived by leaders in the movement included buildings in beautiful natural settings. The minutes of the 1929 session of the General Conference Mennonite Church (GCM) speak to this: "It [a retreat] needs to be of sufficient duration and held under such favorable conditions and surroundings that it may lead to a real re-creation of body, mind, and soul!" And so it was that Mennonite church camps and retreat centers multiplied across North America. Camp facilities and established retreat programs of the Evangelical Mennonite Brethren, Brethren in Christ, Mennonite Brethren, General Conference Mennonite and Mennonite, as of 1982, numbered 90.

Since the mid-1940s church agencies and institutions began to have retreats. The women's organizations of the various Mennonite groups have annual retreats usually planned by district conference committees. The women gather for Bible study, small group work, and deep sharing, always asking, "What does God have *for* me and ask *of* me?" Retreats of this kind for both women and men have been well attended in the Southwest Conference (MC). The Ohio Conference (MC) planned one just for men.

Mission boards find retreats for newly appointed and returning missionaries to be beneficial. The Mennonite Brethren Board of Missions and Services has a policy to fund worker retreats in each of the countries where the board sponsors missionaries. These are annual or biennial, and their purpose is to bring inspiration and fellowship. Business is not to be on the agenda! Mennonite (MC) Board of Missions and Charities (MBM) started conducting missionary orientations with a retreat format in 1943. In 1958, 1964, and 1966 these were held jointly with the Eastern Mennonite Board of Missions and Charities (MC). At times these were held in conjunction with missionary and Bible conferences. In the 1970s these gatherings were renamed Annual Overseas Seminars. They continued to have elements of both input and renewal. In March 1985 the General Conference Mennonite Commission on Overseas Missions (COM), MBM, and Mennonite Central Committee (MCC) joined together to sponsor the first re-entry retreat for those overseas workers who had returned to North America within the year. In 1986 the children of these workers were also invited. Through worship, fellowship, psychodrama and group therapy, participants were helped to readjust to North American culture. COM and MBM also sponsor retreats for their workers when they are living overseas. Workers in Europe gather annually for a "Colloquium." Since the late 1970s mission board and MCC personnel in India, Nepal, and Bangladesh meet together each year for retreat. In Bolivia Mennonite Ministries retreat annually; COM and MBM workers in the Tokyo area do also. Since the early 1960s MCC has been having annual retreats for workers on or near overseas MCC locations. These agencies cooperate in sharing leaders for these events.

Over the years many able persons have also given of themselves in leading retreats for °voluntary service (VS) workers in the United States. In 1973 when these in-service training seminars began they were held in retreat centers from Florida to California, some in the spring, some in the summer, and some in the fall. More recently there is one orientation retreat for all the workers while the project directors of the Mennonite Church (MC) VS units are given an additional time for a contemplative retreat.

Mennonite educational institutions frequently start the school year by having a retreat for staff members plus a wide variety of retreats for student groups. Individual congregations or groups within congregations retreat together as do interest and professional groups of many kinds across the church. Congregational and youth retreats are very common among most European Mennonite groups.

Throughout the General Conference Mennonite Church and the Mennonite Church (MC) congregations people with gifts to enable spiritual renewal are being affirmed and sought out to lead meetings and retreats. In 1986 the Mennonite Church (MC) printed a booklet entitled, "Resource Persons for Spiritual Renewal." Seventy people are listed as involved in this ministry; certainly others are as yet unnoted. The Spiritual Emphasis Committee (GCM) is working at a similar listing. These persons desire to lead participants to a closer fellowship and walk with God. The trend now is to continue retreats focused on particular needs and tasks *and* to have retreats with the central focus being spiritual growth. Those who lead retreats of this kind describe the interest among Mennonites as moderate or low, but growing. TMG

Jess Kauffman, *Guideposts to Camp Programming,* a manual prepared in 1958 for the Mennonite Commission for Education, copy in Mennonite Historical Library, Goshen; Jess Kauffman, *A Vision and a Legacy: The Story of Mennonite Camping, 1920-80* (Newton, 1984); *Men-O-Lan,* 40th Anniversary of Retreats at Men-O-Lan, 1941-81 (Eastern District Conference, GCM); John L. Casteel, *Renewal in Retreats* (Association Press, New York, 1959); Samuel F. Pannabecker, *Faith in Ferment* (Newton, 1968), see ch. "Retreats and the Retreat Movement"; *Minutes* (GCM) (1929), vol. 2, pp. 188-89; Northern District Conference reports in *Minutes* (GCM) (1931); Western District Retreat Committee report in Western District Conference minutes, 48th session, Oct. 18-19, 1939; Education Committee, of the Middle District report in *Minutes* (GCM) (1939).

Reublin, Wilhelm (ME IV:304), was one of the most widely connected figures in early Swiss and South German Anabaptism. His career demonstrates the close relation between believers baptism and social protest.

Born in Rottenburg on the Neckar, educated at Freiburg and Tübingen, Reublin was a priest whose sphere of activity in the diocese of Constance overlapped Swabia (sw. Germany) and Switzerland. His °tithe resistance in the Reformation and Peasants' War may have been inspired by the Tübingen master Conrad Summenhart (d. 1502), who taught that the tithe had no basis in divine law.

Expelled from his charge in Basel in 1522 for zealous advocacy of the Reformation, at the end of that year he was made priest by the village of Witikon in Zürich territories. In June 1523 he led six villages south and east of Zürich in resisting payment of tithes to the major ecclesiastical chapter in the city. In his sermons at the time he praised godly peasants and attacked clerics, patricians, and burgomasters. Conrad °Grebel sided with the rural tithe resisters against Zwingli and the Zürich Council in what seems to have been the beginning of the rupture between Zwingli and the Reformation radicals in Zürich. In early 1524 rural followers of Reublin were the first Zürich subjects to refuse infant baptism. Reublin, Grebel, and °°Mantz were the chief advocates of adult baptism in debates before the Zürich Council in January 1525.

Exiled from Zürich in Jan. 1525 because of their opposition to Zwingli on the baptism issue, Reublin and Johannes °°Brötli took refuge in Hallau for the rest of the year. Hallau was the center of rural resistance to the government of Schaffhausen during the °Peasants' War. Reublin and Brötli replaced the Hallau pastor and enjoyed armed protection by the villagers when the Schaffhausen government tried to arrest them. Reublin established contact with two nearby Reformers sympathetic to Anabaptism: the Schaffhausen pastor Sebastian °°Hofmeister, and the Waldshut pastor, Balthasar °Hubmaier. Reublin baptized Hubmaier, who initiated an Anabaptist Reformation in Waldshut at Easter 1525. During the

Peasants' War Reublin was the leading figure in temporarily establishing a territorial base for Anabaptism in the Swiss-Swabian border lands. The village of Schleitheim, very close to Hallau, refused its tithes in 1525 and afterward. It was in Reublin's sphere of activity and he led Michael °Sattler to Schleitheim in February 1527, almost as certainly as he led him to Horb, where Sattler was arrested. This link of Reublin with Schleitheim lends credibility to interpreting the Seven Articles of Schleitheim as an expression, in radically altered form, of the Peasant War's rejection of established society.

Active in Switzerland, Swabia, Alsace, and Moravia, Reublin, in less than 10 years as an Anabaptist, had intimate connections with most of the important leaders of Swiss-South German Anabaptism: with Conrad Grebel, Felix Mantz, Balthasar Hubmaier, Michael Sattler, Hans °°Denck, Jakob °°Kautz, Hans °°Bünderlin, Pilgram °Marpeck, Jakob °°Widemann, and Jakob °°Hutter. He eventually renounced Anabaptism and lived for more than 30 years afterward, dying at an advanced age. JMS

J. F. G. Goeters, "Die Vorgeschichte des Täufertums in Zürich," in *Studien zur Geschichte und Theologie der Reformation: Festschrift für Ernst Bizer,* ed. Luise Abramowski and J. F. G. Goeters (Neukirchen-Vluyn: Neukirchner Verlag, 1969), 239-81; Martin Haas, "Der Weg der Täufer in die Absonderung: Zur Interdependenz von Theologie und sozialem Verhalten," in *Umstrittenes Täufertum* (1975), 50-78; Heiko A. Oberman, *Masters of the Reformation* (Cambridge: Cambridge U. Press, 1981; originally published in German 1977), 113-27, 187-209; Arnold Snyder, "The Schleitheim Articles in Light of the Revolution of the Common Man: Continuation or Departure?," *Sixteenth Century J.,* 16 (1985), 419-30; James M. Stayer, "Reublin and Brötli: The Revolutionary Beginnings of Swiss Anabaptism," in *The Origins and Characteristics of Anabaptism,* ed. Marc Lienhard (The Hague: Nijhoff, 1977), 83-102.

Revivalism (ME IV:308, 312). The word "revival" is commonly used in both the sense of renewal, or awakening, and to describe a technique developed during the Second Great Awakening (ca. 1795-1810) and its aftermath. This article is concerned primarily with the latter, but will give cross references to renewal movements as well. Revival meetings were a pervasive technique for evangelism and spiritual renewal in American Protestant churches for a century and a quarter, from ca. 1830 to 1955, although they both preceded and followed these dates. Revival meetings commonly consisted of consecutive nightly meetings, together with weekend services, which extended over a week or more. Emotional messages stressing sin and salvation called for repentance expressed by an individual response to a personal invitation to accept salvation. Gospel songs reinforced this message (°°hymnology). Beginning late in the 19th c., Mennonites widely adopted this form of revivalism.

In the 1950s mass revivals held in tents, stadiums, or large auditoriums became common throughout America. Mass tent revivals were begun in the Mennonite churches when George R. Brunk II, a graduate of Union Theological Seminary (Richmond, Va.) and ordained preacher, joined forces with his brother Lawrence, who served as business manager and song leader for their campaigns until 1953. Their first series of meetings began in June 1951 at

East Chestnut Street in Lancaster, Pa., and continued for seven weeks. It was followed that summer and fall by campaigns at Souderton, Pa.; Orrville, Ohio; Manheim, Pa.; and, during the winter, in Sarasota, Fla. The meetings quickly became inter-Mennonite. A spring 1952 campaign in Johnstown, Pa., was followed by a July campaign in Kitchener, Ont., cooperatively sponsored by the Ontario Mennonite Conference (MC) and local churches, including the Amish Mennonites, Mennonite Brethren, the Stirling Avenue and United Mennonite congregations (GCM), the United Missionary Church, and the Brethren in Christ.

A second Mennonite tent revival unit was sponsored in 1952 by Christian Laymen's Tent Evangelism, Inc. (CLTE), with headquarters in Orrville, Ohio. Howard Hammer, formerly a United Brethren in Christ minister, was the first evangelist, followed in 1955 by Myron Augsburger, when Hammer went to South America as a missionary. Andrew Jantzi, an evangelist from the Conservative Amish Mennonite Church, led a third organization which was largely confined to his own denomination. A fourth organization, Mennonite Evangelical Crusades (sponsored by the Virginia Mennonite Conference [MC]) held four campaigns in 1956 and one in 1957 with A. Don Augsburger as speaker.

In 1955 the Brunk Revivals, with Lawrence no longer a part of the team, went to Rosthern, Sask. The series was initially sponsored by the General Conference Mennonite Church, but soon other groups were cooperating. In the summer of 1956 Brunk Revivals returned to Saskatchewan to hold meetings at Osler and Swift Current, followed by additional series in Dolton, S.D., and Mountain Lake, Minn. In the summer of 1957 tent meetings were held in southern Manitoba and sponsorship included the Mennonite Brethren, Evangelical Mennonite Brethren, Evangelical Mennonite Conference (Kleine Gemeinde), General Conference Mennonites, Bergthal Mennonites, Rudnerweide Mennonites (Evangelical Mennonite Mission Conference), Blumenorter Mennonite, and two non-Mennonite groups, the Evangelical Free Church and the Emmanuel Church. In the summer of 1958 the Brunk Revivals went to British Columbia, with the meetings under the sponsorship of the General Conference Mennonite Church, Mennonite Brethren, and Evangelical Mennonite Brethren. In the late 1950s, under the leadership of Myron Augsburger, CLTE began holding meetings in large urban auditoriums as well as tents. Renamed Crusade for Christ, the operation elicited interdenominational sponsorship. The summer of 1958 began with a city-wide campaign in Harrisburg, Pa., followed by another in Fort Wayne, Ind., in August. A March 1959 series in Convention Hall, Hutchinson, Ks., was sponsored by 70 churches in the city together with the Christian Business Men's Association, Youth for Christ, and the Gideons organization. In January 1959, the parent organization modified its name to Christian Laymen's Evangelical Association, since it was no longer holding meetings in tents, and the public name of the meetings became Augsburger Crusades. In 1962 the organization disbanded, the tent was sold, and the monies distributed to Mennonite missions. The last Brunk campaign was held in Landisville, Pa., in July 1982, after which the tent and equipment were sold, and a foundation was formed to allocate the proceeds to continuing evangelistic work.

The mass revivals elicited widespread response in church periodicals from 1951 to 1953. Initial affirmative reports of the meetings were followed by articles endeavoring to associate the revivals with a renewed emphasis on evangelism in the Mennonite churches. By the end of 1953 it became apparent that although the meetings were stimulating renewal, they were not primarily evangelistic, i.e., reaching unchurched, non-Mennonite individuals.

The General Council of Mennonite Church [MC] General Conference adopted "A Statement of Concerns on Revivalism and Evangelism" in April 1953. The statement was basically supportive of the mass revivals, but concerns were also in evidence, including the primary-junior age of °baptism that was becoming common. The concern over child evangelism prompted a formal study beginning in 1953, and a subsequent statement, entitled "Position on the Nurture and Evangelism of Children." It was adopted by Mennonite Church [MC] General Conference in 1955. Additional revivalistic emphases that made Mennonites uncomfortable were: (1) the prominence given to the confrontation of the individual with the devil and to the theme of the wrath of God; (2) the focus on the individual; and (3) conversions that did not result in °church membership. Mennonites traditionally believed that God's love, not his wrath, shaped his relationship with mankind. Furthermore, although the cooperation of local community churches was solicited for the mass campaigns, the setting essentially removed the experience from the congregational context. Whereas traditionally conversion and church membership were closely associated, in revivalism the individual's relationship to the church was considered secondary. Revivalism, its critics charged, aimed at crisis commitment to faith in Christ, while giving little attention to full °discipleship.

Mennonites had always considered the new birth essential, but repentance and the will were held to be more important than experience or feeling. From its beginning phases in the First Great Awakening (1730s-1770s), revivalism caused divisions among Mennonites, drawing off its most enthusiastic supporters into new denominations (ME IV:309). As the Pennsylvania German Revival climaxed in the late 18th c., it was responded to by Christian Burkholder in Nützliche und Erbauliche Anrede an die Jugend (Useful and Edifying Address to the Young), 1804. A few decades later, during the Second Great Awakening, Abraham °°Godschalk wrote on Becoming A New Creature (1838). In the late 19th c., during the Third Great Awakening, the influential leader John M. °°Brenneman published Hope, Sanctification, and a Noble Determination. Both Brenneman and Godschalk presented the Mennonite understanding of obedience and commitment in opposition to revivalist teachings.

The Mennonite Brethren Church grew out of a °pietistic revival in Russia, and itinerant evangelism has characterized this group in both Russia and

America. Multiple lay evangelists served the church extensively from 1910 to 1954. With a decline in their availability at midcentury, evangelists from interdenominational organizations began to be used. Concern over this trend prompted the appointment of conference evangelists from 1954 to 1972. Among the persons serving in this program were Loyal A. Funk as chairman of the Board of Evangelism, with Waldo Wiebe, David J. Wiens, Henry J. Schmidt (and in Canada H. H. Epp) serving as conference evangelists. Elmo Warkentine, as executive secretary of the board, implemented a church wide program of training for evangelism.

For the first six decades of the 20th c. revivalism and resultant "quickening" in Mennonite churches was viewed positively by historians. Since the mid-1970s new scholarship has observed both that Mennonites had more interaction with the First and Second Great Awakenings than was formerly supposed and that revivalism altered Mennonite understandings of the Gospel (Schlabach, Sutter, and Hostetler).

William G. McLoughlin in his book, *Revivals, Awakenings, and Reform*, has closely associated widespread religious awakenings with profound cultural transformation. As areas of the Mennonite church embraced revivalism in the 19th and early 20th c., major adjustments were being made to American cultural patterns. Similarly, in the 1950s and 1960s the Mennonite Church (MC) was experiencing profound transformation in religious forms, structured programs, and cultural interaction. The mass revivals brought spiritual revival for many and the unleashing of energies which found expression in new programs.

Revivalism in the Mennonite churches waned by the late 1950s, although some tent meetings continued to be held. Many congregations discontinued °°revival meetings. Some of the functions of revival meetings were taken over by the burgeoning °camping movement where fireside services often functioned as revival meetings, frequently with a very young age group. By 1970 the °charismatic movement was also providing a base for renewal. BSH

Dale Franklin Dickey, "The Tent Evangelism Movement in the Mennonite Church: A Dramatic Analysis," (PhD diss., Bowling Green State U. 1980), although shaped toward the discipline of speech and communications, this is the most complete account of the Mennonite mass tent revival movement; Theron F. Schlabach, "Reveille for die Stillen im Lande: A Stir Among Mennonites in the Late Nineteenth Century," *MQR*, 51 (1977), 213-26; idem, "Mennonites, Revivalism, Modernity, 1683-1850," *Church History*, 48 (1979), 298-415; idem, *Gospel Versus Gospel* (Scottdale, 1980; George Brunk II, "Which Gospel Is It," *GH* (May 26, 1981), 409-11; Carlton O. Wittlinger, "The Impact of Wesleyan Holiness on the Brethren in Christ to 1910," *MQR*, 49 (1975), 259-83; idem, "The Advance in Wesleyan Holiness Among the Brethren in Christ since 1910," *MQR*, 50 (1976), 21-36; Beulah S. Hostetler, *American Mennonites and Protestant Awakenings* (Scottdale, 1987), 150-75, 279-87; William G. McLoughlin, *Revivals, Awakenings, and Reforms* (Chicago: U. of Chicago Press, 1978); Paul M. Lederach, "Revival in Franconia," *GH* (Sept. 18, 1951), 902-3; Maurice E. Lehman, "The Lancaster Revival," *GH* (Sept. 4, 1951), 852-53; Nelson E. Kauffman, "Report of the First Annual Meeting of Christian Laymen's Evangelism, Inc." *GH* (Feb. 3, 1953), 102-103; Peter Penner, "Reflections on Mass Evangelism," *Chr. Leader* (July 1961), 4, 5, and 19; John A. Toews, *History MB* (1975); "Position on the Nurture and Evangelism of Children," *Mennonite General Conference*

[MC] Proceedings, (Hesston, Ks.), 1955, 53-55; "A Statement of Concerns on Revival and Evangelism, Adopted by the General Council of General Conference, *GH* (Aug. 18, 1953), 777; Sandra Lee Cronk, "*Gelassenheit*: The Rites of the Redemptive Process in Old Order Amish and Old Order Mennonite Communities" (PhD diss., U. of Chicago, 1977), esp. 270-80, cf. *MQR*, 55 (1981), 5-44; Sem C. Sutter, "Mennonites and the Pennsylvania German Revival," *MQR*, 50 (1976), 37-57; Joseph S. Miller, "The Pennsylvania Mennonite Church Near Zimmerdale, Kansas," *PMH*, 5, no. 3 (July 1982), 14-19; idem, "The Kansas Movement: Paul Erb's Viewpoint," *PMH*, 5, no. 3 (July 1982), 20-22; Frank H. Epp, *Mennonites in Canada I*, ch. 6; idem, ed., *Revival Fires in Manitoba* (Denbigh, Va.: Brunk Revivals, Inc., 1957); Mark R. Wenger, "Ripe Harvest: A. D. Wenger and the Birth of the Revival Movement in Lancaster Conference," *PMH*, 4, no. 2 (April 1981), 2-14; Sarah Stambaugh, *I Hear the Reaper's Song* (Intercourse, Pa.: Good Books, 1984); Katie F. Shank, *Revival Fires* (Broadway, Va.: the author, 1952); A. J. Klassen, ed., *Revival Fires in British Columbia* (Denbigh, Va.: Brunk Revivals, Inc., 1958); Clyde G. Kratz, "Mixed Blessings" (unpublished term paper, Eastern Mennonite College, 1985), an analysis of the Brunk campaign in Souderton, Pa., in 1951 (copy at Menno Simons Historical Library, Harrisonburg, Va.); Harry A. Brunk, *History of Mennonites in Virginia, 1900-1960* (Verona: McClure Printing Co., Inc. 1972), 447-49.

See also Altar Call; Camp Meetings; Evangelism; Prayer Meetings.

Revolution. Mennonites, throughout most of their history, have been suspicious of sociopolitical revolution. This was also true of many Anabaptists, after the initial involvement of some in revolutionary movements at °Münster and in the °Peasants' War. During the 18th and 19th c. Mennonites were often tolerated by virtue of °privileges granted by kings and princes and hesitated to support movements calling for the overthrow of aristocratic governments in Russia, Germany, or colonial America.

Theologically, however, Anabaptism was revolutionary in its attitude toward the existing, traditional church. Anabaptist °restitutionism, in its zeal to restore the pristine apostolic church, scoffed at calls for reform in favor of a radical new creation. Anabaptist studies during the 1970s and 1980s have increasingly pointed to the revolutionary °apocalypticism, anticlericalism, antisacramentalism, and antitraditionalism that formed the matrix for Anabaptism of all varieties (°history, °tradition, °Anabaptism).

This dual inheritance—a Mennonite inclination to be the "quiet in the land" in return for privileged toleration and an Anabaptist apocalyptic zeal for radical change—has led to widely divergent attitudes toward revolution in the 20th c. Some Mennonites involved in °sociopolitical activism have favored various forms of °liberation theologies or radical social protest in North and South America, Europe, South Africa and elsewhere. The issue of violent revolution which is closely connected with many of these movements has, as a result, been debated. Other Mennonites have decried these developments as a betrayal of Mennonite ethical dualism (°°nonconformity). In the latter view, Christians are not to seek sociopolitical change by "worldly" methods, including various forms of nonviolent pressure politics, and certainly not by any form of violent revolution.

Throughout much of the 20th c., Mennonites have found themselves confronted directly by the disruption and polarization that accompanies revolutionary situations, most recently in Indonesia, Zaire, Central America, and Ethiopia. The story of Mennonite responses to these situations has not been recorded or studied. Mennonite responses to the Russian Revolution have been the object of some study and °historical writing during the 1970s and 1980s. DDM

Lowell H. Zuck, ed., *Christianity and Revolution: Christian Testimonies, 1520-1650* (Philadelphia: Temple U. Press, 1975); John Ruth, *'Twas Seeding Time* (Scottdale, 1976); John B. Toews, *Czars, Soviets, and Mennonites* (Newton, 1982); Dietrich Neufeld, *A Russian Dance of Death*, trans. and ed. Al Reimer (Winnipeg: Hyperion, 1977); Vincent Harding, "The Peace Witness and Modern Revolutionary Movements," *The Witness of the Holy Spirit: Proceedings of the Eighth Mennonite World Conference Amsterdam, The Netherlands, July 23-30, 1967*, ed. C. J. Dyck (Elkhart, Ind.: Mennonite World Conference, n.d.); Melvin Gingerich, *The Christian and Revolution* (Scottdale, 1968); consultation on "The Christian Worker in Revolutionary Situations" (Council of Mission Board Secretaries, 1971); *MQR*, 58 (Aug. 1984), sp. issue on liberation theologies; Walter Klaassen, "Doperdom als revolutie: een voorbeeld van 'confessionalisme' in de doopsgezinde geschiedschrijving," *Doops. Bijdr.*, n.r. 7 (1981), 109-15 (additional literature is cited under °Anabaptism, °Historiography, °Peasants' War, °Münster, Müntzer); John B. Toews, *The Mennonite Brethren Church in Zaire* (Fresno: Board of Christian Literature, MB Churches, 1978), 143-53; C. Arnold Snyder, "The Relevance of Anabaptist Nonviolence for Nicaragua Today," *CGR*, 2 (1984), 123-37; idem,, "Anabaptism and Revolution: The Case of Michael Sattler," *Church History*, 50 (1981), 276-87; Leonard Friesen, "Mennonites in Russia and the Revolution of 1905: Experiences, Perceptions, and Responses," *MQR*, 62 (1988), 42-55; idem, "The Russian Revolution of 1917 Reconsidered: New Light on an Old Subject," *CGR*, 5 (1987), 135-46; James M. Stayer, "Reublin and Brötli: the Revolutionary Beginnings of Swiss Anabaptism," in *The Origins and Characteristics of Anabaptism*, ed. Marc Lienhard (The Hague: Martinus Nijhoff, 1977), 83-102; Arthur Gish, "Eine Theologie für die Revolution," *Menn. Geschbl.*, Jg. 29, n.F. 24 (1972), 13-34; Dennis D. Martin, "Nothing New Under the Sun?: Mennonites and History," *CGR*, 5 (1987), 1-27; Levi Keidel, *Caught in the Crossfire* (Scottdale, 1979).

See also Authority; Church-State Relations; Nonresistance; Political Attitudes.

Rheinland-Pfalz (Rhenish Palatinate) Federal State, Germany.

After World War II, the influx of refugees from °West Prussia led to the establishment of the Mennonite congregation in Enkenbach, the largest Mennonite church in Rheinland-Pfalz (496 members). The congregational life of the °°Palatinate churches was enriched by American sisters and brethren, who assisted in every respect, including the construction of housing for Mennonite refugees at Enkenbach. In the 1960s a more intense coordination of the work of local congregations began. The salaried preachers meet six times a year and, besides other services, have compiled several publications: a manual for baptisms, burials and other ceremonies, and statements on biblical interpretation, etc., the mode of baptism, and the understanding of ministry. In most churches lay preachers are serving in addition to the salaried preachers. This indicates a shift toward more emphasis on the °priesthood of all believers. While most efforts during the 1950s and 1960s were centered on the congregations, interest in outreach has grown in recent years, as is evident in the missions at Neumühle (1977) and Kaiserslautern (1982). The retirement and nursing home at Enkenbach is regarded as commitment of love towards a society

neglecting senior people. The boarding school at the °Weierhof offers opportunity for educational ministry by church members. The third Mennonite European Regional Conference was held at Enkenbach in 1981.   K-DW

Menn. Jahrbuch; congregational publications from Enkenbach, Ibersheim, Ludwigshafen, and Weierhof.

Rhodesia. See Zimbabwe, Zambia.

Rhymes.

Warren Kliewer and Bertha Fast Harder have collected children's rhymes used by Mennonite speakers of the Low German °dialect in Minnesota. Many represent nursery lore; that is, rhymes used by adults with pre-school °children. Among these are verses used while counting the child's fingers, naming parts of the face and body, and bouncing the child on the knee. Others are childlore; that is, verses used by children while playing with other children. Chief among these are game and counting off rhymes, jokes, satiric narratives, and holiday poems. Although no comparative data is supplied, these rhymes are probably also found in non-Mennonite Low German cultures.

The same is apparently true of the *Plautdietsch* rhymes and songs collected by Victor Carl Friesen among the Western Canadian Mennonites. One of the most interesting of these is the 19-stanza "Brummels Song," a nonsense song about a man who found a louse in his shirt while washing it. The 11-stanza "Brummtopp Song" must have many variant stanzas, since the young people who sing it while performing the New Year's mummers' play typically compose or alter stanzas to make the song fit the household in which they are performing.

A distinctively Mennonite use of rhyming has been identified by Doreen Klassen among Russian Mennonite immigrants to North America since the 1870s. In this living tradition, individual community members, using traditional Germanic and English tunes, compose verses for songs that are then sung and passed on by ear by other community members.

The subject matter is varied, including nonsense songs, work songs, satires of deviant members of the community, game songs, love songs, laments, religious songs and narratives (ballads). Typical contexts for singing these songs are while doing farm chores and other work or at family evening singings. In earlier times, such songs were composed and sung at meetings on the streets (*Gausseshlinyels* songs), meetings of hired hands on Saturday nights or Sunday afternoons, and young peoples' evenings (*Schlüsselbund* songs). Two newer contexts for performing these songs are evenings of entertainment used for fund-raising in rural Manitoba (*Plautdietsha Ohvent* [Low German evenings]) and commemorative events such as village reunions and centennial celebrations.   EB

Victor Carl Friesen, *The Windmill Turning: Nursery Rhymes, Maxims, and Other Expressions of Western Canadian Mennonites* (Edmonton: U. of Alberta Press, 1988); Bertha Fast Harder, "Low German for Children—Rhymes, and Poems," *Menn. Life*, 36, no. 3 (Sept. 1981), 12-16; Doreen Klassen, "Low German Songs? Ohba yo!" *Menn. Life*, 33, no. 4 (Dec. 1978), 23-26; idem, *Singing Mennonite: Low German Songs among the Mennonites* (Winnipeg: U. of Manitoba Press, 1988); Warren Kliewer, "Low German Children's Rimes,"

Menn. Life, 14, no. 3 (July 1959), 141-42; idem, "More Low German Children's Rhymes," *Menn. Life*, 15, no. 4 (Oct. 1960), 173-74, 180.

See also Dialect Literature and Speech; Folklore.

Richmond Hill Colony, Belize Close to Orange Walk, this colony was started in 1960 by Old Colony Mennonite settlers from the Peace River area of Alberta. It had disbanded by 1965.   JBL

Righteousness. The Biblical terminology for "righteousness" carries rich and varied meanings. Sometimes righteousness consists primarily in conformity to a legal or ethical standard (Lv 19:15, 36; Ex 23:6-8). At other times, righteousness denotes the subjective moral and spiritual character of individuals and groups (Prv 21:25, Lk 1:6). In other instances, righteousness is the activity through which God overcomes his enemies, vindicates his people, and establishes them in peace (Ps 98:7-9, Is 62:1-2). Differing theological understandings of righteousness, °justification, °atonement and ethics are often rooted in decisions as to which of these meanings is dominant.

In the era of the Protestant Reformation, the issue of righteousness was closely tied to that of justification. Roman Catholics maintained that individuals can be justified only when God imparts to them a moral and spiritual righteousness which actually makes them righteous. Protestants, however, argued that righteousness is the acceptance and forgiveness which God imputes to individuals who are not yet personally righteous.

Subsequently, Protestant orthodoxy developed the formal concept of righteousness as divine legal standards for human behavior. Those who fulfill these perfectly merit eternal life, while those who break them deserve eternal death. But since no one has fulfilled these standards and everyone has broken them, Christ's righteousness is his legal fulfillment of God's requirements and his legal payment of their penalties in our place. Imputation of this righteousness is God's assigning these accomplishments to an individual's account, apart from any impartation of subjective righteousness. Many Fundamentalists hold this view today.

The Anabaptists understood righteousness in several ways. Sometimes it meant those violated divine requirements which Christ satisfied on our behalf. Anabaptists also spoke of Christ's righteousness being imputed (although not in a strictly legal way) to cover the sinfulness of infants and of the corrupt "flesh" of Christians.

More often, Anabaptists regarded righteousness as a moral and spiritual energy. Its inmost character and the scope of its effects, however, often transcended the Catholic notion of a quality which God imparts. Righteousness often means the divine activity and life itself. Leonhard °°Schiemer emphasized "the birth, death, and resurrection in us of Christ who is our righteousness" (CRR 3: 54). For Peter °°Riedemann, "Christ is our righteousness" meant that through "his actual strength or working, he guideth us into his nature, essence and character" (*Confession of Faith*, p. 36). Since the Anabaptists experienced this righteousness to be in con-

tinual conflict with the world, the flesh, and the devil and expected God to shortly vindicate his righteous people, its deepest character may also correspond to the biblical notion of that activity whereby God overcomes his enemies and establishes his people in peace.   TNF

CRR 3:41-71, 211-31; John Reumann, *Righteousness in the New Testament* (Philadelphia: Fortress, 1982); Manfred Brauch, "Perspectives on 'God's Righteousness' in Recent German Discussion" in E. P. Sanders, *Paul and Palestinian Judaism* (Philadelphia: Fortress, 1977), 526-42; Peter Riedemann (Ridemann), *Account of Our Religion, Doctrine, and Faith*, trans. Kathleen E. Hasenberg (London and Rifton, N.Y.: Plough, 1938, 1950, 1970), 34-48, 61-86, 165-88; Menno Simons, "The True Christian Faith" in Menno *Writings*, esp. 335-43; "Brief and Clear Confession" in Menno, *Writings*, esp. 422-440; Michael Sattler, "Two Kinds of Obedience" in CRR 1: 121-25, and "Schleitheim Confession" in CRR 1: 28-43.

See also Salvation; Sanctification.

Rio Corrientes Colony, Paraguay, located 255 km. (158 mi.) from Asunción on 1,500 hectares, is the sister colony to °Agua Azul. These settlements work closely with each other and also with the °Luz y Esperanza Colony. These three settlements are the only ones in which mixed marriages with Paraguayans are welcomed and in which Paraguayan believers are received into the congregation and the colony as full members. They call themselves the Mennonite Christian Brotherhood. In 1986 the Rio Corrientes Colony contained 167 persons in 18 families, of whom 12 were English-speaking and 6 were Spanish-speaking. Fifty-three were members of the congregation (40 English-speaking, 13 Spanish-speaking).   GR

Rio Verde Colony, Paraguay, lies 350 km. (217 mi.) ne. of Asunción on highway 3. Old Colony Reinländer Mennonites from Mexico purchased 20,526 hectares (50,700 acres) of land. An additional 6,000 hectares (14,820 acres), on the opposite side of the highway, were purchased by private investors. The colony's name means Green River. The first 14 families (106 persons) arrived in 1969 from Chihuahua, Mexico. A shortage of suitable land in Mexico was the reason for migration. Gradually additional families came from Mexico as well as from Belize and Canada. Eighteen villages have been planned; 13 have already been occupied. The population in 1986 was 2,397, of whom 802 were members of the congregation.

The settlement has made much progress economically. With the use of modern machinery large tracts of land were quickly cleared for cultivation. Soybeans, beans, and wheat are primary crops, but milk production is also carried on. Blacksmiths, sawmills, carpentry shops, and stores are available to provide the settlers with most of the things they need for daily life.

The importance of °tradition and separation from the world is strongly emphasized. Uniformity of °dress is immediately apparent. The express desire of the leaders of the colony is that it remain as it is. Cars and motorcycles, as well as pocket watches, radios, and belts (instead of suspenders), are not permitted.   GR

Riva Palacios Colony, Bolivia, located 60 km. (37 mi.) south of Santa Cruz. It was started in 1967 by ca. 50 Old Colony Mennonite families from Mexico with 100 more families arriving in 1968. In 1986 Riva Palacios had a population of 5,686 with 1,900 baptized church members. It is the largest Mennonite settlement in Bolivia, and its church affiliation is with the Old Colony Mennonites. Ben Peters is the bishop. There are five church buildings in different parts of the colony. Schools are found in most of the 39 villages. The colony owns about 33,000 hectares (81,500 acres) of land.

The colonists left Mexico to begin a new life in the jungle of Bolivia because of population pressures and scarcity of land, a desire to return to a more conservative life-style, and a desire for a new experience and adventure.

As in all the other Mennonite colonies in Bolivia farming is the main activity of the colonists. This colony consists of many well-to-do farmers who have nice farmyards, spacious houses and barns or sheds, machinery (tractors with steel wheels), and large areas of cultivated land; but there are also many poor people, both young and old. Small gas motors or windmills are used to pump the water from good wells into water reservoirs which serve as pressure tanks. Electricity is used only for welding and for small electric motors in the shops.

No bicycles, motorcycles, cars, pickup trucks, or other trucks are permitted. Neither does the church permit the use of °radios, record players, or tape recorders. Church rules are very strictly enforced with the °°ban being applied freely. Higher education is prohibited. There are, however, self-taught dentists, doctors, midwives, and chiropractors.   IHie

Rocky Mountain Mennonite Conference (MC) was organized as a conference district in Sept. 1961, at the first annual meeting in La Junta, Col. In a Colorado Springs meeting the previous July steps were taken to form a district conference with the encouragement of Harold S. °Bender, guest speaker. Christian workers conferences and regular ministers meetings preceded the conference organization. Fourteen congregations formed Rocky Mountain Conference with eleven congregations in Colorado and one each in Nebraska, Kansas, and Texas. These congregations had earlier been a part of South Central Mennonite Conference with E. M. Yost as area overseer. Yost became the first overseer of Rocky Mountain Conference.

Health care and human services have been important in the witness and ministry of Mennonites in the Rocky Mountain region. Six communities in Colorado have been served by Mennonite-operated °hospitals and nursing homes. Frontier Boys Village, a facility for emotionally disturbed boys, emerged from the Rocky Mountain Camp ministry. The Prince of Peace Chapel in Aspen and the Mennonite Urban Ministry in Denver also provide significant ministries. Voluntary service workers from across the Mennonite Church have served in these settings with most congregations including former voluntary service workers among their members.

In 1987 the district had 19 congregations in Colorado, New Mexico, and Texas. One congregation is also affiliated with the Brethren in Christ; 2 congregations are also members of the General Conference Mennonite Church. Membership in the conference is 1,308. The official organ of the conference is the *Echo*.   WJ

MC Yearbook (1988-89), 77-78.

Roman Catholic Church (ME I:532). The opening statement in the article on "Catholicism and Anabaptism," namely, "this is a theme which has not yet been thoroughly studied," remains as valid in 1988 as it was in 1955. Anabaptist studies have given some attention to medieval and Catholic roots of Anabaptism but most interpreters have continued to work with medieval Catholicism as "background to the Reformation" rather than a subject in its own right, leading to a degree of misinterpretation. Readers should consult articles on °Anabaptism, °historiography, °monasticism, °mysticism, and Michael °Sattler for information about these studies.

The Roman Catholic Church emerged out of medieval Catholicism by way of the Catholic °Reformation (Council of Trent, 1545-63). Mennonites generally continued the strong anti-Catholicism that was evident in the polemical writings of the 16th-c. Anabaptists. Anabaptists survived primarily in Protestant lands, owing to the ruthless re-Catholicization of Hutterites in Moravia and the presecution-induced exodus of Anabaptists from Bavaria, Austria, Tirol, etc. Mennonites thus had little contact with Catholics until their resettlement in parts of Alsace and Bavaria in the 17th-19th c., their immigration to and missionary work in Latin America in the 20th c., and their late-20th-c. migration to the °urban centers of North America.

Mennonite missionary memoirs and publicity literature of the early and mid-20th c. were often written in an anti-Catholic tone. Catholics were portrayed as superstitious and idolatrous at best and, occasionally as lazy and dirty. Like the 16th-c. Anabaptists, Mennonites were convinced that the Roman Catholic church was an apostate form of Christianity.

This has changed slightly in the later 20th c. Internal changes in Catholicism are responsible in part; the Mennonite exodus from rural subcultures and entry into businesses and professions in large cities has also played a role. A professor at Mennonite Biblical Seminary, C. J. Dyck, was an observer at the Second Vatican Council (1963-65), the reform council that symbolizes the most significant changes in Roman Catholic life and thought. Some Mennonite periodicals reported on these events (partially analyzed by Bertsche). Roman Catholic leaders in North America have become active in discussions of the issues of war and °peace, often drawing on Mennonite theologians' and activists' work, sometimes working cooperatively in peace organizations. North American Mennonite interest in °spiritual formation and °worship renewal have drawn to some degree on Roman Catholic resources. Mennonites in Paraguay and Colombia have had limited conversations with Roman Catholic leaders; Mennonite missionaries and Mennonite Central Committee workers in many countries have worked with Roman Catholics in a variety of projects. Mennonite World Conference was represented at the international interreligious day of prayer called by Pope John Paul II at Assisi in 1986. Some Mennonites have interacted extensively with Latin American proponents of °liberation theologies. (These theologies are viewed by the official teaching office of the Roman Catholic Church as potentially un-Catholic.)

Despite these changes, in many Mennonite circles, rural as well as urban, lay as well as theologically trained, considerable residual suspicion of Catholicism remains. Theologically literate Mennonites are suspicious of Catholic understandings of priesthood, sacrament, tradition, and teaching office; grass-roots Mennonites continue elements of the traditional Protestant rejection of Catholicism as idolatrous and apostate.

Exceptions to the above generalizations are illustrated by the pamphlet by H. Goerz. Goerz passes over the "Constantinian Fall" theory of church history, places the "fall of the church" in the Gregorian Reform of the 11th c. (a viewpoint remarkably similar to recent scholarship on the growth of the papacy), and maintains a tone of cautious openness toward a wide variety of Catholic teachings.

Roman Catholicism has a high view of the institutional church, her °tradition, and her teaching office. Mennonites have similarly held a high view of the visible church, depending, however, on unwritten rules and structures, in contrast to the highly developed theology, priesthood, and canon law of the Roman Catholics. Similarly, since the Anabaptist movement, Anabaptists and Mennonites have taught a memorialistic view of °baptism and °communion as mere signs rather than sacraments (dynamic °symbols), which places Mennonites at the opposite extreme from the Roman Catholic understanding of the use of visible and physical things in sacral worship. Practically speaking Mennonites have also made use of created things in a sacralized way, failing however, to develop a theology of sacrament to explain the relationship of spirit and matter.   DDM

H. Goerz, *Die Urgemeinde: Die Katholische Kirche; Die Reformation—Drei kurze kirchengeschichtliche Studien* (Yarrow, B.C.: Columbia Press for the author, n.d. [ca. 1980]; Janeen Bertsche [Johnson], "What Mennonites Have Been Saying About Catholics" (student paper, Bluffton College, 1986); Kauffman/Harder, *Anabaptists Four C. Later* (1975), 248-52; *MWR* (Feb. 19, 1987), 6; *Menn. Rep.* (Apr. 25, 1988), 12; Winfried Eisenblätter, "Die katholische Auseinandersetzung mit dem Täufertum," *Menn. Geschbl.,* Jg. 22, n.F. 17 (1965), 47-53; Peter C. Erb, "A Reflection on Mennonite Theology in Canada," *JMS*, 1 (1983), 179-90; idem, "Between Presumption and Despair," in *Why I Am a Mennonite,*, ed. Harry Loewen (Scottdale, 1988), 62-76; Dennis D. Martin, "Anabaptist Discipleship and Anabaptist and Mennonite Spirituality," *MQR*, 62 (1988), 5-25; Juhnke, *Mission* (1979), 150-58; Horst Gerlach, "Die Mennoniten in katholischer Sicht" (Karlsruhe: H. Schneider, ca. 1964), 8pp; C. J. Dyck, "The Literature of Vatican Council II:A Bibliographical Commentary," *Anglican Theological Review,* 49 (1967), 263-80, does not deal with Mennonites.

See also Bolivia; History; Restitutionism; Zaire.

Rosedale Mennonite Missions. See Conservative Mennonite Conference.

Rosenort Colony, Bolivia, is located about 80 km. (50 mi.) east of Santa Cruz, east of the Rio Grande

river. It was started in 1975 by a portion of the Canadian settlers of the Reinland colony near Santa Cruz. Land shortage had become more and more a problem and they wanted to be farther away from the city. Growing tensions between the two groups in the Reinland colony also contributed to the decision. The church in Rosenort is considered part of the Reinländer Mennonites. Its bishop was Corny Nickel, who moved to Rosenort from the Reinland colony only in 1986. Three ministers and one deacon (1985) also served the church.

Besides a small cheese factory there are no businesses in Rosenort, not even a store. Each farmer does all his business in Santa Cruz. Farmers in Rosenort use rubber tires on their tractors, but motorized vehicles (cars, pickups, trucks, and motorcycles) are not permitted, neither are radios, tape recorders, or phonographs. In 1986 Rosenort had approximately 350 inhabitants, of whom ca. 140 were church members.   IHie

Ross, Jeremiah (b. 1905), is the Cree Indian pastor of the Elim Mennonite Church at Cross Lake, Man. Jeremiah's call to the ministry came through the reading of the Scriptures and by receiving a special dream while he and his wife Fanny were on a hunting trip in 1942. It was not until 25 years later that Jeremiah Ross trusted Mennonite missionary Ernie Sawatzky with the story of his dream. When Sawatzky then invited Jeremiah to tell that dream to the congregation, they unanimously acclaimed him as their minister. Jeremiah was ordained as a Mennonite pastor on Feb. 4, 1968, with Henry Funk, chairman of the Mennonite Pioneer Mission Board, officiating. Since his ordination, Ross has given excellent pastoral leadership within his Cree community and beyond. He has done so without relinquishing his role as a traditional Indian elder and while maintaining his vocation as an outstanding hunter and trapper.   MW

Rothmann, Bernhard (ME IV:367), began preaching ca. 1529 and had become the key reformer of °Münster by 1531. While retaining friendly relations with Lutherans for the sake of appeasing the Münster city council and to achieve a political alliance with the Schmalkaldic League, Rothmann's proposed reforms dovetailed with the civic communal ideology of the urban Reformation. His ideal of "a community of faith under God" meshed with the aspirations of guild leaders who hoped to wrest political control from the city's ruling elite. At the same time he made himself a spokesman for local autonomy vis-à-vis the city's overlord, the bishop. Attempts to remove Rothmann were therefore met by popular opposition. Theologically Rothmann remained eclectic, borrowing, as his "Confession" of 1532 indicates, from °°Campanus' "Restitution," °°Zwingli's "Fidei ratio," and °°Melancthon's "Loci."

Rothmann's gradual rejection of infant baptism, starting in the summer of 1533, was not only a logical consequence of his sacramental theology, but related also to his resistance to external pressure from Luther and the Schmalkaldic league to revise his *Church Order* of April 1533 along more orthodox Wittenberg lines. Adopting a more separatist conception of church structure, Rothmann joined forces with the °°"Wassenberg preachers," becoming the leader of a small radical group.

In the milieu spawned by the arrival of apostles of °°Jan Matthijs in Jan. 1534, Rothmann allowed himself to be baptized. The crisis of Feb. 9-10, 1534, during which the small band of Anabaptists was delivered from their Catholic and Lutheran opponents, led to the triumph of Rothmann's faction. With the arrival of Jan Matthijs himself on Feb. 23, 1534 (the same day Anabaptists gained legal control of the city council), Rothmann lost direct leadership of the Münster Reformation and became little more than the propagandist for the besieged community. His most important tracts date from this period. Three of them, "Restitution," "Concerning Vengeance," and "The Hiddenness of the Word of God," helped to shape the ideological development of Dutch Anabaptism. While Rothmann initially disagreed with some of °Jan van Leiden's innovations, such as polygamy, he had little choice but to acquiesce and to rationalize the new practice. Destruction of the kingdom on June 25, 1535, ended Rothmann's reform career, and probably his life, although there are reports that he was seen in Lübeck and Rostock in 1537.   GKW

The most important source for Rothmann's theological development is the critical edition of all his extant works (letters, disputations, confessions and tracts) edited by Robert Stupperich, *Die Schriften der Münsterischen Täufer und ihrer Gegner*, part 1: *Die Schriften Bernhard Rothmanns* (Münster: Aschendorff, 1970). Selections from documents relating to Münster are found in Richard van Dülmen, ed., *Das Täuferreich zu Münster* (München: Deutscher Taschenbuch Verlag, 1974). Recent literature on Rothmann and Münster was reviewed by James M. Stayer, "Was Dr. Kuehler's Conception of Early Dutch Anabaptism Historically Sound? The Historical Discussion of Anabaptist Münster 450 Years After," *MQR*, 60 (1986), 261-88. See also Stayer, "The Münsterite Rationalization of Bernhard Rothmann," *Journal of the History of Ideas*, 28 (1967), 179-92 and idem, Sword (1972, 1976). The "Reformed" nature of Rothmann's early theology is noted by W. J. de Bakker, in *Profiles of Radical Reformers*, ed. H.-J. Goertz and Walter Klaassen (Scottdale, 1982), 191-202. Se also Goertz, "De vroege Theologie van Bernhard Rothmann: De gereformeerde Achtergrond van het Munsterse Doperrijk," *Doops. Bijdr.*, n.r. 3 (1977), 9-20. Martin Brecht has discovered many of the sources used by Rothmann in his early writings and has made several corrections to Stupperich's notes in "Die Theologie Bernhard Rothmanns," *Jb. für westfälische Kg.*, 78 (1985), 49-82. The best discussion to date of the reasons behind Rothmann's rejection of infant baptism and espousal of Anabaptism is found in Tara Kuratsuka, "Gesamtgilde und Täufer: Der Radikalisierungsprozess in der Reformation Münsters: Von der reformatorischen Bewegung zum Täuferreich 1534/35" *ARG*, 76 (1985) 231-70. Hans Galen, ed., *Die Wiedertäufer in Münster* (Münster: Stadmuseum Münster, 2nd edition, 1982) contains useful illustrations and texts regarding the Münster kingdom.

Roy, Surendra N. (1928-85), was the second child and eldest son in a family of eight children. His father, Rev. Samuel Roy, was employed, first as a "Bible teacher" (°lay evangelist) and later as a pastor, by the Brethren in Christ Church, India.

Surendra received his theological training at the Allahabad Bible Seminary. In 1950 he returned to serve the Brethren in Christ Church, located in Bihar State. During his 35 years of ministry, Roy was involved in all levels of Christian service. For many years, he provided leadership for the Brethren in Christ Church Society of India, frequently alternat-

ing between the positions of chairman and treasurer. At the same time, he served as the regional superintendent of the Saharsa District, helped to develop and manage Jiwan Jyoti (Light of Life Bookstore) and was long-term pastor of the Saharsa congregation. Roy had a unique ministry to upper class Hindus. He moved with ease among local government officials and was respected by the secular and business leaders of Saharsa.

Roy filled a vital role in the transitional period, 1955-75, when the Indian church assumed responsibility for what had been a North American mission program. He also enjoyed broader church life, involving himself in such groups as the Evangelical Fellowship of India, the °Mennonite Christian Service Fellowship of India, and the Evangelical Trust Association of North India. His wife, Dorothy Mary, served during many of these years as the headmistress of the local mission (church) school. They were the parents of five children.   HRS

Rudnerweide Mennonite Church. See Evangelical Mennonite Mission Conference.

Rural Life (ME II:303). Most Mennonites of European origin, until well into the 20th c., have assumed that the Christian life is best lived in a rural °°community, one composed of fellow believers, friends, and in many cases relatives, who will support one's faith and one's family as fellow Christians should. The rural community was thought to provide some protection from threatening "worldly" forces seen as pervasive and inherent in city life but less problematic and somewhat controllable from the safety of the rural community.

This rural bias was not present at the beginning of the Anabaptist movement, and is losing its grip on Mennonites in the late 20th c., as many Mennonites no longer are or want to be rural residents. Some in the church are embarrassed by the traditional Mennonite rural bias, and see it as an impediment to the growth and witness of the church in the city and the larger world today (°church growth; °urban church).

The first generation of Mennonites in 16th-c. Switzerland and The Netherlands were largely city people and did not display any bias for rural life. (Cities in 16th-c. Europe usually had no more than 20,000-50,000 residents, with a few as large as 100,000 or 200,000. They were more like 20th-c. small towns than modern industrial cities.) Some Anabaptists were highly educated teachers, medical doctors, artists, and engineers, as well as pastors and evangelists. Less educated urban Mennonites were often artisans, skilled in one of the crafts common in late medieval and early modern Europe.

Intense and long-lasting °persecution drove Swiss, South German, and Austrian Mennonites, Amish, and Hutterites to seek refuge in isolated rural areas, often somewhat out of the reach of the city-based magistrates and state church officials who held in their hands the power of life and death, or at least banishment, for religious dissenters. Persecution, which lasted 300 years among the Swiss Mennonites and Amish and which nearly exterminated the Hutterites, drove them to find even temporary refuge wherever they could. This was often on the rural estate of a sympathetic nobleman or prince. Sometimes the offer of protection was extended in exchange for the Mennonites' and Hutterites' agreement to work the estate as farmhands and artisans.

These formerly urban people found it necessary to develop productive agricultural practices, which they passed down from one generation to the next. Crop rotation, use of legumes, manuring of crop land, and careful husbandry of livestock all proved productive, especially when practiced with Mennonite diligence. Rarely permitted and rarely wanting to own land at first, Mennonites depended on agricultural skills to keep them in the good graces of their protectors and employers. In this way Swiss-German Mennonites and Austrian Hutterites were transformed from an urban to an almost totally rural people. Agricultural and related occupations in a small, close-knit community provided a commonality and stability to both church life and social life of Mennonites, even in the face of varying degrees of persecution and hostility.

The experience of the Dutch and North German Mennonites was markedly different. A relatively short period of intense persecution ended in 1579 with the Union of Utrecht, after which relative toleration developed. Some Mennonites, particularly those in Friesland, were, and preferred to stay, rural, but others in The Netherlands and North Germany were relatively prosperous and respected urbanites: merchants, doctors, and even artists. They were a much more cosmopolitan people than the Swiss, partly due to social acceptance and partly due to the geography and commercial development of their area. Very few of the Dutch and North German Mennonites came to North America directly, however. A notable exception were those from Krefeld who came to Germantown, Pa. (1683).

Some of the Dutch and North German Mennonites, most of whom remained in Europe, were attracted by offers of land, or at least the chance to develop and farm land in Prussia in the 17th c. and later in Russia and the Ukraine (18th and 19th cs.) The offer to come to Prussia was extended by Frederick I and that to Russia by Catherine the Great. In each case the Mennonites were welcomed because of their agricultural and technical skills (°water technology). In Prussia, however, they remained under certain civil and social restrictions, so some left for Russia when that invitation came.

The *Privilegium* (°privilege) granted those who went to Russia was particularly attractive. In included complete religious freedom, exemption from military service, and the right to control their own religious, educational, and civic affairs. The Mennonites were allowed to settle in colonies separate from the native Russians. Each family was given ca. 176 acres of land. This offer was unprecedented for Mennonites. In effect they were granted not only land and precious religious freedom, but the right to have a state within a state.

Settlement was in line-villages (*Straßendorfer*) with narrow lots and houses along the main village street. Additional land and pasture lay further away from the villages. The Mennonites prospered. They developed an extremely productive agriculture and accompanying agricultural industries (e.g., flour mills, creameries, farm implement factories). At one time six percent of total Russian industrial production was in the Mennonite colonies.

Elementary and secondary schools, a business schools, girls schools, and a school for the deaf were founded. Homes for the aged, orphanages, hospitals, and mental hospitals were founded. The Mennonites developed a rural society where music and cultural learning were valued. Theirs was an island of peace and prosperity in a sea of poverty and imminent revolution.

As the provisions of the *Privilegium* were gradually withdrawn from 1874 to 1917, the Russian Mennonites frantically tried to renegotiate their privileges, but with little success. Some 18,000 emigrated to North America in the 1870s. After pillaging, famine, and epidemics, thousands more managed to leave in the 1920s, largely to Paraguay, Brazil, and Canada. Forced collectivization, imprisonment, and exile to Siberia awaited those who had stayed. The rural Mennonite paradise in Russia had ended.

But the ideal of the nearly autonomous Mennonite rural community lived for a time in Canada among the most conservative of the 1870s Russian immigrants, the °°Kleine Gemeinde and the Old Colony Mennonites. They first attempted to recreate the Russian colonies on the °°East Reserve and °°West Reserve in Manitoba. In the wake of controversy over °public and private schools, what became known as Old Colony Mennonites moved to Chihuahua State, Mexico, to follow the dream another step. Other Russian Mennonites have attempted to recreate the Russian colony model in Paraguay, Brazil, and Bolivia with some success, but nowhere matching the wealth and success of the original Russian colonies.

The Swiss Mennonites, Amish, and Hutterites have also, each in their own way, tried to recreate the rural community in the New World, in Canada, the United States, and in a few new settlements in Central America, notably Belize. Lacking the Russian Mennonite experience of governing themselves in a Mennonite commonwealth, the Swiss-origin Amish and Mennonites were relatively content to be left alone, avoiding conflict wherever possible. They became the "quiet ones in the country," content to live out their lives in peaceful rural communities. (Rural Mennonite communities, whether of Swiss or Russian Mennonite origin, may have been less successful in avoiding internal conflict than they were in avoiding conflict with the non-Mennonite world around them. See, for example, Rudy Wiebe, *Peace Shall Destroy Many*, 1962).

The Hutterites, who had been helped in reestablishing their *Bruderhof* pattern in Russia by the Russian Mennonites, introduced it to the Dakotas and prairie provinces of Canada upon emigration, although with periodic harassment by state and provincial authorities and resentful neighbors, especially during and after World War I and in the 1940s in South Dakota and Alberta.

The ideal for all the Mennonite groups (Swiss-German Amish and Mennonites, Hutterites, Russian-origin Low-Germans) was close to Tönnies' concept of the *Gemeinschaft*, a rural community based on close, intimate ties of blood, land, and kinship; a community where people respect °tradition and prefer to remain and interact with kin and friends of their own group, rather than with strangers in a more urban, cosmopolitan, and less rooted community.

In North America in the period after World War II, however, progressive Mennonites, those now more open to contact with outsiders and who exercise little collective °discipline any longer (Mennonite Church [MC], General Conference Mennonites, Mennonite Brethren, Evangelical Mennonite Church), have seen many of their members leave the rural community for the opportunities of the city. Often these moves are associated with higher education and upward social mobility. In some cases members of these groups retain something of the rural ideal by maintaining a rural or semi-rural residence but an urban occupation, or by maintaining a large garden on a lot in suburbia, as, for example, the Kansas Mennonite who moved to the Washington, D.C., suburbs and grew a patch of Kansas wheat descended from the Turkey Red wheat brought to Kansas by his ancestors from Russia. His rural heritage is still precious to him and alive in his consciousness. Whether it will be for his children and grandchildren is highly questionable.

More culturally °conservative Mennonite groups (Amish, Hutterites, Old Colony, Church of God in Christ Mennonite, Old Order Mennonites), who are less open to outsiders, who retain a higher degree of control over individual members, and who take pains to maintain clearer boundaries between themselves and the larger society around them, hold more firmly to tradition in general and to the ideal of maintaining the rural community, although this differs in practice from group to group. Even these groups have not been immune from the forces of °urbanization and °modernity, especially in Canada and the United States. But they have resisted change more vigorously than the progressive groups and have been more resourceful in meeting the challenges and threats to rural community life.

Change is present in the community life of all Mennonite groups. But the rural ideal is most strongly fixed, and will likely remain so, in the more culturally conservative groups. Whether it can be kept alive by the more progressive groups remains open to question. They are less willing to pay as high a price to preserve and maintain the rural community, and more likely to let individual members make their own individual adaptations to economic and social pressures. The net result is a weaker commitment to rural life and the rural community in the more progressive groups, some of which are now consciously putting first priority on urban mission efforts and church and community life in urban as opposed to rural areas.

Recent empirical studies document the increasing urbanization of the progressive Mennonite groups, as well as the slightly less radical move from rural farm to rural nonfarm residence, which in some cases is accomplished simply by giving up farming as a livelihood but without a change in actual residence. In the Mennonite Church (MC) in Canada and the United States, the percentage of persons with rural farm residence declined from 51 to 21 percent from 1963 to 1982. Those with rural nonfarm residence increased from 25 to 46 percent, and those with an urban residence increased from 24 to 33 percent in the same period.

Among the more highly urbanized Mennonite Brethren in North America the percentage living in cities of 25,000 population or more was already 36 percent in 1972 and increased further to 41 percent by 1982. And even for those North American Mennonites remaining in rural areas, the city increasingly intrudes and changes the pattern of rural life through °mass communication, efficient transportation, and commercial, educational, and cultural influence.

For Mennonites in other areas of the world, firm data are unavailable, but it would appear that except for the still fairly rural ethnic Mennonites in Latin America, many Mennonites are now also urban, especially in Europe and Japan. This is perhaps less true in Africa, India, and Indonesia, where many Mennonites are found in rural areas and small towns.   MLY

Leo Driedger and J. Howard Kauffman, "Urbanization of Mennonites: Canadian and American Comparisons," *MQR,* 56 (1982), 269-90; Frank H. Epp, *Mennonites in Canada 1;* John A. Hostetler, *Hutterite Society* (1974); *MB Profile, 1972-1982,* in *Direction,* 14, no. 2 (1985), sp. issue; Yoder, *MC Census* (1985); Kauffman/Harder, *Anabaptists Four C. Later* (1975), 203ff.

See also Acculturation; Automobile; Dialect Literature and Speech; German Language; Sociological Studies.

Rural Mission (Mennonite Church [MC]).

Rural mission is the counterpart of °urban and foreign °missions. The Mennonite disposition to rural missions is rooted in the early Anabaptist experience of °persecution which changed them from an urban to a rural orientation, encouraged lay rather than professional leadership, engendered the development of quietism, and stimulated an attachment to the °frontier.

In America, being an agricultural people, Mennonites felt more at home and more competent working with the rural culture and were often attracted to the poor and disadvantaged people in rural areas. For 200 years of the Mennonite sojourn in America there was no overt mission outreach. When, near the close of the 19th c. there finally came an awakening (°renaissance), Mennonites thought of missions in terms of city or foreign work. During the middle third of the 20th c., however, Mennonites made a great effort to evangelize rural America.

There are, however, several outstanding examples of rural outreach following the American Civil War, though they were not thought of as "mission" work at the time. The most notable was the effort of the Mennonites of the Shenandoah Valley to plant churches in the adjoining highlands of Virginia and West Virginia. A traditional story told about the beginning of this work describes John Heatwole, a potter (°ceramics), who hid in the forested foothills to avoid being forced into the Confederate Army. On being warned that Confederate scouts had located his hideout, he walked backward in the snow to the top of the ridge behind his cabin, then turned and fled into the mountains to the west. He was given refuge by a kindly mountain family. After the war he urged Mennonite ministers to go into the area with the gospel. Men from the highlands regularly came to the farms in the Shenandoah Valley for the grain and fruit harvest, often working for the Mennonites, whom they invited to come into the mountains to hold religious services.

Mennonite ministers began regularly scheduled trips of two or three days in duration, holding services in homes, schoolhouses, and lumber camps in the highlands of Virginia and West Virginia. Groups of believers were consolidated into congregations and meetinghouses were built. As transportation improved, °°Sunday schools were organized. °Summer Bible schools also aided the development of active congregations.

Mennonites who settled the Great Plains of the West following the American Civil War found the distances great and settlements scattered. Almost as a matter of survival they made greater effort to reach their neighbors with the gospel than had earlier Mennonite settlers of the East. So again, without a specific consciousness of mission they carried on a significant work of outreach. In Canada, the Mennonites of Ontario rather early attracted to their fellowship a significant number of non-Mennonite neighbors and called from this out-group numerous able leaders. By about 1874 Bishop H. H. Blough of Allegheny Conference was promoting work in the mountains of Maryland.

In 1882 the °°Mennonite Evangelizing Committee was formed at Elkhart, Ind., becoming the °°Mennonite Evangelizing Board of America in 1892. Also in 1892 the Virginia Home Mission Board was formed and in 1894 the Home Missions Advocates of Lancaster (Pa.). These groups primarily raised funds to send out evangelists and pastors to the places where there were small and struggling congregations of Mennonite settlers.

During the first third of the 20th c. almost all the district conferences of the Mennonite Church (MC) organized their own mission boards. A few undertook foreign or urban work but most of them concentrated on rural missions with a new understanding of mission and a zeal to reach the lost for Christ.

Virginia Mennonite Conference (MC) continued to expand into the Virginia and West Virginia highlands and later into Kentucky. Lancaster Mennonite Conference (MC) began the first community betterment mission project in 1898 with the opening of Welsh Mountain Industrial Mission. Later they encouraged groups of Mennonites to settle in colonies in the South, notably in Alabama and Mississippi. The Indiana-Michigan Conference (MC) established churches in the northern peninsula of Michigan. South Central Mennonite Conference (MC) expanded into the Osage River country of Arkansas and the Alberta-Saskatchewan Conference (MC) expanded into the Peace River country to the north. Franconia Mennonite Conference (MC) sent her rural mission workers to New England, particularly Vermont.

In the nine-year period, 1945-53, the Mennonite Church (MC) opened 132 rural missions in North America. In 1948 students of the rural mission movement estimated that in Virginia Mennonite Conference 37 percent of the membership was made up of out-group converts and their descendents. In South Central Conference the figure was 23 percent. In the northern District of the Virginia Conference, located in the center of the mission movement to the highlands, 50 percent of the membership and 33 percent of the ordained leadership was of highland extraction.

These efforts were not always successful numerically. Some which were begun in hope were later abandoned. Many have remained as small and struggling congregations. But from the standpoint of breaking out of the old Swiss-German Mennonite culture the rural mission movement was one of the most significant things which happened in the Mennonite Church (MC).   LMW

Linden M. Wenger, "A Study of Rural Missions in the Mennonite Church" (ThM thesis, Union Theological Seminary, Richmond, Va., 1955); Theron F. Schlabach, *Gospel Versus Gospel* (Scottdale, 1980), 262-89; John A. Lapp, *India* (1972), ch. 15; Wittlinger, *Piety and Obedience* (1978), 447-53.

See also Shank, Clara Brubaker; Steiner, Clara Daisy Eby.

Russia. See Union of Soviet Socialist Republics.

Russian Revolution and Civil War. Many Mennonites, especially younger people, greeted the resignation of the Tsar of Russia, Nicholas II in February 1917 with consent and considerable relief. The tremendous anti-German pressures of the war years had taken their toll even among former patriots, while the strident voices calling for fundamental changes in Russian society had found ears in Mennonite communities as well. Others realized, to be sure, that violent revolution, if it came, would exact a heavy price of all people in Russia. Mennonites would be no more exempt than any others.

The overthrow of the provisional government, led by Alexander Kerensky in October 1917, quickly bore out the truth of this analysis. In only a few months Halbstadt and other villages of the southern Ukrainian Mennonite settlements came to feel the full impact of terror and bloodshed that would soon engulf the entire country. Outlying °estates were attacked and burned while their owners fled to the safety of the main Mennonite colonies nearby. The first village soviets (revolutionary councils) were formed and the requisition of foodstuffs began throughout the area.

The German invasion of Ukraine, and the entry of these troops into the Mennonite settlements in April 1918 seemed to promise a great change for the better. Churches were opened, and properties were restored, and normal community life began to function again. But the respite was short-lived. By the fall of the year the occupying forces needed to leave as the armistice officially ended World War I and the Germans had to retreat. They deposited weapons in the colonies for the villagers to use to defend themselves, and in the surrounding countryside Ukrainian peasants under Nestor Makhno (ME III:430) prepared to move in.

In a desperate effort to help themselves during the absence of central governing authority, the majority of Ukrainian Mennonite settlements set up military self-defense units (°*Selbstschutz*) to protect their families and homes from attacks by Makhno's forces. In the view of some this move saved the Molotschna villages at least from more serious damage. Others felt, however, that there were then and would be later negative consequences, and that this decision was a serious tactical error. In any case, it was hardly consistent with the traditionally pacifist Mennonite faith.

By now restorationist White armies had gathered energies to counterattack. Admiral Kolchak, in eastern Russia, and the generals Denikin and Wrangel in the Caucasus and the Ukraine, hoped to stall the Red takeover of the country, and to squelch the revolution as such, if possible. Civil war became a brutal and all-engulfing sequel, then, to the revolution in Petrograd (St. Petersburg) and Moscow. For a time it seemed that the Leninist-inspired thrust to the south, southeast, and other parts of the country would be pushed back.

Many young Mennonite men, often those from former *Selbstschutz* units, volunteered for service in the White army. Others were conscripted, and fought with these forces as long as they could. Several fronts of the Red-White military clashes moved back and forth between the Mennonite villages, resulting in further property destruction and loss of life. This was less true in such areas as °Orenburg or Slavgorod/Omsk where the Whites moved through some of the settlements but serious battles tended to be fought outside Mennonite communities, or not at all.

The final defeat of the White armies under Wrangel in the fall of 1920 terminated all effective opposition to the revolution. A number of Mennonites who had fought with the Whites were evacuated from Crimean ports to Constantinople at the end of the war. They made their way eventually to the United States. Russian Mennonites now were forced to come to terms with the new regime.   LK

William H. Chamberlain, *The Russian Revolution, 1917-1921*, 2 vols. (New York: Macmillan, 1952); John P. Dyck, ed., *Troubles and Triumphs, 1914-1924: Excerpts from the Diary of P. J. Dyck* (Springstein, Man.: the editor, 1981); David Footman, *Civil War in Russia* (London: Faber and Faber, 1961); Taras Hunczak, ed., *The Ukraine, 1917-1921: A Study in Revolution* (Cambridge, Mass.: Harvard Ukrainian Research Institute, 1977); A. N. Ipatov, *Wer Sind die Mennoniten?* (Alma Ata: Verlag Kazachstan, 1977); Lawrence Klippenstein, "Mennonite Pacifism and State Service in Russia: A Case Study in State Church Relations, 1789-1936" (PhD diss., U. of Minnesota, 1984); Dietrich Neufeld, *A Russian Dance of Death: Revolution and Civil War in the Ukraine*, trans. and ed. Al Reimer (Winnipeg: Hyperion, 1977); J. P. Nickel, ed., *Thy Kingdom Come: The Diary of Johann J. Nickel of Rosenhof, 1918-1919* (Saskatoon, Sask.: the editor, n.d.); Michael Palij, *The Anarchism of Nestor Makhno, 1918-1921: An Aspect of the Ukrainian Revolution* (Seattle: U. of Washington Press, 1976); Gerald Peters, ed. and trans., *Diary of Anna Baerg, 1916-1924* (Winnipeg: CMBC, 1985); George P. Schroeder, *Miracles of Grace and Judgement: A Family Strives for Survival during the Russian Revolution* (Lodi, Cal.: the author, 1974); [B. Unruh, ed.,] *Die Mennoniten Gemeinden in Russland waehrend der Kriegs- und Revolutionsjahre, 1914-1920* (Heilbronn: Kommissions-Verlag der Mennonitischen Fluechtlingsfürsorge, 1921); Leonard G. Friesen, "The Russian Revolution of 1917 Reconsidered: New Light on an Old Subject," *CGR*, 5 (1987), 135-46.

See also Communism.

Russian Soviet Federated Socialist Republic (RSFSR). In the 20th c. the focus of Soviet Mennonite activity has shifted from the Ukraine to the RSFSR, an administrative unit covering three fourths of all Soviet territory and containing half the population of the USSR. Following the liquidation of the settlements in the Ukraine (1943) what remained as Mennonite settlement areas were the Orenburg settlements (formerly the Samara and Trakt settlements), a chain of villages along a railroad line from Omsk to Novosibirsk, and extensive settlements of Mennonites in the Altai region of Western Siberia, including such cities as Slavgorod, Pavlodar, and Barnaul. All of these areas received more Mennonites through the forcible repatriation of refugees after World War II and Deportation Regime (°Spetskomandantura).

Repatriated Germans including Mennonites were sent into the forests ne. of Moscow, especially in Vologodskaia, Permskaia, Arkhangel'skaia Oblasts (provinces of the RSFSR) and in the Karelian and Komi Autonomous Soviet Socialist Republics (ASSRs). These included such places as Vologda, Sokol, Arkhangel'sk, Syktyvkar, Ukhta, Krasnovishersk, Solikamsk, Perm, Sverdlovsk, Novaiia Lialia, Krasnoturinsk, Severoural'sk, Cheliabinsk. These names signify hardship and became the grave for loved ones. Many of these settlements were abandoned when the Deportation Regime was lifted (after 1955) as Mennonites moved farther south into the industrial cities in the Ural mountain range and still farther to ne. °Kazakhstan where relatives had been sent to work in the mines. The Karaganda region of Kazakhstan is now (1988) the largest center for Mennonites in the USSR. Many others moved in the early 1960s to southern Kazakhstan (Alma Ata) or nearby °Kirgizia.

In the RSFSR the Novosibirsk °Kirchliche Mennonite congregation had been functioning openly since 1960 but was only registered in 1973. By that date a few congregations of Mennonite Brethren (MB) and Kirchliche Mennonites were functioning in the Orenburg settlements, but the Donskoi church (MB) was the first to be registered in 1978. There are now 31 registered congregations in Orenburg Oblast, of which 6 belong to the °All-Union Council of Evangelical Christians - Baptists (AUCECB), 14 are Mennonite Brethren, and 11 are Kirchliche Mennonites, representing about 3,000 and 750 members for the latter two groups. Little is known about congregations in the Altai region.

Revival came to isolated settlements when preachers of the gospel, often just released from prison, came by, sometimes also performing baptisms for dozens at a time. Such heroes, most of them still unnamed, braved the elements and the long arm of the law as they sought to encourage lonely, isolated Mennonite people. Others came to rely on shortwave radio broadcasts. A meeting of Kirchliche Mennonite elders and preachers in 1957 in Solikamsk (northern Urals) to organize a conference was broken up by the authorities. There is still no system of regular communication for either Mennonite Brethren or Kirchliche Mennonites. In 1979,

the AUCECB organized a centralized senior presbyter structure for the RSFSR, naming Jakob Fast as
one of two deputy senior presbyters, with special
duties to visit Mennonite congregations in the
RSFSR.   WWS

Richard Pipes, *The Formation of the Soviet Union,* rev. ed.
(New York: Atheneum, 1964); Gerd Stricker, "Mennoniten
in der Sowjetunion nach 1941," *Kirche im Osten,* 27 (1984);
Walter Sawatsky, "Mennonite Congregations in the Soviet
Union Today," *Menn. Life,* 33 (March 1978), 12-26; idem,
"From Russian to Soviet Mennonites 1945-1985" forthcom-
ing in *Russian Mennonites,* ed. John Friesen.

Rußländer. The term *Rußländer* developed in
Canada. It identified the 1920s Mennonite immigrants from the Soviet Union, and distinguished
them from the 1870s immigrants who were called
°*Kanadier.* The differences between the two groups
sometimes caused suspicion and tension. The differences were created by the two groups' widely differing experiences. The Rußländer in Russia had
been part of the Mennonite commonwealth which
up to the Bolshevik Revolution (1917) was wealthy,
and had created an impressive array of churches,
schools, health care, and financial institutions. They
had worked out an arrangement with the Russian
government whereby their young men performed alternative service either in forestry work or in the
°Red Cross. The Rußländer had experienced World
War I, the °Russian Revolution and Civil War, and
anarchy. Some had used arms to defend themselves.
All had lost their possessions.

In Canada Rußländer tended to see Kanadier as
less cultured, less well-educated, and not as progressive economically. During the 1930s and 1940s the
Rußländer established Bible schools, high schools,
colleges, and other institutions across Canada. Their
members also took control or at least exercised
strong influence in some of the organizations
founded by Kanadier, for example the Conference of
Mennonites in Canada, the Mennonite Collegiate Institute at Gretna, Man., and various Mennonite
Brethren institutions.   JF

F. H. Epp, *Mennonites in Canada II,* 242-45, 416-17.

S

Sabbatarianism. *Sabbatarianism* refers both to an emphasis on strict Sunday rest and to the practice among some Christians of a return to the Jewish-Christian seventh day (Saturday) as the day of worship. Only the latter will be discussed here.

Sabbatarianism has been a perennial, even if peripheral, issue among radical Protestants since the 16th c. In the 20th century, it is vigorously taught by the °Seventh-Day Adventists and the Seventh-Day Baptists. Among Anabaptists it appeared between 1527 and 1529 at Liegnitz, Silesia, under the leadership of Oswald °°Glaidt and Andreas °Fischer. These men then carried the teaching into the Nikolsburg area in Moravia about 1532, provoking, among other things, a written reaction from Martin Luther (*Wider die Sabbather*, 1538). It appeared late in the century among radical Unitarians in Transylvania, but was never widely accepted by either Anabaptists or Unitarians. The teaching died out by about 1540 among Anabaptists and was completely marginalized among Unitarians by about 1620.

Anabaptist Sabbatarianism does have interpretive significance in modern research. For, although the teaching was clearly rooted in biblical primitivism, the fact that most Anabaptists considered it a peripheral issue indicated that these Anabaptists employed other criteria alongside °restitutionism in °biblical interpretation.   DL

Daniel Liechty, *Andreas Fischer and Sabbatarian Anabaptism* (Scottdale, 1988); Samuele Bacchiocchi, *From Sabbath to Sunday* (Rome, 1977); Gerhard Hasel, "The Anabaptists of the Sixteenth Century and their Relationship to the Sabbath" (MA thesis, Andrews U., 1960); Richard Mueller, *Adventisten, Sabbat, Reformation* (Lund, 1979); *Menn. Bib. II*, p. 623 (on Sunday rest).

Sacapano, Felonito A. (Apr. 29, 1919-Oct. 6, 1987), was the founder of Missions Now, an Anabaptist and Mennonite church group in the Philippines. The independent group was formed in 1949 to engage in rural church planting, leadership training, and economic development in the congregations. Felonito served as the chairperson of Missions Now from its incorporation in 1965 until his death.

In 1971 he visited the United States looking for an American agency willing to share in the work of Missions Now while respecting its integrity as a Filipino church. The Lord led him to the Eastern Mennonite Board of Missions (MC), which had opened a work in the Philippines earlier that year for that very purpose. Thus began a fraternal relationship which has continued through the years.

Sacapano was a strong yet compassionate, sacrificial leader. He was trained in several Baptist Bible schools, but also studied business and political science in the university. Born in Romblon, central

Philippines, he lived in the hometown of his wife, Maria, in Laguna (south of Manila) where they raised their seven children.   JEM

Sacraments. See Ordinances.

St. Joseph Co., Mich., Old Order Amish Settlement. See Centreville, Mich., Old Order Amish Settlement.

Sakakibara Gan and Mano Chiyo. Gan Sakakibara is a leading Japanese Anabaptist historian and socio-economist. He has written six books on Anabaptism and translated five from English. His collection of 5,000 books and magazines, which included part of Robert °Friedmann's library, was donated to the Friedmann-Sakakibara Library (established in 1981), a branch of the Japan Anabaptist Center, Tokyo. For his 25-year effort at introduction and reevaluation of Anabaptism in Japan, he was given an award by the Christian Culture Association in 1982.

Gan was born into an ardent Buddhist family on Nov. 17, 1898, near Nagoya City. In 1918, while a student at Kobe Higher School of Commerce, he was baptized in a Presbyterian Church in Kobe. In 1927 he married Chiyo *Mano*, (1898-Apr. 28, 1987), a Christian woman, then a reporter for *Fujin no Tomo* (*The Friend of Women*), a monthly magazine for intellectual women. Gan and Chiyo became parents of four children.

After graduation from Tokyo Commercial College in 1924, Gan became a professor at Fukushima Higher School of Commerce, run by the government. In 1930 he joined the Social Christianity Movement. In *Rejection of Introspective Christianity* (1931, a pamphlet in Japanese written under the pseudonym Itsushi *Fukuda*), he insisted that faith should include deeds in the true Christian life. He was an Anabaptist at heart.

In the summer of 1932, he studied under Georg Wünsch at Marburg U. in Germany. His *Christian Socio-Economic Ethics* (English equiv.), which won first prize in a Christian Thought Essay Contest, was published the same year. Nine years later the book was barred from circulation because of its liberal tendency. The trends of the time did not allow him to stay in a government school, so he resigned from Fukushima School in 1939. He was without a job during the war years. His friends and former students helped his family. Most of his time was used in preparation of *A Study of British Classical Economics* (English equivalent), eventually published in 1961.

In the first election of the House of Councilors, April 1947, Chiyo Sakakibara was a candidate of the Japan Socialist Party and won a seat. She served as the Parliamentary Vice-Minister of Justice in 1948. She also served as a board member and administrator of Ferris Women's College and on the alumni board of Aoyama University. She was a member of the founding committee of the International Christian University and served as an honorary member of the board of that school until her death. Meanwhile Gan became a professor in the Economic Department of Aoyama Gakuin University in 1949, and taught history of socioeconomic thought until 1967, when he was made a professor emeritus.

After attending a World Council of Churches conference in Greece in 1959, as a delegate of the United Church of Christ in Japan, he and his wife made a six-month trip in Europe and the United States. Knowing his interest in intentional communities, Paul Peachey, then a Mennonite Central Committee representative in Japan, introduced Gan to the Hutterian Society of Brothers in New York and Koinonia Farms in Georgia. There he learned for the first time that intentional communities, which he thought had died out in the 19th c., still existed, that there were actually Christians who practiced their faith in a communal way of life. He also visited Reba Place in Chicago and a Hutterite community in South Dakota. Here at last he found the contact point between his academic interest and belief in a practical Christianity. The encounter with those communal groups led him to his second conversion—into Anabaptism.

Upon his return to Japan, he energetically began writing essays on Anabaptism in the *Aoyama Keizai Ronshu* (*Aoyama Economics Review*). The first book in the Sakakibara Anabaptist Thought Series appeared in 1967. An autobiography is underway. He (as well as his wife until her death) is a member of the Honan-cho Mennonite Church in Tokyo.   MO

Menn. Life, 28 (March 1973), 13; *MWR* (June 18, 1987), 3, for obituary of Chiyo Mano; English equivalent titles of book written by Sakakibara Gan are: *A Study of Present Day Christian Community of Goods* (1967), *Martyrdom and Exodus: 450 Years of Hutterites* (1967), *A Historical Study of Classical Age Anabaptism* (1972), *Anabaptist Heritage of Conscientious Objectors* (1974), *A Study of Church Communities* (1976), and *The Life of Conrad Grebel* (1982); translations: Arthur Gish, *The New Left and Christian Radicalism* (1973), Robert Friedmann, *The Theology of Anabaptism* (1975), Peter Riedemann, *Hutterite Confession of Faith* (1977), Hans Georg Fischer, *The Life of Jakob Hutter* (1978), Myron Augsburger, *Pilgrim Aflame* (1979); Sakakibara Gan, *My Pilgrimage to Anabaptism* (unpublished; Japanese and English).

Salatiga, Indonesia, a retirement community and military town of about 100,000 inhabitants, is located in the highlands of Central Java, about 50 km. (30 mi.) south of the provincial capital, °Semarang. Salatiga is the home of Satya Wacana Christian University, an interdenominational university of strong reputation. The two Mennonite conferences of Central Java have cooperated in the development of the school and have held key positions on the board of trustees and faculty. In the late 1980s it has 6,000 students.

In the late 1960s the conference of the Persatuan Gereja-Gereja Kristen Muria Indonesia (Muria Christian Church of Indonesia) launched an effort to begin a congregation in Salatiga. That congregation grew out of a student fellowship but intentionally spread into the wider community. In less than a decade it had grown to well over 600 members and has developed a number of branches in and around the city of Salatiga.   LMY

Salvation. The basic elements of the historical teaching of the Christian church on salvation are reiterated by the Anabaptists: that all people have sinned in Adam and are therefore unworthy of the favor of God; that through the death of Christ the way of salvation is provided for all; that the way of salvation is effective only if and when individuals respond appropriately. If there is a major divergence theologically between Anabaptists and other Christians, it focuses on the way in which Anabaptists generally understand the last of these elements, the human response. This will be discussed below.

Of the various theories of the °atonement, the satisfaction theory is prominent among 16th-c. Anabaptists. That is not to say that they consciously chose one theory over another, but that they tended to accept the dominant emphasis of the day. Thus they held that in order for sinners to be rescued from the clutches of Satan, a perfect sacrifice was required. Christ, as the sinless one, provided this sacrifice and in this way satisfied the justice of God. Some Anabaptists, such as Melchior °Hoffman, °Menno Simons and °°Dirk Philips, go so far as to support this view with the teaching that Christ had "celestial flesh" despite his human birth (°°incarnation). Yet this never becomes a matter for refined and prolonged debate. The Anabaptists move beyond a narrow and objective application of the satisfaction notion.

As noted above, the major discussion concerning salvation does not focus on the theory of the atonement, but rather on the appropriate human response. That is, there was widespread consensus that one cannot lay claim to salvation on the basis of forgiveness alone. Rather, repentance must be followed by amendment of life. In other words, °discipleship (*Nachfolge*) belongs constitutively and integrally to the work of salvation.

Regarding the place of good works within salvation, the Anabaptists are quick to point out that good deeds are not to be offered as merit before God. Righteousness on the basis of good works is completely out of the question. Rather, the good deeds of the believer are an extension of the gracious work of God in the life of the believer; indeed, they are an extension of the salvific work of God as such. This means that if good works are not in evidence it is questionable whether the saving work of God has taken root in the person.

Basic to this viewpoint is a particular theology of °grace. Menno Simons holds that grace does not make its original entrance with the Fall; it is present already in the act of °creation. Inasmuch as the divine act of creation establishes the works of God, grace is therefore integral to works. It follows that the good works of God done by people belong to the gracious work of God. Thus salvation, as the work of grace, includes not only the justification of the sinner, but also what is sometimes called °sanctification. This explains as well why the Anabaptists could speak somewhat unreservedly of the positive place of the °law in the Christian life. This is also the reason why "works righteousness" is not seen as a danger provided that good works maintain their basis in grace.

This theology of grace provides the basis for regarding all people as called to salvation. The human race was created with the potential for grace. That is, grace is universal in the sense that God offers grace to all people, not only to the so-called elect. Thus salvation is preached to all with a sense of urgency and with the assumption that from God's side no one is excluded from the invitation to believe.

This basic approach to a theology of salvation has critical implications for a number of questions. First, what is the place of °°original sin in Anabaptist theology? Anabaptists have a unique approach to original sin, an approach that supports their understanding of salvation. They affirm the historical reality of original sin, but deny that its power over the individual is final and absolute. That is, they hold that evil has entered the world through the first human parents and that all people are sinners because of the ongoing effects of that act. Yet the effect is not understood as total and debilitating. Something of the image of God, given with creation, remains. This provides a point of entrance for the Spirit of God. As well, this gives the person as such the capacity to exercise a free decision with respect to the invitation to salvation. In the light of the above it is understandable that Anabaptists have had some appreciation for the position of Pelagius (fl. 400-418) rather than Augustine (354-430) on the question of free will.

Second, what is the view of Anabaptists regarding the salvation of children? Generally it is held that while children are conceived and born in sin, they are protected by the grace of God until such a time as they are able to take a conscious and informed stand, in confession and action, for or against the saving work of Christ. In this connection it is therefore not appropriate to baptize °infants. While children are certainly not considered to be Christians by virtue of their natural birth into believing families, neither are they destined to eternal punishment if not baptized as infants. Rather, they are considered safe in the grace of God until they are able to exercise their free will in response to the offer of salvation.

Third, will some be saved and others not? As mentioned above, the Anabaptists do not subscribe to that doctrine of °predestination which held that some are chosen to be saved while others are destined for damnation. They insist only that Christ died for all. With this they do not imply a universalism, as though all would inevitably and eventually be saved. Rather, their intent is to uphold the graciousness of God toward all people and the freedom of all to choose God. The choice between life and death is the responsibility of the one to whom grace is offered.

It should be added that while the Anabaptists do not promote predestinationism or °°universalism, they are advocates of °°religious liberty or toleration. People should be allowed to believe as they wish without coercion. This implies a graciousness toward all people, especially the powerless. Such graciousness is not based on a lax attitude toward the unbeliever or toward those who hold a contrary view. Rather, it is based both on a theological conviction and on a practical concern: the conviction that God is truly a God of grace toward all, and the concern that they and others be allowed to follow their conscience in matters of faith, and not be coerced by force and even by threat of death to comply with a particular form of religion or with the official religion of the state.

Fourth, how is the salvation of the sinner experienced? The Anabaptists tend toward a wholistic view. This can be understood in two senses. Firstly, salvation encompasses the entire person, impinging upon every dimension of life. The person becomes a "new creation" through repentance and amendment of life. Secondly, it is the whole Christ that saves. That is, the work of justification is understood as the incarnation of the life, the death, and the resurrection of Christ in the disciple. One cannot find in Anabaptism the typical Protestant distinction between justification and sanctification. Nor can one find an exclusive concentration on the atoning death of Christ distinct from the salvific power of his life and ministry. In short, salvation is the original and ongoing experience of new birth, understood as the transformaiton of the whole person into the likeness of Christ. Salvation is experienced through the interplay of forgiveness and discipleship.

Finally, what is the context in which salvation is experienced and affirmed? The Anabaptists place great emphasis upon the faithful church as the experiential °community of salvation. If salvation means incorporation into Christ, this implies incorporation into the °church, the body of Christ. The Anabaptists do not make salvation an individualistic matter, but see its earthly culmination in the experience of voluntary participation in the visible church.

To this point we have sought to outline in broad terms the view of salvation generally held by 16th-c. Anabaptists. The question now arises: have these predominant features been upheld among Mennonites since that time? This is a difficult question to answer since historical developments are complex. Yet some observations are possible on the basis of major °confessions of faith that have been formulated and accepted from time to time throughout Mennonite history.

The Dordrecht Confession of 1632 carries forward the essential features of Anabaptism from the previous century. For example, here repentance and "amendment of life" are integrally related (art. 6; Loewen, *Confessions*, 65). However in the centuries that followed, significant changes are noticeable. While an overt dedication to a biblical basis continued, this basis proved broad enough to allow for rather diverse and divergent developments.

One variation can be noted in the Ris Confession of 1766. Here one notes a fortification against a legalistic view of salvation. This is accomplished by highlighting grace alone, with works understood as only an outward proof of an inward grace (Art. 20: Loewen, *Confessions*, 94/92). With reference to works the major concern is that self-righteousness and legalism be avoided.

Another variation comes to light in the soteriology which accompanied the rise of the Mennonite Brethren church in Russia around 1860. This movement reacted against the growing assumption within the mother church that salvation is a natural birthright for Mennonite colonists, and that personal holiness is secondary in salvation. The Mennonite Brethren focused on the salvation experience as a radical turning from sin to a life of personal holiness. The influence of European °Pietism of the 18th and 19th c. can also be seen in the Mennonite Brethren emphasis.

Some of the Mennonites in North America were influenced noticeably by °Fundamentalism during the first half of the 20th c. The Mennonite Church's (MC) confession of 1921, entitled "Christian Fundamentals," reflects this (Loewen, *Confessions*, 71-72). Here the human condition is stated in terms of helpless fallenness, and the work of Christ is presented unequivocally in terms of the substitutionary atonement alone (art. 4-6). The 1921 statement also discounts the possibility of reforming society independent of the merits of Christ and the experience of the new birth (art. 10). This reflects the typical reaction of Fundamentalism against the °social gospel. When brought to bear on Mennonite theology the emphasis results in an unfortunate disjunction of salvation from discipleship.

Mennonite scholarship during the past 40 years has given some attention to a theology of salvation. Spearheaded by the discovery and interpretation of Anabaptist sources, theologians have suggested guidelines for a faithful application of an Anabaptist-Mennonite perspective to this theme. One finds in these writings a call for the wholesome integration of nurture with evangelism, a recovery of the integral relationship between soteriology and discipleship, and an affirmation of the integration of salvation with the doctrine of the church. HHa

Myron S. Augsburger, "Conversion in Anabaptist Thought," *MQR*, 36 (1962), 243-55; Alvin J. Beachy, "The Grace of God in Christ as Understood by Five Major Anabaptist Writers," *MQR*, 37 (1963), 5-33; John Driver, *Understanding the Atonement for the Mission of the Church* (Scottdale, 1986); Cornelius J. Dyck, "Sinners and Saints," and J. A. Oosterbaan, "Grace in Dutch Mennonite Theology," in *A Legacy of Faith*, by C. J. Dyck (Newton, 1962), 87-102; 69-85; Robert Friedmann, *A Theology of Anabaptism* (Scottdale, 1973), 78-101; CRR 3: 41-71; John A. Toews, *History MB* (1975), 361-79; John C., Wenger, "Concerning the Satisfaction of Christ: An Anabaptist Tract on True Christianity," *MQR*, 20 (1946), 243-54; idem, "Grace and Discipleship in Anabaptism," *MQR*, 35 (1961), 50-69; Gideon G. Yoder, *The Nurture and Evangelism of Children* (Scottdale, 1959); John Howard Yoder, *The Politics of Jesus* (Grand Rapids: Eerdmans, 1972), ch. 11.

See also Conversion; Regeneration.

Samenwerkingsverband van "de Vier Instellingen" in de Doopsgezinde Broederschap (Cooperative Union of the Four Mennonite Institutions. In November 1981 the °Doopsgezinde Vredesgroep (Dutch Mennonite Peace Group), the °Doopsgezinde Zendingsraad (Dutch Mennonite Mission Board), the °Stichting voor Bijzondere Noden (Foundation for Relief Needs), and the Werkverband Doopsgezinden en Ontwikkelingssamenwerking (Work Group for Cooperation between Mennonites and Development Work) united to form this one agency. The purpose of this union was primarily to emphasize to the congregations that each of these activities are a part of the total assignment of our churches, that is, service of the Christian church to the world. The intent was to make clear that this work must have a place in the programs of every congregation.

Steps taken to achieve this include the publishing of an annual project book; several announcements throughout the year in the church weekly paper, *Algemeen Doopsgezind Weekblad*; and coordination of the annual meetings of these agencies. Each of these keeps the others informed of their plans and activities also. LLau

Samida, John Wellington (Apr. 3, 1903-Oct. 22, 1986), was born in Chunar, Mirzapur Dist., Uttar Pradesh, India, the son of an Anglican minister, Henry Samida. J. W. was a graduate of Allahabad U. where he received a BA degree (ca. 1927) and later completed his BT degree from the U. of Jabalpur.

In 1932 he accepted an appointment under the American Mennonite Mission, °Dhamtari, Madhya Pradesh, to teach in the normal school. He later became headmaster of the Mennonite high school. In 1941 he married Alice Ebbu, also a teacher in the Mennonite mission schools. They had three children, Vimla, Vimal, and Dipak. J. W. Samida's gifts in leadership were recognized both in the educational field as well as in the church. He became the first national to be appointed principal of the academy (later Mennonite Higher Secondary School), a post he held until his retirement in 1962. He was a regular member of both the Mennonite Educational Board and the Mennonite Medical Board, was an active member of the Sundarganj Mennonite church, and was frequently elected a member of the church *panchayat* (council). He was a man of impartial judgment and helped steer the church into channels of peace and mutual understanding.

Alice Ebbu Samida died in 1962. Both J. W. and Alice are buried in the Christian cemetery in Dhamtari. JAF

Biographical information supplied by V. K. Samida, E. P. Bachan, Sam M. King, and S. Paul Miller; John A. Lapp, *India* (1972), index.

San José de Pequina Colony, Bolivia, is located about 340 km. (212 mi.) east of Santa Cruz. This is 40 km. (25 mi.) north of the town of San José de Chiquitos. This colony was started in 1974 when about 70 Old Colony Mennonite families from the Shipyard and Blue Creek Mennonite colonies in Belize, and about 20 families from Santa Rita colony, Mexico, moved to Bolivia. Bishop Jacob Harms was the colony's spiritual leader in 1986 when the colony had a total population of 1,668 with 543 baptized church members. The distance from the city and transportation problems have made marketing difficult, and the colony has not prospered very much. IHie

Sanctification (ME IV:414). The article on this subject in ME IV covers the meanings of the term, some of the various ways in which it has been stressed, and some controversies that emerged on the subject. The present revision touches on some applications of the concept, developments in the °holiness movement, and developments in the holiness-pentecostal-°charismatic movements related to sanctification.

The concept "sanctification" derives from New Testament Greek terms translated variously as "be holy," "hallow," "sanctify," "holiness," "sanctification," "holy," and "purify." The terms generally imply a purified, separated life given wholly to God for his service. It may safely be said that all Christian groups believe in sanctification; Scripture declares that "without holiness no one will see the Lord" (Heb 12:14). Differences among people and groups come at points of understanding regarding time, extent, and expression. Although most believe that Christians improve toward sanctification throughout life; many within the holiness movement maintain that entire sanctification is possible at once.

Differing views on sanctification of persons include the following: Roman Catholics maintain that most persons attain lasting holiness only after death and in most cases, after an experience of purgation. In life on earth sanctification is experienced through the sacraments of °baptism, confirmation (in which the gifts of the Holy Spirit are received), penance and the Eucharist (°communion). Most Protestants teach that sanctification is complete at the moment of death when the °Holy Spirit fully cleanses and prepares the believer to stand before God in purity and true holiness. People grow in sanctification and vary in the extent of realization to that point. People within the Holiness Movement take a position that humans may be entirely sanctified in this life, cleansed from the sinful nature (°°original °sin) and set apart for God. Entire sanctification occurs at a point subsequent to °regeneration; the exact meaning and extent of this work varies among people endorsing this general position. Some maintain that the sin nature is eradicated and the Christian no longer commits deliberate acts of sin. Others hold that the motive area of the Christian is cleansed, so that the Christian wills only to do God's will.

The modern holiness movement is generally associated with the teaching of John Wesley. Current scholarship holds that the tenor of Wesley's teaching was that sanctification is dynamic in nature, that it is proportional to the degree of commitment to God and surrender to the Holy Spirit. Some "Wesleyans," on another hand, hold a more static position, maintaining that entire sanctification is momentary, fixed, and final.

What is known as the "holiness revival" arose in America following the Civil War and swept across the nation through the camp meeting movement (°holiness camps). The revival moved with varying degrees of intensity. In one aspect it finally found expression in the beginnings of the pentecostal movement, usually associated with Charles Parham at Bethel Bible College in Topeka, Ks., Jan. 1, 1901. This was a holiness-pentecostal movement at first, emphasizing sanctification as well as the gifts of the Holy Spirit, including tongue speaking. As the

Pentecostal movement spread it was taken up by persons of other theological views; for instance, the Assemblies of God represented a synthesis of Baptism with the Spirit and a traditional view of sanctification as progressive. The neo-pentecostal movement, or °charismatic movement from about 1960 and forward places primary emphasis upon the Holy Spirit and the gifts (*charismata*) and does not generally emphasize sanctification in relation to charismatic renewal. The same can be said of the Roman Catholic charismatic renewal beginning in 1966.

Mennonites began early to be affected by charismatic renewal of the 1960s. Interest in these matters was widespread by the 1980s. Research by denominational officials in 1986 indicated that the numbers of Mennonites describing themselves as charismatic doubled every five years from 1974; in 1984 approximately 14,000 Mennonites were involved in charismatic renewal. One-fourth to one-third of pastors responsible for the primary leadership of congregations may have been charismatic, while approximately 43 percent of church-planting pastors had charismatic commitments. Organized groups such as Mennonite Renewal Services promote this position. Publications such as *Empowered* seek to encourage charismatic interest without being divisive. Technically, the primary interest of charismatic expression among Mennonites is not on sanctification as such, but on the person, power, and gifts of the Holy Spirit.   OHA

MQR, 35, no. 2 (Apr. 1961), sp. issue on the Anabaptist and Weslayan traditions; Leo G. Cox, *John Wesley's Concept of Perfection* (Kansas City, Mo.: Beacon Hill Press, 1964); Luke L. Keefer, Jr., *Everything Necessary* (Nappanee, 1984); Harald G. Lindstrom, *Wesley and Sanctification* (Wilmore, Ky.: Francis Asbury Press, 1984); Richard Quebedeaux, *The New Charismatics* (Garden City, N.Y.: Doubleday, 1976); Vinson Synan, ed., *Aspects of Pentecostal-Charismatic Origins* (Plainfield, N.J.: Logos International, 1975); idem, *The Holiness-Pentecostal Movement in the United States* (Grand Rapids, Mich.: Eerdmans, 1976); various articles in *BIC Hist. Life*, (Dec. 1983).

Santa Clara Colony, Mexico. See Sommerfeld Mennonites.

Santa Clara Colony, Paraguay, is a small settlement located some 385 km. (238 mi.) ne. of Asunción. It was established by Sommerfeld Mennonite immigrants from Santa Clara Colony, Mexico. The primary reason for the coming of these settlers was scarcity of land in Mexico and the availability of good, cheap land in Paraguay. In 1971 they bought 2,700 hectares (6,670 acres) of heavily wooded jungle land for 900 Guaranies (seven dollars U.S. per hectare). Forty families came originally, but 19 found pioneering too difficult and left. In 1986 there were a total of 26 families (133 persons), of whom 50 were members of the congregation. While this group must also be classified as conservative, they do use motorized vehicles and wear contemporary clothing.   GR

Santa Rita Colony, Bolivia, also referred to as Paurito, is located 35 km. (20 mi.) se. of Santa Cruz, 6 km. south of the town of Pauritos. The colony was established in 1967 by a group of Old Colony Men-

SASKATCHEWAN

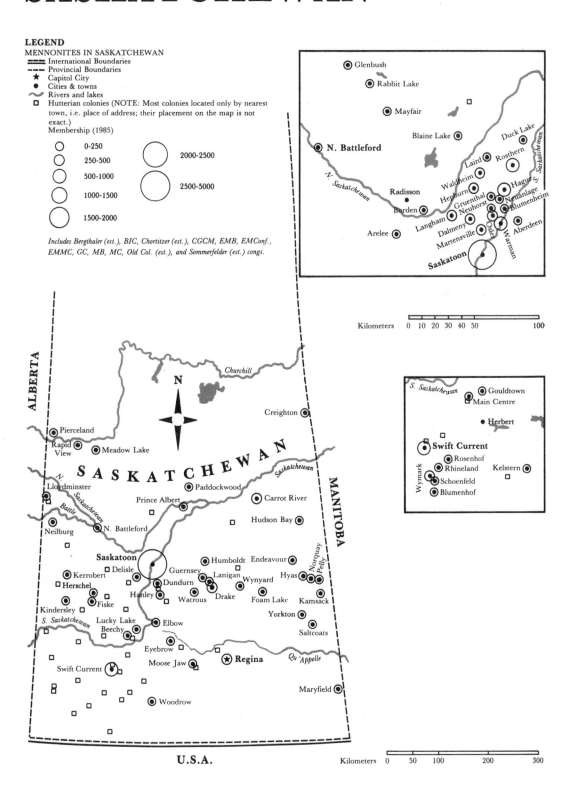

nonites from Mexico with minister Ben Penner as their spiritual leader. It had 482 baptized members and a total population of 1,505 in 1986.　　　IHie

Santa Rita Colony, Mexico. See Nord Colony, Mexico.

Santa Rosa Colony, Argentina. See Remecó-Guatrache Colony, Argentina.

Sardjo Djojodihardjo (d. 1948) was chosen to serve as secretary of the synod of the Gergeja Injili di Tanah Jawa (Evangelical Church of Java), Indonesia, at the time of its formation in May 1940 in a time of crisis. Two years later, to deal with the chaos and spiritual destruction resulting from the Muslim uprising of March 1942, Sardjo was appointed to one of the two teams of two selected to visit each congregation and assess their condition and needs. At the same time he became the chairman of the synod, a responsibility he held intermittently during the following years of Japanese occupation, persecution, famine, and revolution. Hurried removal from the hospital after an operation to escape Dutch military action brought about his untimely death in 1948 in Surakarta.

By that time Sardjo Djojodihardjo had served the mission and then the independent national church for 35 years. Part of that time he was a teacher in the teacher training school in Margorejo. Part of it was spent as a Bible translator working with Pieter Anton °°Jansz on the revsion of the Javanese Bible. In 1941 he was appointed to carry on the administration of the mission's 22 elementary and secondary schools when missionary activities were increasingly limited. He also maintained contacts in circles of teachers of Javanese mystical philosophy and their disciples to challenge them with the Christian gospel. Perhaps his most significant ministry was as pastor of the Pati congregation for more than a decade until the time of his death.　　　LMY

Doopsgezinde Zendingsvereeniging, *Verslag van de Staat en de Verrigtingen der Doopsgezinde Vereeniging to Bevordering der Evangelieverbreiding in di Nederlandsche Overzeesche Bezittingen* (the annual reports of the Dutch Mennonite Mission Union published in Amsterdam beginning in 1848); Th. E. Jensma, *Doopsgezinde Zending in Indonesia* ('s-Gravenhage: Boekcentrum N. V. 1968); Martati Ins. Kumaat, *Benih yang Tumbuh*, V [A survey of the Evangelical Church of Java] (Jakarta: Lembaga Penelitian dan Studi-DGI 1973); Sigit Heru Soekotjo and Lawrence M. Yoder. "Sejarah Gereja Kristen Muria Indonesia" [History of the Evangelical Church of Java] (unpubl. ms.); Lawrence M. Yoder, ed., *Bahan Sejarah Gereja Injili di Tanah Jawa* [Historical Resources on the History of the Evangelical Church of Java] (Pati, Indonesia: Komisi Sejarah Gereja GITD, 1977); idem, "Sejara Margorejo," *Wiyata Wacana*, 7, no. 1 (1977), 18-25.

Sarya, Nyamuko (Hezekiah) (b. 1922), was baptized Jan. 23, 1943 at Mukgango, Tanzania. He married Perusi on Mar. 1, 1941. They have (1988) the following children: Greshom, Boniface, Neema, Agness, Joshua, Magoma, Jude, Phebe, Joseph, John, Paulo, and Hilda. Several are deceased. They invested in the education of their children (three are accountants, two are engineers, and the others serve as manager, economist, teacher, businessman, electrician and sportsman. The youngest is a student (1988).

Hezekiah and Perusi built a temporary house near the church's first boarding school in 1951 so that Hezekiah could complete primary education. By 1955 he had completed Bukiroba Bible School and in 1965 he graduated from Mennonite Theological College. He was called as teacher and evangelist in 1944 and was ordained as deacon (1955), minister (1960), and bishop (1979). For 25 years he served in the Musoma area in Mugango, Butata, Tegeruka, Wanyere, and Kabasa and then for 10 years in Dar es Salaam. As bishop, he lives at Bukiroba, Musoma. At Dar es Salaam he inaugurated regular offerings towards a large church building and got the project underway. He also served as government contact for the Mennonites. He was chairman of the Dar es Salaam ministerial group and served on committees of the Christian Council of Tanzania and on the board of Tanzania Bible Society. He has strengthened the life of the church at the district level as bishop. He planted congregations in Tabora, Dodoma, Sumbawanga, and Morogoro.　　　MMH

Hezekiah N. Sarya, "Testimony," *Miss. Mess.* (Dec. 1964), 16; idem, "The Church Must Plan," *Miss. Mess.* (Jan. 1971), 6; Mahlon M. Hess, *The Pilgrimage of Faith of Tanzania Mennonite Church, 1934-83* (Salunga, Pa.: EMBMC, 1985), 71, 75, 76, 77, 96, 107, 114, 132, 160, 162; also Hess files at Mennonite Historical Library, Lancaster, Pa.; John E. Leatherman, "The Grace of God in Tanganyika," segments on "The Church" and "Bible School," in *Miss., Mess.* (July 1956), 6.

Saskatchewan (ME IV:425). The pressures Mennonites felt in Manitoba and other parts of the world brought many settlers to what became Saskatchewan, beginning in the 1890s. In addition to the initial settlement at Rosthern, reserves of land were established for the Old Colony Mennonites in the Osler-Hague area (1895) between Saskatoon and Rosthern, and se. of Swift Current (1904). They established 29 villages in the two reserves. Settlements of Mennonite Brethren, General Conference Mennonites, Evangelical Mennonite Brethren, and Krimmer Mennonite Brethren were also established. Most of these groups settled in districts adjoining or in close proximity to the two reserves. Some of the settlements, however, were more isolated. Members of the Mennonite Church (MC) settled at Guernsey, some Mennonite Brethren settled at Woodrow and Fox Valley, a General Conference community emerged at Drake, and a Sommerfeld group was established at Carrot River.

The 1920s brought compulsory elementary school education to Saskatchewan, and ca. 3,000 Old Colony, Bergthal, and Sommerfeld Mennonites from Saskatchewan joined 4,000 from Manitoba to establish new communities in Latin America. The new wave of Mennonite immigrants from Russia from 1923 to 1930 filled many of the vacant farms left by the Latin American emigrants. Many new settlements were also established. In the 1920s communities were established in Dundurn, Hanley, Herschel, Fiske, Colonsay, Holdfast, Jansen, and Wilden. Many of these settlements were established on large estates of from 1,000 to 10,000 acres (400-4,000 hectares).

The third major influx of Mennonites to Saskatchewan occurred after World War II. Those who made up this group of immigrants had suffered through the dispersion in the Soviet Union and other effects of World War II. Many had fled to western Germany at the end of the war, and upon arrival in Canada, settled mainly in the existing Mennonite communities and in the larger cities, particularly Saskatoon.

In 1987 the largest concentration of Mennonites in Saskatchewan was in Saskatoon with eight General Conference (GCM) congregations, three Mennonite Brethren congregations, and one each of Evangelical Mennonite Conference, Evangelical Mennonite Mission Conference, and Brethren in Christ. In addition, the surrounding rural area north to Rosthern, nw. to Borden, sw. to Herschel, east to Aberdeen, and south to Hanley made the general Saskatoon area a very concentrated inter-Mennonite community. The second largest concentration of Mennonites was to be in the Swift Current area.

Schools have been developed by both the General Conference (GCM) and the Mennonite Brethren (MB) since shortly after their arrival. Still in operation are the Rosthern Junior College (high school), Hepburn Bible Institute (MB), and the Swift Current Bible Institute (GCM). An elementary school has been developed by the Saskatchewan Bergthal community (°Sommerfeld Mennonites) at Osler.

Mennonite Central Committee (MCC) Saskatchewan has become a strong unifying force in the Mennonite communities. Numerous programs and services have been established, particularly in the Saskatoon area. The MCC °relief sales in Saskatoon and Swift Current have become important annual events. Outreach in mission and service includes a strong person-to-person program at the Prince Albert Penitentiary. Many Saskatchewan Mennonites also serve as volunteers internationally through MCC.

Mennonite Central Committee is an example of the importance of combining faith and service, but is not the only example. Homes for senior citizens and nursing homes have been developed in Saskastoon, Rosthern, Warman, and Herbert. Group homes are serving youth and handicapped in Saskatoon and Swift Current. The Brethren in Christ Church operates a home for Native school children in Timber Bay (northern Saskatchewan). Home care community-based services for seniors are available through province-wide services. Prior to the province-wide service which developed in the early 1970s, the Mennonite communities north of Saskatchewan had already developed such services, open to both Mennonites and non-Mennonites in their communities.

The °urbanization of Mennonites in Saskatchewan is increasing. Since World War II increasing numbers of Mennonites entered °professions such as °nursing, teaching, and social work. Large numbers entered the trades and worked in the cities. This movement has broadened so that by the late 1980s, Mennonites are involved in a wide range of professions, trades, and °businesses. Involvement in the civil service of Saskatchewan and Canada has developed. Many work as professionals in research; in services related to agriculture, social services, °health and °mental health, and in senior management and policy positions in °government. Political involvement—on municipal, provincial, and federal levels—has increased greatly since the time of Gerhardt Ens, who was the first Mennonite member of the Saskatchewan Legislature (early 20th c.).

The integration of the Mennonite communities into the mainstream of provincial life has been increasing greatly. Participation in public life, politically as well as in public service; involvement in economic structures and systems (business, trades, professions, as well as farming); extensive involvement in education (as students and educators at every level including a number of professors in the universities at Saskatoon and Regina); and an almost total use of English as the first language have had a major impact on the nature and identity of Mennonites in Saskatchewan.

Some implications of these changes are that many who grow up in Mennonite homes, churches, and communities shift to non-Mennonite denominations. The Christian and Missionary Alliance Church, for example, has many members who come from Mennonite background. Some shift to mainline churches, e.g., United Church of Canada, is also occurring. On the other hand, many of non-Mennonite background are joining Mennonite churches. These new Mennonites come from mainline Protestant and Catholic churches and various evangelical communities. Chinese and Vietnamese Mennonite churches are developing in Saskatoon and Regina. Major developments with reformulations of identity and theological orientation are in process. Many Mennonite pastors have received their professional theological education in Mennonite schools and seminaries such as those at Fresno, Cal. (MB), and at Elkhart, Ind. (MC, GCM), but many pastors and leaders also are graduates from interdenominational schools such as Briercrest Bible Institute or Canadian Bible College, or take seminary training on a part-time basis from Lutheran Seminary in Saskatoon.

Membership in the conferences has shifted toward a greater urban base. Membership in 1987 was as follows: General Conference Mennonite Church, 5,400; Mennonite Brethren, 3,250; Mennonite Church, 130; Bergthal [Saskatchewan], 1,000; Old Colony, 800; Evangelical Mennonite Mission Conference, 650; Evangelical Mennonite Conference, 615. The total baptized membership was ca. 11,000.   OD

MC Yearbook (1988-89), 17-18; Leonard Doell, *The Bergthaler Mennonite Church of Saskatchewan 1892-1975* (Winnipeg: CMBC, 1987); F. H. Epp, *Mennonites in Canada I*; idem, *Mennonites in Canada II*; Howard J. Richards, *Atlas of Saskatchewan* (Modern Press, Saskatoon, c. 1969), p. V.; Daniel Hertzler, *From Germantown to Steinbach* (Scottdale, 1981), 211-24.

Satan. In biblical literature Satan appears in later Old Testament writings as an angelic "son of God" within the heavenly court, as God's prosecuting attorney (Job 1-2; Zec 3:1-2; 1 Chr 21:1). In intertestamental and New Testament literature Satan appears as the head of evil—rebellious, defiant and in opposition to God. Lucifer's fall from heaven (Is 14:14) is usually employed to explain this change in Satan's status. One Mennonite writer uses this text together with Ez 28:12-16, 2 Pet 2:4, and Jude 6 to explain how Satan became the Devil (Hostetter, 15-20). Rev 12:9 identifies Satan as the devil and "ancient serpent" (Gn 3:1-5). It speaks also of war in heaven, the archangel Michael's victory over the dragon, and Satan's fall from heaven. The gospel news is that Christ destroys the works of the devil (1 Jn 3:8; Heb 2:14-15). Proclaiming the gospel dethrones Satan (Lk 10:18); Christ's death and resurrection disarms the powers (Col 2:15). Through new birth and freedom not to °sin, God through Christ keeps the believer from Satan, while the world is under Satan's power (1 Jn 5:18-19). By wearing the full armor of God, the believer victoriously battles against the invisible evil forces which attack, deceive, and seduce believers personally and through structures (Eph 6:10-18).

Anabaptist writings show frequent use of the words *devil* and *Satan*. Though no doctrinal treatises are devoted to the nature and work of Satan, many pages mention the word or contain cognate ideas. In Menno's writings Catholic priests and sacramental abuses are often castigated with vituperate language, such as, the "people [who] have . . . deserted the one God-pleasing position as to doctrine, sacraments, and life . . . [and are] rather devils than Christians (Menno, *Writings*, 302). Menno regarded the writings of his opponents to be prompted by the evil one, for Satan has always been opposed to the truth (*Writings*, 838-39). Of the 14 references under *Satan* or *Devil* (possessed) in the index to Menno's *Complete Writings*, many contain Menno's polemic against the accusers of the Anabaptists (180, 269, 838-39). Several texts describe the deceitful, lying nature of Satan (469, 838-39, 994); one deals with church °discipline, i.e., handing over to Satan (469); two admonish believers to be vigilant against the devil (1,028, 1,046); two defend against the accusation that the Anabaptists were demon-possessed (535, 571); and two emphasize Christ's destruction of, trampling upon, and power over the serpent (324, 838). Menno's "Hymn of Discipleship" (1,065) speaks of his and the believer's past experience: "Enmeshed was I in Satan's gauze, My life abomination was, Right well I served the devil's cause."

The index to the letters of Conrad Grebel and related writings (CRR 4) lists 29 references under *devil*. Ten of these are connected explicitly to disputes over baptism in which Anabaptists said or were reported to have said that "infant baptism is of the devil." Most uses are name-calling, though five of Zwingli's uses describe the devil's nature briefly, usually to extend the same to the nature of his opponents. Five times also Zwingli identified the Anabaptists as devil-inspired and four more times cited their claim that infant baptism is of the devil. *The Writings of Pilgram Marpeck* (CRR 2) has no entry for either Satan or devil in the subject index; a spot reading shows recurring references to Satan as seeking to beguile and lead astray the believers (91, 94). The evil one is often referred to as "the serpent" (108, 114-15).

Robert °Friedmann's classic work on Anabaptist theology regards "The Doctrine of the Two Worlds" and °discipleship as constituent elements of Anabaptism, though an eschatological emphasis is the heart of Anabaptist theology in his view. He cites the light-darkness dualism in the third and fourth articles of the °Schleitheim Confession. Thus, "All who follow the devil and the world have no part with those who are called unto God out of the world" (art. 3, Friedmann, 39). Hutterite theology has the same Christ/world dualism, he argues.

Peter Riedemann's *Confession of Faith* (1565) includes a brief 10-line statement "On the Likeness of the Devil;" it emphasizes the devil's lying nature, pointing out that those who lie, sin, and do injustice are of the devil (54). Of the 33 Mennonite confessions of faith in Loewen's, *Confessions*, none has an article on Satan or the Devil, although the 1961 Church of God in Christ Mennonite statement has an article on "The Fall of the Angels" (Loewen, 209/207). Most contain an article on "The Fall of Man" in which the serpent's (devil's, Satan's) beguiling work is mentioned. Similarly, Walter Klaassen's *Anabaptism in Outline* (CRR 3) has no section on evil, Satan, world or nonconformity. Of its 28,155 entries, *Mennonite Bibliography: 1631-1961* lists twelve under *devil*. ME I-IV contains no article on Satan or Devil and no article on evil; it does contain a short article on °°worldliness and a lengthy article on °nonconformity, both of which assert the Mennonite belief that evil is to be resisted in its sociocultural expression (see also J. C. Wenger's *Separated Unto God*).

Several Dutch Mennonite writings address the topic in sustained form. In a 15-page treatise, *Korte Verhandeling van de Duyvelen . . .* (1676), the °°Collegient Frans °°Kuyper sought to prove that demons (devils) do exist as independent sense beings different from humans and animals. Again in 1678, in the hope of convincing atheists, he published a 38-page booklet of exceptional true stories which clearly prove that demons do exist. A 47-page treatise published in 1700 focused on the temptatations of Jesus, exposing the crafty, beguiling nature of the devil (C. Tirion, *De versoekinge onses Heeren Jesu Christi in de Woestijne . . .*). In 1856 Douwe Simon °°Gorter's lectures included a 36-page treatise on "The Higher World." In it he said he came to believe in the personal existence of the devil, as well as good and evil spirits, through his own study of the Bible. He was not taught it in church or in his theological studies. He said further that he believed that belief in the personal existence of the devil is the real Doopsgezind (Mennonite) view though it was not part of the confessions. A shorter essay appeared in 1896 by Bauke Haga, "Satan in de gedaante van een engel des lichts" (*Zondagsbote*, 9 [1896], 103, 107-08).

Daniel °Kauffman's *Bible Doctrine* (1914) devoted Part II to "Satan and His Works" (143-80). George R. °°Brunk (d. 1938) wrote the section on *Satan*, A. D. Wenger on *Temptation*, and J. S. Hartzler on *Sin*. Brunk's treatment was comprehensive, succinct, and perceptive—perhaps a classic Mennonite statement. He began with definitions for Satan and devil, and then distinguished between demons and devil which the King James translation of the Bible fails to do. He then warned against the modern tendency to rid the world of mystery and hence to eliminate both devil and God by holding that *evil* is the only *devil*. He then discussed the devil under six headings:

"His Personality, The Author of Evil, His Power and Influence, His Unfathomable Enmity, His Devices, and His Limitations and Destiny." Brunk ended the section on "Enmity" saying, "He seems to be the fountain of every vice heated white hot by unquenchable hate, stirred up to the most intense and ceaseless activity to undermine the throne of God and to damn the whole world to eternal wretchedness and oblivion." Under devices he listed 10: "Fall of Man, Temptation of Christ, Blindness, Unbelief, 'Lying Wonders,' Hypnotic Power, False Christs, Religious Wars, Perverting the Truth, and Heresies." In the 1929 edition, *Doctrines of the Bible*, a similar section appears as part IV and was titled "The Realms of Darkness" (202-35). While much of the earlier content reappeared in modified form, the content of the 1914 sections titled "His Power and Influences" and "His Devices," is largely missing. The hellish work of Satan is less evident. The section is divided into four parts: Satan (or Devil), Satan—His Dominion, Sin, and Unbelief. Daniel Kauffman, new author of this section, said that "it is important that we recognize this adversary as having a real personality, not as a mere evil influence or evil propensity working in man" (205). The chapter portrays Satan as "a roaring lion, . . . seeking whom he may devour" (1 Pet 5:8), "the prince of the power of the air" (Eph 2:2), "the god of this world" (2 Cor 4:4), and "the prince of this world" (Jn 14:30). He is "prince of the demons" (Mt 12:28; 2 Cor 4:4) and seeks to seduce believers as an angel of light (2 Cor 11:14).

Der Bote carried a two-part essay, "Die alte Schlange, ihr Ursprung, Sein and Ende" by H. Lepp-Reesor in 1932. In 1941 *Die Mennonitsche Rundschau* carried a four-part series on "Das Satanische Reich" by N. N. Hiebert. These essays expound the biblical teaching. The former connects Satan's end to a premillennial view of end-times; the latter strongly warns Christians of Satan's seducing power and points also to Christ's victory over Satan and to God's keeping power. Two related studies appeared in the next few years: Arthur G. Willems' master's thesis at Dallas Theological Seminary, "The Eschatology of Satan" (1944) and a textual study by Abraham H. Unruh, "Das Geheimnis der Bosheit: 2 Thess. 2:4-10" (*Menn. Rundschau* 70, no. 41-43, [Oct. 8-22, 1947]). Addressing directly and amply the topic of Satan, B. Charles Hostetter gave nine Mennonite Hour radio sermons, printed under the title *Satan and His Strategy* (1953). This booklet not only exposed the deceptive, seductive tactics of Satan, but urgently calls men and women to turn from Satan's kingdom to Jesus Christ in whom is salvation and security.

J. C. Wenger's *Introduction to Theology* (1954) contains a four-page section on Satan which comes at the end of his chapter on "God as Creator" and follows a section on "Angels." He notes the minor role of Satan in the Old Testament and points to Is 14 and Ez 28 as texts referring to more than just the pagan kings of Tyre and Babylon (note the phrases: "How you are fallen from heaven, O Day Star, son of Dawn!" and "You were the signet of perfection, full of wisdom, and perfect in beauty. You were in Eden, the garden of God"). Wenger says further that the biblical view of Satan and his hosts is not that of the medieval concept "of playful and malicious imps" but that Satan works in respectable ways, wanting people "of social status and upright lives to represent the cause of morality, humanistic philosophy, and perhaps even religion if divorced from the blood of Christ" (117). Further, Satan puts forth greatest effort not upon unbelievers, who are already in his grip, but upon the Christian to lead "into discouragement or sin, and to provoke hostility and opposition . . . ." (117). Satan's deception is also the focus of Myron A. King's 1958 essay, "The Working of Deception" (*Sword Trumpet*, 26, no. 3, pp. 29-34).

With the publication of H. Berkhof's *Christ and Power* (Scottdale, 1962) Mennonite discussion of evil has focused mostly on sociopolitical dimensions, i.e., the principalities and the powers. J. H. Yoder's *Politics of Jesus* (chs. 8 and 12 especially) have further developed this emphasis. This led to a fresh emphasis in Mennonite higher education on the *Christus victor* view of the °atonement, emphasizing Christ's conquest of Satan, the powers and demons through his death and resurrection (see Driver, ch. 3). Thomas N. Finger's *Christian Theology* addresses the larger topic of evil, Satan and the devil extensively: in his treatment of atonement in which Christ defeats Satan and the powers of evil and in his treatment of sin (vol. 1, 291-367; vol. 2, ch. 7).

Edmund G. Kaufman's *Basic Christian Convictions* (1972) considers numerous ways to explain the origin of evil, among them the devil. He says this explanation raises more problems than it solves (88-89); he thus opts for the view that evil originates in the human will (90). Gordon D. Kaufman's *Systematic Theology* (1968) does not discuss Satan or the devil; he addresses the problem of evil (theodicy) in discussing God's goodness (162, 309-12).

In the midst of popular American sensationalized attention to the demonic in the 1970s, Paul M. Miller wrote *The Devil Did Not Make Me Do It* in an effort to save personal responsibility for human sin against the trend to easily blame sins and sickness on the devil. With influences from the charismatic movement and missionary experience overseas, Mennonites studied anew the topic of the demonic (Jacobs, *Demons*). In 1987 Finger and Swartley coauthored a study of the biblical teaching on "bondage and deliverance," investigating the topics of evil, Satan, devil, °exorcism, and Christ's victory. Other essays prepared for the same consultation (as was the Finger/Swartley paper) addressed the topics of evil and Satan from various perspectives—historical, Roman Catholic and Evangelical theology, psychological, anthropological, and pastoral (see °exorcism).

The Kauffman-Harder survey of Mennonite beliefs (*Anabaptism Four C. Later*, 1975) reports 93 percent of sampled North American Mennonites believing in a personal devil (p. 106), 71 percent experiencing a sense of being tempted by the devil, 15 percent feeling that some personal misfortune was caused by the devil, and 11 percent feeling that the devil used them as his agent (p. 94).   WMS

See also Apocalypticism.

John Driver, *Understanding the Atonement for the Mission of the Church* (Scottdale, 1986), esp. 71-86; Thomas N. Finger, *Christian Theology: An Eschatological Approach*, vol. 1 (Nashville: Nelson, 1985; Scottdale, 1987), vol. 2; Robert Friedmann, *The Theology of Anabaptism* (Scottdale, 1973), part II; D. S. Gorter "De Hoogere Wereld" in *Doopsgezinde Lektuur* 2 (1856), 199-235; Nicholas N. Hiebert, "Das satanische Reich," *Mennonitische Rundschau*, 64, no. 5, 9-11 (Jan. 29, Feb. 26, Mar. 5, 12, 1941); B. Charles Hostetter, *Satan and His Strategy* (Harrisonburg, Va.: Mennonite Hour, ca. 1953), nine radio sermons, 64 pp.; Daniel Kauffman, ed., *Bible Doctrine* (Scottdale, 1914), 145-80, and idem, *Doctrines of the Bible* (Scottdale, 1929), 201-35; Frans Kuyper, *Korte Verhandeling van de Duyvelen . . .* (1676); idem, *Filosofisch en Historiaal Bewijz dat 'er Duyvelen Zijn . . .* (Rotterdam: Isaak Naeranus, 1678); Herman Lepp-Reesor, "Die alte Schlange, ihr Ursprung, Sein und Ende," *Der Bote*, 9, no. 50, and 51 (Dec. 14 and 21, 1932); Willard M. Swartley, ed., *Essays on Spiritual Bondage and Deliverance*, Occasional Papers, 11 (Elkhart, Ind.: IMS, 1988); John Christian Wenger, *Introduction to Theology*, 2nd ed. (Scottdale, 1954), 114-18; Walter Wink, *Unmasking the Powers: The Invisible Forces That Determine Human Existence* (Philadelphia: Fortress, 1986); John Howard Yoder, *The Politics of Jesus* (Grand Rapids: Eerdmans, 1972).

See also Apocalypticism.

Sattler, Michael (ME IV:427). As attention has shifted away from the Zürich "origins" of °Anabaptism to its regional developments, the life and work of Michael Sattler have been recognized as pivotal to the self-definition and subsequent survival of Swiss Anabaptism. The °Schleitheim Confession, for which Sattler carried primary responsibility as author, circulated widely together with vivid accounts of his heroic martyrdom on May 20, 1527, at Rottenburg am Neckar. These writings did much to publicize the nascent Anabaptist movement.

Recent scholarship has concentrated on clarifying formative influences on Michael Sattler. In particular, given the fact that he had been prior of the Benedictine monastery St. Peter's of the Black Forest, near Freiburg im Breisgau, the question arises: Were there elements of the °monastic experience that carried over to Sattler's later Anabaptism? Further critical attention also has been given to the primary and secondary sources documenting Michael Sattler's contact with the rebellious °peasants of 1525 and with the Swiss Anabaptist movement in and around Zürich, Strasbourg, and Württemberg. Among the more significant conclusions are the following:

A critical examination of the sources has not sustained the conclusion that Sattler knew Greek and Hebrew, contrary to the report in the *Hutterite Chronicle*.

In 1519, St. Peter's of the Black Forest initiated a process of monastic reform through the Benedictine Bursfeld Union. While this reform was never fully instituted, internal evidence indicates a relatively high level of monastic observance at St. Peter's.

Monastic records fail to mention Michael Sattler by name. However, the priors of the monastery are named through the year 1518. Sattler's tenure as prior, as mentioned by Valerius Anshelm's *Chronicle*, would therefore fall after this date.

Close comparison of reformed Benedictine literature with Sattler's writings has led one historian to the conclusion that Sattler's christocentric emphasis, as well as his stress on the church as the pure and separated community of saints, have significant intellectual roots in Sattler's monastic experience.

Reformation ideas in the area surrounding Freiburg were carried by the peasants, who combined an emphasis on Scripture alone with socioeconomic demands. Peasants living on lands owned by St. Peter's participated in the Peasants' War of 1525; the monastery itself was taken by the Black Forest troop of peasants on May 12, 1525. This troop included Anabaptist volunteers from Waldshut and Hallau. This invasion of St. Peter's may well have provided the occasion for Sattler's departure from the monastery, for he appears subsequently in the archival record in the company of Anabaptists of the Waldshut/Hallau region.

Some fundamental grievances championed by the peasants continue to be articulated in the Schleitheim Articles, suggesting that Schleitheim is in some significant ways a continuation of, rather than a total break with, the movement of the common people (Peasants' War).

It is not certain exactly when Michael Sattler joined the Anabaptist movement. Sattler had certainly joined the Anabaptists by June 1526, but whether he was already baptized by November 1525 is open to question. The documents relating to the subject are limited, and debate about their significance continues.

Sattler's documented activity as an Anabaptist missionary took place in the dependent territories north of Zürich and near Strasbourg, in the town of Lahr. Early in 1525 he had a friendly debate with °°Bucer and °°Capito in Strasbourg, where he pleaded for the release of imprisoned brethren. Sources indicate that Wilhelm °°Reublin, not Michael Sattler, was the primary Anabaptist missionary in Württemberg (Horb and Rottenburg) during 1526 and 1527.

Following the Schleitheim meeting of Feb. 24, 1527, Sattler travelled to Württemberg, apparently to pastor the congregation at Horb. Michael Sattler was arrested in Horb along with other Anabaptists sometime before Mar. 18, 1527.

It is not known when Michael Sattler married Margaretha, a former Beguine sister. She was arrested with him, imprisoned, tried, and executed by drowning on May 22, 1527, two days following Sattler's death by burning at the stake. Margaretha resolutely declined all offers of mercy in return for her °recantation.

Critical examination of trial documents has shown that there are three independent accounts of the trial. In addition, the official charges read at the trial (which mention Margaretha by name), as well as a record of Michael Sattler's pretrial questioning, have come to light.   CAS

English translations of Sattler's Writings in CRR 1; German text of the Schleitheim Articles ("Brüderliche Vereinigung") in *TA Schweiz II*, 26-36; C. Arnold Snyder, *Life and Thought of Michael Sattler* (Scottdale, 1984); Martin Haas, "Michael Sattler: Auf dem Weg der Täufer in die Absonderung," in *Radikale Reformatoren*, ed. Hans-Jürgen Goertz (Munich: C. H. Beck, 1978), 115-24 (Engl. trans., Scottdale, 1982); C. Arnold Snyder, "Anabaptism and Revolution: The Case of Michael Sattler," *Church History*, 50 (1981), 276-87; idem, in *MQR*, 53 (1978), 328-32, 57 (1983), 5-26, 54 (1980), 208-28; Hans-Jürgen Goertz, *Die Taufer: Geschichte und Deutung* (Munich: C. H. Beck, 1980), 20-23; C. Arnold

Snyder, "The Schleitheim Articles in Light of the Revolution of the Common Man: Continuation or Departure?" *Sixteenth Century J.*, 16 (1985), 419-30; critiques of Snyder's book and articles by Dennis Martin and Heinold Fast, with responses by Snyder in *MQR*, 60 (1986), 139-64, 364-73, 61 (1987), 262-73, 62 (1988), 496-506; Myron Augsburger, "Michael Sattler, d. 1527: Theologian of the Swiss Brethren Movement." (ThD diss., Union Theological Seminary, Richmond, Va., 1964); Jean Seguy, "Sattler et Loyola: Ou Deux Formes de Radicalisme Religieux au XVI Siècle," in *The Origins and Characteristics of Anabaptism*, ed. Marc Lienhard (The Hague: M. Nijhoff, 1977), 105-25; Hans Stricker, "Michael Sattler als Verfasser der Schleitheimer Artikel," *Menn. Geschbl.*, Jg. 21, n.F. 16 (1964), 15-18.

See also Schleitheim Confession.

Schaefer, Paul J. (1899-1969), was an outstanding Manitoba Mennonite educator and church leader. He was born of Lutheran parents in the Russian Caucasus region. After elementary schooling in his native village he studied for nine years at the *Gymnasium* (secondary school) in Tarutino, Bessarabia. Schaefer then became a teacher in the Mennonite village of Alexandrodar (Alexanderfeld) in the Kuban valley. He married a colleague, Margaretha Wiebe, and was received into the Mennonite congregation. In 1925 the couple emigrated to Canada. They joined the Blumenort Mennonite church, a southern Manitoba congregation of newly-arrived immigrants from Russia. Paul and Margaretha Schaefer had four children. In 1948 Margaretha died. In 1949 Paul married Louise Wiebe Neufeld, whose daughter then also joined the family circle.

Schaefer earned a Manitoba teaching certificate and a bachelor's degree. From 1928 to 1943 he taught school in Gnadenthal. Then followed 25 years of teaching, 19 of them as principal, at the Mennonite Collegiate Institute, Gretna. He authored the history series *Woher? Wohin? Mennoniten!*, a biography of Mennonite educator H. H. °°Ewert, and numerous shorter articles.

A minister since 1942, Schaefer was elected °elder (bishop) in 1954. The former Lutheran, who had become a persuaded Anabaptist, thus made a momentous decision—he received baptism upon confession of faith and then accepted the call to congregational leadership. Schaefer gained prominence on the wider Canadian Mennonite scene. He served in Sunday school leadership, on youth and education committees, on the Canadian Mennonite Bible College board, and as moderator of the Conference of Mennonites in Manitoba. PDZ

Menn. Bib. II, p. 498.

Schaep, Jan Claes (June 12, 1640-ca. 1676), son of Griete Cornelis and Claes Jansz, an oilmiller at Wormerveer. Schaep was most probably a merchant and belonged to the Frisian Mennonites. As a poet with the intention to publish "to the glory of God" he published only one—rather successful—volume: *Bloem-Tuyntje, Bestaende in Inderlycke Bedenckingen, Gelyckenissen, ofte Exempelen: midsgaders eenige Sang-Rymen, ofte Liedekens*. Part 1 consists of rather moralistic and symbolical poems about everyday events. Part 2 contains hymns and topical songs. Style and content reflect a simple but sincere piety. The booklet was revised in 1671 (Amsterdam), with reprints in 1686, 1697, and 1724, edited by his father who added five poems of his own. All editions are illustrated. The one of 1724 has 15 extra engravings by J. Lamsveldt. One of Schaep's hymns is found in *'t Groot Achter-Hofken* (1664) and C. Stapel's *Lusthof der Zielen* (1681). His *Bloem-Tuyntje* has often been awarded to exceptional students in school and as a present in catechism classes in Mennonite congregations. PVis

Jan Aten, *De Wormerveersche Dichter Jan Claasz. Schaap geboren 12 juni 1640* (n.p., 1940); offprint from the daily 'De Zaanlander' (biography); John Landwehr, *Emblem Books in the Low Countries 1554-1949* (Utrecht, 1970), 598-602, includes bibliography; P. J. Meertens and Hilary Sayles, *Nederlandse Emblemata: Bloemlezing uit de Noord- en Zuidnederlandse Emblemata-literatuur van de 16de en 17de eeuw* (Leiden, 1983), 153-155, an anthology.

Schellenberg, Katharina Lohrenz (Nov. 28, 1870-Jan. 1, 1945). At the age of 34, following four years of training at a homeopathic school of medicine in Kansas City, Ks., Katharina Schellenberg, daughter of Elder Abraham and Katharina Lohrenz Schellenberg, became the first woman doctor in the Mennonite Brethren Church. She was also trained as a nurse and served for a short period as the first supervisor of the Goessel [Ks.] Hospital. She discontinued her medical practice in her home town of Buhler, Ks., to leave for India in 1906 and begin a medical work at the Mulkapet station in 1907, transferring to other areas later on. She took only two furloughs during nearly 38 years of service in India (1914 and 1923). When she returned in 1926 to work in the new hospital at Shamshabad, she trained her own nurses and worked tirelessly, taking few vacations in the hills during the hot seasons. Although she never married, she adopted a foster child. During World War II she and Helen Warkentin served alone on the mission station for two years. She died while in service at Shamshabad in 1945. KFW

Esther Jost in *Women Among the Brethren* (1979), 82-94; Katie Funk Wiebe, "The Life and Work of Dr. K. L. Schellenberg," *The Youth Worker*, 6 (1959).

Schirmer, Amy Talasnemptewa (1904-77), was a General Conference Mennonite (GCM) missionary among the Hopi people in Arizona and the Northern Cheyenne people in Montana. She was born into the Bear Clan, from which the chiefs of Oraibi came. Her parents were among the first Christians at Oraibi, Ariz. Amy entered the Bible Institute of Los Angeles in 1933. While a student, she began Thursday and Sunday afternoon meetings with Indian girls (and their boy friends) working in Los Angeles. The group grew to about 30 or 40 young people by 1935 and later became a church. After her graduation in 1936, Amy returned to the Hopi reservation and married Daniel Schirmer. Together they served as missionaries in Bacavi and Hotevilla, Ariz., until 1949; in Birney and Busby, Mont., among the Northern Cheyenne, until 1964; and again among the Hopi in Moencopi and Bacavi until 1974. In Montana, she worked especially with Cheyenne girls, helping them feel at ease away from their own communities and helping them prepare programs and music to perform. LB

Barrett, *Vision* (1983), 44, 71, 72.

Schirmer, Daniel (b. 1908), was a Mennonite missionary and minister among the Hopi people in Arizona and the Northern Cheyenne people in Montana. He was named Siwinainiwa (Young Cedar Sprout) by his relatives, who were preparing for his burial because his mother had died after childbirth. Hopi custom assumed that such a baby was an evil spirit because it had caused its mother's death. Mary Schirmer, a General Conference Mennonite (GCM) missionary in Hotevilla, adopted the baby and renamed him Daniel.

From 1934 to 1949, Daniel Schirmer served as minister of the Mennonite congregations in Bacavi and Hotevilla, Ariz. He and his wife, Amy Tales-nemptewa Schirmer, later were missionaries in Birney and Busby, Mont., among the Northern Cheyenne. He returned to the Hopi reservation in 1964 to serve the churches in Moencopi and Bacavi until his retirment in 1974. He was ordained as a minister of the gospel in 1951.   LB

Barrett, *Vision* (1983), 44, 71, 72.

Schisms. The Anabaptist movement very early developed a concept of the church in which a voluntary personal commitment to Christ and to the body of fellow believers was expected. This visible community developed a common body of beliefs and a common set of ethical expectations. Members were expected to encourage each other in maintaining these and to admonish one another when someone departed from them (°discipline). This meant that the primary form of "church" was the local congregation.

With this understanding of church, it was quite possible for Anabaptist groups developing in different parts of Europe to differ in aspects of faith and practice. When these differences were perceived by one group or the other to be unacceptable, a separation or schism took place. If the relationship between the two groups had been a close one at an earlier time, then the schism might be formalized by pronouncing the ban on the entire group deemed to hold the unacceptable ethical or doctrinal position.

With this emphasis on a personal commitment as basis for membership in the local church, members also had a much larger role in the discerning and upholding of the common beliefs and practices than had been the case in the hierarchical pattern of the Roman Catholic Church. When this process of arriving at a consensus broke down within a local congregation, a schism might result. If the issues separating the two portions were deemed to be serious enough, mutual excommunication might result.

The Anabaptist understanding of church also included a separation from the state and a renunciation of any coercive means of punishing dissidents. Beyond personal and group admonition, the °°ban was the only step available. Among some groups it therefore became the means to ensure unity within the church. During the first several generations of the movement, the more or less intense °persecution created an atmosphere in which it was difficult both to develop consensus and to maintain a consistent practice of the faith. The rather frequent schisms that resulted from these factors in the early years of Anabaptism, led to the expression "Täuferkrankheit" (Anabaptist disease).

Most of the schisms which took place in Anabaptist and Mennonite history are described in ME I-IV. The following survey illustrates the various reasons for schisms and attempts to assess the mood in the 1980s.

Moravian-Hutterian. The 1527 separation of the °°Stäbler, led by Hans °Hut, and the °°Schwertler, led by Balthasar °Hubmaier, in °°Nikolsburg, reflected a difference in the view of the church's relation to the state, and hence, to such issues as the paying of war °taxes and the legitimate use of the sword (°church-state relations).

There have been no formal schisms among the Hutterian Brethren, as the Stäbler group came to be known, since that early split. Internal tensions over the issue of their historic communal living pattern have led to the loss of individuals or families. Following the emigration of the entire Hutterite church from Russia to America in the 1870s, a large number of its members chose to abandon communal living, many of them joining the Mennonites. The process of incorporating the Society of Brothers (ME IV:1126) into the °Hutterian Brethren was accompanied by some "schisms" between the initial acceptance in 1930 and the reincorporation in 1974.

Swiss-South German. The deepest rift in this group was the separation of the followers of Jacob °°Ammann, who insisted on stricter discipline in the church and on shunning (°°avoidance) of those excommunicated. Hans °°Reist, whom Ammann criticized for being too tolerant, did not accept shunning. Attempts at reconciliation failed and by 1693 the °°Amish division was final. In the 19th c. some Mennonites of the Emmental region of Switzerland joined a movement led by Samuel °°Fröhlich because they were dissatisfied with the low level of spiritual life in their church.

Dutch Mennonites. Menno's emphasis on the idea of a "church without spot or wrinkle" opened the door for his zealous colleagues to push him into using the ban to maintain a pure church. Those groups which continued to hold that the primary use of church discipline should be the correction of erring members, such as the °°Waterlander and the °°High German, by 1557 distanced themselves from those practicing the "hard" ban. A more long-lasting schism took place in 1567 with the mutual banning of the °°Flemish and °°Frisian groups. The issues dividing them were to a large extent cultural and personal. Both experienced subsequent divisions into "Old" and "Young" factions. By the middle of the 17th c. a process of reunification of the various Dutch groups had begun, leading to the formation of the °Algemene Doopsgezinde Sociëteit in 1811.

Russian Mennonites. Mennonites in the Vistula delta area of Prussia (later Poland) maintained close relations with the Dutch church. As a result the Flemish-Frisian division took root among them and was still strong enough to be transferred to Russia with the first emigration in 1789. While that rift was gradually being overcome in Russia, a new division began about 1812. Klaas °Reimer objected to the low level of morality and spirituality in the church in the Molotschna colony, and his objections led to the separation of the °°Kleine Gemeinde (°Evangelical Mennonite Conference).

A °pietistic revival in the Mennonite colonies around the middle of the 19th c. and several other kinds of outside influence, led to the separation of the °°Mennonite Brethren in 1860, the °Templer movement in 1863, and the °°Krimmer Mennonite Brethren in 1869. An attempt to mediate between the Mennonite Brethren and the Mennonite church (°Kirchliche Mennoniten) led instead to yet another group, the °°Allianzgemeinde in 1905.

North American Mennonites. Frontier °revivalism and pressure to conform to society proved to be divisive among Mennonites in North America. The 1775 excommunication of Martin °°Boehm for revivalist tendencies, and that of Bishop Christian °°Funk in 1778 for his support of war tax, are samples. Both John °°Herr in 1812 and John °Holdeman in 1859 claimed to be more Anabaptist in their emphasis on discipline than the groups from which they separated. Holdeman also emphasized the necessity of the new birth and separation from the world.

The 1847 division in the Franconia (Pa.) Conference was precipitated by the insistence of John H. °Oberholtzer on a written constitution and the keeping of minutes in the conference. Oberholtzer's °°East Pennsylvania Conference of Mennonites in 1860 joined with other "new" Mennonite groups to form the °General Conference Mennonite Church, which became the second largest Mennonite group in North America.

An emphasis on the new birth led Bishop Henry °°Egli's group to separate from the Amish in Indiana in 1866, resulting eventually in the °Evangelical Mennonite Church. In the 1880s Bishop Isaac °°Peters in Nebraska and Bishop Aaron °°Wall in Minnesota separated from their respective churches over issues of personal regeneration and strict discipline, and founded the Conference of United Mennonite Brethren in North America in 1889 (since 1937 the Evangelical Mennonite Brethren; since 1987, the °Fellowship of Evangelical Bible Churches).

The increasing adaptation of the main body of Mennonites to current North American ways (°acculturation) led to divisions of another kind. Certain groups, wishing to preserve traditional customs of °worship and church life, separated from conferences which had introduced such new pratices as °Sunday schools, evangelistic services, and °°singing in harmony. These came to be known collectively as °Old Order Mennonites, although they originated in various places at different times and are not formally associated in one organization. Locally they are sometimes known by their founding leader; e.g., Jacob °°Wisler, 1872, Indiana and Ohio; Abraham Martin (1834-1902), 1889 Ontario (°°Martin Old Order Mennonite Church); Jonas °Martin, 1893, Pennsylvania. Old Order °Amish, characterized by worship in homes, "plain" dress, horse-and-buggy culture, and a strictly rural way of life, are similarly distinct from "Church Amish" or Amish Mennonites (e.g., °Beachy Amish Mennonite Fellowship). But

their origin is less directly the result of specific schisms.

Among the Mennonites who came to Canada from Russia in the 1870s, the promotion of secondary school education led to a separation in the °Bergthal group, with a large majority opposing this move. In Manitoba the small pro-education group retained the name Bergthaler, with the larger conservative blocks, geographically separated by the Red River became the °Chortitzer conference and °Sommerfeld Mennonites.

Disagreements in several Canadian groups over the seriousness of the governments' violation of Mennonite rights or °privileges during and after World War I led to separations of another kind. In the 1920s parts of the Chortitzer, Sommerfelder, and °Old Colony churches emigrated to Mexico and Paraguay over this issue. Where the decision to emigrate was made by the church as a total body, those who remained behind were in several cases functionally excommunicated. As a result, the non-emigrating portions of the Old Colony Church in Manitoba and the Saskatchewan Valley had to be reorganized with the help of leadership from non-Old Colony churches.

Just as a number of European divisions were transported to North America by immigration, so mission activity by European and North American Mennonites resulted in new churches in Asia and Africa separated from each other through their ties with different "parent" churches. For example, Japan has four different Mennonite and Brethren in Christ conferences and Zaire has three.

Among smaller groups, especially the culturally more conservative ones, schisms continue to take place. In the larger conferences this is no longer the case, although occasionally individual congregations withdraw from affiliation with regional or national conferences. Such withdrawals have been most characteristic of the Mennonite Church (MC), where a number of independent local conferences have emerged since the late 1960s (°conservative Mennonites). In general, however, among the largest Mennonite conferences in North America and Europe, there are signs of increasing cooperation and, in some cases even merger (°Conference of Mennonites in Eastern Canada; °Arbeitsgemeinschaft deutcher Mennonitengemeinden; °inter-Mennonite cooperation). Ironically, mergers themselves can produce schisms if minority portions of the merging groups choose not to go along with the merger. **AE**

Calvin Redekop, *Brotherhood and Schism* (Scottdale, 1963); Harold E. Bauman, *The Price of Church Unity* (Scottdale, 1962); Elmer P. Weaver, Jr., in *Guidelines for Today* (July-Aug. 1985) 20-21; *PMH*, 7 (Oct. 1984), 2-10.

See also Conservative Mennonites.

Schleitheim Confession (ME I:447). The *Schleitheim Confession* (also known as the *Brüderliche Vereinigung* or the *Schleitheim Brotherly Union*) has come to be recognized as a watershed articulation of certain Swiss Anabaptist distinctives. Michael °Sattler is now accepted as being the primary author of the seven articles. These were ratified on Feb. 24,

1527, during an assembly of Anabaptists in the northern Swiss village of Schleitheim.

The significance of the Brotherly Union was evident immediately: the articles were copied and circulated quickly and extensively in the Swiss and South German Anabaptist communities. Reaction within those communities was not exclusively positive. Some of the articles were contested within Anabaptist circles (e.g., art. 6 by Balthasar °Hubmaier); Ulrich °°Zwingli and John °°Calvin wrote refutations of the confession as a whole.

While Schleitheim's immediate influence on the Anabaptism of the Swiss and South German areas is undeniable, the historical connections linking Schleitheim to the later confessional tradition have yet to be clarified. Schleitheim's teaching on the sword and the oath (Art. 6 and 7) became increasingly normative in the Mennonite and Hutterite traditions, but the articles themselves seem not to have been preserved in a confessional sense: there is no obvious direct line of descent from Schleitheim to the later Mennonite °confessions such as Dordrecht. The Schleitheim Confession has received significant denominational attention again only following its recovery in the modern period, with particular attention paid to Schleitheim's teaching on the sword.

Some scholarly difference of opinion exists concerning Schleitheim's historical status as a confessional delineator: was it directed primarily against the Protestant reformers, and that only after °°Bucer and °°Capito rejected the ecumenical overtures of Michael Sattler? Or was Schleitheim a further development of prior °sectarian impulses, and directed primarily to the Anabaptist community? Some historians have noted further that although Schleitheim explicitly rejects social rebellion, it also preserves important demands first enunciated in the °Peasants' War of 1525.   CAS

Critical edition of the *Brüderliche Vereinigung* in *TA Schweiz II*, 26-36; earliest known Dutch edition *Broederlicke vereeninge sommighe kinderen Gods . . . Item eenen Sendbrief van Michael Sattler. . . .* (n.p., 1560); English trans. in CRR 1: 27-43; C. Arnold Snyder, *The Life and Thought of Michael Sattler* (Scottdale, 1984); Loewen, *Confessions*; Martin Haas, "Der Weg der Taufer in die Absonderung," in *Umstrittenes Täufertum*, ed. H.-J. Goertz (Göttingen: Vandenhoeck and Ruprecht, 1977), 50-78; Richard Stauffer, "Zwingli et Calvin, Critiques de la Confession de Schleitheim," in *The Origins and Characteristics of Anabaptism*, ed. Marc Lienhard (The Hague: M. Nijhoff, 1977), 126-47; Leland Harder, "Zwingli's Reaction to the Schleitheim Confession of Faith of the Anabaptists," *Sixteenth Century J.*, 11 (1980), 51-66; Balthasar Hubmaier, "Von dem Schwert," in *Hubmaier, Schriften*, 434-57; John H. Yoder, "Der Kristallisationspunkt des Täufertums," *Menn. Geschbl.*, Jg. 29, n.F. 24 (1972), 35-47; Klaus Deppermann, "Die Strassburger Reformatoren und die Krise des oberdeutschen Täufertums im Jahre 1527," *Menn. Geschbl.*, Jg. 30, n.F. 25 (1973), 24-41; Hans J. Goertz, *Die Täufer: Geschichte und Deutung* (Munich: C. H. Beck, 1980), 20-23; C. Arnold Snyder, "The Schleitheim Articles in Light of the Revolution of the Common Man: Continuation or Departure?" *Sixteenth Century J.*, 16 (1985), 419-30; James M. Stayer, *Anabaptists and the Sword* (Lawrence, Ks.: Coronado Press, 1972, 1976); John H. Yoder, " 'Anabaptists and the Sword' Revisited: Systematic Historiography and Undogmatic Nonresistants," *Z. für Kg.*, 85 (1974), 126-139; John W. Miller, "Schleitheim Pacifism and Modernity," *CGR*, 3 (1985), 155-63; *GH* (Feb. 22, 1977), sp. issue; Beulah Stauffer Hostetler, *American Mennonites and Protestant Movements* (Scottdale, 1987); H. W. Meihuizen, "Who were the 'False Brethren' mentioned in the Schleitheim Articles?" *MQR*, 41

(1967), 200-222; Hans Stricker, "Michael Sattler als Verfasser der Schleitheimer Artikel," *Menn. Geschbl.*, Jg. 21, n.F. 16 (1964), 15-18; Hans Quiring, "Das Schleitheimer Täuferbekenntnis von 1527," *Menn. Geschbl.*, Jg. 15, n.F. 9 (1957), 34-40; H. W. Meihuizen, J. A. Oosterbaan, and H. B. Kossen, *Broederlijke Vereniging* (Amsterdam: Doopsgezinde Historische Kring, 1974).

Schmidt, Augusta (b. Mar. 3, 1894), was born in Goessel, Ks., and was well prepared to become a General Conference Mennonite missionary. She taught in rural schools for three years, received a BA degree from Bethel College (1922), spent one term at Witmarsum Seminary (Bluffton, Ohio), and earned a nursing degree from Bethel Deaconess Hospital (Newton, Ks., 1927)

Augusta was ordained a missionary, Aug. 4, 1927, and left for India on October 10, arriving in Bombay on Nov. 24, 1927. Stationed at Korba where medical facilities were almost nonexistent, she engaged in a widespread healing ministry. She earned the title "Sadhuni" (the holy one) because of her devotion to her task. Her life was a personification of obedience to Christ.

From November 1935 to 1938, and from February 1945 to March 1950, Augusta was principal of Funk Memorial Girls School and manager of the girls' hostel in Janjgir. From 1938 to 1945 she was principal of the Jagdeeshpur Mission Middle School. When the male teachers refused to work under a woman administrator, she hired substitutes until the regular staff returned. Later she served as superintendent of nursing at Sewa Bhavan Hospital and was also busy as a midwife. She also became active in a cooperative to enable weavers to improve their economic status. From August 1951 to 1956 Augusta was superintendent of nursing at the Bethesda Leprosy Hospital and Homes in Champa and principal of Kirkham School there.

Augusta retired from India in August 1956 and helped start what later became the "Northview Development Center" in Newton, Ks., where she taught weaving. She entered the Bethel Home for the Aged in 1978 and continues there (1988).   HR/RR

Notes from Augusta's mother's diary submitted by Martha F. Graber; Kathryn Jantzen, "In Remembrance," *India Calling* (summer 1957); Augusta Schmidt, "School Fees," *India Calling* (Christmas Issue, 1940); *Augusta Schmidt*, a leaflet issued by Literature Committee of the Women's Home and Foreign Missionary Association (GCM); India [GCM] missionaries, *Twenty-Five Years With God in India*; Mrs. Harold [Ruth R.] Ratzlaff, ed., *Fellowship in the Gospel, India: 1900-1950* (Newton: MPO, 1950), 48-51, 132.

Schmidt, Clara and John. See Hansen's Disease ("Pioneers of a Better Way" [feature]).

Scholarship. Anabaptism as a lay movement, inherited and passed on to its descendants suspicion of scholarship common to lay people in the Middle Ages. Nevertheless, scholarship has been part of the Anabaptist and Mennonite tradition, culminating in intense scholarly attention given to its own history in the 20th c.

A number of early Anabaptist leaders had university and para-university (humanist) education and were acquainted with the methods of scholarship. °Menno Simons specifically said that he understood the value of "learnedness and the languages." The writings of °Hubmaier, °°Denck, °°Dirk Philips and others were average works of scholarship in their time.

But Menno Simons and the other educated leaders rejected scholarly devices such as syllogisms (logic) and synecdoche (literature, hermeneutics) since they saw them as contrivances to blunt the clear, literal meaning and demands of Scripture. Scholarship was increasingly rejected as lay leaders replaced the early (educated) leadership. Lay leaders tended to regard scholarship as a mark of pride and social preferment. Perhaps equally important was the fact that those who interrogated Anabaptists during persecution, and on whose testimony they suffered penalties including death, were trained theologians and Scripture scholars. The belief that theological and Scripture scholarship led to pride, unbelief, and unprincipled compromise for the sake of financial gain, thus destroying the simplicity of faith, became the dominant view in all the Mennonite communities.

However, since the late 16th c. there is visible among the followers of Menno a gradual °acculturation, which also produced changing attitudes toward scholarship. Beginning in The Netherlands in the 17th c., Mennonites have seen the economic advantages as well as the service opportunities in scholarship which was part of professional training. Studies leading to °medicine, teaching, engineering, (°water technology), and commerce (°business), for example, could be reconciled without much difficulty with a simple faith. That view has survived despite the tensions that developed between Christian faith and science in the last two centuries. Simple faith could remain unassailed inasmuch as, at least in recent decades, all disciplines are taught without recourse to religious categories.

With the notable exception of the Mennonite seminary in Amsterdam (established in 1735), Mennonites in Europe have received their scholarly education in the universities. In North America they have established their own schools beginning late in the 19th c., staffed with Mennonite graduates from the secular universities and the °seminaries of the major denominations. These colleges aligned themselves consciously with the American tradition of liberal arts education including its critical approach to every subject not excluding the Bible and Christian belief. Growing numbers of educated Mennonite church members demanded an educated clergy who, in their own schools, had to come to terms with the post-Enlightenment historical and literary criticism of the Bible.

Formal studies in theology and church history were from their beginnings in the 18th and 19th c. put into the service of doctrinal orthodoxy and apologetics. Traditionally the study of Christian doctrine and the view of human history as history of salvation was thought to be of one piece with faith oriented upon the Bible. When doctrine began to be studied developmentally, however, and historical study assumed relativity also in the study of Anabaptism and even Scripture, it became more difficult to maintain the simplicity of faith. Mennonites, as also many other Christians, responded by exempting at least the Bible from the accepted criteria for scholarly study. Gradually, however, this exemption too was surrendered on the grounds of consistency. And so, in addition to their trained professionals, theologians and historians, Mennonites also produced Scripture scholars.

It is at this point that the tensions remain high among Mennonites, the Doopsgezinde (Dutch Mennonites) and some German Mennonites excepted. Scholarship in all disciplines is not a fact of Mennonite life. As it has always done before, scholarship tends to separate academics and trained clergy from lay people, and Scripture scholars and theologians become professional experts. The suspicion remains that scholarship will cause the loss of simple belief in God and undermine resort to the Bible as the lodestone of faith which can be effectively used by the simplest Christian. WKlaa

In addition to references at the end of the article "colleges" (ME I:639), see James C. Juhnke, *Dialogue with a Heritage: Cornelius H. Wedel and the Beginnings of Bethel College* (North Newton: Bethel College, 1987).

Schools, Christian. See Private Christian Schools.

Schowalter, Paul (Aug. 28, 1912-Aug. 28, 1984), preacher, church leader, and historian, was born at °°Kaplaneihof. Baptized at °°Deutschhof he graduated in 1932 from the *Gymnasium* (secondary school) at °°Landau in the Palatinate. The gifted youth studied theology at Greifswald, Erlangen and Tübingen, 1932-36. From 1937-39 he served as vicar under the guidance of Pastor Christian °°Neff in the °°Weierhof and °°Uffhofen congregations, and was ordained as Neff's successor in 1939. The same year he was drafted and served as an accountant and sergeant in a medical unit in France and Russia until 1945. From then on he served the two congregations until 1971 and lived at Weierhof until his death.

Schowalter reorganized after World War II youth work, baptismal instructions, and conference meetings. He helped to distribute Mennonite Central Committee material aid to refugees from Russia and East and °West Prussia. During this time the Weierhof congregation's fellowship and education building was erected. He taught religion at the °Weierhof Mennonite-founded secondary school, served as treasurer for the Konferenz der Süddeutschen Mennoniten, 1951-68, and edited the *Gemeindekalender*, 1951-67. He also served in the Youth Commission, °Deutsches Mennonitisches Friedenskomitee, as a secretary in the Vereinigung Deutscher Mennonitengemeinden, and as secretary of the Mennonitischer Geschichtsverein (°historical society), 1947-74. From 1959-1964 he was a member of the Mennonite World Conference committee and in this capacity he twice visited North America.

Schowalter also hosted many North American tour groups at Weierhof and aided them and others in genealogical research. He helped to set up the Mennonitische Forschungsstelle Weierhof (°historical and genealogical library) after it had moved there from Krefeld. He wrote approximately 100 articles (history, sermons, book reviews, reports, financial statements), which showed his tremendous knowledge, and ability to interpret history combined with theology. About from 1967 on he suffered from deep mental depressions, was often hospitalized, but still succeeded in better days to publish a book, *Stammbuch der Familie Schowalter* (Weierhof, 1979).   HG

H. Fast, "P. Schowalter (1912-1984)," *Menn. Geschbl.,* Jg. 42, n.F. 37 (1985), 128-29; Theo Glück in *Gemeinde Unterwegs* (Nov. 1984), 129; Horst Quiring in *Mennonitische Blätter* (Oct. 1984), 152; Gary Waltner, *300 Jahre Mennonitengemeinde Weierhof 1682-1982* (Weierhof, 1982). In addition to Schowalter's articles in *ML* and *ME,* see "Ein Predigerverzeichnis vom Jahre 1766," *Menn. Geschbl.,* Jg. 4 (1939), 88-89; "Zum Gedenken an Chr. Neff," *Menn. Geschbl.,* Jg. 6, n.F. 1 (1949), 2-13; "Mennoniten auf dem Haftelhof in der Pfalz," *Menn. Geschbl.,* Jg. 28, n.F. 23 (1971), 39-50; "Zum Gedächtnis N. v. d. Zijpp," *Menn. Geschbl.,* Jg. 22, n.F. 17 (1965), 7-9; "Johann Eimann (1964-1847), Ein Mennonit der keiner mehr sein durfte," *Menn. Jahrbuch* (1980), 37-40; "Wer gab die erste Anregung zu einer Mennonitischen Weltkonferenz," *Der Mennonit,* 15 (1962), 8-9, 102.

Schrag, Menno (Mar. 23, 1904-June 12, 1987), was born to Andrew G. and Freni (Strausz) Schrag in Harvey Co., Ks. He studied at Hesston Academy, Bethel College and Wheaton College (ll.), graduating from the latter in 1931. He also met Gertrude Aeberhard there. They were married in 1933.

In 1925 Schrag began newspaper work as typesetter at the °°Herald Publishing Co., Newton, Ks., which published *Der Herold* and, from 1923, the °°*Mennonite Weekly Review.* He was named assistant editor of the *Review* in 1927, and became editor in 1935, a position he held until 1969. He believed that the *Review* could become an instrument of unity among Mennonites. Under his leadership the paper grew from a 4-page issue with fewer than 1,000 subscribers to a 12-page weekly that reaches readers in most Mennonite groups in North America. He traveled widely (37 countries) and wrote more than 2,500 editorials.

Schrag served the church in many ways in addition to journalism. He was a member of many church boards and committees, including the Bethel College Board of Directors (1951-63), the Board of Education and Publication of the General Conference Mennonite Church, and the Historical Committee of that conference (chairman).   CJD

MWR (June 18, 1987), 1-2, 4.

Schroeder, Susanna Theresa Nickel (1888-1966). Although Susanna Nickel, born to Russian Mennonite parents in Mountain Lake, Minn., "always felt like a missionary at heart" and dreamed of service in India, she never left North America. In 1910 Susanna, known as Susie, married Peter Reuben °°Schroeder, who was later to become a prominent General Conference Mennonite Church leader and vocal critic of "modernism." The Schroeders were married while studying at Bethel College in Newton, Ks., the first married couple to attend the school. After Peter's graduation, Susie threw her energies into Christian service as a pastor's spouse. They served congregations in Berne, Ind., Freeman, S.D., and Mountain Lake, Minn. Since Peter traveled a great deal on behalf of the conference, Susie carried heavier responsibility for parenting their four daughters—Celeste (d. 1968), Vernelle, Louise (d. 1943) and Esther Ruth.

Shortly after moving to Mountain Lake Peter died

at age 52 after a brief illness (1941). Besides facing the loss of a spouse, Susie had to face the loss of her "vocation" as pastor's wife. The following year the Bethel congregation in Mountain Lake invited her to serve as a paid "church worker." For the next ten years she visited the sick and young mothers, wrote conference reports for the pastors, taught adult Bible school, Sunday school, and teacher training classes and updated church records.

Throughout her life her commitment to missions remained strong. She served as secretary of the Women's Missionary Association of the General Conference Mennonite Church from 1926 to 1928; encouraged her sister, Helen, and daughter, Vernelle, who were able to serve in India; assisted the relief committee in Mountain Lake in sending huge shipments of food and clothing to those in need; and wrote in her will, "And girls, remember missions."   GGK

Naomi Lehman, *Pilgrimage of a Congregation* (Berne, Ind.: First Mennonite Church, 1982); Celeste Schroeder Dehnert, "Peter R. Schroeder—Pastor and Conference Worker," *Menn. Life,* 4 (July 1949); Bessie B. Koontz, *Refreshing Rays from Western Slopes* (Newton, Ks.: Allen Publishing Co., 1965); Mrs. P. R. Schroeder, "My Memoirs" (manuscript compiled by Celeste Schroeder Dehnert, MLA [North Newton], 1964); Ruth Unrau, *Encircled* (1986), 101-14.

Schultz, George P. (May 30, 1880-Oct. 21, 1957), an Evangelical Mennonite Brethren pastor and evangelist, was born in Mountain Lake, Minn., a son of Peter °°Schultz. George Schultz graduated from Moody Bible Institute and held degrees from Chicago Theological Seminary and Northern Baptist Theological Seminary. From 1908 to 1916 Schultz was superintendent of the Happy Hour Mission in Chicago, and from 1916 to 1951 pastor of Brighton Park Mennonite (Grace Community) Church in Chicago. He held revival meetings throughout the United States and Canada. He served as editor of his Conference paper for many years and published a book and pamphlet.   ACS

George P. Schultz, *Short Talks on Live Themes* (Scottdale: MPH, 1924), 96pp.; idem, *The Making of a Home* (Chicago: Glad Tidings Publishing Company, Chicago, 1928); Arnold C. Schultz, "George P. Schultz: Pioneer Chicago Mennonite Churchman," *Mennonite Heritage* (Illinois), 9, no. 4 (Dec. 1982) 37, 39-42; *Who's Who Menn.* (1943), 216, 217; Smith, *Illinois* (1983); Weber, *Illinois,* (1931).

See also Urban Church.

Schulz, David (1897-1976). Born near Altona, Man., David Schulz attended the Mennonite Educational Institute at Altona and began his public life as teacher in the Mennonite private and emerging public schools. He became a farmer and was called to the ministry in 1920. His theological direction was influenced by time spent at the Mennonite Brethren Bible School in Winkler, Man.

Schulz was picked by Elder Jacob Hoeppner of the °Bergthal Mennonite church of Manitoba to succeed him. In 1926 the church affirmed both Schulz and Hoeppner by choosing Schulz to be the elder and leader of this multicongregation church. He served faithfully and well until illness forced him to retire. Schulz worked in the tradition of the Mennonite °elder as it had developed through several centuries. He was rather authoritarian. He was well-liked by young and old. Bridal couples sought him for their weddings and bereaved families wanted him for the burial of their loved ones. He preached consistently good sermons with an emphasis on family living and °discipleship. He was a consistent supporter of °evangelistic efforts.

Schulz was largely responsible for the founding of Elim Bible School (1929, 1936). He regretted that the Winkler Bible School had become a Mennonite Brethren denominational school. He was also active in helping to establish the Altona hospital, the Ebenezer Home for the Aged, the Eden Mental Health Center in Winkler, and the CFAM radio station in Altona.

Schulz was an active supporter of the Conference of Mennonites in Manitoba and the Conference of Mennonites in Canada and served on many committees. Negative experiences with the General Conference Mennonite Church during the earlier history of the Bergthal Mennonites made him suspicious and he did not favor joining that conference.

Schulz was solidly rooted in the Anabaptist tradition of °nonresistance. Consequently when World War II came, he was a strong advocate for an active °peace position. He, together with the other elders of the churches of the 1870s migration (°Kanadier) worked for a meaningful °alternative to military service.

David Schulz was married in 1919 to Tina Friesen and was the father of seven sons and two daughters.   HJG

Henry J. Gerbrandt, *Adventure in Faith* (Altona: D. W. Friesen and Son's Ltd., 1970), 116-18, 128-37, 157-58, 164, 170, 177, 271ff, 305ff, 345ff.

Schweizerisches Mennonitisches Evangelisationskomitee (SMEK; Swiss Mennonite Mission Committee), was founded in 1951 as a commission of the Conférence Mennonite Suisse/Konferenz der Mennoniten in der Schweiz (Swiss Mennonite Conference). From its inception SMEK has worked closely with °Europäisches Mennonitisches Evangelisations-Komitee. By 1987 10 missionaries have been sent to Indonesia (medical and general church work in Irian Jaya since 1957), Ecuador (Bible translation into the Quechua language since 1967), and the Chad (1963-84, concentrating on child care, youth work and congregational assistance). These workers were all sent to assist non-Mennonite projects. From 1955 to 1980 SMEK worked in Austria with Mennonite Central Committee, later with the Mennonite Brethren congregations in Austria. In 1987 discussions are in process with the relief agency of the Swiss Mennonite Conference, the °Schweizerische Mennonitische Organisation, to achieve closer integration of work and objectives.   JBau

Menn. Jahrbuch (1984), 154.

Schweizerisches Mennonitisches Friedenskomitee/Comité Mennonite suisse pour la paix (SMFK/CMSP; Swiss Mennonite Peace Committee). While the question of military service for the Swiss Mennonites was dormant between 1945 and 1965, it became an issue after this period of time because of increasing contacts with North-American Menno-

nites and general sociocultural developments in Europe. A mandate from the Conférence Mennonite Suisse/Konferenz der Mennoniten in der Schweiz (Swiss Mennonite Conference) led in 1970 to the founding of a "Study Commission on Military Issues" (Studienkommission für Militärfragen). This commission became an official organ of the conference in 1974 with the task of pursuing and deepening awareness of the question of military service and °°nonresistance (*Wehrlosigkeit*) through regular updating of information and recommendations for the congregations.

According to the new statutes of the conference (1983), this committee, which in the process of extending its range of activities has adopted the new name of Swiss Mennonite Peace Committee (Schweizerisches Mennonitisches Friedenskomitee/Comité Mennonite Suisse pour la Paix) has the mandate to further the peace witness within and beyond the Mennonite congregations.

Chairpersons of the SMFK have been Paul Hofer (1970-83), Hanspeter Jecker (1983-87), and Paul Gerber (1987-). SMFK is a member of both °Church and Peace and the European Mennonite Peace Committee (°Europäisches Mennonitisches Friedenskomitee).   HJeck

Schwenckfeld, Caspar von (ME IV:1120). Born into a noble family in Ossig, Silesia, Caspar Schwenckfeld began service as advisor to Friedrich II, Duke of Liegnitz in 1518. In the same year, having read Luther's works, he underwent a religious awakening which drew him into humanist and Reformation circles.

Few documents from Schwenckfeld's early period remain, but in his major work, the *Admonition* of 1524, he maintains on essentially ethical grounds, that Luther's teaching on justification, the bondage of the will, the role of works, the law, and Christ's satisfaction result in immoral libertarianism.

In 1525 Schwenckfeld arrived at a spiritualist interpretation of the Lord's Supper, teaching that flesh can never participate in spirit, nor serve as a means in the work of the Spirit. His conclusions, supported by a vision experienced by his colleague Valentine °Crautwald, was that the words of institution are to be understood as saying, "My body is this, namely, food." Such food, he believed, was the glorified body of Christ, of which the individual became a spiritual partaker. Since all Christendom was in turmoil, in 1526 Schwenckfeld and his followers called for a *Stillstand*, a suspension of the observation of the Lord's Supper, until God should make his will known in the matter. This interpretation was fiercely rejected by Luther in 1526.

Schwenckfeld's theological debates continued throughout the next several years and in 1529, to save his Duke embarrassment, Schwenckfeld went into voluntary exile in Strasbourg. There he soon came into conflict with °°Bucer and by 1534 had begun what was to continue in large part a peripatetic life throughout the south German regions in and around Augsburg and Ulm until his death.

Just prior to his self-exile, he and Crautwald encountered Silesian Sabbatarian Anabaptism as propounded by Oswald °°Glait and Andreas °Fischer, and in Strasbourg he met other proponents of Anabaptism, among whom were Hans °°Denck, Melchior °Hoffman and Pilgram °Marpeck. (Schwenckfeld was initially on friendly terms with the latter but debated openly with him in the early 1540s.) These contacts directed him to consider the matter of baptism. Following his Spiritualist framework, Schwenckfeld insisted that by inner washing alone one is united with the body of Christ. Baptism should be for adults who understand its significance, but infant baptism although attacked by him, was not rejected.

Christological concerns, already with Schwenckfeld in 1525, were settled for him by 1538 when he composed his *Great Confession*. Schwenckfeld insisted that Jesus' humanity was not that of a creature but, rather, of heavenly origin, a celestial flesh in which a progressive deification took place, the divine nature more and more divinizing it.

By the grace of God fallen human beings may participate in the new creation through faith. Faith not only declares that one is justified but is knowledge (*Erkenntniss Christi*). Implanted in the believer, faith develops parallel to the way the divine progressed in Christ's celestial flesh, leading one through suffering into glory, if it is allowed free reign.

This distinction between the physical and the spiritual was the controlling force, as well, in Schwenckfeld's approach to the Scriptures and to the doctrine of the church. For him the outer voice is subordinated to the inner, the letter of the Scriptures to the spirit, words to the Word. The church too is understood as a spiritual entity. Salvation is ultimately a private matter, for which no institution can be responsible. Thus, the state is to play no role in the life of the church, nor is the church to insist that the state must maintain particular theological positions.　　PCE

Peter C. Erb, ed., *Schwenckfeld and Early Schwenckfeldianism* (Pennsburg, Pa.: Schwenkfelder Library, 1986); R. Emmet McLaughlin, *Caspar Schwenckfeld, Reluctant Radical: His Life to 1540* (New Haven: Yale U. Press, 1986); Selina Gerhard Schultz, *Caspar Schwenckfeld von Ossig (1489-1561)*, 4th ed., with introduction by Peter C. Erb (Pennsburg, The Board of Publication of the Schwenkfelder Church, 1977); Horst Weigelt, *The Schwenkfelders in Silesia*, trans. by Peter C. Erb (Pennsburg, Pa.: Schwenkfelder Library, 1985).

Sciences, Natural. From its origins, Mennonite thought has given scant attention to either the doctrine of °creation, natural theology, or the natural sciences. Scientific pursuits among Mennonites typically have reflected the ambient culture rather than elements intrinsic to the Anabaptist or Mennonite tradition (°acculturation). The history of Mennonite scientific pursuits thus parallels the vicissitudes of Mennonite involvement in other aspects of high culture, for example, the fine arts.

The magisterial reformers of the 16th c. did not count the natural sciences among their primary concerns, and the lack of interest in science among the early Anabaptist leaders is not unusual when viewed in that light. The Anabaptist movement labored under exceptional circumstances, however. Whatever incipient interest in scientific pursuits existed among Anabaptists was undermined by the rapid demise of the first generation of highly-educated leaders, the appeal of Anabaptism predominantly to peasants and artisans, and intensive °persecution. The free city of Strasbourg, a context in which such interests might have flourished, illustrates the problems peculiar to Anabaptism. Strasbourg initially served as a haven for dissenters of every stripe. During the tumultuous years of the 1520s, scientific activity (as gauged by publications and university enrollments) declined. By the time it eventually resumed in the 1530s and 1540s, however, the city had banished all Anabaptists, including Pilgram °Marpeck, the only first-generation Anabaptist leader with highly-developed "scientific" (engineering) skills. Thanks to the demand for his expertise, Marpeck lived to a ripe old age despite his Anabaptist faith. The extensive knowledge of natural phenomena presupposed by his work in mining, metallurgy, and city water works has, however, left scarcely a trace in his writings. The radical biblicism that characterizes the Anabaptist movement is illustrated by Menno Simons's theory of the °°incarnation. Wrongly linked with Aristotelianism, Menno's understanding of conception rejected all contemporary naturalistic explanations in favor of the only view he considered biblical, namely that the mother contributed no flesh to the foetus.

In the tolerant and prosperous atmosphere of the northern Netherlands of the 17th c., Mennonite interest in the natural sciences blossomed, at the level of reflection as well as in practice. The first article of the Dordrecht Confession (1632) opens with God and creation, in contrast to the °Schleitheim Confession (1527), which omits these topics altogether. During this period, many Dutch Mennonites entered the medical profession (°°medicine). To conclude their formal training, these physicians often wrote Latin dissertations on physiological or anatomical topics. The Bidloo family stands out with special prominence. Govert °°Bidloo wrote a splendid book of human anatomy and served as personal physician to William III, first in Holland and later in England, where he was elected a Fellow of the Royal Society of London. His nephew Nicolaas °°Bidloo founded the first medical school in Moscow under Tsar Peter the Great. In the physical sciences, the cobbler Dirk °°Rembrandtz van Nierop published books on navigation, mathematics, and astronomy. In addition to his technical interests, he sought to reconcile the sun-centered Copernican system of the universe with Scripture, and defended the new Cartesian natural philosophy.

In the 18th c., several Dutch Mennonites gave institutional form to their intellectual interests. Founded in 1735 to train preachers, the °°Amsterdam Mennonite Theological Seminary also offered courses in physics, mathematics, and natural philosophy taught by Klaas de °°Vries, Heere °°Oosterbaan, and Gerrit °°Hesselink. English natural theology also left an imprint on Mennonite circles. The Harlingen preachers Johannes °°Stinstra and Jan °°Boelaart translated into Dutch the works of Samuel °°Clarke, a prominent exponent of Newtonian natural theology in England. The wealthy merchant Pieter °°Teyler endowed the Teyler Foundation to encourage work in both science and religion. The Mennonite pastor Jan °°Nieuwenhuizen and his son Martin founded the °°Maatschappij tot Nut van 't Algemeen to make education accessible to the poor. Characterized by a strong Christian Enlightenment flavor, the society published many introductory works on a wide variety of topics, including physical geography, geology, and natural history. Both societies remain active in the late 1980s. The most prominent Dutch scientist of Mennonite descent was the geneticist Hugo de Vries (d. 1935), who proposed the "mutation theory" that laid the foundations of modern genetics.

In contrast to acculturation in The Netherlands, the cultural isolation of the Alsatian Mennonites of the late 18th and 19th c. not only preserved a sympathetic-magical worldview rooted in popular culture, traditional botanical lore, and °folk medicine, but also stimulated a highly-developed empirical science of agriculture. Similar successes characterize the Mennonite colonies of Russia, where the °°Agricultural Association promoted scientific cattle breeding.

Outside The Netherlands before the late 19th c., Mennonites rarely studied beyond grammar and secondary school, and seldom had the leisure to teach themselves science. In this respect, the Philadelphia astronomer and clock-maker David °°Rittenhouse, who came from a Mennonite background, was the exception rather than the rule. He not only made the best American calculation of solar parallax based on the transit of Venus for 1769, but also was active in Pennsylvania politics.

Outside The Netherlands and northern Germany, it was not until the turn of the 20th c. that Mennonites took a significant interest in higher education. The Halstead (Ks.) School, founded in 1883 as a teacher-training and college preparatory school, included several science courses in its four-year curriculum. Bethel College (Ks.) was founded in 1887-88; the Elkhart (Ind.) Institute of Science, Industry and the Arts (later Goshen College) in 1894. During the following decades, North American Mennonite higher education felt the influence of °Fundamentalism. Leaders like H. P. °°Krehbiel (GCM) and George R. °°Brunk (MC) sought to preserve their church conferences from the scientific outlook they saw embodied in the twin dangers of Darwinian °evolution and critical methods of °biblical scholarship. The Articles of Faith adopted by the Mennonite Church (MC) General Conference at Garden City, Mo. (1921), asserted the historicity and literal truth of Gn 1. Although related tensions closed Goshen College, 1923-24, such problems evidently had little long-term effect on the intellectual orientation of Mennonite students. At Bluffton College, for example, one fourth to one fifth of the students majored in science between the 1920s and 1960s. For most other Mennonite institutions, the growth of interest in science was a post-World War II phenomenon. Increases in the number of majors did not always translate into PhD degrees, however, for the service motif of Mennonite ethics channeled many students with scientific interests into secondary education and medical practice rather than research. Around 1960, one third to one half of Mennonites involved in nontheological graduate work were studying medicine.

In recent years, science programs in Mennonite colleges have given more emphasis to basic research. Although science majors represent a small proportion of the total number of graduates, the quality is high. Research-oriented professors in Mennonite undergraduate colleges have inspired "schools" of PhD students in such fields as plant pathology and solid state physics.

Although theological °pluralism, °urbanization, a decentralized church °polity, and opportunities for studying science at non-Mennonite schools make reliable figures difficult to obtain, scientists of Mennonite background have made their way onto the faculties and research staffs of major universities and scientific laboratories, and have served in the leadership of major scientific societies.

At the level of policy implications, Mennonite Central Committee (MCC) has been involved in matters of scientific import in at least two ways. Since the 1950s, the MCC Peace Section has coordinated efforts to think about the consequences of nuclear weapons. Between 1962 and 1976, the Teachers Abroad Program of MCC sent many science teachers to secondary schools in sub-Sahara Africa. **MHSh**

Michael Shank, "Mennonites and the Natural Sciences," forthcoming in *MQR*; Kenneth Thibodeau, "Science and the Reformation," *Sixteenth Century J.*, 7 (1976) 35-50; Cornelius Krahn, "Anabaptism and the Culture of the Netherlands," *Recovery*, 219-36; Maarten Schagen, *Naamlijst der Doopsgesinde Schrijveren en Schriften, 1539-1745* (Amsterdam, 1745); Dirk Rembrandtz van Nierop, *Des aertrijks beweging* (Amsterdam, 1661); W. W. Mijnhardt, "Veertig Jaar Cultuurbevordering: Teylers Stichting 1778-1815," in *Teyler' 1778-1978: Studies en bijdragen over Teylers Stichting naar aanleiding van het tweede eeuwfest* (Haarlem/Antwerpen: Schuyt, 1978); *Dictionary of Scientific Biography*, vol. 14 (New York, 1979), 95-105 (De Vries); vol. 15 (1980), 28-30 (Bidloo); Jean Séguy, "Religion and Agricultural Success," *MQR*, 47 (1973), 179-224; Brooke Hindle, *David Rittenhouse* (Princeton, 1964); George R. Brunk, "The Present Apostasy, *GH*, (Mar. 21, 1918), 931-32; James Juhnke, *People of Two Kingdoms* (Newton, 1975); Erwin Hiebert, *The Impact of Atomic Energy* (Newton, 1961).

See also Technology.

Sculpture. The following Mennonite artists have worked primarily in sculpture: Esther Augsburger, Robert S. Brunk, Norman Epp, Gathie Falk, Milton S. Good, Rod Harder, David Hostetler, Leslie Leupp (metalworking), John Mishler, Arlie J.Regier, Steven Simcox, Duane Wiens. For additional information about shows in which their work has been exhibited and for Mennonite artists in ceramics, see the entries on °Painting and °Ceramics. **RK**

Second Work of Grace. See Grace; Holiness Movement; Sanctification.

Secondary Schools (ME II:740). In the United States and Canada secondary schools are more commonly called high schools and usually contain grades 9-12, although some high schools may have only grades 10-12 and Canadian schools may include grade 13. Secondary schools, both °public and °private (church), have been established in other parts of the world but this article will deal only with those located in Canada, United States, and Puerto Rico (see also °mission schools, °education).

In North America the first secondary schools were religiously oriented although today most of the secondary schools are public schools. In the United States, public secondary schools developed largely after the Civil War. During the latter half of the 19th c., as state governments established public elementary schools, Mennonites endeavored to meet the next need, secondary education. Therefore, the first era for the establishment of Mennonite secondary schools was in the 1890-1920 period when academies were begun. Most of these later became colleges.

The second era for the development of Mennonite high schools began about 1940 and lasted approximately 20 years. The high schools of this era were established in direct opposition to public high schools. This differed from the earlier era which established academies because there were no public high schools. The schools founded after World War II were usually located in large Mennonite communities and were often organized and controlled by district conferences. The support for Mennonite high schools developed because of the pressures brought on by World War II, compulsory school attendance laws, and the gradual assimilation of Mennonites into society.

Most of the more recent Mennonite high schools were designed to protect, safeguard, and isolate Mennonite youth from secular society. If students were placed in a carefully controlled environment during the impressionable and formative teenage years, there was a better chance that they would remain in the Mennonite church. In addition, the Mennonite high schools were established as a reaction to the decline of the religious or moral element in public education. In many rural Mennonite communities the public high school student body was greatly influenced by Mennonites. However, with an increasingly industrialized society, with a growing mobility, and with the importation of threatening ideas into the Mennonite community there developed a greater need for Mennonite high schools. One school's stated purpose as it began early in this era was, "to counteract the influence of the public school on the youth, especially the far-reaching effects of militarism." Later this same school stated its purpose in a more positive way, as did most Mennonite high schools: "to correlate the teachings of the Bible with all other subjects, to provide a proper learning environment, to foster an evangelistic spirit, and to prepare young people for future service in the church and community." Although General Conference Mennonites in Canada are involved in a variety of secondary schools, in the United States, it is primarily the Mennonite Church (MC) and, to a lesser extent, the Mennonite Brethren, who have been involved with private Christian secondary schools.

Since the 1970s a national movement for the establishment of Christian schools has not left Mennonites unaffected. Even though every school is established for unique reasons, these latter schools were often formed as a reaction to public school conditions. None of these schools were established by conferences but by congregations or special interest groups.

The 25-year record of the enrollment in Mennonite Church (MC) high schools, 1961-86, shows almost constant growth, despite a declining Mennonite Church (MC) high school population pool in the

SECONDARY SCHOOLS
William Hooley

Table 1. Academies (secondary schools) which later became colleges, 1893-1920

School	Location	Established	Control
Bethel College	North Newton, Ks.	1893	General Conference Mennonite Church
Bluffton College	Bluffton, Ohio	1914	General Conference Mennonite Church
Eastern Mennonite College	Harrisonburg, Va.	1917	Mennonite Church Board of Education
Freeman Junior College	Freeman, S.D.	1903	Corp. of Mennonite Churches of S.D.
Goshen College	Goshen, Ind.	1903	Mennonite Church Board of Education
Messiah College	Grantham, Pa.	1909	Brethren in Christ
Tabor College	Hillsboro, Ks.	1908	Mennonite Brethren
Upland College	Upland, Cal.	1920	Brethren in Christ

SECONDARY SCHOOLS

Table 2. North American Mennonite Secondary Schools, 1987

School	Location	Established	Control
Academia Menonita Betania	Aibonito, P.R.	1947	Convention of Mennonite Churches of Puerto Rico
°Academia Menonita Summit Hills	San Juan, P.R.	1961	Summit Hills Mennonite Church
Anchor Christian High School	Shippensburg, Pa.	1972	Anchor Christian School Bd. of Directors
°Belleville Mennonite High School	Belleville, Pa.	1945	Belleville Mennonite School Bd. of Trustees
°Bethany Christian High School	Goshen, Ind.	1954	Ind.-Mich. Mennonite Conference
°Central Christian High School	Kidron, Ohio	1961	Ohio Conference of the Mennonite Church
°Christopher Dock Mennonite High School	Lansdale, Pa.	1953	Franconia Mennonite Conference
Clinton Christian High School	Goshen, Ind.	1950	Clinton Christian School Association
Conestoga Christian School	Morgantown, Pa.	1952	Conestoga Christian School Bd. of Trustees
°Eastern Mennonite High School	Harrisonburg, Pa.	1917	Virginia Mennonite Conference
Elliott Prairie Christian School	Woodburn, Ore.	1948	Hopewell Mennonite Church
Faith Mennonite High School	Kinzers, Pa.	1975	Faith Mennonite High School Bd. of Directors
°Freeman Academy	Freeman, S.D.	1903	Freeman Academy Board of Trustees
Greenwood Mennonite Church School	Greenwood, Del.	1928	Greenwood Mennonite Churches
Hartville Christian High School	Hartville, Ohio	1956	Hartville Conservative Mennonite Church
°Iowa Mennonite School	Kalona, Iowa	1944	Iowa-Nebraska Mennonite Conference
Johnstown Christian School	Hollsopple, Pa.	1944	Johnstown Christian School Board
Kraybill High School	Mt. Joy, Pa.	1948	Lancaster Mennonite Conference
°Lancaster Mennonite High School	Lancaster, Pa.	1942	Lancaster Mennonite Conference
Maranatha Christian School	Watsontown, Pa.	1971	Maranatha Christian School Corp.
Mennonite Brethren Collegiate Institute	Winnipeg, Man.	1945	Mennonite Brethren
Mennonite Collegiate Institute	Gretna, Man.	1889	Assoc. of Mennonite Churches of Manitoba
Mennonite Educational Institute	Clearbrook, B.C.	1944	Mennonite Brethren
Mountain View Christian School	Springs, Pa.	1973	Beachy Amish Mountain View Church
Paradise Mennonite School	Hagerstown, Pa.	1958	Washington County, Md. Mennonite
Plumstead Christian School	Plumsteadville, Pa.	1948	Plumstead Christian School Bd. of Trustees
°Rockway Mennonite Collegiate	Kitchener, Ont.	1945	Rockway Mennonite School Association
°Sarasota Christian School	Sarasota, Fla.	1958	Sarasota Mennonite Churches
Shalom Christian Academy High School	Chambersburg, Pa.	1976	Shalom Christian Academy High School
Terre Hill Mennonite High School	Terre Hill, Pa.	1985	Terre Hill Mennonite High School Board
°United Mennonite Educational Institute	Leamington, Ont.	1945	General Conference Mennonites of Ontario
°Western Mennonite School	Salem, Ore.	1945	Pacific Coast Mennonite Conference

°Member of Mennonite Secondary Education Council.

1970s and 1980s. By the 1980s one out of three Mennonite Church (MC) youth is in a Mennonite high school. From 25 percent in 1961-62, the percentage of Mennonite Church adherents of high-school-age who attended Mennonite high schools dropped to 20 percent in 1969-70, but has risen steadily since that year, reaching 36.6 percent in 1986.

Mennonite secondary schools of the 1980s have a range of philosophies and emphases. However, most would not philosophically support the earlier premise of existing primarily to protect Mennonite young people. The emphases would be much more on integrating faith with all other dimensions of life and to prepare for service in the church and world. The Mennonite Board of Education's (MC) philosophy of education states, "The people of God are a distinct people with a distinct calling and unique educational goals. They must educate to transmit their history and make their identity clear; train in the skills needed to carry on the work they consider important; teach the values they consider important; help the young develop his/her own personal view of reality."

The Mennonite Secondary Educational Council was officially organized in 1961 as the body to which many of the Mennonite high schools belong. MSEC has established the following goals for itself: (1) to stimulate long-range planning and goal setting; (2) to promote understanding of and growth in Christian education with a Mennonite-Anabaptist perspective; (3) to provide and/or direct eductional research on behalf of the member schools; (4) to stimulate curriculum development efforts; (5) to provide for personal fellowship of chief school administrators; (6) to establish and maintain a strong relationship with Mennonite Board of Education in order to coordinate the educational efforts of the schools as they relate to the colleges and congregations, and (7) to organize and carry out efforts beneficial to the individual schools, administrators, board members, faculties, and students. These purposes are regularly carried out through a number of programs and activities including an annual Mennonite high school music festival, a biennial teachers' convention, biennial Mennonite high school board workshop, and regular reports to and meetings with the Mennonite Board of Education (MC). WDH

Harold E. Bauman, "Why Do We Have Church High Schools?" paper presented at the meeting of the Mennonite Board of Education, Lansdale, Pa., Oct., 1965; "Census of Mennonite High-School-Age Youth, 1962-87" and "Mennonite High School Enrollments, 1961-87," unpublished material compiled by Mennonite Board of Education (MC), 1987; John E. Hartzler, Education Among the Mennonites of America (Danvers, Ill.: Central Publishing Board, 1925); Silas Hertzler, "Attendance in Mennonite Secondary Schools and Colleges," MQR, 27 (1952), 280-98; idem, "Mennonite Parochial Schools," in Proceedings of the Seventh Annual Conference on Mennonite Cultural Problems (Tabor College, Hillsboro, Ks., 1949), 68-79; William D. Hooley, "A Comparison of the Values, Attitudes, and Beliefs of Mennonite Youth Who Attended A Church-Related High School and Those Who Attended Public High Schools" (DEd diss., Western Michigan U., 1974); Donald B. Kraybill, Ethnic Education: The Impact of Mennonite Schooling (San Francisco: R and E Research Associates, Inc., 1977); Ira E. Miller, "The Development and the Present Status of Mennonite Secondary and Higher Education in the United States and Canada" (DEd diss., Temple U., 1953); A. D. Wenger, Who Should Educate Our Children? (pamphlet, n.p., Mar. 24, 1926); current statistics are found in MC Yearbook (biennial); addresses of GCM schools are found in GCM Handbook.

See also Weierhof.

Sectarianism and Cultural Mandate. Mennonites have, possibly from almost the beginning, been concerned about their identity in relationship to the world, and especially the cultural forms it takes. Separation from the world, the idea of two kingdoms, °nonconformity to the world, and rejection of domination by state and state church, are only a few of the emphases which have expressed this concern. A central theological and normative thrust therefore has been how the "colony of heaven" or the "people of God" has been expressed in history and what God really desires of his covenanted °community.

Non-Mennonite scholars and church officials have been less unsure about what the Mennonite °tradition really was: (1) The Roman Catholic tradition has defined the Anabaptist-Mennonite stream as heretical, irrelevant, and hence a sect. (2) Protestant scholars and ecclesiastics have been less sanguine, but have still maintained that it was a sectarian movement, emphasizing marginal and deviant factors at the expense of central historical Christian teachings. (3) Sociologists and church historians have attempted to be more neutral and objective, defining sectarian in neutral terms and in fact proposing that the sectarian may be closer to the essence of Christianity than the "mainstream churches" of Christendom.

The essential difference between sect and church was that the church expresses God's design through cultural forms and by dominance while the sect is defined as expressing God's design though rejection of cultural dominance by forming voluntary congregations of believers (Troeltsch; B. Johnson).

One of the most trenchant sociological and theological analyses of the sectarian-culture debate has been H. Richard °Niebuhr's "Christ and culture" typology in which he designates the Mennonites as desiring a "Christ against culture" (Niebuhr). His thesis that the Mennonites have opposed culture is, however, a thorough misunderstanding of Mennonites, because they never have rejected culture as such, only those expressions which they think hinder the kingdom of God expressing itself. Hence "selective °acculturation" is a far better analysis of Mennonite attitude toward culture (Eaton). Mennonites have always subordinated specific cultural forms to the primacy of community life (Redekop, 1976). The wide range of selective acculturation by Mennonite groups, and the significance they attach to the subtle variations proves the point.

The sectarian image, stance and identification has been more of an occupation of outsiders, the domain of academics and ecclesiastics. "Entering the mainstream culture" is hence not a self-conscious Mennonite relinquishment of the "sectarian" stance, rather the process of the continual adoption of cultural forms in its life. But the question remains—how does cultural adaptation affect the "spiritual covenant"?

The enduring debate for Mennonites has been, "What does it mean to be faithful to God's Kingdom?" The inevitable development of particular subcultural forms, i.e., ethnic traits (Redekop, "Ethnic", 1984) has been a major dilemma for Mennonites, for they have been unable to rest easy with the fact that any religious life expresses itself in a particular cultural form. Hence the debate about Mennonites being a sectarian or ethnic group or a religious church, expecially as exacerbated by the inroads of °Fundamentalism and °evangelicalism (Kraus), has intensified in recent years. This debate has of course been to a large extent the result of adopting the prevailing Christian popular theology. This is doubly ironic because while this debate and self-doubt is going on, Anabaptist-Mennonite theology and belief system is being increasingly propounded by non-Mennonites as the most relevant and exciting system of theology, especially by proponents of °liberation and feminist theologies.

How do Mennonites today understand themselves and what is their °identity? Using the scholarly literature of North American analysis as our guide, though that may be an inadequate base, we find that earlier researchers have indeed adopted the view that Mennonites were a sect group, and that the beginning of the missionary thrust signaled the end of the sectarian stance (Kauffman, 1931). More subsequent research and theorizing attempted to analyse and describe the loss of sectarianism on the part of Mennonites (Harder, Redekop, Kyle).

This was followed by an understanding, spearheaded by E. K. Francis, of the Mennonites as a religious movement becoming an ethnic group. Many rank-and-file Mennonites as well as religious leaders, influenced by evangelical Christianity, accepted this description as fact, and actively began to oppose and reject the ethnic nature of Christianity, not aware of the fact that they were saying thereby that Christianity could be 100 percent American and be Christian, but could not be some unusual mixture of European and American and still be Christian.

Recent Mennonite analysis of self-identity proposes that the Anabaptists and Mennonites were a movement, and that the identifying traits or boundaries of the group are not the cultural forms, but the ideology (the "Anabaptist Vision") which served and serves to orient the Mennonites to their true heritage. Thus there can be a pluralism among Mennonite communities because the cultural forms are not as important as the "unifying" vision of the "radical covenant." Hence the entrance of Mennonites into the professions, and urban living is possible without destroying the Mennonite "colony of heaven."

There is a considerable crisis in Mennonite identity in the late 1980s, as indicated by the literature on it (Redekop and Steiner, 1988). A recent conference on Mennonite self-identity (1986) attests to the importance of the issue. Participants proposed that sect and ethnicity are not adequate to define Mennonitism, that we must look at the ideology (the covenant) to understand what it means to be a Mennonite. In the realm of theology and Christian faith, Mennonites are increasingly engaging the larger Christian community and challenging many presuppositions but on the sociocultural level, Mennonites still tend to remain isolated.

Does the attempt at total faithfulness result in a particular life-style and cultural form, or does life-style have little or nothing to do with faith? If the former answer is taken, the ethnic question will continue to plague Mennonites (Redekop, "Ethic", 1984). If the latter is taken, the issue of identity will fade as the impact of this belief makes itself felt in the congregation. Mennonite understanding of the implications of the "two kingdom" theology for cultural expression and forms has never been clear, because of the anti-intellectualism that has developed, and precisely because of the way "separation from the world" itself affects the analysis. This issue remains one of the most urgent problems in Mennonite life and thought. For additional theological analysis see the works by Yoder, Erb, and Burkholder as listed below. CWR

J. Lawrence Burkholder, "The Problem of Social Responsibility from the Perspective of the Mennonite Church," (PhD diss., Princeton Theological Seminary, 1958; published Elkhart, Ind.: IMS, 1988); Joseph Eaton, "Controlled Acculturation," American Sociological Review, 17 (June 1952); Peter C. Erb, "A Reflection on Mennonite Theology in Canada" JMS, 1 (1983), 179-90; D. K. Francis, In Search of Utopia (Glencoe: Free Press, 1955); Leland Harder, "The Quest for Equilibrium in an Established Sect" (PhD diss., Northwestern U., 1962); Benton Johnson, "A Critical Appraisal of the Church-Sect Typology," American Sociological Review, 17 (June 1952); E. G. Kauffman, Mennonite Missionary Interest (Berne: Mennonite Book Concern, 1931); C. Norman Kraus, ed., Evangelicalism and Anabaptism (Scottdale, 1979); Richard G. Kyle, From Sect to Denomination (Hillsboro: Center for Mennonite Brethren Studies, 1985); H. Richard Niebuhr, Christ and Culture (New York: Harper and Brothers, 1951; Calvin Redekop, "The Mennonite Identity Crisis" JMS, 2 (1984), 87-103, "The Sectarian Black and White World" (PhD diss., U. of Chicago, 1959), Free Church and Seductive Culture (Scottdale, 1976), and "Anabaptism and the Ethnic Ghost" MQR, 58 (1984), 133-46; Calvin Redekop and Sam J. Steiner, Mennonite Identity: Historical and Contemporary Perspectives (Lanham, Md.: University Press of America, 1988); Ernst Troeltsch, The Social Teachings of the Christian Churches (New York: MacMillan, 1931); Joachim Wach, Church, Denomination and Sect (Evanston: Seabury-Western, 1946); John H. Yoder, The Priestly Kingdom (Notre Dame U. Press, 1984).

See also Church-State Relations; Government; Literature; Nonconformity; Political Attitudes; Restitutionism; Sociopolitical Activism.

Selbstschutz (ME IV:1124). The Selbstschutz (self-defense) began as a spontaneous movement by the Mennonites in the Ukraine to protect lives and property during the period of violent anarchy following the °Russian Revolution. During the German occupation (April-November, 1918) hitherto secret Selbstschutz units were trained openly under German supervision mainly in Molotschna, Chortitza, Nikolaipol, and Sagradovka. If and when the German troops withdrew, these militia units were to become operative.

The Molotschna Selbstschutz proved to be the only one of any military significance. As the largest and wealthiest Mennonite colony, Molotschna had the most to lose from terrorist depredations. Fear of imminent disaster grew as local acts of looting and murder multiplied and refugees from nearby Schönfeld-Brazol reported harrowing experiences. The more militant Mennonites were further influenced by the glamorous presence of German troops and by the militancy of nearby non-Mennonite German colonists. They also welcomed the compromise resolution approved at the Lichtenau °°Allgemeine Mennonitische Bundeskonferenz (July 1918) which affirmed the ideal of °non-resistance but refused to condemn Mennonites who took up arms. The centuries-old principle of non-resistance seemed suddenly irrelevant in a life-and-death crisis.

Aided and abetted by the White Army, the Molotschna *Selbstschutz* took the field with a successful attack against Makhnovite (ME III:430) forces at Chernigovka (Dec. 6, 1918). During the winter of 1918-19 the *Selbstschutz*, now an "army" of 2,700 infantry divided into 20 companies (of which 7 were non-Mennonite Germans from Prischib) and 300 cavalry, held a thinly-stretched "front" against Makhno's forces at Blumental, 20 mi. (33 km.) north of Molotschna. In early March 1919, Makhno combined with the advancing Red Army to force the *Selbstschutz* to retreat and disband in Halbstadt.

What had begun as a police action ended, in the eyes of the Bolshevik government, as rebellious fighting against the Red Army. Having opted out of the political process four centuries earlier, the Mennonites had opted back in militarily and shown that "the logic of circumstances spoke more strongly than the logic of theology," according to one historian. In tragically provocative conditions and against the will of the majority, Mennonites had sacrificed the concept of the suffering church to the instinct for self-preservation.   AR

John B. Toews, "The Origins and Activities of the Mennonite *Selbstschutz* in the Ukraine (1918-1919)," *MQR*, 46 (1972), 5-39, the most comprehensive and analytical treatment of the *Selbstschutz* to date, summarized in idem, *Czars, Soviets and Mennonites* (Newton, 1982), 79-94; J. P. Epp, "The Mennonite Selbstschutz in the Ukraine: An Eyewitness Account," intro. and trans. by J. B. Toews in *Menn. Life*, 26 (July 1971), 138-42; Dietrich Neufeld, *A Russian Dance of Death: Revolution and Civil War in the Ukraine*, trans. and ed. by Al Reimer (Winnipeg: Hyperion Press, 1977), 69-80, 133-36; Bernhard J. Dick, "Something About the Selbstschutz of the Nonresistant Mennonites in South Russia," trans. and ed. by Harry Loewen and Al Reimer in *JMS*, 4 (1986), 135-42; George G. Thielman, "The Mennonite *Selbstschutz* in the Ukraine During the Revolution," *The New Review: A Journal of East-European History*, 10 (March 1970), 50-60, weakened by factual errors and imprecise generalizations.

Self-Education. With the exception of the °°Amsterdam Mennonite Theological Seminary in The Netherlands which began in 1735 and the °°Witmarsum Theological Seminary (1921-31), graduate-level °seminary education for Mennonite pastors did not arise until after World War II. In the 18th, 19th, and first half of the 20th c., North American Mennonite pastors were chosen out of the congregation without the benefit of formal theological or biblical education. However, those chosen were recognized spiritual leaders who often had formal training equal to or a little beyond the average congregational member. In the late 19th and early 20th c. °Bible institute training became accessible to some, especially among Mennonite Brethren and General Conference Mennonites.

These pastors educated themselves in the pastoral ministry. They found ways to increase their knowledge and skills for ministry. Like Orie O. °Miller, a dedicated lay leader and executive for Mennonite Central Committee and the Eastern Mennonite Board of Missions and Charities, these pastors read

their Bible through each year. Others memorized Scripture while resting horses in the midst of farm work. A few educated themselves by extensive reading. For example, Christian E. Charles and John W. Burkholder of the Lancaster Mennonite Conference read 300 pages a week throughout their lives. J. B. Smith, the first president of Eastern Mennonite College, gained much of his training through correspondence courses.

As a rural people in the 19th c., Mennonite farmers had more time available for reading during the winter months. North American Mennonite pastors read available books during the evening hours. As a result they were highly esteemed leaders in the community. They observed other pastors at work and learned by listening. They related their learnings to the context of their ministry.

Following World War II graduate-level seminary education gained momentum in the Mennonite churches of North America. However, as late as 1980 only 25 percent of Mennonite Church (MC) pastors and 35 percent of General Conference Mennonite Church pastors were seminary graduates. To provide training for the others, seminars and ministers' week programs emerged. In the Mennonite Conference of Ontario and Quebec (MC) a "Conference-Based Theological Education" program began in 1977. The Atlantic Coast, Franconia, and Lancaster conferences developed a Conference-Based Theological Education program in 1980. A similar program emerged in Kansas. In Central America, South America, Africa, and Asia, Mennonites began adapting °Theological Education by Extension as a means of training pastors without seminary education.   PMZ

See also Bible Colleges and Institutes; Pastoral Education.

SELFHELP Crafts, a program sponsored by the Mennonite Central Committee (MCC) and designed to provide employment for people in developing countries by marketing internationally handicraft items these people can make but are unable to sell locally. In earlier years it was referred to as the "Needlework Program" and in the 1970s it was called "MCC Self Help Program." In 1980 the name was officially changed to "SELFHELP Crafts."

The program has an organization structure loosely parallel to that of MCC with international, Canadian, and United States divisions. This allows for greater flexibility in purchasing and marketing of crafts from various countries and from certain overseas projects not permitted to be imported into both countries. The international office, at Akron, Pa., provides guidelines and researches and approves overseas projects. The headquarters and warehouse for the Canadian program are in New Hamburg, Ont., and the United States program's headquarters and warehouse are at Akron, Pa.

The program is operated on a nonprofit basis but is not subsidized by MCC funds. Markup to cover the costs of shipping, customs and overhead expenses is added to the basic price paid to the producer. Special care is taken to select projects where local artisans are treated fairly and paid reasonable wages in relation to their community wage scale. The program works closely with MCC overseas development programs, church, and mission projects. The SELFHELP Crafts idea began in 1946 when Edna Ruth °Byler was asked by poverty-stricken women in Puerto Rico and by MCC workers Mary Lauver and Olga Martens to take needlework items back to the United States to sell so the Puerto Rican women could buy food and clothing for their families. Edna Byler operated it as a private undertaking until 1962 when it became part of the total relief, rehabilitation, and development program of MCC. She continued on a part-time basis until retirement in 1970. Since 1971 MCC-appointed full-time directors have been Janet Yoder (1971-74), Nick Dyck (1975-77), and Paul Leatherman (1977-). Herman Neff has served as director of the Canadian program since 1981, when Canadian operations were centralized from provincial centers.

From a small beginning the program has grown very rapidly with yearly sales increases as high as 69 percent. Direct purchases of crafts from producers (excluding all costs of distribution), totalled $53,000 in 1971 and grew by 1987 to more than two million dollars paid to more than 100 producer groups in 30 countries. The income benefited more than 30,000 people.

One of the factors contributing to the rapid growth was the SELFHELP and Thrift Shop outlets established locally in various communities throughout the United States and Canada. In 1987 there were more than 120 outlets; they accounted for more than 50 percent of the total sales and provided people with a tangible opportunity for involvement in the work of MCC. Volunteers are an invaluable part of all aspects of the program. SELFHELP Crafts also markets items through sales to other nonprofit shops and to commercial customers, through a large showroom in Ephrata, Pa., through °relief sales, through displays at churches and organizations, and through local SELFHELP representatives.

A significant side effect of the program is that it helps to preserve traditional handicraft skills which might otherwise be lost. SELFHELP Crafts is primarily concerned with the needs and welfare of the producers rather than the consumers and considers the educational aspects dealing with injustice, poverty and international understanding to be an integral part of the program. It seeks to carry out the goals of MCC by trying to meet human need serving in the name of Christ. JY

MCC Workbooks, 1971-87 (Akron, Pa.: MCC); brochures and filmstrips available from SELFHELP Crafts offices in Akron, Pa., and New Hamburg, Ont.; lists of Thrift Shop and SELFHELP Crafts stores are published biennially in MC Yearbook.

Semarang, Indonesia, is a port city with an estimated population of 1,026,671 (1988) located on the ne. coast of the island of Java, roughly 500 km. (308 mi.) east of °Jakarta, the capital city of Indonesia. As the capital city of the province of Central Java, Semarang has many important roles to play.

The synod offices of the Persatuan Gereja-Gereja Kristen Muria Indonesia (Muria [Mennonite] Christian Church of Indonesia) are located in Semarang,

as are three of its congregations. The formation of the first Muria congregation in Semarang in 1958 represented the first major push of the church beyond the Muria area.

The most prominent ministry of the Muria church based in Semarang is their ICHTHUS ratio station. A congregation of the Gereja Injili di Tanah Java (Javanese Mennonite Conference) has also been established in Semarang. LMY

Seminaries (ME IV:499). The first Mennonite theological seminary was the Doopsgezind Seminarie (°°Amsterdam Mennonite Theological Seminary) begun in 1735 to educate for ministry in Doopsgezind congregations, in cooperation with the Theological Faculty of the U. of Amsterdam, where Reformed and Lutheran churches also were involved. Before 1811 this seminary was sponsored by the Mennonite Church in Amsterdam, and since then by the °Algemeene Doopsgezinde Sociëteit (general conference of Dutch Mennonites). Through using university resources, work is offered toward master's and doctoral degrees. Currently (1987) three Mennonite professors, in pastoral theology, practical theology, and systematic theology and Anabaptist studies, together with the university faculty serve approximately 35 students, including a growing number of women and students pursuing lay ministry preparation.

The largest center of Mennonite theological studies currently is the program called the Associated Mennonite Biblical Seminaries in Elkhart, Ind. This association since 1958 includes Goshen Biblical Seminary, formerly Goshen College Biblical Seminary, of the Mennonite Church (MC), which developed first as a Bible school that was part of Goshen College. By 1946 it was called a seminary and began to offer a graduate-level seminary program. The other partner is Mennonite Biblical Seminary of the General Conference Mennonite Church (GCM), preceded by the "Christliche Bildungsanstalt der Mennoniten-Gemeinschaft" at Wadsworth, Ohio (1868-78), the Witmarsum Theological Seminary at Bluffton College, Ohio (1921-31), and then Mennonite Biblical Seminary as affiliated with Bethany Biblical Seminary in Chicago (1945-58). Since 1969 the two schools use a common campus in Elkhart, Ind. This program offers courses leading to a variety of master's degrees, including the Master of Divinity (MDiv), the Master of Arts (MA) in Peace Studies, and the Master of Arts in Theological Studies. Courses include biblical, historical, theological, and ethical studies, as well as studies in missions and evangelism and various pastoral leadership ministries. Twenty-eight regular faculty members serve approximately 200 students, including a growing number of women and some who do not anticipate pastoral ministry. An Institute of Mennonite Studies provides sponsorship and supervision for numerous research projects and some publications relating to Mennonite faith, life, and work. A Mission Training Center gives special impetus to equipping people in mission, evangelism, church planting, and transcultural ministries.

Eastern Mennonite Seminary at Harrisonburg, Va., is an outgrowth of the Bible curriculum of °°Eastern Mennonite College. By 1948 postgraduate courses were being offered, by 1960 a full three-year graduate program was operating, and by 1968 the MDiv degree was offered. Master of Arts in Religion and the Master of Arts in Church Ministries degrees were added later. Fifteen full-time or part-time faculty members serve ca. 100 students. A Center for Evangelism and Church Planting is an added feature.

The Mennonite Brethren Biblical Seminary at Fresno, Cal. serves the Mennonite Brethren since 1955. It offers MDiv and various MA degrees. Twenty-one full-time and part-time faculty members serve ca. 150 students. A Center for Mennonite Brethren Studies (1974) and a Center for Training in Mission/Evangelism (1985) are adjunct programs.

In 1965 a Council of Mennonite Seminaries was convened and organized as a channel of communication among Mennonite seminaries in the United States.

Canadian graduate-level Mennonite theological studies are offered at Conrad Grebel College in Waterloo, Ont., at Canadian Mennonite Bible College, Mennonite Brethren Bible College, and the Mennonite Studies Center in Winnipeg; and at the Mennonite Center of Regent College in Vancouver, B.C.

Mennonites of Indonesia are served by the Akademi Kristen Wiyata Wacana (AKWW) Theological College and Seminary at Pati. This was originally a cooperative venture (founded 1965) of the Gereja Injili de Tanah Jawa (GITJ; Evangelical Church of Java) and the Persatuan Gereja-Gereja Kristen Muria Indonesia (GKMI, United Muria Indonesia Christian Church) with the support of the Europäisches Mennonitisches Evangelisationskomitee (EMEK) and Mennonite Central Committee. The GITJ had first opened a Bible school in Pati in 1950 which later developed into the larger seminary vision, which in turn encountered both problematic internal differences and external government regulation.

The Universitas Kristen Duta Wacana (Messenger of the Word Christian University) until recently incorporated the Bale Wiyata Institute of Malang, East Java, which a number of Indonesian pastors had attended. Since 1988 it is known as Sekolah Tinggi Agama Kristen Wiyata Wacana (Disciple of the Word Upper School for the Christian Religion). Both GITJ and GKMI are constituent members of this university with each supplying several board members, numerous students, and at least one faculty member in Old Testament. This school is located in °Yogyakarta, and is a cooperative venture with other denominations. (See Alle G. Hoekema, "Developments in the Education of Preachers in the Indonesian Mennonite Churches," *MQR*, 59 (1985), 398-409.)

Mennonites in South America, with some external assistance from North American Mennonite Church and General Conference Mennonite mission boards developed the Seminario Evangélico Menonita de Teología (Mennonite Theological Seminary, °°ME IV:1106) in Montevideo, Uruguay, in 1955. While not functioning at full graduate levels it served in the training of congregational leaders, both in Spanish and in German, for Mennonites in Paraguay, Argentina, Uruguay, and Brazil. For political reasons this seminary, after 20 years of significant ministry,

was closed in 1974. In a modified form, under Paraguayan Mennonite leadership, another seminary has emerged in Asunción, and functions there in a theological training program known as Centro Evangélico Menonita de Teología Asunción (Mennonite Theological Center). Its 5 professors were serving 35 students in 1986.

The École de Théologie Evangélique de Kinshasa (ETEK, Kinshasa Protestant School of Theology) first opened in 1968 to serve theological and pastoral training needs, especially in Zaire, "with the purpose of edifying the Protestant Church that it may respond to African and universal needs." In 1970 it moved to its own new campus. This has developed into the Institute Supérieur Théologique de Kinshasa (ISTK, Kinshasa Higher Institute of Theology) sponsored by six constituent conferences of which two are Mennonite (1986). Served by an international faculty, it seeks to offer authentically African Christian training in biblical studies, theology, history, practical theology, and Christian education. It emphasizes African studies, psychology and counseling, language studies, and modern methods of communication. It has university level courses leading to a Bachelor of Theology degree. Since 1982 it offers courses in library science leading to the Master in Library Science, and it has a Women's School offering "a comprehensive program preparing women for church-related ministries." Eleven full-time professors plus visiting professors and five teachers in the Women's School instruct nearly 100 students in Theology, 5 in Library Science and 55 in Women's School (1987). A discerned trend in this school is some shift from focus on pastoral education to a more general scope of training. Mennonites of Zaire are involved in faculty leadership as well as in the student body.

The Osaka Biblical Seminary in Japan was established in 1960 by the Baptist General Conference mission, the North American Baptist mission, and the Mennonite Brethren mission, its forerunner having been the Mennonite Brethren Bible School founded in 1957. It focused on the training of pastors, evangelists, Christian educators, and missionaries with much of its work done as in-service training. In 1971, however, the Mennonite Brethren Conference of Japan having decided to withdraw from OBS, began, with one student, their own school in the Ishibashi Church, calling it Evangelical Biblical Seminary. In 1987 it had a student body of 6-8 and a faculty of two, one of whom is an expatriate. It is notable that of about 25 pastors serving MB churches in Japan, all are graduates of this school, a base for remarkable unity. The seminary maintains a strong emphasis on spirituality and evangelism, and exhibits a unique blend of North American and Japanese characteristics in its program.

Listing Mennonite and Brethren in Christ leadership training programs covering Africa, Asia, Latin America, and the Caribbean in 1986, Donald R. Jacobs makes it clear that the training of Mennonites for church leadership has become a worldwide phenomenon, that much of this is done at a °Bible college or Bible institute level, that the development of °theological education by extension (TEE) has become a useful design, and that such programs among Mennonites are to be found in Central African Republic, Kenya, Tanzania, Zambia, and Zimbabwe as well as in Zaire in Africa; in India, the Philippines, and Taiwan, as well as Indonesia and Japan in Asia; and in Argentina, Boliva, Chile, Colombia, Ecuador, Peru, Uruguay, Venezuela, Belize, Costa Rica, Dominican Republic, El Salvador, Guatemala, Haiti, Honduras, Jamaica, Mexico, Nicaragua, Panama, Puerto Rico, and Trinidad as well as in Paraguay in Central and South America. Especially notable is the work of Seminario Ministerial de Liderazgo Anabautista (SEMILLA; Anabaptist Ministerial Leaders Seminary). EW

MC Yearbook (1986-87), 126; GMC Handbook (1987), 140-43; Wittlinger, Piety and Obedience (1978). 436ff; MQR, 59 (1985), 398; Menn. Rep. (May 23, 1988), 10.

See also Pastoral Education.

Seminario Ministerial de Liderazgo Anabautista (SEMILLA; Anabaptist Ministerial Leaders Seminary). See Consulta Anabautista Menonita Centroamericana.

Sermon on the Mount (Mt 5:1-7; cf. Lk 6:17-49). These passages of Scripture are often seen as pointing to the essence of the Anabaptist understanding of the Christian way, especially in contrast to mainstream Protestantism with its roots in the Lutheran and Calvinist °reformations. Whereas Luther emphasized salvation by °faith and °grace alone, the Anabaptists placed emphasis on the °obedience of faith. To their critics this meant the introduction of a new °legalism and works righteousness and therefore made them just as guilty of error as the Catholics. The Anabaptists, of course, did not treat the Sermon on the Mount as a separate or special category of Scripture, elevating some New Testament writings above others the way Luther did with some of the writings of Paul and John's gospel. They did have a clear understanding of the priority of the New Testament over the Old and of the centrality of Christ. This understanding derived in part from the Sermon on the Mount. But the sermon did not become a canon within the canon of the New Testament in any explicit sense.

Nevertheless the references to the Sermon on the Mount by various Anabaptist writers are frequent. The Beatitudes are cited quite frequently, especially Mt 5:10-12 (in relation to the Anabaptists' experience of °suffering and °persecution). Other references which are cited most frequently are 5:33-37 (integrity and the °°oath); 5:38-48 (°nonresistance and °love of enemies); 6:24 (serving God or mammon); 6:33 (seeking first the °kingdom of God); 7:13-14 (the narrow way); 7:15-20 (false prophets are known by their fruits); and 7:21-23 (doing the will of the Father). These references demonstrate a heavy Anabaptist emphasis on the teachings of the Sermon on the Mount. Howard Loewen has demonstrated the predominance of citations of Matthew in most Mennonite °confessions of faith. Within Matthew the Sermon on the Mount is most extensively referred to and within the Sermon the references to love for one's enemies (5:38-48) and the section on integrity and the oath (5:33-37) predominate (Loewen, Confessions, 35, 250-57/58). These citations are perhaps not surprising because

they focus on doctrinal distinctives of Mennonites. On the other hand, the references to persecution and suffering tend to fall away in the confessions of faith, perhaps because of changing circumstances.

One of the most significant threats to the central role of the Sermon on the Mount in Mennonite thought and practice has been the influence of °dispensational theology, especially in North America but also to a considerable degree among the Russian Mennonites at the beginning of the 20th century. Dispensational theology created a method of °biblical interpretation (hermeneutic) which seriously undermined the central role of the Sermon on the Mount. In this view history was divided into a series of seven ages or dispensations. God was seen as working in different ways in each dispensation. The age of the law preceded the age of grace, which was the age of the New Testament church. Characteristically the dividing point between the two ages was seen as coming with the crucifixion. Christ, at the beginning of his ministry, offered the kingdom of God to the Jews until they rejected it, and Matthew 11 was often viewed as marking the point of rejection. Christ's earlier ministry, including the Sermon on the Mount, was therefore still kingdom preaching with an emphasis on the law rather than on gospel.

The impact of dispensational teaching was very clearly felt by various Mennonite groups, although it was not always taken to extremes sufficient to counter directly Mennonite teachings on nonresistance and °discipleship, which were strongly rooted in the sermon. Nevertheless, some of the foremost exponents of dispensationalism did undermine Mennonite theology implicitly or explicitly. The °Selbstschutz (self-defense) movement in Russia in 1918-19, for example, was supported or tolerated by prominent individuals who had accepted a dispensationalist °eschatology. In North America, William °Bestvater was perhaps the best-known exponent of dispensationalism among Mennonite Brethren. He regarded the Sermon on the Mount as a proclamation of the kingdom which was essentially postponed until the millennium. In the meantime, Bestvater maintained, Paul was given a new gospel to proclaim—a gospel of grace. Nevertheless Bestvater asserted that the Sermon on the Mount is instructive for the Christian life.

Among other Mennonite groups the interpretation of the Sermon on the Mount often became part of the larger °Fundamentalist-Modernist controversy. In the 1930s a number of pamphlets and articles appeared questioning whether the Sermon on the Mount remained applicable to the church. One of the clearest statements was given by John Horsch in an article entitled, "The Postponement Theory." Attempting to refute the substance of a book by Donald G. Barnhouse, Horsch argued strongly that Jesus did not offer an earthly kingdom to the Jews at the beginning of his reign and that the Sermon on the Mount was intended for our day. Horsch was particularly concerned about the implications of the theory for the doctrine of nonresistance because, according to Barnhouse, Jesus later in his ministry had declared himself against the principle of nonresistance.

Other Mennonite expositions, such as Jacob Nickel's Betrachtungen über die Bergpredigt, have often echoed Horsch's concern about setting aside the Sermon on the Mount in such a manner.

The Fundamentalist-Modernist controversy of the early 20th c. in many ways set the stage for the Mennonite and Anabaptist renewal signaled especially by Harold Bender's essay, "The Recovery of the °Anabaptist Vision." Bender's concluding statement in the essay was, "We shall not believe [the Anabaptists said], that the Sermon on the Mount or any other vision that He had is only a heavenly vision meant but to keep His followers in tension until the last great day, but we shall practice what He taught, believing that where He walked we can by his grace follow in His steps." (*Recovery*, 54). The impact of this restatement of vision and the associated emphasis on discipleship, following of Christ (*Nachfolge Christi*), kingdom ethics, and the doctrine of the °church generated more interest and literature on the Sermon on the Mount. The sermon was seen as setting forth in the most beautiful way the ideal society of °love and was contrasted to the magisterial Reformers' emphasis on faith alone. In a similar way the (Hutterian) Society of Brothers under Eberhard Arnold was inspired by the story of the Anabaptists toward an emphasis on the Sermon on the Mount.

In subsequent decades the appreciation for the Sermon on the Mount has been manifested in a variety of ways among Mennonites, including the popularity of Dietrich °Bonhoeffer's *The Cost of Discipleship*. A number of recent books by Mennonite authors on the Sermon on the Mount have appeared, including John W. Miller, *The Christian Way;* John Driver, *Kingdom Citizens;* and Clarence Bauman, *The Sermon on the Mount: The Modern Quest for its Meaning.* While the authors do not make any special claim to be writing solely from an Anabaptist or Mennonite theological perspective, it is nevertheless clear that they view themselves in that tradition. Mennonite ethical reflection today continues to see the Sermon on the Mount as foundational for much of its work.   AJD

Guy F. Hershberger, ed., *The Recovery of the Anabaptist Vision* (Scottdale, 1957); Eberhard Arnold, *Salt and Light: Talks and Writings on the Sermon on the Mount* (Rifton, NY: Plough, 1967); John Horsch, "The Postponement Theory," *GH* (Nov. 23, 1933), 722-23, 731-32; William J. Bestvater, "Dispensationelle Lehren aus dem Evangelium Mattaei," *Zeugnis der Schrift* (n.d. [May, 1919?]), 9-18; Jacob J. Nickel, *Betrachtungen über die Bergpredigt unsers Herrn Jesu Christi* (Rosthern, Sask., 1959); John W. Miller, *The Christian Way: A Guide to the Christian Life Based on the Sermon on the Mount* (Scottdale, 1969); John Driver, *Kingdom Citizens* (Scottdale, 1980); Clarence Bauman, *The Sermon on the Mount: The Modern Quest for its Meaning* (Macon, Ga.: Mercer U. Press, 1985); Jason Martin, *The Sermon on the Mount: A Guide for Practical Faith* (Scottdale, MPH, 1986), 197; William McGrath, *The Sermon on the Mount* (Minerva, Ohio: A[mish]-M[ennonite] Publications, 1985).

Servants (Russia). Some prosperous Mennonite immigrants to Russia in the late 18th and early 19th c. brought servants with them. These were youths, or more often young girls, related by ties of kinship or marriage to their employers. Occasionally, however, they were non-Mennonites, some of whom later joined the Mennonite faith. From the outset of settlement servants thus were accepted as normal members of prosperous Mennonite households. Female servants, who often came from poor families,

assisted with domestic chores, while male servants were employed in farm work, especially herding and shepherding in the early years. As incomes increased and the area cultivated expanded in the colonies, additional labor was required on colony farms and for domestic duties in the homes. In the Molotschna colony in 1855, 1,598 people were employed as laborers and servants, 737 of whom were Mennonite, 681 were Russian (usually local Ukrainians), and 180 were "German" colonists, Tatars, etc. Increasingly Russian peasants were employed, either local Ukrainians or Great Russians who were seasonal migrants from central Russia.

By 1914 it was common for established colony farmers in New Russia to employ a farm laborer for the main agricultural season (May to October) or for the entire year; additional labor at ploughing and harvest time; and contract labor for building, etc. In the house a maid or maids assisted with housework, washing, cooking, and childcare. In richer households a child's maid was also employed to care for very young children. As a consequence, young Mennonites learned to speak Ukrainian at an early age. Male farm workers slept in the barn or in special quarters away from the house; female servants in their own quarters or in the house. While farm workers and servants were occasionally ill-treated, many served Mennonites for long periods, sometimes members of the same family for a number of generations. Female servants, because they were more closely identified with the domestic sphere, were more integrated into Mennonite families and Mennonite ways than most male farm laborers. Some servants were taught basic literacy skills by the employers or their children and maintained close connections with their Mennonite families even after they had married and returned home.

Mennonite °estate owners and industrialists employed a large labor force and their more extensive households required more servants than colony homes, servants whose roles were also more clearly defined. Mennonites living in urban areas, often professional people or businessmen, also employed such servants. The treatment of laborers and servants varied greatly in these situations, but again there are reports of close connections being established.

The employment of servants and laborers came to an end with the °Russian Revolution and Civil War (1917-20) but not before servants had occasionally defended their employers against attacks by marauding bands, neighboring peasants, and troops.   JU

Service, living for others rather than self, received new emphasis and importance for Mennonites and Brethren in Christ people in the 20th c., especially since 1950. In that year, the Mennonite Central Committee (MCC), which had understood itself primarily as a °relief (food and fiber) agency, added a second emphasis—service. The challenge to give not only things, but also oneself, in glad service to others, met a ready response as hundreds of volunteers left home to serve the needy through special organizations: TAP (Teachers Abroad Program), °°Pax, °Voluntary Service (VS), and others.

Inevitably there followed a flood of literature, mostly articles in denominational periodicals, on various aspects of service (educational, medical, agricultural, social, etc.) with all having in common the emphasis on motivation and following the example of Jesus who "went about doing good" (Acts 10:38). Then came the concern that Jesus might be regarded merely as a good example to be followed rather than as Lord and Saviour of life. As more persons entered service assignments one heard it said that "there is no greater treason, than to do the right thing for the wrong reason." There was some call for the development of a theology of service.

In time it was recognized that motivation for service might start at any number of places, e.g., an awareness of world needs, especially the plight of people in countries of the "Two-Thirds World"; a vision of Jesus and his call to be like the good Samaritan (Lk 10:29-37); or a desire to be obedient to Scripture and "go into all the world." It also became evident that in the process of service the motivation frequently changed, motives were upgraded or purified. One might enter service simply to help the poor but end up realizing one's own poverty and thus take a significant and often first step to authentic self-awareness and spiritual growth.

For Mennonites in the 20th c. service became a restatement in rather tangible and practical ways that God is a God of life, not death. "Say to them, 'As I live,' says the Lord God, 'I have no pleasure in the death of the wicked, but that the wicked turn from his way and live'" (Ez 33:11). Jesus confirmed this in his teaching and ministry saying, "I came that they may have life, and have it abundantly" (Jn 10:10). Whether thus articulated or not, service came to be identified with the will of God for his people. In service men and women confirmed God's abiding principle of life and also pointed others to God, the source of life. Service became a new way of saying that the gospel is indeed good news, it is a message of life. It was a way of making visible outwardly what was felt inwardly in conversion, a way to put flesh on the sometimes dry bones of theological statements about being born again.

Service for others in a consumer-oriented, narcissistic and self-destructive society was perceived as a clear message of liberation from the enslaving powers, a proof that Christ had indeed made all things new. Instead of insisting on one's own way and instead of dominating other people, for whatever reason, the emphasis on service was a way of saying that just as "the Son of man came not to be served but to serve" (Mt 20:28), so his 20th-c. disciples also seek the welfare of others above their own.

Somewhere along the road of service 20th-c. Mennonites discovered that people often resist, or at least resent, being served and thus Mennonites were forced to rethink Jesus' statement as quoted by the Apostle Paul: "It is more blessed to give than to receive" (Acts 20:35). It was a humbling experience for a people eager to do good in the name of Christ. It was an experience that pointed up the cheapness of paternalistic service, the need for less sympathy and more empathy, and a calling for the highest degree of identification with the recipient of the service. It was, therefore, no academic question to ask how an affluent people like North American

Mennonites could bring wholeness and healing to poverty-stricken people around the world. A seemingly inseparable gulf separated the two. Whenever this question was raised in the printed page, at conferences, or at seminars, numerous possible solutions were offered but never the radical step suggested by Jesus to the rich young ruler to "go, sell what you possess and give it to the poor" (Mt 19:21). Instead the call was for the practice of good °stewardship rather than for divesting oneself of all possessions and thus standing on an equal footing with the poor. That was left for the idealists like Francis of Assisi, Waldo (Waldenses), Leo Tolstoy, and Jesus.

A major shift in service emphasis came with the careful articulation of the marriage between word and deed. It became increasingly clear that bread and the bread of life belong together, that mission boards and MCC, for example, are basically engaged in the same task of serving God by serving humans. This was made clear, for example, by the appointment and funding of workers for Botswana by mission boards and MCC serving together in *one* agency known there simply as Mennonite Ministries (MM). It is an attempt to do what used to be called the "comprehensive approach," an attempt to unite "diakonia" and "kerygma," service and proclamation.

However, just when it appeared that the pieces were coming together with the fusion of word and deed, and the joining of mission with service, various Muslim countries, as well as Communist countries like China, permitted Mennonite service but did not permit the spoken word. This raised the question about the validity and value of what is called "Christian presence," a silent service without proclamation.

Meanwhile in the North American Mennonite churches emphasis was placed on service as a lifestyle. The service motif was to permeate all of life. At the same time an attempt was made to go to the root causes of hunger, violence, and despair. As the linkage between militarism and poverty for example became evident, as structural evil was seen as the "powers and principalities" that the Apostle Paul talked about (Rom 8:38; Eph 3:10, 6:12; Col 1:16, 2:15), service began to take on ever new and specialized forms.

Service, the speaking, writing and doing of it, has energized the church and provided it with a clear biblical mandate to "be steadfast, immovable, always abounding in the work of the Lord" (1 Cor 15:58). Emphasis on service has helped to make eschatalogical hope visible. It is being understood as rooted in salvation history which looks two ways, back to the "finished work" of Christ, and forward to the fullness and completion by the return of Christ. Because Mennonites believe that the kingdom of God is already here, that the believer is already in it and is to "occupy till I come" (Lk 19:13), he goes about his work, serving with the gifts given him, carrying something of the greatness and solemnity of eternity into his daily routine. She knows that her service is contributing to the completion of Christ's triumph, when "He shall reign forever and ever."   PJD

Peter J. Dyck, "A Theology of Service," *MQR,* 44 (1970), 262-80; Robert Kreider, "The Impact of MCC Service on American Mennonites," *ibid.,* 245-61.

See also Development Work; Health Services; Humanitarianism; Mutual Aid; Relief Work; Work Camps.

Seventh-Day Adventists, stand with Mennonites and other denominations in the long tradition of believers baptism, a practice reinstituted by the Anabaptists on the basis of their study of the Scriptures and the example of the apostolic church (°restitutionism).

The seventh-day Adventist Church traces its start as an evangelical denomination to 1844 when a congregation in New Hampshire began observing the seventh day, Saturday, as the Sabbath. God's intention for the Sabbath, Adventists maintain, was to meet the needs of created man and woman, as expressed in Gn 2:2, 3; Ex 20:8-11; the prophets; and in New Testament passages. Adventists base their restoration of Saturday as the day of rest and worship on the word and example of the apostolic church.

Some Anabaptists did keep the Sabbath. The best known °Sabbatarian Anabaptists were Oswald °°Glaidt and Andreas °Fischer. While the two are seen as spiritual forbears, the Adventist's primary reason for Sabbath-keeping is that it is scriptural.

Adventists maintain numerous colleges, secondary schools, publishing houses, and some 270 medical institutions in the United States and worldwide. North American membership in 1987 was 687,000 (worldwide, ca. 3,000,000 in 1985). The church's headquarters are in Washington, D.C.　　JMB

Richard Müller, "Identifying the True Church," *Ministry* (Sept. 1986) 17-19, an article by a Seventh-Day Adventist in a SDA journal about 16th-c. Anabaptists; Samuele Bacchiocchi, *From Sabbath to Sunday* (Rome, 1977).

See also Manitoba Colony, Mexico.

Sewel (Zeenwel), Jacob. See Zinspenning, Judith.

Sex Education includes instruction in biological, psychological, sociological, and value concepts. It is a necessary aspect of every human life, since humans, unlike animals, are without specific instincts to serve as a guide in reproduction and expression of °sexuality.

Sex education remains a controversial topic which is often avoided in the Mennonite community, both within the family as well as at the congregational level. Who should accept responsibility for instruction of the young on sexuality? Avoidance of the problem has often led to default. Churches may state that sex education is a private concern for parents and children; parents may feel uncomfortable with the subject and procrastinate.

Historically, sex education among Mennonites appears to have been largely a matter of self-education. Children would learn by observation of animals and adults, communication with peers and sympathetic adults, or by reading available, often inferior, literature. In solid village communities this form of self-education may have been reasonably effective, even if not comprehensive (Wiebe, *Salvation*).

While Mennonite churches did not concern themselves with sex education, they directly censured such irresponsible expressions of sexuality as extramarital sex and adultery. Emphasis on salvation of souls often led to downgrading of the mortal body, also a gift of God. Nevertheless, marriage was the almost universal adult condition among Mennonites, and children were considered evidence of divine blessing and obedience to His will.

Mennonite principles, including the stress on Christian discipleship and pacifism, with its emphasis on the sanctity of human life, can readily lead to the awareness that life, lived as male or female, should be equally good and satisfying. The Church as the custodian and teacher of values and absolutes, should affect lives within families, including the expressions of humanity and sexuality.

Good family values and attitudes are the essential formative forces for children. Families where parents feel free and happy to express affection and love for each other will have happy children, accepting themselves and their being, and their sexuality, with joy. In contrast, families affected by violence and anger will produce permanently scarred children (Behrends, *Der Steppenhengst*). The role of Mennonite parents in sex education of their children has varied, and often has been haphazard (Konrad, *The Blue Jar*).

The middle of the 20th c. has brought increased interaction between Mennonites and the larger society, and this was reflected by changed attitudes regarding the family, children and values. While sex education is usually thought of in terms of children and young adults, it, like all learning, is really a lifetime process. Thus, in Western Canada, public health nurses taught Mennonite "immigrant" women about child spacing, with health and social benefits.

While the historic attitudes to sex education have continued among the most traditional Mennonite groups, the more progressive churches have taken more overt approaches to education about good family relationships. Premarital counseling, including sexual aspects, by ministers is widespread. Seminars, retreats, and Mennonite Marriage Encounters are available for improving the quality of relationships within families and strengthening feelings of self-worth and responsibility. There are groups receiving less attention: °single adults, the elderly, and the people with special problems. It is hoped that the awareness and compassion developed in present efforts will lead to further extension.

Currently, Mennonite schools include sex education in their curricula, with special attention to the 12-15-year-old age group. Mennonite manuals, books, church policy statements, and specialists are widely available. Mennonite pastoral education includes stress on the pastoral role in counseling and sex education. Concerned Mennonite teachers and health professionals are often able to witness effectively to the wholeness of the person, including sexuality, far beyond their own congregations.

Mennonite sex educators of the 20th c. cite the following goals: The first objective is the acquisition of accurate information. Sex education should provide individuals with basic facts about sexuality and clear up misconceptions.

A second objective is the development of greater self-awareness and understanding. When individuals acquire more information regarding sexuality, it enables them to develop a greater insight into their own sexuality. This can lead to a reduction in anxieties about their own sexual development and help young people better manage their own sexual problems.

A third objective is to help the Mennonite people clarify their own sexual values so they are less dependent on the standards of their peers and the society, and less likely to engage in promiscuous sexual relations.

A fourth objective is the improvement of communication skills. It is a myth that people are open in their discussions of sex. Most of the openness is carried out in a superficial way and sex education can provide the opportunity to discuss sex in a serious manner. However, it must be emphasized that many aspects of sex are personal and private. Open communication can only occur in a setting where the individual's opinions are valued and respected. Communication cannot take place if individuals are afraid to express their opinions because of being ridiculed by parents, sex educator, or peers. Given a supportive atmosphere, individuals will be able to discuss sexual topics in a serious manner.

Being more knowledgeable about sexual issues, having greater self-understanding and being able to communicate more effectively, can increase one's self-esteem. A very important objective of sex education is the fostering of positive feelings of self-worth which sex educators find lacking among Mennonites.

A fifth objective of sex education is the development of toleration for those whose opinions differ from our own. Mennonite history reveals persecution for conscience sake. During persecution the Mennonite people were tolerant of differences due to the universal persecution. As a respected denomination in North America the tolerance is less visible and hostility is often manifested in relation to sexual differences and education.

Finally, the sixth goal of sex education should be the increasing of communication and closeness between parents and their children. Sex education courses in °private and °public schools provide for an opportunity for parents to discuss openly with their children sexual matters, fostering a feeling of closeness to parents.

Given the conflicting values about sex among Mennonites, choosing a sexual standard is a serious and difficult matter. When it comes to values, Mennonite Christians look to the Bible and the Mennonite heritage for direction and guidance. Though sexuality is not a major theme of the Mennonite witness, the Bible and the Mennonite heritage do give attention to personal living. It can be seen how prone individuals are to miss the mark and how easily life can be distorted. Yet Jesus Christ offers a liberation from those powers that disfigure God's intent for his children.

Sexuality has within it those elements, both physical and spiritual, that can be used to fulfill God's will for individual lives.   SG

Hilda Enns, Sue Goerzen, Lois Paff Bergen, *Teens and Sexuality* (Newton, 1984); Ernst Behrends, *Der Steppenhengst* (Hohenstaufer Verlag, 1969); Anne Konrad, *The Blue Jar* (Winnipeg: Queenston House, 1985); Sue Goerzen, Wilmer Martin, and the Task Force on Sexuality (GCM, MC), *Human Sexuality in the Christian Life* (1986); Armin Wiebe, *The Salvation of Yasch Siemens* (Winnipeg: Turnstone Press, 1984); C. F. Derstine, *Manual of Sex Education for Parents, Teachers, and Students* (Kitchener, 1942; Grand Rapids: Zondervan, 1943); idem, *The Path to Beautiful Womanhood* (Kitchener, 1942; Grand Rapids: Zondervan, 1944); idem, *The Path to Noble Manhood* (Kitchener, 1942; Grand Rapids: Zondervan, 1944); Jacob H. Janzen, *Das Sexuelle Problem* (Waterloo, Ont., 1941-46); Merle W. Eshleman and Noah K. Mack, *Christian Manhood* (Scottdale, 1948); H. Clair Amstutz, *Growing Up to Love: A Guide to Sex Education for Parents* (Scottdale, 1956); F. H. Epp, *Mennonites in Canada II*, pp. 476-78.

Sexuality. Few written records exist to shed light on Mennonite sexual attitudes and behavior before the early 20th c. This might be surprising when one considers how pervasive an aspect of the human personality and how important a dimension of human interaction sexuality is. However, Mennonites were apparently following the societal reluctance to acknowledge their sexuality explicitly and certainly to talk (or write) much about it. Those who can remember Mennonite congregational life in the 1920s or 1930s have witnessed a remarkable change in the openness with which sexuality is discussed. Articles in church papers, as well as conference proceedings, deal with sexuality concerns much more explicitly, again reflecting the trends in society.

Written material from earlier periods referred to aspects of genital sexual behavior much more than to sexuality as a broad dimension of personal identity and overall male-female interaction.

There was widespread Christian bias against sex solely for pleasure—the bias was that sex is for procreation only. An understanding of this requires a look at the ancient mind-body dualism derived from Greek thought. There are some hints of this in some of the Apostle Paul's writings, especially when he writes about carnal-mindedness. The mind-body dualism was applied by the early Christians in an anti-flesh manner. That attitude stems from the early centuries of the Christian church and was carried through the Middle Ages into modern times. Part of the reason for this attitude on the part of the early Christians may have been their reaction against the licentiousness of the ruling class in Roman society. This anti-sex, anti-flesh attitude also contributed to the rise of monasticism and the affirmation of total celibacy as the most devout life-style to which Christians could aspire.

The overall mind-body dualism persisted well into the 20th c. Overcoming this dualism was made more difficult because human physical bodies were sexual bodies, and sexuality has always been a source of anxiety to society. The present writer remembers clearly the attitudes conveyed from the pulpit when he was a lad: an attitude suggesting that one almost needed to be ashamed of one's body; the body was identified with "the flesh"—the body was seen as a major source of temptation which would lead to sin. In recent years, however, these attitudes are changing and the church is beginning to affirm the goodness of God's marvelous creation, the human body. The mind-body dichotomy is also lessening as we begin to focus on and understand the meaning of wholeness and shalom.

Because of the scarcity of Anabaptist writing on sexuality, we know very little about the Anabaptists' sexual attitudes. What they did write was standard condemnation of sexual immorality. Their attitudes seem to have been common to the Christians of their times, but their practice was that of a more consistent following of those attitudes, a greater adherence to their beliefs and standards. Evidence of their exceptional practice (e.g., less sexual promiscuity) is gleaned from the writings of those who opposed them. One Reformed pastor, Georg Thormann, author of °°*Probier-Stein* (1696) found it necessary, in order to be credible, to praise Swiss Brethren for their higher-than-average Christian morality.

We also have record of their prohibition of behaviors such as adultery. In the congregational records at Montbéliard in Alsace there is reference to certain members who were excommunicated "for reasons of adultery." In the early 1800s church rules of congregations in the Palatinate included prohibitions against adultery and prostitution.

As part of the Radical Reformation Anabaptists experienced some acute and perhaps unique sexual problems. In some cases there were sexual irregularities. For example, when a mate would not go along with a spouse in joining the Anabaptists, the issue of fidelity to one's unbelieving spouse came into question. In some cases a form of bigamy developed in which a "spiritual marriage" formed with fellow Anabaptist adherents coexisted alongside a previous marriage. Such irregularities probably involved only a handful however. In °Münster there apparently were instances of polygamy, not as a demonstration of sexual license but for purposes of procreation only, there being more women than men in the movement, a situation exacerbated by persecution.

For the last 50 years a steadily increasing amount of information is available because Mennonites have begun to speak and write a great deal more about sexual attitudes and practices. In Aug. 1929, C. D. Esch spoke at the Mennonite Church (MC) general conference on Christian standards of social purity. In 1941, in Ontario, an article appeared entitled "The Sexual Problem"(!) In the early 1950s a medical doctor, H. Clair Amstutz became a prolific and well-known writer on sexual, marriage, and °family topics, concluding with his *Marriage in Today's World* in 1978. C. F. °Derstine, George R. Brunk (b. 1911), John W. Miller, Howard Charles, and Merle Eshleman also wrote on sexual issues and consistently upheld traditional standards of sexual morality.

In the late 1960s, with the development of the "free speech movement" and the Vietnam War protests with their attack on the establishment and its tenets, a societal loosening of sexual values evolved which came to be known as "the new morality." Characteristics of the new morality included generally greater permissiveness, less commitment to marriage, and an abandonment of the standard of genital intercourse within marriage only. Articles condemning "the new morality" began to appear in many Mennonite church papers. Then in Aug. 1968, a "Conference on Christianity and Sexuality" was convened on the campus of the Mennonite Biblical Seminary in Elkhart, Ind. The conference came about as a result of Mennonites attending several ecumenical church meetings on sexuality. The World Council of Churches conducted a "Consultation on Sexual Ethics" in Switzerland in 1964. The participants at that meeting were unable to formulate a theology of sexuality acceptable to those present and they acknowledged that the churches must accept some responsibility for the chaos which existed. Following this, in May 1966, the second North American Conference on Church and Family was held in Hamilton, Ont. The Mennonites attending the Hamilton conference met one evening to raise the question of what the conference had to say to Mennonites. It was acknowledged that the Mennonite denominations had given little attention to the issues raised, that more attention was needed, and that a conference should be held; hence the 1968 Elkhart meeting. At the Elkhart "Conference on Christianity and Sexuality," 91 participants engaged in dialogue, debate, and study of the papers presented by various participants. The conference was descriptive and analytical, and it was helpful to hear each other, but no unified statement on sexuality emerged.

In the late 1970s Mennonites became increasingly aware of the homosexually-oriented persons among them, and as people with same-sex orientation became more visible and more assertive the churches reacted (generally in a strongly negative way). Issues such as homosexuality, the growing °divorce rate, elective °abortions among Mennonites, and an increasing incidence of non-marital sexual intercourse led a number of Mennonite leaders from various conferences to request the Mennonite Medical Association (an inter-Mennonite organization of physicians and dentists) to sponsor a *Symposium on Human Sexuality*. This symposium met in two sessions (Sept. 1978 and Apr. 1979) to study a variety of sexuality issues. Inasmuch as homosexuality was the major stimulus for the symposium, most of the presentations had both sessions address the issues surrounding same-sex orientation.

In May 1980 another seminar on human sexuality was held at Laurelville Mennonite Church Center as a follow-up to the two Mennonite Medical Association consultations in Chicago. In this meeting, as well as in the Chicago consultations, the Mennonite denominations were called upon to articulate a theology of the body, i.e., a sexual theology. The need for broad-based °sex education programs in the local congregation was emphasized; and the church was challenged to do more by way of understanding homosexuality, to affirm °singleness as a valid option, and to articulate meaningful statements on sexual ethics in the context of the new challenges presented by society. The church was also called upon to be a healing community for the many who are victimized by a variety of sexual abuses and coercion. Mennonites were becoming increasingly aware that all forms of sexual exploitation existed within Mennonite congregations.

In 1981, the General Conference Mennonites (GCM) and the Mennonite Church (MC) jointly appointed a Human Sexuality Study Committee. This committee met three times a year from Jan. 1982 to Jan. 1987. It developed a study guide entitled *Human Sexuality in the Christian Life* which was submitted to the congregations of both denominations for study over the period from 1984 to 1987. The General Conference Mennonite Church at Saskatoon in 1986 and the Mennonite Church General Assembly at Purdue in 1987 adopted similar statements reaffirming the goodness of sexuality and its place of honor and joy in the human family. Both called their members to confession and to covenant. Both groups reiterated their understanding that the Bible teaches that genital intercourse is reserved for heterosexual marriage and teaches the sanctity of the marriage covenant. The need to continue the study and dialogue on sexuality issues was also emphasized.

Meanwhile, as in the rest of North American society, sex roles and °gender expectations were rapidly changing and women were moving out into the work place and into positions of leadership in the church as well. In some congregations women have been ordained and in most they have begun to serve on church boards and in other leadership positions of various kinds. This change has not been without accompanying dissension. In many denominational settings, feelings have been intense as the issue has been debated as to whether equality of the sexes should necessarily mean similar roles for men and women in church life.

In conclusion, especially with regard to sexuality, Mennonites have always been a great deal more reactive than proactive, reacting to the mores and practices of the society in which they lived. The increased activity and study of sexuality in the last 20 years particularly, was stimulated more by an increasingly permissive society, the feminist movement, and the gay rights movement than by a growing awareness that Mennonites have inadequately understood and addressed the biblical understandings of the sexual dimensions of human personality and life. We have still not formulated a theology of the body nor of sexuality which can effectively undergird an ongoing program of Christian sexuality education. We have made a step in reuniting sexuality and spirituality, but what has transpired in the last several years should be seen as the beginning of a new era in Christian male-female relationships and not as the ending of a project which articulates all that we need to say on this subject for the next generation.   WSK

See also Lederach, Mary Mensch.

Shalom Covenant Communities (SCC) is an association of local churches emphasizing renewal, °community and °mission, formed in 1974. Seeking a more faithful Christian °discipleship, all of the founding groups originally practiced complete sharing of financial resources among all members. Many other aspects of community life and Christian discipleship were pursued with equal vigor. Founding members of SCC were Fellowship of Hope (Elkhart, Ind.), New Creation Fellowship (Newton, Ks.), Plow Creek Fellowship (Tiskilwa, Ill.), and Reba Place Fellowship (Evanston, Ill.). Rediscovery of the °Anabaptist vision provided much of the original impetus. The communities were also shaped significantly by °charismatic renewal and contact with other renewal groups. Local church membership eventually changed to allow both communal and non-communal

economic patterns. Other groups with similar vision have actively associated with SCC. With the Mennonite Board of Missions (MC) they jointly sponsor an outreach to Burgos, Spain. In 1983 the Fellowship of Hope began publishing for the SCC, a magazine, *Coming Together*.   VV

See also Concern Pamphlets Movement; House Churches; Restitutionism.

Shambuyuyu Emmanuel. A child born to a slave couple among the Chokwe people in southern Kwilu province of the Belgian Congo (Zaire), near the Angolan border, was named Nduwa. When a new outpost of the Unevangelized Tribes Mission was started near his village, Nduwa was one of the first boys admitted, after hesitation on the part of the village fathers, to the mission school. He was among the first to accept Christ and to be baptized, at which time he took a new name, Emmanuel. Later when his first child was born he became known as Shambuyuyu, the father of Mbuyuyu.

After finishing the training available at the mission post, Shambuyuyu was chosen to go to Vanga, a Baptist station far to the northwest to take a short term Bible course. When he returned he became one of the church's first itinerant evangelists. In 1952 the Congo Inland Mission took over the area for mission work and in due time ordained Shambuyuyu as pastor in the Église du Christ au Zaire, Communauté Mennonite (CMZA; Zaire Mennonite Church). In the 1960s Emmanuel was asked to leave Kamayala to open a new work among a group of isolated people between the Loange and Kasai Rivers. He became one of the first missionaries of the Zaire Mennonite Church. When he and his family returned five years later a church had been planted in the new area. Back in Kamayala, Emmanuel was again allocated a rural area which he served faithfully for another 15 years until his sudden death in July 1985.   JEB

Shank, Clara May Brubaker (May 21, 1869-Sept. 21, 1958), teacher, lay leader, °rural missionary, and writer, was born to pioneering church planters in Missouri. Through the influence of John S. °°Coffman she attended the Elkhart Institute and then returned home to the Ozark region of Missouri to undertake mission work with her family. Brubaker's message and mission were rooted in late 19th-c. Mennonite-evangelical stirrings. She wrote 78 articles for the *Herald of Truth* and the *Gospel Herald* between 1886 and 1927. Many of them urged personal °conversion followed by °nonresistance and °nonconformity. She emphasized church unity and Christian witness through daily life. She evangelized through teaching, leadership in Sunday school, and pastoral °visitation. At the age of 55 she married church planter John R. °°Shank and continued in lay ministry in Missouri until her death.   PS-K

Priscilla Stuckey-Kauffman, "A Woman's Ministry: Clara Brubaker Shank, 1869-1958," *MQR*, 60 (1986), 404-28.

Shank, Crissie Yoder (Jan. 7, 1888-Oct. 12, 1929), the oldest of three children of John A. and Sadie Yoder, was born near Holden, Mo. In early childhood she moved with her parents to Wayne County,

Ohio, where she grew up and taught in the public school system. After receiving a BA degree from Goshen College (1909), she taught English and was dean of women at Bethel College, Ks. In 1914 she married Charles L. Shank.

In 1915 the Shanks went to °Dhamtari, Madhya Pradesh, India, under appointment by the Mennonite Board of Missions and Charities (MC). Due to a daughter's illness they returned to the United States after only four years of service. Crissie captured the drama and meaning of these years in a book for young readers, *Letters from Mary*. She was a gifted speaker and writer with global and ecumenical concerns and she used her gifts to promote missions. She helped organize the Mennonite General Women's and Girl's Missionary Society and edited its publication, *Monthly Letter* (later *Voice*).   JAF

Crissie Shank, *Letters from Mary* (Scottdale: MPH, 1924); Sharon Klingelsmith, "Women in the Mennonite Church, 1900-1930," *MQR*, 54 (1980), 163-207; Rich, *Mennonite Women* (1983), 138-40; *GH* (Oct. 24, 1929), 623; American Mennonite MC Mission, Dhamtari, India, *Building on the Rock* (Scottdale: MPH, 1926), 184; *Menn. Bib.*, 24328, 24379; interview with Mary Royer.

Shank, Emma Elizabeth Hershey (Aug. 11, 1881-Dec. 1939). The daughter of Jacob M. and Mary (Eby) Hershey, Emma Elizabeth Hershey Shank was the first Mennonite Church (MC) missionary to die in South America. She is buried at Pehuajo. She lived in central Argentina 22 years with her husband J. W. Shank whom she married in 1910. She was a public school teacher for 11 years in Missouri and Colorado.

Noted for homemaking skills and loyalty to her family (Elsie, Robert, and Paul), Emma also provided care for boarding students living in her home and, as matron, for orphanage girls. Weakened by typhoid fever, she also endured multiple family separations.

Emma began and managed a kindergarten, inspired Argentine Bible readers during home visits, and prepared with care to lead women's meetings. Her descriptions of Argentine life are picturesque. She wished North Americans to read about mission efforts in order to be good neighbors, to sense spiritual kinship, and to be informed in prayer.   DYN

Selena Gamber, "In Memoriam—Emma Hershey Shank," *Missionary Sewing Circle Letter*, 10, no. 11 (May 1940); Emma Hershey Shank, "From South America," *Missionary Sewing Circle Letter*, 2, no. 3 (Mar. 1932); J. W. Shank, "Autobiographical Notes" [also titled: "Establishing Christ's Church Under the Southern Cross" (typescript, Hesston, Ks., 1969); Emma Hershey Shank, "Scenes from our Window," *GH*, (Aug. 1, 1918), 321.

Shank, Josephus Wenger (Oct. 10, 1881-May 17, 1970). Identified by one historian as the father of Mennonite missions in Argentina, J. W. Shank was born at Versailles, Mo. He was a Mennonite Church (MC) missionary in Argentina for 33 years. Prior to J. W. and Emma Hershey Shank's arrival in 1917, he had carefully researched five South American countries and contacted 60 missionaries to decide where a Mennonite witness should be centered. He then solicited more than $20,000 for the mission cause.

J. W. loved to study literature; while awaiting coworkers, he taught in Nebraska and at Goshen College (from which he graduated in 1910). His hobby was writing; numerous articles gave North American Mennonite readers extensive information about how new Sunday schools were begun, peoples' characteristics, business and industry, and the °Roman Catholic church in Argentina.

As part of his missionary task J. W. preached, taught Argentine Christians (especially at the Bible institute), trained new missionaries, created a catechism, served as mission treasurer, investigated and developed new locations, assisted Indians with legal matters, and wrote. Family experience included frequent moves, periods of separation from his spouse or three children, Emma Shank's death, and a second marriage (to Selena Gamber) in 1942. J. W. and Selena worked primarily with Chaco Indians from 1943-50, a more isolated but rigorous effort.

Active retirement years found J. W. in deputation work, as a pastor, recording history, teaching four years at Eastern Mennonite College, working as a handyman at the La Junta (Col.) center for retirees. He was privileged to return to Argentina for the 40th anniversary for Mennonite mission. He died when living at Showalter Villa, Hesston, Ks.   DYN

J. W. Shank, "Autobiographical Notes" [also titled "Establishing Christ's Church Under the Southern Cross] (typescript, Hesston, Ks., 1969); idem, "Central Argentina as a Background for Christian Evangelism," (BD thesis, Bethany Biblical Seminary, Chicago, 1933); idem, "Mennonite Missions in Argentina," *GH*, 39 (1946), 784-86; idem and others, *The Gospel under the Southern Cross*, A History of the Argentine Mennonite Mission of South America Celebrating its 25th Anniversary 1917-1942 (Scottdale: MPH, 1943); idem, a series of articles about Argentina in *Christian Monitor*, 7 (Apr.-Aug. 1921), 109-10, 140-42, 172-74, 202-03, 236-37; idem, "We Enter the Chaco Indian Work," part of Latin America Mission Study Kit (Elkhart, Ind.: MBM, 1951); idem, "To the Land of the Southern Cross," *Chr. Living*, 7 (Jan. 1960), 14-17, 32-33, 37 (Feb. 1960), 24-27.

Shank, Selena Gamber (b. 1893). Selena Gamber graduated from Lancaster General Hospital's nursing school in 1919 and from Toronto Bible College in 1923. In five articles about nursing (1921), she encouraged young women to respond to health needs. Two years later she was a Mennonite Church (MC) missionary in central Argentina.

She wrote descriptively of home life among poor, middle class, and wealthy people; she wrote about nursing opportunities. When a mission family was on furlough, she left an orphanage assignment to be general superintendent at the Carlos Casares station, doing a wide variety of tasks, except preaching. During an extended furlough (1933-37) she supervised nursing work at Mennonite Hospital, La Junta, Col.

In 1942 Selena married veteran Argentina missionary J. W. Shank. Together they ventured into new work among Chaco Indians, she with tasks as nurse, teacher, cook. After 1950 Shanks had assignments at the Chicago Spanish Mission, Eastern Mennonite College, in Puerto Rico, and at La Junta, Col. Selena substituted as school nurse, created a course of study and trained nurse aides, and was nurse in charge of a retirement nursing home. She moved to Kansas in her retirement.   DYN

Selena Gamber, "Nursing as a Vocation," in *YCC*, 2 (July 3-21, 1921), 522, 534, 540, 546, 557; idem, a series titled: "Home Life in the Argentine," *YCC*, 7 (Feb. 6-21, 1926), 45, 53, 57; idem, "Medical Mission in South America," *YCC*, (July 11, 1926), 217-18; J. W. Shank, "Autobiographical Notes" [also titled: "Establishing Christ's Church Under the Southern Cross"] (typescript, Hesston, Ks., 1969).

Shantz, Elven (1893-1984). The son of Menno and Susannah (Bowman) Shantz, Elven Shantz was born at Breslau, Ont. In 1920 he married Mabel Weber, a sister of Urias K. °Weber, then minister at Eby's Mennonite Church, which later became known as First Mennonite Church, Kitchener. Elven and Mabel Shantz returned from homesteading in Saskatchewan and joined the Stirling Avenue Mennonite Church, Kitchener, in 1929. He became an active lay leader in that congregation. Shantz was always considered a "liberal" Mennonite but had a great rapport with all Mennonites.

He served as secretary of the Military Problems Committee of the °°Conference of Historic Peace Churches, 1943-64. Shantz organized the Ontario unit of Mennonite Disaster Service in 1958 and was interim secretary of Mennonite Central Committee Ontario in the 1960s.

As a result of these activities, his farm background, his ability to speak the Pennsylvania-German dialect and his fine rapport with the Old Order, Amish, and Conservative Mennonites, Shantz was asked to be their spokesman to government in their requests for exemption from government health insurance, Family Allowance, Old Age Security, Workmen's Compensation, and the Canada Pension Plan, and in gaining recognition of their right to establish °private Christian schools. Shantz was active in the founding of Conrad Grebel College in 1961, the Mennonite Historical Society of Ontario, and the Ontario Mennonite °relief sale in 1966. The members of many branches of Mennonites who attended and participated at his funeral attested to his commitment and service to Mennonite unity. LBe

Minutes of the Military Problems Committee of Conference of Historic Peace Churches, 1940-64; minutes of MCC (Ontario), 1964-; minutes of Ontario Mennonite Relief Sale board, 1966-; minutes of Conrad Grebel College board; minutes of the Mennonite Historical Society of Ontario (all located in Conrad Grebel College Archives [Waterloo]).

Shantz, Jacob Yost (ME IV:511). Although best known for his role in promoting the immigration of Mennonites from Russia to Manitoba in the 1870s, more recent research has provided a fuller picture of this enigmatic lay Mennonite leader.

Shantz was easily the wealthiest Mennonite entrepreneur in Ontario in the early 1880s, with more than 300 people on the payroll of his Dominion Button Works alone. Overexpansion and possible mismanagement in a declining market led to virtual bankruptcy by 1886. Shantz spent the rest of his life paying his debts, and died a man of moderate means.

In 1882 Shantz was elected mayor of Berlin (Kitchener) in an uncontested election. Inexplicably he resigned four days after taking office, though the town council briefly considered not accepting the resignation. The fact that J. Y. Shantz's son, Moses, was also elected as a member of the council may have generated pressure for one of the family to resign. Shantz's letter of resignation has not survived.

In 1898 Shantz joined the local Christian Science congregation, and remained a member in good standing until his death, although evidence is inconclusive on the question of whether he remained

actively involved to the time of his death in 1909. He was still an active member, serving on the congregation's board of directors, at age 81 (1903). Four factors help to explain Shantz's interest in the then-new Christian Science movement. (1) Shantz had a life-long interest in the innovative, whether in °business, land settlement, or religious thought—though he always believed himself to be orthodox. (2) The emphasis in Christian Science on a rigorous, healthful life-style was appealing. Shantz was active in the temperance movement, and was a vegetarian at least part of his life. (3) Jacob Y. Shantz was a "healer" with a reputation for curing cancer. Although his approach differed from that of Christian Science, enough common interest existed to prove attractive. (4) Shantz probably felt rejected by the Mennonite Brethren in Christ (°°United Missionary) denomination as he was phased out of all leadership roles by 1896. SSt

Samuel J. Steiner, *Vicarious Pioneer: the Life of Jacob Y. Shantz* (Winnipeg: Hyperion Press, 1988).

Shenk, Alta Barge (Mar. 24, 1912-July 21, 1969). The daughter of Witmer and Elnora (Ebenshade) Barge, Alta Barge married J. Clyde Shenk on Aug. 14, 1935; in July of the next year, they sailed to Tanganyika (Tanzania). In addition to parenting five children (David, Joseph, Anna Kathryn, John, Daniel), Alta was active in opening three mission stations with the Eastern Mennonite Board of Missions and Charities (MC). During their 33rd year in Africa, she died in a plane crash near Nairobi, Kenya.

Through language study, Bible study sessions with women or girls, visits to homes, supervision of Bible instruction in church schools, beginner and advanced reading classes, dispensing medicines, or teaching sewing classes, Alta knew strength through prayer. She knew subjected and abused women; she regretted when young girls were sold or married to old men. She wrote about both evil and Holy Spirit activity among people. With trust in her own children, she attended to their varied needs. To suggest that her life blended into the background would be unfortunate. DYN

Mahlon M. Hess, "'Chips of Gold' in Memory of Alta B. Shenk," *Miss. Mess.* 46, no. 9 (Jan. 1970), 6-9; Africa Circle Letters, letters from EMBMC Africa workers that were mimeographed and sent to their friends every 6-8 weeks, copies at MHL (Goshen) and EMBMC (Salunga, Pa.); George Ronald Anchak, "An Experience in the Paradox of Indigenous Church Building: A History of the Eastern Mennonite Mission in Tanganyika 1934-1961" (PhD diss. Michigan State U., 1975); Alta and J. Clyde Shenk, frequent short articles in *GH*, e.g. (Apr. 3, 1941), 25-26, (Nov. 4, 1943), 660, (Dec. 2, 1943), 740-41, and *GH, Christian Missions* supplement (Aug. 1943), 400-401, (Mar. 1944), 1051, (Apr. 1944), 20, 25; Dorothy Smoker and Merle Eshleman, *God Led Us to Tanganyika*, (Salunga, Pa.: EMBMC, 1956, 47pp.; David W. Shenk, "Pioneering in Africa," *Chr. Living* (May 1988), 2-9.

Shidi Lazalo (b. ca. 1918) was the son of a Mupende slave wife of a Muchoke chief in south central Belgian Congo (Zaire), Africa. At birth his arms and legs were underdeveloped with badly deformed ankles and wrists which did not permit normal function. Since his mother thought the deformity was due to witchcraft she would have had her son thrown in the river except for the father's intervention. Shidi means "animosity."

About 1926 Shidi and several relatives were redeemed by fellow clansmen from Tshingila, their home village far to the north. Shidi was carried all of the way by his relatives. A year later missionary Frank Enns from the Nyanga Station of the °°Congo Inland Mission (later known as the Africa Inter-Mennonite Mission) brought a teacher-evangelist who befriended Shidi. The following year Shidi was taken to Nyanga where he did odd jobs in the Enns house yard in exchange for food, shelter, and further schooling. Shidi responded eagerly to the opportunity for study and accepted Christ. At his baptism he chose the new name Lazarus, for, as he explained, he truly was as one who had risen from the dead.

In 1930 Presbyterian Mission doctors offered to take him to Bulape hoping to correct some of the deformity. Shidi lived there for 22 years, graduated from the Bible School, and plunged into the work of village evangelist. He had a working knowledge of several African languages and became increasingly effective.

In 1952 he returned to Nyanga where he soon received invitations from far and near to preach. Sometimes he traveled with missionaries and other times rode on a special two-wheeled cart pushed by students. After assurance that he would not transmit his deformity to any children he might have, he found a Christian woman who would accept him and he married Biabo Esete in 1953. They have five lovely daughters. He never allowed his handicap to limit his ministry and embitter him and immeasurably enriched the Mennonite Church in Zaire by his life, spirit and ministry.   JEB

Shintoism is a Japanese religion whose name is derived from *shinto*, meaning literally "way of the gods." The term was first used in the *Nihonshoki*, a chronology compiled in A.D. 720 in response to an imperial ordinance. The appearance of the word in such a document suggests Shinto's relationship to the imperial system.

Shintoism is °animistic in origin. Its deities are the natural world, spiritual powers, rulers and heroes, and °ancestors. The Shinto term for god is *kami* but it does not necessarily mean a transcendent being. Anything worthy of respect (a rock, animal, plant) can be called *kami*. (In regard to the origins of *kami*, the term *Kojiki* is also of interest).

Shintoism does not have an articulate theology, although it is doctrinally influenced by °Buddhism and Confucianism. It does, however, have concepts of heaven, eternal world, sin, defilement, and cleansing. Anything associated with death is considered "defiled." So while Shinto weddings or purification rites of children, for example, are common, Japanese funerals are usually a Buddhist ceremony.

Throughout its history Shintoism has almost always been closely identified with the imperial system. In 1867 the government finally made Shintoism the state religion. Twenty-three years later it issued an "Edict on Education," which was to become the doctrine of state Shintoism. The edict supported the "holy" imperial system founded by legendary imperial ancestors, and demanded that people give

their lives to the emperor should an emergency arise. The state Shinto system and the edict eventually made the emperor a *kami*. It was actually taught that the emperor was a "manifest god" until he made a public denial of his deity in January 1946, after World War II.

People in Japan and throughout Asia, especially Christians, suffered unbearable agony under the state Shinto system. People were forced to visit shrines to show their allegiance to the emperor. There was a law forbidding the use of irreverant words and behavior against the imperial family and the Ise Shrine, which enshrines the mythical Sun-goddess, the professed ancestor of the emperor. Many people were arrested on charges of violating the law. Prosecuted Christians were forced to answer the question, "Who do you think is greater, Christ or the Emperor?" and the answer determined their fate.

Shintoism was deprived of all its privileges at the collapse of the Japanese Empire in 1945. However, in recent years there has been a revival of the Shintoistic traditions in Japanese society, exemplified by the call for · nationalization of the Yasukuni Shrine (which enshrines the war dead "who laid down their lives for the emperor") and the incorporation of Shinto ideology into the public education system. It is cause for concern to Christians.   HY

See also Civil Religion; Patriotism.

Shipyard Colony, Belize, was founded in April 1958 by Old Colony Mennonites from Chihuahua and Durango States in Mexico. Clearing the forest was begun immediately, but by hand only. Thirty years later the ax had been replaced by the bulldozer and the chainsaw, and grain was harvested with a combine instead of a scythe. Sorghum, corn and, more recently, rice have been primary grain crops. Several thousand broiler hens are sold weekly in surrounding towns, as are tomatoes, melons, cucumbers, sweet peppers, and other vegetables. Livestock is also a major source of income. Several sawmills have ·been built and provide necessary lumber for houses and furniture. Carpenters and blacksmiths, several retail stores, and two dentists are also part of the settlement. The 1987 the colony's population was 1,966, including children.   DKF/JBL

MWH (1978), 278; *MWR* (March 14, 1985), 2.

Shoulderblade, Julia Yellow Horse. See Cheyenne (Julia Yellow Horse Shoulderblade: Cheyenne Minister [feature].

Showalter, Elizabeth Anna (b. Jan. 11, 1907), was born in the Shenandoah Valley near Broadway, Va., the twelfth child in the family of George B. and Elizabeth Blosser Showalter. She graduated from Harrisonburg State Normal School (James Madison University) and received an MA degree in journalism from Syracuse U. She taught at Iowa Mennonite School, Goshen College, and Eastern Mennonite College. From 1949 to 1960 she edited *Words of Cheer* for the Mennonite Publishing House and was known as "Aunt Beth" to her readers. She worked for two years for Laubach Literacy, Inc., including teaching short-term writing courses in Africa. In 1961 she began "Books Abroad," a project to furnish donated used books for institutions and persons overseas; it later became a part of the Women's Missionary and Service Commission (MC). In retirement she moved to Harrisonburg, Va., moving to Heritage Haven when it opened in 1981.   HA

Siemens, Jacob John (May 23, 1896-July 12, 1963). Born near Altona, Man., and baptized and married in the °Bergthal Mennonite Church, Jake Siemens was the primary idealogue of the consumer and producer °cooperatives, °credit unions and agricultural societies among the southern Manitoba Mennonites in the 1930s and 1940s. For Siemens cooperatives were °mutual aid and Christian °love in practice. He communicated his vision through a great variety of adult education programs, e.g., the Rhineland Agricultural Institute in Altona, which taught Christian ethics and Mennonite history alongside agriculture courses. He also inspired numerous young Mennonites to become missionaries for cooperatives in Manitoba and beyond. The Bergthal Mennonite leadership rejected his vision as too °socialistic and insufficiently orthodox. The resulting pro- and anti-cooperative division in much of the area between Altona and Winkler influenced both church and community very negatively. He left the Mennonites and moved to Winnipeg. He died after an unsuccessful venture into politics as a member of the New Democratic Party (NDP), filled with a growing sense that the cooperative movement was weakening in its prophetic and educational task. He was buried from a Unitarian church. J. W. Fretz credited him for best exemplifying rural mutual aid and Frank H. °Epp eulogized him as a latter-day Johann °°Cornies. RJS

Henry Dyck, "Jacob John Siemens and the Co-operative Movement in Southern Manitoba 1929-1955" (MA thesis, U. of Manitoba, 1982); F. H. Epp, *Mennonites in Canada II,* pp. 363-67.

Sin (ME IV:79). Reinhold Niebuhr (1892-1971) was fond of saying that the Christian doctrine of sin is the most empirical of all doctrines. The reality of sin needs no proof. It is demonstrated again and again in our human experience: we both sin against others and are sinned against.

But what is sin essentially? And what is its source or origin? its symptoms? What is meant by original sin? This article will attempt to answer some of these questions from the perspective of the Bible and historical theology, the latter including especially Anabaptism.

The Old Testament. In the Old Testament there are several word clusters which refer to sin. The predominant word is *chattath,* which means to miss the mark (Ex 32:30). Perhaps a more fundamental root word for developing a biblical view of sin, however, is that of *peshar,* which means rebellion (Is 43:27). Another somewhat common Hebrew word for sin is *ayin,* implying a state of guilt or corruption attendant with sin (Jer 30:14-15).

A word study on sin does not probe the depths of the Old Testament's understanding. Indeed, the story of the Fall of humankind (Gn 3) attempts to give a narrative account of the origin of sin in

human experience without even using the word "sin." According to this account of Adam and Eve in the Garden of Eden, sin is prototypically at one and the same time rebellion against the will of God and a breech in relationship with God.

Sin, then, represents both a turning away from covenant relationship with God and a turning to other gods (idolatry). The other gods can either be religious (pagan gods or occultism, Is 2:6ff.) or they can be political (human rulers or military might, Hos 14:3).

The prophet Jeremiah presages the New Testament in looking inward for the source of sin and evil: an evil or corrupted heart is the cause of willful acts of disobedience against God (11:8). And whereas the Mosaic law had said the consequences of sin would be visited upon the children to the third and fourth generations (Ex 20:5), Ezekiel clarified that the guilt of sin rests with the perpetrator: "The soul that sins shall die" (Ez 18:4, 20).

The New Testament. The key words for the concept of sin in the New Testament are *hamartolos* ("sinners"), *hamartano* (to miss the mark) and *hamartia* (sin). In Jesus' context the "sinners" were the godless, those who were disobedient to the law (e.g., the publicans, Lk 7:37), those who didn't hold to the Pharisaic interpretation of the law, the heathen and those separated from God.

Jesus seems not to have rejected these distinctions between the righteous and the sinners, but he did reject the idea that sinners are a unique class of people. In fact, Jesus gave an ironic twist to these distinctions: it was the so-called "righteous" who were the most corrupted by sin (Mt 23:27-28); and it was for the "sinners" that Jesus gave his life (Mt 9:10-13).

Like Jeremiah before him, Jesus was not merely concerned with outward acts (either of righteousness or of sin), but was also concerned with an inward attitude, disposition, or motivation (Mk 7:6-8). Not only is murder wrong but the anger which motivates it (Mt 5:21ff.); adultery alone is not at fault but the lust which drives it (Mt 5:27ff.).

Unlike modern-day evangelists, Jesus neither encouraged people to wallow in the guilt of their sin nor to resort to self-condemnation on the basis of their sin. He called them rather to repent of (turn from) their sin and follow him (discipleship, Mk 1:14ff.).

For the apostle Paul, sin appears to be a suprapersonal (cosmic) force which nevertheless holds power over persons and enslaves them (Rom 5:12; 6:12, 17, 20, 7:14, 23). This force he refers to as "flesh," which is not to be associated with the physical body but rather is to be contrasted with the spirit of God against which the flesh contends. The result of sin for Paul is death—spiritual and physical (Rom 6:23; 7:5; 1 Cor 15:56)—both of which entered human experience through the disobedience of our first parents, Adam and Eve (Rom 5:12-14).

Sin is not the final word for Paul. The keys are that Jesus dies for our sins (Rom 5:8; 1 Cor 15:3) and that through the Spirit we are able to overcome the power of sin. The law convicts us of our sin—that is, shows us what sin is (Rom 3:20; 7:7). But because of the seductiveness of the flesh the law incites us to sin (Rom 7:5). It is only in the power of the resurrection and the indwelling of the Spirit that one can be rescued from the flesh which enslaves and the law which condemns (Rom 8:1-17; Gal 5:16-26).

In John's gospel sin is portrayed as a quality of life expressed in word, deed, and thought (Jn 8:21, 24, 34). As in Paul there is a dualism involving the forces of good and evil. John uses different terminology to describe this dualism—not spirit-flesh but light-darkness (1:4-9). More explicitly than other New Testament writers, John links sin with the Devil (8:34, 44; cf. 1 Jn 3:8). It was Jesus' mission to destroy the works of the Devil, however, and to take away sins (1 Jn 3:5-9). At the heart of sin is lack of faith in Jesus Christ (Jn 16:8f.; 15:22, 24).

"World" (cosmos) is used in a twofold sense in John. First, it was through Christ that the world was created (1:10) and it was for the world that Jesus gave himself (3:16-17). Second, the world has come under the sway of the Evil One and as such opposes God (8:23) and is the source of persecution of Jesus and his disciples (15:18-20). Jesus' own death and resurrection are portrayed as a struggle against the world as enslaved by the devil and an overcoming of the world (16:33).

In his first epistle, John does talk about sin as transgression, lawlessness, and unrighteousness (1:9; 3:4; 5:17). In this context, however, he was addressing a believing community both to counteract the notion that believers could not sin and to confess that Jesus forgives and overcomes sin. Oftentimes Christians have associated sin with this narrower sense of transgression against God's law, rather than seeing it in the deeper biblical sense of yielding to and being enslaved by the forces of evil.

Historical Developments. Throughout the first several centuries of the Christian church there was earnest teaching about what it meant to be a follower of Jesus. Indeed, some would later accuse the early church of moralism, that is, a doctrine of salvation by human works. Generally the early church believed in the freedom of the will, that is, the ability of humans to choose between and do either good or evil.

Some of the early church theologians could somewhat naively perceive sin to be ignorance about what is good and right, the antidote of which is correct teaching and training. Irenaeus, for example, could explain the sin of Adam and Eve as childlike immaturity. The whole purpose of both creation and redemption is to bring human beings to the level of spiritual and moral maturity which God intends for them.

By the time Christianity was legitimized by the state during the reign of Emperor Constantine (306-37), however, the problem of the church was not moralism but rather moral laxness. Not only the common Christians but also many leaders in the church lived carnal lives. Except for a few ascetics, there was not much emphasis on the teachings of Jesus or on discipleship. It is in this context, then, that the debates between Pelagius and Augustine (d. 430) must be understood.

Pelagius, a 5th-c. British monk, was concerned about the breakdown in the moral quality of the church. In part, he blamed this on some of the teachings of his contemporaries, including Augus-

tine. He reacted, for example, to a famous line from Augustine's *Confessions*: "Thou commandest continence; grant what Thou commandest and command what thou wilt." This, he thought, amounted to a lack of moral responsibility (what Bonhoeffer called "cheap grace" in the 20th c.).

Pelagius was also concerned about an influx of pessimism into Christian theology which he attributed to the influence of the dualistic religion of Manichaeism, popular at the time. (Augustine himself was a Manichee before becoming Christian.) One source of this pessimism was a commentary on Paul's epistles attributed to Ambrose (a bishop who was instrumental in Augustine's conversion). One of the problem spots, said Pelagius, was the comment on Rom 5:12 which maintained that: "in Adam all sinned as in a lump"; that human souls were derived from parents like bodies; and that thereby sin was transmitted.

Pelagius responded with his own commentary on Pauline epistles. He asserted that there is no hereditary transmission of sin through reproduction but that rather we voluntarily sin by following Adam's example. True, we are corrupted by a sinful environment and increasingly our sinful decisions weaken our will; but we don't come into the world inherently sinful.

It was important to Pelagius to assert that both in doing good as well as in sinning personal assent is involved. He maintained that newborn babies were without evil—though he didn't reject infant baptism—and that Adam didn't become a mortal, he was created that way. Pelagius was misrepresented in the ensuing controversy, perhaps most of all by one of his overly-zealous disciples, Celestius. It was said of Pelagius that he denied the need for grace. Yet for Pelagius forgiveness was unmerited favor (grace, in other words). Furthermore, grace for him was divine aid for doing the good which comes through moral exhortation and the example of Christ. Pelagius himself was condemned at several church councils.

Augustine attempted to clarify his own position on human nature and grace in response to Pelagius and his followers. He based his thoughts on a Latin translation of Rom 5:12 which said "the entire race fell with Adam." The conclusion which he reached from this was that sin was hereditary and that its transmission was associated with sexual reproduction. Hence, Augustine could say that virginity was a higher ideal than marriage and that sex even within marriage is tainted by concupiscence (desire or appetite of the lower nature).

Augustine assumed the propriety of infant baptism and concluded from it that babies are polluted by sin, since they couldn't have committed actual sin. They have a sinful nature from birth, in other words, for which they receive remission of sins through baptism. (He said that unbaptized infants receive only a mild form of damnation, however, if they die in infancy—they eternally are in a state of "limbo.") Humankind is really by nature collectively sinful; the so-called good acts of pagans are actually sinful. Without redeeming grace no one is capable of acts of pure will.

It would be justice if all of us were to be condemned to hell, according to Augustine; but God in his mercy elected to save a substantial minority by a decree of predestination. If you think that is not justice, think of the guilt attached to original and actual sin. None deserves unmerited favor. This unconditional grace is irresistible. Since men and women are so corrupt they cannot will the good, grace must do it; further, if grace were not irresistible, God's decree of predestination would be thwarted. Verification of this operation of grace within a person is through consistent goodness of character to a "final perseverance" which is also a gift of God, not a matter of merit.

In sum, Augustine's position on sin and grace was: (a) The acknowledgement that we are dependent upon God for our creation leads to the acknowledgement that we are dependent upon God for our redemption. (b) He could not conceive of a free will and a natural delight in the good (after the Fall), nor could he conceive of achieving the good even if humans delighted in it. The good can come about only through the Holy Spirit's empowerment. (c) Nature and will are not separate for Augustine. All expressions of the will are really expressions of human nature which is sinful. (d) His psychological realism prevented him from perceiving simple choices between the good and the evil; all our decisions are tainted by mixed motives and sinful desires. (e) Freedom means power to choose and do good but this is the very power which humanity lacks because of its fallen nature.

It must be added that Augustine definitely did not want to attribute any kind of ultimate status to evil. In raising the question as to what the nature of evil is, he would want to say that it has no status of its own—i.e., it hasn't the status of ultimate reality; rather, evil is the privation of the good, or a falling away from the good, or an inordinate desire for the (relative) good (not the ultimate Good). God is a good God, and evil cannot be attributed to God. Also, God's creation was good, and evil cannot be attributed to some flaw in creation. (Here Augustine is breaking away from Platonic and Manichaeistic dualisms which claim that matter is evil.)

So whence comes evil? It came from a misuse of the freedom of the will on that part of our first parents. As he said in his *Confessions*, "To climb against [God] was your [i.e., Adam and Eve's] fall." Thenceforward none of their progeny has the freedom to choose between good and evil; all of us were born with the propensity to sin subsequent to their sin. Before the fall Adam and Eve had the power to not sin; after the Fall all humans have not the power to not sin; only in the next life will we not have the power to sin: *posse non peccare, non posse non peccare, non posse peccare.*

It can be said in many respects that the Reformation was actually a revival of Augustinianism, especially Augustine's understanding of human nature, the bondage of the will and predestination. (Luther had been a monk in the Augustinian order.) In the Middle Ages a distinction was made between the image and likeness of human beings (Gen 1:26). The *image* had to do with the natural endowment of reason and will which humans have; *likeness*, on the other hand, referred to moral (or supernatural) characteristics which were given to humans when first created but were then lost due to sin, although the image remained intact. Only by divine grace can the likeness be restored.

This led to the two-story theology of Thomas Aquinas, the first story based upon reason and leading to a natural knowledge of God and the second story based upon supernatural revelation which resulted in knowledge of a specific Christian and salvific nature.

Luther rejected a distinction between image and likeness. He understood the image and likeness to be what is called Hebrew parallelism—they are synonyms with the same referent. But while he added this corrective to the interpretation of Gen 1:26, he made another kind of assumption which the text itself does not: for Luther not only is the likeness corrupted by the fall but also the image. This is called total depravity.

Luther could say that there are relics of the image left; e.g., Gen 9:6 seems to imply that the image is still intact even after the fall. But Luther understood that to mean that the divine intention for the *imago dei* in humankind is still there but it is not *actually* in human beings.

Calvin also rejected the distinction between image and likeness, and saw that both were corrupted with the fall. He was more optimistic about remnants of the *imago dei*, however. For this reason he could say that self-knowledge and knowledge of God are interrelated. True knowledge of self will lead to knowledge of God since we are created in the image of God and that image has specifically to do with the faculty of knowledge or reason. However, this true self-knowledge which leads to knowledge of God will show us to be corrupt and sinful in the light of knowledge of God who is holy.

The will was the dominant human faculty in mainline Protestant's understanding of sin and human nature. The will, being corrupted by sin, could not will the good nor turn to God even if one wished to with the emotions or knew that one should with the reason. That could come about only through God's "irresistible grace."

In the development of his doctrine of predestination Calvin said that it was by eternal decree that God had willed that some should be saved and others condemned. Here he goes beyond Augustine (as well as Luther). Augustine wouldn't have said that God actively predestined some to eternal damnation; rather he said that those who were condemned were simply passed over; they were left to stew in their juices and they thereby got what all humans rightly deserve. But Calvin went that further step to say that God actually decreed that some would be saved and others damned. (That is why this is called the doctrine of "double predestination.")

The Anabaptists were in agreement with the mainline reformers that before the Fall humankind was in a state of blessedness with the ability to choose between good and evil. In what God had created there was no evil. They believed that through Adam's sin the whole human race had fallen into a state of corruption and condemnation. Thenceforth, human nature was corrupted by sin.

Where the Anabaptists differed with the mainline reformers was in the extent of the Fall's effects, especially with regard to the divine image in human beings. For many of the Anabaptists there was a remaining vestige of the divine image in human beings after the fall. It was through this vestige of the divine image that God could appeal to human beings to turn from sin and turn to Christ for their redemption.

There were, of course, differences between the Anabaptists themselves. There were four different understandings of what original sin was: "It is described as inborn incurable sickness, as the loss of the power to distinguish between good and evil, as a poison which has wrought a corruption within a nature originally good, and as the mature man which over-extends itself into the realm of the supernatural" (Beachy, 38).

The Anabaptists also rejected the idea of the bondage of the will and predestination. Predestination seemed to them to suggest that God was the source of evil. The bondage of the will seemed to suggest that human beings are excused from making a decision for faith in Jesus Christ and a life of discipleship. They believed in the freedom of the will though not in the Pelagian sense; rather, it was their view that with the aid of divine grace the tendency toward evil in humans could be overcome. "Without this freedom of the will discipleship, the heart of Anabaptism, loses its meaning" (Friedmann, 207).

The Anabaptists did not deny the reality of sin nor did they even deny the inheritance of a tendency to sin from our first parents. But they did not accept this tendency toward sinning as being an inevitable fate. A favorite passage was Ez 18:4, 20: "The soul that sins shall die. The son shall not suffer for the iniquity of the father, nor the father suffer for the iniquity of the son; the righteousness of the righteous shall be upon himself, and the wickedness of the wicked shall be upon himself" (v. 20).

The Anabaptists made a distinction between two problems: that of the problem of original sin as it affects infants who do not yet know the difference between good and evil; and the problem with original sin in adults (either before or after conversion). They universally rejected the Roman Catholic notion that infant baptism was a necessary sacrament to take care of the effects of original sin and to assure that an infant would not be damned. They believed that the wages of sin is death, physical death, but this did not mean for them eternal death or condemnation on account of the death of Christ which reconciles God and humanity. They further believed that Christ's death was efficacious for those who do not yet know the difference between good and evil—infants and children.

Some Anabaptists drew an interesting parallel between the unrighteousness of Adam and the righteousness of Christ. The righteousness of Christ is of no avail to anyone unless it is appropriated through faith; likewise, the sin of Adam does not impair one except through that person choosing to make it a part of his own being. "For, as foreign righteousness does not save anybody, so will foreign sin not condemn anybody either" (Friedmann, p. 210).

The backside of this argument is that if Adam's sin would condemn all because all share inherently in his sinful nature, then it would necessarily follow that Christ's righteousness would also save everyone also apart from faith. Here is an implicit argument against universalism—or the universal conferring of sin from Adam and righteousness from Christ. What

condemns people is choosing to live in the sin of Adam and bearing, therefore, the fruits of sharing in the Adamic nature.

Another key for the Anabaptist understanding of sin has to do with their belief in the possibility of rebirth or spiritual transformation in which the natural person is transformed into a spiritual person. This is in contrast to Luther's understanding of the status of the justified person as being *simul justus et peccator* (at once righteous and a sinner). On the basis of faith in the grace of Jesus Christ the believer is deemed righteous, according to Luther, but on the basis of his own nature and deeds he is a sinner.

For the Anabaptists, however, justification does not only change a person's standing before God in a legal sense but also brings about a change within the person in a moral sense. In Pauline terms, it can be said that the mainline reformers tended to emphasize Paul's comment in Rom 7:18, "For I know that nothing good dwells within me," whereas the Anabaptist emphasis would be accounted for by Paul's teaching on death to sin and new life in the spirit (Rom 8).

This is not to suggest that there is still not a struggle between the two natures or that the individual cannot backslide into the old nature. They did not deny the power or presence of sin in believers and were fully cognizant of the temptations of sin. This was partly due to the fact that they acknowledged the radical dualism of the New Testament (between the kingdom of God and the kingdom of earth; or between the powers of light and darkness or spirit and the flesh). It was only against this radical dualism that the idea of conversion or spiritual rebirth made any sense at all.

Concluding Theses on Sin. (1) Sin, though it does not have ultimate reality, is nevertheless a phenomenon which must be reckoned with. The cross is both *because* of our sins and *for* our sins; no theology of the cross can take lightly the possibility nor the consequences of sin. The cross, in other words, is an indication of the depths to which men and women had fallen in their sin; but the cross was also an indication of the seriousness with which God takes sin and the extent to which God is willing to do something about it.

(2) Sin is a phenomenon which has more than individual dimensions or consequences; there is also a corporate and systemic dimension which must be reckoned with. This may be one of the weaknesses of the Anabaptist perspective built upon Ez 18 and their reading of Rom 5:12. Even though they understood the corporate dimension of God's redemptive project through their doctrine of the church, sin was interpreted too much as a voluntary and willful act of the individual. Some emphases in contemporary biblical scholarship and theology can ameliorate this tendency such as: (a) Another reading of Rom 5:12 which interprets sin as not being transmitted from generation to generation through procreation or physical means but rather interprets Adam in terms of the Hebrew concept of corporate personality: what Adam does is representative of us all—the whole human family chooses to use its freedom in willful disobedience against God. Sin,

therefore has social and environmental implications. Sin is not simply transmitted from generations but because of sin there is a social environment in which we are conditioned towards sin. (b) An understanding of the principalities and powers as being overcome by evil and that therefore there are forces beyond our immediate control with which we must contend (Eph 6:12; cf. Col 1:16; Rom 8:28). Sin must be understood in part as being in collusion with or in bondage to these evil principalities. (c) The °Social Gospel, which helped to bring to forefront the social and cultural aspects of sin (and the heirs of the Social Gospel—feminist and liberation theologies). With the insights gained through these various contemporary understandings, a doctrine of sin needs to be understood in a dialectic framework between the individual and the corporate or the structural. On the one hand it is individuals who create the environment in which we live—human culture and society. On the other, once that environment is created, it turns around and shapes us as individuals. Due to the sin of our forebears and our own, our environment conditions us towards sin against others, God and ourselves. Salvation, then, cannot merely be the saving of individual souls nor even simply the rescuing of individuals from a sinful environment but it must also include the shaping of a new environment which conditions people toward the will of God and righteousness. Here is where sin, salvation and the church intersect.

(3) Sin takes different forms, and we must be attentive to those different forms, not viewing it in monolithic terms. Sin is not merely pride (*hubris*) as it has been defined or understood in much of Western thought nor is it simply sensuousness or evil desire as in eastern thought. A corollary to an understanding of sin as multi-formed is that salvation must be viewed as multi-formed; that is, the gospel too comes to people in different forms. Salvation addresses the particular sins of an individual or people or culture.

We might generally speak of two categories of sin (following Kierkegaard): sins of infinitude and sins of finitude. Sins of infinitude are those in which an individual or a people try to make of themselves more than they were intended to be—they try to be as gods. Sins of finitude, then, are the converse: those in which individuals or a people do not claim their rightful place in God's creation—as persons created in God's image, beings just a little lower than the angels who are charged with the stewardship of this earth and of their own endowments (giftedness).

(4) There is forgiveness for our sins but grace does not treat merely the symptoms of human sin; it also treats the cause. Grace is more than pardon for human sins and shortcomings; grace also is transformative, recreative power. Popular Protestant understandings of sin and grace tend toward a never ending cul de sac of grace: we sin, we ask forgiveness of God, God forgives. Sin, however, is not the last word where God's grace and Spirit are active. Regeneration and new life in Christ are possible (2 Cor 3:17-18; Eph 2:8-10, esp. v. 10).   RAK

Alvin J. Beachy, *The Concept of Grace in the Radical Reformation* (Nieuwkoop: B. De Graaf, 1977), ch. 2; C. J.

Dyck, ed., *A Legacy of Faith* (Newton, 1962), 87ff.; Thomas N. Finger, *Christian Theology: An Eschatological Perspective*, vol. 2 (Scottdale, 1989), ch. 6; Thomas N. Finger and Willard Swartley, "Bondage and Deliverance: Biblical and Theological Perspectives," in *Essays on Spiritual Bondage and Deliverance*, ed. Willard Swartley, Occasional Papers, 11 (Elkhart, Ind.: IMS, 1988), 10-38; Robert Friedmann, "The Doctrine of Original Sin as Held by the Anabaptists of the 16th C.," *MQR*, 33 (1959), 206-14; CRR 3, ch. 2; Richard E. Weingart, "The Meaning of Sin in the Theology of Menno Simons," *MQR*, 41 (1967), 25-39.

See also Creation; Exorcism; Forgiveness; Grace; Salvation; Satan.

Singing (ME IV:533). The earliest known writing by an Anabaptist on the subject of singing is that of Conrad °Grebel, who expressed his opposition to singing in 1524 with the same argument as did his teacher Zwingli: all that was needed (in °worship) was the Word; but also because Grebel understood singing to be forbidden by the Apostle Paul (Ephesians and Colossians), and because he thought singing might cause either vexation or conceit. Another early Anabaptist leader, Balthasar °Hubmaier, was not opposed to singing, but cautioned, in 1526, that unless people sang with understanding and from the heart and with the Holy Spirit, God would not accept their songs. The same thought was echoed by the Hutterite leader, Peter °°Riedemann, somewhat later, when he said that singing spiritual songs is pleasing to God only if people sing attentively, in the fear of God, and as inspired by the spirit of Christ. Singing for carnal pleasure (*aus Fleisches Lust*) or for the beauty of the sound, according to Riedemann, is a serious sin. He also noted that the Hutterites allowed singing of spiritual songs only. °Menno Simons had virtually nothing to say about singing other than that hymns should not be sung thoughtlessly or frivolously. The Dutch Mennonite, Hans de °°Ries, in his preface to the hymnal °°*Liedtboeck* (1582), wrote the most detailed critique of and instructions regarding singing. He decried singing without a spirit of true devotion, taking pleasure in the sound of human voices and of the melody, not paying heed to the meaning of the words, and singing hymns while living unregenerate lives, without having experienced the truths of the songs, or without a spirit of gratitude. He then continued with admonitions that spiritual songs must be sung to the glory of God in a true spirit of devotion and with a heart that has turned from all earthly things; that they must be sung for edification of oneself and one's neighbor, and be accompanied by a life reflecting the faith of the singer.

In the 18th c., influenced by North German °Pietist hymnals, Prussian Mennonite reflection on singing gave more attention to the power of music. In the preface to a hymnal of 1752, edifying singing is described as capable of causing the sinner to be converted, bringing the wrongdoer onto the right path, admonishing the unruly, comforting mourners, instructing the ignorant, and making the zealous stronger amd more godly.

Some 20th-c. North American Mennonite hymnals contain prefaces with comments on historical, aesthetic, and practical considerations of hymns, whereas the Mennonite Brethren have continued to emphasize that singing of hymns be done from the heart and that the singer must repent if he is unable to do so; in addition, as did the Pietists of old, they caution that art is not to overshadow content and truth, and that hymns are a powerful witness to visitors.

The Practice of Singing. Early Anabaptist and Hutterite songs give accounts of men and women singing while going to their deaths by fire or water (the earliest being the account of Felix °°Mantz singing "Into thy hands, Lord, I commend my spirit" before he was drowned in 1527) and of prisoners in separate dungeons in the same castles very loudly singing spiritual songs to comfort and encourage one another in the faith and to let the brethren on the outside know where they were imprisoned.

The earliest known account of Anabaptists singing when they met to worship was that of the singing of a communion hymn in Franconia in 1527. During interrogation at trials in the next decade Anabaptists stated that they sang psalms in their meetings. The earliest Anabaptist hymnal was published in 1564 (°°Ausbund), but Anabaptists wrote and sang many hundreds of songs to the tunes of popular songs, the new Lutheran and Reformed Church hymns, some ancient Roman Catholic chants, and other melodies.

The publication of a great number of hymnals, at first in the Dutch language, and then in German in Prussia and Russia, is evidence that singing became a very important part of worship among the Dutch-Prussian-Russian Mennonites. In the 18th c. a hymnal used a great deal by the Mennonites of Prussia was °°*Geistreiches Gesangbuch* (1767), based on the Pietist hymnal of the same name that was compiled by Freylinghausen. When the Mennonites left Prussia for Russia after 1788, they took two hymnals, containing both the older Lutheran chorales and newer Pietist hymns with them. An account of a worship service in the Chortitza colony in 1840, written much later, describes the unaccompanied unison singing of a congregation of some 50 persons led by a *Vorsänger* (cantor); it is described as having been so energetic and strong that it seemed as if they wanted to "topple the walls of Jericho." According to the account, most sang from memory. Singing was an important activity among the Russian Mennonites at occasions other than worship services; for instance, at weddings the young couple was greeted by a °choir as they entered the sanctuary, and the congregation sang numerous hymns during the service. After the church service, the single young people and young married couples sang during the ritual of replacing the bride's myrtle wreath and veil, and for the rest of the evening the younger people played singing games while the older generation looked on. At other informal social gatherings young people in Russian Mennonite villages sang, often with guitar accompaniment, and played the same singing games as at weddings. At the turn of the century, a minister in one village, Jacob Martens, instituted Sunday afternoon gatherings in his home for the youth, at which, in addition to studying the Bible and other great literature, they sang and made instrumental °music. Somewhat later, the *Gesanggottesdienst* (song service), comprising solo, ensemble, and choral singing, together with readings from the Bible and intended as a type of evangelistic service, became an important musical

genre in Russian Mennonite villages. When they migrated to America, the Russian Mennonites brought along the hymnals they had used in Russia and soon also instituted large choral festivals which became major musical and social events for young and old.

One of the most striking aspects of congregational singing in all but the conservative branches of the Mennonite churches is four-part singing. This was greatly facilitated in what eventually became the Mennonite Church (MC) by singing schools modeled by Joseph °°Funk, on those formed at the beginning of the 19th c. in the eastern United States. Funk published *Genuine Church Music* (1832; renamed °°*Harmonia Sacra* in 1851), for use in the singing schools.

In Russia, four-part congregational singing in the Mennonite churches was greatly aided by the fact that at the end of the 19th c. virtually every young person became a member of the church choir, singing with numbers (*Ziffern*), and that they continued to do so after emigration to America. In the United States part-singing by the congregation was encouraged in the General Conference Mennonite Church (GCM) by the publication in 1890 of a hymnal which contained both text and four-part harmony in one volume.

During the 20th c. the use of instruments has been resisted in the Mennonite Church (MC) because they were "worldly" and because of fear that the tradition of four-part congregational singing would suffer. Although Russian Mennonites have made use of organs and pianos in worship, their harmonized congregational singing has not declined. A significant change that has taken place in the Mennonite Church beginning in the 1960s, was the addition of pianos or organs or both; however, many congregations still prefer to sing without instruments and use the organ or piano only for preludes and postludes and as accompaniment for the occasional duets or other small vocal ensembles. Occasionally they have instrumental music as "special music." Furthermore, in many urban churches a choir may sing for special occasions. Whereas in the past, the only music at worship services in Mennonite Church (MC) congregations was congregational singing and an occasional male quartet, and at weddings, only congregational singing and male quartets, a wedding at an urban MC church in the late 1980s is very much like that of other Mennonite churches.

Most Old Colony Mennonites, Old Order Mennonites, and Amish continue to sing in unison and in the German language in their worship services and have no music other than unaccompanied congregational singing in their religious services. Most Old Colony Mennonites in Canada and Mexico still sing the hymns of the 18th-c. *Gesangbuch* based on the German *Geistreiches Gesangbuch* of 1767. The Evangelical Mennonite Mission Conference (EMMC), which comes out of that tradition, has English and Low German worship services and has adopted the *Worship Hymnal* of the Mennonite Brethren church for use in English-language worship. They sing in harmony; choirs composed of young people and small vocal ensembles sing in EMMC worship services.

Most of the Amish continue to sing from the *Aus-*

bund in worship services, but the Amish at Aylmer, Ont. sing from the 1892 edition of °°*Unpartheyische Liedersammlung,* which contains some *Ausbund* songs. Most Amish young people sing the hymns from *Unpartheyische Liedersammlung* (first ed., 1820) and secular songs, e.g., country and western music, at their °°"singings," which provide the main opportunities for courting. But at Aylmer, the young people sing from the *Sunday School Hymnal with Supplement,* which contains many gospel songs. The use of instruments is forbidden.

Some Old Order Mennonites conduct singing schools in which they use a book with shaped notes, such as *Philharmonia* (1875), which contains many of the standard old hymns, but in the 1980s they have also adopted *Christian Hymnal* (1959), which consists mainly of gospel songs. This is the official songbook for use in the Sunday evening "singings" of the young people, but they also sing from books such as *Radio Favorites* in four-part harmony. Old Order Mennonites in Canada use °°*Gemeinschaftliche Liedersammlung* (first ed., 1936) in their worship services; in the United States they sing from *Unpartheyische Liedersammlung.* The church does not allow use of instruments. Some, like the Markham Mennonites in Ontario, who left the Old Order Mennonite Church, sing two German and two English hymns in their worship services, from *Gemeinschaftliche Liedersammlung* and *Mennonite Hymns* (1953) respectively. Part-singing is not forbidden in their worship services, except for the more conservative Old Order groups in the United States. At Old Order Mennonite singing schools and Sunday evening "singings," the young people sing gospel songs in harmony but without instrumental accompaniment.

The singing of gospel songs has been the cause for considerable controversy in the Mennonite church. It is said that Joseph Funk published *Harmonia Sacra* because he was opposed to gospel songs; however, many Mennonite Church (MC) congregations have sung almost exclusively gospel songs for considerable periods in their history. When the Russian Mennonite church divided in 1860, the new branch, called the Mennonite Brethren, sang almost exclusively translations of American gospel songs. Today virtually all Mennonite churches sing some gospel songs, even in Europe. Since 1969 the Mennonite Church and General Conference Mennonites share a hymnal (*Mennonite Hymnal*), and sing the hymns of the various ethnic groups: Swiss psalms; German chorales and Pietist hymns; and American folk hymns, gospel songs, and spirituals. The hymns of the hymnal to be published in the 1990s will be shared by General Conference, Mennonite Church (MC), and the Church of the °°Brethren, among others.

There is lively debate in the 1980s among the Mennonite Brethren about the trend, in many of their congregations, towards the use of choruses, Christian "pop" (popular) music, aided by amplifiers, microphones, and body movements imitating the general North American entertainment industry in worship services. Some General Conference churches, particularly on the West Coast, are following this trend also.

Unaccompanied singing at the unison and octave (but sometimes, unknowingly, in parallel fourths) has always been an important part of Hutterite life: in daily worship, for recreation, as a means of inculcating the articles of faith, and, very importantly, to keep their history alive. The latter is done by singing the historical songs which Anabaptists and Hutterites wrote in the 16th and 17th c. and which comprise a large part of their *Lieder der Hutterischen Brüder.* Just as the school curriculum of the Hutterites in the 18th c. consisted of (memorizing) prayers, singing, and writing (songs), so it has continued in their Saturday school under the direction of a Hutterite teacher. Hutterites still take Riedemann's thoughts about singing very seriously—they are fearful of singing *"aus Fleisches Lust,"* and sing their old songs at the beginning and end of worship services in order to awaken a spirit of devotion and to give encouragement, in accordance with Riedemann's precepts. They have aurally transmitted the melodies of their 16th and 17th-c. songs, and most of them sing in the shrill, nasal style that they have employed throughout their history. In addition to singing at their worship services and at home, Hutterites also sing for three or four hours on four evenings before the one wedding day of the year. Many of the songs on these occasions are gospel songs. There have been dramatic changes in many of the Hutterite colonies of late: fraternal relations with the (Hutterian) Society of Brothers (ME IV:1126) in the eastern United States have been reestablished, some Hutterite colonies are very open to evangelists, some of them watch a Canadian Christian television program at school. Thus they are exposed to much new music and in some colonies the young poeple sing these new songs in harmony.

The eastern Hutterites (formerly the Society of Brothers) practice both sacred and secular choral and instrumental music. They have a unique hymnal which contains original settings, by Marlys Swinger, of numerous texts by their founder, Eberhard °°Arnold, as well as a variety of songs by the major composers, some Negro spirituals, and hymns found in other hymnals. Before their weddings, they have several evenings of singing and musical performances of such major works as Vivaldi's *Gloria* with their own orchestral accompaniment.   HMa

Charles Burkhart, "Music of the Old Colony Mennonites," *Menn. Life,* 7, no. 1 (July 1952), 20-21, 47; Robert Friedmann, *Hutterite Studies,* ed. Harold Bender (Goshen, Ind.: Mennonite Historical Society, 1961); Orland Gingerich, *The Amish of Canada* (Waterloo, Ont.: Conrad Press, 1972); George Pullen Jackson, "The Strange Music of the Old Order Amish," *The Musical Quarterly,* vol. 31, pp. 275-88; Rufus M. Jones, *Studies in Mystical Religion* (London: Macmillan, 1909); Walter Jost, "The Hymn Tune Tradition of the General Conference Mennonite Church (PhD diss., U. of Southern California, 1966); Peter Letkemann, "The Hymnody and Choral Music of the Mennonites in Russia, 1789-1915 (PhD diss., U. of Toronto, 1985); Helen Martens, "Hutterite Songs: The Origins and Aural Transmission of their Melodies from the Sixteenth Century (PhD diss., Columbia U., 1968); idem, "Music of Some Religious Minorities in Canada," *Ethnomusicology* (Sept. 1972); idem, "Mennonite Music," "Amish Music," "Hutterite Music," in *Encyclopedia of Music in Canada* (1981); W. Wiswedel, *Bilder and Führergestalten aus dem Täufertum,* vol. 3 (Kassel, 1952); Joseph W. Yoder, "The Church Music of the Old Order Amish and the Old Colony Mennonites," *MQR,* 27 (1953), 34-54.

See also Eastern Pennsylvania Mennonite Church; Hymnology; Menno Colony; Music; Old Order River Brethren; Worship.

Singleness. Increased singleness among the North American adult population is bringing increased awareness of the needs and contributions of unmarried people to society. According to 1985 U.S. Census Bureau figures, 40 percent of the U.S. adult population was single as compared to 31 percent in 1975. It has been predicted that this percentage will increase beyond 50 percent by the turn of the century and that society will become single-oriented rather than couple-oriented in the process.

The percentage of Mennonites who are single is somewhat smaller than the population at-large. It was reported by Kauffman and Harder in *Anabaptists Four Centuries Later* (1975) that 27.3 percent of all Mennonite and Brethren in Christ members were single. In the 1982 Mennonite Church census conducted by Michael Yoder, 26 percent of all Mennonite Church adult members were single as compared to 35 percent from 1982 U.S. Census Bureau reports.

Never-married Mennonite women have tended to outnumber never-married Mennonite men. For example, Kauffman and Harder found that of those Mennonites and Brethren in Christ members 45 years and over, 1.6 percent of the men and 9.3 percent of the women never married. Apparently, single Mennonite men have found spouses outside Mennonite denominations more frequently than have single Mennonite women.

Single adults fall into many different categories. They are young, old, never-married, divorced, separated, widowed, parents, and childless. Some are single by choice and others by circumstance. Two factors which have contributed to increased singleness in the 1980s have been rising age of first °marriage and a higher °divorce rate.

As singleness increases in North America, denominational attitudes towards singles are more accepting, however, marriage and family-centeredness are still considered the norm. Activities, sermon topics, and special events often reflect support for couples rather than singles. Singles want affirmation that they are whole people without marriage, and they desire equal consideration of their problems and concerns.

One step toward a broader acceptance of singles would be a more clearly articulated theology of singleness. John Howard Yoder concluded an article entitled "Singleness in Ethical and Pastoral Perspective" with the statement that singleness represents unfinished theological and ethical agenda. (This article appeared in a publication entitled *Being Single: Resources on Singleness,* published as a cooperative effort of the Episcopal Church, Association of Evangelical Lutheran Churches, American Lutheran Church, Lutheran Church in America and the U.S. Roman Catholic Conference of Bishops, 1986.) One example of unfinished theological agenda derives from the assumption held since the Protestant Reformation's rejection of °monasticism: that singleness is a temporary state before marriage. Such a concept feeds into the stereotyped opinion that older never-married women are to be pitied and that older never-married men are suspect.

Biblical support for singleness as a life-long option is modeled by several key New Testament persons, including Jesus, Paul, John the Baptist, Martha and Mary and their brother Lazarus. Jesus suggested three reasons for remaining single (Mt 19:12) including circumstance by birth, circumstance by incapacitation or mutilation, and circumstance of religious commitment. However Jesus did not force singleness upon his followers. Paul advised against marriage because of impending hard times facing the church and the imminence of Christ's return (1 Cor 7:26), but he called compulsory celibacy a heresy (1 Tim 4:13). In balance, neither the expectation of singleness or marriage have been required of followers of Jesus according to the Bible. A commitment to celibacy was required of all baptized believers in the Syriac church of 2nd c.; from the 3rd to the 16th c. the monastic vocation was a prominent aspect of church life, and continues as such for Eastern Orthodox and Roman Catholic Christians. It is has been a less prominent but viable choice for Lutheran and Mennonite women (°°deaconesses) and for Anglican men and women.

Another area of unfinished theological and ethical agenda relates to the expectation that single people in the church remain celibate until marriage. An unstated uneasiness with life-long singleness is that singles cannot be trusted to remain celibate even if they are committed to doing so. A clearly stated theology of sexuality that expresses trust in the never-married person would also affirm singleness as a choice.

Other issues for singles with theological implications include coping with loneliness and needing intimacy. Loneliness can be understood as the underside of intimacy. A theme which often appears in literature on singleness is the need to value friendship as a source of intimacy. Jesus modeled relationships with his disciples and others which were intimate but based on friendship.

Single people among Mennonites and Brethren in Christ began to express need for acceptance in the late 1960s and early 1970s through articles in church periodicals and books on the topic of singleness. Most of these were written by women. Books of this type included Frances Bontrager (later Frances Bontrager Greaser), *The Church and the Single Person* (Scottdale, 1969); Evelyn King (later Evelyn King Mumaw), *Women Alone* (Scottdale, 1970; and Katie Funk Wiebe, *A Widow's Search for Joy* (Wheaton, Ill.: Tyndale Press, 1976). Another book on a related topic published in this decade is G. Edwin Bontrager, *Divorce and the Faithful Church* (Scottdale, 1978).

In the 1980s more was written about singleness and singles ministry. *Single Voices* was co-edited by Bruce Yoder and Imo Jeanne Yoder, (Scottdale, 1982). It included contributions from seven different writers, a discussion guide, and a bibliography. A booklet entitled *Ministry to Single Adults,* edited by Ed Toews, was published by Pacific District Conference of the Mennonite Brethren Churches (Fresno, Cal., 1985). *Human Sexuality in the Christian Life: A Working Document for Study and Dialogue* (Scottdale and Newton, 1985) includes a chapter on singleness. *Being Brothers and Sisters:*

Stories of Personal Need in the Church (Newton, 1984) also includes a chapter on singleness.

Scattered efforts at programs for singles are developing in Mennonite denominations. Activities include single young adult Sunday school classes, ad hoc regional organizations for young adult singles, conference-sponsored activities for young singles, support groups and retreats for divorced and widowed persons, support groups for single parents, and the publication by churchwide agencies of printed resources in singles ministry.

Before it was acceptable for married women to pursue both a career and raising a family, a place was made for single women in the church to work in the mission field and church educational institutions. For example, in a booklet entitled *Missionaries Home and Abroad* published by Women's Society of the Krimmer Mennonite Brethren Conference in 1960, 36 couples and 24 single women were listed as having been missionaries for that conference between 1869 and 1960. (No single men were listed. Five of the single women married at a later date.) The establishment of the various deaconess sisterhoods in the 19th and early 20th c., mentioned above, is another example of the opportunities for single women in mission.

Stories and biographies of single women can be found in several books including Mary Lou Cummings, ed. (Newton, 1978), Ruth Unrau, *Encircled: Stories of Mennonite Women* (Newton, 1986), and E. S. Rich, *Mennonite Women* (Scottdale, 1983). Articles focusing on issues for single women were incuded in Dorothy Yoder Nyce, ed., *Which Way Women?* (Akron: MCC, 1980). MB

Kauffman/Harder, *Anabaptists Four C. Later* (1975); Yoder, *MC Census* (1985); Peter C. Erb, "A Reflection on Mennonite Theology in Canada," *JMS*, 1 (1983), 179-90, at 186-87.

See also Marriage; Ordinances.

Sioux People. See Indians, North America.

Slagel, Arthur W. (1891-Apr. 22, 1943), early Mennonite relief worker, served in famine-stricken southern Russia under the auspices of the fledgling Mennonite Central Committee (MCC). In Sept. 1920, Slagel, Orie °Miller, and Clayton °°Kratz reached Constantinople, where Slagel assembled relief shipments bound for Russia. Eighteen months later, American Mennonite Relief, the Russia-based arm of MCC, established kitchens in the Ukraine. From 1922 to 1923 Slagel supervised a feeding program for 75,000 people, including 60,000 Mennonites.

Slagel was born at Flanagan, Ill. In 1919-20, upon graduating from Goshen College, he taught at Hesston College, Hesston, Ks. In 1925, two years after returning from Russia, Slagel married former MCC worker Vesta Zook. He joined a printing firm in Chicago. In 1932 the family moved to a farm near Topeka, Ind. RWG

P. C. Hiebert and Orie O. Miller, *Feeding the Hungry: Russia Famine 1919-1925* (Scottdale: MCC, 1929); John D. Unruh, *In the Name of Christ: A History of the Mennonite Central Committee and Its Service 1920-1951* (Scottdale, 1952), 16-22; *MCC Story*, vol. 5, ch 2; Geraldine Gross Harder, *When Apples Are Ripe: The Story of Clayton Kratz* (Scottdale, 1971), 153-57; files of Arthur Slagel at MC Archives (Goshen).

Slavgorod (Altai). See Russian Soviet Federated Socialist Republic (RSFSR).

Smicksburg, Pa, Old Order Amish Settlement is located in Indiana Co. about 65 mi. (105 km.) ne. of Pittsburgh. Founded in 1962 by families seeking cheaper farm land and motivated by a sincere desire to establish a "purer" Amish community, the settlement has experienced steady growth. In the 25 years of its existence, the Smicksburg community has seven church districts (congregations) with a total population of approximately 1,200, making it the fourth largest among the 40 Amish settlements in Pennsylvania. The Smicksburg community is representative of many of the newer settlements populated by younger and middle-aged Amish families seeking change within the traditional Amish customs of °°nonconformity to the outside world. SLY

Smith, Henry L. (1888-1924), was the leader of the party that established continuing Brethren in Christ missionary work in India in 1914. Included in the party was his wife, Katie Burkholder Smith, and Effie Rohrer. The location was northern Bihar. Born in Harrisburg, Pa., Smith married in 1911 and was ordained to the ministry in 1913. He earned his undergraduate degree at Elizabethtown College (1909), his master's degree from Potomac U., Washington, D.C., and was working on his doctorate (theology) at the time of his death. His educational experience also included teaching at what eventually became Messiah College (1910-13) and at Beulah (later Upland) College (1921). He wrote *Bible Doctrine*, the first systematic theology by a member of the Brethren in Christ Church.

Smith was the superintendent of the missionary work in India. The avenues of outreach were evangelism (village and bazaar work), orphanages, medical dispensaries, and relief for the poor and famine-stricken. By 1918 he had helped to organize three mission stations: Madhipura, Saharsa, and Supaul. Response to the gospel was limited, given the strong Hinduism of the area. Smith was a man of missionary zeal, gifted in presenting doctrinal truth, and talented in administration. He died of confluent smallpox at the age of 36. MHS

Anna R. Engle, John A. Climenhaga, and Leoda A. Buckwalter, *There Is No Difference* (Nappanee, 1950); Wittlinger, *Piety and Obedience* (1978); H. L. Smith in *EV* (July 21, 1924), 13-14, and (July 7, 1924), 1; obituary in *EV* (May 12, 1924), 3; H. L. Smith, *Bible Doctrine* (Upland, Cal.: the author, 1921); *Second Annual Catalog Messiah Bible School and Missionary Training Home* (Grantham, Pa., 1911-1912); *The Poinsettia* (Upland, Cal.: Beulah College, 1922).

Smith, Samuel Roger (1853-1916), was a businessman, educator, and a noted leader in the Brethren in Christ Church. For several years he taught in a local school near Hershey, Pa. Later he operated a feed mill and dealt in stocks. Following the failure of his business, he moved to Harrisburg and began to manufacture noodles. In 1909 he moved the operation to Grantham, Pa., where he constructed the largest factory of its kind east of the Mississippi River.

In 1896 he and his wife became members of the Brethren in Christ Church. Ten years later he was elected to the ministry. In 1896 he helped to found Messiah Rescue Home and Orphanage in Harrisburg (later Messiah Village near Mechanicsburg, Pa.). In 1916 he brought the orphanage to Grantham where it was known as Messiah Orphanage. He was elected secretary of General Conference in 1899 and retained that office until his death in 1916. As General Conference secretary he had the major part in drafting the constitution and bylaws of his denomination when it was incorporated in 1904. With John R. Zook he produced the first Brethren in Christ hymnal that utilized musical notation. From 1905 to 1916 he was a member of the denomination's General Executive Committee, in which position he traveled widely in the United States and Canada to deal with major denominational problems. In 1913, when the Brethren in Christ in the Grantham area organized into a district, Smith was elected its first bishop.

Smith is best remembered as the leader in the founding of Messiah Bible School and Missionary Training Home (later Messiah College). Against much opposition and largely from his own financial resources, he obtained a charter for the school in 1909. During the first academic year, classes were held in his house in Harrisburg. When the campus followed Smith and his noodle company to Grantham in 1911, it was to a large building on land donated by Smith behind his newly constructed house. He taught Bible in the school and served as its first president until his death.

Smith was an avid amateur scientist and astronomer. Through the years he collected an excellent laboratory which he eventually gave to the science department of the college he had helped to found.   EMS

E. Morris Sider, *Messiah College: A History* (Nappanee, Ind., 1984); Wittlinger, *Piety and Obedience* (1978), 289-99 passim; *EV* (Sept. 18, 1916), 20.

Smith, Verna Graber (b. Nov. 30, 1902). Born near Noble, Iowa, Verna Graber was one of nine children of Daniel and Fanny Conrad Graber. On Sept. 13, 1930, she married Willard Harvey Smith. She was educated at Hesston Academy (graduated 1922), Goshen College, Ind. (BA, 1928), the U. of Iowa, Indiana U., and the U. of Wisconsin (MA, 1951). After teaching in elementary schools (1923-25, 1928-30), Smith taught Latin (1930-38, 1938-44, part-time), English (1931-32), and Spanish (1947-71) at Goshen College. In the summer of 1964 she and her husband led a pilot Study-Service Trimester in El Salvador. She was with the Mennonite Central Committee in Paraguay, 1944-45 and in Mexico, 1954-55. In 1949 Smith collaborated with her husband in writing *Paraguayan Interlude: Observations and Impressions* (Scottdale, 1950). In 1976 Verna and Willard Smith established the Smith-Graber Scholarship in American History and Studies at Goshen College and in 1982 the Willard and Verna Smith Chair in American History and Culture. In 1985 they also provided general scholarships for students in any field of study.   SRE

Menn. Bib. II, p. 505; Rich, *Mennonite Women* (1983), 123; Willard H. Smith, *The Trail to Santa Fe: A Pilgrim's Progress* (Goshen: the author, 1985).

Smith, Willard Harvey (b. Oct. 15, 1900), North American Mennonite historian, was born near Eureka, Ill., the eldest child of John J. and Katie E. Smith Smith. After graduating from Hesston Academy in 1920, his education included: Hesston College (1920-21), Goshen College, (BA, 1928), the U. of Michigan (MA, 1929), the U. of Chicago, and Indiana U. (PhD, 1939). Teaching at Goshen College, 1929-72, he became full professor of history and political science in 1942, served as dean of men (1932-35), and chaired the social sciences division from 1949 to 1968. He directed Mennonite Central Committee work in Paraguay (1944-45). Smith was a member and officer of a variety of professional historical, political science, and teachers' associations. His writings include: *Paraguayan Interlude* (Scottdale, 1950); *Schuyler Colfax: The Changing Fortunes of a Political Idol* (1952); *William Jennings Bryan, Christian Reformer* (1969); *The Social and Religious Thought of William Jennings Bryan* (1975); *Mennonites in Illinois* (Scottdale, 1983); and his autobiography, *The Trail to Santa Fe: A Pilgrim's Progress* (1985).   SRE

Willard H. Smith, *The Trail to Santa Fe: A Pilgrim's Progress* (Goshen, Ind.: author, 1985); *Who's Who Mennonites* (1943), 226; *Menn. Bib. II*, p. 505.

Smyth, John (ME IV:554). An English Puritan and a Cambridge U. graduate, Smyth was city lecturer in Lincoln 1600-1602, losing his job in a local political dispute. Disillusioned by the anti-Puritan policies of James I and unable to obtain employment in the Church of England, he became a Separatist about 1606. (English Separatists advocated a church composed only of committed believers but retained infant baptism.) Smyth became a leader among Separatists near Gainsborough, Lincolnshire, and Scrooby, Nottinghamshire. These Separatists fled to Amsterdam in the spring of 1608, where they quarreled with the Ancient Church of Separatists. In *The Differences of the Churches of the seperation* [sic] (1608) Smyth criticized the Ancient Church for using "man-made" books (including Scripture translations) in worship services; for distinguishing between pastors, teachers, and elders and limiting their numbers in a congregation; and for receiving money from nonmembers.

At least half of the Smyth congregation, led by John Robinson, moved on to Leiden early in 1609. About the same time, Smyth decided that infant baptism was wrong and rebaptized himself and his congregation. He published *The Character of the Beast* (1609) as a defense of believer's baptism. Coming into contact with a °°Waterlander-°°Frisian Mennonite congregation, Smyth decided that they were a true church and he should have sought baptism from them. Thirty-two members of the congregation sought union with the Mennonites, having accepted Mennonite positions on the state, free will and possibly the °°incarnation. An alliance was achieved in 1610, which alienated other Mennonite groups and contributed to the breakup of the Mennonite alliance, the °°Bevredigde Broederschap. William Bradford of the Robinson faction described Smyth as gifted but unstable, a description which has been widely accepted by historians. In his "Last Booke," written shortly before his death, Smyth repented of his uncharitable attitude toward theological opponents, while repudiating none of his theology.

Smyth died in 1612, survived by his wife Mary and their children. Mary evidently shared his theological views and signed the application to join the Mennonites, but little else is known of Smyth's family. JRC

James R. Coggins, "John Smyth's Congregation: English Separatism, Dutch Mennonites and the Elect Nation" (PhD diss., U. of Waterloo, 1986); William Bradford, *Of Plymouth Plantation* (New York: Knopf, 1959), 9-17; Walter H. Burgess, *John Robinson, Pastor of the Pilgrim Fathers* (London: William A. Norgate, 1920), 409-17. A series of articles in *The Baptist Quarterly*, 30 (1984) debated Smyth's theology.

See also Baptists.

Snyder, Elvin Valores (Apr. 1, 1900-Dec. 6, 1985), missionary. Born near Breslau, Ont. to Ozias and Barbara Snyder, Elvin Snyder studied at Toronto Bible College (1925), Goshen College (BA, 1927), and Southwest Texas State Teachers College (MA, 1952). He married Mary Adah Fretz in 1928 and, after her death in 1974, married Esther Brunk Fadner in 1978. Snyder served in a wide variety of mission projects including those in Toronto (1922-25); Canton, Ohio (1927-28); Trenque Lauquen, America, and Carlos Casares, Argentina (1928-47); Chicago (1947-49); Lost Creek, Ky. (1949-50); Mathis, Tex. (1950-53); Puerto Rico (1953-65); and Corpus Christi, Tex. (1966-67). In his later years he taught in the Spanish department at Eastern Mennonite College (1971-73) and provided pastoral leadership to the Milwaukee Mennonite Church (1973-75). Snyder served variously as an orphanage director, language instructer, Bible institute director, editor, and pastor. SSt

Elvin V. Snyder collection, MC Archives (Goshen); "Snyder, Elvin Valores," *Who's Who in Texas Today* (Austin: Pemberton Press, 1967), 338; "Elvin Valores Snyder," in *The Gospel under the Southern Cross* (Scottdale: MPH, 1943), 186-87; *GH* Dec. 31, 1985), 928.

Social Class. Rural agricultural societies tend to be more homogenous, that is, members of such societies are not greatly differentiated by status, prestige, income, and occupation because almost everyone does the same agricultural work for a living. However, as °industrialization sets in and °urbanization begins, occupational specialties and differential rewards develop, increasing the gap between the rich and the poor. Differential social strata emerge so that a society becomes layered into higher and lower classes. Most industrialized countries of Europe and North America, as well as Japan and others have become highly stratified. Whereas many Mennonites in the recent past were agriculturalists (some in The Netherlands have been urban longer), they too are beginning to urbanize greatly in North America and Europe. To what extent are they also stratified into social classes?

We can examine the social class of Mennonites by using indicators of socioeconomic status such as education, income, and °occupation, or we can also examine class as economic and political power groups which may be in conflict. We expect that Mennonites in developing countries of Latin America, Asia, and Africa will still be less stratified than Mennonites in industrial countries of North America and Europe. Since comparative data on world Mennonites are limited, let us concentrate on the half (46.1 percent in 1984) of the Mennonites of the

SOCIAL CLASS CHART
Leo Driedger compiler

Table 1. Comparison of Educational, Income, and Occupational Status
of Canadians by Religious Groups, 1981

Religious Denomination	Education (Post Secondary)	Income (Mean)	Occupation (Professional)	Composite Rank
Jewish	55.6%	$19,529	45.5%	1
No Religion	50.8	14,854	30.4	2
All Other Religions	59.7	12,734	36.2	3
Anglican	41.4	13,661	27.1	4
United Church	40.7	13,693	25.6	5
Other Protestant	46.6	12,586	27.8	6
Presbyterian	39.5	13,334	24.4	7
Morman	48.3	12,412	24.4	8
Lutheran	40.4	13,303	22.3	9
Ukrainian Catholic	32.8	12,421	22.9	10
Reformed Bodies	40.6	12,306	21.6	11
Baptist	37.5	11,740	22.4	12
Roman Catholic	35.9	12,293	22.4	13
Eastern Orthodox	32.0	12,395	18.9	14
Mennonite	**31.8**	**11,809**	**21.0**	**15**
Pentecostal	32.1	10,782	17.7	16
Salvation Army	26.2	10,317	17.3	17
Jehovah's Witness	26.8	10,317	11.9	18
Hutterite	1.1	11,392	10.4	19
Total Population	**39.1**	**$12,993**	**24.4**	

world living in industrialized North America where some data are available.

Socioeconomic Status. Canada is one of the few countries which collects data about religion as part of its census and, fortunately, the Mennonites (.8 percent of the population are included. Using education, income, and occupation as socioeconomic indicators, we compare 19 religious groupings in Table 1, and find that on each of the three indicators Mennonites rank in the third and lowest stratum. One third (31.8 percent) of them had more than high school education, their income averaged $11,809 in 1984, and one fifth worked in the professions. Many Mennonites in Canada may be upwardly mobile, but compared to other Canadians, Mennonites are still below the national average socioeconomically.

Findings in the United States suggest that Mennonites there may be more comparable to the American national average. The Kaufman and Harder study comparing five Mennonite groups in the United States and Canada in the 1970s shows that 31.9 percent had studied beyond high school, 15.9 percent were professional and technical workers, and that the median income was $9,608. Mennonites are still more heavily involved in agriculture and this tends to bring the socioeconomic status down. However, Kauffman and Harder found that socioeconomic status varied considerably by Mennonite groups, with General Conference Mennonites scoring highest on education, and Mennonites of the Evangelical Mennonite Church earning the highest incomes. Michael Yoder's survey of members of the Mennonite Church in the United States (1982) showed that 37.1 percent had studied beyond high school, and 21.1 percent were in °professional and technical occupations (only 11.8 percent in farming). Because the present analysis includes data from 1972 (Kauffman/Harder), 1981 (Canadian census), and 1982, figures are not always comparable.

Influence and Power. Studies of the socioeconomic status of Mennonites in North America suggest that they are moving from mostly agricultural occupations to higher educational, income, and occupational levels especially as industrialization and urbanization sets in. Karl Marx was interested in social class as power; he concluded that the capitalists wielded too much power over the laboring masses, and a greater balance was necessary. Since historically the Anabaptists were usually the persecuted underdogs in Europe, they were for the most part powerless. Some scholars contend that they were a part of the mass movement of the peasant wars in the 16th c. although Harold Bender and Paul Peachey do not think so (°historiography).

The studies of Coenen and Krahn suggest that the Dutch Anabaptist movement was more urban, more professional, and more dominated by artisans (who were relatively more mobile socially) than was the Swiss and South German Anabaptist movement. Persecution did not eradicate the Anabaptists from Dutch cities as much as was the case in Switzerland, and toleration set in more quickly, possibly because of the more lenient, commercial, industrial, pluralist, tendencies in the north. Thus, the Dutch-North

German Anabaptists were a movement of higher social status. A number of Dutch Mennonites entered politics and became cabinet ministers with considerable power. This pro-urban predilection, according to Penner, seemed to remain when Dutch Anabaptists settled in the Vistula area in Prussia. Agricultural work involved considerable skills in engineering and building of dams and drainage, often near such large commercial cities as Danzig and Elbing (°water technology). Some Mennonites became influential in °business.

Migrations from Prussia to Russia, and later to Canada and the United States, seemed to involve a social class selection process. The first Mennonites who moved to the Chortitza colony in Russia (1789), were largely leaderless artisans who, according to D. H. Epp, had little experience in farming. They were followed by more educated Mennonites who established the Molotschna colony in 1803. John B. Toews documents the considerable extent of industrialization of Mennonites in Russia later, including the emergence of some wealthy entrepreneurs. There is some debate on the extent to which Russian Mennonites became wealthy, and whether they brought on themselves the wrath of Russian peasants during the °Russian Revolution and Civil War, 1917-1920. This requires more research.

The early Mennonite migrants from Russia to North America in the 1870s were often landless and less well-to-do. They seemed to value education less than those who remained in Russia, as indicated by the Old Colony Mennonites in Canada and Mexico. The more educated, landowners migrated to Canada only in the 1920s, after many had obtained higher education, and undertaken professions and industrial and commercial enterprises. Some Mennonites in North America today are becoming more wealthy and some are also entering °politics. Mennonite economic and political power is still minimal, but it seems to be increasing. This too requires more study.   LDr

Tim B. Heaton, "Socio-Demographic Characteristics of Religious Groups in Canada," *Sociological Analysis*, 47 (1986), 54-65; Kauffman/Harder, *Anabaptists Four C. Later* (1975); Michael L. Yoder, "Findings from the 1982 Mennonite Census," *MQR*, 59 (1985), 307-49; Calvin W. Redekop, *Old Colony Mennonites* (Baltimore: Johns Hopkins U. Press, 1969), 93ff.

See also Demography; Sociological Studies.

Social Gospel, a term which came into use in North America soon after 1900, refers to a movement concerned with the unequal distribution of wealth through capitalism, with the exploitation of the poor, and with a christianizing of society in all areas of life. Its goal was to help bring in the °kingdom of God, which it believed to be "humanity organized according to the will of God." In the United States its influence spanned the years from the Civil War (1861-65) to World War I, peaking in the first two decades of the 20th c., but it was also influential in England (Charles Kingsley [1819-75]), and in Canada (J. S. Woodsworth [1874-1942]).

The roots of the Social Gospel grew, in part, in °liberal theology with its idealism and optimistic view of progress, but also in °Evangelicalism (°Pietism) and °sectarianism (Anabaptism). Those standing primarily in the liberal tradition were social evolutionists with unbounded optimism. The end of slavery now meant that God had opened the way "for the redemption and sanctification of our whole social system." Progress against evil would be inevitable. Henry Ward Beecher (1813-87) gave his endorsement to the soap advertisement: "Cleanliness is next to Godliness. Soap must be considered a means of grace and a clergyman who recommends moral things should be willing to recommend soap." Winthrop Hudson was to write later: "It was as if God had been 'naturalized' and invited. . . 'to give a weekly editorial commentary' on the vagaries of a society, in the image of which he had been made." For these clergy Christ was a moral example, a loving presence whose vision was now finally being realized. There was little mention of the cross of Christ.

A different mood and theology prevailed among those who stood more in the evangelical activist tradition of Jonathan Edwards (1703-58), Charles Finney (1792-1875), and the Great Awakening (1730s and 1740s). The foremost spokesman of this emphasis was Walter Rauschenbusch (1861-1918), a Baptist minister and professor of church history at Rochester [N.Y.] Divinity School. Rauschenbusch knew both Anabaptism and the Mennonites well, as did his father August, an immigrant German Lutheran Pietist, later a Baptist minister, who made a return trip to Germany to study the history of the Anabaptist Hubmaier at Waldshut. Walter not only had a personal conversion experience at age 17, and what he called a "discipleship experience" at 21 ("I wanted to do hard work for God"), but translated a volume of gospel songs into German (*Evangeliums Lieder*) and believed that "the social order cannot be saved without regenerate men."

Walter Rauschenbusch saw himself standing in the tradition of the Old Testament prophets and of Jesus. He opposed the private, otherworldly piety promoted by most churches. We rarely sin against God alone, he said, but also against our fellow human beings. Adam's opportunities to sin real good were rather limited in comparison to the opportunities in modern society. Sins which are real sins need social room to develop, but the churches have lost sight of the kingdom and concentrate on small personal sins. Yet we crucified Jesus with religious bigotry, graft, and political power, corruption of justice, mob spirit, and militarism. Jesus died as much for social sins as for individual sins; it was the social sins, in fact, that killed him. As a social sin "war is the most sinful thing there is." Its root is greed and deceit. Rauschenbusch was a pacifist.

For Rauschenbusch sin was at the heart of national decay but he was not a Calvinist. The Fall had not robbed humans of the ability to change things. Free will had not been lost. Christians could make society more Christlike. "I have entire sympathy with the conservative instinct which shrinks from giving up any of the dear possessions which have made life holy for us. We have none too much of them left. . . . The social gospel calls for an expansion in the scope of salvation. . . . It is able to create a more searching sense of sin and to preach repentance to the respectable and mighty who have

ridden humanity to the mouth of hell. . . ." "Does Calvinism deal adequately with a man who appears before the judgment seat of Christ with $50,000,000 and its human corollaries to his credit, and then pleads a free pardon through faith in the atoning sacrifice? . . . If we can trust the Bible, God is against capitalism, its method, spirit, and results." Rauschenbusch considered himself a Christian Socialist but never joined the Socialist Party.

Rauschenbusch was a lonely prophet. Initially the Social Gospel was more a movement of the clergy than the people. His vision of social justice included industrial democracy, fair wages and decent working hours, an end to child labor, the nationalization of huge industries, e.g., coal and iron. Yet he did not share the optimism of the liberals: "The continents are strewn with the ruins of dead nations and civilizations. History laughs at the optimistic illusion that 'nothing can stand in the way of human progress' . . . What guarantee have we, then, that our modern civilization with its pomp will not be 'one with Nineveh and Tyre?'" He died a disappointed and misunderstood man with "brother fighting brother" in 1914-18. Perhaps he had been too optimistic after all, even with his strong emphasis on sin.

The great depression of the 1930s, two world wars, Stalinism, Hitler, and the holocaust put an end to the optimistic theology of liberalism and of the Social Gospel. The "realism" of °Neo-orthodoxy took its place. It is surprizing that in their concern to overcome capitalism the Social Gospelers failed to be alert to other social issues like racism and women's rights. But they clearly did alert the churches to many issues of justice and the dangers of a private piety unaccountable to anyone. In identifying with the needs of the poor, and seeing the demonic potential of corporate, economic or political power, they anticipated some aspects of 20th-c. °liberation theology. They gave strong impetus to fledgling peace movements. Woodsworth was also a pacifist. His mother was of Mennonite background. The New Democratic Party (NDP) in Canada is a political continuation of the Social Gospel vision of S. G. Bland (1859-1950) and J. S. Woodsworth. The latter was the founder (1932) of the Cooperative Commonwealth Federation (CCF) party, which preceded the NDP and its policies.

Most Mennonites in Canada, particularly those who came from Russia, have had a deep-seated fear of socialism as being too much like Communism. Yet it was the CCF which first had a vision for Canada-wide health care and pension plans. These were partly put in place by the CCF party under Thomas (Tommy) Clement Douglas who, as premier of Saskatchewan (1944-61), was leader of the first socialist government elected in North America. Douglas later served as leader of the NDP until 1971.

In the United States many Mennonites were also opposed to the Social Gospel because socialism for them meant Communism. The Social Gospel, they believed, is liberalism and modernism, which undercuts biblical authority, trades individual for social salvation, promotes witnessing to the state about bad laws and evil structures, and finally leads to social action which is "identical with that of humanists and socialists who have embraced the Marxist philosophy." Eschatology is also at issue since "Christians do not believe. . ." that changing social structures will make a better world. "For the Bible message of *personal* reconstruction the social gospel substitutes the call to *social* reconstruction." For these persons the only key to social improvement was individual conversion. The issue was thus joined since the Social Gospel did indeed challenge individualism in all areas of social and religious life.

Yet most Mennonites in North America, and globally, were part of a vast worldwide social aid program through the Mennonite Central Committee (MCC). Concerns were heard occasionally that MCC workers were not witnessing effectively to the Good News of Jesus Christ, but generally MCC received broad support. So also a concern for world peace led to the founding of a committee for peace concerns under Mennonite World Conference in Curitiba, Brazil (1972). Mennonites carried on large social programs in the fields of °mental health, service to the elderly, inner city °voluntary service units, etc.

With this new concern for society new terms entered the Mennonite vocabulary, including concern for °*justice*, particularly after the civil rights movement of the 1960s. With this came the struggle of how best to reconcile justice with the traditional Mennonite preference for the word °*love*. Such terms as "direct action," "nonviolent resistance," "confronting in love," and "conflict resolution" also entered the Mennonite vocabulary and, at times, practice. It appeared that many Mennonites believed in working at both individual and social change at the same time, believing this to be the way of Christ. CJD

Sidney E. Ahlstrom, *A Religious History of the American People* (New Haven, 1972); Richard Allen, *The Social Passion: Religion and Social Reform in Canada, 1914-1928* (Toronto, 1973); Lloyd J. Averill, *American Theology in the Liberal Tradition* (Philadelphia, 1967); *Encyclopedia Canadiana*, vol. 10 (Ottawa, 1963). Paul A. Carter, *The Decline and Revival of the Social Gospel* (New York, 1954); Edwin S. Gaustad, *A Documentary History of Religion in America Since 1865* (Grand Rapids, 1983). Robert T. Handy, ed., *The Social Gospel in America 1870-1920* (New York, 1966); idem, *A History of the Churches in the United States and Canada* (New York, 1977); Guy F. Hershberger, "The Modern Social Gospel and the Way of the Cross," *MQR*, 30 (1956), 83-103; John Horsch, *Modern Religious Liberalism* (Scottdale, 1924); Winthrop S. Hudson, *The Great Tradition in the American Churches* (New York, 1953); Benson Y. Landis, ed., *A Rauschenbusch Reader* (New York, 1957); James H. Nichols, *History of Christianity 1650-1950* (New York, 1956); H. Richard Niebuhr, *Christ and Culture* (New York, 1951); Walter Rauschenbusch, *Christianity and the Social Crisis* (New York, 1907; idem, *Christianizing the Social Order* (New York, 1912); idem, *Dare We Be Christians?* (Boston, 1914); idem, *The Social Principles of Jesus* (New York, 1916); idem, *A Theology for the Social Gospel* (New York, 1917); Theron F. Schlabach, *Gospel versus Gospel* (Scottdale, 1980); Donovan E. Smucker, "The Origins of Walter Rauschenbusch's Social Ethics" (PhD thesis, U. of Chicago, 1957); idem, "Multiple Motifs in the Thought of Rauschenbusch: A Study in the Origins of the Social Gospel," *Encounter*, 19 (1958), 14-20; Ronald C. White and others, *The Social Gospel* (Philadelphia, 1976).

See also Development Work; Fundamentalism; Relief Work; Service; Sociopolitical Activism.

Social Meetings. One aspect of °revivalism and °Pietism in North America and Europe was the development of °prayer meetings, revival services (protracted meetings), "testimony" ("experience")

meetings, hymn sings, missionary conventions, and other assemblies alongside traditional Sunday morning °worship services. Most early 19th-c. Mennonites and Amish resisted such meetings as they resisted the revivalistic movements in general. With the acceptance of revivalism, Sunday schools, and prayer meetings among the more °acculturated Mennonite groups, opposition to social meetings and evening meetings faded. Since Mennonites and Amish have acculturated at varied rates, social meetings, evening meetings, hymn sings, and Bible study groups were divisive issues for groups as diverse as the Evangelical Mennonite Mission Conference (Rudnerweider Mennonites) and the Old Order Amish in the mid and late 20th c. Even as this was happening, some congregations among the more acculturated groups in North America (MC, GCMC etc.) had begun, by the 1980s, to abandon the revival meetings, prayer meetings, and Sunday evening church services they accepted in the early 20th c. This trend gave rise to criticism from members for whom these aspects of evangelical revivalism had become part of "traditional" Mennonite life since the 19th c. DDM

Wittlinger, *Piety and Obedience* (1978), 82; F. H. Epp, *Mennonites in Canada II*, 427-29; John A. Hostetler, *Amish Society* (1980), 280-83, 399-304, 344-45.

See also Bible Conferences; Conservative Mennonites; Recreation; Sommerfeld Colony, Paraguay; Sommerfeld Mennonites.

Socialism developed in the 19th c. as a response to injustice and inequality. It called for the public ownership and control of the means of production. The mines and mills of Europe operated in surroundings of intense squalor and ugliness. Karl Marx (1818-93) and Friedrich Engels (1820-95) proclaimed deterministic laws of social development which were yoked to an affirmation of violent revolution. Simultaneously, democratic socialism emerged principally in the British Labour Party and the German Social Democrats.

Democratic Socialism was embraced by Christian socialists in England (F. D. Maurice and Charles Kingsley), Switzerland (Herman Kutter [Emil Brunner's predecessor in the chair of theology at Zurich], and Leonhard Ragaz), the United States (Washington Gladden, Walter Rauschenbusch, and Norman Thomas), and Canada (J. S. Woodsworth).

The democratic Christian socialists rejected antireligious, materialistic, violent, dogmatic, bureaucratic, centralized, and deterministic °communism. They saw the °kingdom of God as a powerful historical reality providing the dynamic for social change in the direction of a welfare state and a just democratic society thus correcting the abuses of capitalism and using a qualified form of public ownership already tested in the post office, railroads, and public utilities.

Later socialist revisionists chastened by communist totalitarianism further emphasized people power instead of class analysis, rejected public ownership as a first principle, and made a strong emphasis on pluralism and tolerance.

When the New Deal program of Franklin Roosevelt in the United States and the Liberal Party in Canada embraced welfare legislation it lessened the appeal of socialism since the new social legislation covered social needs from the cradle to the grave.

Socialism outside north America and Europe is an ambivalent mixture of primordial relations of tribalism, language, religion, blood and a quest for modernization and °industrialization. The old socialists talked about social equality and political freedom. The new governing socialist elites of the Two-Thirds World talk about economic development and political power.

In the Hispanic world socialism has been reaffirmed mainly by Catholic Christians under the rubric of °liberation theology in which the God of the Bible blesses the poor, rejects unjust economic and political establishments, and urges the church to be a prophetic voice. Violence is accepted reluctantly as a necessity after the failure of peaceful means. Gustavo Gutiérrez, José Miguel Bonino, and Camillo Torres are representative voices of Hispanic liberation theology. South American Mennonites have not accepted liberation theology.

Mennonites in the Soviet Union in the 1980s appreciate the Soviet welfare system with its free education and free medicine, pensions and cheap housing. They are pleased they can buy houses and save money in the bank. But there is always the feeling of alienation because of a state which precariously tolerates but does not accept religious faith and life.

In Canada the New Democratic Party (NDP) is a viable, effective socialist party which has organized provincial governments in British Columbia, Saskatchewan, and Manitoba, and is gaining momentum federally in Ottawa. In Manitoba, Vic Schroeder, a member of the Winnipeg Charleswood Mennonite Church served as Minister of Finance in the NDP government (1987). Other Mennonites have held portfolios in the western Canadian socialist governments. J. J. °Siemens of Altona, Man. was a major figure in the prairie °cooperative movements who unsuccessfully ran for office with the NDP.   DES

See also Political Attitudes.

Socialization is the complex learning process through which people develop selfhood and acquire the knowledge, skills, and motivations required for participation in society. This process links individuals to groups and society. Surprisingly little Mennonite research has been done on this process, although John Hostetler and others have written about Hutterite and Amish socialization. Studies of Mennonite social psychological processes in general are meagre, and the process of socialization into a Mennonite identity, ideology, or community are scarce. Much more research is required.

Development of the Self. There is a long-standing debate as to whether nature or nurture contributes more to the development of personality and self. In rural Mennonite communities one often hears the assertion that "Johnny behaves just like his father," implying that there is a biological gene connection which accounts for similar behavior. More recently, with the development of the social sciences, imitation and social learning are given much more emphasis. In this view Johnny is a product of his social environment, and behaves like his father because of imitation and learning.

Theorists such as Cooley and Mead have developed the nurture thesis. Charles Cooley proposed that the self develops through a socialization process, and used the metaphor of the looking-glass (mirror) to illustrate his point. The self is social in that it emerges out of interaction with others, as the individual looks into the mirror of those around her, and learns how her actions are received by others. In this process the individual adjusts her behavior so that it is acceptable to the group and thus becomes a valued member. The individual imagines how her behavior appears to others, imagines how others judge her behavior, and on this basis is happy or unhappy with herself. The self or personality becomes largely a product of society.

George Herbert Mead elaborated on Cooley's insights and expanded them in his book, *Mind, Self and Society*. He thought the development of the self is dependent upon the capacity to use language. Both depend on "taking the role of the other," where it is necessary to place oneself into the shoes of the other in order to communicate. Mead elaborated on the need to role-play, which is such an important part of play for children. Children learn to imagine that they are parents and that dolls are their children, etc. In the process the self emerges as distinct from yet linked to groups and to other people. Both Cooley and Mead claim that the self is largely a product of the parents, relatives, friends, and others with whom a child associates. They claim nurture is more important than nature.

According to Erik Erikson the ego, around which the individual integrates a sense of identity, develops in the process of socialization. He too thinks society plays an important role in molding personality. He emphasized that socialization is a lifelong process which goes through cycles from infancy to adolescence to various states of young, middle, and elderly adulthood. The individual has different needs in the various stages of life.

Agents of Socialization. Both informal and formal agents are involved in the socialization of individuals. The family and peers are typical informal agents of socialization and the school and °mass media represent formal agents.

Research on the Mennonite °family is more common, but emphasis on the socialization process is still limited. In his book *Amish Society* John Hostetler elaborates on children and how they grow up in the home where love and discipline are important to develop responsibility. In Hostetler's *Hutterite Society*, he devotes a whole chapter to family socialization in preparation for initiation (baptism) into adult life and training to identify with the colony, where deviancy is rare. Here he enlarges upon the early stages of socialization, especially infancy, kindergarten, and the school years. Hostetler and Huntington, in their book *Hutterites in North America* also enlarge on the family and socialization, including age patterns, formal schooling, and socialization of youth.

In these relatively closed Hutterite and Amish societies peers are but one of a number of controlling agents and adults tend to dominate socialization. In more open societies, especially where urban Mennonites find themselves a part of numerous networks, peers become especially influential in schools. Peers provide opportunities to practice social roles, are an important source of information, and greatly influence values and attitudes in mate selection, sex relations, and forms of expression in music, sports and the like. Paul Lederach studied a variety of beliefs and attitudes of Mennonite youth and concluded that young people from unbroken families had great advantages.

While informal agents such as the family and peers are influential, more formal agents such as the school and the media also influence modern Mennonite socialization. Teachers, textbooks, and peers vary in °public schools, and many Mennonites send their children to °private schools hoping that Mennonite beliefs, values, and norms will be encouraged. °Radio, °television, and newspapers increasingly influence Mennonite values, so that Mennonite periodicals and some radio stations have emerged to help socialize children and youth. Increasing evidence of violence in the media, certainly influences Mennonite values of non-resistance. Too little research is available to evaluate the extent of media influence, and the effectiveness of alternative schools, and media.

Problems of Resocialization. One might expect that Anabaptists, who have migrated so often to new countries, where they again and again had to learn new languages, new customs and cultures, would have studied this resocialization process. Yet little research has been carried out. Mennonites work frequently with °refugees who also face resocialization in new countries, but little work has been done in this area as well. Many parents came from other countries and thus know at first hand the generation gaps which developed as children of immigrant parents learned new ways. Again, too little research has been done. Old world °authority patterns were very different than in North America, with its more libertarian society, but these changing authority patterns also need study. Recently °gender roles have begun to change, and Mennonites too are beginning to discuss the role of women in the °ministry, the church, at work, and in the home. Again, these resocialization processes need study. Much research is needed in the Mennonite socialization and resocialization areas.   LDr

John A. Hostetler, *Amish Society,* (1980); idem, *Hutterite Society* (1974); John A. Hostetler and Gertrude Huntington, *The Hutterites in North America* (New York: Holt, Rinehart and Winston, 1967); Paul M. Lederach, *Mennonite Youth* (Scottdale, 1971); Marlene Mackie, "Socialization," in *Sociology,* ed. Robert Hagedorn (Toronto: Holt, Rinehart and Winston, 1986); George H. Mead, *Mind, Self and Society* (Chicago, 1934).

Society of Brothers. See Hutterian Brethren.

Socioeconomic Tensions. See Community; Land Distribution; Social Class; Wealth.

Sociological Studies. Sociology is a relatively young discipline beginning roughly a century ago, with European founders such as Karl Marx (1818-83), Emil Durkheim (1858-1917), and Max Weber (1864-1920). Because of °industrialization and °urbanization, Europe was fast changing from traditional aristocratic and village (peasant) societies to middle class (bourgeois) societies. Increasingly there was a need to understand better the influence of industrial °capitalism upon society and social solidarity, to understand the influence of these changes on economic, political and religious ideology, and to assess the processes of revolution, industrialization and urbanization. What was happening to the foundation of European civilization?

Early American sociologists, similar to European sociologists, were interested in what was happening to °tradition, culture, °communities, social institutions (e.g., °family, religion, °economics, °politics), in a changing environment. Some were more interested in structural analysis and change, others more interested in processes and conflicts. All were faced with finding ways and methods of collecting information, and developing theories to guide their research and help explain their findings.

If early European and American sociologists were concerned with change in their communities and societies, we would expect the same for minorities such as the Mennonites. Mennonite roots began in Europe where sociology was born. As Mennonites found themselves moving from rural communities to urban environments, we would expect such a minority group to be concerned with separation, °ethnicity, maintenance of community, coinflict, urbanization, family solidarity, °socialization, ideology and identity.

While Mennonites were confined to rural settlements, struggling as pioneers to survive, non-Mennonites began to study them. C. A. Dawson studied Mennonites in western Canada as early as 1936. E. K. Francis began Mennonite studies in 1945 and published a book on Manitoba Mennonites in 1955, while Eaton and Weil also puiblished a book on Hutterites in 1955. World War II scattered many Mennonites as they served in alternative service camps and Civilian Public Service. Soon thereafter many trained as sociologists. In 1941 Winfield Fretz finished a PhD degree, and others such as John Hostetler (1954), Paul Peachey (1954), Calvin Redekop (1954, 1959), Leland Harder (1954), Leo Driedger (1955), and J. Howard Kaufmann (1960) completed graduate degrees in sociology in the 1950s. Since then many more Mennonites have taken degrees in sociology and study of Mennonites has now continued for about 30 years.

A major review of more than 100 publications about Mennonites, written by 50 different scholars, in an article by Driedger and Redekop (1983) gives bibliographic details that are omitted in the present summary. A review of the major works shows that sectarian research has by and large given way to intersystemic and conflict research, reflecting the prevailing theories of the day. Almost all of the studies reviewed concern themselves with isolating the basic features of the Mennonite community.

Winfield Fretz was the first Mennonite to publish a volume on the rural Mennonite community (*Pilgrims in Paraguay,* 1953). John Hostetler followed with volumes on the rural Amish (1963) and Hutterites (1967) in North America. It is not surprising that the first Mennonite scholars would concentrate on rural communities using mainly in-depth qualitative and ethnographical methods. Surprisingly, no community studies in the traditional manner which approach the thoroughness of the Lynds, Dollard, Warner, Redfield, Loomis, and Vidich and Benson have been done on Mennonites in North America.

E. K. Francis clearly led the way in the ethnic research of Mennonites, beginning in southern Manitoba in 1945 and culminating in his volume *In Search of Utopia* (1955). Francis used the study of the Mennonite community to generate ethnic theory which has stimulated sophisticated work comparing Mennonites with numerous other groups. These studies have exposed Mennonite research to the broader sociological arena, because increasingly they have dealt with general sociological issues, of solidarity, boundaries, institutions, networks, identity and the like.

Calvin Redekop, stimulated by the works of Francis led out in sectarian research with his dissertation in 1959, and his volume *The Old Colony Mennonites* (1969). The sect-church continuum of Weber and Troeltsch provided the focus for rural-urban, gemeinschaft-gesellschaft study, and the movement of Mennonites from sect to church-like characteristics. Concern with loss of community in the process of modernization and industrialization has continued to the present in studies carried out by Mennonites.

While Anabaptists in Europe (especially The Netherlands) have been urban from the beginning, Mennonites in North America have moved to the city more recently. Paul Peachey was among the first to study this phenomenon (*The Church in the City*, 1963). Since then Leo Driedger, located in Winnipeg, the largest urban concentration of Mennonites, has published extensively on urbanization of Mennonites. Studies so far have mostly documented the degree of urbanization. What happens to the quest for community when urbanization increases? The influence of modernization, the role of technology, and resulting changes need to be studied more. The role of socialization, identity, and formation of networks is an important part of this research. A whole new research agenda has developed.

Qualitative ethnological and community methods of sociological research are increasingly supplemented by quantitative survey research. The most extensive survey of Mennonites in North America was done by J. Howard Kauffman and Leland Harder (*Anabaptists Four Centuries Later*, 1975). Many others used their data; a supplemental survey was underway in 1988. Leland Harder also carried out three surveys of North American General Conference Mennonites in 1960, 1970, and 1980, and Leo Driedger and others conducted a national survey of Mennonites in Canada in 1977. A census of the Mennonite Church (MC) by Michael Yoder and a similar survey of Mennonite Brethren, updating the 1972 Kauffman/Harder study, were completed in 1982 and published in 1985. Survey research is increasing and numerous other surveys have been done.

With increasing industrialization and urbanization of Mennonites in North America and Europe, more attention will be given to identity, socialization, social networks and social conflict. Such economic factors as the struggle for use of land in developing countries, will require more research. Questions about the place of Christianity in °capitalism and °communism are also opening up new areas of conflict. Questions of what it means to be a "remnant" in a changing world of poverty will likely lead Mennonite sociologists more to a study of social change and conflict in the future. LD/CWR

Leo Driedger and J. Howard Kauffman, "Urbanization of Mennonites: Canadian and American Comparisons," *MQR*, 56 (1982), 269-90; Leo Driedger and Calvin Redekop, "Sociology of Mennonites," *JMS*, 1 (1983), 33-63; J. W. Fretz, *Pilgrims in Paraguay* (Scottdale, 1953); E. K. Francis, *In Search of Utopia: The Mennonites in Manitoba* (Altona: D. W. Friesen, 1955); Peter M. Hamm, *Continuity and Change Among Canadian Mennonite Brethren* (Waterloo, Ont.: Wilfrid Laurier U. Press, 1987); Leland Harder and J. Howard Kauffman, *Anabaptists Four Centuries Later: A Profile of Five Mennonite and Brethren in Christ Denominations* (Scottdale, 1975); J. Howard Kauffman, "Report on Mennonite Sociological Research," *MQR*, 37 (1963), 126-31; idem, "Toward a Sociology of Mennonites," *MQR*, 30 (1956), 163-212; Richard G. Kyle, *From Sect to Denomination: Church Types and their Implications for Mennonite Brethren History* (1985); Paul Peachey, *The Church in the City* (Newton, 1963); Calvin Redekop, *The Old Colony Mennonites: Dilemmas of Ethnic Minority Life* (Baltimore: Johns Hopkins U. Press, 1969); Michael L. Yoder, "Findings from the 1982 Mennonite [MC] Census," *MQR*, 59 (1985), 307-49; John E. Toews, Abraham Konrad, and Alvin Dueck, "Mennonite Brethren Church Membership Survey, 1972-1982," *Direction*, 14, no. 2 (Fall 1985), 3-89.

See also Anthropology; Church Growth Movement; Geography; Mennonite Studies; Social Class; Statistics.

Sociopolitical Activism refers to citizen actions intended to influence public policy or change social structures. From their beginnings, Anabaptist and Mennonite groups have petitioned governments on matters of religious toleration, exemption from military service, immigration rights, and other concerns essential to maintaining the identity and integrity of the church community (°lobbying).

During most of their history, Mennonites have been reluctant to act publicly on broader questions of °justice and civil order. It should be noted, however, that the first generation of Anabaptists dared to challenge the policies of contemporary rulers. °Menno Simons did not hesitate to argue against capital punishment and to call persons in authority to obey the will of God for their office. With his forthright, almost defiant, exhortations to magistrates, Menno stands as a prototype of prophetic witness to the state.

Severe persecution and subsequent immigration muted the aggressiveness of the early Anabaptists. When they found refuge in America and in Russia, Mennonites tended to isolate themselves from the social and political system around them, becoming "the quiet in the land." After the American Colonial period, voting in elections came to be viewed negatively by many Mennonites.

The 19th-c. awakening of North American Mennonites created new interest in outreach beyond their isolated communities. This renewal was accompanied by external events—famine in India, war in Europe, revolution in Russia—that brought sweeping changes in the church's relation to society and state.

Early in the 20th c., the temperance question became the occasion for otherwise nonvoting Mennonites to advocate prohibition of alcoholic beverages. Members of the Virginia Conference (MC), for example, in 1915 resolved to "use our influence by vote or otherwise, against the use or sale of strong drink." Some church leaders advocated the alternative of personal witness to saloon-keepers in local communities.

In the period after World War II, the expanding global °mission, °relief, and °service activities of church agencies brought human needs to the attention of Mennonite people. Through their ministry to suffering people, Mennonites discovered the pervasive impact of government policies, for good or for evil. Race relations also became an issue for Mennonites as they learned of the evils of racial segregation and discrimination.

Mennonite °voluntary service units and °church planting projects in °urban places brought awareness of the massive dimensions of economic injustice and inspired public efforts to bring about reform at both local and national levels. Outreach through prison ministries and concern for criminal offenders led to official testimony against °capital punishment, along with working toward constructive alternatives to conventional prison punishment.

Responding to these concerns, official Mennonite bodies began to address government officials regarding issues of justice and social welfare, along with continuing their public witness on °peace and military concerns. Among many examples of bolder and more comprehensive political pronouncements are the 1959 General Conference Mennonite Church resolution on surplus food and the international °refugee year, and the 1964 Franconia Conference (MC) letter to United States senators encouraging a "practical, workable Civil Rights Bill."

The growing activism of the 1960s resulted in many denominational study processes, conference resolutions, and major position statements on social concerns. Such writers as Peter Ediger, Frank °Epp, John A. Lapp, John H. Redekop and John H. Yoder provided theological reflection on political witness and activity. During the same decade, a number of Mennonites joined in demonstrations, boycotts, and other controversial public actions. Most claimed to be acting from the same motives of Christian compassion and concern for justice that inspired the more conventional approaches.

Although traditional Mennonite teaching has warned against the temptations of power and political office, some Mennonite individuals have launched election campaigns based on platforms that explicitly expressed Christian values. Prominent recent examples include Frank Epp in Ontario (1979, 1980), James Juhnke in Kansas (1970), LeRoy Kennel in Illinois (1980, 1982), and Terry Miller in South Dakota. Canadian Mennonites have accepted political involvement much more readily than the U.S. churches. A significant number of Canadian provincial and national posts were held by persons of Mennonite background in the late 1980s (°politics; °government).

The agencies and committees created by the Mennonite churches to deal with public issues have generally included other social problems along with continuing peace concerns. Typical agenda items for the Mennonite Central Committee Peace Section and the Mennonite Central Committee Canada Peace and Social Concerns Committee, for example,

have included °abortion, acid rain, agriculture problems, East-West exchange, war °taxes and °conscription.

The Washington office of MCC, established in 1968, and the Ottawa office of MCC Canada, represent deliberate efforts to engage the national political scene (lobbying). These offices, through the *Washington Memo*, the *Ottawa Report*, and other means, provide information on a wide range of issues and enable constituents to communicate their concerns to government officials.   JRB

John H. Redekop, "Mennonites and Politics in Canada and the United States," *JMS*, 1 (1983), 79-105, includes a listing of Mennonite politicians and extensive bibliography in the notes; Urbane Peachey, ed., *Mennonite Statements on Peace and Social Concerns, 1900-1978* (1980); General Board, (MC), unpublished papers from "The Church's Relationship to the Political Order," presented at "Conversations on Faith II" at Laurelville, Pa., March 7-9, 1985 (see especially J. R. Burkholder, "Continuity and Change: An Analysis of the Mennonite Experience with the Political Order"; *Washington Memo*, (published bimonthly); *Ottawa Report*; *Justice and the Christian Witness*, statement adopted by both the General Conference Mennonite Church and the Mennonite Church General Assembly at Bethlehem Pa., 1983; John Howard Yoder, *The Christian Witness to the State* (Newton, 1964); Duane K. Friesen, *Mennonite Witness on Peace and Social Concerns: 1900-1980* (Akron Pa.: MCC, 1982); Theron F. Schlabach, "Politics and Peoplehood," *Goshen College Bulletin*, 65, no. 4 (July 1980), 6-7; J. Lawrence Burkholder, "The Problem of Social Responsibility from the Perspective of the Mennonite Church," (ThD diss., Princeton Theological Seminary, 1958; published Elkhart, Ind.: IMS, 1988)); J. R. Burkholder and Calvin Redekop, eds., *Kingdom, Cross, and Community* (Scottdale, 1976), see especially essays by James Juhnke, Calvin Redekop, and John Redekop; James Juhnke, "A Mennonite Runs for Congress," *Menn. Life*, 26, no. 1, (Jan. 1971), 8-11; James C. Juhnke, *A People of Two Kingdoms: The Political Acculturation of Kansas Mennonites* (Newton, 1975); Frank H. Epp, *A Strategy for Peace: Reflections of a Christian Pacifist* (Grand Rapids: Eerdmans, 1973); John H. Redekop, *Making Political Decisions: A Christian Perspective* (Scottdale, 1972); Mennonite Central Committee, "A New Look at the Church and State Issue" (from 1965 study conference, Chicago); General Conference Mennonite Church, "Christian Responsibility to Society," official statement on social issues (Newton, 1963); Mennonite General Conference (MC), "The Christian Witness to the State," official statement adopted in 1961; Guy F. Hershberger, *The Way of the Cross in Human Relations* (Scottdale, 1958); Elmer Neufeld, "Christian Responsibility in the Political Situation," *MQR*, (Apr. 1958); Frank H. Epp and Marlene G. Epp, *The Progressions of the Mennonite Central Committee Peace Section* (Akron Pa.: MCC, 1984); Kauffman/Harder, *Anabaptists Four C. Later* (1975), 166-69.

See also Church-State Relations; Development Work; Institutions, Church; Revolution.

Anarchy and Activism: The Isaak Story

On September 6, 1901, in Buffalo, New York, a young man named Leon Czolgosz shot United States President William McKinley. Czolgosz, a self-proclaimed anarchist, believed his deed was in the interest of the working class. Three days later, McKinley was dead. What followed was the questioning, detention, and arrest of hundreds of anarchists across the country. One of those arrested more than 500 miles away, in Chicago, was Abraham Isaak. He had been born in a Mennonite colony in the Russian Empire.

At the turn of the century anarchism, a movement and doctrine that rejected all government authority, was as popular as it would ever be in the United States. Far from meaning chaos or violence, the doctrine espoused a natural order based on voluntary association in which people would live peaceful and productive lives. Isaak was well-known in late 19th- and early 20th century anarchist circles. He contributed to the American anarchist movement through a publishing career in three different cities, a career that spanned at least 13 years.

After he immigrated in 1890, Isaak with his wife and three children first settled in Portland, Oregon. In 1895, with the help of several friends, the Isaaks launched the publication of an anarchist weekly called *The Firebrand*. This paper was short lived. In 1897, it was suppressed and its associates arrested after they published an issue that contained a poem by Walt Whitman. Portland officials declared that the poem, "A Woman Waits for Me," was "obscene" and that mailing it violated federal law. Sometime between 1898 and 1900 the Isaaks left Portland for San Francisco in search of greater tolerance. Here again they published an anarchist newspaper.

In San Francisco they also met and became close friends with America's most prominent anarchist, Emma Goldman. Goldman warmly described them as "unusual" people. "The particular attraction of the Isaaks for me," she later wrote in her autobiography *Living My Life,* "was the consistency of their lives [and] the harmony between the ideas they professed and their application." The Isaaks, whose family lifestyle was authentically anarchistic, were indeed "unusual." But they were unusual for other reasons.

The Isaaks had roots in the Mennonites, whom Goldman called a "liberal religious sect in Russia, of German origin." Little is known about why they immigrated, why they became anarchists, or their Mennonite background. But in response to a letter that asked whether there has ever existed a true anarchist society, Isaak wrote in 1897 in the pages of *The Firebrand*: "I was born and raised in a community of Mennonites in Russia. . . . These people [had] obtained the privilege from the Russian government to manage their own affairs, and as their religion was against civil laws they lived for about 70 years without laws or officers . . . . These people had been persecuted. . . in western Europe and were considered as the lawless, just as the anarchists are today." But when wheat-raising became profitable and accumulation began, Isaak continued, the "rich and the poor" among Russia's Mennonites had become distinct. Hence, "government stepped in, and today there are beggars, thieves and drunkards among them, but I have not heard of a murder yet."

By 1901, at the time of McKinley's assassination, the Isaaks were living and publishing yet another anarchist newspaper in Chicago. Incidentally, there they met the would-be assassin Czolgosz, whose constant espousal of violence evoked Abraham Isaak's suspicion. These suspicions would soon prove well-founded.

As of this writing, nothing is known of the Isaaks after their arrest. It is possible that they moved on to New York. It is also possible that they were deported back to Russia in 1919 at the peak of the "red scare." As anarchists, the Isaaks were social and political "gadflies." They rejected the authoritarianism of organized religion and government. As ethnic Mennonites (although they stepped beyond Mennonites' religious, political, and social

perimeters) they participated in a heritage from which they could not divorce themselves. Their history reveals a most rare and controversial "Mennonite response" to an age of turbulence and transition.   SKS

Soedjono Harsosoedirdjo. See Gereja Injili di Tanah Jawa.

Soehadiweko Djojodihardjo (Oct. 4, 1918-Sept. 16, 1988). No one person has had a more profound influence in the growth and development of the Gereja Injili di Tanah Jawa (Evangelical Church of Java) from the time of its formation in 1940 to the present than Soehadiweko Djojodihardjo. As the son of another extraordinary church leader, °Sardjoe Djojodihardjo, Soehadiweko as a youth already demonstrated remarkable capabilities. Mission policy in the 1930s provided for only limited leadership training. The normal school in Margorejo, which earlier served a key role in leadership training, was closed in the 1920s because of financial pressure. In 1937 two promising young leaders, Soewignjo Harsosoedirdjo and Siswojo were sent to Bale Wiyoto Theological Institute in Malang, East Java. Soehadiweko Djojodihardjo was the only person sent to study at the Hogere Theologische School (Higher Theological School) in Batavia (Jakarta).

All of Soehadiweko's books and notes from his study in Batavia were destroyed when the train on which he returned to his home was set on fire and destroyed. This experience inaugurated for him personally the baptism in fire—martyrdom, mob violence in Muslim uprisings, oppressive occupation, famine, revolutionary struggle—that his church was to experience in the decade of the 1940s. Soon Soehadiweko was standing with his father, carrying key church leadership responsibilities. After the uprisings in 1942 Soehadiweko was among the two teams of two sent to ascertain the consequenses of violence for the churches. In 1943 he was chosen as synod secretary. During the tense days of the revolution (1945-50), by virtue of their affiliation with the allegedly Dutch religion, Javanese Christians were accused of complicity with the Dutch effort to retake Indonesia as a colony. Thus the church lived under the constant threat of violence at the hands of radical Muslim nationalists. In this situation the synod appointed Soehadiweko to the intelligence office of the revolutionary forces while other younger members of the church engaged in other aspects of the struggle.

Soehadiweko was still quite young when he was called to take over pastoral responsibilities at the point of his father's untimely death in 1948. Shortly thereafter he was also chosen to serve as chairman of the synod, a position he filled for more than 30 years. During this period the congregation he copastored (for a time together with Esther Soesanto) spawned dozens of branch fellowships more than a dozen of which have since become mature congregations. The number of congregations in the synod expanded during this time from 18 to 52. His rich pastoral ministry has gone far beyond the circles of his congregation and synod. Sometimes this ministry was carried out in the midst of violent political and religious upheaval such as during the aftermath of the failed coup attempt in 1965.

Soehadiweko also played key roles at the board level in developing many of the synod's ministering agencies. One of the most significant of these has been the theological college in Pati, Akademi Kristen Wiyata Wacana. At the same time Soehadiweko for decades has been chairman of the board of ecumenical institutions like Satya Wacana Christian University in Salatiga and Duta Wacana Theological Seminary in Yogyakarta with his fellow churchman from the Pati congregation, Pirenamoelja, serving as secretary. These complement a long-term role as a key participant in the activities of the Council (now Fellowship) of Churches in Indonesia and involvement in the Asian Mennonite Conference and the Mennonite World Conference beginning in 1952.   LMY

Doopsgezinde Zendingsvereeniging, *Verslag van de Staat en de Verrigtingen der Doopsgezinde Vereeniging to Bevordering der Evangelieverbreiding in di Nederlandsche Overzeesche Bezittingen* the annual reports of the Dutch Mennonite Mission Union published in Amsterdam beginning in 1848; Th. E. Jensma, *Doopsgezinde Zending in Indonesia* ('s Gravenhage: Boekcentrum N. V., 1968); *Jerih dan Juang,* National Survey on the Church in Indonesia, (Jakarta, Indonesia: Lembaga Penelitian dan Studi-DGI, 1979); Martati Ins. Kumaat, *Benih yang Tumbuh, V,* a survey of the Evangelical Church of Java (Jakarta: Lembaga Penelitian dan Studi-DGI, 1973); Sigit Heru Soekotjo and Lawrence M. Yoder, "Sejarah Gereja Kristen Muria Indonesia" [History of the Evangelical Church of Java], unpublished manuscript; Lawrence M. Yoder, ed. *Bahan Serjarah Gereja Injili di Tanah Jawa* [Historical Resources on the History of the Evangelical Church of Java] (Pati, Indonesia: Komisi Sejarah Gereja GITD, 1977); idem, "The Introduction and Expression of Islam and Christianity in the Cultural Context of North Central Java" (PhD diss., Fuller Theological Seminary, 1987); idem, "Sejarah Margorejo," *Wiyata Wacana,* 7, no. 1, (1977), 18-25; *Miss. Focus,* 13 (1985), 20-21.

Solomon, Phoebe Sheela (Bisahu (b. Jan. 8, 1917), deaconess in the Mennonite Church in India, and teacher in the °Dhamtari municipal schools, was born in Lohara District, Rajnandgaon, Madhya Pradesh, India. She was the oldest child of Bisahu and Pyari Bai Prasad, °lay evangelists employed by the Pentecostal Missionary Bands Mission. After her mother died in 1920 her father remarried and moved to Korba to work for the General Conference Mennonite Mission. In 1926 the family moved to Dhamtari where both parents served in rural evangelism. Phoebe completed her primary and middle school in American Mennonite Mission schools at Balodgahan and high school in Jabalpur. She graduated from Isabella Thoburn College, Lucknow, Uttar Pradesh, the first woman graduate in the Mennonite Church in India.

Phoebe taught in the Garjan Memorial Middle School in Balodgahan from 1940 until her marriage to Stephen N. Solomon in 1942. Then she transferred to the mission schools in Dhamtari where she taught both in high school and in the normal school. In 1954 she began teaching in the municipal higher secondary school where she remained until retirement in 1972. In 1942 she was ordained deaconess for the Sundarganj congregation and in 1962 represented the Mahila Sabha (Women's Fellowship) of the Mennonite Church in India at the Mennonite World Conference in Kitchener, Ont.   JAF

Solomon, Stephen N. (b. Apr. 14, 1914), teacher in Mennonite schools in °Dhamtari, Madhya Pradesh (M.P.), and minister in the Mennonite Church in India, was born in Jagdalpur, Bastar District, M.P., India. He was the son of Samedas and Bitawan Solomon. His father died when Stephen was very young and his mother took him to Dhamtari where he was admitted to the boys' orphanage of the American Mennonite Mission. Stephen completed high school in 1935, taught for two years in the mission normal school and tutored new missionaries in language study. In 1946 he received BA and BEd degrees from the U. of Calcutta. He returned to Dhamtari and taught Hindi at the Mennonite Higher Secondary School until his retirement in 1976. He married Phoebe Bisahu in 1942. They had four daughters and one son.

Stephen was a prolific writer and a good musician, composing songs, writing dramas, and translating ca. 60 books and booklets for the North India Christian Tract and Book Society and the Masihi Sahitya Sanstha. He edited the conference paper, *Mennonait Mandli Samachar Patrika* for several years, and was a regular member of the Mennonite Literature and Audio Visual Board. He served on the panel of translators for the Bible Society of India's new Hindi translation of the Bible. In 1947 he was ordained deacon in the Sundarganj congregation and in 1970 was ordained a minister to serve as co-pastor. In retirement he has assisted as pastor in several congregations. He was conference secretary for two terms and in 1948 was delegate for the Mennonite Church in India (MC) at the Mennonite World Conference in the United States.   JAF

Somalia (ME IV:572). Missionaries from the Eastern Mennonite [MC] Board of Missions and Charities (EMBMC) first arrived in Somalia in January 1953. This venture represented the first Protestant witness in that country since the Swedish Lutheran Mission was asked to leave in 1935.

For the first 16 years the mission programs expanded rapidly to include five locations and more than 30 missionaries. Emphasis was given to establishing service ministries which were requested by the Somali people and government. This included several schools, a clinic and hospital, and other small community development programs. The coming of independence in July 1960, spawned a search for new understandings of truth, faith, the will and peace of God.

The military takeover in October 1969 and eventual nationalization of all mission properties and programs in 1972 significantly altered mission involvement in Somalia. Educational personnel were reassigned to teaching positions in various government schools. Changing government policies eventually led to all mission personnel being asked to leave in 1976.

In 1979 Mennonite Central Committee (MCC) formed an agreement with the Somali government to give assistance to refugee needs. A year later workers from Eastern Mennonite Board of Missions and Charities were able to return to Somalia. As of December 1986 there were 13 EMBMC workers (plus children) assigned to educational and medical programs. The MCC team of 7 persons works with long-term development needs of refugees.

The local Christian fellowship has continued under national leadership, although in a less structured way. Despite the changes of the past decade EMBMC, MCC, and other workers support and encourage the fellowship by their presence, service, and witness.   KMN

MWH (1978), 99; *MWH* (1984), 15; *MC Yearbook* (1988-89), 160.

Somali Mennonite Believers Fellowship is located mostly in Mogadishu, the capital city of the Democratic Republic of Somalia. The fellowship has weekly worship services every Friday morning. The Fellowship is minimally organized with leadership given by a council chosen by the members.

The involvement of Eastern Mennonite Board of Missions and Charities was initiated in 1953. In the past the work of the Sudan Interior Mission also contributed to the Christian witness in Somalia. Since 1980, several other Christian agencies have become involved in relief and development programs and, by their presence in the country, give encouragement and support to this small fellowship. Roman Catholics, mostly from Italy, have been active in health, education, and orphanage ministries since 1935.

This Mogadishu fellowship is probably the only active group in the country with predominately Somali leadership. There are no official membership lists and attendance at weekly worship services varies from 20 to 40. There has been slow growth in the fellowship the last five years.   KMN

MWH (1978), 99; *MWH* (1984), 15; *MC Yearbook* (1988-89), 163.

Somerset Co., Pa., Old Order Amish Settlement. See Meyersdale-Springs, Pa., Old Order Amish Settlement.

Sommerfeld Colony, Bolivia, located 55 km. (35 mi.) se. of Santa Cruz, east of the Swift Current colony. Sommerfeld was established in 1968 by a group of about 50 Mennonite families from the Santa Clara colony in Mexico. This is the only group that has moved from Mexico to Bolivia that does not belong to the Old Colony Mennonites. It is a °Sommerfeld Mennonite church with bishop Peter Wiebe as their leader. One church building and two schools are located in the colony. The colony consists of four villages. Due to financial hardships and squatters it has lost some of its land; some land has also been sold to the neighboring Swift Current colony. In 1986 the population of Sommerfeld colony consisted of 419 people with 132 baptized church members.   IHie

See also Bergthal Mennonites.

Sommerfeld Colony, Paraguay (ME IV:576). Located 210 km. (130 mi.) east of Asunción along the highway connecting that city with Presidente Stroessner on the Brazilian border. The total land purchased included 31,428 hectares (77,627 acres), inhabited by 1,750 persons (1986) of whom 586 were church members. Two Mennonite villages,

Neuhoffnung (Campo 9) and Altona (Campo 8) lie directly along the highway. °Bergthal Colony is approximately 20 km. (12 mi.) north of Sommerfeld. The settlers for both colonies came from Canada in 1948, 740 from Manitoba's °°East Reserve, 764 from the °°West Reserve, and 140 from Saskatchewan. Those from the East Reserve founded Bergthal Colony. All of them were descendents of the immigrants from Russia to Canada in 1874-1918 (°Berthal Mennonites; °Sommerfeld Mennonites).

The reasons given for their leaving Canada are the inroads of secular society into their congregations and the possibility Paraguay offered to live a separated life with closed settlements in which to train their children and young people in their own schools in the German language.

The group boarded the ship *Volendam* at Quebec City on June 25, 1948, except for a small group which had flown to Paraguay earlier to make preparations. The Volendam had already made two trips with refugees from Europe to Paraguay. In Buenos Aires all their belongings were loaded onto a riverboat on which they traveled to Asunción. From there they traveled by train to Villarica, arriving there on July 23, 1948.

Since there was no road to most of the land they had purchased they began building this themselves, usually through heavy forest. Difficulties were also encountered with the owners of adjoining land. After months of waiting, while the road was being built, approximately one-third of the emigrants returned to Canada. Those who remained, however, succeeded in establishing two flourishing settlements i.e. Sommerfeld and Bergthal. Sommerfeld is considered to be one of the most prosperous Mennonite settlements in Paraguay today (1986). Its inhabitants' primary sources of income are from wood products, agriculture, and dairy products.

Little change has occurred in congregational life. Sermons are usually read. There is no youth work and no Bible study meetings or prayer meetings are held (°social meetings). The ministers have not received special training for their duties. Baptismal instruction is given annually from Easter to Pentecost, at which time the baptism itself occurs. Unbaptized adults are not allowed to live in the settlement.

The congregation has assumed responsibility for the welfare of the settlement. A well-equipped hospital has now been built. Schools continue in the traditional manner, with the teachers receiving no special training for their task. Primary textbooks for the schools are a reader, catechism, hymnbook, and the Bible. Attendance is required to age 14.   GR

See also Bergthal Mennonites.

Sommerfeld Mennonites [and Saskatchewan Bergthal Mennonites]
(ME IV:576) are Mennonites of the Bergthal Colony in Russia who settled in the °°West Reserve of Manitoba in the 1880s. Originally part of the Bergthal congregation, they took the name *Sommerfelder* after 1894. In that year Abraham Doerksen of the village of Sommerfeld was ordained °elder for the large majority of the West Reserve Bergthaler, who had since 1889 resisted aspects of the leadership of

Bergthal elder Johann Funk (°acculturation: "Funk and Funk" [feature]).

Funk promoted activities in higher education, foreign missions, and pulpit exchange with other churches which many of his members resisted as an "Americanization" of the church. The outside persons through whom these emphases were introduced came largely from the United States, especially from the General Conference Mennonite Church (GCM). The coming of H. H. °°Ewert from Kansas to serve as principal of the newly organized Mennonite Educational Institute in Gretna precipitated the separation of the large majority of the church, who wished to remain in solidarity with the Bergthal group on the East Reserve (now known as the °Chortitzer Conference), from Funk's °Bergthal Mennonites [Manitoba] who eventually merged with the Conference of Mennonites in Canada [GCM]). Accordingly, it was Elder David Stoesz of the Chortitzer who ordained Doerksen as elder of the "Sommerfelder" in 1894.

This separation did not mean the end of cooperation. The °°*Waisenamt* was not divided until 1907, when the West Reserve Bergthaler wanted to incorporate it legally and the majority of the Sommerfelder did not. In many villages the two groups continued to cooperate in the operation of elementary schools, both private and public. In 1913 the Sommerfelder took the initiative in organizing a *Schulkommission* (school commission) whose goals were to improve instruction in the schools, especially in German and religion, and to represent Mennonite educational concerns before the government. H. H. Ewert urged the other Manitoba churches to support this initiative.

Sommerfelder Mennonites were part of the westward migration to what later became Saskatchewan beginning in the 1890s. Elders Stoesz and Doerksen served these groups from time to time. In 1902 Doerksen ordained Kornelius Epp and in 1908 Aron Zacharias as elder of the group at Rosthern. He conducted ministerial elections for the group at Herbert in 1907 and four years later ordained his brother, David Doerksen, as elder of that group. The Rosthern group took the name *Bergthaler* (usually referred to as Saskatchewan Bergthaler to distinguish them from the Manitoba West Reserve Bergthal group that eventually merged with the Conference of Mennonites in Canada [GCM]). The Herbert-Swift Current group remained Sommerfelder.

By the mid-1920s Sommerfelder resistance to secondary education had diminished to the point where almost the entire board of the Mennonite Educational Institute in Altona consisted of Sommerfeld Mennonites. During the school crisis precipitated by Manitoba legislation brought in during World War I (1916), the Sommerfelder cooperated with other Mennonite groups in attempting to negotiate a compromise. Similarly, the Sommerfelder church cooperated with other Mennonite churches in representations to Ottawa in relation to °nonresistance issues during both wars, in the raising of °relief and Red Cross funds, and in the administration of °alternative service activities.

In the context of the migration of Old Colony Mennonites to Mexico after World War I, Elder Abraham Doerksen and some 600 Sommerfelder (8 percent of the Manitoba church) moved to the colony of Santa Clara. Another group of 357 together with 227 Saskatchewan Bergthaler led by Elder Aron Zacharias, joined the East Reserve Chortitzer in founding Menno Colony in Paraguay in 1927. (The 1948 founding of °Sommerfeld and °Bergthal colonies in east Paraguay by Manitoba Sommerfelder and Chortitzer and Saskatchewan Bergthaler is noted in ME IV.) Some 15 Canadian families, mostly Saskatchewan Bergthaler, were involved in the 1963 founding of the Bergthal Colony in Bolivia, together with immigrants from the Canadiense Colony of Paraguay. During the 1970s a congregation was begun in Aylmer, Ont. among Mennonites who had immigrated to the area from Mexico.

Joint conferences of the elders and ministers of various "Sommerfelder" groups (including Manitoba, Herbert, and Vanderhoof [British Columbia] Sommerfelder; Chortitzer Conference; and Saskatchewan Bergthaler from Aberdeen and Carrot River) were held periodically (1934, 1952, 1955, 1957, 1982) to agree on issues common to all and to coordinate church practices.

°Urbanization and °acculturation affected the Sommerfelder groups more slowly than it did other Mennonite groups in Canada. The language transition from German to English was still in progress in the 1980s. In 1952 the Sommerfelder and Chortitzer began to hold regular church srvices in Winnipeg, giving rise to a joint congregation. Since about 1980 the two groups meet separately.

In social services, such as the construction and operating of senior citizens' homes, Mennonite Central Committee overseas relief and service, and other such areas, the Sommerfelder cooperate with other Mennonite groups. In the 1980s ministers were still elected for life and served without remuneration. Each one served the entire church, preaching at the various locations according to a set rotation.

The decade of the 1950s was a difficult one for the Manitoba Sommerfelder Church. Accommodation to Canadian society during the 1940s was resisted by some and welcomed by others. Some of the more conservative people emigrated to Paraguay; many who looked for more rapid changes joined the Manitoba Bergthaler or Rudnerweider (Evangelical Mennonite Mission Conference) churches. Failing eyesight brought the retirement of Bishop Peter A. °Toews in 1951, but not before three ministers had been defrocked for supporting unacceptable innovations in wedding dress. His successors struggled to find a new equilibrium. This, however, was not achieved before the separation in 1958 of some 800 (of 2,800) members and 12 (of 16) ministers to form the Reinländer Mennoniten Gemeinde of Manitoba.

The 1970s were marked by rapid changes. Sunday school had been introduced in the 1950s. Young people's meetings, the use of some English in church (including the decision to purchase English hymnals), and formal involvement with Mennonite Central Committee, began in the 1970s and 1980s. By 1987 there were signs that even this pace of change was not enough to satisfy all segments of the church.

Membership of the Sommerfelder Church in Manitoba in 1985 was 3,981. Its elders have been Abraham Doerksen (1894-1922), Heinrich J. Friesen (1922-31), Peter A. Toews (1931-51), Peter M. Friesen, (1951-57), and Johann A. Friesen (1955-). Elders serving the Saskatchewan Bergthaler Church (ca. 1,000 members in 1985) have been Kornelius Epp (1902-08), Aron Zacharias (1908-26), Cornelius Hamm (1928-47), Abram J. Buhler (1947-75), and John D. Reddekopp (1975-). Groups separating in 1979 and 1983 sought affiliation with Carrot River-area Bergthaler and Herbert-area Sommerfelder respectively. The Sommerfelder in southern Saskatchewan (ca. 400 members in 1985) were led by David F. Doerksen from 1911 until his move to Paraguay in 1948. David Wall, Swift Current (1935-71), and David Wiebe (1971-).

The following Sommerfelder/Bergthaler colonies existed in Latin America as of 1987. They are grouped by country with year of founding, origin of colonists, population, membership, and name of elder (1987) in that order. MEXICO: °°*Santa Clara Colony* [1922], Manitoba Sommerfelder (1700, 616), Jacob F. Doerksen. PARAGUAY: °*Santa Clara Colony* [1972], Mexico (133, 50), Abram Friesen; °*Bergthal Colony* [1948], Manitoba Chortitzer (1478, 555), Jacob R. Funk; °*Reinfeld Colony* [1966], Bergthal (119, 64), Jacob R. Funk; °*Sommerfeld Colony* [1948], Manitoba Sommerfelder (1752, 678), Jacob Heinrichs. BOLIVIA: °*Canadiense Colony* [1956], from Menno Colony in Paraguay (807, 329), Dietrich Dueck; °*Morgenland Colony* [1975], branch colony of Candiense (280, 104), Dietrich Dueck; °*Bergthal Colony* [1963], from Canadiense Colony (306, 127), Johann Guenter; °*Sommerfeld Colony* [1968], Mexico (419, 132), Peter Wiebe; °*Nueva Holanda Colony* [1983], from Canadiense Colony (394, 157), Peter Giesbrecht. °Menno Colony in Paraguay (origin of Canadiense Colony above) was founded in 1927 by Chortitzer and Sommerfelder from Manitoba and Bergthaler from Saskatchewan, has 3,050 members and a population of 6,650. It is now affiliated with the General Conference Mennonite Church (GCM). AE/JP

Leonard Doell, *The Bergthaler Mennonite Church of Saskatchewan, 1892-1975* (Winnipeg: CMBC Publications, 1987); Jacob Giesbrecht, "In the 'Nachfolge Tradition': The Sommerfelder Mennonites of Manitoba, Canada," (unpubl. paper, Winnipeg, 1983), copy at Mennonite Heritage Centre, (Winnipeg); Reimer, *Quilt* (1983), 36-40; Jake Peters, "An Annotated Bibliography of Materials Relating to the Sommerfelder Mennonite Church" (unpublished, 1979) Mennonite Heritage Centre Archives; idem, Mennonite Private Schools in Manitoba and Saskatchewan, 1874-1925 (Steinbach: Mennonite Village Museum, 1985); idem, *The Waisenamt: A History of Mennonite Inheritance Custom* (Steinbach: Mennonite Village Museum, 1985); Abe Warkentin, *Strangers and Pilgrims* (Steinbach: *Mennonitische Post* (1987); *Der Mitarbeiter*, 1905-34; David Stoesz and Abraham Doerksen archival collections in Mennonite Heritage Centre Archives; *MWH* (1978), 323; *MWH* (1984), 135.

See also Conservative Mennonites; Old Colony Mennonites.

Sona, Nicodemus Rupdhar (b. 1926) was born in a Christian home in the village of Dongania in India. He graduated from Allahabad Agricultural College in Northern Province, took teachers training in Jabalpur, M.P. and received a MA degree in Raipur, Madhya Pradesh (M.P).

From 1957 to 1978 he taught and lectured in the Janzen Memorial Higher Secondary School in upper division. In 1979 he became principal of Joyti Higher Secondary School in Korba, M.P., and later also manager of the Mission Hindi Medium schools there. He married Ukiya Gardia in February 1943. They have three sons and two daughters.

Nicodemus was baptized in 1943 and has served the church faithfully as Sunday school teacher, church council member, treasurer of his local congregation and the Bhartiya General Conference Mennonite Conference. In 1972 he attended the Mennonite World Conference in Curitiba, Brazil; visited churches in the United States; and attended the Goals, Priority and Strategy Conference in Chicago. His influence as teacher and churchman continues today (1988). HR/RR

Soteriology. See Justification; Salvation.

South Africa. See Republic of South Africa.

South America (ME IV:583). The first 50 years of Mennonite experience in South America took place predominantly in immigrant, German-speaking communities. In the last 30 years indigenous churches of Native American and Latino people numbering about 12,300 members in 10 countries have taken prominence. This indigenous church has grown out of North American Mennonite mission effort and the witness of the immigrant Mennonite communities. By 1988 the immigrant communities number about 19,000 baptized members and still largely live in colonies. In 1957 there were about 1,000 indigenous and 7,150 immigrant Mennonite church members in five South American countries (ME IV:583).

Since 1957 the indigenous churches have grown mostly by evangelism while the immigrant communities grew through major migrations from Mexico and Belize along with smaller migrations from Canada and the United States. The immigrants went primarily to Bolivia and Paraguay (in 1986 also to Argentina). In the immigrant colonies established earlier, rapid natural growth has been largely offset by return migration to Canada and to Europe. In 1988 there were at least 10 North American Mennonite and Brethren in Christ mission agencies operating in South America. The agencies support the work of the established churches and in a number of cases expatriate missionaries work under national leadership. In the 1980s the mission agencies initiated work in Venezuela, Ecuador, Peru, and Chile. At the end of the 1980s a major concern is to find ways for the national churches and mission agencies to work in partnership.

Growing contacts between the indigenous and immigrant streams of Mennonites in recent years and the revolutionary political climate in the region painfully highlight the growing economic gap between the two streams. Prosperous Mennonite colonies on the one hand are deeply involved in international economics through import and export while on the other hand a substantial number of indigenous Mennonites struggle for survival. The dis-

SOUTH AMERICA

LEGEND
MENNONITE CHURCHES IN SOUTH AMERICA
■ Organized bodies
★ MCC involvement
□ Other missions and programs (not including those
   relating to organized bodies)
● 500 members (approx. locations)

Kilometers   0   500   1000   1500

TABLE

Organized bodies	Membership (1986 unless noted)
ARGENTINA	
Altkolonier Mennoniten (Old Col. Menn.)	ca. 200 (1987)
Evangelische Mennonitische Bruderschaft (Evan. Menn. Br. Ch.)	
Iglesia Evangelica Menonite Argentina (Argentine Evan. Menn. Ch.)	1516
Iglesia Evangelica Unida (United Evan. Ch.)	62
BOLIVIA	
Altkolonier Mennoniten Gemeinden (Old Colony Mennonites)	ca. 5800
Bergthaler Mennonite Gemeinden (Bergthaler Mennonites)	185
Iglesia Menonita de Bolivia (Bolivian Menn. Ch.)	90
Mision Evangelica Menonita (Evan. Menn. Miss.)	48
Reinlaender Mennoniten Gemeinde (Reinlaender Mennonites)	ca. 380
Sommerfelder Mennoniten Gemeinde (Sommerfelder Mennonites)	618
BRAZIL	
Associacao das Igrejas Irmaos Menonitas do Brazil (Assoc. of the Menn. Br. Churches of Brazil)	1790
Associacao das Igrejas Menonitas do Brazil (Assoc. of the Menn. Churches of Brazil)	719
Associacao Evangelica Menonita (Evan. Menn. Assoc.)	895
Convencao Brasileira das Igrejas Irmaos Menonitas (Brazilian Conv. of the Menn. Br. Ch.)	1600
COLOMBIA	
Asociacion de Iglesias Hermanos Menonitas (Assoc. of Menn. Br. Churches)	2000 (1987)
Iglesia Evangelica Menonita (Evan. Menn. Ch.)	890 (1987)
ECUADOR	
Mision Evangelica Menonita en Ecuador (Menn. Miss. in Ecuador)	80
PARAGUAY	
Altkolonier Mennoniten Gemeinden (Old Colony Mennonites)	1249
Beachy Amish Mennonite Fellowship	71
Bergthaler Mennonite Gemeinden (Bergthaler Menn. Ch.)	780
Convencion de las Iglesias Evangelicas Chulupi (Chulupi Evan. Conv.)	1500
Convencion de las Iglesias Evangelicas de los Hermanos Lengua (Lengua Evan. Conv.)	1300
Convencion de las Iglesias Evangelicas de las Indigenas (United Evan. Conv.)	1500
Convencion de las Iglesias Evangelicas Unidas Menonitas (United Evan. Churches)	500
Convencion Evangelica de los Hermanos Menonitas (Evan. Conv. of Menn. Br.)	1520
Evangelische Mennonitische Bruderschaft (Evan. Menn. Br. Ch.)	359
Evangelische Mennonitische Gemeinde (Evan. Menn. Ch.)	200
Konferenz der Mennonitischen Brudergemeinden von Paraguay (Conf. of the Menn. Br. Churches of P.)	2300 (1987)
Mennonite Christian Brotherhood	114
Sommerfelder Mennoniten Gemeinde (Somm. Menn. Ch.)	600
Vereinigung der Mennonitengemeinden von Paraguay (Assoc. of Menn. Churches in Paraguay)	4947
TRINIDAD & TOBAGO	
Mennonite Church of Trinidad & Tobago	850
URUGUAY	
Convencion de Iglesias Menonitas en Uruguay (Uruguayan Menn. Conv.)	216 (1987)
Consejo de las Congregaciones de los Hermanos Menonitas (Council of Menn. Br. Congs.)	170 (1987)
Konferenz de Mennonitengemeinden in Uruguay (Conf. of Mennonites in Uruguay)	521
VENEZUELA	
Concilio de las Iglesias Evangelicas Menonitas en Venezuela (Council of Evan. Menn. Churches in V.)	121

Other programs and missions (not incl. those relating to organized bodies)
BRAZIL: Ch. of God in Christ, Menn.
CHILE: Menn. B. of Miss.
ECUADOR: Euro. Menn. Evan.-komm.
PARAGUAY: E. Penn. Menn. Ch., Evan. Menn. Conf. B. of Miss.
PERU: Menn. B. of Miss., Menn. Br. Miss./Services
VENEZUELA: Evan. Menn. Ch. Comm. on Overseas Miss.

parities raise questions whether a common identity can be forged. At the same time common efforts in mission and service result in notable integration of the two streams in some places, e.g., in Uruguay.

Mennonites, Amish, and Brethren in Christ in South America today range from (1) the religiously conservative and culturally isolated to (2) middle class professionals integrated into larger society to (3) those suffering due to their work for social justice. Immigrant Mennonite communities are still obvious subcultures in terms of language, church polity, the arts, and occupations. However, third-generation immigrants are showing signs of integration with the larger society through pursuit of higher education, employment choices, and more relationship with indigenous churches.

The Mennonite Central Committee (MCC) assisted some of the first immigrants to settle in Paraguay, Uruguay, and Brazil. As the colonies became economically self-sufficient and as the indigenous churches became established, North American Mennonites via MCC shifted from supporting immigrant colonies to joining them in service ministries. Local Mennonite conferences now operate social assistance programs in Paraguay, Brazil, Colombia, Uruguay, and Argentina. International Mennonite Organization (IMO) of Europe assists South American Mennonites in service ministries, especially in Brazil, Uruguay, and Paraguay.

In 1974, the Mennonite Biblical Seminary moved from Montevideo to Asunción, where, renamed Centro Evangélico Menonita de Teologia Asunción (CEMTA), it provides biblical and theological training in both German and Spanish serving the Southern Cone countries. The Instituto e Seminário Bíblico dos Irmãos Menonitas (ISBIM; Mennonite Brethren Seminary and Bible Institute) in Curitiba, Brazil, serves both immigrant and indigenous churches, primarily in the Portuguese language. Bible institutes or °theological education by extension programs operate in most of the countries. The German-speaking Mennonite communities operate their own elementary and secondary schools.

Most of the conferences publish church papers in Spanish, Portuguese, or German. The German-language papers, *Menno Blatt* (Paraguay), and *Bibel und Pflug* (Brazil), have subscribers in North America and Europe. *Die Mennonitsche Post* (Steinbach, Man.) serves as an important communications link between °Kanadier immigrant Mennonites throughout Latin America.

Mennonite ecclesiology and theology have been heavily influenced by conservative evangelical Protestantism. However, Anabaptist emphases on °community, °discipleship, °service, and °peace are increasingly prominent as the Latin American Mennonites and Brethren in Christ live out their faith in the context of economic disparities and social ferment. The churches are known as peace churches both through their service in conflict situations and °conscientious objection positions. °Worship patterns vary widely, reflecting borrowings from both Pentecostal and European Protestant traditions. Since Vatican II there is some interaction with °Roman Catholics, albeit limited.

Brazilian Mennonites hosted the Mennonite World

MENNONITES AND BRETHREN IN CHRIST
IN SOUTH AMERICA

Compiler: Herman Bontrager (author of article)

Country	Total Members	Indigenous Members	Immigrant [1]		Groups, Conferences
			Members	Population	
Argentina	1,816	1,516	300	600	3
Bolivia	6,297	100	6,197	17,688	6
Brazil	4,992	2,407	2,585		5
Chile[2]					
Colombia	2,633	2,633			3
Ecuador	84	84			1
Paraguay	14,950	5,186	9,764	22,570	15
Peru	65	65			1
Uruguay	971	371	600		3
Venezuela	256	256			3
Totals	**32,064**	**12,618**	**19,446**		

Sources: *MWH* (1984), *MC Yearbook*, (1986-87), Abe Warkentin, *Strangers and Pilgrims* Winnipeg: *Die Mennonitische Post*, 1987).

[1] Immigrants from Canada, Russia, Poland, Mexico, Belize, and USA, plus their descendants.
[2] Mennonite Board of Missions and MCC have programs; no local church members.

Conference general assembly in Curitiba in 1972. In the 1960s and 1970s the Congreso Menonita Latino-americano promoted continent-wide inter-Mennonite study and fellowship events. Those events discontinued in the 1970s due to distance and diversity, but °regional consultations for the Southern Cone and the Andean Region countries emerged in the late 1980s. Latin American Mennonites maintain connections with the global Mennonite community and many have family connections in Canada. The Latin American churches are providing growing numbers of church and theological leaders to the larger Mennonite church.   HBon

MWH (1978), 45-48.

South American Conference of Mennonite Brethren Congregations. See Südamerikanische Konferenz der Mennonitischen Brüdergemeinden.

South Carolina. Since the 1950s Mennonites have moved into South Carolina and established a number of congregations and outreach centers. In 1988 the Beachy Amish Mennonite Fellowship had two congregations with a membership of 174. The Southeast Conference (MC) had two congregations (one of which also belonged to the Afro-American Mennonite Association), with membership of 56, and the Southeastern Conference (MC) had one congregation with membership of 79. In addition to these churches there were three Mennonite congregations that were not affiliated with any conference. Their total membership was 216.   RSa

MC Yearbook (1988-89), 41, 79, 97-99, 166-68.

South Central Mennonite Conference (MC) (ME III:149, IV:584). South Central Mennonite Conference (SCMC) can trace its roots to two 19th-c. con-

ferences, Missouri-Iowa (1873) and Kansas-Nebraska (1876). In a merger of (Old) Mennonite conferences in 1920, Kansas-Nebraska (after 1946 South Central) became one of five conferences west of the Illinois and Indiana border. Between 1923 and 1986 the SCMC operated under six constitutions. In the preamble of the early constitutions the functions of conference were to promote the cause of Christ, to maintain and strengthen the work of the church, and to promulgate the doctrines of the word and church.

Few major changes in °polity occurred in the SCMC until 1955 when the office of °bishop was discontinued and replaced with that of area overseer, which later gave way to the office of conference minister. The 1975 constitution helped clarify the growing autonomy of congregations with less emphasis on the authority of the conference delegate body. At this time conference functions were divided among three commissions under the leadership of the conference Executive Committee: Leadership, Church Planning and Development, and Congregational Life.

An unofficial de facto district structure was developed between 1983 and 1986 in which the conference was divided into four geographic districts under the leadership of a Conference Coordinating Council composed of members from each district. The districts (Arkansas-Missouri, Kansas-Oklahoma, Texas-Mexico, and Mid-Texas) each had a district minister and three commissions. This plan of organization was officially accepted in the 1986 delegate session.

The conference was made up of 50 congregations with a membership of 4,291 in 1986. The official conference publication is the *Conference Messenger*. The conference office is located in Hesston, Ks. JGH

Paul Erb, *South Central Frontiers* (Scottdale, 1974).

South Dakota (ME IV:585). Several changes have occurred among Mennonite institutions in South Dakota within the last 30 years. Due to declining enrollments, increased costs of operation, and increasing debt brought on at least partly by the depressed farm economy, the Freeman Junior College Corporation decided on Oct. 17, 1985, to close the college program in May 1986, and concentrate efforts on the academy. At the same time, plans were initiated to add grades seven and eight to the academy beginning with the 1986-87 school year. Another important institution developed over the last 30 years is Swan Lake Christian Camp near Viborg. Owned and operated by the Northern District Conference (GCM), the camp has a full summer program for youth and many winter weekend retreats. The Salem Mennonite Home for the Aged in Freeman has expanded its capacity to 52 beds and four low-rental apartments for the elderly. This supervised personal living facility operates at full capacity.

Membership in the area Mennonite churches appears to be declining, perhaps by 10 percent or more in the last 30 years. Several factors contribute to this including smaller-size families and out-migration of young people seeking employment. Freeman, S.D., continues to be a Mennonite center and is the home of the Mennonite Historical Archives and Heritage Hall Museum, located on the Freeman Academy campus. Also located on campus is the annual spring Schmeckfest, a "festival of tasting" that features foods and exhibits from the various local Mennonite ethnic groups.　　　LDS

MC Yearbook (1988-89), 41.

South Korea. See Korea, Republic of.

South Pacific Mennonite Conference. See Southwest Mennonite Conference; Pacific Coast Mennonite Conference.

Southeast Mennonite Conference (MC). From 1927 to 1967 Mennonite churches in the Southeastern United States belonged to the Indiana-Michigan, Ohio, Lancaster, Virginia, or Conservative Mennonite conferences (MC) and had few ties to one another.

The Southeast Mennonite Convention was born on Aug. 9-10, 1967, when a group of 13 ministers and a few lay people representing Mennonite churches in Florida, Georgia, and South Carolina met in Tampa, Fla., to discuss mission strategy for Mennonites in the Southeast. For six years the convention was an informal fellowship for Mennonite churches in the Southeast.

In 1973 the convention affirmed a plan to become a regional conference affiliated with the Mennonite Church (MC) General Assembly. Except for those affiliated with the Conservative Mennonite Conference, the congregations eventually chose to discontinue formal ties to the parent conferences.

In 1987 the convention changed its name to Southeast Mennonite Conference. It had 23 congregations totaling approximately 2,000 members. Major conference components are the Board of Congregational Outreach, Board of Congregational Life,

Southeast Mennonite Mutual Aid Board, Women's Mission and Service Commission, Congregational Leadership Committee, and Peace and Social Concerns Committee. An executive committee oversees the conference's work. The conference office is in Sarasota, Fla. The official publication is *Proclamation*, published 10 times each year.

The Sarasota Christian School, Sunnyside Properties and Nursing Home, World's Attic (°SELFHELP Crafts), and the Southern Mennonite Camp Association are affiliated institutions which report to the conference.　　　MWL

MC Yearbook (1988-89), 79-80.

Southeastern Mennonite Conference was officially organized in June 1972 by a group concerned about deviations from Bible doctrine and practices espoused by the Anabaptist movement. Formerly part of the West Valley District of the Virginia Mennonite Conference, Southeastern Conference initially consisted of 12 congregations, 559 members, and 37 ordained men. The conference publishes a bimonthly periodical, *Life Lines* of the Southeastern Mennonite Conference. It meets semiannually in regular session during the last full week of January and June. In June 1979 the conference took action to form two districts, designated as Virginia-West Virginia District and Georgia-Carolina District. In 1981 the conference opened a mission in Anasco, Puerto Rico. In 1986 Southeastern Conference consisted of 17 congregations, with 3 in Georgia, 1 in Puerto Rico, 1 in South Carolina, 9 in Virginia, and 3 in West Virginia. There were a total of 837 members and a ministerial body numbering 54 members (5 bishops, 32 ministers, and 18 deacons).　　　JDRi

MC Yearbook (1988-89), 97.

See also Conservative Mennonites.

Southern District Conference (MB) consists of 40 congregations in the following states: Kansas, Oklahoma, Colorado, Texas, and Arkansas. In 1960 the °°Krimmer Mennonite Brethren Churches in these five states joined the Southern District Conference through merger. The total membership of the Southern District in 1987 was 6,598.

The Southern District Conference has five commissions: Stewardship; Youth; Church Extension and Evangelism; Christian Education; and Faith and Life. They are coordinated through a Coordinating Board, an executive committee, and a district minister.

In addition to the commissions there is an active Women's Missionary Service organization. Tabor College, a regional Christian liberal arts college, is owned by four districts: Southern, Central, Latin American, and North Carolina districts. The Tabor College Senate, with representatives from the churches of the four districts, operates the college. The college makes annual reports to the four district conferences.

Other Southern District ministries are managed through cooperative arrangements with the United States Conference of the Mennonite Brethren and the General Conference of the Mennonite Brethren Churches in North America. The records of the

Southern District Conference are housed in the archival center at the Center for Mennonite Brethren Studies at Tabor College. The Southern District Conference maintains an office in Hillsboro, Ks. WP

MB Yearbook (1981), 174, 192-95.

Southern Rhodesia. See Zambia.

Southwest Mennonite Conference (MC). On Sept. 6, 1948, the California and Arizona congregations of the Pacific Coast Mennonite Conference (MC) formed the South Pacific Mennonite Conference (MC). On Nov. 24, 1966, the name was changed to Southwest Mennonite Conference.

As of November 1987 the conference had 21 congregations and a membership of 1,482. Five congregations were members of both the Mennonite Church (MC) and the General Conference Mennonite Church (GCM). Nine congregations were in Arizona, 12 in California, and one in Tijuana, Mexico. The largest concentrations of Mennonites were in the Phoenix (748) and Los Angeles (503) areas. Other congregations in Arizona were located in Tuscon, Prescott, and on the Navaho Indian reservation. There was one congregation in San Francisco, and one in Fresno, Cal.

There is a rich cultural and ethnic diversity in the conference including Navaho congregations, Afro-Americans, and persons from Belize, Guatamala, and El Salvador, as well as those of European origin. An Indonesian congregation is an associate member of the conference. A conference paper, *Southwest Messenger*, is published quarterly.   DWM

MC Yearbook, (1988-89), 81.

Soviet Central Asia. About one quarter (the western portion) of the Soviet land mass is commonly regarded as being part of Europe. The rest is often spoken of as °°Asiatic Russia, i.e., the eastern three quarters which fit geographically into Asia. Soviet Central Asia refers then to a group of republics in the south central part of the Soviet Union. Their population is largely Muslim. The republics of °Kazakhstan, °Kirgizia, Tadzhikistan, Uzbekistan, and Turkmenia form the core of this region.

The entire area came under firm tsarist control in the later decades of the 19th c. Some Mennonites came to settle in the vicinity of Khiva in the present republic of Uzbekistan around 1885 when Claasz °°Epp of the Trakt settlement led a group to settle near Ak Metchet. Many of the families who came here soon moved on to North America, or returned to their home communities in Russia. Those who remained eventually had to relocate near the border of China further east and south. Descendants of the group reside there today (1987).

Soviet Central Asia became the home for hundreds of thousands of Germans when they were forced to relocate during World War II as "enemies of the people," and placed under a "special regime" (°Spetskomandantura). Others who had been consigned to prisons and work camps farther north during this time joined families and acquaintances in the more climatically congenial cities and larger towns of the south when the restrictions on ethnic Germans ended in 1955. Most of the major cities of

Central Asia—Tselinograd, Karaganda, Pavlodar, Dzhambul, and Alma Ata in Kazakhstan; Frunze in Kirgizia; Tashkent in Uzbekistan; Dushanbe in Tadzhikistan—have sizable German Catholic, Lutheran, or Mennonite communities in their vicinity today.

During the early years of reconstruction following World War II, many Mennonites, scattered as they were, simply joined growing Baptist congregations which were registered with the government right after the war (°All-Union Council of Evangelical Christians - Baptists). When the *Initiativniki* schism came in the early 1960s (°Council of Churches of Evangelical Christians - Baptists), some Mennonites joined the new unregistered groups, and have continued, often in leadership positions, to participate this way right to the present. Several of the largest registered Baptist congregations in Central Asia, e.g., those at Karaganda, Kant, Alma Ata, Frunze, and Tashkent, retain significant German segments in their memberships. Sometimes separate services are held to accommodate these families, and former Mennonites are finding leadership posts here as well.

The foremost Mennonite Brethren congregations of Soviet Central Asia are found in Karaganda and Novopavlovka near Frunze, with some unregistered congregations also at Dzhambul and other places. The °Kirchliche Mennonite groups have been strongest in Karaganda (400 members, 1987), Alma Ata (150 members), and Tokmak, near Frunze (225 members). They have additional registered groups meeting at Politotdel, near Alma Ata; Dzhambul; and several other places, e.g., Romanovka, near Frunze. Many families of these groups emigrated to West Germany in the 1970s and a growing number have left in recent years as well.   LK

Serguisz Bankowski, *Die Katholiken in der Sowjetunion* (Zollikon, Switzerland: Glaube in den 2. Welt, 1981); Rudolf Bohren, *Lutheraner in der Sowjetunion* (Zollikon, Switzerland: Glaube in der 2. Welt, 1981); Walter Sawatsky, *Soviet Evangelicals Since World War II* (Scottdale, 1981); *MWH* (1978), 63-71; Gerd Stricker, "Die Mennoniten in der Sowjetunion nach 1941. Ein Facette russlanddeutschen Kirchenwesens," *Kirche im Osten*, 27 (1984), 57-98; idem, with Walter Sawatsky, "Mennonites in Russia and the Soviet Union: An Aspect of the Church History of the Germans in Russia," *Religion in Communist Lands*, 12 (Winter, 1984), 293-311; Gerd Stricker, "German Protestants in Tsarist Russia and the Soviet Union," *Religion in Communist Lands*, 15, no. 2 (Summer 1987), 32-53.

Soviet Union. See Union of Soviet Socialist Republics.

Spain. Before 1976 the sporadic presence of Spanish Mennonite Christians was due to contacts by emigrated Spaniards with Mennonite congregations in Switzerland, France, Belgium, and Germany. Once these few Christians returned to Spain, they either associated with the existing Protestant congregations, especially °Baptists and Plymouth Brethren, or they remained anonymous.

After the death of the dictator Francisco Franco in 1975, many mission boards began to see that Spain had open doors for them. In 1976 the Mennonite Brethren Board of Missions and Services and the Mennonite Board of Missions (MC) sent missionaries to Spain. The Mennonite Board of Missions (MBM) initiated work in Barcelona as an intentional community while the Mennonite Brethren began forming a church in Madrid.

Ten years later, the Mennonite presence in Barcelona had developed a congregation and a senior citizens home. In Madrid the Mennonite Brethren had one congregation with three meeting places. After 1981 the work of the Christian Community in Quintaladueña, Burgos, helped by MBM, was consolidated with a congregation and a ministry working with prisoners and drug addicts.

There also are some groups who identified in a general way with the Anabaptist testimony. This is the case of the congregations in Fuenlabrada and in Vallecas, Madrid. In general terms, after ten years of Mennonite testimony in Spain a combined membership of 120 persons can be estimated.   HZ

MWH (1984), 124; Marcelino Menendez-Pelayo, *Historia de los Heterodoxos Españoles*, 2 vols. (Madrid: Biblioteca de autores cristianos, 1978); Ricardo García-Villoslada, director, *Historia de la Iglesia en España*, vol. 3 (Madrid: Biblioteca de autores cristianos, 1975); José Gallardo, Freedom for the Captives: How Love is Rebuilding Lives in Spain (Scottdale, 1988).

See also Comunidad Cristiana; Comunidad Christiana de los Hermanos Menonitas de España.

Spanish Lookout Colony, Belize, was settled in 1978 by approximately 75 families of °°Kleine Gemeinde Mennonites from the Quellen Colony, Chihuahua, Mexico. They left Mexico because land was not readily available, and because they objected to the social welfare law. Spanish Lookout comprises 18,500 acres (7,500 hectares) in the Cayo District and is situated on the north side of the Belize River. This area was jungle when the settlers arrived. Products are eggs, broiler hens, beans, corn, grain sorghum, milk, cheese, and beef cattle. Vegetables were the major source of income during the first 10 years, but they are no longer produced in any sizable quantity. Administration, roads, bridges, and schools are maintained by the colony. The overall impression is that Spanish Lookout is a flourishing community. A number of familes have moved away to the Interlake area in Manitoba, Canada, and an additional 25 families have relocated in the Northfield Mennonite settlement in Nova Scotia, Canada. However, natural growth has maintained population levels despite these migrations. As of 1987 there were 1,108 residents. Refugees from Guatemala and El Salvador have been attracted to the colony for employment. The colony maintains four schools which include an enrollment of 75 refugee children.   DFDueck

Colony Government and Taxation. The taxation system of Spanish Lookout Colony came with the first settlers from Chihuahua, Mexico. An agreed-upon percentage of the different items raised on each farm is deducted at the collection center, often the local store. Many items are taxed at one percent, others at two percent of the selling price. This applies more to eggs, broiler hens, milk, lumber, garden produce, and cattle. For field crops (corn, milo [sorghum], soy beans, etc.) the farmer is responsible to give a trustworthy answer. A direct tax is also levied on other goods.

Two or three days' labor are required yearly of all men over 21 for road maintenance. There are also

taxes on land, residences, vehicles, farm equipment, etc. The government collects land taxes through the settlement administration. Income taxes are filed personally. As a general rule, taxes are paid only on items sold off the settlement. Not all of the taxes were started at the same time, but rather as the need arose. No extra tax is charged to families with school children. Everyone shares in the taxes for education.

A settlement the size of Spanish Lookout requires many different offices, i.e., bishops, ministers, deacons, school board members, teachers, school trustees, song leaders, colony "Vorsteher" (chairman) with two assistants, land committee, road committee, board of directors for °cooperative store, and boards for the dairies, clinic, welfare agency, outreach, "Waisenamt" (orphans bureau, welfare agency), ombudsmen ("Gutmänner"), youth leaders, secretary, cemetery overseer.

Teachers receive one month of training each year before the opening of the school term. Teachers, regardless of experience, are expected to visit other schools in the settlement. Two conferences are held annually, where all teachers, trustees, board members, and parents in the particular school district may attend. The curriculum is bilingual (English and German). Most children attend school for seven years. In the 1980s there have been problems in obtaining teachers.   JBL

MWH (1978), 194-95.

Spartansburg, Pa., Old Order Amish Settlement is located in Crawford Co. in the nw. part of the state. The first Amish family to move to Crawford Co. was the Andrew J. Mast family from °Nappanee, Ind. Settlers from °Geauga Co., Ohio followed, and by 1924 a sizeable group located near the town of Atlantic. The community suffered a severe tornado storm in 1985 bringing hundreds of Amish from other midwest settlements to rebuild the leveled houses and barns.

A second settlement in Crawford Co. began in 1931 near the town of Spartansburg. Most families moved in from Geauga Co. during the Great Depression. Farms were available to rent and land was cheap to buy. Harvests, however, were disappointing and within eight years the entire Amish community moved away. In 1966, nearly 30 years after the first settlement became extinct, a new group of Amish families from Geauga County moved in and in many cases occupied the same farms left behind by the previous Amish settlers. In 1984 there were five church districts (congregations) with 90 families and a population of just under 1,000.   SLY

Spetskomandantura. This "Special Command," also known as the "Deportation Regime," originated with the illegal decree of Aug. 28, 1941, ordering Soviet Germans in the Volga Republic region (but actually applied to all Germans) to be resettled farther east to prevent collaborating with the invading German army. As a peace-time special administration, the *Spetskomandantura* applied to all three categories of Soviet Germans and Mennonites: (1) local Germans (in the °Orenburg settlements, etc.) who had not been uprooted; (2) those repatriated to the Soviet Union after 1945 (whose situation varied between

[a]those scattered across the Soviet Union in labor camps, and [b] those placed in settled areas); and (3) those in the workers' army (*Trud armia*).

A secret administrative directive of Nov. 26, 1948, finally clarified legal points of reference and administrative arrangements. Violations of the special command were punishable under sections 1a-d of Article 58, and also Article 19 of the Soviet Criminal Code. Within the Ministry of the Interior the NKVD established the Main Directorate of Deportations, which had an officer posted to every factory and office and a representative in every large town and village where the deported peoples lived.

There were four major implications for Mennonites and other Germans: (1) loss of all civil rights; (2) the splitting up of families, including the loss of many children to orphanages; (3) rigid controls on travel and correspondence, involving a special identity card and compulsory biweekly reporting (later monthly; annually after 1954); (4) loss of access to education, since they were outside the educational network. In that generation of children a large percentage grew up functionally illiterate. Until 1948, hunger was the major preoccupation, followed by inadequate housing, family separation concerns, and lack of educational access causing the loss of the German and Mennonite culture. After 1948 there were spiritual revivals in some of the *Spetskomandantura* camps, with Mennonites finding Christian fellowship with other Germans with whom they were thrown together.

The *Spetskomandantura* was abolished by decree in December 1955, with Soviet Germans and Mennonites receiving internal passports thereafter. The initial rehabilitation resulted in resumption of correspondence with loved ones, moving and family reunification, access to secondary schools and institutes, but also military service obligations. A further moral rehabilitation followed on Aug. 24, 1964, and restrictions on moving back to the original home areas finally were lifted on Nov. 3, 1972. WWS

Walter Sawatsky, "Spetskomandantura," in *Germans Past and Present*, ed. Ingeborg Fleischhauer and Benjamin Pinkus (London: C. Hurst, 1986); A. Nekrich, *The Punished Peoples: The Deportation and Fate of Soviet Minorities at the End of the Second World War* (New York, 1978); Walter Sawatsky, "From Russian to Soviet Mennonites 1945-1985" (forthcoming in *Russian Mennonites*, ed. John Friesen); Walter Wedel, *Nur Zwanzig Kilometer* (Wuppertal: Brockhaus, 1979).

See also Persecution.

Spiritual Direction and Spiritual Formation.

Although the terms *spiritual formation* and *spiritual direction* initially came from the Eastern Orthodox and Roman Catholic contemplative traditions, these concepts are clearly taught in the Scriptures. Christians are to have the mind of Jesus who was in the form (*morphe*) of God, but also took on the form of a servant in our behalf (Phil 2:6-7). Paul was in travail "until Christ be formed in you!" (Gal 4:19). Christians are to be transformed (*metamorphe*) by the renewal of their minds (Rom 12:2), and "changed (*metamorphometha*) into [God's] likeness from one degree of glory to another" (2 Cor 3:18). The biblical pattern is for Jesus to be formed in believers, as he was in the form of God.

Spiritual direction is a means to enhance spiritual formation in the life of the believer. In the classic sense a spiritual director is one who, as a representative of the church, walks with another as a mentor or guide to facilitate that person's relationship (formation) with God; it is a voluntary relationship between an individual wanting to enhance his or her spiritual growth and a more mature Christian who is able and willing to serve as mentor. Spiritual friendship involves a relationship between two friends for the purpose of enhancing each other's spiritual growth. Certainly Jesus sought to facilitate and give direction to the lives of his disciples, calling them to "follow me and I will make you become fishers of men." Paul said "be imitators of me, as I am of Christ." Throughout the New Testament, Christians are called to admonish and exhort one another to a life of faithfulness in Jesus Christ.

Although, until recently, Mennonites did not use the terms "spiritual formation" and "spiritual direction" to describe their religious experience, concern for formation and direction have been inherent in Mennonite emphasis upon °discipleship. Anabaptist and Mennonite discipleship has been a spirituality shaped by the ethical imperative to follow Jesus at all costs. The Anabaptist understanding of following was characterized by repentance (turning to Jesus) and baptism as a covenant with God and the church. Their covenant was to be obedient disciples, to be yielded to God in daily life (*Gelassenheit*), to live by the "rule of Christ" in mutual accountability and °discipline, to share possessions with any as there was need, to practice °love and °nonresistance with all, to accept "crossbearing" for Christ's sake, and boldly to call others to follow Jesus. This discipleship may be thought of as a covenantal spirituality in which each one is called to personal faith, to accountability in Christian community, and to suffering love in relationship to the world.

°Persecution strengthened Anabaptist resolve to trust and obey God even as Jesus did. Discipleship, crossbearing or martyrdom, love and nonresistance, and *Gelassenheit* became prominent themes of Anabaptist spirituality to which Mennonites in Europe, Russia, and North America later turned as they sought the renewal of the church. However, in a world without intense persecution the dynamics of crossbearing changed. Already in the 16th c. the spirituality of some in The Netherlands and Germany was influenced by Pietism and rationalism. Formation for Dutch Mennonites was largely pursued through education. As Mennonites in North America sought to follow Jesus in their time, the emphasis changed from martyrdom to °humility and, in the early 20th c., to °°nonconformity and °mission.

Several additional themes have also been important in Mennonite history. The sharing of material goods in °mutual aid and °service to others have always been significant expressions of Mennonite spiritual life. Mennonites have historically lived close to nature which often resulted in a sense of being and working with God in vocation, °community, and °worship.

Certainly Mennonite spirituality has been embedded in an ethical and communal way of life more than in self-conscious practices of piety such as meditation, fasting, contemplation, rituals, or keeping of holy days (°Christian calendar). However, throughout their history, Mennonites have also repeatedly experienced a quest for heartfelt devotion to God. Almost from the beginning some were attracted to the piety of religious groups with more emotional expression. Many Mennonites were drawn to Pietism in Europe, North America (17th and 18th c.), and Russia (19th c.); to °revivalism in 19th- and 20th-c. North America, and to °charismatic renewal in mid 20th-c. North America. American Mennonite spirituality has also been influenced in this century by °Fundamentalist and °Evangelical emphases. These various expressions have sometimes been an extension of and sometimes in tension with the emphasis in Mennonite discipleship upon an ethical way of life concerned more with doing the will of God than with religious experience as such.

Various expressions of worship and witness have also emerged in the mix of historic Mennonite doctrine with indigenous Mennonite churches throughout the world. To date there has not been enough study to describe accurately the variety of expressions of spirituality among non-Western Mennonites or even the variety that exists among Mennonites in Europe and North America. However, it is apparent that the worship and prayers of non-Western Mennonites has often been more emotionally expressive and fervent than that of many of their brothers and sisters of Germanic descent in the Western world. Certainly these expressions of spirituality are unique, and not simply extensions of Mennonite experience in the Western world.

Since the mid 20th c., the life of North American Mennonites has become more diffuse and diversified. Missions and °modernity have significantly influenced Mennonite religious experience. During World War II and following, Mennonite missions and service throughout the world greatly increased. At the same time there was also a growing receptivity to modernity. With this involvement in "the world" came increased assimilation, °acculturation, and adaptation, resulting in more diversity of experience and greater individuality in conviction concerning the nature and meaning of following Jesus in contemporary life.

The experience of Christian community, in which Mennonite discipleship has historically been embedded, has been diminishing among Western Mennonites. Therefore, continued attention is being given to means that will help strengthen and sustain personal and corporate spirituality. This includes awareness of expressions of spirituality from other Christian traditions in their use of °symbols, rituals, and liturgy; Scriptures; meditation; contemplation; spiritual direction; journaling and other reflective experiences for personal spiritual growth. These may well serve to facilitate spiritual growth among contemporary Mennonites concerned with following Jesus in daily life.

Spiritual direction in the classic sense has not been practiced among Mennonites until recently. However, the Anabaptists experienced a significant form of corporate spiritual direction through the exercise of the "rule of Christ" in their communal life (°discipline). The baptismal covenant resulting in mutual accountability, mutual discipline, and mutual support was intended to promote faithfulness, devotion, and personal transformation in the individual and the congregation.

Later in Mennonite history, responsibility for spiritual growth and discipline was primarily delegated to a few key leaders in the congregation, to representatives of the church who were to provide direction by safeguarding the spiritual well-being of each one. Contemporary Mennonites in North America are also pursuing the use of certain forms of spiritual direction, along with other practices of pastoral care, to enhance faithfulness to God through personal spiritual growth, corporate worship, mutual accountability, and mutual support. The practice of spiritual direction can help Mennonites pursue the biblical concern for mutual exhortation and the Anabaptist concern for mutual accountability and discipline.   MGS

William A. Barry and William J. Connolly, *The Practice of Spiritual Direction* (New York: Seabury, 1982); Tilden Edwards, *Spiritual Friend* (New York: Paulist Press, 1980); MEA 1: C. J. Dyck, *Intro. Menn. History* (1967, 1981); Theron F. Schlabach, *Gospel Versus Gospel: Mission and the Mennonite Church, 1863-1944* (Scottdale, 1980); Marcus G. Smucker, "Self-Sacrifice and Self-Realization in Mennonite Spirituality" (PhD diss., Union for Experimenting Colleges and Universities, 1987).

See also Christian Education; Pastoral Counseling.

Spiritual Life, or *spirituality,* refers to aspects of Christian life that unite what Mennonites commonly understand as separate topics: doctrine (°theology) and ethics. In the classic Christian tradition of the first twelve centuries, teaching on "spirituality" was no more and no less than teaching and living the Christian message of salvation: the restoration of the sin-corrupted image of God in men and women and participation in the divine nature through the church's sacraments, both being grounded in the reality of the Incarnation. Proclamation and teaching, experience and ethics all emanated from this center.

Anabaptist and Mennonite suspicion of academic (scholastic) theology coupled with emphasis on °discipleship ethics may partly explain why Mennonites are only beginning, late in the 20th c., to explore spirituality, that is, to reflect deliberately on the interrelationships between ethics and doctrine and on the mystery of God becoming human so that men and women could know God intimately and ontologically (in being) as well as ethically (in actions). This is not to say that Mennonites have not had their own spiritualities. It is to say that they have not reflected on the character of their spiritualities in any sustained and systematic way. Much research remains to be carried out in this field. The present article offers a brief overview of two models for understanding Anabaptist and Mennonite spirituality. A large number of articles in the present volume offer insight into Mennonite and Anabaptist spirituality, and the reader is encouraged to consult them as indicated.

The dominant interpretation of Anabaptist and Mennonite spirituality was set forth by Robert °Friedmann in his classic work, *Mennonite Piety through the Centuries* (1949); variations on it have been offered by other scholars. Friedmann understood the reception of °Pietism by Mennonites to be a largely negative development, an abandonment of the heroic, existential, and costly Anabaptist discipleship in favor of a sweet, interiorized piety. This negative image of Pietism has been challenged by a number of scholars, notably Dale Brown from within the Believers Church fold. Whether Pietism is viewed as a negative or positive development, however, most interpreters have used Anabaptism and Pietism as the two poles for analyzing Mennonite spirituality, with "interiorizing" Pietism being continued in °revivalism and the °charismatic and °evangelical movements, and "externalizing" Anabaptism being reborn in the 20th c. "recovery of the °Anabaptist vision," the °Concern movement, °house churches, and the Eberhard °°Arnold Hutterian Brethren, to name only a few examples.

Yet another variation on this dominant framework for understanding Anabaptist and Mennonite spirituality has been offered by Joseph Liechty, Theron Schlabach, and others. In this view, °humility, in part under Pietist influence, replaced the original Anabaptist understanding of °suffering discipleship. Because Mennonite scholars, with a few exceptions, have not explored the pre-Reformation tradition of humility in depth, humility is portrayed as inwardness rather than a comprehensive attitude related to ascetic discipline, martyrdom (both literal and figurative), and crossbearing, as it was understood in the early and medieval church.

An alternative paradigm for interpreting Anabaptist and Mennonite spirituality makes use of "first generation" and "second generation" categories (Martin 1988). As the martyrdom spirituality of the first-generation church (1st-3rd c.) gave way to the monastic-led church of the 4th-12th centuries, the °monastic life inherited the mantle of the martyrs, the apostolic writings were collected in a fixed canon of Scriptures, and charismatic ministries were institutionalized in sacraments and ecclesial offices and tradition. Leaders in this process understood this development to be a legitimate one, a transition in which, by the power of the Holy Spirit, Christ continued to be embodied in the institutions and structures of the church. Thus spirituality in the second generation was characterized by liturgy (°worship), sacraments (°ordinances), offices, rule-centered monastic life, and °tradition.

At first glance, it would appear that Anabaptist and Mennonite history does not fit this model. Anabaptists and Mennonites opposed Catholic teachings on sacraments, liturgy, church offices, and tradition. Yet a closer look reveals that the transition from Anabaptists to °Mennonites involved a similar institutionalization of the initial charismatic fervor. Because their Anabaptist ancestors had originated in a °revolution against corrupted institutions of the church, Mennonites continued to teach against sacraments, priestly and episcopal office, and tradition, even while de facto they were establishing their own sacraments, priestliness (°bishop: "My Good Bishop" feature), and tradition. Mennonite spirituality thus became institutionalized in a manner parallel to the development of Catholicism in the 3rd-12th c.

One advantage of the first- and second-generation model for analyzing the history of spirituality is that it applies to all Christian groups. All movements must originate somewhere and therefore can be viewed as having a first-generation phase. Although this first generation can be prolonged for a while, all movements sooner or later must face the second generation with its need for institutionalization. One can trace this development among Catholics, Puritans, Baptists, and Pentecostal movements, as well as Anabaptists. Indeed, this model offers a way to understand comprehensively the role of revivalism, charismatic renewal, house churches, and the neo-Anabaptist "recovery of the °Anabaptist vision" in Mennonite history. Such renewals are efforts, on the part of a group that claims never to have left the first generation's fervor behind, to prolong or recover the first-generation character that their doctrine requires; the recurrence of such renewal movements indicates that second-generation institutionalization is taking place and that practice is different from theory (doctrine). The conflict and confusion resulting from trying to live in the first generation (in theory) and second generation (in practice) at the same time gives rise to a wide variety of Mennonite spiritualities. Some are quite sacramental and ritualized (Amish, Older Order Mennonites, Hutterites). Others are charismatic, radical, and spontaneous (revivalism, °sociopolitical activism, °civil disobedience, house churches and intentional communities). Some trends in Mennonite spirituality in the 1980s have drawn from Catholic sources, although modifying the borrowings heavily in the process, since Mennonite °polity makes it impossible to establish a traditional, liturgical, and sacramental spirituality in Mennonite circles. Some Catholic elements have been borrowed by abstracting meditation techniques or pastoral approaches from their sacramental and liturgical moorings and then assimilating them to the nonsacramental and nonliturgical Quaker tradition of silence and social activism.

The most significant trend in Mennonite spirituality in the late 20th c. results from the disintegration of traditional Mennonite subcultures in Russia, Europe, and North America. In these second-generation subcultures Mennonite spirituality was routinized and embedded in the patterns of life within the Mennonite communities. Worship followed regular patterns that were in effect liturgies; children were born into the community and "grew into" the church in a manner that closely paralleled infant baptism; ministers and bishops (elders) were ordained and surrounded with an aura of sanctity closely paralleling sacramental ordination in Catholic or Orthodox circles. All that was missing was an articulated theology of these liturgical and sacramental practices. As Mennonites left their subcultures or were forced to leave them by external pressures, the traditional patterned, routinized, ritualized, and sacramentalized practices disappeared. Since there was no articulated and "portable" theology of liturgy or tradition that could be carried from the dissolving subculture into the new mainstream culture, a broad range of practices and theories filled the vacuum. The diversity of these Mennonite spiritualities offers a broad field for future research.   DDM

In addition to the bibliographies for articles on Family Worship; Spiritual Direction and Formation; and Worship, Private, see the following (the list is selective, even arbitrary at points): Dennis D. Martin, "Catholic Spirituality and Anabaptist and Mennonite Discipleship," *MQR* 62 (1988), 5-25; Peter C. Erb, "Anabaptist Spirituality," in *Protestant Spiritual Traditions*, ed. Frank C. Senn (New York: Paulist Press, 1986), 80-124; Sandra Cronk, "Gelassenheit: The Rites of the Redemptive Process in the Old Order Amish and Old Order Mennonite Communities" (PhD diss., U. of Chicago, 1977), cf. *MQR*, 55 (1981), 5-44; Robert Friedmann, *Mennonite Piety Through the Centuries* (Goshen: Mennonite Historical Society, 1949); Timothy George, "Early Anabaptist Spirituality in the Low Countries," *MQR* 62 (1988), 257-75, also published in *Doops. Bijdr.*, n.r. 12-13 (1986-87); Kenneth R. Davis, *Anabaptism and Asceticism* (Scottdale, 1974); idem, "Anabaptism as a Charismatic Movement," *MQR*, 53 (1979), 219-36; Werner O. Packull, *Mysticism and the Early South German-Austrian Anabaptist Movement, 1525-1531* (Scottdale, 1977); C. J. Dyck, "The Life of the Spirit in Anabaptism," *MQR*, 47 (1973), 309-26; Harold S. Bender, Franklin Littell, Walter Klaassen, Gerhard J. Neumann in *MQR*, 35 (April 1961), sp. issue; Harold S. Bender, "The Anabaptist Theology of Discipleship," *MQR*, 24 (1950), 25-32; Walter Klaassen, "Spiritualization in the Reformation," *MQR*, 37 (1963), 67-77; John C. Wenger, "Grace and Discipleship in Anabaptism," *MQR*, 35 (1961), 50-69; John D. Rempel, "Christology and the Lord's Supper in Anabaptism: A Study in the Theology of Balthasar Hubmaier, Pilgram Marpeck, and Dirk Philips" (ThD diss., St. Michael's College, Toronto School of Theology, 1986); Dale W. Brown, *Understanding Pietism* (Grand Rapids: Eerdmans, 1978); Sjouke Voolstra, "True Penitence: The Core of Menno Simons' Theology," *MQR*, 62 (1988), 387-400, also published in *Doops. Bijdr.*, n.r. 12-13 (1986-87); Willis M. Stoesz, "The New Creature: Menno Simon's Understanding of the Christian Faith," *MQR*, 39 (1965), 5-24; Stephen B. Boyd, "Pilgram Marpeck and the Justice of Christ" (PhD dissertation, Harvard University, 1984); A. Orley Swartzendruber, "The Piety and Theology of the Anabaptist Martyrs in Von Braght's Martyrs' Mirror," *MQR*, 28 (1954), 128-42; Jean Runzo, "Hutterite Communal Discipline, 1529-1565," *ARG*, 71 (1980), 160-79; Paul M. Yoder and others, *Four Hundred Years with the Ausbund* (Scottdale, 1964), esp. ch. 2: "Teachings Stressed in the Ausbund" by Elizabeth Bender; Hans-Jürgen Goertz, *Die Täufer: Geschichte und Deutung* (Munich: C. H. Beck, 1980); Joseph C. Liechty, "Humility: The Foundation of the Mennonite Religious Outlook in the 1860s," *MQR*, 54 (1980), 5-31; Heinrich Funck, *Eine Restitution oder Erklärung einiger Hauptpunkte des Gesetzes. . . .* (Philadelphia: Funck family, 1763); [Christian Burkholder], *Nützliche und Erbauliche Anrede an die Jugend* ([Ephrata, Pa.?], 1804); John M. Brenneman, *Pride and Humility: A Discourse, Setting Forth the Characteristics of the Proud and the Humble*, first published as a series of articles in *Herald of Truth* in 1866; or as a separate pamphlet, *Hoffart and Demuth: Einander gegenüber gestellt* (Elkhart, Ind.: John F. Funk, 1867); MEA 1; MEA 2; Theron F. Schlabach, "Mennonites and Pietism in America, 1740-1880: Some Thoughts on the Friedmann Thesis," *MQR*, 57 (1983), 222-40; idem, "Mennonite Revivalism, Modernity — 1683-1850," *Church History* 48 (1979) 398-415; Beulah Stauffer Hostetler, *American Mennonites and Protestant Movements: A Community Paradigm* (Scottdale, 1987); Hans-Jürgen Goertz, ed., *Die Mennoniten*, Die Kirchen der Welt, 8 (Stuttgart: Evangelisches Verlagswerk, 1971); James Urry, "All that Glitters. . .': Delbert Plett and the Place of the Kleine Gemeinde in Russian-Mennonite History," *JMS*, 4 (1986), 228-50; "Letter of Henry Egly to Katherine Amstutz" in Stan Nussbaum, *You Must Be Born Again* (Ft. Wayne, Ind.: EMCh, 1980), 67-68; Martin H. Schrag, "The Brethren in Christ Attitude toward the 'World': A Historical Study of the Movement from Separation to an Increasing Acceptance of American Society," (PhD diss., Temple U., 1967); John R. Martin, *Ventures in Discipleship* (Scottdale, 1984); Marcus G. Smucker, "Self-Sacrifice and Self-Realization in Mennonite Spirituality" (PhD diss., Union for Experimenting Colleges and Universities, 1987); Peter C. Erb, "A Reflection on Mennonite Theology in Canada," *JMS*, 1 (1983), 179-90; Myron Augsburger, *Walking in the Resurrection* (Scottdale, 1976); Chester K. Lehman, *The Holy Spirit and the Holy Life* (Scottdale, 1959); John M. Drescher, *Spirit Fruit* (Scottdale, 1974); Virgil Vogt in *Concern* pamphlet no. 9 (March 1961), pp. 44-47; Alan Kreider, *Journey Towards Holiness: A Way*

of Living for God's Nation (Scottdale, 1987); Rodney J. Sawatsky, *Authority and Identity: The Dynamics of the General Conference Mennonite Church* (North Newton, Ks.: Bethel College, 1987); Ministry of Spirituality Committee (MC), "A Pastoral Letter on Spirituality," *GH* (May 5, 1987), 306-8, cf. response in *GH* (Sept. 22, 1987), 668-69; Marlin E. Miller in *GH* (Aug. 31, 1982), 586; *GH* (May 1982), a series of articles, "Spirituality Reconsidered"; Chester C. Osborne in *GH* (Oct. 28, 1986), 734-35; John R. Mumaw in *GH* (Aug. 7, 1984), 548-51; "Focus on Spiritual Formation," *Builder* (Jan. 1985), sp. issue; William R. McGrath, *How to Find Your Perfection in Christ: A Devotional Study of Hebrews* (Minerva, Ohio: McGrath, [1986]). See also many biographies, autobiographies, and fictional accounts of 19th- and 20th-c. Mennonites, e.g., Tobias K. Hershey, as told to Daniel Hertzler, *I'd Do It Again* (Elkhart: Mennonite Board of Missions and Charities, 1961), esp. 38, 40, 127-28, 151-53; John S. Umble, "Memoirs of an Amish Bishop," *MQR*, 22 (1948) 94-115; Priscilla Stuckey-Kauffman, "A Woman's Ministry: Clara Brubaker Shank, 1869-1958," *MQR*, 60 (1986), 404-28; Peter G. Epp, *Agatchen: A Russian Mennonite Mother's Story*, trans. and edited by Peter Pauls (Winnipeg: Hyperion, 1986; originally published as *Eine Mutter* [1932]).

See also °°Bible; Bible Study; Camps and Retreat Centers; Communion; Conversion; Devotional Literature; Discipline; Family Worship; Feetwashing; Holiness Movement; Holy Spirit; Hospitality; Hymnology; Justice; Love; Mysticism; Nonconformity; *Ordnung*; Philosophy; °°Pietersz., Pieter (1574-1651); Prayer; Retreats; Roman Catholic Church; Sanctification; °°Schabaelje, Jan Philipsz.; Schwenckfeld, Kaspar von; Sermon on the Mount; Symbols; Lesher, Christian.

Sports. Historically Mennonites have stressed the importance of the wise use of their resources, including time, money, and energy. They looked to the Bible for guidance in daily living and placed emphasis upon using any leisure time for productive purposes such as °Bible study to gain a better understanding of the Scriptures. Play and °recreation activities for adults were thought of as wasting time. Many team sports were considered to be activities of the world and were avoided by Christians who had separated themselves from the world (°°nonconformity).

The Industrial Revolution, compulsory education, and a lack of agricultural land brought about an end to the way that Mennonites were able to shield themselves from worldly influence. Entering high school and taking jobs in neighboring cities brought them increasingly into contact with people of other faiths.

This interaction with non-Mennonites exposed young Mennonites to a large variety of "worldly" °amusements including participation in team sports. Individual sports such as hunting and fishing were utilitarian because they put food on the table and thus they did not pose the kind of problem presented by participation in team sports, e.g., football and basketball. Attendance in public high schools brought with it the opportunity for Mennonite youth to participate in sports which frequently caused family disagreements and confrontations in the church. In some churches this actually became a test of membership (°discipline).

The history of team sports and intercollegiate athletics in Mennonite colleges reflects the general attitude of the period. From the beginning students were highly interested in organizing team sports while the schools' supporting constituency generally opposed interschool athletics. The faculty and college boards were cautious, being aware of the desires of the student but fearing negative reactions from conservative and vocal constituents. While some administrators and board members supported the athletic programs, many felt that sports were detrimental to the schools' purposes and objectives. The attitudes of people changed gradually with the passing of time.

Physical education classes, recreation, and intramural sports have been an important part of Mennonite colleges since their inception. Intercollegiate participation in team sports came earlier to Bethel College and Bluffton College than to the other Mennonite colleges.

As early as 1897 a group of 30 students at Bethel College organized a football team. This met with opposition from the faculty and constituency, and the board expressed its hope that every state in the union would soon prohibit football. In 1901 the faculty took the following action: "Realizing the dangers in modern football, some of the objectionable features which have of late been introduced into the game at Bethel College, the faculty at their meeting on the 22nd of November placed the following restrictions on the game, so far as playing football at this institution is concerned: 'Football may be played at Bethel College only on the condition that no running with the ball, interference, or mass plays of any kind be permitted'." Summarizing this turbulent period at Bethel, P. J. Wedel said that "In spite of objections and restrictions, athletic contests gained in favor with the student and assumed a more prominent place in student activities" (Wedel, *Bethel College*, 128). By 1910 athletics, primarily basketball and baseball, had found an important place in student activities at Bethel College. Football was introduced officially in 1914 and intercollegiate competition has continued.

Sports at Bluffton College had a similar history. Hardesty indicates that tennis and baseball were played at Bluffton during the 1904-05 school year with the first official football game being played in 1905 (Hardesty, 16-18). However, it was not until 1908 that intercollegiate games were permitted in all sports. In 1914 a new, more conservative, college board considered football to be "unsavory and barbaric," bringing an end officially to football at Bluffton. However, unofficial games continued to be played by a team named the "Bluffton Collegians" and coached by Professor H. W. Berky. A traditional story relates that a football was buried ceremonially in back of the chapel building after a chapel service. Not until 1922 did the board relent and permit a football game in which Bluffton defeated Toledo.

Intercollegiate athletics came to the Mennonite Church (MC) schools (Goshen, Hesston, and Eastern Mennonite College) much later than to the General Conference schools (Bethel and Bluffton). In 1911 the Mennonite Board of Education (MC) officially discouraged "all games which encourage the spirit of rivalry, intercollegiate contest, etc." There is evidence of participation in intercollegiate sports of basketball, tennis, baseball, and track at Goshen College in 1918-20. In 1920 the Mennonite Board of Education passed a resolution prohibiting all inter-

school athletic events (Umble, 237-38). Before World War II these schools emphasized intramural sports and physical education programs focusing on participation by all students.

The faculty approved an intercollegiate program in 1956 and Goshen College had its first official game with another school in 1957. Hesston College and Eastern Mennonite College had similar histories.

While women were included in the physical education programs of the colleges, it was not until the 1960s that they actively participated in intercollegiate team sports. In the 1950s Mennonite colleges held "Sports Days" to which women from other schools were invited. It was not until 1958 that the Goshen College girls team played its first official basketball game with Grace College and its first season of play was in 1963-64. In 1987 team sports for women at Mennonite colleges include field hockey, tennis, basketball, track, and volleyball.

In the 1980s most Mennonite schools in the United States participate in intercollegiate team sports, many of them in leagues with regularly scheduled games for both men and women. Faculty, school constituency, and students appreciate the way participation in team sports helps develop leadership, teaches cooperation, and unifies and promotes school loyalty. Even so, questions continue to be raised concerning intercollegiate athletics. The newspapers are constantly reminding us of the excesses and recruitment violations in many of the universities with extensive athletic programs. There are questions raised as to the place of highly competitive contact sports in relationship to Mennonite °nonresistance and °peace testimony. There are always questions raised relating to the costs of specific programs. Even though concerns are still being expressed, it is readily apparent that intercollegiate sports are being enthusiastically supported and enjoyed by students, faculty, and the school constituencies.   OHG

Gerhard R. Buhr, "A Historical Study of Men's Intercollegiate Athletics at Bethel College, North Newton, Kansas from 1900 to the Spring of 1960," (Master's thesis, Kansas State Teachers College, Emporia, Ks., 1962); Charles Evan Oswald, "A History of Sports in the Mennonite Church of North America Since 1900," (Master's thesis, U. of Illinois, 1956); Von Hardesty, *A Narrative of Bluffton College* (Bluffton College, 1974); Roman Gingerich, "Campus Recreation and Athletic Program," paper read at the Recreation Study Conference, Elkhart, Indiana, 1956; Peter J. Wedel, *The Story of Bethel College* (North Newton: Mennonite Press, 1954); *Echoes* (Bethel College Annual, 1908); Beth Johnson Ruth, "Goshen Women Playing Through," *Goshen College Bulletin* (Nov. 1982), 5; Rebecca Burkholder, "Today's Athletes Inherit Program Begun by Gingerich," *Goshen College Bulletin* (Nov. 1962), 15; "Minutes of Annual Meeting of the Mennonite Board of Education," held at Goshen College, Goshen, Indiana, June 17, 1911; John Umble, *Goshen College 1894-1954* (Scottdale: MPH, 1955); *School and College Journal* (Bethel College, January 1897); "Minutes," faculty meeting, Bethel College, Nov. 22, 1901; John A. Lapp, *India* (1972), 60.

See also Bolivia; Work Ethic.

Sprunger, Agnes, was born in Berne, Ind., where she early came to faith in Christ and conviction about Christian service. She graduated from Fort Wayne Bible Institute in 1909 and from a nurses training course in Cincinnati in 1911. After engaging in church service in Detroit, she applied to the °°Congo Inland Mission (Africa Inter-Mennonite Mission) with promised support of the Berne Missionary Church, of which she was a life-long member. She was commissioned in 1916 and sailed to the Belgian Congo (Zaire) that same year.

Her first term was spent at Djoko Punda where she learned the Tshiluba language and served in the station dispensary and schools. In 1923 she accompanied Henry and Emma °Moser and Erma Birky to pioneer a new work among the Baphende people west of the Loange River at Mukedi. There she found a language still in process of analysis with only small parts of Scripture translated. While she had no training in linguistics, Agnes decided to do what she could to give the Baphende people the Scriptures in their own tongue. In consultation with the British and Foreign Bible Society of London she began her task. In 1935 the first edition of the Baphende New Testament came off the press at Kinshasa the capital of Zaire. She then turned her attention to the Old Testament. The conclusion of the first manuscript coincided wih her retirement in 1953.   JEB

Sprunger, Lilly Bachman and Vernon. Vernon Sprunger (1904-80) was born at Dalton, Ohio. Following high school he taught for several years and then secured employment with the B. F. Goodrich Rubber Company of Akron, Ohio. Restless at heart he enrolled in Bluffton College (Ohio) to prepare himself for other service. While there he met Lilly Bachman (1901-60) of Pulaski, Iowa, who was pursuing her certification as a teacher. They were married in July 1931 following their graduation.

They applied to the °°Congo Inland Mission in July 1931 and sailed in September for Belgian Congo (Zaire). Upon arrival at Mukedi Station in Kwilu Province they quickly turned their training and energy to upgrading not only the school at their station, but also those of the entire mission. When a new colonial regime in 1948 offered government subsidies to Protestant missions for educational purposes, the Sprungers advocated accepting the offer and a decade of church growth followed as biblical instruction was incorporated into the curriculum of mission schools at every level. Vernon also served as field treasurer and legal representative. In 1951 he was named interim general secretary of the Congo Protestant Council representing all Protestant missions to the Belgian Congo colonial government.

The Sprungers returned to the United States in 1960 when Lilly was diagnosed as having cancer. Vernon was appointed interim executive secretary of the Congo Inland Mission (Africa Inter-Mennonite Mission). After Lilly died he returned to Zaire where his broad experience was needed in the post-independence era. In 1962 he married fellow missionary Irena Liechty of Berne, Ind. In 1972 they retired to Berne, Ind., where they were living when Vernon died.   JEB

State, Anabaptist-Mennonite Attitudes toward. See Church-State Relations.

Statistics are numerical summaries of participation in such aspects of church life as °worship, °Sunday

schools, colleges. On the basis of such data needs and trends in church life are identified. Results are used by church leaders.

Although European Mennonites published lists of preachers, elders, and congregations beginning in 1731 (Naamlijst, ME III:804), the formal collection of data about Mennonites in North America appears to be a 20th-c. development. Before 1900 this work was done by interested individuals who worked informally and independently. One early effort was carried out by John F. Funk between 1895 and 1900. Funk gathered a broad range of data from congregations belonging to Mennonite bodies.

In the United States collection of church data was carried out every 10 years by the U.S. Census Bureau, 1850-90. After that time the census of religious bodies was moved to the middle of the decade with surveys being conducted in 1906, 1916, 1926, and 1936. For the latter census, the data was collected from each congregation directly from lists of congregations supplied to the Bureau by denominational leaders. Included with the census report was a brief historical, doctrinal, organizational, and statistical description of each denominational body included in it. Data gathered included information about membership, church buildings, annual expenditures, church schools, and the pastor. Most Mennonite bodies participated in this census.

When the U.S. Bureau of Census discontinued the gathering of religious data the religious community banded together through ad hoc organizations to gather such information. These studies, which count membership and churches by denomination according to county and state, have been done in 1952, 1971, and 1980. The 1990 study is being sponsored by the Association of Statisticians of American Religious Bodies (ASARB). Results of these studies are published in the volume, *Churches and Church Membership in the United States.*

Annually the *Yearbook of American and Canadian Churches* collects and publishes membership, church school, ministerial, and financial data of all religious bodies in the United States and Canada. A number of Mennonite bodies are listed in this volume.

Statistics Canada is the federal agency that gathers information about Canadian religious bodies in a census every 10 years, (e.g. 1971, 1981). Mennonite is one category in the census. Under it, all Mennonite and Amish data is collected. Age, sex, and metropolitan area are the data requested. Results are published in the volume, *Census of Canada's Population.*

The formal collection of data among Mennonite bodies in North America developed gradually in the 20th c. In most bodies the information is gathered annually by each group from a central office or designated officer. The information is then compiled and published as part of an annual report or as a separate °yearbook which is available to all interested readers. Over the years the degree of detail in the data collected has increased. For example, changes in membership are now analyzed in terms of sources of entrance such as baptism, letter of transfer, and other ways. Reasons for departure from membership are reported through such categories as excommunication, letter of transfer, and other ways.

Lists of ministers, first published in North America in the early part of the 20th c., continue to be created with more detail being added to the later years. In addition to name, address, and office, information now carried often includes telephone number, name of spouse, district conference designation, dates of ordination, degree of responsibility being carried, and name of congregation.

Sociological studies have also been carried out to gather specific information as well as to analyze trends taking place within the membership. One of these was the *MCC Peace Census* (1940). In this survey the number of men and women per age levels, e.g. up to 18; 18-30; 31-45; 46-65, in Mennonite congregations was sought in order to develop alternate plans in view of the impending military °conscription in World War II. The *Mennonite Family Census* was conducted in 1963 by the Historical and Research Committee of the Mennonite Church (MC). The study collected marriage, family, occupational, church membership, educational, and other data about the families surveyed. It was an update of a 1950 study. The 1963 study was later updated in 1982 by Michael L. Yoder. Comparisons to the results of the 1980 census were made in order to gauge developments in relation to the general United States population.

Anabaptists Four Centuries Later (1975) by J. Howard Kauffman and Leland Harder was a 1972 cooperative study of five Mennonite and Brethren in Christ bodies (Mennonite Church, General Conference Mennonite Church, Mennonite Brethren, Brethren in Christ, and Evangelical Mennonite Church). The purpose of the study was to obtain a profile of the beliefs, attitudes, and religious priorities of Mennonite and Brethren in Christ churches. In 1982, the Mennonite Brethren updated this same study in their congregations. A general updating of the Kauffman/Harder study was underway in 1988.

In 1985, the Evangelical Mennonite Conference conducted a variety of surveys to determine family, Christian education, music, and educational needs of their membership. In 1986 the Evangelical Mennonite Brethren Church conducted a survey to determine a future Senior Ministries program for members 50 years and older. The General Conference Mennonite Church has published a *Fact Book of Congregational Membership* in 1970 and 1980. This was preceded by a census in 1960.

The demand for information about congregations and members is growing. Needs addressed include helping Mennonite employers and potential employees get together, helping members with the same interests or vocations find one another, assisting church boards and agencies contact specific interest groups with their services and products, and supporting °church planting efforts. Such varied stimuli are reflected in a proposal made in the mid-1980s by the Council of Mennonite Computer Users to develop a common data base containing information on all members of all Mennonite bodies.

Mennonites in The Netherlands and Germany publish annual yearbooks, with the latter including data on Swiss, French, and German-speaking South American congregations and organizations. Other Mennonite groups around the world publish annual directories, often as supplements to denominational °periodicals. Limited statistics for Mennonites around the world are compiled by Mennonite World Conference (MWC). These were published in the *Mennonite World Handbook* (1978, supplemented in 1984) and are updated regularly in the MWC periodical, *Courier*. A new edition of the *Mennonite World Handbook* is planned for 1990.　　　　JEH

For bibliographical information see Sociological Studies; Yearbooks and Directories.

See also Demography; Sociological Studies.

Stauffer, Elam (Jan. 20, 1899-Jan. 9, 1981), was born to Benjamin R. and Fannie Weidman Stauffer in Lancaster Co., Pa. He married Elizabeth Kauffman on Nov. 25, 1920; she died in Africa on June 25, 1947. Elam married Grace Metzler on June 3, 1949. After study at Millersville State Normal School (Pennsylvania) and teaching two years, he began farming. A chorister and Sunday school teacher in his home congregation, Erisman Mennonite Church, he and Elizabeth also helped in mission outreach at Miners Village.

The Eastern Mennonite Board of Missions and Charities called the Stauffers and John and Ruth °Mosemann to be their first overseas missions team. Elam and John were ordained on Apr. 19, 1933. Elam and Orie °Miller traveled to Africa to look for a field of service. They decided on Tanganyika (Tanzania). The Stauffers and Mosemanns arrived at Shirati on May 26, 1934. On Sept 5, 1938 Elam was ordained bishop of the emerging church. During their first furlough the Stauffers studied at Eastern Mennonite College.

From the beginning Elam Stauffer endeavored to avoid institutional missions and to concentrate on self-supporting, self-propagating, self-governing indigenous churches. Within seven years the mission had reached its goal of five stations, but half of those baptized had already left the church. Elam was the leader of both the missionary team and the head of what became the Kanisa la Mennonite Tanzania (Tanzania Mennonite Church). A major component of both roles was his Bible teaching ministry. His family life, his role as counselor, and his ministry in prayer contributed to his effective leadership. In 1964 he recognized it was time for a new generation of leaders to assume responsibility. Having ordained 18 pastors and deacons, he took steps to call the first Tanzanian bishop.

After his retirement in 1964, Elam had oversight of a few Lancaster Conference congregations. Most of his energies were spent in Bible teaching and promoting missions.　　　　MMH

Mahlon M. Hess, *The Pilgrimage of Faith of Tanzania Mennonite Church, 1934-83* (Salunga, Pa.: Eastern Mennonite Board, 1985); *Miss. Mess*, sp. memorial issue (Oct. 1981), 2-15; Dale Brubaker, "Know Your Bishop," *Youth Mess.* (Mar. 2, 1969), 4-5; Elam W. Stauffer, "Report of Trip to Find a Location," *Miss. Mess.* (May 1934), 16-19, (July 1934), 14-18; idem, "Separate unto Me Ezekiel and Andrea," *Miss. Mess.* (Nov. 1950), 10-11; idem, "Institutions and the Young Indigenous Church," *Miss. Mess.* (May 1953), 6, 8, 11; idem, "I Commend You to God," *Miss. Mess.* (Aug. 1964), 2-4; idem, "Confidence—There Is No Other Way," *Miss. Mess.* (Jan. 1978), 6.

Stauffer, John L. (1888-1959), began his career as

Mennonite churchman and educator at the Altoona, Pa., mission in 1910, the year he married Lydia Kolb and was ordained a minister. In 1918 he accepted a call to teach Bible at Eastern Mennonite School, Harrisonburg, Va., where he filled important roles in academic and administrative work. In 1936, after the death of A. D. °°Wenger, he became the school's third president. He guided the school in its steady growth in all aspects until the end of his tenure in 1948, when it achieved full collegiate status as Eastern Mennonite College. Stauffer's policies kept the college close to its conservative Mennonite constituency, located primarily in the eastern United States. As minister, pastor, and bishop (from 1934 onward), he was a strong leader among Virginia Mennonites. He published articles and tracts on Bible doctrines and spoke frequently at °Bible conferences. He served on important committees in the Mennonite Church (MC) General Conference and as its moderator, 1947-49. He was the father of two daughters and three sons.   HRP

"Stauffer Mennonites" See Old Order Mennonites.

Steigerwald, Henry P. (1870-1929), a Brethren in Christ missionary who served as bishop of the Brethren in Christ church in the Rhodesias (Zimbabwe and Zambia) during his years in Africa (1901-28). Born in Ashland, Ohio, and married to Grace Pugh (1893), Steigerwald was ordained bishop of the fledgling Rhodesian missionary work (begun 1898) before he left the United States. Bishop Steigerwald gave leadership to the first major expansion of the missionary endeavor. Six new stations were opened: Mapane (1904), Mtshabezi (1906), Macha (1906), Mandamabge (1911, but soon abandoned), Sikalongo (1916), and Wanezi (1924). He placed strong emphasis on evangelism and education. The first African Brethren in Christ Conference was held in 1919, the first African overseers were appoointed in 1921, and the first African deacons elected in the following year. The positive response to the gospel is reflected in the fact that, by 1919, there were about 450 church members and approximately 800 in the catechumens' class. Bishop Steigerwald was a man of vision, mature judgment, and humility—all aspects of his leadership gifts.   MHS

Anna R. Engle, John A. Climenhaga, and Leoda A. Buckwalter, *There Is No Difference* (Nappanee, 1950); "Translated," *EV* (Feb. 4, 1929), 15; Frances H. Davidson, *South and South Central Africa* (Elgin, Ill.: Brethren Publishing House, 1915).

Steiner, Clara Daisy Eby (1873-1929), a founder and leader of the Mennonite [MC] Women's Missionary Society (ME III:640). The Society was the result of her conviction that women should and could play an active role in the church.

For years Clara used her considerable abilities behind the scenes as a partner with her husband, Menno Simon °°Steiner in °urban mission work in Chicago, Ill., and Canton, Ohio, and then in churchwide work when M. S. Steiner served on various Mennonite Church (MC) boards. Clara's loss of an active role in the church when M. S. died in 1911 weighed heavily. Not only did she manage the farm and housework and raise her children but she responded to the call she felt from God to establish an organization for women.

A few existent sewing circles served as the base, but Clara's vision went beyond sewing to the entire field of home and foreign °mission endeavor. She wanted the society to diffuse missionary spirit among women and provide opportunity for their significant participation in church work through planning for and supporting women missionaries and mission projects related to women.

The society flourished for a time despite great resistance to any executive role for women in the church. Clara understood the conservative forces and factionalism that kept the society from obtaining any official authorization and tried to work diplomatically but persistently. Finally, in 1926, the Mission Board appointed its own women's committee strictly for sewing work. Although the society attempted to continue the more important aspects of the work, it ceased to exist in 1928 (ME IV:974). In 1929 its influential founder died.   SLK

Rich, *Mennonite Women* (1983), 195-99; Sharon L. Klingelsmith, "Women in the Mennonite Church, 1900-1930," *MQR*, 54 (1980), 163-207 passim; MC Archives (Goshen), Clara Eby Steiner Collection; Melvin Gingerich, "The Mennonite Woman's Missionary Society," *MQR*, 37 (1963), 113-25, 214-33 passim.

Stephen, Balamdas D. (1894-1952), was born in a village near Raipur, Madhya Pradesh, India, just after his mother had been widowed. She died in the famine of 1893-94. B. D. was brought up and educated in the Methodist mission. After teaching in a Methodist school for some time, he entered government service as a contractor and moved his family to Birra near Mauhadih. There he met P. J. Wiens at an open-air preaching service at the weekly market and joined the group with his lusty singing. Wiens invited B. D. and his wife Ruth Bai, to join the General Conference Mennonite mission as °lay evangelists. B. D. pastored a small worshiping group in Taldeori village for 10 years and kept up his enthusiastic witness until his retirement in 1950. He died of a stroke in his son Samuel's home.   HKor

Stephen, Samuel (b. Mar. 28, 1918), son of °Balamdas and Ruth Bai Stephen was born near Mauhadih, Madhya Pradesh, India. He received his education in the Boys School, Mauhadih; St. Paul's Boys School, Raipur; and high school in °Dhamtari. After teaching in Mauhadih (1936-38), he earned a teacher's certificate in 1940 at Jabalpur.

Samuel went to teach at the Janzen Memorial School (JMS) at Jagdeeshpur in 1940. In 1944 JMS became an agricultural high school. Samuel married Helen Pennalal, a member of the Disciples of Christ Church, Bilaspur, and a teacher in Funk Memorial Girls School, Janjgir, in 1944. She joined the staff of JMS. Samuel and Helen have two children, Shireen and Anand. Samuel became headmaster of JMS in 1945; in 1947 he earned a BA degree as a private candidate and an MA in education from Wichita State U. in 1957. In 1958 he became principal of JMS; the school was raised to Higher Secondary status that same year. When he retired from JMS he served as manager for three more years in mission schools in Korba, Champa, Janjgir, and Jagdeeshpur.

Samuel also served as Sunday school teacher and choir director, and served on various church committees. In 1966 he was ordained an evangelist and assisted the pastor of Bethel church, Jagdeeshpur. He gave capable leadership to the Bharatiya General Conference Mennonite Church as chairman, secretary, treasurer, land agent, and on various committees. He was chairman of the General Conference Mennonite Mission and a consultant on education and legal matters. He was chairman of the Rural Economic Development and Community Health Association and vice chairman of the Menno Educational Society. His most recent position is chairman of the Polytechnic School in Mahasamund.   HKor

Stevenson, Alvin (1870-Feb. 16, 1913), was born in Quebec, Canada, but found his way as a young man to New York State where he enrolled in a missionary training program sponsored by the Christian and Missionary Alliance. In 1896 he and his wife set sail to the Congo Free State where they began their missionary service under sponsorship of Christian and Missionary Alliance.

In 1897 his wife and infant son died in Africa. In 1904 Alvin married Mathilde °Kohm who was serving with the Christian and Missionary Alliance under the auspices of the Defenseless Mennonite Church (Evangelical Mennonite Church). After the Stevensons returned to the United States in 1910, Alvin joined his wife's church. When the new inter-Mennonite mission board (Congo Inland Mission, later Africa Inter-Mennonite Mission) was formed in 1911 by the Defenseless Mennonites and the °°Central Conference Mennonite Church, Alvin left his family in Illinois and went to Africa to join Lawrence and Rose °Haigh to explore for a new mission field. They agreed upon two sites in Belgian Congo (Zaire) at Kalamba Mukenge in south central Congo among the Lulua people and Djoko Punda to the north among a mix of Lulua, Baluba, and Bakuba people. Soon after they were established at Djoko, Stevenson became ill with lung congestion and died. He was buried in Africa.   JEB

See bibliography under Kohm, Mathilde.

Stevenson, Mathilde Kohm. See Kohm, Mathilde.

Stewardship. The concept of stewardship emerges out of °creation. The Creator placed our first parents in the garden as caretakers. In the Old Testament people were familiar with the responsibilities and relationships of caretakers and stewards. Joseph was a steward in Potiphar's house. When he became ruler of Egypt, he had a steward (a "man over the house," Gn 43:19) who took care of his household affairs. All Christians are to be *stewards* of God's mysteries (*oikonomous;* 1 Cor 4:1; 1 Pet 4:10). Jesus speaks of the faithful and wise steward (*oikonomos,* Lk 12:42). This is the word from which *economics* is derived (*oikos* — manage + *nomos* — house). Another Greek word translated *steward* is found in the parable of the vineyard. The owner of the vineyard told the steward, or foreman (*epitropos,* i.e., one to whom a thing is committed), to call the workers and pay them their wages (Mt 20:8). From these and many other Scriptures, both the word and

concept of stewardship is clear in biblical usage. *Steward* derives from Old English words meaning the *keeper of a hall.* An English dictionary defines stewardship as "a person entrusted with management of estates or affairs not his own; an administrator" (Funk and Wagnalls).

God is the Creator of the earth and all that is in it, including humankind. Adam and Eve were formed from the dust, just as the creatures of the field. There is one amazing difference! God ". . . breathed into [Adam's] nostrils the breath of life, and [Adam] became a living being" (Gn 2:15). They were given specific responsibilities and commandments. The relationship of caretaker and steward is further established when the birds and beasts were brought to Adam to see what he would name them. God the Creator and owner, and people the caretakers and stewards, is a major theme that flows throughout biblical revelation. God's relationship as owner and lord of the world is constantly reaffirmed in both the Old Testament and New Testament, e.g., Ps 24:1; Jn 3:16.

After disobedience in Eden and after the first couple was evicted from the Garden, redemption becomes a dominant theme of the Old Testament looking forward to the coming of Christ. The covenant with Abraham, the exodus from Egypt, and fulfillment of covenant in a promised land are a confirmation of God to his people that he called them into a special relationship with him. The prophets continually call a disobedient people to return to be faithful to the covenant.

The New Testament is the fulfillment of the promised redemption in Christ. Jesus comes to establish the kingdom of heaven of which he is the king. In one of the many kingdom parables, he says, ". . . it will be like a man going on a journey, who called his servants and entrusted his property to them" (Mt 25:14). Faithfulness is the standard of judgment when the master of the servants returns. The stewardship parables (e.g. Mt 20:8; Lk 12:42; 16:1-3) clearly establish Christ as Lord and Master. His people are called to be stewards and managers of the Master's goods. Jesus' teaching on stewardship is set in the context of managing material possessions. The intent of his teaching clearly goes beyond material goods to show his hearers they have the responsibility of a steward to act on the manager's behalf in his absence, "until I come back" (Lk 19:13).

Stewardship teaching among churches in the Anabaptist tradition carries a strong °discipleship emphasis. H. S. °Bender stated "First and fundamental in the Anabaptist vision was the conception of the essence of Christianity as discipleship." This is not so much the inward experience of God's grace as the outward application in all conduct and relationships. "Following Christ" was the emphasis (Bender, "Anabaptist Vision").

"A new concept of the church with newness of life and applied Christianity" is cited by Bender as a second major element in Anabaptist faith. One of the Swiss martyrs of 1528 said, "If they know of any one who is in need, whether or not he is a member of their church, they believe it their duty, out of love to God, to render help and aid." Swiss Brethren applicants for baptism were asked "whether they would consecrate themselves with all their temporal possessions to the service of God and His people."

Persecution or the threat of it tended to help Anabaptists solve the problem of indifferent members and the demands of church °discipline. By the middle of the 19th c. the political situation shifted in most European countries, and in some of the American colonies there was a relatively free religious climate early in the 18th c. The fervor of faith was kept alive in part by emphasizing responsibility toward one another through °mutual aid. Alms books were more important than records of baptism, marriages, or funerals. The Skippack (Pennsylvania) alms book, for instance, lists assistance to immigrants, maintenance for a poor man, and a pound of sugar for Maria von Fossen; along with church property maintenance, communion supplies and costs for operation of the schools. (MacMaster, 160-64).

Mennonites who followed the °frontier, or came to the frontier as immigrants, found that establishing homes and a livelihood consumed most of their energy and resources. By the 1950s the poverty of the 1930s gave way to growing prosperity. As communities prospered, many church members did not have a clear biblical sense that who they are and what they own is the Lord's. Nor did they understand that their assets belong to God and that they are stewards entrusted to administer these assets until he returns. The baptismal commitment often did not carry the specific expectation to consecrate "themselves with all . . . temporal possessions."

In spite of shortcomings in practice, stewardship became a dominant church concern in the decades after World War II. Practice was ahead of theology. It is easier to respond to tangible need than to abstract mandates. Before the 1950s many congregations had no budget, no systematic plan for giving, and offered little financial support to pastors.

The events surrounding World War II transformed the outlook and economics of the inter-Mennonite and Amish family. By joining efforts under the Mennonite Central Committee umbrella, vast quantities of food and clothing were shipped to war-torn Europe. MCC workers personally distributed these relief supplies "in the name of Christ." The impact on the North American churches was amazing.

In the post-war decades mission and service expanded at home and abroad beyond expectation. Young people were drafted and others volunteered for service in Canada, United States, and around the world. Mennonite colleges added courses of study preparing the young for work in service professions. The colleges were expanding enrollments while church °secondary and elementary schools were being established. °Mental health centers, °hospitals, nursing °homes and retirement communities began to flourish. Inter-Mennonite service programs such as Mennonite °Disaster Service, °Mennonite Economic Development Associates, and church °camping associations were organized.

There was work to be done. Mennonites were *doers*, so they joined forces, organized and developed varied and diverse service programs and ministries. Service projects close to the people found it easy to raise financial support. The post-war cash economy provided new resources to support the op-

portunity offered by the expanding church vision. Congregations and denominational °institutions became interested in budgets, financial planning, and fiscal responsibility for church-sponsored programs. Tithing and stewardship became important issues. It was important for people of financial means to take part in forming the new vision for the emerging ministries. It was not always clear whether the emphasis on tithing and stewardship was a concern to promote biblical principles of faith, or a way to motivate people with means to support expanding programs. The 35 years from the early 1950s to the late 1980s were a time of growth for Mennonites and related groups in North America and beyond. The church faced many problems, but God supplied material and spiritual resources to accomplish ministries important to the life of his kingdom.

A review of denominational °yearbooks indicates that most of the Mennonite and Brethren in Christ conference structures include commissions or directors with responsibility for stewardship ministries. Staff serving under the denominational boards are available to hold workshops and seminars in congregations that want to strengthen their understanding of stewardship. Specialized services are available in estate planning, building congregational budgets, and guidance to families for financial planning and tithing.

As Mennonites move toward the 21st c., there is a growing emphasis on the broader aspects of Christian stewardship in °preaching, °Sunday school literature, and in the church °periodicals. A listing of topics and frequent concerns follow: (1) Spiritual renewal and a re-ordering of life's priorities, often emphasizing the meaning of discipleship in a secular age and seeking Christ's kingdom first (Mt 6:13) are frequent references. (2) Stewardship of time, talents, and vocation are topics people are exploring. Humans are created in God's image. Believers bodies are referred to as God's temple (1 Cor 6:19-20). (3) Care for the environment, global ecology, and concern for the welfare of exploited people are emphasized. As science and technology advance, the potential for destruction of God's creation increases. (4) Personal and family financial management, including an emphasis and study of biblical teaching of the tithe, of the °jubilee principle, and of what constitutes an appropriate life-style are discussed. Estate planning and planned giving are increasingly important to people who wish to practice biblical stewardship.

The biblical themes of creation, redemption and discipleship, which include the call to holy living, are the lofty base on which stewardship practices are built. Management of money is an issue that never quite goes away. It is still the scorecard that shows how we understand the Christian gospel. Ultimately, however, money is not the issue. The issue is how one gets it, what one does with it, and what one lets money do to oneself.   LP

MEA 1: 160-64; H. S. Bender, "Vision"; Milo Kauffman, *The Challenge of Christian Stewardship* (Scottdale, 1955); idem, *Stewards of God* (Scottdale, 1975); Robert A. Yoder, *Seeking First the Kingdom: Called to Faithful Stewardship* (Scottdale, 1983); Ray Bair and Lillian Bair, *God's Managers: A Budget Guide and Daily Financial Record Book for Christians* (Scottdale, 1985); Kauffman/Harder, *Anabaptists Four C. Later* (1975), 233ff.

See also Jacob Engle Foundation (BIC); Kauffman, Milo; Mennonite Foundation; Stichtung: voor Bijzondere Noden.

Stichting: Stuw-Kracht-10 (Foundation Reserve Power 10). See Stichting voor Bijzondere Nooden.

Stichting Tabor (Foundation Tabor). See Stichting voor Bijzondere Nooden.

Stichting voor Bijzondere Noden in de Doopsgezinde Broederschap en Daarbuiten (Foundation for Special Needs within the Mennonite Brotherhood and Beyond) (ME II:344, IV:632). Since the state has taken increasing responsibility for welfare affairs in many areas the church could withdraw from aspects of its earlier work, e.g., the children's home in Schoorl and the home Patria in Baarn for repatriated Dutch people from Indonesia. Consequently increasing interest focused on overseas, with the intention of cooperating with the Mennonite congregations there. Thus 30 percent of the 1986 budget of the foundation went to Latin America in support of the work carried on among the Indians by Mennonite congregations. Short- and long-term volunteers have also been sent. Adoption programs for school children in Bangladesh and Indonesia have also been initiated.

In Germany help has been given to Mennonites returning from Latin America and from Russia, including material, pastoral, and educational support. The Mennonite congregations in Europe have formed the °International Mennonite Organization (IMO) to coordinate these efforts. The foundation was particularly active in forming this coordinating agency.

Stichting Stuwkracht 10 (Foundation Power Reservoir 10) is an organization of anonymous donors pledged to tithe their income in behalf of the needs of the world. The organization arose as a result of the inspiration received at the Mennonite World Conference in Amsterdam in 1967. In 1985 there were 60 members.

Stichting Tabor (Foundation Tabor) was founded to give help and support to children and young people, both in The Netherlands and beyond, in their educational and developmental needs to the end that they may become self-sufficient persons finding their place in society. This organization originated out of the *Stichting voor Bijzondere Noden in de Doopsgezinde Broederschap en Daarbuiten* and several other funds designated specifically for help to Mennonite children in the Dutch brotherhood. LLau

R. de Zeeuw, "De vlucht van Bijzondere Noden," *Doops. Jaar.* (1987), 22-32.

See also Algemene Doopsgezinde Sociëteit; Relief Work; Development Work; Mennonite Central Committee; Relief Work; Samenwerkingsverband van "de Vier Instellingen" in de Doopsgezinde Broederschap.

Stoltzfus, Grant Moses (Feb. 12, 1916-July 21, 1974), professor of sociology and church history at Eastern Mennonite College and Seminary, 1957-74.

Born at Elverson, Pa., he was the son of Sylvanus and Lydia Hartz Stoltzfus. He married Ruth Brunk of Denbigh, Va., June 17, 1941. Together they raised a family of three daughters and two sons.

A graduate of Goshen College (BA), U. of Pittsburgh (MA), and Union Theological Seminary in Richmond, Va. (BD and ThD), Stoltzfus served the church as a teacher in the classroom and in numerous conferences, frequently with Ruth, on the theme of strengthening family life; as a historian and the author of the well-regarded *Mennonites of the Ohio and Eastern Conference* (1969); as a member of several local and binational committees including Park View Mennonite Church and the Historical Committee (MC); as editor of the *Mennonite Community Magazine* (1947-53); and as administrator of °°Civilian Public Service units for Mennonite Central Committee (1941-46).

Stoltzfus pioneered in recovering the early history of the Amish in colonial Pennsylvania. His concern for religious freedom and civil liberties inspired his work for °conscientious objectors and the mentally handicapped during World War II. At the time of his death he was writing a history of the origins of °alternative service for conscientious objectors in the United States. He was active in the National Committee for Amish Religious Freedom and the civil rights movement in Virginia. As the inscription on his tombstone observes, he indeed "loved the truth and peace." JAL

Menn. Bib. II, p. 507; *Who's Who Mennonites* (1943), 235.

Stoltzfus, John A. (Oct. 22, 1870-Apr. 3, 1957), was a lifelong resident of Lancaster Co., Pa., and a farmer by occupation. He was married to Anna K. Stoltzfus, and they had nine children. After Anna's death, he married Amanda Beachy. John was ordained minister (Apr. 28, 1911) and bishop (Apr. 25, 1926).

John had been a leader of a group involuntarily leaving the Old Order Amish church over disagreements about application of the *Meidung* (°°avoidance) in 1909. By 1930 his congregation came to be known as the Weavertown Amish Mennonite Church and affiliated with the Beachy Amish Mennonite fellowship. John was an influential and widely known leader, and was one of the principal conveners of the meeting in which Amish Mennonite Aid was organized. John was noted for his executive ability and statesmanship in church matters, giving assistance to many congregations. He had a deep faith in God and this was reflected in the evangelical fervor of his messages. More than 30 Beachy Amish ministers were present at his funeral. ESY

Strickler, Jacob, Jr. (1788-1859), was a bishop in the River Brethren church (later known as Brethren in Christ) in York Co., Pa. He is recognized as a leader in the movement which separated from the main body of River Brethren (Brethren in Christ) to form the Old Order River Brethren. Jacob was born in York Co., the son of Jacob (1755-1837) and Elizabeth (Miller) Strickler (this was not Bishop Jacob Strickler). He operated a mill with his father near Wrightsville, Pa. Jacob Jr. married Nancy Gerber (1791-1884); they had eight children. SES

Laban T. Brechbill, *History Old Order River Brethren* (n.p.: Brechbill and Strickler, 1972), 79-81; Alice Strickler, *Stricklers of Pennsylvania* (Scottdale: MPH, 1942), 106.

Strickler, Joseph (1797-1879), was born in York Co., Pa., the son of Bishop Jacob Strickler (1768-1842) and Catherine Cormeny Strickler (1765-1841). In 1819 he married Mary Leib, to whom eight children were born. He was a miller and farmer near Goldsboro, Pa. He was a member of the River Brethren (later known as Brethren in Christ). He later became a leader among the Old Order River Brethren. It appears that Joseph moved to Manor Twp. in Lancaster Co. in the 1860s. He was called upon to give bishop oversight to the recently organized congregation of Old Order River Brethren in that county. SES

Laban T. Brechbill, *History Old Order River Brethren* (n.p.: Brechbill and Strickler, 1972), 38-39, 78-79; Alice Strickler, *Stricklers of Pennsylvania* (Scottdale, MPH, 1942), 243.

Student and Young Adult Services (SYAS). The Student Services Committee was formed by the Mennonite Board of Missions (MC) in August 1958. It adopted a policy statement in August 1959, which stated that it was to provide "services" rather than administer a program for Mennonite students on non-Mennonite college and university campuses. That policy was still in effect in 1987. In 1978 the Student Services Committee became Student and Young Adult Services to reflect inclusion of urban young adults in its work. In 1985 SYAS was given a mandate to develop churchwide young adult ministry resources.

Most SYAS programs are co-sponsored with the Commission on Education (COE) of the General Conference Mennonite Church. In 1986 COE contracted with SYAS to administer for COE on an interim basis jointly sponsored SYAS/COE activities.

Aspects of the program include the census of "scattered" (mostly °urban) young adults and graduate and undergraduate students at non-Mennonite schools, a network of contact persons for these students and young adults, resources for student fellowship groups and urban young adults, congregations oriented toward special events for students and young adults, *in search* (a newsletter for students and young adults), *Feedback* (a resource newsletter on congregational ministry with young adults), and special research projects.

Student Services executive secretaries were Virgil Brenneman (1958-1973) and Hubert Brown (1974-1981). Directors of SYAS were Richard Mojonnier (1980-81) and Myrna Burkholder (1981-).   MB

S. F. Pannabecker, *Open Doors* (1975), 232-33; 435; Mennonite Board of Missions, Student and Young Adult Services, SYAS/COE *Study Project, Congregational Study Profile,* vol 1; *It Matters Where You Scatter,* vol 2; (Elkhart, Ind.: Student and Young Adult Services, Mennonite Board of Missions, 1986).

Student Exchanges. See International Exchanges.

Suckau, Cornelius H. (Jan. 23, 1881-Nov.12, 1951). Born to John and Marie Andres Suckau on a farm near Newton, Ks. Suckau graduated from Bethel College Academy. His call to mission work came while he taught school in the Newton area.

After three years of training at the Union Mission-ary Training Institute of Brooklyn, N.Y., he married fellow graduate Lulu Johnson, in June 1909. In August 1909 they entered General Conference Mennonite mission work in India; in 1914 they were appointed to open the mission station at Korba, Madhya Pradesh, India.

Suckau was an energetic, but independent missionary evangelist. After the family's furlough in 1928 he was not reappointed, at least in part because of a health problem.

His 15-year tenure at First Mennonite Church in Berne, Ind. was marked by a strong but controversial emphasis on °dispensationalism, premillennialism, and eternal security. The congregation gained 270 members.

In October 1943 Suckau resigned to become the president of the newly founded Grace Bible Institute (Grace College of the Bible), Omaha, Nebr., 1943-50.   NEL

Eva F. Sprunger, *The First Hundred Years: A History of the Mennonite Church in Adams Co., Ind., 1838-1938* (Berne, 1938), 236-38; Juhnke, *Mission* (1979), 28, 94-96, 240; Paul Kuhlmann, *The Story of Grace,* 71; Naomi Lehman, *Pilgrimage of a Congregation* (Berne: First Mennonite Church, 1982), ch. 7; yearbooks of First Mennonite Church, Berne, Ind.

See also Fundamentalism.

Südamerikanische Konferenz der Mennonitischen Brüdergemeinden (South American Conference of Mennonite Brethren Congregations). This includes the Mennonite Brethren congregations, mostly of Russian immigrant background in Brazil, Paraguay, and Uruguay. The first meeting of this conference was in Friesland Colony in 1962. The purpose of the conference was to promote unity among the congregations and increase faithfulness in doctrine and practice. Ideological and doctrinal differences had become apparent among the congregations since World War II. °Nonresistance had been neglected. A sense of failure prevailed among the leaders and members, with a desire to change things but uncertainty about how to do this. Relationships with the German congregations, which had been so helpful before the war, had been broken. It was not surprising, therefore, that contact with North American Mennonite Brethren developed into very fruitful interdependence.

From the beginning strong emphasis was placed upon the need for Bible schools, mission work, Sunday school, youth work, and singing. A Bible study course to promote this was begun in 1956. In 1961 this course was located in Brazil with the founding of a Bible institute (Instituto e Seminário Bíblico Irmãos Menonitas, Curitiba). Questions raised at early conferences included the definition of love relationships, marriage with unbelievers, reception of members who had not been baptized by °immersion, and remarriage of persons whose spouse had been lost in the war but who might still be alive somewhere.

National conferences were founded in Paraguay, Brazil, and Uruguay in 1961 but by 1979 most members of the Mennonite Brethren church had left Uruguay, leaving only Brazil and Paraguay in the South American Conference. In its meetings this conference gradually evolved from a work-oriented conference to one centering on issues of faith and life, meeting triennially. In 1984 there were 16 congregations in Brazil with 1,834 members, and 8 congregations in Paraguay with 1,243 members, for a total of 3,077 members.

The leaders of the conference have been: Gerhard Balzer (1948-53), Fernheim; Kornelius Voth (1953-57), Friesland; Gerhard Balzer (1958-62), Fernheim; Hans Wiens (1962-67), Asunción; Heinrich Lowen (1967-69), Curitiba; Erich Giesbrecht (1969-73), Fernheim; Willy Janz (1973-79), Curitiba; Gerhard Ratzlaff (1979-85), Asunción; Peter Penner (1985-), Witmarsum.   GR

Willy Janz and Gerhard Ratzlaff, *Gemeinde unter dem Kreuz des Südens: Die Mennonitischen Brüdergemeinden in Brasilien, Paraguay, and Uruguay 1930-1980* (Curitiba, 1980); minutes of the conference, 1948-1985; *MWH* (1984), 109.

Sudan is the largest country in Africa and one of the world's poorest countries. The Nile River, which flows from the south to the north, has secured Sudan's place in world history. In the north, the culture is Arabic, the religion is °Islam, and the landscape is mostly desert. In the south, the culture is African, the religions are °animist and Christian, and the landscape is savannah (subtropical grasslands). The north and south are separated by a large swamp called the Sudd, from which Sudan gets its name. Since independence in 1956, Sudan has suffered from two civil wars, a number of military coups d'état, large-scale drought and famine, as well as political and economic instability.

Mennonites first began their work in Sudan in 1972. The program continues to be a fully seconded one, with all workers supervised not by their "primary" agencies (Mennonite) but rather by "secondary" agencies, in this case the Sudan Council of Churches or ACROSS, an externally based consortium of evangelical development agencies. In 1986 there were 17 Mennonite Central Committee volunteers serving in both the north and south, in relief work with Ugandan and Ethiopian refugees, and in longer term development projects.   CRY

Suffering may be defined as all heavy and striking instances of misfortune, causing physical or mental distress or pain. In most religions suffering raises the profound problem of its relation to divinity. Adherents of primitive religions often viewed it as imposed by the gods, capriciously but also as something to be endured. The gods imposing it, in return needed to be propitiated; rites of passage in these religions often involved suffering. In Islam suffering led to fatalism. The ancient Hebrews viewed suffering as a judgment of God necessitated by human sin; humans suffered because of their own willful behavior, and they ought not to blame God for it. Hebrew suffering was also a probe of the righteous leading them to strengthened faith.

New Testament Christians embraced the supreme form of suffering, martyrdom, as entirely natural, because of the martyrdom of Jesus but also perhaps because of the Stoics' insistent denial of the reality of suffering. New Testament authors emphasized suffering as useful and necessary to strengthen and purify the Christian (Rom 5:3-5; Heb 12:6).

To the ancients suffering raised the problem of the good. Graeco-Romans generally regarded suffering as tragic and even evil, perhaps evidence of the gods' displeasure but more likely the result of divine caprice. It was not necessarily tied to human behavior. Or they regarded wealth as an unmitigated good. New Testament authors, on the other hand, thought that the good led toward the realization of the kingdom of God. Thus material loss or imprisonment or pain or sickness—in short, any form of personal distress—could induce one to reflect more carefully on his own life; it could awaken conscience, helpful in the Christian's life on earth but also finally in her progress toward eternity. And wealth could be an evil. Christians viewed both good and evil from the perspective of °eternity.

Throughout church history there have always been groups of devout Christians who revived and refurbished the New Testament view of suffering, both because they thought the New Testament view (not necessarily the church's °tradition) ought to be the supreme guide to life and also because the New Testament view of suffering conformed to the realities of their existence—suffering, often at the hands of other Christians. Sixteenth-century Anabaptists were such a group.

For the Anabaptists suffering was (1) being in Christ. Suffering denoted following Christ, being engrafted into Christ, participating with him in life in the most intimate possible manner. They expressed gratitude to him, joy in participating with him in suffering, obedience to his commands including taking up the cross (Phil 2:8). Their theology was essentially christological.

(2) Suffering was also redemptive. It led them to a complete identification with Christ, not only in his suffering and death but also in resurrection with him. To Menno suffering was a sign of election, of genuinely belonging to Christ ("Of the Cross of Christ," 1556). For some Anabaptists suffering in the form of martyrdom hastened the approach of Christ's return and thus of their own ultimate redemption. For a few of them martyrdom was itself a certain and positive rite of passage into eternity. Despite their denial of a pelagianist soteriology (works righteousness), all of them thought that suffering was at least a sign of certain redemption.

(3) Suffering was also disciplinary. It led the Christian through the hard school of Christ, in discipleship to Christ, strengthening him for every test, hardening her to endure rack and refute clever inquisitor. It turned the Christian toward obedience to Christ and the fellowship of believers, therefore disobedience to the world. It meant conflict and strife, not contented easy living, because the evil world would not permit the true believer respite or rest. That constant warfare could produce a resolute hardened soldier of the Lord, following Paul's model (Eph 6:13-20).

(4) Anabaptists believed that suffering was inevitable. "It has been so from the beginning, that the righteous must suffer, and that the unrighteous always prevail" (*Martyrs Mirror* [Scottdale, 1951], 668). Evil, willful people and social structures inevitably imposed suffering on those Christians who remained faithful to Christ. Christ's injunction to take up the cross and follow him, a hard saying,

made suffering as he had suffered a universal factual reality (2 Tim 3:12; 1 Pet 2:21). Anabaptists viewed suffering as less the result of one's own sin than Luther, for instance, would have had it; for Anabaptists, suffering was caused by the sins of others. As Christ had found suffering inevitable, so his followers would too. Participation with Christ in suffering included the entire fellowship; the entire body suffered. Inevitability included the perpetual hostility of evil forces in the world toward true believers. Christians were locked in a cosmic struggle between God and the forces of evil.

(5) Suffering was avengable. God would avenge his suffering people. Ultimately the righteous would be victorious and the sinful °persecutors, civil and religious, would be defeated. Most Anabaptists awaiting execution seem to have expected some specific avenging act by God and left the matter of vengeance entirely to the Lord. A few of them seemed eager to predict the time and manner of divine retribution on their persecutors; and a handful vented their spleen in angry outbursts. Most of them were both submissive and bold, and intended their predictions of vengeance as evangelical warnings, a deliberate part of their larger mission.

To some Anabaptists suffering was implicit in both the nature of the universe and soteriology. Anabaptist °mystics, especially those like Hans °Hut and other followers of Thomas °Müntzer who immersed themselves in mystical reflections, explained internal pain and suffering—doubt, indecision, anxiety, guilt—as deriving from the human creaturely condition, imposed by the Creator. As animals suffered under the domination of humans, so also humans suffered under the dominance of fellow humans and even God. They suffered inner anguish that carried through stages of perception of soul condition to complete resignation (*Gelassenheit*), in which condition the Spirit of God could finally enter for its salvific work.

This mystical salvationism bore a physical character for the human, so that physical baptism was a necessary stage in salvation. In believers' baptism with water the Anabaptist mystics partially bridged the gap between internalized mystical suffering and the external suffering via martyrdom of Anabaptists such as the Swiss Brethren.

From approximately 1600 to our own times Mennonites have generally regarded suffering in traditional Anabaptist terms, even when they were not persecuted; the mystical Anabaptist suffering strain fell away. As Mennonites made their peace with the world and °acculturated in various places and times, some leaders recalled them to an earlier pristine Christian condition by publishing martyr tales. The crowning literary achievement of martyr tales was van Braght's °°*Martyrs' Mirror* (1660), with many subsequent editions in Dutch, German, and finally English. The large number of copies of many editions of the *Martyrs' Mirror* found in the older Mennonite °historical libraries is itself mute testimony to the immense spiritual popularity of that work, next to the Bible and some hymnals the most important literary possession of Mennonite families.

Anabaptists and Mennonites after them have emphasized practice more than theory. One is not surprised therefore to discover little or no formal theology of suffering, even in our own times when Mennonites publish far more than any rational human can read. In recent decades Mennonite theologians—writing systematic, biblical, or practical theology—have rarely broached the topic. A few meditations for a radio audience, a few published sermons, an occasional pamphlet, an article in some church paper—these alone provide a forum for Mennonite discourse on the subject. Although the scholars who write systematic theology are generally silent on the topic, there remains a substratum of conviction among many Mennonites, certainly among the more traditional groups, that suffering is salvific, purgative, and inevitable. Such people satisfy their thirst for literary support for their view with the standard writing, the *Martyrs' Mirror*, still a staple in their literary diet, as evidenced by the frequency of recent reprintings.

In the past two decades a growing number of Western-world Mennonites regard suffering as less a theological than a psychoanalytic-therapeutic topic, and read and act accordingly.

If Mennonites have not written recently about suffering, nor reshaped a fresh theology of suffering, they have nonetheless responded to the suffering of others in relief and service activities on a global basis. The impetus, suffering of others inviting °service from Christians for whom suffering is a major motif in life, derives from the Anabaptists' own scriptural emphases and religious experiences. Even a recanted mid 16th-c. Anabaptist found his post-Anabaptist niche as administrator of poor relief for Strasbourg.

Within Mennonite history there have been two major outpourings of material aid to other people. In the 17th and 18th c. the Dutch Mennonites gave immense quantities of money and material aid to religious refugees of differing persuasions, but including also their Swiss co-religionists. In the 20th c. North American Mennonites founded the Mennonite Central Committee for sending material aid to beleaguered Russian Mennonites impoverished by the °Russian Revolution and Civil War. Largely quiescent for several decades, World War II called the MCC back to life, and still more recently European Mennonites added their own relief organization. JSO

David W. Augsburger, *Why, My God, Why?* (Harrisonburg, Va.: Mennonite Hour, 1967); James E. Bertsche, "The Shadow of Suffering," in *A Kingdom of Priests: The Church in the New Nations*, ed., Wilbert R. Shenk (Newton and Scottdale, 1967), 126-39; Jaap Brüsewitz, "Van Deportatie naar Emigratie: een Archiefonderzoek naar de Overkomst van Zwitserse Broeders naar de Republiek der Verenigde Nederlanden in de 18e Eeuw" (typescript, Amsterdam Mennonite Seminary, 1981); J. Lawrence Burkholder, "The Theology of Suffering," in Burkholder, "The Problem of Social Responsibility from the Perspective of the Mennonite Church" (PhD diss., Princeton Theological Seminary, 1958; published at Elkhart, Ind.: IMS, 1988), 69-75; John M. Drescher, *Strength for Suffering* (Scottdale, 1969); idem, *Suffering and God's Presence* (Scottdale, 1971); Cornelius J. Dyck, "The Suffering Church in Anabaptism," *MQR*, 59 (1985), 5-23; Peter J. Dyck, "A Theology of Service," *MQR*, 44 (1970), 213-44; Irvin B. Horst, *Dutch Aid to Swiss Brethren* (Amsterdam: Doops. Hist. Kring, 1984); B. Charles Hostetter, *The School of Suffering* (Harrisonburg, Va.: Mennonite Hour, 1960); Ed G. Kaufman, "The Christian and Suffering," *Bethel College Bulletin*, 36, no. 11 (June 1, 1949); Alan F. Kreider, "The Servant is Not Greater Than

His Master': The Anabaptists and the Suffering Church," *MQR,* 58 (1984), 5-29; W. J. Kühler, "Dutch Mennonite Relief Work in the 17th and 18th Centuries," *MQR,* 17 (1943), 87-94; Nancy S. Lapp, "From Pain and Suffering to Resurrection," *GH,* 76 (1983), 182-83; Ethelbert Stauffer, "Täufertum und Märtyrertheologie," *Z. für KG,* 52 (1933), 545-98.

See also Humility; Relief Work.

Sukhlal, Manohar (ca. 1888-Mar. 24, 1960), a teacher, deacon, evangelist, and minister of the Mennonite Church in India was born to a Hindu Harijan farmer family of Chattisgarh, Madhya Pradesh (M.P.). He was one of the 16 children admitted by William °Page to the American Mennonite Mission orphanage in Dhamtari, M.P., in 1899.

He was assigned to various supervisory tasks at the orphanage, and, after completing his middle school education, he took local normal school (teacher) training. In 1912(?) he married Sukhma Bai, one of the boarding girls. They had four children. In 1917 he was sent to Jabalpur, M.P., for further teacher training at a government school after which he served as supervisor of the mission-operated primary schools in and about °Dhamtari. In 1921 he was appointed to serve as headmaster of the vernacular middle school for girls in Balodgahan (later known as Garjan Memorial School).

Sukhlal early exhibited an interest in village evangelism and outreach. In 1912 he was Hindi recording secretary for the first India Mennonite Conference. In 1913 he was ordained deacon for the Sunderganj congregation and in 1931 became the first ordained Indian minister. He lived a very simple life-style and used unsophisticated language. He was ordained deacon for the Sundarganj congregation in Dhamtari, but served most of his pastoral years in Balodgahan. He also served in pastorates at the Shantipur Leprosy Hospital and at Ghatula. He died in retirement at his village home in Balodgahan.   JAF

Biographical data supplied by P. J. Malagar; American Mennonite MC Mission, Dhamtari, India, *Building on the Rock* (Scottdale: MPH, 1926); American Mennonite Mission Annual Reports (1913, 1931); American Mennonite Mission Educational and Evangelistic Committee files in MC Archives (Goshen), box IV-17-7.

Summer Camps. See Camps and Retreat Centers.

Summer (Vacation) Bible School (ME IV:654). The growth of the summer Bible school program continued in the Mennonite Church (MC) until 1963. In that year there were 835 schools, 11,033 teachers, and 100,786 students. In 1973 there were 744 schools, 7,567 teachers, and 77,256 students. The 1983 records reveal a decline to 599 schools, 6,053 teachers, and 54,210 students. The trend from ten-day material to five-day material went from 95 percent for ten-day in 1954 to only 25 percent in 1985. The enrollment continued to drop even though less time was spent in summer Bible school.

Alternative approaches have been introduced. For example, weekend summer Bible School beginning Sunday afternoon and concluding Monday evening for grades six through ten. Team teaching (usually husband-wife teams) was used for the first time in Scottdale to present the Herald Omnibus Bible curricula. Box lunches were provided by the congregations for Sunday evening. Monday's lunch was served by the women of the church with a hot dog and watermelon cookout in the evening meal. Devotionals consisted of camp-fire programs each evening.

On the denominational level, Paul Clemens succeeded C. F. °Yake as secretary for the summer Bible school program from 1958 through 1963. Maynard W. Shetler served from 1964 through 1967. In 1968 the Commission for Christian Education assumed responsibility for the summer Bible school program. Since 1975 the Mennonite Board of Congregational Ministries has given leadership to the summer Bible school program.

The Herald summer Bible school materials and program were made available in India in Hindi and in Europe in German and French, with a few grades translated into Italian. The Herald Summer Bible School Series was revised in 1958 and again in 1966/67. In 1976/77 the course was rewritten, built mostly on the same Bible texts. A five-day, closely-graded course was developed from the ten-day curriculum to meet the need for shorter schools.

The Herald Omnibus Bible Series was released in 1973 and 1974. Outlines for this closely-graded course were developed by Paul M. Lederach with James E. Horsch as editor and Marjorie Waybill as associate editor. This series explores what the Bible and Jesus have to say about the issues children and youth face. This multi-purpose course was designed for use in five-day vacation Bible schools, church camps, released-time °Christian education, clubs, and week-day or Sunday evening study.

The daily vacation Bible school (*Die Sommerbibel Schularbeit* in the early reports), was initiated among the Mennonite Brethren in Canada by Bethany and Winkler Bible Schools in 1933. The mission to children, as recalled by Henry Warkentin, awakened unprecedented interest and missionary zeal and became the first organized expression of missionary vision. From small beginnings that engendered much enthusiasm in the 1930s and the 1940s daily vacation Bible schools (DVBS) peaked for the Mennonite Brethren between 1957 and 1965. The big question raised about DVBS was what happened to the converts? How many churches developed from this work? John Dyck stated in 1966 that after nearly 25 years of °children's work, they had not established one permanent mission.

The first summer Bible school among General Conference Mennonites was held in the summer of 1921, at Berne, Ind. Affiliation with the Summer Bible School Association at Chester, Pa., was effected and their prescribed course for a five-week term was adopted. In 1925, the four churches of Berne united to make it a union summer Bible school. Cornelius H. °Suckau served as superintendent of the union summer Bible school from 1931 to 1940. From the 1930s onward, daily vacation Bible schools were common throughout the General Conference Church. A wide variety of interdenominational materials were used, including the Herald Summer Bible School Series.

In 1938, the Board of Education (GCM) declared the DVBS program to be of inestimable spiritual value to the cause of Christ and the spreading of God's Word. The board never developed a DVBS curriculum of its own, but twice adopted the Herald Press materials for use in General Conference Bible schools. In 1950, over 70 percent of General Conference Bible schools used the Herald Summer Bible School Series. **MWS**

MC Yearbook (1963-); Mennonite Publishing House records; Eva F. Sprunger, *The First Hundred Years: A History of the Mennonite Church in Adams Co., Ind., 1838-1938* (Berne, 1938), 170; Naomi Lehman, *Pilgrimage of a Congregation* (Berne: First Mennonite Church, 1982), 84; Willard Claassen, "Reflections on the Development of Christian Education Program and Ministries" (unpublished paper); Mary Sprunger, "Education and Publication: The Early Days" (unpublished paper); Peter Penner, *No Longer at Arm's Length: Mennonite Brethren Church Planting in Canada, 1883-1983* (Winnipeg: Kindred Press, 1987); C. F. Yake, *Superintendent Manual, Summer Bible School* (1951), has been reissued three times (1958, 1966, 1978).

See also Christian Education; Derstine, Clayton Freed; Lark, James and Rowena; New England; Sunday Schools.

Sunday School Literature (ME IV:661). The major event in Mennonite °Christian education curriculum since 1958 was the development of the Foundation Series for children, youth, and adults as a cooperative project of five peace churches. Brethren in Christ, the General Conference Mennonite Church (GCM), and the Mennonite Church (MC) were publishing partners for all three units. The Church of the Brethren was a publishing partner for youth and adult and a cooperative user for children's material. The Mennonite Brethren Church was a cooperative user for the youth and adult series.

The Foundation Series replaced the series introduced in 1960 by the Mennonite Church (MC) as the Herald Graded Sunday School Series and by the General Conference Mennonite Church as the Living Faith Graded Sunday School Series. While using the same basic materials for these two curricula, each publisher revised the material to fit its needs. The Foundation Series advanced the level of cooperation by producing the same edition for all users. The children's curriculum, for which Paul M. Lederach was executive director, was introduced in 1977, and a revision was completed in 1986. Helmut Harder served as director for the adult and youth curriculum.

Use of the Foundation Series for children was extended to German-speaking churches by the Conference of Mennonites in South America, who translated the material for congregations in Brazil, Paraguay, and Uruguay. Beginning in 1980, the Hispanic Anabaptist-Mennonite Churches of the Western Hemisphere, with help from the Council of International Ministries, developed a Spanish-language curriculum for adults, based in part on the Foundation Series for Adults (Currículo Anabautista de Educación Bíblica Congregaciónal). Hector Valencia and Marta Quiroga de Alvarez served as editorial directors. In 1985, work was begun to develop a four-year curriculum for children using the basic concepts of the Foundation Series for children. Leticia Stucky served as its coordinator. Executive director for both projects was Arnoldo Casas.

Since 1960, the Mennonite Church (MC) and the General Conference Mennonite Church have published *Builder*, a Christian education monthly with helps for teachers of the *Adult Bible Study Guide* which has served both groups since 1974. In the area of storypapers, the General Conference *Junior Messenger* was combined with the Mennonite Church's *Words of Cheer* in 1971 to become *On the Line*. In 1967 *Der Kinderbote* for German-speaking children was transferred to Brazil, where it was published until the end of 1981, when it was discontinued. *With*, a monthly magazine for youth, was developed in 1968 by the General Conference Mennonite Church and Mennonite Publishing House (MC) to succeed the latter's *Youth's Christian Companion*. In the same year, Mennonite Publishing House introduced *Purpose*, a weekly storypaper for adults.

Since 1964, the Church of God in Christ Mennonite (Holdeman) has published its own Sunday school series. Through Gospel Publishers, Moundridge, Ks., they provide lessons for five age groups, pre-school to adult, using their own outlines to cover the Bible in four years. Some of these lessons are translated into Spanish for mission congregations in South America. The Holdeman church had earlier used materials from Rod and Staff Publishers, Crockett, Ky. (founded in 1958), whose outlines cover the Bible in seven years with lessons for five age groups as well as storypapers. Christian Light Publications, Harrisonburg, Va., founded in 1969, also publishes a full range of lessons based on the Uniform Lesson (International Sunday School Lessons) outlines. **MSh**

The Foundation Series Handbook, edited by Virginia A. Hostetler and Laurence Martin, published by Brethren Press, Evangel Press, Faith and Life Press, and Mennonite Publishing House, 1986.

Sunday Schools (ME IV:657). Three major developments have affected the Sunday school movement among Mennonites in the years since 1955. Sunday schools have become highly organized, extensive work has been accomplished in philosophy and curriculum development, and the educational settings of the congregation have expanded far beyond the confines of Sunday school.

Emphasizing organization and growth, Mennonites followed the example of mainline Protestant Sunday schools in the 1950s and introduced graded classes in all departments. Churches began to make long-range plans for education, train teachers, build proper facilities, and purchase equipment for the school environment. Training events undergirded the educational efforts of the church with courses offered in Bible study methods, teaching strategies, songleading, family life issues, and group leadership dynamics.

Also supporting the organized school was a new publication jointly produced by the Board of Education and Publication of the General Conference Mennonite Church, Newton, Ks., and the Mennonite Publishing House, Scottdale, Pa. Edited by Maynard Shelly, *Builder* was introduced in October 1960, with the purpose of supporting congregational education and providing helps for Sunday school teachers. Monthly columns were prepared with a special focus on adult, youth, and children's education. The magazine also included background biblical essays for Sunday school teachers.

A series of consultations and seminars over the next 20 years provided direction for educational philosophy and ultimately for curriculum development. In 1963, Christian educators, representatives of churchwide boards, pastors, and theologians participated in a study which developed a single objective for °Christian education in the Mennonite Church (MC): "Through Christian education, the church seeks to help all persons to know God as revealed supremely in Jesus Christ and the Scriptures; to become aware of who they are, of what their situation is, and of their alienation, to the end that they may repent of their sin, respond to God's redeeming love in faith, and become members of the body of Christ; to grow in Christ within the community of believers; to walk in the Spirit in every relationship; to fulfill the call to discipleship in the world; and to abide in the Christian hope."

In 1968, Paul M. Lederach, director of curriculum development in the Mennonite Church (MC), called for a clearer educational vision in his book, *Reshaping the Teaching Ministry*. Among the concerns addressed in the book are the inadequacy of Sunday school to educate people for Christian living, the separation of Sunday school from worship, the lack of clarity concerning the pastor's role in education, the need for teacher training, and the need for coordination among church agencies in providing educational resources for congregations.

In an effort to develop common understandings and a unified goal for congregational education, a four-day Christian education seminar at Laurelville Mennonite Church Center, Mt. Pleasant, Pa., in 1970 brought together representatives from all areas of Mennonite Church (MC) and General Conference Mennonite life. The slogan, "Enabling Adults in Mission," became the organizing focus for the years ahead. As a result of the seminar, more attention was given to Christian education as an experience-centered process. The educational ministry of the congregation was expanded to include such settings as decision-making by consensus, formulating congregational covenants, participation in marriage enrichment seminars and retreats, and experiencing growth through small group sharing in study and fellowship. Workshops were promoted in congregations with the purpose of helping adults understand how children, youth, and adults really learn. Laboratory methods of learning which emphasized self-discovery and involvement were promoted as well as responding to the Bible through art, drama, and writing. Elective studies were published to emphasize and develop the mission theme.

A major step was taken toward cooperative curriculum development in 1972 when leaders representing Mennonite, Church of the Brethren, and Brethren in Christ groups participated in a consultation at Camp Amigo, near Sturgis, Mich. After exploring the possibility of developing a new graded Sunday school curriculum for ages two through grade eight, three groups took action to become publishing partners (Mennonite Church [MC], Brethren in Christ, General Conference Mennonite Church) with one group (Church of the Brethren)

deciding to become cooperative users of the curriculum.

A publishing council and an editorial council with Paul M. Lederach as executive director were formed in 1973 to oversee the project. Global objectives for the joint curriculum project were (1) to provide congregations with educational materials containing information, methods, resources, evaluation; (2) to assist adults to share the heritage of the People of God, its history, its present life, and its destiny with children in the midst of the congregation; (3) so that the children, individually and corporately, will freely respond, to the full extent of their ability to Jesus Christ in love, in faith, in obedience. Called the *Foundation Series*, the new curriculum was first used in September 1977 along with new teacher training resources.

In 1976 a similar group met at the United Mennonite Church, Vineland, Ont., to test and develop a proposal for a new curriculum for youth and adults which would enlarge the Foundation Series. Under the oversight of executive director Helmut Harder, the new youth curriculum first began to be used in Sept. 1981. Also introduced in 1981, a two-year course for adults highlighted the faith understandings of Anabaptism. Not intended to replace the Uniform Series (International Sunday School Lessons) which had been the standard study series for adults, but rather to supplement it, the eight-part adult Foundation Series focused on such themes as community, faith development, the family of God, the Kingdom of God, peace, mission, stewardship, and the Word and Spirit.

Intensive teacher training supported these curricular developments. "Project Teach," a week-long, live-in teacher training event, which was first held at Bethel College (Ks.) in 1973, was jointly sponsored by the Commission on Education (GCM), Mennonite Board of Congregational Ministries (MC), and regional conference or district leadership. The week of learning included group studies in Mennonite history, Anabaptist theology, Bible study, and human development as well as classroom training in creative teaching methods. "Project: Teach" was succeeded in 1986 with a four-day weekend version known as ACT (Aid to Christian Teaching).

During the time that the church was investing heavily in Sunday school, other educational settings in the congregation also began to flourish. Midweek small group fellowships often studied the Bible together or reflected on current issues. Intergenerational family clusters experimented with a more flexible, experience-centered style of education. The growth and expansion of Mennonite °camps and weekend retreats added more opportunities for Christian education. The resulting proliferation of educational settings in recent years has tended to make the Sunday school less significant.

Although a desire to integrate worship and the various educational settings had been expressed since the 1960s, a renewed vision for integration was developed in a consultation held in March 1982, at Associated Mennonite Biblical Seminaries in Elkhart, Ind. Two years later leaders from Mennonite, Church of the Brethren, and Brethren in Christ churches met at LaGrange Park, Ill., to continue to discern a vision for congregational education which would meet the challenges of the 1990s. Growing out of these two events in 1982 and 1984, the Inter-Mennonite Task Force on Future Models of Education in the Congregation was appointed to plan for and develop a new model of education that would fulfill the vision for unity of congregational ministries (encompassing worship, community and mission) and enable congregations to be loving signs of God's reign in the world.

Mennonites have also sought to assess the impact of Sunday school participation. The Kauffman-Harder church member profile of 1972 measured this impact in five denominations (Mennonite Church [MC], General Conference Mennonite Church, Mennonite Brethren, Brethren in Christ, Evangelical Mennonite Church). Using criteria suggested by H. S. °Bender in *Mennonite Sunday School Centennial, 1840-1940* (Scottdale, 1940), researchers found that Sunday school has contributed positively to the life of the church and reinforces other types of religious commitment.

Compared to other major American denominations, Mennonites and Brethren ranked high in Sunday school attendance. Among the five groups, however, significant differences were observed in the level of Sunday school participation. The Evangelical Mennonite Church (MC) ranked highest followed by Brethren in Christ, then Mennonite Church, Mennonite Brethren, and finally the General Conference Mennonite Church. The age group least likely to be involved in Sunday school was 20-29 years old whereas those over 30 expressed a higher degree of interest. The more urbanized people are, the less likely they are to be involved in Sunday school.

The Kauffman-Harder study revealed that those who regularly participated in Sunday school scored significantly higher than others in biblical knowledge. They also scored higher on scales measuring personal piety, morality, and evangelistic involvement but not on social ethics.

Although the Sunday school has provided many opportunities for lay leadership in the church, those who regularly participated in Sunday school were slightly less likely than others to be committed to the concept of shared ministry. Kauffman and Harder concluded that one of the most crucial goals of an Anabaptist Christian education apparently has not been achieved by the contemporary Sunday school.

Though their research focused mainly on the Sunday school, Kauffman and Harder suggested that informal nurture in the family and community and corporate discernment among believers have traditionally been the way faith is transmitted among Anabaptist groups. Some evidence suggests that the introduction of Sunday school, a formal agency for Christian education with borrowed assumptions and emphases, has in fact contributed to the decline of corporate discernment as a significant context for Christian education among the descendents of the Anabaptists. In the future, new approaches for nurturing faith undoubtedly will be required to meet the challenge of forming Christians in the world. MKr

Arnold W. Cressman, "Input in the Consideration of a Philosophy of Christian Education for the Congregation" (background paper for the Philosophy of Education Seminar,

Sept. 13-16, 1968); Leland Harder, *Perspectives on the Nurturing of Faith,* Occasional Papers no. 6 (Elkhart: IMS, 1983); Daniel Hertzler, *Mennonite Education: Why and How?* (Scottdale, 1971); James E. Horsch, "The Objectives of a Believers' Church Curriculum," *Builder,* 26, no. 12 (Dec. 1976); Inter-Mennonite Task Force on Future Models of Education, "Growing Into Christ: An Educational Vision" (unpublished position paper, Nov. 1987); Kaufman/Harder, *Anabaptists Four C. Later* (1975); Marlene Kropf, "A New Model of Congregational Education," *Builder,* 37, no. 4 (Apr. 1987); Paul M. Lederach, *Handbook: Mennonite Commission for Christian Education* (Scottdale: MCCE, 1957); idem, Reshaping the Teaching Ministry (Scottdale, 1968); Wittlinger, *Piety and Obedience* (1978), 413ff.

See also Summer Vacation Bible School.

Swartzentruber, Amos (1893-June 2, 1966), with his wife Edna (Litwiller), the first Canadian Amish Mennonite missionaries, serving a short term in Youngstown, Ohio (1923), followed by work in Argentina (1924-63). Born near Baden, Ont., he worked for several farmers following grade school. He found salvation, at about the age of 15, in meetings he attended at a United Brethren Church in Kitchener. He was baptized at the Steinmann (Amish) Mennonite Church a few years later. His first wife, Clara Yantzi, died of cancer after three years of marriage. C. F. °Derstine, Peter Mayer, and other visiting preachers he heard at First Mennonite Church, Kitchener, Ont., and the Baden Mennonite Mission influenced him to attend Bible college. He enrolled at Bethany Bible Training School (CBreth) in Chicago, where he met Edna Litwiller a student from his home community. They were married June 23, 1920. Amos was ordained a minister Feb. 17, 1924, the day before he and Edna left for Argentina.

As a missionary Amos was a good administrator and manager. He was elected bishop in 1934. For most of his term of service he was treasurer of the Argentine mission (1927-58), chairman of the building commitee, and bishop. The family was faced with tragedy in 1947 as their daughter Doris and her husband Clifford Snyder and two children were enroute to missionary service in Argentina; Clifford died of a cerebral hemorrhage on board ship. Health conditions for Amos meant retirement in 1963. The couple moved from Argentina to Kitchener, Ont. JMB

John Bender, ed., *Pilgerleben, Pilgrims, Peragrinos* (Western Ontario Mennonite Conference, 1984); *Menn Bib. II,* p. 509.

Swartzentruber, Edna (d. Dec. 1976), with her husband Amos, the first Canadian Amish Mennonite missionaries. She was born at St. Agatha, Ont., an older sister of Nelson °Litwiller. She studied at Bethany Bible Training School (CBreth) in Chicago. Amos Swartzentruber subsequently enrolled at the same school. They were married on June 23, 1920, at the Steinmann (Amish) Mennonite Church, Baden, Ont. After farming briefly, the couple entered service with Mennonite Board of Missions (MC) Elkhart, Ind., first evaluating and closing its institutional mission at Youngstown, Ohio (1923), and then as missionaries to Argentina (1924-1963). They had three children, Doris, A. Orley, and Anita. In Argentina Edna taught the daily lessons for Bible readers, who in turn did home visitation. She was a good teacher and public speaker, a stern disciplinarian, and one with a sense of humor. While her main role was to manage the home, her oldest daughter comments, "I am sure that in this day she would qualify as a minister." After her husband's death in 1966 she moved back to Argentina and lived close to her youngest daughter and son-in-law, Anita and Raul Garcia, until her death.　　　JMB

YCC, 6 (1925), 765, 771, 781.

Swaziland, a kingdom in southern Africa (17,000 sq. km.; 6,700 sq.mi.; population [1982], 600,000). The first Mennonite Central Committee and Eastern Mennonite [MC] Board of Missions and Charities personnel arrived in Swaziland in 1971 to begin a program which is registered as "The Mennonite Board of Swaziland." The program began with three teachers in the Teachers Abroad Program. By 1976, there were 26 people working in vocational training, health, agriculture, handicapped concerns, Bible education, and church leadership training (mainly with the °African Independent Churches). In 1985 the program consisted of 17 people. There has always been a significant emphasis on working in cooperation with local churches and other established institutions. Due to Swaziland's geographic location, South African and Mozambican refugees have frequently been a major focus of the Swaziland Mennonite program.　　　GN

Sweden. Except for Melchior °Hoffman's visits to Sweden, Anabaptists seemed to have bypassed Scandinavia. Later the Lutheran state church suppressed all free church movements until the mid-19th c. Mennonite contact with Sweden has been largely circumstantial: participating in international church gatherings; young people attending Torchbearer's Bible School; Mennonite Central Committee (MCC) volunteers marrying Swedish spouses and settling there. Several books by Mennonite and Brethren in Christ authors have been translated into Swedish. Since 1983 Thomas and Disa Rutschman work in Jokkmokk as overseas missions associates with the Mennonite Board of Missions (MC). Their work consists of pastoring a small free church and related outreach efforts.　　　TR

Ronald J. Sider, *Kristus och våldet* (SKEAB, 1981); John H. Yoder, *Jesu Politik* (Verbum, 1984); articles about Anabaptism in *Nytt Liv* (1978, 1986) and *Kristna Freds* (1986).

Swift Current Colony, Bolivia, is located 50 km. (30 mi.) south of Santa Cruz, adjacent to the north edge of Riva Palacios colony. Swift Current colony was established in 1967 by Mennonites from the Swift [Current] colony in Mexico. There are 20 villages in the Bolivian colony. This Old Colony Mennonite group is under the leadership of bishop Peter Klassen. In 1986 the church consisted of 840 members within a total population of 2,510.　　　IHie

Swift Current Colony, Mexico. See Manitoba Colony, Mexico; Mexico (see also ME IV:669).

Switzerland. See Bern; Basel; Emmental; Schweizerisches Mennonitisches Evangelisationskomitee (SMEK; Swiss Mennonite Mission Committee); Schweizerisches Mennonitisches Friedenskomitee/Comité Mennonite suisse pour la paix (SMFK/CMSP; Swiss Mennonite Peace Committee).

Symbols (ME II:194) are words, images, sounds, objects, concepts, or actions which represent some other entities or realities. They have the power to unite different human feelings, thoughts, and experiences into coherent meanings. Symbols are polyvalent, carrying multiple meanings, and must be distinguished from signs. Signs give information and are limited to specific contexts, e.g., stop signs have no meaning outside of situations of potential danger and function only as warnings. Symbols, however, reveal realities beyond the context in which they are found and beyond the limits of their physical or conceptual boundaries, e.g., a gun is a symbol of violence, danger, coercion, or sport no matter where it is found. The realities discerned through symbols can only be apprehended by means of the symbols. Thus, they function as windows onto the unseen. Symbols share in realities they represent. Therefore, the basic characteristics or qualities of a symbol can be extended so as to "re-present" other realities. (To use an earlier example, a gun's structure and purpose is to stop movement or to intimidate a victim, thus the realities of death, fear, and power which it represents can be understood.)

Symbols cannot be created by manipulation. Words, objects, and actions may first emerge as signs in certain settings. Later, they may become symbols as they are repeated and more meanings and experiences cluster around them. Symbols emerge within communities which share a common worldview, common experiences, and common goals.

Religious symbols most often represent some aspect of the sacred presence which infuses life. (God is this presence in Judaeo-Christian traditions.) While this sacred presence cannot be directly perceived with human senses, it can be discerned and experienced symbolically. Many religious symbols are highly stylized and recur in the history of the tradition. They evoke certain feelings and memories in those who understand the objects or words to be symbols. A cross, an apple, a serpent, a lamb, the Bible, baptism, feetwashing, bread, and wine are examples of such symbols prominent in Christian faith. To understand these symbols is to know something of the nature of God and the experience of faith. Other religious symbols are more diffuse and less structured. They are generally not considered to be at the center of Chrisitan faith and experience; their meanings are contextually or culturally bounded. The °prayer veil, wedding bands, the dove, and various ceremonial artifacts are examples of diffuse symbols. Yet, in specific settings, these symbols have the power to represent to and for the community something of God's essence.

Since symbols arise from human experience, their meanings can only be discerned through the activities of human life. Religious symbols can communicate their meanings only as the realities they represent have been experienced by believers. The identity of a believer in any religious tradition results from being taught its primary symbols and from competently using or understanding them. °Worship is the primary setting where the religious symbols of a faith tradition are presented, experienced and appropriated. They reveal the worshiping community's basic beliefs. While these symbols may be taught and explained in other settings, it is in worship that they are lived. Through them the community of faith represents itself to God and to the world, and the Godhead is represented to the community. Thus, religious symbols have a reflexive character; through them two-way communication is possible.

Each religious community or tradition reinforces certain symbols, consciously or unconsciously, according to the frequency of their presentation in worship. Among Roman Catholics, for example, the symbol of the eucharist is essential to worship. For contemporary Mennonites the eucharist (°communion) is not an essential symbol for worship, even though it is an important observance. Congregational °singing, hearing God's word, and °preaching are essential symbols. The symbols which are repeatedly presented in the worship context will shape the °spiritual life of that community. Attention will be focused on certain aspects of the sacred realities represented in these symbols while other aspects may be forgotten or ignored. This process, in part, accounts for the distinctions found among various Christian traditions.

While it may be assumed that the community of faith selects and regulates the symbols presented in worship, it may also be presumed that each individual believer has certain symbols which are particularly meaningful for private devotion. These symbols may correspond to the believer's tradition or community. The symbol(s) may be borrowed from other traditions or emerge from a significant experience in the believer's life. These private symbols will shape the spirituality of the individual, providing a point of orientation for his or her decisions, ethics, and life-style.

Anabaptists and Mennonites have been particularly suspicious of religious symbols ever since their beginnings in the 16th c. Ulrich Zwingli's restricted view of symbolism in worship was shared by most Anabaptists. A symbol, in their view, functioned essentially as a sign with obvious and unambiguous meanings. Zwingli's ideas about symbols were a reaction to the stylization and excessive manipulation of symbols found in the Catholic Mass. He and the Anabaptists failed to grasp the fact that human beings are symbol-making and symbol-utilizing creatures. Human activity or interaction is impossible without the use of symbols. Only through the medium of symbols can the gathered community encounter the presence of the persons of God in worship.

There is a tendency in °modern culture and among Mennonites in general to limit the meanings of commonly used religious symbols and symbolic activities. The temptation to concretize the symbol's meaning or to create a one-to-one correspondence between symbol and meaning is strong. However, the meaning of symbols, particularly religious symbols are polyvalent, expressing a variety of meanings. This multiplicity provides for richness in personal and corporate religious experience. This fact explains how common symbols, like communion, can stir controversy within congregations and between churches when certain meanings are emphasized over other possible meanings. Many of the recent °ecumenical discussions with regard to baptism, eucharist (communion), and ministry have emphasized expanding and incorporating the various traditional meanings clustered around these symbolic actions and coming to agreement on the range of possible meanings.

At the risk of exclusion, the following religious symbols may be said to be primary for Mennonites. (1) The *person of Jesus*—a symbol of God revealing God's nature and relationship to humankind. (2) The *Word of God*—a symbol of the incarnated Christ, the written biblical text revealing the activity of God in the world and the authoritative and creative power of preaching. (3) The *Cross*—a symbol revealing the means of human salvation, a life of suffering, submission, and discipleship. (4) The *community of faith, the church*—a symbol revealing the presence of Christ in the world, the reality of God's kingdom, the mission of evangelization, the locus of Christian fellowship, mutual accountability, and support. (5) *Baptism*—a symbol revealing personal salvation, new spiritual life, a commitment to Christianity, fellowship in the community, accountability, and discipleship. (6) *Communion*—a symbol revealing the covenant of salvation between God and humanity, fellowship, reconciliation, gratitude, and the memorial of Christ's passion. (7) *Congregational singing*—a symbol revealing congregational unity, personal submission to the community, public affirmation of faith, and spiritual vitality. (8)*Bible study*—a symbol revealing the desire for faithfulness and moral living, congregational unity, democracy, fellowship, and belief in the authoritative power of God's word. (9) *Prayer Veiling*—a symbol (for some Mennonite women) representing humility, submission to Christ's headship, and separation from the world. RSl

"Religious Symbolism and Iconography," *Encyclopedia Britannica*, 15th ed. (1985); Evelyn Underhill, *Worship* (New York: Crossroad Books, 1937; reprinted 1982) 3-59; *Symbol: The Language of Liturgy* (Federation of Dioceses Liturgy Conference Study Book, Washington, D. C., n.d.); Adrien Nocent, "Gestures, Symbols and Words in Present-day Western Liturgy," in *Symbol and Art in Worship*, ed. Luis Maldonado and David Power, Concilium Series, 132 (New York: Seabury, 1980), 19-27; Susanne Langer, *Philosophy in a New Key* (Cambridge, Mass: Harvard, 1960); Rollo May, *Symbolism in Religion and Literature* (New York: George Braziller, 1960); Mary Douglas, *Natural Symbols: Explorations in Cosmology* (New York: Pantheon Books, 1982); *GH* (Nov. 17, 1987), 806.

See also Confessions of Faith; Folk Arts; Folklore; Graphic Design; Ordinances; Ordnung; Worship, Public; Worship, Private.

T

Taipei, Taiwan. Located in northern °Taiwan, Taipei is not only the administrative seat of the government of the Republic of China, but also the principal cultural and economic center and transportation hub. With a 1986 population of 5.5 million, it is the fastest growing city in Asia. Taipei is an international-class city, and combines the best of old China and modern Taiwan.

Taipei is also the center for many Christian churches, mission agencies, and theological seminaries. The central offices and guest centers for both the General Conference Mennonite mission in Taiwan and the Fellowship of Mennonite Churches in Taiwan are located in Taipei. Seven of the 17 Mennonite churches in Taiwan are in Taipei.   SVS

Taiwan is an island located 100 miles (160 km.) off the se. coast of China, opposite Fukien Province, astride the Tropic of Cancer halfway between Japan and the Philippines. Two-thirds of the island of 13,885 sq. mi. (35,962 sq. km.) is mountainous. Formerly known as Formosa (Portuguese for "beautiful island"), Taiwan (Chinese for "terraced bay") is governed by the Nationalist Chinese party (Kuomingtang) as the Republic of China. In its history, the island was occupied by the Spanish, Dutch, Chinese, and Japanese (1895-1945), reverting to China in 1945.

With a 1986 population of 19.5 million, it is the second most densely populated country in the world. Seventy percent of the population resides in the urban areas. Eighty-three percent of the population is Taiwanese, southern Chinese who immigrated to Taiwan in the early 17th c. Ten aboriginal tribes of Malayo-Polynesian background along with refugees from the Chinese mainland are minority groups. Mandarin Chinese is the official language, though the Taiwanese dialect is the mother tongue of the majority.

Economically, Taiwan is highly developed, ranking among the six largest exporting countries in the world. Per capita gross national product is expected to surpass $13,000 (US) by the year 2000. Since 1950 Taiwan has moved from agrarian land reform through labor-intensive industry to high technology industry. Infrastructure development projects have made Taiwan a country with modern and efficient transportation and telecommunication.

°Buddhism, Taoism, and religious Confucianism along with popular folk religion are practiced by the people of Taiwan. Only three percent of the population is considered Christian. The Presbyterian Church of England began mission work in southern Taiwan in 1865 under James Maxwell, and in 1872 George MacKay from the Presbyterian Church of Canada began medical and evangelistic work in northern Taiwan. Today the Presbyterian Church is the largest and oldest Taiwanese Christian church. Following World War II, numerous other mission groups entered Taiwan to establish churches.

Mennonite Central Committee (MCC) was invited by the Presbyterian Church to begin relief and medical work in Taiwan in 1948, and the General

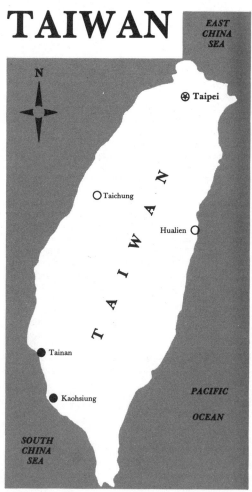

TAIWAN

LEGEND:
MENNONITE CHURCHES IN TAIWAN
○ Centers of the Fellowship of Mennonite Churches in Taiwan
★ Capitol city
● Other cities

Kilometers   0   25   50   100

870

Conference Mennonite mission followed with church planting work in 1954. In 1986 there were 17 Mennonite congregations of the Fellowship of Mennonite Churches in Taiwan located in three major cities of Taiwan. In addition the Mennonite Christian Hospital is located on the east coast.   SVS

MWH (1978) 183-87, (1984) 41; Sheldon V. Sawatzky, "The Gateway of Promise: A Study of the Taiwan Mennonite Church and the Factors Affecting Its Growth," (MA thesis, Fuller Theological Seminary, 1970).

Takeda Jiro (b. 1932), first pastor of the Nihon Menonaito Burezaren Kyoden (Japan Mennonite Brethren Conference), was born in Kyushu. His father was a casualty of World War II, which greatly prejudiced Jiro *Takeda* against foreigners. But while seeking employment in Osaka, to fill a void in his life he visited various churches and the former Mennonite Central Committee center which had become the Konohana church (MB). The peace position greatly appealed to him. He was baptized on June 23, 1955.

In April 1957 he entered the Mennonite Brethren Bible Institute's first class. The following year he married a fellow student, Sumiko *Yagi*. Upon graduation, he assisted missionary Jonathan Bartel and subsequently became pastor of the Konohana church, later relocated at Tamagawa, where he was serving in 1986. In April 1969, he was ordained to the ministry. He has served as chairman of the Mennonite Brethren Conference, and has been active in cooperating with other evangelicals, having served as vice-chairman of the Osaka Crusade, office manager for the Billy Graham Crusade, and chairman of the Kansai area Japan Protestant Conference.

Two sons were born into the family and the elder, Shinji, is the first second-generation pastor among the Mennonite Brethren. Pastor Takeda's younger brother is also a pastor with the conference.   HaFr

Tan King Ien. See Persatuan Gereja-Gereja Kristen Muria Indonesia.

Tanase Takio (b. Mar. 14, 1929), a leading minister and teacher of the Nihon Menonaito Kirisuto Kyokai Kyogikai, Hokkaido (Japan Mennonite Christian Church Conference, Hokkaido), was born in Tokyo. Later he moved to Hokkaido where he met Ralph and Genevieve °Buckwalter. He was baptized in Kushiro in 1952, while helping them with mission work.

After study at Hesston College and Goshen College (1954-57), he became pastor of the Tsurugadai congregation in Kushiro. The following year he married Aiko *Harada*. They became parents of two children. Except for one year at the Hombetsu congregation in 1959, he continued to serve the Tsurugadai congregation, largely in a self-supporting capacity. He again went to Goshen in 1969, receiving a BA degree from Goshen College and an MRE degree from Goshen Biblical Seminary in 1972.

In 1965 he helped to organize the Eastern Hokkaido Bible School, where he served for many years as director and head teacher. Later the school moved to Obihiro, and there, besides teaching, he served on the pastoral team of the Obihiro congregation.

In the spring of 1987, he moved back to Tokyo and began serving part-time as pastor of the Honancho Christian Church. He is also involved in writing and translation work with the Japan Mennonite Literature Association.   HMo

Takio Tanase, "How My Understanding of Mission Has Developed," *Miss. Focus,* 15 (Sept. 1987), 39-40.

Tanganyika. See Tanzania.

Tanzania, United Republic of. Formerly known as Tanganyika, Tanzania is located in East Africa along the Indian Ocean and is bounded to the north by Kenya and Uganda, to the west by Rwanda, Burundi, and Zaire, and to the south by Zambia, Malawi, and Mozambique. Its topography includes Africa's highest peak (Kilimanjaro), Africa's largest lake (Victoria [Nyanza]), and Africa's deepest and longest lake (Tanganyika). The Great Rift Valley bisects the nation from north to south. The climate is low-latitude wet and dry, with heavy rains from March to May, a dry season from June to October, short rains from November to December, and a short dry season in January and February. The natural vegetation is savanna grassland with scattered thorn forest. Several national parks with wild animals have been established.

The people, comprising more than 120 tribes, are mostly Bantu. There are also Nilo-Hamites (e.g., the Masai and Luo), a few groups related to Khoisan of southern Africa, and some Asian and European peoples. In 1978 the population was 17 million.

From the 12th to the 15th c. the Arabs had a flourishing trade on the east coast. The Portuguese in the 16th c. ravaged the main port city Kilwa and other coastal cities, but the Arabs continued the slave trade from Bagamoyo. In the 19th c. two German missionary explorers, Krapf and Rebmann, gave Germany a basis for its claim to Tanganyika. Great Britain recognized this claim in return for Zanzibar and Heligoland. After World I the territory was mandated to Great Britain under the League of Nations. After World War II it became a trust territory under United Nations.

Julius Nyerere launched the movement for independence in 1954; in 1961 he became the nation's first prime minister. In 1963 he was chosen as president of the republic. In 1964 Tanganyika united with the islands of Zanzibar and Pemba to form the new nation Tanzania. It is a one-party state with a parliamentary form of government. Nyerere, a Christian from the mainland, was head of government, 1961-87. He was succeeded by Mwinyi, a Muslim from Zanzibar.

The capital is being transferred from Dar es Salaam inland to Dodoma. The socialist economy is being relaxed in the 1980s to allow for more private enterprise. Tanzania is one of the poorest nations in the world, but is determined to fend for itself. Its war with Uganda to drive Idi Amin from power (1978-79) increased the poverty; shortages of fuel and basic supplies were commonplace. The government changed its socialist policies beginning in 1986 and devalued its currency. It has depended on sisal, coffee, cotton, tea, gold, diamonds, and tourism for income. In spite of poverty Tanzania has the highest literacy rate in Black Africa. Universal primary

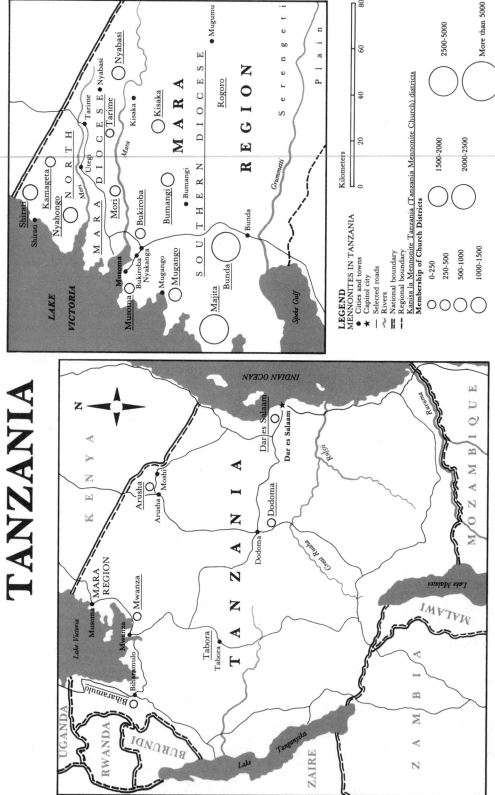

TANZANIA

Membership data as of 1982. From Mahlon M. Hess, Pilgrimage of Faith of Tanzania Mennonite Church 1934-83 (Musoma: Tanzania Mennonite Church, 1985).

LEGEND
MENNONITES IN TANZANIA
- Cities and towns
★ Capitol city
Selected roads
≈ Rivers
National boundary
Regional boundary
Kanisa la Mennonite Tanzania (Tanzania Mennonite Church districts

Membership of Church Districts
- 0-250
- 250-500
- 500-1000
- 1000-1500
- 1500-2000
- 2000-2500
- 2500-5000
- More than 5000

education was undertaken in 1977 and adult literacy programs have helped increase literacy to over 50 percent.

Mennonite mission efforts date from 1934, and resulted in the Kanisa la Mennonite Tanzania (Tanzania Mennonite Church) whose autonomy was recognized in 1960. After the church received government recognition, the mission was dissolved. Lancaster Mennonite Conference (MC) and its mission board (Eastern Mennonite Board of Missions and Charities) now relate directly to the Tanzania church assisting with limited personnel and finance. In 1961 Mennonite Central Committee (MCC) established its Teachers Abroad Program in Tanganyika, providing teachers in schools managed by government and other denominations. The MCC program has been enlarged to include medical and community development personnel. DLW

Mahlon M. Hess, *Pilgrimage of Faith: Tanzania Mennonite Church, 1934-83* (Salunga, Pa.: Eastern Mennonite Board of Missions and Charities, 1985), originally appeared in Swahili as *Safari Ya Imani*); *MWH* (1984), 16; George R. Anchak, "Experience in the Paradox of Indigenous Church Building: History of the Eastern Mennonite Mission in Tanganyika, 1934-1961 (PhD thesis, Michigan State U., 1975).

See also Kanisa la Mennonite Tanzania; Kenya Mennonite Church.

Tanzania Mennonite Church. See Kanisa la Mennonite Tanzania.

TAP (Teachers Abroad Program). See Development Work; Inter-Mennonite Cooperation; International Relations; Mennonite Central Committee.

Taxes (ME IV:687) and war are inextricably linked together. When governments wage war, they eventually levy taxes to pay for them. The taxes may be explicit or indirect. Unfortunately most citizens find themselves implicated in making payments to a military leviathan, regardless of which century or country they live in. Anabaptists almost consistently avoided °military service but, with the exception of the Hutterites, expressly urged payment of tax money which made war possible. Can Mennonites still be °conscientious objectors when the primary tool of war is money?

For 16th-c. Hutterites the issue of "blood money" was clear and unequivocal. They could see no significant difference between fighting a war and supporting it with taxes. Still Anabaptist and Mennonite histories reveal a lot of indecision about the propriety of paying military-related taxes. Much of this is due to the widespread assumption that there was a biblical mandate to pay all taxes much like other financial obligations. These assumptions are being challenged again by scholars and others in the 20th c.

Conscience was alive among Mennonites and Dunkers (Church of the Brethren) on Nov. 7, 1775, when they submitted a joint declaration to the General Assembly of the Commonwealth of Pennsylvania, saying that they were ready at all times to help those in need, but that they were "not at Liberty in Conscience to take up Arms to conquer our Enemies." Drafters of the U.S. constitution (1783-89) recognized the equivalence of con-

scientious objection to war taxes as well as military service, by the °historic peace churches. Recognition of this connection failed to remain in the final draft of the second amendment to the constitution. As a result, states then required payment in lieu of military service.

In Prussia Mennonites were disinclined to pay the military and church taxes based on land ownership. By the 1780s they were apprehensive about the growing military preparations, particularly the annual tax of 5,000 *thaler* required for the support of military schools. This factor prompted many to relocate in southern Russia and was among the factors leading others to form the °°Kleine Gemeinde by 1814.

There were no income taxes in the United States until 1862, when they were imposed to pay for the °Civil War. Americans were outraged at the imposition of war taxes, which were lifted again in 1872. It is notable that the first proposal of a general federal government income tax was made in 1815, in part to pay for the expenses of the war of 1812-14.

When Mennonites were migrating to Kansas an existing law (1865) required the payment annually of a $30 fine for the privilege of exemption from military service. In response to recommendations from the governor, the legislature repealed the "onerous tax" on Mar. 9, 1874.

Income taxes reappeared in the United States in 1913 just in time to pay for °World War I. It was a "class tax" upon the wealthy. Most Mennonites were not affected by it. However, they cooperated with patriotic expectations as best they could, "developing their own programs of voluntary benevolence and relief to provide a moral equivalent of military service and war bond drives." With increased pressure practically everyone "bought a few bonds." Bond drives were a problem in that they were designed not only to finance the war but also to foster patriotism. The bonds did focus the money aspect of war (Margaret Entz in *Menn. Life* [Sept 1975], 4-9), and some Mennonites who refused to buy bonds suffered violence as a result.

World War I proved to be a watershed experience for the Mennonites. Their confrontation with the government's military authorities on the draft was so traumatic that the peace churches turned almost the whole of their attention to military duty requirements and forgot their testimony against taxes for war.

World War II saw the Victory Tax of 1943 established as the first "mass tax" through withholding at the source of income, the employer. Continued uneasiness with governmental pressure to purchase war bonds led to a Mennonite Central Committee effort to substitute "Civilian Bonds." However, U.S. Treasury officials did not clearly commit themselves to use the proceeds strictly for civilian purposes.

The war tax issue remained largely dormant during World War II. The first Mennonite to mention the subject was Austin Regier, a nonregistrant, who was sentenced to a federal penitentiary for refusing to comply with the draft. He firmly believed that "the consistent pacifist would refuse war taxes." The idea of organizing war tax resistance in the United States seems to have begun with the Peacemaker Movement which was formed by a heterogenous group of pacifists in Chicago early in 1948.

An increasingly larger portion of the U.S. federal budget has gone to finance past, present, and future wars in the 1970s and 1980s. Numerous statements have been issued as part of a new wave of concern beginning in 1958. "A Call to Action" was issued by Mennonites and Brethren in Christ meeting in Minneapolis on Nov. 21, 1970. *The Way of Peace,* a Christian declaration supporting war tax refusal, was adopted by the General Conference Mennonite Church at Fresno, Cal., on Aug. 19, 1971. Other statements and resolutions followed in 1974, 1977, 1980, and 1983. The Mennonite Church (MC) issued resolutions in 1979, 1981, 1985, and 1987. A special conference (GCM) was held in Minneapolis in February 1979 specifically to discuss and explore war tax options. The General Board was mandated "to use all legal, legislative, and administrative avenues for achieving a conscientious objector exemption." This followed the Inter-Mennonite/Brethren in Christ War Tax Conference held in Kitchener, Ont., Oct. 30-Nov. 1, 1975. In response to the growing war tax concern, the Commission on Home Ministries (GCM) began publishing the *God and Caesar* newsletter in January of 1975.

As early as 1959 the °°Society of Friends introduced into the U.S. Congress the "People's Program for Peace" bill. They also circulated a proposal called the "Civilian Income Tax Fund." Other peace tax fund legislation was formulated in 1973. Many Mennonites had refused to pay the telephone excise tax during the Vietnam War.

In March 1974 a Mennonite pastor, Michio Ohno, refused to pay his allotment for Japanese military expenses. Out of the protest, Japanese Fellowship of Reconciliation members, Quakers, Mennonites, and other nonviolent activists worked together to form a group called COMIT (Conscientious Objection to Military Tax). Within 10 years COMIT grew to 400 members, half of whom have filed to refuse payment to the military. Since 1981 22 members have brought their appeal to the Tokyo Local Court to challenge the Japanese Government and its tax offices for collecting and spending tax funds unconstitutionally. Hearings have been held 23 times during a five-year period. The judges seem to be avoiding their responsibility. The issue of national defense is so political that the courts refrain from making a decision.

In 1975 Cornelia Lehn (a Canadian citizen) requested her employer, the General Conference Mennonite Church, to refuse to withhold taxes from her salary. Months of intense, agonizing debate followed. In the 1980s similar requests by church employees came before both the Mennonite Church and the Mennonite Central Committee. Both institutions declined to comply with employee requests and continued to withhold taxes and forward the money to the government. Finally, on Sept. 1, 1983, the General Conference Mennonite Church honored such requests. By official conference action "the employees of the Church administration are given the power to be true to the high demands of Christ's Law of Love, in that they can decline to remit withholding taxes from employees that have requested it and therefore open up the possibility to resist for

reasons of conscience to pay for the preparation of war." The conference reported these decisions to the federal government's Internal Revenue Service (IRS) but as of Sept. 21, 1987, no action had been taken against the conference. Because of this shift of attention to the corporate level new opportunities for witness have opened up. It is believed that never before in U.S. history have employers refused to withhold taxes for those employees who request this action for reasons of conscience.

In 1978 "Conscience Canada" was organized at the instigation of a few Quakers in Victoria, B.C. John R. °Dyck of Saskatoon, Sask., is among the Mennonites who invested energy in this peace education effort. In 1980, Canadians learned that "freedom of conscience" was to be included in the new constitution. Since 1982 this recognition of conscience has become the basis for a new wave of action to create a legal alternative to paying taxes for war. (Peace tax legislation was introduced in 1983 and 1985. The first nationwide meeting was held in April 1987 at Ottawa). Citizens are preparing a test case.

An increase in open tax resistance is evident despite the Tax Equity and Fiscal Responsibility Act of 1982 which provides that, in the United States, an individual "shall pay a penalty of $500" if he or she files an income-tax return that is incorrect due either to taking a frivolous position or to seeking to delay or impede administration of the tax law. The 1982 tax law is unique in that there is an automatic penalty imposed on taxpayers. Futhermore, the penalty is assessed before opportunity for appeal is given. This is quite discriminatory and suggests that the IRS may be guilty of violating the fourth amendment of the United States Constitution.

Italy has demonstrated that legislation can remove the burden of military taxes. Italians accused of propagating the Peace Tax Campaign since 1981 have been fully acquitted on "grounds of particular moral and social value," or "the act did not amount to a crime." Peace tax campaigns have emerged, not only in Japan, Canada, Italy, and the United States, but also in Germany, Spain, Switzerland, France, Great Britain, Belgium, New Zealand, Australia, Luxembourg, Austria, Norway, South Africa, Sri Lanka, and The Netherlands. This movement has gathered such momentum that an International Peace Tax Campaign Conference was held for the first time in Tübingen, West Germany, Sept. 18-21, 1986. Marian Claassen Franz of Washington, D.C., was among the 100 people who met to share information with War Resisters International in London. In 1987 the IRS approved tax deductible status for the Peace Tax Foundation. The campaign for a Peace Tax Fund in the United States now can focus its limited resources on °lobbying, while the foundation expands its outreach and research programs.

Conscientious objectors to war in the United States recognize that the solution to their dilemma of conscience concerning the government's tax demands lies in the United States Congress. "So long as the Internal Revenue Code is deficient in recognizing freedom of conscience as protected by the first and ninth amendments, we shall be journeying through this dungeon of IRS levies, summonses and court trials. *The origin and the solution to our problem lie most immediately with Congress,* and ultimately with a restored public community of conscience" (Robert Hull, 1987). Today's combat soldier is the taxpayer—the person who provides the money to produce and deploy the push-button hardware and software for mass annihilation. Individuals shoulder great responsibility for warfare and for peace. At times the most effective way to take responsibility is to refuse to collaborate. The task is progressively to make the coercion of conscience unthinkable by the majority who put their faith in military solutions.   DDK

Bibl. on War and Peace (1987), 185-200; Linda B. Coffin, Peter Goldberger, Robert Hull, Jay E. McNeil, *Fear God and Honor the Emperor: a Manual for Military Tax Withholding for Religious Employers* (Philadelphia and Elkhart: Friends Committee on War Tax Concerns and New Call to Peacemaking); Donald D. Kaufman, "War Taxes: Should They Be Paid?" *Program Guide 1971* (Scottdale), 38-42; Wolfgang Kraus, ed., *Was Gehört dem Kaiser? Das Problem der Kriegssteuern* (Weisenheim am Berg, West Germany: Agape Verlag, 1984), 127 pp. and response by Victor Janzen, "Gebt dem Kaiser was des Kaiser's ist," *Der Bote,* 60, no. 21 (May 25, 1983), 21; Dale W. Brown and Vernard M. Eller, eds., "Symposium on Tax Resistance," *Brethren Life and Thought,* 19 (1974), 101-24; Richard K. MacMaster, Samuel L. Horst, and Robert F. Ulle, *Conscience in Crisis* (Scottdale, 1979), 29-31, 68, 78-80, 113-15, 247-49, 354-62; C. J. Dyck, ed., *Intro. to, Menn. Hist.* (1967), 52-53, 106, 120-34, 295-98; John L. Ruth, *'Twas Seeding Time: A Mennonite View of the American Revolution* (Scottdale, 1976), 59-88, 162-63; idem, *Maintaining the Right Fellowship* (Scottdale, 1984), 150-58; Margaret Entz, "War Bond Drives and the Kansas Mennonite Response," *Menn. Life,* 30 (Sept. 1975), 4-9; Melvin D. Schmidt, "Tax Refusal as Conscientious Objection to War," *MQR,* 43, (1969), 234-46; John Howard Yoder, "Why I Don't Pay All My Income Tax," *GH* (Jan. 22, 1963), 81, 92, cf. *Mennonite* (Feb. 126, 1963), 132-34, and *Sojourners,* 6, no. 3 (Mar. 1977), 11-12; John Howard Yoder, *The Christian Witness to the State* (Newton, 1964), esp. p. 54; Duane K. Friesen, *Christian Peacemaking and International Conflict: A Realist Pacifist Perspective* (Scottdale, 1986), 134-40; Richard J. Goossen, "An Examination of the Legal Justification for War Tax Resistance: The Scope of Freedom of Conscience under the Canadian Charter of Rights and Freedoms," *CGR,* 4 (1986), 21-42 with response 4 (1986), 158-60; Guy F. Hershberger, *The Mennonite Church in the Second World War* (Scottdale: MPH, 1951), ch. 11, pp. 138-148, on "Civilian Bonds"; idem, *The Way of the Cross in Human Relations* (Scottdale, 1958), 167, 178, 184, 196-97; *Consultation on Civil Responsibility*—a resource packet of 15 papers presented at Elkhart, Ind. (June 1-4, 1978) under the auspices of the General Conference Mennonite Church; *The Way of Peace,*—position statement (GCM), Aug. 1971 (Newton, 1972); Robert Hull, "1040 Peace Tax Form," (Newton: Commission on Home Ministries, Peace and Justice, GCM, 1987), 1-8; E. Stanley Bohn, "The Missionary and the War Tax Refuser," *Mennonite* (June 11, 1985), 308; Howard H. Charles, "The Troublesome Tax Question," *Builder* (Nov. 1972), 19-20, 30; Leo Driedger, "Positions on Tax Dollars for War Purposes," a 6-page compilation circulated by the Board of Christian Service (GCM) (Newton, 1960); Edith Adamson and Marian Franz, "Struggling with Taxes for Military Force," *Mennonite* (Mar. 10, 1987), 104; *MWR* (Aug. 31, 1978), 6 (Japan); Levi Keidel, "The Mennonite Credibility Gap," *Mennonite* (Dec. 23, 1975), 730-31; Elmer Neufeld and John Unruh, report of MCC Peace Section meeting held in Chicago, Ill., Jan. 21, 1960 (Akron, Pa.: MCC), 1-5; Ernie Regehr, *Making a Killing* (Toronto: McClelland and Stewart, 1975); Eugene K. Souder, "Nonresistant People and the Federal Income Tax," *GH* (Dec. 27, 1960), 1103; Ruth C. Stoltzfus, "War Tax Research Report: Challenging Withholding Law on First Amendment Grounds," a special study prepared for Commission on Home Ministries (GCM)," (Aug. 1975), 1-16; John E. Toews, "Paul's View of the State," *Chr. Leader* (Apr. 25, 1978), 5-7; Edward Yoder, "Christianity and the State," *MQR,* 11, no. 3 (July 1937), 171-95; idem, "The Obligation of the Christian to the State and Community—'Render to Caesar'," *MQR,* 13, no. 2 (Apr. 1939), 104-22; LaVernae J.

Dick, "A Noose for the Minister," *Mennonite* (Apr. 21, 1964), 263-65; Marian C. Franz, "Conscience is Contagious," *Mennonite* (July 28, 1987), 316-19; Robert Kreider and Mary S. Sprunger, *Sourcebook: Oral History Interviews with World War One Conscientious Objectors* (Akron, Pa.: MCC, 1986), esp. pp. 116, 128ff.; United States Comptroller General, *Illegal Tax Protesters Threaten Tax System* (Gaithersburg, Md.: U.S. General Accounting Office, Document Handling and Information Services Facility, July 8, 1981), 70pp; Juhnke, *Mission* (1979), 123 (Japan); *Minutes* (BIC) (1986) 40-41; *MWR* (Jan. 8, 1987) 5 (on Japanese war tax trial, 1986); *Menn. Rep* (May 11, 1987), 1.

See also Church-State Relations; Nonresistance; Peace; Spanish Lookout Colony, Belize; Tithes.

Teachers Abroad Program (TAP). See Development Work; Inter-Mennonite Cooperation; International Relations; Mennonite Central Committee.

Technology. Most Mennonites have accepted technological advances. They have contributed to these advances and benefited from them.

  Agriculture. Mennonites were known as excellent farmers throughout their history. They generally used the same technology as other farmers but put in extra effort to get the best results with the technology available. Mennonites in southern Germany and the Alsace have been viewed by some scholars as innovators in livestock breeding and crop rotation techniques; the claim is disputed by others. In the 19th c. better quality steel led to improvements in agricultural machinery. In Russia, in the 19th c., this meant production of higher quality wagons, plows, mowers, reapers, and threshing machines. The Russian Mennonites made improvements on this agricultural machinery to adapt it to local conditions and make it easier to repair and maintain. Often, also they were able to produce such machines cheaper than imported models. In North America, Mennonites were making similar improvements in agricultural machinery in the 19th and on into the 20th c. Examples would be the production of straw blowers, self-feeders for threshing machines, and refinements in other harvesting machinery.

  Mills. The Dutch had become very adept at building and using mills powered by wind to pump °water so that land could be drained for agricultural use. The Dutch Mennonites used this technology in The Netherlands and took this skill with them across northern Europe as they moved eastward. They not only built and operated the mills but also engineered the drainage systems. In Prussia mills were also used for producing flour from the grain grown on the drained soil. On the Russian steppes and on the prairies of North America the mills were used more as grist mills and saw mills. This particular skill has helped make Mennonites more welcome in each of the locales where they have been.

  Transportation. Mennonites generally accepted the transportation technology that was available to them. The Dutch people were adept sailors; Dutch Mennonites were active in various maritime endeavors. Horses and wagons were used by European Mennonites when this was the common mode of transportation. Especially in Russia, the Mennonites became very good wagon manufacturers. Later, when steam and internal combustion engines made tractors, trains, automobiles, bigger ships, and airplanes available, Mennonites generally accepted these as well. There were some exceptions, however (see below).

Manufacturing. The Dutch Mennonites were active in shipbuilding, the related lumber business, food industry, and the textile industry. These industries carried over to Prussia and Russia. New modes of power like steam made large flour mills possible in Russia, much bigger than those powered by the windmills of the previous centuries. Agricultural machinery was manufactured on a large scale in Russia, including wagons, mowers, plows, and threshing machines. In North America, Mennonites have been involved in many areas of manufacturing, including as in previous centuries, the food industry, lumber business, flour mills, and agricultural machinery. Some of the °plain people are still excellent wagon manufacturers.

Communication. European Mennonites used the same means of communication as transportation made possible. Publishing was also done by the available technology. In the 19th and 20th c., when newer technologies came into common use, the Mennonites used these as well. These included the telephone, telegraph, television, offset press, photocopying, laser printing, and other computer-generated technologies. These recent technologies have raised many questions even though they have been commonly accepted and used by Mennonites. They threaten to introduce many undesirable values into the home through °television and related technologies. For Mennonite businesses and institutions it raises questions of the right to privacy and the use of information to manipulate or take advantage of other people. There is a concern that people remain able to control technology and not vice versa.

Not all Mennonites have adapted to changes in technology. Old Order Mennonites, Old Order Amish, Old Colony Mennonites, some Sommerfeld Mennonites, Old Order River Brethren and others have been very cautious in adopting any technology which potentially threatened their traditional way of life. Some have accepted a non-rubber-tired tractor as something that was an asset, and, if kept under control, would not threaten their way of life. Some have not accepted the °radio or television because they would be a liability and would threaten their way of life. These technologies would allow a direct invasion of the outside world into their homes which could potentially bring unacceptable changes. Their basic motivations are both religious and pragmatic. They prefer to retain the old and tried technology which has not threatened their ways of life.

Mennonites have always tried to help members of their own community in need (°mutual aid). In the 20th c. they have also begun helping others. This has brought them in contact with peoples of other cultures who use other technologies. It has raised the question whether one should place a higher value on one technolgy over another. The approach taken by Mennonite °development workers has generally been that one does not categorize technologies in a way that makes one better than another. Rather they have sought to adapt available technologies to local situations. For example, Eric Rempel of Manitoba, Canada, helped Africans develop a farm implement using local materials and skills

which they could easily manufacture and maintain. European or North American Mennonites might categorize this farm machinery as less efficient than their own machinery. However, they were quite willing to support Rempel in his work. The same Rempel helped North American native peoples develop a wild rice harvester which they could use for their local needs. This piece of machinery is much more complex than the one Rempel developed for the Africans but it met the needs using locally available and understood technologies. In both cases, technology was used to benefit people rather than imposing supposedly superior technologies which would not have been adaptable (°appropriate technology).

Technology needs to remain a tool for individuals, the church, and society to use. If it becomes a master or is imposed from the outside, Mennonites would generally deem it inappropriate technology. Therefore, technology will continue to be viewed, adapted, and used in the broader context of the ultimate purpose for people on this earth.   BF

Jean Séguy, "Religion and Agricultural Success: The Vocational Life of the French Anabaptists from the 17th to the 19th C.," *MQR*, 47 (1973), 179-224, cf. idem, *Les Assemblées anabaptistes-mennonites de France* (The Hague: Mouton, 1977); Dominique Varry, "Jacques Klopfenstein and the Almanacs of Belfort and Montbéliard in the 19th C.," *MQR*, 58 (1984), 241-57; James Urry, "Through the Eye of a Needle: Wealth and the Mennonite Experience in Imperial Russia," *JMS*, 3 (1985), 7-35; C. J. Dyck, ed., *Intr. Menn. Hist.* (Scottdale, 1967); W. H. G. Armytage, *A Social History of Engineering* (London: Faber and Faber, 1961); J. Ellul, *The Technological Society* (New York: Alfred A. Knopf, Inc., 1964, 1976); George Grant, *Technology and Empire* (Toronto, 1969); *Unterhaltungsblatt für die deutchen Ansiedler im Südlichen Rußland*; this periodical contains a series of articles which mention Mennonite technological contributions, 1849-61, copies at Centre for Mennonite Brethren Studies, Winnipeg; *Odessaer Zeitung* 1876-88; Calvin W. Redekop, *Old Colony Mennonites* (Baltimore: Johns Hopkins U. Press, 1969), e.g., 137ff; John A. Hostetler, *Amish Society* (1980); idem, *Hutterite Society* (1974).

See also Ecology; Industrialization; Modernity.

He Drove a Ford

On °Java, one of °Indonesia's 3,000 islands, lived a wealthy Chinese businessman, Tee Siem Tat. This talented and determined man ran several businesses—he sold office machines and supplies, he sold dairy products, he sold car tires and oil, and he did printing for a cigarette company. But Tee had a problem. He was sick. His body was sick and his mind was anxious, and nothing helped him get well. He had asked the Chinese temple priests for help. He had also tried six different Dutch doctors. (It was the Dutch who controlled Indonesia at that time.) Not one could find anything wrong with him.

Mrs. Tee said, "Why don't you see if the Christians can help you?" Now nearly all Indonesians who weren't Chinese like Tee (and thus of the Buddhist and Confucian religions), were Muslims. As for Christians, there were very few, only some of the Dutch plus some missionaries who had come to Indonesia when the Dutch came. The Tees did know a little about Christianity already. They knew that the Christians had some good schools. For that reason Mr. Tee had enrolled his three children in a Catholic school, even though they had to be baptized to enter the school. Baptism meant nothing to him if his children could get a good education there.

Mrs. Tee knew a little more about Christianity than her husband. Her aunt had gotten a Bible to find out more about Christianity. Then she had decided she wasn't interested after all and gave the Bible to her niece. Mrs. Tee would read it sometimes late at night, crying when she read about Jesus dying on the cross. Tee didn't want her to read the Bible and said, "Why do you read this book? It belongs to the Dutch religion."

So Tee had tried everything he knew of to get well—except to try Christianity as his wife suggested. He began to seek out and to talk to Christians to find out what they believed. He began to study Christianity and the Bible. In his searching he became acquainted with missionaries from different missions, but none seemed to him to follow the Bible. Finally Tee talked to a Dutch Mennonite missionary and found that his teaching on baptism agreed with what Tee was learning from the Bible.

Tee, who had been busy studying and learning and thinking, suddenly realized that he was well again! His sickness had gradually gone away.

Tee began to give his time and money to sharing his beliefs with his family and with the other Chinese. At first they avoided him. To them becoming a Christian was treachery. It was betraying all their customs and beliefs.

But Tee was a persuasive person, and God was with him. On Dec. 6, 1920, Tee and 25 other Chinese were baptized in Tee's home. By October more than 100 had been baptized. Tee then asked the Dutch Mennonite missionaries to help in this work with the Chinese. "We really can't do that," they said, "we have been sent to work with the Indonesian people, not the Chinese."

Not too long after cars had been invented and were being manufactured, Tee had bought a Ford. Now Tee began to use this Ford to travel out from °Kudus, where he lived, witnessing wherever he went. Mrs. Tee always went along with him. She could talk to those whom Mr. Tee, because of Chinese customs, could not talk to—the women.

From town to town they drove, seeking out the Chinese and beginning to have gatherings. They would meet in someone's home, or in a school room, or on the veranda of a hotel, or in a tobacco warehouse—wherever they could get permission to meet. Later on the groups, as they became large enough, built church buildings.

For 20 years Tee worked faithfully as God's witness to the Chinese in Java. When he died in 1940, there were 300 Chinese Christians in eight churches. In Chinese families the sons usually followed the fathers in their work. So it was in Tee's family. His son and son-in-law became leaders in the church. Later his grandson, Herman Tan, was the first from their church to study overseas.

By 1982 Muria Christian Church of Indonesia, as it's now called, had 6,750 Christians in 50 congregations, and in 1984 one of its leaders, Charles Cristano, was president of Mennonite World Conference.   MH

Excerpted from "The Witness Who Drove a Ford," in "God's Witnesses" (unpublished). Used by permission of Mennonite Board of Missions (Elkhart, Ind.). Also published in *On the Line* © 1988, Mennonite Publishing House. Used by permission.

See also Persatuan Gereja-Gereja Kristen Muria Indonesia.

Television has been accepted by most Mennonites but with uneasiness caused by its images of violence, immorality, and materialism. Most recognize it as a powerful medium of communication that should be used for evangelism and Christian teaching.

The Brethren in Christ, whose General Conference had once banned photography, opted in 1951 to use education to control the negative power of television, warning its members to use television with care.

A survey of church leaders by the *Mennonite Weekly Review* in 1968 found that 68 percent in the General Conference Mennonite Church, 42 percent in the Mennonite Church (MC) and 34 percent among Mennonite Brethren approved of television. In contrast 100 percent of Amish and Church of God in Christ Mennonite (Holdeman), leaders disapproved of television. Holdeman teaching aims to keep television, °radio, and "mind-corrupting" books and periodicals, as carriers of North American culture, out of the home. Hutterites find radio and television destructive of the discipline of colony life and therefore avoid it.

Kauffman and Harder in the 1972 study of Mennonite and Brethren in Christ life found that adult church members were watching television 1.2 hours a day and 27 percent admitted that television ads influenced their buying practices. In 1976, Joe Bridges, media consultant for the United States Mennonite Brethren conference, said that the negative impact of television could be overcome "if we realize the potential of television and use it to reach people where they are."

Discussion of the use of television during the last quarter century has focused on its disciplined use. In 1961, Mennonite Broadcasts asked its people to commend the television industry for "its constructive programs in religious and educational fields and in reducing objectionable features such as hard liquor advertising" and to ask for "further steps to improve its programming." In early 1977 the *Mennonite* (GCM) and *Gospel Herald* (MC) sponsored a series of critical articles by Larry Kehler who urged concern for "the battle between the beautiful potential of our children and the wild beast which lurks within an untamed television set."   MSh

Kauffman/Harder, *Anabaptists Four C. Later* (1975), 123-24, 240-41, 287-88; Henry Weaver, "Television: Friend or Foe?" Focal Pamphlet Series, 8 (Scottdale, 1962); *MWR* (Apr. 4, 1968), 4-6; *GH* (Jan. 3, 1961), 19, (May 14, 1968), 432-34, (June 11, 1968), editorial, (Nov. 3, 1970), 925-26, (Mar. 20, 1973), 245, (Mar. 1, 1977), 192, (Sept. 2, 1980), 693; *Mennonite* (Feb. 18, 1964), 110-11, (Oct. 17, 1967), 628, (Apr. 30, 1968), 320, (Mar. 14, 1972), 184; S. Roy Kauffman, "Life Without Television," *The Other Side* (Oct. 1987), 36-40; Wittlinger, *Piety and Obedience* (1978), 347; LaVerna Klippenstein in *Chr. Living* (April 1987), 13.

See also Amusements and Entertainment; Broadcasting, Radio and Television; Conservative Mennonite Church of Ontario; Eastern Pennsylvania Mennonite Church; Mass Media; Nonconformity; Old Order River Brethren; Radio (opposition to).

Templar Movement (ME IV:693). The German Temple movement grew out of the religious ferment in mid-19th c. Württemberg. Under the influence of the Swabian Lutheran theologian J. A. Bengel (1687-1752) and the popular writings of J. H. Jung-Stilling (1740-1817) the °Pietist reaction against the modern historical-critical theology of David Friedrich Strauss (1808-74) was both strong and varied. Christoph Hoffmann (1815-85), the theologically trained son of the founder of the separatist Pietist community at Korntal near Stuttgart (Wilhelm Hoffmann), was among the more vocal critics. He defeated Strauss in the election to the German constitutional assembly, the Frankfurt Parliament, of 1848, but lost faith in the political process there and returned to his other interest—teaching and missions. Together with the Paulus brothers (grandsons of Philipp Matthäus Hahn), he operated a school which attracted the attention of Nikolai Schmidt, a prominent Mennonite from Gnadenfeld (Molotschna), who in turn sent a young student, Johannes Lange, to this school.

At this school, located at the Kirschenhardthof (a property near Stuttgart), Lange, together with others, became a "friend of Jerusalem" (*Jerusalemsfreund*), as members of the movement came to be known. Hoffman had determined that the circumstances, bad economic times combined with new religious doubts, called for a drastic restitution of the "people of God" that would in effect constitute a rebuilding of the temple in Jerusalem. How literally or figuratively this was to be understood never became completely clear.

Earlier (around 1817) whole Swabian settlements had relocated to southern Russia and other eastern points, motivated by both hard times and eschatological teachings. The Temple idea appeared to be in line with these and, apparently, with the thinking of some Russian Mennonites, whose pilgrim theology led several groups to "places of refuge" (see Claasz °°Epp). The educational emphasis of the German Templars should not be overlooked. It undoubtedly attracted some of the more intelligent young Mennonites and helped to bring about a second division within the "large" church at Gnadenfeld (the Mennonite Brethren had separated in 1860). Like the Mennonite Brethren, the Templars, who did not use the "Temple" name at the outset but were known as the "Evangelical Mennonite Church of Gnadenfeld," had to relocate along with these into the Kuban and Caucasus areas. In the Temple settlements which arose at Wohldemfürst, Alexanderfeld (Kuban) and Tempelhof and Orbelyanovka (Caucasus) Mennonites and non-Mennonites mingled, though Mennonites like the Schmidts and the Langes continued to play an important role and the Mennonite Templars continued to think of themselves as Mennonites, claiming from the Russian government the °privileges of that group.

Friedrich Lange, brother of Johannes, became the first major historian of the Temple Society. The family of Nikolai Schmidt eventually built a house on the outskirts of Jerusalem. In later periods Russian Mennonite names (e.g., Dyck, Fast, Arndt) played a role in the all-too-eventful future of the Temple Society, as it came to be known. Severe dislocations resulted from the two World Wars and eventually the Templars were removed from the "Holy Land" to Australia and Germany, where they maintain a minor presence.   VGD

N[ikolas] Arndt, "Erinnerungen eines Olginoers" (110-page typescript, Melbourne, 1977); P. M. Friesen, *Brotherhood*, index; Heinrich Sawatzky, *Templer Mennonitischer Herkunft* (Winnipeg: Echo Verlag, 1955; translation in progress); Victor G. Doerksen, "Mennonite Templers in Russia," *JMS*, 3 (1985), 128-37; idem, "Eduard Wüst and Jerusalem," *MQR* 56 (1982), 169-78; Paul Sauer, *Uns rief das Heilige Land. Die Tempel gesellschaft im Wandel der Zeit* (1985); James Urry, "The Closed and the Open: Social and Religious Change Amongst the Mennonites in Russia (1789-1889)" (diss., Oxford U., 1978), esp ch. IX, 2.

See also Apocalypticism.

Tennessee (ME IV:694). In 1988 there were congregations representing six different Mennonite and Brethren in Christ conferences. The Beachy Amish Mennonite Fellowship had seven congregations with a total membership of 419. Several conferences of the Mennonite Church (MC) had established congregations as follows: Virginia (2 congregations, 67 members); Atlantic Coast (1, 20). Indiana-Michigan conference had a new church planting effort in Nashville. The Brethren in Christ Central Regional Conference had three congregations with total membership of 154. There was also one congregation of the Church of God in Christ Mennonite (Holdeman), at Monterey. In 1985 there were four Old Order Amish settlements with a total of seven congregations (districts). Three of these settlements were established after 1974.   RSa

MC Yearbook (1988-89), 41-42; Luthy, *Amish Settlements* (1985), 2, 12; Wittlinger, *Piety and Obedience* (1978), 452.

See also Ethridge, Tenn., Old Order Amish Settlement.

Texas (ME IV:701). Since 1957 membership in Texas Mennonite churches has more than doubled, growing from 500 to more than 1,000 in 1987. Eight congregations affiliated with the Mennonite Church (MC) had a membership of 282. A Conservative Mennonite Conference congregation in San Antonio had 33 members. Five congregations dually affiliated with the General Conference Mennonite Church (GCM) and the Mennonite Church (MC) in Dallas, Fort Worth, and Houston had 174 members. The Houston Chinese church (GCM) had 28 members. Eight Mennonite Brethren congregations had 241 members. One congregation was dually affiliated (MB, MC) and had 35 members. A congregation in Paris (42 members) was affiliated with the Mid-West Mennonite Fellowship. Three unaffiliated Mennonite congregations had 44 members. Two Brethren in Christ congregations numbered 49 members. A Beachy Amish Mennonite congregation of 61 members and a group of German-speaking Mennonites from Mexico and Canada near Seminole (1977) with ties to the Evangelical Mennonite Mission Conference (62 members) complete the roster.

Employment opportunities in dairy and poultry farming attracted Old Order Amish families to the areas of Gonzales, Boling, and Dublin between 1980 and 1983. Many of the Amish intended to work just long enough to acquire funds for purchasing farms in their home communities located throughout the Midwest. Not all families regard their stay in Texas as temporary, however. The three communities, totaling 42 households, appear stable and permanent.

As many as eight °voluntary service units in Texas have been affiliated with the Mennonite Board of Missions (MC) in the past 25 years. In 1987 active units were located only in San Antonio and Brownsville. Additional voluntary service units are located in Dallas (GCM) and San Antonio (Conservative Mennonite Board of Missions).   JHU

MC Yearbook (1988-89), 42; William P. Kuvlesky, "Ethnic Subculture and Social Change: The Case of the Old Order Amish in Texas" (paper presented at the Annual Meeting of the Southern Association of Agricultural Scientists, Biloxi, Mississippi, February 1985); idem, "Some Amish Move a Lot: The Old Order Amish in Texas" (paper presented at the 1987 meetings of the Southern Association of Agricultural Scientists, Nashville, Tennessee); Anna Hiebert Esau, *What God Has Wrought* (Winnipeg and Hillsboro: Kindred Press, 1988); Luthy, *Amish Settlements* (1985), 12.

Thailand (formerly Siam), a country in Southeast Asia. Mennonite Central Committee (MCC) began involvement in Thailand in 1960 by placing workers at the Prae Christian Hospital. Later that year, two °°Pax volunteers began work at an experimental farm in Chiang Rai. From 1963 to 1975 MCC had no programs in Thailand. In 1975 two MCC workers from Vietnam began working in Thailand with the Church of Christ in Thailand. In 1979 MCC began working with Indochinese refugees flooding into Thailand (job creation, social services, peace concerns, agriculture and education). The MCC office in Bangkok also provides logistical support for MCC work in Indochina. There were eight MCC volunteers in Thailand in 1987.   BS

Theological Education by Extension (TEE) is a ministry-oriented model of church leadership training whose primary purpose is to provide training for people who are already serving in church leadership positions. One author has called it "simply decentralized theological education. It is a field-based approach which does not interrupt the learner's productive relationship to society" (Mulholland, p. 66). TEE is distinguished from traditional models of leadership training by several factors, of which the most obvious is the "extension" element. As an extension program, the training is offered at a location near the student's home eliminating the need to spend months or years in preparation at a °Bible school or °seminary. One of the main visions of the TEE model is "to encourage and enable local leaders to develop their gifts and ministries without leaving their homes, jobs, communities, and local congregations" (Kinsler, p. 30). TEE is a flexible program which is able to adjust to the needs and abilities of the students and can be developed and adapted to the local situation and meet particular needs. For this reason it has been finding increasing acceptance over the past few years, particularly by the growing churches in developing countries.

In 1963 the Presbyterian Seminary in Guatemala began a new leadership training program which became known as Theological Education by Extension (TEE). This program was in response to the observation that the conventional theological curriculum which they offered was not meeting the needs of the young, growing church. They observed that many of the rural churches were without pastors while a high percentage of the seminary graduates did not remain in ministry, but were engaged in other occupations. The original educational model consisted of home study materials, weekly classes with an instructor at several regional centers near the students' homes, and monthly meetings of all students together at the central campus. The program continued to develop and adapt in the following years and soon spread to other parts of Latin America and the world.

Since its beginning in 1963, TEE has become increasingly popular in the young, growing churches of Africa and Latin America. According to the "World Directory of Theological Education by Extension" the total enrollment in TEE programs worldwide grew to 14,000 by 1972, and to more than 55,000 by 1980 (Youngblood, p. 13).

In general, the TEE model of leadership training is a response to the following problems: (a) Conventional residential Bible schools and seminaries have not provided enough church leaders to keep up with the needs of rapidly growing churches. (b) Many people, including some already serving as pastors, would like to study theology and leadership but are unable to enroll at a residential school because of the high cost of training or because of commitments to family, jobs, and church leadership. (c) Students who attend the residential schools tend to be young and inexperienced and have not proven themselves in church leadership roles. Also, many of the seminaries are in urban settings, and it is difficult for the students to return to ministries in rural, agricultural areas and to adjust to life in these areas, which are often economically depressed. As a result of these factors, a high percentage of the students do not continue as pastors following graduation, but often obtain other employment in urban areas. (d) Conventional theological education tends to be isolated from actual involvement in ministry and too often the students are not prepared to apply the concepts they have learned to the needs they encounter in the local churches. (e) The high cost of operating and maintaining a conventional Bible school increases the dependence on outside resources, since many of the younger churches do not have the ability to administer that kind of program without outside assistance.

The typical TEE program has three main parts. (a) Lesson materials are prepared for individual study by the student at home. Through these materials, the student gains the facts and knowledge relating to the course of study. Many of the materials are in the form of programmed instruction. This form of instruction, with its well-defined objectives and instructions for self-study, seems to be most appropriate considering the educational background of many of the students. (b) *"Seminar" meetings* are held weekly, several times a month, or monthly so that the students can discuss the material they learned in their individual studies and consider how it applies to their life and church work. The seminar meetings are usually held in existing church buildings or schools in regional centers near the homes of the students. (c) Because TEE is training for ministry, *field experience* is an important part of a TEE program. The lesson materials are written to include work assignments which relate in practical ways to the student's own ministry. Since the students are normally involved in leadership positions, the knowledge gained in the lesson materials and through sharing in the seminars can be applied almost immediately.

According to information published by the Mennonite Christian Leadership Foundation in 1986, there were at least 27 different Mennonite-related TEE programs in 20 different countries of Africa, Latin America, and the Caribbean. The Eastern Hokkaido Bible School in Japan is a similar nonresidential program. There is at least one TEE program among the Indian Mennonites of Northern Ontario. More than 2,600 students are enrolled in the various Mennonite-related TEE programs.

The first TEE program in the Tanzania Mennonite Church was started late in 1982 in the North Mara Diocese. In 1985, a similar program was started in the South Mara Diocese. The Mennonite Theological College in Musoma had been closed in 1981 because of the small percentage of graduates who entered church ministries and the general feeling among church leadership that the overall benefit to the church was not enough to justify the cost of operation. The TEE program began with 5 regional centers (seminar locations) and approximately 75 students enrolled. By 1987, in both dioceses, there was a total of 18 regional centers and approximately 450 students enrolled. Most of the students were lay church leaders who were in charge of small, local congregations. The teaching staff included two expatriate missionaries and six local pastors. Besides the benefits of providing training in biblical studies and church leadership, the TEE program has also encouraged a sense of community and mutual support among the church leaders of Tanzania Mennonite Church.

In Central America, a program with a vision similar to TEE is SEMILLA (Seminario Ministerial de Liderazgo Anabautista [Anabaptist Ministerial Seminary for Leaders]), which has more than 100 students enrolled from eight Central American countries. In this program, the instructors travel to the various countries to hold classes for the students from that country. The students engage in individual study during the intervals between the classes, which are held for several days at a time and several months apart. The studies offered through SEMILLA are on a higher academic level than those generally offered through TEE. SEMILLA is administered by representatives from Mennonite and Mennonite-related churches in each of the Central American countries involved.

In recent years, there is increasing interest among North American Mennonite regional conferences in developing educational programs with a format similar to TEE, in order to provide preparation and in-service training for church leaders ("conference-based theological education"). JB

Agustin and Rosario Batle, *Theological Education by Extension: A Guide for T.E.E. Workers in Developing Countries* (Nairobi: Uzima Press, 1983); Fred Holland, *Teaching Through T.E.E.* (Nairobi: Evangel Publishing House, 1975); Jonathan Hogarth, Kiranga Gatimu, and David Barrett, *Theological Education in Context: 100 Extension Programs in Contemporary Africa* (Nairobi: Uzima Press, 1983); Donald R. Jacobs, *Leadership Training Programs: Mennonite and Brethren in Christ, Covering Africa, Asia, Latin America and the Caribbean* (Landisville, Pa.: Mennonite Christian Leadership Foundation, 1986); Ross F. Kinsler, *The Extension Movement in Theological Education*, rev. ed. (Pasadena: William Carey Library, 1981); Kenneth B. Mulholland, *Adventures in Training the Ministry* (Presbyterian and Reformed Publishing Company, 1976); W. Frederic Sprunger, *TEE in Japan: A Realistic Vision* (Pasadena, Cal.: William Carey Library, 1981); Robert L. Youngblood, ed., *Cypress: TEE Comes of Age* (Exeter: The Paternoster Press, n.d. [ca. 1985]).

See also Indian Ministries, North America; Pastoral Education.

Theologies from the Two-Thirds World.

In the 1970s and 1980s theologies have arisen within social, economical, and political situations in the impoverished countries (also called Third World or Two-Thirds World) where there is a scandalous and frightening contrast between the Christian faith and the practice of that faith. People in Africa, Latin America, and Asia have lived and experienced the use of the Christian faith as the ideology of Europe and North America. The repressed peoples have felt manipulated by a theology of dominion that has been used by the dominating countries to exploit, colonize, and impoverish other peoples.

From the early 1960s, various social, economic, and political circumstances favored the development of new ways to interpret the Scriptures and to live out the Christian faith. Christians in exploited and dependent countries began asking how one could best be a Christian in the midst of so much misery, exploitation, and violence. In the wisdom of the Asiatic peoples, the vitality of the African nations, and the poetic aggressiveness of the Latin Americans, cultures are observed which have not lost their religious values. These peoples have been able to integrate in their world of magic their autochthonous values with the values of a Christianity brought to them from Catholic or Protestant centers.

While missionary movements coming from rich countries expanded in the impoverished nations (especially since World War II), a clear sense of dependence, marginality, and increased misery arose, and with this, revolutionary, nationalistic and decolonization movements became stronger. National Christians recovered for the church the meaning that history is the place where God works. But it is a history seen through the eyes of the poor and oppressed: not that of the dominating first (democratic-capitalist West) or second (socialist-communist Eastern Bloc) worlds. Thus the °kingdom of God not only incorporates the biblical idea of this history, but also gives meaning to the Christian faith as the future of this record in favor of the poor.

Inasmuch as the history of the various rich nations has been lived in cultures and norms that differ from life in Africa, Asia, and Latin America and has been a chronicle of dehumanization, slavery, and all forms of violence, a salvation is needed that is not atomistic and individualistic as modern Western Christian theology teaches. Salvation must be seen not only as salvation from personal sin but must shed light on a historicized concept of sin, that is also part of social and political structures that create poverty and dehumanization. From this perspective, salvation is revealed as an experience of liberation from all injustice.

The church movements in areas of poverty and injustice (which also include social groups and marginalized areas within the wealthy countries) are of such complexity and variety that it is not possible to formulate a global vision of the problem. Only the most characteristic features and emphasis in the historic process of Christians reflecting theologically in situations of injustice are noted here: (a) The theological discourse is oriented toward a critique of the dominant ideology of development, capital, and the values of a rich world conveyed with a Christian covering. (b) Underdevelopment is discovered to be the result of causes emanating from developed countries that seek to keep less developed countries dependent and indebted. Reflection through the Bible makes people aware of these structures. (c) This context of social injustice and biblical interpretation promotes a concern with pastoral practice. (d) The orientation and practice of the believing communities differ from that of the missions which, in a great part, has been mere expansion of the Western, North American, and European world. (e) The universality of the gospel is not expressed in a dominant culture but rather in the peculiarity of each culture. Capitalistic imperialism and international socialism are less universal in character than the gospel. Therefore traditions, autonomous cultures, and a genuine spirituality are elevated above Western secularization. (f) The poor are considered to be the focus of God and all Christian practice is directed toward them. It is among the poor where the faith is lived and theological reflection is organized as an evangelizing announcement as well as a condemnation of all injustice. (g) The fundamental theological topics or emphasis arise from the sociocultural characteristics and the human needs of each area. In Latin America the practice of the historic Jesus and his preference for the poor is emphasized. The African theologies combine the belief in the Great God with respect for °ancestors, with the Spirit and with the christological experience of an "Adam-redivivus" (Adam renewed or restored in Christ). In Asia, voluntary renunciation in favor of the poor is taken as a search for God and as a profound spiritual answer against imposed misery and western secularization.

The basic question in the theologies of the impoverished peoples is not a matter of absolute content but it is a way of doing theology. It is a problem of praxis and obedience.

Traditional theology uses philosophy as the instrument for analysis and promotes an interiorization of the faith, then subsequently tries to apply it to the needs of life. That is, first is theology, then putting it into practice.

In the theologies of impoverished peoples, obedient practice is first. This Christian praxis uses the social sciences as an instrument for analysis since the problems of the community have to do with social and economic situations and structures. From the praxis and in dialogue with the biblical text, theological creation and doctrinal discourse come forth as second in importance. In other words, these theologies, rather than offering content, show a new way to interpret, to re-read the biblical text, starting from an unjust reality which is known and in which the Christian faith in suffering love is practiced as the solution. The Bible is interpreted from a concrete situation of suppression, a re-reading that produces a fresh look at the biblical text.

The Mennonite churches in the evangelized nations have inherited the virtues and defects of the theologies brought by the Mennonite mssionaries from the power centers. Some brought a clear understanding of the Anabaptist vision of missions while others copied and brought °dispensationalist models from North America. Although some Mennonite communities in Asia, Africa, and Latin America have inherited non-Mennonite theological content, it has been the contact with reality and a deepening of the faith that has caused them to be creative in their way of living the faith.

Mennonite churches in the impoverished nations owe their theological creation and depth to the efforts of mission agencies; nationalism and social, political and above all, ideological independence from the North American and central European power centers; and to the search for Christian identity in the midst of violent and unjust societies. The role of the missionary has changed so that the direction and theological reflection are in the hands of those who make up the sociocultural context where they live the faith. Each national church convention is autonomous, establishing a fraternal relationship as equals with any church in the rich countries, without inferiority complexes or a colonialistic spirit. In these churches Anabaptist content coincides with some of the theological concerns of impoverished countries (kingdom of God, °peace and °justice, the lordship of Christ, pardon, repentance, °reconciliation and °suffering as signs of the cross and the testimony of the presence of the Spirit, the Christian community as a sign of the kingdom). HZ

MQR, 58, supplement (Aug. 1984), sp. issue; Julio de Santa Ana, *Towards A Church of the Poor* (Geneva: World Council of Churches, 1979); idem, *Separation Without Hope?* (Geneva: World Council of Churches, 1978); Cyril H. Powles, "Christianity in the Third World: How Do We Study History?" *Studies in Religion*, 13 (1984), 131-44; José Miguez Bonino, *Doing Theology in a Revolutionary Situation* (Philadelphia: Fortress Press, 1975); LaVerne A. Rutschman, "Latin American Liberation Theology and Radical Anabaptism," *Journal of Ecumenical Studies*, 19, no. 1 (1982), 38-56; Jon Sobrino, "Teología de la liberación y teología europea progresista," *Misión abierta*, 77 (1984), 395-410; Adrian Hastings, "On African Theology," *Scottish Journal of Theology*, 37 (1984), 359-74; Aloysius Pieris, "L'Asie non sémitique face aux modèles occidentaux d'inculturation," *Orientierung*, 49 (1985), 102-6; Harold W. Fehderau, "Missions and the Younger Churches," in *The Church in Mission*, ed. A. J. Klassen (Fresno: MB Board of Christian Literature, 1967, 266-85; Wilbert R. Shenk, ed., *A Kingdom of Priests: The Church in the New Nations* (Newton and Scottdale, 1967).

See also Liberation Theologies; Mission.

Theology (ME IV:704). In classical Greek theology meant the knowledge of God or teaching about °God and divine matters (*theo*, God; *logos*, word or study). The New Testament does not use the concept "theology." But the Bible knows and teaches about the one God who has created the world, called Israel and the Church, and seeks to redeem humankind through Jesus Christ and the Holy Spirit. The Scriptures therefore contain theology understood as a distinctive knowledge and language about God, about God's speaking and acting in relation to humankind and the world, and about human responses to God's acting and speaking.

For definitional reasons, it is useful to distinguish theology from doctrine. Doctrines are teachings regarding Christian beliefs and practices, which are considered normative for the Christian church, such as the doctrine of °salvation through Jesus Christ, the Son of God. Judgements on which teachings should be normative for the Christian church, however, frequently differ among various groups and communities. Mennonites, for example, consider believers °baptism and the rejection of violence as well as salvation through Jesus Christ normative doctrines. Such doctrines are normally correlated with theology, but are not identical with it. Theology usually seeks to interpret, justify, correct, and defend commonly held doctrines, their assumptions, and their potential implications. Theologies also frequently try to deal with everything which is desirable to teach as well as that which is essential. They may therefore range more widely and vary more greatly than would normally be the case for doctrines. For example, the doctrine of believers baptism may be interpreted and defended primarily in terms of the nature of the °church or of the reality of faith or of following Jesus' example. And it may be related to and explained in terms of a general theory of °ordinances or °symbols or sacraments.

Both theology and doctrine may be explicitly stated and formulated in spoken or written forms. Or they may be implicit and operative in °worship, church °traditions and practices, patterns of personal and group piety, or standards of Christian conduct. Implicit and operative doctrines frequently, and perhaps even normally, become explicit and official through disagreements and disputes about what should be acknowledged as °authoritative or normative. For example, controversy about the baptism of °°infants during the Protestant Reformation contributed to the development of explicit doctrines of believers baptism (by Anabaptists and Mennonites) and of infant baptism (by Lutherans and the Reformed) and their accompanying theologies. Or, controversy about the °°Incarnation contributed to the "heavenly flesh" doctrine, which was in turn later disputed and modified among the Dutch Mennonites.

In its explicit forms, theology can be understood as disciplined, discriminating, and comprehensive reflection on and articulation of normative Christian teachings and practices in a particular time and place. Christian theology arises and is carried out primarily within the community of faith in the attempt to articulate the presuppositions, content, and consequences of faith in Jesus Christ for the doctrine, practices, and spirituality of the Church and of individual believers.

In Western Christianity, theology as a discipline of study and teaching has frequently been further differentiated at least into systematic or dogmatic theology, apologetic or foundational theology, and practical theology. Systematic theology is primarily concerned with faithfulness to normative beliefs and practices. Apologetic theology seeks primarily to defend and explain Christian beliefs and practices in terms which can be intelligible to those who have not (yet) come to faith. Practical theology focuses on the application of normative beliefs and practices in the life of the Church and the believer.

In its concern for faithfulness, theology draws from specific sources and renders itself accountable to specific criteria. These usually include the Bible, learnings from tradition, contemporary experiences and insights of the faith community, and disciplined thought. Theologies differ considerably, depending on the relative weight granted to these sources and criteria.

Theologies also differ significantly in the degree to which they seek to be comprehensive (summarizing normative beliefs and practices as a whole) or occasional (focusing on specific issues). With the exception of the Dutch Mennonites in the 19th c. and some contemporary North American Mennonites, most theological reflection and articulation among Mennonites has been occasional *rather than* comprehensive and has claimed to be rigorously biblical *rather than* also drawing significantly upon the resources of tradition, experience, and logic as appropriate.

Mennonites have frequently viewed "theology" with suspicion and distrust (ME IV:704). Their emphasis on the importance of °discipleship and ethics most likely contributed significantly to Anabaptist and Mennonite suspicions of theology since the 16th c. as they found it in the Roman Catholic tradition and the emerging Protestant groups. To some degree their distrust of theology was also conditioned by their experience of °persecution and theological justification of persecution by both Protestants and Catholics. To a minor degree, their suspicions may have reflected an anti-intellectual stance. But in spite of these suspicions, one should not overlook the fact that early Anabaptist and Mennonite teachers were in conversation, through their writings and debate, with leading theological voices of their time.

The major reason for their suspicions of the dominant theologies was based on the ways they saw theological interpretation used to detract from the hard sayings of Scripture (for example, in relation to baptism or the rejection of violence), or to justify doctrines which appeared to make no demands (faith apart from discipleship), or to perpetuate a form of °legalism by putting all doctrines on the same level. They also decried what seemed to be a lack of careful controls for interpreting the sense of Scriptures and the reservation of theology for the experts only. For them the true test of a theological statement was its compatibility with the life and doctrine of Jesus Christ and the apostles. The measure of true theological understanding depended not primarily upon the level of intellectual ability but upon the openness and abandonment to God's will as revealed in Jesus Christ and the teaching and example of the apostles. Throughout their subsequent history, Mennonites have frequently dogmatized this critique and expanded it into a general anti-theological stance rather than discriminating between good and bad theology.

Contemporary scholarship has characterized the

theological orientation of 16th-c. Anabaptism in several ways. These models represent attempts to understand 16th-c. Anabaptist theology better and to articulate a distinctively Mennonite theological perspective in theology in the 20th c.

According to one view, Anabaptism represents a radicalized version of the Protestant °Reformation. The Anabaptists pushed biblical authority to more consistent conclusions than did the Protestant reformers on matters such as baptism, °nonresistance, and the authority of the congregation (rather than the civil authorities or the church hierarchy) to decide normative doctrine. H. S. °Bender adopted a variation of this view and held that Anabaptist theology basically agrees with such major orthodox Christian doctrines as the Trinity, Christ, Scripture, justification by faith, and °°original °sin. But it also constitutes a major theological type alongside Calvinist and Lutheran theologies with a distinctive focus in ecclesiology and discipleship.

Another variation of this view was proposed by Robert °Friedmann. Anabaptists adopted an implicit and "existential theology" with a focus on the two kingdoms. This focus had implications for many traditional doctrines. Thus, the Anabaptists remained orthodox in their understandings of the Trinity and °Christology, with the addition of seeing Christ not only as savior but also as the model for Christian life. But they differed radically from the Protestant orientation in their theological anthropology, soteriology, quiet eschatology, and ecclesiology.

A second view holds that the theological orientation of the earliest South German Anabaptism amounted to a radicalization of Catholic °mysticism in a Reformation context. Werner Packull contends that the legacy of late medieval mysticism rather than the radicalization of the Reformation explains the early synergism and the later moralism of the Anabaptists, and their differences with Luther on anthropology, christology, and the outer Word. This orientation was modified in the Hutterites and the groups around °Marpeck. According to Packull the Hutterites gave °community priority over theology and remained theologically confused. Marpeck sought to clarify, purify, and systematize the theological convictions of the movement rather than choosing communitarian conformity or Swiss parochialism. He was thereby driven to accept a more or less Protestantized position on many theological issues, including the doctrines of justification and the Word of God. Blough has challenged this interpretation of Marpeck and argues that Marpeck was influenced by Luther in his anti-spiritualist emphasis on the humanity of Christ, but not in his understanding of °justification.

A third interpretation of the Anabaptist theological orientation holds that it represents a position in its own right which is neither Catholic nor Protestant, but combines some of the strengths of both. Walter Klaassen notes that the Anabaptists brought faith and works together. They incorporated the concerns of Catholic monastic movement while leaving aside its emphases on celibacy and restricted Christian vocation. They emphasized with the Protestants that the church rather than the hierarchy or the scholars alone interprets Scripture.

A fourth view has been proposed by Hans-Jürgen Goertz. He rejects the attempt to characterize the essence of Anabaptist theology in normative confessional terms and describes the various Anabaptists as "in, with, and under" the Reformation context. They represented a diversity of positions because they took up varying impulses in the context of the Reformation. The Anabaptist theological positions arose out of quite different attempts to implement the vision of an alternative Christianity. The concrete shape of this vision frequently was first developed in practice. Goertz further characterizes the life context of these Anabaptist movements as the milieu of anticlericalism in the Radical Reformation.

A variation on this view may be Durnbaugh's "believers church" thesis. Believers churches understand the Christian church to be a covenanted and disciplined community of those walking in the way of Jesus. Such groups, including Anabaptists and Mennonites have articulated a variable set of common convictions on ecclesiology, eschatology, and following Jesus (discipleship) in somewhat diverse theological ways which are dependent to a significant degree on the particular context and the nature of the renewal they project.

Less scholarly attention has been devoted to theological developments among Mennonites since the 16th c. In contrast to the explicit elaboration of Protestant theology into comprehensive summaries of Orthodox beliefs, Mennonite theologies have traditionally been more implicit, operational, and occasional than explicit, formal, and systematic. With the exception of the Dutch Mennonites since the 18th c. and North American Mennonites in the 20th c., theological statements have frequently taken the form of °confessional summaries, inspirational tracts, narrative accounts of history for internal use, or occasional essays rather than either extensive or comprehensive accounts of normative teaching.

The implicit theology of many North American Mennonites includes elements of traditional orthodoxy, pieces of °Fundamentalist and °Evangelical tenets, and selected practices of their 16th-c. forebears. According to Kauffman's and Harder's survey (*Anabaptists Four C. Later* [1975]), American Mennonites scored higher in general orthodoxy (beliefs in the personal existence of God, the Incarnation, the divinity and humanity of Jesus Christ, two kingdoms, the return of Christ, life after death, heaven and hell) than the national average for Protestants and Roman Catholics. Mennonites have also frequently affirmed key Fundamentalist and Evangelical doctrines (biblical °inerrancy, the Virgin Birth, a six-day creation, etc.). They also support their forebears' teachings on discipleship, °suffering for the Gospel, baptism of believers, congregational discipline, rejection of the oath, practicing nonresistance, and separation from the world (°nonconformity) to varying degrees.

The search for a theological perspective rooted in the renewal of the Anabaptist-Mennonite heritage among North American Mennonites in the 20th c. has thus been conditioned by a varied mix of doctrinal and ethical currents and undercurrents. The general lack of adherence to a specific doctrinal structure and the fragmentation of what seemed to be an implicit theological consensus has produced increasing theological diversity among Mennonites as well as proposals for Mennonites to formulate an explicit theology or at least a distinctive theological perspective.

One such proposal finds a common theological core in the Mennonite confessional tradition (Loewen). This proposal is based on the assumption that Mennonite confessional statements revolve around the three-fold axis of christology, the doctrine of the church (ecclesiology), and the doctrine of "last things" (eschatology), with Christ as the foundation for each. Accordingly, christology and soteriology focus on redemption and regeneration; ecclesiology and mission emphasize the life of the church, its mission, and the life of discipleship; and eschatology centers on judgement and resurrection hope.

Other proposals emphasize distinctive perspectives in christology, ecclesiology, eschatology, and ethics. These perspectives would be informed by an understanding of Christian faith which includes following Christ in life, a concept of the church as a disciplined and missionary community of believers, the belief that the rule of God has already begun but is yet to be consummated, and the concern to incorporate normative Christian practices as well as beliefs into theological reflection and formulation. In spite of these proposals and the current discussions they represent, most contemporary Mennonite theological literature has remained occasional and thematic rather than systematic and comprehensive.

Nevertheless, at least three efforts to elaborate more comprehensive and systematic accounts of theology which are fundamentally informed by an Anabaptist perspective or take it into account are underway. C. Norman Kraus' *Jesus Christ Our Lord* is meant to be the introductory volume of a full systematic theology. Thomas N. Finger's *Christian Theology* draws on Anabaptist-Mennonite perspectives. The Baptist theologian James Wm. McClendon, Jr.'s volume on *Systematic Theology: Ethics* is to be followed by a volume on doctrine and one on apologetics.   MEM

Neal Blough, *Christologie Anabaptiste: Pilgram Marpeck et l'humanité du Christ* (Geneva: Labor et Fides, 1984); Donald F. Durnbaugh, *The Believers Church: The History and Character of Radical Protestantism* (New York: Macmillan, 1969; Scottdale, 1985); Thomas N. Finger, *Christian Theology, An Eschatological Approach* (Nashville: Thomas Nelson, 1985; Scottdale, 1985ff.); Robert Friedmann, *The Theology of Anabaptism* (Scottdale, 1973); Kauffman/Harder, *Anabaptists Four C. Later* (1975), 101-17; Hans-Jürgen Goertz, *Die Täufer: Geschichte und Deutung* (Munich: C. H. Beck, 1980), 161ff.; Walter Klaassen, *Anabaptism: Neither Catholic nor Protestant* (Waterloo: Conrad Press, 1973); C. Norman Kraus, *Jesus Christ Our Lord: Christology from a Disciple's Perspective* (Scottdale, 1987); Loewen, *Confessions*; James Wm. McClendon, *Systematic Theology*, vol. 1: *Ethics* (Nashville: Abingdon, 1986), 17-46; *MB Profile, 1972-1982* IN *Direction*, 14, no. 2 (1985), sp. issue; Werner O. Packull, *Mysticism and the Early South German-Austrian Anabaptist Movement, 1525-1531* (Scottdale, 1977); James Reimer, "The Nature and Possibility of a Mennonite Theology," *CGR*, 1, no. 1 (Winter 1983), 33-55; Willard M. Swartley, ed., *Explorations of Systematic Theology From Mennonite Perspectives*, Occasional Papers No. 7 (Elkhart: IMS, 1984).

See also °°Catechisms; Discipleship; Pastoral Education; Seminaries.

Thiessen, Anna J. (Jan. 26, 1892-Apr. 1, 1977), was the oldest of 13 children born to Jacob W. and Helena Siemens Thiessen at Wassieljewka, Russia. She emigrated with her parents to Manitoba in 1903. In 1906 the family moved to Herbert, Sask., where Anna attended Bible school for two years. In 1915 she went to Winnipeg, where she devoted the rest of her working life (except for two years, 1923-25, attending the Bible Institute of Los Angeles) to city mission work with Mennonite refugees from the Soviet Union and to the °°Girls' Home program.

The girls' home was an effort to assist Mennonite young women who came to Winnipeg to work in domestic service. Thiessen furnished a home-away-from-home at her "Martha-Mary" center, where gatherings were held on Sundays and during the Thursday afternoon "day off" for domestic servants in the city. She was a surrogate mother but also a friend and sister. On occasion she intervened to curb exploitation by employers. In these and other ways Anna Thiessen took care of physical and spiritual needs (Sunday schools, Dorcas Circle, and other challenges to service). In 1932 the "Martha-Mary" Home was permanently housed in a 16-room house at 427 Mountain Ave. The work continued at that location for 27 years and included following up on the women after they left domestic service as well as annual reports to the Conference of Mennonites in Canada.   RSa

K. F. Wiebe, ed., *Women Among the Brethren* (1979), 118-28; Marlene Epp, "The Mennonite Girls' Homes of Winnipeg: A Home away from Home," *JMS*, 6 (1988), 100-14 passim.

Thiessen, Franz C. (July 25, 1881-Feb. 24, 1950). Born at Rueckenau, Molotschna, Ukraine, Thiessen was educated at the Ohrloff Zentralschule (high school) and at teacher training institutions in Halbstadt, Sevastopol, and Kharkov. He joined the Mennonite Brethren church. Thiessen married Lydia Wieler in 1901; after she died in 1908, he married Margaretha Wieler in 1910. He had eight children, three sons and five daughters. He served in the medical corps in Yalta, Crimea, 1915-17. Thiessen emigrated to Rosthern, Sask., in 1925. Ordained in 1937, he served as pastor at the North-End Mennonite Brethren Church, Winnipeg.

Thiessen taught at the elementary school in Rheinfeld in the Zagradovka Colony; at the high school in Alexanderkrone, Molotschna Colony (1906-08); and was principal of the high school at Davlekanovo, Ufa Province. In Canada he taught in the German-English Academy at Rosthern, Sask. (1925-32), and in Bible school and elementary German school programs in three churches in Winnipeg (1932-43). From 1943 to 1950 he taught in the Bible institute and high school (Mennonite Educational Institute) at Abbotsford and Clearbrook, B.C., teaching religion, German, and music. He was active in conference affairs, youth work, missions, and in the publication of songs and textbooks. He organized and conducted choirs and choir director workshops in churches, school, and community, and promoted classical music and oratorios.   CTK

Kaethe Klassen, *My Father Franz C. Thiessen* (Winnipeg: Centre for MB Studies, 1986), 70; Frank H. Epp, *Education with a Plus: The Story of Rosthern Junior College* (Waterloo, Ont.: Conrad Grebel Press); letters and correspondence, Centre for MB Studies, Winnipeg.

Thiessen, Jacob Johann (Aug. 31, 1893-Aug. 25, 1977), was born in Klippenfeld, Molotschna Colony, South Russia, and taught in Tiegenhagen and Fischau. In 1917 he married Katherine Kornelsen, with whom he shared life for 60 years. During the emigration of 1923-25 he assisted three transports of Mennonite emigrants to leave for Canada, and in October 1926, he and his family also left for Canada. In July 1930 he became a mission worker in Saskatoon, Sask. This led to the establishment of the °°Girls Home in 1931, with the Thiessens as houseparents (1931-56), and the organization of First Mennonite Church. He was ordained to the ministry (1932) and as bishop (°elder, 1938) and served that congregation until his retirement in 1964.

Interest in and concern for °refugees ran like a red cord through his life activities. He was secretary (1927-46) and chairman (1946-64) of the °°Canadian Mennonite Board of [Immigration and] Colonization. When that board merged into Mennonite Central Committee he became a member of MCC Canada. From 1947 to 1964 he served on the executive committee of MCC (Akron, Pa.), and in 1948 he visited refugee camps in Europe, seeking to open doors to bring displaced persons to Canada. In 1950 he traveled to South America in search of his brothers and sisters in the faith, encouraging, strengthening, preaching, and counseling wherever he went.

He was deeply involved in the work of the Conference of Mennonites in Canada, attending its sessions from 1927, participating in various committees until 1943 when he was elected moderator of the conference, a position he held until 1959. In 1941 he was appointed to a committee to study the need for a theological training institute in Canada, served as its chairman, and helped establish Canadian Mennonite Bible College in Winnipeg in 1947. He was the chairman of the college's board of directors until 1966. Thiessen was also a member of the Board of Foreign Missions (GCM), 1947-58, and of the editorial board for *Der Bote*, 1955-77 (17 years as chairman). In 1955 he received an honorary DD degree from Bethany Biblical Seminary, with which Mennonite Biblical Seminary (GCM) was associated.

Records indicate that he ordained 21 missionaries, 22 ministers, and 12 elders, officiated at 356 weddings and 290 funerals, and baptized more than 600 people as part of his work in the ministry. He was a man with a love for people, who helped to weld the General Conference Mennonite congregations in Canada into a strong, unified body, and laid a solid foundation of training pastoral and lay leaders for the Canadian churches.   EP

MCC Story, 4; F. H. Epp, *Mennonite Exodus: The Rescue and Resettlement of the Russian Mennonites since the Communist Revolution* (Altona, Man.: D. W. Friesen, 1962); Esther Patkau, *First Mennonite Church in Saskatoon 1923-1982* (Altona, Man.: D. W. Friesen, 1982); idem, "J. J. Thiessen's Ministry in Saskatoon" (MTh Thesis, Lutheran Theological Seminary, Saskatoon, 1979); J. G. Rempel, *Fünfzig Jahre Konferenzbestrebungen 1902-1952*, pt. 2 (Steinbach, Man.: Derksen Printers for Conference of Mennonites in Canada, 1952); *Who's Who Mennonites* (1943), 241; *Menn. Bib. II*, p. 510.

Thiessen, John (May 25, 1893-Feb. 16, 1967). Born near Inman, Ks., John Thiessen was the son of Jacob

and Sara Janzen Thiessen. He attended German school, 1899-1902; public school, 1902-08; Bethel Academy, 1912-16; Bethel College, 1916-19 (AB); the U. of Chicago, 1919-20; McCormick Seminary, 1920-21; Witmarsum Seminary 1929-30 (BD); Garrett Biblical Institute, 1930; and Bluffton College, 1931 (AM). He married Elizabeth R. Wiens, May 4, 1921. Thiessen was an educational and pastoral missionary at Mauhadih and Jagdeeshpur, India, 1921-49, and was executive secretary of the General Conference Mennonite Mission Board, 1952-58. He was a member of the Bethel Congregation, Inman, Ks. Thiessen was pastor of congregations at Pandora, Ohio; Henderson, Neb.; and Newton, Goessel, and Hillsboro, Ks. The children of John and Elizabeth Wiens Thiessen are Harold (1922-86), Arthur (1923-), Eleanor Ewert (1926-1980), Muriel T. Stackley (1937-), and Dorothy Alpert (1941-).   MTS

Juhnke, *Mission* (1979).

Third-World Theologies. See Theologies from the Two-Thirds World.

Tithes. A church tax of one tenth on all produce, used for the support of the clergy, became mandatory for all Christians in the 9th c. It was based on the Old Testament tithe law of Dt 14:22-23. When peasants determined to take control of church affairs during 1522-1526, there were tithe refusals on the ground that tithes went to support indolent and greedy clergy. Peasants demanded that the tithes be used to support the clergy they chose and, beyond that, the poor of the parish (the second of the Twelve Articles of the Peasants). There were some tithe refusals in Zürich in 1522, articulated by the radical priest Simon Stumpf, and continued controversy over their use in 1523. Zwingli and the city council insisted on payment, but adopted the popular program of using tithes to support parish clergy and the poor. Anabaptists insisted from the beginning that the tithe, being a tax of the government, should be paid since the New Testament made it mandatory.   WKlaa

J. F. G. Goeters, "Die Vorgeschichte des Täufertums in Zürich," in *Studien zur Geschichte und Theologie der Reformation*, ed. L. Abramowski und J. F. G. Goeters (Neukirchen-Vluyn: Neukirchener Verlag, 1969), 239-81, at 246-9; James M. Stayer, "Neue Modelle eines gemeinsamen Lebens: Gütergemeinschaft im Täufertum," *Alles Gehört Allen: Das Experiment der Gütergemeinschaft vom 16. Jahrhundert bis heute*, ed. H. J. Goertz (Munich: C. H. Beck, 1984), 25ff; CRR 4: 207-20 passim and index.

See also Peasants' War; Reublin, Wilhelm.

Toews, Gerhard (Georg de Brecht) (1897-1986), novelist and historian, was born in Schönfeld-Brazol, Ukraine. He attended Kommerzschule (business school) in Halbstadt and university in Kharkov, where his studies were interrupted by World War I. Toews served as an officer in the Molotschna °Selbstschutz and after its collapse fled to the Crimea, where he joined the White Army and later eluded the Soviet authorities by escaping through Turkey to Germany. He emigrated to Canada in 1923 and farmed in Saskatchewan while trying to establish himself as a writer. His novels *Heimat in Flamen* (Homeland Aflame, 1933) and its sequel

Heimat in Trümmern (Homeland in Rubble, 1936) which portray the dramatic experiences of Mennonite soldiers, were well received but had limited sales. Disappointed, Toews moved back to Germany in 1939, hoping to improve his writing fortunes. He returned to Canada in 1951 and settled in St. Catherines, Ont.

In his novels Toews generates strong narrative energy and depicts actions and pathos through believable if somewhat stereotyped characters. He never really stands above his fictional world, and he accepts Russian-Mennonite attitudes and values uncritically. Nevertheless, his novels are important firsthand fictional accounts of a tragic chapter in Mennonite history. AR

Georg de Brecht, *Die Heimat in Flammen* (Regina: Sonderabdruck aus *Der Courier,* n.d.); Gerhard Toews, *Die Heimat in Trümmern* (Steinbach: Warte Verlag, 1936); idem, *Schönfeld: Werde und Opfergang einer deutschen Siedlung in der Ukraine* (Winnipeg: Rundschau Publishing House, 1939); Al Reimer, "The Russian-Mennonite Experience in Fiction," in *Mennonite Images: Historical, Cultural and Literary Essays Dealing with Mennonite Issues,* ed. Harry Loewen (Winnipeg: Hyperion Press Ltd., 1980), 227-29; J. H. Janzen, "The Literature of the Russian-Canadian Mennonites," *Menn. Life,* 1 (Jan. 1946), 22-25.

See also Literature.

Toews, John Aron (Aug. 15, 1912-1979), was a respected teacher, preacher, and conference leader of the Mennonite Brethren Church in North America. He was born in Rückenau, South Russia to Aron A. and Agnes (Harms) Toews. The family fled the Soviet Union in 1926 and settled in Namaka, Alta. Later Toews attended a variety of intitutions including the Coaldale Bible Institute, the Prophetic Bible Institute led by William Aberhard, Tabor College (BTh, 1940), and the U. of Minnesota (PhD, 1964). In 1935 he was married to Nettie Willms and five children were born to them.

Most of Toews' life was spent in a teaching career, especially at the Mennonite Brethren Bible College (1947-67; 1976-79) where he served as president for seven years (1956-63). He also taught at Trinity Western College in British Columbia, served three years in a pastoral ministry in British Columbia, and spent shorter periods of teaching and ministry in Europe and South America. He served his denomination in a variety of committees and leadership roles and at the time of his death was moderator of the General Conference of Mennonite Brethren Churches. Toews had a special concern for cooperation with other Mennonite bodies, which was expressed by active involvement in the Mennonite World Conference, Mennonite Central Committee, and in other activities. He was the author of a number of books and numerous articles, many of which focused on Anabaptist and Mennonite concerns, including a definitive history of his own denomination (1975). He was probably the most effective interpreter and spokesman for the °Anabaptist vision in the Mennonite Brethren Church in his generation. AJD

John A. Toews, *People of the Way: Selected Essays and Addresses by John A. Toews,* ed. by Abe J. Dueck, Herbert Giesbrecht, and Allen R. Guenther (Winnipeg: Historical Committee of the Board of Higher Education, Canadian Conference of Mennonite Brethren Churches, 1981); idem, *A History of the Mennonite Brethren Church: Pilgrims and Pioneers,* ed. by A. J. Klassen (Fresno: MB Board of Chris-

tian Literature, 1975); idem, *True Nonresistance through Christ: A Study of Biblical Principles* (Winnipeg: MB Board of General Welfare and Public Relations, 1955).

Toews, John B. (b. 1906), a teacher, pastor, school administrator, missions executive, and theologian from the General Conference of Mennonite Brethren Churches. He was born at Alexandertal, Ukraine, Russia, and attended the Zentralschule in Gnadenfeld and the Mittelschule in Halbstadt, Molotschna. He graduated from the U. of Ukraine in 1926 and continued studies at the U. of Amsterdam (1926-28). He immigrated to Coaldale, Alta., in 1928 and studied at Tabor College, (Ks., STD); Western Baptist Theological Seminary (BD and ThM); and Southern Baptist Theological Seminary, Louisville, Ky. (summers 1941-44).

Toews taught New Testament theology and doctrine at Bethany Bible School in Hepburn, Sask., and served as president of the school (1932-38). He was director of the Bible department at Freeman College, Freeman, S.D. (1940-42), president of Mennonite Brethren Bible College, Winnipeg (1945-48), professor of missions and practical theology, Mennonite Brethren Biblical Seminary, Fresno, Cal. (1964-78), and president of the seminary in Fresno for eight years. He was pastor of the Hepburn Mennonite Brethren Church (1937-38), and also pastored Mennonite Brethren churches at Buhler, Ks. (1942-45) and Reedley, Cal. (1948-53).

One of Toews' major contributions to his denomination was a 10-year term of service as general secretary of the Mennonite Brethren Board of Missions and Services (1953-63). Together with his previous interest in missions, his travels for the board established him as a missionary statesman among Mennonites. He has also been prominent in other Mennonite Brethren activities, serving on the Educational Committee (1942-48), Program Committee (1948-51, 1954-57), Board of Missions (1948-53, 1966-72), Board of Reference and Counsel (1948-60), and as General Conference vice-chairman (1948-51).

Having taught history and theology until his retirement in 1980, he remains active in the Fresno seminary community in historical research and writing. He gave impetus to and served as director of the Center for Mennonite Brethren Studies. Toews was a long-time supporter of the Institute of Mennonite Studies, Elkhart, Ind.

Among his published writings are *The Key to Fruitful Christian Service* (Back to the Bible Publications, 1959); *The Mennonite Brethren Church in Zaire* (MB Board of Christian Literature, 1978). He helped translate P. M. Friesen's *Mennonite Brotherhood in Russia, 1789-1910* (MB Board of Christian Literature, 1980). MHein

Toews, Peter A. (July 23, 1877-Mar. 6, 1961), was born in Chortitza, South Russia and came to Canada in 1892. He settled in Kleinstadt, on the Manitoba °°West Reserve. In Altona he was a farmer, businessman (cattle-buying, farm machinery sales), educator, civic politician, and a spiritual leader in the Sommerfelder Mennonite Church. He served as reeve of the rural municipality of Rhineland (1920-29) and was chairman of the board of directors for the Mennonite Educational Institute (1922-26). He encouraged unsuccessfully (1925) the passage of a provincial bill to establish a separate Mennonite school division. He was elected minister (1929), ordained (1930), and confirmed as elder (1931). He retired from the ministry in 1951. In the work of the ministry he visited northern Alberta (1930) in search of land suitable for resettlement. He dealt with congregational difficulties that led to the formation of the Rudnerweider Mennonite Church (1937). He served as co-chairman of the *Ältesterkomitee* (Committee of Elders) created to negotiate °alternatives to military service and helped raise funds for Red Cross and assistance to widows and orphans. In 1958 he became part of the conservative group that left the Sommerfelder Church to form the Reinländer Mennoniten Gemeinde (Reinland Mennonite Church). He was buried in Schoenthal, Man.   JGies

E. Bergen, "Pioneer Portrait of the Past (196)," *Red River Valley Echo*, 40 (July 30, 1980,) 11; Frank H. Epp, *Mennonites in Canada II*; H. J. Gerbrandt, "Wealth is Rooted in People," *MM*, 1 (May 1972), 11-12; J. J. Kehler, "Lebensverzeichnis," *Steinbach Post*, 48 (March 28, 1961), 5; D. P. Reimer, ed., *Experiences of the Mennonites of Canada during the Second World War, 1939-1945* (Altona, Man., 1946); Peter D. Zacharias, *Reinland: An Experience in Community* (Reinland, Man., 1976).

Tojo Takanobu (b. 1942) was born in Osaka during World War II. He was saved and baptized in The Evangelical Alliance Mission (TEAM) Christian church in December 1965, then went to Shimonoseki City in °Yamaguchi Prefecture as a teacher of economics in the city college in 1969. Since that time he has been teaching "Economic Policy" as a full professor, having received his PhD in economics in 1985.

In 1970, he met Doyle Book, a Brethren in Christ missionary, and this was the beginning of a close working relationship with the Anabaptists. Together they began a house meeting in the home of the missionary, which later developed into a growing and thriving Japanese church, the Yamanota Christian Church. From its conception, he has carried leadership responsibilities. In 1986 he was senior lay pastor. He was also chairman of the Nihon Kirisutokyo Keiteidan (Japan Brethren in Christ Conference) and a representative to the Nihon Menonaito Senkyokai (Japan Mennonite Fellowship).

In 1981 he married Yuko *Nagao*, a member of the Oita Mennonite church (Nihon Menonaito Kirisutokyo Kyokai Kaigi, GCM). They have two sons. Takanobu *Tojo* is known for his sense of humor, scholarly approach to the Scriptures, training of lay leaders, and evangelism of young men from his university contacts.   JGray

Tokyo, the capital of Japan, with a population of 11,829,363 (1985), is one of the world's largest cities. It covers an area of 2,145 sq. km. (828 sq. mi.). Tokyo is Japan's political, financial, business, educational, transportation, and fashion center. In 1868, Emperor Meiji, grandfather of present (1986) Emperor Hirohito, declared a change of the capital from Kyoto to Tokyo ("eastern capital"), which was formerly called Edo ("estuary"). At the heart of the city one can see the Imperial Palace, the residence of the emperor and empress, and its grounds (1457). From about 1600 the Tokugawa shoguns resided at this castle.

Rebuilt after nearly total destruction in World War II, the city hosted the Olympic Games in 1964. Some pollution problems exist, but the residents of this giant modern city are proud of its general cleanliness, safety, skyscrapers, universities and museums, and public transportation system (including super-express bullet trains which run north, south, and west from Tokyo). Its central location also contributes to its influence on the nation. Tokyo is where East meets West with much westernization on the one hand, and oriental traditions on the other. An increasing number of tourists and businessmen visit from all parts of the world. Mennonite work began in 1953.   MS

Tokyo Chiku Menonaito Kyokai Rengo (Tokyo Area Fellowship of Mennonite Churches) consists of five churches scattered from central Tokyo to three surrounding prefectures. The groups are small with fewer than 100 members total, but are growing slowly into ongoing Mennonite churches. Four Japanese workers (largely self-supporting), two expatriate missionary couples, and one short-term couple were providing leadership in 1986. Two churches have their own buildings; the other three are house churches. More than 20,000,000 people live in the Greater Tokyo area.

The first Mennonite missionaries came to Japan in 1949 and the early 1950s. They began pioneer evangelism in Hokkaido, Osaka, Yamaguchi (southern Honshu), and Kyushu. As churches were formed, seekers and new believers, especially students, from the outlying areas gradually found their way to Tokyo.

In August 1953, the Mennonite Board of Missions (MC) sent a missionary couple to Tokyo. The present Honan-cho church center purchased property and began work in 1954. On Jan. 15, 1956, the first three baptisms took place. Mennonite Central Committee opened a peace witness in Tokyo that same year, providing personnel thereafter for 13 years. By 1963 there were three missionary couples in the city, representing the Brethren in Christ, General Conference Mennonite Church (GCM), and Mennonite Church (MC).

In 1964 the Mennonite-related churches in Tokyo formed an official conference under the name *Keihin Dendo Kyoryokukai* (Greater Tokyo Evangelism Cooperative Association). That existed until 1979 when the Brethren in Christ groups withdrew to form their own organization.

The remaining groups then formed a new conference (GCM/MC) called *Tokyo Chiku Menonaito Kyokai Rengo* with continued cooperation from both the Commission on Overseas Missions (GCM) and Mennonite Board of Missions (MC) in North America. The reorganized conference also cooperates with the two boards in sponsoring the Japan Anabaptist Center (guesthouse and study center), plus the newly built Friedmann-Sakakibara Library with more than 5,000 Mennonite publications.

Tokyo Area Fellowship members pray and remain confident that many more churches will emerge in the Tokyo area with the increasing maturity of its present body of believers.   YI

MWH (1978), 157-160; *MWH* (1984), 39.

See also Urban Church.

Tourism. For the middle classes, tourism is a recent phenomenon made possible by °mass communication, high speed transit and the leisure and resources generated by industrial and post-industrial societies. As Mennonites have assimilated (°acculturation) into °modern life they have also begun to travel to commercial tourist sites as well as to landmarks related to Anabaptist and Mennonite history. This article focuses on the development and impact of tourism on Amish and Mennonite communities. In the middle of the 20th c., the most conservative Amish and Mennonite communities attracted the interest of tourists since many of these communities lagged behind the larger society in their willingness to adapt to modern life. Amish and Old Order Mennonite groups with their distinctive clothing and the use of horse-and-buggy transportation provided a glimpse of an earlier epoch of North American life for urban residents caught in the fast pace of modern life. The Mennonite Church (MC) and the General Conference Mennonite Church were assimilating into mainstream culture at the same time that tourism was developing in North America. Thus these groups never became the primary focus of tourist attention. Old Order groups, both Amish and Mennonite, who dared not to be modern, were the ones that caught the curiosity of tourists with their distinctive life-styles. Tourist industries in Ohio, Indiana, Iowa, Manitoba, Ontario, and Pennsylvania, although not completely dependent on these plain groups, were nevertheless spurred by the presence of Old Order groups.

Lancaster County, Pa., home of the earliest and oldest tourist industry accentuating the °plain groups, hosted approximately 5 million visitors annually in the 1980s—350 for each Amish person in the county. The tourists spent more than 400 million dollars per year. Amish historian David Luthy dates the origin of Amish tourism in Lancaster Co. to the publication of a tourist booklet by Steinfeldt in 1937. By 1965, 2 million tourists were flocking to Lancaster Co. each year to see the Amish and the Mennonites. In 1958 the Mennonites opened a Mennonite Information Center and by 1974 an estimated 40,000 tourists visited the center annually (°interpretation and information centers). The same pattern of evolution has occurred in other communities in North America who host a high concentration of Amish and Old Order Mennonites in close proximity to urban centers.

Tourist establishments for hospitality, entertainment, and education were owned primarily by non-Mennonite entrepreneurs in the early stage of tourism. Since 1970 Mennonites themselves have become increasingly involved in commercial hospitality as owners of motels and restaurants as well as bed-and-breakfast facilities. These commercial enterprises cater to local clientele as well as to tourists. Prior to the 1980s the Amish remained rather aloof from tourist establishments which were characterized by one Amishman as "leisure-lust playgrounds." Since then some Amish have become directly involved by opening hundreds of small roadside stands on the edge of their farms and lawns to sell produce and homemade crafts. These small native stands represent a negotiated compromise between the Amish and the tourists. On the one hand they provide tourists with a rare, but controlled, peek into genuine Amish life and the tourists, in turn, respond by purchasing Amish-made products which bolsters the Amish economy especially in areas faced with shrinking farmland. Tourist industries also provide a major source of jobs and income for non-Mennonite and Mennonite people in several local communities.

Formal tourist sites play several important roles in structuring the encounter between plain groups and the modern world. They provide a buffer zone of sorts that protects the natives from the tourists. Tour guides and simulated attractions occupy the tourists' time and keep them a respectable distance from Old Order groups. Tourist sites and tour guides provide a structured restraint that permits daily Amish and Mennonite life to continue largely undisturbed backstage. For the most part tourists and their tour guides follow established routes and stop at designated places pinpointed on tourist maps. The guides and sites serve as a curtain that insulates Old Order groups from what would otherwise be a chaotic intrusion on their life. Tourist establishments also offer an educational setting where questions can be asked without fear of embarrassment and insult. They also provide descriptive information and an overview of Amish and Mennonite life that would be difficult to obtain from many rank and file members. Tourist sites in these ways are "front stage" operations which protect Old Order life backstage from the questions and intrusions of thousands of visitors.

A series of paradoxes thread their way through the phenomenon of tourism. To begin with, the European Anabaptists were violently persecuted and exterminated because they dared to be different. Paradoxically the defiance of modern culture by Old Order groups has brought them not °persecution, but admiration and respect. The course of history has converted them from despised heretics into esteemed objects of modern curiosity. Moreover, the world which these Old Order groups have tried so hard to keep at arms length, is now reaching out to them. Oddly enough, the more separate and unique they become the more they entice modern curiosity. Furthermore, the tourists come to see the distinctively dressed Old Order people, not the progressive Mennonites who operate the information centers and serve as tour guides. In fact, if all Mennonites and Amish were as assimilated as those who operate the motels and information centers, tourists would pay scant attention to the Mennonites. The prime objects of tourist interest, the Old Order groups, show little interest in tourism, which they often consider a nuisance.

As a traditionally agrarian folk, Mennonites were somewhat slow to begin °urban missions. The tourist phenomenon ironically brought urbanites to the front door of Mennonites and the more progressive and evangelical ones saw the tourists as a mission field which the Lord had brought to them. Mennonite information centers combine an attempt to provide reliable factual information with a witness to the gospel of Jesus Christ and the beliefs of the Mennonites and Amish. Indeed, involvement in the tourist industry has served to sharpen Mennonite convictions and beliefs. Tour guides and information center personnel have been forced to study their own history and that of related groups in order to answer the incessant questions that tourists bring. Brochures on Amish and Mennonite beliefs and films and video interpretations targeted on tourists have also clarified and strengthened Mennonite beliefs among members themselves. The encounter with tourism has thus served to hone Mennonite identity and historical consciousness.

Among Old Order groups, tourism which appears to threaten solitude and privacy, may in fact bolster cultural identity. An Old Order Amish person noted that, "Today we get loads of praise for our way of life." Another Amish leader said, "We are no longer looked down upon." The fact that tourists from around the world have come to learn of their way of life has brought quiet satisfaction and enhanced Amish collective self-esteem. Tourism with its clicking cameras and staring visitors, like persecution of bygone days, reinforces the cultural boundaries and reminds the Amish that they are indeed different from the rest of the world. Tourism also creates expectations for Old Order behavior since the tourists come to see a horse-and-buggy people who have turned their backs on electricity. Old Order behavior, thus in part, fulfills the expectations created by the tourist industry. Such external expectations may indeed fortify rather than endanger the Old Order way of life.

Perhaps the greatest irony lies in the new relationship that tourism has created between Amish and Mennonites and their surrounding communities. The larger culture from which the Old Order groups have fervently sought to remain independent, has now come to depend on them financially in order to sustain the tourist industries. The image and identity of Lancaster Co., Pa., for instance, is highly dependent on the presence of the Amish community. Although they are not assertive politically, their importance for tourism has given the Amish a newfound power and leverage to negotiate with modern officials over issues ranging from schools to zoning laws—all of which are essential to their survival as as people.

The negative consequences of tourism are many: congested roads, commercial development of prime farmland, disruption of normal social life, distorted images of many plain groups, commercialization of religious and cultural symbols, and rampant greed. Tourism, with all its ironies however, may indeed strengthen the cultural vitality of Old Order groups. It provides a mobile mission field for Mennonite evangelistic efforts, increases the profits of Mennonite entrepreneurs in the hospitality industry, and sharpens Mennonite historical and theological consciousness. It has indeed been a fascinating and profitable encounter with the modern world.   DBK

Dean MacCannell, *The Tourist: A New Theory of the Leisure Class* (New York: Schocken Books, 1976); Roy C. Buck, "Bloodless Theatre: Images of the Old Order Amish in Tourism Literature," *PMH*, 2 (July 1979), 2-11; idem, "Boundary Maintenance Revisited: Tourist Experience in an Old Order Amish Community," *Rural Sociology*, 43 (Summer 1978) 221-34; J. A. Hostetler, *Amish Society* (1980), 307-10; Donald B. Kraybill, *The Riddle of Amish Culture* (Baltimore: Johns Hopkins U. Press, 1989), 227-234; David Luthy, "The Origin of Amish Tourism in Lancaster County, Pennsylvania," *Family Life* (Nov. 1980), 31-34; Bernice Steinfeldt, *The Amish of Lancaster County* (Lancaster: Arthur G. Steinfeldt, 1937); Joseph F. Beiler, "The Tourist Season," *GH* (June 8, 1976), 482; Esther Eby Glass, "Fifty Thousand Questions," *Chr. Living* (June 1967), 8-10; Anna R. Denlinger, "Just Ordinary People: The Growth of Tourism in Lancaster County," *Miss. Mess.* (April 1972), 12-13; A. Martha Denlinger, "Mennonite Encounter with Tourists," *GH* (Sep. 16, 1975), 652-53; "Life or Lifestyle: What Do Tourists See?" *Miss. Mess.* (Aug. 1975), 12-13; Eugene Witmer, "What Do Tourists Come to See?" *Miss. Mess.* (Oct. 1977), 10-11; Milo D. Stahl, "Tourism as Mission and Presence: A Serious Call to the Church," *Miss. Focus*, 16 (Mar. 1988), 8-10.

See also Literature; Motion Pictures.

Tradition. Anabaptism originated in a revolt against tradition because Anabaptists, more than other Protestant Reformers, were convinced that many "human traditions" had been illegitimately added to the Scriptures since the time of the apostles. These corruptions of the pure church included °°infant baptism; priesthood; false, exaggerated, externalized sacraments; religious coercion; and °military participation. Often the distinction between legitimate tradition and false tradition was blurred. Defenders of tradition as legitimate in principle would point out that even the Bible in its present form is the product of tradition, of "handing down" from Christ to the apostles to the rest of the church, since Christ himself, instead of writing Scriptures, entrusted his message to his disciples. Ironically the legitimacy of extra-scriptural tradition in worship and church life was pointed out by none other than Tertullian, the rigorist North African church leader [fl. ca. 200], in the same tract that is frequently used to support Mennonite and Anabaptist opposition to military service, namely, *On the Chaplet*, also known as *On the Soldier's Crown* (ch. 3-4.) All Protestants attacked Catholic traditionalism, but the Anabaptists were among the most extreme. In the process tradition itself frequently was declared illegitimate, that is, all tradition was branded false tradition and Scripture and tradition were viewed as mutually exclusive. The goal of radical reformers, and, to a certain degree, of all Protestants, was to restore the pristine church, uncorrupted by tradition (°restitutionism).

Yet °Mennonites have often been very traditional. Modern sociologists have confirmed an ancient theological and philosophical insight: tradition is an essential aspect of human existence (Shils). As children are born to men and women in a religious or political movement, the parents naturally seek structures and °institutions by which to pass on their beliefs and convictions. The Latin word *tradere*, from which *tradition* is derived, simply means "handing to," "passing on." Tradition as an °authority for Mennonite life emerged very quickly (Dyck). The most traditional members of the Mennonite family in the 20th c. are the Amish, Hutterites, Old Order Mennonites, Sommerfeld Mennonites, and Old Colony Mennonites. In these groups it is accepted that children grow up within the Christian community and embrace the handed-down faith, making it authentically their own when they decide to be baptized and "join the church." Some tension remains where it is apparent that some have joined with less inner conviction than might be hoped for, but a minimal degree of inner conviction is evident simply by being willing to obey the practices and customs of the group. In this way all those who remain Amish, Hutterite, Old Order Mennonite, Sommerfelder, or Old Colony in their daily life are continually saying yes with inner conviction to the faith they have accepted. It is a verbally unarticulated but genuine assent to faith—a faith transmitted through tradition. This pattern was also characteristic of the °°Kirchen-Gemeinden Mennonites of 19th-c. Russia.

At various points, the more °acculturated, progressive, and °revivalist Mennonites have become uneasy about the degree to which custom and tradition had become authoritative. Like the early Anabaptists, they feared that the faith being passed on was not authentic, was "merely traditional," and therefore was false faith. In these groups genuine, authentic faith was equated with articulated, expressive °conversion to and acceptance of baptism, °church membership, and °discipleship. In place of a theology of tradition, leaders in these groups affirm the principle that the church must be reestablished in every generation ("the °Believers Church is always only one generation away from extinction"). In movements advocating revivalism, Pietism, higher education, missions, social activism, feminism, and °charismatic experience, various Mennonite groups have carried out renewed revolts against Mennonite tradition in a manner parallel to the original Anabaptist revolt against Catholic tradition. These groups include the °°Kleine Gemeinde, Mennonite Brethren, Church of God in Christ Mennonite (Holdeman), Mennonite Church (MC), General Conference Mennonite Church, Brethren in Christ, the group led by Eberhard and Emmy °Arnold (eastern °Hutterian Brethren). Within the larger Mennonite groups since World War II, the °Concern movement of the 1950s and 1960s, the °house church movement, the charismatic movement, and other developments represent similar reactions against a perceived empty and illegitimate traditionalism.

Each of these new movements or denominations, if they are to survive very long, in turn must face the need to establish institutions and structures to pass on their vision for special gifts of the Holy Spirit, decentralized authority, small-group dynamics, women's equality, mission work, or revivalism. Some have succeeded (e.g. the Church of God in Christ Mennonite [Holdeman] and the Arnold portion of the Hutterian Brethren since the early 1970s). Those who either have tried and failed or, out of principle, not even tried to establish second-generation structures, have disappeared (e.g., revivalism, Pietism, classic missionary enthusiasm—replaced by °relief and °service work and social activism) or will eventually disappear unless they find a way to become traditionalists in the future. This would be viewed differently by members of the restitutionist groups—what is here described as "disappearing" would be described by advocates of Believers Church renewal as "continuation" by way of rebirth in every generation. Traditionalists and restitutionists thus would disagree over the nature of "continuity" itself. Much of the Mennonite confusion in regard to °sectarianism and cultural involvement can be traced to confused intuitions about the positive and negative aspects of tradition.

Contrary to the popular perception, traditionalism is not static. A theology of tradition is a theology of change, but it is a theology of change that is deliberately slowed down and controlled. Traditionalists seek to be faithful to tradition, and innovations are always measured against the authority of tradition. Students of Amish or Hutterite society see clearly how these groups have slowly changed over the decades. What traditionalist groups do not permit is revolutionary or radical change, change that would entirely overthrow existing structures and institutions. The same observations can be made of non-Protestant traditionalist Christians, namely °Roman Catholics and °Eastern Orthodox. Change does occur in these groups (after all, it was the supposed corrupting changes made by these groups that so angered Anabaptists and Protestants in the first place) but it occurs through existing structures and institutions. Traditionalism as a theology says that institutions and structures are legitimate ways the Holy Spirit works in the church, basing this principle in God's choice to become incarnate in Christ. Thus the canon of Scripture, the office of bishop, the liturgy and sacraments of the church are all institutionalized through divine leading. Antitraditionalists (restitutionists), whether the Concern movement or leaders of the Mennonite °Renaissance of the late 19th c., call for rapid, immediate change to eliminate tradition-induced corruptions, yet, because their goal is a pristine, pure, and uncorrupted church, they are ill-prepared to cope with change in the second generation. As described above, the best "renewal within every generation" would be the one that "corrupts" the original ideal as little as possible. If complete faithfulness to the original ideal were actually achieved, there would be no change at all. In practice, "renewal within each generation" never corresponds precisely to the original ideal and thus, the antitraditional theology is in fact a form of tradition that remains in unresolved tension with its principle of avoiding changes in the original ideal. Ironically, it seems that the more one achieves a pure, uncorrupted, restored church, the less one is prepared to admit that it can and must change and develop as it is handed on to the next generation, i.e., that some "corruption" is in fact legitimate development and that the goal is to distinguish legitimate from illegitimate change.   DDM

Cornelius J. Dyck, "The Place of Tradition in Dutch Anabaptism" *Church History*, 43 (1974), 34-49; Walter Klaassen, "Menno Simons: Molder of a Tradition," *MQR*, 62 (1988), 368-86, cf. *Doops. Bijdragen*, n.r. 12-13 (1986-87), 226-47; Hans-Jürgen Goertz, "Der Fremde Menno Simons: Antiklerikale Argumentation im Werk eines melchioritischen Täufers," *Menn. Geschbl.*, 42 (1985), 24-42, at 34; Menno, *Writings*, 90-91, 128-29, 238-39, 300-302 etc.; Marpeck in *CRR* 2: 46-59, 127-30, 155-56, 215-16, 253-54, 281-82 etc.; John H. Yoder, *Priestly Kingdom* (Notre Dame U. Press, 1984), ch. 3, 6; idem, "Anabaptist Vision and Mennonite Reality," in *Consultation on Anabaptist-Mennonite Theology*, ed. A. J. Klassen (Fresno: MBBS for Council of Mennonite Seminaries, 1970), 1-46; idem, "The Authority of the Canon," in *Essays on Biblical Interpretation*, ed. W. M. Swartley (Elkhart: IMS, 1984), 265-90; Alan Kreider, *Journey toward Holiness* (Scottdale, 1987); Gordon Kaufman, *Systematic Theology: A Historicist Perspective*, 2nd ed. (New York: Scribners, 1978), xiv-xx; Dennis D. Martin, "Nothing New Under the Sun? Mennonites and History," *CGR*, 5 (1987), 1-27, responses 147-53, 260-62; Peter C. Erb, "Reflections on Mennonite Theology in Canada," *JMS*, 1 (1983), 179-95, esp. 182; A. James Reimer, "The Nature and

Possibility of a Mennonite Theology," *CGR*, 1 (1983) 33-55; idem, "Theological Method, Modernity, and the Role of Tradition," in *Prophetic Vision Applied to One's Academic Discipline*, 1978 Mennonite Graduate Seminar (Waterloo, Ontario), 109-21; Marlin Jeschke, *Believers Baptism for Children of the Church* (Scottdale, 1983); Rodney J. Sawatsky, *Authority and Identity: The Dynamics of the General Conference Mennonite Church*, Cornelius H. Wedel Historical Series, 1-2 (North Newton: Bethel College, 1987); Levi Miller, "I Am a Mennonite, Not an Anabaptist," *GH* (July 7, 1987), 482-84; Alvin Dueck, "North American Psychology: Gospel of Modernity?" *CGR*, 3 (1985), 165-78; Wolfgang Eggers, *Community for Life* (Scottdale, 1988), 252-65; *Menn. Life*, 19 (Apr. 1964), sp. issue on the Bible and its authority; Paul E. Whitmer, "Autobiography" (n.d., ca. 1952), 91-96, copy in AMBS library and MHL (Goshen); James Urry, "'All that Glitters. . .': Delbert Plett and the Place of the Kleine Gemeinde in Russian-Mennonite History," *JMS* 4 (1986) 228-50; Miriam E. Warner, *Mennonite Brethren: The Maintenance of Continuity in a Religious Ethnic Group* (PhD diss. U. of California, Berkeley (1987); Thomas N. Finger, "The Way to Nicea: Reflections from a Mennonite Perspective," *CGR*, 3 (1985), 231-49, with responses in *CGR*, 4 (1986), 57-60, 160-61; J. W. Fretz in *MWR* (June 23, 1988), 8, (June 30, 1988), 6, (July 7, 1988), 6, critical of the role of tradition among Old Colony Mennonites. On tradition outside Mennonite circles, see Edward Shils. *Tradition* (U. of Chicago Press, 1981); Karl F. Morrison, *The Mimetic Tradition of Reform in the West* (Princeton U. Press, 1982); idem, *Tradition and Authority in the Western Church, 300-1140* (Princeton U. Press, 1969); Arthur C. Cochrane, "The Mystery of the Continuity of the Church: A Study in Reformed Symbolics," *J. of Ecumenical Studies*, 2 (1965), 81-96; John M. Headley, "The Reformation as Crisis in the Understanding of Tradition," *ARG*, 78 (1987), 5-23; John Henry Newman, *An Essay on the Development of Christian Doctrine* (1845; reprinted Garden City, N.Y: Doubleday, 1960); Heiko A. Oberman, "Quo Vadis? Tradition from Irenaeus to Humani Generis," *Scottish J. of Theology*, 16 (1963), 225-55; Eugene Fairweather, ed., *The Oxford Movement* (New York: Oxford U. Press, 1964), esp. pp. 60-89; Tertullian, *The Chaplet, or De Corona*, in Ante-Nicene Fathers series, vol. 3, pp. 94-95.

See also Conservative Mennonites; History, Theology of; Modernity; *Ordnung*; Revolution.

Transcendence. See God, Doctrine of.

Transkei. See Republic of South Africa.

Travel. See Tourism.

I Have No Fear: Annie C. Funk and the *Titanic*

Annie Funk perished with 1,500 other people when the "unsinkable" ocean liner, *Titanic*, sank on the night of April 15, 1912. A General Conference Mennonite woman who went to Janjgir, India, in 1906 at the age of 32, Annie Funk was born on April 12, 1874. She was the daughter of James B. and Susanna Clemmer Funk, and grew up in Eastern Pennsylvania in the beautiful Butter Valley, about three miles from the Hereford Mennonite Church, located at Bally in Berks County.

She received her training at the West Chester State Normal School and at the Northfield [Mass.] Training School founded by D. L. Moody. Before going to India in November 1906, she had served among the blacks in Chattanooga, Tenn., and with the Young Women's Christian Association at Paterson, N.J.

Her faith was symbolized by a reply she made to a concerned friend who reminded her of the dangerous ocean voyage in 1906: "Our heavenly Father is as near to us on sea as on land. My trust is in Him. I have no fear."

She was a dedicated and beloved worker in India. The girls' school at Janjgir, which she founded in 1908, was later named the Annie C. Funk Memorial School.

In 1912 she was called home to Pennsylvania because of the illness of her mother. In England she unexpectedly secured passage on the *Titanic* because a coal strike had delayed the *S.S. Haverford* on which she was booked.

When the *Titanic* struck an iceberg in the North Atlantic and began to sink, there were not enough lifeboats to accommodate all of the passengers. Annie, according to a confirmed report, unselfishly relinquished her place in a lifeboat to a mother with children. When Annie's friends back in Pennsylvania heard of this incident they said, "It was just like Annie to do something like that."   RRK

Juhnke, *Mission* (1979), 229, index; John Ruth, *Maintaining the Right Fellowship* (Scottdale, 1984), 412-14; *MWR* (Jan. 19, 1986), 4; *Menn. Life*, 12 (Jan. 1957), 44-46; *GCM Yearbook* (1913), 17-21; *Mennonite* (Apr. 18-June 13, 1912).

Tres Cruces Colony, Bolivia, is located approximately 100 km. (60 mi.) east of Santa Cruz, close to the railroad. It was established in 1982 mainly by settlers from Belize, with several families each from Riva Palacios and Swift Current colonies in Bolivia. This Old Colony group is being served by Bishop Ben Peters of the Riva Palacios colony. In 1986 the church had 285 members and the total population was 785.   IHie

Tres Palmas Colony, Bolivia. The first Mennonite settlement in Bolivia, Tres Palmas was started in 1954 by several Mennonite families from the °Fernheim colony in Paraguay who were looking for a better climate and for better living conditions. Tres Palmas was located several km. ne. of the city of Santa Cruz. It was dissolved in 1986 when the few remaining families either moved back to Paraguay or to Canada.   IHie

Tres Palmas Colony, Paraguay, is located some 20 km.(12 mi.) north of the °Bergthal Colony, and ca. 40 km. (25 mi.) north of the °Sommerfeld Colony. The origin of Tres Palmas was somewhat unusual. A renewal movement came to several families in the Bergthal Colony in 1961 through listening to radio station HCJB of Quito, Ecuador. They were encouraged by peoples who had worked outside the colony, e.g., at the Centro de Salud Menonita Kilometer 81, a hospital for victims of °Hansen's disease (leprosy).. This renewal could not fit its desire for new forms e.g., Sunday schools and better elementary education, into the existing situation. They consequently moved to the land of Jacob Braun, naming their new village Lucero (Light).

Adjoining Lucero was the large land holding of John Janzen, likewise a °Bergthal Mennonite, who pursued lumbering and furniture production on his property. He made 14,000 hectares (34,580 acres) available to the new colony. With this land available at reasonable price settlers came from numerous other colonies in Paraguay, Mexico, Brazil, Uruguay,

Bolivia, the United States, Germany, and Russia. Many also left almost as quickly as they came, particularly from 1984 to 1986. This emigration, coupled with the diverse backgrounds of the settlers, has hindered the rapid development of the colony. Three villages have been established.

Education is available through grade 9 with the first six years primarily in German, but the following three accommodated to the national educational program of Paraguay. Spiritually the Evangelische Mennonitische Gemeinde (which relates to the Evangelical Mennonite Conference, formerly Kleine Gemeinde, in Canada) is the only established congregation. Its membership in 1986 was 60. Population of the colony was 220.   GR

Trinidad and Tobago is a lovely tropical Caribbean twin island nation of 1,980 sq. mi. (5,100 sq. km.) just seven miles from Venezuela. Arawak and Carib Indians inhabited these islands when Christopher Columbus landed there in 1498. African and Indian slaves and indentured servants arrived in these British colonies, which became independent in 1962. A Commonwealth-type parliamentary government was retained with elections held every five years.

The 1980 census revealed a population of 1,055,800 with 41 percent Negro, 41 percent East Indian, and 16 percent mixed. The four major religious groups are Roman Catholic (34 percent), Hindu (25 percent), Anglican (15 percent), and Muslim (6 percent). Trinidad's major trading partner is the United States (petroleum, sugar). The nation is moving from a primarily rural orientation toward an urban one, and from an agricultural society toward a technological society. Most agricultural work is still performed with hand labor, however. Primary school education is available to all children, but limited facilities and teachers do not permit all children to go on to secondary school. Part of the U. of the West Indies is located in Trinidad. In the 1970s educational and health facilities and services were expanded with funds from the oil boom.

Mennonite Church (MC) °broadcasting and medical work, beginning in 1969, led to the formation of the °Mennonite Church of Trinidad and Tobago. RFK

Trinity. See God, Doctrine of.

Troyer, George D. (1890-1969), was a missionary physician in India (Madhya Pradesh, 1923-36) and Puerto Rico (1944-67) with Mennonite Board of Missions (MC). He was born in Kokomo, Ind., the last of 29 siblings. He was the only one in his family to attend college. He graduated from the Chicago Medical School in 1922. He married Kathryn Sommers in July, 1914. Their four children, B. Nortell Troyer, Dana O. Troyer, Annabelle Troyer Greaser, and G. Weldon Troyer, all served overseas with Mennonite Board of Missions. George and Kathryn had significant leadership roles in the development of Mennonite General Hospital (ME IV:1057, 1107) and the Convención de las Iglesias Evangélicas Menonitas, Puerto Rico.   LHG

Troyer, Kathryn Sommers (1893-1973), was a missionary in India (Madhya Pradesh, 1923-1936) and Puerto Rico (1944-1967), with the Mennonite Board of Missions and Charities (MC). She was born in Kokomo, Ind., and married George D. Troyer on July 12, 1914. Even though her formal education was limited she became a capable Bible student and linguist. She was particularly effective in Bible studies and other ministries among women in India and Puerto Rico.

Following the Troyers' return to Goshen, Ind., in 1967, Kathryn became actively involved with Hispanic people and assisted in the beginning of the Hispanic Mennonite congregation in Goshen.   LHG

Trud Armia. See Spetskomandantura.

Trumbull Co., Ohio, Old Order Amish Settlement. See Geauga-Trumbull Counties, Ohio, Old Order Amish Settlement.

Tshikapa, Zaire. Situated at the confluence of the Kasai and Tshikapa Rivers, Tshikapa has been known since earliest Belgian colonial days as a diamond mining center as well as the traditional boundary between a cluster of ethnic groups: the Lulua to the east; the Baphende to the west; and the Chokwe, Lunda, and Babindi to the south.

Because the town was planned and built as the administrative center of the Belgian Forminiere Mining Company, local people were viewed primarily as a source of labor and the providers of needed food supplies. Thus they were regimented and closely supervised. While company money was freely used to develop housing for the expatriate personnel, a well-appointed Roman Catholic chaplaincy, a large hospital complex, and extensive camps for workers, Mennonite missionaries were for years tolerated in the camps only on an occasional visitation basis.

In the early 1950s, after much effort, the °°Congo Inland Mission (CIM) was at last able to secure clearance to build a station near Kalonda village on a hillside overlooking the Kasai River at a distance of some five miles from the town of Tshikapa. The Église du Christ au Zaire, Communauté Mennonite (CMZA, Zaire Mennonite Church) has since secured choice land at Tshikapa, adjacent to the government airport, where central administrative offices have been built to house the officers and department heads of the church.

In 1986 the CMZA counted nine churches in the Tshikapa area. It offers significant medical service on both sides of the river and sponsors a variety of schools as well as several book shops.

Lying approximately 640 air miles (1050 km.) to the se. of Kinshasa, the population of the Tshikapa area in 1986 was rapidly approaching 150,000.   JEB

Tshimika Mutondo (b. 1918). Born at the village of Shakalongo in the Belgian Congo (Zaire), Tshimika Mutondo attended primary school at the Shambungu Baptist Mission (1930) and was baptized in 1934. He worked as a cook in a missionary home and completed primary school in 1942. Later he completed Emmaus correspondence courses and extension theology courses. He married Makeka in 1942 and they both began teaching the Bible. Tshimika was ordained as a deacon in the Mennonite Brethren (MB) conference in 1945 and began preaching in the villages. From 1946 to 1957 he and his wife were houseparents for the girls in the school dormitory and Tshimaka was foreman of the mission workmen. In 1957 he was ordained as Mennonite Brethren pastor and church leader. Tshimika and his wife are the parents of seven living children.   AP

Tshinyama Katoko (Jean) (1911-Sept. 16, 1987) was born to Chief Tshenda and his wife Namevadi in the Belgian Congo (Zaire). He attended the Shambungu Baptist mission school in 1931 and the next year accepted Christ. From 1934 to 1935 he worked as a cook in a missionary's home. He was married in 1935 to Thumba and together they had several children. After completing primary school Tshinyama taught at Tshenda and later (until 1940) served as a preacher-evangelist at Tambwe.

In 1941 Tshinyama began nurses training at the Vanga Baptist Station and after completion of the training he worked in Iwungu, Nkara, and Kajiji. In the latter place he also preached to the patients as well as working as a nurse. After 1956 until his death he worked full-time as hospital evangelist at the Kajiji Mennonite Brethren Hospital.   AP

Tunggul Wulung (Tunggulwulung), Ibrahim (d. 1885). As something of a folk hero Tunggul Wulung's early life is enshrouded in legends that are difficult to confirm or deny. These include birth as a scion of the Javanese royal line (in about 1800), participation in the Java War (1825-30) against colonial rule, change of identity and relocation in the Juana area to hide from his past, spiritual dissatisfaction despite of material success, arrest for horse theft, and finally escape to become a hermit mystic on Mount Kelud in East Java. One scholar suggests that he is the author of the inflammatory 19th-c. Javanistic tract, Serat Darmogandul.

The mysterious discovery of the Ten Commandments on a scrap of paper under his mat, his mystic partner and wife Endang Sampurnowati, the indigenous Javanese Christian movement in Nogoro, and a Nederlandsch Zendelingengenootschaft (Dutch Missionary Board) missionary, Jellesma, in Mojowarno all seem to have influenced Tunggul Wulung's conversion to Christian faith in about 1852 (and baptism by Jellesma on July 6, 1857 with the Christian name Ibrahim). He also used the honorific title of a traditional Javanese teacher of religion, Kyai.

Early in 1853 Tunggul Wulung sought partnership with Mennonite missionary Pieter °°Jansz in Jepara. Unfortunately the terms Jansz set for such a partnership were too domineering and presumptuous in Tunggul Wulung's mind, and he ultimately saw no option but to form an indigenous Christian movement based in remote villages independent of any mission. He traveled the length and breadth of Java gathering his converts and some dissatisfied members of mission congregations into his remote Christian villages. His first settlement (1856) in the Muria area was Ujung Watu (near present day Margokerto). Soon his center of activity in this area shifted a short distance south to Bondo, where, after more than 30 years of ministry, he died and was buried. His second and third settlements in the Muria area were in Banyutowo and Tegalombo.

Though sharply criticized by the missionaries for his allegedly syncretistic teachings and practices Tunggul Wulung clearly had a stronger appeal among the Javanese people than the missionaries. He was able to facilitate the engagement of the gospel with the real world of the Javanese people in a very direct way. He seemed to relish challenging in the name of Jesus Christ the evil spiritual powers that the Javanese knew to be dominating their lives. And he did not hesitate to nourish the hope in his followers that the Christian teaching about the coming of the kingdom of God would in some measure correspond to their hoped-for deliverance from oppressive foreign rule and the debilitating influence of Islamic belief. Perhaps these things help to explain why he had nearly 10 times as many followers in the Muria area by the end of his ministry as did the Mennonite missionaries.

Tunggul Wulung's first wife was Endang Sampurnowati. He later lived with another woman, the widow of one of his followers, though his first wife was still alive and living in Ujung Watu. Claims of biological descent from Tunggul Wulung are very difficult to confirm. His spiritual heritage is much more clearly evident in the life of the Gereja Injili di Tanah Jawa (Evangelical Church of Java).

In his estrangement from most missionaries Tunggul Wulung found a friend and supporter in the high government official and promoter of indigenous Christian movements, Anthing. However, Anthing's later involvement with the Irvingite Apostolic movement left little imprint on Tunggul Wulung and his movement. Tunggul Wulung was an early teacher of the leader of the south Central Javanese indigenous Christian movement, Kyai Sadrach.   LMY

Philip van Akkeren, Sri and Christ (New York: Friendship Press, 1970); S. Coolsma, De Zendingseeuw voor Nederlandsch Oost-Indie (Utrecht: C. H. E. Breijer, 1901); Doopsgezinde Zendingsvereeniging, Verslag van de Staat en de Verrigtingen der Doopsgezinde Vereeniging to Bevordering der Evangelieverbreiding in di Nederlandsche Overzeesche Bezittingen the annual reports of the Dutch Mennonite Mission Union published in Amsterdam beginning in 1848; A. G. Hoekema, "Kyai Ibrahim Tunggul Wulung (1800-1885), 'Apollos Jawa,'" Peninjau, 7 (1978), 3-23; idem, "Pieter Jansz (1820-1904), First Mennonite Missionary to Java," MQR, 52 (1978), 58-76; idem, "De Tijd is Vervuld," Doops. Bijdr., n.r. 2 (1976), 144-59; P. Jansz, manuscripts of annual reports to the Doopsgezinde Zendingsvereeniging, in the archives of the Evangelical Church of Java in Pati, Indonesia; idem, personal correspondence and journal (Daagboek) in three handwritten vols. covering 1852-60 in archives of the Doopsgezinde Zendingsraad in Amsterdam; Th. E. Jensma, Doopsgezinde Zending in Indonesia ('s Gravenhage: Boekcentrum N. V., 1968); Martati Ins. Kumaat, Benih yang Tumbuh, V, a survey of the Evangelical Church of Java, (Jakarta: Lembaga Penelitian dan Studi—DGI, 1973); Sigit Heru Soekotjo and Lawrence M. Yoder, "Sejarah Gereja Kristen Muria Indonesia" [History of the Evangelical Church of Java], unpublished manuscript; J. D. Wolterbeek, Babad Zending ing Tanah Jawi (Purwokerto, Indonesia: De Boer, 1939); Lawrence M. Yoder, ed., Bahan Serjarah Gereja Injili di Tanah Jawa [Historical Resources on the History of the Evangelical Church of Java] (Pati, Indonesia: Komisi Sejarah Gereja GITD, 1977); idem, "The Introduction and Expression of Islam and Christianity in the Cultural Context of North Central Java" (PhD diss., Fuller Theological Seminary, 1987); idem, "Sejarah Margorejo," Wiyata Wacana, 7, no. 1 (1977), 18-25; idem, "Tunggul Wulung," Wiyata Wacana, 3, no. 2 (1974), 24-36.

Turkey. Members of the Conservative Mennonite Conference first entered Turkey as self-supporting "tentmakers" (Acts 18:3) in 1982. One individual was enrolled in the university as a student. The other was hired as a university teacher of English. Conscious of the fact that the Turkish government finds the presence of western missionaries offensive in a country where 99 percent of the people are Muslim, the Mennonite personnel were sensitive about how they shared their faith and worked to make responsible professional contributions to the country.

The Turkish constitution grants complete freedom of religion to all individuals. Christians are sometimes arrested and called in for questioning, but when brought to trial have always been acquitted.

One Mennonite worker was thus tried, acquitted but eventually evicted.

The harassment and societal pressure make conversion to Christianity extremely difficult but a small, national Christian fellowship is growing. Mennonite workers are contributing to this effort. They hope to maintain a low-key presence in the country.   JShow

Tuscarawas Co., Ohio, Old Order Amish Settlement. See Holmes-Wayne-Tuscarawas Counties, Ohio, Old Order Amish Settlement.

U

Uganda. Mennonite Central Committee (MCC) began work in Uganda in 1979 in what was intended as a short-term war reconstruction effort. It related primarily to the Church of Uganda because there was no Mennonite or Brethren in Christ Church in Uganda, and because, until late in 1986, there was no active ecumenical council. The MCC program has shifted from war reconstruction to a reconciliation effort. It has spread to various parts of the country working with a variety of ethnic and church groups in an attempt to manifest a peace witness in a society wracked by unending conflict. In 1986 there were six MCC workers in Uganda. Six others had to be reassigned to other countries because of unsafe conditions. Administration of the Uganda program, previously centered in °Nairobi, Kenya, was transferred to Uganda in 1986, with full-time program administrators based in Kampala.   DM/JM

Ulery, Orville B. (1880-1945), was a Brethren in Christ leader and businessman. He developed a greenhouse business in Springfield, Ohio, and with income from this business liberally supported many church activities, especially missions.

In 1910 he was elected to the ministry and in 1914 he became bishop of the Clark County district of southern Ohio. He served his denomination as evangelist and became known for illustrating his sermons with fluorescent rocks. He was chairman of the Publication Board from 1917 to 1944; under his leadership, the church paper, the *Evangelical Visitor*, became a °holiness paper. From 1923 to 1927 he served as acting editor of the *Evangelical Visitor*. At the same time, from 1928 to 1943, he was secretary of General Conference. He was twice moderator of that body.

Ulery was a strong °peace advocate. When General Conference in 1938 created a Nonresistance Committee, he served it first as secretary and then as chairman. As its chairman, he was the liaison between the Brethren in Christ and the Mennonite Central Committee (MCC) during the war years. He served on the subcommittee of MCC that was concerned with the °°Civilian Public Service camps. He was also chairman of the Committee on Labor Union Affiliation (BIC) which considered cases of conflict between members of the denomination and °labor unions.   EMS

E. Morris Sider, *Nine Portraits* (Nappanee, Ind., 1978), 308-36; Wittlinger, *Piety and Obedience* (1978), 325-327, 333, 335, 349, 402; *EV supplement* (Sept. 24, 1945), I-VIII.

Umsiedler (Resettlers.) Before the 1970s a few Russian Mennonites emigrated into the Bundesrepublik Deutschland (Federal Republic of Germany) within the scope of family reunification programs. Then the numbers of "resettlers" increased dramatically, came to a peak in 1978, and slowed down to almost none in the early 1980s. Some of those who had been members of Mennoniten-Kirchengemeinden (°Kirchliche Mennoniten) in the Soviet Union established new congregations with their own church buildings (°Bielefeld, °Neuwied, Wolfsburg), others joined existing congregations, especially those established by refugees from °West Prussia and the Soviet Union (Bechterdissen, Backnang, Espelkamp, Freiburg, Göttingen, Neuwied-Torney).

The ecclesiology of the resettlers is determined by the now fading tradition of Mennonite church life in Russia and by their consciousness as persecuted Christians. They prefer lay preaching; they do not expect their elders and preachers to have a theological education and to receive a salary. Their sermons have a evangelistic stamp. Choirs and church music play an important role. Ecumenical relations are upheld mostly with evangelical groups and the World Council of Churches in Geneva is regarded as fatal for Christendom. The resettler churches are growing, primarily due to missionary outreach.

Preferring to solve issues among themselves rather than joining the existing German Mennonite conferences, they established in Bechterdissen (°Bielefeld) in 1978 what became the Arbeitsgemeinschaft zur geistlichen Unterstützung in Mennonitengemeinden (AGUM), a task force for spiritual assistance in Mennonite churches. It takes care of the continuing education for preachers, makes Sunday school material available, assists smaller churches, attends to scattered sisters and brothers, and conducts evangelization. The Conference of Mennonites in Canada and the Algemene Doopsgezinde Sociëteit support the work of the AGUM with finances and personnel. A productive cooperation of the Vereinigung Deutscher Mennonitengemeinden with the resettler churches has not developed, despite many efforts. The resettlers find too little biblical rigor and church discipline in the *Vereinigung*; they object to the use of cosmetics and display of jewelry, and the wearing of fashionable dresses; and they also resist the salaried ministry by one pastor (one pastor system) among the *Vereinigung* congregations.   GHil

During the 1970s many members of the *Mennonite Brethren* church of Russia also entered the Bundesrepublik. The principal motive for leaving Russia was a deep longing for religious freedom and a serious concern for the future of their children.

Some of the resettlers joined the existing Mennonite Brethren congregations. The difference in understanding of the attitudes of personal piety, however, led the resettlers to establish four churches of their own between 1976 and 1979. A few years

895

later, the largest congregation was divided by controversy. In 1986 there were five independent resettler Mennonite Brethren congregations amounting to 1,400 members (Espelkamp [2], Waldbröl, Neuwied, Frankenthal). After the influx from Russia stopped, the churches grew more slowly. In the mid-1980s the annual increase in members was ca. 4-5 percent. Although these congregations have not joined a conference, they maintain close connections by visiting each other, by exchanging their preachers, and by conducting occasional seminars for preachers. Since the beginning, these churches have been concerned about integration and identity. Resolution of the tension arising from these concerns would be significant for the Mennonite brotherhood in West Germany. After almost 10 years the Brethren remain "resettler churches" and have no contact with other German churches. The Frankenthal congregation is an exception in its openness to outside visitors at worship services and its readiness to accept members who were not born in Russia. Children of resettlers do accept Mennonite religious instruction among the denominational options in German public schools. They maintain a Bible school, to train members for congregational work.

Since these churches are still developing and have to live in difficult circumstances, the question of foreign mission first arose in 1985. Both in Russia and Germany the Baptist Church seeks to gain influence in Mennonite Brethren churches. A clarification of the biblical well-founded differences between the Mennonite Brethren Church and the Baptist Church is most essential.   GWö

Return *emigrants,* or *Rückwanderer,* are Russian Mennonites who settled in South America in 1930-32 or 1947-48, then came to the Bundesrepublik beginning in the late 1950s. In Latin America they lived in the Paraguayan colonies of Neuland, Volendam, Fernheim, Friesland, and Menno; in El Ombu, Gartenthal and Delta in Uruguay; in the metropolitan areas of Buenos Aires, Argentina, and Curitiba, Brazil; and near Santa Cruz in Bolivia. The relief agencies Stichting voor Bjzondere Noden (Dutch) and Hilfswerk der Vereinigung Deutscher Mennonitengemeinden (German) commissioned Rie Hoogeveen, a Dutch social worker (1960-67), and Jakob Redekopp, manager of the retirement home at Enkenbach, (1967-72) as part-time workers to assist the *Rückwanderer.* The °International Mennonite organization (IMO) established in November 1972 the *Mennonitische Umsiedlerbetreuung* and employed Hans von Niessen to take care of the *Rückwanderer* and the *Umsiedler* from the Soviet Union as well. Since 1973 yearly meetings have been held for Rückwanderer and Umsiedler in Bechterdissen, Neuwied, °Espelkamp and °Bielefeld. In 1986 about 2,400 return emigrants were living in West Germany especially in the Bielefeld, Espelkamp, Gronau, Neuwied, and Stuttgart areas. Most return emigrants settled where they could find Mennonite congregations and jobs. Reasons for their coming were economic difficulties, social insecurities, and health problems in South America and the presence of relatives in the Bundesrepublik. A *Landsmannschaft der Südamerika-Heimkehrer* (Fellowship of the Return Emigrants from South America) was established in 1979; it had 270 members in 1986.   HvN

H. Dürksen, "Mennonitische Rückwanderer aus Paraguay," (unpublished thesis at the U. of Cologne, 1975, written with support from IMO); Heinrich Wölk and Gerhard Wölk, *Die Mennoniten-Brüdergemeinde in Rußland 1925-1980* (Fresno: Center for MB Studies, 1981), Engl. trans. as *A Wilderness Journey* (Fresno, 1982); *Menn. Jahrbuch* (1976-86; Hans v. Niessen, "Betreuungsdienst mennonitischer Aussiedler aus der UdSSR" in *Die Kirchen und das religiöse Leben der Rußlanddeutschen,* ed. Joseph Schnurr (Stuttgart, 1978).

See also Migration; Refugees.

Union of Mennonite Churches in Germany. See Verband deutscher Mennoniten-Gemeinden.

Union of Soviet Socialist Republics (USSR) (ME IV:381). An estimated 55,000 practicing Mennonites, or about 100,000 ethnic Mennonites, now live in this vast country that has become a nuclear superpower second only to the United States. They constitute about seven percent of the world population of Mennonites. If during the second half of the 19th c. the Russian Mennonites were leaders in the Mennonite world in °education, °wealth, in conference organization, and even in missionary vision, their condition during the Soviet period has been in sharp contrast. Soviet Mennonites are unorganized, poorly educated, dependent on other groups, and uncertain of their identity.

The USSR was initially quite restricted geographically and politically. Many Mennonites found themselves within the borders of the Ukrainian Republic which was considerably independent of Moscow until 1923. Other Mennonites in the Asiatic· part of the former Russian Empire encountered a variety of political administrations before Soviet power could gradually extend its reach. During the first decade of Soviet power, the major impact on the Mennonites was the experience of the civil war at close range. During the famine of 1921-23, many Mennonites suffered privation and death. For those living in the Ukraine, the USSR had come to mean the triumph of anarchy, the senseless destruction of property and people, and disregard for civilized values.

During their first decade in the new USSR, Mennonite leaders were preoccupied with helping their people adjust from being a special people with the °privilege of self-government, to one of equality with the rest of the Soviet population, and to finding an acceptable future there, particularly by emphasizing Mennonite expertise in agriculture. At the same time, those leaders were negotiating with Soviet authorities to secure permission to emigrate. At first emigration was envisioned for the relatively small number of displaced persons. The Soviet authorities were taken aback when B. B. °Janz, key organizer in the Ukraine, informed them that 20,000 Mennonites wished to emigrate. About 20,000 did indeed emigrate, mainly to Canada, from 1924-26, with an additional 6,000 (out of a much larger number gathered at the gates of Moscow) leaving via Germany in 1929. This emigration represented a major loss of leadership.

Mennonites and Soviet Religious Policy.
Mennonites had developed some experience in

cooperation across denominational lines through the forestry service (°*Forsteidienst*), broader evangelical efforts at evangelism (sometimes sharing the services of a full-time evangelist with Baptists and Evangelical Christians), and the review boards for °conscientious objectors (1919-30). In 1925 Mennonites met at an all-union conference, where they approved an eight-point appeal to the Soviet authorities, spelling out the minimum requirements for religious liberty: (1) undisturbed religious meetings and discussions in churches and private homes for adults and children; (2) unrestricted religious societies, choirs; (3) unrestricted erection of new church buildings, and tax exemption for churches and ministers; (4) unrestricted creation of Christian orphanages; (5) undisturbed acquisition of Bibles and other Christian literature, including periodicals; (6) undisturbed Bible courses for the training of ministers; (7) recognition of schools as a place for neither religious nor anti-religious propaganda; (8) exemption from military service and training, and granting of useful alternative service. This appeal was, of course, rejected by the Soviet authorities, who at that time were engaged in a concerted effort to secure the loyalty of religious bodies. The conference came to be known as a "martyrs' conference" since so many of the delegates disappeared in the prisons and camps later. In 1926 the Baptists, the Evangelical Christians, and the Pentecostals all met in national congress to approve a declaration of loyalty to Soviet power and to reject pacifism as a doctrinal position. The following year the Orthodox church's acting Patriarch Sergei issued a statement of full support for Soviet power. Since the Mennonites were never able to meet in conference again, they were never able to issue such formal statements, although in practice it made no difference then. Subsequently it has prevented their legal recognition as a denomination.

The new legislation on religion of April 1929, together with the renewed stress on ideology necessary to carry out large scale collectivization, represented the beginning of the worst attack on religion that all religious confessions have experienced in the USSR. The Stalinist purges came in waves, that of 1937-38 (the so-called *Yezhovschina*) probably having the most devastating impact. By 1938 virtually all leaders, whether clergy, teachers, or other civil leaders had been killed or imprisoned.

Mennonites experienced the second major campaign to eliminate religion, the Khrushchev campaign of 1959-64, with less severity than did the Orthodox and Baptists because few Mennonite congregations had been registered by then. Nevertheless, Mennonites were affected by needing to choose between two conflicting unions—the °All-Union Council of Evangelical Christians - Baptists (AUCECB) and the °Council of Churches of Evangelical Christians - Baptists (CCECB). Many Mennonites took this antireligious campaign as further impetus to move either to the °Baltic Soviet Socialist Republics, or to the °Kirgizian Soviet Socialist Republic, where the antireligious pressure was less severe.

With a somewhat more moderate revision of the basic legislation on religion in 1975, and the new emphasis on Soviet legality, as well as an apparent desire by local authorities to dampen emigration fever, Mennonite congregations began obtaining state registration as local autonomous societies. There are currently (1988) 25 independent Mennonite Brethren and 21 °Kirchliche Mennonite congregations with either full registration, registration as a branch of another group, or merely verbal permission to act as if registered.

Mennonites and Policy toward Soviet Germans. Under the tsars there was a clear sense of difference between (German) *kolonisty* and *Mennonity*. During the Soviet period Mennonites became fused with other Germans through common experiences. Like all Soviet Germans Mennonites experienced the forcible deportation to the east in 1941, or the forcible repatriation after the war. Together with all Soviet Germans they submitted to the °*Spetskomandantura* (Deportation Regime) until it was lifted in December 1955, and the subsequent three stages of gradual rehabilitation. Together with the Germans they experienced thoroughgoing russianization. Since educational and literary opportunities were so drastically restricted during the Deportation Regime, their knowledge of language and culture declined greatly. When Harold Bender visited in 1956 he predicted the loss of many Mennonite young people, some of them to other groups, if the Mennonite churches would not embrace the Russian language and culture. In 1986 another Mennonite World Conference delegation voiced concern not only about the lost generation, recognizing that now the churches would soon be required to adopt Russian as language of worship in order to survive, but also voiced concern about the general loss of a sense of Anabaptist-Mennonite distinctives. Yet the congregations revealed spiritual vibrancy, active children and youth programs (though not yet legal), and committed leaders handicapped due to lack of training and literature.

Soviet Mennonites have been confronting an identity crisis in several ways. With somewhat over half of the practicing Mennonites now part of an integrated union of Evangelical Christians-Baptists (the new common name for Soviet evangelicals including Pentecostals and Mennonites), there is uncertainty about a separate identity, yet a desire to retain links with Mennonites abroad. Loss of theological uniqueness (all registered independent Mennonite congregations were unable to include the nonresistance clause in their constitutions) has meant that Mennonite uniqueness was expressed culturally through language, and to a less tangible degree in a deliberately more eirenic style of decision-making.

Still another approach to retaining a separate identity has been to seek emigration to Germany. Many Mennonites were among the 40,000 Germans who applied for emigration when that was rumored to be possible in 1956. A modest program of reunification of families separated during the war developed from 1970-85, during which time more than 13,000 Mennonites came to West Germany (°*Umsiedler*). A second such movement began in February 1987, including more than 1,000 Mennonites and Baptists (mainly ethnic Mennonites) within the first 12 months. Once again leadership ranks have been decimated and families are uncertain what to do. The majority of Mennonites are likely to remain in the USSR after their second century of sojourn in the Russian lands, but the challenges to new and younger leaders are certainly daunting.   WWS

Gerd Stricker, "Mennoniten in der Sowjetunion nach 1941," *Kirche im Osten*, 27 (1984); John B. Toews, *Czars, Soviets and Mennonites* (Newton, 1982); Walter Sawatsky, *Soviet Evangelicals Since World War II* (Scottdale, 1981); idem, "From Russian to Soviet Mennonites 1945-1985" (forthcoming in *Russian Mennonites*, ed. John Friesen; *MWH* (1978), 63-71; Heinrich Wölk and Gerhard Wölk, *A Wilderness Journey. Glimpses of the Mennonite Brethren Church in Russia 1925-1980* (Fresno: Center for MB Studies, 1982; also published in German, Fresno, 1981); James Urry, *None But Saints: The Transformation of Mennonite Life in Russia, 1789-1889* (Winnipeg: Hyperion, 1988); *MWH* (1978), 63-71, 310; *MWH* (1984), 126.

See also German Language; Kazakhstan Soviet Socialist Republic; Moldavian Soviet Socialist Republic; Orenburg Region; Pleshanov Settlement; Russian Revolution and Civil War; Russian Soviet Federated Socialist Republic; Soviet Central Asia.

United Evangelical Church, Panama. See Iglesia Evangélica Unida, Panama.

United Evangelical Church, Vietnam. See Giáo Hôi Tin Lành (Hê-phái Mê-nô-nít), Vietnam.

United Evangelical Mennonite Churches, Paraguay. See Convención de las Iglesias Evangélicas Unidas Menonitas, Paraguay.

United German Mennonite Congregations. See Vereinigung der deutschen Mennonitengemeinden.

United Kingdom Conference of Mennonites. See London Mennonite Fellowship.

United Mennonite Conference of Ontario. See Conference of United Mennonite Churches of Ontario.

United Muria Indonesia Christian Church. See Persatuan Gereja-Gereja Kristen Muria Indonesia.

United States. See Amish; Beachy Amish Mennonite Fellowship; Brethren in Christ; Church of God in Christ Mennonite; Evangelical Mennonite Church; Fellowship of Evangelical Bible Churches (Evangelical Mennonite Brethren Conference); General Conference Mennonite Church; Hutterian Brethren; Mennonite Brethren Church of North America; Mennonite Church (MC); Old Order Mennonites; Old Order River Brethren; Reformed Mennonites.

United Zion Church (United Zion's Children). In February 1853 "The United Zion's Children" was organized by Mathias Brinser. This group was located mostly in eastern Pennsylvania, and was formerly a part of the "River Brethren" (Brethren in Christ). One of the issues in the formation of the United Zion's Children was whether meetinghouses were acceptable or whether Christians should only meet in homes. Brinser favored the use of a meetinghouse.

The church incorporated in 1953, and, in 1986, had 13 congregations and 880 members. The United Zion Church operates a nursing home, a campgrove (°holiness camps), and a youth center. It supports missionaries in Africa, Chile, and the United States.   JPM

Paul R. Hollinger, *UZ: A History of the United Zion Church, 1853-1980* (n.p.: the author, 1981); S. H. Brinser, and others, *Brief History of the United Zion's Children Church* (n.p., n.d.), 1-8; Wittlinger, *Piety and Obedience* (1979), 133-39, 379, 412, 466, 514, 549.

Universal Military Training is a response to modern warfare, i.e., warfare carried out by mass conscripted citizen armies. Universal Military Training (UMT) was invented to organize and manage the °conscription process. Typically it requires a period of full-time training followed by a longer reserve status punctuated by brief retraining sessions. In some cases the reserve status may last for two or three decades.

In the United States the first concerted effort to create a UMT followed World War I. In 1919 several bills were submitted to Congress. Most called for a two-year training period for all men between 18 and 26 years of age, followed by membership in a national reserve force.

The specter of wartime conscription transformed into peacetime conscription generated enormous concern among the °historic peace churches. Henry C. Early, moderator of the Church of the °°Brethren, called enactment of UMT a "calamity" and the Brethren in Virginia, under his leadership, issued a strong statement condemning the idea. The Mennonites launched an aggressive petition campaign which garnered 20,000 Mennonite signatures (25 percent of United States Mennonites in 1919) protesting passage of the UMT legislation. Americans viewed UMT as a form of European militarism and the legislative initiatives did not get out of congressional committees.

In January 1945 President Roosevelt announced his intention to propose a UMT program after the war. He hoped such a plan would circumvent the American people's reluctance to support a large peacetime military force, which Roosevelt believed was necessary. The plan was designed to create a reservoir of trained men who could be available for service. All men between 18 and 20 would undergo a period of military training and then become a part of a reserve pool of manpower for five years. Hearings were held on the bill in 1945 but the proposal never got out of the congressional committee. A second effort to create UMT failed in 1947, largely because important congressmen believed it impinged on personal freedom.

In 1951 the Universal Military Training Service Act was passed to raise personnel for the Korean War, but the UMT provision of the act could only be implemented after additional legislative action. That action was attempted in 1952, but was defeated. In its place Congress enacted a much more modest plan embodied in the Armed Forces Reserve Act which utilized regular inductees, who after five years of active service could opt for reserve status, with certain special privileges, and specified obligations with regard to recall to active service in the event of war.

A last effort to pass a UMT bill was made in 1955. It failed largely because of controversial amendments dealing with racial segregation in the National Guard. The bill would have inducted all young men for six months of training and membership in the reserves for six and one-half years. With the defeat of UMT in 1955, it was never again a serious legislative possibility. The idea was raised from time to time by military administrators, but fears about the militarization of American society, strong resistance to the sweeping compulsory quality of UMT, and the reliance, in the 1950s, on airpower as the centerpiece of American readiness (the air force, with its highly technical demands had little need for a generally trained reserve), all conspired to reduce UMT to a dead issue, although during the Vietnam War, UMT surfaced briefly.

Throughout these years the Mennonites consistently testified against UMT whenever the issue appeared. In June 1945 Harold °Bender made an eloquent argument against UMT to the House of Representatives Committee on Post-War Military Policy. He spoke for the Mennonite Central Committee. Over the next 10 years he appeared before numerous congressional committees on the same issue, as did Brethren and Friends (Quakers) leaders.

In other countries UMT laws are very common. Some notable exceptions of interest to Mennonites have been Canada, Zaire, Costa Rica, India, and Japan. The best, if somewhat dated, survey of international conscription policies is found in Prasad and Smyth, *Conscription: A World Survey* (1968).   ANK

See also Alternative Service; Conscientious Objection.

Unruh, Abraham H. (Apr. 5, 1878-Jan. 15, 1961), an outstanding Mennonite Brethren minister, teacher, and Bible expositor, was born in the village of Timir-Bulat, Crimea, South Russia. His father died when Abraham was only five. He was brought up by his uncle, Cornelius Unruh, a teacher who provided many educational opportunities for Abraham. He received his teacher's certificate at the age of 17 and began his teaching career in the elementary school of Menlertschik, 1895-1903. During this time, in 1900, he married Katharina Toews who was born on Oct. 8, 1876, in Klippenfeld, South Russia, but grew up in the town of Spat. Unruh taught in both the Barvenkovo elementary school and Kommerz-schule (business school), 1903-1915. It was here that most of the Unruhs' six children were born. In 1904, at the age of 26, he was ordained to the ministry.

Following two years of Red Cross service, 1915-17, he moved back to Barvenkovo, but anti-German sentiment ran high, and so he moved his family back to the Crimea where he accepted the position of principal of the *Zentralschule* (secondary school) in Karassan. In 1920 Abraham was asked to join the new-founded Bible School in Tschongraw. He taught Bible in this school until it was forced by Soviet authorities to close in 1924.

The closing of the school convinced him to mi-

grate to Canada in January 1925. That fall, inspired by the Tschongraw experience, he rented several rooms in Winkler, Man., and began a Bible school. He was soon joined by two other Tschongraw teachers, Gerhard Reimer and Johann G. Wiens. For 19 years Abraham led what became the Winkler Bible Institute, edited a small paper titled *Die Antwort* (The Answer), and taught the Bible and preached in Mennonite communities both in Canada and the United States. He also had a concern for quality Sunday School materials and wrote many materials himself. Conference educational concerns soon led to the call for a school of higher education for Mennonite Brethren in Canada.

In 1944 the Canadian Mennonite Brethren Conference established a new school in Winnipeg: Mennonite Brethren Bible College. Abraham Unruh was asked to be its first president. Concerned that the school needed a president who could relate more to English-speaking members of the MB churches, he resigned after one year as president, though he continued as professor of biblical studies for 10 years. Upon retirement at age 76, Abraham had served the church for some 50 years. His wife followed him in death on Nov. 7, 1963.

During his years of ministry Abraham wrote numerous books. Among them were: *Die Mennonitische Bibleschule in Tschongraw; Eine Einleitung für die Lehrer des Sontagsschule; Leitfaden für den Religionsunterricht; Nikodemus; Gottes Wort als Wegweiser fuer die Gemeindezucht; Des Herrn Mahnung an die Gemeinde der Endzeit; Der ewige Sohn Gottes; Der Prophet Jesaja; Die Geschichte der Mennoniten-Brüdergemeinde.*   KR

For additional writings see *Menn. Bib. II*, p. 512. In addition, see H. P. Toews, *A. H. Unruh, DD: Lebensgeschichte 1878-1961* (Winnipeg: The Christian Press, 1961); David Ewert, *Stalwart for the Truth: The Life and Legacy of A. H. Unruh* (Winnipeg: Board of Christian Literature, 1975); Peggy Regehr, "Abraham H. and Tina Unruh: A Granddaughter's Biography," *Mennonite Brethren Historical Society Newsletter*, 2, no. 3 (1984), 1-4; J. A. Toews, *Hist. MB* (1975), index.

Unruh, Abram A. (b. Oct. 20, 1903). Born in Barvenkovo, South Russia, to Abraham H. and Katharina Toews Unruh, A. A. Unruh was a missionary in India for 32 years (1935-67). Having attended high school and polytechnical school at Simferopol, Crimea, Russia, he migrated to Canada with his parents in 1925, where he attended Winkler Bible School for four years, Ontario Bible College for one year, and Tabor College (BA, ThB). He taught at Dalmeny [Sask.] Bible School for four years and Winkler Bible School for one year before being appointed to India and ordained in 1935 by Mennonite Brethren. He married Annie J. Enns of Winkler (Oct. 21, 1926), with whom he had five children. In India he served mainly in Gadwal and Wanaparty with shorter terms at Nagarkurnool and Shamshabad. His entire missionary ministry of evangelism and nurture was dominated by an overarching concern for the development of an indigenous church and training its leadership, as seen in his establishing of elders institutes. In 1975, following the death of Annie J. Enns Unruh (1972) he married Mrs. Agatha Friesen (nee Klassen) of Waldheim, Sask., who died on Aug. 31, 1983.   PMH

Unruh, Annie Enns (Mar. 17, 1900-Aug. 21, 1972). Born at Hoffnungsfeld near Winkler, Man., to John and Aganetha Wiens Enns, Annie Enns Unruh was a missionary in India for 32 years (1935-67). Having completed a Normal School education and one year at Winkler Bible School, she taught for seven years in public schools near Winkler. She married Abram A. Unruh (Oct. 21, 1926) and became the mother of five children: Peggy (m. Walter Regehr), Kathryn (m. Robert Des Roches), Helen (m. Oscar Epp), Louise (m. George Block), and Donald (m. Margie Unruh). All the children attended British, and later American, boarding schools in India. Serving with her husband at Gadwal, Wanaparty, Nagarkurnool, and Shamshabad, Annie Unruh was uniquely gifted in a ministry to women and was an effective teacher, readily winning the confidence of students who came for counsel.   PMH

Upper Barton Creek Colony, Belize, is a settlement of reformers from different backgrounds which was established in 1969 in the hills of western Belize. Because of convictions against the modernistic trends and for other reasons, several Low German families left the colonies of Spanish Lookout and Shipyard and were joined by some Mennonites from Pennsylvania who came to Belize via Arkansas. After some years of difficulty 11 families and a few native Belizian members joined a church at Scottsville, Ky. (USA) in 1984. These members who remained at Upper Barton Creek settlement live simply and in nonconformity to the world. They do not own any equipment with motors and do not use electricity. They oppose education above elementary school and the influence of worldly literature. They believe in strict discipline and religious teaching for children and also practice strict °discipline among adults to avoid "erring doctrines" and carnal-mindedness. Members are accepted from any nationality but only upon evidence of a change of heart and life. They do not smoke or drink, they dress plainly, and the men wear beards. They farm on a small scale using horses, producing vegetables, cattle, honey, etc. The colony is more self-sufficient than many. Total population in 1988 was 157 including 45 church members and 2 ministers.   HPF

Upper Volta. See Burkina Faso.

Urban Church (ME I:603). Some 16th-c. Anabaptist congregations were located in urban areas, and some Mennonite congregations in subsequent centuries were also located in urban areas. The period since World War II has seen a rapid increase in the number of urban Mennonite churches worldwide. As urbanization has increased around the world, Mennonites also have migrated from °rural areas to cities, and Mennonites have established new churches in cities.

In 16th-c. Europe, the Anabaptist movement began in (preindustrial) cities. But as persecution increased, many of those who survived withdrew to rural areas. Large groups of Mennonites in the intervening centuries (especially those in Switzerland, Prussia, Russia, and North and South America) maintained their separate identity and beliefs by living in relative isolation from the people and cultures around them.

North America. Although the Germantown Mennonite congregation, established in 1683, is technically the oldest North American Mennonite church in a city, it is a city church because Germantown later became incorporated into the city of Philadelphia. Most of the early Mennonite immigrants from Europe settled in rural areas, and, until World War II, Mennonites were still predominantly rural, more rural than Americans or Canadians as a whole.

The first major impulse for city churches came in the 1890s as congregations were established for eastern Pennsylvania Mennonites moving to such urban areas as Philadelphia or Souderton. During the period from 1890 to 1930, Mennonites were also influenced by the broader Protestant missionary movement. While overseas missions were beginning among Mennonites during that time, Mennonites were also looking to establish "foreign missions at home," that is, missions aimed toward recent immigrants from eastern Europe and other ethnic minorities in the large cities. Such missions were begun by Mennonite Church (MC) workers in Chicago in 1893; by Mennonite Brethren in Christ in Dayton, Ohio, in 1894; by Mennonite Brethren in Hurley, Wis., in 1907; and by the General Conference Mennonite Church in Los Angeles in 1909 (although earlier city churches had been started by its Middle District and Eastern District). Most city missions during that period were directed toward uplifting the poor or lower middle class and bringing them into the North American mainstream. Rural Mennonites often viewed the city as a den of wickedness and a place as much in need of the gospel as a "pagan tribe" overseas.

Beginning with the migration of Russian Mennonites to Canada in the 1920s, the city became a home for Mennonites much more rapidly. Immigrants not only settled on farms but in cities like Kitchener (Berlin) and Winnipeg. In addition, daughters of those who settled on farms often came to the cities to find work. The °°girls' homes, social, spiritual, and residential centers established for these young women, often served as bases for new congregations in cities like Winnipeg, Vancouver, and Saskatoon.

Until World War II, however, North American Mennonites were still predominantly rural. In 1943, 54 percent of General Conference Mennonites, for example, were farmers. By 1964, only 30.7 percent of General Conference Mennonites earned a living through farming.

Beginning about 1940 in Canada and after World War II in the United States, all the major Mennonite groups experienced a spurt in urban church planting. (This was also the experience of other American denominations.) In the United States, the Mennonite migration to the cities was encouraged by the military draft. As °conscientious objectors to military service, many Mennonite young men did °alternative service in hospitals and other institutions in cities. Many of them adjusted to urban ways, found jobs after the terms of service, and stayed in the cities. Mennonite mission boards and district conferences followed these and other migrating Mennonites to the cities and founded churches. From 1956 to 1968 more new Mennonite churches were founded than in any previous decade in the century, and almost all of these churches were in towns and cities. Issues of this new push for city churches were discussed in the newsletter *The Mennonite Church in the City.*

Another stimulus for new Mennonites churches began in the late 1970s. Within the Mennonite Church (MC) and the General Conference Mennonite Church (GCM), about 270 congregations were established between 1970 and 1985, and 60 percent of these were in cities of more than 30,000 population. This represents a much higher percentage of urban congregations than among the 587 mission churches founded by the Mennonite Church between 1890 and 1960. Of these, 26 percent were in towns and 12 percent in cities and suburbs. Of the 71 MC city congregations founded 1890-1960, 46 were begun after World War II. The Mennonite Brethren (MB), in 1986, had 48 congregations out of 117 in the United States conference that were located in towns and cities of over 20,000 population. In 1983 there were 412 Mennonite congregations (MC, GC, MB, Brethren in Christ (BIC)) in North America in counties with populations greater than 500,000. Their average attendance was 120.

Urban churches were more likely to experience high mobility and to include °house churches or small groups within the church to replace the natural social contacts with other church members often found in rural areas. Urban congregations were also more likely to be affiliated with more than one Mennonite conference. Almost all dually affiliated congregations (usually GCM and MC, occasionally also Church of the Brethren or other group) were located in larger towns and cities, where Mennonite divisions were less important than in the rural churches from which many members came.

Urban Mennonite churches in North America were more likely to have a higher percentage of members not of Mennonite background. It was estimated that 55 percent of Mennonite Brethren members in MB city congregations in 1986 were of non-German, non-Mennonite background. In addition, a growing number of urban churches were established for non-English-speaking groups, serving large groups of new immigrants. In 1986, the General Conference Mennonite Church had urban congregations for the following language groups: Spanish, Chinese, Vietnamese, and Laotian. A quarterly newsletter for urban Mennonite churches, *Urban Connections,* began publication in 1985.

Central and South America. Urban Mennonite churches in Latin America have also been primarily a post-World-War-II phenomenon. The first German-speaking Mennonites in Latin America settled in rural areas. Mennonites began moving to the isolated Chaco area of Paraguay in 1926. But the first Mennonite church in the capital city of Asunción was founded in 1949. Most of its early members were urban immigrants from the Mennonite colonies, and a large part of them were students. A German-speaking congregation, Vilardebo, began in Montevideo, Uruguay, in 1952. Its members are primarily managers, artisans, and students, and it attracts

many young people from the Mennonite colonies. In Brazil, Mennonite dairy farmers settled near the city of Curitiba and both General Conference Mennonite and Mennonite Brethren German-speaking churches have existed in that city since the 1950s. The movement from settlement to city or suburb is bringing about changes in Mennonite life in Brazil. The education level of church members is rising. There is more °acculturation to Brazilian life and the Portuguese language.

The earliest North American Mennonite mission work in South America was the Mennonite Church (MC) effort in Argentina, beginning in 1917. As in most Mennonite foreign mission work, the missionaries began in rural towns and villages. Work was begun in the city of Buenos Aires in 1949, initially to serve recent Russian Mennonite immigrants and then to serve Spanish-speaking people.

Even in the early post-World-War-II period, with its rapid expansion in mission work, most new Mennonite work began in rural areas. The General Conference Mennonite mission in Colombia began in 1945 with a school for children of °Hansen's Disease (leprosy) patients near Cachipay. Within the next 15 years, both the GCM and the MB conferences in Colombia began work in cities—the Mennonite Brethren in Cali, a city of over 700,000 (1958), and the General Conference in the capital city of Bogota, to follow up people from rural areas who moved to the city for studies. In 1986, that conference also had a second church in °Bogotá and another in the city of Ibague.

Initial rural strategies were also followed by Eastern Mennonite Board of Missions (MC) in Honduras (beginning in 1950), the Evangelical Mennonite Church in the Dominican Republic (1949), the Mennonite Board of Missions (MC) in Puerto Rico (1946), and the Brethren in Christ in Nicaragua (1965). Urban Mennonite churches were later established in all of these countries.

Mission work which began later has included both rural and urban churches at the beginning (Belize, Eastern Board, 1965; Guatemala, Eastern Board, 1971; Costa Rica, Rosedale Mennonite Missions [Conservative Mennonite Conference], 1965). In some instances work has begun in cities (Mexico City, 1960; Caracas, Venezuela, 1979).

Europe. Urban Mennonite churches have existed in The Netherlands and northern Germany since the time of the Reformation (Amsterdam, Danzig, Elbing, Hamburg, Emden, and later Krefeld). But in recent times across Europe, urbanization is affecting the shape of the church. Only a small proportion of European Mennonites are farmers.

In the Federal Republic of Germany, for example, congregations like Ludwigshafen and Würzburg changed already in the 19th c. from completely rural to almost completely urban congregations, with a shift to a new location for worship or a change in name, or both. Toward the end of the 19th c., new congregations were founded in a few of the larger cities of Germany (Berlin, Munich, Hannover, Kaiserslautern, and Stuttgart) because Mennonites had migrated to the cities in the wake of °industrialization.

The Mennonite refugees from West Prussia who

came to West Germany after World War II settled mostly in cities, even though almost all of them had been farmers before emigration. They either joined existing city congregations or formed new congregations in settlements, but even these did not have a rural character. A similar pattern is evident in the more recent groups of resettlers (°*Umsiedler*) from the Soviet Union. Where they have built congregations, they are city congregations and have members with urban °occupations.

In 1986, all the larger Mennonite congregations in Germany were city congregations. Their membership, however, has either stayed the same or declined. Many Mennonites in the latest decades have trickled away because they live where there is no Mennonite church. The loss for Mennonites from the younger generation has been estimated at 30 to 40 percent. Another phenomenon resulting from urban mobility is nonresident membership over a long period of time. People want to remain true to their home congregation and, even if a nearby congregation is available, often do not transfer membership.

In Switzerland before World War II, the only urban congregation was Schänzli near Basel, in which a majority of the members still lived in the country. Since World War II, congregations have started in Bern (1959), Biel-Brügg (1966), and Liestal (1975). Les Bulles, a French-speaking congregation, was founded in 1894 with a membership composed largely of farmers. By 1986, more than half lived and worked in the city. More Swiss Mennonite congregations are becoming French-speaking, an effect of industrialization.

Asia. Early North American mission efforts in India and China were mostly rural, although the Brethren in Christ early established a church in Saharsa, India. In India, the four Mennonite groups began work in rural areas about the turn of the century. In more recent years, Mennonite people have been moving from the older, established congregations to new industrial sites for employment. These form the core of the Aaga-harra, Bailadila, and Durg-Bhilai congregations of the Mennonite Church in India and the Raipur and Korba congregations of the Bharatiya General Conference Mennonite Church.

Even the mission work that began shortly after World War II did not start in the cities. The Mennonite groups that came to Japan in the early 1950s did not intend to start churches in the bigger cities. Rather, they went to rural areas, e.g. Hokkaido (MC) and Kyushu (GCM). As people moved from rural areas for education or work, Mennonite pastors followed them up. In this way the first congregation in Tokyo was established in the 1960s. The Tokyo congregations in 1987 were small (10 to 20 people) and experienced high mobility. One of the first Mennonite city congregations in Japan began unintentionally as an outgrowth of General Conference Mennonite missionaries in language study in Kobe, far from their intended area of work on the southern island of Kyushu (°mission: "A Young Church Leads the Way").

In Taiwan and Hong Kong, Mennonite churches have been urban from the beginning, although in Taiwan there has also been work with mountain tribal people. The Fellowship of Mennonite Churches in Taiwan has 17 congregations in the three urban centers of Taipei, Taichung, and Hwalien.

Africa. In Africa, most of the Mennonite mission work was first carried out among °animistic rural people, such as those in areas that became Tanzania, Rhodesia, Zaire, and Zambia. The major initiative toward Mennonite urban witness in Africa came from the local African churches. Frequently, missionaries were invited to participate and supplement the local effort. Much of the urban membership is comprised of rural people who had Mennonite connections before migrating to the city. This often results in small urban congregations with a rural or tribal mentality. Most African Mennonite congregations are rural or town-oriented rather than urban. However, they are affected by urbanization as men leave the villages to work in the cities, leaving women and children at home.

Some Mennonites had migrated to Nairobi, Kenya, as early as the 1950s. But a congregation did not start until 1973. Missionaries from the Eastern Mennonite Board began meeting for Sunday services with African Mennonite leaders living in Nairobi. A second congregation was opened in 1977 in a Nairobi slum.   LB

Lois Barrett, *The Vision and the Reality* (Newton, 1983); Ronald J. Dueck, "The Development of Canadian City Missions" (unpublished paper, Conference of Mennonites in Canada Archives, Winnipeg, 1966); J. Winfield Fretz, "A Study of Mennonite Religious Institutions in Chicago," (BD thesis, Chicago Theological Seminary, 1940); Juhnke, *Mission* (1979); A. J. Klassen, ed., *The Church in Mission: A Sixtieth Anniversary Tribute to J. B. Toews* (Fresno, Cal.: MB Board of Christian Literature, 1967); *MWH* (1978), (1984); Robert Kreider, "Vocations of Swiss and South German Anabaptists," *Menn. Life*, 8, no. 1 (Jan. 1953), 39-42; *The Mennonite Church in the City* (1956-68), a newsletter published by the Board of Missions, GCM, Newton; *Menn. Life*, 19, no. 1 (Jan. 1964), sp. issue; "Mennonites in Urban Canada," Proceedings of the 1968 Conference on Urbanization of Mennonites in Canada, U. of Manitoba, Winnipeg," *Menn. Life*, 23, no. 4 (Oct. 1968); John T. Neufeld, et al., "Mennonite Work in Chicago Prior to 1960," (unpublished paper, MLA [North Newton]; *Our Continuing Mission in the City: A Brief History of Western District Conference [GCM] Home Mission Churches* (Home Mission Committee, Oct. 1969); Paul Peachey, *The Church in the City*, Menn. Life, no. 2 (Newton, 1963); Simon Pellew, "Urban Strategy Questionnaire; Report of Analysis," (Elkhart, Ind.: MBM, Apr. 5, 1986); Theron F. Schlabach, *Gospel versus Gospel: Mission and the Mennonite Church 1963-1944* (Scottdale, 1980); Harvey Sider, *The Church in Mission* (Nappanee, 1975); *Urban Connections*, an inter-Mennonite urban newsletter, (Elkhart, Ind.: MBM, 1985-); Kauffman/Harder, *Anabaptists Four C. Later* (1975), 283-96; Yoder, *MC Census* (1985); Wittlinger, *Piety and Obedience* (1979), 174-77, 453-56; Stan Nussbaum, *You Must Be Born Again* (Ft. Wayne: EMCh, 1980), 21-22.

See also Bert, Sarah; England; Evangelism; Grubb, Elmer F; Hawaii; Kaufman, Elsie; Lapp, Sarah Hahn; Lapp, Fannie Hershey; Mission; Rescue Missions; Rural Mission; Schultz, George P.; Sociological Studies.

A Seventeenth-Century Mennonite Pioneer in the Bronx

Becoming mission aggressive in the last half of the 20th c. in New York State and New York City would indeed be an act of God's grace and power. For New York City is where the Mennonites first arrived in North America—in 1621 and following years, long before the Germantown, Pa., settlement of 1683. Why did the first Dutch Mennonite traders fail to establish a permanent Mennonite mission or church in New Amsterdam?

One reason is that Dutch Mennonites came for commercial purposes, not mission. Furthermore, under the Dutch government in New Amsterdam (1621-1664), Mennonites apparently worshiped with Quakers and Baptists but neither were tolerated by the Dutch. Fear of political reprisal from the Dutch government, which labeled Mennonites in New York City as "Anabaptist" along with other deviants may also have made them hesitant about proselytizing. (Mennonites in Holland were still being harassed at the time, although overt °persecution had ceased.) The Dutch Mennonites in The Netherlands had lost much of their evangelistic fervor since their assertive Anabaptist mission days of a century before. All of these factors may have inclined them to associate with Quakers and Baptist dissenters without making themselves distinctive and vulnerable.

Mennonites were not in New Amsterdam very long. Some recent research identifies Jonas Bronck, the founder of the Bronx as a Mennonite Anabaptist who lived only four years in New Amsterdam (1639-43) and then died, some think at the hands of the Indians. Bronck was the first white man to settle the Bronx. He built a house and established a farm at what is now 132nd Street and Lincoln Ave. He paid the Dutch West India Company and the Indians, with whom he sought to live in peace, for the Bronx land. He believed God led him to this Bronx wilderness which was a "veritable paradise" that needed only the industrious hand of man to make it the finest region in all the world. There is a famous painting in the Bronx Historical library of Dutch governor Kieft signing a peace treaty with the Indians in Bronck's house on April 22, 1642. Bronck refused to arm himself against the Indians and said "God is my defense." Bronck scolded the Dutch Governor Kieft once for treating the Indians too harshly. Bronck was an educated man who is credited for having the first library in New York City with volumes in Dutch, German, and Danish, mostly dealing with law and theology.

If Bronck had had more time would he have established a mission to the Indians? Would he have founded the first Mennonite Church in New York City? With such strong faith in God and a determination to live in peace could it not have been possible? Up to this time no research has shown that other 17th-c. Dutch Mennonite traders in New York City had a strong conviction about aggressive mission and pioneering permanence. Mennonites in New York City 345 years later have established 15 small churches, but still need to recover fully the aggressive urban mission of their 16th-c. Anabaptist forebears, as an impetus to establish strong permanent indigenous, urban Mennonite churches. **JIS**

J. Franklin Jameson, ed., *Original Narratives of Early American History* (New York: Barnes and Noble, 1949), 260; George L. Smith, *Religion and Trade in New Netherlands* (Ithaca: Cornell U. Press, 1973), 13, 237; Ann Lowry, *The Story of the Flushing Meeting House*, p. 13; Kessler and Rachler, *Peter Stuyvesant and His New York* (Bronx, N.Y., at the Bronx Historical Library); Esther Singleton, *Dutch New York*, pp. 130-71, 186; Henry T. Cook, *The Borough of the Bronx (1639-1913)* (New York: Bronx Historical Society), 10; C. Henry Smith, *Story of the Mennonites* (Newton, 1950), 179; Irvin B. Horst, "Report on New York City Survey Study and Investigation" (Salunga, Pa., Aug. 16, 1949), pp. 8-9; Pamphlet no. 4, "An Old Library" in section of *The Spirit of '76*, vol. 8, no. 3, Nov. 1901, printed by Louis H. Cornish, Nassau and Beekman, Morse Building, R. no. 27 and 28, N. Y.; John I. Smucker, "Reflections and Implications of Urban Mennonite Mission in the South Bronx" (PhD diss., Union for Experimenting Colleges and Universities, 1985), 14-16; John L. Ruth, *Maintaining the Right Fellowship* (Scottdale, 1984), 31, 52; Joust Dahlerup, "A Bronx Tercentary," in *Scandinavian*, Bronx Historical Library, N.Y., *Review*, vol. 29 (1939), 129-30; Wells, Haffen, and Briggs, *The Bronx and Its People (1609-1927)*, vol. 1 (New York: Louis Historical Publishing Co., 1927), 126.

Urbanization. During the 16th c. Christopher Columbus and many others explored new worlds. Feudalism was declining and nationalism was on the rise. New ideas were spawned, the old structures could no longer hold the new ideas, discoveries and religious ferment. It was a changing economic, political and religious environment, and new canopies had to be built to integrate new discoveries and traditional values. Urbanization was an important part of this process. The Anabaptist-Mennonite movement started primarily in cities such as Zurich, Bern, Strasbourg, Emden, Amsterdam, Leewarden, Groningen, Leyden, Rotterdam, Antwerp, Brussels, Münster and Cologne. In the Swiss, South German, and Austrian cities, the Anabaptist movement was crushed and survived only in remote areas. It was different in The Netherlands. Of the thirteen cities listed by Cornelius Krahn, only two were Swiss; the majority were north European, often members of the Hanseatic commercial league. While Anabaptists in central Europe fled the cities, in the northern cities they survived first as an underground movement, later as a tolerated minority and finally as a recognized religious group. (It must be remembered that these cities were relatively small and nonindustrialized. The largest of them had 100,000-200,000 inhabitants, many had between 20,000 and 50,000. They were dominated by commerce and artisan crafts rather than large industries and factories. Many urban dwellers maintained small livestock; city neighborhoods retained some elements of rural life.)

Paul Peachey's study, published as *Die Soziale Herkunft der Schweizerischen Täufer* (The Social Origins of the Swiss Anabaptists), of 762 Swiss individuals who were connected with the Anabaptist movement in central Europe, shows that 150 of these were urban (20 percent). There were 612 villagers and peasants (80 percent), whom he classified as rural. Of the 150 who were urban, 20 had been clergy (14 priests and 6 monks), 20 more were urban lay intellectuals (including °Grebel, °°Manz, °°Denck and °°Hugwald), 10 came from the nobility, and 100 were citizens, often urban artisans. Among the artisans, tailors and bakers were most common. Peasants (460) constituted about three-fifths of the total number of persons listed. Combining them with the villagers we conclude that four-fifths of the people appearing in court records belonged to the nonurban population. Most of the urban Anabaptist leaders disappeared within two years (1525-27) through martyrdom, early death, recantation, exile or other unknown destiny. Thus, the Swiss Anabaptist movement was only one-fifth urban to begin with, and almost completely rural two years later. Severe persecution made an urban foothold impossible.

Urbanism among Mennonites of the northern Low Countries is as old as Mennonitism itself. There are some 1,500 Mennonites in Amsterdam, and some 1,300 in Haarlem in 1986 as well as more than 1,000 in a number of other cities. In the 16th c. Amsterdam and Rotterdam were part of the Hanseatic League, whose ships plied the Baltic sea between such ports as Bergen, Oslo, Stockholm, Copenhagen, Danzig, Amsterdam, Rotterdam, and London. While °Menno Simons himself emerged out of rural Friesland, he nevertheless served Mennonites in many urban centers of the 16th c.

W. L. C. Coenen made a study of the Anabaptist martyrs in The Netherlands and found that not one out of 161 martyrs was a farmer. Among the 58 °occupations were weavers (27), tailors (17), shoemakers (13), sailors (6), carpenters (5), goldsmiths (5), hatmakers (5), bricklayers (4), bakers (3), leather dealers (3), teachers (3), saddlers (3), and potters (3). There were also Mennonites in rural areas in North Holland, Friesland, and Groningen. °Persecution also drove some to the east into Prussia, mostly into the countryside as well as the suburbs of cities such as Altona, Hamburg, Danzig, Marienburg, Elbing and Koenigsburg. Many moved upward into the middle class.

Thus, two major Mennonite branches emerged in Europe: The Swiss and South German rural farmers, and the Dutch, North German Russian entrepreneurs with roots in the commerce and artisan manufacturing of northern Europe. While many Dutch Anabaptists have always remained urban, most others turned to safer rural environs and became farmers because of persecution. Thus, for hundreds of years, these rural Mennonites have been known as the "Stillen im Lande" (peaceful country folk). However, in the 20th c. Mennonites in some parts of the world are moving to cities.

World Mennonite Urbanization. A °Mennonite World Conference map shows that in 1984 there were 724,000 Mennonite members in 57 countries. Almost half (46.1 percent) resided in two countries of North America, (333,704 members) and the other half (53.9 percent) were located roughly in equal numbers on the four continents of Asia (7 countries, 113,504 members), Africa (11 countries, 107,221 members), Europe (13 countries, 92,368 members), and Latin America (23 countries, 76,938 members). Only one eighth (12.7 percent) live in Europe, the place of Anabaptist beginnings. About two-thirds (most in Europe and North America, and some in South America) are descendants of European Caucasians, and one third are now mostly of Asian and African origins (°demography).

In 1984, 90 percent of all Mennonites in the world lived in eleven countries. In Table 1 we see that one third (32 percent) live in the United States; only about 5 percent live in the original countries of The Netherlands (2.8 percent), Germany (1.6 percent) and Switzerland (.4 percent). The range of urbanization of these countries varies enormously from a high of 82 percent in The Netherlands, to a low of 14 percent in Tanzania.

While statistics on Mennonite urbanization for the United States and Canada are available, it is very difficult to assemble data on urban Mennonites in the Soviet Union and most of the other countries. Estimates by Mennonites who live in these coun-

URBANIZATION
Compiler: Leo Driedger (author of article)

Table 1. Mennonites in Eleven Countries and Degree of Urbanization of These Countries, 1974-83

Countries	% of Nation Urban	Number of Mennonite Members	% of Total World Mennonites
United States	73.1	232,192	32.1
Canada	75.7	101,512	14.0
Zaire	34.2	66,408	9.2
Indonesia	22.4	62,911	8.7
Russia	64.1	55,000	7.6
India	22.1	43,998	6.1
Mexico	66.0	31,161	4.3
Netherlands	81.7	20,200	2.8
Paraguay	38.6	13,939	1.9
Tanzania	13.8	13,614	1.9
West Germany	77.0	11,688	1.6
Totals		**652,623**	**90.2**

Source: United Nations Demographic Yearbook, 1983, and Mennonite World Conference map, 1984.

URBANIZATION

Table 2. Comparison of American and Canadian Mennonites by Rural and Rural Differentiations

Country and Region	Size of Community							
	Farm	Rural Non-Farm	Village/ Town 2,500	2,500- 25,000	25,000- 250,000	Over 250,000	Total %	N
USA								
East	35%	31	13	16	4	1	100	(895)
Midwest	36	20	15	19	9	2	100	(792)
Prairies	39	4	26	15	7	10	100	(760)
Pacific	13	9	4	28	25	21	100	(326)
Total USA %	34	18	16	18	9	6	100	
N	(933)	(491)	(447)	(492)	(241)	(169)		(2773)
Canada								
Ontario	29	11	15	13	29	2	100	(299)
Prairies	42	2	12	5	4	35	100	(373)
British Columbia	17	21	10	19	19	4	100	(93)
Total Canada %	34	8	14	10	16	18	100	
N	(258)	(62)	(108)	(76)	(120)	(139)		(763)
North American								
Sample %	34	16	16	16	10	9	100	
N	(1191)	(553)	(555)	(568)	(361)	(308)		(3536)

Source: Kauffman/Harder, *Anabaptists Four Centuries Later* (1975); Driedger and Kauffman in *MQR*, 56 (1982).

tries, show that usually Mennonites are more rural than respective national urban figures; in no case were Mennonites more urban than respective national averages. Mennonites still are urban in The Netherlands, where they have always lived in cities, and where they remain the largest original Anabaptist group (20,000). Mennonites have also moved very heavily into cities in the Soviet Union after World War II, and Mennonite urbanization is also escalating in North America so that about half of Canadian Mennonites are urban.

Urban Mennonites in North America. Since almost half (46.1 percent) of all Mennonites live in the United States and Canada, and since the best urban data are available from there, we shall examine North American Mennonite urbanization in more detail. Howard Kauffman and Leland Harder made the most extensive survey of North American Mennonites in 1972; Driedger and Kauffman published a paper on urbanization using some of these data in 1982. They found that two thirds of the total sample of Mennonites taken in North America were rural, and one third were urban, living in cities of more than 2,500 people. They found that Canadian Mennonites were significantly more urban (44 percent) than American Mennonites (32 percent). However, there are many interesting variations by region and by size of community.

We find Canadian and American Mennonites are similar in the farm and village/town categories. However, there are twice as many rural nonfarm Mennonites in the United States (18 percent) as in Canada (8 percent). This greater proportion of nonfarm American Mennonites accounts for the higher total rural proportion.

The basic difference between the two countries in the three urban categories (small city, medium, and large metropolitan centers), is that American Mennonites reside twice as frequently in small cities and Canadian Mennonites are two to three times more likely to reside in larger metropolitan centers. There were also important regional variations. Only 20 percent of the Mennonites in the American East, 23 percent in the Midwest, 32 percent in the American prairie states, and 74 percent of the Pacific Coast Mennonites were urban. Mennonites in the western United States, who were largely of Dutch-Russian background were roughly twice as urban as the Mennonites in eastern America, who were largely of Swiss (Pennsylvania-German) background. These urban distinctions by region are not apparent in Canada. Roughly 40 to 45 percent of the Mennonites were urban in all parts of Canada in 1972. Since then urbanization has increased.

A closer examination of Mennonites in some of the major metropolitan centers of North America shows that there are 1,000 or more members in six centers in Canada. The largest numbers are located in Winnipeg (9,400), Saskatoon (2,300), Kitchener-Waterloo (2,300), and Vancouver (4,800) in 1985. These Mennonites worship in more than a dozen churches in each of five of the centers (3 dozen in Winnipeg). Canadian urban Mennonites are mostly of European heritage who have moved to the cities from rural hinterlands, or who have entered cities as immigrants especially after World War II. Each of the eight cities listed have substantial rural Mennonite hinterlands which feed into these cities. While Mennonites of Asian backgrounds are also starting urban churches, they still represent a small proportion of urban Mennonites in Canada; African origin Mennonites hardly exist in Canada.

The patterns of Mennonite urbanization tend to be different in the United States. Rural Mennonites have not so much moved from hinterlands into large metropolitan centers as they have been attracted more to small cities (Lancaster, Harrisonburg, Elkhart). Mennonite congregations in larger cities are more often the result of mission and church planting efforts and represent a greater variety of ethnic and racial backgrounds. Table 3 indicates that there are relatively small numbers of Mennonites in the very large American metropolitan centers of three million or more. The 2,754 Mennonites who worship in 60 congregations located in Chicago (1,006 members), Los Angeles (534), Washington (437), New York City (406), and Philadelphia (371), comprise groups averaging fewer than 50 members, compared to Canadian urban churches with average memberships of 325. Eastern American Swiss Mennonites are attracted more to smaller urban centers of 50,000 or less: Lancaster, Pa. (9 churches, plus others outside the city itself), Goshen, Ind. (12 churches, with 9 more in adjoining rural areas), and Harrisonburg, Va. (10 churches, plus several located in adjoining rural areas). Western Russian-background Mennonites in Fresno, Cal, (7 churches), and Wichita, Ks. (6 churches), follow the Canadian pattern more.

Amsterdam was the world urban Mennonite center for more than 400 years, with Mennonite membership as high as 10,000. By 1986 this had declined to 1,500 members worshiping in five places. This was part of a general decline in membership in The Netherlands from 31,000 in 1972 to 20,200 in 1984. Thus, after World War II, Winnipeg has emerged as the largest urban Mennonite center in the world with 19,100 Mennonites (1981 census), representing about 9,400 adult members who worshiped in 44 churches in the city in 1988.

There are many Mennonite institutions in Winnipeg, including two colleges, two high schools, the Mennonite Central Committee headquarters for Canada and for Manitoba, two offender ministries half-way houses for former prisoners, a hospital, many homes for the elderly, several credit unions, 44 churches, six newspapers, several musical and

URBANIZATION

Table 3. Mennonites Located in Selected Metropolitan Centers of Canada and the USA, 1985

Metropolitan Centers (100,000 plus)	Size of Metropolitan Population (Census 1980/81)	Number of Mennonites (all ages, 1981 Census)	Number of Mennonite Churches	Mennonite Adult Membership
CANADA				
Winnipeg	578,625	19,105	36	10,000
Saskatoon	152,265	9,915	14	5,000
Kitchener/Waterloo	285,145	9,760	14	4,900
Vancouver	1,250,610	9,515	16	4,800
St. Catherines	301,565	5,985	6	3,000
Calgary	587,025	3,635	12	1,900
Toronto	2,975,495	2,950	4	1,500
Edmonton	650,895	1,920	7	1,000
USA				
Lancaster, Pa.	54,725	(non-metro)	23	3,100
Harrisonburg, Va.	53,264	(non-metro)	10	1,784
Fresno, Cal.	515,013		7	1,249
Elkhart, Ind.	46,515	(non-metro)	9	1,144
Chicago, Ill.	7,102,328		18	1,006
Wichita, Ks.	411,313		6	978
Los Angeles, Cal.	7,477,657		10	534
Washington, D.C.	3,060,240		9	437
New York, N.Y.	9,119,737		14	406
Philadelphia, Pa.	4,716,818		9	371

Source: 1980 USA Census, 1981 Canadian Census, and Mennonite conference yearbooks.

drama societies, two national conference offices (GCM and MB), and scores of Mennonite businesses and companies. A variety of conferences, associations, corporations, organizations, and societies keep information flowing between Winnipeg Mennonites and other Mennonite communities.

Leadership of Mennonite churches in Winnipeg has been entirely Mennonite. About 150 ministers have served the 44 Mennonite churches in Winnipeg over the past fifty years, and all of them (except four to six) were Mennonite. Many were well educated and were heavily involved in provincial, national, and international Mennonite conference activities. Most of the leaders in the 44 churches are graduates of Mennonite Bible schools, high schools, colleges and seminaries. Thus they come in constant contact with networks of leaders from all over Canada, the United States and the world. Mennonite leadership also extends to editors of Mennonite and non-Mennonite Winnipeg papers; businessmen in influential places; teachers and professors at elementary, secondary, and university levels; social workers; medical professionals; and virtually all other °professions and °occupations. These positions have given them the means to inform and promote their identity at all levels of society. More importantly, they are active in their Mennonite churches and they are committed to their heritage and perceived by their fellow Mennonites as committed members. The degree of integration between Winnipeg Mennonites in their Mennonite structures and their everyday occupations is considerable. It is a natural outflow of their faith, life and work. Similar activities are happening in many other cities, but usually not on the same scale.

Urban Mennonite Beliefs and Attitudes. To what extent do beliefs and attitudes of Mennonites change as they urbanize? The early Anabaptists believed in adult °baptism, and they could not take part in war. They also believed in the °priesthood of all believers, a °disciplined church and the importance of °evangelism. They did not swear the oath, and they could not serve in °governments. Studies show that these beliefs are still held by urban and rural North American Mennonites alike. However, Driedger and Kauffman found more rural-urban differences when they examined social issues of the day. There was a great deal of consensus against issues such as use of hard drugs, and becoming drunk. However, many more rural than metropolitan Mennonites thought that it was wrong to gamble (80 to 69 percent), smoke tobacco (67 to 56 percent), remarry when the first spouse is still living (66 to 49 percent), drink alcohol moderately (57 to 34 percent), °divorce when the cause is not adultery (55 to 39 percent), attend for-adults-only movies (54 to 32 percent), engage in social °dancing (50 to 30 percent), masturbate (49 to 37 percent), and divorce when the cause is adultery (39 to 24 percent).

Fewer metropolitan Mennonites hold to some present and past norms of personal morality, but there is somewhat more urban flexibility on °family breakdown. More research is required to document the quality of urban Mennonite beliefs, attitudes and behavior especially in other parts of the world. LDr

W. L. C. Coenen, *Bijdrage tot de Kennis van de Maatschappelijke Verhoudingen van de Zestiendeeeuwische Doopers* (Amsterdam, 1920), 1-90; Leo Driedger and J. Howard Kauffman, "Urbanization of Mennonites: Canadian and American Comparisons," *MQR*, 56 (1982), 269-90; Leo Driedger, "Canadian Mennonite Urbanism: Ethnic Villagers or Metropolitan Remnant?", *MQR*, 49 (1975), 150-62; idem, "Post-War Canadian Mennonites: From Rural to Urban Dominance," *JMS*, 6 (1988), 70-88; Cornelius Krahn, *Dutch Anabaptism: Origin, Spread, Life and Thought* (Scottdale, 1981), 90-100; Kauffman/Harder, *Anabaptists Four C. Later* (1975); Paul Peachey, *Die Soziale Herkunft der Schweizerischen Täufer in der Reformationszeit* (Karlsruhe, 1954), 102-27; Paul Peachey, *The Church in the City* (Newton, 1963).

See also Acculturation; Kinshasa, Zaire; Migrations; Modernity; Professions.

Uruguay. According to the 1986 census, almost half of the less than 3 million inhabitants of Uruguay live in the capital city of Montevideo. Only 4 percent claim active membership in any religious community, including the Roman Catholic church, the largest denomination.

During the first half of the 20th c. Uruguay experienced a period of extraordinary economic, civic, social, and cultural growth. Signs of deterioration began to show thereafter and the country gradually ceased to be known as "the Switzerland of America." In 1973 the country came under the control of a military junta in response to a subversive guerrilla movement which had arisen to protest corrupt administrative practices. The years which followed saw a people long-accustomed to political liberty subjected to suffering, oppression and self-repression. Individual liberties were suspended and human rights violated. By 1980 a major movement of civic opposition developed which led eventually to democratic elections in 1984 and a constitutionally elected president in 1985. Social and economic conditions reflected the turmoil of recent years: in Montevideo, 40 percent of the families live below the poverty level with incomes that are less than twice the cost of food; 13 percent are indigent; 25 percent of the children admitted to hospitals are found to be suffering from malnutrition. The quality and reach of education has dropped.

In 1986, the total baptized Mennonite membership was 1,000. Of these, 525 belong to the four congregations of the Konferenz der Mennonitengemeinden, 295 belong to the seven congregations affiliated with the Convención de las Iglesias Menonitas, and 180 belong to the seven congregations organized under the Consejo de las Congregaciones de los Hermanos Menonitas (MB)). In 1960, the °Evangelization Board of the Mennonite Churches of Uruguay was organized, to take care of local needs. These included the Seminario Evangélico Menonita de Teología (1956-73), which was replaced by Centro de estudios y retiros (Study and Retreat Center) of the Mennonite Churches in Uruguay in 1974. In 1986 it offered a three-year certificate program and regular schedule of weekend fellowship and study retreats. The Consejo also operates a training center in Montevideo. The two institutions have carried on some parts of their programs cooperatively.

The °cooperative practices of the German-speaking Mennonite colonies (Konferenz der Mennonitengemeinden) are a modern adaptation of

Christian brotherhood economic principles (°mutual aid). These practices have made it possible for the colonies to survive economically, whereas many individuals would not have been able to do so. In 1984 the Inter-Mennonite Council for Social Services was formed with representatives from the Convención, the Konferenz and the Consejo. It provides a channel through which congregations can share with brothers and sisters in need, as well as in the wider community. A similar concern has led the Convención and the Konferenz to operate Hogar Siquem, a home for children and adolescents. The Mennonite Central Committee participates in both of these programs.

Undoubtedly, first the Seminario, and later the Centro de estudios y retiros, have both played an important role in articulating Anabaptist principles of °biblical interpretation. A peoplehood ecclesiology and a vision of the church as a family of brothers and sisters may well be one of the most important contributions of the Mennonite Churches in Uruguay. And even though military service is not obligatory in Uruguay, pacifist convictions and teaching on °peace and °justice are to be found among the Mennonite congregations. There is an Anabaptist ferment abroad in the church which calls for moving from theory to a practice which is more radically biblical.   MR

MWH (1978) 264-71; *MWH* (1984); H. Wall, "Drei Jahre in Uruguay," *Menn. Geschbl.*, Jg. 9, n.F. 4 (1952), 18-26; G. E. Reimer, "Die Mennoniten in Uruguay," *Menn. Geschbl.*, Jg. 11, n.F. 6 (1954), 55-60.

Uruguay Mennonite Conference. See Convención de las Iglesias Menonitas en Uruguay.

V

Vacation Bible School. See Summer (Vacation) Bible School.

Valle Esperanza Colony, Bolivia, also referred to as Hoffnungsthal, is located about 140 km. (90 mi.) ne. of Santa Cruz. It was established by Old Colony Mennonite settlers from Mexico in 1975. Bishop Johann Loewen is the colony's church leader. In 1986 the colony had 1,400 inhabitants, of whom 607 were baptized church members. This colony is one of the most prosperous Old Colony settlements in Bolivia, partly due to good land.   IHie

Venezuela. See Concilio de las Iglesias Evangélicas Menonitas, Venezuela.

Verband der Mennonitengemeinden in Baden-Württemberg (Association of Mennonite Churches in Baden-Württemberg). See Baden-Württemberg.

Verband deutscher Mennonitengemeinden (Federation of Mennonite Churches) (ME IV:809; I:211). In 1986 the following 22 congregations belonged to the "Verband": Augsburg, Backnang, Bad Königshofen, Deutschhof, Eichstock, Freiburg, Hasselbach, Heidelberg, Heidenheim, Heilbronn, Ingolstadt, Karlsruhe-Thomashof, Möckmühl, Neustadt-Branchweilerhof, Nürnberg, Regensburg (jointly with a membership of the Vereinigung der Deutschen Mennonitengemeinden), Reutlingen, Sinsheim, Stuttgart, Überlingen and Würzburg. The churches are mostly situated in cities of the Federal states of °Baden-Württemberg, °Bayern, and °Rheinland-Pfalz. They number 1,632 baptized members. Nineteen elders, 42 preachers, 20 deacons, and many volunteers care for duties and services. Although the Verband keeps strictly to its principle of non-professional preachers, 7 preachers and one congregational assistant for the church work are employed on a half-time or full-time basis. They have been educated at universities, seminaries, or Bible schools.

Formerly, the Verband was meant to be a single congregation under common leadership of the elders (°°*Ältestenrat*); in the 1980s each local congregation determines its own matters independently. Matters of more general concern are discussed and decided in the conference of the elders, preachers, and deacons, (*Ältesten-, Prediger-, und Diakonenversammlung*, ÄPDV), which is composed of brothers and sisters selected by the churches. Meetings are held quarterly for the purpose of fellowship and discussions; voting is avoided wherever possible. A member of the Verband's general board or an authorized deputy chairs these meetings.

The Verband's most important tasks are preaching the gospel in worship, pastoral care, evangelization, and missionary work. Mission is carried out together with the °Deutsches Mennonitisches Missionskomitee. The Verband is engaged in relief work through the Mennonitische Hilfswerk Christenpflicht, in youth work together with the Arbeitsgemeinschaft süddeutscher Mennonitengemeinden, and in °peace witness jointly with the °Deutsches Mennonitisches Friedenskomitee. The Verband arranges for meetings, retreats, and seminars to prepare its members for a living in faith and service. Its purpose is to foster °discipleship; to promote faith, love and hope in the churches and in every individual person; and to challenge and prepare for a missionary and peacemaking service to neighbors.

All churches of the Verband also support the Bibelheim der Mennoniten-Thomashof near Karlsruhe, which was founded in 1924 as a home for the aged, as headquarters for the Verband, and a place for retreats. The official organ of the Verband, °°*Gemeindeblatt der Mennoniten,* was replaced by *Gemeinde Unterwegs* from 1974-85. Since 1985 both the Verband and Vereinigung der deutschen Mennonitengemeinden are served by *Brücke.*

When founded in 1904, the task of the °°Diakonissenwerk of the Verband (deaconess program) was to care for the Verband's families and the Hospital Adelsheim. Later deaconesses served at the Bibelheim Thomashof. Lack of trainees, however, has brought deaconess work to an end. The system of itinerant preachers (°°*Reiseprediger*) established in 1871 gradually shifted to a church building program. Twice a year, before the observance of °communion, the preachers exchange visits with the neighboring churches. Compared to former times, the congregations meet more often for the Lord's Supper. In accordance with a resolution of the ÄPDV, baptism by immersion as well as by pouring is being practiced.

All churches of the Verband are also members of the Mennonitische Hilfswerk Christenpflicht, founded in 1920 for the support of the needy, particularly of the Mennonite refugees from Russia. After 1945 their challenges were great. The Hilfswerk works closely with the °International Mennonite Organization (IMO) and maintains a home for the elderly in Burgweinting near Regensburg.

The Verband maintains relationships with other German Mennonite conferences and to the Mennonite World Conference in particular. It is an associate member of the Vereinigung Evangelischer Freikirchen (Union of Protestant Free Churches). It also contributes in every respect to the realization of the purposes of the recently established Arbeitsgemeinschaft deutscher Mennonitengemeinden. All churches of the Verband are encouraged to extend fellowship toward other denominations at local levels.

909

The general board of the Verband is at the same time both leading and executive body of the ÄPDV. Chairmen of the Verband were Christian Landes of Lautenbach (ME IV:809), Kurt Lichdi of Heilbronn (1962-73), and Heinrich Funck of Ingolstadt (1974-82). Since 1983 Adolf Schnebele of Karlsruhe, is chairman of the Verband.

In 1966 the 12 churches located in Baden-Württemberg incorporated as Verband der Mennoniten-Gemeinden in Baden-Württemberg, giving the Verband corporate legal status with the state, e.g., in issues pertaining to Mennonite °conscientious objectors.   ASchn

Menn. Jahrbuch (1984) 99-100; Diether Götz Lichdi, *Über Zürich und Witmarsum nach Addis Abeba: Die Mennoniten in Geschichte und Gegenwart* (Maxdorf, 1983); *MWH* (1978), 293-94; *MWH* (1984) 116.

See also Vereinigung der deutschen Mennonitengemeinden; Konferenz süddeutscher Mennonitengemeinden.

Vereinigung bayerischer Mennonitengemeinden (Union of Bavarian Mennonite Churches) is an association of all Mennonite congregations located in °Bayern (Bavaria) in 1922, with the exception of the Ingolstadt congregation but including the congregations in what at that time was the Bavarian-Palatinate area. It was incorporated in 1926 and 1928. The 19 members in 1928 were Branchweilerhof, Deutschhof, Donauwörth (today: Augsburg) Eichstock, Eppstein, Ernstweiler (today: Zweibrücken), Friedelsheim, Kohlhof, Kühbörncheshof, Ludwigshafen, München, Neudorferhof, Obersülzen, Regensburg, Sembach, Trappstadt (today: Bad Königshofen im Grabfeld), Weierhof, Würzburg (Würzburg-Giebelstadt) and Ixheim (today: Zweibrücken). The association was joined by the Nürnberg congregation in 1972 and the Ingolstadt congregation in 1979. According to a new constitution (1987) only the churches located in Bavaria, i.e., Augsburg, Bad Königshofen im Grabfeld, Eichstock, Ingolstadt, München, Nürnberg, Regensburg, and Würzburg will be members of the association. The association is an associate member of the *Argbeitsgemeinschaft christlicher Kirchen in Bayern* (Task Force of Christian Churches in Bavaria).   ThSchm

Menn. Jahrbuch.

Vereinigung der deutschen Mennonitengemeinden (Union of German Mennonite Congregations) (ME IV:811). Four different traditions are united in the Vereinigung: old north-German city congregations; old Palatinate rural congregations; Mennonites who came from East and °West Prussia and from the Soviet Union after 1945 as °refugees, who in part formed new congregations; and resettlers (°*Umsiedler*) from the Soviet Union in the 1970s and late 1980s. The integration of these resettlers into the Mennonite conferences and services has not yet been successful; only the congregation of resettlers of Wolfsburg has joined the Vereinigung. The relationship of the Vereinigung to the Arbeitsgemeinschaft deutscher Mennonitengemeinden in which resettler congregations participate, has to this date (1986) not been clarified.

Since about 1978 the Vereinigung and the Verband deutscher Mennonitengemeinden (Federation of German Mennonite Churches) have, for various reasons, drawn closer. A task force was established for mutual endeavors. At present considerable movement is taking place, and the 100th anniversary of the Vereinigung took place without great fuss for just this reason. The main underlying and unanswered question within the Vereinigung is: How can German Mennonites really become a spiritual unity with the huge span in theological and social positions they hold? Not of little concern, the differences in the education of ministers still creates "centrifugal" tendencies in the Vereinigung.

An aid towards better integration within the Vereinigung, since 1966, are the annual *Mitgliederversammlungen* (members' assemblies) which promote a consciousness of identity and unity. Outwardly the Vereinigung represents its congregations to other churches and to government offices, and it is often erroneously seen as a representative of all German Mennonites. Inwardly the Vereinigung without a full-time chairperson or secretary, is more weak than strong in giving stimulus and leadership, and more often than not its congregations each choose their own way. Finances play a lesser role in the work of the Vereinigung than they did before World War II; the Vereinigung has changed from a more business-oriented to a more theologically-oriented body. Subjects of discussion are: °peace witness, °ecumenical participation (attendance at the World Council of Churches assemblies in 1968, 1975, 1983; response to the 1982 "Lima Document" on baptism, eucharist, and ministry), and youth work, in particular the encouragement of the theology students. A seminar for pastors (together with the Verband is held annually. A further main point of emphasis is the social welfare work which has moved from a welfare for our own German people in the time after 1945 to a commitment for the needy outside Europe and North America. Contact with the Mennonites in the Deutsche Demokratische Republik (German Democratic Republic) and in the Soviet Union is also a concern of the Vereinigung.   PJFo

Menn. Jahrbuch, esp. (1986); Diether Götz Lichdi, *Über Zürich und Witmarsum nach Addis Abeba: Die Mennoniten in Geschichte und Gegenwart* (Maxdorf, 1983); *MWH* (1978) 295-99; *MWH* (1984), 117.

Vereinigung der Mennonitengemeinden, Paraguay (Association of Mennonite Churches) (ME II:323). From July 4, 1930 to May 1932, ca. 2,000 people came to Paraguay to form Fernheim Colony in the heart of the °°Chaco region. In 1937 ca. one-third of these moved to the east side of the Paraguay River and founded Friesland Colony. This temporary separation was soon bridged through conferences and mutual visitation. The two groups were strengthened in 1947 with the coming of additional refugees to found Volendam and Neuland colonies.

In 1948 these congregations joined the General Conference Mennonite Church of North America and received both spiritual and financial help from it. In 1950 a congregation was founded in Asunción. On Jan. 10, 1967, leaders of these congregations met to found the Conference of Mennonite Congregations in Paraguay. Peter Wiens of Fernheim was elected president, Johann Regehr of Friesland was chosen vice-chairman, and Dietrich Klassen of Neuland became secretary. The conference adopted the "Mennonite confession of faith" as its foundation. The original annual meetings of the conference were later changed to biennial meetings.

The purpose of the conference was (1) to promote and deepen the Christian faith in life and work; (2) to promote among Mennonites biblical knowledge concerning doctrine and practice, including baptism, nonresistance and holiness; and (3) to coordinate work in mission, evangelism, education, the production of literature, peace teaching, and Christian service. (4) A particular concern of the new conference has been to promote missionary activity among the Indians in the °Chaco and in east Paraguay. This also involves cooperation with other Mennonite conferences. Inter-Mennonite cooperation is also evident in continuing support for the Centro Evangélico Menonita de Teología, Asunción (CEMTA), a Bible institute and seminary. PW

MWH (1978), 258-60; *MWH* (1984), 99; *GCM Handbook* (1988), 39-40.

Vermittlungskomitee. When the Mennonite churches in Paraguay joined the General Conference Mennonite Church (GCM) of North America in 1948 the latter sent a representative to Paraguay to supervise the distribution of financial and other resources supplied from North America. The congregations in Paraguay thereupon formed a *Vermittlungskomitee* (liaison committee) to promote spiritual life, to distribute funds equitably, and to select young people for further education.

Through this committee the congregations in Paraguay were united in a new way, including those in °Neuland and °Volendam who were in particular need of financial help. Select students received help to study in theology and in medicine. The school in °Menno Colony received support and the congregation in Asunción received several ministers from North America. Teachers were also sent to Paraguay, as were subscriptions to *Der Bote* and *Der Kinderbote*. Mission work was begun in Cambyreta, in Villa Hayes and at Kilometer 81 (Centro de Salud Menonita, a hospital for victims of Hansen's Disease [leprosy]). The Vermittlungskomitee was also responsible for the founding of the Vereinigung der Mennonitengemeinden in Paraguay (GCM) in 1967, after which the Vermittlungskomitee ceased to function. The committee had only one chairman, Elder Jacob Isaak of Fernheim (1950-67). PW

S. F. Pannabecker, *Open Doors* (1975), 240.

Vermont. See New England.

Victim-Offender Reconciliation Program (VORP). See Reconciliation.

Vietnam (ME IV:820). Mennonites began work in Vietnam in 1954, when France lost its Indochina colony and the United States supported a new government in Saigon. Mennonite Central Committee (MCC) aided refugees resettling in the south, but soon focused on medical and agricultural work in the central highlands. They staffed a leprosarium in Banmethuot (1955) and a hospital in Nhatrang (1960).

MCC worked closely with the Evangelical Church of Vietnam (ECVN), whose 50,000 members resulted from Christian and Missionary Alliance (CMA) missions since 1911. They also worked in student services and hosted several °work camps. An early tragedy was the capture of Danny Gerber with other CMA staff in 1962, never to be heard of again. By 1964 the U.S. was directly involved in the fighting.

In 1965 MCC joined Church World Service and Lutheran World Relief to form Vietnam Christian Service (VNCS), a joint program administered by MCC at the others' request. This built on the good rapport MCC had created, but the pros and cons of such a large agency were often debated. MCC's work grew along with the engulfing war and the United States' entrenchment. By 1968, when the Tet Offensive brought the destruction to the cities, MCC staff had peaked at 42 and U.S. troops at a half million.

Under VNCS the program moved into community development with a range of social services. Use of the military for transportation and security for work in the provinces caused constant concern, producing repeated discussions with United States and Vietnamese officials to maintain a reconciliation stance in their civil strife. After seven years MCC left VNCS to work more closely with its own purposes and identify more with the suffering. By 1974 its main objective was defined as peace and reconciliation.

In the 20 years prior to the change of government in 1975, 117 persons served with MCC in Vietnam. The value of material aid and the costs of personnel and program totaled nearly $1.5 million (U.S.). Of this, $216,000 was given to war victims of "the other side" in both North and South.

The Eastern Mennonite Board of Missions and Charities responded to the invitation of MCC and ECVN by sending two missionary couples in 1957. They began the Vietnám Mennonite Mission (VNMM), which was not granted official registration until 1964 because of the strong Roman Catholic position of the Diem government. By then the staff had increased to 10, the average number in the country for the next decade.

Half of the mission staff were long-term teacher-evangelists and half were short-term associates. The question of how to relate to the ECVN remained central. Through the years the two agencies were able to keep an open, supportive association while developing a separate program and church group.

Missionaries developed various outreach programs, with two major projects. A large student center in Saigon reflected the opportunity to work with students everywhere. Through its English classes, reading room, and study facilities, the Mennonite Center became a popular place for thousands of students. Often biblical materials were used in the classes and public programs.

Community evangelism utilized a variety of services and programs, often carried out jointly with MCC. This was especially effective among resettled refugees in Gia Dinh, at the northern edge of

Saigon. Here the clinics, sewing classes, day-care, primary school, family-child assistance, and the rebuilding of several hundred houses gave concrete expression to the gospel. This became the primary congregation for the 150 Vietnamese who identified themselves as Mennonite Christians by 1975.

Most Mennonites who served in Vietnam with both MCC and EMBMC saw their witness for peace as a major purpose of their presence. In friendships and in contacts with the government and the press they tried to share with the Vietnamese people their concern about United States policy. They also gave a significant witness back to North America in their writing and speaking. Several statements received wide distribution.

A less publicized witness for peace was the series of contacts with officials of North Vietnam and the Provisional Revolutionary Government of the South. Repeated visits were made to foreign capitals for such contacts, preparing the way for continued relationships and assistance following the war.

Four MCC workers were among the few foreigners who deliberately stayed for the transition period after May 1, 1975. Two of them, after their departure in 1976, wrote books about their experiences. Some MCC and EMBMC staff members have returned briefly for official visits in the decade since. Emergency and medical aid has been given for specific projects, visited by staff members from Bangkok. The United States government has repeatedly denied permission for MCC (U.S.) to ship any aid to Vietnam; so this assistance has been given by MCC Canada, which also sells °SELFHELP Crafts from Vietnamese workers.   JEM

Luke S. Martin, "An Evaluation of a Generation of Mennonite Mission, Service and Peacemaking in Vietnam 1954-1976" (unpub. study sponsored by MCC and EMBMC, 1977); Atlee and Winifred Beechy, *Vietnam: Who Cares* (Scottdale, 1968); James R. Klassen, *Jimshoes in Vietnam* (Scottdale, 1986); Earl S. Martin, *Reaching the Other Side* (New York: Crown, 1978); James E. Metzler, *From Saigon to Shalom* (Scottdale, 1985); *MWH* (1978), 188; *MWH* (1984) 42.

See also Giáo Hội Tín Lành (Hệ-phái Mê-nô-nít), Vietnam.

Missing in Action: The Daniel Gerber Story

The death of Daniel Gerber—if indeed the long-missing Mennonite Central Committee Vietnam volunteer is dead—was not in vain. That was the message Ha Jimmy Cillpam brought in May 1987 to Elvina Gerber of Kidron, Ohio, a mother waiting with uncertainty for 25 years.

Cillpam, a Montagnard tribesman, knew Daniel Gerber as a leprosarium worker in Ban Me Thuot, Vietnam. "I was about 12 years old when I got acquainted with your son and brother," he told Elvina Gerber, her son David, and her daughter-in-law, Leora, during that visit to their Kidron farm. "I will never forget how he came to live in our village. He ate with other people and played with us boys. But most important, he was a 'white angel' who came to tell us of a God that loves us and forgives our sins." Gerber, 22 years old at the time of his abduction, grew up on the family farm. In lieu of military service he had chosen to serve a three-year term with MCC in a Vietnamese hospital. The night of his capture, Gerber was walking on the hospital grounds with his fiancée, Ruth Wilting of Cleveland, Ohio. Wilting watched as Gerber's hands were bound and he was led away.

That happened on May 31, 1962, and Gerber's family never heard from him again. Later, Wilting came to visit the people in Kidron who might have become her in-laws. She told them, Elvina Gerber said, that she felt called to return to Vietnam. Wilting kept in contact with the family until 1968, when she was herself killed by Viet Cong forces at the hospital where she continued to work. She now lies buried in the highlands with other missionaries killed in Vietnam.

Captured along with Daniel Gerber were two Christian and Missionary Alliance workers, Eleanor A. Vietti of Houston, Texas, and Archie Mitchell of Ellensberg, Washington. The three volunteers are the longest-missing Americans in Vietnam.

Gerber was the second MCC worker to be lost through wartime violence. An earlier volunteer, Clayton Kratz, was killed in the Russian Ukraine in 1922.

Gerber's attitude about war and peace was stated simply in his application to MCC: "Christ taught love and that is what his children must do" (MCC News Service, Akron, Pa., May 29, 1987).

Earliest reports on the abduction claimed the three missionaries were being forced to treat wounded Viet Cong soldiers. Through the years since then there were both promising and disappointing reports regarding Gerber's whereabouts. Nothing could ever be confirmed.

Later his mother came to the conclusion that Gerber had died. "For many years we had hope that he was alive," she said. "Then one day a friend of Daniel's, who is now a missionary to Japan, came to see me. He told how he prayed for Daniel every day. One day the Lord told him, 'Daniel is with me.' When he told me that, I believed that my son went to be with the Lord" (*The Daily Record*, Wooster, Ohio, May 20, 1987).

A strong faith in God helped the Gerber family through the difficult times. One of the hardest things to accept was a 1968 farm accident that killed Daniel's father, Nathan Gerber.

In addition to sharing reminiscences of Daniel Gerber, Cillpam shared his own story with the family. The Montagnard tribe is an ethnic minority group of rural people who live in villages separated from the mainstream of Vietnamese life. The tribal group had never heard of a Christian God until the first missionaries came to the village in 1940.

Cillpam's father was an early believer who became an ordained minister. Many people, sometimes whole villages, responded to the gospel, and Cillpam reported that on one day his father baptized 327 people. Churches sprang up all over the countryside.

In 1975, he found himself trying to help other Montagnards and Vietnamese escape from Saigon, which was on the verge of falling to the communists. He was able to jump on an airplane in a United States airlift to the Philippines, two days before Saigon fell.

After arriving in the United States, Cillpam dedicated himself to helping people, aiding those fleeing their homeland for a new life in America. He was instrumental in saving many "boat people" on the North China Sea, and at the time he met with the Gerbers he was working with 213 Asian refugees in Greensboro, North Carolina. He hoped, eventually, to be able to return to his homeland and preach the gospel to his own people.

"The world may say that Daniel's life was wasted," he said. "Well, it was not wasted. Christ came to the world and the people killed him, but his life was not wasted. Neither is Daniel's." DSh

The Daily Record, Wooster, Ohio, May 20; cf. *MWR* (June 11, 1987), 1-2.

Vietnam Mennonite Church. See Giáo Hội Tin Lành (Hệ-phái Mê-nô-nít), Vietnam (Evangelical Church [Mennonite Branch]).

Vietnam War (1954-75). *Trinh* Cong Son wrote a war protest song in Vietnamese titled, "A Mother's Legacy." The song summarizes Vietnam's history: "A thousand years of slavery to the Chinese, a hundred years of domination by the French, twenty years of civil war." Americans call the latter "the Vietnam War." Some Vietnamese now call it "the American War."

At the end of World War II, *Ho* Chi Minh declared Vietnam independent and then appealed to the United States president and secretary of state for support. Instead of answering *Ho* Chi Minh, the United States supported the return of France to rule Vietnam as a colony. By 1954, the United States aid to France totaled 80 percent of French expenses for her war in Vietnam.

After Vietnam militarily defeated the French at Dien Bien Phu in 1954, the Geneva Peace Accords temporarily divided Vietnam, allowing Vietnam time to reorganize for national elections in 1956. The United States immediately began a rumor campaign against the North and then helped evacuate people moving to the South. Later the former president of the United States, Dwight Eisenhower, acknowledged that, if the 1956 election had been held, 80 percent of the people would have voted for *Ho* Chi Minh rather than *Ngo* Dinh Diem. Both *Ngo* Dinh Diem and United States leaders disliked that prospect and consequently thwarted the election and majority rule. With those roots, war's bitter fruit loomed ahead.

In 1964, the United States began taking unpublicized, provocative actions against the Democratic Government of (North) Vietnam (DRVN), including kidnapping citizens and sending U.S. warships deep into the Gulf of Tonkin. In 1965, the U.S. secretary of state falsely claimed that 400 troops from North Vietnam had invaded South Vietnam; soon the U.S. bombed North Vietnam and sent 3,500 Marines to South Vietnam. The major resistance to the Republic of (South) Vietnam (RVN), however, lay in the South. In 1968, at BenTre, South Vietnam (population 35,000), a U.S. army major said, "It became necessary to destroy the town in order to save it." That year, the number of U.S. troops in Vietnam to-

taled more than 500,000. In 1969, the opposition in the South organized the Provisional Revolutionary Government (PRG).

In October 1972, U.S. president Richard Nixon agreed to sign a peace treaty, then reneged and ordered a massive bombing of North Vietnam at Christmas. Although the Paris Peace Accords were signed in January 1973, the war dragged on until the Republic of Vietnam collapsed in April 1975. Vietnam held national elections in April 1976.

Mennonite Central Committee (MCC) work in Vietnam began with refugee relief work in 1954 in the South. The first workers included Delbert Wiens, Roy Eby, Adam Ewert, and Eva °Harshbarger. Besides being a friend, *Nguyen* Van Ninh served as translator, administrative assistant, and advisor through the years of foreign Mennonite presence in Vietnam. Sponsored by the Eastern Mennonite [MC] Board of Missions and Charities (EMBMC), James and Arlene Stauffer started the Vietnam Mennonite Mission in 1957. Luke and Mary Martin (1962) and Don and Doris Sensenig (1963) came later. Mennonite Central Committee and the Vietnam Mennonite Mission shared personnel and cooperated on many projects: evangelism and service went hand-in-hand.

Attempting to maintain a balanced perspective, MCC contacted the Democratic Republic of Vietnam in 1966. MCC delegations headed by Atlee Beechy met representatives of the DRVN and the forerunner of the PRG in 1968; medical shipments to them followed. As the PRG picked up the pieces after the collapse of the Republic of Vietnam, the four foreign MCC workers who stayed in Vietnam through the change of governments in April 1975 (Earl Martin, Yoshihiro Ichikawa, Max Ediger, and James Klassen) continued the dialogue with some of the same representatives. Although MCC delegations have visited Vietnam, no long-term foreign Mennonite personnel have stayed in Vietnam since Yoshihiro Ichikawa left in 1976. One MCC worker in Central Veitnam, Dan Gerber, has been missing since May 1962, just prior to intense military action in the area where he lived.

Foreign Mennonites working in Vietnam during the war faced many ambiguities: helping refugees appeared to help the Thieu government which officially condemned peace (or neutralism) as illegal and procommunist. MCC medical shipments to the opposition also raised questions. Vietnamese Mennonites agonized over the war and military conscription. One active member of the Gia Dinh Mennonite congregation was a draft resister.

North American Mennonites needed to confront warmongering in their own countries. Mennonite publications carried a steady flow of information and discussion about the basic issues of the war with more accuracy and more clarity than the U.S. government provided. In the U.S., responses to the draft, income °tax, telephone surtax, and federal elections involved difficult decisions. U.S. history is clear: income taxes were established to support wars. Mennonite response to income tax was blurred; many paid the tax, some paid under protest, some refused to pay, some avoided paying. °Conscription in the United States also prompted many responses: some Mennonites protested, some burned their selective service (draft) cards, some resisted the draft and were imprisoned, many Mennonite men requested °conscientious objector status, a small percentage served in the military. Unrest and fragmentation in the U.S. society permeated the church: Mennonites debated the validity of peace walks and prayer vigils. Some Mennonite participated, many did not. Some received national media attention, most did not. Some Mennonites traveled to Washington, D.C., to protest; MCC established a Peace Section office there.

Faithful discipleship challenged Canadian Mennonites, too. Some helped U.S. draft dodgers resettle in Canada. The need to protest Canadian production of military supplies for U.S. use in Vietnam was just as clear, but the response was weaker. Many Mennonite churches in Canada, as well as in the U.S., have helped Vietnamese war refugees and refugees from the economic collapse which hit Vietnam when U.S. economic aid was terminated in 1975.

The war in Vietnam taught many Mennonites that every stance carries political overtones: paying taxes or joining the military are neither more nor less political than refusing to pay taxes or refusing to join the military. Regarding Vietnam, the record of the Mennonite church—like that of her members—reflects a continuum of faithfulness, from clear to blurred. To this day, forgiveness and reconciliation are needed to heal the wounds of that war. The U.S. still deals with Vietnam under the Trading-with-the-Enemy Act. Canada, however, has established diplomatic relations with Vietnam. The war in Vietnam—like all war—caused untold suffering and created more problems than it solved.   JRKla

Bibl. On War and Peace (1987), 679-706; Joseph Buttinger, Vietnam: A Political History (New York: Praeger, 1968); Frances Fitzgerald, Fire in the Lake: The Vietnamese and Americans in Vietnam (New York: Vintage, 1972); Don Luce and John Sommer, Viet Nam: The Unheard Voices (Ithaca: Cornell U. Press, 1969); Robert Scheer, How the United States Got Involved in Vietnam (Santa Barbara, California: Center for the Study of Democratic Institutions, 1965); Sam Brown and Len Ackland, eds., Why Are We Still in Vietnam? (New York: Vintage, 1970); American Friends Service Committee, Peace in Vietnam: A New Approach to Southeast Asia (New York: Hill and Wang, 1966); Robert McAfee Brown, Abraham J. Heschel, and Michael Novak, Vietnam: Crisis of Conscience (New York: Association Press, 1967); Gareth Porter, A Peace Denied: The United States, Vietnam, and the Paris Agreement (Bloomington: Indiana U. Press, 1975); Tiziano Terzani, Giai Phong! The Fall and Liberation of Saigon (New York: St. Martin's Press, 1976); Noam Chomsky and Edward S. Herman, After the Cataclysm: Postwar Indochina and the Reconstruction of Imperial Ideology (Boston: South End Press, 1979); Atlee and Winifred Beechy, Vietnam: Who Cares? (Scottdale, 1968); Omar Eby, A House in Hue (Scottdale, 1968); Earl S. Martin, Reaching the Other Side: The Journal of an American Who Stayed to Witness Vietnam's Postwar Transition (New York: Crown Publishers, Inc., 1978); James R. Klassen, Jimshoes in Vietnam: Orienting a Westerner (Scottdale, 1986); Frank H. Epp, ed., I Would Like to Dodge the Draft-Dodgers, But . . . (Waterloo: Conrad Press, 1970); idem, The Glory and the Shame: Editorials on the Past, Present, and Future of the Mennonite Church (Winnipeg: Canadian Mennonite Publishing Association, Inc., 1968), 41-49; Wilbert R. Shenk, Mission Focus: Current Issues (Scottdale, 1980), 313-66; Milton Viorst, Fire in the Streets: America in the 1960s (New York: Simon and Schuster, 1979); Arthur G. Gish, The New Left and Christian Radicalism (Grand Rapids: Eerdmans, 1970); Jacqui Chagnon and Don Luce, eds., Of Quiet Courage: Poems from Viet Nam (Washington, D.C.: Indochina Mobile Education Project, 1974); Trinh Cong Son, Ca Khuc Da Vang (Vietnam: Nhan Ban, ca. 1970), 26-27; Jerry Elmer, "A U.S. Policy that Creates Refugees," The Pawtucket Evening Times (June 30, 1980); Walter Gormly, "Americans Can't Name Vietnam Enemy," Mennonite (July 5, 1966), 448; Linda Gibson Hiebert, "The Roots of Uprootedness," Sojourners 8, (Sept. 1979), 7; Flora Lewis in The New York Times (Jan. 25, 1973), C23; David Rosenbaum in The New York Times (Dec. 26, 1972), 10.

See also Church-State Relations; Peace; Peace Activism; Relief Work.

Virginia (ME IV:829) is the 13th most populous state in the nation, numbering 5,787,000 in 1987, which was 2.4 percent of the total population of the United States. Between 1980 and 1986 Virginia's population increased by 8.2 percent compared with 6.4 percent growth for the nation. Mennonites in Virginia also increased in number. In 1957 there were six groups comprising a total membership of 4,429 in 54 congregations. Thirty years later there were nine conferences and groups, 94 congregations, and 7,332 members. When Brethren in Christ totals are added, the total membership of all Mennonite branches in Virginia and West Virginia was 8,017 distributed among 102 congregations as follows: Virginia Mennonite Conference (MC), 65 congregations, 5,501 members (not including 12 VMC congregations of 392 members in Kentucky, North Carolina, Tennessee, and Ohio); Atlantic Coast Conference (MC) 1, 38; Southeastern Mennonite Conference, 12, 837; Old Order Mennonites, 3, 584; Beachy Amish Mennonites, 8, 460; Mennonite Christian Brotherhood, 1, 26; Horning Mennonites (°Old Order Mennonites, Weaverland Conference), 1, 53; unaffiliated congregations 2, 93; Fellowship Churches, 1, 75; Brethren in Christ, 8, 350.

The Old Order Amish settlements in the Stuarts Draft (Augusta Co.) and Catlett (Fauquier Co.) areas have disbanded. The Stuarts Draft settlement, begun in 1942, ended in 1981. Those families who did not become a part of the Beachy Amish Mennonites moved to Tennessee. By 1977, the Catlett settlement, which had begun in 1946, had also disappeared. Those who did not join the Beachy fellowship churches migrated to Kentucky. Loss of leadership seems to have been the main reason for the disbanding of these settlements.

With the disappearance of the Old Order Amish from Virginia, the most conservative Mennonites are the Old Order Mennonites of Dayton in Rockingham Co. Like the Old Order Amish, they prohibit the use of automobiles and commercial electricity, and like them, they experience external pressures. Scarcity and expensiveness of land makes it increasingly difficult for parents to provide children with farms, and farm technology imposes standards which require the use of diesel generators for electricity. Old Order children receive no more than an eighth-grade education, and after successfully defending this tradition in court in 1970, the leaders established their own schools. Teachers who lack a high school education are drawn from within the church. However, consideration is being given to hiring certified teachers. Since the 1950s when a division occurred within the Old Order community, there have been two groups (Wenger and Showalter). They alternate between two of the three meetinghouses for their worship services. The Horning Mennonites in the same area are an offshoot of the Old Order groups. They broke away in 1957 and use automobiles, but they paint the bumpers black. Therefore, they are often called Black Bumper Mennonites.

The seven Beachy Amish Mennonite Fellowship congregations are found at Catlett (Fauquier Co.), Stuarts Draft (Augusta Co.), Madison (Madison Co.), Farmville (Prince Edward Co.), and Kempsville in the Norfolk-Chesapeake area. Some are more conservative than others. For example, the Mt. Zion congregation in Stuarts Draft continued the use of the German language in its worship services until 1985, whereas the Faith Christian Fellowship at Catlett is a very outgoing congregation which holds revival meetings and whose bishop is director of Choice Books of Northern Virginia, an extensive bookrack evangelism program begun in 1968. Faith Mission Home in Madison, founded in 1965, is a residential home and training center for children who are mentally retarded. In 1983 a lawsuit regarding the use of corporal punishment was filed against the home in an attempt to close it, but the judge granted a temporary stay which was based on appeals to a higher court. No verdict had yet been rendered by the summer of 1986.

Until 1972, the only major division among Virginia Mennonites took place in 1900 when a group of Old Order Mennonites left the main Virginia Conference body. On June 30, 1972, the second division occurred when a number of congregations again left the Virginia Mennonite Conference to form the Southeastern Mennonite Conference. The main concerns were modern dress and education. Most of the Virginia churches affiliated with the Southeastern Conference are located in Rockingham Co. One congregation is at Stanardsville (Greene Co.), and another is located at South Boston (Halifax Co.). Other churches of the conference are scattered as widely as West Virginia, South Carolina, Georgia, and Puerto Rico. Christian Light Publications, founded in 1969 in Harrisonburg, publishes the Southeastern Conference periodical *Life Lines* and other materials used by the conference. One of the pastors owns and operates Park View Press, which prints Southeastern Conference materials and also serves the wider community. The Southeasten Conference has two Christian day schools, one in West Virginia and one near Dayton, Va. Two groups, one at Mount Crawford and the other at Timberville, are offshoots of the Southeastern Conference.

The Virginia Mennonite Conference has experienced much change since the 1950s. Most striking has been the shift from agricultural to °business and °professional °occupations. The best example is the Warwick River congregation in Newport News which in 1987 had only one member who had retained his tract of farmland in what was once a colony of Mennonite farmers. Mennonites in the Newport News-Norfolk area are in the middle of a military-industrial complex. Some are employed in the naval shipyards and other military bases, but most are involved in the thriving building industry of the Tidewater area. Members of the larger congregations in the Shenandoah Valley also consist mainly of business and professional persons. Change has also come about through various types of expansion. New congregations have been established in the cities of Roanoke, Christiansburg, Fredericksburg, Waynesboro, and Hampton. Attempts at church planting have been made among the Spanish- and Vietnamese-speaking people of the Washington, D.C., area. A group which is not yet an established congregation is developing in Woodstock.

Institutions too have grown. In 1965 Eastern Mennonite Seminary was established, so that what was once Eastern Mennonite College is now Eastern Mennonite College and Seminary. The college added a science center in 1965, a library and archives in 1971, and a discipleship center in 1974. In 1975 a renovation of the chapel was completed. Four dormitories were added, and when the administration building burned down in 1984, a new campus center was erected two years later in its place. Eastern Mennonite High School (EMHS) has become independent from the college and seminary and has recently added cafeteria and industrial arts wings to its structure. Two other church schools are located in Newport News and Chesapeake. Retirement and nursing °homes have also increased in number and function. What was once the Virginia Mennonite Home for the Aged in Harrisonburg is now a part of the large Virginia Mennonite Retirement Community which includes Heritage Haven, Woodland, and Park Village for senior adults, and Oak Lea Health Care Center. In Newport News the Warwick River congregation operates Menno Wood, a retirement home. Pleasant View Homes in Broadway, begun in 1970, has facilities for the handicapped and mentally retarded at that location as well as in Harrisonburg. In 1958 Highland Retreat, a church camp was begun near Bergton. A retreat center, founded in 1984, is being developed near Williamsburg. A °SELFHELP Crafts gift and thrift shop in Harrisonburg and the annual °relief sale near Waynesboro help provide funds for Mennonite Central Committee. A voluntary service unit under Mennonite Board of Missions is located in Richmond. Harrisonburg is the headquarters of Mennonite Board of Missions (MC) Media Ministries, formerly known as Mennonite Broadcasts. In 1969 the Park View Federal Credit Union was founded to provide financial services to members of Mennonite organizations in Park View and members of Mennonite churches in Harrisonburg and Rockingham Co.   GRB

MC Yearbook (1988-89), 42-43; *Minutes (BIC)* (1986), 206-7, 236-39; Gail Nardi, "The Old Order," *Richmond Times-Dispatch* (Nov. 9, 1986), F 1-3; idem, "The Changing Mennonites," *Richmond Times-Dispatch* (Nov. 16, 1986), F 1, 3, 4; Elmer S. Yoder, *The Beachy Amish Mennonite Fellowship Churches* (Hartville, Ohio: Diakonia Ministries, 1987), 253-54, 311-12, 360-67; Luthy, *Amish Settlements* (1985), 1-2; Wittlinger, *Piety and Obedience* (1978), 146, 447-48; Daniel Hertzler, *From Germantown to Steinbach* (Scottdale, 1981), 41-53; Harry A. Brunk, *History of Mennonites in Virginia, 1727-1900* (Staunton: McClure Printing Co., 1959); idem, *History of Mennonites in Virginia, 1900-1960* (Verona: McClure Printing Co., Inc., 1972).

See also Voluntary Service.

Virginia Mennonite Conference (MC) (ME IV:833). In 1987 Virginia Mennonite Conference (VMC) was made up of 77 congregations scattered throughout Virginia, West Virginia, Tennessee, Ohio, Kentucky, and North Carolina. Two were Afro-American. One was Hispanic. There were 10 clusters of congregations called *districts*. Their combined membership was 5,893.

The conference had some sizeable losses in the 1970s when 12 congregations (559) members) withdrew to form the Southeastern Mennonite Conference (1972). Three congregations in Florida (431 members) transferred in 1975 to the new Southeast Mennonite Convention (Conference after 1986); and the Sonnenburg congregation (216 members) joined the Ohio Conference (1976).

The Virginia Conference has eight agencies: VM Retirement Community, VM Board of Missions, VM Auto Aid, VM Property Aid, Pleasant View Homes (for the handicapped), VM Conference Center, Eastern Mennonite High School (transferred from Eastern Mennonite College governance in 1982), and Family Life Resource Center. Eastern Mennonite College and Seminary was released from VMC governance in 1984 to operate under the Mennonite Board of Education (MC).

Virginia Mennonite Board of Missions (VMBM) began its first overseas work in Sicily, Italy, in 1951. Later it expanded to Jamaica (1954), Guyana (1969-72), and Trinidad (1971), all located in the Caribbean Sea. Since 1977, the Jamaica Mennonite Church has functioned without the full-time presence of missionaries and is recognized as a fraternal conference. Between 1950 and 1987 VMBM was also involved in planting 40 new congregations in Virginia, West Virginia, North Carolina, and Ohio.

The conference publicizes the activities of its agencies through a weekly broadcast, "Missions in our Changing World"; a monthly paper, *The Bridge*; and a bimonthly magazine, *Missionary Light*.   PLK

MC Yearbook (1988-89), 82-84.

Visiting, Pastoral. See Pastoral Visiting.

Visiting, Social. See Hospitality.

Visual Arts. See Ceramics; Painting and Printmaking; Photography.

Vogt, Esther (Mar. 25, 1905-Jan. 3, 1988). Esther Kulp was the second of six children born at Isaac and Lizzie (Bergey) Kulp. She was born at Philadelphia and while very young moved with her parents to Cheraw, Col. Esther went to high school at Cheraw and La Junta, Col. transferring to Hesston Academy, (Ks.) for her last year, receiving her diploma in 1923. She received her college degree in 1927 from Hesston College. While in college she served as secretary to the dean and the president of the college, 1924-27. On July 24, 1927, she was married to Milton C. Vogt; they arrived in India on Nov. 25, 1927. They served with the American Mennonite Mission (MC), °Dhamtari, until 1941 when they were transferred to Bihar. She served there until the death of her husband in 1968.

The Vogts had six children. Soon after the birth of her fourth child, Bernard, in 1937 Esther suffered a stroke which paralyzed her left side. She never completely recovered from this. Seven months later, in

January 1938, diphtheria claimed the life of baby Bernard.

She shared with her husband the concern for building the church and was very active with the Bible women (°lay evangelists), especially before her stroke. Soon after the death of her husband in 1968 she returned to the United States where she retired in Colorado. She later moved to Chicago to live with her son, Virgil. She died at Beth-haven Nursing Home, Hannibal, Mo.   SPM

GH (Mar. 5, 1968), 194, 195; *GH* (Feb. 9, 1988), 102; Esther Rose Graber compiler, "MBM Missionary Directory" (1983, 1984).

Vogt, Milton Christian (Aug. 14, 1901-Jan. 1968), was born near Moundridge, Ks. He was the oldest of eight children born to Christian A. and Barbra Ruth Vogt. He completed high school at Hesston Academy in 1922 and then taught school for one year. Following the year of teaching he enrolled at Hesston College. He transferred to Goshen College for his senior year (BA, 1927). After his graduation he was appointed, along with his fiancée, Esther Kulp, to serve as a missionary in India, and was ordained to the ministry at Hesston Mennonite Church on June 26, 1927.

Milton and Esther Vogt served as missionaries, 1927-68. The first 14 years were spent in the mission at °Dhamtari. In 1941 they were transferred to Bihar to work in the evangelistic program that was starting there. Milton's last 18 years in Palamau District were most fruitful and satisfying. The main concern and passion of his life was building the church. No effort was too much to visit small groups of Christians for prayer meetings and Sunday services. Milton's abilities and responsibilities were many. He was effective as an evangelist and pastor and on committees. He was secretary and treasurer of the Bihar Mennonite Mission for 18 years and also for a number of years went about 60 miles three days each week to oversee the work at Satbarwa Hospital. He served with famine relief in West Bengal, 1943-44. His qualities of openness, simplicity, diligence, fearlessness, and cheerfulness, and his deep devotion and sense of purpose combined to make him a person loved and respected by all who knew him.

Milton Vogt apparently suffered a stroke while riding his motorcycle on his way to work. This led to his death at Satbarwa Hospital. He was buried near his home at Bathet, Palamau District, Bihar.   SPM

See Vogt, Esther Kulp, for bibliography.

Volendam Colony, Paraguay (ME IV:843), was founded in 1947 by immigrants from Russia via Germany. The landscape is slightly rolling with forest and lowland alternating. The forest lands, when cleared, are well suited to the cultivation of wheat, soya beans, and feed grains, while the lowlands are used for grazing of cattle herds. The colony possesses a total of 32,700 hectares (80,800 acres) which is divided into 100 hectares (250 acres) per family. In 1987 the colony's population of 676 people lived in twelve villages.

Administrative patterns closely resemble those developed in Russia, with an administrator (mayor—°°*Oberschulze*) and four advisers responsible for colony affairs. A hospital as well as an elementary and a secondary school serve the colony, as does a retirement home and a producer-consumer °cooperative. The latter is responsible for the sale of colony products as well as the supplying of necessary items for colony life through its cooperative store.

In the spiritual realm two congregations have been organized, the Mennonite congregation (GCM) with 269 members and the Mennonite Brethren congregation with 52 members. These congregations are not only gathered for worship, but are also responsible for the education and training of young people and for missionary activity. Both congregations work closely together and are also related to their South American and North American conferences and to Mennonite World Conference.   AF

Menn. Jahrbuch (1984), 158; *GCM Handbook* (1988), 40; Abram Funk, ed., *25 Jahre Volendam, 1947-1972* (Curitiba, Brazil, 1972).

Vologda. See Russian Soviet Federated Socialist Republic (RSFSR).

Voluntary Service (ME IV:848) describes the programs of the Mennonite and Brethren in Christ churches in which, for a limited period of time, people live and work sacrificially in the name of Christ in a needy location, often a place other than their home community. The concept of voluntary service (VS) originated in Verdun, France, in 1920 when Pierre Ceresole organized a voluntary work group to rebuild houses in an area damaged by World War I. As early as 1943 the °°Society of Friends (Quakers) sponsored the first recorded °work camp in the United States near Westmoreland, Pa. Three years later at Quaker Bridge, N.Y., Mennonites participated in a Friends work camp. These activities contributed to the emerging Mennonite vision.

Mennonites, who found themselves heirs to a heritage of °suffering and understood their human relationships in a way that led to °service, remembered the tragedy of war and efforts of famine °relief. Those who served in °°Civilian Public Service (CPS) projects during World War II found human need in unsuspecting dimensions. The rediscovery that Christian love in action is indeed giving to your neighbor in the name of Christ moved people to dream new dreams.

Early in World War II the Virginia Mennonites living in the area of Hampton Roads were being pressured to participate in the civil defense program. At about the same time the churches in Indiana were confronted with a similar problem in the form of the High School Victory Corps. On the one hand stood the growing hostility of non-Mennonite neighbors calling for involvement in the military and civil defense programs. Pulling from the other direction was an awakened conscience about human need and the real possibilities of giving help with limited resources. These stimuli precipitated several kindred voluntary service programs.

The recommendation that some form of Mennonite voluntary service be formed was adopted by committees of the *Mennonite Church* (MC) on Feb. 12, 1943. The first voluntary service unit was organized during the summer of 1944 and was administered in connection with the Mennonite missions in Chicago. Long-term voluntary service, in which workers served for at least a year, was initiated by the Mennonite Church in Sept. 1948, when four volunteers were assigned to the Kansas City, Mo., General Hospital. A significant development in the VS program of the Mennonite Church was the beginning of overseas VS in °Dhamtari, India, in 1952, the year the national draft of conscientious objectors began. The program in the US continued at various levels throughout the 1960s and 1970s—in 1986 MC volunteers in the United States numbered 69.

The *Conservative Mennonite Conference* began voluntary service in Espelkamp, Germany, in 1950. In 1958 the conference opened its first long-term VS unit at a state mental hospital in Meridian, Miss. An overseas program was launched in the Cohuita area of Costa Rica in 1963. In 1984 41 volunteers served with the Conservative Mennonite Conference in nine locations in the United States. A distinct *Lancaster Conference* (MC) VS program was officially launched in 1952. In 1986, 51 volunteers served in 11 program locations. They worked with local Mennonite congregations to strengthen the relationship between the volunteers' work assignments and the outreach goals of the congregations.

The first of the *Mennonite Central Committee (MCC)* inter-Mennonite voluntary service units emerged as a parallel to MCC-administered °°Civilian Public Service (CPS) projects. Summer service units for women, who were not part of the CPS program, were begun in 1944 at the Ypsilanti (Mich.) State Hospital and the State Hospital for Mental Diseases at Howard, R.I. MCC officially began a VS program on Jan. 1, 1947, with a builders unit on the island of Walcheren, Holland. The first international short-term °work camps were conducted in 1948 in Hamburg and Frankfurt; that year the first Canadian service units were opened. In 1949 MCC opened a long-term unit in Topeka, Ks., that was designed to expose youth to the best in the field of °mental health care as a prelude to a Mennonite mental health effort. That year 10 long-term VSers went to Europe and two to Paraguay; they were forerunners of the MCC °°Pax program. Teaching and nursing assignments were made in Newfoundland in 1956. In 1986 103 volunteers served in 13 MCC program locations in the USA. *Mennonite Central Committee Canada (MCCC)* was organized in 1963; by 1965, it assumed direction of the summer voluntary service program in Canada. A long-term VS program was begun in Toronto in 1966. In 1974, MCCC assumed full responsibility for the MCC program in Canada. In 1986 there were 143 VSers in service with MCCC. Fifty-two of those were involved in local voluntary service—serving in a sacrificial way in their home communities.

The *General Conference Mennonite Church* (GCM) created a voluntary service program on Feb. 20, 1946. Nine volunteers were assigned for a period of summer service in the Woodlawn area of Chicago in a community service project providing Bible school teachers and youth activity leaders. The first overseas summer service assignment began in 1950 with the sending of four short-term workers to the Mennonite mission in Cachipay, Colombia. The first of the long-term GCM projects was launched in 1955 with the assignment of two missions Pax volunteers to the Congo (Zaire) to work with the °°Congo Inland Mission, (later renamed Africa Inter-Mennonite Mission). Long-term volunteers in North America were not assigned until 1957, the same year that the conference initiated summer high shool VS. At the end of 1986 there were 98 persons in the GCM program in 30 program locations in North America.

Voluntary service was initiated in the *Brethren in Christ* Church in 1947 with the assignment of a person for a short term of service at the Navajo mission in New Mexico, which until 1954 was the only Brethren in Christ project using volunteers. That year volunteers were assigned to Rhodesia (Zambia, Zimbabwe). Over the years volunteers in such diverse locations as San Francisco, Timber Bay, Sask., and the Bronx, N.Y., worked with local congregational activities. Eighty-five people participated in the Brethren in Christ VS program in 1986. They were located in nine program units in North America, staffing community service organizations and °camps as well as providing administrative support to the program.

In the fall of 1950 MCC asked the Mennonite churches in Europe to choose youth representatives who would be responsible to plan and operate a voluntary service program in Europe. At their first meeting in December 1950, the representatives assumed the name of *Mennonitischer Freiwilligendienst* (MFD, Mennonite Voluntary Service). The first activity was to create an international Mennonite youth team to help in the resettlement of several Mennonite families in south Germany at the close of 1951. The following year MFD involved 154 volunteers in summer work camps and a winter caravan contributed some 20,000 hours of labor to help refugees, displaced persons, Mennonites, and others in need, and to help build a youth center, three church buildings, and five housing projects in Germany and Austria.

The challenge to develop a Christian voluntary service program among the churches in Paraguay came from MCC which resulted in the creation of *Christlicher Dienst* (CD; Christian Service). In 1951 the first workers were placed at Kilometer 81, a clinic for victims of Hansen's Disease (leprosy), to help patients and to introduce the concept of voluntary service to the churches. In 1957 two volunteers began serving in the government psychiatric hospital in Asunción—the location which, in 1987, had the most CD workers. Other CD volunteers helped to construct the Trans-Chaco Road and worked in children's homes, at a home for the aged, in a radio station, and at a school for children of Paraguayan ranchers in the Chaco. The first project outside Paraguay was in Chile, following the earthquake and tidal wave in May 1960, where they worked in reconstruction and distributed material aid donated by the Paraguayan churches. In 1976 CD sent workers to Guatemala following an earthquake there. As of 1987 15 people had served abroad with CD. During the period 1980-85, 507 people participated in work camps in Paraguay—an activity which promoted voluntary service and challenged the spiritual life of the congregations in Paraguay. The first volunteers from abroad came from Brazil in 1958 and later from Canada, West Germany, Holland, and Switzerland.

The *Mennonite Brethren General Conference* (North America) approved the creation of a Christian Service Program in 1960 to provide opportunities for short-term service for members of the conference as an expression of Christian discipleship and an oportunity to serve conference outreach in a needy world. In 1963 38 workers were in Christian Service assignments in the United States, Colombia, Paraguay, Zaire, and India. In 1986 27 volunteers served people to help build the church in 12 locations in the United States.

The *Associação Menonita de Assistência Social* (AMAS; Mennonite Association for Social Assistance) is the Christian service organization of the Mennonite churches in Brazil. Applications by Brazilian young people participating in the International Visitor Exchange Program of MCC since 1966 have been processed by AMAS. Since 1983 AMAS administers a program called Serving and Learning Together (SALT), in which youth from North America live and work for a year in Brazil. Under the sponsorship of the International Mennonite Organization (IMO), German volunteers serve with AMAS in Brazil in a program which began in 1972. In 1987 AMAS assigned the first Brazilian volunteers to Germany and Paraguay. Each year AMAS volunteers serve with the love of Christ in the interior of Brazil.

Although there are other Mennonite voluntary service activities around the world and relatively modest numbers of people have participated in voluntary service over the years, the concept has gained wide acceptance in the churches as a way for persons, especially youth, to commit their lives voluntarily and sacrificially for a period of Christian service in situations of human need. As a result, significant learning about the world, the meaning of Christian °discipleship and servanthood has ensued—a process both enlightening and enriching the churches around the world.   HAP

J. D. Unruh, *In The Name Of Christ* (Scottdale, 1952), 294-309; Wilfred J. Unruh, "Study of Mennonite Service Programs," (Elkhart, Ind.: IMS, 1965); files of the voluntary service directors' meetings, MC Archives (Goshen); biennial listings of some VS programs are found in *MC Yearbook*.

See also Alternative Service; Development Work.

Voth, Catherine (Oct. 2, 1878-Aug. 19, 1926), was born near Inman, Ks., to Cornelius and Cornelia (Heidebrecht) Voth. Early in life she showed unusual poise, dignity of character, and powers of concentration. She was a very able student. In 1897 she confessed faith in Christ, joining and remaining a life-long member of the Hoffnungsau Mennonite Church near Inman.

Her love of God and people led her into the nursing career for which she showed great ability. It also led her to become one of the first three Mennonite deaconesses in North America (1908). She was soon given major responsibility at the Bethel Deaconess Hospital in Newton, Ks., becoming the first director of the new Nurses Training School, including supervision of operating room, laboratory, and X-ray procedures.

In 1912 she helped found the Kansas Nurses Association, of which she served as president (1916-19). From 1915 to the time of her death she was a member of the Kansas State Board for the Examination and Registration of Nurses. She was also a member of the board of directors of the American Nurses' Association. Her life motto was Ps 37:4-5. WHD

Edmund G. Kaufman, *General Conference Mennonite Pioneers* (North Newton, 1973), 399-404.

Voth, Mathilda Kliewer (1899-April 1, 1986), missionary under the General Conference Mennonite Church (GCM) in China (1919-39), Japan (1951-55), and Taiwan (1955-58). Born at Whitewater, Ks., to John P. and Eva Jantz Kliewer, she attended Bethel College (1916-17), Denver U. (summer, 1927), and Witmarsum Seminary (1927-28). She taught school at Vona, Col. (1917-18). She married William C. Voth in 1918. They were ordained for missionary service in June 1919. Four children were born to them.

In China Mathilda was director of the Girls' Mission School at Taming (1923-27), then held literacy and evangelism classes and home study Bible courses for women in the villages. From 1942 to 1950 she was secretary for the Women's Missionary Association of the General Conference Mennonite Church. After retirement she remained active in church, community, and family affairs, teaching and writing. Her book *Clear Shining After Rain* (Newton,

1980) is an account of her missionary experiences. VU

Juhnke, *Mission* (1979), 113, 115ff, 242, and index; *Menn. Rep.* (Apr. 28, 1986), 23; *MWR* (Apr. 10, 1986), 12.

Voth, William Cornelius (Mar. 10, 1888-May 13, 1962), missionary under the General Conference Mennonite Church (GCM), in China (1919-39; 1948-50), Japan (1951-55), and Taiwan (1955-58). In 1943-44 he helped survey South America for new mission work.

Born at Lehigh, Ks., to Cornelius C. and Sarah Duerksen Voth, at age three Voth moved with his family to Oklahoma. He attended Mennonite Preparatory Academy in Hillsboro., Ks.; Bethel College, Newton, Ks. (BA, 1918); and Colorado State Teachers' College. He also studied architecture and engineering at the U. of Oklahoma. On furlough (1927-28) he also studied at Iliff Seminary in Denver, Col., and at Witmarsum Seminary in Bluffton, Ohio.

He married Mathilda Kliewer in 1918. They were ordained for missionary service and left for China in July 1919. Four children were born to them. The first term he supervised building construction but was also involved in developing policies for nationalization of the church. During his subsequent terms he was engaged in rural evangelism. In Japan and Taiwan he assisted in opening new fields. VU

Juhnke, *Mission* (1979), 113, 115ff, 242, and index; *Mennonite* (May 22, 1962), 348, (May 30, 1961), 357-59.

Voting. See Government; Political Attitudes; Politics; Sociopolitical Activism.

W

Wall, Cornelius (Sept. 25, 1893-Nov. 17, 1985), knew early in adulthood that his heart was in studying and teaching the Bible. From this clear vision grew a life which nurtured the development of °Bible schools from Russia to the United States, Canada and Switzerland.

Wall taught at Zoar Academy, Inman, Ks.; Hesston College, Ks.; and at Bible schools in Henderson, Nebr., and Mountain Lake, Minn., before accepting a Mennonite Central Committee assignment to Gronau, Germany, in 1948. In Gronau he led Bible conferences and youth retreats for Mennonite °refugees fleeing from the Soviet army after World War II. Through this refugee work Wall and his wife Agnes did much to awaken interest for European Bible school. Wall later helped organize the European Mennonite Bible School at Bienenberg near Basel, Switzerland.   CRW

Cornelius Wall and Agnes Wall, *As We Remember* (Hillsboro, Ks., Mennonite Brethren Publishing House, 1979); Christine Wiebe, "Cornelius Wall," in *MCC Story*, 4: 194-214; Obituary in *Chr. Leader* (Dec. 10, 1985).

Walters, John (1884-Mar. 1, 1962), a citizen of India, was born in the home of a Methodist minister. He was baptized in the Methodist Church as a young man. He was educated in or near Jabalpur, Madhya Pradesh, India. After high school he went to the Hardoi Bible Institute. After finishing there, he took normal teachers training. In 1904 he married an orphan girl from the Mukti Bai Mission.

He accepted a position in the Karbala Mission in Raipur. However he was not happy in Karbala so in 1930 when the Bible school in Janjgir opened he accepted a position in that school. There he taught church history, religions, Bible geography, Christian doctrines and Old Testament prophets. He continued in this school until about 1948.

While teaching he was also very active in the church, serving as Sunday school teacher, member of the church council, and as treasurer. For some years he was treasurer of the Bharatiya General Conference Mennonite Church.

In 1949 he was called to be the pastor of the church in Jagdeeshpur. He was then ordained as an elder in the General Conference Mennonite Church and he served that church until 1951. He then returned to Janjgir and became the pastor there. Besides his pastoral work he translated many tracts from English to Hindi and actively distributed them. He also wrote a number of dramas on the lives of Jeremiah and St. Paul.

His life was characterized by a deep faith in Jesus Christ and wherever one would meet him one could sense his dedication to Christ and the church.   HR

See also Lay Evangelists ("A Woman of the Bible" [feature]).

Wang, Stephen (Wang Xin-fu) (b. 1905), the oldest of three sons, was born into the home of a poor peasant family in Henan (Honan) Province of China. His father, a Confucian scholar and teacher, became a Christian and later was employed as an evangelist in the General Conference Mennonite Church mission at Kaizhou ([Kai Chow] Puyang). Stephen studied in the Mennonite mission schools at Kaizhou. There he became a close friend of classmate James °Liu. In 1928 with assistance from E. G. °Kaufman, Liu and Wang entered Yenching University in Beijing where they studied for two years. From 1930 to 1932 they studied at Bluffton College and Bethel College, graduating from the latter school.

When Liu and Wang returned to China as the first American-trained Chinese in the Chinese Mennonite Church, Wang became director of youth work on the mission staff at Damingfu (Taming-fu), 1932-33. On July 13, 1934, he married Zhang Zhang Ruiling (Margaret), headmistress of a nearby Christian girls' school. In 1934 they moved to Kaizhou where both taught in the Mennonite high school and led in the church program.

With the Japanese invasion of China in 1937, Wang and his family fled south with the intention of returning soon to Kaizhou. As the war continued, the Wang family moved westward, ending in Lanzhou, Ganzu Province, where Stephen taught physical science in several universities (1943-50). Three of the Wang children died on the westward trek.

In 1950 the Wangs moved to Northeastern Normal University in Zhangchun in Jilin Province, where Stephen taught chemistry until the 1980s. During the Cultural Revolution (1966-69), Stephen was sent with his family to work for four years in the countryside. Stephen and Margaret Wang have two daughters and three sons.

It had long been assumed that, when communications were broken off during World War II, Stephen Wang had died. In 1980 he renewed contact in Hengyang with his old friends, James and Hazel Liu. In 1982, on the 50th anniversary of his graduation from Bethel College, he was invited by Bluffton and Bethel Colleges to visit churches and mission and college friends in the United States.   RK

Robert Kreider, ed., *Christians True in China* (Newton, 1988), autobiographical accounts.

War Bonds. See Investments.

920

War Taxes. See Taxes.

Washington (ME IV:892) had Amish Mennonites and Swiss Mennonites in its Columbia plateau for 15 years before they organized a (GCM) congregation at Colfax in 1893. The Jacob Kauffman family moved from Kansas to Washington in 1878 by covered wagon, but most Menonites arrived after °railroads opened the area, and some at Ritzville and Newport settled on railroad land.

After 1957 new congregations formed at Pasco (unaffiliated but initially MC-related) in 1967, Seattle (GCM, later also MC) in 1968, Ferndale (MB) in 1980, Spokane (GCM) in 1981, and Othello (CGC) in 1987. Washington had 797 Mennonites in 1987, including 454 from the General Conference Mennonite Church; 229 Mennonite Brethren; 64 unaffiliated Mennonites; 28 Church of God in Christ Mennonite (Holdeman); and 22 from the Mennonite Church (MC). General Conference Mennonites own Camrac, a retreat center near Leavenworth. Eastern Washington Mennonites began an MCC °relief sale in 1977. Congregations withdrew from Mennonite affiliation or disbanded at Colfax (GCM), Monroe (GCM), Seattle (MB), and Federal Way (MB).   HKL

Lee Price Campbell, "Seventy-Five Years on the Shore of the Peaceful Sea; A History of the Pacific District Conference of the General Conference Mennonite Church of North America" (MDiv thesis, Western Evangelical Seminary, Portland, Ore., 1973), 31-36, 55-73; H. D. Burkholder, *The Story of Our Conference and Churches* (North Newton: Mennonite Press, 1951), 22-36; Pacific Coast Conference (MC), Annual Report, 1986, 9; Pacific District Conference (GCM), Annual Report, 1986, 12-13; *MC Yearbook* (1986-87), 45, 83, 102; Hope Kauffman Lind, "Mennonites in Oregon and Related Congregations in Neighboring States (1876-1976)" (unpublished manuscript); Daniel Hertzler, *From Germantown to Steinbach* (Scottdale, 1981), 173-85.

***Washington Memo.* See Lobbying; Sociopolitical Activism.**

Washington-Franklin Mennonite Conference consists of 10 congregations with a membership of 900. Five congregations were formed since 1959: Pondsville and Pinesburg in Washington Co., Md.; Waynecastle in Franklin Co., Pa.; Flintstone in Allegany Co., Md.; and Lockards Creek in Clay Co., Ky. The conference has one bishop, 13 ministers, and six deacons. Conference sessions are held annually on the second Thursday of September at the Reiff's Meeting House. The conference rules and discipline of 1957 were revised in 1978.

The conference mission board operates the Mennonite Old Peoples Home at Maugansville, Md. The conference Mennonite Mutual Aid Plan provides help to those who experience fire or lightning damage. The Washington County Mennonite Church Association gives aid in case of liability in vehicle accidents. The conference operates the Paradise Mennonite School, Flintstone Mennonite School, and the Lockards Creek Mennonite School.   DRM

MC Yearbook (1988-89), MC Yrbk (1984) 100.

Water Technology. Dike building was not new when the Mennonites arrived in the Vistula Delta of °West Prussia. The Teutonic Knights had built a circular dike around 1320. But the system had decayed under Polish rule after the Second Peace of Thorn (1466). When the Anabaptist refugees arrived in the 16th c. those dikes along the Vistula and Nogat existed, but the lower parts lacked drainage, because they lay one and one-half to two meters below sea level. The Dutch refugees erected a dike several miles long east of this old dam towards the Frische Haff and dug a network of ditches through which the excess water was pumped up into the Linau, Tiege, and Jungfersche Lake, which drained into the Haff. Mennonites imported new wind-propelled watermills, using a winding staircase to pump the water into those rivers. (Articles on many of the people and places mentioned here are found in ME I-IV.)

In the same fashion they drained the Drausensee (west of Elbing and the Ellerwald swamps). Mennonites owned river boats (*"Mennoniten Kähne"*) in the centuries that followed. They were well-suited to transport dirt for dike building. Since the dikes had to be inspected annually, Mennonites were often chosen as "Deichhauptmann" (dike inspector). Gustav Fieguth (Kunzendorf) and Hermann Froese (Klakendorf) were dike inspectors in 1936. The same year, Gustav Zimmermann (Tiegenhof) is mentioned as captain of a ship. Others worked for the Schichau shipyards in Elbing and Danzig. The book by Hermann Thiessen, and Bartholomäus Tiessen, *300 Jahre Familientradition* (Burgdorf 1986), lists a number of Mennonites and descendents who were involved with ships.

In 1740 about 300 Mennonites under King Frederick II of Prussia moved to Labiau, east of Königsberg and received land in the "Elbings-Kolonie" (*East Prussia*), which had been started in 1728. The group did some draining of land, but could not make a fair living, so they left before 1748. An old dike was still called "Mennonitendamm" in 1921.

Mennonites in the 17th c. Netherlands played an important part in the whaling industry, especially those from the strict Mennonite traditions who wouldn't sail in ships to the Dutch East Indies because those ships carried arms. Mennonites involved in whaling included men from Ameland and the Zaanstreek (Dirk Hiddes Kat, *Dagboek*, Haarlem 1818; C. P. Sorghdrager, *Memorie-boek: De wereld van C. P. Sorghdrager 1779-1824*, Ameland, n.d.; S. Lootsma, *Nederlandse walvisvaart, meer speciaal de zaanse*, Wormerveer, 1937).

From the beginning Mennonites were interested in fighting Holland's number one foe, water. They were members of the boards of polders, and they were builders of mills. Well known were Jan Andrieszoon (Leeghwater) and Pieter Pieters (M. A. Verkade, *Den derden Dach: ontstaan en ontwikkeling van de Polder Westzaan*, Wormerveer, 1982; J. G. de Roever, *Jan Adriaenszoon Leeghwater*, Amsterdam, 1944; S. Groenveld and others, *Wederdopers, menisten en doopsgezinden*, Zutphen 1981).

In the early 20th c. Cornelis Lely (1854-1929), a minister in several government cabinets, improved the Noordzee Canal and planned the reclaiming of the Zuiderzee. (K. Jansma, *Lely de bewinger van de Zuiderzee*, (Amsterdam, 1948)). In all cities of the Netherlands Mennonites were shipowners, the best known being members of the van Eeghen family. (J. Rogge, *Het handelshuis van Eeghen,* Amsterdam 1949; S. Groenveld, *Wederdopers*).

Mennonites of Hamburg-Altona were, from the 17th c. onward, leading shipowners, shipbuilders, and traders along sea routes. A Mennonite was the first to send a ship to Archangel, Russia. The leading family in Hamburg-Altona was descended from the Mennonite deacon Paul Roosen (1582-1649). His son, Gerrit (1612-1711) traveled to Russia to buy moose hides. His grandson Berend I (1705-1788) became the most outstanding Mennonite shipowner trading in ports such as Amsterdam, Bordeaux, and London. He built his own ships at his shipyards at Reiherstieg, which he inherited from his father-in-law Lucas Kramer. He owned 20 ships. One got lost with one million marks worth of linen, wax, and manufactured goods. In 1673, of the 53 ships in Hamburg's Greenland whaling industry, 46 were owned by Mennonites. The trade was so good that in 1674 the first Mennonite church in Hamburg was built and financed by a contribution of 5 percent of the proceeds of the whaling industry for one year. Emil Greve of Hamburg was from around 1900 on, owner of a port business and had in his possession tugs and barges.

Three Mennonite families who had lived under oppressive Polish noblemen in Jesiorka and 35 other families who had lived under the jurisdiction of Anton von Wipschinsky near Danzig came to the *Netzebruch*, a swampy area near Driesen and founded the colonies Brenkenhoffswalde, Franzthal, and Neu-Dessau. In the "Kiewitzwinkel" and a section of pasture belonging to the village of Trebitsch, which had not been used for ages, they brought the land, after draining it, into an arable condition. Here they could settle fourteen families, each having lots of 10-15 hectares (25-37 acres). They drained the Carleische Hütung and the "Elsenbruch" (Rudolf März-Vorbruch, "Neues von den Mennoniten in Netzebruch," *Heimatkalender,* Friedeberg, 1929, 19-26; "Franz Balthasar Schönberg von Brenkenhoff," *Heimatkalender,* Friedeberg, 1929), 39-43).

The *Mennonitisches Adressbuch 1936* mentions under Hamburg, Fritz and Knut Claassen of Wedel as shipbuilders, and retired Admiral Siegfried Claassen (1884-1951) an elder in the Hamburg church. At the beginning of World War II he was chairman of the prize court of the German Navy in Hamburg. Walter Greve and Kurt Greve, father and uncle of present (1987) church councillor, Helmut Greve, spent a few years as wholesale traders in Paris, London, and Bangkok and as such had many connections with the shipping industry. Helmut got his practical experience with the Stülchen and Son Shipyards (Blohm and Voss).

The above mentioned *Adressbuch* of 1936 mentions under *Emden* a seaport in northwest Germany, a number of Mennonite shipbuilders, shipowners, the widow of a navy officer, and Willem Mennen, "merchant and shipowner". The widow of Admiral Breusing, Martha, nee Brons lived in Berlin. The father of the famous reformer of Mennonite agriculture in the Ukraine, Johann Cornies, had been a sailor prior to his moving to Russia. He likely learned to be a self-trained doctor while on mer-

chant ships traveling to Lisbon in 1755 and India. Thus he could treat his native neighbors in the steppe of the Ukraine and make them friends.

The Kuban settlement in Russia, which was begun in 1867, had difficuilties finding good drinking water. Spring water was of low quality. The village Wohldemfürst had to draw water from the Kuban River. Only after wealth increased and straw-thatched roofs could be replaced by tile and sheet metal, could rain water be piped into cisterns for household usage. (*Die Kubaner Siedlung,* Historische Schriftenreihe des Echo-Verlages, 9, Steinbach, Manitoba, 1953). When Mennonites settled in Crimea they also had water problems. In Toultschak they built a water system for the village in the 1890s. In Saribasch the water was not sufficient although the well was 80 meters deep. They built a reserve well, but sold the village in the 1890s to Lutheran Christians. In the village of Spat they found good water at the River Salquier. (Martin Durksen, *Die Krim war unsere Heimat,* Winnipeg, Manitoba, 1980, pp. 26-30.) The artist Ernst Dyck, displaced by the events of World War II, was employed in Leninpol, Kirgizia, to construct irrigation systems at the River Talos in order to make the cultivation of cotton, apples, and grapes possible.

In Bavaria, at the invitation of Duke Maximilian Josef (King of Bavaria after 1805) invited Mennonites to settle, in part because they could drain the "Donaumoos" area near Neuburg on the Danube, where they established the settlement of Maxweiler (1802ff). However, they left after 1852 in order to avoid military training, for Lee Co., Iowa. After World War II Mennonites of the Kohlhof congregation in the Palatinate used irrigation water to raise vegetables.

Mennonites were often busy operating water-propelled mills. Johannes Wohlgemuth (1720-1798) received an *Erbbestandsbrief* (hereditary contract) in 1755 from Carl, Prince of Nassau, to operate a regular mill and an oil mill in Albisheim/Pfrimm near Kirchheimbolanden. The mill was in the same family for seven generations. The Brubacher family operated the Obere Schmelzmühle in the same village. (Ludwig Wasem, *1150 Jahre Albisheim 835-1985,* Kirchheimbolanden, 1985, 87-88).

The book by Friedrich Wilhelm Weber, *Die Geschichte der Mühlen und des Müllerhandwerks der Pfalz,* (Otterbach 1978), mentions more than 20 families with Mennonite names who operated various watermills after the Thirty Years War (1618-48). The Brubacher family had the tanning mill in Albisheim (1843-1916). In the paper mill of Alt-leiningen the Göbel, Eymann, and Hertzler families were involved in the 19th c. Joseph Hauter ground limestone in Zweibrücken in 1791. It is very likely that Mennonites brought the idea of "limeing" to Pennsylvania. According to *Mennonitisches Adressbuch 1936,* the following Mennonite families had mills: Heinrich Reidiger, "Strohbrücker Mill"; Heinrich Guth, "Bärbrunnermühle"; Schertz, "Bettinger Mühle"; Heinrich and Adolf Hauter, Kirschbachermühle; Emil Hauter, "Eichelsbachermühle"; Adolf Eyer, "Faustermühle; Jakob Hauter, "Grossstein-hausermühle; Otto Schertz, "Haustadtermühle; Emil Eyer, "Rosselmühle; Joseph Schertz, "Schartermühle;

Joseph Guth family, "Stampermühle/Giessen" and Adolf Guth, the "Stampermühle". All of them belonged to the Ixheim (Amish) or Ernstweiler (Mennonite) congregations, united in 1937 into the Zweibrücken congregation.

The "Schlossmühle of Altleiningen was in the hands of Krehbiel, Johannes Ummel and later Heinrich Krehbiel (1700-1750 had the "Wartenberg Mill." The "Winnweiler Mill" was run by Jakob Würtz. He had the later the "Untermühle" in St. Alban near Rockenhausen. Before 1870 he migrated to New York and worked there in a big mill. Christian Eichelberger (1772-1830) had the "Neumühle" near Sembach after 1811. The family had it for over 100 years until ca. 1916. The "Untere Mühle" near Enkenbach (now a retirement home for the Protestant Church) was run by the Krehbiel and Würtz families in the 19th c. The "Diemerstein Mill" was in the hands of the Engel, Eymann, and Goebel families in the 18th and 19th c. The owners of the "Weissmühle" near Eisenberg left for America about 1830-40. Practically all Mennonite families quit the milling business before or soon after World War II when legislation favored bigger mills. However, some like in Lauterborn (Luxembourg) and Hornbach (Reidiger-Hauter) are using the water turbine to generate electricity. Many more examples of Mennonites involved in water-driven milling businesses could be cited.

In Alsace Pilgram Marpeck greatly aided the city of Strasbourg by suggesting that wood should be cut in the Black Forest and Vosges Mountains and brought by river to Strasbourg. Even in 1600 this wood was called "Pilgerholz" after *Pilgram* Marpeck. In the Markirchen Valley the Anabaptists cultivated unused ground and at the ends of their fields they excavated a ditch that could be used as drainage. They also irrigated the pastures with a special type of equipment. When Peter Hege came in 1912 from Branchweilerhof to Schafbusch near Wissemburg, Alsace, he put drainage pipes 1,20 m. (about 4 ft.) deep into parallel ditches, 12 m.(40 ft.) apart. Gilles Pelsy developed a perfectly working drainage machine and is now (1987) receiving orders for it from all over France. At the same time Paul Oesch of Toul (Lorraine) was draining a sizeable piece of land. In the Colmar and Neuf-Brisach area of Alsace, which has rainfall of only 500-600 mm. (19-23 inches) per year, Mennonites together with other neighbors installed after World War II an irrigation system that raised the grain production. The Bon Homme Hutterite Bruderhof in South Dakota used irrigation water from the Gavis Point Dam of the Lewis and Clark Lake since the 1960s and has certain water rights. In a similar way the Hutterite colonies of Reardan, Espinola, and Warden, west of Spokane, Wash., use large irrigation rigs and raise fantastic crops of barley, alfalfa, and seed potatoes. Mennonites in the north central and northwestern states of the United States frequently depend on irrigation systems to farm otherwise nonarable lands.

European Mennonite Evangelism Committee and Mennonite Central Committee (MCC) workers have supervised well-digging operations in Chad, Burkina Faso and other areas of the Sahel region since 1964. In Chad the wells were combined with desert-adapted techniques for planting trees (developed in Israel) and simple pumps. In Indonesia, MCC helped build dams to irrigate rice fields during dry periods (1971-77).

In 1985 MCC workers and local laborers in southern Bangladesh installed up to 40 tube wells a day and cleaned a number of flooded *pukurs*, normally used for fresh water wells, which had been filled by salt water during the flood, caused by a cyclone.

When the first Mennonites arrived in the Gran Chaco, Paraguay in 1926-27, their biggest problem was the lack of drinking water. In some villages they found no potable water at all. In Gnadenheim they dug 20 wells before finding one with good water. From these bad experiences the Mennonites learned better methods of well-digging, e.g., using sheet-iron to buttress walls against the sandy soil. In °Filadelfia they did not have enough water for the settlers, soldiers, and the newly installed steam engine. So in 1932 they built a reservoir on the "Wasserkamp." In 1986 each Mennonite family had its own cistern with plenty of good water.

In Brazil the situation was better. When Mennonites arrived in 1930 they found many creeks and rivers, and the elevated land around °Witmarsum, Paraná State, had many springs. These were improved and houses connected with pipes. Later artesian wells and a central water system was built.   HG

Otto Schowalter, "Kulturleistungen der Hamburger Mennoniten," *Menn. Geschbl.*, 3 (Dec. 1938) 33-48; Samuel A. Yoder, *Middle East Sojourn*, (Scottdale 1951) 169-70; Horst Gerlach, *Bildband zur Geschichte der Mennoniten* (Uelzen, 1980), 160-62; Bertram La Baume-Kloeppel, *Das Weichsel-Nogat-Delta* (Danzig, 1924); Ernst W. Schepansky, "Mennoniten in Hamburg und Altona zur Zeit des Merkantilismus," *Menn. Geschbl.* 54-73; Hans Szymanski, *Brandenburg-Preußen zur See* (Berlin, 1938); Horst Gerlach, "Johann Cornies: Ein Westpreuße reformiert die russische Landwirtschaft," *Westpreussiches Jahrbuch* (1975), 137-44; Edward Carstenn, *Geschichte der Hansestadt Elbing* (Elbing 1937); Ed Wiens, "New Method Taps Wells in Bangladesh," *MWR* (July 11, 1985), 6; Jean Séguy, *Les assemblées anabaptistes-mennonites de France* (The Hague: Mouton, 1977), 491-97; Ludwig Wasem, *1150 Jahre Albisheim, 835-1985* (Kirchheimbolanden, 1985), 87-88; Peter P. Klassen, *Kaputi Mennonita*, 2nd. ed. (Filadelfia, 1976); Peter Wiens and Peter Klassen, *Jubiläumsschrift zum 25 jährigen Bestehen der Kolonie Fernheim* (Chaco, Paraguay, and Winnipeg, 1955).

See also India.

Wayindama Emmanuel was born to Chokwe parents in the mid-1920s near the Angola border in Kahemba Territory of Kwilu Province, the Belgian Congo (Zaire), Africa. Wayindama came as a boy to Kamayala, a pioneer mission post of the Unevangelized Tribes Mission where he enrolled in primary school. After graduating and teaching several years, he was sent ca. 300 km. (186 mi.) north to Mukedi, a station of the °°Congo Inland Mission (Africa Inter-Mennonite Mission), where, in the early 1950s, he took a special two-year teacher training course. Returning to Kamayala, he became the first African director of the station school.

In 1956 he was chosen with his family to go to Tshikapa in the West Kasai to take a three-year course in the Mennonite Bible Institute (by then Kamayala was part of the Congo Inland Mission field). Finishing at the top of his class, Wayindama was invited back to Tshikapa in 1962 to become the first African instructor at this school. In 1963 the Bible Institute was relocated west of the Loange River at Kandala in Kwilu Province. In the rebellion in 1964 the Kandala station was an early target. While fleeing south on foot with his family, Wayindama was intercepted by suspicious government soldiers, but spared from execution by intervention of a Christian soldier.

At home in Kamayala Wayindama was promptly appointed lead pastor of the Mennonite church. Upon completing his tenure there he accepted an itinerant teaching pastor assignment in the sprawling church district. Today Mennonite congregations are to be found established in a number of isolated rural settings which were Wayindama's responsibility.　　　　　　　　　　　　　　HEid

Wayne Co., Ohio, Old Order Amish Settlement. See Holmes-Wayne-Tuscarawas Counties, Ohio, Old Order Amish Settlement.

Wealth. The use of wealth in worship and the church is as old as Gn 4: 3-4 and as recent as the offering last Sunday morning. Likewise wealth has been sought after as early as Gn 26: 13, 14 and as recently as the reader's latest investment. The Scripture is full of references to good and bad uses of wealth in the lives of God's people.

In the Mennonite Churches it seems there has been greater emphasis on the temptations and evils of wealth, rather than the faithful and effective use of wealth to continue the work Christ began. This negative teaching on wealth has divided families, inspired some to join communal groups, and led some successful business persons to leave the Mennonite fold and join the Presbyterians, Methodists, or other Christian denominations.

The Bible speaks forthrightly about wealth being one of the tools in the hands of the Christian to advance the kingdom. From creation (birth), we are gifted with about 75 years (time), with intellect (ability and talents), and we are born into a material world (property, money, wealth). With these three gifts at birth (time, talent and treasure), we are given freedom and independence to use them to achieve our goals in life—whether selfish or humanitarian.

When we become Christians we become new persons, as the apostle Paul says. We are entrusted with the gospel and given new goals and new purposes in life. At that moment our gifts from creation (time, talent, wealth) become the tools we use in continuing the work that Christ began, namely, communicating the gospel. Our mission and our °stewardship is to use our gifts received at the time of our birth to advance and promote our gift of redemption.

For example, a carpenter is not hired to take selfish care of tools. They are to be used, even worn out, in building a house. Likewise, Christians are to use their wealth, as well as their time and intellect, in building the kingdom of God. In fact there is a very close relationship between quality and excellence of the church's program and the adequacy of money to support it. This can be shown diagrammatically as follows:

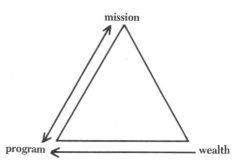

The mission statement of a church agency is the controlling document for its board of trustees. But the mission statement is powerless until that mission is expressed through a program. For instance, a mission board has home and foreign missions with personnel, travel, salaries, facilities, furloughs, etc. Not one aspect of the progrm can be put into action without money (wealth). Wealth makes possible a program which puts into action the mission of the church. Note the flow of the arrows in the diagram. The perceived and accepted mission of the church is primary to any group or agency but the church's mission is frequently poorly executed through its program because of the inadequacy of financial resources to undergird it.

This inadequacy of financial resources has occurred because of the church's failure to keep together the triad of creation gifts (time, talent and wealth). The church "overemphasized" the importance of service, study, and use of time, and has spoken negatively on money. We have emphasized the "go sell" [your wealth] portions of the Scriptures over the "effective use of" [wealth] portions of the Scripture. For instance, rarely does a pastor speak on the dishonest steward passage (Lk 16). Here Jesus is clearly saying that the people of the world know what money is for—they use it to gain their purposes (mission). Likewise Christians should be just as wise as the people of the world, by using their money for the purposes (mission) of the church. Through our teaching and emphasis, we have separated what God intended to be together—mission and its means of accomplishment (wealth).

One way to teach this concept is to show that money (wages) are a person's mind and energy expressed in portable form. For instance, a smile will not purchase a suit from a clothing store. Yet one can work at some job and be paid wages for brawn, ability and even charm (personality), then go to the clothing merchant and write a check to receive a suit of clothes.

Translating this concept of wealth to the triangular diagram above, everyone through his or her wealth can be a part of the church's mission. The one who "goes" is no more important than the one who "supports." This links the entrepreneur to the church's mission in a creative way. People of wealth begin to see they are just as important to the church as the teachers, ministers, missionaries, or service workers.

This concept of the role of wealth is clearly described by a famous preacher of a past generation. "Money is a miraculous thing. It is your personal energy reduced to portable form and endowed with power you do not possess. It can go where you cannot go, speak languages you cannot speak, lift burdens you cannot touch with your fingers, save lives with which you cannot deal directly."

God certainly did not intend the church to be poor. Through a two-step plan, first fruits and °jubilee, adequate provisions for stewardship have been made. Through first fruits, we give regularly from current income throughout our life. Secondly, at the end of life (after 50 years) we leave a portion of our accumulated assets to the church. The problem has been with our unfaithfulness in teaching the importance of wealth in carrying out our kingdom responsibilities. We have indeed separated what God intended to be together—time, ability, wealth. DEK

Kaufman/Harder, *Anabaptists Four C. Later* (1975), 275-77; James Urry, "Through the Eye of a Needle: Wealth and the Mennonite Experience in Imperial Russia," *JMS* 3 (1985) 7-35.

See also Business; Capitalism; Discipleship; Land Distribution; Materialism; Mutual Aid; Nicaragua; Nonconformity; Property; Socialism; Theologies from the Two-Thirds World.

Weaverland Conference. See Old Order Mennonites.

Weber, Max (1864-1920). See Sociological Studies.

Weber, Urias K. (1879-1971), was the son of Menno S. Weber and the former Sarah Knipe. He was married to the former Magdalena Shoemaker. In 1907 Urias Weber was chosen a minister by lot in the First Mennonite Church at Berlin (Kitchener), Ont. The lot had earlier fallen on his father, who had refused to accept the call. Urias Weber's only formal pastoral education occurred during part of one year spent at Moody Bible Institute (1910). At First Mennonite Church he preached in the English services only.

In 1924 a controversy arose over whether members must wear uniform "plain °dress" while working in factories and offices. After Weber admitted to communion some who did not wear the prescribed garb (an action taken contrary to instructions from Ontario bishops), he was silenced until the next session of conference. Approximately half of the congregation chose to form a new, unaffiliated congregation and asked Weber to be the minister. He served as pastor of the Stirling Avenue Mennonite Church, 1924-42, and as pastor emeritus from 1942 until his death. AEM

Weddings (ME IV:1134) are related to °marriage as an initiatory ceremony is related to an ongoing reality. The belated inclusion of an article on weddings in the supplement section of ME IV and the complete absence of such in the still earlier °°*Mennonite Cyclopedic Dictionary* illustrate the much greater attention which Mennonites have given marriage as compared to the wedding. This initiatory rite has received little studied attention to date and the present article will center primarily upon the North American Mennonite experience. Amish and Hutterite practices are described in two books by John A. Hostetler.

Virtually no light is thrown by the Scriptures upon the wedding service itself. Anabaptists shared with the Reformers a rejection of the sacramental concept of marriage (°ordinances), though Anabaptists lifted the consecrated view of marriage to a considerable height in contrast to the Reformers. Concern for the wedding apparently expressed itself in the assumption that the ceremony would be consistent with the general teachings of the New Testament concerning the appropriate words, attitudes, and actions of a disciple of Christ.

There is a diversity of practice among the various Mennonite branches, conferences, and communities in North America on the several aspects of the wedding. The specifics included in the present entry simply signal the need to examine more closely the understanding and practices of each particular branch, conference, and community.

The strong sense of commitment to Christ and to one's fellow believers that characterizes Mennonites means that wedding practices are a matter of concern to the congregation and the wider Mennonite fellowship.

Historically, weddings involving Mennonites had to be between members of the Mennonite church in order to have the approval of the congregation(s) involved. Until early in the 20th c., weddings were generally performed by a °bishop or °elder, or rarely, by a minister with the bishop's (elder's) permission.

In those congregations where people did not become members of the Mennonite church until after marriage, it was customary for the couple to be married by a non-Mennonite minister or by a civil servant. A marriage between a Mennonite and a non-Mennonite was for centuries a matter calling for congregational °discipline.

Within the consensus that weddings are an expression of congregational life and should reflect the beliefs and practices of the Body of Christ, Mennonite attitudes vary with regard to whether a wedding is primarily a congregational event or a private and a more personal affair. This difference has grown since the removing of the ban against marriage between persons of different Christian traditions. Most Mennonite ministers refuse to marry non-Christians or couples where only one is a Christian though this attitude may be fading.

Since the mid-1900s most Mennonite pastors insist on counseling sessions before the wedding takes place. Many congregations have either formal or informal guidelines regarding weddings. These may address such details as use of the meetinghouse, choice of a date, what music is to be used, the nature of the service, the number of attendants, the use of °symbols such as rings and candles, the dress of the wedding party, decoration of the meetinghouse, the reception following the wedding, and the manner of reporting the event in the local newspapers. In earlier decades weddings were held either in the home of the bishop or the bride or in the meetinghouse at the close of a regular worship service. In the late 1980s they are held at a separate hour and day in the meetinghouse. The entire congregation is generally invited to the wedding, but only a smaller number of friends and family are invited to the reception, which may be held either in the meetinghouse or in a community facility.

There is a growing concern among Mennonite leaders over many new practices that are being introduced into Mennonite weddings as a result of generally increasing °acculturation, inter-marriage with people of other Christian traditions, and affluence (°wealth). The former full-length sermon is now replaced with a brief meditation given while the wedding party remains standing before the congregation. Some practices characteristic of the wider culture, e.g., the "giving away of the bride" and the custom of the congregation rising while the bride enters, are being questioned as to whether they are congruent with Christian faith. The rising number of °divorces in Western society is generating a more serious look at both premarital and postmarital counseling.

Attempts are being made to bring the wedding into the mainstream of the congregation's life along with baptism and parent-child dedications. Church periodicals are addressing this matter in articles and editorials. Some conferences are appointing committees for the specific purpose of examining wedding practices with the intent of developing a greater consistency among the congregations. Mennonite °secondary schools are giving instruction regarding the planning of Christian weddings as a part of courses on family life. Special retreats for those engaged to be married are held by some conferences and church retreat centers.   GCS

John A. Hostetler, *Amish Society* (1980), 191-98; idem, *Hutterite Society* (1974), 239-40, 339-41; *Menn. Life*, 28 (Sept.1973), 72-75, on Old Colony Mennonites; Lois G. Clemens, "15. Marriage as Community Concern," *Issues to Discuss* (1973), 92-97; Paul Erb, "Christian Weddings," *GH* (July 21, 1959), 643; Gary and Lydia Harder, *Celebrating Christian Marriage* (Newton, 1980; Scottdale: MPH, 1980), 1-48; Waldo Hiebert, "Wanted—A Christian Philosophy of Weddings," *GH* (Sept. 23, 1958), 902, 911; John H. Redekop, "What Makes a Wedding Christian?" *MB Herald*, 25, no. 16 (Sept. 5, 1986, 12; Stephen Scott, *The Amish Wedding and Other Special Occasions of the Old Order Communities* (Good Books, 1988); Gerald C. Studer, "34. A Look at Weddings," *1966 Program Guide for Sunday Evening Services* (Scottdale: MPH), 131-33, 37; idem, "Weddings, A Significant Aspect of Community," *Chr. Living*, 34, no. 6 (June, 1987), 24-28; *Minister's Manual* (Steinbach, Manitoba: The Evangelical Mennonite Conference, 1983), 25-31; Church Polity Committee, John L. Horst, Secretary, *Mennonite Church Polity* (Scottdale, 1944), 130-33; John S. Coffman and John F. Funk, *Confession of Faith and Ministers' Manual* (Scottdale, 1952), 91-95; Heinz and Dorothea Janzen, *Minister's Manual* (Newton, 1983; Scottdale: MPH, 1983), 81-93; E. F. Bittinger, "Wedding Customs," *Brethren Encyclopedia* (1983), 1324-26.

See also Bergthal Mennonites (Saskatchewan); Courtship; Folklore; Kaufman, Edmund G.; Mennonite Church in India.

Weierhof, Germany

Weierhof, Germany (ME IV:911). After World War II Mennonite congregational life at the Weierhof was considerably enriched with the reception of many refugees. The congregation at Ulffhofen joined Weierhof in 1972. A new orientation and the involvement of numerous members led to a stronger contribution of laity in worship; the establishment of cell groups; and the holding of a variety of events. A community center was built, 1965-66. °Peace witness became an important concern of the congregation. Preachers were Paul Schowalter (1938-71), Hans Werner Janzen (1972-81), and Willi Wiedemann

(1982-). Christian Galle (1946-69), Eckbert Driedger (1969-87), and Gerhard Wiehler (1987-) served as chairmen of the congregation.

The "Gymnasium am Donnersberg" (°°Realanstalt am Donnersberg) was reopened in 1959. In 1986 this secondary school had 684 students. Helmut Haury was the principal until 1975, when he was followed by Georg Ballod. The school building houses the following institutions: (1) From 1959 to 1988 the "Weierhöfer Stelle" was headquarters for various administrative and relief programs of the °Vereinigung der deutschen Mennonitengemeinden. In 1972 Hanspeter Bergtholdt replaced Richard Hertzler as administrator. (2) The Mennonitische Forschungsstelle, a Mennonite °historical and genealogical research library has been administered by Paul Schowalter (to 1975) and Gary Waltner (since 1975). (3) The offices of the youth work of the Konferenz Süddeutscher Mennonitengemeinden, administered by Ruth Raab and Anita Hein (since 1985-1988/89).   HHau

Gary J. Waltner, ed., *300 Jahre Mennonitengemeinde Weierhof 1682-1982*; Eckbert Driedger, "Vom Weierhöfer Antrag bis zum Emder Beschluß," *Brücke* (1986), 88-89; Helmut Haury, "Schwierige Weichenstellungen: Die Weierhof-Jahre 1979 bis 1985 aus der Sicht des Trägervereins," *Schriften des Gymnasiums Weierhof*, 1 (1985), 9ff.; Richard Hertzler, "Das Hilfswerk der Vereinigung der Deutschen Mennonitengemeinden - Weierhöfer Stelle," *Der Mennonit* (1961), 138-39; Gary J. Waltner, "Vorgestellt: Die Mennonitische Forschungsstelle," *Mennonitische Blätter* (1978), 43; Peter Hege, "Jugendwerk der Konferenz Süddeutscher Mennonitengemeinden (Juwe)," *Menn. Jahrbuch* (1986), 110-11.

Wenger, Adah Frances Good Burkhalter

Wenger, Adah Frances Good Burkhalter (Sept. 23, 1889-Jan. 4, 1985). Born at Elida, Ohio, Ada Good graduated from Bluffton Academy in 1918. She married Noah L. Burkhalter, Aug. 6, 1918. She served as a missionary (GCM) and Bible teacher in India, 1919-52. Noah died in India, 1920, two months before the birth of their son Lawrence. Adah Burkhalter's study leave in the United States, 1922-25, led to a BTh degree from Witmarsum Seminary, Bluffton, Ohio, in 1925. She returned to India with her son in 1925. On Mar. 3, 1926, she married Paul A. Wenger. She helped with evangelistic work in four areas, including 19 years at Korba, Madhya Pradesh. She was hostess at the Mennonite Mission Center, Chicago, 1953-57. After Paul Wenger's death she lived at Greencroft Center, Goshen, Ind. Adah loved music, wrote poetry, and composed poems for scrapbooks for each of five grandchildren. She enjoyed six great-grandchildren.   KLJ

In addition to literature cited under Paul Wenger, see Ruth R. Ratzlaff, ed., *Fellowship in the Gospel, India: 1900-1950* (Newton: MPO, 1950), 103-5, 128; Samuel T. Moyer, *They Heard the Call* (Newton, 1970), 103-5; Adah B. Wenger, "Sarguja," *India Calling* 15, no. 1 (Spring, 1952), 1, 2; *Menn. Rep.* (Feb. 4, 1985), 15.

Wenger, Paul A.

Wenger, Paul A. (Mar. 22, 1889-Jan. 22, 1969). Born at Fortuna, Mo., Wenger studied at the U. of Idaho Agriculture College (1912-16); the Bible Institute of Los Angeles (1920-22); Bethel College, Ks. (BA, 1933); and the Biblical Seminary in New York (1943-44). He was a seed analyst and assistant field agronomist for the State of Idaho, 1916-18, and a missionary to India, 1923-52. From 1953-57 he administered the Mennonite Mission Center, Chicago. A minister (GCM), elder, deacon, and Sunday School teacher, he was a member of First Mennonite Church, Aberdeen, Idaho; and First Mennonite Church, Bluffton, Ohio. He married Adah Frances Good Burkhalter on Mar. 3, 1926, at Mauhadih, Madhya Pradesh, India. In Jagdeeshpur (1925-31) he introduced the flying shuttle to speed up hand-loom weaving and organized the Christian Cooperative Bank and Christian Weavers' Association of Basna. He and Adah Wenger served many years in evangelistic work in Korba, Madhya Pradesh State, and opened mission work in Sarguja State, 1949. He died at Bluffton, Ohio. KLJ

Twenty-five Years with God in India (Berne, Ind.: Mennonite Book Concern, 1929), 198-99; Ruth R. Ratzlaff, ed., *Fellowship in the Gospel, India: 1900-1950* (Newton: MPO, 1950), 130; William Beery and Judith Beery Garber, *The Beery Family History* (Elgin, Ill: Brethren Publishing House, 1957), 371-72; Samuel T. Moyer, *They Heard the Call* (Newton, 1970), 7, 137-40; Juhnke, *Mission* (1979), 165; Paul A. Wenger, "The Road to Sarguja," *India Calling,* 15, no. 1 (Mission Press, Jubbulpore, Madhya Pradesh, India, Spring, 1952), 3; Kathryn L. Jantzen, "Wengers Leave India," *India Calling,* 15, no. 3 (Fall, 1953), 1; *Who's Who Mennonites* (1943), 271.

West, Daniel, (1893-1971) was a teacher and principal in Ohio and Indiana public schools for 10 years following graduation from Manchester College in 1917. He then became national director of youth work in the Church of the Brethren. In this capacity he was noted for his successful work with young people in camp and discussion settings. West's noncombatant service in the US Army (1917-18) intensified his peace convictions; he was responsible for Brethren peace education, 1938-59. During 1936 he visited college campuses for the Emergency Peace Campaign and in 1937 was called by the American Friends Service Committee to administer relief in Spain during the Civil War. It was there that West envisioned the program for which he is best known—the Heifer Project, designed to send young cows to stricken areas; recipients agreed to "pass on the gift" by donating offspring of these animals to others in need. Still attracting Mennonite support in the 1980s, the interfaith agency Heifer Project Inc. has sent thousands of animals to more than 100 countries. DFD

Glee Yoder, *Passing on the Gift* (Elgin, Ill.: Brethren Press, 1978), a biography; Roger E. Sappington, *Brethren Social Policy* (Elgin, Ill.: Brethren Press, 1961); Rufus D. Bowman, *Church of the Brethren and War, 1708-1941* (Elgin, Ill.: Brethren Publishing House, 1944); Kenneth I. Morse in *Brethren Encyclopedia* (1983), 1330-32 and *Biographical Dictionary of Modern Peace Leaders,* ed. Harold Josephson (Westport, Conn.: Greenwood Press, 1985), 1013-14; *Messenger* [CBreth] (Oct. 15, 1971), 12-16, 26.

West Bank, Jordan River. Following the creation of the State of Israel by the United Nations in 1948, Mennonite Central Committee (MCC) began work in 1950 among the Palestinians on the West Bank annexed by the government of Jordan. Initial involvements were with refugees and people in border villages, involving mainly food, clothing, education, and rural development. MCC began two boarding schools for boys in Hebron and Beit Jala, plus a needlework program among rural women in the Hebron area.

Following the June 1967 Israeli occupation of the West Bank, Israel revalidated MCC's agreement with the government of Jordan governing MCC's West Bank activities. During the 1970s MCC shifted to rural development because of the absence of any governmental support and services for the Palestinians as a people. Access and rights to land and water became important issues. In 1980 the MCC director (Paul Quiring) was refused permission to return as MCC representative when he publicly articulated the Palestinians' increasing inaccessibility to West Bank land and water resources. In the 1980s peace and justice concerns have been increasingly emphasized through additional staff, a peace resource center, and through teaching and interpretation. In 1987 there are six MCC volunteers and seven Palestinian staff members.

Since 1950 frequent dialogue between MCC workers on the West Bank and Mennonite Board of Missions (MC) workers in Israel has taken place. PM

West Prussia (ME IV:920). The Mennonites who had to leave their ancestral home in West Prussia, East Prussia, and Danzig (Gdansk) between 1945 and 1947, today live predominantly in three countries: in the Bundesrepublik Deutschland (BRD; Federal Republic of Germany), Uruguay, and Canada. Approximately 250 live in the Deutsche Demokratische Republik (German Democratic Republic). At first these refugees lived mainly in the northern part of Germany (BRD), but then moved because of available jobs to the Ruhr Valley in the west-central BRD and partly also to the southern part of the country. The emigration to Canada happened mostly through the initiative of individuals, whereas two emigrant transports went to Uruguay. As a result of family relationships a heavy exchange of visiting takes place between these countries.

Very few of these originally agrarian people still live on farms in Germany today. Most of the former refugee families now work at urban jobs. Many children from these families have become lost to the Anabaptist faith because they live in areas without a Mennonite congregation, or they have changed their membership to another church. Some of the Mennonite refugees found new homes in largely Mennonite settlements, e.g., Bechterdissen, Espelkamp, °Neuwied, Enkenbach, and Backnang. Two further settlements in Wedel near Hamburg and Lübeck did not develop into autonomous Mennonite congregations. In these settlement churches something of the old mode of life (closed living situation, far-reaching unity of family, neighborhood, church) has survived. Other Mennonite congregations which were founded by refugees after 1945 today are very small, threatened by dissolution, and their members live scattered far and wide. This is especially true whenever a congregation has no full-time minister and no meetingplace or building of its own (e.g., Kiel, Lübeck, Göttingen, Bremen). Whenever refugees joined already existing Mennonite congregations (e.g., Hamburg, Krefeld, Weierhof) they enlivened and enriched these in spite of initial adjustment problems; thus it is in large part through West-Prussian Mennonite influence that the lay ministry (frequently alongside a full-time minister) is blooming again in German Mennonite churches today.

The integration of refugees in West German

society happened gradually, and many refugees at first nourished hopes for a return. Therefore they joined existing Mennonite congregations only with hesitation, or they formed their own new congregations. It was the economic upswing in the Federal Republic of Germany, above all in the late 1950s, which very much eased the integration of Mennonite refugees. A memorandum of the German Lutheran Church in 1965, which advised reconciliation with Poland and a renunciation of the "old country" in East and West Prussia, set loose some intense debating in Mennonite congregations. Exactly when individuals gave up hope of a return to West Prussia varies—for some this occurred already in the 1950s, for others in 1961 (building of the Wall in Berlin, climax of the East-West conflict), for others not until the 1970s (Moscow and Warsaw Treaty between the BRD and the Soviet Union and Poland respectively).

In West Prussia itself where Mennonites lived for 400 years, their traces are fading. The old farmhouses, frequently built of wood, are disappearing more and more with the passing of time. The people who live there today are refugees from the former East Poland which was ceded to the Soviet Union at the end of the war. The fields are cultivated and well-kept, and, after initial difficulties, the marshlands, whose °water drainage systems were destroyed during the war, are dry again. Some of the Mennonite church buildings still stand. Some serve Catholic congregations (Elbing-Ellerwald, Montau, Obernessau, Preussisch-Rosengart) or a Protestant congregation (Danzig) as meetingplaces; others are used as storage buildings (Fürstenwerderfeld, Thiensdorf). Still other Mennonite church buildings have vanished. Cemeteries of the former Mennonite congregations, for 35 years hidden in the countryside and abandoned and overgrown, are being cleared away since the 1970s. Occasionally visitors from the west have taken souvenirs. Private efforts to bring the "Nickelstone" (Abraham °°Nickel) into the Bundesrepublik Deutschland have been without success.

Since approximately 1970 Poland is making visits of refugees to their former residential areas possible and, among others, many Mennonites have gone there and so made their peace with the past. For the younger generation of former West-Prussian Mennonites, Prussia is no longer a special, living memory; they are at home in West Germany. Through these visits, many individual contacts with people in present-day Poland have been made, including occasional contact with Polish maids or coachmen who still live there. It was especially these former West-Prussians who in the early 1980s, sent many parcels to Poland when it was experiencing its worst economic distress—this was also a symbol of reconciliation and solidarity with the old country as well as with its present population. In the years 1973, 1974, and 1980 groups of young Mennonites drove to Poland under the auspices of the Protestant *Aktion Sühnezeichen* (Movement of Reconciliation), to visit the former concentration camp Stutthof near Gdansk and Majdanek near Lublin, thus contributing to the reconciliation.   PJFo

Menn. Jahrbuch (1985), 17-24.

West Virginia (ME IV:929). The population of West Virginia declined during the 1950s through the 1980s, especially in coal mining and lumbering areas. The exodus from the highlands encouraged several Mennonite congregations to consolidate. By 1987 there were 13 Mennonite congregations with a total membership of 384. Eight of these congregations are affiliated with the Virginia Mennonite Conference (MC), three with Southeastern Mennonite conference, and two with Allegheny Mennonite Conference (MC).

Mennonites in the Appalachian regions of West Virginia have promoted craft production, a medical clinic at Harman, a campground (Harman Mountain Farm), and, for a time, a Discipleship Center (also at Harman), sponsored by Mennonite Board of Missions (MC).

Mennonite Disaster Service made a significant contribution following the flood disasters at Man (1971) and Petersburg (1985).   PLK

MC Yearbook (1988-89), 44.

Western Conservative Mennonite Fellowship was first listed in the *Mennonite Yearbook* of 1978. It was a group of nine congregations of like faith and practice who chose to be recognized as a fellowship for the purpose of identity and to have a larger base for counseling, fellowship, and mission outreach. In 1987 the fellowship consisted of nine congregations in Alberta, Idaho, Montana, Oregon, and Arizona with a total membership of 315 in 113 households. The ministerial body numbered 8 bishops, 10 ministers, and 6 deacons.

The fellowship sponsors a mission in Belize with two families and four supported workers. A church has been organized there with attendance averaging 75. The mission also has a school with 3 teachers and 50 students.   RMG

MC Yearbook (1988-89), 100.

Western District Conference (GCM) (ME IV:933) was organized Oct. 26-28, 1892, in Newton, Ks., as an enlargement of the °°Kansas Conference. In 1987 there were 77 congregations with a membership of 13,628 located in Kansas (48), Oklahoma (16), Colorado (6), Texas (5), and Nebraska (2).

A major development of the past 30 years has been the enlargement of program and the establishment of a central office with paid staff. The office has been located since 1965 on the Bethel College campus in North Newton, Ks. The staff began with a part-time field worker in 1946 in the person of Bernhard H. Janzen. This developed into the position of district minister and the following persons have served: William F. Unruh, 1949-59; Elmer R. Friesen, 1961-67; Elbert Koontz, 1967-78; and Frank Keller, 1978-. Other full-time staff in 1987 were an office secretary, a church planting and program coordinator, a youth coordinator, and a camp director. Three part-time positions were: treasurer, loan librarian, and assistant camp director.

Standing committees in 1987 were: Executive, Board of Trustees, Education, Evangelism, Historical, Home Mission, Life Enrichment, Ministerial, Peace and Social Concerns, Program, and Retreat. Appointed committees were: Coordinating, Personnel, Tournament, and Spirituality Taskforce. A newsletter, *Western District Edition*, is incorporated into *The Mennonite*.

The movement of Mennonites from farms to °urban areas was matched by a growing effort to start new churches in the cities. The effort that began in the 1950s gained momentum so that 11 new churches joined the conference in the 1970s, and 12 joined 1980-86.

Cooperative efforts with the two sister district conferences of the Mennonite Church (MC), South Central and Rocky Mountain, have increased. In 1964 the Rainbow Mennonite Church, Kansas City, Ks., became the first congregation with dual affiliation. In 1987 there are 16 urban congregations with dual affiliation (MC, GCM). In 1965 the first joint high school retreat was held at Rocky Mountain Mennonite Camp. The Peace and Social Concerns Committee and the Education Committee have sponsored joint programs.

The Western District has been at the forefront in the involvement of women in pastoral ministry, ordaining Marilyn Miller on Sept. 19, 1976. In 1987 there were five women serving as sole pastors, two as associate pastors, and six as copastors.   DHa

David A. Haury, *Prairie People: A History of the Western District Conference* (Newton, 1981); *GCM Handbook* (1988), 116-18, 142, 44.

Western Ontario Mennonite Conference (MC) (ME IV:65). The conference had its beginning in 1963 when the Amish Mennonite Conference of Ontario (MC) decided to drop the term *Amish* from its title. The word *Western* is primarily a geographic designation to distinguish it from the Mennonite Conference of Ontario (MC).

However a number of other changes had occurred in the 1950s and early 1960s. The conference received its first official charter in 1956, had discontinued its Sunday School Conference for a much broader Christian Nurture Council, and became a full-fledged member of the General Conference (General Assembly) of the Mennonite Church (MC). In 1961 a joint church planting agreement with the Mennonite Conference of Ontario was approved, as was the decision to appoint three members to the Board of Governors of the emerging Conrad Grebel College.

In 1964 the first official lay representatives took part in conference proceedings. Acting on a proposal brought to conference by a study committee appointed in 1963, approval was given for all ministers to perform marriages, baptism, and serve communion without a bishop present. The same document provided guidelines for pastoral changes and the appointment of a "ministerial superintendent" to oversee such changes and serve as a pastor to pastors. The term "conference minister" was adopted a few years later when that designation became common.

A new constitution was approved by the conference in 1970 as an ever greater involvement in mission outreach with both the Mennonite Conference of Ontario and the Conference of United Mennonite Churches in Ontario (GCM). This development led in the early 1970s to the formation of a full-fledged inter-Mennonite conference (1973), with all three conferences, however, continuing their separate

organizations. In March 1987 members of the Western Ontario Mennonite Conference voted to disband their separate organization in favor of becoming a part of the Mennonite Conference of Eastern Canada (1988).   OG

MC Yearbook (1986-87), 92-93.

Whiteman, Milton (d. 1958), was the first Northern Cheyenne to be ordained as a Mennonite °elder. (He was ordained to that office in 1950 at the Petter Memorial Mennonite Church in Lame Deer, Mont.) He also served as a minister of the Birney Mennonite Church. Both congregations are on the Northern Cheyenne Reservation in se. Montana and are among those begun by the Board of Foreign Missions (GCM). Whiteman also worked for the United States Bureau of Indian Affairs as a policeman on the reservation. For a time he was chief of the Indian police. In Lame Deer, numerous members of the church were armed policemen. However, Whiteman was known for not carrying weapons because of his peacemaking convictions. He silenced those who criticized his not carrying weapons by telling them of the time when he needed to arrest a man charged with murder. Whitemen had had no gun but succeeded in bringing the man out from his hideout. LB

Barrett, *Vision* (1983), 69, 72.

Whiteshield, Harvey (Heskovetseso) (1860-1941), was an early mission worker in the General Conference Mennonite mission to the Southern Cheyenne people in what is now Oklahoma. His Cheyenne name was Heskovetseso (Little Porcupine).

Educated in English at the Carlisle Institute in Pennsylvania, he collaborated with missionary Rodolphe °°Petter on the initial linguistic work committing the Cheyenne language to writing. By 1894 Whiteshield was teaching a Cheyenne reading class along with Petter. In 1904 Whiteshield's translation of John Bunyan's *Pilgrim's Progress* and some Bible portions, edited by Rodolphe Petter and Bertha Kinsinger [°Petter], were published.

Whiteshield also served as a paid mission worker ("native helper," °lay evangelists) in the Oklahoma Indian churches beginning in 1892 in the Cantonment area. By the 1930s, Whiteshield and John Heap of Birds were promoting hymns with traditional Cheyenne music as well as Cheyenne words. This was the first major effort to incorporate Cheyenne culture into the Christian community. Until then, Cheyenne Mennonite churches had been singing Cheyenne translations of English or German hymns. In the 1970s, some of these Cheyenne spiritual songs were recorded and given musical notation by David Graber. One song composed by Whiteshield is included in Graber's book.

In his theology as well as his music, Whiteshield also attempted to build bridges between the biblical story and Cheyenne culture. At a native helpers' conference in 1930, he made a presentation on the meaning of the blood in the atonement, comparing its significance in Jewish, Christian, and traditional Indian religions.   LB

Barrett, *Vision* (1983), 25, 30-31, 60, 70; David Graber, ed., *Tsese-Ma' Heone-Nemeototse (Cheyenne Spiritual Songs)* (Newton, 1982); *Miss. News and Notes*, 5, no. 4 (Dec. 1930), 3; Rodolphe Petter, "Some Reminiscences of Past Years in

My Mission Service among the Cheyenne," *Mennonite*, 51, no. 44 (Nov. 10, 1936), 3; Harvey Whiteshield, trans., with Rodolphe Petter and Bertha Kinsinger, *Pilgrim's Progress* (Berne, Ind.: Witness Print., 1904).

See also Hymnology.

Whosoever Will Mission. See Grubb, Elmer F.

Wichert, Johann J., (Oct. 1, 1897-Nov. 12, 1983), was born in Mariawohl, Molotschna colony, Russia, the son of Jacob and Maria Peters Wichert. He received his elementary education in Mariawohl, secondary education in Gnadenfeld, and teacher training in the University of Kharkov in 1914. He taught in Mariawohl (1915-16) and in Rudnerweide (1917-22), where he was baptized by Elder David Nickel in 1918.

Wichert emigrated to Waterloo, Ont. in 1925. He was ordained as minister, May 20, 1928, and as elder Sept. 3, 1944 (by Jacob H. Janzen). He married Lydia Koop, Aug. 20, 1944. Wichert served the Vineland United Mennonite Church, Vineland, Ont. as minister from 1927 and as elder (1944-66), where he remained active as a member till his death. He was an outstanding teacher, was active in conference committees, and, together with Lydia, served Mennonite immigrants in Europe under MCC in 1947.   DJ

Obituary by Nikolai N. Franzen and Lydia Wichert in *Der Bote* (December 7, 1983), 1-2; John Giesbrecht, and others, *50th Anniversary Highlights of the Vineland United Mennonite Church, 1936-1986* (Vineland: n.p., 1986), 1-91; Johann G. Rempel, *Fuenfzig Jahre Konferenzbestrebungen, 1902-1952*, Part II (Steinbach: Derksen Printers, n.d.), 327.

Wiebe, Elizabeth (Lizzie) Pauls (1876-1957) and **Henry V.** (1871-1943), were the first Mennonite missionaries in America to work among southern blacks. Under the sponsorship of the Krimmer Mennonite Brethren Church, they began a mission and an orphanage and school for black children at Elk Park, N.C. (1900-1908), in a climate of racial hostility and rigid segregation. For five years of their stay in North Carolina the Wiebes and their growing family shared their house with another missionary family and 20 black orphans, which resulted in an integrated school, illegal at the time. The missionaries suffered verbal abuse and physical harassment, but persisted. They expanded their school work to Sunday school and youth work and continued with church services. In 1908 the Wiebes returned to Kansas where Henry pastored the Lehigh Krimmer Mennonite Brethren Church. The work in North Carolina developed into a small conference of churches that became part of the United States Mennonite Brethren Conference in 1960 when the Mennonite Brethren and Krimmer Mennonite Brethren merged.   KFW

Connie Isaac in *Women Among Brethren*, ed. K. F. Wiebe (1979) 105-17; Elizabeth Wiebe, "The Founding and Pioneer Work of the Krimmer Mennonite Brethren Mountain Mission in North Carolina," *Christian Witness* (March 15, 1950), 5-7; Leroy Bechler, *Black Mennonite Church in North America* (Scottdale, 1986), 37-40; Don Ratzlaff in *Miss. Focus*, 10 (Dec.1982), 36-38.

Wiebe, John A., (Mar. 30, 1900-Dec. 28, 1963). Born at Bingham Lake, Minn., to Mr. and Mrs. A. J.

Wiebe, John A. Wiebe was a missionary in India for 36 years. A graduate of Tabor College (BA), he studied theology at Dallas Theological Seminary, Winona Lake School of Theology, and Northwestern Theological Seminary (BD), and completed his MA at Minnesota State U. Married to Viola Bergthold on June 1, 1926, he was engaged in an evangelism ministry before beginning work in India in 1927 under Mennonite Brethren. Especially gifted in diplomacy, Wiebe was instrumental in registering properties, forming the governing council of the India Mennonite Brethren church, beginning a hospital, high school, and printing press, and building local churches—mostly from Mahabubnagar where the Wiebes lived more than half their years in India. As the former president of the Hyderabad State Christian Council, Wiebe had an ecumenical vision, and at the time of his tragic death by drowning, he was teaching at Ramapatnam Baptist Seminary. The Wiebes had seven children, most of whom have chosen cross-cultural vocations.   PMH

Wiebe, Viola Bergthold (b. Aug. 17, 1903). Born at Buhler, Ks., to Daniel F. and Katharina Mandtler °°Bergthold, Viola Bergthold Wiebe was a missionary in India for 43 years. A graduate of Hebron Girls School at Ootacamund in India, where her parents were Mennonite Brethren missionaries, and of Tabor College in Kansas (BA), she married John A. Wiebe on June 1, 1926, and began ministry in India in 1927, serving with her husband in Nagarkurnool, Wanaparty, Kalvakurthy, and Devarakonda during the first years. Her longest periods of service were at Mahabubnagar (18 years) and Ramapatnam Baptist Seminary (10 years), continuing some seven years after her husband's death. With her roots in India, Viola Wiebe was especially sensitized to identify with the Indian people and was instrumental in organizing women's and girls' associations. She was the mother of seven children, Esther, John (m. Carol Hiebert), Ruth (m. Herb Friesen), Irene (m. Don Janzen), David (m. Lorma Kroeker), Paul (m. Donna Kliewer), and Marilyn (m. Cole Dodge). Viola Wiebe traveled and ministered widely during her retirement years, visiting her children who frequently were to be found active in ministries in Africa and Asia.   PMH

Wiens, Agnes (Aganetha) Harder (Jan. 24, 1884-Aug. 17, 1951). The daughter of Abraham John (1840-1924) and Anna Fast (1841-98) Harder, Aganetha Harder was born at Alexanderwohl in the Molotschna Colony, Russia. Her father and stepmother brought her from Russia to attend Bethel College, North Newton, Ks. She graduated from Bethel Academy in 1904. Planning to be a °°deaconess, she took nurse's training in Cincinnati with Martha Richert °Penner. She married Peter Jacob Wiens on Feb. 14, 1906, at West Swamp Mennonite Church, Quakertown, Pa.

As a General Conference Mennonite missionary in Mauhadih and Basna (later known as Jagdeeshpur), India, 1906-15, 1917-25, 1927-37, she supervised educational, medical, and nutritional aspects of °mission boarding schools, inspecting students every morning. Because of the °caste system, whole groups came for baptism into the Christian faith, as many as

90 at one time. The children of Agnes and Peter Wiens were Ferdinand Jacob (1907-80), Rudolf Peter (1909-72), Agnes Mieka Willis Bailey (1913-), Martha Elizabeth Koehn (1919-), and Frieda Esther Epp Krehbiel (1919-).   MTS

Wiens, Peter Jacob (Apr. 15, 1877-June 7, 1945). Born at Neu-Schönsee, Chortitza Colony, Russia, Peter Wiens was the son of Jacob J. and Maria Quapp Wiens. (Maria was daughter of Johann Wiens [1814-91], and Helen Quapp [1818-82]. Peter attended the Zentralschule at Neu-Schoensee. He was one of four Russian Mennonite young people who were encouraged by David Goerz to come to Bethel College in 1901; he graduated from Bethel Academy in 1904, then studied medicine in Brooklyn, N.Y. In 1906 Wiens married Agnes Harder, with whom he served as a missionary in Mauhadih and Basna (Jagdeeshpur), India, 1906-15, 1917-25, 1927-37, working as an evangelist, educator, builder, and horticulturist. Wiens frequently joked that he was a PhD, a "poor Hindi doctor." He was pastor at Upland, Cal. (1915), and Hutchinson, Ks., (1926), during furloughs. He worked in the Mennonite Historical Library at Bethel College and preached in congregations, 1937-45.   MTS

Winger, John (Hans) (ca. 1756-1828), was a pioneer leader of the River Brethren (later Brethren in Christ, or Tunkers) in Canada. Born probably of Mennonite parents, he became one of the first members of the River Brethren at their place of origin in Lancaster Co., Pa. He may have been one of the founders of that group, along with Jacob °Engel.

In 1788, with his wife (the former Elizabeth Eschlemann), their six children, and his sister Anna, her husband (Jacob Sider), and their three children, and possibly others, John Winger emigrated to Canada. The small group settled first in the Short Hills near what later became Welland, Ont. They did not find the land suitable for farming, and in 1792 their buildings and crops were destroyed by a violent storm. This led Winger and Sider to petition successfully for crown land lying farther to the east, near the later town of Fort Erie.

Here they established the first permanent Brethren in Christ congregation in what later became Ontario. Winger was pastor of this small group and later was made overseer (°bishop), possibly when Jacob Engel first visited Ontario. Winger helped to organize River Brethren congregations near Waterloo and Markham.

With Mennonites and Quakers, Winger petitioned the government of Upper Canada for release of church members from militia duty. The petition was granted by the legislature in 1793, but members of these groups were required to pay fines in order to retain their exemption.

John Winger was the father of ten children, one of whom, Jacob, succeeded him as minister and overseer.   EMS

Asa Bearss, *Origin and History of the Tunker Church in Canada* (Ridgeway, Ont.: M. V. Disher, 1918), 1-7; Wittlinger, *Piety and Obedience* (1978) 15-39 passim; Asa W. Climenhaga, *History of the Brethren in Christ Church* (Nappanee, Ind., 1942), 25-27; E. Morris Sider, *Brethren in Christ in Canada: Two Hundred Years of Tradition and Change* (Nappanee, 1988), esp. 7-12, 37-39.

Wisconsin (ME IV:964). In 1988 there were 18 Mennonite congregations in Wisconsin, including a church planting effort by the Central District Conference (GCM) in Milwaukee. The Church of God in Christ Mennonite (Holdeman), had one congregation. There were four Fellowship Churches with a total membership of 179, and one congregation (24 members) with dual membership in the Illinois Mennonite Conference (MC) and Central District Conference (GCM). The other conferences represented (number of congregations and members) were: North Central Mennonite Conference (MC; 2, 65); Midwest Mennonite Fellowship (2, 84); Brethren in Christ (1, 34); Conservative Mennonite Conference (MC; 1, 33). Four unaffiliated congregations had a total membership of 143. The Conservative Mennonite Mission Board (Rosedale) administered a voluntary service unit at Northwoods Beach Home, Hayward, Wis.

In 1985 there were 14 Old Order Amish settlements in the state with a total of 25 congregations. Rapid expansion of Amish settlement in Wisconsin followed the 1972 Supreme Court decision in *Wisconsin versus Yoder,* which declared that no state could require Amish children to go to high school.   .   RSa

See also Medford, Wis., Old Order Amish Settlement; Cashton, Wis., Old Order Amish Settlement.

MC Yearbook (1988-89), 44, 52, 72, 85, 88, 95-96, 98-99, 152; Luthy, *Amish Settlements* (1985), 3, 12; *GCM Handbook* (1988), 13, 140.

"Wisler Mennonites." See Old Order Mennonites.

Witmarsum Colony, Paraná State, Brazil. The history of Witmarsum begins on June 7, 1951, when the families who had not yet left the °°Krauel Colony in Santa Catarina State, bought the Cancela ranch (17,000 acres; 7,600 hectares), located on the highlands of Paraná State, 70 km. (45 mi.) west of Curitiba. During the next five years the Krauel settlement, whose central civil district was also called °°Witmarsum, was terminated and the settlers moved to Paraná. The purchase of this land was made possible by a North American loan of $30,000.

Witmarsum is divided into five villages. Each family was allowed to purchase 100-200 acres of land. Through the purchase of ca. 1,000 acres of land in 1980, a new settlement called Colônia Primavera was added to the Witmarsum community though it lies 35 km. (21 mi.) from the main center. This land accommodated nine families.

The buildings of the original owner of the ranch became the center of colony activities. It is there that a creamery, shopping center, hospital, school, administration offices, silos, feed factories, and other necessary institutions were established. The settlement is operated as a producer-consumer °cooperative.

There is one Mennonite Brethren (Associação das Igrejas Irmãos Menonitas do Brasil, AIIMB) congregation and one Mennonite church (GCM; Associação Das Igrejas Menonitas do Brasil; AIMB) in Witmarsum. Both congregations are active in evangelism and social welfare. There is much poverty in the area. A Portuguese-speaking congregation has been established in Witmarsum. The Fritz Kliewer School includes students from kindergarten to grade eleven. In the senior high classes agricultural training is available, as is general education and special courses in teacher training and in music.

Witmarsum has made significant economic progress in recent years. The dairy industry has been modernized, and pedigreed livestock is in great demand throughout the land, yielding significant additional income. In 1986 over 5,000 tons of wheat, ca. 4,000 tons of soybeans, 8,000 tons of corn, and 2,500 tons of barley were harvested; 1,650 head of cattle were sold. Milk production exceeded 5 million gallons. The cooperative is responsible for these activities and employs 350 people. In 1987 190 families lived in Witmarsum, most of them also employing additional workers. There are no marketing problems for the products of the settlement. Paved roads, electricity, telephone, and plumbing help to make the settlement progressive and fully modern.   PP,Jr./HenEns

New Settlements Related to Witmarsum. *Núcleo Leiteiro,* near Lapa. In 1970 a new settlement was founded some 60 km. (37 mi.) from Curitiba, near the town of Lapa, to provide milk and dairy products for the rapidly growing city of Curitiba. By 1987 26 farms had been established, all with full modern conveniences. The limited number of settlers, however, has allowed the establishing of only the first four years of elementary school. Other German-speaking settlers have also moved into the area. It has become a flourishing settlement. In addition to a Mennonite Brethren congregation Lutheran, Reformed, and Church of God congregations have also been established.   PP,Jr.

Clevelândia. A Mennonite settlement was established 20 km. (12 mi.) south of the town of Clevelândia, Paraná State, in 1953, with 44 farms, concentrating primarily on dairy production. The school, Mennonite Brethren congregation, and Sunday school were terminated already within the first eight years, in part because of the early death of the founder and teacher Franz Hübert, in part because of crop failures and marketing difficulties. The settlers have left the colony for Curitiba, Witmarsum, Bagé, and Canada. A thriving missionary congregation remains active in the area. PP,Jr./HenEns

Guarituba. A settlement founded 1948 in a suburb of Curitiba, Guarituba flourished especially in the late 1950s. Circa 35 dairy farms were established with a daily production of ca. 2,000 gallons of milk. A Mennonite Brethren (AIIMB) congregation as well as an AIMB congregation (GCM) and a school were established. With the founding of the Clevelândia settlement in sw. Paraná, however, some of the strongest farmers left for that community, followed by others moving to Boqueirão, Witmarsum, and Canada. The farms were sold to non-Mennonites. By 1966 the settlement had been dissolved.   PP,Jr./HenEns

Fazenda Modelo at Ponta Grossa. In the late 1950s an attempt was made to purchase a model experimental farm comprising ca. 7,500 acres (3,040 hectares) from the state of Paraná. It was conveniently located along a main route between Curitiba and Ponta Grossa, some 40 km. (25 mi.) from Witmar-

sum. Negotiations with the department of agriculture in Rio de Janeiro seemed promising and the Witmarsum administration waited for further state action, but nothing happened. In 1977, when Brazil's president, Ernesto Geisel, visited Witmarsum, the need for more land and the request for purchasing this farm was mentioned to him. He showed much interest in the plan and promised to pursue this, but nothing has happened since. Bureaucratic and political considerations seem to be blocking progress of this plan.

Colônia Primavera near Palmeira. A small but successful settlement was begun in 1980 when ca. 1,100 acres (450 hectares) lying 35 km. (22 mi.) from Witmarsum near the city of Palmeira were purchased. Nine young farm families from Witmarsum were located on this land. It is in fact an extension of Witmarsum itself and considered a part of that settlement in every way.

Colônia Concórdia in Bahia State. The need for more land for young Witmarsum farmers continues. Early in the 1980s a large suitable tract was located some 700 km. (435 mi.) north of Brazilia, some 2,000 km (1,250 mi.) from Witmarsum. The land itself seemed promising, the climate fully acceptable, the price seemed reasonable, and credits with low interest rates were available. Consequently an area of nearly 50,000 acres (20,000 hectares) was purchased in April 1984 by 48 Mennonites coming not only from Witmarsum but also Curitiba, Lapa, and São Paulo. It was agreed that the settlement would be autonomous and independent of Witmarsum. The land was subdivided, wells were drilled, and farming began.

The big surprise came in September 1987 when colonists from the adjacent state of Goiás, accompanied by police, came and occupied a good part of the land. Discussions and study indicated that the states of Bahia and Goiás could not agree on the boundary line between them and the disputed area ran right through the purchased acreage. Negotiations were unsuccessful and the Mennonite settlers were not willing to let the situation climax to a crisis through coercion. Consequently they abandoned the land they had purchased in Goiás and relocated in Bahia, a move which scattered the settlement far beyond what they had earlier anticipated. Some of the participants withdrew from the project, but others were determined to continue realizing their vision. An excellent crop was harvested in 1987. In that year more than 30,000 acres (12,000 hectares) were already being cultivated, with expectations that this acreage would soon double and triple. The undertaking has remained a private venture however, with Mennonites from other parts of Brazil not participating in the project. It is clear that this area presents excellent opportunities for young families seeking to establish themselves.

Fazenda Santa Rita near Palmeira. In 1985 it became possible to purchase ca. 1,100 acres (450 hectares) adjoining village number 4 in Witmarsum. However, since the price of this land was very high, its purchase benefited the established farmers more than the young couples who were unable to finance the venture.   HGK

Women (ME IV:972). In the midst of the 16th-c. patriarchal society *Anabaptist women* held worship services, taught the Scriptures, distributed the sacraments, were elders and prophets, went on evangelistic tours, debated with theologians—and died for their faith. About one-third of the 930 martyrs listed in *Martyrs' Mirror* are women.

The trial records of both the ecclesiastical and civil courts, and the letters exchanged between husbands and wives, give us the accounts of the activities of Anabaptist women. Some noteworthy women martyrs should be remembered. °°Elisabeth Dirks learned Latin in a convent, studied the Latin Bible and became a respected teacher before her martyrdom by drowning on Mar. 27, 1549. °°Lysken Dirks exchanged letters of mutual encouragement with her husband, °°Jeronimus Segersz., from separate prisons in Antwerp in 1551. Both were later tortured and killed. Jeronimus wrote to Lijsken, "And though they tell you to attend to your sewing, this does not hinder us, for Christ has called us all, and commanded us to search the Scriptures, since they testify of him and Christ also said that Magdalene had chosen the better part, because she searched the Scriptures." Margarette Pruess, the daughter of a Strasbourg printer, survived her three printer husbands and became known for publishing Anabaptist works. Veronika °°Gross, baptized in 1525, and Anna Salminger were well-known for their evangelistic work and their contribution to the establishment of the congregation in Augsburg. Others include, Ruth Kunstel, a minister; Ruth Hagen, an elder; Argula von °°Grumbach, who wrote on ecclesiastical affairs; and Goetken Gerrits, a composer of hymns.

Protestant Reformers and Anabaptist leaders dealt with the scandal of clerical concubinage by eliminating mandatory clerical celibacy and accenting the married life of the pastor. (Some Anabaptists made marriage mandatory for the office of elder or bishop, excluding unmarried men from this office on the basis of 1 Tim 3:2.) As Christian preachers had done for centuries, °Menno Simons urged laymen to make the sexual relationship contractual. Just as Christian men were to fulfill their moral obligations and marry, so Christian women were responsible to be good wives. The majority of Anabaptists held to a traditional marriage structure, but the emphasis on voluntary church membership, adult baptism, and personal commitment to Christ, demanded each individual's response. At times it was impossible for Anabaptist women to follow the wishes of their nonbelieving husbands. Claus-Peter Clasen suggests that the Hutterite belief in the unique true church as grounds for divorce threatened to cause 'wild havoc' in 16th-c. Europe. The Hutterites refused to appear in marriage courts; rather, they encouraged their converts to leave their unbelieving spouses.

In the political and theological milieu of the 16th c., Anabaptist fathers were often fugitives ministering to churches in far-flung groups and the husbands of Anabaptist women were often apostates and hence excommunicated from the church community. Consequently much of the responsibility for survival and °childrearing fell on the shoulders of the mothers.   MGP

Mennonite Women: The Netherlands. After the initial trauma of the 16th c., Mennonite family life reverted to a more traditional structure, and by the 17th-19th c. women did not vote and were not eligible to be members of church boards. Since ca. 1865 women have slowly gained the privilege of voting in various congregations and at the present time (1987), women in all Dutch Mennonite congregations have full voting rights and are eligible to be members of the church boards.

In 1911, when the first Mennonite sister, Annie Zernike, completed training at the Mennonite Seminary at the University in Amsterdam, it seemed a logical conclusion that her qualifications for interpreting God's Word in the fellowship of believers be honored. Three congregations offered her a position. She chose Bovenknijpe, a small rural congregation near Heerenveen, and this Dutch Mennonite congregation ordained her as their minister. Since then sisters have been recognized as having the same opportunities of service in Dutch Mennonite congregations as brothers.

Depending on their qualifications and experience, women have responsibility at all levels in the congregations and in the denomination at large. In 1987, of a total of 93 ordained pastors, 33 are women. One woman has chaired the Algemene Doopsgezinde Sociëteit (General Mennonite Conference), and a larger number have been in executive positions. Not all Dutch women serving in churches are theologians; some are theologically trained, but there are a large number of lay sisters doing part-time or full-time work, some as pastoral assistants, because of their leadership gifts.

The Dutch Mennonites were the first denomination in The Netherlands to ordain women ministers. When the larger feminist movement reached the other Dutch denominations, the Dutch Mennonite sisters were called upon to present their roles and leadership experiences to Christian women who had traditionally had less freedom in representative positions.

Dutch Mennonite women who attend local congregational women's organizations have been nationally organized in a central federation called Landelijke Federatie van Doopsgezinde Zusters since 1952. The local organizations called "Zusterkringen" (sisters' circles) date from the last part of the 19th c. A smaller group of women calling themselves "Vrouwen in de Broederschap" (Women in the Brotherhood) were active in the years 1978-85, trying to stimulate a deeper awareness of women's issues. However, because of female integration in the conference on equal basis with men, this group ceased functioning as a separate feminist group.   MGP/AW/MMMat

Mennonite Women: North America. Traditionally, homemaking has been the major interest of Mennonite women in North America, but by the middle of the 19th c. the education of women was seen as a means of fighting poverty, and women began to attend denominational Bible schools and colleges. By 1883 articles dealing with women praying, testifying, or preaching in public meetings are found in Mennonite publications in America, and by the late 19th c., interest in women's rights appears.

During the latter half of the 20th c. commissions were formed to study women's issues and relate them to the faith, and an effort was made to give women recognition for their ministry, especially in the foreign mission field, where they contributed greatly to the spread of the gospel. The Task Force on Women of the Mennonite Central Committee Peace Section began the *Mennonite Central Committee on Women's Concerns Report,* a publication covering current women's issues.

The three largest groups, comprising 85 percent of North American Mennonites, are the Mennonite Church (MC), the General Conference Mennonite Church, and the Mennonite Brethren Church. These three groups have vastly different understandings and practices regarding women. During the first half of the 20th c., the Mennonite Church was considerably more interested in the dress of women, especially the head-covering or prayer cap which was distinctive to that denomination. A study of their denominational publications also reveals an interest in missions, motherhood, the work of the sewing circle, and woman's role in church and society. The General Conference Mennonites put their energies into the development of the °°deaconess movement, which became an avenue for ministry by women. Interest was also shown in missions and in the role of women in church and society, women in ministry, and women pastors. Mennonite Brethren showed an interest in the home and marriage, as well as a concentrated interest in the Scripture passages regarding biblical women and the exegesis of passages about women. From 1960 forward, there has been an intensified interest by the Mennonite Brethren in the role of women in church and society, women's ministry, women in seminary, and women as pastors. Here too, we find a continued interest in missions.

Mennonite women of all branches consistently hold to a conservative theological position, but because of their very divergent backgrounds (some coming to North America directly from Germany and Switzerland and others from Holland via Prussia and Russia), Mennonite women have developed distinct personalities as well as distinct ways of living out their theology. This is particularly so in the development of the role of women within the church. Women hold conference board positions in all three denominations. Both the Mennonite Church and the General Conference Mennonite Church have ordained women as pastors since 1978 and 1980, respectively, and employ women as professors in their colleges and seminaries. The Mennonite Brethren do not ordain women as pastors, but a growing number of women have completed seminary training and are serving in various capacities, including pastoral staff positions. Mennonite Brethren women also hold faculty positions at denominational colleges and at the Mennonite Brethren Biblical Seminary.

At the local church level, a women's organization, variously titled Women's Missionary and Service Commission, Women in Mission, Women's Ministries, etc.) is significant in all Mennonite denominations, and until recently, perhaps the majority of Mennonite women participated. This organization was originally dedicated to the task of providing for the needs of missionary families. Today it typically takes

on the financial support of various mission projects, including social work programs (orphanages, schools, retirement homes). Mission sales were a chief means of producing revenue for mission work, and in the process, the Mennonite women have become famous for the art of quilting.

The 20th c. has been a time of rapid change for Mennonite women in North America. In addition to their traditional interest in the home and the Mennonite community, there is a growing emphasis on education and activities outside the home. At the close of the 1980s the most distinguishing feature of American Mennonite women is no longer their rural communities or their plain dress, but rather their strong faith in Jesus Christ.   MGP

Roland H. Bainton, *Women of the Reformation in Germany and Italy* (Boston: Augsburg Publishing House and Beacon Press, 1977), 145-58; M. Lucille Marr, "Anabaptist Women of the North: Peers in the Faith, Subordinates in Marriage," *MQR,* 61 (1987), 347-362; Marion Kobelt-Groch, "Why Did Petronella Leave Her Husband? Reflections on Marital Avoidance among the Halberstadt Anabaptists," *MQR,* 62 (1988), 26-41, cf. *Menn. Geschbl.* Jg. 43-44 (1986-87); Clause-Peter Clasen, *Anabaptism: A Social History 1525-1618* (Ithaca: Cornell U. Press, 1972), 200-209; Keith L. Sprunger, *Triumph Over Silence: Women in Protestant History* (Westport, Conn.: Greenwood Press, 1985), 45-74; Miriam Chrisman, "Women and the Reformation in Strasbourg 1490-1530," *ARG,* 63 (1972), 143-67; Herta Funk, ed., *Study Guide,* Pt. 1: *Women in the Bible and Early Anabaptism;* Pt. 2: *Lesson Helps for "All We're Meant to Be* (Newton, 1975), 33-38; M. M. Matthijssen-Berkman, "Women in the World-Wide Mennonite Church," Address given at the Mennonite World Conference, General Council Meeting, Nairobi, Kenya, July 22, 1981; Marilyn G. Peters, "History of Mennonite Women in the 19th and 20th C.: A Comparison between [sic] The Mennonite Church, The General Conference Mennonite Church and the Mennonite Brethren Church" (PhD diss. Research, Center for Mennonite Studies, Fresno Pacific College, Fresno, Cal., 1987); Sharon Klingelsmith, "Women in the Mennonite Church, 1900-1930" *MQR,* 54 (1980), 163-207; Mary Lou Cummings, *Full Circle: Stories of Mennonite Women* (Newton, 1978); Rich, *Mennonite Women* (1983); Gladys V. Goering, *Women in Search of Mission: a History of the General Conference Mennonite Women's Organization* (Newton, 1980); Katie Funk Wiebe, *Women Among the Brethren* (Hillsboro, Ks.: Board of Christian Literature [MB], 1979); Perry and Elizabeth Yoder, *New Men; New Roles. A Study Guide for Christian People in Social Change* (Newton, 1977); Kauffman/Harder, *Anabaptists Four C. Later* (Scottdale, 1975), 194-97; Calvin W. Redekop, *Old Colony Mennonites* (Baltimore: Johns Hopkins U. Press, 1969), 97ff.; Wittlinger, *Piety and Obedience* (1978), 522ff.; *Resource List of Mennonite and Brethren in Christ Women* regular editions available from MCC in Akron, Pa.

See also All-India Mennonite Women's Conference; Evangelical Mennonite Church; Iglesia Hermanos en Cristo, Nicaragua; Iglesia Menonita de Bolivia; Lay Evangelists; Men's Work; Occupations; Polity; Women in Mission (GCM); Women's Auxiliary (EMCh); Women's Ministries (EMB); Women's Missionary and Service Commission (MC).

Women in Mission (GCM) (ME IV:975), formerly Women's Missionary Association (name changed in 1974), an auxiliary of the General Conference Mennonite Church, meets in a delegated session once every three years. It was organized in 1917 at Reedley, Cal., with informal meetings dating back to 1902. In 1986 Women in Mission gave its first report to the triennial meeting of the General Conference Mennonite Church at Saskatoon, Sask.

Between conference sessions the work of Women

in Mission is carried on by an advisory council, composed of president, United States and Canadian vice-presidents, secretary, the chairman of the Literature Committee, and district and provincial advisors and presidents. The coordinator for Women in Mission and the editor of the bimonthly publication, *Window to Mission*, are appointed by the Advisory Council. The annual budget for 1986 was $252,500.

The purpose of the organization is to help women become involved effectively in the mission of the church and to develop and use the diversity of women's talents. From the early purpose of sewing for mission projects, the emphasis has been enlarged to include the support of missionary, relief, and educational projects. Women in Mission also contributes to the support of Mennonite Biblical Seminary, Mennonite Central Committee, and Africa Inter-Mennonite Mission. It has subsidized the printing of publications in the areas of peace, mission, and women's biographies, and it has published its own history, *Women in Search of Mission*, by Gladys Goering. RU

Gladys V. Goering, *Women in Search of Mission: A History of the General Conference Mennonite Women's Organization* (Newton, 1980); Hillegonda van der Smissen, *The History of Our Mission Societies*, (n.p.: Literature Committee of Women's Home and Foreign Missions, 1929); *GCM Handbook* (1988), 96; Manitoba Mennonite Women in Mission, *History of Manitoba Mennonite Women in Mission, 1942-1977* (Winnipeg: Manitoba Mennonite Women in Mission, 1977).

See also Mennonite Men.

Women's Auxiliary (EMCh). Although many congregations within the Evangelical Mennonite Church had active women's groups, the first denominational report of women's work was a 1934 orphanage report. In 1935 the "Ladies of the conference" donated $62.90 to the conference budget. Officers were first listed in 1941. The following year the Ladies Missionary Society reported to the delegate body.

Throughout the years, Women's Auxiliary has supported with both money and handwork the Salem Children's Home, Flanagan, Ill.: Africa Inter-Mennonite Mission; Miracle Camp, Lawton, Mich.; and the Evangelical Mennonite Church's general budget. Women's Auxiliary conducts annual °retreats and encourages community outreach by local groups.

To meet the challenges of the 21st c., the Evangelical Mennonite Church has recently restructured its women's work, designating it "Women's Ministry," and appointing a Director of Women's Ministry. RLG

Women's Ministries (EMB). The Evangelical Mennonite Brethren (°Fellowship of Evangelical Bible Churches) Women's Mission Society was established in 1943 as an auxiliary organization of the conference. A variety of programs were developed involving missionary and relief work centering in the local church women's groups. Devotions and Bible studies are an important part of these meetings. At the annual meeting of the organization during conference time, special projects such as love offerings to a selected group of missionaries, are determined. The

appearance at these annual meetings of missionaries on furlough offers opportunity for better understanding and appreciation of the missionary program. At the conference in 1986 the name of the society was changed to the Evangelical Mennonite Brethren Women's Ministries "to better portray all the different kinds of ministries our women are involved in." ACS

Women's Missionary and Service Commission (MC) (ME IV:974) is a churchwide organization with a special interest in women's and girls' activities in the church. It is recognized for its many years of significant ministry as a mission and service agency of the church. It seeks to involve the women and the girls in the church through its conference and congregational organizations and activities. In the Mennonite Church reorganization in 1971, the Women's Missionary and Service commission (WMSC, formerly Women's Missionary and Service Auxiliary) was placed in an adjunct relationship with the newly formed Mennonite Board of Congregational Ministries.

Executive secretaries have included Beulah Kauffman, Barbara (Bender) Reber (1978-88), and Marian Hostetler (1988-). Velorus (Gingrich) Shearer of Wilkes-Barre, Pa., has served as editor of the monthly publication, *Voice*, since 1978, replacing Lois Gunden Clemens (1960-78). During the 1980s a concerted effort has been made to involve women in business and the professions as well as homemakers. In 1979 a committee composed of Alice (Weber) Lapp, Jocele (Thut) Meyer, Emma (Sommers) Richards, Barbara K. (Bender) Reber (chairperson), and Leonard Gross (consultant) was formed to begin writing the history of Mennonite Church (MC) women. *Mennonite Women 1683-1983: A Story of God's Faithfulness*, ed. by Elaine (Sommers) Rich, was released in the spring of 1983.

In 1983 the Bylaws Revision Task Force presented to the General Assembly (MC) recommendations for some structure changes. This was approved on Aug. 5, 1983, at the Bethlehem, Pa., General Assembly. This placed the WMSC as an Associate Group in the Mennonite Church. The General Assembly's constitution permits special interest groups to request recognition by the General Board as associate groups, with their guidelines subject to approval by the General Board. Such associate groups continue to maintain primary relationships in the regional conferences. Organizations which qualify as associate groups appoint up to six delegates to the General Assembly and members to the General Board. BKR

Woodworking. See Furniture and Woodworking.

Work Camps (Asia), the outgrowth of the Christian Youth Peace Seminars sponsored in Japan by Mennonite Central Committee (MCC) Peace Section. In the 1964 seminar Japanese youth learned of the earlier Japanese atrocities perpetrated against Koreans. Several Mennonite youth sought a way to show repentance and effect °reconciliation. August of 1965 saw 39 Japanese and Korean youth working on a farm-improvement project near Taegu, Korea, at a time, 20 years after wartime hostilities ceased, when Japanese and Korean Christians were not yet talking with each other and Korean students were rioting in Seoul's streets against a proposed Japan-Korea peace treaty. One rough evening, after long pent-up feelings broke out, reconciliation on a deep level occurred. A 12-year series of MCC-sponsored Reconciliation Seminars conducted by Japanese and Korean church leaders also resulted from the 1965 work camp. Korean youth asked for another camp, which was held at Obirin University near Tokyo, Japan in 1966.

Taiwan Mennonite Church sent representatives who participated in the third camp at a hospital in Taegu. Mennonite youth from India and Indonesia joined the fourth camp, held at a mountain-farm project near Taipei. Hong Kong Mennonite youth were represented at a fifth camp held in Sapporo, Japan, bringing together for the first time in history representatives from all Asian Mennonite churches.

Church leaders as well as youth from seven Asian Mennonite churches joined the sixth work camp at Faith-Love Children's home, Fanling, Hong Kong, expressly to prepare for the first Asia Mennonite Conference (AMC) at °Dhamtari, India, in 1971.

Subsequent camps were held under AMC sponsorship in India, (1971); Vietnam (1972); Bangladesh (1974); Philippines (1977); Hong Kong (1982); and Korea, (1985). All-India Mennonite camps took place near Calcutta and Jadcherla in 1980 and 1987. All of these camps follow much the same format as other European and North American Work camps, with work projects during the day and Anabaptist-related seminars in the evening.   CCB

III Asia Mennonite Conference Report Book (May 14-18, 1986), p. 26; Carl C. Beck, "God Reconciles," in *A Kingdom of Priests: The Church in the New Nations*, ed., Wilbert R. Shenk (Newton and Scottdale, 1967), 96-109.

See also Camps; Development Work; Peace Education; Relief Work; Service.

Work Camps, Europe. The Mennonite work camp movement is a particular adaptation of a phenomenon which has numerous precedents, including the following: (1) the idealistic flank of many °socialist movements (e.g., the Israeli Kibbutzim and European socialists), as well as the labor movements related to socialism; (2) national political parties and governments which attempted to enlist especially the young; (3) religious movements (e.g., the Student Volunteer Movement and the InterVarsity Christian Fellowship, more recently, such new religious groups as the Unification Church); (4) other religious groups, e.g., the Unitarians and the Society of Friends (Quakers), who, through the °°American Friends Service Committee, conducted various types of work camps since World War I. This latter provided the closest connection for Mennonite activities (Lehman, Unruh, Kehler).

The central dynamic of the international work camp movement was the expression of idealism through practical assistance and a learning-growing experience for the participants (Gillette). The work project was normally clean-up work in parks, recreation areas, or war-torn communities; reconstruction of damaged or destroyed buildings (schools, church-es, recreation centers); and various aspects of community organization and service (Gillette). The work camp movement received its main impetus from World War I and World War II, especially in Europe, but it spread to other parts of the world as well, e.g., Asia. These were religious and humanist responses to human need. The burgeoning of the work camp movement after World War II is illustrated by the existence of the "Coordination Committee for International Voluntary Work Camps," sponsored by the youth Section of the United Nations Educational Scientific, and Cultural Organization (UNESCO), headquartered at Paris for many years in the 1950s and 1960s. In 1963 for example, this coordination committee assisted more than 20 work camp organizations operating in Europe to conduct more than 100 work camps. Among these camps were some sponsored by Mennonitischer Freiwilligendienst (Mennonite Voluntary Service, MVS), an inter-Mennonite program organized by Dutch, French, German, and Swiss Mennonites (Redekop).

Although it has often been assumed that Mennonite youth serving on a °voluntary service basis was a rather pure Mennonite idea, Mennonite participation in the work camp movement undoubtedly received some inspiration from the worldwide movement, especially through connections with Friends Service Committee activities. The idea was in the air during and after World War I. The Friends Ambulance Unit in France in World War I, the Friends Reconstruction Unit in France, and the Near East Relief, in which Mennonites participated, provided some connection. During and after World War II, the emergence of °°Civilian Public Service Camps and the voluntary service program in °mental hospitals were also a direct result of developments not limited to Mennonites.

But the work camps sponsored by MVS developed most fully toward the work camp movement. It began with Mennonite Central Committee's program to send Mennonite youth from Mennonite colleges to Europe in 1948. These volunteers helped in projects like the one at °Espelkamp in Germany (Brunk). The °°Pax program (1951) sparked more support (Bender). As many as five or six work camps were conducted for a number of years, beginning in 1950 and continuing on into the 1970s. Projects were supported not only in Germany, but also in The Netherlands, France, Switzerland, Austria, Italy, Spain, and other countries.

These camps were composed mainly of non-Mennonite youth, but the goals reflected MCC's serving "in the name of Christ." The objectives included the desire to serve human need in a practical way and to interact with youth of other backgrounds and cultures to witness to the Anabaptist and Mennonite faith and to learn from other perspectives as well. Hundreds of young people benefitted greatly from the program, and the program was finally terminated because of lack of pressing human needs. Mennonite work camps are still occasionally organized on a very specific basis, such as assisting in a building renovation or rebuilding of an inner-city church building and the like.   CWR

Emily Brunk, *Espelkamp* (Frankfort a. M.: MCC, 1951); Urie Bender, *Soldiers of Compassion* (Scottdale, 1969); Arthur Gillette, *One Million Volunteers* (New York: Penguin Books, 1968); Larry Kehler, "The Many Activities of Mennonite Central Committee," *MQR* 54 (1970), 298-315; Martin C. Lehman, *The History and Principles of Mennonite Relief Work: An Introduction* (Akron: MCC, 1945); Calvin Redekop, "Development of Voluntary Service in Europe," *GH* (Jan. 22, 1952); John D. Unruh, *In the Name of Christ* (Scottdale, 1952); Wilfrid J. Unruh, "A Study of Mennonite Voluntary Service Programs," report prepared for Institute of Mennonite Studies, Associated Mennonite Biblical Seminaries, Elkhart, Ind., 1965.

See also Camps; Development Work; Peace Education; Relief Work; Service.

Work Ethic. Work in its many aspects is central to Anabaptist and Mennonite history and theology, but practically no discussion exists on the subject, while leisure has an extensive bibliography. This disparity indicates the implicit and unreflective acceptance of work. Work has physical, psychological, social, cultural, and religious foundations. Elements of work included the job (the economic aspects of living), career (the personal-psychological history of work), °occupation (the social structure of work), vocation (the value cluster of work), and calling (the religious dimension and purpose of work). The cultural aspect of work pertains to how work, i.e., labor, has been utilized in a society, e.g., whether work is slave or free, whether it has been directed mainly to survival as over against leisure, whether it is regulated or not.

Work has great relevance for Anabaptist-Mennonites since they too are °economic creatures and have been involved in economic and °business activities. That Mennonites have not developed a theology of work is consistent with their practice of stressing ethics rather than abstract belief (Erb, Burkholder).

For the Anabaptists, work became a means by which toleration and the right to exist was guaranteed by the authorities of Switzerland, France, Germany, Austria, and Prussia. Thus, for example, the emigrating Dutch Mennonites earned toleration by reclaiming areas of the Vistula Delta in Prussia (cf. Séguy, Hostetler, Penner, °water technology). The subsequent toleration of Mennonites in the above-named countries; and the establishment of the Mennonite colonies in Russia, Canada, Latin America; and the vast and prosperous agricultural area in Europe, Canada, and United States, attest to the massive amounts of labor Mennonites have done. "Hard work" has always been an important element in Mennonite identity along with sobriety, honesty, dependability and the other virtues. Troeltsch insists that Mennonites came from the masses and represent the revolt against oppression of the laboring strata, hence the emphasis on work is genuinely inherited.

As Troeltsch avers, Mennonites in time "capitulated" to the "Protestant calling" (p. 705) and forsook their ideal. This is the direct consequence of interaction with the Germanic and Protestant work ethic, a concept described and popularized by Weber and others. Hence, by the end of the 19th c., Mennonite attitudes toward, and involvement in, work can be said to be rather similar to that of Protestantism. The phenomenal achievements of the Hutterite colonies; Mennonite agriculturalists in Europe; Mennonite colonies in Russia, Canada, and Latin America; and the Menonite settlements in various parts of the United States; not to overlook the achievements of Mennonites in business, are well established facts.

In the late 20th c. Mennonites can be classed in two groups regarding the work ethic: Germanically-derived Mennonites and non-Germanic Mennonites. For the first-mentioned group, work is a means to security, to social status, self-expression, and all the other general functions of work defined above. It became justified as a means to freedom alluded to above and also as a natural consequence of life on the land—to subdue, dominate and make land productive takes much labor, the God-ordained sweat of the brow! (Gn 3:19). Mennonite life on the land thus dignified work and made it inherently necessary, as most Mennonite novels indicate (e.g., Arnold Dyck and Rudy Wiebe [Dill]). Sociological accounts of Mennonites in general (Correll) or groups such as Russian Mennonites (Rempel), Hutterites (Hostetler), Amish (Hostetler. Cronk), Old Colony Mennonites (Redekop), Old Order Mennonites (Cronk), Church of God in Christ Mennonite [Holdeman] (Hiebert), the town of Altona, Manitoba (Epp), implicitly stress the centrality of hard work in establishing Mennonite settlements and, in a few cases, explicitly discuss the relevance of work especially on the land (Hostetler, Redekop, Cronk).

Non-Germanic Mennonites, the "new" Mennonites in Africa, Asia, Japan, and Latin America, to name just a few areas, have attitudes toward work that reflect the values of their respective societies. The "New" and "Old" Mennonites of Latin America (e.g., the Germanic-background Mennonites and the Mennonites of Indian background in the Chaco), sometimes living side-by-side, reflect radically differing work ethics, which often create tensions and misunderstandings (cf. Redekop, 1980). The implications for proselytizing non-Germanic members is obvious and is creating serious problems, with more to come. It is thus possible to say there are two attitudes toward work, existing together, sometimes in the same congregation.

With the present juxtaposition of several theologies and ethics of work, their reconciliation is possible only by recovering and adapting the earlier Anabaptist and Mennonite theology and ethic of work.

As indicated above, an informed Mennonite theology regarding work came by default, since there was little reflection on work as a part of the °kingdom of God. Work became a means to gain acceptance and tolerance and the practice emerged which expressed Mennonite theology. This practice was based on strongly held convictions about following Christ and becoming part of the kingdom of God.

Thus, the understandings of work inherent in the Anabaptist tradition is ultimately derived from its utopian vision of the restoration of the primitive church (°restitutionism), the 16th-c. movements to liberate the °peasants and artisans from oppression, and the creation of the community of believers, which implied voluntary care and support for those who had committed themselves to take on the yoke of Christ (Peachey, Nafziger).

The channel, or medium, by which this was to be achieved was the voluntary congregation, where the communal ethic took precedence over selfish goals, as Nafziger has shown. Stewardship of God's °creation was thus the "theology" by which the needs of members were met through °mutual aid, one's neighbor was to be served with one's own resources, and personal consumption was to be managed by the norms of simplicity and °°nonconformity to worldly opulence and self-indulgence. This can be termed the "communal ethic,," or "Gelassenheit ethic" (Cronk), and is distinct from both the "capitalistic" and the "communistic" ethic, which have been so broadly debated in modern times.

The integration, or at least reconciliation, of the two Mennonite work ethics is possible only if both converge to the original utopian vision of the role of work in the kingdom of God. Work was not a means of grace or salvation, nor was it irrelevant; rather it was to be the means of helping to restore the pure church. Work was the basis for providing help and care directly to people in need, and for providing the resources needed to share with others. It is strange that Anabaptists rarely spoke of the role of work in following Christ, in achieving fraternity in the congregation and in serving the broader world. This is understandable only if we realize that the expressions of their concerns were the result of the specific debates and conflicts with their accusers and persecutors: the accusation of communism was a major contention, and thus the focus was on property, not on work which makes property, resources, and stewardship basically possible.

The "communal" or "Gelassenheit" ethic has rarely been fully expressed in the Anabaptist-Mennonite tradition, but it has been present in varying degrees over the centuries, e.g., among Hutterian Brethren, semicommunal Mennonites like the Old Colony Mennonites (church ownership of land and a certain amount of resources set aside for the poor), and the contempory Mennonite intentional communities, especially in North America (Cronk, Smucker). Modern Mennonites, especially of those of the Germanic stream, have gradually been co-opted by the capitalistic ethic. Thus, even though there are still strong indications of a communal practice, Mennonites are now predominantly motivated by the work ethic of capitalism, in which work is the means of achieving wealth and status, but not all work, rather "smart work," where one uses training, expertise, financial clout, or other means to work in a way that will bring fast returns. No specific research on the meaning and function of work has been conducted within the Mennonite framework, although the Mennonite relation to capitalism has received some attention. This is an area of most serious neglect and if investigated, promises great rewards for the fulfillment of the Anabaptist-Menonite vision. Contemporary discussions and analysis of work, especially in reference to its ethical and religious meaning among Mennonites is relatively dormant. °Mennonite Economic Development Associates is promoting studies of work and *The Marketplace*, its official publication, is taking the lead in promoting the discussion. °Sunday School curricula and other publications deal with work, but not in a concerted fashion.   CWR

J. L. Burkholder, "Ethics," *ME IV*, 1079-83; Sandra Cronk, "Gelassenheit: The Rites of the Redemptive Process in the Old Order Amish and Old Order Mennonite Communities" (PhD diss., U. of Chicago, 1977), cf. *MQR*, 55 (1981), 5-44; Vicky Schreiber Dill, "Land Relatedness in the Mennonite Novels of Rudy Wiebe," *MQR*, 58 (1984), 50-69; Arnold Dyck, *Lost in the Steppes* (Steinbach, 1974); Peter C. Erb, "A Reflection on Mennonite Theology in Canada," *JMS*, 1 (1983), 179-90; Esther Epp-Tiessen, *Altona: The Story of a Prairie Town* (Altona: D. W. Friesen and Sons, 1982); Clarence Hiebert, *The Holdeman People* (Pasadena: William Carey Library, 1973); John A. Hostetler, *Amish Society* (1980); idem, *Hutterite Society* (1974); Estel Wayne Nafziger, "The Mennonite Ethic in the Weberian Framework" *Explorations in Entrepreneurial History*, 2, no. 1 (Spring/Summer 1965); Paul Peachey, "Social Background and Social Philosophy of the Swiss Anabaptists 1525-1540, *MQR*, 28 (1954), 102-27; Horst Penner, *Anseidlung Mennonitischer Niederlander im Weichselmündungsgebiet* (Weierhof: Mennonitischer Geschichtsverein, 1940); Calvin Redekop, *The Old Colony Mennonites* (Baltimore: Johns Hopkins Press, 1969); idem, *Strangers Become Neighbors* (Scottdale, 1980); Calvin Redekop and Urie A. Bender, *Who Am I? What Am I?: Searching for Meaning in Your Work* (Grand Rapids: Zondervan, 1988); David G. Rempel, "The Mennonite Commonwealth in Russia: A Sketch of its Founding and Endurance, 1789-1919," *MQR*, 47 (1973), 259-308, and 48 (1974), 5-54; Jean Séguy, *Les Assemblées Anabaptistes-Mennonites de France* (The Hague: Mouton and Co., 1977); Donovan Smucker, "Gelassenheit, Entrepreneurs, and Remnants: Socio-economic Models among the Mennonites," in *Kingdom, Cross and Community*, ed. J. R. Burkholder and C. Redekop (Scottdale, 1976); Ernst Troeltsch, *The Social Teachings of the Christian Churches* (New York: Harper and Row, 1960); Max Weber, *The Protestant Ethic and the Spirit of Capitalism* (New York: Charles Scribner's Sons, 1958).

See also Idleness; Professions; Recreation.

Works. See Grace; Legalism; Salvation.

World War I. The great war in 1914-18 was a dramatic turning point for Mennonites in Europe and North America, as it was for Western civilization generally. In central and western Europe (Switzerland, The Netherlands, Germany, and Galicia) Mennonites had largely abandoned the teaching of °nonresistance in previous decades. A Prussian Cabinet Order of 1868, still in effect in 1914, allowed for noncombatant military service, but this service was not significantly different from regular service. By September 1915 some 2,000 young Mennonites were in German military service. About 400 died during the war. The military destruction, defeat, and ultimate dismemberment of Germany wrought havoc for Mennonite life as well as for the prospects of German Mennonite unity. The Versailles treaty separated about half the formerly German Mennonites into the countries of France (Alsace), Poland, and the Danzig Free State.

A comparison and contrast of the Mennonite war experiences in Russia and the United States illustrates the variety of possible nonresistant responses within totalitarian and democratic nations involved in total war. Church membership in both countries was about 75,000 and growing; both enjoyed unusual vitality in church and community life in the prewar years. Mennonites in Russia and in North America had maintained their commitment to the doctrine of nonresistance and had benefited from functional agreements with their governments which exempted them from direct military service. In Russia the Mennonite involvement with the war was immediate, intense, and purposeful, but ultimately tragic in its results. In America the Mennonite involvement was delayed, diffused, and confusing, but ultimately invigorating for Mennonite peoplehood. The Russian Empire suffered humiliating international invasion and defeat (1,700,000 dead), domestic political revolution, civil anarchy and war, and the inauguration of a new °Communist order. The United States entered the war late (April 1917), lost relatively less treasure or manpower (115,000 dead) and emerged as a victorious world power with stable government. After the war Russian Mennonitism declined while North American Mennonites played an increasingly dominant role in world Mennonite affairs.

When Russia declared war on Germany in August 1914 the German-speaking Mennonites in Russia moved quickly to declare allegiance to their Russian fatherland and to offer noncombatant goods and services which would aid the war effort. About 14,000 Mennonite men were mobilized during the war. Half of these served in forestry service (°*Forsteidienst*), an alternative service program which Mennonites had funded and administered since 1881. Others worked in the °Red Cross or medical corps to provide health care for wounded soldiers on the western front and the Turkish front. Mennonites established hospital faciliites and collected funds for relief of soldiers' families. The expenses of the service program reached a peak of 1,000,000 rubles per month. Perhaps 100 or more Mennonites in the medical corps died at the battlefront or were victims of disease. Factors contributing to the success of the Mennonite noncombatant contribution included patriotic feelings for the Fatherland in peril, a desire to be of Christian service as Good Samaritans to those who were suffering, and the need to deflect criticism of German-speaking colonists and to demonstrate that Mennonites were worthy to keep their special °privileges. The relative cultural homogeneity and administrative unity of Mennonites in Russia made it possible to organize quickly and efficiently, although it was in behalf of a losing cause. By mid-April 1918 the victorious German armies occupied the Ukraine area where the original Mennonite settlements were located.

American Mennonites confronted the war belatedly, after the Russian armies had surrendered and the Russian Mennonite contribution to the Fatherland was concluded. American Mennonites were culturally diverse and administratively decentralized. They had no generally accepted alternative service program for draftees and no generally recognized war-related but non-military service agencies to make use of benevolent wartime contributions. The United States government prosecuted the war as a righteous democratic crusade and depended upon local communities to inspire patriotic fervor. The government raised money for the war not primarily through °taxes but rather through a series of "voluntary" war bond drives. Mennonites often resisted war bond purchases, but they also often bought bonds either willingly or after severe local pressure. Mennonite young men were °conscripted into military training

camps upon the government's promise that they would not be coerced into combatant service against their conscience. The War Department in fact intended to persuade as many pacifists as possible to join the war crusade. Secretary of War Newton D. °°Baker deliberately delayed the provision of noncombatant service opportunities for the men in training camps to allow time for °conscientious objectors to be converted to the military crusade. Although reliable figures are unavailable, it is likely that more American Mennonite young men abandoned their nonresistant heritage and joined regular national military service than did Russian Mennonite young men before the Russian defeat. About 150 American Mennonite young men were court-martialed and imprisoned for refusing military orders. Some accepted noncombatant service in the medical corps or quartermaster corps (supply and support services). Late in war a few were allowed to work on farm furloughs. The war ended before a satisfactory alternative system could be worked out, but the steadfast witness of the young men who refused to take up weapons in World War I paved the way for the more favorable °°Civilian Public Service Program in World War II. Civilian Public Service was remarkably similar to the Russian Mennonite forestry service under the Tsars.

As German-speaking pacifist people, Mennonites in both Russia and the United States were unfairly attacked for alleged treasonous identification with the German enemy. Some Mennonites in both countries indeed had been drawn to German cultural nationalism in decades before the war, but seldom to German militarism and imperialism. A group of Russian Mennonite intellectuals had been to Germany for higher education. In the war years before America declared war on Germany, some American Mennonites who had immigrated in the 1870s and 1880s expressed German sympathies by collecting war relief funds for the German Red Cross. Other American Mennonites, e.g., historian C. Henry °°Smith, were outspokenly anti-German and blamed Prussian militarism for starting the war.

The Russian government's anti-Germanism campaigns demonstrated that Mennonite °alternative service programs, no matter how generous, could not bridge the cultural gap and win the trust of the Russian people. The government closed German-language publications, forbade German-language advertising or public speaking, outlawed meetings of Germans outside churches, and required russianization of place names. Most alarming was a series of land liquidation laws, made increasingly stringent from 1915 to 1917, which seemed to threaten the legal basis for Mennonite acquisition and ownership of land. Military defeats at the front accelerated the Germanophobia and fostered local attacks on Mennonite interests. Mennonites protested that they were loyal Russian citizens, that they were contributing sacrificially to the national effort, and that they were originally of Dutch, rather than German, background. By the time of the German occupation of the Ukraine (mid-April 1918) the Mennonites had suffered so severely under the anti-Germanic attacks of anarchists and Bolsheviks that they welcomed the German army as liberators. This imprudent fraternization with the enemy, together with the subsequent Mennonite organization of a military self-defense (°*Selbstchutz*) force to protect local villages in the civil war and anarchy that followed the Russian surrender to Germany, compromised Mennonite claims to Russian citizenship and to the practice of nonresistance in the coming years.

America's wartime anti-Germanism was more diffused. President Woodrew Wilson's policies fostered anti-Germanism even as he maintained an official pose of enlightened democratic liberalism. German-speaking Mennonites might have suffered as greatly as did their Russian counterparts if Germany had militarily defeated and invaded the United States in a manner similar to the German defeat and invasion of Russia. A national "Committee on Public Information" whipped up public hatred of all things German, and an Espionage Act (1917) and Sedition Act (1918) set the stage for restriction of civil liberties. Two Mennonite leaders, Samuel H. Miller of Ohio and Lewis J. °°Heatwole of Virginia, were tried and convicted under the Sedition Act. At the local level American superpatriots forced Mennonite schools to stop teaching German, terrorized pacifists into purchasing war bonds, burned church buildings (Oklahoma and Michigan), and a college administration building (Tabor College in Kansas, though arson was not conclusively proven), and forced Mennonites to fly the American °flag. The Hutterites were especially victimized in military prisons and war bond drives. About 1,000 Hutterites migrated to Canada as a result. An additional 600-800 Mennonites, nearly all of Dutch-Russian background, migrated to Canada to escape wartime pressures. Anti-German and antipacifist sentiments were less severe in Pennsylvania and among Mennonites who had immigrated earlier and had °acculturated more fully to American ways.

While the war devastated the Russian Mennonite economy, it enriched American Mennonites through high prices for agricultural products. American Mennonites gave money, including war bonds, to church agencies in unprecedented amounts. Church institutions and °relief and missions programs thus benefited from the war. Some Mennonite young men joined postwar Quaker reconstruction units in France. A famine after the °Russian Revolution and civil war (early 1920s) led to the creation of a Mennonite Central Committee (MCC), whose prodigious relief efforts in the Ukraine were in part a product of pent-up energies and resources generated by the war.

The American Mennonite experience showed that war could be invigorating for a nonresistant people whose nation triumphed and who suffered enough persecution to remind them of the first principles of their religious heritage. But excessive persecution could destroy a people. Russian Mennonite wartime experience revealed the vulnerability of an ethnic pacifist subculture in a country which lost a war and which was convulsed by revolution and anarchy. Even in countries where Mennonites had abandoned their pacifism by the 20th c., the moral bankruptcy of Western civilization represented by World Wars I and II and the nuclear arms race helped ensure that the issue of nonresistance in the Anabaptist-

Mennonite heritage would be relevant on the world scene and critical for Mennonite identity in the future. JCJ

J. S. Hartzler, *Mennonites in the World War* (Scottdale: MPH, 1921); James C. Juhnke, *Building the Denomination* (Scottdale, 1988), ch. 8 (= MEA 3); Lawrence Klippenstein, "Mennonite Pacifism and State Service in Russia, A Case Study in Church Relations 1789-1936" (PhD diss. U. of Minnesota, 1984); Federick C. Luebke, *Bonds of Loyalty: German Americans and World War I* (DeKalb: Northern Illinois U. Press, 1974); Keith L. Sprunger and others eds., *Voices Against War: A Guide to the Schowalter Oral History Collection on World War I Conscientious Objectors* (North Newton: Bethel College, 1973, 1981); Allan Teichroew, "World War I and the Mennonite Migration to Canada to Avoid the Draft," *MQR*, 45 (1971), 219-49; John B. Toews, *Csars, Soviets and Mennonites* (Newton, 1982); Mary Sprunger, *Sourcebook: Oral History Interviews with World War One Conscientious Objectors* [n.p.: Mennonite Central Committee, 1986).

World War II (Germany). Under the totalitarianism of the Nazi regime (°National Socialism) men and women were drafted to various duties expected by the state and the Nazi party. Those duties were enlarged in the course of the war and their observance was carefully surveyed by the Gestapo (secret service). These orders were obeyed partly by conviction, partly by fear, partly by indifference. The obedience was smoothed by the continued propaganda. No Mennonites resisted conscription. After the war Mennonites, as most Germans, withdrew into their privacy, the enthusiasm for any kind of public service or any kind of political utopia was low. The "skeptical generation" became predominant for 20 years.

Unlike the experience of World War I there were no food shortages or epidemics. The people suffered from the devastation of air raids. In the summer of 1943 the Anglo-American forces gained superiority in the air. Saturation bombing began with Hamburg that year and continued until the bombing of Dresden in 1945. They dropped more than 1,500,000 metric tons of bombs; about half a million people, mostly women and children, died. Two million apartments were destroyed and about 7.5 million became homeless. Notwithstanding, experts agree that the *Bombenterror* (terror from bombs) supported the Allies' victory minimally. Since most of the Mennonites were rural people they did not experience air raids as a rule. However, the Mennonites in Hamburg, Berlin, Ludwigshafen, Emden, Krefeld, and Heilbronn suffered from the bombing. Their congregational centers were destroyed, or heavily damaged and many of their members lost their housing and had to seek shelter in the countryside.

The occupation of Germany began with the conquest of Aachen in October 1944 and was concluded with the cease fire on May 8, 1945. The West Prussian catastrophe was assured when intense cold allowed the Soviet tanks to cross fields and frozen rivers beginning Jan. 12, 1945. The population, poorly informed and not prepared for evacuation, began a desperate attempt to reach safety somewhere in the West. Among them were about 35,000 Mennonites: (1) 12,000 West Prussians and (2) more than 20,000 Ukrainian °refugees who had been temporarily settled in the Warthegau. Most refugees trekked with wagons, hay racks, and bicycles. Many were sooner or later overtaken by the Soviet army. An unknown number, mostly children and aged died from starvation, exhaustion, and diseases. A few were killed by the invading soldiers—victims of cruelty. Some refugees crossed the Baltic Sea by boat and landed in Denmark or Schleswig-Holstein. Some of the Red Cross boats were torpedoed, taking their passengers to their deaths. The refugees lived for up to seven years in camps and some suffered extreme hardships before they received new homes and subsistence income. The Mennonites in southwestern Germany were able to remain in their homes, and, although they suffered some material losses, their base of livelihood remained intact. Most of them tried individually to render assistance to refugees and victims of air raids.

The reconstruction started very slowly. °Relief organizations such as the Mennonite Central Committee (MCC) were allowed into Germany only in the spring of 1946. MCC started with feeding programs for children; continued with the distribution of food and clothing, organized the emigration to Canada, Paraguay, and Uruguay; assisted with the construction of settlements for West Prussian refugees in Wedel, °Espelkamp, Bechterdissen, Enkenbach, °Neuwied, and Backnang and established neighborhood centers at Heilbronn, Kaiserslautern and Berlin. About two-thirds of the German Mennonites were refugees seeking new homes, new congregations, new livelihoods, and new spiritual nurturing. About 2,000 West Prussian (one-sixth of the total number of refugees) found new homes in those settlements. In addition 10 new congregations were established by mostly West Prussian refugees. Older West German congregations, e.g., Hamburg, Emden, Krefeld, and Neuwied experienced new life through the West Prussians. Not all newcomers settled in the neighborhood of a congregation. Many of them joined another denomination. Very few West Prussians were able to resume farming; most of them had to make their living outside the traditional Mennonite limits and visions.

The general impact of the war in the postwar period were: (1) Anxiety about survival and coping with hardships during a time of breakdown not only of the nation and people, but also of ideals. The prewar way of life was replaced by conflicting feelings of survival—guilt and shame; (2) The punishment period of the allied victors ceased in 1947 with the approaching Cold War. The West Germans as well as other Europeans received help and encouragement from the United States. Europeans' energy awakened and eventually they thought less about their catastrophic experiences and repressed individual and collective guilt and began to look forward gladly to stability and material success.

The Mennonites had unique experiences in addition to those of the general population: (1) The various influences from the American Mennonites were stimulating; the MCC relief work drew forth, besides gratitude for assistance, a sense of commonality and awareness of shared models for the Christian life. Personal contacts via church leaders and MCC and °°Pax volunteers; international exchanges, including the Intermenno trainee program for young adults; and student exchanges that brought German students to North American Mennonite colleges and seminaries all helped to open minds and to teach some kind of solidarity. (2) The "°Anabaptist Vision" with its *Nachfolge* ("following after," °discipleship) theology had a constructive and consolidating impact. It was suited to encourge Mennonite identity and activate the members' involvement in the church. (3) Due to the emerging Cold War and the American influence the °peace witness became a major issue in the 1950s. After the war the overwhelming attitude of the Germans was: never war again, never an army, never any weapons! This changed gradually with the Cold War. With American assistance German Mennonites began to take a stand in the ongoing discussion. (4) The debate concerning the Mennonite attitudes towards Nazism stirred heavy emotions but helped Mennonites realize that as Christians they could not rid themselves of the past. To acknowledge that most Mennonites had sympathized with the regime was painful. (5) The Mennonite World Conference fostered a desire to take part in the worldwide Mennonite fellowship. (6) The °urbanization of most Mennonites caused a far-reaching social change. They now have to learn how to resist the temptations of pluralistic ideologies and to contextualize their Anabaptist-Mennonite tradition in a non-Christian environment.　　　DGL

Heinold Fast, "Die Eidesverweigerung bei den Mennoniten," *Menn. Geschibl.*, Jg. 22, n.F. 17 (1965); Hans-Jürgen Goertz, "Nationale Erhebung und religiöser Niedergang," *Menn Geschbl.*, Jg. 31, n.F. 27 (1974); Diether Götz Lichdi, *Mennoniten im Dritten Reich: Dokumentation und Deutung* (Weierhof, 1977); idem, *Über Zürich und Witmarsum nach Addis Abeba: Mennoniten in Geschichte und Gegenwart* (Maxdorf, 1983); idem, "The Story of Nazism and its Reception Today," *Menn. Life*, 36 (March 1981); "The Fourth of December," *Menn. Life*, 38 (Sept. 1983); idem, "Vergegenwärtigung und Auftrag—zum 8 Mai 1945," *Gemeinde Unterwegs* (May, 1985); idem, "Das Friedenszeugnis der deutschen Mennoniten im 20. Jahrhundert," in *30 Jahre D[eutsches] M[ennonitisches] F[riedens]-K[omitee], 1956-1986* (Bammental, 1986); *Menn. Jahr.* (1985); Horst Penner, *Die ost- und westpreußischen Mennoniten*, vol. 2 (Kirchheimbolanden, 1987).

World War II (Soviet Union). World War II is commonly described as the period of armed conflict between September 1939 and May 1945. However, for the peoples of central and eastern Europe the beginning of that tragic period is not quite as distinctly set off from the "state of peace." In the two largest European dictatorships (Germany and the Soviet Union), the war against the individual citizen started in the early 1930s, and in the Soviet Union that war was as costly in human lives as the later international conflict. The impact of the Stalin terror on Soviet society was devastating. In the Ukraine especially the German, Ukrainian, and Mennonite minorities suffered, but Stalin had alienated the majority of his people and even his army just before the war started.

The tragedy of the Mennonite experience during these years is not yet fully documented. All Mennonite churches were closed by 1934-35, and by 1938, in the Chortitza colony, 43.5 percent of all Mennonite fathers were in prisons or in forced labor camps (concentration camps). In Zagradovka 51.5 percent of the fathers were missing, and in the Baratov villages 70.2 percent were missing. On the average we can say that 50 percent of Mennonite families lost their provider during these years. The spiritual leadership perished and the few isolated church leaders who survived, lived a life of constant fear.

In Western Europe the Mennonite community was relatively well informed about the suffering of Mennonites in the Soviet Union, and there is no doubt that that knowledge influenced the mood of the Mennonite community when it faced the polarization of European politics before the war. The issue of military service was no longer a serious object for discussion, but political affiliation was something else. A few Mennonites were impressed by the social programs of the Right, some decided that the political Right was the lesser evil, but the options were very limited. Thus, most European Mennonites were caught by the turmoil of the events and were dragged along.

When World War II started, all Mennonites were shocked, because on the Rhine and on the Volga they realized that this would be a very trying experience. The Mennonites in the Soviet Union feared for the lives of their loved ones in the labor camps and prisons. Furthermore, although Mennonites in the Soviet Union had stubbornly and successfully defended their nonresistance position until 1935, with the closing of all churches they had no institution to influence their young men, and 50 percent of their families were without fathers. The impact of this situation was frightening. It became obvious that individual families were not equipped to hold out against the impact of the flood of atheistic propaganda. Morals were declining in spite of the really courageous and admirable effort of Mennonite mothers. And thus, when in early 1940, for the first time large numbers of Mennonite young men were drafted into the army, there was no longer any resistance. The spirit of the Russian Mennonite community had been broken, and when, on June 22, 1941, Germany and the Soviet Union faced each other at war, Mennonites knew that they were confronting the greatest danger since the 16th c.

On Aug. 16, 1941, 70 Mennonite villages of the Crimean Peninsula were evacuated by train with a few hours notice. On the same day all Mennonite communities west of the Dniepr River were evacuated under NKVD (People's Commissariat of Internal Affairs) "protection." However, the majority were overrun by the fast-advancing German army before they could cross the Dniepr bridges. On August 19, 1941, all villages on the west bank of the Dniepr River were in German hands.

The 56 Molotschna villages and other settlements on the east side of the Dniepr suffered more severely than those on the west bank of the Dniepr. In September, before the German army overran this area, all Mennonite men between 16 and 65 were rounded up and marched off to unknown destinations. Then the evacuation of women and children began, but only 23 villages were evacuated before the arrival of the German army. At this point we estimate that at least 50 percent of the men perished, but the loss of life was also high among the evacuated women and children.

The advancing German army gave the impression of calm and order. This army had worship services on Sundays and permitted churches to open their doors again. Hope grew that the Mennonite community could survive. Between August 1941 and October 1943 an active church life developed in the villages that had survived. Young people were baptized in large numbers, the church came alive and it was amazing how a community whose leadership potential had been depleted to the bare bones, suddenly found renewed strength. The reality of the nature of Hitler's regime came to these communities slowly, when the political arm of the system reached the occupied territory.

For two years the Mennonite villages west and east of the Dniepr River lived between hope and fear. When they began to recognize the evil aspects of Hitler's outrageous policies, their fears only multiplied. They realized that under the circumstances their only hope to save their lives was in deserting everything that had been dear to them. In September 1943 the remaining inhabitants of the Molotschna villages took to the road. The Chortitza villages followed in October. Thirty-five thousand Mennonites, as well as 350,000 ethnic Germans, and well over a million Ukrainians and other nationalities attempted to save their lives by escaping to western Europe. They reached the eastern frontier of Germany and were temporarily given shelter, but, in 1945 they had to run again. This time their fate was rape, death, and deportation. Circa 23,000 Mennonites were returned to the Soviet Union, where they were exiled to the distant cold regions of northeastern Europe and Siberia. Many were sentenced to 10 and 25 years of hard labor. Thousands perished and were never heard of again.

However, the westward offensive of the Soviet army into Germany, which started in January 1945, affected not only the refugees from Russia. All the Mennonite villages east of the Elbe River were now deserted as the mother communities of the Russian Mennonites—Danzig, West Prussia, and East Prussia—also were lost in this tragic war. And thus, all Russian, Polish, and Prussian Mennonite communities between Volga and Elbe were wiped off the map.

After the war, those who had escaped founded the colonies °Volendam and °Neuland in Paraguay; El Ombu, Delta, and Gartental in Uruguay; and a small colony in Buenos Aires, Argentina. Eventually ca. 8,000 emigrated to Canada, and the rest settled in Germany. Since 1970 ca. 20,000 Mennonites were permitted to leave the Soviet Union and resettle in West Germany. These °Umsiedler may well play a significant role in the rejuvenation of the Mennonite church in Europe.

It has also become obvious that the remnant of the Mennonite church in the Soviet Union is not dead, and that the church actually experienced a revival. In the late 1980s there are approximately 55,000 Mennonites in the Union of Soviet Socialist Republics. Many of them live in areas of their original exile, but several large colonies have also survived in the Ural region and in Siberia. In the °Orenburg and New-Samara (°Pleshanov) colonies, with 23 and 13 villages respectively, the church has come alive and is growing. The people have rediscovered their heritage and they are clinging to it. Two other colonies, Slavgorod (56 villages) and Barnaul (13 villages) are not yet open to tourists in 1988. A number of strong Mennonite churches have developed in °Soviet Central Asia: Karaganda, Dzhambul, Dushanbe, Frunse, Alma-Ata, and a number of other towns and villages.

Mennonites in the Soviet Union and in Western Europe have entered a new era, and it can only be hoped that the traumatic experience of World War II will not be forgotten. GKE

Arnold Bachmann, *Galiziens Mennoniten im Wandel der Zeiten* (Bachnang, 1984); George K. Epp, "Die große Flucht," in *Menn. Jahrbuch* (1985); Peter Epp, *Ob Tausend fallen. . . .* (Weichs: MEMRA Verlag, 1987); Gerhard Fast, *Das Ende von Chortitza* (Winnipeg: Regehr's Printing, 1973); Abram Funk, ed., *25 Jahre Volendam, 1947-1972* (Curitiba, 1972); Christian Hege, "Die Mennoniten in den Kriegsgebieten 1939/40," *Menn. Geschbl.*, Jg. 5 (1940), 6-9; Peter Hildebrand, *Odyssee Wider Willen: Das Schicksal eines Auslandsdeutschen* (Oldenburg: Heinz Holzberg Verlag, 1984); Diether Götz Lichdi, *Mennoniten im Dritten Reich: Dokumentation und Deutung* (Heilbronn: Gustav Hölbe GmbH, 1977); Gerhard Lohrenz, *The Lost Generation and other Stories* (Steinbach, 1982); idem, *The Odyssey of the Bergen Family* (Steinbach, 1978); M. Martens, *Stormy Tides: Religious Persecutions in Soviet Russia* (Winnipeg, 1940); Jacob A. Neufeld, *Tiefenwege: Erfahrungen und Erlebnisse von Russland-Mennoniten in zwei Jahrsehnten bis 1949* (Virgil, Ont.: Niagara Press, 1949); Erich L. Ratzlaff, *Im Weichselbogen: Mennoniten-Siedlungen in Zentralpolen* (Winnipeg: Christian Press, 1971); Hans Rempel, ed., *Waffen der Wehrlosen: Ersatzdienst der Mennoniten in der USSR* (Winnipeg: CMBC Publications, 1980); Walter Sawatsky, *Soviet Evangelicals Since World War II* (Scottdale, 1981); Walter Wedel, *Nur zwanzig Kilometer: Eine Jugend in den russischen Wäldern* (Wuppertal: R. Brockhaus Verlag, 1979); Heinrich Wölk, and Gerhard Wölk, *Die Mennoniten Brüdergemeinde in Rußland 1925-1980* (Fresno: Center for MB Studies, 1981; Winnipeg, Christian Press, 1981), Engl. trans. as *A Wilderness Journey* (Fresno, 1982); Rainer Zacharias, ed., *Neues Marienburger Heimatbuch* (Herford: Verlag Wendt Groll GmbH, 1967). Countless articles on this subject have appeared in *Der Bote* and *Mennonite Life*. Papers from a symposium on the impact of World War II on Canadian Mennonites held at Winnipeg, May 1987, were published in *JMS*, 6 (1988); Benjamin Pinkus, and Ingeborg Fleischhauer, *Die Deutschen in der Sowjetunion: Geschichte einer nationalen Minderheit im 20. Jahrhundert* (Baden-Baden: Nomos Verlagsgesellschaft, 1987).

Worship, Private, is the concern to make faith operative in daily life. It runs like a silver thread through the Mennonite story. As Kauffman and Harder point out in their book *Anabaptists Four Centuries Later*, "personal acts of Bible meditation, prayer and devotion are the religious practices usually conceived to be the well-spring of faithful living" (p. 96).

The beginnings of the Mennonite heritage of private worship are with the Anabaptists. Kauffman and Harder write, "Even with their emphases on corporate assembly and community, early Anabaptists didn't overlook the importance of the personal devotional discipline. One of their earliest documents admonished, 'Read the Psalter daily at home'" (CRR 1:44). Robert Friedman in his article on °°devotional literature concurs, saying, "The main devotional book of the Anabaptists and Mennonites was and still is, the Bible; all the rest are auxiliary to it." His article does, however, describe the auxiliary literature that was used and how it defines what was of importance to the Anabaptists of the 16th, 17th,

and 18th c. Books containing confessions (testimonies) of outstanding Anabaptists (some of them martyrs) were very popular for devotional reading through the ages, and were handed down to children and grandchildren. Then too, for their hymns, sermons, and devotional books, Anabaptists and Mennonites borrowed heavily from other traditions, e.g., °Pietists, °°Moravians, and °°Brethren (Dunkers). The emphasis of Count °°Zinzendorf and the Moravians, for example, on Jesus as loving and kind, left its mark on Mennonites. The Mennonite and non-Mennonite sources of the °°*Ernsthafte Christenpflicht*, the first Mennonite prayer book (1739) are described in ME II:244. Since 1984 selections from this prayer book are available in English under the title *A Devoted Christian's Prayer Book* (Aylmer, Ont. and Lagrange, Ind.: Pathway Publishing Corporation).

Anabaptists did not describe just how they carried on their private prayer nor give any evaluation of its depth and meaning. Something of the quality of Anabaptist private prayer can be inferred by noting how outsiders saw them. Georg Thormann, a Swiss Reformed pastor, in *The Touchstone* (1690) assured his readers that "it is not necessary to become an Anabaptist to be saved!" Hans de °°Ries was known for his fervent audible prayers which he must have prayed out of a life of meaningful private worship. It is also safe to assume that Anabaptist public worship reflected Anabaptist private worship and vice versa, in both meaning and form. As to form, Anabaptist worship was to be without embellishment and simple, so that form would not crowd God out. Silent prayer was the general practice until about the 18th or 19th c. Until the 20th c. aspects of the traditional °Christian calendar were followed. As to meaning, for Mennonites and Anabaptists to worship was to be in fellowship with the Divine, to have a repentant attitude, and to yield to God (°°*Gelassenheit*). It was also to take Jesus' life for one's personal example, to show opposition to evil, and to express °love. These must certainly have been some of the expectations they brought also to their private worship.

Some sense of Mennonite private worship can also be inferred by taking note of what was happening in the world around them. The impact of their rural environment, wars and revolutions, revival meetings, and Pietism, shaped Mennonites in the 19th c. and into the early 20th c. One of the tasks of prayer was to discern how best to live out their faith in the midst of these experiences.

Then came World Wars I and II with the options to do military, noncombatant, or °alternative service. There were also greater opportunities in higher °education and in world °mission. These led to what later became the °°Women's Missionary and Service organization (MC) to publish a *Monthly Prayer Cycle* (1921) with the stated purpose of "encouraging intelligent and effectual prayer for missions in the Sunday school, sewing circles, prayer meetings, family worship and private prayer." Each page of the leaflet had a Bible verse such as Prv 15:8 or Jas 5:16 at the top and a particular prayer request for each day. On day 24, for example, participants were asked to pray for high school and college girls "that they may give us their new ideas and we may learn from them because the church needs them." On day 20 readers were asked to pray "that America will be worthy of being called a 'Christian nation.'" In 1935 a modest sheet entitled *The Voluntary Prayer Link* was printed in Ontario. Its editor, Oscar Burkholder (ME IV:1069), wrote, "It will be my purpose to place a sheet in the hands of every person who will agree to use it as an aid in their regular devotions." For almost five years it collected both items for prayer and answers to prayer, both locally and from foreign fields. The General Sewing Circle (MC) again took up the task of calling people to prayer for missions in 1946 by publishing *The Daily Prayer Calendar.* The first day of each month was to be prayer for the Mennonite Church "that she may receive an enlarged vision of her true mission in the world" and "that mothers and fathers in the church may have divine wisdom to lead their children in the way of the Lord." Four years later this booklet was enlarged to include a daily Bible reading, prayers for children, and suggested book lists for personal and family spiritual growth as well as specific prayer requests for missionaries, relief workers, those serving Mennonite institutions, the government, and the United Nations. It was then called *The Daily Prayer Guide.* It, and its successor known as *Voice*, had and have a quiet but definite influence on the development and regularity of private worship in the church.

Interest in personal devotions kept growing. John R. °Mumaw, General Secretary for the Mennonite Commission for Christian Education and Young People's work, wrote that "worship is a real necessity of the soul," and that "One of the vital aspects of Christian living is a consciousness of God's presence with us" (*Worship in the Home*, ca. 1941). Likewise Ernest Bohn in his speech in 1947 at the sixth conference on "Mennonite Cultural Problems" links piety to the deepening concern for the Christian family. He says, "As we now come to the consideration of definite techniques of teaching religion in the home, may we suggest as number one, a pair of parents who have thoroughly committed themselves to Christ and his way of life."

By and large Mennonites see private worship as affecting daily living. Paul °Erb, the editor of the *Gospel Herald* (MC) during the 1940s and 1950s, judged reader interest in personal spiritual growth to be high. He ran a series entitled, "To Be Near to God," and printed numerous articles of this kind. Mennonite leaders as a whole in those decades and the ones to follow urged members to live as they pray and pray as they live. Christian living, including prayer, is to deal with the issues of the day: the meaning of °°nonconformity in the 1950s, of being Christian in relationships and making the church relevant in the 1960s, of being responsible politically and socially for peace and justice in the 1970s and 1980s, and of resisting the indulgence of the 1980s.

Included in Kauffman and Harder's profile of five Mennonite and Brethren in Christ denominations is a description of their devotionalism and °sanctification. They found, for example, that 77 percent of respondents had a "sense of being loved by Christ," 71 percent "a sense of being tempted by the devil,"

and 72 percent "a feeling . . . [of being] in the presence of God." Further, 77 percent of the subjects in the study as over against 75 percent of American Protestants who "generally pray at least once a week," prayed daily or more. Thirty-two percent, as over against 13 percent of American Protestants who "read the Bible at home," studied the Bible daily. Yet the authors concluded with the observation that "twentieth century Anabaptists have not been able to achieve fully a synthesis of the worshiping heart and the helping hand."

A person's concept of God and of God's desired responses from humans does affect private worship. The °°Dordrecht Confession's (1632) view of God as Eternal, Almighty, Creator of all things visible and invisible, at work in all, present for comfort and protection continues with Mennonites as a people scattered throughout the world. Contemporary American Mennonites, along with East Indian, African, and Japanese Mennonites frequently address God as Father. Members of Spanish-speaking Mennonite churches in Paraguay more often call God, "our Owner." Can it be that non-Western (in an ideological rather than a geographical sense) Mennonites know for a fact that in God alone exists all hope? North Americans who have lived abroad say that fellow Mennonites there seem to see prayer as central to living and are ready to speak to this. It appears that Mennonites worldwide want to respond to God in commitment and in obedience which is the fruit of love.

Mennonites continue to be influenced by and borrow from various other Christian groups. Beginning in the 1970s this is particularly true of the °charismatic influence. One of the benefits which has come to the Mennonites through this is a deepening hunger for fellowship with God in prayer and Bible reading. In the hope of helping Mennonites "borrow" wisely, the Ministry of Spirituality Committee (MC) called a consultation in August of 1986 at Ashland, Ohio, to consider carefully six streams of spirituality which presently influence the church. The "streams" studied were charismatic, relational, feminist, Anabaptist, conservative evangelical, and contemplative. Over 70 persons attended and then spelled out what influences can be seen to contribute to a stronger Mennonite spirituality.

Interest in Christian spirituality (an intimate relationship between God and people which enables them to love God, follow Christ, and walk in the Spirit) continues strong within the denomination. The General Conference Mennonite Church also, in 1985, appointed a Spiritual Emphasis Committee to encourage the intentional giving of self to spiritual growth in private worship. Mennonite seminaries and colleges do include courses on the spiritual disciplines and private prayer, and report continuing interest in and sincere commitment to these studies. TMG

Menn Bib II, index under Devotional Literature, Family Prayer; Kauffman/Harder, *Anabaptists Four C. Later* (1975); Robert Friedmann, *Mennonite Piety Through the Centuries*; idem, "Devotional Literature of the Swiss Brethren 1600-1800," *MQR*, 16 (1942), 199-220; idem, "Mennonite Prayer Books," *MQR*, 17 (1943), 179-206; idem, "Devotional Literature of the Mennonites in Danzig and East Prussia to 1800," *MQR*, 18 (1944), 162-73; idem, "Dutch Mennonite

Devotional Literature from Peter Peters to Johannes Deknatel, 1625-1753," *MQR*, 25 (1951), 187-207; Paul M. Miller, "Worship among the Early Anabaptists," *MQR*, 30 (1956), 235-46; Abraham P. Toews, *American Mennonite Worship: Its Roots, Development and Application* (New York: Exposition Press, 1960); *Family Worship* (Scottdale, 1961-), a quarterly; *Our Family Worships* (Newton, 1961-), a quarterly; A. Donald Augsburger, "Parental Roles in the Development of Attitudinal Patterns in the Family Worship Experience" (MRE Thesis, Eastern Baptist Theological Seminary, 1956); Ernest Bohn, "Religion in the Home" in *Proceedings* of the 6th Annual Conference on Mennonite Cultural Problems, held at Goshen College, August 1-2, 1947, pp. 87-94; *Christian Family Relationships*, Proceedings of the Study Conference on Home Interests . . . Held at Goshen College, . . . August 28-31, 1959 (Mennonite Commission for Christian Education, 1960), various articles; John R. Mumaw, *Worship in the Home* (Scottdale: MPH, ca. 1941); Nelson E. Kauffman, ed., *For Family Worship: A Series of Doctrinal Meditations based on Scripture Selections for the Family Worship Hour*. . . (Scottdale, 1949); John R. Mumaw, "Vital Experiences at the Family Altar," in *Christian Ministry* 5 (1952), 216-19; Harold E. Bauman, "The Family Aids Spiritual Maturity," *Chr. Living*, 7 (October 1960) 8-10; Paul M. Yoder, et al, *Four Hundred Years with the Ausbund* (Scottdale, 1964); Paul Erb, *Don't Park Here* (Scottdale, 1962) in part IV; "The Voluntary Prayer Link," sent out by L. J. Burkholder, Markham, Ont., Nov. 1935-Oct 1940; papers at "The Mennonite Church Consultation on Spirituality" at Ashland, Ohio, Aug. 1986 (Mennonite Board of Congregational Ministries [MC]); Katie Funk Wiebe *Who Are the Mennonite Brethren* (Winnipeg and Hillsboro: Kindred Press, 1984, 14-15; "Spirituality Reconsidered," a series of articles *GH* (May, 1982).

See also Family Worship.

Worship, Public (North America) (ME IV:984). The words "variety" and "diversity" best characterize public worship among North American Mennonites in the 1960s, 1970s, and 1980s. Few recurring patterns of worship can be detected in the churches across the continent, except, perhaps among the °Amish and °Hutterites. There are a host of reasons why such a variety of patterns exist. Some of these reasons stem from forces within Mennonite groups and others from outside.

Particularly in the late 1960s a cynicism about the purpose and nature of Christian worship seemed to erode earlier worship understandings and practices. Several Mennonite scholars began researching and writing on worship as a form of covenant renewal between God and the community of faith. They followed the biblical notion of covenant through the testaments and developed a coherent theology of worship. These writings helped to clarify the purpose of worship among Mennonites and to articulate how God was present in the midst of the worshiping community. The covenant renewal pattern has reoriented Mennonite worship theology and has given rise to various forms of covenant renewal services. As more early Anabaptist writings have been translated into English, the worship theology and practice of various Anabaptist groups are coming to light. Various liturgical forms and understandings of the church °ordinances have informed current practices. However, a careful articulation of Anabaptist worship theology has not yet been elaborated.

Hymn °singing, °prayer, and °preaching are the primary elements of nearly all Mennonite worship services. All other worship activities are of secondary importance.

The *Mennonite Hymnal* of 1968 brought together the hymnody traditions of the General Conference

Mennonites and the Mennonite Church (MC). While preferences for certain hymn types and styles persist for worship in each group, the hymnal made all of the dominant styles available to both of these major groups (°hymnology). This merger has brought some musical standardization facilitating more intergroup worship. The 1942 *Gesangbuch der Mennoniten* was republished in Canada in 1965 and is used in worship among some of the Russian Mennonites there. The Mennonite Brethren *Worship Hymnal* of 1971 shares many standard hymns with the *Mennonite Hymnal*, but also contains many 19th c. American gospel hymns. Other nontraditional music sources are being used in most Mennonite groups, including 20th-c. evangelical gospel songs, Scripture songs, folk songs (often displayed on overhead projectors in the meeting room), Gelineau psalmody, and music from various monastic communities. These songs and hymns may require various forms of instrumental accompaniment, though pianos, organs, and guitars are most often used. This diversity creates an array of new styles and different theologies in the course of a worship service.

Among the Mennonite Church (MC) congregations four-part unaccompanied singing still dominates, though many congregations use pianos, or organs, or both, on occasion. The Amish continue to sing in an ornamented a capella style. Their hymns, taken from the *Ausbund*, are sung quite slowly. Among the General Conference Mennonites and Mennonite Brethren, accompanied hymn singing is preferred. More church °choirs have been organized in recent years to provide additional music for the worship service or to support congregational singing.

Various styles of public °prayer have been in evidence in recent decades. The pastoral prayer remains a popular style. The pastor or worship leader prays on behalf of the community, offering statements of thanksgiving, confession, petition, and intercession. These prayers may be composed extemporaneously and may become quite lengthy. Often the pastoral prayer is the only prayer found in the service. It is generally used in large congregations and in more formal worship settings. Another style of prayer, feasible for small congregations, is spontaneous, voluntary prayers by individual members on behalf of the community. The pastor or worship leader may begin or end the period of prayer with short summary prayers. This style may reflect, in part, the influence of the °charismatic movement of the 1970s. Silent prayer is growing in prominence in many churches, in part as the result of increased contact with Quaker and contemplative spiritualities, but also reflecting earlier Anabaptist and Mennonite practice. Long periods of silence are observed in which one may pray aloud if so moved, but generally no one prays audibly. In all of these cases, a period of sharing "joys and concerns" or general announcements may precede the time of prayer. Among Mennonites, a reluctance to pray shorter prayers more often throughout the service persists as does the reluctance to repeat prayers from service to service. Generally speaking, the Lord's Prayer is not said as a regular part of Sunday worship in most congregations.

Preaching remains the central element of Mennonite worship, requiring most of the time allotted for worship. The sermon is usually the orienting point of the service, influencing the selection of hymns, prayer themes, Scripture readings, etc. In some places the sermon has been renamed "teaching," and the lecture style has been borrowed as a model for delivery. Ethical issues and life-style concerns have provided the primary themes. Sermons using biblical themes or having proclamatory intentions have been less frequent. In recent years preaching has seemed to be at a low ebb in many congregations. Generally, preaching has tended to appeal primarily to the minds of the worshipers and has not stirred their hearts. A renewal of preaching is currently underway which must integrate the skills of biblical exegesis and public speaking with the needs of Mennonites in the contemporary world.

With regard to other Mennonite worship practices the following general observations may be made. (1) German is the language of worship in a very small number of Mennonite congregations, predominantly in Canada. Amish, Hutterite, and Old Order Mennonite services are carried out in German in the United States and Canada. (2) In North America Mennonite worship services are being carried on in Spanish, Chinese dialects, Vietnamese dialects, Creole, various North American Indian dialects, and other ethnic languages. (3) The influence of Afro-American, Hispanic, Asian, and Indian cultures can be seen in these Mennonite worship settings, particularly in hymns and musical styles.

(4) While most congregations continue to meet in church buildings or meetinghouses, small groups, primarily in urban areas, are meeting in homes, schools, or storefronts. The worship space used by these groups influences the activities of worship chosen and their level of formality and informality.

(5) In most congregations the Bible is not read extensively during worship. Usually short portions of Scripture are read which provide a base for the sermon. In some congregations a predetermined cycle of readings (lectionary) is followed, often prescribing two or three passages for each Sunday. This practice ensures that larger portions of Scripture are read in the course of a season or year.

(6) Diverse patterns of worship leadership can be found, expressing the theology of the °priesthood of all believers. The primary patterns are: (a) a pastor leads the service except the singing; a song leader leads music; (b) a "worship leader" leads all of the activities except singing and preaching, a song leader leads music, a pastor preaches; (c) a "worship leader" leads some of the activities, a song leader leads music, a pastor preaches, congregational members read Scripture, pray, give announcements, tell a children's story, etc. In most cases worship leaders and song leaders may be men or women. However preaching is done predominantly by men; in a few congregations women may occupy the pulpit.

(7) Overall, the confession of sin and the acknowledgement of grace are elements of worship which have not been emphasized in recent Mennonite worship. In some congregations preparation sermons and services prior to infrequent °communion services serve this purpose. Righteous living and morality, however, are highly stressed in worship.

(8) Most Mennonite congregations lack a sound theology for the activity of collecting a monetary °offering. It is assumed that an offering should be taken, but this activity is not linked in any coherent way with other worship activities. It is not viewed generally as an expression of personal commitment or thanksgiving.

(9) In many Mennonite congregations children and youth present a problem in worship. Developmental studies have shown that the highly verbal style of Mennonite worship cannot usually meet the cognitive, emotional, or spiritual needs of children and youth. As a partial remedy to this problem children's sermons or stories have sometimes been included in the structure of worship.

(10) Communion is observed with varying degrees of frequency in Mennonite congregations. Some groups observe the celebration twice a year; other groups have a quarterly observance. In a few congregations, communion is celebrated more than four times a year. °Feetwashing may be practiced in conjunction with communion in some congregations, but most groups no longer observe this service.

(11) Worship in many congregations is coordinated by a worship committee leading to a more °democratic approach to worship and reflecting a desire to meet the needs of the majority of the members.

Overall, a wide variety of worship patterns exist among contemporary Mennonites and Brethren in Christ. A distrust of ritual or highly patterned worship has persisted in the last decades, coinciding with the cynicism in society over the role and efficacy of ritual and °symbolic activity in human life. This has led to extreme individualism in society and in worship. Many worshipers rejected those traditional religious expressions which they personally cannot believe or do not understand. At various times attention to the transcendence of God has been minimized while the presence of the Spirit in the community's fellowship has been central. At these times, worship has had a "horizontal" orientation and has lacked a sense of "vertical" focus. There has been some attempt to restore some earlier forms of Anabaptist and Mennonite worship particularly with regard to communion. The recovery of some early Anabaptist prayers has provided a renewed sense of Anabaptist worship spirituality. As the self-identity of North American Mennonites changes, more coherent and stable worship patterns will need to emerge if the essentials of Anabaptist and Mennonite faith and practice are to persist.

(1) Since the early 1960s there has been more dialogue among all Christian traditions, particularly with regard to baptism, communion, and ministry. This discussion has reshaped some questions which affect worship practices, e.g. the question of how Christ is present in the Lord's Supper according to biblical and theological traditions. The °Roman Catholic liturgical renewal of the 19th and early 20th c., which was encouraged by the Second Vatican Council (1962-65), has made worship resources and other theologies of worship more accessible to Mennonites. Some of these have been incorporated in Mennonite practice.

(2) During the era of the United States' war in

°Vietnam American public with regard to government, authority, and public life resulted in the erosion of faith in the power of symbols and rituals to join people in activities expressing common beliefs. This suspicion of ritual, which was also fostered by 18th-, 19th-, and early 20-c. philosophers, has always been present in the Mennonite tradition to a greater or lesser degree. The period of the 1960s heightened the cynicism of many Mennonite young adults and intellectuals and was particularly evident in the individualism expressed in public worship.

(3) The charismatic movement of the 1970s reclaimed the power of the Holy Spirit in religious experience and brought believers together from various denominations. New forms of singing, spontaneous and patterned prayers, and ecstatic utterances found their way into the worship services of all denominations. The influences of this movement are still felt among Mennonites.

(4) The civil rights and women's movements of the 1960s and 1970s brought with them the awareness that language shapes the way people perceive themselves and their world. As a result the language of hymns and biblical texts came under attack. Attempts to be inclusive of all members of the Christian community have required the elimination of racist references as well as the elimination of "man" when referring to humanity. The most embattled issue remains whether references to God can be only masculine or whether feminine images of and references to God are biblically and theologically acceptable.

(5) The impact of television evangelists of the 1970s and 1980s, with their slick and highly choreographed "services," is felt in many congregations. These shows present, for many, a model of what worship could be. The language of the evangelists, their musical texts and styles, and their formulas of prayer and confession are being taken over into congregational worship. The preaching styles of these evangelists are influencing the expectations of Mennonite preaching.

(6) North American culture may be most accurately described as a salad bowl, not a melting pot. Ethnic and personal distinctives are flaunted and encouraged by the society. As Mennonites carry out the °evangelistic task, they are integrating patterns of expression which have not been characteristically Mennonite. The worship context is the most likely place where these complementary and conflicting modes of expression are integrated or refined.   RSL

Alvin J. Beachy, *Worship as Celebration of Covenant and Incarnation* (Newton and Scottdale, 1968); Walter Klaassen, *Biblical and Theological Bases for Worship in the Believers' Church* (Newton, 1978); Millard C. Lind, *Biblical Foundations for Christian Worship* (Scottdale, 1973); Abraham P. Toews, *American Mennonite Worship* (New York: Exposition Press, 1960); Werner Enninger and Joachim Raith, *An Ethnography-of-Communication Approach to Ceremonial Situations: A Study on Communication in Institutionalized Social Contexts: The Old Order Amish Church Service* (Wiesbaden: Franz Steiner Verlag GMBH, 1982); John Rempel. "Forum: Baptism, Eucharist and Ministry," *Worship*, 57 (1983), 451-54. a believers church i.e., not specifically Mennonite, response to the World Council of Churches statement on Baptism, Eucharist and Ministry; J. Ward Shank, "Formality and Informality in Public Worship," (April 4, 1961), 305; Ronald A. Krehbiel, "A Study and Proposal of Congregational Involvement in Worship for a General Conference Mennonite Church' (DMin diss., San Francisco Theological Seminary, 1977); *Issues in Congregational Formation: Builder Reprints for Adult Discussion Groups* (Scottdale and Newton, 1985), 34-55; John Rempel, "Worship and Spiritual Gifts" (unpublished); idem, "Christian Worship: Surely the Lord Is in this Place," *CGR*, 6 (1988), 101-17; Peter C. Erb, "A Reflection on a Mennonite Theology in Canada," *JMS*, 1 (1983), 179-90; C. J. Dyck and others, "Theology and Practice of Anabaptist Worship," *MQR*, 40 (1966), 163-78.

See also Architecture; House Churches; Music, Instrumental.

Worship Aids refers, among nonliturgical churches, to written or sung texts utilized for different worship activities, e.g., calls-to-worship, invocations, offertory prayers, benedictions, hymns. Broadly speaking, worship aids may also include symbolic movements (°dance) and environmental designs.

Among Mennonites in the 1980s emphasis is placed on creativity and variety in the worship materials. The expression of local and current needs in contemporary language is considered essential in composing or selecting texts. As a result of these tendencies, classical prayer texts, litanies, confessions, benedictions, and some hymns are seldom used. The repetition of texts is not valued. Worship planners need a vast reservoir of materials available for various types of worship services. However, among other Anabaptist-related groups the texts for worship are more defined. Generally in groups where oral tradition is active and printed worship materials are used minimally, worship texts are only slightly varied and tend toward formulaic structure (Amish, Old Order Mennonites, Hutterites, Old Colony Mennonites, etc.).

Worship aids may be structured and performed in a variety of ways. Texts may be sung in unison or sung antiphonally between choir (or solo singer) and congregation. Texts may be read or sung by a single person. Some texts require congregational interaction and are structured to be performed antiphonally, responsively or chorically. Movements or dances may be done by an individual or a group while simple gestures or postures may be carried out by the entire congregation.

Worship aids must be selected carefully. The following evaluations must be made in writing for selecting materials for congregational worship. (1) Does the text witness to or support the biblical or theological traditions of Christianity and Anabaptism? (2) Does the text contribute to the flow of the worship activity? (3) Does the text say and do what is necessary for the specific worship activity for which it is chosen, e.g., is a call-to-worship text addressed to the congregation or is it actually an opening prayer directed to God? (4) Does the text have literary and linguistic integrity? (5) What is the intention of the text? (6) How does the text provide for a response from or by the congregation?

The primary sources for worship aids are: denominational hymnals (for hymns and printed congregational texts); canticles, psalms, and hymns from the Bible; items written by worship leaders; bulletin covers produced by denominational publishing houses; the pamphlets in the "Worship Series" published jointly by the Mennonite Church and the

General Conference Mennonite publishing houses (18 pamphlets as of 1986); denominational ministers' manuals; lectionaries compiled by non-Mennonite denominations; worship books from other traditions (e.g., Roman Catholic *Missals, Lutheran Book of Worship,* Episcopal and Anglican *Book of Common Prayer,* Presbyterian *Worship Book,* the translation of the Taizé liturgy, *Common Praise,* etc.); other denominational music collections and hymnals; supplemental books of worship materials published by other religious publishing houses (e. g., *Ventures in Worship,* lectionary supplements, *Oxford Book of Prayer,* etc.); and materials from nonreligious literature, music and dance.   RSl

Wung Tien-Min and Chuang Chang. *Wung* (b. Oct. 8, 1905), the son of *Wung* Yi and *Wung* Chen Mo, was born in Changhua, Taiwan. His father died when he was 12 years old. Although he was the best student in the class, he could not continue with his high school education but left home to work on a farm to support the family. He was married on Nov. 19, 1925, to *Chuang* Chang. To them were born 12 children—six sons and six daughters.

At the age of 27 Wung opened a mill for husking rice and the economic situation of the family improved. With the outbreak of World War II, the Japanese government did not permit anyone to own a private mill. He gave up the mill and became a civil servant while at the same time farming two acres (one hectare) of rice.

At age 24 he turned from worshiping idols to worship God. The Japanese tried to force Christians to worship the emperor, but Wung and Chuang refused. He and his family were insulted and abused by neighbors as well as relatives. Inspired by Dr. John Soong's life and testimony, Wung witnessed to his relatives and some of them became Christians.

In the 1950s the Presbyterian church in Taiwan needed more pastors and Wung answered the call from God. Three years later he was asked by the Mennonite Central Committee (MCC) workers to assist them. (MCC came to Taiwan in 1948.) After working with them for a short time, he opened his house to begin worship services. The Hsi-tun Mennonite Church, located in Taichung, Taiwan, had its beginning in the Wung's home.

During his 17 years in the pastoral ministry, Wung has served four Mennonite churches. His most significant experience was to see many people converted to the Lord from the worship of idols and also to see four of his sons enter the pastoral ministry. His most traumatic experience was to see some church members leave the Lord and go back to idol worship. He believes more Menonite youth should be encouraged to enter seminary to prepare themselves for the gospel ministry. His wisdom and counsel have been much appreciated by the younger pastors.   PK

Y

Yaguchi Yorifumi (b. Nov. 1, 1935), professor, poet, and Japanese Mennonite leader was born in Miyagi Prefecture. As a churchman, he is leader of the Sapporo Shalom house church, a member of the Hokkaido Conference Peace Committee (Nihon Menonaito Kirisuto Kyokai Kyogikai), and secretary of the Asia Mennonite Conference. He aims to build a vital small-scale church, in which every member takes a positive role in its activities, and whose vocation is to offer the biblical alternative of shalom and °justice to contemporary society.

As a poet, he has published eight books and has translated several others, including a collection of Ralph °Buckwalter's poems. His °poetry reflects a strong biblical motif, especially that of the prophets. As a scholar, he teaches literature and Bible at Hokusei Gakuen College in Sapporo. He holds degrees from Tohoku-Gakuin University, International Christian University, and Goshen Biblical Seminary (1962-65). He was a visiting scholar at the State University of New York in Buffalo in 1977. He has written numerous articles on poetry and Anabaptism. He is married to Mitsuko *Mori*; they have two sons.　　　　　　　　　　　　　　　　　　　KK

Yorifumi Yaguchi, *How To Eat Loaches* (Dumaguete City, Philippines: n.p., 1984); Jean Janzen, David Waltner-Toews, Yorifumi Yaguchi, *Three Mennonite Poets* (Intercourse, Pa.: Good Books, 1986); *MWR* (Aug. 6, 1987), 12.

Yake, Clayton Franklin (Nov. 25, 1889-May 22, 1974). Clayton F. Yake was born near Lititz, Pa., in 1920 and died at Mt. Pleasant, Pa. After a brief career in educational work, he came to Mennonite Publishing House (MC) at Scottdale, Pa., to serve as founding editor of *Youth's Christian Companion*, a weekly publication for Mennonite young people. He continued as editor until his retirement in 1954.

In addition, he edited and wrote Sunday school lessons for children, and, after his retirement, for adults. He was editor of Mennonite Summer Bible School materials appearing in 1928 and 1934. He also edited a comprehensive series of summer Bible school materials, first published in 1948. His superintendent's manual for the last-mentioned series served as the thesis for his master's degree in Christian education, received from Winona Lake School of Theology in 1956.

He was a member of the Mennonite Board of Education (MC) from 1935 to 1953 and was involved in a wide variety of activities for young people. He was a charter member and first secretary of what has become Laurelville Mennonite Church Center, Mt. Pleasant, Pa. He was superintendent of East Scottdale Sunday School, 1922-39.

In 1918 he married Martha Eby. She died Jan. 1, 1988. There are six living children.　　　　　　DH

Who's Who Mennonites (1943), 281; *Menn. Bib. II,* p. 522; Kenneth Reed in *GH* (Dec. 28, 1976), 984.

Yamada Takashi (b. Mar. 29, 1926), a leader and pioneer in both church and research work for Japan Mennonites, was born in Kobe. Educated and trained at Kobe Commercial High School and Japan's Navy school, he served in World War II. He was baptized in the "unofficial" Kobe congregation (see °mission: "A Young Church Leads the Way" feature) in 1952 and was ordained a pastor in 1959. The same year he married Yoshiko *Oiwani*. They have five children.

In 1956 he became pastor of the Aburatsu Church in Nichinan, °Miyazaki Prefecture, and in 1959 moved to the Kobayashi church, where he was still serving as leader of the larger Kirishima Christian Brotherhood in 1986. He has been chairman of the Nihon Menonaito Kirisuto Kyokai Kaigi (Japan Mennonite Christian Church Conference, GCM), vice-chairman of Asia Mennonite Conference and Mennonite World Conference, and helped organize the Nihon Menonaito Senkyokai (Japan Mennonite Fellowship).

In 1969 he lectured at the Associated Mennonite Biblical Seminaries, where he was the first Theological Center guest. He has done extensive research on evangelism and Anabaptism. One theme emerging from that research is the need for critical reflection on how western churches have conducted mission work in the Asian situation, just as Anabaptism was a critique of Christianity in 16th c. Europe.　　HKaw

Neil Braun, Paul W. Boschman, Takashi Yamada, *Experiments in Church Growth: Japan* (Tokyo: New Life League, 1968), 72-110; Takashi Yamada, "Integrating Critique and Formation," *Mennonite* (Jan. 13, 1981), 17-20.

Yamaguchi Prefecture, Honshu, Japan, is located at the western tip of Honshu Island, Japan. To the north is the Sea of Japan, and to the south, the Inland Sea. A bridge and tunnel connect Shimonoseki City with the island of Kyushu. The size of the prefecture is 6,095 sq. km. (2,353 sq. mi.). The average low temperature in January is about 3 degrees C. (38 degrees F.); the average high in August, 30 degrees C. (86 degrees F.). Annual precipitation is approximately 1,700 mm (67 in.). Population is 1,587,000 (1980). The capital is Yamaguchi City. An industrial area extends along the Inland Sea, and a rural area along the Japan Sea, with rice and citrus as major crops. Hagi pottery is famous, and there are many tourist attractions such as the coasts, caves, and hot springs. The Korean peninsula lies only about 150 km (95 mi.) away.

In 1953, the first Brethren in Christ congregation was founded in Hagi City. In 1986 there is also a congregation in Nagato City, and two in Shimono-seki. These congregations were all started by or together with a missionary, but are now guided by self-supporting Japanese lay leaders. The Yamaguchi Prefectural Brethren in Christ Church Conference was organized in 1971.   MOk

"Yamaguchi Prefecture" in *Kodansha Encyclopedia of Japan,* vol. 8, (Tokyo: Kodansha, 1983), 295; *MWH* (1978), 161-63.

See also Nihon Kirisutokyo Keiteidan (Japan Brethren in Christ Church).

Yanada Hiroshi (b. Dec. 23, 1934), one of the first leaders of the Nihon Menonaito Kirisutokyo Kyokai Kaigi (Japan Mennonite Christian Church Conference, GCM), was born in Tokyo. His father, an engineer, influenced his entering Kobe Institute of Technology. But his baptism on Oct. 5, 1952, in the "unofficial" Kobe congregation (°mission: "A Young Church Leads the Way" feature) prompted a change. He attended Japan Christian College (1956-60), then went to the °Miyazaki area to work with literature. In 1960 he married Takako *Ushijima.* Their two daughters later attended Bethel College, North Newton, Ks., and both married American Mennonites.

The family moved to Miyakonojo in 1961, continuing with the Literature Committee work and pastoring the Namiki congregation there. In 1962 he became pastor of the Aburatsu congregation in Nichinan, and, in 1964, of the Oyodo congregation in Miyazaki, where he was serving in 1986. In 1975-76 he studied at Associated Mennonite Biblical Seminaries, Elkhart, Ind.

He is widely known and respected as a pastor, interpreter, translator, and leader. Some of the posts he has held are: chairman of the Japan Mennonite Christian Church Conference, executive committee member of the Mennonite World Conference, and chairman of the Asia Mennonite Conference (1984-86). His translation work includes the article "The Anabaptist Vision," by H. S. Bender, and the book *Evangelicalism and Anabaptism,* C. Norman Kraus (Scottdale, 1979).   AD

Yearbooks and Directories (ME IV:1002). The present article seeks to describe changes which have occurred since 1959. Titles that have begun or ceased publication are included. The general purpose and use of yearbooks remain much the same. However, attention should be called to a few developments over the past 30 years.

The general classification of directory material published by various bodies remains much the same. No official body publishes almanac information along with directory material. Privately published almanacs do contain directory material; e.g., *Der Neue Amerikanische Calendar* by Raber and its English equivalent. This almanac in revised form was first issued in 1970 and contains Old Order Amish ministerial and congregational directory. (A large number of unofficial local Amish directories have begun to appear [°Amish].) European Mennonite yearbooks continue to include literary material such as biographical and historical articles.

The titles of these publications have not changed and include words such as "yearbook," "handbook," "directory," or "report." The name depends usually on the content and purpose of the publication. The frequency of publication varies depending upon the publication policy of the respective body. Some have changed from annual to biennial; e.g., since 1986 the *Mennonite Yearbook* (MC), even though still containing the word "yearbook" in its title. When minutes of proceedings are included the frequency depends upon the general meetings of the body, whether annual, biennial, or triennial. Frequency also is determined in some instances on the cost of collecting, compiling, editing, and publishing the directory.

The purpose and use of these publications remain much the same in that they provide useful information for members, lay leaders, ministers, and personnel in organizations and institutions.

The most important change in these publications is the greatly increased amount of information published. Several reasons for this trend are: (1) the growth in the membership, organizations, and activities of the various Mennonite groups; (2) the inclusion of both current and historical statistical material having to do with membership, finances, and enrollments in Christian education agencies; (3) the reporting of information on the °inter-Mennonite organizations, such as Mennonite Central Committee, Mennonite Mutual Aid and others; (4) and the inclusion of information on bodies and organizations not aligned with the official body but closely affiliated wih it, such as closely affiliated conferences, Christian day schools, campgrounds, publications, and similar material. Examples of this expanded coverage can be found in *Handbook of Information* (GCM) and especially in *Mennonite Yearbook* (MC).

Three general organizational groupings may be listed as issuing yearbooks and directories: (1) Some congregations issue directories or yearbooks, in some instances containing pictures of members; these directories list ministerial staff, organizations, membership, and activities of the congregation. (2) District and regional conferences, mission boards, and education, publication, and inter-Mennonite agencies also publish directories. (3) Some Mennonite churches in India, Africa, South America, Central America, Japan, and elsewhere, publish booklets containing conference proceedings with or without directory material. (4) Most Mennonite and Brethren in Christ conferences in North America and Europe publish yearbooks or directories. This article is concerned with the fourth group.

Directory publications that were not listed in ME IV or which have been changed or newly established include the following: *Minutes of the General Conference* (BIC, 1871-); *Proceedings of Mennonite World Conference* (issued for the eleven assemblies held since 1925); *Mennonite World Handbook* (issued first in 1978 with supplement 1984; projected new edition in 1990; annual updating of some data in MWC *Courier*); *EMC Yearbook* (EMCon); *Mennonitischer Gemeinde-Kalender* (1950-70, South German Mennonite Conference); *Directory* (Eastern Pennsylvania Mennonite Church, 1970-); *Yearbook* (Conference of Mennonites in Canada, 1903-); *Year-*

book (MB General Conference). In Europe the following directories continue to be published: *Mennonitisches Jahrbuch*, containing information about German-speaking Mennonites in Germany, Switzerland, France, Austria, and Latin America; *Doopsgezind Jaarboekje* (The Netherlands). French Mennonites publish an annual directory as part of their °periodical, *Christ Seul* (Christ Only). EDZ

MWH (1978), (1984) lists official yearbooks for various Mennonite groups.

See also Publishing.

Yemen Arab Republic, located on the southern Red Sea coast of the Arabian Peninsula, had a population of 6,159,000 in 1985. The population is 100 percent Muslim, 50 percent Sunni and 50 percent Shiite. A relatively poor country, three-fourths of the labor force is employed in agriculture. The literacy rate is 20 percent; life expectancy is 42.7 years for men and 44.8 for women. Population growth is 2.6 percent per year. The government maintains a highly restrictive policy with regard to Christian ministry. Since 1981 one Mennonite has taught in a school for children of the international community and is an Overseas Mission Associate with the Mennonite Board of Missions (MC). WRS

Yoder, David A. See Bishop ("My Good Bishop" [feature]).

Yoder, Phoebe Ethel (Jan. 26, 1903-Sept. 9, 1981), served as an administrator, nurse, and educator in Tanganyika (Tanzania) under the Eastern Mennonite Board of Missions and Charities (MC) for 35 years. She was born in McPherson County, Ks., to C. D. and Susanna (Heatwole) Yoder and died at Schowalter Villa in Hesston, Ks. At age 12 Phoebe felt God's call to Africa. She attended Hesston College and Goshen College (BA 1934 and ThB). In 1937 she received her RN from the La Junta [Col.] Mennonite School of Nursing and went to Tanganyika, where she set up a nursing station in a garage, started schools, supervised the construction of 10 school buildings, taught, served as a nurse-doctor, and assisted in translating the New Testament into Jita and Swahili. ESR

David W. Shenk, *Mennonite Safari* (Scottdale, 1974), 19-21; Carol Duerksen in Hesston College *Alumni News* (Feb., 1974); Rich, *Mennonite Women* (1983), 140-42.

Yoder, Sanford Calvin (1879-1975), was born to Christian S. and Anna Swartzendruber Yoder, near Iowa City, Iowa. In 1903 he married Emma Stutzman from the same community. Their three children were Myron, Marguerite, and LaVerne.

Yoder graduated from the Clarion, Iowa, high school (1901) and Hamilton College of Law (LLB, 1926), U. of Iowa (BA, 1927), Winona Lake School of Theology (MA, 1933), Northern Baptist Seminary (BD, 1934; DD, 1937), and Gordon College Divinity School (STD, 1939). He taught in the public schools of Iowa and Washington. In Washington he was also a rancher.

Yoder was ordained to the ministry in the Mennonite Church (MC) at Chappell, Nebr., in 1911.

When he returned with his family to Kalona, Iowa, in 1913, he was ordained bishop at the East Union congregation. His most significant work was as secretary of the Mennonite Board of Missions (MC), 1921-44, and as president of Goshen College, Goshen, Ind. (1923-40). His statesmanship and leadership served as a reconciling influence in the Mennonite Church (MC) during the troubled decade of the 1920s and the years following. WHS

Sanford C. Yoder, *The Days of My Years* (Scottdale, 1959); J. S. Umble, *Goshen College, 1894-1954* (Goshen College, Goshen, Ind., 1955); J. Lawrence Burkholder, ed., *An Evening to Honor Sanford Calvin Yoder* (Goshen College, Goshen, Ind., 1974); *Goshen College Bulletin* (July 1975); *Who's Who Mennonites* (1943), 287; *The National Cyclopedia of American Biography*, vol. 59 (Clifton, N.J., 1980).

Yogyakarta, an Indonesian city of 398,000, is the capital of a special region in south Central Java designated as a sultanate of Yogyakarta. This special city recalls the days in the precolonial era when Java was under the rule of a succession of independent kingdoms. As one of the two key centers of Javanese culture, Yogyakarta still exhibits much of the heritage of those ancient kingdoms. That cultural heritage contributes greatly to the creativity of the present-day cultural and artistic world of Yogyakarta, as does the memory of its role as capitol of Indonesia during the revolution.

The ecumenical Duta Wacana Theological Seminary, recently also a university, is located in Yogyakarta. The seminary has enjoyed the strong involvement of both of the Mennonite conferences of Indonesia at the student, faculty and trustee level. A congregation of the Persatuan Gereja-Gereja Kristen Muria Indonesia (the Muria Christian Church of Indonesia) has also been established in Yogyakarta. LMY

Yordy, Anna M. (Mar. 9, 1885-Jan. 1, 1975), offered dedicated continuity to the Chicago Home Mission from 1915 to 1945. Even though Mennonite Church (MC) exposure to city experience was then limited, she believed in the mission's intents and efforts. She wrote about °urban realities in church papers.

Tasks to which Anna gave energy and attention included: superintendent of the Junior Sunday School Department; two evenings a week to teach Scriptures and work with crafts; organizing the "Fresh Air" program in which 100-200 children (regular mission attendees) spent a least two summer weeks with rural Mennonite families; weekly visits in homes to look up absentees, solicit new people, win parent trust; assisting with the annual Christmas dinner (begun in 1896) which seated 160 at a time until all were fed; teaching Bible school; distributing clothing sent by Mennonite church women; leading a women's or girls' group attending sewing school; treating 100 patients a year, having earned chiropractic degrees in 1918 and 1943.

Anna's congenial spirit continued with her as a matron of Coffman Hall at Goshen College, 1945-51. DYN

Emma Oyer, *What God Hath Wrought in a Half Century at the Mennonite Home Mission* (Elkhart, Ind.: MBM, 1949); Harry F. Weber, *Centennial History of the Mennonites of Illinois, 1829-1919* (Goshen: Mennonite Historical Society,

1931), 275-91; Anna Yordy, "Mennonite Home Mission," *GH* (Aug. 7, 1930), 427-28; idem, a number of articles between 1930 and 1940 in *Missionary Sewing Circle Letter.*

York and Adams Counties, Pa., Conservative Mennonite Churches of. See Conservative Mennonite Churches of York and Adams Counties, Pa.

"Yorkers." See Old Order River Brethren.

Young, Sarah Alice Troyer (Apr. 3, 1871-July 16, 1900), was one of the first Mennonite women to go overseas as a foreign missionary. She went to China in 1896 under the auspices of the China Inland Mission and served there for four and a half years until she was killed during the Boxer Rebellion. Sarah ("Sade") was born in Clinton Twp., Elkhart Co., Ind., the eighth of eleven children of John D. and Cathrine (Egli) Troyer. In her late teens the family moved to Milford, Nebr. Sarah left for China in January 1896 and worked in Shanxi [Shansi] province in northern China. On April 1, 1899 she married John Young, a Scottish missionary. They were killed July 16, 1900, and their bodies were thrown into the Yellow River. A memorial stone was erected in her memory in 1901 in Kih-Cheo, China. She was a sister of D. J. Troyer, attorney, Goshen, Ind.   EmSR

MHB, 44, no. 1 (Jan. 1984), 1-5; Marshall Bromhall, ed., *Martyred Missionaries of China Inland Mission* (Toronto, 1901); Rich, *Mennonite Women* (1983), 129.

Youth Homes (ME IV:86) are organized as members of the Mennonite Child Care Association (MCCA), a program entity of Mennonite Health Association. The Mennonite Health Association aims to promote an integrating philosophy of health care within the church, in that church-sponsored health care programs both demonstrate and proclaim the wholeness of the healing Christ.

Agencies affiliated with the Mennonite Child Care Association seek to provide a range of services to troubled children and their families. Services range from counseling to residential treatment. Residential services provide group settings in which children can live and work on the problems that caused them to be separated from their families. Day treatment, foster care, independent living for older youth, and group homes are also offered.

The management board of a Mennonite-related youth home usually is made up of local church and community people in the service area. Support for the programs comes from service payments, government grants, and private contributions from both within and beyond the service area.

Members or eligible for membership of the MCCA are: Zenith Camp of the Ozarks, Ozark, Ark.; Salem Children's Home, Flanagan, Ill.; Argentine Youth Services, Kansas City, Ks.; Edgewood Children's Center, Webster Groves, Mo.; Grace Children's Home, Henderson, Nebr.; The Adriel School, West Liberty, Ohio; Craigwood Youth Services, Ailsa Craig, Ont.; Nairn Family Homes, Ailsa Craig, Ont.; Red Lake Children's Homes, Red Lake, Ont.; The Lighthouse Youth Center, Inc., Marion, Pa.; and Millersville Youth Village, Millersville, Pa.   JMB

MC Yearbook (1988-89), 125-26.

See also Disabilities; Indian Ministries, North America.

Yugoslavia, "Land of the South Slavs," became a monarchy in 1918, but fell to foreign invasion in World War II. Josip Broz Tito led Partisan resistance, then broke with the Soviet bloc in 1948 to pursue policies of nonalignment and worker self-management. Large religious groups (Eastern Orthodox, Catholic, Islamic) lost former privileges, but eventually benefited from the society's increasing openness and improved personal liberties. Traditional religion reinforced ethnic separatism; only the Protestant minority (less than one percent) bridges among numerous ethnic groups. Mennonite involvement began with earthquake relief in Skopje, Macedonia (1963), and contacts with the indigenous °Nazarene movement. In the 1970s Eastern Mennonite Board of Missions and Charities (MC) and later Mennonite Central Committee began supporting volunteers for university studies and fraternal relations with other Protestants in the free-church tradition, notably in cooperation with the Biblical Theological Institute of Zagreb (1987-).   NGS

Trevor Beeson, *Discretion and Valour: Religious Conditions in Russia and Eastern Europe,* 2nd ed. (London and Philadelphia: Fount Paperbacks, and Fortress Press, 1982), 288-321; Stella Alexander, *Church and State in Yugoslavia since 1945* (Cambridge: Cambridge U. Press, 1979); N. Gerald Shenk, "How Should Christians Respond to Communism?" in *What about the Russians? A Christian Approach to US-Soviet Conflict,* ed. Dale W. Brown (Elgin, Ill.: The Brethren Press, 1984); idem, "Social Expectations of Christians in a Marxist State," *MQR,* 55 (1981), 231-39; Paul Mojzes, *Christian-Marxist Dialogue in Eastern Europe* (Minneapolis: Augsburg, 1981), 128-58; Vekoslav Grmič, "Socialism as it Actually Exists in the Light of Christian Theology," *Concilium,* 154 (1982), 64-69; "Church and Religion in the Self-Managing Society," *Socialist Thought and Practice,* 23 (1983), 60-127.

Z

Zacatecas Colonies, Mexico (La Batea, La Honda, Campeche).

La Batea Colony originated in the early 1960s when a group of 75 Old Colony settlers from the Nuevo Ideál colony, Durango State, together with 5 from the Chihuahua colonies under the leadership of Diedrich Braun, was able to buy 3,000 hectares (7,400 acres) of land at $72 (US) per hectare in Zacatecas State, 90 km. (55 mi.) nw. of Fresnillo. After the transactions were made the Durango colony approved of the move and promised moral support, since land shortage had become acute. Later more land was bought, bringing the total to 4,685 hectares (11,500 acres). With an altitude of ca. 2,600 m. (8,500 ft.) above sea level, from 300 to 600 m. higher than colonies in Durango State or Chihuahua State (°Manitoba Colony), but farther south, the physical conditions of soil and climate are similar to those of the mother colonies, therefore agricultural practices remained much the same. Oats, beans, barley, and wheat mature well. Cheese is being produced.

Only three families began the settlement in 1961 but by 1962 there were 518 inhabitants. By 1986 the population stood at 1,786, of these 352 were baptized members. The colony has four schools where four teachers instruct. About half of the membership attends worship services in the one meeting-house of the colony on Sunday mornings. Both Low and High German languages are used in worship services. Only High German is taught in the schools. Some 113 persons left for a new colony in Campeche State in 1986.

La Honda Colony began in 1964 when the Nuevo Ideál Colony bought another tract of land, 17,000 hectares (42,000 acres), in Zacatecas, at only $16 (US) per hectare. An additional 4,000 hectares (9,880 acres) were bought and given to the landless Mexican population as a gesture of kindness. The La Honda hacienda complex was bought complete with buildings that had housed owner and workers. These served as temporary shelter while the land for 11 villages was surveyed and farmsteads were laid out. Here, as in La Batea, climate and soil conditions at an altitude of 2,300 m. (7,545 ft.) are similar to those in Durango. Corn, beans, and oats seem to be the better crops; wheat and barley mature. Fruit for home use, such as peaches, pears, and plums can be raised since all farmsteads have sufficient water. The settlement began with 176 landless families from Durango. J. K. Guenther and David Wall provided leadership. By 1986 total population numbered 4,063, of which 1,452 were baptized members. The colony has 18 schools with as many teachers, and 4 meetinghouses where Sunday morning worship ser-

vices are conducted. Both Low and High German are used. High German only is taught in the schools.

In 1987 the La Honda colony began a settlement in *Campeche* State. Both the La Batea and La Honda settlements have had problems with the "agraristas," landless Mexican farmers who may claim untitled, uncultivated land anywhere in the Republic. This has led Mennonites to procure proper documentation of landholdings and to be willing to help poorer nationals. HEns

Zaire, The Republic of (ME I:269, 690), known as the Congo Free State (1885-1908), Belgian Congo (1908-60), and as the Democratic Republic of the Congo (1960-71) has been an area of major Mennonite interest and ministry in the 20th c.

The Congo inland Mission (CIM), known since 1971 as the Africa Inter-Mennonite Mission (AIMM), placed its first missionaries in the West Kasai region of south central Congo in 1912.

Already in 1913, Aaron A. and Ernestina °Janzen, a Mennonite Brethren couple from Mountain Lake, Minn., applied for service with the CIM and served until 1920. Upon returning to the Congo, they opened an independent work at Kafumba, a location south of °Kikwit along the Kwilu River in an un-evangelized area later known as Bandundu Province. Following World War II, some small faith missions of that region were no longer able to keep pace with the changes and demands of work of the post-war era and appealed to other missions to assume responsibility for the ministries they had launched. It was at this juncture that the Mennonite Brethren Board of Missions and Services (BOMAS) decided to assume responsibility for the Kafumba work pioneered by the Janzens, and at the same time, to broaden their ministry to cover some of the areas which were being relinquished by other missions. From its administrative base at Kikwit, the BOMAS ministry was eventually extended to incorporate mission posts at Matende, Kipungu, Lusemvu, Kajiji, and Panzi, all of which were located in the southern part of Kwilu Province.

CIM ministry began at a place called Djoko Punda (known during the Belgian era as Charlesville). Located at the farthest navigable point inland on the Kasai River, among a mix of Lulua and Baluba people, it quickly became the post of supply for the new CIM work as well as its first point of evangelism. A primary school was early established; it was quickly followed by the mission's first Bible school. A second CIM mission post was also immediately established several days trek south of Djoko near a village called Kalamba. This location was deliberately selected since it was adjacent to the home village of the king of the Lulua people.

In 1946 the decision was made to move the station some 11 mi. (18 km.) to the nw. where it was renamed Mutena. This post remains an important center of the Église du Christ au Zaire, Communauté Mennonite au Zaire (CMZA; Zaire Mennonite Church).

With the end of World War I and the arrival of new missionaries, high priority was given to a ministry among the Baphende people to the south and west of Djoko. A hardy, industrious, and agrarian people, they had no resident witness to the gospel among them. After some exploratory evangelistic trips made by missionaries and national Christians, a site was chosen near Nyanga village some 100 mi. (160 km.) southwest of Djoko. By 1920 the first new missionaries took up residence at this third post. Following the pattern established at the previous two stations, primary education and the dispensing of basic medications soon became part of the ministry along with Bible instruction and apprenticeship in evangelism for new converts.

Since the majority of the Baphende people lived to the west of the Loange River in neighboring Kwilu Province (later known as Bandundu Province), plans were early laid to situate a fourth post somewhere in the tribal area west of the river. By 1923 further missionary personnel arrived and the first team was placed adjacent to a large village called Mukedi, the location of an influential paramount chief of the area. Thus by the late 1920s the CIM work was based at four stations in two provinces.

A notable feature of the broader Zaire mission scene by this time was the emergence of a strong and influential inter-mission organization known as the Congo Protestant Council (CPC). A large country with a great variety of ethnic groups, Congo early attracted a growing number of Protestant missions. This mission community eventually reached a total of some 55 different organizations sponsored by a mix of European and North American Protestant church groups. Of whatever origin or theological stance, all quickly encountered the aggressive and combative personnel of the Roman Catholic missions. The Protestant missions, of whatever origin or persuasion, early discovered that there was much to be gained by closing ranks and in dealing with the government and the favored Roman Catholic Church from a stance of solidarity.

A CPC office was soon established in the capital of the Belgian Congo, Leopoldville (known as °Kinshasa after political independence), as annual consultative assemblies became traditional. CIM and the Mennonite Brethren Mission early joined this council and participated actively in meetings and special commissions.

World War II brought with it several far-reaching changes for mission work in Zaire. The colonial administrators had recruited Congolese troops who were sent to fight in North Africa. As these troops were eventually brought back home and discharged, they returned to their home villages with greatly broadened understandings and aspirations. Some even dared to express the opinion that the Belgian colonial rule under which they lived was not something to be simply accepted forever.

In Belgium also there was dramatic postwar change. Angered by what they considered to have been collaboration on the part of King Leopold III with the German occupation forces during the war, the Belgians not only insisted that he yield his throne to his son but on the occasion of the first elections they repudiated the Catholic party which had long dominated the Belgian political scene replacing it with a new coalition government made up of Socialists and Liberals. Among the changes which the new administration introduced was the offer to Protestant missions in the Congo of government subsidies for medical and educational work which met government standards. After some debate, the great majority of the Protestant missions in Congo opted to apply for these funds. There promptly followed a major expansion of Protestant educational and medical work across the land, an expansion in which the CIM and BOMAS fully shared. Not only was this a time of new financial resources from a new and sympathetic colonial regime, but it was also the time of a surge of new missionary recruits. In the West Kasai, CIM had already pinpointed areas where its ministry was still inadequate. Some 75 mi. (120 km) nw. of Djoko was a large ethnic group known as the Bashilele. Until the late 1940s, CIM's ministry among them had been largely limited to regional school centers and periodic evangelistic trips. With much encouragement from the Congolese believers of the area, the decision was made in 1950 to establish a fifth station at a place called Banga.

At the same time, there was growing concern for a rapidly expanding diamond mining center called °Tshikapa that was located along the Kasai River between Djoko and Mutena. Already the site of a large Catholic mission, CIM efforts to minister to the steadily growing number of Mennonite Christians living in work camps at Tshikapa consistently encountered frustrating limitations. Parallel requests to secure a plot of ground in the vicinity were also denied. Finally, in 1950, through the intervention of the CPC secretary in Kinshasa, government permission to occupy a hillside five miles across the river from the diamond center was granted. Taking its name from an adjacent village, the sixth CIM station was called Kalonda.

To the west in Bandundu Province, where a cluster of small faith missions were having difficulty coping with the new postwar era, opportunity also came to the CIM to acquire two new mission posts. Near the Angolan border in Kahemba territory was Kamayala, a mission post established under the auspices of the Unevangelized Tribes Mission in 1930 by two extraordinary sisters, Bertha and Mary Miller. This mission, like others, also made an appeal to other organizations to assume responsibility for ongoing ministry. The CIM responded in 1952, thus beginning its first ministry among Chokwe and Lunda people.

Between Kamayala and Mukedi was Kandala, a station which had been started in 1926 by a pioneering Canadian Baptist couple, Percy and Rosalie Near, and was also situated among the Baphende people. The Nears approached CIM about assuming leadership for the work. Terms were agreed upon and the first CIM personnel arrived on the station in 1954.

ZAIRE-ANGOLA

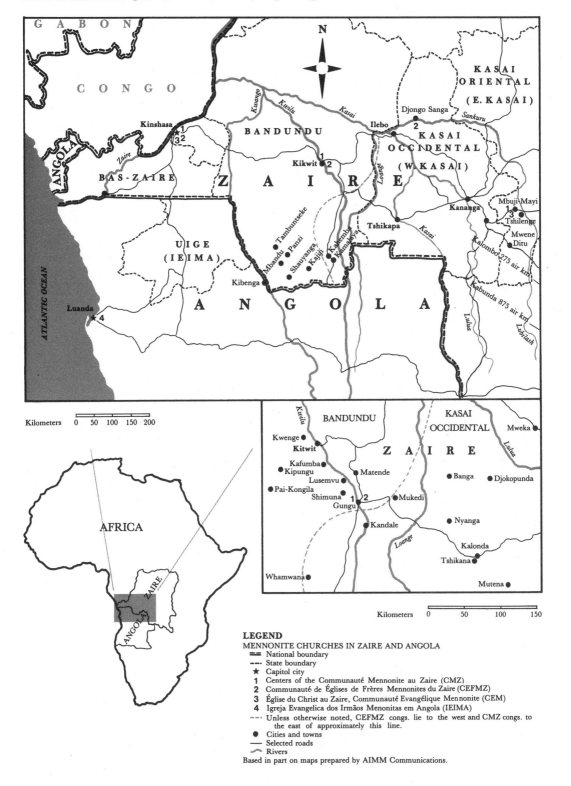

AFRICA

Kilometers   0   50   100   150

LEGEND
MENNONITE CHURCHES IN ZAIRE AND ANGOLA
≡≡ National boundary
--- State boundary
★ Capitol city
1 Centers of the Communauté Mennonite au Zaire (CMZ)
2 Communauté de Églises de Frères Mennonites du Zaire (CEFMZ)
3 Église du Christ au Zaire, Communauté Evangélique Mennonite (CEM)
4 Igreja Evangelica dos Irmãos Menonitas em Angola (IEIMA)
--- Unless otherwise noted, CEFMZ congs. lie to the west and CMZ congs. to the east of approximately this line.
● Cities and towns
— Selected roads
〰 Rivers
Based in part on maps prepared by AIMM Communications.

CIM and Mennonite Brethren (MB) areas lay side-by-side in Congo and eventually gave rise to three autonomous Mennonite churches. All are part of the national Zairian church, the Église du Christ au Zaire (ECZ). Stemming from the work of the CIM were the ECZ: Communauté Mennonite (CMZA) and ECZ: Communauté Evangélique Mennonite (CEM). The church which grew out of the work of the Mennonite Brethren came to be known as ECZ: Communauté des Frères Mennonites (CFMZA).

CIM and MB missionaries were partners in several cooperative ventures across the years, notably in a four-year teacher training school at Nyanga in the early 1950s; a missionary children's school at Kajiji, 1954-60; and a pastoral training school, also at Kajiji, 1963-68. Both Mennonite missions were founding partners of the Theological Institute of Kinshasa (Institut Supérieur Théologique de Kinshasa; ISTK), a venture in which 10 other mission groups originally shared. Both CIM and BOMAS have provided teaching staff for this school since it opened. All three Mennonite churches send pastoral candidates there for training.

Mennonite Central Committee (MCC) first became involved in Congo in the 1950s, when a few North American °conscientious objectors were sent as °alternative service volunteers. In the aftermath of political independence (1960), MCC teamed with the Congo Protestant Council to form the Congo Protestant Relief Association (CPRA), which became a channel for relief supplies for various areas where local populations were displaced by political unrest. Known as ZPRA, this cooperative project with Zaire mission and church communities continues.

It was also in the 1960s that Zaire became one of the areas selected by MCC administrators for service for °°Pax and Teachers Abroad Program (TAP) personnel. During that decade a steady stream of young people came to Zaire, where they served in a wide variety of roles with Mennonite and other missons. MCC eventually moved beyond construction sites and schoolrooms to cooperative efforts with Zaire Mennonite churches in various rural °development projects.

In more recent years, MCC has collaborated with the three Zaire churches in helping to sponsor seminars for pastors on a variety of topics including issues of peace, justice, and development. French-speaking Mennonites from Europe and North America have been resource people for these much appreciated sessions.

The three Mennonite churches in Zaire are situated in a land of great potential, and they are confronted by formidable problems. Economic inflation and devaluation of national currency have been steady since the 1970s; dishonesty and graft have surfaced at many levels of public life. All of this exerts tremendous pressure upon the Christian community of the country. In the midst of grievous social and economic problems, however, it is heartening to note that wherever pockets of stability and integrity are found, invariably they are church-related. Both in terms of political development and church growth on the continent of Africa, more will be heard from Zaire and its Mennonite churches in coming years. JEB

Juhnke, *Mission* (1979); *MWH* (1978), 104-16; *MWH* (1984), 19-21; John B. Toews, *The Mennonite Brethren Church in Zaire* (Fresno: Board of Christian Literature, 1978); Levi Keidel, *Caught in the Crossfire* (Scottdale, 1979).

See also Angola.

Ngongo David's Strong Heart

We learned to pray more than ever before when independence came to the Congo in 1960. Suddenly the Belgian government was gone and there was much confusion. There were many leaders and no unity. Then the revolution came. All the white men were in danger of being killed, as well as many of us. We told the missionaries to leave. One morning they gave me the keys to all the buildings at Nyanga station, including their own houses, and fled across the border into Angola. We were thankful they were not killed as many others were. We prayed much for them.

When the missionaries went, they left their hunting guns here. I took them to the attic of the big house, together with all the ammunition, and hid them. When fighting started, the village people came and asked for the guns of the missionaries. I said, "No, they are not yours. Besides, you want to use them to kill people, but the Bible says that is a great sin."

Then they brought a man to me who was dying because his arm had been cut off by the enemy. They said, "Give us the guns or we will chop your arm off, too."

I said, "No. You can kill me if you wish, but I will not give you the guns to kill other people."

They left and said they would come back in the morning to kill me.

My friends told me to give the guns to the people. When night came I hid. I prayed all night. I sang my favorite song softly to myself over and over as part of my prayer for help: "What a friend we have in Jesus. . . ." I knew I was doing the will of God. He gave me peace and courage. He helped me. The men did not return in the morning. My friends said, "Ngongo David has a strong heart." It was an answer to prayer.

Those were hard days. The missionaries were gone and I was responsible for everything—the school, the church services, visiting the sick, and also caring for the mission property. The rebels came to steal and kill. We never knew when they might kill us, too. Refugees came asking for help. Many people said we were spies and traitors because we were Christians. The members of our churches were scattered all over what was then called the Congo. Those were hard times.

But in all this God heard my prayers. We learned to trust him more. When the missionaries returned, they said we had grown strong and free in spirit. They said they would no longer be our leaders in the mission; we should lead and they would help us as we had earlier helped them. We agreed because we knew we needed each other and loved each other. CJD

Adapted from a story in Cornelius J. Dyck, *Twelve Becoming,* copyright by Faith and Life Press, Newton, Ks., 1973, pp. 89-95. Used by permission.

ZAMBIA

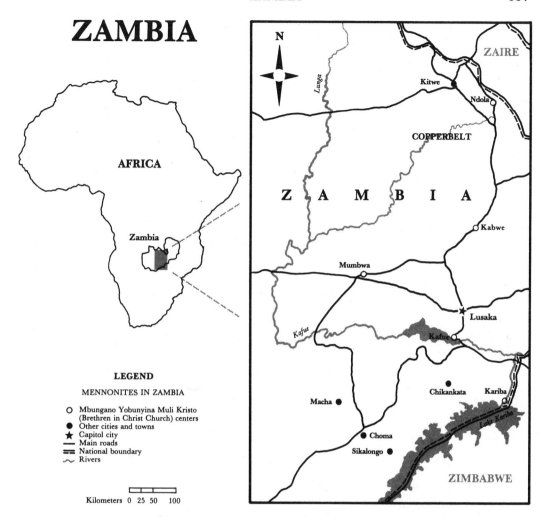

AFRICA

Zambia

LEGEND

MENNONITES IN ZAMBIA

- ○ Mbungano Yobunyina Muli Kristo (Brethren in Christ Church) centers
- ● Other cities and towns
- ★ Capitol city
- — Main roads
- ══ National boundary
- ∼ Rivers

Kilometers 0 25 50 100

Zambia. Before its independence the central African nation of Zambia, known as Northern Rhodesia, was part of the Federation of Rhodesia and Nyasaland (which included also what became Zimbabwe and Malawi). Mennonite work beyond that of the Mbungano Yabunyina Muli Kristo (Brethren in Christ Church) began in Northern Rhodesia in 1962. In the middle of that year two Mennonite Central Committee (MCC) Teachers Abroad Program (TAP) workers were assigned, under the direction of the bishop of the Brethren in Christ Church in Africa. Both teachers were placed near the capital city of Lusaka at Chipembi Secondary School, one of seven secondary schools operating in northern Rhodesia at that time.

In October 1964 Zambia received its independence from Great Britain, and the ensuing emphasis on national development included a strong push for more education. A favorable economic situation due in large part to high prices for copper, Zambia's chief export, made possible rapid expansion to 98 secondary schools by 1970. In response the number of personnel increased to 14 by 1966 and to 30 by 1970. These workers continued to work in church-related (including one BIC) secondary schools in central Zambia. The MCC program expanded in 1967 with the placement of two °°Pax volunteers. In the following years Pax personnel were assigned as maintenance workers at the Brethren in Christ hospital at Macha and at two other church-related farm training institutes. In 1970 two teachers were placed at David Livingstone Teacher Training College, an institution of the Christian Council of Zambia (CCZ).

After nine years of administration by Brethren in Christ field staff, MCC appointed its first full-time director for the Zambia program in 1971. While numbers of teachers remained high, assignments in locations such as the University of Zambia and the African Literature Centre (an inter-church adult education program) increased the diversity of the program. Teachers were also spread out in remote schools from one end of Zambia to the other. With close to 80 percent of teachers in Zambia still expatriates in the early 1970s, it was clear that the training of Zambian teachers was not being accomplished as quickly as hoped. Nevertheless MCC administration began to discuss ways to become involved more broadly than in formal education. While no single program direction replaced the education thrust, workers were seconded to a post-secondary agricultural institution, the YWCA, a Zambian organization promoting women's groups in urban squatter areas, and the government district nutrition office. By the end of the decade Zambia could provide most of its own teaching staff; along with that came a growing call to hire Zambians in positions formerly held by expatriates. MCC workers during this time became aware of the needs of school leavers, those who for lack of means or space were excluded from the education ladder.

During the 1970s Zambia became home to thousands of °refugees fleeing the war being fought with increasing ferocity against the white minority government of its neighbor (Southern) Rhodesia (later Zimbabwe). The conflict with colonial powers in Angola and Mozambique also affected Zambia, since all but one of its transport links to the ocean passed through these three neighboring countries. In 1979, after contacting representatives of one of the Zimbabwean liberation movements in Lusaka, MCC began providing material aid to refugees in Zambia through an arm of the CCZ. Rhodesian raids on refugee and other targets in Zambia kept the level of tension high until an agreement to end the war was signed and independence came to Zimbabwe in 1980.

Relationships between MCC and the Brethren in Christ church took on a renewed importance in the 1980s. From 1981 to 1983 a missionary couple sent to Zambia by the United Church of Christ (US) mission board were placed through MCC in a Brethren in Christ rural development and nutrition program. Later, in 1986, conversations were renewed on ways of working jointly in those areas. In 1981 the first two Zambian young people selected by the Brethren in Christ church went to North America through the MCC Visitor Exchange program, and several others have participated each year since then (°international exchanges). In 1983 the church, assisted by MCC, organized a visit by Messiah College professor Martin Schrag to spend time teaching on biblical peacemaking and reconciliation. While the end of the war in Zimbabwe had eased some tension, Zambia's role as a "frontline state" in relation to South Africa was a critical issue for many church people, who shared with all Africans a strong desire for an end to white minority rule in South Africa.

In the 1980s MCC also began working with the African Methodist Episcopal Church in education, community agriculture, women's work, and technical training. Research into the region's agricultural potential led to involvement in a government soya bean research and extension project in one district, and to the appointment in 1986 of full-time coordinators for the MCC agricultural program in both Zambia and Zimbabwe.　　　NRH

MCC Workbooks, 1961-1986, and MCC Africa administrator trip reports, 1963-1986, in MCC files, Akron, Pa; *MWH* (1978), 117-20; *MWH* (1984), 22.

Zeenwal (Sewel), Jacob. See Zinspenning, Judith.

Zentralschule (Secondary School). Despite cross references throughout ME I-IV to this topic, no article was included. Readers interested in the range of secondary schools included under this name in the Mennonite colonies in Russia should consult ME II:155-57.　　　Staff

T. D. Regehr, *For Everything a Season: A History of the Alexanderkrone Zentralschule* (CMBC, 1988).

Zigler, Michael Robert (Nov. 9, 1891-Oct. 25, 1985), peace activist, church executive, ecumenical leader. After undergraduate and graduate study, M. R. Zigler was a YMCA secretary during World War I (1917-1918). He was then called to the Church of the Brethren headquarters at Elgin, Ill., where he served in various leadership capacities until 1948. Chief among these was his direction of the Brethren Service Committee (BSC) during World War II. He led in the development of the °°Civilian Public Service program for °conscientious objectors as the chairman of the °°National Service Board for Religious Objectors, which coordinated the activities of the °historic peace churches. Zigler was one of the initiators of Church World Service, an ecumenical relief agency. In 1948 he went to Geneva as director of BSC work in Europe and as Brethren representative to the World Council of Churches, until his retirement in 1958. After returning to the United States he initiated the On Earth Peace program (1974) and sought closer relationships among several Brethren bodies, including a role as catalyst for *The Brethren Encyclopedia*. Zigler worked closely with Mennonites, especially Harold S. °Bender and Orie O. °Miller, a warm personal friend.　　　DFD

Inez G. Long, *One Man's Peace* (New Windsor, Md.: On Earth Peace Assembly, 1983), a biography; Roger E. Sappington, *Brethren Social Policy* (Elgin, Ill.: Brethren Press, 1961); D. F. Durnbaugh, ed., *To Serve the Present Age* (Elgin, 1975); Leslie Eisan, *Pathways of Peace* (Elgin, 1948); Rufus D. Bowman, *Church of the Brethren and War, 1708-1941* (Elgin, 1944); D. F. Durnbaugh in *Brethren Encyclopedia* (1983), 1398-99; *Messenger* [CBreth] (December, 1985), 12-13; *MWR* (Nov. 7, 1985), 6; Melvin Gingerich, *Service for Peace* (Akron, Pa.: Mennonite Central Committee, 1949), 50, 54ff., 62ff., 439; Paul Erb, *Orie O. Miller* (Scottdale, 1969);, 11, 222, 223; John C. Wenger and others, *Harold S. Bender* (Scottdale, 1964), 119-120.

Zijpp, Nanne van der (Apr. 2, 1900-Jan. 22, 1965), studied theology at the Amsterdam Mennonite Seminary and the U. of Amsterdam (1920-25). In 1961 he was awarded an honorary doctorate by the U. of Amsterdam. He served as pastor in Zijldijk (1926-), Joure (1928-), Almelo (1940-), and Rotterdam (1946-64). He also began lecturing in Anabaptist and Mennonite history at the Mennonite seminary in 1948, being appointed professor in 1964.

In his first congregation van der Zijpp became acquainted with Karel Vos, a Mennonite historian, who stimulated van der Zijpp's interest in Anabaptism in The Netherlands. He also developed contacts with Quakers and American Mennonites which further encouraged him in his work, particularly in nonresistance. In 1928 he published his first brochure *De vroege doopsgezinden en de krijgsdienst* (The Early Anabaptists and Military Service). After the initial volumes of Anabaptist sources were published he concentrated increasingly on his historical work, particularly on Menno Simons, about whom he read a major paper at the Mennonite World Conference in Karlsruhe in 1936.

During World War II Van der Zijpp developed a filing system which became the foundation for his future publications in Anabaptism and Mennonitism, particularly also for the four-volume *Mennonite Encyclopedia.* He wrote 480 articles, totaling nearly 10,000 inches of print, for the encyclopedia. His *Geschiedenis der Doopsgezinden in Nederland* (History of the Mennonites in the Netherlands) appeared in 1952 as the first comprehensive work of this kind. Two years later he presented a major lecture on the confessions of the Dutch Menonites. He was also instrumental in initiating the publication of *Stemmen uit de Doopsgezinde Broederschap* (Voices from the Mennonite Brotherhood; 1952-63).

Van der Zijpp was definitely not an armchair scholar. He was an excellent pastor, worked intensely with the Russian Mennonite refugees during and following World War II, gave outstanding guidance to the Mennonite youth work in The Netherlands and to the retreat center at Elspeet. Though his publications centered primarily on Anabaptist and Mennonite themes, his total interest was much broader., For example, he gave occasional lectures on philosophy at the U. of Rotterdam.   SBJZ

A list of van der Zijpp's writings is found in "Uit het werk van N. van der Zijpp 1900-1965," in *Jaarboek van de Maatschappij der Nederlandse Letterkunde te Leiden* (Amsterdam, 1968). See also *Nederlands Archief voor Kerkgeschiedenis,* 46 (1964-65), 255; *Jaarboek van de Maatschappij der Nederlandse Letterkunde te Leiden* (1965-66), 133-41; *Rotterdams Jaarboekje* (1966), 285-288; D. Nauta, ed., *Biografisch lexicon voor de geschiedenis van het Nederlandse Protestantisme* (Kampen, 1978), vol. 2, pp. 476-77; H. W. Meihuizen, "In memoriam N. van der Zijpp," *Menn. Geschbl.,* Jg. 22, n.F. 17 (1965), 5-7; Paul Schowalter, "Zum Gedächtnis an N. van der Zijpp," *Menn. Geschbl.,* Jg. 22, n.F. 17 (1965), 7-9; *Menn. Life,* 24 (1969), 174-78.

Zimbabwe is a landlocked republic in south central Africa, located on the southern African plateau and surrounded by Mozambique, Zambia, Botswana, and South Africa. It has a population of 8.5 million (1986) with a 4.4 percent annual growth rate, and it covers an area of 150,804 sq. mi. (390,582 sq. km.; making it slightly larger than Montana). Its people, basically of Bantu background, consist of 30 ethnic groups, of which the largest is the Shona people (66 percent) and second largest the Ndebele people (18 percent). Zimbabwe became independent in 1980 after 14 years of warfare by black nationalists against the white minority government. The two Anabaptist-oriented organizations that have been active in Zimbabwe are the Brethren in Christ Church (since 1898) and Mennonite Central Committee (since 1976).

The Ndebele people, a branch of the Zulu tribe, moved north in the first half of the 19th c., partly because of the intransigence of Zulu leadership, partly because of the expansion of the Dutch Boers, and partly as an expression of their expanionistic ambition. They took possession of much of what is today Zimbabwe, subduing local tribes and gaining some domination over the Shona people. They called their new homeland Amandebeleland (anglicized as Matebeleland). Subsequently, the British under Cecil Rhodes and his British South Africa Company

claimed the territory and secured it through two wars (1893-1894, and 1896), in which they defeated the Ndebele and allied forces, driving the last of the warriors into the Matopo Hills. It was in those hills that the Brethren in Christ began their missionary work in 1898.

The first Protestant missionary in the area was the famous Robert Moffat of the London Mission Society. He visited the land in 1829 and later in 1859 he and members of his family established a permanent work. It was not, however, until the activity of Cecil Rhodes that the missionary movement sharply focused its attention on what came to be called Southern Rhodesia. The early mission societies to work in the country included the Church Mission Society (1890, British), Wesleyan Methodists (1890, British), Salvation Army (1891), American Board of Commissioners for Foreign Missions (1893), Seventh Day Adventists (1895), Methodist Episcopal Church (1895, American), South Africa General Mission (1897), and the Brethren in Christ (1898).

Zimbabwe became independent as a part of the world-wide nationalistic independence movement following World War II. In 1923 the claims of the British South Africa Company were turned over to the British government and Southern Rhodesia became a self-governing British colony with a white minority government. The Federation of the Rhodesias and Nyasaland, which was formed in 1953, broke up in 1963 when majority (black) rule was established in Nyasaland (Malawi) and in Northern Rhodesia (Zambia). In 1965 Southern Rhodesia's prime minister, Ian Smith, seceded from the British Empire and declared [Southern] Rhodesia as an independent nation. The growing ferment for independence within the black majority issued in a long and intense guerrilla war waged by the black nationalistic Patriotic Front against the government. The Patriotic Front consisted of a number of political and military parties; the largest groups were Robert Mugabe's Zimbabwe African National Union (called ZANU, Shona-based) and Joshua Nkomo's Zimbabwe African People's Union (known as ZAPU; Ndebele-based). The relationship between these two groups was tenuous and fraught with tension. On April 18, 1980, independence came and Southern Rhodesia became Zimbabwe. Mugabe was elected prime minister. The result has been, rooted in pre-British Ndebele domination of the Shona people, that the Ndebele minority has not always fared so well. Although the Brethren in Christ (BIC) membership is largely Ndebele in background, the BIC has grown significantly in the last few years. Able Brethren leadership has helped the church to transcend tribal loyalties.

It was the relief needs caused by the guerrilla war that brought the Mennonite Central Committee (MCC) to Zimbabwe in 1980. The aim was to deal first with the emergency needs and then move on to resettlement and reconstruction projects. MCC worked closely and in consultation with the Brethren in Christ Church of Zimbabwe. The first emergency efforts consisted of aiding Zimbabwean refugees living in the surrounding countries of Zambia, Botswana, and Mozambique. Further activities involved providing maize and beans for needy people in Zimbabwe, such food being distributed by the Christian Care network (the service arm of the Christian Council of Zimbabwe). MCC also gave some money to Christian Care for the purchasing of seed, tools, and fertilizer, and funded the salary for a Brethren in Christ national serving on the Christian Care staff. The emergency phase of the work was coming to an end when Zimbabwe, along with much of sub-Sahara Africa, experienced drought and famine (1981-84)

In response, MCC sent a large shipment of wheat, powdered milk, vegetable oil, and beans from North America to Zimbabwe; the material was distributed by Christian Care. Subsequently, 5,000 metric tons of wheat was shipped, exchanged for maize, and passed on by the same organization. In addition, a shipment of clothing and blankets was sent and shared through the BIC and Christian Care. Sheets, towels, and blankets were provided for the Brethren in Christ hospitals. The widespread rains of 1985 resulted in a record harvest meeting the food needs of the nation, but the limited rain in southeast Zimbabwe in 1986 caused a food shortage there.

The war for independence disrupted many aspects of the Zimbabwean BIC schools, hospitals, and churches which were closed; white missionaries had to leave the country. MCC assisted the BIC by providing professional staff for the social services of the brotherhood. During 1981 and 1982, an MCC medical administrator worked with the church in reopening and staffing two hospitals. Subsequently, two MCC nurses worked in a Brethren in Christ hospital and aided in some medical clinics. One MCC volunteer worked in the area of nutrition, and a physiotherapist was placed at the National Rehabilitation Center near Harare for a short period of time. MCC also provided funding to Disabled Persons International and made a further contribution by providing teachers for Brethren in Christ schools, central for secondary schools. The projection is to continue to supply teachers as needed. MCC, through its child sponsorship program, paid the school fees for needy students (65 students were sponsored 1982-85).

Food shortages brought into focus the need for improved agriculture. Brethren in Christ farms were not adequately staffed because of the war. MCC provided one agriculturalist from 1982 to 1986. An agriculturalist, assigned to animal husbandry, began work in 1987. MCC aided the BIC in other ways: funding repair of a water dam at a church station; funds to improve water, communications, and housing at another station; funding the salary of an administrator for one year to reinstate BIC religious programming; helping in the BIC central office in Bulawayo; assisting office staff at the BIC Ekuphileni Bible Institute; and providing resource people to conduct peace seminars in BIC churches in the Bulawayo area. MCC continues to work in Zimbabwe.   LBo/MHS

David B. Barrett, ed. World Christian Encyclopedia (Oxford Press, 1982); Richard W. Hull, "Zimbabwe's Elusive Quest for Unity," Current History, 85 (May 1986), 209-12; Patrick Johnson, Operation World (W.E.C. Publications, 1986); J. Herbert Kane, A Global View of Christian Missions (Grand Rapids, Mich.: Baker Book House, 1971); Virginia Curtin

Knight, "Zimbabwe," Encyclopedia Americana, pp. 776-77; Jack Shepherd, "Zimbabwe: Poised on the Brink," Harpers (July 1987), 26-31; MWH (1978), 93-98.

See also Ibandla Labazalwane Kukristu e-Zimbabwe.

Zinspenning, Judith (ME IV:508), daughter of the Mennonite tradesman Conrad Zinspenning and Catharina de Mol, was married in 1652 to the physician Jacob Willemsz Sewel. She showed such a deep religious inclination that her father said: "It is a pity that this girl is not a boy, who then in time might become an eminent instrument in the church." Judith found the Flemish Mennonite worship dry and lifeless; the Collegiants were little better. In 1657 missionary William Ames won her to Quakerism. Here she found the lively inner "Spirit." The Sewels left the Mennonites and became ardent "instruments" of Quakerism. The Sewel home became a place for Quaker meetings. She was the first woman to lead worship services.

In 1663 she traveled to England with William Ames' successor William Caton, where she developed further intimate contacts with the Quakers. She preached and wrote several books, including Een ernstige Berispinge (An Earnest Reproof, 1660). She became a victim of a plague epidemic on her return to The Netherlands. Years later her son Willem °°Sewel published her writings in Eenige schriften en zendbrieven. . . nu tot verderen dienst gemeen gemaakt (1684). He also included a warm tribute to her in his Historie.   SBJZ/KLS

W. I. Hull, William Sewel of Amsterdam 1653-1720, the first Quaker historian of Quakerism (Swarthmore, 1934, 3-19, 212-13; C. W. Roldanus, Zeventiende-eeuwse geestesbloei, 2nd ed. (Utrecht-Antwerpen, 1961), 111-13; J. Z. Kannegieter, Geschiedenis van de vroegere Quakergemeenschap te Amsterdam, 1656 tot begin negentiende eeuw (Amsterdam-Haarlem: Scheltema and Holkema, 1971), 13-24.

Zion Mennonite Church, a southern Manitoba congregation which grew out of the Old Colony Mennonites in November 1980. Its charter membership of 156 included two ministers, Wilhelm Thiessen and Jacob Wiebe. The congregation built a new house of worship at Schanzenfeld, south of Winkler in 1981. Henry K. Schellenberg, Chortitzer Mennonite Church elder (bishop), served the Zion congregation with baptism and communion until March 1982, when Wilhelm Thiessen was chosen as the first elder. Henry Wall and Frank Unrau became ministers in 1981 and 1985 respectively. In 1987 the congregation numbered 256 members and 161 unbaptized children; Sunday school enrollment was 150 (ages 3-16), and 70-75 young people attended an active youth organization.   PDZ

MWR (Mar. 7, 1984), 5.

Zook, John Roel (1857-1919), was an evangelist and °holiness advocate in the Brethren in Christ Church. He was born near Morrison, Ill. He taught school for several years and studied law briefly. Around 1896 he was ordained a minister. In the same year he moved to Des Moines, Iowa, to take charge of a mission which had been turned over to the Brethren in Christ by Charles Good, a member of a small group similar to Zook's church.

Zook early gained prominence in the Brethren in

Christ Church as an evangelist. He conducted numerous revival meetings each year in the United States and Canada. Children's meetings were a marked feature of these services, with the result that child conversions, in addition to adult conversions, became common in the denomintion.

He was a strong advocate of the doctrine of holiness that was beginning to make its way into the denomination in Zook's time. He was the leader of those who persuaded General Conference in 1910 to declare holiness to be a doctrine taught by the Brethren in Christ Church.

Zook also had a prominent role in his church as a member of the Foreign Mission Board. He served on that board from 1896 to 1919, the last fifteen years as chairman. At the time of his death he was leading a fund-raising campaign for missions and was preparing to travel to the church's mission areas.

He also campaigned for a church school. He wanted to establish one in Des Moines as a training school for future mission workers. In this, however, he failed, and the school, Messiah Bible College and Missionary Training Home (now Messiah College), was established in Pennsylvania. Zook, however, served as chairman of its first Board of Managers.   EMS

E. Morris Sider, *Nine Portraits* (Nappanee, Ind., 1978), 120-155; Wittlinger, *Piety and Obedience* (1978), 240-241, 291-294; Asa W. Climenhaga, *History of the Brethren in Christ Church* (Nappanee, Ind., 1942), 170-171; *EV* (Dec. 22, 1919), 9.

Zook, Noah (1841-1912). Born near Chambersburg, Pa., Noah Zook and his family became a part of the Brethren in Christ movement to Dickinson Co., Ks., in 1881. In 1872 he was called to the ministry and during the 1880s became one of the leading evangelists in the church. He explored Chicago (1888) as a possible °urban mission field. Then with another evangelist he engaged in church planting evangelism in Michigan (1888-1889). A few years later (1893-1894) Zook gave his energies to a gospel tent ministry in Kansas. For 13 years, beginning in 1896, he and his wife, Mary Snoke Zook, became full-time evangelists traveling among the Brethren in Christ congregations proclaiming justification, second work °sanctification, missions, divine healing, and the second coming of Christ. They were undeterred by resistance to their approach and teachings and lived to see the fruit of their labor. Four of their children became foreign missionaries. By 1910 revival meetings were an integral part of Brethren life, and in that year the denomination adopted a Wesleyan-oriented statement on sanctification (°holiness movement). Divine healing was practiced and the Brethren became versed in °dispensational premillennialism.   MHS

Owen H. Alderfer, "The Mind of the Brethren in Christ" (PhD diss., Clarement Graduate School, 1964); Wittlinger, *Piety and Obedience* (1978), 167-70, 348-49; Martin H. Schrag, "Societies Influencing the Brethren in Christ Toward a Missionary Program," *MQR*, 42 (1968), 117-31.